Pastor Wesley Baker
2389 Deeds Road
Granville, OH 43023
740 587-2027

D1085192

PRESENTED

TO _____

_____

BY _____

_____

ON _____

_____

YOUR WORD IS A LAMP FOR MY FEET,
A LIGHT ON MY PATH.

PSALM 119:105

NEW INTERNATIONAL VERSION

HOLY BIBLE

ZONDERVAN®

Library of Congress Catalog Card Number 2010939329

Printed in China

N101210

13 14 15 16 17 18 19 20 /DSC/ 15 14 13 12 11 10 9 8 7 6 5 4

A portion of the purchase price of your NIV® Bible is provided to Biblica so together we support the mission of *Transforming lives through God's Word.*

Biblica provides God's Word to people through translation, publishing and Bible engagement in Africa, Asia Pacific, Europe, Latin America, Middle East, and North America. Through its worldwide reach, Biblica engages people with God's Word so that their lives are transformed through a relationship with Jesus Christ.

Table of Contents

The Old Testament

The New Testament

Alphabetical Order of the Books of the Bible

The books of the New Testament are indicated by *italics*.

Preface

vi · PREFACE

The goal of the New International Version (NIV) is to enable English-speaking
people from around the world to read and hear God's eternal Word in their own
language. Our work as translators is motivated by our conviction that the Bible
is God's Word in written form. We believe that the Bible contains the divine answer to the deepest needs of humanity, sheds unique light on our path in a dark
world and sets forth the way to our eternal well-being. Out of these deep convictions, we have sought to recreate as far as possible the experience of the original
audience — blending transparency to the original text with accessibility for the
millions of English speakers around the world. We have prioritized accuracy,
clarity and literary quality with the goal of creating a translation suitable for
public and private reading, evangelism, teaching, preaching, memorizing and
liturgical use. We have also sought to preserve a measure of continuity with the
long tradition of translating the Scriptures into English.

The complete NIV Bible was first published in 1978. It was a completely
new translation made by over a hundred scholars working directly from the
best available Hebrew, Aramaic and Greek texts. The translators came from the
United States, Great Britain, Canada, Australia and New Zealand, giving the
translation an international scope. They were from many denominations and
churches — including Anglican, Assemblies of God, Baptist, Brethren, Christian
Reformed, Church of Christ, Evangelical Covenant, Evangelical Free, Lutheran,
Mennonite, Methodist, Nazarene, Presbyterian, Wesleyan and others. This
breadth of denominational and theological perspective helped to safeguard the
translation from sectarian bias. For these reasons, and by the grace of God, the
NIV has gained a wide readership in all parts of the English-speaking world.

The work of translating the Bible is never finished. As good as they are, English translations must be regularly updated so that they will continue to communicate accurately the meaning of God's Word. Updates are needed in order
to reflect the latest developments in our understanding of the biblical world and
its languages and to keep pace with changes in English usage. Recognizing,
then, that the NIV would retain its ability to communicate God's Word accurately only if it were regularly updated, the original translators established The
Committee on Bible Translation (CBT). The committee is a self-perpetuating
group of biblical scholars charged with keeping abreast of advances in biblical
scholarship and changes in English and issuing periodic updates to the NIV.
CBT is an independent, self-governing body and has sole responsibility for the
NIV text. The committee mirrors the original group of translators in its diverse
international and denominational makeup and in its unifying commitment to
the Bible as God's inspired Word.

In obedience to its mandate, the committee has issued periodic updates to the NIV. An initial revision was released in 1984. A more thorough revision process was completed in 2005, resulting in the separately published Today's New International Version (TNIV). The updated NIV you now have in your hands builds on both the original NIV and the TNIV and represents the latest effort of the committee to articulate God's unchanging Word in the way the original authors might have said it had they been speaking in English to the global English-speaking audience today.

The first concern of the translators has continued to be the accuracy of the translation and its faithfulness to the intended meaning of the biblical writers. This has moved the translators to go beyond a formal word-for-word rendering of the original texts. Because thought patterns and syntax differ from language to language, accurate communication of the meaning of the biblical authors demands constant regard for varied contextual uses of words and idioms and for frequent modifications in sentence structures.

As an aid to the reader, sectional headings have been inserted. They are not to be regarded as part of the biblical text and are not intended for oral reading. It is the committee's hope that these headings may prove more helpful to the reader than the traditional chapter divisions, which were introduced long after the Bible was written.

For the Old Testament the standard Hebrew text, the Masoretic Text as published in the latest edition of *Biblia Hebraica*, has been used throughout. The Masoretic Text tradition contains marginal notations that offer variant readings. These have sometimes been followed instead of the text itself. Because such instances involve variants within the Masoretic tradition, they have not been indicated in the textual notes. In a few cases, words in the basic consonantal text have been divided differently than in the Masoretic Text. Such cases are usually indicated in the textual footnotes. The Dead Sea Scrolls contain biblical texts that represent an earlier stage of the transmission of the Hebrew text. They have been consulted, as have been the Samaritan Pentateuch and the ancient scribal traditions concerning deliberate textual changes. The translators also consulted the more important early versions — the Greek Septuagint, Aquila, Symmachus and Theodotion, the Latin Vulgate, the Syriac Peshitta, the Aramaic Targums and, for the Psalms, the *Juxta Hebraica* of Jerome. Readings from these versions, the Dead Sea Scrolls and the scribal traditions were occasionally followed where the Masoretic Text seemed doubtful and where accepted principles of textual criticism showed that one or more of these textual witnesses appeared to provide the correct reading. In rare cases, the committee has emended the Hebrew text where it appears to have become corrupted at an even earlier stage of its transmission. These departures from the Masoretic Text are also indicated in the textual footnotes. Sometimes the vowel indicators (which are later additions to the basic consonantal text) found in the Masoretic Text did not, in the judgment of the committee, represent the correct vowels for the original text. Accordingly, some words have been read with a different set of vowels. These instances are usually not indicated in the footnotes.

The Greek text used in translating the New Testament is an eclectic one, based on the latest editions of the Nestle-Aland/United Bible Societies' Greek New Testament. The committee has made its choices among the variant readings in accordance with widely accepted principles of New Testament textual criticism. Footnotes call attention to places where uncertainty remains.

The New Testament authors, writing in Greek, often quote the Old Testament from its ancient Greek version, the Septuagint. This is one reason why some of the Old Testament quotations in the NIV New Testament are not identical to the corresponding passages in the NIV Old Testament. Such quotations in the New Testament are indicated with the footnote "(see Septuagint)."

Other footnotes in this version are of several kinds, most of which need no explanation. Those giving alternative translations begin with "Or" and generally introduce the alternative with the last word preceding it in the text, except when it is a single-word alternative. When poetry is quoted in a footnote, a slash mark indicates a line division.

It should be noted that references to diseases, minerals, flora and fauna, architectural details, clothing, jewelry, musical instruments and other articles cannot always be identified with precision. Also, linear measurements and measures of capacity can only be approximated (see the Table of Weights and Measures). Although *Selah,* used mainly in the Psalms, is probably a musical term, its meaning is uncertain. Since it may interrupt reading and distract the reader, this word has not been kept in the English text, but every occurrence has been signaled by a footnote.

One of the main reasons the task of Bible translation is never finished is the change in our own language, English. Although a basic core of the language remains relatively stable, many diverse and complex linguistic factors continue to bring about subtle shifts in the meanings and/or connotations of even old, well-established words and phrases. One of the shifts that creates particular challenges to writers and translators alike is the manner in which gender is presented. The original NIV (1978) was published in a time when "a man" would naturally be understood, in many contexts, to be referring to a person, whether male of female. But most English speakers today tend to hear a distinctly male connotation in this word. In recognition of this change in English, this edition of the NIV, along with almost all other recent English translations, substitutes other expressions when the original text intends to refer generically to men and women equally. Thus, for instance, the NIV (1984) rendering of 1 Corinthians 8:3, "But the man who loves God is known by God" becomes in this edition "But whoever loves God is known by God." On the other hand, "man" and "mankind," as ways of denoting the human race, are still widely used. This edition of the NIV therefore continues to use these words, along with other expressions, in this way.

A related shift in English creates a greater challenge for modern translations: the move away from using the third-person masculine singular pronouns — "he/him/his" — to refer to men and women equally. This usage does persist at a low level in some forms of English, and this revision therefore occasionally uses these pronouns in a generic sense. But the tendency, recognized in day-to-day usage and confirmed by extensive research, is away from the generic use of "he," "him" and "his." In recognition of this shift in language and in an effort to translate into the "common" English that people are actually using, this revision of the NIV generally uses other constructions when the biblical text is plainly addressed to men and women equally. The reader will frequently encounter a "they," "them" or "their" to express a generic singular idea. Thus, for instance, Mark 8:36 reads: "What good is it for someone to gain the whole world, yet forfeit their soul?" This generic use of the "indefinite" or "singular" "they/them/their" has a venerable place in English idiom and has quickly become established as standard English, spoken and written, all over the world. Where an individual emphasis is deemed to be present, "anyone" or "everyone" or some other equivalent is generally used as the antecedent of such pronouns.

Sometimes the chapter and/or verse numbering in English translations of the Old Testament differs from that found in published Hebrew texts. This is particularly the case in the Psalms, where the traditional titles are often included in the Hebrew verse numbering. Such differences are indicated in the footnotes at the bottom of the page. In the New Testament, verse numbers that marked off portions of the traditional English text not supported by the best Greek manuscripts now appear in brackets, with a footnote indicating the text that has been omitted (see, for example, Matthew 17:[21]).

Mark 16:9–20 and John 7:53–8:11, although long accorded virtually equal status with the rest of the Gospels in which they stand, have a very questionable — and confused — standing in the textual history of the New Testament, as noted in the bracketed annotations with which they are set off. A different typeface has been chosen for these passages to indicate even more clearly their uncertain status.

Basic formatting of the text, such as lining the poetry, paragraphing (both prose and poetry), setting up of (administrative-like) lists, indenting letters and lengthy prayers within narratives and the insertion of sectional headings, has been the work of the committee. However, the choice between single-column and double-column formats has been left to the publishers. Also the issuing of "red-letter" editions is a publisher's choice — one the committee does not endorse.

The committee has again been reminded that every human effort is flawed — including this revision of the NIV. We trust, however, that many will find in it an improved representation of the Word of God, through which they hear his call to faith in our Lord Jesus Christ and to service in his kingdom. We offer this version of the Bible to him in whose name and for whose glory it has been made.

The Committee on Bible Translation
September 2010

The Old Testament

Genesis

The Beginning

1 In the beginning God created the heavens and the earth. ²Now the earth was formless and empty, darkness was over the surface of the deep, and the Spirit of God was hovering over the waters. Jn 1:1-2; Isa 45:12,18

³And God said, "Let there be light," and there was light. ⁴God saw that the light was good, and he separated the light from the darkness. ⁵God called the light "day," and the darkness he called "night." And there was evening, and there was morning—the first day. 2Co 4:66

⁶And God said, "Let there be a vault between the waters to separate water from water." ⁷So God made the vault and separated the water under the vault from the water above it. And it was so. ⁸God called the vault "sky." And there was evening, and there was morning—the second day. Ps 148:4; Jer 10:12

⁹And God said, "Let the water under the sky be gathered to one place, and let dry ground appear." And it was so. ¹⁰God called the dry ground "land," and the gathered waters he called "seas." And God saw that it was good. Ps 104:6-9; Jer 5:22; 2Pe 3:5

¹¹Then God said, "Let the land produce vegetation: seed-bearing plants and trees on the land that bear fruit with seed in it, according to their various kinds." And it was so. ¹²The land produced vegetation: plants bearing seed according to their kinds and trees bearing fruit with seed in it according to their kinds. And God saw that it was good. ¹³And there was evening, and there was morning—the third day. Ps 65:9-13

¹⁴And God said, "Let there be lights in the vault of the sky

to separate the day from the night, and let them serve as signs to mark sacred times, and days and years, ¹⁵and let them be lights in the vault of the sky to give light on the earth." And it was so. ¹⁶God made two great lights—the greater light to govern the day and the lesser light to govern the night. He also made the stars. ¹⁷God set them in the vault of the sky to give light on the earth, ¹⁸to govern the day and the night, and to separate light from darkness. And God saw that it was good. ¹⁹And there was evening, and there was morning—the fourth day.   Ps 74:16

²⁰And God said, "Let the water teem with living creatures, and let birds fly above the earth across the vault of the sky." ²¹So God created the great creatures of the sea and every living thing with which the water teems and that moves about in it, according to their kinds, and every winged bird according to its kind. And God saw that it was good. ²²God blessed them and said, "Be fruitful and increase in number and fill the water in the seas, and let the birds increase on the earth." ²³And there was evening, and there was morning—the fifth day.   Ge 8:17

²⁴And God said, "Let the land produce living creatures according to their kinds: the livestock, the creatures that move along the ground, and the wild animals, each according to its kind." And it was so. ²⁵God made the wild animals according to their kinds, the livestock according to their kinds, and all the creatures that move along the ground according to their kinds. And God saw that it was good.

²⁶Then God said, "Let us make mankind in our image, in our likeness, so that they may rule over the fish in the sea and the birds in the sky, over the livestock and all the wild animals,ᵃ and over all the creatures that move along the ground."   Ge 29:6

²⁷So God created mankind in
　　his own image,   1Co 11:7
in the image of God he
　　created them;
male and female he created
　　them.   Ge 5:2; Mk 10:6

²⁸God blessed them and said to them, "Be fruitful and increase in number; fill the earth and subdue it. Rule over the fish in the sea and the birds in the sky and over every living creature that moves on the ground." Ge 9:1,7

²⁹Then God said, "I give

ᵃ 26 Probable reading of the original Hebrew text (see Syriac); Masoretic Text *the earth* you every seed-bearing plant on the face of the whole earth and every tree that has fruit with seed in it. They will be yours for food. ³⁰And to all the beasts of the earth and all the birds in the sky and all the creatures that move along the ground—everything that has the breath of life in it—I give every green plant for food." And it was so. Ps 104:14

³¹God saw all that he had made, and it was very good. And there was evening, and there was morning—the sixth day. Ps 104:24

2 Thus the heavens and the earth were completed in all their vast array. Isa 44:24

²By the seventh day God had finished the work he had been doing; so on the seventh day he rested from all his work. ³Then God blessed the seventh day and made it holy, because on it he rested from all the work of creating that he had done. Ex 20:11; Heb 4:4

Adam and Eve

⁴This is the account of the heavens and the earth when they were created, when the LORD God made the earth and the heavens.

⁵Now no shrub had yet appeared on the earthᵃ and no plant had yet sprung up, for the LORD God had not sent rain on the earth and there was no one to work the ground, ⁶but streamsᵇ came up from the earth and watered the whole surface of the ground. ⁷Then the LORD God formed a manᶜ from the dust of the ground and breathed into his nostrils the breath of life, and the man became a living being. 1Co 15:45; Ge 3:19; Ps 103:14

⁸Now the LORD God had planted a garden in the east, in Eden; and there he put the man he had formed. ⁹The LORD God made all kinds of trees grow out of the ground—trees that were pleasing to the eye and good for food. In the middle of the garden were the tree of life and the tree of the knowledge of good and evil. Ge 3:22,24; Rev 2:7; 22:2,14,19

¹⁰A river watering the garden flowed from Eden; from there it was separated into four headwaters. ¹¹The name of the first is the Pishon; it winds through the entire land of Havilah, where there is gold. ¹²(The gold of that land is good; aromatic resinᵈ and onyx are also there.) ¹³The name of the second river is the Gihon; it winds through the entire land of Cush.ᵉ ¹⁴The name of the third river is the Tigris; it runs along the east

---

ᵃ 5 Or land; also in verse 6   ᵇ 6 Or mist   ᶜ 7 The Hebrew for man (adam) sounds like and may be related to the Hebrew for ground (adamah); it is also the name Adam (see verse 20).   ᵈ 12 Or good; pearls   ᵉ 13 Possibly southeast Mesopotamia side of Ashur. And the fourth river is the Euphrates. Da 10:4 ¹⁵The LORD God took the man and put him in the Garden of Eden to work it and take care of it. ¹⁶And the LORD God commanded the man, "You are free to eat from any tree in the garden; ¹⁷but you must not eat from the tree of the knowledge of good and evil, for when you eat from it you will certainly die." Ro 5:12; 6:23

¹⁸The LORD God said, "It is not good for the man to be alone. I will make a helper suitable for him." 1Co 11:9

¹⁹Now the LORD God had formed out of the ground all the wild animals and all the birds in the sky. He brought them to the man to see what he would name them; and whatever the man called each living creature, that was its name. ²⁰So the man gave names to all the livestock, the birds in the sky and all the wild animals. Ps 8:7

But for Adam[a] no suitable helper was found. ²¹So the LORD God caused the man to fall into a deep sleep; and while he was sleeping, he took one of the man's ribs[b] and then closed up the place with flesh. ²²Then the LORD God made a woman from the rib[c] he had taken out of the man, and he brought her to the man. 1Co 11:8-9

²³The man said,

"This is now bone of my bones
  and flesh of my flesh;

she shall be called 'woman,'
  for she was taken out of
    man."

²⁴That is why a man leaves his father and mother and is united to his wife, and they become one flesh. Mt 19:5; Eph 5:31; Mal 2:15

²⁵Adam and his wife were both naked, and they felt no shame.

The Fall

3 Now the serpent was more crafty than any of the wild animals the LORD God had made. He said to the woman, "Did God really say, 'You must not eat from any tree in the garden'?" 2Co 11:3; Rev 12:9; 20:2

²The woman said to the serpent, "We may eat fruit from the trees in the garden, ³but God did say, 'You must not eat fruit from the tree that is in the middle of the garden, and you must not touch it, or you will die.'"

⁴"You will not certainly die," the serpent said to the woman. ⁵"For God knows that when you eat from it your eyes will be opened, and you will be like God, knowing good and evil." Jn 8:44

⁶When the woman saw that the fruit of the tree was good for food and pleasing to the eye, and also desirable for gaining wisdom, she took some and ate it. She also gave some to her husband, who was with her, and he ate it. ⁷Then the eyes of both

---

[a] 20 Or *the man*   [b] 21 Or *took part of the man's side*   [c] 22 Or *part*

of them were opened, and they realized they were naked; so they sewed fig leaves together and made coverings for themselves. 1Ti 2:14; Jas 1:14-15; 1Jn 2:16

⁸Then the man and his wife heard the sound of the LORD God as he was walking in the garden in the cool of the day, and they hid from the LORD God among the trees of the garden. ⁹But the LORD God called to the man, "Where are you?" Job 31:33

¹⁰He answered, "I heard you in the garden, and I was afraid because I was naked; so I hid."

¹¹And he said, "Who told you that you were naked? Have you eaten from the tree that I commanded you not to eat from?"

¹²The man said, "The woman you put here with me — she gave me some fruit from the tree, and I ate it."

¹³Then the LORD God said to the woman, "What is this you have done?"

The woman said, "The serpent deceived me, and I ate." 2Co 11:3

¹⁴So the LORD God said to the serpent, "Because you have done this,

"Cursed are you above all
    livestock   Dt 28:15-20
and all wild animals!
You will crawl on your belly
    and you will eat dust Isa 65:25
    all the days of your life.
¹⁵And I will put enmity

between you and the
    woman,
and between your offspringᵃ
    and hers;   Rev 12:17; 1Jn 3:8
he will crushᵇ your head,
    and you will strike his
    heel."

¹⁶To the woman he said,

"I will make your pains in
    childbearing very
    severe;
with painful labor you will
    give birth to children.
Your desire will be for your
    husband,
and he will rule over
    you."   1Co 11:3

¹⁷To Adam he said, "Because you listened to your wife and ate fruit from the tree about which I commanded you, 'You must not eat from it,'

"Cursed is the ground
    because of you; Ro 8:20-22
through painful toil you
    will eat food from it
all the days of your
    life.   Job 5:7; Ecc 2:23
¹⁸It will produce thorns and
    thistles for you,   Job 31:40
    and you will eat the plants
    of the field.   Ps 104:14
¹⁹By the sweat of your brow
    you will eat your food
until you return to the
    ground,
since from it you were
    taken;

ᵃ 15 Or *seed*   ᵇ 15 Or *strike*

for dust you are
   and to dust you will
      return." Ge 2:7; Ps 90:3

[20] Adam[a] named his wife Eve,[b] because she would become the mother of all the living. 1Ti 2:13

[21] The LORD God made garments of skin for Adam and his wife and clothed them. [22] And the LORD God said, "The man has now become like one of us, knowing good and evil. He must not be allowed to reach out his hand and take also from the tree of life and eat, and live forever." [23] So the LORD God banished him from the Garden of Eden to work the ground from which he had been taken. [24] After he drove the man out, he placed on the east side[c] of the Garden of Eden cherubim and a flaming sword flashing back and forth to guard the way to the tree of life. Ge 2:9; Rev 22:14; Ex 25:18-22

Cain and Abel

4 Adam[a] made love to his wife Eve, and she became pregnant and gave birth to Cain.[d] She said, "With the help of the LORD I have brought forth[e] a man." [2] Later she gave birth to his brother Abel. Lk 11:51

Now Abel kept flocks, and Cain worked the soil. [3] In the course of time Cain brought some of the fruits of the soil as an offering to the LORD. [4] And Abel also brought an offering — fat portions from some of the firstborn of his flock. The LORD looked with favor on Abel and his offering, [5] but on Cain and his offering he did not look with favor. So Cain was very angry, and his face was downcast. Heb 11:4; Ex 13:2,12; Nu 18:12

[6] Then the LORD said to Cain, "Why are you angry? Why is your face downcast? [7] If you do what is right, will you not be accepted? But if you do not do what is right, sin is crouching at your door; it desires to have you, but you must rule over it." Ro 6:16; Nu 32:23

[8] Now Cain said to his brother Abel, "Let's go out to the field."[f] While they were in the field, Cain attacked his brother Abel and killed him. Mt 23:35; 1Jn 3:12

[9] Then the LORD said to Cain, "Where is your brother Abel?"

"I don't know," he replied. "Am I my brother's keeper?"

[10] The LORD said, "What have you done? Listen! Your brother's blood cries out to me from the ground. [11] Now you are under a curse and driven from the ground, which opened its mouth to receive your brother's blood from your hand. [12] When you work the ground, it will no longer yield its crops for you. You

---

[a] 20,1 Or The man   [b] 20 Eve probably means living.   [c] 24 Or placed in front
[d] 1 Cain sounds like the Hebrew for brought forth or acquired.   [e] 1 Or have acquired
[f] 8 Samaritan Pentateuch, Septuagint, Vulgate and Syriac; Masoretic Text does not have "Let's go out to the field."

will be a restless wanderer on the earth." _{Heb 12:24; Rev 6:9-10}

¹³ Cain said to the LORD, "My punishment is more than I can bear. ¹⁴ Today you are driving me from the land, and I will be hidden from your presence; I will be a restless wanderer on the earth, and whoever finds me will kill me." _{Ps 51:11; Nu 35:19,21,27,33}

¹⁵ But the LORD said to him, "Not so[a]; anyone who kills Cain will suffer vengeance seven times over." Then the LORD put a mark on Cain so that no one who found him would kill him. ¹⁶ So Cain went out from the LORD's presence and lived in the land of Nod,[b] east of Eden. _{Eze 9:4,6; Ge 2:8}

¹⁷ Cain made love to his wife, and she became pregnant and gave birth to Enoch. Cain was then building a city, and he named it after his son Enoch. ¹⁸ To Enoch was born Irad, and Irad was the father of Mehujael, and Mehujael was the father of Methushael, and Methushael was the father of Lamech. _{Ps 49:11}

¹⁹ Lamech married two women, one named Adah and the other Zillah. ²⁰ Adah gave birth to Jabal; he was the father of those who live in tents and raise livestock. ²¹ His brother's name was Jubal; he was the father of all who play stringed instruments and pipes. ²² Zillah also had a son, Tubal-Cain, who forged all kinds of tools out of[c] bronze and iron. Tubal-Cain's sister was Naamah. _{Ex 35:35}

²³ Lamech said to his wives,

"Adah and Zillah, listen to me;
    wives of Lamech, hear my
    words.
I have killed a man for
    wounding me, _{Ex 20:13}
a young man for injuring
    me.
²⁴ If Cain is avenged seven
    times,
    then Lamech seventy-seven
    times." _{ver 15; Mt 18:22}

²⁵ Adam made love to his wife again, and she gave birth to a son and named him Seth,[d] saying, "God has granted me another child in place of Abel, since Cain killed him." ²⁶ Seth also had a son, and he named him Enosh. _{Ge 5:3}

At that time people began to call on[e] the name of the LORD.

From Adam to Noah

5 This is the written account of Adam's family line.

When God created mankind, he made them in the likeness of God. ²He created them male and female and blessed them. And he named them "Mankind"[f] when they were created. _{Ge 1:27; Eph 4:24}

³ When Adam had lived 130

---

^a 15 Septuagint, Vulgate and Syriac; Hebrew *Very well*   ^b 16 *Nod* means *wandering* (see verses 12 and 14).   ^c 22 Or *who instructed all who work in*   ^d 25 *Seth* probably means *granted.*   ^e 26 Or *to proclaim*   ^f 2 Hebrew *adam*

years, he had a son in his own likeness, in his own image; and he named him Seth. ⁴After Seth was born, Adam lived 800 years and had other sons and daughters. ⁵Altogether, Adam lived a total of 930 years, and then he died. Ge 3:19

⁶When Seth had lived 105 years, he became the father*a* of Enosh. ⁷After he became the father of Enosh, Seth lived 807 years and had other sons and daughters. ⁸Altogether, Seth lived a total of 912 years, and then he died. Ge 4:26

⁹When Enosh had lived 90 years, he became the father of Kenan. ¹⁰After he became the father of Kenan, Enosh lived 815 years and had other sons and daughters. ¹¹Altogether, Enosh lived a total of 905 years, and then he died. 1Ch 1:2

¹²When Kenan had lived 70 years, he became the father of Mahalalel. ¹³After he became the father of Mahalalel, Kenan lived 840 years and had other sons and daughters. ¹⁴Altogether, Kenan lived a total of 910 years, and then he died. Lk 3:37

¹⁵When Mahalalel had lived 65 years, he became the father of Jared. ¹⁶After he became the father of Jared, Mahalalel lived 830 years and had other sons and daughters. ¹⁷Altogether, Mahalalel lived a total of 895 years, and then he died. 1Ch 1:2

¹⁸When Jared had lived 162 years, he became the father of Enoch. ¹⁹After he became the father of Enoch, Jared lived 800 years and had other sons and daughters. ²⁰Altogether, Jared lived a total of 962 years, and then he died. Jude 14

²¹When Enoch had lived 65 years, he became the father of Methuselah. ²²After he became the father of Methuselah, Enoch walked faithfully with God 300 years and had other sons and daughters. ²³Altogether, Enoch lived a total of 365 years. ²⁴Enoch walked faithfully with God; then he was no more, because God took him away. Ge 6:9; Mic 6:8

²⁵When Methuselah had lived 187 years, he became the father of Lamech. ²⁶After he became the father of Lamech, Methuselah lived 782 years and had other sons and daughters. ²⁷Altogether, Methuselah lived a total of 969 years, and then he died.

²⁸When Lamech had lived 182 years, he had a son. ²⁹He named him Noah*b* and said, "He will comfort us in the labor and painful toil of our hands caused by the ground the LORD has cursed." ³⁰After Noah was born, Lamech lived 595 years and had other sons and daughters. ³¹Altogether, Lamech lived a total of 777 years, and then he died. Ro 8:20

³²After Noah was 500 years

---

a 6 *Father* may mean *ancestor*; also in verses 7-26.   *b* 29 *Noah* sounds like the Hebrew for *comfort*.

old, he became the father of Shem, Ham and Japheth. Ge 10:1

Wickedness in the World

6 When human beings began to increase in number on the earth and daughters were born to them, ²the sons of God saw that the daughters of humans were beautiful, and they married any of them they chose. ³Then the LORD said, "My Spirit will not contend with*a* humans forever, for they are mortal*b*; their days will be a hundred and twenty years." Ps 78:39; Isa 57:16 ⁴The Nephilim were on the earth in those days — and also afterward — when the sons of God went to the daughters of humans and had children by them. They were the heroes of old, men of renown. Nu 13:33 ⁵The LORD saw how great the wickedness of the human race had become on the earth, and that every inclination of the thoughts of the human heart was only evil all the time. ⁶The LORD regretted that he had made human beings on the earth, and his heart was deeply troubled. ⁷So the LORD said, "I will wipe from the face of the earth the human race I have created — and with them the animals, the birds and the creatures that move along the ground — for I regret that I have made them." ⁸But Noah found favor in the eyes of the LORD. Isa 63:10; Ge 8:21; 19:19

Noah and the Flood

⁹This is the account of Noah and his family.

Noah was a righteous man, blameless among the people of his time, and he walked faithfully with God. ¹⁰Noah had three sons: Shem, Ham and Japheth. Ge 5:22; Heb 11:7; 2Pe 2:5 ¹¹Now the earth was corrupt in God's sight and was full of violence. ¹²God saw how corrupt the earth had become, for all the people on earth had corrupted their ways. ¹³So God said to Noah, "I am going to put an end to all people, for the earth is filled with violence because of them. I am surely going to destroy both them and the earth. ¹⁴So make yourself an ark of cypress*c* wood; make rooms in it and coat it with pitch inside and out. ¹⁵This is how you are to build it: The ark is to be three hundred cubits long, fifty cubits wide and thirty cubits high.*d* ¹⁶Make a roof for it, leaving below the roof an opening one cubit*e* high all around.*f* Put a door in the side of the ark and make lower, middle

---

a 3 Or *My spirit will not remain in*   *b 3* Or *corrupt*   *c 14* The meaning of the Hebrew for this word is uncertain.   *d 15* That is, about 450 feet long, 75 feet wide and 45 feet high or about 135 meters long, 23 meters wide and 14 meters high   *e 16* That is, about 18 inches or about 45 centimeters   *f 16* The meaning of the Hebrew for this clause is uncertain.

and upper decks. ¹⁷I am going to bring floodwaters on the earth to destroy all life under the heavens, every creature that has the breath of life in it. Everything on earth will perish. ¹⁸But I will establish my covenant with you, and you will enter the ark — you and your sons and your wife and your sons' wives with you. ¹⁹You are to bring into the ark two of all living creatures, male and female, to keep them alive with you. ²⁰Two of every kind of bird, of every kind of animal and of every kind of creature that moves along the ground will come to you to be kept alive. ²¹You are to take every kind of food that is to be eaten and store it away as food for you and for them." Ge 9:9-16; Ps 14:1-3; 2Pe 2:5

²²Noah did everything just as God commanded him. Ge 7:5,9,16

7 The LORD then said to Noah, "Go into the ark, you and your whole family, because I have found you righteous in this generation. ²Take with you seven pairs of every kind of clean animal, a male and its mate, and one pair of every kind of unclean animal, a male and its mate, ³and also seven pairs of every kind of bird, male and female, to keep their various kinds alive throughout the earth. ⁴Seven days from now I will send rain on the earth for forty days and forty nights, and I will wipe from the face of the earth every living creature I have made." Ge 6:9; Heb 11:7; Lev 10:10

⁵And Noah did all that the LORD commanded him. Ge 6:22

⁶Noah was six hundred years old when the floodwaters came on the earth. ⁷And Noah and his sons and his wife and his sons' wives entered the ark to escape the waters of the flood. ⁸Pairs of clean and unclean animals, of birds and of all creatures that move along the ground, ⁹male and female, came to Noah and entered the ark, as God had commanded Noah. ¹⁰And after the seven days the floodwaters came on the earth. Ge 5:32

¹¹In the six hundredth year of Noah's life, on the seventeenth day of the second month — on that day all the springs of the great deep burst forth, and the floodgates of the heavens were opened. ¹²And rain fell on the earth forty days and forty nights. Ge 8:2; Eze 26:19

¹³On that very day Noah and his sons, Shem, Ham and Japheth, together with his wife and the wives of his three sons, entered the ark. ¹⁴They had with them every wild animal according to its kind, all livestock according to their kinds, every creature that moves along the ground according to its kind and every bird according to its kind, everything with wings. ¹⁵Pairs of all creatures that have the breath of life in them came to Noah and

entered the ark. [16]The animals going in were male and female of every living thing, as God had commanded Noah. Then the LORD shut him in.   Ge 6:19

[17]For forty days the flood kept coming on the earth, and as the waters increased they lifted the ark high above the earth. [18]The waters rose and increased greatly on the earth, and the ark floated on the surface of the water. [19]They rose greatly on the earth, and all the high mountains under the entire heavens were covered. [20]The waters rose and covered the mountains to a depth of more than fifteen cubits.[a,b] [21]Every living thing that moved on land perished—birds, livestock, wild animals, all the creatures that swarm over the earth, and all mankind. [22]Everything on dry land that had the breath of life in its nostrils died. [23]Every living thing on the face of the earth was wiped out; people and animals and the creatures that move along the ground and the birds were wiped from the earth. Only Noah was left, and those with him in the ark.   2Pe 2:5; Mt 24:39

[24]The waters flooded the earth for a hundred and fifty days.   Ge 8:3

8 But God remembered Noah and all the wild animals and the livestock that were with him in the ark, and he sent a wind over the earth, and the waters receded. [2]Now the springs of the deep and the floodgates of the heavens had been closed, and the rain had stopped falling from the sky. [3]The water receded steadily from the earth. At the end of the hundred and fifty days the water had gone down, [4]and on the seventeenth day of the seventh month the ark came to rest on the mountains of Ararat. [5]The waters continued to recede until the tenth month, and on the first day of the tenth month the tops of the mountains became visible.   Ge 19:29; 9:15

[6]After forty days Noah opened a window he had made in the ark [7]and sent out a raven, and it kept flying back and forth until the water had dried up from the earth. [8]Then he sent out a dove to see if the water had receded from the surface of the ground. [9]But the dove could find nowhere to perch because there was water over all the surface of the earth; so it returned to Noah in the ark. He reached out his hand and took the dove and brought it back to himself in the ark. [10]He waited seven more days and again sent out the dove from the ark. [11]When the dove returned to him in the evening, there in its beak was a freshly plucked olive leaf! Then Noah knew that the water had receded

---

[a] 20 That is, about 23 feet or about 6.8 meters the mountains were covered

[b] 20 Or rose more than fifteen cubits, and

from the earth. ¹²He waited seven more days and sent the dove out again, but this time it did not return to him.   Ge 7:12

¹³By the first day of the first month of Noah's six hundred and first year, the water had dried up from the earth. Noah then removed the covering from the ark and saw that the surface of the ground was dry. ¹⁴By the twenty-seventh day of the second month the earth was completely dry.   Ge 7:11

¹⁵Then God said to Noah, ¹⁶"Come out of the ark, you and your wife and your sons and their wives. ¹⁷Bring out every kind of living creature that is with you — the birds, the animals, and all the creatures that move along the ground — so they can multiply on the earth and be fruitful and increase in number on it." Ge 1:22

¹⁸So Noah came out, together with his sons and his wife and his sons' wives. ¹⁹All the animals and all the creatures that move along the ground and all the birds — everything that moves on land — came out of the ark, one kind after another.

²⁰Then Noah built an altar to the LORD and, taking some of all the clean animals and clean birds, he sacrificed burnt offerings on it. ²¹The LORD smelled the pleasing aroma and said in his heart: "Never again will I curse the ground because of humans, even though[a] every inclination of the human heart is evil from childhood. And never again will I destroy all living creatures, as I have done. Ge 9:11,15; 12:7-8; 22:2

²²"As long as the earth
        endures,
    seedtime and harvest,
    cold and heat,
    summer and winter,
    day and night
    will never cease."   Jer 33:20,25

God's Covenant With Noah

9 Then God blessed Noah and his sons, saying to them, "Be fruitful and increase in number and fill the earth. ²The fear and dread of you will fall on all the beasts of the earth, and on all the birds in the sky, on every creature that moves along the ground, and on all the fish in the sea; they are given into your hands. ³Everything that lives and moves about will be food for you. Just as I gave you the green plants, I now give you everything. Ge 1:22,29

⁴"But you must not eat meat that has its lifeblood still in it. ⁵And for your lifeblood I will surely demand an accounting. I will demand an accounting from every animal. And from each human being, too, I will demand an accounting for the life of another human being. Ge 4:10; Lev 3:17; 17:10

⁶"Whoever sheds human
        blood,

---

[a] 21 Or humans, for

by humans shall their blood
  be shed; Ex 21:12,14; Mt 26:52
for in the image of God
  has God made
  mankind. Ge 1:26

⁷As for you, be fruitful and increase in number; multiply on the earth and increase upon it."Ge 1:22

⁸Then God said to Noah and to his sons with him: ⁹"I now establish my covenant with you and with your descendants after you ¹⁰and with every living creature that was with you—the birds, the livestock and all the wild animals, all those that came out of the ark with you—every living creature on earth. ¹¹I establish my covenant with you: Never again will all life be destroyed by the waters of a flood; never again will there be a flood to destroy the earth." Ge 6:18; 8:21; Isa 54:9

¹²And God said, "This is the sign of the covenant I am making between me and you and every living creature with you, a covenant for all generations to come: ¹³I have set my rainbow in the clouds, and it will be the sign of the covenant between me and the earth. ¹⁴Whenever I bring clouds over the earth and the rainbow appears in the clouds, ¹⁵I will remember my covenant between me and you and all living creatures of every kind. Never again will the waters become a flood to destroy

all life. ¹⁶Whenever the rainbow appears in the clouds, I will see it and remember the everlasting covenant between God and all living creatures of every kind on the earth." Ge 17:7,13,19; Lev 26:42,45

¹⁷So God said to Noah, "This is the sign of the covenant I have established between me and all life on the earth." ver 12; Ge 17:11

The Sons of Noah

¹⁸The sons of Noah who came out of the ark were Shem, Ham and Japheth. (Ham was the father of Canaan.) ¹⁹These were the three sons of Noah, and from them came the people who were scattered over the whole earth. Ge 10:32

²⁰Noah, a man of the soil, proceeded*a* to plant a vineyard. ²¹When he drank some of its wine, he became drunk and lay uncovered inside his tent. ²²Ham, the father of Canaan, saw his father naked and told his two brothers outside. ²³But Shem and Japheth took a garment and laid it across their shoulders; then they walked in backward and covered their father's naked body. Their faces were turned the other way so that they would not see their father naked. Hab 2:15

²⁴When Noah awoke from his wine and found out what his youngest son had done to him, ²⁵he said,

a 20 Or *soil, was the first*

"Cursed be Canaan!   ver 18
The lowest of slaves
will he be to his brothers."

²⁶He also said,

"Praise be to the LORD, the
God of Shem!
May Canaan be the slave of
Shem.   1Ki 9:21
²⁷May God extend Japheth's*ᵃ
territory;   Ge 10:2-5
may Japheth live in the
tents of Shem,   Eph 2:13-14
and may Canaan be the
slave of Japheth."

²⁸After the flood Noah lived 350
years. ²⁹Noah lived a total of 950
years, and then he died.   Ge 2:17

The Table of Nations

10 This is the account of
Shem, Ham and Japheth,
Noah's sons, who themselves
had sons after the flood.   Ge 2:4

The Japhethites
10:2-5pp — 1Ch 1:5-7

²The sonsᵇ of Japheth:
Gomer, Magog, Madai, Ja-
van, Tubal, Meshek and
Tiras.   Eze 38:2,6; Rev 20:8
³The sons of Gomer:
Ashkenaz, Riphath and
Togarmah.   Eze 38:6; Jer 51:27
⁴The sons of Javan:
Elishah, Tarshish, the Kit-

tites and the Rodanites.ᶜ
⁵(From these the mari-
time peoples spread out
into their territories by
their clans within their
nations, each with its own
language.)   1Ch 1:5-7; Jnh 1:3

The Hamites
10:6-20pp — 1Ch 1:8-16

⁶The sons of Ham:
Cush, Egypt, Put and Ca-
naan.   ver 15; Ge 9:18
⁷The sons of Cush:
Seba, Havilah, Sabtah, Ra-
amah and Sabteka.
The sons of Raamah:
Sheba and Dedan.

⁸Cush was the fatherᵈ of Nimrod, who became a mighty warrior on the earth. ⁹He was a
mighty hunter before the LORD;
that is why it is said, "Like Nimrod, a mighty hunter before the
LORD." ¹⁰The first centers of his
kingdom were Babylon, Uruk,
Akkad and Kalneh, inᵉ Shinar.ᶠ
¹¹From that land he went to Assyria, where he built Nineveh,
Rehoboth Ir,ᵍ Calah ¹²and Re-
sen, which is between Nineveh
and Calah—which is the great
city.   Ge 11:9; Mic 5:6; Jnh 1:2

¹³Egypt was the father of
the Ludites, Anamites,

ᵃ 27 *Japheth* sounds like the Hebrew for *extend.*   ᵇ 2 *Sons* may mean *descendants* or
successors or *nations*; also in verses 3, 4, 6, 7, 20-23, 29 and 31.   ᶜ 4 Some manuscripts
of the Masoretic Text and Samaritan Pentateuch (see also Septuagint and 1 Chron. 1:7);
most manuscripts of the Masoretic Text *Dodanites*   ᵈ 8 *Father* may mean *ancestor* or
predecessor or *founder*; also in verses 13, 15, 24 and 26.   ᵉ 10 Or *Uruk and Akkad—all of
them in*   ᶠ 10 That is, Babylonia   ᵍ 11 Or *Nineveh with its city squares*

Lehabites, Naphtuhites, ¹⁴Pathrusites, Kasluhites (from whom the Philistines came) and Caphtorites. Ge 21:32,34

¹⁵Canaan was the father of
Sidon his firstborn,ᵃ and
of the Hittites, ¹⁶Jebusites,
Amorites, Girgashites, ¹⁷Hivites, Arkites, Sinites, ¹⁸Arvadites, Zemarites and
Hamathites. Ge 9:18; Eze 28:21

Later the Canaanite clans scattered ¹⁹and the borders of Canaan reached from Sidon toward Gerar as far as Gaza, and then toward Sodom, Gomorrah, Admah and Zeboyim, as far as Lasha. Ge 13:12

²⁰These are the sons of Ham by their clans and languages, in their territories and nations.

The Semites
10:21-31pp — Ge 11:10-27; 1Ch 1:17-27

²¹Sons were also born to Shem, whose older brother wasᵇ Japheth; Shem was the ancestor of all the sons of Eber. Nu 24:24

²²The sons of Shem:
Elam, Ashur, Arphaxad,
Lud and Aram. Jer 49:34
²³The sons of Aram:
Uz, Hul, Gether and Meshek.ᶜ Job 1:1
²⁴Arphaxad was the father ofᵈ
Shelah,

and Shelah the father of
Eber. Lk 3:35
²⁵Two sons were born to Eber:
One was named Peleg,ᵉ
because in his time the
earth was divided; his
brother was named Joktan.
²⁶Joktan was the father of
Almodad, Sheleph, Hazarmaveth, Jerah, ²⁷Hadoram, Uzal, Diklah, ²⁸Obal,
Abimael, Sheba, ²⁹Ophir,
Havilah and Jobab. All
these were sons of Joktan.

³⁰The region where they lived stretched from Mesha toward Sephar, in the eastern hill country.

³¹These are the sons of Shem by their clans and languages, in their territories and nations. Ge 11:10-27

³²These are the clans of Noah's sons, according to their lines of descent, within their nations. From these the nations spread out over the earth after the flood. Ge 9:19

The Tower of Babel

11 Now the whole world had one language and a common speech. ²As people moved eastward,ᶠ they found a plain in Shinarᵍ and settled there. Ge 10:10

³They said to each other, "Come, let's make bricks and bake them

---

ᵃ 15 Or *of the Sidonians, the foremost*   ᵇ 21 Or *Shem, the older brother of*
ᶜ 23 See Septuagint and 1 Chron. 1:17; Hebrew *Mash*.   ᵈ 24 Hebrew; Septuagint *father of*
Cainan, and Cainan was the father of   ᵉ 25 *Peleg* means *division*.   ᶠ 2 Or *from the east*;
or *in the east*   ᵍ 2 That is, Babylonia

thoroughly." They used brick instead of stone, and tar for mortar. ⁴Then they said, "Come, let us build ourselves a city, with a tower that reaches to the heavens, so that we may make a name for ourselves; otherwise we will be scattered over the face of the whole earth." Dt 1:28; Ge 6:4; Dt 4:27

⁵But the LORD came down to see the city and the tower the people were building. ⁶The LORD said, "If as one people speaking the same language they have begun to do this, then nothing they plan to do will be impossible for them. ⁷Come, let us go down and confuse their language so they will not understand each other." Ge 18:21; 42:23

⁸So the LORD scattered them from there over all the earth, and they stopped building the city. ⁹That is why it was called Babel[a]—because there the LORD confused the language of the whole world. From there the LORD scattered them over the face of the whole earth. Lk 1:51; Ge 10:10

From Shem to Abram
11:10-27pp — Ge 10:21-31; 1Ch 1:17-27

¹⁰This is the account of Shem's family line.

Two years after the flood, when Shem was 100 years old, he became the father[b] of Arphaxad. ¹¹And after he became the father of Arphaxad, Shem lived 500 years and had other sons and daughters.

¹²When Arphaxad had lived 35 years, he became the father of Shelah. ¹³And after he became the father of Shelah, Arphaxad lived 403 years and had other sons and daughters.[c] Lk 3:35

¹⁴When Shelah had lived 30 years, he became the father of Eber. ¹⁵And after he became the father of Eber, Shelah lived 403 years and had other sons and daughters. Lk 3:35

¹⁶When Eber had lived 34 years, he became the father of Peleg. ¹⁷And after he became the father of Peleg, Eber lived 430 years and had other sons and daughters.

¹⁸When Peleg had lived 30 years, he became the father of Reu. ¹⁹And after he became the father of Reu, Peleg lived 209 years and had other sons and daughters.

²⁰When Reu had lived 32 years, he became the father of Serug. ²¹And after he became the father of Serug, Reu lived 207 years and had other sons and daughters.

²²When Serug had lived 30 years, he became the father of

---

[a] 9 That is, Babylon; *Babel* sounds like the Hebrew for *confused.*   [b] 10 *Father* may mean *ancestor;* also in verses 11-25.   [c] 12,13 Hebrew; Septuagint (see also Luke 3:35, 36 and note at Gen. 10:24) *35 years, he became the father of Cainan. ¹³And after he became the father of Cainan, Arphaxad lived 430 years and had other sons and daughters, and then he died. When Cainan had lived 130 years, he became the father of Shelah. And after he became the father of Shelah, Cainan lived 330 years and had other sons and daughters*

Nahor. ²³ And after he became the father of Nahor, Serug lived 200 years and had other sons and daughters.

²⁴ When Nahor had lived 29 years, he became the father of Terah. ²⁵ And after he became the father of Terah, Nahor lived 119 years and had other sons and daughters. Lk 3:34

²⁶ After Terah had lived 70 years, he became the father of Abram, Nahor and Haran. Ge 10:21

Abram's Family

²⁷ This is the account of Terah's family line.

Terah became the father of Abram, Nahor and Haran. And Haran became the father of Lot. ²⁸ While his father Terah was still alive, Haran died in Ur of the Chaldeans, in the land of his birth. ²⁹ Abram and Nahor both married. The name of Abram's wife was Sarai, and the name of Nahor's wife was Milkah; she was the daughter of Haran, the father of both Milkah and Iskah. ³⁰ Now Sarai was childless because she was not able to conceive. Ge 12:4

³¹ Terah took his son Abram, his grandson Lot son of Haran, and his daughter-in-law Sarai, the wife of his son Abram, and together they set out from Ur of the Chaldeans to go to Canaan. But when they came to Harran, they settled there. Ge 15:7; Ac 7:4

³² Terah lived 205 years, and he died in Harran.

The Call of Abram

12 The Lord had said to Abram, "Go from your country, your people and your father's household to the land I will show you. Ac 7:3; Heb 11:8

² "I will make you into a great
    nation, Ge 17:2,4; 18:18
  and I will bless you; Ge 24:1,35
I will make your name
    great,
  and you will be a blessing.ᵃ
³ I will bless those who bless
    you,
  and whoever curses you I
    will curse; Ge 27:29; Nu 24:9
and all peoples on earth
  will be blessed through
    you."ᵇ Ge 22:18; Ac 3:25

⁴ So Abram went, as the Lord had told him; and Lot went with him. Abram was seventy-five years old when he set out from Harran. ⁵ He took his wife Sarai, his nephew Lot, all the possessions they had accumulated and the people they had acquired in Harran, and they set out for the land of Canaan, and they arrived there. Ge 11:31; 14:14

⁶ Abram traveled through the land as far as the site of the great tree of Moreh at Shechem. At that time the Canaanites were in the land. ⁷ The Lord appeared to Abram and said, "To your

ᵃ 2 Or *be seen as blessed*   ᵇ 3 Or *earth / will use your name in blessings* (see 48:20) offspring*a* I will give this land." So he built an altar there to the LORD, who had appeared to him.   Ge 13:15,17; 17:1; Ps 105:9-11

⁸From there he went on toward the hills east of Bethel and pitched his tent, with Bethel on the west and Ai on the east. There he built an altar to the LORD and called on the name of the LORD.

⁹Then Abram set out and continued toward the Negev.   Ge 4:26

Abram in Egypt
12:10-20Ref — Ge 20:1-18; 26:1-11

¹⁰Now there was a famine in the land, and Abram went down to Egypt to live there for a while because the famine was severe. ¹¹As he was about to enter Egypt, he said to his wife Sarai, "I know what a beautiful woman you are. ¹²When the Egyptians see you, they will say, 'This is his wife.' Then they will kill me but will let you live. ¹³Say you are my sister, so that I will be treated well for your sake and my life will be spared because of you."   Ge 20:2

¹⁴When Abram came to Egypt, the Egyptians saw that Sarai was a very beautiful woman. ¹⁵And when Pharaoh's officials saw her, they praised her to Pharaoh, and she was taken into his palace. ¹⁶He treated Abram well for her sake, and Abram acquired sheep and cattle, male and female donkeys, male and female servants, and camels.   Ge 24:35; Job 1:3

¹⁷But the LORD inflicted serious diseases on Pharaoh and his household because of Abram's wife Sarai. ¹⁸So Pharaoh summoned Abram. "What have you done to me?" he said. "Why didn't you tell me she was your wife? ¹⁹Why did you say, 'She is my sister,' so that I took her to be my wife? Now then, here is your wife. Take her and go!" ²⁰Then Pharaoh gave orders about Abram to his men, and they sent him on his way, with his wife and everything he had.   Ge 20:1-18; 26:1-11; 1Ch 16:21

Abram and Lot Separate

13 So Abram went up from Egypt to the Negev, with his wife and everything he had, and Lot went with him. ²Abram had become very wealthy in livestock and in silver and gold. Ge 12:5

³From the Negev he went from place to place until he came to Bethel, to the place between Bethel and Ai where his tent had been earlier ⁴and where he had first built an altar. There Abram called on the name of the LORD.   Ge 12:7-8

⁵Now Lot, who was moving about with Abram, also had flocks and herds and tents. ⁶But the land could not support them while they stayed together, for their possessions were so great that they were not able to stay together. ⁷And quarreling arose between Abram's herders and Lot's. The Canaanites and Periz-

a 7 Or *seed*

zites were also living in the land at that time. Ge 26:20-21; 36:7; 12:6

⁸ So Abram said to Lot, "Let's not have any quarreling between you and me, or between your herders and mine, for we are close relatives. ⁹ Is not the whole land before you? Let's part company. If you go to the left, I'll go to the right; if you go to the right, I'll go to the left." Ps 133:1; Pr 15:18

¹⁰ Lot looked around and saw that the whole plain of the Jordan toward Zoar was well watered, like the garden of the LORD, like the land of Egypt. (This was before the LORD destroyed Sodom and Gomorrah.) ¹¹ So Lot chose for himself the whole plain of the Jordan and set out toward the east. The two men parted company: ¹² Abram lived in the land of Canaan, while Lot lived among the cities of the plain and pitched his tents near Sodom. ¹³ Now the people of Sodom were wicked and were sinning greatly against the LORD. Ge 18:20; 19:17-29; 2Pe 2:8

¹⁴ The LORD said to Abram after Lot had parted from him, "Look around from where you are, to the north and south, to the east and west. ¹⁵ All the land that you see I will give to you and your offspring[a] forever. ¹⁶ I will make your offspring like the dust of the earth, so that if anyone could count the dust, then your offspring could be counted. ¹⁷ Go, walk through the length and

breadth of the land, for I am giving it to you." Ge 12:7; Nu 13:17-25

¹⁸ So Abram went to live near the great trees of Mamre at Hebron, where he pitched his tents. There he built an altar to the LORD. Ge 8:20; 14:13,24

Abram Rescues Lot

14 At the time when Amraphel was king of Shinar,[b] Arioch king of Ellasar, Kedorlaomer king of Elam and Tidal king of Goyim, ² these kings went to war against Bera king of Sodom, Birsha king of Gomorrah, Shinab king of Admah, Shemeber king of Zeboyim, and the king of Bela (that is, Zoar). ³ All these latter kings joined forces in the Valley of Siddim (that is, the Dead Sea Valley). ⁴ For twelve years they had been subject to Kedorlaomer, but in the thirteenth year they rebelled. Nu 34:3,12; Jos 3:16

⁵ In the fourteenth year, Kedorlaomer and the kings allied with him went out and defeated the Rephaites in Ashteroth Karnaim, the Zuzites in Ham, the Emites in Shaveh Kiriathaim ⁶ and the Horites in the hill country of Seir, as far as El Paran near the desert. ⁷ Then they turned back and went to En Mishpat (that is, Kadesh), and they conquered the whole territory of the Amalekites, as well as the Amorites who were living in Hazezon Tamar. Dt 2:12,22; Ge 21:21

---

[a] 15 Or seed; also in verse 16   [b] 1 That is, Babylonia; also in verse 9

⁸Then the king of Sodom, the king of Gomorrah, the king of Admah, the king of Zeboyim and the king of Bela (that is, Zoar) marched out and drew up their battle lines in the Valley of Siddim ⁹against Kedorlaomer king of Elam, Tidal king of Goyim, Amraphel king of Shinar and Arioch king of Ellasar—four kings against five. ¹⁰Now the Valley of Siddim was full of tar pits, and when the kings of Sodom and Gomorrah fled, some of the men fell into them and the rest fled to the hills. ¹¹The four kings seized all the goods of Sodom and Gomorrah and all their food; then they went away. ¹²They also carried off Abram's nephew Lot and his possessions, since he was living in Sodom.   Ge 13:10; 19:17-29; Dt 29:23

¹³A man who had escaped came and reported this to Abram the Hebrew. Now Abram was living near the great trees of Mamre the Amorite, a brotherᵃ of Eshkol and Aner, all of whom were allied with Abram. ¹⁴When Abram heard that his relative had been taken captive, he called out the 318 trained men born in his household and went in pursuit as far as Dan. ¹⁵During the night Abram divided his men to attack them and he routed them, pursuing them as far as Hobah, north of Damascus. ¹⁶He recovered all the goods and brought back his relative Lot and his possessions,

together with the women and the other people.   Ge 13:18; 15:3

¹⁷After Abram returned from defeating Kedorlaomer and the kings allied with him, the king of Sodom came out to meet him in the Valley of Shaveh (that is, the King's Valley).

¹⁸Then Melchizedek king of Salem brought out bread and wine. He was priest of God Most High, ¹⁹and he blessed Abram, saying,   Ps 110:4; Heb 7:2,6

"Blessed be Abram by God
        Most High,
    Creator of heaven and
        earth.
²⁰And praise be to God Most
        High,
    who delivered your enemies
        into your hand."   Ge 24:27

Then Abram gave him a tenth of everything.   Heb 7:4

²¹The king of Sodom said to Abram, "Give me the people and keep the goods for yourself."

²²But Abram said to the king of Sodom, "With raised hand I have sworn an oath to the LORD, God Most High, Creator of heaven and earth, ²³that I will accept nothing belonging to you, not even a thread or the strap of a sandal, so that you will never be able to say, 'I made Abram rich.' ²⁴I will accept nothing but what my men have eaten and the share that belongs to the men who went with me—to Aner,

ᵃ 13 Or a relative; or an ally

Eshkol and Mamre. Let them have their share." Ex 6:8; Rev 10:5-6

The LORD's Covenant With Abram

15 After this, the word of the LORD came to Abram in a vision: Nu 12:6

"Do not be afraid,
    Abram. Ge 21:17; 26:24
I am your shield,[a] Dt 33:29
your very great reward.[b]"

[2] But Abram said, "Sovereign LORD, what can you give me since I remain childless and the one who will inherit[c] my estate is Eliezer of Damascus?" [3] And Abram said, "You have given me no children; so a servant in my household will be my heir." Ac 7:5 [4] Then the word of the LORD came to him: "This man will not be your heir, but a son who is your own flesh and blood will be your heir." [5] He took him outside and said, "Look up at the sky and count the stars — if indeed you can count them." Then he said to him, "So shall your offspring[d] be." Gal 4:28; Ro 4:18 [6] Abram believed the LORD, and he credited it to him as righteousness. Ro 4:3,20-24; Gal 3:6; Jas 2:23 [7] He also said to him, "I am the LORD, who brought you out of Ur of the Chaldeans to give you this land to take possession of it." Ge 13:17

[8] But Abram said, "Sovereign LORD, how can I know that I will gain possession of it?" Lk 1:18 [9] So the LORD said to him, "Bring me a heifer, a goat and a ram, each three years old, along with a dove and a young pigeon." Nu 19:2; Dt 21:3 [10] Abram brought all these to him, cut them in two and arranged the halves opposite each other; the birds, however, he did not cut in half. [11] Then birds of prey came down on the carcasses, but Abram drove them away. Lev 1:17; Jer 34:18 [12] As the sun was setting, Abram fell into a deep sleep, and a thick and dreadful darkness came over him. [13] Then the LORD said to him, "Know for certain that for four hundred years your descendants will be strangers in a country not their own and that they will be enslaved and mistreated there. [14] But I will punish the nation they serve as slaves, and afterward they will come out with great possessions. [15] You, however, will go to your ancestors in peace and be buried at a good old age. [16] In the fourth generation your descendants will come back here, for the sin of the Amorites has not yet reached its full measure." Ex 12:32-38,40; Ge 25:8 [17] When the sun had set and darkness had fallen, a smoking firepot with a blazing torch appeared and passed between the

---

[a] 1 Or *sovereign*   [b] 1 Or *shield; / your reward will be very great*   [c] 2 The meaning of the Hebrew for this phrase is uncertain.   [d] 5 Or *seed*

pieces. ¹⁸On that day the LORD made a covenant with Abram and said, "To your descendants I give this land, from the Wadi*a* of Egypt to the great river, the Euphrates— ¹⁹the land of the Kenites, Kenizzites, Kadmonites, ²⁰Hittites, Perizzites, Rephaites, ²¹Amorites, Canaanites, Girgashites and Jebusites." Ge 17:2,4,7

Hagar and Ishmael

16 Now Sarai, Abram's wife, had borne him no children. But she had an Egyptian slave named Hagar; ²so she said to Abram, "The LORD has kept me from having children. Go, sleep with my slave; perhaps I can build a family through her." Ge 11:30; 30:3-4

Abram agreed to what Sarai said. ³So after Abram had been living in Canaan ten years, Sarai his wife took her Egyptian slave Hagar and gave her to her husband to be his wife. ⁴He slept with Hagar, and she conceived. Ge 12:5

When she knew she was pregnant, she began to despise her mistress. ⁵Then Sarai said to Abram, "You are responsible for the wrong I am suffering. I put my slave in your arms, and now that she knows she is pregnant, she despises me. May the LORD judge between you and me." Ge 31:53

⁶"Your slave is in your hands," Abram said. "Do with her whatever you think best." Then Sarai mistreated Hagar; so she fled from her. Jos 9:25

⁷The angel of the LORD found Hagar near a spring in the desert; it was the spring that is beside the road to Shur. ⁸And he said, "Hagar, slave of Sarai, where have you come from, and where are you going?" Ge 21:17; 22:11,15

"I'm running away from my mistress Sarai," she answered.

⁹Then the angel of the LORD told her, "Go back to your mistress and submit to her." ¹⁰The angel added, "I will increase your descendants so much that they will be too numerous to count." Ge 13:16; 17:20

¹¹The angel of the LORD also said to her:

"You are now pregnant
    and you will give birth to a
        son.
You shall name him Ishmael,*b*
    for the LORD has heard of
        your misery. Ex 2:24; 3:7,9
¹²He will be a wild donkey of a
    man;
    his hand will be against
        everyone
    and everyone's hand
        against him,
and he will live in hostility
    toward*c* all his
        brothers." Ge 25:18

¹³She gave this name to the LORD who spoke to her: "You are the God who sees me," for she said, "I have now seen*d* the One

---

a 18 Or *river*   *b* 11 *Ishmael* means *God hears.*   *c* 12 Or *live to the east / of*   *d* 13 Or *seen*
the back of

who sees me." ¹⁴That is why the well was called Beer Lahai Roi*ᵃ*; it is still there, between Kadesh and Bered. Ge 32:30

¹⁵So Hagar bore Abram a son, and Abram gave the name Ishmael to the son she had borne. ¹⁶Abram was eighty-six years old when Hagar bore him Ishmael. Gal 4:22

The Covenant of Circumcision

17 When Abram was ninety-nine years old, the LORD appeared to him and said, "I am God Almighty*ᵇ*; walk before me faithfully and be blameless. ²Then I will make my covenant between me and you and will greatly increase your numbers." Ge 15:18; 28:3

³Abram fell facedown, and God said to him, ⁴"As for me, this is my covenant with you: You will be the father of many nations. ⁵No longer will you be called Abram*ᶜ*; your name will be Abraham,*ᵈ* for I have made you a father of many nations. ⁶I will make you very fruitful; I will make nations of you, and kings will come from you. ⁷I will establish my covenant as an everlasting covenant between me and you and your descendants after you for the generations to come, to be your God and the God of your descendants after you. ⁸The whole land of Canaan, where you now reside as a foreigner, I will give as an everlasting possession to you and your descendants after you; and I will be their God." Ge 12:2; 35:11; Ro 4:17

⁹Then God said to Abraham, "As for you, you must keep my covenant, you and your descendants after you for the generations to come. ¹⁰This is my covenant with you and your descendants after you, the covenant you are to keep: Every male among you shall be circumcised. ¹¹You are to undergo circumcision, and it will be the sign of the covenant between me and you. ¹²For the generations to come every male among you who is eight days old must be circumcised, including those born in your household or bought with money from a foreigner — those who are not your offspring. ¹³Whether born in your household or bought with your money, they must be circumcised. My covenant in your flesh is to be an everlasting covenant. ¹⁴Any uncircumcised male, who has not been circumcised in the flesh, will be cut off from his people; he has broken my covenant." Ro 4:11

¹⁵God also said to Abraham, "As for Sarai your wife, you are no longer to call her Sarai; her name will be Sarah. ¹⁶I will bless her and will surely give you a son by her. I will bless her so that she will be the mother of nations;

ᵃ 14 *Beer Lahai Roi* means *well of the Living One who sees me.*   *ᵇ* 1 Hebrew *El-Shaddai*
ᶜ 5 *Abram* means *exalted father.*   *ᵈ* 5 *Abraham* probably means *father of many.*

kings of peoples will come from her." Ge 18:10; Gal 4:31

¹⁷Abraham fell facedown; he laughed and said to himself, "Will a son be born to a man a hundred years old? Will Sarah bear a child at the age of ninety?" ¹⁸And Abraham said to God, "If only Ishmael might live under your blessing!" Ge 21:11; 18:12

¹⁹Then God said, "Yes, but your wife Sarah will bear you a son, and you will call him Isaac.ᵃ I will establish my covenant with him as an everlasting covenant for his descendants after him. ²⁰And as for Ishmael, I have heard you: I will surely bless him; I will make him fruitful and will greatly increase his numbers. He will be the father of twelve rulers, and I will make him into a great nation. ²¹But my covenant I will establish with Isaac, whom Sarah will bear to you by this time next year." ²²When he had finished speaking with Abraham, God went up from him. Ge 16:10; 21:18; 25:12-16

²³On that very day Abraham took his son Ishmael and all those born in his household or bought with his money, every male in his household, and circumcised them, as God told him. ²⁴Abraham was ninety-nine years old when he was circumcised, ²⁵and his son Ishmael was thirteen; ²⁶Abraham and his son Ishmael were both circum-cised on that very day. ²⁷And every male in Abraham's household, including those born in his household or bought from a foreigner, was circumcised with him. Ro 4:11

The Three Visitors

18 The LORD appeared to Abraham near the great trees of Mamre while he was sitting at the entrance to his tent in the heat of the day. ²Abraham looked up and saw three men standing nearby. When he saw them, he hurried from the entrance of his tent to meet them and bowed low to the ground. ver 16,22; Heb 13:2

³He said, "If I have found favor in your eyes, my lord,ᵇ do not pass your servant by. ⁴Let a little water be brought, and then you may all wash your feet and rest under this tree. ⁵Let me get you something to eat, so you can be refreshed and then go on your way—now that you have come to your servant." Ge 43:24; Jdg 13:15

"Very well," they answered, "do as you say."

⁶So Abraham hurried into the tent to Sarah. "Quick," he said, "get three seahsᶜ of the finest flour and knead it and bake some bread."

⁷Then he ran to the herd and selected a choice, tender calf and gave it to a servant, who hurried

---

ᵃ 19 *Isaac* means *he laughs.*   ᵇ 3 Or *eyes, Lord*   ᶜ 6 That is, probably about 36 pounds or about 16 kilograms to prepare it. ⁸He then brought some curds and milk and the calf that had been prepared, and set these before them. While they ate, he stood near them under a tree. Ge 19:3

⁹"Where is your wife Sarah?" they asked him.

"There, in the tent," he said.

¹⁰Then one of them said, "I will surely return to you about this time next year, and Sarah your wife will have a son." Ro 9:9

Now Sarah was listening at the entrance to the tent, which was behind him. ¹¹Abraham and Sarah were already very old, and Sarah was past the age of childbearing. ¹²So Sarah laughed to herself as she thought, "After I am worn out and my lord is old, will I now have this pleasure?" Ge 17:17; Ro 4:19; 1Pe 3:6

¹³Then the LORD said to Abraham, "Why did Sarah laugh and say, 'Will I really have a child, now that I am old?' ¹⁴Is anything too hard for the LORD? I will return to you at the appointed time next year, and Sarah will have a son." Jer 32:17,27; Lk 1:37; Ro 4:21

¹⁵Sarah was afraid, so she lied and said, "I did not laugh."

But he said, "Yes, you did laugh."

Abraham Pleads for Sodom

¹⁶When the men got up to leave, they looked down toward Sodom, and Abraham walked along with them to see them on their way. ¹⁷Then the LORD said, "Shall I hide from Abraham what I am about to do? ¹⁸Abraham will surely become a great and powerful nation, and all nations on earth will be blessed through him.ᵃ ¹⁹For I have chosen him, so that he will direct his children and his household after him to keep the way of the LORD by doing what is right and just, so that the LORD will bring about for Abraham what he has promised him." Gal 3:8; Dt 4:9-10

²⁰Then the LORD said, "The outcry against Sodom and Gomorrah is so great and their sin so grievous ²¹that I will go down and see if what they have done is as bad as the outcry that has reached me. If not, I will know." Ge 19:13; Eze 16:46

²²The men turned away and went toward Sodom, but Abraham remained standing before the LORD.ᵇ ²³Then Abraham approached him and said: "Will you sweep away the righteous with the wicked? ²⁴What if there are fifty righteous people in the city? Will you really sweep it away and not spareᶜ the place for the sake of the fifty righteous people in it? ²⁵Far be it from you to do such a thing—to kill the righteous with the wicked,

---

ᵃ 18 Or *will use his name in blessings* (see 48:20)   ᵇ 22 Masoretic Text; an ancient Hebrew scribal tradition *but the LORD remained standing before Abraham*   ᶜ 24 Or *forgive*; also in verse 26 treating the righteous and the wicked alike. Far be it from you! Will not the Judge of all the earth do right?" ^{Nu 16:22; Ro 3:6}

²⁶ The LORD said, "If I find fifty righteous people in the city of Sodom, I will spare the whole place for their sake." ^{Jer 5:1}

²⁷ Then Abraham spoke up again: "Now that I have been so bold as to speak to the Lord, though I am nothing but dust and ashes, ²⁸ what if the number of the righteous is five less than fifty? Will you destroy the whole city for lack of five people?" ^{Ge 2:7}

"If I find forty-five there," he said, "I will not destroy it."

²⁹ Once again he spoke to him, "What if only forty are found there?"

He said, "For the sake of forty, I will not do it."

³⁰ Then he said, "May the Lord not be angry, but let me speak. What if only thirty can be found there?"

He answered, "I will not do it if I find thirty there."

³¹ Abraham said, "Now that I have been so bold as to speak to the Lord, what if only twenty can be found there?"

He said, "For the sake of twenty, I will not destroy it."

³² Then he said, "May the Lord not be angry, but let me speak just once more. What if only ten can be found there?" ^{Jdg 6:39}

He answered, "For the sake of ten, I will not destroy it."

³³ When the LORD had finished speaking with Abraham, he left, and Abraham returned home. ^{Ge 17:22}

Sodom and Gomorrah Destroyed

19 The two angels arrived at Sodom in the evening, and Lot was sitting in the gateway of the city. When he saw them, he got up to meet them and bowed down with his face to the ground. ² "My lords," he said, "please turn aside to your servant's house. You can wash your feet and spend the night and then go on your way early in the morning." ^{Ge 18:22}

"No," they answered, "we will spend the night in the square."

³ But he insisted so strongly that they did go with him and entered his house. He prepared a meal for them, baking bread without yeast, and they ate. ⁴ Before they had gone to bed, all the men from every part of the city of Sodom — both young and old — surrounded the house. ⁵ They called to Lot, "Where are the men who came to you tonight? Bring them out to us so that we can have sex with them." ^{Jdg 19:22; Ro 1:24-27}

⁶ Lot went outside to meet them and shut the door behind him ⁷ and said, "No, my friends. Don't do this wicked thing. ⁸ Look, I have two daughters who have never slept with a man. Let me bring them out to

you, and you can do what you like with them. But don't do anything to these men, for they have come under the protection of my roof." Jdg 19:24; 2Pe 2:7-8

⁹ "Get out of our way," they replied. "This fellow came here as a foreigner, and now he wants to play the judge! We'll treat you worse than them." They kept bringing pressure on Lot and moved forward to break down the door. Ac 7:27

¹⁰ But the men inside reached out and pulled Lot back into the house and shut the door. ¹¹ Then they struck the men who were at the door of the house, young and old, with blindness so that they could not find the door. Dt 28:28-29

¹² The two men said to Lot, "Do you have anyone else here — sons-in-law, sons or daughters, or anyone else in the city who belongs to you? Get them out of here, ¹³ because we are going to destroy this place. The outcry to the LORD against its people is so great that he has sent us to destroy it." 1Ch 21:15

¹⁴ So Lot went out and spoke to his sons-in-law, who were pledged to marry[a] his daughters. He said, "Hurry and get out of this place, because the LORD is about to destroy the city!" But his sons-in-law thought he was joking. Nu 16:21

¹⁵ With the coming of dawn, the angels urged Lot, saying, "Hurry! Take your wife and your two daughters who are here, or you will be swept away when the city is punished." Nu 16:26; Rev 18:4

¹⁶ When he hesitated, the men grasped his hand and the hands of his wife and of his two daughters and led them safely out of the city, for the LORD was merciful to them. ¹⁷ As soon as they had brought them out, one of them said, "Flee for your lives! Don't look back, and don't stop anywhere in the plain! Flee to the mountains or you will be swept away!" ver 26

¹⁸ But Lot said to them, "No, my lords,[b] please! ¹⁹ Your[c] servant has found favor in your[c] eyes, and you[c] have shown great kindness to me in sparing my life. But I can't flee to the mountains; this disaster will overtake me, and I'll die. ²⁰ Look, here is a town near enough to run to, and it is small. Let me flee to it — it is very small, isn't it? Then my life will be spared." Ge 6:8; 24:12

²¹ He said to him, "Very well, I will grant this request too; I will not overthrow the town you speak of. ²² But flee there quickly, because I cannot do anything until you reach it." (That is why the town was called Zoar.[d]) Ge 13:10

²³ By the time Lot reached Zoar, the sun had risen over the land. ²⁴ Then the LORD rained down

---

ᵃ 14 Or *were married to*   ᵇ 18 Or *No, Lord*; or *No, my lord*   ᶜ 19 The Hebrew is singular.
ᵈ 22 *Zoar* means *small*.

burning sulfur on Sodom and Gomorrah — from the LORD out of the heavens. ²⁵Thus he overthrew those cities and the entire plain, destroying all those living in the cities — and also the vegetation in the land. ²⁶But Lot's wife looked back, and she became a pillar of salt. ver 17; Lk 17:29,32

²⁷Early the next morning Abraham got up and returned to the place where he had stood before the LORD. ²⁸He looked down toward Sodom and Gomorrah, toward all the land of the plain, and he saw dense smoke rising from the land, like smoke from a furnace. Ge 18:22; Rev 18:9

²⁹So when God destroyed the cities of the plain, he remembered Abraham, and he brought Lot out of the catastrophe that overthrew the cities where Lot had lived. 2Pe 2:7

Lot and His Daughters

³⁰Lot and his two daughters left Zoar and settled in the mountains, for he was afraid to stay in Zoar. He and his two daughters lived in a cave. ³¹One day the older daughter said to the younger, "Our father is old, and there is no man around here to give us children — as is the custom all over the earth. ³²Let's get our father to drink wine and then sleep with him and preserve our family line through our father." Ge 14:10

³³That night they got their father to drink wine, and the older daughter went in and slept with him. He was not aware of it when she lay down or when she got up.

³⁴The next day the older daughter said to the younger, "Last night I slept with my father. Let's get him to drink wine again tonight, and you go in and sleep with him so we can preserve our family line through our father." ³⁵So they got their father to drink wine that night also, and the younger daughter went in and slept with him. Again he was not aware of it when she lay down or when she got up.

³⁶So both of Lot's daughters became pregnant by their father. ³⁷The older daughter had a son, and she named him Moab*a*; he is the father of the Moabites of today. ³⁸The younger daughter also had a son, and she named him Ben-Ammi*b*; he is the father of the Ammonites*c* of today. Dt 2:9,19

Abraham and Abimelek

20:1-18Ref — Ge 12:10-20; 26:1-11

20 Now Abraham moved on from there into the region of the Negev and lived between Kadesh and Shur. For a while he stayed in Gerar, ²and there Abraham said of his wife Sarah, "She is my sister." Then Abimelek king of Gerar sent for Sarah and took her. ver 12; Ge 12:13; 26:7

---

a 37 Moab sounds like the Hebrew for *from father*.   *b 38* Ben-Ammi means *son of my father's people.*   *c 38* Hebrew *Bene-Ammon*

³But God came to Abimelek in a dream one night and said to him, "You are as good as dead because of the woman you have taken; she is a married woman." Ge 26:11

⁴Now Abimelek had not gone near her, so he said, "Lord, will you destroy an innocent nation? ⁵Did he not say to me, 'She is my sister,' and didn't she also say, 'He is my brother'? I have done this with a clear conscience and clean hands."

⁶Then God said to him in the dream, "Yes, I know you did this with a clear conscience, and so I have kept you from sinning against me. That is why I did not let you touch her. ⁷Now return the man's wife, for he is a prophet, and he will pray for you and you will live. But if you do not return her, you may be sure that you and all who belong to you will die." 1Sa 7:5; 25:26,34; Job 42:8

⁸Early the next morning Abimelek summoned all his officials, and when he told them all that had happened, they were very much afraid. ⁹Then Abimelek called Abraham in and said, "What have you done to us? How have I wronged you that you have brought such great guilt upon me and my kingdom? You have done things to me that should never be done." ¹⁰And Abimelek asked Abraham, "What was your reason for doing this?" Ge 12:18

¹¹Abraham replied, "I said to myself, 'There is surely no fear of God in this place, and they will kill me because of my wife.' ¹²Besides, she really is my sister, the daughter of my father though not of my mother; and she became my wife. ¹³And when God had me wander from my father's household, I said to her, 'This is how you can show your love to me: Everywhere we go, say of me, "He is my brother."'" Ps 36:1; Ge 12:12; 26:7

¹⁴Then Abimelek brought sheep and cattle and male and female slaves and gave them to Abraham, and he returned Sarah his wife to him. ¹⁵And Abimelek said, "My land is before you; live wherever you like."

¹⁶To Sarah he said, "I am giving your brother a thousand shekels*ᵃ* of silver. This is to cover the offense against you before all who are with you; you are completely vindicated." Ge 12:16; 13:9

¹⁷Then Abraham prayed to God, and God healed Abimelek, his wife and his female slaves so they could have children again, ¹⁸for the LORD had kept all the women in Abimelek's household from conceiving because of Abraham's wife Sarah. Ge 12:10-20; 26:1-11

The Birth of Isaac

21 Now the LORD was gracious to Sarah as he had said, and the LORD did for Sarah what he had promised. ²Sarah

---

ᵃ 16 That is, about 25 pounds or about 12 kilograms

became pregnant and bore a son to Abraham in his old age, at the very time God had promised him. ³Abraham gave the name Isaac[a] to the son Sarah bore him. ⁴When his son Isaac was eight days old, Abraham circumcised him, as God commanded him. ⁵Abraham was a hundred years old when his son Isaac was born to him. Ge 17:10,12,19; Gal 4:22

⁶Sarah said, "God has brought me laughter, and everyone who hears about this will laugh with me." ⁷And she added, "Who would have said to Abraham that Sarah would nurse children? Yet I have borne him a son in his old age." Ge 17:17; Isa 54:1

Hagar and Ishmael Sent Away

⁸The child grew and was weaned, and on the day Isaac was weaned Abraham held a great feast. ⁹But Sarah saw that the son whom Hagar the Egyptian had borne to Abraham was mocking, ¹⁰and she said to Abraham, "Get rid of that slave woman and her son, for that woman's son will never share in the inheritance with my son Isaac." Gal 4:30; Ge 16:15

¹¹The matter distressed Abraham greatly because it concerned his son. ¹²But God said to him, "Do not be so distressed about the boy and your slave woman. Listen to whatever Sarah tells you, because it is through Isaac that your offspring[b] will be reckoned. ¹³I will make the son of the slave into a nation also, because he is your offspring." Ro 9:7; Heb 11:18; Ge 17:18

¹⁴Early the next morning Abraham took some food and a skin of water and gave them to Hagar. He set them on her shoulders and then sent her off with the boy. She went on her way and wandered in the Desert of Beersheba. ver 31,32

¹⁵When the water in the skin was gone, she put the boy under one of the bushes. ¹⁶Then she went off and sat down about a bowshot away, for she thought, "I cannot watch the boy die." And as she sat there, she[c] began to sob.

¹⁷God heard the boy crying, and the angel of God called to Hagar from heaven and said to her, "What is the matter, Hagar? Do not be afraid; God has heard the boy crying as he lies there. ¹⁸Lift the boy up and take him by the hand, for I will make him into a great nation." Ge 17:20; Ex 3:7

¹⁹Then God opened her eyes and she saw a well of water. So she went and filled the skin with water and gave the boy a drink. Nu 22:31

²⁰God was with the boy as he grew up. He lived in the desert and became an archer. ²¹While he was living in the Desert of Paran, his mother got a wife for him from Egypt. Ge 28:15; Lk 1:66; Ge 24:4,38

---

[a] 3 *Isaac* means *he laughs.*   [b] 12 Or *seed*   [c] 16 Hebrew; Septuagint *the child*

The Treaty at Beersheba

22At that time Abimelek and Phicol the commander of his forces said to Abraham, "God is with you in everything you do. 23Now swear to me here before God that you will not deal falsely with me or my children or my descendants. Show to me and the country where you now reside as a foreigner the same kindness I have shown to you." Ge 26:28; 39:2,3

24Abraham said, "I swear it."

25Then Abraham complained to Abimelek about a well of water that Abimelek's servants had seized. 26But Abimelek said, "I don't know who has done this. You did not tell me, and I heard about it only today."Ge 26:15,18,20-22

27So Abraham brought sheep and cattle and gave them to Abimelek, and the two men made a treaty. 28Abraham set apart seven ewe lambs from the flock, 29and Abimelek asked Abraham, "What is the meaning of these seven ewe lambs you have set apart by themselves?" Ge 26:28,31

30He replied, "Accept these seven lambs from my hand as a witness that I dug this well."Ge 31:44,47

31So that place was called Beersheba,a because the two men swore an oath there. Ge 26:33

32After the treaty had been made at Beersheba, Abimelek and Phicol the commander of his forces returned to the land of the Philistines. 33Abraham planted a tamarisk tree in Beersheba, and there he called on the name of the LORD, the Eternal God. 34And Abraham stayed in the land of the Philistines for a long time. Ge 4:26; Dt 33:27

Abraham Tested

22 Some time later God tested Abraham. He said to him, "Abraham!" Dt 8:2,16; Heb 11:17

"Here I am," he replied.

2Then God said, "Take your son, your only son, whom you love— Isaac—and go to the region of Moriah. Sacrifice him there as a burnt offering on a mountain I will show you."Jn 3:16; Heb 11:17; 1Jn 4:9

3Early the next morning Abraham got up and loaded his donkey. He took with him two of his servants and his son Isaac. When he had cut enough wood for the burnt offering, he set out for the place God had told him about. 4On the third day Abraham looked up and saw the place in the distance. 5He said to his servants, "Stay here with the donkey while I and the boy go over there. We will worship and then we will come back to you."

6Abraham took the wood for the burnt offering and placed it on his son Isaac, and he himself carried the fire and the knife. As the two of them went on together,

---

a 31 Beersheba can mean *well of seven* and *well of the oath*.

⁷Isaac spoke up and said to his father Abraham, "Father?" Jn 19:17 "Yes, my son?" Abraham replied.

"The fire and wood are here," Isaac said, "but where is the lamb for the burnt offering?" Lev 1:10 ⁸Abraham answered, "God himself will provide the lamb for the burnt offering, my son." And the two of them went on together.

⁹When they reached the place God had told him about, Abraham built an altar there and arranged the wood on it. He bound his son Isaac and laid him on the altar, on top of the wood. ¹⁰Then he reached out his hand and took the knife to slay his son. ¹¹But the angel of the LORD called out to him from heaven, "Abraham! Abraham!" Heb 11:17-19; Jas 2:21

"Here I am," he replied.

¹²"Do not lay a hand on the boy," he said. "Do not do anything to him. Now I know that you fear God, because you have not withheld from me your son, your only son." 1Sa 15:22; Jn 3:16; 1Jn 4:9 ¹³Abraham looked up and there in a thicket he saw a ramᵃ caught by its horns. He went over and took the ram and sacrificed it as a burnt offering instead of his son. ¹⁴So Abraham called that place The LORD Will Provide. And to this day it is said, "On the mountain of the LORD it will be provided." Ro 8:32

¹⁵The angel of the LORD called to Abraham from heaven a second time ¹⁶and said, "I swear by myself, declares the LORD, that because you have done this and have not withheld your son, your only son, ¹⁷I will surely bless you and make your descendants as numerous as the stars in the sky and as the sand on the seashore. Your descendants will take possession of the cities of their enemies, ¹⁸and through your offspringᵇ all nations on earth will be blessed,ᶜ because you have obeyed me." Ac 3:25; Heb 6:14

¹⁹Then Abraham returned to his servants, and they set off together for Beersheba. And Abraham stayed in Beersheba.

Nahor's Sons

²⁰Some time later Abraham was told, "Milkah is also a mother; she has borne sons to your brother Nahor: ²¹Uz the firstborn, Buz his brother, Kemuel (the father of Aram), ²²Kesed, Hazo, Pildash, Jidlaph and Bethuel." ²³Bethuel became the father of Rebekah. Milkah bore these eight sons to Abraham's brother Nahor. ²⁴His concubine, whose name was Reumah, also had sons: Tebah, Gaham, Tahash and Maakah. Ge 24:15

ᵃ 13 Many manuscripts of the Masoretic Text, Samaritan Pentateuch, Septuagint and Syriac; most manuscripts of the Masoretic Text *a ram behind him*   ᵇ 18 Or *seed*   ᶜ 18 Or *and all nations on earth will use the name of your offspring in blessings* (see 48:20)

The Death of Sarah

23 Sarah lived to be a hundred and twenty-seven years old. ²She died at Kiriath Arba (that is, Hebron) in the land of Canaan, and Abraham went to mourn for Sarah and to weep over her. Ge 13:18; Jos 14:15

³Then Abraham rose from beside his dead wife and spoke to the Hittites.ᵃ He said, ⁴"I am a foreigner and stranger among you. Sell me some property for a burial site here so I can bury my dead." Ps 105:12; Heb 11:9,13

⁵The Hittites replied to Abraham, ⁶"Sir, listen to us. You are a mighty prince among us. Bury your dead in the choicest of our tombs. None of us will refuse you his tomb for burying your dead." Ge 14:14-16; 24:35

⁷Then Abraham rose and bowed down before the people of the land, the Hittites. ⁸He said to them, "If you are willing to let me bury my dead, then listen to me and intercede with Ephron son of Zohar on my behalf ⁹so he will sell me the cave of Machpelah, which belongs to him and is at the end of his field. Ask him to sell it to me for the full price as a burial site among you." Ge 25:9

¹⁰Ephron the Hittite was sitting among his people and he replied to Abraham in the hearing of all the Hittites who had come to the gate of his city. ¹¹"No, my lord," he said. "Listen to me; I giveᵇ you the field, and I giveᵇ you the cave that is in it. I giveᵇ it to you in the presence of my people. Bury your dead." Ru 4:4

¹²Again Abraham bowed down before the people of the land ¹³and he said to Ephron in their hearing, "Listen to me, if you will. I will pay the price of the field. Accept it from me so I can bury my dead there."

¹⁴Ephron answered Abraham, ¹⁵"Listen to me, my lord; the land is worth four hundred shekelsᶜ of silver, but what is that between you and me? Bury your dead." Eze 45:12

¹⁶Abraham agreed to Ephron's terms and weighed out for him the price he had named in the hearing of the Hittites: four hundred shekels of silver, according to the weight current among the merchants. Jer 32:9

¹⁷So Ephron's field in Machpelah near Mamre—both the field and the cave in it, and all the trees within the borders of the field—was deeded ¹⁸to Abraham as his property in the presence of all the Hittites who had come to the gate of the city. ¹⁹Afterward Abraham buried his wife Sarah in the cave in the field of Machpelah near Mamre (which is at Hebron) in the land of Canaan. ²⁰So the field and the cave in it were deeded to

---

ᵃ 3 Or *the descendants of Heth*; also in verses 5, 7, 10, 16, 18 and 20   ᵇ 11 Or *sell*
ᶜ 15 That is, about 10 pounds or about 4.6 kilograms

Abraham by the Hittites as a burial site. Ge 25:9; 50:13

Isaac and Rebekah

24 Abraham was now very old, and the LORD had blessed him in every way. ²He said to the senior servant in his household, the one in charge of all that he had, "Put your hand under my thigh. ³I want you to swear by the LORD, the God of heaven and the God of earth, that you will not get a wife for my son from the daughters of the Canaanites, among whom I am living, ⁴but will go to my country and my own relatives and get a wife for my son Isaac." Ge 12:1; 28:2

⁵The servant asked him, "What if the woman is unwilling to come back with me to this land? Shall I then take your son back to the country you came from?" Heb 11:15

⁶"Make sure that you do not take my son back there," Abraham said. ⁷"The LORD, the God of heaven, who brought me out of my father's household and my native land and who spoke to me and promised me on oath, saying, 'To your offspring[a] I will give this land' — he will send his angel before you so that you can get a wife for my son from there. ⁸If the woman is unwilling to come back with you, then you will be released from this oath of mine. Only do not take my son back there." ⁹So the servant put his hand under the thigh of his master Abraham and swore an oath to him concerning this matter. Ge 12:7; 13:15; Gal 3:16

¹⁰Then the servant left, taking with him ten of his master's camels loaded with all kinds of good things from his master. He set out for Aram Naharaim[b] and made his way to the town of Nahor. ¹¹He had the camels kneel down near the well outside the town; it was toward evening, the time the women go out to draw water. 1Sa 9:11

¹²Then he prayed, "LORD, God of my master Abraham, make me successful today, and show kindness to my master Abraham. ¹³See, I am standing beside this spring, and the daughters of the townspeople are coming out to draw water. ¹⁴May it be that when I say to a young woman, 'Please let down your jar that I may have a drink,' and she says, 'Drink, and I'll water your camels too' — let her be the one you have chosen for your servant Isaac. By this I will know that you have shown kindness to my master." Ge 26:24; Jdg 6:17,37

¹⁵Before he had finished praying, Rebekah came out with her jar on her shoulder. She was the daughter of Bethuel son of Milkah, who was the wife of Abraham's brother Nahor. ¹⁶The woman was very beautiful, a

---

ᵃ 7 Or *seed*   ᵇ 10 That is, Northwest Mesopotamia

virgin; no man had ever slept with her. She went down to the spring, filled her jar and came up again. Ge 22:23; 26:7

¹⁷The servant hurried to meet her and said, "Please give me a little water from your jar."

¹⁸"Drink, my lord," she said, and quickly lowered the jar to her hands and gave him a drink.

¹⁹After she had given him a drink, she said, "I'll draw water for your camels too, until they have had enough to drink." ²⁰So she quickly emptied her jar into the trough, ran back to the well to draw more water, and drew enough for all his camels. ²¹Without saying a word, the man watched her closely to learn whether or not the LORD had made his journey successful. Ge 12:14

²²When the camels had finished drinking, the man took out a gold nose ring weighing a beka[a] and two gold bracelets weighing ten shekels.[b] ²³Then he asked, "Whose daughter are you? Please tell me, is there room in your father's house for us to spend the night?" Ge 47

²⁴She answered him, "I am the daughter of Bethuel, the son that Milkah bore to Nahor." ²⁵And she added, "We have plenty of straw and fodder, as well as room for you to spend the night." Ge 11:29

²⁶Then the man bowed down and worshiped the LORD, ²⁷saying, "Praise be to the LORD, the God of my master Abraham, who has not abandoned his kindness and faithfulness to my master. As for me, the LORD has led me on the journey to the house of my master's relatives." ver 48,52; Ge 32:10

²⁸The young woman ran and told her mother's household about these things. ²⁹Now Rebekah had a brother named Laban, and he hurried out to the man at the spring. ³⁰As soon as he had seen the nose ring, and the bracelets on his sister's arms, and had heard Rebekah tell what the man said to her, he went out to the man and found him standing by the camels near the spring. ³¹"Come, you who are blessed by the LORD," he said. "Why are you standing out here? I have prepared the house and a place for the camels." Ge 26:29; 29:5,12,13

³²So the man went to the house, and the camels were unloaded. Straw and fodder were brought for the camels, and water for him and his men to wash their feet. ³³Then food was set before him, but he said, "I will not eat until I have told you what I have to say." Ge 43:24

"Then tell us," Laban said.

³⁴So he said, "I am Abraham's servant. ³⁵The LORD has blessed my master abundantly, and he has become wealthy. He has given him sheep and cattle, silver

---

[a] 22 That is, about 1/5 ounce or about 5.7 grams   [b] 22 That is, about 4 ounces or about 115 grams

and gold, male and female servants, and camels and donkeys. ³⁶My master's wife Sarah has borne him a son in her old age, and he has given him everything he owns. ³⁷And my master made me swear an oath, and said, 'You must not get a wife for my son from the daughters of the Canaanites, in whose land I live, ³⁸but go to my father's family and to my own clan, and get a wife for my son.'   ver 1; Ge 25:5

³⁹"Then I asked my master, 'What if the woman will not come back with me?'   ver 5

⁴⁰"He replied, 'The LORD, before whom I have walked faithfully, will send his angel with you and make your journey a success, so that you can get a wife for my son from my own clan and from my father's family. ⁴¹You will be released from my oath if, when you go to my clan, they refuse to give her to you—then you will be released from my oath.'   ver 7-8

⁴²"When I came to the spring today, I said, 'LORD, God of my master Abraham, if you will, please grant success to the journey on which I have come. ⁴³See, I am standing beside this spring. If a young woman comes out to draw water and I say to her, "Please let me drink a little water from your jar," ⁴⁴and if she says to me, "Drink, and I'll draw water for your camels too," let her be the one the LORD has chosen for my master's son.'   ver 12-14

⁴⁵"Before I finished praying in my heart, Rebekah came out, with her jar on her shoulder. She went down to the spring and drew water, and I said to her, 'Please give me a drink.'   1Sa 1:13

⁴⁶"She quickly lowered her jar from her shoulder and said, 'Drink, and I'll water your camels too.' So I drank, and she watered the camels also.   ver 18-19

⁴⁷"I asked her, 'Whose daughter are you?'   ver 23

"She said, 'The daughter of Bethuel son of Nahor, whom Milkah bore to him.'   ver 24

"Then I put the ring in her nose and the bracelets on her arms, ⁴⁸and I bowed down and worshiped the LORD. I praised the LORD, the God of my master Abraham, who had led me on the right road to get the granddaughter of my master's brother for his son. ⁴⁹Now if you will show kindness and faithfulness to my master, tell me; and if not, tell me, so I may know which way to turn."   Ge 47:29; Jos 2:14; Eze 16:11-12

⁵⁰Laban and Bethuel answered, "This is from the LORD; we can say nothing to you one way or the other. ⁵¹Here is Rebekah; take her and go, and let her become the wife of your master's son, as the LORD has directed."   Ps 118:23; Ge 31:7,24,29,42

⁵²When Abraham's servant heard what they said, he bowed down to the ground before the LORD. ⁵³Then the servant

brought out gold and silver jewelry and articles of clothing and gave them to Rebekah; he also gave costly gifts to her brother and to her mother. ⁵⁴ Then he and the men who were with him ate and drank and spent the night there. ver 26

When they got up the next morning, he said, "Send me on my way to my master." ver 56,59

⁵⁵ But her brother and her mother replied, "Let the young woman remain with us ten days or so; then you^a may go." Jdg 19:4

⁵⁶ But he said to them, "Do not detain me, now that the LORD has granted success to my journey. Send me on my way so I may go to my master." ver 12

⁵⁷ Then they said, "Let's call the young woman and ask her about it." ⁵⁸ So they called Rebekah and asked her, "Will you go with this man?" Jdg 19:3

"I will go," she said. Ru 1:16

⁵⁹ So they sent their sister Rebekah on her way, along with her nurse and Abraham's servant and his men. ⁶⁰ And they blessed Rebekah and said to her, Ge 35:8

"Our sister, may you increase
    to thousands upon
        thousands; Ge 17:16
may your offspring possess
    the cities of their
        enemies." Ge 22:17

⁶¹ Then Rebekah and her attendants got ready and mounted the camels and went back with the man. So the servant took Rebekah and left.

⁶² Now Isaac had come from Beer Lahai Roi, for he was living in the Negev. ⁶³ He went out to the field one evening to meditate,^{b} and as he looked up, he saw camels approaching. ⁶⁴ Rebekah also looked up and saw Isaac. She got down from her camel ⁶⁵ and asked the servant, "Who is that man in the field coming to meet us?" Ps 1:2; Ge 16:14; 25:11

"He is my master," the servant answered. So she took her veil and covered herself.

⁶⁶ Then the servant told Isaac all he had done. ⁶⁷ Isaac brought her into the tent of his mother Sarah, and he married Rebekah. So she became his wife, and he loved her; and Isaac was comforted after his mother's death. Ge 25:20; 29:18,20

The Death of Abraham

25:1-4pp — 1Ch 1:32-33

25 Abraham had taken another wife, whose name was Keturah. ² She bore him Zimran, Jokshan, Medan, Midian, Ishbak and Shuah. ³ Jokshan was the father of Sheba and Dedan; the descendants of Dedan were the Ashurites, the Letushites and the Leummites. ⁴ The sons of Midian were Ephah, Epher, Hanok, Abida and

---

^{a} 55 Or *she* ^{b} 63 The meaning of the Hebrew for this word is uncertain.

Eldaah. All these were descendants of Keturah. 1Ch 1:32-33

[5] Abraham left everything he owned to Isaac. [6] But while he was still living, he gave gifts to the sons of his concubines and sent them away from his son Isaac to the land of the east. Ge 24:36; 21:10

[7] Abraham lived a hundred and seventy-five years. [8] Then Abraham breathed his last and died at a good old age, an old man and full of years; and he was gathered to his people. [9] His sons Isaac and Ishmael buried him in the cave of Machpelah near Mamre, in the field of Ephron son of Zohar the Hittite, [10] the field Abraham had bought from the Hittites.[a] There Abraham was buried with his wife Sarah. [11] After Abraham's death, God blessed his son Isaac, who then lived near Beer Lahai Roi. Ge 15:15; 23:16; 49:29,33

Ishmael's Sons
25:12-16pp — 1Ch 1:29-31

[12] This is the account of the family line of Abraham's son Ishmael, whom Sarah's slave, Hagar the Egyptian, bore to Abraham. Ge 16:15

[13] These are the names of the sons of Ishmael, listed in the order of their birth: Nebaioth the firstborn of Ishmael, Kedar, Adbeel, Mibsam, [14] Mishma, Dumah, Massa, [15] Hadad, Tema, Jetur, Naphish and Kedemah. [16] These were the sons of Ishmael, and these are the names of the twelve tribal rulers according to their settlements and camps. [17] Ishmael lived a hundred and thirty-seven years. He breathed his last and died, and he was gathered to his people. [18] His descendants settled in the area from Havilah to Shur, near the eastern border of Egypt, as you go toward Ashur. And they lived in hostility toward[b] all the tribes related to them. 1Ch 1:29-31; Ge 16:12

Jacob and Esau

[19] This is the account of the family line of Abraham's son Isaac.

Abraham became the father of Isaac, [20] and Isaac was forty years old when he married Rebekah daughter of Bethuel the Aramean from Paddan Aram[c] and sister of Laban the Aramean. Ge 24:29

[21] Isaac prayed to the LORD on behalf of his wife, because she was childless. The LORD answered his prayer, and his wife Rebekah became pregnant. [22] The babies jostled each other within her, and she said, "Why is this happening to me?" So she went to inquire of the LORD. 1Ch 5:20; 1Sa 9:9

[23] The LORD said to her,

"Two nations are in your
    womb, Ge 17:4

---

[a] 10 Or the descendants of Heth   [b] 18 Or lived to the east of   [c] 20 That is, Northwest Mesopotamia

and two peoples from
 within you will be
 separated;
one people will be stronger
 than the other,
and the older will serve the
 younger." Ge 27:29,40

²⁴When the time came for her to give birth, there were twin boys in her womb. ²⁵The first to come out was red, and his whole body was like a hairy garment; so they named him Esau.ᵃ ²⁶After this, his brother came out, with his hand grasping Esau's heel; so he was named Jacob.ᵇ Isaac was sixty years old when Rebekah gave birth to them. Hos 12:3; Ge 27:11,36

²⁷The boys grew up, and Esau became a skillful hunter, a man of the open country, while Jacob was content to stay at home among the tents. ²⁸Isaac, who had a taste for wild game, loved Esau, but Rebekah loved Jacob. Ge 27:3,5

²⁹Once when Jacob was cooking some stew, Esau came in from the open country, famished. ³⁰He said to Jacob, "Quick, let me have some of that red stew! I'm famished!" (That is why he was also called Edom.ᶜ) Ge 32:3

³¹Jacob replied, "First sell me your birthright." Dt 21:16-17

³²"Look, I am about to die," Esau said. "What good is the birthright to me?"

³³But Jacob said, "Swear to me first." So he swore an oath to him, selling his birthright to Jacob. Heb 12:16

³⁴Then Jacob gave Esau some bread and some lentil stew. He ate and drank, and then got up and left.

So Esau despised his birthright.

Isaac and Abimelek

26:1-11Ref — Ge 12:10-20; 20:1-18

26 Now there was a famine in the land—besides the previous famine in Abraham's time—and Isaac went to Abimelek king of the Philistines in Gerar. ²The Lᴏʀᴅ appeared to Isaac and said, "Do not go down to Egypt; live in the land where I tell you to live. ³Stay in this land for a while, and I will be with you and will bless you. For to you and your descendants I will give all these lands and will confirm the oath I swore to your father Abraham. ⁴I will make your descendants as numerous as the stars in the sky and will give them all these lands, and through your offspringᵈ all nations on earth will be blessed,ᵉ ⁵because Abraham obeyed me and did everything I required of him, keeping my commands, my decrees and my instructions." ⁶So Isaac stayed in Gerar. Ge 12:1,7,10

ᵃ 25 Esau may mean hairy.   ᵇ 26 Jacob means he grasps the heel, a Hebrew idiom for he deceives.   ᶜ 30 Edom means red.   ᵈ 4 Or seed   ᵉ 4 Or and all nations on earth will use the name of your offspring in blessings (see 48:20)

⁷When the men of that place asked him about his wife, he said, "She is my sister," because he was afraid to say, "She is my wife." He thought, "The men of this place might kill me on account of Rebekah, because she is beautiful." Ge 12:13; 20:2,12

⁸When Isaac had been there a long time, Abimelek king of the Philistines looked down from a window and saw Isaac caressing his wife Rebekah. ⁹So Abimelek summoned Isaac and said, "She is really your wife! Why did you say, 'She is my sister'?"

Isaac answered him, "Because I thought I might lose my life on account of her."

¹⁰Then Abimelek said, "What is this you have done to us? One of the men might well have slept with your wife, and you would have brought guilt upon us."

¹¹So Abimelek gave orders to all the people: "Anyone who harms this man or his wife shall surely be put to death." Ge 12:10-20; 20:1-18

¹²Isaac planted crops in that land and the same year reaped a hundredfold, because the LORD blessed him. ¹³The man became rich, and his wealth continued to grow until he became very wealthy. ¹⁴He had so many flocks and herds and servants that the Philistines envied him. ¹⁵So all the wells that his father's servants had dug in the time of his father Abraham, the Philis-tines stopped up, filling them with earth. ver 3; Ge 21:30

¹⁶Then Abimelek said to Isaac, "Move away from us; you have become too powerful for us."

¹⁷So Isaac moved away from there and encamped in the Valley of Gerar, where he settled. ¹⁸Isaac reopened the wells that had been dug in the time of his father Abraham, which the Philistines had stopped up after Abraham died, and he gave them the same names his father had given them. Ge 21:30

¹⁹Isaac's servants dug in the valley and discovered a well of fresh water there. ²⁰But the herders of Gerar quarreled with those of Isaac and said, "The water is ours!" So he named the well Esek,ᵃ because they disputed with him. ²¹Then they dug another well, but they quarreled over that one also; so he named it Sitnah.ᵇ ²²He moved on from there and dug another well, and no one quarreled over it. He named it Rehoboth,ᶜ saying, "Now the LORD has given us room and we will flourish in the land." Ge 17:6

²³From there he went up to Beersheba. ²⁴That night the LORD appeared to him and said, "I am the God of your father Abraham. Do not be afraid, for I am with you; I will bless you and will increase the number of your descendants for the sake of my servant Abraham." Ge 17:7; 24:12

ᵃ 20 Esek means dispute.   ᵇ 21 Sitnah means opposition.   ᶜ 22 Rehoboth means room.

25 Isaac built an altar there and called on the name of the LORD. There he pitched his tent, and there his servants dug a well. Ge 12:7

26 Meanwhile, Abimelek had come to him from Gerar, with Ahuzzath his personal adviser and Phicol the commander of his forces. 27 Isaac asked them, "Why have you come to me, since you were hostile to me and sent me away?" Ge 21:22

28 They answered, "We saw clearly that the LORD was with you; so we said, 'There ought to be a sworn agreement between us' — between us and you. Let us make a treaty with you 29 that you will do us no harm, just as we did not harm you but always treated you well and sent you away peacefully. And now you are blessed by the LORD." Ge 21:22; 24:31

30 Isaac then made a feast for them, and they ate and drank. 31 Early the next morning the men swore an oath to each other. Then Isaac sent them on their way, and they went away peacefully. Ge 21:31

32 That day Isaac's servants came and told him about the well they had dug. They said, "We've found water!" 33 He called it Shibah,a and to this day the name of the town has been Beersheba.b Ge 21:14

Jacob Takes Esau's Blessing

34 When Esau was forty years old, he married Judith daughter of Beeri the Hittite, and also Basemath daughter of Elon the Hittite. 35 They were a source of grief to Isaac and Rebekah. Ge 27:46; 36:2

27 When Isaac was old and his eyes were so weak that he could no longer see, he called for Esau his older son and said to him, "My son." Ge 25:25; 48:10

"Here I am," he answered.

2 Isaac said, "I am now an old man and don't know the day of my death. 3 Now then, get your equipment — your quiver and bow — and go out to the open country to hunt some wild game for me. 4 Prepare me the kind of tasty food I like and bring it to me to eat, so that I may give you my blessing before I die." Ge 49:28; Dt 33:1; Heb 11:20

5 Now Rebekah was listening as Isaac spoke to his son Esau. When Esau left for the open country to hunt game and bring it back, 6 Rebekah said to her son Jacob, "Look, I overheard your father say to your brother Esau, 7 'Bring me some game and prepare me some tasty food to eat, so that I may give you my blessing in the presence of the LORD before I die.' 8 Now, my son, listen carefully and do what I tell you: 9 Go out to the flock and bring me two choice young goats, so I can prepare some tasty food for

---

a 33 Shibah can mean oath or seven.   b 33 Beersheba can mean well of the oath and well of seven.

your father, just the way he likes it. ¹⁰Then take it to your father to eat, so that he may give you his blessing before he dies." ver 13,43

¹¹Jacob said to Rebekah his mother, "But my brother Esau is a hairy man while I have smooth skin. ¹²What if my father touches me? I would appear to be tricking him and would bring down a curse on myself rather than a blessing." ver 22; Ge 25:25

¹³His mother said to him, "My son, let the curse fall on me. Just do what I say; go and get them for me." Mt 27:25

¹⁴So he went and got them and brought them to his mother, and she prepared some tasty food, just the way his father liked it. ¹⁵Then Rebekah took the best clothes of Esau her older son, which she had in the house, and put them on her younger son Jacob. ¹⁶She also covered his hands and the smooth part of his neck with the goatskins. ¹⁷Then she handed to her son Jacob the tasty food and the bread she had made. ver 27

¹⁸He went to his father and said, "My father."

"Yes, my son," he answered. "Who is it?"

¹⁹Jacob said to his father, "I am Esau your firstborn. I have done as you told me. Please sit up and eat some of my game, so that you may give me your blessing." ver 4

²⁰Isaac asked his son, "How did you find it so quickly, my son?"

"The LORD your God gave me success," he replied. Ge 24:12

²¹Then Isaac said to Jacob, "Come near so I can touch you, my son, to know whether you really are my son Esau or not." ver 12

²²Jacob went close to his father Isaac, who touched him and said, "The voice is the voice of Jacob, but the hands are the hands of Esau." ²³He did not recognize him, for his hands were hairy like those of his brother Esau; so he proceeded to bless him. ²⁴"Are you really my son Esau?" he asked. ver 16; Ge 45:4

"I am," he replied.

²⁵Then he said, "My son, bring me some of your game to eat, so that I may give you my blessing." ver 4

Jacob brought it to him and he ate; and he brought some wine and he drank. ²⁶Then his father Isaac said to him, "Come here, my son, and kiss me."

²⁷So he went to him and kissed him. When Isaac caught the smell of his clothes, he blessed him and said, Heb 11:20; SS 4:11

"Ah, the smell of my son
    is like the smell of a field
    that the LORD has blessed.
²⁸May God give you heaven's
        dew Dt 33:13
    and earth's richness —
    an abundance of grain and
        new wine. Dt 33:28
²⁹May nations serve you Isa 49:7,23
    and peoples bow down to
        you. Ge 9:25; 25:23

Be lord over your brothers,
and may the sons of your
mother bow down to
you.
May those who curse you be
cursed
and those who bless you be
blessed." Ge 12:3

³⁰ After Isaac finished blessing him, and Jacob had scarcely left his father's presence, his brother Esau came in from hunting. ³¹ He too prepared some tasty food and brought it to his father. Then he said to him, "My father, please sit up and eat some of my game, so that you may give me your blessing." ver 4

³² His father Isaac asked him, "Who are you?"

"I am your son," he answered, "your firstborn, Esau."

³³ Isaac trembled violently and said, "Who was it, then, that hunted game and brought it to me? I ate it just before you came and I blessed him — and indeed he will be blessed!" Ge 28:3,4; Ro 11:29

³⁴ When Esau heard his father's words, he burst out with a loud and bitter cry and said to his father, "Bless me — me too, my father!" Heb 12:17

³⁵ But he said, "Your brother came deceitfully and took your blessing." Jer 9:4

³⁶ Esau said, "Isn't he rightly named Jacobᵃ? This is the second time he has taken advantage of me: He took my birthright, and now he's taken my blessing!" Then he asked, "Haven't you reserved any blessing for me?" Ge 25:26,33

³⁷ Isaac answered Esau, "I have made him lord over you and have made all his relatives his servants, and I have sustained him with grain and new wine. So what can I possibly do for you, my son?" ver 28

³⁸ Esau said to his father, "Do you have only one blessing, my father? Bless me too, my father!" Then Esau wept aloud. Heb 12:17

³⁹ His father Isaac answered him,

"Your dwelling will be
away from the earth's
richness,
away from the dew of
heaven above. ver 28
⁴⁰ You will live by the sword
and you will serve your
brother. Ge 25:23
But when you grow restless,
you will throw his yoke
from off your neck." 2Ki 8:20-22

⁴¹ Esau held a grudge against Jacob because of the blessing his father had given him. He said to himself, "The days of mourning for my father are near; then I will kill my brother Jacob." Ge 32:11

⁴² When Rebekah was told what her older son Esau had said, she sent for her younger son Jacob and said to him, "Your brother

ᵃ 36 Jacob means he grasps the heel, a Hebrew idiom for he takes advantage of or he deceives.

Esau is planning to avenge himself by killing you. ⁴³Now then, my son, do what I say: Flee at once to my brother Laban in Harran. ⁴⁴Stay with him for a while until your brother's fury subsides. ⁴⁵When your brother is no longer angry with you and forgets what you did to him, I'll send word for you to come back from there. Why should I lose both of you in one day?" ver 8; Ge 11:31

⁴⁶Then Rebekah said to Isaac, "I'm disgusted with living because of these Hittite women. If Jacob takes a wife from among the women of this land, from Hittite women like these, my life will not be worth living." Ge 26:35

28 So Isaac called for Jacob and blessed him. Then he commanded him: "Do not marry a Canaanite woman. ²Go at once to Paddan Aram,ᵃ to the house of your mother's father Bethuel. Take a wife for yourself there, from among the daughters of Laban, your mother's brother. ³May God Almightyᵇ bless you and make you fruitful and increase your numbers until you become a community of peoples. ⁴May he give you and your descendants the blessing given to Abraham, so that you may take possession of the land where you now reside as a foreigner, the land God gave to Abraham." ⁵Then Isaac sent Jacob on his way, and he went to Paddan Aram, to Laban son of Bethuel the Aramean, the brother of Rebekah, who was the mother of Jacob and Esau. Ge 12:2-3; 17:8; 24:3

⁶Now Esau learned that Isaac had blessed Jacob and had sent him to Paddan Aram to take a wife from there, and that when he blessed him he commanded him, "Do not marry a Canaanite woman," ⁷and that Jacob had obeyed his father and mother and had gone to Paddan Aram. ⁸Esau then realized how displeasing the Canaanite women were to his father Isaac; ⁹so he went to Ishmael and married Mahalath, the sister of Nebaioth and daughter of Ishmael son of Abraham, in addition to the wives he already had. Ge 26:34-35

Jacob's Dream at Bethel

¹⁰Jacob left Beersheba and set out for Harran. ¹¹When he reached a certain place, he stopped for the night because the sun had set. Taking one of the stones there, he put it under his head and lay down to sleep. ¹²He had a dream in which he saw a stairway resting on the earth, with its top reaching to heaven, and the angels of God were ascending and descending on it. ¹³There above itᶜ stood the LORD, and he said: "I am the LORD, the God of your father Abraham and the God of Isaac.

ᵃ 2 That is, Northwest Mesopotamia; also in verses 5, 6 and 7   ᵇ 3 Hebrew *El-Shaddai*
ᶜ 13 Or *There beside him*

I will give you and your descendants the land on which you are lying. **14**Your descendants will be like the dust of the earth, and you will spread out to the west and to the east, to the north and to the south. All peoples on earth will be blessed through you and your offspring.*ᵃ* **15**I am with you and will watch over you wherever you go, and I will bring you back to this land. I will not leave you until I have done what I have promised you." Jn 1:51; Ge 12:3

16When Jacob awoke from his sleep, he thought, "Surely the LORD is in this place, and I was not aware of it." **17**He was afraid and said, "How awesome is this place! This is none other than the house of God; this is the gate of heaven." Ex 3:5; Jos 5:15

18Early the next morning Jacob took the stone he had placed under his head and set it up as a pillar and poured oil on top of it. **19**He called that place Bethel,*ᵇ* though the city used to be called Luz. Jdg 1:23,26

20Then Jacob made a vow, saying, "If God will be with me and will watch over me on this journey I am taking and will give me food to eat and clothes to wear **21**so that I return safely to my father's household, then the LORD*ᶜ* will be my God **22**and*ᵈ* this stone that I have set up as a pillar will be God's house, and of all that you give me I will give you a tenth." Dt 26:17; Ge 14:20; 31:13

Jacob Arrives in Paddan Aram

29 Then Jacob continued on his journey and came to the land of the eastern peoples. **2**There he saw a well in the open country, with three flocks of sheep lying near it because the flocks were watered from that well. The stone over the mouth of the well was large. **3**When all the flocks were gathered there, the shepherds would roll the stone away from the well's mouth and water the sheep. Then they would return the stone to its place over the mouth of the well. Jdg 6:3,33

4Jacob asked the shepherds, "My brothers, where are you from?"

"We're from Harran," they replied. Ge 28:10

5He said to them, "Do you know Laban, Nahor's grandson?"

"Yes, we know him," they answered. Ge 11:29

6Then Jacob asked them, "Is he well?"

"Yes, he is," they said, "and here comes his daughter Rachel with the sheep."

7"Look," he said, "the sun is still high; it is not time for the flocks to be gathered. Water the

---

ᵃ 14 Or *will use your name and the name of your offspring in blessings* (see 48:20)   *ᵇ 19 Bethel* means *house of God.*   *ᶜ 20,21* Or *Since God . . . father's household, the LORD*   *ᵈ 21,22* Or *household, and the LORD will be my God,* ²²*then* sheep and take them back to pasture." Ex 2:16

⁸"We can't," they replied, "until all the flocks are gathered and the stone has been rolled away from the mouth of the well. Then we will water the sheep." Ge 24:13

⁹While he was still talking with them, Rachel came with her father's sheep, for she was a shepherd. ¹⁰When Jacob saw Rachel daughter of his uncle Laban, and Laban's sheep, he went over and rolled the stone away from the mouth of the well and watered his uncle's sheep. ¹¹Then Jacob kissed Rachel and began to weep aloud. ¹²He had told Rachel that he was a relative of her father and a son of Rebekah. So she ran and told her father. Ge 24:28

¹³As soon as Laban heard the news about Jacob, his sister's son, he hurried to meet him. He embraced him and kissed him and brought him to his home, and there Jacob told him all these things. ¹⁴Then Laban said to him, "You are my own flesh and blood." Ge 24:29; Jdg 9:2

Jacob Marries Leah and Rachel

After Jacob had stayed with him for a whole month, ¹⁵Laban said to him, "Just because you are a relative of mine, should you work for me for nothing? Tell me what your wages should be." Ge 31:7,41

¹⁶Now Laban had two daughters; the name of the older was Leah, and the name of the younger was Rachel. ¹⁷Leah had weak^a eyes, but Rachel had a lovely figure and was beautiful. ¹⁸Jacob was in love with Rachel and said, "I'll work for you seven years in return for your younger daughter Rachel." Hos 12:12

¹⁹Laban said, "It's better that I give her to you than to some other man. Stay here with me." ²⁰So Jacob served seven years to get Rachel, but they seemed like only a few days to him because of his love for her. Ge 31:15; Hos 12:12

²¹Then Jacob said to Laban, "Give me my wife. My time is completed, and I want to make love to her." Jdg 15:1

²²So Laban brought together all the people of the place and gave a feast. ²³But when evening came, he took his daughter Leah and brought her to Jacob, and Jacob made love to her. ²⁴And Laban gave his servant Zilpah to his daughter as her attendant. Jdg 14:10; Jn 2:1-2

²⁵When morning came, there was Leah! So Jacob said to Laban, "What is this you have done to me? I served you for Rachel, didn't I? Why have you deceived me?" Ge 12:18; 27:36

²⁶Laban replied, "It is not our custom here to give the younger daughter in marriage before the older one. ²⁷Finish this daughter's bridal week; then we will give you the younger one also, in

^{a} 17 Or delicate

return for another seven years of work." Jdg 14:12

²⁸ And Jacob did so. He finished the week with Leah, and then Laban gave him his daughter Rachel to be his wife. ²⁹ Laban gave his servant Bilhah to his daughter Rachel as her attendant. ³⁰ Jacob made love to Rachel also, and his love for Rachel was greater than his love for Leah. And he worked for Laban another seven years. Ge 31:41

Jacob's Children

³¹ When the LORD saw that Leah was not loved, he enabled her to conceive, but Rachel remained childless. ³² Leah became pregnant and gave birth to a son. She named him Reuben,ᵃ for she said, "It is because the LORD has seen my misery. Surely my husband will love me now." Dt 21:15-17; Ps 127:3; Ge 16:11

³³ She conceived again, and when she gave birth to a son she said, "Because the LORD heard that I am not loved, he gave me this one too." So she named him Simeon.ᵇ Ge 34:25

³⁴ Again she conceived, and when she gave birth to a son she said, "Now at last my husband will become attached to me, because I have borne him three sons." So he was named Levi.ᶜ Ge 49:5-7

³⁵ She conceived again, and when she gave birth to a son she said, "This time I will praise the LORD." So she named him Judah.ᵈ Then she stopped having children. Ge 49:8; Mt 1:2-3

30 When Rachel saw that she was not bearing Jacob any children, she became jealous of her sister. So she said to Jacob, "Give me children, or I'll die!" Ge 29:31

² Jacob became angry with her and said, "Am I in the place of God, who has kept you from having children?" Ge 16:2

³ Then she said, "Here is Bilhah, my servant. Sleep with her so that she can bear children for me and I too can build a family through her." Ge 16:2

⁴ So she gave him her servant Bilhah as a wife. Jacob slept with her, ⁵ and she became pregnant and bore him a son. ⁶ Then Rachel said, "God has vindicated me; he has listened to my plea and given me a son." Because of this she named him Dan.ᵉ Ge 16:3-4; 49:16-17

⁷ Rachel's servant Bilhah conceived again and bore Jacob a second son. ⁸ Then Rachel said, "I have had a great struggle with my sister, and I have won." So she named him Naphtali.ᶠ Ge 49:21

ᵃ 32 *Reuben* sounds like the Hebrew for *he has seen my misery*; the name means *see, a son.*   ᵇ 33 *Simeon* probably means *one who hears.*   ᶜ 34 *Levi* sounds like and may be derived from the Hebrew for *attached.*   ᵈ 35 *Judah* sounds like and may be derived from the Hebrew for *praise.*   ᵉ 6 *Dan* here means *he has vindicated.*   ᶠ 8 *Naphtali* means *my struggle.*

⁹When Leah saw that she had stopped having children, she took her servant Zilpah and gave her to Jacob as a wife. ¹⁰Leah's servant Zilpah bore Jacob a son. ¹¹Then Leah said, "What good fortune!"ᵃ So she named him Gad.ᵇ   ver 4

¹²Leah's servant Zilpah bore Jacob a second son. ¹³Then Leah said, "How happy I am! The women will call me happy." So she named him Asher.ᶜ   Lk 1:48

¹⁴During wheat harvest, Reuben went out into the fields and found some mandrake plants, which he brought to his mother Leah. Rachel said to Leah, "Please give me some of your son's mandrakes."   SS 7:13

¹⁵But she said to her, "Wasn't it enough that you took away my husband? Will you take my son's mandrakes too?"   Nu 16:9,13

"Very well," Rachel said, "he can sleep with you tonight in return for your son's mandrakes."

¹⁶So when Jacob came in from the fields that evening, Leah went out to meet him. "You must sleep with me," she said. "I have hired you with my son's mandrakes." So he slept with her that night.

¹⁷God listened to Leah, and she became pregnant and bore Jacob a fifth son. ¹⁸Then Leah said, "God has rewarded me for giving my servant to my husband." So she named him Issachar.ᵈ   Ge 46:13; 49:14

¹⁹Leah conceived again and bore Jacob a sixth son. ²⁰Then Leah said, "God has presented me with a precious gift. This time my husband will treat me with honor, because I have borne him six sons." So she named him Zebulun.ᵉ   1Pe 3:7

²¹Some time later she gave birth to a daughter and named her Dinah.   Ge 34:1

²²Then God remembered Rachel; he listened to her and enabled her to conceive. ²³She became pregnant and gave birth to a son and said, "God has taken away my disgrace." ²⁴She named him Joseph,ᶠ and said, "May the Lord add to me another son."   Ge 35:17; Isa 4:1; Lk 1:25

Jacob's Flocks Increase

²⁵After Rachel gave birth to Joseph, Jacob said to Laban, "Send me on my way so I can go back to my own homeland. ²⁶Give me my wives and children, for whom I have served you, and I will be on my way. You know how much work I've done for you."   Ge 24:54; 29:20,30

²⁷But Laban said to him, "If I have found favor in your eyes, please stay. I have learned by divination that the Lord has

ᵃ 11 Or "A troop is coming!"   ᵇ 11 Gad can mean good fortune or a troop.   ᶜ 13 Asher means happy.   ᵈ 18 Issachar sounds like the Hebrew for reward.   ᵉ 20 Zebulun probably means honor.   ᶠ 24 Joseph means may he add.

blessed me because of you." ²⁸He added, "Name your wages, and I will pay them." Ge 26:24; 29:15; 39:3,5

²⁹Jacob said to him, "You know how I have worked for you and how your livestock has fared under my care. ³⁰The little you had before I came has increased greatly, and the Lᴏʀᴅ has blessed you wherever I have been. But now, when may I do something for my own household?" Ge 31:38-40; 1Ti 5:8

³¹"What shall I give you?" he asked.

"Don't give me anything," Jacob replied. "But if you will do this one thing for me, I will go on tending your flocks and watching over them: ³²Let me go through all your flocks today and remove from them every speckled or spotted sheep, every dark-colored lamb and every spotted or speckled goat. They will be my wages. ³³And my honesty will testify for me in the future, whenever you check on the wages you have paid me. Any goat in my possession that is not speckled or spotted, or any lamb that is not dark-colored, will be considered stolen." Ge 31:8,12

³⁴"Agreed," said Laban. "Let it be as you have said." ³⁵That same day he removed all the male goats that were streaked or spotted, and all the speckled or spotted female goats (all that had white on them) and all the dark-colored lambs, and he placed them in the care of his sons.

³⁶Then he put a three-day journey between himself and Jacob, while Jacob continued to tend the rest of Laban's flocks. Ge 31:1

³⁷Jacob, however, took fresh-cut branches from poplar, almond and plane trees and made white stripes on them by peeling the bark and exposing the white inner wood of the branches. ³⁸Then he placed the peeled branches in all the watering troughs, so that they would be directly in front of the flocks when they came to drink. When the flocks were in heat and came to drink, ³⁹they mated in front of the branches. And they bore young that were streaked or speckled or spotted. ⁴⁰Jacob set apart the young of the flock by themselves, but made the rest face the streaked and dark-colored animals that belonged to Laban. Thus he made separate flocks for himself and did not put them with Laban's animals. ⁴¹Whenever the stronger females were in heat, Jacob would place the branches in the troughs in front of the animals so they would mate near the branches, ⁴²but if the animals were weak, he would not place them there. So the weak animals went to Laban and the strong ones to Jacob. ⁴³In this way the man grew exceedingly prosperous and came to own large flocks, and female and male servants, and camels and donkeys. Ge 12:16; 13:2; 26:13-14

Jacob Flees From Laban

31 Jacob heard that Laban's sons were saying, "Jacob has taken everything our father owned and has gained all this wealth from what belonged to our father." ²And Jacob noticed that Laban's attitude toward him was not what it had been. Ge 30:42

³Then the LORD said to Jacob, "Go back to the land of your fathers and to your relatives, and I will be with you." Ge 21:22; 26:3; 32:9

⁴So Jacob sent word to Rachel and Leah to come out to the fields where his flocks were. ⁵He said to them, "I see that your father's attitude toward me is not what it was before, but the God of my father has been with me. ⁶You know that I've worked for your father with all my strength, ⁷yet your father has cheated me by changing my wages ten times. However, God has not allowed him to harm me. ⁸If he said, 'The speckled ones will be your wages,' then all the flocks gave birth to speckled young; and if he said, 'The streaked ones will be your wages,' then all the flocks bore streaked young. ⁹So God has taken away your father's livestock and has given them to me. Ge 21:22; 30:32,42

¹⁰"In breeding season I once had a dream in which I looked up and saw that the male goats mating with the flock were streaked, speckled or spotted. ¹¹The angel of God said to me in the dream, 'Jacob.' I answered, 'Here I am.' ¹²And he said, 'Look up and see that all the male goats mating with the flock are streaked, speckled or spotted, for I have seen all that Laban has been doing to you. ¹³I am the God of Bethel, where you anointed a pillar and where you made a vow to me. Now leave this land at once and go back to your native land.' " Ge 28:10-22; Ex 3:7

¹⁴Then Rachel and Leah replied, "Do we still have any share in the inheritance of our father's estate? ¹⁵Does he not regard us as foreigners? Not only has he sold us, but he has used up what was paid for us. ¹⁶Surely all the wealth that God took away from our father belongs to us and our children. So do whatever God has told you." Ge 29:20

¹⁷Then Jacob put his children and his wives on camels, ¹⁸and he drove all his livestock ahead of him, along with all the goods he had accumulated in Paddan Aram,ᵃ to go to his father Isaac in the land of Canaan. Ge 35:27

¹⁹When Laban had gone to shear his sheep, Rachel stole her father's household gods. ²⁰Moreover, Jacob deceived Laban the Aramean by not telling him he was running away. ²¹So he fled with all he had, crossed the Euphrates River, and headed for the hill country of Gilead. Ge 27:36; 35:2

ᵃ 18 That is, Northwest Mesopotamia

Laban Pursues Jacob

²²On the third day Laban was told that Jacob had fled. ²³Taking his relatives with him, he pursued Jacob for seven days and caught up with him in the hill country of Gilead. ²⁴Then God came to Laban the Aramean in a dream at night and said to him, "Be careful not to say anything to Jacob, either good or bad." Ge 20:3; 24:50

²⁵Jacob had pitched his tent in the hill country of Gilead when Laban overtook him, and Laban and his relatives camped there too. ²⁶Then Laban said to Jacob, "What have you done? You've deceived me, and you've carried off my daughters like captives in war. ²⁷Why did you run off secretly and deceive me? Why didn't you tell me, so I could send you away with joy and singing to the music of timbrels and harps? ²⁸You didn't even let me kiss my grandchildren and my daughters goodbye. You have done a foolish thing. ²⁹I have the power to harm you; but last night the God of your father said to me, 'Be careful not to say anything to Jacob, either good or bad.' ³⁰Now you have gone off because you longed to return to your father's household. But why did you steal my gods?" ver 19,55

³¹Jacob answered Laban, "I was afraid, because I thought you would take your daughters away from me by force. ³²But if you find anyone who has your gods, that person shall not live. In the presence of our relatives, see for yourself whether there is anything of yours here with me; and if so, take it." Now Jacob did not know that Rachel had stolen the gods. Ge 44:9

³³So Laban went into Jacob's tent and into Leah's tent and into the tent of the two female servants, but he found nothing. After he came out of Leah's tent, he entered Rachel's tent. ³⁴Now Rachel had taken the household gods and put them inside her camel's saddle and was sitting on them. Laban searched through everything in the tent but found nothing. ver 37; Ge 44:12

³⁵Rachel said to her father, "Don't be angry, my lord, that I cannot stand up in your presence; I'm having my period." So he searched but could not find the household gods. Lev 19:3,32

³⁶Jacob was angry and took Laban to task. "What is my crime?" he asked Laban. "How have I wronged you that you hunt me down? ³⁷Now that you have searched through all my goods, what have you found that belongs to your household? Put it here in front of your relatives and mine, and let them judge between the two of us. ver 23

³⁸"I have been with you for twenty years now. Your sheep and goats have not miscarried, nor have I eaten rams from your flocks. ³⁹I did not bring you

animals torn by wild beasts; I bore the loss myself. And you demanded payment from me for whatever was stolen by day or night. ⁴⁰This was my situation: The heat consumed me in the daytime and the cold at night, and sleep fled from my eyes. ⁴¹It was like this for the twenty years I was in your household. I worked for you fourteen years for your two daughters and six years for your flocks, and you changed my wages ten times. ⁴²If the God of my father, the God of Abraham and the Fear of Isaac, had not been with me, you would surely have sent me away empty-handed. But God has seen my hardship and the toil of my hands, and last night he rebuked you." Ge 29:30,32; Ex 22:13

⁴³Laban answered Jacob, "The women are my daughters, the children are my children, and the flocks are my flocks. All you see is mine. Yet what can I do today about these daughters of mine, or about the children they have borne? ⁴⁴Come now, let's make a covenant, you and I, and let it serve as a witness between us." Ge 21:27; Jos 24:27

⁴⁵So Jacob took a stone and set it up as a pillar. ⁴⁶He said to his relatives, "Gather some stones." So they took stones and piled them in a heap, and they ate there by the heap. ⁴⁷Laban called it Jegar Sahadutha, and Jacob called it Galeed.ᵃ Ge 28:18

⁴⁸Laban said, "This heap is a witness between you and me today." That is why it was called Galeed. ⁴⁹It was also called Mizpah,ᵇ because he said, "May the LORD keep watch between you and me when we are away from each other. ⁵⁰If you mistreat my daughters or if you take any wives besides my daughters, even though no one is with us, remember that God is a witness between you and me." Jdg 11:29; 1Sa 7:5-6

⁵¹Laban also said to Jacob, "Here is this heap, and here is this pillar I have set up between you and me. ⁵²This heap is a witness, and this pillar is a witness, that I will not go past this heap to your side to harm you and that you will not go past this heap and pillar to my side to harm me. ⁵³May the God of Abraham and the God of Nahor, the God of their father, judge between us." Ge 16:5

So Jacob took an oath in the name of the Fear of his father Isaac. ⁵⁴He offered a sacrifice there in the hill country and invited his relatives to a meal. After they had eaten, they spent the night there. ver 42

⁵⁵Early the next morning Laban kissed his grandchildren and his daughters and blessed them. Then he left and returned home.ᶜ Ge 18:33

ᵃ 47 The Aramaic *Jegar Sahadutha* and the Hebrew *Galeed* both mean *witness heap.*
ᵇ 49 *Mizpah* means *watchtower.*   ᶜ 55 In Hebrew texts this verse (31:55) is numbered 32:1.

Jacob Prepares to Meet Esau

32 *a* Jacob also went on his way, and the angels of God met him. ²When Jacob saw them, he said, "This is the camp of God!" So he named that place Mahanaim.*b*   Ps 34:7; 91:11

³Jacob sent messengers ahead of him to his brother Esau in the land of Seir, the country of Edom. ⁴He instructed them: "This is what you are to say to my lord Esau: 'Your servant Jacob says, I have been staying with Laban and have remained there till now. ⁵I have cattle and donkeys, sheep and goats, male and female servants. Now I am sending this message to my lord, that I may find favor in your eyes.'"   Ge 12:16; 33:8,10,15

⁶When the messengers returned to Jacob, they said, "We went to your brother Esau, and now he is coming to meet you, and four hundred men are with him."   Ge 33:1

⁷In great fear and distress Jacob divided the people who were with him into two groups,*c* and the flocks and herds and camels as well. ⁸He thought, "If Esau comes and attacks one group,*d* the group*d* that is left may escape."   ver 11

⁹Then Jacob prayed, "O God of my father Abraham, God of my father Isaac, LORD, you who said to me, 'Go back to your country and your relatives, and I will make you prosper,' ¹⁰I am unworthy of all the kindness and faithfulness you have shown your servant. I had only my staff when I crossed this Jordan, but now I have become two camps. ¹¹Save me, I pray, from the hand of my brother Esau, for I am afraid he will come and attack me, and also the mothers with their children. ¹²But you have said, 'I will surely make you prosper and will make your descendants like the sand of the sea, which cannot be counted.'"   Hos 1:10; Ge 24:27; 31:13

¹³He spent the night there, and from what he had with him he selected a gift for his brother Esau: ¹⁴two hundred female goats and twenty male goats, two hundred ewes and twenty rams, ¹⁵thirty female camels with their young, forty cows and ten bulls, and twenty female donkeys and ten male donkeys. ¹⁶He put them in the care of his servants, each herd by itself, and said to his servants, "Go ahead of me, and keep some space between the herds."   Ge 43:11,15,25-26; Pr 18:16

¹⁷He instructed the one in the lead: "When my brother Esau meets you and asks, 'Who do you belong to, and where are you going, and who owns all these animals in front of you?' ¹⁸then you are to say, 'They belong to your

---

a In Hebrew texts 32:1-32 is numbered 32:2-33.   *b* 2 *Mahanaim* means *two camps.*
c 7 Or *camps*   *d* 8 Or *camp*

servant Jacob. They are a gift sent to my lord Esau, and he is coming behind us.'" Ge 18:3

¹⁹He also instructed the second, the third and all the others who followed the herds: "You are to say the same thing to Esau when you meet him. ²⁰And be sure to say, 'Your servant Jacob is coming behind us.'" For he thought, "I will pacify him with these gifts I am sending on ahead; later, when I see him, perhaps he will receive me." ²¹So Jacob's gifts went on ahead of him, but he himself spent the night in the camp. Ge 33:10; Pr 21:14

Jacob Wrestles With God

²²That night Jacob got up and took his two wives, his two female servants and his eleven sons and crossed the ford of the Jabbok. ²³After he had sent them across the stream, he sent over all his possessions. ²⁴So Jacob was left alone, and a man wrestled with him till daybreak. ²⁵When the man saw that he could not overpower him, he touched the socket of Jacob's hip so that his hip was wrenched as he wrestled with the man. ²⁶Then the man said, "Let me go, for it is daybreak."

But Jacob replied, "I will not let you go unless you bless me." Hos 12:4

²⁷The man asked him, "What is your name?"

"Jacob," he answered.

²⁸Then the man said, "Your name will no longer be Jacob, but Israel,ᵃ because you have struggled with God and with humans and have overcome." Ge 17:5; 35:10

²⁹Jacob said, "Please tell me your name." Jdg 13:17

But he replied, "Why do you ask my name?" Then he blessed him there. Ge 35:9

³⁰So Jacob called the place Peniel,ᵇ saying, "It is because I saw God face to face, and yet my life was spared." Ge 16:13; Ex 24:11; Jdg 6:22

³¹The sun rose above him as he passed Peniel,ᶜ and he was limping because of his hip. ³²Therefore to this day the Israelites do not eat the tendon attached to the socket of the hip, because the socket of Jacob's hip was touched near the tendon. ver 25

Jacob Meets Esau

33 Jacob looked up and there was Esau, coming with his four hundred men; so he divided the children among Leah, Rachel and the two female servants. ²He put the female servants and their children in front, Leah and her children next, and Rachel and Joseph in the rear. ³He himself went on ahead and bowed down to the ground seven times as he approached his brother. Ge 32:6; 42:6

⁴But Esau ran to meet Jacob

ᵃ 28 *Israel* probably means *he struggles with God.*   ᵇ 30 *Peniel* means *face of God.*
ᶜ 31 Hebrew *Penuel,* a variant of *Peniel*

and embraced him; he threw his arms around his neck and kissed him. And they wept. ⁵Then Esau looked up and saw the women and children. "Who are these with you?" he asked. Ge 45:14-15

Jacob answered, "They are the children God has graciously given your servant." Ge 48:9; Ps 127:3; Isa 8:18

⁶Then the female servants and their children approached and bowed down. ⁷Next, Leah and her children came and bowed down. Last of all came Joseph and Rachel, and they too bowed down.

⁸Esau asked, "What's the meaning of all these flocks and herds I met?" Ge 32:14-16

"To find favor in your eyes, my lord," he said. Ge 24:9

⁹But Esau said, "I already have plenty, my brother. Keep what you have for yourself."

¹⁰"No, please!" said Jacob. "If I have found favor in your eyes, accept this gift from me. For to see your face is like seeing the face of God, now that you have received me favorably. ¹¹Please accept the present that was brought to you, for God has been gracious to me and I have all I need." And because Jacob insisted, Esau accepted it. Ge 32:20; 1Sa 25:27

¹²Then Esau said, "Let us be on our way; I'll accompany you."

¹³But Jacob said to him, "My lord knows that the children are tender and that I must care for the ewes and cows that are nursing their young. If they are driven hard just one day, all the animals will die. ¹⁴So let my lord go on ahead of his servant, while I move along slowly at the pace of the flocks and herds before me and the pace of the children, until I come to my lord in Seir." Ge 32:3

¹⁵Esau said, "Then let me leave some of my men with you."

"But why do that?" Jacob asked. "Just let me find favor in the eyes of my lord." Ge 34:11

¹⁶So that day Esau started on his way back to Seir. ¹⁷Jacob, however, went to Sukkoth, where he built a place for himself and made shelters for his livestock. That is why the place is called Sukkoth.ᵃ Jdg 8:4-5,8,14-16

¹⁸After Jacob came from Paddan Aram,ᵇ he arrived safely at the city of Shechem in Canaan and camped within sight of the city. ¹⁹For a hundred pieces of silver,ᶜ he bought from the sons of Hamor, the father of Shechem, the plot of ground where he pitched his tent. ²⁰There he set up an altar and called it El Elohe Israel.ᵈ Jos 24:1,32; Jn 4:5

Dinah and the Shechemites

34 Now Dinah, the daughter Leah had borne to Jacob, went out to visit the women

ᵃ 17 Sukkoth means shelters. ᵇ 18 That is, Northwest Mesopotamia ᶜ 19 Hebrew hundred kesitahs; a kesitah was a unit of money of unknown weight and value. ᵈ 20 El Elohe Israel can mean El is the God of Israel or mighty is the God of Israel.

of the land. ²When Shechem son of Hamor the Hivite, the ruler of that area, saw her, he took her and raped her. ³His heart was drawn to Dinah daughter of Jacob; he loved the young woman and spoke tenderly to her. ⁴And Shechem said to his father Hamor, "Get me this girl as my wife." Ge 30:21

⁵When Jacob heard that his daughter Dinah had been defiled, his sons were in the fields with his livestock; so he did nothing about it until they came home.

⁶Then Shechem's father Hamor went out to talk with Jacob. ⁷Meanwhile, Jacob's sons had come in from the fields as soon as they heard what had happened. They were shocked and furious, because Shechem had done an outrageous thing in[a] Israel by sleeping with Jacob's daughter—a thing that should not be done. Dt 22:21; Jdg 20:6; 2Sa 13:12

⁸But Hamor said to them, "My son Shechem has his heart set on your daughter. Please give her to him as his wife. ⁹Intermarry with us; give us your daughters and take our daughters for yourselves. ¹⁰You can settle among us; the land is open to you. Live in it, trade[b] in it, and acquire property in it." Ge 13:9; 42:34; 47:6,27

¹¹Then Shechem said to Dinah's father and brothers, "Let me find favor in your eyes, and I will give you whatever you ask. ¹²Make the price for the bride and the gift I am to bring as great as you like, and I'll pay whatever you ask me. Only give me the young woman as my wife." Ex 22:16; Dt 22:29; 1Sa 18:25

¹³Because their sister Dinah had been defiled, Jacob's sons replied deceitfully as they spoke to Shechem and his father Hamor. ¹⁴They said to them, "We can't do such a thing; we can't give our sister to a man who is not circumcised. That would be a disgrace to us. ¹⁵We will enter into an agreement with you on one condition only: that you become like us by circumcising all your males. ¹⁶Then we will give you our daughters and take your daughters for ourselves. We'll settle among you and become one people with you. ¹⁷But if you will not agree to be circumcised, we'll take our sister and go." Ge 17:14; Ex 12:48

¹⁸Their proposal seemed good to Hamor and his son Shechem. ¹⁹The young man, who was the most honored of all his father's family, lost no time in doing what they said, because he was delighted with Jacob's daughter. ²⁰So Hamor and his son Shechem went to the gate of their city to speak to the men of their city. ²¹"These men are friendly toward us," they said. "Let them live in our land and trade

---

[a] 7 Or against   [b] 10 Or move about freely; also in verse 21

in it; the land has plenty of room for them. We can marry their daughters and they can marry ours. ²²But the men will agree to live with us as one people only on the condition that our males be circumcised, as they themselves are. ²³Won't their livestock, their property and all their other animals become ours? So let us agree to their terms, and they will settle among us." ver 3; Ru 4:1

²⁴All the men who went out of the city gate agreed with Hamor and his son Shechem, and every male in the city was circumcised. Ge 23:10

²⁵Three days later, while all of them were still in pain, two of Jacob's sons, Simeon and Levi, Dinah's brothers, took their swords and attacked the unsuspecting city, killing every male. ²⁶They put Hamor and his son Shechem to the sword and took Dinah from Shechem's house and left. ²⁷The sons of Jacob came upon the dead bodies and looted the city where[a] their sister had been defiled. ²⁸They seized their flocks and herds and donkeys and everything else of theirs in the city and out in the fields. ²⁹They carried off all their wealth and all their women and children, taking as plunder everything in the houses. Ge 49:5,7

³⁰Then Jacob said to Simeon and Levi, "You have brought trouble on me by making me obnoxious to the Canaanites and Perizzites, the people living in this land. We are few in number, and if they join forces against me and attack me, I and my household will be destroyed." Ex 5:21; 1Ch 16:19

³¹But they replied, "Should he have treated our sister like a prostitute?"

Jacob Returns to Bethel

35 Then God said to Jacob, "Go up to Bethel and settle there, and build an altar there to God, who appeared to you when you were fleeing from your brother Esau." Ge 27:43; 28:19

²So Jacob said to his household and to all who were with him, "Get rid of the foreign gods you have with you, and purify yourselves and change your clothes. ³Then come, let us go up to Bethel, where I will build an altar to God, who answered me in the day of my distress and who has been with me wherever I have gone." ⁴So they gave Jacob all the foreign gods they had and the rings in their ears, and Jacob buried them under the oak at Shechem. ⁵Then they set out, and the terror of God fell on the towns all around them so that no one pursued them. Ge 28:15,20-22; 32:7; Ex 19:10

⁶Jacob and all the people with him came to Luz (that is, Bethel) in the land of Canaan. ⁷There he built an altar, and he called the place El Bethel,[b] because it was

---

[a] 27 Or *because*   [b] 7 *El Bethel* means *God of Bethel*.

there that God revealed himself to him when he was fleeing from his brother. Ge 28:13,19

⁸Now Deborah, Rebekah's nurse, died and was buried under the oak outside Bethel. So it was named Allon Bakuth.ᵃ Ge 24:59

⁹After Jacob returned from Paddan Aram,ᵇ God appeared to him again and blessed him. ¹⁰God said to him, "Your name is Jacob,ᶜ but you will no longer be called Jacob; your name will be Israel.ᵈ" So he named him Israel. Ge 17:5; 32:29

¹¹And God said to him, "I am God Almightyᵉ; be fruitful and increase in number. A nation and a community of nations will come from you, and kings will be among your descendants. ¹²The land I gave to Abraham and Isaac I also give to you, and I will give this land to your descendants after you." ¹³Then God went up from him at the place where he had talked with him. Ge 13:15; 17:6

¹⁴Jacob set up a stone pillar at the place where God had talked with him, and he poured out a drink offering on it; he also poured oil on it. ¹⁵Jacob called the place where God had talked with him Bethel.ᶠ Ge 28:18-19

The Deaths of Rachel and Isaac
35:23-26pp — 1Ch 2:1-2

¹⁶Then they moved on from Bethel. While they were still some distance from Ephrath, Rachel began to give birth and had great difficulty. ¹⁷And as she was having great difficulty in childbirth, the midwife said to her, "Don't despair, for you have another son." ¹⁸As she breathed her last—for she was dying—she named her son Ben-Oni.ᵍ But his father named him Benjamin.ʰ Ge 30:24

¹⁹So Rachel died and was buried on the way to Ephrath (that is, Bethlehem). ²⁰Over her tomb Jacob set up a pillar, and to this day that pillar marks Rachel's tomb. 1Sa 10:2

²¹Israel moved on again and pitched his tent beyond Migdal Eder. ²²While Israel was living in that region, Reuben went in and slept with his father's concubine Bilhah, and Israel heard of it. Ge 49:4

Jacob had twelve sons:
²³The sons of Leah:
  Reuben the firstborn of Jacob, Ge 46:8
  Simeon, Levi, Judah, Issachar and Zebulun. Ge 29:35
²⁴The sons of Rachel:
  Joseph and Benjamin. ver 18
²⁵The sons of Rachel's servant Bilhah:
  Dan and Naphtali.

ᵃ 8 *Allon Bakuth* means *oak of weeping.*   ᵇ 9 That is, Northwest Mesopotamia; also in verse 26   ᶜ 10 *Jacob* means *he grasps the heel,* a Hebrew idiom for *he deceives.*   ᵈ 10 *Israel* probably means *he struggles with God.*   ᵉ 11 Hebrew *El-Shaddai*   ᶠ 15 *Bethel* means *house of God.*   ᵍ 18 *Ben-Oni* means *son of my trouble.*   ʰ 18 *Benjamin* means *son of my right hand.*

²⁶The sons of Leah's servant Zilpah:

Gad and Asher. Ge 30:11,13

These were the sons of Jacob, who were born to him in Paddan Aram. 1Ch 2:1-2

²⁷Jacob came home to his father Isaac in Mamre, near Kiriath Arba (that is, Hebron), where Abraham and Isaac had stayed. ²⁸Isaac lived a hundred and eighty years. ²⁹Then he breathed his last and died and was gathered to his people, old and full of years. And his sons Esau and Jacob buried him. Ge 15:15; 25:8-9

Esau's Descendants

36:10-14pp — 1Ch 1:35-37
36:20-28pp — 1Ch 1:38-42

36 This is the account of the family line of Esau (that is, Edom). Ge 25:30

²Esau took his wives from the women of Canaan: Adah daughter of Elon the Hittite, and Oholibamah daughter of Anah and granddaughter of Zibeon the Hivite— ³also Basemath daughter of Ishmael and sister of Nebaioth. Ge 26:34; 28:8-9

⁴Adah bore Eliphaz to Esau, Basemath bore Reuel, ⁵and Oholibamah bore Jeush, Jalam and Korah. These were the sons of Esau, who were born to him in Canaan. 1Ch 1:35

⁶Esau took his wives and sons and daughters and all the members of his household, as well as his livestock and all his other animals and all the goods he had acquired in Canaan, and moved to a land some distance from his brother Jacob. ⁷Their possessions were too great for them to remain together; the land where they were staying could not support them both because of their livestock. ⁸So Esau (that is, Edom) settled in the hill country of Seir. Ge 13:6; 32:3

⁹This is the account of the family line of Esau the father of the Edomites in the hill country of Seir.

¹⁰These are the names of Esau's sons:

Eliphaz, the son of Esau's wife Adah, and Reuel, the son of Esau's wife Basemath.

¹¹The sons of Eliphaz:

Teman, Omar, Zepho, Gatam and Kenaz. Am 1:12

¹²Esau's son Eliphaz also had a concubine named Timna, who bore him Amalek. These were grandsons of Esau's wife Adah. Ex 17:8,16

¹³The sons of Reuel:

Nahath, Zerah, Shammah and Mizzah. These were grandsons of Esau's wife Basemath.

14 The sons of Esau's wife Oholibamah daughter of Anah and granddaughter of Zibeon, whom she bore to Esau:

Jeush, Jalam and Korah.

15 These were the chiefs among Esau's descendants: Ex 15:15

The sons of Eliphaz the firstborn of Esau:

Chiefs Teman, Omar, Zepho, Kenaz, 16 Korah,*a* Gatam and Amalek. These were the chiefs descended from Eliphaz in Edom; they were grandsons of Adah.

17 The sons of Esau's son Reuel:

Chiefs Nahath, Zerah, Shammah and Mizzah. These were the chiefs descended from Reuel in Edom; they were grandsons of Esau's wife Basemath.

18 The sons of Esau's wife Oholibamah:

Chiefs Jeush, Jalam and Korah. These were the chiefs descended from Esau's wife Oholibamah daughter of Anah.

19 These were the sons of Esau (that is, Edom), and these were their chiefs.   Ge 25:30

20 These were the sons of Seir the Horite, who were living in the region: Ge 14:6; Dt 2:12,22

Lotan, Shobal, Zibeon, Anah, 21 Dishon, Ezer and Dishan. These sons of Seir in Edom were Horite chiefs.

22 The sons of Lotan:

Hori and Homam.*b* Timna was Lotan's sister.

23 The sons of Shobal:

Alvan, Manahath, Ebal, Shepho and Onam.

24 The sons of Zibeon:

Aiah and Anah. This is the Anah who discovered the hot springs*c* in the desert while he was grazing the donkeys of his father Zibeon.

25 The children of Anah:

Dishon and Oholibamah daughter of Anah.

26 The sons of Dishon*d*:

Hemdan, Eshban, Ithran and Keran.

27 The sons of Ezer:

Bilhan, Zaavan and Akan.

28 The sons of Dishan:

Uz and Aran.   1Ch 1:38-42

29 These were the Horite chiefs:

Lotan, Shobal, Zibeon, Anah, 30 Dishon, Ezer and Dishan. These were the Horite chiefs, according to their divisions, in the land of Seir.

a 16 Masoretic Text; Samaritan Pentateuch (also verse 11 and 1 Chron. 1:36) does not have *Korah*.   *b* 22 Hebrew *Hemam*, a variant of *Homam* (see 1 Chron. 1:39)   *c* 24 Vulgate; Syriac *discovered water;* the meaning of the Hebrew for this word is uncertain.
d 26 Hebrew *Dishan*, a variant of *Dishon*

The Rulers of Edom
36:31-43pp — 1Ch 1:43-54

31 These were the kings who reigned in Edom before any Israelite king reigned:

32 Bela son of Beor became king of Edom. His city was named Dinhabah. 1Ch 1:43

33 When Bela died, Jobab son of Zerah from Bozrah succeeded him as king. Jer 49:13

34 When Jobab died, Husham from the land of the Temanites succeeded him as king. Eze 25:13

35 When Husham died, Hadad son of Bedad, who defeated Midian in the country of Moab, succeeded him as king. His city was named Avith. Ge 19:37

36 When Hadad died, Samlah from Masrekah succeeded him as king.

37 When Samlah died, Shaul from Rehoboth on the river succeeded him as king.

38 When Shaul died, Baal-Hanan son of Akbor succeeded him as king.

39 When Baal-Hanan son of Akbor died, Hadad*a* succeeded him as king. His city was named Pau, and his wife's name was Mehetabel daughter of Matred, the daughter of Me-Zahab.

40 These were the chiefs descended from Esau, by name, according to their clans and regions:

Timna, Alvah, Jetheth, **41** Oholibamah, Elah, Pinon, **42** Kenaz, Teman, Mibzar, **43** Magdiel and Iram. These were the chiefs of Edom, according to their settlements in the land they occupied.

This is the family line of Esau, the father of the Edomites. 1Ch 1:43

Joseph's Dreams

37 Jacob lived in the land where his father had stayed, the land of Canaan. Ge 17:8

2 This is the account of Jacob's family line.

Joseph, a young man of seventeen, was tending the flocks with his brothers, the sons of Bilhah and the sons of Zilpah, his father's wives, and he brought their father a bad report about them. 1Sa 2:24; Ps 78:71

3 Now Israel loved Joseph more than any of his other sons, because he had been born to him in his old age; and he made an ornate*b* robe for him. **4** When his brothers saw that their father loved him more than any of them, they hated him and

---

a 39 Many manuscripts of the Masoretic Text, Samaritan Pentateuch and Syriac (see also 1 Chron. 1:50); most manuscripts of the Masoretic Text *Hadar*   *b 3* The meaning of the Hebrew for this word is uncertain; also in verses 23 and 32.

could not speak a kind word to him. Ge 27:41; 44:20

⁵Joseph had a dream, and when he told it to his brothers, they hated him all the more. ⁶He said to them, "Listen to this dream I had: ⁷We were binding sheaves of grain out in the field when suddenly my sheaf rose and stood upright, while your sheaves gathered around mine and bowed down to it." Ge 42:6,9; 44:14; 50:18

⁸His brothers said to him, "Do you intend to reign over us? Will you actually rule us?" And they hated him all the more because of his dream and what he had said. Ge 49:26

⁹Then he had another dream, and he told it to his brothers. "Listen," he said, "I had another dream, and this time the sun and moon and eleven stars were bowing down to me." Ge 28:12

¹⁰When he told his father as well as his brothers, his father rebuked him and said, "What is this dream you had? Will your mother and I and your brothers actually come and bow down to the ground before you?" ¹¹His brothers were jealous of him, but his father kept the matter in mind. Ge 27:29; Lk 2:19,51; Ac 7:9

Joseph Sold by His Brothers

¹²Now his brothers had gone to graze their father's flocks near Shechem, ¹³and Israel said to Joseph, "As you know, your brothers are grazing the flocks near Shechem. Come, I am going to send you to them."

"Very well," he replied.

¹⁴So he said to him, "Go and see if all is well with your brothers and with the flocks, and bring word back to me." Then he sent him off from the Valley of Hebron. Ge 13:18

When Joseph arrived at Shechem, ¹⁵a man found him wandering around in the fields and asked him, "What are you looking for?"

¹⁶He replied, "I'm looking for my brothers. Can you tell me where they are grazing their flocks?"

¹⁷"They have moved on from here," the man answered. "I heard them say, 'Let's go to Dothan.'" 2Ki 6:13

So Joseph went after his brothers and found them near Dothan. ¹⁸But they saw him in the distance, and before he reached them, they plotted to kill him. Mk 14:1

¹⁹"Here comes that dreamer!" they said to each other. ²⁰"Come now, let's kill him and throw him into one of these cisterns and say that a ferocious animal devoured him. Then we'll see what comes of his dreams." Ge 50:20

²¹When Reuben heard this, he tried to rescue him from their hands. "Let's not take his life," he said. ²²"Don't shed any blood. Throw him into this cistern here in the wilderness, but don't lay a

hand on him." Reuben said this to rescue him from them and take him back to his father. Ge 42:22

²³ So when Joseph came to his brothers, they stripped him of his robe—the ornate robe he was wearing— ²⁴ and they took him and threw him into the cistern. The cistern was empty; there was no water in it. Jer 41:7

²⁵ As they sat down to eat their meal, they looked up and saw a caravan of Ishmaelites coming from Gilead. Their camels were loaded with spices, balm and myrrh, and they were on their way to take them down to Egypt. ver 28

²⁶ Judah said to his brothers, "What will we gain if we kill our brother and cover up his blood? ²⁷ Come, let's sell him to the Ishmaelites and not lay our hands on him; after all, he is our brother, our own flesh and blood." His brothers agreed. Ge 4:10; 42:21

²⁸ So when the Midianite merchants came by, his brothers pulled Joseph up out of the cistern and sold him for twenty shekels[a] of silver to the Ishmaelites, who took him to Egypt. Ge 45:4-5; Ps 105:17

²⁹ When Reuben returned to the cistern and saw that Joseph was not there, he tore his clothes. ³⁰ He went back to his brothers and said, "The boy isn't there! Where can I turn now?" ver 22; Ge 42:13,36

³¹ Then they got Joseph's robe, slaughtered a goat and dipped the robe in the blood. ³² They took the ornate robe back to their father and said, "We found this. Examine it to see whether it is your son's robe." ver 3,23

³³ He recognized it and said, "It is my son's robe! Some ferocious animal has devoured him. Joseph has surely been torn to pieces." ver 20; Ge 44:20,28

³⁴ Then Jacob tore his clothes, put on sackcloth and mourned for his son many days. ³⁵ All his sons and daughters came to comfort him, but he refused to be comforted. "No," he said, "I will continue to mourn until I join my son in the grave." So his father wept for him. Ge 42:38; 44:22,29,31

³⁶ Meanwhile, the Midianites[b] sold Joseph in Egypt to Potiphar, one of Pharaoh's officials, the captain of the guard. Ge 39:1

Judah and Tamar

38 At that time, Judah left his brothers and went down to stay with a man of Adullam named Hirah. ² There Judah met the daughter of a Canaanite man named Shua. He married her and made love to her; ³ she became pregnant and gave birth to a son, who was named Er. ⁴ She conceived again and gave birth to a son and named him Onan. ⁵ She gave birth to still another son and named him Shelah. It

---

[a] 28 That is, about 8 ounces or about 230 grams   [b] 36 Samaritan Pentateuch, Septuagint, Vulgate and Syriac (see also verse 28); Masoretic Text *Medanites*

was at Kezib that she gave birth to him. 1Ch 2:3; 4:21

⁶Judah got a wife for Er, his firstborn, and her name was Tamar. ⁷But Er, Judah's firstborn, was wicked in the LORD's sight; so the LORD put him to death.

⁸Then Judah said to Onan, "Sleep with your brother's wife and fulfill your duty to her as a brother-in-law to raise up offspring for your brother." ⁹But Onan knew that the child would not be his; so whenever he slept with his brother's wife, he spilled his semen on the ground to keep from providing offspring for his brother. ¹⁰What he did was wicked in the LORD's sight; so the LORD put him to death also. Dt 25:5-6; Mt 22:24-28; Ge 46:12

¹¹Judah then said to his daughter-in-law Tamar, "Live as a widow in your father's household until my son Shelah grows up." For he thought, "He may die too, just like his brothers." So Tamar went to live in her father's household. Ru 1:13

¹²After a long time Judah's wife, the daughter of Shua, died. When Judah had recovered from his grief, he went up to Timnah, to the men who were shearing his sheep, and his friend Hirah the Adullamite went with him. Jos 15:10,57

¹³When Tamar was told, "Your father-in-law is on his way to Timnah to shear his sheep," ¹⁴she took off her widow's clothes, covered herself with a veil to disguise herself, and then sat down at the entrance to Enaim, which is on the road to Timnah. For she saw that, though Shelah had now grown up, she had not been given to him as his wife. Ge 31:19

¹⁵When Judah saw her, he thought she was a prostitute, for she had covered her face. ¹⁶Not realizing that she was his daughter-in-law, he went over to her by the roadside and said, "Come now, let me sleep with you." Lev 18:15; 20:12

"And what will you give me to sleep with you?" she asked.

¹⁷"I'll send you a young goat from my flock," he said. Eze 16:33

"Will you give me something as a pledge until you send it?" she asked.

¹⁸He said, "What pledge should I give you?"

"Your seal and its cord, and the staff in your hand," she answered. So he gave them to her and slept with her, and she became pregnant by him. ¹⁹After she left, she took off her veil and put on her widow's clothes again.

²⁰Meanwhile Judah sent the young goat by his friend the Adullamite in order to get his pledge back from the woman, but he did not find her. ²¹He asked the men who lived there, "Where is the shrine prostitute who was beside the road at Enaim?" Lev 19:29; Hos 4:14

"There hasn't been any shrine prostitute here," they said.

²²So he went back to Judah and said, "I didn't find her. Besides, the men who lived there said, 'There hasn't been any shrine prostitute here.' "

²³Then Judah said, "Let her keep what she has, or we will become a laughingstock. After all, I did send her this young goat, but you didn't find her."

²⁴About three months later Judah was told, "Your daughter-in-law Tamar is guilty of prostitution, and as a result she is now pregnant."

Judah said, "Bring her out and have her burned to death!" Lev 21:9

²⁵As she was being brought out, she sent a message to her father-in-law. "I am pregnant by the man who owns these," she said. And she added, "See if you recognize whose seal and cord and staff these are." ver 18

²⁶Judah recognized them and said, "She is more righteous than I, since I wouldn't give her to my son Shelah." And he did not sleep with her again. 1Sa 24:17

²⁷When the time came for her to give birth, there were twin boys in her womb. ²⁸As she was giving birth, one of them put out his hand; so the midwife took a scarlet thread and tied it on his wrist and said, "This one came out first." ²⁹But when he drew back his hand, his brother came out, and she said, "So this is how you have broken out!" And he was named Perez.ᵃ ³⁰Then his brother, who had the scarlet thread on his wrist, came out. And he was named Zerah.ᵇ Ge 46:12; Nu 26:20-21

Joseph and Potiphar's Wife

39 Now Joseph had been taken down to Egypt. Potiphar, an Egyptian who was one of Pharaoh's officials, the captain of the guard, bought him from the Ishmaelites who had taken him there. Ge 37:25,36; Ps 105:17

²The LORD was with Joseph so that he prospered, and he lived in the house of his Egyptian master. ³When his master saw that the LORD was with him and that the LORD gave him success in everything he did, ⁴Joseph found favor in his eyes and became his attendant. Potiphar put him in charge of his household, and he entrusted to his care everything he owned. ⁵From the time he put him in charge of his household and of all that he owned, the LORD blessed the household of the Egyptian because of Joseph. The blessing of the LORD was on everything Potiphar had, both in the house and in the field. ⁶So Potiphar left everything he had in Joseph's care; with Joseph in charge, he did not concern himself with anything except the food he ate. Ge 21:22; 26:28; Ps 1:3

Now Joseph was well-built and handsome, ⁷and after a while his master's wife took notice of

ᵃ 29 Perez means breaking out.   ᵇ 30 Zerah can mean scarlet or brightness.

Joseph and said, "Come to bed with me!" Pr 7:15-18

⁸But he refused. "With me in charge," he told her, "my master does not concern himself with anything in the house; everything he owns he has entrusted to my care. ⁹No one is greater in this house than I am. My master has withheld nothing from me except you, because you are his wife. How then could I do such a wicked thing and sin against God?" ¹⁰And though she spoke to Joseph day after day, he refused to go to bed with her or even be with her. Ge 20:6; 42:18; Pr 6:23-24

¹¹One day he went into the house to attend to his duties, and none of the household servants was inside. ¹²She caught him by his cloak and said, "Come to bed with me!" But he left his cloak in her hand and ran out of the house. Pr 7:13

¹³When she saw that he had left his cloak in her hand and had run out of the house, ¹⁴she called her household servants. "Look," she said to them, "this Hebrew has been brought to us to make sport of us! He came in here to sleep with me, but I screamed. ¹⁵When he heard me scream for help, he left his cloak beside me and ran out of the house." Dt 22:24,27

¹⁶She kept his cloak beside her until his master came home. ¹⁷Then she told him this story: "That Hebrew slave you brought us came to me to make sport of

me. ¹⁸But as soon as I screamed for help, he left his cloak beside me and ran out of the house." Ex 23:1,7

¹⁹When his master heard the story his wife told him, saying, "This is how your slave treated me," he burned with anger. ²⁰Joseph's master took him and put him in prison, the place where the king's prisoners were confined. Ps 105:18

But while Joseph was there in the prison, ²¹the LORD was with him; he showed him kindness and granted him favor in the eyes of the prison warden. ²²So the warden put Joseph in charge of all those held in the prison, and he was made responsible for all that was done there. ²³The warden paid no attention to anything under Joseph's care, because the LORD was with Joseph and gave him success in whatever he did. ver 3; Ex 3:21

The Cupbearer and the Baker

40 Some time later, the cupbearer and the baker of the king of Egypt offended their master, the king of Egypt. ²Pharaoh was angry with his two officials, the chief cupbearer and the chief baker, ³and put them in custody in the house of the captain of the guard, in the same prison where Joseph was confined. ⁴The captain of the guard assigned them to Joseph, and he attended them. Ge 39:4,20

After they had been in custody

for some time, [5] each of the two men — the cupbearer and the baker of the king of Egypt, who were being held in prison — had a dream the same night, and each dream had a meaning of its own.   Ge 41:11

[6] When Joseph came to them the next morning, he saw that they were dejected. [7] So he asked Pharaoh's officials who were in custody with him in his master's house, "Why do you look so sad today?"   Ne 2:2

[8] "We both had dreams," they answered, "but there is no one to interpret them."   Ge 41:8,15

Then Joseph said to them, "Do not interpretations belong to God? Tell me your dreams." Ge 41:16

[9] So the chief cupbearer told Joseph his dream. He said to him, "In my dream I saw a vine in front of me, [10] and on the vine were three branches. As soon as it budded, it blossomed, and its clusters ripened into grapes. [11] Pharaoh's cup was in my hand, and I took the grapes, squeezed them into Pharaoh's cup and put the cup in his hand."

[12] "This is what it means," Joseph said to him. "The three branches are three days. [13] Within three days Pharaoh will lift up your head and restore you to your position, and you will put Pharaoh's cup in his hand, just as you used to do when you were his cupbearer. [14] But when all goes

well with you, remember me and show me kindness; mention me to Pharaoh and get me out of this prison. [15] I was forcibly carried off from the land of the Hebrews, and even here I have done nothing to deserve being put in a dungeon."   Da 2:36; 4:19; Jos 2:12

[16] When the chief baker saw that Joseph had given a favorable interpretation, he said to Joseph, "I too had a dream: On my head were three baskets of bread.[a] [17] In the top basket were all kinds of baked goods for Pharaoh, but the birds were eating them out of the basket on my head."

[18] "This is what it means," Joseph said. "The three baskets are three days. [19] Within three days Pharaoh will lift off your head and impale your body on a pole. And the birds will eat away your flesh."   ver 12-13

[20] Now the third day was Pharaoh's birthday, and he gave a feast for all his officials. He lifted up the heads of the chief cupbearer and the chief baker in the presence of his officials: [21] He restored the chief cupbearer to his position, so that he once again put the cup into Pharaoh's hand — [22] but he impaled the chief baker, just as Joseph had said to them in his interpretation.   ver 13; Ps 105:19

[23] The chief cupbearer, however, did not remember Joseph; he forgot him.   Job 19:14

---

[a] 16 Or *three wicker baskets*

Pharaoh's Dreams

41 When two full years had passed, Pharaoh had a dream: He was standing by the Nile, ²when out of the river there came up seven cows, sleek and fat, and they grazed among the reeds. ³After them, seven other cows, ugly and gaunt, came up out of the Nile and stood beside those on the riverbank. ⁴And the cows that were ugly and gaunt ate up the seven sleek, fat cows. Then Pharaoh woke up. Ge 20:3; Isa 19:6

⁵He fell asleep again and had a second dream: Seven heads of grain, healthy and good, were growing on a single stalk. ⁶After them, seven other heads of grain sprouted — thin and scorched by the east wind. ⁷The thin heads of grain swallowed up the seven healthy, full heads. Then Pharaoh woke up; it had been a dream.

⁸In the morning his mind was troubled, so he sent for all the magicians and wise men of Egypt. Pharaoh told them his dreams, but no one could interpret them for him. Da 2:1,3; 4:5,19; Ex 7:11,22

⁹Then the chief cupbearer said to Pharaoh, "Today I am reminded of my shortcomings. ¹⁰Pharaoh was once angry with his servants, and he imprisoned me and the chief baker in the house of the captain of the guard. ¹¹Each of us had a dream the same night, and each dream had a meaning of its own. ¹²Now a young Hebrew was there with us, a servant of the captain of the guard. We told him our dreams, and he interpreted them for us, giving each man the interpretation of his dream. ¹³And things turned out exactly as he interpreted them to us: I was restored to my position, and the other man was impaled." Ge 40:2,5,12,22

¹⁴So Pharaoh sent for Joseph, and he was quickly brought from the dungeon. When he had shaved and changed his clothes, he came before Pharaoh. Ps 105:20

¹⁵Pharaoh said to Joseph, "I had a dream, and no one can interpret it. But I have heard it said of you that when you hear a dream you can interpret it." Da 15:16

¹⁶"I cannot do it," Joseph replied to Pharaoh, "but God will give Pharaoh the answer he desires." Ge 40:8; Da 2:30; 2Co 3:5

¹⁷Then Pharaoh said to Joseph, "In my dream I was standing on the bank of the Nile, ¹⁸when out of the river there came up seven cows, fat and sleek, and they grazed among the reeds. ¹⁹After them, seven other cows came up — scrawny and very ugly and lean. I had never seen such ugly cows in all the land of Egypt. ²⁰The lean, ugly cows ate up the seven fat cows that came up first. ²¹But even after they ate them, no one could tell that they had done so; they looked just as ugly as before. Then I woke up.

²²"In my dream I saw seven

heads of grain, full and good, growing on a single stalk. ²³ After them, seven other heads sprouted — withered and thin and scorched by the east wind. ²⁴ The thin heads of grain swallowed up the seven good heads. I told this to the magicians, but none of them could explain it to me." ver 8

²⁵ Then Joseph said to Pharaoh, "The dreams of Pharaoh are one and the same. God has revealed to Pharaoh what he is about to do. ²⁶ The seven good cows are seven years, and the seven good heads of grain are seven years; it is one and the same dream. ²⁷ The seven lean, ugly cows that came up afterward are seven years, and so are the seven worthless heads of grain scorched by the east wind: They are seven years of famine. Da 2:45; 2Ki 8:1

²⁸ "It is just as I said to Pharaoh: God has shown Pharaoh what he is about to do. ²⁹ Seven years of great abundance are coming throughout the land of Egypt, ³⁰ but seven years of famine will follow them. Then all the abundance in Egypt will be forgotten, and the famine will ravage the land. ³¹ The abundance in the land will not be remembered, because the famine that follows it will be so severe. ³² The reason the dream was given to Pharaoh in two forms is that the matter has been firmly decided by God, and God will do it soon. ver 47,54; Ge 47:13

³³ "And now let Pharaoh look for a discerning and wise man and put him in charge of the land of Egypt. ³⁴ Let Pharaoh appoint commissioners over the land to take a fifth of the harvest of Egypt during the seven years of abundance. ³⁵ They should collect all the food of these good years that are coming and store up the grain under the authority of Pharaoh, to be kept in the cities for food. ³⁶ This food should be held in reserve for the country, to be used during the seven years of famine that will come upon Egypt, so that the country may not be ruined by the famine." ver 48,56

³⁷ The plan seemed good to Pharaoh and to all his officials. ³⁸ So Pharaoh asked them, "Can we find anyone like this man, one in whom is the spirit of God[a]?" Nu 27:18; Da 4:8-9,18; 5:11,14

³⁹ Then Pharaoh said to Joseph, "Since God has made all this known to you, there is no one so discerning and wise as you. ⁴⁰ You shall be in charge of my palace, and all my people are to submit to your orders. Only with respect to the throne will I be greater than you." Ps 105:21-22; Ac 7:10

Joseph in Charge of Egypt

⁴¹ So Pharaoh said to Joseph, "I hereby put you in charge of the

^a 38 Or *of the gods*

whole land of Egypt." ⁴²Then Pharaoh took his signet ring from his finger and put it on Joseph's finger. He dressed him in robes of fine linen and put a gold chain around his neck. ⁴³He had him ride in a chariot as his second-in-command,^a and people shouted before him, "Make way^b!" Thus he put him in charge of the whole land of Egypt. Ge 42:6; Est 3:10; Da 5:7,16,29

⁴⁴Then Pharaoh said to Joseph, "I am Pharaoh, but without your word no one will lift hand or foot in all Egypt." ⁴⁵Pharaoh gave Joseph the name Zaphenath-Paneah and gave him Asenath daughter of Potiphera, priest of On,^c to be his wife. And Joseph went throughout the land of Egypt. Ps 105:22

⁴⁶Joseph was thirty years old when he entered the service of Pharaoh king of Egypt. And Joseph went out from Pharaoh's presence and traveled throughout Egypt. ⁴⁷During the seven years of abundance the land produced plentifully. ⁴⁸Joseph collected all the food produced in those seven years of abundance in Egypt and stored it in the cities. In each city he put the food grown in the fields surrounding it. ⁴⁹Joseph stored up huge quantities of grain, like the sand of the sea; it was so much that he stopped keeping records because it was beyond measure. Da 1:19

⁵⁰Before the years of famine came, two sons were born to Joseph by Asenath daughter of Potiphera, priest of On. ⁵¹Joseph named his firstborn Manasseh^d and said, "It is because God has made me forget all my trouble and all my father's household." ⁵²The second son he named Ephraim^e and said, "It is because God has made me fruitful in the land of my suffering." Ge 17:6; 49:22

⁵³The seven years of abundance in Egypt came to an end, ⁵⁴and the seven years of famine began, just as Joseph had said. There was famine in all the other lands, but in the whole land of Egypt there was food. ⁵⁵When all Egypt began to feel the famine, the people cried to Pharaoh for food. Then Pharaoh told all the Egyptians, "Go to Joseph and do what he tells you." ver 30; Ps 105:11; Ac 7:11

⁵⁶When the famine had spread over the whole country, Joseph opened all the storehouses and sold grain to the Egyptians, for the famine was severe throughout Egypt. ⁵⁷And all the world came to Egypt to buy grain from Joseph, because the famine was severe everywhere. Ge 12:10; 42:5

^a 43 Or *in the chariot of his second-in-command*; or *in his second chariot*   ^b 43 Or *Bow down*   ^c 45 That is, Heliopolis; also in verse 50   ^d 51 *Manasseh* sounds like and may be derived from the Hebrew for *forget*.   ^e 52 *Ephraim* sounds like the Hebrew for *twice fruitful*.

Joseph's Brothers Go to Egypt

42 When Jacob learned that there was grain in Egypt, he said to his sons, "Why do you just keep looking at each other?" ²He continued, "I have heard that there is grain in Egypt. Go down there and buy some for us, so that we may live and not die." Ge 43:8; Ac 7:12

³Then ten of Joseph's brothers went down to buy grain from Egypt. ⁴But Jacob did not send Benjamin, Joseph's brother, with the others, because he was afraid that harm might come to him. ⁵So Israel's sons were among those who went to buy grain, for there was famine in the land of Canaan also. ver 38; Ac 7:11

⁶Now Joseph was the governor of the land, the person who sold grain to all its people. So when Joseph's brothers arrived, they bowed down to him with their faces to the ground. ⁷As soon as Joseph saw his brothers, he recognized them, but he pretended to be a stranger and spoke harshly to them. "Where do you come from?" he asked. Ge 37:7-10; 41:41

"From the land of Canaan," they replied, "to buy food."

⁸Although Joseph recognized his brothers, they did not recognize him. ⁹Then he remembered his dreams about them and said to them, "You are spies! You have come to see where our land is unprotected." Ge 37:7

¹⁰"No, my lord," they answered.

"Your servants have come to buy food. ¹¹We are all the sons of one man. Your servants are honest men, not spies."

¹²"No!" he said to them. "You have come to see where our land is unprotected."

¹³But they replied, "Your servants were twelve brothers, the sons of one man, who lives in the land of Canaan. The youngest is now with our father, and one is no more." Ge 37:30,33; 44:20

¹⁴Joseph said to them, "It is just as I told you: You are spies! ¹⁵And this is how you will be tested: As surely as Pharaoh lives, you will not leave this place unless your youngest brother comes here. ¹⁶Send one of your number to get your brother; the rest of you will be kept in prison, so that your words may be tested to see if you are telling the truth. If you are not, then as surely as Pharaoh lives, you are spies!" ¹⁷And he put them all in custody for three days. Ge 40:4; 1Sa 17:55

¹⁸On the third day, Joseph said to them, "Do this and you will live, for I fear God: ¹⁹If you are honest men, let one of your brothers stay here in prison, while the rest of you go and take grain back for your starving households. ²⁰But you must bring your youngest brother to me, so that your words may be verified and that you may not die." This they proceeded to do. ver 15,34; Ge 43:5; Lev 25:43

²¹ They said to one another, "Surely we are being punished because of our brother. We saw how distressed he was when he pleaded with us for his life, but we would not listen; that's why this distress has come on us." Hos 5:15

²² Reuben replied, "Didn't I tell you not to sin against the boy? But you wouldn't listen! Now we must give an accounting for his blood." ²³ They did not realize that Joseph could understand them, since he was using an interpreter. Ge 9:5; 37:21-22

²⁴ He turned away from them and began to weep, but then came back and spoke to them again. He had Simeon taken from them and bound before their eyes. Ge 45:14-15

²⁵ Joseph gave orders to fill their bags with grain, to put each man's silver back in his sack, and to give them provisions for their journey. After this was done for them, ²⁶ they loaded their grain on their donkeys and left. Ro 12:17,20-21

²⁷ At the place where they stopped for the night one of them opened his sack to get feed for his donkey, and he saw his silver in the mouth of his sack. ²⁸ "My silver has been returned," he said to his brothers. "Here it is in my sack." Ge 43:21-22

Their hearts sank and they turned to each other trembling and said, "What is this that God has done to us?" Ge 43:23

²⁹ When they came to their father Jacob in the land of Canaan, they told him all that had happened to them. They said, ³⁰ "The man who is lord over the land spoke harshly to us and treated us as though we were spying on the land. ³¹ But we said to him, 'We are honest men; we are not spies. ³² We were twelve brothers, sons of one father. One is no more, and the youngest is now with our father in Canaan.' ver 7

³³ "Then the man who is lord over the land said to us, 'This is how I will know whether you are honest men: Leave one of your brothers here with me, and take food for your starving households and go. ³⁴ But bring your youngest brother to me so I will know that you are not spies but honest men. Then I will give your brother back to you, and you can trade*a* in the land.' " Ge 34:10

³⁵ As they were emptying their sacks, there in each man's sack was his pouch of silver! When they and their father saw the money pouches, they were frightened. ³⁶ Their father Jacob said to them, "You have deprived me of my children. Joseph is no more and Simeon is no more, and now you want to take Benjamin. Everything is against me!" Ge 43:14

³⁷ Then Reuben said to his father, "You may put both of my sons to death if I do not bring him back to you. Entrust him

---

a 34 Or *move about freely*

to my care, and I will bring him back."

³⁸But Jacob said, "My son will not go down there with you; his brother is dead and he is the only one left. If harm comes to him on the journey you are taking, you will bring my gray head down to the grave in sorrow." Ge 37:33,35

The Second Journey to Egypt

43 Now the famine was still severe in the land. ²So when they had eaten all the grain they had brought from Egypt, their father said to them, "Go back and buy us a little more food." Ge 12:10; 41:56-57

³But Judah said to him, "The man warned us solemnly, 'You will not see my face again unless your brother is with you.' ⁴If you will send our brother along with us, we will go down and buy food for you. ⁵But if you will not send him, we will not go down, because the man said to us, 'You will not see my face again unless your brother is with you.'"Ge 42:15

⁶Israel asked, "Why did you bring this trouble on me by telling the man you had another brother?"

⁷They replied, "The man questioned us closely about ourselves and our family. 'Is your father still living?' he asked us. 'Do you have another brother?' We simply answered his questions. How were we to know he would

say, 'Bring your brother down here'?" Ge 42:13

⁸Then Judah said to Israel his father, "Send the boy along with me and we will go at once, so that we and you and our children may live and not die. ⁹I myself will guarantee his safety; you can hold me personally responsible for him. If I do not bring him back to you and set him here before you, I will bear the blame before you all my life. ¹⁰As it is, if we had not delayed, we could have gone and returned twice." Ge 42:37; 44:32; Phm 18-19

¹¹Then their father Israel said to them, "If it must be, then do this: Put some of the best products of the land in your bags and take them down to the man as a gift—a little balm and a little honey, some spices and myrrh, some pistachio nuts and almonds. ¹²Take double the amount of silver with you, for you must return the silver that was put back into the mouths of your sacks. Perhaps it was a mistake. ¹³Take your brother also and go back to the man at once. ¹⁴And may God Almighty^a grant you mercy before the man so that he will let your other brother and Benjamin come back with you. As for me, if I am bereaved, I am bereaved." Ge 32:20; 37:25; 42:25

¹⁵So the men took the gifts and double the amount of silver, and Benjamin also. They hurried

^a 14 Hebrew *El-Shaddai*

down to Egypt and presented themselves to Joseph. ¹⁶When Joseph saw Benjamin with them, he said to the steward of his house, "Take these men to my house, slaughter an animal and prepare a meal; they are to eat with me at noon." Ge 44:1,4,12

¹⁷The man did as Joseph told him and took the men to Joseph's house. ¹⁸Now the men were frightened when they were taken to his house. They thought, "We were brought here because of the silver that was put back into our sacks the first time. He wants to attack us and overpower us and seize us as slaves and take our donkeys."

¹⁹So they went up to Joseph's steward and spoke to him at the entrance to the house. ²⁰"We beg your pardon, our lord," they said, "we came down here the first time to buy food. ²¹But at the place where we stopped for the night we opened our sacks and each of us found his silver — the exact weight — in the mouth of his sack. So we have brought it back with us. ²²We have also brought additional silver with us to buy food. We don't know who put our silver in our sacks." ver 15; Ge 42:27,35

²³"It's all right," he said. "Don't be afraid. Your God, the God of your father, has given you treasure in your sacks; I received your silver." Then he brought Simeon out to them. Ge 42:28

²⁴The steward took the men into Joseph's house, gave them water to wash their feet and provided fodder for their donkeys. ²⁵They prepared their gifts for Joseph's arrival at noon, because they had heard that they were to eat there. ver 16; Ge 18:4; 24:32

²⁶When Joseph came home, they presented to him the gifts they had brought into the house, and they bowed down before him to the ground. ²⁷He asked them how they were, and then he said, "How is your aged father you told me about? Is he still living?" Ge 37:7,10; Mt 2:11

²⁸They replied, "Your servant our father is still alive and well." And they bowed down, prostrating themselves before him. Ge 37:7

²⁹As he looked about and saw his brother Benjamin, his own mother's son, he asked, "Is this your youngest brother, the one you told me about?" And he said, "God be gracious to you, my son." ³⁰Deeply moved at the sight of his brother, Joseph hurried out and looked for a place to weep. He went into his private room and wept there. Ge 42:13,24; 45:2,14,15

³¹After he had washed his face, he came out and, controlling himself, said, "Serve the food." Ge 45:1

³²They served him by himself, the brothers by themselves, and the Egyptians who ate with him by themselves, because Egyptians could not eat with Hebrews, for that is detestable to

Egyptians. [33] The men had been seated before him in the order of their ages, from the firstborn to the youngest; and they looked at each other in astonishment. [34] When portions were served to them from Joseph's table, Benjamin's portion was five times as much as anyone else's. So they feasted and drank freely with him.   Ge 37:3; 45:22; 46:34

A Silver Cup in a Sack

44 Now Joseph gave these instructions to the steward of his house: "Fill the men's sacks with as much food as they can carry, and put each man's silver in the mouth of his sack. [2] Then put my cup, the silver one, in the mouth of the youngest one's sack, along with the silver for his grain." And he did as Joseph said.   Ge 42:25

[3] As morning dawned, the men were sent on their way with their donkeys. [4] They had not gone far from the city when Joseph said to his steward, "Go after those men at once, and when you catch up with them, say to them, 'Why have you repaid good with evil? [5] Isn't this the cup my master drinks from and also uses for divination? This is a wicked thing you have done.'"   Ge 30:27; Ps 35:12

[6] When he caught up with them, he repeated these words to them. [7] But they said to him, "Why does my lord say such things? Far be it from your servants to do any-

thing like that! [8] We even brought back to you from the land of Canaan the silver we found inside the mouths of our sacks. So why would we steal silver or gold from your master's house? [9] If any of your servants is found to have it, he will die; and the rest of us will become my lord's slaves."   Ge 31:32

[10] "Very well, then," he said, "let it be as you say. Whoever is found to have it will become my slave; the rest of you will be free from blame."

[11] Each of them quickly lowered his sack to the ground and opened it. [12] Then the steward proceeded to search, beginning with the oldest and ending with the youngest. And the cup was found in Benjamin's sack. [13] At this, they tore their clothes. Then they all loaded their donkeys and returned to the city. Ge 37:29; Nu 14:6

[14] Joseph was still in the house when Judah and his brothers came in, and they threw themselves to the ground before him. [15] Joseph said to them, "What is this you have done? Don't you know that a man like me can find things out by divination?"   ver 5

[16] "What can we say to my lord?" Judah replied. "What can we say? How can we prove our innocence? God has uncovered your servants' guilt. We are now my lord's slaves — we ourselves and the one who was found to have the cup."   ver 9; Ge 43:18

[17] But Joseph said, "Far be it

from me to do such a thing! Only the man who was found to have the cup will become my slave. The rest of you, go back to your father in peace."

¹⁸ Then Judah went up to him and said: "Pardon your servant, my lord, let me speak a word to my lord. Do not be angry with your servant, though you are equal to Pharaoh himself. ¹⁹ My lord asked his servants, 'Do you have a father or a brother?' ²⁰ And we answered, 'We have an aged father, and there is a young son born to him in his old age. His brother is dead, and he is the only one of his mother's sons left, and his father loves him.' Ge 37:33; 42:13

²¹ "Then you said to your servants, 'Bring him down to me so I can see him for myself.' ²² And we said to my lord, 'The boy cannot leave his father; if he leaves him, his father will die.' ²³ But you told your servants, 'Unless your youngest brother comes down with you, you will not see my face again.' ²⁴ When we went back to your servant my father, we told him what my lord had said. Ge 42:15; 43:5

²⁵ "Then our father said, 'Go back and buy a little more food.' ²⁶ But we said, 'We cannot go down. Only if our youngest brother is with us will we go. We cannot see the man's face unless our youngest brother is with us.' Ge 43:2

²⁷ "Your servant my father said to us, 'You know that my wife bore me two sons. ²⁸ One of them went away from me, and I said, "He has surely been torn to pieces." And I have not seen him since. ²⁹ If you take this one from me too and harm comes to him, you will bring my gray head down to the grave in misery.' Ge 37:33; 42:38; 46:19

³⁰ "So now, if the boy is not with us when I go back to your servant my father, and if my father, whose life is closely bound up with the boy's life, ³¹ sees that the boy isn't there, he will die. Your servants will bring the gray head of our father down to the grave in sorrow. ³² Your servant guaranteed the boy's safety to my father. I said, 'If I do not bring him back to you, I will bear the blame before you, my father, all my life!' Ge 43:9; 1Sa 18:1

³³ "Now then, please let your servant remain here as my lord's slave in place of the boy, and let the boy return with his brothers. ³⁴ How can I go back to my father if the boy is not with me? No! Do not let me see the misery that would come on my father." Jn 15:13

Joseph Makes Himself Known

45 Then Joseph could no longer control himself before all his attendants, and he cried out, "Have everyone leave my presence!" So there was no one with Joseph when he made himself known to his brothers. ² And he wept so loudly that the Egyp-

tians heard him, and Pharaoh's household heard about it. Ge 29:11

³Joseph said to his brothers, "I am Joseph! Is my father still living?" But his brothers were not able to answer him, because they were terrified at his presence. Ac 7:13

⁴Then Joseph said to his brothers, "Come close to me." When they had done so, he said, "I am your brother Joseph, the one you sold into Egypt! ⁵And now, do not be distressed and do not be angry with yourselves for selling me here, because it was to save lives that God sent me ahead of you. ⁶For two years now there has been famine in the land, and for the next five years there will be no plowing and reaping. ⁷But God sent me ahead of you to preserve for you a remnant on earth and to save your lives by a great deliverance.ᵃ Ge 37:28; 50:20; Ps 105:17

⁸"So then, it was not you who sent me here, but God. He made me father to Pharaoh, lord of his entire household and ruler of all Egypt. ⁹Now hurry back to my father and say to him, 'This is what your son Joseph says: God has made me lord of all Egypt. Come down to me; don't delay. ¹⁰You shall live in the region of Goshen and be near me — you, your children and grandchildren, your flocks and herds, and all you have. ¹¹I will provide for you there, because five years of famine are still to come. Otherwise you and your household and all who belong to you will become destitute.' Ge 41:41; Jdg 17:10

¹²"You can see for yourselves, and so can my brother Benjamin, that it is really I who am speaking to you. ¹³Tell my father about all the honor accorded me in Egypt and about everything you have seen. And bring my father down here quickly." Ac 7:14

¹⁴Then he threw his arms around his brother Benjamin and wept, and Benjamin embraced him, weeping. ¹⁵And he kissed all his brothers and wept over them. Afterward his brothers talked with him. Lk 15:20

¹⁶When the news reached Pharaoh's palace that Joseph's brothers had come, Pharaoh and all his officials were pleased. ¹⁷Pharaoh said to Joseph, "Tell your brothers, 'Do this: Load your animals and return to the land of Canaan, ¹⁸and bring your father and your families back to me. I will give you the best of the land of Egypt and you can enjoy the fat of the land.' Ge 27:28; 46:34

¹⁹"You are also directed to tell them, 'Do this: Take some carts from Egypt for your children and your wives, and get your father and come. ²⁰Never mind about your belongings, because the best of all Egypt will be yours.'" Ge 46:5

²¹So the sons of Israel did

ᵃ 7 Or *save you as a great band of survivors*

this. Joseph gave them carts, as Pharaoh had commanded, and he also gave them provisions for their journey. ²²To each of them he gave new clothing, but to Benjamin he gave three hundred shekels*a* of silver and five sets of clothes. ²³And this is what he sent to his father: ten donkeys loaded with the best things of Egypt, and ten female donkeys loaded with grain and bread and other provisions for his journey. ²⁴Then he sent his brothers away, and as they were leaving he said to them, "Don't quarrel on the way!" Ge 42:21-22

²⁵So they went up out of Egypt and came to their father Jacob in the land of Canaan. ²⁶They told him, "Joseph is still alive! In fact, he is ruler of all Egypt." Jacob was stunned; he did not believe them. ²⁷But when they told him everything Joseph had said to them, and when he saw the carts Joseph had sent to carry him back, the spirit of their father Jacob revived. ²⁸And Israel said, "I'm convinced! My son Joseph is still alive. I will go and see him before I die." ver 19; Ge 44:28

Jacob Goes to Egypt

46 So Israel set out with all that was his, and when he reached Beersheba, he offered sacrifices to the God of his father Isaac. Ge 31:42

²And God spoke to Israel in a vision at night and said, "Jacob! Jacob!" Ge 15:1; Job 33:14-15

"Here I am," he replied. Ge 22:1

³"I am God, the God of your father," he said. "Do not be afraid to go down to Egypt, for I will make you into a great nation there. ⁴I will go down to Egypt with you, and I will surely bring you back again. And Joseph's own hand will close your eyes." Ge 12:2; 50:1,24

⁵Then Jacob left Beersheba, and Israel's sons took their father Jacob and their children and their wives in the carts that Pharaoh had sent to transport him. ⁶So Jacob and all his offspring went to Egypt, taking with them their livestock and the possessions they had acquired in Canaan. ⁷Jacob brought with him to Egypt his sons and grandsons and his daughters and granddaughters — all his offspring. Dt 26:5; Jos 24:4

⁸These are the names of the sons of Israel (Jacob and his descendants) who went to Egypt:

Reuben the firstborn of Jacob.
⁹The sons of Reuben: 1Ch 5:3
Hanok, Pallu, Hezron and Karmi.
¹⁰The sons of Simeon: Ge 29:33
Jemuel, Jamin, Ohad, Jakin, Zohar and Shaul the son of a Canaanite woman. Ex 6:15
¹¹The sons of Levi: Ge 29:34
Gershon, Kohath and Merari.

---

a 22 That is, about 7 1/2 pounds or about 3.5 kilograms

¹²The sons of Judah: Ge 29:35
Er, Onan, Shelah, Perez
and Zerah (but Er and
Onan had died in the land
of Canaan).
The sons of Perez: 1Ch 2:5
Hezron and Hamul.
¹³The sons of Issachar: Ge 30:18
Tola, Puah,ᵃ Jashubᵇ and
Shimron.
¹⁴The sons of Zebulun: Ge 30:20
Sered, Elon and Jahleel.
¹⁵These were the sons Leah
bore to Jacob in Paddan Aram,ᶜ
besides his daughter Dinah.
These sons and daughters of his
were thirty-three in all.
¹⁶The sons of Gad: Ge 30:11
Zephon,ᵈ Haggi, Shuni,
Ezbon, Eri, Arodi and Are-
li.   Nu 26:15
¹⁷The sons of Asher: Ge 30:13
Imnah, Ishvah, Ishvi and
Beriah.
Their sister was Serah.
The sons of Beriah:
Heber and Malkiel.
¹⁸These were the children
born to Jacob by Zilpah, whom
Laban had given to his daughter
Leah — sixteen in all.

¹⁹The sons of Jacob's wife Rachel:
Joseph and Benjamin.
²⁰In Egypt, Manasseh and
Ephraim were born to Jo-
seph by Asenath daugh-
ter of Potiphera, priest of
On.ᵉ   Ge 41:51-52; 44:27
²¹The sons of Benjamin: 1Ch 7:6
Bela, Beker, Ashbel, Gera,
Naaman, Ehi, Rosh, Mup-
pim, Huppim and Ard.
²²These were the sons of Rachel who were born to Jacob —
fourteen in all.

²³The son of Dan:
Hushim.
²⁴The sons of Naphtali:
Jahziel, Guni, Jezer and
Shillem.
²⁵These were the sons born to
Jacob by Bilhah, whom Laban
had given to his daughter Rachel — seven in all.   Ge 29:29; 30:8

²⁶All those who went to Egypt
with Jacob — those who were his
direct descendants, not counting
his sons' wives — numbered sixty-
six persons. ²⁷With the two sonsᶠ
who had been born to Joseph in
Egypt, the members of Jacob's
family, which went to Egypt, were
seventyᵍ in all.   Ac 7:14; Ex 1:5; Dt 10:22

²⁸Now Jacob sent Judah ahead
of him to Joseph to get directions
to Goshen. When they arrived in
the region of Goshen, ²⁹Joseph
had his chariot made ready and

ᵃ 13 Samaritan Pentateuch and Syriac (see also 1 Chron. 7:1); Masoretic Text *Puvah*
ᵇ 13 Samaritan Pentateuch and some Septuagint manuscripts (see also Num. 26:24 and
1 Chron. 7:1); Masoretic Text *Iob*   ᶜ 15 That is, Northwest Mesopotamia   ᵈ 16 Samaritan
Pentateuch and Septuagint (see also Num. 26:15); Masoretic Text *Ziphion*   ᵉ 20 That is,
Heliopolis   ᶠ 27 Hebrew; Septuagint *the nine children*   ᵍ 27 Hebrew (see also Exodus 1:5
and note); Septuagint (see also Acts 7:14) *seventy-five*

went to Goshen to meet his father Israel. As soon as Joseph appeared before him, he threw his arms around his father[a] and wept for a long time. Ge 45:14-15

[30] Israel said to Joseph, "Now I am ready to die, since I have seen for myself that you are still alive."

[31] Then Joseph said to his brothers and to his father's household, "I will go up and speak to Pharaoh and will say to him, 'My brothers and my father's household, who were living in the land of Canaan, have come to me. [32] The men are shepherds; they tend livestock, and they have brought along their flocks and herds and everything they own.' [33] When Pharaoh calls you in and asks, 'What is your occupation?' [34] you should answer, 'Your servants have tended livestock from our boyhood on, just as our fathers did.' Then you will be allowed to settle in the region of Goshen, for all shepherds are detestable to the Egyptians." Ge 43:32; Ex 8:26

47 Joseph went and told Pharaoh, "My father and brothers, with their flocks and herds and everything they own, have come from the land of Canaan and are now in Goshen." [2] He chose five of his brothers and presented them before Pharaoh. Ge 46:31

[3] Pharaoh asked the brothers, "What is your occupation?"

"Your servants are shepherds," they replied to Pharaoh, "just as our fathers were." [4] They also said to him, "We have come to live here for a while, because the famine is severe in Canaan and your servants' flocks have no pasture. So now, please let your servants settle in Goshen." Ge 46:34

[5] Pharaoh said to Joseph, "Your father and your brothers have come to you, [6] and the land of Egypt is before you; settle your father and your brothers in the best part of the land. Let them live in Goshen. And if you know of any among them with special ability, put them in charge of my own livestock." Ge 45:18; Ex 18:21,25

[7] Then Joseph brought his father Jacob in and presented him before Pharaoh. After Jacob blessed[b] Pharaoh, [8] Pharaoh asked him, "How old are you?"

[9] And Jacob said to Pharaoh, "The years of my pilgrimage are a hundred and thirty. My years have been few and difficult, and they do not equal the years of the pilgrimage of my fathers." [10] Then Jacob blessed[c] Pharaoh and went out from his presence. ver 7; Ge 25:7

[11] So Joseph settled his father and his brothers in Egypt and gave them property in the best part of the land, the district of Rameses, as Pharaoh directed. [12] Joseph also provided his father and his brothers and all his father's household with food, ac-

cording to the number of their children. Ex 1:11; 12:37

Joseph and the Famine

¹³There was no food, however, in the whole region because the famine was severe; both Egypt and Canaan wasted away because of the famine. ¹⁴Joseph collected all the money that was to be found in Egypt and Canaan in payment for the grain they were buying, and he brought it to Pharaoh's palace. ¹⁵When the money of the people of Egypt and Canaan was gone, all Egypt came to Joseph and said, "Give us food. Why should we die before your eyes? Our money is all gone." Ge 41:30,56

¹⁶"Then bring your livestock," said Joseph. "I will sell you food in exchange for your livestock, since your money is gone." ¹⁷So they brought their livestock to Joseph, and he gave them food in exchange for their horses, their sheep and goats, their cattle and donkeys. And he brought them through that year with food in exchange for all their livestock. Ex 14:9

¹⁸When that year was over, they came to him the following year and said, "We cannot hide from our lord the fact that since our money is gone and our livestock belongs to you, there is nothing left for our lord except our bodies and our land. ¹⁹Why should we perish before your eyes — we and our land as well? Buy us and our land in exchange for food, and we with our land will be in bondage to Pharaoh. Give us seed so that we may live and not die, and that the land may not become desolate." Ge 42:2

²⁰So Joseph bought all the land in Egypt for Pharaoh. The Egyptians, one and all, sold their fields, because the famine was too severe for them. The land became Pharaoh's, ²¹and Joseph reduced the people to servitude,[a] from one end of Egypt to the other. ²²However, he did not buy the land of the priests, because they received a regular allotment from Pharaoh and had food enough from the allotment Pharaoh gave them. That is why they did not sell their land. Dt 14:28-29; Ezr 7:24

²³Joseph said to the people, "Now that I have bought you and your land today for Pharaoh, here is seed for you so you can plant the ground. ²⁴But when the crop comes in, give a fifth of it to Pharaoh. The other four-fifths you may keep as seed for the fields and as food for yourselves and your households and your children." Ge 41:34

²⁵"You have saved our lives," they said. "May we find favor in the eyes of our lord; we will be in bondage to Pharaoh." Ge 32:5

---

a 21 Samaritan Pentateuch and Septuagint (see also Vulgate); Masoretic Text *and he moved the people into the cities*

²⁶So Joseph established it as a law concerning land in Egypt—still in force today—that a fifth of the produce belongs to Pharaoh. It was only the land of the priests that did not become Pharaoh's.   ver 22

²⁷Now the Israelites settled in Egypt in the region of Goshen. They acquired property there and were fruitful and increased greatly in number.   Ge 17:6

²⁸Jacob lived in Egypt seventeen years, and the years of his life were a hundred and forty-seven. ²⁹When the time drew near for Israel to die, he called for his son Joseph and said to him, "If I have found favor in your eyes, put your hand under my thigh and promise that you will show me kindness and faithfulness. Do not bury me in Egypt, ³⁰but when I rest with my fathers, carry me out of Egypt and bury me where they are buried."   Ge 49:29-32; 24:2

"I will do as you say," he said.

³¹"Swear to me," he said. Then Joseph swore to him, and Israel worshiped as he leaned on the top of his staff.ᵃ   Heb 11:21

Manasseh and Ephraim

48 Some time later Joseph was told, "Your father is ill." So he took his two sons Manasseh and Ephraim along with him. ²When Jacob was told, "Your son Joseph has come to you," Israel rallied his strength and sat up on the bed.   Ge 41:52

³Jacob said to Joseph, "God Almightyᵇ appeared to me at Luz in the land of Canaan, and there he blessed me ⁴and said to me, 'I am going to make you fruitful and increase your numbers. I will make you a community of peoples, and I will give this land as an everlasting possession to your descendants after you.'   Ge 28:13,19; 35:9-12

⁵"Now then, your two sons born to you in Egypt before I came to you here will be reckoned as mine; Ephraim and Manasseh will be mine, just as Reuben and Simeon are mine. ⁶Any children born to you after them will be yours; in the territory they inherit they will be reckoned under the names of their brothers. ⁷As I was returning from Paddan,ᶜ to my sorrow Rachel died in the land of Canaan while we were still on the way, a little distance from Ephrath. So I buried her there beside the road to Ephrath" (that is, Bethlehem).   Ge 35:19; 41:50-52

⁸When Israel saw the sons of Joseph, he asked, "Who are these?"

⁹"They are the sons God has given me here," Joseph said to his father.   Ge 33:5

Then Israel said, "Bring them to me so I may bless them."Ge 27:4

¹⁰Now Israel's eyes were failing

ᵃ 31 Or Israel bowed down at the head of his bed   ᵇ 3 Hebrew El-Shaddai   ᶜ 7 That is, Northwest Mesopotamia because of old age, and he could hardly see. So Joseph brought his sons close to him, and his father kissed them and embraced them. _{Ge 27:1,27}

¹¹ Israel said to Joseph, "I never expected to see your face again, and now God has allowed me to see your children too."

¹² Then Joseph removed them from Israel's knees and bowed down with his face to the ground. ¹³ And Joseph took both of them, Ephraim on his right toward Israel's left hand and Manasseh on his left toward Israel's right hand, and brought them close to him. ¹⁴ But Israel reached out his right hand and put it on Ephraim's head, though he was the younger, and crossing his arms, he put his left hand on Manasseh's head, even though Manasseh was the firstborn. _{Ge 41:51}

¹⁵ Then he blessed Joseph and said, _{Ge 17:1}

"May the God before whom
    my fathers
  Abraham and Isaac walked
    faithfully,
the God who has been my
    shepherd _{Ge 49:24}
  all my life to this day,
¹⁶ the Angel who has delivered
    me from all harm
  — may he bless these
    boys. _{Heb 11:21}
May they be called by my name

and the names of my fathers
    Abraham and
  Isaac, _{Ge 28:13}
and may they increase greatly
    on the earth."

¹⁷ When Joseph saw his father placing his right hand on Ephraim's head he was displeased; so he took hold of his father's hand to move it from Ephraim's head to Manasseh's head. ¹⁸ Joseph said to him, "No, my father, this one is the firstborn; put your right hand on his head." _{ver 14; Ge 25:23}

¹⁹ But his father refused and said, "I know, my son, I know. He too will become a people, and he too will become great. Nevertheless, his younger brother will be greater than he, and his descendants will become a group of nations." ²⁰ He blessed them that day and said,

"In your^a name will Israel
    pronounce this
    blessing:
'May God make you
  like Ephraim and
  Manasseh.'" _{Nu 2:20; Ru 4:11}

So he put Ephraim ahead of Manasseh.

²¹ Then Israel said to Joseph, "I am about to die, but God will be with you^b and take you^b back to the land of your^b fathers. ²² And to you I give one more ridge of land^c than to your brothers, the ridge I

---

^{a} 20 The Hebrew is singular. ^{b} 21 The Hebrew is plural. ^{c} 22 The Hebrew for *ridge of land* is identical with the place name Shechem.

took from the Amorites with my sword and my bow." Jn 4:5; Ge 26:3

Jacob Blesses His Sons

49:1-28Ref — Dt 33:1-29

49 Then Jacob called for his sons and said: "Gather around so I can tell you what will happen to you in days to come. Nu 24:14

2 "Assemble and listen, sons of Jacob;
listen to your father Israel.

3 "Reuben, you are my firstborn, Ge 29:32
my might, the first sign of my strength, Dt 21:17
excelling in honor, excelling in power.
4 Turbulent as the waters, you will no longer excel,
for you went up onto your father's bed,
onto my couch and defiled it. Ge 35:22; Dt 27:20

5 "Simeon and Levi are brothers —
their swords[a] are weapons of violence. Ge 34:25
6 Let me not enter their council,
let me not join their assembly, Pr 1:15; Eph 5:11
for they have killed men in their anger Ge 34:26
and hamstrung oxen as they pleased.

7 Cursed be their anger, so fierce,
and their fury, so cruel!
I will scatter them in Jacob
and disperse them in Israel. Jos 19:1,9

8 "Judah,[b] your brothers will praise you;
your hand will be on the neck of your enemies;
your father's sons will bow down to you. 1Ch 5:2
9 You are a lion's cub, Judah; Nu 24:9
you return from the prey, my son.
Like a lion he crouches and lies down,
like a lioness — who dares to rouse him?
10 The scepter will not depart from Judah, Nu 24:17,19
nor the ruler's staff from between his feet,[c]
until he to whom it belongs[d] shall come
and the obedience of the nations shall be his. Ps 2:9; Isa 42:1,4
11 He will tether his donkey to a vine,
his colt to the choicest branch;
he will wash his garments in wine,
his robes in the blood of grapes.

---

[a] 5 The meaning of the Hebrew for this word is uncertain.   [b] 8 *Judah* sounds like and may be derived from the Hebrew for *praise*.   [c] 10 Or *from his descendants*   [d] 10 Or *to whom tribute belongs*; the meaning of the Hebrew for this phrase is uncertain.

¹²His eyes will be darker than
    wine,
    his teeth whiter than milk.ᵃ

¹³"Zebulun will live by the
    seashore   Dt 33:18-19
    and become a haven for
    ships;
    his border will extend
    toward Sidon.

¹⁴"Issachar is a rawbonedᵇ
    donkey
    lying down among the
    sheep pens.ᶜ
¹⁵When he sees how good is his
    resting place
    and how pleasant is his
    land,
    he will bend his shoulder to
    the burden
    and submit to forced labor.

¹⁶"Danᵈ will provide justice for
    his people   Dt 33:22
    as one of the tribes of
    Israel.
¹⁷Dan will be a snake by the
    roadside,   Jdg 18:27
    a viper along the path,
    that bites the horse's heels
    so that its rider tumbles
    backward.

¹⁸"I look for your deliverance,
    LORD.

¹⁹"Gadᵉ will be attacked by a
    band of raiders,   Dt 33:20
    but he will attack them at
    their heels.

²⁰"Asher's food will be
    rich;   Dt 33:24
    he will provide delicacies fit
    for a king.

²¹"Naphtali is a doe set
    free   Dt 33:23
    that bears beautiful fawns.ᶠ

²²"Joseph is a fruitful
    vine,   Dt 33:13-17
    a fruitful vine near a spring,
    whose branches climb over
    a wall.ᵍ
²³With bitterness archers
    attacked him;
    they shot at him with
    hostility.
²⁴But his bow remained steady,
    his strong arms stayedʰ
    limber,   Ps 18:34
    because of the hand of the
    Mighty One of
    Jacob,   Ps 132:2,5; Isa 1:24
    because of the Shepherd,
    the Rock of
    Israel,   Isa 28:16
²⁵because of your father's God,
    who helps you,   Ge 28:13
    because of the Almighty,ⁱ
    who blesses you
    with blessings of the skies
    above,
    blessings of the deep
    springs below,

ᵃ 12 Or *will be dull from wine, / his teeth white from milk*   ᵇ 14 Or *strong*   ᶜ 14 Or *the
campfires*; or *the saddlebags*   ᵈ 16 *Dan* here means *he provides justice.*   ᵉ 19 *Gad*
sounds like the Hebrew for *attack* and also for *band of raiders.*   ᶠ 21 Or *free; / he utters
beautiful words*   ᵍ 22 Or *Joseph is a wild colt, / a wild colt near a spring, / a wild donkey
on a terraced hill*   ʰ 23,24 Or *archers will attack . . . will shoot . . . will remain . . . will stay*
ⁱ 25 Hebrew *Shaddai*

blessings of the breast and
womb.
26 Your father's blessings are
greater
than the blessings of the
ancient mountains,
than*a* the bounty of the age-
old hills.
Let all these rest on the head
of Joseph,
on the brow of the prince
among*b* his
brothers. Dt 33:15-16

27 "Benjamin is a ravenous wolf;
in the morning he devours
the prey,
in the evening he divides
the plunder."

28 All these are the twelve tribes
of Israel, and this is what their father said to them when he blessed
them, giving each the blessing
appropriate to him. Dt 33:1-29

The Death of Jacob

29 Then he gave them these
instructions: "I am about to be
gathered to my people. Bury me
with my fathers in the cave in
the field of Ephron the Hittite,
30 the cave in the field of Machpelah, near Mamre in Canaan,
which Abraham bought along
with the field as a burial place
from Ephron the Hittite. 31 There
Abraham and his wife Sarah
were buried, there Isaac and his
wife Rebekah were buried, and

there I buried Leah. 32 The field
and the cave in it were bought
from the Hittites.*c*" Ge 25:9; 35:29

33 When Jacob had finished
giving instructions to his sons,
he drew his feet up into the bed,
breathed his last and was gathered to his people. Ge 25:8

50 Joseph threw himself on
his father and wept over
him and kissed him. 2 Then Joseph directed the physicians in
his service to embalm his father
Israel. So the physicians embalmed him, 3 taking a full forty
days, for that was the time required for embalming. And the
Egyptians mourned for him seventy days. Ge 46:4; 2Ch 16:14

4 When the days of mourning
had passed, Joseph said to Pharaoh's court, "If I have found favor in your eyes, speak to Pharaoh for me. Tell him, 5 'My father
made me swear an oath and
said, "I am about to die; bury me
in the tomb I dug for myself in
the land of Canaan." Now let me
go up and bury my father; then I
will return.'" Ge 47:31; Isa 22:16

6 Pharaoh said, "Go up and
bury your father, as he made you
swear to do."

7 So Joseph went up to bury his
father. All Pharaoh's officials accompanied him—the dignitaries of his court and all the dignitaries of Egypt— 8 besides all
the members of Joseph's house-

---

a 26 Or *of my progenitors, / as great as*   *b* 26 Or *of the one separated from*   *c* 32 Or *the*
descendants of Heth

hold and his brothers and those belonging to his father's household. Only their children and their flocks and herds were left in Goshen. ⁹Chariots and horsemen*a* also went up with him. It was a very large company.

¹⁰When they reached the threshing floor of Atad, near the Jordan, they lamented loudly and bitterly; and there Joseph observed a seven-day period of mourning for his father. ¹¹When the Canaanites who lived there saw the mourning at the threshing floor of Atad, they said, "The Egyptians are holding a solemn ceremony of mourning." That is why that place near the Jordan is called Abel Mizraim.*b*   1Sa 31:13

¹²So Jacob's sons did as he had commanded them: ¹³They carried him to the land of Canaan and buried him in the cave in the field of Machpelah, near Mamre, which Abraham had bought along with the field as a burial place from Ephron the Hittite. ¹⁴After burying his father, Joseph returned to Egypt, together with his brothers and all the others who had gone with him to bury his father.   Ge 23:20; Ac 7:16

Joseph Reassures His Brothers

¹⁵When Joseph's brothers saw that their father was dead, they said, "What if Joseph holds a grudge against us and pays us back for all the wrongs we did to him?" ¹⁶So they sent word to Joseph, saying, "Your father left these instructions before he died: ¹⁷'This is what you are to say to Joseph: I ask you to forgive your brothers the sins and the wrongs they committed in treating you so badly.' Now please forgive the sins of the servants of the God of your father." When their message came to him, Joseph wept.   Ge 37:28

¹⁸His brothers then came and threw themselves down before him. "We are your slaves," they said.   Ge 37:7

¹⁹But Joseph said to them, "Don't be afraid. Am I in the place of God? ²⁰You intended to harm me, but God intended it for good to accomplish what is now being done, the saving of many lives. ²¹So then, don't be afraid. I will provide for you and your children." And he reassured them and spoke kindly to them.   Ro 8:28; 12:19; Ge 45:5

The Death of Joseph

²²Joseph stayed in Egypt, along with all his father's family. He lived a hundred and ten years ²³and saw the third generation of Ephraim's children. Also the children of Makir son of Manasseh were placed at birth on Joseph's knees.*c*   Nu 32:39-40

²⁴Then Joseph said to his

---

a 9 Or *charioteers*   *b* 11 *Abel Mizraim* means *mourning of the Egyptians.*   *c* 23 That is, were counted as his brothers, "I am about to die. But God will surely come to your aid and take you up out of this land to the land he promised on oath to Abraham, Isaac and Jacob." [25] And Joseph made the Israelites swear an oath and said, "God will surely come to your aid, and then you must carry my bones up from this place." Ge 12:7; 26:3

[26] So Joseph died at the age of a hundred and ten. And after they embalmed him, he was placed in a coffin in Egypt.

Exodus

The Israelites Oppressed

1 These are the names of the sons of Israel who went to Egypt with Jacob, each with his family: ²Reuben, Simeon, Levi and Judah; ³Issachar, Zebulun and Benjamin; ⁴Dan and Naphtali; Gad and Asher. ⁵The descendants of Jacob numbered seventy*a* in all; Joseph was already in Egypt. Ge 46:8,26

⁶Now Joseph and all his brothers and all that generation died, ⁷but the Israelites were exceedingly fruitful; they multiplied greatly, increased in numbers and became so numerous that the land was filled with them. Ge 46:3; Ac 7:17; Ge 50:26

⁸Then a new king, to whom Joseph meant nothing, came to power in Egypt. ⁹"Look," he said to his people, "the Israelites have become far too numerous for us. ¹⁰Come, we must deal shrewdly with them or they will become even more numerous and, if war breaks out, will join our enemies, fight against us and leave the country." Ps 105:24-25; Ac 7:17-19

¹¹So they put slave masters over them to oppress them with forced labor, and they built Pithom and Rameses as store cities for Pharaoh. ¹²But the more they were oppressed, the more they multiplied and spread; so the Egyptians came to dread the Israelites ¹³and worked them ruthlessly. ¹⁴They made their lives bitter with harsh labor in brick and mortar and with all kinds of work in the fields; in all their harsh labor the Egyptians worked them ruthlessly. Ex 3:7; 2:23; Nu 20:15

¹⁵The king of Egypt said to the Hebrew midwives, whose names were Shiphrah and Puah, ¹⁶"When you are helping the Hebrew women during childbirth on the delivery stool, if you see that the baby is a boy, kill him; but if it is a girl, let her live." ¹⁷The midwives, however, feared God and did not do what the king of Egypt had told them to do; they

---

a 5 Masoretic Text (see also Gen. 46:27); Dead Sea Scrolls and Septuagint (see also Acts 7:14 and note at Gen. 46:27) *seventy-five* let the boys live. ¹⁸Then the king of Egypt summoned the midwives and asked them, "Why have you done this? Why have you let the boys live?" <small>ver 21; Pr 16:6</small>

¹⁹The midwives answered Pharaoh, "Hebrew women are not like Egyptian women; they are vigorous and give birth before the midwives arrive." <small>Jos 2:4-6</small>

²⁰So God was kind to the midwives and the people increased and became even more numerous. ²¹And because the midwives feared God, he gave them families of their own. <small>1Sa 2:35</small>

²²Then Pharaoh gave this order to all his people: "Every Hebrew boy that is born you must throw into the Nile, but let every girl live." <small>Ac 7:19</small>

The Birth of Moses

2 Now a man of the tribe of Levi married a Levite woman, ²and she became pregnant and gave birth to a son. When she saw that he was a fine child, she hid him for three months. ³But when she could hide him no longer, she got a papyrus basket^a for him and coated it with tar and pitch. Then she placed the child in it and put it among the reeds along the bank of the Nile. ⁴His sister stood at a distance to see what would happen to him. <small>Heb 11:23; Ex 15:20; 6:20</small>

⁵Then Pharaoh's daughter went down to the Nile to bathe, and her attendants were walking along the riverbank. She saw the basket among the reeds and sent her female slave to get it. ⁶She opened it and saw the baby. He was crying, and she felt sorry for him. "This is one of the Hebrew babies," she said. <small>Ex 7:15</small>

⁷Then his sister asked Pharaoh's daughter, "Shall I go and get one of the Hebrew women to nurse the baby for you?"

⁸"Yes, go," she answered. So the girl went and got the baby's mother. ⁹Pharaoh's daughter said to her, "Take this baby and nurse him for me, and I will pay you." So the woman took the baby and nursed him. ¹⁰When the child grew older, she took him to Pharaoh's daughter and he became her son. She named him Moses,^b saying, "I drew him out of the water."

Moses Flees to Midian

¹¹One day, after Moses had grown up, he went out to where his own people were and watched them at their hard labor. He saw an Egyptian beating a Hebrew, one of his own people. ¹²Looking this way and that and seeing no one, he killed the Egyptian and hid him in the sand. ¹³The next day he went out and saw two Hebrews fighting. He asked the one in the wrong,

---

^a 3 The Hebrew can also mean *ark*, as in Gen. 6:14.   ^b 10 *Moses* sounds like the Hebrew for *draw out.*

"Why are you hitting your fellow Hebrew?" Ac 7:23; Heb 11:24-26

[14] The man said, "Who made you ruler and judge over us? Are you thinking of killing me as you killed the Egyptian?" Then Moses was afraid and thought, "What I did must have become known." Ac 7:27

[15] When Pharaoh heard of this, he tried to kill Moses, but Moses fled from Pharaoh and went to live in Midian, where he sat down by a well. [16] Now a priest of Midian had seven daughters, and they came to draw water and fill the troughs to water their father's flock. [17] Some shepherds came along and drove them away, but Moses got up and came to their rescue and watered their flock. Ex 3:1; Ge 29:10

[18] When the girls returned to Reuel their father, he asked them, "Why have you returned so early today?" Nu 10:29

[19] They answered, "An Egyptian rescued us from the shepherds. He even drew water for us and watered the flock."

[20] "And where is he?" Reuel asked his daughters. "Why did you leave him? Invite him to have something to eat." Ge 31:54

[21] Moses agreed to stay with the man, who gave his daughter Zipporah to Moses in marriage. [22] Zipporah gave birth to a son, and Moses named him Gershom,[a]

saying, "I have become a foreigner in a foreign land." Ex 18:2; Heb 11:13

[23] During that long period, the king of Egypt died. The Israelites groaned in their slavery and cried out, and their cry for help because of their slavery went up to God. [24] God heard their groaning and he remembered his covenant with Abraham, with Isaac and with Jacob. [25] So God looked on the Israelites and was concerned about them. Ex 3:7; Ps 105:10,42

Moses and the Burning Bush

3 Now Moses was tending the flock of Jethro his father-in-law, the priest of Midian, and he led the flock to the far side of the wilderness and came to Horeb, the mountain of God. [2] There the angel of the LORD appeared to him in flames of fire from within a bush. Moses saw that though the bush was on fire it did not burn up. [3] So Moses thought, "I will go over and see this strange sight—why the bush does not burn up." Dt 33:16; Ac 7:30

[4] When the LORD saw that he had gone over to look, God called to him from within the bush, "Moses! Moses!"

And Moses said, "Here I am." Ge 31:11

[5] "Do not come any closer," God said. "Take off your sandals, for the place where you are standing is holy ground." [6] Then he said, "I am the God of your

---

[a] 22 *Gershom* sounds like the Hebrew for *a foreigner there.*

father,^a the God of Abraham, the God of Isaac and the God of Jacob." At this, Moses hid his face, because he was afraid to look at God. Ac 7:32-33; Mt 22:32

⁷The LORD said, "I have indeed seen the misery of my people in Egypt. I have heard them crying out because of their slave drivers, and I am concerned about their suffering. ⁸So I have come down to rescue them from the hand of the Egyptians and to bring them up out of that land into a good and spacious land, a land flowing with milk and honey—the home of the Canaanites, Hittites, Amorites, Perizzites, Hivites and Jebusites. ⁹And now the cry of the Israelites has reached me, and I have seen the way the Egyptians are oppressing them. ¹⁰So now, go. I am sending you to Pharaoh to bring my people the Israelites out of Egypt." Mic 6:4; Ex 2:25

¹¹But Moses said to God, "Who am I that I should go to Pharaoh and bring the Israelites out of Egypt?" Ex 6:12,30; 1Sa 18:18

¹²And God said, "I will be with you. And this will be the sign to you that it is I who have sent you: When you have brought the people out of Egypt, you^b will worship God on this mountain." Ro 8:31

¹³Moses said to God, "Suppose I go to the Israelites and say to them, 'The God of your fathers has sent me to you,' and they ask me, 'What is his name?' Then what shall I tell them?"

¹⁴God said to Moses, "I AM WHO I AM.^c This is what you are to say to the Israelites: 'I AM has sent me to you.'" Ex 6:2-3; Jn 8:58; Heb 13:8

¹⁵God also said to Moses, "Say to the Israelites, 'The LORD,^d the God of your fathers—the God of Abraham, the God of Isaac and the God of Jacob—has sent me to you.'

"This is my name forever,
  the name you shall
    call me
  from generation to
    generation. Ps 135:13

¹⁶"Go, assemble the elders of Israel and say to them, 'The LORD, the God of your fathers—the God of Abraham, Isaac and Jacob—appeared to me and said: I have watched over you and have seen what has been done to you in Egypt. ¹⁷And I have promised to bring you up out of your misery in Egypt into the land of the Canaanites, Hittites, Amorites, Perizzites, Hivites and Jebusites—a land flowing with milk and honey.' Ge 15:16

¹⁸"The elders of Israel will listen to you. Then you and the elders are to go to the king of Egypt and say to him, 'The LORD, the God of the Hebrews, has met

---

^a 6 Masoretic Text; Samaritan Pentateuch (see Acts 7:32) *fathers*   ^b 12 The Hebrew is plural.   ^c 14 Or *I WILL BE WHAT I WILL BE*   ^d 15 The Hebrew for LORD sounds like and may be related to the Hebrew for *I AM* in verse 14.

with us. Let us take a three-day journey into the wilderness to offer sacrifices to the LORD our God.' ¹⁹But I know that the king of Egypt will not let you go unless a mighty hand compels him. ²⁰So I will stretch out my hand and strike the Egyptians with all the wonders that I will perform among them. After that, he will let you go. Ex 6:1,6; 12:31-33; Dt 6:22

²¹"And I will make the Egyptians favorably disposed toward this people, so that when you leave you will not go empty-handed. ²²Every woman is to ask her neighbor and any woman living in her house for articles of silver and gold and for clothing, which you will put on your sons and daughters. And so you will plunder the Egyptians." Ps 105:37; Ex 11:2

Signs for Moses

4 Moses answered, "What if they do not believe me or listen to me and say, 'The LORD did not appear to you'?" Ex 3:18

²Then the LORD said to him, "What is that in your hand?"

"A staff," he replied. ver 17,20

³The LORD said, "Throw it on the ground."

Moses threw it on the ground and it became a snake, and he ran from it. ⁴Then the LORD said to him, "Reach out your hand and take it by the tail." So Moses reached out and took hold of the snake and it turned back into a staff in his hand. ⁵"This," said the LORD, "is so that they may believe that the LORD, the God of their fathers — the God of Abraham, the God of Isaac and the God of Jacob — has appeared to you." Ex 19:9

⁶Then the LORD said, "Put your hand inside your cloak." So Moses put his hand into his cloak, and when he took it out, the skin was leprous[a] — it had become as white as snow. Nu 12:10; 2Ki 5:1,27

⁷"Now put it back into your cloak," he said. So Moses put his hand back into his cloak, and when he took it out, it was restored, like the rest of his flesh.

⁸Then the LORD said, "If they do not believe you or pay attention to the first sign, they may believe the second. ⁹But if they do not believe these two signs or listen to you, take some water from the Nile and pour it on the dry ground. The water you take from the river will become blood on the ground." Ex 7:17-21

¹⁰Moses said to the LORD, "Pardon your servant, Lord. I have never been eloquent, neither in the past nor since you have spoken to your servant. I am slow of speech and tongue." Ex 6:12; Jer 1:6

¹¹The LORD said to him, "Who gave human beings their mouths? Who makes them deaf or mute? Who gives them sight or makes them blind? Is it not I, the LORD? ¹²Now go; I will help you

---

a 6 The Hebrew word for *leprous* was used for various diseases affecting the skin.

speak and will teach you what to say." Isa 50:4; Jer 1:9; Lk 12:12

¹³But Moses said, "Pardon your servant, Lord. Please send someone else." Jnh 1:1-3

¹⁴Then the LORD's anger burned against Moses and he said, "What about your brother, Aaron the Levite? I know he can speak well. He is already on his way to meet you, and he will be glad to see you. ¹⁵You shall speak to him and put words in his mouth; I will help both of you speak and will teach you what to do. ¹⁶He will speak to the people for you, and it will be as if he were your mouth and as if you were God to him. ¹⁷But take this staff in your hand so you can perform the signs with it." Ex 7:1-2,9-21; Nu 23:5

Moses Returns to Egypt

¹⁸Then Moses went back to Jethro his father-in-law and said to him, "Let me return to my own people in Egypt to see if any of them are still alive."

Jethro said, "Go, and I wish you well."

¹⁹Now the LORD had said to Moses in Midian, "Go back to Egypt, for all those who wanted to kill you are dead." ²⁰So Moses took his wife and sons, put them on a donkey and started back to Egypt. And he took the staff of God in his hand. Ex 2:15,23

²¹The LORD said to Moses, "When you return to Egypt, see that you perform before Pharaoh all the wonders I have given you the power to do. But I will harden his heart so that he will not let the people go. ²²Then say to Pharaoh, 'This is what the LORD says: Israel is my firstborn son, ²³and I told you, "Let my son go, so he may worship me." But you refused to let him go; so I will kill your firstborn son.'" Ex 12:12,29; Jer 31:9

²⁴At a lodging place on the way, the LORD met Moses[a] and was about to kill him. ²⁵But Zipporah took a flint knife, cut off her son's foreskin and touched Moses' feet with it.[b] "Surely you are a bridegroom of blood to me," she said. ²⁶So the LORD let him alone. (At that time she said "bridegroom of blood," referring to circumcision.) Jos 5:2-3

²⁷The LORD said to Aaron, "Go into the wilderness to meet Moses." So he met Moses at the mountain of God and kissed him. ²⁸Then Moses told Aaron everything the LORD had sent him to say, and also about all the signs he had commanded him to perform. Ex 3:1

²⁹Moses and Aaron brought together all the elders of the Israelites, ³⁰and Aaron told them everything the LORD had said to Moses. He also performed the signs before the people, ³¹and they believed. And when they heard that the LORD was con-

---

a 24 Hebrew *him*   b 25 The meaning of the Hebrew for this clause is uncertain.

cerned about them and had seen their misery, they bowed down and worshiped. Ex 3:16,18

Bricks Without Straw

5 Afterward Moses and Aaron went to Pharaoh and said, "This is what the LORD, the God of Israel, says: 'Let my people go, so that they may hold a festival to me in the wilderness.'" Ex 4:23

²Pharaoh said, "Who is the LORD, that I should obey him and let Israel go? I do not know the LORD and I will not let Israel go." Ex 3:19; Job 21:15

³Then they said, "The God of the Hebrews has met with us. Now let us take a three-day journey into the wilderness to offer sacrifices to the LORD our God, or he may strike us with plagues or with the sword." Ex 3:18-19; Job 21:15

⁴But the king of Egypt said, "Moses and Aaron, why are you taking the people away from their labor? Get back to your work!" ⁵Then Pharaoh said, "Look, the people of the land are now numerous, and you are stopping them from working." Ex 1:11

⁶That same day Pharaoh gave this order to the slave drivers and overseers in charge of the people: ⁷"You are no longer to supply the people with straw for making bricks; let them go and gather their own straw. ⁸But require them to make the same number of bricks as before; don't reduce the quota. They are lazy;

that is why they are crying out, 'Let us go and sacrifice to our God.' ⁹Make the work harder for the people so that they keep working and pay no attention to lies." Ge 15:13

¹⁰Then the slave drivers and the overseers went out and said to the people, "This is what Pharaoh says: 'I will not give you any more straw. ¹¹Go and get your own straw wherever you can find it, but your work will not be reduced at all.'" ¹²So the people scattered all over Egypt to gather stubble to use for straw. ¹³The slave drivers kept pressing them, saying, "Complete the work required of you for each day, just as when you had straw." ¹⁴And Pharaoh's slave drivers beat the Israelite overseers they had appointed, demanding, "Why haven't you met your quota of bricks yesterday or today, as before?" Isa 10:24

¹⁵Then the Israelite overseers went and appealed to Pharaoh: "Why have you treated your servants this way? ¹⁶Your servants are given no straw, yet we are told, 'Make bricks!' Your servants are being beaten, but the fault is with your own people."

¹⁷Pharaoh said, "Lazy, that's what you are — lazy! That is why you keep saying, 'Let us go and sacrifice to the LORD.' ¹⁸Now get to work. You will not be given any straw, yet you must produce your full quota of bricks."

[19] The Israelite overseers realized they were in trouble when they were told, "You are not to reduce the number of bricks required of you for each day." [20] When they left Pharaoh, they found Moses and Aaron waiting to meet them, [21] and they said, "May the LORD look on you and judge you! You have made us obnoxious to Pharaoh and his officials and have put a sword in their hand to kill us."   Ge 34:30; Ex 14:11

God Promises Deliverance

[22] Moses returned to the LORD and said, "Why, Lord, why have you brought trouble on this people? Is this why you sent me? [23] Ever since I went to Pharaoh to speak in your name, he has brought trouble on this people, and you have not rescued your people at all."   Jer 4:10

6 Then the LORD said to Moses, "Now you will see what I will do to Pharaoh: Because of my mighty hand he will let them go; because of my mighty hand he will drive them out of his country."   Ex 3:19; 12:31,33,39

[2] God also said to Moses, "I am the LORD. [3] I appeared to Abraham, to Isaac and to Jacob as God Almighty,[a] but by my name the LORD[b] I did not make myself fully known to them. [4] I also established my covenant with them to give them the land of Canaan, where they resided as foreigners. [5] Moreover, I have heard the groaning of the Israelites, whom the Egyptians are enslaving, and I have remembered my covenant.   Ex 2:23; 3:14; Ge 15:18

[6] "Therefore, say to the Israelites: 'I am the LORD, and I will bring you out from under the yoke of the Egyptians. I will free you from being slaves to them, and I will redeem you with an outstretched arm and with mighty acts of judgment. [7] I will take you as my own people, and I will be your God. Then you will know that I am the LORD your God, who brought you out from under the yoke of the Egyptians. [8] And I will bring you to the land I swore with uplifted hand to give to Abraham, to Isaac and to Jacob. I will give it to you as a possession. I am the LORD.'"   Ge 15:18; Dt 7:8; Ps 136:21-22

[9] Moses reported this to the Israelites, but they did not listen to him because of their discouragement and harsh labor.

[10] Then the LORD said to Moses, [11] "Go, tell Pharaoh king of Egypt to let the Israelites go out of his country."

[12] But Moses said to the LORD, "If the Israelites will not listen to me, why would Pharaoh listen to me, since I speak with faltering lips[c]?"   Ex 4:10

---

[a] 3 Hebrew *El-Shaddai*   [b] 3 See note at 3:15. also in verse 30   [c] 12 Hebrew *I am uncircumcised of lips*;

Family Record of Moses and Aaron

¹³ Now the LORD spoke to Moses and Aaron about the Israelites and Pharaoh king of Egypt, and he commanded them to bring the Israelites out of Egypt. Ex 3:10

¹⁴ These were the heads of their families[a]: Ge 46:9

The sons of Reuben the firstborn son of Israel were Hanok and Pallu, Hezron and Karmi. These were the clans of Reuben.

¹⁵ The sons of Simeon were Jemuel, Jamin, Ohad, Jakin, Zohar and Shaul the son of a Canaanite woman. These were the clans of Simeon. 1Ch 4:24

¹⁶ These were the names of the sons of Levi according to their records: Gershon, Kohath and Merari. Levi lived 137 years. Ge 46:11; Nu 3:17

¹⁷ The sons of Gershon, by clans, were Libni and Shimei. 1Ch 6:17

¹⁸ The sons of Kohath were Amram, Izhar, Hebron and Uzziel. Kohath lived 133 years. 1Ch 6:2,18

¹⁹ The sons of Merari were Mahli and Mushi. 1Ch 6:19

These were the clans of Levi according to their records.

²⁰ Amram married his father's sister Jochebed, who bore him Aaron and Moses. Amram lived 137 years. Ex 2:1-2

²¹ The sons of Izhar were Korah, Nepheg and Zikri.

²² The sons of Uzziel were Mishael, Elzaphan and Sithri. Lev 10:4

²³ Aaron married Elisheba, daughter of Amminadab and sister of Nahshon, and she bore him Nadab and Abihu, Eleazar and Ithamar. Lev 10:1; Nu 3:2,32

²⁴ The sons of Korah were Assir, Elkanah and Abiasaph. These were the Korahite clans. Nu 26:11

²⁵ Eleazar son of Aaron married one of the daughters of Putiel, and she bore him Phinehas. Nu 25:7,11; Jos 24:33

These were the heads of the Levite families, clan by clan.

²⁶ It was this Aaron and Moses to whom the LORD said, "Bring the Israelites out of Egypt by their divisions." ²⁷ They were the ones who spoke to Pharaoh king of Egypt about bringing the Israelites out of Egypt—this same Moses and Aaron. Ex 7:4

Aaron to Speak for Moses

²⁸ Now when the LORD spoke to Moses in Egypt, ²⁹ he said to him, "I am the LORD. Tell Pharaoh king of Egypt everything I tell you." ver 2,11

a 14 The Hebrew for families here and in verse 25 refers to units larger than clans.

³⁰But Moses said to the LORD, "Since I speak with faltering lips, why would Pharaoh listen to me?" ver 12

7 Then the LORD said to Moses, "See, I have made you like God to Pharaoh, and your brother Aaron will be your prophet. ²You are to say everything I command you, and your brother Aaron is to tell Pharaoh to let the Israelites go out of his country. ³But I will harden Pharaoh's heart, and though I multiply my signs and wonders in Egypt, ⁴he will not listen to you. Then I will lay my hand on Egypt and with mighty acts of judgment I will bring out my divisions, my people the Israelites. ⁵And the Egyptians will know that I am the LORD when I stretch out my hand against Egypt and bring the Israelites out of it." Ex 3:20; 4:16,21

⁶Moses and Aaron did just as the LORD commanded them. ⁷Moses was eighty years old and Aaron eighty-three when they spoke to Pharaoh. Dt 34:7; Ac 7:23,30

Aaron's Staff Becomes a Snake

⁸The LORD said to Moses and Aaron, ⁹"When Pharaoh says to you, 'Perform a miracle,' then say to Aaron, 'Take your staff and throw it down before Pharaoh,' and it will become a snake."

¹⁰So Moses and Aaron went to Pharaoh and did just as the LORD commanded. Aaron threw his staff down in front of Pharaoh and his officials, and it became a snake. ¹¹Pharaoh then summoned wise men and sorcerers, and the Egyptian magicians also did the same things by their secret arts: ¹²Each one threw down his staff and it became a snake. But Aaron's staff swallowed up their staffs. ¹³Yet Pharaoh's heart became hard and he would not listen to them, just as the LORD had said. Ge 41:8; Ex 4:2-5; Isa 7:11

The Plague of Blood

¹⁴Then the LORD said to Moses, "Pharaoh's heart is unyielding; he refuses to let the people go. ¹⁵Go to Pharaoh in the morning as he goes out to the river. Confront him on the bank of the Nile, and take in your hand the staff that was changed into a snake. ¹⁶Then say to him, 'The LORD, the God of the Hebrews, has sent me to say to you: Let my people go, so that they may worship me in the wilderness. But until now you have not listened. ¹⁷This is what the LORD says: By this you will know that I am the LORD: With the staff that is in my hand I will strike the water of the Nile, and it will be changed into blood. ¹⁸The fish in the Nile will die, and the river will stink; the Egyptians will not be able to drink its water.' " Ex 3:18; 4:9; Rev 16:4

¹⁹The LORD said to Moses, "Tell Aaron, 'Take your staff and stretch out your hand over the waters of Egypt—over the

streams and canals, over the ponds and all the reservoirs — and they will turn to blood.' Blood will be everywhere in Egypt, even in vessels*a* of wood and stone." Ex 14:21

²⁰ Moses and Aaron did just as the LORD had commanded. He raised his staff in the presence of Pharaoh and his officials and struck the water of the Nile, and all the water was changed into blood. ²¹ The fish in the Nile died, and the river smelled so bad that the Egyptians could not drink its water. Blood was everywhere in Egypt. Ps 78:44; 105:29

²² But the Egyptian magicians did the same things by their secret arts, and Pharaoh's heart became hard; he would not listen to Moses and Aaron, just as the LORD had said. ²³ Instead, he turned and went into his palace, and did not take even this to heart. ²⁴ And all the Egyptians dug along the Nile to get drinking water, because they could not drink the water of the river. ver 11

The Plague of Frogs

²⁵ Seven days passed after the LORD struck the Nile. ¹ Then the LORD said to Moses, "Go to Pharaoh and say to him, 'This is what the LORD says: Let my people go, so that they may worship me. ² If you refuse to let them go, I will send a plague of frogs on your whole country. ³ The Nile will teem with frogs. They will come up into your palace and your bedroom and onto your bed, into the houses of your officials and on your people, and into your ovens and kneading troughs. ⁴ The frogs will come up on you and your people and all your officials.'" Ex 3:12,18; 10:6

⁵ Then the LORD said to Moses, "Tell Aaron, 'Stretch out your hand with your staff over the streams and canals and ponds, and make frogs come up on the land of Egypt.'" Ex 7:19

⁶ So Aaron stretched out his hand over the waters of Egypt, and the frogs came up and covered the land. ⁷ But the magicians did the same things by their secret arts; they also made frogs come up on the land of Egypt. Ex 7:11; Ps 78:45

⁸ Pharaoh summoned Moses and Aaron and said, "Pray to the LORD to take the frogs away from me and my people, and I will let your people go to offer sacrifices to the LORD." Ex 9:28; 10:17

⁹ Moses said to Pharaoh, "I leave to you the honor of setting the time for me to pray for you and your officials and your people that you and your houses may be rid of the frogs, except for those that remain in the Nile."

¹⁰ "Tomorrow," Pharaoh said. Moses replied, "It will be as you

---

a 19 Or *even on their idols*   *b* In Hebrew texts 8:1-4 is numbered 7:26-29, and 8:5-32 is numbered 8:1-28.

say, so that you may know there is no one like the LORD our God. [11] The frogs will leave you and your houses, your officials and your people; they will remain only in the Nile." Ex 9:14; Dt 33:26

[12] After Moses and Aaron left Pharaoh, Moses cried out to the LORD about the frogs he had brought on Pharaoh. [13] And the LORD did what Moses asked. The frogs died in the houses, in the courtyards and in the fields. [14] They were piled into heaps, and the land reeked of them. [15] But when Pharaoh saw that there was relief, he hardened his heart and would not listen to Moses and Aaron, just as the LORD had said. Ex 7:14

The Plague of Gnats

[16] Then the LORD said to Moses, "Tell Aaron, 'Stretch out your staff and strike the dust of the ground,' and throughout the land of Egypt the dust will become gnats." [17] They did this, and when Aaron stretched out his hand with the staff and struck the dust of the ground, gnats came on people and animals. All the dust throughout the land of Egypt became gnats. [18] But when the magicians tried to produce gnats by their secret arts, they could not.

Since the gnats were on people and animals everywhere, [19] the magicians said to Pharaoh,

"This is the finger of God." But Pharaoh's heart was hard and he would not listen, just as the LORD had said. Ex 7:5; 9:11; Ps 8:3; 105:31

The Plague of Flies

[20] Then the LORD said to Moses, "Get up early in the morning and confront Pharaoh as he goes to the river and say to him, 'This is what the LORD says: Let my people go, so that they may worship me. [21] If you do not let my people go, I will send swarms of flies on you and your officials, on your people and into your houses. The houses of the Egyptians will be full of flies; even the ground will be covered with them. Ex 3:18; 7:15

[22] "'But on that day I will deal differently with the land of Goshen, where my people live; no swarms of flies will be there, so that you will know that I, the LORD, am in this land. [23] I will make a distinction[a] between my people and your people. This sign will occur tomorrow.'" Ex 7:5; 9:4,6,26

[24] And the LORD did this. Dense swarms of flies poured into Pharaoh's palace and into the houses of his officials; throughout Egypt the land was ruined by the flies. Ps 78:45; 105:31

[25] Then Pharaoh summoned Moses and Aaron and said, "Go, sacrifice to your God here in the land." Ex 9:27; 10:16

[26] But Moses said, "That would not be right. The sacrifices we of-

[a] 23 Septuagint and Vulgate; Hebrew *will put a deliverance*

fer the LORD our God would be detestable to the Egyptians. And if we offer sacrifices that are detestable in their eyes, will they not stone us? [27] We must take a three-day journey into the wilderness to offer sacrifices to the LORD our God, as he commands us." Ge 43:32; Ex 3:18

[28] Pharaoh said, "I will let you go to offer sacrifices to the LORD your God in the wilderness, but you must not go very far. Now pray for me." ver 8

[29] Moses answered, "As soon as I leave you, I will pray to the LORD, and tomorrow the flies will leave Pharaoh and his officials and his people. Only let Pharaoh be sure that he does not act deceitfully again by not letting the people go to offer sacrifices to the LORD."

[30] Then Moses left Pharaoh and prayed to the LORD, [31] and the LORD did what Moses asked. The flies left Pharaoh and his officials and his people; not a fly remained. [32] But this time also Pharaoh hardened his heart and would not let the people go. ver 12; Ex 4:21

The Plague on Livestock

9 Then the LORD said to Moses, "Go to Pharaoh and say to him, 'This is what the LORD, the God of the Hebrews, says: "Let my people go, so that they may worship me." [2] If you refuse to let them go and continue to hold them back, [3] the hand of the LORD will bring a terrible plague on your livestock in the field — on your horses, donkeys and camels and on your cattle, sheep and goats. [4] But the LORD will make a distinction between the livestock of Israel and that of Egypt, so that no animal belonging to the Israelites will die.' " Ex 8:1,22

[5] The LORD set a time and said, "Tomorrow the LORD will do this in the land." [6] And the next day the LORD did it: All the livestock of the Egyptians died, but not one animal belonging to the Israelites died. [7] Pharaoh investigated and found that not even one of the animals of the Israelites had died. Yet his heart was unyielding and he would not let the people go. Ex 7:14; 8:32

The Plague of Boils

[8] Then the LORD said to Moses and Aaron, "Take handfuls of soot from a furnace and have Moses toss it into the air in the presence of Pharaoh. [9] It will become fine dust over the whole land of Egypt, and festering boils will break out on people and animals throughout the land." Rev 16:2

[10] So they took soot from a furnace and stood before Pharaoh. Moses tossed it into the air, and festering boils broke out on people and animals. [11] The magicians could not stand before Moses because of the boils that were on them and on all the Egyptians.

[12]But the LORD hardened Pharaoh's heart and he would not listen to Moses and Aaron, just as the LORD had said to Moses.   Ex 4:21

The Plague of Hail

[13]Then the LORD said to Moses, "Get up early in the morning, confront Pharaoh and say to him, 'This is what the LORD, the God of the Hebrews, says: Let my people go, so that they may worship me, [14]or this time I will send the full force of my plagues against you and against your officials and your people, so you may know that there is no one like me in all the earth. [15]For by now I could have stretched out my hand and struck you and your people with a plague that would have wiped you off the earth. [16]But I have raised you up[a] for this very purpose, that I might show you my power and that my name might be proclaimed in all the earth. [17]You still set yourself against my people and will not let them go. [18]Therefore, at this time tomorrow I will send the worst hailstorm that has ever fallen on Egypt, from the day it was founded till now. [19]Give an order now to bring your livestock and everything you have in the field to a place of shelter, because the hail will fall on every person and animal that has not been brought in and is still out in the field, and they will die.' "   Ro 9:17; Ex 8:10

[20]Those officials of Pharaoh who feared the word of the LORD hurried to bring their slaves and their livestock inside. [21]But those who ignored the word of the LORD left their slaves and livestock in the field.   Pr 13:13

[22]Then the LORD said to Moses, "Stretch out your hand toward the sky so that hail will fall all over Egypt—on people and animals and on everything growing in the fields of Egypt." [23]When Moses stretched out his staff toward the sky, the LORD sent thunder and hail, and lightning flashed down to the ground. So the LORD rained hail on the land of Egypt; [24]hail fell and lightning flashed back and forth. It was the worst storm in all the land of Egypt since it had become a nation. [25]Throughout Egypt hail struck everything in the fields—both people and animals; it beat down everything growing in the fields and stripped every tree. [26]The only place it did not hail was the land of Goshen, where the Israelites were.   ver 4; Ps 105:32-33; Jos 10:11

[27]Then Pharaoh summoned Moses and Aaron. "This time I have sinned," he said to them. "The LORD is in the right, and I and my people are in the wrong. [28]Pray to the LORD, for we have had enough thunder and hail. I will let you go; you don't have to stay any longer."   Ex 8:8; 10:16; 2Ch 12:6

[29]Moses replied, "When I have

___
[a] 16 Or *have spared you*

gone out of the city, I will spread out my hands in prayer to the LORD. The thunder will stop and there will be no more hail, so you may know that the earth is the LORD's. [30] But I know that you and your officials still do not fear the LORD God." 1Ki 8:22,38; Ps 24:1

[31] (The flax and barley were destroyed, since the barley had headed and the flax was in bloom. [32] The wheat and spelt, however, were not destroyed, because they ripen later.) Ru 1:22

[33] Then Moses left Pharaoh and went out of the city. He spread out his hands toward the LORD; the thunder and hail stopped, and the rain no longer poured down on the land. [34] When Pharaoh saw that the rain and hail and thunder had stopped, he sinned again: He and his officials hardened their hearts. [35] So Pharaoh's heart was hard and he would not let the Israelites go, just as the LORD had said through Moses. Ex 4:21

The Plague of Locusts

10 Then the LORD said to Moses, "Go to Pharaoh, for I have hardened his heart and the hearts of his officials so that I may perform these signs of mine among them [2] that you may tell your children and grandchildren how I dealt harshly with the Egyptians and how I performed my signs among them, and that you may know that I am the LORD." Dt 4:9; Ps 44:1

[3] So Moses and Aaron went to Pharaoh and said to him, "This is what the LORD, the God of the Hebrews, says: 'How long will you refuse to humble yourself before me? Let my people go, so that they may worship me. [4] If you refuse to let them go, I will bring locusts into your country tomorrow. [5] They will cover the face of the ground so that it cannot be seen. They will devour what little you have left after the hail, including every tree that is growing in your fields. [6] They will fill your houses and those of all your officials and all the Egyptians — something neither your parents nor your ancestors have ever seen from the day they settled in this land till now.'" Then Moses turned and left Pharaoh. Joel 1:4; Jas 4:10

[7] Pharaoh's officials said to him, "How long will this man be a snare to us? Let the people go, so that they may worship the LORD their God. Do you not yet realize that Egypt is ruined?" Ex 8:19; 23:33

[8] Then Moses and Aaron were brought back to Pharaoh. "Go, worship the LORD your God," he said. "But tell me who will be going." Ex 8:8

[9] Moses answered, "We will go with our young and our old, with our sons and our daughters, and with our flocks and herds, because we are to celebrate a festival to the LORD."

[10] Pharaoh said, "The LORD be with you — if I let you go, along

with your women and children! Clearly you are bent on evil.[a] [11]No! Have only the men go and worship the LORD, since that's what you have been asking for." Then Moses and Aaron were driven out of Pharaoh's presence.

[12]And the LORD said to Moses, "Stretch out your hand over Egypt so that locusts swarm over the land and devour everything growing in the fields, everything left by the hail." Ex 7:19

[13]So Moses stretched out his staff over Egypt, and the LORD made an east wind blow across the land all that day and all that night. By morning the wind had brought the locusts; [14]they invaded all Egypt and settled down in every area of the country in great numbers. Never before had there been such a plague of locusts, nor will there ever be again. [15]They covered all the ground until it was black. They devoured all that was left after the hail—everything growing in the fields and the fruit on the trees. Nothing green remained on tree or plant in all the land of Egypt. Joel 2:1-11,25

[16]Pharaoh quickly summoned Moses and Aaron and said, "I have sinned against the LORD your God and against you. [17]Now forgive my sin once more and pray to the LORD your God to take this deadly plague away from me." Ex 9:27

[18]Moses then left Pharaoh and prayed to the LORD. [19]And the LORD changed the wind to a very strong west wind, which caught up the locusts and carried them into the Red Sea.[b] Not a locust was left anywhere in Egypt. [20]But the LORD hardened Pharaoh's heart, and he would not let the Israelites go. Ex 4:21

The Plague of Darkness

[21]Then the LORD said to Moses, "Stretch out your hand toward the sky so that darkness spreads over Egypt—darkness that can be felt." [22]So Moses stretched out his hand toward the sky, and total darkness covered all Egypt for three days. [23]No one could see anyone else or move about for three days. Yet all the Israelites had light in the places where they lived. Ps 105:28; Rev 16:10

[24]Then Pharaoh summoned Moses and said, "Go, worship the LORD. Even your women and children may go with you; only leave your flocks and herds behind." ver 8-10

[25]But Moses said, "You must allow us to have sacrifices and burnt offerings to present to the LORD our God. [26]Our livestock too must go with us; not a hoof is to be left behind. We have to use some of them in worshiping the LORD our God, and until we get there we will not know what we are to use to worship the LORD."

---

[a] 10 Or *Be careful, trouble is in store for you!*   [b] 19 Or *the Sea of Reeds*

²⁷But the LORD hardened Pharaoh's heart, and he was not willing to let them go. ²⁸Pharaoh said to Moses, "Get out of my sight! Make sure you do not appear before me again! The day you see my face you will die."

²⁹"Just as you say," Moses replied. "I will never appear before you again." Heb 11:27

The Plague on the Firstborn

11 Now the LORD had said to Moses, "I will bring one more plague on Pharaoh and on Egypt. After that, he will let you go from here, and when he does, he will drive you out completely. ²Tell the people that men and women alike are to ask their neighbors for articles of silver and gold." ³(The LORD made the Egyptians favorably disposed toward the people, and Moses himself was highly regarded in Egypt by Pharaoh's officials and by the people.) Dt 34:11; Ex 3:21-22

⁴So Moses said, "This is what the LORD says: 'About midnight I will go throughout Egypt. ⁵Every firstborn son in Egypt will die, from the firstborn son of Pharaoh, who sits on the throne, to the firstborn son of the female slave, who is at her hand mill, and all the firstborn of the cattle as well. ⁶There will be loud wailing throughout Egypt — worse than there has ever been or ever will be again. ⁷But among the Is-raelites not a dog will bark at any person or animal.' Then you will know that the LORD makes a distinction between Egypt and Israel. ⁸All these officials of yours will come to me, bowing down before me and saying, 'Go, you and all the people who follow you!' After that I will leave." Then Moses, hot with anger, left Pharaoh. Ex 8:22; 12:31-33

⁹The LORD had said to Moses, "Pharaoh will refuse to listen to you — so that my wonders may be multiplied in Egypt." ¹⁰Moses and Aaron performed all these wonders before Pharaoh, but the LORD hardened Pharaoh's heart, and he would not let the Israelites go out of his country. Ex 4:21; 7:4

The Passover and the Festival of Unleavened Bread

12:14-20pp — Lev 23:4-8; Nu 28:16-25; Dt 16:1-8

12 The LORD said to Moses and Aaron in Egypt, ²"This month is to be for you the first month, the first month of your year. ³Tell the whole community of Israel that on the tenth day of this month each man is to take a lamb^a for his family, one for each household. ⁴If any household is too small for a whole lamb, they must share one with their nearest neighbor, having taken into account the number of people there are. You are to determine the amount of lamb needed in

---

^a 3 The Hebrew word can mean *lamb* or *kid*; also in verse 4.

accordance with what each person will eat. [5]The animals you choose must be year-old males without defect, and you may take them from the sheep or the goats. [6]Take care of them until the fourteenth day of the month, when all the members of the community of Israel must slaughter them at twilight. [7]Then they are to take some of the blood and put it on the sides and tops of the doorframes of the houses where they eat the lambs. [8]That same night they are to eat the meat roasted over the fire, along with bitter herbs, and bread made without yeast. [9]Do not eat the meat raw or boiled in water, but roast it over a fire — with the head, legs and internal organs. [10]Do not leave any of it till morning; if some is left till morning, you must burn it. [11]This is how you are to eat it: with your cloak tucked into your belt, your sandals on your feet and your staff in your hand. Eat it in haste; it is the LORD's Passover. Dt 16:1,3; Lev 22:18-21

[12]"On that same night I will pass through Egypt and strike down every firstborn of both people and animals, and I will bring judgment on all the gods of Egypt. I am the LORD. [13]The blood will be a sign for you on the houses where you are, and when I see the blood, I will pass over you. No destructive plague will touch you when I strike Egypt. Nu 33:4; Heb 11:28

[14]"This is a day you are to commemorate; for the generations to come you shall celebrate it as a festival to the LORD — a lasting ordinance. [15]For seven days you are to eat bread made without yeast. On the first day remove the yeast from your houses, for whoever eats anything with yeast in it from the first day through the seventh must be cut off from Israel. [16]On the first day hold a sacred assembly, and another one on the seventh day. Do no work at all on these days, except to prepare food for everyone to eat; that is all you may do. Ex 13:5,10; 23:15; Lev 23:6

[17]"Celebrate the Festival of Unleavened Bread, because it was on this very day that I brought your divisions out of Egypt. Celebrate this day as a lasting ordinance for the generations to come. [18]In the first month you are to eat bread made without yeast, from the evening of the fourteenth day until the evening of the twenty-first day. [19]For seven days no yeast is to be found in your houses. And anyone, whether foreigner or native-born, who eats anything with yeast in it must be cut off from the community of Israel. [20]Eat nothing made with yeast. Wherever you live, you must eat unleavened bread." Lev 23:4-8; Nu 28:16-25; Dt 16:1-8

[21]Then Moses summoned all the elders of Israel and said to them, "Go at once and select the animals for your families and slaughter the Passover lamb.

²²Take a bunch of hyssop, dip it into the blood in the basin and put some of the blood on the top and on both sides of the doorframe. None of you shall go out of the door of your house until morning. ²³When the LORD goes through the land to strike down the Egyptians, he will see the blood on the top and sides of the doorframe and will pass over that doorway, and he will not permit the destroyer to enter your houses and strike you down. Mk 14:12-16; 1Co 10:10

²⁴"Obey these instructions as a lasting ordinance for you and your descendants. ²⁵When you enter the land that the LORD will give you as he promised, observe this ceremony. ²⁶And when your children ask you, 'What does this ceremony mean to you?' ²⁷then tell them, 'It is the Passover sacrifice to the LORD, who passed over the houses of the Israelites in Egypt and spared our homes when he struck down the Egyptians.'" Then the people bowed down and worshiped. ²⁸The Israelites did just what the LORD commanded Moses and Aaron. ver 11; Jos 4:6

²⁹At midnight the LORD struck down all the firstborn in Egypt, from the firstborn of Pharaoh, who sat on the throne, to the firstborn of the prisoner, who was in the dungeon, and the firstborn of all the livestock as well. ³⁰Pharaoh and all his offi-

cials and all the Egyptians got up during the night, and there was loud wailing in Egypt, for there was not a house without someone dead. Ex 4:23; 11:4,6

The Exodus

³¹During the night Pharaoh summoned Moses and Aaron and said, "Up! Leave my people, you and the Israelites! Go, worship the LORD as you have requested. ³²Take your flocks and herds, as you have said, and go. And also bless me." Ex 10:9,26

³³The Egyptians urged the people to hurry and leave the country. "For otherwise," they said, "we will all die!" ³⁴So the people took their dough before the yeast was added, and carried it on their shoulders in kneading troughs wrapped in clothing. ³⁵The Israelites did as Moses instructed and asked the Egyptians for articles of silver and gold and for clothing. ³⁶The LORD had made the Egyptians favorably disposed toward the people, and they gave them what they asked for; so they plundered the Egyptians. Ex 3:22

³⁷The Israelites journeyed from Rameses to Sukkoth. There were about six hundred thousand men on foot, besides women and children. ³⁸Many other people went up with them, and also large droves of livestock, both flocks and herds. ³⁹With the dough the Israelites had brought

from Egypt, they baked loaves of unleavened bread. The dough was without yeast because they had been driven out of Egypt and did not have time to prepare food for themselves. Nu 11:13,21; 33:3-5

⁴⁰ Now the length of time the Israelite people lived in Egypt[a] was 430 years. ⁴¹ At the end of the 430 years, to the very day, all the LORD's divisions left Egypt. ⁴² Because the LORD kept vigil that night to bring them out of Egypt, on this night all the Israelites are to keep vigil to honor the LORD for the generations to come. Dt 16:1,6; Ac 7:6

Passover Restrictions

⁴³ The LORD said to Moses and Aaron, "These are the regulations for the Passover meal: ver 11

"No foreigner may eat it. ⁴⁴ Any slave you have bought may eat it after you have circumcised him, ⁴⁵ but a temporary resident or a hired worker may not eat it. Ge 17:12

⁴⁶ "It must be eaten inside the house; take none of the meat outside the house. Do not break any of the bones. ⁴⁷ The whole community of Israel must celebrate it. Nu 9:12; Jn 19:36

⁴⁸ "A foreigner residing among you who wants to celebrate the LORD's Passover must have all the males in his household circumcised; then he may take part like one born in the land. No uncircumcised male may

eat it. ⁴⁹ The same law applies both to the native-born and to the foreigner residing among you." Nu 9:14; 15:15-16,29

⁵⁰ All the Israelites did just what the LORD had commanded Moses and Aaron. ⁵¹ And on that very day the LORD brought the Israelites out of Egypt by their divisions. Ex 6:26

Consecration of the Firstborn

13 The LORD said to Moses, ² "Consecrate to me every firstborn male. The first offspring of every womb among the Israelites belongs to me, whether human or animal." Lk 2:23

³ Then Moses said to the people, "Commemorate this day, the day you came out of Egypt, out of the land of slavery, because the LORD brought you out of it with a mighty hand. Eat nothing containing yeast. ⁴ Today, in the month of Aviv, you are leaving. ⁵ When the LORD brings you into the land of the Canaanites, Hittites, Amorites, Hivites and Jebusites—the land he swore to your ancestors to give you, a land flowing with milk and honey—you are to observe this ceremony in this month: ⁶ For seven days eat bread made without yeast and on the seventh day hold a festival to the LORD. ⁷ Eat unleavened bread during those seven days; nothing with yeast

---

[a] 40 Masoretic Text; Samaritan Pentateuch and Septuagint *Egypt and Canaan*

in it is to be seen among you, nor shall any yeast be seen anywhere within your borders. [8]On that day tell your son, 'I do this because of what the LORD did for me when I came out of Egypt.' [9]This observance will be for you like a sign on your hand and a reminder on your forehead that this law of the LORD is to be on your lips. For the LORD brought you out of Egypt with his mighty hand. [10]You must keep this ordinance at the appointed time year after year. Ex 12:15-20; Dt 6:8

[11]"After the LORD brings you into the land of the Canaanites and gives it to you, as he promised on oath to you and your ancestors, [12]you are to give over to the LORD the first offspring of every womb. All the firstborn males of your livestock belong to the LORD. [13]Redeem with a lamb every firstborn donkey, but if you do not redeem it, break its neck. Redeem every firstborn among your sons. Nu 18:15; Lk 2:23

[14]"In days to come, when your son asks you, 'What does this mean?' say to him, 'With a mighty hand the LORD brought us out of Egypt, out of the land of slavery. [15]When Pharaoh stubbornly refused to let us go, the LORD killed the firstborn of both people and animals in Egypt. This is why I sacrifice to the LORD the first male offspring of every womb and redeem each of my firstborn sons.' [16]And it will be like a sign on your hand and a symbol on your forehead that the LORD brought us out of Egypt with his mighty hand." Ex 12:29; Dt 6:20

Crossing the Sea

[17]When Pharaoh let the people go, God did not lead them on the road through the Philistine country, though that was shorter. For God said, "If they face war, they might change their minds and return to Egypt." [18]So God led the people around by the desert road toward the Red Sea.[a] The Israelites went up out of Egypt ready for battle. Ex 14:11

[19]Moses took the bones of Joseph with him because Joseph had made the Israelites swear an oath. He had said, "God will surely come to your aid, and then you must carry my bones up with you from this place."[b] Ge 50:24-25; Jos 24:32

[20]After leaving Sukkoth they camped at Etham on the edge of the desert. [21]By day the LORD went ahead of them in a pillar of cloud to guide them on their way and by night in a pillar of fire to give them light, so that they could travel by day or night. [22]Neither the pillar of cloud by day nor the pillar of fire by night left its place in front of the people. Ex 14:19,24; Ps 78:14; 1Co 10:1

14 Then the LORD said to Moses, [2]"Tell the Israelites to turn back and encamp near

---

[a] 18 Or *the Sea of Reeds*   [b] 19 See Gen. 50:25.

Pi Hahiroth, between Migdol and the sea. They are to encamp by the sea, directly opposite Baal Zephon. ³Pharaoh will think, 'The Israelites are wandering around the land in confusion, hemmed in by the desert.' ⁴And I will harden Pharaoh's heart, and he will pursue them. But I will gain glory for myself through Pharaoh and all his army, and the Egyptians will know that I am the LORD." So the Israelites did this.   Ro 9:17,22-23; Ex 4:21

⁵When the king of Egypt was told that the people had fled, Pharaoh and his officials changed their minds about them and said, "What have we done? We have let the Israelites go and have lost their services!" ⁶So he had his chariot made ready and took his army with him. ⁷He took six hundred of the best chariots, along with all the other chariots of Egypt, with officers over all of them. ⁸The LORD hardened the heart of Pharaoh king of Egypt, so that he pursued the Israelites, who were marching out boldly. ⁹The Egyptians — all Pharaoh's horses and chariots, horsemen*a* and troops — pursued the Israelites and overtook them as they camped by the sea near Pi Hahiroth, opposite Baal Zephon.   Ex 15:9; Nu 33:3

¹⁰As Pharaoh approached, the Israelites looked up, and there were the Egyptians, marching after them. They were terrified and cried out to the LORD. ¹¹They said to Moses, "Was it because there were no graves in Egypt that you brought us to the desert to die? What have you done to us by bringing us out of Egypt? ¹²Didn't we say to you in Egypt, 'Leave us alone; let us serve the Egyptians'? It would have been better for us to serve the Egyptians than to die in the desert!"   Ne 9:9; Ps 34:17

¹³Moses answered the people, "Do not be afraid. Stand firm and you will see the deliverance the LORD will bring you today. The Egyptians you see today you will never see again. ¹⁴The LORD will fight for you; you need only to be still."   Ps 46:10; Isa 30:15; Ex 15:3

¹⁵Then the LORD said to Moses, "Why are you crying out to me? Tell the Israelites to move on. ¹⁶Raise your staff and stretch out your hand over the sea to divide the water so that the Israelites can go through the sea on dry ground. ¹⁷I will harden the hearts of the Egyptians so that they will go in after them. And I will gain glory through Pharaoh and all his army, through his chariots and his horsemen. ¹⁸The Egyptians will know that I am the LORD when I gain glory through Pharaoh, his chariots and his horsemen."   Ex 4:17; Isa 10:26

¹⁹Then the angel of God, who

---

a 9 Or *charioteers*; also in verses 17, 18, 23, 26 and 28 had been traveling in front of Israel's army, withdrew and went behind them. The pillar of cloud also moved from in front and stood behind them, ²⁰coming between the armies of Egypt and Israel. Throughout the night the cloud brought darkness to the one side and light to the other side; so neither went near the other all night long.　　Ex 13:21

²¹Then Moses stretched out his hand over the sea, and all that night the LORD drove the sea back with a strong east wind and turned it into dry land. The waters were divided, ²²and the Israelites went through the sea on dry ground, with a wall of water on their right and on their left.　　Heb 11:29; Isa 63:12

²³The Egyptians pursued them, and all Pharaoh's horses and chariots and horsemen followed them into the sea. ²⁴During the last watch of the night the LORD looked down from the pillar of fire and cloud at the Egyptian army and threw it into confusion. ²⁵He jammed[a] the wheels of their chariots so that they had difficulty driving. And the Egyptians said, "Let's get away from the Israelites! The LORD is fighting for them against Egypt."　　ver 14; Ex 13:21

²⁶Then the LORD said to Moses, "Stretch out your hand over the sea so that the waters may flow back over the Egyptians and their chariots and horsemen." ²⁷Moses stretched out his hand over the sea, and at daybreak the sea went back to its place. The Egyptians were fleeing toward[b] it, and the LORD swept them into the sea. ²⁸The water flowed back and covered the chariots and horsemen — the entire army of Pharaoh that had followed the Israelites into the sea. Not one of them survived.　　Ex 15:1,21; Ps 106:11

²⁹But the Israelites went through the sea on dry ground, with a wall of water on their right and on their left. ³⁰That day the LORD saved Israel from the hands of the Egyptians, and Israel saw the Egyptians lying dead on the shore. ³¹And when the Israelites saw the mighty hand of the LORD displayed against the Egyptians, the people feared the LORD and put their trust in him and in Moses his servant.　　Jn 2:11; Ps 106:8,10,21

The Song of Moses and Miriam

15 Then Moses and the Israelites sang this song to the LORD:　　Rev 15:3

"I will sing to the LORD, Ps 106:12
　for he is highly exalted.
Both horse and driver
　he has hurled into the sea.

²"The LORD is my strength and
　my defense[c];　　Ps 59:17
　he has become my
　　salvation. Ps 18:2,46; Hab 3:18

[a] 25 See Samaritan Pentateuch, Septuagint and Syriac; Masoretic Text *removed*
[b] 27 Or *from*　[c] 2 Or *song*

He is my God, and I will
 praise him,
my father's God, and I will
 exalt him.   Ex 3:6,15-16
³The LORD is a warrior;   Rev 19:11
 the LORD is his name.
⁴Pharaoh's chariots and his
 army
 he has hurled into the sea.
The best of Pharaoh's officers
 are drowned in the Red
 Sea.ᵃ
⁵The deep waters have covered
 them;
 they sank to the depths like
 a stone.
⁶Your right hand, LORD,   Ps 118:15
 was majestic in power.
Your right hand, LORD,
 shattered the enemy.
⁷"In the greatness of your
 majesty
 you threw down those who
 opposed you.
You unleashed your burning
 anger;
 it consumed them like
 stubble.
⁸By the blast of your nostrils
 the waters piled up.   Ps 78:13
The surging waters stood up
 like a wall;
 the deep waters congealed
 in the heart of the sea.
⁹The enemy boasted,
 'I will pursue, I will
 overtake them.   Ex 14:5-9
I will divide the spoils;
 I will gorge myself on them.

I will draw my sword
 and my hand will destroy
 them.'
¹⁰But you blew with your
 breath,
 and the sea covered them.
They sank like lead
 in the mighty waters.
¹¹Who among the gods
 is like you, LORD?   Ex 8:10
Who is like you —
 majestic in holiness,   Isa 6:3
awesome in glory,   Ps 18:1
 working wonders?

¹²"You stretch out your right
 hand,
 and the earth swallows
 your enemies.
¹³In your unfailing love you will
 lead   Ne 9:12
 the people you have
 redeemed.
In your strength you will
 guide them
 to your holy dwelling.   Ps 78:54
¹⁴The nations will hear and
 tremble;
 anguish will grip the people
 of Philistia.
¹⁵The chiefs of Edom will be
 terrified,
 the leaders of Moab will
 be seized with
 trembling,   Nu 22:3
the peopleᵇ of Canaan will
 melt away;
¹⁶ terror and dread will fall on
 them.
By the power of your arm

___

ᵃ 4 Or the Sea of Reeds; also in verse 22   ᵇ 15 Or rulers

they will be as still as a
stone —
until your people pass by,
Lord,
until the people you
bought[a] pass by. Ps 74:2
[17]You will bring them in and
plant them Ps 44:2
on the mountain of your
inheritance — Ps 78:54,68
the place, Lord, you made for
your dwelling,
the sanctuary, Lord, your
hands established.

[18]"The Lord reigns
for ever and ever."

[19]When Pharaoh's horses, chariots and horsemen[b] went into the sea, the Lord brought the waters of the sea back over them, but the Israelites walked through the sea on dry ground. [20]Then Miriam the prophet, Aaron's sister, took a timbrel in her hand, and all the women followed her, with timbrels and dancing. [21]Miriam sang to them: Ex 14:28; Nu 26:59; 1Sa 18:6

"Sing to the Lord,
for he is highly exalted.
Both horse and driver
he has hurled into the sea."

The Waters of Marah and Elim

[22]Then Moses led Israel from the Red Sea and they went into the Desert of Shur. For three days they traveled in the desert without finding water. [23]When they came to Marah, they could not drink its water because it was bitter. (That is why the place is called Marah.[c]) [24]So the people grumbled against Moses, saying, "What are we to drink?" Nu 33:8

[25]Then Moses cried out to the Lord, and the Lord showed him a piece of wood. He threw it into the water, and the water became fit to drink.

There the Lord issued a ruling and instruction for them and put them to the test. [26]He said, "If you listen carefully to the Lord your God and do what is right in his eyes, if you pay attention to his commands and keep all his decrees, I will not bring on you any of the diseases I brought on the Egyptians, for I am the Lord, who heals you." Ex 23:25-26; Dt 28:27,58-60

[27]Then they came to Elim, where there were twelve springs and seventy palm trees, and they camped there near the water. Nu 33:9

Manna and Quail

16 The whole Israelite community set out from Elim and came to the Desert of Sin, which is between Elim and Sinai, on the fifteenth day of the second month after they had come out of Egypt. [2]In the desert the whole community grumbled against Moses and Aaron. [3]The Israelites said to them, "If only we had died by the Lord's hand in Egypt!

[a] 16 Or created [b] 19 Or charioteers [c] 23 Marah means bitter.

There we sat around pots of meat and ate all the food we wanted, but you have brought us out into this desert to starve this entire assembly to death." Nu 11:4,34; 1Co 10:10

[4]Then the LORD said to Moses, "I will rain down bread from heaven for you. The people are to go out each day and gather enough for that day. In this way I will test them and see whether they will follow my instructions. [5]On the sixth day they are to prepare what they bring in, and that is to be twice as much as they gather on the other days." Dt 8:3; Jn 6:31

[6]So Moses and Aaron said to all the Israelites, "In the evening you will know that it was the LORD who brought you out of Egypt, [7]and in the morning you will see the glory of the LORD, because he has heard your grumbling against him. Who are we, that you should grumble against us?" [8]Moses also said, "You will know that it was the LORD when he gives you meat to eat in the evening and all the bread you want in the morning, because he has heard your grumbling against him. Who are we? You are not grumbling against us, but against the LORD." Nu 16:11; Ro 13:2

[9]Then Moses told Aaron, "Say to the entire Israelite community, 'Come before the LORD, for he has heard your grumbling.' "

[10]While Aaron was speaking to the whole Israelite community, they looked toward the desert, and there was the glory of the LORD appearing in the cloud. Ex 13:21; 1Ki 8:10

[11]The LORD said to Moses, [12]"I have heard the grumbling of the Israelites. Tell them, 'At twilight you will eat meat, and in the morning you will be filled with bread. Then you will know that I am the LORD your God.' "

[13]That evening quail came and covered the camp, and in the morning there was a layer of dew around the camp. [14]When the dew was gone, thin flakes like frost on the ground appeared on the desert floor. [15]When the Israelites saw it, they said to each other, "What is it?" For they did not know what it was. Nu 11:7-9,31; Ps 78:27-28

Moses said to them, "It is the bread the LORD has given you to eat. [16]This is what the LORD has commanded: 'Everyone is to gather as much as they need. Take an omer[a] for each person you have in your tent.' "

[17]The Israelites did as they were told; some gathered much, some little. [18]And when they measured it by the omer, the one who gathered much did not have too much, and the one who gathered little did not have too little. Everyone had gathered just as much as they needed. 2Co 8:15

[19]Then Moses said to them, "No one is to keep any of it until morning." Ex 12:10

---

[a] 16 That is, possibly about 3 pounds or about 1.4 kilograms; also in verses 18, 32, 33 and 36

²⁰However, some of them paid no attention to Moses; they kept part of it until morning, but it was full of maggots and began to smell. So Moses was angry with them.

²¹Each morning everyone gathered as much as they needed, and when the sun grew hot, it melted away. ²²On the sixth day, they gathered twice as much—two omers*ᵃ* for each person—and the leaders of the community came and reported this to Moses. ²³He said to them, "This is what the Lord commanded: 'Tomorrow is to be a day of sabbath rest, a holy sabbath to the Lord. So bake what you want to bake and boil what you want to boil. Save whatever is left and keep it until morning.'"

²⁴So they saved it until morning, as Moses commanded, and it did not stink or get maggots in it. ²⁵"Eat it today," Moses said, "because today is a sabbath to the Lord. You will not find any of it on the ground today. ²⁶Six days you are to gather it, but on the seventh day, the Sabbath, there will not be any." Ge 2:3; Ex 20:8

²⁷Nevertheless, some of the people went out on the seventh day to gather it, but they found none. ²⁸Then the Lord said to Moses, "How long will you*ᵇ* refuse to keep my commands and my instructions? ²⁹Bear in mind that the Lord has given you the Sabbath; that is why on the sixth day he gives you bread for two days. Everyone is to stay where they are on the seventh day; no one is to go out." ³⁰So the people rested on the seventh day. Ps 78:10

³¹The people of Israel called the bread manna.*ᶜ* It was white like coriander seed and tasted like wafers made with honey. ³²Moses said, "This is what the Lord has commanded: 'Take an omer of manna and keep it for the generations to come, so they can see the bread I gave you to eat in the wilderness when I brought you out of Egypt.'"

³³So Moses said to Aaron, "Take a jar and put an omer of manna in it. Then place it before the Lord to be kept for the generations to come." Heb 9:4

³⁴As the Lord commanded Moses, Aaron put the manna with the tablets of the covenant law, so that it might be preserved. ³⁵The Israelites ate manna forty years, until they came to a land that was settled; they ate manna until they reached the border of Canaan. Ex 25:16,21-22; Jos 5:12

³⁶(An omer is one-tenth of an ephah.)

Water From the Rock

17 The whole Israelite community set out from the Desert of Sin, traveling from place to place as the Lord commanded.

ᵃ 22 That is, possibly about 6 pounds or about 2.8 kilograms   *ᵇ 28* The Hebrew is plural.
ᶜ 31 *Manna* sounds like the Hebrew for *What is it?* (see verse 15).

They camped at Rephidim, but there was no water for the people to drink. ²So they quarreled with Moses and said, "Give us water to drink." Nu 20:2

Moses replied, "Why do you quarrel with me? Why do you put the LORD to the test?" Dt 6:16; Ps 78:18

³But the people were thirsty for water there, and they grumbled against Moses. They said, "Why did you bring us up out of Egypt to make us and our children and livestock die of thirst?" Ex 15:24; 16:2

⁴Then Moses cried out to the LORD, "What am I to do with these people? They are almost ready to stone me." Nu 14:10

⁵The LORD answered Moses, "Go out in front of the people. Take with you some of the elders of Israel and take in your hand the staff with which you struck the Nile, and go. ⁶I will stand there before you by the rock at Horeb. Strike the rock, and water will come out of it for the people to drink." So Moses did this in the sight of the elders of Israel. ⁷And he called the place Massah[a] and Meribah[b] because the Israelites quarreled and because they tested the LORD saying, "Is the LORD among us or not?" Nu 20:11; 1Co 10:4

The Amalekites Defeated

⁸The Amalekites came and attacked the Israelites at Rephidim. ⁹Moses said to Joshua, "Choose some of our men and go out to fight the Amalekites. Tomorrow I will stand on top of the hill with the staff of God in my hands." Dt 25:17-19

¹⁰So Joshua fought the Amalekites as Moses had ordered, and Moses, Aaron and Hur went to the top of the hill. ¹¹As long as Moses held up his hands, the Israelites were winning, but whenever he lowered his hands, the Amalekites were winning. ¹²When Moses' hands grew tired, they took a stone and put it under him and he sat on it. Aaron and Hur held his hands up — one on one side, one on the other — so that his hands remained steady till sunset. ¹³So Joshua overcame the Amalekite army with the sword. Jas 5:16

¹⁴Then the LORD said to Moses, "Write this on a scroll as something to be remembered and make sure that Joshua hears it, because I will completely blot out the name of Amalek from under heaven." Ex 34:27

¹⁵Moses built an altar and called it The LORD is my Banner. ¹⁶He said, "Because hands were lifted up against[c] the throne of the LORD,[d] the LORD will be at war against the Amalekites from generation to generation." Ge 22:14; Nu 24:7

---

[a] 7 Massah means testing. [b] 7 Meribah means quarreling. [c] 16 Or to [d] 16 The meaning of the Hebrew for this clause is uncertain.

Jethro Visits Moses

18 Now Jethro, the priest of Midian and father-in-law of Moses, heard of everything God had done for Moses and for his people Israel, and how the LORD had brought Israel out of Egypt. Ex 2:16; 3:1 ² After Moses had sent away his wife Zipporah, his father-in-law Jethro received her ³ and her two sons. One son was named Gershom,ᵃ for Moses said, "I have become a foreigner in a foreign land"; ⁴ and the other was named Eliezer,ᵇ for he said, "My father's God was my helper; he saved me from the sword of Pharaoh." Ex 2:22; 4:25; Ac 7:29 ⁵ Jethro, Moses' father-in-law, together with Moses' sons and wife, came to him in the wilderness, where he was camped near the mountain of God. ⁶ Jethro had sent word to him, "I, your father-in-law Jethro, am coming to you with your wife and her two sons." Ex 3:1 ⁷ So Moses went out to meet his father-in-law and bowed down and kissed him. They greeted each other and then went into the tent. ⁸ Moses told his father-in-law about everything the LORD had done to Pharaoh and the Egyptians for Israel's sake and about all the hardships they had met along the way and how the LORD had saved them. Ge 29:13; 43:28

⁹ Jethro was delighted to hear about all the good things the LORD had done for Israel in rescuing them from the hand of the Egyptians. ¹⁰ He said, "Praise be to the LORD, who rescued you from the hand of the Egyptians and of Pharaoh, and who rescued the people from the hand of the Egyptians. ¹¹ Now I know that the LORD is greater than all other gods, for he did this to those who had treated Israel arrogantly." ¹² Then Jethro, Moses' father-in-law, brought a burnt offering and other sacrifices to God, and Aaron came with all the elders of Israel to eat a meal with Moses' father-in-law in the presence of God. Lk 1:51; Ps 68:19-20

¹³ The next day Moses took his seat to serve as judge for the people, and they stood around him from morning till evening. ¹⁴ When his father-in-law saw all that Moses was doing for the people, he said, "What is this you are doing for the people? Why do you alone sit as judge, while all these people stand around you from morning till evening?"

¹⁵ Moses answered him, "Because the people come to me to seek God's will. ¹⁶ Whenever they have a dispute, it is brought to me, and I decide between the parties and inform them of God's decrees and instructions." Nu 9:6,8; Dt 17:8-13

¹⁷ Moses' father-in-law replied,

ᵃ 3 *Gershom* sounds like the Hebrew for *a foreigner there.*   ᵇ 4 *Eliezer* means *my God is helper.*

"What you are doing is not good. ¹⁸You and these people who come to you will only wear yourselves out. The work is too heavy for you; you cannot handle it alone. ¹⁹Listen now to me and I will give you some advice, and may God be with you. You must be the people's representative before God and bring their disputes to him. ²⁰Teach them his decrees and instructions, and show them the way they are to live and how they are to behave. ²¹But select capable men from all the people—men who fear God, trustworthy men who hate dishonest gain—and appoint them as officials over thousands, hundreds, fifties and tens. ²²Have them serve as judges for the people at all times, but have them bring every difficult case to you; the simple cases they can decide themselves. That will make your load lighter, because they will share it with you. ²³If you do this and God so commands, you will be able to stand the strain, and all these people will go home satisfied." Nu 27:5; Dt 15:1; 16:19

²⁴Moses listened to his father-in-law and did everything he said. ²⁵He chose capable men from all Israel and made them leaders of the people, officials over thousands, hundreds, fifties and tens. ²⁶They served as judges for the people at all times. The difficult cases they brought to Moses, but the simple ones they decided themselves. ver 22; Dt 1:13-15

²⁷Then Moses sent his father-in-law on his way, and Jethro returned to his own country. Nu 10:29

At Mount Sinai

19 On the first day of the third month after the Israelites left Egypt—on that very day—they came to the Desert of Sinai. ²After they set out from Rephidim, they entered the Desert of Sinai, and Israel camped there in the desert in front of the mountain. Ex 17:1

³Then Moses went up to God, and the LORD called to him from the mountain and said, "This is what you are to say to the descendants of Jacob and what you are to tell the people of Israel: ⁴'You yourselves have seen what I did to Egypt, and how I carried you on eagles' wings and brought you to myself. ⁵Now if you obey me fully and keep my covenant, then out of all nations you will be my treasured possession. Although the whole earth is mine, ⁶you*a* will be for me a kingdom of priests and a holy nation.' These are the words you are to speak to the Israelites." Dt 7:6; 1Pe 2:5

⁷So Moses went back and summoned the elders of the people and set before them all the words the LORD had commanded him to speak. ⁸The people all responded together, "We will do

---

a 5,6 Or possession, for the whole earth is mine. ⁶You

everything the LORD has said." So Moses brought their answer back to the LORD. Ex 24:3,7; Dt 5:27

⁹The LORD said to Moses, "I am going to come to you in a dense cloud, so that the people will hear me speaking with you and will always put their trust in you." Then Moses told the LORD what the people had said. ver 16; Ex 24:15-16

¹⁰And the LORD said to Moses, "Go to the people and consecrate them today and tomorrow. Have them wash their clothes ¹¹and be ready by the third day, because on that day the LORD will come down on Mount Sinai in the sight of all the people. ¹²Put limits for the people around the mountain and tell them, 'Be careful that you do not approach the mountain or touch the foot of it. Whoever touches the mountain is to be put to death. ¹³They are to be stoned or shot with arrows; not a hand is to be laid on them. No person or animal shall be permitted to live.' Only when the ram's horn sounds a long blast may they approach the mountain." Lev 11:44; Heb 12:20

¹⁴After Moses had gone down the mountain to the people, he consecrated them, and they washed their clothes. ¹⁵Then he said to the people, "Prepare yourselves for the third day. Abstain from sexual relations." Ge 35:2

¹⁶On the morning of the third day there was thunder and lightning, with a thick cloud over the mountain, and a very loud trumpet blast. Everyone in the camp trembled. ¹⁷Then Moses led the people out of the camp to meet with God, and they stood at the foot of the mountain. ¹⁸Mount Sinai was covered with smoke, because the LORD descended on it in fire. The smoke billowed up from it like smoke from a furnace, and the whole mountain*a* trembled violently. ¹⁹As the sound of the trumpet grew louder and louder, Moses spoke and the voice of God answered him.*b* Ps 81:7; 104:32; Heb 12:18-19

²⁰The LORD descended to the top of Mount Sinai and called Moses to the top of the mountain. So Moses went up ²¹and the LORD said to him, "Go down and warn the people so they do not force their way through to see the LORD and many of them perish. ²²Even the priests, who approach the LORD, must consecrate themselves, or the LORD will break out against them." Lev 10:3; 1Sa 6:19

²³Moses said to the LORD, "The people cannot come up Mount Sinai, because you yourself warned us, 'Put limits around the mountain and set it apart as holy.'" ver 12

²⁴The LORD replied, "Go down and bring Aaron up with you. But the priests and the people must

---

a 18 Most Hebrew manuscripts; a few Hebrew manuscripts and Septuagint *and all the people*
b 19 Or *and God answered him with thunder*

not force their way through to come up to the LORD, or he will break out against them." Ex 24:1,9

25 So Moses went down to the people and told them.

The Ten Commandments

20:1-17pp — Dt 5:6-21

20 And God spoke all these words:

2 "I am the LORD your God, who brought you out of Egypt, out of the land of slavery. Ex 13:3

3 "You shall have no other gods before*a* me. Dt 6:14; Jer 35:15

4 "You shall not make for yourself an image in the form of anything in heaven above or on the earth beneath or in the waters below. 5 You shall not bow down to them or worship them; for I, the LORD your God, am a jealous God, punishing the children for the sin of the parents to the third and fourth generation of those who hate me, 6 but showing love to a thousand generations of those who love me and keep my commandments. Dt 4:24; 7:9; Jer 32:18

7 "You shall not misuse the name of the LORD your God, for the LORD will not hold anyone guilt-less who misuses his name. Lev 19:12

8 "Remember the Sabbath day by keeping it holy. 9 Six days you shall labor and do all your work, 10 but the seventh day is a sabbath to the LORD your God. On it you shall not do any work, neither you, nor your son or daughter, nor your male or female servant, nor your animals, nor any foreigner residing in your towns. 11 For in six days the LORD made the heavens and the earth, the sea, and all that is in them, but he rested on the seventh day. Therefore the LORD blessed the Sabbath day and made it holy. Ex 31:13-16; Ge 2:2

12 "Honor your father and your mother, so that you may live long in the land the LORD your God is giving you. Mt 15:4; Eph 6:2

13 "You shall not murder. Ro 13:9

14 "You shall not commit adultery. Mt 19:18

15 "You shall not steal. Lev 19:11,13

16 "You shall not give false testimony against your neighbor. Ex 23:1,7

17 "You shall not covet your neighbor's house. You shall not covet your neighbor's wife, or his

a 3 Or *besides*

male or female servant, his ox or donkey, or anything that belongs to your neighbor." Dt 5:6-21

¹⁸When the people saw the thunder and lightning and heard the trumpet and saw the mountain in smoke, they trembled with fear. They stayed at a distance ¹⁹and said to Moses, "Speak to us yourself and we will listen. But do not have God speak to us or we will die." Dt 5:5,23-27; Ex 19:16-19

²⁰Moses said to the people, "Do not be afraid. God has come to test you, so that the fear of God will be with you to keep you from sinning." Pr 16:6

²¹The people remained at a distance, while Moses approached the thick darkness where God was. Dt 5:22

Idols and Altars

²²Then the LORD said to Moses, "Tell the Israelites this: 'You have seen for yourselves that I have spoken to you from heaven: ²³Do not make any gods to be alongside me; do not make for yourselves gods of silver or gods of gold. ver 3

²⁴" 'Make an altar of earth for me and sacrifice on it your burnt offerings and fellowship offerings, your sheep and goats and your cattle. Wherever I cause my name to be honored, I will come to you and bless you. ²⁵If you make an altar of stones for me, do not build it with dressed stones, for you will defile it if you use a tool on it. ²⁶And do not go up to my altar on steps, or your private parts may be exposed.' Ge 12:2; Dt 27:5-6

21 "These are the laws you are to set before them: Dt 4:14

Hebrew Servants

21:2-6pp — Dt 15:12-18
21:2-11Ref — Lev 25:39-55

²"If you buy a Hebrew servant, he is to serve you for six years. But in the seventh year, he shall go free, without paying anything. ³If he comes alone, he is to go free alone; but if he has a wife when he comes, she is to go with him. ⁴If his master gives him a wife and she bears him sons or daughters, the woman and her children shall belong to her master, and only the man shall go free. Jer 34:8,14

⁵"But if the servant declares, 'I love my master and my wife and children and do not want to go free,' ⁶then his master must take him before the judges.ᵃ He shall take him to the door or the doorpost and pierce his ear with an awl. Then he will be his servant for life. Dt 15:12-18

⁷"If a man sells his daughter as a servant, she is not to go free as male servants do. ⁸If she does not please the master who

ᵃ 6 Or before God

has selected her for himself,^a he must let her be redeemed. He has no right to sell her to foreigners, because he has broken faith with her. ⁹If he selects her for his son, he must grant her the rights of a daughter. ¹⁰If he marries another woman, he must not deprive the first one of her food, clothing and marital rights. ¹¹If he does not provide her with these three things, she is to go free, without any payment of money.Lev 25:39-55; 1Co 7:3-5

Personal Injuries

¹²"Anyone who strikes a person with a fatal blow is to be put to death. ¹³However, if it is not done intentionally, but God lets it happen, they are to flee to a place I will designate. ¹⁴But if anyone schemes and kills someone deliberately, that person is to be taken from my altar and put to death.   Dt 19:11-12; Nu 35:10-34

¹⁵"Anyone who attacks^b their father or mother is to be put to death.

¹⁶"Anyone who kidnaps someone is to be put to death, whether the victim has been sold or is still in the kidnapper's possession.   Dt 24:7

¹⁷"Anyone who curses their father or mother is to be put to death.   Mk 7:10

¹⁸"If people quarrel and one person hits another with a stone or with their fist^c and the victim does not die but is confined to bed, ¹⁹the one who struck the blow will not be held liable if the other can get up and walk around outside with a staff; however, the guilty party must pay the injured person for any loss of time and see that the victim is completely healed.

²⁰"Anyone who beats their male or female slave with a rod must be punished if the slave dies as a direct result, ²¹but they are not to be punished if the slave recovers after a day or two, since the slave is their property.   Lev 25:44-46

²²"If people are fighting and hit a pregnant woman and she gives birth prematurely^d but there is no serious injury, the offender must be fined whatever the woman's husband demands and the court allows. ²³But if there is serious injury, you are to take life for life, ²⁴eye for eye, tooth for tooth, hand for hand, foot for foot, ²⁵burn for burn, wound for wound, bruise for bruise.   Mt 5:38

²⁶"An owner who hits a male or female slave in the eye and destroys it must let the slave go free to compensate for the eye. ²⁷And an owner who knocks out the tooth of a male or female slave must let the slave go free to compensate for the tooth.

²⁸"If a bull gores a man or woman to death, the bull is to

---

^a 8 Or *master so that he does not choose her*   ^b 15 Or *kills*   ^c 18 Or *with a tool*
^d 22 Or *she has a miscarriage*

be stoned to death, and its meat must not be eaten. But the owner of the bull will not be held responsible. ²⁹ If, however, the bull has had the habit of goring and the owner has been warned but has not kept it penned up and it kills a man or woman, the bull is to be stoned and its owner also is to be put to death. ³⁰ However, if payment is demanded, the owner may redeem his life by the payment of whatever is demanded. ³¹ This law also applies if the bull gores a son or daughter. ³² If the bull gores a male or female slave, the owner must pay thirty shekels*a* of silver to the master of the slave, and the bull is to be stoned to death. Zec 11:12-13; Mt 26:15; Ge 9:5

³³ "If anyone uncovers a pit or digs one and fails to cover it and an ox or a donkey falls into it, ³⁴ the one who opened the pit must pay the owner for the loss and take the dead animal in exchange.

³⁵ "If anyone's bull injures someone else's bull and it dies, the two parties are to sell the live one and divide both the money and the dead animal equally. ³⁶ However, if it was known that the bull had the habit of goring, yet the owner did not keep it penned up, the owner must pay, animal for animal, and take the dead animal in exchange.

Protection of Property

22 *b* "Whoever steals an ox or a sheep and slaughters it or sells it must pay back five head of cattle for the ox and four sheep for the sheep. 2Sa 12:6

² "If a thief is caught breaking in at night and is struck a fatal blow, the defender is not guilty of bloodshed; ³ but if it happens after sunrise, the defender is guilty of bloodshed. Mt 24:43

"Anyone who steals must certainly make restitution, but if they have nothing, they must be sold to pay for their theft. ⁴ If the stolen animal is found alive in their possession — whether ox or donkey or sheep — they must pay back double. Ge 43:12; Ex 21:2

⁵ "If anyone grazes their livestock in a field or vineyard and lets them stray and they graze in someone else's field, the offender must make restitution from the best of their own field or vineyard. ver 1

⁶ "If a fire breaks out and spreads into thornbushes so that it burns shocks of grain or standing grain or the whole field, the one who started the fire must make restitution. Jdg 15:5

⁷ "If anyone gives a neighbor silver or goods for safekeeping and they are stolen from the neighbor's house, the thief, if caught, must pay back double. ⁸ But if the thief is not found, the

---

a 32 That is, about 12 ounces or about 345 grams 21:37, and 22:2-31 is numbered 22:1-30.   *b* In Hebrew texts 22:1 is numbered owner of the house must appear before the judges, and they must[a] determine whether the owner of the house has laid hands on the other person's property. [9] In all cases of illegal possession of an ox, a donkey, a sheep, a garment, or any other lost property about which somebody says, 'This is mine,' both parties are to bring their cases before the judges.[b] The one whom the judges declare[c] guilty must pay back double to the other.   Dt 25:1

[10] "If anyone gives a donkey, an ox, a sheep or any other animal to their neighbor for safekeeping and it dies or is injured or is taken away while no one is looking, [11] the issue between them will be settled by the taking of an oath before the LORD that the neighbor did not lay hands on the other person's property. The owner is to accept this, and no restitution is required. [12] But if the animal was stolen from the neighbor, restitution must be made to the owner. [13] If it was torn to pieces by a wild animal, the neighbor shall bring in the remains as evidence and shall not be required to pay for the torn animal.   Ge 31:39; Heb 6:16

[14] "If anyone borrows an animal from their neighbor and it is injured or dies while the owner is not present, they must make restitution. [15] But if the owner is with the animal, the borrower will not have to pay. If the animal was hired, the money paid for the hire covers the loss.   Lev 19:13

Social Responsibility

[16] "If a man seduces a virgin who is not pledged to be married and sleeps with her, he must pay the bride-price, and she shall be his wife. [17] If her father absolutely refuses to give her to him, he must still pay the bride-price for virgins.   Dt 22:28

[18] "Do not allow a sorceress to live.   Lev 20:27; Dt 18:11

[19] "Anyone who has sexual relations with an animal is to be put to death.   Lev 18:23

[20] "Whoever sacrifices to any god other than the LORD must be destroyed.[d]   Dt 17:2-5

[21] "Do not mistreat or oppress a foreigner, for you were foreigners in Egypt.   Dt 10:19

[22] "Do not take advantage of the widow or the fatherless. [23] If you do and they cry out to me, I will certainly hear their cry. [24] My anger will be aroused, and I will kill you with the sword; your wives will become widows and your children fatherless.   Ps 18:6; 109:9

[25] "If you lend money to one of my people among you who is needy, do not treat it like a business deal; charge no interest. [26] If

---

[a] 8 Or *before God, and he will*   [b] 9 Or *before God*   [c] 9 Or *whom God declares*
[d] 20 The Hebrew term refers to the irrevocable giving over of things or persons to the LORD, often by totally destroying them.

you take your neighbor's cloak as a pledge, return it by sunset, [27] because that cloak is the only covering your neighbor has. What else can they sleep in? When they cry out to me, I will hear, for I am compassionate.   Ex 34:6; Lev 25:35-37

[28] "Do not blaspheme God[a] or curse the ruler of your people.

[29] "Do not hold back offerings from your granaries or your vats.[b]   Ex 23:15-16,19

"You must give me the firstborn of your sons. [30] Do the same with your cattle and your sheep. Let them stay with their mothers for seven days, but give them to me on the eighth day.   Ex 13:2; Lev 22:27

[31] "You are to be my holy people. So do not eat the meat of an animal torn by wild beasts; throw it to the dogs.   Lev 19:2

Laws of Justice and Mercy

23 "Do not spread false reports. Do not help a guilty person by being a malicious witness.   Ex 20:16; Ps 35:11

[2] "Do not follow the crowd in doing wrong. When you give testimony in a lawsuit, do not pervert justice by siding with the crowd, [3] and do not show favoritism to a poor person in a lawsuit.   Dt 16:19

[4] "If you come across your enemy's ox or donkey wandering off, be sure to return it. [5] If you see the donkey of someone who hates you fallen down under its load, do not leave it there; be sure you help them with it.   Dt 22:4

[6] "Do not deny justice to your poor people in their lawsuits. [7] Have nothing to do with a false charge and do not put an innocent or honest person to death, for I will not acquit the guilty.   Eph 4:25

[8] "Do not accept a bribe, for a bribe blinds those who see and twists the words of the innocent.   Dt 10:17

[9] "Do not oppress a foreigner; you yourselves know how it feels to be foreigners, because you were foreigners in Egypt.   Ex 22:21

Sabbath Laws

[10] "For six years you are to sow your fields and harvest the crops, [11] but during the seventh year let the land lie unplowed and unused. Then the poor among your people may get food from it, and the wild animals may eat what is left. Do the same with your vineyard and your olive grove.

[12] "Six days do your work, but on the seventh day do not work, so that your ox and your donkey may rest, and so that the slave born in your household and the foreigner living among you may be refreshed.   Ex 20:9

[13] "Be careful to do everything I have said to you. Do not invoke the names of other gods; do not let them be heard on your lips.   1Ti 4:16

---

a 28 Or *Do not revile the judges*   *b 29* The meaning of the Hebrew for this phrase is uncertain.

The Three Annual Festivals

14 "Three times a year you are to celebrate a festival to me. Ex 34:23-24

15 "Celebrate the Festival of Unleavened Bread; for seven days eat bread made without yeast, as I commanded you. Do this at the appointed time in the month of Aviv, for in that month you came out of Egypt. Ex 12:17

"No one is to appear before me empty-handed. Ex 34:20

16 "Celebrate the Festival of Harvest with the firstfruits of the crops you sow in your field. Ex 34:22

"Celebrate the Festival of Ingathering at the end of the year, when you gather in your crops from the field. Dt 16:13

17 "Three times a year all the men are to appear before the Sovereign LORD. Dt 16:16

18 "Do not offer the blood of a sacrifice to me along with anything containing yeast. Ex 34:25

"The fat of my festival offerings must not be kept until morning. Dt 16:4

19 "Bring the best of the firstfruits of your soil to the house of the LORD your God. Dt 26:2,10

"Do not cook a young goat in its mother's milk. Dt 14:21

God's Angel to Prepare the Way

20 "See, I am sending an angel ahead of you to guard you along the way and to bring you to the place I have prepared. 21 Pay attention to him and listen to what he says. Do not rebel against him; he will not forgive your rebellion, since my Name is in him. 22 If you listen carefully to what he says and do all that I say, I will be an enemy to your enemies and will oppose those who oppose you. 23 My angel will go ahead of you and bring you into the land of the Amorites, Hittites, Perizzites, Canaanites, Hivites and Jebusites, and I will wipe them out. 24 Do not bow down before their gods or worship them or follow their practices. You must demolish them and break their sacred stones to pieces. 25 Worship the LORD your God, and his blessing will be on your food and water. I will take away sickness from among you, 26 and none will miscarry or be barren in your land. I will give you a full life span. Dt 12:30-31

27 "I will send my terror ahead of you and throw into confusion every nation you encounter. I will make all your enemies turn their backs and run. 28 I will send the hornet ahead of you to drive the Hivites, Canaanites and Hittites out of your way. 29 But I will not drive them out in a single year, because the land would become desolate and the wild animals too numerous for you. 30 Little by little I will drive them out before you, until you have increased enough to take possession of the land. Dt 7:23; Jos 24:12

31 "I will establish your bor-

ders from the Red Sea[a] to the Mediterranean Sea,[b] and from the desert to the Euphrates River. I will give into your hands the people who live in the land, and you will drive them out before you. ³²Do not make a covenant with them or with their gods. ³³Do not let them live in your land or they will cause you to sin against me, because the worship of their gods will certainly be a snare to you." Dt 7:16; Jos 21:44

The Covenant Confirmed

24 Then the LORD said to Moses, "Come up to the LORD, you and Aaron, Nadab and Abihu, and seventy of the elders of Israel. You are to worship at a distance, ²but Moses alone is to approach the LORD; the others must not come near. And the people may not come up with him." Nu 11:16

³When Moses went and told the people all the LORD's words and laws, they responded with one voice, "Everything the LORD has said we will do." ⁴Moses then wrote down everything the LORD had said. Ex 19:8; Dt 31:9

He got up early the next morning and built an altar at the foot of the mountain and set up twelve stone pillars representing the twelve tribes of Israel. ⁵Then he sent young Israelite men, and they offered burnt offerings and sacrificed young bulls as fellow-ship offerings to the LORD. ⁶Moses took half of the blood and put it in bowls, and the other half he splashed against the altar. ⁷Then he took the Book of the Covenant and read it to the people. They responded, "We will do everything the LORD has said; we will obey." Heb 9:19; Ex 19:8

⁸Moses then took the blood, sprinkled it on the people and said, "This is the blood of the covenant that the LORD has made with you in accordance with all these words." Heb 9:20; 1Pe 1:2

⁹Moses and Aaron, Nadab and Abihu, and the seventy elders of Israel went up ¹⁰and saw the God of Israel. Under his feet was something like a pavement made of lapis lazuli, as bright blue as the sky. ¹¹But God did not raise his hand against these leaders of the Israelites; they saw God, and they ate and drank. Ge 32:30; Eze 1:26; Rev 4:3

¹²The LORD said to Moses, "Come up to me on the mountain and stay here, and I will give you the tablets of stone with the law and commandments I have written for their instruction." Ex 32:15-16

¹³Then Moses set out with Joshua his aide, and Moses went up on the mountain of God. ¹⁴He said to the elders, "Wait here for us until we come back to you. Aaron and Hur are with you, and anyone involved in a dispute can go to them." Ex 3:1; 17:9

¹⁵When Moses went up on the

---

[a] 31 Or *the Sea of Reeds*   [b] 31 Hebrew *to the Sea of the Philistines*

mountain, the cloud covered it, [16] and the glory of the LORD settled on Mount Sinai. For six days the cloud covered the mountain, and on the seventh day the LORD called to Moses from within the cloud. [17] To the Israelites the glory of the LORD looked like a consuming fire on top of the mountain. [18] Then Moses entered the cloud as he went on up the mountain. And he stayed on the mountain forty days and forty nights.   Heb 12:18,29; Ex 19:9

Offerings for the Tabernacle
25:1-7pp — Ex 35:4-9

25 The LORD said to Moses, [2] "Tell the Israelites to bring me an offering. You are to receive the offering for me from everyone whose heart prompts them to give. [3] These are the offerings you are to receive from them: gold, silver and bronze; [4] blue, purple and scarlet yarn and fine linen; goat hair; [5] ram skins dyed red and another type of durable leather[a]; acacia wood; [6] olive oil for the light; spices for the anointing oil and for the fragrant incense; [7] and onyx stones and other gems to be mounted on the ephod and breastpiece.   Ex 35:4-9; 2Co 8:11-12

[8] "Then have them make a sanctuary for me, and I will dwell among them. [9] Make this taber-nacle and all its furnishings exactly like the pattern I will show you.   Ex 29:45; Rev 21:3

The Ark
25:10-20pp — Ex 37:1-9

[10] "Have them make an ark[b] of acacia wood—two and a half cubits long, a cubit and a half wide, and a cubit and a half high.[c] [11] Overlay it with pure gold, both inside and out, and make a gold molding around it. [12] Cast four gold rings for it and fasten them to its four feet, with two rings on one side and two rings on the other. [13] Then make poles of acacia wood and overlay them with gold. [14] Insert the poles into the rings on the sides of the ark to carry it. [15] The poles are to remain in the rings of this ark; they are not to be removed. [16] Then put in the ark the tablets of the covenant law, which I will give you.   Dt 31:26; Heb 9:4

[17] "Make an atonement cover of pure gold—two and a half cubits long and a cubit and a half wide. [18] And make two cherubim out of hammered gold at the ends of the cover. [19] Make one cherub on one end and the second cherub on the other; make the cherubim of one piece with the cover, at the two ends. [20] The cherubim are to have their wings spread upward, overshadowing the cover with

---

[a] 5 Possibly the hides of large aquatic mammals   [b] 10 That is, a chest   [c] 10 That is, about 3 3/4 feet long and 2 1/4 feet wide and high or about 1.1 meters long and 68 centimeters wide and high; similarly in verse 17

them. The cherubim are to face each other, looking toward the cover. ²¹ Place the cover on top of the ark and put in the ark the tablets of the covenant law that I will give you. ²² There, above the cover between the two cherubim that are over the ark of the covenant law, I will meet with you and give you all my commands for the Israelites.   Ex 37:1-9

The Table

25:23-29pp — Ex 37:10-16

²³ "Make a table of acacia wood—two cubits long, a cubit wide and a cubit and a half high.ᵃ ²⁴ Overlay it with pure gold and make a gold molding around it. ²⁵ Also make around it a rim a handbreadthᵇ wide and put a gold molding on the rim. ²⁶ Make four gold rings for the table and fasten them to the four corners, where the four legs are. ²⁷ The rings are to be close to the rim to hold the poles used in carrying the table. ²⁸ Make the poles of acacia wood, overlay them with gold and carry the table with them. ²⁹ And make its plates and dishes of pure gold, as well as its pitchers and bowls for the pouring out of offerings. ³⁰ Put the bread of the Presence on this table to be before me at all times.   Ex 37:10-16; Nu 4:7

The Lampstand

25:31-39pp — Ex 37:17-24

³¹ "Make a lampstand of pure gold. Hammer out its base and shaft, and make its flowerlike cups, buds and blossoms of one piece with them. ³² Six branches are to extend from the sides of the lampstand—three on one side and three on the other. ³³ Three cups shaped like almond flowers with buds and blossoms are to be on one branch, three on the next branch, and the same for all six branches extending from the lampstand. ³⁴ And on the lampstand there are to be four cups shaped like almond flowers with buds and blossoms. ³⁵ One bud shall be under the first pair of branches extending from the lampstand, a second bud under the second pair, and a third bud under the third pair—six branches in all. ³⁶ The buds and branches shall all be of one piece with the lampstand, hammered out of pure gold.   Zec 4:2; Rev 1:12

³⁷ "Then make its seven lamps and set them up on it so that they light the space in front of it. ³⁸ Its wick trimmers and trays are to be of pure gold. ³⁹ A talentᶜ of pure gold is to be used for the lampstand and all these accessories. ⁴⁰ See that you make them according to the pattern shown you on the mountain.   Ex 37:17-24; Ac 7:44

ᵃ 23 That is, about 3 feet long, 1 1/2 feet wide and 2 1/4 feet high or about 90 centimeters long, 45 centimeters wide and 68 centimeters high   ᵇ 25 That is, about 3 inches or about 7.5 centimeters   ᶜ 39 That is, about 75 pounds or about 34 kilograms

The Tabernacle

26:1-37pp — Ex 36:8-38

26 "Make the tabernacle with ten curtains of finely twisted linen and blue, purple and scarlet yarn, with cherubim woven into them by a skilled worker. [2] All the curtains are to be the same size — twenty-eight cubits long and four cubits wide.[a] [3] Join five of the curtains together, and do the same with the other five. [4] Make loops of blue material along the edge of the end curtain in one set, and do the same with the end curtain in the other set. [5] Make fifty loops on one curtain and fifty loops on the end curtain of the other set, with the loops opposite each other. [6] Then make fifty gold clasps and use them to fasten the curtains together so that the tabernacle is a unit. Ex 36:8-13

[7] "Make curtains of goat hair for the tent over the tabernacle — eleven altogether. [8] All eleven curtains are to be the same size — thirty cubits long and four cubits wide.[b] [9] Join five of the curtains together into one set and the other six into another set. Fold the sixth curtain double at the front of the tent. [10] Make fifty loops along the edge of the end curtain in one set and also along the edge of the end curtain in the other set. [11] Then make fifty bronze clasps and put them in the loops to fasten the tent together as a unit. [12] As for the additional length of the tent curtains, the half curtain that is left over is to hang down at the rear of the tabernacle. [13] The tent curtains will be a cubit[c] longer on both sides; what is left will hang over the sides of the tabernacle so as to cover it. [14] Make for the tent a covering of ram skins dyed red, and over that a covering of the other durable leather.[d] Ex 36:14-19

[15] "Make upright frames of acacia wood for the tabernacle. [16] Each frame is to be ten cubits long and a cubit and a half wide,[e] [17] with two projections set parallel to each other. Make all the frames of the tabernacle in this way. [18] Make twenty frames for the south side of the tabernacle [19] and make forty silver bases to go under them — two bases for each frame, one under each projection. [20] For the other side, the north side of the tabernacle, make twenty frames [21] and forty silver bases — two under each frame. [22] Make six frames for the far end, that is, the west end of the tabernacle, [23] and make two frames for the corners at the far end. [24] At these two corners they must be double from the bottom

---

[a] 2 That is, about 42 feet long and 6 feet wide or about 13 meters long and 1.8 meters wide
[b] 8 That is, about 45 feet long and 6 feet wide or about 13.5 meters long and 1.8 meters wide
[c] 13 That is, about 18 inches or about 45 centimeters   [d] 14 Possibly the hides of large aquatic mammals (see 25:5)   [e] 16 That is, about 15 feet long and 2 1/4 feet wide or about 4.5 meters long and 68 centimeters wide

all the way to the top and fitted into a single ring; both shall be like that. ²⁵ So there will be eight frames and sixteen silver bases — two under each frame. Ex 36:20-30

²⁶ "Also make crossbars of acacia wood: five for the frames on one side of the tabernacle, ²⁷ five for those on the other side, and five for the frames on the west, at the far end of the tabernacle. ²⁸ The center crossbar is to extend from end to end at the middle of the frames. ²⁹ Overlay the frames with gold and make gold rings to hold the crossbars. Also overlay the crossbars with gold. Ex 36:31-34

³⁰ "Set up the tabernacle according to the plan shown you on the mountain. Ex 25:9,40; Ac 7:44; Heb 8:5

³¹ "Make a curtain of blue, purple and scarlet yarn and finely twisted linen, with cherubim woven into it by a skilled worker. ³² Hang it with gold hooks on four posts of acacia wood overlaid with gold and standing on four silver bases. ³³ Hang the curtain from the clasps and place the ark of the covenant law behind the curtain. The curtain will separate the Holy Place from the Most Holy Place. ³⁴ Put the atonement cover on the ark of the covenant law in the Most Holy Place. ³⁵ Place the table outside the curtain on the north side of the tabernacle and put the lampstand opposite it on the south side. Ex 36:35-36; Heb 9:2-3

³⁶ "For the entrance to the tent make a curtain of blue, purple and scarlet yarn and finely twisted linen — the work of an embroiderer. ³⁷ Make gold hooks for this curtain and five posts of acacia wood overlaid with gold. And cast five bronze bases for them. Ex 36:37-38

The Altar of Burnt Offering
27:1-8pp — Ex 38:1-7

27 "Build an altar of acacia wood, three cubits^a high; it is to be square, five cubits long and five cubits wide.^b ² Make a horn at each of the four corners, so that the horns and the altar are of one piece, and overlay the altar with bronze. ³ Make all its utensils of bronze — its pots to remove the ashes, and its shovels, sprinkling bowls, meat forks and firepans. ⁴ Make a grating for it, a bronze network, and make a bronze ring at each of the four corners of the network. ⁵ Put it under the ledge of the altar so that it is halfway up the altar. ⁶ Make poles of acacia wood for the altar and overlay them with bronze. ⁷ The poles are to be inserted into the rings so they will be on two sides of the altar when it is carried. ⁸ Make the altar hollow, out of boards. It is to be made just as you were shown on the mountain. Ex 38:1-7

^a 1 That is, about 4 1/2 feet or about 1.4 meters   ^b 1 That is, about 7 1/2 feet or about 2.3 meters long and wide

The Courtyard

27:9-19pp — Ex 38:9-20

⁹ "Make a courtyard for the tabernacle. The south side shall be a hundred cubits[a] long and is to have curtains of finely twisted linen, ¹⁰ with twenty posts and twenty bronze bases and with silver hooks and bands on the posts. ¹¹ The north side shall also be a hundred cubits long and is to have curtains, with twenty posts and twenty bronze bases and with silver hooks and bands on the posts.

¹² "The west end of the courtyard shall be fifty cubits[b] wide and have curtains, with ten posts and ten bases. ¹³ On the east end, toward the sunrise, the courtyard shall also be fifty cubits wide. ¹⁴ Curtains fifteen cubits[c] long are to be on one side of the entrance, with three posts and three bases, ¹⁵ and curtains fifteen cubits long are to be on the other side, with three posts and three bases.

¹⁶ "For the entrance to the courtyard, provide a curtain twenty cubits[d] long, of blue, purple and scarlet yarn and finely twisted linen — the work of an embroiderer — with four posts and four bases. ¹⁷ All the posts around the courtyard are to have silver bands and hooks, and

bronze bases. ¹⁸ The courtyard shall be a hundred cubits long and fifty cubits wide,[e] with curtains of finely twisted linen five cubits[f] high, and with bronze bases. ¹⁹ All the other articles used in the service of the tabernacle, whatever their function, including all the tent pegs for it and those for the courtyard, are to be of bronze. Ex 38:9-20

Oil for the Lampstand

27:20-21pp — Lev 24:1-3

²⁰ "Command the Israelites to bring you clear oil of pressed olives for the light so that the lamps may be kept burning. ²¹ In the tent of meeting, outside the curtain that shields the ark of the covenant law, Aaron and his sons are to keep the lamps burning before the LORD from evening till morning. This is to be a lasting ordinance among the Israelites for the generations to come. Lev 24:1-3

The Priestly Garments

28 "Have Aaron your brother brought to you from among the Israelites, along with his sons Nadab and Abihu, Eleazar and Ithamar, so they may serve me as priests. ²Make sacred garments for your brother Aaron to give him dignity and

---

[a] 9 That is, about 150 feet or about 45 meters; also in verse 11   [b] 12 That is, about 75 feet or about 23 meters; also in verse 13   [c] 14 That is, about 23 feet or about 6.8 meters; also in verse 15   [d] 16 That is, about 30 feet or about 9 meters   [e] 18 That is, about 150 feet long and 75 feet wide or about 45 meters long and 23 meters wide   [f] 18 That is, about 7 1/2 feet or about 2.3 meters

honor. ³Tell all the skilled workers to whom I have given wisdom in such matters that they are to make garments for Aaron, for his consecration, so he may serve me as priest. ⁴These are the garments they are to make: a breastpiece, an ephod, a robe, a woven tunic, a turban and a sash. They are to make these sacred garments for your brother Aaron and his sons, so they may serve me as priests. ⁵Have them use gold, and blue, purple and scarlet yarn, and fine linen. Ex 31:3,6

The Ephod
28:6-14pp — Ex 39:2-7

⁶"Make the ephod of gold, and of blue, purple and scarlet yarn, and of finely twisted linen—the work of skilled hands. ⁷It is to have two shoulder pieces attached to two of its corners, so it can be fastened. ⁸Its skillfully woven waistband is to be like it—of one piece with the ephod and made with gold, and with blue, purple and scarlet yarn, and with finely twisted linen.

⁹"Take two onyx stones and engrave on them the names of the sons of Israel ¹⁰in the order of their birth—six names on one stone and the remaining six on the other. ¹¹Engrave the names of the sons of Israel on the two stones the way a gem cutter engraves a seal. Then mount the stones in gold filigree settings ¹²and fasten them on the shoulder pieces of the ephod as memorial stones for the sons of Israel. Aaron is to bear the names on his shoulders as a memorial before the Lord. ¹³Make gold filigree settings ¹⁴and two braided chains of pure gold, like a rope, and attach the chains to the settings. Ex 39:2-7

The Breastpiece
28:15-28pp — Ex 39:8-21

¹⁵"Fashion a breastpiece for making decisions—the work of skilled hands. Make it like the ephod: of gold, and of blue, purple and scarlet yarn, and of finely twisted linen. ¹⁶It is to be square—a span[a] long and a span wide—and folded double. ¹⁷Then mount four rows of precious stones on it. The first row shall be carnelian, chrysolite and beryl; ¹⁸the second row shall be turquoise, lapis lazuli and emerald; ¹⁹the third row shall be jacinth, agate and amethyst; ²⁰the fourth row shall be topaz, onyx and jasper.[b] Mount them in gold filigree settings. ²¹There are to be twelve stones, one for each of the names of the sons of Israel, each engraved like a seal with the name of one of the twelve tribes. Rev 21:12

²²"For the breastpiece make braided chains of pure gold,

[a] 16 That is, about 9 inches or about 23 centimeters [b] 20 The precise identification of some of these precious stones is uncertain.

like a rope. ²³Make two gold rings for it and fasten them to two corners of the breastpiece. ²⁴Fasten the two gold chains to the rings at the corners of the breastpiece, ²⁵and the other ends of the chains to the two settings, attaching them to the shoulder pieces of the ephod at the front. ²⁶Make two gold rings and attach them to the other two corners of the breastpiece on the inside edge next to the ephod. ²⁷Make two more gold rings and attach them to the bottom of the shoulder pieces on the front of the ephod, close to the seam just above the waistband of the ephod. ²⁸The rings of the breastpiece are to be tied to the rings of the ephod with blue cord, connecting it to the waistband, so that the breastpiece will not swing out from the ephod.   Ex 39:8-21

²⁹"Whenever Aaron enters the Holy Place, he will bear the names of the sons of Israel over his heart on the breastpiece of decision as a continuing memorial before the Lord. ³⁰Also put the Urim and the Thummim in the breastpiece, so they may be over Aaron's heart whenever he enters the presence of the Lord. Thus Aaron will always bear the means of making decisions for the Israelites over his heart before the Lord.   Lev 8:8; Nu 27:21

Other Priestly Garments
28:31-43pp — Ex 39:22-31

³¹"Make the robe of the ephod entirely of blue cloth, ³²with an opening for the head in its center. There shall be a woven edge like a collar[a] around this opening, so that it will not tear. ³³Make pomegranates of blue, purple and scarlet yarn around the hem of the robe, with gold bells between them. ³⁴The gold bells and the pomegranates are to alternate around the hem of the robe. ³⁵Aaron must wear it when he ministers. The sound of the bells will be heard when he enters the Holy Place before the Lord and when he comes out, so that he will not die.

³⁶"Make a plate of pure gold and engrave on it as on a seal: HOLY TO THE LORD. ³⁷Fasten a blue cord to it to attach it to the turban; it is to be on the front of the turban. ³⁸It will be on Aaron's forehead, and he will bear the guilt involved in the sacred gifts the Israelites consecrate, whatever their gifts may be. It will be on Aaron's forehead continually so that they will be acceptable to the Lord.   Nu 18:1; Zec 14:20

³⁹"Weave the tunic of fine linen and make the turban of fine linen. The sash is to be the work of an embroiderer. ⁴⁰Make tunics, sashes and caps for Aaron's sons to give them dignity and honor.

---

c 32 The meaning of the Hebrew for this word is uncertain.

41 After you put these clothes on your brother Aaron and his sons, anoint and ordain them. Consecrate them so they may serve me as priests. Ex 29:7-9; Lev 18:1-36

42 "Make linen undergarments as a covering for the body, reaching from the waist to the thigh. **43** Aaron and his sons must wear them whenever they enter the tent of meeting or approach the altar to minister in the Holy Place, so that they will not incur guilt and die. Ex 20:26

"This is to be a lasting ordinance for Aaron and his descendants. Ex 39:22-31

Consecration of the Priests

29:1-37pp — Lev 8:1-36

29 "This is what you are to do to consecrate them, so they may serve me as priests: Take a young bull and two rams without defect. **2** And from the finest wheat flour make round loaves without yeast, thick loaves without yeast and with olive oil mixed in, and thin loaves without yeast and brushed with olive oil. **3** Put them in a basket and present them along with the bull and the two rams. **4** Then bring Aaron and his sons to the entrance to the tent of meeting and wash them with water. **5** Take the garments and dress Aaron with the tunic, the robe of the ephod, the ephod itself and the breast-piece. Fasten the ephod on him by its skillfully woven waistband. **6** Put the turban on his head and attach the sacred emblem to the turban. **7** Take the anointing oil and anoint him by pouring it on his head. **8** Bring his sons and dress them in tunics **9** and fasten caps on them. Then tie sashes on Aaron and his sons.*a* The priesthood is theirs by a lasting ordinance.

"Then you shall ordain Aaron and his sons. Nu 18:7; Ex 30:25,30-31

10 "Bring the bull to the front of the tent of meeting, and Aaron and his sons shall lay their hands on its head. **11** Slaughter it in the LORD's presence at the entrance to the tent of meeting. **12** Take some of the bull's blood and put it on the horns of the altar with your finger, and pour out the rest of it at the base of the altar. **13** Then take all the fat on the internal organs, the long lobe of the liver, and both kidneys with the fat on them, and burn them on the altar. **14** But burn the bull's flesh and its hide and its intestines outside the camp. It is a sin offering.*b* Lev 1:4; Heb 13:11

15 "Take one of the rams, and Aaron and his sons shall lay their hands on its head. **16** Slaughter it and take the blood and splash it against the sides of the altar. **17** Cut the ram into pieces and wash the internal organs and the

a 9 Hebrew; Septuagint *on them*   *b 14* Or *purification offering*; also in verse 36 legs, putting them with the head and the other pieces. ¹⁸ Then burn the entire ram on the altar. It is a burnt offering to the Lord, a pleasing aroma, a food offering presented to the Lord. Ge 8:21

¹⁹ "Take the other ram, and Aaron and his sons shall lay their hands on its head. ²⁰ Slaughter it, take some of its blood and put it on the lobes of the right ears of Aaron and his sons, on the thumbs of their right hands, and on the big toes of their right feet. Then splash blood against the sides of the altar. ²¹ And take some blood from the altar and some of the anointing oil and sprinkle it on Aaron and his garments and on his sons and their garments. Then he and his sons and their garments will be consecrated. Heb 9:22

²² "Take from this ram the fat, the fat tail, the fat on the internal organs, the long lobe of the liver, both kidneys with the fat on them, and the right thigh. (This is the ram for the ordination.) ²³ From the basket of bread made without yeast, which is before the Lord, take one round loaf, one thick loaf with olive oil mixed in, and one thin loaf. ²⁴ Put all these in the hands of Aaron and his sons and have them wave them before the Lord as a wave offering. ²⁵ Then take them from their hands and burn them on the altar along with the burnt offering for a pleasing aroma to the Lord,

a food offering presented to the Lord. ²⁶ After you take the breast of the ram for Aaron's ordination, wave it before the Lord as a wave offering, and it will be your share. Lev 7:30

²⁷ "Consecrate those parts of the ordination ram that belong to Aaron and his sons: the breast that was waved and the thigh that was presented. ²⁸ This is always to be the perpetual share from the Israelites for Aaron and his sons. It is the contribution the Israelites are to make to the Lord from their fellowship offerings. Lev 7:31,34

²⁹ "Aaron's sacred garments will belong to his descendants so that they can be anointed and ordained in them. ³⁰ The son who succeeds him as priest and comes to the tent of meeting to minister in the Holy Place is to wear them seven days. Nu 20:26,28

³¹ "Take the ram for the ordination and cook the meat in a sacred place. ³² At the entrance to the tent of meeting, Aaron and his sons are to eat the meat of the ram and the bread that is in the basket. ³³ They are to eat these offerings by which atonement was made for their ordination and consecration. But no one else may eat them, because they are sacred. ³⁴ And if any of the meat of the ordination ram or any bread is left over till morning, burn it up. It must not be eaten, because it is sacred. Lev 22:10,13

³⁵ "Do for Aaron and his sons everything I have commanded you, taking seven days to ordain them. ³⁶ Sacrifice a bull each day as a sin offering to make atonement. Purify the altar by making atonement for it, and anoint it to consecrate it. ³⁷ For seven days make atonement for the altar and consecrate it. Then the altar will be most holy, and whatever touches it will be holy. Lev 8:1-36

³⁸ "This is what you are to offer on the altar regularly each day: two lambs a year old. ³⁹ Offer one in the morning and the other at twilight. ⁴⁰ With the first lamb offer a tenth of an ephah*ᵃ* of the finest flour mixed with a quarter of a hin*ᵇ* of oil from pressed olives, and a quarter of a hin of wine as a drink offering. ⁴¹ Sacrifice the other lamb at twilight with the same grain offering and its drink offering as in the morning — a pleasing aroma, a food offering presented to the LORD. Nu 28:3-8

⁴² "For the generations to come this burnt offering is to be made regularly at the entrance to the tent of meeting, before the LORD. There I will meet you and speak to you; ⁴³ there also I will meet with the Israelites, and the place will be consecrated by my glory. Ex 25:22; 1Ki 8:11

⁴⁴ "So I will consecrate the tent of meeting and the altar and will consecrate Aaron and his sons to serve me as priests. ⁴⁵ Then I will dwell among the Israelites and be their God. ⁴⁶ They will know that I am the LORD their God, who brought them out of Egypt so that I might dwell among them. I am the LORD their God. Ex 25:8; 2Co 6:16; Rev 21:3

The Altar of Incense

30:1-5pp — Ex 37:25-28

30 "Make an altar of acacia wood for burning incense. ² It is to be square, a cubit long and a cubit wide, and two cubits high*ᶜ* — its horns of one piece with it. ³ Overlay the top and all the sides and the horns with pure gold, and make a gold molding around it. ⁴ Make two gold rings for the altar below the molding — two on each of the opposite sides — to hold the poles used to carry it. ⁵ Make the poles of acacia wood and overlay them with gold. ⁶ Put the altar in front of the curtain that shields the ark of the covenant law — before the atonement cover that is over the tablets of the covenant law — where I will meet with you. Ex 37:25-28

⁷ "Aaron must burn fragrant incense on the altar every morning when he tends the lamps. ⁸ He must burn incense again when he lights the lamps at twilight so

---

ᵃ 40 That is, probably about 3 1/2 pounds or about 1.6 kilograms   *ᵇ 40* That is, probably about 1 quart or about 1 liter   *ᶜ 2* That is, about 1 1/2 feet long and wide and 3 feet high or about 45 centimeters long and wide and 90 centimeters high incense will burn regularly before the LORD for the generations to come. ⁹Do not offer on this altar any other incense or any burnt offering or grain offering, and do not pour a drink offering on it. ¹⁰Once a year Aaron shall make atonement on its horns. This annual atonement must be made with the blood of the atoning sin offering*a* for the generations to come. It is most holy to the LORD."   Lev 16:18-19,30

Atonement Money

¹¹Then the LORD said to Moses, ¹²"When you take a census of the Israelites to count them, each one must pay the LORD a ransom for his life at the time he is counted. Then no plague will come on them when you number them. ¹³Each one who crosses over to those already counted is to give a half shekel,*b* according to the sanctuary shekel, which weighs twenty gerahs. This half shekel is an offering to the LORD. ¹⁴All who cross over, those twenty years old or more, are to give an offering to the LORD. ¹⁵The rich are not to give more than a half shekel and the poor are not to give less when you make the offering to the LORD to atone for your lives. ¹⁶Receive the atonement money from the Israelites and use it for the service of the tent of meeting. It will be a memorial for the Israelites before the LORD, making atonement for your lives."   Nu 1:2,49; 31:50

Basin for Washing

¹⁷Then the LORD said to Moses, ¹⁸"Make a bronze basin, with its bronze stand, for washing. Place it between the tent of meeting and the altar, and put water in it. ¹⁹Aaron and his sons are to wash their hands and feet with water from it. ²⁰Whenever they enter the tent of meeting, they shall wash with water so that they will not die. Also, when they approach the altar to minister by presenting a food offering to the LORD, ²¹they shall wash their hands and feet so that they will not die. This is to be a lasting ordinance for Aaron and his descendants for the generations to come."   Ex 27:21; 40:31-32

Anointing Oil

²²Then the LORD said to Moses, ²³"Take the following fine spices: 500 shekels*c* of liquid myrrh, half as much (that is, 250 shekels) of fragrant cinnamon, 250 shekels*d* of fragrant calamus, ²⁴500 shekels of cassia—all according to the sanctuary shekel—and a hin*e* of olive oil. ²⁵Make these into a

a 10 Or *purification offering*   *b 13* That is, about 1/5 ounce or about 5.8 grams; also in verse 15   *c 23* That is, about 12 1/2 pounds or about 5.8 kilograms; also in verse 24   *d 23* That is, about 6 1/4 pounds or about 2.9 kilograms   *e 24* That is, probably about 1 gallon or about 3.8 liters sacred anointing oil, a fragrant blend, the work of a perfumer. It will be the sacred anointing oil. ²⁶Then use it to anoint the tent of meeting, the ark of the covenant law, ²⁷the table and all its articles, the lampstand and its accessories, the altar of incense, ²⁸the altar of burnt offering and all its utensils, and the basin with its stand. ²⁹You shall consecrate them so they will be most holy, and whatever touches them will be holy. *Ex 37:29; Lev 8:10*

³⁰"Anoint Aaron and his sons and consecrate them so they may serve me as priests. ³¹Say to the Israelites, 'This is to be my sacred anointing oil for the generations to come. ³²Do not pour it on anyone else's body and do not make any other oil using the same formula. It is sacred, and you are to consider it sacred. ³³Whoever makes perfume like it and puts it on anyone other than a priest must be cut off from their people.'" *Lev 8:2,12,30*

Incense

³⁴Then the LORD said to Moses, "Take fragrant spices—gum resin, onycha and galbanum—and pure frankincense, all in equal amounts, ³⁵and make a fragrant blend of incense, the work of a perfumer. It is to be salted and pure and sacred. ³⁶Grind some of it to powder and place it in front of the ark of the covenant law in the tent of meeting, where I will meet with

you. It shall be most holy to you. ³⁷Do not make any incense with this formula for yourselves; consider it holy to the LORD. ³⁸Whoever makes incense like it to enjoy its fragrance must be cut off from their people." *Ex 29:37; Lev 2:3*

Bezalel and Oholiab
31:2-6pp — Ex 35:30-35

31 Then the LORD said to Moses, ²"See, I have chosen Bezalel son of Uri, the son of Hur, of the tribe of Judah, ³and I have filled him with the Spirit of God, with wisdom, with understanding, with knowledge and with all kinds of skills — ⁴to make artistic designs for work in gold, silver and bronze, ⁵to cut and set stones, to work in wood, and to engage in all kinds of crafts. ⁶Moreover, I have appointed Oholiab son of Ahisamak, of the tribe of Dan, to help him. Also I have given ability to all the skilled workers to make everything I have commanded you: ⁷the tent of meeting, the ark of the covenant law with the atonement cover on it, and all the other furnishings of the tent — ⁸the table and its articles, the pure gold lampstand and all its accessories, the altar of incense, ⁹the altar of burnt offering and all its utensils, the basin with its stand — ¹⁰and also the woven garments, both the sacred garments for Aaron the priest and the garments for his sons when they serve as priests, [11] and the anointing oil and fragrant incense for the Holy Place. They are to make them just as I commanded you." Ex 35:30-35

The Sabbath

[12] Then the LORD said to Moses, [13] "Say to the Israelites, 'You must observe my Sabbaths. This will be a sign between me and you for the generations to come, so you may know that I am the LORD, who makes you holy. Eze 20:12,20

[14] "'Observe the Sabbath, because it is holy to you. Anyone who desecrates it is to be put to death; those who do any work on that day must be cut off from their people. [15] For six days work is to be done, but the seventh day is a day of sabbath rest, holy to the LORD. Whoever does any work on the Sabbath day is to be put to death. [16] The Israelites are to observe the Sabbath, celebrating it for the generations to come as a lasting covenant. [17] It will be a sign between me and the Israelites forever, for in six days the LORD made the heavens and the earth, and on the seventh day he rested and was refreshed.'" Ex 20:8-11

[18] When the LORD finished speaking to Moses on Mount Sinai, he gave him the two tablets of the covenant law, the tablets of stone inscribed by the finger of God. Ex 32:15-16

The Golden Calf

32 When the people saw that Moses was so long in coming down from the mountain, they gathered around Aaron and said, "Come, make us gods[a] who will go before us. As for this fellow Moses who brought us up out of Egypt, we don't know what has happened to him." Ac 7:40

[2] Aaron answered them, "Take off the gold earrings that your wives, your sons and your daughters are wearing, and bring them to me." [3] So all the people took off their earrings and brought them to Aaron. [4] He took what they handed him and made it into an idol cast in the shape of a calf, fashioning it with a tool. Then they said, "These are your gods,[b] Israel, who brought you up out of Egypt." Dt 9:16

[5] When Aaron saw this, he built an altar in front of the calf and announced, "Tomorrow there will be a festival to the LORD." [6] So the next day the people rose early and sacrificed burnt offerings and presented fellowship offerings. Afterward they sat down to eat and drink and got up to indulge in revelry. 1Co 10:7

[7] Then the LORD said to Moses, "Go down, because your people, whom you brought up out of Egypt, have become corrupt. [8] They have been quick to turn away from what I command-

---

a 1 Or *a god*; also in verses 23 and 31   *b* 4 Or *This is your god*; also in verse 8 ed them and have made themselves an idol cast in the shape of a calf. They have bowed down to it and sacrificed to it and have said, 'These are your gods, Israel, who brought you up out of Egypt.' Dt 9:12

⁹ "I have seen these people," the LORD said to Moses, "and they are a stiff-necked people. ¹⁰ Now leave me alone so that my anger may burn against them and that I may destroy them. Then I will make you into a great nation." Ex 33:3,5; Isa 48:4; Ac 7:51

¹¹ But Moses sought the favor of the LORD his God. "LORD," he said, "why should your anger burn against your people, whom you brought out of Egypt with great power and a mighty hand? ¹² Why should the Egyptians say, 'It was with evil intent that he brought them out, to kill them in the mountains and to wipe them off the face of the earth'? Turn from your fierce anger; relent and do not bring disaster on your people. ¹³ Remember your servants Abraham, Isaac and Israel, to whom you swore by your own self: 'I will make your descendants as numerous as the stars in the sky and I will give your descendants all this land I promised them, and it will be their inheritance forever.'" ¹⁴ Then the LORD relented and did not bring on his people the disaster he had threatened. Nu 14:13-16; Dt 9:18

¹⁵ Moses turned and went down the mountain with the two tablets of the covenant law in his hands. They were inscribed on both sides, front and back. ¹⁶ The tablets were the work of God; the writing was the writing of God, engraved on the tablets. Ex 31:18; Dt 9:15

¹⁷ When Joshua heard the noise of the people shouting, he said to Moses, "There is the sound of war in the camp."

¹⁸ Moses replied:

"It is not the sound of victory,
　it is not the sound of defeat;
it is the sound of singing
　that I hear."

¹⁹ When Moses approached the camp and saw the calf and the dancing, his anger burned and he threw the tablets out of his hands, breaking them to pieces at the foot of the mountain. ²⁰ And he took the calf the people had made and burned it in the fire; then he ground it to powder, scattered it on the water and made the Israelites drink it. Dt 9:16,21

²¹ He said to Aaron, "What did these people do to you, that you led them into such great sin?"

²² "Do not be angry, my lord," Aaron answered. "You know how prone these people are to evil. ²³ They said to me, 'Make us gods who will go before us. As for this fellow Moses who brought us up out of Egypt, we don't know what has happened to him.' ²⁴ So I told them, 'Whoever has any gold jewelry, take it off.' Then they

gave me the gold, and I threw it into the fire, and out came this calf!" Dt 9:24

²⁵Moses saw that the people were running wild and that Aaron had let them get out of control and so become a laughingstock to their enemies. ²⁶So he stood at the entrance to the camp and said, "Whoever is for the LORD, come to me." And all the Levites rallied to him.

²⁷Then he said to them, "This is what the LORD, the God of Israel, says: 'Each man strap a sword to his side. Go back and forth through the camp from one end to the other, each killing his brother and friend and neighbor.' " ²⁸The Levites did as Moses commanded, and that day about three thousand of the people died. ²⁹Then Moses said, "You have been set apart to the LORD today, for you were against your own sons and brothers, and he has blessed you this day." Nu 25:3,5; Dt 33:9

³⁰The next day Moses said to the people, "You have committed a great sin. But now I will go up to the LORD; perhaps I can make atonement for your sin." Lev 1:4

³¹So Moses went back to the LORD and said, "Oh, what a great sin these people have committed! They have made themselves gods of gold. ³²But now, please forgive their sin—but if not, then blot me out of the book you have written." Ro 9:3; Ps 69:28; Da 12:1

³³The LORD replied to Moses,

"Whoever has sinned against me I will blot out of my book. ³⁴Now go, lead the people to the place I spoke of, and my angel will go before you. However, when the time comes for me to punish, I will punish them for their sin." Dt 29:20; 32:35; Ps 99:8

³⁵And the LORD struck the people with a plague because of what they did with the calf Aaron had made.

33 Then the LORD said to Moses, "Leave this place, you and the people you brought up out of Egypt, and go up to the land I promised on oath to Abraham, Isaac and Jacob, saying, 'I will give it to your descendants.' ²I will send an angel before you and drive out the Canaanites, Amorites, Hittites, Perizzites, Hivites and Jebusites. ³Go up to the land flowing with milk and honey. But I will not go with you, because you are a stiff-necked people and I might destroy you on the way." Ex 3:8; 32:10

⁴When the people heard these distressing words, they began to mourn and no one put on any ornaments. ⁵For the LORD had said to Moses, "Tell the Israelites, 'You are a stiff-necked people. If I were to go with you even for a moment, I might destroy you. Now take off your ornaments and I will decide what to do with you.' " ⁶So the Israelites stripped off their ornaments at Mount Horeb. Nu 14:39

The Tent of Meeting

[7]Now Moses used to take a tent and pitch it outside the camp some distance away, calling it the "tent of meeting." Anyone inquiring of the LORD would go to the tent of meeting outside the camp. [8]And whenever Moses went out to the tent, all the people rose and stood at the entrances to their tents, watching Moses until he entered the tent. [9]As Moses went into the tent, the pillar of cloud would come down and stay at the entrance, while the LORD spoke with Moses. [10]Whenever the people saw the pillar of cloud standing at the entrance to the tent, they all stood and worshiped, each at the entrance to their tent. [11]The LORD would speak to Moses face to face, as one speaks to a friend. Then Moses would return to the camp, but his young aide Joshua son of Nun did not leave the tent. Nu 12:8; Dt 34:10; Ps 99:7

Moses and the Glory of the LORD

[12]Moses said to the LORD, "You have been telling me, 'Lead these people,' but you have not let me know whom you will send with me. You have said, 'I know you by name and you have found favor with me.' [13]If you are pleased with me, teach me your ways so I may know you and continue to find favor with you. Remember that this nation is your people." Dt 9:26,29; Ps 25:4

[14]The LORD replied, "My Presence will go with you, and I will give you rest." Jos 21:44; Isa 63:9

[15]Then Moses said to him, "If your Presence does not go with us, do not send us up from here. [16]How will anyone know that you are pleased with me and with your people unless you go with us? What else will distinguish me and your people from all the other people on the face of the earth?" Ex 34:10; Nu 14:14

[17]And the LORD said to Moses, "I will do the very thing you have asked, because I am pleased with you and I know you by name." Jas 5:16

[18]Then Moses said, "Now show me your glory." Ex 16:7; Jn 1:14

[19]And the LORD said, "I will cause all my goodness to pass in front of you, and I will proclaim my name, the LORD, in your presence. I will have mercy on whom I will have mercy, and I will have compassion on whom I will have compassion. [20]But," he said, "you cannot see my face, for no one may see me and live." Ro 9:15

[21]Then the LORD said, "There is a place near me where you may stand on a rock. [22]When my glory passes by, I will put you in a cleft in the rock and cover you with my hand until I have passed by. [23]Then I will remove my hand and you will see my back; but my face must not be seen." Ps 91:4

The New Stone Tablets

34 The LORD said to Moses, "Chisel out two stone tablets like the first ones, and I will write on them the words that were on the first tablets, which you broke. ²Be ready in the morning, and then come up on Mount Sinai. Present yourself to me there on top of the mountain. ³No one is to come with you or be seen anywhere on the mountain; not even the flocks and herds may graze in front of the mountain."   Ex 19:11; 32:19

⁴So Moses chiseled out two stone tablets like the first ones and went up Mount Sinai early in the morning, as the LORD had commanded him; and he carried the two stone tablets in his hands. ⁵Then the LORD came down in the cloud and stood there with him and proclaimed his name, the LORD. ⁶And he passed in front of Moses, proclaiming, "The LORD, the LORD, the compassionate and gracious God, slow to anger, abounding in love and faithfulness, ⁷maintaining love to thousands, and forgiving wickedness, rebellion and sin. Yet he does not leave the guilty unpunished; he punishes the children and their children for the sin of the parents to the third and fourth generation."   Ex 20:6; Ps 103:3

⁸Moses bowed to the ground at once and worshiped. ⁹"Lord," he said, "if I have found favor in your eyes, then let the Lord go with us. Although this is a stiff-necked people, forgive our wickedness and our sin, and take us as your inheritance."   Ps 33:12

¹⁰Then the LORD said: "I am making a covenant with you. Before all your people I will do wonders never before done in any nation in all the world. The people you live among will see how awesome is the work that I, the LORD, will do for you. ¹¹Obey what I command you today. I will drive out before you the Amorites, Canaanites, Hittites, Perizzites, Hivites and Jebusites. ¹²Be careful not to make a treaty with those who live in the land where you are going, or they will be a snare among you. ¹³Break down their altars, smash their sacred stones and cut down their Asherah poles.ᵃ ¹⁴Do not worship any other god, for the LORD, whose name is Jealous, is a jealous God.   Ex 33:2; Dt 5:2-3

¹⁵"Be careful not to make a treaty with those who live in the land; for when they prostitute themselves to their gods and sacrifice to them, they will invite you and you will eat their sacrifices. ¹⁶And when you choose some of their daughters as wives for your sons and those daughters prostitute themselves to their gods, they will lead your sons to do the same.   Nu 25:2; Dt 7:3

ᵃ 13 That is, wooden symbols of the goddess Asherah

¹⁷"Do not make any idols. Ex 32:8

¹⁸"Celebrate the Festival of Unleavened Bread. For seven days eat bread made without yeast, as I commanded you. Do this at the appointed time in the month of Aviv, for in that month you came out of Egypt. Ex 12:2,15,17

¹⁹"The first offspring of every womb belongs to me, including all the firstborn males of your livestock, whether from herd or flock. ²⁰Redeem the firstborn donkey with a lamb, but if you do not redeem it, break its neck. Redeem all your firstborn sons. Ex 13:2

"No one is to appear before me empty-handed. Dt 16:16

²¹"Six days you shall labor, but on the seventh day you shall rest; even during the plowing season and harvest you must rest. Ex 20:9

²²"Celebrate the Festival of Weeks with the firstfruits of the wheat harvest, and the Festival of Ingathering at the turn of the year.ᵃ ²³Three times a year all your men are to appear before the Sovereign LORD, the God of Israel. ²⁴I will drive out nations before you and enlarge your territory, and no one will covet your land when you go up three times each year to appear before the LORD your God. Ex 23:14,16

²⁵"Do not offer the blood of a sacrifice to me along with anything containing yeast, and do not let any of the sacrifice from the Passover Festival remain until morning. Ex 23:18

²⁶"Bring the best of the firstfruits of your soil to the house of the LORD your God. Ex 22:29

"Do not cook a young goat in its mother's milk." Ex 23:19

²⁷Then the LORD said to Moses, "Write down these words, for in accordance with these words I have made a covenant with you and with Israel." ²⁸Moses was there with the LORD forty days and forty nights without eating bread or drinking water. And he wrote on the tablets the words of the covenant—the Ten Commandments. Dt 4:13; 10:4

The Radiant Face of Moses

²⁹When Moses came down from Mount Sinai with the two tablets of the covenant law in his hands, he was not aware that his face was radiant because he had spoken with the LORD. ³⁰When Aaron and all the Israelites saw Moses, his face was radiant, and they were afraid to come near him. ³¹But Moses called to them; so Aaron and all the leaders of the community came back to him, and he spoke to them. ³²Afterward all the Israelites came near him, and he gave them all the commands the LORD had given him on Mount Sinai. Mt 17:2

³³When Moses finished speaking to them, he put a veil over his

---

ᵃ 22 That is, in the autumn

face. [34]But whenever he entered the LORD's presence to speak with him, he removed the veil until he came out. And when he came out and told the Israelites what he had been commanded, [35]they saw that his face was radiant. Then Moses would put the veil back over his face until he went in to speak with the LORD.   2Co 3:13

Sabbath Regulations

35 Moses assembled the whole Israelite community and said to them, "These are the things the LORD has commanded you to do: [2]For six days, work is to be done, but the seventh day shall be your holy day, a day of sabbath rest to the LORD. Whoever does any work on it is to be put to death. [3]Do not light a fire in any of your dwellings on the Sabbath day."   Ex 16:23

Materials for the Tabernacle

35:4-9pp — Ex 25:1-7
35:10-19pp — Ex 39:32-41

[4]Moses said to the whole Israelite community, "This is what the LORD has commanded: [5]From what you have, take an offering for the LORD. Everyone who is willing is to bring to the LORD an offering of gold, silver and bronze; [6]blue, purple and scarlet yarn and fine linen; goat hair; [7]ram skins dyed red and another type of durable leather[a]; acacia wood; [8]olive oil for the light; spices for the anointing oil and for the fragrant incense; [9]and onyx stones and other gems to be mounted on the ephod and breastpiece.   Ex 25:1-7

[10]"All who are skilled among you are to come and make everything the LORD has commanded: [11]the tabernacle with its tent and its covering, clasps, frames, crossbars, posts and bases; [12]the ark with its poles and the atonement cover and the curtain that shields it; [13]the table with its poles and all its articles and the bread of the Presence; [14]the lampstand that is for light with its accessories, lamps and oil for the light; [15]the altar of incense with its poles, the anointing oil and the fragrant incense; the curtain for the doorway at the entrance to the tabernacle; [16]the altar of burnt offering with its bronze grating, its poles and all its utensils; the bronze basin with its stand; [17]the curtains of the courtyard with its posts and bases, and the curtain for the entrance to the courtyard; [18]the tent pegs for the tabernacle and for the courtyard, and their ropes; [19]the woven garments worn for ministering in the sanctuary—both the sacred garments for Aaron the priest and the garments for his sons when they serve as priests."   Ex 39:32-41

[20]Then the whole Israelite

---

[a] 7 Possibly the hides of large aquatic mammals; also in verse 23

community withdrew from Moses' presence, ²¹and everyone who was willing and whose heart moved them came and brought an offering to the LORD for the work on the tent of meeting, for all its service, and for the sacred garments. ²²All who were willing, men and women alike, came and brought gold jewelry of all kinds: brooches, earrings, rings and ornaments. They all presented their gold as a wave offering to the LORD. ²³Everyone who had blue, purple or scarlet yarn or fine linen, or goat hair, ram skins dyed red or the other durable leather brought them. ²⁴Those presenting an offering of silver or bronze brought it as an offering to the LORD, and everyone who had acacia wood for any part of the work brought it. ²⁵Every skilled woman spun with her hands and brought what she had spun—blue, purple or scarlet yarn or fine linen. ²⁶And all the women who were willing and had the skill spun the goat hair. ²⁷The leaders brought onyx stones and other gems to be mounted on the ephod and breastpiece. ²⁸They also brought spices and olive oil for the light and for the anointing oil and for the fragrant incense. ²⁹All the Israelite men and women who were willing brought to the LORD freewill offerings for all the work the LORD through Moses had commanded them to do.   ver 4-9; Ex 25:1-7; 36:3

Bezalel and Oholiab
35:30-35pp — Ex 31:2-6

³⁰Then Moses said to the Israelites, "See, the LORD has chosen Bezalel son of Uri, the son of Hur, of the tribe of Judah, ³¹and he has filled him with the Spirit of God, with wisdom, with understanding, with knowledge and with all kinds of skills— ³²to make artistic designs for work in gold, silver and bronze, ³³to cut and set stones, to work in wood and to engage in all kinds of artistic crafts. ³⁴And he has given both him and Oholiab son of Ahisamak, of the tribe of Dan, the ability to teach others. ³⁵He has filled them with skill to do all kinds of work as engravers, designers, embroiderers in blue, purple and scarlet yarn and fine linen, and weavers—all of them skilled workers and designers.

36 ¹So Bezalel, Oholiab and every skilled person to whom the LORD has given skill and ability to know how to carry out all the work of constructing the sanctuary are to do the work just as the LORD has commanded."   Ex 21:2-6

²Then Moses summoned Bezalel and Oholiab and every skilled person to whom the LORD had given ability and who was willing to come and do the work. ³They received from Moses all the offerings the Israelites had brought to carry out the work of constructing the sanctuary. And

the people continued to bring freewill offerings morning after morning. ⁴So all the skilled workers who were doing all the work on the sanctuary left what they were doing ⁵and said to Moses, "The people are bringing more than enough for doing the work the LORD commanded to be done."   2Ch 24:14; 2Co 8:2-3

⁶Then Moses gave an order and they sent this word throughout the camp: "No man or woman is to make anything else as an offering for the sanctuary." And so the people were restrained from bringing more, ⁷because what they already had was more than enough to do all the work.

The Tabernacle

36:8-38pp — Ex 26:1-37

⁸All those who were skilled among the workers made the tabernacle with ten curtains of finely twisted linen and blue, purple and scarlet yarn, with cherubim woven into them by expert hands. ⁹All the curtains were the same size — twenty-eight cubits long and four cubits wide.ᵃ ¹⁰They joined five of the curtains together and did the same with the other five. ¹¹Then they made loops of blue material along the edge of the end curtain in one set, and the same was done with the end curtain in the other set. ¹²They also made fifty loops on one curtain and fifty loops on the end curtain of the other set, with the loops opposite each other. ¹³Then they made fifty gold clasps and used them to fasten the two sets of curtains together so that the tabernacle was a unit.

¹⁴They made curtains of goat hair for the tent over the tabernacle — eleven altogether. ¹⁵All eleven curtains were the same size — thirty cubits long and four cubits wide.ᵇ ¹⁶They joined five of the curtains into one set and the other six into another set. ¹⁷Then they made fifty loops along the edge of the end curtain in one set and also along the edge of the end curtain in the other set. ¹⁸They made fifty bronze clasps to fasten the tent together as a unit. ¹⁹Then they made for the tent a covering of ram skins dyed red, and over that a covering of the other durable leather.ᶜ

²⁰They made upright frames of acacia wood for the tabernacle. ²¹Each frame was ten cubits long and a cubit and a half wide,ᵈ ²²with two projections set parallel to each other. They made all the frames of the tabernacle in this way. ²³They made twenty frames for the south side of the

---

ᵃ 9 That is, about 42 feet long and 6 feet wide or about 13 meters long and 1.8 meters wide
ᵇ 15 That is, about 45 feet long and 6 feet wide or about 14 meters long and 1.8 meters wide
ᶜ 19 Possibly the hides of large aquatic mammals (see 35:7)   ᵈ 21 That is, about 15 feet long and 2 1/4 feet wide or about 4.5 meters long and 68 centimeters wide

tabernacle [24] and made forty silver bases to go under them — two bases for each frame, one under each projection. [25] For the other side, the north side of the tabernacle, they made twenty frames [26] and forty silver bases — two under each frame. [27] They made six frames for the far end, that is, the west end of the tabernacle, [28] and two frames were made for the corners of the tabernacle at the far end. [29] At these two corners the frames were double from the bottom all the way to the top and fitted into a single ring; both were made alike. [30] So there were eight frames and sixteen silver bases — two under each frame.

[31] They also made crossbars of acacia wood: five for the frames on one side of the tabernacle, [32] five for those on the other side, and five for the frames on the west, at the far end of the tabernacle. [33] They made the center crossbar so that it extended from end to end at the middle of the frames. [34] They overlaid the frames with gold and made gold rings to hold the crossbars. They also overlaid the crossbars with gold.

[35] They made the curtain of blue, purple and scarlet yarn and finely twisted linen, with cherubim woven into it by a skilled worker. [36] They made four posts of acacia wood for it and overlaid them with gold. They made gold hooks for them and cast their four silver bases. [37] For the entrance to the tent they made a curtain of blue, purple and scarlet yarn and finely twisted linen — the work of an embroiderer; [38] and they made five posts with hooks for them. They overlaid the tops of the posts and their bands with gold and made their five bases of bronze.   Ex 26:1-37

The Ark

37:1-9pp — Ex 25:10-20

37 Bezalel made the ark of acacia wood — two and a half cubits long, a cubit and a half wide, and a cubit and a half high.[a] [2] He overlaid it with pure gold, both inside and out, and made a gold molding around it. [3] He cast four gold rings for it and fastened them to its four feet, with two rings on one side and two rings on the other. [4] Then he made poles of acacia wood and overlaid them with gold. [5] And he inserted the poles into the rings on the sides of the ark to carry it.   ver 11,26; Ex 31:2

[6] He made the atonement cover of pure gold — two and a half cubits long and a cubit and a half wide. [7] Then he made two cherubim out of hammered gold at the ends of the cover. [8] He made one cherub on one end and the

---

[a] 1 That is, about 3 1/4 feet long and 2 1/4 feet wide and high or about 1.1 meters long and 68 centimeters wide and high; similarly in verse 6

second cherub on the other; at the two ends he made them of one piece with the cover. ⁹The cherubim had their wings spread upward, overshadowing the cover with them. The cherubim faced each other, looking toward the cover. Ex 25:10-20

The Table
37:10-16pp — Ex 25:23-29

¹⁰They*a* made the table of acacia wood — two cubits long, a cubit wide and a cubit and a half high.*b* ¹¹Then they overlaid it with pure gold and made a gold molding around it. ¹²They also made around it a rim a handbreadth*c* wide and put a gold molding on the rim. ¹³They cast four gold rings for the table and fastened them to the four corners, where the four legs were. ¹⁴The rings were put close to the rim to hold the poles used in carrying the table. ¹⁵The poles for carrying the table were made of acacia wood and were overlaid with gold. ¹⁶And they made from pure gold the articles for the table — its plates and dishes and bowls and its pitchers for the pouring out of drink offerings. Ex 25:23-29

The Lampstand
37:17-24pp — Ex 25:31-39

¹⁷They made the lampstand of pure gold. They hammered out its base and shaft, and made its flowerlike cups, buds and blossoms of one piece with them. ¹⁸Six branches extended from the sides of the lampstand — three on one side and three on the other. ¹⁹Three cups shaped like almond flowers with buds and blossoms were on one branch, three on the next branch and the same for all six branches extending from the lampstand. ²⁰And on the lampstand were four cups shaped like almond flowers with buds and blossoms. ²¹One bud was under the first pair of branches extending from the lampstand, a second bud under the second pair, and a third bud under the third pair — six branches in all. ²²The buds and the branches were all of one piece with the lampstand, hammered out of pure gold. Heb 9:2; Rev 1:12

²³They made its seven lamps, as well as its wick trimmers and trays, of pure gold. ²⁴They made the lampstand and all its accessories from one talent*d* of pure gold. Ex 25:31-39

The Altar of Incense
37:25-28pp — Ex 30:1-5

²⁵They made the altar of incense out of acacia wood. It was square, a cubit long and a cubit

---

a 10 Or *He*; also in verses 11-29   *b 10* That is, about 3 feet long, 1 1/2 feet wide and 2 1/4 feet high or about 90 centimeters long, 45 centimeters wide and 68 centimeters high
c 12 That is, about 3 inches or about 7.5 centimeters   *d 24* That is, about 75 pounds or about 34 kilograms

wide and two cubits high*a* — its horns of one piece with it. ²⁶They overlaid the top and all the sides and the horns with pure gold, and made a gold molding around it. ²⁷They made two gold rings below the molding — two on each of the opposite sides — to hold the poles used to carry it. ²⁸They made the poles of acacia wood and overlaid them with gold. Ex 30:1-5

²⁹They also made the sacred anointing oil and the pure, fragrant incense — the work of a perfumer. Ex 30:1,25; 31:11

The Altar of Burnt Offering

38:1-7pp — Ex 27:1-8

38 They*b* built the altar of burnt offering of acacia wood, three cubits*c* high; it was square, five cubits long and five cubits wide.*d* ²They made a horn at each of the four corners, so that the horns and the altar were of one piece, and they overlaid the altar with bronze. ³They made all its utensils of bronze — its pots, shovels, sprinkling bowls, meat forks and firepans. ⁴They made a grating for the altar, a bronze network, to be under its ledge, halfway up the altar. ⁵They cast bronze rings to hold the poles for the four corners of the bronze grating. ⁶They made the poles of acacia wood and overlaid them with bronze. ⁷They inserted the poles into the rings so they would be on the sides of the altar for carrying it. They made it hollow, out of boards. Ex 27:1-8

The Basin for Washing

⁸They made the bronze basin and its bronze stand from the mirrors of the women who served at the entrance to the tent of meeting. Dt 23:17; 1Sa 2:22

The Courtyard

38:9-20pp — Ex 27:9-19

⁹Next they made the courtyard. The south side was a hundred cubits*e* long and had curtains of finely twisted linen, ¹⁰with twenty posts and twenty bronze bases, and with silver hooks and bands on the posts. ¹¹The north side was also a hundred cubits long and had twenty posts and twenty bronze bases, with silver hooks and bands on the posts.

¹²The west end was fifty cubits*f* wide and had curtains, with ten posts and ten bases, with silver hooks and bands on the posts. ¹³The east end, toward the sunrise, was also fifty cubits wide. ¹⁴Curtains fifteen cubits*g* long were on one side of the entrance, with three posts and three bases,

a 25 That is, about 1 1/2 feet long and wide and 3 feet high or about 45 centimeters long and wide and 90 centimeters high   *b 1* Or *He*; also in verses 2-9   *c 1* That is, about 4 1/2 feet or about 1.4 meters   *d 1* That is, about 7 1/2 feet or about 2.3 meters long and wide   *e 9* That is, about 150 feet or about 45 meters   *f 12* That is, about 75 feet or about 23 meters   *g 14* That is, about 22 feet or about 6.8 meters

¹⁵and curtains fifteen cubits long were on the other side of the entrance to the courtyard, with three posts and three bases. ¹⁶All the curtains around the courtyard were of finely twisted linen. ¹⁷The bases for the posts were bronze. The hooks and bands on the posts were silver, and their tops were overlaid with silver; so all the posts of the courtyard had silver bands.

¹⁸The curtain for the entrance to the courtyard was made of blue, purple and scarlet yarn and finely twisted linen—the work of an embroiderer. It was twenty cubits*ᵃ* long and, like the curtains of the courtyard, five cubits*ᵇ* high, ¹⁹with four posts and four bronze bases. Their hooks and bands were silver, and their tops were overlaid with silver. ²⁰All the tent pegs of the tabernacle and of the surrounding courtyard were bronze. Ex 27:9-19

The Materials Used

²¹These are the amounts of the materials used for the tabernacle, the tabernacle of the covenant law, which were recorded at Moses' command by the Levites under the direction of Ithamar son of Aaron, the priest. ²²(Bezalel son of Uri, the son of Hur, of the tribe of Judah, made everything the LORD commanded Moses; ²³with him was Oholiab son of Ahisamak, of the tribe of Dan—an engraver and designer, and an embroiderer in blue, purple and scarlet yarn and fine linen.) ²⁴The total amount of the gold from the wave offering used for all the work on the sanctuary was 29 talents and 730 shekels,*ᶜ* according to the sanctuary shekel. Nu 1:50,53; 9:15

²⁵The silver obtained from those of the community who were counted in the census was 100 talents*ᵈ* and 1,775 shekels,*ᵉ* according to the sanctuary shekel — ²⁶one beka per person, that is, half a shekel,*ᶠ* according to the sanctuary shekel, from everyone who had crossed over to those counted, twenty years old or more, a total of 603,550 men. ²⁷The 100 talents of silver were used to cast the bases for the sanctuary and for the curtain — 100 bases from the 100 talents, one talent for each base. ²⁸They used the 1,775 shekels to make the hooks for the posts, to overlay the tops of the posts, and to make their bands. Ex 30:12-14

²⁹The bronze from the wave offering was 70 talents and 2,400 shekels.*ᵍ* ³⁰They used it to make the bases for the entrance to the tent of meeting, the bronze altar

---

ᵃ 18 That is, about 30 feet or about 9 meters   *ᵇ 18* That is, about 7 1/2 feet or about 2.3 meters   *ᶜ 24* The weight of the gold was a little over a ton or about 1 metric ton.   *ᵈ 25* That is, about 3 3/4 tons or about 3.4 metric tons; also in verse 27   *ᵉ 25* That is, about 44 pounds or about 20 kilograms; also in verse 28   *ᶠ 26* That is, about 1/5 ounce or about 5.7 grams   *ᵍ 29* The weight of the bronze was about 2 1/2 tons or about 2.4 metric tons.

with its bronze grating and all its utensils, [31] the bases for the surrounding courtyard and those for its entrance and all the tent pegs for the tabernacle and those for the surrounding courtyard.

The Priestly Garments

39 From the blue, purple and scarlet yarn they made woven garments for ministering in the sanctuary. They also made sacred garments for Aaron, as the LORD commanded Moses.   Ex 35:19,23

The Ephod

39:2-7pp — Ex 28:6-14

[2] They[a] made the ephod of gold, and of blue, purple and scarlet yarn, and of finely twisted linen. [3] They hammered out thin sheets of gold and cut strands to be worked into the blue, purple and scarlet yarn and fine linen — the work of skilled hands. [4] They made shoulder pieces for the ephod, which were attached to two of its corners, so it could be fastened. [5] Its skillfully woven waistband was like it — of one piece with the ephod and made with gold, and with blue, purple and scarlet yarn, and with finely twisted linen, as the LORD commanded Moses.

[6] They mounted the onyx stones in gold filigree settings and engraved them like a seal with the names of the sons of Israel. [7] Then they fastened them on the shoulder pieces of the ephod as memorial stones for the sons of Israel, as the LORD commanded Moses.   Ex 28:6-14

The Breastpiece

39:8-21pp — Ex 28:15-28

[8] They fashioned the breastpiece — the work of a skilled craftsman. They made it like the ephod: of gold, and of blue, purple and scarlet yarn, and of finely twisted linen. [9] It was square — a span[b] long and a span wide — and folded double. [10] Then they mounted four rows of precious stones on it. The first row was carnelian, chrysolite and beryl; [11] the second row was turquoise, lapis lazuli and emerald; [12] the third row was jacinth, agate and amethyst; [13] the fourth row was topaz, onyx and jasper.[c] They were mounted in gold filigree settings. [14] There were twelve stones, one for each of the names of the sons of Israel, each engraved like a seal with the name of one of the twelve tribes.

[15] For the breastpiece they made braided chains of pure gold, like a rope. [16] They made two gold filigree settings and two gold rings, and fastened the rings to two of the corners of the breastpiece. [17] They fastened the two gold chains to the rings

---

[a] 2 Or *He*; also in verses 7, 8 and 22   [b] 9 That is, about 9 inches or about 23 centimeters
[c] 13 The precise identification of some of these precious stones is uncertain.

at the corners of the breastpiece, [18] and the other ends of the chains to the two settings, attaching them to the shoulder pieces of the ephod at the front. [19] They made two gold rings and attached them to the other two corners of the breastpiece on the inside edge next to the ephod. [20] Then they made two more gold rings and attached them to the bottom of the shoulder pieces on the front of the ephod, close to the seam just above the waistband of the ephod. [21] They tied the rings of the breastpiece to the rings of the ephod with blue cord, connecting it to the waistband so that the breastpiece would not swing out from the ephod — as the LORD commanded Moses.   Ex 28:15-28

Other Priestly Garments
39:22-31pp — Ex 28:31-43

[22] They made the robe of the ephod entirely of blue cloth — the work of a weaver — [23] with an opening in the center of the robe like the opening of a collar,[a] and a band around this opening, so that it would not tear. [24] They made pomegranates of blue, purple and scarlet yarn and finely twisted linen around the hem of the robe. [25] And they made bells of pure gold and attached them around the hem between the pomegranates. [26] The bells and pomegranates alternated around the hem of the robe to be worn for ministering, as the LORD commanded Moses.

[27] For Aaron and his sons, they made tunics of fine linen — the work of a weaver — [28] and the turban of fine linen, the linen caps and the undergarments of finely twisted linen. [29] The sash was made of finely twisted linen and blue, purple and scarlet yarn — the work of an embroiderer — as the LORD commanded Moses.   Ex 28:4; Lev 6:10

[30] They made the plate, the sacred emblem, out of pure gold and engraved on it, like an inscription on a seal: HOLY TO THE LORD. [31] Then they fastened a blue cord to it to attach it to the turban, as the LORD commanded Moses.   Ex 28:31-43

Moses Inspects the Tabernacle
39:32-41pp — Ex 35:10-19

[32] So all the work on the tabernacle, the tent of meeting, was completed. The Israelites did everything just as the LORD commanded Moses. [33] Then they brought the tabernacle to Moses: the tent and all its furnishings, its clasps, frames, crossbars, posts and bases; [34] the covering of ram skins dyed red and the covering of another durable leather[b] and the shielding curtain; [35] the ark of the covenant law with its poles and the atonement cover; [36] the

---

[a] 23 The meaning of the Hebrew for this word is uncertain.   [b] 34 Possibly the hides of large aquatic mammals

table with all its articles and the bread of the Presence; ³⁷ the pure gold lampstand with its row of lamps and all its accessories, and the olive oil for the light; ³⁸ the gold altar, the anointing oil, the fragrant incense, and the curtain for the entrance to the tent; ³⁹ the bronze altar with its bronze grating, its poles and all its utensils; the basin with its stand; ⁴⁰ the curtains of the courtyard with its posts and bases, and the curtain for the entrance to the courtyard; the ropes and tent pegs for the courtyard; all the furnishings for the tabernacle, the tent of meeting; ⁴¹ and the woven garments worn for ministering in the sanctuary, both the sacred garments for Aaron the priest and the garments for his sons when serving as priests.   Ex 35:10-19

⁴² The Israelites had done all the work just as the Lord had commanded Moses. ⁴³ Moses inspected the work and saw that they had done it just as the Lord had commanded. So Moses blessed them.   Lev 9:22-23; 2Ch 30:27

Setting Up the Tabernacle

40 Then the Lord said to Moses: ² "Set up the tabernacle, the tent of meeting, on the first day of the first month. ³ Place the ark of the covenant law in it and shield the ark with the curtain. ⁴ Bring in the table and set out what belongs on it. Then bring in the lampstand and

set up its lamps. ⁵ Place the gold altar of incense in front of the ark of the covenant law and put the curtain at the entrance to the tabernacle.   Ex 26:33; Nu 1:1

⁶ "Place the altar of burnt offering in front of the entrance to the tabernacle, the tent of meeting; ⁷ place the basin between the tent of meeting and the altar and put water in it. ⁸ Set up the courtyard around it and put the curtain at the entrance to the courtyard.   Ex 30:18; 2Ki 16:14

⁹ "Take the anointing oil and anoint the tabernacle and everything in it; consecrate it and all its furnishings, and it will be holy. ¹⁰ Then anoint the altar of burnt offering and all its utensils; consecrate the altar, and it will be most holy. ¹¹ Anoint the basin and its stand and consecrate them.   Ex 30:26

¹² "Bring Aaron and his sons to the entrance to the tent of meeting and wash them with water. ¹³ Then dress Aaron in the sacred garments, anoint him and consecrate him so he may serve me as priest. ¹⁴ Bring his sons and dress them in tunics. ¹⁵ Anoint them just as you anointed their father, so they may serve me as priests. Their anointing will be to a priesthood that will continue throughout their generations." ¹⁶ Moses did everything just as the Lord commanded him.   Ex 29:9; Nu 25:13

¹⁷ So the tabernacle was set up on the first day of the first month

in the second year. [18]When Moses set up the tabernacle, he put the bases in place, erected the frames, inserted the crossbars and set up the posts. [19]Then he spread the tent over the tabernacle and put the covering over the tent, as the LORD commanded him. Nu 7:1; 2Ch 1:3

[20]He took the tablets of the covenant law and placed them in the ark, attached the poles to the ark and put the atonement cover over it. [21]Then he brought the ark into the tabernacle and hung the shielding curtain and shielded the ark of the covenant law, as the LORD commanded him. Ex 16:34; Heb 9:4

[22]Moses placed the table in the tent of meeting on the north side of the tabernacle outside the curtain [23]and set out the bread on it before the LORD, as the LORD commanded him. Ex 26:35

[24]He placed the lampstand in the tent of meeting opposite the table on the south side of the tabernacle [25]and set up the lamps before the LORD, as the LORD commanded him. Ex 26:35

[26]Moses placed the gold altar in the tent of meeting in front of the curtain [27]and burned fragrant incense on it, as the LORD commanded him.

[28]Then he put up the curtain at the entrance to the tabernacle. [29]He set the altar of burnt offering near the entrance to the tabernacle, the tent of meeting, and offered on it burnt offerings and grain offerings, as the LORD commanded him. ver 6; Ex 29:38-42; 30:6

[30]He placed the basin between the tent of meeting and the altar and put water in it for washing, [31]and Moses and Aaron and his sons used it to wash their hands and feet. [32]They washed whenever they entered the tent of meeting or approached the altar, as the LORD commanded Moses. Ex 30:20

[33]Then Moses set up the courtyard around the tabernacle and altar and put up the curtain at the entrance to the courtyard. And so Moses finished the work. ver 8; Ex 27:9

The Glory of the LORD

[34]Then the cloud covered the tent of meeting, and the glory of the LORD filled the tabernacle. [35]Moses could not enter the tent of meeting because the cloud had settled on it, and the glory of the LORD filled the tabernacle. Nu 9:15-23

[36]In all the travels of the Israelites, whenever the cloud lifted from above the tabernacle, they would set out; [37]but if the cloud did not lift, they did not set out—until the day it lifted. [38]So the cloud of the LORD was over the tabernacle by day, and fire was in the cloud by night, in the sight of all the Israelites during all their travels. Nu 9:17-23

Leviticus

The Burnt Offering

1 The LORD called to Moses and spoke to him from the tent of meeting. He said, 2 "Speak to the Israelites and say to them: 'When anyone among you brings an offering to the LORD, bring as your offering an animal from either the herd or the flock.   Lev 22:18-19

3 " 'If the offering is a burnt offering from the herd, you are to offer a male without defect. You must present it at the entrance to the tent of meeting so that it will be acceptable to the LORD. 4 You are to lay your hand on the head of the burnt offering, and it will be accepted on your behalf to make atonement for you. 5 You are to slaughter the young bull before the LORD, and then Aaron's sons the priests shall bring the blood and splash it against the sides of the altar at the entrance to the tent of meeting. 6 You are to skin the burnt offering and cut it into pieces. 7 The sons of Aaron the priest are to put fire on the altar and arrange wood on the fire.

8 Then Aaron's sons the priests shall arrange the pieces, including the head and the fat, on the wood that is burning on the altar. 9 You are to wash the internal organs and the legs with water, and the priest is to burn all of it on the altar. It is a burnt offering, a food offering, an aroma pleasing to the LORD.   Ge 8:21; Eph 5:2

10 " 'If the offering is a burnt offering from the flock, from either the sheep or the goats, you are to offer a male without defect. 11 You are to slaughter it at the north side of the altar before the LORD, and Aaron's sons the priests shall splash its blood against the sides of the altar. 12 You are to cut it into pieces, and the priest shall arrange them, including the head and the fat, on the wood that is burning on the altar. 13 You are to wash the internal organs and the legs with water, and the priest is to bring all of them and burn them on the altar. It is a burnt offering, a food offering, an aroma pleasing to the LORD.

14 " 'If the offering to the LORD is a burnt offering of birds, you are to offer a dove or a young pigeon. 15 The priest shall bring it to the altar, wring off the head and burn it on the altar; its blood shall be drained out on the side of the altar. 16 He is to remove the crop and the feathers[a] and throw them down east of the altar where the ashes are. 17 He shall tear it open by the wings, not dividing it completely, and then the priest shall burn it on the wood that is burning on the altar. It is a burnt offering, a food offering, an aroma pleasing to the LORD.   Lev 5:7; 6:10

The Grain Offering

2 " 'When anyone brings a grain offering to the LORD, their offering is to be of the finest flour. They are to pour olive oil on it, put incense on it 2 and take it to Aaron's sons the priests. The priest shall take a handful of the flour and oil, together with all the incense, and burn this as a memorial[b] portion on the altar, a food offering, an aroma pleasing to the LORD. 3 The rest of the grain offering belongs to Aaron and his sons; it is a most holy part of the food offerings presented to the LORD.   Lev 6:14-18; 10:12-13

4 " 'If you bring a grain offering baked in an oven, it is to consist of the finest flour: either thick loaves made without yeast and with olive oil mixed in or thin loaves made without yeast and brushed with olive oil. 5 If your grain offering is prepared on a griddle, it is to be made of the finest flour mixed with oil, and without yeast. 6 Crumble it and pour oil on it; it is a grain offering. 7 If your grain offering is cooked in a pan, it is to be made of the finest flour and some olive oil. 8 Bring the grain offering made of these things to the LORD; present it to the priest, who shall take it to the altar. 9 He shall take out the memorial portion from the grain offering and burn it on the altar as a food offering, an aroma pleasing to the LORD. 10 The rest of the grain offering belongs to Aaron and his sons; it is a most holy part of the food offerings presented to the LORD.   Ex 29:2; Lev 7:9

11 " 'Every grain offering you bring to the LORD must be made without yeast, for you are not to burn any yeast or honey in a food offering presented to the LORD. 12 You may bring them to the LORD as an offering of the firstfruits, but they are not to be offered on the altar as a pleasing aroma. 13 Season all your grain offerings with salt. Do not leave the salt of the covenant of your God out of your grain offerings; add salt to all your offerings.   Nu 18:19; Eze 43:24

14 " 'If you bring a grain offer-

---

[a] 16 Or *crop with its contents*; the meaning of the Hebrew for this word is uncertain.
[b] 2 Or *representative*; also in verses 9 and 16

ing of firstfruits to the LORD, offer crushed heads of new grain roasted in the fire. [15] Put oil and incense on it; it is a grain offering. [16] The priest shall burn the memorial portion of the crushed grain and the oil, together with all the incense, as a food offering presented to the LORD.   Lev 23:10

The Fellowship Offering

3 " 'If your offering is a fellowship offering, and you offer an animal from the herd, whether male or female, you are to present before the LORD an animal without defect. [2] You are to lay your hand on the head of your offering and slaughter it at the entrance to the tent of meeting. Then Aaron's sons the priests shall splash the blood against the sides of the altar. [3] From the fellowship offering you are to bring a food offering to the LORD: the internal organs and all the fat that is connected to them, [4] both kidneys with the fat on them near the loins, and the long lobe of the liver, which you will remove with the kidneys. [5] Then Aaron's sons are to burn it on the altar on top of the burnt offering that is lying on the burning wood; it is a food offering, an aroma pleasing to the LORD.   Lev 7:11-34; 22:21

[6] " 'If you offer an animal from the flock as a fellowship offering to the LORD, you are to offer a male or female without defect. [7] If you offer a lamb, you are to pre-

sent it before the LORD, [8] lay your hand on its head and slaughter it in front of the tent of meeting. Then Aaron's sons shall splash its blood against the sides of the altar. [9] From the fellowship offering you are to bring a food offering to the LORD: its fat, the entire fat tail cut off close to the backbone, the internal organs and all the fat that is connected to them, [10] both kidneys with the fat on them near the loins, and the long lobe of the liver, which you will remove with the kidneys. [11] The priest shall burn them on the altar as a food offering presented to the LORD.   Lev 21:6,17

[12] " 'If your offering is a goat, you are to present it before the LORD, [13] lay your hand on its head and slaughter it in front of the tent of meeting. Then Aaron's sons shall splash its blood against the sides of the altar. [14] From what you offer you are to present this food offering to the LORD: the internal organs and all the fat that is connected to them, [15] both kidneys with the fat on them near the loins, and the long lobe of the liver, which you will remove with the kidneys. [16] The priest shall burn them on the altar as a food offering, a pleasing aroma. All the fat is the LORD's.   Lev 1:9; 1Sa 2:16

[17] " 'This is a lasting ordinance for the generations to come, wherever you live: You must not eat any fat or any blood.' "

The Sin Offering

4 The LORD said to Moses, [2] "Say to the Israelites: 'When anyone sins unintentionally and does what is forbidden in any of the LORD's commands —

Lev 5:15-18; Heb 9:7

[3] "'If the anointed priest sins, bringing guilt on the people, he must bring to the LORD a young bull without defect as a sin offering[a] for the sin he has committed. [4] He is to present the bull at the entrance to the tent of meeting before the LORD. He is to lay his hand on its head and slaughter it there before the LORD. [5] Then the anointed priest shall take some of the bull's blood and carry it into the tent of meeting. [6] He is to dip his finger into the blood and sprinkle some of it seven times before the LORD, in front of the curtain of the sanctuary. [7] The priest shall then put some of the blood on the horns of the altar of fragrant incense that is before the LORD in the tent of meeting. The rest of the bull's blood he shall pour out at the base of the altar of burnt offering at the entrance to the tent of meeting. [8] He shall remove all the fat from the bull of the sin offering — all the fat that is connected to the internal organs, [9] both kidneys with the fat on them near the loins, and the long lobe of the liver, which he will remove with the kidneys — [10] just as the fat is removed from the ox[b] sacrificed as a fellowship offering. Then the priest shall burn them on the altar of burnt offering. [11] But the hide of the bull and all its flesh, as well as the head and legs, the internal organs and the intestines — [12] that is, all the rest of the bull — he must take outside the camp to a place ceremonially clean, where the ashes are thrown, and burn it there in a wood fire on the ash heap.

Lev 5:9; Heb 13:11

[13] "'If the whole Israelite community sins unintentionally and does what is forbidden in any of the LORD's commands, even though the community is unaware of the matter, when they realize their guilt [14] and the sin they committed becomes known, the assembly must bring a young bull as a sin offering and present it before the tent of meeting. [15] The elders of the community are to lay their hands on the bull's head before the LORD, and the bull shall be slaughtered before the LORD. [16] Then the anointed priest is to take some of the bull's blood into the tent of meeting. [17] He shall dip his finger into the blood and sprinkle it before the LORD seven times in front of the curtain. [18] He is to put

---

[a] 3 Or *purification offering*; here and throughout this chapter   [b] 10 The Hebrew word can refer to either male or female.

some of the blood on the horns of the altar that is before the LORD in the tent of meeting. The rest of the blood he shall pour out at the base of the altar of burnt offering at the entrance to the tent of meeting. ¹⁹He shall remove all the fat from it and burn it on the altar, ²⁰and do with this bull just as he did with the bull for the sin offering. In this way the priest will make atonement for the community, and they will be forgiven. ²¹Then he shall take the bull outside the camp and burn it as he burned the first bull. This is the sin offering for the community. ver 3; Nu 15:25

²²"'When a leader sins unintentionally and does what is forbidden in any of the commands of the LORD his God, when he realizes his guilt ²³and the sin he has committed becomes known, he must bring as his offering a male goat without defect. ²⁴He is to lay his hand on the goat's head and slaughter it at the place where the burnt offering is slaughtered before the LORD. It is a sin offering. ²⁵Then the priest shall take some of the blood of the sin offering with his finger and put it on the horns of the altar of burnt offering and pour out the rest of the blood at the base of the altar. ²⁶He shall burn all the fat on the altar as he burned the fat of the fellowship offering. In this way the priest will make atonement

for the leader's sin, and he will be forgiven. Lev 9:9; Nu 31:13

²⁷"'If any member of the community sins unintentionally and does what is forbidden in any of the LORD's commands, when they realize their guilt ²⁸and the sin they have committed becomes known, they must bring as their offering for the sin they committed a female goat without defect. ²⁹They are to lay their hand on the head of the sin offering and slaughter it at the place of the burnt offering. ³⁰Then the priest is to take some of the blood with his finger and put it on the horns of the altar of burnt offering and pour out the rest of the blood at the base of the altar. ³¹They shall remove all the fat, just as the fat is removed from the fellowship offering, and the priest shall burn it on the altar as an aroma pleasing to the LORD. In this way the priest will make atonement for them, and they will be forgiven. Ge 8:21; Lev 1:4

³²"'If someone brings a lamb as their sin offering, they are to bring a female without defect. ³³They are to lay their hand on its head and slaughter it for a sin offering at the place where the burnt offering is slaughtered. ³⁴Then the priest shall take some of the blood of the sin offering with his finger and put it on the horns of the altar of burnt offering and pour out the rest of

the blood at the base of the altar. [35]They shall remove all the fat, just as the fat is removed from the lamb of the fellowship offering, and the priest shall burn it on the altar on top of the food offerings presented to the LORD. In this way the priest will make atonement for them for the sin they have committed, and they will be forgiven. Ex 29:38; Lev 1:4; 9:3

5 "'If anyone sins because they do not speak up when they hear a public charge to testify regarding something they have seen or learned about, they will be held responsible. Pr 29:24

[2]"'If anyone becomes aware that they are guilty—if they unwittingly touch anything ceremonially unclean (whether the carcass of an unclean animal, wild or domestic, or of any unclean creature that moves along the ground) and they are unaware that they have become unclean, but then they come to realize their guilt; [3]or if they touch human uncleanness (anything that would make them unclean) even though they are unaware of it, but then they learn of it and realize their guilt; [4]or if anyone thoughtlessly takes an oath to do anything, whether good or evil (in any matter one might carelessly swear about) even though they are unaware of it, but then they learn of it and realize their guilt— [5]when anyone becomes aware that they are guilty in any of these matters, they must confess in what way they have sinned. [6]As a penalty for the sin they have committed, they must bring to the LORD a female lamb or goat from the flock as a sin offering[a]; and the priest shall make atonement for them for their sin. Lev 16:21; 26:40

[7]"'Anyone who cannot afford a lamb is to bring two doves or two young pigeons to the LORD as a penalty for their sin—one for a sin offering and the other for a burnt offering. [8]They are to bring them to the priest, who shall first offer the one for the sin offering. He is to wring its head from its neck, not dividing it completely, [9]and is to splash some of the blood of the sin offering against the side of the altar; the rest of the blood must be drained out at the base of the altar. It is a sin offering. [10]The priest shall then offer the other as a burnt offering in the prescribed way and make atonement for them for the sin they have committed, and they will be forgiven. Lev 12:8; 14:21

[11]"'If, however, they cannot afford two doves or two young pigeons, they are to bring as an offering for their sin a tenth of an ephah[b] of the finest flour for a sin

---

[a] 6 Or *purification offering*; here and throughout this chapter   [b] 11 That is, probably about 3 1/2 pounds or about 1.6 kilograms

offering. They must not put olive oil or incense on it, because it is a sin offering. ¹²They are to bring it to the priest, who shall take a handful of it as a memorial[a] portion and burn it on the altar on top of the food offerings presented to the LORD. It is a sin offering. ¹³In this way the priest will make atonement for them for any of these sins they have committed, and they will be forgiven. The rest of the offering will belong to the priest, as in the case of the grain offering.'" Lev 2:1,3; 4:26

The Guilt Offering

¹⁴The LORD said to Moses: ¹⁵"When anyone is unfaithful to the LORD by sinning unintentionally in regard to any of the LORD's holy things, they are to bring to the LORD as a penalty a ram from the flock, one without defect and of the proper value in silver, according to the sanctuary shekel.[b] It is a guilt offering. ¹⁶They must make restitution for what they have failed to do in regard to the holy things, pay an additional penalty of a fifth of its value and give it all to the priest. The priest will make atonement for them with the ram as a guilt offering, and they will be forgiven. Lev 6:4; 22:14; Nu 5:7

¹⁷"If anyone sins and does what is forbidden in any of the LORD's commands, even though they do not know it, they are guilty and will be held responsible. ¹⁸They are to bring to the priest as a guilt offering a ram from the flock, one without defect and of the proper value. In this way the priest will make atonement for them for the wrong they have committed unintentionally, and they will be forgiven. ¹⁹It is a guilt offering; they have been guilty of[c] wrongdoing against the LORD." Lev 6:6; 14:12

6[d] The LORD said to Moses: ²"If anyone sins and is unfaithful to the LORD by deceiving a neighbor about something entrusted to them or left in their care or about something stolen, or if they cheat their neighbor, ³or if they find lost property and lie about it, or if they swear falsely about any such sin that people may commit— ⁴when they sin in any of these ways and realize their guilt, they must return what they have stolen or taken by extortion, or what was entrusted to them, or the lost property they found, ⁵or whatever it was they swore falsely about. They must make restitution in full, add a fifth of the value to it and give it all to the owner on the day they present their guilt offering. ⁶And as a penalty they must bring to the priest, that is, to the LORD, their guilt offering, a ram from

---

[a] 12 Or representative   [b] 15 That is, about 2/5 ounce or about 12 grams   [c] 19 Or offering; atonement has been made for their   [d] In Hebrew texts 6:1-7 is numbered 5:20-26, and 6:8-30 is numbered 6:1-23.

the flock, one without defect and of the proper value. [7]In this way the priest will make atonement for them before the LORD, and they will be forgiven for any of the things they did that made them guilty." Lev 5:15; Dt 22:1-3

The Burnt Offering

[8]The LORD said to Moses: [9]"Give Aaron and his sons this command: 'These are the regulations for the burnt offering: The burnt offering is to remain on the altar hearth throughout the night, till morning, and the fire must be kept burning on the altar. [10]The priest shall then put on his linen clothes, with linen undergarments next to his body, and shall remove the ashes of the burnt offering that the fire has consumed on the altar and place them beside the altar. [11]Then he is to take off these clothes and put on others, and carry the ashes outside the camp to a place that is ceremonially clean. [12]The fire on the altar must be kept burning; it must not go out. Every morning the priest is to add firewood and arrange the burnt offering on the fire and burn the fat of the fellowship offerings on it. [13]The fire must be kept burning on the altar continuously; it must not go out. Ex 28:39-43; Lev 4:12

The Grain Offering

[14]" 'These are the regulations for the grain offering: Aaron's sons are to bring it before the LORD, in front of the altar. [15]The priest is to take a handful of the finest flour and some olive oil, together with all the incense on the grain offering, and burn the memorial[a] portion on the altar as an aroma pleasing to the LORD. [16]Aaron and his sons shall eat the rest of it, but it is to be eaten without yeast in the sanctuary area; they are to eat it in the courtyard of the tent of meeting. [17]It must not be baked with yeast; I have given it as their share of the food offerings presented to me. Like the sin offering[b] and the guilt offering, it is most holy. [18]Any male descendant of Aaron may eat it. For all generations to come it is his perpetual share of the food offerings presented to the LORD. Whatever touches them will become holy.[c] '" Lev 2:3; Eze 44:29

[19]The LORD also said to Moses, [20]"This is the offering Aaron and his sons are to bring to the LORD on the day he[d] is anointed: a tenth of an ephah[e] of the finest flour as a regular grain offering, half of it in the morning and half in the evening. [21]It must be prepared with oil on a griddle; bring it well-mixed

---

[a] 15 Or representative   [b] 17 Or purification offering; also in verses 25 and 30
[c] 18 Or Whoever touches them must be holy; similarly in verse 27   [d] 20 Or each
[e] 20 That is, probably about 3 1/2 pounds or about 1.6 kilograms

and present the grain offering broken[a] in pieces as an aroma pleasing to the LORD. **22** The son who is to succeed him as anointed priest shall prepare it. It is the LORD's perpetual share and is to be burned completely. **23** Every grain offering of a priest shall be burned completely; it must not be eaten." Ex 29:2; Lev 2:5

The Sin Offering

24 The LORD said to Moses, **25** "Say to Aaron and his sons: 'These are the regulations for the sin offering: The sin offering is to be slaughtered before the LORD in the place the burnt offering is slaughtered; it is most holy. **26** The priest who offers it shall eat it; it is to be eaten in the sanctuary area, in the courtyard of the tent of meeting. **27** Whatever touches any of the flesh will become holy, and if any of the blood is spattered on a garment, you must wash it in the sanctuary area. **28** The clay pot the meat is cooked in must be broken; but if it is cooked in a bronze pot, the pot is to be scoured and rinsed with water. **29** Any male in a priest's family may eat it; it is most holy. **30** But any sin offering whose blood is brought into the tent of meeting to make atonement in the Holy Place must not be eaten; it must be burned up. Ex 29:37; Lev 1:5,11; 11:33

The Guilt Offering

7 " 'These are the regulations for the guilt offering, which is most holy: **2** The guilt offering is to be slaughtered in the place where the burnt offering is slaughtered, and its blood is to be splashed against the sides of the altar. **3** All its fat shall be offered: the fat tail and the fat that covers the internal organs, **4** both kidneys with the fat on them near the loins, and the long lobe of the liver, which is to be removed with the kidneys. **5** The priest shall burn them on the altar as a food offering presented to the LORD. It is a guilt offering. **6** Any male in a priest's family may eat it, but it must be eaten in the sanctuary area; it is most holy. Ex 29:13; Lev 6:18

7 " 'The same law applies to both the sin offering[b] and the guilt offering: They belong to the priest who makes atonement with them. **8** The priest who offers a burnt offering for anyone may keep its hide for himself. **9** Every grain offering baked in an oven or cooked in a pan or on a griddle belongs to the priest who offers it, **10** and every grain offering, whether mixed with olive oil or dry, belongs equally to all the sons of Aaron. Lev 2:5; 16:17,26

The Fellowship Offering

11 " 'These are the regulations

for the fellowship offering anyone may present to the LORD:

12 " 'If they offer it as an expression of thankfulness, then along with this thank offering they are to offer thick loaves made without yeast and with olive oil mixed in, thin loaves made without yeast and brushed with oil, and thick loaves of the finest flour well-kneaded and with oil mixed in. 13 Along with their fellowship offering of thanksgiving they are to present an offering with thick loaves of bread made with yeast. 14 They are to bring one of each kind as an offering, a contribution to the LORD; it belongs to the priest who splashes the blood of the fellowship offering against the altar. 15 The meat of their fellowship offering of thanksgiving must be eaten on the day it is offered; they must leave none of it till morning. Lev 22:30; Am 4:5

16 " 'If, however, their offering is the result of a vow or is a freewill offering, the sacrifice shall be eaten on the day they offer it, but anything left over may be eaten on the next day. 17 Any meat of the sacrifice left over till the third day must be burned up. 18 If any meat of the fellowship offering is eaten on the third day, the one who offered it will not be accepted. It will not be reckoned to their credit, for it has become impure; the person who eats any of it will be held responsible. Lev 19:5-8; Nu 18:27

19 " 'Meat that touches anything ceremonially unclean must not be eaten; it must be burned up. As for other meat, anyone ceremonially clean may eat it. 20 But if anyone who is unclean eats any meat of the fellowship offering belonging to the LORD, they must be cut off from their people. 21 Anyone who touches something unclean — whether human uncleanness or an unclean animal or any unclean creature that moves along the ground[a] — and then eats any of the meat of the fellowship offering belonging to the LORD must be cut off from their people.' " Lev 22:3-7

Eating Fat and Blood Forbidden

22 The LORD said to Moses, 23 "Say to the Israelites: 'Do not eat any of the fat of cattle, sheep or goats. 24 The fat of an animal found dead or torn by wild animals may be used for any other purpose, but you must not eat it. 25 Anyone who eats the fat of an animal from which a food offering may be[b] presented to the LORD must be cut off from their people. 26 And wherever you live, you must not eat the blood of any bird or animal. 27 Anyone who eats blood must be cut off from their people.' " Ge 9:4; Lev 17:10-24

---

a 21 A few Hebrew manuscripts, Samaritan Pentateuch, Syriac and Targum (see 5:2); most Hebrew manuscripts *any unclean, detestable thing*   b 25 Or *offering is*

The Priests' Share

²⁸The LORD said to Moses, ²⁹"Say to the Israelites: 'Anyone who brings a fellowship offering to the LORD is to bring part of it as their sacrifice to the LORD. ³⁰With their own hands they are to present the food offering to the LORD; they are to bring the fat, together with the breast, and wave the breast before the LORD as a wave offering. ³¹The priest shall burn the fat on the altar, but the breast belongs to Aaron and his sons. ³²You are to give the right thigh of your fellowship offerings to the priest as a contribution. ³³The son of Aaron who offers the blood and the fat of the fellowship offering shall have the right thigh as his share. ³⁴From the fellowship offerings of the Israelites, I have taken the breast that is waved and the thigh that is presented and have given them to Aaron the priest and his sons as their perpetual share from the Israelites.'"   Ex 29:27; Nu 18:18-19

³⁵This is the portion of the food offerings presented to the LORD that were allotted to Aaron and his sons on the day they were presented to serve the LORD as priests. ³⁶On the day they were anointed, the LORD commanded that the Israelites give this to them as their perpetual share for the generations to come.   Lev 8:12,30

³⁷These, then, are the regulations for the burnt offering, the grain offering, the sin offering, the guilt offering, the ordination offering and the fellowship offering, ³⁸which the LORD gave Moses at Mount Sinai in the Desert of Sinai on the day he commanded the Israelites to bring their offerings to the LORD.   Lev 1:2; 6:9

The Ordination of Aaron and His Sons

8:1-36pp — Ex 29:1-37

8 The LORD said to Moses, ²"Bring Aaron and his sons, their garments, the anointing oil, the bull for the sin offering,ᵃ the two rams and the basket containing bread made without yeast, ³and gather the entire assembly at the entrance to the tent of meeting." ⁴Moses did as the LORD commanded him, and the assembly gathered at the entrance to the tent of meeting.   Ex 29:2-3; 30:23-25,30

⁵Moses said to the assembly, "This is what the LORD has commanded to be done." ⁶Then Moses brought Aaron and his sons forward and washed them with water. ⁷He put the tunic on Aaron, tied the sash around him, clothed him with the robe and put the ephod on him. He also fastened the ephod with a decorative waistband, which he tied around him. ⁸He placed the breastpiece on him and put

---

ᵃ 2 Or *purification offering*; also in verse 14

the Urim and Thummim in the breastpiece. ⁹Then he placed the turban on Aaron's head and set the gold plate, the sacred emblem, on the front of it, as the LORD commanded Moses. Ex 28:30,36; Ac 22:16

¹⁰Then Moses took the anointing oil and anointed the tabernacle and everything in it, and so consecrated them. ¹¹He sprinkled some of the oil on the altar seven times, anointing the altar and all its utensils and the basin with its stand, to consecrate them. ¹²He poured some of the anointing oil on Aaron's head and anointed him to consecrate him. ¹³Then he brought Aaron's sons forward, put tunics on them, tied sashes around them and fastened caps on them, as the LORD commanded Moses. Ex 30:26,30

¹⁴He then presented the bull for the sin offering, and Aaron and his sons laid their hands on its head. ¹⁵Moses slaughtered the bull and took some of the blood, and with his finger he put it on all the horns of the altar to purify the altar. He poured out the rest of the blood at the base of the altar. So he consecrated it to make atonement for it. ¹⁶Moses also took all the fat around the internal organs, the long lobe of the liver, and both kidneys and their fat, and burned it on the altar. ¹⁷But the bull with its hide and its flesh and its intestines he burned up outside the camp, as the LORD commanded Moses. Ps 66:15; Heb 9:22

¹⁸He then presented the ram for the burnt offering, and Aaron and his sons laid their hands on its head. ¹⁹Then Moses slaughtered the ram and splashed the blood against the sides of the altar. ²⁰He cut the ram into pieces and burned the head, the pieces and the fat. ²¹He washed the internal organs and the legs with water and burned the whole ram on the altar. It was a burnt offering, a pleasing aroma, a food offering presented to the LORD, as the LORD commanded Moses.

²²He then presented the other ram, the ram for the ordination, and Aaron and his sons laid their hands on its head. ²³Moses slaughtered the ram and took some of its blood and put it on the lobe of Aaron's right ear, on the thumb of his right hand and on the big toe of his right foot. ²⁴Moses also brought Aaron's sons forward and put some of the blood on the lobes of their right ears, on the thumbs of their right hands and on the big toes of their right feet. Then he splashed blood against the sides of the altar. ²⁵After that, he took the fat, the fat tail, all the fat around the internal organs, the long lobe of the liver, both kidneys and their fat and the right thigh. ²⁶And from the basket of bread made without yeast, which was before the LORD, he took one

thick loaf, one thick loaf with olive oil mixed in, and one thin loaf, and he put these on the fat portions and on the right thigh. ²⁷He put all these in the hands of Aaron and his sons, and they waved them before the LORD as a wave offering. ²⁸Then Moses took them from their hands and burned them on the altar on top of the burnt offering as an ordination offering, a pleasing aroma, a food offering presented to the LORD. ²⁹Moses also took the breast, which was his share of the ordination ram, and waved it before the LORD as a wave offering, as the LORD commanded Moses. Lev 7:31-34; Heb 9:18-22

³⁰Then Moses took some of the anointing oil and some of the blood from the altar and sprinkled them on Aaron and his garments and on his sons and their garments. So he consecrated Aaron and his garments and his sons and their garments. Nu 3:3

³¹Moses then said to Aaron and his sons, "Cook the meat at the entrance to the tent of meeting and eat it there with the bread from the basket of ordination offerings, as I was commanded: 'Aaron and his sons are to eat it.' ³²Then burn up the rest of the meat and the bread. ³³Do not leave the entrance to the tent of meeting for seven days, until the days of your ordination are completed, for your ordination will last seven days. ³⁴What has been done today was commanded by the LORD to make atonement for you. ³⁵You must stay at the entrance to the tent of meeting day and night for seven days and do what the LORD requires, so you will not die; for that is what I have been commanded."

³⁶So Aaron and his sons did everything the LORD commanded through Moses. Ex 29:1-37; Dt 11:1

The Priests Begin Their Ministry

9 On the eighth day Moses summoned Aaron and his sons and the elders of Israel. ²He said to Aaron, "Take a bull calf for your sin offering[a] and a ram for your burnt offering, both without defect, and present them before the LORD. ³Then say to the Israelites: 'Take a male goat for a sin offering, a calf and a lamb — both a year old and without defect — for a burnt offering, ⁴and an ox[b] and a ram for a fellowship offering to sacrifice before the LORD, together with a grain offering mixed with olive oil. For today the LORD will appear to you.'" Ex 29:43; Eze 43:27

⁵They took the things Moses commanded to the front of the tent of meeting, and the entire assembly came near and stood before the LORD. ⁶Then Moses said, "This is what the LORD has

---

[a] 2 Or *purification offering*; here and throughout this chapter [b] 4 The Hebrew word can refer to either male or female; also in verses 18 and 19.

commanded you to do, so that the glory of the LORD may appear to you." Ex 24:16

7 Moses said to Aaron, "Come to the altar and sacrifice your sin offering and your burnt offering and make atonement for yourself and the people; sacrifice the offering that is for the people and make atonement for them, as the LORD has commanded." Heb 5:1,3; 7:27

8 So Aaron came to the altar and slaughtered the calf as a sin offering for himself. **9** His sons brought the blood to him, and he dipped his finger into the blood and put it on the horns of the altar; the rest of the blood he poured out at the base of the altar. **10** On the altar he burned the fat, the kidneys and the long lobe of the liver from the sin offering, as the LORD commanded Moses; **11** the flesh and the hide he burned up outside the camp. Lev 4:1-12

12 Then he slaughtered the burnt offering. His sons handed him the blood, and he splashed it against the sides of the altar. **13** They handed him the burnt offering piece by piece, including the head, and he burned them on the altar. **14** He washed the internal organs and the legs and burned them on top of the burnt offering on the altar. Lev 1:8

15 Aaron then brought the offering that was for the people. He took the goat for the people's sin offering and slaughtered it and

offered it for a sin offering as he did with the first one. Lev 4:27-31

16 He brought the burnt offering and offered it in the prescribed way. **17** He also brought the grain offering, took a handful of it and burned it on the altar in addition to the morning's burnt offering. Lev 1:1-13; 2:1-2

18 He slaughtered the ox and the ram as the fellowship offering for the people. His sons handed him the blood, and he splashed it against the sides of the altar. **19** But the fat portions of the ox and the ram—the fat tail, the layer of fat, the kidneys and the long lobe of the liver— **20** these they laid on the breasts, and then Aaron burned the fat on the altar. **21** Aaron waved the breasts and the right thigh before the LORD as a wave offering, as Moses commanded. Lev 3:1-11; 7:30-34

22 Then Aaron lifted his hands toward the people and blessed them. And having sacrificed the sin offering, the burnt offering and the fellowship offering, he stepped down. Nu 6:23; Lk 24:50

23 Moses and Aaron then went into the tent of meeting. When they came out, they blessed the people; and the glory of the LORD appeared to all the people. **24** Fire came out from the presence of the LORD and consumed the burnt offering and the fat portions on the altar. And when all the people saw it, they shouted for joy and fell facedown. 1Ki 18:39

The Death of Nadab and Abihu

10 Aaron's sons Nadab and Abihu took their censers, put fire in them and added incense; and they offered unauthorized fire before the LORD, contrary to his command. ²So fire came out from the presence of the LORD and consumed them, and they died before the LORD. ³Moses then said to Aaron, "This is what the LORD spoke of when he said: Lev 16:12; Nu 3:2-4

"'Among those who approach
   me
I will be proved
   holy;   Ex 30:29; Eze 28:22
in the sight of all the people
I will be honored.'"   Isa 49:3

Aaron remained silent.

⁴Moses summoned Mishael and Elzaphan, sons of Aaron's uncle Uzziel, and said to them, "Come here; carry your cousins outside the camp, away from the front of the sanctuary." ⁵So they came and carried them, still in their tunics, outside the camp, as Moses ordered.   Ex 6:22

⁶Then Moses said to Aaron and his sons Eleazar and Ithamar, "Do not let your hair become unkempt*a* and do not tear your clothes, or you will die and the LORD will be angry with the whole community. But your relatives, all the Israelites, may mourn for those the LORD has destroyed by fire. ⁷Do not leave the entrance to the tent of meeting or you will die, because the LORD's anointing oil is on you." So they did as Moses said.   Nu 16:22; Jos 7:1

⁸Then the LORD said to Aaron, ⁹"You and your sons are not to drink wine or other fermented drink whenever you go into the tent of meeting, or you will die. This is a lasting ordinance for the generations to come, ¹⁰so that you can distinguish between the holy and the common, between the unclean and the clean, ¹¹and so you can teach the Israelites all the decrees the LORD has given them through Moses."   Lev 20:25; Eze 44:21

¹²Moses said to Aaron and his remaining sons, Eleazar and Ithamar, "Take the grain offering left over from the food offerings prepared without yeast and presented to the LORD and eat it beside the altar, for it is most holy. ¹³Eat it in the sanctuary area, because it is your share and your sons' share of the food offerings presented to the LORD; for so I have been commanded. ¹⁴But you and your sons and your daughters may eat the breast that was waved and the thigh that was presented. Eat them in a ceremonially clean place; they have been given to you and your children as your share of the Israelites' fellowship offerings. ¹⁵The thigh that was presented

---

a 6 Or *Do not uncover your heads*

and the breast that was waved must be brought with the fat portions of the food offerings, to be waved before the LORD as a wave offering. This will be the perpetual share for you and your children, as the LORD has commanded." Lev 6:14-18; 7:34

16 When Moses inquired about the goat of the sin offering[a] and found that it had been burned up, he was angry with Eleazar and Ithamar, Aaron's remaining sons, and asked, 17 "Why didn't you eat the sin offering in the sanctuary area? It is most holy; it was given to you to take away the guilt of the community by making atonement for them before the LORD. 18 Since its blood was not taken into the Holy Place, you should have eaten the goat in the sanctuary area, as I commanded." Lev 6:26,30; 9:3

19 Aaron replied to Moses, "Today they sacrificed their sin offering and their burnt offering before the LORD, but such things as this have happened to me. Would the LORD have been pleased if I had eaten the sin offering today?" 20 When Moses heard this, he was satisfied. Lev 9:12

Clean and Unclean Food
11:1-23pp — Dt 14:3-20

11 The LORD said to Moses and Aaron, 2 "Say to the Israelites: 'Of all the animals that live on land, these are the ones you may eat: 3 You may eat any animal that has a divided hoof and that chews the cud. Ac 10:12-14

4 " 'There are some that only chew the cud or only have a divided hoof, but you must not eat them. The camel, though it chews the cud, does not have a divided hoof; it is ceremonially unclean for you. 5 The hyrax, though it chews the cud, does not have a divided hoof; it is unclean for you. 6 The rabbit, though it chews the cud, does not have a divided hoof; it is unclean for you. 7 And the pig, though it has a divided hoof, does not chew the cud; it is unclean for you. 8 You must not eat their meat or touch their carcasses; they are unclean for you. Isa 65:4; Heb 9:10

9 " 'Of all the creatures living in the water of the seas and the streams you may eat any that have fins and scales. 10 But all creatures in the seas or streams that do not have fins and scales — whether among all the swarming things or among all the other living creatures in the water — you are to regard as unclean. 11 And since you are to regard them as unclean, you must not eat their meat; you must regard their carcasses as unclean. 12 Anything living in the water that does not have fins and scales is to be regarded as unclean by you. Lev 7:18

---

a 16 Or purification offering; also in verses 17 and 19

13 " 'These are the birds you are to regard as unclean and not eat because they are unclean: the eagle,[a] the vulture, the black vulture, 14 the red kite, any kind of black kite, 15 any kind of raven, 16 the horned owl, the screech owl, the gull, any kind of hawk, 17 the little owl, the cormorant, the great owl, 18 the white owl, the desert owl, the osprey, 19 the stork, any kind of heron, the hoopoe and the bat.

20 " 'All flying insects that walk on all fours are to be regarded as unclean by you. 21 There are, however, some flying insects that walk on all fours that you may eat: those that have jointed legs for hopping on the ground. 22 Of these you may eat any kind of locust, katydid, cricket or grasshopper. 23 But all other flying insects that have four legs you are to regard as unclean.   Dt 14:3-20; Mt 3:4

24 " 'You will make yourselves unclean by these; whoever touches their carcasses will be unclean till evening. 25 Whoever picks up one of their carcasses must wash their clothes, and they will be unclean till evening.   Lev 14:8,47; 15:5; Nu 31:24

26 " 'Every animal that does not have a divided hoof or that does not chew the cud is unclean for you; whoever touches the carcass of any of them will be unclean. 27 Of all the animals that walk on all fours, those that walk on their paws are unclean for you; whoever touches their carcasses will be unclean till evening. 28 Anyone who picks up their carcasses must wash their clothes, and they will be unclean till evening. These animals are unclean for you.

29 " 'Of the animals that move along the ground, these are unclean for you: the weasel, the rat, any kind of great lizard, 30 the gecko, the monitor lizard, the wall lizard, the skink and the chameleon. 31 Of all those that move along the ground, these are unclean for you. Whoever touches them when they are dead will be unclean till evening. 32 When one of them dies and falls on something, that article, whatever its use, will be unclean, whether it is made of wood, cloth, hide or sackcloth. Put it in water; it will be unclean till evening, and then it will be clean. 33 If one of them falls into a clay pot, everything in it will be unclean, and you must break the pot. 34 Any food you are allowed to eat that has come into contact with water from any such pot is unclean, and any liquid that is drunk from such a pot is unclean. 35 Anything that one of their carcasses falls on becomes unclean; an oven or cooking pot must be broken up. They are unclean, and you are to regard them as unclean. 36 A spring, however, or a cistern for collecting water

---

[a] 13 The precise identification of some of the birds, insects and animals in this chapter is uncertain.

remains clean, but anyone who touches one of these carcasses is unclean. [37]If a carcass falls on any seeds that are to be planted, they remain clean. [38]But if water has been put on the seed and a carcass falls on it, it is unclean for you.

Lev 15:12

[39]"'If an animal that you are allowed to eat dies, anyone who touches its carcass will be unclean till evening. [40]Anyone who eats some of its carcass must wash their clothes, and they will be unclean till evening. Anyone who picks up the carcass must wash their clothes, and they will be unclean till evening.

Lev 17:15; 22:8

[41]"'Every creature that moves along the ground is to be regarded as unclean; it is not to be eaten. [42]You are not to eat any creature that moves along the ground, whether it moves on its belly or walks on all fours or on many feet; it is unclean. [43]Do not defile yourselves by any of these creatures. Do not make yourselves unclean by means of them or be made unclean by them. [44]I am the LORD your God; consecrate yourselves and be holy, because I am holy. Do not make yourselves unclean by any creature that moves along the ground. [45]I am the LORD, who brought you up out of Egypt to be your God; therefore be holy, because I am holy.

Ex 19:6; Lev 19:2; 1Pe 1:16

[46]"'These are the regulations concerning animals, birds, every living thing that moves about in the water and every creature that moves along the ground. [47]You must distinguish between the unclean and the clean, between living creatures that may be eaten and those that may not be eaten.'"

Lev 10:10

Purification After Childbirth

12 The LORD said to Moses, [2]"Say to the Israelites: 'A woman who becomes pregnant and gives birth to a son will be ceremonially unclean for seven days, just as she is unclean during her monthly period. [3]On the eighth day the boy is to be circumcised. [4]Then the woman must wait thirty-three days to be purified from her bleeding. She must not touch anything sacred or go to the sanctuary until the days of her purification are over. [5]If she gives birth to a daughter, for two weeks the woman will be unclean, as during her period. Then she must wait sixty-six days to be purified from her bleeding.

Ge 17:12; Lk 1:59

[6]"'When the days of her purification for a son or daughter are over, she is to bring to the priest at the entrance to the tent of meeting a year-old lamb for a burnt offering and a young pigeon or a dove for a sin offering.[a]

---

[a] 6 Or *purification offering*; also in verse 8

[7] He shall offer them before the LORD to make atonement for her, and then she will be ceremonially clean from her flow of blood. " 'These are the regulations for the woman who gives birth to a boy or a girl. [8] But if she cannot afford a lamb, she is to bring two doves or two young pigeons, one for a burnt offering and the other for a sin offering. In this way the priest will make atonement for her, and she will be clean.' " Lev 4:26; 5:7; Lk 2:22-24

Regulations About Defiling Skin Diseases

13 The LORD said to Moses and Aaron, [2] "When anyone has a swelling or a rash or a shiny spot on their skin that may be a defiling skin disease,[a] they must be brought to Aaron the priest or to one of his sons[b] who is a priest. [3] The priest is to examine the sore on the skin, and if the hair in the sore has turned white and the sore appears to be more than skin deep, it is a defiling skin disease. When the priest examines that person, he shall pronounce them ceremonially unclean. [4] If the shiny spot on the skin is white but does not appear to be more than skin deep and the hair in it has not turned white, the priest is to isolate the affected person for seven days. [5] On the seventh day the priest is to examine them, and if he sees that the sore is unchanged and has not spread in the skin, he is to isolate them for another seven days. [6] On the seventh day the priest is to examine them again, and if the sore has faded and has not spread in the skin, the priest shall pronounce them clean; it is only a rash. They must wash their clothes, and they will be clean. [7] But if the rash does spread in their skin after they have shown themselves to the priest to be pronounced clean, they must appear before the priest again. [8] The priest is to examine that person, and if the rash has spread in the skin, he shall pronounce them unclean; it is a defiling skin disease. Lev 11:25; Dt 24:8

[9] "When anyone has a defiling skin disease, they must be brought to the priest. [10] The priest is to examine them, and if there is a white swelling in the skin that has turned the hair white and if there is raw flesh in the swelling, [11] it is a chronic skin disease and the priest shall pronounce them unclean. He is not to isolate them, because they are already unclean. Lev 14:8; Nu 12:10

[12] "If the disease breaks out all over their skin and, so far as the priest can see, it covers all the skin of the affected person from head to foot, [13] the priest is to examine them, and if the disease

---

[a] 2 The Hebrew word for *defiling skin disease*, traditionally translated "leprosy," was used for various diseases affecting the skin; here and throughout verses 3-46.   [b] 2 Or *descendants*

has covered their whole body, he shall pronounce them clean. Since it has all turned white, they are clean. ¹⁴But whenever raw flesh appears on them, they will be unclean. ¹⁵When the priest sees the raw flesh, he shall pronounce them unclean. The raw flesh is unclean; they have a defiling disease. ¹⁶If the raw flesh changes and turns white, they must go to the priest. ¹⁷The priest is to examine them, and if the sores have turned white, the priest shall pronounce the affected person clean; then they will be clean.   ver 2,6

¹⁸"When someone has a boil on their skin and it heals, ¹⁹and in the place where the boil was, a white swelling or reddish-white spot appears, they must present themselves to the priest. ²⁰The priest is to examine it, and if it appears to be more than skin deep and the hair in it has turned white, the priest shall pronounce that person unclean. It is a defiling skin disease that has broken out where the boil was. ²¹But if, when the priest examines it, there is no white hair in it and it is not more than skin deep and has faded, then the priest is to isolate them for seven days. ²²If it is spreading in the skin, the priest shall pronounce them unclean; it is a defiling disease. ²³But if the spot is unchanged and has not spread, it is only a scar from the boil, and

the priest shall pronounce them clean.   Ex 9:9; Lev 14:37

²⁴"When someone has a burn on their skin and a reddish-white or white spot appears in the raw flesh of the burn, ²⁵the priest is to examine the spot, and if the hair in it has turned white, and it appears to be more than skin deep, it is a defiling disease that has broken out in the burn. The priest shall pronounce them unclean; it is a defiling skin disease. ²⁶But if the priest examines it and there is no white hair in the spot and if it is not more than skin deep and has faded, then the priest is to isolate them for seven days. ²⁷On the seventh day the priest is to examine that person, and if it is spreading in the skin, the priest shall pronounce them unclean; it is a defiling skin disease. ²⁸If, however, the spot is unchanged and has not spread in the skin but has faded, it is a swelling from the burn, and the priest shall pronounce them clean; it is only a scar from the burn.   ver 4-5

²⁹"If a man or woman has a sore on their head or chin, ³⁰the priest is to examine the sore, and if it appears to be more than skin deep and the hair in it is yellow and thin, the priest shall pronounce them unclean; it is a defiling skin disease on the head or chin. ³¹But if, when the priest examines the sore, it does not seem to be more than skin deep and

there is no black hair in it, then the priest is to isolate the affected person for seven days. ³²On the seventh day the priest is to examine the sore, and if it has not spread and there is no yellow hair in it and it does not appear to be more than skin deep, ³³then the man or woman must shave themselves, except for the affected area, and the priest is to keep them isolated another seven days. ³⁴On the seventh day the priest is to examine the sore, and if it has not spread in the skin and appears to be no more than skin deep, the priest shall pronounce them clean. They must wash their clothes, and they will be clean. ³⁵But if the sore does spread in the skin after they are pronounced clean, ³⁶the priest is to examine them, and if he finds that the sore has spread in the skin, he does not need to look for yellow hair; they are unclean. ³⁷If, however, the sore is unchanged so far as the priest can see, and if black hair has grown in it, the affected person is healed. They are clean, and the priest shall pronounce them clean. Lev 11:25

³⁸"When a man or woman has white spots on the skin, ³⁹the priest is to examine them, and if the spots are dull white, it is a harmless rash that has broken out on the skin; they are clean.

⁴⁰"A man who has lost his hair and is bald is clean. ⁴¹If he has lost his hair from the front of his scalp and has a bald forehead, he is clean. ⁴²But if he has a reddish-white sore on his bald head or forehead, it is a defiling disease breaking out on his head or forehead. ⁴³The priest is to examine him, and if the swollen sore on his head or forehead is reddish-white like a defiling skin disease, ⁴⁴the man is diseased and is unclean. The priest shall pronounce him unclean because of the sore on his head. 2Ki 2:23; Eze 29:18

⁴⁵"Anyone with such a defiling disease must wear torn clothes, let their hair be unkempt,ᵃ cover the lower part of their face and cry out, 'Unclean! Unclean!' ⁴⁶As long as they have the disease they remain unclean. They must live alone; they must live outside the camp. Nu 5:1-4; La 4:15; Lk 17:12

Regulations About Defiling Molds

⁴⁷"As for any fabric that is spoiled with a defiling mold—any woolen or linen clothing, ⁴⁸any woven or knitted material of linen or wool, any leather or anything made of leather — ⁴⁹if the affected area in the fabric, the leather, the woven or knitted material, or any leather article, is greenish or reddish, it is a defiling mold and must be

ᶜ 45 Or *clothes, uncover their head*

shown to the priest. [50] The priest is to examine the affected area and isolate the article for seven days. [51] On the seventh day he is to examine it, and if the mold has spread in the fabric, the woven or knitted material, or the leather, whatever its use, it is a persistent defiling mold; the article is unclean. [52] He must burn the fabric, the woven or knitted material of wool or linen, or any leather article that has been spoiled; because the defiling mold is persistent, the article must be burned. Mk 1:44; Lev 14:44

[53] "But if, when the priest examines it, the mold has not spread in the fabric, the woven or knitted material, or the leather article, [54] he shall order that the spoiled article be washed. Then he is to isolate it for another seven days. [55] After the article has been washed, the priest is to examine it again, and if the mold has not changed its appearance, even though it has not spread, it is unclean. Burn it, no matter which side of the fabric has been spoiled. [56] If, when the priest examines it, the mold has faded after the article has been washed, he is to tear the spoiled part out of the fabric, the leather, or the woven or knitted material. [57] But if it reappears in the fabric, in the woven or knitted material, or in the leather article, it is a spreading mold; whatever has the mold must be burned. [58] Any fabric, woven or knitted material, or any leather article that has been washed and is rid of the mold, must be washed again. Then it will be clean."

[59] These are the regulations concerning defiling molds in woolen or linen clothing, woven or knitted material, or any leather article, for pronouncing them clean or unclean.

Cleansing From Defiling Skin Diseases

14 The LORD said to Moses, [2] "These are the regulations for any diseased person at the time of their ceremonial cleansing, when they are brought to the priest: [3] The priest is to go outside the camp and examine them. If they have been healed of their defiling skin disease,[a] [4] the priest shall order that two live clean birds and some cedar wood, scarlet yarn and hyssop be brought for the person to be cleansed. [5] Then the priest shall order that one of the birds be killed over fresh water in a clay pot. [6] He is then to take the live bird and dip it, together with the cedar wood, the scarlet yarn and the hyssop, into the blood of the bird that was killed over the fresh water. [7] Seven times he shall sprinkle the one

---

[a] 3 The Hebrew word for *defiling skin disease*, traditionally translated "leprosy," was used for various diseases affecting the skin; also in verses 7, 32, 54 and 57.

to be cleansed of the defiling disease, and then pronounce them clean. After that, he is to release the live bird in the open fields. Mt 8:2-4; Nu 19:6; 2Ki 5:10,14

8 "The person to be cleansed must wash their clothes, shave off all their hair and bathe with water; then they will be ceremonially clean. After this they may come into the camp, but they must stay outside their tent for seven days. 9 On the seventh day they must shave off all their hair; they must shave their head, their beard, their eyebrows and the rest of their hair. They must wash their clothes and bathe themselves with water, and they will be clean. Lev 11:25; 13:6

10 "On the eighth day they must bring two male lambs and one ewe lamb a year old, each without defect, along with three-tenths of an ephah[a] of the finest flour mixed with olive oil for a grain offering, and one log[b] of oil. 11 The priest who pronounces them clean shall present both the one to be cleansed and their offerings before the LORD at the entrance to the tent of meeting. Mt 8:4

12 "Then the priest is to take one of the male lambs and offer it as a guilt offering, along with the log of oil; he shall wave them before the LORD as a wave offering. 13 He is to slaughter the lamb in the sanctuary area where the sin offering[c] and the burnt offering are slaughtered. Like the sin offering, the guilt offering belongs to the priest; it is most holy. 14 The priest is to take some of the blood of the guilt offering and put it on the lobe of the right ear of the one to be cleansed, on the thumb of their right hand and on the big toe of their right foot. 15 The priest shall then take some of the log of oil, pour it in the palm of his own left hand, 16 dip his right forefinger into the oil in his palm, and with his finger sprinkle some of it before the LORD seven times. 17 The priest is to put some of the oil remaining in his palm on the lobe of the right ear of the one to be cleansed, on the thumb of their right hand and on the big toe of their right foot, on top of the blood of the guilt offering. 18 The rest of the oil in his palm the priest shall put on the head of the one to be cleansed and make atonement for them before the LORD. Ex 29:11; Lev 5:18

19 "Then the priest is to sacrifice the sin offering and make atonement for the one to be cleansed from their uncleanness. After that, the priest shall slaughter the burnt offering 20 and offer it on the altar, together with the grain offering, and make atonement for them, and they will be clean.

---

[a] 10 That is, probably about 11 pounds or about 5 kilograms   [b] 10 That is, about 1/3 quart or about 0.3 liter; also in verses 12, 15, 21 and 24   [c] 13 Or *purification offering*; also in verses 19, 22 and 31

21 "If, however, they are poor and cannot afford these, they must take one male lamb as a guilt offering to be waved to make atonement for them, together with a tenth of an ephah[a] of the finest flour mixed with olive oil for a grain offering, a log of oil, 22 and two doves or two young pigeons, such as they can afford, one for a sin offering and the other for a burnt offering. Lev 5:7; 12:8

23 "On the eighth day they must bring them for their cleansing to the priest at the entrance to the tent of meeting, before the LORD. 24 The priest is to take the lamb for the guilt offering, together with the log of oil, and wave them before the LORD as a wave offering. 25 He shall slaughter the lamb for the guilt offering and take some of its blood and put it on the lobe of the right ear of the one to be cleansed, on the thumb of their right hand and on the big toe of their right foot. 26 The priest is to pour some of the oil into the palm of his own left hand, 27 and with his right forefinger sprinkle some of the oil from his palm seven times before the LORD. 28 Some of the oil in his palm he is to put on the same places he put the blood of the guilt offering — on the lobe of the right ear of the one to be cleansed, on the thumb of their right hand and on the big toe of their right foot.

29 The rest of the oil in his palm the priest shall put on the head of the one to be cleansed, to make atonement for them before the LORD. 30 Then he shall sacrifice the doves or the young pigeons, such as the person can afford, 31 one as a sin offering and the other as a burnt offering, together with the grain offering. In this way the priest will make atonement before the LORD on behalf of the one to be cleansed."

32 These are the regulations for anyone who has a defiling skin disease and who cannot afford the regular offerings for their cleansing. Lev 5:7; 13:2; Nu 6:14

Cleansing From Defiling Molds

33 The LORD said to Moses and Aaron, 34 "When you enter the land of Canaan, which I am giving you as your possession, and I put a spreading mold in a house in that land, 35 the owner of the house must go and tell the priest, 'I have seen something that looks like a defiling mold in my house.' 36 The priest is to order the house to be emptied before he goes in to examine the mold, so that nothing in the house will be pronounced unclean. After this the priest is to go in and inspect the house. 37 He is to examine the mold on the walls, and if it has greenish or reddish depressions that

a 21 That is, probably about 3 1/2 pounds or about 1.6 kilograms appear to be deeper than the surface of the wall, ³⁸the priest shall go out the doorway of the house and close it up for seven days. ³⁹On the seventh day the priest shall return to inspect the house. If the mold has spread on the walls, ⁴⁰he is to order that the contaminated stones be torn out and thrown into an unclean place outside the town. ⁴¹He must have all the inside walls of the house scraped and the material that is scraped off dumped into an unclean place outside the town. ⁴²Then they are to take other stones to replace these and take new clay and plaster the house. Ge 17:8; Nu 32:22

⁴³"If the defiling mold reappears in the house after the stones have been torn out and the house scraped and plastered, ⁴⁴the priest is to go and examine it and, if the mold has spread in the house, it is a persistent defiling mold; the house is unclean. ⁴⁵It must be torn down—its stones, timbers and all the plaster—and taken out of the town to an unclean place. Lev 13:51

⁴⁶"Anyone who goes into the house while it is closed up will be unclean till evening. ⁴⁷Anyone who sleeps or eats in the house must wash their clothes. Lev 11:24-25

⁴⁸"But if the priest comes to examine it and the mold has not spread after the house has been plastered, he shall pronounce the house clean, because the defiling mold is gone. ⁴⁹To purify the house he is to take two birds and some cedar wood, scarlet yarn and hyssop. ⁵⁰He shall kill one of the birds over fresh water in a clay pot. ⁵¹Then he is to take the cedar wood, the hyssop, the scarlet yarn and the live bird, dip them into the blood of the dead bird and the fresh water, and sprinkle the house seven times. ⁵²He shall purify the house with the bird's blood, the fresh water, the live bird, the cedar wood, the hyssop and the scarlet yarn. ⁵³Then he is to release the live bird in the open fields outside the town. In this way he will make atonement for the house, and it will be clean." Lev 13:6; Ps 51:7

⁵⁴These are the regulations for any defiling skin disease, for a sore, ⁵⁵for defiling molds in fabric or in a house, ⁵⁶and for a swelling, a rash or a shiny spot, ⁵⁷to determine when something is clean or unclean. Lev 13:2,47-52

These are the regulations for defiling skin diseases and defiling molds. Lev 10:10

Discharges Causing Uncleanness

15 The LORD said to Moses and Aaron, ²"Speak to the Israelites and say to them: 'When any man has an unusual bodily discharge, such a discharge is unclean. ³Whether it continues flowing from his body or is blocked, it will make him unclean. This is how his discharge will bring about uncleanness: Lev 22:4; Mt 9:20

⁴"'Any bed the man with a discharge lies on will be unclean, and anything he sits on will be unclean. ⁵Anyone who touches his bed must wash their clothes and bathe with water, and they will be unclean till evening. ⁶Whoever sits on anything that the man with a discharge sat on must wash their clothes and bathe with water, and they will be unclean till evening. Lev 11:25; 14:8

⁷"'Whoever touches the man who has a discharge must wash their clothes and bathe with water, and they will be unclean till evening. Lev 22:5

⁸"'If the man with the discharge spits on anyone who is clean, they must wash their clothes and bathe with water, and they will be unclean till evening. Nu 12:14

⁹"'Everything the man sits on when riding will be unclean, ¹⁰and whoever touches any of the things that were under him will be unclean till evening; whoever picks up those things must wash their clothes and bathe with water, and they will be unclean till evening. Nu 19:10

¹¹"'Anyone the man with a discharge touches without rinsing his hands with water must wash their clothes and bathe with wa-

ter, and they will be unclean till evening.

¹²"'A clay pot that the man touches must be broken, and any wooden article is to be rinsed with water. Lev 6:28

¹³"'When a man is cleansed from his discharge, he is to count off seven days for his ceremonial cleansing; he must wash his clothes and bathe himself with fresh water, and he will be clean. ¹⁴On the eighth day he must take two doves or two young pigeons and come before the LORD to the entrance to the tent of meeting and give them to the priest. ¹⁵The priest is to sacrifice them, the one for a sin offering*a* and the other for a burnt offering. In this way he will make atonement before the LORD for the man because of his discharge. Lev 8:33; 14:18-19

¹⁶"'When a man has an emission of semen, he must bathe his whole body with water, and he will be unclean till evening. ¹⁷Any clothing or leather that has semen on it must be washed with water, and it will be unclean till evening. ¹⁸When a man has sexual relations with a woman and there is an emission of semen, both of them must bathe with water, and they will be unclean till evening. Lev 22:4; Dt 23:10

¹⁹"'When a woman has her regular flow of blood, the impurity of her monthly period will

---

a 15 Or *purification offering*; also in verse 30

last seven days, and anyone who touches her will be unclean till evening. _{Lev 12:2}

20 "'Anything she lies on during her period will be unclean, and anything she sits on will be unclean. **21** Anyone who touches her bed will be unclean; they must wash their clothes and bathe with water, and they will be unclean till evening. **22** Anyone who touches anything she sits on will be unclean; they must wash their clothes and bathe with water, and they will be unclean till evening. **23** Whether it is the bed or anything she was sitting on, when anyone touches it, they will be unclean till evening.

24 "'If a man has sexual relations with her and her monthly flow touches him, he will be unclean for seven days; any bed he lies on will be unclean. _{Lev 12:2}

25 "'When a woman has a discharge of blood for many days at a time other than her monthly period or has a discharge that continues beyond her period, she will be unclean as long as she has the discharge, just as in the days of her period. **26** Any bed she lies on while her discharge continues will be unclean, as is her bed during her monthly period, and anything she sits on will be unclean, as during her period. **27** Anyone who touches them will be unclean; they must

wash their clothes and bathe with water, and they will be unclean till evening. _{Mt 9:20}

28 "'When she is cleansed from her discharge, she must count off seven days, and after that she will be ceremonially clean. **29** On the eighth day she must take two doves or two young pigeons and bring them to the priest at the entrance to the tent of meeting. **30** The priest is to sacrifice one for a sin offering and the other for a burnt offering. In this way he will make atonement for her before the LORD for the uncleanness of her discharge. _{Lev 14:22}

31 "'You must keep the Israelites separate from things that make them unclean, so they will not die in their uncleanness for defiling my dwelling place,*ᵃ* which is among them.'" _{Nu 19:13,20; Eze 5:11}

32 These are the regulations for a man with a discharge, for anyone made unclean by an emission of semen, **33** for a woman in her monthly period, for a man or a woman with a discharge, and for a man who has sexual relations with a woman who is ceremonially unclean. _{ver 2}

The Day of Atonement

16:2-34pp — Lev 23:26-32; Nu 29:7-11

16 The LORD spoke to Moses after the death of the two sons of Aaron who died when they approached the LORD. **2** The

---

ᵃ 31 Or *my tabernacle*

LORD said to Moses: "Tell your brother Aaron that he is not to come whenever he chooses into the Most Holy Place behind the curtain in front of the atonement cover on the ark, or else he will die. For I will appear in the cloud over the atonement cover. Ex 25:22

³ "This is how Aaron is to enter the Most Holy Place: He must first bring a young bull for a sin offering*a* and a ram for a burnt offering. ⁴ He is to put on the sacred linen tunic, with linen undergarments next to his body; he is to tie the linen sash around him and put on the linen turban. These are sacred garments; so he must bathe himself with water before he puts them on. ⁵ From the Israelite community he is to take two male goats for a sin offering and a ram for a burnt offering. Lev 4:13-21; 2Ch 29:23

⁶ "Aaron is to offer the bull for his own sin offering to make atonement for himself and his household. ⁷ Then he is to take the two goats and present them before the LORD at the entrance to the tent of meeting. ⁸ He is to cast lots for the two goats — one lot for the LORD and the other for the scapegoat.*b* ⁹ Aaron shall bring the goat whose lot falls to the LORD and sacrifice it for a sin offering. ¹⁰ But the goat chosen by lot as the scapegoat shall be presented alive before the LORD to be used for making atonement by sending it into the wilderness as a scapegoat. Lev 9:7; Heb 7:27; 9:7,12

¹¹ "Aaron shall bring the bull for his own sin offering to make atonement for himself and his household, and he is to slaughter the bull for his own sin offering. ¹² He is to take a censer full of burning coals from the altar before the LORD and two handfuls of finely ground fragrant incense and take them behind the curtain. ¹³ He is to put the incense on the fire before the LORD, and the smoke of the incense will conceal the atonement cover above the tablets of the covenant law, so that he will not die. ¹⁴ He is to take some of the bull's blood and with his finger sprinkle it on the front of the atonement cover; then he shall sprinkle some of it with his finger seven times before the atonement cover. Lev 10:1; Heb 9:7,13

¹⁵ "He shall then slaughter the goat for the sin offering for the people and take its blood behind the curtain and do with it as he did with the bull's blood: He shall sprinkle it on the atonement cover and in front of it. ¹⁶ In this way he will make atonement for the Most Holy Place because of the uncleanness and rebellion of the Israelites, whatever their sins have been. He is to do the same for the tent of meeting, which is among them in the midst of their

---

a 3 Or *purification offering*; here and throughout this chapter   *b 8* The meaning of the Hebrew for this word is uncertain; also in verses 10 and 26.

uncleanness. ¹⁷No one is to be in the tent of meeting from the time Aaron goes in to make atonement in the Most Holy Place until he comes out, having made atonement for himself, his household and the whole community of Israel. Ex 29:36; Heb 9:7,12

¹⁸ "Then he shall come out to the altar that is before the LORD and make atonement for it. He shall take some of the bull's blood and some of the goat's blood and put it on all the horns of the altar. ¹⁹He shall sprinkle some of the blood on it with his finger seven times to cleanse it and to consecrate it from the uncleanness of the Israelites. Lev 4:7,25

²⁰ "When Aaron has finished making atonement for the Most Holy Place, the tent of meeting and the altar, he shall bring forward the live goat. ²¹ He is to lay both hands on the head of the live goat and confess over it all the wickedness and rebellion of the Israelites — all their sins — and put them on the goat's head. He shall send the goat away into the wilderness in the care of someone appointed for the task. ²²The goat will carry on itself all their sins to a remote place; and the man shall release it in the wilderness. Lev 5:5; Isa 53:12

²³ "Then Aaron is to go into the tent of meeting and take off the linen garments he put on be-

fore he entered the Most Holy Place, and he is to leave them there. ²⁴He shall bathe himself with water in the sanctuary area and put on his regular garments. Then he shall come out and sacrifice the burnt offering for himself and the burnt offering for the people, to make atonement for himself and for the people. ²⁵He shall also burn the fat of the sin offering on the altar. Eze 42:14; 44:19

²⁶ "The man who releases the goat as a scapegoat must wash his clothes and bathe himself with water; afterward he may come into the camp. ²⁷The bull and the goat for the sin offerings, whose blood was brought into the Most Holy Place to make atonement, must be taken outside the camp; their hides, flesh and intestines are to be burned up. ²⁸The man who burns them must wash his clothes and bathe himself with water; afterward he may come into the camp. Lev 11:25; Heb 13:11

²⁹ "This is to be a lasting ordinance for you: On the tenth day of the seventh month you must deny yourselves^a and not do any work — whether native-born or a foreigner residing among you — ³⁰because on this day atonement will be made for you, to cleanse you. Then, before the LORD, you will be clean from all your sins. ³¹It is a day of sabbath rest, and you must deny yourselves; it is a

---

^a 29 Or must fast; also in verse 31

lasting ordinance. [32]The priest who is anointed and ordained to succeed his father as high priest is to make atonement. He is to put on the sacred linen garments [33]and make atonement for the Most Holy Place, for the tent of meeting and the altar, and for the priests and all the members of the community. Nu 29:7; Eph 5:26

[34]"This is to be a lasting ordinance for you: Atonement is to be made once a year for all the sins of the Israelites." Heb 9:7,25

And it was done, as the LORD commanded Moses. Lev 23:26-32

Eating Blood Forbidden

17 The LORD said to Moses, [2]"Speak to Aaron and his sons and to all the Israelites and say to them: 'This is what the LORD has commanded: [3]Any Israelite who sacrifices an ox,[a] a lamb or a goat in the camp or outside of it [4]instead of bringing it to the entrance to the tent of meeting to present it as an offering to the LORD in front of the tabernacle of the LORD — that person shall be considered guilty of bloodshed; they have shed blood and must be cut off from their people. [5]This is so the Israelites will bring to the LORD the sacrifices they are now making in the open fields. They must bring them to the priest, that is, to the LORD, at the entrance to the tent of meeting and sacrifice them as fellowship offerings. [6]The priest is to splash the blood against the altar of the LORD at the entrance to the tent of meeting and burn the fat as an aroma pleasing to the LORD. [7]They must no longer offer any of their sacrifices to the goat idols[b] to whom they prostitute themselves. This is to be a lasting ordinance for them and for the generations to come.' Ex 34:15; 1Co 10:20

[8]"Say to them: 'Any Israelite or any foreigner residing among them who offers a burnt offering or sacrifice [9]and does not bring it to the entrance to the tent of meeting to sacrifice it to the LORD must be cut off from the people of Israel. Lev 1:3; 3:7

[10]"'I will set my face against any Israelite or any foreigner residing among them who eats blood, and I will cut them off from the people. [11]For the life of a creature is in the blood, and I have given it to you to make atonement for yourselves on the altar; it is the blood that makes atonement for one's life.[c] [12]Therefore I say to the Israelites, "None of you may eat blood, nor may any foreigner residing among you eat blood." Ge 9:4; Heb 9:22

[13]"'Any Israelite or any foreigner residing among you who hunts any animal or bird that may be eaten must drain out the blood and cover it with earth, [14]be-

---

[a] 3 The Hebrew word can refer to either male or female.   [b] 7 Or the demons
[c] 11 Or atonement by the life in the blood

cause the life of every creature is its blood. That is why I have said to the Israelites, "You must not eat the blood of any creature, because the life of every creature is its blood; anyone who eats it must be cut off." Ge 9:4; Dt 12:16

15 " 'Anyone, whether native-born or foreigner, who eats anything found dead or torn by wild animals must wash their clothes and bathe with water, and they will be ceremonially unclean till evening; then they will be clean. 16 But if they do not wash their clothes and bathe themselves, they will be held responsible.' " Ex 22:31; Dt 14:21

Unlawful Sexual Relations

18 The LORD said to Moses, 2 "Speak to the Israelites and say to them: 'I am the LORD your God. 3 You must not do as they do in Egypt, where you used to live, and you must not do as they do in the land of Canaan, where I am bringing you. Do not follow their practices. 4 You must obey my laws and be careful to follow my decrees. I am the LORD your God. 5 Keep my decrees and laws, for the person who obeys them will live by them. I am the LORD. Eze 20:11; Ro 10:5; Gal 3:12

6 " 'No one is to approach any close relative to have sexual relations. I am the LORD.

7 " 'Do not dishonor your father by having sexual relations with your mother. She is your mother; do not have relations with her. Lev 20:11

8 " 'Do not have sexual relations with your father's wife; that would dishonor your father. Lev 20:11; 1Co 5:1

9 " 'Do not have sexual relations with your sister, either your father's daughter or your mother's daughter, whether she was born in the same home or elsewhere. Lev 20:17

10 " 'Do not have sexual relations with your son's daughter or your daughter's daughter; that would dishonor you.

11 " 'Do not have sexual relations with the daughter of your father's wife, born to your father; she is your sister.

12 " 'Do not have sexual relations with your father's sister; she is your father's close relative. Lev 20:19

13 " 'Do not have sexual relations with your mother's sister, because she is your mother's close relative.

14 " 'Do not dishonor your father's brother by approaching his wife to have sexual relations; she is your aunt. Lev 20:20

15 " 'Do not have sexual relations with your daughter-in-law. She is your son's wife; do not have relations with her. Lev 20:12

16 " 'Do not have sexual relations with your brother's wife; that would dishonor your brother. Lev 20:21

17 " 'Do not have sexual relations

with both a woman and her daughter. Do not have sexual relations with either her son's daughter or her daughter's daughter; they are her close relatives. That is wickedness. _{Lev 20:14}

18 " 'Do not take your wife's sister as a rival wife and have sexual relations with her while your wife is living.

19 " 'Do not approach a woman to have sexual relations during the uncleanness of her monthly period. _{Lev 15:24}

20 " 'Do not have sexual relations with your neighbor's wife and defile yourself with her. _{Ex 20:14}

21 " 'Do not give any of your children to be sacrificed to Molek, for you must not profane the name of your God. I am the LORD. _{Lev 19:12; 20:2-5; Dt 12:31}

22 " 'Do not have sexual relations with a man as one does with a woman; that is detestable. _{Lev 20;13; Ro 1:27}

23 " 'Do not have sexual relations with an animal and defile yourself with it. A woman must not present herself to an animal to have sexual relations with it; that is a perversion. _{Lev 20:15}

24 " 'Do not defile yourselves in any of these ways, because this is how the nations that I am going to drive out before you became defiled. 25 Even the land was defiled; so I punished it for its sin, and the land vomited out its inhabitants. 26 But you must keep my decrees and my laws. The native-born and the foreigners residing among you must not do any of these detestable things, 27 for all these things were done by the people who lived in the land before you, and the land became defiled. 28 And if you defile the land, it will vomit you out as it vomited out the nations that were before you. _{Dt 18:12}

29 " 'Everyone who does any of these detestable things — such persons must be cut off from their people. 30 Keep my requirements and do not follow any of the detestable customs that were practiced before you came and do not defile yourselves with them. I am the LORD your God.' " _{Dt 11:1}

Various Laws

19 The LORD said to Moses, 2 "Speak to the entire assembly of Israel and say to them: 'Be holy because I, the LORD your God, am holy. _{Lev 11:44; 1Pe 1:16}

3 " 'Each of you must respect your mother and father, and you must observe my Sabbaths. I am the LORD your God. _{Ex 20:12}

4 " 'Do not turn to idols or make metal gods for yourselves. I am the LORD your God. _{Ps 96:5}

5 " 'When you sacrifice a fellowship offering to the LORD, sacrifice it in such a way that it will be accepted on your behalf. 6 It shall be eaten on the day you sacrifice it or on the next day; anything left over until the third day must be burned up. 7 If any

of it is eaten on the third day, it is impure and will not be accepted. **8**Whoever eats it will be held responsible because they have desecrated what is holy to the LORD; they must be cut off from their people. Lev 7:16-17

9"'When you reap the harvest of your land, do not reap to the very edges of your field or gather the gleanings of your harvest. **10**Do not go over your vineyard a second time or pick up the grapes that have fallen. Leave them for the poor and the foreigner. I am the LORD your God. Dt 24:19-22

11"'Do not steal. Ex 20:15

"'Do not lie. Eph 4:25

"'Do not deceive one another.

12"'Do not swear falsely by my name and so profane the name of your God. I am the LORD. Ex 20:7

13"'Do not defraud or rob your neighbor. Ex 22:15,25-27

"'Do not hold back the wages of a hired worker overnight. Dt 24:15

14"'Do not curse the deaf or put a stumbling block in front of the blind, but fear your God. I am the LORD. Dt 27:18

15"'Do not pervert justice; do not show partiality to the poor or favoritism to the great, but judge your neighbor fairly. Ex 23:2,6; Dt 1:17

16"'Do not go about spreading slander among your people. Ps 15:3

"'Do not do anything that endangers your neighbor's life. I am the LORD. Ex 23:7

17"'Do not hate a fellow Israelite in your heart. Rebuke your neighbor frankly so you will not share in their guilt. Jn 2:9; Mt 18:15

18"'Do not seek revenge or bear a grudge against anyone among your people, but love your neighbor as yourself. I am the LORD. Mt 5:43; Gal 5:14; Ro 12:19

19"'Keep my decrees.

"'Do not mate different kinds of animals.

"'Do not plant your field with two kinds of seed.

"'Do not wear clothing woven of two kinds of material. Dt 22:9,11

20"'If a man sleeps with a female slave who is promised to another man but who has not been ransomed or given her freedom, there must be due punishment.*a* Yet they are not to be put to death, because she had not been freed. **21**The man, however, must bring a ram to the entrance to the tent of meeting for a guilt offering to the LORD. **22**With the ram of the guilt offering the priest is to make atonement for him before the LORD for the sin he has committed, and his sin will be forgiven. Lev 5:15

23"'When you enter the land and plant any kind of fruit tree, regard its fruit as forbidden.*b* For three years you are to consider it forbidden*b*; it must not be eaten. **24**In the fourth year all its fruit will be holy, an offering of praise

a 20 Or *be an inquiry*   *b* 23 Hebrew *uncircumcised*

to the LORD. ²⁵But in the fifth year you may eat its fruit. In this way your harvest will be increased. I am the LORD your God.   Pr 3:9

²⁶ " 'Do not eat any meat with the blood still in it.   Lev 17:10

" 'Do not practice divination or seek omens.   Dt 18:10

²⁷ " 'Do not cut the hair at the sides of your head or clip off the edges of your beard.   Lev 21:5

²⁸ " 'Do not cut your bodies for the dead or put tattoo marks on yourselves. I am the LORD.

²⁹ " 'Do not degrade your daughter by making her a prostitute, or the land will turn to prostitution and be filled with wickedness.   Dt 23:18

³⁰ " 'Observe my Sabbaths and have reverence for my sanctuary. I am the LORD.   Lev 26:2

³¹ " 'Do not turn to mediums or seek out spiritists, for you will be defiled by them. I am the LORD your God.   Lev 20:6; Isa 8:19

³² " 'Stand up in the presence of the aged, show respect for the elderly and revere your God. I am the LORD.   Job 32:4; 1Ti 5:1

³³ " 'When a foreigner resides among you in your land, do not mistreat them. ³⁴The foreigner residing among you must be treated as your native-born. Love them as yourself, for you were foreigners in Egypt. I am the LORD your God.   ver 18; Ex 12:48; Dt 10:19

³⁵ " 'Do not use dishonest standards when measuring length, weight or quantity. ³⁶Use honest scales and honest weights, an honest ephah^a and an honest hin.^b I am the LORD your God, who brought you out of Egypt.

³⁷ " 'Keep all my decrees and all my laws and follow them. I am the LORD.' "   2Ki 17:37

Punishments for Sin

20 The LORD said to Moses, ² "Say to the Israelites: 'Any Israelite or any foreigner residing in Israel who sacrifices any of his children to Molek is to be put to death. The members of the community are to stone him. ³I myself will set my face against him and will cut him off from his people; for by sacrificing his children to Molek, he has defiled my sanctuary and profaned my holy name. ⁴If the members of the community close their eyes when that man sacrifices one of his children to Molek and if they fail to put him to death, ⁵I myself will set my face against him and his family and will cut them off from their people together with all who follow him in prostituting themselves to Molek.   Lev 18:21; Dt 17:2-5

⁶ " 'I will set my face against anyone who turns to mediums and spiritists to prostitute themselves by following them, and

---

^a 36 An ephah was a dry measure having the capacity of about 3/5 of a bushel or about 22 liters.   ^b 36 A hin was a liquid measure having the capacity of about 1 gallon or about 3.8 liters.

will cut them off from their people. Lev 19:31

7 " 'Consecrate yourselves and be holy, because I am the LORD your God. 8 Keep my decrees and follow them. I am the LORD, who makes you holy. Eph 1:4; 1Pe 1:16

9 " 'Anyone who curses their father or mother is to be put to death. Because they have cursed their father or mother, their blood will be on their own head. Ex 21:17; Dt 27:16

10 " 'If a man commits adultery with another man's wife — with the wife of his neighbor — both the adulterer and the adulteress are to be put to death. Ex 20:14

11 " 'If a man has sexual relations with his father's wife, he has dishonored his father. Both the man and the woman are to be put to death; their blood will be on their own heads. Lev 18:7

12 " 'If a man has sexual relations with his daughter-in-law, both of them are to be put to death. What they have done is a perversion; their blood will be on their own heads. Lev 18:15

13 " 'If a man has sexual relations with a man as one does with a woman, both of them have done what is detestable. They are to be put to death; their blood will be on their own heads. Lev 18:22

14 " 'If a man marries both a woman and her mother, it is wicked. Both he and they must be burned in the fire, so that no wickedness will be among you. Dt 27:23

15 " 'If a man has sexual relations with an animal, he is to be put to death, and you must kill the animal. Lev 18:23

16 " 'If a woman approaches an animal to have sexual relations with it, kill both the woman and the animal. They are to be put to death; their blood will be on their own heads.

17 " 'If a man marries his sister, the daughter of either his father or his mother, and they have sexual relations, it is a disgrace. They are to be publicly removed from their people. He has dishonored his sister and will be held responsible. Lev 18:9

18 " 'If a man has sexual relations with a woman during her monthly period, he has exposed the source of her flow, and she has also uncovered it. Both of them are to be cut off from their people. Lev 15:24; 18:19

19 " 'Do not have sexual relations with the sister of either your mother or your father, for that would dishonor a close relative; both of you would be held responsible. Lev 18:12-13

20 " 'If a man has sexual relations with his aunt, he has dishonored his uncle. They will be held responsible; they will die childless. Lev 18:14

21 " 'If a man marries his brother's wife, it is an act of impurity; he has dishonored his brother. They will be childless. Lev 18:16

22 " 'Keep all my decrees and

laws and follow them, so that the land where I am bringing you to live may not vomit you out. 23You must not live according to the customs of the nations I am going to drive out before you. Because they did all these things, I abhorred them. 24But I said to you, "You will possess their land; I will give it to you as an inheritance, a land flowing with milk and honey." I am the LORD your God, who has set you apart from the nations.   Ex 33:16; Lev 18:3,25-28

25"'You must therefore make a distinction between clean and unclean animals and between unclean and clean birds. Do not defile yourselves by any animal or bird or anything that moves along the ground—those that I have set apart as unclean for you. 26You are to be holy to me because I, the LORD, am holy, and I have set you apart from the nations to be my own.   Dt 14:3-21

27"'A man or woman who is a medium or spiritist among you must be put to death. You are to stone them; their blood will be on their own heads.'"   Lev 19:31

Rules for Priests

21 The LORD said to Moses, "Speak to the priests, the sons of Aaron, and say to them: 'A priest must not make himself ceremonially unclean for any of his people who die, 2except for a close relative, such as his mother or father, his son or daughter, his brother, 3or an unmarried sister who is dependent on him since she has no husband—for her he may make himself unclean. 4He must not make himself unclean for people related to him by marriage,[a] and so defile himself.   Eze 44:25

5"'Priests must not shave their heads or shave off the edges of their beards or cut their bodies. 6They must be holy to their God and must not profane the name of their God. Because they present the food offerings to the LORD, the food of their God, they are to be holy.   Lev 18:21; 19:28

7"'They must not marry women defiled by prostitution or divorced from their husbands, because priests are holy to their God. 8Regard them as holy, because they offer up the food of your God. Consider them holy, because I the LORD am holy—I who make you holy.   Eze 44:22

9"'If a priest's daughter defiles herself by becoming a prostitute, she disgraces her father; she must be burned in the fire.   Ge 38:24

10"'The high priest, the one among his brothers who has had the anointing oil poured on his head and who has been ordained to wear the priestly garments, must not let his hair become unkempt[b] or tear his clothes. 11He

---

[a] 4 Or unclean as a leader among his people   [b] 10 Or not uncover his head

must not enter a place where there is a dead body. He must not make himself unclean, even for his father or mother, ¹²nor leave the sanctuary of his God or desecrate it, because he has been dedicated by the anointing oil of his God. I am the LORD. Lev 10:6-7

¹³ " 'The woman he marries must be a virgin. ¹⁴He must not marry a widow, a divorced woman, or a woman defiled by prostitution, but only a virgin from his own people, ¹⁵so that he will not defile his offspring among his people. I am the LORD, who makes him holy.' " Eze 44:22

¹⁶The LORD said to Moses, ¹⁷"Say to Aaron: 'For the generations to come none of your descendants who has a defect may come near to offer the food of his God. ¹⁸No man who has any defect may come near: no man who is blind or lame, disfigured or deformed; ¹⁹no man with a crippled foot or hand, ²⁰or who is a hunchback or a dwarf, or who has any eye defect, or who has festering or running sores or damaged testicles. ²¹No descendant of Aaron the priest who has any defect is to come near to present the food offerings to the LORD. He has a defect; he must not come near to offer the food of his God. ²²He may eat the most holy food of his God, as well as the holy food; ²³yet because of

his defect, he must not go near the curtain or approach the altar, and so desecrate my sanctuary. I am the LORD, who makes them holy.' " Lev 22:19-25; Dt 23:1

²⁴So Moses told this to Aaron and his sons and to all the Israelites.

22 The LORD said to Moses, ²"Tell Aaron and his sons to treat with respect the sacred offerings the Israelites consecrate to me, so they will not profane my holy name. I am the LORD. Lev 19:8

³"Say to them: 'For the generations to come, if any of your descendants is ceremonially unclean and yet comes near the sacred offerings that the Israelites consecrate to the LORD, that person must be cut off from my presence. I am the LORD. Lev 7:20-21

⁴ " 'If a descendant of Aaron has a defiling skin disease[a] or a bodily discharge, he may not eat the sacred offerings until he is cleansed. He will also be unclean if he touches something defiled by a corpse or by anyone who has an emission of semen, ⁵or if he touches any crawling thing that makes him unclean, or any person who makes him unclean, whatever the uncleanness may be. ⁶The one who touches any such thing will be unclean till evening. He must not eat any of the sacred offerings unless he

---

[a] 4 The Hebrew word for *defiling skin disease*, traditionally translated "leprosy," was used for various diseases affecting the skin.

has bathed himself with water. [7]When the sun goes down, he will be clean, and after that he may eat the sacred offerings, for they are his food. [8]He must not eat anything found dead or torn by wild animals, and so become unclean through it. I am the LORD.   Lev 11:24-28,39; Nu 18:11

[9]" 'The priests are to perform my service in such a way that they do not become guilty and die for treating it with contempt. I am the LORD, who makes them holy.   Ex 28:43

[10]" 'No one outside a priest's family may eat the sacred offering, nor may the guest of a priest or his hired worker eat it. [11]But if a priest buys a slave with money, or if slaves are born in his household, they may eat his food. [12]If a priest's daughter marries anyone other than a priest, she may not eat any of the sacred contributions. [13]But if a priest's daughter becomes a widow or is divorced, yet has no children, and she returns to live in her father's household as in her youth, she may eat her father's food. No unauthorized person, however, may eat it.   Ge 17:13; Ex 12:44

[14]" 'Anyone who eats a sacred offering by mistake must make restitution to the priest for the offering and add a fifth of the value to it. [15]The priests must not desecrate the sacred offerings the Israelites present to the LORD [16]by allowing them to eat the sacred offerings and so bring upon them guilt requiring payment. I am the LORD, who makes them holy.' "   Lev 5:15

Unacceptable Sacrifices

[17]The LORD said to Moses, [18]"Speak to Aaron and his sons and to all the Israelites and say to them: 'If any of you — whether an Israelite or a foreigner residing in Israel — presents a gift for a burnt offering to the LORD, either to fulfill a vow or as a freewill offering, [19]you must present a male without defect from the cattle, sheep or goats in order that it may be accepted on your behalf. [20]Do not bring anything with a defect, because it will not be accepted on your behalf. [21]When anyone brings from the herd or flock a fellowship offering to the LORD to fulfill a special vow or as a freewill offering, it must be without defect or blemish to be acceptable. [22]Do not offer to the LORD the blind, the injured or the maimed, or anything with warts or festering or running sores. Do not place any of these on the altar as a food offering presented to the LORD. [23]You may, however, present as a freewill offering an ox[a] or a sheep that is deformed or stunted, but it will not be accepted in fulfillment of

---

[a] 23 The Hebrew word can refer to either male or female.

a vow. ²⁴You must not offer to the LORD an animal whose testicles are bruised, crushed, torn or cut. You must not do this in your own land, ²⁵and you must not accept such animals from the hand of a foreigner and offer them as the food of your God. They will not be accepted on your behalf, because they are deformed and have defects.'" Lev 3:6; Dt 15:21

²⁶The LORD said to Moses, ²⁷"When a calf, a lamb or a goat is born, it is to remain with its mother for seven days. From the eighth day on, it will be acceptable as a food offering presented to the LORD. ²⁸Do not slaughter a cow or a sheep and its young on the same day. Ex 22:30; Dt 22:6-7

²⁹"When you sacrifice a thank offering to the LORD, sacrifice it in such a way that it will be accepted on your behalf. ³⁰It must be eaten that same day; leave none of it till morning. I am the LORD. Lev 7:12; Ps 107:22

³¹"Keep my commands and follow them. I am the LORD. ³²Do not profane my holy name, for I must be acknowledged as holy by the Israelites. I am the LORD, who made you holy ³³and who brought you out of Egypt to be your God. I am the LORD." Dt 4:2,40; Ps 105:45

The Appointed Festivals

23 The LORD said to Moses, ²"Speak to the Israelites and say to them: 'These are my appointed festivals, the appointed festivals of the LORD, which you are to proclaim as sacred assemblies. Nu 29:39

The Sabbath

³"'There are six days when you may work, but the seventh day is a day of sabbath rest, a day of sacred assembly. You are not to do any work; wherever you live, it is a sabbath to the LORD. Ex 20:9-10; 31:13

The Passover and the Festival of Unleavened Bread

23:4-8pp — Ex 12:14-20; Nu 28:16-25; Dt 16:1-8

⁴"'These are the LORD's appointed festivals, the sacred assemblies you are to proclaim at their appointed times: ⁵The LORD's Passover begins at twilight on the fourteenth day of the first month. ⁶On the fifteenth day of that month the LORD's Festival of Unleavened Bread begins; for seven days you must eat bread made without yeast. ⁷On the first day hold a sacred assembly and do no regular work. ⁸For seven days present a food offering to the LORD. And on the seventh day hold a sacred assembly and do no regular work.'" Ex 12:14-20; Nu 28:16-25; Dt 16:1-8

Offering the Firstfruits

⁹The LORD said to Moses, ¹⁰"Speak to the Israelites and say to them: 'When you enter the land I am going to give you and you reap its harvest, bring to the priest a sheaf of the first grain you

harvest. [11] He is to wave the sheaf before the LORD so it will be accepted on your behalf; the priest is to wave it on the day after the Sabbath. [12] On the day you wave the sheaf, you must sacrifice as a burnt offering to the LORD a lamb a year old without defect, [13] together with its grain offering of two-tenths of an ephah[a] of the finest flour mixed with olive oil — a food offering presented to the LORD, a pleasing aroma — and its drink offering of a quarter of a hin[b] of wine. [14] You must not eat any bread, or roasted or new grain, until the very day you bring this offering to your God. This is to be a lasting ordinance for the generations to come, wherever you live. Ex 23:16,19; Ro 11:16

The Festival of Weeks

23:15-22pp — Nu 28:26-31; Dt 16:9-12

[15] " 'From the day after the Sabbath, the day you brought the sheaf of the wave offering, count off seven full weeks. [16] Count off fifty days up to the day after the seventh Sabbath, and then present an offering of new grain to the LORD. [17] From wherever you live, bring two loaves made of two-tenths of an ephah of the finest flour, baked with yeast, as a wave offering of firstfruits to the LORD. [18] Present with this bread seven male lambs, each a year old and without defect, one

young bull and two rams. They will be a burnt offering to the LORD, together with their grain offerings and drink offerings — a food offering, an aroma pleasing to the LORD. [19] Then sacrifice one male goat for a sin offering[c] and two lambs, each a year old, for a fellowship offering. [20] The priest is to wave the two lambs before the LORD as a wave offering, together with the bread of the firstfruits. They are a sacred offering to the LORD for the priest. [21] On that same day you are to proclaim a sacred assembly and do no regular work. This is to be a lasting ordinance for the generations to come, wherever you live. ver 2-3; Ac 2:1

[22] " 'When you reap the harvest of your land, do not reap to the very edges of your field or gather the gleanings of your harvest. Leave them for the poor and for the foreigner residing among you. I am the LORD your God.' " Nu 28:26-31; Dt 16:9-12

The Festival of Trumpets

23:23-25pp — Nu 29:1-6

[23] The LORD said to Moses, [24] "Say to the Israelites: 'On the first day of the seventh month you are to have a day of sabbath rest, a sacred assembly commemorated with trumpet blasts. [25] Do no regular work, but present a food offering to the LORD.' " Nu 29:1-6

---

[a] 13 That is, probably about 7 pounds or about 3.2 kilograms; also in verse 17   [b] 13 That is, about 1 quart or about 1 liter   [c] 19 Or *purification offering*

The Day of Atonement
23:26-32pp — Lev 16:2-34; Nu 29:7-11

²⁶ The LORD said to Moses, ²⁷ "The tenth day of this seventh month is the Day of Atonement. Hold a sacred assembly and deny yourselves,*ᵃ* and present a food offering to the LORD. ²⁸ Do not do any work on that day, because it is the Day of Atonement, when atonement is made for you before the LORD your God. ²⁹ Those who do not deny themselves on that day must be cut off from their people. ³⁰ I will destroy from among their people anyone who does any work on that day. ³¹ You shall do no work at all. This is to be a lasting ordinance for the generations to come, wherever you live. ³² It is a day of sabbath rest for you, and you must deny yourselves. From the evening of the ninth day of the month until the following evening you are to observe your sabbath."   Lev 16:2-34; Nu 29:7-11

The Festival of Tabernacles
23:33-43pp — Nu 29:12-39; Dt 16:13-17

³³ The LORD said to Moses, ³⁴ "Say to the Israelites: 'On the fifteenth day of the seventh month the LORD's Festival of Tabernacles begins, and it lasts for seven days. ³⁵ The first day is a sacred assembly; do no regular work. ³⁶ For seven days present food offerings to the LORD, and on the eighth day hold a sacred assembly and present a food offering to the LORD. It is the closing special assembly; do no regular work.   Ex 23:16; Dt 16:13; Jn 7:2

³⁷ (" 'These are the LORD's appointed festivals, which you are to proclaim as sacred assemblies for bringing food offerings to the LORD — the burnt offerings and grain offerings, sacrifices and drink offerings required for each day. ³⁸ These offerings are in addition to those for the LORD's Sabbaths and*ᵇ* in addition to your gifts and whatever you have vowed and all the freewill offerings you give to the LORD.)   ver 2,4; Eze 45:17

³⁹ " 'So beginning with the fifteenth day of the seventh month, after you have gathered the crops of the land, celebrate the festival to the LORD for seven days; the first day is a day of sabbath rest, and the eighth day also is a day of sabbath rest. ⁴⁰ On the first day you are to take branches from luxuriant trees — from palms, willows and other leafy trees — and rejoice before the LORD your God for seven days. ⁴¹ Celebrate this as a festival to the LORD for seven days each year. This is to be a lasting ordinance for the generations to come; celebrate it in the seventh month. ⁴² Live in temporary shelters for seven days: All native-born Israelites

ᵃ 27 Or *and fast*; similarly in verses 29 and 32 LORD's *Sabbaths, and these offerings are*   *ᵇ 38* Or *These festivals are in addition to the* are to live in such shelters ⁴³so your descendants will know that I had the Israelites live in temporary shelters when I brought them out of Egypt. I am the LORD your God.'" Nu 29:12-39; Dt 16:13-17

⁴⁴So Moses announced to the Israelites the appointed festivals of the LORD.

Olive Oil and Bread Set Before the LORD

24:1-3pp — Ex 27:20-21

24 The LORD said to Moses, ²"Command the Israelites to bring you clear oil of pressed olives for the light so that the lamps may be kept burning continually. ³Outside the curtain that shields the ark of the covenant law in the tent of meeting, Aaron is to tend the lamps before the LORD from evening till morning, continually. This is to be a lasting ordinance for the generations to come. ⁴The lamps on the pure gold lampstand before the LORD must be tended continually. Ex 27:20-21

⁵"Take the finest flour and bake twelve loaves of bread, using two-tenths of an ephah*a* for each loaf. ⁶Arrange them in two stacks, six in each stack, on the table of pure gold before the LORD. ⁷By each stack put some pure incense as a memorial*b* portion to represent the bread and to be a food offering presented to the LORD. ⁸This bread is to be set out before the LORD regularly, Sabbath after Sabbath, on behalf of the Israelites, as a lasting covenant. ⁹It belongs to Aaron and his sons, who are to eat it in the sanctuary area, because it is a most holy part of their perpetual share of the food offerings presented to the LORD." Mt 12:4; Nu 4:7; 2Ch 2:4

A Blasphemer Put to Death

¹⁰Now the son of an Israelite mother and an Egyptian father went out among the Israelites, and a fight broke out in the camp between him and an Israelite. ¹¹The son of the Israelite woman blasphemed the Name with a curse; so they brought him to Moses. (His mother's name was Shelomith, the daughter of Dibri the Danite.) ¹²They put him in custody until the will of the LORD should be made clear to them. Ex 18:16; Nu 15:34

¹³Then the LORD said to Moses: ¹⁴"Take the blasphemer outside the camp. All those who heard him are to lay their hands on his head, and the entire assembly is to stone him. ¹⁵Say to the Israelites: 'Anyone who curses their God will be held responsible; ¹⁶anyone who blasphemes the name of the LORD is to be put to death. The entire assembly must stone them. Whether foreigner

---

a 5 That is, probably about 7 pounds or about 3.2 kilograms   *b* 7 Or *representative* or native-born, when they blaspheme the Name they are to be put to death. Dt 13:9; 1Ki 21:10,13

[17] " 'Anyone who takes the life of a human being is to be put to death. [18] Anyone who takes the life of someone's animal must make restitution — life for life. [19] Anyone who injures their neighbor is to be injured in the same manner: [20] fracture for fracture, eye for eye, tooth for tooth. The one who has inflicted the injury must suffer the same injury. [21] Whoever kills an animal must make restitution, but whoever kills a human being is to be put to death. [22] You are to have the same law for the foreigner and the native-born. I am the LORD your God.' " Ex 21:12; Mt 5:38

[23] Then Moses spoke to the Israelites, and they took the blasphemer outside the camp and stoned him. The Israelites did as the LORD commanded Moses.

The Sabbath Year

25 The LORD said to Moses at Mount Sinai, [2] "Speak to the Israelites and say to them: 'When you enter the land I am going to give you, the land itself must observe a sabbath to the LORD. [3] For six years sow your fields, and for six years prune your vineyards and gather their crops. [4] But in the seventh year the land is to have a year of sabbath rest, a sabbath to the LORD. Do not sow your fields or prune your vineyards. [5] Do not reap what grows of itself or harvest the grapes of your untended vines. The land is to have a year of rest. [6] Whatever the land yields during the sabbath year will be food for you — for yourself, your male and female servants, and the hired worker and temporary resident who live among you, [7] as well as for your livestock and the wild animals in your land. Whatever the land produces may be eaten. Ex 23:10

The Year of Jubilee

25:8-38Ref — Dt 15:1-11
25:39-55Ref — Ex 21:2-11; Dt 15:12-18

[8] " 'Count off seven sabbath years — seven times seven years — so that the seven sabbath years amount to a period of forty-nine years. [9] Then have the trumpet sounded everywhere on the tenth day of the seventh month; on the Day of Atonement sound the trumpet throughout your land. [10] Consecrate the fiftieth year and proclaim liberty throughout the land to all its inhabitants. It shall be a jubilee for you; each of you is to return to your family property and to your own clan. [11] The fiftieth year shall be a jubilee for you; do not sow and do not reap what grows of itself or harvest the untended vines. [12] For it is a jubilee and is to be holy for you; eat only what is taken directly from the fields. Jer 34:8,15,17; Lk 4:19

¹³ " 'In this Year of Jubilee everyone is to return to their own property.   ver 10

¹⁴ " 'If you sell land to any of your own people or buy land from them, do not take advantage of each other. ¹⁵You are to buy from your own people on the basis of the number of years since the Jubilee. And they are to sell to you on the basis of the number of years left for harvesting crops. ¹⁶When the years are many, you are to increase the price, and when the years are few, you are to decrease the price, because what is really being sold to you is the number of crops. ¹⁷Do not take advantage of each other, but fear your God. I am the LORD your God.   Lev 19:14,32

¹⁸ " 'Follow my decrees and be careful to obey my laws, and you will live safely in the land. ¹⁹Then the land will yield its fruit, and you will eat your fill and live there in safety. ²⁰You may ask, "What will we eat in the seventh year if we do not plant or harvest our crops?" ²¹I will send you such a blessing in the sixth year that the land will yield enough for three years. ²²While you plant during the eighth year, you will eat from the old crop and will continue to eat from it until the harvest of the ninth year comes in.   Lev 26:10; Hag 2:19

²³ " 'The land must not be sold permanently, because the land is mine and you reside in my land as foreigners and strangers. ²⁴Throughout the land that you hold as a possession, you must provide for the redemption of the land.   Ge 23:4; Ex 19:5; 1Pe 2:11

²⁵ " 'If one of your fellow Israelites becomes poor and sells some of their property, their nearest relative is to come and redeem what they have sold. ²⁶If, however, there is no one to redeem it for them but later on they prosper and acquire sufficient means to redeem it themselves, ²⁷they are to determine the value for the years since they sold it and refund the balance to the one to whom they sold it; they can then go back to their own property. ²⁸But if they do not acquire the means to repay, what was sold will remain in the possession of the buyer until the Year of Jubilee. It will be returned in the Jubilee, and they can then go back to their property.   Lev 27:13,19,31; Ru 2:20

²⁹ " 'Anyone who sells a house in a walled city retains the right of redemption a full year after its sale. During that time the seller may redeem it. ³⁰If it is not redeemed before a full year has passed, the house in the walled city shall belong permanently to the buyer and the buyer's descendants. It is not to be returned in the Jubilee. ³¹But houses in villages without walls around them are to be considered as belonging to the open country.

They can be redeemed, and they are to be returned in the Jubilee. [32] " 'The Levites always have the right to redeem their houses in the Levitical towns, which they possess. [33] So the property of the Levites is redeemable — that is, a house sold in any town they hold — and is to be returned in the Jubilee, because the houses in the towns of the Levites are their property among the Israelites. [34] But the pastureland belonging to their towns must not be sold; it is their permanent possession. Nu 35:1-8

[35] " 'If any of your fellow Israelites become poor and are unable to support themselves among you, help them as you would a foreigner and stranger, so they can continue to live among you. [36] Do not take interest or any profit from them, but fear your God, so that they may continue to live among you. [37] You must not lend them money at interest or sell them food at a profit. [38] I am the LORD your God, who brought you out of Egypt to give you the land of Canaan and to be your God. Dt 15:1-11; Ex 22:25

[39] " 'If any of your fellow Israelites become poor and sell themselves to you, do not make them work as slaves. [40] They are to be treated as hired workers or temporary residents among you; they are to work for you until the Year of Jubilee. [41] Then they and their children are to be released, and

they will go back to their own clans and to the property of their ancestors. [42] Because the Israelites are my servants, whom I brought out of Egypt, they must not be sold as slaves. [43] Do not rule over them ruthlessly, but fear your God. 1Ki 9:22; Eze 34:4; Col 4:1

[44] " 'Your male and female slaves are to come from the nations around you; from them you may buy slaves. [45] You may also buy some of the temporary residents living among you and members of their clans born in your country, and they will become your property. [46] You can bequeath them to your children as inherited property and can make them slaves for life, but you must not rule over your fellow Israelites ruthlessly.

[47] " 'If a foreigner residing among you becomes rich and any of your fellow Israelites become poor and sell themselves to the foreigner or to a member of the foreigner's clan, [48] they retain the right of redemption after they have sold themselves. One of their relatives may redeem them: [49] An uncle or a cousin or any blood relative in their clan may redeem them. Or if they prosper, they may redeem themselves. [50] They and their buyer are to count the time from the year they sold themselves up to the Year of Jubilee. The price for their release is to be based on the rate paid to a hired worker

for that number of years. ⁵¹ If many years remain, they must pay for their redemption a larger share of the price paid for them. ⁵² If only a few years remain until the Year of Jubilee, they are to compute that and pay for their redemption accordingly. ⁵³ They are to be treated as workers hired from year to year; you must see to it that those to whom they owe service do not rule over them ruthlessly. Ex 21:2-11; Dt 15:12-18

⁵⁴ "'Even if someone is not redeemed in any of these ways, they and their children are to be released in the Year of Jubilee, ⁵⁵ for the Israelites belong to me as servants. They are my servants, whom I brought out of Egypt. I am the LORD your God.

Reward for Obedience

26 "'Do not make idols or set up an image or a sacred stone for yourselves, and do not place a carved stone in your land to bow down before it. I am the LORD your God. Ex 20:4; Dt 5:8

² "'Observe my Sabbaths and have reverence for my sanctuary. I am the LORD. Lev 19:30

³ "'If you follow my decrees and are careful to obey my commands, ⁴ I will send you rain in its season, and the ground will yield its crops and the trees their fruit. ⁵ Your threshing will continue until grape harvest and the grape harvest will continue until planting, and you will eat all the food you want and live in safety in your land. Lev 25:18; Dt 28:1,9

⁶ "'I will grant peace in the land, and you will lie down and no one will make you afraid. I will remove wild beasts from the land, and the sword will not pass through your country. ⁷ You will pursue your enemies, and they will fall by the sword before you. ⁸ Five of you will chase a hundred, and a hundred of you will chase ten thousand, and your enemies will fall by the sword before you. Ps 29:11; 147:14

⁹ "'I will look on you with favor and make you fruitful and increase your numbers, and I will keep my covenant with you. ¹⁰ You will still be eating last year's harvest when you will have to move it out to make room for the new. ¹¹ I will put my dwelling place^a among you, and I will not abhor you. ¹² I will walk among you and be your God, and you will be my people. ¹³ I am the LORD your God, who brought you out of Egypt so that you would no longer be slaves to the Egyptians; I broke the bars of your yoke and enabled you to walk with heads held high. Ge 17:6; 2Co 6:16

Punishment for Disobedience

¹⁴ "'But if you will not listen to me and carry out all these com-

---

^a 11 Or *my tabernacle*

mands, [15] and if you reject my decrees and abhor my laws and fail to carry out all my commands and so violate my covenant, [16] then I will do this to you: I will bring on you sudden terror, wasting diseases and fever that will destroy your sight and sap your strength. You will plant seed in vain, because your enemies will eat it. [17] I will set my face against you so that you will be defeated by your enemies; those who hate you will rule over you, and you will flee even when no one is pursuing you.   Dt 28:15-68; Mal 2:2

[18] " 'If after all this you will not listen to me, I will punish you for your sins seven times over. [19] I will break down your stubborn pride and make the sky above you like iron and the ground beneath you like bronze. [20] Your strength will be spent in vain, because your soil will not yield its crops, nor will the trees of your land yield their fruit.   Dt 28:23; Ps 127:1; Isa 25:11

[21] " 'If you remain hostile toward me and refuse to listen to me, I will multiply your afflictions seven times over, as your sins deserve. [22] I will send wild animals against you, and they will rob you of your children, destroy your cattle and make you so few in number that your roads will be deserted.   Dt 32:24

[23] " 'If in spite of these things

you do not accept my correction but continue to be hostile toward me, [24] I myself will be hostile toward you and will afflict you for your sins seven times over. [25] And I will bring the sword on you to avenge the breaking of the covenant. When you withdraw into your cities, I will send a plague among you, and you will be given into enemy hands. [26] When I cut off your supply of bread, ten women will be able to bake your bread in one oven, and they will dole out the bread by weight. You will eat, but you will not be satisfied.   Ps 105:16; Jer 2:30

[27] " 'If in spite of this you still do not listen to me but continue to be hostile toward me, [28] then in my anger I will be hostile toward you, and I myself will punish you for your sins seven times over. [29] You will eat the flesh of your sons and the flesh of your daughters. [30] I will destroy your high places, cut down your incense altars and pile your dead bodies[a] on the lifeless forms of your idols, and I will abhor you. [31] I will turn your cities into ruins and lay waste your sanctuaries, and I will take no delight in the pleasing aroma of your offerings. [32] I myself will lay waste the land, so that your enemies who live there will be appalled. [33] I will scatter you

---

[a] 30 Or *your funeral offerings*

among the nations and will draw out my sword and pursue you. Your land will be laid waste, and your cities will lie in ruins. ³⁴Then the land will enjoy its sabbath years all the time that it lies desolate and you are in the country of your enemies; then the land will rest and enjoy its sabbaths. ³⁵All the time that it lies desolate, the land will have the rest it did not have during the sabbaths you lived in it.   Dt 4:27; Ps 74:3-7; Jer 9:11

³⁶"'As for those of you who are left, I will make their hearts so fearful in the lands of their enemies that the sound of a windblown leaf will put them to flight. They will run as though fleeing from the sword, and they will fall, even though no one is pursuing them. ³⁷They will stumble over one another as though fleeing from the sword, even though no one is pursuing them. So you will not be able to stand before your enemies. ³⁸You will perish among the nations; the land of your enemies will devour you. ³⁹Those of you who are left will waste away in the lands of their enemies because of their sins; also because of their ancestors' sins they will waste away.   Eze 21:7

⁴⁰"'But if they will confess their sins and the sins of their ancestors—their unfaithfulness and their hostility toward me, ⁴¹which made me hostile toward them so that I sent them into the land of their enemies—then when their uncircumcised hearts are humbled and they pay for their sin, ⁴²I will remember my covenant with Jacob and my covenant with Isaac and my covenant with Abraham, and I will remember the land. ⁴³For the land will be deserted by them and will enjoy its sabbaths while it lies desolate without them. They will pay for their sins because they rejected my laws and abhorred my decrees. ⁴⁴Yet in spite of this, when they are in the land of their enemies, I will not reject them or abhor them so as to destroy them completely, breaking my covenant with them. I am the LORD their God. ⁴⁵But for their sake I will remember the covenant with their ancestors whom I brought out of Egypt in the sight of the nations to be their God. I am the LORD.'"   Dt 4:31; 1Jn 1:9

⁴⁶These are the decrees, the laws and the regulations that the LORD established at Mount Sinai between himself and the Israelites through Moses.   Lev 7:38; 27:34

Redeeming What Is the LORD's

27 The LORD said to Moses, ²"Speak to the Israelites and say to them: 'If anyone makes a special vow to dedicate a person to the LORD by giving the equivalent value, ³set the value of a male between the ages of twenty and sixty at fifty

shekels^a of silver, according to the sanctuary shekel^b; ⁴for a female, set her value at thirty shekels^c; ⁵for a person between the ages of five and twenty, set the value of a male at twenty shekels^d and of a female at ten shekels^e; ⁶for a person between one month and five years, set the value of a male at five shekels^f of silver and that of a female at three shekels^g of silver; ⁷for a person sixty years old or more, set the value of a male at fifteen shekels^h and of a female at ten shekels. ⁸If anyone making the vow is too poor to pay the specified amount, the person being dedicated is to be presented to the priest, who will set the value according to what the one making the vow can afford. Ex 30:13; Nu 18:16

⁹"'If what they vowed is an animal that is acceptable as an offering to the Lord, such an animal given to the Lord becomes holy. ¹⁰They must not exchange it or substitute a good one for a bad one, or a bad one for a good one; if they should substitute one animal for another, both it and the substitute become holy. ¹¹If what they vowed is a ceremonially unclean animal—one that is not acceptable as an offering to the Lord—the animal must

be presented to the priest, ¹²who will judge its quality as good or bad. Whatever value the priest then sets, that is what it will be. ¹³If the owner wishes to redeem the animal, a fifth must be added to its value. Lev 25:25; Dt 15:19

¹⁴"'If anyone dedicates their house as something holy to the Lord, the priest will judge its quality as good or bad. Whatever value the priest then sets, so it will remain. ¹⁵If the one who dedicates their house wishes to redeem it, they must add a fifth to its value, and the house will again become theirs. ver 13,20

¹⁶"'If anyone dedicates to the Lord part of their family land, its value is to be set according to the amount of seed required for it—fifty shekels of silver to a homerⁱ of barley seed. ¹⁷If they dedicate a field during the Year of Jubilee, the value that has been set remains. ¹⁸But if they dedicate a field after the Jubilee, the priest will determine the value according to the number of years that remain until the next Year of Jubilee, and its set value will be reduced. ¹⁹If the one who dedicates the field wishes to redeem it, they must add a fifth to its value, and the field will again become theirs. ²⁰If, however, they do not

---

^a3 That is, about 1 1/4 pounds or about 575 grams; also in verse 16   ^b3 That is, about 2/5 ounce or about 12 grams; also in verse 25   ^c4 That is, about 12 ounces or about 345 grams   ^d5 That is, about 8 ounces or about 230 grams   ^e5 That is, about 4 ounces or about 115 grams; also in verse 7   ^f6 That is, about 2 ounces or about 58 grams   ^g6 That is, about 1 1/4 ounces or about 35 grams   ^h7 That is, about 6 ounces or about 175 grams   ⁱ16 That is, probably about 300 pounds or about 135 kilograms

redeem the field, or if they have sold it to someone else, it can never be redeemed. ²¹When the field is released in the Jubilee, it will become holy, like a field devoted to the LORD; it will become priestly property. Nu 18:14; Eze 44:29

²² "'If anyone dedicates to the LORD a field they have bought, which is not part of their family land, ²³the priest will determine its value up to the Year of Jubilee, and the owner must pay its value on that day as something holy to the LORD. ²⁴In the Year of Jubilee the field will revert to the person from whom it was bought, the one whose land it was. ²⁵Every value is to be set according to the sanctuary shekel, twenty gerahs to the shekel. Ex 30:13; Lev 25:28

²⁶ "'No one, however, may dedicate the firstborn of an animal, since the firstborn already belongs to the LORD; whether an ox[a] or a sheep, it is the LORD's. ²⁷If it is one of the unclean animals, it may be bought back at its set value, adding a fifth of the value to it. If it is not redeemed, it is to be sold at its set value. Ex 13:2,12

²⁸ "'But nothing that a person owns and devotes[b] to the LORD — whether a human being or an animal or family land — may be sold or redeemed; everything so devoted is most holy to the LORD. Jos 6:17-19

²⁹ "'No person devoted to destruction[c] may be ransomed; they are to be put to death.

³⁰ "'A tithe of everything from the land, whether grain from the soil or fruit from the trees, belongs to the LORD; it is holy to the LORD. ³¹Whoever would redeem any of their tithe must add a fifth of the value to it. ³²Every tithe of the herd and flock — every tenth animal that passes under the shepherd's rod — will be holy to the LORD. ³³No one may pick out the good from the bad or make any substitution. If anyone does make a substitution, both the animal and its substitute become holy and cannot be redeemed.'" Ge 28:22; Mal 3:8

³⁴These are the commands the LORD gave Moses at Mount Sinai for the Israelites. Lev 26:46

---

[a] 26 The Hebrew word can refer to either male or female.   [b] 28 The Hebrew term refers to the irrevocable giving over of things or persons to the LORD.   [c] 29 The Hebrew term refers to the irrevocable giving over of things or persons to the LORD, often by totally destroying them.

Numbers

The Census

1 The LORD spoke to Moses in the tent of meeting in the Desert of Sinai on the first day of the second month of the second year after the Israelites came out of Egypt. He said: ² "Take a census of the whole Israelite community by their clans and families, listing every man by name, one by one. ³ You and Aaron are to count according to their divisions all the men in Israel who are twenty years old or more and able to serve in the army. ⁴ One man from each tribe, each of them the head of his family, is to help you. ⁵ These are the names of the men who are to assist you: Ex 30:11-16; Dt 1:15

from Reuben, Elizur son of Shedeur;   Rev 7:5

⁶ from Simeon, Shelumiel son of Zurishaddai;   Nu 25:14

⁷ from Judah, Nahshon son of Amminadab;   Ge 29:35

⁸ from Issachar, Nethanel son of Zuar;   Ge 30:18

⁹ from Zebulun, Eliab son of Helon;   Nu 10:16

¹⁰ from the sons of Joseph:
from Ephraim, Elishama son of Ammihud;   Nu 2:18
from Manasseh, Gamaliel son of Pedahzur;   Nu 10:23

¹¹ from Benjamin, Abidan son of Gideoni;   Nu 10:24

¹² from Dan, Ahiezer son of Ammishaddai;   Nu 2:25

¹³ from Asher, Pagiel son of Okran;   Nu 2:27; 10:26

¹⁴ from Gad, Eliasaph son of Deuel;   Nu 2:14; 10:20

¹⁵ from Naphtali, Ahira son of Enan."   Nu 2:29; 10:27

¹⁶ These were the men appointed from the community, the leaders of their ancestral tribes. They were the heads of the clans of Israel.   Ex 18:25; Nu 7:2

¹⁷ Moses and Aaron took these men whose names had been specified, ¹⁸ and they called the whole community together on the first day of the second month. The people registered their ancestry by their clans and

families, and the men twenty years old or more were listed by name, one by one, ¹⁹as the LORD commanded Moses. And so he counted them in the Desert of Sinai: Ezr 2:59; Heb 7:3

²⁰From the descendants of Reuben the firstborn son of Israel: Nu 26:5-11; Rev 7:5 All the men twenty years old or more who were able to serve in the army were listed by name, one by one, according to the records of their clans and families. ²¹The number from the tribe of Reuben was 46,500.

²²From the descendants of Simeon: Nu 26:12-14; Rev 7:7 All the men twenty years old or more who were able to serve in the army were counted and listed by name, one by one, according to the records of their clans and families. ²³The number from the tribe of Simeon was 59,300.

²⁴From the descendants of Gad: Nu 26:15-18; Rev 7:5 All the men twenty years old or more who were able to serve in the army were listed by name, according to the records of their clans and families. ²⁵The number from the tribe of Gad was 45,650.

²⁶From the descendants of Judah: Nu 26:19-22; Mt 1:2; Rev 7:5 All the men twenty years old or more who were able to serve in the army were listed by name, according to the records of their clans and families. ²⁷The number from the tribe of Judah was 74,600.

²⁸From the descendants of Issachar: Nu 26:23-25; Rev 7:7 All the men twenty years old or more who were able to serve in the army were listed by name, according to the records of their clans and families. ²⁹The number from the tribe of Issachar was 54,400.

³⁰From the descendants of Zebulun: Nu 26:26-27; Rev 7:8 All the men twenty years old or more who were able to serve in the army were listed by name, according to the records of their clans and families. ³¹The number from the tribe of Zebulun was 57,400.

³²From the sons of Joseph: From the descendants of Ephraim: Nu 26:35-37 All the men twenty years old or more who were able to serve in the army were listed by name, according to the records of their clans and families. ³³The

number from the tribe of Ephraim was 40,500.

³⁴From the descendants of Manasseh:Nu 26:28-34; Rev 7:6 All the men twenty years old or more who were able to serve in the army were listed by name, according to the records of their clans and families. ³⁵The number from the tribe of Manasseh was 32,200.

³⁶From the descendants of Benjamin: Nu 26:38-41; Rev 7:8 All the men twenty years old or more who were able to serve in the army were listed by name, according to the records of their clans and families. ³⁷The number from the tribe of Benjamin was 35,400.

³⁸From the descendants of Dan: Nu 26:42-43 All the men twenty years old or more who were able to serve in the army were listed by name, according to the records of their clans and families. ³⁹The number from the tribe of Dan was 62,700.

⁴⁰From the descendants of Asher: Nu 26:44-47; Rev 7:6 All the men twenty years old or more who were able to serve in the army were listed by name, according to the records of their

clans and families. ⁴¹The number from the tribe of Asher was 41,500.

⁴²From the descendants of Naphtali: Nu 26:48-50; Rev 7:6 All the men twenty years old or more who were able to serve in the army were listed by name, according to the records of their clans and families. ⁴³The number from the tribe of Naphtali was 53,400.

⁴⁴These were the men counted by Moses and Aaron and the twelve leaders of Israel, each one representing his family. ⁴⁵All the Israelites twenty years old or more who were able to serve in Israel's army were counted according to their families. ⁴⁶The total number was 603,550. Nu 2:32; 26:64

⁴⁷The ancestral tribe of the Levites, however, was not counted along with the others. ⁴⁸The LORD had said to Moses: ⁴⁹"You must not count the tribe of Levi or include them in the census of the other Israelites. ⁵⁰Instead, appoint the Levites to be in charge of the tabernacle of the covenant law—over all its furnishings and everything belonging to it. They are to carry the tabernacle and all its furnishings; they are to take care of it and encamp around it. ⁵¹Whenever the tabernacle is to move, the Levites are to take it down, and whenever the tabernacle is

to be set up, the Levites shall do it. Anyone else who approaches it is to be put to death. ⁵²The Israelites are to set up their tents by divisions, each of them in their own camp under their standard. ⁵³The Levites, however, are to set up their tents around the tabernacle of the covenant law so that my wrath will not fall on the Israelite community. The Levites are to be responsible for the care of the tabernacle of the covenant law." Nu 2:33; 18:2-4

⁵⁴The Israelites did all this just as the LORD commanded Moses.

The Arrangement of the Tribal Camps

2 The LORD said to Moses and Aaron: ² "The Israelites are to camp around the tent of meeting some distance from it, each of them under their standard and holding the banners of their family." Nu 1:52; Ps 74:4

³On the east, toward the sunrise, the divisions of the camp of Judah are to encamp under their standard. The leader of the people of Judah is Nahshon son of Amminadab. ⁴His division numbers 74,600. Nu 10:14

⁵The tribe of Issachar will camp next to them. The leader of the people of Issachar is Nethanel son of Zuar. ⁶His division numbers 54,400. Nu 1:8; 10:15

⁷The tribe of Zebulun will be next. The leader of the people of Zebulun is Eliab son of Helon. ⁸His division numbers 57,400. Nu 1:9

⁹All the men assigned to the camp of Judah, according to their divisions, number 186,400. They will set out first. Nu 10:14

¹⁰On the south will be the divisions of the camp of Reuben under their standard. The leader of the people of Reuben is Elizur son of Shedeur. ¹¹His division numbers 46,500. Nu 1:5

¹²The tribe of Simeon will camp next to them. The leader of the people of Simeon is Shelumiel son of Zurishaddai. ¹³His division numbers 59,300. Nu 1:6

¹⁴The tribe of Gad will be next. The leader of the people of Gad is Eliasaph son of Deuel.ᵃ ¹⁵His division numbers 45,650. Nu 1:14

¹⁶All the men assigned to the camp of Reuben, according to their divisions, number 151,450. They will set out second. Nu 10:18

¹⁷Then the tent of meeting and the camp of the Levites will set out in the

ᵃ 14 Many manuscripts of the Masoretic Text, Samaritan Pentateuch and Vulgate (see also 1:14); most manuscripts of the Masoretic Text *Reuel* middle of the camps. They will set out in the same order as they encamp, each in their own place under their standard. Nu 10:21

¹⁸On the west will be the divisions of the camp of Ephraim under their standard. The leader of the people of Ephraim is Elishama son of Ammihud. ¹⁹His division numbers 40,500. Ge 48:20

²⁰The tribe of Manasseh will be next to them. The leader of the people of Manasseh is Gamaliel son of Pedahzur. ²¹His division numbers 32,200. Nu 1:10

²²The tribe of Benjamin will be next. The leader of the people of Benjamin is Abidan son of Gideoni. ²³His division numbers 35,400. Nu 1:11; Ps 68:27

²⁴All the men assigned to the camp of Ephraim, according to their divisions, number 108,100. They will set out third. Nu 10:22; Ps 80:2

²⁵On the north will be the divisions of the camp of Dan under their standard. The leader of the people of Dan is Ahiezer son of Ammishaddai. ²⁶His division numbers 62,700. Nu 1:12

²⁷The tribe of Asher will camp next to them. The leader of the people of Asher is Pagiel son of Okran.

²⁸His division numbers 41,500. Nu 1:13

²⁹The tribe of Naphtali will be next. The leader of the people of Naphtali is Ahira son of Enan. ³⁰His division numbers 53,400. Nu 1:15

³¹All the men assigned to the camp of Dan number 157,600. They will set out last, under their standards. Nu 10:25

³²These are the Israelites, counted according to their families. All the men in the camps, by their divisions, number 603,550. ³³The Levites, however, were not counted along with the other Israelites, as the LORD commanded Moses.

³⁴So the Israelites did everything the LORD commanded Moses; that is the way they encamped under their standards, and that is the way they set out, each of them with their clan and family. Ex 38:26; Nu 1:46-47

The Levites

3 This is the account of the family of Aaron and Moses at the time the LORD spoke to Moses at Mount Sinai. Ex 6:27

²The names of the sons of Aaron were Nadab the firstborn and Abihu, Eleazar and Ithamar. ³Those were the names of Aaron's sons, the anointed priests, who were ordained to serve as priests. ⁴Nadab and

Abihu, however, died before the LORD when they made an offering with unauthorized fire before him in the Desert of Sinai. They had no sons, so Eleazar and Ithamar served as priests during the lifetime of their father Aaron. Ex 6:23; Lev 10:1-2

⁵The LORD said to Moses, ⁶"Bring the tribe of Levi and present them to Aaron the priest to assist him. ⁷They are to perform duties for him and for the whole community at the tent of meeting by doing the work of the tabernacle. ⁸They are to take care of all the furnishings of the tent of meeting, fulfilling the obligations of the Israelites by doing the work of the tabernacle. ⁹Give the Levites to Aaron and his sons; they are the Israelites who are to be given wholly to him.ᵃ ¹⁰Appoint Aaron and his sons to serve as priests; anyone else who approaches the sanctuary is to be put to death." Nu 1:51; 8:6-22; 18:1-7

¹¹The LORD also said to Moses, ¹²"I have taken the Levites from among the Israelites in place of the first male offspring of every Israelite woman. The Levites are mine, ¹³for all the firstborn are mine. When I struck down all the firstborn in Egypt, I set apart for myself every firstborn in Israel, whether human or animal. They are to be mine. I am the LORD." Ex 13:12; Nu 8:16,18

¹⁴The LORD said to Moses in the Desert of Sinai, ¹⁵"Count the Levites by their families and clans. Count every male a month old or more." ¹⁶So Moses counted them, as he was commanded by the word of the LORD. Nu 26:62 ¹⁷These were the names of the sons of Levi: Ge 46:11

Gershon, Kohath and Merari. Ex 6:16
¹⁸These were the names of the Gershonite clans:
Libni and Shimei. Ex 6:17
¹⁹The Kohathite clans:
Amram, Izhar, Hebron and Uzziel. Ex 6:18
²⁰The Merarite clans: Ge 46:11
Mahli and Mushi. Ex 6:19
These were the Levite clans, according to their families.

²¹To Gershon belonged the clans of the Libnites and Shimeites; these were the Gershonite clans. ²²The number of all the males a month old or more who were counted was 7,500. ²³The Gershonite clans were to camp on the west, behind the tabernacle. ²⁴The leader of the families of the Gershonites was Eliasaph son of Lael. ²⁵At the tent of meeting the Gershonites were responsible for the care of the tabernacle and tent, its coverings, the curtain at the entrance to the tent of meeting, ²⁶the curtains of the courtyard,

---

ᵃ 9 Most manuscripts of the Masoretic Text; some manuscripts of the Masoretic Text, Samaritan Pentateuch and Septuagint (see also 8:16) *to me* the curtain at the entrance to the courtyard surrounding the tabernacle and altar, and the ropes — and everything related to their use. Ex 6:17; 25:9; Nu 4:25

27 To Kohath belonged the clans of the Amramites, Izharites, Hebronites and Uzzielites; these were the Kohathite clans. 28 The number of all the males a month old or more was 8,600.*a* The Kohathites were responsible for the care of the sanctuary. 29 The Kohathite clans were to camp on the south side of the tabernacle. 30 The leader of the families of the Kohathite clans was Elizaphan son of Uzziel. 31 They were responsible for the care of the ark, the table, the lampstand, the altars, the articles of the sanctuary used in ministering, the curtain, and everything related to their use. 32 The chief leader of the Levites was Eleazar son of Aaron, the priest. He was appointed over those who were responsible for the care of the sanctuary. Ex 25:10-22,31; 1Ch 26:23

33 To Merari belonged the clans of the Mahlites and the Mushites; these were the Merarite clans. 34 The number of all the males a month old or more who were counted was 6,200. 35 The leader of the families of the Merarite clans was Zuriel son of Abihail; they were to camp on the north side of the tabernacle. 36 The Merarites were appointed to take care of the frames of the tabernacle, its crossbars, posts, bases, all its equipment, and everything related to their use, 37 as well as the posts of the surrounding courtyard with their bases, tent pegs and ropes. Ex 6:19; Nu 4:32

38 Moses and Aaron and his sons were to camp to the east of the tabernacle, toward the sunrise, in front of the tent of meeting. They were responsible for the care of the sanctuary on behalf of the Israelites. Anyone else who approached the sanctuary was to be put to death. Nu 18:5

39 The total number of Levites counted at the LORD's command by Moses and Aaron according to their clans, including every male a month old or more, was 22,000. Nu 26:62

40 The LORD said to Moses, "Count all the firstborn Israelite males who are a month old or more and make a list of their names. 41 Take the Levites for me in place of all the firstborn of the Israelites, and the livestock of the Levites in place of all the firstborn of the livestock of the Israelites. I am the LORD." ver 12,15

42 So Moses counted all the

a 28 Hebrew; some Septuagint manuscripts *8,300*

firstborn of the Israelites, as the LORD commanded him. ⁴³The total number of firstborn males a month old or more, listed by name, was 22,273.

⁴⁴The LORD also said to Moses, ⁴⁵"Take the Levites in place of all the firstborn of Israel, and the livestock of the Levites in place of their livestock. The Levites are to be mine. I am the LORD. ⁴⁶To redeem the 273 firstborn Israelites who exceed the number of the Levites, ⁴⁷collect five shekels*ᵃ* for each one, according to the sanctuary shekel, which weighs twenty gerahs. ⁴⁸Give the money for the redemption of the additional Israelites to Aaron and his sons." Ex 13:13; Nu 18:15

⁴⁹So Moses collected the redemption money from those who exceeded the number redeemed by the Levites. ⁵⁰From the firstborn of the Israelites he collected silver weighing 1,365 shekels,*ᵇ* according to the sanctuary shekel. ⁵¹Moses gave the redemption money to Aaron and his sons, as he was commanded by the word of the LORD. ver 46-48

The Kohathites

4 The LORD said to Moses and Aaron: ²"Take a census of the Kohathite branch of the Levites by their clans and families. ³Count all the men from thirty to fifty years of age who come to serve in the work at the tent of meeting. Ex 30:12; Nu 8:25; 1Ch 23:3,24

⁴"This is the work of the Kohathites at the tent of meeting: the care of the most holy things. ⁵When the camp is to move, Aaron and his sons are to go in and take down the shielding curtain and put it over the ark of the covenant law. ⁶Then they are to cover the curtain with a durable leather,*ᶜ* spread a cloth of solid blue over that and put the poles in place. Ex 25:10,16; 26:31,33

⁷"Over the table of the Presence they are to spread a blue cloth and put on it the plates, dishes and bowls, and the jars for drink offerings; the bread that is continually there is to remain on it. ⁸They are to spread a scarlet cloth over them, cover that with the durable leather and put the poles in place. Ex 25:30; Lev 24:6

⁹"They are to take a blue cloth and cover the lampstand that is for light, together with its lamps, its wick trimmers and trays, and all its jars for the olive oil used to supply it. ¹⁰Then they are to wrap it and all its accessories in a covering of the durable leather and put it on a carrying frame. Ex 25:31,37-38

¹¹"Over the gold altar they are to spread a blue cloth and cover that with the durable leather and put the poles in place. Ex 30:1

ᵃ 47 That is, about 2 ounces or about 58 grams   *ᵇ 50* That is, about 35 pounds or about 16 kilograms   *ᶜ 6* Possibly the hides of large aquatic mammals; also in verses 8, 10, 11, 12, 14 and 25

¹² "They are to take all the articles used for ministering in the sanctuary, wrap them in a blue cloth, cover that with the durable leather and put them on a carrying frame.

¹³ "They are to remove the ashes from the bronze altar and spread a purple cloth over it. ¹⁴ Then they are to place on it all the utensils used for ministering at the altar, including the firepans, meat forks, shovels and sprinkling bowls. Over it they are to spread a covering of the durable leather and put the poles in place. Ex 27:1-8

¹⁵ "After Aaron and his sons have finished covering the holy furnishings and all the holy articles, and when the camp is ready to move, only then are the Kohathites to come and do the carrying. But they must not touch the holy things or they will die. The Kohathites are to carry those things that are in the tent of meeting. Nu 1:51; 2Sa 6:6-7

¹⁶ "Eleazar son of Aaron, the priest, is to have charge of the oil for the light, the fragrant incense, the regular grain offering and the anointing oil. He is to be in charge of the entire tabernacle and everything in it, including its holy furnishings and articles." Ex 25:6; 29:41

¹⁷ The LORD said to Moses and Aaron, ¹⁸ "See that the Kohathite tribal clans are not destroyed from among the Levites. ¹⁹ So that they may live and not die when they come near the most holy things, do this for them: Aaron and his sons are to go into the sanctuary and assign to each man his work and what he is to carry. ²⁰ But the Kohathites must not go in to look at the holy things, even for a moment, or they will die." Ex 19:21; 1Sa 6:19

The Gershonites

²¹ The LORD said to Moses, ²² "Take a census also of the Gershonites by their families and clans. ²³ Count all the men from thirty to fifty years of age who come to serve in the work at the tent of meeting.

²⁴ "This is the service of the Gershonite clans in their carrying and their other work: ²⁵ They are to carry the curtains of the tabernacle, that is, the tent of meeting, its covering and its outer covering of durable leather, the curtains for the entrance to the tent of meeting, ²⁶ the curtains of the courtyard surrounding the tabernacle and altar, the curtain for the entrance to the courtyard, the ropes and all the equipment used in the service of the tent. The Gershonites are to do all that needs to be done with these things. ²⁷ All their service, whether carrying or doing other work, is to be done under the direction of Aaron and his sons. You shall assign to them as their responsibility all they are to carry. ²⁸ This

is the service of the Gershonite clans at the tent of meeting. Their duties are to be under the direction of Ithamar son of Aaron, the priest. Ex 27:10-18; Nu 3:25-26

The Merarites

29 "Count the Merarites by their clans and families. 30 Count all the men from thirty to fifty years of age who come to serve in the work at the tent of meeting. 31 As part of all their service at the tent, they are to carry the frames of the tabernacle, its crossbars, posts and bases, 32 as well as the posts of the surrounding courtyard with their bases, tent pegs, ropes, all their equipment and everything related to their use. Assign to each man the specific things he is to carry. 33 This is the service of the Merarite clans as they work at the tent of meeting under the direction of Ithamar son of Aaron, the priest." Ge 46:11; Nu 3:36

The Numbering of the Levite Clans

34 Moses, Aaron and the leaders of the community counted the Kohathites by their clans and families. 35 All the men from thirty to fifty years of age who came to serve in the work at the tent of meeting, 36 counted by clans, were 2,750. 37 This was the total of all those in the Kohathite clans who served at the tent

of meeting. Moses and Aaron counted them according to the LORD's command through Moses. Nu 3:27

38 The Gershonites were counted by their clans and families. 39 All the men from thirty to fifty years of age who came to serve in the work at the tent of meeting, 40 counted by their clans and families, were 2,630. 41 This was the total of those in the Gershonite clans who served at the tent of meeting. Moses and Aaron counted them according to the LORD's command. Ge 46:11

42 The Merarites were counted by their clans and families. 43 All the men from thirty to fifty years of age who came to serve in the work at the tent of meeting, 44 counted by their clans, were 3,200. 45 This was the total of those in the Merarite clans. Moses and Aaron counted them according to the LORD's command through Moses. ver 29

46 So Moses, Aaron and the leaders of Israel counted all the Levites by their clans and families. 47 All the men from thirty to fifty years of age who came to do the work of serving and carrying the tent of meeting 48 numbered 8,580. 49 At the LORD's command through Moses, each was assigned his work and told what to carry. Nu 3:39

Thus they were counted, as the LORD commanded Moses. Nu 1:47

The Purity of the Camp

5 The LORD said to Moses, 2 "Command the Israelites to send away from the camp anyone who has a defiling skin disease[a] or a discharge of any kind, or who is ceremonially unclean because of a dead body. 3 Send away male and female alike; send them outside the camp so they will not defile their camp, where I dwell among them." 4 The Israelites did so; they sent them outside the camp. They did just as the LORD had instructed Moses. Lev 26:12; 2Co 6:16

Restitution for Wrongs

5 The LORD said to Moses, 6 "Say to the Israelites: 'Any man or woman who wrongs another in any way[b] and so is unfaithful to the LORD is guilty 7 and must confess the sin they have committed. They must make full restitution for the wrong they have done, add a fifth of the value to it and give it all to the person they have wronged. 8 But if that person has no close relative to whom restitution can be made for the wrong, the restitution belongs to the LORD and must be given to the priest, along with the ram with which atonement is made for the wrongdoer. 9 All the sacred contributions the Israelites bring to a priest will belong to him. 10 Sacred things belong to their owners, but what they give to the priest will belong to the priest.'" Lev 5:5; 6:2; Lk 19:8

The Test for an Unfaithful Wife

11 Then the LORD said to Moses, 12 "Speak to the Israelites and say to them: 'If a man's wife goes astray and is unfaithful to him 13 so that another man has sexual relations with her, and this is hidden from her husband and her impurity is undetected (since there is no witness against her and she has not been caught in the act), 14 and if feelings of jealousy come over her husband and he suspects his wife and she is impure — or if he is jealous and suspects her even though she is not impure — 15 then he is to take his wife to the priest. He must also take an offering of a tenth of an ephah[c] of barley flour on her behalf. He must not pour olive oil on it or put incense on it, because it is a grain offering for jealousy, a reminder-offering to draw attention to wrongdoing. Eze 29:16

16 "'The priest shall bring her and have her stand before the LORD. 17 Then he shall take some holy water in a clay jar and put some dust from the tabernacle floor into the water. 18 After the priest has had the woman stand

---

[a] 2 The Hebrew word for *defiling skin disease*, traditionally translated "leprosy," was used for various diseases affecting the skin.   [b] 6 Or *woman who commits any wrong common to mankind*   [c] 15 That is, probably about 3 1/2 pounds or about 1.6 kilograms

before the LORD, he shall loosen her hair and place in her hands the reminder-offering, the grain offering for jealousy, while he himself holds the bitter water that brings a curse. [19] Then the priest shall put the woman under oath and say to her, "If no other man has had sexual relations with you and you have not gone astray and become impure while married to your husband, may this bitter water that brings a curse not harm you. [20] But if you have gone astray while married to your husband and you have made yourself impure by having sexual relations with a man other than your husband" — [21] here the priest is to put the woman under this curse — "may the LORD cause you to become a curse[a] among your people when he makes your womb miscarry and your abdomen swell. [22] May this water that brings a curse enter your body so that your abdomen swells or your womb miscarries."   Jos 6:26; Ps 109:18

" 'Then the woman is to say, "Amen. So be it."   Dt 27:15

[23] " 'The priest is to write these curses on a scroll and then wash them off into the bitter water. [24] He shall make the woman drink the bitter water that brings a curse, and this water that brings a curse and causes bitter suffering will enter her. [25] The priest is to take from her hands the grain offering for jealousy, wave it before the LORD and bring it to the altar. [26] The priest is then to take a handful of the grain offering as a memorial[b] offering and burn it on the altar; after that, he is to have the woman drink the water. [27] If she has made herself impure and been unfaithful to her husband, this will be the result: When she is made to drink the water that brings a curse and causes bitter suffering, it will enter her, her abdomen will swell and her womb will miscarry, and she will become a curse. [28] If, however, the woman has not made herself impure, but is clean, she will be cleared of guilt and will be able to have children.   Jer 29:18; 42:18

[29] " 'This, then, is the law of jealousy when a woman goes astray and makes herself impure while married to her husband, [30] or when feelings of jealousy come over a man because he suspects his wife. The priest is to have her stand before the LORD and is to apply this entire law to her. [31] The husband will be innocent of any wrongdoing, but the woman will bear the consequences of her sin.' "   Lev 5:1; 20:17

The Nazirite

6 The LORD said to Moses, [2] "Speak to the Israelites and say to them: 'If a man or woman

---

[a] 21 That is, may he cause your name to be used in cursing (see Jer. 29:22); or, may others see that you are cursed; similarly in verse 27.   [b] 26 Or *representative*

wants to make a special vow, a vow of dedication to the LORD as a Nazirite, [3] they must abstain from wine and other fermented drink and must not drink vinegar made from wine or other fermented drink. They must not drink grape juice or eat grapes or raisins. [4] As long as they remain under their Nazirite vow, they must not eat anything that comes from the grapevine, not even the seeds or skins. Jdg 13:5; Am 2:11-12; Ac 21:23

[5] " 'During the entire period of their Nazirite vow, no razor may be used on their head. They must be holy until the period of their dedication to the LORD is over; they must let their hair grow long.

[6] " 'Throughout the period of their dedication to the LORD, the Nazirite must not go near a dead body. [7] Even if their own father or mother or brother or sister dies, they must not make themselves ceremonially unclean on account of them, because the symbol of their dedication to God is on their head. [8] Throughout the period of their dedication, they are consecrated to the LORD. Nu 9:6; 1Sa 1:11

[9] " 'If someone dies suddenly in the Nazirite's presence, thus defiling the hair that symbolizes their dedication, they must shave their head on the seventh day — the day of their cleansing.

[10] Then on the eighth day they must bring two doves or two young pigeons to the priest at the entrance to the tent of meeting. [11] The priest is to offer one as a sin offering[a] and the other as a burnt offering to make atonement for the Nazirite because they sinned by being in the presence of the dead body. That same day they are to consecrate their head again. [12] They must rededicate themselves to the LORD for the same period of dedication and must bring a year-old male lamb as a guilt offering. The previous days do not count, because they became defiled during their period of dedication. Lev 5:7; 14:22

[13] " 'Now this is the law of the Nazirite when the period of their dedication is over. They are to be brought to the entrance to the tent of meeting. [14] There they are to present their offerings to the LORD: a year-old male lamb without defect for a burnt offering, a year-old ewe lamb without defect for a sin offering, a ram without defect for a fellowship offering, [15] together with their grain offerings and drink offerings, and a basket of bread made with the finest flour and without yeast — thick loaves with olive oil mixed in, and thin loaves brushed with olive oil. Lev 14:10; Ac 21:26

[16] " 'The priest is to present all these before the LORD and make

---

[a] 11 Or *purification offering*; also in verses 14 and 16

the sin offering and the burnt offering. ¹⁷ He is to present the basket of unleavened bread and is to sacrifice the ram as a fellowship offering to the LORD, together with its grain offering and drink offering.   Lev 1:3; 23:13

¹⁸ " 'Then at the entrance to the tent of meeting, the Nazirite must shave off the hair that symbolizes their dedication. They are to take the hair and put it in the fire that is under the sacrifice of the fellowship offering.   ver 9; Ac 21:24

¹⁹ " 'After the Nazirite has shaved off the hair that symbolizes their dedication, the priest is to place in their hands a boiled shoulder of the ram, and one thick loaf and one thin loaf from the basket, both made without yeast. ²⁰ The priest shall then wave these before the LORD as a wave offering; they are holy and belong to the priest, together with the breast that was waved and the thigh that was presented. After that, the Nazirite may drink wine.   Ecc 9:7

²¹ " 'This is the law of the Nazirite who vows offerings to the LORD in accordance with their dedication, in addition to whatever else they can afford. They must fulfill the vows they have made, according to the law of the Nazirite.' "   ver 2,13

The Priestly Blessing

²² The LORD said to Moses, ²³ "Tell Aaron and his sons, 'This is how you are to bless the Israelites. Say to them: 1Ch 23:13

²⁴ " ' "The LORD bless you Dt 28:3-6
and keep you;
²⁵ the LORD make his face shine
on you   Ps 80:3; 119:135
and be gracious to
you;   Ge 43:29; Ps 25:16
²⁶ the LORD turn his face toward
you   Ps 4:6; 44:3
and give you peace." ' Ps 29:11

²⁷ "So they will put my name on the Israelites, and I will bless them."   Dt 28:10; 2Ch 7:14

Offerings at the Dedication of the Tabernacle

7 When Moses finished setting up the tabernacle, he anointed and consecrated it and all its furnishings. He also anointed and consecrated the altar and all its utensils. ² Then the leaders of Israel, the heads of families who were the tribal leaders in charge of those who were counted, made offerings. ³ They brought as their gifts before the LORD six covered carts and twelve oxen — an ox from each leader and a cart from every two. These they presented before the tabernacle.   Ex 40:9,17

⁴ The LORD said to Moses, ⁵ "Accept these from them, that they may be used in the work at the tent of meeting. Give them to the Levites as each man's work requires."

⁶ So Moses took the carts and oxen and gave them to the Le-

vites. ⁷He gave two carts and four oxen to the Gershonites, as their work required, ⁸and he gave four carts and eight oxen to the Merarites, as their work required. They were all under the direction of Ithamar son of Aaron, the priest. ⁹But Moses did not give any to the Kohathites, because they were to carry on their shoulders the holy things, for which they were responsible. Nu 4:15,31-33

¹⁰When the altar was anointed, the leaders brought their offerings for its dedication and presented them before the altar. ¹¹For the LORD had said to Moses, "Each day one leader is to bring his offering for the dedication of the altar." 2Ch 7:9

¹²The one who brought his offering on the first day was Nahshon son of Amminadab of the tribe of Judah.

¹³His offering was one silver plate weighing a hundred and thirty shekels*a* and one silver sprinkling bowl weighing seventy shekels,*b* both according to the sanctuary shekel, each filled with the finest flour mixed with olive oil as a grain offering; ¹⁴one gold dish weighing ten shekels,*c* filled with incense; ¹⁵one young bull, one ram and one male lamb a year old for a burnt offering; ¹⁶one male goat for a sin offering*d*; ¹⁷and two oxen, five rams, five male goats and five male lambs a year old to be sacrificed as a fellowship offering. This was the offering of Nahshon son of Amminadab. Lev 3:1; 4:3,23

¹⁸On the second day Nethanel son of Zuar, the leader of Issachar, brought his offering. Nu 1:8

¹⁹The offering he brought was one silver plate weighing a hundred and thirty shekels and one silver sprinkling bowl weighing seventy shekels, both according to the sanctuary shekel, each filled with the finest flour mixed with olive oil as a grain offering; ²⁰one gold dish weighing ten shekels, filled with incense; ²¹one young bull, one ram and one male lamb a year old for a burnt offering; ²²one male goat for a sin offering; ²³and two oxen, five rams, five male goats and five male lambs a year old to be sacrificed as a fellowship offering. This was the offering of Nethanel son of Zuar.

²⁴On the third day, Eliab son of Helon, the leader of the people

---

a 13 That is, about 3 1/4 pounds or about 1.5 kilograms; also elsewhere in this chapter
b 13 That is, about 1 3/4 pounds or about 800 grams; also elsewhere in this chapter
c 14 That is, about 4 ounces or about 115 grams; also elsewhere in this chapter
d 16 Or *purification offering*; also elsewhere in this chapter

of Zebulun, brought his offering. Nu 1:9

25His offering was one silver plate weighing a hundred and thirty shekels and one silver sprinkling bowl weighing seventy shekels, both according to the sanctuary shekel, each filled with the finest flour mixed with olive oil as a grain offering; 26one gold dish weighing ten shekels, filled with incense; 27one young bull, one ram and one male lamb a year old for a burnt offering; 28one male goat for a sin offering; 29and two oxen, five rams, five male goats and five male lambs a year old to be sacrificed as a fellowship offering. This was the offering of Eliab son of Helon.

30On the fourth day Elizur son of Shedeur, the leader of the people of Reuben, brought his offering. Nu 1:5

31His offering was one silver plate weighing a hundred and thirty shekels and one silver sprinkling bowl weighing seventy shekels, both according to the sanctuary shekel, each filled with the finest flour mixed with olive oil as a grain offering; 32one gold dish weighing ten shekels, filled with incense; 33one young bull, one ram and one male lamb a year old for a burnt offering; 34one male goat for a sin offering; 35and two oxen, five rams, five male goats and five male lambs a year old to be sacrificed as a fellowship offering. This was the offering of Elizur son of Shedeur.

36On the fifth day Shelumiel son of Zurishaddai, the leader of the people of Simeon, brought his offering. Nu 1:6

37His offering was one silver plate weighing a hundred and thirty shekels and one silver sprinkling bowl weighing seventy shekels, both according to the sanctuary shekel, each filled with the finest flour mixed with olive oil as a grain offering; 38one gold dish weighing ten shekels, filled with incense; 39one young bull, one ram and one male lamb a year old for a burnt offering; 40one male goat for a sin offering; 41and two oxen, five rams, five male goats and five male lambs a year old to be sacrificed as a fellowship offering. This was the offering of Shelumiel son of Zurishaddai.

42On the sixth day Eliasaph son of Deuel, the leader of the people of Gad, brought his offering. Nu 1:14

43His offering was one silver plate weighing a hundred and thirty shekels and one silver sprinkling bowl weighing seventy shekels, both according to the sanctuary shekel, each filled with the finest flour mixed with olive oil as a grain offering; ⁴⁴one gold dish weighing ten shekels, filled with incense; ⁴⁵one young bull, one ram and one male lamb a year old for a burnt offering; ⁴⁶one male goat for a sin offering; ⁴⁷and two oxen, five rams, five male goats and five male lambs a year old to be sacrificed as a fellowship offering. This was the offering of Eliasaph son of Deuel.

⁴⁸On the seventh day Elishama son of Ammihud, the leader of the people of Ephraim, brought his offering.   Nu 1:10
⁴⁹His offering was one silver plate weighing a hundred and thirty shekels and one silver sprinkling bowl weighing seventy shekels, both according to the sanctuary shekel, each filled with the finest flour mixed with olive oil as a grain offering; ⁵⁰one gold dish weighing ten shekels, filled with incense; ⁵¹one young bull, one ram and one male lamb a year old for a burnt offering; ⁵²one male goat for a sin offering; ⁵³and two oxen, five rams, five male goats and five male lambs a year old to

be sacrificed as a fellowship offering. This was the offering of Elishama son of Ammihud.

⁵⁴On the eighth day Gamaliel son of Pedahzur, the leader of the people of Manasseh, brought his offering.   Nu 1:10; 2:20
⁵⁵His offering was one silver plate weighing a hundred and thirty shekels and one silver sprinkling bowl weighing seventy shekels, both according to the sanctuary shekel, each filled with the finest flour mixed with olive oil as a grain offering; ⁵⁶one gold dish weighing ten shekels, filled with incense; ⁵⁷one young bull, one ram and one male lamb a year old for a burnt offering; ⁵⁸one male goat for a sin offering; ⁵⁹and two oxen, five rams, five male goats and five male lambs a year old to be sacrificed as a fellowship offering. This was the offering of Gamaliel son of Pedahzur.

⁶⁰On the ninth day Abidan son of Gideoni, the leader of the people of Benjamin, brought his offering.   Nu 1:11
⁶¹His offering was one silver plate weighing a hundred and thirty shekels and one silver sprinkling bowl weighing seventy shekels, both according to the sanctuary

shekel, each filled with the finest flour mixed with olive oil as a grain offering; 62 one gold dish weighing ten shekels, filled with incense; 63 one young bull, one ram and one male lamb a year old for a burnt offering; 64 one male goat for a sin offering; 65 and two oxen, five rams, five male goats and five male lambs a year old to be sacrificed as a fellowship offering. This was the offering of Abidan son of Gideoni.

66 On the tenth day Ahiezer son of Ammishaddai, the leader of the people of Dan, brought his offering. Nu 1:12; 2:25
67 His offering was one silver plate weighing a hundred and thirty shekels and one silver sprinkling bowl weighing seventy shekels, both according to the sanctuary shekel, each filled with the finest flour mixed with olive oil as a grain offering; 68 one gold dish weighing ten shekels, filled with incense; 69 one young bull, one ram and one male lamb a year old for a burnt offering; 70 one male goat for a sin offering; 71 and two oxen, five rams, five male goats and five male lambs a year old to be sacrificed as a fellowship offering. This was the offering of Ahiezer son of Ammishaddai.

72 On the eleventh day Pagiel son of Okran, the leader of the people of Asher, brought his offering. Nu 1:13
73 His offering was one silver plate weighing a hundred and thirty shekels and one silver sprinkling bowl weighing seventy shekels, both according to the sanctuary shekel, each filled with the finest flour mixed with olive oil as a grain offering; 74 one gold dish weighing ten shekels, filled with incense; 75 one young bull, one ram and one male lamb a year old for a burnt offering; 76 one male goat for a sin offering; 77 and two oxen, five rams, five male goats and five male lambs a year old to be sacrificed as a fellowship offering. This was the offering of Pagiel son of Okran.

78 On the twelfth day Ahira son of Enan, the leader of the people of Naphtali, brought his offering. Nu 1:15; 2:29
79 His offering was one silver plate weighing a hundred and thirty shekels and one silver sprinkling bowl weighing seventy shekels, both according to the sanctuary shekel, each filled with the finest flour mixed with olive oil as a grain offering; 80 one gold dish weighing

ten shekels, filled with incense; [81] one young bull, one ram and one male lamb a year old for a burnt offering; [82] one male goat for a sin offering; [83] and two oxen, five rams, five male goats and five male lambs a year old to be sacrificed as a fellowship offering. This was the offering of Ahira son of Enan.

[84] These were the offerings of the Israelite leaders for the dedication of the altar when it was anointed: twelve silver plates, twelve silver sprinkling bowls and twelve gold dishes. [85] Each silver plate weighed a hundred and thirty shekels, and each sprinkling bowl seventy shekels. Altogether, the silver dishes weighed two thousand four hundred shekels,[a] according to the sanctuary shekel. [86] The twelve gold dishes filled with incense weighed ten shekels each, according to the sanctuary shekel. Altogether, the gold dishes weighed a hundred and twenty shekels.[b] [87] The total number of animals for the burnt offering came to twelve young bulls, twelve rams and twelve male lambs a year old, together with their grain offering. Twelve male goats were used for the sin offering. [88] The total number of animals for the sacrifice of the fellowship offering came to twenty-four oxen, sixty rams, sixty male goats and sixty male lambs a year old. These were the offerings for the dedication of the altar after it was anointed. ver 1,10

[89] When Moses entered the tent of meeting to speak with the LORD, he heard the voice speaking to him from between the two cherubim above the atonement cover on the ark of the covenant law. In this way the LORD spoke to him. Ex 25:21-22; Ps 80:1; 99:1

Setting Up the Lamps

8 The LORD said to Moses, [2] "Speak to Aaron and say to him, 'When you set up the lamps, see that all seven light up the area in front of the lampstand.'"

[3] Aaron did so; he set up the lamps so that they faced forward on the lampstand, just as the LORD commanded Moses. [4] This is how the lampstand was made: It was made of hammered gold—from its base to its blossoms. The lampstand was made exactly like the pattern the LORD had shown Moses. Ex 25:36-37

The Setting Apart of the Levites

[5] The LORD said to Moses: [6] "Take the Levites from among all the Israelites and make them ceremonially clean. [7] To purify them, do this: Sprinkle the water of cleansing on them; then

---

[a] 85 That is, about 60 pounds or about 28 kilograms   [b] 86 That is, about 3 pounds or about 1.4 kilograms

have them shave their whole bodies and wash their clothes. And so they will purify themselves. [8]Have them take a young bull with its grain offering of the finest flour mixed with olive oil; then you are to take a second young bull for a sin offering.[a] [9]Bring the Levites to the front of the tent of meeting and assemble the whole Israelite community. [10]You are to bring the Levites before the LORD, and the Israelites are to lay their hands on them. [11]Aaron is to present the Levites before the LORD as a wave offering from the Israelites, so that they may be ready to do the work of the LORD.   Lev 8:3; Isa 52:11; Ac 6:6

[12]"Then the Levites are to lay their hands on the heads of the bulls, using one for a sin offering to the LORD and the other for a burnt offering, to make atonement for the Levites. [13]Have the Levites stand in front of Aaron and his sons and then present them as a wave offering to the LORD. [14]In this way you are to set the Levites apart from the other Israelites, and the Levites will be mine.   Nu 3:12

[15]"After you have purified the Levites and presented them as a wave offering, they are to come to do their work at the tent of meeting. [16]They are the Israelites who are to be given wholly to me. I have taken them as my own in place of the firstborn, the first male offspring from every Israelite woman. [17]Every firstborn male in Israel, whether human or animal, is mine. When I struck down all the firstborn in Egypt, I set them apart for myself. [18]And I have taken the Levites in place of all the firstborn sons in Israel. [19]From among all the Israelites, I have given the Levites as gifts to Aaron and his sons to do the work at the tent of meeting on behalf of the Israelites and to make atonement for them so that no plague will strike the Israelites when they go near the sanctuary."   Ex 13:2; Nu 3:12

[20]Moses, Aaron and the whole Israelite community did with the Levites just as the LORD commanded Moses. [21]The Levites purified themselves and washed their clothes. Then Aaron presented them as a wave offering before the LORD and made atonement for them to purify them. [22]After that, the Levites came to do their work at the tent of meeting under the supervision of Aaron and his sons. They did with the Levites just as the LORD commanded Moses.   Ge 35:2; Nu 16:47

[23]The LORD said to Moses, [24]"This applies to the Levites: Men twenty-five years old or more shall come to take part in the work at the tent of meet-

ing, [25] but at the age of fifty, they must retire from their regular service and work no longer. [26] They may assist their brothers in performing their duties at the tent of meeting, but they themselves must not do the work. This, then, is how you are to assign the responsibilities of the Levites." Nu 4:3; 1Ch 23:3

The Passover

9 The LORD spoke to Moses in the Desert of Sinai in the first month of the second year after they came out of Egypt. He said, [2] "Have the Israelites celebrate the Passover at the appointed time. [3] Celebrate it at the appointed time, at twilight on the fourteenth day of this month, in accordance with all its rules and regulations." Ex 12:2-11,43-49; Nu 1:1

[4] So Moses told the Israelites to celebrate the Passover, [5] and they did so in the Desert of Sinai at twilight on the fourteenth day of the first month. The Israelites did everything just as the LORD commanded Moses. Ex 12:1-13; Jos 5:10

[6] But some of them could not celebrate the Passover on that day because they were ceremonially unclean on account of a dead body. So they came to Moses and Aaron that same day [7] and said to Moses, "We have become unclean because of a dead body, but why should we be kept from presenting the LORD's offer-

ing with the other Israelites at the appointed time?" Ex 18:15; Nu 27:2

[8] Moses answered them, "Wait until I find out what the LORD commands concerning you."

[9] Then the LORD said to Moses, [10] "Tell the Israelites: 'When any of you or your descendants are unclean because of a dead body or are away on a journey, they are still to celebrate the LORD's Passover, [11] but they are to do it on the fourteenth day of the second month at twilight. They are to eat the lamb, together with unleavened bread and bitter herbs. [12] They must not leave any of it till morning or break any of its bones. When they celebrate the Passover, they must follow all the regulations. [13] But if anyone who is ceremonially clean and not on a journey fails to celebrate the Passover, they must be cut off from their people for not presenting the LORD's offering at the appointed time. They will bear the consequences of their sin. Ge 17:14; Ex 12:8,15,46

[14] "'A foreigner residing among you is also to celebrate the LORD's Passover in accordance with its rules and regulations. You must have the same regulations for both the foreigner and the native-born.'" Ex 12:48-49

The Cloud Above the Tabernacle

[15] On the day the tabernacle, the tent of the covenant law, was

set up, the cloud covered it. From evening till morning the cloud above the tabernacle looked like fire. [16] That is how it continued to be; the cloud covered it, and at night it looked like fire. [17] Whenever the cloud lifted from above the tent, the Israelites set out; wherever the cloud settled, the Israelites encamped. [18] At the LORD's command the Israelites set out, and at his command they encamped. As long as the cloud stayed over the tabernacle, they remained in camp. [19] When the cloud remained over the tabernacle a long time, the Israelites obeyed the LORD's order and did not set out. [20] Sometimes the cloud was over the tabernacle only a few days; at the LORD's command they would encamp, and then at his command they would set out. [21] Sometimes the cloud stayed only from evening till morning, and when it lifted in the morning, they set out. Whether by day or by night, whenever the cloud lifted, they set out. [22] Whether the cloud stayed over the tabernacle for two days or a month or a year, the Israelites would remain in camp and not set out; but when it lifted, they would set out. [23] At the LORD's command they encamped, and at the LORD's command they set out. They obeyed the LORD's order, in accordance with his command through Moses. Ex 13:21; 40:36-38; 1Co 10:1

The Silver Trumpets

10 The LORD said to Moses: [2] "Make two trumpets of hammered silver, and use them for calling the community together and for having the camps set out. [3] When both are sounded, the whole community is to assemble before you at the entrance to the tent of meeting. [4] If only one is sounded, the leaders — the heads of the clans of Israel — are to assemble before you. [5] When a trumpet blast is sounded, the tribes camping on the east are to set out. [6] At the sounding of a second blast, the camps on the south are to set out. The blast will be the signal for setting out. [7] To gather the assembly, blow the trumpets, but not with the signal for setting out. Ps 47:5; Jer 4:5,19; Joel 2:1,15

[8] "The sons of Aaron, the priests, are to blow the trumpets. This is to be a lasting ordinance for you and the generations to come. [9] When you go into battle in your own land against an enemy who is oppressing you, sound a blast on the trumpets. Then you will be remembered by the LORD your God and rescued from your enemies. [10] Also at your times of rejoicing — your appointed festivals and New Moon feasts — you are to sound the trumpets over your burnt offerings and fellowship offerings, and they will be a memorial for you be-

fore your God. I am the LORD your God." Lev 23:24; Ps 106:4

The Israelites Leave Sinai

[11] On the twentieth day of the second month of the second year, the cloud lifted from above the tabernacle of the covenant law. [12] Then the Israelites set out from the Desert of Sinai and traveled from place to place until the cloud came to rest in the Desert of Paran. [13] They set out, this first time, at the LORD's command through Moses. Nu 9:17; Dt 1:6

[14] The divisions of the camp of Judah went first, under their standard. Nahshon son of Amminadab was in command. [15] Nethanel son of Zuar was over the division of the tribe of Issachar, [16] and Eliab son of Helon was over the division of the tribe of Zebulun. [17] Then the tabernacle was taken down, and the Gershonites and Merarites, who carried it, set out. Nu 2:3-9; 4:21-32

[18] The divisions of the camp of Reuben went next, under their standard. Elizur son of Shedeur was in command. [19] Shelumiel son of Zurishaddai was over the division of the tribe of Simeon, [20] and Eliasaph son of Deuel was over the division of the tribe of Gad. [21] Then the Kohathites set out, carrying the holy things. The tabernacle was to be set up before they arrived. Nu 2:10-16; 4:20

[22] The divisions of the camp of Ephraim went next, under their standard. Elishama son of Ammihud was in command. [23] Gamaliel son of Pedahzur was over the division of the tribe of Manasseh, [24] and Abidan son of Gideoni was over the division of the tribe of Benjamin. Nu 1:10-11; 2:24

[25] Finally, as the rear guard for all the units, the divisions of the camp of Dan set out under their standard. Ahiezer son of Ammishaddai was in command. [26] Pagiel son of Okran was over the division of the tribe of Asher, [27] and Ahira son of Enan was over the division of the tribe of Naphtali. [28] This was the order of march for the Israelite divisions as they set out. Nu 2:31; Jos 6:9

[29] Now Moses said to Hobab son of Reuel the Midianite, Moses' father-in-law, "We are setting out for the place about which the LORD said, 'I will give it to you.' Come with us and we will treat you well, for the LORD has promised good things to Israel." Ge 12:7; Ex 2:18

[30] He answered, "No, I will not go; I am going back to my own land and my own people." Mt 21:29

[31] But Moses said, "Please do not leave us. You know where we should camp in the wilderness, and you can be our eyes. [32] If you come with us, we will share with you whatever good things the LORD gives us." Dt 10:18; Ps 22:27-31

[33] So they set out from the mountain of the LORD and traveled for three days. The ark of the covenant of the LORD went

before them during those three days to find them a place to rest. ³⁴The cloud of the LORD was over them by day when they set out from the camp. Nu 9:15-23; Jos 3:3

³⁵Whenever the ark set out, Moses said,

"Rise up, LORD!
 May your enemies be
  scattered; Ps 68:1
 may your foes flee before
  you." Dt 7:10; 32:41

³⁶Whenever it came to rest, he said,

"Return, LORD,
 to the countless thousands
  of Israel." Dt 1:10

Fire From the LORD

11 Now the people complained about their hardships in the hearing of the LORD, and when he heard them his anger was aroused. Then fire from the LORD burned among them and consumed some of the outskirts of the camp. ²When the people cried out to Moses, he prayed to the LORD and the fire died down. ³So that place was called Taberah,ᵃ because fire from the LORD had burned among them. Lev 10:2; Nu 21:7

Quail From the LORD

⁴The rabble with them began to crave other food, and again the Israelites started wailing and said,

"If only we had meat to eat! ⁵We remember the fish we ate in Egypt at no cost—also the cucumbers, melons, leeks, onions and garlic. ⁶But now we have lost our appetite; we never see anything but this manna!" Ex 16:3; Ps 78:18

⁷The manna was like coriander seed and looked like resin. ⁸The people went around gathering it, and then ground it in a hand mill or crushed it in a mortar. They cooked it in a pot or made it into loaves. And it tasted like something made with olive oil. ⁹When the dew settled on the camp at night, the manna also came down. Ex 16:13,31

¹⁰Moses heard the people of every family wailing at the entrance to their tents. The LORD became exceedingly angry, and Moses was troubled. ¹¹He asked the LORD, "Why have you brought this trouble on your servant? What have I done to displease you that you put the burden of all these people on me? ¹²Did I conceive all these people? Did I give them birth? Why do you tell me to carry them in my arms, as a nurse carries an infant, to the land you promised on oath to their ancestors? ¹³Where can I get meat for all these people? They keep wailing to me, 'Give us meat to eat!' ¹⁴I cannot carry all these people by myself; the burden is too heavy for me. ¹⁵If this

---

ᵃ 3 *Taberah* means *burning.*

is how you are going to treat me, please go ahead and kill me—if I have found favor in your eyes—and do not let me face my own ruin." Ex 5:22; 18:18; 1Ki 19:4

16The LORD said to Moses: "Bring me seventy of Israel's elders who are known to you as leaders and officials among the people. Have them come to the tent of meeting, that they may stand there with you. 17I will come down and speak with you there, and I will take some of the power of the Spirit that is on you and put it on them. They will share the burden of the people with you so that you will not have to carry it alone. Ex 18:18; 1Sa 10:6

18"Tell the people: 'Consecrate yourselves in preparation for tomorrow, when you will eat meat. The LORD heard you when you wailed, "If only we had meat to eat! We were better off in Egypt!" Now the LORD will give you meat, and you will eat it. 19You will not eat it for just one day, or two days, or five, ten or twenty days, 20but for a whole month—until it comes out of your nostrils and you loathe it—because you have rejected the LORD, who is among you, and have wailed before him, saying, "Why did we ever leave Egypt?"'" Ex 19:10; 1Sa 10:19; Ac 7:39

21But Moses said, "Here I am among six hundred thousand men on foot, and you say, 'I will give them meat to eat for a whole month!' 22Would they have enough if flocks and herds were slaughtered for them? Would they have enough if all the fish in the sea were caught for them?"Mt 15:33

23The LORD answered Moses, "Is the LORD's arm too short? Now you will see whether or not what I say will come true for you." Isa 50:2; 59:1

24So Moses went out and told the people what the LORD had said. He brought together seventy of their elders and had them stand around the tent. 25Then the LORD came down in the cloud and spoke with him, and he took some of the power of the Spirit that was on him and put it on the seventy elders. When the Spirit rested on them, they prophesied—but did not do so again. Nu 12:5; 1Sa 10:10; Ac 2:17

26However, two men, whose names were Eldad and Medad, had remained in the camp. They were listed among the elders, but did not go out to the tent. Yet the Spirit also rested on them, and they prophesied in the camp. 27A young man ran and told Moses, "Eldad and Medad are prophesying in the camp."

28Joshua son of Nun, who had been Moses' aide since youth, spoke up and said, "Moses, my lord, stop them!" Mk 9:38-40

29But Moses replied, "Are you jealous for my sake? I wish that all the LORD's people were prophets and that the LORD would put his Spirit on them!" 30Then Moses and the elders of Israel returned to the camp. 1Co 14:5

³¹Now a wind went out from the LORD and drove quail in from the sea. It scattered them up to two cubits*a* deep all around the camp, as far as a day's walk in any direction. ³²All that day and night and all the next day the people went out and gathered quail. No one gathered less than ten homers.*b* Then they spread them out all around the camp. ³³But while the meat was still between their teeth and before it could be consumed, the anger of the LORD burned against the people, and he struck them with a severe plague. ³⁴Therefore the place was named Kibroth Hattaavah,*c* because there they buried the people who had craved other food. Ex 16:13; Ps 78:30; 106:15

³⁵From Kibroth Hattaavah the people traveled to Hazeroth and stayed there. Nu 33:17

Miriam and Aaron Oppose Moses

12 Miriam and Aaron began to talk against Moses because of his Cushite wife, for he had married a Cushite. ²"Has the LORD spoken only through Moses?" they asked. "Hasn't he also spoken through us?" And the LORD heard this. Ex 2:21; Nu 11:1

³(Now Moses was a very hum-ble man, more humble than anyone else on the face of the earth.) Mt 11:29

⁴At once the LORD said to Moses, Aaron and Miriam, "Come out to the tent of meeting, all three of you." So the three of them went out. ⁵Then the LORD came down in a pillar of cloud; he stood at the entrance to the tent and summoned Aaron and Miriam. When the two of them stepped forward, ⁶he said, "Listen to my words: Nu 11:25

"When there is a prophet among you,
I, the LORD, reveal myself to them in visions, Ge 15:1
I speak to them in dreams. Ge 31:10; Heb 1:1
⁷But this is not true of my servant Moses; Ps 105:26
he is faithful in all my house. Heb 3:2,5
⁸With him I speak face to face, clearly and not in riddles; Dt 34:10
he sees the form of the LORD. Ps 17:15
Why then were you not afraid to speak against my servant Moses?"

⁹The anger of the LORD burned against them, and he left them.

¹⁰When the cloud lifted from above the tent, Miriam's skin was leprous*d*—it became as white

---

a 31 That is, about 3 feet or about 90 centimeters   *b* 32 That is, possibly about 1 3/4 tons or about 1.6 metric tons   *c* 34 *Kibroth Hattaavah* means *graves of craving.*
d 10 The Hebrew for *leprous* was used for various diseases affecting the skin.

as snow. Aaron turned toward her and saw that she had a defiling skin disease, ¹¹ and he said to Moses, "Please, my lord, I ask you not to hold against us the sin we have so foolishly committed. ¹² Do not let her be like a stillborn infant coming from its mother's womb with its flesh half eaten away." Dt 24:9; 2Sa 19:19; 2Ki 5:1,27

¹³ So Moses cried out to the LORD, "Please, God, heal her!"

¹⁴ The LORD replied to Moses, "If her father had spit in her face, would she not have been in disgrace for seven days? Confine her outside the camp for seven days; after that she can be brought back." ¹⁵ So Miriam was confined outside the camp for seven days, and the people did not move on till she was brought back. Lev 13:46

¹⁶ After that, the people left Hazeroth and encamped in the Desert of Paran. Nu 11:35

Exploring Canaan

13 The LORD said to Moses, ² "Send some men to explore the land of Canaan, which I am giving to the Israelites. From each ancestral tribe send one of its leaders." Dt 1:22

³ So at the LORD's command Moses sent them out from the Desert of Paran. All of them were leaders of the Israelites. ⁴ These are their names: Nu 1:16

from the tribe of Reuben,
   Shammua son of Zakkur;
⁵ from the tribe of Simeon,
   Shaphat son of Hori;
⁶ from the tribe of Judah, Caleb
   son of Jephunneh; Nu 14:6,24
⁷ from the tribe of Issachar,
   Igal son of Joseph;
⁸ from the tribe of Ephraim,
   Hoshea son of Nun; Nu 11:28
⁹ from the tribe of Benjamin,
   Palti son of Raphu;
¹⁰ from the tribe of Zebulun,
   Gaddiel son of Sodi;
¹¹ from the tribe of Manasseh
   (a tribe of Joseph), Gaddi
   son of Susi;
¹² from the tribe of Dan, Ammiel son of Gemalli;
¹³ from the tribe of Asher, Sethur son of Michael;
¹⁴ from the tribe of Naphtali,
   Nahbi son of Vophsi;
¹⁵ from the tribe of Gad, Geuel
   son of Maki.

¹⁶ These are the names of the men Moses sent to explore the land. (Moses gave Hoshea son of Nun the name Joshua.) Dt 32:44

¹⁷ When Moses sent them to explore Canaan, he said, "Go up through the Negev and on into the hill country. ¹⁸ See what the land is like and whether the people who live there are strong or weak, few or many. ¹⁹ What kind of land do they live in? Is it good or bad? What kind of towns do they live in? Are they unwalled or fortified? ²⁰ How is the soil? Is it fertile or poor? Are there trees in it or not? Do your best to bring

back some of the fruit of the land." (It was the season for the first ripe grapes.)   Ge 12:9; Dt 1:25

²¹So they went up and explored the land from the Desert of Zin as far as Rehob, toward Lebo Hamath. ²²They went up through the Negev and came to Hebron, where Ahiman, Sheshai and Talmai, the descendants of Anak, lived. (Hebron had been built seven years before Zoan in Egypt.) ²³When they reached the Valley of Eshkol,ᵃ they cut off a branch bearing a single cluster of grapes. Two of them carried it on a pole between them, along with some pomegranates and figs. ²⁴That place was called the Valley of Eshkol because of the cluster of grapes the Israelites cut off there. ²⁵At the end of forty days they returned from exploring the land.   Jos 15:13-14; Ps 78:12,43

Report on the Exploration

²⁶They came back to Moses and Aaron and the whole Israelite community at Kadesh in the Desert of Paran. There they reported to them and to the whole assembly and showed them the fruit of the land. ²⁷They gave Moses this account: "We went into the land to which you sent us, and it does flow with milk and honey! Here is its fruit. ²⁸But the people who live there are powerful, and the cities are fortified

and very large. We even saw descendants of Anak there. ²⁹The Amalekites live in the Negev; the Hittites, Jebusites and Amorites live in the hill country; and the Canaanites live near the sea and along the Jordan."   Ex 3:8; Dt 1:25,28

³⁰Then Caleb silenced the people before Moses and said, "We should go up and take possession of the land, for we can certainly do it."

³¹But the men who had gone up with him said, "We can't attack those people; they are stronger than we are." ³²And they spread among the Israelites a bad report about the land they had explored. They said, "The land we explored devours those living in it. All the people we saw there are of great size. ³³We saw the Nephilim there (the descendants of Anak come from the Nephilim). We seemed like grasshoppers in our own eyes, and we looked the same to them."   Dt 1:28; 9:1; Jos 14:8

The People Rebel

14 That night all the members of the community raised their voices and wept aloud. ²All the Israelites grumbled against Moses and Aaron, and the whole assembly said to them, "If only we had died in Egypt! Or in this wilderness! ³Why is the LORD bringing us to this land only to let us fall by

---

ᵃ 23 *Eshkol* means *cluster*; also in verse 24.

the sword? Our wives and children will be taken as plunder. Wouldn't it be better for us to go back to Egypt?" ⁴And they said to each other, "We should choose a leader and go back to Egypt." Nu 11:1; Dt 1:39

⁵Then Moses and Aaron fell facedown in front of the whole Israelite assembly gathered there. ⁶Joshua son of Nun and Caleb son of Jephunneh, who were among those who had explored the land, tore their clothes ⁷and said to the entire Israelite assembly, "The land we passed through and explored is exceedingly good. ⁸If the LORD is pleased with us, he will lead us into that land, a land flowing with milk and honey, and will give it to us. ⁹Only do not rebel against the LORD. And do not be afraid of the people of the land, because we will devour them. Their protection is gone, but the LORD is with us. Do not be afraid of them." Dt 1:21; 9:7,23,24; 10:15

¹⁰But the whole assembly talked about stoning them. Then the glory of the LORD appeared at the tent of meeting to all the Israelites. ¹¹The LORD said to Moses, "How long will these people treat me with contempt? How long will they refuse to believe in me, in spite of all the signs I have performed among them? ¹²I will strike them down with a plague and destroy them, but I will make you into a nation greater and stronger than they." Ex 32:10; Lev 9:23

¹³Moses said to the LORD, "Then the Egyptians will hear about it! By your power you brought these people up from among them. ¹⁴And they will tell the inhabitants of this land about it. They have already heard that you, LORD, are with these people and that you, LORD, have been seen face to face, that your cloud stays over them, and that you go before them in a pillar of cloud by day and a pillar of fire by night. ¹⁵If you put all these people to death, leaving none alive, the nations who have heard this report about you will say, ¹⁶'The LORD was not able to bring these people into the land he promised them on oath, so he slaughtered them in the wilderness.' Ex 13:21; 15:14; 32:11-14

¹⁷"Now may the Lord's strength be displayed, just as you have declared: ¹⁸'The LORD is slow to anger, abounding in love and forgiving sin and rebellion. Yet he does not leave the guilty unpunished; he punishes the children for the sin of the parents to the third and fourth generation.' ¹⁹In accordance with your great love, forgive the sin of these people, just as you have pardoned them from the time they left Egypt until now." Ex 20:5; 34:6,9

²⁰The LORD replied, "I have forgiven them, as you asked. ²¹Nevertheless, as surely as I live and as surely as the glory of the LORD fills the whole earth,

[22]not one of those who saw my glory and the signs I performed in Egypt and in the wilderness but who disobeyed me and tested me ten times— [23]not one of them will ever see the land I promised on oath to their ancestors. No one who has treated me with contempt will ever see it. [24]But because my servant Caleb has a different spirit and follows me wholeheartedly, I will bring him into the land he went to, and his descendants will inherit it. [25]Since the Amalekites and the Canaanites are living in the valleys, turn back tomorrow and set out toward the desert along the route to the Red Sea.[a]"   Nu 32:12; Jos 14:8,14; Heb 3:18

[26]The LORD said to Moses and Aaron: [27]"How long will this wicked community grumble against me? I have heard the complaints of these grumbling Israelites. [28]So tell them, 'As surely as I live, declares the LORD, I will do to you the very thing I heard you say: [29]In this wilderness your bodies will fall—every one of you twenty years old or more who was counted in the census and who has grumbled against me. [30]Not one of you will enter the land I swore with uplifted hand to make your home, except Caleb son of Jephunneh and Joshua son of Nun. [31]As for your children

that you said would be taken as plunder, I will bring them in to enjoy the land you have rejected. [32]But as for you, your bodies will fall in this wilderness. [33]Your children will be shepherds here for forty years, suffering for your unfaithfulness, until the last of your bodies lies in the wilderness. [34]For forty years—one year for each of the forty days you explored the land—you will suffer for your sins and know what it is like to have me against you.' [35]I, the LORD, have spoken, and I will surely do these things to this whole wicked community, which has banded together against me. They will meet their end in this wilderness; here they will die."   Nu 13:25; 23:19; 1Co 10:5

[36]So the men Moses had sent to explore the land, who returned and made the whole community grumble against him by spreading a bad report about it— [37]these men who were responsible for spreading the bad report about the land were struck down and died of a plague before the LORD. [38]Of the men who went to explore the land, only Joshua son of Nun and Caleb son of Jephunneh survived.   Nu 13:32; 1Co 10:10

[39]When Moses reported this to all the Israelites, they mourned bitterly. [40]Early the next morning they set out for the highest point in the hill country, saying, "Now

[a] 25 Or the Sea of Reeds

we are ready to go up to the land the LORD promised. Surely we have sinned!" Dt 1:41

⁴¹But Moses said, "Why are you disobeying the LORD's command? This will not succeed! ⁴²Do not go up, because the LORD is not with you. You will be defeated by your enemies, ⁴³for the Amalekites and the Canaanites will face you there. Because you have turned away from the LORD, he will not be with you and you will fall by the sword." Dt 1:42; 2Ch 24:20

⁴⁴Nevertheless, in their presumption they went up toward the highest point in the hill country, though neither Moses nor the ark of the LORD's covenant moved from the camp. ⁴⁵Then the Amalekites and the Canaanites who lived in that hill country came down and attacked them and beat them down all the way to Hormah. Nu 21:3; Dt 1:43-44

Supplementary Offerings

15 The LORD said to Moses, ²"Speak to the Israelites and say to them: 'After you enter the land I am giving you as a home ³and you present to the LORD food offerings from the herd or the flock, as an aroma pleasing to the LORD — whether burnt offerings or sacrifices, for special vows or freewill offerings or festival offerings — ⁴then the person who brings an offering shall present to the LORD a grain offering of a tenth of an ephah*a* of the finest flour mixed with a quarter of a hin*b* of olive oil. ⁵With each lamb for the burnt offering or the sacrifice, prepare a quarter of a hin of wine as a drink offering. Lev 1:2; 6:14; 23:1-44

⁶" 'With a ram prepare a grain offering of two-tenths of an ephah*c* of the finest flour mixed with a third of a hin*d* of olive oil, ⁷and a third of a hin of wine as a drink offering. Offer it as an aroma pleasing to the LORD. Nu 28:12

⁸" 'When you prepare a young bull as a burnt offering or sacrifice, for a special vow or a fellowship offering to the LORD, ⁹bring with the bull a grain offering of three-tenths of an ephah*e* of the finest flour mixed with half a hin*f* of olive oil, ¹⁰and also bring half a hin of wine as a drink offering. This will be a food offering, an aroma pleasing to the LORD. ¹¹Each bull or ram, each lamb or young goat, is to be prepared in this manner. ¹²Do this for each one, for as many as you prepare. Lev 1:3; 14:10

¹³" 'Everyone who is native-born must do these things in this way when they present a food of-

---

a 4 That is, probably about 3 1/2 pounds or about 1.6 kilograms   *b 4* That is, about 1 quart or about 1 liter; also in verse 5   *c 6* That is, probably about 7 pounds or about 3.2 kilograms *d 6* That is, about 1 1/3 quarts or about 1.3 liters; also in verse 7   *e 9* That is, probably about 11 pounds or about 5 kilograms   *f 9* That is, about 2 quarts or about 1.9 liters; also in verse 10 fering as an aroma pleasing to the LORD. ¹⁴For the generations to come, whenever a foreigner or anyone else living among you presents a food offering as an aroma pleasing to the LORD, they must do exactly as you do. ¹⁵The community is to have the same rules for you and for the foreigner residing among you; this is a lasting ordinance for the generations to come. You and the foreigner shall be the same before the LORD: ¹⁶The same laws and regulations will apply both to you and to the foreigner residing among you.' " ver 29; Nu 9:14

¹⁷The LORD said to Moses, ¹⁸"Speak to the Israelites and say to them: 'When you enter the land to which I am taking you ¹⁹and you eat the food of the land, present a portion as an offering to the LORD. ²⁰Present a loaf from the first of your ground meal and present it as an offering from the threshing floor. ²¹Throughout the generations to come you are to give this offering to the LORD from the first of your ground meal. Jos 5:11-12; Ro 11:16

Offerings for Unintentional Sins

²²" 'Now if you as a community unintentionally fail to keep any of these commands the LORD gave Moses— ²³any of the LORD's commands to you through him, from the day the LORD gave them and continuing through the generations to come— ²⁴and if this is done unintentionally without the community being aware of it, then the whole community is to offer a young bull for a burnt offering as an aroma pleasing to the LORD, along with its prescribed grain offering and drink offering, and a male goat for a sin offering.ᵃ ²⁵The priest is to make atonement for the whole Israelite community, and they will be forgiven, for it was not intentional and they have presented to the LORD for their wrong a food offering and a sin offering. ²⁶The whole Israelite community and the foreigners residing among them will be forgiven, because all the people were involved in the unintentional wrong. Lev 4:2,14,20

²⁷" 'But if just one person sins unintentionally, that person must bring a year-old female goat for a sin offering. ²⁸The priest is to make atonement before the LORD for the one who erred by sinning unintentionally, and when atonement has been made, that person will be forgiven. ²⁹One and the same law applies to everyone who sins unintentionally, whether a native-born Israelite or a foreigner residing among you. Lev 4:27,35

³⁰" 'But anyone who sins defiantly, whether native-born or foreigner, blasphemes the LORD

and must be cut off from the people of Israel. [31]Because they have despised the LORD's word and broken his commands, they must surely be cut off; their guilt remains on them.'" Lev 5:1; Dt 17:13

The Sabbath-Breaker Put to Death

[32]While the Israelites were in the wilderness, a man was found gathering wood on the Sabbath day. [33]Those who found him gathering wood brought him to Moses and Aaron and the whole assembly, [34]and they kept him in custody, because it was not clear what should be done to him. [35]Then the LORD said to Moses, "The man must die. The whole assembly must stone him outside the camp." [36]So the assembly took him outside the camp and stoned him to death, as the LORD commanded Moses. Ex 31:14-15; Lev 24:14

Tassels on Garments

[37]The LORD said to Moses, [38]"Speak to the Israelites and say to them: 'Throughout the generations to come you are to make tassels on the corners of your garments, with a blue cord on each tassel. [39]You will have these tassels to look at and so you will remember all the commands of the LORD, that you may obey them and not prosti-

tute yourselves by chasing after the lusts of your own hearts and eyes. [40]Then you will remember to obey all my commands and will be consecrated to your God. [41]I am the LORD your God, who brought you out of Egypt to be your God. I am the LORD your God.'" Lev 11:44; Ro 12:1; Col 1:22

Korah, Dathan and Abiram

16 Korah son of Izhar, the son of Kohath, the son of Levi, and certain Reubenites — Dathan and Abiram, sons of Eliab, and On son of Peleth — became insolent[a] [2]and rose up against Moses. With them were 250 Israelite men, well-known community leaders who had been appointed members of the council. [3]They came as a group to oppose Moses and Aaron and said to them, "You have gone too far! The whole community is holy, every one of them, and the LORD is with them. Why then do you set yourselves above the LORD's assembly?" Ex 19:6; Ps 106:16

[4]When Moses heard this, he fell facedown. [5]Then he said to Korah and all his followers: "In the morning the LORD will show who belongs to him and who is holy, and he will have that person come near him. The man he chooses he will cause to come near him. [6]You, Korah, and all your followers are to do this:

---

[a] 1 Or Peleth — took men

Take censers [7] and tomorrow put burning coals and incense in them before the LORD. The man the LORD chooses will be the one who is holy. You Levites have gone too far!" Nu 14:5; 17:5

[8] Moses also said to Korah, "Now listen, you Levites! [9] Isn't it enough for you that the God of Israel has separated you from the rest of the Israelite community and brought you near himself to do the work at the LORD's tabernacle and to stand before the community and minister to them? [10] He has brought you and all your fellow Levites near himself, but now you are trying to get the priesthood too. [11] It is against the LORD that you and all your followers have banded together. Who is Aaron that you should grumble against him?" Dt 10:8; 1Co 10:10

[12] Then Moses summoned Dathan and Abiram, the sons of Eliab. But they said, "We will not come! [13] Isn't it enough that you have brought us up out of a land flowing with milk and honey to kill us in the wilderness? And now you also want to lord it over us! [14] Moreover, you haven't brought us into a land flowing with milk and honey or given us an inheritance of fields and vineyards. Do you want to treat these men like slaves[a]? No, we will not come!" Lev 20:24; Ac 7:27,35

[15] Then Moses became very angry and said to the LORD, "Do not accept their offering. I have not taken so much as a donkey from them, nor have I wronged any of them." 1Sa 12:3

[16] Moses said to Korah, "You and all your followers are to appear before the LORD tomorrow—you and they and Aaron. [17] Each man is to take his censer and put incense in it—250 censers in all—and present it before the LORD. You and Aaron are to present your censers also." [18] So each of them took his censer, put burning coals and incense in it, and stood with Moses and Aaron at the entrance to the tent of meeting. [19] When Korah had gathered all his followers in opposition to them at the entrance to the tent of meeting, the glory of the LORD appeared to the entire assembly. [20] The LORD said to Moses and Aaron, [21] "Separate yourselves from this assembly so I can put an end to them at once." Ex 32:10; Nu 14:10

[22] But Moses and Aaron fell facedown and cried out, "O God, the God who gives breath to all living things, will you be angry with the entire assembly when only one man sins?" Ge 18:23; Job 21:20

[23] Then the LORD said to Moses, [24] "Say to the assembly, 'Move away from the tents of Korah, Dathan and Abiram.'"

[25] Moses got up and went to

---

[a] 14 Or *to deceive these men*; Hebrew *Will you gouge out the eyes of these men*

Dathan and Abiram, and the elders of Israel followed him. ²⁶He warned the assembly, "Move back from the tents of these wicked men! Do not touch anything belonging to them, or you will be swept away because of all their sins." ²⁷So they moved away from the tents of Korah, Dathan and Abiram. Dathan and Abiram had come out and were standing with their wives, children and little ones at the entrances to their tents. Ge 19:15; Isa 52:11

²⁸Then Moses said, "This is how you will know that the LORD has sent me to do all these things and that it was not my idea: ²⁹If these men die a natural death and suffer the fate of all mankind, then the LORD has not sent me. ³⁰But if the LORD brings about something totally new, and the earth opens its mouth and swallows them, with everything that belongs to them, and they go down alive into the realm of the dead, then you will know that these men have treated the LORD with contempt." Ex 3:12; Jn 5:36; 6:38

³¹As soon as he finished saying all this, the ground under them split apart ³²and the earth opened its mouth and swallowed them and their households, and all those associated with Korah, together with their possessions. ³³They went down alive into the realm of the dead, with everything they owned; the earth closed over them, and they per-ished and were gone from the community. ³⁴At their cries, all the Israelites around them fled, shouting, "The earth is going to swallow us too!" Nu 26:11; Mic 1:3-4

³⁵And fire came out from the LORD and consumed the 250 men who were offering the incense. Nu 11:1-3; 26:10

³⁶The LORD said to Moses, ³⁷"Tell Eleazar son of Aaron, the priest, to remove the censers from the charred remains and scatter the coals some distance away, for the censers are holy — ³⁸the censers of the men who sinned at the cost of their lives. Hammer the censers into sheets to overlay the altar, for they were presented before the LORD and have become holy. Let them be a sign to the Israelites." Nu 26:10; Pr 20:2; Eze 14:8

³⁹So Eleazar the priest collected the bronze censers brought by those who had been burned to death, and he had them hammered out to overlay the altar, ⁴⁰as the LORD directed him through Moses. This was to remind the Israelites that no one except a descendant of Aaron should come to burn incense before the LORD, or he would become like Korah and his followers. Nu 3:10; 2Ch 26:18; Ex 30:7-10

⁴¹The next day the whole Israelite community grumbled against Moses and Aaron. "You have killed the LORD's people," they said.

⁴²But when the assembly gathered in opposition to Moses and Aaron and turned toward the tent of meeting, suddenly the cloud covered it and the glory of the LORD appeared. ⁴³Then Moses and Aaron went to the front of the tent of meeting, ⁴⁴and the LORD said to Moses, ⁴⁵"Get away from this assembly so I can put an end to them at once." And they fell facedown. ver 19; Nu 20:6

⁴⁶Then Moses said to Aaron, "Take your censer and put incense in it, along with burning coals from the altar, and hurry to the assembly to make atonement for them. Wrath has come out from the LORD; the plague has started." ⁴⁷So Aaron did as Moses said, and ran into the midst of the assembly. The plague had already started among the people, but Aaron offered the incense and made atonement for them. ⁴⁸He stood between the living and the dead, and the plague stopped. ⁴⁹But 14,700 people died from the plague, in addition to those who had died because of Korah. ⁵⁰Then Aaron returned to Moses at the entrance to the tent of meeting, for the plague had stopped.ᵃ Ps 106:30; Nu 8:19; 25:13

The Budding of Aaron's Staff

17ᵇ The LORD said to Moses, ²"Speak to the Israelites and get twelve staffs from them, one from the leader of each of their ancestral tribes. Write the name of each man on his staff. ³On the staff of Levi write Aaron's name, for there must be one staff for the head of each ancestral tribe. ⁴Place them in the tent of meeting in front of the ark of the covenant law, where I meet with you. ⁵The staff belonging to the man I choose will sprout, and I will rid myself of this constant grumbling against you by the Israelites." Nu 16:5; Ex 16:7; 25:22

⁶So Moses spoke to the Israelites, and their leaders gave him twelve staffs, one for the leader of each of their ancestral tribes, and Aaron's staff was among them. ⁷Moses placed the staffs before the LORD in the tent of the covenant law. Ex 38:21; Ac 7:44

⁸The next day Moses entered the tent and saw that Aaron's staff, which represented the tribe of Levi, had not only sprouted but had budded, blossomed and produced almonds. ⁹Then Moses brought out all the staffs from the LORD's presence to all the Israelites. They looked at them, and each of the leaders took his own staff. Eze 17:24; Heb 9:4

¹⁰The LORD said to Moses, "Put back Aaron's staff in front of the ark of the covenant law, to be kept as a sign to the rebellious. This will put an end to their grumbling against me, so

---

ᵃ 50 In Hebrew texts 16:36-50 is numbered 17:1-15.   ᵇ In Hebrew texts 17:1-13 is numbered 17:16-28.

that they will not die." [11] Moses did just as the LORD commanded him. Dt 9:24

[12] The Israelites said to Moses, "We will die! We are lost, we are all lost! [13] Anyone who even comes near the tabernacle of the LORD will die. Are we all going to die?" Nu 1:51

Duties of Priests and Levites

18 The LORD said to Aaron, "You, your sons and your family are to bear the responsibility for offenses connected with the sanctuary, and you and your sons alone are to bear the responsibility for offenses connected with the priesthood. [2] Bring your fellow Levites from your ancestral tribe to join you and assist you when you and your sons minister before the tent of the covenant law. [3] They are to be responsible to you and are to perform all the duties of the tent, but they must not go near the furnishings of the sanctuary or the altar. Otherwise both they and you will die. [4] They are to join you and be responsible for the care of the tent of meeting — all the work at the tent — and no one else may come near where you are. Nu 3:10; 4:15

[5] "You are to be responsible for the care of the sanctuary and the altar, so that my wrath will not fall on the Israelites again. [6] I myself have selected your fellow Levites from among the Israelites as a gift to you, dedicated to the LORD to do the work at the tent of meeting. [7] But only you and your sons may serve as priests in connection with everything at the altar and inside the curtain. I am giving you the service of the priesthood as a gift. Anyone else who comes near the sanctuary is to be put to death." Ex 29:9; Nu 3:9; Heb 9:3,6

Offerings for Priests and Levites

[8] Then the LORD said to Aaron, "I myself have put you in charge of the offerings presented to me; all the holy offerings the Israelites give me I give to you and your sons as your portion, your perpetual share. [9] You are to have the part of the most holy offerings that is kept from the fire. From all the gifts they bring me as most holy offerings, whether grain or sin[a] or guilt offerings, that part belongs to you and your sons. [10] Eat it as something most holy; every male shall eat it. You must regard it as holy. Lev 6:16,25

[11] "This also is yours: whatever is set aside from the gifts of all the wave offerings of the Israelites. I give this to you and your sons and daughters as your perpetual share. Everyone in your household who is ceremonially clean may eat it. Ex 29:26; Lev 22:1-16

[12] "I give you all the finest olive

a 9 Or purification

oil and all the finest new wine and grain they give the LORD as the firstfruits of their harvest. ¹³All the land's firstfruits that they bring to the LORD will be yours. Everyone in your household who is ceremonially clean may eat it. Ex 23:19; Ne 10:35

¹⁴"Everything in Israel that is devoted[a] to the LORD is yours. ¹⁵The first offspring of every womb, both human and animal, that is offered to the LORD is yours. But you must redeem every firstborn son and every firstborn male of unclean animals. ¹⁶When they are a month old, you must redeem them at the redemption price set at five shekels[b] of silver, according to the sanctuary shekel, which weighs twenty gerahs. Ex 13:2; Lev 27:6,28

¹⁷"But you must not redeem the firstborn of a cow, a sheep or a goat; they are holy. Splash their blood against the altar and burn their fat as a food offering, an aroma pleasing to the LORD. ¹⁸Their meat is to be yours, just as the breast of the wave offering and the right thigh are yours. ¹⁹Whatever is set aside from the holy offerings the Israelites present to the LORD I give to you and your sons and daughters as your perpetual share. It is an everlasting covenant of salt before the LORD for both you and your offspring." 2Ch 13:5; Lev 3:2

²⁰The LORD said to Aaron, "You will have no inheritance in their land, nor will you have any share among them; I am your share and your inheritance among the Israelites. Dt 10:9; 18:1-2; Jos 13:33

²¹"I give to the Levites all the tithes in Israel as their inheritance in return for the work they do while serving at the tent of meeting. ²²From now on the Israelites must not go near the tent of meeting, or they will bear the consequences of their sin and will die. ²³It is the Levites who are to do the work at the tent of meeting and bear the responsibility for any offenses they commit against it. This is a lasting ordinance for the generations to come. They will receive no inheritance among the Israelites. ²⁴Instead, I give to the Levites as their inheritance the tithes that the Israelites present as an offering to the LORD. That is why I said concerning them: 'They will have no inheritance among the Israelites.'" Lev 27:30-33; Nu 1:51

²⁵The LORD said to Moses, ²⁶"Speak to the Levites and say to them: 'When you receive from the Israelites the tithe I give you as your inheritance, you must present a tenth of that tithe as the LORD's offering. ²⁷Your offering will be reckoned to you as grain from the threshing floor or juice from the winepress. ²⁸In this way

[a] 14 The Hebrew term refers to the irrevocable giving over of things or persons to the LORD.
[b] 16 That is, about 2 ounces or about 58 grams

you also will present an offering to the LORD from all the tithes you receive from the Israelites. From these tithes you must give the LORD's portion to Aaron the priest. ²⁹You must present as the LORD's portion the best and holiest part of everything given to you.' Ne 10:38; Mal 3:8

³⁰ "Say to the Levites: 'When you present the best part, it will be reckoned to you as the product of the threshing floor or the winepress. ³¹You and your households may eat the rest of it anywhere, for it is your wages for your work at the tent of meeting. ³²By presenting the best part of it you will not be guilty in this matter; then you will not defile the holy offerings of the Israelites, and you will not die.'" Lev 19:8; 22:15

The Water of Cleansing

19 The LORD said to Moses and Aaron: ² "This is a requirement of the law that the LORD has commanded: Tell the Israelites to bring you a red heifer without defect or blemish and that has never been under a yoke. ³Give it to Eleazar the priest; it is to be taken outside the camp and slaughtered in his presence. ⁴Then Eleazar the priest is to take some of its blood on his finger and sprinkle it seven times toward the front of the tent of meeting. ⁵While he watches, the heifer is to be burned—its hide, flesh, blood and intestines. ⁶The priest is to take some cedar wood, hyssop and scarlet wool and throw them onto the burning heifer. ⁷After that, the priest must wash his clothes and bathe himself with water. He may then come into the camp, but he will be ceremonially unclean till evening. ⁸The man who burns it must also wash his clothes and bathe with water, and he too will be unclean till evening. Ex 29:14; Lev 4:12,21; Dt 21:3

⁹ "A man who is clean shall gather up the ashes of the heifer and put them in a ceremonially clean place outside the camp. They are to be kept by the Israelite community for use in the water of cleansing; it is for purification from sin. ¹⁰The man who gathers up the ashes of the heifer must also wash his clothes, and he too will be unclean till evening. This will be a lasting ordinance both for the Israelites and for the foreigners residing among them. ver 13; Nu 8:7; Heb 9:13

¹¹ "Whoever touches a human corpse will be unclean for seven days. ¹²They must purify themselves with the water on the third day and on the seventh day; then they will be clean. But if they do not purify themselves on the third and seventh days, they will not be clean. ¹³If they fail to purify themselves after touching a human corpse, they defile the

LORD's tabernacle. They must be cut off from Israel. Because the water of cleansing has not been sprinkled on them, they are unclean; their uncleanness remains on them. Lev 7:20; 21:1; Nu 31:19

14 "This is the law that applies when a person dies in a tent: Anyone who enters the tent and anyone who is in it will be unclean for seven days, 15 and every open container without a lid fastened on it will be unclean.

16 "Anyone out in the open who touches someone who has been killed with a sword or someone who has died a natural death, or anyone who touches a human bone or a grave, will be unclean for seven days. Nu 31:19; Mt 23:27

17 "For the unclean person, put some ashes from the burned purification offering into a jar and pour fresh water over them. 18 Then a man who is ceremonially clean is to take some hyssop, dip it in the water and sprinkle the tent and all the furnishings and the people who were there. He must also sprinkle anyone who has touched a human bone or a grave or anyone who has been killed or anyone who has died a natural death. 19 The man who is clean is to sprinkle those who are unclean on the third and seventh days, and on the seventh day he is to purify them. Those who are being cleansed must wash their clothes and bathe with water, and that eve-

ning they will be clean. 20 But if those who are unclean do not purify themselves, they must be cut off from the community, because they have defiled the sanctuary of the LORD. The water of cleansing has not been sprinkled on them, and they are unclean. 21 This is a lasting ordinance for them. Eze 36:25; Heb 10:22

"The man who sprinkles the water of cleansing must also wash his clothes, and anyone who touches the water of cleansing will be unclean till evening. 22 Anything that an unclean person touches becomes unclean, and anyone who touches it becomes unclean till evening." Lev 5:2

Water From the Rock

20 In the first month the whole Israelite community arrived at the Desert of Zin, and they stayed at Kadesh. There Miriam died and was buried. Ex 15:20; Nu 33:36

2 Now there was no water for the community, and the people gathered in opposition to Moses and Aaron. 3 They quarreled with Moses and said, "If only we had died when our brothers fell dead before the LORD! 4 Why did you bring the LORD's community into this wilderness, that we and our livestock should die here? 5 Why did you bring us up out of Egypt to this terrible place? It has no grain or

figs, grapevines or pomegranates. And there is no water to drink!" Ex 14:11; 17:1-2

⁶Moses and Aaron went from the assembly to the entrance to the tent of meeting and fell facedown, and the glory of the LORD appeared to them. ⁷The LORD said to Moses, ⁸"Take the staff, and you and your brother Aaron gather the assembly together. Speak to that rock before their eyes and it will pour out its water. You will bring water out of the rock for the community so they and their livestock can drink." Ex 17:6; Isa 43:20; Nu 14:5

⁹So Moses took the staff from the LORD's presence, just as he commanded him. ¹⁰He and Aaron gathered the assembly together in front of the rock and Moses said to them, "Listen, you rebels, must we bring you water out of this rock?" ¹¹Then Moses raised his arm and struck the rock twice with his staff. Water gushed out, and the community and their livestock drank. Ex 17:6; Nu 17:10; Ps 106:32-33

¹²But the LORD said to Moses and Aaron, "Because you did not trust in me enough to honor me as holy in the sight of the Israelites, you will not bring this community into the land I give them." Nu 27:14; Dt 1:37

¹³These were the waters of Meribah,ᵃ where the Israelites quarreled with the LORD and where he was proved holy among them. Ex 17:7

Edom Denies Israel Passage

¹⁴Moses sent messengers from Kadesh to the king of Edom, saying: Dt 2:4; Jdg 11:16-17

"This is what your brother Israel says: You know about all the hardships that have come on us. ¹⁵Our ancestors went down into Egypt, and we lived there many years. The Egyptians mistreated us and our ancestors, ¹⁶but when we cried out to the LORD, he heard our cry and sent an angel and brought us out of Egypt. Ex 2:23; 14:19

"Now we are here at Kadesh, a town on the edge of your territory. ¹⁷Please let us pass through your country. We will not go through any field or vineyard, or drink water from any well. We will travel along the King's Highway and not turn to the right or to the left until we have passed through your territory." Nu 21:22

¹⁸But Edom answered:

"You may not pass through here; if you try, we will march out and attack you with the sword." Nu 21:23

ᵃ 13 Meribah means quarreling.

¹⁹The Israelites replied:

"We will go along the main road, and if we or our livestock drink any of your water, we will pay for it. We only want to pass through on foot—nothing else." Dt 2:6,28

²⁰Again they answered:

"You may not pass through."

Then Edom came out against them with a large and powerful army. ²¹Since Edom refused to let them go through their territory, Israel turned away from them. Dt 2:8; Jdg 11:18

The Death of Aaron

²²The whole Israelite community set out from Kadesh and came to Mount Hor. ²³At Mount Hor, near the border of Edom, the LORD said to Moses and Aaron, ²⁴"Aaron will be gathered to his people. He will not enter the land I give the Israelites, because both of you rebelled against my command at the waters of Meribah. ²⁵Get Aaron and his son Eleazar and take them up Mount Hor. ²⁶Remove Aaron's garments and put them on his son Eleazar, for Aaron will be gathered to his people; he will die there." ver 10; Ge 25:8

²⁷Moses did as the LORD commanded: They went up Mount Hor in the sight of the whole community. ²⁸Moses removed Aaron's garments and put them on his son Eleazar. And Aaron died there on top of the mountain. Then Moses and Eleazar came down from the mountain, ²⁹and when the whole community learned that Aaron had died, all the Israelites mourned for him thirty days. Ex 29:29; Nu 33:38; Dt 34:8

Arad Destroyed

21 When the Canaanite king of Arad, who lived in the Negev, heard that Israel was coming along the road to Atharim, he attacked the Israelites and captured some of them. ²Then Israel made this vow to the LORD: "If you will deliver these people into our hands, we will totally destroy^a their cities." ³The LORD listened to Israel's plea and gave the Canaanites over to them. They completely destroyed them and their towns; so the place was named Hormah.^b Ex 22:20; Nu 33:40

The Bronze Snake

⁴They traveled from Mount Hor along the route to the Red Sea,^c to go around Edom. But the people grew impatient on the way; ⁵they spoke against God and against Moses, and said, "Why have you brought us up out of Egypt to die in the wilder-

---

^a 2 The Hebrew term refers to the irrevocable giving over of things or persons to the LORD, often by totally destroying them; also in verse 3.   ^b 3 Hormah means destruction.
^c 4 Or the Sea of Reeds

ness? There is no bread! There is no water! And we detest this miserable food!"   Ps 78:19; Nu 20:22

⁶Then the LORD sent venomous snakes among them; they bit the people and many Israelites died. ⁷The people came to Moses and said, "We sinned when we spoke against the LORD and against you. Pray that the LORD will take the snakes away from us." So Moses prayed for the people.   Dt 8:15; Ps 78:34; Ac 8:24

⁸The LORD said to Moses, "Make a snake and put it up on a pole; anyone who is bitten can look at it and live." ⁹So Moses made a bronze snake and put it up on a pole. Then when anyone was bitten by a snake and looked at the bronze snake, they lived.   Jn 3:14-15; 2Ki 18:4

The Journey to Moab

¹⁰The Israelites moved on and camped at Oboth. ¹¹Then they set out from Oboth and camped in Iye Abarim, in the wilderness that faces Moab toward the sunrise. ¹²From there they moved on and camped in the Zered Valley. ¹³They set out from there and camped alongside the Arnon, which is in the wilderness extending into Amorite territory. The Arnon is the border of Moab, between Moab and the Amorites. ¹⁴That is why the Book of the Wars of the LORD says: Nu 33:44; Dt 2:13-14

". . . Zahab^a in Suphah and the
     ravines,
   the Arnon ¹⁵and^b the slopes
     of the ravines
that lead to the settlement
     of Ar   Dt 2:9,18
and lie along the border of
     Moab."

¹⁶From there they continued on to Beer, the well where the LORD said to Moses, "Gather the people together and I will give them water."

¹⁷Then Israel sang this song:

"Spring up, O well!
   Sing about it,
¹⁸about the well that the princes
     dug,
   that the nobles of the people
     sank—
   the nobles with scepters
     and staffs."

Then they went from the wilderness to Mattanah, ¹⁹from Mattanah to Nahaliel, from Nahaliel to Bamoth, ²⁰and from Bamoth to the valley in Moab where the top of Pisgah overlooks the wasteland.

Defeat of Sihon and Og

²¹Israel sent messengers to say to Sihon king of the Amorites: Dt 1:4; Jdg 11:19-21

²²"Let us pass through your country. We will not turn aside into any field or

---

^{a} 14 Septuagint; Hebrew *Waheb* ^{b} 14,15 Or *"I have been given from Suphah and the ravines / of the Arnon* ¹⁵*to* vineyard, or drink water from any well. We will travel along the King's Highway until we have passed through your territory." Nu 20:17

²³ But Sihon would not let Israel pass through his territory. He mustered his entire army and marched out into the wilderness against Israel. When he reached Jahaz, he fought with Israel. ²⁴ Israel, however, put him to the sword and took over his land from the Arnon to the Jabbok, but only as far as the Ammonites, because their border was fortified. ²⁵ Israel captured all the cities of the Amorites and occupied them, including Heshbon and all its surrounding settlements. ²⁶ Heshbon was the city of Sihon king of the Amorites, who had fought against the former king of Moab and had taken from him all his land as far as the Arnon. Dt 2:32; 29:7; Ps 135:10-11

²⁷ That is why the poets say:

"Come to Heshbon and let it
    be rebuilt;
  let Sihon's city be restored.

²⁸ "Fire went out from Heshbon,
    a blaze from the city of
      Sihon. Jer 48:45
  It consumed Ar of Moab,
    the citizens of Arnon's
      heights. Isa 15:2
²⁹ Woe to you, Moab!
  You are destroyed, people of
    Chemosh! Jdg 11:24

He has given up his sons as
    fugitives
  and his daughters as
    captives
  to Sihon king of the
    Amorites.
³⁰ "But we have overthrown
    them;
  Heshbon's dominion has
    been destroyed all the
    way to Dibon. Nu 32:3
We have demolished them as
    far as Nophah,
  which extends to
    Medeba."

³¹ So Israel settled in the land of the Amorites.

³² After Moses had sent spies to Jazer, the Israelites captured its surrounding settlements and drove out the Amorites who were there. ³³ Then they turned and went up along the road toward Bashan, and Og king of Bashan and his whole army marched out to meet them in battle at Edrei. Nu 32:1,3,35; Dt 13:1,10

³⁴ The LORD said to Moses, "Do not be afraid of him, for I have delivered him into your hands, along with his whole army and his land. Do to him what you did to Sihon king of the Amorites, who reigned in Heshbon." Dt 3:2

³⁵ So they struck him down, together with his sons and his whole army, leaving them no survivors. And they took possession of his land.

Balak Summons Balaam

22 Then the Israelites traveled to the plains of Moab and camped along the Jordan across from Jericho. Nu 33:48 ² Now Balak son of Zippor saw all that Israel had done to the Amorites, ³ and Moab was terrified because there were so many people. Indeed, Moab was filled with dread because of the Israelites. Ex 15:15

⁴ The Moabites said to the elders of Midian, "This horde is going to lick up everything around us, as an ox licks up the grass of the field."

So Balak son of Zippor, who was king of Moab at that time, ⁵ sent messengers to summon Balaam son of Beor, who was at Pethor, near the Euphrates River, in his native land. Balak said: Dt 23:4; 2Pe 2:15

"A people has come out of Egypt; they cover the face of the land and have settled next to me. ⁶ Now come and put a curse on these people, because they are too powerful for me. Perhaps then I will be able to defeat them and drive them out of the land. For I know that whoever you bless is blessed, and whoever you curse is cursed." Nu 23:7,11,13

⁷ The elders of Moab and Midian left, taking with them the fee for divination. When they came to Balaam, they told him what Balak had said. Ge 30:27

⁸ "Spend the night here," Balaam said to them, "and I will report back to you with the answer the LORD gives me." So the Moabite officials stayed with him.

⁹ God came to Balaam and asked, "Who are these men with you?" Ge 20:3

¹⁰ Balaam said to God, "Balak son of Zippor, king of Moab, sent me this message: ¹¹ 'A people that has come out of Egypt covers the face of the land. Now come and put a curse on them for me. Perhaps then I will be able to fight them and drive them away.'"

¹² But God said to Balaam, "Do not go with them. You must not put a curse on those people, because they are blessed." Ge 12:2; 22:17

¹³ The next morning Balaam got up and said to Balak's officials, "Go back to your own country, for the LORD has refused to let me go with you."

¹⁴ So the Moabite officials returned to Balak and said, "Balaam refused to come with us."

¹⁵ Then Balak sent other officials, more numerous and more distinguished than the first. ¹⁶ They came to Balaam and said:

"This is what Balak son of Zippor says: Do not let anything keep you from coming to me, ¹⁷ because I will reward you handsomely and do whatever you say. Come and put a curse on these people for me."

¹⁸But Balaam answered them, "Even if Balak gave me all the silver and gold in his palace, I could not do anything great or small to go beyond the command of the LORD my God. ¹⁹Now spend the night here so that I can find out what else the LORD will tell me."   Nu 24:13; 1Ki 22:14; 2Ch 18:13

²⁰That night God came to Balaam and said, "Since these men have come to summon you, go with them, but do only what I tell you."   Nu 23:5,12,16,26

Balaam's Donkey

²¹Balaam got up in the morning, saddled his donkey and went with the Moabite officials. ²²But God was very angry when he went, and the angel of the LORD stood in the road to oppose him. Balaam was riding on his donkey, and his two servants were with him. ²³When the donkey saw the angel of the LORD standing in the road with a drawn sword in his hand, it turned off the road into a field. Balaam beat it to get it back on the road.   Ex 23:20

²⁴Then the angel of the LORD stood in a narrow path through the vineyards, with walls on both sides. ²⁵When the donkey saw the angel of the LORD, it pressed close to the wall, crushing Balaam's foot against it. So he beat the donkey again.

²⁶Then the angel of the LORD moved on ahead and stood in a narrow place where there was no room to turn, either to the right or to the left. ²⁷When the donkey saw the angel of the LORD, it lay down under Balaam, and he was angry and beat it with his staff. ²⁸Then the LORD opened the donkey's mouth, and it said to Balaam, "What have I done to you to make you beat me these three times?"   Jas 1:19; 2Pe 2:16

²⁹Balaam answered the donkey, "You have made a fool of me! If only I had a sword in my hand, I would kill you right now."   Pr 12:10

³⁰The donkey said to Balaam, "Am I not your own donkey, which you have always ridden, to this day? Have I been in the habit of doing this to you?"

"No," he said.

³¹Then the LORD opened Balaam's eyes, and he saw the angel of the LORD standing in the road with his sword drawn. So he bowed low and fell facedown.   Ge 21:19

³²The angel of the LORD asked him, "Why have you beaten your donkey these three times? I have come here to oppose you because your path is a reckless one before me.ᵃ ³³The donkey saw me and turned away from me these three times. If it had not

ᵃ 32 The meaning of the Hebrew for this clause is uncertain.

turned away, I would certainly have killed you by now, but I would have spared it."

³⁴Balaam said to the angel of the LORD, "I have sinned. I did not realize you were standing in the road to oppose me. Now if you are displeased, I will go back." Nu 14:40

³⁵The angel of the LORD said to Balaam, "Go with the men, but speak only what I tell you." So Balaam went with Balak's officials.

³⁶When Balak heard that Balaam was coming, he went out to meet him at the Moabite town on the Arnon border, at the edge of his territory. ³⁷Balak said to Balaam, "Did I not send you an urgent summons? Why didn't you come to me? Am I really not able to reward you?" Nu 21:13

³⁸"Well, I have come to you now," Balaam replied. "But I can't say whatever I please. I must speak only what God puts in my mouth." Nu 23:5,16,26

³⁹Then Balaam went with Balak to Kiriath Huzoth. ⁴⁰Balak sacrificed cattle and sheep, and gave some to Balaam and the officials who were with him. ⁴¹The next morning Balak took Balaam up to Bamoth Baal, and from there he could see the outskirts of the Israelite camp. Nu 21:28; 23:13

Balaam's First Message

23 Balaam said, "Build me seven altars here, and prepare seven bulls and seven rams for me." ²Balak did as Balaam said, and the two of them offered a bull and a ram on each altar. ver 14,30; Nu 22:40

³Then Balaam said to Balak, "Stay here beside your offering while I go aside. Perhaps the LORD will come to meet with me. Whatever he reveals to me I will tell you." Then he went off to a barren height. ver 15

⁴God met with him, and Balaam said, "I have prepared seven altars, and on each altar I have offered a bull and a ram."

⁵The LORD put a word in Balaam's mouth and said, "Go back to Balak and give him this word." Dt 18:18; Jer 1:9

⁶So he went back to him and found him standing beside his offering, with all the Moabite officials. ⁷Then Balaam spoke his message: ver 18; Nu 24:3,21

"Balak brought me from
    Aram,
  the king of Moab from the
    eastern mountains.
'Come,' he said, 'curse Jacob
    for me;
  come, denounce
    Israel.' Nu 22:6
⁸How can I curse
  those whom God has not
    cursed? Nu 22:12
How can I denounce
  those whom the LORD has
    not denounced?
⁹From the rocky peaks I see
    them,

from the heights I view
them.
I see a people who live apart
and do not consider
themselves one of the
nations. Dt 32:8; 33:28
[10] Who can count the dust of
Jacob
or number even a fourth of
Israel?
Let me die the death of the
righteous,
and may my final end be
like theirs!" Ps 37:37

[11] Balak said to Balaam, "What have you done to me? I brought you to curse my enemies, but you have done nothing but bless them!" Nu 24:10; Ne 13:2

[12] He answered, "Must I not speak what the LORD puts in my mouth?" Nu 22:20,38

Balaam's Second Message

[13] Then Balak said to him, "Come with me to another place where you can see them; you will not see them all but only the outskirts of their camp. And from there, curse them for me." [14] So he took him to the field of Zophim on the top of Pisgah, and there he built seven altars and offered a bull and a ram on each altar.

[15] Balaam said to Balak, "Stay here beside your offering while I meet with him over there."

[16] The LORD met with Balaam and put a word in his mouth and said, "Go back to Balak and give him this word." Nu 22:38

[17] So he went to him and found him standing beside his offering, with the Moabite officials. Balak asked him, "What did the LORD say?"

[18] Then he spoke his message:

"Arise, Balak, and listen;
hear me, son of Zippor.
[19] God is not human, that he
should lie, Isa 55:9; Hos 11:9
not a human being, that
he should change his
mind. 1Sa 15:29; Mal 3:6
Does he speak and then not
act?
Does he promise and not
fulfill?
[20] I have received a command to
bless;
he has blessed, and I cannot
change it. Ge 22:17; Nu 22:12

[21] "No misfortune is seen in
Jacob, Ps 32:2,5; Ro 4:7-8
no misery observed[a] in
Israel.
The LORD their God is with
them;
the shout of the King is
among them. Ps 89:15-18
[22] God brought them out of
Egypt;
they have the strength of a
wild ox. Nu 24:8; Dt 33:17
[23] There is no divination
against[b] Jacob,

---

[a] 21 Or *He has not looked on Jacob's offenses / or on the wrongs found* [b] 23 Or *in*

no evil omens against[a]
    Israel.   Nu 24:1; Jos 13:22
It will now be said of Jacob
    and of Israel, 'See what God
    has done!'
24 The people rise like a lioness;
    they rouse themselves like a
    lion   Ge 49:9
that does not rest till it
    devours its prey
and drinks the blood of its
    victims."

25 Then Balak said to Balaam, "Neither curse them at all nor bless them at all!"

26 Balaam answered, "Did I not tell you I must do whatever the LORD says?"

Balaam's Third Message

27 Then Balak said to Balaam, "Come, let me take you to another place. Perhaps it will please God to let you curse them for me from there." 28 And Balak took Balaam to the top of Peor, overlooking the wasteland.   Ps 106:28

29 Balaam said, "Build me seven altars here, and prepare seven bulls and seven rams for me." 30 Balak did as Balaam had said, and offered a bull and a ram on each altar.

24 Now when Balaam saw that it pleased the LORD to bless Israel, he did not resort to divination as at other times, but turned his face toward the wilderness. 2 When Balaam looked out and saw Israel encamped tribe by tribe, the Spirit of God came on him 3 and he spoke his message: Nu 11:25-26; 1Sa 10:10; 19:20

"The prophecy of Balaam son
    of Beor,
the prophecy of one whose
    eye sees clearly,
4 the prophecy of one who
    hears the words of God,
who sees a vision from the
    Almighty,[b]   Ge 15:1
who falls prostrate, and
    whose eyes are opened:

5 "How beautiful are your tents,
    Jacob,
    your dwelling places, Israel!

6 "Like valleys they spread
    out,
    like gardens beside a river,
like aloes planted by the
    LORD,
    like cedars beside the
    waters.   Ps 1:3; 104:16
7 Water will flow from their
    buckets;
    their seed will have
    abundant water.

"Their king will be greater
    than Agag;
    their kingdom will be
    exalted.   2Sa 5:12; 1Ch 14:2
8 "God brought them out of
    Egypt;
    they have the strength of a
    wild ox.
They devour hostile nations

a 23 Or in   b 4 Hebrew *Shaddai*; also in verse 16

and break their bones in
pieces;   Ps 2:9; Jer 50:17
with their arrows they
pierce them.   Ps 45:5
⁹Like a lion they crouch and lie
down,
like a lioness — who dares
to rouse them?

"May those who bless you be
blessed
and those who curse you be
cursed!"   Ge 12:3

¹⁰Then Balak's anger burned against Balaam. He struck his hands together and said to him, "I summoned you to curse my enemies, but you have blessed them these three times. ¹¹Now leave at once and go home! I said I would reward you handsomely, but the LORD has kept you from being rewarded."   Nu 22:17; 23:11

¹²Balaam answered Balak, "Did I not tell the messengers you sent me, ¹³'Even if Balak gave me all the silver and gold in his palace, I could not do anything of my own accord, good or bad, to go beyond the command of the LORD — and I must say only what the LORD says'? ¹⁴Now I am going back to my people, but come, let me warn you of what this people will do to your people in days to come."   Nu 22:18,20; Mic 6:5

Balaam's Fourth Message

¹⁵Then he spoke his message:

"The prophecy of Balaam son
of Beor,
the prophecy of one whose
eye sees clearly,
¹⁶the prophecy of one who
hears the words of God,
who has knowledge from
the Most High,
who sees a vision from the
Almighty,
who falls prostrate, and
whose eyes are opened:

¹⁷"I see him, but not now;
I behold him, but not
near.   Rev 1:7
A star will come out of
Jacob;   Mt 2:2
a scepter will rise out of
Israel.   Ge 49:10
He will crush the foreheads of
Moab,
the skulls*a* of*b* all the people
of Sheth.*c*
¹⁸Edom will be conquered;
Seir, his enemy, will be
conquered,
but Israel will grow strong.
¹⁹A ruler will come out of Jacob
and destroy the survivors of
the city."   Ge 49:10; Mic 5:2

Balaam's Fifth Message

²⁰Then Balaam saw Amalek and spoke his message:

"Amalek was first among the
nations,
but their end will be utter
destruction."   Dt 25:19

---

a 17 Samaritan Pentateuch (see also Jer. 48:45); the meaning of the word in the Masoretic Text is uncertain.   *b 17* Or possibly *Moab, / batter*   *c 17* Or *all the noisy boasters*

Balaam's Sixth Message

²¹ Then he saw the Kenites and spoke his message:

"Your dwelling place is
    secure,
  your nest is set in a rock;
²² yet you Kenites will be
    destroyed
  when Ashur takes you
    captive."   Ge 10:22

Balaam's Seventh Message

²³ Then he spoke his message:

"Alas! Who can live when God
    does this?ᵃ
²⁴   Ships will come from the
    shores of Cyprus;
  they will subdue Ashur and
    Eber,
  but they too will come to
    ruin."   Ge 10:4,21

²⁵ Then Balaam got up and returned home, and Balak went his own way.   Nu 31:8

Moab Seduces Israel

25 While Israel was staying in Shittim, the men began to indulge in sexual immorality with Moabite women, ² who invited them to the sacrifices to their gods. The people ate the sacrificial meal and bowed down before these gods. ³ So Israel yoked themselves to the Baal of Peor. And the LORD's anger burned against them.   Ex 20:5; Nu 31:16; Ps 106:28

⁴ The LORD said to Moses, "Take all the leaders of these people, kill them and expose them in broad daylight before the LORD, so that the LORD's fierce anger may turn away from Israel."   Dt 4:3; 13:17

⁵ So Moses said to Israel's judges, "Each of you must put to death those of your people who have yoked themselves to the Baal of Peor."

⁶ Then an Israelite man brought into the camp a Midianite woman right before the eyes of Moses and the whole assembly of Israel while they were weeping at the entrance to the tent of meeting. ⁷ When Phinehas son of Eleazar, the son of Aaron, the priest, saw this, he left the assembly, took a spear in his hand ⁸ and followed the Israelite into the tent. He drove the spear into both of them, right through the Israelite man and into the woman's stomach. Then the plague against the Israelites was stopped; ⁹ but those who died in the plague numbered 24,000.   Nu 14:37; 1Co 10:8

¹⁰ The LORD said to Moses, ¹¹ "Phinehas son of Eleazar, the son of Aaron, the priest, has turned my anger away from the Israelites. Since he was as zealous for my honor among them as I am, I did not put an end to them in my zeal. ¹² Therefore tell him I am making my covenant of

---

ᵃ 23 Masoretic Text; with a different word division of the Hebrew *The people from the islands will gather from the north.*

peace with him. [13]He and his descendants will have a covenant of a lasting priesthood, because he was zealous for the honor of his God and made atonement for the Israelites." Isa 54:10; Mal 2:4-5; Ex 20:5

[14]The name of the Israelite who was killed with the Midianite woman was Zimri son of Salu, the leader of a Simeonite family. [15]And the name of the Midianite woman who was put to death was Kozbi daughter of Zur, a tribal chief of a Midianite family. Nu 31:8; Jos 13:21

[16]The LORD said to Moses, [17]"Treat the Midianites as enemies and kill them. [18]They treated you as enemies when they deceived you in the Peor incident involving their sister Kozbi, the daughter of a Midianite leader, the woman who was killed when the plague came as a result of that incident." Nu 31:1-3,16

The Second Census

26 After the plague the LORD said to Moses and Eleazar son of Aaron, the priest, [2]"Take a census of the whole Israelite community by families—all those twenty years old or more who are able to serve in the army of Israel." [3]So on the plains of Moab by the Jordan across from Jericho, Moses and Eleazar the priest spoke with them and said, [4]"Take a census of the men twenty years old or more, as the LORD commanded Moses." Ex 30:11-16; Nu 22:1

These were the Israelites who came out of Egypt:

[5]The descendants of Reuben, the firstborn son of Israel, were:

through Hanok, the Hanokite clan;

through Pallu, the Palluite clan;

[6]through Hezron, the Hezronite clan;

through Karmi, the Karmite clan. Nu 1:20; 1Ch 5:3

[7]These were the clans of Reuben; those numbered were 43,730.

[8]The son of Pallu was Eliab, [9]and the sons of Eliab were Nemuel, Dathan and Abiram. The same Dathan and Abiram were the community officials who rebelled against Moses and Aaron and were among Korah's followers when they rebelled against the LORD. [10]The earth opened its mouth and swallowed them along with Korah, whose followers died when the fire devoured the 250 men. And they served as a warning sign. [11]The line of Korah, however, did not die out. Ex 6:24; Nu 16:2; Dt 24:16

[12]The descendants of Simeon by their clans were:

through Nemuel, the Nemuelite clan;

through Jamin, the Jaminite clan; 1Ch 4:24

through Jakin, the Jakinite clan;

[13]through Zerah, the Zerahite clan; Ge 46:10

through Shaul, the Shaulite clan.

[14] These were the clans of Simeon; those numbered were 22,200.

[15] The descendants of Gad by their clans were:

through Zephon, the Zephonite clan; Ge 46:16

through Haggi, the Haggite clan;

through Shuni, the Shunite clan;

[16] through Ozni, the Oznite clan;

through Eri, the Erite clan;

[17] through Arodi,[a] the Arodite clan;

through Areli, the Arelite clan.

[18] These were the clans of Gad; those numbered were 40,500.

[19] Er and Onan were sons of Judah, but they died in Canaan.

[20] The descendants of Judah by their clans were:

through Shelah, the Shelanite clan; 1Ch 2:3

through Perez, the Perezite clan;

through Zerah, the Zerahite clan.

[21] The descendants of Perez were:

through Hezron, the Hezronite clan;

through Hamul, the Hamulite clan.

[22] These were the clans of Judah; those numbered were 76,500.

[23] The descendants of Issachar by their clans were:

through Tola, the Tolaite clan; Ge 46:13

through Puah, the Puite[b] clan;

[24] through Jashub, the Jashubite clan;

through Shimron, the Shimronite clan.

[25] These were the clans of Issachar; those numbered were 64,300. Nu 1:29

[26] The descendants of Zebulun by their clans were:

through Sered, the Seredite clan;

through Elon, the Elonite clan;

through Jahleel, the Jahleelite clan.

[27] These were the clans of Zebulun; those numbered were 60,500. Nu 1:31

[28] The descendants of Joseph by their clans through Manasseh and Ephraim were:

[29] The descendants of Manasseh:

through Makir, the Makirite clan (Makir was the father of Gilead); Jos 17:1

through Gilead, the Gileadite clan.

---

[a] 17 Samaritan Pentateuch and Syriac (see also Gen. 46:16); Masoretic Text *Arod*

[b] 23 Samaritan Pentateuch, Septuagint, Vulgate and Syriac (see also 1 Chron. 7:1); Masoretic Text *through Puvah, the Punite*

³⁰These were the descendants of Gilead:

through Iezer, the Iezerite clan;   Jos 17:2; Jdg 6:11

through Helek, the Helek-ite clan;

³¹through Asriel, the Asriel-ite clan;

through Shechem, the She-chemite clan;

³²through Shemida, the She-midaite clan;

through Hepher, the He-pherite clan.

³³(Zelophehad son of He-pher had no sons; he had only daughters, whose names were Mahlah, Noah, Hoglah, Milkah and Tirzah.)   Nu 27:1; 36:11

³⁴These were the clans of Manasseh; those numbered were 52,700.

³⁵These were the descendants of Ephraim by their clans:

through Shuthelah, the Shu-thelahite clan;

through Beker, the Bekerite clan;

through Tahan, the Tahan-ite clan.

³⁶These were the descendants of Shuthelah:

through Eran, the Eranite clan.

³⁷These were the clans of Ephraim; those numbered were 32,500.   Nu 1:33

These were the descendants of Joseph by their clans.

³⁸The descendants of Benjamin by their clans were: Ge 46:21

through Bela, the Belaite clan;

through Ashbel, the Ashbel-ite clan;

through Ahiram, the Ahi-ramite clan;

³⁹through Shupham,ᵃ the Shu-phamite clan;

through Hupham, the Hu-phamite clan.

⁴⁰The descendants of Bela through Ard and Naaman were:

through Ard,ᵇ the Ardite clan;

through Naaman, the Na-amite clan.

⁴¹These were the clans of Benjamin; those numbered were 45,600.   Nu 1:37

⁴²These were the descendants of Dan by their clans:

through Shuham, the Shu-hamite clan.   Ge 46:23

These were the clans of Dan:
⁴³All of them were Shuhamite clans; and those numbered were 64,400.

⁴⁴The descendants of Asher by their clans were:

through Imnah, the Imnite clan;

ᵃ 39 A few manuscripts of the Masoretic Text, Samaritan Pentateuch, Vulgate and Syriac (see also Septuagint); most manuscripts of the Masoretic Text *Shephupham* ᵇ 40 Samaritan Pentateuch and Vulgate (see also Septuagint); Masoretic Text does not have *through Ard*.

through Ishvi, the Ishvite clan;

through Beriah, the Beriite clan;

⁴⁵and through the descendants of Beriah:

through Heber, the Heberite clan;

through Malkiel, the Malkielite clan.

⁴⁶(Asher had a daughter named Serah.)

⁴⁷These were the clans of Asher; those numbered were 53,400.

⁴⁸The descendants of Naphtali by their clans were:

through Jahzeel, the Jahzeelite clan;

through Guni, the Gunite clan;

⁴⁹through Jezer, the Jezerite clan;

through Shillem, the Shillemite clan.

⁵⁰These were the clans of Naphtali; those numbered were 45,400.

⁵¹The total number of the men of Israel was 601,730.   Ex 12:37; 38:26

⁵²The LORD said to Moses, ⁵³"The land is to be allotted to them as an inheritance based on the number of names. ⁵⁴To a larger group give a larger inheritance, and to a smaller group a smaller one; each is to receive its inheritance according to the number of those listed. ⁵⁵Be sure that the land is distributed by lot. What each group inherits will be according to the names for its ancestral tribe. ⁵⁶Each inheritance is to be distributed by lot among the larger and smaller groups."   Nu 33:54; 34:14; Jos 11:23

⁵⁷These were the Levites who were counted by their clans:

through Gershon, the Gershonite clan;

through Kohath, the Kohathite clan;

through Merari, the Merarite clan.

⁵⁸These also were Levite clans:

the Libnite clan,

the Hebronite clan,

the Mahlite clan,

the Mushite clan,

the Korahite clan.

(Kohath was the forefather of Amram; ⁵⁹the name of Amram's wife was Jochebed, a descendant of Levi, who was born to the Levites*a* in Egypt. To Amram she bore Aaron, Moses and their sister Miriam. ⁶⁰Aaron was the father of Nadab and Abihu, Eleazar and Ithamar. ⁶¹But Nadab and Abihu died when they made an offering before the LORD with unauthorized fire.)   Ex 6:20; Lev 10:1-2; Nu 3:2

⁶²All the male Levites a month old or more numbered 23,000.

<hr />

a 59 Or *Jochebed, a daughter of Levi, who was born to Levi*

They were not counted along with the other Israelites because they received no inheritance among them. Nu 1:47; 18:23

⁶³These are the ones counted by Moses and Eleazar the priest when they counted the Israelites on the plains of Moab by the Jordan across from Jericho. ⁶⁴Not one of them was among those counted by Moses and Aaron the priest when they counted the Israelites in the Desert of Sinai. ⁶⁵For the LORD had told those Israelites they would surely die in the wilderness, and not one of them was left except Caleb son of Jephunneh and Joshua son of Nun. Nu 14:28; Dt 2:14-15; Heb 3:17

Zelophehad's Daughters

27:1-11pp — Nu 36:1-12

27 The daughters of Zelophehad son of Hepher, the son of Gilead, the son of Makir, the son of Manasseh, belonged to the clans of Manasseh son of Joseph. The names of the daughters were Mahlah, Noah, Hoglah, Milkah and Tirzah. They came forward ²and stood before Moses, Eleazar the priest, the leaders and the whole assembly at the entrance to the tent of meeting and said, ³"Our father died in the wilderness. He was not among Korah's followers, who banded together against the LORD, but he died for his own sin and left no sons. ⁴Why should our father's name disappear from his clan because he had no son? Give us property among our father's relatives." Nu 16:2; 26:65; 36:1

⁵So Moses brought their case before the LORD, ⁶and the LORD said to him, ⁷"What Zelophehad's daughters are saying is right. You must certainly give them property as an inheritance among their father's relatives and give their father's inheritance to them. Nu 9:8; Jos 17:4

⁸"Say to the Israelites, 'If a man dies and leaves no son, give his inheritance to his daughter. ⁹If he has no daughter, give his inheritance to his brothers. ¹⁰If he has no brothers, give his inheritance to his father's brothers. ¹¹If his father had no brothers, give his inheritance to the nearest relative in his clan, that he may possess it. This is to have the force of law for the Israelites, as the LORD commanded Moses.'" Nu 36:1-12

Joshua to Succeed Moses

¹²Then the LORD said to Moses, "Go up this mountain in the Abarim Range and see the land I have given the Israelites. ¹³After you have seen it, you too will be gathered to your people, as your brother Aaron was, ¹⁴for when the community rebelled at the waters in the Desert of Zin, both of you disobeyed my command to honor me as holy before their eyes." (These were the waters of

Meribah Kadesh, in the Desert of Zin.) Nu 20:12; 33:47; Dt 32:48-52

¹⁵Moses said to the LORD, ¹⁶"May the LORD, the God who gives breath to all living things, appoint someone over this community ¹⁷to go out and come in before them, one who will lead them out and bring them in, so the LORD's people will not be like sheep without a shepherd." Nu 16:22; Dt 31:2; Mt 9:36

¹⁸So the LORD said to Moses, "Take Joshua son of Nun, a man in whom is the spirit of leadership,ᵃ and lay your hand on him. ¹⁹Have him stand before Eleazar the priest and the entire assembly and commission him in their presence. ²⁰Give him some of your authority so the whole Israelite community will obey him. ²¹He is to stand before Eleazar the priest, who will obtain decisions for him by inquiring of the Urim before the LORD. At his command he and the entire community of the Israelites will go out, and at his command they will come in." Nu 11:25-29; Dt 34:9

²²Moses did as the LORD commanded him. He took Joshua and had him stand before Eleazar the priest and the whole assembly. ²³Then he laid his hands on him and commissioned him, as the LORD instructed through Moses.

Daily Offerings

28 The LORD said to Moses, ²"Give this command to the Israelites and say to them: 'Make sure that you present to me at the appointed time my food offerings, as an aroma pleasing to me.' ³Say to them: 'This is the food offering you are to present to the LORD: two lambs a year old without defect, as a regular burnt offering each day. ⁴Offer one lamb in the morning and the other at twilight, ⁵together with a grain offering of a tenth of an ephahᵇ of the finest flour mixed with a quarter of a hinᶜ of oil from pressed olives. ⁶This is the regular burnt offering instituted at Mount Sinai as a pleasing aroma, a food offering presented to the LORD. ⁷The accompanying drink offering is to be a quarter of a hin of fermented drink with each lamb. Pour out the drink offering to the LORD at the sanctuary. ⁸Offer the second lamb at twilight, along with the same kind of grain offering and drink offering that you offer in the morning. This is a food offering, an aroma pleasing to the LORD. Ex 29:38; Lev 2:1; 3:11

Sabbath Offerings

⁹"'On the Sabbath day, make an offering of two lambs a year old without defect, together with

---

ᵃ 18 Or the Spirit ᵇ 5 That is, probably about 3 1/2 pounds or about 1.6 kilograms; also in verses 13, 21 and 29 ᶜ 5 That is, about 1 quart or about 1 liter; also in verses 7 and 14 its drink offering and a grain offering of two-tenths of an ephah[a] of the finest flour mixed with olive oil. [10]This is the burnt offering for every Sabbath, in addition to the regular burnt offering and its drink offering. Lev 23:13; Mt 12:5

Monthly Offerings

[11]"'On the first of every month, present to the LORD a burnt offering of two young bulls, one ram and seven male lambs a year old, all without defect. [12]With each bull there is to be a grain offering of three-tenths of an ephah[b] of the finest flour mixed with oil; with the ram, a grain offering of two-tenths of an ephah of the finest flour mixed with oil; [13]and with each lamb, a grain offering of a tenth of an ephah of the finest flour mixed with oil. This is for a burnt offering, a pleasing aroma, a food offering presented to the LORD. [14]With each bull there is to be a drink offering of half a hin[c] of wine; with the ram, a third of a hin[d]; and with each lamb, a quarter of a hin. This is the monthly burnt offering to be made at each new moon during the year. [15]Besides the regular burnt offering with its drink offering, one male goat is to be presented to the LORD as a sin offering.[e] Lev 4:3; Nu 10:10

The Passover

28:16-25pp — Ex 12:14-20; Lev 23:4-8; Dt 16:1-8

[16]"'On the fourteenth day of the first month the LORD's Passover is to be held. [17]On the fifteenth day of this month there is to be a festival; for seven days eat bread made without yeast. [18]On the first day hold a sacred assembly and do no regular work. [19]Present to the LORD a food offering consisting of a burnt offering of two young bulls, one ram and seven male lambs a year old, all without defect. [20]With each bull offer a grain offering of three-tenths of an ephah of the finest flour mixed with oil; with the ram, two-tenths; [21]and with each of the seven lambs, one-tenth. [22]Include one male goat as a sin offering to make atonement for you. [23]Offer these in addition to the regular morning burnt offering. [24]In this way present the food offering every day for seven days as an aroma pleasing to the LORD; it is to be offered in addition to the regular burnt offering and its drink offering. [25]On the seventh day hold a sacred assembly and do no regular work. Ex 12:14-20; Lev 23:4-8; Dt 16:1-8

The Festival of Weeks

28:26-31pp — Lev 23:15-22; Dt 16:9-12

[26]"'On the day of firstfruits, when you present to the LORD

---

[a] 9 That is, probably about 7 pounds or about 3.2 kilograms; also in verses 12, 20 and 28
[b] 12 That is, probably about 11 pounds or about 5 kilograms; also in verses 20 and 28
[c] 14 That is, about 2 quarts or about 1.9 liters   [d] 14 That is, about 1 1/3 quarts or about 1.3 liters   [e] 15 Or purification offering; also in verse 22

an offering of new grain during the Festival of Weeks, hold a sacred assembly and do no regular work. ²⁷Present a burnt offering of two young bulls, one ram and seven male lambs a year old as an aroma pleasing to the Lord. ²⁸With each bull there is to be a grain offering of three-tenths of an ephah of the finest flour mixed with oil; with the ram, two-tenths; ²⁹and with each of the seven lambs, one-tenth. ³⁰Include one male goat to make atonement for you. ³¹Offer these together with their drink offerings, in addition to the regular burnt offering and its grain offering. Be sure the animals are without defect. Lev 23:15-22; Dt 16:9-12

The Festival of Trumpets
29:1-6pp — Lev 23:23-25

29 "'On the first day of the seventh month hold a sacred assembly and do no regular work. It is a day for you to sound the trumpets. ²As an aroma pleasing to the Lord, offer a burnt offering of one young bull, one ram and seven male lambs a year old, all without defect. ³With the bull offer a grain offering of three-tenths of an ephah[a] of the finest flour mixed with olive oil; with the ram, two-tenths[b]; ⁴and with each of the seven lambs,

one-tenth.[c] ⁵Include one male goat as a sin offering[d] to make atonement for you. ⁶These are in addition to the monthly and daily burnt offerings with their grain offerings and drink offerings as specified. They are food offerings presented to the Lord, a pleasing aroma. Lev 23:23-25

The Day of Atonement
29:7-11pp — Lev 16:2-34; 23:26-32

⁷"'On the tenth day of this seventh month hold a sacred assembly. You must deny yourselves[e] and do no work. ⁸Present as an aroma pleasing to the Lord a burnt offering of one young bull, one ram and seven male lambs a year old, all without defect. ⁹With the bull offer a grain offering of three-tenths of an ephah of the finest flour mixed with oil; with the ram, two-tenths; ¹⁰and with each of the seven lambs, one-tenth. ¹¹Include one male goat as a sin offering, in addition to the sin offering for atonement and the regular burnt offering with its grain offering, and their drink offerings. Lev 16:2-34; 23:26-32

The Festival of Tabernacles
29:12-39pp — Lev 23:33-43; Dt 16:13-17

¹²"'On the fifteenth day of the seventh month, hold a sacred assembly and do no regular work. Celebrate a festival to the Lord

---

[a] 3 That is, probably about 11 pounds or about 5 kilograms; also in verses 9 and 14
[b] 3 That is, probably about 7 pounds or about 3.2 kilograms; also in verses 9 and 14
[c] 4 That is, probably about 3 1/2 pounds or about 1.6 kilograms; also in verses 10 and 15
[d] 5 Or *purification offering*; also elsewhere in this chapter   [e] 7 Or *must fast*

for seven days. [13]Present as an aroma pleasing to the LORD a food offering consisting of a burnt offering of thirteen young bulls, two rams and fourteen male lambs a year old, all without defect. [14]With each of the thirteen bulls offer a grain offering of three-tenths of an ephah of the finest flour mixed with oil; with each of the two rams, two-tenths; [15]and with each of the fourteen lambs, one-tenth. [16]Include one male goat as a sin offering, in addition to the regular burnt offering with its grain offering and drink offering.   Lev 23:24; 1Ki 8:2

[17]" 'On the second day offer twelve young bulls, two rams and fourteen male lambs a year old, all without defect. [18]With the bulls, rams and lambs, offer their grain offerings and drink offerings according to the number specified. [19]Include one male goat as a sin offering, in addition to the regular burnt offering with its grain offering, and their drink offerings.   Nu 28:3,15

[20]" 'On the third day offer eleven bulls, two rams and fourteen male lambs a year old, all without defect. [21]With the bulls, rams and lambs, offer their grain offerings and drink offerings according to the number specified. [22]Include one male goat as a sin offering, in addition to the regular burnt offering with its grain offering and drink offering.

[23]" 'On the fourth day offer ten bulls, two rams and fourteen male lambs a year old, all without defect. [24]With the bulls, rams and lambs, offer their grain offerings and drink offerings according to the number specified. [25]Include one male goat as a sin offering, in addition to the regular burnt offering with its grain offering and drink offering.

[26]" 'On the fifth day offer nine bulls, two rams and fourteen male lambs a year old, all without defect. [27]With the bulls, rams and lambs, offer their grain offerings and drink offerings according to the number specified. [28]Include one male goat as a sin offering, in addition to the regular burnt offering with its grain offering and drink offering.

[29]" 'On the sixth day offer eight bulls, two rams and fourteen male lambs a year old, all without defect. [30]With the bulls, rams and lambs, offer their grain offerings and drink offerings according to the number specified. [31]Include one male goat as a sin offering, in addition to the regular burnt offering with its grain offering and drink offering.

[32]" 'On the seventh day offer seven bulls, two rams and fourteen male lambs a year old, all without defect. [33]With the bulls, rams and lambs, offer their grain offerings and drink offerings according to the number specified. [34]Include one male goat as a sin

offering, in addition to the regular burnt offering with its grain offering and drink offering.

³⁵ " 'On the eighth day hold a closing special assembly and do no regular work. ³⁶ Present as an aroma pleasing to the LORD a food offering consisting of a burnt offering of one bull, one ram and seven male lambs a year old, all without defect. ³⁷ With the bull, the ram and the lambs, offer their grain offerings and drink offerings according to the number specified. ³⁸ Include one male goat as a sin offering, in addition to the regular burnt offering with its grain offering and drink offering.   Lev 1:9; 23:36

³⁹ " 'In addition to what you vow and your freewill offerings, offer these to the LORD at your appointed festivals: your burnt offerings, grain offerings, drink offerings and fellowship offerings.' "   Lev 23:33-43; Dt 16:13-17

⁴⁰ Moses told the Israelites all that the LORD commanded him.ᵃ

Vows

30 ᵇ Moses said to the heads of the tribes of Israel: "This is what the LORD commands: ² When a man makes a vow to the LORD or takes an oath to obligate himself by a pledge, he must not break his word but must do everything he said.   Dt 23:21-23

³ "When a young woman still living in her father's household makes a vow to the LORD or obligates herself by a pledge ⁴ and her father hears about her vow or pledge but says nothing to her, then all her vows and every pledge by which she obligated herself will stand. ⁵ But if her father forbids her when he hears about it, none of her vows or the pledges by which she obligated herself will stand; the LORD will release her because her father has forbidden her.

⁶ "If she marries after she makes a vow or after her lips utter a rash promise by which she obligates herself ⁷ and her husband hears about it but says nothing to her, then her vows or the pledges by which she obligated herself will stand. ⁸ But if her husband forbids her when he hears about it, he nullifies the vow that obligates her or the rash promise by which she obligates herself, and the LORD will release her.   Ge 3:16; Lev 5:4

⁹ "Any vow or obligation taken by a widow or divorced woman will be binding on her.

¹⁰ "If a woman living with her husband makes a vow or obligates herself by a pledge under oath ¹¹ and her husband hears about it but says nothing to her and does not forbid her, then all her vows or the pledges by which she obligated herself will stand. ¹² But if her husband nullifies

---

ᵃ 40 In Hebrew texts this verse (29:40) is numbered 30:1.   ᵇ In Hebrew texts 30:1-16 is numbered 30:2-17.

them when he hears about them, then none of the vows or pledges that came from her lips will stand. Her husband has nullified them, and the LORD will release her. [13] Her husband may confirm or nullify any vow she makes or any sworn pledge to deny herself.[a] [14] But if her husband says nothing to her about it from day to day, then he confirms all her vows or the pledges binding on her. He confirms them by saying nothing to her when he hears about them. [15] If, however, he nullifies them some time after he hears about them, then he must bear the consequences of her wrongdoing." Eph 5:22; Col 3:18

[16] These are the regulations the LORD gave Moses concerning relationships between a man and his wife, and between a father and his young daughter still living at home.

Vengeance on the Midianites

31 The LORD said to Moses, [2] "Take vengeance on the Midianites for the Israelites. After that, you will be gathered to your people." Nu 20:26; 27:13

[3] So Moses said to the people, "Arm some of your men to go to war against the Midianites so that they may carry out the LORD's vengeance on them. [4] Send into battle a thousand men from each of the tribes of Israel." [5] So twelve thousand men armed for battle, a thousand from each tribe, were supplied from the clans of Israel. [6] Moses sent them into battle, a thousand from each tribe, along with Phinehas son of Eleazar, the priest, who took with him articles from the sanctuary and the trumpets for signaling. Nu 10:9; Jdg 11:36; Ps 94:1

[7] They fought against Midian, as the LORD commanded Moses, and killed every man. [8] Among their victims were Evi, Rekem, Zur, Hur and Reba—the five kings of Midian. They also killed Balaam son of Beor with the sword. [9] The Israelites captured the Midianite women and children and took all the Midianite herds, flocks and goods as plunder. [10] They burned all the towns where the Midianites had settled, as well as all their camps. [11] They took all the plunder and spoils, including the people and animals, [12] and brought the captives, spoils and plunder to Moses and Eleazar the priest and the Israelite assembly at their camp on the plains of Moab, by the Jordan across from Jericho. Dt 20:13; Jdg 21:11; Jos 13:21-22

[13] Moses, Eleazar the priest and all the leaders of the community went to meet them outside the camp. [14] Moses was angry with the officers of the army—the commanders of thousands and commanders of hundreds—who returned from the battle. Ex 18:21; Dt 1:15

a 13 Or to fast

[15] "Have you allowed all the women to live?" he asked them. [16] "They were the ones who followed Balaam's advice and enticed the Israelites to be unfaithful to the LORD in the Peor incident, so that a plague struck the LORD's people. [17] Now kill all the boys. And kill every woman who has slept with a man, [18] but save for yourselves every girl who has never slept with a man.   2Pe 2:15; Nu 25:1-9; Jdg 21:11

[19] "Anyone who has killed someone or touched someone who was killed must stay outside the camp seven days. On the third and seventh days you must purify yourselves and your captives. [20] Purify every garment as well as everything made of leather, goat hair or wood."   Nu 19:12,16

[21] Then Eleazar the priest said to the soldiers who had gone into battle, "This is what is required by the law that the LORD gave Moses: [22] Gold, silver, bronze, iron, tin, lead [23] and anything else that can withstand fire must be put through the fire, and then it will be clean. But it must also be purified with the water of cleansing. And whatever cannot withstand fire must be put through that water. [24] On the seventh day wash your clothes and you will be clean. Then you may come into the camp."   1Co 3:13; Nu 19:9,17; Lev 11:25

Dividing the Spoils

[25] The LORD said to Moses, [26] "You and Eleazar the priest and the family heads of the community are to count all the people and animals that were captured. [27] Divide the spoils equally between the soldiers who took part in the battle and the rest of the community. [28] From the soldiers who fought in the battle, set apart as tribute for the LORD one out of every five hundred, whether people, cattle, donkeys or sheep. [29] Take this tribute from their half share and give it to Eleazar the priest as the LORD's part. [30] From the Israelites' half, select one out of every fifty, whether people, cattle, donkeys, sheep or other animals. Give them to the Levites, who are responsible for the care of the LORD's tabernacle." [31] So Moses and Eleazar the priest did as the LORD commanded Moses.   Nu 3:7; 18:21; Jos 22:8

[32] The plunder remaining from the spoils that the soldiers took was 675,000 sheep, [33] 72,000 cattle, [34] 61,000 donkeys [35] and 32,000 women who had never slept with a man.

[36] The half share of those who fought in the battle was:

337,500 sheep, [37] of which the tribute for the LORD was 675;

[38] 36,000 cattle, of which the tribute for the LORD was 72;

[39] 30,500 donkeys, of which

the tribute for the LORD was 61; [40] 16,000 people, of whom the tribute for the LORD was 32.

[41] Moses gave the tribute to Eleazar the priest as the LORD's part, as the LORD commanded Moses. Nu 18:8 [42] The half belonging to the Israelites, which Moses set apart from that of the fighting men — [43] the community's half — was 337,500 sheep, [44] 36,000 cattle, [45] 30,500 donkeys [46] and 16,000 people. [47] From the Israelites' half, Moses selected one out of every fifty people and animals, as the LORD commanded him, and gave them to the Levites, who were responsible for the care of the LORD's tabernacle.

[48] Then the officers who were over the units of the army — the commanders of thousands and commanders of hundreds — went to Moses [49] and said to him, "Your servants have counted the soldiers under our command, and not one is missing. [50] So we have brought as an offering to the LORD the gold articles each of us acquired — armlets, bracelets, signet rings, earrings and necklaces — to make atonement for ourselves before the LORD." Ex 30:16; Jer 23:4 [51] Moses and Eleazar the priest accepted from them the gold — all the crafted articles. [52] All the gold from the commanders of thousands and commanders of hundreds that Moses and Eleazar presented as a gift to the LORD weighed 16,750 shekels.[a] [53] Each soldier had taken plunder for himself. [54] Moses and Eleazar the priest accepted the gold from the commanders of thousands and commanders of hundreds and brought it into the tent of meeting as a memorial for the Israelites before the LORD. Ex 28:12; Dt 20:14

The Transjordan Tribes

32 The Reubenites and Gadites, who had very large herds and flocks, saw that the lands of Jazer and Gilead were suitable for livestock. [2] So they came to Moses and Eleazar the priest and to the leaders of the community, and said, [3] "Ataroth, Dibon, Jazer, Nimrah, Heshbon, Elealeh, Sebam, Nebo and Beon — [4] the land the LORD subdued before the people of Israel — are suitable for livestock, and your servants have livestock. [5] If we have found favor in your eyes," they said, "let this land be given to your servants as our possession. Do not make us cross the Jordan." Ex 12:38; Nu 21:32,34 [6] Moses said to the Gadites and Reubenites, "Should your fellow Israelites go to war while you sit

---

[a] 52 That is, about 420 pounds or about 190 kilograms

here? [7] Why do you discourage the Israelites from crossing over into the land the LORD has given them? [8] This is what your fathers did when I sent them from Kadesh Barnea to look over the land. [9] After they went up to the Valley of Eshkol and viewed the land, they discouraged the Israelites from entering the land the LORD had given them. [10] The LORD's anger was aroused that day and he swore this oath: [11] 'Because they have not followed me wholeheartedly, not one of those who were twenty years old or more when they came up out of Egypt will see the land I promised on oath to Abraham, Isaac and Jacob — [12] not one except Caleb son of Jephunneh the Kenizzite and Joshua son of Nun, for they followed the LORD wholeheartedly.' [13] The LORD's anger burned against Israel and he made them wander in the wilderness forty years, until the whole generation of those who had done evil in his sight was gone.   Nu 13:27-14:4; Dt 1:19-25; Ps 63:8

[14] "And here you are, a brood of sinners, standing in the place of your fathers and making the LORD even more angry with Israel. [15] If you turn away from following him, he will again leave all this people in the wilderness, and you will be the cause of their destruction."   Dt 30:17-18; 2Ch 7:20

[16] Then they came up to him and said, "We would like to build pens here for our livestock and cities for our women and children. [17] But we will arm ourselves for battle[a] and go ahead of the Israelites until we have brought them to their place. Meanwhile our women and children will live in fortified cities, for protection from the inhabitants of the land. [18] We will not return to our homes until each of the Israelites has received their inheritance. [19] We will not receive any inheritance with them on the other side of the Jordan, because our inheritance has come to us on the east side of the Jordan."   Jos 4:12-13; 12:1; 22:1-4

[20] Then Moses said to them, "If you will do this — if you will arm yourselves before the LORD for battle [21] and if all of you who are armed cross over the Jordan before the LORD until he has driven his enemies out before him — [22] then when the land is subdued before the LORD, you may return and be free from your obligation to the LORD and to Israel. And this land will be your possession before the LORD.   Dt 3:18-20

[23] "But if you fail to do this, you will be sinning against the LORD; and you may be sure that your sin will find you out. [24] Build cities for your women and children, and pens for your flocks, but do what you have promised."   Ge 4:7

---

[a] 17 Septuagint; Hebrew *will be quick to arm ourselves*

²⁵The Gadites and Reubenites said to Moses, "We your servants will do as our lord commands. ²⁶Our children and wives, our flocks and herds will remain here in the cities of Gilead. ²⁷But your servants, every man who is armed for battle, will cross over to fight before the LORD, just as our lord says." Jos 1:14

²⁸Then Moses gave orders about them to Eleazar the priest and Joshua son of Nun and to the family heads of the Israelite tribes. ²⁹He said to them, "If the Gadites and Reubenites, every man armed for battle, cross over the Jordan with you before the LORD, then when the land is subdued before you, you must give them the land of Gilead as their possession. ³⁰But if they do not cross over with you armed, they must accept their possession with you in Canaan." Dt 3:18-20; Jos 1:13

³¹The Gadites and Reubenites answered, "Your servants will do what the LORD has said. ³²We will cross over before the LORD into Canaan armed, but the property we inherit will be on this side of the Jordan."

³³Then Moses gave to the Gadites, the Reubenites and the half-tribe of Manasseh son of Joseph the kingdom of Sihon king of the Amorites and the kingdom of Og king of Bashan — the whole land with its cities and the territory around them. Nu 21:24; Jos 12:6

³⁴The Gadites built up Dibon, Ataroth, Aroer, ³⁵Atroth Shophan, Jazer, Jogbehah, ³⁶Beth Nimrah and Beth Haran as fortified cities, and built pens for their flocks. ³⁷And the Reubenites rebuilt Heshbon, Elealeh and Kiriathaim, ³⁸as well as Nebo and Baal Meon (these names were changed) and Sibmah. They gave names to the cities they rebuilt. ver 3; Dt 2:36

³⁹The descendants of Makir son of Manasseh went to Gilead, captured it and drove out the Amorites who were there. ⁴⁰So Moses gave Gilead to the Makirites, the descendants of Manasseh, and they settled there. ⁴¹Jair, a descendant of Manasseh, captured their settlements and called them Havvoth Jair.ᵇ ⁴²And Nobah captured Kenath and its surrounding settlements and called it Nobah after himself. Ge 50:23; Dt 3:14; 2Sa 18:18

Stages in Israel's Journey

33 Here are the stages in the journey of the Israelites when they came out of Egypt by divisions under the leadership of Moses and Aaron. ²At the LORD's command Moses recorded the stages in their journey. This is their journey by stages: Ps 77:20; Mic 6:4

ᵃ 41 Or them the settlements of Jair

³The Israelites set out from Rameses on the fifteenth day of the first month, the day after the Passover. They marched out defiantly in full view of all the Egyptians, ⁴who were burying all their firstborn, whom the LORD had struck down among them; for the LORD had brought judgment on their gods. Ex 12:12; 14:8

⁵The Israelites left Rameses and camped at Sukkoth.

⁶They left Sukkoth and camped at Etham, on the edge of the desert. Ex 13:20

⁷They left Etham, turned back to Pi Hahiroth, to the east of Baal Zephon, and camped near Migdol. Ex 14:2

⁸They left Pi Hahiroth*a* and passed through the sea into the desert, and when they had traveled for three days in the Desert of Etham, they camped at Marah. Ex 14:22

⁹They left Marah and went to Elim, where there were twelve springs and seventy palm trees, and they camped there. Ex 15:27

¹⁰They left Elim and camped by the Red Sea.*b*

¹¹They left the Red Sea and camped in the Desert of Sin. Ex 16:1

¹²They left the Desert of Sin and camped at Dophkah.

¹³They left Dophkah and camped at Alush.

¹⁴They left Alush and camped at Rephidim, where there was no water for the people to drink.

¹⁵They left Rephidim and camped in the Desert of Sinai. Ex 17:1; 19:1

¹⁶They left the Desert of Sinai and camped at Kibroth Hattaavah. Nu 11:34

¹⁷They left Kibroth Hattaavah and camped at Hazeroth. Nu 11:35

¹⁸They left Hazeroth and camped at Rithmah.

¹⁹They left Rithmah and camped at Rimmon Perez.

²⁰They left Rimmon Perez and camped at Libnah.

²¹They left Libnah and camped at Rissah.

²²They left Rissah and camped at Kehelathah.

²³They left Kehelathah and camped at Mount Shepher.

²⁴They left Mount Shepher and camped at Haradah.

²⁵They left Haradah and camped at Makheloth.

²⁶They left Makheloth and camped at Tahath.

²⁷They left Tahath and camped at Terah.

a 8 Many manuscripts of the Masoretic Text, Samaritan Pentateuch and Vulgate; most manuscripts of the Masoretic Text *left from before Hahiroth*   *b 10* Or *the Sea of Reeds*; also in verse 11

²⁸They left Terah and camped at Mithkah.

²⁹They left Mithkah and camped at Hashmonah.

³⁰They left Hashmonah and camped at Moseroth.

³¹They left Moseroth and camped at Bene Jaakan.

³²They left Bene Jaakan and camped at Hor Haggidgad.

³³They left Hor Haggidgad and camped at Jotbathah.

³⁴They left Jotbathah and camped at Abronah.

³⁵They left Abronah and camped at Ezion Geber. Dt 2:8

³⁶They left Ezion Geber and camped at Kadesh, in the Desert of Zin. Nu 20:1

³⁷They left Kadesh and camped at Mount Hor, on the border of Edom. ³⁸At the LORD's command Aaron the priest went up Mount Hor, where he died on the first day of the fifth month of the fortieth year after the Israelites came out of Egypt. ³⁹Aaron was a hundred and twenty-three years old when he died on Mount Hor. Nu 20:22,25-28; Dt 10:6

⁴⁰The Canaanite king of Arad, who lived in the Negev of Canaan, heard that the Israelites were coming. Nu 21:1

⁴¹They left Mount Hor and camped at Zalmonah.

⁴²They left Zalmonah and camped at Punon.

⁴³They left Punon and camped at Oboth. Nu 21:10

⁴⁴They left Oboth and camped at Iye Abarim, on the border of Moab.

⁴⁵They left Iye Abarim and camped at Dibon Gad.

⁴⁶They left Dibon Gad and camped at Almon Diblathaim.

⁴⁷They left Almon Diblathaim and camped in the mountains of Abarim, near Nebo.

⁴⁸They left the mountains of Abarim and camped on the plains of Moab by the Jordan across from Jericho. ⁴⁹There on the plains of Moab they camped along the Jordan from Beth Jeshimoth to Abel Shittim. Nu 22:1; 25:1

⁵⁰On the plains of Moab by the Jordan across from Jericho the LORD said to Moses, ⁵¹"Speak to the Israelites and say to them: 'When you cross the Jordan into Canaan, ⁵²drive out all the inhabitants of the land before you. Destroy all their carved images and their cast idols, and demolish all their high places. ⁵³Take possession of the land and settle in it, for I have given you the land to possess. ⁵⁴Distribute the land by lot, according to your clans. To a larger group give a larger inheritance, and to a smaller group a smaller one. Whatever falls to them by lot will be theirs. Distrib-

ute it according to your ancestral tribes. Ex 23:24; Ps 106:34-36; Nu 26:54

⁵⁵ "'But if you do not drive out the inhabitants of the land, those you allow to remain will become barbs in your eyes and thorns in your sides. They will give you trouble in the land where you will live. ⁵⁶ And then I will do to you what I plan to do to them.'" Jos 23:13; Jdg 2:3; Ps 106:36

Boundaries of Canaan

34 The LORD said to Moses, ² "Command the Israelites and say to them: 'When you enter Canaan, the land that will be allotted to you as an inheritance is to have these boundaries: Ge 17:8; Dt 1:7-8; Ps 78:54-55

³ "'Your southern side will include some of the Desert of Zin along the border of Edom. Your southern boundary will start in the east from the southern end of the Dead Sea, ⁴ cross south of Scorpion Pass, continue on to Zin and go south of Kadesh Barnea. Then it will go to Hazar Addar and over to Azmon, ⁵ where it will turn, join the Wadi of Egypt and end at the Mediterranean Sea. Ge 15:18; Nu 32:8; Jos 15:1-3

⁶ "'Your western boundary will be the coast of the Mediterranean Sea. This will be your boundary on the west.

⁷ "'For your northern boundary, run a line from the Mediterranean Sea to Mount Hor ⁸ and from Mount Hor to Lebo Hamath. Then the boundary will go to Zedad, ⁹ continue to Ziphron and end at Hazar Enan. This will be your boundary on the north. Eze 47:15-17; Nu 13:21

¹⁰ "'For your eastern boundary, run a line from Hazar Enan to Shepham. ¹¹ The boundary will go down from Shepham to Riblah on the east side of Ain and continue along the slopes east of the Sea of Galilee.ᵃ ¹² Then the boundary will go down along the Jordan and end at the Dead Sea. Dt 3:17; 2Ki 23:33

"'This will be your land, with its boundaries on every side.'"

¹³ Moses commanded the Israelites: "Assign this land by lot as an inheritance. The LORD has ordered that it be given to the nine and a half tribes, ¹⁴ because the families of the tribe of Reuben, the tribe of Gad and the half-tribe of Manasseh have received their inheritance. ¹⁵ These two and a half tribes have received their inheritance east of the Jordan across from Jericho, toward the sunrise." Nu 32:33; Jos 14:1-5

¹⁶ The LORD said to Moses, ¹⁷ "These are the names of the men who are to assign the land for you as an inheritance: Eleazar the priest and Joshua son of Nun. ¹⁸ And appoint one leader from each tribe to help as-

ᵃ 11 Hebrew Kinnereth

sign the land. ¹⁹These are their names: Nu 1:4,16; Jos 14:1

Caleb son of Jephunneh,
from the tribe of Judah;
²⁰Shemuel son of Ammihud,
from the tribe of Simeon;
²¹Elidad son of Kislon,
from the tribe of Benjamin; Ge 49:27; Ps 68:27
²²Bukki son of Jogli,
the leader from the tribe of Dan;
²³Hanniel son of Ephod,
the leader from the tribe of Manasseh son of Joseph;
²⁴Kemuel son of Shiphtan,
the leader from the tribe of Ephraim son of Joseph;
²⁵Elizaphan son of Parnak,
the leader from the tribe of Zebulun;
²⁶Paltiel son of Azzan,
the leader from the tribe of Issachar;
²⁷Ahihud son of Shelomi,
the leader from the tribe of Asher; Nu 1:40
²⁸Pedahel son of Ammihud,
the leader from the tribe of Naphtali."

²⁹These are the men the LORD commanded to assign the inheritance to the Israelites in the land of Canaan.

Towns for the Levites

35 On the plains of Moab by the Jordan across from Jericho, the LORD said to Moses, ²"Command the Israelites to give the Levites towns to live in from the inheritance the Israelites will possess. And give them pasturelands around the towns. ³Then they will have towns to live in and pasturelands for the cattle they own and all their other animals. Lev 25:32-34; Jos 14:3-4 ⁴"The pasturelands around the towns that you give the Levites will extend a thousand cubits^a from the town wall. ⁵Outside the town, measure two thousand cubits^b on the east side, two thousand on the south side, two thousand on the west and two thousand on the north, with the town in the center. They will have this area as pastureland for the towns.

Cities of Refuge

35:6-34Ref — Dt 4:41-43; 19:1-14; Jos 20:1-9

⁶"Six of the towns you give the Levites will be cities of refuge, to which a person who has killed someone may flee. In addition, give them forty-two other towns. ⁷In all you must give the Levites forty-eight towns, together with their pasturelands. ⁸The towns you give the Levites from the land the Israelites possess are to be given in proportion to the inheritance of each tribe: Take many towns from a tribe that has many, but few from one that has few." Nu 26:54; Jos 20:7-9

^{a} 4 That is, about 1,500 feet or about 450 meters meters

^{b} 5 That is, about 3,000 feet or about 900

⁹Then the LORD said to Moses: ¹⁰"Speak to the Israelites and say to them: 'When you cross the Jordan into Canaan, ¹¹select some towns to be your cities of refuge, to which a person who has killed someone accidentally may flee. ¹²They will be places of refuge from the avenger, so that anyone accused of murder may not die before they stand trial before the assembly. ¹³These six towns you give will be your cities of refuge. ¹⁴Give three on this side of the Jordan and three in Canaan as cities of refuge. ¹⁵These six towns will be a place of refuge for Israelites and for foreigners residing among them, so that anyone who has killed another accidentally can flee there. Ex 21:13; Jos 20:3

¹⁶"'If anyone strikes someone a fatal blow with an iron object, that person is a murderer; the murderer is to be put to death. ¹⁷Or if anyone is holding a stone and strikes someone a fatal blow with it, that person is a murderer; the murderer is to be put to death. ¹⁸Or if anyone is holding a wooden object and strikes someone a fatal blow with it, that person is a murderer; the murderer is to be put to death. ¹⁹The avenger of blood shall put the murderer to death; when the avenger comes upon the murderer, the avenger shall put the murderer to death. ²⁰If anyone with malice aforethought shoves another or throws something at them intentionally so that they die ²¹or if out of enmity one person hits another with their fist so that the other dies, that person is to be put to death; that person is a murderer. The avenger of blood shall put the murderer to death when they meet. Ex 21:12,14; Lev 24:17

²²"'But if without enmity someone suddenly pushes another or throws something at them unintentionally ²³or, without seeing them, drops on them a stone heavy enough to kill them, and they die, then since that other person was not an enemy and no harm was intended, ²⁴the assembly must judge between the accused and the avenger of blood according to these regulations. ²⁵The assembly must protect the one accused of murder from the avenger of blood and send the accused back to the city of refuge to which they fled. The accused must stay there until the death of the high priest, who was anointed with the holy oil. Ex 21:13; 29:7

²⁶"'But if the accused ever goes outside the limits of the city of refuge to which they fled ²⁷and the avenger of blood finds them outside the city, the avenger of blood may kill the accused without being guilty of murder. ²⁸The accused must stay in the city of refuge until the death of the high priest; only after the death of the high priest may they return to their own property.

²⁹"'This is to have the force of

law for you throughout the generations to come, wherever you live.

30 " 'Anyone who kills a person is to be put to death as a murderer only on the testimony of witnesses. But no one is to be put to death on the testimony of only one witness. Dt 17:6; Mt 18:16; 2Co 13:1

31 " 'Do not accept a ransom for the life of a murderer, who deserves to die. They are to be put to death.

32 " 'Do not accept a ransom for anyone who has fled to a city of refuge and so allow them to go back and live on their own land before the death of the high priest. 33 " 'Do not pollute the land where you are. Bloodshed pollutes the land, and atonement cannot be made for the land on which blood has been shed, except by the blood of the one who shed it. 34 Do not defile the land where you live and where I dwell, for I, the LORD, dwell among the Israelites.' " Dt 4:41-43; 19:1-14; Jos 20:1-9

Inheritance of Zelophehad's Daughters

36:1-12pp — Nu 27:1-11

36 The family heads of the clan of Gilead son of Makir, the son of Manasseh, who were from the clans of the descendants of Joseph, came and spoke before Moses and the leaders, the heads of the Israelite families. 2 They said, "When the LORD commanded my lord to give the land as an inheritance to the Israelites by lot, he ordered you to give the inheritance of our brother Zelophehad to his daughters. 3 Now suppose they marry men from other Israelite tribes; then their inheritance will be taken from our ancestral inheritance and added to that of the tribe they marry into. And so part of the inheritance allotted to us will be taken away. 4 When the Year of Jubilee for the Israelites comes, their inheritance will be added to that of the tribe into which they marry, and their property will be taken from the tribal inheritance of our ancestors." Lev 25:10; Nu 26:33; 26:29

5 Then at the LORD's command Moses gave this order to the Israelites: "What the tribe of the descendants of Joseph is saying is right. 6 This is what the LORD commands for Zelophehad's daughters: They may marry anyone they please as long as they marry within their father's tribal clan. 7 No inheritance in Israel is to pass from one tribe to another, for every Israelite shall keep the tribal inheritance of their ancestors. 8 Every daughter who inherits land in any Israelite tribe must marry someone in her father's tribal clan, so that every Israelite will possess the inheritance of their ancestors. 9 No inheritance may pass from one tribe to another, for each Israelite tribe is to keep the land it inherits." 1Ki 21:3; 1Ch 23:22

¹⁰So Zelophehad's daughters did as the LORD commanded Moses. ¹¹Zelophehad's daughters—Mahlah, Tirzah, Hoglah, Milkah and Noah—married their cousins on their father's side. ¹²They married within the clans of the descendants of Manasseh son of Joseph, and their inheritance remained in their father's tribe and clan.   Nu 27:1-11

¹³These are the commands and regulations the LORD gave through Moses to the Israelites on the plains of Moab by the Jordan across from Jericho. Lev 26:46

Deuteronomy

The Command to Leave Horeb

1 These are the words Moses spoke to all Israel in the wilderness east of the Jordan — that is, in the Arabah — opposite Suph, between Paran and Tophel, Laban, Hazeroth and Dizahab. ²(It takes eleven days to go from Horeb to Kadesh Barnea by the Mount Seir road.)   Dt 19:23

³In the fortieth year, on the first day of the eleventh month, Moses proclaimed to the Israelites all that the LORD had commanded him concerning them. ⁴This was after he had defeated Sihon king of the Amorites, who reigned in Heshbon, and at Edrei had defeated Og king of Bashan, who reigned in Ashtaroth.   Nu 21:33-35; 33:38; Jos 13:12

⁵East of the Jordan in the territory of Moab, Moses began to expound this law, saying:

⁶The LORD our God said to us at Horeb, "You have stayed long enough at this mountain. ⁷Break camp and advance into the hill country of the Amorites; go to all the neighboring peoples in the Arabah, in the mountains, in the western foothills, in the Negev and along the coast, to the land of the Canaanites and to Lebanon, as far as the great river, the Euphrates. ⁸See, I have given you this land. Go in and take possession of the land the LORD swore he would give to your fathers — to Abraham, Isaac and Jacob — and to their descendants after them."   Ge 12:7; Dt 11:24; Nu 10:13

The Appointment of Leaders

⁹At that time I said to you, "You are too heavy a burden for me to carry alone. ¹⁰The LORD your God has increased your numbers so that today you are as numerous as the stars in the sky. ¹¹May the LORD, the God of your ancestors, increase you a thousand times and bless you as he has promised! ¹²But how can I bear your problems and your burdens and your disputes all by myself? ¹³Choose

some wise, understanding and respected men from each of your tribes, and I will set them over you." Ex 18:18; Ge 15:5; Dt 10:22 ¹⁴You answered me, "What you propose to do is good."

¹⁵So I took the leading men of your tribes, wise and respected men, and appointed them to have authority over you — as commanders of thousands, of hundreds, of fifties and of tens and as tribal officials. ¹⁶And I charged your judges at that time, "Hear the disputes between your people and judge fairly, whether the case is between two Israelites or between an Israelite and a foreigner residing among you. ¹⁷Do not show partiality in judging; hear both small and great alike. Do not be afraid of anyone, for judgment belongs to God. Bring me any case too hard for you, and I will hear it." ¹⁸And at that time I told you everything you were to do. Ex 18:25; Dt 16:18; Jas 2:1

Spies Sent Out

¹⁹Then, as the LORD our God commanded us, we set out from Horeb and went toward the hill country of the Amorites through all that vast and dreadful wilderness that you have seen, and so we reached Kadesh Barnea. ²⁰Then I said to you, "You have reached the hill country of the Amorites, which the LORD our God is giving us. ²¹See, the LORD your God has given you the land. Go up and take possession of it as the LORD, the God of your ancestors, told you. Do not be afraid; do not be discouraged." Jos 1:6,9,18; Dt 8:15

²²Then all of you came to me and said, "Let us send men ahead to spy out the land for us and bring back a report about the route we are to take and the towns we will come to." Nu 13:1-3

²³The idea seemed good to me; so I selected twelve of you, one man from each tribe. ²⁴They left and went up into the hill country, and came to the Valley of Eshkol and explored it. ²⁵Taking with them some of the fruit of the land, they brought it down to us and reported, "It is a good land that the LORD our God is giving us." Nu 13:21-25

Rebellion Against the LORD

²⁶But you were unwilling to go up; you rebelled against the command of the LORD your God. ²⁷You grumbled in your tents and said, "The LORD hates us; so he brought us out of Egypt to deliver us into the hands of the Amorites to destroy us. ²⁸Where can we go? Our brothers have made our hearts melt in fear. They say, 'The people are stronger and taller than we are; the cities are large, with walls up to the sky. We even saw the Anakites there.'" Nu 14:1-4; Dt 9:28; Nu 13:33

²⁹Then I said to you, "Do not be terrified; do not be afraid of them. ³⁰The LORD your God, who

is going before you, will fight for you, as he did for you in Egypt, before your very eyes, **31** and in the wilderness. There you saw how the LORD your God carried you, as a father carries his son, all the way you went until you reached this place." Dt 32:10-12; Ac 13:18; Ex 14:14

32 In spite of this, you did not trust in the LORD your God, **33** who went ahead of you on your journey, in fire by night and in a cloud by day, to search out places for you to camp and to show you the way you should go. Ps 106:24; Ex 13:21

34 When the LORD heard what you said, he was angry and solemnly swore: **35** "No one from this evil generation shall see the good land I swore to give your ancestors, **36** except Caleb son of Jephunneh. He will see it, and I will give him and his descendants the land he set his feet on, because he followed the LORD wholeheartedly." Nu 14:23,28-30

37 Because of you the LORD became angry with me also and said, "You shall not enter it, either. **38** But your assistant, Joshua son of Nun, will enter it. Encourage him, because he will lead Israel to inherit it. **39** And the little ones that you said would be taken captive, your children who do not yet know good from bad — they will enter the land. I will give it to them and they will take possession of it. **40** But as for you,

turn around and set out toward the desert along the route to the Red Sea.*a"* Nu 20:12; 14:3; Dt 3:26

41 Then you replied, "We have sinned against the LORD. We will go up and fight, as the LORD our God commanded us." So every one of you put on his weapons, thinking it easy to go up into the hill country.

42 But the LORD said to me, "Tell them, 'Do not go up and fight, because I will not be with you. You will be defeated by your enemies.'" Nu 14:41-43

43 So I told you, but you would not listen. You rebelled against the LORD's command and in your arrogance you marched up into the hill country. **44** The Amorites who lived in those hills came out against you; they chased you like a swarm of bees and beat you down from Seir all the way to Hormah. **45** You came back and wept before the LORD, but he paid no attention to your weeping and turned a deaf ear to you. **46** And so you stayed in Kadesh many days — all the time you spent there. Job 27:9; Ps 118:12; Nu 20:1

Wanderings in the Wilderness

2 Then we turned back and set out toward the wilderness along the route to the Red Sea,*a* as the LORD had directed me. For a long time we made our way around the hill country of Seir.

a 40,1 Or the Sea of Reeds

²Then the LORD said to me, ³"You have made your way around this hill country long enough; now turn north. ⁴Give the people these orders: 'You are about to pass through the territory of your relatives the descendants of Esau, who live in Seir. They will be afraid of you, but be very careful. ⁵Do not provoke them to war, for I will not give you any of their land, not even enough to put your foot on. I have given Esau the hill country of Seir as his own. ⁶You are to pay them in silver for the food you eat and the water you drink.'" Jos 24:4; Nu 20:14-21

⁷The LORD your God has blessed you in all the work of your hands. He has watched over your journey through this vast wilderness. These forty years the LORD your God has been with you, and you have not lacked anything. Dt 8:2-4

⁸So we went on past our relatives the descendants of Esau, who live in Seir. We turned from the Arabah road, which comes up from Elath and Ezion Geber, and traveled along the desert road of Moab. 1Ki 9:26; Dt 1:1

⁹Then the LORD said to me, "Do not harass the Moabites or provoke them to war, for I will not give you any part of their land. I have given Ar to the descendants of Lot as a possession." Ge 19:36-38

¹⁰(The Emites used to live there — a people strong and numerous, and as tall as the Anakites. ¹¹Like the Anakites, they too were considered Rephaites, but the Moabites called them Emites. ¹²Horites used to live in Seir, but the descendants of Esau drove them out. They destroyed the Horites from before them and settled in their place, just as Israel did in the land the LORD gave them as their possession.) ver 22; Ge 14:5

¹³And the LORD said, "Now get up and cross the Zered Valley." So we crossed the valley.

¹⁴Thirty-eight years passed from the time we left Kadesh Barnea until we crossed the Zered Valley. By then, that entire generation of fighting men had perished from the camp, as the LORD had sworn to them. ¹⁵The LORD's hand was against them until he had completely eliminated them from the camp. Nu 14:29-35; Dt 1:34-35

¹⁶Now when the last of these fighting men among the people had died, ¹⁷the LORD said to me, ¹⁸"Today you are to pass by the region of Moab at Ar. ¹⁹When you come to the Ammonites, do not harass them or provoke them to war, for I will not give you possession of any land belonging to the Ammonites. I have given it as a possession to the descendants of Lot." ver 9; Ge 19:38

²⁰(That too was considered a land of the Rephaites, who used to live there; but the Ammonites called them Zamzummites.

²¹ They were a people strong and numerous, and as tall as the Anakites. The LORD destroyed them from before the Ammonites, who drove them out and settled in their place. ²² The LORD had done the same for the descendants of Esau, who lived in Seir, when he destroyed the Horites from before them. They drove them out and have lived in their place to this day. ²³ And as for the Avvites who lived in villages as far as Gaza, the Caphtorites coming out from Caphtor*ᵃ* destroyed them and settled in their place.) Ge 10:14; Jos 13:3; Am 9:7

Defeat of Sihon King of Heshbon

²⁴ "Set out now and cross the Arnon Gorge. See, I have given into your hand Sihon the Amorite, king of Heshbon, and his country. Begin to take possession of it and engage him in battle. ²⁵ This very day I will begin to put the terror and fear of you on all the nations under heaven. They will hear reports of you and will tremble and be in anguish because of you." Ex 15:14-16; Dt 11:25

²⁶ From the Desert of Kedemoth I sent messengers to Sihon king of Heshbon offering peace and saying, ²⁷ "Let us pass through your country. We will stay on the main road; we will not turn aside to the right or to the left. ²⁸ Sell us food to eat and water to drink for their price in silver. Only let us pass through on foot — ²⁹ as the descendants of Esau, who live in Seir, and the Moabites, who live in Ar, did for us — until we cross the Jordan into the land the LORD our God is giving us." ³⁰ But Sihon king of Heshbon refused to let us pass through. For the LORD your God had made his spirit stubborn and his heart obstinate in order to give him into your hands, as he has now done. Ex 4:21; Nu 21:21-22

³¹ The LORD said to me, "See, I have begun to deliver Sihon and his country over to you. Now begin to conquer and possess his land." Dt 1:8

³² When Sihon and all his army came out to meet us in battle at Jahaz, ³³ the LORD our God delivered him over to us and we struck him down, together with his sons and his whole army. ³⁴ At that time we took all his towns and completely destroyed*ᵇ* them — men, women and children. We left no survivors. ³⁵ But the livestock and the plunder from the towns we had captured we carried off for ourselves. ³⁶ From Aroer on the rim of the Arnon Gorge, and from the town in the gorge, even as far as Gilead, not one town was too strong for us. The LORD our God gave us all of them. ³⁷ But in accordance with the command of

---

ᵃ 23 That is, Crete   *ᵇ 34* The Hebrew term refers to the irrevocable giving over of things or persons to the LORD, often by totally destroying them.

the LORD our God, you did not encroach on any of the land of the Ammonites, neither the land along the course of the Jabbok nor that around the towns in the hills. Dt 3:6; 7:2; Ge 32:22

Defeat of Og King of Bashan

3 Next we turned and went up along the road toward Bashan, and Og king of Bashan with his whole army marched out to meet us in battle at Edrei. [2] The LORD said to me, "Do not be afraid of him, for I have delivered him into your hands, along with his whole army and his land. Do to him what you did to Sihon king of the Amorites, who reigned in Heshbon." Nu 21:33

[3] So the LORD our God also gave into our hands Og king of Bashan and all his army. We struck them down, leaving no survivors. [4] At that time we took all his cities. There was not one of the sixty cities that we did not take from them — the whole region of Argob, Og's kingdom in Bashan. [5] All these cities were fortified with high walls and with gates and bars, and there were also a great many unwalled villages. [6] We completely destroyed[a] them, as we had done with Sihon king of Heshbon, destroying[a] every city — men, women and children. [7] But

all the livestock and the plunder from their cities we carried off for ourselves. Dt 2:24,34; 1Ki 4:13

[8] So at that time we took from these two kings of the Amorites the territory east of the Jordan, from the Arnon Gorge as far as Mount Hermon. [9] (Hermon is called Sirion by the Sidonians; the Amorites call it Senir.) [10] We took all the towns on the plateau, and all Gilead, and all Bashan as far as Salekah and Edrei, towns of Og's kingdom in Bashan. [11] (Og king of Bashan was the last of the Rephaites. His bed was decorated with iron and was more than nine cubits long and four cubits wide.[b] It is still in Rabbah of the Ammonites.) Ge 14:5; 2Sa 12:26; Ps 29:6

Division of the Land

[12] Of the land that we took over at that time, I gave the Reubenites and the Gadites the territory north of Aroer by the Arnon Gorge, including half the hill country of Gilead, together with its towns. [13] The rest of Gilead and also all of Bashan, the kingdom of Og, I gave to the half-tribe of Manasseh. (The whole region of Argob in Bashan used to be known as a land of the Rephaites. [14] Jair, a descendant of Manasseh, took the whole region of Argob as far as the border of the Geshurites and the Maakathites; it was

---

[a] 6 The Hebrew term refers to the irrevocable giving over of things or persons to the LORD, often by totally destroying them.   [b] 11 That is, about 14 feet long and 6 feet wide or about 4 meters long and 1.8 meters wide

named after him, so that to this day Bashan is called Havvoth Jair.*) [15] And I gave Gilead to Makir. [16] But to the Reubenites and the Gadites I gave the territory extending from Gilead down to the Arnon Gorge (the middle of the gorge being the border) and out to the Jabbok River, which is the border of the Ammonites. [17] Its western border was the Jordan in the Arabah, from Kinnereth to the Sea of the Arabah (that is, the Dead Sea), below the slopes of Pisgah.   Nu 32:32-38; Nu 34:11; Dt 2:36

[18] I commanded you at that time: "The LORD your God has given you this land to take possession of it. But all your able-bodied men, armed for battle, must cross over ahead of the other Israelites. [19] However, your wives, your children and your livestock (I know you have much livestock) may stay in the towns I have given you, [20] until the LORD gives rest to your fellow Israelites as he has to you, and they too have taken over the land that the LORD your God is giving them across the Jordan. After that, each of you may go back to the possession I have given you."   Nu 32:17; Jos 1:14

Moses Forbidden to Cross the Jordan

[21] At that time I commanded Joshua: "You have seen with your own eyes all that the LORD your God has done to these two kings. The LORD will do the same to all the kingdoms over there where you are going. [22] Do not be afraid of them; the LORD your God himself will fight for you." Ex 14:14; Dt 1:29

[23] At that time I pleaded with the LORD: [24] "Sovereign LORD, you have begun to show to your servant your greatness and your strong hand. For what god is there in heaven or on earth who can do the deeds and mighty works you do? [25] Let me go over and see the good land beyond the Jordan — that fine hill country and Lebanon."   Dt 4:22; Ex 15:11; Dt 11:2

[26] But because of you the LORD was angry with me and would not listen to me. "That is enough," the LORD said. "Do not speak to me anymore about this matter. [27] Go up to the top of Pisgah and look west and north and south and east. Look at the land with your own eyes, since you are not going to cross this Jordan. [28] But commission Joshua, and encourage and strengthen him, for he will lead this people across and will cause them to inherit the land that you will see." [29] So we stayed in the valley near Beth Peor.   Dt 1:37; Nu 27:12; Dt 34:6

Obedience Commanded

4 Now, Israel, hear the decrees and laws I am about to teach you. Follow them so that you may

---

a 14 Or *called the settlements of Jair*

live and may go in and take possession of the land the LORD, the God of your ancestors, is giving you. ²Do not add to what I command you and do not subtract from it, but keep the commands of the LORD your God that I give you. <small>Dt 30:15-20; 12:32; Rev 22:18-19</small>

³You saw with your own eyes what the LORD did at Baal Peor. The LORD your God destroyed from among you everyone who followed the Baal of Peor, ⁴but all of you who held fast to the LORD your God are still alive today. <small>Ps 106:28</small>

⁵See, I have taught you decrees and laws as the LORD my God commanded me, so that you may follow them in the land you are entering to take possession of it. ⁶Observe them carefully, for this will show your wisdom and understanding to the nations, who will hear about all these decrees and say, "Surely this great nation is a wise and understanding people." ⁷What other nation is so great as to have their gods near them the way the LORD our God is near us whenever we pray to him? ⁸And what other nation is so great as to have such righteous decrees and laws as this body of laws I am setting before you today? <small>2Sa 7:23; Isa 55:6; 2Ti 3:15</small>

⁹Only be careful, and watch yourselves closely so that you do not forget the things your eyes have seen or let them fade from your heart as long as you live. Teach them to your children and to their children after them. ¹⁰Remember the day you stood before the LORD your God at Horeb, when he said to me, "Assemble the people before me to hear my words so that they may learn to revere me as long as they live in the land and may teach them to their children." ¹¹You came near and stood at the foot of the mountain while it blazed with fire to the very heavens, with black clouds and deep darkness. ¹²Then the LORD spoke to you out of the fire. You heard the sound of words but saw no form; there was only a voice. ¹³He declared to you his covenant, the Ten Commandments, which he commanded you to follow and then wrote them on two stone tablets. ¹⁴And the LORD directed me at that time to teach you the decrees and laws you are to follow in the land that you are crossing the Jordan to possess. <small>Pr 4:23; Eph 6:4; Ex 34:28</small>

Idolatry Forbidden

¹⁵You saw no form of any kind the day the LORD spoke to you at Horeb out of the fire. Therefore watch yourselves very carefully, ¹⁶so that you do not become corrupt and make for yourselves an idol, an image of any shape, whether formed like a man or a woman, ¹⁷or like any animal on earth or any bird that flies in the air, ¹⁸or like any creature that moves along the ground or any

fish in the waters below. ¹⁹And when you look up to the sky and see the sun, the moon and the stars — all the heavenly array — do not be enticed into bowing down to them and worshiping things the LORD your God has apportioned to all the nations under heaven. ²⁰But as for you, the LORD took you and brought you out of the iron-smelting furnace, out of Egypt, to be the people of his inheritance, as you now are.   Ex 20:4-5; Dt 5:8; 1Ki 8:51

²¹The LORD was angry with me because of you, and he solemnly swore that I would not cross the Jordan and enter the good land the LORD your God is giving you as your inheritance. ²²I will die in this land; I will not cross the Jordan; but you are about to cross over and take possession of that good land. ²³Be careful not to forget the covenant of the LORD your God that he made with you; do not make for yourselves an idol in the form of anything the LORD your God has forbidden. ²⁴For the LORD your God is a consuming fire, a jealous God.   Heb 12:29; Dt 1:37; 3:25

²⁵After you have had children and grandchildren and have lived in the land a long time — if you then become corrupt and make any kind of idol, doing evil in the eyes of the LORD your God and arousing his anger, ²⁶I call the heavens and the earth as witnesses against you this day that you will quickly perish from the land that you are crossing the Jordan to possess. You will not live there long but will certainly be destroyed. ²⁷The LORD will scatter you among the peoples, and only a few of you will survive among the nations to which the LORD will drive you. ²⁸There you will worship man-made gods of wood and stone, which cannot see or hear or eat or smell. ²⁹But if from there you seek the LORD your God, you will find him if you seek him with all your heart and with all your soul. ³⁰When you are in distress and all these things have happened to you, then in later days you will return to the LORD your God and obey him. ³¹For the LORD your God is a merciful God; he will not abandon or destroy you or forget the covenant with your ancestors, which he confirmed to them by oath.   Dt 30:18-19; 2Ki 17:2,17; 2Ch 15:4

The LORD Is God

³²Ask now about the former days, long before your time, from the day God created human beings on the earth; ask from one end of the heavens to the other. Has anything so great as this ever happened, or has anything like it ever been heard of? ³³Has any other people heard the voice of God*a* speaking out of fire, as you have, and lived? ³⁴Has any

ᵃ 33 Or *of a god*

god ever tried to take for himself one nation out of another nation, by testings, by signs and wonders, by war, by a mighty hand and an outstretched arm, or by great and awesome deeds, like all the things the LORD your God did for you in Egypt before your very eyes? Dt 5:24-26; 7:19; Mt 24:31

³⁵You were shown these things so that you might know that the LORD is God; besides him there is no other. ³⁶From heaven he made you hear his voice to discipline you. On earth he showed you his great fire, and you heard his words from out of the fire. ³⁷Because he loved your ancestors and chose their descendants after them, he brought you out of Egypt by his Presence and his great strength, ³⁸to drive out before you nations greater and stronger than you and to bring you into their land to give it to you for your inheritance, as it is today. Ex 19:9,19; Dt 10:15; 1Sa 2:2

³⁹Acknowledge and take to heart this day that the LORD is God in heaven above and on the earth below. There is no other. ⁴⁰Keep his decrees and commands, which I am giving you today, so that it may go well with you and your children after you and that you may live long in the land the LORD your God gives you for all time. Jos 2:11; Lev 22:31; Dt 5:16

Cities of Refuge

4:41-43Ref — Nu 35:6-34; Dt 19:1-14; Jos 20:1-9

⁴¹Then Moses set aside three cities east of the Jordan, ⁴²to which anyone who had killed a person could flee if they had unintentionally killed a neighbor without malice aforethought. They could flee into one of these cities and save their life. ⁴³The cities were these: Bezer in the wilderness plateau, for the Reubenites; Ramoth in Gilead, for the Gadites; and Golan in Bashan, for the Manassites. Nu 35:6-34; Dt 19:1-14

Introduction to the Law

⁴⁴This is the law Moses set before the Israelites. ⁴⁵These are the stipulations, decrees and laws Moses gave them when they came out of Egypt ⁴⁶and were in the valley near Beth Peor east of the Jordan, in the land of Sihon king of the Amorites, who reigned in Heshbon and was defeated by Moses and the Israelites as they came out of Egypt. ⁴⁷They took possession of his land and the land of Og king of Bashan, the two Amorite kings east of the Jordan. ⁴⁸This land extended from Aroer on the rim of the Arnon Gorge to Mount Sirion*a* (that is, Hermon), ⁴⁹and included all the Arabah east of the Jordan, as far as the Dead Sea,*b* below the slopes of Pisgah. Nu 21:26

---

a 48 Syriac (see also 3:9); Hebrew *Siyon*   *b* 49 Hebrew *the Sea of the Arabah*

The Ten Commandments

5:6-21pp — Ex 20:1-17

5 Moses summoned all Israel and said:

Hear, Israel, the decrees and laws I declare in your hearing today. Learn them and be sure to follow them. ²The LORD our God made a covenant with us at Horeb. ³It was not with our ancestors[a] that the LORD made this covenant, but with us, with all of us who are alive here today. ⁴The LORD spoke to you face to face out of the fire on the mountain. ⁵(At that time I stood between the LORD and you to declare to you the word of the LORD, because you were afraid of the fire and did not go up the mountain.) And he said: *Ex 19:5; 20:18,21; Dt 4:12,33,36*

⁶"I am the LORD your God, who brought you out of Egypt, out of the land of slavery. *Lev 26:1*

⁷"You shall have no other gods before[b] me.

⁸"You shall not make for yourself an image in the form of anything in heaven above or on the earth beneath or in the waters below. ⁹You shall not bow down to them or worship them; for I, the LORD your God, am a jealous God, punishing the children for the sin of the parents to the third and fourth generation of those who hate me, ¹⁰but showing love to a thousand generations of those who love me and keep my commandments. *Ex 34:7*

¹¹"You shall not misuse the name of the LORD your God, for the LORD will not hold anyone guiltless who misuses his name. *Lev 19:12*

¹²"Observe the Sabbath day by keeping it holy, as the LORD your God has commanded you. ¹³Six days you shall labor and do all your work, ¹⁴but the seventh day is a sabbath to the LORD your God. On it you shall not do any work, neither you, nor your son or daughter, nor your male or female servant, nor your ox, your donkey or any of your animals, nor any foreigner residing in your towns, so that your male and female servants may rest, as you do. ¹⁵Remember that you were slaves in Egypt and that the LORD your God brought you out of there with a mighty hand and an outstretched arm.

---

a 3 Or *not only with our parents*   *b 7* Or *besides*

Therefore the LORD your God has commanded you to observe the Sabbath day. Ge 2:2; Heb 4:4

¹⁶ "Honor your father and your mother, as the LORD your God has commanded you, so that you may live long and that it may go well with you in the land the LORD your God is giving you. Lev 19:3; Eph 6:2-3

¹⁷ "You shall not murder. Ge 9:6

¹⁸ "You shall not commit adultery. Mt 5:27-30; Jas 2:11

¹⁹ "You shall not steal. Lev 19:11

²⁰ "You shall not give false testimony against your neighbor. Mk 10:19

²¹ "You shall not covet your neighbor's wife. You shall not set your desire on your neighbor's house or land, his male or female servant, his ox or donkey, or anything that belongs to your neighbor." Ex 20:1-17; Ro 7:7

²² These are the commandments the LORD proclaimed in a loud voice to your whole assembly there on the mountain from out of the fire, the cloud and the deep darkness; and he added nothing more. Then he wrote them on two stone tablets and gave them to me. Ex 31:18; Dt 4:13

²³ When you heard the voice out of the darkness, while the mountain was ablaze with fire,

all the leaders of your tribes and your elders came to me. ²⁴ And you said, "The LORD our God has shown us his glory and his majesty, and we have heard his voice from the fire. Today we have seen that a person can live even if God speaks with them. ²⁵ But now, why should we die? This great fire will consume us, and we will die if we hear the voice of the LORD our God any longer. ²⁶ For what mortal has ever heard the voice of the living God speaking out of fire, as we have, and survived? ²⁷ Go near and listen to all that the LORD our God says. Then tell us whatever the LORD our God tells you. We will listen and obey." Dt 4:33; 18:16; Ex 19:19

²⁸ The LORD heard you when you spoke to me, and the LORD said to me, "I have heard what this people said to you. Everything they said was good. ²⁹ Oh, that their hearts would be inclined to fear me and keep all my commands always, so that it might go well with them and their children forever! Ps 81:8,13; Isa 48:18

³⁰ "Go, tell them to return to their tents. ³¹ But you stay here with me so that I may give you all the commands, decrees and laws you are to teach them to follow in the land I am giving them to possess." Ex 24:12

³² So be careful to do what the LORD your God has commanded you; do not turn aside to the right or to the left. ³³ Walk in obedience

to all that the LORD your God has commanded you, so that you may live and prosper and prolong your days in the land that you will possess. Dt 17:11,20; Jos 1:7; Jer 7:23

Love the LORD Your God

6 These are the commands, decrees and laws the LORD your God directed me to teach you to observe in the land that you are crossing the Jordan to possess, ²so that you, your children and their children after them may fear the LORD your God as long as you live by keeping all his decrees and commands that I give you, and so that you may enjoy long life. ³Hear, Israel, and be careful to obey so that it may go well with you and that you may increase greatly in a land flowing with milk and honey, just as the LORD, the God of your ancestors, promised you. Ex 3:8; 20:20; Dt 10:12-13

⁴Hear, O Israel: The LORD our God, the LORD is one.ᵃ ⁵Love the LORD your God with all your heart and with all your soul and with all your strength. ⁶These commandments that I give you today are to be on your hearts. ⁷Impress them on your children. Talk about them when you sit at home and when you walk along the road, when you lie down and when you get up. ⁸Tie them as symbols on your hands and bind them on your foreheads. ⁹Write them on the doorframes of your houses and on your gates. Mt 22:37; Dt 11:18; Eph 6:4

¹⁰When the LORD your God brings you into the land he swore to your fathers, to Abraham, Isaac and Jacob, to give you—a land with large, flourishing cities you did not build, ¹¹houses filled with all kinds of good things you did not provide, wells you did not dig, and vineyards and olive groves you did not plant—then when you eat and are satisfied, ¹²be careful that you do not forget the LORD, who brought you out of Egypt, out of the land of slavery. Dt 8:10; Jos 24:13; Ps 103:2

¹³Fear the LORD your God, serve him only and take your oaths in his name. ¹⁴Do not follow other gods, the gods of the peoples around you; ¹⁵for the LORD your God, who is among you, is a jealous God and his anger will burn against you, and he will destroy you from the face of the land. ¹⁶Do not put the LORD your God to the test as you did at Massah. ¹⁷Be sure to keep the commands of the LORD your God and the stipulations and decrees he has given you. ¹⁸Do what is right and good in the LORD's sight, so that it may go well with you and you may go in and take over the good land the LORD promised on oath to your ancestors, ¹⁹thrusting out all

ᵃ 4 Or The LORD our God is one LORD; or The LORD is our God, the LORD is one; or The LORD is our God, the LORD alone your enemies before you, as the LORD said.   Mt 4:7; Dt 4:24; Ps 119:4

²⁰In the future, when your son asks you, "What is the meaning of the stipulations, decrees and laws the LORD our God has commanded you?" ²¹tell him: "We were slaves of Pharaoh in Egypt, but the LORD brought us out of Egypt with a mighty hand. ²²Before our eyes the LORD sent signs and wonders—great and terrible—on Egypt and Pharaoh and his whole household. ²³But he brought us out from there to bring us in and give us the land he promised on oath to our ancestors. ²⁴The LORD commanded us to obey all these decrees and to fear the LORD our God, so that we might always prosper and be kept alive, as is the case today. ²⁵And if we are careful to obey all this law before the LORD our God, as he has commanded us, that will be our righteousness."   Ex 13:14; Jer 32:39; Ro 10:3,5

Driving Out the Nations

7 When the LORD your God brings you into the land you are entering to possess and drives out before you many nations—the Hittites, Girgashites, Amorites, Canaanites, Perizzites, Hivites and Jebusites, seven nations larger and stronger than you— ²and when the LORD your God has delivered them over to you and you have defeated them, then you must destroy them totally.^a Make no treaty with them, and show them no mercy. ³Do not intermarry with them. Do not give your daughters to their sons or take their daughters for your sons, ⁴for they will turn your children away from following me to serve other gods, and the LORD's anger will burn against you and will quickly destroy you. ⁵This is what you are to do to them: Break down their altars, smash their sacred stones, cut down their Asherah poles^b and burn their idols in the fire. ⁶For you are a people holy to the LORD your God. The LORD your God has chosen you out of all the peoples on the face of the earth to be his people, his treasured possession.   Ex 23:32; Dt 14:2; 31:3

⁷The LORD did not set his affection on you and choose you because you were more numerous than other peoples, for you were the fewest of all peoples. ⁸But it was because the LORD loved you and kept the oath he swore to your ancestors that he brought you out with a mighty hand and redeemed you from the land of slavery, from the power of Pharaoh king of Egypt. ⁹Know therefore that the LORD your God is God; he is the faithful God,

---

^a 2 The Hebrew term refers to the irrevocable giving over of things or persons to the LORD, often by totally destroying them; also in verse 26.   ^b 5 That is, wooden symbols of the goddess Asherah; here and elsewhere in Deuteronomy

keeping his covenant of love to a thousand generations of those who love him and keep his commandments. [10] But

those who hate him he will repay to their face by destruction;
he will not be slow to repay to their face those who hate him.

[11] Therefore, take care to follow the commands, decrees and laws I give you today.

[12] If you pay attention to these laws and are careful to follow them, then the LORD your God will keep his covenant of love with you, as he swore to your ancestors. [13] He will love you and bless you and increase your numbers. He will bless the fruit of your womb, the crops of your land — your grain, new wine and olive oil — the calves of your herds and the lambs of your flocks in the land he swore to your ancestors to give you. [14] You will be blessed more than any other people; none of your men or women will be childless, nor will any of your livestock be without young. [15] The LORD will keep you free from every disease. He will not inflict on you the horrible diseases you knew in Egypt, but he will inflict them on all who hate you. [16] You must destroy all the peoples the LORD your God gives over to you. Do not look on them with pity and do not serve their gods, for that will be a snare to you. Dt 28:1-14; Ex 23:26; 15:26

[17] You may say to yourselves, "These nations are stronger than we are. How can we drive them out?" [18] But do not be afraid of them; remember well what the LORD your God did to Pharaoh and to all Egypt. [19] You saw with your own eyes the great trials, the signs and wonders, the mighty hand and outstretched arm, with which the LORD your God brought you out. The LORD your God will do the same to all the peoples you now fear. [20] Moreover, the LORD your God will send the hornet among them until even the survivors who hide from you have perished. [21] Do not be terrified by them, for the LORD your God, who is among you, is a great and awesome God. [22] The LORD your God will drive out those nations before you, little by little. You will not be allowed to eliminate them all at once, or the wild animals will multiply around you. [23] But the LORD your God will deliver them over to you, throwing them into great confusion until they are destroyed. [24] He will give their kings into your hand, and you will wipe out their names from under heaven. No one will be able to stand up against you; you will destroy them. [25] The images of their gods you are to burn in the fire. Do not covet the silver and gold on them, and do not take it for yourselves,

or you will be ensnared by it, for it is detestable to the LORD your God. ²⁶ Do not bring a detestable thing into your house or you, like it, will be set apart for destruction. Regard it as vile and utterly detest it, for it is set apart for destruction. Dt 4:34; Ex 23:28-30; Ps 105:5

Do Not Forget the LORD

8 Be careful to follow every command I am giving you today, so that you may live and increase and may enter and possess the land the LORD promised on oath to your ancestors. ² Remember how the LORD your God led you all the way in the wilderness these forty years, to humble and test you in order to know what was in your heart, whether or not you would keep his commands. ³ He humbled you, causing you to hunger and then feeding you with manna, which neither you nor your ancestors had known, to teach you that man does not live on bread alone but on every word that comes from the mouth of the LORD. ⁴ Your clothes did not wear out and your feet did not swell during these forty years. ⁵ Know then in your heart that as a man disciplines his son, so the LORD your God disciplines you. Dt 4:1; Mt 4:4; Heb 12:5-11

⁶ Observe the commands of the LORD your God, walking in obedience to him and revering him. ⁷ For the LORD your God is bringing you into a good land — a land with brooks, streams, and deep springs gushing out into the valleys and hills; ⁸ a land with wheat and barley, vines and fig trees, pomegranates, olive oil and honey; ⁹ a land where bread will not be scarce and you will lack nothing; a land where the rocks are iron and you can dig copper out of the hills. Dt 11:9-12; Jer 2:7

¹⁰ When you have eaten and are satisfied, praise the LORD your God for the good land he has given you. ¹¹ Be careful that you do not forget the LORD your God, failing to observe his commands, his laws and his decrees that I am giving you this day. ¹² Otherwise, when you eat and are satisfied, when you build fine houses and settle down, ¹³ and when your herds and flocks grow large and your silver and gold increase and all you have is multiplied, ¹⁴ then your heart will become proud and you will forget the LORD your God, who brought you out of Egypt, out of the land of slavery. ¹⁵ He led you through the vast and dreadful wilderness, that thirsty and waterless land, with its venomous snakes and scorpions. He brought you water out of hard rock. ¹⁶ He gave you manna to eat in the wilderness, something your ancestors had never known, to humble and test you so that in the end it might go well with you. ¹⁷ You may say to yourself, "My power and the

strength of my hands have produced this wealth for me." ¹⁸But remember the LORD your God, for it is he who gives you the ability to produce wealth, and so confirms his covenant, which he swore to your ancestors, as it is today.   Dt 6:10-12; Pr 10:22; Hos 2:8

¹⁹If you ever forget the LORD your God and follow other gods and worship and bow down to them, I testify against you today that you will surely be destroyed. ²⁰Like the nations the LORD destroyed before you, so you will be destroyed for not obeying the LORD your God.   Dt 4:26; 30:18

Not Because of Israel's Righteousness

9 Hear, Israel: You are now about to cross the Jordan to go in and dispossess nations greater and stronger than you, with large cities that have walls up to the sky. ²The people are strong and tall — Anakites! You know about them and have heard it said: "Who can stand up against the Anakites?" ³But be assured today that the LORD your God is the one who goes across ahead of you like a devouring fire. He will destroy them; he will subdue them before you. And you will drive them out and annihilate them quickly, as the LORD has promised you.   Nu 13:22,28,32-33; Dt 7:23-24; 31:3

⁴After the LORD your God has driven them out before you, do not say to yourself, "The LORD has brought me here to take possession of this land because of my righteousness." No, it is on account of the wickedness of these nations that the LORD is going to drive them out before you. ⁵It is not because of your righteousness or your integrity that you are going in to take possession of their land; but on account of the wickedness of these nations, the LORD your God will drive them out before you, to accomplish what he swore to your fathers, to Abraham, Isaac and Jacob. ⁶Understand, then, that it is not because of your righteousness that the LORD your God is giving you this good land to possess, for you are a stiff-necked people.   Ge 12:7; Lev 18:21,24-30; Dt 8:17

The Golden Calf

⁷Remember this and never forget how you aroused the anger of the LORD your God in the wilderness. From the day you left Egypt until you arrived here, you have been rebellious against the LORD. ⁸At Horeb you aroused the LORD's wrath so that he was angry enough to destroy you. ⁹When I went up on the mountain to receive the tablets of stone, the tablets of the covenant that the LORD had made with you, I stayed on the mountain forty days and forty nights; I ate no bread and drank no water. ¹⁰The LORD gave me two stone

tablets inscribed by the finger of God. On them were all the commandments the Lord proclaimed to you on the mountain out of the fire, on the day of the assembly. Ps 106:19; Ex 24:12,15,18

¹¹At the end of the forty days and forty nights, the Lord gave me the two stone tablets, the tablets of the covenant. ¹²Then the Lord told me, "Go down from here at once, because your people whom you brought out of Egypt have become corrupt. They have turned away quickly from what I commanded them and have made an idol for themselves." Ex 32:7-8; Jdg 2:17

¹³And the Lord said to me, "I have seen this people, and they are a stiff-necked people indeed! ¹⁴Let me alone, so that I may destroy them and blot out their name from under heaven. And I will make you into a nation stronger and more numerous than they." Ex 32:10

¹⁵So I turned and went down from the mountain while it was ablaze with fire. And the two tablets of the covenant were in my hands. ¹⁶When I looked, I saw that you had sinned against the Lord your God; you had made for yourselves an idol cast in the shape of a calf. You had turned aside quickly from the way that the Lord had commanded you. ¹⁷So I took the two tablets and threw them out of my hands, breaking them to pieces before your eyes. Ex 32:15

¹⁸Then once again I fell prostrate before the Lord for forty days and forty nights; I ate no bread and drank no water, because of all the sin you had committed, doing what was evil in the Lord's sight and so arousing his anger. ¹⁹I feared the anger and wrath of the Lord, for he was angry enough with you to destroy you. But again the Lord listened to me. ²⁰And the Lord was angry enough with Aaron to destroy him, but at that time I prayed for Aaron too. ²¹Also I took that sinful thing of yours, the calf you had made, and burned it in the fire. Then I crushed it and ground it to powder as fine as dust and threw the dust into a stream that flowed down the mountain. Ex 34:28; Heb 12:21; Ex 32:20

²²You also made the Lord angry at Taberah, at Massah and at Kibroth Hattaavah. Nu 11:3; Ex 17:7

²³And when the Lord sent you out from Kadesh Barnea, he said, "Go up and take possession of the land I have given you." But you rebelled against the command of the Lord your God. You did not trust him or obey him. ²⁴You have been rebellious against the Lord ever since I have known you. Dt 31:27; Ps 106:24

²⁵I lay prostrate before the Lord those forty days and forty nights because the Lord had said he would destroy you. ²⁶I prayed to the Lord and said, "Sovereign Lord, do not destroy your

people, your own inheritance that you redeemed by your great power and brought out of Egypt with a mighty hand. [27] Remember your servants Abraham, Isaac and Jacob. Overlook the stubbornness of this people, their wickedness and their sin. [28] Otherwise, the country from which you brought us will say, 'Because the LORD was not able to take them into the land he had promised them, and because he hated them, he brought them out to put them to death in the wilderness.' [29] But they are your people, your inheritance that you brought out by your great power and your outstretched arm."   Ex 32:11; Dt 4:20; 1Ki 8:51

Tablets Like the First Ones

10 At that time the LORD said to me, "Chisel out two stone tablets like the first ones and come up to me on the mountain. Also make a wooden ark.[a] [2] I will write on the tablets the words that were on the first tablets, which you broke. Then you are to put them in the ark."   Ex 25:16,21; 34:1-2

[3] So I made the ark out of acacia wood and chiseled out two stone tablets like the first ones, and I went up on the mountain with the two tablets in my hands. [4] The LORD wrote on these tablets what he had written before,

the Ten Commandments he had proclaimed to you on the mountain, out of the fire, on the day of the assembly. And the LORD gave them to me. [5] Then I came back down the mountain and put the tablets in the ark I had made, as the LORD commanded me, and they are there now.   Ex 20:1; 40:20

[6] (The Israelites traveled from the wells of Bene Jaakan to Moserah. There Aaron died and was buried, and Eleazar his son succeeded him as priest. [7] From there they traveled to Gudgodah and on to Jotbathah, a land with streams of water. [8] At that time the LORD set apart the tribe of Levi to carry the ark of the covenant of the LORD, to stand before the LORD to minister and to pronounce blessings in his name, as they still do today. [9] That is why the Levites have no share or inheritance among their fellow Israelites; the LORD is their inheritance, as the LORD your God told them.)   Nu 33:30-31,38; Dt 18:5; 21:5

[10] Now I had stayed on the mountain forty days and forty nights, as I did the first time, and the LORD listened to me at this time also. It was not his will to destroy you. [11] "Go," the LORD said to me, "and lead the people on their way, so that they may enter and possess the land I swore to their ancestors to give them."   Ex 34:28; Dt 9:18-19,25

---

[a] 1 That is, a chest

Fear the LORD

¹²And now, Israel, what does the LORD your God ask of you but to fear the LORD your God, to walk in obedience to him, to love him, to serve the LORD your God with all your heart and with all your soul, ¹³and to observe the LORD's commands and decrees that I am giving you today for your own good? Mic 6:8; Dt 6:5

¹⁴To the LORD your God belong the heavens, even the highest heavens, the earth and everything in it. ¹⁵Yet the LORD set his affection on your ancestors and loved them, and he chose you, their descendants, above all the nations—as it is today. ¹⁶Circumcise your hearts, therefore, and do not be stiff-necked any longer. ¹⁷For the LORD your God is God of gods and Lord of lords, the great God, mighty and awesome, who shows no partiality and accepts no bribes. ¹⁸He defends the cause of the fatherless and the widow, and loves the foreigner residing among you, giving them food and clothing. ¹⁹And you are to love those who are foreigners, for you yourselves were foreigners in Egypt. ²⁰Fear the LORD your God and serve him. Hold fast to him and take your oaths in his name. ²¹He is the one you praise; he is your God, who performed for you those great and awesome wonders you saw with your own eyes.

²²Your ancestors who went down into Egypt were seventy in all, and now the LORD your God has made you as numerous as the stars in the sky. Lev 19:34; Dt 4:37; 1Ki 8:27

Love and Obey the LORD

11 Love the LORD your God and keep his requirements, his decrees, his laws and his commands always. ²Remember today that your children were not the ones who saw and experienced the discipline of the LORD your God: his majesty, his mighty hand, his outstretched arm; ³the signs he performed and the things he did in the heart of Egypt, both to Pharaoh king of Egypt and to his whole country; ⁴what he did to the Egyptian army, to its horses and chariots, how he overwhelmed them with the waters of the Red Sea*a* as they were pursuing you, and how the LORD brought lasting ruin on them. ⁵It was not your children who saw what he did for you in the wilderness until you arrived at this place, ⁶and what he did to Dathan and Abiram, sons of Eliab the Reubenite, when the earth opened its mouth right in the middle of all Israel and swallowed them up with their households, their tents and every living thing that belonged to them. ⁷But it was your own eyes that saw all these great things the LORD has done. Nu 16:1-35; Dt 5:24; 10:12

---

a 4 Or *the Sea of Reeds*

⁸Observe therefore all the commands I am giving you today, so that you may have the strength to go in and take over the land that you are crossing the Jordan to possess, ⁹and so that you may live long in the land the LORD swore to your ancestors to give to them and their descendants, a land flowing with milk and honey. ¹⁰The land you are entering to take over is not like the land of Egypt, from which you have come, where you planted your seed and irrigated it by foot as in a vegetable garden. ¹¹But the land you are crossing the Jordan to take possession of is a land of mountains and valleys that drinks rain from heaven. ¹²It is a land the LORD your God cares for; the eyes of the LORD your God are continually on it from the beginning of the year to its end. Jos 1:7; Dt 4:40; 8:7

¹³So if you faithfully obey the commands I am giving you today—to love the LORD your God and to serve him with all your heart and with all your soul— ¹⁴then I will send rain on your land in its season, both autumn and spring rains, so that you may gather in your grain, new wine and olive oil. ¹⁵I will provide grass in the fields for your cattle, and you will eat and be satisfied. Dt 4:29; Joel 2:23; Ps 104:14

¹⁶Be careful, or you will be enticed to turn away and worship other gods and bow down to them. ¹⁷Then the LORD's anger will burn against you, and he will shut up the heavens so that it will not rain and the ground will yield no produce, and you will soon perish from the good land the LORD is giving you. ¹⁸Fix these words of mine in your hearts and minds; tie them as symbols on your hands and bind them on your foreheads. ¹⁹Teach them to your children, talking about them when you sit at home and when you walk along the road, when you lie down and when you get up. ²⁰Write them on the doorframes of your houses and on your gates, ²¹so that your days and the days of your children may be many in the land the LORD swore to give your ancestors, as many as the days that the heavens are above the earth. Dt 4:9-10; 6:6-8; 1Ki 8:35

²²If you carefully observe all these commands I am giving you to follow—to love the LORD your God, to walk in obedience to him and to hold fast to him— ²³then the LORD will drive out all these nations before you, and you will dispossess nations larger and stronger than you. ²⁴Every place where you set your foot will be yours: Your territory will extend from the desert to Lebanon, and from the Euphrates River to the Mediterranean Sea. ²⁵No one will be able to stand against you. The LORD your God, as he promised you, will put the terror and fear of

you on the whole land, wherever you go. Ge 15:18; Dt 7:24; 9:1

²⁶See, I am setting before you today a blessing and a curse— ²⁷the blessing if you obey the commands of the LORD your God that I am giving you today; ²⁸the curse if you disobey the commands of the LORD your God and turn from the way that I command you today by following other gods, which you have not known. ²⁹When the LORD your God has brought you into the land you are entering to possess, you are to proclaim on Mount Gerizim the blessings, and on Mount Ebal the curses. ³⁰As you know, these mountains are across the Jordan, westward, toward the setting sun, near the great trees of Moreh, in the territory of those Canaanites living in the Arabah in the vicinity of Gilgal. ³¹You are about to cross the Jordan to enter and take possession of the land the LORD your God is giving you. When you have taken it over and are living there, ³²be sure that you obey all the decrees and laws I am setting before you today. Dt 28:1-14; 30:1,15,19; 27:12-13

The One Place of Worship

12 These are the decrees and laws you must be careful to follow in the land that the LORD, the God of your ancestors, has given you to possess—as long as you live in the land. ²Destroy completely all the places on the high mountains, on the hills and under every spreading tree, where the nations you are dispossessing worship their gods. ³Break down their altars, smash their sacred stones and burn their Asherah poles in the fire; cut down the idols of their gods and wipe out their names from those places. Dt 4:9-10; Nu 33:52; Ex 23:13

⁴You must not worship the LORD your God in their way. ⁵But you are to seek the place the LORD your God will choose from among all your tribes to put his Name there for his dwelling. To that place you must go; ⁶there bring your burnt offerings and sacrifices, your tithes and special gifts, what you have vowed to give and your freewill offerings, and the firstborn of your herds and flocks. ⁷There, in the presence of the LORD your God, you and your families shall eat and shall rejoice in everything you have put your hand to, because the LORD your God has blessed you. Dt 14:26; 2Ch 7:12,16

⁸You are not to do as we do here today, everyone doing as they see fit, ⁹since you have not yet reached the resting place and the inheritance the LORD your God is giving you. ¹⁰But you will cross the Jordan and settle in the land the LORD your God is giving you as an inheritance, and he will give you rest from all your enemies around you so that you will live in safety. ¹¹Then

to the place the LORD your God will choose as a dwelling for his Name — there you are to bring everything I command you: your burnt offerings and sacrifices, your tithes and special gifts, and all the choice possessions you have vowed to the LORD. [12] And there rejoice before the LORD your God — you, your sons and daughters, your male and female servants, and the Levites from your towns who have no allotment or inheritance of their own. [13] Be careful not to sacrifice your burnt offerings anywhere you please. [14] Offer them only at the place the LORD will choose in one of your tribes, and there observe everything I command you. Dt 10:9; 15:20; 3:20

[15] Nevertheless, you may slaughter your animals in any of your towns and eat as much of the meat as you want, as if it were gazelle or deer, according to the blessing the LORD your God gives you. Both the ceremonially unclean and the clean may eat it. [16] But you must not eat the blood; pour it out on the ground like water. [17] You must not eat in your own towns the tithe of your grain and new wine and olive oil, or the firstborn of your herds and flocks, or whatever you have vowed to give, or your freewill offerings or special gifts. [18] Instead, you are to eat them in the presence of the LORD your God at the place the LORD your God will choose — you, your sons and daughters, your male and female servants, and the Levites from your towns — and you are to rejoice before the LORD your God in everything you put your hand to. [19] Be careful not to neglect the Levites as long as you live in your land.   Lev 17:10-12; Dt 14:5,27

[20] When the LORD your God has enlarged your territory as he promised you, and you crave meat and say, "I would like some meat," then you may eat as much of it as you want. [21] If the place where the LORD your God chooses to put his Name is too far away from you, you may slaughter animals from the herds and flocks the LORD has given you, as I have commanded you, and in your own towns you may eat as much of them as you want. [22] Eat them as you would gazelle or deer. Both the ceremonially unclean and the clean may eat. [23] But be sure you do not eat the blood, because the blood is the life, and you must not eat the life with the meat. [24] You must not eat the blood; pour it out on the ground like water. [25] Do not eat it, so that it may go well with you and your children after you, because you will be doing what is right in the eyes of the LORD.   Ge 15:18; Lev 17:11,14; Dt 4:40

[26] But take your consecrated things and whatever you have vowed to give, and go to the place the LORD will choose. [27] Present

your burnt offerings on the altar of the LORD your God, both the meat and the blood. The blood of your sacrifices must be poured beside the altar of the LORD your God, but you may eat the meat. ²⁸ Be careful to obey all these regulations I am giving you, so that it may always go well with you and your children after you, because you will be doing what is good and right in the eyes of the LORD your God.   Lev 1:5,9,13

²⁹ The LORD your God will cut off before you the nations you are about to invade and dispossess. But when you have driven them out and settled in their land, ³⁰ and after they have been destroyed before you, be careful not to be ensnared by inquiring about their gods, saying, "How do these nations serve their gods? We will do the same." ³¹ You must not worship the LORD your God in their way, because in worshiping their gods, they do all kinds of detestable things the LORD hates. They even burn their sons and daughters in the fire as sacrifices to their gods.   Dt 9:5; 18:10

³² See that you do all I command you; do not add to it or take away from it.ᵃ   Dt 4:2

Worshiping Other Gods

13 ᵇ If a prophet, or one who foretells by dreams, appears among you and announc-es to you a sign or wonder, ² and if the sign or wonder spoken of takes place, and the prophet says, "Let us follow other gods" (gods you have not known) "and let us worship them," ³ you must not listen to the words of that prophet or dreamer. The LORD your God is testing you to find out whether you love him with all your heart and with all your soul. ⁴ It is the LORD your God you must follow, and him you must revere. Keep his commands and obey him; serve him and hold fast to him. ⁵ That prophet or dreamer must be put to death for inciting rebellion against the LORD your God, who brought you out of Egypt and redeemed you from the land of slavery. That prophet or dreamer tried to turn you from the way the LORD your God commanded you to follow. You must purge the evil from among you.   Dt 8:2,16; 2Ki 23:3; Mt 24:24

⁶ If your very own brother, or your son or daughter, or the wife you love, or your closest friend secretly entices you, saying, "Let us go and worship other gods" (gods that neither you nor your ancestors have known, ⁷ gods of the peoples around you, whether near or far, from one end of the land to the other), ⁸ do not yield to them or listen to them. Show them no pity. Do not spare them or shield them. ⁹ You must

ᵃ 32 In Hebrew texts this verse (12:32) is numbered 13:1.   ᵇ In Hebrew texts 13:1-18 is numbered 13:2-19.

certainly put them to death. Your hand must be the first in putting them to death, and then the hands of all the people. **10**Stone them to death, because they tried to turn you away from the LORD your God, who brought you out of Egypt, out of the land of slavery. **11**Then all Israel will hear and be afraid, and no one among you will do such an evil thing again. Dt 17:2-7; 17:13; Pr 1:10

12If you hear it said about one of the towns the LORD your God is giving you to live in **13**that troublemakers have arisen among you and have led the people of their town astray, saying, "Let us go and worship other gods" (gods you have not known), **14**then you must inquire, probe and investigate it thoroughly. And if it is true and it has been proved that this detestable thing has been done among you, **15**you must certainly put to the sword all who live in that town. You must destroy it completely,*a* both its people and its livestock. **16**You are to gather all the plunder of the town into the middle of the public square and completely burn the town and all its plunder as a whole burnt offering to the LORD your God. That town is to remain a ruin forever, never to be rebuilt, **17**and none of the condemned things*a* are to be found

in your hands. Then the LORD will turn from his fierce anger, will show you mercy, and will have compassion on you. He will increase your numbers, as he promised on oath to your ancestors— **18**because you obey the LORD your God by keeping all his commands that I am giving you today and doing what is right in his eyes. Jos 8:28; Nu 25:4; Dt 7:25-26

Clean and Unclean Food

14:3-20pp — Lev 11:1-23

14 You are the children of the LORD your God. Do not cut yourselves or shave the front of your heads for the dead, **2**for you are a people holy to the LORD your God. Out of all the peoples on the face of the earth, the LORD has chosen you to be his treasured possession. Lev 21:5; Ro 8:14; Dt 7:6

3Do not eat any detestable thing. **4**These are the animals you may eat: the ox, the sheep, the goat, **5**the deer, the gazelle, the roe deer, the wild goat, the ibex, the antelope and the mountain sheep.*b* **6**You may eat any animal that has a divided hoof and that chews the cud. **7**However, of those that chew the cud or that have a divided hoof you may not eat the camel, the rabbit or the hyrax. Although they chew the cud, they do not have a divided hoof;

a 15,17 The Hebrew term refers to the irrevocable giving over of things or persons to the LORD, often by totally destroying them. *b 5* The precise identification of some of the birds and animals in this chapter is uncertain.

are ceremonially unclean for you. [8] The pig is also unclean; although it has a divided hoof, it does not chew the cud. You are not to eat their meat or touch their carcasses. Lev 11:2-45; Eze 4:14

[9] Of all the creatures living in the water, you may eat any that has fins and scales. [10] But anything that does not have fins and scales you may not eat; for you it is unclean.

[11] You may eat any clean bird. [12] But these you may not eat: the eagle, the vulture, the black vulture, [13] the red kite, the black kite, any kind of falcon, [14] any kind of raven, [15] the horned owl, the screech owl, the gull, any kind of hawk, [16] the little owl, the great owl, the white owl, [17] the desert owl, the osprey, the cormorant, [18] the stork, any kind of heron, the hoopoe and the bat.

[19] All flying insects are unclean to you; do not eat them. [20] But any winged creature that is clean you may eat. Lev 11:1-23

[21] Do not eat anything you find already dead. You may give it to the foreigner residing in any of your towns, and they may eat it, or you may sell it to any other foreigner. But you are a people holy to the LORD your God. Lev 17:15

Do not cook a young goat in its mother's milk. Ex 34:26

Tithes

[22] Be sure to set aside a tenth of all that your fields produce each year. [23] Eat the tithe of your grain, new wine and olive oil, and the firstborn of your herds and flocks in the presence of the LORD your God at the place he will choose as a dwelling for his Name, so that you may learn to revere the LORD your God always. [24] But if that place is too distant and you have been blessed by the LORD your God and cannot carry your tithe (because the place where the LORD will choose to put his Name is so far away), [25] then exchange your tithe for silver, and take the silver with you and go to the place the LORD your God will choose. [26] Use the silver to buy whatever you like: cattle, sheep, wine or other fermented drink, or anything you wish. Then you and your household shall eat there in the presence of the LORD your God and rejoice. [27] And do not neglect the Levites living in your towns, for they have no allotment or inheritance of their own. Lev 27:30; Nu 18:20; Dt 12:5

[28] At the end of every three years, bring all the tithes of that year's produce and store it in your towns, [29] so that the Levites (who have no allotment or inheritance of their own) and the foreigners, the fatherless and the widows who live in your towns may come and eat and be satisfied, and so that the LORD your God may bless you in all the work of your hands. Dt 15:10; 26:12

The Year for Canceling Debts

15:1-11Ref — Lev 25:8-38

15 At the end of every seven years you must cancel debts. [2]This is how it is to be done: Every creditor shall cancel any loan they have made to a fellow Israelite. They shall not require payment from anyone among their own people, because the LORD's time for canceling debts has been proclaimed. [3]You may require payment from a foreigner, but you must cancel any debt your fellow Israelite owes you. [4]However, there need be no poor people among you, for in the land the LORD your God is giving you to possess as your inheritance, he will richly bless you, [5]if only you fully obey the LORD your God and are careful to follow all these commands I am giving you today. [6]For the LORD your God will bless you as he has promised, and you will lend to many nations but will borrow from none. You will rule over many nations but none will rule over you. Dt 31:10; 23:20; 28:12-13,44

[7]If anyone is poor among your fellow Israelites in any of the towns of the land the LORD your God is giving you, do not be hardhearted or tightfisted toward them. [8]Rather, be openhanded and freely lend them whatever they need. [9]Be careful not to harbor this wicked thought: "The seventh year, the year for canceling debts, is near," so that you do not show ill will toward the needy among your fellow Israelites and give them nothing. They may then appeal to the LORD against you, and you will be found guilty of sin. [10]Give generously to them and do so without a grudging heart; then because of this the LORD your God will bless you in all your work and in everything you put your hand to. [11]There will always be poor people in the land. Therefore I command you to be openhanded toward your fellow Israelites who are poor and needy in your land. Lev 25:8-38; Mt 26:11; 1Jn 3:17

Freeing Servants

15:12-18pp — Ex 21:2-6
15:12-18Ref — Lev 25:38-55

[12]If any of your people — Hebrew men or women — sell themselves to you and serve you six years, in the seventh year you must let them go free. [13]And when you release them, do not send them away empty-handed. [14]Supply them liberally from your flock, your threshing floor and your winepress. Give to them as the LORD your God has blessed you. [15]Remember that you were slaves in Egypt and the LORD your God redeemed you. That is why I give you this command today. Ex 21:2-6; Lev 25:38-55

[16]But if your servant says to you, "I do not want to leave you," because he loves you and your family and is well off with you,

¹⁷then take an awl and push it through his earlobe into the door, and he will become your servant for life. Do the same for your female servant.

¹⁸Do not consider it a hardship to set your servant free, because their service to you these six years has been worth twice as much as that of a hired hand. And the LORD your God will bless you in everything you do.

The Firstborn Animals

¹⁹Set apart for the LORD your God every firstborn male of your herds and flocks. Do not put the firstborn of your cows to work, and do not shear the firstborn of your sheep. ²⁰Each year you and your family are to eat them in the presence of the LORD your God at the place he will choose. ²¹If an animal has a defect, is lame or blind, or has any serious flaw, you must not sacrifice it to the LORD your God. ²²You are to eat it in your own towns. Both the ceremonially unclean and the clean may eat it, as if it were gazelle or deer. ²³But you must not eat the blood; pour it out on the ground like water. Ex 13:2; Lev 22:19-25; Dt 12:5-7,17

The Passover

16:1-8pp — Ex 12:14-20; Lev 23:4-8; Nu 28:16-25

16 Observe the month of Aviv and celebrate the Passover of the LORD your God, because in the month of Aviv he brought you out of Egypt by night. ²Sacrifice as the Passover to the LORD your God an animal from your flock or herd at the place the LORD will choose as a dwelling for his Name. ³Do not eat it with bread made with yeast, but for seven days eat unleavened bread, the bread of affliction, because you left Egypt in haste — so that all the days of your life you may remember the time of your departure from Egypt. ⁴Let no yeast be found in your possession in all your land for seven days. Do not let any of the meat you sacrifice on the evening of the first day remain until morning. Ex 12:2; 34:25

⁵You must not sacrifice the Passover in any town the LORD your God gives you ⁶except in the place he will choose as a dwelling for his Name. There you must sacrifice the Passover in the evening, when the sun goes down, on the anniversary*ᵃ* of your departure from Egypt. ⁷Roast it and eat it at the place the LORD your God will choose. Then in the morning return to your tents. ⁸For six days eat unleavened bread and on the seventh day hold an assembly to the LORD your God and do no work. Ex 12:14-20; Lev 23:4-8; Nu 28:16-25

The Festival of Weeks

16:9-12pp — Lev 23:15-22; Nu 28:26-31

⁹Count off seven weeks from

ᵃ 6 Or down, at the time of day

the time you begin to put the sickle to the standing grain. [10]Then celebrate the Festival of Weeks to the LORD your God by giving a freewill offering in proportion to the blessings the LORD your God has given you. [11]And rejoice before the LORD your God at the place he will choose as a dwelling for his Name—you, your sons and daughters, your male and female servants, the Levites in your towns, and the foreigners, the fatherless and the widows living among you. [12]Remember that you were slaves in Egypt, and follow carefully these decrees. Lev 23:15-22; Nu 28:26-31

The Festival of Tabernacles

16:13-17pp — Lev 23:33-43; Nu 29:12-39

[13]Celebrate the Festival of Tabernacles for seven days after you have gathered the produce of your threshing floor and your winepress. [14]Be joyful at your festival—you, your sons and daughters, your male and female servants, and the Levites, the foreigners, the fatherless and the widows who live in your towns. [15]For seven days celebrate the festival to the LORD your God at the place the LORD will choose. For the LORD your God will bless you in all your harvest and in all the work of your hands, and your joy will be complete. Lev 23:34

[16]Three times a year all your men must appear before the LORD your God at the place he will choose: at the Festival of Unleavened Bread, the Festival of Weeks and the Festival of Tabernacles. No one should appear before the LORD empty-handed: [17]Each of you must bring a gift in proportion to the way the LORD your God has blessed you. Lev 23:33-43; Nu 29:12-39; Ex 34:20

Judges

[18]Appoint judges and officials for each of your tribes in every town the LORD your God is giving you, and they shall judge the people fairly. [19]Do not pervert justice or show partiality. Do not accept a bribe, for a bribe blinds the eyes of the wise and twists the words of the innocent. [20]Follow justice and justice alone, so that you may live and possess the land the LORD your God is giving you. Ex 23:2,8; Dt 1:17

Worshiping Other Gods

[21]Do not set up any wooden Asherah pole beside the altar you build to the LORD your God, [22]and do not erect a sacred stone, for these the LORD your God hates. Lev 26:1

17 Do not sacrifice to the LORD your God an ox or a sheep that has any defect or flaw in it, for that would be detestable to him. Dt 15:21

[2]If a man or woman living among you in one of the towns the LORD gives you is found doing evil in the eyes of the LORD your

God in violation of his covenant, ³and contrary to my command has worshiped other gods, bowing down to them or to the sun or the moon or the stars in the sky, ⁴and this has been brought to your attention, then you must investigate it thoroughly. If it is true and it has been proved that this detestable thing has been done in Israel, ⁵take the man or woman who has done this evil deed to your city gate and stone that person to death. ⁶On the testimony of two or three witnesses a person is to be put to death, but no one is to be put to death on the testimony of only one witness. ⁷The hands of the witnesses must be the first in putting that person to death, and then the hands of all the people. You must purge the evil from among you.   Nu 35:30; Dt 13:6-11; Mt 18:16

Law Courts

⁸If cases come before your courts that are too difficult for you to judge — whether bloodshed, lawsuits or assaults — take them to the place the Lᴏʀᴅ your God will choose. ⁹Go to the Levitical priests and to the judge who is in office at that time. Inquire of them and they will give you the verdict. ¹⁰You must act according to the decisions they give you at the place the Lᴏʀᴅ will choose. Be careful to do everything they instruct you to do. ¹¹Act according to whatever they teach you and the decisions they give you. Do not turn aside from what they tell you, to the right or to the left. ¹²Anyone who shows contempt for the judge or for the priest who stands ministering there to the Lᴏʀᴅ your God is to be put to death. You must purge the evil from Israel. ¹³All the people will hear and be afraid, and will not be contemptuous again.   Dt 12:5; 19:17; Nu 15:30

The King

¹⁴When you enter the land the Lᴏʀᴅ your God is giving you and have taken possession of it and settled in it, and you say, "Let us set a king over us like all the nations around us," ¹⁵be sure to appoint over you a king the Lᴏʀᴅ your God chooses. He must be from among your fellow Israelites. Do not place a foreigner over you, one who is not an Israelite. ¹⁶The king, moreover, must not acquire great numbers of horses for himself or make the people return to Egypt to get more of them, for the Lᴏʀᴅ has told you, "You are not to go back that way again." ¹⁷He must not take many wives, or his heart will be led astray. He must not accumulate large amounts of silver and gold.   1Sa 8:5,19-20; 1Ki 10:26; Jer 30:21

¹⁸When he takes the throne of his kingdom, he is to write for himself on a scroll a copy of this law, taken from that of the Levitical priests. ¹⁹It is to be with him,

and he is to read it all the days of his life so that he may learn to revere the Lord his God and follow carefully all the words of this law and these decrees ²⁰ and not consider himself better than his fellow Israelites and turn from the law to the right or to the left. Then he and his descendants will reign a long time over his kingdom in Israel. Jos 1:8; 1Ki 15:5

Offerings for Priests and Levites

18 The Levitical priests — indeed, the whole tribe of Levi — are to have no allotment or inheritance with Israel. They shall live on the food offerings presented to the Lord, for that is their inheritance. ²They shall have no inheritance among their fellow Israelites; the Lord is their inheritance, as he promised them. Dt 10:9; 1Co 9:13

³This is the share due the priests from the people who sacrifice a bull or a sheep: the shoulder, the internal organs and the meat from the head. ⁴You are to give them the firstfruits of your grain, new wine and olive oil, and the first wool from the shearing of your sheep, ⁵for the Lord your God has chosen them and their descendants out of all your tribes to stand and minister in the Lord's name always. Lev 7:28-34; Nu 18:12; Dt 10:8

⁶If a Levite moves from one of your towns anywhere in Israel where he is living, and comes in all earnestness to the place the Lord will choose, ⁷he may minister in the name of the Lord his God like all his fellow Levites who serve there in the presence of the Lord. ⁸He is to share equally in their benefits, even though he has received money from the sale of family possessions. Ne 12:44,47

Occult Practices

⁹When you enter the land the Lord your God is giving you, do not learn to imitate the detestable ways of the nations there. ¹⁰Let no one be found among you who sacrifices their son or daughter in the fire, who practices divination or sorcery, interprets omens, engages in witchcraft, ¹¹or casts spells, or who is a medium or spiritist or who consults the dead. ¹²Anyone who does these things is detestable to the Lord; because of these same detestable practices the Lord your God will drive out those nations before you. ¹³You must be blameless before the Lord your God. Dt 12:31; Lev 18:24

The Prophet

¹⁴The nations you will dispossess listen to those who practice sorcery or divination. But as for you, the Lord your God has not permitted you to do so. ¹⁵The Lord your God will raise up for you a prophet like me from among you, from your fellow Is-

raelites. You must listen to him. [16]For this is what you asked of the LORD your God at Horeb on the day of the assembly when you said, "Let us not hear the voice of the LORD our God nor see this great fire anymore, or we will die." Ex 20:19; Jn 1:21; Ac 3:22

[17]The LORD said to me: "What they say is good. [18]I will raise up for them a prophet like you from among their fellow Israelites, and I will put my words in his mouth. He will tell them everything I command him. [19]I myself will call to account anyone who does not listen to my words that the prophet speaks in my name. [20]But a prophet who presumes to speak in my name anything I have not commanded, or a prophet who speaks in the name of other gods, is to be put to death." Isa 51:16; Jn 4:25-26; Ac 3:23

[21]You may say to yourselves, "How can we know when a message has not been spoken by the LORD?" [22]If what a prophet proclaims in the name of the LORD does not take place or come true, that is a message the LORD has not spoken. That prophet has spoken presumptuously, so do not be alarmed. Jer 28:9

Cities of Refuge

19:1-14Ref — Nu 35:6-34; Dt 4:41-43; Jos 20:1-9

19 When the LORD your God has destroyed the nations whose land he is giving you, and when you have driven them out and settled in their towns and houses, [2]then set aside for yourselves three cities in the land the LORD your God is giving you to possess. [3]Determine the distances involved and divide into three parts the land the LORD your God is giving you as an inheritance, so that a person who kills someone may flee for refuge to one of these cities. Dt 12:29

[4]This is the rule concerning anyone who kills a person and flees there for safety—anyone who kills a neighbor unintentionally, without malice aforethought. [5]For instance, a man may go into the forest with his neighbor to cut wood, and as he swings his ax to fell a tree, the head may fly off and hit his neighbor and kill him. That man may flee to one of these cities and save his life. [6]Otherwise, the avenger of blood might pursue him in a rage, overtake him if the distance is too great, and kill him even though he is not deserving of death, since he did it to his neighbor without malice aforethought. [7]This is why I command you to set aside for yourselves three cities.

[8]If the LORD your God enlarges your territory, as he promised on oath to your ancestors, and gives you the whole land he promised them, [9]because you carefully follow all these laws I command you today—to love the LORD

your God and to walk always in obedience to him — then you are to set aside three more cities. [10] Do this so that innocent blood will not be shed in your land, which the LORD your God is giving you as your inheritance, and so that you will not be guilty of bloodshed. Dt 21:1-9

[11] But if out of hate someone lies in wait, assaults and kills a neighbor, and then flees to one of these cities, [12] the killer shall be sent for by the town elders, be brought back from the city, and be handed over to the avenger of blood to die. [13] Show no pity. You must purge from Israel the guilt of shedding innocent blood, so that it may go well with you.

[14] Do not move your neighbor's boundary stone set up by your predecessors in the inheritance you receive in the land the LORD your God is giving you to possess. Nu 35:6-34; Dt 4:41-43; Jos 20:1-9

Witnesses

[15] One witness is not enough to convict anyone accused of any crime or offense they may have committed. A matter must be established by the testimony of two or three witnesses.

[16] If a malicious witness takes the stand to accuse someone of a crime, [17] the two people involved in the dispute must stand in the presence of the LORD before the priests and the judges who are in office at the time. [18] The judges must make a thorough investigation, and if the witness proves to be a liar, giving false testimony against a fellow Israelite, [19] then do to the false witness as that witness intended to do to the other party. You must purge the evil from among you. [20] The rest of the people will hear of this and be afraid, and never again will such an evil thing be done among you. [21] Show no pity: life for life, eye for eye, tooth for tooth, hand for hand, foot for foot. Mt 5:38; Ps 27:12; Pr 19:5,9

Going to War

20 When you go to war against your enemies and see horses and chariots and an army greater than yours, do not be afraid of them, because the LORD your God, who brought you up out of Egypt, will be with you. [2] When you are about to go into battle, the priest shall come forward and address the army. [3] He shall say: "Hear, Israel: Today you are going into battle against your enemies. Do not be fainthearted or afraid; do not panic or be terrified by them. [4] For the LORD your God is the one who goes with you to fight for you against your enemies to give you victory." Dt 1:30; 31:6,8; 2Ch 32:7-8

[5] The officers shall say to the army: "Has anyone built a new house and not yet begun to live in it? Let him go home, or he may die in battle and someone

else may begin to live in it. ⁶Has anyone planted a vineyard and not begun to enjoy it? Let him go home, or he may die in battle and someone else enjoy it. ⁷Has anyone become pledged to a woman and not married her? Let him go home, or he may die in battle and someone else marry her." ⁸Then the officers shall add, "Is anyone afraid or fainthearted? Let him go home so that his fellow soldiers will not become disheartened too." ⁹When the officers have finished speaking to the army, they shall appoint commanders over it. Dt 24:5; Jdg 7:3

¹⁰When you march up to attack a city, make its people an offer of peace. ¹¹If they accept and open their gates, all the people in it shall be subject to forced labor and shall work for you. ¹²If they refuse to make peace and they engage you in battle, lay siege to that city. ¹³When the LORD your God delivers it into your hand, put to the sword all the men in it. ¹⁴As for the women, the children, the livestock and everything else in the city, you may take these as plunder for yourselves. And you may use the plunder the LORD your God gives you from your enemies. ¹⁵This is how you are to treat all the cities that are at a distance from you

and do not belong to the nations nearby. Nu 31:7; Jos 8:2; 1Ki 9:21

¹⁶However, in the cities of the nations the LORD your God is giving you as an inheritance, do not leave alive anything that breathes. ¹⁷Completely destroy[a] them — the Hittites, Amorites, Canaanites, Perizzites, Hivites and Jebusites — as the LORD your God has commanded you. ¹⁸Otherwise, they will teach you to follow all the detestable things they do in worshiping their gods, and you will sin against the LORD your God. Ex 23:33; Dt 7:2; Jos 11:14

¹⁹When you lay siege to a city for a long time, fighting against it to capture it, do not destroy its trees by putting an ax to them, because you can eat their fruit. Do not cut them down. Are the trees people, that you should besiege them?[b] ²⁰However, you may cut down trees that you know are not fruit trees and use them to build siege works until the city at war with you falls.

Atonement for an Unsolved Murder

21 If someone is found slain, lying in a field in the land the LORD your God is giving you to possess, and it is not known who the killer was, ²your elders and judges shall go out and measure the distance from the body

---

[a] 17 The Hebrew term refers to the irrevocable giving over of things or persons to the LORD, often by totally destroying them. [b] 19 Or down to use in the siege, for the fruit trees are for the benefit of people.

to the neighboring towns. ³Then the elders of the town nearest the body shall take a heifer that has never been worked and has never worn a yoke ⁴and lead it down to a valley that has not been plowed or planted and where there is a flowing stream. There in the valley they are to break the heifer's neck. ⁵The Levitical priests shall step forward, for the LORD your God has chosen them to minister and to pronounce blessings in the name of the LORD and to decide all cases of dispute and assault. ⁶Then all the elders of the town nearest the body shall wash their hands over the heifer whose neck was broken in the valley, ⁷and they shall declare: "Our hands did not shed this blood, nor did our eyes see it done. ⁸Accept this atonement for your people Israel, whom you have redeemed, LORD, and do not hold your people guilty of the blood of an innocent person." Then the bloodshed will be atoned for, ⁹and you will have purged from yourselves the guilt of shedding innocent blood, since you have done what is right in the eyes of the LORD.   Dt 17:8-11; 19:13; Mt 27:24

Marrying a Captive Woman

¹⁰When you go to war against your enemies and the LORD your God delivers them into your hands and you take captives, ¹¹if you notice among the captives a beautiful woman and are attracted to her, you may take her as your wife. ¹²Bring her into your home and have her shave her head, trim her nails ¹³and put aside the clothes she was wearing when captured. After she has lived in your house and mourned her father and mother for a full month, then you may go to her and be her husband and she shall be your wife. ¹⁴If you are not pleased with her, let her go wherever she wishes. You must not sell her or treat her as a slave, since you have dishonored her.   Lev 14:9; Ps 45:10; Jos 21:44

The Right of the Firstborn

¹⁵If a man has two wives, and he loves one but not the other, and both bear him sons but the firstborn is the son of the wife he does not love, ¹⁶when he wills his property to his sons, he must not give the rights of the firstborn to the son of the wife he loves in preference to his actual firstborn, the son of the wife he does not love. ¹⁷He must acknowledge the son of his unloved wife as the firstborn by giving him a double share of all he has. That son is the first sign of his father's strength. The right of the firstborn belongs to him.   Ge 29:33; 49:3; 1Ch 26:10

A Rebellious Son

¹⁸If someone has a stubborn and rebellious son who does

not obey his father and mother and will not listen to them when they discipline him, [19]his father and mother shall take hold of him and bring him to the elders at the gate of his town. [20]They shall say to the elders, "This son of ours is stubborn and rebellious. He will not obey us. He is a glutton and a drunkard." [21]Then all the men of his town are to stone him to death. You must purge the evil from among you. All Israel will hear of it and be afraid. Dt 13:11; Eph 6:1-3

Various Laws

[22]If someone guilty of a capital offense is put to death and their body is exposed on a pole, [23]you must not leave the body hanging on the pole overnight. Be sure to bury it that same day, because anyone who is hung on a pole is under God's curse. You must not desecrate the land the LORD your God is giving you as an inheritance. Gal 3:13; Jos 8:29; Jn 19:31

22 If you see your fellow Israelite's ox or sheep straying, do not ignore it but be sure to take it back to its owner. [2]If they do not live near you or if you do not know who owns it, take it home with you and keep it until they come looking for it. Then give it back. [3]Do the same if you find their donkey or cloak or anything else they have lost. Do not ignore it. Ex 23:4-5

[4]If you see your fellow Israelite's donkey or ox fallen on the road, do not ignore it. Help the owner get it to its feet.

[5]A woman must not wear men's clothing, nor a man wear women's clothing, for the LORD your God detests anyone who does this.

[6]If you come across a bird's nest beside the road, either in a tree or on the ground, and the mother is sitting on the young or on the eggs, do not take the mother with the young. [7]You may take the young, but be sure to let the mother go, so that it may go well with you and you may have a long life. Lev 22:28; Dt 4:40

[8]When you build a new house, make a parapet around your roof so that you may not bring the guilt of bloodshed on your house if someone falls from the roof.

[9]Do not plant two kinds of seed in your vineyard; if you do, not only the crops you plant but also the fruit of the vineyard will be defiled.[a] Lev 19:19

[10]Do not plow with an ox and a donkey yoked together. 2Co 6:14

[11]Do not wear clothes of wool and linen woven together.

[12]Make tassels on the four corners of the cloak you wear. Nu 15:37

Marriage Violations

[13]If a man takes a wife and, after sleeping with her, dislikes

---

[a] 9 Or *be forfeited to the sanctuary*

her [14] and slanders her and gives her a bad name, saying, "I married this woman, but when I approached her, I did not find proof of her virginity," [15] then the young woman's father and mother shall bring to the town elders at the gate proof that she was a virgin. [16] Her father will say to the elders, "I gave my daughter in marriage to this man, but he dislikes her. [17] Now he has slandered her and said, 'I did not find your daughter to be a virgin.' But here is the proof of my daughter's virginity." Then her parents shall display the cloth before the elders of the town, [18] and the elders shall take the man and punish him. [19] They shall fine him a hundred shekels[a] of silver and give them to the young woman's father, because this man has given an Israelite virgin a bad name. She shall continue to be his wife; he must not divorce her as long as he lives.   Ex 18:21; Dt 1:9-18

[20] If, however, the charge is true and no proof of the young woman's virginity can be found, [21] she shall be brought to the door of her father's house and there the men of her town shall stone her to death. She has done an outrageous thing in Israel by being promiscuous while still in her father's house. You must purge the evil from among you.   Ge 34:7; Dt 13:5

[22] If a man is found sleeping with another man's wife, both the man who slept with her and the woman must die. You must purge the evil from Israel.   Lev 20:10

[23] If a man happens to meet in a town a virgin pledged to be married and he sleeps with her, [24] you shall take both of them to the gate of that town and stone them to death—the young woman because she was in a town and did not scream for help, and the man because he violated another man's wife. You must purge the evil from among you.

[25] But if out in the country a man happens to meet a young woman pledged to be married and rapes her, only the man who has done this shall die. [26] Do nothing to the woman; she has committed no sin deserving death. This case is like that of someone who attacks and murders a neighbor, [27] for the man found the young woman out in the country, and though the betrothed woman screamed, there was no one to rescue her.

[28] If a man happens to meet a virgin who is not pledged to be married and rapes her and they are discovered, [29] he shall pay her father fifty shekels[b] of silver. He must marry the young woman, for he has violated her. He can never divorce her as long as he lives.   Ex 22:16

[a] 19 That is, about 2 1/2 pounds or about 1.2 kilograms   [b] 29 That is, about 1 1/4 pounds or about 575 grams

³⁰A man is not to marry his father's wife; he must not dishonor his father's bed.ᵃ   Lev 18:8; Dt 27:20

Exclusion From the Assembly

23ᵇ No one who has been emasculated by crushing or cutting may enter the assembly of the LORD.

²No one born of a forbidden marriageᶜ nor any of their descendants may enter the assembly of the LORD, not even in the tenth generation.

³No Ammonite or Moabite or any of their descendants may enter the assembly of the LORD, not even in the tenth generation. ⁴For they did not come to meet you with bread and water on your way when you came out of Egypt, and they hired Balaam son of Beor from Pethor in Aram Naharaimᵈ to pronounce a curse on you. ⁵However, the LORD your God would not listen to Balaam but turned the curse into a blessing for you, because the LORD your God loves you. ⁶Do not seek a treaty of friendship with them as long as you live.   Nu 22:5-6; Ezr 9:12; Ne 13:2

⁷Do not despise an Edomite, for the Edomites are related to you. Do not despise an Egyptian, because you resided as foreigners in their country. ⁸The third generation of children born to them may enter the assembly of the LORD.   Ge 25:26; Ex 22:21

Uncleanness in the Camp

⁹When you are encamped against your enemies, keep away from everything impure. ¹⁰If one of your men is unclean because of a nocturnal emission, he is to go outside the camp and stay there. ¹¹But as evening approaches he is to wash himself, and at sunset he may return to the camp.   Lev 15:16

¹²Designate a place outside the camp where you can go to relieve yourself. ¹³As part of your equipment have something to dig with, and when you relieve yourself, dig a hole and cover up your excrement. ¹⁴For the LORD your God moves about in your camp to protect you and to deliver your enemies to you. Your camp must be holy, so that he will not see among you anything indecent and turn away from you.   Lev 26:12

Miscellaneous Laws

¹⁵If a slave has taken refuge with you, do not hand them over to their master. ¹⁶Let them live among you wherever they like and in whatever town they choose. Do not oppress them.   1Sa 30:15

¹⁷No Israelite man or woman is to become a shrine prostitute. ¹⁸You must not bring the earn-

ᵃ 30 In Hebrew texts this verse (22:30) is numbered 23:1.   ᵇ In Hebrew texts 23:1-25 is numbered 23:2-26.   ᶜ 2 Or one of illegitimate birth   ᵈ 4 That is, Northwest Mesopotamia ings of a female prostitute or of a male prostitute[a] into the house of the LORD your God to pay any vow, because the LORD your God detests them both. Lev 19:29; 20:13

19 Do not charge a fellow Israelite interest, whether on money or food or anything else that may earn interest. **20** You may charge a foreigner interest, but not a fellow Israelite, so that the LORD your God may bless you in everything you put your hand to in the land you are entering to possess. Ex 22:25; Lev 25:35-37

21 If you make a vow to the LORD your God, do not be slow to pay it, for the LORD your God will certainly demand it of you and you will be guilty of sin. **22** But if you refrain from making a vow, you will not be guilty. **23** Whatever your lips utter you must be sure to do, because you made your vow freely to the LORD your God with your own mouth. Nu 30:1-2; Mt 5:33

24 If you enter your neighbor's vineyard, you may eat all the grapes you want, but do not put any in your basket. **25** If you enter your neighbor's grainfield, you may pick kernels with your hands, but you must not put a sickle to their standing grain. Mt 12:1; Mk 2:23

24 If a man marries a woman who becomes displeasing to him because he finds some-thing indecent about her, and he writes her a certificate of divorce, gives it to her and sends her from his house, **2** and if after she leaves his house she becomes the wife of another man, **3** and her second husband dislikes her and writes her a certificate of divorce, gives it to her and sends her from his house, or if he dies, **4** then her first husband, who divorced her, is not allowed to marry her again after she has been defiled. That would be detestable in the eyes of the LORD. Do not bring sin upon the land the LORD your God is giving you as an inheritance. Jer 3:1; Mt 5:31; 19:7-9

5 If a man has recently married, he must not be sent to war or have any other duty laid on him. For one year he is to be free to stay at home and bring happiness to the wife he has married. Dt 20:7

6 Do not take a pair of millstones — not even the upper one — as security for a debt, because that would be taking a person's livelihood as security.

7 If someone is caught kidnapping a fellow Israelite and treating or selling them as a slave, the kidnapper must die. You must purge the evil from among you. Ex 21:16

8 In cases of defiling skin diseases,[b] be very careful to do exactly as the Levitical priests

---

[a] 18 Hebrew *of a dog*   [b] 8 The Hebrew word for *defiling skin diseases*, traditionally translated "leprosy," was used for various diseases affecting the skin.

instruct you. You must follow carefully what I have commanded them. [9] Remember what the LORD your God did to Miriam along the way after you came out of Egypt. Lev 13:1-46; Nu 12:10

[10] When you make a loan of any kind to your neighbor, do not go into their house to get what is offered to you as a pledge. [11] Stay outside and let the neighbor to whom you are making the loan bring the pledge out to you. [12] If the neighbor is poor, do not go to sleep with their pledge in your possession. [13] Return their cloak by sunset so that your neighbor may sleep in it. Then they will thank you, and it will be regarded as a righteous act in the sight of the LORD your God. Ex 22:26; Dt 6:25; Da 4:27

[14] Do not take advantage of a hired worker who is poor and needy, whether that worker is a fellow Israelite or a foreigner residing in one of your towns. [15] Pay them their wages each day before sunset, because they are poor and are counting on it. Otherwise they may cry to the LORD against you, and you will be guilty of sin. Lev 19:13; Jas 5:4

[16] Parents are not to be put to death for their children, nor children put to death for their parents; each will die for their own sin. Jer 31:29-30; Eze 18:20

[17] Do not deprive the foreigner or the fatherless of justice, or take the cloak of the widow as a pledge. [18] Remember that you were slaves in Egypt and the LORD your God redeemed you from there. That is why I command you to do this.

[19] When you are harvesting in your field and you overlook a sheaf, do not go back to get it. Leave it for the foreigner, the fatherless and the widow, so that the LORD your God may bless you in all the work of your hands. [20] When you beat the olives from your trees, do not go over the branches a second time. Leave what remains for the foreigner, the fatherless and the widow. [21] When you harvest the grapes in your vineyard, do not go over the vines again. Leave what remains for the foreigner, the fatherless and the widow. [22] Remember that you were slaves in Egypt. That is why I command you to do this. Lev 19:9; 23:22

25 When people have a dispute, they are to take it to court and the judges will decide the case, acquitting the innocent and condemning the guilty. [2] If the guilty person deserves to be beaten, the judge shall make them lie down and have them flogged in his presence with the number of lashes the crime deserves, [3] but the judge must not impose more than forty lashes. If the guilty party is flogged more than that, your fellow Israelite will be degraded in your eyes. Dt 17:8-13; 19:17; 2Co 11:24

[4]Do not muzzle an ox while it is treading out the grain. 1Ti 5:18

[5]If brothers are living together and one of them dies without a son, his widow must not marry outside the family. Her husband's brother shall take her and marry her and fulfill the duty of a brother-in-law to her. [6]The first son she bears shall carry on the name of the dead brother so that his name will not be blotted out from Israel. Ru 4:5,10; Mt 22:24; Lk 20:28

[7]However, if a man does not want to marry his brother's wife, she shall go to the elders at the town gate and say, "My husband's brother refuses to carry on his brother's name in Israel. He will not fulfill the duty of a brother-in-law to me." [8]Then the elders of his town shall summon him and talk to him. If he persists in saying, "I do not want to marry her," [9]his brother's widow shall go up to him in the presence of the elders, take off one of his sandals, spit in his face and say, "This is what is done to the man who will not build up his brother's family line." [10]That man's line shall be known in Israel as The Family of the Unsandaled. Ru 4:1-2,5-6

[11]If two men are fighting and the wife of one of them comes to rescue her husband from his assailant, and she reaches out and seizes him by his private parts, [12]you shall cut off her hand. Show her no pity.

[13]Do not have two differing weights in your bag—one heavy, one light. [14]Do not have two differing measures in your house—one large, one small. [15]You must have accurate and honest weights and measures, so that you may live long in the land the LORD your God is giving you. [16]For the LORD your God detests anyone who does these things, anyone who deals dishonestly. Lev 19:35-37; Pr 11:1

[17]Remember what the Amalekites did to you along the way when you came out of Egypt. [18]When you were weary and worn out, they met you on your journey and attacked all who were lagging behind; they had no fear of God. [19]When the LORD your God gives you rest from all the enemies around you in the land he is giving you to possess as an inheritance, you shall blot out the name of Amalek from under heaven. Do not forget! Ex 17:8; Ps 36:1; 1Sa 15:2-3

Firstfruits and Tithes

26 When you have entered the land the LORD your God is giving you as an inheritance and have taken possession of it and settled in it, [2]take some of the firstfruits of all that you produce from the soil of the land the LORD your God is giving you and put them in a basket. Then go to the place the LORD your God will choose as a dwelling for his Name [3]and say to the priest in office at the time, "I declare today to the LORD

your God that I have come to the land the LORD swore to our ancestors to give us." ⁴The priest shall take the basket from your hands and set it down in front of the altar of the LORD your God. ⁵Then you shall declare before the LORD your God: "My father was a wandering Aramean, and he went down into Egypt with a few people and lived there and became a great nation, powerful and numerous. ⁶But the Egyptians mistreated us and made us suffer, subjecting us to harsh labor. ⁷Then we cried out to the LORD, the God of our ancestors, and the LORD heard our voice and saw our misery, toil and oppression. ⁸So the LORD brought us out of Egypt with a mighty hand and an outstretched arm, with great terror and with signs and wonders. ⁹He brought us to this place and gave us this land, a land flowing with milk and honey; ¹⁰and now I bring the firstfruits of the soil that you, LORD, have given me." Place the basket before the LORD your God and bow down before him. ¹¹Then you and the Levites and the foreigners residing among you shall rejoice in all the good things the LORD your God has given to you and your household. Ex 3:8; 23:16,19; Dt 4:34

¹²When you have finished setting aside a tenth of all your produce in the third year, the year of the tithe, you shall give it to the Levite, the foreigner, the fatherless and the widow, so that they may eat in your towns and be satisfied. ¹³Then say to the LORD your God: "I have removed from my house the sacred portion and have given it to the Levite, the foreigner, the fatherless and the widow, according to all you commanded. I have not turned aside from your commands nor have I forgotten any of them. ¹⁴I have not eaten any of the sacred portion while I was in mourning, nor have I removed any of it while I was unclean, nor have I offered any of it to the dead. I have obeyed the LORD my God; I have done everything you commanded me. ¹⁵Look down from heaven, your holy dwelling place, and bless your people Israel and the land you have given us as you promised on oath to our ancestors, a land flowing with milk and honey." Dt 14:28-29; Ps 119:141,153,176

Follow the LORD's Commands

¹⁶The LORD your God commands you this day to follow these decrees and laws; carefully observe them with all your heart and with all your soul. ¹⁷You have declared this day that the LORD is your God and that you will walk in obedience to him, that you will keep his decrees, commands and laws — that you will listen to him. ¹⁸And the LORD has declared this day that

you are his people, his treasured possession as he promised, and that you are to keep all his commands. ¹⁹He has declared that he will set you in praise, fame and honor high above all the nations he has made and that you will be a people holy to the LORD your God, as he promised. Dt 7:6; 28:1,13,44; 4:7-8

The Altar on Mount Ebal

27 Moses and the elders of Israel commanded the people: "Keep all these commands that I give you today. ²When you have crossed the Jordan into the land the LORD your God is giving you, set up some large stones and coat them with plaster. ³Write on them all the words of this law when you have crossed over to enter the land the LORD your God is giving you, a land flowing with milk and honey, just as the LORD, the God of your ancestors, promised you. ⁴And when you have crossed the Jordan, set up these stones on Mount Ebal, as I command you today, and coat them with plaster. ⁵Build there an altar to the LORD your God, an altar of stones. Do not use any iron tool on them. ⁶Build the altar of the LORD your God with fieldstones and offer burnt offerings on it to the LORD your God. ⁷Sacrifice fellowship offerings there, eating them and rejoicing in the presence of the LORD your God. ⁸And you shall write very clearly all the words of this law on these stones you have set up." Ex 20:25; Dt 26:9

Curses From Mount Ebal

⁹Then Moses and the Levitical priests said to all Israel, "Be silent, Israel, and listen! You have now become the people of the LORD your God. ¹⁰Obey the LORD your God and follow his commands and decrees that I give you today."

¹¹On the same day Moses commanded the people:

¹²When you have crossed the Jordan, these tribes shall stand on Mount Gerizim to bless the people: Simeon, Levi, Judah, Issachar, Joseph and Benjamin. ¹³And these tribes shall stand on Mount Ebal to pronounce curses: Reuben, Gad, Asher, Zebulun, Dan and Naphtali. Jos 8:35

¹⁴The Levites shall recite to all the people of Israel in a loud voice:

¹⁵"Cursed is anyone who makes an idol—a thing detestable to the LORD, the work of skilled hands—and sets it up in secret." Ex 20:4; 34:17
Then all the people shall say, "Amen!"

¹⁶"Cursed is anyone who dishonors their father or mother." Ex 21:17
Then all the people shall say, "Amen!"

¹⁷"Cursed is anyone who

moves their neighbor's boundary stone." Pr 22:28

Then all the people shall say, "Amen!"

¹⁸ "Cursed is anyone who leads the blind astray on the road." Lev 19:14

Then all the people shall say, "Amen!"

¹⁹ "Cursed is anyone who withholds justice from the foreigner, the fatherless or the widow." Dt 10:18; 24:19

Then all the people shall say, "Amen!"

²⁰ "Cursed is anyone who sleeps with his father's wife, for he dishonors his father's bed." Lev 18:7; Dt 22:30

Then all the people shall say, "Amen!"

²¹ "Cursed is anyone who has sexual relations with any animal." Lev 18:23

Then all the people shall say, "Amen!"

²² "Cursed is anyone who sleeps with his sister, the daughter of his father or the daughter of his mother."

Then all the people shall say, "Amen!"

²³ "Cursed is anyone who sleeps with his mother-in-law."

Then all the people shall say, "Amen!"

²⁴ "Cursed is anyone who kills their neighbor secretly."

Then all the people shall say, "Amen!"

²⁵ "Cursed is anyone who accepts a bribe to kill an innocent person." Ex 23:7-8

Then all the people shall say, "Amen!"

²⁶ "Cursed is anyone who does not uphold the words of this law by carrying them out." Gal 3:10

Then all the people shall say, "Amen!"

Blessings for Obedience

28 If you fully obey the LORD your God and carefully follow all his commands I give you today, the LORD your God will set you high above all the nations on earth. ² All these blessings will come on you and accompany you if you obey the LORD your God: Dt 26:19; Lev 26:3

³ You will be blessed in the city and blessed in the country. Ge 39:5

⁴ The fruit of your womb will be blessed, and the crops of your land and the young of your livestock — the calves of your herds and the lambs of your flocks. Ge 49:25

⁵ Your basket and your kneading trough will be blessed.

⁶ You will be blessed when you come in and blessed when you go out. Ps 121:8

⁷ The LORD will grant that the enemies who rise up against you will be defeated before you.

They will come at you from one direction but flee from you in seven. Lev 26:8,17

⁸The LORD will send a blessing on your barns and on everything you put your hand to. The LORD your God will bless you in the land he is giving you.

⁹The LORD will establish you as his holy people, as he promised you on oath, if you keep the commands of the LORD your God and walk in obedience to him. ¹⁰Then all the peoples on earth will see that you are called by the name of the LORD, and they will fear you. ¹¹The LORD will grant you abundant prosperity—in the fruit of your womb, the young of your livestock and the crops of your ground—in the land he swore to your ancestors to give you. Ex 19:6

¹²The LORD will open the heavens, the storehouse of his bounty, to send rain on your land in season and to bless all the work of your hands. You will lend to many nations but will borrow from none. ¹³The LORD will make you the head, not the tail. If you pay attention to the commands of the LORD your God that I give you this day and carefully follow them, you will always be at the top, never at the bottom. ¹⁴Do not turn aside from any of the commands I give you today, to the right or to the left, following other gods and serving them. Lev 26:4; Dt 5:32; 15:3,6

Curses for Disobedience

¹⁵However, if you do not obey the LORD your God and do not carefully follow all his commands and decrees I am giving you today, all these curses will come on you and overtake you: Lev 26:14; Jos 23:15

¹⁶You will be cursed in the city and cursed in the country.

¹⁷Your basket and your kneading trough will be cursed.

¹⁸The fruit of your womb will be cursed, and the crops of your land, and the calves of your herds and the lambs of your flocks.

¹⁹You will be cursed when you come in and cursed when you go out.

²⁰The LORD will send on you curses, confusion and rebuke in everything you put your hand to, until you are destroyed and come to sudden ruin because of the evil you have done in forsaking him.ᵃ ²¹The LORD will plague you with diseases until he has destroyed you from the land you are entering to possess. ²²The LORD will strike you with wasting disease, with fever and inflammation, with scorching heat and drought, with blight and mildew, which will plague you until you perish.

ᵃ 20 Hebrew me

²³ The sky over your head will be bronze, the ground beneath you iron. ²⁴ The LORD will turn the rain of your country into dust and powder; it will come down from the skies until you are destroyed. Isa 51:20; Am 4:9; Mal 2:2

²⁵ The LORD will cause you to be defeated before your enemies. You will come at them from one direction but flee from them in seven, and you will become a thing of horror to all the kingdoms on earth. ²⁶ Your carcasses will be food for all the birds and the wild animals, and there will be no one to frighten them away. ²⁷ The LORD will afflict you with the boils of Egypt and with tumors, festering sores and the itch, from which you cannot be cured. ²⁸ The LORD will afflict you with madness, blindness and confusion of mind. ²⁹ At midday you will grope about like a blind person in the dark. You will be unsuccessful in everything you do; day after day you will be oppressed and robbed, with no one to rescue you. Jer 15:4; 7:33; 1Sa 5:6

³⁰ You will be pledged to be married to a woman, but another will take her and rape her. You will build a house, but you will not live in it. You will plant a vineyard, but you will not even begin to enjoy its fruit. ³¹ Your ox will be slaughtered before your eyes, but you will eat none of it. Your donkey will be forcibly taken from you and will not be returned. Your sheep will be given to your enemies, and no one will rescue them. ³² Your sons and daughters will be given to another nation, and you will wear out your eyes watching for them day after day, powerless to lift a hand. ³³ A people that you do not know will eat what your land and labor produce, and you will have nothing but cruel oppression all your days. ³⁴ The sights you see will drive you mad. ³⁵ The LORD will afflict your knees and legs with painful boils that cannot be cured, spreading from the soles of your feet to the top of your head. Jer 5:15-17; 8:10; Am 5:11

³⁶ The LORD will drive you and the king you set over you to a nation unknown to you or your ancestors. There you will worship other gods, gods of wood and stone. ³⁷ You will become a thing of horror, a byword and an object of ridicule among all the peoples where the LORD will drive you. Dt 4:28; Jer 16:13; 24:9

³⁸ You will sow much seed in the field but you will harvest little, because locusts will devour it. ³⁹ You will plant vineyards and cultivate them but you will not drink the wine or gather the grapes, because worms will eat them. ⁴⁰ You will have olive trees throughout your country but you will not use the oil, because the olives will drop off. ⁴¹ You will have sons and daughters but you

will not keep them, because they will go into captivity. ⁴²Swarms of locusts will take over all your trees and the crops of your land. Joel 1:4; Mic 6:15; Hag 1:6,9

⁴³The foreigners who reside among you will rise above you higher and higher, but you will sink lower and lower. ⁴⁴They will lend to you, but you will not lend to them. They will be the head, but you will be the tail.

⁴⁵All these curses will come on you. They will pursue you and overtake you until you are destroyed, because you did not obey the LORD your God and observe the commands and decrees he gave you. ⁴⁶They will be a sign and a wonder to you and your descendants forever. ⁴⁷Because you did not serve the LORD your God joyfully and gladly in the time of prosperity, ⁴⁸therefore in hunger and thirst, in nakedness and dire poverty, you will serve the enemies the LORD sends against you. He will put an iron yoke on your neck until he has destroyed you. Ne 9:35; Isa 8:18; Jer 28:13-14

⁴⁹The LORD will bring a nation against you from far away, from the ends of the earth, like an eagle swooping down, a nation whose language you will not understand, ⁵⁰a fierce-looking nation without respect for the old or pity for the young. ⁵¹They will devour the young of your livestock and the crops of your land until you are destroyed. They

will leave you no grain, new wine or olive oil, nor any calves of your herds or lambs of your flocks until you are ruined. ⁵²They will lay siege to all the cities throughout your land until the high fortified walls in which you trust fall down. They will besiege all the cities throughout the land the LORD your God is giving you. Isa 47:6; Jer 48:40; Zep 1:14-17

⁵³Because of the suffering that your enemy will inflict on you during the siege, you will eat the fruit of the womb, the flesh of the sons and daughters the LORD your God has given you. ⁵⁴Even the most gentle and sensitive man among you will have no compassion on his own brother or the wife he loves or his surviving children, ⁵⁵and he will not give to one of them any of the flesh of his children that he is eating. It will be all he has left because of the suffering your enemy will inflict on you during the siege of all your cities. ⁵⁶The most gentle and sensitive woman among you—so sensitive and gentle that she would not venture to touch the ground with the sole of her foot—will begrudge the husband she loves and her own son or daughter ⁵⁷the afterbirth from her womb and the children she bears. For in her dire need she intends to eat them secretly because of the suffering your enemy will inflict

on you during the siege of your cities. Lev 26:29; Jer 19:9; La 2:20

⁵⁸ If you do not carefully follow all the words of this law, which are written in this book, and do not revere this glorious and awesome name—the LORD your God— ⁵⁹ the LORD will send fearful plagues on you and your descendants, harsh and prolonged disasters, and severe and lingering illnesses. ⁶⁰ He will bring on you all the diseases of Egypt that you dreaded, and they will cling to you. ⁶¹ The LORD will also bring on you every kind of sickness and disaster not recorded in this Book of the Law, until you are destroyed. ⁶² You who were as numerous as the stars in the sky will be left but few in number, because you did not obey the LORD your God. ⁶³ Just as it pleased the LORD to make you prosper and increase in number, so it will please him to ruin and destroy you. You will be uprooted from the land you are entering to possess. Dt 10:22; Ne 9:23; Pr 1:26

⁶⁴ Then the LORD will scatter you among all nations, from one end of the earth to the other. There you will worship other gods—gods of wood and stone, which neither you nor your ancestors have known. ⁶⁵ Among those nations you will find no repose, no resting place for the sole of your foot. There the LORD will give you an anxious mind, eyes weary with longing, and a despairing heart. ⁶⁶ You will live in constant suspense, filled with dread both night and day, never sure of your life. ⁶⁷ In the morning you will say, "If only it were evening!" and in the evening, "If only it were morning!"—because of the terror that will fill your hearts and the sights that your eyes will see. ⁶⁸ The LORD will send you back in ships to Egypt on a journey I said you should never make again. There you will offer yourselves for sale to your enemies as male and female slaves, but no one will buy you. Dt 4:27; Lev 26:16,36; Job 7:4

Renewal of the Covenant

29 *ᵃ* These are the terms of the covenant the LORD commanded Moses to make with the Israelites in Moab, in addition to the covenant he had made with them at Horeb. Dt 5:2-3

² Moses summoned all the Israelites and said to them:

Your eyes have seen all that the LORD did in Egypt to Pharaoh, to all his officials and to all his land. ³ With your own eyes you saw those great trials, those signs and great wonders. ⁴ But to this day the LORD has not given you a mind that understands or eyes that see or ears that hear. ⁵ Yet the LORD says, "During the forty

---

ᵃ In Hebrew texts 29:1 is numbered 28:69, and 29:2-29 is numbered 29:1-28.

years that I led you through the wilderness, your clothes did not wear out, nor did the sandals on your feet. ⁶You ate no bread and drank no wine or other fermented drink. I did this so that you might know that I am the LORD your God." Dt 8:4; Isa 6:10; Ro 11:8

⁷When you reached this place, Sihon king of Heshbon and Og king of Bashan came out to fight against us, but we defeated them. ⁸We took their land and gave it as an inheritance to the Reubenites, the Gadites and the half-tribe of Manasseh. Nu 21:21-24,33-35; 32:33

⁹Carefully follow the terms of this covenant, so that you may prosper in everything you do. ¹⁰All of you are standing today in the presence of the LORD your God—your leaders and chief men, your elders and officials, and all the other men of Israel, ¹¹together with your children and your wives, and the foreigners living in your camps who chop your wood and carry your water. ¹²You are standing here in order to enter into a covenant with the LORD your God, a covenant the LORD is making with you this day and sealing with an oath, ¹³to confirm you this day as his people, that he may be your God as he promised you and as he swore to your fathers, Abraham, Isaac and Jacob. ¹⁴I am making this covenant, with its oath, not only with you ¹⁵who are standing here with us today in the presence of the LORD our God but also with those who are not here today. Ge 17:7; Jos 1:7; Ac 2:39

¹⁶You yourselves know how we lived in Egypt and how we passed through the countries on the way here. ¹⁷You saw among them their detestable images and idols of wood and stone, of silver and gold. ¹⁸Make sure there is no man or woman, clan or tribe among you today whose heart turns away from the LORD our God to go and worship the gods of those nations; make sure there is no root among you that produces such bitter poison. Dt 28:36; Heb 12:15

¹⁹When such a person hears the words of this oath and they invoke a blessing on themselves, thinking, "I will be safe, even though I persist in going my own way," they will bring disaster on the watered land as well as the dry. ²⁰The LORD will never be willing to forgive them; his wrath and zeal will burn against them. All the curses written in this book will fall on them, and the LORD will blot out their names from under heaven. ²¹The LORD will single them out from all the tribes of Israel for disaster, according to all the curses of the covenant written in this Book of the Law. Dt 9:14; Ps 74:1; 79:5

²²Your children who follow you in later generations and foreigners who come from distant lands will see the calamities that have

fallen on the land and the diseases with which the LORD has afflicted it. ²³ The whole land will be a burning waste of salt and sulfur—nothing planted, nothing sprouting, no vegetation growing on it. It will be like the destruction of Sodom and Gomorrah, Admah and Zeboyim, which the LORD overthrew in fierce anger. ²⁴ All the nations will ask: "Why has the LORD done this to this land? Why this fierce, burning anger?" Jer 19:8; 22:8-9; Zep 2:9

²⁵ And the answer will be: "It is because this people abandoned the covenant of the LORD, the God of their ancestors, the covenant he made with them when he brought them out of Egypt. ²⁶ They went off and worshiped other gods and bowed down to them, gods they did not know, gods he had not given them. ²⁷ Therefore the LORD's anger burned against this land, so that he brought on it all the curses written in this book. ²⁸ In furious anger and in great wrath the LORD uprooted them from their land and thrust them into another land, as it is now." 1Ki 14:15; 2Ki 17:23; Da 9:11,13-14

²⁹ The secret things belong to the LORD our God, but the things revealed belong to us and to our children forever, that we may follow all the words of this law. 2Ti 3:16

Prosperity After Turning to the LORD

30 When all these blessings and curses I have set before you come on you and you take them to heart wherever the LORD your God disperses you among the nations, ²and when you and your children return to the LORD your God and obey him with all your heart and with all your soul according to everything I command you today, ³then the LORD your God will restore your fortunes[a] and have compassion on you and gather you again from all the nations where he scattered you. ⁴Even if you have been banished to the most distant land under the heavens, from there the LORD your God will gather you and bring you back. ⁵He will bring you to the land that belonged to your ancestors, and you will take possession of it. He will make you more prosperous and numerous than your ancestors. ⁶The LORD your God will circumcise your hearts and the hearts of your descendants, so that you may love him with all your heart and with all your soul, and live. ⁷The LORD your God will put all these curses on your enemies who hate and persecute you. ⁸You will again obey the LORD and follow all his commands I am giving you today. ⁹Then the LORD your God

---

a 3 Or *will bring you back from captivity*

will make you most prosperous in all the work of your hands and in the fruit of your womb, the young of your livestock and the crops of your land. The LORD will again delight in you and make you prosperous, just as he delighted in your ancestors, [10]if you obey the LORD your God and keep his commands and decrees that are written in this Book of the Law and turn to the LORD your God with all your heart and with all your soul.   Dt 11:26; Ps 126:4; Jer 32:39

The Offer of Life or Death

[11]Now what I am commanding you today is not too difficult for you or beyond your reach. [12]It is not up in heaven, so that you have to ask, "Who will ascend into heaven to get it and proclaim it to us so we may obey it?" [13]Nor is it beyond the sea, so that you have to ask, "Who will cross the sea to get it and proclaim it to us so we may obey it?" [14]No, the word is very near you; it is in your mouth and in your heart so you may obey it.   Isa 45:19,23; Ro 10:6

[15]See, I set before you today life and prosperity, death and destruction. [16]For I command you today to love the LORD your God, to walk in obedience to him, and to keep his commands, decrees and laws; then you will live and increase, and the LORD your God will bless you in the land you are entering to possess.   Dt 4:1; 11:26

[17]But if your heart turns away and you are not obedient, and if you are drawn away to bow down to other gods and worship them, [18]I declare to you this day that you will certainly be destroyed. You will not live long in the land you are crossing the Jordan to enter and possess.   Dt 8:19

[19]This day I call the heavens and the earth as witnesses against you that I have set before you life and death, blessings and curses. Now choose life, so that you and your children may live [20]and that you may love the LORD your God, listen to his voice, and hold fast to him. For the LORD is your life, and he will give you many years in the land he swore to give to your fathers, Abraham, Isaac and Jacob.   Dt 4:26; Ps 27:1

Joshua to Succeed Moses

31 Then Moses went out and spoke these words to all Israel: [2]"I am now a hundred and twenty years old and I am no longer able to lead you. The LORD has said to me, 'You shall not cross the Jordan.' [3]The LORD your God himself will cross over ahead of you. He will destroy these nations before you, and you will take possession of their land. Joshua also will cross over ahead of you, as the LORD said. [4]And the LORD will do to them what he did to Sihon and Og, the kings of the Amorites, whom he destroyed along with their land. [5]The LORD will deliver them to you, and you

must do to them all that I have commanded you. ⁶Be strong and courageous. Do not be afraid or terrified because of them, for the LORD your God goes with you; he will never leave you nor forsake you." Dt 3:23,26; 7:2; Jos 10:25

⁷Then Moses summoned Joshua and said to him in the presence of all Israel, "Be strong and courageous, for you must go with this people into the land that the LORD swore to their ancestors to give them, and you must divide it among them as their inheritance. ⁸The LORD himself goes before you and will be with you; he will never leave you nor forsake you. Do not be afraid; do not be discouraged." Dt 1:38; 3:28; Ex 13:21

Public Reading of the Law

⁹So Moses wrote down this law and gave it to the Levitical priests, who carried the ark of the covenant of the LORD, and to all the elders of Israel. ¹⁰Then Moses commanded them: "At the end of every seven years, in the year for canceling debts, during the Festival of Tabernacles, ¹¹when all Israel comes to appear before the LORD your God at the place he will choose, you shall read this law before them in their hearing. ¹²Assemble the people — men, women and children, and the foreigners residing in your towns — so they can listen and learn to fear the LORD your God and follow carefully all the words

of this law. ¹³Their children, who do not know this law, must hear it and learn to fear the LORD your God as long as you live in the land you are crossing the Jordan to possess." Nu 4:15; Dt 15:1; Jos 8:34-35

Israel's Rebellion Predicted

¹⁴The LORD said to Moses, "Now the day of your death is near. Call Joshua and present yourselves at the tent of meeting, where I will commission him." So Moses and Joshua came and presented themselves at the tent of meeting. Nu 27:13; Dt 32:49-50

¹⁵Then the LORD appeared at the tent in a pillar of cloud, and the cloud stood over the entrance to the tent. ¹⁶And the LORD said to Moses: "You are going to rest with your ancestors, and these people will soon prostitute themselves to the foreign gods of the land they are entering. They will forsake me and break the covenant I made with them. ¹⁷And in that day I will become angry with them and forsake them; I will hide my face from them, and they will be destroyed. Many disasters and calamities will come on them, and in that day they will ask, 'Have not these disasters come on us because our God is not with us?' ¹⁸And I will certainly hide my face in that day because of all their wickedness in turning to other gods. Ex 33:9; Nu 14:42; Jdg 10:6,13

¹⁹"Now write down this song

and teach it to the Israelites and have them sing it, so that it may be a witness for me against them. [20] When I have brought them into the land flowing with milk and honey, the land I promised on oath to their ancestors, and when they eat their fill and thrive, they will turn to other gods and worship them, rejecting me and breaking my covenant. [21] And when many disasters and calamities come on them, this song will testify against them, because it will not be forgotten by their descendants. I know what they are disposed to do, even before I bring them into the land I promised them on oath." [22] So Moses wrote down this song that day and taught it to the Israelites.   Dt 32:15-17; Jn 2:24-25

[23] The LORD gave this command to Joshua son of Nun: "Be strong and courageous, for you will bring the Israelites into the land I promised them on oath, and I myself will be with you."   Jos 1:6

[24] After Moses finished writing in a book the words of this law from beginning to end, [25] he gave this command to the Levites who carried the ark of the covenant of the LORD: [26] "Take this Book of the Law and place it beside the ark of the covenant of the LORD your God. There it will remain as a witness against you. [27] For I know how rebellious and stiff-necked you are. If you have been rebellious against the LORD while I am still alive and with you, how much more will you rebel after I die! [28] Assemble before me all the elders of your tribes and all your officials, so that I can speak these words in their hearing and call the heavens and the earth to testify against them. [29] For I know that after my death you are sure to become utterly corrupt and to turn from the way I have commanded you. In days to come, disaster will fall on you because you will do evil in the sight of the LORD and arouse his anger by what your hands have made."   Dt 4:26; 9:6,24; 32:1

The Song of Moses

[30] And Moses recited the words of this song from beginning to end in the hearing of the whole assembly of Israel:

32

Listen, you heavens, and
    I will speak;
hear, you earth, the words
    of my mouth.   Dt 4:26; Isa 1:2
[2] Let my teaching fall like rain
    and my words descend like
    dew,
like showers on new grass,
    like abundant rain on
    tender plants.   Isa 55:11

[3] I will proclaim the name of
    the LORD.   Ex 33:19
Oh, praise the greatness of
    our God!   Dt 3:24
[4] He is the Rock, his works are
    perfect,   2Sa 22:31

and all his ways are just.
A faithful God who does no
wrong,
upright and just is he.   Dt 7:9

⁵They are corrupt and not his
children;
to their shame they are a
warped and crooked
generation. Dt 31:29; Mt 17:17
⁶Is this the way you repay the
LORD,
you foolish and unwise
people?   Ps 74:2; 116:12
Is he not your Father, your
Creator,ᵃ
who made you and formed
you?   Dt 1:31; Isa 63:16

⁷Remember the days of old;
consider the generations
long past.   Ps 44:1; Job 8:8
Ask your father and he will
tell you,
your elders, and they will
explain to you.   Ex 13:14
⁸When the Most High gave
the nations their
inheritance,
when he divided all
mankind,
he set up boundaries for the
peoples
according to the number
of the sons of
Israel.ᵇ   Ge 11:8; Ac 17:26
⁹For the LORD's portion is his
people,
Jacob his allotted
inheritance.   Jer 10:16

¹⁰In a desert land he found him,
in a barren and howling
waste.   Jer 2:6
He shielded him and cared for
him;
he guarded him as the
apple of his eye,   Ps 17:8
¹¹like an eagle that stirs up its
nest
and hovers over its young,
that spreads its wings to catch
them
and carries them aloft. Ex 19:4
¹²The LORD alone led him;
no foreign god was with
him.   Dt 4:35; Isa 43:12

¹³He made him ride on the
heights of the land
and fed him with the fruit of
the fields.
He nourished him with honey
from the rock,
and with oil from the flinty
crag,   Dt 8:8; Job 29:6
¹⁴with curds and milk from
herd and flock
and with fattened lambs
and goats,
with choice rams of Bashan
and the finest kernels of
wheat.
You drank the foaming blood
of the grape. Ps 81:16; 147:14

¹⁵Jeshurunᶜ grew fat and
kicked;
filled with food, they
became heavy and
sleek.   Dt 31:20

ᵃ 6 Or *Father, who bought you*   ᵇ 8 Masoretic Text; Dead Sea Scrolls (see also Septuagint)
sons of God   ᶜ 15 *Jeshurun* means *the upright one*, that is, Israel.

They abandoned the God who
made them
and rejected the Rock their
Savior.   Isa 1:4,28

¹⁶They made him jealous
with their foreign
gods
and angered him with
their detestable
idols.   1Co 10:22; Ps 78:58

¹⁷They sacrificed to false
gods, which are not
God —
gods they had not known,
gods that recently
appeared,
gods your ancestors did not
fear.   Dt 28:64; Jdg 5:8

¹⁸You deserted the Rock, who
fathered you;
you forgot the God who
gave you birth.   Ps 106:21

¹⁹The LORD saw this and
rejected them   Jer 44:21-23
because he was angered
by his sons and
daughters.   Ps 106:40

²⁰"I will hide my face from
them," he said,   Dt 31:17,29
"and see what their end
will be;
for they are a perverse
generation,
children who are
unfaithful.

²¹They made me jealous by
what is no god
and angered me with
their worthless
idols.   1Ki 16:13,26

I will make them envious by
those who are not a
people;
I will make them angry by
a nation that has no
understanding.   Ro 10:19

²²For a fire will be kindled by
my wrath,
one that burns down to
the realm of the dead
below.
It will devour the earth and its
harvests
and set afire the
foundations of the
mountains.   Jer 15:14; La 4:11

²³"I will heap calamities on
them
and spend my arrows
against them.   Dt 29:21

²⁴I will send wasting famine
against them,
consuming pestilence and
deadly plague;   Dt 28:22
I will send against them
the fangs of wild
beasts,   Lev 26:22
the venom of vipers that
glide in the dust.   Am 5:18

²⁵In the street the sword will
make them childless;
in their homes terror will
reign.
The young men and young
women will perish,
the infants and those with
gray hair.   2Ch 36:17; Eze 7:15

²⁶I said I would scatter them
and erase their name from
human memory,   Dt 4:27

²⁷but I dreaded the taunt of the
enemy,
lest the adversary
misunderstand
and say, 'Our hand has
triumphed;
the LORD has not done all
this.' " Isa 10:13
²⁸They are a nation without
sense,
there is no discernment in
them. Isa 1:3; 27:11
²⁹If only they were wise and
would understand this
and discern what their end
will be! Ps 81:13
³⁰How could one man chase a
thousand,
or two put ten thousand to
flight,
unless their Rock had sold them,
unless the LORD had given
them up? Lev 26:8; Ps 44:12
³¹For their rock is not like our
Rock,
as even our enemies
concede. Ge 49:24
³²Their vine comes from the
vine of Sodom
and from the fields of
Gomorrah.
Their grapes are filled with
poison,
and their clusters with
bitterness. Dt 29:18
³³Their wine is the venom of
serpents,
the deadly poison of
cobras. Ps 58:4

³⁴"Have I not kept this in
reserve
and sealed it in my vaults?
³⁵It is mine to avenge; I will
repay.
In due time their foot will
slip;
their day of disaster is near
and their doom rushes
upon them." Ro 12:19
³⁶The LORD will vindicate his
people
and relent concerning his
servants
when he sees their strength is
gone
and no one is left, slave or
free.^a Ps 135:14; Joel 2:14
³⁷He will say: "Now where are
their gods,
the rock they took
refuge in, Jdg 10:14; Jer 2:28
³⁸the gods who ate the fat of
their sacrifices
and drank the wine of their
drink offerings?
Let them rise up to help
you!
Let them give you shelter!
³⁹"See now that I myself am he!
There is no god
besides me. Isa 41:4; 45:5
I put to death and I bring to
life,
I have wounded and I will
heal,
and no one can deliver out
of my hand. Ps 50:22

^a 36 Or *and they are without a ruler or leader*

⁴⁰I lift my hand to heaven and
    solemnly swear:
  As surely as I live forever,
⁴¹when I sharpen my flashing
    sword
  and my hand grasps it in
    judgment,   Isa 66:16
  I will take vengeance on my
    adversaries
  and repay those who
    hate me.   Jer 50:29
⁴²I will make my arrows drunk
    with blood,
  while my sword devours
    flesh:
  the blood of the slain and the
    captives,
  the heads of the enemy
    leaders."   Jer 12:12; 46:10,14
⁴³Rejoice, you nations, with his
    people,ᵃ,ᵇ   Ro 15:10
  for he will avenge the blood
    of his servants;
  he will take vengeance on his
    enemies
  and make atonement for his
    land and people.   Ps 85:1

⁴⁴Moses came with Joshuaᶜ
son of Nun and spoke all the
words of this song in the hearing
of the people. ⁴⁵When Moses finished reciting all these words to
all Israel, ⁴⁶he said to them, "Take
to heart all the words I have solemnly declared to you this day,
so that you may command your
children to obey carefully all the
words of this law. ⁴⁷They are not
just idle words for you — they are
your life. By them you will live
long in the land you are crossing
the Jordan to possess." Eze 40:4; Dt
30:20

Moses to Die on Mount Nebo

⁴⁸On that same day the LORD
told Moses, ⁴⁹"Go up into the
Abarim Range to Mount Nebo
in Moab, across from Jericho,
and view Canaan, the land I
am giving the Israelites as their
own possession. ⁵⁰There on the
mountain that you have climbed
you will die and be gathered to
your people, just as your brother Aaron died on Mount Hor
and was gathered to his people.
⁵¹This is because both of you
broke faith with me in the presence of the Israelites at the waters
of Meribah Kadesh in the Desert of Zin and because you did
not uphold my holiness among
the Israelites. ⁵²Therefore, you
will see the land only from a
distance; you will not enter the
land I am giving to the people of
Israel."   Ge 25:8; Nu 20:11-13; 27:12

Moses Blesses the Tribes

33:1-29Ref — Ge 49:1-28

33 This is the blessing that
Moses the man of God
pronounced on the Israelites before his death. ²He said: Jos 14:6

ᵃ 43 Or *Make his people rejoice, you nations*   ᵇ 43 Masoretic Text; Dead Sea Scrolls (see
also Septuagint) *people, / and let all the angels worship him, /*   ᶜ 44 Hebrew *Hoshea*, a
variant of *Joshua*

"The LORD came from Sinai
and dawned over them
from Seir;
he shone forth from Mount
Paran. Ps 50:2; 68:8; Hab 3:3
He came with[a] myriads of
holy ones
from the south, from
his mountain
slopes.[b] Da 7:10; Rev 5:11
³Surely it is you who love the
people;
all the holy ones are in your
hand.
At your feet they all bow
down,
and from you receive
instruction, Lk 10:39
⁴the law that Moses gave us,
the possession of the
assembly of
Jacob. Ps 119:111; Jn 1:17
⁵He was king over Jeshurun[c]
when the leaders of the
people assembled,
along with the tribes of
Israel. Nu 23:21

⁶"Let Reuben live and not die,
nor[d] his people be few."

⁷And this he said about Judah:

"Hear, LORD, the cry of Judah;
bring him to his people.
With his own hands he
defends his cause.
Oh, be his help against his
foes!" Ge 49:10

⁸About Levi he said:

"Your Thummim and Urim
belong
to your faithful
servant. Ex 28:30
You tested him at Massah;
you contended with him
at the waters of
Meribah. Ex 17:7
⁹He said of his father and
mother,
'I have no regard for them.'
He did not recognize his
brothers
or acknowledge his own
children,
but he watched over your
word
and guarded your
covenant. Ex 32:26-29
¹⁰He teaches your precepts to
Jacob
and your law to Israel.
He offers incense before you
and whole burnt
offerings on your
altar. Ps 51:19; Lev 10:11
¹¹Bless all his skills, LORD,
and be pleased with the
work of his hands.
Strike down those who rise
against him,
his foes till they rise no
more."

¹²About Benjamin he said:

"Let the beloved of the LORD
rest secure in him,
for he shields him all day
long,

---

[a] 2 Or from   [b] 2 The meaning of the Hebrew for this phrase is uncertain.   [c] 5 Jeshurun
means the upright one, that is, Israel; also in verse 26.   [d] 6 Or but let

and the one the LORD
 loves rests between his
 shoulders." Ex 28:12; Dt 12:10

¹³ About Joseph he said:

"May the LORD bless his land
 with the precious dew from
 heaven above
 and with the deep
 waters that lie
 below;   Ge 27:28; 49:25
¹⁴ with the best the sun brings
 forth
 and the finest the moon can
 yield;
¹⁵ with the choicest gifts of the
 ancient mountains
 and the fruitfulness of the
 everlasting hills;   Hab 3:6
¹⁶ with the best gifts of the earth
 and its fullness
 and the favor of him who
 dwelt in the burning
 bush.
Let all these rest on the head
 of Joseph,
 on the brow of the prince
 among*ᵃ* his
 brothers.   Ex 3:2
¹⁷ In majesty he is like a
 firstborn bull;
 his horns are the horns of a
 wild ox.
With them he will gore the
 nations,
 even those at the ends of the
 earth.   Nu 23:22; 1Ki 22:11
Such are the ten thousands of
 Ephraim;

such are the thousands of
 Manasseh."

¹⁸ About Zebulun he said:

"Rejoice, Zebulun, in your
 going out,
 and you, Issachar, in your
 tents.   Ge 49:13-15
¹⁹ They will summon peoples to
 the mountain
 and there offer the
 sacrifices of the
 righteous;   Ps 4:5; Isa 2:3
they will feast on the
 abundance of the seas,
 on the treasures hidden in
 the sand."   Isa 60:5,11

²⁰ About Gad he said:

"Blessed is he who enlarges
 Gad's domain!
Gad lives there like a lion,
 tearing at arm or
 head.   Ge 30:11; 49:19
²¹ He chose the best land for
 himself;
 the leader's portion was kept
 for him.   Nu 32:1-5,31-32
When the heads of the people
 assembled,
 he carried out the LORD's
 righteous will,
 and his judgments
 concerning
 Israel."   Jos 4:12

²² About Dan he said:

"Dan is a lion's cub,
 springing out of Bashan."

ᵃ 16 Or of the one separated from

²³ About Naphtali he said:

"Naphtali is abounding with
    the favor of the LORD
and is full of his blessing;
he will inherit southward to
    the lake."   Ge 30:8

²⁴ About Asher he said:

"Most blessed of sons is Asher;
let him be favored by his
    brothers,
and let him bathe his feet in
    oil.   Ge 49:21; Job 29:6
²⁵ The bolts of your gates will be
    iron and bronze,   Ne 3:3
and your strength will
    equal your days.   Dt 4:40

²⁶ "There is no one like the God
    of Jeshurun,
who rides across the
    heavens to help you
and on the clouds in his
    majesty.   Ex 15:11; 2Sa 22:10
²⁷ The eternal God is your
    refuge,
and underneath are the
    everlasting arms.   Ps 90:1
He will drive out your
    enemies before you,
saying, 'Destroy them!'   Dt 7:2
²⁸ So Israel will live in safety;
Jacob will dwell^a secure
in a land of grain and new
    wine,
where the heavens drop
    dew.   Ge 27:28; Jer 23:6
²⁹ Blessed are you, Israel!
Who is like you,

a people saved by the
    LORD?   2Sa 7:23; Ps 144:15
He is your shield and helper
    and your glorious sword.
Your enemies will cower
    before you,
and you will tread on their
    heights."   Ex 18:4; Ps 115:9-11

The Death of Moses

34 Then Moses climbed Mount Nebo from the plains of Moab to the top of Pisgah, across from Jericho. There the LORD showed him the whole land—from Gilead to Dan, ² all of Naphtali, the territory of Ephraim and Manasseh, all the land of Judah as far as the Mediterranean Sea, ³ the Negev and the whole region from the Valley of Jericho, the City of Palms, as far as Zoar. ⁴ Then the LORD said to him, "This is the land I promised on oath to Abraham, Isaac and Jacob when I said, 'I will give it to your descendants.' I have let you see it with your eyes, but you will not cross over into it."   Ge 12:7; Dt 32:52; 2Ch 28:15

⁵ And Moses the servant of the LORD died there in Moab, as the LORD had said. ⁶ He buried him^b in Moab, in the valley opposite Beth Peor, but to this day no one knows where his grave is. ⁷ Moses was a hundred and twenty years old when he died, yet his eyes were not weak nor

---

^a 28 Septuagint; Hebrew *Jacob's spring is*   ^b 6 Or *He was buried*

his strength gone. [8]The Israelites grieved for Moses in the plains of Moab thirty days, until the time of weeping and mourning was over.   Jos 1:1-2; Jude 9; Ge 27:1

[9]Now Joshua son of Nun was filled with the spirit[a] of wisdom because Moses had laid his hands on him. So the Israelites listened to him and did what the LORD had commanded Moses.   Nu 27:18,23; Isa 11:2

[10]Since then, no prophet has risen in Israel like Moses, whom the LORD knew face to face, [11]who did all those signs and wonders the LORD sent him to do in Egypt — to Pharaoh and to all his officials and to his whole land. [12]For no one has ever shown the mighty power or performed the awesome deeds that Moses did in the sight of all Israel.   Dt 18:15,18; Ex 33:11; Nu 12:6,8

---

[a] 9 Or Spirit

Joshua

Joshua Installed as Leader

1 After the death of Moses the servant of the LORD, the LORD said to Joshua son of Nun, Moses' aide: [2] "Moses my servant is dead. Now then, you and all these people, get ready to cross the Jordan River into the land I am about to give to them — to the Israelites. [3] I will give you every place where you set your foot, as I promised Moses. [4] Your territory will extend from the desert to Lebanon, and from the great river, the Euphrates — all the Hittite country — to the Mediterranean Sea in the west. [5] No one will be able to stand against you all the days of your life. As I was with Moses, so I will be with you; I will never leave you nor forsake you. [6] Be strong and courageous, because you will lead these people to inherit the land I swore to their ancestors to give them. Dt 7:24; 11:24; 31:6-8

[7] "Be strong and very coura- geous. Be careful to obey all the law my servant Moses gave you; do not turn from it to the right or to the left, that you may be suc- cessful wherever you go. [8] Keep this Book of the Law always on your lips; meditate on it day and night, so that you may be care- ful to do everything written in it. Then you will be prosper- ous and successful. [9] Have I not commanded you? Be strong and courageous. Do not be afraid; do not be discouraged, for the LORD your God will be with you wher- ever you go." Dt 31:23; Ps 1:1-3; Jer 1:8

[10] So Joshua ordered the offi- cers of the people: [11] "Go through the camp and tell the people, 'Get your provisions ready. Three days from now you will cross the Jordan here to go in and take possession of the land the LORD your God is giving you for your own.'" Jos 3:2; Joel 3:2

[12] But to the Reubenites, the Gadites and the half-tribe of

Manasseh, Joshua said, ¹³ "Remember the command that Moses the servant of the LORD gave you after he said, 'The LORD your God will give you rest by giving you this land.' ¹⁴Your wives, your children and your livestock may stay in the land that Moses gave you east of the Jordan, but all your fighting men, ready for battle, must cross over ahead of your fellow Israelites. You are to help them ¹⁵until the LORD gives them rest, as he has done for you, and until they too have taken possession of the land the LORD your God is giving them. After that, you may go back and occupy your own land, which Moses the servant of the LORD gave you east of the Jordan toward the sunrise." Nu 32:20-22; Jos 22:1-4; Dt 3:18

¹⁶Then they answered Joshua, "Whatever you have commanded us we will do, and wherever you send us we will go. ¹⁷Just as we fully obeyed Moses, so we will obey you. Only may the LORD your God be with you as he was with Moses. ¹⁸Whoever rebels against your word and does not obey it, whatever you may command them, will be put to death. Only be strong and courageous!" ver 5,9; Nu 27:20

Rahab and the Spies

2 Then Joshua son of Nun secretly sent two spies from Shittim. "Go, look over the land," he said, "especially Jericho." So they went and entered the house of a prostitute named Rahab and stayed there. Heb 11:31; Jas 2:25

²The king of Jericho was told, "Look, some of the Israelites have come here tonight to spy out the land." ³So the king of Jericho sent this message to Rahab: "Bring out the men who came to you and entered your house, because they have come to spy out the whole land."

⁴But the woman had taken the two men and hidden them. She said, "Yes, the men came to me, but I did not know where they had come from. ⁵At dusk, when it was time to close the city gate, they left. I don't know which way they went. Go after them quickly. You may catch up with them." ⁶(But she had taken them up to the roof and hidden them under the stalks of flax she had laid out on the roof.) ⁷So the men set out in pursuit of the spies on the road that leads to the fords of the Jordan, and as soon as the pursuers had gone out, the gate was shut. 2Sa 17:19-20; Nu 22:1; Jos 6:22

⁸Before the spies lay down for the night, she went up on the roof ⁹and said to them, "I know that the LORD has given you this land and that a great fear of you has fallen on us, so that all who live in this country are melting in fear because of you. ¹⁰We have heard how

the LORD dried up the water of the Red Sea[a] for you when you came out of Egypt, and what you did to Sihon and Og, the two kings of the Amorites east of the Jordan, whom you completely destroyed.[b] [11]When we heard of it, our hearts melted in fear and everyone's courage failed because of you, for the LORD your God is God in heaven above and on the earth below. Ex 14:21; 23:27; Nu 21:21,24,34-35

[12]"Now then, please swear to me by the LORD that you will show kindness to my family, because I have shown kindness to you. Give me a sure sign [13]that you will spare the lives of my father and mother, my brothers and sisters, and all who belong to them — and that you will save us from death."

[14]"Our lives for your lives!" the men assured her. "If you don't tell what we are doing, we will treat you kindly and faithfully when the LORD gives us the land." Jdg 1:24; Mt 5:7

[15]So she let them down by a rope through the window, for the house she lived in was part of the city wall. [16]She said to them, "Go to the hills so the pursuers will not find you. Hide yourselves there three days until they return, and then go on your way." Ac 9:25; Jer 38:6,11

[17]Now the men had said to her,

"This oath you made us swear will not be binding on us [18]unless, when we enter the land, you have tied this scarlet cord in the window through which you let us down, and unless you have brought your father and mother, your brothers and all your family into your house. [19]If any of them go outside your house into the street, their blood will be on their own heads; we will not be responsible. As for those who are in the house with you, their blood will be on our head if a hand is laid on them. [20]But if you tell what we are doing, we will be released from the oath you made us swear." Ge 24:8; Mt 27:25; Eze 33:4

[21]"Agreed," she replied. "Let it be as you say."

So she sent them away, and they departed. And she tied the scarlet cord in the window.

[22]When they left, they went into the hills and stayed there three days, until the pursuers had searched all along the road and returned without finding them. [23]Then the two men started back. They went down out of the hills, forded the river and came to Joshua son of Nun and told him everything that had happened to them. [24]They said to Joshua, "The LORD has surely given the whole land into our hands; all the people are melting in fear because of us." ver 9

[a] 10 Or *the Sea of Reeds*   [b] 10 The Hebrew term refers to the irrevocable giving over of things or persons to the LORD, often by totally destroying them.

Crossing the Jordan

3 Early in the morning Joshua and all the Israelites set out from Shittim and went to the Jordan, where they camped before crossing over. ²After three days the officers went throughout the camp, ³giving orders to the people: "When you see the ark of the covenant of the LORD your God, and the Levitical priests carrying it, you are to move out from your positions and follow it. ⁴Then you will know which way to go, since you have never been this way before. But keep a distance of about two thousand cubits[a] between you and the ark; do not go near it." Dt 31:9; Jos 2:1; 1:11

⁵Joshua told the people, "Consecrate yourselves, for tomorrow the LORD will do amazing things among you." Ex 19:10,14; Jos 7:13

⁶Joshua said to the priests, "Take up the ark of the covenant and pass on ahead of the people." So they took it up and went ahead of them.

⁷And the LORD said to Joshua, "Today I will begin to exalt you in the eyes of all Israel, so they may know that I am with you as I was with Moses. ⁸Tell the priests who carry the ark of the covenant: 'When you reach the edge of the Jordan's waters, go and stand in the river.'" Jos 1:5; 1Ch 29:25

⁹Joshua said to the Israelites, "Come here and listen to the words of the LORD your God. ¹⁰This is how you will know that the living God is among you and that he will certainly drive out before you the Canaanites, Hittites, Hivites, Perizzites, Girgashites, Amorites and Jebusites. ¹¹See, the ark of the covenant of the Lord of all the earth will go into the Jordan ahead of you. ¹²Now then, choose twelve men from the tribes of Israel, one from each tribe. ¹³And as soon as the priests who carry the ark of the LORD — the Lord of all the earth — set foot in the Jordan, its waters flowing downstream will be cut off and stand up in a heap." Dt 5:26; Jos 4:2,4; Zec 6:5

¹⁴So when the people broke camp to cross the Jordan, the priests carrying the ark of the covenant went ahead of them. ¹⁵Now the Jordan is at flood stage all during harvest. Yet as soon as the priests who carried the ark reached the Jordan and their feet touched the water's edge, ¹⁶the water from upstream stopped flowing. It piled up in a heap a great distance away, at a town called Adam in the vicinity of Zarethan, while the water flowing down to the Sea of the Arabah (that is, the Dead Sea) was completely cut off. So the people crossed over opposite Jericho. ¹⁷The priests who carried the ark of the covenant of the LORD stopped in the middle of the Jordan and stood on dry

a 4 That is, about 3,000 feet or about 900 meters

ground, while all Israel passed by until the whole nation had completed the crossing on dry ground. Ex 14:22,29; Jos 4:18; Ac 7:44-45

4 When the whole nation had finished crossing the Jordan, the LORD said to Joshua, ²"Choose twelve men from among the people, one from each tribe, ³and tell them to take up twelve stones from the middle of the Jordan, from right where the priests are standing, and carry them over with you and put them down at the place where you stay tonight." Dt 27:2; Jos 3:12; ver 20

⁴So Joshua called together the twelve men he had appointed from the Israelites, one from each tribe, ⁵and said to them, "Go over before the ark of the LORD your God into the middle of the Jordan. Each of you is to take up a stone on his shoulder, according to the number of the tribes of the Israelites, ⁶to serve as a sign among you. In the future, when your children ask you, 'What do these stones mean?' ⁷tell them that the flow of the Jordan was cut off before the ark of the covenant of the LORD. When it crossed the Jordan, the waters of the Jordan were cut off. These stones are to be a memorial to the people of Israel forever." Ex 12:26; 13:14; Jos 3:13

⁸So the Israelites did as Joshua commanded them. They took twelve stones from the middle of the Jordan, according to the number of the tribes of the Israelites, as the LORD had told Joshua; and they carried them over with them to their camp, where they put them down. ⁹Joshua set up the twelve stones that had been*ᵃ* in the middle of the Jordan at the spot where the priests who carried the ark of the covenant had stood. And they are there to this day. Ex 28:21; 1Sa 7:12

¹⁰Now the priests who carried the ark remained standing in the middle of the Jordan until everything the LORD had commanded Joshua was done by the people, just as Moses had directed Joshua. The people hurried over, ¹¹and as soon as all of them had crossed, the ark of the LORD and the priests came to the other side while the people watched. ¹²The men of Reuben, Gad and the half-tribe of Manasseh crossed over, ready for battle, in front of the Israelites, as Moses had directed them. ¹³About forty thousand armed for battle crossed over before the LORD to the plains of Jericho for war. Ex 13:18; Nu 32:27

¹⁴That day the LORD exalted Joshua in the sight of all Israel; and they stood in awe of him all the days of his life, just as they had stood in awe of Moses. Jos 3:7

¹⁵Then the LORD said to Joshua, ¹⁶"Command the priests carrying the ark of the covenant law to come up out of the Jordan." Ex 25:22

ᵃ 9 Or Joshua also set up twelve stones

17 So Joshua commanded the priests, "Come up out of the Jordan."

18 And the priests came up out of the river carrying the ark of the covenant of the LORD. No sooner had they set their feet on the dry ground than the waters of the Jordan returned to their place and ran at flood stage as before. Jos 3:15

19 On the tenth day of the first month the people went up from the Jordan and camped at Gilgal on the eastern border of Jericho. 20 And Joshua set up at Gilgal the twelve stones they had taken out of the Jordan. 21 He said to the Israelites, "In the future when your descendants ask their parents, 'What do these stones mean?' 22 tell them, 'Israel crossed the Jordan on dry ground.' 23 For the LORD your God dried up the Jordan before you until you had crossed over. The LORD your God did to the Jordan what he had done to the Red Sea[a] when he dried it up before us until we had crossed over. 24 He did this so that all the peoples of the earth might know that the hand of the LORD is powerful and so that you might always fear the LORD your God." Ex 15:16; 1Ki 8:42-43; Ps 106:8

5 Now when all the Amorite kings west of the Jordan and all the Canaanite kings along the coast heard how the LORD had dried up the Jordan before the Israelites until they[b] had crossed over, their hearts melted in fear and they no longer had the courage to face the Israelites. Nu 13:29

Circumcision and Passover at Gilgal

2 At that time the LORD said to Joshua, "Make flint knives and circumcise the Israelites again." 3 So Joshua made flint knives and circumcised the Israelites at Gibeath Haaraloth.[c] Ex 4:25

4 Now this is why he did so: All those who came out of Egypt — all the men of military age — died in the wilderness on the way after leaving Egypt. 5 All the people that came out had been circumcised, but all the people born in the wilderness during the journey from Egypt had not. 6 The Israelites had moved about in the wilderness forty years until all the men who were of military age when they left Egypt had died, since they had not obeyed the LORD. For the LORD had sworn to them that they would not see the land he had solemnly promised their ancestors to give us, a land flowing with milk and honey. 7 So he raised up their sons in their place, and these were the ones Joshua circumcised. They were still uncircumcised because they had not been circum-

---

[a] 23 Or *the Sea of Reeds*   [b] 1 Another textual tradition *we*   [c] 3 *Gibeath Haaraloth* means *the hill of foreskins.*

cised on the way. ⁸And after the whole nation had been circumcised, they remained where they were in camp until they were healed.   Dt 2:7,14; Nu 14:23,29-35

⁹Then the LORD said to Joshua, "Today I have rolled away the reproach of Egypt from you." So the place has been called Gilgal*ᵃ* to this day.

¹⁰On the evening of the fourteenth day of the month, while camped at Gilgal on the plains of Jericho, the Israelites celebrated the Passover. ¹¹The day after the Passover, that very day, they ate some of the produce of the land: unleavened bread and roasted grain. ¹²The manna stopped the day after*ᵇ* they ate this food from the land; there was no longer any manna for the Israelites, but that year they ate the produce of Canaan.   Ex 12:6; 16:35; Nu 15:19

The Fall of Jericho

¹³Now when Joshua was near Jericho, he looked up and saw a man standing in front of him with a drawn sword in his hand. Joshua went up to him and asked, "Are you for us or for our enemies?"   Ge 18:2; 32:24

¹⁴"Neither," he replied, "but as commander of the army of the LORD I have now come." Then Joshua fell facedown to the ground in reverence, and asked him, "What message does my Lord*ᶜ* have for his servant?"Ge 17:3

¹⁵The commander of the LORD's army replied, "Take off your sandals, for the place where you are standing is holy." And Joshua did so.   Ex 3:5; Ac 7:33

6 Now the gates of Jericho were securely barred because of the Israelites. No one went out and no one came in.   Jos 24:11

²Then the LORD said to Joshua, "See, I have delivered Jericho into your hands, along with its king and its fighting men. ³March around the city once with all the armed men. Do this for six days. ⁴Have seven priests carry trumpets of rams' horns in front of the ark. On the seventh day, march around the city seven times, with the priests blowing the trumpets. ⁵When you hear them sound a long blast on the trumpets, have the whole army give a loud shout; then the wall of the city will collapse and the army will go up, everyone straight in."   Dt 7:24; Lev 25:9; Isa 42:13

⁶So Joshua son of Nun called the priests and said to them, "Take up the ark of the covenant of the LORD and have seven priests carry trumpets in front of it." ⁷And he ordered the army, "Advance! March around the city, with an armed guard going ahead of the ark of the LORD."   Ex 14:15; 1Sa 4:3

⁸When Joshua had spoken to the people, the seven priests carrying the seven trumpets before the LORD went forward, blowing

---

ᵃ 9 Gilgal sounds like the Hebrew for *roll*.   *ᵇ 12* Or *the day*   *ᶜ 14* Or *lord* their trumpets, and the ark of the LORD's covenant followed them. ⁹The armed guard marched ahead of the priests who blew the trumpets, and the rear guard followed the ark. All this time the trumpets were sounding. ¹⁰But Joshua had commanded the army, "Do not give a war cry, do not raise your voices, do not say a word until the day I tell you to shout. Then shout!" ¹¹So he had the ark of the LORD carried around the city, circling it once. Then the army returned to camp and spent the night there. Isa 52:12

¹²Joshua got up early the next morning and the priests took up the ark of the LORD. ¹³The seven priests carrying the seven trumpets went forward, marching before the ark of the LORD and blowing the trumpets. The armed men went ahead of them and the rear guard followed the ark of the LORD, while the trumpets kept sounding. ¹⁴So on the second day they marched around the city once and returned to the camp. They did this for six days.

¹⁵On the seventh day, they got up at daybreak and marched around the city seven times in the same manner, except that on that day they circled the city seven times. ¹⁶The seventh time around, when the priests sounded the trumpet blast, Joshua commanded the army, "Shout! For the LORD has given you the city! ¹⁷The city and all that is in it are to be devoted*a* to the LORD. Only Rahab the prostitute and all who are with her in her house shall be spared, because she hid the spies we sent. ¹⁸But keep away from the devoted things, so that you will not bring about your own destruction by taking any of them. Otherwise you will make the camp of Israel liable to destruction and bring trouble on it. ¹⁹All the silver and gold and the articles of bronze and iron are sacred to the LORD and must go into his treasury." Lev 27:28; Jos 2:4; 7:1

²⁰When the trumpets sounded, the army shouted, and at the sound of the trumpet, when the men gave a loud shout, the wall collapsed; so everyone charged straight in, and they took the city. ²¹They devoted the city to the LORD and destroyed with the sword every living thing in it—men and women, young and old, cattle, sheep and donkeys. Dt 20:16; Am 2:2

²²Joshua said to the two men who had spied out the land, "Go into the prostitute's house and bring her out and all who belong to her, in accordance with your oath to her." ²³So the young men who had done the spying went in and brought out Rahab, her father and mother, her brothers and sisters and all who be-

---

a 17 The Hebrew term refers to the irrevocable giving over of things or persons to the LORD, often by totally destroying them; also in verses 18 and 21.

longed to her. They brought out her entire family and put them in a place outside the camp of Israel. Jos 2:14; Heb 11:31 [24]Then they burned the whole city and everything in it, but they put the silver and gold and the articles of bronze and iron into the treasury of the LORD's house. [25]But Joshua spared Rahab the prostitute, with her family and all who belonged to her, because she hid the men Joshua had sent as spies to Jericho — and she lives among the Israelites to this day. Jdg 1:25 [26]At that time Joshua pronounced this solemn oath: "Cursed before the LORD is the one who undertakes to rebuild this city, Jericho:

"At the cost of his firstborn son
    he will lay its foundations;
at the cost of his youngest
    he will set up its gates."

[27]So the LORD was with Joshua, and his fame spread throughout the land. Jos 1:5; 9:1

Achan's Sin

7 But the Israelites were unfaithful in regard to the devoted things[a]; Achan son of Karmi, the son of Zimri,[b] the son of Zerah, of the tribe of Judah, took some of them. So the LORD's anger burned against Israel. Jos 6:18

[2]Now Joshua sent men from Jericho to Ai, which is near Beth Aven to the east of Bethel, and told them, "Go up and spy out the region." So the men went up and spied out Ai. Jos 18:12

[3]When they returned to Joshua, they said, "Not all the army will have to go up against Ai. Send two or three thousand men to take it and do not weary the whole army, for only a few people live there." [4]So about three thousand went up; but they were routed by the men of Ai, [5]who killed about thirty-six of them. They chased the Israelites from the city gate as far as the stone quarries and struck them down on the slopes. At this the hearts of the people melted in fear and became like water. Lev 26:17; Dt 28:25

[6]Then Joshua tore his clothes and fell facedown to the ground before the ark of the LORD, remaining there till evening. The elders of Israel did the same, and sprinkled dust on their heads. [7]And Joshua said, "Alas, Sovereign LORD, why did you ever bring this people across the Jordan to deliver us into the hands of the Amorites to destroy us? If only we had been content to stay on the other side of the Jordan! [8]Pardon your servant, Lord. What can I say, now that Israel has been routed by its enemies?

---

a 1 The Hebrew term refers to the irrevocable giving over of things or persons to the LORD, often by totally destroying them; also in verses 11, 12, 13 and 15.   *b 1* See Septuagint and 1 Chron. 2:6; Hebrew *Zabdi*; also in verses 17 and 18.

⁹The Canaanites and the other people of the country will hear about this and they will surround us and wipe out our name from the earth. What then will you do for your own great name?" Ex 32:12; Job 2:12; Rev 18:19

¹⁰The LORD said to Joshua, "Stand up! What are you doing down on your face? ¹¹Israel has sinned; they have violated my covenant, which I commanded them to keep. They have taken some of the devoted things; they have stolen, they have lied, they have put them with their own possessions. ¹²That is why the Israelites cannot stand against their enemies; they turn their backs and run because they have been made liable to destruction. I will not be with you anymore unless you destroy whatever among you is devoted to destruction. Jos 6:17-19; Ac 5:1-2; Dt 29:27

¹³"Go, consecrate the people. Tell them, 'Consecrate yourselves in preparation for tomorrow; for this is what the LORD, the God of Israel, says: There are devoted things among you, Israel. You cannot stand against your enemies until you remove them. Jos 3:5; 6:18

¹⁴"'In the morning, present yourselves tribe by tribe. The tribe the LORD chooses shall come forward clan by clan; the clan the LORD chooses shall come forward family by family; and the family the LORD chooses shall come forward man by man. ¹⁵Whoever is caught with the devoted things shall be destroyed by fire, along with all that belongs to him. He has violated the covenant of the LORD and has done an outrageous thing in Israel!'" Ge 34:7; 1Sa 14:39; Pr 16:33

¹⁶Early the next morning Joshua had Israel come forward by tribes, and Judah was chosen. ¹⁷The clans of Judah came forward, and the Zerahites were chosen. He had the clan of the Zerahites come forward by families, and Zimri was chosen. ¹⁸Joshua had his family come forward man by man, and Achan son of Karmi, the son of Zimri, the son of Zerah, of the tribe of Judah, was chosen. Nu 26:20

¹⁹Then Joshua said to Achan, "My son, give glory to the LORD, the God of Israel, and honor him. Tell me what you have done; do not hide it from me." Jer 13:16; Jn 9:24

²⁰Achan replied, "It is true! I have sinned against the LORD, the God of Israel. This is what I have done: ²¹When I saw in the plunder a beautiful robe from Babylonia,ᵃ two hundred shekelsᵇ of silver and a bar of gold weighing fifty shekels,ᶜ I coveted them and took them. They are hidden in the ground inside my tent, with the silver underneath." Eph 5:5; 1Ti 6:10

ᵃ 21 Hebrew Shinar   ᵇ 21 That is, about 5 pounds or about 2.3 kilograms   ᶜ 21 That is, about 1 1/4 pounds or about 575 grams

²²So Joshua sent messengers, and they ran to the tent, and there it was, hidden in his tent, with the silver underneath. ²³They took the things from the tent, brought them to Joshua and all the Israelites and spread them out before the LORD.

²⁴Then Joshua, together with all Israel, took Achan son of Zerah, the silver, the robe, the gold bar, his sons and daughters, his cattle, donkeys and sheep, his tent and all that he had, to the Valley of Achor. ²⁵Joshua said, "Why have you brought this trouble on us? The LORD will bring trouble on you today." Jos 6:18; 15:7

Then all Israel stoned him, and after they had stoned the rest, they burned them. ²⁶Over Achan they heaped up a large pile of rocks, which remains to this day. Then the LORD turned from his fierce anger. Therefore that place has been called the Valley of Achor*a* ever since. Dt 13:17; 17:5

Ai Destroyed

8 Then the LORD said to Joshua, "Do not be afraid; do not be discouraged. Take the whole army with you, and go up and attack Ai. For I have delivered into your hands the king of Ai, his people, his city and his land. ²You shall do to Ai and its king as you did to Jericho and its king, except that you may carry off their plunder and livestock for

yourselves. Set an ambush behind the city." Jos 1:9; 6:2; Dt 1:21

³So Joshua and the whole army moved out to attack Ai. He chose thirty thousand of his best fighting men and sent them out at night ⁴with these orders: "Listen carefully. You are to set an ambush behind the city. Don't go very far from it. All of you be on the alert. ⁵I and all those with me will advance on the city, and when the men come out against us, as they did before, we will flee from them. ⁶They will pursue us until we have lured them away from the city, for they will say, 'They are running away from us as they did before.' So when we flee from them, ⁷you are to rise up from ambush and take the city. The LORD your God will give it into your hand. ⁸When you have taken the city, set it on fire. Do what the LORD has commanded. See to it; you have my orders." Jdg 7:7; 20:29-38

⁹Then Joshua sent them off, and they went to the place of ambush and lay in wait between Bethel and Ai, to the west of Ai — but Joshua spent that night with the people. 2Ch 13:13

¹⁰Early the next morning Joshua mustered his army, and he and the leaders of Israel marched before them to Ai. ¹¹The entire force that was with him marched up and approached the city and arrived in front of it. They set up

---

a 26 Achor means *trouble.*

camp north of Ai, with the valley between them and the city. [12] Joshua had taken about five thousand men and set them in ambush between Bethel and Ai, to the west of the city. [13] So the soldiers took up their positions — with the main camp to the north of the city and the ambush to the west of it. That night Joshua went into the valley. Ge 22:3

[14] When the king of Ai saw this, he and all the men of the city hurried out early in the morning to meet Israel in battle at a certain place overlooking the Arabah. But he did not know that an ambush had been set against him behind the city. [15] Joshua and all Israel let themselves be driven back before them, and they fled toward the wilderness. [16] All the men of Ai were called to pursue them, and they pursued Joshua and were lured away from the city. [17] Not a man remained in Ai or Bethel who did not go after Israel. They left the city open and went in pursuit of Israel. Jos 15:61; 18:12; Jdg 20:34

[18] Then the Lord said to Joshua, "Hold out toward Ai the javelin that is in your hand, for into your hand I will deliver the city." So Joshua held out toward the city the javelin that was in his hand. [19] As soon as he did this, the men in the ambush rose quickly from their position and rushed forward. They entered the city and captured it and quickly set it on fire. Ex 14:16; 17:9-12

[20] The men of Ai looked back and saw the smoke of the city rising up into the sky, but they had no chance to escape in any direction; the Israelites who had been fleeing toward the wilderness had turned back against their pursuers. [21] For when Joshua and all Israel saw that the ambush had taken the city and that smoke was going up from it, they turned around and attacked the men of Ai. [22] Those in the ambush also came out of the city against them, so that they were caught in the middle, with Israelites on both sides. Israel cut them down, leaving them neither survivors nor fugitives. [23] But they took the king of Ai alive and brought him to Joshua. Dt 7:2; 1Sa 15:8

[24] When Israel had finished killing all the men of Ai in the fields and in the wilderness where they had chased them, and when every one of them had been put to the sword, all the Israelites returned to Ai and killed those who were in it. [25] Twelve thousand men and women fell that day — all the people of Ai. [26] For Joshua did not draw back the hand that held out his javelin until he had destroyed[a] all who lived in Ai. [27] But Israel did carry off for themselves the livestock and plunder of this

---

[a] 26 The Hebrew term refers to the irrevocable giving over of things or persons to the Lord, often by totally destroying them.

city, as the LORD had instructed Joshua. Ex 17:12; Dt 20:16-18 ²⁸So Joshua burned Ai[a] and made it a permanent heap of ruins, a desolate place to this day. ²⁹He impaled the body of the king of Ai on a pole and left it there until evening. At sunset, Joshua ordered them to take the body from the pole and throw it down at the entrance of the city gate. And they raised a large pile of rocks over it, which remains to this day. Dt 13:16; 21:23; Jn 19:31

The Covenant Renewed at Mount Ebal

³⁰Then Joshua built on Mount Ebal an altar to the LORD, the God of Israel, ³¹as Moses the servant of the LORD had commanded the Israelites. He built it according to what is written in the Book of the Law of Moses—an altar of uncut stones, on which no iron tool had been used. On it they offered to the LORD burnt offerings and sacrificed fellowship offerings. ³²There, in the presence of the Israelites, Joshua wrote on stones a copy of the law of Moses. ³³All the Israelites, with their elders, officials and judges, were standing on both sides of the ark of the covenant of the LORD, facing the Levitical priests who carried it. Both the foreigners living among them and the native-born were there. Half of the people stood in front of Mount Gerizim and half of them in front of Mount Ebal, as Moses the servant of the LORD had formerly commanded when he gave instructions to bless the people of Israel. Ex 20:25; Dt 27:6-7; 11:29

³⁴Afterward, Joshua read all the words of the law—the blessings and the curses—just as it is written in the Book of the Law. ³⁵There was not a word of all that Moses had commanded that Joshua did not read to the whole assembly of Israel, including the women and children, and the foreigners who lived among them. Dt 31:12; Jos 1:8

The Gibeonite Deception

9 Now when all the kings west of the Jordan heard about these things—the kings in the hill country, in the western foothills, and along the entire coast of the Mediterranean Sea as far as Lebanon (the kings of the Hittites, Amorites, Canaanites, Perizzites, Hivites and Jebusites)— ²they came together to wage war against Joshua and Israel. Nu 34:6; Ex 3:17

³However, when the people of Gibeon heard what Joshua had done to Jericho and Ai, ⁴they resorted to a ruse: They went as a delegation whose donkeys were loaded[b] with worn-out sacks and old wineskins, cracked and mended. ⁵They put worn and patched sandals on their feet and wore old

---

[a] 28 Ai means the ruin. [b] 4 Most Hebrew manuscripts; some Hebrew manuscripts, Vulgate and Syriac (see also Septuagint) They prepared provisions and loaded their donkeys

clothes. All the bread of their food supply was dry and moldy. ⁶Then they went to Joshua in the camp at Gilgal and said to him and the Israelites, "We have come from a distant country; make a treaty with us." Jos 5:10; 10:2

⁷The Israelites said to the Hivites, "But perhaps you live near us, so how can we make a treaty with you?" Ex 23:32; Jos 11:19

⁸"We are your servants," they said to Joshua.

But Joshua asked, "Who are you and where do you come from?"

⁹They answered: "Your servants have come from a very distant country because of the fame of the LORD your God. For we have heard reports of him: all that he did in Egypt, ¹⁰and all that he did to the two kings of the Amorites east of the Jordan — Sihon king of Heshbon, and Og king of Bashan, who reigned in Ashtaroth. ¹¹And our elders and all those living in our country said to us, 'Take provisions for your journey; go and meet them and say to them, "We are your servants; make a treaty with us." ' ¹²This bread of ours was warm when we packed it at home on the day we left to come to you. But now see how dry and moldy it is. ¹³And these wineskins that we filled were new, but see how cracked they are. And our clothes and sandals are worn out by the very long journey." Dt 20:15; Jos 2:9; Nu 21:24,35

¹⁴The Israelites sampled their provisions but did not inquire of the LORD. ¹⁵Then Joshua made a treaty of peace with them to let them live, and the leaders of the assembly ratified it by oath.

¹⁶Three days after they made the treaty with the Gibeonites, the Israelites heard that they were neighbors, living near them. ¹⁷So the Israelites set out and on the third day came to their cities: Gibeon, Kephirah, Beeroth and Kiriath Jearim. ¹⁸But the Israelites did not attack them, because the leaders of the assembly had sworn an oath to them by the LORD, the God of Israel. Jos 18:25; Ps 15:4

The whole assembly grumbled against the leaders, ¹⁹but all the leaders answered, "We have given them our oath by the LORD, the God of Israel, and we cannot touch them now. ²⁰This is what we will do to them: We will let them live, so that God's wrath will not fall on us for breaking the oath we swore to them." ²¹They continued, "Let them live, but let them be woodcutters and water carriers in the service of the whole assembly." So the leaders' promise to them was kept. Ex 15:24; Dt 29:11

²²Then Joshua summoned the Gibeonites and said, "Why did you deceive us by saying, 'We live a long way from you,' while actually you live near us? ²³You are now under a curse: You will never be released from service as

woodcutters and water carriers for the house of my God." Ge 9:25

²⁴They answered Joshua, "Your servants were clearly told how the LORD your God had commanded his servant Moses to give you the whole land and to wipe out all its inhabitants from before you. So we feared for our lives because of you, and that is why we did this. ²⁵We are now in your hands. Do to us whatever seems good and right to you." Ge 16:6; Jer 26:14

²⁶So Joshua saved them from the Israelites, and they did not kill them. ²⁷That day he made the Gibeonites woodcutters and water carriers for the assembly, to provide for the needs of the altar of the LORD at the place the LORD would choose. And that is what they are to this day. Dt 12:5

The Sun Stands Still

10 Now Adoni-Zedek king of Jerusalem heard that Joshua had taken Ai and totally destroyed[a] it, doing to Ai and its king as he had done to Jericho and its king, and that the people of Gibeon had made a treaty of peace with Israel and had become their allies. ²He and his people were very much alarmed at this, because Gibeon was an important city, like one of the royal cities; it was larger than Ai, and all its men were good fight-

ers. ³So Adoni-Zedek king of Jerusalem appealed to Hoham king of Hebron, Piram king of Jarmuth, Japhia king of Lachish and Debir king of Eglon. ⁴"Come up and help me attack Gibeon," he said, "because it has made peace with Joshua and the Israelites." Ge 13:18; Jos 8:22; Jdg 1:7

⁵Then the five kings of the Amorites — the kings of Jerusalem, Hebron, Jarmuth, Lachish and Eglon — joined forces. They moved up with all their troops and took up positions against Gibeon and attacked it. Nu 13:29

⁶The Gibeonites then sent word to Joshua in the camp at Gilgal: "Do not abandon your servants. Come up to us quickly and save us! Help us, because all the Amorite kings from the hill country have joined forces against us."

⁷So Joshua marched up from Gilgal with his entire army, including all the best fighting men. ⁸The LORD said to Joshua, "Do not be afraid of them; I have given them into your hand. Not one of them will be able to withstand you." Jos 1:9; 8:1

⁹After an all-night march from Gilgal, Joshua took them by surprise. ¹⁰The LORD threw them into confusion before Israel, so Joshua and the Israelites defeated them completely at Gibeon. Israel pursued them along the

---

a 1 The Hebrew term refers to the irrevocable giving over of things or persons to the LORD, often by totally destroying them; also in verses 28, 35, 37, 39 and 40.

road going up to Beth Horon and cut them down all the way to Azekah and Makkedah. ¹¹As they fled before Israel on the road down from Beth Horon to Azekah, the LORD hurled large hailstones down on them, and more of them died from the hail than were killed by the swords of the Israelites. Dt 7:23; Jdg 5:20; Ps 18:12

¹²On the day the LORD gave the Amorites over to Israel, Joshua said to the LORD in the presence of Israel:

"Sun, stand still over Gibeon,
  and you, moon, over the
    Valley of Aijalon." Am 2:9
¹³So the sun stood still,
  and the moon stopped,
    till the nation avenged itself
      on*a* its enemies,

as it is written in the Book of Jashar. 2Sa 1:18; Hab 3:11

The sun stopped in the middle of the sky and delayed going down about a full day. ¹⁴There has never been a day like it before or since, a day when the LORD listened to a human being. Surely the LORD was fighting for Israel! Ex 14:14; Isa 38:8

¹⁵Then Joshua returned with all Israel to the camp at Gilgal.

Five Amorite Kings Killed

¹⁶Now the five kings had fled and hidden in the cave at Makkedah. ¹⁷When Joshua was told that the five kings had been found hiding in the cave at Makkedah, ¹⁸he said, "Roll large rocks up to the mouth of the cave, and post some men there to guard it. ¹⁹But don't stop; pursue your enemies! Attack them from the rear and don't let them reach their cities, for the LORD your God has given them into your hand."

²⁰So Joshua and the Israelites defeated them completely, but a few survivors managed to reach their fortified cities. ²¹The whole army then returned safely to Joshua in the camp at Makkedah, and no one uttered a word against the Israelites. Dt 20:16

²²Joshua said, "Open the mouth of the cave and bring those five kings out to me." ²³So they brought the five kings out of the cave—the kings of Jerusalem, Hebron, Jarmuth, Lachish and Eglon. ²⁴When they had brought these kings to Joshua, he summoned all the men of Israel and said to the army commanders who had come with him, "Come here and put your feet on the necks of these kings." So they came forward and placed their feet on their necks. Dt 7:24; Mal 4:3

²⁵Joshua said to them, "Do not be afraid; do not be discouraged. Be strong and courageous. This is what the LORD will do to all the enemies you are going to fight." ²⁶Then Joshua put the kings to death and exposed their bodies on five poles, and they were left

___
a 13 Or *nation triumphed over*

hanging on the poles until evening. ²⁷ At sunset Joshua gave the order and they took them down from the poles and threw them into the cave where they had been hiding. At the mouth of the cave they placed large rocks, which are there to this day. Dt 21:23

Southern Cities Conquered

²⁸ That day Joshua took Makkedah. He put the city and its king to the sword and totally destroyed everyone in it. He left no survivors. And he did to the king of Makkedah as he had done to the king of Jericho. Dt 20:16; Jos 6:21

²⁹ Then Joshua and all Israel with him moved on from Makkedah to Libnah and attacked it. ³⁰ The LORD also gave that city and its king into Israel's hand. The city and everyone in it Joshua put to the sword. He left no survivors there. And he did to its king as he had done to the king of Jericho. Nu 33:20

³¹ Then Joshua and all Israel with him moved on from Libnah to Lachish; he took up positions against it and attacked it. ³² The LORD gave Lachish into Israel's hands, and Joshua took it on the second day. The city and everyone in it he put to the sword, just as he had done to Libnah. ³³ Meanwhile, Horam king of Gezer had come up to help Lachish, but Joshua defeated him and his army — until no survivors were left.

³⁴ Then Joshua and all Israel with him moved on from Lachish to Eglon; they took up positions against it and attacked it. ³⁵ They captured it that same day and put it to the sword and totally destroyed everyone in it, just as they had done to Lachish. ³⁶ Then Joshua and all Israel with him went up from Eglon to Hebron and attacked it. ³⁷ They took the city and put it to the sword, together with its king, its villages and everyone in it. They left no survivors. Just as at Eglon, they totally destroyed it and everyone in it. Jos 14:13; 15:13; Jdg 1:10

³⁸ Then Joshua and all Israel with him turned around and attacked Debir. ³⁹ They took the city, its king and its villages, and put them to the sword. Everyone in it they totally destroyed. They left no survivors. They did to Debir and its king as they had done to Libnah and its king and to Hebron. Jos 15:15; Jdg 1:11

⁴⁰ So Joshua subdued the whole region, including the hill country, the Negev, the western foothills and the mountain slopes, together with all their kings. He left no survivors. He totally destroyed all who breathed, just as the LORD, the God of Israel, had commanded. ⁴¹ Joshua subdued them from Kadesh Barnea to Gaza and from the whole region of Goshen to Gibeon. ⁴² All these kings and their lands Joshua conquered in one campaign, because the

LORD, the God of Israel, fought for Israel. Dt 7:24; Jos 11:16; ver 14

⁴³ Then Joshua returned with all Israel to the camp at Gilgal.

Northern Kings Defeated

11 When Jabin king of Hazor heard of this, he sent word to Jobab king of Madon, to the kings of Shimron and Akshaph, ² and to the northern kings who were in the mountains, in the Arabah south of Kinnereth, in the western foothills and in Naphoth Dor on the west; ³ to the Canaanites in the east and west; to the Amorites, Hittites, Perizzites and Jebusites in the hill country; and to the Hivites below Hermon in the region of Mizpah. ⁴ They came out with all their troops and a large number of horses and chariots — a huge army, as numerous as the sand on the seashore. ⁵ All these kings joined forces and made camp together at the Waters of Merom to fight against Israel. Jdg 7:12; Jos 12:3; Dt 7:1

⁶ The LORD said to Joshua, "Do not be afraid of them, because by this time tomorrow I will hand all of them, slain, over to Israel. You are to hamstring their horses and burn their chariots." Jos 10:8; 2Sa 8:4

⁷ So Joshua and his whole army came against them suddenly at the Waters of Merom and attacked them, ⁸ and the LORD gave them into the hand of Israel. They defeated them and pursued them all the way to Greater Sidon, to Misrephoth Maim, and to the Valley of Mizpah on the east, until no survivors were left. ⁹ Joshua did to them as the LORD had directed: He hamstrung their horses and burned their chariots. Jos 13:6

¹⁰ At that time Joshua turned back and captured Hazor and put its king to the sword. (Hazor had been the head of all these kingdoms.) ¹¹ Everyone in it they put to the sword. They totally destroyed[a] them, not sparing anyone that breathed, and he burned Hazor itself. Dt 20:16-17

¹² Joshua took all these royal cities and their kings and put them to the sword. He totally destroyed them, as Moses the servant of the LORD had commanded. ¹³ Yet Israel did not burn any of the cities built on their mounds — except Hazor, which Joshua burned. ¹⁴ The Israelites carried off for themselves all the plunder and livestock of these cities, but all the people they put to the sword until they completely destroyed them, not sparing anyone that breathed. ¹⁵ As the LORD commanded his servant Moses, so Moses commanded Joshua, and Joshua did it; he left nothing undone of all that the LORD commanded Moses. Ex 34:11; Nu 33:50-52; Jos 1:7

ᵃ 11 The Hebrew term refers to the irrevocable giving over of things or persons to the LORD, often by totally destroying them; also in verses 12, 20 and 21.

¹⁶So Joshua took this entire land: the hill country, all the Negev, the whole region of Goshen, the western foothills, the Arabah and the mountains of Israel with their foothills, ¹⁷from Mount Halak, which rises toward Seir, to Baal Gad in the Valley of Lebanon below Mount Hermon. He captured all their kings and put them to death. ¹⁸Joshua waged war against all these kings for a long time. ¹⁹Except for the Hivites living in Gibeon, not one city made a treaty of peace with the Israelites, who took them all in battle. ²⁰For it was the LORD himself who hardened their hearts to wage war against Israel, so that he might destroy them totally, exterminating them without mercy, as the LORD had commanded Moses. Ex 14:17; Jos 9:3; 10:41

²¹At that time Joshua went and destroyed the Anakites from the hill country: from Hebron, Debir and Anab, from all the hill country of Judah, and from all the hill country of Israel. Joshua totally destroyed them and their towns. ²²No Anakites were left in Israelite territory; only in Gaza, Gath and Ashdod did any survive.

²³So Joshua took the entire land, just as the LORD had directed Moses, and he gave it as an inheritance to Israel according to their tribal divisions. Then the land had rest from war. Ex 33:14; Nu 13:22,33; Jos 21:43-45

List of Defeated Kings

12 These are the kings of the land whom the Israelites had defeated and whose territory they took over east of the Jordan, from the Arnon Gorge to Mount Hermon, including all the eastern side of the Arabah: Dt 3:8

²Sihon king of the Amorites, who reigned in Heshbon.

He ruled from Aroer on the rim of the Arnon Gorge — from the middle of the gorge — to the Jabbok River, which is the border of the Ammonites. This included half of Gilead. ³He also ruled over the eastern Arabah from the Sea of Galilee^a to the Sea of the Arabah (that is, the Dead Sea), to Beth Jeshimoth, and then southward below the slopes of Pisgah. Jos 11:2; 13:20; Jdg 11:19

⁴And the territory of Og king of Bashan, one of the last of the Rephaites, who reigned in Ashtaroth and Edrei. ⁵He ruled over Mount Hermon, Salekah, all of Bashan to the border of the people of Geshur and Maakah, and half of Gilead to the border of Sihon king of Heshbon. Nu 21:21,33; Dt 1:4

⁶Moses, the servant of the LORD, and the Israelites conquered

^a 3 Hebrew *Kinnereth*

them. And Moses the servant of the LORD gave their land to the Reubenites, the Gadites and the half-tribe of Manasseh to be their possession. Nu 32:29,33

7 Here is a list of the kings of the land that Joshua and the Israelites conquered on the west side of the Jordan, from Baal Gad in the Valley of Lebanon to Mount Halak, which rises toward Seir. Joshua gave their lands as an inheritance to the tribes of Israel according to their tribal divisions. 8 The lands included the hill country, the western foothills, the Arabah, the mountain slopes, the wilderness and the Negev. These were the lands of the Hittites, Amorites, Canaanites, Perizzites, Hivites and Jebusites. These were the kings: Jos 11:17; Ezr 9:1

9 the king of Jericho	one
the king of Ai (near Bethel)	one
10 the king of Jerusalem	one
the king of Hebron	one
11 the king of Jarmuth	one
the king of Lachish	one
12 the king of Eglon	one
the king of Gezer	one
13 the king of Debir	one
the king of Geder	one
14 the king of Hormah	one
the king of Arad	one
15 the king of Libnah	one
the king of Adullam	one
16 the king of Makkedah	one
the king of Bethel	one
17 the king of Tappuah	one

the king of Hepher	one
18 the king of Aphek	one
the king of Lasharon	one
19 the king of Madon	one
the king of Hazor	one
20 the king of Shimron Meron	one
the king of Akshaph	one
21 the king of Taanach	one
the king of Megiddo	one
22 the king of Kedesh	one
the king of Jokneam in Carmel	one
23 the king of Dor (in Naphoth Dor)	one
the king of Goyim in Gilgal	one
24 the king of Tirzah	one
thirty-one kings in all.	

Land Still to Be Taken

13 When Joshua had grown old, the LORD said to him, "You are now very old, and there are still very large areas of land to be taken over. Jos 14:10

2 "This is the land that remains: all the regions of the Philistines and Geshurites, 3 from the Shihor River on the east of Egypt to the territory of Ekron on the north, all of it counted as Canaanite though held by the five Philistine rulers in Gaza, Ashdod, Ashkelon, Gath and Ekron; the territory of the Avvites 4 on the south; all the land of the Canaanites, from Arah of the Sidonians as far

as Aphek and the border of the Amorites; [5] the area of Byblos; and all Lebanon to the east, from Baal Gad below Mount Hermon to Lebo Hamath.   Dt 2:23; Jdg 3:3; Am 2:10

[6] "As for all the inhabitants of the mountain regions from Lebanon to Misrephoth Maim, that is, all the Sidonians, I myself will drive them out before the Israelites. Be sure to allocate this land to Israel for an inheritance, as I have instructed you, [7] and divide it as an inheritance among the nine tribes and half of the tribe of Manasseh."   Jos 11:8; Nu 33:54

Division of the Land East of the Jordan

[8] The other half of Manasseh,[a] the Reubenites and the Gadites had received the inheritance that Moses had given them east of the Jordan, as he, the servant of the LORD, had assigned it to them.   Jos 12:6

[9] It extended from Aroer on the rim of the Arnon Gorge, and from the town in the middle of the gorge, and included the whole plateau of Medeba as far as Dibon, [10] and all the towns of Sihon king of the Amorites, who ruled in Heshbon, out to the border of the Ammonites. [11] It also included Gilead, the territory of the

people of Geshur and Maakah, all of Mount Hermon and all Bashan as far as Salekah — [12] that is, the whole kingdom of Og in Bashan, who had reigned in Ashtaroth and Edrei. (He was the last of the Rephaites.) Moses had defeated them and taken over their land. [13] But the Israelites did not drive out the people of Geshur and Maakah, so they continue to live among the Israelites to this day.   Dt 2:36; 3:11; Jos 12:4

[14] But to the tribe of Levi he gave no inheritance, since the food offerings presented to the LORD, the God of Israel, are their inheritance, as he promised them.   Dt 18:1-2

[15] This is what Moses had given to the tribe of Reuben, according to its clans:

[16] The territory from Aroer on the rim of the Arnon Gorge, and from the town in the middle of the gorge, and the whole plateau past Medeba [17] to Heshbon and all its towns on the plateau, including Dibon, Bamoth Baal, Beth Baal Meon, [18] Jahaz, Kedemoth, Mephaath, [19] Kiriathaim, Sibmah, Zereth Shahar on the hill in the valley, [20] Beth Peor, the slopes of Pisgah, and Beth

---

[a] 8 Hebrew *With it* (that is, with the other half of Manasseh)

Jeshimoth — [21] all the towns on the plateau and the entire realm of Sihon king of the Amorites, who ruled at Heshbon. Moses had defeated him and the Midianite chiefs, Evi, Rekem, Zur, Hur and Reba — princes allied with Sihon — who lived in that country. [22] In addition to those slain in battle, the Israelites had put to the sword Balaam son of Beor, who practiced divination. [23] The boundary of the Reubenites was the bank of the Jordan. These towns and their villages were the inheritance of the Reubenites, according to their clans. Nu 21:23; 31:8; 32:37

[24] This is what Moses had given to the tribe of Gad, according to its clans:

[25] The territory of Jazer, all the towns of Gilead and half the Ammonite country as far as Aroer, near Rabbah; [26] and from Heshbon to Ramath Mizpah and Betonim, and from Mahanaim to the territory of Debir; [27] and in the valley, Beth Haram, Beth Nimrah, Sukkoth and Zaphon with the rest of the realm of Sihon king of Heshbon (the east side of the Jordan, the territory up to the end of the Sea of Galilee[a]). [28] These towns and their villages were the inheritance of the Gadites, according to their clans. Nu 21:32; 34:11

[29] This is what Moses had given to the half-tribe of Manasseh, that is, to half the family of the descendants of Manasseh, according to its clans:

[30] The territory extending from Mahanaim and including all of Bashan, the entire realm of Og king of Bashan — all the settlements of Jair in Bashan, sixty towns, [31] half of Gilead, and Ashtaroth and Edrei (the royal cities of Og in Bashan). This was for the descendants of Makir son of Manasseh — for half of the sons of Makir, according to their clans. Nu 32:41; Jos 12:4

[32] This is the inheritance Moses had given when he was in the plains of Moab across the Jordan east of Jericho. [33] But to the tribe of Levi, Moses had given no inheritance; the Lord, the God of Israel, is their inheritance, as he promised them. Nu 18:20

Division of the Land West of the Jordan

14 Now these are the areas the Israelites received as an inheritance in the land of Canaan, which Eleazar the priest, Joshua son of Nun and the heads of the tribal clans of Israel allot-

---

[a] 27 Hebrew *Kinnereth*

ted to them. ²Their inheritances were assigned by lot to the nine and a half tribes, as the LORD had commanded through Moses. ³Moses had granted the two and a half tribes their inheritance east of the Jordan but had not granted the Levites an inheritance among the rest, ⁴for Joseph's descendants had become two tribes — Manasseh and Ephraim. The Levites received no share of the land but only towns to live in, with pasturelands for their flocks and herds. ⁵So the Israelites divided the land, just as the LORD had commanded Moses. Nu 32:33; 34:17-18; Jos 13:14

Allotment for Caleb

⁶Now the people of Judah approached Joshua at Gilgal, and Caleb son of Jephunneh the Kenizzite said to him, "You know what the LORD said to Moses the man of God at Kadesh Barnea about you and me. ⁷I was forty years old when Moses the servant of the LORD sent me from Kadesh Barnea to explore the land. And I brought him back a report according to my convictions, ⁸but my fellow Israelites who went up with me made the hearts of the people melt in fear. I, however, followed the LORD my God wholeheartedly. ⁹So on that day Moses swore to me, 'The land on which your feet have walked will be your inheritance and that of your children forever, because you have followed the LORD my God wholeheartedly.'ᵃ Nu 13:30; 14:6-9,24,30; Dt 1:36

¹⁰"Now then, just as the LORD promised, he has kept me alive for forty-five years since the time he said this to Moses, while Israel moved about in the wilderness. So here I am today, eighty-five years old! ¹¹I am still as strong today as the day Moses sent me out; I'm just as vigorous to go out to battle now as I was then. ¹²Now give me this hill country that the LORD promised me that day. You yourself heard then that the Anakites were there and their cities were large and fortified, but, the LORD helping me, I will drive them out just as he said." Nu 13:33; Dt 34:7

¹³Then Joshua blessed Caleb son of Jephunneh and gave him Hebron as his inheritance. ¹⁴So Hebron has belonged to Caleb son of Jephunneh the Kenizzite ever since, because he followed the LORD, the God of Israel, wholeheartedly. ¹⁵(Hebron used to be called Kiriath Arba after Arba, who was the greatest man among the Anakites.) Jos 22:6-7 Then the land had rest from war. Jos 11:23

Allotment for Judah

15:15-19pp — Jdg 1:11-15

15 The allotment for the tribe of Judah, according to its clans, extended down to the

ᵃ 9 Deut. 1:36

territory of Edom, to the Desert of Zin in the extreme south. Nu 34:3 ²Their southern boundary started from the bay at the southern end of the Dead Sea, ³crossed south of Scorpion Pass, continued on to Zin and went over to the south of Kadesh Barnea. Then it ran past Hezron up to Addar and curved around to Karka. ⁴It then passed along to Azmon and joined the Wadi of Egypt, ending at the Mediterranean Sea. This is their^a southern boundary.

⁵The eastern boundary is the Dead Sea as far as the mouth of the Jordan. Ge 14:3

The northern boundary started from the bay of the sea at the mouth of the Jordan, ⁶went up to Beth Hoglah and continued north of Beth Arabah to the Stone of Bohan son of Reuben. ⁷The boundary then went up to Debir from the Valley of Achor and turned north to Gilgal, which faces the Pass of Adummim south of the gorge. It continued along to the waters of En Shemesh and came out at En Rogel. ⁸Then it ran up the Valley of Ben Hinnom along the southern slope of the Jebusite city (that is, Jerusalem). From there it climbed to the top of the hill west of the Hinnom Valley at the northern end of the Valley of Rephaim. ⁹From the hilltop the boundary headed toward the spring of the waters of Nephtoah, came out at the towns of Mount Ephron and went down toward Baalah (that is, Kiriath Jearim). ¹⁰Then it curved westward from Baalah to Mount Seir, ran along the northern slope of Mount Jearim (that is, Kesalon), continued down to Beth Shemesh and crossed to Timnah. ¹¹It went to the northern slope of Ekron, turned toward Shikkeron, passed along to Mount Baalah and reached Jabneel. The boundary ended at the sea. Jos 7:24; 18:17; 1Ch 13:6 ¹²The western boundary is the coastline of the Mediterranean Sea. Nu 34:6

These are the boundaries around the people of Judah by their clans.

¹³In accordance with the LORD's command to him, Joshua gave to Caleb son of Jephunneh a portion in Judah — Kiriath Arba, that is, Hebron. (Arba was the forefather of Anak.) ¹⁴From Hebron Caleb drove out the three Anakites — Sheshai, Ahiman and Talmai, the sons of Anak. ¹⁵From there he marched against the people living in Debir

^a 4 Septuagint; Hebrew *your*

(formerly called Kiriath Sepher). [16] And Caleb said, "I will give my daughter Aksah in marriage to the man who attacks and captures Kiriath Sepher." [17] Othniel son of Kenaz, Caleb's brother, took it; so Caleb gave his daughter Aksah to him in marriage.

[18] One day when she came to Othniel, she urged him[a] to ask her father for a field. When she got off her donkey, Caleb asked her, "What can I do for you?" Jos 14:13

[19] She replied, "Do me a special favor. Since you have given me land in the Negev, give me also springs of water." So Caleb gave her the upper and lower springs. Jdg 1:11-15

[20] This is the inheritance of the tribe of Judah, according to its clans:

[21] The southernmost towns of the tribe of Judah in the Negev toward the boundary of Edom were:

Kabzeel, Eder, Jagur, [22] Kinah, Dimonah, Adadah, [23] Kedesh, Hazor, Ithnan, [24] Ziph, Telem, Bealoth, [25] Hazor Hadattah, Kerioth Hezron (that is, Hazor), [26] Amam, Shema, Moladah, [27] Hazar Gaddah, Heshmon, Beth Pelet, [28] Hazar Shual, Beersheba, Biziothiah, [29] Baalah, Iyim, Ezem, [30] Eltolad, Kesil, Hormah, [31] Ziklag, Madmannah, Sansannah, [32] Lebaoth, Shilhim, Ain and Rimmon — a total of twenty-nine towns and their villages. Ge 21:31; 35:21; 1Sa 27:6

[33] In the western foothills:

Eshtaol, Zorah, Ashnah, [34] Zanoah, En Gannim, Tappuah, Enam, [35] Jarmuth, Adullam, Sokoh, Azekah, [36] Shaaraim, Adithaim and Gederah (or Gederothaim)[b] — fourteen towns and their villages. Jdg 13:25; 16:31

[37] Zenan, Hadashah, Migdal Gad, [38] Dilean, Mizpah, Joktheel, [39] Lachish, Bozkath, Eglon, [40] Kabbon, Lahmas, Kitlish, [41] Gederoth, Beth Dagon, Naamah and Makkedah — sixteen towns and their villages. Jos 10:3; 2Ki 14:7,19

[42] Libnah, Ether, Ashan, [43] Iphtah, Ashnah, Nezib, [44] Keilah, Akzib and Mareshah — nine towns and their villages. 1Ch 6:59

[45] Ekron, with its surrounding settlements and villages; [46] west of Ekron, all that were in the vicinity of Ashdod, together with their villages; [47] Ashdod, its surrounding settlements and villages; and Gaza, its settlements and villages, as far as the Wadi of Egypt and the coastline of the Mediterranean Sea. Nu 34:6

---

[a] 18 Hebrew and some Septuagint manuscripts; other Septuagint manuscripts (see also note at Judges 1:14) *Othniel, he urged her*   [b] 36 Or *Gederah and Gederothaim*

⁴⁸In the hill country:

Shamir, Jattir, Sokoh, ⁴⁹Dannah, Kiriath Sannah (that is, Debir), ⁵⁰Anab, Eshtemoh, Anim, ⁵¹Goshen, Holon and Giloh—eleven towns and their villages. Jos 10:41; Jdg 10:1

⁵²Arab, Dumah, Eshan, ⁵³Janim, Beth Tappuah, Aphekah, ⁵⁴Humtah, Kiriath Arba (that is, Hebron) and Zior—nine towns and their villages. Ge 25:14

⁵⁵Maon, Carmel, Ziph, Juttah, ⁵⁶Jezreel, Jokdeam, Zanoah, ⁵⁷Kain, Gibeah and Timnah—ten towns and their villages. Jdg 10:12; 1Ch 11:31

⁵⁸Halhul, Beth Zur, Gedor, ⁵⁹Maarath, Beth Anoth and Eltekon—six towns and their villages.ᵃ

⁶⁰Kiriath Baal (that is, Kiriath Jearim) and Rabbah—two towns and their villages. Dt 3:11; Jos 18:14

⁶¹In the wilderness:

Beth Arabah, Middin, Sekakah, ⁶²Nibshan, the City of Salt and En Gedi—six towns and their villages. Jos 8:15; Eze 47:10

⁶³Judah could not dislodge the Jebusites, who were living in Jerusalem; to this day the Jebusites live there with the people of Judah. Jdg 1:21; 2Sa 5:6

Allotment for Ephraim and Manasseh

16 The allotment for Joseph began at the Jordan, east of the springs of Jericho, and went up from there through the desert into the hill country of Bethel. ²It went on from Bethel (that is, Luz),ᵇ crossed over to the territory of the Arkites in Ataroth, ³descended westward to the territory of the Japhletites as far as the region of Lower Beth Horon and on to Gezer, ending at the Mediterranean Sea. Jos 8:15; 18:13

⁴So Manasseh and Ephraim, the descendants of Joseph, received their inheritance. Jos 18:5

⁵This was the territory of Ephraim, according to its clans:

The boundary of their inheritance went from Ataroth Addar in the east to Upper Beth Horon ⁶and continued to the Mediterranean Sea. From Mikmethath on the north it curved eastward to Taanath Shiloh, passing by it to Janoah on the east. ⁷Then it went down from Janoah to Ataroth and Naarah, touched Jericho and came out at the Jordan. ⁸From Tappuah the border went west to the Kanah Ravine and ended at the Medi-

---

ᵃ 59 The Septuagint adds another district of eleven towns, including Tekoa and Ephrathah (Bethlehem). ᵇ 2 Septuagint; Hebrew *Bethel to Luz* terranean Sea. This was the inheritance of the tribe of the Ephraimites, according to its clans. ⁹It also included all the towns and their villages that were set aside for the Ephraimites within the inheritance of the Manassites. Jos 17:7,9; 2Ki 15:29; 1Ch 7:28

¹⁰They did not dislodge the Canaanites living in Gezer; to this day the Canaanites live among the people of Ephraim but are required to do forced labor. Jos 17:13

17 This was the allotment for the tribe of Manasseh as Joseph's firstborn, that is, for Makir, Manasseh's firstborn. Makir was the ancestor of the Gileadites, who had received Gilead and Bashan because the Makirites were great soldiers. ²So this allotment was for the rest of the people of Manasseh—the clans of Abiezer, Helek, Asriel, Shechem, Hepher and Shemida. These are the other male descendants of Manasseh son of Joseph by their clans. Ge 41:51; 50:23; Nu 26:30

³Now Zelophehad son of Hepher, the son of Gilead, the son of Makir, the son of Manasseh, had no sons but only daughters, whose names were Mahlah, Noah, Hoglah, Milkah and Tirzah. ⁴They went to Eleazar the priest, Joshua son of Nun, and the leaders and said, "The LORD commanded Moses to give us an inheritance among our relatives." So Joshua gave

them an inheritance along with the brothers of their father, according to the LORD's command. ⁵Manasseh's share consisted of ten tracts of land besides Gilead and Bashan east of the Jordan, ⁶because the daughters of the tribe of Manasseh received an inheritance among the sons. The land of Gilead belonged to the rest of the descendants of Manasseh. Nu 27:1,5-7; Jos 13:30-31

⁷The territory of Manasseh extended from Asher to Mikmethath east of Shechem. The boundary ran southward from there to include the people living at En Tappuah. ⁸(Manasseh had the land of Tappuah, but Tappuah itself, on the boundary of Manasseh, belonged to the Ephraimites.) ⁹Then the boundary continued south to the Kanah Ravine. There were towns belonging to Ephraim lying among the towns of Manasseh, but the boundary of Manasseh was the northern side of the ravine and ended at the Mediterranean Sea. ¹⁰On the south the land belonged to Ephraim, on the north to Manasseh. The territory of Manasseh reached the Mediterranean Sea and bordered Asher on the north and Issachar on the east. Jos 16:8

¹¹Within Issachar and Asher, Manasseh also had

Beth Shan, Ibleam and the people of Dor, Endor, Taanach and Megiddo, together with their surrounding settlements (the third in the list is Naphoth*a*). Jos 11:2; 1Sa 31:10

¹²Yet the Manassites were not able to occupy these towns, for the Canaanites were determined to live in that region. ¹³However, when the Israelites grew stronger, they subjected the Canaanites to forced labor but did not drive them out completely. Jos 16:10

¹⁴The people of Joseph said to Joshua, "Why have you given us only one allotment and one portion for an inheritance? We are a numerous people, and the LORD has blessed us abundantly."

¹⁵"If you are so numerous," Joshua answered, "and if the hill country of Ephraim is too small for you, go up into the forest and clear land for yourselves there in the land of the Perizzites and Rephaites."

¹⁶The people of Joseph replied, "The hill country is not enough for us, and all the Canaanites who live in the plain have chariots fitted with iron, both those in Beth Shan and its settlements and those in the Valley of Jezreel." Jdg 1:19; 1Sa 29:1

¹⁷But Joshua said to the tribes of Joseph — to Ephraim and Manasseh — "You are numerous and very powerful. You will have not only one allotment ¹⁸but the for-

ested hill country as well. Clear it, and its farthest limits will be yours; though the Canaanites have chariots fitted with iron and though they are strong, you can drive them out."

Division of the Rest of the Land

18 The whole assembly of the Israelites gathered at Shiloh and set up the tent of meeting there. The country was brought under their control, ²but there were still seven Israelite tribes who had not yet received their inheritance. Jos 19:51; Jer 7:12

³So Joshua said to the Israelites: "How long will you wait before you begin to take possession of the land that the LORD, the God of your ancestors, has given you? ⁴Appoint three men from each tribe. I will send them out to make a survey of the land and to write a description of it, according to the inheritance of each. Then they will return to me. ⁵You are to divide the land into seven parts. Judah is to remain in its territory on the south and the tribes of Joseph in their territory on the north. ⁶After you have written descriptions of the seven parts of the land, bring them here to me and I will cast lots for you in the presence of the LORD our God. ⁷The Levites, however, do not get a portion among you, because the priestly service of the LORD is their inheritance. And Gad, Reuben and the

---

a 11 That is, Naphoth Dor

half-tribe of Manasseh have already received their inheritance on the east side of the Jordan. Moses the servant of the LORD gave it to them." _{Jos 13:33; 15:1; 16:1-4}

⁸As the men started on their way to map out the land, Joshua instructed them, "Go and make a survey of the land and write a description of it. Then return to me, and I will cast lots for you here at Shiloh in the presence of the LORD." ⁹So the men left and went through the land. They wrote its description on a scroll, town by town, in seven parts, and returned to Joshua in the camp at Shiloh. ¹⁰Joshua then cast lots for them in Shiloh in the presence of the LORD, and there he distributed the land to the Israelites according to their tribal divisions. _{Jos 19:51; Jer 7:12}

Allotment for Benjamin

¹¹The first lot came up for the tribe of Benjamin according to its clans. Their allotted territory lay between the tribes of Judah and Joseph:

¹²On the north side their boundary began at the Jordan, passed the northern slope of Jericho and headed west into the hill country, coming out at the wilderness of Beth Aven. ¹³From there it crossed to the south slope of Luz (that is, Bethel) and went down to Ataroth Addar on the hill south of Lower Beth Horon. _{Ge 28:19; Jos 16:1; Jdg 1:23}

¹⁴From the hill facing Beth Horon on the south the boundary turned south along the western side and came out at Kiriath Baal (that is, Kiriath Jearim), a town of the people of Judah. This was the western side.

¹⁵The southern side began at the outskirts of Kiriath Jearim on the west, and the boundary came out at the spring of the waters of Nephtoah. ¹⁶The boundary went down to the foot of the hill facing the Valley of Ben Hinnom, north of the Valley of Rephaim. It continued down the Hinnom Valley along the southern slope of the Jebusite city and so to En Rogel. ¹⁷It then curved north, went to En Shemesh, continued to Geliloth, which faces the Pass of Adummim, and ran down to the Stone of Bohan son of Reuben. ¹⁸It continued to the northern slope of Beth Arabah^a and on down into the Arabah. ¹⁹It then went to the northern slope of Beth Hoglah and came out at the northern bay of the Dead Sea, at the mouth of the Jordan in the south. This was the southern boundary. _{Ge 14:3; Jos 15:9}

---

^a 18 Septuagint; Hebrew *slope facing the Arabah*

20The Jordan formed the boundary on the eastern side.

These were the boundaries that marked out the inheritance of the clans of Benjamin on all sides. 1Sa 9:1

21The tribe of Benjamin, according to its clans, had the following towns:

Jericho, Beth Hoglah, Emek Keziz, **22**Beth Arabah, Zemaraim, Bethel, **23**Avvim, Parah, Ophrah, **24**Kephar Ammoni, Ophni and Geba — twelve towns and their villages. 2Ch 13:4; Isa 10:29

25Gibeon, Ramah, Beeroth, **26**Mizpah, Kephirah, Mozah, **27**Rekem, Irpeel, Taralah, **28**Zelah, Haeleph, the Jebusite city (that is, Jerusalem), Gibeah and Kiriath — fourteen towns and their villages. Jos 15:8; Jdg 4:5; 2Sa 21:14

This was the inheritance of Benjamin for its clans. Eze 48:23

Allotment for Simeon

19:2-10pp — 1Ch 4:28-33

19 The second lot came out for the tribe of Simeon according to its clans. Their inheritance lay within the territory of Judah. **2**It included: Ge 49:7

Beersheba (or Sheba),[a] Moladah, **3**Hazar Shual, Balah, Ezem, **4**Eltolad, Bethul, Hormah, **5**Ziklag, Beth Mar-

kaboth, Hazar Susah, **6**Beth Lebaoth and Sharuhen — thirteen towns and their villages; Ge 21:14

7Ain, Rimmon, Ether and Ashan — four towns and their villages — **8**and all the villages around these towns as far as Baalath Beer (Ramah in the Negev). Jos 15:32

This was the inheritance of the tribe of the Simeonites, according to its clans. **9**The inheritance of the Simeonites was taken from the share of Judah, because Judah's portion was more than they needed. So the Simeonites received their inheritance within the territory of Judah. Ge 49:7

Allotment for Zebulun

10The third lot came up for Zebulun according to its clans: 1Ch 4:28

The boundary of their inheritance went as far as Sarid. **11**Going west it ran to Maralah, touched Dabbesheth, and extended to the ravine near Jokneam. **12**It turned east from Sarid toward the sunrise to the territory of Kisloth Tabor and went on to Daberath and up to Japhia. **13**Then it continued eastward to Gath Hepher and Eth Kazin; it came out at Rimmon and turned toward Neah. **14**There the boundary went around on the north to Hannathon and

---

a 2 Or *Beersheba, Sheba;* 1 Chron. 4:28 does not have *Sheba.*

ended at the Valley of Iphtah El. ¹⁵ Included were Kattath, Nahalal, Shimron, Idalah and Bethlehem. There were twelve towns and their villages. Ge 35:19; Jos 12:22; 1Ch 6:72 ¹⁶ These towns and their villages were the inheritance of Zebulun, according to its clans. Eze 48:26

Allotment for Issachar

¹⁷ The fourth lot came out for Issachar according to its clans. ¹⁸ Their territory included: Ge 30:18 Jezreel, Kesulloth, Shunem, ¹⁹ Hapharaim, Shion, Anaharath, ²⁰ Rabbith, Kishion, Ebez, ²¹ Remeth, En Gannim, En Haddah and Beth Pazzez. ²² The boundary touched Tabor, Shahazumah and Beth Shemesh, and ended at the Jordan. There were sixteen towns and their villages. 1Sa 28:4; 2Ki 4:8; Ps 89:12 ²³ These towns and their villages were the inheritance of the tribe of Issachar, according to its clans.

Allotment for Asher

²⁴ The fifth lot came out for the tribe of Asher according to its clans. ²⁵ Their territory included: Jos 17:7 Helkath, Hali, Beten, Akshaph, ²⁶ Allammelek, Amad and Mishal. On the west the boundary touched Carmel and Shihor Libnath. ²⁷ It then turned east toward Beth Dagon, touched Zebulun and the Valley of Iphtah El, and went north to Beth Emek and Neiel, passing Kabul on the left. ²⁸ It went to Abdon,^a Rehob, Hammon and Kanah, as far as Greater Sidon. ²⁹ The boundary then turned back toward Ramah and went to the fortified city of Tyre, turned toward Hosah and came out at the Mediterranean Sea in the region of Akzib, ³⁰ Ummah, Aphek and Rehob. There were twenty-two towns and their villages. Ge 10:19; Jdg 1:31; 1Ki 9:13 ³¹ These towns and their villages were the inheritance of the tribe of Asher, according to its clans.

Allotment for Naphtali

³² The sixth lot came out for Naphtali according to its clans: ³³ Their boundary went from Heleph and the large tree in Zaanannim, passing Adami Nekeb and Jabneel to Lakkum and ending at the Jordan. ³⁴ The boundary ran west through Aznoth Tabor and came out at Hukkok. It touched Zebulun on the south, Asher on the west and the Jordan^b on the east. ³⁵ The fortified towns were Ziddim, Zer, Hammath, Rakkath, Kinnereth, ³⁶ Adamah,

---

^a 28 Some Hebrew manuscripts (see also 21:30); most Hebrew manuscripts *Ebron*
^b 34 Septuagint; Hebrew *west, and Judah, the Jordan,*

Ramah, Hazor, ³⁷Kedesh, Edrei, En Hazor, ³⁸Iron, Migdal El, Horem, Beth Anath and Beth Shemesh. There were nineteen towns and their villages. Jos 11:1; Jdg 4:11

³⁹These towns and their villages were the inheritance of the tribe of Naphtali, according to its clans. Dt 33:23

Allotment for Dan

⁴⁰The seventh lot came out for the tribe of Dan according to its clans. ⁴¹The territory of their inheritance included:

Zorah, Eshtaol, Ir Shemesh, ⁴²Shaalabbin, Aijalon, Ithlah, ⁴³Elon, Timnah, Ekron, ⁴⁴Eltekeh, Gibbethon, Baalath, ⁴⁵Jehud, Bene Berak, Gath Rimmon, ⁴⁶Me Jarkon and Rakkon, with the area facing Joppa. Jdg 1:35; Jnh 1:3

⁴⁷(When the territory of the Danites was lost to them, they went up and attacked Leshem, took it, put it to the sword and occupied it. They settled in Leshem and named it Dan after their ancestor.) Jdg 18:1,27,29

⁴⁸These towns and their villages were the inheritance of the tribe of Dan, according to its clans.

Allotment for Joshua

⁴⁹When they had finished dividing the land into its allotted portions, the Israelites gave Joshua son of Nun an inheritance among them, ⁵⁰as the LORD had commanded. They gave him the town he asked for—Timnath Serah*ᵃ* in the hill country of Ephraim. And he built up the town and settled there. Jos 24:30

⁵¹These are the territories that Eleazar the priest, Joshua son of Nun and the heads of the tribal clans of Israel assigned by lot at Shiloh in the presence of the LORD at the entrance to the tent of meeting. And so they finished dividing the land. Jos 14:1; 18:10

Cities of Refuge

20:1-9Ref — Nu 35:9-34; Dt 4:41-43; 19:1-14

20 Then the LORD said to Joshua: ²"Tell the Israelites to designate the cities of refuge, as I instructed you through Moses, ³so that anyone who kills a person accidentally and unintentionally may flee there and find protection from the avenger of blood. ⁴When they flee to one of these cities, they are to stand in the entrance of the city gate and state their case before the elders of that city. Then the elders are to admit the fugitive into their city and provide a place to live among them. ⁵If the avenger of blood comes in pursuit, the elders must not surrender the fugitive, because the fugitive killed their neighbor unintentionally and without malice aforethought. ⁶They are to stay

---

ᵃ 50 Also known as *Timnath Heres* (see Judges 2:9)

in that city until they have stood trial before the assembly and until the death of the high priest who is serving at that time. Then they may go back to their own home in the town from which they fled." Lev 4:2; Nu 35:12; Ru 4:1

[7] So they set apart Kedesh in Galilee in the hill country of Naphtali, Shechem in the hill country of Ephraim, and Kiriath Arba (that is, Hebron) in the hill country of Judah. [8] East of the Jordan (on the other side from Jericho) they designated Bezer in the wilderness on the plateau in the tribe of Reuben, Ramoth in Gilead in the tribe of Gad, and Golan in Bashan in the tribe of Manasseh. [9] Any of the Israelites or any foreigner residing among them who killed someone accidentally could flee to these designated cities and not be killed by the avenger of blood prior to standing trial before the assembly. Nu 35:9-34; Dt 4:41-43; 19:1-14

Towns for the Levites
21:4-39pp — 1Ch 6:54-80

21 Now the family heads of the Levites approached Eleazar the priest, Joshua son of Nun, and the heads of the other tribal families of Israel [2] at Shiloh in Canaan and said to them, "The LORD commanded through Moses that you give us towns to live in, with pasturelands for our livestock." [3] So, as the LORD had commanded, the Israelites gave the Levites the following towns and pasturelands out of their own inheritance: Nu 35:2-3; Jos 14:1; Lev 25:32

[4] The first lot came out for the Kohathites, according to their clans. The Levites who were descendants of Aaron the priest were allotted thirteen towns from the tribes of Judah, Simeon and Benjamin. [5] The rest of Kohath's descendants were allotted ten towns from the clans of the tribes of Ephraim, Dan and half of Manasseh. Nu 3:17

[6] The descendants of Gershon were allotted thirteen towns from the clans of the tribes of Issachar, Asher, Naphtali and the half-tribe of Manasseh in Bashan. Ge 30:18

[7] The descendants of Merari, according to their clans, received twelve towns from the tribes of Reuben, Gad and Zebulun. Ex 6:16

[8] So the Israelites allotted to the Levites these towns and their pasturelands, as the LORD had commanded through Moses.

[9] From the tribes of Judah and Simeon they allotted the following towns by name [10] (these towns were assigned to the descendants of Aaron who were from the Kohathite clans of the Levites, because the first lot fell to them): [11] They gave them Kiriath Arba (that is, Hebron), with its surrounding pastureland, in the hill country of Judah.

(Arba was the forefather of Anak.) ¹²But the fields and villages around the city they had given to Caleb son of Jephunneh as his possession. Jos 15:13; 1Ch 6:55; Ge 23:2

¹³So to the descendants of Aaron the priest they gave Hebron (a city of refuge for one accused of murder), Libnah, ¹⁴Jattir, Eshtemoa, ¹⁵Holon, Debir, ¹⁶Ain, Juttah and Beth Shemesh, together with their pasturelands— nine towns from these two tribes. Jos 15:42; 1Ch 6:57; Nu 33:20

¹⁷And from the tribe of Benjamin they gave them Gibeon, Geba, ¹⁸Anathoth and Almon, together with their pasturelands—four towns. Jos 18:24; Ne 11:32; Jer 32:7

¹⁹The total number of towns for the priests, the descendants of Aaron, came to thirteen, together with their pasturelands. 2Ch 31:15

²⁰The rest of the Kohathite clans of the Levites were allotted towns from the tribe of Ephraim:

²¹In the hill country of Ephraim they were given Shechem (a city of refuge for one accused of murder) and Gezer, ²²Kibzaim and Beth Horon, together with their pasturelands—four towns. Jos 20:7; 1Sa 1:1

²³Also from the tribe of Dan they received Eltekeh, Gibbethon, ²⁴Aijalon and Gath Rimmon, together with their pasturelands—four towns.

²⁵From half the tribe of Manasseh they received Taanach and Gath Rimmon, together with their pasturelands—two towns.

²⁶All these ten towns and their pasturelands were given to the rest of the Kohathite clans.

²⁷The Levite clans of the Gershonites were given:

from the half-tribe of Manasseh,
Golan in Bashan (a city of refuge for one accused of murder) and Be Eshterah, together with their pasturelands—two towns; Nu 35:6
²⁸from the tribe of Issachar,
Kishion, Daberath, ²⁹Jarmuth and En Gannim, together with their pasturelands—four towns; Ge 30:18
³⁰from the tribe of Asher,
Mishal, Abdon, ³¹Helkath and Rehob, together with their pasturelands—four towns; Jos 17:7
³²from the tribe of Naphtali,
Kedesh in Galilee (a city of refuge for one accused of murder), Hammoth Dor and Kartan, together with their pasturelands—three towns. Jos 20:7; Nu 35:6
³³The total number of towns of the Gershonite clans came to thirteen, together with their pasturelands.

³⁴The Merarite clans (the rest of the Levites) were given:
from the tribe of Zebulun, Jokneam, Kartah, ³⁵Dimnah and Nahalal, together with their pasturelands—four towns; 1Ch 6:77; Jos 12:22
³⁶from the tribe of Reuben, Bezer, Jahaz, ³⁷Kedemoth and Mephaath, together with their pasturelands—four towns; Jos 20:8; Nu 21:23
³⁸from the tribe of Gad, Ramoth in Gilead (a city of refuge for one accused of murder), Mahanaim, ³⁹Heshbon and Jazer, together with their pasturelands—four towns in all. 1Ch 6:54-80; Dt 4:43
⁴⁰The total number of towns allotted to the Merarite clans, who were the rest of the Levites, came to twelve.

⁴¹The towns of the Levites in the territory held by the Israelites were forty-eight in all, together with their pasturelands. ⁴²Each of these towns had pasturelands surrounding it; this was true for all these towns. Nu 35:7

⁴³So the LORD gave Israel all the land he had sworn to give their ancestors, and they took possession of it and settled there. ⁴⁴The LORD gave them rest on every side, just as he had sworn to their ancestors. Not one of their enemies withstood them; the LORD gave all their enemies into their hands. ⁴⁵Not one of all the LORD's good promises to Israel failed; every one was fulfilled. Dt 11:31; Jos 1:13; 23:14

Eastern Tribes Return Home

22 Then Joshua summoned the Reubenites, the Gadites and the half-tribe of Manasseh ²and said to them, "You have done all that Moses the servant of the LORD commanded, and you have obeyed me in everything I commanded. ³For a long time now—to this very day—you have not deserted your fellow Israelites but have carried out the mission the LORD your God gave you. ⁴Now that the LORD your God has given them rest as he promised, return to your homes in the land that Moses the servant of the LORD gave you on the other side of the Jordan. ⁵But be very careful to keep the commandment and the law that Moses the servant of the LORD gave you: to love the LORD your God, to walk in obedience to him, to keep his commands, to hold fast to him and to serve him with all your heart and with all your soul." Dt 3:20; 5:29; Nu 32:18

⁶Then Joshua blessed them and sent them away, and they went to their homes. ⁷(To the half-tribe of Manasseh Moses had given land in Bashan, and to the other half of the tribe Joshua gave land on the west side of the Jordan along with their fellow Israelites.) When Joshua sent

them home, he blessed them, [8]saying, "Return to your homes with your great wealth — with large herds of livestock, with silver, gold, bronze and iron, and a great quantity of clothing — and divide the plunder from your enemies with your fellow Israelites." Ex 39:43; Nu 31:27; 1Sa 30:16

[9]So the Reubenites, the Gadites and the half-tribe of Manasseh left the Israelites at Shiloh in Canaan to return to Gilead, their own land, which they had acquired in accordance with the command of the LORD through Moses. Nu 32:26,29

[10]When they came to Geliloth near the Jordan in the land of Canaan, the Reubenites, the Gadites and the half-tribe of Manasseh built an imposing altar there by the Jordan. [11]And when the Israelites heard that they had built the altar on the border of Canaan at Geliloth near the Jordan on the Israelite side, [12]the whole assembly of Israel gathered at Shiloh to go to war against them. Jos 18:1

[13]So the Israelites sent Phinehas son of Eleazar, the priest, to the land of Gilead — to Reuben, Gad and the half-tribe of Manasseh. [14]With him they sent ten of the chief men, one from each of the tribes of Israel, each the head of a family division among the Israelite clans. Nu 1:4; 25:7

[15]When they went to Gilead — to Reuben, Gad and the half-tribe of Manasseh — they said to them: [16]"The whole assembly of the LORD says: 'How could you break faith with the God of Israel like this? How could you turn away from the LORD and build yourselves an altar in rebellion against him now? [17]Was not the sin of Peor enough for us? Up to this very day we have not cleansed ourselves from that sin, even though a plague fell on the community of the LORD! [18]And are you now turning away from the LORD? Nu 25:1-9; Dt 12:13-14

"'If you rebel against the LORD today, tomorrow he will be angry with the whole community of Israel. [19]If the land you possess is defiled, come over to the LORD's land, where the LORD's tabernacle stands, and share the land with us. But do not rebel against the LORD or against us by building an altar for yourselves, other than the altar of the LORD our God. [20]When Achan son of Zerah was unfaithful in regard to the devoted things,[a] did not wrath come on the whole community of Israel? He was not the only one who died for his sin.'" Nu 16:22; Jos 7:1

[21]Then Reuben, Gad and the half-tribe of Manasseh replied to the heads of the clans of Israel: [22]"The Mighty One, God, the

---

[a] 20 The Hebrew term refers to the irrevocable giving over of things or persons to the LORD, often by totally destroying them.

LORD! The Mighty One, God, the LORD! He knows! And let Israel know! If this has been in rebellion or disobedience to the LORD, do not spare us this day. ²³ If we have built our own altar to turn away from the LORD and to offer burnt offerings and grain offerings, or to sacrifice fellowship offerings on it, may the LORD himself call us to account. Dt 10:17; 18:19; 1Ki 8:39

²⁴ "No! We did it for fear that some day your descendants might say to ours, 'What do you have to do with the LORD, the God of Israel? ²⁵ The LORD has made the Jordan a boundary between us and you—you Reubenites and Gadites! You have no share in the LORD.' So your descendants might cause ours to stop fearing the LORD.

²⁶ "That is why we said, 'Let us get ready and build an altar—but not for burnt offerings or sacrifices.' ²⁷ On the contrary, it is to be a witness between us and you and the generations that follow, that we will worship the LORD at his sanctuary with our burnt offerings, sacrifices and fellowship offerings. Then in the future your descendants will not be able to say to ours, 'You have no share in the LORD.' Dt 12:6; Jos 24:27

²⁸ "And we said, 'If they ever say this to us, or to our descendants, we will answer: Look at the replica of the LORD's altar, which our ancestors built, not for burnt offerings and sacrifices, but as a witness between us and you.'

²⁹ "Far be it from us to rebel against the LORD and turn away from him today by building an altar for burnt offerings, grain offerings and sacrifices, other than the altar of the LORD our God that stands before his tabernacle." Dt 12:13-14; Jos 24:16

³⁰ When Phinehas the priest and the leaders of the community—the heads of the clans of the Israelites—heard what Reuben, Gad and Manasseh had to say, they were pleased. ³¹ And Phinehas son of Eleazar, the priest, said to Reuben, Gad and Manasseh, "Today we know that the LORD is with us, because you have not been unfaithful to the LORD in this matter. Now you have rescued the Israelites from the LORD's hand." Lev 26:11-12; 2Ch 15:2

³² Then Phinehas son of Eleazar, the priest, and the leaders returned to Canaan from their meeting with the Reubenites and Gadites in Gilead and reported to the Israelites. ³³ They were glad to hear the report and praised God. And they talked no more about going to war against them to devastate the country where the Reubenites and the Gadites lived. 1Ch 29:20; Da 2:19

³⁴ And the Reubenites and the Gadites gave the altar this name: A Witness Between Us—that the LORD is God. Ge 21:30

Joshua's Farewell to the Leaders

23 After a long time had passed and the LORD had given Israel rest from all their enemies around them, Joshua, by then a very old man, ²summoned all Israel—their elders, leaders, judges and officials—and said to them: "I am very old. ³You yourselves have seen everything the LORD your God has done to all these nations for your sake; it was the LORD your God who fought for you. ⁴Remember how I have allotted as an inheritance for your tribes all the land of the nations that remain—the nations I conquered—between the Jordan and the Mediterranean Sea in the west. ⁵The LORD your God himself will push them out for your sake. He will drive them out before you, and you will take possession of their land, as the LORD your God promised you. Jos 13:1; 21:44; Nu 33:53

⁶"Be very strong; be careful to obey all that is written in the Book of the Law of Moses, without turning aside to the right or to the left. ⁷Do not associate with these nations that remain among you; do not invoke the names of their gods or swear by them. You must not serve them or bow down to them. ⁸But you are to hold fast to the LORD your God, as you have until now. Ex 23:13; Dt 10:20; Jos 1:7

⁹"The LORD has driven out before you great and powerful nations; to this day no one has been able to withstand you. ¹⁰One of you routs a thousand, because the LORD your God fights for you, just as he promised. ¹¹So be very careful to love the LORD your God. Dt 3:22; 11:23; Lev 26:8

¹²"But if you turn away and ally yourselves with the survivors of these nations that remain among you and if you intermarry with them and associate with them, ¹³then you may be sure that the LORD your God will no longer drive out these nations before you. Instead, they will become snares and traps for you, whips on your backs and thorns in your eyes, until you perish from this good land, which the LORD your God has given you. Ex 34:16; Dt 7:3; Ps 106:34-35

¹⁴"Now I am about to go the way of all the earth. You know with all your heart and soul that not one of all the good promises the LORD your God gave you has failed. Every promise has been fulfilled; not one has failed. ¹⁵But just as all the good things the LORD your God has promised you have come to you, so he will bring on you all the evil things he has threatened, until the LORD your God has destroyed you from this good land he has given you. ¹⁶If you violate the covenant of the LORD your God, which he commanded you, and go and serve other gods and bow down to them, the LORD's anger will burn against you, and you will quickly perish

from the good land he has given you."   Dt 28:15; Jos 21:45; 1Ki 2:2

The Covenant Renewed at Shechem

24 Then Joshua assembled all the tribes of Israel at Shechem. He summoned the elders, leaders, judges and officials of Israel, and they presented themselves before God. Jos 23:2 ²Joshua said to all the people, "This is what the LORD, the God of Israel, says: 'Long ago your ancestors, including Terah the father of Abraham and Nahor, lived beyond the Euphrates River and worshiped other gods. ³But I took your father Abraham from the land beyond the Euphrates and led him throughout Canaan and gave him many descendants. I gave him Isaac, ⁴and to Isaac I gave Jacob and Esau. I assigned the hill country of Seir to Esau, but Jacob and his family went down to Egypt.   Ge 11:32; 25:26; 46:5-6

⁵"'Then I sent Moses and Aaron, and I afflicted the Egyptians by what I did there, and I brought you out. ⁶When I brought your people out of Egypt, you came to the sea, and the Egyptians pursued them with chariots and horsemen*a* as far as the Red Sea.*b* ⁷But they cried to the LORD for help, and he put darkness between you and the Egyptians; he brought the sea over them and covered them. You saw with your own eyes what I did to the Egyptians. Then you lived in the wilderness for a long time.   Ex 3:10; 14:9; Dt 1:46

⁸"'I brought you to the land of the Amorites who lived east of the Jordan. They fought against you, but I gave them into your hands. I destroyed them from before you, and you took possession of their land. ⁹When Balak son of Zippor, the king of Moab, prepared to fight against Israel, he sent for Balaam son of Beor to put a curse on you. ¹⁰But I would not listen to Balaam, so he blessed you again and again, and I delivered you out of his hand.   Ex 23:23; Nu 22:2; Dt 23:5

¹¹"'Then you crossed the Jordan and came to Jericho. The citizens of Jericho fought against you, as did also the Amorites, Perizzites, Canaanites, Hittites, Girgashites, Hivites and Jebusites, but I gave them into your hands. ¹²I sent the hornet ahead of you, which drove them out before you — also the two Amorite kings. You did not do it with your own sword and bow. ¹³So I gave you a land on which you did not toil and cities you did not build; and you live in them and eat from vineyards and olive groves that you did not plant.'   Dt 6:10-11; Jos 3:16-17; Ps 44:3,6-7

¹⁴"Now fear the LORD and serve him with all faithfulness. Throw away the gods your

a 6 Or *charioteers*   *b* 6 Or *the Sea of Reeds*

ancestors worshiped beyond the Euphrates River and in Egypt, and serve the LORD. ¹⁵But if serving the LORD seems undesirable to you, then choose for yourselves this day whom you will serve, whether the gods your ancestors served beyond the Euphrates, or the gods of the Amorites, in whose land you are living. But as for me and my household, we will serve the LORD." Dt 10:12; Ru 1:16; 1Sa 12:24

¹⁶Then the people answered, "Far be it from us to forsake the LORD to serve other gods! ¹⁷It was the LORD our God himself who brought us and our parents up out of Egypt, from that land of slavery, and performed those great signs before our eyes. He protected us on our entire journey and among all the nations through which we traveled. ¹⁸And the LORD drove out before us all the nations, including the Amorites, who lived in the land. We too will serve the LORD, because he is our God."

¹⁹Joshua said to the people, "You are not able to serve the LORD. He is a holy God; he is a jealous God. He will not forgive your rebellion and your sins. ²⁰If you forsake the LORD and serve foreign gods, he will turn and bring disaster on you and make an end of you, after he has been good to you." Ex 23:21; Jos 23:15; 1Ch 28:9

²¹But the people said to Joshua, "No! We will serve the LORD."

²²Then Joshua said, "You are witnesses against yourselves that you have chosen to serve the LORD." Ru 4:10; Ps 119:30,173

"Yes, we are witnesses," they replied. Dt 25:9

²³"Now then," said Joshua, "throw away the foreign gods that are among you and yield your hearts to the LORD, the God of Israel." 1Ki 8:58

²⁴And the people said to Joshua, "We will serve the LORD our God and obey him." Ex 19:8; 24:3,7

²⁵On that day Joshua made a covenant for the people, and there at Shechem he reaffirmed for them decrees and laws. ²⁶And Joshua recorded these things in the Book of the Law of God. Then he took a large stone and set it up there under the oak near the holy place of the LORD. Ex 24:8; Dt 31:24

²⁷"See!" he said to all the people. "This stone will be a witness against us. It has heard all the words the LORD has said to us. It will be a witness against you if you are untrue to your God." Jos 22:27; Pr 30:9; Hab 2:11

²⁸Then Joshua dismissed the people, each to their own inheritance. Jdg 21:23-24

Buried in the Promised Land
24:29-31pp — Jdg 2:6-9

²⁹After these things, Joshua son of Nun, the servant of the LORD, died at the age of a hundred and ten. ³⁰And they buried

him in the land of his inheritance, at Timnath Serah[a] in the hill country of Ephraim, north of Mount Gaash. Jos 19:50; Jdg 1:1

[31] Israel served the LORD throughout the lifetime of Joshua and of the elders who outlived him and who had experienced everything the LORD had done for Israel. Jdg 2:6-9

[32] And Joseph's bones, which the Israelites had brought up from Egypt, were buried at Shechem in the tract of land that Jacob bought for a hundred pieces of silver[b] from the sons of Hamor, the father of Shechem. This became the inheritance of Joseph's descendants. Ge 33:19; 50:25; Ex 13:19

[33] And Eleazar son of Aaron died and was buried at Gibeah, which had been allotted to his son Phinehas in the hill country of Ephraim. Jos 22:13; 1Sa 9:4

---

[a] 30 Also known as *Timnath Heres* (see Judges 2:9)   [b] 32 Hebrew *hundred kesitahs*; a kesitah was a unit of money of unknown weight and value.

Judges

Israel Fights the Remaining Canaanites

1:11-15pp — Jos 15:15-19

1 After the death of Joshua, the Israelites asked the LORD, "Who of us is to go up first to fight against the Canaanites?" ^{Nu 27:21; Jos 24:29; Jdg 3:1-6}

²The LORD answered, "Judah shall go up; I have given the land into their hands." Ge 49:8

³The men of Judah then said to the Simeonites their fellow Israelites, "Come up with us into the territory allotted to us, to fight against the Canaanites. We in turn will go with you into yours." So the Simeonites went with them.

⁴When Judah attacked, the LORD gave the Canaanites and Perizzites into their hands, and they struck down ten thousand men at Bezek. ⁵It was there that they found Adoni-Bezek and fought against him, putting to rout the Canaanites and Perizzites. ⁶Adoni-Bezek fled, but they chased him and caught him, and cut off his thumbs and big toes. Ge 13:7; Jos 3:10

⁷Then Adoni-Bezek said, "Seventy kings with their thumbs and big toes cut off have picked up scraps under my table. Now God has paid me back for what I did to them." They brought him to Jerusalem, and he died there. Lev 24:19

⁸The men of Judah attacked Jerusalem also and took it. They put the city to the sword and set it on fire. Jos 15:63

⁹After that, Judah went down to fight against the Canaanites living in the hill country, the Negev and the western foothills. ¹⁰They advanced against the Canaanites living in Hebron (formerly called Kiriath Arba) and defeated Sheshai, Ahiman and Talmai. ¹¹From there they advanced against the people living in Debir (formerly called Kiriath Sepher). Nu 13:17; Jos 15:14

¹²And Caleb said, "I will give my daughter Aksah in marriage

to the man who attacks and captures Kiriath Sepher." ¹³Othniel son of Kenaz, Caleb's younger brother, took it; so Caleb gave his daughter Aksah to him in marriage.

¹⁴One day when she came to Othniel, she urged him*a* to ask her father for a field. When she got off her donkey, Caleb asked her, "What can I do for you?"

¹⁵She replied, "Do me a special favor. Since you have given me land in the Negev, give me also springs of water." So Caleb gave her the upper and lower springs.   Jos 15:15-19

¹⁶The descendants of Moses' father-in-law, the Kenite, went up from the City of Palms*b* with the people of Judah to live among the inhabitants of the Desert of Judah in the Negev near Arad.   Nu 10:29; Dt 34:3; Jdg 4:11

¹⁷Then the men of Judah went with the Simeonites their fellow Israelites and attacked the Canaanites living in Zephath, and they totally destroyed*c* the city. Therefore it was called Hormah.*d* ¹⁸Judah also took*e* Gaza, Ashkelon and Ekron—each city with its territory.   Nu 21:3; Jos 11:22

¹⁹The LORD was with the men of Judah. They took possession of the hill country, but they were unable to drive the people from the plains, because they had chariots fitted with iron. ²⁰As Moses had promised, Hebron was given to Caleb, who drove from it the three sons of Anak. ²¹The Benjamites, however, did not drive out the Jebusites, who were living in Jerusalem; to this day the Jebusites live there with the Benjamites.   Jos 14:9; 15:63; 17:16

²²Now the tribes of Joseph attacked Bethel, and the LORD was with them. ²³When they sent men to spy out Bethel (formerly called Luz), ²⁴the spies saw a man coming out of the city and they said to him, "Show us how to get into the city and we will see that you are treated well." ²⁵So he showed them, and they put the city to the sword but spared the man and his whole family. ²⁶He then went to the land of the Hittites, where he built a city and called it Luz, which is its name to this day.   Ge 28:19; Jos 2:12,14; 6:25

²⁷But Manasseh did not drive out the people of Beth Shan or Taanach or Dor or Ibleam or Megiddo and their surrounding settlements, for the Canaanites were determined to live in that land. ²⁸When Israel became strong, they pressed the Canaanites into forced labor but never drove them out completely. ²⁹Nor did Ephraim drive

---

a 14 Hebrew; Septuagint and Vulgate *Othniel, he urged her*   *b* 16 That is, Jericho
c 17 The Hebrew term refers to the irrevocable giving over of things or persons to the LORD, often by totally destroying them.   *d* 17 *Hormah* means *destruction.*   *e* 18 Hebrew; Septuagint *Judah did not take*

out the Canaanites living in Gezer, but the Canaanites continued to live there among them. [30]Neither did Zebulun drive out the Canaanites living in Kitron or Nahalol, so these Canaanites lived among them, but Zebulun did subject them to forced labor. [31]Nor did Asher drive out those living in Akko or Sidon or Ahlab or Akzib or Helbah or Aphek or Rehob. [32]The Asherites lived among the Canaanite inhabitants of the land because they did not drive them out. [33]Neither did Naphtali drive out those living in Beth Shemesh or Beth Anath; but the Naphtalites too lived among the Canaanite inhabitants of the land, and those living in Beth Shemesh and Beth Anath became forced laborers for them. [34]The Amorites confined the Danites to the hill country, not allowing them to come down into the plain. [35]And the Amorites were determined also to hold out in Mount Heres, Aijalon and Shaalbim, but when the power of the tribes of Joseph increased, they too were pressed into forced labor. [36]The boundary of the Amorites was from Scorpion Pass to Sela and beyond.   Jos 15:3; 16:10; 17:11

The Angel of the Lord at Bokim

2 The angel of the Lord went up from Gilgal to Bokim and said, "I brought you up out of Egypt and led you into the land I swore to give to your ancestors. I said, 'I will never break my covenant with you, [2]and you shall not make a covenant with the people of this land, but you shall break down their altars.' Yet you have disobeyed me. Why have you done this? [3]And I have also said, 'I will not drive them out before you; they will become traps for you, and their gods will become snares to you.'"   Ex 20:2; Jos 23:13; Ps 106:36

[4]When the angel of the Lord had spoken these things to all the Israelites, the people wept aloud, [5]and they called that place Bokim.[a] There they offered sacrifices to the Lord.

Disobedience and Defeat

2:6-9pp — Jos 24:29-31

[6]After Joshua had dismissed the Israelites, they went to take possession of the land, each to their own inheritance. [7]The people served the Lord throughout the lifetime of Joshua and of the elders who outlived him and who had seen all the great things the Lord had done for Israel.

[8]Joshua son of Nun, the servant of the Lord, died at the age of a hundred and ten. [9]And they buried him in the land of his inheritance, at Timnath Heres[b] in the hill country of Ephraim, north of Mount Gaash.   Jos 24:29-31; 19:50

[10]After that whole generation

---

[a] 5 *Bokim* means *weepers.*   [b] 9 Also known as *Timnath Serah* (see Joshua 19:50 and 24:30)

had been gathered to their ancestors, another generation grew up who knew neither the LORD nor what he had done for Israel. [11] Then the Israelites did evil in the eyes of the LORD and served the Baals. [12] They forsook the LORD, the God of their ancestors, who had brought them out of Egypt. They followed and worshiped various gods of the peoples around them. They aroused the LORD's anger [13] because they forsook him and served Baal and the Ashtoreths. [14] In his anger against Israel the LORD gave them into the hands of raiders who plundered them. He sold them into the hands of their enemies all around, whom they were no longer able to resist. [15] Whenever Israel went out to fight, the hand of the LORD was against them to defeat them, just as he had sworn to them. They were in great distress. Dt 28:25; 31:16; 1Sa 2:12 [16] Then the LORD raised up judges,[a] who saved them out of the hands of these raiders. [17] Yet they would not listen to their judges but prostituted themselves to other gods and worshiped them. They quickly turned from the ways of their ancestors, who had been obedient to the LORD's commands. [18] Whenever the LORD raised up a judge for them, he was with the judge and saved them out of the hands of their enemies as long as the judge

lived; for the LORD relented because of their groaning under those who oppressed and afflicted them. [19] But when the judge died, the people returned to ways even more corrupt than those of their ancestors, following other gods and serving and worshiping them. They refused to give up their evil practices and stubborn ways. Jos 1:5; Jdg 3:12; Ac 13:20 [20] Therefore the LORD was very angry with Israel and said, "Because this nation has violated the covenant I ordained for their ancestors and has not listened to me, [21] I will no longer drive out before them any of the nations Joshua left when he died. [22] I will use them to test Israel and see whether they will keep the way of the LORD and walk in it as their ancestors did." [23] The LORD had allowed those nations to remain; he did not drive them out at once by giving them into the hands of Joshua. Dt 8:2,16; Jos 23:16; Jdg 3:1,14

3 These are the nations the LORD left to test all those Israelites who had not experienced any of the wars in Canaan [2] (he did this only to teach warfare to the descendants of the Israelites who had not had previous battle experience): [3] the five rulers of the Philistines, all the Canaanites, the Sidonians, and the Hivites living in the Lebanon mountains from Mount Baal

[a] 16 Or *leaders*; similarly in verses 17-19

Hermon to Lebo Hamath. ⁴They were left to test the Israelites to see whether they would obey the LORD's commands, which he had given their ancestors through Moses.   Ex 15:25; Jos 13:3; Jdg 2:21-22

⁵The Israelites lived among the Canaanites, Hittites, Amorites, Perizzites, Hivites and Jebusites. ⁶They took their daughters in marriage and gave their own daughters to their sons, and served their gods.   Ex 34:16; Dt 7:3-4

Othniel

⁷The Israelites did evil in the eyes of the LORD; they forgot the LORD their God and served the Baals and the Asherahs. ⁸The anger of the LORD burned against Israel so that he sold them into the hands of Cushan-Rishathaim king of Aram Naharaim,ᵃ to whom the Israelites were subject for eight years. ⁹But when they cried out to the LORD, he raised up for them a deliverer, Othniel son of Kenaz, Caleb's younger brother, who saved them. ¹⁰The Spirit of the LORD came on him, so that he became Israel's judgeᵇ and went to war. The LORD gave Cushan-Rishathaim king of Aram into the hands of Othniel, who overpowered him. ¹¹So the land had peace for forty years, until Othniel son of Kenaz died.   Nu 11:25,29; Dt 4:9; Jdg 6:34

Ehud

¹²Again the Israelites did evil in the eyes of the LORD, and because they did this evil the LORD gave Eglon king of Moab power over Israel. ¹³Getting the Ammonites and Amalekites to join him, Eglon came and attacked Israel, and they took possession of the City of Palms.ᶜ ¹⁴The Israelites were subject to Eglon king of Moab for eighteen years.   Jdg 1:16; 2:11,14

¹⁵Again the Israelites cried out to the LORD, and he gave them a deliverer—Ehud, a left-handed man, the son of Gera the Benjamite. The Israelites sent him with tribute to Eglon king of Moab. ¹⁶Now Ehud had made a double-edged sword about a cubitᵈ long, which he strapped to his right thigh under his clothing. ¹⁷He presented the tribute to Eglon king of Moab, who was a very fat man. ¹⁸After Ehud had presented the tribute, he sent on their way those who had carried it. ¹⁹But on reaching the stone images near Gilgal he himself went back to Eglon and said, "Your Majesty, I have a secret message for you."   1Ch 12:2; Ps 78:34

The king said to his attendants, "Leave us!" And they all left.

²⁰Ehud then approached him while he was sitting alone in the upper room of his palaceᵉ and said, "I have a message from God

---

ᵃ 8 That is, Northwest Mesopotamia   ᵇ 10 Or leader   ᶜ 13 That is, Jericho   ᵈ 16 That is, about 18 inches or about 45 centimeters is uncertain; also in verse 24.   ᵉ 20 The meaning of the Hebrew for this word for you." As the king rose from his seat, [21] Ehud reached with his left hand, drew the sword from his right thigh and plunged it into the king's belly. [22] Even the handle sank in after the blade, and his bowels discharged. Ehud did not pull the sword out, and the fat closed in over it. [23] Then Ehud went out to the porch[a]; he shut the doors of the upper room behind him and locked them. Am 3:15

[24] After he had gone, the servants came and found the doors of the upper room locked. They said, "He must be relieving himself in the inner room of the palace." [25] They waited to the point of embarrassment, but when he did not open the doors of the room, they took a key and unlocked them. There they saw their lord fallen to the floor, dead. 1Sa 24:3; 2Ki 2:17 [26] While they waited, Ehud got away. He passed by the stone images and escaped to Seirah. [27] When he arrived there, he blew a trumpet in the hill country of Ephraim, and the Israelites went down with him from the hills, with him leading them. Jdg 6:34 [28] "Follow me," he ordered, "for the LORD has given Moab, your enemy, into your hands." So they followed him down and took possession of the fords of the Jordan that led to Moab; they allowed no one to cross over. [29] At that time they struck down about ten thousand Moabites, all vigorous and strong; not one escaped. [30] That day Moab was made subject to Israel, and the land had peace for eighty years. Jdg 7:9,15,24; 12:5

Shamgar

[31] After Ehud came Shamgar son of Anath, who struck down six hundred Philistines with an oxgoad. He too saved Israel. Jdg 5:6

Deborah

4 Again the Israelites did evil in the eyes of the LORD, now that Ehud was dead. [2] So the LORD sold them into the hands of Jabin king of Canaan, who reigned in Hazor. Sisera, the commander of his army, was based in Harosheth Haggoyim. [3] Because he had nine hundred chariots fitted with iron and had cruelly oppressed the Israelites for twenty years, they cried to the LORD for help. Jdg 1:19; 2:19; Jos 11:1

[4] Now Deborah, a prophet, the wife of Lappidoth, was leading[b] Israel at that time. [5] She held court under the Palm of Deborah between Ramah and Bethel in the hill country of Ephraim, and the Israelites went up to her to have their disputes decided. [6] She sent for Barak son of Abinoam from Kedesh in Naphtali and said to him, "The LORD, the God of Israel, commands you: 'Go, take with you ten thousand men of Naphtali and Zebulun and

---

[a] 23 The meaning of the Hebrew for this word is uncertain.   [b] 4 Traditionally *judging*

lead them up to Mount Tabor. [7] I will lead Sisera, the commander of Jabin's army, with his chariots and his troops to the Kishon River and give him into your hands.'" Heb 11:32; Ps 83:9; Ge 35:8

[8] Barak said to her, "If you go with me, I will go; but if you don't go with me, I won't go."

[9] "Certainly I will go with you," said Deborah. "But because of the course you are taking, the honor will not be yours, for the LORD will deliver Sisera into the hands of a woman." So Deborah went with Barak to Kedesh. [10] There Barak summoned Zebulun and Naphtali, and ten thousand men went up under his command. Deborah also went up with him. Jdg 5:15,18

[11] Now Heber the Kenite had left the other Kenites, the descendants of Hobab, Moses' brother-in-law,[a] and pitched his tent by the great tree in Zaanannim near Kedesh. Jdg 1:16

[12] When they told Sisera that Barak son of Abinoam had gone up to Mount Tabor, [13] Sisera summoned from Harosheth Haggoyim to the Kishon River all his men and his nine hundred chariots fitted with iron.

[14] Then Deborah said to Barak, "Go! This is the day the LORD has given Sisera into your hands. Has not the LORD gone ahead of you?" So Barak went down Mount Tabor, with ten thousand men following him. [15] At Barak's advance, the LORD routed Sisera and all his chariots and army by the sword, and Sisera got down from his chariot and fled on foot. Dt 9:3; Jos 10:10; 2Sa 5:24

[16] Barak pursued the chariots and army as far as Harosheth Haggoyim, and all Sisera's troops fell by the sword; not a man was left. [17] Sisera, meanwhile, fled on foot to the tent of Jael, the wife of Heber the Kenite, because there was an alliance between Jabin king of Hazor and the family of Heber the Kenite.

[18] Jael went out to meet Sisera and said to him, "Come, my lord, come right in. Don't be afraid." So he entered her tent, and she covered him with a blanket.

[19] "I'm thirsty," he said. "Please give me some water." She opened a skin of milk, gave him a drink, and covered him up. Jdg 5:25

[20] "Stand in the doorway of the tent," he told her. "If someone comes by and asks you, 'Is anyone in there?' say 'No.'"

[21] But Jael, Heber's wife, picked up a tent peg and a hammer and went quietly to him while he lay fast asleep, exhausted. She drove the peg through his temple into the ground, and he died.

[22] Just then Barak came by in pursuit of Sisera, and Jael went out to meet him. "Come," she said, "I will show you the man you're looking for." So he went

---

[a] 11 Or *father-in-law*

in with her, and there lay Sisera with the tent peg through his temple — dead.

²³On that day God subdued Jabin king of Canaan before the Israelites. ²⁴And the hand of the Israelites pressed harder and harder against Jabin king of Canaan until they destroyed him. Ne 9:24; Ps 18:47

The Song of Deborah

5 On that day Deborah and Barak son of Abinoam sang this song: Ex 15:1

² "When the princes in Israel
    take the lead,
  when the people willingly
    offer themselves —
  praise the LORD!

³ "Hear this, you kings! Listen,
    you rulers!
  I, even I, will sing to*a* the
    LORD;
  I will praise the LORD,
    the God of Israel, in
    song. Ps 27:6

⁴ "When you, LORD, went out
    from Seir,
  when you marched from
    the land of Edom, Dt 33:2
  the earth shook, the heavens
    poured,
  the clouds poured down
    water. Ps 68:8
⁵ The mountains quaked before
    the LORD, the One of
    Sinai,

before the LORD, the God of
    Israel. Ex 19:18

⁶ "In the days of Shamgar son of
    Anath, Jdg 3:31
  in the days of Jael, the
    highways were
    abandoned; Jdg 4:17
  travelers took to winding
    paths.
⁷ Villagers in Israel would not
    fight;
  they held back until I,
    Deborah, arose,
  until I arose, a mother in
    Israel.
⁸ God chose new leaders Dt 32:17
  when war came to the city
    gates,
  but not a shield or spear was
    seen
  among forty thousand in
    Israel.
⁹ My heart is with Israel's
    princes,
  with the willing volunteers
    among the people.
  Praise the LORD!

¹⁰ "You who ride on white
    donkeys, Jdg 10:4
  sitting on your saddle
    blankets,
  and you who walk along the
    road,
  consider ¹¹the voice of the
    singers*b* at the watering
    places.
  They recite the victories of
    the LORD, 1Sa 12:7; Mic 6:5

a 3 Or *of*   *b 11* The meaning of the Hebrew for this word is uncertain.

the victories of his villagers
in Israel.

"Then the people of the LORD
went down to the city gates.
12 'Wake up, wake up,
Deborah!   Ps 57:8
Wake up, wake up, break
out in song!
Arise, Barak!
Take captive your captives,
son of Abinoam.' Ps 68:18

13 "The remnant of the nobles
came down;
the people of the LORD
came down to me
against the mighty.
14 Some came from Ephraim,
whose roots were in
Amalek;
Benjamin was with the
people who followed
you.
From Makir captains came
down,
from Zebulun those who
bear a commander's*a*
staff.
15 The princes of Issachar were
with Deborah;   Jdg 4:10
yes, Issachar was with
Barak,
sent under his command
into the valley.
In the districts of Reuben
there was much searching
of heart.
16 Why did you stay among the
sheep pens*b*

to hear the whistling for the
flocks?   Nu 32:1
In the districts of Reuben
there was much searching
of heart.
17 Gilead stayed beyond the
Jordan.
And Dan, why did he linger
by the ships?
Asher remained on the coast
and stayed in his coves.
18 The people of Zebulun risked
their very lives;
so did Naphtali on the
terraced fields.   Jdg 4:6,10

19 "Kings came, they fought,
the kings of Canaan
fought.
At Taanach, by the waters of
Megiddo,   Jdg 1:27
they took no plunder of
silver.
20 From the heavens the stars
fought,
from their courses they
fought against Sisera.
21 The river Kishon swept them
away,
the age-old river, the river
Kishon.
March on, my soul; be
strong!
22 Then thundered the horses'
hooves —
galloping, galloping go his
mighty steeds.
23 'Curse Meroz,' said the angel
of the LORD.

---

a 14 The meaning of the Hebrew for this word is uncertain.   *b* 16 Or *the campfires*; or *the saddlebags*

'Curse its people bitterly,
    because they did not come to
        help the LORD,
    to help the LORD against the
        mighty.'

24 "Most blessed of women be
    Jael,   Jdg 4:17
    the wife of Heber the
        Kenite,
    most blessed of tent-
        dwelling women.
25 He asked for water, and she
        gave him milk;
    in a bowl fit for nobles she
        brought him curdled
        milk.
26 Her hand reached for the tent
        peg,
    her right hand for the
        workman's hammer.
    She struck Sisera, she crushed
        his head,
    she shattered and pierced
        his temple.
27 At her feet he sank,
    he fell; there he lay.
    At her feet he sank, he fell;
    where he sank, there he
        fell — dead.

28 "Through the window peered
        Sisera's mother;
    behind the lattice she cried
        out,   Pr 7:6
    'Why is his chariot so long in
        coming?
    Why is the clatter of his
        chariots delayed?'
29 The wisest of her ladies
    answer her;

    indeed, she keeps saying to
        herself,
30 'Are they not finding and
        dividing the
        spoils: Ex 15:9; 1Sa 30:24
    a woman or two for each
        man,
    colorful garments as plunder
        for Sisera,
    colorful garments
        embroidered,
    highly embroidered garments
        for my neck —
    all this as plunder?'

31 "So may all your enemies
        perish, LORD!
    But may all who love you be
        like the sun   Ps 19:4; 89:36
    when it rises in its strength."

Then the land had peace forty
years.   Jdg 3:11

Gideon

6 The Israelites did evil in the
eyes of the LORD, and for sev-
en years he gave them into the
hands of the Midianites. 2 Because
the power of Midian was so oppressive, the Israelites prepared
shelters for themselves in mountain clefts, caves and strongholds.
3 Whenever the Israelites planted
their crops, the Midianites, Amalekites and other eastern peoples invaded the country. 4 They
camped on the land and ruined
the crops all the way to Gaza and
did not spare a living thing for Israel, neither sheep nor cattle nor

donkeys. ⁵They came up with their livestock and their tents like swarms of locusts. It was impossible to count them or their camels; they invaded the land to ravage it. ⁶Midian so impoverished the Israelites that they cried out to the LORD for help.   Lev 26:16; Jdg 7:12

⁷When the Israelites cried out to the LORD because of Midian, ⁸he sent them a prophet, who said, "This is what the LORD, the God of Israel, says: I brought you up out of Egypt, out of the land of slavery. ⁹I rescued you from the hand of the Egyptians. And I delivered you from the hand of all your oppressors; I drove them out before you and gave you their land. ¹⁰I said to you, 'I am the LORD your God; do not worship the gods of the Amorites, in whose land you live.' But you have not listened to me."   Jdg 2:1; Ps 44:2; Jer 10:2

¹¹The angel of the LORD came and sat down under the oak in Ophrah that belonged to Joash the Abiezrite, where his son Gideon was threshing wheat in a winepress to keep it from the Midianites. ¹²When the angel of the LORD appeared to Gideon, he said, "The LORD is with you, mighty warrior."   Jos 1:5; Heb 11:32

¹³"Pardon me, my lord," Gideon replied, "but if the LORD is with us, why has all this happened to us? Where are all his wonders that our ancestors told us about when they said, 'Did not the LORD bring us up out of Egypt?' But now the LORD has abandoned us and given us into the hand of Midian."   Ps 44:1

¹⁴The LORD turned to him and said, "Go in the strength you have and save Israel out of Midian's hand. Am I not sending you?"   Heb 11:34

¹⁵"Pardon me, my lord," Gideon replied, "but how can I save Israel? My clan is the weakest in Manasseh, and I am the least in my family."   1Sa 9:21

¹⁶The LORD answered, "I will be with you, and you will strike down all the Midianites, leaving none alive."   Ex 3:12

¹⁷Gideon replied, "If now I have found favor in your eyes, give me a sign that it is really you talking to me. ¹⁸Please do not go away until I come back and bring my offering and set it before you."   Ge 24:14

And the LORD said, "I will wait until you return."

¹⁹Gideon went inside, prepared a young goat, and from an ephah*ᵃ* of flour he made bread without yeast. Putting the meat in a basket and its broth in a pot, he brought them out and offered them to him under the oak.   Ge 18:7-8

²⁰The angel of God said to him, "Take the meat and the unleavened bread, place them on this rock, and pour out the broth." And Gideon did so. ²¹Then the angel of the LORD touched the

---

ᵃ 19 That is, probably about 36 pounds or about 16 kilograms meat and the unleavened bread with the tip of the staff that was in his hand. Fire flared from the rock, consuming the meat and the bread. And the angel of the LORD disappeared. ²²When Gideon realized that it was the angel of the LORD, he exclaimed, "Alas, Sovereign LORD! I have seen the angel of the LORD face to face!" Jdg 13:16,19,21; Lev 9:24; Ge 32:30 ²³But the LORD said to him, "Peace! Do not be afraid. You are not going to die." Da 10:19 ²⁴So Gideon built an altar to the LORD there and called it The LORD Is Peace. To this day it stands in Ophrah of the Abiezrites. Jdg 8:32 ²⁵That same night the LORD said to him, "Take the second bull from your father's herd, the one seven years old.ᵃ Tear down your father's altar to Baal and cut down the Asherah poleᵇ beside it. ²⁶Then build a proper kind ofᶜ altar to the LORD your God on the top of this height. Using the wood of the Asherah pole that you cut down, offer the secondᵈ bull as a burnt offering." Ex 34:13 ²⁷So Gideon took ten of his servants and did as the LORD told him. But because he was afraid of his family and the townspeople, he did it at night rather than in the daytime.

²⁸In the morning when the people of the town got up, there was Baal's altar, demolished, with the Asherah pole beside it cut down and the second bull sacrificed on the newly built altar! 1Ki 16:32 ²⁹They asked each other, "Who did this?"

When they carefully investigated, they were told, "Gideon son of Joash did it."

³⁰The people of the town demanded of Joash, "Bring out your son. He must die, because he has broken down Baal's altar and cut down the Asherah pole beside it."

³¹But Joash replied to the hostile crowd around him, "Are you going to plead Baal's cause? Are you trying to save him? Whoever fights for him shall be put to death by morning! If Baal really is a god, he can defend himself when someone breaks down his altar." ³²So because Gideon broke down Baal's altar, they gave him the name Jerub-Baalᵉ that day, saying, "Let Baal contend with him." Jdg 7:1; 1Sa 12:11

³³Now all the Midianites, Amalekites and other eastern peoples joined forces and crossed over the Jordan and camped in the Valley of Jezreel. ³⁴Then the Spirit of the LORD came on

ᵃ 25 Or Take a full-grown, mature bull from your father's herd   ᵇ 25 That is, a wooden symbol of the goddess Asherah; also in verses 26, 28 and 30   ᶜ 26 Or build with layers of stone an   ᵈ 26 Or full-grown; also in verse 28   ᵉ 32 Jerub-Baal probably means let Baal contend.

Gideon, and he blew a trumpet, summoning the Abiezrites to follow him. ³⁵He sent messengers throughout Manasseh, calling them to arms, and also into Asher, Zebulun and Naphtali, so that they too went up to meet them. Jos 17:16; Jdg 3:10,27; 4:6

³⁶Gideon said to God, "If you will save Israel by my hand as you have promised— ³⁷look, I will place a wool fleece on the threshing floor. If there is dew only on the fleece and all the ground is dry, then I will know that you will save Israel by my hand, as you said." ³⁸And that is what happened. Gideon rose early the next day; he squeezed the fleece and wrung out the dew—a bowlful of water. Ge 24:14

³⁹Then Gideon said to God, "Do not be angry with me. Let me make just one more request. Allow me one more test with the fleece, but this time make the fleece dry and let the ground be covered with dew." ⁴⁰That night God did so. Only the fleece was dry; all the ground was covered with dew. Ge 18:32

Gideon Defeats the Midianites

7 Early in the morning, Jerub-Baal (that is, Gideon) and all his men camped at the spring of Harod. The camp of Midian was north of them in the valley near the hill of Moreh. ²The LORD said to Gideon, "You have too many men. I cannot deliver Midian into their hands, or Israel would boast against me, 'My own strength has saved me.' ³Now announce to the army, 'Anyone who trembles with fear may turn back and leave Mount Gilead.'" So twenty-two thousand men left, while ten thousand remained. Dt 8:17; 20:8; Jdg 6:32

⁴But the LORD said to Gideon, "There are still too many men. Take them down to the water, and I will thin them out for you there. If I say, 'This one shall go with you,' he shall go; but if I say, 'This one shall not go with you,' he shall not go." 1Sa 14:6

⁵So Gideon took the men down to the water. There the LORD told him, "Separate those who lap the water with their tongues as a dog laps from those who kneel down to drink." ⁶Three hundred of them drank from cupped hands, lapping like dogs. All the rest got down on their knees to drink.

⁷The LORD said to Gideon, "With the three hundred men that lapped I will save you and give the Midianites into your hands. Let all the others go home." ⁸So Gideon sent the rest of the Israelites home but kept the three hundred, who took over the provisions and trumpets of the others. Jos 8:7

Now the camp of Midian lay below him in the valley. ⁹During that night the LORD said to Gideon, "Get up, go down against the camp, because I am going to give it into your hands. ¹⁰If you are afraid to attack, go down to the camp with your servant Purah ¹¹and listen to what they are saying. Afterward, you will be encouraged to attack the camp." So he and Purah his servant went down to the outposts of the camp. ¹²The Midianites, the Amalekites and all the other eastern peoples had settled in the valley, thick as locusts. Their camels could no more be counted than the sand on the seashore. Jos 2:24; 11:4; Jdg 8:10

¹³Gideon arrived just as a man was telling a friend his dream. "I had a dream," he was saying. "A round loaf of barley bread came tumbling into the Midianite camp. It struck the tent with such force that the tent overturned and collapsed."

¹⁴His friend responded, "This can be nothing other than the sword of Gideon son of Joash, the Israelite. God has given the Midianites and the whole camp into his hands."

¹⁵When Gideon heard the dream and its interpretation, he bowed down and worshiped. He returned to the camp of Israel and called out, "Get up! The LORD has given the Midianite camp into your hands." ¹⁶Dividing the three hundred men into three companies, he placed trumpets and empty jars in the hands of all of them, with torches inside. 1Sa 15:31

¹⁷"Watch me," he told them. "Follow my lead. When I get to the edge of the camp, do exactly as I do. ¹⁸When I and all who are with me blow our trumpets, then from all around the camp blow yours and shout, 'For the LORD and for Gideon.'" Jdg 3:27

¹⁹Gideon and the hundred men with him reached the edge of the camp at the beginning of the middle watch, just after they had changed the guard. They blew their trumpets and broke the jars that were in their hands. ²⁰The three companies blew the trumpets and smashed the jars. Grasping the torches in their left hands and holding in their right hands the trumpets they were to blow, they shouted, "A sword for the LORD and for Gideon!" ²¹While each man held his position around the camp, all the Midianites ran, crying out as they fled. 2Ki 7:7

²²When the three hundred trumpets sounded, the LORD caused the men throughout the camp to turn on each other with their swords. The army fled to Beth Shittah toward Zererah as far as the border of Abel Meholah near Tabbath. ²³Israelites from Naphtali, Asher and all Manasseh were called out, and they pursued the Midianites. ²⁴Gideon sent messengers throughout the hill country of Ephraim, saying, "Come down against the Midianites and seize the waters of the

Jordan ahead of them as far as Beth Barah." Jdg 3:28; 6:35; 1Sa 14:20

So all the men of Ephraim were called out and they seized the waters of the Jordan as far as Beth Barah. ²⁵They also captured two of the Midianite leaders, Oreb and Zeeb. They killed Oreb at the rock of Oreb, and Zeeb at the winepress of Zeeb. They pursued the Midianites and brought the heads of Oreb and Zeeb to Gideon, who was by the Jordan. Jdg 8:4; Ps 83:11; Isa 10:26

Zebah and Zalmunna

8 Now the Ephraimites asked Gideon, "Why have you treated us like this? Why didn't you call us when you went to fight Midian?" And they challenged him vigorously. Jdg 12:1

²But he answered them, "What have I accomplished compared to you? Aren't the gleanings of Ephraim's grapes better than the full grape harvest of Abiezer? ³God gave Oreb and Zeeb, the Midianite leaders, into your hands. What was I able to do compared to you?" At this, their resentment against him subsided. Jdg 7:25; Pr 15:1

⁴Gideon and his three hundred men, exhausted yet keeping up the pursuit, came to the Jordan and crossed it. ⁵He said to the men of Sukkoth, "Give my troops some bread; they are worn out, and I am still pursuing Zebah and Zalmunna, the kings of Midian." Ge 33:17

⁶But the officials of Sukkoth said, "Do you already have the hands of Zebah and Zalmunna in your possession? Why should we give bread to your troops?" 1Sa 25:11

⁷Then Gideon replied, "Just for that, when the LORD has given Zebah and Zalmunna into my hand, I will tear your flesh with desert thorns and briers." Jdg 7:15

⁸From there he went up to Peniel[a] and made the same request of them, but they answered as the men of Sukkoth had. ⁹So he said to the men of Peniel, "When I return in triumph, I will tear down this tower." Ge 32:30; 1Ki 12:25

¹⁰Now Zebah and Zalmunna were in Karkor with a force of about fifteen thousand men, all that were left of the armies of the eastern peoples; a hundred and twenty thousand swordsmen had fallen. ¹¹Gideon went up by the route of the nomads east of Nobah and Jogbehah and attacked the unsuspecting army. ¹²Zebah and Zalmunna, the two kings of Midian, fled, but he pursued them and captured them, routing their entire army. Jdg 7:12; Nu 32:42; Isa 9:4

¹³Gideon son of Joash then returned from the battle by the Pass of Heres. ¹⁴He caught a young man of Sukkoth and questioned him, and the young man wrote down for him the names of the seventy-seven officials of Sukkoth, the el-

ª 8 Hebrew *Penuel*, a variant of *Peniel*; also in verses 9 and 17 ders of the town. ¹⁵Then Gideon came and said to the men of Sukkoth, "Here are Zebah and Zalmunna, about whom you taunted me by saying, 'Do you already have the hands of Zebah and Zalmunna in your possession? Why should we give bread to your exhausted men?'" ¹⁶He took the elders of the town and taught the men of Sukkoth a lesson by punishing them with desert thorns and briers. ¹⁷He also pulled down the tower of Peniel and killed the men of the town. Jdg 6:11

¹⁸Then he asked Zebah and Zalmunna, "What kind of men did you kill at Tabor?" Jdg 4:6

"Men like you," they answered, "each one with the bearing of a prince."

¹⁹Gideon replied, "Those were my brothers, the sons of my own mother. As surely as the LORD lives, if you had spared their lives, I would not kill you." ²⁰Turning to Jether, his oldest son, he said, "Kill them!" But Jether did not draw his sword, because he was only a boy and was afraid.

²¹Zebah and Zalmunna said, "Come, do it yourself. 'As is the man, so is his strength.'" So Gideon stepped forward and killed them, and took the ornaments off their camels' necks. Ps 83:11

Gideon's Ephod

²²The Israelites said to Gideon, "Rule over us — you, your son and your grandson — because you have saved us from the hand of Midian."

²³But Gideon told them, "I will not rule over you, nor will my son rule over you. The LORD will rule over you." ²⁴And he said, "I do have one request, that each of you give me an earring from your share of the plunder." (It was the custom of the Ishmaelites to wear gold earrings.) 1Sa 8:7; 12:12; Ge 25:13

²⁵They answered, "We'll be glad to give them." So they spread out a garment, and each of them threw a ring from his plunder onto it. ²⁶The weight of the gold rings he asked for came to seventeen hundred shekels,ᵃ not counting the ornaments, the pendants and the purple garments worn by the kings of Midian or the chains that were on their camels' necks. ²⁷Gideon made the gold into an ephod, which he placed in Ophrah, his town. All Israel prostituted themselves by worshiping it there, and it became a snare to Gideon and his family. Jdg 17:5; Dt 7:16; Ps 106:39

Gideon's Death

²⁸Thus Midian was subdued before the Israelites and did not raise its head again. During Gideon's lifetime, the land had peace forty years. Jdg 5:31

²⁹Jerub-Baal son of Joash went back home to live. ³⁰He had seventy sons of his own, for he had

---

ᵃ 26 That is, about 43 pounds or about 20 kilograms

many wives. [31] His concubine, who lived in Shechem, also bore him a son, whom he named Abimelek. [32] Gideon son of Joash died at a good old age and was buried in the tomb of his father Joash in Ophrah of the Abiezrites.

Jdg 7:1; 9:2,5,18,24

[33] No sooner had Gideon died than the Israelites again prostituted themselves to the Baals. They set up Baal-Berith as their god [34] and did not remember the LORD their God, who had rescued them from the hands of all their enemies on every side. [35] They also failed to show any loyalty to the family of Jerub-Baal (that is, Gideon) in spite of all the good things he had done for them.

Jdg 2:11,13,19; 9:16; Dt 4:9

Abimelek

9 Abimelek son of Jerub-Baal went to his mother's brothers in Shechem and said to them and to all his mother's clan, [2] "Ask all the citizens of Shechem, 'Which is better for you: to have all seventy of Jerub-Baal's sons rule over you, or just one man?' Remember, I am your flesh and blood."

Ge 29:14; Jdg 8:31

[3] When the brothers repeated all this to the citizens of Shechem, they were inclined to follow Abimelek, for they said, "He is related to us." [4] They gave him seventy shekels[a] of silver from the temple of Baal-Berith, and Abimelek used it to hire reckless scoundrels, who became his followers. [5] He went to his father's home in Ophrah and on one stone murdered his seventy brothers, the sons of Jerub-Baal. But Jotham, the youngest son of Jerub-Baal, escaped by hiding. [6] Then all the citizens of Shechem and Beth Millo gathered beside the great tree at the pillar in Shechem to crown Abimelek king.

Jdg 8:33; 2Ki 11:2

[7] When Jotham was told about this, he climbed up on the top of Mount Gerizim and shouted to them, "Listen to me, citizens of Shechem, so that God may listen to you. [8] One day the trees went out to anoint a king for themselves. They said to the olive tree, 'Be our king.'

Dt 11:29; Jn 4:20

[9] "But the olive tree answered, 'Should I give up my oil, by which both gods and humans are honored, to hold sway over the trees?'

[10] "Next, the trees said to the fig tree, 'Come and be our king.'

[11] "But the fig tree replied, 'Should I give up my fruit, so good and sweet, to hold sway over the trees?'

[12] "Then the trees said to the vine, 'Come and be our king.'

[13] "But the vine answered, 'Should I give up my wine, which cheers both gods and humans, to hold sway over the trees?'

Ecc 2:3

[14] "Finally all the trees said to

---

a 4 That is, about 1 3/4 pounds or about 800 grams

the thornbush, 'Come and be our king.'

¹⁵ "The thornbush said to the trees, 'If you really want to anoint me king over you, come and take refuge in my shade; but if not, then let fire come out of the thornbush and consume the cedars of Lebanon!' Isa 30:2

¹⁶ "Have you acted honorably and in good faith by making Abimelek king? Have you been fair to Jerub-Baal and his family? Have you treated him as he deserves? ¹⁷ Remember that my father fought for you and risked his life to rescue you from the hand of Midian. ¹⁸ But today you have revolted against my father's family. You have murdered his seventy sons on a single stone and have made Abimelek, the son of his female slave, king over the citizens of Shechem because he is related to you. ¹⁹ So have you acted honorably and in good faith toward Jerub-Baal and his family today? If you have, may Abimelek be your joy, and may you be his, too! ²⁰ But if you have not, let fire come out from Abimelek and consume you, the citizens of Shechem and Beth Millo, and let fire come out from you, the citizens of Shechem and Beth Millo, and consume Abimelek!" Jdg 8:30

²¹ Then Jotham fled, escaping to Beer, and he lived there because he was afraid of his brother Abimelek.

²² After Abimelek had governed Israel three years, ²³ God stirred up animosity between Abimelek and the citizens of Shechem so that they acted treacherously against Abimelek. ²⁴ God did this in order that the crime against Jerub-Baal's seventy sons, the shedding of their blood, might be avenged on their brother Abimelek and on the citizens of Shechem, who had helped him murder his brothers. ²⁵ In opposition to him these citizens of Shechem set men on the hilltops to ambush and rob everyone who passed by, and this was reported to Abimelek. Nu 35:33; Dt 27:25; 1Sa 16:14

²⁶ Now Gaal son of Ebed moved with his clan into Shechem, and its citizens put their confidence in him. ²⁷ After they had gone out into the fields and gathered the grapes and trodden them, they held a festival in the temple of their god. While they were eating and drinking, they cursed Abimelek. ²⁸ Then Gaal son of Ebed said, "Who is Abimelek, and why should we Shechemites be subject to him? Isn't he Jerub-Baal's son, and isn't Zebul his deputy? Serve the family of Hamor, Shechem's father! Why should we serve Abimelek? ²⁹ If only this people were under my command! Then I would get rid of him. I would say to Abimelek, 'Call out your whole army!' " ᵃ 2Sa 15:4

ᵃ 29 Septuagint; Hebrew *him.*" Then he said to Abimelek, "Call out your whole army!"

³⁰When Zebul the governor of the city heard what Gaal son of Ebed said, he was very angry. ³¹Under cover he sent messengers to Abimelek, saying, "Gaal son of Ebed and his clan have come to Shechem and are stirring up the city against you. ³²Now then, during the night you and your men should come and lie in wait in the fields. ³³In the morning at sunrise, advance against the city. When Gaal and his men come out against you, seize the opportunity to attack them." 1Sa 10:7

³⁴So Abimelek and all his troops set out by night and took up concealed positions near Shechem in four companies. ³⁵Now Gaal son of Ebed had gone out and was standing at the entrance of the city gate just as Abimelek and his troops came out from their hiding place. Ps 32:7; Jer 49:10

³⁶When Gaal saw them, he said to Zebul, "Look, people are coming down from the tops of the mountains!"

Zebul replied, "You mistake the shadows of the mountains for men."

³⁷But Gaal spoke up again: "Look, people are coming down from the central hill,ᵃ and a company is coming from the direction of the diviners' tree."

³⁸Then Zebul said to him, "Where is your big talk now, you who said, 'Who is Abimelek that we should be subject to him?' Aren't these the men you ridiculed? Go out and fight them!"

³⁹So Gaal led outᵇ the citizens of Shechem and fought Abimelek. ⁴⁰Abimelek chased him all the way to the entrance of the gate, and many were killed as they fled. ⁴¹Then Abimelek stayed in Arumah, and Zebul drove Gaal and his clan out of Shechem.

⁴²The next day the people of Shechem went out to the fields, and this was reported to Abimelek. ⁴³So he took his men, divided them into three companies and set an ambush in the fields. When he saw the people coming out of the city, he rose to attack them. ⁴⁴Abimelek and the companies with him rushed forward to a position at the entrance of the city gate. Then two companies attacked those in the fields and struck them down. ⁴⁵All that day Abimelek pressed his attack against the city until he had captured it and killed its people. Then he destroyed the city and scattered salt over it. Dt 29:23; 2Ki 3:25

⁴⁶On hearing this, the citizens in the tower of Shechem went into the stronghold of the temple of El-Berith. ⁴⁷When Abimelek heard that they had assembled there, ⁴⁸he and all his men went up Mount Zalmon. He took an

---

ᵃ 37 The Hebrew for this phrase means *the navel of the earth.*   ᵇ 39 Or *Gaal went out in the sight of* ax and cut off some branches, which he lifted to his shoulders. He ordered the men with him, "Quick! Do what you have seen me do!" ⁴⁹ So all the men cut branches and followed Abimelek. They piled them against the stronghold and set it on fire with the people still inside. So all the people in the tower of Shechem, about a thousand men and women, also died. Ps 68:14

⁵⁰ Next Abimelek went to Thebez and besieged it and captured it. ⁵¹ Inside the city, however, was a strong tower, to which all the men and women — all the people of the city — had fled. They had locked themselves in and climbed up on the tower roof. ⁵² Abimelek went to the tower and attacked it. But as he approached the entrance to the tower to set it on fire, ⁵³ a woman dropped an upper millstone on his head and cracked his skull. 2Sa 11:21

⁵⁴ Hurriedly he called to his armor-bearer, "Draw your sword and kill me, so that they can't say, 'A woman killed him.'" So his servant ran him through, and he died. ⁵⁵ When the Israelites saw that Abimelek was dead, they went home. 1Sa 31:4

⁵⁶ Thus God repaid the wickedness that Abimelek had done to his father by murdering his seventy brothers. ⁵⁷ God also made the people of Shechem pay for all their wickedness. The curse of

Jotham son of Jerub-Baal came on them.

Tola

10 After the time of Abimelek, a man of Issachar named Tola son of Puah, the son of Dodo, rose to save Israel. He lived in Shamir, in the hill country of Ephraim. ² He led^a Israel twenty-three years; then he died, and was buried in Shamir. Jdg 2:16; Ge 46:13

Jair

³ He was followed by Jair of Gilead, who led Israel twenty-two years. ⁴ He had thirty sons, who rode thirty donkeys. They controlled thirty towns in Gilead, which to this day are called Havvoth Jair.^b ⁵ When Jair died, he was buried in Kamon. Nu 32:41

Jephthah

⁶ Again the Israelites did evil in the eyes of the LORD. They served the Baals and the Ashtoreths, and the gods of Aram, the gods of Sidon, the gods of Moab, the gods of the Ammonites and the gods of the Philistines. And because the Israelites forsook the LORD and no longer served him, ⁷ he became angry with them. He sold them into the hands of the Philistines and the Ammonites, ⁸ who that year shattered and crushed them. For eighteen years they oppressed all the Israelites

^a 2 Traditionally *judged*; also in verse 3   ^b 4 Or *called the settlements of Jair*

on the east side of the Jordan in Gilead, the land of the Amorites. [9]The Ammonites also crossed the Jordan to fight against Judah, Benjamin and Ephraim; Israel was in great distress. [10]Then the Israelites cried out to the LORD, "We have sinned against you, forsaking our God and serving the Baals." Jdg 2:13; Dt 31:17; 1Sa 12:10

[11]The LORD replied, "When the Egyptians, the Amorites, the Ammonites, the Philistines, [12]the Sidonians, the Amalekites and the Maonites[a] oppressed you and you cried to me for help, did I not save you from their hands? [13]But you have forsaken me and served other gods, so I will no longer save you. [14]Go and cry out to the gods you have chosen. Let them save you when you are in trouble!" Dt 32:37; Jdg 3:13; Ps 106:42

[15]But the Israelites said to the LORD, "We have sinned. Do with us whatever you think best, but please rescue us now." [16]Then they got rid of the foreign gods among them and served the LORD. And he could bear Israel's misery no longer. Jos 24:23; 1Sa 3:18; Isa 63:9

[17]When the Ammonites were called to arms and camped in Gilead, the Israelites assembled and camped at Mizpah. [18]The leaders of the people of Gilead said to each other, "Whoever will take the lead in attacking the Ammonites will be head over all who live in Gilead." Jdg 11:8,9,29

11 Jephthah the Gileadite was a mighty warrior. His father was Gilead; his mother was a prostitute. [2]Gilead's wife also bore him sons, and when they were grown up, they drove Jephthah away. "You are not going to get any inheritance in our family," they said, "because you are the son of another woman." [3]So Jephthah fled from his brothers and settled in the land of Tob, where a gang of scoundrels gathered around him and followed him. Heb 11:32; 2Sa 10:6,8

[4]Some time later, when the Ammonites were fighting against Israel, [5]the elders of Gilead went to get Jephthah from the land of Tob. [6]"Come," they said, "be our commander, so we can fight the Ammonites." Jdg 10:9

[7]Jephthah said to them, "Didn't you hate me and drive me from my father's house? Why do you come to me now, when you're in trouble?" Ge 26:27

[8]The elders of Gilead said to him, "Nevertheless, we are turning to you now; come with us to fight the Ammonites, and you will be head over all of us who live in Gilead." Jdg 10:18

[9]Jephthah answered, "Suppose you take me back to fight the Ammonites and the LORD gives them to me—will I really be your head?"

[10]The elders of Gilead replied, "The LORD is our witness; we

---

[a] 12 Hebrew; some Septuagint manuscripts *Midianites*

will certainly do as you say." ¹¹ So Jephthah went with the elders of Gilead, and the people made him head and commander over them. And he repeated all his words before the LORD in Mizpah.   Jer 42:5

¹² Then Jephthah sent messengers to the Ammonite king with the question: "What do you have against me that you have attacked my country?"

¹³ The king of the Ammonites answered Jephthah's messengers, "When Israel came up out of Egypt, they took away my land from the Arnon to the Jabbok, all the way to the Jordan. Now give it back peaceably."   Nu 21:24

¹⁴ Jephthah sent back messengers to the Ammonite king, ¹⁵ saying:

"This is what Jephthah says: Israel did not take the land of Moab or the land of the Ammonites. ¹⁶ But when they came up out of Egypt, Israel went through the wilderness to the Red Sea*a* and on to Kadesh. ¹⁷ Then Israel sent messengers to the king of Edom, saying, 'Give us permission to go through your country,' but the king of Edom would not listen. They sent also to the king of Moab, and he refused. So Israel stayed at Kadesh.   Nu 20:14; Dt 1:40; 2:19

¹⁸ "Next they traveled through the wilderness, skirted the lands of Edom and Moab, passed along the eastern side of the country of Moab, and camped on the other side of the Arnon. They did not enter the territory of Moab, for the Arnon was its border.   Nu 21:4; Dt 2:8

¹⁹ "Then Israel sent messengers to Sihon king of the Amorites, who ruled in Heshbon, and said to him, 'Let us pass through your country to our own place.' ²⁰ Sihon, however, did not trust Israel*b* to pass through his territory. He mustered all his troops and encamped at Jahaz and fought with Israel.   Nu 21:21-22; Dt 2:32

²¹ "Then the LORD, the God of Israel, gave Sihon and his whole army into Israel's hands, and they defeated them. Israel took over all the land of the Amorites who lived in that country, ²² capturing all of it from the Arnon to the Jabbok and from the desert to the Jordan.   Dt 2:36

²³ "Now since the LORD, the God of Israel, has driven the Amorites out before his people Israel, what right have you to take it over? ²⁴ Will you not take what your god Chemosh gives you? Likewise, whatever the

---

a 16 Or *the Sea of Reeds*   *b* 20 Or *however, would not make an agreement for Israel*

Lord our God has given us, we will possess. [25] Are you any better than Balak son of Zippor, king of Moab? Did he ever quarrel with Israel or fight with them? [26] For three hundred years Israel occupied Heshbon, Aroer, the surrounding settlements and all the towns along the Arnon. Why didn't you retake them during that time? [27] I have not wronged you, but you are doing me wrong by waging war against me. Let the Lord, the Judge, decide the dispute this day between the Israelites and the Ammonites." Ge 16:5; 18:25

[28] The king of Ammon, however, paid no attention to the message Jephthah sent him.

[29] Then the Spirit of the Lord came on Jephthah. He crossed Gilead and Manasseh, passed through Mizpah of Gilead, and from there he advanced against the Ammonites. [30] And Jephthah made a vow to the Lord: "If you give the Ammonites into my hands, [31] whatever comes out of the door of my house to meet me when I return in triumph from the Ammonites will be the Lord's, and I will sacrifice it as a burnt offering." Jdg 3:10; Ge 28:20; Lev 1:3

[32] Then Jephthah went over to fight the Ammonites, and the Lord gave them into his hands. [33] He devastated twenty towns from Aroer to the vicinity of Minnith, as far as Abel Keramim. Thus Israel subdued Ammon. Eze 27:17

[34] When Jephthah returned to his home in Mizpah, who should come out to meet him but his daughter, dancing to the sound of timbrels! She was an only child. Except for her he had neither son nor daughter. [35] When he saw her, he tore his clothes and cried, "Oh no, my daughter! You have brought me down and I am devastated. I have made a vow to the Lord that I cannot break." Nu 30:2; Ecc 5:2,4-5; Jer 31:4

[36] "My father," she replied, "you have given your word to the Lord. Do to me just as you promised, now that the Lord has avenged you of your enemies, the Ammonites. [37] But grant me this one request," she said. "Give me two months to roam the hills and weep with my friends, because I will never marry."

[38] "You may go," he said. And he let her go for two months. She and her friends went into the hills and wept because she would never marry. [39] After the two months, she returned to her father, and he did to her as he had vowed. And she was a virgin.

From this comes the Israelite tradition [40] that each year the young women of Israel go out for four days to commemorate the daughter of Jephthah the Gileadite.

Jephthah and Ephraim

12 The Ephraimite forces were called out, and they crossed over to Zaphon. They said to Jephthah, "Why did you go to fight the Ammonites without calling us to go with you? We're going to burn down your house over your head." Jdg 8:1

² Jephthah answered, "I and my people were engaged in a great struggle with the Ammonites, and although I called, you didn't save me out of their hands. ³ When I saw that you wouldn't help, I took my life in my hands and crossed over to fight the Ammonites, and the LORD gave me the victory over them. Now why have you come up today to fight me?" 1Sa 19:5

⁴ Jephthah then called together the men of Gilead and fought against Ephraim. The Gileadites struck them down because the Ephraimites had said, "You Gileadites are renegades from Ephraim and Manasseh." ⁵ The Gileadites captured the fords of the Jordan leading to Ephraim, and whenever a survivor of Ephraim said, "Let me cross over," the men of Gilead asked him, "Are you an Ephraimite?" If he replied, "No," ⁶ they said, "All right, say 'Shibboleth.'" If he said, "Sibboleth," because he could not pronounce the word correctly, they seized him and killed him at the fords of the Jordan. Forty-two thousand Ephraimites were killed at that time. Jdg 3:28

⁷ Jephthah led*ᵃ* Israel six years. Then Jephthah the Gileadite died and was buried in a town in Gilead.

Ibzan, Elon and Abdon

⁸ After him, Ibzan of Bethlehem led Israel. ⁹ He had thirty sons and thirty daughters. He gave his daughters away in marriage to those outside his clan, and for his sons he brought in thirty young women as wives from outside his clan. Ibzan led Israel seven years. ¹⁰ Then Ibzan died and was buried in Bethlehem. Ge 35:19

¹¹ After him, Elon the Zebulunite led Israel ten years. ¹² Then Elon died and was buried in Aijalon in the land of Zebulun. Jos 10:12

¹³ After him, Abdon son of Hillel, from Pirathon, led Israel. ¹⁴ He had forty sons and thirty grandsons, who rode on seventy donkeys. He led Israel eight years. ¹⁵ Then Abdon son of Hillel died and was buried at Pirathon in Ephraim, in the hill country of the Amalekites. Jdg 5:10,14

The Birth of Samson

13 Again the Israelites did evil in the eyes of the LORD, so the LORD delivered them into the hands of the Philistines for forty years. Jdg 2:11; 14:4

ᵃ 7 Traditionally *judged*; also in verses 8-14

²A certain man of Zorah, named Manoah, from the clan of the Danites, had a wife who was childless, unable to give birth. ³The angel of the LORD appeared to her and said, "You are barren and childless, but you are going to become pregnant and give birth to a son. ⁴Now see to it that you drink no wine or other fermented drink and that you do not eat anything unclean. ⁵You will become pregnant and have a son whose head is never to be touched by a razor because the boy is to be a Nazirite, dedicated to God from the womb. He will take the lead in delivering Israel from the hands of the Philistines."   Nu 6:2,13; 1Sa 1:11; Lk 1:13

⁶Then the woman went to her husband and told him, "A man of God came to me. He looked like an angel of God, very awesome. I didn't ask him where he came from, and he didn't tell me his name. ⁷But he said to me, 'You will become pregnant and have a son. Now then, drink no wine or other fermented drink and do not eat anything unclean, because the boy will be a Nazirite of God from the womb until the day of his death.'"

⁸Then Manoah prayed to the LORD: "Pardon your servant, Lord. I beg you to let the man of God you sent to us come again to teach us how to bring up the boy who is to be born."

⁹God heard Manoah, and the angel of God came again to the woman while she was out in the field; but her husband Manoah was not with her. ¹⁰The woman hurried to tell her husband, "He's here! The man who appeared to me the other day!"

¹¹Manoah got up and followed his wife. When he came to the man, he said, "Are you the man who talked to my wife?"

"I am," he said.

¹²So Manoah asked him, "When your words are fulfilled, what is to be the rule that governs the boy's life and work?"

¹³The angel of the LORD answered, "Your wife must do all that I have told her. ¹⁴She must not eat anything that comes from the grapevine, nor drink any wine or other fermented drink nor eat anything unclean. She must do everything I have commanded her."   Nu 6:4

¹⁵Manoah said to the angel of the LORD, "We would like you to stay until we prepare a young goat for you."   Jdg 6:19

¹⁶The angel of the LORD replied, "Even though you detain me, I will not eat any of your food. But if you prepare a burnt offering, offer it to the LORD." (Manoah did not realize that it was the angel of the LORD.)

¹⁷Then Manoah inquired of the angel of the LORD, "What is your name, so that we may honor you when your word comes true?"   Ge 32:29

¹⁸He replied, "Why do you ask my name? It is beyond understanding.^a" ¹⁹Then Manoah took a young goat, together with the grain offering, and sacrificed it on a rock to the LORD. And the LORD did an amazing thing while Manoah and his wife watched: ²⁰As the flame blazed up from the altar toward heaven, the angel of the LORD ascended in the flame. Seeing this, Manoah and his wife fell with their faces to the ground. ²¹When the angel of the LORD did not show himself again to Manoah and his wife, Manoah realized that it was the angel of the LORD. Lev 9:24; 1Ch 21:16

²²"We are doomed to die!" he said to his wife. "We have seen God!" Dt 5:26

²³But his wife answered, "If the LORD had meant to kill us, he would not have accepted a burnt offering and grain offering from our hands, nor shown us all these things or now told us this." Ps 25:14

²⁴The woman gave birth to a boy and named him Samson. He grew and the LORD blessed him, ²⁵and the Spirit of the LORD began to stir him while he was in Mahaneh Dan, between Zorah and Eshtaol. 1Sa 3:19; Heb 11:32; Jdg 18:12

Samson's Marriage

14 Samson went down to Timnah and saw there a young Philistine woman. ²When he returned, he said to his father and mother, "I have seen a Philistine woman in Timnah; now get her for me as my wife." Ge 21:21; 34:4

³His father and mother replied, "Isn't there an acceptable woman among your relatives or among all our people? Must you go to the uncircumcised Philistines to get a wife?" Ge 24:4; Ex 34:16

But Samson said to his father, "Get her for me. She's the right one for me." ⁴(His parents did not know that this was from the LORD, who was seeking an occasion to confront the Philistines; for at that time they were ruling over Israel.) Jos 11:20

⁵Samson went down to Timnah together with his father and mother. As they approached the vineyards of Timnah, suddenly a young lion came roaring toward him. ⁶The Spirit of the LORD came powerfully upon him so that he tore the lion apart with his bare hands as he might have torn a young goat. But he told neither his father nor his mother what he had done. ⁷Then he went down and talked with the woman, and he liked her. Jdg 3:10; 13:1

⁸Some time later, when he went back to marry her, he turned aside to look at the lion's carcass, and in it he saw a swarm of bees and some honey. ⁹He scooped out the honey with his hands and ate as he went along.

---

^a 18 Or *is wonderful*

When he rejoined his parents, he gave them some, and they too ate it. But he did not tell them that he had taken the honey from the lion's carcass.

¹⁰ Now his father went down to see the woman. And there Samson held a feast, as was customary for young men. ¹¹ When the people saw him, they chose thirty men to be his companions.

¹² "Let me tell you a riddle," Samson said to them. "If you can give me the answer within the seven days of the feast, I will give you thirty linen garments and thirty sets of clothes. ¹³ If you can't tell me the answer, you must give me thirty linen garments and thirty sets of clothes."   Eze 17:2; Ge 29:27; 2Ki 5:5

"Tell us your riddle," they said. "Let's hear it."

¹⁴ He replied,

"Out of the eater, something
     to eat;
   out of the strong, something
     sweet."

For three days they could not give the answer.

¹⁵ On the fourth[a] day, they said to Samson's wife, "Coax your husband into explaining the riddle for us, or we will burn you and your father's household to death. Did you invite us here to steal our property?"   Jdg 15:6; 16:5; Ecc 7:26

¹⁶ Then Samson's wife threw herself on him, sobbing, "You hate me! You don't really love me. You've given my people a riddle, but you haven't told me the answer."   Jdg 16:15

"I haven't even explained it to my father or mother," he replied, "so why should I explain it to you?" ¹⁷ She cried the whole seven days of the feast. So on the seventh day he finally told her, because she continued to press him. She in turn explained the riddle to her people.

¹⁸ Before sunset on the seventh day the men of the town said to him,

"What is sweeter than
     honey?
   What is stronger than a
     lion?"

Samson said to them,

"If you had not plowed with
     my heifer,
   you would not have solved
     my riddle."

¹⁹ Then the Spirit of the LORD came powerfully upon him. He went down to Ashkelon, struck down thirty of their men, stripped them of everything and gave their clothes to those who had explained the riddle. Burning with anger, he returned to his father's home. ²⁰ And Samson's wife was given to one of his companions who had attended him at the feast.   Jdg 6:34; 1Sa 11:6; Isa 11:2

---

[a] 15 Some Septuagint manuscripts and Syriac; Hebrew *seventh*

Samson's Vengeance on the Philistines

15 Later on, at the time of wheat harvest, Samson took a young goat and went to visit his wife. He said, "I'm going to my wife's room." But her father would not let him go in.   Ge 38:17

[2] "I was so sure you hated her," he said, "that I gave her to your companion. Isn't her younger sister more attractive? Take her instead."   Jdg 14:20

[3] Samson said to them, "This time I have a right to get even with the Philistines; I will really harm them." [4] So he went out and caught three hundred foxes and tied them tail to tail in pairs. He then fastened a torch to every pair of tails, [5] lit the torches and let the foxes loose in the standing grain of the Philistines. He burned up the shocks and standing grain, together with the vineyards and olive groves.

[6] When the Philistines asked, "Who did this?" they were told, "Samson, the Timnite's son-in-law, because his wife was given to his companion."

So the Philistines went up and burned her and her father to death. [7] Samson said to them, "Since you've acted like this, I swear that I won't stop until I get my revenge on you." [8] He attacked them viciously and slaughtered many of them. Then he went down and stayed in a cave in the rock of Etam.   Jdg 14:15; Ge 38:24

[9] The Philistines went up and camped in Judah, spreading out near Lehi. [10] The people of Judah asked, "Why have you come to fight us?"

"We have come to take Samson prisoner," they answered, "to do to him as he did to us."

[11] Then three thousand men from Judah went down to the cave in the rock of Etam and said to Samson, "Don't you realize that the Philistines are rulers over us? What have you done to us?"   Jdg 13:1; 14:4

He answered, "I merely did to them what they did to me."

[12] They said to him, "We've come to tie you up and hand you over to the Philistines."

Samson said, "Swear to me that you won't kill me yourselves."   Ge 47:31

[13] "Agreed," they answered. "We will only tie you up and hand you over to them. We will not kill you." So they bound him with two new ropes and led him up from the rock. [14] As he approached Lehi, the Philistines came toward him shouting. The Spirit of the LORD came powerfully upon him. The ropes on his arms became like charred flax, and the bindings dropped from his hands. [15] Finding a fresh jawbone of a donkey, he grabbed it and struck down a thousand men.   Lev 26:8; Jos 23:10; Jdg 14:19

[16] Then Samson said,

"With a donkey's jawbone
    I have made donkeys of
    them.[a]
With a donkey's jawbone
    I have killed a thousand
    men."

[17] When he finished speaking, he threw away the jawbone; and the place was called Ramath Lehi.[b]

[18] Because he was very thirsty, he cried out to the LORD, "You have given your servant this great victory. Must I now die of thirst and fall into the hands of the uncircumcised?" [19] Then God opened up the hollow place in Lehi, and water came out of it. When Samson drank, his strength returned and he revived. So the spring was called En Hakkore,[c] and it is still there in Lehi.   Ge 45:27; Jdg 16:28; Isa 40:29

[20] Samson led[d] Israel for twenty years in the days of the Philistines.   Jdg 13:1; 16:31

Samson and Delilah

16 One day Samson went to Gaza, where he saw a prostitute. He went in to spend the night with her. [2] The people of Gaza were told, "Samson is here!" So they surrounded the place and lay in wait for him all night at the city gate. They made no move during the night, saying, "At dawn we'll kill him."   1Sa 19:11; Ps 118:10-12

[3] But Samson lay there only until the middle of the night. Then he got up and took hold of the doors of the city gate, together with the two posts, and tore them loose, bar and all. He lifted them to his shoulders and carried them to the top of the hill that faces Hebron.

[4] Some time later, he fell in love with a woman in the Valley of Sorek whose name was Delilah. [5] The rulers of the Philistines went to her and said, "See if you can lure him into showing you the secret of his great strength and how we can overpower him so we may tie him up and subdue him. Each one of us will give you eleven hundred shekels[e] of silver."   Ge 24:67; Jos 13:3; Jdg 14:15

[6] So Delilah said to Samson, "Tell me the secret of your great strength and how you can be tied up and subdued."

[7] Samson answered her, "If anyone ties me with seven fresh bowstrings that have not been dried, I'll become as weak as any other man."

[8] Then the rulers of the Philistines brought her seven fresh bowstrings that had not been dried, and she tied him with them. [9] With men hidden in the room, she called to him, "Samson, the Philistines are upon you!" But he snapped the bow-

---

[a] 16 Or *made a heap or two*; the Hebrew for *donkey* sounds like the Hebrew for *heap*.
[b] 17 *Ramath Lehi* means *jawbone hill*.   [c] 19 *En Hakkore* means *caller's spring*.
[d] 20 Traditionally *judged*   [e] 5 That is, about 28 pounds or about 13 kilograms

strings as easily as a piece of string snaps when it comes close to a flame. So the secret of his strength was not discovered.

¹⁰ Then Delilah said to Samson, "You have made a fool of me; you lied to me. Come now, tell me how you can be tied."

¹¹ He said, "If anyone ties me securely with new ropes that have never been used, I'll become as weak as any other man." Jdg 15:13

¹² So Delilah took new ropes and tied him with them. Then, with men hidden in the room, she called to him, "Samson, the Philistines are upon you!" But he snapped the ropes off his arms as if they were threads.

¹³ Delilah then said to Samson, "All this time you have been making a fool of me and lying to me. Tell me how you can be tied."

He replied, "If you weave the seven braids of my head into the fabric on the loom and tighten it with the pin, I'll become as weak as any other man." So while he was sleeping, Delilah took the seven braids of his head, wove them into the fabric ¹⁴ and ᵃ tightened it with the pin.

Again she called to him, "Samson, the Philistines are upon you!" He awoke from his sleep and pulled up the pin and the loom, with the fabric.

¹⁵ Then she said to him, "How can you say, 'I love you,' when you won't confide in me? This is the third time you have made a fool of me and haven't told me the secret of your great strength." ¹⁶ With such nagging she prodded him day after day until he was sick to death of it. Jdg 14:16

¹⁷ So he told her everything. "No razor has ever been used on my head," he said, "because I have been a Nazirite dedicated to God from my mother's womb. If my head were shaved, my strength would leave me, and I would become as weak as any other man." Nu 6:2,5; Mic 7:5

¹⁸ When Delilah saw that he had told her everything, she sent word to the rulers of the Philistines, "Come back once more; he has told me everything." So the rulers of the Philistines returned with the silver in their hands. ¹⁹ After putting him to sleep on her lap, she called for someone to shave off the seven braids of his hair, and so began to subdue him.ᵇ And his strength left him. Pr 7:26-27

²⁰ Then she called, "Samson, the Philistines are upon you!"

He awoke from his sleep and thought, "I'll go out as before and shake myself free." But he did not know that the Lord had left him. Nu 14:42; Jos 7:12; 1Sa 16:14

²¹ Then the Philistines seized

ᵃ 13,14 Some Septuagint manuscripts; Hebrew *replied, "I can if you weave the seven braids of my head into the fabric on the loom." ¹⁴So she* ᵇ 19 Hebrew; some Septuagint manuscripts *and he began to weaken* him, gouged out his eyes and took him down to Gaza. Binding him with bronze shackles, they set him to grinding grain in the prison. ²²But the hair on his head began to grow again after it had been shaved.   Jer 47:1

The Death of Samson

²³Now the rulers of the Philistines assembled to offer a great sacrifice to Dagon their god and to celebrate, saying, "Our god has delivered Samson, our enemy, into our hands."   1Sa 5:2
²⁴When the people saw him, they praised their god, saying,

"Our god has delivered our
          enemy
into our hands,   1Sa 31:9
the one who laid waste our
          land
     and multiplied our slain."

²⁵While they were in high spirits, they shouted, "Bring out Samson to entertain us." So they called Samson out of the prison, and he performed for them.   Jdg 9:27; Ru 3:7

When they stood him among the pillars, ²⁶Samson said to the servant who held his hand, "Put me where I can feel the pillars that support the temple, so that I may lean against them." ²⁷Now the temple was crowded with men and women; all the rulers of the Philistines were there, and on the roof were about three thousand men and wom-

en watching Samson perform. ²⁸Then Samson prayed to the LORD, "Sovereign LORD, remember me. Please, God, strengthen me just once more, and let me with one blow get revenge on the Philistines for my two eyes." ²⁹Then Samson reached toward the two central pillars on which the temple stood. Bracing himself against them, his right hand on the one and his left hand on the other, ³⁰Samson said, "Let me die with the Philistines!" Then he pushed with all his might, and down came the temple on the rulers and all the people in it. Thus he killed many more when he died than while he lived.   Jdg 15:18; Jer 15:15

³¹Then his brothers and his father's whole family went down to get him. They brought him back and buried him between Zorah and Eshtaol in the tomb of Manoah his father. He had led*a* Israel twenty years.   Jdg 13:2; Ru 1:1

Micah's Idols

17 Now a man named Micah from the hill country of Ephraim ²said to his mother, "The eleven hundred shekels*b* of silver that were taken from you and about which I heard you utter a curse—I have that silver with me; I took it."

Then his mother said, "The LORD bless you, my son!"   Ru 2:20
³When he returned the elev-

---

a 31 Traditionally *judged*   *b 2* That is, about 28 pounds or about 13 kilograms en hundred shekels of silver to his mother, she said, "I solemnly consecrate my silver to the LORD for my son to make an image overlaid with silver. I will give it back to you." Ex 20:4,23

[4] So after he returned the silver to his mother, she took two hundred shekels[a] of silver and gave them to a silversmith, who used them to make the idol. And it was put in Micah's house. Ex 32:4; Isa 17:8 [5] Now this man Micah had a shrine, and he made an ephod and some household gods and installed one of his sons as his priest. [6] In those days Israel had no king; everyone did as they saw fit. Dt 12:8; Jdg 8:27; 19:1

[7] A young Levite from Bethlehem in Judah, who had been living within the clan of Judah, [8] left that town in search of some other place to stay. On his way[b] he came to Micah's house in the hill country of Ephraim. Jdg 19:1; Mic 5:2; Mt 2:1 [9] Micah asked him, "Where are you from?"

"I'm a Levite from Bethlehem in Judah," he said, "and I'm looking for a place to stay."

[10] Then Micah said to him, "Live with me and be my father and priest, and I'll give you ten shekels[c] of silver a year, your clothes and your food." [11] So the Levite agreed to live with him, and the young man became like one of his sons to him. [12] Then Micah in-

stalled the Levite, and the young man became his priest and lived in his house. [13] And Micah said, "Now I know that the LORD will be good to me, since this Levite has become my priest." Nu 18:7; Jdg 18:19

The Danites Settle in Laish

18 In those days Israel had no king. Jdg 17:6 And in those days the tribe of the Danites was seeking a place of their own where they might settle, because they had not yet come into an inheritance among the tribes of Israel. [2] So the Danites sent five of their leading men from Zorah and Eshtaol to spy out the land and explore it. These men represented all the Danites. They told them, "Go, explore the land." Jos 2:1; 19:47; Jdg 13:25

So they entered the hill country of Ephraim and came to the house of Micah, where they spent the night. [3] When they were near Micah's house, they recognized the voice of the young Levite; so they turned in there and asked him, "Who brought you here? What are you doing in this place? Why are you here?" Jdg 17:1

[4] He told them what Micah had done for him, and said, "He has hired me and I am his priest."

[5] Then they said to him, "Please inquire of God to learn whether our journey will be successful." Ge 25:22; 2Sa 5:19; 1Ki 22:5

---

[a] 4 That is, about 5 pounds or about 2.3 kilograms   [b] 8 Or *To carry on his profession*
[c] 10 That is, about 4 ounces or about 115 grams

⁶The priest answered them, "Go in peace. Your journey has the LORD's approval."

⁷So the five men left and came to Laish, where they saw that the people were living in safety, like the Sidonians, at peace and secure. And since their land lacked nothing, they were prosperous.ᵃ Also, they lived a long way from the Sidonians and had no relationship with anyone else.ᵇ   Ge 34:25; Jos 19:47

⁸When they returned to Zorah and Eshtaol, their fellow Danites asked them, "How did you find things?"

⁹They answered, "Come on, let's attack them! We have seen the land, and it is very good. Aren't you going to do something? Don't hesitate to go there and take it over. ¹⁰When you get there, you will find an unsuspecting people and a spacious land that God has put into your hands, a land that lacks nothing whatever."   Nu 13:30; Dt 8:9; 1Ki 22:3

¹¹Then six hundred men of the Danites, armed for battle, set out from Zorah and Eshtaol. ¹²On their way they set up camp near Kiriath Jearim in Judah. This is why the place west of Kiriath Jearim is called Mahaneh Danᶜ to this day. ¹³From there they went on to the hill country of Ephraim and came to Micah's house.   Jdg 13:25

¹⁴Then the five men who had spied out the land of Laish said to their fellow Danites, "Do you know that one of these houses has an ephod, some household gods and an image overlaid with silver? Now you know what to do." ¹⁵So they turned in there and went to the house of the young Levite at Micah's place and greeted him. ¹⁶The six hundred Danites, armed for battle, stood at the entrance of the gate. ¹⁷The five men who had spied out the land went inside and took the idol, the ephod and the household gods while the priest and the six hundred armed men stood at the entrance of the gate.   Ge 31:19; Jdg 17:5; Mic 5:13

¹⁸When the five men went into Micah's house and took the idol, the ephod and the household gods, the priest said to them, "What are you doing?"

¹⁹They answered him, "Be quiet! Don't say a word. Come with us, and be our father and priest. Isn't it better that you serve a tribe and clan in Israel as priest rather than just one man's household?" ²⁰The priest was very pleased. He took the ephod, the household gods and the idol and went along with the people. ²¹Putting their little children, their livestock and their possessions in front of them, they turned away and left.   Jdg 17:10; Job 21:5; 29:9

²²When they had gone some

ᵃ 7 The meaning of the Hebrew for this clause is uncertain.   ᵇ 7 Hebrew; some Septuagint manuscripts *with the Arameans*   ᶜ 12 *Mahaneh Dan* means *Dan's camp*.

distance from Micah's house, the men who lived near Micah were called together and overtook the Danites. ²³As they shouted after them, the Danites turned and said to Micah, "What's the matter with you that you called out your men to fight?"

²⁴He replied, "You took the gods I made, and my priest, and went away. What else do I have? How can you ask, 'What's the matter with you?'"

²⁵The Danites answered, "Don't argue with us, or some of the men may get angry and attack you, and you and your family will lose your lives." ²⁶So the Danites went their way, and Micah, seeing that they were too strong for him, turned around and went back home. Ps 18:17

²⁷Then they took what Micah had made, and his priest, and went on to Laish, against a people at peace and secure. They attacked them with the sword and burned down their city. ²⁸There was no one to rescue them because they lived a long way from Sidon and had no relationship with anyone else. The city was in a valley near Beth Rehob. Jos 19:47; 2Sa 10:6

The Danites rebuilt the city and settled there. ²⁹They named it Dan after their ancestor Dan, who was born to Israel — though the city used to be called Laish.

³⁰There the Danites set up for themselves the idol, and Jonathan son of Gershom, the son of Moses,ᵃ and his sons were priests for the tribe of Dan until the time of the captivity of the land. ³¹They continued to use the idol Micah had made, all the time the house of God was in Shiloh. Ex 2:22; Jos 19:47; 18:1

A Levite and His Concubine

19 In those days Israel had no king.

Now a Levite who lived in a remote area in the hill country of Ephraim took a concubine from Bethlehem in Judah. ²But she was unfaithful to him. She left him and went back to her parents' home in Bethlehem, Judah. After she had been there four months, ³her husband went to her to persuade her to return. He had with him his servant and two donkeys. She took him into her parents' home, and when her father saw him, he gladly welcomed him. ⁴His father-in-law, the woman's father, prevailed on him to stay; so he remained with him three days, eating and drinking, and sleeping there. Ex 32:6

⁵On the fourth day they got up early and he prepared to leave, but the woman's father said to his son-in-law, "Refresh yourself with something to eat; then you can go." ⁶So the two of them sat

ᵃ 30 Many Hebrew manuscripts, some Septuagint manuscripts and Vulgate; many other Hebrew manuscripts and some other Septuagint manuscripts *Manasseh* down to eat and drink together. Afterward the woman's father said, "Please stay tonight and enjoy yourself." ⁷ And when the man got up to go, his father-in-law persuaded him, so he stayed there that night. ⁸ On the morning of the fifth day, when he rose to go, the woman's father said, "Refresh yourself. Wait till afternoon!" So the two of them ate together.

⁹ Then when the man, with his concubine and his servant, got up to leave, his father-in-law, the woman's father, said, "Now look, it's almost evening. Spend the night here; the day is nearly over. Stay and enjoy yourself. Early tomorrow morning you can get up and be on your way home." ¹⁰ But, unwilling to stay another night, the man left and went toward Jebus (that is, Jerusalem), with his two saddled donkeys and his concubine.   1Ch 11:4-5

¹¹ When they were near Jebus and the day was almost gone, the servant said to his master, "Come, let's stop at this city of the Jebusites and spend the night."

¹² His master replied, "No. We won't go into any city whose people are not Israelites. We will go on to Gibeah." ¹³ He added, "Come, let's try to reach Gibeah or Ramah and spend the night in one of those places." ¹⁴ So they went on, and the sun set as they neared Gibeah in Benjamin. ¹⁵ There they stopped to spend the night. They went and sat in the city square, but no one took them in for the night.   Ge 19:2; 1Sa 10:26

¹⁶ That evening an old man from the hill country of Ephraim, who was living in Gibeah (the inhabitants of the place were Benjamites), came in from his work in the fields. ¹⁷ When he looked and saw the traveler in the city square, the old man asked, "Where are you going? Where did you come from?"   Ps 104:23

¹⁸ He answered, "We are on our way from Bethlehem in Judah to a remote area in the hill country of Ephraim where I live. I have been to Bethlehem in Judah and now I am going to the house of the LORD.^a No one has taken me in for the night. ¹⁹ We have both straw and fodder for our donkeys and bread and wine for ourselves your servants — me, the woman and the young man with us. We don't need anything."   Jdg 18:31

²⁰ "You are welcome at my house," the old man said. "Let me supply whatever you need. Only don't spend the night in the square." ²¹ So he took him into his house and fed his donkeys. After they had washed their feet, they had something to eat and drink.   Ge 24:32-33; Lk 7:44

²² While they were enjoying themselves, some of the wicked men of the city surrounded the house. Pounding on the door, they shouted to the old man who

^a 18 Hebrew, Vulgate, Syriac and Targum; Septuagint *going home*

owned the house, "Bring out the man who came to your house so we can have sex with him." Ge 19:4

²³The owner of the house went outside and said to them, "No, my friends, don't be so vile. Since this man is my guest, don't do this outrageous thing. ²⁴Look, here is my virgin daughter, and his concubine. I will bring them out to you now, and you can use them and do to them whatever you wish. But as for this man, don't do such an outrageous thing." Ge 34:7; Dt 22:21; 2Sa 13:12

²⁵But the men would not listen to him. So the man took his concubine and sent her outside to them, and they raped her and abused her throughout the night, and at dawn they let her go. ²⁶At daybreak the woman went back to the house where her master was staying, fell down at the door and lay there until daylight. Jdg 20:5; 1Sa 31:4

²⁷When her master got up in the morning and opened the door of the house and stepped out to continue on his way, there lay his concubine, fallen in the doorway of the house, with her hands on the threshold. ²⁸He said to her, "Get up; let's go." But there was no answer. Then the man put her on his donkey and set out for home.

²⁹When he reached home, he took a knife and cut up his concubine, limb by limb, into twelve parts and sent them into all the areas of Israel. ³⁰Everyone who saw it was saying to one another, "Such a thing has never been seen or done, not since the day the Israelites came up out of Egypt. Just imagine! We must do something! So speak up!" Jdg 20:7; 1Sa 11:7

The Israelites Punish the Benjamites

20 Then all Israel from Dan to Beersheba and from the land of Gilead came together as one and assembled before the LORD in Mizpah. ²The leaders of all the people of the tribes of Israel took their places in the assembly of God's people, four hundred thousand men armed with swords. ³(The Benjamites heard that the Israelites had gone up to Mizpah.) Then the Israelites said, "Tell us how this awful thing happened." Jdg 8:10; 21:5; 1Sa 7:5

⁴So the Levite, the husband of the murdered woman, said, "I and my concubine came to Gibeah in Benjamin to spend the night. ⁵During the night the men of Gibeah came after me and surrounded the house, intending to kill me. They raped my concubine, and she died. ⁶I took my concubine, cut her into pieces and sent one piece to each region of Israel's inheritance, because they committed this lewd and outrageous act in Israel. ⁷Now, all you Israelites, speak up and tell me what you have decided to do." Jos 7:15; Jdg 19:25-26

⁸All the men rose up together as one, saying, "None of us will go home. No, not one of us will return to his house. ⁹But now this is what we'll do to Gibeah: We'll go up against it in the order decided by casting lots. ¹⁰We'll take ten men out of every hundred from all the tribes of Israel, and a hundred from a thousand, and a thousand from ten thousand, to get provisions for the army. Then, when the army arrives at Gibeah*a* in Benjamin, it can give them what they deserve for this outrageous act done in Israel." ¹¹So all the Israelites got together and united as one against the city.

¹²The tribes of Israel sent messengers throughout the tribe of Benjamin, saying, "What about this awful crime that was committed among you? ¹³Now turn those wicked men of Gibeah over to us so that we may put them to death and purge the evil from Israel." Dt 13:13

But the Benjamites would not listen to their fellow Israelites. ¹⁴From their towns they came together at Gibeah to fight against the Israelites. ¹⁵At once the Benjamites mobilized twenty-six thousand swordsmen from their towns, in addition to seven hundred able young men from those living in Gibeah. ¹⁶Among all these soldiers there were sev-

en hundred select troops who were left-handed, each of whom could sling a stone at a hair and not miss. Jdg 3:15; 1Ch 12:2

¹⁷Israel, apart from Benjamin, mustered four hundred thousand swordsmen, all of them fit for battle.

¹⁸The Israelites went up to Bethel*b* and inquired of God. They said, "Who of us is to go up first to fight against the Benjamites?" Jos 12:9; Jdg 18:5

The LORD replied, "Judah shall go first."

¹⁹The next morning the Israelites got up and pitched camp near Gibeah. ²⁰The Israelites went out to fight the Benjamites and took up battle positions against them at Gibeah. ²¹The Benjamites came out of Gibeah and cut down twenty-two thousand Israelites on the battlefield that day. ²²But the Israelites encouraged one another and again took up their positions where they had stationed themselves the first day. ²³The Israelites went up and wept before the LORD until evening, and they inquired of the LORD. They said, "Shall we go up again to fight against the Benjamites, our fellow Israelites?" Nu 14:1; Jos 7:6

The LORD answered, "Go up against them."

²⁴Then the Israelites drew near to Benjamin the second

---

a 10 One Hebrew manuscript; most Hebrew manuscripts *Geba*, a variant of *Gibeah*
b 18 Or *to the house of God*; also in verse 26

day. ²⁵This time, when the Benjamites came out from Gibeah to oppose them, they cut down another eighteen thousand Israelites, all of them armed with swords.

²⁶Then all the Israelites, the whole army, went up to Bethel, and there they sat weeping before the LORD. They fasted that day until evening and presented burnt offerings and fellowship offerings to the LORD. ²⁷And the Israelites inquired of the LORD. (In those days the ark of the covenant of God was there, ²⁸with Phinehas son of Eleazar, the son of Aaron, ministering before it.) They asked, "Shall we go up again to fight against the Benjamites, our fellow Israelites, or not?" Dt 18:5; Jdg 21:4

The LORD responded, "Go, for tomorrow I will give them into your hands." Jdg 7:9

²⁹Then Israel set an ambush around Gibeah. ³⁰They went up against the Benjamites on the third day and took up positions against Gibeah as they had done before. ³¹The Benjamites came out to meet them and were drawn away from the city. They began to inflict casualties on the Israelites as before, so that about thirty men fell in the open field and on the roads — the one leading to Bethel and the other to Gibeah. ³²While the Benjamites were saying, "We are defeating them as before," the Israelites were saying, "Let's retreat and draw them away from the city to the roads." Jos 8:2,4

³³All the men of Israel moved from their places and took up positions at Baal Tamar, and the Israelite ambush charged out of its place on the west[a] of Gibeah.[b] ³⁴Then ten thousand of Israel's able young men made a frontal attack on Gibeah. The fighting was so heavy that the Benjamites did not realize how near disaster was. ³⁵The LORD defeated Benjamin before Israel, and on that day the Israelites struck down 25,100 Benjamites, all armed with swords. ³⁶Then the Benjamites saw that they were beaten. Jos 8:19; 1Sa 9:21

Now the men of Israel had given way before Benjamin, because they relied on the ambush they had set near Gibeah. ³⁷Those who had been in ambush made a sudden dash into Gibeah, spread out and put the whole city to the sword. ³⁸The Israelites had arranged with the ambush that they should send up a great cloud of smoke from the city, ³⁹and then the Israelites would counterattack. Jos 8:15

The Benjamites had begun to inflict casualties on the Israelites (about thirty), and they said, "We are defeating them as in the first

---

^a 33 Some Septuagint manuscripts and Vulgate; the meaning of the Hebrew for this word is uncertain.   ^b 33 Hebrew *Geba,* a variant of *Gibeah*

battle." **40** But when the column of smoke began to rise from the city, the Benjamites turned and saw the whole city going up in smoke. **41** Then the Israelites counterattacked, and the Benjamites were terrified, because they realized that disaster had come on them. **42** So they fled before the Israelites in the direction of the wilderness, but they could not escape the battle. And the Israelites who came out of the towns cut them down there. **43** They surrounded the Benjamites, chased them and easily*a* overran them in the vicinity of Gibeah on the east. **44** Eighteen thousand Benjamites fell, all of them valiant fighters. **45** As they turned and fled toward the wilderness to the rock of Rimmon, the Israelites cut down five thousand men along the roads. They kept pressing after the Benjamites as far as Gidom and struck down two thousand more. Jos 15:32; Jdg 21:13

46 On that day twenty-five thousand Benjamite swordsmen fell, all of them valiant fighters. **47** But six hundred of them turned and fled into the wilderness to the rock of Rimmon, where they stayed four months. **48** The men of Israel went back to Benjamin and put all the towns to the sword, including the animals and everything else they found. All the towns they came across they set on fire. 1Sa 9:21

Wives for the Benjamites

21 The men of Israel had taken an oath at Mizpah: "Not one of us will give his daughter in marriage to a Benjamite." Jos 9:18; Jdg 20:1

2 The people went to Bethel,*b* where they sat before God until evening, raising their voices and weeping bitterly. **3** "LORD, God of Israel," they cried, "why has this happened to Israel? Why should one tribe be missing from Israel today?"

4 Early the next day the people built an altar and presented burnt offerings and fellowship offerings. Jdg 20:26; 2Sa 24:25

5 Then the Israelites asked, "Who from all the tribes of Israel has failed to assemble before the LORD?" For they had taken a solemn oath that anyone who failed to assemble before the LORD at Mizpah was to be put to death. Jdg 5:23

6 Now the Israelites grieved for the tribe of Benjamin, their fellow Israelites. "Today one tribe is cut off from Israel," they said. **7** "How can we provide wives for those who are left, since we have taken an oath by the LORD not to give them any of our daughters in marriage?" **8** Then they asked, "Which one of the tribes of Israel failed to assemble before the LORD at Mizpah?" They discovered that no one from Jabesh Gil-

---

a 43 The meaning of the Hebrew for this word is uncertain.   *b* 2 Or *to the house of God* ead had come to the camp for the assembly. ⁹For when they counted the people, they found that none of the people of Jabesh Gilead were there. 1Sa 11:1

¹⁰So the assembly sent twelve thousand fighting men with instructions to go to Jabesh Gilead and put to the sword those living there, including the women and children. ¹¹"This is what you are to do," they said. "Kill every male and every woman who is not a virgin." ¹²They found among the people living in Jabesh Gilead four hundred young women who had never slept with a man, and they took them to the camp at Shiloh in Canaan. Nu 31:17-18; Jos 18:1

¹³Then the whole assembly sent an offer of peace to the Benjamites at the rock of Rimmon. ¹⁴So the Benjamites returned at that time and were given the women of Jabesh Gilead who had been spared. But there were not enough for all of them. Jdg 20:47

¹⁵The people grieved for Benjamin, because the LORD had made a gap in the tribes of Israel. ¹⁶And the elders of the assembly said, "With the women of Benjamin destroyed, how shall we provide wives for the men who are left? ¹⁷The Benjamite survivors must have heirs," they said, "so that a tribe of Israel will not be wiped out. ¹⁸We can't give them our daughters as wives, since we

Israelites have taken this oath: 'Cursed be anyone who gives a wife to a Benjamite.' ¹⁹But look, there is the annual festival of the LORD in Shiloh, which lies north of Bethel, east of the road that goes from Bethel to Shechem, and south of Lebonah." Jos 16:1; 1Sa 1:3

²⁰So they instructed the Benjamites, saying, "Go and hide in the vineyards ²¹and watch. When the young women of Shiloh come out to join in the dancing, rush from the vineyards and each of you seize one of them to be your wife. Then return to the land of Benjamin. ²²When their fathers or brothers complain to us, we will say to them, 'Do us the favor of helping them, because we did not get wives for them during the war. You will not be guilty of breaking your oath because you did not give your daughters to them.'" Ex 15:20; Jdg 11:34

²³So that is what the Benjamites did. While the young women were dancing, each man caught one and carried her off to be his wife. Then they returned to their inheritance and rebuilt the towns and settled in them. Jdg 20:48

²⁴At that time the Israelites left that place and went home to their tribes and clans, each to his own inheritance.

²⁵In those days Israel had no king; everyone did as they saw fit. Jdg 17:6; 18:1; 19:1

Ruth

Naomi Loses Her Husband and Sons

1 In the days when the judges ruled,[a] there was a famine in the land. So a man from Bethlehem in Judah, together with his wife and two sons, went to live for a while in the country of Moab. [2]The man's name was Elimelek, his wife's name was Naomi, and the names of his two sons were Mahlon and Kilion. They were Ephrathites from Bethlehem, Judah. And they went to Moab and lived there. Ge 35:19; Jdg 2:16-18; 3:30

[3]Now Elimelek, Naomi's husband, died, and she was left with her two sons. [4]They married Moabite women, one named Orpah and the other Ruth. After they had lived there about ten years, [5]both Mahlon and Kilion also died, and Naomi was left without her two sons and her husband. Mt 1:5

Naomi and Ruth Return to Bethlehem

[6]When Naomi heard in Moab that the LORD had come to the aid of his people by providing food for them, she and her daughters-in-law prepared to return home from there. [7]With her two daughters-in-law she left the place where she had been living and set out on the road that would take them back to the land of Judah. Ex 4:31; Mt 6:11

[8]Then Naomi said to her two daughters-in-law, "Go back, each of you, to your mother's home. May the LORD show you kindness, as you have shown kindness to your dead husbands and to me. [9]May the LORD grant that each of you will find rest in the home of another husband." Ru 2:20; 3:1; 2Ti 1:16

Then she kissed them goodbye and they wept aloud [10]and said to her, "We will go back with you to your people."

[11]But Naomi said, "Return home, my daughters. Why would you come with me? Am I going to have any more sons, who could become your husbands? [12]Return home, my daughters; I am too old to have another husband.

Even if I thought there was still hope for me — even if I had a husband tonight and then gave birth to sons — [13] would you wait until they grew up? Would you remain unmarried for them? No, my daughters. It is more bitter for me than for you, because the LORD's hand has turned against me!" Ge 38:11; Jdg 2:15; Job 19:21

[14] At this they wept aloud again. Then Orpah kissed her mother-in-law goodbye, but Ruth clung to her. Pr 17:17; 18:24

[15] "Look," said Naomi, "your sister-in-law is going back to her people and her gods. Go back with her." Jos 24:14; Jdg 11:24

[16] But Ruth replied, "Don't urge me to leave you or to turn back from you. Where you go I will go, and where you stay I will stay. Your people will be my people and your God my God. [17] Where you die I will die, and there I will be buried. May the LORD deal with me, be it ever so severely, if even death separates you and me." [18] When Naomi realized that Ruth was determined to go with her, she stopped urging her. 1Sa 3:17; 2Ki 2:2; Ac 21:14

[19] So the two women went on until they came to Bethlehem. When they arrived in Bethlehem, the whole town was stirred because of them, and the women exclaimed, "Can this be Naomi?" Mt 21:10

[20] "Don't call me Naomi,[a]" she told them. "Call me Mara,[b] because the Almighty[c] has made my life very bitter. [21] I went away full, but the LORD has brought me back empty. Why call me Naomi? The LORD has afflicted[d] me; the Almighty has brought misfortune upon me." Job 1:21

[22] So Naomi returned from Moab accompanied by Ruth the Moabite, her daughter-in-law, arriving in Bethlehem as the barley harvest was beginning. Ex 9:31

Ruth Meets Boaz in the Grain Field

2 Now Naomi had a relative on her husband's side, a man of standing from the clan of Elimelek, whose name was Boaz. Ru 1:2; 3:2,12

[2] And Ruth the Moabite said to Naomi, "Let me go to the fields and pick up the leftover grain behind anyone in whose eyes I find favor." Lev 19:9; Dt 24:19

Naomi said to her, "Go ahead, my daughter." [3] So she went out, entered a field and began to glean behind the harvesters. As it turned out, she was working in a field belonging to Boaz, who was from the clan of Elimelek.

[4] Just then Boaz arrived from Bethlehem and greeted the harvesters, "The LORD be with you!"

"The LORD bless you!" they answered. Ps 129:7-8

---

[a] 20 Naomi means pleasant. [b] 20 Mara means bitter. [c] 20 Hebrew Shaddai; also in verse 21 [d] 21 Or has testified against

⁵Boaz asked the overseer of his harvesters, "Who does that young woman belong to?"

⁶The overseer replied, "She is the Moabite who came back from Moab with Naomi. ⁷She said, 'Please let me glean and gather among the sheaves behind the harvesters.' She came into the field and has remained here from morning till now, except for a short rest in the shelter." Ru 1:22

⁸So Boaz said to Ruth, "My daughter, listen to me. Don't go and glean in another field and don't go away from here. Stay here with the women who work for me. ⁹Watch the field where the men are harvesting, and follow along after the women. I have told the men not to lay a hand on you. And whenever you are thirsty, go and get a drink from the water jars the men have filled."

¹⁰At this, she bowed down with her face to the ground. She asked him, "Why have I found such favor in your eyes that you notice me—a foreigner?" 1Sa 25:23

¹¹Boaz replied, "I've been told all about what you have done for your mother-in-law since the death of your husband—how you left your father and mother and your homeland and came to live with a people you did not know before. ¹²May the LORD repay you for what you have done. May you be richly rewarded by the LORD,

the God of Israel, under whose wings you have come to take refuge." Ru 1:14; 1Sa 24:19; Ps 17:8

¹³"May I continue to find favor in your eyes, my lord," she said. "You have put me at ease by speaking kindly to your servant—though I do not have the standing of one of your servants." Ge 18:3

¹⁴At mealtime Boaz said to her, "Come over here. Have some bread and dip it in the wine vinegar."

When she sat down with the harvesters, he offered her some roasted grain. She ate all she wanted and had some left over. ¹⁵As she got up to glean, Boaz gave orders to his men, "Let her gather among the sheaves and don't reprimand her. ¹⁶Even pull out some stalks for her from the bundles and leave them for her to pick up, and don't rebuke her."

¹⁷So Ruth gleaned in the field until evening. Then she threshed the barley she had gathered, and it amounted to about an ephah.ᵃ ¹⁸She carried it back to town, and her mother-in-law saw how much she had gathered. Ruth also brought out and gave her what she had left over after she had eaten enough.

¹⁹Her mother-in-law asked her, "Where did you glean today? Where did you work? Blessed be the man who took notice of you!" Ps 41:1

Then Ruth told her mother-in-

ᵃ 17 That is, probably about 30 pounds or about 13 kilograms law about the one at whose place she had been working. "The name of the man I worked with today is Boaz," she said.

²⁰"The LORD bless him!" Naomi said to her daughter-in-law. "He has not stopped showing his kindness to the living and the dead." She added, "That man is our close relative; he is one of our guardian-redeemers.^a" Ru 3:10

²¹Then Ruth the Moabite said, "He even said to me, 'Stay with my workers until they finish harvesting all my grain.'"

²²Naomi said to Ruth her daughter-in-law, "It will be good for you, my daughter, to go with the women who work for him, because in someone else's field you might be harmed."

²³So Ruth stayed close to the women of Boaz to glean until the barley and wheat harvests were finished. And she lived with her mother-in-law. Dt 16:9

Ruth and Boaz at the Threshing Floor

3 One day Ruth's mother-in-law Naomi said to her, "My daughter, I must find a home^b for you, where you will be well provided for. ²Now Boaz, with whose women you have worked, is a relative of ours. Tonight he will be winnowing barley on the threshing floor. ³Wash, put on perfume, and get dressed in your best clothes. Then go down to the threshing floor, but don't let him know you are there until he has finished eating and drinking. ⁴When he lies down, note the place where he is lying. Then go and uncover his feet and lie down. He will tell you what to do." Ru 2:1; 2Sa 14:2

⁵"I will do whatever you say," Ruth answered. ⁶So she went down to the threshing floor and did everything her mother-in-law told her to do. Eph 6:1; Col 3:20

⁷When Boaz had finished eating and drinking and was in good spirits, he went over to lie down at the far end of the grain pile. Ruth approached quietly, uncovered his feet and lay down. ⁸In the middle of the night something startled the man; he turned—and there was a woman lying at his feet! Jdg 19:6,9,22; 2Sa 13:28; 1Ki 21:7

⁹"Who are you?" he asked.

"I am your servant Ruth," she said. "Spread the corner of your garment over me, since you are a guardian-redeemer^c of our family." Ru 2:20

¹⁰"The LORD bless you, my daughter," he replied. "This kindness is greater than that which you showed earlier: You have not run after the younger men,

^a 20 The Hebrew word for *guardian-redeemer* is a legal term for one who has the obligation to redeem a relative in serious difficulty (see Lev. 25:25-55). ^b 1 Hebrew *find rest* (see 1:9) ^c 9 The Hebrew word for *guardian-redeemer* is a legal term for one who has the obligation to redeem a relative in serious difficulty (see Lev. 25:25-55); also in verses 12 and 13.

whether rich or poor. ¹¹And now, my daughter, don't be afraid. I will do for you all you ask. All the people of my town know that you are a woman of noble character. ¹²Although it is true that I am a guardian-redeemer of our family, there is another who is more closely related than I. ¹³Stay here for the night, and in the morning if he wants to do his duty as your guardian-redeemer, good; let him redeem you. But if he is not willing, as surely as the LORD lives I will do it. Lie here until morning." Dt 25:5; Pr 12:4; Mt 22:24

¹⁴So she lay at his feet until morning, but got up before anyone could be recognized; and he said, "No one must know that a woman came to the threshing floor." Ro 14:16; 2Co 8:21

¹⁵He also said, "Bring me the shawl you are wearing and hold it out." When she did so, he poured into it six measures of barley and placed the bundle on her. Then he^a went back to town.

¹⁶When Ruth came to her mother-in-law, Naomi asked, "How did it go, my daughter?"

Then she told her everything Boaz had done for her ¹⁷and added, "He gave me these six measures of barley, saying, 'Don't go back to your mother-in-law empty-handed.'"

¹⁸Then Naomi said, "Wait, my daughter, until you find out what happens. For the man will not rest until the matter is settled today." Ps 37:3-5

Boaz Marries Ruth

4 Meanwhile Boaz went up to the town gate and sat down there just as the guardian-redeemer^b he had mentioned came along. Boaz said, "Come over here, my friend, and sit down." So he went over and sat down. Ru 3:12

²Boaz took ten of the elders of the town and said, "Sit here," and they did so. ³Then he said to the guardian-redeemer, "Naomi, who has come back from Moab, is selling the piece of land that belonged to our relative Elimelek. ⁴I thought I should bring the matter to your attention and suggest that you buy it in the presence of these seated here and in the presence of the elders of my people. If you will redeem it, do so. But if you^c will not, tell me, so I will know. For no one has the right to do it except you, and I am next in line." Lev 25:25; Jer 32:7-8; 1Ki 21:8

"I will redeem it," he said.

⁵Then Boaz said, "On the day you buy the land from Naomi, you also acquire Ruth the Moabite,

---

^a 15 Most Hebrew manuscripts; many Hebrew manuscripts, Vulgate and Syriac *she*
^b 1 The Hebrew word for *guardian-redeemer* is a legal term for one who has the obligation to redeem a relative in serious difficulty (see Lev. 25:25-55); also in verses 3, 6, 8 and 14.
^c 4 Many Hebrew manuscripts, Septuagint, Vulgate and Syriac; most Hebrew manuscripts *he*

the[a] dead man's widow, in order to maintain the name of the dead with his property." Ge 38:8; Dt 25:5-6

⁶At this, the guardian-redeemer said, "Then I cannot redeem it because I might endanger my own estate. You redeem it yourself. I cannot do it." Ru 3:13

⁷(Now in earlier times in Israel, for the redemption and transfer of property to become final, one party took off his sandal and gave it to the other. This was the method of legalizing transactions in Israel.) Dt 25:7-9

⁸So the guardian-redeemer said to Boaz, "Buy it yourself." And he removed his sandal.

⁹Then Boaz announced to the elders and all the people, "Today you are witnesses that I have bought from Naomi all the property of Elimelek, Kilion and Mahlon. ¹⁰I have also acquired Ruth the Moabite, Mahlon's widow, as my wife, in order to maintain the name of the dead with his property, so that his name will not disappear from among his family or from his hometown. Today you are witnesses!"

¹¹Then the elders and all the people at the gate said, "We are witnesses. May the LORD make the woman who is coming into your home like Rachel and Leah, who together built up the family of Israel. May you have standing in Ephrathah and be famous in Bethlehem. ¹²Through the offspring the LORD gives you by this young woman, may your family be like that of Perez, whom Tamar bore to Judah." Ps 127:3; 128:3; Ge 38:29

Naomi Gains a Son

¹³So Boaz took Ruth and she became his wife. When he made love to her, the LORD enabled her to conceive, and she gave birth to a son. ¹⁴The women said to Naomi: "Praise be to the LORD, who this day has not left you without a guardian-redeemer. May he become famous throughout Israel! ¹⁵He will renew your life and sustain you in your old age. For your daughter-in-law, who loves you and who is better to you than seven sons, has given him birth." Ge 29:31; Ru 1:16-17; 1Sa 1:8

¹⁶Then Naomi took the child in her arms and cared for him. ¹⁷The women living there said, "Naomi has a son!" And they named him Obed. He was the father of Jesse, the father of David. 1Sa 16:1,18

The Genealogy of David

4:18-22pp — 1Ch 2:5-15; Mt 1:3-6; Lk 3:31-33

¹⁸This, then, is the family line of Perez: Mt 1:3-6

Perez was the father of Hezron,
¹⁹Hezron the father of Ram,
Ram the father of Amminadab,

---

[a] 5 Vulgate and Syriac; Hebrew (see also Septuagint) *Naomi and from Ruth the Moabite, you acquire the*

20Amminadab the father of Nahshon,
Nahshon the father of Salmon,a
21Salmon the father of Boaz,
Boaz the father of Obed,
22Obed the father of Jesse,
and Jesse the father of David.

---

a 20 A few Hebrew manuscripts, some Septuagint manuscripts and Vulgate (see also verse 21 and Septuagint of 1 Chron. 2:11); most Hebrew manuscripts *Salma*

1 Samuel

The Birth of Samuel

1 There was a certain man from Ramathaim, a Zuphite[a] from the hill country of Ephraim, whose name was Elkanah son of Jeroham, the son of Elihu, the son of Tohu, the son of Zuph, an Ephraimite. ²He had two wives; one was called Hannah and the other Peninnah. Peninnah had children, but Hannah had none. 1Ch 6:27,34; Dt 21:15-17

³Year after year this man went up from his town to worship and sacrifice to the LORD Almighty at Shiloh, where Hophni and Phinehas, the two sons of Eli, were priests of the LORD. ⁴Whenever the day came for Elkanah to sacrifice, he would give portions of the meat to his wife Peninnah and to all her sons and daughters. ⁵But to Hannah he gave a double portion because he loved her, and the LORD had closed her womb. ⁶Because the LORD had closed Hannah's womb, her rival kept provoking her in order to irritate her. ⁷This went on year after year. Whenever Hannah went up to the house of the LORD, her rival provoked her till she wept and would not eat. ⁸Her husband Elkanah would say to her, "Hannah, why are you weeping? Why don't you eat? Why are you downhearted? Don't I mean more to you than ten sons?" Ge 16:1; Ru 4:15; Job 24:21

⁹Once when they had finished eating and drinking in Shiloh, Hannah stood up. Now Eli the priest was sitting on his chair by the doorpost of the LORD's house. ¹⁰In her deep anguish Hannah prayed to the LORD, weeping bitterly. ¹¹And she made a vow, saying, "LORD Almighty, if you will only look on your servant's misery and remember me, and not forget your servant but give her a son, then I will give him to the LORD for all the days of his life, and no razor will ever be used on his head." Nu 6:1-21; Jdg 13:5; 1Sa 3:3

¹²As she kept on praying to the LORD, Eli observed her mouth.

a 1 See Septuagint and 1 Chron. 6:26-27,33-35; or *from Ramathaim Zuphim*.

¹³Hannah was praying in her heart, and her lips were moving but her voice was not heard. Eli thought she was drunk ¹⁴and said to her, "How long are you going to stay drunk? Put away your wine."

¹⁵"Not so, my lord," Hannah replied, "I am a woman who is deeply troubled. I have not been drinking wine or beer; I was pouring out my soul to the LORD. ¹⁶Do not take your servant for a wicked woman; I have been praying here out of my great anguish and grief." Ps 42:4; 62:8

¹⁷Eli answered, "Go in peace, and may the God of Israel grant you what you have asked of him." Jdg 18:6; Ps 20:3-5; Mk 5:34

¹⁸She said, "May your servant find favor in your eyes." Then she went her way and ate something, and her face was no longer downcast. Ru 2:13; Ro 15:13

¹⁹Early the next morning they arose and worshiped before the LORD and then went back to their home at Ramah. Elkanah made love to his wife Hannah, and the LORD remembered her. ²⁰So in the course of time Hannah became pregnant and gave birth to a son. She named him Samuel,ᵃ saying, "Because I asked the LORD for him." Ge 30:22; Ex 2:10,22

Hannah Dedicates Samuel

²¹When her husband Elkanah went up with all his family to offer the annual sacrifice to the LORD and to fulfill his vow, ²²Hannah did not go. She said to her husband, "After the boy is weaned, I will take him and present him before the LORD, and he will live there always."ᵇ Dt 12:11; Lk 2:22

²³"Do what seems best to you," her husband Elkanah told her. "Stay here until you have weaned him; only may the LORD make good hisᶜ word." So the woman stayed at home and nursed her son until she had weaned him.

²⁴After he was weaned, she took the boy with her, young as he was, along with a three-year-old bull,ᵈ an ephahᵉ of flour and a skin of wine, and brought him to the house of the LORD at Shiloh. ²⁵When the bull had been sacrificed, they brought the boy to Eli, ²⁶and she said to him, "Pardon me, my lord. As surely as you live, I am the woman who stood here beside you praying to the LORD. ²⁷I prayed for this child, and the LORD has granted me what I asked of him. ²⁸So now I give him to the LORD. For his whole life he will be given over to the LORD." And he worshiped the LORD there. Nu 15:8-10; Dt 12:5; Ge 24:26,52

ᵃ 20 *Samuel* sounds like the Hebrew for *heard by God.* ᵇ 22 Masoretic Text; Dead Sea Scrolls *always. I have dedicated him as a Nazirite—all the days of his life."* ᶜ 23 Masoretic Text; Dead Sea Scrolls, Septuagint and Syriac *your* ᵈ 24 Dead Sea Scrolls, Septuagint and Syriac; Masoretic Text *with three bulls* ᵉ 24 That is, probably about 36 pounds or about 16 kilograms

Hannah's Prayer

2 Then Hannah prayed and said:

Lk 1:46-55

"My heart rejoices in the
　LORD;
　in the LORD my horn[a] is
　lifted high.
My mouth boasts over my
　enemies,
　for I delight in your
　deliverance.

Isa 12:2-3

[2] "There is no one holy like the
　LORD;
　there is no one besides you;
　there is no Rock like our
　God.

Ex 15:11

Dt 32:30-31

[3] "Do not keep talking so
　proudly
　or let your mouth speak
　such arrogance,
for the LORD is a God who
　knows,
　and by him deeds are
　weighed.

Pr 8:13

1Sa 16:7; 1Ki 8:39

[4] "The bows of the warriors are
　broken,
　but those who stumbled are
　armed with strength.

Ps 37:15

[5] Those who were full hire
　themselves out for food,
　but those who were hungry
　are hungry no more.
She who was barren has
　borne seven children,
　but she who has had
　many sons pines
　away.

Ps 113:9; Jer 15:9

[6] "The LORD brings death and
　makes alive;
　he brings down to the grave
　and raises up.

Dt 32:39

[7] The LORD sends poverty and
　wealth;
　he humbles and he exalts.
[8] He raises the poor from the
　dust
　and lifts the needy from the
　ash heap;
he seats them with princes
　and has them inherit a
　throne of honor.

Job 36:7

"For the foundations of the
　earth are the LORD's;
　on them he has set the
　world.

Job 38:4

[9] He will guard the feet of his
　faithful servants,
　but the wicked will be
　silenced in the place of
　darkness.

Ps 91:12

Mt 8:12

"It is not by strength that one
　prevails;
[10]　those who oppose the LORD
　will be broken.
The Most High will thunder
　from heaven;
　the LORD will judge the
　ends of the earth.

Ex 15:6

2Sa 22:14

Ps 96:13

"He will give strength to his
　king
　and exalt the horn of his
　anointed."

Ps 89:24

[11] Then Elkanah went home to
Ramah, but the boy ministered

---

a 1 *Horn* here symbolizes strength; also in verse 10.

before the LORD under Eli the priest. 1Sa 3:1

Eli's Wicked Sons

¹²Eli's sons were scoundrels; they had no regard for the LORD. ¹³Now it was the practice of the priests that, whenever any of the people offered a sacrifice, the priest's servant would come with a three-pronged fork in his hand while the meat was being boiled ¹⁴and would plunge the fork into the pan or kettle or caldron or pot. Whatever the fork brought up the priest would take for himself. This is how they treated all the Israelites who came to Shiloh. ¹⁵But even before the fat was burned, the priest's servant would come and say to the person who was sacrificing, "Give the priest some meat to roast; he won't accept boiled meat from you, but only raw." Lev 7:29-34; Jer 2:8

¹⁶If the person said to him, "Let the fat be burned first, and then take whatever you want," the servant would answer, "No, hand it over now; if you don't, I'll take it by force."

¹⁷This sin of the young men was very great in the LORD's sight, for they*a* were treating the LORD's offering with contempt. Mal 2:7-9

¹⁸But Samuel was ministering before the LORD — a boy wearing a linen ephod. ¹⁹Each year his mother made him a little robe and took it to him when she went up with her husband to offer the annual sacrifice. ²⁰Eli would bless Elkanah and his wife, saying, "May the LORD give you children by this woman to take the place of the one she prayed for and gave to*b* the LORD." Then they would go home. ²¹And the LORD was gracious to Hannah; she gave birth to three sons and two daughters. Meanwhile, the boy Samuel grew up in the presence of the LORD. Ge 21:1; Jdg 13:24; 1Sa 1:3

²²Now Eli, who was very old, heard about everything his sons were doing to all Israel and how they slept with the women who served at the entrance to the tent of meeting. ²³So he said to them, "Why do you do such things? I hear from all the people about these wicked deeds of yours. ²⁴No, my sons; the report I hear spreading among the LORD's people is not good. ²⁵If one person sins against another, God*c* may mediate for the offender; but if anyone sins against the LORD, who will intercede for them?" His sons, however, did not listen to their father's rebuke, for it was the LORD's will to put them to death. Ex 38:8; Nu 15:30; Jos 11:20

²⁶And the boy Samuel continued to grow in stature and in favor with the LORD and with people. Lk 2:52

---

a 17 Dead Sea Scrolls and Septuagint; Masoretic Text *people*   *b* 20 Dead Sea Scrolls; Masoretic Text *and asked from*   *c* 25 Or *the judges*

Prophecy Against the House of Eli

[27] Now a man of God came to Eli and said to him, "This is what the LORD says: 'Did I not clearly reveal myself to your ancestor's family when they were in Egypt under Pharaoh? [28] I chose your ancestor out of all the tribes of Israel to be my priest, to go up to my altar, to burn incense, and to wear an ephod in my presence. I also gave your ancestor's family all the food offerings presented by the Israelites. [29] Why do you[a] scorn my sacrifice and offering that I prescribed for my dwelling? Why do you honor your sons more than me by fattening yourselves on the choice parts of every offering made by my people Israel?' Ex 4:14-16; 28:1; Dt 12:5

[30] "Therefore the LORD, the God of Israel, declares: 'I promised that members of your family would minister before me forever.' But now the LORD declares: 'Far be it from me! Those who honor me I will honor, but those who despise me will be disdained. [31] The time is coming when I will cut short your strength and the strength of your priestly house, so that no one in it will reach old age, [32] and you will see distress in my dwelling. Although good will be done to Israel, no one in your family line will ever reach old age. [33] Every one of you that I do not cut off from serving at my altar I will spare only to destroy your sight and sap your strength, and all your descendants will die in the prime of life. Ex 29:9; 1Sa 4:11-18; Zec 8:4

[34] "'And what happens to your two sons, Hophni and Phinehas, will be a sign to you — they will both die on the same day. [35] I will raise up for myself a faithful priest, who will do according to what is in my heart and mind. I will firmly establish his priestly house, and they will minister before my anointed one always. [36] Then everyone left in your family line will come and bow down before him for a piece of silver and a loaf of bread and plead, "Appoint me to some priestly office so I can have food to eat."'" 1Sa 4:11; 2Sa 7:11,27; 1Ki 11:38

The LORD Calls Samuel

3 The boy Samuel ministered before the LORD under Eli. In those days the word of the LORD was rare; there were not many visions. Ps 74:9; Am 8:11; 1Sa 2:11

[2] One night Eli, whose eyes were becoming so weak that he could barely see, was lying down in his usual place. [3] The lamp of God had not yet gone out, and Samuel was lying down in the house of the LORD, where the ark of God was. [4] Then the LORD called Samuel. Lev 24:1-4; 1Sa 4:15

Samuel answered, "Here I am." [5] And he ran to Eli and said, "Here I am; you called me." Isa 6:8

[a] 29 The Hebrew is plural.

But Eli said, "I did not call; go back and lie down." So he went and lay down.

⁶Again the LORD called, "Samuel!" And Samuel got up and went to Eli and said, "Here I am; you called me."

"My son," Eli said, "I did not call; go back and lie down."

⁷Now Samuel did not yet know the LORD: The word of the LORD had not yet been revealed to him. Ac 19:12

⁸A third time the LORD called, "Samuel!" And Samuel got up and went to Eli and said, "Here I am; you called me."

Then Eli realized that the LORD was calling the boy. ⁹So Eli told Samuel, "Go and lie down, and if he calls you, say, 'Speak, LORD, for your servant is listening.'" So Samuel went and lay down in his place.

¹⁰The LORD came and stood there, calling as at the other times, "Samuel! Samuel!"

Then Samuel said, "Speak, for your servant is listening."

¹¹And the LORD said to Samuel: "See, I am about to do something in Israel that will make the ears of everyone who hears about it tingle. ¹²At that time I will carry out against Eli everything I spoke against his family—from beginning to end. ¹³For I told him that I would judge his family forever because of the sin he knew about; his sons blasphemed God,ᵃ and he failed to restrain them. ¹⁴Therefore I swore to the house of Eli, 'The guilt of Eli's house will never be atoned for by sacrifice or offering.'" 1Sa 2:27-36; 2Ki 21:12; Isa 22:14

¹⁵Samuel lay down until morning and then opened the doors of the house of the LORD. He was afraid to tell Eli the vision, ¹⁶but Eli called him and said, "Samuel, my son."

Samuel answered, "Here I am."

¹⁷"What was it he said to you?" Eli asked. "Do not hide it from me. May God deal with you, be it ever so severely, if you hide from me anything he told you." ¹⁸So Samuel told him everything, hiding nothing from him. Then Eli said, "He is the LORD; let him do what is good in his eyes." 2Sa 3:35; Isa 39:8

¹⁹The LORD was with Samuel as he grew up, and he let none of Samuel's words fall to the ground. ²⁰And all Israel from Dan to Beersheba recognized that Samuel was attested as a prophet of the LORD. ²¹The LORD continued to appear at Shiloh, and there he revealed himself to Samuel through his word. Ge 39:2; 1Sa 9:6; 2:21

4 And Samuel's word came to all Israel.

The Philistines Capture the Ark

Now the Israelites went out to fight against the Philistines. The

---

ᵃ 13 An ancient Hebrew scribal tradition (see also Septuagint); Masoretic Text *sons made themselves contemptible*

Israelites camped at Ebenezer, and the Philistines at Aphek. ²The Philistines deployed their forces to meet Israel, and as the battle spread, Israel was defeated by the Philistines, who killed about four thousand of them on the battlefield. ³When the soldiers returned to camp, the elders of Israel asked, "Why did the LORD bring defeat on us today before the Philistines? Let us bring the ark of the LORD's covenant from Shiloh, so that he may go with us and save us from the hand of our enemies."   Nu 10:35; Jos 7:7; 1Sa 7:12

⁴So the people sent men to Shiloh, and they brought back the ark of the covenant of the LORD Almighty, who is enthroned between the cherubim. And Eli's two sons, Hophni and Phinehas, were there with the ark of the covenant of God.   2Sa 6:2

⁵When the ark of the LORD's covenant came into the camp, all Israel raised such a great shout that the ground shook. ⁶Hearing the uproar, the Philistines asked, "What's all this shouting in the Hebrew camp?"   Jos 6:5,10

When they learned that the ark of the LORD had come into the camp, ⁷the Philistines were afraid. "A god has[a] come into the camp," they said. "Oh no! Nothing like this has happened before. ⁸We're doomed! Who will deliver us from the hand of these mighty gods? They are the gods who struck the Egyptians with all kinds of plagues in the wilderness. ⁹Be strong, Philistines! Be men, or you will be subject to the Hebrews, as they have been to you. Be men, and fight!"   Ex 15:14; Jdg 13:1; 1Co 16:13

¹⁰So the Philistines fought, and the Israelites were defeated and every man fled to his tent. The slaughter was very great; Israel lost thirty thousand foot soldiers. ¹¹The ark of God was captured, and Eli's two sons, Hophni and Phinehas, died.   Dt 28:25; 1Sa 2:34

Death of Eli

¹²That same day a Benjamite ran from the battle line and went to Shiloh with his clothes torn and dust on his head. ¹³When he arrived, there was Eli sitting on his chair by the side of the road, watching, because his heart feared for the ark of God. When the man entered the town and told what had happened, the whole town sent up a cry.   Jos 7:6

¹⁴Eli heard the outcry and asked, "What is the meaning of this uproar?"

The man hurried over to Eli, ¹⁵who was ninety-eight years old and whose eyes had failed so that he could not see. ¹⁶He told Eli, "I have just come from the battle line; I fled from it this very day."   1Sa 3:2

Eli asked, "What happened, my son?"

---

[a] 7 Or "Gods have (see Septuagint)

[17]The man who brought the news replied, "Israel fled before the Philistines, and the army has suffered heavy losses. Also your two sons, Hophni and Phinehas, are dead, and the ark of God has been captured."

[18]When he mentioned the ark of God, Eli fell backward off his chair by the side of the gate. His neck was broken and he died, for he was an old man, and he was heavy. He had led[a] Israel forty years.   Jdg 2:16

[19]His daughter-in-law, the wife of Phinehas, was pregnant and near the time of delivery. When she heard the news that the ark of God had been captured and that her father-in-law and her husband were dead, she went into labor and gave birth, but was overcome by her labor pains. [20]As she was dying, the women attending her said, "Don't despair; you have given birth to a son." But she did not respond or pay any attention.

[21]She named the boy Ichabod,[b] saying, "The Glory has departed from Israel" — because of the capture of the ark of God and the deaths of her father-in-law and her husband. [22]She said, "The Glory has departed from Israel, for the ark of God has been captured."   Ps 106:20

The Ark in Ashdod and Ekron

5 After the Philistines had captured the ark of God, they took it from Ebenezer to Ashdod. [2]Then they carried the ark into Dagon's temple and set it beside Dagon. [3]When the people of Ashdod rose early the next day, there was Dagon, fallen on his face on the ground before the ark of the LORD! They took Dagon and put him back in his place. [4]But the following morning when they rose, there was Dagon, fallen on his face on the ground before the ark of the LORD! His head and hands had been broken off and were lying on the threshold; only his body remained. [5]That is why to this day neither the priests of Dagon nor any others who enter Dagon's temple at Ashdod step on the threshold. Jdg 16:23; Isa 46:7; Eze 6:6

[6]The LORD's hand was heavy on the people of Ashdod and its vicinity; he brought devastation on them and afflicted them with tumors.[c] [7]When the people of Ashdod saw what was happening, they said, "The ark of the god of Israel must not stay here with us, because his hand is heavy on us and on Dagon our god." [8]So they called together all the rulers of the Philistines and asked them, "What shall we do with the ark of the god of Israel?" Ex 9:3; Ps 78:66; 1Sa 6:5

---

[a] 18 Traditionally *judged*   [b] 21 *Ichabod* means *no glory*.   [c] 6 Hebrew; Septuagint and Vulgate *tumors. And rats appeared in their land, and there was death and destruction throughout the city*

They answered, "Have the ark of the god of Israel moved to Gath." So they moved the ark of the God of Israel.

[9]But after they had moved it, the Lord's hand was against that city, throwing it into a great panic. He afflicted the people of the city, both young and old, with an outbreak of tumors.[a] [10]So they sent the ark of God to Ekron. 1Sa 7:13

As the ark of God was entering Ekron, the people of Ekron cried out, "They have brought the ark of the god of Israel around to us to kill us and our people." [11]So they called together all the rulers of the Philistines and said, "Send the ark of the god of Israel away; let it go back to its own place, or it[b] will kill us and our people." For death had filled the city with panic; God's hand was very heavy on it. [12]Those who did not die were afflicted with tumors, and the outcry of the city went up to heaven. 1Sa 4:8

The Ark Returned to Israel

6 When the ark of the Lord had been in Philistine territory seven months, [2]the Philistines called for the priests and the diviners and said, "What shall we do with the ark of the Lord? Tell us how we should send it back to its place." Ge 41:8; Ex 7:11

[3]They answered, "If you return the ark of the god of Israel, do not send it back to him without a gift; by all means send a guilt offering to him. Then you will be healed, and you will know why his hand has not been lifted from you." Ex 23:15; Lev 5:15; Dt 16:16

[4]The Philistines asked, "What guilt offering should we send to him?"

They replied, "Five gold tumors and five gold rats, according to the number of the Philistine rulers, because the same plague has struck both you and your rulers. [5]Make models of the tumors and of the rats that are destroying the country, and give glory to Israel's god. Perhaps he will lift his hand from you and your gods and your land. [6]Why do you harden your hearts as the Egyptians and Pharaoh did? When Israel's god dealt harshly with them, did they not send the Israelites out so they could go on their way? Ex 12:31,33; Jos 7:19; 13:3

[7]"Now then, get a new cart ready, with two cows that have calved and have never been yoked. Hitch the cows to the cart, but take their calves away and pen them up. [8]Take the ark of the Lord and put it on the cart, and in a chest beside it put the gold objects you are sending back to him as a guilt offering. Send it on its way, [9]but keep watching it. If it goes up to its own territory, toward Beth Shemesh, then the Lord has brought this great disaster on us. But if it

a 9 Or *with tumors in the groin* (see Septuagint)   b 11 Or *he* does not, then we will know that it was not his hand that struck us but that it happened to us by chance." 2Sa 6:3; Nu 19:2; Jos 15:10

¹⁰So they did this. They took two such cows and hitched them to the cart and penned up their calves. ¹¹They placed the ark of the LORD on the cart and along with it the chest containing the gold rats and the models of the tumors. ¹²Then the cows went straight up toward Beth Shemesh, keeping on the road and lowing all the way; they did not turn to the right or to the left. The rulers of the Philistines followed them as far as the border of Beth Shemesh.

¹³Now the people of Beth Shemesh were harvesting their wheat in the valley, and when they looked up and saw the ark, they rejoiced at the sight. ¹⁴The cart came to the field of Joshua of Beth Shemesh, and there it stopped beside a large rock. The people chopped up the wood of the cart and sacrificed the cows as a burnt offering to the LORD. ¹⁵The Levites took down the ark of the LORD, together with the chest containing the gold objects, and placed them on the large rock. On that day the people of Beth Shemesh offered burnt offerings and made sacrifices to the LORD. ¹⁶The five rulers of the Philistines saw all this and then returned that same day to Ekron. 2Sa 24:22; 1Ki 19:21

¹⁷These are the gold tumors the Philistines sent as a guilt offering to the LORD — one each for Ashdod, Gaza, Ashkelon, Gath and Ekron. ¹⁸And the number of the gold rats was according to the number of Philistine towns belonging to the five rulers — the fortified towns with their country villages. The large rock on which the Levites set the ark of the LORD is a witness to this day in the field of Joshua of Beth Shemesh.

¹⁹But God struck down some of the inhabitants of Beth Shemesh, putting seventy[a] of them to death because they looked into the ark of the LORD. The people mourned because of the heavy blow the LORD had dealt them. ²⁰And the people of Beth Shemesh asked, "Who can stand in the presence of the LORD, this holy God? To whom will the ark go up from here?" Ex 19:21; Lev 11:45; Mal 3:2

²¹Then they sent messengers to the people of Kiriath Jearim, saying, "The Philistines have returned the ark of the LORD. Come down and take it up to your town." ¹So the men of Kiriath Jearim came and took up the ark of the LORD. They brought it to Abinadab's house on the hill and consecrated Eleazar his son to guard the ark of the LORD. ²The ark remained at Kiriath Jearim a long time — twenty years in all. 2Sa 6:3

[a] 19 A few Hebrew manuscripts; most Hebrew manuscripts and Septuagint 50,070

Samuel Subdues the Philistines at Mizpah

Then all the people of Israel turned back to the LORD. ³So Samuel said to all the Israelites, "If you are returning to the LORD with all your hearts, then rid yourselves of the foreign gods and the Ashtoreths and commit yourselves to the LORD and serve him only, and he will deliver you out of the hand of the Philistines." ⁴So the Israelites put away their Baals and Ashtoreths, and served the LORD only.   Jos 24:14; Joel 2:12; Lk 4:8

⁵Then Samuel said, "Assemble all Israel at Mizpah, and I will intercede with the LORD for you." ⁶When they had assembled at Mizpah, they drew water and poured it out before the LORD. On that day they fasted and there they confessed, "We have sinned against the LORD." Now Samuel was serving as leader*a* of Israel at Mizpah.   Jdg 10:10; Ne 9:1; La 2:19

⁷When the Philistines heard that Israel had assembled at Mizpah, the rulers of the Philistines came up to attack them. When the Israelites heard of it, they were afraid because of the Philistines. ⁸They said to Samuel, "Do not stop crying out to the LORD our God for us, that he may rescue us from the hand of the Philistines." ⁹Then Samuel took a suckling lamb and sacrificed it as a whole burnt offering to the LORD. He cried out to the LORD on Israel's behalf, and the LORD answered him.   1Sa 17:11; Isa 37:4; Ps 99:6

¹⁰While Samuel was sacrificing the burnt offering, the Philistines drew near to engage Israel in battle. But that day the LORD thundered with loud thunder against the Philistines and threw them into such a panic that they were routed before the Israelites. ¹¹The men of Israel rushed out of Mizpah and pursued the Philistines, slaughtering them along the way to a point below Beth Kar.   Jos 10:10; 1Sa 2:10; 2Sa 22:14-15

¹²Then Samuel took a stone and set it up between Mizpah and Shen. He named it Ebenezer,*b* saying, "Thus far the LORD has helped us."   Jos 4:9; Jdg 13:1,5; 1Sa 13:5

¹³So the Philistines were subdued and they stopped invading Israel's territory. Throughout Samuel's lifetime, the hand of the LORD was against the Philistines. ¹⁴The towns from Ekron to Gath that the Philistines had captured from Israel were restored to Israel, and Israel delivered the neighboring territory from the hands of the Philistines. And there was peace between Israel and the Amorites.   Jdg 13:1,5; 1Sa 13:5

¹⁵Samuel continued as Israel's leader all the days of his life. ¹⁶From year to year he went on a circuit from Bethel to Gilgal to Mizpah, judging Israel in all those places. ¹⁷But he always went back to Ramah, where his home was,

---

a 6 Traditionally *judge*; also in verse 15   *b* 12 *Ebenezer* means *stone of help.*

and there he also held court for Israel. And he built an altar there to the LORD. 1Sa 12:11; Jdg 21:4

Israel Asks for a King

8 When Samuel grew old, he appointed his sons as Israel's leaders.*a* ²The name of his firstborn was Joel and the name of his second was Abijah, and they served at Beersheba. ³But his sons did not follow his ways. They turned aside after dishonest gain and accepted bribes and perverted justice. Dt 16:18-19; Ps 15:5

⁴So all the elders of Israel gathered together and came to Samuel at Ramah. ⁵They said to him, "You are old, and your sons do not follow your ways; now appoint a king to lead*b* us, such as all the other nations have." Dt 17:14-20

⁶But when they said, "Give us a king to lead us," this displeased Samuel; so he prayed to the LORD. ⁷And the LORD told him: "Listen to all that the people are saying to you; it is not you they have rejected, but they have rejected me as their king. ⁸As they have done from the day I brought them up out of Egypt until this day, forsaking me and serving other gods, so they are doing to you. ⁹Now listen to them; but warn them solemnly and let them know what the king who will reign over them will claim as his rights." Ex 16:8; 1Sa 10:19; 15:11

¹⁰Samuel told all the words of the LORD to the people who were asking him for a king. ¹¹He said, "This is what the king who will reign over you will claim as his rights: He will take your sons and make them serve with his chariots and horses, and they will run in front of his chariots. ¹²Some he will assign to be commanders of thousands and commanders of fifties, and others to plow his ground and reap his harvest, and still others to make weapons of war and equipment for his chariots. ¹³He will take your daughters to be perfumers and cooks and bakers. ¹⁴He will take the best of your fields and vineyards and olive groves and give them to his attendants. ¹⁵He will take a tenth of your grain and of your vintage and give it to his officials and attendants. ¹⁶Your male and female servants and the best of your cattle*c* and donkeys he will take for his own use. ¹⁷He will take a tenth of your flocks, and you yourselves will become his slaves. ¹⁸When that day comes, you will cry out for relief from the king you have chosen, but the LORD will not answer you in that day." 1Sa 14:52; 1Ki 21:7,15; Mic 3:4

¹⁹But the people refused to listen to Samuel. "No!" they said. "We want a king over us. ²⁰Then we will be like all the other nations, with a king to lead us and

a 1 Traditionally *judges*   *b 5* Traditionally *judge*; also in verses 6 and 20
c 16 Septuagint; Hebrew *young men*

to go out before us and fight our battles." _{Isa 66:4; Jer 44:16}

²¹ When Samuel heard all that the people said, he repeated it before the LORD. ²² The LORD answered, "Listen to them and give them a king." _{Jdg 11:11}

Then Samuel said to the Israelites, "Everyone go back to your own town."

Samuel Anoints Saul

9 There was a Benjamite, a man of standing, whose name was Kish son of Abiel, the son of Zeror, the son of Bekorath, the son of Aphiah of Benjamin. ² Kish had a son named Saul, as handsome a young man as could be found anywhere in Israel, and he was a head taller than anyone else. _{1Sa 10:23; 14:51; 1Ch 9:39}

³ Now the donkeys belonging to Saul's father Kish were lost, and Kish said to his son Saul, "Take one of the servants with you and go and look for the donkeys." ⁴ So he passed through the hill country of Ephraim and through the area around Shalisha, but they did not find them. They went on into the district of Shaalim, but the donkeys were not there. Then he passed through the territory of Benjamin, but they did not find them. _{Jos 24:33; 2Ki 4:42}

⁵ When they reached the district of Zuph, Saul said to the servant who was with him, "Come, let's go back, or my father will stop thinking about the donkeys and start worrying about us." _{1Sa 10:2}

⁶ But the servant replied, "Look, in this town there is a man of God; he is highly respected, and everything he says comes true. Let's go there now. Perhaps he will tell us what way to take." _{Dt 33:1; 1Sa 3:19}

⁷ Saul said to his servant, "If we go, what can we give the man? The food in our sacks is gone. We have no gift to take to the man of God. What do we have?" _{1Ki 14:3}

⁸ The servant answered him again. "Look," he said, "I have a quarter of a shekel[a] of silver. I will give it to the man of God so that he will tell us what way to take." ⁹ (Formerly in Israel, if someone went to inquire of God, they would say, "Come, let us go to the seer," because the prophet of today used to be called a seer.) _{2Sa 24:11; 1Ch 26:28; Isa 30:10}

¹⁰ "Good," Saul said to his servant. "Come, let's go." So they set out for the town where the man of God was.

¹¹ As they were going up the hill to the town, they met some young women coming out to draw water, and they asked them, "Is the seer here?"

¹² "He is," they answered. "He's ahead of you. Hurry now; he has just come to our town today, for the people have a sacrifice at the high place. ¹³ As soon as you enter the town, you will find him

---

_{a 8 That is, about 1/10 ounce or about 3 grams}

before he goes up to the high place to eat. The people will not begin eating until he comes, because he must bless the sacrifice; afterward, those who are invited will eat. Go up now; you should find him about this time." Ge 31:54; Nu 28:11-15; Mt 14:19

¹⁴They went up to the town, and as they were entering it, there was Samuel, coming toward them on his way up to the high place.

¹⁵Now the day before Saul came, the LORD had revealed this to Samuel: ¹⁶"About this time tomorrow I will send you a man from the land of Benjamin. Anoint him ruler over my people Israel; he will deliver them from the hand of the Philistines. I have looked on my people, for their cry has reached me." Ex 3:7-9; 1Sa 10:1

¹⁷When Samuel caught sight of Saul, the LORD said to him, "This is the man I spoke to you about; he will govern my people." 1Sa 16:12

¹⁸Saul approached Samuel in the gateway and asked, "Would you please tell me where the seer's house is?"

¹⁹"I am the seer," Samuel replied. "Go up ahead of me to the high place, for today you are to eat with me, and in the morning I will send you on your way and will tell you all that is in your heart. ²⁰As for the donkeys you lost three days ago, do not worry about them; they have been found. And to whom is all the desire of Israel turned, if not to you and your whole family line?" 1Sa 8:5; 12:13; Ezr 6:8

²¹Saul answered, "But am I not a Benjamite, from the smallest tribe of Israel, and is not my clan the least of all the clans of the tribe of Benjamin? Why do you say such a thing to me?" Jdg 20:35,46

²²Then Samuel brought Saul and his servant into the hall and seated them at the head of those who were invited—about thirty in number. ²³Samuel said to the cook, "Bring the piece of meat I gave you, the one I told you to lay aside."

²⁴So the cook took up the thigh with what was on it and set it in front of Saul. Samuel said, "Here is what has been kept for you. Eat, because it was set aside for you for this occasion from the time I said, 'I have invited guests.'" And Saul dined with Samuel that day.

²⁵After they came down from the high place to the town, Samuel talked with Saul on the roof of his house. ²⁶They rose about daybreak, and Samuel called to Saul on the roof, "Get ready, and I will send you on your way." When Saul got ready, he and Samuel went outside together. ²⁷As they were going down to the edge of the town, Samuel said to Saul, "Tell the servant to go on ahead of us"—and the servant did so—"but you stay here for a while, so that I may give you a message from God." Dt 22:8; Ac 10:9

10

Then Samuel took a flask of olive oil and poured it on Saul's head and kissed him, saying, "Has not the LORD anointed you ruler over his inheritance?[a] ²When you leave me today, you will meet two men near Rachel's tomb, at Zelzah on the border of Benjamin. They will say to you, 'The donkeys you set out to look for have been found. And now your father has stopped thinking about them and is worried about you. He is asking, "What shall I do about my son?"' 2Ki 9:1,3,6; Dt 32:9

³"Then you will go on from there until you reach the great tree of Tabor. Three men going up to worship God at Bethel will meet you there. One will be carrying three young goats, another three loaves of bread, and another a skin of wine. ⁴They will greet you and offer you two loaves of bread, which you will accept from them. Ge 35:7-8; Pr 18:16

⁵"After that you will go to Gibeah of God, where there is a Philistine outpost. As you approach the town, you will meet a procession of prophets coming down from the high place with lyres, timbrels, pipes and harps being played before them, and they will be prophesying. ⁶The Spirit of the LORD will come powerfully upon you, and you will prophesy with them; and you will be changed into a different person. ⁷Once these signs are fulfilled, do whatever your hand finds to do, for God is with you. Nu 11:25; 1Sa 19:23-24; Jdg 6:12

⁸"Go down ahead of me to Gilgal. I will surely come down to you to sacrifice burnt offerings and fellowship offerings, but you must wait seven days until I come to you and tell you what you are to do." 1Sa 11:14-15; 13:8

Saul Made King

⁹As Saul turned to leave Samuel, God changed Saul's heart, and all these signs were fulfilled that day. ¹⁰When he and his servant arrived at Gibeah, a procession of prophets met him; the Spirit of God came powerfully upon him, and he joined in their prophesying. ¹¹When all those who had formerly known him saw him prophesying with the prophets, they asked each other, "What is this that has happened to the son of Kish? Is Saul also among the prophets?" 1Sa 19:20,24; Mt 13:54

¹²A man who lived there answered, "And who is their father?" So it became a saying: "Is Saul also among the prophets?" ¹³After Saul stopped prophesying, he went to the high place.

¹⁴Now Saul's uncle asked him and his servant, "Where have you been?" 1Sa 14:50

[a] 1 Hebrew; Septuagint and Vulgate *over his people Israel? You will reign over the LORD's people and save them from the power of their enemies round about. And this will be a sign to you that the LORD has anointed you ruler over his inheritance:*

"Looking for the donkeys," he said. "But when we saw they were not to be found, we went to Samuel."

¹⁵Saul's uncle said, "Tell me what Samuel said to you."

¹⁶Saul replied, "He assured us that the donkeys had been found." But he did not tell his uncle what Samuel had said about the kingship.   1Sa 9:20

¹⁷Samuel summoned the people of Israel to the LORD at Mizpah ¹⁸and said to them, "This is what the LORD, the God of Israel, says: 'I brought Israel up out of Egypt, and I delivered you from the power of Egypt and all the kingdoms that oppressed you.' ¹⁹But you have now rejected your God, who saves you out of all your disasters and calamities. And you have said, 'No, appoint a king over us.' So now present yourselves before the LORD by your tribes and clans."   Jdg 6:8-9; 1Sa 7:5; 8:5-7

²⁰When Samuel had all Israel come forward by tribes, the tribe of Benjamin was taken by lot. ²¹Then he brought forward the tribe of Benjamin, clan by clan, and Matri's clan was taken. Finally Saul son of Kish was taken. But when they looked for him, he was not to be found. ²²So they inquired further of the

LORD, "Has the man come here yet?"   1Sa 23:2,4,9-11

And the LORD said, "Yes, he has hidden himself among the supplies."

²³They ran and brought him out, and as he stood among the people he was a head taller than any of the others. ²⁴Samuel said to all the people, "Do you see the man the LORD has chosen? There is no one like him among all the people."   Dt 17:15; 2Sa 21:6

Then the people shouted, "Long live the king!"   1Ki 1:25,34,39

²⁵Samuel explained to the people the rights and duties of kingship. He wrote them down on a scroll and deposited it before the LORD. Then Samuel dismissed the people to go to their own homes.   Dt 17:14-20; 1Sa 8:11-18

²⁶Saul also went to his home in Gibeah, accompanied by valiant men whose hearts God had touched. ²⁷But some scoundrels said, "How can this fellow save us?" They despised him and brought him no gifts. But Saul kept silent. 1Sa 11:4; 1Ki 10:25; 2Ch 17:5

Saul Rescues the City of Jabesh

11 Nahash[a] the Ammonite went up and besieged Jabesh Gilead. And all the men of Jabesh said to him, "Make a trea-

---

a 1 Masoretic Text; Dead Sea Scrolls *gifts. Now Nahash king of the Ammonites oppressed the Gadites and Reubenites severely. He gouged out all their right eyes and struck terror and dread in Israel. Not a man remained among the Israelites beyond the Jordan whose right eye was not gouged out by Nahash king of the Ammonites, except that seven thousand men fled from the Ammonites and entered Jabesh Gilead. About a month later,* ¹*Nahash* ty with us, and we will be subject to you." Jdg 21:8; 1Sa 12:12 ²But Nahash the Ammonite replied, "I will make a treaty with you only on the condition that I gouge out the right eye of every one of you and so bring disgrace on all Israel." Nu 16:14; 1Sa 17:26 ³The elders of Jabesh said to him, "Give us seven days so we can send messengers throughout Israel; if no one comes to rescue us, we will surrender to you." 1Sa 8:4 ⁴When the messengers came to Gibeah of Saul and reported these terms to the people, they all wept aloud. ⁵Just then Saul was returning from the fields, behind his oxen, and he asked, "What is wrong with everyone? Why are they weeping?" Then they repeated to him what the men of Jabesh had said. 1Sa 10:5,26; Jdg 2:4; 1Sa 30:4 ⁶When Saul heard their words, the Spirit of God came powerfully upon him, and he burned with anger. ⁷He took a pair of oxen, cut them into pieces, and sent the pieces by messengers throughout Israel, proclaiming, "This is what will be done to the oxen of anyone who does not follow Saul and Samuel." Then the terror of the LORD fell on the people, and they came out together as one. ⁸When Saul mustered them at Bezek, the men of Israel numbered three hundred thousand and those of Judah thirty thousand. Jdg 3:10; 19:29; 21:5

⁹They told the messengers who had come, "Say to the men of Jabesh Gilead, 'By the time the sun is hot tomorrow, you will be rescued.'" When the messengers went and reported this to the men of Jabesh, they were elated. ¹⁰They said to the Ammonites, "Tomorrow we will surrender to you, and you can do to us whatever you like."

¹¹The next day Saul separated his men into three divisions; during the last watch of the night they broke into the camp of the Ammonites and slaughtered them until the heat of the day. Those who survived were scattered, so that no two of them were left together. Jdg 7:16

Saul Confirmed as King

¹²The people then said to Samuel, "Who was it that asked, 'Shall Saul reign over us?' Turn these men over to us so that we may put them to death." 1Sa 10:27; Lk 19:27 ¹³But Saul said, "No one will be put to death today, for this day the LORD has rescued Israel." 1Sa 19:5; 2Sa 19:22 ¹⁴Then Samuel said to the people, "Come, let us go to Gilgal and there renew the kingship." ¹⁵So all the people went to Gilgal and made Saul king in the presence of the LORD. There they sacrificed fellowship offerings before the LORD, and Saul and all the Israelites held a great celebration. 1Sa 10:8,17,25

Samuel's Farewell Speech

12 Samuel said to all Israel, "I have listened to everything you said to me and have set a king over you. ²Now you have a king as your leader. As for me, I am old and gray, and my sons are here with you. I have been your leader from my youth until this day. ³Here I stand. Testify against me in the presence of the LORD and his anointed. Whose ox have I taken? Whose donkey have I taken? Whom have I cheated? Whom have I oppressed? From whose hand have I accepted a bribe to make me shut my eyes? If I have done any of these things, I will make it right." 1Sa 8:7; 24:6; 2Sa 1:14

⁴"You have not cheated or oppressed us," they replied. "You have not taken anything from anyone's hand." Ex 22:4; Ac 23:9

⁵Samuel said to them, "The LORD is witness against you, and also his anointed is witness this day, that you have not found anything in my hand."

"He is witness," they said.

⁶Then Samuel said to the people, "It is the LORD who appointed Moses and Aaron and brought your ancestors up out of Egypt. ⁷Now then, stand here, because I am going to confront you with evidence before the LORD as to all the righteous acts performed by the LORD for you and your ancestors. Ex 6:26; Eze 20:35; Mic 6:1-5

⁸"After Jacob entered Egypt, they cried to the LORD for help, and the LORD sent Moses and Aaron, who brought your ancestors out of Egypt and settled them in this place. Ex 2:23; 3:10; 4:16

⁹"But they forgot the LORD their God; so he sold them into the hand of Sisera, the commander of the army of Hazor, and into the hands of the Philistines and the king of Moab, who fought against them. ¹⁰They cried out to the LORD and said, 'We have sinned; we have forsaken the LORD and served the Baals and the Ashtoreths. But now deliver us from the hands of our enemies, and we will serve you.' ¹¹Then the LORD sent Jerub-Baal,ᵃ Barak,ᵇ Jephthah and Samuel,ᶜ and he delivered you from the hands of your enemies all around you, so that you lived in safety. Jdg 3:7; 4:2; 6:14,32

¹²"But when you saw that Nahash king of the Ammonites was moving against you, you said to me, 'No, we want a king to rule over us'—even though the LORD your God was your king. ¹³Now here is the king you have chosen, the one you asked for; see, the LORD has set a king over you. ¹⁴If you fear the LORD and serve and obey him and do not rebel against his commands, and if both you and the king who reigns over you follow the LORD your God—

ᵃ 11 Also called *Gideon*   ᵇ 11 Some Septuagint manuscripts and Syriac; Hebrew *Bedan*
ᶜ 11 Hebrew; some Septuagint manuscripts and Syriac *Samson*

good! ¹⁵But if you do not obey the LORD, and if you rebel against his commands, his hand will be against you, as it was against your ancestors. Jdg 8:23; Jos 24:14; Hos 13:11

¹⁶"Now then, stand still and see this great thing the LORD is about to do before your eyes! ¹⁷Is it not wheat harvest now? I will call on the LORD to send thunder and rain. And you will realize what an evil thing you did in the eyes of the LORD when you asked for a king." Ex 14:13; 1Sa 8:6-7; Pr 26:1

¹⁸Then Samuel called on the LORD, and that same day the LORD sent thunder and rain. So all the people stood in awe of the LORD and of Samuel. Ex 14:31

¹⁹The people all said to Samuel, "Pray to the LORD your God for your servants so that we will not die, for we have added to all our other sins the evil of asking for a king." Ex 9:28

²⁰"Do not be afraid," Samuel replied. "You have done all this evil; yet do not turn away from the LORD, but serve the LORD with all your heart. ²¹Do not turn away after useless idols. They can do you no good, nor can they rescue you, because they are useless. ²²For the sake of his great name the LORD will not reject his people, because the LORD was pleased to make you his own. ²³As for me, far be it from me that

I should sin against the LORD by failing to pray for you. And I will teach you the way that is good and right. ²⁴But be sure to fear the LORD and serve him faithfully with all your heart; consider what great things he has done for you. ²⁵Yet if you persist in doing evil, both you and your king will perish." Dt 31:6; Hab 2:18; Col 1:9

Samuel Rebukes Saul

13 Saul was thirtyᵃ years old when he became king, and he reigned over Israel forty-ᵇ two years.

²Saul chose three thousand men from Israel; two thousand were with him at Mikmash and in the hill country of Bethel, and a thousand were with Jonathan at Gibeah in Benjamin. The rest of the men he sent back to their homes.

³Jonathan attacked the Philistine outpost at Geba, and the Philistines heard about it. Then Saul had the trumpet blown throughout the land and said, "Let the Hebrews hear!" ⁴So all Israel heard the news: "Saul has attacked the Philistine outpost, and now Israel has become obnoxious to the Philistines." And the people were summoned to join Saul at Gilgal. 1Sa 10:5; Jdg 3:27

⁵The Philistines assembled to fight Israel, with three thousandᶜ

ᵃ 1 A few late manuscripts of the Septuagint; Hebrew does not have *thirty*. ᵇ 1 Probable reading of the original Hebrew text (see Acts 13:21); Masoretic Text does not have *forty-*.
ᶜ 5 Some Septuagint manuscripts and Syriac; Hebrew *thirty thousand*

chariots, six thousand charioteers, and soldiers as numerous as the sand on the seashore. They went up and camped at Mikmash, east of Beth Aven. [6]When the Israelites saw that their situation was critical and that their army was hard pressed, they hid in caves and thickets, among the rocks, and in pits and cisterns. [7]Some Hebrews even crossed the Jordan to the land of Gad and Gilead. Jos 11:4; Jdg 6:2; Nu 32:33

Saul remained at Gilgal, and all the troops with him were quaking with fear. [8]He waited seven days, the time set by Samuel; but Samuel did not come to Gilgal, and Saul's men began to scatter. [9]So he said, "Bring me the burnt offering and the fellowship offerings." And Saul offered up the burnt offering. [10]Just as he finished making the offering, Samuel arrived, and Saul went out to greet him. 1Sa 10:8; 15:13; 2Sa 24:25

[11]"What have you done?" asked Samuel.

Saul replied, "When I saw that the men were scattering, and that you did not come at the set time, and that the Philistines were assembling at Mikmash, [12]I thought, 'Now the Philistines will come down against me at Gilgal, and I have not sought the LORD's favor.' So I felt compelled to offer the burnt offering."

[13]"You have done a foolish thing," Samuel said. "You have not kept the command the LORD your God gave you; if you had, he would have established your kingdom over Israel for all time. [14]But now your kingdom will not endure; the LORD has sought out a man after his own heart and appointed him ruler of his people, because you have not kept the LORD's command." 2Ch 16:9; Ac 7:46

[15]Then Samuel left Gilgal[a] and went up to Gibeah in Benjamin, and Saul counted the men who were with him. They numbered about six hundred. 1Sa 14:2

Israel Without Weapons

[16]Saul and his son Jonathan and the men with them were staying in Gibeah[b] in Benjamin, while the Philistines camped at Mikmash. [17]Raiding parties went out from the Philistine camp in three detachments. One turned toward Ophrah in the vicinity of Shual, [18]another toward Beth Horon, and the third toward the borderland overlooking the Valley of Zeboyim facing the wilderness. Jos 18:23; Ne 11:34

[19]Not a blacksmith could be found in the whole land of Israel, because the Philistines had said, "Otherwise the Hebrews will make swords or spears!" [20]So all Israel went down to the Philis-

---

a 15 Hebrew; Septuagint *Gilgal and went his way; the rest of the people went after Saul to meet the army, and they went out of Gilgal*   *b* 16 Two Hebrew manuscripts; most Hebrew manuscripts *Geba,* a variant of *Gibeah* tines to have their plow points, mattocks, axes and sickles*a* sharpened. [21] The price was two-thirds of a shekel*b* for sharpening plow points and mattocks, and a third of a shekel*c* for sharpening forks and axes and for repointing goads.   2Ki 24:14

[22] So on the day of the battle not a soldier with Saul and Jonathan had a sword or spear in his hand; only Saul and his son Jonathan had them.   Jdg 5:8

Jonathan Attacks the Philistines

[23] Now a detachment of Philistines had gone out to the pass at Mikmash. **14** [1] One day Jonathan son of Saul said to his young armor-bearer, "Come, let's go over to the Philistine outpost on the other side." But he did not tell his father.

[2] Saul was staying on the outskirts of Gibeah under a pomegranate tree in Migron. With him were about six hundred men, [3] among whom was Ahijah, who was wearing an ephod. He was a son of Ichabod's brother Ahitub son of Phinehas, the son of Eli, the LORD's priest in Shiloh. No one was aware that Jonathan had left.   1Sa 4:21; 13:15; 22:11,20

[4] On each side of the pass that Jonathan intended to cross to reach the Philistine outpost was a cliff; one was called Bozez and the other Seneh. [5] One cliff stood to the north toward Mikmash, the other to the south toward Geba.

[6] Jonathan said to his young armor-bearer, "Come, let's go over to the outpost of those uncircumcised men. Perhaps the LORD will act in our behalf. Nothing can hinder the LORD from saving, whether by many or by few."   Jdg 7:4; 1Sa 17:46-47; Jer 9:26

[7] "Do all that you have in mind," his armor-bearer said. "Go ahead; I am with you heart and soul."

[8] Jonathan said, "Come on, then; we will cross over toward them and let them see us. [9] If they say to us, 'Wait there until we come to you,' we will stay where we are and not go up to them. [10] But if they say, 'Come up to us,' we will climb up, because that will be our sign that the LORD has given them into our hands."   Ge 24:14; Jdg 6:36-37

[11] So both of them showed themselves to the Philistine outpost. "Look!" said the Philistines. "The Hebrews are crawling out of the holes they were hiding in." [12] The men of the outpost shouted to Jonathan and his armor-bearer, "Come up to us and we'll teach you a lesson." 1Sa 13:6; 17:43-44

So Jonathan said to his armor-bearer, "Climb up after me; the LORD has given them into the hand of Israel."   2Sa 5:24

[13] Jonathan climbed up, using

---

a 20 Septuagint; Hebrew *plow points*   *b 21* That is, about 1/4 ounce or about 8 grams
c 21 That is, about 1/8 ounce or about 4 grams

his hands and feet, with his armor-bearer right behind him. The Philistines fell before Jonathan, and his armor-bearer followed and killed behind him. ¹⁴In that first attack Jonathan and his armor-bearer killed some twenty men in an area of about half an acre.

Israel Routs the Philistines

¹⁵Then panic struck the whole army—those in the camp and field, and those in the outposts and raiding parties—and the ground shook. It was a panic sent by God.ᵃ   Ge 35:5; 2Ki 7:5-7; 1Sa 13:17

¹⁶Saul's lookouts at Gibeah in Benjamin saw the army melting away in all directions. ¹⁷Then Saul said to the men who were with him, "Muster the forces and see who has left us." When they did, it was Jonathan and his armor-bearer who were not there.

¹⁸Saul said to Ahijah, "Bring the ark of God." (At that time it was with the Israelites.)ᵇ ¹⁹While Saul was talking to the priest, the tumult in the Philistine camp increased more and more. So Saul said to the priest, "Withdraw your hand."   Nu 27:21; 1Sa 30:7

²⁰Then Saul and all his men assembled and went to the battle. They found the Philistines in total confusion, striking each other with their swords. ²¹Those Hebrews who had previously been with the Philistines and had gone up with them to their camp went over to the Israelites who were with Saul and Jonathan. ²²When all the Israelites who had hidden in the hill country of Ephraim heard that the Philistines were on the run, they joined the battle in hot pursuit. ²³So on that day the LORD saved Israel, and the battle moved on beyond Beth Aven.   Ex 14:30; Jdg 7:22; 1Sa 13:6

Jonathan Eats Honey

²⁴Now the Israelites were in distress that day, because Saul had bound the people under an oath, saying, "Cursed be anyone who eats food before evening comes, before I have avenged myself on my enemies!" So none of the troops tasted food.   Jos 6:26

²⁵The entire army entered the woods, and there was honey on the ground. ²⁶When they went into the woods, they saw the honey oozing out; yet no one put his hand to his mouth, because they feared the oath. ²⁷But Jonathan had not heard that his father had bound the people with the oath, so he reached out the end of the staff that was in his hand and dipped it into the honeycomb. He raised his hand to his mouth, and his eyes brightened.ᶜ ²⁸Then one of the soldiers told him, "Your father bound the army under a strict oath, saying,

---

ᵃ 15 Or *a terrible panic*   ᵇ 18 Hebrew; Septuagint *"Bring the ephod." (At that time he wore the ephod before the Israelites.)*   ᶜ 27 Or *his strength was renewed*; similarly in verse 29

'Cursed be anyone who eats food today!' That is why the men are faint." 1Sa 30:12; Ps 19:10; Pr 16:24

²⁹ Jonathan said, "My father has made trouble for the country. See how my eyes brightened when I tasted a little of this honey. ³⁰ How much better it would have been if the men had eaten today some of the plunder they took from their enemies. Would not the slaughter of the Philistines have been even greater?" 1Ki 18:18

³¹ That day, after the Israelites had struck down the Philistines from Mikmash to Aijalon, they were exhausted. ³² They pounced on the plunder and, taking sheep, cattle and calves, they butchered them on the ground and ate them, together with the blood. ³³ Then someone said to Saul, "Look, the men are sinning against the LORD by eating meat that has blood in it." Ge 9:4; Lev 17:10-14; 1Sa 15:19

"You have broken faith," he said. "Roll a large stone over here at once." ³⁴ Then he said, "Go out among the men and tell them, 'Each of you bring me your cattle and sheep, and slaughter them here and eat them. Do not sin against the LORD by eating meat with blood still in it.'"

So everyone brought his ox that night and slaughtered it there. ³⁵ Then Saul built an altar to the LORD; it was the first time he had done this. 1Sa 7:17

³⁶ Saul said, "Let us go down and pursue the Philistines by night and plunder them till dawn, and let us not leave one of them alive."

"Do whatever seems best to you," they replied.

But the priest said, "Let us inquire of God here."

³⁷ So Saul asked God, "Shall I go down and pursue the Philistines? Will you give them into Israel's hand?" But God did not answer him that day. 1Sa 10:22; 28:6,15

³⁸ Saul therefore said, "Come here, all you who are leaders of the army, and let us find out what sin has been committed today. ³⁹ As surely as the LORD who rescues Israel lives, even if the guilt lies with my son Jonathan, he must die." But not one of them said a word. 2Sa 12:5

⁴⁰ Saul then said to all the Israelites, "You stand over there; I and Jonathan my son will stand over here."

"Do what seems best to you," they replied.

⁴¹ Then Saul prayed to the LORD, the God of Israel, "Why have you not answered your servant today? If the fault is in me or my son Jonathan, respond with Urim, but if the men of Israel are at fault,ᵃ respond with Thummim." Jonathan and Saul were taken by lot, and the men were cleared. ⁴² Saul said, "Cast the lot between me and Jonathan my son." And Jonathan was taken. Ac 1:24; Pr 16:33

ᵃ 41 Septuagint; Hebrew does not have "Why . . . at fault.

43 Then Saul said to Jonathan, "Tell me what you have done."

So Jonathan told him, "I tasted a little honey with the end of my staff. And now I must die!"

44 Saul said, "May God deal with me, be it ever so severely, if you do not die, Jonathan." Ru 1:17

45 But the men said to Saul, "Should Jonathan die — he who has brought about this great deliverance in Israel? Never! As surely as the LORD lives, not a hair of his head will fall to the ground, for he did this today with God's help." So the men rescued Jonathan, and he was not put to death. 2Sa 14:11; 1Ki 1:52

46 Then Saul stopped pursuing the Philistines, and they withdrew to their own land.

47 After Saul had assumed rule over Israel, he fought against their enemies on every side: Moab, the Ammonites, Edom, the kings*a* of Zobah, and the Philistines. Wherever he turned, he inflicted punishment on them.*b* 48 He fought valiantly and defeated the Amalekites, delivering Israel from the hands of those who had plundered them. 1Sa 11:1-13; 15:2,7

Saul's Family

49 Saul's sons were Jonathan, Ishvi and Malki-Shua. The name of his older daughter was Merab, and that of the younger was Michal. 50 His wife's name was Ahinoam daughter of Ahimaaz. The name of the commander of Saul's army was Abner son of Ner, and Ner was Saul's uncle. 51 Saul's father Kish and Abner's father Ner were sons of Abiel. 1Sa 9:1; 18:17-20

52 All the days of Saul there was bitter war with the Philistines, and whenever Saul saw a mighty or brave man, he took him into his service. 1Sa 8:11

The LORD Rejects Saul as King

15 Samuel said to Saul, "I am the one the LORD sent to anoint you king over his people Israel; so listen now to the message from the LORD. 2 This is what the LORD Almighty says: 'I will punish the Amalekites for what they did to Israel when they waylaid them as they came up from Egypt. 3 Now go, attack the Amalekites and totally destroy*c* all that belongs to them. Do not spare them; put to death men and women, children and infants, cattle and sheep, camels and donkeys.'" Ex 17:8-14; Nu 24:20; 1Sa 9:16

4 So Saul summoned the men and mustered them at Telaim — two hundred thousand foot soldiers and ten thousand from Judah. 5 Saul went to the city of Amalek and set an ambush in the ravine. 6 Then he said to the Kenites, "Go away, leave the Ama-

---

a 47 Masoretic Text; Dead Sea Scrolls and Septuagint *king*   *b 47* Hebrew; Septuagint *he was victorious*   *c 3* The Hebrew term refers to the irrevocable giving over of things or persons to the LORD, often by totally destroying them; also in verses 8, 9, 15, 18, 20 and 21.

lekites so that I do not destroy you along with them; for you showed kindness to all the Israelites when they came up out of Egypt." So the Kenites moved away from the Amalekites. Ex 18:10,19; Nu 10:29-32

⁷Then Saul attacked the Amalekites all the way from Havilah to Shur, near the eastern border of Egypt. ⁸He took Agag king of the Amalekites alive, and all his people he totally destroyed with the sword. ⁹But Saul and the army spared Agag and the best of the sheep and cattle, the fat calves*a* and lambs — everything that was good. These they were unwilling to destroy completely, but everything that was despised and weak they totally destroyed. Ge 16:7; 25:17-18; 1Sa 14:48

¹⁰Then the word of the LORD came to Samuel: ¹¹"I regret that I have made Saul king, because he has turned away from me and has not carried out my instructions." Samuel was angry, and he cried out to the LORD all that night. Ge 6:6; Jos 22:16; 1Ki 9:6-7

¹²Early in the morning Samuel got up and went to meet Saul, but he was told, "Saul has gone to Carmel. There he has set up a monument in his own honor and has turned and gone on down to Gilgal." Jos 15:55

¹³When Samuel reached him, Saul said, "The LORD bless you! I have carried out the LORD's instructions."

¹⁴But Samuel said, "What then is this bleating of sheep in my ears? What is this lowing of cattle that I hear?"

¹⁵Saul answered, "The soldiers brought them from the Amalekites; they spared the best of the sheep and cattle to sacrifice to the LORD your God, but we totally destroyed the rest."

¹⁶"Enough!" Samuel said to Saul. "Let me tell you what the LORD said to me last night."

"Tell me," Saul replied.

¹⁷Samuel said, "Although you were once small in your own eyes, did you not become the head of the tribes of Israel? The LORD anointed you king over Israel. ¹⁸And he sent you on a mission, saying, 'Go and completely destroy those wicked people, the Amalekites; wage war against them until you have wiped them out.' ¹⁹Why did you not obey the LORD? Why did you pounce on the plunder and do evil in the eyes of the LORD?" 1Sa 9:21; 14:32

²⁰"But I did obey the LORD," Saul said. "I went on the mission the LORD assigned me. I completely destroyed the Amalekites and brought back Agag their king. ²¹The soldiers took sheep and cattle from the plunder, the best of what was devoted to God, in order to sacrifice them to the LORD your God at Gilgal."

²²But Samuel replied:

---

a 9 Or *the grown bulls*; the meaning of the Hebrew for this phrase is uncertain.

"Does the Lord delight in
    burnt offerings and
    sacrifices
  as much as in obeying the
    Lord?
To obey is better than
    sacrifice,
  and to heed is better than
    the fat of rams.   Isa 1:11-15
23 For rebellion is like the sin of
    divination,
  and arrogance like the evil
    of idolatry.
Because you have rejected the
    word of the Lord,
  he has rejected you as
    king."   1Sa 13:13

24 Then Saul said to Samuel, "I have sinned. I violated the Lord's command and your instructions. I was afraid of the men and so I gave in to them. 25 Now I beg you, forgive my sin and come back with me, so that I may worship the Lord."   Ex 10:17; 2Sa 12:13; Isa 51:12-13

26 But Samuel said to him, "I will not go back with you. You have rejected the word of the Lord, and the Lord has rejected you as king over Israel!"   1Sa 13:14

27 As Samuel turned to leave, Saul caught hold of the hem of his robe, and it tore. 28 Samuel said to him, "The Lord has torn the kingdom of Israel from you today and has given it to one of your neighbors — to one better than you. 29 He who is the Glory of Israel does not lie or change his mind; for he is not a human being, that he should change his mind."   Eze 24:14; 1Sa 28:17; 1Ki 11:11,31

30 Saul replied, "I have sinned. But please honor me before the elders of my people and before Israel; come back with me, so that I may worship the Lord your God." 31 So Samuel went back with Saul, and Saul worshiped the Lord.   Jn 12:43

32 Then Samuel said, "Bring me Agag king of the Amalekites."

Agag came to him in chains.[a] And he thought, "Surely the bitterness of death is past."

33 But Samuel said,

"As your sword has made
    women childless,
  so will your mother be
    childless among
    women."   Ge 9:6; Jdg 1:7

And Samuel put Agag to death before the Lord at Gilgal.

34 Then Samuel left for Ramah, but Saul went up to his home in Gibeah of Saul. 35 Until the day Samuel died, he did not go to see Saul again, though Samuel mourned for him. And the Lord regretted that he had made Saul king over Israel.   1Sa 11:4; 16:1; 19:24

Samuel Anoints David

16 The Lord said to Samuel, "How long will you mourn for Saul, since I have rejected him as king over Israel? Fill your horn with oil and be on your way; I

a 32 The meaning of the Hebrew for this phrase is uncertain.

am sending you to Jesse of Bethlehem. I have chosen one of his sons to be king." Ac 13:22; Ru 4:17

²But Samuel said, "How can I go? If Saul hears about it, he will kill me."

The LORD said, "Take a heifer with you and say, 'I have come to sacrifice to the LORD.' ³Invite Jesse to the sacrifice, and I will show you what to do. You are to anoint for me the one I indicate." Ex 4:15; Dt 17:15; 1Sa 9:16

⁴Samuel did what the LORD said. When he arrived at Bethlehem, the elders of the town trembled when they met him. They asked, "Do you come in peace?" 1Ki 2:13; 2Ki 9:17

⁵Samuel replied, "Yes, in peace; I have come to sacrifice to the LORD. Consecrate yourselves and come to the sacrifice with me." Then he consecrated Jesse and his sons and invited them to the sacrifice. Ex 19:10,22

⁶When they arrived, Samuel saw Eliab and thought, "Surely the LORD's anointed stands here before the LORD." 1Sa 17:13

⁷But the LORD said to Samuel, "Do not consider his appearance or his height, for I have rejected him. The LORD does not look at the things people look at. People look at the outward appearance, but the LORD looks at the heart." 1Ki 8:39; 1Ch 28:9

⁸Then Jesse called Abinadab and had him pass in front of Samuel. But Samuel said, "The LORD has not chosen this one either." ⁹Jesse then had Shammah pass by, but Samuel said, "Nor has the LORD chosen this one." ¹⁰Jesse had seven of his sons pass before Samuel, but Samuel said to him, "The LORD has not chosen these." ¹¹So he asked Jesse, "Are these all the sons you have?" 1Sa 17:12

"There is still the youngest," Jesse answered. "He is tending the sheep."

Samuel said, "Send for him; we will not sit down until he arrives."

¹²So he sent for him and had him brought in. He was glowing with health and had a fine appearance and handsome features. Ge 39:6; 1Sa 9:17

Then the LORD said, "Rise and anoint him; this is the one."

¹³So Samuel took the horn of oil and anointed him in the presence of his brothers, and from that day on the Spirit of the LORD came powerfully upon David. Samuel then went to Ramah. 1Sa 10:1,6,9-10

David in Saul's Service

¹⁴Now the Spirit of the LORD had departed from Saul, and an evil*a* spirit from the LORD tormented him. Jdg 16:20; 9:23

¹⁵Saul's attendants said to him, "See, an evil spirit from God is tormenting you. ¹⁶Let our lord command his servants here to search for someone who can play the lyre.

---

a 14 Or *and a harmful*; similarly in verses 15, 16 and 23

He will play when the evil spirit from God comes on you, and you will feel better." 1Sa 18:10; 2Ki 3:15

¹⁷So Saul said to his attendants, "Find someone who plays well and bring him to me."

¹⁸One of the servants answered, "I have seen a son of Jesse of Bethlehem who knows how to play the lyre. He is a brave man and a warrior. He speaks well and is a fine-looking man. And the LORD is with him." 1Sa 3:19; 17:32-37

¹⁹Then Saul sent messengers to Jesse and said, "Send me your son David, who is with the sheep." ²⁰So Jesse took a donkey loaded with bread, a skin of wine and a young goat and sent them with his son David to Saul. 1Sa 10:27; Pr 18:16

²¹David came to Saul and entered his service. Saul liked him very much, and David became one of his armor-bearers. ²²Then Saul sent word to Jesse, saying, "Allow David to remain in my service, for I am pleased with him." Ge 41:46; Pr 22:29

²³Whenever the spirit from God came on Saul, David would take up his lyre and play. Then relief would come to Saul; he would feel better, and the evil spirit would leave him. Jdg 9:23

David and Goliath

17 Now the Philistines gathered their forces for war and assembled at Sokoh in Ju-

dah. They pitched camp at Ephes Dammim, between Sokoh and Azekah. ²Saul and the Israelites assembled and camped in the Valley of Elah and drew up their battle line to meet the Philistines. ³The Philistines occupied one hill and the Israelites another, with the valley between them. 1Sa 13:5; Jos 15:35

⁴A champion named Goliath, who was from Gath, came out of the Philistine camp. His height was six cubits and a span.ᵃ ⁵He had a bronze helmet on his head and wore a coat of scale armor of bronze weighing five thousand shekelsᵇ; ⁶on his legs he wore bronze greaves, and a bronze javelin was slung on his back. ⁷His spear shaft was like a weaver's rod, and its iron point weighed six hundred shekels.ᶜ His shield bearer went ahead of him. Jos 11:21-22; 2Sa 21:19

⁸Goliath stood and shouted to the ranks of Israel, "Why do you come out and line up for battle? Am I not a Philistine, and are you not the servants of Saul? Choose a man and have him come down to me. ⁹If he is able to fight and kill me, we will become your subjects; but if I overcome him and kill him, you will become our subjects and serve us." ¹⁰Then the Philistine said, "This day I defy the armies of Israel! Give me a man and let us fight each other." ¹¹On

---

ᵃ 4 That is, about 9 feet 9 inches or about 3 meters   ᵇ 5 That is, about 125 pounds or about 58 kilograms   ᶜ 7 That is, about 15 pounds or about 6.9 kilograms hearing the Philistine's words, Saul and all the Israelites were dismayed and terrified. 1Sa 8:17

¹²Now David was the son of an Ephrathite named Jesse, who was from Bethlehem in Judah. Jesse had eight sons, and in Saul's time he was very old. ¹³Jesse's three oldest sons had followed Saul to the war: The firstborn was Eliab; the second, Abinadab; and the third, Shammah. ¹⁴David was the youngest. The three oldest followed Saul, ¹⁵but David went back and forth from Saul to tend his father's sheep at Bethlehem. 1Ch 2:13-15; Ge 35:19; 1Sa 16:6

¹⁶For forty days the Philistine came forward every morning and evening and took his stand.

¹⁷Now Jesse said to his son David, "Take this ephah*a* of roasted grain and these ten loaves of bread for your brothers and hurry to their camp. ¹⁸Take along these ten cheeses to the commander of their unit. See how your brothers are and bring back some assurance*b* from them. ¹⁹They are with Saul and all the men of Israel in the Valley of Elah, fighting against the Philistines." Ge 37:14; 1Sa 25:18

²⁰Early in the morning David left the flock in the care of a shepherd, loaded up and set out, as Jesse had directed. He reached the camp as the army was going out to its battle positions, shouting the war cry. ²¹Israel and the Philistines were drawing up their lines facing each other. ²²David left his things with the keeper of supplies, ran to the battle lines and asked his brothers how they were. ²³As he was talking with them, Goliath, the Philistine champion from Gath, stepped out from his lines and shouted his usual defiance, and David heard it. ²⁴Whenever the Israelites saw the man, they all fled from him in great fear.

²⁵Now the Israelites had been saying, "Do you see how this man keeps coming out? He comes out to defy Israel. The king will give great wealth to the man who kills him. He will also give him his daughter in marriage and will exempt his family from taxes in Israel." Jos 15:16; 1Sa 18:17

²⁶David asked the men standing near him, "What will be done for the man who kills this Philistine and removes this disgrace from Israel? Who is this uncircumcised Philistine that he should defy the armies of the living God?" 1Sa 11:2; 14:6; Dt 5:26

²⁷They repeated to him what they had been saying and told him, "This is what will be done for the man who kills him."

²⁸When Eliab, David's oldest brother, heard him speaking with the men, he burned with anger at him and asked, "Why have you come down here? And

---

a 17 That is, probably about 36 pounds or about 16 kilograms   *b* 18 Or *some token;* or *some pledge of spoils* with whom did you leave those few sheep in the wilderness? I know how conceited you are and how wicked your heart is; you came down only to watch the battle." Ge 37:4,8,11; Pr 18:19

29 "Now what have I done?" said David. "Can't I even speak?" 30 He then turned away to someone else and brought up the same matter, and the men answered him as before. 31 What David said was overheard and reported to Saul, and Saul sent for him.

32 David said to Saul, "Let no one lose heart on account of this Philistine; your servant will go and fight him." Dt 20:3; 1Sa 16:18

33 Saul replied, "You are not able to go out against this Philistine and fight him; you are only a young man, and he has been a warrior from his youth." Nu 13:31

34 But David said to Saul, "Your servant has been keeping his father's sheep. When a lion or a bear came and carried off a sheep from the flock, 35 I went after it, struck it and rescued the sheep from its mouth. When it turned on me, I seized it by its hair, struck it and killed it. 36 Your servant has killed both the lion and the bear; this uncircumcised Philistine will be like one of them, because he has defied the armies of the living God. 37 The LORD who rescued me from the paw of the lion and the paw of the bear will rescue me from the hand of this Philistine." Jer 49:19; 2Co 1:10; 2Ti 4:17

Saul said to David, "Go, and the LORD be with you." 1Sa 20:13; 1Ch 22:11

38 Then Saul dressed David in his own tunic. He put a coat of armor on him and a bronze helmet on his head. 39 David fastened on his sword over the tunic and tried walking around, because he was not used to them. Ge 41:42

"I cannot go in these," he said to Saul, "because I am not used to them." So he took them off. 40 Then he took his staff in his hand, chose five smooth stones from the stream, put them in the pouch of his shepherd's bag and, with his sling in his hand, approached the Philistine.

41 Meanwhile, the Philistine, with his shield bearer in front of him, kept coming closer to David. 42 He looked David over and saw that he was little more than a boy, glowing with health and handsome, and he despised him. 43 He said to David, "Am I a dog, that you come at me with sticks?" And the Philistine cursed David by his gods. 44 "Come here," he said, "and I'll give your flesh to the birds and the wild animals!" 1Sa 24:14; 1Ki 20:10-11; Pr 16:18

45 David said to the Philistine, "You come against me with sword and spear and javelin, but I come against you in the name of the LORD Almighty, the God of the armies of Israel, whom you have defied. 46 This day the LORD will deliver you into my hands, and I'll strike you down and cut

off your head. This very day I will give the carcasses of the Philistine army to the birds and the wild animals, and the whole world will know that there is a God in Israel. ⁴⁷All those gathered here will know that it is not by sword or spear that the LORD saves; for the battle is the LORD's, and he will give all of you into our hands." 1Ki 18:36; 2Ch 14:11; 32:8

⁴⁸As the Philistine moved closer to attack him, David ran quickly toward the battle line to meet him. ⁴⁹Reaching into his bag and taking out a stone, he slung it and struck the Philistine on the forehead. The stone sank into his forehead, and he fell facedown on the ground.

⁵⁰So David triumphed over the Philistine with a sling and a stone; without a sword in his hand he struck down the Philistine and killed him.

⁵¹David ran and stood over him. He took hold of the Philistine's sword and drew it from the sheath. After he killed him, he cut off his head with the sword. Heb 11:34

When the Philistines saw that their hero was dead, they turned and ran. ⁵²Then the men of Israel and Judah surged forward with a shout and pursued the Philistines to the entrance of Gathᵃ and to the gates of Ekron. Their dead were strewn along the Shaaraim road to Gath and Ekron.

⁵³When the Israelites returned from chasing the Philistines, they plundered their camp. Jos 15:36

⁵⁴David took the Philistine's head and brought it to Jerusalem; he put the Philistine's weapons in his own tent.

⁵⁵As Saul watched David going out to meet the Philistine, he said to Abner, commander of the army, "Abner, whose son is that young man?" 1Sa 16:21

Abner replied, "As surely as you live, Your Majesty, I don't know."

⁵⁶The king said, "Find out whose son this young man is."

⁵⁷As soon as David returned from killing the Philistine, Abner took him and brought him before Saul, with David still holding the Philistine's head.

⁵⁸"Whose son are you, young man?" Saul asked him.

David said, "I am the son of your servant Jesse of Bethlehem." Ru 4:17

Saul's Growing Fear of David

18 After David had finished talking with Saul, Jonathan became one in spirit with David, and he loved him as himself. ²From that day Saul kept David with him and did not let him return home to his family. ³And Jonathan made a covenant with David because he loved him as himself. ⁴Jonathan took off the robe he was wearing and gave it to David, along with his tunic, and even his sword, his bow and his belt. Ge 41:42; 44:30; 2Sa 1:26

⁵Whatever mission Saul sent him on, David was so successful that Saul gave him a high rank in the army. This pleased all the troops, and Saul's officers as well.
⁶When the men were returning home after David had killed the Philistine, the women came out from all the towns of Israel to meet King Saul with singing and dancing, with joyful songs and with timbrels and lyres. ⁷As they danced, they sang: Ex 15:20; Jdg 11:34

"Saul has slain his thousands,
    and David his tens of
    thousands." 1Sa 21:11

⁸Saul was very angry; this refrain displeased him greatly. "They have credited David with tens of thousands," he thought, "but me with only thousands. What more can he get but the kingdom?" ⁹And from that time on Saul kept a close eye on David. 1Sa 15:8

¹⁰The next day an evil[a] spirit from God came forcefully on Saul. He was prophesying in his house, while David was playing the lyre, as he usually did. Saul had a spear in his hand ¹¹and he hurled it, saying to himself, "I'll pin David to the wall." But David eluded him twice. 1Sa 16:14; 19:7; 20:7,33

¹²Saul was afraid of David, because the LORD was with Da-vid but had departed from Saul. ¹³So he sent David away from him and gave him command over a thousand men, and David led the troops in their campaigns. ¹⁴In everything he did he had great success, because the LORD was with him. ¹⁵When Saul saw how successful he was, he was afraid of him. ¹⁶But all Israel and Judah loved David, because he led them in their campaigns. Ge 39:3; Nu 27:17; Jos 6:27

¹⁷Saul said to David, "Here is my older daughter Merab. I will give her to you in marriage; only serve me bravely and fight the battles of the LORD." For Saul said to himself, "I will not raise a hand against him. Let the Philistines do that!" 1Sa 17:25; 25:28

¹⁸But David said to Saul, "Who am I, and what is my family or my clan in Israel, that I should become the king's son-in-law?" ¹⁹So[b] when the time came for Merab, Saul's daughter, to be given to David, she was given in marriage to Adriel of Meholah. 2Sa 7:18; 21:8

²⁰Now Saul's daughter Michal was in love with David, and when they told Saul about it, he was pleased. ²¹"I will give her to him," he thought, "so that she may be a snare to him and so that the hand of the Philistines may be against him." So Saul said to David, "Now you have a second opportunity to become my son-in-law."

---

[a] 10 Or a harmful   [b] 19 Or However,

²²Then Saul ordered his attendants: "Speak to David privately and say, 'Look, the king likes you, and his attendants all love you; now become his son-in-law.'"

²³They repeated these words to David. But David said, "Do you think it is a small matter to become the king's son-in-law? I'm only a poor man and little known."

²⁴When Saul's servants told him what David had said, ²⁵Saul replied, "Say to David, 'The king wants no other price for the bride than a hundred Philistine foreskins, to take revenge on his enemies.'" Saul's plan was to have David fall by the hands of the Philistines. $\quad$ Ex 22:17; Jer 20:10

²⁶When the attendants told David these things, he was pleased to become the king's son-in-law. So before the allotted time elapsed, ²⁷David took his men with him and went out and killed two hundred Philistines and brought back their foreskins. They counted out the full number to the king so that David might become the king's son-in-law. Then Saul gave him his daughter Michal in marriage. $\quad$ 2Sa 3:14

²⁸When Saul realized that the LORD was with David and that his daughter Michal loved David, ²⁹Saul became still more afraid of him, and he remained his enemy the rest of his days.

³⁰The Philistine commanders continued to go out to battle, and as often as they did, David met with more success than the rest of Saul's officers, and his name became well known.

Saul Tries to Kill David

19 Saul told his son Jonathan and all the attendants to kill David. But Jonathan had taken a great liking to David ²and warned him, "My father Saul is looking for a chance to kill you. Be on your guard tomorrow morning; go into hiding and stay there. ³I will go out and stand with my father in the field where you are. I'll speak to him about you and will tell you what I find out." $\quad$ 1Sa 18:9; 20:12

⁴Jonathan spoke well of David to Saul his father and said to him, "Let not the king do wrong to his servant David; he has not wronged you, and what he has done has benefited you greatly. ⁵He took his life in his hands when he killed the Philistine. The LORD won a great victory for all Israel, and you saw it and were glad. Why then would you do wrong to an innocent man like David by killing him for no reason?" $\quad$ Ge 42:22; 1Sa 11:13; Mt 27:4

⁶Saul listened to Jonathan and took this oath: "As surely as the LORD lives, David will not be put to death."

⁷So Jonathan called David and told him the whole conversation. He brought him to Saul, and David was with Saul as before.

⁸Once more war broke out, and David went out and fought the Philistines. He struck them with such force that they fled before him.

⁹But an evil*ᵃ* spirit from the LORD came on Saul as he was sitting in his house with his spear in his hand. While David was playing the lyre, ¹⁰Saul tried to pin him to the wall with his spear, but David eluded him as Saul drove the spear into the wall. That night David made good his escape.   1Sa 16:14; 18:10-11

¹¹Saul sent men to David's house to watch it and to kill him in the morning. But Michal, David's wife, warned him, "If you don't run for your life tonight, tomorrow you'll be killed." ¹²So Michal let David down through a window, and he fled and escaped. ¹³Then Michal took an idol and laid it on the bed, covering it with a garment and putting some goats' hair at the head.   Jos 2:15; Ac 9:25

¹⁴When Saul sent the men to capture David, Michal said, "He is ill."   Jos 2:4

¹⁵Then Saul sent the men back to see David and told them, "Bring him up to me in his bed so that I may kill him." ¹⁶But when the men entered, there was the idol in the bed, and at the head was some goats' hair.

¹⁷Saul said to Michal, "Why did you deceive me like this and send my enemy away so that he escaped?"

Michal told him, "He said to me, 'Let me get away. Why should I kill you?'"

¹⁸When David had fled and made his escape, he went to Samuel at Ramah and told him all that Saul had done to him. Then he and Samuel went to Naioth and stayed there. ¹⁹Word came to Saul: "David is in Naioth at Ramah"; ²⁰so he sent men to capture him. But when they saw a group of prophets prophesying, with Samuel standing there as their leader, the Spirit of God came on Saul's men, and they also prophesied. ²¹Saul was told about it, and he sent more men, and they prophesied too. Saul sent men a third time, and they also prophesied. ²²Finally, he himself left for Ramah and went to the great cistern at Seku. And he asked, "Where are Samuel and David?"   Nu 11:25; 1Sa 10:5

"Over in Naioth at Ramah," they said.

²³So Saul went to Naioth at Ramah. But the Spirit of God came even on him, and he walked along prophesying until he came to Naioth. ²⁴He stripped off his garments, and he too prophesied in Samuel's presence. He lay naked all that day and all that night. This is why people say, "Is Saul also among the prophets?"   1Sa 15:35

ᵃ 9 Or *But a harmful*

David and Jonathan

20 Then David fled from Naioth at Ramah and went to Jonathan and asked, "What have I done? What is my crime? How have I wronged your father, that he is trying to kill me?" 1Sa 24:9

² "Never!" Jonathan replied. "You are not going to die! Look, my father doesn't do anything, great or small, without letting me know. Why would he hide this from me? It isn't so!"

³ But David took an oath and said, "Your father knows very well that I have found favor in your eyes, and he has said to himself, 'Jonathan must not know this or he will be grieved.' Yet as surely as the LORD lives and as you live, there is only a step between me and death." Dt 6:13

⁴ Jonathan said to David, "Whatever you want me to do, I'll do for you."

⁵ So David said, "Look, tomorrow is the New Moon feast, and I am supposed to dine with the king; but let me go and hide in the field until the evening of the day after tomorrow. ⁶ If your father misses me at all, tell him, 'David earnestly asked my permission to hurry to Bethlehem, his hometown, because an annual sacrifice is being made there for his whole clan.' ⁷ If he says, 'Very well,' then your servant is safe. But if he loses his temper, you can be sure that he is determined to harm me. ⁸ As for you, show kindness to your servant, for you have brought him into a covenant with you before the LORD. If I am guilty, then kill me yourself! Why hand me over to your father?" 1Sa 18:3; 2Sa 14:32; Nu 10:10

⁹ "Never!" Jonathan said. "If I had the least inkling that my father was determined to harm you, wouldn't I tell you?"

¹⁰ David asked, "Who will tell me if your father answers you harshly?"

¹¹ "Come," Jonathan said, "let's go out into the field." So they went there together.

¹² Then Jonathan said to David, "I swear by the LORD, the God of Israel, that I will surely sound out my father by this time the day after tomorrow! If he is favorably disposed toward you, will I not send you word and let you know? ¹³ But if my father intends to harm you, may the LORD deal with Jonathan, be it ever so severely, if I do not let you know and send you away in peace. May the LORD be with you as he has been with my father. ¹⁴ But show me unfailing kindness like the LORD's kindness as long as I live, so that I may not be killed, ¹⁵ and do not ever cut off your kindness from my family — not even when the LORD has cut off every one of David's enemies from the face of the earth." Ru 1:17; 1Sa 3:17; 2Sa 9:7

¹⁶ So Jonathan made a covenant with the house of David, saying, "May the LORD call David's

enemies to account." ¹⁷And Jonathan had David reaffirm his oath out of love for him, because he loved him as he loved himself.   1Sa 25:22

¹⁸Then Jonathan said to David, "Tomorrow is the New Moon feast. You will be missed, because your seat will be empty. ¹⁹The day after tomorrow, toward evening, go to the place where you hid when this trouble began, and wait by the stone Ezel. ²⁰I will shoot three arrows to the side of it, as though I were shooting at a target. ²¹Then I will send a boy and say, 'Go, find the arrows.' If I say to him, 'Look, the arrows are on this side of you; bring them here,' then come, because, as surely as the LORD lives, you are safe; there is no danger. ²²But if I say to the boy, 'Look, the arrows are beyond you,' then you must go, because the LORD has sent you away. ²³And about the matter you and I discussed—remember, the LORD is witness between you and me forever."   Ge 31:50; 1Sa 19:2

²⁴So David hid in the field, and when the New Moon feast came, the king sat down to eat. ²⁵He sat in his customary place by the wall, opposite Jonathan,ᵃ and Abner sat next to Saul, but David's place was empty. ²⁶Saul said nothing that day, for he thought, "Something must have happened to David to make him ceremonially unclean—surely he is un-

clean." ²⁷But the next day, the second day of the month, David's place was empty again. Then Saul said to his son Jonathan, "Why hasn't the son of Jesse come to the meal, either yesterday or today?"   Lev 7:20-21; 15:5; 1Sa 16:5

²⁸Jonathan answered, "David earnestly asked me for permission to go to Bethlehem. ²⁹He said, 'Let me go, because our family is observing a sacrifice in the town and my brother has ordered me to be there. If I have found favor in your eyes, let me get away to see my brothers.' That is why he has not come to the king's table."

³⁰Saul's anger flared up at Jonathan and he said to him, "You son of a perverse and rebellious woman! Don't I know that you have sided with the son of Jesse to your own shame and to the shame of the mother who bore you? ³¹As long as the son of Jesse lives on this earth, neither you nor your kingdom will be established. Now send someone to bring him to me, for he must die!"

³²"Why should he be put to death? What has he done?" Jonathan asked his father. ³³But Saul hurled his spear at him to kill him. Then Jonathan knew that his father intended to kill David.   Ge 31:36; 1Sa 18:11,17; 19:4

³⁴Jonathan got up from the table in fierce anger; on that second day of the feast he did not

ᵃ 25 Septuagint; Hebrew wall. Jonathan arose

eat, because he was grieved at his father's shameful treatment of David.

³⁵In the morning Jonathan went out to the field for his meeting with David. He had a small boy with him, ³⁶and he said to the boy, "Run and find the arrows I shoot." As the boy ran, he shot an arrow beyond him. ³⁷When the boy came to the place where Jonathan's arrow had fallen, Jonathan called out after him, "Isn't the arrow beyond you?" ³⁸Then he shouted, "Hurry! Go quickly! Don't stop!" The boy picked up the arrow and returned to his master. ³⁹(The boy knew nothing about all this; only Jonathan and David knew.) ⁴⁰Then Jonathan gave his weapons to the boy and said, "Go, carry them back to town."

⁴¹After the boy had gone, David got up from the south side of the stone and bowed down before Jonathan three times, with his face to the ground. Then they kissed each other and wept together—but David wept the most.

⁴²Jonathan said to David, "Go in peace, for we have sworn friendship with each other in the name of the LORD, saying, 'The LORD is witness between you and me, and between your descendants and my descendants forever.'" Then David left, and Jonathan went back to the town.ᵃ 1Sa 1:17; 2Sa 1:26; Pr 18:24

David at Nob

21 ᵇ David went to Nob, to Ahimelek the priest. Ahimelek trembled when he met him, and asked, "Why are you alone? Why is no one with you?" 1Sa 14:3; 16:4

²David answered Ahimelek the priest, "The king sent me on a mission and said to me, 'No one is to know anything about the mission I am sending you on.' As for my men, I have told them to meet me at a certain place. ³Now then, what do you have on hand? Give me five loaves of bread, or whatever you can find."

⁴But the priest answered David, "I don't have any ordinary bread on hand; however, there is some consecrated bread here—provided the men have kept themselves from women." Mt 12:4; Lev 24:8-9

⁵David replied, "Indeed women have been kept from us, as usual wheneverᶜ I set out. The men's bodies are holy even on missions that are not holy. How much more so today!" ⁶So the priest gave him the consecrated bread, since there was no bread there except the bread of the Presence that had been removed from before the LORD and replaced by hot bread on the day it was taken away. Ex 25:30; 1Th 4:4

⁷Now one of Saul's servants was there that day, detained be-

ᵃ 42 In Hebrew texts this sentence (20:42b) is numbered 21:1.   ᵇ In Hebrew texts 21:1-15 is numbered 21:2-16.   ᶜ 5 Or *from us in the past few days since* fore the LORD; he was Doeg the Edomite, Saul's chief shepherd.

⁸David asked Ahimelek, "Don't you have a spear or a sword here? I haven't brought my sword or any other weapon, because the king's mission was urgent."

⁹The priest replied, "The sword of Goliath the Philistine, whom you killed in the Valley of Elah, is here; it is wrapped in a cloth behind the ephod. If you want it, take it; there is no sword here but that one."   1Sa 17:51

David said, "There is none like it; give it to me."

David at Gath

¹⁰That day David fled from Saul and went to Achish king of Gath. ¹¹But the servants of Achish said to him, "Isn't this David, the king of the land? Isn't he the one they sing about in their dances:

" 'Saul has slain his
      thousands,
   and David his tens of
      thousands'?"   1Sa 18:7; 29:5

¹²David took these words to heart and was very much afraid of Achish king of Gath. ¹³So he pretended to be insane in their presence; and while he was in their hands he acted like a madman, making marks on the doors of the gate and letting saliva run down his beard.

¹⁴Achish said to his servants, "Look at the man! He is insane!

Why bring him to me? ¹⁵Am I so short of madmen that you have to bring this fellow here to carry on like this in front of me? Must this man come into my house?"

David at Adullam and Mizpah

22 David left Gath and escaped to the cave of Adullam. When his brothers and his father's household heard about it, they went down to him there. ²All those who were in distress or in debt or discontented gathered around him, and he became their commander. About four hundred men were with him.   1Sa 25:13; 2Sa 23:13; Ps 57 Title

³From there David went to Mizpah in Moab and said to the king of Moab, "Would you let my father and mother come and stay with you until I learn what God will do for me?" ⁴So he left them with the king of Moab, and they stayed with him as long as David was in the stronghold.

⁵But the prophet Gad said to David, "Do not stay in the stronghold. Go into the land of Judah." So David left and went to the forest of Hereth.   2Sa 24:11; 1Ch 21:9

Saul Kills the Priests of Nob

⁶Now Saul heard that David and his men had been discovered. And Saul was seated, spear in hand, under the tamarisk tree on the hill at Gibeah, with all his officials standing at his side. ⁷He said to them, "Listen, men

of Benjamin! Will the son of Jesse give all of you fields and vineyards? Will he make all of you commanders of thousands and commanders of hundreds? **8**Is that why you have all conspired against me? No one tells me when my son makes a covenant with the son of Jesse. None of you is concerned about me or tells me that my son has incited my servant to lie in wait for me, as he does today." 1Sa 8:14; 18:3; Jdg 4:5

9But Doeg the Edomite, who was standing with Saul's officials, said, "I saw the son of Jesse come to Ahimelek son of Ahitub at Nob. **10**Ahimelek inquired of the LORD for him; he also gave him provisions and the sword of Goliath the Philistine." 1Sa 17:51; 21:7; Nu 27:21

11Then the king sent for the priest Ahimelek son of Ahitub and all the men of his family, who were the priests at Nob, and they all came to the king. **12**Saul said, "Listen now, son of Ahitub."

"Yes, my lord," he answered.

13Saul said to him, "Why have you conspired against me, you and the son of Jesse, giving him bread and a sword and inquiring of God for him, so that he has rebelled against me and lies in wait for me, as he does today?"

14Ahimelek answered the king, "Who of all your servants is as loyal as David, the king's son-in-law, captain of your bodyguard and highly respected in your household? **15**Was that day

the first time I inquired of God for him? Of course not! Let not the king accuse your servant or any of his father's family, for your servant knows nothing at all about this whole affair."

16But the king said, "You will surely die, Ahimelek, you and your whole family."

17Then the king ordered the guards at his side: "Turn and kill the priests of the LORD, because they too have sided with David. They knew he was fleeing, yet they did not tell me."

But the king's officials were unwilling to raise a hand to strike the priests of the LORD. Ex 1:17

18The king then ordered Doeg, "You turn and strike down the priests." So Doeg the Edomite turned and struck them down. That day he killed eighty-five men who wore the linen ephod. **19**He also put to the sword Nob, the town of the priests, with its men and women, its children and infants, and its cattle, donkeys and sheep. 1Sa 2:18,31; 15:3

20But one son of Ahimelek son of Ahitub, named Abiathar, escaped and fled to join David. **21**He told David that Saul had killed the priests of the LORD. **22**Then David said to Abiathar, "That day, when Doeg the Edomite was there, I knew he would be sure to tell Saul. I am responsible for the death of your whole family. **23**Stay with me; don't be afraid. The man who wants to kill you is trying to kill me too. You will be safe with me." 1Sa 2:32; 23:6,9; 1Ki 2:26

David Saves Keilah

23 When David was told, "Look, the Philistines are fighting against Keilah and are looting the threshing floors," [2] he inquired of the LORD, saying, "Shall I go and attack these Philistines?" Jos 15:44; 1Sa 30:8

The LORD answered him, "Go, attack the Philistines and save Keilah."

[3] But David's men said to him, "Here in Judah we are afraid. How much more, then, if we go to Keilah against the Philistine forces!"

[4] Once again David inquired of the LORD, and the LORD answered him, "Go down to Keilah, for I am going to give the Philistines into your hand." [5] So David and his men went to Keilah, fought the Philistines and carried off their livestock. He inflicted heavy losses on the Philistines and saved the people of Keilah. [6] (Now Abiathar son of Ahimelek had brought the ephod down with him when he fled to David at Keilah.) Jos 8:7; Jdg 7:7; 1Sa 22:20

Saul Pursues David

[7] Saul was told that David had gone to Keilah, and he said, "God has delivered him into my hands, for David has imprisoned himself by entering a town with gates and bars." [8] And Saul called up all his forces for battle, to go down to Keilah to besiege David and his men.

[9] When David learned that Saul was plotting against him, he said to Abiathar the priest, "Bring the ephod." [10] David said, "LORD, God of Israel, your servant has heard definitely that Saul plans to come to Keilah and destroy the town on account of me. [11] Will the citizens of Keilah surrender me to him? Will Saul come down, as your servant has heard? LORD, God of Israel, tell your servant."

And the LORD said, "He will."

[12] Again David asked, "Will the citizens of Keilah surrender me and my men to Saul?"

And the LORD said, "They will."

[13] So David and his men, about six hundred in number, left Keilah and kept moving from place to place. When Saul was told that David had escaped from Keilah, he did not go there. 1Sa 22:2; 25:13

[14] David stayed in the wilderness strongholds and in the hills of the Desert of Ziph. Day after day Saul searched for him, but God did not give David into his hands. Ps 32:7; 54:3-4

[15] While David was at Horesh in the Desert of Ziph, he learned that[a] Saul had come out to take his life. [16] And Saul's son Jonathan went to David at Horesh and

---

[a] 15 Or he was afraid because

helped him find strength in God. [17] "Don't be afraid," he said. "My father Saul will not lay a hand on you. You will be king over Israel, and I will be second to you. Even my father Saul knows this." [18] The two of them made a covenant before the LORD. Then Jonathan went home, but David remained at Horesh. 1Sa 20:16,42; 24:20; 2Sa 21:7

[19] The Ziphites went up to Saul at Gibeah and said, "Is not David hiding among us in the strongholds at Horesh, on the hill of Hakilah, south of Jeshimon? [20] Now, Your Majesty, come down whenever it pleases you to do so, and we will be responsible for giving him into your hands." 1Sa 26:1

[21] Saul replied, "The LORD bless you for your concern for me. [22] Go and get more information. Find out where David usually goes and who has seen him there. They tell me he is very crafty. [23] Find out about all the hiding places he uses and come back to me with definite information. Then I will go with you; if he is in the area, I will track him down among all the clans of Judah." 1Sa 22:8

[24] So they set out and went to Ziph ahead of Saul. Now David and his men were in the Desert of Maon, in the Arabah south of Jeshimon. [25] Saul and his men began the search, and when David was told about it, he went down to the rock and stayed in the Desert of Maon. When Saul heard this, he went into the Desert of Maon in pursuit of David. Jos 15:55; 1Sa 25:2

[26] Saul was going along one side of the mountain, and David and his men were on the other side, hurrying to get away from Saul. As Saul and his forces were closing in on David and his men to capture them, [27] a messenger came to Saul, saying, "Come quickly! The Philistines are raiding the land." [28] Then Saul broke off his pursuit of David and went to meet the Philistines. That is why they call this place Sela Hammahlekoth.[a] [29] And David went up from there and lived in the strongholds of En Gedi.[b] 1Sa 24:22; Ps 17:9; 2Ch 20:2

David Spares Saul's Life

24 [c] After Saul returned from pursuing the Philistines, he was told, "David is in the Desert of En Gedi." [2] So Saul took three thousand able young men from all Israel and set out to look for David and his men near the Crags of the Wild Goats. 1Sa 23:28-29; 26:2

[3] He came to the sheep pens along the way; a cave was there, and Saul went in to relieve himself. David and his men were far back in the cave. [4] The men said, "This is the day the LORD spoke of when he said[d] to you, 'I

---

[a] 28 *Sela Hammahlekoth* means *rock of parting.* [b] 29 In Hebrew texts this verse (23:29) is numbered 24:1. [c] In Hebrew texts 24:1-22 is numbered 24:2-23. [d] 4 Or *"Today the LORD is saying*

will give your enemy into your hands for you to deal with as you wish.'" Then David crept up unnoticed and cut off a corner of Saul's robe. 1Sa 25:28-30; Jdg 3:24

⁵Afterward, David was conscience-stricken for having cut off a corner of his robe. ⁶He said to his men, "The LORD forbid that I should do such a thing to my master, the LORD's anointed, or lay my hand on him; for he is the anointed of the LORD." ⁷With these words David sharply rebuked his men and did not allow them to attack Saul. And Saul left the cave and went his way. 1Sa 26:11; 2Sa 24:10

⁸Then David went out of the cave and called out to Saul, "My lord the king!" When Saul looked behind him, David bowed down and prostrated himself with his face to the ground. ⁹He said to Saul, "Why do you listen when men say, 'David is bent on harming you'? ¹⁰This day you have seen with your own eyes how the LORD delivered you into my hands in the cave. Some urged me to kill you, but I spared you; I said, 'I will not lay my hand on my lord, because he is the LORD's anointed.' ¹¹See, my father, look at this piece of your robe in my hand! I cut off the corner of your robe but did not kill you. See that there is nothing in my hand to indicate that I am guilty of wrongdoing or rebellion. I have not wronged you, but you are hunting me down to take my life.

¹²May the LORD judge between you and me. And may the LORD avenge the wrongs you have done to me, but my hand will not touch you. ¹³As the old saying goes, 'From evildoers come evil deeds,' so my hand will not touch you. Ge 16:5; Jdg 11:27; Mt 7:20

¹⁴"Against whom has the king of Israel come out? Who are you pursuing? A dead dog? A flea? ¹⁵May the LORD be our judge and decide between us. May he consider my cause and uphold it; may he vindicate me by delivering me from your hand." 1Sa 17:43; Ps 35:1,23; Mic 7:9

¹⁶When David finished saying this, Saul asked, "Is that your voice, David my son?" And he wept aloud. ¹⁷"You are more righteous than I," he said. "You have treated me well, but I have treated you badly. ¹⁸You have just now told me about the good you did to me; the LORD delivered me into your hands, but you did not kill me. ¹⁹When a man finds his enemy, does he let him get away unharmed? May the LORD reward you well for the way you treated me today. ²⁰I know that you will surely be king and that the kingdom of Israel will be established in your hands. ²¹Now swear to me by the LORD that you will not kill off my descendants or wipe out my name from my father's family." Ge 38:26; 2Sa 21:1-9; Mt 5:44

²²So David gave his oath to Saul. Then Saul returned home,

but David and his men went up to the stronghold. 1Sa 23:29

David, Nabal and Abigail

25 Now Samuel died, and all Israel assembled and mourned for him; and they buried him at his home in Ramah. Then David moved down into the Desert of Paran.ᵃ   Dt 34:8; 1Sa 28:3 ²A certain man in Maon, who had property there at Carmel, was very wealthy. He had a thousand goats and three thousand sheep, which he was shearing in Carmel. ³His name was Nabal and his wife's name was Abigail. She was an intelligent and beautiful woman, but her husband was surly and mean in his dealings—he was a Calebite.   Jos 15:55; Pr 31:10; Ge 31:19 ⁴While David was in the wilderness, he heard that Nabal was shearing sheep. ⁵So he sent ten young men and said to them, "Go up to Nabal at Carmel and greet him in my name. ⁶Say to him: 'Long life to you! Good health to you and your household! And good health to all that is yours!   1Ch 12:18; Ps 122:7; Lk 10:5 ⁷"'Now I hear that it is sheep-shearing time. When your shepherds were with us, we did not mistreat them, and the whole time they were at Carmel nothing of theirs was missing. ⁸Ask your own servants and they will tell you. Therefore be favorable toward my men, since we come at a festive time. Please give your servants and your son David whatever you can find for them.'"

⁹When David's men arrived, they gave Nabal this message in David's name. Then they waited.

¹⁰Nabal answered David's servants, "Who is this David? Who is this son of Jesse? Many servants are breaking away from their masters these days. ¹¹Why should I take my bread and water, and the meat I have slaughtered for my shearers, and give it to men coming from who knows where?"   Jdg 8:6; 9:28

¹²David's men turned around and went back. When they arrived, they reported every word. ¹³David said to his men, "Each of you strap on your sword!" So they did, and David strapped his on as well. About four hundred men went up with David, while two hundred stayed with the supplies.   1Sa 23:13; 30:24

¹⁴One of the servants told Abigail, Nabal's wife, "David sent messengers from the wilderness to give our master his greetings, but he hurled insults at them. ¹⁵Yet these men were very good to us. They did not mistreat us, and the whole time we were out in the fields near them nothing was missing. ¹⁶Night and day they were a wall around us the whole time we were herding our sheep near them. ¹⁷Now think it over and see what you can do, because

ᵃ 1 Hebrew and some Septuagint manuscripts; other Septuagint manuscripts *Maon* disaster is hanging over our master and his whole household. He is such a wicked man that no one can talk to him." Ex 14:22; 1Sa 20:7

¹⁸Abigail acted quickly. She took two hundred loaves of bread, two skins of wine, five dressed sheep, five seahs*a* of roasted grain, a hundred cakes of raisins and two hundred cakes of pressed figs, and loaded them on donkeys. ¹⁹Then she told her servants, "Go on ahead; I'll follow you." But she did not tell her husband Nabal. Ge 32:20; 2Sa 16:1; 1Ch 12:40

²⁰As she came riding her donkey into a mountain ravine, there were David and his men descending toward her, and she met them. ²¹David had just said, "It's been useless—all my watching over this fellow's property in the wilderness so that nothing of his was missing. He has paid me back evil for good. ²²May God deal with David,*b* be it ever so severely, if by morning I leave alive one male of all who belong to him!" 1Sa 3:17; 1Ki 14:10; Ps 109:5

²³When Abigail saw David, she quickly got off her donkey and bowed down before David with her face to the ground. ²⁴She fell at his feet and said: "Pardon your servant, my lord, and let me speak to you; hear what your servant has to say. ²⁵Please pay no attention, my lord, to that wicked man Nabal. He is just like his name—his name means Fool, and folly goes with him. And as for me, your servant, I did not see the men my lord sent. ²⁶And now, my lord, as surely as the LORD your God lives and as you live, since the LORD has kept you from bloodshed and from avenging yourself with your own hands, may your enemies and all who are intent on harming my lord be like Nabal. ²⁷And let this gift, which your servant has brought to my lord, be given to the men who follow you. 1Sa 20:41; Pr 14:16; 17:12

²⁸"Please forgive your servant's presumption. The LORD your God will certainly make a lasting dynasty for my lord, because you fight the LORD's battles, and no wrongdoing will be found in you as long as you live. ²⁹Even though someone is pursuing you to take your life, the life of my lord will be bound securely in the bundle of the living by the LORD your God, but the lives of your enemies he will hurl away as from the pocket of a sling. ³⁰When the LORD has fulfilled for my lord every good thing he promised concerning him and has appointed him ruler over Israel, ³¹my lord will not have on his conscience the staggering burden of needless bloodshed or of having avenged himself. And when the LORD your God has brought my lord

---

a 18 That is, probably about 60 pounds or about 27 kilograms   *b* 22 Some Septuagint manuscripts; Hebrew *with David's enemies* success, remember your servant." 2Sa 7:11,26; 18:32; Jer 10:18 ³²David said to Abigail, "Praise be to the LORD, the God of Israel, who has sent you today to meet me. ³³May you be blessed for your good judgment and for keeping me from bloodshed this day and from avenging myself with my own hands. ³⁴Otherwise, as surely as the LORD, the God of Israel, lives, who has kept me from harming you, if you had not come quickly to meet me, not one male belonging to Nabal would have been left alive by daybreak." Ge 24:27; Ex 18:10; Lk 1:68 ³⁵Then David accepted from her hand what she had brought him and said, "Go home in peace. I have heard your words and granted your request." Ge 19:21

³⁶When Abigail went to Nabal, he was in the house holding a banquet like that of a king. He was in high spirits and very drunk. So she told him nothing at all until daybreak. ³⁷Then in the morning, when Nabal was sober, his wife told him all these things, and his heart failed him and he became like a stone. ³⁸About ten days later, the LORD struck Nabal and he died. Pr 20:1; Ecc 10:17; 1Sa 26:10

³⁹When David heard that Nabal was dead, he said, "Praise be to the LORD, who has upheld my cause against Nabal for treating me with contempt. He has kept his servant from doing wrong and has brought Nabal's wrongdoing down on his own head."

Then David sent word to Abigail, asking her to become his wife. ⁴⁰His servants went to Carmel and said to Abigail, "David has sent us to you to take you to become his wife."

⁴¹She bowed down with her face to the ground and said, "I am your servant and am ready to serve you and wash the feet of my lord's servants." ⁴²Abigail quickly got on a donkey and, attended by her five female servants, went with David's messengers and became his wife. ⁴³David had also married Ahinoam of Jezreel, and they both were his wives. ⁴⁴But Saul had given his daughter Michal, David's wife, to Paltiel[a] son of Laish, who was from Gallim. Ge 24:61-67; Jos 15:56; 2Sa 3:15

David Again Spares Saul's Life

26 The Ziphites went to Saul at Gibeah and said, "Is not David hiding on the hill of Hakilah, which faces Jeshimon?" ²So Saul went down to the Desert of Ziph, with his three thousand select Israelite troops, to search there for David. ³Saul made his camp beside the road on the hill of Hakilah facing Jeshimon, but David stayed in the wilderness. When he saw that Saul had followed him there, ⁴he sent out scouts and learned that Saul had definitely arrived.

a 44 Hebrew *Palti*, a variant of *Paltiel*

[5] Then David set out and went to the place where Saul had camped. He saw where Saul and Abner son of Ner, the commander of the army, had lain down. Saul was lying inside the camp, with the army encamped around him. 1Sa 17:55

[6] David then asked Ahimelek the Hittite and Abishai son of Zeruiah, Joab's brother, "Who will go down into the camp with me to Saul?" 2Sa 10:10; Jdg 7:10-11; 1Ch 2:16

"I'll go with you," said Abishai. [7] So David and Abishai went to the army by night, and there was Saul, lying asleep inside the camp with his spear stuck in the ground near his head. Abner and the soldiers were lying around him.

[8] Abishai said to David, "Today God has delivered your enemy into your hands. Now let me pin him to the ground with one thrust of the spear; I won't strike him twice."

[9] But David said to Abishai, "Don't destroy him! Who can lay a hand on the LORD's anointed and be guiltless? [10] As surely as the LORD lives," he said, "the LORD himself will strike him, or his time will come and he will die, or he will go into battle and perish. [11] But the LORD forbid that I should lay a hand on the LORD's anointed. Now get the spear and water jug that are near his head, and let's go." 1Sa 31:6; 2Sa 1:14; Dt 31:14

[12] So David took the spear and water jug near Saul's head, and they left. No one saw or knew about it, nor did anyone wake up. They were all sleeping, because the LORD had put them into a deep sleep. Ge 2:21; 15:12

[13] Then David crossed over to the other side and stood on top of the hill some distance away; there was a wide space between them. [14] He called out to the army and to Abner son of Ner, "Aren't you going to answer me, Abner?"

Abner replied, "Who are you who calls to the king?"

[15] David said, "You're a man, aren't you? And who is like you in Israel? Why didn't you guard your lord the king? Someone came to destroy your lord the king. [16] What you have done is not good. As surely as the LORD lives, you and your men must die, because you did not guard your master, the LORD's anointed. Look around you. Where are the king's spear and water jug that were near his head?"

[17] Saul recognized David's voice and said, "Is that your voice, David my son?" 1Sa 24:16

David replied, "Yes it is, my lord the king." [18] And he added, "Why is my lord pursuing his servant? What have I done, and what wrong am I guilty of? [19] Now let my lord the king listen to his servant's words. If the LORD has incited you against me, then may he accept an offering. If, however, people have done it, may they be cursed before the LORD! They have driven me today from my share in the LORD's inheritance and have said, 'Go, serve other gods.' ²⁰ Now do not let my blood fall to the ground far from the presence of the LORD. The king of Israel has come out to look for a flea — as one hunts a partridge in the mountains." 1Sa 24:9,11-14; 2Sa 14:16

²¹ Then Saul said, "I have sinned. Come back, David my son. Because you considered my life precious today, I will not try to harm you again. Surely I have acted like a fool and have been terribly wrong." Ex 9:27; 1Sa 15:24; 24:17

²² "Here is the king's spear," David answered. "Let one of your young men come over and get it. ²³ The LORD rewards everyone for their righteousness and faithfulness. The LORD delivered you into my hands today, but I would not lay a hand on the LORD's anointed. ²⁴ As surely as I valued your life today, so may the LORD value my life and deliver me from all trouble." Ps 7:8; 54:7; 62:12

²⁵ Then Saul said to David, "May you be blessed, David my son; you will do great things and surely triumph."

So David went on his way, and Saul returned home.

David Among the Philistines

27 But David thought to himself, "One of these days I will be destroyed by the hand of Saul. The best thing I can do is to escape to the land of the Philistines. Then Saul will give up searching for me anywhere in Israel, and I will slip out of his hand."

² So David and the six hundred men with him left and went over to Achish son of Maok king of Gath. ³ David and his men settled in Gath with Achish. Each man had his family with him, and David had his two wives: Ahinoam of Jezreel and Abigail of Carmel, the widow of Nabal. ⁴ When Saul was told that David had fled to Gath, he no longer searched for him. 1Sa 25:13; 21:10; 1Ki 2:39

⁵ Then David said to Achish, "If I have found favor in your eyes, let a place be assigned to me in one of the country towns, that I may live there. Why should your servant live in the royal city with you?"

⁶ So on that day Achish gave him Ziklag, and it has belonged to the kings of Judah ever since. ⁷ David lived in Philistine territory a year and four months. Jos 15:31; 19:5

⁸ Now David and his men went up and raided the Geshurites, the Girzites and the Amalekites. (From ancient times these peoples had lived in the land extending to Shur and Egypt.) ⁹ Whenever David attacked an area, he did not leave a man or woman alive, but took sheep and cattle, donkeys and camels, and clothes. Then he returned to Achish. Jos 13:2,13; Ex 17:8; 1Sa 15:3

¹⁰ When Achish asked, "Where

did you go raiding today?" David would say, "Against the Negev of Judah" or "Against the Negev of Jerahmeel" or "Against the Negev of the Kenites." [11] He did not leave a man or woman alive to be brought to Gath, for he thought, "They might inform on us and say, 'This is what David did.'" And such was his practice as long as he lived in Philistine territory. [12] Achish trusted David and said to himself, "He has become so obnoxious to his people, the Israelites, that he will be my servant for life." Jdg 1:16; 1Ch 2:9,25

28 In those days the Philistines gathered their forces to fight against Israel. Achish said to David, "You must understand that you and your men will accompany me in the army." 1Sa 29:1

[2] David said, "Then you will see for yourself what your servant can do."

Achish replied, "Very well, I will make you my bodyguard for life."

Saul and the Medium at Endor

[3] Now Samuel was dead, and all Israel had mourned for him and buried him in his own town of Ramah. Saul had expelled the mediums and spiritists from the land. Lev 19:31; Dt 18:10-11

[4] The Philistines assembled and came and set up camp at Shunem, while Saul gathered all Israel and set up camp at Gilboa. [5] When Saul saw the Philistine army, he was afraid; terror filled his heart. [6] He inquired of the LORD, but the LORD did not answer him by dreams or Urim or prophets. [7] Saul then said to his attendants, "Find me a woman who is a medium, so I may go and inquire of her." Ex 28:30; 1Ch 10:13-14; 2Ki 4:8

"There is one in Endor," they said. Jos 17:11

[8] So Saul disguised himself, putting on other clothes, and at night he and two men went to the woman. "Consult a spirit for me," he said, "and bring up for me the one I name." Dt 18:10-11; 2Ch 18:29; Isa 8:19

[9] But the woman said to him, "Surely you know what Saul has done. He has cut off the mediums and spiritists from the land. Why have you set a trap for my life to bring about my death?"

[10] Saul swore to her by the LORD, "As surely as the LORD lives, you will not be punished for this."

[11] Then the woman asked, "Whom shall I bring up for you?"

"Bring up Samuel," he said.

[12] When the woman saw Samuel, she cried out at the top of her voice and said to Saul, "Why have you deceived me? You are Saul!"

[13] The king said to her, "Don't be afraid. What do you see?"

The woman said, "I see a ghostly figure[a] coming up out of the earth."

[a] 13 Or see spirits; or see gods

¹⁴ "What does he look like?" he asked.

"An old man wearing a robe is coming up," she said. 1Sa 15:27

Then Saul knew it was Samuel, and he bowed down and prostrated himself with his face to the ground.

¹⁵ Samuel said to Saul, "Why have you disturbed me by bringing me up?"

"I am in great distress," Saul said. "The Philistines are fighting against me, and God has departed from me. He no longer answers me, either by prophets or by dreams. So I have called on you to tell me what to do." 1Sa 18:12

¹⁶ Samuel said, "Why do you consult me, now that the LORD has departed from you and become your enemy? ¹⁷ The LORD has done what he predicted through me. The LORD has torn the kingdom out of your hands and given it to one of your neighbors — to David. ¹⁸ Because you did not obey the LORD or carry out his fierce wrath against the Amalekites, the LORD has done this to you today. ¹⁹ The LORD will deliver both Israel and you into the hands of the Philistines, and tomorrow you and your sons will be with me. The LORD will also give the army of Israel into the hands of the Philistines." 1Sa 15:28; 31:2; 1Ki 20:42

²⁰ Immediately Saul fell full length on the ground, filled with fear because of Samuel's words. His strength was gone, for he had eaten nothing all that day and all that night.

²¹ When the woman came to Saul and saw that he was greatly shaken, she said, "Look, your servant has obeyed you. I took my life in my hands and did what you told me to do. ²² Now please listen to your servant and let me give you some food so you may eat and have the strength to go on your way." Jdg 12:3; 1Sa 19:5

²³ He refused and said, "I will not eat."

But his men joined the woman in urging him, and he listened to them. He got up from the ground and sat on the couch. 2Ki 5:13

²⁴ The woman had a fattened calf at the house, which she butchered at once. She took some flour, kneaded it and baked bread without yeast. ²⁵ Then she set it before Saul and his men, and they ate. That same night they got up and left.

Achish Sends David Back to Ziklag

29 The Philistines gathered all their forces at Aphek, and Israel camped by the spring in Jezreel. ² As the Philistine rulers marched with their units of hundreds and thousands, David and his men were marching at the rear with Achish. ³ The commanders of the Philistines asked, "What about these Hebrews?" 1Sa 4:1; 28:1; 2Ki 9:30

Achish replied, "Is this not David, who was an officer of Saul king of Israel? He has already been with me for over a year, and from the day he left Saul until now, I have found no fault in him." 1Sa 27:7; Da 6:5

⁴But the Philistine commanders were angry with Achish and said, "Send the man back, that he may return to the place you assigned him. He must not go with us into battle, or he will turn against us during the fighting. How better could he regain his master's favor than by taking the heads of our own men? ⁵Isn't this the David they sang about in their dances: 1Sa 14:21; 1Ch 12:19

> " 'Saul has slain his
>   thousands,
> and David his tens of
>   thousands'?" 1Sa 18:7; 21:11

⁶So Achish called David and said to him, "As surely as the LORD lives, you have been reliable, and I would be pleased to have you serve with me in the army. From the day you came to me until today, I have found no fault in you, but the rulers don't approve of you. ⁷Now turn back and go in peace; do nothing to displease the Philistine rulers." 1Sa 27:8-12

⁸"But what have I done?" asked David. "What have you found against your servant from the day I came to you until now? Why can't I go and fight against the enemies of my lord the king?"

⁹Achish answered, "I know that you have been as pleasing in my eyes as an angel of God; nevertheless, the Philistine commanders have said, 'He must not go up with us into battle.' ¹⁰Now get up early, along with your master's servants who have come with you, and leave in the morning as soon as it is light." 2Sa 14:17,20; 19:27; 1Ch 12:19

¹¹So David and his men got up early in the morning to go back to the land of the Philistines, and the Philistines went up to Jezreel.

David Destroys the Amalekites

30 David and his men reached Ziklag on the third day. Now the Amalekites had raided the Negev and Ziklag. They had attacked Ziklag and burned it, ²and had taken captive the women and everyone else in it, both young and old. They killed none of them, but carried them off as they went on their way. 1Sa 15:7; 27:8

³When David and his men reached Ziklag, they found it destroyed by fire and their wives and sons and daughters taken captive. ⁴So David and his men wept aloud until they had no strength left to weep. ⁵David's two wives had been captured—Ahinoam of Jezreel and Abigail, the widow of Nabal of Carmel. ⁶David was greatly distressed because the men were talking of stoning him; each one was bitter in spirit because of his sons and daughters.

But David found strength in the LORD his God. Ex 17:4; Ps 56:3-4,11

[7] Then David said to Abiathar the priest, the son of Ahimelek, "Bring me the ephod." Abiathar brought it to him, [8] and David inquired of the LORD, "Shall I pursue this raiding party? Will I overtake them?" 1Sa 22:20; 23:2

"Pursue them," he answered. "You will certainly overtake them and succeed in the rescue."

[9] David and the six hundred men with him came to the Besor Valley, where some stayed behind. [10] Two hundred of them were too exhausted to cross the valley, but David and the other four hundred continued the pursuit. 1Sa 27:2

[11] They found an Egyptian in a field and brought him to David. They gave him water to drink and food to eat — [12] part of a cake of pressed figs and two cakes of raisins. He ate and was revived, for he had not eaten any food or drunk any water for three days and three nights. Jdg 15:19

[13] David asked him, "Who do you belong to? Where do you come from?"

He said, "I am an Egyptian, the slave of an Amalekite. My master abandoned me when I became ill three days ago. [14] We raided the Negev of the Kerethites, some territory belonging to Judah and the Negev of Caleb. And we burned Ziklag." Jos 14:13; 2Sa 8:18; Eze 25:16

[15] David asked him, "Can you lead me down to this raiding party?"

He answered, "Swear to me before God that you will not kill me or hand me over to my master, and I will take you down to them."

[16] He led David down, and there they were, scattered over the countryside, eating, drinking and reveling because of the great amount of plunder they had taken from the land of the Philistines and from Judah. [17] David fought them from dusk until the evening of the next day, and none of them got away, except four hundred young men who rode off on camels and fled. [18] David recovered everything the Amalekites had taken, including his two wives. [19] Nothing was missing: young or old, boy or girl, plunder or anything else they had taken. David brought everything back. [20] He took all the flocks and herds, and his men drove them ahead of the other livestock, saying, "This is David's plunder." Ge 14:16; 1Sa 15:3; Lk 12:19

[21] Then David came to the two hundred men who had been too exhausted to follow him and who were left behind at the Besor Valley. They came out to meet David and the men with him. As David and his men approached, he asked them how they were. [22] But all the evil men and troublemakers among David's followers said, "Because they did not go out

with us, we will not share with them the plunder we recovered. However, each man may take his wife and children and go."

²³ David replied, "No, my brothers, you must not do that with what the LORD has given us. He has protected us and delivered into our hands the raiding party that came against us. ²⁴ Who will listen to what you say? The share of the man who stayed with the supplies is to be the same as that of him who went down to the battle. All will share alike." ²⁵ David made this a statute and ordinance for Israel from that day to this. Nu 31:27; Jos 22:8

²⁶ When David reached Ziklag, he sent some of the plunder to the elders of Judah, who were his friends, saying, "Here is a gift for you from the plunder of the LORD's enemies." Ge 33:11

²⁷ David sent it to those who were in Bethel, Ramoth Negev and Jattir; ²⁸ to those in Aroer, Siphmoth, Eshtemoa ²⁹ and Rakal; to those in the towns of the Jerahmeelites and the Kenites; ³⁰ to those in Hormah, Bor Ashan, Athak ³¹ and Hebron; and to those in all the other places where he and his men had roamed. Jos 13:16; 14:13; Jdg 1:17

Saul Takes His Life

31:1-13pp — 2Sa 1:4-12; 1Ch 10:1-12

31 Now the Philistines fought against Israel; the Israelites fled before them, and many fell dead on Mount Gilboa. ² The Philistines were in hot pursuit of Saul and his sons, and they killed his sons Jonathan, Abinadab and Malki-Shua. ³ The fighting grew fierce around Saul, and when the archers overtook him, they wounded him critically. 1Sa 28:4

⁴ Saul said to his armor-bearer, "Draw your sword and run me through, or these uncircumcised fellows will come and run me through and abuse me." Jdg 9:54

But his armor-bearer was terrified and would not do it; so Saul took his own sword and fell on it. ⁵ When the armor-bearer saw that Saul was dead, he too fell on his sword and died with him. ⁶ So Saul and his three sons and his armor-bearer and all his men died together that same day.

⁷ When the Israelites along the valley and those across the Jordan saw that the Israelite army had fled and that Saul and his sons had died, they abandoned their towns and fled. And the Philistines came and occupied them.

⁸ The next day, when the Philistines came to strip the dead, they found Saul and his three sons fallen on Mount Gilboa. ⁹ They cut off his head and stripped off his armor, and they sent messengers throughout the land of the Philistines to proclaim the news in the temple of their idols and among their people. ¹⁰ They put his armor in the temple of the Ashtoreths

and fastened his body to the wall of Beth Shan. Jos 17:11; Jdg 2:12-13; 2Sa 1:20

[11] When the people of Jabesh Gilead heard what the Philistines had done to Saul, [12] all their valiant men marched through the night to Beth Shan. They took down the bodies of Saul and his sons from the wall of Beth Shan and went to Jabesh, where they burned them. [13] Then they took their bones and buried them under a tamarisk tree at Jabesh, and they fasted seven days. 1Ch 10:1-12; 2Sa 1:4-12; 21:12-14

bodies of Saul and his sons from
the wall of Beth Shan and went to
Jabesh, where they burned them.
[13] Then they took their bones and
buried them under a tamarisk
tree at Jabesh, and they fasted sev-
en days.   1Ch 10:12; 1Sa 4:12; 2Sa 2:4

and fastened his body to the wall of
Beth Shan.   1Sa 14:16; 2:4; 2Sa 21:12
[12] When the people of Jabesh
Gilead heard what the Philistines
had done to Saul, [12] all their valiant
men marched through the night
to Beth Shan. They took down the

2 Samuel

David Hears of Saul's Death

1:4-12pp — 1Sa 31:1-13; 1Ch 10:1-12

1 After the death of Saul, David returned from striking
down the Amalekites and stayed
in Ziklag two days. [2] On the third
day a man arrived from Saul's
camp with his clothes torn and
dust on his head. When he came
to David, he fell to the ground to
pay him honor.   1Sa 4:12; 30:17; 31:6
   [3] "Where have you come from?"
David asked him.

He answered, "I have escaped
from the Israelite camp."

[4] "What happened?" David
asked. "Tell me."

"The men fled from the battle," he replied. "Many of them
fell and died. And Saul and his
son Jonathan are dead."

[5] Then David said to the young
man who brought him the report,
"How do you know that Saul and
his son Jonathan are dead?"

[6] "I happened to be on Mount
Gilboa," the young man said,
"and there was Saul, leaning
on his spear, with the chariots
and their drivers in hot pursuit.

[7] When he turned around and
saw me, he called out to me, and
I said, 'What can I do?'   1Sa 31:2-4
   [8] "He asked me, 'Who are you?'

" 'An Amalekite,' I answered.

[9] "Then he said to me, 'Stand
here by me and kill me! I'm in
the throes of death, but I'm still
alive.'

[10] "So I stood beside him and
killed him, because I knew that
after he had fallen he could not
survive. And I took the crown that
was on his head and the band on
his arm and have brought them
here to my lord."   Jdg 9:54; 2Ki 11:12

[11] Then David and all the
men with him took hold of their
clothes and tore them. [12] They
mourned and wept and fasted
till evening for Saul and his son
Jonathan, and for the army of the
LORD and for the nation of Israel, because they had fallen by the
sword.   1Sa 31:1-13; 1Ch 10:1-12; Ge 37:29

[13] David said to the young man
who brought him the report,
"Where are you from?"

"I am the son of a foreigner, an
Amalekite," he answered.

¹⁴David asked him, "Why weren't you afraid to lift your hand to destroy the LORD's anointed?" 1Sa 24:6

¹⁵Then David called one of his men and said, "Go, strike him down!" So he struck him down, and he died. ¹⁶For David had said to him, "Your blood be on your own head. Your own mouth testified against you when you said, 'I killed the LORD's anointed.'" 2Sa 4:10; Lev 20:9; Mt 27:24-25

David's Lament for Saul and Jonathan

¹⁷David took up this lament concerning Saul and his son Jonathan, ¹⁸and he ordered that the people of Judah be taught this lament of the bow (it is written in the Book of Jashar): Jos 10:13

¹⁹"A gazelle*ᵃ* lies slain on your heights, Israel.
How the mighty have fallen! 2Sa 3:38

²⁰"Tell it not in Gath, Mic 1:10
proclaim it not in the streets of Ashkelon,
lest the daughters of the Philistines be glad,
lest the daughters of the uncircumcised rejoice. Ex 15:20; 1Sa 18:6; 31:8

²¹"Mountains of Gilboa, 1Sa 31:1
may you have neither dew nor rain,

may no showers fall on your terraced fields.*ᵇ* Eze 31:15
For there the shield of the mighty was despised,
the shield of Saul — no longer rubbed with oil. Isa 21:5

²²"From the blood of the slain,
from the flesh of the mighty, Isa 34:3,7
the bow of Jonathan did not turn back,
the sword of Saul did not return unsatisfied.

²³Saul and Jonathan —
in life they were loved and admired,
and in death they were not parted.
They were swifter than eagles, Jer 4:13
they were stronger than lions. Jdg 14:18

²⁴"Daughters of Israel, weep for Saul,
who clothed you in scarlet and finery,
who adorned your garments with ornaments of gold.

²⁵"How the mighty have fallen in battle!
Jonathan lies slain on your heights.

²⁶I grieve for you, Jonathan my brother; 1Sa 20:42
you were very dear to me.

ᵃ 19 Gazelle *here symbolizes a human dignitary.*   *ᵇ 21* Or / *nor fields that yield grain for offerings*

Your love for me was
    wonderful,
    more wonderful than that
        of women.　　　1Sa 18:1

²⁷ "How the mighty have fallen!
    The weapons of war have
        perished!"

David Anointed King Over Judah

2 In the course of time, David inquired of the LORD. "Shall I go up to one of the towns of Judah?" he asked.　　1Sa 23:2,11-12

The LORD said, "Go up."

David asked, "Where shall I go?"

"To Hebron," the LORD answered.　　Ge 13:18; 1Sa 30:31

² So David went up there with his two wives, Ahinoam of Jezreel and Abigail, the widow of Nabal of Carmel. ³ David also took the men who were with him, each with his family, and they settled in Hebron and its towns. ⁴ Then the men of Judah came to Hebron, and there they anointed David king over the tribe of Judah.　　1Sa 25:42; 27:2; 2Sa 5:3-5

When David was told that it was the men from Jabesh Gilead who had buried Saul, ⁵ he sent messengers to them to say to them, "The LORD bless you for showing this kindness to Saul your master by burying him. ⁶ May the LORD now show you kindness and faithfulness, and I too will show you the same favor because you have done this. ⁷ Now then, be strong and brave, for Saul your master is dead, and the people of Judah have anointed me king over them."　　Ex 34:6; 1Sa 23:21; 1Ti 1:16

War Between the Houses of David and Saul

3:2-5pp — 1Ch 3:1-4

⁸ Meanwhile, Abner son of Ner, the commander of Saul's army, had taken Ish-Bosheth son of Saul and brought him over to Mahanaim. ⁹ He made him king over Gilead, Ashuri and Jezreel, and also over Ephraim, Benjamin and all Israel.　　Jdg 1:32; 1Sa 14:50; 1Ch 12:29

¹⁰ Ish-Bosheth son of Saul was forty years old when he became king over Israel, and he reigned two years. The tribe of Judah, however, remained loyal to David. ¹¹ The length of time David was king in Hebron over Judah was seven years and six months.　　2Sa 5:5

¹² Abner son of Ner, together with the men of Ish-Bosheth son of Saul, left Mahanaim and went to Gibeon. ¹³ Joab son of Zeruiah and David's men went out and met them at the pool of Gibeon. One group sat down on one side of the pool and one group on the other side.　　Jos 18:25; 2Sa 8:16; 1Ch 2:16

¹⁴ Then Abner said to Joab, "Let's have some of the young men get up and fight hand to hand in front of us."

"All right, let them do it," Joab said.

[15] So they stood up and were counted off—twelve men for Benjamin and Ish-Bosheth son of Saul, and twelve for David. [16] Then each man grabbed his opponent by the head and thrust his dagger into his opponent's side, and they fell down together. So that place in Gibeon was called Helkath Hazzurim.[a]

[17] The battle that day was very fierce, and Abner and the Israelites were defeated by David's men. 2Sa 3:1

[18] The three sons of Zeruiah were there: Joab, Abishai and Asahel. Now Asahel was as fleet-footed as a wild gazelle. [19] He chased Abner, turning neither to the right nor to the left as he pursued him. [20] Abner looked behind him and asked, "Is that you, Asahel?" 1Ch 2:16; 12:8

"It is," he answered.

[21] Then Abner said to him, "Turn aside to the right or to the left; take on one of the young men and strip him of his weapons." But Asahel would not stop chasing him.

[22] Again Abner warned Asahel, "Stop chasing me! Why should I strike you down? How could I look your brother Joab in the face?" 2Sa 3:27

[23] But Asahel refused to give up the pursuit; so Abner thrust the butt of his spear into Asahel's stomach, and the spear came out through his back. He fell there and died on the spot. And every man stopped when he came to the place where Asahel had fallen and died. 2Sa 3:27; 20:12

[24] But Joab and Abishai pursued Abner, and as the sun was setting, they came to the hill of Ammah, near Giah on the way to the wasteland of Gibeon. [25] Then the men of Benjamin rallied behind Abner. They formed themselves into a group and took their stand on top of a hill.

[26] Abner called out to Joab, "Must the sword devour forever? Don't you realize that this will end in bitterness? How long before you order your men to stop pursuing their fellow Israelites?" Dt 32:42

[27] Joab answered, "As surely as God lives, if you had not spoken, the men would have continued pursuing them until morning."

[28] So Joab blew the trumpet, and all the troops came to a halt; they no longer pursued Israel, nor did they fight anymore. 2Sa 18:16

[29] All that night Abner and his men marched through the Arabah. They crossed the Jordan, continued through the morning hours[b] and came to Mahanaim.

[30] Then Joab stopped pursuing Abner and assembled the whole army. Besides Asahel, nineteen of David's men were found missing. [31] But David's men had killed

---

[a] 16 *Helkath Hazzurim* means *field of daggers* or *field of hostilities.*   [b] 29 See Septuagint; the meaning of the Hebrew for this phrase is uncertain.

three hundred and sixty Benjamites who were with Abner. [32] They took Asahel and buried him in his father's tomb at Bethlehem. Then Joab and his men marched all night and arrived at Hebron by daybreak. Ge 49:29

3 The war between the house of Saul and the house of David lasted a long time. David grew stronger and stronger, while the house of Saul grew weaker and weaker. 2Sa 2:17; 5:10; 1Ki 14:30

[2] Sons were born to David in Hebron:

His firstborn was Amnon the son of Ahinoam of Jezreel; 1Sa 25:43; 1Ch 3:1-3

[3] his second, Kileab the son of Abigail the widow of Nabal of Carmel; 1Sa 25:42

the third, Absalom the son of Maakah daughter of Talmai king of Geshur; 1Sa 27:8

[4] the fourth, Adonijah the son of Haggith; 1Ki 1:5,11

the fifth, Shephatiah the son of Abital;

[5] and the sixth, Ithream the son of David's wife Eglah.

These were born to David in Hebron.

Abner Goes Over to David

[6] During the war between the house of Saul and the house of David, Abner had been strengthening his own position in the house of Saul. [7] Now Saul had had a concubine named Rizpah daughter of Aiah. And Ish-Bosheth said to Abner, "Why did you sleep with my father's concubine?" 2Sa 16:21-22; 21:8-11

[8] Abner was very angry because of what Ish-Bosheth said. So he answered, "Am I a dog's head — on Judah's side? This very day I am loyal to the house of your father Saul and to his family and friends. I haven't handed you over to David. Yet now you accuse me of an offense involving this woman! [9] May God deal with Abner, be it ever so severely, if I do not do for David what the LORD promised him on oath [10] and transfer the kingdom from the house of Saul and establish David's throne over Israel and Judah from Dan to Beersheba." [11] Ish-Bosheth did not dare to say another word to Abner, because he was afraid of him. 2Sa 9:8; 1Ki 19:2; Jdg 20:1

[12] Then Abner sent messengers on his behalf to say to David, "Whose land is it? Make an agreement with me, and I will help you bring all Israel over to you."

[13] "Good," said David. "I will make an agreement with you. But I demand one thing of you: Do not come into my presence unless you bring Michal daughter of Saul when you come to see me." [14] Then David sent messengers to Ish-Bosheth son of Saul, demanding, "Give me my wife Michal, whom I betrothed to myself for the price of a hundred Philistine foreskins." Ge 43:5; 1Sa 18:27

[15] So Ish-Bosheth gave orders

and had her taken away from her husband Paltiel son of Laish. ¹⁶Her husband, however, went with her, weeping behind her all the way to Bahurim. Then Abner said to him, "Go back home!" So he went back. Dt 24:1-4; 1Sa 25:44

¹⁷Abner conferred with the elders of Israel and said, "For some time you have wanted to make David your king. ¹⁸Now do it! For the LORD promised David, 'By my servant David I will rescue my people Israel from the hand of the Philistines and from the hand of all their enemies.'" Jdg 11:11; 1Sa 9:16

¹⁹Abner also spoke to the Benjamites in person. Then he went to Hebron to tell David everything that Israel and the whole tribe of Benjamin wanted to do. ²⁰When Abner, who had twenty men with him, came to David at Hebron, David prepared a feast for him and his men. ²¹Then Abner said to David, "Let me go at once and assemble all Israel for my lord the king, so that they may make a covenant with you, and that you may rule over all that your heart desires." So David sent Abner away, and he went in peace. 1Sa 10:20-21; 1Ki 11:37; 1Ch 12:2,16

Joab Murders Abner

²²Just then David's men and Joab returned from a raid and brought with them a great deal of plunder. But Abner was no longer with David in Hebron, because David had sent him away, and he had gone in peace. ²³When Joab and all the soldiers with him arrived, he was told that Abner son of Ner had come to the king and that the king had sent him away and that he had gone in peace.

²⁴So Joab went to the king and said, "What have you done? Look, Abner came to you. Why did you let him go? Now he is gone! ²⁵You know Abner son of Ner; he came to deceive you and observe your movements and find out everything you are doing."

²⁶Joab then left David and sent messengers after Abner, and they brought him back from the cistern at Sirah. But David did not know it. ²⁷Now when Abner returned to Hebron, Joab took him aside into an inner chamber, as if to speak with him privately. And there, to avenge the blood of his brother Asahel, Joab stabbed him in the stomach, and he died. 2Sa 2:22; 20:9-10; 1Ki 2:5

²⁸Later, when David heard about this, he said, "I and my kingdom are forever innocent before the LORD concerning the blood of Abner son of Ner. ²⁹May his blood fall on the head of Joab and on his whole family! May Joab's family never be without someone who has a running sore or leprosy^a or who leans on a crutch or who falls by the sword or who lacks food." Dt 21:9; Lev 15:2; 1Ki 2:31-33

³⁰(Joab and his brother Abishai

^a 29 The Hebrew for *leprosy* was used for various diseases affecting the skin.

murdered Abner because he had killed their brother Asahel in the battle at Gibeon.)

³¹ Then David said to Joab and all the people with him, "Tear your clothes and put on sackcloth and walk in mourning in front of Abner." King David himself walked behind the bier. ³² They buried Abner in Hebron, and the king wept aloud at Abner's tomb. All the people wept also. Ge 37:34; Pr 24:17; Isa 20:2 ³³ The king sang this lament for Abner: 2Sa 1:17

"Should Abner have died as
the lawless die?
³⁴   Your hands were not bound,
your feet were not fettered.
You fell as one falls before the
wicked."

And all the people wept over him again.

³⁵ Then they all came and urged David to eat something while it was still day; but David took an oath, saying, "May God deal with me, be it ever so severely, if I taste bread or anything else before the sun sets!" Ru 1:17; 2Sa 1:12; 12:17 ³⁶ All the people took note and were pleased; indeed, everything the king did pleased them. ³⁷ So on that day all the people there and all Israel knew that the king had no part in the murder of Abner son of Ner.

³⁸ Then the king said to his men, "Do you not realize that a commander and a great man has fallen in Israel this day? ³⁹ And today, though I am the anointed king, I am weak, and these sons of Zeruiah are too strong for me. May the Lᴏʀᴅ repay the evildoer according to his evil deeds!" 2Sa 19:5-7; 1Ki 2:5-6,33-34; Ps 41:10

Ish-Bosheth Murdered

4 When Ish-Bosheth son of Saul heard that Abner had died in Hebron, he lost courage, and all Israel became alarmed. ² Now Saul's son had two men who were leaders of raiding bands. One was named Baanah and the other Rekab; they were sons of Rimmon the Beerothite from the tribe of Benjamin — Beeroth is considered part of Benjamin, ³ because the people of Beeroth fled to Gittaim and have resided there as foreigners to this day. 2Sa 3:27; Jos 9:17; Ne 11:33

⁴ (Jonathan son of Saul had a son who was lame in both feet. He was five years old when the news about Saul and Jonathan came from Jezreel. His nurse picked him up and fled, but as she hurried to leave, he fell and became disabled. His name was Mephibosheth.) 1Sa 18:1; 2Sa 9:3,6; 1Ch 8:34

⁵ Now Rekab and Baanah, the sons of Rimmon the Beerothite, set out for the house of Ish-Bosheth, and they arrived there in the heat of the day while he was taking his noonday rest. ⁶ They went into the inner part of the house as if to get some wheat, and

they stabbed him in the stomach. Then Rekab and his brother Baanah slipped away. 2Sa 2:23

⁷They had gone into the house while he was lying on the bed in his bedroom. After they stabbed and killed him, they cut off his head. Taking it with them, they traveled all night by way of the Arabah. ⁸They brought the head of Ish-Bosheth to David at Hebron and said to the king, "Here is the head of Ish-Bosheth son of Saul, your enemy, who tried to kill you. This day the LORD has avenged my lord the king against Saul and his offspring." 1Sa 24:4; 25:29

⁹David answered Rekab and his brother Baanah, the sons of Rimmon the Beerothite, "As surely as the LORD lives, who has delivered me out of every trouble, ¹⁰when someone told me, 'Saul is dead,' and thought he was bringing good news, I seized him and put him to death in Ziklag. That was the reward I gave him for his news! ¹¹How much more — when wicked men have killed an innocent man in his own house and on his own bed — should I not now demand his blood from your hand and rid the earth of you!" 1Ki 1:29; 2Sa 1:2-16; Ge 9:5

¹²So David gave an order to his men, and they killed them. They cut off their hands and feet and hung the bodies by the pool in Hebron. But they took the head of Ish-Bosheth and buried it in Abner's tomb at Hebron. 2Sa 1:15

David Becomes King Over Israel

5:1-3pp — 1Ch 11:1-3

5 All the tribes of Israel came to David at Hebron and said, "We are your own flesh and blood. ²In the past, while Saul was king over us, you were the one who led Israel on their military campaigns. And the LORD said to you, 'You will shepherd my people Israel, and you will become their ruler.'" 1Sa 16:1; 18:5,13,16

³When all the elders of Israel had come to King David at Hebron, the king made a covenant with them at Hebron before the LORD, and they anointed David king over Israel. 1Ch 11:1-3; 2Sa 2:4; 3:21

⁴David was thirty years old when he became king, and he reigned forty years. ⁵In Hebron he reigned over Judah seven years and six months, and in Jerusalem he reigned over all Israel and Judah thirty-three years. Lk 3:23

David Conquers Jerusalem

5:6-10pp — 1Ch 11:4-9
5:11-16pp — 1Ch 3:5-9; 14:1-7

⁶The king and his men marched to Jerusalem to attack the Jebusites, who lived there. The Jebusites said to David, "You will not get in here; even the blind and the lame can ward you off." They thought, "David cannot get in here." ⁷Nevertheless, David captured the fortress of Zion — which is the City of David. Jos 15:8; Jdg 1:8; 1Ki 2:10

[8]On that day David had said, "Anyone who conquers the Jebusites will have to use the water shaft to reach those 'lame and blind' who are David's enemies.[a]" That is why they say, "The 'blind and lame' will not enter the palace."

[9]David then took up residence in the fortress and called it the City of David. He built up the area around it, from the terraces[b] inward. [10]And he became more and more powerful, because the LORD God Almighty was with him.   1Ch 11:4-9; 2Sa 3:1; 1Ki 9:15,24

[11]Now Hiram king of Tyre sent envoys to David, along with cedar logs and carpenters and stonemasons, and they built a palace for David. [12]Then David knew that the LORD had established him as king over Israel and had exalted his kingdom for the sake of his people Israel.   1Ki 5:1,18; 1Ch 14:1

[13]After he left Hebron, David took more concubines and wives in Jerusalem, and more sons and daughters were born to him. [14]These are the names of the children born to him there: Shammua, Shobab, Nathan, Solomon, [15]Ibhar, Elishua, Nepheg, Japhia, [16]Elishama, Eliada and Eliphelet.   1Ch 3:5-9; 14:1-7; Dt 17:17

David Defeats the Philistines
5:17-25pp — 1Ch 14:8-17

[17]When the Philistines heard that David had been anointed king over Israel, they went up in full force to search for him, but David heard about it and went down to the stronghold. [18]Now the Philistines had come and spread out in the Valley of Rephaim; [19]so David inquired of the LORD, "Shall I go and attack the Philistines? Will you deliver them into my hands?"   1Sa 23:2; 2Sa 23:14; Jos 15:8

The LORD answered him, "Go, for I will surely deliver the Philistines into your hands."

[20]So David went to Baal Perazim, and there he defeated them. He said, "As waters break out, the LORD has broken out against my enemies before me." So that place was called Baal Perazim.[c] [21]The Philistines abandoned their idols there, and David and his men carried them off.   1Ch 14:12; Isa 28:21

[22]Once more the Philistines came up and spread out in the Valley of Rephaim; [23]so David inquired of the LORD, and he answered, "Do not go straight up, but circle around behind them and attack them in front of the poplar trees. [24]As soon as you hear the sound of marching in the tops of the poplar trees, move quickly, because that will mean the LORD has gone out in front of you to strike the Philistine army." [25]So David did as the LORD commanded him, and he struck down the Philistines

---

[a] 8 Or are hated by David   [b] 9 Or the Millo breaks out.   [c] 20 Baal Perazim means the lord who

all the way from Gibeon[a] to Gezer.   1Ch 14:8-17; Jdg 4:14; 2Ki 7:6

The Ark Brought to Jerusalem

6:1-11pp — 1Ch 13:1-14
6:12-19pp — 1Ch 15:25–16:3

6 David again brought together all the able young men of Israel — thirty thousand. [2]He and all his men went to Baalah[b] in Judah to bring up from there the ark of God, which is called by the Name,[c] the name of the LORD Almighty, who is enthroned between the cherubim on the ark. [3]They set the ark of God on a new cart and brought it from the house of Abinadab, which was on the hill. Uzzah and Ahio, sons of Abinadab, were guiding the new cart [4]with the ark of God on it,[d] and Ahio was walking in front of it. [5]David and all Israel were celebrating with all their might before the LORD, with castanets,[e] harps, lyres, timbrels, sistrums and cymbals.   Lev 24:16; 1Sa 4:4; 6:7

[6]When they came to the threshing floor of Nakon, Uzzah reached out and took hold of the ark of God, because the oxen stumbled. [7]The LORD's anger burned against Uzzah because of his irreverent act; therefore God struck him down, and he died there beside the ark of God.   Ex 19:22; Nu 4:15,19-20; 1Ch 15:13

[8]Then David was angry because the LORD's wrath had broken out against Uzzah, and to this day that place is called Perez Uzzah.[f]   Ps 7:11

[9]David was afraid of the LORD that day and said, "How can the ark of the LORD ever come to me?" [10]He was not willing to take the ark of the LORD to be with him in the City of David. Instead, he took it to the house of Obed-Edom the Gittite. [11]The ark of the LORD remained in the house of Obed-Edom the Gittite for three months, and the LORD blessed him and his entire household.   1Ch 13:1-14; Ge 39:5

[12]Now King David was told, "The LORD has blessed the household of Obed-Edom and everything he has, because of the ark of God." So David went to bring up the ark of God from the house of Obed-Edom to the City of David with rejoicing. [13]When those who were carrying the ark of the LORD had taken six steps, he sacrificed a bull and a fattened calf. [14]Wearing a linen ephod, David was dancing before the LORD with all his might, [15]while he and all Israel were bringing up the ark of the LORD with shouts and the sound of trumpets.   Ex 15:20; 1Ki 8:1,5,62

[16]As the ark of the LORD was

---

[a] 25 Septuagint (see also 1 Chron. 14:16); Hebrew *Geba* (see 1 Chron. 13:6)   [b] 2 That is, Kiriath Jearim (see 1 Chron. 13:6)   [c] 2 Hebrew; Septuagint and Vulgate do not have *the Name.*   [d] 3,4 Dead Sea Scrolls and some Septuagint manuscripts; Masoretic Text *cart* [4]*and they brought it with the ark of God from the house of Abinadab, which was on the hill*   [e] 5 Masoretic Text; Dead Sea Scrolls and Septuagint (see also 1 Chron. 13:8) *songs*   [f] 8 *Perez Uzzah* means *outbreak against Uzzah.*

entering the City of David, Michal daughter of Saul watched from a window. And when she saw King David leaping and dancing before the LORD, she despised him in her heart.

¹⁷They brought the ark of the LORD and set it in its place inside the tent that David had pitched for it, and David sacrificed burnt offerings and fellowship offerings before the LORD. ¹⁸After he had finished sacrificing the burnt offerings and fellowship offerings, he blessed the people in the name of the LORD Almighty. ¹⁹Then he gave a loaf of bread, a cake of dates and a cake of raisins to each person in the whole crowd of Israelites, both men and women. And all the people went to their homes. 1Ch 15:25–16:3; 2Ch 1:4; Hos 3:1

²⁰When David returned home to bless his household, Michal daughter of Saul came out to meet him and said, "How the king of Israel has distinguished himself today, going around half-naked in full view of the slave girls of his servants as any vulgar fellow would!"

²¹David said to Michal, "It was before the LORD, who chose me rather than your father or anyone from his house when he appointed me ruler over the LORD's people Israel—I will celebrate before the LORD. ²²I will become even more undignified than this, and I will be humiliated in my own eyes. But by these slave girls you spoke of, I will be held in honor." 1Sa 13:14

²³And Michal daughter of Saul had no children to the day of her death.

God's Promise to David

7:1-17pp — 1Ch 17:1-15

7 After the king was settled in his palace and the LORD had given him rest from all his enemies around him, ²he said to Nathan the prophet, "Here I am, living in a house of cedar, while the ark of God remains in a tent." Ex 26:1; 2Sa 5:11; 1Ch 17:1

³Nathan replied to the king, "Whatever you have in mind, go ahead and do it, for the LORD is with you."

⁴But that night the word of the LORD came to Nathan, saying:

⁵"Go and tell my servant David, 'This is what the LORD says: Are you the one to build me a house to dwell in? ⁶I have not dwelt in a house from the day I brought the Israelites up out of Egypt to this day. I have been moving from place to place with a tent as my dwelling. ⁷Wherever I have moved with all the Israelites, did I ever say to any of their rulers whom I commanded to shepherd my people Israel, "Why have you not built me a house of cedar?"' Ex 40:18,34; Lev 26:11-12

⁸"Now then, tell my ser-

vant David, 'This is what the LORD Almighty says: I took you from the pasture, from tending the flock, and appointed you ruler over my people Israel. ⁹I have been with you wherever you have gone, and I have cut off all your enemies from before you. Now I will make your name great, like the names of the greatest men on earth. ¹⁰And I will provide a place for my people Israel and will plant them so that they can have a home of their own and no longer be disturbed. Wicked people will not oppress them anymore, as they did at the beginning ¹¹and have done ever since the time I appointed leaders*ᵃ* over my people Israel. I will also give you rest from all your enemies. 1Sa 16:11; Ps 18:37-42; Isa 5:1-7

" 'The LORD declares to you that the LORD himself will establish a house for you: ¹²When your days are over and you rest with your ancestors, I will raise up your offspring to succeed you, your own flesh and blood, and I will establish his kingdom. ¹³He is the one who will build a house for my Name, and I will establish the throne of his kingdom forever. ¹⁴I will be his father, and he will be my son. When he does wrong, I will punish him with a rod wielded by men, with floggings inflicted by human hands. ¹⁵But my love will never be taken away from him, as I took it away from Saul, whom I removed from before you. ¹⁶Your house and your kingdom will endure forever before me*ᵇ*; your throne will be established forever.' " 1Ch 17:1-15; 1Sa 15:23,28

¹⁷Nathan reported to David all the words of this entire revelation.

David's Prayer
7:18-29pp — 1Ch 17:16-27

¹⁸Then King David went in and sat before the LORD, and he said:

"Who am I, Sovereign LORD, and what is my family, that you have brought me this far? ¹⁹And as if this were not enough in your sight, Sovereign LORD, you have also spoken about the future of the house of your servant—and this decree, Sovereign LORD, is for a mere human!*ᶜ* 1Sa 18:18; Isa 55:8-9

²⁰"What more can David say to you? For you know your servant, Sovereign LORD. ²¹For the sake of your

---

ᵃ 11 Traditionally *judges*   *ᵇ 16* Some Hebrew manuscripts and Septuagint; most Hebrew manuscripts *you*   *ᶜ 19* Or *for the human race* word and according to your will, you have done this great thing and made it known to your servant. 1Sa 16:7; Jn 21:17

22 "How great you are, Sovereign Lord! There is no one like you, and there is no God but you, as we have heard with our own ears. 23 And who is like your people Israel — the one nation on earth that God went out to redeem as a people for himself, and to make a name for himself, and to perform great and awesome wonders by driving out nations and their gods from before your people, whom you redeemed from Egypt?ᵃ 24 You have established your people Israel as your very own forever, and you, Lord, have become their God. Dt 3:24; 4:32-38; 26:18

25 "And now, Lord God, keep forever the promise you have made concerning your servant and his house. Do as you promised, 26 so that your name will be great forever. Then people will say, 'The Lord Almighty is God over Israel!' And the house of your servant David will be established in your sight.

27 "Lord Almighty, God of Israel, you have revealed this to your servant, saying, 'I will build a house for you.' So your servant has found courage to pray this prayer to you. 28 Sovereign Lord, you are God! Your covenant is trustworthy, and you have promised these good things to your servant. 29 Now be pleased to bless the house of your servant, that it may continue forever in your sight; for you, Sovereign Lord, have spoken, and with your blessing the house of your servant will be blessed forever." 1Ch 17:16-27; Nu 6:23-27

David's Victories
8:1-14pp — 1Ch 18:1-13

8 In the course of time, David defeated the Philistines and subdued them, and he took Metheg Ammah from the control of the Philistines.

2 David also defeated the Moabites. He made them lie down on the ground and measured them off with a length of cord. Every two lengths of them were put to death, and the third length was allowed to live. So the Moabites became subject to David and brought him tribute. Nu 24:17

3 Moreover, David defeated Hadadezer son of Rehob, king of Zobah, when he went to restore his monument atᵇ the Euphrates Riv-

---

ᵃ 23 See Septuagint and 1 Chron. 17:21; Hebrew *wonders for your land and before your people, whom you redeemed from Egypt, from the nations and their gods.*   ᵇ 3 Or *his control along* er. ⁴David captured a thousand of his chariots, seven thousand charioteers*a* and twenty thousand foot soldiers. He hamstrung all but a hundred of the chariot horses. Jos 11:9; 1Sa 14:47

⁵When the Arameans of Damascus came to help Hadadezer king of Zobah, David struck down twenty-two thousand of them. ⁶He put garrisons in the Aramean kingdom of Damascus, and the Arameans became subject to him and brought tribute. The LORD gave David victory wherever he went. 2Sa 3:18; 1Ki 11:24

⁷David took the gold shields that belonged to the officers of Hadadezer and brought them to Jerusalem. ⁸From Tebah*b* and Berothai, towns that belonged to Hadadezer, King David took a great quantity of bronze. 1Ki 10:16; Eze 47:16

⁹When Tou*c* king of Hamath heard that David had defeated the entire army of Hadadezer, ¹⁰he sent his son Joram*d* to King David to greet him and congratulate him on his victory in battle over Hadadezer, who had been at war with Tou. Joram brought with him articles of silver, of gold and of bronze.

¹¹King David dedicated these articles to the LORD, as he had done with the silver and gold from all the nations he had subdued: ¹²Edom*e* and Moab, the Ammonites and the Philistines, and Amalek. He also dedicated the plunder taken from Hadadezer son of Rehob, king of Zobah. 1Ki 7:51

¹³And David became famous after he returned from striking down eighteen thousand Edomites*f* in the Valley of Salt. 2Ki 14:7

¹⁴He put garrisons throughout Edom, and all the Edomites became subject to David. The LORD gave David victory wherever he went. 1Ch 18:1-13; Ge 27:29,37-40

David's Officials
8:15-18pp — 1Ch 18:14-17

¹⁵David reigned over all Israel, doing what was just and right for all his people. ¹⁶Joab son of Zeruiah was over the army; Jehoshaphat son of Ahilud was recorder; ¹⁷Zadok son of Ahitub and Ahimelek son of Abiathar were priests; Seraiah was secretary; ¹⁸Benaiah son of Jehoiada was over the Kerethites and Pelethites; and David's sons were priests.*g* Ge 18:19; 1Sa 30:14; 1Ch 24:3

---

a 4 Septuagint (see also Dead Sea Scrolls and 1 Chron. 18:4); Masoretic Text *captured seventeen hundred of his charioteers* *b 8* See some Septuagint manuscripts (see also 1 Chron. 18:8); Hebrew *Betah.* *c 9* Hebrew *Toi*, a variant of *Tou*; also in verse 10 *d 10* A variant of *Hadoram* *e 12* Some Hebrew manuscripts, Septuagint and Syriac (see also 1 Chron. 18:11); most Hebrew manuscripts *Aram* *f 13* A few Hebrew manuscripts, Septuagint and Syriac (see also 1 Chron. 18:12); most Hebrew manuscripts *Aram* (that is, Arameans) *g 18* Or *were chief officials* (see Septuagint and Targum; see also 1 Chron. 18:17)

David and Mephibosheth

9 David asked, "Is there anyone still left of the house of Saul to whom I can show kindness for Jonathan's sake?" 1Sa 20:14-17,42

²Now there was a servant of Saul's household named Ziba. They summoned him to appear before David, and the king said to him, "Are you Ziba?" 2Sa 16:1-4; 19:17

"At your service," he replied.

³The king asked, "Is there no one still alive from the house of Saul to whom I can show God's kindness?"

Ziba answered the king, "There is still a son of Jonathan; he is lame in both feet." 2Sa 4:4

⁴"Where is he?" the king asked.

Ziba answered, "He is at the house of Makir son of Ammiel in Lo Debar." 2Sa 17:27-29

⁵So King David had him brought from Lo Debar, from the house of Makir son of Ammiel.

⁶When Mephibosheth son of Jonathan, the son of Saul, came to David, he bowed down to pay him honor.

David said, "Mephibosheth!"

"At your service," he replied.

⁷"Don't be afraid," David said to him, "for I will surely show you kindness for the sake of your father Jonathan. I will restore to you all the land that belonged to your grandfather Saul, and you will always eat at my table." 1Ki 2:7

⁸Mephibosheth bowed down and said, "What is your servant, that you should notice a dead dog like me?" 2Sa 16:9

⁹Then the king summoned Ziba, Saul's steward, and said to him, "I have given your master's grandson everything that belonged to Saul and his family. ¹⁰You and your sons and your servants are to farm the land for him and bring in the crops, so that your master's grandson may be provided for. And Mephibosheth, grandson of your master, will always eat at my table." (Now Ziba had fifteen sons and twenty servants.)

¹¹Then Ziba said to the king, "Your servant will do whatever my lord the king commands his servant to do." So Mephibosheth ate at David's*a* table like one of the king's sons.

¹²Mephibosheth had a young son named Mika, and all the members of Ziba's household were servants of Mephibosheth. ¹³And Mephibosheth lived in Jerusalem, because he always ate at the king's table; he was lame in both feet. 1Ch 8:34

David Defeats the Ammonites

10:1-19pp — 1Ch 19:1-19

10 In the course of time, the king of the Ammonites died, and his son Hanun succeeded him as king. ²David thought, "I will show kindness to Hanun son of Nahash, just as

---

a 11 Septuagint; Hebrew *my*

his father showed kindness to me." So David sent a delegation to express his sympathy to Hanun concerning his father. 1Sa 11:1

When David's men came to the land of the Ammonites, ³the Ammonite commanders said to Hanun their lord, "Do you think David is honoring your father by sending envoys to you to express sympathy? Hasn't David sent them to you only to explore the city and spy it out and overthrow it?" ⁴So Hanun seized David's envoys, shaved off half of each man's beard, cut off their garments at the buttocks, and sent them away. Isa 15:2; 20:4

⁵When David was told about this, he sent messengers to meet the men, for they were greatly humiliated. The king said, "Stay at Jericho till your beards have grown, and then come back."

⁶When the Ammonites realized that they had become obnoxious to David, they hired twenty thousand Aramean foot soldiers from Beth Rehob and Zobah, as well as the king of Maakah with a thousand men, and also twelve thousand men from Tob. Ge 34:30; 2Sa 8:5

⁷On hearing this, David sent Joab out with the entire army of fighting men. ⁸The Ammonites came out and drew up in battle formation at the entrance of their city gate, while the Arameans of Zobah and Rehob and the men of Tob and Maakah were by themselves in the open country.

⁹Joab saw that there were battle lines in front of him and behind him; so he selected some of the best troops in Israel and deployed them against the Arameans. ¹⁰He put the rest of the men under the command of Abishai his brother and deployed them against the Ammonites. ¹¹Joab said, "If the Arameans are too strong for me, then you are to come to my rescue; but if the Ammonites are too strong for you, then I will come to rescue you. ¹²Be strong, and let us fight bravely for our people and the cities of our God. The LORD will do what is good in his sight." Dt 31:6; 1Sa 3:18; 1Co 16:13

¹³Then Joab and the troops with him advanced to fight the Arameans, and they fled before him. ¹⁴When the Ammonites realized that the Arameans were fleeing, they fled before Abishai and went inside the city. So Joab returned from fighting the Ammonites and came to Jerusalem.

¹⁵After the Arameans saw that they had been routed by Israel, they regrouped. ¹⁶Hadadezer had Arameans brought from beyond the Euphrates River; they went to Helam, with Shobak the commander of Hadadezer's army leading them.

¹⁷When David was told of this, he gathered all Israel, crossed the Jordan and went to Helam. The Arameans formed their battle lines to meet David and fought against him. ¹⁸But they fled before

Israel, and David killed seven hundred of their charioteers and forty thousand of their foot soldiers.[a] He also struck down Shobak the commander of their army, and he died there. ¹⁹When all the kings who were vassals of Hadadezer saw that they had been routed by Israel, they made peace with the Israelites and became subject to them.　2Sa 8:6

So the Arameans were afraid to help the Ammonites anymore.　1Ch 19:1-19; 1Ki 11:25

David and Bathsheba

11 In the spring, at the time when kings go off to war, David sent Joab out with the king's men and the whole Israelite army. They destroyed the Ammonites and besieged Rabbah. But David remained in Jerusalem.　1Ki 20:22,26; 1Ch 20:1

²One evening David got up from his bed and walked around on the roof of the palace. From the roof he saw a woman bathing. The woman was very beautiful, ³and David sent someone to find out about her. The man said, "She is Bathsheba, the daughter of Eliam and the wife of Uriah the Hittite." ⁴Then David sent messengers to get her. She came to him, and he slept with her. (Now she was purifying herself from her monthly uncleanness.) Then she went back home. ⁵The

woman conceived and sent word to David, saying, "I am pregnant."　Ps 51 Title; Mt 5:28; Jas 1:14-15

⁶So David sent this word to Joab: "Send me Uriah the Hittite." And Joab sent him to David. ⁷When Uriah came to him, David asked him how Joab was, how the soldiers were and how the war was going. ⁸Then David said to Uriah, "Go down to your house and wash your feet." So Uriah left the palace, and a gift from the king was sent after him. ⁹But Uriah slept at the entrance to the palace with all his master's servants and did not go down to his house.　1Ch 11:41

¹⁰David was told, "Uriah did not go home." So he asked Uriah, "Haven't you just come from a military campaign? Why didn't you go home?"

¹¹Uriah said to David, "The ark and Israel and Judah are staying in tents,[b] and my commander Joab and my lord's men are camped in the open country. How could I go to my house to eat and drink and make love to my wife? As surely as you live, I will not do such a thing!"　2Sa 7:2

¹²Then David said to him, "Stay here one more day, and tomorrow I will send you back." So Uriah remained in Jerusalem that day and the next. ¹³At David's invitation, he ate and drank with him, and David made him

---

[a] 18 Some Septuagint manuscripts (see also 1 Chron. 19:18); Hebrew *horsemen*
[b] 11 Or *staying at Sukkoth*

drunk. But in the evening Uriah went out to sleep on his mat among his master's servants; he did not go home.

¹⁴ In the morning David wrote a letter to Joab and sent it with Uriah. ¹⁵ In it he wrote, "Put Uriah out in front where the fighting is fiercest. Then withdraw from him so he will be struck down and die." 1Ki 21:8; 2Sa 12:12

¹⁶ So while Joab had the city under siege, he put Uriah at a place where he knew the strongest defenders were. ¹⁷ When the men of the city came out and fought against Joab, some of the men in David's army fell; moreover, Uriah the Hittite died.

¹⁸ Joab sent David a full account of the battle. ¹⁹ He instructed the messenger: "When you have finished giving the king this account of the battle, ²⁰ the king's anger may flare up, and he may ask you, 'Why did you get so close to the city to fight? Didn't you know they would shoot arrows from the wall? ²¹ Who killed Abimelek son of Jerub-Besheth ᵃ? Didn't a woman drop an upper millstone on him from the wall, so that he died in Thebez? Why did you get so close to the wall?' If he asks you this, then say to him, 'Moreover, your servant Uriah the Hittite is dead.'" Jdg 9:50-54

²² The messenger set out, and when he arrived he told David everything Joab had sent him to say. ²³ The messenger said to David, "The men overpowered us and came out against us in the open, but we drove them back to the entrance of the city gate. ²⁴ Then the archers shot arrows at your servants from the wall, and some of the king's men died. Moreover, your servant Uriah the Hittite is dead."

²⁵ David told the messenger, "Say this to Joab: 'Don't let this upset you; the sword devours one as well as another. Press the attack against the city and destroy it.' Say this to encourage Joab."

²⁶ When Uriah's wife heard that her husband was dead, she mourned for him. ²⁷ After the time of mourning was over, David had her brought to his house, and she became his wife and bore him a son. But the thing David had done displeased the LORD. 2Sa 12:9; Ps 51:4-5

Nathan Rebukes David

11:1; 12:29-31pp — 1Ch 20:1-3

12 The LORD sent Nathan to David. When he came to him, he said, "There were two men in a certain town, one rich and the other poor. ² The rich man had a very large number of sheep and cattle, ³ but the poor man had nothing except one little ewe lamb he had bought. He raised it, and it grew up with him and his children. It shared his food, drank

---

ᵃ 21 Also known as *Jerub-Baal* (that is, Gideon)

from his cup and even slept in his arms. It was like a daughter to him. 2Sa 14:4; 1Ki 20:35-41

⁴"Now a traveler came to the rich man, but the rich man refrained from taking one of his own sheep or cattle to prepare a meal for the traveler who had come to him. Instead, he took the ewe lamb that belonged to the poor man and prepared it for the one who had come to him."

⁵David burned with anger against the man and said to Nathan, "As surely as the LORD lives, the man who did this must die! ⁶He must pay for that lamb four times over, because he did such a thing and had no pity." Ex 22:1

⁷Then Nathan said to David, "You are the man! This is what the LORD, the God of Israel, says: 'I anointed you king over Israel, and I delivered you from the hand of Saul. ⁸I gave your master's house to you, and your master's wives into your arms. I gave you all Israel and Judah. And if all this had been too little, I would have given you even more. ⁹Why did you despise the word of the LORD by doing what is evil in his eyes? You struck down Uriah the Hittite with the sword and took his wife to be your own. You killed him with the sword of the Ammonites. ¹⁰Now, therefore, the sword will never depart from your house, because you despised me and took

the wife of Uriah the Hittite to be your own.' 2Sa 11:15; 13:28; 1Ki 20:42

¹¹"This is what the LORD says: 'Out of your own household I am going to bring calamity on you. Before your very eyes I will take your wives and give them to one who is close to you, and he will sleep with your wives in broad daylight. ¹²You did it in secret, but I will do this thing in broad daylight before all Israel.'" Dt 28:30

¹³Then David said to Nathan, "I have sinned against the LORD." 1Sa 15:24; 2Sa 24:10

Nathan replied, "The LORD has taken away your sin. You are not going to die. ¹⁴But because by doing this you have shown utter contempt for[a] the LORD, the son born to you will die." Pr 28:13; Isa 52:5

¹⁵After Nathan had gone home, the LORD struck the child that Uriah's wife had borne to David, and he became ill. ¹⁶David pleaded with God for the child. He fasted and spent the nights lying in sackcloth[b] on the ground. ¹⁷The elders of his household stood beside him to get him up from the ground, but he refused, and he would not eat any food with them. 1Sa 25:38; 2Sa 13:31; Ps 5:7

¹⁸On the seventh day the child died. David's attendants were afraid to tell him that the child was dead, for they thought, "While the child was still living, he wouldn't listen to us when we

---

[a] 14 An ancient Hebrew scribal tradition; Masoretic Text *for the enemies of*   [b] 16 Dead Sea Scrolls and Septuagint; Masoretic Text does not have *in sackcloth*.

spoke to him. How can we now tell him the child is dead? He may do something desperate."

¹⁹David noticed that his attendants were whispering among themselves, and he realized the child was dead. "Is the child dead?" he asked.

"Yes," they replied, "he is dead."

²⁰Then David got up from the ground. After he had washed, put on lotions and changed his clothes, he went into the house of the LORD and worshiped. Then he went to his own house, and at his request they served him food, and he ate. Job 1:20

²¹His attendants asked him, "Why are you acting this way? While the child was alive, you fasted and wept, but now that the child is dead, you get up and eat!" Jdg 20:26

²²He answered, "While the child was still alive, I fasted and wept. I thought, 'Who knows? The LORD may be gracious to me and let the child live.' ²³But now that he is dead, why should I go on fasting? Can I bring him back again? I will go to him, but he will not return to me." Jnh 3:9; Ge 37:35

²⁴Then David comforted his wife Bathsheba, and he went to her and made love to her. She gave birth to a son, and they named him Solomon. The LORD loved him; ²⁵and because the LORD loved him, he sent word through Nathan the prophet to name him Jedidiah.ᵃ 1Ki 1:11; 1Ch 22:9; Mt 1:6

²⁶Meanwhile Joab fought against Rabbah of the Ammonites and captured the royal citadel. ²⁷Joab then sent messengers to David, saying, "I have fought against Rabbah and taken its water supply. ²⁸Now muster the rest of the troops and besiege the city and capture it. Otherwise I will take the city, and it will be named after me." Dt 3:11

²⁹So David mustered the entire army and went to Rabbah, and attacked and captured it. ³⁰David took the crown from their king'sᵇ head, and it was placed on his own head. It weighed a talentᶜ of gold, and it was set with precious stones. David took a great quantity of plunder from the city ³¹and brought out the people who were there, consigning them to labor with saws and with iron picks and axes, and he made them work at brickmaking.ᵈ David did this to all the Ammonite towns. Then he and his entire army returned to Jerusalem. 1Ch 20:1-3; 1Sa 14:47

Amnon and Tamar

13 In the course of time, Amnon son of David fell in love with Tamar, the beautiful sister of Absalom son of David. 2Sa 3:2; 1Ch 3:9

ᵃ 25 *Jedidiah* means *loved by the LORD.* ᵇ 30 Or *from Milkom's* (that is, Molek's) ᶜ 30 That is, about 75 pounds or about 34 kilograms ᵈ 31 The meaning of the Hebrew for this clause is uncertain.

²Amnon became so obsessed with his sister Tamar that he made himself ill. She was a virgin, and it seemed impossible for him to do anything to her.

³Now Amnon had an adviser named Jonadab son of Shimeah, David's brother. Jonadab was a very shrewd man. ⁴He asked Amnon, "Why do you, the king's son, look so haggard morning after morning? Won't you tell me?"

Amnon said to him, "I'm in love with Tamar, my brother Absalom's sister."

⁵"Go to bed and pretend to be ill," Jonadab said. "When your father comes to see you, say to him, 'I would like my sister Tamar to come and give me something to eat. Let her prepare the food in my sight so I may watch her and then eat it from her hand.'"

⁶So Amnon lay down and pretended to be ill. When the king came to see him, Amnon said to him, "I would like my sister Tamar to come and make some special bread in my sight, so I may eat from her hand."

⁷David sent word to Tamar at the palace: "Go to the house of your brother Amnon and prepare some food for him." ⁸So Tamar went to the house of her brother Amnon, who was lying down. She took some dough, kneaded it, made the bread in his sight and baked it. ⁹Then she took the pan and served him the bread, but he refused to eat.

"Send everyone out of here," Amnon said. So everyone left him. ¹⁰Then Amnon said to Tamar, "Bring the food here into my bedroom so I may eat from your hand." And Tamar took the bread she had prepared and brought it to her brother Amnon in his bedroom. ¹¹But when she took it to him to eat, he grabbed her and said, "Come to bed with me, my sister." Ge 39:12; 45:1

¹²"No, my brother!" she said to him. "Don't force me! Such a thing should not be done in Israel! Don't do this wicked thing. ¹³What about me? Where could I get rid of my disgrace? And what about you? You would be like one of the wicked fools in Israel. Please speak to the king; he will not keep me from being married to you." ¹⁴But he refused to listen to her, and since he was stronger than she, he raped her. Lev 18:9; Dt 22:25; Jdg 19:23

¹⁵Then Amnon hated her with intense hatred. In fact, he hated her more than he had loved her. Amnon said to her, "Get up and get out!"

¹⁶"No!" she said to him. "Sending me away would be a greater wrong than what you have already done to me."

But he refused to listen to her. ¹⁷He called his personal servant and said, "Get this woman out of my sight and bolt the door after her." ¹⁸So his servant put her out and bolted the door after her. She was wearing an ornate[a] robe, for this was the kind of garment the virgin daughters of the king wore. [19]Tamar put ashes on her head and tore the ornate robe she was wearing. She put her hands on her head and went away, weeping aloud as she went. Ge 37:23; Jos 7:6; Est 4:1

[20]Her brother Absalom said to her, "Has that Amnon, your brother, been with you? Be quiet for now, my sister; he is your brother. Don't take this thing to heart." And Tamar lived in her brother Absalom's house, a desolate woman.

[21]When King David heard all this, he was furious. [22]And Absalom never said a word to Amnon, either good or bad; he hated Amnon because he had disgraced his sister Tamar. Ge 31:24; Lev 19:17-18

Absalom Kills Amnon

[23]Two years later, when Absalom's sheepshearers were at Baal Hazor near the border of Ephraim, he invited all the king's sons to come there. [24]Absalom went to the king and said, "Your servant has had shearers come. Will the king and his attendants please join me?" 1Sa 25:7

[25]"No, my son," the king replied. "All of us should not go; we would only be a burden to you." Although Absalom urged him, he still refused to go but gave him his blessing.

[26]Then Absalom said, "If not, please let my brother Amnon come with us."

The king asked him, "Why should he go with you?" [27]But Absalom urged him, so he sent with him Amnon and the rest of the king's sons.

[28]Absalom ordered his men, "Listen! When Amnon is in high spirits from drinking wine and I say to you, 'Strike Amnon down,' then kill him. Don't be afraid. Haven't I given you this order? Be strong and brave." [29]So Absalom's men did to Amnon what Absalom had ordered. Then all the king's sons got up, mounted their mules and fled. Jdg 19:6,9,22; 1Sa 25:36

[30]While they were on their way, the report came to David: "Absalom has struck down all the king's sons; not one of them is left." [31]The king stood up, tore his clothes and lay down on the ground; and all his attendants stood by with their clothes torn.

[32]But Jonadab son of Shimeah, David's brother, said, "My lord should not think that they killed all the princes; only Amnon is dead. This has been Absalom's express intention ever since the day Amnon raped his sister Tamar. [33]My lord the king should not be concerned about the report that all the king's sons are dead. Only Amnon is dead."

[34]Meanwhile, Absalom had fled.

---

[a] 18 The meaning of the Hebrew for this word is uncertain; also in verse 19.

Now the man standing watch looked up and saw many people on the road west of him, coming down the side of the hill. The watchman went and told the king, "I see men in the direction of Horonaim, on the side of the hill."[a]

[35] Jonadab said to the king, "See, the king's sons have come; it has happened just as your servant said."

[36] As he finished speaking, the king's sons came in, wailing loudly. The king, too, and all his attendants wept very bitterly.

[37] Absalom fled and went to Talmai son of Ammihud, the king of Geshur. But King David mourned many days for his son. 2Sa 3:3; 14:23

[38] After Absalom fled and went to Geshur, he stayed there three years. [39] And King David longed to go to Absalom, for he was consoled concerning Amnon's death.

Absalom Returns to Jerusalem

14 Joab son of Zeruiah knew that the king's heart longed for Absalom. [2] So Joab sent someone to Tekoa and had a wise woman brought from there. He said to her, "Pretend you are in mourning. Dress in mourning clothes, and don't use any cosmetic lotions. Act like a woman who has spent many days grieving for the dead. [3] Then go to the king and speak these words to him." And Joab put the words in her mouth. 2Sa 12:20; 20:16; 2Ch 11:6

[4] When the woman from Tekoa went[b] to the king, she fell with her face to the ground to pay him honor, and she said, "Help me, Your Majesty!"

[5] The king asked her, "What is troubling you?"

She said, "I am a widow; my husband is dead. [6] I your servant had two sons. They got into a fight with each other in the field, and no one was there to separate them. One struck the other and killed him. [7] Now the whole clan has risen up against your servant; they say, 'Hand over the one who struck his brother down, so that we may put him to death for the life of his brother whom he killed; then we will get rid of the heir as well.' They would put out the only burning coal I have left, leaving my husband neither name nor descendant on the face of the earth." Dt 19:10-13; Nu 35:19; Mt 21:38

[8] The king said to the woman, "Go home, and I will issue an order in your behalf." 1Sa 25:35

[9] But the woman from Tekoa said to him, "Let my lord the king pardon me and my family, and let the king and his throne be without guilt." 1Sa 25:24; 1Ki 2:33; Mt 27:25

[10] The king replied, "If anyone says anything to you, bring them to me, and they will not bother you again."

---

[a] 34 Septuagint; Hebrew does not have this sentence.   [b] 4 Many Hebrew manuscripts, Septuagint, Vulgate and Syriac; most Hebrew manuscripts *spoke*

[11]She said, "Then let the king invoke the LORD his God to prevent the avenger of blood from adding to the destruction, so that my son will not be destroyed." Nu 35:12,21

"As surely as the LORD lives," he said, "not one hair of your son's head will fall to the ground."

[12]Then the woman said, "Let your servant speak a word to my lord the king."

"Speak," he replied.

[13]The woman said, "Why then have you devised a thing like this against the people of God? When the king says this, does he not convict himself, for the king has not brought back his banished son? [14]Like water spilled on the ground, which cannot be recovered, so we must die. But that is not what God desires; rather, he devises ways so that a banished person does not remain banished from him. 2Sa 12:7; Nu 35:15,25-28

[15]"And now I have come to say this to my lord the king because the people have made me afraid. Your servant thought, 'I will speak to the king; perhaps he will grant his servant's request. [16]Perhaps the king will agree to deliver his servant from the hand of the man who is trying to cut off both me and my son from God's inheritance.'

[17]"And now your servant says, 'May the word of my lord the king secure my inheritance, for my lord the king is like an angel of God in discerning good and evil. May the LORD your God be with you.'" 2Sa 19:27; 1Ki 3:9

[18]Then the king said to the woman, "Don't keep from me the answer to what I am going to ask you."

"Let my lord the king speak," the woman said.

[19]The king asked, "Isn't the hand of Joab with you in all this?"

The woman answered, "As surely as you live, my lord the king, no one can turn to the right or to the left from anything my lord the king says. Yes, it was your servant Joab who instructed me to do this and who put all these words into the mouth of your servant. [20]Your servant Joab did this to change the present situation. My lord has wisdom like that of an angel of God — he knows everything that happens in the land." 2Sa 18:13; Isa 28:6

[21]The king said to Joab, "Very well, I will do it. Go, bring back the young man Absalom."

[22]Joab fell with his face to the ground to pay him honor, and he blessed the king. Joab said, "Today your servant knows that he has found favor in your eyes, my lord the king, because the king has granted his servant's request." Ge 47:7

[23]Then Joab went to Geshur and brought Absalom back to Jerusalem. [24]But the king said, "He must go to his own house;

he must not see my face." So Absalom went to his own house and did not see the face of the king.

²⁵In all Israel there was not a man so highly praised for his handsome appearance as Absalom. From the top of his head to the sole of his foot there was no blemish in him. ²⁶Whenever he cut the hair of his head—he used to cut his hair once a year because it became too heavy for him—he would weigh it, and its weight was two hundred shekels*a* by the royal standard. Eze 44:20

²⁷Three sons and a daughter were born to Absalom. His daughter's name was Tamar, and she became a beautiful woman.

²⁸Absalom lived two years in Jerusalem without seeing the king's face. ²⁹Then Absalom sent for Joab in order to send him to the king, but Joab refused to come to him. So he sent a second time, but he refused to come. ³⁰Then he said to his servants, "Look, Joab's field is next to mine, and he has barley there. Go and set it on fire." So Absalom's servants set the field on fire.

³¹Then Joab did go to Absalom's house, and he said to him, "Why have your servants set my field on fire?" Jdg 15:5

³²Absalom said to Joab, "Look, I sent word to you and said, 'Come here so I can send you to the king to ask, "Why have I come from Geshur? It would be better for me

if I were still there!"' Now then, I want to see the king's face, and if I am guilty of anything, let him put me to death." 1Sa 20:8; 2Sa 3:3

³³So Joab went to the king and told him this. Then the king summoned Absalom, and he came in and bowed down with his face to the ground before the king. And the king kissed Absalom. Ge 33:4

Absalom's Conspiracy

15 In the course of time, Absalom provided himself with a chariot and horses and with fifty men to run ahead of him. ²He would get up early and stand by the side of the road leading to the city gate. Whenever anyone came with a complaint to be placed before the king for a decision, Absalom would call out to him, "What town are you from?" He would answer, "Your servant is from one of the tribes of Israel." ³Then Absalom would say to him, "Look, your claims are valid and proper, but there is no representative of the king to hear you." ⁴And Absalom would add, "If only I were appointed judge in the land! Then everyone who has a complaint or case could come to me and I would see that they receive justice." Jdg 9:29; 2Sa 19:8; Pr 12:2

⁵Also, whenever anyone approached him to bow down before him, Absalom would reach out his hand, take hold of him and kiss him. ⁶Absalom behaved in

a 26 That is, about 5 pounds or about 2.3 kilograms

this way toward all the Israelites who came to the king asking for justice, and so he stole the hearts of the people of Israel. Ro 16:18

⁷At the end of four*ᵃ* years, Absalom said to the king, "Let me go to Hebron and fulfill a vow I made to the LORD. ⁸While your servant was living at Geshur in Aram, I made this vow: 'If the LORD takes me back to Jerusalem, I will worship the LORD in Hebron.ᵇ'" Ge 28:20; 2Sa 13:37-38

⁹The king said to him, "Go in peace." So he went to Hebron.

¹⁰Then Absalom sent secret messengers throughout the tribes of Israel to say, "As soon as you hear the sound of the trumpets, then say, 'Absalom is king in Hebron.'" ¹¹Two hundred men from Jerusalem had accompanied Absalom. They had been invited as guests and went quite innocently, knowing nothing about the matter. ¹²While Absalom was offering sacrifices, he also sent for Ahithophel the Gilonite, David's counselor, to come from Giloh, his hometown. And so the conspiracy gained strength, and Absalom's following kept on increasing. 2Sa 16:15,23; 1Ki 1:34,39; Ps 3:1

David Flees

¹³A messenger came and told David, "The hearts of the people of Israel are with Absalom."

¹⁴Then David said to all his officials who were with him in Jerusalem, "Come! We must flee, or none of us will escape from Absalom. We must leave immediately, or he will move quickly to overtake us and bring ruin on us and put the city to the sword." 2Sa 19:9

¹⁵The king's officials answered him, "Your servants are ready to do whatever our lord the king chooses."

¹⁶The king set out, with his entire household following him; but he left ten concubines to take care of the palace. ¹⁷So the king set out, with all the people following him, and they halted at the edge of the city. ¹⁸All his men marched past him, along with all the Kerethites and Pelethites; and all the six hundred Gittites who had accompanied him from Gath marched before the king. 2Sa 8:18; 16:21-22

¹⁹The king said to Ittai the Gittite, "Why should you come along with us? Go back and stay with King Absalom. You are a foreigner, an exile from your homeland. ²⁰You came only yesterday. And today shall I make you wander about with us, when I do not know where I am going? Go back, and take your people with you. May the LORD show you kindness and faithfulness."ᶜ 1Sa 23:13; 2Sa 2:6; 18:2

ᵃ 7 Some Septuagint manuscripts, Syriac and Josephus; Hebrew *forty*   *ᵇ 8* Some Septuagint manuscripts; Hebrew does not have *in Hebron.*   *ᶜ 20* Septuagint; Hebrew *May kindness and faithfulness be with you*

²¹But Ittai replied to the king, "As surely as the LORD lives, and as my lord the king lives, wherever my lord the king may be, whether it means life or death, there will your servant be." Ru 1:16-17; Pr 17:17

²²David said to Ittai, "Go ahead, march on." So Ittai the Gittite marched on with all his men and the families that were with him.

²³The whole countryside wept aloud as all the people passed by. The king also crossed the Kidron Valley, and all the people moved on toward the wilderness. 1Sa 11:4

²⁴Zadok was there, too, and all the Levites who were with him were carrying the ark of the covenant of God. They set down the ark of God, and Abiathar offered sacrifices until all the people had finished leaving the city. Nu 4:15; 1Sa 22:20; 2Sa 8:17

²⁵Then the king said to Zadok, "Take the ark of God back into the city. If I find favor in the LORD's eyes, he will bring me back and let me see it and his dwelling place again. ²⁶But if he says, 'I am not pleased with you,' then I am ready; let him do to me whatever seems good to him." Ex 15:13; 1Sa 3:18; Ps 43:3

²⁷The king also said to Zadok the priest, "Do you understand? Go back to the city with my blessing. Take your son Ahimaaz with you, and also Abiathar's son Jonathan. You and Abiathar return with your two sons. ²⁸I will wait at the fords in the wilderness until word comes from you to inform me." ²⁹So Zadok and Abiathar took the ark of God back to Jerusalem and stayed there. 1Sa 9:9

³⁰But David continued up the Mount of Olives, weeping as he went; his head was covered and he was barefoot. All the people with him covered their heads too and were weeping as they went up. ³¹Now David had been told, "Ahithophel is among the conspirators with Absalom." So David prayed, "LORD, turn Ahithophel's counsel into foolishness." 2Sa 16:23; Est 6:12; Isa 20:2-4

³²When David arrived at the summit, where people used to worship God, Hushai the Arkite was there to meet him, his robe torn and dust on his head. ³³David said to him, "If you go with me, you will be a burden to me. ³⁴But if you return to the city and say to Absalom, 'Your Majesty, I will be your servant; I was your father's servant in the past, but now I will be your servant,' then you can help me by frustrating Ahithophel's advice. ³⁵Won't the priests Zadok and Abiathar be there with you? Tell them anything you hear in the king's palace. ³⁶Their two sons, Ahimaaz son of Zadok and Jonathan son of Abiathar, are there with them. Send them to me with anything you hear." 2Sa 17:15-16; 19:35

³⁷So Hushai, David's confidant, arrived at Jerusalem as Absalom was entering the city. 1Ch 27:33

David and Ziba

16 When David had gone a short distance beyond the summit, there was Ziba, the steward of Mephibosheth, waiting to meet him. He had a string of donkeys saddled and loaded with two hundred loaves of bread, a hundred cakes of raisins, a hundred cakes of figs and a skin of wine. 2Sa 9:1-13; 1Sa 25:18

2The king asked Ziba, "Why have you brought these?"

Ziba answered, "The donkeys are for the king's household to ride on, the bread and fruit are for the men to eat, and the wine is to refresh those who become exhausted in the wilderness."2Sa 17:27

3The king then asked, "Where is your master's grandson?"

Ziba said to him, "He is staying in Jerusalem, because he thinks, 'Today the Israelites will restore to me my grandfather's kingdom.'"

4Then the king said to Ziba, "All that belonged to Mephibosheth is now yours."

"I humbly bow," Ziba said. "May I find favor in your eyes, my lord the king."

Shimei Curses David

5As King David approached Bahurim, a man from the same clan as Saul's family came out from there. His name was Shimei son of Gera, and he cursed as he came out. 6He pelted David and all the king's officials with stones, though all the troops and the special guard were on David's right and left. 7As he cursed, Shimei said, "Get out, get out, you murderer, you scoundrel! 8The LORD has repaid you for all the blood you shed in the household of Saul, in whose place you have reigned. The LORD has given the kingdom into the hands of your son Absalom. You have come to ruin because you are a murderer!" 2Sa 19:16-23; 1Ki 2:8-9,36,44

9Then Abishai son of Zeruiah said to the king, "Why should this dead dog curse my lord the king? Let me go over and cut off his head." Ex 22:28; 2Sa 9:8

10But the king said, "What does this have to do with you, you sons of Zeruiah? If he is cursing because the LORD said to him, 'Curse David,' who can ask, 'Why do you do this?'" 2Sa 19:22; Ro 9:20

11David then said to Abishai and all his officials, "My son, my own flesh and blood, is trying to kill me. How much more, then, this Benjamite! Leave him alone; let him curse, for the LORD has told him to. 12It may be that the LORD will look upon my misery and restore to me his covenant blessing instead of his curse today." Dt 23:5; 2Sa 12:11; Ro 8:28

13So David and his men continued along the road while Shimei was going along the hillside opposite him, cursing as he went and throwing stones at him and showering him with dirt.

¹⁴The king and all the people with him arrived at their destination exhausted. And there he refreshed himself. 2Sa 17:2

The Advice of Ahithophel and Hushai

¹⁵Meanwhile, Absalom and all the men of Israel came to Jerusalem, and Ahithophel was with him. ¹⁶Then Hushai the Arkite, David's confidant, went to Absalom and said to him, "Long live the king! Long live the king!"

¹⁷Absalom said to Hushai, "So this is the love you show your friend? If he's your friend, why didn't you go with him?" 2Sa 19:25

¹⁸Hushai said to Absalom, "No, the one chosen by the LORD, by these people, and by all the men of Israel—his I will be, and I will remain with him. ¹⁹Furthermore, whom should I serve? Should I not serve the son? Just as I served your father, so I will serve you." 2Sa 15:34

²⁰Absalom said to Ahithophel, "Give us your advice. What should we do?"

²¹Ahithophel answered, "Sleep with your father's concubines whom he left to take care of the palace. Then all Israel will hear that you have made yourself obnoxious to your father, and the hands of everyone with you will be more resolute." ²²So they pitched a tent for Absalom on the roof, and he slept with his fa-

ther's concubines in the sight of all Israel. 2Sa 12:11-12

²³Now in those days the advice Ahithophel gave was like that of one who inquires of God. That was how both David and Absalom regarded all of Ahithophel's advice. 2Sa 15:12; 17:14,23

17 Ahithophel said to Absalom, "I would*ᵃ* choose twelve thousand men and set out tonight in pursuit of David. ²I would attack him while he is weary and weak. I would strike him with terror, and then all the people with him will flee. I would strike down only the king ³and bring all the people back to you. The death of the man you seek will mean the return of all; all the people will be unharmed." ⁴This plan seemed good to Absalom and to all the elders of Israel. 2Sa 16:14; 1Ki 22:31

⁵But Absalom said, "Summon also Hushai the Arkite, so we can hear what he has to say as well." ⁶When Hushai came to him, Absalom said, "Ahithophel has given this advice. Should we do what he says? If not, give us your opinion." 2Sa 15:32

⁷Hushai replied to Absalom, "The advice Ahithophel has given is not good this time. ⁸You know your father and his men; they are fighters, and as fierce as a wild bear robbed of her cubs. Besides, your father is an experienced fighter; he will not spend

ᵃ 1 Or Let me

the night with the troops. [9]Even now, he is hidden in a cave or some other place. If he should attack your troops first,[a] whoever hears about it will say, 'There has been a slaughter among the troops who follow Absalom.' [10]Then even the bravest soldier, whose heart is like the heart of a lion, will melt with fear, for all Israel knows that your father is a fighter and that those with him are brave. Jos 2:9,11; 1Sa 16:18; Hos 13:8

[11]"So I advise you: Let all Israel, from Dan to Beersheba — as numerous as the sand on the seashore — be gathered to you, with you yourself leading them into battle. [12]Then we will attack him wherever he may be found, and we will fall on him as dew settles on the ground. Neither he nor any of his men will be left alive. [13]If he withdraws into a city, then all Israel will bring ropes to that city, and we will drag it down to the valley until not so much as a pebble is left." Ge 12:2; 22:17; Mic 1:6

[14]Absalom and all the men of Israel said, "The advice of Hushai the Arkite is better than that of Ahithophel." For the LORD had determined to frustrate the good advice of Ahithophel in order to bring disaster on Absalom. 2Sa 15:34; Ne 4:15; Ps 9:16

[15]Hushai told Zadok and Abiathar, the priests, "Ahithophel has advised Absalom and the elders of Israel to do such and such, but I have advised them to do so and so. [16]Now send a message at once and tell David, 'Do not spend the night at the fords in the wilderness; cross over without fail, or the king and all the people with him will be swallowed up.' "

[17]Jonathan and Ahimaaz were staying at En Rogel. A female servant was to go and inform them, and they were to go and tell King David, for they could not risk being seen entering the city. [18]But a young man saw them and told Absalom. So the two of them left at once and went to the house of a man in Bahurim. He had a well in his courtyard, and they climbed down into it. [19]His wife took a covering and spread it out over the opening of the well and scattered grain over it. No one knew anything about it. Jos 2:6; 15:7; 2Sa 3:16

[20]When Absalom's men came to the woman at the house, they asked, "Where are Ahimaaz and Jonathan?"

The woman answered them, "They crossed over the brook."[b] The men searched but found no one, so they returned to Jerusalem. Ex 1:19; Jos 2:3-5; 1Sa 19:12-17

[21]After they had gone, the two climbed out of the well and went to inform King David. They said to him, "Set out and cross the river at once; Ahithophel has advised such and such against you." [22]So

---

[a] 9 Or *When some of the men fall at the first attack toward the water.*   [b] 20 Or *"They passed by the sheep pen*

David and all the people with him set out and crossed the Jordan. By daybreak, no one was left who had not crossed the Jordan.

²³When Ahithophel saw that his advice had not been followed, he saddled his donkey and set out for his house in his hometown. He put his house in order and then hanged himself. So he died and was buried in his father's tomb. 2Sa 15:12; Mt 27:5; 2Ki 20:1

Absalom's Death

²⁴David went to Mahanaim, and Absalom crossed the Jordan with all the men of Israel. ²⁵Absalom had appointed Amasa over the army in place of Joab. Amasa was the son of Jether,ᵃ an Ishmaeliteᵇ who had married Abigal, the daughter of Nahash and sister of Zeruiah the mother of Joab. ²⁶The Israelites and Absalom camped in the land of Gilead. Ge 32:2; 2Sa 19:13; 1Ch 2:13-17

²⁷When David came to Mahanaim, Shobi son of Nahash from Rabbah of the Ammonites, and Makir son of Ammiel from Lo Debar, and Barzillai the Gileadite from Rogelim ²⁸brought bedding and bowls and articles of pottery. They also brought wheat and barley, flour and roasted grain, beans and lentils,ᶜ ²⁹honey and curds, sheep, and cheese from cows' milk for David and his people to eat. For they said, "The people have become exhausted and hungry and thirsty in the wilderness." 2Sa 10:1-2; 16:2; 19:31-39

18 David mustered the men who were with him and appointed over them commanders of thousands and commanders of hundreds. ²David sent out his troops, a third under the command of Joab, a third under Joab's brother Abishai son of Zeruiah, and a third under Ittai the Gittite. The king told the troops, "I myself will surely march out with you." 1Sa 11:11; 26:6; 2Sa 15:19

³But the men said, "You must not go out; if we are forced to flee, they won't care about us. Even if half of us die, they won't care; but you are worth ten thousand of us.ᵈ It would be better now for you to give us support from the city." 1Sa 18:7; 2Sa 21:17

⁴The king answered, "I will do whatever seems best to you."

So the king stood beside the gate while all his men marched out in units of hundreds and of thousands. ⁵The king commanded Joab, Abishai and Ittai, "Be gentle with the young man Absalom for my sake." And all the troops heard the king giving orders concerning Absalom to each of the commanders.

ᵃ 25 Hebrew *Ithra*, a variant of *Jether*   ᵇ 25 Some Septuagint manuscripts (see also 1 Chron. 2:17); Hebrew and other Septuagint manuscripts *Israelite*   ᶜ 28 Most Septuagint manuscripts and Syriac; Hebrew *lentils, and roasted grain*   ᵈ 3 Two Hebrew manuscripts, some Septuagint manuscripts and Vulgate; most Hebrew manuscripts *care; for now there are ten thousand like us*

⁶David's army marched out of the city to fight Israel, and the battle took place in the forest of Ephraim. ⁷There Israel's troops were routed by David's men, and the casualties that day were great—twenty thousand men. ⁸The battle spread out over the whole countryside, and the forest swallowed up more men that day than the sword.   Jos 17:18

⁹Now Absalom happened to meet David's men. He was riding his mule, and as the mule went under the thick branches of a large oak, Absalom's hair got caught in the tree. He was left hanging in midair, while the mule he was riding kept on going.   2Sa 14:26

¹⁰When one of the men saw what had happened, he told Joab, "I just saw Absalom hanging in an oak tree."

¹¹Joab said to the man who had told him this, "What! You saw him? Why didn't you strike him to the ground right there? Then I would have had to give you ten shekels[a] of silver and a warrior's belt."

¹²But the man replied, "Even if a thousand shekels[b] were weighed out into my hands, I would not lay a hand on the king's son. In our hearing the king commanded you and Abishai and Ittai, 'Protect the young man Absalom for my sake.'[c] ¹³And if I had put my life in jeopardy[d]—and nothing is hidden from the king—you would have kept your distance from me."   2Sa 14:19-20

¹⁴Joab said, "I'm not going to wait like this for you." So he took three javelins in his hand and plunged them into Absalom's heart while Absalom was still alive in the oak tree. ¹⁵And ten of Joab's armor-bearers surrounded Absalom, struck him and killed him.   2Sa 14:30; 12:10

¹⁶Then Joab sounded the trumpet, and the troops stopped pursuing Israel, for Joab halted them. ¹⁷They took Absalom, threw him into a big pit in the forest and piled up a large heap of rocks over him. Meanwhile, all the Israelites fled to their homes. 2Sa 2:28; 20:22; Jos 7:26

¹⁸During his lifetime Absalom had taken a pillar and erected it in the King's Valley as a monument to himself, for he thought, "I have no son to carry on the memory of my name." He named the pillar after himself, and it is called Absalom's Monument to this day. Ge 14:17; 1Sa 15:12; 2Sa 14:27

David Mourns

¹⁹Now Ahimaaz son of Zadok said, "Let me run and take the news to the king that the LORD has vindicated him by delivering

---

a 11 That is, about 4 ounces or about 115 grams   *b 12* That is, about 25 pounds or about 12 kilograms   *c 12* A few Hebrew manuscripts, Septuagint, Vulgate and Syriac; most Hebrew manuscripts may be translated *Absalom, whoever you may be.*   *d 13* Or *Otherwise, if I had acted treacherously toward him*

him from the hand of his enemies." Jdg 11:36; 2Sa 15:36

²⁰"You are not the one to take the news today," Joab told him. "You may take the news another time, but you must not do so today, because the king's son is dead."

²¹Then Joab said to a Cushite, "Go, tell the king what you have seen." The Cushite bowed down before Joab and ran off.

²²Ahimaaz son of Zadok again said to Joab, "Come what may, please let me run behind the Cushite."

But Joab replied, "My son, why do you want to go? You don't have any news that will bring you a reward."

²³He said, "Come what may, I want to run."

So Joab said, "Run!" Then Ahimaaz ran by way of the plainᵃ and outran the Cushite.

²⁴While David was sitting between the inner and outer gates, the watchman went up to the roof of the gateway by the wall. As he looked out, he saw a man running alone. ²⁵The watchman called out to the king and reported it. 2Sa 19:8; 2Ki 9:17

The king said, "If he is alone, he must have good news." And the runner came closer and closer.

²⁶Then the watchman saw another runner, and he called down to the gatekeeper, "Look, another man running alone!"

The king said, "He must be bringing good news, too." 1Ki 1:42

²⁷The watchman said, "It seems to me that the first one runs like Ahimaaz son of Zadok."

"He's a good man," the king said. "He comes with good news."

²⁸Then Ahimaaz called out to the king, "All is well!" He bowed down before the king with his face to the ground and said, "Praise be to the LORD your God! He has delivered up those who lifted their hands against my lord the king."

²⁹The king asked, "Is the young man Absalom safe?"

Ahimaaz answered, "I saw great confusion just as Joab was about to send the king's servant and me, your servant, but I don't know what it was."

³⁰The king said, "Stand aside and wait here." So he stepped aside and stood there.

³¹Then the Cushite arrived and said, "My lord the king, hear the good news! The LORD has vindicated you today by delivering you from the hand of all who rose up against you."

³²The king asked the Cushite, "Is the young man Absalom safe?"

The Cushite replied, "May the enemies of my lord the king and all who rise up to harm you be like that young man." Jdg 5:31; 1Sa 25:26

³³The king was shaken. He

ᵃ23 That is, the plain of the Jordan

went up to the room over the gateway and wept. As he went, he said: "O my son Absalom! My son, my son Absalom! If only I had died instead of you—O Absalom, my son, my son!"*a* Ex 32:32; Ro 9:3

19b Joab was told, "The king is weeping and mourning for Absalom." ²And for the whole army the victory that day was turned into mourning, because on that day the troops heard it said, "The king is grieving for his son." ³The men stole into the city that day as men steal in who are ashamed when they flee from battle. ⁴The king covered his face and cried aloud, "O my son Absalom! O Absalom, my son, my son!"

⁵Then Joab went into the house to the king and said, "Today you have humiliated all your men, who have just saved your life and the lives of your sons and daughters and the lives of your wives and concubines. ⁶You love those who hate you and hate those who love you. You have made it clear today that the commanders and their men mean nothing to you. I see that you would be pleased if Absalom were alive today and all of us were dead. ⁷Now go out and encourage your men. I swear by the LORD that if you don't go out, not a man will be left with you by nightfall. This will be worse for you than all the calamities that

have come on you from your youth till now." Pr 14:28

⁸So the king got up and took his seat in the gateway. When the men were told, "The king is sitting in the gateway," they all came before him. 2Sa 15:2

Meanwhile, the Israelites had fled to their homes.

David Returns to Jerusalem

⁹Throughout the tribes of Israel, all the people were arguing among themselves, saying, "The king delivered us from the hand of our enemies; he is the one who rescued us from the hand of the Philistines. But now he has fled the country to escape from Absalom; ¹⁰and Absalom, whom we anointed to rule over us, has died in battle. So why do you say nothing about bringing the king back?" 2Sa 8:1-14

¹¹King David sent this message to Zadok and Abiathar, the priests: "Ask the elders of Judah, 'Why should you be the last to bring the king back to his palace, since what is being said throughout Israel has reached the king at his quarters? ¹²You are my relatives, my own flesh and blood. So why should you be the last to bring back the king?' ¹³And say to Amasa, 'Are you not my own flesh and blood? May God deal with me, be it ever so severely, if you are not the commander

---

a 33 In Hebrew texts this verse (18:33) is numbered 19:1. *b* In Hebrew texts 19:1-43 is numbered 19:2-44.

of my army for life in place of Joab.' " Ge 29:14; 2Sa 2:13; 17:25

¹⁴He won over the hearts of the men of Judah so that they were all of one mind. They sent word to the king, "Return, you and all your men." ¹⁵Then the king returned and went as far as the Jordan.

Now the men of Judah had come to Gilgal to go out and meet the king and bring him across the Jordan. ¹⁶Shimei son of Gera, the Benjamite from Bahurim, hurried down with the men of Judah to meet King David. ¹⁷With him were a thousand Benjamites, along with Ziba, the steward of Saul's household, and his fifteen sons and twenty servants. They rushed to the Jordan, where the king was. ¹⁸They crossed at the ford to take the king's household over and to do whatever he wished. Jos 5:9; 2Sa 16:1-2; 1Ki 2:8

When Shimei son of Gera crossed the Jordan, he fell prostrate before the king ¹⁹and said to him, "May my lord not hold me guilty. Do not remember how your servant did wrong on the day my lord the king left Jerusalem. May the king put it out of his mind. ²⁰For I your servant know that I have sinned, but today I have come here as the first from the tribes of Joseph to come down and meet my lord the king." 1Sa 22:15; 2Sa 16:6-8

²¹Then Abishai son of Zeruiah said, "Shouldn't Shimei be put to death for this? He cursed the LORD's anointed." Ex 22:28

²²David replied, "What does this have to do with you, you sons of Zeruiah? What right do you have to interfere? Should anyone be put to death in Israel today? Don't I know that today I am king over Israel?" ²³So the king said to Shimei, "You shall not die." And the king promised him on oath. 1Sa 11:13; 2Sa 16:10; 1Ki 2:8,42

²⁴Mephibosheth, Saul's grandson, also went down to meet the king. He had not taken care of his feet or trimmed his mustache or washed his clothes from the day the king left until the day he returned safely. ²⁵When he came from Jerusalem to meet the king, the king asked him, "Why didn't you go with me, Mephibosheth?" 2Sa 4:4

²⁶He said, "My lord the king, since I your servant am lame, I said, 'I will have my donkey saddled and will ride on it, so I can go with the king.' But Ziba my servant betrayed me. ²⁷And he has slandered your servant to my lord the king. My lord the king is like an angel of God; so do whatever you wish. ²⁸All my grandfather's descendants deserved nothing but death from my lord the king, but you gave your servant a place among those who eat at your table. So what right do I have to make any more appeals to the king?" 2Sa 14:17,20; 21:6-9

²⁹The king said to him, "Why

say more? I order you and Ziba to divide the land."

30 Mephibosheth said to the king, "Let him take everything, now that my lord the king has returned home safely."

31 Barzillai the Gileadite also came down from Rogelim to cross the Jordan with the king and to send him on his way from there. **32** Now Barzillai was very old, eighty years of age. He had provided for the king during his stay in Mahanaim, for he was a very wealthy man. **33** The king said to Barzillai, "Cross over with me and stay with me in Jerusalem, and I will provide for you." 2Sa 17:27; 1Ki 2:7

34 But Barzillai answered the king, "How many more years will I live, that I should go up to Jerusalem with the king? **35** I am now eighty years old. Can I tell the difference between what is enjoyable and what is not? Can your servant taste what he eats and drinks? Can I still hear the voices of male and female singers? Why should your servant be an added burden to my lord the king? **36** Your servant will cross over the Jordan with the king for a short distance, but why should the king reward me in this way? **37** Let your servant return, that I may die in my own town near the tomb of my father and mother. But here is your servant Kimham. Let him cross over with my lord the king. Do for him whatever you wish." 1Ki 2:7; Ps 90:10; Jer 41:17

38 The king said, "Kimham shall cross over with me, and I will do for him whatever you wish. And anything you desire from me I will do for you."

39 So all the people crossed the Jordan, and then the king crossed over. The king kissed Barzillai and bid him farewell, and Barzillai returned to his home. Ge 31:55

40 When the king crossed over to Gilgal, Kimham crossed with him. All the troops of Judah and half the troops of Israel had taken the king over.

41 Soon all the men of Israel were coming to the king and saying to him, "Why did our brothers, the men of Judah, steal the king away and bring him and his household across the Jordan, together with all his men?" Jdg 8:1; 12:1

42 All the men of Judah answered the men of Israel, "We did this because the king is closely related to us. Why are you angry about it? Have we eaten any of the king's provisions? Have we taken anything for ourselves?"

43 Then the men of Israel answered the men of Judah, "We have ten shares in the king; so we have a greater claim on David than you have. Why then do you treat us with contempt? Weren't we the first to speak of bringing back our king?"

But the men of Judah pressed their claims even more forcefully than the men of Israel.

Sheba Rebels Against David

20 Now a troublemaker named Sheba son of Bikri, a Benjamite, happened to be there. He sounded the trumpet and shouted,

"We have no share in David,
no part in Jesse's son! 1Ki 12:16
Every man to his tent, Israel!"

²So all the men of Israel deserted David to follow Sheba son of Bikri. But the men of Judah stayed by their king all the way from the Jordan to Jerusalem.

³When David returned to his palace in Jerusalem, he took the ten concubines he had left to take care of the palace and put them in a house under guard. He provided for them but had no sexual relations with them. They were kept in confinement till the day of their death, living as widows. 2Sa 15:16; 16:21-22

⁴Then the king said to Amasa, "Summon the men of Judah to come to me within three days, and be here yourself." ⁵But when Amasa went to summon Judah, he took longer than the time the king had set for him. 2Sa 19:13

⁶David said to Abishai, "Now Sheba son of Bikri will do us more harm than Absalom did. Take your master's men and pursue him, or he will find fortified cities and escape from us."ᵃ ⁷So Joab's men and the Kerethites and Pele-

thites and all the mighty warriors went out under the command of Abishai. They marched out from Jerusalem to pursue Sheba son of Bikri. 2Sa 8:18; 1Ki 1:38

⁸While they were at the great rock in Gibeon, Amasa came to meet them. Joab was wearing his military tunic, and strapped over it at his waist was a belt with a dagger in its sheath. As he stepped forward, it dropped out of its sheath. Jos 9:3; 2Sa 2:18

⁹Joab said to Amasa, "How are you, my brother?" Then Joab took Amasa by the beard with his right hand to kiss him. ¹⁰Amasa was not on his guard against the dagger in Joab's hand, and Joab plunged it into his belly, and his intestines spilled out on the ground. Without being stabbed again, Amasa died. Then Joab and his brother Abishai pursued Sheba son of Bikri. 2Sa 2:23

¹¹One of Joab's men stood beside Amasa and said, "Whoever favors Joab, and whoever is for David, let him follow Joab!" ¹²Amasa lay wallowing in his blood in the middle of the road, and the man saw that all the troops came to a halt there. When he realized that everyone who came up to Amasa stopped, he dragged him from the road into a field and threw a garment over him. ¹³After Amasa had been removed from the road,

ᵃ 6 Or *and do us serious injury*

everyone went on with Joab to pursue Sheba son of Bikri. 2Sa 2:23

14 Sheba passed through all the tribes of Israel to Abel Beth Maakah and through the entire region of the Bikrites,ª who gathered together and followed him. 15 All the troops with Joab came and besieged Sheba in Abel Beth Maakah. They built a siege ramp up to the city, and it stood against the outer fortifications. While they were battering the wall to bring it down, 16 a wise woman called from the city, "Listen! Listen! Tell Joab to come here so I can speak to him." 17 He went toward her, and she asked, "Are you Joab?" 2Sa 14:2; 2Ki 19:32; 1Ki 15:20

"I am," he answered.

She said, "Listen to what your servant has to say."

"I'm listening," he said.

18 She continued, "Long ago they used to say, 'Get your answer at Abel,' and that settled it. 19 We are the peaceful and faithful in Israel. You are trying to destroy a city that is a mother in Israel. Why do you want to swallow up the LORD's inheritance?" Dt 2:26; 1Sa 26:19; 2Sa 21:3

20 "Far be it from me!" Joab replied, "Far be it from me to swallow up or destroy! 21 That is not the case. A man named Sheba son of Bikri, from the hill country of Ephraim, has lifted up his hand against the king, against David. Hand over this one man, and I'll withdraw from the city."

The woman said to Joab, "His head will be thrown to you from the wall." 2Sa 4:8

22 Then the woman went to all the people with her wise advice, and they cut off the head of Sheba son of Bikri and threw it to Joab. So he sounded the trumpet, and his men dispersed from the city, each returning to his home. And Joab went back to the king in Jerusalem. Ecc 9:13

David's Officials

23 Joab was over Israel's entire army; Benaiah son of Jehoiada was over the Kerethites and Pelethites; 24 Adoniramᵇ was in charge of forced labor; Jehoshaphat son of Ahilud was recorder; 25 Sheva was secretary; Zadok and Abiathar were priests; 26 and Ira the Jairiteᶜ was David's priest. 2Sa 8:16-18; 1Ki 4:3,6

The Gibeonites Avenged

21 During the reign of David, there was a famine for three successive years; so David sought the face of the LORD. The LORD said, "It is on account of Saul and his blood-stained house; it is because he put the Gibeonites to death." Ge 12:10; Ex 32:11

2 The king summoned the

ª 14 See Septuagint and Vulgate; Hebrew *Berites*. also 1 Kings 4:6 and 5:14); Hebrew *Adoram* and Syriac (see also 23:38) *Ithrite*   ᵇ 24 Some Septuagint manuscripts (see   ᶜ 26 Hebrew; some Septuagint manuscripts

Gibeonites and spoke to them. (Now the Gibeonites were not a part of Israel but were survivors of the Amorites; the Israelites had sworn to spare them, but Saul in his zeal for Israel and Judah had tried to annihilate them.) [3]David asked the Gibeonites, "What shall I do for you? How shall I make atonement so that you will bless the LORD's inheritance?" Jos 9:15; 1Sa 26:19

[4]The Gibeonites answered him, "We have no right to demand silver or gold from Saul or his family, nor do we have the right to put anyone in Israel to death." Nu 35:33-34

"What do you want me to do for you?" David asked.

[5]They answered the king, "As for the man who destroyed us and plotted against us so that we have been decimated and have no place anywhere in Israel, [6]let seven of his male descendants be given to us to be killed and their bodies exposed before the LORD at Gibeah of Saul—the LORD's chosen one." Nu 25:4; 1Sa 10:24

So the king said, "I will give them to you."

[7]The king spared Mephibosheth son of Jonathan, the son of Saul, because of the oath before the LORD between David and Jonathan son of Saul. [8]But the king took Armoni and Mephibosheth, the two sons of Aiah's daughter Rizpah, whom she had borne to Saul, together with the five sons of Saul's daughter Merab,[a] whom she had borne to Adriel son of Barzillai the Meholathite. [9]He handed them over to the Gibeonites, who killed them and exposed their bodies on a hill before the LORD. All seven of them fell together; they were put to death during the first days of the harvest, just as the barley harvest was beginning. 1Sa 20:8,15; 2Sa 3:7; 4:4

[10]Rizpah daughter of Aiah took sackcloth and spread it out for herself on a rock. From the beginning of the harvest till the rain poured down from the heavens on the bodies, she did not let the birds touch them by day or the wild animals by night. [11]When David was told what Aiah's daughter Rizpah, Saul's concubine, had done, [12]he went and took the bones of Saul and his son Jonathan from the citizens of Jabesh Gilead. (They had stolen their bodies from the public square at Beth Shan, where the Philistines had hung them after they struck Saul down on Gilboa.) [13]David brought the bones of Saul and his son Jonathan from there, and the bones of those who had been killed and exposed were gathered up. Dt 21:23; 1Sa 31:11-13

[14]They buried the bones of Saul and his son Jonathan in the tomb of Saul's father Kish, at Zela

---

[a] 8 Two Hebrew manuscripts, some Septuagint manuscripts and Syriac (see also 1 Samuel 18:19); most Hebrew and Septuagint manuscripts *Michal*

in Benjamin, and did everything the king commanded. After that, God answered prayer in behalf of the land. Jos 7:26; 18:28; 2Sa 24:25

Wars Against the Philistines

21:15-22pp — 1Ch 20:4-8

15 Once again there was a battle between the Philistines and Israel. David went down with his men to fight against the Philistines, and he became exhausted. 16 And Ishbi-Benob, one of the descendants of Rapha, whose bronze spearhead weighed three hundred shekels[a] and who was armed with a new sword, said he would kill David. 17 But Abishai son of Zeruiah came to David's rescue; he struck the Philistine down and killed him. Then David's men swore to him, saying, "Never again will you go out with us to battle, so that the lamp of Israel will not be extinguished." 2Sa 18:3; 20:6; 1Ki 11:36

18 In the course of time, there was another battle with the Philistines, at Gob. At that time Sibbekai the Hushathite killed Saph, one of the descendants of Rapha. 1Ch 11:29; 20:4

19 In another battle with the Philistines at Gob, Elhanan son of Jair[b] the Bethlehemite killed the brother of[c] Goliath the Gittite, who had a spear with a shaft like a weaver's rod. 1Sa 17:7

20 In still another battle, which took place at Gath, there was a huge man with six fingers on each hand and six toes on each foot — twenty-four in all. He also was descended from Rapha. 21 When he taunted Israel, Jonathan son of Shimeah, David's brother, killed him. 1Ch 20:4-8; 1Sa 16:9

22 These four were descendants of Rapha in Gath, and they fell at the hands of David and his men.

David's Song of Praise

22:1-51pp — Ps 18:1-50

22 David sang to the LORD the words of this song when the LORD delivered him from the hand of all his enemies and from the hand of Saul. 2 He said: Ex 15:1; Jdg 5:1

"The LORD is my rock,
    my fortress and my
      deliverer; Dt 32:4; Ps 31:3
3 my God is my rock, in
    whom I take
      refuge, Dt 32:37; Jer 16:19
my shield[d] and the
    horn[e] of my
      salvation. Ge 15:1; Lk 1:69
He is my stronghold, my
    refuge and my
      savior — Ps 9:9
from violent people you
    save me.

4 "I called to the LORD, who is
    worthy of praise, Ps 48:1

---

[a] 16 That is, about 7 1/2 pounds or about 3.5 kilograms   [b] 19 See 1 Chron. 20:5; Hebrew Jaare-Oregim.   [c] 19 See 1 Chron. 20:5; Hebrew does not have the brother of.   [d] 3 Or sovereign   [e] 3 Horn here symbolizes strength.

and have been saved from
my enemies.
⁵The waves of death swirled
about me; Ps 69:14-15; 93:4
the torrents of destruction
overwhelmed me.
⁶The cords of the grave coiled
around me; Ps 116:3
the snares of death
confronted me.

⁷"In my distress I called to the
LORD;
I called out to my God.
From his temple he heard my
voice;
my cry came to his ears.
⁸The earth trembled and
quaked, Jdg 5:4; Ps 77:18
the foundations of the
heavens*a* shook; Job 26:11
they trembled because he
was angry.
⁹Smoke rose from his
nostrils;
consuming fire came from
his mouth, Ps 97:3
burning coals blazed out
of it.
¹⁰He parted the heavens and
came down;
dark clouds were under his
feet. 1Ki 8:12; Na 1:3
¹¹He mounted the cherubim
and flew;
he soared*b* on the wings of
the wind. Ps 104:3
¹²He made darkness his canopy
around him —

the dark*c* rain clouds of the
sky.
¹³Out of the brightness of his
presence
bolts of lightning blazed
forth. ver 9
¹⁴The LORD thundered from
heaven; 1Sa 2:10
the voice of the Most High
resounded.
¹⁵He shot his arrows and
scattered the enemy,
with great bolts of lightning
he routed them.
¹⁶The valleys of the sea were
exposed
and the foundations of the
earth laid bare
at the rebuke of the LORD, Na 1:4
at the blast of breath from
his nostrils.

¹⁷"He reached down from on
high and took hold
of me; Ps 144:7
he drew me out of deep
waters. Ex 2:10
¹⁸He rescued me from my
powerful enemy,
from my foes, who were too
strong for me.
¹⁹They confronted me in the
day of my disaster,
but the LORD was my
support. Ps 23:4
²⁰He brought me out into a
spacious place; Ps 31:8
he rescued me because he
delighted in me. 2Sa 15:26

a 8 Hebrew; Vulgate and Syriac (see also Psalm 18:7) *mountains*   *b 11* Many Hebrew
manuscripts (see also Psalm 18:10); most Hebrew manuscripts *appeared*   *c 12* Septuagint
(see also Psalm 18:11); Hebrew *massed*

²¹ "The LORD has dealt with
me according to my
righteousness; 1Sa 26:23
according to the cleanness
of my hands he has
rewarded me. Ps 24:4
²² For I have kept the ways of the
LORD; Ge 18:19; Ps 128:1
I am not guilty of turning
from my God.
²³ All his laws are before me;
I have not turned away from
his decrees. Ps 119:102
²⁴ I have been blameless before
him Ge 6:9; Eph 1:4
and have kept myself from
sin.
²⁵ The LORD has rewarded
me according to my
righteousness, ver 21
according to my cleanness*a*
in his sight.
²⁶ "To the faithful you show
yourself faithful,
to the blameless you show
yourself blameless,
²⁷ to the pure you show yourself
pure, Mt 5:8
but to the devious you show
yourself shrewd. Lev 26:23
²⁸ You save the humble, Ps 72:12-13
but your eyes are on the
haughty to bring them
low. Isa 2:12,17; 5:15
²⁹ You, LORD, are my lamp; Ps 27:1
the LORD turns my
darkness into light.

³⁰ With your help I can advance
against a troop*b*;
with my God I can scale a
wall.
³¹ "As for God, his way is
perfect: Dt 32:4; Mt 5:48
The LORD's word is
flawless; Ps 12:6; 119:140
he shields all who take
refuge in him. Ge 15:1
³² For who is God besides the
LORD?
And who is the Rock except
our God? 1Sa 2:2
³³ It is God who arms me with
strength*c*
and keeps my way
secure.
³⁴ He makes my feet like the feet
of a deer; Hab 3:19
he causes me to stand on
the heights. Dt 32:13
³⁵ He trains my hands for
battle; Ps 144:1
my arms can bend a bow of
bronze.
³⁶ You make your saving help
my shield; Eph 6:16
your help has made*d* me
great.
³⁷ You provide a broad path for
my feet, Pr 4:11
so that my ankles do not
give way.
³⁸ "I pursued my enemies and
crushed them;

<hr>

a 25 Hebrew; Septuagint and Vulgate (see also Psalm 18:24) *to the cleanness of my
hands* *b* 30 Or *can run through a barricade* *c* 33 Dead Sea Scrolls, some Septuagint
manuscripts, Vulgate and Syriac (see also Psalm 18:32); Masoretic Text *who is my strong
refuge* *d* 36 Dead Sea Scrolls; Masoretic Text *shield; / you stoop down to make*

I did not turn back till they
    were destroyed.
³⁹I crushed them completely,
    and they could not
    rise;   Mal 4:3
  they fell beneath my feet.
⁴⁰You armed me with strength
    for battle;
  you humbled my
    adversaries before me.
⁴¹You made my enemies
    turn their backs in
    flight,   Ex 23:27
  and I destroyed my foes.
⁴²They cried for help, but there
    was no one to save
    them —   Ps 50:22; Isa 1:15
  to the LORD, but he did not
    answer.
⁴³I beat them as fine as the dust
    of the earth;
  I pounded and trampled
    them like mud in the
    streets.   Isa 10:6; Mic 7:10

⁴⁴"You have delivered me
    from the attacks of the
    peoples;   2Sa 3:1
  you have preserved me
    as the head of
    nations.   Dt 28:13
  People I did not know now
    serve me,   Isa 55:3-5
⁴⁵ foreigners cower
    before me; Ps 66:3; 81:15
  as soon as they hear of me,
    they obey me.
⁴⁶They all lose heart;
  they come trembling[a] from
    their strongholds. Mic 7:17

⁴⁷"The LORD lives! Praise be to
    my Rock!
  Exalted be my God, the
    Rock, my Savior! Ps 89:26
⁴⁸He is the God who avenges me,
  who puts the nations
    under me,   Ps 144:2
⁴⁹ who sets me free from my
    enemies.   Ps 140:1,4
  You exalted me above my
    foes;
  from a violent man you
    rescued me.
⁵⁰Therefore I will praise you,
    LORD, among the
    nations;
  I will sing the praises of
    your name.   Ro 15:9
⁵¹"He gives his king great
    victories; Ps 144:9-10
  he shows unfailing
    kindness to his
    anointed,   Ps 89:20
  to David and his
    descendants forever."

David's Last Words

23 These are the last words
of David:

"The inspired utterance of
    David son of Jesse,
  the utterance of the man
    exalted by the Most
    High,   Ps 78:70-71; 89:27
  the man anointed by the God
    of Jacob,   1Sa 16:12-13
  the hero of Israel's songs:

---

[a] 46 Some Septuagint manuscripts and Vulgate (see also Psalm 18:45); Masoretic Text *they arm themselves*

² "The Spirit of the LORD spoke
   through me; Mt 22:43
   his word was on my tongue.
³ The God of Israel spoke,
   the Rock of Israel said
   to me: Dt 32:4; 2Sa 22:2,32
   'When one rules over people
      in righteousness, Ps 72:2
   when he rules in the fear of
      God, 2Ch 19:7,9; Isa 11:1-5
⁴ he is like the light of morning
      at sunrise Jdg 5:31; Ps 89:36
   on a cloudless morning,
   like the brightness after rain
      that brings grass from the
      earth.'

⁵ "If my house were not right
      with God,
   surely he would not have
      made with me an
      everlasting covenant,
      arranged and secured in
      every part;
   surely he would not bring to
      fruition my salvation
   and grant me my every
      desire.
⁶ But evil men are all to be cast
      aside like thorns, Mt 13:40
   which are not gathered with
      the hand.
⁷ Whoever touches thorns
      uses a tool of iron or the
      shaft of a spear;
   they are burned up where
      they lie."

David's Mighty Warriors
23:8-39pp — 1Ch 11:10-41

⁸ These are the names of David's mighty warriors: 2Sa 17:10

Josheb-Basshebeth,^a a Tahkemonite,^b was chief of the Three; he raised his spear against eight hundred men, whom he killed^c in one encounter. 1Ch 27:2

⁹ Next to him was Eleazar son of Dodai the Ahohite. As one of the three mighty warriors, he was with David when they taunted the Philistines gathered at Pas Dammim^d for battle. Then the Israelites retreated, ¹⁰ but Eleazar stood his ground and struck down the Philistines till his hand grew tired and froze to the sword. The LORD brought about a great victory that day. The troops returned to Eleazar, but only to strip the dead. 1Ch 8:4; 27:4

¹¹ Next to him was Shammah son of Agee the Hararite. When the Philistines banded together at a place where there was a field full of lentils, Israel's troops fled from them. ¹² But Shammah took his stand in the middle of the field. He defended it and struck the Philistines down, and the LORD brought about a great victory.

¹³ During harvest time, three of the thirty chief warriors came down to David at the cave of

---

^a 8 Hebrew; some Septuagint manuscripts suggest *Ish-Bosheth,* that is, *Esh-Baal* (see also 1 Chron. 11:11 *Jashobeam*).   ^b 8 Probably a variant of *Hakmonite* (see 1 Chron. 11:11)   ^c 8 Some Septuagint manuscripts (see also 1 Chron. 11:11); Hebrew and other Septuagint manuscripts *Three; it was Adino the Eznite who killed eight hundred men*   ^d 9 See 1 Chron. 11:13; Hebrew *gathered there.*

Adullam, while a band of Philistines was encamped in the Valley of Rephaim. [14]At that time David was in the stronghold, and the Philistine garrison was at Bethlehem. [15]David longed for water and said, "Oh, that someone would get me a drink of water from the well near the gate of Bethlehem!" [16]So the three mighty warriors broke through the Philistine lines, drew water from the well near the gate of Bethlehem and carried it back to David. But he refused to drink it; instead, he poured it out before the LORD. [17]"Far be it from me, LORD, to do this!" he said. "Is it not the blood of men who went at the risk of their lives?" And David would not drink it. 1Sa 22:4-5; 2Sa 5:18

Such were the exploits of the three mighty warriors.

[18]Abishai the brother of Joab son of Zeruiah was chief of the Three.[a] He raised his spear against three hundred men, whom he killed, and so he became as famous as the Three. [19]Was he not held in greater honor than the Three? He became their commander, even though he was not included among them. 2Sa 10:10,14; 1Ch 11:20

[20]Benaiah son of Jehoiada, a valiant fighter from Kabzeel, performed great exploits. He struck down Moab's two mightiest warriors. He also went down into a pit on a snowy day and killed a lion. [21]And he struck down a huge Egyptian. Although the Egyptian had a spear in his hand, Benaiah went against him with a club. He snatched the spear from the Egyptian's hand and killed him with his own spear. [22]Such were the exploits of Benaiah son of Jehoiada; he too was as famous as the three mighty warriors. [23]He was held in greater honor than any of the Thirty, but he was not included among the Three. And David put him in charge of his bodyguard. 2Sa 8:18; Jos 15:21

[24]Among the Thirty were:
   Asahel the brother of Joab,
   Elhanan son of Dodo from Bethlehem,
[25]Shammah the Harodite,
   Elika the Harodite,
[26]Helez the Paltite, 1Ch 27:10
   Ira son of Ikkesh from Tekoa,
[27]Abiezer from Anathoth,
   Sibbekai[b] the Hushathite,
[28]Zalmon the Ahohite,
   Maharai the Netophathite,
[29]Heled[c] son of Baanah the Netophathite,
   Ithai son of Ribai from Gibeah in Benjamin,
[30]Benaiah the Pirathonite,
   Hiddai[d] from the ravines of Gaash, Jos 24:30

a 18 Most Hebrew manuscripts (see also 1 Chron. 11:20); two Hebrew manuscripts and Syriac *Thirty*   *b 27* Some Septuagint manuscripts (see also 21:18; 1 Chron. 11:29); Hebrew *Mebunnai*   *c 29* Some Hebrew manuscripts and Vulgate (see also 1 Chron. 11:30); most Hebrew manuscripts *Heleb*   *d 30* Hebrew; some Septuagint manuscripts (see also 1 Chron. 11:32) *Hurai*

31 Abi-Albon the Arbathite,
Azmaveth the Barhumite,
32 Eliahba the Shaalbonite,
the sons of Jashen,
Jonathan 33 son of *a* Shammah the Hararite,
Ahiam son of Sharar*b* the Hararite,
34 Eliphelet son of Ahasbai the Maakathite, Dt 3:14
Eliam son of Ahithophel the Gilonite, 2Sa 11:3; 15:12
35 Hezro the Carmelite,
Paarai the Arbite,
36 Igal son of Nathan from Zobah, 1Sa 14:47
the son of Hagri,*c*
37 Zelek the Ammonite,
Naharai the Beerothite, the armor-bearer of Joab son of Zeruiah,
38 Ira the Ithrite, 1Ch 2:53
Gareb the Ithrite
39 and Uriah the Hittite.
There were thirty-seven in all.

David Enrolls the Fighting Men

24:1-17pp — 1Ch 21:1-17

24 Again the anger of the LORD burned against Israel, and he incited David against them, saying, "Go and take a census of Israel and Judah."

2 So the king said to Joab and the army commanders*d* with him, "Go throughout the tribes of Israel from Dan to Beersheba and enroll the fighting men, so that I may know how many there are." Jdg 20:1; 2Sa 3:10; 2Ch 2:17

3 But Joab replied to the king, "May the LORD your God multiply the troops a hundred times over, and may the eyes of my lord the king see it. But why does my lord the king want to do such a thing?" Dt 1:11

4 The king's word, however, overruled Joab and the army commanders; so they left the presence of the king to enroll the fighting men of Israel.

5 After crossing the Jordan, they camped near Aroer, south of the town in the gorge, and then went through Gad and on to Jazer. 6 They went to Gilead and the region of Tahtim Hodshi, and on to Dan Jaan and around toward Sidon. 7 Then they went toward the fortress of Tyre and all the towns of the Hivites and Canaanites. Finally, they went on to Beersheba in the Negev of Judah. Jos 13:9; 19:29; Nu 21:32

8 After they had gone through the entire land, they came back to Jerusalem at the end of nine months and twenty days.

9 Joab reported the number of the fighting men to the king: In Israel there were eight hundred thousand able-bodied men who

---

a 33 Some Septuagint manuscripts (see also 1 Chron. 11:34); Hebrew does not have *son of.* *b* 33 Hebrew; some Septuagint manuscripts (see also 1 Chron. 11:35) *Sakar* *c* 36 Some Septuagint manuscripts (see also 1 Chron. 11:38); Hebrew *Haggadi* *d* 2 Septuagint (see also verse 4 and 1 Chron. 21:2); Hebrew *Joab the army commander* could handle a sword, and in Judah five hundred thousand.

¹⁰David was conscience-stricken after he had counted the fighting men, and he said to the LORD, "I have sinned greatly in what I have done. Now, LORD, I beg you, take away the guilt of your servant. I have done a very foolish thing." 1Sa 13:13; 24:5; 2Sa 12:13

¹¹Before David got up the next morning, the word of the LORD had come to Gad the prophet, David's seer: ¹²"Go and tell David, 'This is what the LORD says: I am giving you three options. Choose one of them for me to carry out against you.'" 1Sa 9:9; 22:5; 1Ch 29:29

¹³So Gad went to David and said to him, "Shall there come on you three*a* years of famine in your land? Or three months of fleeing from your enemies while they pursue you? Or three days of plague in your land? Now then, think it over and decide how I should answer the one who sent me." Eze 14:21; Lev 26:25

¹⁴David said to Gad, "I am in deep distress. Let us fall into the hands of the LORD, for his mercy is great; but do not let me fall into human hands." Ps 51:1; 103:8,13

¹⁵So the LORD sent a plague on Israel from that morning until the end of the time designated, and seventy thousand of the people from Dan to Beersheba died. ¹⁶When the angel stretched out his hand to destroy Jerusalem, the LORD relented concerning the disaster and said to the angel who was afflicting the people, "Enough! Withdraw your hand." The angel of the LORD was then at the threshing floor of Araunah the Jebusite. Ge 6:6; Ex 12:23; 1Ch 27:24

¹⁷When David saw the angel who was striking down the people, he said to the LORD, "I have sinned; I, the shepherd,*b* have done wrong. These are but sheep. What have they done? Let your hand fall on me and my family." 1Ch 21:1-17; Ps 74:1; Jer 49:20

David Builds an Altar
24:18-25pp — 1Ch 21:18-26

¹⁸On that day Gad went to David and said to him, "Go up and build an altar to the LORD on the threshing floor of Araunah the Jebusite." ¹⁹So David went up, as the LORD had commanded through Gad. ²⁰When Araunah looked and saw the king and his officials coming toward him, he went out and bowed down before the king with his face to the ground.

²¹Araunah said, "Why has my lord the king come to his servant?"

"To buy your threshing floor," David answered, "so I can build an altar to the LORD, that the plague on the people may be stopped."

²²Araunah said to David, "Let my lord the king take whatever

a 13 Septuagint (see also 1 Chron. 21:12); Hebrew *seven*   *b 17* Dead Sea Scrolls and Septuagint; Masoretic Text does not have *the shepherd.*

he wishes and offer it up. Here are oxen for the burnt offering, and here are threshing sledges and ox yokes for the wood. ²³ Your Majesty, Araunah*a* gives all this to the king." Araunah also said to him, "May the LORD your God accept you." 1Ki 19:21; Eze 20:40-41; 1Sa 6:14

²⁴ But the king replied to Araunah, "No, I insist on paying you for it. I will not sacrifice to the LORD my God burnt offerings that cost me nothing." Mal 1:13-14

So David bought the threshing floor and the oxen and paid fifty shekels*b* of silver for them. ²⁵ David built an altar to the LORD there and sacrificed burnt offerings and fellowship offerings. Then the LORD answered his prayer in behalf of the land, and the plague on Israel was stopped.

---

a 23 Some Hebrew manuscripts and Septuagint; most Hebrew manuscripts *King Araunah*
b 24 That is, about 1 1/4 pounds or about 575 grams

1 Kings

Adonijah Sets Himself Up as King

1 When King David was very old, he could not keep warm even when they put covers over him. **2** So his attendants said to him, "Let us look for a young virgin to serve the king and take care of him. She can lie beside him so that our lord the king may keep warm."

3 Then they searched throughout Israel for a beautiful young woman and found Abishag, a Shunammite, and brought her to the king. **4** The woman was very beautiful; she took care of the king and waited on him, but the king had no sexual relations with her.

5 Now Adonijah, whose mother was Haggith, put himself forward and said, "I will be king." So he got chariots and horses*a* ready, with fifty men to run ahead of him. **6** (His father had never rebuked him by asking, "Why do you behave as you do?" He was also very handsome and was born next after Absalom.)   2Sa 3:4; 15:1

7 Adonijah conferred with Joab son of Zeruiah and with Abiathar the priest, and they gave him their support. **8** But Zadok the priest, Benaiah son of Jehoiada, Nathan the prophet, Shimei and Rei and David's special guard did not join Adonijah.   2Sa 20:25; 23:8; 1Ki 2:22,28

9 Adonijah then sacrificed sheep, cattle and fattened calves at the Stone of Zoheleth near En Rogel. He invited all his brothers, the king's sons, and all the royal officials of Judah, **10** but he did not invite Nathan the prophet or Benaiah or the special guard or his brother Solomon.   2Sa 12:24

11 Then Nathan asked Bathsheba, Solomon's mother, "Have you not heard that Adonijah, the son of Haggith, has become king, and our lord David knows

a 5 Or charioteers

nothing about it? ¹²Now then, let me advise you how you can save your own life and the life of your son Solomon. ¹³Go in to King David and say to him, 'My lord the king, did you not swear to me your servant: "Surely Solomon your son shall be king after me, and he will sit on my throne"? Why then has Adonijah become king?' ¹⁴While you are still there talking to the king, I will come in and add my word to what you have said." 2Sa 3:4; 1Ch 22:9-13; Pr 15:22

¹⁵So Bathsheba went to see the aged king in his room, where Abishag the Shunammite was attending him. ¹⁶Bathsheba bowed down, prostrating herself before the king.

"What is it you want?" the king asked.

¹⁷She said to him, "My lord, you yourself swore to me your servant by the Lord your God: 'Solomon your son shall be king after me, and he will sit on my throne.' ¹⁸But now Adonijah has become king, and you, my lord the king, do not know about it. ¹⁹He has sacrificed great numbers of cattle, fattened calves, and sheep, and has invited all the king's sons, Abiathar the priest and Joab the commander of the army, but he has not invited Solomon your servant. ²⁰My lord the king, the eyes of all Israel are on you, to learn from you who will sit on the throne of my lord the king after him. ²¹Otherwise, as

soon as my lord the king is laid to rest with his ancestors, I and my son Solomon will be treated as criminals." ver 13,30; Dt 31:16; 1Ki 2:10

²²While she was still speaking with the king, Nathan the prophet arrived. ²³And the king was told, "Nathan the prophet is here." So he went before the king and bowed with his face to the ground.

²⁴Nathan said, "Have you, my lord the king, declared that Adonijah shall be king after you, and that he will sit on your throne? ²⁵Today he has gone down and sacrificed great numbers of cattle, fattened calves, and sheep. He has invited all the king's sons, the commanders of the army and Abiathar the priest. Right now they are eating and drinking with him and saying, 'Long live King Adonijah!' ²⁶But me your servant, and Zadok the priest, and Benaiah son of Jehoiada, and your servant Solomon he did not invite. ²⁷Is this something my lord the king has done without letting his servants know who should sit on the throne of my lord the king after him?"

David Makes Solomon King
1:28-53pp — 1Ch 29:21-25

²⁸Then King David said, "Call in Bathsheba." So she came into the king's presence and stood before him.

²⁹The king then took an oath: "As surely as the Lord lives, who

has delivered me out of every trouble, [30]I will surely carry out this very day what I swore to you by the LORD, the God of Israel: Solomon your son shall be king after me, and he will sit on my throne in my place." ver 13,17; 2Sa 4:9

[31]Then Bathsheba bowed down with her face to the ground, prostrating herself before the king, and said, "May my lord King David live forever!"

[32]King David said, "Call in Zadok the priest, Nathan the prophet and Benaiah son of Jehoiada." When they came before the king, [33]he said to them: "Take your lord's servants with you and have Solomon my son mount my own mule and take him down to Gihon. [34]There have Zadok the priest and Nathan the prophet anoint him king over Israel. Blow the trumpet and shout, 'Long live King Solomon!' [35]Then you are to go up with him, and he is to come and sit on my throne and reign in my place. I have appointed him ruler over Israel and Judah." 1Sa 10:1; 2Sa 15:10; 20:6-7

[36]Benaiah son of Jehoiada answered the king, "Amen! May the LORD, the God of my lord the king, so declare it. [37]As the LORD was with my lord the king, so may he be with Solomon to make his throne even greater than the throne of my lord King David!" ver 47; Jos 1:5,17; 1Sa 20:13

[38]So Zadok the priest, Nathan the prophet, Benaiah son of Je-

hoiada, the Kerethites and the Pelethites went down and had Solomon mount King David's mule, and they escorted him to Gihon. [39]Zadok the priest took the horn of oil from the sacred tent and anointed Solomon. Then they sounded the trumpet and all the people shouted, "Long live King Solomon!" [40]And all the people went up after him, playing pipes and rejoicing greatly, so that the ground shook with the sound. 1Sa 10:24; 2Sa 8:18; Ps 89:20

[41]Adonijah and all the guests who were with him heard it as they were finishing their feast. On hearing the sound of the trumpet, Joab asked, "What's the meaning of all the noise in the city?"

[42]Even as he was speaking, Jonathan son of Abiathar the priest arrived. Adonijah said, "Come in. A worthy man like you must be bringing good news." 2Sa 18:26

[43]"Not at all!" Jonathan answered. "Our lord King David has made Solomon king. [44]The king has sent with him Zadok the priest, Nathan the prophet, Benaiah son of Jehoiada, the Kerethites and the Pelethites, and they have put him on the king's mule, [45]and Zadok the priest and Nathan the prophet have anointed him king at Gihon. From there they have gone up cheering, and the city resounds with it. That's the noise you hear. [46]Moreover, Solomon has taken his seat on

the royal throne. [47]Also, the royal officials have come to congratulate our lord King David, saying, 'May your God make Solomon's name more famous than yours and his throne greater than yours!' And the king bowed in worship on his bed [48]and said, 'Praise be to the LORD, the God of Israel, who has allowed my eyes to see a successor on my throne today.'" ver 37; 1Ki 3:6

[49]At this, all Adonijah's guests rose in alarm and dispersed. [50]But Adonijah, in fear of Solomon, went and took hold of the horns of the altar. [51]Then Solomon was told, "Adonijah is afraid of King Solomon and is clinging to the horns of the altar. He says, 'Let King Solomon swear to me today that he will not put his servant to death with the sword.'" 1Ki 2:28

[52]Solomon replied, "If he shows himself to be worthy, not a hair of his head will fall to the ground; but if evil is found in him, he will die." [53]Then King Solomon sent men, and they brought him down from the altar. And Adonijah came and bowed down to King Solomon, and Solomon said, "Go to your home." 1Ch 29:21-25; 1Sa 14:45

David's Charge to Solomon

2:10-12pp — 1Ch 29:26-28

2 When the time drew near for David to die, he gave a charge to Solomon his son.

[2]"I am about to go the way of all the earth," he said. "So be strong, act like a man, [3]and observe what the LORD your God requires: Walk in obedience to him, and keep his decrees and commands, his laws and regulations, as written in the Law of Moses. Do this so that you may prosper in all you do and wherever you go [4]and that the LORD may keep his promise to me: 'If your descendants watch how they live, and if they walk faithfully before me with all their heart and soul, you will never fail to have a successor on the throne of Israel.' 2Sa 7:13,25; 2Ki 20:3; 1Ch 22:13

[5]"Now you yourself know what Joab son of Zeruiah did to me — what he did to the two commanders of Israel's armies, Abner son of Ner and Amasa son of Jether. He killed them, shedding their blood in peacetime as if in battle, and with that blood he stained the belt around his waist and the sandals on his feet. [6]Deal with him according to your wisdom, but do not let his gray head go down to the grave in peace. 2Sa 2:18; 20:10

[7]"But show kindness to the sons of Barzillai of Gilead and let them be among those who eat at your table. They stood by me when I fled from your brother Absalom. 2Sa 9:7; 17:27; 19:31-39

[8]"And remember, you have with you Shimei son of Gera, the Benjamite from Bahurim, who called down bitter curses on me the day I went to Mahanaim. When he came down to

meet me at the Jordan, I swore to him by the LORD: 'I will not put you to death by the sword.' ⁹But now, do not consider him innocent. You are a man of wisdom; you will know what to do to him. Bring his gray head down to the grave in blood." 2Sa 16:5-13; 19:18-23

¹⁰Then David rested with his ancestors and was buried in the City of David. ¹¹He had reigned forty years over Israel—seven years in Hebron and thirty-three in Jerusalem. ¹²So Solomon sat on the throne of his father David, and his rule was firmly established. 1Ch 29:26-28; 2Ch 1:1; 2Sa 5:7

Solomon's Throne Established

¹³Now Adonijah, the son of Haggith, went to Bathsheba, Solomon's mother. Bathsheba asked him, "Do you come peacefully?" 1Sa 16:4

He answered, "Yes, peacefully." ¹⁴Then he added, "I have something to say to you."

"You may say it," she replied.

¹⁵"As you know," he said, "the kingdom was mine. All Israel looked to me as their king. But things changed, and the kingdom has gone to my brother; for it has come to him from the LORD. ¹⁶Now I have one request to make of you. Do not refuse me."

"You may make it," she said.

¹⁷So he continued, "Please ask King Solomon—he will not refuse you—to give me Abishag the Shunammite as my wife." 1Ki 1:3

¹⁸"Very well," Bathsheba replied, "I will speak to the king for you."

¹⁹When Bathsheba went to King Solomon to speak to him for Adonijah, the king stood up to meet her, bowed down to her and sat down on his throne. He had a throne brought for the king's mother, and she sat down at his right hand. Ps 45:9; 1Ki 15:13

²⁰"I have one small request to make of you," she said. "Do not refuse me."

The king replied, "Make it, my mother; I will not refuse you."

²¹So she said, "Let Abishag the Shunammite be given in marriage to your brother Adonijah." 1Ki 1:3

²²King Solomon answered his mother, "Why do you request Abishag the Shunammite for Adonijah? You might as well request the kingdom for him—after all, he is my older brother—yes, for him and for Abiathar the priest and Joab son of Zeruiah!" 2Sa 12:8; 1Ki 1:3

²³Then King Solomon swore by the LORD: "May God deal with me, be it ever so severely, if Adonijah does not pay with his life for this request! ²⁴And now, as surely as the LORD lives—he who has established me securely on the throne of my father David and has founded a dynasty for me as he promised—Adonijah shall be put to death today!" ²⁵So King Solomon gave orders to Benaiah son of Jehoiada, and

he struck down Adonijah and he died. 2Sa 7:11; 8:18; Ru 1:17

²⁶To Abiathar the priest the king said, "Go back to your fields in Anathoth. You deserve to die, but I will not put you to death now, because you carried the ark of the Sovereign LORD before my father David and shared all my father's hardships." ²⁷So Solomon removed Abiathar from the priesthood of the LORD, fulfilling the word the LORD had spoken at Shiloh about the house of Eli. 1Sa 2:27-36; 22:20; 2Sa 15:24

²⁸When the news reached Joab, who had conspired with Adonijah though not with Absalom, he fled to the tent of the LORD and took hold of the horns of the altar. ²⁹King Solomon was told that Joab had fled to the tent of the LORD and was beside the altar. Then Solomon ordered Benaiah son of Jehoiada, "Go, strike him down!" ver 25; 1Ki 1:7,50

³⁰So Benaiah entered the tent of the LORD and said to Joab, "The king says, 'Come out!'" Ex 21:14
But he answered, "No, I will die here."
Benaiah reported to the king, "This is how Joab answered me."

³¹Then the king commanded Benaiah, "Do as he says. Strike him down and bury him, and so clear me and my whole family of the guilt of the innocent blood that Joab shed. ³²The LORD will repay him for the blood he shed, because without my father David knowing it he attacked two men and killed them with the sword. Both of them—Abner son of Ner, commander of Israel's army, and Amasa son of Jether, commander of Judah's army—were better men and more upright than he. ³³May the guilt of their blood rest on the head of Joab and his descendants forever. But on David and his descendants, his house and his throne, may there be the LORD's peace forever." Dt 19:13; Jdg 9:24; 2Ch 21:13

³⁴So Benaiah son of Jehoiada went up and struck down Joab and killed him, and he was buried at his home out in the country. ³⁵The king put Benaiah son of Jehoiada over the army in Joab's position and replaced Abiathar with Zadok the priest. 1Ki 4:4; 1Ch 29:22

³⁶Then the king sent for Shimei and said to him, "Build yourself a house in Jerusalem and live there, but do not go anywhere else. ³⁷The day you leave and cross the Kidron Valley, you can be sure you will die; your blood will be on your own head." 2Sa 1:16; 15:23

³⁸Shimei answered the king, "What you say is good. Your servant will do as my lord the king has said." And Shimei stayed in Jerusalem for a long time.

³⁹But three years later, two of Shimei's slaves ran off to Achish son of Maakah, king of Gath, and Shimei was told, "Your slaves are in Gath." ⁴⁰At this, he saddled his donkey and went to Achish

at Gath in search of his slaves. So Shimei went away and brought the slaves back from Gath. 1Sa 27:2

⁴¹When Solomon was told that Shimei had gone from Jerusalem to Gath and had returned, ⁴²the king summoned Shimei and said to him, "Did I not make you swear by the LORD and warn you, 'On the day you leave to go anywhere else, you can be sure you will die'? At that time you said to me, 'What you say is good. I will obey.' ⁴³Why then did you not keep your oath to the LORD and obey the command I gave you?"

⁴⁴The king also said to Shimei, "You know in your heart all the wrong you did to my father David. Now the LORD will repay you for your wrongdoing. ⁴⁵But King Solomon will be blessed, and David's throne will remain secure before the LORD forever." 2Sa 7:13; 16:5-13; Pr 25:5

⁴⁶Then the king gave the order to Benaiah son of Jehoiada, and he went out and struck Shimei down and he died.

The kingdom was now established in Solomon's hands. ver 12

Solomon Asks for Wisdom

3:4-15pp — 2Ch 1:2-13

3 Solomon made an alliance with Pharaoh king of Egypt and married his daughter. He brought her to the City of David until he finished building his palace and the temple of the LORD, and the wall around Jerusalem.

²The people, however, were still sacrificing at the high places, because a temple had not yet been built for the Name of the LORD. ³Solomon showed his love for the LORD by walking according to the instructions given him by his father David, except that he offered sacrifices and burned incense on the high places. Dt 6:5; 12:2,4-5; 1Ki 2:3

⁴The king went to Gibeon to offer sacrifices, for that was the most important high place, and Solomon offered a thousand burnt offerings on that altar. ⁵At Gibeon the LORD appeared to Solomon during the night in a dream, and God said, "Ask for whatever you want me to give you." Nu 12:6; 1Ki 9:2; 1Ch 16:39

⁶Solomon answered, "You have shown great kindness to your servant, my father David, because he was faithful to you and righteous and upright in heart. You have continued this great kindness to him and have given him a son to sit on his throne this very day. 1Ki 1:48; 2:4; 9:4

⁷"Now, LORD my God, you have made your servant king in place of my father David. But I am only a little child and do not know how to carry out my duties. ⁸Your servant is here among the people you have chosen, a great people, too numerous to count or number. ⁹So give your servant a discerning heart to govern your people and to distinguish between right and wrong. For who

is able to govern this great people of yours?" Nu 27:17; Pr 2:3-9; Jas 1:5 [10] The Lord was pleased that Solomon had asked for this. [11] So God said to him, "Since you have asked for this and not for long life or wealth for yourself, nor have asked for the death of your enemies but for discernment in administering justice, [12] I will do what you have asked. I will give you a wise and discerning heart, so that there will never have been anyone like you, nor will there ever be. [13] Moreover, I will give you what you have not asked for — both wealth and honor — so that in your lifetime you will have no equal among kings. [14] And if you walk in obedience to me and keep my decrees and commands as David your father did, I will give you a long life." [15] Then Solomon awoke — and he realized it had been a dream. 1Ki 4:20-34; Pr 3:1-2,16

He returned to Jerusalem, stood before the ark of the Lord's covenant and sacrificed burnt offerings and fellowship offerings. Then he gave a feast for all his court. 2Ch 1:2-13; 1Ki 8:65

A Wise Ruling

[16] Now two prostitutes came to the king and stood before him. [17] One of them said, "Pardon me, my lord. This woman and I live in the same house, and I had a baby while she was there with me. [18] The third day after my child was born, this woman also had a baby. We were alone; there was no one in the house but the two of us.

[19] "During the night this woman's son died because she lay on him. [20] So she got up in the middle of the night and took my son from my side while I your servant was asleep. She put him by her breast and put her dead son by my breast. [21] The next morning, I got up to nurse my son — and he was dead! But when I looked at him closely in the morning light, I saw that it wasn't the son I had borne."

[22] The other woman said, "No! The living one is my son; the dead one is yours."

But the first one insisted, "No! The dead one is yours; the living one is mine." And so they argued before the king.

[23] The king said, "This one says, 'My son is alive and your son is dead,' while that one says, 'No! Your son is dead and mine is alive.'"

[24] Then the king said, "Bring me a sword." So they brought a sword for the king. [25] He then gave an order: "Cut the living child in two and give half to one and half to the other."

[26] The woman whose son was alive was deeply moved out of love for her son and said to the king, "Please, my lord, give her the living baby! Don't kill him!" Ge 43:30; Isa 49:15; Jer 31:20

But the other said, "Neither I

nor you shall have him. Cut him in two!"

²⁷Then the king gave his ruling: "Give the living baby to the first woman. Do not kill him; she is his mother."

²⁸When all Israel heard the verdict the king had given, they held the king in awe, because they saw that he had wisdom from God to administer justice. ver 9,11-12; Col 2:3

Solomon's Officials and Governors

4 So King Solomon ruled over all Israel. ²And these were his chief officials:

Azariah son of Zadok—the priest;   1Ch 6:10
³Elihoreph and Ahijah, sons of Shisha—secretaries;
Jehoshaphat son of Ahilud—recorder;   .   2Sa 8:16
⁴Benaiah son of Jehoiada—commander in chief;
Zadok and Abiathar—priests;   1Ki 2:27
⁵Azariah son of Nathan—in charge of the district governors;
Zabud son of Nathan—a priest and adviser to the king;
⁶Ahishar—palace administrator;
Adoniram son of Abda—in charge of forced labor.

⁷Solomon had twelve district governors over all Israel, who supplied provisions for the king and the royal household. Each one had to provide supplies for one month in the year. ⁸These are their names:

Ben-Hur—in the hill country of Ephraim;   Jos 24:33
⁹Ben-Deker—in Makaz, Shaalbim, Beth Shemesh and Elon Bethhanan;   Jdg 1:35
¹⁰Ben-Hesed—in Arubboth (Sokoh and all the land of Hepher were his);   Jos 12:17
¹¹Ben-Abinadab—in Naphoth Dor (he was married to Taphath daughter of Solomon);   Jos 11:2
¹²Baana son of Ahilud—in Taanach and Megiddo, and in all of Beth Shan next to Zarethan below Jezreel, from Beth Shan to Abel Meholah across to Jokmeam;   Jos 17:11; 1Ki 19:16; 1Ch 6:68
¹³Ben-Geber—in Ramoth Gilead (the settlements of Jair son of Manasseh in Gilead were his, as well as the region of Argob in Bashan and its sixty large walled cities with bronze gate bars);   Nu 32:41; Dt 3:4
¹⁴Ahinadab son of Iddo—in Mahanaim;   Jos 13:26
¹⁵Ahimaaz—in Naphtali (he had married Basemath daughter of Solomon);
¹⁶Baana son of Hushai—in Asher and in Aloth; 2Sa 15:32
¹⁷Jehoshaphat son of Paruah—in Issachar;

¹⁸Shimei son of Ela — in Benjamin;   1Ki 1:8
¹⁹Geber son of Uri — in Gilead (the country of Sihon king of the Amorites and the country of Og king of Bashan). He was the only governor over the district.

Solomon's Daily Provisions

²⁰The people of Judah and Israel were as numerous as the sand on the seashore; they ate, they drank and they were happy. ²¹And Solomon ruled over all the kingdoms from the Euphrates River to the land of the Philistines, as far as the border of Egypt. These countries brought tribute and were Solomon's subjects all his life.   2Ch 9:26; Ps 72:8; Ge 15:18

²²Solomon's daily provisions were thirty cors[a] of the finest flour and sixty cors[b] of meal, ²³ten head of stall-fed cattle, twenty of pasture-fed cattle and a hundred sheep and goats, as well as deer, gazelles, roebucks and choice fowl. ²⁴For he ruled over all the kingdoms west of the Euphrates River, from Tiphsah to Gaza, and had peace on all sides. ²⁵During Solomon's lifetime Judah and Israel, from Dan to Beersheba, lived in safety, everyone under their own vine and under their own fig tree.   Jer 23:6; Mic 4:4; Zec 3:10
²⁶Solomon had four[c] thousand stalls for chariot horses, and twelve thousand horses.[d]   1Ki 10:26

²⁷The district governors, each in his month, supplied provisions for King Solomon and all who came to the king's table. They saw to it that nothing was lacking. ²⁸They also brought to the proper place their quotas of barley and straw for the chariot horses and the other horses.

Solomon's Wisdom

²⁹God gave Solomon wisdom and very great insight, and a breadth of understanding as measureless as the sand on the seashore. ³⁰Solomon's wisdom was greater than the wisdom of all the people of the East, and greater than all the wisdom of Egypt. ³¹He was wiser than anyone else, including Ethan the Ezrahite — wiser than Heman, Kalkol and Darda, the sons of Mahol. And his fame spread to all the surrounding nations. ³²He spoke three thousand proverbs and his songs numbered a thousand and five. ³³He spoke about plant life, from the cedar of Lebanon to the hyssop that grows out of walls. He also spoke about animals and birds, reptiles and fish. ³⁴From all nations people came to listen to Solomon's wisdom, sent by all the kings of the world, who had heard of his wisdom.[e] 1Ki 3:12; Pr 1:1; 2Ch 9:23

---

a 22 That is, probably about 5 1/2 tons or about 5 metric tons   *b 22* That is, probably about 11 tons or about 10 metric tons   *c 26* Some Septuagint manuscripts (see also 2 Chron. 9:25); Hebrew *forty*   *d 26* Or *charioteers*   *e 34* In Hebrew texts 4:21-34 is numbered 5:1-14.

Preparations for Building the Temple

5:1-16pp — 2Ch 2:1-18

5 [a] When Hiram king of Tyre heard that Solomon had been anointed king to succeed his father David, he sent his envoys to Solomon, because he had always been on friendly terms with David. ²Solomon sent back this message to Hiram: 2Sa 5:11

³ "You know that because of the wars waged against my father David from all sides, he could not build a temple for the Name of the LORD his God until the LORD put his enemies under his feet. ⁴But now the LORD my God has given me rest on every side, and there is no adversary or disaster. ⁵I intend, therefore, to build a temple for the Name of the LORD my God, as the LORD told my father David, when he said, 'Your son whom I will put on the throne in your place will build the temple for my Name.' 2Sa 7:13; 1Ch 17:12; 22:9 ⁶ "So give orders that cedars of Lebanon be cut for me. My men will work with yours, and I will pay you for your men whatever wages you set. You know that we have no one so skilled in felling timber as the Sidonians."

⁷When Hiram heard Solomon's message, he was greatly pleased and said, "Praise be to the LORD today, for he has given David a wise son to rule over this great nation."

⁸So Hiram sent word to Solomon:

"I have received the message you sent me and will do all you want in providing the cedar and juniper logs. ⁹My men will haul them down from Lebanon to the Mediterranean Sea, and I will float them as rafts by sea to the place you specify. There I will separate them and you can take them away. And you are to grant my wish by providing food for my royal household." Ezr 3:7; Eze 27:17; Ac 12:20

¹⁰In this way Hiram kept Solomon supplied with all the cedar and juniper logs he wanted, ¹¹and Solomon gave Hiram twenty thousand cors[b] of wheat as food for his household, in addition to twenty thousand baths[c,d] of pressed olive oil. Solomon continued to do this for Hiram year after year. ¹²The LORD gave Solomon wisdom, just as he had promised him. There were peaceful relations between Hiram and Solomon, and the two of them made a treaty. 1Ki 3:12; Am 1:9

---

[a] In Hebrew texts 5:1-18 is numbered 5:15-32.   [b] 11 That is, probably about 3,600 tons or about 3,250 metric tons   [c] 11 Septuagint (see also 2 Chron. 2:10); Hebrew *twenty cors*
[d] 11 That is, about 120,000 gallons or about 440,000 liters

¹³King Solomon conscripted laborers from all Israel — thirty thousand men. ¹⁴He sent them off to Lebanon in shifts of ten thousand a month, so that they spent one month in Lebanon and two months at home. Adoniram was in charge of the forced labor. ¹⁵Solomon had seventy thousand carriers and eighty thousand stonecutters in the hills, ¹⁶as well as thirty-three hundred[a] foremen who supervised the project and directed the workers. ¹⁷At the king's command they removed from the quarry large blocks of high-grade stone to provide a foundation of dressed stone for the temple. ¹⁸The craftsmen of Solomon and Hiram and workers from Byblos cut and prepared the timber and stone for the building of the temple.   1Ki 4:6; 1Ch 22:2

Solomon Builds the Temple

6:1-29pp — 2Ch 3:1-14

6 In the four hundred and eightieth[b] year after the Israelites came out of Egypt, in the fourth year of Solomon's reign over Israel, in the month of Ziv, the second month, he began to build the temple of the LORD.

²The temple that King Solomon built for the LORD was sixty cubits long, twenty wide and thirty high.[c] ³The portico at the front of the main hall of the temple extended the width of the temple, that is twenty cubits,[d] and projected ten cubits[e] from the front of the temple. ⁴He made narrow windows high up in the temple walls. ⁵Against the walls of the main hall and inner sanctuary he built a structure around the building, in which there were side rooms. ⁶The lowest floor was five cubits[f] wide, the middle floor six cubits[g] and the third floor seven.[h] He made offset ledges around the outside of the temple so that nothing would be inserted into the temple walls.   Eze 40:16; 41:5-6

⁷In building the temple, only blocks dressed at the quarry were used, and no hammer, chisel or any other iron tool was heard at the temple site while it was being built.   Ex 20:25; Dt 27:5

⁸The entrance to the lowest[i] floor was on the south side of the temple; a stairway led up to the middle level and from there to the third. ⁹So he built the temple and completed it, roofing it with beams and cedar planks. ¹⁰And he built the side rooms all along

---

a 16 Hebrew; some Septuagint manuscripts (see also 2 Chron. 2:2,18) *thirty-six hundred*
b 1 Hebrew; Septuagint *four hundred and fortieth*   *c 2* That is, about 90 feet long, 30 feet wide and 45 feet high or about 27 meters long, 9 meters wide and 14 meters high   *d 3* That is, about 30 feet or about 9 meters; also in verses 16 and 20   *e 3* That is, about 15 feet or about 4.5 meters; also in verses 23-26   *f 6* That is, about 7 1/2 feet or about 2.3 meters; also in verses 10 and 24   *g 6* That is, about 9 feet or about 2.7 meters   *h 6* That is, about 11 feet or about 3.2 meters   *i 8* Septuagint; Hebrew *middle*

the temple. The height of each was five cubits, and they were attached to the temple by beams of cedar. ver 14,38

¹¹ The word of the LORD came to Solomon: ¹² "As for this temple you are building, if you follow my decrees, observe my laws and keep all my commands and obey them, I will fulfill through you the promise I gave to David your father. ¹³ And I will live among the Israelites and will not abandon my people Israel." Dt 31:6; 2Sa 7:12-16

¹⁴ So Solomon built the temple and completed it. ¹⁵ He lined its interior walls with cedar boards, paneling them from the floor of the temple to the ceiling, and covered the floor of the temple with planks of juniper. ¹⁶ He partitioned off twenty cubits at the rear of the temple with cedar boards from floor to ceiling to form within the temple an inner sanctuary, the Most Holy Place. ¹⁷ The main hall in front of this room was forty cubits[a] long. ¹⁸ The inside of the temple was cedar, carved with gourds and open flowers. Everything was cedar; no stone was to be seen. Ex 26:33; Ps 74:6

¹⁹ He prepared the inner sanctuary within the temple to set the ark of the covenant of the LORD there. ²⁰ The inner sanctuary was twenty cubits long, twenty wide and twenty high. He overlaid the inside with pure gold, and he also overlaid the altar of cedar.

²¹ Solomon covered the inside of the temple with pure gold, and he extended gold chains across the front of the inner sanctuary, which was overlaid with gold. ²² So he overlaid the whole interior with gold. He also overlaid with gold the altar that belonged to the inner sanctuary. 1Sa 3:3; Eze 41:3-4

²³ For the inner sanctuary he made a pair of cherubim out of olive wood, each ten cubits high. ²⁴ One wing of the first cherub was five cubits long, and the other wing five cubits — ten cubits from wing tip to wing tip. ²⁵ The second cherub also measured ten cubits, for the two cherubim were identical in size and shape. ²⁶ The height of each cherub was ten cubits. ²⁷ He placed the cherubim inside the innermost room of the temple, with their wings spread out. The wing of one cherub touched one wall, while the wing of the other touched the other wall, and their wings touched each other in the middle of the room. ²⁸ He overlaid the cherubim with gold. Ex 25:20; 37:1-9

²⁹ On the walls all around the temple, in both the inner and outer rooms, he carved cherubim, palm trees and open flowers. ³⁰ He also covered the floors of both the inner and outer rooms of the temple with gold. 2Ch 3:1-14

³¹ For the entrance to the inner sanctuary he made doors out of olive wood that were one

---

[a] 17 That is, about 60 feet or about 18 meters

fifth of the width of the sanctuary. ³²And on the two olive-wood doors he carved cherubim, palm trees and open flowers, and overlaid the cherubim and palm trees with hammered gold. ³³In the same way, for the entrance to the main hall he made door-frames out of olive wood that were one fourth of the width of the hall. ³⁴He also made two doors out of juniper wood, each having two leaves that turned in sockets. ³⁵He carved cherubim, palm trees and open flowers on them and overlaid them with gold hammered evenly over the carvings.

³⁶And he built the inner court-yard of three courses of dressed stone and one course of trimmed cedar beams.   1Ki 7:12; Ezr 6:4

³⁷The foundation of the temple of the LORD was laid in the fourth year, in the month of Ziv. ³⁸In the eleventh year in the month of Bul, the eighth month, the temple was finished in all its details according to its specifications. He had spent seven years building it.   Heb 8:5

Solomon Builds His Palace

7 It took Solomon thirteen years, however, to complete the construction of his palace. ²He built the Palace of the Forest of Lebanon a hundred cubits long, fifty wide and thirty high,ᵃ with four rows of cedar columns supporting trimmed cedar beams. ³It was roofed with cedar above the beams that rested on the columns — forty-five beams, fifteen to a row. ⁴Its windows were placed high in sets of three, facing each other. ⁵All the doorways had rectangular frames; they were in the front part in sets of three, facing each other.ᵇ 1Ki 9:10; 10:17; 2Ch 8:1

⁶He made a colonnade fifty cubits long and thirty wide.ᶜ In front of it was a portico, and in front of that were pillars and an overhanging roof.

⁷He built the throne hall, the Hall of Justice, where he was to judge, and he covered it with cedar from floor to ceiling.ᵈ ⁸And the palace in which he was to live, set farther back, was similar in design. Solomon also made a palace like this hall for Pharaoh's daughter, whom he had married.   1Ki 3:1; 6:15; 2Ch 8:11

⁹All these structures, from the outside to the great courtyard and from foundation to eaves, were made of blocks of high-grade stone cut to size and smoothed on their inner and outer faces. ¹⁰The foundations were laid with large stones of good quality, some measuring ten cubitsᵉ and

---

ᵃ 2 That is, about 150 feet long, 75 feet wide and 45 feet high or about 45 meters long, 23 meters wide and 14 meters high   ᵇ 5 The meaning of the Hebrew for this verse is uncertain.   ᶜ 6 That is, about 75 feet long and 45 feet wide or about 23 meters long and 14 meters wide   ᵈ 7 Vulgate and Syriac; Hebrew *floor*   ᵉ 10 That is, about 15 feet or about 4.5 meters; also in verse 23 some eight.[a] [11]Above were high-grade stones, cut to size, and cedar beams. [12]The great courtyard was surrounded by a wall of three courses of dressed stone and one course of trimmed cedar beams, as was the inner courtyard of the temple of the LORD with its portico. 1Ki 6:36

The Temple's Furnishings
7:23-26pp — 2Ch 4:2-5
7:38-51pp — 2Ch 4:6,10–5:1

[13]King Solomon sent to Tyre and brought Huram,[b] [14]whose mother was a widow from the tribe of Naphtali and whose father was from Tyre and a skilled craftsman in bronze. Huram was filled with wisdom, with understanding and with knowledge to do all kinds of bronze work. He came to King Solomon and did all the work assigned to him. Ex 31:2-5; 2Ch 2:14; 4:11-16

[15]He cast two bronze pillars, each eighteen cubits high and twelve cubits in circumference.[c] [16]He also made two capitals of cast bronze to set on the tops of the pillars; each capital was five cubits[d] high. [17]A network of interwoven chains adorned the capitals on top of the pillars, seven for each capital. [18]He made pomegranates in two rows[e] encircling each network to decorate the capitals on top of the pillars.[f] He did the same for each capital. [19]The capitals on top of the pillars in the portico were in the shape of lilies, four cubits[g] high. [20]On the capitals of both pillars, above the bowl-shaped part next to the network, were the two hundred pomegranates in rows all around. [21]He erected the pillars at the portico of the temple. The pillar to the south he named Jakin[h] and the one to the north Boaz.[i] [22]The capitals on top were in the shape of lilies. And so the work on the pillars was completed. 2Ki 25:17; 2Ch 3:16-17

[23]He made the Sea of cast metal, circular in shape, measuring ten cubits from rim to rim and five cubits high. It took a line of thirty cubits[j] to measure around it. [24]Below the rim, gourds encircled it—ten to a cubit. The gourds were cast in two rows in one piece with the Sea. 2Ki 25:13; 1Ch 18:8; Jer 52:17

[25]The Sea stood on twelve bulls, three facing north, three facing west, three facing south and three facing east. The Sea rested on top of them, and their

---

[a] 10 That is, about 12 feet or about 3.6 meters also in verses 40 and 45   [c] 15 That is, about 27 feet high and 18 feet in circumference or about 8.1 meters high and 5.4 meters in circumference   [d] 16 That is, about 7 1/2 feet or about 2.3 meters; also in verse 23   [e] 18 Two Hebrew manuscripts and Septuagint; most Hebrew manuscripts made the pillars, and there were two rows   [f] 18 Many Hebrew manuscripts and Syriac; most Hebrew manuscripts pomegranates   [g] 19 That is, about 6 feet or about 1.8 meters; also in verse 38   [h] 21 Jakin probably means he establishes.   [i] 21 Boaz probably means in him is strength.   [j] 23 That is, about 45 feet or about 14 meters

[b] 13 Hebrew Hiram, a variant of Huram;

hindquarters were toward the center. ²⁶It was a handbreadth[a] in thickness, and its rim was like the rim of a cup, like a lily blossom. It held two thousand baths.[b] 2Ch 4:2-5; Jer 52:20

²⁷He also made ten movable stands of bronze; each was four cubits long, four wide and three high.[c] ²⁸This is how the stands were made: They had side panels attached to uprights. ²⁹On the panels between the uprights were lions, bulls and cherubim—and on the uprights as well. Above and below the lions and bulls were wreaths of hammered work. ³⁰Each stand had four bronze wheels with bronze axles, and each had a basin resting on four supports, cast with wreaths on each side. ³¹On the inside of the stand there was an opening that had a circular frame one cubit[d] deep. This opening was round, and with its basework it measured a cubit and a half.[e] Around its opening there was engraving. The panels of the stands were square, not round. ³²The four wheels were under the panels, and the axles of the wheels were attached to the stand. The diameter of each wheel was a cu-

bit and a half. ³³The wheels were made like chariot wheels; the axles, rims, spokes and hubs were all of cast metal. 2Ki 16:17; 2Ch 4:14

³⁴Each stand had four handles, one on each corner, projecting from the stand. ³⁵At the top of the stand there was a circular band half a cubit[f] deep. The supports and panels were attached to the top of the stand. ³⁶He engraved cherubim, lions and palm trees on the surfaces of the supports and on the panels, in every available space, with wreaths all around. ³⁷This is the way he made the ten stands. They were all cast in the same molds and were identical in size and shape.

³⁸He then made ten bronze basins, each holding forty baths[g] and measuring four cubits across, one basin to go on each of the ten stands. ³⁹He placed five of the stands on the south side of the temple and five on the north. He placed the Sea on the south side, at the southeast corner of the temple. ⁴⁰He also made the pots[h] and shovels and sprinkling bowls. 2Ch 4:6

So Huram finished all the work he had undertaken for King Solomon in the temple of the LORD:

---

[a] 26 That is, about 3 inches or about 7.5 centimeters   [b] 26 That is, about 12,000 gallons or about 44,000 liters; the Septuagint does not have this sentence.   [c] 27 That is, about 6 feet long and wide and about 4 1/2 feet high or about 1.8 meters long and wide and 1.4 meters high   [d] 31 That is, about 18 inches or about 45 centimeters   [e] 31 That is, about 2 1/4 feet or about 68 centimeters; also in verse 32   [f] 35 That is, about 9 inches or about 23 centimeters   [g] 38 That is, about 240 gallons or about 880 liters   [h] 40 Many Hebrew manuscripts, Septuagint, Syriac and Vulgate (see also verse 45 and 2 Chron. 4:11); many other Hebrew manuscripts *basins*

⁴¹the two pillars;

the two bowl-shaped capitals on top of the pillars;

the two sets of network decorating the two bowl-shaped capitals on top of the pillars;

⁴²the four hundred pomegranates for the two sets of network (two rows of pomegranates for each network decorating the bowl-shaped capitals on top of the pillars);   ver 20

⁴³the ten stands with their ten basins;

⁴⁴the Sea and the twelve bulls under it;

⁴⁵the pots, shovels and sprinkling bowls.   Ex 27:3

All these objects that Huram made for King Solomon for the temple of the LORD were of burnished bronze. ⁴⁶The king had them cast in clay molds in the plain of the Jordan between Sukkoth and Zarethan. ⁴⁷Solomon left all these things unweighed, because there were so many; the weight of the bronze was not determined.   1Ch 22:3

⁴⁸Solomon also made all the furnishings that were in the LORD's temple:

the golden altar;

the golden table on which was the bread of the Presence;   Ex 25:30; 37:10

⁴⁹the lampstands of pure gold (five on the right and five on the left, in front of the inner sanctuary);   Ex 25:31-38

the gold floral work and lamps and tongs;

⁵⁰the pure gold basins, wick trimmers, sprinkling bowls, dishes and censers;   2Ki 25:13

and the gold sockets for the doors of the innermost room, the Most Holy Place, and also for the doors of the main hall of the temple.

⁵¹When all the work King Solomon had done for the temple of the LORD was finished, he brought in the things his father David had dedicated—the silver and gold and the furnishings—and he placed them in the treasuries of the LORD's temple.   2Ch 4:6,10-5:1

The Ark Brought to the Temple

8:1-21pp — 2Ch 5:2-6:11

8 Then King Solomon summoned into his presence at Jerusalem the elders of Israel, all the heads of the tribes and the chiefs of the Israelite families, to bring up the ark of the LORD's covenant from Zion, the City of David. ²All the Israelites came together to King Solomon at the time of the festival in the month of Ethanim, the seventh month.   Lev 23:34; 2Sa 5:7

³When all the elders of Israel had arrived, the priests took up the ark, ⁴and they brought up the ark of the LORD and the tent of meeting and all the sacred furnishings in it. The priests and Levites carried them up, ⁵and King

Solomon and the entire assembly of Israel that had gathered about him were before the ark, sacrificing so many sheep and cattle that they could not be recorded or counted. 2Sa 6:13; 2Ch 1:3

⁶The priests then brought the ark of the LORD's covenant to its place in the inner sanctuary of the temple, the Most Holy Place, and put it beneath the wings of the cherubim. ⁷The cherubim spread their wings over the place of the ark and overshadowed the ark and its carrying poles. ⁸These poles were so long that their ends could be seen from the Holy Place in front of the inner sanctuary, but not from outside the Holy Place; and they are still there today. ⁹There was nothing in the ark except the two stone tablets that Moses had placed in it at Horeb, where the LORD made a covenant with the Israelites after they came out of Egypt. Ex 25:13-15,21; Dt 10:2-5; 1Ki 6:19

¹⁰When the priests withdrew from the Holy Place, the cloud filled the temple of the LORD. ¹¹And the priests could not perform their service because of the cloud, for the glory of the LORD filled his temple. Ex 40:34-35

¹²Then Solomon said, "The LORD has said that he would dwell in a dark cloud; ¹³I have indeed built a magnificent temple for you, a place for you to dwell forever." Ps 132:13

¹⁴While the whole assembly of Israel was standing there, the king turned around and blessed them. ¹⁵Then he said: 2Sa 6:18

"Praise be to the LORD, the God of Israel, who with his own hand has fulfilled what he promised with his own mouth to my father David. For he said, ¹⁶'Since the day I brought my people Israel out of Egypt, I have not chosen a city in any tribe of Israel to have a temple built so that my Name might be there, but I have chosen David to rule my people Israel.' 1Sa 16:1; Lk 1:68

¹⁷"My father David had it in his heart to build a temple for the Name of the LORD, the God of Israel. ¹⁸But the LORD said to my father David, 'You did well to have it in your heart to build a temple for my Name. ¹⁹Nevertheless, you are not the one to build the temple, but your son, your own flesh and blood—he is the one who will build the temple for my Name.' 2Sa 7:2,5,13; 1Ki 5:3,5

²⁰"The LORD has kept the promise he made: I have succeeded David my father and now I sit on the throne of Israel, just as the LORD promised, and I have built the temple for the Name of the LORD, the God of Israel. ²¹I have provided a place there for the ark, in which is the covenant of the

LORD that he made with our ancestors when he brought them out of Egypt." 1Ch 28:6

Solomon's Prayer of Dedication
8:22-53pp — 2Ch 6:12-40

²²Then Solomon stood before the altar of the LORD in front of the whole assembly of Israel, spread out his hands toward heaven ²³and said: Ezr 9:5

"LORD, the God of Israel, there is no God like you in heaven above or on earth below—you who keep your covenant of love with your servants who continue wholeheartedly in your way. ²⁴You have kept your promise to your servant David my father; with your mouth you have promised and with your hand you have fulfilled it—as it is today. Dt 7:9,12; Ne 1:5 ²⁵"Now LORD, the God of Israel, keep for your servant David my father the promises you made to him when you said, 'You shall never fail to have a successor to sit before me on the throne of Israel, if only your descendants are careful in all they do to walk before me faithfully as you have done.' ²⁶And now, God of Israel, let your word that you promised your servant David my father come true. 2Sa 7:25; 1Ki 2:4

²⁷"But will God really dwell on earth? The heavens, even the highest heaven, cannot contain you. How much less this temple I have built! ²⁸Yet give attention to your servant's prayer and his plea for mercy, LORD my God. Hear the cry and the prayer that your servant is praying in your presence this day. ²⁹May your eyes be open toward this temple night and day, this place of which you said, 'My Name shall be there,' so that you will hear the prayer your servant prays toward this place. ³⁰Hear the supplication of your servant and of your people Israel when they pray toward this place. Hear from heaven, your dwelling place, and when you hear, forgive. Dt 12:11; 2Ch 2:6; Isa 66:1

³¹"When anyone wrongs their neighbor and is required to take an oath and they come and swear the oath before your altar in this temple, ³²then hear from heaven and act. Judge between your servants, condemning the guilty by bringing down on their heads what they have done, and vindicating the innocent by treating them in accordance with their innocence. Ex 22:11; Dt 25:1

³³"When your people Israel have been defeated by

an enemy because they have sinned against you, and when they turn back to you and give praise to your name, praying and making supplication to you in this temple, [34] then hear from heaven and forgive the sin of your people Israel and bring them back to the land you gave to their ancestors. Lev 26:17; Dt 28:25

[35] "When the heavens are shut up and there is no rain because your people have sinned against you, and when they pray toward this place and give praise to your name and turn from their sin because you have afflicted them, [36] then hear from heaven and forgive the sin of your servants, your people Israel. Teach them the right way to live, and send rain on the land you gave your people for an inheritance. Lev 26:19

[37] "When famine or plague comes to the land, or blight or mildew, locusts or grasshoppers, or when an enemy besieges them in any of their cities, whatever disaster or disease may come, [38] and when a prayer or plea is made by anyone among your people Israel—being aware of the afflictions of their own hearts, and spreading out their hands toward this temple— [39] then hear from heaven, your dwelling place.

Forgive and act; deal with everyone according to all they do, since you know their hearts (for you alone know every human heart), [40] so that they will fear you all the time they live in the land you gave our ancestors. 1Sa 16:7; 1Ch 28:9

[41] "As for the foreigner who does not belong to your people Israel but has come from a distant land because of your name— [42] for they will hear of your great name and your mighty hand and your outstretched arm—when they come and pray toward this temple, [43] then hear from heaven, your dwelling place. Do whatever the foreigner asks of you, so that all the peoples of the earth may know your name and fear you, as do your own people Israel, and may know that this house I have built bears your Name. Dt 3:24; 1Sa 17:46

[44] "When your people go to war against their enemies, wherever you send them, and when they pray to the LORD toward the city you have chosen and the temple I have built for your Name, [45] then hear from heaven their prayer and their plea, and uphold their cause. Ps 9:4; 140:12

[46] "When they sin against you—for there is no one who does not sin—and you become angry with them and

give them over to their enemies, who take them captive to their own lands, far away or near; [47]and if they have a change of heart in the land where they are held captive, and repent and plead with you in the land of their captors and say, 'We have sinned, we have done wrong, we have acted wickedly'; [48]and if they turn back to you with all their heart and soul in the land of their enemies who took them captive, and pray to you toward the land you gave their ancestors, toward the city you have chosen and the temple I have built for your Name; [49]then from heaven, your dwelling place, hear their prayer and their plea, and uphold their cause. [50]And forgive your people, who have sinned against you; forgive all the offenses they have committed against you, and cause their captors to show them mercy; [51]for they are your people and your inheritance, whom you brought out of Egypt, out of that iron-smelting furnace. Dt 9:29; Ps 106:6; Da 6:10

[52] "May your eyes be open to your servant's plea and to the plea of your people Israel, and may you listen to them whenever they cry out to you. [53]For you singled them out from all the nations of the world to be your own inheritance, just as you declared through your servant Moses when you, Sovereign LORD, brought our ancestors out of Egypt." 2Ch 6:12-40; Ex 19:5

[54]When Solomon had finished all these prayers and supplications to the LORD, he rose from before the altar of the LORD, where he had been kneeling with his hands spread out toward heaven. [55]He stood and blessed the whole assembly of Israel in a loud voice, saying: ver 14; 2Sa 6:18

[56] "Praise be to the LORD, who has given rest to his people Israel just as he promised. Not one word has failed of all the good promises he gave through his servant Moses. [57]May the LORD our God be with us as he was with our ancestors; may he never leave us nor forsake us. [58]May he turn our hearts to him, to walk in obedience to him and keep the commands, decrees and laws he gave our ancestors. [59]And may these words of mine, which I have prayed before the LORD, be near to the LORD our God day and night, that he may uphold the cause of his servant and the cause of his people Israel according to each day's need, [60]so that all the peoples of the earth may know that the LORD is God and that

there is no other. [61] And may your hearts be fully committed to the LORD our God, to live by his decrees and obey his commands, as at this time." 1Ki 11:4; Ps 119:36; Heb 13:5

The Dedication of the Temple
8:62-66pp — 2Ch 7:1-10

[62] Then the king and all Israel with him offered sacrifices before the LORD. [63] Solomon offered a sacrifice of fellowship offerings to the LORD: twenty-two thousand cattle and a hundred and twenty thousand sheep and goats. So the king and all the Israelites dedicated the temple of the LORD.

[64] On that same day the king consecrated the middle part of the courtyard in front of the temple of the LORD, and there he offered burnt offerings, grain offerings and the fat of the fellowship offerings, because the bronze altar that stood before the LORD was too small to hold the burnt offerings, the grain offerings and the fat of the fellowship offerings. 2Ch 4:1

[65] So Solomon observed the festival at that time, and all Israel with him — a vast assembly, people from Lebo Hamath to the Wadi of Egypt. They celebrated it before the LORD our God for seven days and seven days more, fourteen days in all. [66] On the following day he sent the people away. They blessed the

king and then went home, joyful and glad in heart for all the good things the LORD had done for his servant David and his people Israel. 2Ch 7:1-10; Ge 15:18; Nu 34:8

The LORD Appears to Solomon
9:1-9pp — 2Ch 7:11-22

9 When Solomon had finished building the temple of the LORD and the royal palace, and had achieved all he had desired to do, [2] the LORD appeared to him a second time, as he had appeared to him at Gibeon. [3] The LORD said to him: 1Ki 3:5

"I have heard the prayer and plea you have made before me; I have consecrated this temple, which you have built, by putting my Name there forever. My eyes and my heart will always be there. Dt 11:12; 1Ki 8:29; 2Ki 20:5

[4] "As for you, if you walk before me faithfully with integrity of heart and uprightness, as David your father did, and do all I command and observe my decrees and laws, [5] I will establish your royal throne over Israel forever, as I promised David your father when I said, 'You shall never fail to have a successor on the throne of Israel.' 1Ki 2:4; 15:5; 1Ch 22:10

[6] "But if you[a] or your descendants turn away from me

---

[a] 6 The Hebrew is plural.

and do not observe the commands and decrees I have given you[a] and go off to serve other gods and worship them, [7]then I will cut off Israel from the land I have given them and will reject this temple I have consecrated for my Name. Israel will then become a byword and an object of ridicule among all peoples. [8]This temple will become a heap of rubble. All[b] who pass by will be appalled and will scoff and say, 'Why has the LORD done such a thing to this land and to this temple?' [9]People will answer, 'Because they have forsaken the LORD their God, who brought their ancestors out of Egypt, and have embraced other gods, worshiping and serving them—that is why the LORD brought all this disaster on them.'" 2Ch 7:11-22; 2Ki 17:23; Jer 7:14

Solomon's Other Activities

9:10-28pp — 2Ch 8:1-18

[10]At the end of twenty years, during which Solomon built these two buildings—the temple of the LORD and the royal palace— [11]King Solomon gave twenty towns in Galilee to Hiram king of Tyre, because Hiram had supplied him with all the cedar and juniper and gold he wanted. [12]But when Hiram went from Tyre to see the towns that Solomon had given him, he was not pleased with them. [13]"What kind of towns are these you have given me, my brother?" he asked. And he called them the Land of Kabul,[c] a name they have to this day. [14]Now Hiram had sent to the king 120 talents[d] of gold. Jos 19:27; 2Ch 8:2

[15]Here is the account of the forced labor King Solomon conscripted to build the LORD's temple, his own palace, the terraces,[e] the wall of Jerusalem, and Hazor, Megiddo and Gezer. [16](Pharaoh king of Egypt had attacked and captured Gezer. He had set it on fire. He killed its Canaanite inhabitants and then gave it as a wedding gift to his daughter, Solomon's wife. [17]And Solomon rebuilt Gezer.) He built up Lower Beth Horon, [18]Baalath, and Tadmor[f] in the desert, within his land, [19]as well as all his store cities and the towns for his chariots and for his horses[g]—whatever he desired to build in Jerusalem, in Lebanon and throughout all the territory he ruled. 2Sa 5:9; 1Ki 4:26; 5:13

[20]There were still people left from the Amorites, Hittites, Perizzites, Hivites and Jebusites (these peoples were not Israel-

---

[a] 6 The Hebrew is plural.   [b] 8 See some Septuagint manuscripts, Old Latin, Syriac, Arabic and Targum; Hebrew *And though this temple is now imposing, all*   [c] 13 *Kabul* sounds like the Hebrew for *good-for-nothing.*   [d] 14 That is, about 4 1/2 tons or about 4 metric tons   [e] 15 Or *the Millo*; also in verse 24   [f] 18 The Hebrew may also be read *Tamar.*   [g] 19 Or *charioteers*

ites). [21]Solomon conscripted the descendants of all these peoples remaining in the land—whom the Israelites could not extermi-nate[a]—to serve as slave labor, as it is to this day. [22]But Solomon did not make slaves of any of the Israelites; they were his fighting men, his government officials, his officers, his captains, and the commanders of his chariots and charioteers. [23]They were also the chief officials in charge of Sol-omon's projects—550 officials supervising those who did the work.   Lev 25:39; Jos 15:63; Ezr 2:55,58

[24]After Pharaoh's daughter had come up from the City of David to the palace Solomon had built for her, he constructed the terraces.   1Ki 3:1; 11:27; 2Ch 32:5

[25]Three times a year Solomon sacrificed burnt offerings and fel-lowship offerings on the altar he had built for the LORD, burning in-cense before the LORD along with them, and so fulfilled the temple obligations.   Ex 23:14; 2Ch 8:12-13,16

[26]King Solomon also built ships at Ezion Geber, which is near Elath in Edom, on the shore of the Red Sea.[b] [27]And Hiram sent his men—sailors who knew the sea—to serve in the fleet with Solomon's men. [28]They sailed to Ophir and brought back 420 tal-ents[c] of gold, which they delivered to King Solomon.   Nu 33:35; 1Ki 10:11

The Queen of Sheba Visits Solomon
10:1-13pp — 2Ch 9:1-12

10 When the queen of Sheba heard about the fame of Solomon and his relationship to the LORD, she came to test Solo-mon with hard questions. [2]Arriv-ing at Jerusalem with a very great caravan—with camels carrying spices, large quantities of gold, and precious stones—she came to Solomon and talked with him about all that she had on her mind. [3]Solomon answered all her questions; nothing was too hard for the king to explain to her. [4]When the queen of Sheba saw all the wisdom of Solomon and the palace he had built, [5]the food on his table, the seating of his of-ficials, the attending servants in their robes, his cupbearers, and the burnt offerings he made at[d] the temple of the LORD, she was overwhelmed.   Mt 12:42; Jdg 14:12

[6]She said to the king, "The re-port I heard in my own coun-try about your achievements and your wisdom is true. [7]But I did not believe these things un-til I came and saw with my own eyes. Indeed, not even half was told me; in wisdom and wealth you have far exceeded the re-port I heard. [8]How happy your people must be! How happy your officials, who continually stand

---

[a] 21 The Hebrew term refers to the irrevocable giving over of things or persons to the LORD, often by totally destroying them.   [b] 26 Or the Sea of Reeds   [c] 28 That is, about 16 tons or about 14 metric tons   [d] 5 Or the ascent by which he went up to

before you and hear your wisdom! [9] Praise be to the LORD your God, who has delighted in you and placed you on the throne of Israel. Because of the LORD's eternal love for Israel, he has made you king to maintain justice and righteousness." 2Sa 8:15; Ps 72:2; Pr 8:34

[10] And she gave the king 120 talents[a] of gold, large quantities of spices, and precious stones. Never again were so many spices brought in as those the queen of Sheba gave to King Solomon.

[11] (Hiram's ships brought gold from Ophir; and from there they brought great cargoes of almugwood[b] and precious stones. [12] The king used the almugwood to make supports[c] for the temple of the LORD and for the royal palace, and to make harps and lyres for the musicians. So much almugwood has never been imported or seen since that day.) 1Ki 9:27-28

[13] King Solomon gave the queen of Sheba all she desired and asked for, besides what he had given her out of his royal bounty. Then she left and returned with her retinue to her own country. 2Ch 9:1-12

Solomon's Splendor
10:14-29pp — 2Ch 1:14-17; 9:13-28

[14] The weight of the gold that Solomon received yearly was 666 talents,[d] [15] not including the revenues from merchants and traders and from all the Arabian kings and the governors of the territories. 1Ki 9:28

[16] King Solomon made two hundred large shields of hammered gold; six hundred shekels[e] of gold went into each shield. [17] He also made three hundred small shields of hammered gold, with three minas[f] of gold in each shield. The king put them in the Palace of the Forest of Lebanon. 1Ki 7:2; 14:26-28

[18] Then the king made a great throne covered with ivory and overlaid with fine gold. [19] The throne had six steps, and its back had a rounded top. On both sides of the seat were armrests, with a lion standing beside each of them. [20] Twelve lions stood on the six steps, one at either end of each step. Nothing like it had ever been made for any other kingdom. [21] All King Solomon's goblets were gold, and all the household articles in the Palace of the Forest of Lebanon were pure gold. Nothing was made of silver, because silver was considered of little value in Solomon's days. [22] The king had a fleet of trading ships[g] at sea along with the ships of Hiram. Once every

---

[a] 10 That is, about 4 1/2 tons or about 4 metric tons   [b] 11 Probably a variant of algumwood; also in verse 12   [c] 12 The meaning of the Hebrew for this word is uncertain.   [d] 14 That is, about 25 tons or about 23 metric tons   [e] 16 That is, about 15 pounds or about 6.9 kilograms; also in verse 29   [f] 17 That is, about 3 3/4 pounds or about 1.7 kilograms; or perhaps reference is to double minas, that is, about 7 1/2 pounds or about 3.5 kilograms.   [g] 22 Hebrew of ships of Tarshish

three years it returned, carrying gold, silver and ivory, and apes and baboons. 1Ki 9:26; Isa 60:17

²³King Solomon was greater in riches and wisdom than all the other kings of the earth. ²⁴The whole world sought audience with Solomon to hear the wisdom God had put in his heart. ²⁵Year after year, everyone who came brought a gift—articles of silver and gold, robes, weapons and spices, and horses and mules. 1Ki 3:13; 4:30

²⁶Solomon accumulated chariots and horses; he had fourteen hundred chariots and twelve thousand horses,ᵃ which he kept in the chariot cities and also with him in Jerusalem. ²⁷The king made silver as common in Jerusalem as stones, and cedar as plentiful as sycamore-fig trees in the foothills. ²⁸Solomon's horses were imported from Egypt and from Kueᵇ—the royal merchants purchased them from Kue at the current price. ²⁹They imported a chariot from Egypt for six hundred shekels of silver, and a horse for a hundred and fifty.ᶜ They also exported them to all the kings of the Hittites and of the Arameans. 2Ch 1:14-17; 9:13-28; 1Ki 4:26

Solomon's Wives

11 King Solomon, however, loved many foreign women besides Pharaoh's daughter—

Moabites, Ammonites, Edomites, Sidonians and Hittites. ²They were from nations about which the LORD had told the Israelites, "You must not intermarry with them, because they will surely turn your hearts after their gods." Nevertheless, Solomon held fast to them in love. ³He had seven hundred wives of royal birth and three hundred concubines, and his wives led him astray. ⁴As Solomon grew old, his wives turned his heart after other gods, and his heart was not fully devoted to the LORD his God, as the heart of David his father had been. ⁵He followed Ashtoreth the goddess of the Sidonians, and Molek the detestable god of the Ammonites. ⁶So Solomon did evil in the eyes of the LORD; he did not follow the LORD completely, as David his father had done. Ne 13:26; Dt 7:3-4

⁷On a hill east of Jerusalem, Solomon built a high place for Chemosh the detestable god of Moab, and for Molek the detestable god of the Ammonites. ⁸He did the same for all his foreign wives, who burned incense and offered sacrifices to their gods. Nu 21:29; Jdg 11:24

⁹The LORD became angry with Solomon because his heart had turned away from the LORD, the God of Israel, who had appeared to him twice. ¹⁰Although he had forbidden Solomon to follow other gods, Solomon did not keep

ᵃ 26 Or *charioteers*   ᵇ 28 Probably *Cilicia*
1.7 kilograms
ᶜ 29 That is, about 3 3/4 pounds or about

the LORD's command. [11] So the LORD said to Solomon, "Since this is your attitude and you have not kept my covenant and my decrees, which I commanded you, I will most certainly tear the kingdom away from you and give it to one of your subordinates. [12] Nevertheless, for the sake of David your father, I will not do it during your lifetime. I will tear it out of the hand of your son. [13] Yet I will not tear the whole kingdom from him, but will give him one tribe for the sake of David my servant and for the sake of Jerusalem, which I have chosen." 2Sa 7:15

Solomon's Adversaries

[14] Then the LORD raised up against Solomon an adversary, Hadad the Edomite, from the royal line of Edom. [15] Earlier when David was fighting with Edom, Joab the commander of the army, who had gone up to bury the dead, had struck down all the men in Edom. [16] Joab and all the Israelites stayed there for six months, until they had destroyed all the men in Edom. [17] But Hadad, still only a boy, fled to Egypt with some Edomite officials who had served his father. [18] They set out from Midian and went to Paran. Then taking people from Paran with them, they went to Egypt, to Pharaoh king of Egypt, who gave Hadad a house and land and provided him with food. 2Sa 8:14; 1Ch 18:12

[19] Pharaoh was so pleased with Hadad that he gave him a sister of his own wife, Queen Tahpenes, in marriage. [20] The sister of Tahpenes bore him a son named Genubath, whom Tahpenes brought up in the royal palace. There Genubath lived with Pharaoh's own children.

[21] While he was in Egypt, Hadad heard that David rested with his ancestors and that Joab the commander of the army was also dead. Then Hadad said to Pharaoh, "Let me go, that I may return to my own country."

[22] "What have you lacked here that you want to go back to your own country?" Pharaoh asked.

"Nothing," Hadad replied, "but do let me go!"

[23] And God raised up against Solomon another adversary, Rezon son of Eliada, who had fled from his master, Hadadezer king of Zobah. [24] When David destroyed Zobah's army, Rezon gathered a band of men around him and became their leader; they went to Damascus, where they settled and took control. [25] Rezon was Israel's adversary as long as Solomon lived, adding to the trouble caused by Hadad. So Rezon ruled in Aram and was hostile toward Israel. 2Sa 8:3; 10:8,18-19

Jeroboam Rebels Against Solomon

[26] Also, Jeroboam son of Nebat rebelled against the king. He was

one of Solomon's officials, an Ephraimite from Zeredah, and his mother was a widow named Zeruah. 2Sa 20:21; 1Ki 12:2; 2Ch 13:6 ²⁷Here is the account of how he rebelled against the king: Solomon had built the terraces*a* and had filled in the gap in the wall of the city of David his father. ²⁸Now Jeroboam was a man of standing, and when Solomon saw how well the young man did his work, he put him in charge of the whole labor force of the tribes of Joseph. Ru 2:1; 1Ki 9:24; Pr 22:29

²⁹About that time Jeroboam was going out of Jerusalem, and Ahijah the prophet of Shiloh met him on the way, wearing a new cloak. The two of them were alone out in the country, ³⁰and Ahijah took hold of the new cloak he was wearing and tore it into twelve pieces. ³¹Then he said to Jeroboam, "Take ten pieces for yourself, for this is what the LORD, the God of Israel, says: 'See, I am going to tear the kingdom out of Solomon's hand and give you ten tribes. ³²But for the sake of my servant David and the city of Jerusalem, which I have chosen out of all the tribes of Israel, he will have one tribe. ³³I will do this because they have*b* forsaken me and worshiped Ashtoreth the goddess of the Sidonians, Chemosh the god of the Moabites, and Molek the god of the Ammonites, and have not walked in obedience to

me, nor done what is right in my eyes, nor kept my decrees and laws as David, Solomon's father, did. 1Sa 15:27; 1Ki 3:3; 14:2

³⁴"'But I will not take the whole kingdom out of Solomon's hand; I have made him ruler all the days of his life for the sake of David my servant, whom I chose and who obeyed my commands and decrees. ³⁵I will take the kingdom from his son's hands and give you ten tribes. ³⁶I will give one tribe to his son so that David my servant may always have a lamp before me in Jerusalem, the city where I chose to put my Name. ³⁷However, as for you, I will take you, and you will rule over all that your heart desires; you will be king over Israel. ³⁸If you do whatever I command you and walk in obedience to me and do what is right in my eyes by obeying my decrees and commands, as David my servant did, I will be with you. I will build you a dynasty as enduring as the one I built for David and will give Israel to you. ³⁹I will humble David's descendants because of this, but not forever.'" Jos 1:5; 2Sa 7:11,27

⁴⁰Solomon tried to kill Jeroboam, but Jeroboam fled to Egypt, to Shishak the king, and stayed there until Solomon's death. 2Ch 12:2

Solomon's Death
11:41-43pp — 2Ch 9:29-31

⁴¹As for the other events of Solomon's reign — all he did and the

---

a 27 Or *the Millo*   *b 33* Hebrew; Septuagint, Vulgate and Syriac *because he has* wisdom he displayed — are they not written in the book of the annals of Solomon? ⁴²Solomon reigned in Jerusalem over all Israel forty years. ⁴³Then he rested with his ancestors and was buried in the city of David his father. And Rehoboam his son succeeded him as king. 2Ch 9:29-31; Mt 1:7

Israel Rebels Against Rehoboam
12:1-24pp — 2Ch 10:1-11:4

12 Rehoboam went to Shechem, for all Israel had gone there to make him king. ²When Jeroboam son of Nebat heard this (he was still in Egypt, where he had fled from King Solomon), he returned from*ᵃ* Egypt. ³So they sent for Jeroboam, and he and the whole assembly of Israel went to Rehoboam and said to him: ⁴"Your father put a heavy yoke on us, but now lighten the harsh labor and the heavy yoke he put on us, and we will serve you." 1Sa 8:11-18; 1Ki 4:20-28; 11:40

⁵Rehoboam answered, "Go away for three days and then come back to me." So the people went away.

⁶Then King Rehoboam consulted the elders who had served his father Solomon during his lifetime. "How would you advise me to answer these people?" he asked. 1Ki 4:2

⁷They replied, "If today you will be a servant to these people and serve them and give them a favorable answer, they will always be your servants." Pr 15:1

⁸But Rehoboam rejected the advice the elders gave him and consulted the young men who had grown up with him and were serving him. ⁹He asked them, "What is your advice? How should we answer these people who say to me, 'Lighten the yoke your father put on us'?"

¹⁰The young men who had grown up with him replied, "These people have said to you, 'Your father put a heavy yoke on us, but make our yoke lighter.' Now tell them, 'My little finger is thicker than my father's waist. ¹¹My father laid on you a heavy yoke; I will make it even heavier. My father scourged you with whips; I will scourge you with scorpions.'"

¹²Three days later Jeroboam and all the people returned to Rehoboam, as the king had said, "Come back to me in three days." ¹³The king answered the people harshly. Rejecting the advice given him by the elders, ¹⁴he followed the advice of the young men and said, "My father made your yoke heavy; I will make it even heavier. My father scourged you with whips; I will scourge you with scorpions." ¹⁵So the king did not listen to the people, for this turn of events was from the LORD, to fulfill the word the LORD had spoken to Jeroboam

---

ᵃ 2 Or he remained in

son of Nebat through Ahijah the Shilonite. Dt 2:30; 1Ki 11:29; 2Ch 25:20 ¹⁶When all Israel saw that the king refused to listen to them, they answered the king:

"What share do we have in David,
 what part in Jesse's son?
To your tents, Israel! 2Sa 20:1
 Look after your own house, David!"

So the Israelites went home. ¹⁷But as for the Israelites who were living in the towns of Judah, Rehoboam still ruled over them. 1Ki 11:13,36 ¹⁸King Rehoboam sent out Adoniram,ᵃ who was in charge of forced labor, but all Israel stoned him to death. King Rehoboam, however, managed to get into his chariot and escape to Jerusalem. ¹⁹So Israel has been in rebellion against the house of David to this day. 1Ki 4:6; 5:14; 2Ki 17:21 ²⁰When all the Israelites heard that Jeroboam had returned, they sent and called him to the assembly and made him king over all Israel. Only the tribe of Judah remained loyal to the house of David. 1Ki 11:13,32 ²¹When Rehoboam arrived in Jerusalem, he mustered all Judah and the tribe of Benjamin— a hundred and eighty thousand able young men—to go to war against Israel and to regain the kingdom for Rehoboam son of Solomon. 2Ch 11:1 ²²But this word of God came to Shemaiah the man of God: ²³"Say to Rehoboam son of Solomon king of Judah, to all Judah and Benjamin, and to the rest of the people, ²⁴'This is what the LORD says: Do not go up to fight against your brothers, the Israelites. Go home, every one of you, for this is my doing.'" So they obeyed the word of the LORD and went home again, as the LORD had ordered. 2Ch 10:1-11:4

Golden Calves at Bethel and Dan

²⁵Then Jeroboam fortified Shechem in the hill country of Ephraim and lived there. From there he went out and built up Peniel.ᵇ Jdg 8:8,17; 9:45 ²⁶Jeroboam thought to himself, "The kingdom will now likely revert to the house of David. ²⁷If these people go up to offer sacrifices at the temple of the LORD in Jerusalem, they will again give their allegiance to their lord, Rehoboam king of Judah. They will kill me and return to King Rehoboam." Dt 12:5-6 ²⁸After seeking advice, the king made two golden calves. He said to the people, "It is too much for you to go up to Jerusalem. Here are your gods, Israel, who brought you up out of Egypt." ²⁹One he set

ᵃ 18 Some Septuagint manuscripts and Syriac (see also 4:6 and 5:14); Hebrew *Adoram*
ᵇ 25 Hebrew *Penuel,* a variant of *Peniel*

up in Bethel, and the other in Dan. [30] And this thing became a sin; the people came to worship the one at Bethel and went as far as Dan to worship the other.[a]   1Ki 13:34; 2Ki 17:21

[31] Jeroboam built shrines on high places and appointed priests from all sorts of people, even though they were not Levites. [32] He instituted a festival on the fifteenth day of the eighth month, like the festival held in Judah, and offered sacrifices on the altar. This he did in Bethel, sacrificing to the calves he had made. And at Bethel he also installed priests at the high places he had made. [33] On the fifteenth day of the eighth month, a month of his own choosing, he offered sacrifices on the altar he had built at Bethel. So he instituted the festival for the Israelites and went up to the altar to make offerings.   Nu 29:12; 1Ki 13:32

The Man of God From Judah

13 By the word of the Lord a man of God came from Judah to Bethel, as Jeroboam was standing by the altar to make an offering. [2] By the word of the Lord he cried out against the altar: "Altar, altar! This is what the Lord says: 'A son named Josiah will be born to the house of David. On you he will sacrifice the priests of the high places who make offerings here, and human bones will be burned on you.'" [3] That same day the man of God gave a sign:

"This is the sign the Lord has declared: The altar will be split apart and the ashes on it will be poured out."   2Ki 23:15-16,20; Jn 2:11

[4] When King Jeroboam heard what the man of God cried out against the altar at Bethel, he stretched out his hand from the altar and said, "Seize him!" But the hand he stretched out toward the man shriveled up, so that he could not pull it back. [5] Also, the altar was split apart and its ashes poured out according to the sign given by the man of God by the word of the Lord.

[6] Then the king said to the man of God, "Intercede with the Lord your God and pray for me that my hand may be restored." So the man of God interceded with the Lord, and the king's hand was restored and became as it was before.   Ex 8:8; Ac 8:24

[7] The king said to the man of God, "Come home with me for a meal, and I will give you a gift."

[8] But the man of God answered the king, "Even if you were to give me half your possessions, I would not go with you, nor would I eat bread or drink water here. [9] For I was commanded by the word of the Lord: 'You must not eat bread or drink water or return by the way you came.'" [10] So he took another road and did not return by the way he had come to Bethel.   Nu 22:18; 24:13

[11] Now there was a certain old

---

[a] 30 Probable reading of the original Hebrew text; Masoretic Text *people went to the one as far as Dan*

prophet living in Bethel, whose sons came and told him all that the man of God had done there that day. They also told their father what he had said to the king. [12] Their father asked them, "Which way did he go?" And his sons showed him which road the man of God from Judah had taken. [13] So he said to his sons, "Saddle the donkey for me." And when they had saddled the donkey for him, he mounted it [14] and rode after the man of God. He found him sitting under an oak tree and asked, "Are you the man of God who came from Judah?"

"I am," he replied.

[15] So the prophet said to him, "Come home with me and eat."

[16] The man of God said, "I cannot turn back and go with you, nor can I eat bread or drink water with you in this place. [17] I have been told by the word of the LORD: 'You must not eat bread or drink water there or return by the way you came.' " ver 8

[18] The old prophet answered, "I too am a prophet, as you are. And an angel said to me by the word of the LORD: 'Bring him back with you to your house so that he may eat bread and drink water.' " (But he was lying to him.) [19] So the man of God returned with him and ate and drank in his house. Dt 13:3

[20] While they were sitting at the table, the word of the LORD came to the old prophet who had brought him back. [21] He cried out to the man of God who had come from Judah, "This is what the LORD says: 'You have defied the word of the LORD and have not kept the command the LORD your God gave you. [22] You came back and ate bread and drank water in the place where he told you not to eat or drink. Therefore your body will not be buried in the tomb of your ancestors.' " ver 26; 1Ki 20:35

[23] When the man of God had finished eating and drinking, the prophet who had brought him back saddled his donkey for him. [24] As he went on his way, a lion met him on the road and killed him, and his body was left lying on the road, with both the donkey and the lion standing beside it. [25] Some people who passed by saw the body lying there, with the lion standing beside the body, and they went and reported it in the city where the old prophet lived. 1Ki 20:36

[26] When the prophet who had brought him back from his journey heard of it, he said, "It is the man of God who defied the word of the LORD. The LORD has given him over to the lion, which has mauled him and killed him, as the word of the LORD had warned him."

[27] The prophet said to his sons, "Saddle the donkey for me," and they did so. [28] Then he went out and found the body lying on the road, with the donkey and

the lion standing beside it. The lion had neither eaten the body nor mauled the donkey. ²⁹So the prophet picked up the body of the man of God, laid it on the donkey, and brought it back to his own city to mourn for him and bury him. ³⁰Then he laid the body in his own tomb, and they mourned over him and said, "Alas, my brother!" Jer 22:18

³¹After burying him, he said to his sons, "When I die, bury me in the grave where the man of God is buried; lay my bones beside his bones. ³²For the message he declared by the word of the LORD against the altar in Bethel and against all the shrines on the high places in the towns of Samaria will certainly come true." Lev 26:30; 1Ki 16:24,28; 2Ki 23:16,18

³³Even after this, Jeroboam did not change his evil ways, but once more appointed priests for the high places from all sorts of people. Anyone who wanted to become a priest he consecrated for the high places. ³⁴This was the sin of the house of Jeroboam that led to its downfall and to its destruction from the face of the earth. 1Ki 12:30-31; 14:10

Ahijah's Prophecy Against Jeroboam

14 At that time Abijah son of Jeroboam became ill, ²and Jeroboam said to his wife, "Go, disguise yourself, so you won't be recognized as the wife of Jeroboam. Then go to Shiloh. Ahijah the prophet is there—the one who told me I would be king over this people. ³Take ten loaves of bread with you, some cakes and a jar of honey, and go to him. He will tell you what will happen to the boy." ⁴So Jeroboam's wife did what he said and went to Ahijah's house in Shiloh. 1Sa 9:7; 1Ki 11:29

Now Ahijah could not see; his sight was gone because of his age. ⁵But the LORD had told Ahijah, "Jeroboam's wife is coming to ask you about her son, for he is ill, and you are to give her such and such an answer. When she arrives, she will pretend to be someone else."

⁶So when Ahijah heard the sound of her footsteps at the door, he said, "Come in, wife of Jeroboam. Why this pretense? I have been sent to you with bad news. ⁷Go, tell Jeroboam that this is what the LORD, the God of Israel, says: 'I raised you up from among the people and appointed you ruler over my people Israel. ⁸I tore the kingdom away from the house of David and gave it to you, but you have not been like my servant David, who kept my commands and followed me with all his heart, doing only what was right in my eyes. ⁹You have done more evil than all who lived before you. You have made for yourself other gods, idols made of metal; you have aroused my anger and turned your back on me. 1Ki 11:31,33,38; 2Ch 11:15; Ps 50:17

10 " 'Because of this, I am going to bring disaster on the house of Jeroboam. I will cut off from Jeroboam every last male in Israel — slave or free.*a* I will burn up the house of Jeroboam as one burns dung, until it is all gone. 11 Dogs will eat those belonging to Jeroboam who die in the city, and the birds will feed on those who die in the country. The LORD has spoken!'   1Ki 15:29; 16:4; 21:24

12 "As for you, go back home. When you set foot in your city, the boy will die. 13 All Israel will mourn for him and bury him. He is the only one belonging to Jeroboam who will be buried, because he is the only one in the house of Jeroboam in whom the LORD, the God of Israel, has found anything good.   2Ch 12:12; 19:3

14 "The LORD will raise up for himself a king over Israel who will cut off the family of Jeroboam. Even now this is beginning to happen.*b* 15 And the LORD will strike Israel, so that it will be like a reed swaying in the water. He will uproot Israel from this good land that he gave to their ancestors and scatter them beyond the Euphrates River, because they aroused the LORD's anger by making Asherah poles.*c* 16 And he will give Israel up because of the sins Jeroboam has committed and has caused Israel to commit."   Dt 12:3; Jos 23:15-16; 1Ki 12:30

17 Then Jeroboam's wife got up and left and went to Tirzah. As soon as she stepped over the threshold of the house, the boy died. 18 They buried him, and all Israel mourned for him, as the LORD had said through his servant the prophet Ahijah.   1Ki 16:6-9

19 The other events of Jeroboam's reign, his wars and how he ruled, are written in the book of the annals of the kings of Israel. 20 He reigned for twenty-two years and then rested with his ancestors. And Nadab his son succeeded him as king.

Rehoboam King of Judah
14:21,25-31pp — 2Ch 12:9-16

21 Rehoboam son of Solomon was king in Judah. He was forty-one years old when he became king, and he reigned seventeen years in Jerusalem, the city the LORD had chosen out of all the tribes of Israel in which to put his Name. His mother's name was Naamah; she was an Ammonite.   1Ki 11:1; 2Ch 12:13

22 Judah did evil in the eyes of the LORD. By the sins they committed they stirred up his jealous anger more than those who were before them had done. 23 They also set up for themselves high places, sacred stones and Asherah poles on every high hill and under every spreading tree. 24 There were even male shrine

---

a 10 Or *Israel — every ruler or leader*   *b* 14 The meaning of the Hebrew for this sentence is uncertain.   *c* 15 That is, wooden symbols of the goddess Asherah; here and elsewhere in 1 Kings prostitutes in the land; the people engaged in all the detestable practices of the nations the LORD had driven out before the Israelites. Dt 23:17; 32:21; 2Ch 12:1

²⁵ In the fifth year of King Rehoboam, Shishak king of Egypt attacked Jerusalem. ²⁶ He carried off the treasures of the temple of the LORD and the treasures of the royal palace. He took everything, including all the gold shields Solomon had made. ²⁷ So King Rehoboam made bronze shields to replace them and assigned these to the commanders of the guard on duty at the entrance to the royal palace. ²⁸ Whenever the king went to the LORD's temple, the guards bore the shields, and afterward they returned them to the guardroom. 1Ki 10:17; 2Ch 12:2

²⁹ As for the other events of Rehoboam's reign, and all he did, are they not written in the book of the annals of the kings of Judah? ³⁰ There was continual warfare between Rehoboam and Jeroboam. ³¹ And Rehoboam rested with his ancestors and was buried with them in the City of David. His mother's name was Naamah; she was an Ammonite. And Abijah[a] his son succeeded him as king. 2Ch 12:9-16; 1Ki 12:21

Abijah King of Judah
15:1-2,6-8pp — 2Ch 13:1-2,22–14:1

15 In the eighteenth year of the reign of Jeroboam son of Nebat, Abijah[b] became king of Judah, ² and he reigned in Jerusalem three years. His mother's name was Maakah daughter of Abishalom.[c] 2Ch 11:20; 13:2

³ He committed all the sins his father had done before him; his heart was not fully devoted to the LORD his God, as the heart of David his forefather had been. ⁴ Nevertheless, for David's sake the LORD his God gave him a lamp in Jerusalem by raising up a son to succeed him and by making Jerusalem strong. ⁵ For David had done what was right in the eyes of the LORD and had not failed to keep any of the LORD's commands all the days of his life — except in the case of Uriah the Hittite. 2Sa 11:2-27; 12:9; 1Ki 11:4; 2Ch 21:7

⁶ There was war between Abijah[d] and Jeroboam throughout Abijah's lifetime. ⁷ As for the other events of Abijah's reign, and all he did, are they not written in the book of the annals of the kings of Judah? There was war between Abijah and Jeroboam. ⁸ And Abijah rested with his ancestors and was buried in the City of David. And Asa his son succeeded him as king. 2Ch 13:1-2,22-14:1

Asa King of Judah

15:9-22pp — 2Ch 14:2-3; 15:16 – 16:6
15:23-24pp — 2Ch 16:11 – 17:1

[9] In the twentieth year of Jeroboam king of Israel, Asa became king of Judah, [10] and he reigned in Jerusalem forty-one years. His grandmother's name was Maakah daughter of Abishalom. ver 2 [11] Asa did what was right in the eyes of the LORD, as his father David had done. [12] He expelled the male shrine prostitutes from the land and got rid of all the idols his ancestors had made. [13] He even deposed his grandmother Maakah from her position as queen mother, because she had made a repulsive image for the worship of Asherah. Asa cut it down and burned it in the Kidron Valley. [14] Although he did not remove the high places, Asa's heart was fully committed to the LORD all his life. [15] He brought into the temple of the LORD the silver and gold and the articles that he and his father had dedicated. 1Ki 7:51; 14:24; 22:43

[16] There was war between Asa and Baasha king of Israel throughout their reigns. [17] Baasha king of Israel went up against Judah and fortified Ramah to prevent anyone from leaving or entering the territory of Asa king of Judah. Jos 18:25; 1Ki 12:27

[18] Asa then took all the silver and gold that was left in the treasuries of the LORD's temple and of his own palace. He entrusted it to his officials and sent them to Ben-Hadad son of Tabrimmon, the son of Hezion, the king of Aram, who was ruling in Damascus. [19] "Let there be a treaty between me and you," he said, "as there was between my father and your father. See, I am sending you a gift of silver and gold. Now break your treaty with Baasha king of Israel so he will withdraw from me." 1Ki 11:23-24; 14:26

[20] Ben-Hadad agreed with King Asa and sent the commanders of his forces against the towns of Israel. He conquered Ijon, Dan, Abel Beth Maakah and all Kinnereth in addition to Naphtali. [21] When Baasha heard this, he stopped building Ramah and withdrew to Tirzah. [22] Then King Asa issued an order to all Judah — no one was exempt — and they carried away from Ramah the stones and timber Baasha had been using there. With them King Asa built up Geba in Benjamin, and also Mizpah. 2Ch 14:2-3; 15:16-16:6

[23] As for all the other events of Asa's reign, all his achievements, all he did and the cities he built, are they not written in the book of the annals of the kings of Judah? In his old age, however, his feet became diseased. [24] Then Asa rested with his ancestors and was buried with them in the city of his father David. And Jehoshaphat his son succeeded him as king. Mt 1:8

Nadab King of Israel

[25] Nadab son of Jeroboam

became king of Israel in the second year of Asa king of Judah, and he reigned over Israel two years. [26] He did evil in the eyes of the LORD, following the ways of his father and committing the same sin his father had caused Israel to commit. 1Ki 12:30

[27] Baasha son of Ahijah from the tribe of Issachar plotted against him, and he struck him down at Gibbethon, a Philistine town, while Nadab and all Israel were besieging it. [28] Baasha killed Nadab in the third year of Asa king of Judah and succeeded him as king. Jos 19:44; 1Ki 14:14

[29] As soon as he began to reign, he killed Jeroboam's whole family. He did not leave Jeroboam anyone that breathed, but destroyed them all, according to the word of the LORD given through his servant Ahijah the Shilonite. [30] This happened because of the sins Jeroboam had committed and had caused Israel to commit, and because he aroused the anger of the LORD, the God of Israel. 1Ki 14:9-10,14,16

[31] As for the other events of Nadab's reign, and all he did, are they not written in the book of the annals of the kings of Israel? [32] There was war between Asa and Baasha king of Israel throughout their reigns. ver 16

Baasha King of Israel

[33] In the third year of Asa king of Judah, Baasha son of Ahijah became king of all Israel in Tirzah, and he reigned twenty-four years. [34] He did evil in the eyes of the LORD, following the ways of Jeroboam and committing the same sin Jeroboam had caused Israel to commit.

16 Then the word of the LORD came to Jehu son of Hanani concerning Baasha: [2] "I lifted you up from the dust and appointed you ruler over my people Israel, but you followed the ways of Jeroboam and caused my people Israel to sin and to arouse my anger by their sins. [3] So I am about to wipe out Baasha and his house, and I will make your house like that of Jeroboam son of Nebat. [4] Dogs will eat those belonging to Baasha who die in the city, and birds will feed on those who die in the country." 1Ki 14:7-11

[5] As for the other events of Baasha's reign, what he did and his achievements, are they not written in the book of the annals of the kings of Israel? [6] Baasha rested with his ancestors and was buried in Tirzah. And Elah his son succeeded him as king. 1Ki 15:31,33

[7] Moreover, the word of the LORD came through the prophet Jehu son of Hanani to Baasha and his house, because of all the evil he had done in the eyes of the LORD, arousing his anger by the things he did, becoming like the house of Jeroboam—and also because he destroyed it. 1Ki 15:27,29

Elah King of Israel

[8] In the twenty-sixth year of Asa king of Judah, Elah son of Baasha became king of Israel, and he reigned in Tirzah two years. [9] Zimri, one of his officials, who had command of half his chariots, plotted against him. Elah was in Tirzah at the time, getting drunk in the home of Arza, the palace administrator at Tirzah. [10] Zimri came in, struck him down and killed him in the twenty-seventh year of Asa king of Judah. Then he succeeded him as king. 1Ki 18:3; 2Ki 9:30-33

[11] As soon as he began to reign and was seated on the throne, he killed off Baasha's whole family. He did not spare a single male, whether relative or friend. [12] So Zimri destroyed the whole family of Baasha, in accordance with the word of the LORD spoken against Baasha through the prophet Jehu — [13] because of all the sins Baasha and his son Elah had committed and had caused Israel to commit, so that they aroused the anger of the LORD, the God of Israel, by their worthless idols. Dt 32:21; 1Sa 12:21; Isa 41:29

[14] As for the other events of Elah's reign, and all he did, are they not written in the book of the annals of the kings of Israel?

Zimri King of Israel

[15] In the twenty-seventh year of Asa king of Judah, Zimri reigned in Tirzah seven days. The army was encamped near Gibbethon, a Philistine town. [16] When the Israelites in the camp heard that Zimri had plotted against the king and murdered him, they proclaimed Omri, the commander of the army, king over Israel that very day there in the camp. [17] Then Omri and all the Israelites with him withdrew from Gibbethon and laid siege to Tirzah. [18] When Zimri saw that the city was taken, he went into the citadel of the royal palace and set the palace on fire around him. So he died, [19] because of the sins he had committed, doing evil in the eyes of the LORD and following the ways of Jeroboam and committing the same sin Jeroboam had caused Israel to commit. Jos 19:44; 1Ki 15:27

[20] As for the other events of Zimri's reign, and the rebellion he carried out, are they not written in the book of the annals of the kings of Israel?

Omri King of Israel

[21] Then the people of Israel were split into two factions; half supported Tibni son of Ginath for king, and the other half supported Omri. [22] But Omri's followers proved stronger than those of Tibni son of Ginath. So Tibni died and Omri became king.

[23] In the thirty-first year of Asa king of Judah, Omri became king of Israel, and he reigned twelve

years, six of them in Tirzah. ²⁴He bought the hill of Samaria from Shemer for two talents*ᵃ* of silver and built a city on the hill, calling it Samaria, after Shemer, the name of the former owner of the hill. 1Ki 13:32; 15:21; Jn 4:4

²⁵But Omri did evil in the eyes of the LORD and sinned more than all those before him. ²⁶He followed completely the ways of Jeroboam son of Nebat, committing the same sin Jeroboam had caused Israel to commit, so that they aroused the anger of the LORD, the God of Israel, by their worthless idols. Dt 4:25; 32:21; Mic 6:16

²⁷As for the other events of Omri's reign, what he did and the things he achieved, are they not written in the book of the annals of the kings of Israel? ²⁸Omri rested with his ancestors and was buried in Samaria. And Ahab his son succeeded him as king.

Ahab Becomes King of Israel

²⁹In the thirty-eighth year of Asa king of Judah, Ahab son of Omri became king of Israel, and he reigned in Samaria over Israel twenty-two years. ³⁰Ahab son of Omri did more evil in the eyes of the LORD than any of those before him. ³¹He not only considered it trivial to commit the sins of Jeroboam son of Nebat, but he also married Jezebel daughter of Ethbaal king of the Sidonians, and began to serve Baal and worship him. ³²He set up an altar for Baal in the temple of Baal that he built in Samaria. ³³Ahab also made an Asherah pole and did more to arouse the anger of the LORD, the God of Israel, than did all the kings of Israel before him. 1Ki 14:9; 21:25; 2Ki 10:18,21,27

³⁴In Ahab's time, Hiel of Bethel rebuilt Jericho. He laid its foundations at the cost of his firstborn son Abiram, and he set up its gates at the cost of his youngest son Segub, in accordance with the word of the LORD spoken by Joshua son of Nun. Jos 6:26

Elijah Announces a Great Drought

17 Now Elijah the Tishbite, from Tishbe*ᵇ* in Gilead, said to Ahab, "As the LORD, the God of Israel, lives, whom I serve, there will be neither dew nor rain in the next few years except at my word." 2Ki 3:14; Lk 4:25; Jas 5:17

Elijah Fed by Ravens

²Then the word of the LORD came to Elijah: ³"Leave here, turn eastward and hide in the Kerith Ravine, east of the Jordan. ⁴You will drink from the brook, and I have directed the ravens to supply you with food there." Ge 8:7

⁵So he did what the LORD had told him. He went to the Kerith Ravine, east of the Jordan, and stayed there. ⁶The ravens brought him bread and meat in

---

ᵃ 24 That is, about 150 pounds or about 68 kilograms   *ᵇ* 1 Or *Tishbite, of the settlers* the morning and bread and meat in the evening, and he drank from the brook. Ex 16:8

Elijah and the Widow at Zarephath

⁷Some time later the brook dried up because there had been no rain in the land. ⁸Then the word of the LORD came to him: ⁹"Go at once to Zarephath in the region of Sidon and stay there. I have directed a widow there to supply you with food." ¹⁰So he went to Zarephath. When he came to the town gate, a widow was there gathering sticks. He called to her and asked, "Would you bring me a little water in a jar so I may have a drink?" ¹¹As she was going to get it, he called, "And bring me, please, a piece of bread." Ge 24:17; Ob 20; Lk 4:26

¹²"As surely as the LORD your God lives," she replied, "I don't have any bread — only a handful of flour in a jar and a little olive oil in a jug. I am gathering a few sticks to take home and make a meal for myself and my son, that we may eat it — and die." 2Ki 4:2

¹³Elijah said to her, "Don't be afraid. Go home and do as you have said. But first make a small loaf of bread for me from what you have and bring it to me, and then make something for yourself and your son. ¹⁴For this is what the LORD, the God of Israel, says: 'The jar of flour will not be used up and the jug of oil will not run dry until the day the LORD sends rain on the land.'"

¹⁵She went away and did as Elijah had told her. So there was food every day for Elijah and for the woman and her family. ¹⁶For the jar of flour was not used up and the jug of oil did not run dry, in keeping with the word of the LORD spoken by Elijah.

¹⁷Some time later the son of the woman who owned the house became ill. He grew worse and worse, and finally stopped breathing. ¹⁸She said to Elijah, "What do you have against me, man of God? Did you come to remind me of my sin and kill my son?" 2Ki 3:13; Lk 5:8

¹⁹"Give me your son," Elijah replied. He took him from her arms, carried him to the upper room where he was staying, and laid him on his bed. ²⁰Then he cried out to the LORD, "LORD my God, have you brought tragedy even on this widow I am staying with, by causing her son to die?" ²¹Then he stretched himself out on the boy three times and cried out to the LORD, "LORD my God, let this boy's life return to him!" 2Ki 4:34; Ac 20:10

²²The LORD heard Elijah's cry, and the boy's life returned to him, and he lived. ²³Elijah picked up the child and carried him down from the room into the house. He gave him to his mother and said, "Look, your son is alive!"

24 Then the woman said to Elijah, "Now I know that you are a man of God and that the word of the LORD from your mouth is the truth." Jn 3:2; 16:30; Ps 119:43

Elijah and Obadiah

18 After a long time, in the third year, the word of the LORD came to Elijah: "Go and present yourself to Ahab, and I will send rain on the land." 2 So Elijah went to present himself to Ahab. Dt 28:12; Lk 4:25; Jas 5:17

Now the famine was severe in Samaria, 3 and Ahab had summoned Obadiah, his palace administrator. (Obadiah was a devout believer in the LORD. 4 While Jezebel was killing off the LORD's prophets, Obadiah had taken a hundred prophets and hidden them in two caves, fifty in each, and had supplied them with food and water.) 5 Ahab had said to Obadiah, "Go through the land to all the springs and valleys. Maybe we can find some grass to keep the horses and mules alive so we will not have to kill any of our animals." 6 So they divided the land they were to cover, Ahab going in one direction and Obadiah in another. 2Ki 9:7; Ne 7:2; Isa 16:3

7 As Obadiah was walking along, Elijah met him. Obadiah recognized him, bowed down to the ground, and said, "Is it really you, my lord Elijah?" 2Ki 1:8

8 "Yes," he replied. "Go tell your master, 'Elijah is here.'"

9 "What have I done wrong," asked Obadiah, "that you are handing your servant over to Ahab to be put to death? 10 As surely as the LORD your God lives, there is not a nation or kingdom where my master has not sent someone to look for you. And whenever a nation or kingdom claimed you were not there, he made them swear they could not find you. 11 But now you tell me to go to my master and say, 'Elijah is here.' 12 I don't know where the Spirit of the LORD may carry you when I leave you. If I go and tell Ahab and he doesn't find you, he will kill me. Yet I your servant have worshiped the LORD since my youth. 13 Haven't you heard, my lord, what I did while Jezebel was killing the prophets of the LORD? I hid a hundred of the LORD's prophets in two caves, fifty in each, and supplied them with food and water. 14 And now you tell me to go to my master and say, 'Elijah is here.' He will kill me!" 2Ki 2:16; Eze 3:14; Ac 8:39

15 Elijah said, "As the LORD Almighty lives, whom I serve, I will surely present myself to Ahab today." 1Ki 17:1

Elijah on Mount Carmel

16 So Obadiah went to meet Ahab and told him, and Ahab went to meet Elijah. 17 When he saw Elijah, he said to him, "Is that you, you troubler of Israel?" 18 "I have not made trouble for

Israel," Elijah replied. "But you and your father's family have. You have abandoned the LORD's commands and have followed the Baals. ¹⁹Now summon the people from all over Israel to meet me on Mount Carmel. And bring the four hundred and fifty prophets of Baal and the four hundred prophets of Asherah, who eat at Jezebel's table." Jos 19:26; 1Ki 16:31,33

²⁰So Ahab sent word throughout all Israel and assembled the prophets on Mount Carmel. ²¹Elijah went before the people and said, "How long will you waver between two opinions? If the LORD is God, follow him; but if Baal is God, follow him." Jos 24:15; 2Ki 17:41

But the people said nothing.

²²Then Elijah said to them, "I am the only one of the LORD's prophets left, but Baal has four hundred and fifty prophets. ²³Get two bulls for us. Let Baal's prophets choose one for themselves, and let them cut it into pieces and put it on the wood but not set fire to it. I will prepare the other bull and put it on the wood but not set fire to it. ²⁴Then you call on the name of your god, and I will call on the name of the LORD. The god who answers by fire—he is God." 1Ki 19:10; 1Ch 21:26

Then all the people said, "What you say is good."

²⁵Elijah said to the prophets of Baal, "Choose one of the bulls and prepare it first, since there are so many of you. Call on the name of your god, but do not light the fire." ²⁶So they took the bull given them and prepared it.

Then they called on the name of Baal from morning till noon. "Baal, answer us!" they shouted. But there was no response; no one answered. And they danced around the altar they had made.

²⁷At noon Elijah began to taunt them. "Shout louder!" he said. "Surely he is a god! Perhaps he is deep in thought, or busy, or traveling. Maybe he is sleeping and must be awakened." ²⁸So they shouted louder and slashed themselves with swords and spears, as was their custom, until their blood flowed. ²⁹Midday passed, and they continued their frantic prophesying until the time for the evening sacrifice. But there was no response, no one answered, no one paid attention. Lev 19:28; Hab 2:19

³⁰Then Elijah said to all the people, "Come here to me." They came to him, and he repaired the altar of the LORD, which had been torn down. ³¹Elijah took twelve stones, one for each of the tribes descended from Jacob, to whom the word of the LORD had come, saying, "Your name shall be Israel." ³²With the stones he built an altar in the name of the LORD, and he dug a trench around it large enough to hold two seahs*a* of seed. ³³He arranged the wood, cut

---

a 32 That is, probably about 24 pounds or about 11 kilograms the bull into pieces and laid it on the wood. Then he said to them, "Fill four large jars with water and pour it on the offering and on the wood." 1Ki 19:10; 2Ki 17:34; Col 3:17

34 "Do it again," he said, and they did it again.

"Do it a third time," he ordered, and they did it the third time. **35** The water ran down around the altar and even filled the trench.

36 At the time of sacrifice, the prophet Elijah stepped forward and prayed: "LORD, the God of Abraham, Isaac and Israel, let it be known today that you are God in Israel and that I am your servant and have done all these things at your command. **37** Answer me, LORD, answer me, so these people will know that you, LORD, are God, and that you are turning their hearts back again." Nu 16:28; Jos 4:24

38 Then the fire of the LORD fell and burned up the sacrifice, the wood, the stones and the soil, and also licked up the water in the trench. Lev 9:24; 1Ch 21:26; 2Ch 7:1

39 When all the people saw this, they fell prostrate and cried, "The LORD—he is God! The LORD—he is God!" ver 24; Ps 46:10

40 Then Elijah commanded them, "Seize the prophets of Baal. Don't let anyone get away!" They seized them, and Elijah had them brought down to the Kishon Valley and slaughtered there. Dt 13:5; 18:20; 2Ki 10:24-25

41 And Elijah said to Ahab, "Go, eat and drink, for there is the sound of a heavy rain." **42** So Ahab went off to eat and drink, but Elijah climbed to the top of Carmel, bent down to the ground and put his face between his knees. Jas 5:18

43 "Go and look toward the sea," he told his servant. And he went up and looked.

"There is nothing there," he said.

Seven times Elijah said, "Go back."

44 The seventh time the servant reported, "A cloud as small as a man's hand is rising from the sea." Lk 12:54

So Elijah said, "Go and tell Ahab, 'Hitch up your chariot and go down before the rain stops you.'"

45 Meanwhile, the sky grew black with clouds, the wind rose, a heavy rain started falling and Ahab rode off to Jezreel. **46** The power of the LORD came on Elijah and, tucking his cloak into his belt, he ran ahead of Ahab all the way to Jezreel. 2Ki 3:15; 4:29

Elijah Flees to Horeb

19 Now Ahab told Jezebel everything Elijah had done and how he had killed all the prophets with the sword. **2** So Jezebel sent a messenger to Elijah to say, "May the gods deal with me, be it ever so severely, if by this time tomorrow I do not make your life like that of one of them." 1Ki 18:40; 20:10; 2Ki 6:31

³Elijah was afraid[a] and ran for his life. When he came to Beersheba in Judah, he left his servant there, ⁴while he himself went a day's journey into the wilderness. He came to a broom bush, sat down under it and prayed that he might die. "I have had enough, Lord," he said. "Take my life; I am no better than my ancestors." ⁵Then he lay down under the bush and fell asleep. Nu 11:15; Jnh 4:8; Ge 31:21

All at once an angel touched him and said, "Get up and eat." ⁶He looked around, and there by his head was some bread baked over hot coals, and a jar of water. He ate and drank and then lay down again. Ge 16:7

⁷The angel of the Lord came back a second time and touched him and said, "Get up and eat, for the journey is too much for you." ⁸So he got up and ate and drank. Strengthened by that food, he traveled forty days and forty nights until he reached Horeb, the mountain of God. ⁹There he went into a cave and spent the night. Ex 3:1; 34:28; Mt 4:2

The Lord Appears to Elijah

And the word of the Lord came to him: "What are you doing here, Elijah?"

¹⁰He replied, "I have been very zealous for the Lord God Almighty. The Israelites have rejected your covenant, torn down your altars, and put your prophets to death with the sword. I am the only one left, and now they are trying to kill me too." 1Ki 18:4,22

¹¹The Lord said, "Go out and stand on the mountain in the presence of the Lord, for the Lord is about to pass by." Ex 24:12

Then a great and powerful wind tore the mountains apart and shattered the rocks before the Lord, but the Lord was not in the wind. After the wind there was an earthquake, but the Lord was not in the earthquake. ¹²After the earthquake came a fire, but the Lord was not in the fire. And after the fire came a gentle whisper. ¹³When Elijah heard it, he pulled his cloak over his face and went out and stood at the mouth of the cave. Zec 4:6; Ex 3:6; Eze 1:4

Then a voice said to him, "What are you doing here, Elijah?"

¹⁴He replied, "I have been very zealous for the Lord God Almighty. The Israelites have rejected your covenant, torn down your altars, and put your prophets to death with the sword. I am the only one left, and now they are trying to kill me too." Ro 11:3

¹⁵The Lord said to him, "Go back the way you came, and go to the Desert of Damascus. When you get there, anoint Hazael king over Aram. ¹⁶Also, anoint Jehu son of Nimshi king over Israel, and anoint Elisha son of Shaphat from Abel Meholah to succeed

---

a 3 Or *Elijah saw*

you as prophet. [17] Jehu will put to death any who escape the sword of Hazael, and Elisha will put to death any who escape the sword of Jehu. [18] Yet I reserve seven thousand in Israel—all whose knees have not bowed down to Baal and whose mouths have not kissed him." Ro 11:4; 2Ki 8:7-15; 9:14

The Call of Elisha

[19] So Elijah went from there and found Elisha son of Shaphat. He was plowing with twelve yoke of oxen, and he himself was driving the twelfth pair. Elijah went up to him and threw his cloak around him. [20] Elisha then left his oxen and ran after Elijah. "Let me kiss my father and mother goodbye," he said, "and then I will come with you." 2Ki 2:8,14; Mt 8:21-22; Lk 9:61

"Go back," Elijah replied. "What have I done to you?"

[21] So Elisha left him and went back. He took his yoke of oxen and slaughtered them. He burned the plowing equipment to cook the meat and gave it to the people, and they ate. Then he set out to follow Elijah and became his servant. 2Sa 24:22

Ben-Hadad Attacks Samaria

20 Now Ben-Hadad king of Aram mustered his entire army. Accompanied by thirty-two kings with their horses and chariots, he went up and besieged Samaria and attacked it. [2] He sent messengers into the city to Ahab king of Israel, saying, "This is what Ben-Hadad says: [3] 'Your silver and gold are mine, and the best of your wives and children are mine.'" 1Ki 15:18; 22:31; 2Ki 6:24

[4] The king of Israel answered, "Just as you say, my lord the king. I and all I have are yours."

[5] The messengers came again and said, "This is what Ben-Hadad says: 'I sent to demand your silver and gold, your wives and your children. [6] But about this time tomorrow I am going to send my officials to search your palace and the houses of your officials. They will seize everything you value and carry it away.'"

[7] The king of Israel summoned all the elders of the land and said to them, "See how this man is looking for trouble! When he sent for my wives and my children, my silver and my gold, I did not refuse him." 2Ki 5:7

[8] The elders and the people all answered, "Don't listen to him or agree to his demands."

[9] So he replied to Ben-Hadad's messengers, "Tell my lord the king, 'Your servant will do all you demanded the first time, but this demand I cannot meet.'" They left and took the answer back to Ben-Hadad.

[10] Then Ben-Hadad sent another message to Ahab: "May the gods deal with me, be it ever so severely, if enough dust remains in Samaria to give each of my men a handful." 1Ki 19:2

¹¹ The king of Israel answered, "Tell him: 'One who puts on his armor should not boast like one who takes it off.'" Pr 27:1

¹² Ben-Hadad heard this message while he and the kings were drinking in their tents,ᵃ and he ordered his men: "Prepare to attack." So they prepared to attack the city. 1Ki 16:9

Ahab Defeats Ben-Hadad

¹³ Meanwhile a prophet came to Ahab king of Israel and announced, "This is what the LORD says: 'Do you see this vast army? I will give it into your hand today, and then you will know that I am the LORD.'" ver 28; Ex 6:7

¹⁴ "But who will do this?" asked Ahab.

The prophet replied, "This is what the LORD says: 'The junior officers under the provincial commanders will do it.'"

"And who will start the battle?" he asked. Jdg 1:1

The prophet answered, "You will."

¹⁵ So Ahab summoned the 232 junior officers under the provincial commanders. Then he assembled the rest of the Israelites, 7,000 in all. ¹⁶ They set out at noon while Ben-Hadad and the 32 kings allied with him were in their tents getting drunk. ¹⁷ The junior officers under the provincial commanders went out first. ver 12; 1Ki 16:9

Now Ben-Hadad had dispatched scouts, who reported, "Men are advancing from Samaria."

¹⁸ He said, "If they have come out for peace, take them alive; if they have come out for war, take them alive."

¹⁹ The junior officers under the provincial commanders marched out of the city with the army behind them ²⁰ and each one struck down his opponent. At that, the Arameans fled, with the Israelites in pursuit. But Ben-Hadad king of Aram escaped on horseback with some of his horsemen. ²¹ The king of Israel advanced and overpowered the horses and chariots and inflicted heavy losses on the Arameans.

²² Afterward, the prophet came to the king of Israel and said, "Strengthen your position and see what must be done, because next spring the king of Aram will attack you again." 2Sa 11:1

²³ Meanwhile, the officials of the king of Aram advised him, "Their gods are gods of the hills. That is why they were too strong for us. But if we fight them on the plains, surely we will be stronger than they. ²⁴ Do this: Remove all the kings from their commands and replace them with other officers. ²⁵ You must also raise an army like the one you lost — horse for horse and chariot for chariot — so we can fight Israel

---

ᵃ 12 Or *in Sukkoth*; also in verse 16

on the plains. Then surely we will be stronger than they." He agreed with them and acted accordingly.   1Ki 14:23; Ro 1:21-23

26The next spring Ben-Hadad mustered the Arameans and went up to Aphek to fight against Israel. 27When the Israelites were also mustered and given provisions, they marched out to meet them. The Israelites camped opposite them like two small flocks of goats, while the Arameans covered the countryside.   Jdg 6:6; 1Sa 13:6; 2Ki 13:17

28The man of God came up and told the king of Israel, "This is what the LORD says: 'Because the Arameans think the LORD is a god of the hills and not a god of the valleys, I will deliver this vast army into your hands, and you will know that I am the LORD.'"   ver 13

29For seven days they camped opposite each other, and on the seventh day the battle was joined. The Israelites inflicted a hundred thousand casualties on the Aramean foot soldiers in one day. 30The rest of them escaped to the city of Aphek, where the wall collapsed on twenty-seven thousand of them. And Ben-Hadad fled to the city and hid in an inner room.   1Ki 22:25; 2Ch 18:24

31His officials said to him, "Look, we have heard that the kings of Israel are merciful. Let us go to the king of Israel with sackcloth around our waists and ropes around our heads. Perhaps he will spare your life."   Ge 37:34

32Wearing sackcloth around their waists and ropes around their heads, they went to the king of Israel and said, "Your servant Ben-Hadad says: 'Please let me live.'"

The king answered, "Is he still alive? He is my brother."

33The men took this as a good sign and were quick to pick up his word. "Yes, your brother Ben-Hadad!" they said.

"Go and get him," the king said. When Ben-Hadad came out, Ahab had him come up into his chariot.

34"I will return the cities my father took from your father," Ben-Hadad offered. "You may set up your own market areas in Damascus, as my father did in Samaria."   1Ki 15:20; Jer 49:23-27

Ahab said, "On the basis of a treaty I will set you free." So he made a treaty with him, and let him go.   Ex 23:32

A Prophet Condemns Ahab

35By the word of the LORD one of the company of the prophets said to his companion, "Strike me with your weapon," but he refused.   1Ki 13:20; 2Ki 2:3-7

36So the prophet said, "Because you have not obeyed the LORD, as soon as you leave me a lion will kill you." And after the man went away, a lion found him and killed him.   1Ki 13:24

³⁷The prophet found another man and said, "Strike me, please." So the man struck him and wounded him. ³⁸Then the prophet went and stood by the road waiting for the king. He disguised himself with his headband down over his eyes. ³⁹As the king passed by, the prophet called out to him, "Your servant went into the thick of the battle, and someone came to me with a captive and said, 'Guard this man. If he is missing, it will be your life for his life, or you must pay a talent*ᵃ* of silver.' ⁴⁰While your servant was busy here and there, the man disappeared."   2Ki 10:24

"That is your sentence," the king of Israel said. "You have pronounced it yourself."

⁴¹Then the prophet quickly removed the headband from his eyes, and the king of Israel recognized him as one of the prophets. ⁴²He said to the king, "This is what the LORD says: 'You have set free a man I had determined should die.*ᵇ* Therefore it is your life for his life, your people for his people.' " ⁴³Sullen and angry, the king of Israel went to his palace in Samaria.   1Ki 21:4; 22:31-37

Naboth's Vineyard

21 Some time later there was an incident involving a vineyard belonging to Naboth the Jezreelite. The vineyard was in Jezreel, close to the palace of Ahab king of Samaria. ²Ahab said to Naboth, "Let me have your vineyard to use for a vegetable garden, since it is close to my palace. In exchange I will give you a better vineyard or, if you prefer, I will pay you whatever it is worth."   1Ki 18:45-46; 2Ki 9:21

³But Naboth replied, "The LORD forbid that I should give you the inheritance of my ancestors."   Lev 25:23; Nu 36:7; Eze 46:18

⁴So Ahab went home, sullen and angry because Naboth the Jezreelite had said, "I will not give you the inheritance of my ancestors." He lay on his bed sulking and refused to eat.   1Ki 20:43

⁵His wife Jezebel came in and asked him, "Why are you so sullen? Why won't you eat?"

⁶He answered her, "Because I said to Naboth the Jezreelite, 'Sell me your vineyard; or if you prefer, I will give you another vineyard in its place.' But he said, 'I will not give you my vineyard.' "

⁷Jezebel his wife said, "Is this how you act as king over Israel? Get up and eat! Cheer up. I'll get you the vineyard of Naboth the Jezreelite."   1Sa 8:14

⁸So she wrote letters in Ahab's name, placed his seal on them, and sent them to the elders and nobles who lived in Naboth's city with him. ⁹In those letters she wrote: Ge 38:18; Est 3:12; 8:8,10

ᵃ 39 That is, about 75 pounds or about 34 kilograms   *ᵇ 42* The Hebrew term refers to the irrevocable giving over of things or persons to the LORD, often by totally destroying them.

"Proclaim a day of fasting and seat Naboth in a prominent place among the people. ¹⁰But seat two scoundrels opposite him and have them bring charges that he has cursed both God and the king. Then take him out and stone him to death." Ac 6:11

¹¹So the elders and nobles who lived in Naboth's city did as Jezebel directed in the letters she had written to them. ¹²They proclaimed a fast and seated Naboth in a prominent place among the people. ¹³Then two scoundrels came and sat opposite him and brought charges against Naboth before the people, saying, "Naboth has cursed both God and the king." So they took him outside the city and stoned him to death. ¹⁴Then they sent word to Jezebel: "Naboth has been stoned to death." 2Ki 9:26; Isa 58:4

¹⁵As soon as Jezebel heard that Naboth had been stoned to death, she said to Ahab, "Get up and take possession of the vineyard of Naboth the Jezreelite that he refused to sell you. He is no longer alive, but dead." ¹⁶When Ahab heard that Naboth was dead, he got up and went down to take possession of Naboth's vineyard. 1Sa 8:14

¹⁷Then the word of the LORD came to Elijah the Tishbite: ¹⁸"Go down to meet Ahab king of Israel, who rules in Samaria. He is now in Naboth's vineyard, where he has gone to take possession of it. ¹⁹Say to him, 'This is what the LORD says: Have you not murdered a man and seized his property?' Then say to him, 'This is what the LORD says: In the place where dogs licked up Naboth's blood, dogs will lick up your blood—yes, yours!'" 1Ki 22:38; 2Ki 9:26; Ps 9:12

²⁰Ahab said to Elijah, "So you have found me, my enemy!"

"I have found you," he answered, "because you have sold yourself to do evil in the eyes of the LORD. ²¹He says, 'I am going to bring disaster on you. I will wipe out your descendants and cut off from Ahab every last male in Israel—slave or free.ᵃ ²²I will make your house like that of Jeroboam son of Nebat and that of Baasha son of Ahijah, because you have aroused my anger and have caused Israel to sin.' 1Ki 12:30; 14:10

²³"And also concerning Jezebel the LORD says: 'Dogs will devour Jezebel by the wall ofᵇ Jezreel.' 2Ki 9:10,34-36

²⁴"Dogs will eat those belonging to Ahab who die in the city, and the birds will feed on those who die in the country." 1Ki 14:11

²⁵(There was never anyone like Ahab, who sold himself to do evil in the eyes of the LORD, urged on by Jezebel his wife. ²⁶He behaved in the vilest man-

---

ᵃ 21 Or *Israel—every ruler or leader*   ᵇ 23 Most Hebrew manuscripts; a few Hebrew manuscripts, Vulgate and Syriac (see also 2 Kings 9:26) *the plot of ground at* ner by going after idols, like the Amorites the LORD drove out before Israel.) _{Ge 15:16; 1Ki 16:33}

²⁷When Ahab heard these words, he tore his clothes, put on sackcloth and fasted. He lay in sackcloth and went around meekly. _{Ge 37:34; 2Sa 3:31; 2Ki 6:30}

²⁸Then the word of the LORD came to Elijah the Tishbite: ²⁹"Have you noticed how Ahab has humbled himself before me? Because he has humbled himself, I will not bring this disaster in his day, but I will bring it on his house in the days of his son." _{2Ki 9:26}

Micaiah Prophesies Against Ahab

22:1-28pp — 2Ch 18:1-27

22 For three years there was no war between Aram and Israel. ²But in the third year Jehoshaphat king of Judah went down to see the king of Israel. ³The king of Israel had said to his officials, "Don't you know that Ramoth Gilead belongs to us and yet we are doing nothing to retake it from the king of Aram?" _{Dt 4:43; Jos 21:38}

⁴So he asked Jehoshaphat, "Will you go with me to fight against Ramoth Gilead?" _{2Ki 3:7}

Jehoshaphat replied to the king of Israel, "I am as you are, my people as your people, my horses as your horses." ⁵But Jehoshaphat also said to the king of Israel, "First seek the counsel of the LORD." _{Ex 33:7; 2Ki 3:11}

⁶So the king of Israel brought together the prophets — about four hundred men — and asked them, "Shall I go to war against Ramoth Gilead, or shall I refrain?"

"Go," they answered, "for the Lord will give it into the king's hand." _{1Ki 18:19}

⁷But Jehoshaphat asked, "Is there no longer a prophet of the LORD here whom we can inquire of?" _{2Ki 3:11}

⁸The king of Israel answered Jehoshaphat, "There is still one prophet through whom we can inquire of the LORD, but I hate him because he never prophesies anything good about me, but always bad. He is Micaiah son of Imlah." _{Isa 5:20; Am 5:10}

"The king should not say such a thing," Jehoshaphat replied.

⁹So the king of Israel called one of his officials and said, "Bring Micaiah son of Imlah at once."

¹⁰Dressed in their royal robes, the king of Israel and Jehoshaphat king of Judah were sitting on their thrones at the threshing floor by the entrance of the gate of Samaria, with all the prophets prophesying before them. ¹¹Now Zedekiah son of Kenaanah had made iron horns and he declared, "This is what the LORD says: 'With these you will gore the Arameans until they are destroyed.'" _{Dt 33:17; Zec 1:18-21}

¹²All the other prophets were prophesying the same thing. "At-

tack Ramoth Gilead and be victorious," they said, "for the LORD will give it into the king's hand."

¹³The messenger who had gone to summon Micaiah said to him, "Look, the other prophets without exception are predicting success for the king. Let your word agree with theirs, and speak favorably."

¹⁴But Micaiah said, "As surely as the LORD lives, I can tell him only what the LORD tells me."

¹⁵When he arrived, the king asked him, "Micaiah, shall we go to war against Ramoth Gilead, or not?"

"Attack and be victorious," he answered, "for the LORD will give it into the king's hand."

¹⁶The king said to him, "How many times must I make you swear to tell me nothing but the truth in the name of the LORD?"

¹⁷Then Micaiah answered, "I saw all Israel scattered on the hills like sheep without a shepherd, and the LORD said, 'These people have no master. Let each one go home in peace.'"   Nu 27:17; Mt 9:36

¹⁸The king of Israel said to Jehoshaphat, "Didn't I tell you that he never prophesies anything good about me, but only bad?"

¹⁹Micaiah continued, "Therefore hear the word of the LORD: I saw the LORD sitting on his throne with all the multitudes of heaven standing around him on his right and on his left. ²⁰And

the LORD said, 'Who will entice Ahab into attacking Ramoth Gilead and going to his death there?'   Job 1:6; Isa 6:1; Da 7:9

"One suggested this, and another that. ²¹Finally, a spirit came forward, stood before the LORD and said, 'I will entice him.'

²² "'By what means?' the LORD asked.

"'I will go out and be a deceiving spirit in the mouths of all his prophets,' he said.   Jdg 9:23; 2Th 2:11

"'You will succeed in enticing him,' said the LORD. 'Go and do it.'

²³"So now the LORD has put a deceiving spirit in the mouths of all these prophets of yours. The LORD has decreed disaster for you."   Eze 14:9

²⁴Then Zedekiah son of Kenaanah went up and slapped Micaiah in the face. "Which way did the spirit from*a* the LORD go when he went from me to speak to you?" he asked.   ver 11; Ac 23:2

²⁵Micaiah replied, "You will find out on the day you go to hide in an inner room."   1Ki 20:30

²⁶The king of Israel then ordered, "Take Micaiah and send him back to Amon the ruler of the city and to Joash the king's son ²⁷and say, 'This is what the king says: Put this fellow in prison and give him nothing but bread and water until I return safely.'"   2Ch 16:10

²⁸Micaiah declared, "If you

---

a 24 Or *Spirit of*

ever return safely, the LORD has not spoken through me." Then he added, "Mark my words, all you people!" 2Ch 18:1-27; Dt 18:22

Ahab Killed at Ramoth Gilead
22:29-36pp — 2Ch 18:28-34

²⁹So the king of Israel and Jehoshaphat king of Judah went up to Ramoth Gilead. ³⁰The king of Israel said to Jehoshaphat, "I will enter the battle in disguise, but you wear your royal robes." So the king of Israel disguised himself and went into battle. 2Ch 35:32

³¹Now the king of Aram had ordered his thirty-two chariot commanders, "Do not fight with anyone, small or great, except the king of Israel." ³²When the chariot commanders saw Jehoshaphat, they thought, "Surely this is the king of Israel." So they turned to attack him, but when Jehoshaphat cried out, ³³the chariot commanders saw that he was not the king of Israel and stopped pursuing him. 2Sa 17:2

³⁴But someone drew his bow at random and hit the king of Israel between the sections of his armor. The king told his chariot driver, "Wheel around and get me out of the fighting. I've been wounded." ³⁵All day long the battle raged, and the king was propped up in his chariot facing the Arameans. The blood from his wound ran onto the floor of the chariot, and that evening he died. ³⁶As the sun was setting, a cry spread through the army: "Every man to his town. Every man to his land!" 2Ki 14:12; 2Ch 35:23

³⁷So the king died and was brought to Samaria, and they buried him there. ³⁸They washed the chariot at a pool in Samaria (where the prostitutes bathed),^a and the dogs licked up his blood, as the word of the LORD had declared. 1Ki 21:19

³⁹As for the other events of Ahab's reign, including all he did, the palace he built and adorned with ivory, and the cities he fortified, are they not written in the book of the annals of the kings of Israel? ⁴⁰Ahab rested with his ancestors. And Ahaziah his son succeeded him as king. 2Ch 9:17; Am 3:15

Jehoshaphat King of Judah
22:41-50pp — 2Ch 20:31–21:1

⁴¹Jehoshaphat son of Asa became king of Judah in the fourth year of Ahab king of Israel. ⁴²Jehoshaphat was thirty-five years old when he became king, and he reigned in Jerusalem twenty-five years. His mother's name was Azubah daughter of Shilhi. ⁴³In everything he followed the ways of his father Asa and did not stray from them; he did what was right in the eyes of the LORD. The high places, however, were not removed, and the people continued to

---

^a 38 Or *Samaria and cleaned the weapons*

offer sacrifices and burn incense there.*a* 44 Jehoshaphat was also at peace with the king of Israel. 1Ki 15:14; 2Ki 12:3; 2Ch 17:3

45 As for the other events of Jehoshaphat's reign, the things he achieved and his military exploits, are they not written in the book of the annals of the kings of Judah? 46 He rid the land of the rest of the male shrine prostitutes who remained there even after the reign of his father Asa. 47 There was then no king in Edom; a provincial governor ruled. 2Sa 8:14; 1Ki 15:12; 2Ki 3:9

48 Now Jehoshaphat built a fleet of trading ships*b* to go to Ophir for gold, but they never set sail — they were wrecked at Ezion Geber. 49 At that time Ahaziah son of Ahab said to Jehoshaphat,

"Let my men sail with yours," but Jehoshaphat refused. 1Ki 9:26

50 Then Jehoshaphat rested with his ancestors and was buried with them in the city of David his father. And Jehoram his son succeeded him as king. 2Ch 20:31-21:1

Ahaziah King of Israel

51 Ahaziah son of Ahab became king of Israel in Samaria in the seventeenth year of Jehoshaphat king of Judah, and he reigned over Israel two years. 52 He did evil in the eyes of the LORD, because he followed the ways of his father and mother and of Jeroboam son of Nebat, who caused Israel to sin. 53 He served and worshiped Baal and aroused the anger of the LORD, the God of Israel, just as his father had done. 1Ki 15:26; 16:30-32

---

a 43 In Hebrew texts this sentence (22:43b) is numbered 22:44, and 22:44-53 is numbered 22:45-54. *b 48* Hebrew *of ships of Tarshish*

2 Kings

The Lord's Judgment on Ahaziah

1 After Ahab's death, Moab rebelled against Israel. ² Now Ahaziah had fallen through the lattice of his upper room in Samaria and injured himself. So he sent messengers, saying to them, "Go and consult Baal-Zebub, the god of Ekron, to see if I will recover from this injury." 2Sa 8:2; 2Ki 3:5

³ But the angel of the LORD said to Elijah the Tishbite, "Go up and meet the messengers of the king of Samaria and ask them, 'Is it because there is no God in Israel that you are going off to consult Baal-Zebub, the god of Ekron?' ⁴ Therefore this is what the LORD says: 'You will not leave the bed you are lying on. You will certainly die!'" So Elijah went. Ge 16:7

⁵ When the messengers returned to the king, he asked them, "Why have you come back?"

⁶ "A man came to meet us," they replied. "And he said to us, 'Go back to the king who sent you and tell him, "This is what the LORD says: Is it because there is no God in Israel that you are sending messengers to consult Baal-Zebub, the god of Ekron? Therefore you will not leave the bed you are lying on. You will certainly die!"'"

⁷ The king asked them, "What kind of man was it who came to meet you and told you this?"

⁸ They replied, "He had a garment of hair^a and had a leather belt around his waist." Zec 13:4

The king said, "That was Elijah the Tishbite."

⁹ Then he sent to Elijah a captain with his company of fifty men. The captain went up to Elijah, who was sitting on the top of a hill, and said to him, "Man of God, the king says, 'Come down!'" Ex 18:25; 2Ki 6:14; Isa 3:3

¹⁰ Elijah answered the captain, "If I am a man of God, may fire come down from heaven

a 8 Or *He was a hairy man*

and consume you and your fifty men!" Then fire fell from heaven and consumed the captain and his men. 1Ki 18:38; Lk 9:54

¹¹At this the king sent to Elijah another captain with his fifty men. The captain said to him, "Man of God, this is what the king says, 'Come down at once!'"

¹²"If I am a man of God," Elijah replied, "may fire come down from heaven and consume you and your fifty men!" Then the fire of God fell from heaven and consumed him and his fifty men.

¹³So the king sent a third captain with his fifty men. This third captain went up and fell on his knees before Elijah. "Man of God," he begged, "please have respect for my life and the lives of these fifty men, your servants! ¹⁴See, fire has fallen from heaven and consumed the first two captains and all their men. But now have respect for my life!" 1Sa 26:21; Ps 72:14

¹⁵The angel of the LORD said to Elijah, "Go down with him; do not be afraid of him." So Elijah got up and went down with him to the king. Isa 51:12; Jer 1:17; Eze 2:6

¹⁶He told the king, "This is what the LORD says: Is it because there is no God in Israel for you to consult that you have sent messengers to consult Baal-Zebub, the god of Ekron? Because you have done this, you will never leave the bed you are lying on. You will certainly die!" ¹⁷So he died, according to the word of the LORD that Elijah had spoken. 2Ki 8:15; Jer 20:6

Because Ahaziah had no son, Joram*ᵃ* succeeded him as king in the second year of Jehoram son of Jehoshaphat king of Judah. ¹⁸As for all the other events of Ahaziah's reign, and what he did, are they not written in the book of the annals of the kings of Israel? 2Ki 3:1; 8:16

Elijah Taken Up to Heaven

2 When the LORD was about to take Elijah up to heaven in a whirlwind, Elijah and Elisha were on their way from Gilgal. ²Elijah said to Elisha, "Stay here; the LORD has sent me to Bethel." Ge 5:24; 1Ki 19:16,21; Heb 11:5

But Elisha said, "As surely as the LORD lives and as you live, I will not leave you." So they went down to Bethel. Ru 1:16; 1Sa 1:26

³The company of the prophets at Bethel came out to Elisha and asked, "Do you know that the LORD is going to take your master from you today?" 1Sa 10:5; 2Ki 4:1,38

"Yes, I know," Elisha replied, "so be quiet."

⁴Then Elijah said to him, "Stay here, Elisha; the LORD has sent me to Jericho." Jos 3:16; 6:26

And he replied, "As surely as the LORD lives and as you live, I will not leave you." So they went to Jericho.

⁵The company of the prophets at Jericho went up to Elisha and

---

ᵃ 17 Hebrew *Jehoram,* a variant of *Joram*

asked him, "Do you know that the LORD is going to take your master from you today?"

"Yes, I know," he replied, "so be quiet."

⁶ Then Elijah said to him, "Stay here; the LORD has sent me to the Jordan." Jos 3:15

And he replied, "As surely as the LORD lives and as you live, I will not leave you." So the two of them walked on. Ru 1:16

⁷ Fifty men from the company of the prophets went and stood at a distance, facing the place where Elijah and Elisha had stopped at the Jordan. ⁸ Elijah took his cloak, rolled it up and struck the water with it. The water divided to the right and to the left, and the two of them crossed over on dry ground. Ex 14:21-22,29; 1Ki 19:19

⁹ When they had crossed, Elijah said to Elisha, "Tell me, what can I do for you before I am taken from you?"

"Let me inherit a double portion of your spirit," Elisha replied.

¹⁰ "You have asked a difficult thing," Elijah said, "yet if you see me when I am taken from you, it will be yours — otherwise, it will not."

¹¹ As they were walking along and talking together, suddenly a chariot of fire and horses of fire appeared and separated the two of them, and Elijah went up to heaven in a whirlwind. ¹² Elisha saw this and cried out, "My father! My father! The chariots and horsemen of Israel!" And Elisha saw him no more. Then he took hold of his garment and tore it in two. Ge 5:24; 2Ki 13:14; Ps 104:3-4

¹³ Elisha then picked up Elijah's cloak that had fallen from him and went back and stood on the bank of the Jordan. ¹⁴ He took the cloak that had fallen from Elijah and struck the water with it. "Where now is the LORD, the God of Elijah?" he asked. When he struck the water, it divided to the right and to the left, and he crossed over. 1Ki 19:19

¹⁵ The company of the prophets from Jericho, who were watching, said, "The spirit of Elijah is resting on Elisha." And they went to meet him and bowed to the ground before him. ¹⁶ "Look," they said, "we your servants have fifty able men. Let them go and look for your master. Perhaps the Spirit of the LORD has picked him up and set him down on some mountain or in some valley." 1Ki 18:12; Ac 8:39

"No," Elisha replied, "do not send them."

¹⁷ But they persisted until he was too embarrassed to refuse. So he said, "Send them." And they sent fifty men, who searched for three days but did not find him. ¹⁸ When they returned to Elisha, who was staying in Jericho, he said to them, "Didn't I tell you not to go?" 2Ki 8:11

Healing of the Water

¹⁹ The people of the city said to

Elisha, "Look, our lord, this town is well situated, as you can see, but the water is bad and the land is unproductive."

²⁰ "Bring me a new bowl," he said, "and put salt in it." So they brought it to him.

²¹ Then he went out to the spring and threw the salt into it, saying, "This is what the LORD says: 'I have healed this water. Never again will it cause death or make the land unproductive.'" ²² And the water has remained pure to this day, according to the word Elisha had spoken.   Ex 15:25; 2Ki 4:41; 6:6

Elisha Is Jeered

²³ From there Elisha went up to Bethel. As he was walking along the road, some boys came out of the town and jeered at him. "Get out of here, baldy!" they said. "Get out of here, baldy!" ²⁴ He turned around, looked at them and called down a curse on them in the name of the LORD. Then two bears came out of the woods and mauled forty-two of the boys. ²⁵ And he went on to Mount Carmel and from there returned to Samaria.   1Ki 18:20; Ge 4:11; Ne 13:25-27

Moab Revolts

3 Joram*ᵃ* son of Ahab became king of Israel in Samaria in the eighteenth year of Jehoshaphat king of Judah, and he reigned twelve years. ² He did evil in the eyes of the LORD, but not as his father and mother had done. He got rid of the sacred stone of Baal that his father had made. ³ Nevertheless he clung to the sins of Jeroboam son of Nebat, which he had caused Israel to commit; he did not turn away from them.   1Ki 12:28-32; 14:9,16; 16:30-32

⁴ Now Mesha king of Moab raised sheep, and he had to pay the king of Israel a tribute of a hundred thousand lambs and the wool of a hundred thousand rams. ⁵ But after Ahab died, the king of Moab rebelled against the king of Israel. ⁶ So at that time King Joram set out from Samaria and mobilized all Israel. ⁷ He also sent this message to Jehoshaphat king of Judah: "The king of Moab has rebelled against me. Will you go with me to fight against Moab?"   1Ki 22:4; 2Ki 1:1; Isa 16:1

"I will go with you," he replied. "I am as you are, my people as your people, my horses as your horses."

⁸ "By what route shall we attack?" he asked.

"Through the Desert of Edom," he answered.

⁹ So the king of Israel set out with the king of Judah and the king of Edom. After a roundabout march of seven days, the army had no more water for themselves or for the animals with them.   1Ki 22:47

¹⁰ "What!" exclaimed the king

ᵃ 1 Hebrew *Jehoram*, a variant of *Joram*; also in verse 6

of Israel. "Has the LORD called us three kings together only to deliver us into the hands of Moab?"

¹¹But Jehoshaphat asked, "Is there no prophet of the LORD here, through whom we may inquire of the LORD?" 1Ki 22:7

An officer of the king of Israel answered, "Elisha son of Shaphat is here. He used to pour water on the hands of Elijah.ᵃ" Ge 20:7

¹²Jehoshaphat said, "The word of the LORD is with him." So the king of Israel and Jehoshaphat and the king of Edom went down to him. Nu 11:17

¹³Elisha said to the king of Israel, "Why do you want to involve me? Go to the prophets of your father and the prophets of your mother."

"No," the king of Israel answered, "because it was the LORD who called us three kings together to deliver us into the hands of Moab."

¹⁴Elisha said, "As surely as the LORD Almighty lives, whom I serve, if I did not have respect for the presence of Jehoshaphat king of Judah, I would not pay any attention to you. ¹⁵But now bring me a harpist." 1Sa 16:23

While the harpist was playing, the hand of the LORD came on Elisha ¹⁶and he said, "This is what the LORD says: I will fill this valley with pools of water. ¹⁷For this is what the LORD says: You will see neither wind nor rain, yet this valley will be filled with water, and you, your cattle and your other animals will drink. ¹⁸This is an easy thing in the eyes of the LORD; he will also deliver Moab into your hands. ¹⁹You will overthrow every fortified city and every major town. You will cut down every good tree, stop up all the springs, and ruin every good field with stones." Ge 18:14; Jer 32:17,27

²⁰The next morning, about the time for offering the sacrifice, there it was—water flowing from the direction of Edom! And the land was filled with water. Ex 29:39

²¹Now all the Moabites had heard that the kings had come to fight against them; so every man, young and old, who could bear arms was called up and stationed on the border. ²²When they got up early in the morning, the sun was shining on the water. To the Moabites across the way, the water looked red—like blood. ²³"That's blood!" they said. "Those kings must have fought and slaughtered each other. Now to the plunder, Moab!"

²⁴But when the Moabites came to the camp of Israel, the Israelites rose up and fought them until they fled. And the Israelites invaded the land and slaughtered the Moabites. ²⁵They destroyed the towns, and each man threw a stone on every good field until it was covered. They stopped up all the springs and cut down every

ᵃ 11 That is, he was Elijah's personal servant.

good tree. Only Kir Hareseth was left with its stones in place, but men armed with slings surrounded it and attacked it. Isa 16:7; Jer 48:31 ²⁶When the king of Moab saw that the battle had gone against him, he took with him seven hundred swordsmen to break through to the king of Edom, but they failed. ²⁷Then he took his firstborn son, who was to succeed him as king, and offered him as a sacrifice on the city wall. The fury against Israel was great; they withdrew and returned to their own land. Am 2:1; Mic 6:7

The Widow's Olive Oil

4 The wife of a man from the company of the prophets cried out to Elisha, "Your servant my husband is dead, and you know that he revered the LORD. But now his creditor is coming to take my two boys as his slaves." Lev 25:39-43; Ne 5:3-5; Job 22:6

²Elisha replied to her, "How can I help you? Tell me, what do you have in your house?"

"Your servant has nothing there at all," she said, "except a small jar of olive oil." 1Ki 17:12

³Elisha said, "Go around and ask all your neighbors for empty jars. Don't ask for just a few. ⁴Then go inside and shut the door behind you and your sons. Pour oil into all the jars, and as each is filled, put it to one side."

⁵She left him and shut the door behind her and her sons.

They brought the jars to her and she kept pouring. ⁶When all the jars were full, she said to her son, "Bring me another one."

But he replied, "There is not a jar left." Then the oil stopped flowing.

⁷She went and told the man of God, and he said, "Go, sell the oil and pay your debts. You and your sons can live on what is left."

The Shunammite's Son Restored to Life

⁸One day Elisha went to Shunem. And a well-to-do woman was there, who urged him to stay for a meal. So whenever he came by, he stopped there to eat. ⁹She said to her husband, "I know that this man who often comes our way is a holy man of God. ¹⁰Let's make a small room on the roof and put in it a bed and a table, a chair and a lamp for him. Then he can stay there whenever he comes to us." Jos 19:18; Mt 10:41; Ro 12:13

¹¹One day when Elisha came, he went up to his room and lay down there. ¹²He said to his servant Gehazi, "Call the Shunammite." So he called her, and she stood before him. ¹³Elisha said to him, "Tell her, 'You have gone to all this trouble for us. Now what can be done for you? Can we speak on your behalf to the king or the commander of the army?'" 2Ki 8:1

She replied, "I have a home among my own people."

¹⁴ "What can be done for her?" Elisha asked.

Gehazi said, "She has no son, and her husband is old."

¹⁵ Then Elisha said, "Call her." So he called her, and she stood in the doorway. ¹⁶ "About this time next year," Elisha said, "you will hold a son in your arms." Ge 18:10

"No, my lord!" she objected. "Please, man of God, don't mislead your servant!"

¹⁷ But the woman became pregnant, and the next year about that same time she gave birth to a son, just as Elisha had told her.

¹⁸ The child grew, and one day he went out to his father, who was with the reapers. ¹⁹ He said to his father, "My head! My head!" Ru 2:3

His father told a servant, "Carry him to his mother." ²⁰ After the servant had lifted him up and carried him to his mother, the boy sat on her lap until noon, and then he died. ²¹ She went up and laid him on the bed of the man of God, then shut the door and went out. ver 32

²² She called her husband and said, "Please send me one of the servants and a donkey so I can go to the man of God quickly and return."

²³ "Why go to him today?" he asked. "It's not the New Moon or the Sabbath." Nu 10:10; 1Ch 23:31

"That's all right," she said.

²⁴ She saddled the donkey and said to her servant, "Lead on; don't slow down for me un-less I tell you." ²⁵ So she set out and came to the man of God at Mount Carmel. 1Ki 18:20; 2Ki 2:25

When he saw her in the distance, the man of God said to his servant Gehazi, "Look! There's the Shunammite! ²⁶ Run to meet her and ask her, 'Are you all right? Is your husband all right? Is your child all right?' "

"Everything is all right," she said.

²⁷ When she reached the man of God at the mountain, she took hold of his feet. Gehazi came over to push her away, but the man of God said, "Leave her alone! She is in bitter distress, but the LORD has hidden it from me and has not told me why." 1Sa 1:15

²⁸ "Did I ask you for a son, my lord?" she said. "Didn't I tell you, 'Don't raise my hopes'?"

²⁹ Elisha said to Gehazi, "Tuck your cloak into your belt, take my staff in your hand and run. Don't greet anyone you meet, and if anyone greets you, do not answer. Lay my staff on the boy's face." Ex 7:19; 1Ki 18:46

³⁰ But the child's mother said, "As surely as the LORD lives and as you live, I will not leave you." So he got up and followed her.

³¹ Gehazi went on ahead and laid the staff on the boy's face, but there was no sound or response. So Gehazi went back to meet Elisha and told him, "The boy has not awakened."

³² When Elisha reached the

house, there was the boy lying dead on his couch. ³³He went in, shut the door on the two of them and prayed to the LORD. ³⁴Then he got on the bed and lay on the boy, mouth to mouth, eyes to eyes, hands to hands. As he stretched himself out on him, the boy's body grew warm. ³⁵Elisha turned away and walked back and forth in the room and then got on the bed and stretched out on him once more. The boy sneezed seven times and opened his eyes.   1Ki 17:20-21; 2Ki 8:5; Ac 20:10

³⁶Elisha summoned Gehazi and said, "Call the Shunammite." And he did. When she came, he said, "Take your son." ³⁷She came in, fell at his feet and bowed to the ground. Then she took her son and went out.   Heb 11:35

Death in the Pot

³⁸Elisha returned to Gilgal and there was a famine in that region. While the company of the prophets was meeting with him, he said to his servant, "Put on the large pot and cook some stew for these prophets."   2Ki 2:1; 8:1

³⁹One of them went out into the fields to gather herbs and found a wild vine and picked as many of its gourds as his garment could hold. When he returned, he cut them up into the pot of stew, though no one knew what they were. ⁴⁰The stew was

poured out for the men, but as they began to eat it, they cried out, "Man of God, there is death in the pot!" And they could not eat it.

⁴¹Elisha said, "Get some flour." He put it into the pot and said, "Serve it to the people to eat." And there was nothing harmful in the pot.   Ex 15:25; 2Ki 2:21

Feeding of a Hundred

⁴²A man came from Baal Shalishah, bringing the man of God twenty loaves of barley bread baked from the first ripe grain, along with some heads of new grain. "Give it to the people to eat," Elisha said.   1Sa 9:4,7; Mt 14:17; 15:36

⁴³"How can I set this before a hundred men?" his servant asked.

But Elisha answered, "Give it to the people to eat. For this is what the LORD says: 'They will eat and have some left over.'" ⁴⁴Then he set it before them, and they ate and had some left over, according to the word of the LORD.   Lk 9:13

Naaman Healed of Leprosy

5 Now Naaman was commander of the army of the king of Aram. He was a great man in the sight of his master and highly regarded, because through him the LORD had given victory to Aram. He was a valiant soldier, but he had leprosy.ᵃ   Lk 4:27; 2Sa 10:19

²Now bands of raiders from

ᵃ 1 The Hebrew for *leprosy* was used for various diseases affecting the skin; also in verses 3, 6, 7, 11 and 27.

Aram had gone out and had taken captive a young girl from Israel, and she served Naaman's wife. [3] She said to her mistress, "If only my master would see the prophet who is in Samaria! He would cure him of his leprosy." Ge 20:7; 2Ki 6:23

[4] Naaman went to his master and told him what the girl from Israel had said. [5] "By all means, go," the king of Aram replied. "I will send a letter to the king of Israel." So Naaman left, taking with him ten talents[a] of silver, six thousand shekels[b] of gold and ten sets of clothing. [6] The letter that he took to the king of Israel read: "With this letter I am sending my servant Naaman to you so that you may cure him of his leprosy." 1Sa 9:7

[7] As soon as the king of Israel read the letter, he tore his robes and said, "Am I God? Can I kill and bring back to life? Why does this fellow send someone to me to be cured of his leprosy? See how he is trying to pick a quarrel with me!" Ge 30:2; 1Sa 2:6; 1Ki 20:7

[8] When Elisha the man of God heard that the king of Israel had torn his robes, he sent him this message: "Why have you torn your robes? Have the man come to me and he will know that there is a prophet in Israel." [9] So Naaman went with his horses and chariots and stopped at the door of Elisha's house. [10] Elisha sent a messenger to say to him, "Go, wash yourself seven times in the Jordan, and your flesh will be restored and you will be cleansed." Jn 9:7; Lev 14:7; 1Ki 22:7

[11] But Naaman went away angry and said, "I thought that he would surely come out to me and stand and call on the name of the LORD his God, wave his hand over the spot and cure me of my leprosy. [12] Are not Abana and Pharpar, the rivers of Damascus, better than all the waters of Israel? Couldn't I wash in them and be cleansed?" So he turned and went off in a rage. Pr 14:17,29; 19:11; 29:11

[13] Naaman's servants went to him and said, "My father, if the prophet had told you to do some great thing, would you not have done it? How much more, then, when he tells you, 'Wash and be cleansed'!" [14] So he went down and dipped himself in the Jordan seven times, as the man of God had told him, and his flesh was restored and became clean like that of a young boy. Jos 6:15; Job 33:25

[15] Then Naaman and all his attendants went back to the man of God. He stood before him and said, "Now I know that there is no God in all the world except in Israel. So please accept a gift from your servant." Jos 4:24; 1Sa 17:46

[16] The prophet answered, "As surely as the LORD lives, whom I serve, I will not accept a thing."

---

[a] 5 That is, about 750 pounds or about 340 kilograms   [b] 5 That is, about 150 pounds or about 69 kilograms

And even though Naaman urged him, he refused. ver 20,26; Ge 14:23

¹⁷ "If you will not," said Naaman, "please let me, your servant, be given as much earth as a pair of mules can carry, for your servant will never again make burnt offerings and sacrifices to any other god but the LORD. ¹⁸ But may the LORD forgive your servant for this one thing: When my master enters the temple of Rimmon to bow down and he is leaning on my arm and I have to bow there also — when I bow down in the temple of Rimmon, may the LORD forgive your servant for this." Ex 20:24; 2Ki 7:2

¹⁹ "Go in peace," Elisha said.

After Naaman had traveled some distance, ²⁰ Gehazi, the servant of Elisha the man of God, said to himself, "My master was too easy on Naaman, this Aramean, by not accepting from him what he brought. As surely as the LORD lives, I will run after him and get something from him." Ex 20:7

²¹ So Gehazi hurried after Naaman. When Naaman saw him running toward him, he got down from the chariot to meet him. "Is everything all right?" he asked.

²² "Everything is all right," Gehazi answered. "My master sent me to say, 'Two young men from the company of the prophets have just come to me from the hill country of Ephraim. Please give them a talent[a] of silver and two sets of clothing.' " ver 5; Ge 45:22

²³ "By all means, take two talents," said Naaman. He urged Gehazi to accept them, and then tied up the two talents of silver in two bags, with two sets of clothing. He gave them to two of his servants, and they carried them ahead of Gehazi. ²⁴ When Gehazi came to the hill, he took the things from the servants and put them away in the house. He sent the men away and they left.

²⁵ When he went in and stood before his master, Elisha asked him, "Where have you been, Gehazi?"

"Your servant didn't go anywhere," Gehazi answered.

²⁶ But Elisha said to him, "Was not my spirit with you when the man got down from his chariot to meet you? Is this the time to take money or to accept clothes — or olive groves and vineyards, or flocks and herds, or male and female slaves? ²⁷ Naaman's leprosy will cling to you and to your descendants forever." Then Gehazi went from Elisha's presence and his skin was leprous — it had become as white as snow. ver 16; Ex 4:6

An Axhead Floats

6 The company of the prophets said to Elisha, "Look, the place where we meet with you is too small for us. ²Let us go to the

---

a 22 That is, about 75 pounds or about 34 kilograms

Jordan, where each of us can get a pole; and let us build a place there for us to meet." 1Sa 10:5; 2Ki 4:38

And he said, "Go."

³Then one of them said, "Won't you please come with your servants?"

"I will," Elisha replied. ⁴And he went with them.

They went to the Jordan and began to cut down trees. ⁵As one of them was cutting down a tree, the iron axhead fell into the water. "Oh no, my lord!" he cried out. "It was borrowed!"

⁶The man of God asked, "Where did it fall?" When he showed him the place, Elisha cut a stick and threw it there, and made the iron float. ⁷"Lift it out," he said. Then the man reached out his hand and took it.   Ex 15:25; 2Ki 2:21

Elisha Traps Blinded Arameans

⁸Now the king of Aram was at war with Israel. After conferring with his officers, he said, "I will set up my camp in such and such a place."

⁹The man of God sent word to the king of Israel: "Beware of passing that place, because the Arameans are going down there." ¹⁰So the king of Israel checked on the place indicated by the man of God. Time and again Elisha warned the king, so that he was on his guard in such places.   ver 12; Jer 11:18

¹¹This enraged the king of Aram. He summoned his officers and demanded of them, "Tell me! Which of us is on the side of the king of Israel?"

¹²"None of us, my lord the king," said one of his officers, "but Elisha, the prophet who is in Israel, tells the king of Israel the very words you speak in your bedroom."

¹³"Go, find out where he is," the king ordered, "so I can send men and capture him." The report came back: "He is in Dothan." ¹⁴Then he sent horses and chariots and a strong force there. They went by night and surrounded the city.   Ge 37:17; 2Ki 1:9

¹⁵When the servant of the man of God got up and went out early the next morning, an army with horses and chariots had surrounded the city. "Oh no, my lord! What shall we do?" the servant asked.

¹⁶"Don't be afraid," the prophet answered. "Those who are with us are more than those who are with them."   2Ch 32:7; Ps 55:18; 1Jn 4:4

¹⁷And Elisha prayed, "Open his eyes, LORD, so that he may see." Then the LORD opened the servant's eyes, and he looked and saw the hills full of horses and chariots of fire all around Elisha.   2Ki 2:11-12; Ps 68:17; Zec 6:1-7

¹⁸As the enemy came down toward him, Elisha prayed to the LORD, "Strike this army with blindness." So he struck them with blindness, as Elisha had asked.   Ge 19:11; Ac 13:11

¹⁹Elisha told them, "This is not the road and this is not the city. Follow me, and I will lead you to the man you are looking for." And he led them to Samaria.

²⁰After they entered the city, Elisha said, "LORD, open the eyes of these men so they can see." Then the LORD opened their eyes and they looked, and there they were, inside Samaria.

²¹When the king of Israel saw them, he asked Elisha, "Shall I kill them, my father? Shall I kill them?" 2Ki 5:13

²²"Do not kill them," he answered. "Would you kill those you have captured with your own sword or bow? Set food and water before them so that they may eat and drink and then go back to their master." ²³So he prepared a great feast for them, and after they had finished eating and drinking, he sent them away, and they returned to their master. So the bands from Aram stopped raiding Israel's territory. Dt 20:11; 2Ki 5:2; Ro 12:20

Famine in Besieged Samaria

²⁴Some time later, Ben-Hadad king of Aram mobilized his entire army and marched up and laid siege to Samaria. ²⁵There was a great famine in the city; the siege lasted so long that a donkey's head sold for eighty

shekels*a* of silver, and a quarter of a cab*b* of seed pods*c* for five shekels.*d* Lev 26:26; 1Ki 15:18; Isa 36:12

²⁶As the king of Israel was passing by on the wall, a woman cried to him, "Help me, my lord the king!"

²⁷The king replied, "If the LORD does not help you, where can I get help for you? From the threshing floor? From the winepress?" ²⁸Then he asked her, "What's the matter?"

She answered, "This woman said to me, 'Give up your son so we may eat him today, and tomorrow we'll eat my son.' ²⁹So we cooked my son and ate him. The next day I said to her, 'Give up your son so we may eat him,' but she had hidden him." Lev 26:29; Dt 28:53-55

³⁰When the king heard the woman's words, he tore his robes. As he went along the wall, the people looked, and they saw that, under his robes, he had sackcloth on his body. ³¹He said, "May God deal with me, be it ever so severely, if the head of Elisha son of Shaphat remains on his shoulders today!" Ge 37:34; 1Ki 21:27

³²Now Elisha was sitting in his house, and the elders were sitting with him. The king sent a messenger ahead, but before he arrived, Elisha said to the elders, "Don't you see how this murderer is sending someone to cut off my

a 25 That is, about 2 pounds or about 920 grams or about 100 grams *c 25* Or *of doves' dung* *b 25* That is, probably about 1/4 pound *d 25* That is, about 2 ounces or about 58 grams head? Look, when the messenger comes, shut the door and hold it shut against him. Is not the sound of his master's footsteps behind him?" [33] While he was still talking to them, the messenger came down to him. 1Ki 18:4; Eze 8:1

The king said, "This disaster is from the LORD. Why should I wait for the LORD any longer?" Job 2:9

7 Elisha replied, "Hear the word of the LORD. This is what the LORD says: About this time tomorrow, a seah[a] of the finest flour will sell for a shekel[b] and two seahs[c] of barley for a shekel at the gate of Samaria." ver 16

[2] The officer on whose arm the king was leaning said to the man of God, "Look, even if the LORD should open the floodgates of the heavens, could this happen?" 2Ki 5:18; Mal 3:10

"You will see it with your own eyes," answered Elisha, "but you will not eat any of it!" ver 17

The Siege Lifted

[3] Now there were four men with leprosy[d] at the entrance of the city gate. They said to each other, "Why stay here until we die? [4] If we say, 'We'll go into the city' — the famine is there, and we will die. And if we stay here, we will die. So let's go over to the camp of the Arameans and surrender. If

they spare us, we live; if they kill us, then we die." Lev 13:45-46; Nu 5:1-4

[5] At dusk they got up and went to the camp of the Arameans. When they reached the edge of the camp, no one was there, [6] for the Lord had caused the Arameans to hear the sound of chariots and horses and a great army, so that they said to one another, "Look, the king of Israel has hired the Hittite and Egyptian kings to attack us!" [7] So they got up and fled in the dusk and abandoned their tents and their horses and donkeys. They left the camp as it was and ran for their lives. 2Sa 5:24; Ps 48:4-6; Pr 28:1

[8] The men who had leprosy reached the edge of the camp, entered one of the tents and ate and drank. Then they took silver, gold and clothes, and went off and hid them. They returned and entered another tent and took some things from it and hid them also. Isa 33:23; 35:6

[9] Then they said to each other, "What we're doing is not right. This is a day of good news and we are keeping it to ourselves. If we wait until daylight, punishment will overtake us. Let's go at once and report this to the royal palace."

[10] So they went and called out to the city gatekeepers and told

---

[a] 1 That is, probably about 12 pounds or about 5.5 kilograms of flour; also in verses 16 and 18   [b] 1 That is, about 2/5 ounce or about 12 grams; also in verses 16 and 18
[c] 1 That is, probably about 20 pounds or about 9 kilograms of barley; also in verses 16 and 18   [d] 3 The Hebrew for *leprosy* was used for various diseases affecting the skin; also in verse 8.

them, "We went into the Aramean camp and no one was there — not a sound of anyone — only tethered horses and donkeys, and the tents left just as they were." [11] The gatekeepers shouted the news, and it was reported within the palace.

[12] The king got up in the night and said to his officers, "I will tell you what the Arameans have done to us. They know we are starving; so they have left the camp to hide in the countryside, thinking, 'They will surely come out, and then we will take them alive and get into the city.'" Jos 8:4

[13] One of his officers answered, "Have some men take five of the horses that are left in the city. Their plight will be like that of all the Israelites left here — yes, they will only be like all these Israelites who are doomed. So let us send them to find out what happened."

[14] So they selected two chariots with their horses, and the king sent them after the Aramean army. He commanded the drivers, "Go and find out what has happened." [15] They followed them as far as the Jordan, and they found the whole road strewn with the clothing and equipment the Arameans had thrown away in their headlong flight. So the messengers returned and reported to the king. [16] Then the people went out and plundered the camp of the Arameans. So a seah of the finest flour sold for a shekel, and two seahs of barley sold for a shekel, as the LORD had said. ver 1; Isa 33:4,23

[17] Now the king had put the officer on whose arm he leaned in charge of the gate, and the people trampled him in the gateway, and he died, just as the man of God had foretold when the king came down to his house. [18] It happened as the man of God had said to the king: "About this time tomorrow, a seah of the finest flour will sell for a shekel and two seahs of barley for a shekel at the gate of Samaria." ver 2; 2Ki 6:32

[19] The officer had said to the man of God, "Look, even if the LORD should open the floodgates of the heavens, could this happen?" The man of God had replied, "You will see it with your own eyes, but you will not eat any of it!" [20] And that is exactly what happened to him, for the people trampled him in the gateway, and he died. ver 2

The Shunammite's Land Restored

8 Now Elisha had said to the woman whose son he had restored to life, "Go away with your family and stay for a while wherever you can, because the LORD has decreed a famine in the land that will last seven years." [2] The woman proceeded to do as the man of God said. She and her family went away and stayed in the land of the Philistines seven years. 2Ki 4:8-37; Ps 105:16; Hag 1:11 ³At the end of the seven years she came back from the land of the Philistines and went to appeal to the king for her house and land. ⁴The king was talking to Gehazi, the servant of the man of God, and had said, "Tell me about all the great things Elisha has done." ⁵Just as Gehazi was telling the king how Elisha had restored the dead to life, the woman whose son Elisha had brought back to life came to appeal to the king for her house and land. 2Ki 4:35

Gehazi said, "This is the woman, my lord the king, and this is her son whom Elisha restored to life." ⁶The king asked the woman about it, and she told him.

Then he assigned an official to her case and said to him, "Give back everything that belonged to her, including all the income from her land from the day she left the country until now."

Hazael Murders Ben-Hadad

⁷Elisha went to Damascus, and Ben-Hadad king of Aram was ill. When the king was told, "The man of God has come all the way up here," ⁸he said to Hazael, "Take a gift with you and go to meet the man of God. Consult the LORD through him; ask him, 'Will I recover from this illness?' " 1Sa 9:7; 1Ki 19:15; 2Ki 1:2

⁹Hazael went to meet Elisha, taking with him as a gift forty camel-loads of all the finest wares of Damascus. He went in and stood before him, and said, "Your son Ben-Hadad king of Aram has sent me to ask, 'Will I recover from this illness?' "

¹⁰Elisha answered, "Go and say to him, 'You will certainly recover.' Nevertheless,ᵃ the LORD has revealed to me that he will in fact die." ¹¹He stared at him with a fixed gaze until Hazael was embarrassed. Then the man of God began to weep. Jdg 3:25; Isa 38:1; Lk 19:41

¹²"Why is my lord weeping?" asked Hazael.

"Because I know the harm you will do to the Israelites," he answered. "You will set fire to their fortified places, kill their young men with the sword, dash their little children to the ground, and rip open their pregnant women." 2Ki 10:32; 12:17; 13:3,7

¹³Hazael said, "How could your servant, a mere dog, accomplish such a feat?" 1Sa 17:43; 2Sa 3:8

"The LORD has shown me that you will become king of Aram," answered Elisha. 1Ki 19:15

¹⁴Then Hazael left Elisha and returned to his master. When Ben-Hadad asked, "What did Elisha say to you?" Hazael replied, "He told me that you would certainly recover." ¹⁵But the next day he took a thick cloth, soaked it in water and spread it over

---

ᵃ 10 The Hebrew may also be read *Go and say, 'You will certainly not recover,' for.*

the king's face, so that he died. Then Hazael succeeded him as king. 2Ki 1:17

Jehoram King of Judah
8:16-24pp — 2Ch 21:5-10,20

¹⁶ In the fifth year of Joram son of Ahab king of Israel, when Jehoshaphat was king of Judah, Jehoram son of Jehoshaphat began his reign as king of Judah. ¹⁷ He was thirty-two years old when he became king, and he reigned in Jerusalem eight years. ¹⁸ He followed the ways of the kings of Israel, as the house of Ahab had done, for he married a daughter of Ahab. He did evil in the eyes of the LORD. ¹⁹ Nevertheless, for the sake of his servant David, the LORD was not willing to destroy Judah. He had promised to maintain a lamp for David and his descendants forever. 2Sa 7:13; 2Ki 1:17

²⁰ In the time of Jehoram, Edom rebelled against Judah and set up its own king. ²¹ So Jehoram*a* went to Zair with all his chariots. The Edomites surrounded him and his chariot commanders, but he rose up and broke through by night; his army, however, fled back home. ²² To this day Edom has been in rebellion against Judah. Libnah revolted at the same time. Ge 27:40; Jos 21:13; 1Ki 22:47

²³ As for the other events of Jehoram's reign, and all he did, are they not written in the book of the annals of the kings of Judah? ²⁴ Jehoram rested with his ancestors and was buried with them in the City of David. And Ahaziah his son succeeded him as king. 2Ch 21:5-10,20

Ahaziah King of Judah
8:25-29pp — 2Ch 22:1-6

²⁵ In the twelfth year of Joram son of Ahab king of Israel, Ahaziah son of Jehoram king of Judah began to reign. ²⁶ Ahaziah was twenty-two years old when he became king, and he reigned in Jerusalem one year. His mother's name was Athaliah, a granddaughter of Omri king of Israel. ²⁷ He followed the ways of the house of Ahab and did evil in the eyes of the LORD, as the house of Ahab had done, for he was related by marriage to Ahab's family. 1Ki 15:26; 16:23,30

²⁸ Ahaziah went with Joram son of Ahab to war against Hazael king of Aram at Ramoth Gilead. The Arameans wounded Joram; ²⁹ so King Joram returned to Jezreel to recover from the wounds the Arameans had inflicted on him at Ramoth*b* in his battle with Hazael king of Aram. 1Ki 19:15,17; 22:3,29; 2Ki 9:15

Then Ahaziah son of Jehoram king of Judah went down to Jezreel to see Joram son of Ahab, because he had been wounded.

a 21 Hebrew *Joram*, a variant of *Jehoram*; also in verses 23 and 24   *b 29* Hebrew *Ramah*, a variant of *Ramoth*

Jehu Anointed King of Israel

9 The prophet Elisha summoned a man from the company of the prophets and said to him, "Tuck your cloak into your belt, take this flask of olive oil with you and go to Ramoth Gilead. ²When you get there, look for Jehu son of Jehoshaphat, the son of Nimshi. Go to him, get him away from his companions and take him into an inner room. ³Then take the flask and pour the oil on his head and declare, 'This is what the LORD says: I anoint you king over Israel.' Then open the door and run; don't delay!" 1Ki 19:16; 2Ki 4:29; 8:28

⁴So the young prophet went to Ramoth Gilead. ⁵When he arrived, he found the army officers sitting together. "I have a message for you, commander," he said.

"For which of us?" asked Jehu.

"For you, commander," he replied.

⁶Jehu got up and went into the house. Then the prophet poured the oil on Jehu's head and declared, "This is what the LORD, the God of Israel, says: 'I anoint you king over the LORD's people Israel. ⁷You are to destroy the house of Ahab your master, and I will avenge the blood of my servants the prophets and the blood of all the LORD's servants shed by Jezebel. ⁸The whole house of Ahab will perish. I will cut off from Ahab every last male in Israel—slave or free.ᵃ ⁹I will make the house of Ahab like the house of Jeroboam son of Nebat and like the house of Baasha son of Ahijah. ¹⁰As for Jezebel, dogs will devour her on the plot of ground at Jezreel, and no one will bury her.'" Then he opened the door and ran. 1Ki 14:10; 15:29; 21:23

¹¹When Jehu went out to his fellow officers, one of them asked him, "Is everything all right? Why did this maniac come to you?" Jer 29:26; Jn 10:20; Ac 26:24

"You know the man and the sort of things he says," Jehu replied.

¹²"That's not true!" they said. "Tell us."

Jehu said, "Here is what he told me: 'This is what the LORD says: I anoint you king over Israel.'"

¹³They quickly took their cloaks and spread them under him on the bare steps. Then they blew the trumpet and shouted, "Jehu is king!" Mt 21:8; 2Sa 15:10

Jehu Kills Joram and Ahaziah

9:21-29pp — 2Ch 22:7-9

¹⁴So Jehu son of Jehoshaphat, the son of Nimshi, conspired against Joram. (Now Joram and all Israel had been defending Ramoth Gilead against Hazael king of Aram, ¹⁵but King Joramᵇ had returned to Jezreel to recover from

---

ᵃ 8 Or *Israel—every ruler or leader*   ᵇ 15 Hebrew *Jehoram*, a variant of *Joram*; also in verses 17 and 21-24 the wounds the Arameans had inflicted on him in the battle with Hazael king of Aram.) Jehu said, "If you desire to make me king, don't let anyone slip out of the city to go and tell the news in Jezreel." [16]Then he got into his chariot and rode to Jezreel, because Joram was resting there and Ahaziah king of Judah had gone down to see him. 2Ki 8:28-29; 2Ch 22:7

[17]When the lookout standing on the tower in Jezreel saw Jehu's troops approaching, he called out, "I see some troops coming." Isa 21:6

"Get a horseman," Joram ordered. "Send him to meet them and ask, 'Do you come in peace?'" 1Sa 16:4

[18]The horseman rode off to meet Jehu and said, "This is what the king says: 'Do you come in peace?'"

"What do you have to do with peace?" Jehu replied. "Fall in behind me."

The lookout reported, "The messenger has reached them, but he isn't coming back."

[19]So the king sent out a second horseman. When he came to them he said, "This is what the king says: 'Do you come in peace?'"

Jehu replied, "What do you have to do with peace? Fall in behind me."

[20]The lookout reported, "He has reached them, but he isn't coming back either. The driving is like that of Jehu son of Nimshi—he drives like a maniac." 2Sa 18:27

[21]"Hitch up my chariot," Joram ordered. And when it was hitched up, Joram king of Israel and Ahaziah king of Judah rode out, each in his own chariot, to meet Jehu. They met him at the plot of ground that had belonged to Naboth the Jezreelite. [22]When Joram saw Jehu he asked, "Have you come in peace, Jehu?" 1Ki 21:1-7,15-19

"How can there be peace," Jehu replied, "as long as all the idolatry and witchcraft of your mother Jezebel abound?" 1Ki 18:19; 2Ch 21:13

[23]Joram turned about and fled, calling out to Ahaziah, "Treachery, Ahaziah!" 2Ki 11:14

[24]Then Jehu drew his bow and shot Joram between the shoulders. The arrow pierced his heart and he slumped down in his chariot. [25]Jehu said to Bidkar, his chariot officer, "Pick him up and throw him on the field that belonged to Naboth the Jezreelite. Remember how you and I were riding together in chariots behind Ahab his father when the LORD spoke this prophecy against him: [26]'Yesterday I saw the blood of Naboth and the blood of his sons, declares the LORD, and I will surely make you pay for it on this plot of ground, declares the LORD.'[a] Now then, pick him up and throw him on that plot, in

---

[a] 26 See 1 Kings 21:19.

accordance with the word of the LORD." 1Ki 21:19-22,24-29; 22:34

²⁷When Ahaziah king of Judah saw what had happened, he fled up the road to Beth Haggan.ᵃ Jehu chased him, shouting, "Kill him too!" They wounded him in his chariot on the way up to Gur near Ibleam, but he escaped to Megiddo and died there. ²⁸His servants took him by chariot to Jerusalem and buried him with his ancestors in his tomb in the City of David. ²⁹(In the eleventh year of Joram son of Ahab, Ahaziah had become king of Judah.) 2Ch 22:7-9; 2Ki 23:30; 8:25

Jezebel Killed

³⁰Then Jehu went to Jezreel. When Jezebel heard about it, she put on eye makeup, arranged her hair and looked out of a window. ³¹As Jehu entered the gate, she asked, "Have you come in peace, you Zimri, you murderer of your master?"ᵇ 1Ki 16:9-10; Jer 4:30; Eze 23:40

³²He looked up at the window and called out, "Who is on my side? Who?" Two or three eunuchs looked down at him. ³³"Throw her down!" Jehu said. So they threw her down, and some of her blood spattered the wall and the horses as they trampled her underfoot. Ps 7:5

³⁴Jehu went in and ate and drank. "Take care of that cursed woman," he said, "and bury her, for she was a king's daughter." ³⁵But when they went out to bury her, they found nothing except her skull, her feet and her hands. ³⁶They went back and told Jehu, who said, "This is the word of the LORD that he spoke through his servant Elijah the Tishbite: On the plot of ground at Jezreel dogs will devour Jezebel's flesh.ᶜ ³⁷Jezebel's body will be like dung on the ground in the plot at Jezreel, so that no one will be able to say, 'This is Jezebel.' " 1Ki 21:23; Ps 83:10

Ahab's Family Killed

10 Now there were in Samaria seventy sons of the house of Ahab. So Jehu wrote letters and sent them to Samaria: to the officials of Jezreel,ᵈ to the elders and to the guardians of Ahab's children. He said, ²"You have your master's sons with you and you have chariots and horses, a fortified city and weapons. Now as soon as this letter reaches you, ³choose the best and most worthy of your master's sons and set him on his father's throne. Then fight for your master's house." 1Ki 13:32; 21:1

⁴But they were terrified and said, "If two kings could not resist him, how can we?"

⁵So the palace administrator, the city governor, the elders and

---

ᵃ 27 Or *fled by way of the garden house* ᵇ 31 Or *"Was there peace for Zimri, who murdered*
his master?" ᶜ 36 See 1 Kings 21:23. *his master?"* ᵈ 1 Hebrew; some Septuagint manuscripts and
Vulgate *of the city*

the guardians sent this message to Jehu: "We are your servants and we will do anything you say. We will not appoint anyone as king; you do whatever you think best." Jos 9:8; 1Ki 20:4,32

⁶Then Jehu wrote them a second letter, saying, "If you are on my side and will obey me, take the heads of your master's sons and come to me in Jezreel by this time tomorrow."

Now the royal princes, seventy of them, were with the leading men of the city, who were rearing them. ⁷When the letter arrived, these men took the princes and slaughtered all seventy of them. They put their heads in baskets and sent them to Jehu in Jezreel. ⁸When the messenger arrived, he told Jehu, "They have brought the heads of the princes." 2Sa 4:8; 1Ki 21:21

Then Jehu ordered, "Put them in two piles at the entrance of the city gate until morning."

⁹The next morning Jehu went out. He stood before all the people and said, "You are innocent. It was I who conspired against my master and killed him, but who killed all these? ¹⁰Know, then, that not a word the LORD has spoken against the house of Ahab will fail. The LORD has done what he announced through his servant Elijah." ¹¹So Jehu killed everyone in Jezreel who remained of the house of Ahab, as well as all his chief men, his close friends and his priests, leaving him no survivor. 1Ki 21:29; 2Ki 9:7-10

¹²Jehu then set out and went toward Samaria. At Beth Eked of the Shepherds, ¹³he met some relatives of Ahaziah king of Judah and asked, "Who are you?"

They said, "We are relatives of Ahaziah, and we have come down to greet the families of the king and of the queen mother."

¹⁴"Take them alive!" he ordered. So they took them alive and slaughtered them by the well of Beth Eked—forty-two of them. He left no survivor.

¹⁵After he left there, he came upon Jehonadab son of Rekab, who was on his way to meet him. Jehu greeted him and said, "Are you in accord with me, as I am with you?" 1Ch 2:55; Jer 35:6,14-19

"I am," Jehonadab answered.

"If so," said Jehu, "give me your hand." So he did, and Jehu helped him up into the chariot. ¹⁶Jehu said, "Come with me and see my zeal for the LORD." Then he had him ride along in his chariot. 1Ki 19:10; Ezr 10:19; Eze 17:18

¹⁷When Jehu came to Samaria, he killed all who were left there of Ahab's family; he destroyed them, according to the word of the LORD spoken to Elijah. 2Ki 9:8

Servants of Baal Killed

¹⁸Then Jehu brought all the people together and said to them, "Ahab served Baal a little; Jehu will serve him much. ¹⁹Now

summon all the prophets of Baal, all his servants and all his priests. See that no one is missing, because I am going to hold a great sacrifice for Baal. Anyone who fails to come will no longer live." But Jehu was acting deceptively in order to destroy the servants of Baal. 1Ki 16:31-32; 18:19

20 Jehu said, "Call an assembly in honor of Baal." So they proclaimed it. 21 Then he sent word throughout Israel, and all the servants of Baal came; not one stayed away. They crowded into the temple of Baal until it was full from one end to the other. 22 And Jehu said to the keeper of the wardrobe, "Bring robes for all the servants of Baal." So he brought out robes for them. Ex 32:5; Joel 1:14

23 Then Jehu and Jehonadab son of Rekab went into the temple of Baal. Jehu said to the servants of Baal, "Look around and see that no one who serves the LORD is here with you—only servants of Baal." 24 So they went in to make sacrifices and burnt offerings. Now Jehu had posted eighty men outside with this warning: "If one of you lets any of the men I am placing in your hands escape, it will be your life for his life." 1Ki 20:39

25 As soon as Jehu had finished making the burnt offering, he ordered the guards and officers: "Go in and kill them; let no one escape." So they cut them down with the sword. The guards and officers threw the bodies out and then entered the inner shrine of the temple of Baal. 26 They brought the sacred stone out of the temple of Baal and burned it. 27 They demolished the sacred stone of Baal and tore down the temple of Baal, and people have used it for a latrine to this day. 1Ki 14:23; 18:40

28 So Jehu destroyed Baal worship in Israel. 29 However, he did not turn away from the sins of Jeroboam son of Nebat, which he had caused Israel to commit— the worship of the golden calves at Bethel and Dan. 1Ki 12:28-29; 19:17

30 The LORD said to Jehu, "Because you have done well in accomplishing what is right in my eyes and have done to the house of Ahab all I had in mind to do, your descendants will sit on the throne of Israel to the fourth generation." 31 Yet Jehu was not careful to keep the law of the LORD, the God of Israel, with all his heart. He did not turn away from the sins of Jeroboam, which he had caused Israel to commit. 2Ki 15:12; Pr 4:23

32 In those days the LORD began to reduce the size of Israel. Hazael overpowered the Israelites throughout their territory 33 east of the Jordan in all the land of Gilead (the region of Gad, Reuben and Manasseh), from Aroer by the Arnon Gorge through Gilead to Bashan. 2Ki 8:12; 13:25

34 As for the other events of Jehu's reign, all he did, and all his achievements, are they not

written in the book of the annals of the kings of Israel? 1Ki 15:31 ³⁵Jehu rested with his ancestors and was buried in Samaria. And Jehoahaz his son succeeded him as king. ³⁶The time that Jehu reigned over Israel in Samaria was twenty-eight years.

Athaliah and Joash

11:1-21pp — 2Ch 22:10 – 23:21

11 When Athaliah the mother of Ahaziah saw that her son was dead, she proceeded to destroy the whole royal family. ²But Jehosheba, the daughter of King Jehoram*a* and sister of Ahaziah, took Joash son of Ahaziah and stole him away from among the royal princes, who were about to be murdered. She put him and his nurse in a bedroom to hide him from Athaliah; so he was not killed. ³He remained hidden with his nurse at the temple of the LORD for six years while Athaliah ruled the land. 2Ki 12:1; Jdg 9:5

⁴In the seventh year Jehoiada sent for the commanders of units of a hundred, the Carites and the guards and had them brought to him at the temple of the LORD. He made a covenant with them and put them under oath at the temple of the LORD. Then he showed them the king's son. ⁵He commanded them, saying, "This is what you are to do: You who are in the three companies that are going on duty on the Sabbath —

a third of you guarding the royal palace, ⁶a third at the Sur Gate, and a third at the gate behind the guard, who take turns guarding the temple — ⁷and you who are in the other two companies that normally go off Sabbath duty are all to guard the temple for the king. ⁸Station yourselves around the king, each of you with weapon in hand. Anyone who approaches your ranks*b* is to be put to death. Stay close to the king wherever he goes." 1Ch 9:25

⁹The commanders of units of a hundred did just as Jehoiada the priest ordered. Each one took his men — those who were going on duty on the Sabbath and those who were going off duty — and came to Jehoiada the priest. ¹⁰Then he gave the commanders the spears and shields that had belonged to King David and that were in the temple of the LORD. ¹¹The guards, each with weapon in hand, stationed themselves around the king — near the altar and the temple, from the south side to the north side of the temple. 2Sa 8:7; 1Ch 18:7

¹²Jehoiada brought out the king's son and put the crown on him; he presented him with a copy of the covenant and proclaimed him king. They anointed him, and the people clapped their hands and shouted, "Long live the king!" Ex 25:16; 1Sa 10:24; 1Ki 1:39 ¹³When Athaliah heard the

---

a 2 Hebrew *Joram*, a variant of *Jehoram*   *b* 8 Or *approaches the precincts* noise made by the guards and the people, she went to the people at the temple of the LORD. ¹⁴She looked and there was the king, standing by the pillar, as the custom was. The officers and the trumpeters were beside the king, and all the people of the land were rejoicing and blowing trumpets. Then Athaliah tore her robes and called out, "Treason! Treason!" Ge 37:29; 1Ki 1:39; 2Ki 9:23

¹⁵Jehoiada the priest ordered the commanders of units of a hundred, who were in charge of the troops: "Bring her out between the ranks^a and put to the sword anyone who follows her." For the priest had said, "She must not be put to death in the temple of the LORD." ¹⁶So they seized her as she reached the place where the horses enter the palace grounds, and there she was put to death. Ge 4:14; 1Ki 2:30

¹⁷Jehoiada then made a covenant between the LORD and the king and people that they would be the LORD's people. He also made a covenant between the king and the people. ¹⁸All the people of the land went to the temple of Baal and tore it down. They smashed the altars and idols to pieces and killed Mattan the priest of Baal in front of the altars. 1Ki 18:40; 2Ki 10:25; 23:3

Then Jehoiada the priest post-ed guards at the temple of the LORD. ¹⁹He took with him the commanders of hundreds, the Carites, the guards and all the people of the land, and together they brought the king down from the temple of the LORD and went into the palace, entering by way of the gate of the guards. The king then took his place on the royal throne. ²⁰All the people of the land rejoiced, and the city was calm, because Athaliah had been slain with the sword at the palace. Pr 11:10; 28:12

²¹Joash^b was seven years old when he began to reign.^c 2Ch 22:10

Joash Repairs the Temple
12:1-21pp — 2Ch 24:1-14; 24:23-27

12^d In the seventh year of Jehu, Joash^e became king, and he reigned in Jerusalem forty years. His mother's name was Zibiah; she was from Beersheba. ²Joash did what was right in the eyes of the LORD all the years Jehoiada the priest instructed him. ³The high places, however, were not removed; the people continued to offer sacrifices and burn incense there. 2Ki 14:4; 15:35; 18:4

⁴Joash said to the priests, "Collect all the money that is brought as sacred offerings to the temple of the LORD — the money collected in the census, the money received from personal vows and

---

^a 15 Or *out from the precincts*   ^b 21 Hebrew *Jehoash,* a variant of *Joash*   ^c 21 In Hebrew texts this verse (11:21) is numbered 12:1.   ^d In Hebrew texts 12:1-21 is numbered 12:2-22.
^e 1 Hebrew *Jehoash,* a variant of *Joash*; also in verses 2, 4, 6, 7 and 18

the money brought voluntarily to the temple. [5]Let every priest receive the money from one of the treasurers, then use it to repair whatever damage is found in the temple." Ex 35:5; 2Ki 22:4; 1Ch 29:3-9

[6]But by the twenty-third year of King Joash the priests still had not repaired the temple. [7]Therefore King Joash summoned Jehoiada the priest and the other priests and asked them, "Why aren't you repairing the damage done to the temple? Take no more money from your treasurers, but hand it over for repairing the temple." [8]The priests agreed that they would not collect any more money from the people and that they would not repair the temple themselves.

[9]Jehoiada the priest took a chest and bored a hole in its lid. He placed it beside the altar, on the right side as one enters the temple of the LORD. The priests who guarded the entrance put into the chest all the money that was brought to the temple of the LORD. [10]Whenever they saw that there was a large amount of money in the chest, the royal secretary and the high priest came, counted the money that had been brought into the temple of the LORD and put it into bags. [11]When the amount had been determined, they gave the money to the men appointed to supervise the work on the temple. With it they paid those who worked on the temple of the LORD — the carpenters and builders, [12]the masons and stonecutters. They purchased timber and blocks of dressed stone for the repair of the temple of the LORD, and met all the other expenses of restoring the temple. Mk 12:41; Lk 21:1

[13]The money brought into the temple was not spent for making silver basins, wick trimmers, sprinkling bowls, trumpets or any other articles of gold or silver for the temple of the LORD; [14]it was paid to the workers, who used it to repair the temple. [15]They did not require an accounting from those to whom they gave the money to pay the workers, because they acted with complete honesty. [16]The money from the guilt offerings and sin offerings[a] was not brought into the temple of the LORD; it belonged to the priests. Lev 7:7; 2Ki 22:7; 2Ch 24:14

[17]About this time Hazael king of Aram went up and attacked Gath and captured it. Then he turned to attack Jerusalem. [18]But Joash king of Judah took all the sacred objects dedicated by his predecessors — Jehoshaphat, Jehoram and Ahaziah, the kings of Judah — and the gifts he himself had dedicated and all the gold found in the treasuries of the temple of the LORD and of the royal palace, and he sent them to Hazael king of Aram,

---

[a] 16 Or *purification offerings*

who then withdrew from Jerusalem. 1Ki 15:18; 2Ki 8:12

¹⁹As for the other events of the reign of Joash, and all he did, are they not written in the book of the annals of the kings of Judah? ²⁰His officials conspired against him and assassinated him at Beth Millo, on the road down to Silla. ²¹The officials who murdered him were Jozabad son of Shimeath and Jehozabad son of Shomer. He died and was buried with his ancestors in the City of David. And Amaziah his son succeeded him as king. 2Ch 24:1-14; 24:23-27

Jehoahaz King of Israel

13 In the twenty-third year of Joash son of Ahaziah king of Judah, Jehoahaz son of Jehu became king of Israel in Samaria, and he reigned seventeen years. ²He did evil in the eyes of the LORD by following the sins of Jeroboam son of Nebat, which he had caused Israel to commit, and he did not turn away from them. ³So the LORD's anger burned against Israel, and for a long time he kept them under the power of Hazael king of Aram and Ben-Hadad his son. Jdg 2:14; 1Ki 12:26-33

⁴Then Jehoahaz sought the LORD's favor, and the LORD listened to him, for he saw how severely the king of Aram was oppressing Israel. ⁵The LORD provided a deliverer for Israel,

and they escaped from the power of Aram. So the Israelites lived in their own homes as they had before. ⁶But they did not turn away from the sins of the house of Jeroboam, which he had caused Israel to commit; they continued in them. Also, the Asherah pole[a] remained standing in Samaria. 1Ki 16:33; 2Ki 14:26

⁷Nothing had been left of the army of Jehoahaz except fifty horsemen, ten chariots and ten thousand foot soldiers, for the king of Aram had destroyed the rest and made them like the dust at threshing time. 2Ki 10:32-33

⁸As for the other events of the reign of Jehoahaz, all he did and his achievements, are they not written in the book of the annals of the kings of Israel? ⁹Jehoahaz rested with his ancestors and was buried in Samaria. And Jehoash[b] his son succeeded him as king.

Jehoash King of Israel

¹⁰In the thirty-seventh year of Joash king of Judah, Jehoash son of Jehoahaz became king of Israel in Samaria, and he reigned sixteen years. ¹¹He did evil in the eyes of the LORD and did not turn away from any of the sins of Jeroboam son of Nebat, which he had caused Israel to commit; he continued in them.

¹²As for the other events of the reign of Jehoash, all he did and his

---

[a] 6 That is, a wooden symbol of the goddess Asherah; here and elsewhere in 2 Kings
[b] 9 Hebrew Joash, a variant of Jehoash; also in verses 12-14 and 25

achievements, including his war against Amaziah king of Judah, are they not written in the book of the annals of the kings of Israel? [13]Jehoash rested with his ancestors, and Jeroboam succeeded him on the throne. Jehoash was buried in Samaria with the kings of Israel. 2Ki 14:15,23; 14:23; Hos 1:1

[14]Now Elisha had been suffering from the illness from which he died. Jehoash king of Israel went down to see him and wept over him. "My father! My father!" he cried. "The chariots and horsemen of Israel!" 2Ki 2:12

[15]Elisha said, "Get a bow and some arrows," and he did so. [16]"Take the bow in your hands," he said to the king of Israel. When he had taken it, Elisha put his hands on the king's hands.

[17]"Open the east window," he said, and he opened it. "Shoot!" Elisha said, and he shot. "The LORD's arrow of victory, the arrow of victory over Aram!" Elisha declared. "You will completely destroy the Arameans at Aphek."

[18]Then he said, "Take the arrows," and the king took them. Elisha told him, "Strike the ground." He struck it three times and stopped. [19]The man of God was angry with him and said, "You should have struck the ground five or six times; then you would have defeated Aram and completely destroyed it. But now you will defeat it only three times."

[20]Elisha died and was buried.

Now Moabite raiders used to enter the country every spring. [21]Once while some Israelites were burying a man, suddenly they saw a band of raiders; so they threw the man's body into Elisha's tomb. When the body touched Elisha's bones, the man came to life and stood up on his feet. Mt 27:52; 2Ki 3:7; 24:2

[22]Hazael king of Aram oppressed Israel throughout the reign of Jehoahaz. [23]But the LORD was gracious to them and had compassion and showed concern for them because of his covenant with Abraham, Isaac and Jacob. To this day he has been unwilling to destroy them or banish them from his presence. Ex 2:24; 1Ki 19:17; 2Ki 8:12

[24]Hazael king of Aram died, and Ben-Hadad his son succeeded him as king. [25]Then Jehoash son of Jehoahaz recaptured from Ben-Hadad son of Hazael the towns he had taken in battle from his father Jehoahaz. Three times Jehoash defeated him, and so he recovered the Israelite towns. ver 18-19; 2Ki 10:32

Amaziah King of Judah

14:1-7pp — 2Ch 25:1-4,11-12
14:8-22pp — 2Ch 25:17-26:2

14 In the second year of Jehoash[a] son of Jehoahaz king of Israel, Amaziah son of Joash king of Judah began to

---

[a] 1 Hebrew *Joash*, a variant of *Jehoash*; also in verses 13, 23 and 27

reign. [2] He was twenty-five years old when he became king, and he reigned in Jerusalem twenty-nine years. His mother's name was Jehoaddan; she was from Jerusalem. [3] He did what was right in the eyes of the LORD, but not as his father David had done. In everything he followed the example of his father Joash. [4] The high places, however, were not removed; the people continued to offer sacrifices and burn incense there.

[5] After the kingdom was firmly in his grasp, he executed the officials who had murdered his father the king. [6] Yet he did not put the children of the assassins to death, in accordance with what is written in the Book of the Law of Moses where the LORD commanded: "Parents are not to be put to death for their children, nor children put to death for their parents; each will die for their own sin." [a]   Jer 31:30; Eze 18:4,20

[7] He was the one who defeated ten thousand Edomites in the Valley of Salt and captured Sela in battle, calling it Joktheel, the name it has to this day.   2Ch 25:1-4,11

[8] Then Amaziah sent messengers to Jehoash son of Jehoahaz, the son of Jehu, king of Israel, with the challenge: "Come, let us face each other in battle."

[9] But Jehoash king of Israel replied to Amaziah king of Judah: "A thistle in Lebanon sent a message to a cedar in Lebanon, 'Give your daughter to my son in marriage.' Then a wild beast in Lebanon came along and trampled the thistle underfoot. [10] You have indeed defeated Edom and now you are arrogant. Glory in your victory, but stay at home! Why ask for trouble and cause your own downfall and that of Judah also?"   Dt 8:14; Jdg 9:8-15; 2Ch 26:16

[11] Amaziah, however, would not listen, so Jehoash king of Israel attacked. He and Amaziah king of Judah faced each other at Beth Shemesh in Judah. [12] Judah was routed by Israel, and every man fled to his home. [13] Jehoash king of Israel captured Amaziah king of Judah, the son of Joash, the son of Ahaziah, at Beth Shemesh. Then Jehoash went to Jerusalem and broke down the wall of Jerusalem from the Ephraim Gate to the Corner Gate—a section about four hundred cubits long. [b] [14] He took all the gold and silver and all the articles found in the temple of the LORD and in the treasuries of the royal palace. He also took hostages and returned to Samaria.   Jos 15:10; Jer 31:38; Zec 14:10

[15] As for the other events of the reign of Jehoash, what he did and his achievements, including his war against Amaziah king of Judah, are they not written in the book of the annals of the kings of Israel? [16] Jehoash rested with his ancestors and was buried in

---

[a] 6 Deut. 24:16   [b] 13 That is, about 600 feet or about 180 meters

Samaria with the kings of Israel. And Jeroboam his son succeeded him as king. 2Ki 13:12

17 Amaziah son of Joash king of Judah lived for fifteen years after the death of Jehoash son of Jehoahaz king of Israel. **18** As for the other events of Amaziah's reign, are they not written in the book of the annals of the kings of Judah?

19 They conspired against him in Jerusalem, and he fled to Lachish, but they sent men after him to Lachish and killed him there. **20** He was brought back by horse and was buried in Jerusalem with his ancestors, in the City of David. 2Ki 9:28; 18:14,17

21 Then all the people of Judah took Azariah,*a* who was sixteen years old, and made him king in place of his father Amaziah. **22** He was the one who rebuilt Elath and restored it to Judah after Amaziah rested with his ancestors. 2Ch 25:17-26:2

Jeroboam II King of Israel

23 In the fifteenth year of Amaziah son of Joash king of Judah, Jeroboam son of Jehoash king of Israel became king in Samaria, and he reigned forty-one years. **24** He did evil in the eyes of the LORD and did not turn away from any of the sins of Jeroboam son of Nebat, which he had caused Israel

to commit. **25** He was the one who restored the boundaries of Israel from Lebo Hamath to the Dead Sea,*b* in accordance with the word of the LORD, the God of Israel, spoken through his servant Jonah son of Amittai, the prophet from Gath Hepher. Jnh 1:1; Mt 12:39; Dt 3:17

26 The LORD had seen how bitterly everyone in Israel, whether slave or free, was suffering;*c* there was no one to help them. **27** And since the LORD had not said he would blot out the name of Israel from under heaven, he saved them by the hand of Jeroboam son of Jehoash. 2Ki 13:4; Ps 18:41

28 As for the other events of Jeroboam's reign, all he did, and his military achievements, including how he recovered for Israel both Damascus and Hamath, which had belonged to Judah, are they not written in the book of the annals of the kings of Israel? **29** Jeroboam rested with his ancestors, the kings of Israel. And Zechariah his son succeeded him as king. 2Sa 8:5; 1Ki 11:24; 2Ch 8:3

Azariah King of Judah
15:1-7pp — 2Ch 26:3-4,21-23

15 In the twenty-seventh year of Jeroboam king of Israel, Azariah*d* son of Amaziah king of Judah began to reign. **2** He was sixteen years old when he became king, and he reigned

a 21 Also called *Uzziah*   *b 25* Hebrew *the Sea of the Arabah*   *c 26* Or *Israel was suffering. They were without a ruler or leader, and*   *d 1* Also called *Uzziah*; also in verses 6, 7, 8, 17, 23 and 27 in Jerusalem fifty-two years. His mother's name was Jekoliah; she was from Jerusalem. ³He did what was right in the eyes of the LORD, just as his father Amaziah had done. ⁴The high places, however, were not removed; the people continued to offer sacrifices and burn incense there. 2Ki 14:21

⁵The LORD afflicted the king with leprosy*a* until the day he died, and he lived in a separate house.*b* Jotham the king's son had charge of the palace and governed the people of the land. Lev 13:46

⁶As for the other events of Azariah's reign, and all he did, are they not written in the book of the annals of the kings of Judah? ⁷Azariah rested with his ancestors and was buried near them in the City of David. And Jotham his son succeeded him as king. 2Ch 26:3-4,21-23

Zechariah King of Israel

⁸In the thirty-eighth year of Azariah king of Judah, Zechariah son of Jeroboam became king of Israel in Samaria, and he reigned six months. ⁹He did evil in the eyes of the LORD, as his predecessors had done. He did not turn away from the sins of Jeroboam son of Nebat, which he had caused Israel to commit. 1Ki 15:26

¹⁰Shallum son of Jabesh conspired against Zechariah. He attacked him in front of the people,*c* assassinated him and succeeded him as king. ¹¹The other events of Zechariah's reign are written in the book of the annals of the kings of Israel. ¹²So the word of the LORD spoken to Jehu was fulfilled: "Your descendants will sit on the throne of Israel to the fourth generation."*d* 1Ki 15:31; 2Ki 10:30

Shallum King of Israel

¹³Shallum son of Jabesh became king in the thirty-ninth year of Uzziah king of Judah, and he reigned in Samaria one month. ¹⁴Then Menahem son of Gadi went from Tirzah up to Samaria. He attacked Shallum son of Jabesh in Samaria, assassinated him and succeeded him as king. 1Ki 14:17; 2Ki 12:20

¹⁵The other events of Shallum's reign, and the conspiracy he led, are written in the book of the annals of the kings of Israel. 1Ki 15:31

¹⁶At that time Menahem, starting out from Tirzah, attacked Tiphsah and everyone in the city and its vicinity, because they refused to open their gates. He sacked Tiphsah and ripped open all the pregnant women. 1Ki 4:24

Menahem King of Israel

¹⁷In the thirty-ninth year of Azariah king of Judah, Menahem son of Gadi became king of

---

a 5 The Hebrew for *leprosy* was used for various diseases affecting the skin.   *b 5* Or *in a house where he was relieved of responsibilities in Ibleam*   *c 10* Hebrew; some Septuagint manuscripts   *d 12* 2 Kings 10:30

Israel, and he reigned in Samaria ten years. [18]He did evil in the eyes of the LORD. During his entire reign he did not turn away from the sins of Jeroboam son of Nebat, which he had caused Israel to commit.

[19]Then Pul[a] king of Assyria invaded the land, and Menahem gave him a thousand talents[b] of silver to gain his support and strengthen his own hold on the kingdom. [20]Menahem exacted this money from Israel. Every wealthy person had to contribute fifty shekels[c] of silver to be given to the king of Assyria. So the king of Assyria withdrew and stayed in the land no longer. 2Ki 12:18; 1Ch 5:6

[21]As for the other events of Menahem's reign, and all he did, are they not written in the book of the annals of the kings of Israel? [22]Menahem rested with his ancestors. And Pekahiah his son succeeded him as king.

Pekahiah King of Israel

[23]In the fiftieth year of Azariah king of Judah, Pekahiah son of Menahem became king of Israel in Samaria, and he reigned two years. [24]Pekahiah did evil in the eyes of the LORD. He did not turn away from the sins of Jeroboam son of Nebat, which he had caused Israel to commit. [25]One of his chief officers, Pekah son of Remaliah, conspired against

him. Taking fifty men of Gilead with him, he assassinated Pekahiah, along with Argob and Arieh, in the citadel of the royal palace at Samaria. So Pekah killed Pekahiah and succeeded him as king. 2Ki 12:20; 2Ch 28:6; Isa 7:1,4

[26]The other events of Pekahiah's reign, and all he did, are written in the book of the annals of the kings of Israel.

Pekah King of Israel

[27]In the fifty-second year of Azariah king of Judah, Pekah son of Remaliah became king of Israel in Samaria, and he reigned twenty years. [28]He did evil in the eyes of the LORD. He did not turn away from the sins of Jeroboam son of Nebat, which he had caused Israel to commit. 2Ch 28:6; Isa 7:1,4

[29]In the time of Pekah king of Israel, Tiglath-Pileser king of Assyria came and took Ijon, Abel Beth Maakah, Janoah, Kedesh and Hazor. He took Gilead and Galilee, including all the land of Naphtali, and deported the people to Assyria. [30]Then Hoshea son of Elah conspired against Pekah son of Remaliah. He attacked and assassinated him, and then succeeded him as king in the twentieth year of Jotham son of Uzziah. 2Ki 16:9

[31]As for the other events of Pekah's reign, and all he did, are they not written in the book of the annals of the kings of Israel?

---

[a] 19 Also called *Tiglath-Pileser*   [b] 19 That is, about 38 tons or about 34 metric tons
[c] 20 That is, about 1 1/4 pounds or about 575 grams

Jotham King of Judah

15:33-38pp — 2Ch 27:1-4,7-9

[32] In the second year of Pekah son of Remaliah king of Israel, Jotham son of Uzziah king of Judah began to reign. [33] He was twenty-five years old when he became king, and he reigned in Jerusalem sixteen years. His mother's name was Jerusha daughter of Zadok. [34] He did what was right in the eyes of the LORD, just as his father Uzziah had done. [35] The high places, however, were not removed; the people continued to offer sacrifices and burn incense there. Jotham rebuilt the Upper Gate of the temple of the LORD.   ver 3; 2Ch 26:4-5

[36] As for the other events of Jotham's reign, and what he did, are they not written in the book of the annals of the kings of Judah? [37] (In those days the LORD began to send Rezin king of Aram and Pekah son of Remaliah against Judah.) [38] Jotham rested with his ancestors and was buried with them in the City of David, the city of his father. And Ahaz his son succeeded him as king.   2Ch 27:1-4,7-9

Ahaz King of Judah

16:1-20pp — 2Ch 28:1-27

16 In the seventeenth year of Pekah son of Remaliah, Ahaz son of Jotham king of Judah began to reign. [2] Ahaz was twenty years old when he became king, and he reigned in Jerusalem sixteen years. Unlike David his father, he did not do what was right in the eyes of the LORD his God. [3] He followed the ways of the kings of Israel and even sacrificed his son in the fire, engaging in the detestable practices of the nations the LORD had driven out before the Israelites. [4] He offered sacrifices and burned incense at the high places, on the hilltops and under every spreading tree.   Lev 18:21; Dt 12:2,31

[5] Then Rezin king of Aram and Pekah son of Remaliah king of Israel marched up to fight against Jerusalem and besieged Ahaz, but they could not overpower him. [6] At that time, Rezin king of Aram recovered Elath for Aram by driving out the people of Judah. Edomites then moved into Elath and have lived there to this day.   2Ki 14:22; Isa 7:1,4

[7] Ahaz sent messengers to say to Tiglath-Pileser king of Assyria, "I am your servant and vassal. Come up and save me out of the hand of the king of Aram and of the king of Israel, who are attacking me." [8] And Ahaz took the silver and gold found in the temple of the LORD and in the treasuries of the royal palace and sent it as a gift to the king of Assyria. [9] The king of Assyria complied by attacking Damascus and capturing it. He deported its inhabitants to Kir and put Rezin to death.   2Ki 12:18; 15:29; Am 1:5

[10] Then King Ahaz went to

Damascus to meet Tiglath-Pileser king of Assyria. He saw an altar in Damascus and sent to Uriah the priest a sketch of the altar, with detailed plans for its construction. [11] So Uriah the priest built an altar in accordance with all the plans that King Ahaz had sent from Damascus and finished it before King Ahaz returned. [12] When the king came back from Damascus and saw the altar, he approached it and presented offerings[a] on it. [13] He offered up his burnt offering and grain offering, poured out his drink offering, and splashed the blood of his fellowship offerings against the altar. [14] As for the bronze altar that stood before the LORD, he brought it from the front of the temple — from between the new altar and the temple of the LORD — and put it on the north side of the new altar. 2Ch 4:1; 26:16; Isa 8:2

[15] King Ahaz then gave these orders to Uriah the priest: "On the large new altar, offer the morning burnt offering and the evening grain offering, the king's burnt offering and his grain offering, and the burnt offering of all the people of the land, and their grain offering and their drink offering. Splash against this altar the blood of all the burnt offerings and sacrifices. But I will use the bronze altar for seeking guidance." [16] And Uriah the priest did just as King Ahaz had ordered. Ex 29:38-41; 1Sa 9:9

[17] King Ahaz cut off the side panels and removed the basins from the movable stands. He removed the Sea from the bronze bulls that supported it and set it on a stone base. [18] He took away the Sabbath canopy[b] that had been built at the temple and removed the royal entryway outside the temple of the LORD, in deference to the king of Assyria.

[19] As for the other events of the reign of Ahaz, and what he did, are they not written in the book of the annals of the kings of Judah? [20] Ahaz rested with his ancestors and was buried with them in the City of David. And Hezekiah his son succeeded him as king. 2Ch 28:1-27

Hoshea Last King of Israel

17:3-7pp — 2Ki 18:9-12

17 In the twelfth year of Ahaz king of Judah, Hoshea son of Elah became king of Israel in Samaria, and he reigned nine years. [2] He did evil in the eyes of the LORD, but not like the kings of Israel who preceded him.

[3] Shalmaneser king of Assyria came up to attack Hoshea, who had been Shalmaneser's vassal and had paid him tribute. [4] But the king of Assyria discovered that Hoshea was a traitor, for he had sent envoys to So[c] king of Egypt,

---

[a] 12 Or and went up   [b] 18 Or the dais of his throne (see Septuagint)   [c] 4 So is probably an abbreviation for Osorkon.

and he no longer paid tribute to the king of Assyria, as he had done year by year. Therefore Shalmaneser seized him and put him in prison. [5] The king of Assyria invaded the entire land, marched against Samaria and laid siege to it for three years. [6] In the ninth year of Hoshea, the king of Assyria captured Samaria and deported the Israelites to Assyria. He settled them in Halah, in Gozan on the Habor River and in the towns of the Medes.   2Ki 18:9-12; Hos 10:14

Israel Exiled Because of Sin

[7] All this took place because the Israelites had sinned against the LORD their God, who had brought them up out of Egypt from under the power of Pharaoh king of Egypt. They worshiped other gods [8] and followed the practices of the nations the LORD had driven out before them, as well as the practices that the kings of Israel had introduced. [9] The Israelites secretly did things against the LORD their God that were not right. From watchtower to fortified city they built themselves high places in all their towns. [10] They set up sacred stones and Asherah poles on every high hill and under every spreading tree. [11] At every high place they burned incense, as the nations whom the LORD had driven out before them had done. They did wicked things that aroused the LORD's anger. [12] They worshiped idols, though the LORD had said, "You shall not do this."[a] [13] The LORD warned Israel and Judah through all his prophets and seers: "Turn from your evil ways. Observe my commands and decrees, in accordance with the entire Law that I commanded your ancestors to obey and that I delivered to you through my servants the prophets." 1Sa 9:9; Jer 18:11

[14] But they would not listen and were as stiff-necked as their ancestors, who did not trust in the LORD their God. [15] They rejected his decrees and the covenant he had made with their ancestors and the statutes he had warned them to keep. They followed worthless idols and themselves became worthless. They imitated the nations around them although the LORD had ordered them, "Do not do as they do."   Dt 12:30-31; 29:25; 32:21

[16] They forsook all the commands of the LORD their God and made for themselves two idols cast in the shape of calves, and an Asherah pole. They bowed down to all the starry hosts, and they worshiped Baal. [17] They sacrificed their sons and daughters in the fire. They practiced divination and sought omens and sold themselves to do evil in the eyes of the LORD, arousing his anger.   1Ki 21:20; Ro 7:14

[18] So the LORD was very angry

a 12 Exodus 20:4,5

with Israel and removed them from his presence. Only the tribe of Judah was left, [19]and even Judah did not keep the commands of the LORD their God. They followed the practices Israel had introduced. [20]Therefore the LORD rejected all the people of Israel; he afflicted them and gave them into the hands of plunderers, until he thrust them from his presence. 2Ki 15:29; 16:3

[21]When he tore Israel away from the house of David, they made Jeroboam son of Nebat their king. Jeroboam enticed Israel away from following the LORD and caused them to commit a great sin. [22]The Israelites persisted in all the sins of Jeroboam and did not turn away from them [23]until the LORD removed them from his presence, as he had warned through all his servants the prophets. So the people of Israel were taken from their homeland into exile in Assyria, and they are still there. 1Ki 11:11; 12:20

Samaria Resettled

[24]The king of Assyria brought people from Babylon, Kuthah, Avva, Hamath and Sepharvaim and settled them in the towns of Samaria to replace the Israelites. They took over Samaria and lived in its towns. [25]When they first lived there, they did not worship the LORD; so he sent lions among them and they killed some of the people. [26]It was reported to the king of Assyria: "The people you deported and resettled in the towns of Samaria do not know what the god of that country requires. He has sent lions among them, which are killing them off, because the people do not know what he requires." Ge 37:20; 2Ki 18:34

[27]Then the king of Assyria gave this order: "Have one of the priests you took captive from Samaria go back to live there and teach the people what the god of the land requires." [28]So one of the priests who had been exiled from Samaria came to live in Bethel and taught them how to worship the LORD.

[29]Nevertheless, each national group made its own gods in the several towns where they settled, and set them up in the shrines the people of Samaria had made at the high places. [30]The people from Babylon made Sukkoth Benoth, those from Kuthah made Nergal, and those from Hamath made Ashima; [31]the Avvites made Nibhaz and Tartak, and the Sepharvites burned their children in the fire as sacrifices to Adrammelek and Anammelek, the gods of Sepharvaim. [32]They worshiped the LORD, but they also appointed all sorts of their own people to officiate for them as priests in the shrines at the high places. [33]They worshiped the LORD, but they also served their own gods in accordance with the customs

of the nations from which they had been brought. ver 24; 1Ki 12:31

³⁴To this day they persist in their former practices. They neither worship the LORD nor adhere to the decrees and regulations, the laws and commands that the LORD gave the descendants of Jacob, whom he named Israel. ³⁵When the LORD made a covenant with the Israelites, he commanded them: "Do not worship any other gods or bow down to them, serve them or sacrifice to them. ³⁶But the LORD, who brought you up out of Egypt with mighty power and outstretched arm, is the one you must worship. To him you shall bow down and to him offer sacrifices. ³⁷You must always be careful to keep the decrees and regulations, the laws and commands he wrote for you. Do not worship other gods. ³⁸Do not forget the covenant I have made with you, and do not worship other gods. ³⁹Rather, worship the LORD your God; it is he who will deliver you from the hand of all your enemies." Dt 44:23; 5:32

⁴⁰They would not listen, however, but persisted in their former practices. ⁴¹Even while these people were worshiping the LORD, they were serving their idols. To this day their children and grandchildren continue to do as their ancestors did. 1Ki 18:21; Mt 6:24

Hezekiah King of Judah

18:2-4pp — 2Ch 29:1-2; 31:1
18:5-7pp — 2Ch 31:20-21
18:9-12pp — 2Ki 17:3-7

18 In the third year of Hoshea son of Elah king of Israel, Hezekiah son of Ahaz king of Judah began to reign. ²He was twenty-five years old when he became king, and he reigned in Jerusalem twenty-nine years. His mother's name was Abijah[a] daughter of Zechariah. ³He did what was right in the eyes of the LORD, just as his father David had done. ⁴He removed the high places, smashed the sacred stones and cut down the Asherah poles. He broke into pieces the bronze snake Moses had made, for up to that time the Israelites had been burning incense to it. (It was called Nehushtan.[b]) 2Ch 29:1-2; 31:1

⁵Hezekiah trusted in the LORD, the God of Israel. There was no one like him among all the kings of Judah, either before him or after him. ⁶He held fast to the LORD and did not stop following him; he kept the commands the LORD had given Moses. ⁷And the LORD was with him; he was successful in whatever he undertook. He rebelled against the king of Assyria and did not serve him. ⁸From watchtower to fortified city, he defeated the Philistines, as far as Gaza and its territory. 2Ch 31:20-21

⁹In King Hezekiah's fourth

---

[a] 2 Hebrew *Abi,* a variant of *Abijah*   [b] 4 *Nehushtan* sounds like the Hebrew for both *bronze* and *snake.*

year, which was the seventh year of Hoshea son of Elah king of Israel, Shalmaneser king of Assyria marched against Samaria and laid siege to it. ¹⁰ At the end of three years the Assyrians took it. So Samaria was captured in Hezekiah's sixth year, which was the ninth year of Hoshea king of Israel. ¹¹ The king of Assyria deported Israel to Assyria and settled them in Halah, in Gozan on the Habor River and in towns of the Medes. ¹² This happened because they had not obeyed the LORD their God, but had violated his covenant — all that Moses the servant of the LORD commanded. They neither listened to the commands nor carried them out.   2Ki 17:3-7; Da 9:6,10; 1Ki 9:6

¹³ In the fourteenth year of King Hezekiah's reign, Sennacherib king of Assyria attacked all the fortified cities of Judah and captured them. ¹⁴ So Hezekiah king of Judah sent this message to the king of Assyria at Lachish: "I have done wrong. Withdraw from me, and I will pay whatever you demand of me." The king of Assyria exacted from Hezekiah king of Judah three hundred talents*ᵃ* of silver and thirty talents*ᵇ* of gold. ¹⁵ So Hezekiah gave him all the silver that was found in the temple of the LORD and in the treasuries of the royal palace.   1Ki 15:18; 2Ki 16:8

¹⁶ At this time Hezekiah king of Judah stripped off the gold with which he had covered the doors and doorposts of the temple of the LORD, and gave it to the king of Assyria.

Sennacherib Threatens Jerusalem

18:13, 17-37pp — Isa 36:1-22
18:17-35pp — 2Ch 32:9-19

¹⁷ The king of Assyria sent his supreme commander, his chief officer and his field commander with a large army, from Lachish to King Hezekiah at Jerusalem. They came up to Jerusalem and stopped at the aqueduct of the Upper Pool, on the road to the Washerman's Field. ¹⁸ They called for the king; and Eliakim son of Hilkiah the palace administrator, Shebna the secretary, and Joah son of Asaph the recorder went out to them.   2Ki 19:2; Isa 20:1; 22:15

¹⁹ The field commander said to them, "Tell Hezekiah:

"'This is what the great king, the king of Assyria, says: On what are you basing this confidence of yours? ²⁰ You say you have the counsel and the might for war — but you speak only empty words. On whom are you depending, that you rebel against me? ²¹ Look, I know you are depending on Egypt, that splint-

---

ᵃ 14 That is, about 11 tons or about 10 metric tons 1 metric ton   *ᵇ 14* That is, about 1 ton or about ered reed of a staff, which pierces the hand of anyone who leans on it! Such is Pharaoh king of Egypt to all who depend on him. ²²But if you say to me, "We are depending on the LORD our God" — isn't he the one whose high places and altars Hezekiah removed, saying to Judah and Jerusalem, "You must worship before this altar in Jerusalem"? Isa 30:5,7; Eze 29:6

²³ "'Come now, make a bargain with my master, the king of Assyria: I will give you two thousand horses — if you can put riders on them! ²⁴How can you repulse one officer of the least of my master's officials, even though you are depending on Egypt for chariots and horsemen*a*? ²⁵Furthermore, have I come to attack and destroy this place without word from the LORD? The LORD himself told me to march against this country and destroy it.'" 2Ki 19:6,22

²⁶Then Eliakim son of Hilkiah, and Shebna and Joah said to the field commander, "Please speak to your servants in Aramaic, since we understand it. Don't speak to us in Hebrew in the hearing of the people on the wall." Ezr 4:7

²⁷But the commander replied, "Was it only to your master and you that my master sent me to say these things, and not to the people sitting on the wall — who, like you, will have to eat their own excrement and drink their own urine?"

²⁸Then the commander stood and called out in Hebrew, "Hear the word of the great king, the king of Assyria! ²⁹This is what the king says: Do not let Hezekiah deceive you. He cannot deliver you from my hand. ³⁰Do not let Hezekiah persuade you to trust in the LORD when he says, 'The LORD will surely deliver us; this city will not be given into the hand of the king of Assyria.'

³¹"Do not listen to Hezekiah. This is what the king of Assyria says: Make peace with me and come out to me. Then each of you will eat fruit from your own vine and fig tree and drink water from your own cistern, ³²until I come and take you to a land like your own — a land of grain and new wine, a land of bread and vineyards, a land of olive trees and honey. Choose life and not death!

"Do not listen to Hezekiah, for he is misleading you when he says, 'The LORD will deliver us.' ³³Has the god of any nation ever delivered his land from the hand of the king of Assyria? ³⁴Where are the gods of Hamath and Arpad? Where are the gods of Sepharvaim, Hena and Ivvah? Have they rescued Samaria from

a 24 Or *charioteers*

my hand? ³⁵Who of all the gods of these countries has been able to save his land from me? How then can the LORD deliver Jerusalem from my hand?" 2Ch 32:9-19

³⁶But the people remained silent and said nothing in reply, because the king had commanded, "Do not answer him."

³⁷Then Eliakim son of Hilkiah the palace administrator, Shebna the secretary, and Joah son of Asaph the recorder went to Hezekiah, with their clothes torn, and told him what the field commander had said. Isa 36:1-22

Jerusalem's Deliverance Foretold

19:1-13pp — Isa 37:1-13

19 When King Hezekiah heard this, he tore his clothes and put on sackcloth and went into the temple of the LORD. ²He sent Eliakim the palace administrator, Shebna the secretary and the leading priests, all wearing sackcloth, to the prophet Isaiah son of Amoz. ³They told him, "This is what Hezekiah says: This day is a day of distress and rebuke and disgrace, as when children come to the moment of birth and there is no strength to deliver them. ⁴It may be that the LORD your God will hear all the words of the field commander, whom his master, the king of Assyria, has sent to ridicule the living God, and that he will rebuke him for the words the LORD your God has heard. Therefore pray for the remnant that still survives." 2Sa 16:12; 2Ki 18:35

⁵When King Hezekiah's officials came to Isaiah, ⁶Isaiah said to them, "Tell your master, 'This is what the LORD says: Do not be afraid of what you have heard—those words with which the underlings of the king of Assyria have blasphemed me. ⁷Listen! When he hears a certain report, I will make him want to return to his own country, and there I will have him cut down with the sword.'" ver 37; 2Ki 18:25

⁸When the field commander heard that the king of Assyria had left Lachish, he withdrew and found the king fighting against Libnah. 2Ki 18:14

⁹Now Sennacherib received a report that Tirhakah, the king of Cush,^a was marching out to fight against him. So he again sent messengers to Hezekiah with this word: ¹⁰"Say to Hezekiah king of Judah: Do not let the god you depend on deceive you when he says, 'Jerusalem will not be given into the hands of the king of Assyria.' ¹¹Surely you have heard what the kings of Assyria have done to all the countries, destroying them completely. And will you be delivered? ¹²Did the gods of the nations that were destroyed by my predecessors deliver them—the gods of Gozan,

^a 9 That is, the upper Nile region

Harran, Rezeph and the people of Eden who were in Tel Assar? ¹³Where is the king of Hamath or the king of Arpad? Where are the kings of Lair, Sepharvaim, Hena and Ivvah?" Isa 37:1-13

Hezekiah's Prayer

19:14-19pp — Isa 37:14-20

¹⁴Hezekiah received the letter from the messengers and read it. Then he went up to the temple of the LORD and spread it out before the LORD. ¹⁵And Hezekiah prayed to the LORD: "LORD, the God of Israel, enthroned between the cherubim, you alone are God over all the kingdoms of the earth. You have made heaven and earth. ¹⁶Give ear, LORD, and hear; open your eyes, LORD, and see; listen to the words Sennacherib has sent to ridicule the living God.

¹⁷"It is true, LORD, that the Assyrian kings have laid waste these nations and their lands. ¹⁸They have thrown their gods into the fire and destroyed them, for they were not gods but only wood and stone, fashioned by human hands. ¹⁹Now, LORD our God, deliver us from his hand, so that all the kingdoms of the earth may know that you alone, LORD, are God." Isa 37:14-20; Ps 83:18

Isaiah Prophesies Sennacherib's Fall

19:20-37pp — Isa 37:21-38
19:35-37pp — 2Ch 32:20-21

²⁰Then Isaiah son of Amoz sent a message to Hezekiah: "This is what the LORD, the God of Israel, says: I have heard your prayer concerning Sennacherib king of Assyria. ²¹This is the word that the LORD has spoken against him: 2Ki 20:5; Isa 10:5

" 'Virgin Daughter Zion La 2:13
   despises you and mocks
     you. Ps 22:7-8
Daughter Jerusalem
   tosses her head as you
     flee. Ps 109:25
²²Who is it you have ridiculed
   and blasphemed?
Against whom have you
   raised your voice
and lifted your eyes in pride?
   Against the Holy One of
     Israel! Ps 71:22; Isa 5:24
²³By your messengers
   you have ridiculed the Lord.
And you have said, Isa 10:18
"With my many chariots
I have ascended the heights of
   the mountains,
   the utmost heights of
     Lebanon.
I have cut down its tallest
   cedars, Isa 10:34
   the choicest of its junipers.
I have reached its remotest
   parts,
   the finest of its forests.
²⁴I have dug wells in foreign
   lands
   and drunk the water there.
With the soles of my feet
   I have dried up all the
     streams of Egypt."

25 " 'Have you not heard?   Isa 40:21
    Long ago I ordained it.
In days of old I planned it;
    now I have brought it to
        pass,
that you have turned fortified
    cities
    into piles of stone.   Mic 1:6
26 Their people, drained of
    power,
    are dismayed and put to
        shame.   Ps 6:10
They are like plants in the
    field,
    like tender green shoots,
like grass sprouting on the
    roof,
    scorched before it
        grows up.   Ps 129:6

27 " 'But I know where you are
    and when you come and go
    and how you rage
        against me.
28 Because you rage against me
    and because your insolence
        has reached my ears,
I will put my hook in your
        nose   Eze 29:4
    and my bit in your mouth,
and I will make you return
    by the way you came.'

29 "This will be the sign for you,
Hezekiah:
        Lk 2:12

"This year you will eat what
        grows by itself,   Lev 25:5
and the second year what
        springs from that.
But in the third year sow and
        reap,

plant vineyards and eat
        their fruit.   Ps 107:37
30 Once more a remnant of the
        kingdom of Judah
    will take root below and
        bear fruit above.   2Ch 32:22
31 For out of Jerusalem will come
        a remnant,   Ge 45:7
    and out of Mount Zion a
        band of survivors.

"The zeal of the LORD Almighty
will accomplish this.   Isa 9:7

32 "Therefore this is what the
LORD says concerning the king
of Assyria:

" 'He will not enter this city
    or shoot an arrow here.
He will not come before it
        with shield
    or build a siege ramp
        against it.
33 By the way that he came he
        will return;   ver 28
    he will not enter this city,
        declares the LORD.
34 I will defend this city and
        save it,   2Ki 20:6
    for my sake and for the sake
        of David my servant.' "

35 That night the angel of the
LORD went out and put to death
a hundred and eighty-five thousand in the Assyrian camp. When
the people got up the next morning—there were all the dead
bodies! 36 So Sennacherib king
of Assyria broke camp and withdrew. He returned to Nineveh and
stayed there. Ex 12:23; Job 24:24; Jnh 1:2

37 One day, while he was worshiping in the temple of his god Nisrok, his sons Adrammelek and Sharezer killed him with the sword, and they escaped to the land of Ararat. And Esarhaddon his son succeeded him as king. 2Ch 32:20-21; Isa 37:21-38

Hezekiah's Illness

20:1-11pp — 2Ch 32:24-26; Isa 38:1-8

20 In those days Hezekiah became ill and was at the point of death. The prophet Isaiah son of Amoz went to him and said, "This is what the LORD says: Put your house in order, because you are going to die; you will not recover."

2 Hezekiah turned his face to the wall and prayed to the LORD, 3 "Remember, LORD, how I have walked before you faithfully and with wholehearted devotion and have done what is good in your eyes." And Hezekiah wept bitterly. 2Ki 18:3-6; Ne 13:22

4 Before Isaiah had left the middle court, the word of the LORD came to him: 5 "Go back and tell Hezekiah, the ruler of my people, 'This is what the LORD, the God of your father David, says: I have heard your prayer and seen your tears; I will heal you. On the third day from now you will go up to the temple of the LORD. 6 I will add fifteen years to your life. And I will deliver you and this city from the hand of the king of Assyria. I will defend this city for

my sake and for the sake of my servant David.'" 2Ki 19:20,34; Ps 39:12

7 Then Isaiah said, "Prepare a poultice of figs." They did so and applied it to the boil, and he recovered. Isa 38:21

8 Hezekiah had asked Isaiah, "What will be the sign that the LORD will heal me and that I will go up to the temple of the LORD on the third day from now?"

9 Isaiah answered, "This is the LORD's sign to you that the LORD will do what he has promised: Shall the shadow go forward ten steps, or shall it go back ten steps?" Dt 13:2; Jer 44:29

10 "It is a simple matter for the shadow to go forward ten steps," said Hezekiah. "Rather, have it go back ten steps."

11 Then the prophet Isaiah called on the LORD, and the LORD made the shadow go back the ten steps it had gone down on the stairway of Ahaz. 2Ch 32:24-26; Isa 38:1-8

Envoys From Babylon

20:12-19pp — Isa 39:1-8
20:20-21pp — 2Ch 32:32-33

12 At that time Marduk-Baladan son of Baladan king of Babylon sent Hezekiah letters and a gift, because he had heard of Hezekiah's illness. 13 Hezekiah received the envoys and showed them all that was in his storehouses — the silver, the gold, the spices and the fine olive oil — his armory and everything found among his treasures. There was

nothing in his palace or in all his kingdom that Hezekiah did not show them.

[14] Then Isaiah the prophet went to King Hezekiah and asked, "What did those men say, and where did they come from?"

"From a distant land," Hezekiah replied. "They came from Babylon."

[15] The prophet asked, "What did they see in your palace?"

"They saw everything in my palace," Hezekiah said. "There is nothing among my treasures that I did not show them."

[16] Then Isaiah said to Hezekiah, "Hear the word of the LORD: [17] The time will surely come when everything in your palace, and all that your predecessors have stored up until this day, will be carried off to Babylon. Nothing will be left, says the LORD. [18] And some of your descendants, your own flesh and blood who will be born to you, will be taken away, and they will become eunuchs in the palace of the king of Babylon." 2Ki 24:15; 2Ch 33:11

[19] "The word of the LORD you have spoken is good," Hezekiah replied. For he thought, "Will there not be peace and security in my lifetime?" Isa 39:1-8

[20] As for the other events of Hezekiah's reign, all his achievements and how he made the pool and the tunnel by which he brought water into the city, are they not written in the book of the annals of the kings of Judah? [21] Hezekiah rested with his ancestors. And Manasseh his son succeeded him as king. Ne 3:16

Manasseh King of Judah

21:1-10pp — 2Ch 33:1-10
21:17-18pp — 2Ch 33:18-20

21 Manasseh was twelve years old when he became king, and he reigned in Jerusalem fifty-five years. His mother's name was Hephzibah. [2] He did evil in the eyes of the LORD, following the detestable practices of the nations the LORD had driven out before the Israelites. [3] He rebuilt the high places his father Hezekiah had destroyed; he also erected altars to Baal and made an Asherah pole, as Ahab king of Israel had done. He bowed down to all the starry hosts and worshiped them. [4] He built altars in the temple of the LORD, of which the LORD had said, "In Jerusalem I will put my Name." [5] In the two courts of the temple of the LORD, he built altars to all the starry hosts. [6] He sacrificed his own son in the fire, practiced divination, sought omens, and consulted mediums and spiritists. He did much evil in the eyes of the LORD, arousing his anger. Jer 15:4; Lev 18:21

[7] He took the carved Asherah pole he had made and put it in the temple, of which the LORD had said to David and to his son Solomon, "In this temple and in Jerusalem, which I have chosen

out of all the tribes of Israel, I will put my Name forever. **8**I will not again make the feet of the Israelites wander from the land I gave their ancestors, if only they will be careful to do everything I commanded them and will keep the whole Law that my servant Moses gave them." **9**But the people did not listen. Manasseh led them astray, so that they did more evil than the nations the LORD had destroyed before the Israelites. 2Ch 33:1-10

10The LORD said through his servants the prophets: **11**"Manasseh king of Judah has committed these detestable sins. He has done more evil than the Amorites who preceded him and has led Judah into sin with his idols. **12**Therefore this is what the LORD, the God of Israel, says: I am going to bring such disaster on Jerusalem and Judah that the ears of everyone who hears of it will tingle. **13**I will stretch out over Jerusalem the measuring line used against Samaria and the plumb line used against the house of Ahab. I will wipe out Jerusalem as one wipes a dish, wiping it and turning it upside down. **14**I will forsake the remnant of my inheritance and give them into the hands of enemies. They will be looted and plundered by all their enemies; **15**they have done evil in my eyes and have aroused my anger from the day their ances-

tors came out of Egypt until this day." 2Ki 19:4; Ps 78:58-60; Isa 34:11

16Moreover, Manasseh also shed so much innocent blood that he filled Jerusalem from end to end — besides the sin that he had caused Judah to commit, so that they did evil in the eyes of the LORD. 2Ki 24:4

17As for the other events of Manasseh's reign, and all he did, including the sin he committed, are they not written in the book of the annals of the kings of Judah? **18**Manasseh rested with his ancestors and was buried in his palace garden, the garden of Uzza. And Amon his son succeeded him as king.

Amon King of Judah
21:19-24pp — 2Ch 33:21-25

19Amon was twenty-two years old when he became king, and he reigned in Jerusalem two years. His mother's name was Meshullemeth daughter of Haruz; she was from Jotbah. **20**He did evil in the eyes of the LORD, as his father Manasseh had done. **21**He followed completely the ways of his father, worshiping the idols his father had worshiped, and bowing down to them. **22**He forsook the LORD, the God of his ancestors, and did not walk in obedience to him. ver 2-6; 1Ki 11:33

23Amon's officials conspired against him and assassinated the king in his palace. **24**Then the people of the land killed all who had plotted against King Amon, and they made Josiah his son king in his place. 2Ch 33:21-25

²⁵As for the other events of Amon's reign, and what he did, are they not written in the book of the annals of the kings of Judah? ²⁶He was buried in his tomb in the garden of Uzza. And Josiah his son succeeded him as king.

The Book of the Law Found
22:1-20pp — 2Ch 34:1-2,8-28

22 Josiah was eight years old when he became king, and he reigned in Jerusalem thirty-one years. His mother's name was Jedidah daughter of Adaiah; she was from Bozkath. ²He did what was right in the eyes of the LORD and followed completely the ways of his father David, not turning aside to the right or to the left. Dt 5:32; 17:19; Jos 15:39

³In the eighteenth year of his reign, King Josiah sent the secretary, Shaphan son of Azaliah, the son of Meshullam, to the temple of the LORD. He said: ⁴"Go up to Hilkiah the high priest and have him get ready the money that has been brought into the temple of the LORD, which the doorkeepers have collected from the people. ⁵Have them entrust it to the men appointed to supervise the work on the temple. And have these men pay the workers who repair the temple of the LORD— ⁶the carpenters, the builders and the masons. Also have them purchase

timber and dressed stone to repair the temple. ⁷But they need not account for the money entrusted to them, because they are honest in their dealings." 2Ki 12:4-5,11-15

⁸Hilkiah the high priest said to Shaphan the secretary, "I have found the Book of the Law in the temple of the LORD." He gave it to Shaphan, who read it. ⁹Then Shaphan the secretary went to the king and reported to him: "Your officials have paid out the money that was in the temple of the LORD and have entrusted it to the workers and supervisors at the temple." ¹⁰Then Shaphan the secretary informed the king, "Hilkiah the priest has given me a book." And Shaphan read from it in the presence of the king. Dt 31:24

¹¹When the king heard the words of the Book of the Law, he tore his robes. ¹²He gave these orders to Hilkiah the priest, Ahikam son of Shaphan, Akbor son of Micaiah, Shaphan the secretary and Asaiah the king's attendant: ¹³"Go and inquire of the LORD for me and for the people and for all Judah about what is written in this book that has been found. Great is the LORD's anger that burns against us because those who have gone before us have not obeyed the words of this book; they have not acted in accordance with all that is written there concerning us." Dt 29:24-28; 2Ki 25:22

¹⁴Hilkiah the priest, Ahikam, Akbor, Shaphan and Asa-

iah went to speak to the prophet Huldah, who was the wife of Shallum son of Tikvah, the son of Harhas, keeper of the wardrobe. She lived in Jerusalem, in the New Quarter.

[15] She said to them, "This is what the LORD, the God of Israel, says: Tell the man who sent you to me, [16] 'This is what the LORD says: I am going to bring disaster on this place and its people, according to everything written in the book the king of Judah has read. [17] Because they have forsaken me and burned incense to other gods and aroused my anger by all the idols their hands have made,[a] my anger will burn against this place and will not be quenched.' [18] Tell the king of Judah, who sent you to inquire of the LORD, 'This is what the LORD, the God of Israel, says concerning the words you heard: [19] Because your heart was responsive and you humbled yourself before the LORD when you heard what I have spoken against this place and its people—that they would become a curse[b] and be laid waste—and because you tore your robes and wept in my presence, I also have heard you, declares the LORD. [20] Therefore I will gather you to your ancestors, and you will be buried in peace. Your eyes will not see all the disaster I am going to bring on this place.'" 2Ch 34:1-2,8-28

So they took her answer back to the king.

Josiah Renews the Covenant

23:1-3pp — 2Ch 34:29-32
23:4-20Ref — 2Ch 34:3-7,33
23:21-23pp — 2Ch 35:1,18-19
23:28-30pp — 2Ch 35:20–36:1

23 Then the king called together all the elders of Judah and Jerusalem. [2] He went up to the temple of the LORD with the people of Judah, the inhabitants of Jerusalem, the priests and the prophets—all the people from the least to the greatest. He read in their hearing all the words of the Book of the Covenant, which had been found in the temple of the LORD. [3] The king stood by the pillar and renewed the covenant in the presence of the LORD—to follow the LORD and keep his commands, statutes and decrees with all his heart and all his soul, thus confirming the words of the covenant written in this book. Then all the people pledged themselves to the covenant. 2Ch 34:29-32; 2Ki 22:8

[4] The king ordered Hilkiah the high priest, the priests next in rank and the doorkeepers to remove from the temple of the LORD all the articles made for Baal and Asherah and all the starry hosts. He burned them outside Jerusalem in the fields of the Kidron Valley and took the ashes to Bethel. [5] He did away with the idolatrous priests appointed by the

---

[a] 17 Or by everything they have done   [b] 19 That is, their names would be used in cursing (see Jer. 29:22); or, others would see that they are cursed.

kings of Judah to burn incense on the high places of the towns of Judah and on those around Jerusalem—those who burned incense to Baal, to the sun and moon, to the constellations and to all the starry hosts. ⁶He took the Asherah pole from the temple of the LORD to the Kidron Valley outside Jerusalem and burned it there. He ground it to powder and scattered the dust over the graves of the common people. ⁷He also tore down the quarters of the male shrine prostitutes that were in the temple of the LORD, the quarters where women did weaving for Asherah. 1Ki 14:24; 15:12; Eze 16:16

⁸Josiah brought all the priests from the towns of Judah and desecrated the high places, from Geba to Beersheba, where the priests had burned incense. He broke down the gateway at the entrance of the Gate of Joshua, the city governor, which was on the left of the city gate. ⁹Although the priests of the high places did not serve at the altar of the LORD in Jerusalem, they ate unleavened bread with their fellow priests. 1Ki 15:22; Eze 44:10-14

¹⁰He desecrated Topheth, which was in the Valley of Ben Hinnom, so no one could use it to sacrifice their son or daughter in the fire to Molek. ¹¹He removed from the entrance to the temple of the LORD the horses that the kings of Judah had dedicated to the sun. They were in the court*ᵃ* near the room of an official named Nathan-Melek. Josiah then burned the chariots dedicated to the sun. Isa 30:33; Jer 7:31-32; 19:6

¹²He pulled down the altars the kings of Judah had erected on the roof near the upper room of Ahaz, and the altars Manasseh had built in the two courts of the temple of the LORD. He removed them from there, smashed them to pieces and threw the rubble into the Kidron Valley. ¹³The king also desecrated the high places that were east of Jerusalem on the south of the Hill of Corruption—the ones Solomon king of Israel had built for Ashtoreth the vile goddess of the Sidonians, for Chemosh the vile god of Moab, and for Molek the detestable god of the people of Ammon. ¹⁴Josiah smashed the sacred stones and cut down the Asherah poles and covered the sites with human bones. Dt 7:5,25; 1Ki 11:7

¹⁵Even the altar at Bethel, the high place made by Jeroboam son of Nebat, who had caused Israel to sin—even that altar and high place he demolished. He burned the high place and ground it to powder, and burned the Asherah pole also. ¹⁶Then Josiah looked around, and when he saw the tombs that were there on the hillside, he had the bones removed from them and burned on the altar to defile it, in accor-

---

ᵃ 11 The meaning of the Hebrew for this word is uncertain.

dance with the word of the LORD proclaimed by the man of God who foretold these things. 1Ki 13:2

¹⁷ The king asked, "What is that tombstone I see?"

The people of the city said, "It marks the tomb of the man of God who came from Judah and pronounced against the altar of Bethel the very things you have done to it."

¹⁸ "Leave it alone," he said. "Don't let anyone disturb his bones." So they spared his bones and those of the prophet who had come from Samaria. 1Ki 13:31

¹⁹ Just as he had done at Bethel, Josiah removed all the shrines at the high places that the kings of Israel had built in the towns of Samaria and that had aroused the LORD's anger. ²⁰ Josiah slaughtered all the priests of those high places on the altars and burned human bones on them. Then he went back to Jerusalem. 2Ch 34:3-7

²¹ The king gave this order to all the people: "Celebrate the Passover to the LORD your God, as it is written in this Book of the Covenant." ²² Neither in the days of the judges who led Israel nor in the days of the kings of Israel and the kings of Judah had any such Passover been observed. ²³ But in the eighteenth year of King Josiah, this Passover was celebrated to the LORD in Jerusalem. 2Ch 35:1,18

²⁴ Furthermore, Josiah got rid of the mediums and spir-

itists, the household gods, the idols and all the other detestable things seen in Judah and Jerusalem. This he did to fulfill the requirements of the law written in the book that Hilkiah the priest had discovered in the temple of the LORD. ²⁵ Neither before nor after Josiah was there a king like him who turned to the LORD as he did — with all his heart and with all his soul and with all his strength, in accordance with all the Law of Moses. Dt 18:11; 2Ki 18:5

²⁶ Nevertheless, the LORD did not turn away from the heat of his fierce anger, which burned against Judah because of all that Manasseh had done to arouse his anger. ²⁷ So the LORD said, "I will remove Judah also from my presence as I removed Israel, and I will reject Jerusalem, the city I chose, and this temple, about which I said, 'My Name shall be there.'[a]" 2Ki 18:11; 21:13

²⁸ As for the other events of Josiah's reign, and all he did, are they not written in the book of the annals of the kings of Judah?

²⁹ While Josiah was king, Pharaoh Necho king of Egypt went up to the Euphrates River to help the king of Assyria. King Josiah marched out to meet him in battle, but Necho faced him and killed him at Megiddo. ³⁰ Josiah's servants brought his body in a chariot from Megiddo to Jerusalem and buried him in his own

^a 27 1 Kings 8:29

tomb. And the people of the land took Jehoahaz son of Josiah and anointed him and made him king in place of his father. 2Ch 35:20-36:1

Jehoahaz King of Judah
23:31-34pp — 2Ch 36:2-4

³¹Jehoahaz was twenty-three years old when he became king, and he reigned in Jerusalem three months. His mother's name was Hamutal daughter of Jeremiah; she was from Libnah. ³²He did evil in the eyes of the LORD, just as his predecessors had done. ³³Pharaoh Necho put him in chains at Riblah in the land of Hamath so that he might not reign in Jerusalem, and he imposed on Judah a levy of a hundred talents*ᵃ* of silver and a talent*ᵇ* of gold. ³⁴Pharaoh Necho made Eliakim son of Josiah king in place of his father Josiah and changed Eliakim's name to Jehoiakim. But he took Jehoahaz and carried him off to Egypt, and there he died. ³⁵Jehoiakim paid Pharaoh Necho the silver and gold he demanded. In order to do so, he taxed the land and exacted the silver and gold from the people of the land according to their assessments. 2Ch 36:2-4; Jer 22:12; Eze 19:3-4

Jehoiakim King of Judah
23:36–24:6pp — 2Ch 36:5-8

³⁶Jehoiakim was twenty-five years old when he became king, and he reigned in Jerusalem

eleven years. His mother's name was Zebidah daughter of Pedaiah; she was from Rumah. ³⁷And he did evil in the eyes of the LORD, just as his predecessors had done. Jer 26:1

24 During Jehoiakim's reign, Nebuchadnezzar king of Babylon invaded the land, and Jehoiakim became his vassal for three years. But then he turned against Nebuchadnezzar and rebelled. ²The LORD sent Babylonian,*ᶜ* Aramean, Moabite and Ammonite raiders against him to destroy Judah, in accordance with the word of the LORD proclaimed by his servants the prophets. ³Surely these things happened to Judah according to the LORD's command, in order to remove them from his presence because of the sins of Manasseh and all he had done, ⁴including the shedding of innocent blood. For he had filled Jerusalem with innocent blood, and the LORD was not willing to forgive. 2Ki 21:16; 23:26

⁵As for the other events of Jehoiakim's reign, and all he did, are they not written in the book of the annals of the kings of Judah? ⁶Jehoiakim rested with his ancestors. And Jehoiachin his son succeeded him as king. 2Ch 36:5-8

⁷The king of Egypt did not march out from his own country again, because the king of Babylon had taken all his territory,

ᵃ 33 That is, about 3 3/4 tons or about 3.4 metric tons   *ᵇ 33* That is, about 75 pounds or about 34 kilograms   *ᶜ 2* Or *Chaldean* from the Wadi of Egypt to the Euphrates River. Jer 37:5-7; 46:2

Jehoiachin King of Judah
24:8-17pp — 2Ch 36:9-10

⁸Jehoiachin was eighteen years old when he became king, and he reigned in Jerusalem three months. His mother's name was Nehushta daughter of Elnathan; she was from Jerusalem. ⁹He did evil in the eyes of the LORD, just as his father had done. 1Ch 3:16

¹⁰At that time the officers of Nebuchadnezzar king of Babylon advanced on Jerusalem and laid siege to it, ¹¹and Nebuchadnezzar himself came up to the city while his officers were besieging it. ¹²Jehoiachin king of Judah, his mother, his attendants, his nobles and his officials all surrendered to him. Jer 24:1; 29:2; Da 1:1

In the eighth year of the reign of the king of Babylon, he took Jehoiachin prisoner. ¹³As the LORD had declared, Nebuchadnezzar removed the treasures from the temple of the LORD and from the royal palace, and cut up the gold articles that Solomon king of Israel had made for the temple of the LORD. ¹⁴He carried all Jerusalem into exile: all the officers and fighting men, and all the skilled workers and artisans—a total of ten thousand. Only the poorest people of the land were left. 2Ki 25:12; Jer 40:7; 52:16

¹⁵Nebuchadnezzar took Jehoiachin captive to Babylon. He also took from Jerusalem to Babylon the king's mother, his wives, his officials and the prominent people of the land. ¹⁶The king of Babylon also deported to Babylon the entire force of seven thousand fighting men, strong and fit for war, and a thousand skilled workers and artisans. ¹⁷He made Mattaniah, Jehoiachin's uncle, king in his place and changed his name to Zedekiah. 2Ch 36:9-10

Zedekiah King of Judah
24:18-20pp — 2Ch 36:11-16; Jer 52:1-3

¹⁸Zedekiah was twenty-one years old when he became king, and he reigned in Jerusalem eleven years. His mother's name was Hamutal daughter of Jeremiah; she was from Libnah. ¹⁹He did evil in the eyes of the LORD, just as Jehoiakim had done. ²⁰It was because of the LORD's anger that all this happened to Jerusalem and Judah, and in the end he thrust them from his presence. 2Ch 36:11-16; Jer 52:1-3; 2Ki 23:31

The Fall of Jerusalem
25:1-12pp — Jer 39:1-10
25:1-21pp — 2Ch 36:17-20; Jer 52:4-27
25:22-26pp — Jer 40:7-9; 41:1-3, 16-18

Now Zedekiah rebelled against the king of Babylon.

25 So in the ninth year of Zedekiah's reign, on the tenth day of the tenth month, Nebuchadnezzar king of Babylon marched against Jerusalem with his whole army. He encamped outside the city and built siege works all around it. ²The city was kept under siege until the eleventh year of King Zedekiah.

³By the ninth day of the fourth[a] month the famine in the city had become so severe that there was no food for the people to eat. ⁴Then the city wall was broken through, and the whole army fled at night through the gate between the two walls near the king's garden, though the Babylonians[b] were surrounding the city. They fled toward the Arabah,[c] ⁵but the Babylonian[d] army pursued the king and overtook him in the plains of Jericho. All his soldiers were separated from him and scattered, ⁶and he was captured.   Jer 34:21-22

He was taken to the king of Babylon at Riblah, where sentence was pronounced on him. ⁷They killed the sons of Zedekiah before his eyes. Then they put out his eyes, bound him with bronze shackles and took him to Babylon.   2Ki 23:33; Eze 33:21

⁸On the seventh day of the fifth month, in the nineteenth year of Nebuchadnezzar king of Babylon, Nebuzaradan commander of the imperial guard, an official of the king of Babylon, came to Jerusalem. ⁹He set fire to the temple of the LORD, the

royal palace and all the houses of Jerusalem. Every important building he burned down. ¹⁰The whole Babylonian army under the commander of the imperial guard broke down the walls around Jerusalem. ¹¹Nebuzaradan the commander of the guard carried into exile the people who remained in the city, along with the rest of the populace and those who had deserted to the king of Babylon. ¹²But the commander left behind some of the poorest people of the land to work the vineyards and fields.   Jer 39:1-10; 2Ki 24:14

¹³The Babylonians broke up the bronze pillars, the movable stands and the bronze Sea that were at the temple of the LORD and they carried the bronze to Babylon. ¹⁴They also took away the pots, shovels, wick trimmers, dishes and all the bronze articles used in the temple service. ¹⁵The commander of the imperial guard took away the censers and sprinkling bowls — all that were made of pure gold or silver.   Ex 27:3; 1Ki 7:47-50

¹⁶The bronze from the two pillars, the Sea and the movable stands, which Solomon had made for the temple of the LORD, was more than could be weighed. ¹⁷Each pillar was eighteen cubits[e] high. The bronze

---

[a] 3 Probable reading of the original Hebrew text (see Jer. 52:6); Masoretic Text does not have *fourth*.   [b] 4 Or *Chaldeans*; also in verses 13, 25 and 26   [c] 4 Or *the Jordan Valley*
[d] 5 Or *Chaldean*; also in verses 10 and 24   [e] 17 That is, about 27 feet or about 8.1 meters

capital on top of one pillar was three cubits*a* high and was decorated with a network and pomegranates of bronze all around. The other pillar, with its network, was similar.   1Ki 7:15-22

¹⁸The commander of the guard took as prisoners Seraiah the chief priest, Zephaniah the priest next in rank and the three doorkeepers. ¹⁹Of those still in the city, he took the officer in charge of the fighting men, and five royal advisers. He also took the secretary who was chief officer in charge of conscripting the people of the land and sixty of the conscripts who were found in the city. ²⁰Nebuzaradan the commander took them all and brought them to the king of Babylon at Riblah. ²¹There at Riblah, in the land of Hamath, the king had them executed.   Jer 21:1; 29:25

So Judah went into captivity, away from her land.   2Ch 36:17-20

²²Nebuchadnezzar king of Babylon appointed Gedaliah son of Ahikam, the son of Shaphan, to be over the people he had left behind in Judah. ²³When all the army officers and their men heard that the king of Babylon had appointed Gedaliah as governor, they came to Gedaliah at Mizpah—Ishmael son of Nethaniah, Johanan son of Kareah, Seraiah son of Tanhumeth the Netophathite, Jaazaniah the son of the Maakathite, and their men.

²⁴Gedaliah took an oath to reassure them and their men. "Do not be afraid of the Babylonian officials," he said. "Settle down in the land and serve the king of Babylon, and it will go well with you."   Jer 40:5,7

²⁵In the seventh month, however, Ishmael son of Nethaniah, the son of Elishama, who was of royal blood, came with ten men and assassinated Gedaliah and also the men of Judah and the Babylonians who were with him at Mizpah. ²⁶At this, all the people from the least to the greatest, together with the army officers, fled to Egypt for fear of the Babylonians.   Jer 40:7-9; 41:1-3,16-18

Jehoiachin Released
25:27-30pp — Jer 52:31-34

²⁷In the thirty-seventh year of the exile of Jehoiachin king of Judah, in the year Awel-Marduk became king of Babylon, he released Jehoiachin king of Judah from prison. He did this on the twenty-seventh day of the twelfth month. ²⁸He spoke kindly to him and gave him a seat of honor higher than those of the other kings who were with him in Babylon. ²⁹So Jehoiachin put aside his prison clothes and for the rest of his life ate regularly at the king's table. ³⁰Day by day the king gave Jehoiachin a regular allowance as long as he lived.   Jer 52:31-3

---

a 17 That is, about 4 1/2 feet or about 1.4 meters

1 Chronicles

Historical Records From Adam to Abraham

To Noah's Sons

1 Adam, Seth, Enosh, ²Kenan, Mahalalel, Jared, ³Enoch, Methuselah, Lamech, Noah.

⁴The sons of Noah:ᵃ
Shem, Ham and Japheth.

The Japhethites

1:5-7pp — Ge 10:2-5

⁵The sonsᵇ of Japheth:
Gomer, Magog, Madai, Javan, Tubal, Meshek and Tiras.
⁶The sons of Gomer:
Ashkenaz, Riphathᶜ and Togarmah.
⁷The sons of Javan:
Elishah, Tarshish, the Kittites and the Rodanites.   Ge 10:2-5

The Hamites

1:8-16pp — Ge 10:6-20

⁸The sons of Ham:
Cush, Egypt, Put and Canaan.
⁹The sons of Cush:
Seba, Havilah, Sabta, Raamah and Sabteka.
The sons of Raamah:
Sheba and Dedan.
¹⁰Cush was the fatherᵈ of Nimrod, who became a mighty warrior on earth.
¹¹Egypt was the father of the Ludites, Anamites, Lehabites, Naphtuhites, ¹²Pathrusites, Kasluhites (from whom the Philistines came) and Caphtorites.
¹³Canaan was the father of Sidon his firstborn,ᵉ and of the Hittites, ¹⁴Jebusites,

---

ᵃ 4 Septuagint; Hebrew does not have this line.   ᵇ 5 Sons may mean descendants or
successors or nations; also in verses 6-9, 17 and 23.   ᶜ 6 Many Hebrew manuscripts
and Vulgate (see also Septuagint and Gen. 10:3); most Hebrew manuscripts Diphath
ᵈ 10 Father may mean ancestor or predecessor or founder; also in verses 11, 13, 18 and 20.
ᵉ 13 Or of the Sidonians, the foremost

Amorites, Girgashites, ¹⁵Hivites, Arkites, Sinites, ¹⁶Arvadites, Zemarites and Hamathites. Ge 10:6-20

The Semites
1:17-23pp — Ge 10:21-31; 11:10-27

¹⁷The sons of Shem:
Elam, Ashur, Arphaxad,
Lud and Aram.
The sons of Aram:*ᵃ*
Uz, Hul, Gether and Meshek.
¹⁸Arphaxad was the father of
Shelah,
and Shelah the father of
Eber.
¹⁹Two sons were born to Eber:
One was named Peleg,*ᵇ*
because in his time the
earth was divided; his
brother was named Joktan.
²⁰Joktan was the father of
Almodad, Sheleph, Hazarmaveth, Jerah, ²¹Hadoram, Uzal, Diklah,
²²Obal,*ᶜ* Abimael, Sheba,
²³Ophir, Havilah and Jobab. All these were sons of
Joktan. Ge 10:21-31; 11:10-27

²⁴Shem, Arphaxad,*ᵈ* Shelah,
²⁵Eber, Peleg, Reu,
²⁶Serug, Nahor, Terah
²⁷and Abram (that is, Abraham).

The Family of Abraham
²⁸The sons of Abraham:
Isaac and Ishmael.

Descendants of Hagar
1:29-31pp — Ge 25:12-16

²⁹These were their descendants:
Nebaioth the firstborn of
Ishmael, Kedar, Adbeel,
Mibsam, ³⁰Mishma, Dumah, Massa, Hadad, Tema,
³¹Jetur, Naphish and Kedemah. These were the sons
of Ishmael. Ge 25:12-16

Descendants of Keturah
1:32-33pp — Ge 25:1-4

³²The sons born to Keturah,
Abraham's concubine:
Zimran, Jokshan, Medan,
Midian, Ishbak and Shuah.
The sons of Jokshan:
Sheba and Dedan. Ge 10:7
³³The sons of Midian:
Ephah, Epher, Hanok, Abida and Eldaah.
All these were descendants
of Keturah. Ge 25:1-4

Descendants of Sarah
1:35-37pp — Ge 36:10-14

³⁴Abraham was the father of
Isaac. Ge 21:2-3; Mt 1:2; Ac 7:8
The sons of Isaac:
Esau and Israel. Ge 17:5; 25:25

ᵃ 17 One Hebrew manuscript and some Septuagint manuscripts (see also Gen. 10:23); most Hebrew manuscripts do not have this line. *ᵇ 19 Peleg* means *division.* *ᶜ 22* Some Hebrew manuscripts and Syriac (see also Gen. 10:28); most Hebrew manuscripts *Ebal* *ᵈ 24* Hebrew; some Septuagint manuscripts *Arphaxad, Cainan* (see also note at Gen. 11:10)

Esau's Sons

³⁵The sons of Esau: Ge 36:19
Eliphaz, Reuel, Jeush, Jalam and Korah. Ge 36:4
³⁶The sons of Eliphaz:
Teman, Omar, Zepho,[a]
Gatam and Kenaz;
by Timna: Amalek.[b] Ex 17:14
³⁷The sons of Reuel: Ge 36:17
Nahath, Zerah, Shammah
and Mizzah. Ge 36:10-14

The People of Seir in Edom
1:38-42pp — Ge 36:20-28

³⁸The sons of Seir:
Lotan, Shobal, Zibeon,
Anah, Dishon, Ezer and
Dishan.
³⁹The sons of Lotan:
Hori and Homam. Timna
was Lotan's sister.
⁴⁰The sons of Shobal:
Alvan,[c] Manahath, Ebal,
Shepho and Onam.
The sons of Zibeon:
Aiah and Anah. Ge 36:2
⁴¹The son of Anah:
Dishon.
The sons of Dishon:
Hemdan,[d] Eshban, Ithran
and Keran.
⁴²The sons of Ezer:
Bilhan, Zaavan and Akan.[e]
The sons of Dishan[f]:
Uz and Aran. Ge 36:20-28

The Rulers of Edom
1:43-54pp — Ge 36:31-43

⁴³These were the kings who
reigned in Edom before any
Israelite king reigned:
Bela son of Beor, whose
city was named Dinhabah.
⁴⁴When Bela died, Jobab son
of Zerah from Bozrah succeeded him as king.
⁴⁵When Jobab died, Husham
from the land of the Temanites succeeded him as
king. Ge 36:11
⁴⁶When Husham died, Hadad
son of Bedad, who defeated Midian in the country of Moab, succeeded
him as king. His city was
named Avith.
⁴⁷When Hadad died, Samlah
from Masrekah succeeded him as king.
⁴⁸When Samlah died, Shaul from Rehoboth on the
river[g] succeeded him as
king.
⁴⁹When Shaul died, Baal-Hanan son of Akbor succeeded him as king.
⁵⁰When Baal-Hanan died,
Hadad succeeded him as
king. His city was named

---

[a] *36* Many Hebrew manuscripts, some Septuagint manuscripts and Syriac (see also Gen. 36:11); most Hebrew manuscripts *Zephi*   [b] *36* Some Septuagint manuscripts (see also Gen. 36:12); Hebrew *Gatam, Kenaz, Timna and Amalek*   [c] *40* Many Hebrew manuscripts and some Septuagint manuscripts (see also Gen. 36:23); most Hebrew manuscripts *Alian*   [d] *41* Many Hebrew manuscripts and some Septuagint manuscripts (see also Gen. 36:26); most Hebrew manuscripts *Hamran*   [e] *42* Many Hebrew and Septuagint manuscripts (see also Gen. 36:27); most Hebrew manuscripts *Zaavan, Jaakan*   [f] *42* See Gen. 36:28; Hebrew *Dishon,* a variant of *Dishan*   [g] *48* Possibly the Euphrates

Pau,^a and his wife's name was Mehetabel daughter of Matred, the daughter of Me-Zahab. ⁵¹Hadad also died.

The chiefs of Edom were:
Timna, Alvah, Jetheth, ⁵²Oholibamah, Elah, Pinon, ⁵³Kenaz, Teman, Mibzar, ⁵⁴Magdiel and Iram. These were the chiefs of Edom. Ge 36:31-43

Israel's Sons
2:1-2pp — Ge 35:23-26

2 These were the sons of Israel:
Reuben, Simeon, Levi, Judah, Issachar, Zebulun, ²Dan, Joseph, Benjamin, Naphtali, Gad and Asher.

Judah
2:5-15pp — Ru 4:18-22; Mt 1:3-6
To Hezron's Sons

³The sons of Judah: Ge 38:2-10
Er, Onan and Shelah. These three were born to him by a Canaanite woman, the daughter of Shua. Er, Judah's firstborn, was wicked in the LORD's sight; so the LORD put him to death. ⁴Judah's daughter-in-law Tamar bore Perez and Ze-

rah to Judah. He had five sons in all. Ge 38:11-30

⁵The sons of Perez: Ge 46:12
Hezron and Hamul. Nu 26:21
⁶The sons of Zerah:
Zimri, Ethan, Heman, Kalkol and Darda^b—five in all.
⁷The son of Karmi:
Achar,^c who brought trouble on Israel by violating the ban on taking devoted things.^d Jos 6:18; 7:1
⁸The son of Ethan:
Azariah.
⁹The sons born to Hezron were:
Jerahmeel, Ram and Caleb.^e Nu 26:21

From Ram Son of Hezron
¹⁰Ram was the father of Lk 3:32
Amminadab, and Amminadab the father of Nahshon, the leader of the people of Judah. ¹¹Nahshon was the father of Salmon,^f Salmon the father of Boaz, ¹²Boaz the father of Obed and Obed the father of Jesse. Ru 2:1; 4:17
¹³Jesse was the father of Ru 4:17
Eliab his firstborn; the second son was Abinadab, the third Shimea, ¹⁴the fourth

^a 50 Many Hebrew manuscripts, some Septuagint manuscripts, Vulgate and Syriac (see also Gen. 36:39); most Hebrew manuscripts *Pai*   ^b 6 Many Hebrew manuscripts, some Septuagint manuscripts and Syriac (see also 1 Kings 4:31); most Hebrew manuscripts *Dara*   ^c 7 *Achar* means *trouble*; *Achar* is called *Achan* in Joshua.   ^d 7 The Hebrew term refers to the irrevocable giving over of things or persons to the LORD, often by totally destroying them.   ^e 9 Hebrew *Kelubai*, a variant of *Caleb*   ^f 11 Septuagint (see also Ruth 4:21); Hebrew *Salma*

Nethanel, the fifth Raddai, ¹⁵the sixth Ozem and the seventh David. ¹⁶Their sisters were Zeruiah and Abigail. Zeruiah's three sons were Abishai, Joab and Asahel. ¹⁷Abigail was the mother of Amasa, whose father was Jether the Ishmaelite. Ru 4:18-22; Mt 1:3-6

Caleb Son of Hezron

¹⁸Caleb son of Hezron had children by his wife Azubah (and by Jerioth). These were her sons: Jesher, Shobab and Ardon. ¹⁹When Azubah died, Caleb married Ephrath, who bore him Hur. ²⁰Hur was the father of Uri, and Uri the father of Bezalel. ver 42,50

²¹Later, Hezron, when he was sixty years old, married the daughter of Makir the father of Gilead. He made love to her, and she bore him Segub. ²²Segub was the father of Jair, who controlled twenty-three towns in Gilead. ²³(But Geshur and Aram captured Havvoth Jair,ᵃ as well as Kenath with its surrounding settlements—sixty towns.) All these were descendants of Makir the father of Gilead. Nu 32:41; Dt 3:14; Jos 13:30

²⁴After Hezron died in Caleb Ephrathah, Abijah the wife of Hezron bore him Ashhur the fatherᵇ of Tekoa. 1Ch 4:5

Jerahmeel Son of Hezron

²⁵The sons of Jerahmeel the firstborn of Hezron:
Ram his firstborn, Bunah, Oren, Ozem andᶜ Ahijah. ²⁶Jerahmeel had another wife, whose name was Atarah; she was the mother of Onam.

²⁷The sons of Ram the firstborn of Jerahmeel:
Maaz, Jamin and Eker.
²⁸The sons of Onam:
Shammai and Jada.
The sons of Shammai:
Nadab and Abishur.
²⁹Abishur's wife was named Abihail, who bore him Ahban and Molid.
³⁰The sons of Nadab:
Seled and Appaim. Seled died without children.
³¹The son of Appaim:
Ishi, who was the father of Sheshan.
Sheshan was the father of Ahlai.
³²The sons of Jada, Shammai's brother:
Jether and Jonathan. Jether died without children.
³³The sons of Jonathan:
Peleth and Zaza.

ᵃ 23 Or captured the settlements of Jair; also in verses 42, 45, 49-52 and possibly elsewhere.   ᵇ 24 Father may mean civic leader or military leader.   ᶜ 25 Or Oren and Ozem, by

These were the descendants of Jerahmeel.

³⁴Sheshan had no sons—only daughters.

He had an Egyptian servant named Jarha. ³⁵Sheshan gave his daughter in marriage to his servant Jarha, and she bore him Attai.

³⁶Attai was the father of Nathan,

Nathan the father of Zabad,   1Ch 11:41

³⁷Zabad the father of Ephlal,
Ephlal the father of Obed,

³⁸Obed the father of Jehu,
Jehu the father of Azariah,

³⁹Azariah the father of Helez,

Helez the father of Eleasah,

⁴⁰Eleasah the father of Sismai,

Sismai the father of Shallum,

⁴¹Shallum the father of Jekamiah,

and Jekamiah the father of Elishama.

The Clans of Caleb

⁴²The sons of Caleb the brother of Jerahmeel: ver 19

Mesha his firstborn, who was the father of Ziph, and his son Mareshah,ᵃ who was the father of Hebron.

⁴³The sons of Hebron:

Korah, Tappuah, Rekem and Shema. ⁴⁴Shema was the father of Raham, and Raham the father of Jorkeam. Rekem was the father of Shammai. ⁴⁵The son of Shammai was Maon, and Maon was the father of Beth Zur.   Jos 15:55,58

⁴⁶Caleb's concubine Ephah was the mother of Haran, Moza and Gazez. Haran was the father of Gazez.

⁴⁷The sons of Jahdai:

Regem, Jotham, Geshan, Pelet, Ephah and Shaaph.

⁴⁸Caleb's concubine Maakah was the mother of Sheber and Tirhanah. ⁴⁹She also gave birth to Shaaph the father of Madmannah and to Sheva the father of Makbenah and Gibea. Caleb's daughter was Aksah.

⁵⁰These were the descendants of Caleb.   Jos 15:16,31

The sons of Hur the firstborn of Ephrathah: 1Ch 4:4

Shobal the father of Kiriath Jearim, ⁵¹Salma the father of Bethlehem, and Hareph the father of Beth Gader.   ver 19

⁵²The descendants of Shobal the father of Kiriath Jearim were:

Haroeh, half the Manahathites, ⁵³and the clans of Kiriath Jearim: the Ithrites, Puthites, Shumathites and

---

ᵃ 42 The meaning of the Hebrew for this phrase is uncertain.

Mishraites. From these descended the Zorathites and Eshtaolites. 2Sa 23:38

54 The descendants of Salma:

Bethlehem, the Netophathites, Atroth Beth Joab, half the Manahathites, the Zorites, 55 and the clans of scribes*a* who lived at Jabez: the Tirathites, Shimeathites and Sucathites. These are the Kenites who came from Hammath, the father of the Rekabites.*b* Jdg 1:16; Jer 35:2-19

The Sons of David

3:1-4pp — 2Sa 3:2-5
3:5-8pp — 2Sa 5:14-16; 1Ch 14:4-7

3 These were the sons of David born to him in Hebron:

The firstborn was Amnon the son of Ahinoam of Jezreel; Jos 15:56

the second, Daniel the son of Abigail of Carmel;

2 the third, Absalom the son of Maakah daughter of Talmai king of Geshur; the fourth, Adonijah the son of Haggith; 1Ki 2:22

3 the fifth, Shephatiah the son of Abital; and the sixth, Ithream, by his wife Eglah.

4 These six were born to David in Hebron, where he reigned seven years and six months. 2Sa 3:2-5

David reigned in Jerusalem thirty-three years, 5 and these were the children born to him there:

Shammua,*c* Shobab, Nathan and Solomon. These four were by Bathsheba*d* daughter of Ammiel. 6 There were also Ibhar, Elishua,*e* Eliphelet, 7 Nogah, Nepheg, Japhia, 8 Elishama, Eliada and Eliphelet — nine in all. 9 All these were the sons of David, besides his sons by his concubines. And Tamar was their sister. 2Sa 5:14-16; 1Ch 14:4-7

The Kings of Judah

10 Solomon's son was Rehoboam, 1Ki 11:43; 14:21-31
Abijah his son,
Asa his son,
Jehoshaphat his son, 2Ch 17:1
11 Jehoram*f* his son, 2Ki 8:16-24
Ahaziah his son, 2Ch 22:1-10
Joash his son, 2Ki 11:1-12:21
12 Amaziah his son, 2Ki 14:1-22
Azariah his son,
Jotham his son, Isa 1:1; Hos 1:1
13 Ahaz his son, Isa 7:1
Hezekiah his son, Jer 26:19
Manasseh his son, 2Ch 33:1
14 Amon his son, 2Ki 21:19-26
Josiah his son. Jer 1:2; 25:3

---

a 55 Or *of the Sopherites*   *b* 55 Or *father of Beth Rekab*   *c* 5 Hebrew *Shimea,* a variant of *Shammua*   *d* 5 One Hebrew manuscript and Vulgate (see also Septuagint and 2 Samuel 11:3); most Hebrew manuscripts *Bathshua*   *e* 6 Two Hebrew manuscripts (see also 2 Samuel 5:15 and 1 Chron. 14:5); most Hebrew manuscripts *Elishama*   *f* 11 Hebrew *Joram,* a variant of *Jehoram*

¹⁵The sons of Josiah:
Johanan the firstborn,
Jehoiakim the second son,
Zedekiah the third, Jer 37:1
Shallum the fourth. 2Ki 23:31
¹⁶The successors of Jehoiakim:
Jehoiachin*a* his son, Mt 1:11
and Zedekiah. 2Ki 24:18

The Royal Line After the Exile

¹⁷The descendants of Jehoia-
chin the captive:
Shealtiel his son, ¹⁸Malki-
ram, Pedaiah, Shenazzar,
Jekamiah, Hoshama and
Nedabiah. Ezr 1:8; 5:14; Jer 22:30
¹⁹The sons of Pedaiah:
Zerubbabel and Shimei.
The sons of Zerubbabel:
Meshullam and Hananiah.
Shelomith was their sister.
²⁰There were also five oth-
ers:
Hashubah, Ohel, Bereki-
ah, Hasadiah and Jushab-
Hesed.
²¹The descendants of Hanani-
ah:
Pelatiah and Jeshaiah, and
the sons of Rephaiah, of
Arnan, of Obadiah and of
Shekaniah.
²²The descendants of Sheka-
niah:
Shemaiah and his sons:
Hattush, Igal, Bariah, Ne-
ariah and Shaphat — six in
all. Ezr 8:2-3

²³The sons of Neariah:
Elioenai, Hizkiah and Az-
rikam — three in all.
²⁴The sons of Elioenai:
Hodaviah, Eliashib, Pela-
iah, Akkub, Johanan, De-
laiah and Anani — seven
in all.

Other Clans of Judah

4 The descendants of Judah:
Perez, Hezron, Karmi, Hur
and Shobal. Nu 26:21
²Reaiah son of Shobal was
the father of Jahath, and
Jahath the father of Ahu-
mai and Lahad. These
were the clans of the Zo-
rathites.
³These were the sons*b* of
Etam:
Jezreel, Ishma and Idbash.
Their sister was named
Hazzelelponi. ⁴Penuel was
the father of Gedor, and
Ezer the father of Hushah.
These were the descendants
of Hur, the firstborn of
Ephrathah and father*c* of
Bethlehem. Ru 1:19; 1Ch 2:50
⁵Ashhur the father of Tekoa
had two wives, Helah and
Naarah. 1Ch 2:24
⁶Naarah bore him Ahuzzam,
Hepher, Temeni and Haa-
hashtari. These were the
descendants of Naarah.
⁷The sons of Helah:

---

a 16 Hebrew *Jeconiah,* a variant of *Jehoiachin;* also in verse 17   *b* 3 Some Septuagint
manuscripts (see also Vulgate); Hebrew *father*   *c* 4 *Father* may mean *civic leader* or
military leader; also in verses 12, 14, 17, 18 and possibly elsewhere.

Zereth, Zohar, Ethnan, [8] and Koz, who was the father of Anub and Hazzobebah and of the clans of Aharhel son of Harum.

[9] Jabez was more honorable than his brothers. His mother had named him Jabez,[a] saying, "I gave birth to him in pain." [10] Jabez cried out to the God of Israel, "Oh, that you would bless me and enlarge my territory! Let your hand be with me, and keep me from harm so that I will be free from pain." And God granted his request.

[11] Kelub, Shuhah's brother, was the father of Mehir, who was the father of Eshton. [12] Eshton was the father of Beth Rapha, Paseah and Tehinnah the father of Ir Nahash.[b] These were the men of Rekah.

[13] The sons of Kenaz:
Othniel and Seraiah. Jos 15:17
The sons of Othniel:
Hathath and Meonothai.[c]
[14] Meonothai was the father of Ophrah.
Seraiah was the father of Joab,
the father of Ge Harashim.[d] It was called this because its people were skilled workers.

[15] The sons of Caleb son of Jephunneh:
Iru, Elah and Naam.
The son of Elah:
Kenaz.
[16] The sons of Jehallelel:
Ziph, Ziphah, Tiria and Asarel.
[17] The sons of Ezrah:
Jether, Mered, Epher and Jalon. One of Mered's wives gave birth to Miriam, Shammai and Ishbah the father of Eshtemoa. [18] (His wife from the tribe of Judah gave birth to Jered the father of Gedor, Heber the father of Soko, and Jekuthiel the father of Zanoah.) These were the children of Pharaoh's daughter Bithiah, whom Mered had married. Ex 15:20; Jos 15:34
[19] The sons of Hodiah's wife, the sister of Naham:
the father of Keilah the Garmite, and Eshtemoa the Maakathite. Dt 3:14; Jos 15:44
[20] The sons of Shimon:
Amnon, Rinnah, Ben-Hanan and Tilon.
The descendants of Ishi:
Zoheth and Ben-Zoheth.
[21] The sons of Shelah son of Judah:
Er the father of Lekah, Laadah the father of Mareshah and the clans of the linen

---

[a] 9 *Jabez* sounds like the Hebrew for *pain*.   [b] 12 Or *of the city of Nahash*   [c] 13 Some Septuagint manuscripts and Vulgate; Hebrew does not have *and Meonothai*.
[d] 14 *Ge Harashim* means *valley of skilled workers*.

workers at Beth Ashbea, [22] Jokim, the men of Kozeba, and Joash and Saraph, who ruled in Moab and Jashubi Lehem. (These records are from ancient times.) [23] They were the potters who lived at Netaim and Gederah; they stayed there and worked for the king. Ge 38:5

Simeon

4:28-33pp — Jos 19:2-10

[24] The descendants of Simeon: Nemuel, Jamin, Jarib, Zerah and Shaul; Nu 26:12

[25] Shallum was Shaul's son, Mibsam his son and Mishma his son.

[26] The descendants of Mishma: Hammuel his son, Zakkur his son and Shimei his son.

[27] Shimei had sixteen sons and six daughters, but his brothers did not have many children; so their entire clan did not become as numerous as the people of Judah. [28] They lived in Beersheba, Moladah, Hazar Shual, [29] Bilhah, Ezem, Tolad, [30] Bethuel, Hormah, Ziklag, [31] Beth Markaboth, Hazar Susim, Beth Biri and Shaaraim. These were their towns until the reign of David. [32] Their surrounding villages were Etam, Ain, Rimmon, Token and Ashan — five towns — [33] and all the villages around these towns as far as Baalath.[a] These were their settlements. And they kept a genealogical record. Jos 19:2-10

[34] Meshobab, Jamlech, Joshah son of Amaziah, [35] Joel, Jehu son of Joshibiah, the son of Seraiah, the son of Asiel, [36] also Elioenai, Jaakobah, Jeshohaiah, Asaiah, Adiel, Jesimiel, Benaiah, [37] and Ziza son of Shiphi, the son of Allon, the son of Jedaiah, the son of Shimri, the son of Shemaiah.

[38] The men listed above by name were leaders of their clans. Their families increased greatly, [39] and they went to the outskirts of Gedor to the east of the valley in search of pasture for their flocks. [40] They found rich, good pasture, and the land was spacious, peaceful and quiet. Some Hamites had lived there formerly. Jdg 18:7-10

[41] The men whose names were listed came in the days of Hezekiah king of Judah. They attacked the Hamites in their dwellings and also the Meunites who were there and completely destroyed[b] them, as is evident to this day. Then they settled in their place, because there was pasture for their flocks. [42] And five hundred of these Simeonites, led by

---

a 33 Some Septuagint manuscripts (see also Joshua 19:8); Hebrew *Baal*   *b 41* The Hebrew term refers to the irrevocable giving over of things or persons to the LORD, often by totally destroying them.

Pelatiah, Neariah, Rephaiah and Uzziel, the sons of Ishi, invaded the hill country of Seir. ⁴³They killed the remaining Amalekites who had escaped, and they have lived there to this day. 1Sa 15:8; 30:17

Reuben

5 The sons of Reuben the firstborn of Israel (he was the firstborn, but when he defiled his father's marriage bed, his rights as firstborn were given to the sons of Joseph son of Israel; so he could not be listed in the genealogical record in accordance with his birthright, ²and though Judah was the strongest of his brothers and a ruler came from him, the rights of the firstborn belonged to Joseph) — ³the sons of Reuben the firstborn of Israel: Ps 60:7; Mic 5:2; Mt 2:6

Hanok, Pallu, Hezron and Karmi. Nu 26:5

⁴The descendants of Joel:
Shemaiah his son, Gog his son,
Shimei his son, ⁵Micah his son,
Reaiah his son, Baal his son,
⁶and Beerah his son, whom Tiglath-Pileser*a* king of Assyria took into exile. Beerah was a leader of the Reubenites. 2Ki 15:19; 16:10
⁷Their relatives by clans, listed according to their genealogical records: ver 17

Jeiel the chief, Zechariah, ⁸and Bela son of Azaz, the son of Shema, the son of Joel. They settled in the area from Aroer to Nebo and Baal Meon. ⁹To the east they occupied the land up to the edge of the desert that extends to the Euphrates River, because their livestock had increased in Gilead. Nu 32:26; Jos 22:9

¹⁰During Saul's reign they waged war against the Hagrites, who were defeated at their hands; they occupied the dwellings of the Hagrites throughout the entire region east of Gilead. ver 18-21

Gad

¹¹The Gadites lived next to them in Bashan, as far as Salekah: Jos 13:11,24-28
¹²Joel was the chief, Shapham the second, then Janai and Shaphat, in Bashan.
¹³Their relatives, by families, were:
Michael, Meshullam, Sheba, Jorai, Jakan, Zia and Eber — seven in all.
¹⁴These were the sons of Abihail son of Huri, the son of Jaroah, the son of Gilead, the son of Michael, the son of Jeshishai, the son of Jahdo, the son of Buz.
¹⁵Ahi son of Abdiel, the son

a 6 Hebrew *Tilgath-Pilneser*, a variant of *Tiglath-Pileser*; also in verse 26 of Guni, was head of their family.

¹⁶ The Gadites lived in Gilead, in Bashan and its outlying villages, and on all the pasturelands of Sharon as far as they extended.

¹⁷ All these were entered in the genealogical records during the reigns of Jotham king of Judah and Jeroboam king of Israel.

¹⁸ The Reubenites, the Gadites and the half-tribe of Manasseh had 44,760 men ready for military service — able-bodied men who could handle shield and sword, who could use a bow, and who were trained for battle. ¹⁹ They waged war against the Hagrites, Jetur, Naphish and Nodab. ²⁰ They were helped in fighting them, and God delivered the Hagrites and all their allies into their hands, because they cried out to him during the battle. He answered their prayers, because they trusted in him. ²¹ They seized the livestock of the Hagrites — fifty thousand camels, two hundred fifty thousand sheep and two thousand donkeys. They also took one hundred thousand people captive, ²² and many others fell slain, because the battle was God's. And they occupied the land until the exile. 2Ki 15:29; 17:6; Da 6:23

The Half-Tribe of Manasseh

²³ The people of the half-tribe of Manasseh were numerous; they settled in the land from Bashan to Baal Hermon, that is, to Senir (Mount Hermon). Dt 3:8-9; SS 4:8

²⁴ These were the heads of their families: Epher, Ishi, Eliel, Azriel, Jeremiah, Hodaviah and Jahdiel. They were brave warriors, famous men, and heads of their families. ²⁵ But they were unfaithful to the God of their ancestors and prostituted themselves to the gods of the peoples of the land, whom God had destroyed before them. ²⁶ So the God of Israel stirred up the spirit of Pul king of Assyria (that is, Tiglath-Pileser king of Assyria), who took the Reubenites, the Gadites and the half-tribe of Manasseh into exile. He took them to Halah, Habor, Hara and the river of Gozan, where they are to this day. 2Ki 15:29; 17:6; 18:11

Levi

6 *ᵃ* The sons of Levi: Ge 46:11
  Gershon, Kohath and Merari.
² The sons of Kohath:
  Amram, Izhar, Hebron and Uzziel.
³ The children of Amram:
  Aaron, Moses and Miriam.
  The sons of Aaron:
  Nadab, Abihu, Eleazar and Ithamar. Lev 10:1
⁴ Eleazar was the father of Phinehas,
  Phinehas the father of Abishua,

ᵃ In Hebrew texts 6:1-15 is numbered 5:27-41, and 6:16-81 is numbered 6:1-66.

⁵Abishua the father of Bukki,
Bukki the father of Uzzi,
⁶Uzzi the father of Zerahiah,
Zerahiah the father of Meraioth,
⁷Meraioth the father of Amariah,
Amariah the father of Ahitub,
⁸Ahitub the father of Zadok,   2Sa 8:17; 15:27; Ezr 7:2
Zadok the father of Ahimaaz,
⁹Ahimaaz the father of Azariah,
Azariah the father of Johanan,
¹⁰Johanan the father of Azariah (it was he who served as priest in the temple Solomon built in Jerusalem),   1Ki 6:1; 2Ch 3:1; 26:17-18
¹¹Azariah the father of Amariah,
Amariah the father of Ahitub,
¹²Ahitub the father of Zadok,
Zadok the father of Shallum,
¹³Shallum the father of Hilkiah,   2Ki 22:1-20; 2Ch 34:9; 35:8
Hilkiah the father of Azariah,
¹⁴Azariah the father of Seraiah,
and Seraiah the father of Jozadak.ᵃ   Ezr 2:2; Ne 11:11
¹⁵Jozadak was deported when the Lᴏʀᴅ sent Judah and Jerusalem into exile by the hand of Nebuchadnezzar.   2Ki 25:18; Hag 1:1,14; Zec 6:11

¹⁶The sons of Levi: Ge 29:34
Gershon,ᵇ Kohath and Merari.   Nu 26:57
¹⁷These are the names of the sons of Gershon:
Libni and Shimei.
¹⁸The sons of Kohath:
Amram, Izhar, Hebron and Uzziel.
¹⁹The sons of Merari: 1Ch 23:21
Mahli and Mushi.
These are the clans of the Levites listed according to their fathers:
²⁰Of Gershon:
Libni his son, Jahath his son,
Zimmah his son, ²¹Joah his son,
Iddo his son, Zerah his son and Jeatherai his son.
²²The descendants of Kohath:
Amminadab his son, Korah his son,   Ex 6:24
Assir his son, ²³Elkanah his son,
Ebiasaph his son, Assir his son,
²⁴Tahath his son, Uriel his son,   1Ch 15:5
Uzziah his son and Shaul his son.
²⁵The descendants of Elkanah:
Amasai, Ahimoth,

²⁶ Elkanah his son,ª Zophai his son,
Nahath his son, ²⁷ Eliab his son,
Jeroham his son, Elkanah his son ¹Sa 1:1
and Samuel his son.ᵇ ¹Sa 1:20

²⁸ The sons of Samuel:
Joelᶜ the firstborn ver 33
and Abijah the second son.

²⁹ The descendants of Merari:
Mahli, Libni his son,
Shimei his son, Uzzah his son,

³⁰ Shimea his son, Haggiah his son
and Asaiah his son.

The Temple Musicians
6:54-80pp — Jos 21:4-39

³¹ These are the men David put in charge of the music in the house of the Lord after the ark came to rest there. ³² They ministered with music before the tabernacle, the tent of meeting, until Solomon built the temple of the Lord in Jerusalem. They performed their duties according to the regulations laid down for them. 1Ch 15:19; Ezr 3:10; Ps 68:25

³³ Here are the men who served, together with their sons:

From the Kohathites:
Heman, the musician,
the son of Joel, the son of Samuel,

³⁴ the son of Elkanah, the son of Jeroham, ¹Sa 1:1
the son of Eliel, the son of Toah,

³⁵ the son of Zuph, the son of Elkanah,
the son of Mahath, the son of Amasai,

³⁶ the son of Elkanah, the son of Joel,
the son of Azariah, the son of Zephaniah,

³⁷ the son of Tahath, the son of Assir,
the son of Ebiasaph, the son of Korah, Ex 6:24

³⁸ the son of Izhar, the son of Kohath, Ex 6:21
the son of Levi, the son of Israel;

³⁹ and Heman's associate Asaph, who served at his right hand: 1Ch 25:1,9; 2Ch 29:13
Asaph son of Berekiah, the son of Shimea, 1Ch 15:17

⁴⁰ the son of Michael, the son of Baaseiah,ᵈ
the son of Malkijah, ⁴¹ the son of Ethni,
the son of Zerah, the son of Adaiah,

⁴² the son of Ethan, the son of Zimmah,

ª 26 Some Hebrew manuscripts, Septuagint and Syriac; most Hebrew manuscripts *Ahimoth* ²⁶*and Elkanah. The sons of Elkanah:*   ᵇ 27 Some Septuagint manuscripts (see also 1 Samuel 1:19,20 and 1 Chron. 6:33,34); Hebrew does not have *and Samuel his son.*   ᶜ 28 Some Septuagint manuscripts and Syriac (see also 1 Samuel 8:2 and 1 Chron. 6:33); Hebrew does not have *Joel.*   ᵈ 40 Most Hebrew manuscripts; some Hebrew manuscripts, one Septuagint manuscript and Syriac *Maaseiah*

the son of Shimei, [43]the son of Jahath,
the son of Gershon, the son of Levi;

[44]and from their associates, the Merarites, at his left hand:
Ethan son of Kishi, the son of Abdi,
the son of Malluk, [45]the son of Hashabiah,
the son of Amaziah, the son of Hilkiah,
[46]the son of Amzi, the son of Bani,
the son of Shemer, [47]the son of Mahli,
the son of Mushi, the son of Merari,
the son of Levi.

[48]Their fellow Levites were assigned to all the other duties of the tabernacle, the house of God. [49]But Aaron and his descendants were the ones who presented offerings on the altar of burnt offering and on the altar of incense in connection with all that was done in the Most Holy Place, making atonement for Israel, in accordance with all that Moses the servant of God had commanded. Ex 27:1-8; 30:1-7,10; 1Ch 23:32

[50]These were the descendants of Aaron:
Eleazar his son, Phinehas his son,
Abishua his son, [51]Bukki his son,
Uzzi his son, Zerahiah his son,
[52]Meraioth his son, Amariah his son,
Ahitub his son, [53]Zadok his son 2Sa 8:17
and Ahimaaz his son.

[54]These were the locations of their settlements allotted as their territory (they were assigned to the descendants of Aaron who were from the Kohathite clan, because the first lot was for them): Nu 31:10
[55]They were given Hebron in Judah with its surrounding pasturelands. [56]But the fields and villages around the city were given to Caleb son of Jephunneh. Jos 14:13
[57]So the descendants of Aaron were given Hebron (a city of refuge), and Libnah,[a] Jattir, Eshtemoa, [58]Hilen, Debir, [59]Ashan, Juttah[b] and Beth Shemesh, together with their pasturelands. [60]And from the tribe of Benjamin they were given Gibeon,[c] Geba, Alemeth and Anathoth, together with their pasturelands. Jos 10:3; Jer 1:1
The total number of towns distributed among the Ko-

---

[a] 57 See Joshua 21:13; Hebrew *given the cities of refuge: Hebron, Libnah.*   [b] 59 Syriac (see also Septuagint and Joshua 21:16); Hebrew does not have *Juttah.*   [c] 60 See Joshua 21:17; Hebrew does not have *Gibeon.*

hathite clans came to thirteen.

⁶¹ The rest of Kohath's descendants were allotted ten towns from the clans of half the tribe of Manasseh.

⁶² The descendants of Gershon, clan by clan, were allotted thirteen towns from the tribes of Issachar, Asher and Naphtali, and from the part of the tribe of Manasseh that is in Bashan.

⁶³ The descendants of Merari, clan by clan, were allotted twelve towns from the tribes of Reuben, Gad and Zebulun.

⁶⁴ So the Israelites gave the Levites these towns and their pasturelands. ⁶⁵ From the tribes of Judah, Simeon and Benjamin they allotted the previously named towns.   Nu 35:1-8; Jos 21:3,41

⁶⁶ Some of the Kohathite clans were given as their territory towns from the tribe of Ephraim.

⁶⁷ In the hill country of Ephraim they were given Shechem (a city of refuge), and Gezer,ᵃ ⁶⁸ Jokmeam, Beth Horon, ⁶⁹ Aijalon and Gath Rimmon, together with their pasturelands.   Jos 10:10,12

⁷⁰ And from half the tribe of Manasseh the Israelites gave Aner and Bileam, together with their pasturelands, to the rest of the Kohathite clans.

⁷¹ The Gershonites received the following: 1Ch 23:7

From the clan of the half-tribe of Manasseh they received Golan in Bashan and also Ashtaroth, together with their pasturelands;   Jos 20:8

⁷² from the tribe of Issachar they received Kedesh, Daberath, ⁷³ Ramoth and Anem, together with their pasturelands;   Jos 19:12

⁷⁴ from the tribe of Asher they received Mashal, Abdon, ⁷⁵ Hukok and Rehob, together with their pasturelands;   Nu 13:21

⁷⁶ and from the tribe of Naphtali they received Kedesh in Galilee, Hammon and Kiriathaim, together with their pasturelands.   Nu 32:37

⁷⁷ The Merarites (the rest of the Levites) received the following:

From the tribe of Zebulun they received Jokneam, Kartah,ᵇ Rimmono and Tabor, together with their pasturelands;

⁷⁸ from the tribe of Reuben across the Jordan east of Jericho they received Bezer in the wilderness, Jahzah, ⁷⁹ Kedemoth and Mephaath,

---

ᵃ 67 See Joshua 21:21; Hebrew *given the cities of refuge: Shechem, Gezer.*
ᵇ 77 See Septuagint and Joshua 21:34; Hebrew does not have *Jokneam, Kartah.*

together with their pasturelands; Dt 2:26; Jos 20:8
[80] and from the tribe of Gad they received Ramoth in Gilead, Mahanaim, [81] Heshbon and Jazer, together with their pasturelands. Jos 21:4-39; 2Ch 11:14

Issachar

7 The sons of Issachar: Nu 26:23 Tola, Puah, Jashub and Shimron — four in all.
[2] The sons of Tola:
Uzzi, Rephaiah, Jeriel, Jahmai, Ibsam and Samuel — heads of their families. During the reign of David, the descendants of Tola listed as fighting men in their genealogy numbered 22,600.
[3] The son of Uzzi:
Izrahiah.
The sons of Izrahiah:
Michael, Obadiah, Joel and Ishiah. All five of them were chiefs. [4] According to their family genealogy, they had 36,000 men ready for battle, for they had many wives and children.
[5] The relatives who were fighting men belonging to all the clans of Issachar, as listed in their genealogy, were 87,000 in all.

Benjamin

[6] Three sons of Benjamin:
Bela, Beker and Jediael.
[7] The sons of Bela:
Ezbon, Uzzi, Uzziel, Jerimoth and Iri, heads of families — five in all. Their genealogical record listed 22,034 fighting men.
[8] The sons of Beker:
Zemirah, Joash, Eliezer, Elioenai, Omri, Jeremoth, Abijah, Anathoth and Alemeth. All these were the sons of Beker. [9] Their genealogical record listed the heads of families and 20,200 fighting men.
[10] The son of Jediael:
Bilhan.
The sons of Bilhan:
Jeush, Benjamin, Ehud, Kenaanah, Zethan, Tarshish and Ahishahar. [11] All these sons of Jediael were heads of families. There were 17,200 fighting men ready to go out to war.
[12] The Shuppites and Huppites were the descendants of Ir, and the Hushites[a] the descendants of Aher.

Naphtali

[13] The sons of Naphtali: Ge 30:8 Jahziel, Guni, Jezer and Shillem[b] — the descendants of Bilhah.

---

[a] 12 Or *Ir. The sons of Dan: Hushim,* (see Gen. 46:23); Hebrew does not have *The sons of Dan.*
[b] 13 Some Hebrew and Septuagint manuscripts (see also Gen. 46:24 and Num. 26:49); most Hebrew manuscripts *Shallum*

Manasseh

¹⁴The descendants of Manasseh: Ge 41:51; Jos 17:1; 1Ch 5:23

Asriel was his descendant through his Aramean concubine. She gave birth to Makir the father of Gilead. ¹⁵Makir took a wife from among the Huppites and Shuppites. His sister's name was Maakah.

Another descendant was named Zelophehad, who had only daughters. Nu 36:1-12 ¹⁶Makir's wife Maakah gave birth to a son and named him Peresh. His brother was named Sheresh, and his sons were Ulam and Rakem.

¹⁷The son of Ulam:

Bedan.

These were the sons of Gilead son of Makir, the son of Manasseh. ¹⁸His sister Hammoleketh gave birth to Ishhod, Abiezer and Mahlah. 1Sa 12:11; Jos 17:2

¹⁹The sons of Shemida were:

Ahian, Shechem, Likhi and Aniam.

Ephraim

²⁰The descendants of Ephraim: Nu 1:33; 26:35

Shuthelah, Bered his son, Tahath his son, Eleadah his son,

Tahath his son, ²¹Zabad his son

and Shuthelah his son.

Ezer and Elead were killed by the native-born men of Gath, when they went down to seize their livestock. ²²Their father Ephraim mourned for them many days, and his relatives came to comfort him. ²³Then he made love to his wife again, and she became pregnant and gave birth to a son. He named him Beriah,ᵃ because there had been misfortune in his family. ²⁴His daughter was Sheerah, who built Lower and Upper Beth Horon as well as Uzzen Sheerah. Jos 16:3,5

²⁵Rephah was his son, Resheph his son,ᵇ

Telah his son, Tahan his son,

²⁶Ladan his son, Ammihud his son,

Elishama his son, ²⁷Nun his son

and Joshua his son.

²⁸Their lands and settlements included Bethel and its surrounding villages, Naaran to the east, Gezer and its villages to the west, and Shechem and its villages all the way to Ayyah and its villages. ²⁹Along the borders of Manasseh were Beth Shan, Taanach, Megiddo and Dor, together with their villages. The descendants of Joseph son of Israel lived in these towns. Jos 16:7; 17:11

ᵃ 23 *Beriah* sounds like the Hebrew for *misfortune*.   ᵇ 25 Some Septuagint manuscripts; Hebrew does not have *his son*.

Asher

30 The sons of Asher: Ge 46:17
Imnah, Ishvah, Ishvi and
Beriah. Their sister was
Serah. 31 The sons of Beriah:
Heber and Malkiel, who
was the father of Birzaith.
32 Heber was the father of Japhlet, Shomer and Hotham
and of their sister Shua.
33 The sons of Japhlet:
Pasak, Bimhal and Ashvath.
These were Japhlet's sons.
34 The sons of Shomer:
Ahi, Rohgah,*a* Hubbah
and Aram.
35 The sons of his brother Helem:
Zophah, Imna, Shelesh
and Amal.
36 The sons of Zophah:
Suah, Harnepher, Shual,
Beri, Imrah, 37 Bezer, Hod,
Shamma, Shilshah, Ithran*b* and Beera.
38 The sons of Jether:
Jephunneh, Pispah and
Ara.
39 The sons of Ulla:
Arah, Hanniel and Rizia.
40 All these were descendants
of Asher—heads of families,
choice men, brave warriors and
outstanding leaders. The number of men ready for battle, as
listed in their genealogy, was
26,000.

The Genealogy of Saul the Benjamite

8:28-38pp — 1Ch 9:34-44

8 Benjamin was the father of
Bela his firstborn,   Ge 46:21
Ashbel the second son,
Aharah the third,
2 Nohah the fourth and Rapha the fifth.
3 The sons of Bela were:
Addar, Gera, Abihud,*c*
4 Abishua, Naaman, Ahoah, 5 Gera, Shephuphan
and Huram.   2Sa 23:9
6 These were the descendants
of Ehud, who were heads
of families of those living
in Geba and were deported to Manahath: 1Ch 2:52
7 Naaman, Ahijah, and
Gera, who deported them
and who was the father of
Uzza and Ahihud.
8 Sons were born to Shaharaim in Moab after he had
divorced his wives Hushim and Baara. 9 By his
wife Hodesh he had Jobab,
Zibia, Mesha, Malkam,
10 Jeuz, Sakia and Mirmah.
These were his sons, heads
of families. 11 By Hushim
he had Abitub and Elpaal.
12 The sons of Elpaal:
Eber, Misham, Shemed
(who built Ono and Lod
with its surrounding villages), 13 and Beriah and
Shema, who were heads of

---

a 34 Or *of his brother Shomer: Rohgah*   *b* 37 Possibly a variant of *Jether*   *c* 3 Or *Gera the father of Ehud* families of those living in Aijalon and who drove out the inhabitants of Gath.

¹⁴Ahio, Shashak, Jeremoth, ¹⁵Zebadiah, Arad, Eder, ¹⁶Michael, Ishpah and Joha were the sons of Beriah.

¹⁷Zebadiah, Meshullam, Hizki, Heber, ¹⁸Ishmerai, Izliah and Jobab were the sons of Elpaal.

¹⁹Jakim, Zikri, Zabdi, ²⁰Elienai, Zillethai, Eliel, ²¹Adaiah, Beraiah and Shimrath were the sons of Shimei.

²²Ishpan, Eber, Eliel, ²³Abdon, Zikri, Hanan, ²⁴Hananiah, Elam, Anthothijah, ²⁵Iphdeiah and Penuel were the sons of Shashak.

²⁶Shamsherai, Shehariah, Athaliah, ²⁷Jaareshiah, Elijah and Zikri were the sons of Jeroham.

²⁸All these were heads of families, chiefs as listed in their genealogy, and they lived in Jerusalem.

²⁹Jeiel*ᵃ* the father*ᵇ* of Gibeon lived in Gibeon.   Jos 9:3

His wife's name was Maakah, ³⁰and his firstborn son was Abdon, followed by Zur, Kish, Baal, Ner,*ᶜ* Nadab, ³¹Gedor, Ahio, Zeker ³²and Mikloth, who

was the father of Shimeah. They too lived near their relatives in Jerusalem.

³³Ner was the father of Kish, Kish the father of Saul, and Saul the father of Jonathan, Malki-Shua, Abinadab and Esh-Baal.*ᵈ*   1Sa 9:1

³⁴The son of Jonathan: 2Sa 9:12
Merib-Baal,*ᵉ* who was the father of Micah.   2Sa 4:4

³⁵The sons of Micah:
Pithon, Melek, Tarea and Ahaz.

³⁶Ahaz was the father of Jehoaddah, Jehoaddah was the father of Alemeth, Azmaveth and Zimri, and Zimri was the father of Moza. ³⁷Moza was the father of Binea; Raphah was his son, Eleasah his son and Azel his son.

³⁸Azel had six sons, and these were their names:
Azrikam, Bokeru, Ishmael, Sheariah, Obadiah and Hanan. All these were the sons of Azel.   1Ch 9:34-44

³⁹The sons of his brother Eshek:
Ulam his firstborn, Jeush the second son and Eliphelet the third. ⁴⁰The sons of Ulam were brave warriors who could handle the bow. They had many

---

ᵃ 29 Some Septuagint manuscripts (see also 9:35); Hebrew does not have *Jeiel.*   *ᵇ 29 Father* may mean *civic leader* or *military leader.*   *ᶜ 30* Some Septuagint manuscripts (see also 9:36); Hebrew does not have *Ner.*   *ᵈ 33* Also known as *Ish-Bosheth*   *ᵉ 34* Also known as *Mephibosheth* sons and grandsons — 150 in all.

All these were the descendants of Benjamin. Nu 26:38

9 All Israel was listed in the genealogies recorded in the book of the kings of Israel and Judah. They were taken captive to Babylon because of their unfaithfulness.

The People in Jerusalem

9:1-17pp — Ne 11:3-19

²Now the first to resettle on their own property in their own towns were some Israelites, priests, Levites and temple servants. 1Ch 5:25; Ezr 2:43,58,70

³Those from Judah, from Benjamin, and from Ephraim and Manasseh who lived in Jerusalem were:

⁴Uthai son of Ammihud, the son of Omri, the son of Imri, the son of Bani, a descendant of Perez son of Judah. Ge 46:12

⁵Of the Shelanites[a]:

Asaiah the firstborn and his sons.

⁶Of the Zerahites:

Jeuel.

The people from Judah numbered 690.

⁷Of the Benjamites:

Sallu son of Meshullam, the son of Hodaviah, the son of Hassenuah;

⁸Ibneiah son of Jeroham;

Elah son of Uzzi, the son of Mikri; and Meshullam son of Shephatiah, the son of Reuel, the son of Ibnijah.

⁹The people from Benjamin, as listed in their genealogy, numbered 956. All these men were heads of their families.

¹⁰Of the priests:

Jedaiah; Jehoiarib; Jakin;

¹¹Azariah son of Hilkiah, the son of Meshullam, the son of Zadok, the son of Meraioth, the son of Ahitub, the official in charge of the house of God;

¹²Adaiah son of Jeroham, the son of Pashhur, the son of Malkijah; and Maasai son of Adiel, the son of Jahzerah, the son of Meshullam, the son of Meshillemith, the son of Immer. Ezr 2:38

¹³The priests, who were heads of families, numbered 1,760. They were able men, responsible for ministering in the house of God.

¹⁴Of the Levites:

Shemaiah son of Hasshub, the son of Azrikam, the son of Hashabiah, a Merarite; ¹⁵Bakbakkar, Heresh, Galal and Mattaniah son of Mika, the son of Zikri, the son of Asaph; ¹⁶Obadiah son of Shemaiah, the son of Galal, the son of Je-

---

ᵃ 5 See Num. 26:20; Hebrew *Shilonites*.

duthun; and Berekiah son of Asa, the son of Elkanah, who lived in the villages of the Netophathites. 2Ch 20:14

¹⁷The gatekeepers: ver 22; 1Ch 26:1 Shallum, Akkub, Talmon, Ahiman and their fellow Levites, Shallum their chief ¹⁸being stationed at the King's Gate on the east, up to the present time. These were the gatekeepers belonging to the camp of the Levites. ¹⁹Shallum son of Kore, the son of Ebiasaph, the son of Korah, and his fellow gatekeepers from his family (the Korahites) were responsible for guarding the thresholds of the tent just as their ancestors had been responsible for guarding the entrance to the dwelling of the Lord. ²⁰In earlier times Phinehas son of Eleazar was the official in charge of the gatekeepers, and the Lord was with him. ²¹Zechariah son of Meshelemiah was the gatekeeper at the entrance to the tent of meeting. Ne 11:3-19; 1Ch 26:2,14

²²Altogether, those chosen to be gatekeepers at the thresholds numbered 212. They were registered by genealogy in their villages. The gatekeepers had been assigned to their positions of trust by David and Samuel the seer. ²³They and their descendants were in charge of guarding the gates of the house of the Lord — the house called the tent of meeting. ²⁴The gatekeepers were on the four sides: east, west, north and south. ²⁵Their fellow Levites in their villages had to come from time to time and share their duties for seven-day periods. ²⁶But the four principal gatekeepers, who were Levites, were entrusted with the responsibility for the rooms and treasuries in the house of God. ²⁷They would spend the night stationed around the house of God, because they had to guard it; and they had charge of the key for opening it each morning. 1Ch 23:8,30-32; 26:22

²⁸Some of them were in charge of the articles used in the temple service; they counted them when they were brought in and when they were taken out. ²⁹Others were assigned to take care of the furnishings and all the other articles of the sanctuary, as well as the special flour and wine, and the olive oil, incense and spices. ³⁰But some of the priests took care of mixing the spices. ³¹A Levite named Mattithiah, the firstborn son of Shallum the Korahite, was entrusted with the responsibility for baking the offering bread. ³²Some of the Kohathites, their fellow Levites, were in charge of preparing for every Sabbath the bread set out on the table. Lev 24:5-8; 1Ch 23:29

³³Those who were musicians, heads of Levite families, stayed in the rooms of the temple and were exempt from other duties because they were responsible for the work day and night. 1Ch 6:31; Ps 134:1

³⁴All these were heads of Levite families, chiefs as listed in their genealogy, and they lived in Jerusalem.

The Genealogy of Saul

9:34-44pp — 1Ch 8:28-38

³⁵Jeiel the father[a] of Gibeon lived in Gibeon. 1Ch 8:29

His wife's name was Maakah, ³⁶and his firstborn son was Abdon, followed by Zur, Kish, Baal, Ner, Nadab, ³⁷Gedor, Ahio, Zechariah and Mikloth. ³⁸Mikloth was the father of Shimeam. They too lived near their relatives in Jerusalem.

³⁹Ner was the father of Kish, Kish the father of Saul, and Saul the father of Jonathan, Malki-Shua, Abinadab and Esh-Baal.[b] 1Sa 9:1

⁴⁰The son of Jonathan:

Merib-Baal,[c] who was the father of Micah. 2Sa 4:4

⁴¹The sons of Micah:

Pithon, Melek, Tahrea and Ahaz.[d]

⁴²Ahaz was the father of Jadah, Jadah[e] was the father of Alemeth, Azmaveth and Zimri, and Zimri was the father of Moza. ⁴³Moza was the father of Binea; Rephaiah was his son, Eleasah his son and Azel his son.

⁴⁴Azel had six sons, and these were their names:

Azrikam, Bokeru, Ishmael, Sheariah, Obadiah and Hanan. These were the sons of Azel. 1Ch 8:28-38

Saul Takes His Life

10:1-12pp — 1Sa 31:1-13; 2Sa 1:4-12

10 Now the Philistines fought against Israel; the Israelites fled before them, and many fell dead on Mount Gilboa. ²The Philistines were in hot pursuit of Saul and his sons, and they killed his sons Jonathan, Abinadab and Malki-Shua. ³The fighting grew fierce around Saul, and when the archers overtook him, they wounded him.

⁴Saul said to his armor-bearer, "Draw your sword and run me through, or these uncircumcised fellows will come and abuse me."

But his armor-bearer was terrified and would not do it; so Saul took his own sword and fell on it. ⁵When the armor-bearer saw that Saul was dead, he too fell on

---

[a] 35 *Father* may mean *civic leader* or *military leader.*   [b] 39 Also known as *Ish-Bosheth*
[c] 40 Also known as *Mephibosheth*   [d] 41 Vulgate and Syriac (see also Septuagint and 8:35); Hebrew does not have *and Ahaz.*   [e] 42 Some Hebrew manuscripts and Septuagint (see also 8:36); most Hebrew manuscripts *Jarah, Jarah*

his sword and died. ⁶ So Saul and his three sons died, and all his house died together.

⁷ When all the Israelites in the valley saw that the army had fled and that Saul and his sons had died, they abandoned their towns and fled. And the Philistines came and occupied them.

⁸ The next day, when the Philistines came to strip the dead, they found Saul and his sons fallen on Mount Gilboa. ⁹ They stripped him and took his head and his armor, and sent messengers throughout the land of the Philistines to proclaim the news among their idols and their people. ¹⁰ They put his armor in the temple of their gods and hung up his head in the temple of Dagon. Jdg 16:23

¹¹ When all the inhabitants of Jabesh Gilead heard what the Philistines had done to Saul, ¹² all their valiant men went and took the bodies of Saul and his sons and brought them to Jabesh. Then they buried their bones under the great tree in Jabesh, and they fasted seven days. 1Sa 31:1-13; 2Sa 1:4-12

¹³ Saul died because he was unfaithful to the LORD; he did not keep the word of the LORD and even consulted a medium for guidance, ¹⁴ and did not inquire of the LORD. So the LORD put him to death and turned the kingdom over to David son of Jesse. 1Sa 15:28; 2Sa 1:1; 1Ch 12:23

David Becomes King Over Israel
11:1-3pp — 2Sa 5:1-3

11 All Israel came together to David at Hebron and said, "We are your own flesh and blood. ² In the past, even while Saul was king, you were the one who led Israel on their military campaigns. And the LORD your God said to you, 'You will shepherd my people Israel, and you will become their ruler.'" 1Sa 18:5,16; 1Ch 5:2; Mt 2:6

³ When all the elders of Israel had come to King David at Hebron, he made a covenant with them at Hebron before the LORD, and they anointed David king over Israel, as the LORD had promised through Samuel. 2Sa 5:1-3

David Conquers Jerusalem
11:4-9pp — 2Sa 5:6-10

⁴ David and all the Israelites marched to Jerusalem (that is, Jebus). The Jebusites who lived there ⁵ said to David, "You will not get in here." Nevertheless, David captured the fortress of Zion—which is the City of David. Jdg 1:21; 19:10

⁶ David had said, "Whoever leads the attack on the Jebusites will become commander-in-chief." Joab son of Zeruiah went up first, and so he received the command. 2Sa 8:16

⁷ David then took up residence in the fortress, and so it was called the City of David. ⁸ He built up the city around it, from

the terraces[a] to the surrounding wall, while Joab restored the rest of the city. [9]And David became more and more powerful, because the LORD Almighty was with him.   2Sa 3:1; 4:6-10

David's Mighty Warriors
11:10-41pp — 2Sa 23:8-39

[10]These were the chiefs of David's mighty warriors — they, together with all Israel, gave his kingship strong support to extend it over the whole land, as the LORD had promised — [11]this is the list of David's mighty warriors: ver 3; 2Sa 17:10

Jashobeam,[b] a Hakmonite, was chief of the officers[c]; he raised his spear against three hundred men, whom he killed in one encounter.

[12]Next to him was Eleazar son of Dodai the Ahohite, one of the three mighty warriors. [13]He was with David at Pas Dammim when the Philistines gathered there for battle. At a place where there was a field full of barley, the troops fled from the Philistines. [14]But they took their stand in the middle of the field. They defended it and struck the Philistines down, and the LORD brought about a great victory.   Ex 14:30; 1Sa 11:13

[15]Three of the thirty chiefs came down to David to the rock at the cave of Adullam, while a band of Philistines was en-

camped in the Valley of Rephaim. [16]At that time David was in the stronghold, and the Philistine garrison was at Bethlehem. [17]David longed for water and said, "Oh, that someone would get me a drink of water from the well near the gate of Bethlehem!" [18]So the Three broke through the Philistine lines, drew water from the well near the gate of Bethlehem and carried it back to David. But he refused to drink it; instead, he poured it out to the LORD. [19]"God forbid that I should do this!" he said. "Should I drink the blood of these men who went at the risk of their lives?" Because they risked their lives to bring it back, David would not drink it.   2Sa 5:17; 1Ch 14:9; Isa 17:5

Such were the exploits of the three mighty warriors.

[20]Abishai the brother of Joab was chief of the Three. He raised his spear against three hundred men, whom he killed, and so he became as famous as the Three. [21]He was doubly honored above the Three and became their commander, even though he was not included among them.   1Sa 26:6

[22]Benaiah son of Jehoiada, a valiant fighter from Kabzeel, performed great exploits. He struck down Moab's two mightiest warriors. He also went down into a pit on a snowy day and killed a lion. [23]And he struck down an Egyp-

---

[a] 8 Or the Millo   [b] 11 Possibly a variant of Jashob-Baal   [c] 11 Or Thirty; some Septuagint manuscripts Three (see also 2 Samuel 23:8)

tian who was five cubits[a] tall. Although the Egyptian had a spear like a weaver's rod in his hand, Benaiah went against him with a club. He snatched the spear from the Egyptian's hand and killed him with his own spear. ²⁴Such were the exploits of Benaiah son of Jehoiada; he too was as famous as the three mighty warriors. ²⁵He was held in greater honor than any of the Thirty, but he was not included among the Three. And David put him in charge of his bodyguard. 1Sa 17:7,36; Jos 15:21

²⁶The mighty warriors were:
Asahel the brother of Joab,
Elhanan son of Dodo from Bethlehem,
²⁷Shammoth the Harorite,
Helez the Pelonite,
²⁸Ira son of Ikkesh from Tekoa,
Abiezer from Anathoth,
²⁹Sibbekai the Hushathite,
Ilai the Ahohite,
³⁰Maharai the Netophathite,
Heled son of Baanah the Netophathite,
³¹Ithai son of Ribai from Gibeah in Benjamin,
Benaiah the Pirathonite,
³²Hurai from the ravines of Gaash,
Abiel the Arbathite,
³³Azmaveth the Baharumite,
Eliahba the Shaalbonite,
³⁴the sons of Hashem the Gizonite,

Jonathan son of Shagee the Hararite,
³⁵Ahiam son of Sakar the Hararite,
Eliphal son of Ur,
³⁶Hepher the Mekerathite,
Ahijah the Pelonite,
³⁷Hezro the Carmelite,
Naarai son of Ezbai,
³⁸Joel the brother of Nathan,
Mibhar son of Hagri,
³⁹Zelek the Ammonite,
Naharai the Berothite, the armor-bearer of Joab son of Zeruiah,
⁴⁰Ira the Ithrite,
Gareb the Ithrite,
⁴¹Uriah the Hittite, 2Sa 11:6
Zabad son of Ahlai, 2Sa 23:8
⁴²Adina son of Shiza the Reubenite, who was chief of the Reubenites, and the thirty with him,
⁴³Hanan son of Maakah,
Joshaphat the Mithnite,
⁴⁴Uzzia the Ashterathite,
Shama and Jeiel the sons of Hotham the Aroerite,
⁴⁵Jediael son of Shimri,
his brother Joha the Tizite,
⁴⁶Eliel the Mahavite,
Jeribai and Joshaviah the sons of Elnaam,
Ithmah the Moabite,
⁴⁷Eliel, Obed and Jaasiel the Mezobaite.

Warriors Join David

12 These were the men who came to David at Ziklag,

---

[a] 23 That is, about 7 feet 6 inches or about 2.3 meters

while he was banished from the presence of Saul son of Kish (they were among the warriors who helped him in battle; ²they were armed with bows and were able to shoot arrows or to sling stones right-handed or left-handed; they were relatives of Saul from the tribe of Benjamin): Jdg 3:15; 20:16

³Ahiezer their chief and Joash the sons of Shemaah the Gibeathite; Jeziel and Pelet the sons of Azmaveth; Berakah, Jehu the Anathothite, ⁴and Ishmaiah the Gibeonite, a mighty warrior among the Thirty, who was a leader of the Thirty; Jeremiah, Jahaziel, Johanan, Jozabad the Gederathite,ᵃ ⁵Eluzai, Jerimoth, Bealiah, Shemariah and Shephatiah the Haruphite; ⁶Elkanah, Ishiah, Azarel, Joezer and Jashobeam the Korahites; ⁷and Joelah and Zebadiah the sons of Jeroham from Gedor. Jos 15:36,58

⁸Some Gadites defected to David at his stronghold in the wilderness. They were brave warriors, ready for battle and able to handle the shield and spear. Their faces were the faces of lions, and they were as swift as gazelles in the mountains. 2Sa 2:18; 17:10

⁹Ezer was the chief,
Obadiah the second in command, Eliab the third,

¹⁰Mishmannah the fourth,
Jeremiah the fifth,
¹¹Attai the sixth, Eliel the seventh,
¹²Johanan the eighth, Elzabad the ninth,
¹³Jeremiah the tenth and Makbannai the eleventh.

¹⁴These Gadites were army commanders; the least was a match for a hundred, and the greatest for a thousand. ¹⁵It was they who crossed the Jordan in the first month when it was overflowing all its banks, and they put to flight everyone living in the valleys, to the east and to the west. Dt 32:30; Jos 3:15

¹⁶Other Benjamites and some men from Judah also came to David in his stronghold. ¹⁷David went out to meet them and said to them, "If you have come to me in peace to help me, I am ready for you to join me. But if you have come to betray me to my enemies when my hands are free from violence, may the God of our ancestors see it and judge you." 2Sa 3:19

¹⁸Then the Spirit came on Amasai, chief of the Thirty, and he said: Jdg 6:34; 2Sa 17:25

"We are yours, David!
We are with you, son of Jesse!
Success, success to you, 1Sa 25:5
and success to those who help you,

ᵃ 4 In Hebrew texts the second half of this verse (Jeremiah . . . Gederathite) is numbered 12:5, and 12:5-40 is numbered 12:6-41.

for your God will help you."

So David received them and made them leaders of his raiding bands.

[19] Some of the tribe of Manasseh defected to David when he went with the Philistines to fight against Saul. (He and his men did not help the Philistines because, after consultation, their rulers sent him away. They said, "It will cost us our heads if he deserts to his master Saul.") [20] When David went to Ziklag, these were the men of Manasseh who defected to him: Adnah, Jozabad, Jediael, Michael, Jozabad, Elihu and Zillethai, leaders of units of a thousand in Manasseh. [21] They helped David against raiding bands, for all of them were brave warriors, and they were commanders in his army. [22] Day after day men came to help David, until he had a great army, like the army of God.[a]   1Sa 27:6; 29:2-11

Others Join David at Hebron

[23] These are the numbers of the men armed for battle who came to David at Hebron to turn Saul's kingdom over to him, as the LORD had said: 1Sa 16:1; 2Sa 2:3-4; 1Ch 10:14
[24] from Judah, carrying shield and spear — 6,800 armed for battle;
[25] from Simeon, warriors ready for battle — 7,100;
[26] from Levi — 4,600, [27] including Jehoiada, leader of the family of Aaron, with 3,700 men, [28] and Zadok, a brave young warrior, with 22 officers from his family; 2Sa 8:17
[29] from Benjamin, Saul's tribe — 3,000, most of whom had remained loyal to Saul's house until then;   2Sa 2:8-9; 3:19
[30] from Ephraim, brave warriors, famous in their own clans — 20,800;
[31] from half the tribe of Manasseh, designated by name to come and make David king — 18,000;
[32] from Issachar, men who understood the times and knew what Israel should do — 200 chiefs, with all their relatives under their command;   Est 1:13
[33] from Zebulun, experienced soldiers prepared for battle with every type of weapon, to help David with undivided loyalty — 50,000;
[34] from Naphtali — 1,000 officers, together with 37,000 men carrying shields and spears;
[35] from Dan, ready for battle — 28,600;
[36] from Asher, experienced soldiers prepared for battle — 40,000;
[37] and from east of the Jordan,

a 22 Or a great and mighty army

from Reuben, Gad and the half-tribe of Manasseh, armed with every type of weapon — 120,000.

[38] All these were fighting men who volunteered to serve in the ranks. They came to Hebron fully determined to make David king over all Israel. All the rest of the Israelites were also of one mind to make David king. [39] The men spent three days there with David, eating and drinking, for their families had supplied provisions for them. [40] Also, their neighbors from as far away as Issachar, Zebulun and Naphtali came bringing food on donkeys, camels, mules and oxen. There were plentiful supplies of flour, fig cakes, raisin cakes, wine, olive oil, cattle and sheep, for there was joy in Israel. 1Sa 25:18; 2Sa 5:1-3

Bringing Back the Ark

13:1-14pp — 2Sa 6:1-11

13 David conferred with each of his officers, the commanders of thousands and commanders of hundreds. [2] He then said to the whole assembly of Israel, "If it seems good to you and if it is the will of the LORD our God, let us send word far and wide to the rest of our people throughout the territories of Israel, and also to the priests and Levites who are with them in their towns and pasturelands, to come and join us. [3] Let us bring

the ark of our God back to us, for we did not inquire of[a] it[b] during the reign of Saul." [4] The whole assembly agreed to do this, because it seemed right to all the people. 1Sa 7:1-2; 2Ch 1:5

[5] So David assembled all Israel, from the Shihor River in Egypt to Lebo Hamath, to bring the ark of God from Kiriath Jearim. [6] David and all Israel went to Baalah of Judah (Kiriath Jearim) to bring up from there the ark of God the LORD, who is enthroned between the cherubim — the ark that is called by the Name. Jos 15:9; 2Ki 19:15

[7] They moved the ark of God from Abinadab's house on a new cart, with Uzzah and Ahio guiding it. [8] David and all the Israelites were celebrating with all their might before God, with songs and with harps, lyres, timbrels, cymbals and trumpets. Nu 4:15; 1Sa 7:1

[9] When they came to the threshing floor of Kidon, Uzzah reached out his hand to steady the ark, because the oxen stumbled. [10] The LORD's anger burned against Uzzah, and he struck him down because he had put his hand on the ark. So he died there before God. Lev 10:2; 1Ch 15:13,15

[11] Then David was angry because the LORD's wrath had broken out against Uzzah, and to this day that place is called Perez Uzzah.[c] 1Ch 15:13; Ps 7:11

[12] David was afraid of God that day and asked, "How can I ever

---

a 3 Or *we neglected*   *b 3* Or *him*   *c 11 Perez Uzzah* means *outbreak against Uzzah.*

bring the ark of God to me?" ¹³He did not take the ark to be with him in the City of David. Instead, he took it to the house of Obed-Edom the Gittite. ¹⁴The ark of God remained with the family of Obed-Edom in his house for three months, and the Lord blessed his household and everything he had. 2Sa 6:1-11; 1Ch 26:4-5

David's House and Family
14:1-7pp — 2Sa 5:11-16; 1Ch 3:5-8

14 Now Hiram king of Tyre sent messengers to David, along with cedar logs, stonemasons and carpenters to build a palace for him. ²And David knew that the Lord had established him as king over Israel and that his kingdom had been highly exalted for the sake of his people Israel. Nu 24:7; Dt 26:19

³In Jerusalem David took more wives and became the father of more sons and daughters. ⁴These are the names of the children born to him there: Shammua, Shobab, Nathan, Solomon, ⁵Ibhar, Elishua, Elpelet, ⁶Nogah, Nepheg, Japhia, ⁷Elishama, Beeliadaᵃ and Eliphelet. 2Sa 5:11-16; 1Ch 3:5-8

David Defeats the Philistines
14:8-17pp — 2Sa 5:17-25

⁸When the Philistines heard that David had been anointed king over all Israel, they went up in full force to search for him, but David heard about it and went out to meet them. ⁹Now the Philistines had come and raided the Valley of Rephaim; ¹⁰so David inquired of God: "Shall I go and attack the Philistines? Will you deliver them into my hands?" 1Ch 11:1,15

The Lord answered him, "Go, I will deliver them into your hands."

¹¹So David and his men went up to Baal Perazim, and there he defeated them. He said, "As waters break out, God has broken out against my enemies by my hand." So that place was called Baal Perazim.ᵇ ¹²The Philistines had abandoned their gods there, and David gave orders to burn them in the fire. Ex 32:20; Jos 7:15

¹³Once more the Philistines raided the valley; ¹⁴so David inquired of God again, and God answered him, "Do not go directly after them, but circle around them and attack them in front of the poplar trees. ¹⁵As soon as you hear the sound of marching in the tops of the poplar trees, move out to battle, because that will mean God has gone out in front of you to strike the Philistine army." ¹⁶So David did as God commanded him, and they struck down the Philistine army, all the way from Gibeon to Gezer. ver 9; Jos 9:3; 10:33

¹⁷So David's fame spread throughout every land, and the Lord made all the nations fear him. 2Sa 5:17-25

ᵃ 7 A variant of *Eliada*   ᵇ 11 *Baal Perazim* means *the lord who breaks out.*

The Ark Brought to Jerusalem

15:25–16:3pp — 2Sa 6:12-19

15 After David had constructed buildings for himself in the City of David, he prepared a place for the ark of God and pitched a tent for it. [2] Then David said, "No one but the Levites may carry the ark of God, because the LORD chose them to carry the ark of the LORD and to minister before him forever." Nu 4:15; Dt 10:8; 1Ch 16:1

[3] David assembled all Israel in Jerusalem to bring up the ark of the LORD to the place he had prepared for it. [4] He called together the descendants of Aaron and the Levites: 1Ki 8:1; 1Ch 13:5

[5] From the descendants of Kohath,

Uriel the leader and 120 relatives;

[6] from the descendants of Merari,

Asaiah the leader and 220 relatives;

[7] from the descendants of Gershon,[a]

Joel the leader and 130 relatives;

[8] from the descendants of Elizaphan, Ex 6:22

Shemaiah the leader and 200 relatives;

[9] from the descendants of Hebron, Ex 6:18

Eliel the leader and 80 relatives;

[10] from the descendants of Uzziel,

Amminadab the leader and 112 relatives.

[11] Then David summoned Zadok and Abiathar the priests, and Uriel, Asaiah, Joel, Shemaiah, Eliel and Amminadab the Levites. [12] He said to them, "You are the heads of the Levitical families; you and your fellow Levites are to consecrate yourselves and bring up the ark of the LORD, the God of Israel, to the place I have prepared for it. [13] It was because you, the Levites, did not bring it up the first time that the LORD our God broke out in anger against us. We did not inquire of him about how to do it in the prescribed way." [14] So the priests and Levites consecrated themselves in order to bring up the ark of the LORD, the God of Israel. [15] And the Levites carried the ark of God with the poles on their shoulders, as Moses had commanded in accordance with the word of the LORD. Ex 25:14; 2Sa 6:3; 1Ch 13:7-10

[16] David told the leaders of the Levites to appoint their fellow Levites as musicians to make a joyful sound with musical instruments: lyres, harps and cymbals. 1Ch 25:1

[17] So the Levites appointed Heman son of Joel; from his relatives, Asaph son of Berekiah; and from their relatives the Merarites, Ethan son of Kushaiah; [18] and with them their relatives

---

[a] 7 Hebrew *Gershom*, a variant of *Gershon*

next in rank: Zechariah,[a] Jaaziel, Shemiramoth, Jehiel, Unni, Eliab, Benaiah, Maaseiah, Mattithiah, Eliphelehu, Mikneiah, Obed-Edom and Jeiel,[b] the gatekeepers.   1Ch 6:33,39,44; 26:4-5

[19] The musicians Heman, Asaph and Ethan were to sound the bronze cymbals; [20] Zechariah, Jaaziel,[c] Shemiramoth, Jehiel, Unni, Eliab, Maaseiah and Benaiah were to play the lyres according to *alamoth,*[d] [21] and Mattithiah, Eliphelehu, Mikneiah, Obed-Edom, Jeiel and Azaziah were to play the harps, directing according to *sheminith.*[d] [22] Kenaniah the head Levite was in charge of the singing; that was his responsibility because he was skillful at it. 1Ch 25:6

[23] Berekiah and Elkanah were to be doorkeepers for the ark. [24] Shebaniah, Joshaphat, Nethanel, Amasai, Zechariah, Benaiah and Eliezer the priests were to blow trumpets before the ark of God. Obed-Edom and Jehiah were also to be doorkeepers for the ark.   ver 28; 1Ch 16:6

[25] So David and the elders of Israel and the commanders of units of a thousand went to bring up the ark of the covenant of the LORD from the house of Obed-Edom, with rejoicing. [26] Because God had helped the Levites who were carrying the ark of the covenant of the LORD, seven bulls and seven rams were sacrificed. [27] Now David was clothed in a robe of fine linen, as were all the Levites who were carrying the ark, and as were the musicians, and Kenaniah, who was in charge of the singing of the choirs. David also wore a linen ephod. [28] So all Israel brought up the ark of the covenant of the LORD with shouts, with the sounding of rams' horns and trumpets, and of cymbals, and the playing of lyres and harps.   1Ch 13:8,13; 2Ch 1:4

[29] As the ark of the covenant of the LORD was entering the City of David, Michal daughter of Saul watched from a window. And when she saw King David dancing and celebrating, she despised him in her heart.

Ministering Before the Ark

16:8-22pp — Ps 105:1-15
16:23-33pp — Ps 96:1-13
16:34-36pp — Ps 106:1,47-48

16 They brought the ark of God and set it inside the tent that David had pitched for it, and they presented burnt offerings and fellowship offerings before God. [2] After David had finished sacrificing the burnt offerings and fellowship offerings, he blessed the people in the name of the LORD. [3] Then he gave a loaf of

---

[a] *18* Three Hebrew manuscripts and most Septuagint manuscripts (see also verse 20 and 16:5); most Hebrew manuscripts *Zechariah son and* or *Zechariah, Ben and*   [b] *18* Hebrew; Septuagint (see also verse 21) *Jeiel and Azaziah*   [c] *20* See verse 18; Hebrew *Aziel,* a variant of *Jaaziel.*   [d] *20,21* Probably a musical term

bread, a cake of dates and a cake of raisins to each Israelite man and woman. 2Sa 6:12-19; 1Ch 15:1

⁴He appointed some of the Levites to minister before the ark of the LORD, to extol,ᵃ thank, and praise the LORD, the God of Israel: ⁵Asaph was the chief, and next to him in rank were Zechariah, then Jaaziel,ᵇ Shemiramoth, Jehiel, Mattithiah, Eliab, Benaiah, Obed-Edom and Jeiel. They were to play the lyres and harps, Asaph was to sound the cymbals, ⁶and Benaiah and Jahaziel the priests were to blow the trumpets regularly before the ark of the covenant of God. 1Ch 15:2

⁷That day David first appointed Asaph and his associates to give praise to the LORD in this manner: 2Sa 23:1

⁸Give praise to the LORD,
    proclaim his name; ver 34
  make known among the
      nations what he has
      done. 2Ki 19:19
⁹Sing to him, sing praise to him;
    tell of all his wonderful
      acts. Ex 15:1
¹⁰Glory in his holy name;
    let the hearts of those who
      seek the LORD rejoice.
¹¹Look to the LORD and his
      strength;
    seek his face always. Ps 24:6

¹²Remember the wonders he
      has done, Ps 77:11
  his miracles, and the
      judgments he
      pronounced, Ps 78:43
¹³you his servants, the
      descendants of Israel,
  his chosen ones, the
      children of Jacob.
¹⁴He is the LORD our God;
  his judgments are in all the
      earth. Isa 26:9

¹⁵He remembersᶜ his covenant
      forever,
  the promise he made, for a
      thousand generations,
¹⁶the covenant he made with
      Abraham, Ge 17:2; 26:3
  the oath he swore to
      Isaac.
¹⁷He confirmed it to Jacob as a
      decree, Ge 35:9-12
  to Israel as an everlasting
      covenant:
¹⁸"To you I will give the land of
      Canaan Ge 13:14-17
  as the portion you will
      inherit."

¹⁹When they were but few in
      number, Ge 34:30; Dt 7:7
  few indeed, and strangers
      in it,
²⁰theyᵈ wandered from nation
      to nation,
  from one kingdom to
      another.

ᵃ 4 Or petition; or invoke ᵇ 5 See 15:18,20; Hebrew Jeiel, possibly another name for Jaaziel. ᶜ 15 Some Septuagint manuscripts (see also Psalm 105:8); Hebrew Remember ᵈ 18-20 One Hebrew manuscript, Septuagint and Vulgate (see also Psalm 105:12); most Hebrew manuscripts inherit, / ¹⁹though you are but few in number, / few indeed, and strangers in it." / ²⁰They

²¹He allowed no one to oppress
them;
for their sake he rebuked
kings: Ge 12:17; 20:3; Ex 7:15
²²"Do not touch my anointed
ones;
do my prophets no
harm." Ps 105:1-15; Ge 20:7

²³Sing to the Lord, all the earth;
proclaim his salvation day
after day.
²⁴Declare his glory among the
nations,
his marvelous deeds among
all peoples.

²⁵For great is the Lord and
most worthy of praise;
he is to be feared above all
gods. Ps 89:7
²⁶For all the gods of the nations
are idols,
but the Lord made the
heavens. Lev 19:4; Ps 102:25
²⁷Splendor and majesty are
before him;
strength and joy are in his
dwelling place.

²⁸Ascribe to the Lord, all you
families of nations,
ascribe to the Lord glory
and strength. Ps 29:1-2
²⁹Ascribe to the Lord the glory
due his name;
bring an offering and come
before him.
Worship the Lord in the
splendor of hisᵃ
holiness.

³⁰ Tremble before him, all the
earth! Ps 114:7
The world is firmly
established; it cannot
be moved.

³¹Let the heavens rejoice, let the
earth be glad; Isa 49:13
let them say among the
nations, "The Lord
reigns!" Ps 93:1
³²Let the sea resound, and all
that is in it; Ps 98:7
let the fields be jubilant,
and everything in
them!
³³Let the trees of the forest sing,
let them sing for joy before
the Lord,
for he comes to judge the
earth. Ps 96:1-13

³⁴Give thanks to the Lord, for
he is good;
his love endures forever.
³⁵Cry out, "Save us, God our
Savior; Mic 7:7
gather us and deliver us
from the nations,
that we may give thanks to
your holy name,
and glory in your praise."
³⁶Praise be to the Lord, the
God of Israel,
from everlasting to
everlasting.

Then all the people said "Amen"
and "Praise the Lord." Ps 106:1,47

³⁷David left Asaph and his associates before the ark of the

ᵃ 29 Or Lord with the splendor of

covenant of the LORD to minister there regularly, according to each day's requirements. [38]He also left Obed-Edom and his sixty-eight associates to minister with them. Obed-Edom son of Jeduthun, and also Hosah, were gatekeepers. 1Ch 13:13; 26:10; 2Ch 8:14

[39]David left Zadok the priest and his fellow priests before the tabernacle of the LORD at the high place in Gibeon [40]to present burnt offerings to the LORD on the altar of burnt offering regularly, morning and evening, in accordance with everything written in the Law of the LORD, which he had given Israel. [41]With them were Heman and Jeduthun and the rest of those chosen and designated by name to give thanks to the LORD, "for his love endures forever." [42]Heman and Jeduthun were responsible for the sounding of the trumpets and cymbals and for the playing of the other instruments for sacred song. The sons of Jeduthun were stationed at the gate. Ex 29:38; 2Ch 5:13; 7:6

[43]Then all the people left, each for their own home, and David returned home to bless his family.

God's Promise to David

17:1-15pp — 2Sa 7:1-17

17 After David was settled in his palace, he said to Nathan the prophet, "Here I am, living in a house of cedar, while the ark of the covenant of the LORD is under a tent." 1Ch 15:1

[2]Nathan replied to David, "Whatever you have in mind, do it, for God is with you." 2Ch 6:7

[3]But that night the word of God came to Nathan, saying:

[4]"Go and tell my servant David, 'This is what the LORD says: You are not the one to build me a house to dwell in. [5]I have not dwelt in a house from the day I brought Israel up out of Egypt to this day. I have moved from one tent site to another, from one dwelling place to another. [6]Wherever I have moved with all the Israelites, did I ever say to any of their leaders[a] whom I commanded to shepherd my people, "Why have you not built me a house of cedar?"' 1Ch 28:3

[7]"Now then, tell my servant David, 'This is what the LORD Almighty says: I took you from the pasture, from tending the flock, and appointed you ruler over my people Israel. [8]I have been with you wherever you have gone, and I have cut off all your enemies from before you. Now I will make your name like the names of the greatest men on earth. [9]And I will provide a place for my people Israel and will plant

---

[a] 6 Traditionally *judges*; also in verse 10

them so that they can have a home of their own and no longer be disturbed. Wicked people will not oppress them anymore, as they did at the beginning ¹⁰and have done ever since the time I appointed leaders over my people Israel. I will also subdue all your enemies. Jdg 2:16; 2Sa 6:21

" 'I declare to you that the LORD will build a house for you: ¹¹When your days are over and you go to be with your ancestors, I will raise up your offspring to succeed you, one of your own sons, and I will establish his kingdom. ¹²He is the one who will build a house for me, and I will establish his throne forever. ¹³I will be his father, and he will be my son. I will never take my love away from him, as I took it away from your predecessor. ¹⁴I will set him over my house and my kingdom forever; his throne will be established forever.' " 1Ki 2:12

¹⁵Nathan reported to David all the words of this entire revelation. 2Sa 7:1-17

David's Prayer
17:16-27pp — 2Sa 7:18-29

¹⁶Then King David went in and sat before the LORD, and he said:

"Who am I, LORD God, and what is my family, that you have brought me this far? ¹⁷And as if this were not enough in your sight, my God, you have spoken about the future of the house of your servant. You, LORD God, have looked on me as though I were the most exalted of men.

¹⁸"What more can David say to you for honoring your servant? For you know your servant, ¹⁹LORD. For the sake of your servant and according to your will, you have done this great thing and made known all these great promises.

²⁰"There is no one like you, LORD, and there is no God but you, as we have heard with our own ears. ²¹And who is like your people Israel—the one nation on earth whose God went out to redeem a people for himself, and to make a name for yourself, and to perform great and awesome wonders by driving out nations from before your people, whom you redeemed from Egypt? ²²You made your people Israel your very own forever, and you, LORD, have become their God. Ex 9:14; 19:5-6; Isa 44:6

²³"And now, LORD, let the promise you have made concerning your servant and his house be established forever. Do as you promised,

[24] so that it will be established and that your name will be great forever. Then people will say, 'The LORD Almighty, the God over Israel, is Israel's God!' And the house of your servant David will be established before you. 1Ki 8:25

[25] "You, my God, have revealed to your servant that you will build a house for him. So your servant has found courage to pray to you. [26] You, LORD, are God! You have promised these good things to your servant. [27] Now you have been pleased to bless the house of your servant, that it may continue forever in your sight; for you, LORD, have blessed it, and it will be blessed forever." 2Sa 7:18-29; Ps 21:6

David's Victories

18:1-13pp — 2Sa 8:1-14

18 In the course of time, David defeated the Philistines and subdued them, and he took Gath and its surrounding villages from the control of the Philistines.

[2] David also defeated the Moabites, and they became subject to him and brought him tribute.

[3] Moreover, David defeated Hadadezer king of Zobah, in the vicinity of Hamath, when he went to set up his monument at[a] the Euphrates River. [4] David captured a thousand of his chariots, seven thousand charioteers and twenty thousand foot soldiers. He hamstrung all but a hundred of the chariot horses. Ge 2:14; 49:6; 1Ch 19:6

[5] When the Arameans of Damascus came to help Hadadezer king of Zobah, David struck down twenty-two thousand of them. [6] He put garrisons in the Aramean kingdom of Damascus, and the Arameans became subject to him and brought him tribute. The LORD gave David victory wherever he went. 1Ch 19:6

[7] David took the gold shields carried by the officers of Hadadezer and brought them to Jerusalem. [8] From Tebah[b] and Kun, towns that belonged to Hadadezer, David took a great quantity of bronze, which Solomon used to make the bronze Sea, the pillars and various bronze articles. 1Ki 7:23; 2Ch 4:12,15-16

[9] When Tou king of Hamath heard that David had defeated the entire army of Hadadezer king of Zobah, [10] he sent his son Hadoram to King David to greet him and congratulate him on his victory in battle over Hadadezer, who had been at war with Tou. Hadoram brought all kinds of articles of gold, of silver and of bronze.

[11] King David dedicated these articles to the LORD, as he had done with the silver and gold he

---

[a] 3 Or *to restore his control over*   [b] 8 Hebrew *Tibhath*, a variant of *Tebah*

had taken from all these nations: Edom and Moab, the Ammonites and the Philistines, and Amalek. Nu 24:18,20

¹²Abishai son of Zeruiah struck down eighteen thousand Edomites in the Valley of Salt. ¹³He put garrisons in Edom, and all the Edomites became subject to David. The LORD gave David victory wherever he went. 2Sa 8:1-14; 1Ki 11:15

David's Officials

18:14-17pp — 2Sa 8:15-18

¹⁴David reigned over all Israel, doing what was just and right for all his people. ¹⁵Joab son of Zeruiah was over the army; Jehoshaphat son of Ahilud was recorder; ¹⁶Zadok son of Ahitub and Ahimelek[a] son of Abiathar were priests; Shavsha was secretary; ¹⁷Benaiah son of Jehoiada was over the Kerethites and Pelethites; and David's sons were chief officials at the king's side. 2Sa 8:15-18; 1Ch 29:26

David Defeats the Ammonites

19:1-19pp — 2Sa 10:1-19

19 In the course of time, Nahash king of the Ammonites died, and his son succeeded him as king. ²David thought, "I will show kindness to Hanun son of Nahash, because his father showed kindness to me." So David sent a delegation to express his sympathy to Hanun concerning his father. Ge 19:38; Jdg 10:17-11:33

When David's envoys came to Hanun in the land of the Ammonites to express sympathy to him, ³the Ammonite commanders said to Hanun, "Do you think David is honoring your father by sending envoys to you to express sympathy? Haven't his envoys come to you only to explore and spy out the country and overthrow it?" ⁴So Hanun seized David's envoys, shaved them, cut off their garments at the buttocks, and sent them away. Nu 21:32

⁵When someone came and told David about the men, he sent messengers to meet them, for they were greatly humiliated. The king said, "Stay at Jericho till your beards have grown, and then come back."

⁶When the Ammonites realized that they had become obnoxious to David, Hanun and the Ammonites sent a thousand talents[b] of silver to hire chariots and charioteers from Aram Naharaim,[c] Aram Maakah and Zobah. ⁷They hired thirty-two thousand chariots and charioteers, as well as the king of Maakah with his troops, who came and camped near Medeba, while the Ammonites were mustered from their towns and moved out for battle. Jos 13:9,16; 1Ch 18:3,5,9

⁸On hearing this, David sent Joab out with the entire army of

---

[a] 16 Some Hebrew manuscripts, Vulgate and Syriac (see also 2 Samuel 8:17); most Hebrew manuscripts *Abimelek*   [b] 6 That is, about 38 tons or about 34 metric tons   [c] 6 That is, Northwest Mesopotamia

fighting men. ⁹The Ammonites came out and drew up in battle formation at the entrance to their city, while the kings who had come were by themselves in the open country.

¹⁰Joab saw that there were battle lines in front of him and behind him; so he selected some of the best troops in Israel and deployed them against the Arameans. ¹¹He put the rest of the men under the command of Abishai his brother, and they were deployed against the Ammonites. ¹²Joab said, "If the Arameans are too strong for me, then you are to rescue me; but if the Ammonites are too strong for you, then I will rescue you. ¹³Be strong, and let us fight bravely for our people and the cities of our God. The LORD will do what is good in his sight."   1Sa 26:6

¹⁴Then Joab and the troops with him advanced to fight the Arameans, and they fled before him. ¹⁵When the Ammonites realized that the Arameans were fleeing, they too fled before his brother Abishai and went inside the city. So Joab went back to Jerusalem.

¹⁶After the Arameans saw that they had been routed by Israel, they sent messengers and had Arameans brought from beyond the Euphrates River, with Shophak the commander of Hadadezer's army leading them.

¹⁷When David was told of this, he gathered all Israel and crossed the Jordan; he advanced against them and formed his battle lines opposite them. David formed his lines to meet the Arameans in battle, and they fought against him. ¹⁸But they fled before Israel, and David killed seven thousand of their charioteers and forty thousand of their foot soldiers. He also killed Shophak the commander of their army.

¹⁹When the vassals of Hadadezer saw that they had been routed by Israel, they made peace with David and became subject to him.

So the Arameans were not willing to help the Ammonites anymore.   2Sa 10:1-19

The Capture of Rabbah
20:1-3pp — 2Sa 11:1; 12:29-31

20 In the spring, at the time when kings go off to war, Joab led out the armed forces. He laid waste the land of the Ammonites and went to Rabbah and besieged it, but David remained in Jerusalem. Joab attacked Rabbah and left it in ruins. ²David took the crown from the head of their king[a] — its weight was found to be a talent[b] of gold, and it was set with precious stones — and it was placed on David's head. He took a great quantity of plunder from the city ³and brought out the people who were

---

[a] 2 Or *of Milkom,* that is, Molek   [b] 2 That is, about 75 pounds or about 34 kilograms

there, consigning them to labor with saws and with iron picks and axes. David did this to all the Ammonite towns. Then David and his entire army returned to Jerusalem. 2Sa 11:1; 12:29-31

War With the Philistines
20:4-8pp — 2Sa 21:15-22

⁴In the course of time, war broke out with the Philistines, at Gezer. At that time Sibbekai the Hushathite killed Sippai, one of the descendants of the Rephaites, and the Philistines were subjugated.

⁵In another battle with the Philistines, Elhanan son of Jair killed Lahmi the brother of Goliath the Gittite, who had a spear with a shaft like a weaver's rod.

⁶In still another battle, which took place at Gath, there was a huge man with six fingers on each hand and six toes on each foot—twenty-four in all. He also was descended from Rapha. ⁷When he taunted Israel, Jonathan son of Shimea, David's brother, killed him.

⁸These were descendants of Rapha in Gath, and they fell at the hands of David and his men.

David Counts the Fighting Men
21:1-26pp — 2Sa 24:1-25

21 Satan rose up against Israel and incited David to take a census of Israel. ²So David said to Joab and the commanders of the troops, "Go and count

the Israelites from Beersheba to Dan. Then report back to me so that I may know how many there are." 1Ch 27:23-24; 2Ch 18:21

³But Joab replied, "May the LORD multiply his troops a hundred times over. My lord the king, are they not all my lord's subjects? Why does my lord want to do this? Why should he bring guilt on Israel?" Dt 1:11

⁴The king's word, however, overruled Joab; so Joab left and went throughout Israel and then came back to Jerusalem. ⁵Joab reported the number of the fighting men to David: In all Israel there were one million one hundred thousand men who could handle a sword, including four hundred and seventy thousand in Judah. 1Ch 9:1

⁶But Joab did not include Levi and Benjamin in the numbering, because the king's command was repulsive to him. ⁷This command was also evil in the sight of God; so he punished Israel.

⁸Then David said to God, "I have sinned greatly by doing this. Now, I beg you, take away the guilt of your servant. I have done a very foolish thing."

⁹The LORD said to Gad, David's seer, ¹⁰"Go and tell David, 'This is what the LORD says: I am giving you three options. Choose one of them for me to carry out against you.'" 1Sa 9:9; 22:5

¹¹So Gad went to David and said to him, "This is what the

LORD says: 'Take your choice: ¹²three years of famine, three months of being swept away*a* before your enemies, with their swords overtaking you, or three days of the sword of the LORD — days of plague in the land, with the angel of the LORD ravaging every part of Israel.' Now then, decide how I should answer the one who sent me." Dt 32:24; Eze 30:25

¹³David said to Gad, "I am in deep distress. Let me fall into the hands of the LORD, for his mercy is very great; but do not let me fall into human hands." Ps 130:4,7

¹⁴So the LORD sent a plague on Israel, and seventy thousand men of Israel fell dead. ¹⁵And God sent an angel to destroy Jerusalem. But as the angel was doing so, the LORD saw it and relented concerning the disaster and said to the angel who was destroying the people, "Enough! Withdraw your hand." The angel of the LORD was then standing at the threshing floor of Araunah*b* the Jebusite. Ge 6:6; Ex 32:14; 1Ch 27:24

¹⁶David looked up and saw the angel of the LORD standing between heaven and earth, with a drawn sword in his hand extended over Jerusalem. Then David and the elders, clothed in sackcloth, fell facedown. Nu 14:5; Jos 7:6

¹⁷David said to God, "Was it not I who ordered the fighting men to be counted? I, the shepherd,*c* have sinned and done wrong. These are but sheep. What have they done? LORD my God, let your hand fall on me and my family, but do not let this plague remain on your people." 2Sa 7:8; Ps 74:1

David Builds an Altar

¹⁸Then the angel of the LORD ordered Gad to tell David to go up and build an altar to the LORD on the threshing floor of Araunah the Jebusite. ¹⁹So David went up in obedience to the word that Gad had spoken in the name of the LORD. 2Ch 3:1

²⁰While Araunah was threshing wheat, he turned and saw the angel; his four sons who were with him hid themselves. ²¹Then David approached, and when Araunah looked and saw him, he left the threshing floor and bowed down before David with his face to the ground. Jdg 6:11

²²David said to him, "Let me have the site of your threshing floor so I can build an altar to the LORD, that the plague on the people may be stopped. Sell it to me at the full price."

²³Araunah said to David, "Take it! Let my lord the king do whatever pleases him. Look, I will give the oxen for the burnt offerings, the threshing sledges for the wood, and the wheat for

a 12 Hebrew; Septuagint and Vulgate (see also 2 Samuel 24:13) *of fleeing*   *b* 15 Hebrew *Ornan,* a variant of *Araunah;* also in verses 18-28   *c* 17 Probable reading of the original Hebrew text (see 2 Samuel 24:17 and note); Masoretic Text does not have *the shepherd.*

the grain offering. I will give all this."

²⁴But King David replied to Araunah, "No, I insist on paying the full price. I will not take for the LORD what is yours, or sacrifice a burnt offering that costs me nothing."

²⁵So David paid Araunah six hundred shekels*ᵃ* of gold for the site. ²⁶David built an altar to the LORD there and sacrificed burnt offerings and fellowship offerings. He called on the LORD, and the LORD answered him with fire from heaven on the altar of burnt offering.   2Sa 24:1-25

²⁷Then the LORD spoke to the angel, and he put his sword back into its sheath. ²⁸At that time, when David saw that the LORD had answered him on the threshing floor of Araunah the Jebusite, he offered sacrifices there. ²⁹The tabernacle of the LORD, which Moses had made in the wilderness, and the altar of burnt offering were at that time on the high place at Gibeon. ³⁰But David could not go before it to inquire of God, because he was afraid of the sword of the angel of the LORD.   1Ki 3:4; 1Ch 16:39

22 Then David said, "The house of the LORD God is to be here, and also the altar of burnt offering for Israel." 1Ch 21:18-29

Preparations for the Temple

²So David gave orders to assemble the foreigners residing in Israel, and from among them he appointed stonecutters to prepare dressed stone for building the house of God. ³He provided a large amount of iron to make nails for the doors of the gateways and for the fittings, and more bronze than could be weighed. ⁴He also provided more cedar logs than could be counted, for the Sidonians and Tyrians had brought large numbers of them to David.   1Ki 5:6; 9:21

⁵David said, "My son Solomon is young and inexperienced, and the house to be built for the LORD should be of great magnificence and fame and splendor in the sight of all the nations. Therefore I will make preparations for it." So David made extensive preparations before his death.   1Ch 29:1

⁶Then he called for his son Solomon and charged him to build a house for the LORD, the God of Israel. ⁷David said to Solomon: "My son, I had it in my heart to build a house for the Name of the LORD my God. ⁸But this word of the LORD came to me: 'You have shed much blood and have fought many wars. You are not to build a house for my Name, because you have shed much blood on the earth in my sight. ⁹But you will have a son who will be a man of peace and rest, and I will give him rest from all his enemies on every side. His name will be

---

ᵃ 25 That is, about 15 pounds or about 6.9 kilograms

Solomon,[a] and I will grant Israel peace and quiet during his reign. [10]He is the one who will build a house for my Name. He will be my son, and I will be his father. And I will establish the throne of his kingdom over Israel forever.'   2Sa 7:13; 1Ch 17:12

[11]"Now, my son, the LORD be with you, and may you have success and build the house of the LORD your God, as he said you would. [12]May the LORD give you discretion and understanding when he puts you in command over Israel, so that you may keep the law of the LORD your God. [13]Then you will have success if you are careful to observe the decrees and laws that the LORD gave Moses for Israel. Be strong and courageous. Do not be afraid or discouraged.   Jos 1:6-9; 1Ki 3:9-12

[14]"I have taken great pains to provide for the temple of the LORD a hundred thousand talents[b] of gold, a million talents[c] of silver, quantities of bronze and iron too great to be weighed, and wood and stone. And you may add to them. [15]You have many workers: stonecutters, masons and carpenters, as well as those skilled in every kind of work [16]in gold and silver, bronze and iron—craftsmen beyond number. Now begin the work, and the LORD be with you."   ver 11; 2Ch 2:7

[17]Then David ordered all the leaders of Israel to help his son Solomon. [18]He said to them, "Is not the LORD your God with you? And has he not granted you rest on every side? For he has given the inhabitants of the land into my hands, and the land is subject to the LORD and to his people. [19]Now devote your heart and soul to seeking the LORD your God. Begin to build the sanctuary of the LORD God, so that you may bring the ark of the covenant of the LORD and the sacred articles belonging to God into the temple that will be built for the Name of the LORD."   2Ch 5:7; 1Ch 23:25; 28:1-6

The Levites

23 When David was old and full of years, he made his son Solomon king over Israel.

[2]He also gathered together all the leaders of Israel, as well as the priests and Levites. [3]The Levites thirty years old or more were counted, and the total number of men was thirty-eight thousand. [4]David said, "Of these, twenty-four thousand are to be in charge of the work of the temple of the LORD and six thousand are to be officials and judges. [5]Four thousand are to be gatekeepers and four thousand are to praise the LORD with the musical instruments I have provided for that purpose."   1Ch 15:16; 2Ch 19:8

[6]David separated the Levites

---

[a] 9 *Solomon* sounds like and may be derived from the Hebrew for *peace*.   [b] 14 That is, about 3,750 tons or about 3,400 metric tons   [c] 14 That is, about 37,500 tons or about 34,000 metric tons

into divisions corresponding to the sons of Levi: Gershon, Kohath and Merari.   2Ch 8:14; 29:25

Gershonites

⁷Belonging to the Gershonites: Ladan and Shimei.

⁸The sons of Ladan:
Jehiel the first, Zetham and Joel — three in all.

⁹The sons of Shimei:
Shelomoth, Haziel and Haran — three in all.
These were the heads of the families of Ladan.

¹⁰And the sons of Shimei:
Jahath, Ziza,ᵃ Jeush and Beriah.
These were the sons of Shimei — four in all.

¹¹Jahath was the first and Ziza the second, but Jeush and Beriah did not have many sons; so they were counted as one family with one assignment.

Kohathites

¹²The sons of Kohath:
Amram, Izhar, Hebron and Uzziel — four in all.

¹³The sons of Amram: Ex 6:20
Aaron and Moses.
Aaron was set apart, he and his descendants forever, to consecrate the most holy things, to offer sacrifices before the LORD, to minister before him and to pro-

nounce blessings in his name forever. ¹⁴The sons of Moses the man of God were counted as part of the tribe of Levi.   Ex 30:7-10; Dt 33:1

¹⁵The sons of Moses:
Gershom and Eliezer.

¹⁶The descendants of Gershom: 1Ch 26:24-28
Shubael was the first.

¹⁷The descendants of Eliezer:
Rehabiah was the first.
Eliezer had no other sons, but the sons of Rehabiah were very numerous.

¹⁸The sons of Izhar:
Shelomith was the first.

¹⁹The sons of Hebron: 1Ch 24:23
Jeriah the first, Amariah the second, Jahaziel the third and Jekameam the fourth.

²⁰The sons of Uzziel:
Micah the first and Ishiah the second.

Merarites

²¹The sons of Merari: 1Ch 24:26
Mahli and Mushi.
The sons of Mahli:
Eleazar and Kish.

²²Eleazar died without having sons: he had only daughters. Their cousins, the sons of Kish, married them.

²³The sons of Mushi:
Mahli, Eder and Jerimoth — three in all.

ᵃ 10 One Hebrew manuscript, Septuagint and Vulgate (see also verse 11); most Hebrew manuscripts *Zina*

24These were the descendants of Levi by their families—the heads of families as they were registered under their names and counted individually, that is, the workers twenty years old or more who served in the temple of the LORD. 25For David had said, "Since the LORD, the God of Israel, has granted rest to his people and has come to dwell in Jerusalem forever, 26the Levites no longer need to carry the tabernacle or any of the articles used in its service." 27According to the last instructions of David, the Levites were counted from those twenty years old or more. Nu 4:5,15; Dt 10:8

28The duty of the Levites was to help Aaron's descendants in the service of the temple of the LORD: to be in charge of the courtyards, the side rooms, the purification of all sacred things and the performance of other duties at the house of God. 29They were in charge of the bread set out on the table, the special flour for the grain offerings, the thin loaves made without yeast, the baking and the mixing, and all measurements of quantity and size. 30They were also to stand every morning to thank and praise the LORD. They were to do the same in the evening 31and whenever burnt offerings were presented to the LORD on the Sabbaths, at the New Moon feasts and at the appointed festivals. They were to serve before the LORD regularly in the proper number and in the way prescribed for them. Ex 25:30; Lev 19:35-36; 23:4

32And so the Levites carried out their responsibilities for the tent of meeting, for the Holy Place and, under their relatives the descendants of Aaron, for the service of the temple of the LORD. Nu 1:53; 3:6-8,38

The Divisions of Priests

24 These were the divisions of the descendants of Aaron: Nu 3:2-4; 1Ch 23:6

The sons of Aaron were Nadab, Abihu, Eleazar and Ithamar. 2But Nadab and Abihu died before their father did, and they had no sons; so Eleazar and Ithamar served as the priests. 3With the help of Zadok a descendant of Eleazar and Ahimelek a descendant of Ithamar, David separated them into divisions for their appointed order of ministering. 4A larger number of leaders were found among Eleazar's descendants than among Ithamar's, and they were divided accordingly: sixteen heads of families from Eleazar's descendants and eight heads of families from Ithamar's descendants. 5They divided them impartially by casting lots, for there were officials of the sanctuary and officials of God among the descendants of both Eleazar and Ithamar. Ex 6:23; Lev 10:1-2; Nu 3:4

6The scribe Shemaiah son of Nethanel, a Levite, recorded

their names in the presence of the king and of the officials: Zadok the priest, Ahimelek son of Abiathar and the heads of families of the priests and of the Levites — one family being taken from Eleazar and then one from Ithamar. 1Ch 18:16

⁷The first lot fell to Jehoiarib,
  the second to Jedaiah, Ezr 2:36
⁸the third to Harim, Ezr 2:39
  the fourth to Seorim,
⁹the fifth to Malkijah,
  the sixth to Mijamin,
¹⁰the seventh to Hakkoz,
  the eighth to Abijah, Ne 12:4,17
¹¹the ninth to Jeshua,
  the tenth to Shekaniah,
¹²the eleventh to Eliashib,
  the twelfth to Jakim,
¹³the thirteenth to Huppah,
  the fourteenth to Jeshebeab,
¹⁴the fifteenth to Bilgah,
  the sixteenth to Immer, Jer 20:1
¹⁵the seventeenth to Hezir,
  the eighteenth to Happizzez,
¹⁶the nineteenth to Pethahiah,
  the twentieth to Jehezkel,
¹⁷the twenty-first to Jakin,
  the twenty-second to Gamul,
¹⁸the twenty-third to Delaiah
  and the twenty-fourth to Maaziah.

¹⁹This was their appointed order of ministering when they entered the temple of the LORD, according to the regulations prescribed for them by their ances-tor Aaron, as the LORD, the God of Israel, had commanded him.

The Rest of the Levites

²⁰As for the rest of the descendants of Levi: 1Ch 23:6
  from the sons of Amram:
    Shubael;
  from the sons of Shubael:
    Jehdeiah.
²¹As for Rehabiah, from his sons: 1Ch 23:17
  Ishiah was the first.
²²From the Izharites: Shelomoth;
  from the sons of Shelomoth: Jahath.
²³The sons of Hebron: Jeriah the first,ᵃ Amariah the second, Jahaziel the third and Jekameam the fourth. 1Ch 23:19
²⁴The son of Uzziel: Micah;
  from the sons of Micah: Shamir.
²⁵The brother of Micah: Ishiah;
  from the sons of Ishiah: Zechariah.
²⁶The sons of Merari: Mahli and Mushi. 1Ch 6:19; 23:21
  The son of Jaaziah: Beno.
²⁷The sons of Merari:
  from Jaaziah: Beno, Shoham, Zakkur and Ibri.
²⁸From Mahli: Eleazar, who had no sons.
²⁹From Kish: the son of Kish: Jerahmeel.

ᵃ 23 Two Hebrew manuscripts and some Septuagint manuscripts (see also 23:19); most Hebrew manuscripts *The sons of Jeriah:*

30 And the sons of Mushi: Mahli, Eder and Jerimoth.

These were the Levites, according to their families. 31 They also cast lots, just as their relatives the descendants of Aaron did, in the presence of King David and of Zadok, Ahimelek, and the heads of families of the priests and of the Levites. The families of the oldest brother were treated the same as those of the youngest.

The Musicians

25 David, together with the commanders of the army, set apart some of the sons of Asaph, Heman and Jeduthun for the ministry of prophesying, accompanied by harps, lyres and cymbals. Here is the list of the men who performed this service: 1Sa 10:5; 1Ch 6:33,39; 15:16

2 From the sons of Asaph:
Zakkur, Joseph, Nethaniah and Asarelah. The sons of Asaph were under the supervision of Asaph, who prophesied under the king's supervision.

3 As for Jeduthun, from his sons: 1Ch 16:41-42
Gedaliah, Zeri, Jeshaiah, Shimei,[a] Hashabiah and Mattithiah, six in all, under the supervision of their father Jeduthun, who prophesied, using the harp in thanking and praising the LORD. Ge 4:21; Ps 33:2

4 As for Heman, from his sons:
Bukkiah, Mattaniah, Uzziel, Shubael and Jerimoth; Hananiah, Hanani, Eliathah, Giddalti and Romamti-Ezer; Joshbekashah, Mallothi, Hothir and Mahazioth. 5 (All these were sons of Heman the king's seer. They were given him through the promises of God to exalt him. God gave Heman fourteen sons and three daughters.)

6 All these men were under the supervision of their father for the music of the temple of the LORD, with cymbals, lyres and harps, for the ministry at the house of God.

Asaph, Jeduthun and Heman were under the supervision of the king. 7 Along with their relatives — all of them trained and skilled in music for the LORD — they numbered 288. 8 Young and old alike, teacher as well as student, cast lots for their duties.

9 The first lot, which was for Asaph, fell to Joseph,
his sons and relatives[b] 12[c]
the second to Gedaliah,
him and his relatives
and sons 12

---

[a] 3 One Hebrew manuscript and some Septuagint manuscripts (see also verse 17); most Hebrew manuscripts do not have Shimei.   [b] 9 See Septuagint; Hebrew does not have his sons and relatives.   [c] 9 See the total in verse 7; Hebrew does not have twelve.

¹⁰the third to Zakkur,
his sons and relatives 12
¹¹the fourth to Izri,^a
his sons and relatives 12
¹²the fifth to Nethaniah,
his sons and relatives 12
¹³the sixth to Bukkiah,
his sons and relatives 12
¹⁴the seventh to Jesarelah,^b
his sons and relatives 12
¹⁵the eighth to Jeshaiah,
his sons and relatives 12
¹⁶the ninth to Mattaniah,
his sons and relatives 12
¹⁷the tenth to Shimei,
his sons and relatives 12
¹⁸the eleventh to Azarel,^c
his sons and relatives 12
¹⁹the twelfth to Hashabiah,
his sons and relatives 12
²⁰the thirteenth to Shubael,
his sons and relatives 12
²¹the fourteenth to
Mattithiah,
his sons and relatives 12
²²the fifteenth to Jerimoth,
his sons and relatives 12
²³the sixteenth to Hananiah,
his sons and relatives 12
²⁴the seventeenth to
Joshbekashah,
his sons and relatives 12
²⁵the eighteenth to Hanani,
his sons and relatives 12
²⁶the nineteenth to Mallothi,
his sons and relatives 12
²⁷the twentieth to Eliathah,
his sons and relatives 12
²⁸the twenty-first to Hothir,
his sons and relatives 12

²⁹the twenty-second to
Giddalti,
his sons and relatives 12
³⁰the twenty-third to
Mahazioth,
his sons and relatives 12
³¹the twenty-fourth to
Romamti-Ezer,
his sons and relatives 12.

The Gatekeepers

26 The divisions of the gatekeepers: 1Ch 9:17

From the Korahites: Meshelemiah son of Kore, one of the sons of Asaph.

²Meshelemiah had sons:
Zechariah the firstborn,
Jediael the second,
Zebadiah the third,
Jathniel the fourth,
³Elam the fifth,
Jehohanan the sixth
and Eliehoenai the seventh.

⁴Obed-Edom also had sons:
Shemaiah the firstborn,
Jehozabad the second,
Joah the third,
Sakar the fourth,
Nethanel the fifth,
⁵Ammiel the sixth,
Issachar the seventh
and Peullethai the eighth.
(For God had blessed
Obed-Edom.)   2Sa 6:10

⁶Obed-Edom's son Shemaiah also had sons, who were leaders in their father's

^a 11 A variant of *Zeri*   ^b 14 A variant of *Asarelah*   ^c 18 A variant of *Uzziel*

family because they were very capable men. ⁷The sons of Shemaiah: Othni, Rephael, Obed and Elzabad; his relatives Elihu and Semakiah were also able men. ⁸All these were descendants of Obed-Edom; they and their sons and their relatives were capable men with the strength to do the work—descendants of Obed-Edom, 62 in all.

⁹Meshelemiah had sons and relatives, who were able men—18 in all.

¹⁰Hosah the Merarite had sons: Shimri the first (although he was not the firstborn, his father had appointed him the first), ¹¹Hilkiah the second, Tabaliah the third and Zechariah the fourth. The sons and relatives of Hosah were 13 in all. Dt 21:16; 1Ch 5:1

¹²These divisions of the gatekeepers, through their leaders, had duties for ministering in the temple of the LORD, just as their relatives had. ¹³Lots were cast for each gate, according to their families, young and old alike. 1Ch 24:5

¹⁴The lot for the East Gate fell to Shelemiah.ᵃ Then lots were cast for his son Zechariah, a wise counselor, and the lot for the North Gate fell to him. ¹⁵The lot for the South Gate fell to Obed-Edom, and the lot for the storehouse fell to his sons. ¹⁶The lots for the West Gate and the Shalleketh Gate on the upper road fell to Shuppim and Hosah. 1Ch 9:18,21

Guard was alongside of guard: ¹⁷There were six Levites a day on the east, four a day on the north, four a day on the south and two at a time at the storehouse. ¹⁸As for the courtᵇ to the west, there were four at the road and two at the courtᵇ itself.

¹⁹These were the divisions of the gatekeepers who were descendants of Korah and Merari.

The Treasurers and Other Officials

²⁰Their fellow Levites wereᶜ in charge of the treasuries of the house of God and the treasuries for the dedicated things. 1Ch 28:12

²¹The descendants of Ladan, who were Gershonites through Ladan and who were heads of families belonging to Ladan the Gershonite, were Jehieli, ²²the sons of Jehieli, Zetham and his brother Joel. They were in charge of the treasuries of the temple of the LORD. 1Ch 23:7; 29:8

²³From the Amramites, the Izharites, the Hebronites and the Uzzielites: Nu 3:27

²⁴Shubael, a descendant of Gershom son of Moses,

was the official in charge of the treasuries. ²⁵His relatives through Eliezer: Rehabiah his son, Jeshaiah his son, Joram his son, Zikri his son and Shelomith his son. ²⁶Shelomith and his relatives were in charge of all the treasuries for the things dedicated by King David, by the heads of families who were the commanders of thousands and commanders of hundreds, and by the other army commanders. ²⁷Some of the plunder taken in battle they dedicated for the repair of the temple of the LORD. ²⁸And everything dedicated by Samuel the seer and by Saul son of Kish, Abner son of Ner and Joab son of Zeruiah, and all the other dedicated things were in the care of Shelomith and his relatives. 1Sa 9:9; 2Sa 8:11; 1Ch 23:18

²⁹From the Izharites: Kenaniah and his sons were assigned duties away from the temple, as officials and judges over Israel. 1Ch 23:4; Ne 11:16

³⁰From the Hebronites: Hashabiah and his relatives — seventeen hundred able men — were responsible in Israel west of the Jordan for all the work of the LORD and for the king's service. ³¹As for the He-bronites, Jeriah was their chief according to the genealogical records of their families. In the fortieth year of David's reign a search was made in the records, and capable men among the Hebronites were found at Jazer in Gilead. ³²Jeriah had twenty-seven hundred relatives, who were able men and heads of families, and King David put them in charge of the Reubenites, the Gadites and the half-tribe of Manasseh for every matter pertaining to God and for the affairs of the king. 1Ch 23:19; 27:17

Army Divisions

27 This is the list of the Israelites — heads of families, commanders of thousands and commanders of hundreds, and their officers, who served the king in all that concerned the army divisions that were on duty month by month throughout the year. Each division consisted of 24,000 men.

²In charge of the first division, for the first month, was Jashobeam son of Zabdiel. There were 24,000 men in his division. ³He was a descendant of Perez and chief of all the army officers for the first month. 2Sa 23:8; 1Ch 11:11

⁴In charge of the division for the second month was Dodai the Ahohite; Mikloth was the leader of his division. There were 24,000 men in his division. 2Sa 23:9

⁵The third army commander, for the third month, was Benaiah son of Jehoiada the priest. He was chief and there were 24,000 men in his division. ⁶This was the Benaiah who was a mighty warrior among the Thirty and was over the Thirty. His son Ammizabad was in charge of his division.

⁷The fourth, for the fourth month, was Asahel the brother of Joab; his son Zebadiah was his successor. There were 24,000 men in his division. 2Sa 2:18; 1Ch 11:26

⁸The fifth, for the fifth month, was the commander Shamhuth the Izrahite. There were 24,000 men in his division.

⁹The sixth, for the sixth month, was Ira the son of Ikkesh the Tekoite. There were 24,000 men in his division. 2Sa 23:26

¹⁰The seventh, for the seventh month, was Helez the Pelonite, an Ephraimite. There were 24,000 men in his division. 2Sa 23:26; 1Ch 11:27

¹¹The eighth, for the eighth month, was Sibbekai the Hushathite, a Zerahite. There were 24,000 men in his division. 2Sa 21:18

¹²The ninth, for the ninth month, was Abiezer the Anathothite, a Benjamite. There were 24,000 men in his division. 2Sa 23:27; 1Ch 11:28

¹³The tenth, for the tenth month, was Maharai the Netophathite, a Zerahite. There were 24,000 men in his division. 2Sa 23:28; 1Ch 11:30

¹⁴The eleventh, for the eleventh month, was Benaiah the Pirathonite, an Ephraimite. There were 24,000 men in his division. 1Ch 11:31

¹⁵The twelfth, for the twelfth month, was Heldai the Netophathite, from the family of Othniel. There were 24,000 men in his division. Jos 15:17

Leaders of the Tribes

¹⁶The leaders of the tribes of Israel:

over the Reubenites: Eliezer son of Zikri;

over the Simeonites: Shephatiah son of Maakah;

¹⁷over Levi: Hashabiah son of Kemuel; 1Ch 26:30

over Aaron: Zadok; 1Ch 12:28

¹⁸over Judah: Elihu, a brother of David;

over Issachar: Omri son of Michael;

¹⁹over Zebulun: Ishmaiah son of Obadiah;

over Naphtali: Jerimoth son of Azriel;

²⁰over the Ephraimites: Hoshea son of Azaziah;

over half the tribe of Manasseh: Joel son of Pedaiah;
²¹ over the half-tribe of Manasseh in Gilead: Iddo son of Zechariah;

over Benjamin: Jaasiel son of Abner;
²² over Dan: Azarel son of Jeroham.

These were the leaders of the tribes of Israel.

²³ David did not take the number of the men twenty years old or less, because the LORD had promised to make Israel as numerous as the stars in the sky. ²⁴ Joab son of Zeruiah began to count the men but did not finish. God's wrath came on Israel on account of this numbering, and the number was not entered in the book*a* of the annals of King David.   Ge 15:5; 2Sa 24:15

The King's Overseers

²⁵ Azmaveth son of Adiel was in charge of the royal storehouses.

Jonathan son of Uzziah was in charge of the storehouses in the outlying districts, in the towns, the villages and the watchtowers.
²⁶ Ezri son of Kelub was in charge of the workers who farmed the land.
²⁷ Shimei the Ramathite was in charge of the vineyards.

Zabdi the Shiphmite was in charge of the produce of the vineyards for the wine vats.

²⁸ Baal-Hanan the Gederite was in charge of the olive and sycamore-fig trees in the western foothills.   1Ki 10:27

Joash was in charge of the supplies of olive oil.

²⁹ Shitrai the Sharonite was in charge of the herds grazing in Sharon.

Shaphat son of Adlai was in charge of the herds in the valleys.
³⁰ Obil the Ishmaelite was in charge of the camels.

Jehdeiah the Meronothite was in charge of the donkeys.
³¹ Jaziz the Hagrite was in charge of the flocks.   1Ch 5:10

All these were the officials in charge of King David's property.

³² Jonathan, David's uncle, was a counselor, a man of insight and a scribe. Jehiel son of Hakmoni took care of the king's sons.
³³ Ahithophel was the king's counselor.   2Sa 15:12

Hushai the Arkite was the king's confidant. ³⁴ Ahithophel was succeeded by Jehoiada son of Benaiah and by Abiathar.

Joab was the commander of the royal army.   1Ch 11:6

David's Plans for the Temple

28 David summoned all the officials of Israel to assemble at Jerusalem: the officers over the tribes, the commanders of the divisions in the service of the king, the commanders of thousands

a 24 Septuagint; Hebrew *number*

and commanders of hundreds, and the officials in charge of all the property and livestock belonging to the king and his sons, together with the palace officials, the warriors and all the brave fighting men. 1Ch 27:1-31

[2] King David rose to his feet and said: "Listen to me, my fellow Israelites, my people. I had it in my heart to build a house as a place of rest for the ark of the covenant of the LORD, for the footstool of our God, and I made plans to build it. [3] But God said to me, 'You are not to build a house for my Name, because you are a warrior and have shed blood.' 1Ch 22:8; Ps 132:7

[4] "Yet the LORD, the God of Israel, chose me from my whole family to be king over Israel forever. He chose Judah as leader, and from the tribe of Judah he chose my family, and from my father's sons he was pleased to make me king over all Israel. [5] Of all my sons—and the LORD has given me many—he has chosen my son Solomon to sit on the throne of the kingdom of the LORD over Israel. [6] He said to me: 'Solomon your son is the one who will build my house and my courts, for I have chosen him to be my son, and I will be his father. [7] I will establish his kingdom forever if he is unswerving in carrying out my commands and laws, as is being done at this time.' 2Sa 7:13; 1Ch 22:13

[8] "So now I charge you in the sight of all Israel and of the assembly of the LORD, and in the hearing of our God: Be careful to follow all the commands of the LORD your God, that you may possess this good land and pass it on as an inheritance to your descendants forever. Dt 4:1; 6:1

[9] "And you, my son Solomon, acknowledge the God of your father, and serve him with wholehearted devotion and with a willing mind, for the LORD searches every heart and understands every desire and every thought. If you seek him, he will be found by you; but if you forsake him, he will reject you forever. [10] Consider now, for the LORD has chosen you to build a house as the sanctuary. Be strong and do the work." 1Sa 16:7; 2Ch 15:2

[11] Then David gave his son Solomon the plans for the portico of the temple, its buildings, its storerooms, its upper parts, its inner rooms and the place of atonement. [12] He gave him the plans of all that the Spirit had put in his mind for the courts of the temple of the LORD and all the surrounding rooms, for the treasuries of the temple of God and for the treasuries for the dedicated things. [13] He gave him instructions for the divisions of the priests and Levites, and for all the work of serving in the temple of the LORD, as well as for all the articles to be used in its service. [14] He designated the weight of gold for all the gold articles to be used in various kinds

of service, and the weight of silver for all the silver articles to be used in various kinds of service: [15]the weight of gold for the gold lampstands and their lamps, with the weight for each lampstand and its lamps; and the weight of silver for each silver lampstand and its lamps, according to the use of each lampstand; [16]the weight of gold for each table for consecrated bread; the weight of silver for the silver tables; [17]the weight of pure gold for the forks, sprinkling bowls and pitchers; the weight of gold for each gold dish; the weight of silver for each silver dish; [18]and the weight of the refined gold for the altar of incense. He also gave him the plan for the chariot, that is, the cherubim of gold that spread their wings and overshadow the ark of the covenant of the LORD.   Ex 25:18-22; 30:1-10; 1Ch 24:1

[19]"All this," David said, "I have in writing as a result of the LORD's hand on me, and he enabled me to understand all the details of the plan." Ex 25:9; 1Ki 6:38

[20]David also said to Solomon his son, "Be strong and courageous, and do the work. Do not be afraid or discouraged, for the LORD God, my God, is with you. He will not fail you or forsake you until all the work for the service of the temple of the LORD is finished. [21]The divisions of the priests and Levites are ready for all the work on the temple of God, and every willing person skilled in any craft will help you in all the work. The officials and all the people will obey your every command." Ex 35:25-36:5; Dt 31:6

Gifts for Building the Temple

29 Then King David said to the whole assembly: "My son Solomon, the one whom God has chosen, is young and inexperienced. The task is great, because this palatial structure is not for man but for the LORD God. [2]With all my resources I have provided for the temple of my God—gold for the gold work, silver for the silver, bronze for the bronze, iron for the iron and wood for the wood, as well as onyx for the settings, turquoise,[a] stones of various colors, and all kinds of fine stone and marble—all of these in large quantities. [3]Besides, in my devotion to the temple of my God I now give my personal treasures of gold and silver for the temple of my God, over and above everything I have provided for this holy temple: [4]three thousand talents[b] of gold (gold of Ophir) and seven thousand talents[c] of refined silver, for the overlaying of the walls of the buildings, [5]for the gold work and the silver work, and for all the work to be done by the craftsmen. Now, who is willing to

---

[a] 2 The meaning of the Hebrew for this word is uncertain.   [b] 4 That is, about 110 tons or about 100 metric tons   [c] 4 That is, about 260 tons or about 235 metric tons

consecrate themselves to the LORD today?" 1Ch 22:14; Isa 54:11 ⁶Then the leaders of families, the officers of the tribes of Israel, the commanders of thousands and commanders of hundreds, and the officials in charge of the king's work gave willingly. ⁷They gave toward the work on the temple of God five thousand talents*ᵃ* and ten thousand darics*ᵇ* of gold, ten thousand talents*ᶜ* of silver, eighteen thousand talents*ᵈ* of bronze and a hundred thousand talents*ᵉ* of iron. ⁸Anyone who had precious stones gave them to the treasury of the temple of the LORD in the custody of Jehiel the Gershonite. ⁹The people rejoiced at the willing response of their leaders, for they had given freely and wholeheartedly to the LORD. David the king also rejoiced greatly. 1Ki 8:61; 1Ch 26:21; 2Co 9:7

David's Prayer

¹⁰David praised the LORD in the presence of the whole assembly, saying,

"Praise be to you, LORD,
    the God of our father Israel,
    from everlasting to
    everlasting.
¹¹Yours, LORD, is the greatness
    and the power Ps 24:8; 59:17
    and the glory and the
    majesty and the
    splendor,

for everything in heaven and
    earth is yours. Ps 89:11
Yours, LORD, is the
    kingdom;
you are exalted as head
    over all. Rev 5:12-13
¹²Wealth and honor come from
    you; 2Ch 1:12
you are the ruler of all
    things. 2Ch 20:6; Ro 11:36
In your hands are strength
    and power
to exalt and give strength to
    all.
¹³Now, our God, we give you
    thanks,
    and praise your glorious
    name.

¹⁴"But who am I, and who are my people, that we should be able to give as generously as this? Everything comes from you, and we have given you only what comes from your hand. ¹⁵We are foreigners and strangers in your sight, as were all our ancestors. Our days on earth are like a shadow, without hope. ¹⁶LORD our God, all this abundance that we have provided for building you a temple for your Holy Name comes from your hand, and all of it belongs to you. ¹⁷I know, my God, that you test the heart and are pleased with integrity. All these things I have given willingly and with honest intent. And now I have seen with joy how

---

ᵃ 7 That is, about 190 tons or about 170 metric tons   *ᵇ* 7 That is, about 185 pounds or about 84 kilograms   *ᶜ* 7 That is, about 380 tons or about 340 metric tons   *ᵈ* 7 That is, about 675 tons or about 610 metric tons   *ᵉ* 7 That is, about 3,800 tons or about 3,400 metric tons willingly your people who are here have given to you. ¹⁸LORD, the God of our fathers Abraham, Isaac and Israel, keep these desires and thoughts in the hearts of your people forever, and keep their hearts loyal to you. ¹⁹And give my son Solomon the wholehearted devotion to keep your commands, statutes and decrees and to do everything to build the palatial structure for which I have provided." 1Ch 22:14; 28:9; Ps 72:1

²⁰Then David said to the whole assembly, "Praise the LORD your God." So they all praised the LORD, the God of their fathers; they bowed down, prostrating themselves before the LORD and the king.

Solomon Acknowledged as King
29:21-25pp — 1Ki 1:28-53

²¹The next day they made sacrifices to the LORD and presented burnt offerings to him: a thousand bulls, a thousand rams and a thousand male lambs, together with their drink offerings, and other sacrifices in abundance for all Israel. ²²They ate and drank with great joy in the presence of the LORD that day. 1Ki 8:62; 1Ch 23:1

Then they acknowledged Solomon son of David as king a second time, anointing him before the LORD to be ruler and Zadok to be priest. ²³So Solomon sat on the throne of the LORD as king in place of his father David. He prospered and all Israel obeyed him. ²⁴All the officers and warriors, as well as all of King David's sons, pledged their submission to King Solomon. 1Ki 1:33-39; 2:12

²⁵The LORD highly exalted Solomon in the sight of all Israel and bestowed on him royal splendor such as no king over Israel ever had before. 1Ki 1:28-53; 3:13

The Death of David
29:26-28pp — 1Ki 2:10-12

²⁶David son of Jesse was king over all Israel. ²⁷He ruled over Israel forty years—seven in Hebron and thirty-three in Jerusalem. ²⁸He died at a good old age, having enjoyed long life, wealth and honor. His son Solomon succeeded him as king. Ge 15:15; 1Ki 2:10

²⁹As for the events of King David's reign, from beginning to end, they are written in the records of Samuel the seer, the records of Nathan the prophet and the records of Gad the seer, ³⁰together with the details of his reign and power, and the circumstances that surrounded him and Israel and the kingdoms of all the other lands. 1Sa 9:9; 22:5; 2Sa 7:2

2 Chronicles

Solomon Asks for Wisdom

1:2-13pp — 1Ki 3:4-15
1:14-17pp — 1Ki 10:26-29; 2Ch 9:25-28

1 Solomon son of David established himself firmly over his kingdom, for the LORD his God was with him and made him exceedingly great. Ge 39:2; 1Ki 2:12,26

²Then Solomon spoke to all Israel — to the commanders of thousands and commanders of hundreds, to the judges and to all the leaders in Israel, the heads of families — ³and Solomon and the whole assembly went to the high place at Gibeon, for God's tent of meeting was there, which Moses the LORD's servant had made in the wilderness. ⁴Now David had brought up the ark of God from Kiriath Jearim to the place he had prepared for it, because he had pitched a tent for it in Jerusalem. ⁵But the bronze altar that Bezalel son of Uri, the son of Hur, had made was in Gibeon in front of the tabernacle of the LORD; so Solomon and the assembly inquired of him there. ⁶Solomon went up to the bronze altar before the LORD in the tent of meeting and offered a thousand burnt offerings on it. Ex 36:8; 38:2; 2Sa 6:17

⁷That night God appeared to Solomon and said to him, "Ask for whatever you want me to give you." 2Ch 7:12

⁸Solomon answered God, "You have shown great kindness to David my father and have made me king in his place. ⁹Now, LORD God, let your promise to my father David be confirmed, for you have made me king over a people who are as numerous as the dust of the earth. ¹⁰Give me wisdom and knowledge, that I may lead this people, for who is able to govern this great people of yours?" Nu 27:17; 1Ch 28:5

¹¹God said to Solomon, "Since this is your heart's desire and you have not asked for wealth, possessions or honor, nor for the death of your enemies, and since you have not asked for a long life but for wisdom and knowledge to govern my people over whom

I have made you king, [12]therefore wisdom and knowledge will be given you. And I will also give you wealth, possessions and honor, such as no king who was before you ever had and none after you will have." 1Ch 29:25; 2Ch 9:22

[13]Then Solomon went to Jerusalem from the high place at Gibeon, from before the tent of meeting. And he reigned over Israel.

[14]Solomon accumulated chariots and horses; he had fourteen hundred chariots and twelve thousand horses,[a] which he kept in the chariot cities and also with him in Jerusalem. [15]The king made silver and gold as common in Jerusalem as stones, and cedar as plentiful as sycamore-fig trees in the foothills. [16]Solomon's horses were imported from Egypt and from Kue[b] — the royal merchants purchased them from Kue at the current price. [17]They imported a chariot from Egypt for six hundred shekels[c] of silver, and a horse for a hundred and fifty.[d] They also exported them to all the kings of the Hittites and of the Arameans. 1Ki 3:4-15; 10:26-29

Preparations for Building the Temple

2:1-18pp — 1Ki 5:1-16

2 [e] Solomon gave orders to build a temple for the Name of the LORD and a royal palace for himself. [2]He conscripted 70,000 men as carriers and 80,000 as stonecutters in the hills and 3,600 as foremen over them. ver 18; 2Ch 10:4

[3]Solomon sent this message to Hiram[f] king of Tyre:

"Send me cedar logs as you did for my father David when you sent him cedar to build a palace to live in. [4]Now I am about to build a temple for the Name of the LORD my God and to dedicate it to him for burning fragrant incense before him, for setting out the consecrated bread regularly, and for making burnt offerings every morning and evening and on the Sabbaths, at the New Moons and at the appointed festivals of the LORD our God. This is a lasting ordinance for Israel. Ex 25:30; Nu 28:9-10; Dt 12:5

[5]"The temple I am going to build will be great, because our God is greater than all other gods. [6]But who is able to build a temple for him, since the heavens, even the highest heavens, cannot contain him? Who then am I to build a temple for him, except as a place to burn sacrifices before him? 1Ki 8:27; 1Ch 16:25

[7]"Send me, therefore, a man skilled to work in gold

---

a 14 Or *charioteers*   *b 16* Probably Cilicia   *c 17* That is, about 15 pounds or about 6.9 kilograms   *d 17* That is, about 3 3/4 pounds or about 1.7 kilograms   *e* In Hebrew texts 2:1 is numbered 1:18, and 2:2-18 is numbered 2:1-17.   *f 3* Hebrew *Huram,* a variant of *Hiram*; also in verses 11 and 12 and silver, bronze and iron, and in purple, crimson and blue yarn, and experienced in the art of engraving, to work in Judah and Jerusalem with my skilled workers, whom my father David provided. 1Ch 22:16

⁸ "Send me also cedar, juniper and algum*a* logs from Lebanon, for I know that your servants are skilled in cutting timber there. My servants will work with yours ⁹ to provide me with plenty of lumber, because the temple I build must be large and magnificent. ¹⁰ I will give your servants, the woodsmen who cut the timber, twenty thousand cors*b* of ground wheat, twenty thousand cors*c* of barley, twenty thousand baths*d* of wine and twenty thousand baths of olive oil." Ezr 3:7

¹¹ Hiram king of Tyre replied by letter to Solomon:

"Because the LORD loves his people, he has made you their king." 1Ki 10:9; 2Ch 9:8

¹² And Hiram added:

"Praise be to the LORD, the God of Israel, who made heaven and earth! He has given King David a wise son, endowed with intelligence and discernment, who will build a temple for the LORD and a palace for himself. Ps 33:6; 102:25

¹³ "I am sending you Huram-Abi, a man of great skill, ¹⁴ whose mother was from Dan and whose father was from Tyre. He is trained to work in gold and silver, bronze and iron, stone and wood, and with purple and blue and crimson yarn and fine linen. He is experienced in all kinds of engraving and can execute any design given to him. He will work with your skilled workers and with those of my lord, David your father. Ex 31:6

¹⁵ "Now let my lord send his servants the wheat and barley and the olive oil and wine he promised, ¹⁶ and we will cut all the logs from Lebanon that you need and will float them as rafts by sea down to Joppa. You can then take them up to Jerusalem." Jos 19:46; Jnh 1:3

¹⁷ Solomon took a census of all the foreigners residing in Israel, after the census his father David had taken; and they were found to be 153,600. ¹⁸ He assigned 70,000 of them to be carriers and 80,000 to be stonecutters in the hills, with 3,600 foremen over

a 8 Probably a variant of *almug*   *b 10* That is, probably about 3,600 tons or about 3,200 metric tons of wheat   *c 10* That is, probably about 3,000 tons or about 2,700 metric tons of barley   *d 10* That is, about 120,000 gallons or about 440,000 liters them to keep the people working. 1Ki 5:1-16; 1Ch 22:2

Solomon Builds the Temple

3:1-14pp — 1Ki 6:1-29

3 Then Solomon began to build the temple of the LORD in Jerusalem on Mount Moriah, where the LORD had appeared to his father David. It was on the threshing floor of Araunah[a] the Jebusite, the place provided by David. [2] He began building on the second day of the second month in the fourth year of his reign. 1Ch 21:18; Ac 7:47

[3] The foundation Solomon laid for building the temple of God was sixty cubits long and twenty cubits wide[b] (using the cubit of the old standard). [4] The portico at the front of the temple was twenty cubits[c] long across the width of the building and twenty[d] cubits high. Eze 41:2

He overlaid the inside with pure gold. [5] He paneled the main hall with juniper and covered it with fine gold and decorated it with palm tree and chain designs. [6] He adorned the temple with precious stones. And the gold he used was gold of Parvaim. [7] He overlaid the ceiling beams, doorframes, walls and doors of the temple with gold,

and he carved cherubim on the walls. Ge 3:24; 1Ki 6:29-35; Eze 40:16

[8] He built the Most Holy Place, its length corresponding to the width of the temple — twenty cubits long and twenty cubits wide. He overlaid the inside with six hundred talents[e] of fine gold. [9] The gold nails weighed fifty shekels.[f] He also overlaid the upper parts with gold. Ex 26:32-33

[10] For the Most Holy Place he made a pair of sculptured cherubim and overlaid them with gold. [11] The total wingspan of the cherubim was twenty cubits. One wing of the first cherub was five cubits[g] long and touched the temple wall, while its other wing, also five cubits long, touched the wing of the other cherub. [12] Similarly one wing of the second cherub was five cubits long and touched the other temple wall, and its other wing, also five cubits long, touched the wing of the first cherub. [13] The wings of these cherubim extended twenty cubits. They stood on their feet, facing the main hall.[h] Ex 25:18

[14] He made the curtain of blue, purple and crimson yarn and fine linen, with cherubim worked into it. 1Ki 6:1-29

[15] For the front of the temple he made two pillars, which

---

[a] 1 Hebrew Ornan, a variant of Araunah [b] 3 That is, about 90 feet long and 30 feet wide or about 27 meters long and 9 meters wide [c] 4 That is, about 30 feet or about 9 meters; also in verses 8, 11 and 13 [d] 4 Some Septuagint and Syriac manuscripts; Hebrew and a hundred and twenty [e] 8 That is, about 23 tons or about 21 metric tons [f] 9 That is, about 1 1/4 pounds or about 575 grams [g] 11 That is, about 7 1/2 feet or about 2.3 meters; also in verse 15 [h] 13 Or facing inward

together were thirty-five cubits[a] long, each with a capital five cubits high. [16] He made interwoven chains[b] and put them on top of the pillars. He also made a hundred pomegranates and attached them to the chains. [17] He erected the pillars in the front of the temple, one to the south and one to the north. The one to the south he named Jakin[c] and the one to the north Boaz.[d]   1Ki 7:15,17,20

The Temple's Furnishings
4:2-6,10 – 5:1pp — 1Ki 7:23-26,38-51

4 He made a bronze altar twenty cubits long, twenty cubits wide and ten cubits high.[e] [2] He made the Sea of cast metal, circular in shape, measuring ten cubits from rim to rim and five cubits[f] high. It took a line of thirty cubits[g] to measure around it. [3] Below the rim, figures of bulls encircled it — ten to a cubit.[h] The bulls were cast in two rows in one piece with the Sea.   Ex 27:1-2; 2Ki 16:14
[4] The Sea stood on twelve bulls, three facing north, three facing west, three facing south and three facing east. The Sea rested on top of them, and their hindquarters were toward the center. [5] It was a handbreadth[i] in thickness, and its rim was like the rim of a cup, like a lily blossom. It held three thousand baths.[j]

[6] He then made ten basins for washing and placed five on the south side and five on the north. In them the things to be used for the burnt offerings were rinsed, but the Sea was to be used by the priests for washing.   1Ki 7:23-26,38-51

[7] He made ten gold lampstands according to the specifications for them and placed them in the temple, five on the south side and five on the north.   Ex 25:31,40

[8] He made ten tables and placed them in the temple, five on the south side and five on the north. He also made a hundred gold sprinkling bowls.   Ex 25:23; Nu 4:14

[9] He made the courtyard of the priests, and the large court and the doors for the court, and overlaid the doors with bronze. [10] He placed the Sea on the south side, at the southeast corner.   1Ki 6:36

[11] And Huram also made the pots and shovels and sprinkling bowls.

So Huram finished the work he had undertaken for King Solomon in the temple of God: 1Ki 7:14

[12] the two pillars;

the two bowl-shaped capitals on top of the pillars;

the two sets of network dec-

---

[a] 15 That is, about 53 feet or about 16 meters   [b] 16 Or possibly *made chains in the inner sanctuary*; the meaning of the Hebrew for this phrase is uncertain.   [c] 17 *Jakin* probably means *he establishes*.   [d] 17 *Boaz* probably means *in him is strength*.   [e] 1 That is, about 30 feet long and wide and 15 feet high or about 9 meters long and wide and 4.5 meters high   [f] 2 That is, about 7 1/2 feet or about 2.3 meters   [g] 2 That is, about 45 feet or about 14 meters   [h] 3 That is, about 18 inches or about 45 centimeters   [i] 5 That is, about 3 inches or about 7.5 centimeters   [j] 5 That is, about 18,000 gallons or about 66,000 liters

orating the two bowl-shaped capitals on top of the pillars;

[13] the four hundred pomegranates for the two sets of network (two rows of pomegranates for each network, decorating the bowl-shaped capitals on top of the pillars);

[14] the stands with their basins;

[15] the Sea and the twelve bulls under it;

[16] the pots, shovels, meat forks and all related articles.

All the objects that Huram-Abi made for King Solomon for the temple of the LORD were of polished bronze. [17] The king had them cast in clay molds in the plain of the Jordan between Sukkoth and Zarethan.[a] [18] All these things that Solomon made amounted to so much that the weight of the bronze could not be calculated.   1Ki 7:13,23

[19] Solomon also made all the furnishings that were in God's temple:

the golden altar;

the tables on which was the bread of the Presence;

[20] the lampstands of pure gold with their lamps, to burn in front of the inner sanctuary as prescribed; Ex 25:31

[21] the gold floral work and lamps and tongs (they were solid gold);

[22] the pure gold wick trimmers, sprinkling bowls, dishes and censers; and the gold doors of the temple: the inner doors to the Most Holy Place and the doors of the main hall.   Lev 10:1; Nu 7:14

5 When all the work Solomon had done for the temple of the LORD was finished, he brought in the things his father David had dedicated—the silver and gold and all the furnishings—and he placed them in the treasuries of God's temple.   2Sa 8:11; 1Ki 6:14

The Ark Brought to the Temple
5:2 – 6:11pp — 1Ki 8:1-21

[2] Then Solomon summoned to Jerusalem the elders of Israel, all the heads of the tribes and the chiefs of the Israelite families, to bring up the ark of the LORD's covenant from Zion, the City of David. [3] And all the Israelites came together to the king at the time of the festival in the seventh month.   2Sa 6:12; 1Ch 9:1; 15:25

[4] When all the elders of Israel had arrived, the Levites took up the ark, [5] and they brought up the ark and the tent of meeting and all the sacred furnishings in it. The Levitical priests carried them up; [6] and King Solomon and the entire assembly of Israel that had gathered about him were before the ark, sacrificing so many sheep and cattle that they could not be recorded or counted.   Nu 3:31

[a] 17 Hebrew Zeredatha, a variant of Zarethan

⁷The priests then brought the ark of the LORD's covenant to its place in the inner sanctuary of the temple, the Most Holy Place, and put it beneath the wings of the cherubim. ⁸The cherubim spread their wings over the place of the ark and covered the ark and its carrying poles. ⁹These poles were so long that their ends, extending from the ark, could be seen from in front of the inner sanctuary, but not from outside the Holy Place; and they are still there today. ¹⁰There was nothing in the ark except the two tablets that Moses had placed in it at Horeb, where the LORD made a covenant with the Israelites after they came out of Egypt.   Dt 10:2; Ge 3:24; Rev 11:19

¹¹The priests then withdrew from the Holy Place. All the priests who were there had consecrated themselves, regardless of their divisions. ¹²All the Levites who were musicians — Asaph, Heman, Jeduthun and their sons and relatives — stood on the east side of the altar, dressed in fine linen and playing cymbals, harps and lyres. They were accompanied by 120 priests sounding trumpets. ¹³The trumpeters and musicians joined in unison to give praise and thanks to the LORD. Accompanied by trumpets, cymbals and other instruments, the singers raised their voices in praise to the LORD and sang: 1Ch 15:24; 25:1

"He is good;
  his love endures forever."

Then the temple of the LORD was filled with the cloud, ¹⁴and the priests could not perform their service because of the cloud, for the glory of the LORD filled the temple of God.   Ex 29:43; 2Ch 7:2

6 Then Solomon said, "The LORD has said that he would dwell in a dark cloud; ²I have built a magnificent temple for you, a place for you to dwell forever."   1Ki 8:12-50; Ps 135:21

³While the whole assembly of Israel was standing there, the king turned around and blessed them. ⁴Then he said:

"Praise be to the LORD, the God of Israel, who with his hands has fulfilled what he promised with his mouth to my father David. For he said, ⁵'Since the day I brought my people out of Egypt, I have not chosen a city in any tribe of Israel to have a temple built so that my Name might be there, nor have I chosen anyone to be ruler over my people Israel. ⁶But now I have chosen Jerusalem for my Name to be there, and I have chosen David to rule my people Israel.' 1Ch 28:4; 2Ch 12:13

⁷"My father David had it in his heart to build a temple for the Name of the LORD, the God of Israel. ⁸But the LORD said to my father David, 'You

did well to have it in your heart to build a temple for my Name. [9] Nevertheless, you are not the one to build the temple, but your son, your own flesh and blood—he is the one who will build the temple for my Name.' 1Sa 10:7; Ac 7:46

[10] "The LORD has kept the promise he made. I have succeeded David my father and now I sit on the throne of Israel, just as the LORD promised, and I have built the temple for the Name of the LORD, the God of Israel. [11] There I have placed the ark, in which is the covenant of the LORD that he made with the people of Israel." 1Ki 8:1-21; 2Ch 5:10

Solomon's Prayer of Dedication

6:12-40pp — 1Ki 8:22-53
6:41-42pp — Ps 132:8-10

[12] Then Solomon stood before the altar of the LORD in front of the whole assembly of Israel and spread out his hands. [13] Now he had made a bronze platform, five cubits long, five cubits wide and three cubits high,[a] and had placed it in the center of the outer court. He stood on the platform and then knelt down before the whole assembly of Israel and spread out his hands toward heaven. [14] He said: Ne 8:4; Ps 95:6

"LORD, the God of Israel, there is no God like you in heaven or on earth—you who keep your covenant of love with your servants who continue wholeheartedly in your way. [15] You have kept your promise to your servant David my father; with your mouth you have promised and with your hand you have fulfilled it—as it is today. Dt 7:9; 1Ch 22:10

[16] "Now, LORD, the God of Israel, keep for your servant David my father the promises you made to him when you said, 'You shall never fail to have a successor to sit before me on the throne of Israel, if only your descendants are careful in all they do to walk before me according to my law, as you have done.' [17] And now, LORD, the God of Israel, let your word that you promised your servant David come true. 2Sa 7:13,15; 1Ki 2:4; 2Ch 7:18

[18] "But will God really dwell on earth with humans? The heavens, even the highest heavens, cannot contain you. How much less this temple I have built! [19] Yet, LORD my God, give attention to your servant's prayer and his plea for mercy. Hear the cry and the prayer that your servant is praying in your presence. [20] May your eyes be open toward this temple day and

---

[a] 13 That is, about 7 1/2 feet long and wide and 4 1/2 feet high or about 2.3 meters long and wide and 1.4 meters high

night, this place of which you said you would put your Name there. May you hear the prayer your servant prays toward this place. [21] Hear the supplications of your servant and of your people Israel when they pray toward this place. Hear from heaven, your dwelling place; and when you hear, forgive.

[22] "When anyone wrongs their neighbor and is required to take an oath and they come and swear the oath before your altar in this temple, [23] then hear from heaven and act. Judge between your servants, condemning the guilty and bringing down on their heads what they have done, and vindicating the innocent by treating them in accordance with their innocence. Ex 22:11; Isa 3:11

[24] "When your people Israel have been defeated by an enemy because they have sinned against you and when they turn back and give praise to your name, praying and making supplication before you in this temple, [25] then hear from heaven and forgive the sin of your people Israel and bring them back to the land you gave to them and their ancestors. Lev 26:17

[26] "When the heavens are shut up and there is no rain because your people have sinned against you, and when they pray toward this place and give praise to your name and turn from their sin because you have afflicted them, [27] then hear from heaven and forgive the sin of your servants, your people Israel. Teach them the right way to live, and send rain on the land you gave your people for an inheritance. 1Ki 17:1

[28] "When famine or plague comes to the land, or blight or mildew, locusts or grasshoppers, or when enemies besiege them in any of their cities, whatever disaster or disease may come, [29] and when a prayer or plea is made by anyone among your people Israel—being aware of their afflictions and pains, and spreading out their hands toward this temple— [30] then hear from heaven, your dwelling place. Forgive, and deal with everyone according to all they do, since you know their hearts (for you alone know the human heart), [31] so that they will fear you and walk in obedience to you all the time they live in the land you gave our ancestors. 1Sa 16:7; 1Ch 28:9; 2Ch 20:9

[32] "As for the foreigner who does not belong to your people Israel but has come from a distant land because of your great name and your

mighty hand and your outstretched arm — when they come and pray toward this temple, ³³ then hear from heaven, your dwelling place. Do whatever the foreigner asks of you, so that all the peoples of the earth may know your name and fear you, as do your own people Israel, and may know that this house I have built bears your Name.   2Ch 7:14; Jn 12:20

³⁴ "When your people go to war against their enemies, wherever you send them, and when they pray to you toward this city you have chosen and the temple I have built for your Name, ³⁵ then hear from heaven their prayer and their plea, and uphold their cause.   Dt 28:7; 1Ch 5:20

³⁶ "When they sin against you — for there is no one who does not sin — and you become angry with them and give them over to the enemy, who takes them captive to a land far away or near; ³⁷ and if they have a change of heart in the land where they are held captive, and repent and plead with you in the land of their captivity and say, 'We have sinned, we have done wrong and acted wickedly'; ³⁸ and if they turn back to you with all their heart and soul in the land of their captivity where they were taken, and pray toward the land you gave their ancestors, toward the city you have chosen and toward the temple I have built for your Name; ³⁹ then from heaven, your dwelling place, hear their prayer and their pleas, and uphold their cause. And forgive your people, who have sinned against you.   Job 15:14; Jas 3:1; 1Jn 1:8-10

⁴⁰ "Now, my God, may your eyes be open and your ears attentive to the prayers offered in this place.   1Ki 8:22-53

⁴¹ "Now arise, LORD God,
　and come to your
　resting place, 1Ch 28:2
you and the ark of your
　might.
May your priests, LORD
　God, be clothed
　with salvation,
may your faithful
　people rejoice in
　your goodness.
⁴² LORD God, do not reject
　your anointed one.
Remember the great
　love promised
　to David your
　servant."   Ps 132:8-10

The Dedication of the Temple
7:1-10pp — 1Ki 8:62-66

7 When Solomon finished praying, fire came down from heaven and consumed the burnt offering and the sacrifices, and the glory of the LORD filled the temple. ² The priests could not

enter the temple of the LORD because the glory of the LORD filled it. ³When all the Israelites saw the fire coming down and the glory of the LORD above the temple, they knelt on the pavement with their faces to the ground, and they worshiped and gave thanks to the LORD, saying,   Ex 29:43; 40:35; 2Ch 5:14

"He is good;
his love endures forever."

⁴Then the king and all the people offered sacrifices before the LORD. ⁵And King Solomon offered a sacrifice of twenty-two thousand head of cattle and a hundred and twenty thousand sheep and goats. So the king and all the people dedicated the temple of God. ⁶The priests took their positions, as did the Levites with the LORD's musical instruments, which King David had made for praising the LORD and which were used when he gave thanks, saying, "His love endures forever." Opposite the Levites, the priests blew their trumpets, and all the Israelites were standing.   1Ch 15:16; 2Ch 5:12-13

⁷Solomon consecrated the middle part of the courtyard in front of the temple of the LORD, and there he offered burnt offerings and the fat of the fellowship offerings, because the bronze altar he had made could not hold the burnt offerings, the grain offerings and the fat portions.

⁸So Solomon observed the festival at that time for seven days, and all Israel with him—a vast assembly, people from Lebo Hamath to the Wadi of Egypt. ⁹On the eighth day they held an assembly, for they had celebrated the dedication of the altar for seven days and the festival for seven days more. ¹⁰On the twenty-third day of the seventh month he sent the people to their homes, joyful and glad in heart for the good things the LORD had done for David and Solomon and for his people Israel.   Lev 23:36; 2Ch 30:26

The LORD Appears to Solomon

7:11-22pp — 1Ki 9:1-9

¹¹When Solomon had finished the temple of the LORD and the royal palace, and had succeeded in carrying out all he had in mind to do in the temple of the LORD and in his own palace, ¹²the LORD appeared to him at night and said:

"I have heard your prayer and have chosen this place for myself as a temple for sacrifices.   Dt 12:5

¹³"When I shut up the heavens so that there is no rain, or command locusts to devour the land or send a plague among my people, ¹⁴if my people, who are called by my name, will humble themselves and pray and seek my face and turn from their wicked ways, then I will hear from heaven, and

I will forgive their sin and will heal their land. ¹⁵ Now my eyes will be open and my ears attentive to the prayers offered in this place. ¹⁶ I have chosen and consecrated this temple so that my Name may be there forever. My eyes and my heart will always be there. 2Ch 6:27,37,40

¹⁷ "As for you, if you walk before me faithfully as David your father did, and do all I command, and observe my decrees and laws, ¹⁸ I will establish your royal throne, as I covenanted with David your father when I said, 'You shall never fail to have a successor to rule over Israel.' 1Ki 9:4

¹⁹ "But if you[a] turn away and forsake the decrees and commands I have given you[a] and go off to serve other gods and worship them, ²⁰ then I will uproot Israel from my land, which I have given them, and will reject this temple I have consecrated for my Name. I will make it a byword and an object of ridicule among all peoples. ²¹ This temple will become a heap of rubble. All[b] who pass by will be appalled and say, 'Why has the LORD done such a thing to this land and to this temple?' ²² People

will answer, 'Because they have forsaken the LORD, the God of their ancestors, who brought them out of Egypt, and have embraced other gods, worshiping and serving them — that is why he brought all this disaster on them.'" 1Ki 9:1-9; Dt 29:24

Solomon's Other Activities
8:1-18pp — 1Ki 9:10-28

8 At the end of twenty years, during which Solomon built the temple of the LORD and his own palace, ²Solomon rebuilt the villages that Hiram[c] had given him, and settled Israelites in them. ³Solomon then went to Hamath Zobah and captured it. ⁴He also built up Tadmor in the desert and all the store cities he had built in Hamath. ⁵He rebuilt Upper Beth Horon and Lower Beth Horon as fortified cities, with walls and with gates and bars, ⁶as well as Baalath and all his store cities, and all the cities for his chariots and for his horses[d] — whatever he desired to build in Jerusalem, in Lebanon and throughout all the territory he ruled. 1Ch 7:24; 2Ch 14:7

⁷There were still people left from the Hittites, Amorites, Perizzites, Hivites and Jebusites (these people were not Israelites). ⁸Solomon conscripted the descendants of

---

a 19 The Hebrew is plural.   *b 21* See some Septuagint manuscripts, Old Latin, Syriac, Arabic and Targum; Hebrew *And though this temple is now so imposing, all*   *c 2* Hebrew *Huram,* a variant of *Hiram;* also in verse 18   *d 6* Or *charioteers* all these people remaining in the land—whom the Israelites had not destroyed—to serve as slave labor, as it is to this day. [9]But Solomon did not make slaves of the Israelites for his work; they were his fighting men, commanders of his captains, and commanders of his chariots and charioteers. [10]They were also King Solomon's chief officials—two hundred and fifty officials supervising the men. Ge 10:16; 1Ki 4:6; 9:21

[11]Solomon brought Pharaoh's daughter up from the City of David to the palace he had built for her, for he said, "My wife must not live in the palace of David king of Israel, because the places the ark of the LORD has entered are holy." 1Ki 3:1; 7:8

[12]On the altar of the LORD that he had built in front of the portico, Solomon sacrificed burnt offerings to the LORD, [13]according to the daily requirement for offerings commanded by Moses for the Sabbaths, the New Moons and the three annual festivals—the Festival of Unleavened Bread, the Festival of Weeks and the Festival of Tabernacles. [14]In keeping with the ordinance of his father David, he appointed the divisions of the priests for their duties, and the Levites to lead the praise and to assist the priests according to each day's requirement. He also appointed the gatekeepers by divisions for the various gates, because this was what David the man of God had ordered. [15]They did not deviate from the king's commands to the priests or to the Levites in any matter, including that of the treasuries. Nu 28:3; 1Ch 25:1; Ne 12:24,36

[16]All Solomon's work was carried out, from the day the foundation of the temple of the LORD was laid until its completion. So the temple of the LORD was finished.

[17]Then Solomon went to Ezion Geber and Elath on the coast of Edom. [18]And Hiram sent him ships commanded by his own men, sailors who knew the sea. These, with Solomon's men, sailed to Ophir and brought back four hundred and fifty talents[a] of gold, which they delivered to King Solomon. 1Ki 9:10-28; 2Ch 9:9

The Queen of Sheba Visits Solomon
9:1-12pp — 1Ki 10:1-13

9 When the queen of Sheba heard of Solomon's fame, she came to Jerusalem to test him with hard questions. Arriving with a very great caravan—with camels carrying spices, large quantities of gold, and precious stones—she came to Solomon and talked with him about all she had on her mind. [2]Solomon answered all her questions; nothing was too hard for him to explain to her. [3]When the queen of Sheba

---

[a]18 That is, about 17 tons or about 15 metric tons

saw the wisdom of Solomon, as well as the palace he had built, ⁴the food on his table, the seating of his officials, the attending servants in their robes, the cupbearers in their robes and the burnt offerings he made at*a* the temple of the LORD, she was overwhelmed. 1Ki 5:12; Mt 12:42; Lk 11:31

⁵She said to the king, "The report I heard in my own country about your achievements and your wisdom is true. ⁶But I did not believe what they said until I came and saw with my own eyes. Indeed, not even half the greatness of your wisdom was told me; you have far exceeded the report I heard. ⁷How happy your people must be! How happy your officials, who continually stand before you and hear your wisdom! ⁸Praise be to the LORD your God, who has delighted in you and placed you on his throne as king to rule for the LORD your God. Because of the love of your God for Israel and his desire to uphold them forever, he has made you king over them, to maintain justice and righteousness." 1Ch 28:5; 29:23; 2Ch 2:11

⁹Then she gave the king 120 talents*b* of gold, large quantities of spices, and precious stones. There had never been such spices as those the queen of Sheba gave to King Solomon. 2Ch 8:18

¹⁰(The servants of Hiram and the servants of Solomon brought gold from Ophir; they also brought algumwood*c* and precious stones. ¹¹The king used the algumwood to make steps for the temple of the LORD and for the royal palace, and to make harps and lyres for the musicians. Nothing like them had ever been seen in Judah.) 2Ch 8:18

¹²King Solomon gave the queen of Sheba all she desired and asked for; he gave her more than she had brought to him. Then she left and returned with her retinue to her own country. 1Ki 10:1-13

Solomon's Splendor
9:13-28pp — 1Ki 10:14-29; 2Ch 1:14-17

¹³The weight of the gold that Solomon received yearly was 666 talents,*d* ¹⁴not including the revenues brought in by merchants and traders. Also all the kings of Arabia and the governors of the territories brought gold and silver to Solomon. 2Ch 17:11; Isa 21:13; Jer 25:24

¹⁵King Solomon made two hundred large shields of hammered gold; six hundred shekels*e* of hammered gold went into each shield. ¹⁶He also made three hundred small shields of hammered gold, with three hundred shekels*f* of gold in each shield. The king put them in the Palace of the Forest of Lebanon. 1Ki 7:2; 2Ch 12:9

a 4 Or *and the ascent by which he went up to* tons   *c 10* Probably a variant of *almugwood*   *b 9* That is, about 4 1/2 tons or about 4 metric tons   *d 13* That is, about 25 tons or about 23 metric tons   *e 15* That is, about 15 pounds or about 6.9 kilograms   *f 16* That is, about 7 1/2 pounds or about 3.5 kilograms

¹⁷Then the king made a great throne covered with ivory and overlaid with pure gold. ¹⁸The throne had six steps, and a footstool of gold was attached to it. On both sides of the seat were armrests, with a lion standing beside each of them. ¹⁹Twelve lions stood on the six steps, one at either end of each step. Nothing like it had ever been made for any other kingdom. ²⁰All King Solomon's goblets were gold, and all the household articles in the Palace of the Forest of Lebanon were pure gold. Nothing was made of silver, because silver was considered of little value in Solomon's day. ²¹The king had a fleet of trading ships*a* manned by Hiram's*b* servants. Once every three years it returned, carrying gold, silver and ivory, and apes and baboons. 1Ki 22:39

²²King Solomon was greater in riches and wisdom than all the other kings of the earth. ²³All the kings of the earth sought audience with Solomon to hear the wisdom God had put in his heart. ²⁴Year after year, everyone who came brought a gift—articles of silver and gold, and robes, weapons and spices, and horses and mules. 1Ki 3:13; 2Ch 1:12

²⁵Solomon had four thousand stalls for horses and chariots, and twelve thousand horses,*c* which he kept in the chariot cities and also with him in Jerusalem. ²⁶He ruled over all the kings from the Euphrates River to the land of the Philistines, as far as the border of Egypt. ²⁷The king made silver as common in Jerusalem as stones, and cedar as plentiful as sycamore-fig trees in the foothills. ²⁸Solomon's horses were imported from Egypt and from all other countries. 1Ki 10:14-29; 2Ch 1:14-17

Solomon's Death
9:29-31pp — 1Ki 11:41-43

²⁹As for the other events of Solomon's reign, from beginning to end, are they not written in the records of Nathan the prophet, in the prophecy of Ahijah the Shilonite and in the visions of Iddo the seer concerning Jeroboam son of Nebat? ³⁰Solomon reigned in Jerusalem over all Israel forty years. ³¹Then he rested with his ancestors and was buried in the city of David his father. And Rehoboam his son succeeded him as king. 1Ki 2:10; 11:41-43; 1Ch 29:29

Israel Rebels Against Rehoboam
10:1–11:4pp — 1Ki 12:1-24

10 Rehoboam went to Shechem, for all Israel had gone there to make him king. ²When Jeroboam son of Nebat heard this (he was in Egypt, where he had fled from King Solomon), he returned from Egypt. ³So they sent for Jeroboam, and

a 21 Hebrew *of ships that could go to Tarshish*
c 25 Or *charioteers*
b 21 Hebrew *Huram,* a variant of *Hiram*

he and all Israel went to Rehoboam and said to him: [4]"Your father put a heavy yoke on us, but now lighten the harsh labor and the heavy yoke he put on us, and we will serve you." 1Ki 11:40; 1Ch 9:1

[5]Rehoboam answered, "Come back to me in three days." So the people went away.

[6]Then King Rehoboam consulted the elders who had served his father Solomon during his lifetime. "How would you advise me to answer these people?" he asked. Job 8:8-9; 12:12

[7]They replied, "If you will be kind to these people and please them and give them a favorable answer, they will always be your servants." Pr 15:1

[8]But Rehoboam rejected the advice the elders gave him and consulted the young men who had grown up with him and were serving him. [9]He asked them, "What is your advice? How should we answer these people who say to me, 'Lighten the yoke your father put on us'?" 2Sa 17:14; Pr 13:20

[10]The young men who had grown up with him replied, "The people have said to you, 'Your father put a heavy yoke on us, but make our yoke lighter.' Now tell them, 'My little finger is thicker than my father's waist. [11]My father laid on you a heavy yoke; I will make it even heavier. My father scourged you with whips; I will scourge you with scorpions.'"

[12]Three days later Jeroboam and all the people returned to Rehoboam, as the king had said, "Come back to me in three days." [13]The king answered them harshly. Rejecting the advice of the elders, [14]he followed the advice of the young men and said, "My father made your yoke heavy; I will make it even heavier. My father scourged you with whips; I will scourge you with scorpions." [15]So the king did not listen to the people, for this turn of events was from God, to fulfill the word the LORD had spoken to Jeroboam son of Nebat through Ahijah the Shilonite. 1Ki 11:29; 2Ch 25:16-20

[16]When all Israel saw that the king refused to listen to them, they answered the king: 1Ch 9:1

"What share do we have in
   David,   2Sa 20:1
 what part in Jesse's son?
To your tents, Israel!
   Look after your own house,
      David!"

So all the Israelites went home. [17]But as for the Israelites who were living in the towns of Judah, Rehoboam still ruled over them.

[18]King Rehoboam sent out Adoniram,[a] who was in charge of forced labor, but the Israelites stoned him to death. King Rehoboam, however, managed to get into his chariot and escape to Jerusalem. [19]So Israel has been

[a] 18 Hebrew Hadoram, a variant of Adoniram

in rebellion against the house of David to this day. 1Ki 5:14

11 When Rehoboam arrived in Jerusalem, he mustered Judah and Benjamin—a hundred and eighty thousand able young men—to go to war against Israel and to regain the kingdom for Rehoboam. 1Ki 12:21

2 But this word of the LORD came to Shemaiah the man of God: 3 "Say to Rehoboam son of Solomon king of Judah and to all Israel in Judah and Benjamin, 4 'This is what the LORD says: Do not go up to fight against your fellow Israelites. Go home, every one of you, for this is my doing.'" So they obeyed the words of the LORD and turned back from marching against Jeroboam. 1Ki 12:1-24; 2Ch 12:5-7,15

Rehoboam Fortifies Judah

5 Rehoboam lived in Jerusalem and built up towns for defense in Judah: 6 Bethlehem, Etam, Tekoa, 7 Beth Zur, Soko, Adullam, 8 Gath, Mareshah, Ziph, 9 Adoraim, Lachish, Azekah, 10 Zorah, Aijalon and Hebron. These were fortified cities in Judah and Benjamin. 11 He strengthened their defenses and put commanders in them, with supplies of food, olive oil and wine. 12 He put shields and spears in all the cities, and made them very strong. So Judah and Benjamin were his. 13 The priests and Levites from all their districts throughout Israel sided with him. 14 The Levites even abandoned their pasturelands and property and came to Judah and Jerusalem, because Jeroboam and his sons had rejected them as priests of the LORD 15 when he appointed his own priests for the high places and for the goat and calf idols he had made. 16 Those from every tribe of Israel who set their hearts on seeking the LORD, the God of Israel, followed the Levites to Jerusalem to offer sacrifices to the LORD, the God of their ancestors. 17 They strengthened the kingdom of Judah and supported Rehoboam son of Solomon three years, following the ways of David and Solomon during this time. 2Ch 12:1; 13:9; 15:9

Rehoboam's Family

18 Rehoboam married Mahalath, who was the daughter of David's son Jerimoth and of Abihail, the daughter of Jesse's son Eliab. 19 She bore him sons: Jeush, Shemariah and Zaham. 20 Then he married Maakah daughter of Absalom, who bore him Abijah, Attai, Ziza and Shelomith. 21 Rehoboam loved Maakah daughter of Absalom more than any of his other wives and concubines. In all, he had eighteen wives and sixty concubines, twenty-eight sons and sixty daughters. Dt 17:17; 1Ki 15:2

22 Rehoboam appointed Abijah son of Maakah as crown prince among his brothers, in order to make him king. 23 He acted wise-

ly, dispersing some of his sons throughout the districts of Judah and Benjamin, and to all the fortified cities. He gave them abundant provisions and took many wives for them. Dt 21:15-17

Shishak Attacks Jerusalem

12:9-16pp — 1Ki 14:21, 25-31

12 After Rehoboam's position as king was established and he had become strong, he and all Israel[a] with him abandoned the law of the LORD. ²Because they had been unfaithful to the LORD, Shishak king of Egypt attacked Jerusalem in the fifth year of King Rehoboam. ³With twelve hundred chariots and sixty thousand horsemen and the innumerable troops of Libyans, Sukkites and Cushites[b] that came with him from Egypt, ⁴he captured the fortified cities of Judah and came as far as Jerusalem. 2Ch 11:10; 16:8

⁵Then the prophet Shemaiah came to Rehoboam and to the leaders of Judah who had assembled in Jerusalem for fear of Shishak, and he said to them, "This is what the LORD says, 'You have abandoned me; therefore, I now abandon you to Shishak.'" 2Ch 11:2

⁶The leaders of Israel and the king humbled themselves and said, "The LORD is just." Ex 9:27

⁷When the LORD saw that they humbled themselves, this word of the LORD came to Shemaiah: "Since they have humbled themselves, I will not destroy them but will soon give them deliverance. My wrath will not be poured out on Jerusalem through Shishak. ⁸They will, however, become subject to him, so that they may learn the difference between serving me and serving the kings of other lands." Dt 28:48; 1Ki 21:29; Ps 78:38

⁹When Shishak king of Egypt attacked Jerusalem, he carried off the treasures of the temple of the LORD and the treasures of the royal palace. He took everything, including the gold shields Solomon had made. ¹⁰So King Rehoboam made bronze shields to replace them and assigned these to the commanders of the guard on duty at the entrance to the royal palace. ¹¹Whenever the king went to the LORD's temple, the guards went with him, bearing the shields, and afterward they returned them to the guardroom. 2Ch 9:16

¹²Because Rehoboam humbled himself, the LORD's anger turned from him, and he was not totally destroyed. Indeed, there was some good in Judah. 2Ch 19:3

¹³King Rehoboam established himself firmly in Jerusalem and continued as king. He was forty-one years old when he became king, and he reigned seventeen years in Jerusalem, the city the LORD had chosen out of all the

---

a 1 That is, Judah, as frequently in 2 Chronicles Nile region   *b 3* That is, people from the upper tribes of Israel in which to put his Name. His mother's name was Naamah; she was an Ammonite. [14] He did evil because he had not set his heart on seeking the LORD. Dt 12:5; 2Ch 6:6

[15] As for the events of Rehoboam's reign, from beginning to end, are they not written in the records of Shemaiah the prophet and of Iddo the seer that deal with genealogies? There was continual warfare between Rehoboam and Jeroboam. [16] Rehoboam rested with his ancestors and was buried in the City of David. And Abijah his son succeeded him as king. 1Ki 14:21,25-31; 2Ch 9:29

Abijah King of Judah
13:1-2,22 – 14:1pp — 1Ki 15:1-2,6-8

13 In the eighteenth year of the reign of Jeroboam, Abijah became king of Judah, [2] and he reigned in Jerusalem three years. His mother's name was Maakah,[a] a daughter[b] of Uriel of Gibeah.

There was war between Abijah and Jeroboam. [3] Abijah went into battle with an army of four hundred thousand able fighting men, and Jeroboam drew up a battle line against him with eight hundred thousand able troops. 1Ki 15:6; 2Ch 11:20

[4] Abijah stood on Mount Zemaraim, in the hill country of Ephraim, and said, "Jeroboam and all Israel, listen to me! [5] Don't you know that the LORD, the God of Israel, has given the kingship of Israel to David and his descendants forever by a covenant of salt? [6] Yet Jeroboam son of Nebat, an official of Solomon son of David, rebelled against his master. [7] Some worthless scoundrels gathered around him and opposed Rehoboam son of Solomon when he was young and indecisive and not strong enough to resist them. Nu 18:19; 1Ki 11:26

[8] "And now you plan to resist the kingdom of the LORD, which is in the hands of David's descendants. You are indeed a vast army and have with you the golden calves that Jeroboam made to be your gods. [9] But didn't you drive out the priests of the LORD, the sons of Aaron, and the Levites, and make priests of your own as the peoples of other lands do? Whoever comes to consecrate himself with a young bull and seven rams may become a priest of what are not gods. 1Ki 12:28; 2Ch 11:15; Jer 2:11

[10] "As for us, the LORD is our God, and we have not forsaken him. The priests who serve the LORD are sons of Aaron, and the Levites assist them. [11] Every morning and evening they present burnt offerings and fragrant incense to the LORD. They set out the bread on the ceremonially clean table and light the lamps

2 CHRONICLES 14:6 | 709

on the gold lampstand every evening. We are observing the requirements of the LORD our God. But you have forsaken him. ¹²God is with us; he is our leader. His priests with their trumpets will sound the battle cry against you. People of Israel, do not fight against the LORD, the God of your ancestors, for you will not succeed." Nu 10:8-9; Ac 5:39

¹³Now Jeroboam had sent troops around to the rear, so that while he was in front of Judah the ambush was behind them. ¹⁴Judah turned and saw that they were being attacked at both front and rear. Then they cried out to the LORD. The priests blew their trumpets ¹⁵and the men of Judah raised the battle cry. At the sound of their battle cry, God routed Jeroboam and all Israel before Abijah and Judah. ¹⁶The Israelites fled before Judah, and God delivered them into their hands. ¹⁷Abijah and his troops inflicted heavy losses on them, so that there were five hundred thousand casualties among Israel's able men. ¹⁸The Israelites were subdued on that occasion, and the people of Judah were victorious because they relied on the LORD, the God of their ancestors. 2Ch 14:11; 16:8; Ps 22:5

¹⁹Abijah pursued Jeroboam and took from him the towns of Bethel, Jeshanah and Ephron, with their surrounding villages.

²⁰Jeroboam did not regain power during the time of Abijah. And the LORD struck him down and he died.

²¹But Abijah grew in strength. He married fourteen wives and had twenty-two sons and sixteen daughters.

²²The other events of Abijah's reign, what he did and what he said, are written in the annotations of the prophet Iddo.

14 ^a And Abijah rested with his ancestors and was buried in the City of David. Asa his son succeeded him as king, and in his days the country was at peace for ten years. 1Ki 15:1-2,6-8

Asa King of Judah
14:2-3pp — 1Ki 15:11-12

²Asa did what was good and right in the eyes of the LORD his God. ³He removed the foreign altars and the high places, smashed the sacred stones and cut down the Asherah poles.^b ⁴He commanded Judah to seek the LORD, the God of their ancestors, and to obey his laws and commands. ⁵He removed the high places and incense altars in every town in Judah, and the kingdom was at peace under him. ⁶He built up the fortified cities of Judah, since the land was at peace. No one was at war with him during those years, for the LORD gave him rest. 1Ki 15:11-12; 2Ch 34:4,7

^a In Hebrew texts 14:1 is numbered 13:23, and 14:2-15 is numbered 14:1-14.   ^b 3 That is, wooden symbols of the goddess Asherah; here and elsewhere in 2 Chronicles

⁷"Let us build up these towns," he said to Judah, "and put walls around them, with towers, gates and bars. The land is still ours, because we have sought the LORD our God; we sought him and he has given us rest on every side." So they built and prospered.

⁸Asa had an army of three hundred thousand men from Judah, equipped with large shields and with spears, and two hundred and eighty thousand from Benjamin, armed with small shields and with bows. All these were brave fighting men.

⁹Zerah the Cushite marched out against them with an army of thousands upon thousands and three hundred chariots, and came as far as Mareshah. ¹⁰Asa went out to meet him, and they took up battle positions in the Valley of Zephathah near Mareshah. 2Ch 11:8; 16:8

¹¹Then Asa called to the LORD his God and said, "LORD, there is no one like you to help the powerless against the mighty. Help us, LORD our God, for we rely on you, and in your name we have come against this vast army. LORD, you are our God; do not let mere mortals prevail against you." 1Sa 17:45; 2Ch 13:14

¹²The LORD struck down the Cushites before Asa and Judah. The Cushites fled, ¹³and Asa and his army pursued them as far as Gerar. Such a great number of Cushites fell that they could not recover; they were crushed before the LORD and his forces. The men of Judah carried off a large amount of plunder. ¹⁴They destroyed all the villages around Gerar, for the terror of the LORD had fallen on them. They looted all these villages, since there was much plunder there. ¹⁵They also attacked the camps of the herders and carried off droves of sheep and goats and camels. Then they returned to Jerusalem. Ge 10:19; 35:5; 2Ch 13:15

Asa's Reform
15:16-19pp — 1Ki 15:13-16

15 The Spirit of God came on Azariah son of Oded. ²He went out to meet Asa and said to him, "Listen to me, Asa and all Judah and Benjamin. The LORD is with you when you are with him. If you seek him, he will be found by you, but if you forsake him, he will forsake you. ³For a long time Israel was without the true God, without a priest to teach and without the law. ⁴But in their distress they turned to the LORD, the God of Israel, and sought him, and he was found by them. ⁵In those days it was not safe to travel about, for all the inhabitants of the lands were in great turmoil. ⁶One nation was being crushed by another and one city by another, because God was troubling them with every kind of distress. ⁷But as for you, be strong and do

not give up, for your work will be rewarded." Jos 1:7,9; Jas 4:8

⁸When Asa heard these words and the prophecy of Azariah son of[a] Oded the prophet, he took courage. He removed the detestable idols from the whole land of Judah and Benjamin and from the towns he had captured in the hills of Ephraim. He repaired the altar of the LORD that was in front of the portico of the LORD's temple. 2Ch 13:19

⁹Then he assembled all Judah and Benjamin and the people from Ephraim, Manasseh and Simeon who had settled among them, for large numbers had come over to him from Israel when they saw that the LORD his God was with him. 2Ch 11:16-17

¹⁰They assembled at Jerusalem in the third month of the fifteenth year of Asa's reign. ¹¹At that time they sacrificed to the LORD seven hundred head of cattle and seven thousand sheep and goats from the plunder they had brought back. ¹²They entered into a covenant to seek the LORD, the God of their ancestors, with all their heart and soul. ¹³All who would not seek the LORD, the God of Israel, were to be put to death, whether small or great, man or woman. ¹⁴They took an oath to the LORD with loud acclamation, with shouting and with trumpets and horns. ¹⁵All Judah rejoiced about the oath because they had sworn it wholeheartedly. They sought God eagerly, and he was found by them. So the LORD gave them rest on every side. Ex 22:20; Dt 13:9-16; 2Ch 14:13

¹⁶King Asa also deposed his grandmother Maakah from her position as queen mother, because she had made a repulsive image for the worship of Asherah. Asa cut it down, broke it up and burned it in the Kidron Valley. ¹⁷Although he did not remove the high places from Israel, Asa's heart was fully committed to the LORD all his life. ¹⁸He brought into the temple of God the silver and gold and the articles that he and his father had dedicated. Ex 34:13; 2Ch 14:2-5

¹⁹There was no more war until the thirty-fifth year of Asa's reign. 1Ki 15:13-16

Asa's Last Years

16:1-6pp — 1Ki 15:17-22
16:11–17:1pp — 1Ki 15:23-24

16 In the thirty-sixth year of Asa's reign Baasha king of Israel went up against Judah and fortified Ramah to prevent anyone from leaving or entering the territory of Asa king of Judah.

²Asa then took the silver and gold out of the treasuries of the LORD's temple and of his own palace and sent it to Ben-Hadad king of Aram, who was ruling in

---

a 8 Vulgate and Syriac (see also Septuagint and verse 1); Hebrew does not have *Azariah son of.*

Damascus. ³"Let there be a treaty between me and you," he said, "as there was between my father and your father. See, I am sending you silver and gold. Now break your treaty with Baasha king of Israel so he will withdraw from me."

⁴Ben-Hadad agreed with King Asa and sent the commanders of his forces against the towns of Israel. They conquered Ijon, Dan, Abel Maimᵃ and all the store cities of Naphtali. ⁵When Baasha heard this, he stopped building Ramah and abandoned his work. ⁶Then King Asa brought all the men of Judah, and they carried away from Ramah the stones and timber Baasha had been using. With them he built up Geba and Mizpah. 1Ki 15:17-22

⁷At that time Hanani the seer came to Asa king of Judah and said to him: "Because you relied on the king of Aram and not on the LORD your God, the army of the king of Aram has escaped from your hand. ⁸Were not the Cushitesᵇ and Libyans a mighty army with great numbers of chariots and horsemenᶜ? Yet when you relied on the LORD, he delivered them into your hand. ⁹For the eyes of the LORD range throughout the earth to strengthen those whose hearts are fully committed to him. You have done a foolish thing, and from now on you will be at war." 1Sa 13:13; Pr 15:3; Zec 4:10

¹⁰Asa was angry with the seer because of this; he was so enraged that he put him in prison. At the same time Asa brutally oppressed some of the people.

¹¹The events of Asa's reign, from beginning to end, are written in the book of the kings of Judah and Israel. ¹²In the thirty-ninth year of his reign Asa was afflicted with a disease in his feet. Though his disease was severe, even in his illness he did not seek help from the LORD, but only from the physicians. ¹³Then in the forty-first year of his reign Asa died and rested with his ancestors. ¹⁴They buried him in the tomb that he had cut out for himself in the City of David. They laid him on a bier covered with spices and various blended perfumes, and they made a huge fire in his honor. Ge 50:2; 2Ch 21:19; Jer 17:5-6

Jehoshaphat King of Judah

17 Jehoshaphat his son succeeded him as king and strengthened himself against Israel. ²He stationed troops in all the fortified cities of Judah and put garrisons in Judah and in the towns of Ephraim that his father Asa had captured. 1Ki 15:23-24

³The LORD was with Jehoshaphat because he followed the ways of his father David before him. He did not consult the Baals ⁴but sought the God of his fa-

ᵃ 4 Also known as *Abel Beth Maakah* ᵇ 8 That is, people from the upper Nile region ᶜ 8 Or *charioteers* ther and followed his commands rather than the practices of Israel. ⁵The LORD established the kingdom under his control; and all Judah brought gifts to Jehoshaphat, so that he had great wealth and honor. ⁶His heart was devoted to the ways of the LORD; furthermore, he removed the high places and the Asherah poles from Judah. 2Ch 15:17; 19:3; 22:9 ⁷In the third year of his reign he sent his officials Ben-Hail, Obadiah, Zechariah, Nethanel and Micaiah to teach in the towns of Judah. ⁸With them were certain Levites — Shemaiah, Nethaniah, Zebadiah, Asahel, Shemiramoth, Jehonathan, Adonijah, Tobijah and Tob-Adonijah — and the priests Elishama and Jehoram. ⁹They taught throughout Judah, taking with them the Book of the Law of the LORD; they went around to all the towns of Judah and taught the people. Dt 6:4-9; 2Ch 15:3; 19:8 ¹⁰The fear of the LORD fell on all the kingdoms of the lands surrounding Judah, so that they did not go to war against Jehoshaphat. ¹¹Some Philistines brought Jehoshaphat gifts and silver as tribute, and the Arabs brought him flocks: seven thousand seven hundred rams and seven thousand seven hundred goats. Ge 35:5; 2Ch 9:14; 26:8 ¹²Jehoshaphat became more and more powerful; he built forts and store cities in Judah ¹³and

had large supplies in the towns of Judah. He also kept experienced fighting men in Jerusalem. ¹⁴Their enrollment by families was as follows: 2Sa 24:2

From Judah, commanders of units of 1,000:
Adnah the commander, with 300,000 fighting men;
¹⁵next, Jehohanan the commander, with 280,000;
¹⁶next, Amasiah son of Zikri, who volunteered himself for the service of the LORD, with 200,000. Jdg 5:9
¹⁷From Benjamin: Nu 1:36
Eliada, a valiant soldier, with 200,000 men armed with bows and shields;
¹⁸next, Jehozabad, with 180,000 men armed for battle.

¹⁹These were the men who served the king, besides those he stationed in the fortified cities throughout Judah. 2Ch 11:10; 25:5

Micaiah Prophesies Against Ahab

18:1-27pp — 1Ki 22:1-28

18 Now Jehoshaphat had great wealth and honor, and he allied himself with Ahab by marriage. ²Some years later he went down to see Ahab in Samaria. Ahab slaughtered many sheep and cattle for him and the people with him and urged him to attack Ramoth Gilead. ³Ahab king of

Israel asked Jehoshaphat king of Judah, "Will you go with me against Ramoth Gilead?" 2Ch 17:5

Jehoshaphat replied, "I am as you are, and my people as your people; we will join you in the war." 4But Jehoshaphat also said to the king of Israel, "First seek the counsel of the LORD."

5So the king of Israel brought together the prophets—four hundred men—and asked them, "Shall we go to war against Ramoth Gilead, or shall I not?"

"Go," they answered, "for God will give it into the king's hand."

6But Jehoshaphat asked, "Is there no longer a prophet of the LORD here whom we can inquire of?"

7The king of Israel answered Jehoshaphat, "There is still one prophet through whom we can inquire of the LORD, but I hate him because he never prophesies anything good about me, but always bad. He is Micaiah son of Imlah."

"The king should not say such a thing," Jehoshaphat replied.

8So the king of Israel called one of his officials and said, "Bring Micaiah son of Imlah at once."

9Dressed in their royal robes, the king of Israel and Jehoshaphat king of Judah were sitting on their thrones at the threshing floor by the entrance of the gate of Samaria, with all the prophets prophesying before them. 10Now Zedekiah son of Kenaa-nah had made iron horns, and he declared, "This is what the LORD says: 'With these you will gore the Arameans until they are destroyed.'"

11All the other prophets were prophesying the same thing. "Attack Ramoth Gilead and be victorious," they said, "for the LORD will give it into the king's hand."

12The messenger who had gone to summon Micaiah said to him, "Look, the other prophets without exception are predicting success for the king. Let your word agree with theirs, and speak favorably."

13But Micaiah said, "As surely as the LORD lives, I can tell him only what my God says." Nu 22:18,20

14When he arrived, the king asked him, "Micaiah, shall we go to war against Ramoth Gilead, or shall I not?"

"Attack and be victorious," he answered, "for they will be given into your hand."

15The king said to him, "How many times must I make you swear to tell me nothing but the truth in the name of the LORD?"

16Then Micaiah answered, "I saw all Israel scattered on the hills like sheep without a shepherd, and the LORD said, 'These people have no master. Let each one go home in peace.'" Nu 27:17

17The king of Israel said to Jehoshaphat, "Didn't I tell you that he never prophesies anything good about me, but only bad?"

¹⁸Micaiah continued, "Therefore hear the word of the LORD: I saw the LORD sitting on his throne with all the multitudes of heaven standing on his right and on his left. ¹⁹And the LORD said, 'Who will entice Ahab king of Israel into attacking Ramoth Gilead and going to his death there?'   Da 7:9

"One suggested this, and another that. ²⁰Finally, a spirit came forward, stood before the LORD and said, 'I will entice him.'

" 'By what means?' the LORD asked.

²¹ " 'I will go and be a deceiving spirit in the mouths of all his prophets,' he said.   Job 1:6; Jn 8:44

" 'You will succeed in enticing him,' said the LORD. 'Go and do it.'

²²"So now the LORD has put a deceiving spirit in the mouths of these prophets of yours. The LORD has decreed disaster for you."   Job 12:16; Eze 14:9

²³Then Zedekiah son of Kenaanah went up and slapped Micaiah in the face. "Which way did the spirit from ͣ the LORD go when he went from me to speak to you?" he asked.   Jer 20:2; Mk 14:65; Ac 23:2

²⁴Micaiah replied, "You will find out on the day you go to hide in an inner room."

²⁵The king of Israel then ordered, "Take Micaiah and send him back to Amon the ruler of the city and to Joash the king's son, ²⁶and say, 'This is what the king says: Put this fellow in prison and give him nothing but bread and water until I return safely.' "   2Ch 16:10; Heb 11:36

²⁷Micaiah declared, "If you ever return safely, the LORD has not spoken through me." Then he added, "Mark my words, all you people!"   1Ki 22:1-28

Ahab Killed at Ramoth Gilead
18:28-34pp — 1Ki 22:29-36

²⁸So the king of Israel and Jehoshaphat king of Judah went up to Ramoth Gilead. ²⁹The king of Israel said to Jehoshaphat, "I will enter the battle in disguise, but you wear your royal robes." So the king of Israel disguised himself and went into battle.

³⁰Now the king of Aram had ordered his chariot commanders, "Do not fight with anyone, small or great, except the king of Israel." ³¹When the chariot commanders saw Jehoshaphat, they thought, "This is the king of Israel." So they turned to attack him, but Jehoshaphat cried out, and the LORD helped him. God drew them away from him, ³²for when the chariot commanders saw that he was not the king of Israel, they stopped pursuing him.

³³But someone drew his bow at random and hit the king of Israel between the breastplate and the scale armor. The king told the chariot driver, "Wheel around and get me out of the fighting.

ͣ **23** Or *Spirit of*

I've been wounded." ³⁴All day long the battle raged, and the king of Israel propped himself up in his chariot facing the Arameans until evening. Then at sunset he died. 1Ki 22:29-36; 2Ch 13:14

19 When Jehoshaphat king of Judah returned safely to his palace in Jerusalem, ²Jehu the seer, the son of Hanani, went out to meet him and said to the king, "Should you help the wicked and love*ᵃ* those who hate the LORD? Because of this, the wrath of the LORD is on you. ³There is, however, some good in you, for you have rid the land of the Asherah poles and have set your heart on seeking God." 2Ch 17:6; 32:25; Ps 139:21-22

Jehoshaphat Appoints Judges

⁴Jehoshaphat lived in Jerusalem, and he went out again among the people from Beersheba to the hill country of Ephraim and turned them back to the LORD, the God of their ancestors. ⁵He appointed judges in the land, in each of the fortified cities of Judah. ⁶He told them, "Consider carefully what you do, because you are not judging for mere mortals but for the LORD, who is with you whenever you give a verdict. ⁷Now let the fear of the LORD be on you. Judge carefully, for with the LORD our God there is no injustice or partiality or bribery." Ge 18:25; Dt 10:17; 16:18-20

⁸In Jerusalem also, Jehoshaphat appointed some of the Levites, priests and heads of Israelite families to administer the law of the LORD and to settle disputes. And they lived in Jerusalem. ⁹He gave them these orders: "You must serve faithfully and wholeheartedly in the fear of the LORD. ¹⁰In every case that comes before you from your people who live in the cities—whether bloodshed or other concerns of the law, commands, decrees or regulations—you are to warn them not to sin against the LORD; otherwise his wrath will come on you and your people. Do this, and you will not sin. Dt 17:8-13; 2Ch 17:8-9

¹¹"Amariah the chief priest will be over you in any matter concerning the LORD, and Zebadiah son of Ishmael, the leader of the tribe of Judah, will be over you in any matter concerning the king, and the Levites will serve as officials before you. Act with courage, and may the LORD be with those who do well." 1Ch 28:20

Jehoshaphat Defeats Moab and Ammon

20 After this, the Moabites and Ammonites with some of the Meunites*ᵇ* came to wage war against Jehoshaphat. ²Some people came and told Jehoshaphat, "A vast army is coming against you from Edom,*ᶜ*

ᵃ 2 Or *and make alliances with*   *ᵇ* 1 Some Septuagint manuscripts; Hebrew *Ammonites*
ᶜ 2 One Hebrew manuscript; most Hebrew manuscripts, Septuagint and Vulgate *Aram*

from the other side of the Dead Sea. It is already in Hazezon Tamar" (that is, En Gedi). [3] Alarmed, Jehoshaphat resolved to inquire of the LORD, and he proclaimed a fast for all Judah. [4] The people of Judah came together to seek help from the LORD; indeed, they came from every town in Judah to seek him. Ge 14:7; 1Sa 7:6; 2Ch 19:3

[5] Then Jehoshaphat stood up in the assembly of Judah and Jerusalem at the temple of the LORD in the front of the new courtyard [6] and said:

"LORD, the God of our ancestors, are you not the God who is in heaven? You rule over all the kingdoms of the nations. Power and might are in your hand, and no one can withstand you. [7] Our God, did you not drive out the inhabitants of this land before your people Israel and give it forever to the descendants of Abraham your friend? [8] They have lived in it and have built in it a sanctuary for your Name, saying, [9] 'If calamity comes upon us, whether the sword of judgment, or plague or famine, we will stand in your presence before this temple that bears your Name and will cry out to you in our distress, and you will hear us and save us.' Dt 4:39; 1Ch 29:11-12

[10] "But now here are men from Ammon, Moab and Mount Seir, whose territory you would not allow Israel to invade when they came from Egypt; so they turned away from them and did not destroy them. [11] See how they are repaying us by coming to drive us out of the possession you gave us as an inheritance. [12] Our God, will you not judge them? For we have no power to face this vast army that is attacking us. We do not know what to do, but our eyes are on you." Ps 25:15; 83:1-12; 121:1-2

[13] All the men of Judah, with their wives and children and little ones, stood there before the LORD.

[14] Then the Spirit of the LORD came on Jahaziel son of Zechariah, the son of Benaiah, the son of Jeiel, the son of Mattaniah, a Levite and descendant of Asaph, as he stood in the assembly. 2Ch 15:1

[15] He said: "Listen, King Jehoshaphat and all who live in Judah and Jerusalem! This is what the LORD says to you: 'Do not be afraid or discouraged because of this vast army. For the battle is not yours, but God's. [16] Tomorrow march down against them. They will be climbing up by the Pass of Ziz, and you will find them at the end of the gorge in the Desert of Jeruel. [17] You will not have to fight this battle. Take up your positions; stand firm and see the

deliverance the LORD will give you, Judah and Jerusalem. Do not be afraid; do not be discouraged. Go out to face them tomorrow, and the LORD will be with you.' " Ex 14:13; 1Sa 17:47; 2Ch 32:7

¹⁸Jehoshaphat bowed down with his face to the ground, and all the people of Judah and Jerusalem fell down in worship before the LORD. ¹⁹Then some Levites from the Kohathites and Korahites stood up and praised the LORD, the God of Israel, with a very loud voice. Ex 4:31

²⁰Early in the morning they left for the Desert of Tekoa. As they set out, Jehoshaphat stood and said, "Listen to me, Judah and people of Jerusalem! Have faith in the LORD your God and you will be upheld; have faith in his prophets and you will be successful." ²¹After consulting the people, Jehoshaphat appointed men to sing to the LORD and to praise him for the splendor of his*a* holiness as they went out at the head of the army, saying: 1Ch 16:29; Isa 7:9

"Give thanks to the LORD,
    for his love endures
        forever." 2Ch 5:13; Ps 136:1

²²As they began to sing and praise, the LORD set ambushes against the men of Ammon and Moab and Mount Seir who were invading Judah, and they were defeated. ²³The Ammonites and Moabites rose up against the men from Mount Seir to destroy and annihilate them. After they finished slaughtering the men from Seir, they helped to destroy one another. Jdg 7:22; 1Sa 14:20; 2Ch 23:13

²⁴When the men of Judah came to the place that overlooks the desert and looked toward the vast army, they saw only dead bodies lying on the ground; no one had escaped. ²⁵So Jehoshaphat and his men went to carry off their plunder, and they found among them a great amount of equipment and clothing*b* and also articles of value — more than they could take away. There was so much plunder that it took three days to collect it. ²⁶On the fourth day they assembled in the Valley of Berakah, where they praised the LORD. This is why it is called the Valley of Berakah*c* to this day.

²⁷Then, led by Jehoshaphat, all the men of Judah and Jerusalem returned joyfully to Jerusalem, for the LORD had given them cause to rejoice over their enemies. ²⁸They entered Jerusalem and went to the temple of the LORD with harps and lyres and trumpets.

²⁹The fear of God came on all the surrounding kingdoms when they heard how the LORD had fought against the enemies of Israel. ³⁰And the kingdom of Jehoshaphat was at peace, for his

---

a 21 Or *him with the splendor of*   *b* 25 Some Hebrew manuscripts and Vulgate; most Hebrew manuscripts *corpses*   *c* 26 *Berakah* means *praise.*

God had given him rest on every side. 2Ch 15:15; 17:10

The End of Jehoshaphat's Reign

20:31–21:1pp — 1Ki 22:41-50

³¹ So Jehoshaphat reigned over Judah. He was thirty-five years old when he became king of Judah, and he reigned in Jerusalem twenty-five years. His mother's name was Azubah daughter of Shilhi. ³² He followed the ways of his father Asa and did not stray from them; he did what was right in the eyes of the LORD. ³³ The high places, however, were not removed, and the people still had not set their hearts on the God of their ancestors. 2Ch 17:6; 19:3

³⁴ The other events of Jehoshaphat's reign, from beginning to end, are written in the annals of Jehu son of Hanani, which are recorded in the book of the kings of Israel. 1Ki 16:1

³⁵ Later, Jehoshaphat king of Judah made an alliance with Ahaziah king of Israel, whose ways were wicked. ³⁶ He agreed with him to construct a fleet of trading ships.ᵃ After these were built at Ezion Geber, ³⁷ Eliezer son of Dodavahu of Mareshah prophesied against Jehoshaphat, saying, "Because you have made an alliance with Ahaziah, the LORD will destroy what you have made." The ships were wrecked and were not able to set sail to trade.ᵇ

21 Then Jehoshaphat rested with his ancestors and was buried with them in the City of David. And Jehoram his son succeeded him as king. ² Jehoram's brothers, the sons of Jehoshaphat, were Azariah, Jehiel, Zechariah, Azariahu, Michael and Shephatiah. All these were sons of Jehoshaphat king of Israel.ᶜ ³ Their father had given them many gifts of silver and gold and articles of value, as well as fortified cities in Judah, but he had given the kingdom to Jehoram because he was his firstborn son. 2Ch 9:21; 11:10

Jehoram King of Judah

21:5-10,20pp — 2Ki 8:16-24

⁴ When Jehoram established himself firmly over his father's kingdom, he put all his brothers to the sword along with some of the officials of Israel. ⁵ Jehoram was thirty-two years old when he became king, and he reigned in Jerusalem eight years. ⁶ He followed the ways of the kings of Israel, as the house of Ahab had done, for he married a daughter of Ahab. He did evil in the eyes of the LORD. ⁷ Nevertheless, because of the covenant the LORD had made with David, the LORD was not willing to destroy the house of David. He had promised to maintain a lamp for him and his descendants forever.

⁸ In the time of Jehoram, Edom rebelled against Judah and set

---

ᵃ 36 Hebrew *of ships that could go to Tarshish* Judah, as frequently in 2 Chronicles   ᵇ 37 Hebrew *sail for Tarshish*   ᶜ 2 That is, up its own king. ⁹So Jehoram went there with his officers and all his chariots. The Edomites surrounded him and his chariot commanders, but he rose up and broke through by night. ¹⁰To this day Edom has been in rebellion against Judah.

Libnah revolted at the same time, because Jehoram had forsaken the LORD, the God of his ancestors. ¹¹He had also built high places on the hills of Judah and had caused the people of Jerusalem to prostitute themselves and had led Judah astray.

¹²Jehoram received a letter from Elijah the prophet, which said: 2Ki 1:16-17

"This is what the LORD, the God of your father David, says: 'You have not followed the ways of your father Jehoshaphat or of Asa king of Judah. ¹³But you have followed the ways of the kings of Israel, and you have led Judah and the people of Jerusalem to prostitute themselves, just as the house of Ahab did. You have also murdered your own brothers, members of your own family, men who were better than you. ¹⁴So now the LORD is about to strike your people, your sons, your wives and everything that is yours, with a heavy blow. ¹⁵You yourself will be

very ill with a lingering disease of the bowels, until the disease causes your bowels to come out.' " 1Ki 16:29-33

¹⁶The LORD aroused against Jehoram the hostility of the Philistines and of the Arabs who lived near the Cushites. ¹⁷They attacked Judah, invaded it and carried off all the goods found in the king's palace, together with his sons and wives. Not a son was left to him except Ahaziah,ᵃ the youngest. 2Ch 17:10-11; 22:1; 26:7

¹⁸After all this, the LORD afflicted Jehoram with an incurable disease of the bowels. ¹⁹In the course of time, at the end of the second year, his bowels came out because of the disease, and he died in great pain. His people made no funeral fire in his honor, as they had for his predecessors. 2Ch 16:14

²⁰Jehoram was thirty-two years old when he became king, and he reigned in Jerusalem eight years. He passed away, to no one's regret, and was buried in the City of David, but not in the tombs of the kings. 2Ki 8:16-24; 2Ch 24:25

Ahaziah King of Judah

22:1-6pp — 2Ki 8:25-29
22:7-9pp — 2Ki 9:21-29

22 The people of Jerusalem made Ahaziah, Jehoram's youngest son, king in his place, since the raiders, who came with the Arabs into the camp,

---

ᵃ 17 Hebrew *Jehoahaz*, a variant of *Ahaziah*

had killed all the older sons. So Ahaziah son of Jehoram king of Judah began to reign.

² Ahaziah was twenty-two[a] years old when he became king, and he reigned in Jerusalem one year. His mother's name was Athaliah, a granddaughter of Omri.

³ He too followed the ways of the house of Ahab, for his mother encouraged him to act wickedly. ⁴ He did evil in the eyes of the LORD, as the house of Ahab had done, for after his father's death they became his advisers, to his undoing. ⁵ He also followed their counsel when he went with Joram[b] son of Ahab king of Israel to wage war against Hazael king of Aram at Ramoth Gilead. The Arameans wounded Joram; ⁶ so he returned to Jezreel to recover from the wounds they had inflicted on him at Ramoth[c] in his battle with Hazael king of Aram. 2Ch 18:1; 21:6

Then Ahaziah[d] son of Jehoram king of Judah went down to Jezreel to see Joram son of Ahab because he had been wounded.

⁷ Through Ahaziah's visit to Joram, God brought about Ahaziah's downfall. When Ahaziah arrived, he went out with Joram to meet Jehu son of Nimshi, whom the LORD had anointed to destroy the house of Ahab. ⁸ While Jehu was executing judgment on the house of Ahab, he found the officials of Judah and the sons of Ahaziah's relatives, who had been attending Ahaziah, and he killed them. ⁹ He then went in search of Ahaziah, and his men captured him while he was hiding in Samaria. He was brought to Jehu and put to death. They buried him, for they said, "He was a son of Jehoshaphat, who sought the LORD with all his heart." So there was no one in the house of Ahaziah powerful enough to retain the kingdom. 2Ki 9:21-29; 2Ch 10:15

Athaliah and Joash
22:10–23:21pp — 2Ki 11:1-21

¹⁰ When Athaliah the mother of Ahaziah saw that her son was dead, she proceeded to destroy the whole royal family of the house of Judah. ¹¹ But Jehosheba,[e] the daughter of King Jehoram, took Joash son of Ahaziah and stole him away from among the royal princes who were about to be murdered and put him and his nurse in a bedroom. Because Jehosheba,[e] the daughter of King Jehoram and wife of the priest Jehoiada, was Ahaziah's sister, she hid the child from Athaliah so she could not kill him. ¹² He remained hidden with them at the temple of God for six years while Athaliah ruled the land.

23 In the seventh year Jehoiada showed his strength. He made a covenant with the commanders of units of a hundred: Azariah son of Jeroham, Ishmael son of Jehohanan, Azariah son of Obed, Maaseiah son of Adaiah, and Elishaphat son of Zikri. ²They went throughout Judah and gathered the Levites and the heads of Israelite families from all the towns. When they came to Jerusalem, ³the whole assembly made a covenant with the king at the temple of God. Nu 35:2-5; 2Ki 11:17

Jehoiada said to them, "The king's son shall reign, as the LORD promised concerning the descendants of David. ⁴Now this is what you are to do: A third of you priests and Levites who are going on duty on the Sabbath are to keep watch at the doors, ⁵a third of you at the royal palace and a third at the Foundation Gate, and all the others are to be in the courtyards of the temple of the LORD. ⁶No one is to enter the temple of the LORD except the priests and Levites on duty; they may enter because they are consecrated, but all the others are to observe the LORD's command not to enter.ᵃ ⁷The Levites are to station themselves around the king, each with weapon in hand. Anyone who enters the temple is to be put to death. Stay close to the king wherever he goes." 2Sa 7:12; 1Ki 2:4; 2Ch 6:16

⁸The Levites and all the men of Judah did just as Jehoiada the priest ordered. Each one took his men—those who were going on duty on the Sabbath and those who were going off duty—for Jehoiada the priest had not released any of the divisions. ⁹Then he gave the commanders of units of a hundred the spears and the large and small shields that had belonged to King David and that were in the temple of God. ¹⁰He stationed all the men, each with his weapon in his hand, around the king—near the altar and the temple, from the south side to the north side of the temple. 2Ki 11:9; 1Ch 24:1

¹¹Jehoiada and his sons brought out the king's son and put the crown on him; they presented him with a copy of the covenant and proclaimed him king. They anointed him and shouted, "Long live the king!" Dt 17:18; 1Sa 10:24

¹²When Athaliah heard the noise of the people running and cheering the king, she went to them at the temple of the LORD. ¹³She looked, and there was the king, standing by his pillar at the entrance. The officers and the trumpeters were beside the king, and all the people of the land were rejoicing and blowing trumpets, and musicians with their instruments were leading the praises. Then Athaliah tore her robes and shouted, "Treason! Treason!" 1Ki 1:41; 7:15

ᵃ 6 Or *are to stand guard where the LORD has assigned them*

¹⁴Jehoiada the priest sent out the commanders of units of a hundred, who were in charge of the troops, and said to them: "Bring her out between the ranks^a and put to the sword anyone who follows her." For the priest had said, "Do not put her to death at the temple of the LORD." ¹⁵So they seized her as she reached the entrance of the Horse Gate on the palace grounds, and there they put her to death.   Ne 3:28; Jer 31:40

¹⁶Jehoiada then made a covenant that he, the people and the king^b would be the LORD's people. ¹⁷All the people went to the temple of Baal and tore it down. They smashed the altars and idols and killed Mattan the priest of Baal in front of the altars.   Dt 13:6-9; 2Ch 29:10

¹⁸Then Jehoiada placed the oversight of the temple of the LORD in the hands of the Levitical priests, to whom David had made assignments in the temple, to present the burnt offerings of the LORD as written in the Law of Moses, with rejoicing and singing, as David had ordered. ¹⁹He also stationed gatekeepers at the gates of the LORD's temple so that no one who was in any way unclean might enter.   1Ch 9:22; 23:6,28-32

²⁰He took with him the commanders of hundreds, the nobles, the rulers of the people and all the people of the land and brought the king down from the temple of the LORD. They went into the palace through the Upper Gate and seated the king on the royal throne. ²¹All the people of the land rejoiced, and the city was calm, because Athaliah had been slain with the sword. 2Ki 11:1-21; 15:35

Joash Repairs the Temple
24:1-14pp — 2Ki 12:1-16
24:23-27pp — 2Ki 12:17-21

24 Joash was seven years old when he became king, and he reigned in Jerusalem forty years. His mother's name was Zibiah; she was from Beersheba. ²Joash did what was right in the eyes of the LORD all the years of Jehoiada the priest. ³Jehoiada chose two wives for him, and he had sons and daughters.   2Ch 26:5

⁴Some time later Joash decided to restore the temple of the LORD. ⁵He called together the priests and Levites and said to them, "Go to the towns of Judah and collect the money due annually from all Israel, to repair the temple of your God. Do it now." But the Levites did not act at once.   Ex 30:16; 1Ch 11:1

⁶Therefore the king summoned Jehoiada the chief priest and said to him, "Why haven't you required the Levites to bring in from Judah and Jerusalem the tax imposed by Moses the servant of the LORD and by the assembly of Israel for the tent of the covenant law?"   Ex 30:12-16; Nu 1:50

^a 14 Or *out from the precincts*   ^b 16 Or *covenant between the LORD and the people and the king that they* (see 2 Kings 11:17)

[7]Now the sons of that wicked woman Athaliah had broken into the temple of God and had used even its sacred objects for the Baals.

[8]At the king's command, a chest was made and placed outside, at the gate of the temple of the LORD. [9]A proclamation was then issued in Judah and Jerusalem that they should bring to the LORD the tax that Moses the servant of God had required of Israel in the wilderness. [10]All the officials and all the people brought their contributions gladly, dropping them into the chest until it was full. [11]Whenever the chest was brought in by the Levites to the king's officials and they saw that there was a large amount of money, the royal secretary and the officer of the chief priest would come and empty the chest and carry it back to its place. They did this regularly and collected a great amount of money. [12]The king and Jehoiada gave it to those who carried out the work required for the temple of the LORD. They hired masons and carpenters to restore the LORD's temple, and also workers in iron and bronze to repair the temple.

[13]The men in charge of the work were diligent, and the repairs progressed under them. They rebuilt the temple of God according to its original design and reinforced it. [14]When they had finished, they brought the rest of the money to the king and Jehoiada, and with it were made articles for the LORD's temple: articles for the service and for the burnt offerings, and also dishes and other objects of gold and silver. As long as Jehoiada lived, burnt offerings were presented continually in the temple of the LORD. 2Ki 12:1-16; 1Ch 29:3,6,9

[15]Now Jehoiada was old and full of years, and he died at the age of a hundred and thirty. [16]He was buried with the kings in the City of David, because of the good he had done in Israel for God and his temple.

The Wickedness of Joash

[17]After the death of Jehoiada, the officials of Judah came and paid homage to the king, and he listened to them. [18]They abandoned the temple of the LORD, the God of their ancestors, and worshiped Asherah poles and idols. Because of their guilt, God's anger came on Judah and Jerusalem. [19]Although the LORD sent prophets to the people to bring them back to him, and though they testified against them, they would not listen. Ex 34:13; 2Ch 19:2; Jer 7:25

[20]Then the Spirit of God came on Zechariah son of Jehoiada the priest. He stood before the people and said, "This is what God says: 'Why do you disobey the LORD's commands? You will not prosper. Because you have forsaken the LORD, he has forsaken you.'" Nu 14:41; 2Ch 15:2; 20:14

²¹ But they plotted against him, and by order of the king they stoned him to death in the courtyard of the LORD's temple. ²² King Joash did not remember the kindness Zechariah's father Jehoiada had shown him but killed his son, who said as he lay dying, "May the LORD see this and call you to account." Ge 9:5; Ne 9:26; Ac 7:58-59

²³ At the turn of the year,ᵃ the army of Aram marched against Joash; it invaded Judah and Jerusalem and killed all the leaders of the people. They sent all the plunder to their king in Damascus. ²⁴ Although the Aramean army had come with only a few men, the LORD delivered into their hands a much larger army. Because Judah had forsaken the LORD, the God of their ancestors, judgment was executed on Joash. ²⁵ When the Arameans withdrew, they left Joash severely wounded. His officials conspired against him for murdering the son of Jehoiada the priest, and they killed him in his bed. So he died and was buried in the City of David, but not in the tombs of the kings. Lev 26:23-25; 2Ki 12:17-18; 2Ch 14:9

²⁶ Those who conspired against him were Zabad,ᵇ son of Shimeath an Ammonite woman, and Jehozabad, son of Shimrithᶜ a Moabite woman. ²⁷ The account of his sons, the many prophecies about him, and the record of the restoration of the temple of God are written in the annotations on the book of the kings. And Amaziah his son succeeded him as king. 2Ki 12:17-21

Amaziah King of Judah

25:1-4pp — 2Ki 14:1-6
25:11-12pp — 2Ki 14:7
25:17-28pp — 2Ki 14:8-20

25 Amaziah was twenty-five years old when he became king, and he reigned in Jerusalem twenty-nine years. His mother's name was Jehoaddan; she was from Jerusalem. ² He did what was right in the eyes of the LORD, but not wholeheartedly. ³ After the kingdom was firmly in his control, he executed the officials who had murdered his father the king. ⁴ Yet he did not put their children to death, but acted in accordance with what is written in the Law, in the Book of Moses, where the LORD commanded: "Parents shall not be put to death for their children, nor children be put to death for their parents; each will die for their own sin."ᵈ 2Ki 14:1-6; Dt 24:16; 28:61

⁵ Amaziah called the people of Judah together and assigned them according to their families to commanders of thousands and commanders of hundreds for all Judah and Benjamin. He then mustered those twenty years old or more and found that there were

---

ᵃ 23 Probably in the spring   ᵇ 26 A variant of *Jozabad*   ᶜ 26 A variant of *Shomer*
ᵈ 4 Deut. 24:16

three hundred thousand men fit for military service, able to handle the spear and shield. ⁶He also hired a hundred thousand fighting men from Israel for a hundred talentsᵃ of silver. Nu 1:3; 1Ch 21:1

⁷But a man of God came to him and said, "Your Majesty, these troops from Israel must not march with you, for the LORD is not with Israel—not with any of the people of Ephraim. ⁸Even if you go and fight courageously in battle, God will overthrow you before the enemy, for God has the power to help or to overthrow." 2Ch 14:11; 20:6

⁹Amaziah asked the man of God, "But what about the hundred talents I paid for these Israelite troops?"

The man of God replied, "The LORD can give you much more than that." Dt 8:18; Pr 10:22

¹⁰So Amaziah dismissed the troops who had come to him from Ephraim and sent them home. They were furious with Judah and left for home in a great rage.

¹¹Amaziah then marshaled his strength and led his army to the Valley of Salt, where he killed ten thousand men of Seir. ¹²The army of Judah also captured ten thousand men alive, took them to the top of a cliff and threw them down so that all were dashed to pieces. 2Ki 14:7; Ps 141:6

¹³Meanwhile the troops that Amaziah had sent back and had not allowed to take part in the war raided towns belonging to Judah from Samaria to Beth Horon. They killed three thousand people and carried off great quantities of plunder.

¹⁴When Amaziah returned from slaughtering the Edomites, he brought back the gods of the people of Seir. He set them up as his own gods, bowed down to them and burned sacrifices to them. ¹⁵The anger of the LORD burned against Amaziah, and he sent a prophet to him, who said, "Why do you consult this people's gods, which could not save their own people from your hand?" Ex 20:3; Ps 96:5; Isa 44:15

¹⁶While he was still speaking, the king said to him, "Have we appointed you an adviser to the king? Stop! Why be struck down?"

So the prophet stopped but said, "I know that God has determined to destroy you, because you have done this and have not listened to my counsel."

¹⁷After Amaziah king of Judah consulted his advisers, he sent this challenge to Jehoashᵇ son of Jehoahaz, the son of Jehu, king of Israel: "Come, let us face each other in battle."

¹⁸But Jehoash king of Israel replied to Amaziah king of Judah: "A thistle in Lebanon sent a message to a cedar in Lebanon,

---

ᵃ 6 That is, about 3 3/4 tons or about 3.4 metric tons; also in verse 9   ᵇ 17 Hebrew Joash, a variant of Jehoash; also in verses 18, 21, 23 and 25

'Give your daughter to my son in marriage.' Then a wild beast in Lebanon came along and trampled the thistle underfoot. ¹⁹You say to yourself that you have defeated Edom, and now you are arrogant and proud. But stay at home! Why ask for trouble and cause your own downfall and that of Judah also?" Jdg 9:8-15

²⁰Amaziah, however, would not listen, for God so worked that he might deliver them into the hands of Jehoash, because they sought the gods of Edom. ²¹So Jehoash king of Israel attacked. He and Amaziah king of Judah faced each other at Beth Shemesh in Judah. ²²Judah was routed by Israel, and every man fled to his home. ²³Jehoash king of Israel captured Amaziah king of Judah, the son of Joash, the son of Ahaziah,ᵃ at Beth Shemesh. Then Jehoash brought him to Jerusalem and broke down the wall of Jerusalem from the Ephraim Gate to the Corner Gate — a section about four hundred cubitsᵇ long. ²⁴He took all the gold and silver and all the articles found in the temple of God that had been in the care of Obed-Edom, together with the palace treasures and the hostages, and returned to Samaria. 1Ki 12:15; 2Ch 22:7; Jer 31:38

²⁵Amaziah son of Joash king of Judah lived for fifteen years after the death of Jehoash son of Jehoahaz king of Israel. ²⁶As for the other events of Amaziah's reign, from beginning to end, are they not written in the book of the kings of Judah and Israel? ²⁷From the time that Amaziah turned away from following the LORD, they conspired against him in Jerusalem and he fled to Lachish, but they sent men after him to Lachish and killed him there. ²⁸He was brought back by horse and was buried with his ancestors in the City of Judah.ᶜ 2Ki 14:8-20

Uzziah King of Judah

26:1-4pp — 2Ki 14:21-22; 15:1-3
26:21-23pp — 2Ki 15:5-7

26 Then all the people of Judah took Uzziah,ᵈ who was sixteen years old, and made him king in place of his father Amaziah. ²He was the one who rebuilt Elath and restored it to Judah after Amaziah rested with his ancestors.

³Uzziah was sixteen years old when he became king, and he reigned in Jerusalem fifty-two years. His mother's name was Jekoliah; she was from Jerusalem. ⁴He did what was right in the eyes of the LORD, just as his father Amaziah had done. ⁵He sought God during the days of Zechariah, who instructed him in the fearᵃ of God. As long as he

ᵃ 23 Hebrew *Jehoahaz*, a variant of *Ahaziah*   ᵇ 23 That is, about 600 feet or about 180 meters   ᶜ 28 Most Hebrew manuscripts; some Hebrew manuscripts, Septuagint, Vulgate and Syriac (see also 2 Kings 14:20) *David*   ᵈ 1 Also called *Azariah* sought the LORD, God gave him success. 2Ki 14:21-22; 15:1-3 ⁶He went to war against the Philistines and broke down the walls of Gath, Jabneh and Ashdod. He then rebuilt towns near Ashdod and elsewhere among the Philistines. ⁷God helped him against the Philistines and against the Arabs who lived in Gur Baal and against the Meunites. ⁸The Ammonites brought tribute to Uzziah, and his fame spread as far as the border of Egypt, because he had become very powerful. 2Ch 17:11; 21:16; Isa 14:29

⁹Uzziah built towers in Jerusalem at the Corner Gate, at the Valley Gate and at the angle of the wall, and he fortified them. ¹⁰He also built towers in the wilderness and dug many cisterns, because he had much livestock in the foothills and in the plain. He had people working his fields and vineyards in the hills and in the fertile lands, for he loved the soil.

¹¹Uzziah had a well-trained army, ready to go out by divisions according to their numbers as mustered by Jeiel the secretary and Maaseiah the officer under the direction of Hananiah, one of the royal officials. ¹²The total number of family leaders over the fighting men was 2,600. ¹³Under their command was an army of 307,500 men trained for war, a powerful force to support the king against his enemies. ¹⁴Uzziah provided shields, spears, helmets, coats of armor, bows and slingstones for the entire army. ¹⁵In Jerusalem he made devices invented for use on the towers and on the corner defenses so that soldiers could shoot arrows and hurl large stones from the walls. His fame spread far and wide, for he was greatly helped until he became powerful. Jer 46:4

¹⁶But after Uzziah became powerful, his pride led to his downfall. He was unfaithful to the LORD his God, and entered the temple of the LORD to burn incense on the altar of incense. ¹⁷Azariah the priest with eighty other courageous priests of the LORD followed him in. ¹⁸They confronted King Uzziah and said, "It is not right for you, Uzziah, to burn incense to the LORD. That is for the priests, the descendants of Aaron, who have been consecrated to burn incense. Leave the sanctuary, for you have been unfaithful; and you will not be honored by the LORD God." Ex 30:7; Dt 32:15

¹⁹Uzziah, who had a censer in his hand ready to burn incense, became angry. While he was raging at the priests in their presence before the incense altar in the LORD's temple, leprosy[b] broke out on his forehead. ²⁰When Az-

---

a 5 Many Hebrew manuscripts, Septuagint and Syriac; other Hebrew manuscripts *vision*
b 19 The Hebrew for *leprosy* was used for various diseases affecting the skin; also in verses 20, 21 and 23.

ariah the chief priest and all the other priests looked at him, they saw that he had leprosy on his forehead, so they hurried him out. Indeed, he himself was eager to leave, because the LORD had afflicted him.   2Ki 5:25-27

²¹King Uzziah had leprosy until the day he died. He lived in a separate house*ᵃ* — leprous, and banned from the temple of the LORD. Jotham his son had charge of the palace and governed the people of the land.

²²The other events of Uzziah's reign, from beginning to end, are recorded by the prophet Isaiah son of Amoz. ²³Uzziah rested with his ancestors and was buried near them in a cemetery that belonged to the kings, for people said, "He had leprosy." And Jotham his son succeeded him as king.   2Ki 15:5-7; Isa 6:1

Jotham King of Judah
27:1-4,7-9pp — 2Ki 15:33-38

27 Jotham was twenty-five years old when he became king, and he reigned in Jerusalem sixteen years. His mother's name was Jerusha daughter of Zadok. ²He did what was right in the eyes of the LORD, just as his father Uzziah had done, but unlike him he did not enter the temple of the LORD. The people, however, continued their corrupt practices. ³Jotham rebuilt the Upper Gate of the temple of the LORD and did extensive work on the wall at the hill of Ophel. ⁴He built towns in the hill country of Judah and forts and towers in the wooded areas.   2Ch 33:14; Ne 3:26; 1Ch 3:12

⁵Jotham waged war against the king of the Ammonites and conquered them. That year the Ammonites paid him a hundred talents*ᵇ* of silver, ten thousand cors*ᶜ* of wheat and ten thousand cors*ᵈ* of barley. The Ammonites brought him the same amount also in the second and third years.   Ge 19:38

⁶Jotham grew powerful because he walked steadfastly before the LORD his God.   2Ch 26:5

⁷The other events in Jotham's reign, including all his wars and the other things he did, are written in the book of the kings of Israel and Judah. ⁸He was twenty-five years old when he became king, and he reigned in Jerusalem sixteen years. ⁹Jotham rested with his ancestors and was buried in the City of David. And Ahaz his son succeeded him as king.   2Ki 15:33-38

Ahaz King of Judah
28:1-27pp — 2Ki 16:1-20

28 Ahaz was twenty years old when he became king, and he reigned in Jerusalem sixteen years. Unlike David his father, he did not do what was right in the

---

ᵃ 21 Or *in a house where he was relieved of responsibilities*   *ᵇ 5* That is, about 3 3/4 tons or about 3.4 metric tons   *ᶜ 5* That is, probably about 1,800 tons or about 1,600 metric tons of wheat   *ᵈ 5* That is, probably about 1,500 tons or about 1,350 metric tons of barley eyes of the LORD. ²He followed the ways of the kings of Israel and also made idols for worshiping the Baals. ³He burned sacrifices in the Valley of Ben Hinnom and sacrificed his children in the fire, engaging in the detestable practices of the nations the LORD had driven out before the Israelites. ⁴He offered sacrifices and burned incense at the high places, on the hilltops and under every spreading tree.   Lev 18:21; 2Ch 33:2,6

⁵Therefore the LORD his God delivered him into the hands of the king of Aram. The Arameans defeated him and took many of his people as prisoners and brought them to Damascus. Isa 7:1

He was also given into the hands of the king of Israel, who inflicted heavy casualties on him. ⁶In one day Pekah son of Remaliah killed a hundred and twenty thousand soldiers in Judah—because Judah had forsaken the LORD, the God of their ancestors. ⁷Zikri, an Ephraimite warrior, killed Maaseiah the king's son, Azrikam the officer in charge of the palace, and Elkanah, second to the king. ⁸The men of Israel took captive from their fellow Israelites who were from Judah two hundred thousand wives, sons and daughters. They also took a great deal of plunder, which they carried back to Samaria.   2Ki 15:25,27; 2Ch 11:4

⁹But a prophet of the LORD named Oded was there, and he went out to meet the army when it returned to Samaria. He said to them, "Because the LORD, the God of your ancestors, was angry with Judah, he gave them into your hand. But you have slaughtered them in a rage that reaches to heaven. ¹⁰And now you intend to make the men and women of Judah and Jerusalem your slaves. But aren't you also guilty of sins against the LORD your God? ¹¹Now listen to me! Send back your fellow Israelites you have taken as prisoners, for the LORD's fierce anger rests on you."   Lev 25:39-46; Ezr 9:6; Isa 47:6

¹²Then some of the leaders in Ephraim—Azariah son of Jehohanan, Berekiah son of Meshillemoth, Jehizkiah son of Shallum, and Amasa son of Hadlai—confronted those who were arriving from the war. ¹³"You must not bring those prisoners here," they said, "or we will be guilty before the LORD. Do you intend to add to our sin and guilt? For our guilt is already great, and his fierce anger rests on Israel."

¹⁴So the soldiers gave up the prisoners and plunder in the presence of the officials and all the assembly. ¹⁵The men designated by name took the prisoners, and from the plunder they clothed all who were naked. They provided them with clothes and sandals, food and drink, and healing balm. All those who were weak they put on donkeys.

So they took them back to their fellow Israelites at Jericho, the City of Palms, and returned to Samaria. 			Jdg 1:16; 2Ki 6:22

[16] At that time King Ahaz sent to the kings[a] of Assyria for help. [17] The Edomites had again come and attacked Judah and carried away prisoners, [18] while the Philistines had raided towns in the foothills and in the Negev of Judah. They captured and occupied Beth Shemesh, Aijalon and Gederoth, as well as Soko, Timnah and Gimzo, with their surrounding villages. [19] The LORD had humbled Judah because of Ahaz king of Israel,[b] for he had promoted wickedness in Judah and had been most unfaithful to the LORD. [20] Tiglath-Pileser[c] king of Assyria came to him, but he gave him trouble instead of help. [21] Ahaz took some of the things from the temple of the LORD and from the royal palace and from the officials and presented them to the king of Assyria, but that did not help him. 		2Ki 16:7; 2Ch 21:2; Eze 16:27,57

[22] In his time of trouble King Ahaz became even more unfaithful to the LORD. [23] He offered sacrifices to the gods of Damascus, who had defeated him; for he thought, "Since the gods of the kings of Aram have helped them, I will sacrifice to them so they will help me." But they were his downfall and the downfall of all Israel. 		2Ch 25:14; Jer 44:17-18

[24] Ahaz gathered together the furnishings from the temple of God and cut them in pieces. He shut the doors of the LORD's temple and set up altars at every street corner in Jerusalem. [25] In every town in Judah he built high places to burn sacrifices to other gods and aroused the anger of the LORD, the God of his ancestors. 		2Ki 16:18; 2Ch 29:7

[26] The other events of his reign and all his ways, from beginning to end, are written in the book of the kings of Judah and Israel. [27] Ahaz rested with his ancestors and was buried in the city of Jerusalem, but he was not placed in the tombs of the kings of Israel. And Hezekiah his son succeeded him as king. 		2Ki 16:1-20

Hezekiah Purifies the Temple

29:1-2pp — 2Ki 18:2-3

29 Hezekiah was twenty-five years old when he became king, and he reigned in Jerusalem twenty-nine years. His mother's name was Abijah daughter of Zechariah. [2] He did what was right in the eyes of the LORD, just as his father David had done. 		2Ki 18:1-3; 2Ch 34:2

[3] In the first month of the first year of his reign, he opened the doors of the temple of the LORD

---

[a] 16 Most Hebrew manuscripts; one Hebrew manuscript, Septuagint and Vulgate (see also 2 Kings 16:7) *king*   [b] 19 That is, Judah, as frequently in 2 Chronicles   [c] 20 Hebrew *Tilgath-Pilneser*, a variant of *Tiglath-Pileser*

and repaired them. ⁴He brought in the priests and the Levites, assembled them in the square on the east side ⁵and said: "Listen to me, Levites! Consecrate yourselves now and consecrate the temple of the LORD, the God of your ancestors. Remove all defilement from the sanctuary. ⁶Our parents were unfaithful; they did evil in the eyes of the LORD our God and forsook him. They turned their faces away from the LORD's dwelling place and turned their backs on him. ⁷They also shut the doors of the portico and put out the lamps. They did not burn incense or present any burnt offerings at the sanctuary to the God of Israel. ⁸Therefore, the anger of the LORD has fallen on Judah and Jerusalem; he has made them an object of dread and horror and scorn, as you can see with your own eyes. ⁹This is why our fathers have fallen by the sword and why our sons and daughters and our wives are in captivity. ¹⁰Now I intend to make a covenant with the LORD, the God of Israel, so that his fierce anger will turn away from us. ¹¹My sons, do not be negligent now, for the LORD has chosen you to stand before him and serve him, to minister before him and to burn incense."   Nu 3:6; 2Ch 23:16; Jer 25:9,18

¹²Then these Levites set to work: Nu 3:17-20
  from the Kohathites,
    Mahath son of Amasai and Joel son of Azariah;

  from the Merarites,
    Kish son of Abdi and Azariah son of Jehallelel;
  from the Gershonites,
    Joah son of Zimmah and Eden son of Joah; 2Ch 31:15
¹³from the descendants of Elizaphan,
    Shimri and Jeiel;
  from the descendants of Asaph,   1Ch 6:39
    Zechariah and Mattaniah;
¹⁴from the descendants of Heman,
    Jehiel and Shimei;
  from the descendants of Jeduthun,
    Shemaiah and Uzziel.

¹⁵When they had assembled their fellow Levites and consecrated themselves, they went in to purify the temple of the LORD, as the king had ordered, following the word of the LORD. ¹⁶The priests went into the sanctuary of the LORD to purify it. They brought out to the courtyard of the LORD's temple everything unclean that they found in the temple of the LORD. The Levites took it and carried it out to the Kidron Valley. ¹⁷They began the consecration on the first day of the first month, and by the eighth day of the month they reached the portico of the LORD. For eight more days they consecrated the temple of the LORD itself, finishing on the sixteenth day of the first month.   1Ch 23:28; 2Ch 30:12

¹⁸Then they went in to King Hezekiah and reported: "We have

purified the entire temple of the LORD, the altar of burnt offering with all its utensils, and the table for setting out the consecrated bread, with all its articles. ¹⁹We have prepared and consecrated all the articles that King Ahaz removed in his unfaithfulness while he was king. They are now in front of the LORD's altar." 2Ch 28:24

²⁰Early the next morning King Hezekiah gathered the city officials together and went up to the temple of the LORD. ²¹They brought seven bulls, seven rams, seven male lambs and seven male goats as a sin offering*a* for the kingdom, for the sanctuary and for Judah. The king commanded the priests, the descendants of Aaron, to offer these on the altar of the LORD. ²²So they slaughtered the bulls, and the priests took the blood and splashed it against the altar; next they slaughtered the rams and splashed their blood against the altar; then they slaughtered the lambs and splashed their blood against the altar. ²³The goats for the sin offering were brought before the king and the assembly, and they laid their hands on them. ²⁴The priests then slaughtered the goats and presented their blood on the altar for a sin offering to atone for all Israel, because the king had ordered the burnt offering and the sin offering for all Israel. Lev 4:13-15,26

²⁵He stationed the Levites in the temple of the LORD with cymbals, harps and lyres in the way prescribed by David and Gad the king's seer and Nathan the prophet; this was commanded by the LORD through his prophets. ²⁶So the Levites stood ready with David's instruments, and the priests with their trumpets. 1Ch 15:24; 23:5; 25:6

²⁷Hezekiah gave the order to sacrifice the burnt offering on the altar. As the offering began, singing to the LORD began also, accompanied by trumpets and the instruments of David king of Israel. ²⁸The whole assembly bowed in worship, while the musicians played and the trumpets sounded. All this continued until the sacrifice of the burnt offering was completed. 2Ch 23:18

²⁹When the offerings were finished, the king and everyone present with him knelt down and worshiped. ³⁰King Hezekiah and his officials ordered the Levites to praise the LORD with the words of David and of Asaph the seer. So they sang praises with gladness and bowed down and worshiped. 2Ch 20:18

³¹Then Hezekiah said, "You have now dedicated yourselves to the LORD. Come and bring sacrifices and thank offerings to the temple of the LORD." So the assembly brought sacrifices and thank offerings, and all whose

a 21 Or *purification offering*; also in verses 23 and 24

hearts were willing brought burnt offerings. Ex 35:22; Heb 13:15-16 [32] The number of burnt offerings the assembly brought was seventy bulls, a hundred rams and two hundred male lambs — all of them for burnt offerings to the LORD. [33] The animals consecrated as sacrifices amounted to six hundred bulls and three thousand sheep and goats. [34] The priests, however, were too few to skin all the burnt offerings; so their relatives the Levites helped them until the task was finished and until other priests had been consecrated, for the Levites had been more conscientious in consecrating themselves than the priests had been. [35] There were burnt offerings in abundance, together with the fat of the fellowship offerings and the drink offerings that accompanied the burnt offerings. Lev 3:16; Nu 15:5-10; 2Ch 30:3,15

So the service of the temple of the LORD was reestablished. [36] Hezekiah and all the people rejoiced at what God had brought about for his people, because it was done so quickly.

Hezekiah Celebrates the Passover

30 Hezekiah sent word to all Israel and Judah and also wrote letters to Ephraim and Manasseh, inviting them to come to the temple of the LORD in Jerusalem and celebrate the Passover to the LORD, the God of Israel. [2] The king and his officials and the whole assembly in Jerusalem decided to celebrate the Passover in the second month. [3] They had not been able to celebrate it at the regular time because not enough priests had consecrated themselves and the people had not assembled in Jerusalem. [4] The plan seemed right both to the king and to the whole assembly. [5] They decided to send a proclamation throughout Israel, from Beersheba to Dan, calling the people to come to Jerusalem and celebrate the Passover to the LORD, the God of Israel. It had not been celebrated in large numbers according to what was written. Jdg 20:1; Nu 9:10; 2Ch 29:34

[6] At the king's command, couriers went throughout Israel and Judah with letters from the king and from his officials, which read:

"People of Israel, return to the LORD, the God of Abraham, Isaac and Israel, that he may return to you who are left, who have escaped from the hand of the kings of Assyria. [7] Do not be like your parents and your fellow Israelites, who were unfaithful to the LORD, the God of their ancestors, so that he made them an object of horror, as you see. [8] Do not be stiff-necked, as your ancestors were; submit to the

LORD. Come to his sanctuary, which he has consecrated forever. Serve the LORD your God, so that his fierce anger will turn away from you. ⁹If you return to the LORD, then your fellow Israelites and your children will be shown compassion by their captors and will return to this land, for the LORD your God is gracious and compassionate. He will not turn his face from you if you return to him." Dt 30:2-5

¹⁰The couriers went from town to town in Ephraim and Manasseh, as far as Zebulun, but people scorned and ridiculed them. ¹¹Nevertheless, some from Asher, Manasseh and Zebulun humbled themselves and went to Jerusalem. ¹²Also in Judah the hand of God was on the people to give them unity of mind to carry out what the king and his officials had ordered, following the word of the LORD. 2Ch 36:16; Jer 32:39

¹³A very large crowd of people assembled in Jerusalem to celebrate the Festival of Unleavened Bread in the second month. ¹⁴They removed the altars in Jerusalem and cleared away the incense altars and threw them into the Kidron Valley. Nu 28:16; 2Ch 28:24

¹⁵They slaughtered the Passover lamb on the fourteenth day of the second month. The priests and the Levites were ashamed and consecrated themselves and brought burnt offerings to the temple of the LORD. ¹⁶Then they took up their regular positions as prescribed in the Law of Moses the man of God. The priests splashed against the altar the blood handed to them by the Levites. ¹⁷Since many in the crowd had not consecrated themselves, the Levites had to kill the Passover lambs for all those who were not ceremonially clean and could not consecrate their lambs[a] to the LORD. ¹⁸Although most of the many people who came from Ephraim, Manasseh, Issachar and Zebulun had not purified themselves, yet they ate the Passover, contrary to what was written. But Hezekiah prayed for them, saying, "May the LORD, who is good, pardon everyone ¹⁹who sets their heart on seeking God — the LORD, the God of their ancestors — even if they are not clean according to the rules of the sanctuary." ²⁰And the LORD heard Hezekiah and healed the people. 2Ch 7:14; Mal 4:2; Jas 5:16

²¹The Israelites who were present in Jerusalem celebrated the Festival of Unleavened Bread for seven days with great rejoicing, while the Levites and priests praised the LORD every day with resounding instruments dedicated to the LORD.[b]

---

[a] 17 Or *consecrate themselves* [b] 21 Or *priests sang to the LORD every day, accompanied by* the LORD's *instruments of praise*

²²Hezekiah spoke encouragingly to all the Levites, who showed good understanding of the service of the LORD. For the seven days they ate their assigned portion and offered fellowship offerings and praised[a] the LORD, the God of their ancestors. Ex 12:15,17; 13:6 ²³The whole assembly then agreed to celebrate the festival seven more days; so for another seven days they celebrated joyfully. ²⁴Hezekiah king of Judah provided a thousand bulls and seven thousand sheep and goats for the assembly, and the officials provided them with a thousand bulls and ten thousand sheep and goats. A great number of priests consecrated themselves. ²⁵The entire assembly of Judah rejoiced, along with the priests and Levites and all who had assembled from Israel, including the foreigners who had come from Israel and also those who resided in Judah. ²⁶There was great joy in Jerusalem, for since the days of Solomon son of David king of Israel there had been nothing like this in Jerusalem. ²⁷The priests and the Levites stood to bless the people, and God heard them, for their prayer reached heaven, his holy dwelling place. Nu 6:23; Dt 26:15

31 When all this had ended, the Israelites who were there went out to the towns of Judah, smashed the sacred stones and cut down the Asherah poles. They destroyed the high places and the altars throughout Judah and Benjamin and in Ephraim and Manasseh. After they had destroyed all of them, the Israelites returned to their own towns and to their own property. 2Ki 18:4

Contributions for Worship
31:20-21pp — 2Ki 18:5-7

²Hezekiah assigned the priests and Levites to divisions — each of them according to their duties as priests or Levites — to offer burnt offerings and fellowship offerings, to minister, to give thanks and to sing praises at the gates of the LORD's dwelling. ³The king contributed from his own possessions for the morning and evening burnt offerings and for the burnt offerings on the Sabbaths, at the New Moons and at the appointed festivals as written in the Law of the LORD. ⁴He ordered the people living in Jerusalem to give the portion due the priests and Levites so they could devote themselves to the Law of the LORD. ⁵As soon as the order went out, the Israelites generously gave the firstfruits of their grain, new wine, olive oil and honey and all that the fields produced. They brought a great amount, a tithe of everything. ⁶The people of Israel and Judah who lived in the towns of Judah also brought a tithe of their herds

[a] 22 Or *and confessed their sins to*

and flocks and a tithe of the holy things dedicated to the LORD their God, and they piled them in heaps. [7] They began doing this in the third month and finished in the seventh month. [8] When Hezekiah and his officials came and saw the heaps, they praised the LORD and blessed his people Israel. Dt 14:28; Ps 144:13-15

[9] Hezekiah asked the priests and Levites about the heaps; [10] and Azariah the chief priest, from the family of Zadok, answered, "Since the people began to bring their contributions to the temple of the LORD, we have had enough to eat and plenty to spare, because the LORD has blessed his people, and this great amount is left over." Mal 3:10-12

[11] Hezekiah gave orders to prepare storerooms in the temple of the LORD, and this was done. [12] Then they faithfully brought in the contributions, tithes and dedicated gifts. Konaniah, a Levite, was the overseer in charge of these things, and his brother Shimei was next in rank. [13] Jehiel, Azaziah, Nahath, Asahel, Jerimoth, Jozabad, Eliel, Ismakiah, Mahath and Benaiah were assistants of Konaniah and Shimei his brother. All these served by appointment of King Hezekiah and Azariah the official in charge of the temple of God. 2Ch 35:9

[14] Kore son of Imnah the Levite, keeper of the East Gate, was in charge of the freewill offerings given to God, distributing the contributions made to the LORD and also the consecrated gifts. [15] Eden, Miniamin, Jeshua, Shemaiah, Amariah and Shekaniah assisted him faithfully in the towns of the priests, distributing to their fellow priests according to their divisions, old and young alike. Jos 21:9-19; 2Ch 29:12

[16] In addition, they distributed to the males three years old or more whose names were in the genealogical records — all who would enter the temple of the LORD to perform the daily duties of their various tasks, according to their responsibilities and their divisions. [17] And they distributed to the priests enrolled by their families in the genealogical records and likewise to the Levites twenty years old or more, according to their responsibilities and their divisions. [18] They included all the little ones, the wives, and the sons and daughters of the whole community listed in these genealogical records. For they were faithful in consecrating themselves. 1Ch 23:3; Ezr 3:4

[19] As for the priests, the descendants of Aaron, who lived on the farmlands around their towns or in any other towns, men were designated by name to distribute portions to every male among them and to all who were recorded in the genealogies of the Levites.

[20] This is what Hezekiah did

throughout Judah, doing what was good and right and faithful before the LORD his God. ²¹In everything that he undertook in the service of God's temple and in obedience to the law and the commands, he sought his God and worked wholeheartedly. And so he prospered. 2Ki 18:5-7

Sennacherib Threatens Jerusalem

32:9-19pp — 2Ki 18:17-35; Isa 36:2-20
32:20-21pp — 2Ki 19:35-37; Isa 37:36-38

32 After all that Hezekiah had so faithfully done, Sennacherib king of Assyria came and invaded Judah. He laid siege to the fortified cities, thinking to conquer them for himself. ²When Hezekiah saw that Sennacherib had come and that he intended to wage war against Jerusalem, ³he consulted with his officials and military staff about blocking off the water from the springs outside the city, and they helped him. ⁴They gathered a large group of people who blocked all the springs and the stream that flowed through the land. "Why should the kings[a] of Assyria come and find plenty of water?" they said. ⁵Then he worked hard repairing all the broken sections of the wall and building towers on it. He built another wall outside that one and reinforced the terraces[b] of the City of David. He also made

large numbers of weapons and shields. 1Ki 9:24; 1Ch 11:8; Isa 22:8

⁶He appointed military officers over the people and assembled them before him in the square at the city gate and encouraged them with these words: ⁷"Be strong and courageous. Do not be afraid or discouraged because of the king of Assyria and the vast army with him, for there is a greater power with us than with him. ⁸With him is only the arm of flesh, but with us is the LORD our God to help us and to fight our battles." And the people gained confidence from what Hezekiah the king of Judah said. 2Ki 6:16; 2Ch 20:17; Jer 17:5

⁹Later, when Sennacherib king of Assyria and all his forces were laying siege to Lachish, he sent his officers to Jerusalem with this message for Hezekiah king of Judah and for all the people of Judah who were there: Jos 10:3,31

¹⁰"This is what Sennacherib king of Assyria says: On what are you basing your confidence, that you remain in Jerusalem under siege? ¹¹When Hezekiah says, 'The LORD our God will save us from the hand of the king of Assyria,' he is misleading you, to let you die of hunger and thirst. ¹²Did not Hezekiah himself remove this god's high places and altars, saying to Judah and Jerusalem,

^a 4 Hebrew; Septuagint and Syriac *king*   ^b 5 Or *the Millo*

'You must worship before one altar and burn sacrifices on it'? 2Ch 31:1; Isa 37:10; Eze 29:16

13 "Do you not know what I and my predecessors have done to all the peoples of the other lands? Were the gods of those nations ever able to deliver their land from my hand? 14 Who of all the gods of these nations that my predecessors destroyed has been able to save his people from me? How then can your god deliver you from my hand? 15 Now do not let Hezekiah deceive you and mislead you like this. Do not believe him, for no god of any nation or kingdom has been able to deliver his people from my hand or the hand of my predecessors. How much less will your god deliver you from my hand!" Ex 5:2; Da 3:15

16 Sennacherib's officers spoke further against the LORD God and against his servant Hezekiah. 17 The king also wrote letters ridiculing the LORD, the God of Israel, and saying this against him: "Just as the gods of the peoples of the other lands did not rescue their people from my hand, so the god of Hezekiah will not rescue his people from my hand." 18 Then they called out in Hebrew to the people of Jerusalem who were on the wall, to terrify them and

make them afraid in order to capture the city. 19 They spoke about the God of Jerusalem as they did about the gods of the other peoples of the world—the work of human hands. 2Ki 18:17-35; Isa 36:2-20

20 King Hezekiah and the prophet Isaiah son of Amoz cried out in prayer to heaven about this. 21 And the LORD sent an angel, who annihilated all the fighting men and the commanders and officers in the camp of the Assyrian king. So he withdrew to his own land in disgrace. And when he went into the temple of his god, some of his sons, his own flesh and blood, cut him down with the sword. 2Ki 19:35-37; Isa 37:36-38

22 So the LORD saved Hezekiah and the people of Jerusalem from the hand of Sennacherib king of Assyria and from the hand of all others. He took care of them*a* on every side. 23 Many brought offerings to Jerusalem for the LORD and valuable gifts for Hezekiah king of Judah. From then on he was highly regarded by all the nations. 2Ch 17:5; Isa 45:14

Hezekiah's Pride, Success and Death

32:24-33pp — 2Ki 20:1-21; Isa 37:21-38; 38:1-8

24 In those days Hezekiah became ill and was at the point of death. He prayed to the LORD, who answered him and gave him a miraculous sign. 25 But Hezekiah's

heart was proud and he did not respond to the kindness shown him; therefore the LORD's wrath was on him and on Judah and Jerusalem. ²⁶Then Hezekiah repented of the pride of his heart, as did the people of Jerusalem; therefore the LORD's wrath did not come on them during the days of Hezekiah. 2Ch 26:16; Jer 26:18-19

²⁷Hezekiah had very great wealth and honor, and he made treasuries for his silver and gold and for his precious stones, spices, shields and all kinds of valuables. ²⁸He also made buildings to store the harvest of grain, new wine and olive oil; and he made stalls for various kinds of cattle, and pens for the flocks. ²⁹He built villages and acquired great numbers of flocks and herds, for God had given him very great riches. 1Ch 29:12

³⁰It was Hezekiah who blocked the upper outlet of the Gihon spring and channeled the water down to the west side of the City of David. He succeeded in everything he undertook. ³¹But when envoys were sent by the rulers of Babylon to ask him about the miraculous sign that had occurred in the land, God left him to test him and to know everything that was in his heart. Dt 8:16; Isa 39:1

³²The other events of Hezekiah's reign and his acts of devotion are written in the vision of the prophet Isaiah son of Amoz in the book of the kings of Judah

and Israel. ³³Hezekiah rested with his ancestors and was buried on the hill where the tombs of David's descendants are. All Judah and the people of Jerusalem honored him when he died. And Manasseh his son succeeded him as king. 2Ki 20:1-21; Isa 37:21-38; 38:1-8

Manasseh King of Judah

33:1-10pp — 2Ki 21:1-10
33:18-20pp — 2Ki 21:17-18

33 Manasseh was twelve years old when he became king, and he reigned in Jerusalem fifty-five years. ²He did evil in the eyes of the LORD, following the detestable practices of the nations the LORD had driven out before the Israelites. ³He rebuilt the high places his father Hezekiah had demolished; he also erected altars to the Baals and made Asherah poles. He bowed down to all the starry hosts and worshiped them. ⁴He built altars in the temple of the LORD, of which the LORD had said, "My Name will remain in Jerusalem forever." ⁵In both courts of the temple of the LORD, he built altars to all the starry hosts. ⁶He sacrificed his children in the fire in the Valley of Ben Hinnom, practiced divination and witchcraft, sought omens, and consulted mediums and spiritists. He did much evil in the eyes of the LORD, arousing his anger. Lev 18:21; 19:31; 1Sa 28:13

⁷He took the image he had made and put it in God's temple, of

which God had said to David and to his son Solomon, "In this temple and in Jerusalem, which I have chosen out of all the tribes of Israel, I will put my Name forever. [8]I will not again make the feet of the Israelites leave the land I assigned to your ancestors, if only they will be careful to do everything I commanded them concerning all the laws, decrees and regulations given through Moses." [9]But Manasseh led Judah and the people of Jerusalem astray, so that they did more evil than the nations the LORD had destroyed before the Israelites. 2Ki 21:1-10; Jer 15:4

[10]The LORD spoke to Manasseh and his people, but they paid no attention. [11]So the LORD brought against them the army commanders of the king of Assyria, who took Manasseh prisoner, put a hook in his nose, bound him with bronze shackles and took him to Babylon. [12]In his distress he sought the favor of the LORD his God and humbled himself greatly before the God of his ancestors. [13]And when he prayed to him, the LORD was moved by his entreaty and listened to his plea; so he brought him back to Jerusalem and to his kingdom. Then Manasseh knew that the LORD is God. 2Ch 32:26; 1Pe 5:6

[14]Afterward he rebuilt the outer wall of the City of David, west of the Gihon spring in the valley, as far as the entrance of the Fish Gate and encircling the hill of Ophel; he also made it much higher. He stationed military commanders in all the fortified cities in Judah. 1Ki 1:33; 2Ch 27:3

[15]He got rid of the foreign gods and removed the image from the temple of the LORD, as well as all the altars he had built on the temple hill and in Jerusalem; and he threw them out of the city. [16]Then he restored the altar of the LORD and sacrificed fellowship offerings and thank offerings on it, and told Judah to serve the LORD, the God of Israel. [17]The people, however, continued to sacrifice at the high places, but only to the LORD their God. ver 3-7; Lev 7:11-18

[18]The other events of Manasseh's reign, including his prayer to his God and the words the seers spoke to him in the name of the LORD, the God of Israel, are written in the annals of the kings of Israel.[a] [19]His prayer and how God was moved by his entreaty, as well as all his sins and unfaithfulness, and the sites where he built high places and set up Asherah poles and idols before he humbled himself — all these are written in the records of the seers.[b] [20]Manasseh rested with his ancestors and was buried in his palace. And Amon his son succeeded him as king. 2Ki 21:17-18

---

[a] 18 That is, Judah, as frequently in 2 Chronicles Septuagint; most Hebrew manuscripts of Hozai   [b] 19 One Hebrew manuscript and

Amon King of Judah

33:21-25pp — 2Ki 21:19-24

²¹ Amon was twenty-two years old when he became king, and he reigned in Jerusalem two years. ²² He did evil in the eyes of the LORD, as his father Manasseh had done. Amon worshiped and offered sacrifices to all the idols Manasseh had made. ²³ But unlike his father Manasseh, he did not humble himself before the LORD; Amon increased his guilt.

²⁴ Amon's officials conspired against him and assassinated him in his palace. ²⁵ Then the people of the land killed all who had plotted against King Amon, and they made Josiah his son king in his place. 2Ki 21:19-24

Josiah's Reforms

34:1-2pp — 2Ki 22:1-2
34:3-7Ref — 2Ki 23:4-20
34:8-13pp — 2Ki 22:3-7

34 Josiah was eight years old when he became king, and he reigned in Jerusalem thirty-one years. ² He did what was right in the eyes of the LORD and followed the ways of his father David, not turning aside to the right or to the left. 2Ki 22:1-2; 1Ch 3:14

³ In the eighth year of his reign, while he was still young, he began to seek the God of his father David. In his twelfth year he began to purge Judah and Jerusalem of high places, Asherah poles and idols. ⁴ Under his direction the altars of the Baals were torn down; he cut to pieces the incense altars that were above them, and smashed the Asherah poles and the idols. These he broke to pieces and scattered over the graves of those who had sacrificed to them. ⁵ He burned the bones of the priests on their altars, and so he purged Judah and Jerusalem. ⁶ In the towns of Manasseh, Ephraim and Simeon, as far as Naphtali, and in the ruins around them, ⁷ he tore down the altars and the Asherah poles and crushed the idols to powder and cut to pieces all the incense altars throughout Israel. Then he went back to Jerusalem. Lev 26:30; 1Ki 13:2; 2Ch 31:1

⁸ In the eighteenth year of Josiah's reign, to purify the land and the temple, he sent Shaphan son of Azaliah and Maaseiah the ruler of the city, with Joah son of Joahaz, the recorder, to repair the temple of the LORD his God.

⁹ They went to Hilkiah the high priest and gave him the money that had been brought into the temple of God, which the Levites who were the gatekeepers had collected from the people of Manasseh, Ephraim and the entire remnant of Israel and from all the people of Judah and Benjamin and the inhabitants of Jerusalem. ¹⁰ Then they entrusted it to the men appointed to supervise the work on the LORD's temple. These men paid the workers who repaired and restored the

temple. [11]They also gave money to the carpenters and builders to purchase dressed stone, and timber for joists and beams for the buildings that the kings of Judah had allowed to fall into ruin. 2Ch 33:4-7; 35:8

[12]The workers labored faithfully. Over them to direct them were Jahath and Obadiah, Levites descended from Merari, and Zechariah and Meshullam, descended from Kohath. The Levites — all who were skilled in playing musical instruments — [13]had charge of the laborers and supervised all the workers from job to job. Some of the Levites were secretaries, scribes and gatekeepers. 2Ki 12:15; 1Ch 23:4; 25:1

The Book of the Law Found

34:14-28pp — 2Ki 22:8-20
34:29-32pp — 2Ki 23:1-3

[14]While they were bringing out the money that had been taken into the temple of the LORD, Hilkiah the priest found the Book of the Law of the LORD that had been given through Moses. [15]Hilkiah said to Shaphan the secretary, "I have found the Book of the Law in the temple of the LORD." He gave it to Shaphan. 2Ki 22:8; Ezr 7:6; Ne 8:1

[16]Then Shaphan took the book to the king and reported to him: "Your officials are doing everything that has been committed to them. [17]They have paid out

the money that was in the temple of the LORD and have entrusted it to the supervisors and workers." [18]Then Shaphan the secretary informed the king, "Hilkiah the priest has given me a book." And Shaphan read from it in the presence of the king.

[19]When the king heard the words of the Law, he tore his robes. [20]He gave these orders to Hilkiah, Ahikam son of Shaphan, Abdon son of Micah,[a] Shaphan the secretary and Asaiah the king's attendant: [21]"Go and inquire of the LORD for me and for the remnant in Israel and Judah about what is written in this book that has been found. Great is the LORD's anger that is poured out on us because those who have gone before us have not kept the word of the LORD; they have not acted in accordance with all that is written in this book." 2Ch 29:8; La 2:4

[22]Hilkiah and those the king had sent with him[b] went to speak to the prophet Huldah, who was the wife of Shallum son of Tokhath,[c] the son of Hasrah,[d] keeper of the wardrobe. She lived in Jerusalem, in the New Quarter. Ex 15:20; Ne 6:14

[23]She said to them, "This is what the LORD, the God of Israel, says: Tell the man who sent you to me, [24]'This is what the LORD says: I am going to bring disaster

on this place and its people — all the curses written in the book that has been read in the presence of the king of Judah. ²⁵ Because they have forsaken me and burned incense to other gods and aroused my anger by all that their hands have made,ᵃ my anger will be poured out on this place and will not be quenched.' ²⁶ Tell the king of Judah, who sent you to inquire of the LORD, 'This is what the LORD, the God of Israel, says concerning the words you heard: ²⁷ Because your heart was responsive and you humbled yourself before God when you heard what he spoke against this place and its people, and because you humbled yourself before me and tore your robes and wept in my presence, I have heard you, declares the LORD. ²⁸ Now I will gather you to your ancestors, and you will be buried in peace. Your eyes will not see all the disaster I am going to bring on this place and on those who live here.' " 2Ch 12:7; 32:26; 35:20-25

So they took her answer back to the king.   2Ki 22:8-20

²⁹ Then the king called together all the elders of Judah and Jerusalem. ³⁰ He went up to the temple of the LORD with the people of Judah, the inhabitants of Jerusalem, the priests and the Levites — all the people from the least to the greatest. He read in their hearing all the words of the Book of the Covenant, which had been found in the temple of the LORD. ³¹ The king stood by his pillar and renewed the covenant in the presence of the LORD — to follow the LORD and keep his commands, statutes and decrees with all his heart and all his soul, and to obey the words of the covenant written in this book.

³² Then he had everyone in Jerusalem and Benjamin pledge themselves to it; the people of Jerusalem did this in accordance with the covenant of God, the God of their ancestors.   2Ki 23:1-3

³³ Josiah removed all the detestable idols from all the territory belonging to the Israelites, and he had all who were present in Israel serve the LORD their God. As long as he lived, they did not fail to follow the LORD, the God of their ancestors.   ver 3-7; Dt 18:9

Josiah Celebrates the Passover
35:1,18-19pp — 2Ki 23:21-23

35 Josiah celebrated the Passover to the LORD in Jerusalem, and the Passover lamb was slaughtered on the fourteenth day of the first month. ² He appointed the priests to their duties and encouraged them in the service of the LORD's temple. ³ He said to the Levites, who instructed all Israel and who had been consecrated to the LORD: "Put the sacred ark in the temple that Solomon son of David king of Israel built. It is not to be carried about

ᵃ 25 Or by everything they have done

on your shoulders. Now serve the LORD your God and his people Israel. [4]Prepare yourselves by families in your divisions, according to the instructions written by David king of Israel and by his son Solomon. Ex 12:1-30; 2Ch 17:7; Ezr 6:18 [5]"Stand in the holy place with a group of Levites for each subdivision of the families of your fellow Israelites, the lay people. [6]Slaughter the Passover lambs, consecrate yourselves and prepare the lambs for your fellow Israelites, doing what the LORD commanded through Moses." Lev 11:44; 2Ch 29:5 [7]Josiah provided for all the lay people who were there a total of thirty thousand lambs and goats for the Passover offerings, and also three thousand cattle — all from the king's own possessions. 2Ch 30:24; 31:3 [8]His officials also contributed voluntarily to the people and the priests and Levites. Hilkiah, Zechariah and Jehiel, the officials in charge of God's temple, gave the priests twenty-six hundred Passover offerings and three hundred cattle. [9]Also Konaniah along with Shemaiah and Nethanel, his brothers, and Hashabiah, Jeiel and Jozabad, the leaders of the Levites, provided five thousand Passover offerings and five hundred head of cattle for the Levites. 2Ch 31:12-13 [10]The service was arranged and the priests stood in their places with the Levites in their divisions as the king had ordered. [11]The Passover lambs were slaughtered, and the priests splashed against the altar the blood handed to them, while the Levites skinned the animals. [12]They set aside the burnt offerings to give them to the subdivisions of the families of the people to offer to the LORD, as it is written in the Book of Moses. They did the same with the cattle. [13]They roasted the Passover animals over the fire as prescribed, and boiled the holy offerings in pots, caldrons and pans and served them quickly to all the people. [14]After this, they made preparations for themselves and for the priests, because the priests, the descendants of Aaron, were sacrificing the burnt offerings and the fat portions until nightfall. So the Levites made preparations for themselves and for the Aaronic priests. Ex 12:2-11; 29:13; 2Ch 29:22,34 [15]The musicians, the descendants of Asaph, were in the places prescribed by David, Asaph, Heman and Jeduthun the king's seer. The gatekeepers at each gate did not need to leave their posts, because their fellow Levites made the preparations for them. 1Ch 25:1; 26:12-19; 2Ch 29:30 [16]So at that time the entire service of the LORD was carried out for the celebration of the Passover and the offering of burnt offerings on the altar of the LORD, as King Josiah had ordered. [17]The

Israelites who were present celebrated the Passover at that time and observed the Festival of Unleavened Bread for seven days. [18] The Passover had not been observed like this in Israel since the days of the prophet Samuel; and none of the kings of Israel had ever celebrated such a Passover as did Josiah, with the priests, the Levites and all Judah and Israel who were there with the people of Jerusalem. [19] This Passover was celebrated in the eighteenth year of Josiah's reign.   2Ki 23:21-23

The Death of Josiah
35:20–36:1pp — 2Ki 23:28-30

[20] After all this, when Josiah had set the temple in order, Necho king of Egypt went up to fight at Carchemish on the Euphrates, and Josiah marched out to meet him in battle. [21] But Necho sent messengers to him, saying, "What quarrel is there, king of Judah, between you and me? It is not you I am attacking at this time, but the house with which I am at war. God has told me to hurry; so stop opposing God, who is with me, or he will destroy you." 1Ki 13:18; Isa 10:9

[22] Josiah, however, would not turn away from him, but disguised himself to engage him in battle. He would not listen to what Necho had said at God's command but went to fight him on the plain of Megiddo.   1Sa 28:8

[23] Archers shot King Josiah, and he told his officers, "Take me away; I am badly wounded." [24] So they took him out of his chariot, put him in his other chariot and brought him to Jerusalem, where he died. He was buried in the tombs of his ancestors, and all Judah and Jerusalem mourned for him.   1Ki 22:34

[25] Jeremiah composed laments for Josiah, and to this day all the male and female singers commemorate Josiah in the laments. These became a tradition in Israel and are written in the Laments.   Jer 22:10,15-16

[26] The other events of Josiah's reign and his acts of devotion in accordance with what is written in the Law of the LORD — [27] all the events, from beginning to end, are written in the book of the kings of Israel and Judah.

36 [1] And the people of the land took Jehoahaz son of Josiah and made him king in Jerusalem in place of his father.

Jehoahaz King of Judah
36:2-4pp — 2Ki 23:31-34

[2] Jehoahaz[a] was twenty-three years old when he became king, and he reigned in Jerusalem three months. [3] The king of Egypt dethroned him in Jerusalem and imposed on Judah a levy of a hundred talents[b] of silver and a talent[c] of gold. [4] The king

a 2 Hebrew Joahaz, a variant of Jehoahaz; also in verse 4   b 3 That is, about 3 3/4 tons or about 3.4 metric tons   c 3 That is, about 75 pounds or about 34 kilograms of Egypt made Eliakim, a brother of Jehoahaz, king over Judah and Jerusalem and changed Eliakim's name to Jehoiakim. But Necho took Eliakim's brother Jehoahaz and carried him off to Egypt. 2Ki 23:31-34

Jehoiakim King of Judah
36:5-8pp — 2Ki 23:36-24:6

⁵Jehoiakim was twenty-five years old when he became king, and he reigned in Jerusalem eleven years. He did evil in the eyes of the LORD his God. ⁶Nebuchadnezzar king of Babylon attacked him and bound him with bronze shackles to take him to Babylon. ⁷Nebuchadnezzar also took to Babylon articles from the temple of the LORD and put them in his temple*a* there. 2Ki 24:13; Jer 26:1; 35:1

⁸The other events of Jehoiakim's reign, the detestable things he did and all that was found against him, are written in the book of the kings of Israel and Judah. And Jehoiachin his son succeeded him as king. 2Ki 23:36-24:6

Jehoiachin King of Judah
36:9-10pp — 2Ki 24:8-17

⁹Jehoiachin was eighteen*b* years old when he became king, and he reigned in Jerusalem three months and ten days. He did evil in the eyes of the LORD. ¹⁰In the spring, King Nebuchadnezzar sent for him and brought him to Babylon, together with articles of value from the temple of the LORD, and he made Jehoiachin's uncle,*c* Zedekiah, king over Judah and Jerusalem. Jer 22:25; 37:1; Eze 17:12

Zedekiah King of Judah
36:11-16pp — 2Ki 24:18-20; Jer 52:1-3

¹¹Zedekiah was twenty-one years old when he became king, and he reigned in Jerusalem eleven years. ¹²He did evil in the eyes of the LORD his God and did not humble himself before Jeremiah the prophet, who spoke the word of the LORD. ¹³He also rebelled against King Nebuchadnezzar, who had made him take an oath in God's name. He became stiff-necked and hardened his heart and would not turn to the LORD, the God of Israel. ¹⁴Furthermore, all the leaders of the priests and the people became more and more unfaithful, following all the detestable practices of the nations and defiling the temple of the LORD, which he had consecrated in Jerusalem. 2Ki 24:18-20; Jer 52:1-3

The Fall of Jerusalem
36:17-20pp — 2Ki 25:1-21; Jer 52:4-27
36:22-23pp — Ezr 1:1-3

¹⁵The LORD, the God of their ancestors, sent word to them through his messengers again and again, because he had pity on his people and on his dwell-

---

a 7 Or *palace*   *b* 9 One Hebrew manuscript, some Septuagint manuscripts and Syriac (see also 2 Kings 24:8); most Hebrew manuscripts *eight*   *c* 10 Hebrew *brother,* that is, relative (see 2 Kings 24:17) ing place. ¹⁶But they mocked God's messengers, despised his words and scoffed at his prophets until the wrath of the LORD was aroused against his people and there was no remedy. ¹⁷He brought up against them the king of the Babylonians,ᵃ who killed their young men with the sword in the sanctuary, and did not spare young men or young women, the elderly or the infirm. God gave them all into the hands of Nebuchadnezzar. ¹⁸He carried to Babylon all the articles from the temple of God, both large and small, and the treasures of the LORD's temple and the treasures of the king and his officials. ¹⁹They set fire to God's temple and broke down the wall of Jerusalem; they burned all the palaces and destroyed everything of value there.   1Ki 9:8-9; Ps 79:1-3

²⁰He carried into exile to Babylon the remnant, who escaped from the sword, and they became servants to him and his successors until the kingdom of Persia came to power. ²¹The land enjoyed its sabbath rests; all the time of its desolation it rested, until the seventy years were completed in fulfillment of the word of the LORD spoken by Jeremiah.   Ezr 1:1-3; Jer 25:11; 29:10

²²In the first year of Cyrus king of Persia, in order to fulfill the word of the LORD spoken by Jeremiah, the LORD moved the heart of Cyrus king of Persia to make a proclamation throughout his realm and also to put it in writing: Isa 44:28; Jer 25:12; 29:10

²³"This is what Cyrus king of Persia says:

" 'The LORD, the God of heaven, has given me all the kingdoms of the earth and he has appointed me to build a temple for him at Jerusalem in Judah. Any of his people among you may go up, and may the LORD their God be with them.' "   Jdg 4:10

Ezra

Cyrus Helps the Exiles to Return
1:1-3pp — 2Ch 36:22-23

1 In the first year of Cyrus king of Persia, in order to fulfill the word of the Lord spoken by Jeremiah, the Lord moved the heart of Cyrus king of Persia to make a proclamation throughout his realm and also to put it in writing: Jer 25:11-12; 29:10-14

² "This is what Cyrus king of Persia says: 2Ch 36:22-23

" 'The Lord, the God of heaven, has given me all the kingdoms of the earth and he has appointed me to build a temple for him at Jerusalem in Judah. ³ Any of his people among you may go up to Jerusalem in Judah and build the temple of the Lord, the God of Israel, the God who is in Jerusalem, and may their God be with them. ⁴ And in any locality where survivors may now be living, the people are to provide them with silver and gold, with goods and livestock, and with freewill offerings for the temple of God in Jerusalem.' " Ezr 4:3; 5:13

⁵ Then the family heads of Judah and Benjamin, and the priests and Levites — everyone whose heart God had moved — prepared to go up and build the house of the Lord in Jerusalem. ⁶ All their neighbors assisted them with articles of silver and gold, with goods and livestock, and with valuable gifts, in addition to all the freewill offerings.

⁷ Moreover, King Cyrus brought out the articles belonging to the temple of the Lord, which Nebuchadnezzar had carried away from Jerusalem and had placed in the temple of his god.ᵃ ⁸ Cyrus king of Persia had them brought by Mithredath the treasurer, who counted them out to Sheshbazzar the prince of Judah. 2Ki 24:13; Ezr 5:14

ᵃ 7 Or gods

⁹This was the inventory:

gold dishes	30
silver dishes	1,000
silver pans*a*	29
¹⁰gold bowls	30
matching silver bowls	410
other articles	1,000

¹¹In all, there were 5,400 articles of gold and of silver. Sheshbazzar brought all these along with the exiles when they came up from Babylon to Jerusalem.

The List of the Exiles Who Returned

2:1-70pp — Ne 7:6-73

2 Now these are the people of the province who came up from the captivity of the exiles, whom Nebuchadnezzar king of Babylon had taken captive to Babylon (they returned to Jerusalem and Judah, each to their own town, ²in company with Zerubbabel, Joshua, Nehemiah, Seraiah, Reelaiah, Mordecai, Bilshan, Mispar, Bigvai, Rehum and Baanah): 2Ch 36:20; Ne 7:6,73

The list of the men of the people of Israel:

³the descendants of Parosh	2,172
⁴of Shephatiah	372
⁵of Arah	775
⁶of Pahath-Moab (through the line of Jeshua and Joab)	2,812
⁷of Elam	1,254
⁸of Zattu	945
⁹of Zakkai	760
¹⁰of Bani	642
¹¹of Bebai	623
¹²of Azgad	1,222
¹³of Adonikam	666
¹⁴of Bigvai	2,056
¹⁵of Adin	454
¹⁶of Ater (through Hezekiah)	98
¹⁷of Bezai	323
¹⁸of Jorah	112
¹⁹of Hashum	223
²⁰of Gibbar	95
²¹the men of Bethlehem	123
²²of Netophah	56
²³of Anathoth	128
²⁴of Azmaveth	42
²⁵of Kiriath Jearim,*b* Kephirah and Beeroth	743
²⁶of Ramah and Geba	621
²⁷of Mikmash	122
²⁸of Bethel and Ai	223
²⁹of Nebo	52
³⁰of Magbish	156
³¹of the other Elam	1,254
³²of Harim	320
³³of Lod, Hadid and Ono	725
³⁴of Jericho	345
³⁵of Senaah	3,630

³⁶The priests:

the descendants of Jedaiah (through the family of Jeshua)	973

a 9 The meaning of the Hebrew for this word is uncertain. *b* 25 See Septuagint (see also Neh. 7:29); Hebrew *Kiriath Arim.*

37 of Immer   1,052
38 of Pashhur   1,247
39 of Harim   1,017

40 The Levites: Ge 29:34; Nu 3:9

the descendants of Jeshua and Kadmiel (of the line of Hodaviah)   74

41 The musicians: 1Ch 15:16

the descendants of Asaph   128

42 The gatekeepers of the temple: 1Sa 3:15; 1Ch 9:17

the descendants of Shallum, Ater, Talmon, Akkub, Hatita and Shobai   139

43 The temple servants: 1Ch 9:2

the descendants of Ziha, Hasupha, Tabbaoth,
44 Keros, Siaha, Padon,
45 Lebanah, Hagabah, Akkub,
46 Hagab, Shalmai, Hanan,
47 Giddel, Gahar, Reaiah,
48 Rezin, Nekoda, Gazzam,
49 Uzza, Paseah, Besai,
50 Asnah, Meunim, Nephusim,
51 Bakbuk, Hakupha, Harhur,
52 Bazluth, Mehida, Harsha,
53 Barkos, Sisera, Temah,
54 Neziah and Hatipha

55 The descendants of the servants of Solomon:

the descendants of Sotai, Hassophereth, Peruda,
56 Jaala, Darkon, Giddel,
57 Shephatiah, Hattil, Pokereth-Hazzebaim and Ami

58 The temple servants and the descendants of the servants of Solomon 392

59 The following came up from the towns of Tel Melah, Tel Harsha, Kerub, Addon and Immer, but they could not show that their families were descended from Israel: Nu 1:18

60 The descendants of Delaiah, Tobiah and Nekoda   652

61 And from among the priests:

The descendants of Hobaiah, Hakkoz and Barzillai (a man who had married a daughter of Barzillai the Gileadite and was called by that name).
62 These searched for their family records, but they could not find them and so were excluded from the priesthood as unclean. **63** The governor ordered them not to eat any of the most sacred

food until there was a priest ministering with the Urim and Thummim. Ex 28:30; Lev 2:3

⁶⁴The whole company numbered 42,360, ⁶⁵besides their 7,337 male and female slaves; and they also had 200 male and female singers. ⁶⁶They had 736 horses, 245 mules, ⁶⁷435 camels and 6,720 donkeys. Isa 66:20

⁶⁸When they arrived at the house of the LORD in Jerusalem, some of the heads of the families gave freewill offerings toward the rebuilding of the house of God on its site. ⁶⁹According to their ability they gave to the treasury for this work 61,000 darics*a* of gold, 5,000 minas*b* of silver and 100 priestly garments. Ex 25:2

⁷⁰The priests, the Levites, the musicians, the gatekeepers and the temple servants settled in their own towns, along with some of the other people, and the rest of the Israelites settled in their towns. Ne 7:6-73; 11:3-4

Rebuilding the Altar

3 When the seventh month came and the Israelites had settled in their towns, the people assembled together as one in Jerusalem. ²Then Joshua son of Jozadak and his fellow priests and Zerubbabel son of Shealtiel and his associates began to build the altar of the God of Israel to sacrifice burnt offerings on it, in accordance with what is written in the Law of Moses the man of God. ³Despite their fear of the peoples around them, they built the altar on its foundation and sacrificed burnt offerings on it to the LORD, both the morning and evening sacrifices. ⁴Then in accordance with what is written, they celebrated the Festival of Tabernacles with the required number of burnt offerings prescribed for each day. ⁵After that, they presented the regular burnt offerings, the New Moon sacrifices and the sacrifices for all the appointed sacred festivals of the LORD, as well as those brought as freewill offerings to the LORD. ⁶On the first day of the seventh month they began to offer burnt offerings to the LORD, though the foundation of the LORD's temple had not yet been laid. Ex 23:16; Nu 29:12-39

Rebuilding the Temple

⁷Then they gave money to the masons and carpenters, and gave food and drink and olive oil to the people of Sidon and Tyre, so that they would bring cedar logs by sea from Lebanon to Joppa, as authorized by Cyrus king of Persia. Ezr 1:2-4; 6:3

⁸In the second month of the second year after their arrival

a 69 That is, about 1,100 pounds or about 500 kilograms   *b 69* That is, about 3 tons or about 2.8 metric tons at the house of God in Jerusalem, Zerubbabel son of Shealtiel, Joshua son of Jozadak and the rest of the people (the priests and the Levites and all who had returned from the captivity to Jerusalem) began the work. They appointed Levites twenty years old and older to supervise the building of the house of the LORD. [9]Joshua and his sons and brothers and Kadmiel and his sons (descendants of Hodaviah[a]) and the sons of Henadad and their sons and brothers — all Levites — joined together in supervising those working on the house of God. 1Ch 23:24; Ezr 2:40

[10]When the builders laid the foundation of the temple of the LORD, the priests in their vestments and with trumpets, and the Levites (the sons of Asaph) with cymbals, took their places to praise the LORD, as prescribed by David king of Israel. [11]With praise and thanksgiving they sang to the LORD: 1Ch 6:31; 25:1; Zec 6:12

"He is good;
his love toward Israel
endures forever." 1Ch 16:34

And all the people gave a great shout of praise to the LORD, because the foundation of the house of the LORD was laid. [12]But many of the older priests and Levites and family heads, who had seen the former temple, wept aloud when they saw the foundation of this temple being laid, while many others shouted for joy. [13]No one could distinguish the sound of the shouts of joy from the sound of weeping, because the people made so much noise. And the sound was heard far away. Ne 12:24; Isa 16:9

Opposition to the Rebuilding

4 When the enemies of Judah and Benjamin heard that the exiles were building a temple for the LORD, the God of Israel, [2]they came to Zerubbabel and to the heads of the families and said, "Let us help you build because, like you, we seek your God and have been sacrificing to him since the time of Esarhaddon king of Assyria, who brought us here." 2Ki 17:24,41

[3]But Zerubbabel, Joshua and the rest of the heads of the families of Israel answered, "You have no part with us in building a temple to our God. We alone will build it for the LORD, the God of Israel, as King Cyrus, the king of Persia, commanded us." Ezr 1:1-4

[4]Then the peoples around them set out to discourage the people of Judah and make them afraid to go on building.[b] [5]They bribed officials to work against them and frustrate their plans during the entire reign of Cyrus king of Persia and down to the reign of Darius king of Persia. Ezr 3:3

a 9 Hebrew *Yehudah*, a variant of *Hodaviah*   b 4 Or *and troubled them as they built*

Later Opposition Under Xerxes and Artaxerxes

[6] At the beginning of the reign of Xerxes,[a] they lodged an accusation against the people of Judah and Jerusalem. Est 1:1; Da 9:1

[7] And in the days of Artaxerxes king of Persia, Bishlam, Mithredath, Tabeel and the rest of his associates wrote a letter to Artaxerxes. The letter was written in Aramaic script and in the Aramaic language.[b,c] 2Ki 18:26; Da 2:4

[8] Rehum the commanding officer and Shimshai the secretary wrote a letter against Jerusalem to Artaxerxes the king as follows:

[9] Rehum the commanding officer and Shimshai the secretary, together with the rest of their associates—the judges, officials and administrators over the people from Persia, Uruk and Babylon, the Elamites of Susa, [10] and the other people whom the great and honorable Ashurbanipal deported and settled in the city of Samaria and elsewhere in Trans-Euphrates. Ezr 5:6; Ne 4:2

[11] (This is a copy of the letter they sent him.)

To King Artaxerxes,

From your servants in Trans-Euphrates:

[12] The king should know that the people who came up to us from you have gone to Jerusalem and are rebuilding that rebellious and wicked city. They are restoring the walls and repairing the foundations. Ezr 5:3,9

[13] Furthermore, the king should know that if this city is built and its walls are restored, no more taxes, tribute or duty will be paid, and eventually the royal revenues will suffer.[d] [14] Now since we are under obligation to the palace and it is not proper for us to see the king dishonored, we are sending this message to inform the king, [15] so that a search may be made in the archives of your predecessors. In these records you will find that this city is a rebellious city, troublesome to kings and provinces, a place with a long history of sedition. That is why this city was destroyed. [16] We inform the king that if this city is built and its walls are restored, you will be left with nothing in Trans-Euphrates. Ezr 7:24; Ne 5:4; Est 3:8

[17] The king sent this reply:

To Rehum the commanding officer, Shimshai the secretary and the rest of their associates living in Samar-

---

[a] 6 Hebrew *Ahasuerus*   [b] 7 Or *written in Aramaic and translated*   [c] 7 The text of 4:8–6:18 is in Aramaic.   [d] 13 The meaning of the Aramaic for this clause is uncertain.

ia and elsewhere in Trans-Euphrates:

Greetings.

[18] The letter you sent us has been read and translated in my presence. [19] I issued an order and a search was made, and it was found that this city has a long history of revolt against kings and has been a place of rebellion and sedition. [20] Jerusalem has had powerful kings ruling over the whole of Trans-Euphrates, and taxes, tribute and duty were paid to them. [21] Now issue an order to these men to stop work, so that this city will not be rebuilt until I so order. [22] Be careful not to neglect this matter. Why let this threat grow, to the detriment of the royal interests? 1Ki 4:21; 2Ki 18:7

[23] As soon as the copy of the letter of King Artaxerxes was read to Rehum and Shimshai the secretary and their associates, they went immediately to the Jews in Jerusalem and compelled them by force to stop.

[24] Thus the work on the house of God in Jerusalem came to a standstill until the second year of the reign of Darius king of Persia. Ne 2:1-8; Da 9:25; Hag 1:1,15

Tattenai's Letter to Darius

5 Now Haggai the prophet and Zechariah the prophet, a descendant of Iddo, prophesied to the Jews in Judah and Jerusalem in the name of the God of Israel, who was over them. [2] Then Zerubbabel son of Shealtiel and Joshua son of Jozadak set to work to rebuild the house of God in Jerusalem. And the prophets of God were with them, supporting them. Ezr 3:2; Zec 1:1

[3] At that time Tattenai, governor of Trans-Euphrates, and Shethar-Bozenai and their associates went to them and asked, "Who authorized you to rebuild this temple and to finish it?" [4] They[a] also asked, "What are the names of those who are constructing this building?" [5] But the eye of their God was watching over the elders of the Jews, and they were not stopped until a report could go to Darius and his written reply be received. Ezr 1:3; 6:6; Ps 33:18

[6] This is a copy of the letter that Tattenai, governor of Trans-Euphrates, and Shethar-Bozenai and their associates, the officials of Trans-Euphrates, sent to King Darius. [7] The report they sent him read as follows:

To King Darius:

Cordial greetings.

[8] The king should know that we went to the district

---

[a] 4 See Septuagint; Aramaic We.

of Judah, to the temple of the great God. The people are building it with large stones and placing the timbers in the walls. The work is being carried on with diligence and is making rapid progress under their direction. ⁹We questioned the elders and asked them, "Who authorized you to rebuild this temple and to finish it?" ¹⁰We also asked them their names, so that we could write down the names of their leaders for your information. Ezr 4:12 ¹¹This is the answer they gave us:

"We are the servants of the God of heaven and earth, and we are rebuilding the temple that was built many years ago, one that a great king of Israel built and finished. ¹²But because our ancestors angered the God of heaven, he gave them into the hands of Nebuchadnezzar the Chaldean, king of Babylon, who destroyed this temple and deported the people to Babylon. 2Ki 24:1; 25:8-9,11; 2Ch 36:16 ¹³"However, in the first year of Cyrus king of Babylon, King Cyrus issued a decree to rebuild this house of God. ¹⁴He even removed from the temple*a* of Babylon the gold and silver articles of the house of God, which Nebuchadnezzar had taken from the temple in Jerusalem and brought to the temple*a* in Babylon. Then King Cyrus gave them to a man named Sheshbazzar, whom he had appointed governor, ¹⁵and he told him, 'Take these articles and go and deposit them in the temple in Jerusalem. And rebuild the house of God on its site.' Ezr 1:7; 6:5

¹⁶"So this Sheshbazzar came and laid the foundations of the house of God in Jerusalem. From that day to the present it has been under construction but is not yet finished." Ezr 3:10; 6:15

¹⁷Now if it pleases the king, let a search be made in the royal archives of Babylon to see if King Cyrus did in fact issue a decree to rebuild this house of God in Jerusalem. Then let the king send us his decision in this matter. Ezr 4:15; 6:1-2

The Decree of Darius

6 King Darius then issued an order, and they searched in the archives stored in the treasury at Babylon. ²A scroll was found in the citadel of Ecbatana in the province of Media, and this was written on it: Ezr 5:17

a 14 Or *palace*

Memorandum:

³ In the first year of King Cyrus, the king issued a decree concerning the temple of God in Jerusalem:

Let the temple be rebuilt as a place to present sacrifices, and let its foundations be laid. It is to be sixty cubits*a* high and sixty cubits wide, ⁴ with three courses of large stones and one of timbers. The costs are to be paid by the royal treasury. ⁵ Also, the gold and silver articles of the house of God, which Nebuchadnezzar took from the temple in Jerusalem and brought to Babylon, are to be returned to their places in the temple in Jerusalem; they are to be deposited in the house of God. Ezr 1:7; 5:14

⁶ Now then, Tattenai, governor of Trans-Euphrates, and Shethar-Bozenai and you other officials of that province, stay away from there. ⁷ Do not interfere with the work on this temple of God. Let the governor of the Jews and the Jewish elders rebuild this house of God on its site. Ezr 5:3

⁸ Moreover, I hereby decree what you are to do for these elders of the Jews in the construction of this house of God:

Their expenses are to be fully paid out of the royal treasury, from the revenues of Trans-Euphrates, so that the work will not stop. ⁹ Whatever is needed — young bulls, rams, male lambs for burnt offerings to the God of heaven, and wheat, salt, wine and olive oil, as requested by the priests in Jerusalem — must be given them daily without fail, ¹⁰ so that they may offer sacrifices pleasing to the God of heaven and pray for the well-being of the king and his sons. Ezr 7:23; 1Ti 2:1-2

¹¹ Furthermore, I decree that if anyone defies this edict, a beam is to be pulled from their house and they are to be impaled on it. And for this crime their house is to be made a pile of rubble. ¹² May God, who has caused his Name to dwell there, overthrow any king or people who lifts a hand to change this decree or to destroy this temple in Jerusalem. Dt 12:5; Ezr 7:26; Da 2:5

I Darius have decreed it. Let it be carried out with diligence.

Completion and Dedication of the Temple

¹³ Then, because of the decree

King Darius had sent, Tattenai, governor of Trans-Euphrates, and Shethar-Bozenai and their associates carried it out with diligence. [14] So the elders of the Jews continued to build and prosper under the preaching of Haggai the prophet and Zechariah, a descendant of Iddo. They finished building the temple according to the command of the God of Israel and the decrees of Cyrus, Darius and Artaxerxes, kings of Persia. [15] The temple was completed on the third day of the month Adar, in the sixth year of the reign of King Darius. Ezr 5:1; 7:1; Zec 1:1

[16] Then the people of Israel — the priests, the Levites and the rest of the exiles — celebrated the dedication of the house of God with joy. [17] For the dedication of this house of God they offered a hundred bulls, two hundred rams, four hundred male lambs and, as a sin offering[a] for all Israel, twelve male goats, one for each of the tribes of Israel. [18] And they installed the priests in their divisions and the Levites in their groups for the service of God at Jerusalem, according to what is written in the Book of Moses. 1Ki 8:63; 2Ch 7:5; 35:4

The Passover

[19] On the fourteenth day of the first month, the exiles celebrated the Passover. [20] The priests and Levites had purified themselves and were all ceremonially clean. The Levites slaughtered the Passover lamb for all the exiles, for their relatives the priests and for themselves. [21] So the Israelites who had returned from the exile ate it, together with all who had separated themselves from the unclean practices of their Gentile neighbors in order to seek the LORD, the God of Israel. [22] For seven days they celebrated with joy the Festival of Unleavened Bread, because the LORD had filled them with joy by changing the attitude of the king of Assyria so that he assisted them in the work on the house of God, the God of Israel. Ex 12:11; Ezr 1:1

Ezra Comes to Jerusalem

7 After these things, during the reign of Artaxerxes king of Persia, Ezra son of Seraiah, the son of Azariah, the son of Hilkiah, [2] the son of Shallum, the son of Zadok, the son of Ahitub, [3] the son of Amariah, the son of Azariah, the son of Meraioth, [4] the son of Zerahiah, the son of Uzzi, the son of Bukki, [5] the son of Abishua, the son of Phinehas, the son of Eleazar, the son of Aaron the chief priest — [6] this Ezra came up from Babylon. He was a teacher well versed in the Law of Moses, which the LORD, the God of Israel, had given. The king had granted him every-

---

[a] 17 Or *purification offering*

thing he asked, for the hand of the LORD his God was on him. [7] Some of the Israelites, including priests, Levites, musicians, gatekeepers and temple servants, also came up to Jerusalem in the seventh year of King Artaxerxes. Ezr 8:1; Ne 12:36; Isa 41:20

[8] Ezra arrived in Jerusalem in the fifth month of the seventh year of the king. [9] He had begun his journey from Babylon on the first day of the first month, and he arrived in Jerusalem on the first day of the fifth month, for the gracious hand of his God was on him. [10] For Ezra had devoted himself to the study and observance of the Law of the LORD, and to teaching its decrees and laws in Israel. Dt 33:10; Ne 8:1-8

King Artaxerxes' Letter to Ezra

[11] This is a copy of the letter King Artaxerxes had given to Ezra the priest, a teacher of the Law, a man learned in matters concerning the commands and decrees of the LORD for Israel:

[12] Artaxerxes, king of kings,

To Ezra the priest, teacher of the Law of the God of heaven:

Greetings.

[13] Now I decree that any of the Israelites in my kingdom, including priests and Levites, who volunteer to go to Jerusalem with you, may go. [14] You are sent by the king and his seven advisers to inquire about Judah and Jerusalem with regard to the Law of your God, which is in your hand. [15] Moreover, you are to take with you the silver and gold that the king and his advisers have freely given to the God of Israel, whose dwelling is in Jerusalem, [16] together with all the silver and gold you may obtain from the province of Babylon, as well as the freewill offerings of the people and priests for the temple of their God in Jerusalem. [17] With this money be sure to buy bulls, rams and male lambs, together with their grain offerings and drink offerings, and sacrifice them on the altar of the temple of your God in Jerusalem. 2Ch 6:2; Zec 6:10

[18] You and your fellow Israelites may then do whatever seems best with the rest of the silver and gold, in accordance with the will of your God. [19] Deliver to the God of Jerusalem all the articles entrusted to you for worship in the temple of your God. [20] And anything else needed for the temple of your God that you are responsible to supply, you may provide from the royal treasury. Ezr 6:4

[21] Now I, King Artaxerxes, decree that all the treasurers of Trans-Euphrates are

to provide with diligence whatever Ezra the priest, the teacher of the Law of the God of heaven, may ask of you— [22] up to a hundred talents[a] of silver, a hundred cors[b] of wheat, a hundred baths[c] of wine, a hundred baths[c] of olive oil, and salt without limit. [23] Whatever the God of heaven has prescribed, let it be done with diligence for the temple of the God of heaven. Why should his wrath fall on the realm of the king and of his sons? [24] You are also to know that you have no authority to impose taxes, tribute or duty on any of the priests, Levites, musicians, gatekeepers, temple servants or other workers at this house of God. *Ezr 6:10; 8:36*

[25] And you, Ezra, in accordance with the wisdom of your God, which you possess, appoint magistrates and judges to administer justice to all the people of Trans-Euphrates—all who know the laws of your God. And you are to teach any who do not know them. [26] Whoever does not obey the law of your God and the law of the king must surely be punished by death,

banishment, confiscation of property, or imprisonment.[d]

[27] Praise be to the LORD, the God of our ancestors, who has put it into the king's heart to bring honor to the house of the LORD in Jerusalem in this way [28] and who has extended his good favor to me before the king and his advisers and all the king's powerful officials. Because the hand of the LORD my God was on me, I took courage and gathered leaders from Israel to go up with me. *Ezr 5:5; 9:9*

List of the Family Heads Returning With Ezra

8 These are the family heads and those registered with them who came up with me from Babylon during the reign of King Artaxerxes: *Ezr 7:7*

[2] of the descendants of Phinehas, Gershom;
of the descendants of Ithamar, Daniel;
of the descendants of David, Hattush [3] of the descendants of Shekaniah; *1Ch 3:22*

of the descendants of Parosh, Zechariah, and with him were registered 150 men; *Ezr 2:3*
[4] of the descendants of Pahath-Moab, Eliehoenai son

of Zerahiah, and with him 200 men; Ezr 2:6

5 of the descendants of Zattu,ᵃ Shekaniah son of Jahaziel, and with him 300 men;

6 of the descendants of Adin, Ebed son of Jonathan, and with him 50 men; Ezr 2:15

7 of the descendants of Elam, Jeshaiah son of Athaliah, and with him 70 men;

8 of the descendants of Shephatiah, Zebadiah son of Michael, and with him 80 men;

9 of the descendants of Joab, Obadiah son of Jehiel, and with him 218 men;

10 of the descendants of Bani,ᵇ Shelomith son of Josiphiah, and with him 160 men;

11 of the descendants of Bebai, Zechariah son of Bebai, and with him 28 men;

12 of the descendants of Azgad, Johanan son of Hakkatan, and with him 110 men;

13 of the descendants of Adonikam, the last ones, whose names were Eliphelet, Jeuel and Shemaiah, and with them 60 men; Ezr 2:13

14 of the descendants of Bigvai, Uthai and Zakkur, and with them 70 men.

The Return to Jerusalem

15 I assembled them at the canal that flows toward Ahava, and we camped there three days. When I checked among the people and the priests, I found no Levites there. 16 So I summoned Eliezer, Ariel, Shemaiah, Elnathan, Jarib, Elnathan, Nathan, Zechariah and Meshullam, who were leaders, and Joiarib and Elnathan, who were men of learning, 17 and I ordered them to go to Iddo, the leader in Kasiphia. I told them what to say to Iddo and his fellow Levites, the temple servants in Kasiphia, so that they might bring attendants to us for the house of our God. 18 Because the gracious hand of our God was on us, they brought us Sherebiah, a capable man, from the descendants of Mahli son of Levi, the son of Israel, and Sherebiah's sons and brothers, 18 in all; 19 and Hashabiah, together with Jeshaiah from the descendants of Merari, and his brothers and nephews, 20 in all. 20 They also brought 220 of the temple servants—a body that David and the officials had established to assist the Levites. All were registered by name. Ezr 2:43; 5:5

21 There, by the Ahava Canal, I proclaimed a fast, so that we might humble ourselves before our God and ask him for a safe journey for us and our children, with all our possessions. 22 I was ashamed to ask the king for soldiers and horsemen to protect

ᵃ 5 Some Septuagint manuscripts (also 1 Esdras 8:32); Hebrew does not have *Zattu*.
ᵇ 10 Some Septuagint manuscripts (also 1 Esdras 8:36); Hebrew does not have *Bani*.

us from enemies on the road, because we had told the king, "The gracious hand of our God is on everyone who looks to him, but his great anger is against all who forsake him." ²³So we fasted and petitioned our God about this, and he answered our prayer. 2Ch 33:13; Ezr 7:6,9,28

²⁴Then I set apart twelve of the leading priests, namely, Sherebiah, Hashabiah and ten of their brothers, ²⁵and I weighed out to them the offering of silver and gold and the articles that the king, his advisers, his officials and all Israel present there had donated for the house of our God. ²⁶I weighed out to them 650 talents*a* of silver, silver articles weighing 100 talents,*b* 100 talents*b* of gold, ²⁷20 bowls of gold valued at 1,000 darics,*c* and two fine articles of polished bronze, as precious as gold. Ezr 7:15-16

²⁸I said to them, "You as well as these articles are consecrated to the LORD. The silver and gold are a freewill offering to the LORD, the God of your ancestors. ²⁹Guard them carefully until you weigh them out in the chambers of the house of the LORD in Jerusalem before the leading priests and the Levites and the family heads of Israel." ³⁰Then the priests and Levites received the silver and gold and sacred articles that had been weighed out to be taken to the house of our God in Jerusalem. Lev 21:6; 22:2-3

³¹On the twelfth day of the first month we set out from the Ahava Canal to go to Jerusalem. The hand of our God was on us, and he protected us from enemies and bandits along the way. ³²So we arrived in Jerusalem, where we rested three days. Ge 40:13; Ne 2:11

³³On the fourth day, in the house of our God, we weighed out the silver and gold and the sacred articles into the hands of Meremoth son of Uriah, the priest. Eleazar son of Phinehas was with him, and so were the Levites Jozabad son of Jeshua and Noadiah son of Binnui. ³⁴Everything was accounted for by number and weight, and the entire weight was recorded at that time. Ne 3:4,21,24

³⁵Then the exiles who had returned from captivity sacrificed burnt offerings to the God of Israel: twelve bulls for all Israel, ninety-six rams, seventy-seven male lambs and, as a sin offering,*d* twelve male goats. All this was a burnt offering to the LORD. ³⁶They also delivered the king's orders to the royal satraps and to the governors of Trans-Euphrates, who then gave assistance to the people and to the house of God. Ezr 7:21-24; Est 9:3

---

a 26 That is, about 24 tons or about 22 metric tons   *b 26* That is, about 3 3/4 tons or about 3.4 metric tons   *c 27* That is, about 19 pounds or about 8.4 kilograms   *d 35* Or *purification offering*

Ezra's Prayer About Intermarriage

9 After these things had been done, the leaders came to me and said, "The people of Israel, including the priests and the Levites, have not kept themselves separate from the neighboring peoples with their detestable practices, like those of the Canaanites, Hittites, Perizzites, Jebusites, Ammonites, Moabites, Egyptians and Amorites. ²They have taken some of their daughters as wives for themselves and their sons, and have mingled the holy race with the peoples around them. And the leaders and officials have led the way in this unfaithfulness." Ex 22:31; 34:16; Ezr 10:2

³When I heard this, I tore my tunic and cloak, pulled hair from my head and beard and sat down appalled. ⁴Then everyone who trembled at the words of the God of Israel gathered around me because of this unfaithfulness of the exiles. And I sat there appalled until the evening sacrifice. Ezr 10:3

⁵Then, at the evening sacrifice, I rose from my self-abasement, with my tunic and cloak torn, and fell on my knees with my hands spread out to the LORD my God ⁶and prayed: Ex 29:41

"I am too ashamed and disgraced, my God, to lift up my face to you, because our sins are higher than our heads and our guilt has reached to the heavens. ⁷From the days of our ancestors until now, our guilt has been great. Because of our sins, we and our kings and our priests have been subjected to the sword and captivity, to pillage and humiliation at the hand of foreign kings, as it is today. Dt 28:37; 2Ch 28:9; Rev 18:5

⁸"But now, for a brief moment, the LORD our God has been gracious in leaving us a remnant and giving us a firm place*ª* in his sanctuary, and so our God gives light to our eyes and a little relief in our bondage. ⁹Though we are slaves, our God has not forsaken us in our bondage. He has shown us kindness in the sight of the kings of Persia: He has granted us new life to rebuild the house of our God and repair its ruins, and he has given us a wall of protection in Judah and Jerusalem. Ne 9:36; Ps 13:3; Isa 22:23

¹⁰"But now, our God, what can we say after this? For we have forsaken the commands ¹¹you gave through your servants the prophets when you said: 'The land you are entering to possess is a land polluted by the corruption of its peoples. By their detestable practices they have filled it

ª 8 Or a foothold

with their impurity from one end to the other. ¹²Therefore, do not give your daughters in marriage to their sons or take their daughters for your sons. Do not seek a treaty of friendship with them at any time, that you may be strong and eat the good things of the land and leave it to your children as an everlasting inheritance.' Dt 7:3; 23:6

¹³"What has happened to us is a result of our evil deeds and our great guilt, and yet, our God, you have punished us less than our sins deserved and have given us a remnant like this. ¹⁴Shall we then break your commands again and intermarry with the peoples who commit such detestable practices? Would you not be angry enough with us to destroy us, leaving us no remnant or survivor? ¹⁵LORD, the God of Israel, you are righteous! We are left this day as a remnant. Here we are before you in our guilt, though because of it not one of us can stand in your presence." 1Ki 8:47; Ps 130:3

The People's Confession of Sin

10 While Ezra was praying and confessing, weeping and throwing himself down before the house of God, a large crowd of Israelites — men, women and children — gathered around him. They too wept bitterly. ²Then Shekaniah son of Jehiel, one of the descendants of Elam, said to Ezra, "We have been unfaithful to our God by marrying foreign women from the peoples around us. But in spite of this, there is still hope for Israel. ³Now let us make a covenant before our God to send away all these women and their children, in accordance with the counsel of my lord and of those who fear the commands of our God. Let it be done according to the Law. ⁴Rise up; this matter is in your hands. We will support you, so take courage and do it." Dt 7:2-3; Ezr 9:4

⁵So Ezra rose up and put the leading priests and Levites and all Israel under oath to do what had been suggested. And they took the oath. ⁶Then Ezra withdrew from before the house of God and went to the room of Jehohanan son of Eliashib. While he was there, he ate no food and drank no water, because he continued to mourn over the unfaithfulness of the exiles. Dt 9:18; Ne 5:12; 13:25

⁷A proclamation was then issued throughout Judah and Jerusalem for all the exiles to assemble in Jerusalem. ⁸Anyone who failed to appear within three days would forfeit all his property, in accordance with the decision of the officials and elders, and would himself be expelled from the assembly of the exiles.

⁹Within the three days, all the men of Judah and Benjamin had gathered in Jerusalem. And on the twentieth day of the ninth month, all the people were sitting in the square before the house of God, greatly distressed by the occasion and because of the rain. ¹⁰Then Ezra the priest stood up and said to them, "You have been unfaithful; you have married foreign women, adding to Israel's guilt. ¹¹Now honor*ᵃ* the Lord, the God of your ancestors, and do his will. Separate yourselves from the peoples around you and from your foreign wives." Dt 24:1; Mal 2:10-16

¹²The whole assembly responded with a loud voice: "You are right! We must do as you say. ¹³But there are many people here and it is the rainy season; so we cannot stand outside. Besides, this matter cannot be taken care of in a day or two, because we have sinned greatly in this thing. ¹⁴Let our officials act for the whole assembly. Then let everyone in our towns who has married a foreign woman come at a set time, along with the elders and judges of each town, until the fierce anger of our God in this matter is turned away from us." ¹⁵Only Jonathan son of Asahel and Jahzeiah son of Tikvah, supported by Meshullam and Shabbethai the Levite, opposed this. 2Ch 29:10; 30:8; Ne 11:16

¹⁶So the exiles did as was proposed. Ezra the priest selected men who were family heads, one from each family division, and all of them designated by name. On the first day of the tenth month they sat down to investigate the cases, ¹⁷and by the first day of the first month they finished dealing with all the men who had married foreign women.

Those Guilty of Intermarriage

¹⁸Among the descendants of the priests, the following had married foreign women: Jdg 3:6

From the descendants of Joshua son of Jozadak, and his brothers: Maaseiah, Eliezer, Jarib and Gedaliah. ¹⁹(They all gave their hands in pledge to put away their wives, and for their guilt they each presented a ram from the flock as a guilt offering.) Lev 5:15; 2Ki 10:15; Ezr 2:2

²⁰From the descendants of Immer: 1Ch 24:14
Hanani and Zebadiah.

²¹From the descendants of Harim: 1Ch 24:8
Maaseiah, Elijah, Shemaiah, Jehiel and Uzziah.

²²From the descendants of Pashhur: 1Ch 9:12
Elioenai, Maaseiah, Ishmael, Nethanel, Jozabad and Elasah.

ᵃ 11 Or *Now make confession to*

²³Among the Levites: Ne 8:7; 9:4

Jozabad, Shimei, Kelaiah (that is, Kelita), Pethahiah, Judah and Eliezer.
²⁴From the musicians:
Eliashib. Ne 3:1; 12:10; 13:7,28
From the gatekeepers:
Shallum, Telem and Uri.

²⁵And among the other Israelites:

From the descendants of Parosh: Ezr 2:3
Ramiah, Izziah, Malkijah, Mijamin, Eleazar, Malkijah and Benaiah.
²⁶From the descendants of Elam:
Mattaniah, Zechariah, Jehiel, Abdi, Jeremoth and Elijah.
²⁷From the descendants of Zattu:
Elioenai, Eliashib, Mattaniah, Jeremoth, Zabad and Aziza.
²⁸From the descendants of Bebai:
Jehohanan, Hananiah, Zabbai and Athlai.
²⁹From the descendants of Bani:
Meshullam, Malluk, Adaiah, Jashub, Sheal and Jeremoth.
³⁰From the descendants of Pahath-Moab:

Adna, Kelal, Benaiah, Maaseiah, Mattaniah, Bezalel, Binnui and Manasseh.
³¹From the descendants of Harim:
Eliezer, Ishijah, Malkijah, Shemaiah, Shimeon, ³²Benjamin, Malluk and Shemariah.
³³From the descendants of Hashum:
Mattenai, Mattattah, Zabad, Eliphelet, Jeremai, Manasseh and Shimei.
³⁴From the descendants of Bani:
Maadai, Amram, Uel, ³⁵Benaiah, Bedeiah, Keluhi, ³⁶Vaniah, Meremoth, Eliashib, ³⁷Mattaniah, Mattenai and Jaasu.
³⁸From the descendants of Binnui:ᵃ
Shimei, ³⁹Shelemiah, Nathan, Adaiah, ⁴⁰Maknadebai, Shashai, Sharai, ⁴¹Azarel, Shelemiah, Shemariah, ⁴²Shallum, Amariah and Joseph.
⁴³From the descendants of Nebo:
Jeiel, Mattithiah, Zabad, Zebina, Jaddai, Joel and Benaiah.

⁴⁴All these had married foreign women, and some of them had children by these wives.ᵇ

ᵃ 37,38 See Septuagint (also 1 Esdras 9:34); Hebrew *Jaasu* ³⁸*and Bani and Binnui,*
ᵇ 44 Or *and they sent them away with their children*

Nehemiah

Nehemiah's Prayer

1 The words of Nehemiah son of Hakaliah:

In the month of Kislev in the twentieth year, while I was in the citadel of Susa, ²Hanani, one of my brothers, came from Judah with some other men, and I questioned them about the Jewish remnant that had survived the exile, and also about Jerusalem.

Ne 10:1; Zec 7:1

³They said to me, "Those who survived the exile and are back in the province are in great trouble and disgrace. The wall of Jerusalem is broken down, and its gates have been burned with fire." Ne 2:3,13,17

⁴When I heard these things, I sat down and wept. For some days I mourned and fasted and prayed before the God of heaven. ⁵Then I said: Ezr 9:4; Ps 137:1; Da 9:3

"LORD, the God of heaven, the great and awesome God, who keeps his covenant of love with those who love him and keep his commandments, ⁶let your ear be attentive and your eyes open to hear the prayer your servant is praying before you day and night for your servants, the people of Israel. I confess the sins we Israelites, including myself and my father's family, have committed against you. ⁷We have acted very wickedly toward you. We have not obeyed the commands, decrees and laws you gave your servant Moses. Dt 28:14-15; Ne 4:14; Da 9:17

⁸"Remember the instruction you gave your servant Moses, saying, 'If you are unfaithful, I will scatter you among the nations, ⁹but if you return to me and obey my commands, then even if your exiled people are at the farthest horizon, I will gather them from there and bring them to the place I have chosen as a dwelling for my Name.' Lev 26:33; Dt 30:4

¹⁰"They are your servants

and your people, whom you redeemed by your great strength and your mighty hand. ¹¹Lord, let your ear be attentive to the prayer of this your servant and to the prayer of your servants who delight in revering your name. Give your servant success today by granting him favor in the presence of this man." Dt 9:29

I was cupbearer to the king.

Artaxerxes Sends Nehemiah to Jerusalem

2 In the month of Nisan in the twentieth year of King Artaxerxes, when wine was brought for him, I took the wine and gave it to the king. I had not been sad in his presence before, ²so the king asked me, "Why does your face look so sad when you are not ill? This can be nothing but sadness of heart." Ezr 7:1

I was very much afraid, ³but I said to the king, "May the king live forever! Why should my face not look sad when the city where my ancestors are buried lies in ruins, and its gates have been destroyed by fire?" Ne 1:3; Da 2:4

⁴The king said to me, "What is it you want?"

Then I prayed to the God of heaven, ⁵and I answered the king, "If it pleases the king and if your servant has found favor in his sight, let him send me to the city in Judah where my ancestors are buried so that I can rebuild it."

⁶Then the king, with the queen sitting beside him, asked me, "How long will your journey take, and when will you get back?" It pleased the king to send me; so I set a time. Ne 5:14; 13:6

⁷I also said to him, "If it pleases the king, may I have letters to the governors of Trans-Euphrates, so that they will provide me safe-conduct until I arrive in Judah? ⁸And may I have a letter to Asaph, keeper of the royal park, so he will give me timber to make beams for the gates of the citadel by the temple and for the city wall and for the residence I will occupy?" And because the gracious hand of my God was on me, the king granted my requests. ⁹So I went to the governors of Trans-Euphrates and gave them the king's letters. The king had also sent army officers and cavalry with me. Ezr 7:6; 8:22,36

¹⁰When Sanballat the Horonite and Tobiah the Ammonite official heard about this, they were very much disturbed that someone had come to promote the welfare of the Israelites. Ne 4:3; 13:4-7; Est 10:3

Nehemiah Inspects Jerusalem's Walls

¹¹I went to Jerusalem, and after staying there three days ¹²I set out during the night with a few others. I had not told any-

one what my God had put in my heart to do for Jerusalem. There were no mounts with me except the one I was riding on. Ge 40:13

[13] By night I went out through the Valley Gate toward the Jackal[a] Well and the Dung Gate, examining the walls of Jerusalem, which had been broken down, and its gates, which had been destroyed by fire. [14] Then I moved on toward the Fountain Gate and the King's Pool, but there was not enough room for my mount to get through; [15] so I went up the valley by night, examining the wall. Finally, I turned back and reentered through the Valley Gate. [16] The officials did not know where I had gone or what I was doing, because as yet I had said nothing to the Jews or the priests or nobles or officials or any others who would be doing the work. Ne 1:3; 3:13,15

[17] Then I said to them, "You see the trouble we are in: Jerusalem lies in ruins, and its gates have been burned with fire. Come, let us rebuild the wall of Jerusalem, and we will no longer be in disgrace." [18] I also told them about the gracious hand of my God on me and what the king had said to me. 2Sa 2:7; Ne 1:3

They replied, "Let us start rebuilding." So they began this good work.

[19] But when Sanballat the Horonite, Tobiah the Ammonite official and Geshem the Arab heard about it, they mocked and ridiculed us. "What is this you are doing?" they asked. "Are you rebelling against the king?" Ps 44:13-16

[20] I answered them by saying, "The God of heaven will give us success. We his servants will start rebuilding, but as for you, you have no share in Jerusalem or any claim or historic right to it." Ezr 4:3

Builders of the Wall

3 Eliashib the high priest and his fellow priests went to work and rebuilt the Sheep Gate. They dedicated it and set its doors in place, building as far as the Tower of the Hundred, which they dedicated, and as far as the Tower of Hananel. [2] The men of Jericho built the adjoining section, and Zakkur son of Imri built next to them. Ne 7:36; 12:39; Jer 31:38

[3] The Fish Gate was rebuilt by the sons of Hassenaah. They laid its beams and put its doors and bolts and bars in place. [4] Meremoth son of Uriah, the son of Hakkoz, repaired the next section. Next to him Meshullam son of Berekiah, the son of Meshezabel, made repairs, and next to him Zadok son of Baana also made repairs. [5] The next section was repaired by the men of Tekoa, but their nobles would not put their shoulders to the work under their supervisors.[b] 2Sa 14:2; Ne 12:39

a 13 Or *Serpent* or *Fig*   b 5 Or *their Lord* or *the governor*

[6]The Jeshanah[a] Gate was repaired by Joiada son of Paseah and Meshullam son of Besodeiah. They laid its beams and put its doors with their bolts and bars in place. [7]Next to them, repairs were made by men from Gibeon and Mizpah — Melatiah of Gibeon and Jadon of Meronoth — places under the authority of the governor of Trans-Euphrates. [8]Uzziel son of Harhaiah, one of the goldsmiths, repaired the next section; and Hananiah, one of the perfume-makers, made repairs next to that. They restored Jerusalem as far as the Broad Wall. [9]Rephaiah son of Hur, ruler of a half-district of Jerusalem, repaired the next section. [10]Adjoining this, Jedaiah son of Harumaph made repairs opposite his house, and Hattush son of Hashabneiah made repairs next to him. [11]Malkijah son of Harim and Hasshub son of Pahath-Moab repaired another section and the Tower of the Ovens. [12]Shallum son of Hallohesh, ruler of a half-district of Jerusalem, repaired the next section with the help of his daughters. Ne 2:7; 12:38-39

[13]The Valley Gate was repaired by Hanun and the residents of Zanoah. They rebuilt it and put its doors with their bolts and bars in place. They also repaired a thousand cubits[b] of the wall as far as the Dung Gate. Ne 2:13; 2Ch 26:9

[14]The Dung Gate was repaired by Malkijah son of Rekab, ruler of the district of Beth Hakkerem. He rebuilt it and put its doors with their bolts and bars in place. Jer 6:1

[15]The Fountain Gate was repaired by Shallun son of Kol-Hozeh, ruler of the district of Mizpah. He rebuilt it, roofing it over and putting its doors and bolts and bars in place. He also repaired the wall of the Pool of Siloam,[c] by the King's Garden, as far as the steps going down from the City of David. [16]Beyond him, Nehemiah son of Azbuk, ruler of a half-district of Beth Zur, made repairs up to a point opposite the tombs[d] of David, as far as the artificial pool and the House of the Heroes. Jos 15:58; Isa 8:6; Ac 2:29

[17]Next to him, the repairs were made by the Levites under Rehum son of Bani. Beside him, Hashabiah, ruler of half the district of Keilah, carried out repairs for his district. [18]Next to him, the repairs were made by their fellow Levites under Binnui[e] son of Henadad, ruler of the other half-district of Keilah. [19]Next to him, Ezer son of Jeshua, ruler of Mizpah, repaired another section,

[a] 6 Or Old   [b] 13 That is, about 1,500 feet or about 450 meters   [c] 15 Hebrew Shelah, a variant of Shiloah, that is, Siloam   [d] 16 Hebrew; Septuagint, some Vulgate manuscripts and Syriac tomb   [e] 18 Two Hebrew manuscripts and Syriac (see also Septuagint and verse 24); most Hebrew manuscripts Bavvai

from a point facing the ascent to the armory as far as the angle of the wall. ²⁰Next to him, Baruch son of Zabbai zealously repaired another section, from the angle to the entrance of the house of Eliashib the high priest. ²¹Next to him, Meremoth son of Uriah, the son of Hakkoz, repaired another section, from the entrance of Eliashib's house to the end of it. Jos 15:44; Ezr 8:33

²²The repairs next to him were made by the priests from the surrounding region. ²³Beyond them, Benjamin and Hasshub made repairs in front of their house; and next to them, Azariah son of Maaseiah, the son of Ananiah, made repairs beside his house. ²⁴Next to him, Binnui son of Henadad repaired another section, from Azariah's house to the angle and the corner, ²⁵and Palal son of Uzai worked opposite the angle and the tower projecting from the upper palace near the court of the guard. Next to him, Pedaiah son of Parosh ²⁶and the temple servants living on the hill of Ophel made repairs up to a point opposite the Water Gate toward the east and the projecting tower. ²⁷Next to them, the men of Tekoa repaired another section, from the great projecting tower to the wall of Ophel. Ne 8:1,3,16; Jer 32:2

²⁸Above the Horse Gate, the priests made repairs, each in front of his own house. ²⁹Next to them, Zadok son of Immer made repairs opposite his house. Next to him, Shemaiah son of Shekaniah, the guard at the East Gate, made repairs. ³⁰Next to him, Hananiah son of Shelemiah, and Hanun, the sixth son of Zalaph, repaired another section. Next to them, Meshullam son of Berekiah made repairs opposite his living quarters. ³¹Next to him, Malkijah, one of the goldsmiths, made repairs as far as the house of the temple servants and the merchants, opposite the Inspection Gate, and as far as the room above the corner; ³²and between the room above the corner and the Sheep Gate the goldsmiths and merchants made repairs. 2Ch 23:15; Jn 5:2

Opposition to the Rebuilding

4 ᵃ When Sanballat heard that we were rebuilding the wall, he became angry and was greatly incensed. He ridiculed the Jews, ²and in the presence of his associates and the army of Samaria, he said, "What are those feeble Jews doing? Will they restore their wall? Will they offer sacrifices? Will they finish in a day? Can they bring the stones back to life from those heaps of rubble — burned as they are?" Ne 2:10; Ps 79:1

³Tobiah the Ammonite, who was at his side, said, "What they are building — even a fox climbing

---

ᵃ In Hebrew texts 4:1-6 is numbered 3:33-38, and 4:7-23 is numbered 4:1-17.

up on it would break down their wall of stones!" Ne 2:10

[4] Hear us, our God, for we are despised. Turn their insults back on their own heads. Give them over as plunder in a land of captivity. [5] Do not cover up their guilt or blot out their sins from your sight, for they have thrown insults in the face of[a] the builders. Ps 69:27-28; Jer 18:23

[6] So we rebuilt the wall till all of it reached half its height, for the people worked with all their heart.

[7] But when Sanballat, Tobiah, the Arabs, the Ammonites and the people of Ashdod heard that the repairs to Jerusalem's walls had gone ahead and that the gaps were being closed, they were very angry. [8] They all plotted together to come and fight against Jerusalem and stir up trouble against it. [9] But we prayed to our God and posted a guard day and night to meet this threat. Ps 2:2; 83:1-18

[10] Meanwhile, the people in Judah said, "The strength of the laborers is giving out, and there is so much rubble that we cannot rebuild the wall." 1Ch 23:4

[11] Also our enemies said, "Before they know it or see us, we will be right there among them and will kill them and put an end to the work."

[12] Then the Jews who lived near them came and told us ten times over, "Wherever you turn, they will attack us."

[13] Therefore I stationed some of the people behind the lowest points of the wall at the exposed places, posting them by families, with their swords, spears and bows. [14] After I looked things over, I stood up and said to the nobles, the officials and the rest of the people, "Don't be afraid of them. Remember the Lord, who is great and awesome, and fight for your families, your sons and your daughters, your wives and your homes." Nu 14:9; Dt 1:29; 2Sa 10:12

[15] When our enemies heard that we were aware of their plot and that God had frustrated it, we all returned to the wall, each to our own work. 2Sa 17:14; Job 5:12

[16] From that day on, half of my men did the work, while the other half were equipped with spears, shields, bows and armor. The officers posted themselves behind all the people of Judah [17] who were building the wall. Those who carried materials did their work with one hand and held a weapon in the other, [18] and each of the builders wore his sword at his side as he worked. But the man who sounded the trumpet stayed with me. Nu 10:2; Ps 149:6

[19] Then I said to the nobles, the officials and the rest of the people, "The work is extensive and spread out, and we are widely separated from each other

along the wall. [20]Wherever you hear the sound of the trumpet, join us there. Our God will fight for us!" Ex 14:14; Dt 1:30; 20:4 [21]So we continued the work with half the men holding spears, from the first light of dawn till the stars came out. [22]At that time I also said to the people, "Have every man and his helper stay inside Jerusalem at night, so they can serve us as guards by night and as workers by day." [23]Neither I nor my brothers nor my men nor the guards with me took off our clothes; each had his weapon, even when he went for water.[a]

Nehemiah Helps the Poor

5 Now the men and their wives raised a great outcry against their fellow Jews. [2]Some were saying, "We and our sons and daughters are numerous; in order for us to eat and stay alive, we must get grain."

[3]Others were saying, "We are mortgaging our fields, our vineyards and our homes to get grain during the famine." Ge 47:23; Ps 109:11 [4]Still others were saying, "We have had to borrow money to pay the king's tax on our fields and vineyards. [5]Although we are of the same flesh and blood as our fellow Jews and though our children are as good as theirs, yet we have to subject our sons and daughters to slavery. Some of our daughters have al-

ready been enslaved, but we are powerless, because our fields and our vineyards belong to others." Lev 25:39-43,47; Ezr 4:13

[6]When I heard their outcry and these charges, I was very angry. [7]I pondered them in my mind and then accused the nobles and officials. I told them, "You are charging your own people interest!" So I called together a large meeting to deal with them [8]and said: "As far as possible, we have bought back our fellow Jews who were sold to the Gentiles. Now you are selling your own people, only for them to be sold back to us!" They kept quiet, because they could find nothing to say. Ex 22:25-27; Lev 25:35-37,47

[9]So I continued, "What you are doing is not right. Shouldn't you walk in the fear of our God to avoid the reproach of our Gentile enemies? [10]I and my brothers and my men are also lending the people money and grain. But let us stop charging interest! [11]Give back to them immediately their fields, vineyards, olive groves and houses, and also the interest you are charging them — one percent of the money, grain, new wine and olive oil." Ex 22:25; Isa 52:5; 58:6

[12]"We will give it back," they said. "And we will not demand anything more from them. We will do as you say."

Then I summoned the priests and made the nobles and officials take an oath to do what they

---

a 23 The meaning of the Hebrew for this clause is uncertain.

had promised. ¹³I also shook out the folds of my robe and said, "In this way may God shake out of their house and possessions anyone who does not keep this promise. So may such a person be shaken out and emptied!"

At this the whole assembly said, "Amen," and praised the LORD. And the people did as they had promised. Ezr 10:5; Mt 10:14; Ac 18:6

¹⁴Moreover, from the twentieth year of King Artaxerxes, when I was appointed to be their governor in the land of Judah, until his thirty-second year—twelve years—neither I nor my brothers ate the food allotted to the governor. ¹⁵But the earlier governors—those preceding me—placed a heavy burden on the people and took forty shekels*a* of silver from them in addition to food and wine. Their assistants also lorded it over the people. But out of reverence for God I did not act like that. ¹⁶Instead, I devoted myself to the work on this wall. All my men were assembled there for the work; we*b* did not acquire any land. Ne 13:6; Jer 40:7; 2Th 3:7-10

¹⁷Furthermore, a hundred and fifty Jews and officials ate at my table, as well as those who came to us from the surrounding nations. ¹⁸Each day one ox, six choice sheep and some poultry were prepared for me, and every ten days an abundant supply of wine of all kinds. In spite of all this, I never demanded the food allotted to the governor, because the demands were heavy on these people. 1Ki 4:23

¹⁹Remember me with favor, my God, for all I have done for these people. Ge 8:1; Ne 1:8; 13:14,22,31

Further Opposition to the Rebuilding

6 When word came to Sanballat, Tobiah, Geshem the Arab and the rest of our enemies that I had rebuilt the wall and not a gap was left in it—though up to that time I had not set the doors in the gates— ²Sanballat and Geshem sent me this message: "Come, let us meet together in one of the villages*c* on the plain of Ono." 1Ch 8:12; Ne 2:10,19

But they were scheming to harm me; ³so I sent messengers to them with this reply: "I am carrying on a great project and cannot go down. Why should the work stop while I leave it and go down to you?" ⁴Four times they sent me the same message, and each time I gave them the same answer.

⁵Then, the fifth time, Sanballat sent his aide to me with the same message, and in his hand was an unsealed letter ⁶in which was written: Ne 2:10

"It is reported among the

---

a 15 That is, about 1 pound or about 460 grams   *b 16* Most Hebrew manuscripts; some Hebrew manuscripts, Septuagint, Vulgate and Syriac *I*   *c 2* Or *in Kephirim* nations — and Geshem[a] says it is true — that you and the Jews are plotting to revolt, and therefore you are building the wall. Moreover, according to these reports you are about to become their king [7] and have even appointed prophets to make this proclamation about you in Jerusalem: 'There is a king in Judah!' Now this report will get back to the king; so come, let us meet together." Ne 2:19

[8] I sent him this reply: "Nothing like what you are saying is happening; you are just making it up out of your head."

[9] They were all trying to frighten us, thinking, "Their hands will get too weak for the work, and it will not be completed." But I prayed, "Now strengthen my hands."

[10] One day I went to the house of Shemaiah son of Delaiah, the son of Mehetabel, who was shut in at his home. He said, "Let us meet in the house of God, inside the temple, and let us close the temple doors, because men are coming to kill you — by night they are coming to kill you." Nu 18:7

[11] But I said, "Should a man like me run away? Or should someone like me go into the temple to save his life? I will not go!" [12] I realized that God had not sent him, but that he had prophesied

against me because Tobiah and Sanballat had hired him. [13] He had been hired to intimidate me so that I would commit a sin by doing this, and then they would give me a bad name to discredit me. Ne 2:10; Eze 13:22-23

[14] Remember Tobiah and Sanballat, my God, because of what they have done; remember also the prophet Noadiah and how she and the rest of the prophets have been trying to intimidate me. [15] So the wall was completed on the twenty-fifth of Elul, in fifty-two days. Ne 13:29; Eze 13:17-23

Opposition to the Completed Wall

[16] When all our enemies heard about this, all the surrounding nations were afraid and lost their self-confidence, because they realized that this work had been done with the help of our God.

[17] Also, in those days the nobles of Judah were sending many letters to Tobiah, and replies from Tobiah kept coming to them. [18] For many in Judah were under oath to him, since he was son-in-law to Shekaniah son of Arah, and his son Jehohanan had married the daughter of Meshullam son of Berekiah. [19] Moreover, they kept reporting to me his good deeds and then telling him what I said. And Tobiah sent letters to intimidate me.

[a] 6 Hebrew *Gashmu*, a variant of *Geshem*

7 After the wall had been rebuilt and I had set the doors in place, the gatekeepers, the musicians and the Levites were appointed. ²I put in charge of Jerusalem my brother Hanani, along with Hananiah the commander of the citadel, because he was a man of integrity and feared God more than most people do. ³I said to them, "The gates of Jerusalem are not to be opened until the sun is hot. While the gatekeepers are still on duty, have them shut the doors and bar them. Also appoint residents of Jerusalem as guards, some at their posts and some near their own houses." Ne 1:2; 8:9; Ps 68:25

The List of the Exiles Who Returned

7:6-73pp — Ezr 2:1-70

⁴Now the city was large and spacious, but there were few people in it, and the houses had not yet been rebuilt. ⁵So my God put it into my heart to assemble the nobles, the officials and the common people for registration by families. I found the genealogical record of those who had been the first to return. This is what I found written there:

⁶These are the people of the province who came up from the captivity of the exiles whom Nebuchadnezzar king of Babylon had taken captive (they returned to Jerusalem and Judah, each to his own town, ⁷in company with Zerubbabel, Joshua, Nehemiah, Azariah, Raamiah, Nahamani, Mordecai, Bilshan, Mispereth, Bigvai, Nehum and Baanah): Ezr 2:1-70

The list of the men of Israel:

⁸the descendants of Parosh	2,172
⁹of Shephatiah	372
¹⁰of Arah	652
¹¹of Pahath-Moab (through the line of Jeshua and Joab)	2,818
¹²of Elam	1,254
¹³of Zattu	845
¹⁴of Zakkai	760
¹⁵of Binnui	648
¹⁶of Bebai	628
¹⁷of Azgad	2,322
¹⁸of Adonikam	667
¹⁹of Bigvai	2,067
²⁰of Adin	655
²¹of Ater (through Hezekiah)	98
²²of Hashum	328
²³of Bezai	324
²⁴of Hariph	112
²⁵of Gibeon	95
²⁶the men of Bethlehem and Netophah	188
²⁷of Anathoth	128
²⁸of Beth Azmaveth	42
²⁹of Kiriath Jearim, Kephirah and Beeroth	743
³⁰of Ramah and Geba	621
³¹of Mikmash	122

³²of Bethel and Ai   123
³³of the other Nebo   52
³⁴of the other Elam   1,254
³⁵of Harim   320
³⁶of Jericho   345
³⁷of Lod, Hadid and
   Ono   721
³⁸of Senaah   3,930

³⁹The priests:

the descendants of
Jedaiah (through the
family of Jeshua)   973
⁴⁰of Immer   1,052
⁴¹of Pashhur   1,247
⁴²of Harim   1,017

⁴³The Levites:

the descendants of Jeshua
(through Kadmiel
through the line of
Hodaviah)   74

⁴⁴The musicians: Ne 11:23

the descendants of
Asaph   148

⁴⁵The gatekeepers: 1Ch 9:17

the descendants of
Shallum, Ater, Talmon,
Akkub, Hatita and
Shobai   138

⁴⁶The temple servants:

the descendants of
Ziha, Hasupha,
Tabbaoth,
⁴⁷Keros, Sia, Padon,
⁴⁸Lebana, Hagaba,
Shalmai,
⁴⁹Hanan, Giddel, Gahar,
⁵⁰Reaiah, Rezin, Nekoda,
⁵¹Gazzam, Uzza, Paseah,
⁵²Besai, Meunim,
Nephusim,
⁵³Bakbuk, Hakupha,
Harhur,
⁵⁴Bazluth, Mehida,
Harsha,
⁵⁵Barkos, Sisera, Temah,
⁵⁶Neziah and Hatipha

⁵⁷The descendants of the
servants of Solomon:

the descendants of
Sotai, Sophereth,
Perida,
⁵⁸Jaala, Darkon, Giddel,
⁵⁹Shephatiah, Hattil,
Pokereth-Hazzebaim
and Amon

⁶⁰The temple servants and
the descendants of the
servants of Solomon 392

⁶¹The following came up
from the towns of Tel Melah,
Tel Harsha, Kerub, Addon
and Immer, but they could
not show that their families
were descended from Israel:

⁶²the descendants of
Delaiah, Tobiah and
Nekoda   642

⁶³And from among the priests:

the descendants of
Hobaiah, Hakkoz
and Barzillai (a man
who had married a
daughter of Barzillai
the Gileadite and was
called by that name).

⁶⁴These searched for their family records, but they could not find them and so were excluded from the priesthood as unclean. ⁶⁵The governor, therefore, ordered them not to eat any of the most sacred food until there should be a priest ministering with the Urim and Thummim. Ex 28:30; Ne 8:9

⁶⁶The whole company numbered 42,360, ⁶⁷besides their 7,337 male and female slaves; and they also had 245 male and female singers. ⁶⁸There were 736 horses, 245 mules,ᵃ ⁶⁹435 camels and 6,720 donkeys.

⁷⁰Some of the heads of the families contributed to the work. The governor gave to the treasury 1,000 daricsᵇ of gold, 50 bowls and 530 garments for priests. ⁷¹Some of the heads of the families gave to the treasury for the work 20,000 daricsᶜ of gold and 2,200 minasᵈ of silver. ⁷²The total given by the rest of the people was 20,000 darics of gold, 2,000 minasᵉ of silver and 67 garments for priests. Ex 25:2; 1Ch 29:7

⁷³The priests, the Levites, the gatekeepers, the musicians and the temple servants, along with certain of the people and the rest of the Israelites, settled in their own towns. Ezr 3:1; Ne 1:10

Ezra Reads the Law

When the seventh month came and the Israelites had settled in their towns, ¹all the people came together as one in the square before the Water Gate. They told Ezra the teacher of the Law to bring out the Book of the Law of Moses, which the LORD had commanded for Israel. Dt 28:61

²So on the first day of the seventh month Ezra the priest brought the Law before the assembly, which was made up of men and women and all who were able to understand. ³He read it aloud from daybreak till noon as he faced the square before the Water Gate in the presence of the men, women and others who could understand. And all the people listened attentively to the Book of the Law. Lev 23:23-25

⁴Ezra the teacher of the Law stood on a high wooden platform built for the occasion. Beside him on his right stood Mattithiah, Shema, Anaiah, Uriah, Hilkiah and Maaseiah; and on his left

---

ᵃ 68 Some Hebrew manuscripts (see also Ezra 2:66); most Hebrew manuscripts do not have this verse.   ᵇ 70 That is, about 19 pounds or about 8.4 kilograms   ᶜ 71 That is, about 375 pounds or about 170 kilograms; also in verse 72   ᵈ 71 That is, about 1 1/3 tons or about 1.2 metric tons   ᵉ 72 That is, about 1 1/4 tons or about 1.1 metric tons were Pedaiah, Mishael, Malkijah, Hashum, Hashbaddanah, Zechariah and Meshullam. 2Ch 6:13

⁵Ezra opened the book. All the people could see him because he was standing above them; and as he opened it, the people all stood up. ⁶Ezra praised the LORD, the great God; and all the people lifted their hands and responded, "Amen! Amen!" Then they bowed down and worshiped the LORD with their faces to the ground. Ex 4:31; Ezr 9:5; 1Ti 2:8

⁷The Levites—Jeshua, Bani, Sherebiah, Jamin, Akkub, Shabbethai, Hodiah, Maaseiah, Kelita, Azariah, Jozabad, Hanan and Pelaiah—instructed the people in the Law while the people were standing there. ⁸They read from the Book of the Law of God, making it clear[a] and giving the meaning so that the people understood what was being read. Lev 10:11; 2Ch 17:7

⁹Then Nehemiah the governor, Ezra the priest and teacher of the Law, and the Levites who were instructing the people said to them all, "This day is holy to the LORD your God. Do not mourn or weep." For all the people had been weeping as they listened to the words of the Law. Ne 7:1,65,70; Dt 12:7,12; 16:14-15

¹⁰Nehemiah said, "Go and enjoy choice food and sweet drinks, and send some to those who have nothing prepared. This day is holy to our Lord. Do not grieve, for the joy of the LORD is your strength." Lev 23:40; Dt 12:18; Lk 14:12-14

¹¹The Levites calmed all the people, saying, "Be still, for this is a holy day. Do not grieve."

¹²Then all the people went away to eat and drink, to send portions of food and to celebrate with great joy, because they now understood the words that had been made known to them. Est 9:22

¹³On the second day of the month, the heads of all the families, along with the priests and the Levites, gathered around Ezra the teacher to give attention to the words of the Law. ¹⁴They found written in the Law, which the LORD had commanded through Moses, that the Israelites were to live in temporary shelters during the festival of the seventh month ¹⁵and that they should proclaim this word and spread it throughout their towns and in Jerusalem: "Go out into the hill country and bring back branches from olive and wild olive trees, and from myrtles, palms and shade trees, to make temporary shelters"—as it is written.[b]

¹⁶So the people went out and brought back branches and built themselves temporary shelters on their own roofs, in their courtyards, in the courts of the house of God and in the square by the Water Gate and the one by the Gate of Ephraim. ¹⁷The whole

[a] 8 Or God, translating it   [b] 15 See Lev. 23:37-40.

company that had returned from exile built temporary shelters and lived in them. From the days of Joshua son of Nun until that day, the Israelites had not celebrated it like this. And their joy was very great. 2Ch 30:21; Ne 12:39

18 Day after day, from the first day to the last, Ezra read from the Book of the Law of God. They celebrated the festival for seven days, and on the eighth day, in accordance with the regulation, there was an assembly. Nu 29:3

The Israelites Confess Their Sins

9 On the twenty-fourth day of the same month, the Israelites gathered together, fasting and wearing sackcloth and putting dust on their heads. 2 Those of Israelite descent had separated themselves from all foreigners. They stood in their places and confessed their sins and the sins of their ancestors. 3 They stood where they were and read from the Book of the Law of the LORD their God for a quarter of the day, and spent another quarter in confession and in worshiping the LORD their God. 4 Standing on the stairs of the Levites were Jeshua, Bani, Kadmiel, Shebaniah, Bunni, Sherebiah, Bani and Kenani. They cried out with loud voices to the LORD their God. 5 And the Levites — Jeshua, Kadmiel, Bani, Hashabneiah, Sherebiah, Hodiah, Shebaniah and Pethahiah — said: "Stand up and praise the LORD your God, who is from everlasting to everlasting.*a* 1Sa 4:12; Ezr 10:11; Ne 13:3,30

"Blessed be your glorious name, and may it be exalted above all blessing and praise. 6 You alone are the LORD. You made the heavens, even the highest heavens, and all their starry host, the earth and all that is on it, the seas and all that is in them. You give life to everything, and the multitudes of heaven worship you. Ge 1:1; 2Ki 19:15; Ps 95:5 7 "You are the LORD God, who chose Abram and brought him out of Ur of the Chaldeans and named him Abraham. 8 You found his heart faithful to you, and you made a covenant with him to give to his descendants the land of the Canaanites, Hittites, Amorites, Perizzites, Jebusites and Girgashites. You have kept your promise because you are righteous. Ge 15:6,18-21; Ezr 9:15 9 "You saw the suffering of our ancestors in Egypt; you heard their cry at the Red Sea.*b* 10 You sent signs and wonders against Pharaoh, against all his officials and all the people of his land, for you knew how arrogantly the Egyptians treated them. You

---

a 5 Or *God for ever and ever*   *b* 9 Or *the Sea of Reeds* made a name for yourself, which remains to this day. ¹¹You divided the sea before them, so that they passed through it on dry ground, but you hurled their pursuers into the depths, like a stone into mighty waters. ¹²By day you led them with a pillar of cloud, and by night with a pillar of fire to give them light on the way they were to take. Ex 13:21; 14:21; 15:4-5,10

¹³"You came down on Mount Sinai; you spoke to them from heaven. You gave them regulations and laws that are just and right, and decrees and commands that are good. ¹⁴You made known to them your holy Sabbath and gave them commands, decrees and laws through your servant Moses. ¹⁵In their hunger you gave them bread from heaven and in their thirst you brought them water from the rock; you told them to go in and take possession of the land you had sworn with uplifted hand to give them. Ex 16:4; 17:6; Dt 1:8,21

¹⁶"But they, our ancestors, became arrogant and stiff-necked, and they did not obey your commands. ¹⁷They refused to listen and failed to remember the miracles you performed among them.

They became stiff-necked and in their rebellion appointed a leader in order to return to their slavery. But you are a forgiving God, gracious and compassionate, slow to anger and abounding in love. Therefore you did not desert them, ¹⁸even when they cast for themselves an image of a calf and said, 'This is your god, who brought you up out of Egypt,' or when they committed awful blasphemies. Ex 32:4; Nu 14:1-4; Ps 78:11

¹⁹"Because of your great compassion you did not abandon them in the wilderness. By day the pillar of cloud did not fail to guide them on their path, nor the pillar of fire by night to shine on the way they were to take. ²⁰You gave your good Spirit to instruct them. You did not withhold your manna from their mouths, and you gave them water for their thirst. ²¹For forty years you sustained them in the wilderness; they lacked nothing, their clothes did not wear out nor did their feet become swollen. Nu 11:17; Dt 2:7; Isa 63:11,14

²²"You gave them kingdoms and nations, allotting to them even the remotest frontiers. They took over the country of Sihon[a] king of

a 22 One Hebrew manuscript and Septuagint; most Hebrew manuscripts Sihon, that is, the country of the

Heshbon and the country of Og king of Bashan. [23]You made their children as numerous as the stars in the sky, and you brought them into the land that you told their parents to enter and possess. [24]Their children went in and took possession of the land. You subdued before them the Canaanites, who lived in the land; you gave the Canaanites into their hands, along with their kings and the peoples of the land, to deal with them as they pleased. [25]They captured fortified cities and fertile land; they took possession of houses filled with all kinds of good things, wells already dug, vineyards, olive groves and fruit trees in abundance. They ate to the full and were well-nourished; they reveled in your great goodness.   Dt 6:10-12; 32:12-15

[26]"But they were disobedient and rebelled against you; they turned their backs on your law. They killed your prophets, who had warned them in order to turn them back to you; they committed awful blasphemies. [27]So you delivered them into the hands of their enemies, who oppressed them. But when they were oppressed they cried out to you. From heaven you heard them, and in your great compassion you gave them deliverers, who rescued them from the hand of their enemies.   Jdg 2:12-14; 1Ki 14:9

[28]"But as soon as they were at rest, they again did what was evil in your sight. Then you abandoned them to the hand of their enemies so that they ruled over them. And when they cried out to you again, you heard from heaven, and in your compassion you delivered them time after time.   Ps 106:43

[29]"You warned them in order to turn them back to your law, but they became arrogant and disobeyed your commands. They sinned against your ordinances, of which you said, 'The person who obeys them will live by them.' Stubbornly they turned their backs on you, became stiff-necked and refused to listen. [30]For many years you were patient with them. By your Spirit you warned them through your prophets. Yet they paid no attention, so you gave them into the hands of the neighboring peoples. [31]But in your great mercy you did not put an end to them or abandon them, for you are a gracious and merciful God.   Dt 30:16; 2Ki 17:13-18; Zec 7:11

[32]"Now therefore, our God, the great God, mighty and awesome, who keeps

his covenant of love, do not let all this hardship seem trifling in your eyes — the hardship that has come on us, on our kings and leaders, on our priests and prophets, on our ancestors and all your people, from the days of the kings of Assyria until today. ³³ In all that has happened to us, you have remained righteous; you have acted faithfully, while we acted wickedly. ³⁴ Our kings, our leaders, our priests and our ancestors did not follow your law; they did not pay attention to your commands or the statutes you warned them to keep. ³⁵ Even while they were in their kingdom, enjoying your great goodness to them in the spacious and fertile land you gave them, they did not serve you or turn from their evil ways. Ge 18:25; Dt 28:45-48; Da 9:7

³⁶ "But see, we are slaves today, slaves in the land you gave our ancestors so they could eat its fruit and the other good things it produces. ³⁷ Because of our sins, its abundant harvest goes to the kings you have placed over us. They rule over our bodies and our cattle as they please. We are in great distress. Dt 28:33,48; Ezr 9:9

The Agreement of the People

³⁸ "In view of all this, we are making a binding agreement, putting it in writing, and our leaders, our Levites and our priests are affixing their seals to it."^a 2Ch 23:16; Isa 44:5

10^b Those who sealed it were:

Nehemiah the governor, the son of Hakaliah.

Zedekiah, ² Seraiah, Azariah, Jeremiah, Ezr 2:2
³ Pashhur, Amariah, Malkijah, 1Ch 9:12
⁴ Hattush, Shebaniah, Malluk,
⁵ Harim, Meremoth, Obadiah, 1Ch 24:8
⁶ Daniel, Ginnethon, Baruch,
⁷ Meshullam, Abijah, Mijamin,
⁸ Maaziah, Bilgai and Shemaiah.
These were the priests.

⁹ The Levites: Ne 12:1

Jeshua son of Azaniah, Binnui of the sons of Henadad, Kadmiel,
¹⁰ and their associates: Shebaniah,
Hodiah, Kelita, Pelaiah, Hanan,
¹¹ Mika, Rehob, Hashabiah,
¹² Zakkur, Sherebiah, Shebaniah,
¹³ Hodiah, Bani and Beninu.

^a 38 In Hebrew texts this verse (9:38) is numbered 10:1. ^b In Hebrew texts 10:1-39 is numbered 10:2-40.

14 The leaders of the people:

> Parosh, Pahath-Moab, Elam, Zattu, Bani,
> 15 Bunni, Azgad, Bebai,
> 16 Adonijah, Bigvai, Adin, Ezr 8:6
> 17 Ater, Hezekiah, Azzur,
> 18 Hodiah, Hashum, Bezai,
> 19 Hariph, Anathoth, Nebai,
> 20 Magpiash, Meshullam, Hezir, 1Ch 24:15
> 21 Meshezabel, Zadok, Jaddua,
> 22 Pelatiah, Hanan, Anaiah,
> 23 Hoshea, Hananiah, Hasshub,
> 24 Hallohesh, Pilha, Shobek,
> 25 Rehum, Hashabnah, Maaseiah,
> 26 Ahiah, Hanan, Anan,
> 27 Malluk, Harim and Baanah.

28 "The rest of the people — priests, Levites, gatekeepers, musicians, temple servants and all who separated themselves from the neighboring peoples for the sake of the Law of God, together with their wives and all their sons and daughters who are able to understand — 29 all these now join their fellow Israelites the nobles, and bind themselves with a curse and an oath to follow the Law of God given through Moses the servant of God and to obey carefully all the commands, regulations and decrees of the LORD our Lord. Ne 9:2

30 "We promise not to give our daughters in marriage to the peoples around us or take their daughters for our sons. Ex 34:16; Dt 7:3

31 "When the neighboring peoples bring merchandise or grain to sell on the Sabbath, we will not buy from them on the Sabbath or on any holy day. Every seventh year we will forgo working the land and will cancel all debts. Ex 23:11; Dt 15:1; Ne 13:16,18

32 "We assume the responsibility for carrying out the commands to give a third of a shekel[a] each year for the service of the house of our God: 33 for the bread set out on the table; for the regular grain offerings and burnt offerings; for the offerings on the Sabbaths, at the New Moon feasts and at the appointed festivals; for the holy offerings; for sin offerings[b] to make atonement for Israel; and for all the duties of the house of our God. Lev 24:6; 2Ch 24:5

34 "We — the priests, the Levites and the people — have cast lots to determine when each of our families is to bring to the house of our God at set times each year a contribution of wood to burn on the altar of the LORD our God, as it is written in the Law. Ne 13:31

---

a 32 That is, about 1/8 ounce or about 4 grams   b 33 Or purification offerings

35 "We also assume responsibility for bringing to the house of the LORD each year the firstfruits of our crops and of every fruit tree.

Ex 23:19; Nu 18:12

36 "As it is also written in the Law, we will bring the firstborn of our sons and of our cattle, of our herds and of our flocks to the house of our God, to the priests ministering there. Ex 13:2; Nu 18:14-16

37 "Moreover, we will bring to the storerooms of the house of our God, to the priests, the first of our ground meal, of our grain offerings, of the fruit of all our trees and of our new wine and olive oil. And we will bring a tithe of our crops to the Levites, for it is the Levites who collect the tithes in all the towns where we work. **38** A priest descended from Aaron is to accompany the Levites when they receive the tithes, and the Levites are to bring a tenth of the tithes up to the house of our God, to the storerooms of the treasury. **39** The people of Israel, including the Levites, are to bring their contributions of grain, new wine and olive oil to the storerooms, where the articles for the sanctuary and for the ministering priests, the gatekeepers and the musicians are also kept. Lev 23:17

"We will not neglect the house of our God." Dt 12:6

The New Residents of Jerusalem

11:3-19pp — 1Ch 9:1-17

11 Now the leaders of the people settled in Jerusalem. The rest of the people cast lots to bring one out of every ten of them to live in Jerusalem, the holy city, while the remaining nine were to stay in their own towns. **2** The people commended all who volunteered to live in Jerusalem. Ne 7:4,73; Isa 48:2

3 These are the provincial leaders who settled in Jerusalem (now some Israelites, priests, Levites, temple servants and descendants of Solomon's servants lived in the towns of Judah, each on their own property in the various towns, **4** while other people from both Judah and Benjamin lived in Jerusalem): 1Ch 9:2-3; Ezr 2:1

From the descendants of Judah:

Athaiah son of Uzziah, the son of Zechariah, the son of Amariah, the son of Shephatiah, the son of Mahalalel, a descendant of Perez; **5** and Maaseiah son of Baruch, the son of Kol-Hozeh, the son of Hazaiah, the son of Adaiah, the son of Joiarib, the son of Zechariah, a descendant of Shelah. **6** The descendants of Perez who lived in Jerusalem totaled 468 men of standing.

⁷From the descendants of Benjamin:

Sallu son of Meshullam, the son of Joed, the son of Pedaiah, the son of Kolaiah, the son of Maaseiah, the son of Ithiel, the son of Jeshaiah, ⁸and his followers, Gabbai and Sallai—928 men. ⁹Joel son of Zikri was their chief officer, and Judah son of Hassenuah was over the New Quarter of the city.

¹⁰From the priests:

Jedaiah; the son of Joiarib; Jakin; ¹¹Seraiah son of Hilkiah, the son of Meshullam, the son of Zadok, the son of Meraioth, the son of Ahitub, the official in charge of the house of God, ¹²and their associates, who carried on work for the temple—822 men; Adaiah son of Jeroham, the son of Pelaliah, the son of Amzi, the son of Zechariah, the son of Pashhur, the son of Malkijah, ¹³and his associates, who were heads of families—242 men; Amashsai son of Azarel, the son of Ahzai, the son of Meshillemoth, the son of Immer, ¹⁴and his*a* associates, who were men of standing—128. Their chief officer was Zabdiel son of Haggedolim. 2Ki 25:18; Ezr 2:2

¹⁵From the Levites:

Shemaiah son of Hasshub, the son of Azrikam, the son of Hashabiah, the son of Bunni; ¹⁶Shabbethai and Jozabad, two of the heads of the Levites, who had charge of the outside work of the house of God; ¹⁷Mattaniah son of Mika, the son of Zabdi, the son of Asaph, the director who led in thanksgiving and prayer; Bakbukiah, second among his associates; and Abda son of Shammua, the son of Galal, the son of Jeduthun. ¹⁸The Levites in the holy city totaled 284. 1Ch 9:15; 25:1; Rev 21:2

¹⁹The gatekeepers:

Akkub, Talmon and their associates, who kept watch at the gates—172 men. 1Ch 9:1-17

²⁰The rest of the Israelites, with the priests and Levites, were in all the towns of Judah, each on their ancestral property.

²¹The temple servants lived on the hill of Ophel, and Ziha and Gishpa were in charge of them. Ezr 2:43; Ne 3:26

²²The chief officer of the Levites in Jerusalem was Uzzi son of Bani, the son of Hashabiah, the son of Mattaniah, the son of Mika. Uzzi was one of Asaph's descendants, who were the musicians responsible for the ser-

a 14 Most Septuagint manuscripts; Hebrew *their*

vice of the house of God. ²³The musicians were under the king's orders, which regulated their daily activity. 1Ch 9:15; Ne 7:44

²⁴Pethahiah son of Meshezabel, one of the descendants of Zerah son of Judah, was the king's agent in all affairs relating to the people. Ge 38:30

²⁵As for the villages with their fields, some of the people of Judah lived in Kiriath Arba and its surrounding settlements, in Dibon and its settlements, in Jekabzeel and its villages, ²⁶in Jeshua, in Moladah, in Beth Pelet, ²⁷in Hazar Shual, in Beersheba and its settlements, ²⁸in Ziklag, in Mekonah and its settlements, ²⁹in En Rimmon, in Zorah, in Jarmuth, ³⁰Zanoah, Adullam and their villages, in Lachish and its fields, and in Azekah and its settlements. So they were living all the way from Beersheba to the Valley of Hinnom. Ge 21:14; Jos 10:3; 1Sa 27:6

³¹The descendants of the Benjamites from Geba lived in Mikmash, Aija, Bethel and its settlements, ³²in Anathoth, Nob and Ananiah, ³³in Hazor, Ramah and Gittaim, ³⁴in Hadid, Zeboim and Neballat, ³⁵in Lod and Ono, and in Ge Harashim. Jos 11:1; 21:17

³⁶Some of the divisions of the Levites of Judah settled in Benjamin.

Priests and Levites

12 These were the priests and Levites who returned with Zerubbabel son of Shealtiel and with Joshua: 1Ch 3:19; Ezr 2:2
Seraiah, Jeremiah, Ezra, Ezr 2:2 ²Amariah, Malluk, Hattush, ³Shekaniah, Rehum, Meremoth, ⁴Iddo, Ginnethon,^a Abijah, ⁵Mijamin,^b Moadiah, Bilgah, ⁶Shemaiah, Joiarib, Jedaiah, ⁷Sallu, Amok, Hilkiah and Jedaiah.

These were the leaders of the priests and their associates in the days of Joshua.

⁸The Levites were Jeshua, Binnui, Kadmiel, Sherebiah, Judah, and also Mattaniah, who, together with his associates, was in charge of the songs of thanksgiving. ⁹Bakbukiah and Unni, their associates, stood opposite them in the services. Ne 11:17

¹⁰Joshua was the father of Joiakim, Joiakim the father of Eliashib, Eliashib the father of Joiada, ¹¹Joiada the father of Jonathan, and Jonathan the father of Jaddua. Ezr 10:24

¹²In the days of Joiakim, these were the heads of the priestly families:
of Seraiah's family, Meraiah; of Jeremiah's, Hananiah; ¹³of Ezra's, Meshullam; of Amariah's, Jehohanan; ¹⁴of Malluk's, Jonathan;

---

^a 4 Many Hebrew manuscripts and Vulgate (see also verse 16); most Hebrew manuscripts *Ginnethoi*   ^b 5 A variant of *Miniamin*

of Shekaniah's,[a] Joseph;
15 of Harim's, Adna;
of Meremoth's,[b] Helkai;
16 of Iddo's, Zechariah;
of Ginnethon's, Meshullam;
17 of Abijah's, Zikri;
of Miniamin's and of Moadiah's, Piltai;
18 of Bilgah's, Shammua;
of Shemaiah's, Jehonathan;
19 of Joiarib's, Mattenai;
of Jedaiah's, Uzzi;
20 of Sallu's, Kallai;
of Amok's, Eber;
21 of Hilkiah's, Hashabiah;
of Jedaiah's, Nethanel.

22 The family heads of the Levites in the days of Eliashib, Joiada, Johanan and Jaddua, as well as those of the priests, were recorded in the reign of Darius the Persian. 23 The family heads among the descendants of Levi up to the time of Johanan son of Eliashib were recorded in the book of the annals. 24 And the leaders of the Levites were Hashabiah, Sherebiah, Jeshua son of Kadmiel, and their associates, who stood opposite them to give praise and thanksgiving, one section responding to the other, as prescribed by David the man of God. Ezr 2:40

25 Mattaniah, Bakbukiah, Obadiah, Meshullam, Talmon and Akkub were gatekeepers who guarded the storerooms at the gates. 26 They served in the days of Joiakim son of Joshua, the son of Jozadak, and in the days of Nehemiah the governor and of Ezra the priest, the teacher of the Law.

Dedication of the Wall of Jerusalem

27 At the dedication of the wall of Jerusalem, the Levites were sought out from where they lived and were brought to Jerusalem to celebrate joyfully the dedication with songs of thanksgiving and with the music of cymbals, harps and lyres. 28 The musicians also were brought together from the region around Jerusalem — from the villages of the Netophathites, 29 from Beth Gilgal, and from the area of Geba and Azmaveth, for the musicians had built villages for themselves around Jerusalem. 30 When the priests and Levites had purified themselves ceremonially, they purified the people, the gates and the wall. 1Ch 25:6; Ps 92:3

31 I had the leaders of Judah go up on top of[c] the wall. I also assigned two large choirs to give thanks. One was to proceed on top of[d] the wall to the right, toward the Dung Gate. 32 Hoshaiah and half the leaders of Judah followed them, 33 along with Azariah, Ezra, Meshullam, 34 Judah,

a 14 Very many Hebrew manuscripts, some Septuagint manuscripts and Syriac (see also verse 3); most Hebrew manuscripts Shebaniah's   b 15 Some Septuagint manuscripts (see also verse 3); Hebrew Meraioth's   c 31 Or go alongside   d 31 Or proceed alongside

Benjamin, Shemaiah, Jeremiah, ³⁵ as well as some priests with trumpets, and also Zechariah son of Jonathan, the son of Shemaiah, the son of Mattaniah, the son of Micaiah, the son of Zakkur, the son of Asaph, ³⁶ and his associates — Shemaiah, Azarel, Milalai, Gilalai, Maai, Nethanel, Judah and Hanani — with musical instruments prescribed by David the man of God. Ezra the teacher of the Law led the procession. ³⁷ At the Fountain Gate they continued directly up the steps of the City of David on the ascent to the wall and passed above the site of David's palace to the Water Gate on the east.   Ne 2:13-14; 3:15,26

³⁸ The second choir proceeded in the opposite direction. I followed them on top of^a the wall, together with half the people — past the Tower of the Ovens to the Broad Wall, ³⁹ over the Gate of Ephraim, the Jeshanah^b Gate, the Fish Gate, the Tower of Hananel and the Tower of the Hundred, as far as the Sheep Gate. At the Gate of the Guard they stopped.   Ne 3:1,3,8,11; 8:16

⁴⁰ The two choirs that gave thanks then took their places in the house of God; so did I, together with half the officials, ⁴¹ as well as the priests — Eliakim, Maaseiah, Miniamin, Micaiah, Elioenai, Zechariah and Hananiah with their trumpets — ⁴² and also Maaseiah, Shemaiah, Eleazar, Uzzi, Jehohanan, Malkijah, Elam and Ezer. The choirs sang under the direction of Jezrahiah. ⁴³ And on that day they offered great sacrifices, rejoicing because God had given them great joy. The women and children also rejoiced. The sound of rejoicing in Jerusalem could be heard far away.

⁴⁴ At that time men were appointed to be in charge of the storerooms for the contributions, firstfruits and tithes. From the fields around the towns they were to bring into the storerooms the portions required by the Law for the priests and the Levites, for Judah was pleased with the ministering priests and Levites. ⁴⁵ They performed the service of their God and the service of purification, as did also the musicians and gatekeepers, according to the commands of David and his son Solomon. ⁴⁶ For long ago, in the days of David and Asaph, there had been directors for the musicians and for the songs of praise and thanksgiving to God. ⁴⁷ So in the days of Zerubbabel and of Nehemiah, all Israel contributed the daily portions for the musicians and the gatekeepers. They also set aside the portion for the other Levites, and the Levites set aside the portion for the descendants of Aaron.   Nu 18:21; Dt 18:8; 1Ch 25:1

^a 38 Or *them alongside*   ^b 39 Or *Old*

Nehemiah's Final Reforms

13 On that day the Book of Moses was read aloud in the hearing of the people and there it was found written that no Ammonite or Moabite should ever be admitted into the assembly of God, ²because they had not met the Israelites with food and water but had hired Balaam to call a curse down on them. (Our God, however, turned the curse into a blessing.) ³When the people heard this law, they excluded from Israel all who were of foreign descent. Dt 23:3; Nu 22:3-11; 23:11

⁴Before this, Eliashib the priest had been put in charge of the storerooms of the house of our God. He was closely associated with Tobiah, ⁵and he had provided him with a large room formerly used to store the grain offerings and incense and temple articles, and also the tithes of grain, new wine and olive oil prescribed for the Levites, musicians and gatekeepers, as well as the contributions for the priests. Nu 18:21; Ne 2:10; 12:44

⁶But while all this was going on, I was not in Jerusalem, for in the thirty-second year of Artaxerxes king of Babylon I had returned to the king. Some time later I asked his permission ⁷and came back to Jerusalem. Here I learned about the evil thing Eliashib had done in providing Tobiah a room in the courts of the house of God. ⁸I was greatly displeased and threw all Tobiah's household goods out of the room. ⁹I gave orders to purify the rooms, and then I put back into them the equipment of the house of God, with the grain offerings and the incense. 2Ch 29:5; Ne 5:14; Mt 21:12-13

¹⁰I also learned that the portions assigned to the Levites had not been given to them, and that all the Levites and musicians responsible for the service had gone back to their own fields. ¹¹So I rebuked the officials and asked them, "Why is the house of God neglected?" Then I called them together and stationed them at their posts. Ne 10:37-39; Hag 1:1-9

¹²All Judah brought the tithes of grain, new wine and olive oil into the storerooms. ¹³I put Shelemiah the priest, Zadok the scribe, and a Levite named Pedaiah in charge of the storerooms and made Hanan son of Zakkur, the son of Mattaniah, their assistant, because they were considered trustworthy. They were made responsible for distributing the supplies to their fellow Levites. Ne 10:37-39; 12:44; Ac 6:1-5

¹⁴Remember me for this, my God, and do not blot out what I have so faithfully done for the house of my God and its services.

¹⁵In those days I saw people in Judah treading winepresses on the Sabbath and bringing in grain and loading it on donkeys, together with wine, grapes,

figs and all other kinds of loads. And they were bringing all this into Jerusalem on the Sabbath. Therefore I warned them against selling food on that day. ¹⁶People from Tyre who lived in Jerusalem were bringing in fish and all kinds of merchandise and selling them in Jerusalem on the Sabbath to the people of Judah. ¹⁷I rebuked the nobles of Judah and said to them, "What is this wicked thing you are doing—desecrating the Sabbath day? ¹⁸Didn't your ancestors do the same things, so that our God brought all this calamity on us and on this city? Now you are stirring up more wrath against Israel by desecrating the Sabbath." Ex 20:8-11; Ne 10:31; Jer 17:21-23

¹⁹When evening shadows fell on the gates of Jerusalem before the Sabbath, I ordered the doors to be shut and not opened until the Sabbath was over. I stationed some of my own men at the gates so that no load could be brought in on the Sabbath day. ²⁰Once or twice the merchants and sellers of all kinds of goods spent the night outside Jerusalem. ²¹But I warned them and said, "Why do you spend the night by the wall? If you do this again, I will arrest you." From that time on they no longer came on the Sabbath. ²²Then I commanded the Levites to purify themselves and go and guard the gates in order to keep the Sabbath day holy. Lev 23:32; Ne 12:30

Remember me for this also, my God, and show mercy to me according to your great love.

²³Moreover, in those days I saw men of Judah who had married women from Ashdod, Ammon and Moab. ²⁴Half of their children spoke the language of Ashdod or the language of one of the other peoples, and did not know how to speak the language of Judah. ²⁵I rebuked them and called curses down on them. I beat some of the men and pulled out their hair. I made them take an oath in God's name and said: "You are not to give your daughters in marriage to their sons, nor are you to take their daughters in marriage for your sons or for yourselves. ²⁶Was it not because of marriages like these that Solomon king of Israel sinned? Among the many nations there was no king like him. He was loved by his God, and God made him king over all Israel, but even he was led into sin by foreign women. ²⁷Must we hear now that you too are doing all this terrible wickedness and are being unfaithful to our God by marrying foreign women?" 1Ki 11:3; 2Ch 1:12; Ezr 10:2

²⁸One of the sons of Joiada son of Eliashib the high priest was son-in-law to Sanballat the Horonite. And I drove him away from me. Ezr 10:24; Ne 2:10

²⁹Remember them, my God, because they defiled the priestly

office and the covenant of the priesthood and of the Levites. Ne 6:14

30 So I purified the priests and the Levites of everything foreign, and assigned them duties, each to his own task. **31** I also made provision for contributions of wood at designated times, and for the firstfruits. Ne 10:30,34-36

Remember me with favor, my God. ver 14,22; Ge 8:1

Esther

Queen Vashti Deposed

1 This is what happened during the time of Xerxes,[a] the Xerxes who ruled over 127 provinces stretching from India to Cush[b]: 2 At that time King Xerxes reigned from his royal throne in the citadel of Susa, 3 and in the third year of his reign he gave a banquet for all his nobles and officials. The military leaders of Persia and Media, the princes, and the nobles of the provinces were present. Est 8:9; 9:30; Da 9:1

4 For a full 180 days he displayed the vast wealth of his kingdom and the splendor and glory of his majesty. 5 When these days were over, the king gave a banquet, lasting seven days, in the enclosed garden of the king's palace, for all the people from the least to the greatest who were in the citadel of Susa. 6 The garden had hangings of white and blue linen, fastened with cords of white linen and purple material to silver rings on marble pillars. There were couches of gold and silver on a mosaic pavement of porphyry, marble, mother-of-pearl and other costly stones. 7 Wine was served in goblets of gold, each one different from the other, and the royal wine was abundant, in keeping with the king's liberality. 8 By the king's command each guest was allowed to drink with no restrictions, for the king instructed all the wine stewards to serve each man what he wished. Est 2:18; 7:7-8; Eze 23:41

9 Queen Vashti also gave a banquet for the women in the royal palace of King Xerxes. 1Ki 3:15

10 On the seventh day, when King Xerxes was in high spirits from wine, he commanded the seven eunuchs who served him — Mehuman, Biztha, Harbona, Bigtha, Abagtha, Zethar and Karkas — 11 to bring before him Queen Vashti, wearing her royal crown, in order to display her beauty to the people and nobles, for she was lovely to look at. 12 But when the attendants delivered the king's command, Queen

---

a 1 Hebrew Ahasuerus; here and throughout Esther   b 1 That is, the upper Nile region

Vashti refused to come. Then the king became furious and burned with anger. ^{Jdg 16:25; Est 2:21}

¹³ Since it was customary for the king to consult experts in matters of law and justice, he spoke with the wise men who understood the times ¹⁴ and were closest to the king—Karshena, Shethar, Admatha, Tarshish, Meres, Marsena and Memukan, the seven nobles of Persia and Media who had special access to the king and were highest in the kingdom. ^{2Ki 25:19; 1Ch 12:32; Jer 10:7}

¹⁵ "According to law, what must be done to Queen Vashti?" he asked. "She has not obeyed the command of King Xerxes that the eunuchs have taken to her."

¹⁶ Then Memukan replied in the presence of the king and the nobles, "Queen Vashti has done wrong, not only against the king but also against all the nobles and the peoples of all the provinces of King Xerxes. ¹⁷ For the queen's conduct will become known to all the women, and so they will despise their husbands and say, 'King Xerxes commanded Queen Vashti to be brought before him, but she would not come.' ¹⁸ This very day the Persian and Median women of the nobility who have heard about the queen's conduct will respond to all the king's nobles in the same way. There will be no end of disrespect and discord. ^{Pr 19:13; 27:15}

¹⁹ "Therefore, if it pleases the king, let him issue a royal decree and let it be written in the laws of Persia and Media, which cannot be repealed, that Vashti is never again to enter the presence of King Xerxes. Also let the king give her royal position to someone else who is better than she. ²⁰ Then when the king's edict is proclaimed throughout all his vast realm, all the women will respect their husbands, from the least to the greatest." ^{Est 8:8; Da 6:8,12}

²¹ The king and his nobles were pleased with this advice, so the king did as Memukan proposed. ²² He sent dispatches to all parts of the kingdom, to each province in its own script and to each people in their own language, proclaiming that every man should be ruler over his own household, using his native tongue. ^{Ne 13:24; Eph 5:22-24}

Esther Made Queen

2 Later when King Xerxes' fury had subsided, he remembered Vashti and what she had done and what he had decreed about her. ² Then the king's personal attendants proposed, "Let a search be made for beautiful young virgins for the king. ³ Let the king appoint commissioners in every province of his realm to bring all these beautiful young women into the harem at the citadel of Susa. Let them be placed under the care of Hegai, the king's eunuch, who is in charge of the women; and let beau-

ty treatments be given to them. ⁴Then let the young woman who pleases the king be queen instead of Vashti." This advice appealed to the king, and he followed it. Est 1:19-20; 7:10

⁵Now there was in the citadel of Susa a Jew of the tribe of Benjamin, named Mordecai son of Jair, the son of Shimei, the son of Kish, ⁶who had been carried into exile from Jerusalem by Nebuchadnezzar king of Babylon, among those taken captive with Jehoiachin*a* king of Judah. ⁷Mordecai had a cousin named Hadassah, whom he had brought up because she had neither father nor mother. This young woman, who was also known as Esther, had a lovely figure and was beautiful. Mordecai had taken her as his own daughter when her father and mother died. 2Ki 24:6,15; 2Ch 36:10,20; Est 3:2

⁸When the king's order and edict had been proclaimed, many young women were brought to the citadel of Susa and put under the care of Hegai. Esther also was taken to the king's palace and entrusted to Hegai, who had charge of the harem. ⁹She pleased him and won his favor. Immediately he provided her with her beauty treatments and special food. He assigned to her seven female attendants selected from the king's palace and moved her and her attendants into the best place in the harem. 2Ki 25:30; Est 1:2

¹⁰Esther had not revealed her nationality and family background, because Mordecai had forbidden her to do so. ¹¹Every day he walked back and forth near the courtyard of the harem to find out how Esther was and what was happening to her. ver 20

¹²Before a young woman's turn came to go in to King Xerxes, she had to complete twelve months of beauty treatments prescribed for the women, six months with oil of myrrh and six with perfumes and cosmetics. ¹³And this is how she would go to the king: Anything she wanted was given her to take with her from the harem to the king's palace. ¹⁴In the evening she would go there and in the morning return to another part of the harem to the care of Shaashgaz, the king's eunuch who was in charge of the concubines. She would not return to the king unless he was pleased with her and summoned her by name. 1Ki 11:3; Est 4:11; Pr 27:9

¹⁵When the turn came for Esther (the young woman Mordecai had adopted, the daughter of his uncle Abihail) to go to the king, she asked for nothing other than what Hegai, the king's eunuch who was in charge of the harem, suggested. And Esther won the favor of everyone who saw her. ¹⁶She was taken to King Xerxes in the royal residence in the tenth month, the month of

a 6 Hebrew *Jeconiah*, a variant of *Jehoiachin*

Tebeth, in the seventh year of his reign. Est 9:29; Ps 45:14

[17] Now the king was attracted to Esther more than to any of the other women, and she won his favor and approval more than any of the other virgins. So he set a royal crown on her head and made her queen instead of Vashti. [18] And the king gave a great banquet, Esther's banquet, for all his nobles and officials. He proclaimed a holiday throughout the provinces and distributed gifts with royal liberality. Est 1:3,7,11

Mordecai Uncovers a Conspiracy

[19] When the virgins were assembled a second time, Mordecai was sitting at the king's gate. [20] But Esther had kept secret her family background and nationality just as Mordecai had told her to do, for she continued to follow Mordecai's instructions as she had done when he was bringing her up. Est 3:2; 4:2; 5:13

[21] During the time Mordecai was sitting at the king's gate, Bigthana[a] and Teresh, two of the king's officers who guarded the doorway, became angry and conspired to assassinate King Xerxes. [22] But Mordecai found out about the plot and told Queen Esther, who in turn reported it to the king, giving credit to Mordecai. [23] And when the report was investigated and found to be true,

the two officials were impaled on poles. All this was recorded in the book of the annals in the presence of the king. Est 6:1-2; Ps 7:14-16

Haman's Plot to Destroy the Jews

3 After these events, King Xerxes honored Haman son of Hammedatha, the Agagite, elevating him and giving him a seat of honor higher than that of all the other nobles. [2] All the royal officials at the king's gate knelt down and paid honor to Haman, for the king had commanded this concerning him. But Mordecai would not kneel down or pay him honor. Nu 24:7; Dt 25:17-19

[3] Then the royal officials at the king's gate asked Mordecai, "Why do you disobey the king's command?" [4] Day after day they spoke to him but he refused to comply. Therefore they told Haman about it to see whether Mordecai's behavior would be tolerated, for he had told them he was a Jew. Ge 39:10; Est 5:9

[5] When Haman saw that Mordecai would not kneel down or pay him honor, he was enraged. [6] Yet having learned who Mordecai's people were, he scorned the idea of killing only Mordecai. Instead Haman looked for a way to destroy all Mordecai's people, the Jews, throughout the whole kingdom of Xerxes. Est 5:9; Ps 83:4

[7] In the twelfth year of King

---

a 21 Hebrew *Bigthan*, a variant of *Bigthana*

Xerxes, in the first month, the month of Nisan, the *pur* (that is, the lot) was cast in the presence of Haman to select a day and month. And the lot fell on[a] the twelfth month, the month of Adar. Est 9:24,26

⁸ Then Haman said to King Xerxes, "There is a certain people dispersed among the peoples in all the provinces of your kingdom who keep themselves separate. Their customs are different from those of all other people, and they do not obey the king's laws; it is not in the king's best interest to tolerate them. ⁹ If it pleases the king, let a decree be issued to destroy them, and I will give ten thousand talents[b] of silver to the king's administrators for the royal treasury." Ezr 4:15; Ac 16:20-21

¹⁰ So the king took his signet ring from his finger and gave it to Haman son of Hammedatha, the Agagite, the enemy of the Jews. ¹¹ "Keep the money," the king said to Haman, "and do with the people as you please." Ge 41:42; Est 7:6; 8:2

¹² Then on the thirteenth day of the first month the royal secretaries were summoned. They wrote out in the script of each province and in the language of each people all Haman's orders to the king's satraps, the governors of the various provinces and the nobles of the various peoples. These were written in the name of King Xer-xes himself and sealed with his own ring. ¹³ Dispatches were sent by couriers to all the king's provinces with the order to destroy, kill and annihilate all the Jews— young and old, women and children—on a single day, the thirteenth day of the twelfth month, the month of Adar, and to plunder their goods. ¹⁴ A copy of the text of the edict was to be issued as law in every province and made known to the people of every nationality so they would be ready for that day. 1Ki 21:8; Est 8:10-14; 9:10

¹⁵ The couriers went out, spurred on by the king's command, and the edict was issued in the citadel of Susa. The king and Haman sat down to drink, but the city of Susa was bewildered. Est 1:10; 8:15

Mordecai Persuades Esther to Help

4 When Mordecai learned of all that had been done, he tore his clothes, put on sackcloth and ashes, and went out into the city, wailing loudly and bitterly. ² But he went only as far as the king's gate, because no one clothed in sackcloth was allowed to enter it. ³ In every province to which the edict and order of the king came, there was great mourning among the Jews, with fasting, weeping and wailing. Many lay in sackcloth and ashes. Nu 14:6; Est 2:19

---

[a] 7 Septuagint; Hebrew does not have *And the lot fell on.*   [b] 9 That is, about 375 tons or about 340 metric tons

[4]When Esther's eunuchs and female attendants came and told her about Mordecai, she was in great distress. She sent clothes for him to put on instead of his sackcloth, but he would not accept them. [5]Then Esther summoned Hathak, one of the king's eunuchs assigned to attend her, and ordered him to find out what was troubling Mordecai and why.

[6]So Hathak went out to Mordecai in the open square of the city in front of the king's gate. [7]Mordecai told him everything that had happened to him, including the exact amount of money Haman had promised to pay into the royal treasury for the destruction of the Jews. [8]He also gave him a copy of the text of the edict for their annihilation, which had been published in Susa, to show to Esther and explain it to her, and he told him to instruct her to go into the king's presence to beg for mercy and plead with him for her people.   Est 3:9; 7:4

[9]Hathak went back and reported to Esther what Mordecai had said. [10]Then she instructed him to say to Mordecai, [11]"All the king's officials and the people of the royal provinces know that for any man or woman who approaches the king in the inner court without being summoned the king has but one law: that they be put to death unless the king extends the gold scepter to them and spares their lives. But thirty days have passed since I was called to go to the king."   Da 2:9; Est 5:1-2; 8:4

[12]When Esther's words were reported to Mordecai, [13]he sent back this answer: "Do not think that because you are in the king's house you alone of all the Jews will escape. [14]For if you remain silent at this time, relief and deliverance for the Jews will arise from another place, but you and your father's family will perish. And who knows but that you have come to your royal position for such a time as this?"   Ge 50:20; Dt 28:29; Am 5:13

[15]Then Esther sent this reply to Mordecai: [16]"Go, gather together all the Jews who are in Susa, and fast for me. Do not eat or drink for three days, night or day. I and my attendants will fast as you do. When this is done, I will go to the king, even though it is against the law. And if I perish, I perish."   Ge 43:14; 2Ch 20:3; Est 9:31

[17]So Mordecai went away and carried out all of Esther's instructions.

Esther's Request to the King

5 On the third day Esther put on her royal robes and stood in the inner court of the palace, in front of the king's hall. The king was sitting on his royal throne in the hall, facing the entrance. [2]When he saw Queen Esther standing in the court, he was pleased with her and held out to her the gold scepter that

was in his hand. So Esther approached and touched the tip of the scepter. Est 4:11,16; 8:4

³ Then the king asked, "What is it, Queen Esther? What is your request? Even up to half the kingdom, it will be given you." Est 7:2

⁴ "If it pleases the king," replied Esther, "let the king, together with Haman, come today to a banquet I have prepared for him."

⁵ "Bring Haman at once," the king said, "so that we may do what Esther asks."

So the king and Haman went to the banquet Esther had prepared. ⁶ As they were drinking wine, the king again asked Esther, "Now what is your petition? It will be given you. And what is your request? Even up to half the kingdom, it will be granted." Est 7:2; 9:12

⁷ Esther replied, "My petition and my request is this: ⁸ If the king regards me with favor and if it pleases the king to grant my petition and fulfill my request, let the king and Haman come tomorrow to the banquet I will prepare for them. Then I will answer the king's question." Est 2:15; 6:14

Haman's Rage Against Mordecai

⁹ Haman went out that day happy and in high spirits. But when he saw Mordecai at the king's gate and observed that he neither rose nor showed fear in his presence, he was filled with rage against Mordecai. ¹⁰ Nevertheless, Haman restrained himself and went home. Est 2:21; 3:3,5; Pr 14:17

Calling together his friends and Zeresh, his wife, ¹¹ Haman boasted to them about his vast wealth, his many sons, and all the ways the king had honored him and how he had elevated him above the other nobles and officials. ¹² "And that's not all," Haman added. "I'm the only person Queen Esther invited to accompany the king to the banquet she gave. And she has invited me along with the king tomorrow. ¹³ But all this gives me no satisfaction as long as I see that Jew Mordecai sitting at the king's gate." Est 6:13; 9:7-10,13

¹⁴ His wife Zeresh and all his friends said to him, "Have a pole set up, reaching to a height of fifty cubits,ᵃ and ask the king in the morning to have Mordecai impaled on it. Then go with the king to the banquet and enjoy yourself." This suggestion delighted Haman, and he had the pole set up. Est 6:4; 7:9

Mordecai Honored

6 That night the king could not sleep; so he ordered the book of the chronicles, the record of his reign, to be brought in and read to him. ² It was found recorded there that Mordecai had exposed Bigthana and Teresh, two of the king's officers who guarded the doorway, who had

---

ᵃ 14 That is, about 75 feet or about 23 meters

conspired to assassinate King Xerxes. Est 2:23; Da 6:18

³ "What honor and recognition has Mordecai received for this?" the king asked.

"Nothing has been done for him," his attendants answered.

⁴ The king said, "Who is in the court?" Now Haman had just entered the outer court of the palace to speak to the king about impaling Mordecai on the pole he had set up for him.

⁵ His attendants answered, "Haman is standing in the court."

"Bring him in," the king ordered.

⁶ When Haman entered, the king asked him, "What should be done for the man the king delights to honor?"

Now Haman thought to himself, "Who is there that the king would rather honor than me?" ⁷ So he answered the king, "For the man the king delights to honor, ⁸ have them bring a royal robe the king has worn and a horse the king has ridden, one with a royal crest placed on its head. ⁹ Then let the robe and horse be entrusted to one of the king's most noble princes. Let them robe the man the king delights to honor, and lead him on the horse through the city streets, proclaiming before him, 'This is what is done for the man the king delights to honor!'" Ge 41:43; 1Ki 1:33

¹⁰ "Go at once," the king commanded Haman. "Get the robe and the horse and do just as you have suggested for Mordecai the Jew, who sits at the king's gate. Do not neglect anything you have recommended."

¹¹ So Haman got the robe and the horse. He robed Mordecai, and led him on horseback through the city streets, proclaiming before him, "This is what is done for the man the king delights to honor!" Ge 41:42

¹² Afterward Mordecai returned to the king's gate. But Haman rushed home, with his head covered in grief, ¹³ and told Zeresh his wife and all his friends everything that had happened to him. 2Sa 15:30; Est 5:10

His advisers and his wife Zeresh said to him, "Since Mordecai, before whom your downfall has started, is of Jewish origin, you cannot stand against him — you will surely come to ruin!" ¹⁴ While they were still talking with him, the king's eunuchs arrived and hurried Haman away to the banquet Esther had prepared. 1Ki 3:15; Est 5:8

Haman Impaled

7 So the king and Haman went to Queen Esther's banquet, ² and as they were drinking wine on the second day, the king again asked, "Queen Esther, what is your petition? It will be given you. What is your request? Even up to half the kingdom, it will be granted." Est 5:3; 9:12; Mt 22:1-14

³Then Queen Esther answered, "If I have found favor with you, Your Majesty, and if it pleases you, grant me my life — this is my petition. And spare my people — this is my request. ⁴For I and my people have been sold to be destroyed, killed and annihilated. If we had merely been sold as male and female slaves, I would have kept quiet, because no such distress would justify disturbing the king.ᵃ" Est 2:15; 3:9

⁵King Xerxes asked Queen Esther, "Who is he? Where is he — the man who has dared to do such a thing?"

⁶Esther said, "An adversary and enemy! This vile Haman!"

Then Haman was terrified before the king and queen. ⁷The king got up in a rage, left his wine and went out into the palace garden. But Haman, realizing that the king had already decided his fate, stayed behind to beg Queen Esther for his life. 2Ki 21:18; Est 1:12

⁸Just as the king returned from the palace garden to the banquet hall, Haman was falling on the couch where Esther was reclining. Est 1:6

The king exclaimed, "Will he even molest the queen while she is with me in the house?" Ge 34:7

As soon as the word left the king's mouth, they covered Haman's face. ⁹Then Harbona, one of the eunuchs attending the king, said, "A pole reaching to a height of fifty cubitsᵇ stands by Haman's house. He had it set up for Mordecai, who spoke up to help the king." Est 1:10; 5:14

The king said, "Impale him on it!" ¹⁰So they impaled Haman on the pole he had set up for Mordecai. Then the king's fury subsided. Ps 7:14-16; Pr 11:5-6

The King's Edict in Behalf of the Jews

8 That same day King Xerxes gave Queen Esther the estate of Haman, the enemy of the Jews. And Mordecai came into the presence of the king, for Esther had told how he was related to her. ²The king took off his signet ring, which he had reclaimed from Haman, and presented it to Mordecai. And Esther appointed him over Haman's estate. Est 2:7; 3:10; Pr 13:22

³Esther again pleaded with the king, falling at his feet and weeping. She begged him to put an end to the evil plan of Haman the Agagite, which he had devised against the Jews. ⁴Then the king extended the gold scepter to Esther and she arose and stood before him. Est 4:11; 5:2

⁵"If it pleases the king," she said, "and if he regards me with favor and thinks it the right thing to do, and if he is pleased with me, let an order be written

---

ᵃ 4 Or *quiet, but the compensation our adversary offers cannot be compared with the loss the king would suffer*   ᵇ 9 That is, about 75 feet or about 23 meters overruling the dispatches that Haman son of Hammedatha, the Agagite, devised and wrote to destroy the Jews in all the king's provinces. **6**For how can I bear to see disaster fall on my people? How can I bear to see the destruction of my family?" Est 7:4; 9:1

7King Xerxes replied to Queen Esther and to Mordecai the Jew, "Because Haman attacked the Jews, I have given his estate to Esther, and they have impaled him on the pole he set up. **8**Now write another decree in the king's name in behalf of the Jews as seems best to you, and seal it with the king's signet ring—for no document written in the king's name and sealed with his ring can be revoked." Est 1:19; 3:12-14; Da 6:15

9At once the royal secretaries were summoned—on the twenty-third day of the third month, the month of Sivan. They wrote out all Mordecai's orders to the Jews, and to the satraps, governors and nobles of the 127 provinces stretching from India to Cush.*a* These orders were written in the script of each province and the language of each people and also to the Jews in their own script and language. **10**Mordecai wrote in the name of King Xerxes, sealed the dispatches with the king's signet ring, and sent them by mounted couriers, who rode fast horses especially bred for the king. Est 1:1,22

11The king's edict granted the Jews in every city the right to assemble and protect themselves; to destroy, kill and annihilate the armed men of any nationality or province who might attack them and their women and children,*b* and to plunder the property of their enemies. **12**The day appointed for the Jews to do this in all the provinces of King Xerxes was the thirteenth day of the twelfth month, the month of Adar. **13**A copy of the text of the edict was to be issued as law in every province and made known to the people of every nationality so that the Jews would be ready on that day to avenge themselves on their enemies. Est 3:14; 9:10,15,16

14The couriers, riding the royal horses, went out, spurred on by the king's command, and the edict was issued in the citadel of Susa.

The Triumph of the Jews

15When Mordecai left the king's presence, he was wearing royal garments of blue and white, a large crown of gold and a purple robe of fine linen. And the city of Susa held a joyous celebration. **16**For the Jews it was a time of happiness and joy, gladness and honor. **17**In every province and in every city to which the edict of the king came, there was joy and gladness among the

---

a 9 That is, the upper Nile region   *b* 11 Or *province, together with their women and children, who might attack them;*

Jews, with feasting and celebrating. And many people of other nationalities became Jews because fear of the Jews had seized them. Est 9:3; Ps 97:10-12

9 On the thirteenth day of the twelfth month, the month of Adar, the edict commanded by the king was to be carried out. On this day the enemies of the Jews had hoped to overpower them, but now the tables were turned and the Jews got the upper hand over those who hated them. ²The Jews assembled in their cities in all the provinces of King Xerxes to attack those determined to destroy them. No one could stand against them, because the people of all the other nationalities were afraid of them. ³And all the nobles of the provinces, the satraps, the governors and the king's administrators helped the Jews, because fear of Mordecai had seized them. ⁴Mordecai was prominent in the palace; his reputation spread throughout the provinces, and he became more and more powerful. 2Sa 3:1; Est 3:12-14; Pr 22:22-23

⁵The Jews struck down all their enemies with the sword, killing and destroying them, and they did what they pleased to those who hated them. ⁶In the citadel of Susa, the Jews killed and destroyed five hundred men. ⁷They also killed Parshandatha, Dalphon, Aspatha, ⁸Poratha, Adalia, Aridatha, ⁹Parmashta, Arisai, Aridai and Vaizatha, ¹⁰the ten sons of Haman son of Hammedatha, the enemy of the Jews. But they did not lay their hands on the plunder. Est 5:11; 8:11

¹¹The number of those killed in the citadel of Susa was reported to the king that same day. ¹²The king said to Queen Esther, "The Jews have killed and destroyed five hundred men and the ten sons of Haman in the citadel of Susa. What have they done in the rest of the king's provinces? Now what is your petition? It will be given you. What is your request? It will also be granted." Est 5:6; 7:2

¹³"If it pleases the king," Esther answered, "give the Jews in Susa permission to carry out this day's edict tomorrow also, and let Haman's ten sons be impaled on poles." Dt 21:22-23; Est 5:11

¹⁴So the king commanded that this be done. An edict was issued in Susa, and they impaled the ten sons of Haman. ¹⁵The Jews in Susa came together on the fourteenth day of the month of Adar, and they put to death in Susa three hundred men, but they did not lay their hands on the plunder. Ge 14:23; Ezr 6:11; Est 8:11

¹⁶Meanwhile, the remainder of the Jews who were in the king's provinces also assembled to protect themselves and get relief from their enemies. They killed seventy-five thousand of them but did not lay their hands on the plunder. ¹⁷This happened on the thirteenth day of the month of

Adar, and on the fourteenth they rested and made it a day of feasting and joy. Dt 25:19; 1Ki 3:15; 1Ch 4:43

[18]The Jews in Susa, however, had assembled on the thirteenth and fourteenth, and then on the fifteenth they rested and made it a day of feasting and joy.

[19]That is why rural Jews — those living in villages — observe the fourteenth of the month of Adar as a day of joy and feasting, a day for giving presents to each other. ver 22; Dt 16:11,14; Ne 8:10,12

Purim Established

[20]Mordecai recorded these events, and he sent letters to all the Jews throughout the provinces of King Xerxes, near and far, [21]to have them celebrate annually the fourteenth and fifteenth days of the month of Adar [22]as the time when the Jews got relief from their enemies, and as the month when their sorrow was turned into joy and their mourning into a day of celebration. He wrote them to observe the days as days of feasting and joy and giving presents of food to one another and gifts to the poor. Ne 8:12

[23]So the Jews agreed to continue the celebration they had begun, doing what Mordecai had written to them. [24]For Haman son of Hammedatha, the Agagite, the enemy of all the Jews, had plotted against the Jews to destroy them and had cast the *pur* (that is, the lot) for their ruin and destruction. [25]But when the plot came to the king's attention,[a] he issued written orders that the evil scheme Haman had devised against the Jews should come back onto his own head, and that he and his sons should be impaled on poles. [26](Therefore these days were called Purim, from the word *pur*.) Because of everything written in this letter and because of what they had seen and what had happened to them, [27]the Jews took it on themselves to establish the custom that they and their descendants and all who join them should without fail observe these two days every year, in the way prescribed and at the time appointed. [28]These days should be remembered and observed in every generation by every family, and in every province and in every city. And these days of Purim should never fail to be celebrated by the Jews — nor should the memory of these days die out among their descendants. Est 3:7

[29]So Queen Esther, daughter of Abihail, along with Mordecai the Jew, wrote with full authority to confirm this second letter concerning Purim. [30]And Mordecai sent letters to all the Jews in the 127 provinces of Xerxes' kingdom — words of goodwill and assurance — [31]to establish these days of Purim at their designated times, as Mordecai the

---

[a] 25 Or *when Esther came before the king*

Jew and Queen Esther had decreed for them, and as they had established for themselves and their descendants in regard to their times of fasting and lamentation. [32] Esther's decree confirmed these regulations about Purim, and it was written down in the records.

Est 4:1-3,16

The Greatness of Mordecai

10 King Xerxes imposed tribute throughout the empire, to its distant shores. [2] And all his acts of power and might, together with a full account of the greatness of Mordecai, whom the king had promoted, are they not written in the book of the annals of the kings of Media and Persia? [3] Mordecai the Jew was second in rank to King Xerxes, preeminent among the Jews, and held in high esteem by his many fellow Jews, because he worked for the good of his people and spoke up for the welfare of all the Jews.

Ne 2:10; Jer 29:4-7; Da 6:3

Job

Prologue

1 In the land of Uz there lived a man whose name was Job. This man was blameless and upright; he feared God and shunned evil. ²He had seven sons and three daughters, ³and he owned seven thousand sheep, three thousand camels, five hundred yoke of oxen and five hundred donkeys, and had a large number of servants. He was the greatest man among all the people of the East. Ge 6:9; 17:1; Ex 18:21

⁴His sons used to hold feasts in their homes on their birthdays, and they would invite their three sisters to eat and drink with them. ⁵When a period of feasting had run its course, Job would make arrangements for them to be purified. Early in the morning he would sacrifice a burnt offering for each of them, thinking, "Perhaps my children have sinned and cursed God in their hearts." This was Job's regular custom. Ge 8:20; 1Ki 21:10,13

⁶One day the angels[a] came to present themselves before the LORD, and Satan[b] also came with them. ⁷The LORD said to Satan, "Where have you come from?"

Satan answered the LORD, "From roaming throughout the earth, going back and forth on it." 1Pe 5:8

⁸Then the LORD said to Satan, "Have you considered my servant Job? There is no one on earth like him; he is blameless and upright, a man who fears God and shuns evil." Jos 1:7; Job 42:7-8

⁹"Does Job fear God for nothing?" Satan replied. ¹⁰"Have you not put a hedge around him and his household and everything he has? You have blessed the work of his hands, so that his flocks and herds are spread throughout the land. ¹¹But now stretch out your hand and strike everything he has, and he will surely curse you to your face." Job 2:5; 29:6; Ps 34:7

¹²The LORD said to Satan, "Very well, then, everything he

_a 6 Hebrew *the sons of God*   _b 6 Hebrew *satan* means *adversary*.

has is in your power, but on the man himself do not lay a finger."

Then Satan went out from the presence of the LORD.

¹³One day when Job's sons and daughters were feasting and drinking wine at the oldest brother's house, ¹⁴a messenger came to Job and said, "The oxen were plowing and the donkeys were grazing nearby, ¹⁵and the Sabeans attacked and made off with them. They put the servants to the sword, and I am the only one who has escaped to tell you!"   Ge 10:7; Job 6:19

¹⁶While he was still speaking, another messenger came and said, "The fire of God fell from the heavens and burned up the sheep and the servants, and I am the only one who has escaped to tell you!"   Lev 10:2; Nu 11:1-3

¹⁷While he was still speaking, another messenger came and said, "The Chaldeans formed three raiding parties and swept down on your camels and made off with them. They put the servants to the sword, and I am the only one who has escaped to tell you!"   Ge 11:28,31

¹⁸While he was still speaking, yet another messenger came and said, "Your sons and daughters were feasting and drinking wine at the oldest brother's house, ¹⁹when suddenly a mighty wind swept in from the desert and struck the four corners of the house. It collapsed on them and they are dead, and I am the only one who has escaped to tell you!"   Jer 4:11; 13:24

²⁰At this, Job got up and tore his robe and shaved his head. Then he fell to the ground in worship ²¹and said: Ge 37:29; 1Pe 5:6

> "Naked I came from my
>   mother's womb,
>   and naked I will
>   depart.ᵃ   Ecc 5:15; 1Ti 6:7
> The LORD gave and the LORD
>   has taken away;
>   may the name of the LORD
>   be praised."   Job 2:10

²²In all this, Job did not sin by charging God with wrongdoing.   Job 2:10

2 On another day the angelsᵇ came to present themselves before the LORD, and Satan also came with them to present himself before him. ²And the LORD said to Satan, "Where have you come from?"   Job 1:6

Satan answered the LORD, "From roaming throughout the earth, going back and forth on it."

³Then the LORD said to Satan, "Have you considered my servant Job? There is no one on earth like him; he is blameless and upright, a man who fears God and shuns evil. And he still maintains his integrity, though you incited me against him to ruin him without any reason."   Job 9:17; 27:6

ᵃ 21 Or *will return there*   ᵇ 1 Hebrew *the sons of God*

4 "Skin for skin!" Satan replied. "A man will give all he has for his own life. 5 But now stretch out your hand and strike his flesh and bones, and he will surely curse you to your face." Job 1:11; 19:20

6 The LORD said to Satan, "Very well, then, he is in your hands; but you must spare his life."

7 So Satan went out from the presence of the LORD and afflicted Job with painful sores from the soles of his feet to the crown of his head. 8 Then Job took a piece of broken pottery and scraped himself with it as he sat among the ashes. Job 42:6; Eze 27:30; Mt 11:21

9 His wife said to him, "Are you still maintaining your integrity? Curse God and die!"

10 He replied, "You are talking like a foolish*a* woman. Shall we accept good from God, and not trouble?" Job 1:21

In all this, Job did not sin in what he said. Jas 1:12; 5:11

11 When Job's three friends, Eliphaz the Temanite, Bildad the Shuhite and Zophar the Naamathite, heard about all the troubles that had come upon him, they set out from their homes and met together by agreement to go and sympathize with him and comfort him. 12 When they saw him from a distance, they could hardly recognize him; they began to weep aloud, and they tore their robes and sprinkled dust on their heads. 13 Then they sat on the ground with him for seven days and seven nights. No one said a word to him, because they saw how great his suffering was. Ge 50:10; Pr 17:28

Job Speaks

3 After this, Job opened his mouth and cursed the day of his birth. 2 He said:

3 "May the day of my birth perish,
    and the night that said, 'A boy is conceived!' Jer 20:14
4 That day — may it turn to darkness;
    may God above not care about it;
    may no light shine on it.
5 May gloom and utter darkness claim it once more; Job 10:21-22; Jer 2:6
    may a cloud settle over it;
    may blackness overwhelm it.
6 That night — may thick darkness seize it; Job 23:17
    may it not be included among the days of the year
    nor be entered in any of the months.
7 May that night be barren;
    may no shout of joy be heard in it.
8 May those who curse days*b* curse that day,
    those who are ready to rouse Leviathan. Job 41:1,8

a 10 The Hebrew word rendered *foolish* denotes moral deficiency.   *b 8* Or *curse the sea*

⁹May its morning stars become
dark;
may it wait for daylight in
vain
and not see the first rays of
dawn,   Job 41:18
¹⁰for it did not shut the doors of
the womb on me
to hide trouble from my
eyes.

¹¹ "Why did I not perish at birth,
and die as I came from the
womb?   Job 10:18
¹²Why were there knees to
receive me Ge 30:3; Isa 66:12
and breasts that I might be
nursed?
¹³For now I would be lying
down in peace;   Job 17:13
I would be asleep and at
rest   Job 7:8-10,21; 14:10-12
¹⁴with kings and rulers of the
earth,   Job 12:17
who built for themselves
places now lying in
ruins,   Job 15:28
¹⁵with princes who had
gold,   Job 12:21
who filled their houses with
silver.   Job 27:17
¹⁶Or why was I not hidden away
in the ground like a
stillborn child,   Ps 58:8
like an infant who never
saw the light of day?
¹⁷There the wicked cease from
turmoil,
and there the weary are at
rest.   Job 17:16
¹⁸Captives also enjoy their ease;

they no longer hear the
slave driver's shout.
¹⁹The small and the great are
there,
and the slaves are freed
from their owners.

²⁰ "Why is light given to those in
misery,
and life to the bitter of
soul,   1Sa 1:10; Jer 20:18
²¹to those who long for death
that does not come,
who search for it more than
for hidden treasure, Pr 2:4
²²who are filled with gladness
and rejoice when they reach
the grave?
²³Why is life given to a man
whose way is hidden,
whom God has
hedged in?   Job 19:6,8,12
²⁴For sighing has become my
daily food;   Job 6:7
my groans pour out like
water.   Ps 42:3-4
²⁵What I feared has come
upon me;
what I dreaded has
happened to me. Job 30:15
²⁶I have no peace, no quietness;
I have no rest, but only
turmoil."   Job 7:4,14

Eliphaz

4 Then Eliphaz the Temanite
replied:

² "If someone ventures a word
with you, will you be
impatient?

But who can keep from
  speaking?   Job 32:20
3 Think how you have
    instructed many,
  how you have
    strengthened feeble
    hands.   Isa 35:3; Heb 12:12
4 Your words have supported
    those who stumbled;
  you have strengthened
    faltering knees.   Isa 35:3
5 But now trouble comes
    to you, and you are
    discouraged;
  it strikes you, and you are
    dismayed.   Job 6:14; 19:21
6 Should not your piety be your
    confidence   Pr 3:26
  and your blameless ways
    your hope?   Job 1:1

7 "Consider now: Who, being
    innocent, has ever
    perished?   Job 36:7
  Where were the upright
    ever destroyed?   Job 8:20
8 As I have observed, those who
    plow evil   Job 15:35
  and those who sow trouble
    reap it.   Pr 22:8; Hos 10:13
9 At the breath of God they
    perish;   Isa 30:33; 2Th 2:8
  at the blast of his anger they
    are no more.   Job 40:13
10 The lions may roar and growl,
  yet the teeth of the great
    lions are broken.   Job 5:15
11 The lion perishes for lack of
    prey,   Ps 34:10
  and the cubs of the lioness
    are scattered.

12 "A word was secretly brought
    to me,
  my ears caught a whisper
    of it.   Job 26:14; 33:14
13 Amid disquieting dreams in
    the night,
  when deep sleep falls on
    people,   Job 33:15
14 fear and trembling seized me
  and made all my bones
    shake.   Jer 23:9; Hab 3:16
15 A spirit glided past my face,
  and the hair on my body
    stood on end.
16 It stopped,
  but I could not tell what it
    was.
  A form stood before my eyes,
  and I heard a hushed
    voice:
17 'Can a mortal be more
    righteous than God?
  Can even a strong man be
    more pure than his
    Maker?   Job 35:10
18 If God places no trust in his
    servants,
  if he charges his angels with
    error,   Job 15:15
19 how much more those
    who live in houses of
    clay,   Job 10:9
  whose foundations are in
    the dust,   Ge 2:7; Job 22:16
  who are crushed more
    readily than a moth!
20 Between dawn and dusk they
    are broken to pieces;
  unnoticed, they perish
    forever.   Job 20:7; Ps 90:5-6

²¹ Are not the cords of their tent
   pulled up,
   so that they die without
   wisdom?'   Job 36:12

5 "Call if you will, but who
   will answer you?
   To which of the holy ones
   will you turn?   Job 15:15
² Resentment kills a fool,
   and envy slays the simple.
³ I myself have seen a fool
   taking root,   Jer 12:2
   but suddenly his house was
   cursed.   Job 24:18
⁴ His children are far from
   safety,   Job 4:11
   crushed in court without a
   defender.   Am 5:12
⁵ The hungry consume his
   harvest,   Job 18:8-10
   taking it even from among
   thorns,
   and the thirsty pant after
   his wealth.
⁶ For hardship does not spring
   from the soil,
   nor does trouble sprout
   from the ground.
⁷ Yet man is born to trouble
   as surely as sparks fly
   upward.

⁸ "But if I were you, I would
   appeal to God;
   I would lay my cause before
   him.   Ps 35:23; 50:15
⁹ He performs wonders that
   cannot be fathomed,
   miracles that cannot be
   counted.

¹⁰ He provides rain for the earth;
   he sends water on the
   countryside.   Job 36:28
¹¹ The lowly he sets on high,
   and those who mourn are
   lifted to safety.
¹² He thwarts the plans of the
   crafty,   Ne 4:15; Ps 33:10
   so that their hands achieve
   no success.
¹³ He catches the wise in their
   craftiness,   1Co 3:19
   and the schemes of the wily
   are swept away.
¹⁴ Darkness comes upon them
   in the daytime;   Job 12:25
   at noon they grope as in the
   night.   Dt 28:29
¹⁵ He saves the needy from the
   sword in their mouth;
   he saves them from
   the clutches of the
   powerful.   Job 4:10
¹⁶ So the poor have hope,
   and injustice shuts its
   mouth.

¹⁷ "Blessed is the one whom God
   corrects;   Jas 1:12
   so do not despise the
   discipline of the
   Almighty.ᵃ   Ps 94:12; Pr 3:11
¹⁸ For he wounds, but he also
   binds up;   Isa 30:26
   he injures, but his hands
   also heal.   1Sa 2:6
¹⁹ From six calamities he will
   rescue you;
   in seven no harm will touch
   you.   Ps 34:19; 91:10

ᵃ 17 Hebrew *Shaddai*; here and throughout Job

²⁰In famine he will deliver you
from death, Ps 33:19
and in battle from the stroke
of the sword. Ps 144:10
²¹You will be protected from the
lash of the tongue, Ps 31:20
and need not fear when
destruction comes. Ps 91:5
²²You will laugh at destruction
and famine,
and need not fear the wild
animals. Ps 91:13
²³For you will have a covenant
with the stones of the
field, Ps 91:12
and the wild animals will be
at peace with you. Isa 11:6
²⁴You will know that your tent is
secure;
you will take stock of your
property and find
nothing missing. Job 8:6
²⁵You will know that your
children will be many,
and your descendants like
the grass of the earth.
²⁶You will come to the grave in
full vigor, Ge 15:15
like sheaves gathered in
season.

²⁷"We have examined this, and
it is true.
So hear it and apply it to
yourself." Job 8:5; 32:10,17

Job

6 Then Job replied:

²"If only my anguish could be
weighed

and all my misery be placed
on the scales! Job 31:6
³It would surely outweigh the
sand of the seas — Pr 27:3
no wonder my words have
been impetuous. Job 23:2
⁴The arrows of the Almighty
are in me, Job 16:12-13
my spirit drinks in their
poison; Job 21:20
God's terrors are marshaled
against me. Ps 88:15-18
⁵Does a wild donkey bray
when it has grass,
or an ox bellow when it has
fodder?
⁶Is tasteless food eaten without
salt,
or is there flavor in the sap
of the mallow*a*?
⁷I refuse to touch it;
such food makes me ill.

⁸"Oh, that I might have my
request,
that God would grant what I
hope for, Job 14:13
⁹that God would be willing to
crush me,
to let loose his hand and cut
off my life! Nu 11:15; 1Ki 19:4
¹⁰Then I would still have this
consolation —
my joy in unrelenting pain —
that I had not denied the
words of the Holy One.

¹¹"What strength do I have, that
I should still hope?
What prospects, that I
should be patient? Job 21:4

---

a 6 The meaning of the Hebrew for this phrase is uncertain.

¹²Do I have the strength of
    stone?
    Is my flesh bronze?
¹³Do I have any power to help
    myself,   Job 26:2
    now that success has been
    driven from me?

¹⁴"Anyone who withholds
    kindness from a friend
    forsakes the fear of the
    Almighty.
¹⁵But my brothers are as
    undependable as
    intermittent streams,
    as the streams that overflow
¹⁶when darkened by thawing
    ice
    and swollen with melting
    snow,
¹⁷but that stop flowing in the
    dry season,
    and in the heat vanish from
    their channels.   Job 24:19
¹⁸Caravans turn aside from
    their routes;
    they go off into the
    wasteland and perish.
¹⁹The caravans of Tema look for
    water,   Ge 25:15; Isa 21:14
    the traveling merchants of
    Sheba look in hope.
²⁰They are distressed, because
    they had been
    confident;
    they arrive there, only to be
    disappointed.   Jer 14:3
²¹Now you too have proved to
    be of no help;
    you see something dreadful
    and are afraid.   Ps 38:11

²²Have I ever said, 'Give
    something on my
    behalf,
    pay a ransom for me from
    your wealth,
²³deliver me from the hand of
    the enemy,
    rescue me from the clutches
    of the ruthless'?
²⁴"Teach me, and I will be quiet;
    show me where I have been
    wrong.
²⁵How painful are honest
    words!   Ecc 12:11
    But what do your
    arguments prove?
²⁶Do you mean to correct what I
    say,
    and treat my desperate
    words as wind?   Job 8:2; 15:3
²⁷You would even cast lots for
    the fatherless   Joel 3:3
    and barter away your friend.
²⁸"But now be so kind as to look
    at me.
    Would I lie to your
    face?   Job 27:4
²⁹Relent, do not be unjust;
    reconsider, for my integrity
    is at stake.ᵃ   Job 23:7,10
³⁰Is there any wickedness on
    my lips?   Job 27:4
    Can my mouth not discern
    malice?   Job 12:11

7 "Do not mortals have hard
        service on earth?   Job 14:14
    Are not their days like those
    of hired laborers?   Job 14:6

ᵃ 29 Or *my righteousness still stands*

²Like a slave longing for the
　　evening shadows,
　　or a hired laborer waiting to
　　be paid,　Lev 19:13
³so I have been allotted
　　months of futility,
　　and nights of misery have
　　been assigned to me.
⁴When I lie down I think, 'How
　　long before I get up?'
　　The night drags on, and
　　I toss and turn until
　　dawn.
⁵My body is clothed with
　　worms and scabs,　Job 17:14
　my skin is broken and
　　festering.

⁶"My days are swifter than a
　　weaver's shuttle,　Job 9:25
　and they come to an end
　　without hope.　Job 13:15
⁷Remember, O God, that my life
　　is but a breath;　Ps 78:39
　my eyes will never see
　　happiness again.　Job 9:25
⁸The eye that now sees me will
　　see me no longer;
　you will look for me, but I
　　will be no more.　Job 20:7,9
⁹As a cloud vanishes and is
　　gone,
　so one who goes down
　　to the grave does not
　　return.　2Sa 12:23; Job 11:8
¹⁰He will never come to his
　　house again;
　his place will know him no
　　more.　Job 8:18; 27:21,23

¹¹"Therefore I will not keep
　　silent;　Ps 40:9

I will speak out in the
　　anguish of my spirit,
　I will complain in the
　　bitterness of my soul.
¹²Am I the sea, or the monster
　　of the deep,　Eze 32:2-3
　that you put me under
　　guard?
¹³When I think my bed will
　　comfort me
　and my couch will ease my
　　complaint,　Job 9:27
¹⁴even then you frighten me
　　with dreams
　and terrify me with visions,
¹⁵so that I prefer strangling and
　　death,　1Ki 19:4
　rather than this body of
　　mine.
¹⁶I despise my life; I would not
　　live forever.　Job 10:1
　Let me alone; my days have
　　no meaning.

¹⁷"What is mankind that you
　　make so much of them,
　that you give them so much
　　attention,　Ps 8:4; 144:3
¹⁸that you examine them every
　　morning
　and test them every
　　moment?　Job 14:3
¹⁹Will you never look away
　　from me,
　or let me alone even for an
　　instant?　Job 9:18
²⁰If I have sinned, what have I
　　done to you,　Job 35:6
　you who sees everything
　　we do?
　Why have you made me your
　　target?　Job 16:12

Have I become a burden to
   you?*a*
²¹ Why do you not pardon my
      offenses
   and forgive my sins?   Job 10:14
For I will soon lie down in the
      dust;   Ps 104:29
   you will search for me, but I
      will be no more."

Bildad

8 Then Bildad the Shuhite replied:

² "How long will you say such
      things?
   Your words are a blustering
      wind.   Job 6:26
³ Does God pervert justice?   Dt 32:4
   Does the Almighty pervert
      what is right?   Ge 18:25
⁴ When your children sinned
      against him,
   he gave them over to the
      penalty of their sin.
⁵ But if you will seek God
      earnestly
   and plead with the
      Almighty,   Job 11:13
⁶ if you are pure and upright,
   even now he will rouse
      himself on your behalf
   and restore you to your
      prosperous state.   Job 5:24
⁷ Your beginnings will seem
      humble,
   so prosperous will your
      future be.   Job 42:12

⁸ "Ask the former generation
   and find out what their
      ancestors learned,
⁹ for we were born only yesterday
   and know nothing,   Ge 47:9
   and our days on earth are
      but a shadow.   1Ch 29:15
¹⁰ Will they not instruct you and
      tell you?
   Will they not bring forth
      words from their
      understanding?   Pr 4:1
¹¹ Can papyrus grow tall where
      there is no marsh?
   Can reeds thrive without
      water?
¹² While still growing and uncut,
   they wither more quickly
      than grass.   Ps 129:6; Jer 17:6
¹³ Such is the destiny of all who
      forget God;   Ps 9:17
   so perishes the hope of the
      godless.   Job 11:20; Pr 10:28
¹⁴ What they trust in is fragile*b*;
   what they rely on is a
      spider's web.   Isa 59:5
¹⁵ They lean on the web, but it
      gives way;   Job 27:18
   they cling to it, but it does
      not hold.   Ps 49:11
¹⁶ They are like a well-watered
      plant in the sunshine,
   spreading its shoots over
      the garden;   Ps 37:35; 80:11
¹⁷ it entwines its roots around a
      pile of rocks
   and looks for a place among
      the stones.

a 20 A few manuscripts of the Masoretic Text, an ancient Hebrew scribal tradition and
Septuagint; most manuscripts of the Masoretic Text *I have become a burden to myself.*
b 14 The meaning of the Hebrew for this word is uncertain.

¹⁸But when it is torn from its
  spot,
    that place disowns it and
      says, 'I never saw you.'
¹⁹Surely its life withers away,
    and*a* from the soil other
      plants grow.   Ecc 1:4
²⁰"Surely God does not reject
    one who is blameless
    or strengthen the hands of
      evildoers.   Job 21:30
²¹He will yet fill your mouth
    with laughter   Job 5:22
    and your lips with shouts of
      joy.   Ps 126:2
²²Your enemies will be clothed
      in shame,   Ps 35:26; 109:29
    and the tents of the wicked
      will be no more."   Job 18:6

Job

9 Then Job replied:

²"Indeed, I know that this is
      true.
    But how can mere mortals
      prove their innocence
      before God?   Ro 3:20
³Though they wished to
      dispute with him,
    they could not answer
      him one time out of a
      thousand.   Job 10:2
⁴His wisdom is profound, his
      power is vast. Job 11:6; 36:5
    Who has resisted him and
      come out unscathed?
⁵He moves mountains without
      their knowing it

and overturns them in his
      anger.   Mic 1:4
⁶He shakes the earth from its
      place   Isa 2:21; Heb 12:26
    and makes its pillars
      tremble.   Job 26:11
⁷He speaks to the sun and it
      does not shine;
    he seals off the light of the
      stars.   Isa 13:10; Eze 32:8
⁸He alone stretches out the
      heavens   Ge 1:6; Ps 104:2-3
    and treads on the waves of
      the sea.   Job 38:16; Ps 77:19
⁹He is the Maker of the Bear*b*
      and Orion,
    the Pleiades and the
      constellations of the
      south.   Ge 1:16; Job 38:31
¹⁰He performs wonders that
      cannot be fathomed,
    miracles that cannot be
      counted.   Job 5:9
¹¹When he passes me, I cannot
      see him;
    when he goes by, I cannot
      perceive him.   Job 23:8-9
¹²If he snatches away, who can
      stop him?   Job 11:10
    Who can say to him, 'What
      are you doing?'   Isa 45:9
¹³God does not restrain his
      anger;
    even the cohorts of Rahab
      cowered at his feet.
¹⁴"How then can I dispute with
      him?
    How can I find words to
      argue with him?

---

a 19 Or *Surely all the joy it has / is that*   *b* 9 Or *of Leo*

¹⁵Though I were innocent, I
  could not answer him;
 I could only plead with my
   Judge for mercy.   Job 8:5
¹⁶Even if I summoned him and
  he responded,
 I do not believe he would
   give me a hearing.
¹⁷He would crush me with a
  storm   Job 16:12; 30:22
 and multiply my wounds for
   no reason.   Job 2:3; 16:14
¹⁸He would not let me catch my
  breath
 but would overwhelm me
   with misery.   Job 7:19
¹⁹If it is a matter of strength, he
  is mighty!   Ne 9:32
 And if it is a matter of
   justice, who can
   challenge him*a*?
²⁰Even if I were innocent, my
  mouth would
   condemn me;
 if I were blameless, it would
   pronounce me guilty.

²¹"Although I am blameless, Job 1:1
 I have no concern for myself;
 I despise my own life. Job 7:16
²²It is all the same; that is why I
  say,
 'He destroys both the
   blameless and the
   wicked.'   Ecc 9:2-3; Eze 21:3
²³When a scourge brings
  sudden death,   Heb 11:36
 he mocks the despair of the
   innocent.   Job 24:1,12
²⁴When a land falls into the
  hands of the wicked,

 he blindfolds its judges.
 If it is not he, then who is it?

²⁵"My days are swifter than a
  runner;   Job 7:6
 they fly away without a
   glimpse of joy.
²⁶They skim past like boats of
  papyrus,   Isa 18:2
 like eagles swooping down
   on their prey.   Hab 1:8
²⁷If I say, 'I will forget my
  complaint,   Job 7:11
 I will change my expression,
   and smile,'
²⁸I still dread all my sufferings,
 for I know you will not hold
   me innocent.   Job 7:21
²⁹Since I am already found
  guilty,
 why should I struggle in
   vain?   Ps 37:33
³⁰Even if I washed myself with
  soap
 and my hands with
   cleansing powder, Jer 2:22
³¹you would plunge me into a
  slime pit
 so that even my clothes
   would detest me.

³²"He is not a mere mortal like
  me that I might answer
  him,   Ro 9:20
 that we might confront each
   other in court.   Ecc 6:10
³³If only there were someone to
  mediate between us,
 someone to bring us together,
³⁴someone to remove God's rod
  from me,   Ps 39:10

---

a 19 See Septuagint; Hebrew *me*.

so that his terror would
frighten me no more.
³⁵Then I would speak up
without fear of him,
but as it now stands with
me, I cannot.   Job 13:21

10 "I loathe my very life;
therefore I will give free
rein to my complaint
and speak out in the
bitterness of my soul.
²I say to God: Do not declare
me guilty,
but tell me what charges
you have against me.
³Does it please you to
oppress me,   Job 9:22
to spurn the work of your
hands,   Job 14:15; Ps 138:8
while you smile on the
plans of the wicked?
⁴Do you have eyes of flesh?
Do you see as a mortal sees?
⁵Are your days like those of a
mortal
or your years like those of a
strong man,   Ps 90:2,4
⁶that you must search out my
faults
and probe after my sin —
⁷though you know that I am
not guilty
and that no one can rescue
me from your hand?
⁸"Your hands shaped me and
made me.   Ps 119:73
Will you now turn and
destroy me?

⁹Remember that you molded
me like clay.   Isa 64:8
Will you now turn me to
dust again?   Ge 2:7
¹⁰Did you not pour me out like
milk
and curdle me like cheese,
¹¹clothe me with skin and flesh
and knit me together with
bones and sinews?
¹²You gave me life and showed
me kindness,   Job 33:4
and in your providence
watched over my spirit.
¹³"But this is what you
concealed in your heart,
and I know that this was in
your mind: Job 23:13
¹⁴If I sinned, you would be
watching me
and would not let my
offense go unpunished.
¹⁵If I am guilty — woe to me!
Even if I am innocent, I
cannot lift my head,
for I am full of shame
and drowned inᵃ my
affliction.
¹⁶If I hold my head high, you
stalk me like a lion
and again display your
awesome power
against me.
¹⁷You bring new witnesses
against me   Job 16:8
and increase your anger
toward me;   Ru 1:21
your forces come against
me wave upon wave.

ᵃ 15 Or *and aware of*

¹⁸ "Why then did you bring me
    out of the womb? Job 3:11
    I wish I had died before any
    eye saw me.
¹⁹ If only I had never come into
    being,
    or had been carried straight
    from the womb to the
    grave!
²⁰ Are not my few days almost
    over? Job 7:19; 14:1
    Turn away from me so I can
    have a moment's joy
²¹ before I go to the place of no
    return, Job 3:13; 16:22
    to the land of gloom and
    utter darkness, Ps 23:4
²² to the land of deepest night,
    of utter darkness and
    disorder,
    where even the light is like
    darkness."

Zophar

11 Then Zophar the Naama-
    thite replied:

² "Are all these words to go
    unanswered? Job 8:2
    Is this talker to be
    vindicated?
³ Will your idle talk reduce
    others to silence?
    Will no one rebuke you
    when you mock? Job 17:2
⁴ You say to God, 'My beliefs are
    flawless Job 6:10
    and I am pure in your sight.'
⁵ Oh, how I wish that God
    would speak,

that he would open his lips
    against you
⁶ and disclose to you the secrets
    of wisdom, Job 9:4
    for true wisdom has two
    sides.
    Know this: God has even
    forgotten some of your
    sin. Ezr 9:13; Job 15:5

⁷ "Can you fathom the
    mysteries of God? Ecc 3:11
    Can you probe the limits of
    the Almighty?
⁸ They are higher than the
    heavens above — what
    can you do? Job 22:12
    They are deeper than the
    depths below — what
    can you know? Ps 139:8
⁹ Their measure is longer than
    the earth
    and wider than the sea.

¹⁰ "If he comes along and
    confines you in prison
    and convenes a court, who
    can oppose him? Job 9:12
¹¹ Surely he recognizes
    deceivers;
    and when he sees evil, does
    he not take note? Job 34:21
¹² But the witless can no more
    become wise
    than a wild donkey's colt
    can be born human.ᵃ

¹³ "Yet if you devote your heart
    to him 1Sa 7:3; Ps 78:8
    and stretch out your hands
    to him, Ps 88:9

ᵃ 12 Or *wild donkey can be born tame*

¹⁴if you put away the sin that is
in your hand
and allow no evil to dwell in
your tent, Job 22:23; Ps 101:4
¹⁵then, free of fault, you will lift
up your face; Jn 3:21
you will stand firm and
without fear.
¹⁶You will surely forget your
trouble, Isa 65:16
recalling it only as waters
gone by. Job 22:11
¹⁷Life will be brighter than
noonday, Ps 37:6; Isa 58:8,10
and darkness will become
like morning.
¹⁸You will be secure, because
there is hope;
you will look about you and
take your rest in safety.
Lev 26:6; Ps 3:5; Pr 3:24
¹⁹You will lie down, with no one
to make you afraid,
and many will court your
favor. Isa 45:14
²⁰But the eyes of the wicked will
fail, Dt 28:65; Job 17:5
and escape will elude them;
their hope will become a
dying gasp." Job 8:13

Job

12 Then Job replied:

²"Doubtless you are the only
people who matter,
and wisdom will die with
you! Job 17:10
³But I have a mind as well as
you;

I am not inferior to you.
Who does not know all
these things? Job 13:2
⁴"I have become a
laughingstock to my
friends, Job 21:3
though I called on God and
he answered— Ps 91:15
a mere laughingstock,
though righteous and
blameless! Job 6:29
⁵Those who are at ease
have contempt for
misfortune
as the fate of those whose
feet are slipping.
⁶The tents of marauders are
undisturbed, Job 22:18
and those who provoke God
are secure— Job 9:24; 21:9
those God has in his hand.ᵃ
⁷"But ask the animals, and
they will teach you,
or the birds in the sky, and
they will tell you; Mt 6:26
⁸or speak to the earth, and it
will teach you,
or let the fish in the sea
inform you.
⁹Which of all these does not
know
that the hand of the LORD
has done this? Isa 41:20
¹⁰In his hand is the life of every
creature
and the breath of all
mankind. Job 27:3; 33:4
¹¹Does not the ear test words
as the tongue tastes food?

ᵃ 6 Or *those whose god is in their own hand*

¹²Is not wisdom found among
　　the aged?　　Job 15:10
　Does not long life bring
　　understanding? Job 32:7,9

¹³"To God belong wisdom and
　　power; 　　Job 9:4
　counsel and understanding
　　are his. 　　Job 32:8
¹⁴What he tears down cannot
　　be rebuilt; 　Job 19:10; 37:7
　those he imprisons cannot
　　be released.
¹⁵If he holds back the waters,
　　there is drought; 1Ki 8:35
　if he lets them loose, they
　　devastate the land. Ge 7:11
¹⁶To him belong strength and
　　insight;
　both deceived and deceiver
　　are his. 　　Job 13:7,9
¹⁷He leads rulers away stripped
　　and makes fools of judges.
¹⁸He takes off the shackles put
　　on by kings 　Ps 116:16
　and ties a loincloth[a] around
　　their waist.
¹⁹He leads priests away stripped
　　and overthrows officials long
　　established. 　Job 24:12,22
²⁰He silences the lips of trusted
　　advisers
　and takes away the
　　discernment of elders.
²¹He pours contempt on nobles
　　and disarms the mighty.
²²He reveals the deep things of
　　darkness 　　1Co 4:5
　and brings utter darkness
　　into the light. 　Job 3:5

²³He makes nations great, and
　　destroys them; 　Jer 25:9
　he enlarges nations, and
　　disperses them. Ps 107:38
²⁴He deprives the leaders of the
　　earth of their reason;
　he makes them wander in a
　　trackless waste.
²⁵They grope in darkness with
　　no light; 　　Job 5:14
　he makes them stagger like
　　drunkards. 　Ps 107:27

13 "My eyes have seen all
　　this,
　my ears have heard and
　　understood it.
²What you know, I also know;
　I am not inferior to you.
³But I desire to speak to the
　　Almighty
　and to argue my case with
　　God. 　　Job 23:3-4
⁴You, however, smear me with
　　lies; 　Ps 119:69; Jer 23:32
　you are worthless
　　physicians, all of you!
⁵If only you would be
　　altogether silent!
　For you, that would be
　　wisdom. 　Pr 17:28
⁶Hear now my argument;
　listen to the pleas of my lips.
⁷Will you speak wickedly on
　　God's behalf?
　Will you speak deceitfully
　　for him? 　Job 36:4
⁸Will you show him partiality?
　Will you argue the case for
　　God?

ᵃ 18 Or *shackles of kings / and ties a belt*

⁹Would it turn out well if he
    examined you?
  Could you deceive him as
      you might deceive a
      mortal?   Job 12:16; Gal 6:7
¹⁰He would surely call you to
      account
  if you secretly showed
      partiality.
¹¹Would not his splendor terrify
      you?   Job 31:23
  Would not the dread of him
      fall on you?
¹²Your maxims are proverbs of
      ashes;
  your defenses are defenses
      of clay.
¹³"Keep silent and let me speak;
  then let come to me what
      may.   Job 9:21
¹⁴Why do I put myself in
      jeopardy
  and take my life in my
      hands?
¹⁵Though he slay me, yet will I
      hope in him;   Job 7:6
  I will surely*a* defend my
      ways to his face.   Job 27:5
¹⁶Indeed, this will turn out for
      my deliverance,   Isa 12:1
  for no godless person would
      dare come before him!
¹⁷Listen carefully to what I say;
  let my words ring in your ears.
¹⁸Now that I have prepared my
      case,   Job 23:4
  I know I will be vindicated.
¹⁹Can anyone bring charges
      against me?   Isa 50:8

If so, I will be silent and
    die.   Job 10:8
²⁰"Only grant me these two
      things, God,
  and then I will not hide
      from you:
²¹Withdraw your hand far
      from me,   Ps 39:10
  and stop frightening me
      with your terrors.
²²Then summon me and I will
      answer,   Job 14:15
  or let me speak, and you
      reply to me.   Job 9:16
²³How many wrongs and sins
      have I committed?
  Show me my offense and
      my sin.
²⁴Why do you hide your face
  and consider me your
      enemy?   Job 19:11; La 2:5
²⁵Will you torment a windblown
      leaf?
  Will you chase after dry
      chaff?   Job 21:18; Isa 42:3
²⁶For you write down bitter
      things against me
  and make me reap the sins
      of my youth.   Ps 25:7
²⁷You fasten my feet in shackles;
  you keep close watch on all
      my paths
  by putting marks on the
      soles of my feet.
²⁸"So man wastes away like
      something rotten,
  like a garment eaten by
      moths.   Isa 50:9; Jas 5:2

---

a 15 Or *He will surely slay me; I have no hope — / yet I will*

14

¹ "Mortals, born of woman,
  are of few days and full of
  trouble. Job 5:7
² They spring up like flowers
    and wither away; Ps 90:5-6
  like fleeting shadows, they
    do not endure. Job 8:9
³ Do you fix your eye on them?
  Will you bring them*ᵃ* before
    you for judgment? Ps 143:2
⁴ Who can bring what is pure
    from the impure? Ps 51:10
  No one! Jn 3:6; Ro 5:12
⁵ A person's days are
    determined;
  you have decreed the
    number of his months
  and have set limits he
    cannot exceed.
⁶ So look away from him and let
    him alone, Job 7:19
  till he has put in his time like
    a hired laborer. Job 7:1-2

⁷ "At least there is hope for a
    tree:
  If it is cut down, it will
    sprout again,
  and its new shoots will not
    fail.
⁸ Its roots may grow old in the
    ground
  and its stump die in the soil,
⁹ yet at the scent of water it will
    bud
  and put forth shoots like a
    plant. Lev 26:4
¹⁰ But a man dies and is laid low;
  he breathes his last and is
    no more. Job 13:19

¹¹ As the water of a lake dries up
  or a riverbed becomes
    parched and dry, Isa 19:5
¹² so he lies down and does not
    rise;
  till the heavens are no
    more, people will not
    awake Rev 20:11; 21:1
  or be roused from their
    sleep. Ac 3:21

¹³ "If only you would hide me in
    the grave
  and conceal me till your
    anger has passed! Isa 26:20
  If only you would set me a time
  and then remember me!
¹⁴ If someone dies, will they live
    again?
  All the days of my hard
    service
  I will wait for my renewal*ᵇ*
    to come.
¹⁵ You will call and I will answer
    you; Job 13:22
  you will long for the
    creature your hands
    have made.
¹⁶ Surely then you will count my
    steps Pr 5:21; Jer 32:19
  but not keep track of my sin.
¹⁷ My offenses will be sealed up
    in a bag; Dt 32:34
  you will cover over my sin.
¹⁸ "But as a mountain erodes
    and crumbles
  and as a rock is moved from
    its place, Job 18:4
¹⁹ as water wears away stones

ᵃ 3 Septuagint, Vulgate and Syriac; Hebrew *me*   *ᵇ 14* Or *release*

and torrents wash away the
soil,   Job 7:6
so you destroy a person's
hope.
²⁰You overpower them once for
all, and they are gone;
you change their
countenance and send
them away.Job 12:19; Jas 1:10
²¹If their children are honored,
they do not know it;
if their offspring are
brought low, they do
not see it.   Ecc 9:5; Isa 63:16
²²They feel but the pain of their
own bodies
and mourn only for
themselves."   Job 21:21

Eliphaz

15 Then Eliphaz the Temanite replied:

²"Would a wise person answer
with empty notions
or fill their belly with the
hot east wind?   Job 6:26
³Would they argue with
useless words,
with speeches that have no
value?
⁴But you even undermine piety
and hinder devotion to God.
⁵Your sin prompts your mouth;
you adopt the tongue of the
crafty.   Job 5:13
⁶Your own mouth condemns
you, not mine;
your own lips testify against
you.   Lk 19:22

⁷"Are you the first man ever
born?   Job 38:21
Were you brought forth
before the hills?   Ps 90:2
⁸Do you listen in on God's
council?   Ro 11:34; 1Co 2:11
Do you have a monopoly on
wisdom?
⁹What do you know that we do
not know?
What insights do you have
that we do not have?
¹⁰The gray-haired and the aged
are on our side,   Job 32:6-7
men even older than your
father.
¹¹Are God's consolations not
enough for you,   2Co 1:3-4
words spoken gently to you?
¹²Why has your heart carried
you away,   Job 11:13
and why do your eyes flash,
¹³so that you vent your rage
against God   Pr 29:11
and pour out such words
from your mouth?
¹⁴"What are mortals, that they
could be pure,
or those born of woman,
that they could be
righteous?   Job 14:4; Pr 20:9
¹⁵If God places no trust in his
holy ones,
if even the heavens are not
pure in his eyes,   Job 25:5
¹⁶how much less mortals, who
are vile and corrupt,
who drink up evil like
water!   Job 34:7; Pr 19:28

17 "Listen to me and I will
    explain to you;
    let me tell you what I have
    seen,
18 what the wise have declared,
    hiding nothing received
    from their ancestors
19 (to whom alone the land was
    given
    when no foreigners moved
    among them):
20 All his days the wicked man
    suffers torment,
    the ruthless man through
    all the years stored up
    for him.   Job 24:1; 27:13-23
21 Terrifying sounds fill his ears;
    when all seems well,
    marauders attack him.
22 He despairs of escaping the
    realm of darkness;
    he is marked for the sword.
23 He wanders about for food
    like a vulture;   Ps 109:10
    he knows the day of
    darkness is at hand.
24 Distress and anguish fill him
    with terror;
    troubles overwhelm him,
    like a king poised to
    attack,
25 because he shakes his fist at
    God
    and vaunts himself against
    the Almighty,   Job 36:9
26 defiantly charging against
    him
    with a thick, strong shield.

27 "Though his face is covered
    with fat

and his waist bulges with
    flesh,   Ps 17:10
28 he will inhabit ruined towns
    and houses where no one
    lives,   Isa 5:9
    houses crumbling to rubble.
29 He will no longer be rich and
    his wealth will not
    endure,   Job 27:16-17
    nor will his possessions
    spread over the land.
30 He will not escape the
    darkness;   Job 5:14
    a flame will wither his
    shoots,   Job 22:20
    and the breath of God's
    mouth will carry him
    away.   Job 4:9
31 Let him not deceive himself
    by trusting what is
    worthless,   Isa 59:4
    for he will get nothing in
    return.
32 Before his time he will
    wither,   Job 22:16; Ps 55:23
    and his branches will not
    flourish.   Job 18:16
33 He will be like a vine
    stripped of its unripe
    grapes,   Hab 3:17
    like an olive tree shedding
    its blossoms.
34 For the company of the
    godless will be barren,
    and fire will consume the
    tents of those who love
    bribes.   Job 8:22
35 They conceive trouble and
    give birth to evil;   Ps 7:14
    their womb fashions
    deceit."

Job

16 Then Job replied:

2 "I have heard many things
like these;
you are miserable
comforters, all of you!
3 Will your long-winded
speeches never end?
What ails you that you keep
on arguing?   Job 6:26
4 I also could speak like you,
if you were in my place;
I could make fine speeches
against you
and shake my head at you.
5 But my mouth would
encourage you;
comfort from my lips would
bring you relief.

6 "Yet if I speak, my pain is not
relieved;
and if I refrain, it does not
go away.
7 Surely, God, you have worn
me out;   Job 7:3
you have devastated my
entire household.
8 You have shriveled me up —
and it has become a
witness;
my gauntness rises up and
testifies against me.
9 God assails me and tears me
in his anger   Hos 6:1
and gnashes his teeth at me;
my opponent fastens on me
his piercing eyes. Job 13:24
10 People open their mouths to
jeer at me;   Ps 22:13

they strike my cheek in
scorn La 3:30; Mic 5:1; Ac 23:2
and unite together
against me.   Ps 35:15
11 God has turned me over to
the ungodly
and thrown me into the
clutches of the wicked.
12 All was well with me, but he
shattered me;
he seized me by the neck
and crushed me.   Job 9:17
He has made me his target;
13   his archers surround me.
Without pity, he pierces my
kidneys   Job 20:24
and spills my gall on the
ground.
14 Again and again he bursts
upon me;   Job 9:17
he rushes at me like a
warrior.   Joel 2:7

15 "I have sewed sackcloth over
my skin   Ge 37:34
and buried my brow in the
dust.
16 My face is red with weeping,
dark shadows ring my eyes;
17 yet my hands have been free
of violence   Isa 59:6; Jnh 3:8
and my prayer is pure.

18 "Earth, do not cover my
blood;
may my cry never be laid to
rest!   Ps 66:18-19
19 Even now my witness is in
heaven;   Ro 1:9; 1Th 2:5
my advocate is on high.
20 My intercessor is my friend[a]

---

[a] 20 Or *My friends treat me with scorn*

as my eyes pour out tears to
God; La 2:19
²¹on behalf of a man he pleads
with God Ps 9:4
as one pleads for a friend.

²²"Only a few years will pass
before I take the path of no
return. Ecc 12:5

17 ¹My spirit is broken, Ps 143:4
my days are cut short,
the grave awaits me. Ps 88:3-4
²Surely mockers surround me;
my eyes must dwell on their
hostility.

³"Give me, O God, the pledge
you demand. Ps 119:122
Who else will put up
security for me? Isa 38:14
⁴You have closed their minds
to understanding;
therefore you will not let
them triumph.
⁵If anyone denounces their
friends for reward,
the eyes of their children
will fail. Job 11:20

⁶"God has made me a byword
to everyone, Job 30:9
a man in whose face people
spit.
⁷My eyes have grown dim with
grief; Job 16:8
my whole frame is but a
shadow.
⁸The upright are appalled at
this;
the innocent are aroused
against the ungodly.
⁹Nevertheless, the righteous
will hold to their ways,

and those with clean hands
will grow stronger.

¹⁰"But come on, all of you, try
again!
I will not find a wise man
among you. Job 12:2
¹¹My days have passed, my
plans are shattered.
Yet the desires of my heart
¹²turn night into day;
in the face of the darkness
light is near.
¹³If the only home I hope for is
the grave, Job 3:13
if I spread out my bed in the
realm of darkness,
¹⁴if I say to corruption, 'You are
my father,' Job 13:28
and to the worm, 'My
mother' or 'My sister,'
¹⁵where then is my hope — Job 7:6
who can see any hope
for me?
¹⁶Will it go down to the gates of
death? Job 3:17-19; Jnh 2:6
Will we descend together
into the dust?"

Bildad

18 Then Bildad the Shuhite
replied:

²"When will you end these
speeches? Job 16:3
Be sensible, and then we
can talk.
³Why are we regarded as cattle
and considered stupid in
your sight? Ps 73:22
⁴You who tear yourself to
pieces in your anger,

is the earth to be abandoned
for your sake?
Or must the rocks be moved
from their place?

5 "The lamp of a wicked man is
snuffed out;   Pr 13:9; 20:20
the flame of his fire stops
burning.
6 The light in his tent becomes
dark;
the lamp beside him goes
out.   Job 11:17
7 The vigor of his step is
weakened;   Pr 4:12
his own schemes throw him
down.   Job 5:13; 15:6
8 His feet thrust him into a net;
he wanders into its mesh.
9 A trap seizes him by the heel;
a snare holds him fast.
10 A noose is hidden for him on
the ground;
a trap lies in his path.
11 Terrors startle him on every side
and dog his every step.   Job 20:8
12 Calamity is hungry for him;
disaster is ready for him
when he falls.
13 It eats away parts of his skin;
death's firstborn devours
his limbs.   Zec 14:12
14 He is torn from the security of
his tent   Job 8:22
and marched off to the king
of terrors.
15 Fire resides[a] in his tent;
burning sulfur is scattered
over his dwelling.   Ps 11:6
16 His roots dry up below   Isa 5:24

and his branches wither
above.   Mal 4:1
17 The memory of him perishes
from the earth;
he has no name in the land.
18 He is driven from light into
the realm of darkness
and is banished from the
world.
19 He has no offspring or
descendants among his
people,   Isa 14:22; Jer 22:30
no survivor where once he
lived.
20 People of the west are
appalled at his fate;
those of the east are seized
with horror.
21 Surely such is the dwelling of
an evil man;
such is the place of one who
does not know God."

Job

19

Then Job replied:

2 "How long will you
torment me
and crush me with words?
3 Ten times now you have
reproached me;
shamelessly you attack me.
4 If it is true that I have gone
astray,
my error remains my
concern alone.   Job 6:24
5 If indeed you would exalt
yourselves above me
and use my humiliation
against me,

---

a 15 Or Nothing he had remains

⁶then know that God has
  wronged me   Job 27:2
and drawn his net
  around me.   Job 18:8
⁷"Though I cry, 'Violence!' I get
  no response;   Job 30:20
though I call for help, there
  is no justice.   Job 9:24
⁸He has blocked my way so I
  cannot pass; Job 3:23; La 3:7
he has shrouded my paths
  in darkness.   Job 30:26
⁹He has stripped me of my
  honor   Job 12:17
and removed the crown
  from my head.   Ps 89:39,44
¹⁰He tears me down on every
  side till I am gone;
he uproots my hope like a
  tree.   Job 7:6; 24:20
¹¹His anger burns against me;
he counts me among his
  enemies.   Job 13:24
¹²His troops advance in force;
they build a siege ramp
  against me   Job 30:12
and encamp around my tent.

¹³"He has alienated my family
  from me;   Ps 69:8
my acquaintances are
  completely estranged
  from me.   Job 16:7; Ps 88:8
¹⁴My relatives have gone away;
my closest friends have
  forgotten me.   Ps 88:18
¹⁵My guests and my female
  servants count me a
  foreigner;

they look on me as on a
  stranger.
¹⁶I summon my servant, but he
  does not answer,
though I beg him with my
  own mouth.
¹⁷My breath is offensive to my
  wife;
I am loathsome to my own
  family.
¹⁸Even the little boys scorn me;
when I appear, they
  ridicule me.
¹⁹All my intimate friends
  detest me;   Ps 38:11; 55:12-13
those I love have turned
  against me.   Jn 13:18
²⁰I am nothing but skin and
  bones;   Job 33:21; Ps 102:5
I have escaped only by the
  skin of my teeth.ᵃ

²¹"Have pity on me, my friends,
  have pity,   Job 6:14
for the hand of God has
  struck me.
²²Why do you pursue me as
  God does?   Job 13:25; 16:11
Will you never get enough
  of my flesh?   Ps 69:26

²³"Oh, that my words were
  recorded,
that they were written on a
  scroll,   Isa 30:8
²⁴that they were inscribed with
  an iron tool onᵇ lead,
or engraved in rock forever!
²⁵I know that my redeemerᶜ
  lives,   Job 16:19; Ps 78:35; Isa 43

ᵃ 20 Or only by my gums   ᵇ 24 Or and   ᶜ 25 Or vindicator

and that in the end he will stand on the earth.*a*
26 And after my skin has been destroyed,
yet*b* in*c* my flesh I will see God;   Mt 5:8; 1Co 13:12; 1Jn 3:2
27 I myself will see him with my own eyes — I, and not another.
How my heart yearns within me!   Ps 73:26

28 "If you say, 'How we will hound him,   Job 13:25
since the root of the trouble lies in him,*d'*
29 you should fear the sword yourselves;
for wrath will bring punishment by the sword,   Job 15:22
and then you will know that there is judgment.*e'*"

Zophar

20 Then Zophar the Naamathite replied: Job 2:11

2 "My troubled thoughts prompt me to answer because I am greatly disturbed.   Ps 42:5
3 I hear a rebuke that dishonors me,   Job 19:3
and my understanding inspires me to reply.

4 "Surely you know how it has been from of old,   Dt 4:32
ever since mankind*f* was placed on the earth,
5 that the mirth of the wicked is brief,
the joy of the godless lasts but a moment.   Ps 37:35-36
6 Though the pride of the godless person reaches to the heavens
and his head touches the clouds,   Isa 14:13-14; Ob 3-4
7 he will perish forever, like his own dung;   Job 4:20
those who have seen him will say, 'Where is he?'
8 Like a dream he flies away, no more to be found,   Ps 73:20
banished like a vision of the night.   Ps 90:5
9 The eye that saw him will not see him again;
his place will look on him no more.   Job 7:8
10 His children must make amends to the poor;
his own hands must give back his wealth.
11 The youthful vigor that fills his bones   Job 13:26
will lie with him in the dust.

12 "Though evil is sweet in his mouth
and he hides it under his tongue,
13 though he cannot bear to let it go
and lets it linger in his mouth,

---

a 25 Or *on my grave*   *b* 26 Or *And after I awake, / though this body has been destroyed, / then*   *c* 26 Or *destroyed, / apart from*   *d* 28 Many Hebrew manuscripts, Septuagint and Vulgate; most Hebrew manuscripts *me*   *e* 29 Or *sword, / that you may come to know the Almighty*   *f* 4 Or *Adam*

¹⁴yet his food will turn sour in
his stomach;
it will become the venom of
serpents within him.
¹⁵He will spit out the riches he
swallowed;
God will make his stomach
vomit them up.
¹⁶He will suck the poison of
serpents;   Dt 32:32
the fangs of an adder will
kill him.
¹⁷He will not enjoy the streams,
the rivers flowing with
honey and cream. Job 29:6
¹⁸What he toiled for he must
give back uneaten;
he will not enjoy the profit
from his trading.
¹⁹For he has oppressed the poor
and left them destitute;
he has seized houses he did
not build.
²⁰"Surely he will have no respite
from his craving;   Ecc 5:12
he cannot save himself by
his treasure.
²¹Nothing is left for him to
devour;
his prosperity will not
endure.   Job 15:29
²²In the midst of his plenty,
distress will overtake
him;
the full force of misery will
come upon him.
²³When he has filled his belly,
God will vent his burning
anger against him

and rain down his blows on
him.   Ps 78:30-31
²⁴Though he flees from an iron
weapon,   Isa 24:18; Am 5:19
a bronze-tipped arrow
pierces him.
²⁵He pulls it out of his back,
the gleaming point out of
his liver.
Terrors will come over him;
²⁶ total darkness lies in wait
for his treasures. Job 18:18
A fire unfanned will consume
him   Ps 21:9
and devour what is left in
his tent.
²⁷The heavens will expose his
guilt;
the earth will rise up
against him.
²⁸A flood will carry off his house,
rushing waters*ᵃ* on the day
of God's wrath. Job 21:17,20
²⁹Such is the fate God allots the
wicked,
the heritage appointed for
them by God."   Job 27:13

Job

21 Then Job replied:

²"Listen carefully to my words;
let this be the consolation
you give me.
³Bear with me while I speak,
and after I have spoken,
mock on.   Job 16:10

⁴"Is my complaint directed to a
human being?

ᵃ 28 Or The possessions in his house will be carried off, / washed away

Why should I not be
impatient?   Job 6:11
5 Look at me and be appalled;
clap your hand over your
mouth.   Jdg 18:19; Job 40:4
6 When I think about this, I am
terrified;
trembling seizes my body.
7 Why do the wicked live on,
growing old and increasing
in power?   Ps 73:3; Jer 12:1
8 They see their children
established around
them,
their offspring before their
eyes.   Ps 17:14
9 Their homes are safe and free
from fear;   Ps 73:5
the rod of God is not on
them.
10 Their bulls never fail to breed;
their cows calve and do not
miscarry.   Ex 23:26
11 They send forth their children
as a flock;
their little ones dance about.
12 They sing to the music of
timbrel and lyre;   Ps 33:2
they make merry to the
sound of the pipe.   Ps 81:2
13 They spend their years in
prosperity   Job 36:11
and go down to the grave in
peace.ᵃ
14 Yet they say to God, 'Leave us
alone!   Job 22:17
We have no desire to know
your ways.   Pr 1:29
15 Who is the Almighty, that we
should serve him?

What would we gain by
praying to him?'   Job 34:9
16 But their prosperity is not in
their own hands,
so I stand aloof from the
plans of the wicked.
17 "Yet how often is the lamp of
the wicked snuffed out?
How often does calamity
come upon them,
the fate God allots in his
anger?
18 How often are they like straw
before the wind,
like chaff swept away by a
gale?   Ps 1:4
19 It is said, 'God stores up
the punishment of
the wicked for their
children.'   Ex 20:5
Let him repay the wicked,
so that they themselves
will experience it!
20 Let their own eyes see their
destruction;
let them drink the cup of the
wrath of the Almighty.
21 For what do they care about
the families they leave
behind
when their allotted months
come to an end?
22 "Can anyone teach knowledge
to God,   Isa 40:13-14; Ro 11:34
since he judges even the
highest?   Ps 82:1
23 One person dies in full vigor,
completely secure and at
ease,

ᵃ 13 Or in an instant

²⁴well nourished in body,ᵃ
bones rich with marrow.
²⁵Another dies in bitterness of
soul,
never having enjoyed
anything good.
²⁶Side by side they lie in the dust,
and worms cover them both.

²⁷"I know full well what you are
thinking,
the schemes by which you
would wrong me.
²⁸You say, 'Where now is the
house of the great,   Job 1:3
the tents where the wicked
lived?'   Job 8:22
²⁹Have you never questioned
those who travel?
Have you paid no regard to
their accounts—
³⁰that the wicked are spared
from the day of calamity,
that they are delivered
fromᵇ the day of wrath?
³¹Who denounces their conduct
to their face?
Who repays them for what
they have done?
³²They are carried to the grave,
and watch is kept over their
tombs.
³³The soil in the valley is sweet
to them; Job 3:22; 17:16; 24:24
everyone follows after them,
and a countless throng goesᶜ
before them.   Job 3:19

³⁴"So how can you console me
with your nonsense?

Nothing is left of your
answers but falsehood!"

Eliphaz

22 Then Eliphaz the Temanite replied:

²"Can a man be of benefit to God?
Can even a wise person
benefit him?
³What pleasure would it give
the Almighty if you
were righteous?   Isa 1:11
What would he gain if your
ways were blameless?

⁴"Is it for your piety that he
rebukes you
and brings charges against
you?   Job 14:3; 19:29
⁵Is not your wickedness great?
Are not your sins endless?
⁶You demanded security from
your relatives for no
reason;   Ex 22:26
you stripped people of their
clothing, leaving them
naked.
⁷You gave no water to the
weary
and you withheld food from
the hungry,   Job 31:17,21,31
⁸though you were a powerful
man, owning land—
an honored man, living on it.
⁹And you sent widows away
empty-handed Job 24:3,21
and broke the strength of
the fatherless.

¹⁰That is why snares are all
    around you,
  why sudden peril terrifies
    you,
¹¹why it is so dark you cannot see,
  and why a flood of water
    covers you. Ps 69:1-2; 124:4-5
¹²"Is not God in the heights of
    heaven? Job 11:8
  And see how lofty are the
    highest stars!
¹³Yet you say, 'What does God
    know? Ps 10:11
  Does he judge through such
    darkness? Eze 8:12
¹⁴Thick clouds veil him, so he
    does not see us Job 26:9
  as he goes about in the
    vaulted heavens.'
¹⁵Will you keep to the old path
  that the wicked have trod?
¹⁶They were carried off before
    their time, Job 15:32
  their foundations washed
    away by a flood. Mt 7:26-27
¹⁷They said to God, 'Leave us
    alone!
  What can the Almighty do
    to us?'
¹⁸Yet it was he who filled their
    houses with good things,
  so I stand aloof from the
    plans of the wicked.
¹⁹The righteous see their ruin
    and rejoice; Ps 58:10; 107:42
  the innocent mock them,
    saying, Ps 52:6
²⁰'Surely our foes are destroyed,
  and fire devours their
    wealth.' Job 15:30

²¹"Submit to God and be at
    peace with him;
  in this way prosperity will
    come to you. Ps 34:8-10
²²Accept instruction from his
    mouth
  and lay up his words in your
    heart.
²³If you return to the Almighty,
    you will be restored:
  If you remove wickedness
    far from your tent Job 11:14
²⁴and assign your nuggets to the
    dust,
  your gold of Ophir to the
    rocks in the ravines,
²⁵then the Almighty will be
    your gold,
  the choicest silver for you.
²⁶Surely then you will find
    delight in the Almighty
  and will lift up your face to
    God.
²⁷You will pray to him, and he
    will hear you, Isa 58:9
  and you will fulfill your
    vows.
²⁸What you decide on will be
    done,
  and light will shine on your
    ways.
²⁹When people are brought
    low and you say, 'Lift
    them up!'
  then he will save the
    downcast. Mt 23:12; 1Pe 5:5
³⁰He will deliver even one who
    is not innocent,
  who will be delivered
    through the cleanness
    of your hands." Job 42:7-8

Job

23

Then Job replied:

2 "Even today my complaint is
  bitter;   Job 6:3
  his hand[a] is heavy in spite
  of[b] my groaning.   Ps 6:6
3 If only I knew where to find
  him;
  if only I could go to his
  dwelling!
4 I would state my case before
  him   Job 13:18
  and fill my mouth with
  arguments.
5 I would find out what he
  would answer me,
  and consider what he would
  say to me.
6 Would he vigorously oppose
  me?   Job 9:4
  No, he would not press
  charges against me.
7 There the upright can
  establish their
  innocence before him,
                              Job 13:3
  and there I would be
  delivered forever from
  my judge.

8 "But if I go to the east, he is
  not there;
  if I go to the west, I do not
  find him.
9 When he is at work in the
  north, I do not see him;
  when he turns to the south,
  I catch no glimpse of
  him.   Job 9:11

10 But he knows the way that I
   take;
   when he has tested me,
   I will come forth as
   gold.   Ps 139:1-3; 1Pe 1:7
11 My feet have closely followed
   his steps;
   I have kept to his way
   without turning aside.
12 I have not departed from the
   commands of his lips;
   I have treasured the words
   of his mouth more than
   my daily bread.   Jn 4:32,34

13 "But he stands alone, and who
   can oppose him?
   He does whatever he pleases.
14 He carries out his decree
   against me,
   and many such plans he
   still has in store.   1Th 3:3
15 That is why I am terrified
   before him;
   when I think of all this, I
   fear him.
16 God has made my heart faint;
   the Almighty has terrified me.
17 Yet I am not silenced by the
   darkness,   Job 19:8
   by the thick darkness that
   covers my face.

24

"Why does the Almighty
   not set times for
   judgment?   Jer 46:10
   Why must those who know
   him look in vain for
   such days?   Ac 1:7
2 There are those who move
  boundary stones;   Dt 19:14

---

a 2 Septuagint and Syriac; Hebrew / the hand on me   b 2 Or heavy on me in

they pasture flocks they
have stolen.
³They drive away the orphan's
donkey
and take the widow's ox in
pledge. Job 22:6
⁴They thrust the needy from
the path
and force all the poor of the
land into hiding. Pr 28:28
⁵Like wild donkeys in the
desert,
the poor go about their
labor of foraging food;
the wasteland provides food
for their children.
⁶They gather fodder in the
fields
and glean in the vineyards
of the wicked. Ru 2:22
⁷Lacking clothes, they spend
the night naked;
they have nothing to cover
themselves in the cold.
⁸They are drenched by
mountain rains
and hug the rocks for lack of
shelter. La 4:5
⁹The fatherless child is snatched
from the breast;
the infant of the poor is
seized for a debt.
¹⁰Lacking clothes, they go about
naked;
they carry the sheaves, but
still go hungry. Lev 19:9
¹¹They crush olives among the
terraces*a*;
they tread the winepresses,
yet suffer thirst.

¹²The groans of the dying rise
from the city,
and the souls of the wounded
cry out for help.
But God charges no one
with wrongdoing. Job 9:23
¹³"There are those who rebel
against the light, Jn 3:19-20
who do not know its ways
or stay in its paths. Isa 5:20
¹⁴When daylight is gone, the
murderer rises up,
kills the poor and needy,
and in the night steals forth
like a thief. Ps 10:9
¹⁵The eye of the adulterer
watches for dusk; Pr 7:8-9
he thinks, 'No eye will
see me,' Ps 10:11
and he keeps his face
concealed.
¹⁶In the dark, thieves break into
houses, Ex 22:2
but by day they shut
themselves in;
they want nothing to do
with the light. Jn 3:20
¹⁷For all of them, midnight is
their morning;
they make friends with the
terrors of darkness.
¹⁸"Yet they are foam on the
surface of the water;
their portion of the land is
cursed,
so that no one goes to the
vineyards.
¹⁹As heat and drought snatch
away the melted snow,

---

a 11 The meaning of the Hebrew for this word is uncertain.

so the grave snatches away
 those who have sinned.
²⁰The womb forgets them,
 the worm feasts on them;
the wicked are no longer
 remembered   Pr 10:7
 but are broken like a tree.
²¹They prey on the barren and
 childless woman,
 and to the widow they show
 no kindness.   Job 22:9
²²But God drags away the
 mighty by his power;
 though they become
 established, they have
 no assurance of life.
²³He may let them rest in a
 feeling of security,
 but his eyes are on their ways.
²⁴For a little while they are
 exalted, and then they
 are gone;   Ps 37:10
 they are brought low and
 gathered up like all
 others;
 they are cut off like heads of
 grain.   Isa 17:5
²⁵"If this is not so, who can
 prove me false
 and reduce my words to
 nothing?"   Job 6:28; 27:4

Bildad

25

Then Bildad the Shuhite
replied:

²"Dominion and awe belong to
 God;   Job 9:4; Rev 1:6
 he establishes order in the
 heights of heaven.

³Can his forces be numbered?
 On whom does his light not
 rise?   Jas 1:17
⁴How then can a mortal be
 righteous before God?
 How can one born of
 woman be pure?   Job 4:17
⁵If even the moon is not bright
 and the stars are not pure in
 his eyes,   Job 15:15
⁶how much less a mortal, who
 is but a maggot—
 a human being, who is only
 a worm!"   Ps 22:6

Job

26

Then Job replied:

²"How you have helped the
 powerless!   Job 6:12
 How you have saved the
 arm that is feeble!   Ps 71:9
³What advice you have offered
 to one without wisdom!
 And what great insight you
 have displayed!   Job 34:35
⁴Who has helped you utter
 these words?
 And whose spirit spoke
 from your mouth?

⁵"The dead are in deep anguish,
 those beneath the waters
 and all that live in
 them.
⁶The realm of the dead is naked
 before God;   Ps 139:8
 Destruction*a* lies
 uncovered.
⁷He spreads out the northern
 skies over empty space;

---

a 6 Hebrew *Abaddon*

he suspends the earth over
nothing.
⁸He wraps up the waters in his
clouds,   Pr 30:4
yet the clouds do not burst
under their weight.
⁹He covers the face of the full
moon,
spreading his clouds over it.
¹⁰He marks out the horizon on
the face of the waters
for a boundary between light
and darkness.   Job 38:8
¹¹The pillars of the heavens
quake,
aghast at his rebuke.
¹²By his power he churned up
the sea;   Isa 51:15; Jer 31:35
by his wisdom he cut Rahab
to pieces.
¹³By his breath the skies
became fair;
his hand pierced the gliding
serpent.   Isa 27:1
¹⁴And these are but the outer
fringe of his works;
how faint the whisper we
hear of him!
Who then can understand
the thunder of his
power?"   Job 36:29

Job's Final Word to His Friends

27 And Job continued his
discourse:

²"As surely as God lives, who
has denied me justice,
the Almighty, who has made
my life bitter,   Job 9:18
³as long as I have life within me,

the breath of God in my
nostrils,   Job 32:8; 33:4
⁴my lips will not say anything
wicked,
and my tongue will not
utter lies.   Job 6:28
⁵I will never admit you are in
the right;
till I die, I will not deny my
integrity.   Job 2:9; 13:15
⁶I will maintain my innocence
and never let go of it;
my conscience will not
reproach me as long as I
live.   Job 2:3

⁷"May my enemy be like the
wicked,
my adversary like the unjust!
⁸For what hope have the
godless when they are
cut off,   Job 8:13
when God takes away their
life?   Job 11:20; Lk 12:20
⁹Does God listen to their cry
when distress comes upon
them?   Job 35:12; Pr 1:28
¹⁰Will they find delight in the
Almighty?   Job 22:26
Will they call on God at all
times?

¹¹"I will teach you about the
power of God;
the ways of the Almighty I
will not conceal.   Job 36:23
¹²You have all seen this
yourselves.
Why then this meaningless
talk?

¹³"Here is the fate God allots to
the wicked,

the heritage a ruthless
man receives from the
Almighty: Job 20:29
[14] However many his children,
their fate is the sword;
his offspring will never have
enough to eat. Job 20:10
[15] The plague will bury those
who survive him,
and their widows will not
weep for them. Ps 78:64
[16] Though he heaps up silver
like dust
and clothes like piles of clay,
[17] what he lays up the righteous
will wear, Pr 28:8; Ecc 2:26
and the innocent will divide
his silver.
[18] The house he builds is like a
moth's cocoon, Job 8:14
like a hut made by a
watchman. Isa 1:8
[19] He lies down wealthy, but will
do so no more; Job 7:8
when he opens his eyes, all
is gone.
[20] Terrors overtake him like a
flood; Job 15:21
a tempest snatches him
away in the night. Job 20:8
[21] The east wind carries him off,
and he is gone;
it sweeps him out of his
place. Job 7:10
[22] It hurls itself against him
without mercy Jer 13:14
as he flees headlong from
its power.
[23] It claps its hands in derision
and hisses him out of his
place." Job 18:18

Interlude: Where Wisdom Is Found

28 There is a mine for silver
and a place where gold is
refined. Ps 12:6
[2] Iron is taken from the earth,
and copper is smelted from
ore. Dt 8:9
[3] Mortals put an end to the
darkness; Ecc 1:13
they search out the farthest
recesses
for ore in the blackest
darkness. Job 26:10
[4] Far from human dwellings
they cut a shaft, 2Sa 5:8
in places untouched by
human feet;
far from other people they
dangle and sway.
[5] The earth, from which food
comes, Ps 104:14
is transformed below as by
fire;
[6] lapis lazuli comes from its
rocks, Isa 54:11
and its dust contains
nuggets of gold. Job 22:24
[7] No bird of prey knows that
hidden path,
no falcon's eye has seen it.
[8] Proud beasts do not set foot
on it, Job 41:34
and no lion prowls there.
[9] People assault the flinty rock
with their hands Dt 8:15
and lay bare the roots of the
mountains. Jnh 2:6
[10] They tunnel through the rock;
their eyes see all its
treasures.

¹¹They search^a the sources of
the rivers   Ge 7:11
and bring hidden things to
light.   Isa 48:6

¹²But where can wisdom be
found?   Pr 1:20; 8:1; Ecc 7:24
Where does understanding
dwell?

¹³No mortal comprehends its
worth;   Pr 3:15; Mt 13:44-46
it cannot be found in the
land of the living.   Dt 29:29

¹⁴The deep says, "It is not in me";
the sea says, "It is not with
me."   Dt 30:13

¹⁵It cannot be bought with the
finest gold,
nor can its price be weighed
out in silver.   Pr 3:13-14

¹⁶It cannot be bought with the
gold of Ophir,   Ge 10:29
with precious onyx or lapis
lazuli.   Ex 24:10

¹⁷Neither gold nor crystal can
compare with it,   Ps 119:72
nor can it be had for jewels
of gold.   Pr 16:16

¹⁸Coral and jasper are not
worthy of mention;
the price of wisdom is
beyond rubies.   Pr 3:15

¹⁹The topaz of Cush cannot
compare with it;   Ex 28:17
it cannot be bought with
pure gold.   Pr 8:19

²⁰Where then does wisdom
come from?
Where does understanding
dwell?   ver 23,28

²¹It is hidden from the eyes of
every living thing,
concealed even from the
birds in the sky.

²²Destruction^b and Death say,
"Only a rumor of it has
reached our ears."

²³God understands the way to it
and he alone knows where
it dwells,   Pr 8:22-31

²⁴for he views the ends of the
earth   Ps 33:13-14
and sees everything under
the heavens.   Pr 15:3

²⁵When he established the force
of the wind
and measured out the waters,

²⁶when he made a decree for
the rain
and a path for the
thunderstorm,   Job 37:3,8,11

²⁷then he looked at wisdom and
appraised it;
he confirmed it and tested it.

²⁸And he said to the human race,
"The fear of the Lord — that
is wisdom,
and to shun evil is
understanding."   Dt 4:6

Job's Final Defense

29 Job continued his discourse: Job 13:12

²"How I long for the months
gone by,
for the days when God
watched over me,   Jer 31:28

³when his lamp shone on my
head

---

^a 11 Septuagint, Aquila and Vulgate; Hebrew *They dam up*   ^b 22 Hebrew *Abaddon*

and by his light I walked
through darkness!
⁴ Oh, for the days when I was in
my prime,
when God's intimate
friendship blessed my
house,   Ps 25:14
⁵ when the Almighty was still
with me
and my children were
around me,
⁶ when my path was drenched
with cream   Job 20:17
and the rock poured out for
me streams of olive oil.

⁷ "When I went to the gate of
the city   Job 31:21
and took my seat in the
public square,
⁸ the young men saw me and
stepped aside
and the old men rose to
their feet;
⁹ the chief men refrained from
speaking
and covered their mouths
with their hands; Job 21:5
¹⁰ the voices of the nobles were
hushed,
and their tongues stuck
to the roof of their
mouths.   Ps 137:6
¹¹ Whoever heard me spoke well
of me,
and those who saw me
commended me,
¹² because I rescued the poor
who cried for help, Job 24:4
and the fatherless who had
none to assist them.

¹³ The one who was dying
blessed me;
I made the widow's heart
sing.   Job 22:9
¹⁴ I put on righteousness as my
clothing;   Isa 59:17; 61:10
justice was my robe and my
turban.
¹⁵ I was eyes to the blind   Nu 10:31
and feet to the lame.
¹⁶ I was a father to the needy;
I took up the case of the
stranger.
¹⁷ I broke the fangs of the wicked
and snatched the victims
from their teeth.   Ps 3:7
¹⁸ "I thought, 'I will die in my
own house,
my days as numerous as the
grains of sand.   Ps 30:6
¹⁹ My roots will reach to the
water,   Jer 17:8
and the dew will lie all
night on my branches.
²⁰ My glory will not fade;
the bow will be ever new in
my hand.' Ge 49:24; Ps 18:34
²¹ "People listened to me
expectantly,
waiting in silence for my
counsel.
²² After I had spoken, they spoke
no more;
my words fell gently on
their ears.   Dt 32:2
²³ They waited for me as for
showers
and drank in my words as
the spring rain.

²⁴When I smiled at them, they
    scarcely believed it;
the light of my face was
    precious to them.ᵃ
²⁵I chose the way for them and
    sat as their chief;
I dwelt as a king among his
    troops;   Job 1:3
I was like one who comforts
    mourners.   Job 4:4

30

"But now they mock me,
men younger than I,
whose fathers I would have
    disdained
    to put with my sheep dogs.
²Of what use was the strength
    of their hands to me,
since their vigor had gone
    from them?
³Haggard from want and
    hunger,
they roamedᵇ the parched
    land   Isa 8:21
in desolate wastelands at
    night.   Job 24:5
⁴In the brush they gathered
    salt herbs,   Job 39:6
and their foodᶜ was the
    root of the broom
    bush.   1Ki 19:4
⁵They were banished from
    human society,
shouted at as if they were
    thieves.
⁶They were forced to live in the
    dry stream beds,
among the rocks and in
    holes in the ground.

⁷They brayed among the bushes
    and huddled in the
    undergrowth.
⁸A base and nameless brood,
they were driven out of the
    land.   Job 18:18
⁹"And now those young men
    mock me in song; Job 12:4
I have become a byword
    among them.   Job 17:6
¹⁰They detest me and keep their
    distance;
they do not hesitate to spit
    in my face. Nu 12:14; Dt 25:9
¹¹Now that God has unstrung my
    bow and afflicted me,
they throw off restraint in
    my presence.   Ps 32:9
¹²On my right the tribeᵈ attacks;
they lay snares for my feet,
they build their siege ramps
    against me.   Job 19:12
¹³They break up my road; Isa 3:12
they succeed in
    destroying me.
'No one can help him,' they
    say.
¹⁴They advance as through a
    gaping breach;
amid the ruins they come
    rolling in.
¹⁵Terrors overwhelm me; Ps 55:4-5
my dignity is driven away as
    by the wind,
my safety vanishes like a
    cloud.   Job 3:25; Hos 13:3
¹⁶"And now my life ebbs away;
days of suffering grip me.

ᵃ 24 The meaning of the Hebrew for this clause is uncertain.   ᵇ 3 Or gnawed
ᶜ 4 Or fuel   ᵈ 12 The meaning of the Hebrew for this word is uncertain.

¹⁷Night pierces my bones;
 my gnawing pains never rest.
¹⁸In his great power God
  becomes like clothing
  to me^a;
 he binds me like the neck of
  my garment.
¹⁹He throws me into the mud,
 and I am reduced to dust
  and ashes.

²⁰"I cry out to you, God, but you
  do not answer;   Job 19:7
 I stand up, but you merely
  look at me.
²¹You turn on me ruthlessly;
 with the might of your hand
  you attack me.
²²You snatch me up and drive
  me before the wind;
 you toss me about in the
  storm.   Job 9:17
²³I know you will bring me
  down to death,   Job 9:22
 to the place appointed for
  all the living.

²⁴"Surely no one lays a hand on
  a broken man
 when he cries for help in his
  distress.   Job 19:7
²⁵Have I not wept for those in
  trouble?
 Has not my soul grieved for
  the poor?   Job 24:4; Ps 35:13
²⁶Yet when I hoped for good,
  evil came;
 when I looked for light, then
  came darkness.   Jer 8:15
²⁷The churning inside me never
  stops;   La 2:11

days of suffering
  confront me.
²⁸I go about blackened, but not
  by the sun;   Ps 42:9
 I stand up in the assembly
  and cry for help.   Job 19:7
²⁹I have become a brother of
  jackals,   Ps 44:19
 a companion of owls.   Mic 1:8
³⁰My skin grows black and peels;
 my body burns with fever.
³¹My lyre is tuned to mourning,
 and my pipe to the sound of
  wailing.

31
"I made a covenant with
  my eyes
 not to look lustfully at a
  young woman.   Mt 5:28
²For what is our lot from God
  above,
 our heritage from the
  Almighty on high?
³Is it not ruin for the wicked,
 disaster for those who do
  wrong?   Job 34:22
⁴Does he not see my ways
 and count my every step?

⁵"If I have walked with
  falsehood
 or my foot has hurried after
  deceit —   Mic 2:11
⁶let God weigh me in honest
  scales   Job 6:2
 and he will know that I am
  blameless —
⁷if my steps have turned from
  the path,   Job 23:11
 if my heart has been led by
  my eyes,

---

^a 18 Hebrew; Septuagint *power he grasps my clothing*

or if my hands have been
defiled,   Job 9:30
⁸then may others eat what I
have sown,   Lev 26:16
and may my crops be
uprooted.   Mic 6:15

⁹"If my heart has been enticed
by a woman,   Job 24:15
or if I have lurked at my
neighbor's door,
¹⁰then may my wife grind
another man's grain,
and may other men sleep
with her.   Jer 8:10
¹¹For that would have been
wicked,
a sin to be judged.   Ge 38:24
¹²It is a fire that burns to
Destructionᵃ;   Job 15:30
it would have uprooted my
harvest.   Job 20:28

¹³"If I have denied justice to any
of my servants,
whether male or female,
when they had a grievance
against me,   Dt 24:14-15
¹⁴what will I do when God
confronts me?
What will I answer when
called to account?   Ps 10:13
¹⁵Did not he who made me in
the womb make them?
Did not the same one form
us both within our
mothers?   Job 10:3

¹⁶"If I have denied the desires of
the poor   Job 5:16
or let the eyes of the widow
grow weary,   Job 22:9

¹⁷if I have kept my bread to
myself,
not sharing it with the
fatherless —   Job 22:7
¹⁸but from my youth I reared
them as a father would,
and from my birth I guided
the widow —
¹⁹if I have seen anyone
perishing for lack of
clothing,   Job 22:6
or the needy without
garments,   Job 24:4
²⁰and their hearts did not
bless me
for warming them with the
fleece from my sheep,
²¹if I have raised my hand
against the fatherless,
knowing that I had
influence in court,
²²then let my arm fall from the
shoulder,
let it be broken off at the
joint.   Job 38:15
²³For I dreaded destruction
from God,
and for fear of his splendor I
could not do such things.

²⁴"If I have put my trust in gold
or said to pure gold, 'You
are my security,'   Mt 6:24
²⁵if I have rejoiced over my
great wealth,   Ps 62:10
the fortune my hands had
gained,
²⁶if I have regarded the sun in
its radiance   Eze 8:16
or the moon moving in
splendor,

ᵃ 12 Hebrew *Abaddon*

27 so that my heart was secretly
    enticed
  and my hand offered them a
    kiss of homage,
28 then these also would be sins
    to be judged,   Dt 17:2-7
  for I would have been
    unfaithful to God on
    high.

29 "If I have rejoiced at my
    enemy's misfortune
  or gloated over the trouble
    that came to him—
30 I have not allowed my mouth
    to sin
  by invoking a curse against
    their life—
31 if those of my household have
    never said,
  'Who has not been filled
    with Job's meat?'—
32 but no stranger had to spend
    the night in the street,
  for my door was always
    open to the traveler—
33 if I have concealed my sin as
    people do,[a]   Pr 28:13
  by hiding my guilt in my
    heart   Ge 3:8
34 because I so feared the crowd
  and so dreaded the
    contempt of the clans
  that I kept silent and would
    not go outside—

35 ("Oh, that I had someone to
    hear me!   Job 19:7; 30:28
  I sign now my defense—let
    the Almighty answer me;

let my accuser put his
    indictment in writing.
36 Surely I would wear it on my
    shoulder,
  I would put it on like a crown.
37 I would give him an account
    of my every step;
  I would present it to him as
    to a ruler.) —   Job 1:3; 29:25

38 "if my land cries out against me
  and all its furrows are wet
    with tears,
39 if I have devoured its yield
    without payment   1Ki 21:19
  or broken the spirit of its
    tenants,   Jas 5:4
40 then let briers come up
    instead of wheat   Ge 3:18
  and stinkweed instead of
    barley."

The words of Job are ended.

Elihu

32 So these three men
    stopped answering Job,
because he was righteous in his
own eyes. 2 But Elihu son of Barakel the Buzite, of the family of
Ram, became very angry with
Job for justifying himself rather
than God. 3 He was also angry
with the three friends, because
they had found no way to refute
Job, and yet had condemned
him.[b] 4 Now Elihu had waited
before speaking to Job because
they were older than he. 5 But
when he saw that the three men

---

[a] 33 Or *as Adam did*   [b] 3 Masoretic Text; an ancient Hebrew scribal tradition *Job, and so*
had condemned God

had nothing more to say, his anger was aroused.   Ge 22:21; Job 33:9

⁶So Elihu son of Barakel the Buzite said:

"I am young in years,
   and you are old;   Job 15:10
that is why I was fearful,
   not daring to tell you what I
      know.
⁷I thought, 'Age should speak;
   advanced years should
      teach wisdom.'
⁸But it is the spirit*ᵃ* in a person,
   the breath of the Almighty,
      that gives them
         understanding.   Job 27:3
⁹It is not only the old*ᵇ* who are
      wise,
         1Co 1:26
   not only the aged who
      understand what is right.

¹⁰"Therefore I say: Listen to me;
   I too will tell you what I
      know.   Job 5:27
¹¹I waited while you spoke,
   I listened to your reasoning;
while you were searching for
      words,
¹²   I gave you my full attention.
But not one of you has proved
      Job wrong;
   none of you has answered
      his arguments.
¹³Do not say, 'We have found
      wisdom;   Jer 9:23
   let God, not a man, refute
      him.'
¹⁴But Job has not marshaled his
   words against me,   Job 23:4

and I will not answer him
   with your arguments.

¹⁵"They are dismayed and have
   no more to say;
   words have failed them.
¹⁶Must I wait, now that they are
      silent,
   now that they stand there
      with no reply?
¹⁷I too will have my say;
   I too will tell what I know.
¹⁸For I am full of words,
   and the spirit within me
      compels me;   Ac 4:20
¹⁹inside I am like bottled-up
      wine,
   like new wineskins ready to
      burst.
²⁰I must speak and find relief;
   I must open my lips and
      reply.
²¹I will show no partiality,   Lev 19:15
   nor will I flatter anyone;
²²for if I were skilled in flattery,
   my Maker would soon take
      me away.   Ps 12:2-4

33 "But now, Job, listen to
   my words;
   pay attention to everything
      I say.   Job 13:6
²I am about to open my mouth;
   my words are on the tip of
      my tongue.
³My words come from an
      upright heart;
   my lips sincerely speak
      what I know.   Job 6:28; 27:4
⁴The Spirit of God has
   made me;   Ge 2:7

ᵃ 8 Or *Spirit*; also in verse 18   ᵇ 9 Or *many*; or *great*

the breath of the Almighty
    gives me life.   Job 27:3
⁵Answer me then, if you can;
    stand up and argue your
    case before me.   Job 13:18
⁶I am the same as you in God's
    sight;
    I too am a piece of clay.
⁷No fear of me should alarm
    you,
    nor should my hand be
    heavy on you.   Job 9:34

⁸"But you have said in my
    hearing —
    I heard the very words —
⁹'I am pure, I have done no
    wrong;   Job 10:7
    I am clean and free from sin.
¹⁰Yet God has found fault
    with me;
    he considers me his enemy.
¹¹He fastens my feet in shackles;
    he keeps close watch on all
    my paths.'   Job 14:16

¹²"But I tell you, in this you are
    not right,
    for God is greater than any
    mortal.   Ecc 7:20
¹³Why do you complain to him
    that he responds to no one's
    words*a*?
¹⁴For God does speak — now
    one way, now another —
    though no one perceives it.
¹⁵In a dream, in a vision of the
    night,   Job 4:13
    when deep sleep falls on
    people

as they slumber in their
    beds,
¹⁶he may speak in their ears
    and terrify them with
    warnings,
¹⁷to turn them from wrongdoing
    and keep them from pride,
¹⁸to preserve them from the pit,
    their lives from perishing by
    the sword.*b*   Job 15:22

¹⁹"Or someone may be chastened
    on a bed of pain
    with constant distress in
    their bones,
²⁰so that their body finds food
    repulsive   Ps 107:18
    and their soul loathes the
    choicest meal.   Job 3:24
²¹Their flesh wastes away to
    nothing,
    and their bones, once
    hidden, now stick out.
²²They draw near to the pit,
    and their life to the
    messengers of death.*c*
²³Yet if there is an angel at their
    side,
    a messenger, one out of a
    thousand,
    sent to tell them how to be
    upright,   Mic 6:8
²⁴and he is gracious to that
    person and says to God,
    'Spare them from going
    down to the pit;   Isa 38:17
    I have found a ransom for
    them —
²⁵let their flesh be renewed like
    a child's;

a 13 Or *that he does not answer for any of his actions*   *b* 18 Or *from crossing the river*
c 22 Or *to the place of the dead*

let them be restored as
    in the days of their
    youth' —   2Ki 5:14
26 then that person can pray to
    God and find favor with
    him,   Job 34:28
they will see God's face and
    shout for joy;   Job 22:26
he will restore them to full
    well-being.   Ps 50:15; 51:12
27 And they will go to others and
    say,
'I have sinned, I have
    perverted what is right,
but I did not get what I
    deserved.   Ro 6:21
28 God has delivered me from
    going down to the pit,
and I shall live to enjoy the
    light of life.'   Job 22:28

29 "God does all these things to a
    person —   Eph 1:11; Php 2:13
    twice, even three times —
30 to turn them back from the pit,
that the light of life may
    shine on them.   Ps 56:13

31 "Pay attention, Job, and listen
    to me;
be silent, and I will speak.
32 If you have anything to say,
    answer me;
speak up, for I want to
    vindicate you.
33 But if not, then listen to me;
be silent, and I will teach
    you wisdom."   Ps 34:11

34

Then Elihu said:

2 "Hear my words, you wise men;
listen to me, you men of
    learning.
3 For the ear tests words
as the tongue tastes food.
4 Let us discern for ourselves
    what is right;
let us learn together what is
    good.   1Th 5:21

5 "Job says, 'I am innocent,   Job 33:9
but God denies me justice.
6 Although I am right,
I am considered a liar;
although I am guiltless,
    his arrow inflicts an
    incurable wound.'   Job 6:4
7 Is there anyone like Job,
who drinks scorn like water?
8 He keeps company with
    evildoers;
he associates with the
    wicked.   Ps 50:18
9 For he says, 'There is no profit
in trying to please God.'

10 "So listen to me, you men of
    understanding.
Far be it from God to do evil,
from the Almighty to do
    wrong.   Dt 32:4; Job 8:3
11 He repays everyone for what
    they have done;   Ps 62:12
he brings on them what
    their conduct deserves.
12 It is unthinkable that God
    would do wrong,
that the Almighty would
    pervert justice.   Job 8:3
13 Who appointed him over the
    earth?
Who put him in charge of
    the whole world?   Job 38:4

¹⁴ If it were his intention
and he withdrew his spirit^a
and breath,   Ps 104:29
¹⁵ all humanity would perish
together
and mankind would return
to the dust. Ge 3:19; Job 9:22

¹⁶ "If you have understanding,
hear this;
listen to what I say.
¹⁷ Can someone who hates
justice govern? 2Sa 23:3-4
Will you condemn the just
and mighty One? Job 40:8
¹⁸ Is he not the One who says
to kings, 'You are
worthless,'
and to nobles, 'You are
wicked,'   Ex 22:28
¹⁹ who shows no partiality to
princes   Dt 10:17; Ac 10:34
and does not favor the rich
over the poor,
for they are all the work of
his hands?   Job 10:3
²⁰ They die in an instant, in the
middle of the night;
the people are shaken and
they pass away; Job 12:19
the mighty are removed
without human hand.

²¹ "His eyes are on the ways of
mortals;
he sees their every step.
²² There is no deep shadow, no
utter darkness, Ps 139:12
where evildoers can hide.
²³ God has no need to examine
people further,

that they should come before
him for judgment. Job 11:11
²⁴ Without inquiry he shatters
the mighty   Job 12:19
and sets up others in their
place.   Da 2:21
²⁵ Because he takes note of their
deeds,
he overthrows them in
the night and they are
crushed.   Pr 5:21-23
²⁶ He punishes them for their
wickedness
where everyone can see
them,
²⁷ because they turned from
following him   Ps 28:5
and had no regard for any of
his ways.   1Sa 15:11
²⁸ They caused the cry of the poor
to come before him,
so that he heard the cry of
the needy.   Ex 22:23; Jas 5:4
²⁹ But if he remains silent, who
can condemn him?
If he hides his face, who can
see him?
Yet he is over individual and
nation alike,
³⁰   to keep the godless from
ruling,
from laying snares for the
people.   Pr 29:2-12

³¹ "Suppose someone says to God,
'I am guilty but will offend
no more.
³² Teach me what I cannot see;
if I have done wrong, I will
not do so again.' Job 33:27

³³Should God then reward you
on your terms,
when you refuse to repent?
You must decide, not I;
so tell me what you know.

³⁴"Men of understanding declare,
wise men who hear me say
to me,
³⁵'Job speaks without
knowledge;   Job 35:16
his words lack insight.'
³⁶Oh, that Job might be tested to
the utmost
for answering like a wicked
man!   Job 22:15
³⁷To his sin he adds rebellion;
scornfully he claps his
hands among us Job 27:23
and multiplies his words
against God."   Job 23:2

35

Then Elihu said:

²"Do you think this is just?
You say, 'I am in the right,
not God.'   Job 32:2
³Yet you ask him, 'What profit
is it to me,^a
and what do I gain by not
sinning?'   Job 9:29-31; 34:9

⁴"I would like to reply to you
and to your friends with you.
⁵Look up at the heavens and see;
gaze at the clouds so high
above you.   Job 22:12
⁶If you sin, how does that affect
him?
If your sins are many, what
does that do to him?

⁷If you are righteous, what do
you give to him,   Ro 11:35
or what does he receive
from your hand? Job 22:2-3
⁸Your wickedness only affects
humans like yourself,
and your righteousness
only other people.

⁹"People cry out under a load
of oppression;   Ex 2:23
they plead for relief from the
arm of the powerful.
¹⁰But no one says, 'Where is
God my Maker,
who gives songs in the night,
¹¹who teaches us more than he
teaches^b the beasts of
the earth   Ps 94:12
and makes us wiser than^c
the birds in the sky?'
¹²He does not answer when
people cry out   Pr 1:28
because of the arrogance of
the wicked.
¹³Indeed, God does not listen to
their empty plea;
the Almighty pays no
attention to it.   Isa 1:15
¹⁴How much less, then, will he
listen
when you say that you do
not see him,   Job 9:11
that your case is before him
and you must wait for him,
¹⁵and further, that his anger
never punishes
and he does not take
the least notice of
wickedness.^d   Ps 10:11

^a 3 Or you   ^b 10,11 Or night, / ¹¹who teaches us by   ^c 11 Or us wise by   ^d 15 Symmachus,
Theodotion and Vulgate; the meaning of the Hebrew for this word is uncertain.

¹⁶So Job opens his mouth with
empty talk;
without knowledge he
multiplies words."

36 Elihu continued:

²"Bear with me a little longer
and I will show you
that there is more to be said
in God's behalf.
³I get my knowledge from afar;
I will ascribe justice to my
Maker.   Job 8:3
⁴Be assured that my words are
not false;   Job 33:3
one who has perfect
knowledge is with you.

⁵"God is mighty, but despises
no one;   Ps 22:24
he is mighty, and firm in his
purpose.   Job 12:13
⁶He does not keep the wicked
alive   Job 8:22
but gives the afflicted their
rights.   Job 5:15
⁷He does not take his eyes off
the righteous;   Ps 33:18
he enthrones them with
kings   Ps 113:8
and exalts them forever.
⁸But if people are bound in
chains,   Ps 107:10,14
held fast by cords of affliction,
⁹he tells them what they have
done —
that they have sinned
arrogantly.   Job 15:25
¹⁰He makes them listen to
correction   Job 33:16
and commands them to
repent of their evil.
¹¹If they obey and serve him,
they will spend the rest of
their days in prosperity
and their years in
contentment.
¹²But if they do not listen,
they will perish by the
sword^a   Job 15:22
and die without knowledge.

¹³"The godless in heart harbor
resentment;   Ro 2:5
even when he fetters them,
they do not cry for help.
¹⁴They die in their youth,
among male prostitutes of
the shrines.   Dt 23:17
¹⁵But those who suffer he delivers
in their suffering;
he speaks to them in their
affliction.

¹⁶"He is wooing you from the
jaws of distress   Hos 2:14
to a spacious place free
from restriction,
to the comfort of your table
laden with choice food.
¹⁷But now you are laden with
the judgment due the
wicked;
judgment and justice have
taken hold of you.   Job 22:11
¹⁸Be careful that no one entices
you by riches;
do not let a large bribe turn
you aside.   Job 34:33
¹⁹Would your wealth or even all
your mighty efforts

^a 12 Or *will cross the river*

sustain you so you would
not be in distress?
²⁰Do not long for the night,
to drag people away from
their homes.ᵃ
²¹Beware of turning to evil,
which you seem to prefer to
affliction.   Heb 11:25
²²"God is exalted in his power.
Who is a teacher like him?
²³Who has prescribed his ways
for him,   Job 34:13
or said to him, 'You have
done wrong'?
²⁴Remember to extol his work,
which people have praised
in song.   Rev 15:3
²⁵All humanity has seen it;
mortals gaze on it from afar.
²⁶How great is God — beyond
our understanding!
The number of his years is
past finding out.   Heb 1:12

²⁷"He draws up the drops of
water,
which distill as rain to the
streamsᵇ;   Job 38:28; Ps 147:8
²⁸the clouds pour down their
moisture
and abundant showers fall
on mankind.   Job 5:10
²⁹Who can understand how he
spreads out the clouds,
how he thunders from his
pavilion?   Job 37:16
³⁰See how he scatters his
lightning about him,

bathing the depths of the sea.
³¹This is the way he governsᶜ
the nations   Job 37:13
and provides food in
abundance.   Ac 14:17
³²He fills his hands with
lightning
and commands it to strike
its mark.   Job 37:12,15
³³His thunder announces the
coming storm;
even the cattle make known
its approach.ᵈ   Job 28:26

37

"At this my heart pounds
and leaps from its place.
²Listen! Listen to the roar of his
voice,   Job 32:10
to the rumbling that comes
from his mouth.   Ps 29:3-9
³He unleashes his lightning
beneath the whole
heaven
and sends it to the ends of
the earth.   Job 36:32
⁴After that comes the sound of
his roar;
he thunders with his
majestic voice.   Ex 20:19
When his voice resounds,
he holds nothing back.
⁵God's voice thunders in
marvelous ways;
he does great things beyond
our understanding.
⁶He says to the snow, 'Fall on
the earth,'   Job 38:22
and to the rain shower, 'Be a
mighty downpour.'

ᵃ 20 The meaning of the Hebrew for verses 18-20 is uncertain.   ᵇ 27 Or distill from the
mist as rain   ᶜ 31 Or nourishes   ᵈ 33 Or announces his coming — / the One zealous
against evil

⁷So that everyone he has made
    may know his work,
  he stops all people from
    their labor.^{*a*}   Job 12:14
⁸The animals take cover;
  they remain in their dens.
⁹The tempest comes out from
    its chamber,
  the cold from the driving
    winds.
¹⁰The breath of God produces ice,
  and the broad waters
    become frozen.   Job 38:29
¹¹He loads the clouds with
    moisture;
  he scatters his lightning
    through them.   Job 36:27,29
¹²At his direction they swirl
    around
  over the face of the whole
    earth
  to do whatever he
    commands them.   Ps 148:8
¹³He brings the clouds to
    punish people,   1Sa 12:17
  or to water his earth and
    show his love.   Ex 9:18

¹⁴"Listen to this, Job;   Job 32:10
  stop and consider God's
    wonders.   Job 5:9
¹⁵Do you know how God
    controls the clouds
  and makes his lightning
    flash?   Job 36:30,32
¹⁶Do you know how the clouds
    hang poised,
  those wonders of him who
    has perfect knowledge?
¹⁷You who swelter in your clothes

when the land lies hushed
    under the south wind,
¹⁸can you join him in spreading
    out the skies,   Isa 44:24
  hard as a mirror of cast
    bronze?   Dt 28:23

¹⁹"Tell us what we should say to
    him;   Ro 8:26
  we cannot draw up our
    case because of our
    darkness.
²⁰Should he be told that I want
    to speak?
  Would anyone ask to be
    swallowed up?
²¹Now no one can look at the sun,
  bright as it is in the skies
  after the wind has swept
    them clean.
²²Out of the north he comes in
    golden splendor;   Ps 19:5
  God comes in awesome
    majesty.
²³The Almighty is beyond our
    reach and exalted in
    power;   Job 9:4; 1Ti 6:16
  in his justice and great
    righteousness, he does
    not oppress.   Isa 63:9
²⁴Therefore, people revere him,
  for does he not have regard for
    all the wise in heart?^{*b*}"

The LORD Speaks

38 Then the LORD spoke to Job
    out of the storm. He said:

²"Who is this that obscures my
    plans

---

^{*a*} 7 Or *work, / he fills all people with fear by his power
for any who think they are wise.*   ^{*b*} 24 Or *for he does not have regard*

with words without
knowledge?   1Ti 1:7
³Brace yourself like a man;
    I will question you,
    and you shall answer me.

⁴"Where were you when I laid
    the earth's foundation?
    Tell me, if you understand.
⁵Who marked off its
    dimensions? Surely you
    know!   Pr 8:29; Isa 40:12
    Who stretched a measuring
    line across it?
⁶On what were its footings set,
    or who laid its cornerstone —
⁷while the morning stars sang
    together
    and all the angelsᵃ shouted
    for joy?

⁸"Who shut up the sea behind
    doors   Jer 5:22
    when it burst forth from the
    womb,   Ge 1:9-10
⁹when I made the clouds its
    garment
    and wrapped it in thick
    darkness,
¹⁰when I fixed limits for it   Ps 33:7
    and set its doors and bars in
    place,   Job 26:10
¹¹when I said, 'This far you may
    come and no farther;
    here is where your proud
    waves halt'?   Ps 89:9

¹²"Have you ever given orders to
    the morning,
    or shown the dawn its
    place,

¹³that it might take the earth by
    the edges
    and shake the wicked out
    of it?   Ps 104:35
¹⁴The earth takes shape like
    clay under a seal;
    its features stand out like
    those of a garment.
¹⁵The wicked are denied their
    light,   Job 18:5
    and their upraised arm is
    broken.   Ps 10:15

¹⁶"Have you journeyed to the
    springs of the sea
    or walked in the recesses of
    the deep?   Ps 77:19
¹⁷Have the gates of death been
    shown to you?   Ps 9:13
    Have you seen the gates of
    the deepest darkness?
¹⁸Have you comprehended the
    vast expanses of the
    earth?   Job 28:24
    Tell me, if you know all this.

¹⁹"What is the way to the abode
    of light?
    And where does darkness
    reside?
²⁰Can you take them to their
    places?
    Do you know the paths to
    their dwellings?   Job 26:10
²¹Surely you know, for you were
    already born!   Job 15:7
    You have lived so many
    years!
²²"Have you entered the
    storehouses of the snow

ᵃ 7 Hebrew *the sons of God*

or seen the storehouses of
the hail,
²³which I reserve for times of
trouble,   Isa 30:30; Eze 13:11
for days of war and battle?
²⁴What is the way to the place
where the lightning is
dispersed,
or the place where the east
winds are scattered
over the earth?
²⁵Who cuts a channel for the
torrents of rain,
and a path for the
thunderstorm,   Job 28:26
²⁶to water a land where no one
lives,   Job 36:27
an uninhabited desert,
²⁷to satisfy a desolate wasteland
and make it sprout with
grass?   Ps 104:14
²⁸Does the rain have a father?
Who fathers the drops of
dew?
²⁹From whose womb comes the
ice?
Who gives birth to the frost
from the heavens Ps 147:16
³⁰when the waters become hard
as stone,
when the surface of the
deep is frozen?   Job 37:10

³¹ "Can you bind the chainsᵃ of
the Pleiades?
Can you loosen Orion's belt?
³²Can you bring forth the
constellations in their
seasonsᵇ

or lead out the Bearᶜ with its
cubs?
³³Do you know the laws of the
heavens?   Ps 148:6; Jer 31:36
Can you set up God'sᵈ
dominion over the
earth?
³⁴ "Can you raise your voice to
the clouds
and cover yourself with a
flood of water?   Job 22:11
³⁵Do you send the lightning
bolts on their way?
Do they report to you, 'Here
we are'?
³⁶Who gives the ibis wisdomᵉ
or gives the rooster
understanding?ᶠ Job 32:8
³⁷Who has the wisdom to count
the clouds?
Who can tip over the water
jars of the heavens Jos 3:16
³⁸when the dust becomes hard
and the clods of earth stick
together?   1Ki 18:45

³⁹ "Do you hunt the prey for the
lioness
and satisfy the hunger of
the lions   Ps 104:21
⁴⁰when they crouch in their
dens
or lie in wait in a thicket?
⁴¹Who provides food for the
raven   Lk 12:24
when its young cry out to
God
and wander about for lack
of food?   Ps 147:9; Mt 6:26

ᵃ 31 Septuagint; Hebrew *beauty*   ᵇ 32 Or *the morning star in its season*   ᶜ 32 Or *out Leo*
ᵈ 33 Or *their*   ᵉ 36 That is, wisdom about the flooding of the Nile   ᶠ 36 That is,
understanding of when to crow; the meaning of the Hebrew for this verse is uncertain.

39

¹"Do you know when the mountain goats give birth?　Dt 14:5
Do you watch when the doe bears her fawn?
²Do you count the months till they bear?
Do you know the time they give birth?
³They crouch down and bring forth their young;
their labor pains are ended.
⁴Their young thrive and grow strong in the wilds;
they leave and do not return.

⁵"Who let the wild donkey go free?　Job 6:5
Who untied its ropes?
⁶I gave it the wasteland as its home,　Job 24:5; Jer 2:24
the salt flats as its habitat.
⁷It laughs at the commotion in the town;
it does not hear a driver's shout.　Job 3:18
⁸It ranges the hills for its pasture and searches for any green thing.

⁹"Will the wild ox consent to serve you?　Nu 23:22; Dt 33:17
Will it stay by your manger at night?
¹⁰Can you hold it to the furrow with a harness?
Will it till the valleys behind you?
¹¹Will you rely on it for its great strength?　Ps 147:10
Will you leave your heavy work to it?

¹²Can you trust it to haul in your grain
and bring it to your threshing floor?

¹³"The wings of the ostrich flap joyfully,
though they cannot compare with the wings and feathers of the stork.　Zec 5:9
¹⁴She lays her eggs on the ground and lets them warm in the sand,
¹⁵unmindful that a foot may crush them,
that some wild animal may trample them.
¹⁶She treats her young harshly, as if they were not hers;
she cares not that her labor was in vain,
¹⁷for God did not endow her with wisdom
or give her a share of good sense.　Job 35:11
¹⁸Yet when she spreads her feathers to run,
she laughs at horse and rider.

¹⁹"Do you give the horse its strength
or clothe its neck with a flowing mane?
²⁰Do you make it leap like a locust,　Joel 2:4-5
striking terror with its proud snorting?　Jer 8:16
²¹It paws fiercely, rejoicing in its strength,
and charges into the fray.
²²It laughs at fear, afraid of nothing;

it does not shy away from
the sword.
23 The quiver rattles against its
side,
along with the flashing
spear and lance.
24 In frenzied excitement it eats
up the ground;
it cannot stand still when
the trumpet sounds.
25 At the blast of the trumpet it
snorts, 'Aha!'   Jos 6:5
It catches the scent of battle
from afar,
the shout of commanders
and the battle cry.
26 "Does the hawk take flight by
your wisdom
and spread its wings toward
the south?
27 Does the eagle soar at your
command
and build its nest on high?
28 It dwells on a cliff and stays
there at night;
a rocky crag is its
stronghold.
29 From there it looks for food;
its eyes detect it from afar.
30 Its young ones feast on blood,
and where the slain are,
there it is."   Mt 24:28

40 The LORD said to Job:

2 "Will the one who contends
with the Almighty
correct him?   Job 9:15
Let him who accuses God
answer him!"   Job 9:3

3 Then Job answered the LORD:

4 "I am unworthy — how can I
reply to you?   Job 42:6
I put my hand over my
mouth.   Job 29:9
5 I spoke once, but I have no
answer —   Job 9:3
twice, but I will say no more."

6 Then the LORD spoke to Job
out of the storm: Job 38:1

7 "Brace yourself like a man;
I will question you,
and you shall answer me.

8 "Would you discredit my
justice?   Ro 3:3
Would you condemn me to
justify yourself?
9 Do you have an arm like God's,
and can your voice thunder
like his?   Job 37:5; Ps 29:3-4
10 Then adorn yourself with
glory and splendor,
and clothe yourself in honor
and majesty.   Ps 93:1; 104:1
11 Unleash the fury of your wrath,
look at all who are proud
and bring them low,
12 look at all who are proud and
humble them,   1Sa 2:7
crush the wicked where
they stand.   Isa 13:11; 63:2-3,6
13 Bury them all in the dust
together;
shroud their faces in the
grave.
14 Then I myself will admit to
you
that your own right hand
can save you.   Ps 20:6

¹⁵ "Look at Behemoth,
which I made along with you
and which feeds on grass
like an ox. *Isa 11:7*
¹⁶ What strength it has in its
loins, *Job 39:11*
what power in the muscles
of its belly! *Job 41:9*
¹⁷ Its tail sways like a cedar;
the sinews of its thighs are
close-knit.
¹⁸ Its bones are tubes of bronze,
its limbs like rods of iron.
¹⁹ It ranks first among the works
of God, *Job 41:33*
yet its Maker can approach
it with his sword.
²⁰ The hills bring it their produce,
and all the wild animals
play nearby. *Ps 104:26*
²¹ Under the lotus plants it lies,
hidden among the reeds in
the marsh.
²² The lotuses conceal it in their
shadow;
the poplars by the stream
surround it. *Isa 44:4*
²³ A raging river does not
alarm it; *Isa 8:7*
it is secure, though the
Jordan should surge
against its mouth. *Jos 3:1*
²⁴ Can anyone capture it by the
eyes,
or trap it and pierce its nose?

41 ^a "Can you pull in
Leviathan with a
fishhook *Ps 104:26; Isa 27:1*

or tie down its tongue with
a rope?
² Can you put a cord through its
nose
or pierce its jaw with a
hook? *Isa 37:29*
³ Will it keep begging you for
mercy?
Will it speak to you with
gentle words?
⁴ Will it make an agreement
with you
for you to take it as your
slave for life? *Ex 21:6*
⁵ Can you make a pet of it like a
bird
or put it on a leash for the
young women in your
house?
⁶ Will traders barter for it?
Will they divide it up among
the merchants?
⁷ Can you fill its hide with
harpoons
or its head with fishing
spears? *Job 40:24*
⁸ If you lay a hand on it,
you will remember the
struggle and never do it
again! *Job 3:8*
⁹ Any hope of subduing it is
false;
the mere sight of it is
overpowering. *Job 40:16*
¹⁰ No one is fierce enough to
rouse it. *Job 3:8*
Who then is able to stand
against me? *Jer 50:44*
¹¹ Who has a claim against me
that I must pay? *Ro 11:35*

^a In Hebrew texts 41:1-8 is numbered 40:25-32, and 41:9-34 is numbered 41:1-26.

Everything under heaven
   belongs to me.   Ex 19:5

¹² "I will not fail to speak of
   Leviathan's limbs,
   its strength and its graceful
      form.   Job 39:11

¹³ Who can strip off its outer
      coat?
   Who can penetrate its
      double coat of armor*a*?

¹⁴ Who dares open the doors of
      its mouth,   Ps 22:13
   ringed about with fearsome
      teeth?

¹⁵ Its back has*b* rows of shields
   tightly sealed together;

¹⁶ each is so close to the next
   that no air can pass
      between.

¹⁷ They are joined fast to one
      another;
   they cling together and
      cannot be parted.

¹⁸ Its snorting throws out flashes
      of light;
   its eyes are like the rays of
      dawn.   Job 3:9

¹⁹ Flames stream from its mouth;
   sparks of fire shoot out.

²⁰ Smoke pours from its nostrils
   as from a boiling pot over
      burning reeds.

²¹ Its breath sets coals ablaze,
   and flames dart from its
      mouth.   Ps 18:8

²² Strength resides in its neck;
   dismay goes before it.

²³ The folds of its flesh are
   tightly joined;

   they are firm and
      immovable.

²⁴ Its chest is hard as rock,
   hard as a lower millstone.

²⁵ When it rises up, the mighty
      are terrified;   Job 39:20
   they retreat before its
      thrashing.   Job 3:8

²⁶ The sword that reaches it has
      no effect,
   nor does the spear or the
      dart or the javelin.   Jos 8:18

²⁷ Iron it treats like straw
   and bronze like rotten wood.

²⁸ Arrows do not make it flee;
   slingstones are like chaff
      to it.

²⁹ A club seems to it but a piece
      of straw;
   it laughs at the rattling of
      the lance.   Job 5:22

³⁰ Its undersides are jagged
      potsherds,
   leaving a trail in the mud
      like a threshing sledge.

³¹ It makes the depths churn
      like a boiling caldron
   and stirs up the sea like a
      pot of ointment.   Eze 32:2

³² It leaves a glistening wake
      behind it;
   one would think the deep
      had white hair.

³³ Nothing on earth is its
      equal —   Job 40:19
   a creature without fear.

³⁴ It looks down on all that are
      haughty;
   it is king over all that are
      proud."   Job 28:8

---

a 13 Septuagint; Hebrew *double bridle*   *b* 15 Or *Its pride is its*

Job

42

Then Job replied to the LORD:

[2] "I know that you can do all
things; Ge 18:14; Mt 19:26
no purpose of yours can be
thwarted. 2Ch 20:6
[3] You asked, 'Who is this that
obscures my plans
without knowledge?'
Surely I spoke of things I did
not understand,
things too wonderful for me
to know. Ps 40:5
[4] "You said, 'Listen now, and I
will speak;
I will question you,
and you shall answer me.'
[5] My ears had heard of you
but now my eyes have seen
you. Jdg 13:22; Isa 6:5
[6] Therefore I despise myself
and repent in dust and ashes."

Epilogue

[7] After the LORD had said these
things to Job, he said to Eliphaz
the Temanite, "I am angry with
you and your two friends, because you have not spoken the
truth about me, as my servant
Job has. [8] So now take seven bulls
and seven rams and go to my servant Job and sacrifice a burnt offering for yourselves. My servant
Job will pray for you, and I will
accept his prayer and not deal
with you according to your folly. You have not spoken the truth
about me, as my servant Job has."
[9] So Eliphaz the Temanite, Bildad
the Shuhite and Zophar the Naamathite did what the LORD told
them; and the LORD accepted
Job's prayer. Job 22:30; Jas 5:15-16
[10] After Job had prayed for his
friends, the LORD restored his
fortunes and gave him twice as
much as he had before. [11] All his
brothers and sisters and everyone who had known him before
came and ate with him in his
house. They comforted and consoled him over all the trouble the
LORD had brought on him, and
each one gave him a piece of silver[a] and a gold ring. Dt 30:3; Ps 14:7
[12] The LORD blessed the lat-
ter part of Job's life more than
the former part. He had fourteen
thousand sheep, six thousand
camels, a thousand yoke of oxen
and a thousand donkeys. [13] And
he also had seven sons and three
daughters. [14] The first daughter
he named Jemimah, the second
Keziah and the third Keren-Hap-
puch. [15] Nowhere in all the land
were there found women as beautiful as Job's daughters, and their
father granted them an inheritance along with their brothers.
[16] After this, Job lived a hundred and forty years; he saw his
children and their children to
the fourth generation. [17] And so
Job died, an old man and full of
years. Ge 25:8

---

[a] 11 Hebrew *him a kesitah*; a kesitah was a unit of money of unknown weight and value.

Psalms

BOOK I

Psalms 1–41

Psalm 1

¹Blessed is the one
who does not walk in step
with the wicked   Pr 4:14
or stand in the way that
sinners take
or sit in the company of
mockers,   Ps 26:4; Jer 15:17
²but whose delight is in the law
of the LORD,   Ps 119:16,35
and who meditates on his
law day and night.   Jos 1:8
³That person is like a tree
planted by streams of
water,   Jer 17:8
which yields its fruit in
season
and whose leaf does not
wither —
whatever they do prospers.

⁴Not so the wicked!
They are like chaff
that the wind blows away.
⁵Therefore the wicked will not
stand in the judgment,
nor sinners in the assembly
of the righteous.

⁶For the LORD watches over the
way of the righteous,
but the way of the wicked
leads to destruction.

Psalm 2

¹Why do the nations conspire*ᵃ*
and the peoples plot in vain?
²The kings of the earth rise up
and the rulers band together
against the LORD and
against his anointed,
saying,   Jn 1:41; Ac 4:25-26
³"Let us break their chains
and throw off their shackles."

⁴The One enthroned in heaven
laughs;
the Lord scoffs at them.
⁵He rebukes them in his anger
and terrifies them in his
wrath, saying,

ᵃ 1 Hebrew; Septuagint *rage*

6 "I have installed my king
on Zion, my holy mountain."

7 I will proclaim the LORD's decree:

He said to me, "You are my son;
today I have become your
father.   Ac 13:33
8 Ask me,
and I will make the nations
your inheritance,
the ends of the earth your
possession.   Ps 22:27
9 You will break them with a
rod of iron[a];
you will dash them to pieces
like pottery."   Ps 89:23

10 Therefore, you kings, be wise;
be warned, you rulers of the
earth.
11 Serve the LORD with fear
and celebrate his rule with
trembling.   Heb 12:28
12 Kiss his son, or he will be angry
and your way will lead to
your destruction,
for his wrath can flare up in a
moment.   Rev 6:16
Blessed are all who take
refuge in him.   Ps 34:8

Psalm 3[b]

A psalm of David. When he fled
from his son Absalom.

1 LORD, how many are my foes!
How many rise up
against me!

2 Many are saying of me,
"God will not deliver him."[c]

3 But you, LORD, are a shield
around me,   Ge 15:1; Ps 28:7
my glory, the One who lifts
my head high.   Ps 27:6
4 I call out to the LORD,
and he answers me from his
holy mountain.
5 I lie down and sleep;   Lev 26:6
I wake again, because the
LORD sustains me.
6 I will not fear though tens of
thousands
assail me on every side. Ps 27:3

7 Arise, LORD!
Deliver me, my God!
Strike all my enemies on the
jaw;
break the teeth of the wicked.
8 From the LORD comes
deliverance.   Isa 43:3,11
May your blessing be on
your people.

Psalm 4[d]

For the director of music.
With stringed instruments.
A psalm of David.

1 Answer me when I call to you,
my righteous God.
Give me relief from my distress;
have mercy on me and hear
my prayer.   Ps 17:6
2 How long will you people turn
my glory into shame?

---

[a] 9 Or *will rule them with an iron scepter* (see Septuagint and Syriac)   [b] In Hebrew texts
3:1-8 is numbered 3:2-9.   [c] 2 The Hebrew has *Selah* (a word of uncertain meaning) here
and at the end of verses 4 and 8.   [d] In Hebrew texts 4:1-8 is numbered 4:2-9.

How long will you love
delusions and seek false
gods[a]?[b]
3 Know that the Lord has
set apart his faithful
servant for himself;
the Lord hears when I call
to him.   Ps 6:8

4 Tremble and[c] do not sin;
when you are on your
beds,   Ps 77:6
search your hearts and be
silent.
5 Offer the sacrifices of the
righteous
and trust in the Lord. Dt 33:19

6 Many, Lord, are asking,
"Who will bring us
prosperity?"
Let the light of your face
shine on us.   Nu 6:25
7 Fill my heart with joy   Isa 9:3
when their grain and new
wine abound.
8 In peace I will lie down and
sleep,   Ps 3:5
for you alone, Lord,
make me dwell in safety.

Psalm 5[d]

For the director of music. For pipes.
A psalm of David.

1 Listen to my words, Lord,
consider my lament.
2 Hear my cry for help,   Ps 3:4
my King and my God,   Ps 84:3
for to you I pray.

3 In the morning, Lord, you
hear my voice;
in the morning I lay my
requests before you
and wait expectantly.
4 For you are not a God
who is pleased with
wickedness;
with you, evil people are not
welcome.   Ps 11:5; 92:15
5 The arrogant cannot stand
in your presence.   Ps 1:5; 73:3
You hate all who do wrong;
6   you destroy those who tell
lies.   Ps 55:23
The bloodthirsty and deceitful
you, Lord, detest.
7 But I, by your great love,
can come into your house;
in reverence I bow down
toward your holy temple.

8 Lead me, Lord, in your
righteousness   Ps 31:1
because of my enemies—
make your way straight
before me.   Ps 27:11
9 Not a word from their mouth
can be trusted;
their heart is filled with
malice.
Their throat is an open grave;
with their tongues they tell
lies.   Ro 3:13
10 Declare them guilty, O God!
Let their intrigues be their
downfall.
Banish them for their many
sins,   Ps 9:16

---

[a] 2 Or seek lies   [b] 2 The Hebrew has Selah (a word of uncertain meaning) here and at
the end of verse 4.   [c] 4 Or In your anger (see Septuagint)   [d] In Hebrew texts 5:1-12 is
numbered 5:2-13.

for they have rebelled
against you.   Ps 107:11
[11] But let all who take refuge in
you be glad;
let them ever sing for joy.
Spread your protection over
them,
that those who love your
name may rejoice in you.

[12] Surely, LORD, you bless the
righteous;
you surround them with your
favor as with a shield.

Psalm 6[a]

For the director of music. With
stringed instruments. According to
sheminith.[b] A psalm of David.

[1] LORD, do not rebuke me in
your anger   Ps 38:1
or discipline me in your
wrath.
[2] Have mercy on me, LORD, for I
am faint;
heal me, LORD, for my bones
are in agony.   Ps 22:14
[3] My soul is in deep anguish.
How long, LORD, how long?

[4] Turn, LORD, and deliver me;
save me because of your
unfailing love.   Ps 17:13
[5] Among the dead no one
proclaims your name.
Who praises you from the
grave?   Ps 30:9; Isa 38:18
[6] I am worn out from my
groaning.

All night long I flood my bed
with weeping
and drench my couch with
tears.   Ps 42:3
[7] My eyes grow weak with
sorrow;   Ps 31:9
they fail because of all my
foes.

[8] Away from me, all you who do
evil,   Ps 119:115
for the LORD has heard my
weeping.
[9] The LORD has heard my cry
for mercy;   Ps 116:1
the LORD accepts my prayer.
[10] All my enemies will be
overwhelmed with
shame and anguish;
they will turn back and
suddenly be put to
shame.   Ps 71:24; 73:19

Psalm 7[c]

A *shiggaion*[d] of David, which he
sang to the LORD concerning Cush,
a Benjamite.

[1] LORD my God, I take refuge in
you;
save and deliver me from all
who pursue me,   Ps 31:15
[2] or they will tear me apart like
a lion
and rip me to pieces with no
one to rescue me.

[3] LORD my God, if I have done this
and there is guilt on my
hands—   1Sa 24:11; Isa 59:3
[4] if I have repaid my ally with evil

---

[a] In Hebrew texts 6:1-10 is numbered 6:2-11.   [b] Title: Probably a musical term
[c] In Hebrew texts 7:1-17 is numbered 7:2-18.   [d] Title: Probably a literary or musical term

or without cause have
   robbed my foe —
[5] then let my enemy pursue and
   overtake me;
let him trample my life to
   the ground
and make me sleep in the
   dust.[a]

[6] Arise, LORD, in your anger;
rise up against the rage of
   my enemies.
Awake, my God; decree
   justice.   Ps 44:23
[7] Let the assembled peoples
   gather around you,
while you sit enthroned
   over them on high.
[8]   Let the LORD judge the
   peoples.
Vindicate me, LORD, according
   to my righteousness,
according to my integrity,
   O Most High.
[9] Bring to an end the violence of
   the wicked
and make the righteous
   secure —
you, the righteous God   Jer 11:20
who probes minds and
   hearts.   Rev 2:23

[10] My shield[b] is God Most High,
who saves the upright in
   heart.   Ps 125:4
[11] God is a righteous judge,
a God who displays his
   wrath every day.
[12] If he does not relent,
he[c] will sharpen his sword;

he will bend and string his
   bow.
[13] He has prepared his deadly
   weapons;
he makes ready his flaming
   arrows.

[14] Whoever is pregnant with evil
conceives trouble and gives
   birth to disillusionment.
[15] Whoever digs a hole and
   scoops it out
falls into the pit they have
   made.   Job 4:8
[16] The trouble they cause recoils
   on them;
their violence comes down
   on their own heads.

[17] I will give thanks to the
   LORD because of his
   righteousness;   Ps 71:15-16
I will sing the praises of the
   name of the LORD Most
   High.

Psalm 8[d]

For the director of music. According
to *gittith.*[e] A psalm of David.

[1] LORD, our Lord,
how majestic is your name
   in all the earth!   1Ch 16:10

You have set your glory
   in the heavens.   Ps 113:4; 148:13
[2] Through the praise of
   children and infants
you have established a
   stronghold against your
   enemies,   Mt 21:16

---

[a] 5   The Hebrew has *Selah* (a word of uncertain meaning) here.   [b] 10   Or *sovereign*
[c] 12   Or *If anyone does not repent, / God*   [d] In Hebrew texts 8:1-9 is numbered 8:2-10.
[e] Title: Probably a musical term

to silence the foe and the
avenger.   Ps 44:16
³When I consider your heavens,
the work of your fingers,
the moon and the stars,
which you have set in place,
⁴what is mankind that you are
mindful of them,
human beings that you care
for them?^a   Job 7:17

⁵You have made them^b a little
lower than the angels^c
and crowned them^b with
glory and honor.   Ps 21:5
⁶You made them rulers over the
works of your hands;
you put everything under
their^d feet: Heb 2:6-8
⁷all flocks and herds,
and the animals of the wild,
⁸the birds in the sky,
and the fish in the sea,
all that swim the paths of
the seas.   Ge 1:26

⁹LORD, our Lord,
how majestic is your name
in all the earth!   ver 1

Psalm 9^{e,f}

For the director of music.
To the tune of "The Death of the Son."
A psalm of David.

¹I will give thanks to you,
LORD, with all my heart;
I will tell of all your
wonderful deeds.

²I will be glad and rejoice in
you;   Ps 5:11
I will sing the praises of
your name, O Most
High.   Ps 83:18

³My enemies turn back;
they stumble and perish
before you.
⁴For you have upheld my right
and my cause,   Ps 140:12
sitting enthroned as the
righteous judge.   1Pe 2:23
⁵You have rebuked the nations
and destroyed the
wicked;
you have blotted out their
name for ever and ever.
⁶Endless ruin has overtaken
my enemies,
you have uprooted their
cities;
even the memory of them
has perished.   Ps 34:16
⁷The LORD reigns forever;
he has established his
throne for judgment.
⁸He rules the world in
righteousness   Ps 96:13
and judges the peoples with
equity.
⁹The LORD is a refuge for the
oppressed,
a stronghold in times of
trouble.   Ps 32:7
¹⁰Those who know your name
trust in you,   Ps 91:14

---

^a 4 Or *what is a human being that you are mindful of him, / a son of man that you care for him?*   ^b 5 Or *him*   ^c 5 Or *than God*   ^d 6 Or *made him ruler . . . ; / . . . his*   ^e Psalms 9 and 10 may originally have been a single acrostic poem in which alternating lines began with the successive letters of the Hebrew alphabet. In the Septuagint they constitute one psalm.   ^f In Hebrew texts 9:1-20 is numbered 9:2-21.

for you, LORD, have never
    forsaken those who
    seek you.

[11] Sing the praises of the LORD,
    enthroned in Zion;
    proclaim among the nations
    what he has done. Ps 105:1
[12] For he who avenges blood
    remembers; Ge 9:5
    he does not ignore the cries
    of the afflicted.

[13] LORD, see how my enemies
    persecute me! Ps 38:19
    Have mercy and lift me up
    from the gates of death,
[14] that I may declare your
    praises Ps 106:2
    in the gates of Daughter
    Zion,
    and there rejoice in your
    salvation. Ps 13:5

[15] The nations have fallen into
    the pit they have dug;
    their feet are caught in the
    net they have hidden.
[16] The LORD is known by his acts
    of justice;
    the wicked are ensnared
    by the work of their
    hands.[a]
[17] The wicked go down to the
    realm of the dead,
    all the nations that forget
    God. Job 8:13
[18] But God will never forget the
    needy;

the hope of the afflicted will
    never perish. Pr 23:18

[19] Arise, LORD, do not let mortals
    triumph;
    let the nations be judged in
    your presence. Ps 110:6
[20] Strike them with terror, LORD;
    let the nations know they
    are only mortal.

Psalm 10[b]

[1] Why, LORD, do you stand far
    off? Ps 22:1,11
    Why do you hide yourself in
    times of trouble? Ps 13:1

[2] In his arrogance the wicked
    man hunts down the
    weak,
    who are caught in the
    schemes he devises.
[3] He boasts about the cravings
    of his heart; Ps 94:4
    he blesses the greedy and
    reviles the LORD.
[4] In his pride the wicked man
    does not seek him;
    in all his thoughts there is
    no room for God. Ps 14:1
[5] His ways are always
    prosperous;
    your laws are rejected by[c]
    him;
    he sneers at all his enemies.
[6] He says to himself, "Nothing
    will ever shake me."

---

[a] 16 The Hebrew has *Higgaion* and *Selah* (words of uncertain meaning) here; *Selah* occurs
also at the end of verse 20.   [b] Psalms 9 and 10 may originally have been a single acrostic
poem in which alternating lines began with the successive letters of the Hebrew alphabet. In
the Septuagint they constitute one psalm.   [c] 5 See Septuagint; Hebrew / *they are haughty,
and your laws are far from*

He swears, "No one will ever
do me harm." Rev 18:7

⁷His mouth is full of lies and
threats; Ro 3:14
trouble and evil are under
his tongue.
⁸He lies in wait near the villages;
from ambush he murders
the innocent. Ps 94:6
His eyes watch in secret for
his victims;
⁹ like a lion in cover he lies in
wait.
He lies in wait to catch the
helpless; Ps 17:12
he catches the helpless and
drags them off in his net.
¹⁰His victims are crushed, they
collapse;
they fall under his strength.
¹¹He says to himself, "God will
never notice; Job 22:13
he covers his face and never
sees."

¹²Arise, LORD! Lift up your
hand, O God. Mic 5:9
Do not forget the helpless.
¹³Why does the wicked man
revile God?
Why does he say to himself,
"He won't call me to
account"?
¹⁴But you, God, see the trouble
of the afflicted; Ps 22:11
you consider their grief and
take it in hand.
The victims commit
themselves to you;
you are the helper of the
fatherless. Ps 68:5

¹⁵Break the arm of the wicked
man; Ps 37:17
call the evildoer to account
for his wickedness
that would not otherwise be
found out.

¹⁶The LORD is King for ever and
ever; Ps 29:10
the nations will perish from
his land. Dt 8:20
¹⁷You, LORD, hear the desire of
the afflicted;
you encourage them, and
you listen to their cry,
¹⁸defending the fatherless and
the oppressed, Ps 9:9; 82:3
so that mere earthly mortals
will never again strike terror.

Psalm 11

For the director of music. Of David.

¹In the LORD I take refuge. Ps 56:11
How then can you say to me:
"Flee like a bird to your
mountain.
²For look, the wicked bend
their bows;
they set their arrows against
the strings Ps 7:13
to shoot from the shadows
at the upright in heart. Ps 64:3-4
³When the foundations are
being destroyed, Ps 82:5
what can the righteous do?"

⁴The LORD is in his holy temple;
the LORD is on his heavenly
throne.
He observes everyone on
earth;

his eyes examine them.
⁵The LORD examines the
righteous,   Ge 22:1
but the wicked, those who
love violence,
he hates with a passion. Ps 5:5
⁶On the wicked he will rain
fiery coals and burning
sulfur;   Eze 38:22
a scorching wind will be
their lot.   Jer 4:11-12

⁷For the LORD is righteous,
he loves justice;
the upright will see his face.

Psalm 12 *ᵃ*

For the director of music. According
to *sheminith.ᵇ* A psalm of David.

¹Help, LORD, for no one is
faithful anymore; Isa 57:1
those who are loyal have
vanished from the
human race.
²Everyone lies to their
neighbor;
they flatter with their lips
but harbor deception in
their hearts.   Ps 10:7
³May the LORD silence all
flattering lips
and every boastful tongue —
⁴those who say,
"By our tongues we will
prevail;
our own lips will defend
us — who is lord
over us?"

⁵"Because the poor are
plundered and the
needy groan,
I will now arise," says the
LORD.
"I will protect them from
those who malign them."
⁶And the words of the LORD are
flawless,   2Sa 22:31; Ps 18:30
like silver purified in a
crucible,
like goldᶜ refined seven
times.

⁷You, LORD, will keep the
needy safe
and will protect us forever
from the wicked, Ps 37:28
⁸who freely strut about
when what is vile is honored
by the human race.

Psalm 13 *ᵈ*

For the director of music.
A psalm of David.

¹How long, LORD? Will you
forget me forever?
How long will you hide your
face from me?   Job 13:24
²How long must I wrestle with
my thoughts   Ps 42:4
and day after day have
sorrow in my heart?
How long will my enemy
triumph over me? Ps 42:9

³Look on me and answer, LORD
my God.

ᵃ In Hebrew texts 12:1-8 is numbered 12:2-9.   ᵇ Title: Probably a musical term
ᶜ 6 Probable reading of the original Hebrew text; Masoretic Text *earth*   ᵈ In Hebrew texts
13:1-6 is numbered 13:2-6.

Give light to my eyes, or I
will sleep in death, *Ezr 9:8*
⁴and my enemy will say, "I
have overcome him,"
and my foes will rejoice
when I fall.

⁵But I trust in your unfailing
love;
my heart rejoices in your
salvation. *Ps 9:14*
⁶I will sing the LORD's praise,
for he has been good to me.

Psalm 14

14:1-7pp — Ps 53:1-6

For the director of music. Of David.

¹The fool[a] says in his heart,
"There is no God." *Ps 10:4*
They are corrupt, their deeds
are vile;
there is no one who does
good.
²The LORD looks down from
heaven *Ps 33:13*
on all mankind
to see if there are any who
understand, *Ps 92:6*
any who seek God.
³All have turned away, all have
become corrupt; *Ps 58:3*
there is no one who does
good,
not even one. *Ro 3:10-12*
⁴Do all these evildoers know
nothing?

They devour my people as
though eating bread;

they never call on the LORD.
⁵But there they are,
overwhelmed with
dread,
for God is present in
the company of the
righteous.
⁶You evildoers frustrate the
plans of the poor,
but the LORD is their refuge.
⁷Oh, that salvation for Israel
would come out of Zion!
When the LORD restores his
people, *Ps 53:6*
let Jacob rejoice and Israel
be glad!

Psalm 15

A psalm of David.

¹LORD, who may dwell in your
sacred tent? *Ps 27:5-6*
Who may live on your holy
mountain? *Ps 24:3-5*
²The one whose walk is
blameless,
who does what is righteous,
who speaks the truth from
their heart; *Eph 4:25*
³whose tongue utters no slander,
who does no wrong to a
neighbor,
and casts no slur on others;
⁴who despises a vile person
but honors those who fear
the LORD; *Ac 28:10*
who keeps an oath even when
it hurts,

---

[a] 1 The Hebrew words rendered *fool* in Psalms denote one who is morally deficient.

and does not change their
mind;
⁵who lends money to the poor
without interest; Ex 22:25
who does not accept a bribe
against the innocent.

Whoever does these things
will never be shaken. 2Pe 1:10

Psalm 16

A *miktam*[a] of David.

¹Keep me safe, my God,
for in you I take refuge. Ps 7:1

²I say to the LORD, "You are my
Lord;
apart from you I have no
good thing." Ps 73:25
³I say of the holy people who
are in the land,
"They are the noble ones in
whom is all my delight."
⁴Those who run after other
gods will suffer more
and more. Ps 32:10
I will not pour out libations
of blood to such gods
or take up their names on
my lips. Ex 23:13

⁵LORD, you alone are my
portion and my cup;
you make my lot secure.
⁶The boundary lines have
fallen for me in pleasant
places;
surely I have a delightful
inheritance. Ps 78:55
⁷I will praise the LORD, who
counsels me; Ps 73:24

even at night my heart
instructs me.
⁸I keep my eyes always on the
LORD.
With him at my right hand,
I will not be shaken.

⁹Therefore my heart is glad
and my tongue rejoices;
my body also will rest
secure,
¹⁰because you will not abandon
me to the realm of the
dead,
nor will you let your
faithful[b] one see decay.
¹¹You make known to me the
path of life; Mt 7:14
you will fill me with joy in
your presence, Ac 2:25-28
with eternal pleasures at
your right hand.

Psalm 17

A prayer of David.

¹Hear me, LORD, my plea is
just;
listen to my cry. Ps 61:1
Hear my prayer —
it does not rise from
deceitful lips. Isa 29:13
²Let my vindication come from
you;
may your eyes see what is
right.
³Though you probe my heart,
though you examine me at
night and test me,

---

a Title: Probably a literary or musical term   *b* 10 Or *holy*

you will find that I have
  planned no evil;   Job 23:10
my mouth has not
  transgressed.
[4] Though people tried to
  bribe me,
I have kept myself from the
  ways of the violent
through what your lips have
  commanded.
[5] My steps have held to your
  paths;   Ps 44:18
my feet have not stumbled.

[6] I call on you, my God, for you
  will answer me;   Ps 86:7
turn your ear to me and
  hear my prayer.   Ps 116:2
[7] Show me the wonders of your
  great love,   Ps 31:21
you who save by your right
  hand
those who take refuge in
  you from their foes.
[8] Keep me as the apple of your
  eye;   Dt 32:10
hide me in the shadow of
  your wings
[9] from the wicked who are out
  to destroy me,
from my mortal enemies
  who surround me.

[10] They close up their callous
  hearts,
  Ps 73:7
and their mouths speak
  with arrogance.   1Sa 2:3
[11] They have tracked me down,
  they now surround me,
with eyes alert, to throw me
  to the ground.

[12] They are like a lion hungry for
  prey,   Ps 7:2
like a fierce lion crouching
  in cover.

[13] Rise up, LORD, confront them,
  bring them down;   Ps 73:18
with your sword rescue me
  from the wicked.
[14] By your hand save me from
  such people, LORD,
from those of this world
  whose reward is in this
  life.   Lk 16:8
May what you have stored up
  for the wicked fill their
  bellies;
may their children gorge
  themselves on it,
and may there be leftovers
  for their little ones.

[15] As for me, I will be vindicated
  and will see your face;
when I awake, I will be
  satisfied with seeing
  your likeness.   Ps 4:6-7

Psalm 18[a]

18:Title – 50pp — 2Sa 22:1-51

For the director of music. Of David
the servant of the LORD. He sang to
the LORD the words of this song when
the LORD delivered him from the
hand of all his enemies and from the
hand of Saul. He said:

[1] I love you, LORD, my strength.

[2] The LORD is my rock, my
  fortress and my
  deliverer;   Ps 19:14

---

[a] In Hebrew texts 18:1-50 is numbered 18:2-51.

my God is my rock, in
whom I take refuge,
my shield*a* and the horn*b*
of my salvation, my
stronghold.   Ps 59:11; 75:10

³I called to the LORD, who is
worthy of praise,   Ps 48:1
and I have been saved from
my enemies.
⁴The cords of death
entangled me;   Ps 116:3
the torrents of destruction
overwhelmed me.Ps 124:4
⁵The cords of the grave coiled
around me;
the snares of death
confronted me.   Ps 116:3

⁶In my distress I called to the
LORD;
I cried to my God for help.
From his temple he heard my
voice;   Ps 34:15
my cry came before him,
into his ears.
⁷The earth trembled and
quaked,   Jdg 5:4
and the foundations of the
mountains shook;
they trembled because he
was angry.   Ps 68:7-8
⁸Smoke rose from his nostrils;
consuming fire came from
his mouth,   Ps 50:3
burning coals blazed out
of it.
⁹He parted the heavens and
came down;   Ps 144:5

dark clouds were under his
feet.
¹⁰He mounted the cherubim
and flew;
he soared on the wings of
the wind.   Ps 104:3
¹¹He made darkness his
covering, his canopy
around him—
the dark rain clouds of the
sky.   Ps 97:2
¹²Out of the brightness of
his presence clouds
advanced,   Ps 104:2
with hailstones and bolts of
lightning.
¹³The LORD thundered from
heaven;
the voice of the Most High
resounded.*c*   Ps 29:3
¹⁴He shot his arrows and
scattered the enemy,
with great bolts of lightning
he routed them.   Ps 144:6
¹⁵The valleys of the sea were
exposed
and the foundations of the
earth laid bare
at your rebuke, LORD,   Ps 76:6
at the blast of breath from
your nostrils.

¹⁶He reached down from on high
and took hold of me;
he drew me out of deep
waters.   Ps 144:7
¹⁷He rescued me from my
powerful enemy,

a 2 Or *sovereign*   *b 2 Horn* here symbolizes strength.   *c 13* Some Hebrew manuscripts
and Septuagint (see also 2 Samuel 22:14); most Hebrew manuscripts *resounded, / amid
hailstones and bolts of lightning*

from my foes, who were too
strong for me.   Ps 35:10
¹⁸They confronted me in the
day of my disaster,
but the LORD was my support.
¹⁹He brought me out into a
spacious place;   Ps 31:8
he rescued me because he
delighted in me.   Ps 118:5

²⁰The LORD has dealt with
me according to my
righteousness;
according to the cleanness
of my hands he has
rewarded me.   Ps 24:4
²¹For I have kept the ways of the
LORD;   2Ch 34:33
I am not guilty of turning
from my God.
²²All his laws are before me;
I have not turned away from
his decrees.   Ps 119:30
²³I have been blameless before
him
and have kept myself from
sin.
²⁴The LORD has rewarded
me according to my
righteousness,   1Sa 26:23
according to the cleanness
of my hands in his sight.

²⁵To the faithful you show
yourself faithful,   1Ki 8:32
to the blameless you show
yourself blameless,
²⁶to the pure you show yourself
pure,   Mt 5:8
but to the devious you show
yourself shrewd.   Pr 3:34

²⁷You save the humble
but bring low those whose
eyes are haughty.   Pr 6:17
²⁸You, LORD, keep my lamp
burning;
my God turns my darkness
into light.   Job 18:6
²⁹With your help I can advance
against a troop*;   Heb 11:34
with my God I can scale a
wall.

³⁰As for God, his way is perfect:
The LORD's word is flawless;
he shields all who take
refuge in him.
³¹For who is God besides the
LORD?   Dt 32:39; Ps 86:8
And who is the Rock except
our God?   Dt 32:31
³²It is God who arms me with
strength
and keeps my way secure.
³³He makes my feet like the feet
of a deer;   Hab 3:19
he causes me to stand on
the heights.   Dt 32:13
³⁴He trains my hands for battle;
my arms can bend a bow of
bronze.
³⁵You make your saving help
my shield,
and your right hand
sustains me;   Ps 119:116
your help has made me
great.
³⁶You provide a broad path for
my feet,
so that my ankles do not
give way.

---

a 29 Or *can run through a barricade*

37 I pursued my enemies and
overtook them;   Ps 37:20
    I did not turn back till they
    were destroyed.
38 I crushed them so that they
could not rise;   Ps 36:12
    they fell beneath my feet.
39 You armed me with strength
for battle;
    you humbled my
    adversaries before me.
40 You made my enemies turn
their backs in flight,
    and I destroyed my foes.
41 They cried for help, but there
was no one to save
    them —   Ps 50:22
    to the Lord, but he did not
    answer.   Pr 1:28
42 I beat them as fine as
windblown dust;
    I trampled them*a* like mud
    in the streets.
43 You have delivered me from
the attacks of the people;
    you have made me the head
    of nations.   2Sa 8:1-14
    People I did not know now
    serve me,   Isa 52:15; 55:5
44   foreigners cower before me;
    as soon as they hear of me,
    they obey me.   Ps 66:3
45 They all lose heart;
    they come trembling from
    their strongholds.   Mic 7:17

46 The Lord lives! Praise be to
my Rock!
    Exalted be God my Savior!

47 He is the God who avenges me,
    who subdues nations
    under me,   Ps 47:3
48   who saves me from my
    enemies.   Ps 59:1
    You exalted me above my foes;
    from a violent man you
    rescued me.
49 Therefore I will praise you,
    Lord, among the
    nations;
    I will sing the praises of
    your name.   Ps 108:1; Ro 15:9

50 He gives his king great
victories;
    he shows unfailing love to
    his anointed,
    to David and to his
    descendants forever.

Psalm 19*b*

For the director of music.
A psalm of David.

1 The heavens declare the glory
of God;   Isa 40:22; Ro 1:19
    the skies proclaim the work
    of his hands.
2 Day after day they pour forth
speech;
    night after night they reveal
    knowledge.   Ps 74:16
3 They have no speech, they use
no words;
    no sound is heard from
    them.
4 Yet their voice*c* goes out into
all the earth,

a 42 Many Hebrew manuscripts, Septuagint, Syriac and Targum (see also 2 Samuel
22:43); Masoretic Text *I poured them out*   *b* In Hebrew texts 19:1-14 is numbered 19:2-15.
c 4 Septuagint, Jerome and Syriac; Hebrew *measuring line*

their words to the ends of
the world. Ro 10:18
In the heavens God has pitched
a tent for the sun.
5   It is like a bridegroom coming
out of his chamber,
like a champion rejoicing to
run his course.
6 It rises at one end of the heavens
and makes its circuit to the
other; Ps 113:3
nothing is deprived of its
warmth.

7 The law of the LORD is perfect,
refreshing the soul. Ps 23:3
The statutes of the LORD are
trustworthy, Ps 93:5; 111:7
making wise the simple.
8 The precepts of the LORD are
right, Ps 119:128
giving joy to the heart.
The commands of the LORD
are radiant,
giving light to the eyes.
9 The fear of the LORD is pure,
enduring forever.
The decrees of the LORD are
firm,
and all of them are
righteous. Ps 119:138,142
10 They are more precious than
gold, Pr 8:10
than much pure gold;
they are sweeter than honey,
than honey from the
honeycomb.
11 By them your servant is
warned;

in keeping them there is
great reward.
12 But who can discern their
own errors?
Forgive my hidden faults.
13 Keep your servant also from
willful sins;
may they not rule over me.
Then I will be blameless,
innocent of great
transgression.

14 May these words of my mouth
and this meditation of
my heart
be pleasing in your sight,
LORD, my Rock and my
Redeemer. Ps 18:2; Isa 47:4

Psalm 20[a]

For the director of music.
A psalm of David.

1 May the LORD answer you
when you are in distress;
may the name of the God of
Jacob protect you. Ps 91:14
2 May he send you help from
the sanctuary
and grant you support from
Zion.
3 May he remember all your
sacrifices Ac 10:4
and accept your burnt
offerings.[b] Ps 51:19
4 May he give you the desire of
your heart Ps 21:2; 145:16,19
and make all your plans
succeed.
5 May we shout for joy over your
victory

---

[a] In Hebrew texts 20:1-9 is numbered 20:2-10.
uncertain meaning) here.

[b] 3 The Hebrew has *Selah* (a word of

and lift up our banners in
  the name of our God.

May the LORD grant all your
  requests. 1Sa 1:17

⁶Now this I know:
  The LORD gives victory to
    his anointed. Ps 28:8
He answers him from his
  heavenly sanctuary
with the victorious power of
  his right hand.
⁷Some trust in chariots and
  some in horses,
but we trust in the name of
  the LORD our God.
⁸They are brought to their
  knees and fall,
but we rise up and stand firm.
⁹LORD, give victory to the king!
  Answer us when we call!

Psalm 21ᵃ

For the director of music.
A psalm of David.

¹The king rejoices in your
  strength, LORD.
How great is his joy in the
  victories you give! Ps 59:16
²You have granted him his
  heart's desire Ps 37:4
and have not withheld the
  request of his lips.ᵇ
³You came to greet him with
  rich blessings
and placed a crown of pure
  gold on his head. 2Sa 12:30
⁴He asked you for life, and you
  gave it to him —

length of days, for ever and
  ever. Ps 133:3
⁵Through the victories you
  gave, his glory is great;
you have bestowed on him
  splendor and majesty.
⁶Surely you have granted him
  unending blessings
and made him glad with the
  joy of your presence.
⁷For the king trusts in the LORD;
  through the unfailing love
    of the Most High
he will not be shaken. Ps 15:5

⁸Your hand will lay hold on all
  your enemies;
  your right hand will seize
    your foes. Isa 10:10
⁹When you appear for battle,
  you will burn them up as in
    a blazing furnace. Ps 50:3
The LORD will swallow them
  up in his wrath,
and his fire will consume
  them.
¹⁰You will destroy their
  descendants from the
    earth,
their posterity from mankind.
¹¹Though they plot evil against
  you Ps 2:1
and devise wicked schemes,
  they cannot succeed.
¹²You will make them turn their
  backs Ps 7:12-13; 18:40
when you aim at them with
  drawn bow.

¹³Be exalted in your strength,
  LORD; Ps 18:46

ᵃ In Hebrew texts 21:1-13 is numbered 21:2-14, uncertain meaning) here.　ᵇ 2 The Hebrew has *Selah* (a word of

we will sing and praise your
might.

Psalm 22[a]

For the director of music. To the tune
of "The Doe of the Morning."
A psalm of David.

¹ My God, my God, why have
you forsaken me?
Why are you so far from
saving me,
so far from my cries of
anguish?
² My God, I cry out by day, but
you do not answer,
by night, but I find no rest.[b]

³ Yet you are enthroned as the
Holy One;   Ps 99:9
you are the one Israel
praises.[c]   Dt 10:21
⁴ In you our ancestors put their
trust;
they trusted and you
delivered them.
⁵ To you they cried out and
were saved;
in you they trusted and
were not put to shame.

⁶ But I am a worm and not a
man,   Job 25:6
scorned by everyone,
despised by the people.
⁷ All who see me mock me;
they hurl insults, shaking
their heads.   Mt 27:39,44
⁸ "He trusts in the LORD," they
say,

"let the LORD rescue him.
Let him deliver him,
since he delights in him."

⁹ Yet you brought me out of the
womb;   Ps 71:6
you made me trust in you,
even at my mother's
breast.
¹⁰ From birth I was cast on you;
from my mother's womb
you have been my God.

¹¹ Do not be far from me,
for trouble is near
and there is no one to help.

¹² Many bulls surround me;
strong bulls of Bashan
encircle me.
¹³ Roaring lions that tear their
prey   Ps 17:12
open their mouths wide
against me.
¹⁴ I am poured out like water,
and all my bones are out of
joint.
My heart has turned to wax;
it has melted within me.
¹⁵ My mouth[d] is dried up like a
potsherd,
and my tongue sticks to the
roof of my mouth;
you lay me in the dust of
death.   Ps 104:29

¹⁶ Dogs surround me,
a pack of villains
encircles me;

---

[a] In Hebrew texts 22:1-31 is numbered 22:2-32.   [b] 2 Or night, and am not silent
[c] 3 Or Yet you are holy, / enthroned on the praises of Israel   [d] 15 Probable reading of the
original Hebrew text; Masoretic Text strength

they pierce*a* my hands and
  my feet.   Isa 53:5; Jn 19:34
17 All my bones are on display;
  people stare and gloat
    over me.   Lk 23:35
18 They divide my clothes
    among them
  and cast lots for my
    garment.   Jn 19:24
19 But you, LORD, do not be far
    from me.
  You are my strength; come
    quickly to help me.
20 Deliver me from the sword,
  my precious life from the
    power of the dogs.   Ps 35:17
21 Rescue me from the mouth of
    the lions;
  save me from the horns of
    the wild oxen.

22 I will declare your name to
    my people;
  in the assembly I will praise
    you.   Heb 2:12
23 You who fear the LORD, praise
    him!   Ps 135:19
  All you descendants of
    Jacob, honor him!
  Revere him, all you
    descendants of Israel!
24 For he has not despised or
    scorned
  the suffering of the afflicted
    one;
  he has not hidden his face
    from him   Ps 69:17
  but has listened to his cry
    for help.   Heb 5:7

25 From you comes the theme of
  my praise in the great
    assembly;   Ps 35:18
  before those who fear you*b* I
    will fulfill my vows.
26 The poor will eat and be
    satisfied;   Ps 107:9
  those who seek the LORD
    will praise him —   Ps 40:16
  may your hearts live
    forever!

27 All the ends of the earth   Ps 2:8
  will remember and turn to
    the LORD,
  and all the families of the
    nations
  will bow down before
    him,   Ps 86:9
28 for dominion belongs to the
    LORD
  and he rules over the
    nations.   Ps 47:7-8

29 All the rich of the earth
  will feast and
    worship;   Ps 45:12
  all who go down to the dust
    will kneel before
    him —   Isa 26:19
  those who cannot keep
    themselves alive.
30 Posterity will serve him;
  future generations will be
    told about the Lord.
31 They will proclaim his
    righteousness,
  declaring to a people yet
    unborn: Ps 78:6
  He has done it!

a 16 Dead Sea Scrolls and some manuscripts of the Masoretic Text, Septuagint and Syriac;
most manuscripts of the Masoretic Text *me, / like a lion*   *b* 25 Hebrew *him*

Psalm 23

A psalm of David.

[1] The LORD is my shepherd, I
lack nothing.   Isa 40:11
[2]   He makes me lie down in
green pastures,
he leads me beside quiet
waters,   Eze 34:14; Rev 7:17
[3]   he refreshes my soul.
He guides me along the right
paths   Ps 5:8
for his name's sake.
[4] Even though I walk
through the darkest valley,[a]
I will fear no evil,   Ps 3:6; 27:1
for you are with me;   Isa 43:2
your rod and your staff,
they comfort me.

[5] You prepare a table before me
in the presence of my
enemies.
You anoint my head with oil;
my cup overflows.   Ps 16:5
[6] Surely your goodness and love
will follow me
all the days of my life,
and I will dwell in the house
of the LORD
forever.

Psalm 24

Of David. A psalm.

[1] The earth is the LORD's, and
everything in it,   Ps 89:11
the world, and all who live
in it;   1Co 10:26

[2] for he founded it on the seas
and established it on the
waters.

[3] Who may ascend the
mountain of the LORD?
Who may stand in his holy
place?   Ps 15:1
[4] The one who has clean hands
and a pure heart,   Job 17:9
who does not trust in an idol
or swear by a false god.[b]

[5] They will receive blessing
from the LORD
and vindication from God
their Savior.   Ps 17:2
[6] Such is the generation of
those who seek him,
who seek your face, God of
Jacob.[c,d]   Ps 27:8

[7] Lift up your heads, you gates;
be lifted up, you ancient
doors,
that the King of glory may
come in.   Ps 97:6; 1Co 2:8
[8] Who is this King of glory?
The LORD strong and
mighty,
the LORD mighty in battle.
[9] Lift up your heads, you gates;
lift them up, you ancient
doors,
that the King of glory may
come in.
[10] Who is he, this King of glory?
The LORD Almighty —
he is the King of glory.

---

[a] 4 Or *the valley of the shadow of death*   [b] 4 Or *swear falsely*   [c] 6 Two Hebrew
manuscripts and Syriac (see also Septuagint); most Hebrew manuscripts *face, Jacob*
[d] 6 The Hebrew has *Selah* (a word of uncertain meaning) here and at the end of verse 10.

Psalm 25[a]

Of David.

¹In you, LORD my God,
  I put my trust.   Ps 86:4

²I trust in you;
  do not let me be put to
    shame,
  nor let my enemies triumph
    over me.
³No one who hopes in you
  will ever be put to shame,
  but shame will come on those
    who are treacherous
      without cause.

⁴Show me your ways, LORD,
  teach me your paths.   Ex 33:13
⁵Guide me in your truth and
    teach me,
  for you are God my Savior,
  and my hope is in you all
    day long.
⁶Remember, LORD, your great
    mercy and love,   Ps 103:17
  for they are from of old.
⁷Do not remember the sins of
    my youth   Job 13:26; Jer 3:25
  and my rebellious ways;
  according to your love
    remember me,   Ps 51:1
  for you, LORD, are good.

⁸Good and upright is the LORD;
  therefore he instructs
    sinners in his ways.
⁹He guides the humble in what
    is right   Ps 23:3
  and teaches them his way.

¹⁰All the ways of the LORD are
    loving and faithful
  toward those who keep
    the demands of his
      covenant.   Ps 103:18
¹¹For the sake of your name,
    LORD,   Ps 31:3; 79:9
  forgive my iniquity, though
    it is great.

¹²Who, then, are those who fear
    the LORD?
  He will instruct them in
    the ways they should
      choose.[b]   Ps 37:23
¹³They will spend their days in
    prosperity,   Pr 19:23
  and their descendants will
    inherit the land.
¹⁴The LORD confides in those
    who fear him;   Pr 3:32
  he makes his covenant
    known to them.
¹⁵My eyes are ever on the LORD,
  for only he will release my
    feet from the snare.

¹⁶Turn to me and be gracious
    to me,   Ps 69:16
  for I am lonely and afflicted.
¹⁷Relieve the troubles of my
    heart
  and free me from my
    anguish.   Ps 107:6
¹⁸Look on my affliction and my
    distress   2Sa 16:12
  and take away all my sins.
¹⁹See how numerous are my
    enemies   Ps 3:1

---

[a] This psalm is an acrostic poem, the verses of which begin with the successive letters of the Hebrew alphabet.   [b] 12 Or *ways he chooses*

and how fiercely they
    hate me!

²⁰Guard my life and rescue me;
    do not let me be put to
      shame,
    for I take refuge in you.
²¹May integrity and uprightness
    protect me,   Ps 41:12
    because my hope, LORD,ᵃ is
      in you.
²²Deliver Israel, O God,
    from all their troubles! Ps 130:8

Psalm 26

Of David.

¹Vindicate me, LORD,
    for I have led a blameless
      life;   Ps 7:8
I have trusted in the LORD
    and have not faltered. 2Ki 20:3
²Test me, LORD, and try me,
    examine my heart and my
      mind;   Ps 7:9
³for I have always been
    mindful of your
      unfailing love
and have lived in reliance
    on your faithfulness.

⁴I do not sit with the deceitful,
    nor do I associate with
      hypocrites.
⁵I abhor the assembly of
    evildoers   Ps 139:21
and refuse to sit with the
    wicked.
⁶I wash my hands in
    innocence,   Ps 73:13

and go about your altar,
    LORD,
⁷proclaiming aloud your praise
    and telling of all your
      wonderful deeds.   Ps 9:1

⁸LORD, I love the house where
    you live,   Ps 27:4
the place where your glory
    dwells.
⁹Do not take away my soul
    along with sinners,
    my life with those who are
      bloodthirsty,   Ps 28:3
¹⁰in whose hands are wicked
    schemes,
    whose right hands are full
      of bribes.   1Sa 8:3
¹¹I lead a blameless life;
    deliver me and be merciful
      to me.   Ps 69:18
¹²My feet stand on level ground;
    in the great congregation I
      will praise the LORD.

Psalm 27

Of David.

¹The LORD is my light and my
    salvation —   Ex 15:2; Isa 60:19
  whom shall I fear?
The LORD is the stronghold of
    my life —
  of whom shall I be afraid?

²When the wicked advance
    against me
  to devourᵇ me,
it is my enemies and my foes
  who will stumble and fall.

ᵃ 21 Septuagint; Hebrew does not have LORD.   ᵇ 2 Or *slander*

³Though an army besiege me,
my heart will not fear; Ps 3:6
though war break out
against me,
even then I will be confident.

⁴One thing I ask from the LORD,
this only do I seek:
that I may dwell in the house
of the LORD
all the days of my life, Ps 26:8
to gaze on the beauty of the
LORD
and to seek him in his
temple.
⁵For in the day of trouble
he will keep me safe in his
dwelling;
he will hide me in the shelter
of his sacred tent Ps 17:8
and set me high upon a rock.
⁶Then my head will be exalted
above the enemies who
surround me;
at his sacred tent I will sacrifice
with shouts of joy;Ps 107:22
I will sing and make music
to the LORD.

⁷Hear my voice when I call,
LORD;
be merciful to me and
answer me. Ps 13:3
⁸My heart says of you, "Seek
his face!"
Your face, LORD, I will seek.
⁹Do not hide your face from me,
do not turn your servant
away in anger;
you have been my helper.
Do not reject me or forsake me,

God my Savior.
¹⁰Though my father and mother
forsake me,
the LORD will receive me.
¹¹Teach me your way, LORD;
lead me in a straight path
because of my oppressors.
¹²Do not turn me over to the
desire of my foes,
for false witnesses rise up
against me, Mt 26:60; Ac 9:1
spouting malicious
accusations.

¹³I remain confident of this:
I will see the goodness of
the LORD Ps 31:19
in the land of the living. Jer 11:19
¹⁴Wait for the LORD;
be strong and take heart
and wait for the LORD. Ps 40:1

Psalm 28

Of David.

¹To you, LORD, I call;
you are my Rock,
do not turn a deaf ear to me.
For if you remain silent, Ps 83:1
I will be like those who go
down to the pit. Ps 88:4
²Hear my cry for mercy Ps 138:2
as I call to you for help,
as I lift up my hands
toward your Most Holy
Place. Ps 5:7

³Do not drag me away with the
wicked,
with those who do evil,
who speak cordially with their
neighbors

but harbor malice in their
　　hearts. Ps 12:2
⁴Repay them for their deeds
　　and for their evil work;
repay them for what their
　　hands have done 2Ti 4:14
and bring back on them what
　　they deserve. Rev 18:6

⁵Because they have no regard
　　for the deeds of the LORD
and what his hands have
　　done, Isa 5:12
he will tear them down
　　and never build them up
　　again.

⁶Praise be to the LORD,
　　for he has heard my cry for
　　mercy.
⁷The LORD is my strength and
　　my shield; Ps 18:1
　　my heart trusts in him, and
　　he helps me. Ps 13:5
My heart leaps for joy,
　　and with my song I praise
　　him. Ps 40:3; 69:30

⁸The LORD is the strength of
　　his people,
a fortress of salvation for his
　　anointed one. Ps 20:6
⁹Save your people and bless
　　your inheritance; Dt 9:29
be their shepherd and carry
　　them forever. Dt 1:31

Psalm 29

A psalm of David.

¹Ascribe to the LORD, you
　　heavenly beings, 1Ch 16:28

ascribe to the LORD glory
　　and strength. Ps 96:7-9
²Ascribe to the LORD the glory
　　due his name;
worship the LORD in
　　the splendor of his[a]
　　holiness. 2Ch 20:21

³The voice of the LORD is over
　　the waters; Job 37:5
the God of glory thunders,
　　the LORD thunders over the
　　mighty waters.
⁴The voice of the LORD is
　　powerful; Ps 68:33
　　the voice of the LORD is
　　majestic.
⁵The voice of the LORD breaks
　　the cedars;
　　the LORD breaks in pieces
　　the cedars of Lebanon.
⁶He makes Lebanon leap like a
　　calf, Ps 114:4
　　Sirion[b] like a young wild ox.
⁷The voice of the LORD strikes
　　with flashes of lightning.
⁸The voice of the LORD shakes
　　the desert;
　　the LORD shakes the Desert
　　of Kadesh. Nu 13:26
⁹The voice of the LORD twists
　　the oaks[c]
and strips the forests bare.
And in his temple all cry,
　　"Glory!" Ps 26:8

¹⁰The LORD sits enthroned over
　　the flood;
　　the LORD is enthroned as
　　King forever. Ps 10:16

---

[a] 2 Or LORD with the splendor of
deer give birth　　[b] 6 That is, Mount Hermon　　[c] 9 Or LORD makes the

11 The LORD gives strength to
    his people;   Ps 28:8
  the LORD blesses his people
    with peace.   Ps 37:11

Psalm 30ᵃ

A psalm. A song. For the dedication
  of the temple.ᵇ Of David.

1 I will exalt you, LORD,
  for you lifted me out of the
    depths
  and did not let my enemies
    gloat over me.   Ps 25:2
2 LORD my God, I called to you
    for help,
  and you healed me.   Ps 6:2
3 You, LORD, brought me up from
    the realm of the dead;
  you spared me from going
    down to the pit.   Ps 86:13

4 Sing the praises of the LORD,
    you his faithful people;
  praise his holy name.
5 For his anger lasts only a
    moment,   Ps 103:9
  but his favor lasts a lifetime;
  weeping may stay for the
    night,
  but rejoicing comes in the
    morning.   2Co 4:17

6 When I felt secure, I said,
  "I will never be shaken."
7 LORD, when you favored me,
  you made my royal
    mountainᶜ stand firm;
  but when you hid your face,
  I was dismayed.   Ps 104:29

8 To you, LORD, I called;
  to the Lord I cried for mercy:
9 "What is gained if I am
    silenced,
  if I go down to the pit?
  Will the dust praise you?
  Will it proclaim your
    faithfulness?   Ps 6:5
10 Hear, LORD, and be merciful
    to me;   Ps 4:1
  LORD, be my help."

11 You turned my wailing into
    dancing;
  you removed my sackcloth
    and clothed me with
    joy,   Ps 4:7; Jer 31:4,13
12 that my heart may sing your
    praises and not be silent.
  LORD my God, I will praise
    you forever.   Ps 16:9; 44:8

Psalm 31ᵈ

31:1-4pp — Ps 71:1-3

For the director of music.
  A psalm of David.

1 In you, LORD, I have taken
    refuge;   Ps 7:1
  let me never be put to shame;
  deliver me in your
    righteousness.
2 Turn your ear to me,
  come quickly to my rescue;
  be my rock of refuge,
  a strong fortress to save me.
3 Since you are my rock and my
    fortress,   Ps 18:2
  for the sake of your name
    lead and guide me. Ps 23:3

ᵃ In Hebrew texts 30:1-12 is numbered 30:2-13.   ᵇ Title: Or *palace*   ᶜ 7 That is, Mount Zion   ᵈ In Hebrew texts 31:1-24 is numbered 31:2-25.

⁴Keep me free from the trap
    that is set for me,
  for you are my refuge. Ps 71:1-3
⁵Into your hands I commit my
    spirit;   Lk 23:46
  deliver me, LORD, my
    faithful God.

⁶I hate those who cling to
    worthless idols;
  as for me, I trust in the LORD.
⁷I will be glad and rejoice in
    your love,
  for you saw my affliction
  and knew the anguish of my
    soul.   Ps 10:14; Jn 10:27
⁸You have not given me into
    the hands of the enemy
  but have set my feet in a
    spacious place.

⁹Be merciful to me, LORD, for I
    am in distress;
  my eyes grow weak with
    sorrow,   Ps 6:7
  my soul and body with grief.
¹⁰My life is consumed by
    anguish
  and my years by groaning;
  my strength fails because of
    my affliction,ᵃ
  and my bones grow weak.
¹¹Because of all my enemies,
  I am the utter contempt of
    my neighbors   Ps 38:11
  and an object of dread to my
    closest friends —
  those who see me on the
    street flee from me.
¹²I am forgotten as though I
    were dead;   Ps 88:4

  I have become like broken
    pottery.
¹³For I hear many whispering,
  "Terror on every side!" Jer 20:3
  They conspire against me
  and plot to take my life.

¹⁴But I trust in you, LORD; Ps 140:6
  I say, "You are my God."
¹⁵My times are in your hands;
  deliver me from the hands
    of my enemies,
  from those who pursue me.
¹⁶Let your face shine on your
    servant;   Ps 4:6
  save me in your unfailing
    love.
¹⁷Let me not be put to shame,
    LORD,   Ps 25:2-3
  for I have cried out to you;
  but let the wicked be put to
    shame
  and be silent in the realm of
    the dead.
¹⁸Let their lying lips be
    silenced,   Ps 120:2
  for with pride and contempt
  they speak arrogantly against
    the righteous.   Ps 94:4

¹⁹How abundant are the good
    things
  that you have stored up for
    those who fear you,
  that you bestow in the sight of
    all,   Isa 64:4
  on those who take refuge in
    you.
²⁰In the shelter of your presence
    you hide them   Ps 27:5
  from all human intrigues;

ᵃ 10 Or *guilt*

you keep them safe in your
    dwelling
  from accusing tongues.

²¹ Praise be to the LORD,
    for he showed me the
      wonders of his love Ps 17:7
  when I was in a city under
    siege. 1Sa 23:7
²² In my alarm I said,   Ps 116:11
    "I am cut off from your sight!"
  Yet you heard my cry for mercy
    when I called to you for help.

²³ Love the LORD, all his faithful
    people! Ps 34:9
  The LORD preserves those
    who are true to him,
  but the proud he pays back
    in full. Ps 94:2
²⁴ Be strong and take heart, Ps 27:14
  all you who hope in the
    LORD.

Psalm 32

Of David. A *maskil.*[a]

¹ Blessed is the one
  whose transgressions are
    forgiven,
  whose sins are covered. Ps 85:2
² Blessed is the one
  whose sin the LORD does
    not count against them
  and in whose spirit is no
    deceit. Jn 1:47

³ When I kept silent,
  my bones wasted away Ps 31:10
    through my groaning all
    day long.

⁴ For day and night
  your hand was heavy
    on me; Job 33:7
  my strength was sapped
    as in the heat of summer.[b]

⁵ Then I acknowledged my sin
    to you
  and did not cover up my
    iniquity.
  I said, "I will confess   Pr 28:13
    my transgressions to the
    LORD."
  And you forgave
    the guilt of my sin.   Lev 26:40

⁶ Therefore let all the faithful
    pray to you
  while you may be found;
  surely the rising of the mighty
    waters
  will not reach them.
⁷ You are my hiding place;
  you will protect me from
    trouble   Ps 9:9
  and surround me with songs
    of deliverance.   Ex 15:1

⁸ I will instruct you and teach
    you in the way you
    should go;
  I will counsel you with my
    loving eye on you. Ps 33:18
⁹ Do not be like the horse or the
    mule,
  which have no
    understanding
  but must be controlled by bit
    and bridle
  or they will not come to you.

---

a Title: Probably a literary or musical term   *b* 4 The Hebrew has *Selah* (a word of uncertain meaning) here and at the end of verses 5 and 7.

¹⁰Many are the woes of the
 wicked, Ro 2:9
 but the LORD's unfailing love
 surrounds the one who
 trusts in him. Pr 16:20

¹¹Rejoice in the LORD and be
 glad, you righteous;
 sing, all you who are
 upright in heart!

Psalm 33

¹Sing joyfully to the LORD, you
 righteous;
 it is fitting for the upright to
 praise him. Ps 32:11; 147:1
²Praise the LORD with the harp;
 make music to him on the
 ten-stringed lyre.
³Sing to him a new song; Ps 96:1
 play skillfully, and shout for
 joy.

⁴For the word of the LORD is
 right and true; Ps 19:8
 he is faithful in all he does.
⁵The LORD loves righteousness
 and justice; Ps 11:7
 the earth is full of his
 unfailing love. Ps 119:64

⁶By the word of the LORD the
 heavens were made,
 their starry host by the
 breath of his mouth.
⁷He gathers the waters of the
 sea into jars^a;
 he puts the deep into
 storehouses.
⁸Let all the earth fear the
 LORD;

let all the people of the world
 revere him. Ps 67:7; 96:9
⁹For he spoke, and it came to be;
 he commanded, and it
 stood firm. Ge 1:3

¹⁰The LORD foils the plans of
 the nations; Isa 8:10
 he thwarts the purposes of
 the peoples.
¹¹But the plans of the LORD
 stand firm forever,
 the purposes of his heart
 through all generations.

¹²Blessed is the nation whose
 God is the LORD,
 the people he chose for his
 inheritance. Ex 19:5; Dt 7:6
¹³From heaven the LORD looks
 down
 and sees all mankind; Job 28:24
¹⁴from his dwelling place he
 watches
 all who live on earth —
¹⁵he who forms the hearts of all,
 who considers everything
 they do. Jer 32:19

¹⁶No king is saved by the size of
 his army;
 no warrior escapes by his
 great strength.
¹⁷A horse is a vain hope for
 deliverance; Ps 20:7
 despite all its great strength
 it cannot save.
¹⁸But the eyes of the LORD are
 on those who fear him,
 on those whose hope is in
 his unfailing love, Ps 147:11

---

^a 7 Or sea as into a heap

¹⁹to deliver them from death
and keep them alive in
famine. Job 5:20

²⁰We wait in hope for the LORD;
he is our help and our shield.
²¹In him our hearts rejoice,
for we trust in his holy
name.
²²May your unfailing love be
with us, LORD,
even as we put our hope in
you. Ps 6:4

Psalm 34^{a,b}

Of David. When he pretended
to be insane before Abimelek, who
drove him away, and he left.

¹I will extol the LORD at all times;
his praise will always be on
my lips. Ps 71:6; Eph 5:20
²I will glory in the LORD; Jer 9:24
let the afflicted hear and
rejoice.
³Glorify the LORD with me;
let us exalt his name
together. Lk 1:46

⁴I sought the LORD, and he
answered me; Mt 7:7
he delivered me from all my
fears.
⁵Those who look to him are
radiant; Ps 36:9
their faces are never
covered with shame.
⁶This poor man called, and the
LORD heard him;
he saved him out of all his
troubles. Ps 25:17

⁷The angel of the LORD
encamps around those
who fear him, Da 6:22
and he delivers them.
⁸Taste and see that the LORD is
good; 1Pe 2:3
blessed is the one who takes
refuge in him. Ps 2:12
⁹Fear the LORD, you his holy
people,
for those who fear him lack
nothing. Ps 23:1
¹⁰The lions may grow weak and
hungry,
but those who seek the LORD
lack no good thing.
¹¹Come, my children, listen
to me;
I will teach you the fear of
the LORD.
¹²Whoever of you loves life 1Pe 3:10
and desires to see many
good days,
¹³keep your tongue from evil
and your lips from telling
lies.
¹⁴Turn from evil and do
good; Ps 37:27
seek peace and pursue it.

¹⁵The eyes of the LORD are on
the righteous, Job 36:7
and his ears are attentive to
their cry;
¹⁶but the face of the LORD is
against those who do
evil,
to blot out their name from
the earth. Pr 10:7

---

^a This psalm is an acrostic poem, the verses of which begin with the successive letters of the
Hebrew alphabet.   ^b In Hebrew texts 34:1-22 is numbered 34:2-23.

¹⁷The righteous cry out, and the
LORD hears them; Ps 145:19
he delivers them from all
their troubles.
¹⁸The LORD is close to the
brokenhearted   Isa 57:15
and saves those who are
crushed in spirit.

¹⁹The righteous person may
have many troubles,
but the LORD delivers him
from them all;   Pr 24:16
²⁰he protects all his bones,
not one of them will be
broken.   Jn 19:36

²¹Evil will slay the wicked; Ps 94:23
the foes of the righteous will
be condemned.
²²The LORD will rescue his
servants;   1Ki 1:29
no one who takes refuge
in him will be
condemned.

Psalm 35

Of David.

¹Contend, LORD, with those
who contend with me;
fight against those who
fight against me.   Ps 43:1
²Take up shield and armor;
arise and come to my aid.
³Brandish spear and javelin^a
against those who pursue
me.
Say to me,
"I am your salvation."

⁴May those who seek my life

be disgraced and put to
shame;   Ps 70:2
may those who plot my ruin
be turned back in dismay.
⁵May they be like chaff before
the wind,   Job 21:18
with the angel of the LORD
driving them away;
⁶may their path be dark and
slippery,
with the angel of the LORD
pursuing them.

⁷Since they hid their net for me
without cause
and without cause dug a pit
for me,   Ps 7:4
⁸may ruin overtake them by
surprise—   1Th 5:3
may the net they hid
entangle them,
may they fall into the pit, to
their ruin.
⁹Then my soul will rejoice in
the LORD   Lk 1:47
and delight in his
salvation.   Isa 61:10
¹⁰My whole being will exclaim,
"Who is like you, LORD?
You rescue the poor from those
too strong for them,
the poor and needy from
those who rob them."

¹¹Ruthless witnesses come
forward;
they question me on things
I know nothing about.
¹²They repay me evil for good
and leave me like one
bereaved.

^a 3 Or *and block the way*

¹³Yet when they were ill, I put
     on sackcloth
   and humbled myself with
     fasting.   Job 30:25
   When my prayers returned to
     me unanswered,
¹⁴   I went about mourning
     as though for my friend or
       brother.
   I bowed my head in grief
     as though weeping for my
       mother.
¹⁵But when I stumbled, they
     gathered in glee;
   assailants gathered
     against me without my
       knowledge.
   They slandered me without
     ceasing.   Job 30:1,8
¹⁶Like the ungodly they
     maliciously mocked;*ᵃ*
   they gnashed their teeth
     at me.   La 2:16

¹⁷How long, Lord, will you
     look on?   Hab 1:13
   Rescue me from their
     ravages,
   my precious life from these
     lions.   Ps 22:20
¹⁸I will give you thanks in the
     great assembly;
   among the throngs I will
     praise you.   Ps 22:22
¹⁹Do not let those gloat over me
     who are my enemies
       without cause;
   do not let those who hate me
     without reason   Ps 38:19
   maliciously wink the eye.

²⁰They do not speak peaceably,
   but devise false accusations
     against those who live
       quietly in the land.
²¹They sneer at me and say,
   "Aha! Aha!   Ps 22:13; 40:15
   With our own eyes we have
     seen it."
²²Lord, you have seen this; do
     not be silent.   Ex 3:7
   Do not be far from me,
     Lord.   Ps 10:1
²³Awake, and rise to my defense!
   Contend for me, my God
     and Lord.
²⁴Vindicate me in your
     righteousness, Lord
       my God;
   do not let them gloat
     over me.   Ps 22:17
²⁵Do not let them think, "Aha,
     just what we wanted!"
   or say, "We have swallowed
     him up."   La 2:16
²⁶May all who gloat over my
     distress
   be put to shame and
     confusion;   Ps 40:14; 109:29
   may all who exalt themselves
     over me
   be clothed with shame and
     disgrace.
²⁷May those who delight in my
     vindication   Ps 9:4
   shout for joy and gladness;
   may they always say, "The
     Lord be exalted,
   who delights in the well-
     being of his servant."

ᵃ 16 Septuagint; Hebrew may mean *Like an ungodly circle of mockers,*

28 My tongue will proclaim your
   righteousness, Ps 51:14
   your praises all day long.

Psalm 36[a]

For the director of music. Of David
the servant of the LORD.

1 I have a message from God in
   my heart
   concerning the sinfulness
   of the wicked:[b]
There is no fear of God
   before their eyes. Ro 3:18

2 In their own eyes they flatter
   themselves
   too much to detect or hate
   their sin.
3 The words of their mouths are
   wicked and deceitful;
   they fail to act wisely or do
   good. Jer 4:22
4 Even on their beds they plot
   evil; Pr 4:16
   they commit themselves to
   a sinful course Isa 65:2
   and do not reject what is
   wrong.

5 Your love, LORD, reaches to
   the heavens,
   your faithfulness to the
   skies. Ps 57:10
6 Your righteousness is like the
   highest mountains,
   your justice like the great
   deep. Ro 11:33
You, LORD, preserve both
   people and animals.

7 How priceless is your
   unfailing love, O God!
People take refuge in the
   shadow of your wings.
8 They feast on the abundance
   of your house; Ps 65:4
   you give them drink from
   your river of delights.
9 For with you is the fountain of
   life; Jer 2:13
   in your light we see light.

10 Continue your love to those
   who know you,
   your righteousness to the
   upright in heart. Ps 7:10
11 May the foot of the proud not
   come against me,
   nor the hand of the wicked
   drive me away. Ps 71:4
12 See how the evildoers lie
   fallen—
   thrown down, not able to rise!

Psalm 37[c]

Of David.

1 Do not fret because of those
   who are evil
   or be envious of those who
   do wrong; Ps 73:3; Pr 23:17-18
2 for like the grass they will
   soon wither,
   like green plants they will
   soon die away. Ps 90:6

3 Trust in the LORD and do
   good;
   dwell in the land and enjoy
   safe pasture.

---

[a] In Hebrew texts 36:1-12 is numbered 36:2-13.
transgression of the wicked / resides in their hearts.
[b] 1 Or *A message from God: The*
[c] This psalm is an acrostic poem, the
stanzas of which begin with the successive letters of the Hebrew alphabet.

⁴Take delight in the LORD,
  and he will give you the
    desires of your heart.

⁵Commit your way to the LORD;
  trust in him and he will do
    this: Ps 55:22
⁶He will make your righteous
  reward shine like the
    dawn,   Job 11:17
  your vindication like the
    noonday sun.

⁷Be still before the LORD
  and wait patiently for him;
  do not fret when people
    succeed in their ways,
  when they carry out their
    wicked schemes.   Ps 40:1

⁸Refrain from anger and turn
  from wrath; Eph 4:31; Col 3:8
  do not fret — it leads only to
    evil.
⁹For those who are evil will be
    destroyed,
  but those who hope in the
    LORD will inherit the
    land.   Isa 57:13; 60:21

¹⁰A little while, and the wicked
    will be no more;   Job 7:10
  though you look for them,
    they will not be found.
¹¹But the meek will inherit the
    land   Mt 5:5
  and enjoy peace and
    prosperity.

¹²The wicked plot against the
    righteous
  and gnash their teeth at
    them;   Ps 35:16

¹³but the Lord laughs at the
    wicked,
  for he knows their day is
    coming.   1Sa 26:10; Ps 2:4

¹⁴The wicked draw the sword
  and bend the bow   Ps 11:2
  to bring down the poor and
    needy,   Ps 35:10
  to slay those whose ways
    are upright.
¹⁵But their swords will pierce
    their own hearts,   Ps 9:16
  and their bows will be
    broken.

¹⁶Better the little that the
    righteous have
  than the wealth of many
    wicked;   Pr 15:16
¹⁷for the power of the wicked
    will be broken,   Ps 10:15
  but the LORD upholds the
    righteous.

¹⁸The blameless spend their days
    under the LORD's care,
  and their inheritance will
    endure forever.
¹⁹In times of disaster they will
    not wither;
  in days of famine they will
    enjoy plenty.

²⁰But the wicked will perish:
  Though the LORD's enemies
    are like the flowers of
    the field,
  they will be consumed, they
    will go up in smoke.

²¹The wicked borrow and do
    not repay,

but the righteous give
   generously;   Ps 112:5
²²those the LORD blesses will
   inherit the land,
   but those he curses will be
      destroyed.   Pr 3:33

²³The LORD makes firm the steps
   of the one who delights in
   him;   1Sa 2:9
²⁴though he may stumble, he
   will not fall,   Pr 24:16
   for the LORD upholds him
      with his hand.

²⁵I was young and now I am old,
   yet I have never seen the
      righteous forsaken
   or their children begging
      bread.
²⁶They are always generous and
   lend freely;
   their children will be a
      blessing.ᵃ   Ps 147:13

²⁷Turn from evil and do
   good;   Ps 34:14
   then you will dwell in the
      land forever.
²⁸For the LORD loves the just
   and will not forsake his
      faithful ones.   Ps 21:10

Wrongdoers will be
   completely destroyedᵇ;
   the offspring of the wicked
      will perish.
²⁹The righteous will inherit the
      land
   and dwell in it forever.

³⁰The mouths of the righteous
   utter wisdom,
   and their tongues speak
      what is just.
³¹The law of their God is in their
   hearts;   Dt 6:6; Ps 40:8
   their feet do not slip.

³²The wicked lie in wait for the
   righteous,   Ps 10:8
   intent on putting them to
      death;
³³but the LORD will not leave
      them in the power of
      the wicked
   or let them be condemned
      when brought to trial.

³⁴Hope in the LORD   Ps 27:14
   and keep his way.
   He will exalt you to inherit the
      land;
   when the wicked are
      destroyed, you will see it.

³⁵I have seen a wicked and
      ruthless man
   flourishing like a luxuriant
      native tree,   Job 5:3
³⁶but he soon passed away and
      was no more;
   though I looked for him, he
      could not be found.

³⁷Consider the blameless,
   observe the upright;
   a future awaits those who
      seek peace.ᶜ   Isa 57:1-2
³⁸But all sinners will be
      destroyed;

ᵃ 26 Or *freely; / the names of their children will be used in blessings* (see Gen. 48:20); or *freely; / others will see that their children are blessed*   ᵇ 28 See Septuagint; Hebrew *They will be protected forever*   ᶜ 37 Or *upright; / those who seek peace will have posterity* there will be no future[a] for the wicked. Ps 1:4

³⁹The salvation of the righteous comes from the LORD; he is their stronghold in time of trouble. Ps 9:9

⁴⁰The LORD helps them and delivers them; 1Ch 5:20 he delivers them from the wicked and saves them, because they take refuge in him.

Psalm 38[b]

A psalm of David. A petition.

¹LORD, do not rebuke me in your anger or discipline me in your wrath. Ps 6:1

²Your arrows have pierced me, and your hand has come down on me.

³Because of your wrath there is no health in my body; there is no soundness in my bones because of my sin.

⁴My guilt has overwhelmed me like a burden too heavy to bear. Ezr 9:6

⁵My wounds fester and are loathsome because of my sinful folly.

⁶I am bowed down and brought very low; all day long I go about mourning. Ps 35:14

⁷My back is filled with searing pain;

there is no health in my body.

⁸I am feeble and utterly crushed; I groan in anguish of heart.

⁹All my longings lie open before you, Lord; my sighing is not hidden from you. Job 3:24

¹⁰My heart pounds, my strength fails me; even the light has gone from my eyes. Ps 6:7

¹¹My friends and companions avoid me because of my wounds; my neighbors stay far away.

¹²Those who want to kill me set their traps, Ps 140:5 those who would harm me talk of my ruin; all day long they scheme and lie. Ps 35:20

¹³I am like the deaf, who cannot hear, like the mute, who cannot speak;

¹⁴I have become like one who does not hear, whose mouth can offer no reply.

¹⁵LORD, I wait for you; Ps 39:7 you will answer, Lord my God.

¹⁶For I said, "Do not let them gloat Ps 35:26 or exalt themselves over me when my feet slip."

^a 38 Or posterity   ^b In Hebrew texts 38:1-22 is numbered 38:2-23.

¹⁷For I am about to fall,
  and my pain is ever with me.
¹⁸I confess my iniquity;   Ps 32:5
  I am troubled by my sin.
¹⁹Many have become my
    enemies without cause^a;
  those who hate me without
    reason are numerous.
²⁰Those who repay my good
    with evil   Ps 35:12
  lodge accusations
    against me,
  though I seek only to do
    what is good.
²¹Lord, do not forsake me;
  do not be far from me, my
    God.   Ps 35:22
²²Come quickly to help me,
  my Lord and my Savior.

Psalm 39^b

For the director of music.
For Jeduthun. A psalm of David.

¹I said, "I will watch my ways
    and keep my tongue from sin;
  I will put a muzzle on my
    mouth
  while in the presence of the
    wicked."
²So I remained utterly silent,
  not even saying anything
    good.
  But my anguish increased;
³ my heart grew hot within me.
  While I meditated, the fire
    burned;   Jer 20:9
  then I spoke with my tongue:

⁴"Show me, Lord, my life's end
  and the number of my days;
  let me know how fleeting
    my life is.   Ps 103:14
⁵You have made my days a mere
    handbreadth;   Ps 89:45
  the span of my years is as
    nothing before you.
  Everyone is but a breath,
    even those who seem secure.^c

⁶"Surely everyone goes around
    like a mere phantom;
  in vain they rush about,
    heaping up wealth Ps 127:2
  without knowing whose it
    will finally be.   Lk 12:20

⁷"But now, Lord, what do I look
    for?
  My hope is in you.
⁸Save me from all my
    transgressions;   Ps 44:13
  do not make me the scorn
    of fools.
⁹I was silent; I would not open
    my mouth,   Job 2:10
  for you are the one who has
    done this.
¹⁰Remove your scourge from me;
  I am overcome by the blow
    of your hand.   Job 9:34
¹¹When you rebuke and
    discipline anyone for
    their sin,
  you consume their wealth
    like a moth —   Job 13:28
  surely everyone is but a
    breath.

^a 19 One Dead Sea Scrolls manuscript; Masoretic Text *my vigorous enemies*   ^b In Hebrew texts 39:1-13 is numbered 39:2-14.   ^c 5 The Hebrew has *Selah* (a word of uncertain meaning) here and at the end of verse 11.

12 "Hear my prayer, LORD,
    listen to my cry for help;
    do not be deaf to my weeping.
  I dwell with you as a foreigner,
    a stranger, as all my
    ancestors were. Heb 11:13
13 Look away from me, that I
    may enjoy life again
    before I depart and am no
    more." Job 10:21

Psalm 40[a]

40:13-17pp — Ps 70:1-5

For the director of music.
Of David. A psalm.

1 I waited patiently for the LORD;
    he turned to me and heard
    my cry.
2 He lifted me out of the slimy
    pit,
    out of the mud and mire;
  he set my feet on a rock Ps 27:5
    and gave me a firm place to
    stand.
3 He put a new song in my
    mouth, Ps 33:3
    a hymn of praise to our God.
  Many will see and fear the
    LORD
    and put their trust in him.

4 Blessed is the one
    who trusts in the LORD, Ps 84:12
  who does not look to the proud,
    to those who turn aside to
    false gods.[b]
5 Many, LORD my God,
    are the wonders you have
    done, Ps 136:4

the things you planned
    for us.
None can compare with you;
    were I to speak and tell of
    your deeds,
    they would be too many to
    declare.

6 Sacrifice and offering you did
    not desire — 1Sa 15:22
    but my ears you have
    opened[c] —
  burnt offerings and sin
    offerings[d] you did not
    require. Isa 1:11
7 Then I said, "Here I am, I have
    come —
    it is written about me in the
    scroll.[e]
8 I desire to do your will, my God;
    your law is within my heart."

9 I proclaim your saving acts in
    the great assembly;
  I do not seal my lips, LORD,
    as you know. Ps 119:13
10 I do not hide your righteousness
    in my heart;
  I speak of your faithfulness
    and your saving help.
  I do not conceal your love and
    your faithfulness
    from the great assembly.

11 Do not withhold your mercy
    from me, LORD;
  may your love and
    faithfulness always
    protect me. Ps 43:3
12 For troubles without number
    surround me;

---

[a] In Hebrew texts 40:1-17 is numbered 40:2-18.   [b] 4 Or to lies   [c] 6 Hebrew; some
Septuagint manuscripts but a body you have prepared for me   [d] 6 Or purification offerings
[e] 7 Or come / with the scroll written for me

my sins have overtaken me,
    and I cannot see.   Ps 38:4
They are more than the hairs
    of my head,
    and my heart fails within me.
[13]Be pleased to save me, LORD;
    come quickly, LORD, to
      help me.   Ps 70:1

[14]May all who want to take my
    life
  be put to shame and
    confusion;
may all who desire my ruin
  be turned back in disgrace.
[15]May those who say to me,
    "Aha! Aha!"
  be appalled at their own
    shame.
[16]But may all who seek you   Ps 9:10
  rejoice and be glad in you;
may those who long for your
    saving help always say,
  "The LORD is great!"   Ps 35:27

[17]But as for me, I am poor and
    needy;
  may the Lord think of me.
You are my help and my
    deliverer;
  you are my God, do not delay.

Psalm 41 [a]

For the director of music.
A psalm of David.

[1]Blessed are those who have
    regard for the weak;
  the LORD delivers them in
    times of trouble.
[2]The LORD protects and
    preserves them —

they are counted among the
    blessed in the land —
  he does not give them over to
    the desire of their foes.
[3]The LORD sustains them on
    their sickbed
  and restores them from
    their bed of illness.

[4]I said, "Have mercy on me,
    LORD;   Ps 6:2
  heal me, for I have sinned
    against you."   Ps 51:4
[5]My enemies say of me in
    malice,
  "When will he die and his
    name perish?"   Ps 38:12
[6]When one of them comes to
    see me,
  he speaks falsely, while his
    heart gathers slander;
then he goes out and
    spreads it around.

[7]All my enemies whisper
    together against me;
  they imagine the worst for
    me, saying,
[8]"A vile disease has afflicted
    him;
  he will never get up from
    the place where he lies."
[9]Even my close friend,
    someone I trusted,   Ps 55:12
one who shared my bread,
  has turned [b] against me.

[10]But may you have mercy on
    me, LORD;
  raise me up, that I may
    repay them.   Ps 3:3

---

[a] In Hebrew texts 41:1-13 is numbered 41:2-14.   [b] 9 Hebrew *has lifted up his heel*

¹¹I know that you are pleased
with me,   Ps 147:11
for my enemy does not
triumph over me.
¹²Because of my integrity you
uphold me   Ps 37:17
and set me in your presence
forever.   Job 36:7

¹³Praise be to the LORD, the
God of Israel,
from everlasting to
everlasting.
Amen and Amen.

BOOK II

Psalms 42 – 72

Psalm 42^{a,b}

For the director of music.
A *maskil*^c of the Sons of Korah.

¹As the deer pants for streams
of water,
so my soul pants for you, my
God.   Ps 119:131
²My soul thirsts for God, for
the living God.   Ps 63:1
When can I go and meet
with God?
³My tears have been my food
day and night,   Ps 80:5
while people say to me all day
long,
"Where is your God?"
⁴These things I remember

as I pour out my soul:
how I used to go to the house
of God   Isa 30:29
under the protection of the
Mighty One^d
with shouts of joy and praise
among the festive throng.

⁵Why, my soul, are you
downcast?   Ps 38:6; 77:3
Why so disturbed within me?
Put your hope in God,   La 3:24
for I will yet praise him,
my Savior and my God.   Ps 44:3

⁶My soul is downcast
within me;
therefore I will remember
you
from the land of the Jordan,
the heights of Hermon —
from Mount Mizar.
⁷Deep calls to deep
in the roar of your
waterfalls;
all your waves and breakers
have swept over me.   Ps 88:7

⁸By day the LORD directs his
love,
at night his song is with me —
a prayer to the God of my
life.

⁹I say to God my Rock,
"Why have you forgotten me?
Why must I go about
mourning,   Ps 38:6
oppressed by the enemy?"
¹⁰My bones suffer mortal agony

^a In many Hebrew manuscripts Psalms 42 and 43 constitute one psalm.   ^b In Hebrew
texts 42:1-11 is numbered 42:2-12.   ^c Title: Probably a literary or musical term
^d 4 See Septuagint and Syriac; the meaning of the Hebrew for this line is uncertain.

as my foes taunt me,
saying to me all day long,
"Where is your God?"

¹¹ Why, my soul, are you
    downcast?
  Why so disturbed within me?
Put your hope in God,
  for I will yet praise him,
  my Savior and my God. Ps 43:5

Psalm 43ᵃ

¹ Vindicate me, my God,
  and plead my cause
  against an unfaithful
    nation. Ps 26:1
Rescue me from those who are
  deceitful and wicked.
² You are God my stronghold.
  Why have you rejected me?
Why must I go about mourning,
  oppressed by the enemy?
³ Send me your light and your
    faithful care, Ps 36:9
  let them lead me;
let them bring me to your holy
    mountain, Ps 42:4
  to the place where you dwell.
⁴ Then I will go to the altar of
    God, Ps 26:6
  to God, my joy and my
    delight.
I will praise you with the lyre,
  O God, my God. Ps 33:2

⁵ Why, my soul, are you
    downcast?
  Why so disturbed within me?
Put your hope in God,

for I will yet praise him,
  my Savior and my God. Ps 42:6

Psalm 44ᵇ

For the director of music.
Of the Sons of Korah. A *maskil*.ᶜ

¹ We have heard it with our
    ears, O God;
  our ancestors have told us
what you did in their days,
  in days long ago.
² With your hand you drove out
    the nations
  and planted our ancestors;
you crushed the peoples
  and made our ancestors
    flourish. Ps 80:9
³ It was not by their sword that
    they won the land,
  nor did their arm bring
    them victory;
it was your right hand, your
    arm,
  and the light of your face, for
    you loved them. Dt 7:7-8

⁴ You are my King and my God,
  who decreesᵈ victories for
    Jacob.
⁵ Through you we push back
    our enemies;
  through your name we
    trample our foes.
⁶ I put no trust in my bow, Ps 33:16
  my sword does not bring me
    victory;
⁷ but you give us victory over
    our enemies, Ps 136:24

ᵃ In many Hebrew manuscripts Psalms 42 and 43 constitute one psalm.   ᵇ In Hebrew
texts 44:1-26 is numbered 44:2-27.   ᶜ Title: Probably a literary or musical term
ᵈ 4 Septuagint, Aquila and Syriac; Hebrew *King, O God; / command*

you put our adversaries to
    shame.   Ps 53:5
⁸In God we make our boast all
    day long,   Ps 34:2
  and we will praise your
    name forever.ᵃ

⁹But now you have rejected
    and humbled us; Ps 60:1,10
  you no longer go out with
    our armies.
¹⁰You made us retreat before
    the enemy,   Lev 26:17
  and our adversaries have
    plundered us.
¹¹You gave us up to be devoured
    like sheep   Ro 8:36
  and have scattered us among
    the nations.   Dt 28:64
¹²You sold your people for a
    pittance,   Isa 52:3; Jer 15:13
  gaining nothing from their
    sale.
¹³You have made us a reproach
    to our neighbors,
  the scorn and derision of
    those around us.   Dt 28:37
¹⁴You have made us a byword
    among the nations;
  the peoples shake their
    heads at us.   Jer 24:9
¹⁵I live in disgrace all day long,
  and my face is covered with
    shame
¹⁶at the taunts of those who
    reproach and revile me,
  because of the enemy, who
    is bent on revenge.

¹⁷All this came upon us,

though we had not forgotten
    you;   Ps 78:7,57
  we had not been false to
    your covenant.
¹⁸Our hearts had not turned
    back;   Job 23:11
  our feet had not strayed
    from your path.
¹⁹But you crushed us and made
    us a haunt for jackals;
  you covered us over with
    deep darkness.

²⁰If we had forgotten the name
    of our God   Ps 78:11
  or spread out our hands to a
    foreign god,   Dt 6:14; Ps 81:9
²¹would not God have
    discovered it,
  since he knows the secrets
    of the heart?   Ps 139:1-2
²²Yet for your sake we face
    death all day long;
  we are considered as sheep
    to be slaughtered.   Ro 8:36

²³Awake, Lord! Why do you
    sleep?   Ps 7:6
  Rouse yourself! Do not
    reject us forever.
²⁴Why do you hide your face
  and forget our misery and
    oppression?

²⁵We are brought down to the
    dust;   Ps 119:25
  our bodies cling to the
    ground.
²⁶Rise up and help us;
  rescue us because of your
    unfailing love.   Ps 25:22

ᵃ 8 The Hebrew has *Selah* (a word of uncertain meaning) here.

Psalm 45 [a]

For the director of music. To the tune of "Lilies." Of the Sons of Korah. A *maskil*. [b] A wedding song.

[1] My heart is stirred by a noble theme
    as I recite my verses for the king;
  my tongue is the pen of a skillful writer.

[2] You are the most excellent of men
    and your lips have been anointed with grace,
  since God has blessed you forever.

[3] Gird your sword on your side, you mighty one;   Isa 9:6
  clothe yourself with splendor and majesty.
[4] In your majesty ride forth victoriously   Rev 6:2
  in the cause of truth, humility and justice;
  let your right hand achieve awesome deeds.   Dt 4:34
[5] Let your sharp arrows pierce the hearts of the king's enemies;
  let the nations fall beneath your feet.
[6] Your throne, O God, [c] will last for ever and ever;   Ps 93:2
  a scepter of justice will be the scepter of your kingdom.

[7] You love righteousness and hate wickedness;   Ps 33:5
  therefore God, your God, has set you above your companions
  by anointing you with the oil of joy.   Heb 1:8-9
[8] All your robes are fragrant with myrrh and aloes and cassia;   SS 1:3
  from palaces adorned with ivory
  the music of the strings makes you glad.
[9] Daughters of kings are among your honored women;
  at your right hand is the royal bride in gold of Ophir.

[10] Listen, daughter, and pay careful attention:
  Forget your people and your father's house.   Dt 21:13
[11] Let the king be enthralled by your beauty;
  honor him, for he is your lord.   Ps 95:6; Isa 54:5
[12] The city of Tyre will come with a gift, [d]
  people of wealth will seek your favor.   Ps 22:29
[13] All glorious is the princess within her chamber;
  her gown is interwoven with gold.
[14] In embroidered garments she is led to the king;   SS 1:4
  her virgin companions follow her —

---

[a] In Hebrew texts 45:1-17 is numbered 45:2-18.   [b] Title: Probably a literary or musical term
[c] 6 Here the king is addressed as God's representative.   [d] 12 Or *A Tyrian robe is among the gifts*

those brought to be with her.
[15] Led in with joy and gladness,
they enter the palace of the
king.

[16] Your sons will take the place
of your fathers;
you will make them princes
throughout the land.

[17] I will perpetuate your
memory through all
generations;   Mal 1:11
therefore the nations will
praise you for ever and
ever.   Ps 138:4

Psalm 46[a]

For the director of music.
Of the Sons of Korah. According
to *alamoth*.[b] A song.

[1] God is our refuge and
strength,
an ever-present help in
trouble.   Dt 4:7
[2] Therefore we will not fear,
though the earth give
way   Ps 23:4; 82:5
and the mountains fall into
the heart of the sea,
[3] though its waters roar and
foam   Ps 93:3
and the mountains quake
with their surging.[c]

[4] There is a river whose streams
make glad the city of
God,   Ps 48:1,8; Isa 60:14
the holy place where the
Most High dwells.

[5] God is within her, she will not
fall;
God will help her at break of   Isa 12:6
day.
[6] Nations are in uproar,
kingdoms fall;   Ps 2:1
he lifts his voice, the earth
melts.

[7] The LORD Almighty is with us;
the God of Jacob is our
fortress.   Ps 9:9

[8] Come and see what the LORD
has done,   Ps 66:5
the desolations he has
brought on the earth.
[9] He makes wars cease
to the ends of the earth.   Isa 2:4
He breaks the bow and
shatters the spear;   Ps 76:3
he burns the shields[d] with
fire.   Eze 39:9
[10] He says, "Be still, and know
that I am God;   Ps 100:3
I will be exalted among the
nations,
I will be exalted in the earth."

[11] The LORD Almighty is with us;
the God of Jacob is our
fortress.   Ps 20:1

Psalm 47[e]

For the director of music.
Of the Sons of Korah. A psalm.

[1] Clap your hands, all you
nations;   Ps 98:8; Isa 55:12
shout to God with cries of
joy.

---

[a] In Hebrew texts 46:1-11 is numbered 46:2-12.   [b] Title: Probably a musical term   [c] 3 The
Hebrew has *Selah* (a word of uncertain meaning) here and at the end of verses 7 and 11.
[d] 9 Or *chariots*   [e] In Hebrew texts 47:1-9 is numbered 47:2-10.

904 | PSALM 47:2

²For the LORD Most High is
    awesome,   Dt 7:21
the great King over all the
    earth.
³He subdued nations under us,
    peoples under our feet.
⁴He chose our inheritance for us,
    the pride of Jacob, whom he
    loved.ᵃ

⁵God has ascended amid
    shouts of joy,
the LORD amid the sounding
    of trumpets.   Ps 68:33; 98:6
⁶Sing praises to God, sing
    praises;
sing praises to our King,
    sing praises.   Ps 68:4
⁷For God is the King of all the
    earth;
sing to him a psalm of praise.

⁸God reigns over the nations;
    God is seated on his holy
    throne.
⁹The nobles of the nations
    assemble
as the people of the God of
    Abraham,
for the kingsᵇ of the earth
    belong to God;   Ps 89:18
    he is greatly exalted.

Psalm 48ᶜ

A song. A psalm of the Sons of Korah.

¹Great is the LORD, and most
    worthy of praise,   Ps 96:4
in the city of our God, his
    holy mountain.   Mic 4:1

²Beautiful in its loftiness, Ps 50:2
    the joy of the whole earth,
like the heights of Zaphonᵈ is
    Mount Zion,
    the city of the Great King.
³God is in her citadels;
    he has shown himself to be
    her fortress.   Ps 46:7

⁴When the kings joined forces,
    when they advanced
    together,   2Sa 10:1-19
⁵they saw her and were
    astounded;
    they fled in terror.   Ex 15:16
⁶Trembling seized them there,
    pain like that of a woman in
    labor.
⁷You destroyed them like ships
    of Tarshish
shattered by an east wind.

⁸As we have heard,
    so we have seen
in the city of the LORD Almighty,
    in the city of our God:
God makes her secure
    forever.ᵃ   Ps 87:5

⁹Within your temple, O God,
    we meditate on your
    unfailing love.   Ps 26:3
¹⁰Like your name, O God, Jos 7:9
    your praise reaches to the
    ends of the earth;
your right hand is filled
    with righteousness.
¹¹Mount Zion rejoices,
    the villages of Judah are glad
because of your judgments.

ᵃ 4,8 The Hebrew has *Selah* (a word of uncertain meaning) here. ᵇ 9 Or *shields* ᶜ In
Hebrew texts 48:1-14 is numbered 48:2-15. ᵈ 2 *Zaphon* was the most sacred mountain of
the Canaanites.

^{12}Walk about Zion, go around her,
count her towers,
^{13}consider well her ramparts,
view her citadels, Ps 122:7
that you may tell of them
to the next generation. Ps 78:6

^{14}For this God is our God for
ever and ever;
he will be our guide even to
the end. Ps 23:4

Psalm 49^a

For the director of music.
Of the Sons of Korah. A psalm.

^{1}Hear this, all you peoples;
listen, all who live in this
world, Ps 33:8
^{2}both low and high,
rich and poor alike:
^{3}My mouth will speak words of
wisdom; Ps 37:30
the meditation of my
heart will give you
understanding.
^{4}I will turn my ear to a proverb;
with the harp I will
expound my riddle:

^{5}Why should I fear when evil
days come, Ps 23:4
when wicked deceivers
surround me —
^{6}those who trust in their
wealth Job 31:24
and boast of their great
riches?
^{7}No one can redeem the life of
another

or give to God a ransom for
them —
^{8}the ransom for a life is costly,
no payment is ever
enough — Mt 16:26
^{9}so that they should live on
forever
and not see decay. Ps 89:48
^{10}For all can see that the wise
die, Ecc 2:16
that the foolish and the
senseless also perish,
leaving their wealth to
others. Ecc 2:18,21
^{11}Their tombs will remain their
houses^b forever,
their dwellings for endless
generations,
though they had^c named
lands after themselves.

^{12}People, despite their wealth,
do not endure;
they are like the beasts that
perish.

^{13}This is the fate of those who
trust in themselves,
and of their followers, who
approve their sayings.^{d}
^{14}They are like sheep and are
destined to die; Job 24:19
death will be their shepherd
(but the upright will prevail
over them in the
morning). Da 7:18; Mal 4:3
Their forms will decay in the
grave,
far from their princely
mansions.

---

^{a} In Hebrew texts 49:1-20 is numbered 49:2-21. ^{b} 11 Septuagint and Syriac; Hebrew *In
their thoughts their houses will remain* ^{c} 11 Or *generations, / for they have* ^{d} 13 The
Hebrew has *Selah* (a word of uncertain meaning) here and at the end of verse 15.

15 But God will redeem me from
the realm of the dead;
he will surely take me to
himself.
16 Do not be overawed when
others grow rich,
when the splendor of their
houses increases;
17 for they will take nothing with
them when they die,
their splendor will not
descend with them.
18 Though while they live they
count themselves
blessed —   Lk 12:19
and people praise you when
you prosper —
19 they will join those who have
gone before them,
who will never again see
the light of life.   Job 33:30

20 People who have wealth but
lack understanding
are like the beasts that perish.

Psalm 50

A psalm of Asaph.

1 The Mighty One, God, the
LORD,
speaks and summons the
earth
from the rising of the sun to
where it sets.   Ps 113:3
2 From Zion, perfect in beauty,
God shines forth.   Dt 33:2
3 Our God comes
and will not be silent;
a fire devours before him, Ps 97:3

and around him a tempest
rages.
4 He summons the heavens
above,
and the earth, that he may
judge his people: Dt 4:26
5 "Gather to me this
consecrated people,
who made a covenant with
me by sacrifice."   Ex 24:7
6 And the heavens proclaim his
righteousness,
for he is a God of justice.[a,b]

7 "Listen, my people, and I will
speak;
I will testify against you,
Israel:
I am God, your God.   Ex 20:2
8 I bring no charges against
you concerning your
sacrifices
or concerning your burnt
offerings, which are
ever before me.   Hos 6:6
9 I have no need of a bull from
your stall
or of goats from your pens,
10 for every animal of the forest
is mine,
and the cattle on a
thousand hills.   Ps 104:24
11 I know every bird in the
mountains,   Mt 6:26
and the insects in the fields
are mine.
12 If I were hungry I would not
tell you,
for the world is mine, and
all that is in it.   Ex 19:5

---

a 6 With a different word division of the Hebrew; Masoretic Text *for God himself is judge*
b 6 The Hebrew has *Selah* (a word of uncertain meaning) here.

¹³Do I eat the flesh of bulls
    or drink the blood of goats?

¹⁴"Sacrifice thank offerings to
    God,   Heb 13:15
    fulfill your vows to the Most
    High,   Dt 23:21
¹⁵and call on me in the day of
    trouble;
    I will deliver you, and you
    will honor me."   Ps 22:23

¹⁶But to the wicked person,
God says:

"What right have you to recite
    my laws
    or take my covenant on
    your lips?   Isa 29:13
¹⁷You hate my instruction
    and cast my words behind
    you.   Ne 9:26; Ro 2:21-22
¹⁸When you see a thief, you join
    with him;   Ro 1:32; 1Ti 5:22
    you throw in your lot with
    adulterers.
¹⁹You use your mouth for evil
    and harness your tongue to
    deceit.   Ps 52:2
²⁰You sit and testify against
    your brother
    and slander your own
    mother's son.
²¹When you did these things
    and I kept silent,   Ecc 8:11
    you thought I was exactly[a]
    like you.
But I now arraign you
    and set my accusations
    before you.   Ps 90:8

²²"Consider this, you who forget
    God,   Job 8:13; Ps 9:17
    or I will tear you to pieces,
    with no one to rescue
    you:
²³Those who sacrifice thank
    offerings honor me,
    and to the blameless[b] I will
    show my salvation."

Psalm 51[c]

For the director of music. A psalm
of David. When the prophet Nathan
came to him after David had
committed adultery with Bathsheba.

¹Have mercy on me, O God,
    according to your unfailing
    love;
    according to your great
    compassion
    blot out my transgressions.
²Wash away all my iniquity
    and cleanse me from my sin.

³For I know my transgressions,
    and my sin is always before
    me.   Isa 59:12
⁴Against you, you only, have I
    sinned
    and done what is evil in
    your sight;   Ge 20:6; Lk 15:21
so you are right in your
    verdict
    and justified when you
    judge.   Ro 3:4
⁵Surely I was sinful at birth,
    sinful from the time my
    mother conceived me.

---

[a] 21 Or *thought the 'I AM' was*   [b] 23 Probable reading of the original Hebrew text; the meaning of the Masoretic Text for this phrase is uncertain.   [c] In Hebrew texts 51:1-19 is numbered 51:3-21.

6 Yet you desired faithfulness
  even in the womb;
 you taught me wisdom in
  that secret place. Ps 15:2

7 Cleanse me with hyssop, and
  I will be clean; Lev 14:4
 wash me, and I will be
  whiter than snow. Isa 1:18
8 Let me hear joy and gladness;
 let the bones you have
  crushed rejoice.
9 Hide your face from my sins
 and blot out all my iniquity.

10 Create in me a pure heart,
  O God, Ac 15:9
 and renew a steadfast spirit
  within me. Eze 18:31
11 Do not cast me from your
  presence
 or take your Holy Spirit
  from me. Eph 4:30
12 Restore to me the joy of your
  salvation Ps 13:5
 and grant me a willing
  spirit, to sustain me.

13 Then I will teach transgressors
  your ways, Ac 9:21-22
 so that sinners will turn
  back to you.
14 Deliver me from the guilt of
  bloodshed, O God, 2Sa 12:9
 you who are God my Savior,
 and my tongue will sing of
  your righteousness.
15 Open my lips, Lord, Ps 9:14
 and my mouth will declare
  your praise.

16 You do not delight in sacrifice,
  or I would bring it;
 you do not take pleasure in
  burnt offerings.
17 My sacrifice, O God, is*a* a
  broken spirit;
 a broken and contrite heart
 you, God, will not despise.

18 May it please you to prosper
  Zion, Ps 102:16; Isa 51:3
 to build up the walls of
  Jerusalem.
19 Then you will delight in
  the sacrifices of the
  righteous, Ps 4:5
 in burnt offerings offered
  whole;
 then bulls will be offered on
  your altar. Ps 66:15

Psalm 52*b*

For the director of music.
A *maskil*c of David. When Doeg
the Edomite had gone to Saul and
told him: "David has gone to
the house of Ahimelek."

1 Why do you boast of evil, you
  mighty hero?
 Why do you boast all day
  long, Ps 94:4
 you who are a disgrace in
  the eyes of God?
2 You who practice deceit,
 your tongue plots
  destruction;
 it is like a sharpened razor.
3 You love evil rather than
  good,

---

a 17 Or *The sacrifices of God are*
Probably a literary or musical term *b* In Hebrew texts 52:1-9 is numbered 52:3-11. *c* Title:

falsehood rather than
    speaking the truth.[a]
[4]You love every harmful word,
    you deceitful tongue! Ps 120:2

[5]Surely God will bring you down
    to everlasting ruin:
He will snatch you up and
    pluck you from your tent;
he will uproot you from the
    land of the living. Pr 2:22
[6]The righteous will see and fear;
    they will laugh at you,
    saying, Job 22:19; Ps 37:34
[7]"Here now is the man
    who did not make God his
    stronghold
but trusted in his great wealth
    and grew strong by
    destroying others!"

[8]But I am like an olive tree
    flourishing in the house of
    God;
I trust in God's unfailing love
    for ever and ever.
[9]For what you have done I will
    always praise you Ps 30:12
in the presence of your
    faithful people.
And I will hope in your name,
    for your name is good. Ps 54:6

Psalm 53[b]

53:1-6pp — Ps 14:1-7

For the director of music. According
to *mahalath*.[c] A *maskil*[d] of David.

[1]The fool says in his heart, Ro 3:10
    "There is no God." Ps 10:4

They are corrupt, and their
    ways are vile;
there is no one who does
    good.
[2]God looks down from
    heaven Ps 33:13
on all mankind
to see if there are any who
    understand,
any who seek God. 2Ch 15:2
[3]Everyone has turned away, all
    have become corrupt;
there is no one who does
    good,
not even one. Ro 3:10-12

[4]Do all these evildoers know
    nothing?
They devour my people as
    though eating bread;
they never call on God.
[5]But there they are,
    overwhelmed with
    dread,
where there was nothing to
    dread. Lev 26:17
God scattered the bones of
    those who attacked
    you; Eze 6:5
you put them to shame, for
    God despised them.

[6]Oh, that salvation for Israel
    would come out of Zion!
When God restores his
    people,
let Jacob rejoice and Israel
    be glad!

[a] 3 The Hebrew has *Selah* (a word of uncertain meaning) here and at the end of verse 5. [b] In Hebrew texts 53:1-6 is numbered 53:2-7. [c] Title: Probably a musical term [d] Title: Probably a literary or musical term

Psalm 54[a]

For the director of music. With stringed instruments. A *maskil*[b] of David. When the Ziphites had gone to Saul and said, "Is not David hiding among us?"

[1] Save me, O God, by your name;   Ps 20:1
   vindicate me by your might.   2Ch 20:6
[2] Hear my prayer, O God;
   listen to the words of my mouth.   Ps 5:1; 55:1

[3] Arrogant foes are attacking me;   Ps 86:14
   ruthless people are trying to kill me —
   people without regard for God.[c]   Ps 36:1

[4] Surely God is my help;   Ps 118:7
   the Lord is the one who sustains me.   Ps 41:12

[5] Let evil recoil on those who slander me;
   in your faithfulness destroy them.   Ps 89:49

[6] I will sacrifice a freewill offering to you;
   I will praise your name, LORD, for it is good.   Ps 52:9
[7] You have delivered me from all my troubles,
   and my eyes have looked in triumph on my foes.   Ps 59:10

Psalm 55[d]

For the director of music. With stringed instruments. A *maskil*[b] of David.

[1] Listen to my prayer, O God,
   do not ignore my plea;   Ps 27:9
[2] hear me and answer me.
   My thoughts trouble me and I am distraught   Isa 38:14
[3] because of what my enemy is saying,
   because of the threats of the wicked;
   for they bring down suffering on me   2Sa 16:6-8
   and assail me in their anger.

[4] My heart is in anguish within me;
   the terrors of death have fallen on me.   Ps 116:3
[5] Fear and trembling have beset me;   Job 21:6; Ps 119:120
   horror has overwhelmed me.
[6] I said, "Oh, that I had the wings of a dove!
   I would fly away and be at rest.
[7] I would flee far away
   and stay in the desert;[e]
[8] I would hurry to my place of shelter,
   far from the tempest and storm."   Isa 4:6
[9] Lord, confuse the wicked, confound their words,

---

[a] In Hebrew texts 54:1-7 is numbered 54:3-9.   [b] Title: Probably a literary or musical term
[c] 3 The Hebrew has *Selah* (a word of uncertain meaning) here.   [d] In Hebrew texts 55:1-23 is numbered 55:2-24.   [e] 7 The Hebrew has *Selah* (a word of uncertain meaning) here and in the middle of verse 19.

for I see violence and strife
    in the city.   Jer 6:7
10 Day and night they prowl
        about on its walls;
    malice and abuse are
        within it.
11 Destructive forces are at work
        in the city;   Ps 5:9
    threats and lies never leave
        its streets.   Ps 10:7

12 If an enemy were insulting me,
        I could endure it;
    if a foe were rising against me,
        I could hide.
13 But it is you, a man like myself,
        my companion, my close
        friend,   Ps 41:9
14 with whom I once enjoyed
        sweet fellowship
    at the house of God,
        as we walked about
        among the worshipers. Ps 42:4

15 Let death take my enemies by
        surprise;
    let them go down alive to the
        realm of the dead,   Nu 16:30
    for evil finds lodging among
        them.

16 As for me, I call to God,
        and the LORD saves me.
17 Evening, morning and noon
        I cry out in distress,
    and he hears my voice.
18 He rescues me unharmed
        from the battle waged
        against me,
    even though many
        oppose me.

19 God, who is enthroned from
        of old,   Dt 33:27
    who does not change —
    he will hear them and humble
        them,
    because they have no fear of
        God.   Ps 36:1
20 My companion attacks his
        friends;   Ps 7:4
    he violates his covenant.
21 His talk is smooth as butter,
        yet war is in his heart;
    his words are more soothing
        than oil,
    yet they are drawn swords.

22 Cast your cares on the LORD
        and he will sustain you;
    he will never let
        the righteous be shaken.
23 But you, God, will bring down
        the wicked
    into the pit of decay;
    the bloodthirsty and deceitful
        will not live out half their
        days.   Job 15:32; Pr 10:27

But as for me, I trust in you.

Psalm 56[a]

For the director of music.
To the tune of "A Dove on Distant
Oaks." Of David. A *miktam*.[b]
When the Philistines had
seized him in Gath.

1 Be merciful to me, my God,
        for my enemies are in hot
        pursuit;   Ps 57:1-3
    all day long they press their
        attack.

[a] In Hebrew texts 56:1-13 is numbered 56:2-14.   [b] Title: Probably a literary or musical term

²My adversaries pursue me all
   day long;   Ps 57:3
   in their pride many are
   attacking me.

³When I am afraid, I put my
   trust in you.   Ps 55:4-5
⁴ In God, whose word I
   praise —
   in God I trust and am not afraid.
   What can mere mortals do
   to me?   Ps 118:6; Heb 13:6

⁵All day long they twist my
   words;   Ps 41:7
   all their schemes are for my
   ruin.
⁶They conspire, they lurk, Ps 59:3
   they watch my steps,
   hoping to take my life.
⁷Because of their wickedness
   do not*ᵃ let them escape;
   in your anger, God, bring the
   nations down.   Ps 36:12

⁸Record my misery;
   list my tears on your scrollᵇ —
   are they not in your record?
⁹Then my enemies will turn
   back   Ps 9:3
   when I call for help.   Ps 102:2
   By this I will know that God
   is for me.   Ro 8:31

¹⁰In God, whose word I praise,
   in the LORD, whose word I
   praise —
¹¹in God I trust and am not
   afraid.
   What can man do to me?

¹²I am under vows to you, my
   God;   Ps 50:14
   I will present my thank
   offerings to you.
¹³For you have delivered me
   from death   Ps 116:8
   and my feet from
   stumbling,
   that I may walk before God
   in the light of life.   Job 33:30

Psalm 57ᶜ

57:7-11pp — Ps 108:1-5

For the director of music.
To the tune of "Do Not Destroy."
Of David. A *miktam.*ᵈ When he had
fled from Saul into the cave.

¹Have mercy on me, my God,
   have mercy on me,
   for in you I take refuge. Ps 2:12
   I will take refuge in the
   shadow of your wings
   until the disaster has passed.

²I cry out to God Most High,
   to God, who vindicates me.
³He sends from heaven and
   saves me,   Ps 18:9,16
   rebuking those who hotly
   pursue me — ᵉ   Ps 56:1
   God sends forth his love
   and his faithfulness.

⁴I am in the midst of lions;
   I am forced to dwell among
   ravenous beasts —
   men whose teeth are spears
   and arrows,

ᵃ 7 Probable reading of the original Hebrew text; Masoretic Text does not have *do not*.
ᵇ 8 Or *misery; / put my tears in your wineskin*   ᶜ In Hebrew texts 57:1-11 is numbered
57:2-12.   ᵈ Title: Probably a literary or musical term   ᵉ 3 The Hebrew has *Selah* (a word
of uncertain meaning) here and at the end of verse 6.

whose tongues are sharp
   swords. Pr 30:14

⁵Be exalted, O God, above the
   heavens;
   let your glory be over all the
      earth. Ps 108:5

⁶They spread a net for my feet—
   I was bowed down in distress.
They dug a pit in my path—
   but they have fallen into it
      themselves. Ps 7:15; Pr 28:10

⁷My heart, O God, is steadfast,
   my heart is steadfast; Ps 108:1
   I will sing and make music.
⁸Awake, my soul!
   Awake, harp and lyre! Ps 16:9
   I will awaken the dawn.

⁹I will praise you, Lord, among
   the nations;
   I will sing of you among the
      peoples.
¹⁰For great is your love, reaching
   to the heavens;
   your faithfulness reaches to
      the skies. Ps 36:5

¹¹Be exalted, O God, above the
   heavens;
   let your glory be over all the
      earth. ver 5

Psalm 58ᵃ

For the director of music.
To the tune of "Do Not Destroy."
Of David. A *miktam*.ᵇ

¹Do you rulers indeed speak
   justly? Ps 82:2

Do you judge people with
   equity?
²No, in your heart you devise
   injustice,
   and your hands mete out
      violence on the earth.

³Even from birth the wicked go
   astray;
   from the womb they are
      wayward, spreading
      lies.
⁴Their venom is like the venom
   of a snake, Ps 140:3; Ecc 10:11
   like that of a cobra that has
      stopped its ears,
⁵that will not heed the tune of
   the charmer,
   however skillful the
      enchanter may be.

⁶Break the teeth in their
   mouths, O God;
   LORD, tear out the fangs of
      those lions! Job 4:10
⁷Let them vanish like water
   that flows away; Jos 7:5
   when they draw the bow, let
      their arrows fall short.
⁸May they be like a slug that
   melts away as it moves
      along,
   like a stillborn child that
      never sees the sun.
⁹Before your pots can feel the
   heat of the thorns—
   whether they be green or
      dry—the wicked will
      be swept away.ᶜ Pr 10:25

ᵃ In Hebrew texts 58:1-11 is numbered 58:2-12. ᵇ Title: Probably a literary or musical term
ᶜ 9 The meaning of the Hebrew for this verse is uncertain.

¹⁰The righteous will be glad
    when they are avenged,
when they dip their feet in
    the blood of the wicked.
¹¹Then people will say,
    "Surely the righteous still
      are rewarded;
    surely there is a God who
      judges the earth."   Ps 9:8

Psalm 59^a

For the director of music.
To the tune of "Do Not Destroy."
Of David. A *miktam.*^b When Saul
sent men to watch David's house
in order to kill him.

¹Deliver me from my enemies,
    O God;   Ps 143:9
    be my fortress against those
      who are attacking me.
²Deliver me from evildoers
    and save me from those
      who are after my blood.

³See how they lie in wait for me!
    Fierce men conspire
      against me   Ps 56:6
    for no offense or sin of
      mine, Lord.
⁴I have done no wrong, yet they
    are ready to attack me.
    Arise to help me; look on my
      plight!
⁵You, Lord God Almighty,
    you who are the God of Israel,
    rouse yourself to punish all
      the nations;
    show no mercy to wicked
      traitors.^c   Jer 18:23

⁶They return at evening,
    snarling like dogs,   ver 14
    and prowl about the city.
⁷See what they spew from their
      mouths —
    the words from their lips are
      sharp as swords,   Ps 57:4
    and they think, "Who can
      hear us?"   Ps 10:11
⁸But you laugh at them, Lord;
    you scoff at all those nations.

⁹You are my strength, I watch
      for you;
    you, God, are my fortress,
¹⁰   my God on whom I can rely.

God will go before me
    and will let me gloat over
      those who slander me.
¹¹But do not kill them, Lord our
      shield,^d   Ps 84:9
    or my people will forget.   Dt 4:9
In your might uproot them
    and bring them down.
¹²For the sins of their mouths,
    for the words of their lips,
    let them be caught in their
      pride.
For the curses and lies they
      utter,
¹³   consume them in your wrath,
    consume them till they are
      no more.   Ps 104:35
Then it will be known to the
      ends of the earth
    that God rules over Jacob.

¹⁴They return at evening,
    snarling like dogs,

---

^a In Hebrew texts 59:1-17 is numbered 59:2-18.   ^b Title: Probably a literary or musical term
^c 5 The Hebrew has *Selah* (a word of uncertain meaning) here and at the end of verse 13.
^d 11 Or *sovereign*

and prowl about the city.
¹⁵They wander about for food
and howl if not satisfied.
¹⁶But I will sing of your
strength,
in the morning I will sing of
your love;   Ps 101:1
for you are my fortress,
my refuge in times of
trouble.   Ps 46:1
¹⁷You are my strength, I sing
praise to you;
you, God, are my fortress,
my God on whom I can
rely.   ver 10

Psalm 60[a]

60:5-12pp — Ps 108:6-13

For the director of music.
To the tune of "The Lily of the
Covenant." A miktam[b] of David.
For teaching. When he fought Aram
Naharaim[c] and Aram Zobah,[d] and
when Joab returned and struck down
twelve thousand Edomites
in the Valley of Salt.

¹You have rejected us, God,
and burst upon us;Ps 44:9
you have been angry — now
restore us!   Ps 79:5; 80:3
²You have shaken the land and
torn it open;   Ps 18:7
mend its fractures, for it is
quaking.   2Ch 7:14
³You have shown your people
desperate times;   Ps 71:20
you have given us wine that
makes us stagger.

⁴But for those who fear you, you
have raised a banner
to be unfurled against the
bow.[e]
⁵Save us and help us with your
right hand,   Ps 108:6
that those you love may be
delivered.
⁶God has spoken from his
sanctuary:
"In triumph I will parcel out
Shechem   Ge 12:6
and measure off the Valley
of Sukkoth.
⁷Gilead is mine, and Manasseh
is mine;   Jos 13:31
Ephraim is my helmet,
Judah is my scepter.   Ge 49:10
⁸Moab is my washbasin,
on Edom I toss my sandal;
over Philistia I shout in
triumph."   2Sa 8:1
⁹Who will bring me to the
fortified city?
Who will lead me to Edom?
¹⁰Is it not you, God, you who
have now rejected us
and no longer go out with
our armies?   Jos 7:12
¹¹Give us aid against the
enemy,
for human help is
worthless.   Ps 146:3
¹²With God we will gain the
victory,
and he will trample down
our enemies.   Nu 24:18

^a In Hebrew texts 60:1-12 is numbered 60:3-14.   ^b Title: Probably a literary or musical term
^c Title: That is, Arameans of Northwest Mesopotamia   ^d Title: That is, Arameans of
central Syria   ^e 4 The Hebrew has Selah (a word of uncertain meaning) here.

Psalm 61[a]

For the director of music. With stringed instruments. Of David.

[1] Hear my cry, O God;   Ps 64:1
    listen to my prayer.

[2] From the ends of the earth I
        call to you,
    I call as my heart grows faint;
    lead me to the rock that is
        higher than I.   Ps 18:2

[3] For you have been my refuge,
    a strong tower against the
        foe.   Pr 18:10

[4] I long to dwell in your tent
        forever
    and take refuge in the
        shelter of your wings.[b]

[5] For you, God, have heard my
        vows;   Ps 56:12
    you have given me the
        heritage of those who
        fear your name.   Ps 86:11

[6] Increase the days of the king's
        life,
    his years for many
        generations.   Ps 21:4

[7] May he be enthroned in God's
        presence forever;   Ps 41:12
    appoint your love and
        faithfulness to protect
        him.

[8] Then I will ever sing in praise
        of your name   Ps 65:1
    and fulfill my vows day
        after day.

Psalm 62[c]

For the director of music. For Jeduthun. A psalm of David.

[1] Truly my soul finds rest in
        God;   Dt 23:21
    my salvation comes from
        him.

[2] Truly he is my rock and my
        salvation;   Ps 89:26
    he is my fortress, I will
        never be shaken.   Ps 59:9

[3] How long will you assault me?
    Would all of you throw me
        down —
    this leaning wall, this
        tottering fence?   Isa 30:13

[4] Surely they intend to topple me
        from my lofty place;
    they take delight in lies.
    With their mouths they bless,
    but in their hearts they
        curse.[d]   Ps 28:3

[5] Yes, my soul, find rest in God;
    my hope comes from him.

[6] Truly he is my rock and my
        salvation;
    he is my fortress, I will not
        be shaken.

[7] My salvation and my honor
        depend on God[e];
    he is my mighty rock, my
        refuge.   Ps 46:1; 85:9

[8] Trust in him at all times, you
        people;
    pour out your hearts to him,
    for God is our refuge.

---

[a] In Hebrew texts 61:1-8 is numbered 61:2-9.   [b] 4 The Hebrew has *Selah* (a word of uncertain meaning) here.   [c] In Hebrew texts 62:1-12 is numbered 62:2-13.   [d] 4 The Hebrew has *Selah* (a word of uncertain meaning) here and at the end of verse 8.
[e] 7 Or / *God Most High is my salvation and my honor*

⁹Surely the lowborn are but a
breath,   Ps 39:5,11
the highborn are but a lie.
If weighed on a balance, they
are nothing;   Isa 40:15
together they are only a
breath.
¹⁰Do not trust in extortion
or put vain hope in stolen
goods;
though your riches increase,
do not set your heart on
them.   Job 31:25; 1Ti 6:6-10

¹¹One thing God has spoken,
two things I have heard:
"Power belongs to you, God,
¹²   and with you, Lord, is
unfailing love";   Ps 86:5
and, "You reward everyone
according to what they have
done."   Mt 16:27

Psalm 63ᵃ

A psalm of David. When he was
in the Desert of Judah.

¹You, God, are my God,
earnestly I seek you;
I thirst for you,   Ps 42:2
my whole being longs for
you,
in a dry and parched land
where there is no water.

²I have seen you in the
sanctuary
and beheld your power and
your glory.
³Because your love is better
than life,   Ps 69:16
my lips will glorify you.

⁴I will praise you as long as I
live,   Ps 104:33
and in your name I will lift
up my hands.
⁵I will be fully satisfied as with
the richest of foods;
with singing lips my mouth
will praise you.

⁶On my bed I remember you;
I think of you through the
watches of the night.
⁷Because you are my help,   Ps 27:9
I sing in the shadow of your
wings.
⁸I cling to you;
your right hand upholds me.

⁹Those who want to kill me
will be destroyed; Ps 40:14
they will go down to the
depths of the earth.
¹⁰They will be given over to the
sword
and become food for jackals.

¹¹But the king will rejoice in God;
all who swear by God will
glory in him,   Dt 6:13
while the mouths of liars
will be silenced.

Psalm 64ᵇ

For the director of music.
A psalm of David.

¹Hear me, my God, as I voice
my complaint;   Ps 55:2
protect my life from the
threat of the enemy.
²Hide me from the conspiracy
of the wicked,   Ps 56:6; 59:2

ᵃ In Hebrew texts 63:1-11 is numbered 63:2-12.   ᵇ In Hebrew texts 64:1-10 is numbered 64:2-11.

from the plots of evildoers.
³They sharpen their tongues
   like swords
and aim cruel words like
   deadly arrows.   Ps 58:7
⁴They shoot from ambush at
   the innocent;   Ps 11:2
they shoot suddenly,
   without fear.   Ps 55:19

⁵They encourage each other in
   evil plans,
they talk about hiding their
   snares;
they say, "Who will see it*ᵃ*?"
⁶They plot injustice and say,
   "We have devised a perfect
   plan!"
Surely the human mind and
   heart are cunning.

⁷But God will shoot them with
   his arrows;
they will suddenly be struck
   down.
⁸He will turn their own
   tongues against them
and bring them to ruin;
all who see them will shake
   their heads in scorn.
⁹All people will fear;
they will proclaim the
   works of God
and ponder what he has
   done.   Jer 51:10
¹⁰The righteous will rejoice in
   the LORD
and take refuge in him;
all the upright in heart will
   glory in him!   Ps 32:11

Psalm 65*ᵇ*

For the director of music.
A psalm of David. A song.

¹Praise awaits*ᶜ* you, our God,
   in Zion;
to you our vows will be
   fulfilled.   Ps 116:18
²You who answer prayer,
   to you all people will come.
³When we were overwhelmed
   by sins,   Ps 38:4
you forgave*ᵈ* our
   transgressions.   Heb 9:14
⁴Blessed are those you choose
and bring near to live in
   your courts!
We are filled with the good
   things of your house,
of your holy temple.

⁵You answer us with awesome
   and righteous deeds,
God our Savior,   Ps 85:4
the hope of all the ends of the
   earth
and of the farthest seas,
⁶who formed the mountains by
   your power,
having armed yourself with
   strength,   Ps 93:1
⁷who stilled the roaring of the
   seas,   Mt 8:26
the roaring of their waves,
and the turmoil of the
   nations.   Isa 17:12-13
⁸The whole earth is filled with
   awe at your wonders;
where morning dawns,
   where evening fades,
you call forth songs of joy.

ᵃ 5 Or *us*   *ᵇ* In Hebrew texts 65:1-13 is numbered 65:2-14.   *ᶜ 1* Or *befits*; the meaning of
the Hebrew for this word is uncertain.   *ᵈ 3* Or *made atonement for*

⁹You care for the land and
    water it;   Ps 68:9-10
  you enrich it abundantly.
The streams of God are filled
    with water
  to provide the people with
    grain,   Ps 46:4; 104:14
  for so you have ordained it.ᵃ
¹⁰You drench its furrows and
    level its ridges;
  you soften it with showers
    and bless its crops.
¹¹You crown the year with your
    bounty,
  and your carts overflow
    with abundance.
¹²The grasslands of the
    wilderness overflow;
  the hills are clothed with
    gladness.
¹³The meadows are covered
    with flocks   Ps 144:13
  and the valleys are mantled
    with grain;   Ps 72:16
  they shout for joy and
    sing.   Ps 98:8; Isa 55:12

Psalm 66

For the director of music.
A song. A psalm.

¹Shout for joy to God, all the
    earth!   Ps 100:1
² Sing the glory of his name;
  make his praise glorious.
³Say to God, "How awesome
    are your deeds!   Ps 65:5
  So great is your power
  that your enemies cringe
    before you.   Ps 18:44

⁴All the earth bows down to you;
  they sing praise to you,
  they sing the praises of your
    name."ᵇ
⁵Come and see what God has
    done,
  his awesome deeds for
    mankind!
⁶He turned the sea into dry land,
  they passed through the
    waters on foot —
  come, let us rejoice in him.
⁷He rules forever by his power,
  his eyes watch the nations —
  let not the rebellious rise up
    against him.   Ps 140:8

⁸Praise our God, all peoples,
  let the sound of his praise
    be heard;
⁹he has preserved our lives
  and kept our feet from
    slipping.   Ps 121:3
¹⁰For you, God, tested us;
  you refined us like silver.
¹¹You brought us into prison
  and laid burdens on our
    backs.   La 1:13
¹²You let people ride over our
    heads;   Isa 51:23
  we went through fire and
    water,
  but you brought us to a place
    of abundance.   Isa 43:2

¹³I will come to your temple
  with burnt offerings
  and fulfill my vows to you —
¹⁴vows my lips promised and
  my mouth spoke

ᵃ 9 Or *for that is how you prepare the land*   ᵇ 4 The Hebrew has *Selah* (a word of uncertain
meaning) here and at the end of verses 7 and 15.

when I was in trouble.
15 I will sacrifice fat animals to
you
and an offering of rams;
I will offer bulls and goats.

16 Come and hear, all you who
fear God;
let me tell you what he has
done for me. Ps 71:15,24
17 I cried out to him with my
mouth;
his praise was on my tongue.
18 If I had cherished sin in my
heart,
the Lord would not have
listened; Jas 4:3
19 but God has surely listened
and has heard my prayer.
20 Praise be to God,
who has not rejected my
prayer Ps 22:24; 68:35
or withheld his love from me!

Psalm 67[a]

For the director of music.
With stringed instruments.
A psalm. A song.

1 May God be gracious to us
and bless us
and make his face shine
on us — [b] Nu 6:24-26
2 so that your ways may be
known on earth,
your salvation among all
nations. Tit 2:11

3 May the peoples praise you,
God;

may all the peoples praise
you.
4 May the nations be glad and
sing for joy, Ps 100:1-2
for you rule the peoples
with equity Ps 96:10-13
and guide the nations of the
earth.
5 May the peoples praise you,
God;
may all the peoples praise
you.

6 The land yields its harvest;
God, our God, blesses us.
7 May God bless us still,
so that all the ends of the
earth will fear him.

Psalm 68[c]

For the director of music.
Of David. A psalm. A song.

1 May God arise, may his
enemies be scattered;
may his foes flee before him.
2 May you blow them away like
smoke — Hos 13:3
as wax melts before the fire,
may the wicked perish
before God.
3 But may the righteous be glad
and rejoice before God;
may they be happy and
joyful.

4 Sing to God, sing in praise of
his name, Ps 66:2
extol him who rides on the
clouds[d]; Dt 33:26

[a] In Hebrew texts 67:1-7 is numbered 67:2-8.   [b] 1 The Hebrew has *Selah* (a word of
uncertain meaning) here and at the end of verse 4.   [c] In Hebrew texts 68:1-35 is numbered
68:2-36.   [d] 4 Or *name, / prepare the way for him who rides through the deserts*

rejoice before him — his
name is the Lord.   Ex 6:3
[5]A father to the fatherless, a
defender of widows,
is God in his holy dwelling.
[6]God sets the lonely in
families,[a]   Ps 113:9
he leads out the prisoners
with singing;   Ac 12:6
but the rebellious live in a
sun-scorched land.

[7]When you, God, went out
before your people,
when you marched through
the wilderness,[b]
[8]the earth shook, the heavens
poured down rain,
before God, the One of Sinai,
before God, the God of Israel.
[9]You gave abundant showers,
O God;   Dt 11:11
you refreshed your weary
inheritance.
[10]Your people settled in it,
and from your bounty, God,
you provided for the
poor.   Ps 74:19

[11]The Lord announces the word,
and the women who
proclaim it are a mighty
throng:
[12]"Kings and armies flee in
haste;   Jos 10:16
the women at home divide
the plunder.
[13]Even while you sleep among
the sheep pens,[c]   Ge 49:14

the wings of my dove are
sheathed with silver,
its feathers with shining
gold."
[14]When the Almighty[d] scattered
the kings in the land,
it was like snow fallen on
Mount Zalmon.

[15]Mount Bashan, majestic
mountain,   ver 22; Nu 21:33
Mount Bashan, rugged
mountain,
[16]why gaze in envy, you rugged
mountain,
at the mountain where God
chooses to reign,   Dt 12:5
where the Lord himself will
dwell forever?
[17]The chariots of God are tens
of thousands
and thousands of
thousands;   Dt 33:2
the Lord has come
from Sinai into his
sanctuary.[e]
[18]When you ascended on high,
you took many captives;
you received gifts from
people,   Eph 4:8
even from[f] the rebellious —
that you,[g] Lord God, might
dwell there.

[19]Praise be to the Lord, to God
our Savior,   Ps 65:5
who daily bears our
burdens.   Ps 55:22
[20]Our God is a God who saves;

---

[a] 6 Or the desolate in a homeland   [b] 7 The Hebrew has Selah (a word of uncertain meaning) here and at the end of verses 19 and 32.   [c] 13 Or the campfires; or the saddlebags
[d] 14 Hebrew Shaddai   [e] 17 Probable reading of the original Hebrew text; Masoretic Text Lord is among them at Sinai in holiness   [f] 18 Or gifts for people, / even   [g] 18 Or they

from the Sovereign LORD
  comes escape from
  death.   Ps 56:13
²¹Surely God will crush the
  heads of his enemies,
  the hairy crowns of those
   who go on in their sins.
²²The Lord says, "I will bring
  them from Bashan;
  I will bring them from the
   depths of the sea, Nu 21:33
²³that your feet may wade in the
  blood of your foes, Ps 58:10
  while the tongues of your
   dogs have their share."

²⁴Your procession, God, has
  come into view,
  the procession of my God
   and King into the
   sanctuary.   Ps 63:2
²⁵In front are the singers, after
  them the musicians;
  with them are the young
   women playing the
   timbrels.   1Ch 13:8
²⁶Praise God in the great
  congregation;
  praise the LORD in the
   assembly of Israel. Isa 48:1
²⁷There is the little tribe of
  Benjamin, leading
  them,   1Sa 9:21
  there the great throng of
   Judah's princes,
  and there the princes
   of Zebulun and of
   Naphtali.   Jdg 5:18

²⁸Summon your power, God*a*;

show us your strength, our
  God, as you have done
  before.
²⁹Because of your temple at
  Jerusalem
  kings will bring you
   gifts.   Ps 72:10
³⁰Rebuke the beast among the
  reeds,
  the herd of bulls among
   the calves of the
   nations.   Ps 22:12
  Humbled, may the beast bring
   bars of silver.
  Scatter the nations who
   delight in war.
³¹Envoys will come from
  Egypt;   Isa 45:14
  Cush*b* will submit herself to
   God.

³²Sing to God, you kingdoms of
  the earth,
  sing praise to the Lord,
³³to him who rides across the
  highest heavens, the
  ancient heavens, Ps 18:10
  who thunders with mighty
   voice.
³⁴Proclaim the power of God,
  whose majesty is over Israel,
  whose power is in the
   heavens.
³⁵You, God, are awesome in
  your sanctuary;
  the God of Israel gives
   power and strength to
   his people.   Ps 29:11

Praise be to God!   Ps 66:20

---

a 28 Many Hebrew manuscripts, Septuagint and Syriac; most Hebrew manuscripts *Your God has summoned power for you*   *b* 31 That is, the upper Nile region

Psalm 69[a]

For the director of music.
To the tune of "Lilies." Of David.

[1] Save me, O God,
for the waters have come up
to my neck.   Jnh 2:5
[2] I sink in the miry depths,
where there is no foothold.
I have come into the deep
waters;
the floods engulf me.
[3] I am worn out calling for help;
my throat is parched.
My eyes fail,   Ps 119:82; Isa 38:14
looking for my God.
[4] Those who hate me without
reason   Jn 15:25
outnumber the hairs of my
head;
many are my enemies without
cause,   Ps 35:19
those who seek to
destroy me.
I am forced to restore
what I did not steal.

[5] You, God, know my folly; Ps 38:5
my guilt is not hidden from
you.   Ps 44:21

[6] Lord, the LORD Almighty,
may those who hope in you
not be disgraced because
of me;
God of Israel,
may those who seek you
not be put to shame
because of me.
[7] For I endure scorn for your
sake,   Jer 15:15
and shame covers my face.
[8] I am a foreigner to my own
family,
a stranger to my own
mother's children; Ps 31:11
[9] for zeal for your house
consumes me,   Jn 2:17
and the insults of those who
insult you fall on me.
[10] When I weep and fast,   Ps 35:13
I must endure scorn;
[11] when I put on sackcloth,
people make sport of me.
[12] Those who sit at the gate
mock me,
and I am the song of the
drunkards.   Job 30:9

[13] But I pray to you, LORD,
in the time of your favor;
in your great love, O God,
answer me with your sure
salvation.
[14] Rescue me from the mire,
do not let me sink;
deliver me from those who
hate me,
from the deep waters. Ps 144:7
[15] Do not let the floodwaters
engulf me
or the depths swallow me up
or the pit close its mouth
over me.
[16] Answer me, LORD, out of the
goodness of your love;
in your great mercy turn
to me.
[17] Do not hide your face from
your servant;   Ps 27:9

[a] In Hebrew texts 69:1-36 is numbered 69:2-37.

answer me quickly, for I am
   in trouble.
¹⁸Come near and rescue me;
   deliver me because of my
      foes.

¹⁹You know how I am scorned,
      disgraced and shamed;
   all my enemies are before
      you.
²⁰Scorn has broken my heart
   and has left me helpless;
I looked for sympathy, but
      there was none,
   for comforters, but I found
      none.   Job 16:2; Isa 63:5
²¹They put gall in my food
   and gave me vinegar for my
      thirst.   Jn 19:28-30

²²May the table set before them
      become a snare;
   may it become retribution
      andᵃ a trap.
²³May their eyes be darkened so
      they cannot see,
   and their backs be bent
      forever.   Ro 11:9-10
²⁴Pour out your wrath on
      them;
   let your fierce anger
      overtake them.
²⁵May their place be deserted;
   let there be no one to dwell
      in their tents.
²⁶For they persecute those you
      wound
   and talk about the pain of
      those you hurt.   Isa 53:4
²⁷Charge them with crime upon
      crime;

do not let them share in
   your salvation.
²⁸May they be blotted out of the
      book of life   Ex 32:32-33
   and not be listed with the
      righteous.
²⁹But as for me, afflicted and in
      pain —
   may your salvation, God,
      protect me.   Ps 59:1; 70:5

³⁰I will praise God's name in
      song
   and glorify him with
      thanksgiving.
³¹This will please the LORD
      more than an ox,
   more than a bull with its
      horns and hooves. Ps 50:9
³²The poor will see and be
      glad —   Ps 34:2
   you who seek God, may
      your hearts live! Ps 22:26
³³The LORD hears the needy
   and does not despise his
      captive people.

³⁴Let heaven and earth praise
      him,
   the seas and all that move
      in them,   Ps 96:11; Isa 44:23
³⁵for God will save Zion
   and rebuild the cities of
      Judah.   Ps 51:18; Isa 44:26
Then people will settle there
      and possess it;
³⁶   the children of his servants
      will inherit it,
   and those who love his
      name will dwell there.

ᵃ 22 Or snare / and their fellowship become

Psalm 70[a]

70:1-5pp — Ps 40:13-17

For the director of music.
Of David. A petition.

[1] Hasten, O God, to save me;
come quickly, LORD, to
help me. Ps 40:13

[2] May those who want to take
my life Ps 35:4
be put to shame and
confusion;
may all who desire my ruin
be turned back in disgrace.

[3] May those who say to me,
"Aha! Aha!"
turn back because of their
shame.

[4] But may all who seek you Ps 9:10
rejoice and be glad in you;
may those who long for your
saving help always say,
"The LORD is great!" Ps 35:27

[5] But as for me, I am poor and
needy; Ps 40:17
come quickly to me, O God.
You are my help and my
deliverer; Ps 18:2
LORD, do not delay.

Psalm 71

71:1-3pp — Ps 31:1-4

[1] In you, LORD, I have taken
refuge;
let me never be put to
shame. Ps 25:2-3; 31:1

[2] In your righteousness, rescue
me and deliver me;

turn your ear to me and
save me. Ps 17:6

[3] Be my rock of refuge,
to which I can always go;
give the command to save me,
for you are my rock and my
fortress. Ps 18:2; 31:2-3

[4] Deliver me, my God, from the
hand of the wicked,
from the grasp of those who
are evil and cruel.

[5] For you have been my hope,
Sovereign LORD,
my confidence since my
youth. Jer 17:7

[6] From birth I have relied on you;
you brought me forth from
my mother's womb.
I will ever praise you. Ps 34:1

[7] I have become a sign to many;
you are my strong refuge.

[8] My mouth is filled with your
praise,
declaring your splendor all
day long. Ps 35:28

[9] Do not cast me away when I
am old; ver 18
do not forsake me when my
strength is gone.

[10] For my enemies speak
against me;
those who wait to kill me
conspire together. Ps 10:8

[11] They say, "God has forsaken
him;
pursue him and seize him,
for no one will rescue him."

[12] Do not be far from me, my
God; Ps 35:22

come quickly, God, to
    help me.   Ps 70:1
[13] May my accusers perish in
    shame;
may those who want to
    harm me
be covered with scorn and
    disgrace.   ver 24

[14] As for me, I will always have
    hope;   Ps 130:7
I will praise you more and
    more.

[15] My mouth will tell of your
    righteous deeds,   Ps 35:28
of your saving acts all day
    long—
though I know not how to
    relate them all.

[16] I will come and proclaim your
    mighty acts, Sovereign
    LORD;   Ps 106:2
I will proclaim your
    righteous deeds, yours
    alone.

[17] Since my youth, God, you
    have taught me,
and to this day I declare
    your marvelous deeds.

[18] Even when I am old and gray,
    do not forsake me, my God,
till I declare your power to the
    next generation,
your mighty acts to all who
    are to come.   Ps 22:30,31

[19] Your righteousness, God,
    reaches to the heavens,
you who have done great
    things.
Who is like you, God? Ps 35:10

[20] Though you have made me
    see troubles,   Ps 60:3
many and bitter,
you will restore my life again;
from the depths of the earth
    you will again bring me up.
[21] You will increase my honor
    and comfort me once more.

[22] I will praise you with the harp
    for your faithfulness, my God;
I will sing praise to you with
    the lyre,
Holy One of Israel.   2Ki 19:22
[23] My lips will shout for joy
    when I sing praise to you—
I whom you have
    delivered.   Ps 103:4
[24] My tongue will tell of your
    righteous acts
all day long,   Ps 35:28
for those who wanted to
    harm me
have been put to shame and
    confusion.

Psalm 72

Of Solomon.

[1] Endow the king with your
    justice, O God,
the royal son with your
    righteousness.
[2] May he judge your people in
    righteousness,   Isa 9:7
your afflicted ones with
    justice.

[3] May the mountains bring
    prosperity to the
    people,
the hills the fruit of
    righteousness.

⁴May he defend the afflicted
among the people
and save the children of the
needy;   Isa 11:4
may he crush the oppressor.
⁵May he endure*ᵃ* as long as the
sun,
as long as the moon,
through all generations.
⁶May he be like rain falling on
a mown field,   Hos 6:3
like showers watering the
earth.
⁷In his days may the righteous
flourish   Ps 92:12; Isa 2:4
and prosperity abound till
the moon is no more.

⁸May he rule from sea to sea
and from the River*ᵇ* to the
ends of the earth. Ex 23:31
⁹May the desert tribes bow
before him
and his enemies lick the dust.
¹⁰May the kings of Tarshish and
of distant shores
bring tribute to him.
May the kings of Sheba and Seba
present him gifts.   2Ch 9:24
¹¹May all kings bow down to him
and all nations serve him.

¹²For he will deliver the needy
who cry out,
the afflicted who have no
one to help.
¹³He will take pity on the weak
and the needy
and save the needy from
death.

¹⁴He will rescue them from
oppression and
violence,
for precious is their blood in
his sight.   Ps 116:15

¹⁵Long may he live!
May gold from Sheba be
given him.   Isa 60:6
May people ever pray for him
and bless him all day long.
¹⁶May grain abound throughout
the land;
on the tops of the hills may
it sway.
May the crops flourish like
Lebanon   Ps 104:16
and thrive*ᶜ* like the grass of
the field.
¹⁷May his name endure forever;
may it continue as long as
the sun.   Ps 89:36

Then all nations will be
blessed through him,*ᵈ*
and they will call him
blessed.   Ge 12:3; Lk 1:48

¹⁸Praise be to the Lᴏʀᴅ God, the
God of Israel,   1Ch 29:10
who alone does marvelous
deeds.
¹⁹Praise be to his glorious name
forever;
may the whole earth be
filled with his glory.
Amen and Amen.

²⁰This concludes the prayers
of David son of Jesse.

ᵃ 5 Septuagint; Hebrew *You will be feared*   *ᵇ 8* That is, the Euphrates   *ᶜ 16* Probable
reading of the original Hebrew text; Masoretic Text *Lebanon, / from the city*   *ᵈ 17* Or *will
use his name in blessings* (see Gen. 48:20)

BOOK III

Psalms 73–89

Psalm 73

A psalm of Asaph.

¹Surely God is good to Israel,
  to those who are pure in
    heart. Mt 5:8

²But as for me, my feet had
    almost slipped;
  I had nearly lost my
    foothold.

³For I envied the arrogant Ps 37:1
  when I saw the prosperity of
    the wicked. Job 21:7

⁴They have no struggles;
  their bodies are healthy and
    strong.ᵃ

⁵They are free from common
    human burdens; Job 21:9
  they are not plagued by
    human ills.

⁶Therefore pride is their
    necklace;
  they clothe themselves with
    violence. Ps 109:18

⁷From their callous hearts
    comes iniquityᵇ; Ps 17:10
  their evil imaginations have
    no limits.

⁸They scoff, and speak with
    malice;
  with arrogance they
    threaten oppression.

⁹Their mouths lay claim to
    heaven,
and their tongues take
    possession of the earth.

¹⁰Therefore their people turn to
    them
  and drink up waters in
    abundance.ᶜ

¹¹They say, "How would God
    know?
  Does the Most High know
    anything?"

¹²This is what the wicked are
    like —
  always free of care, they
    go on amassing
    wealth. Ps 49:6

¹³Surely in vain I have kept my
    heart pure Job 34:9
  and have washed my hands
    in innocence. Ps 26:6

¹⁴All day long I have been
    afflicted,
  and every morning brings
    new punishments.

¹⁵If I had spoken out like that,
  I would have betrayed your
    children.

¹⁶When I tried to understand all
    this,
  it troubled me deeply Ecc 8:17

¹⁷till I entered the sanctuary of
    God; Ps 77:13
  then I understood their
    final destiny. Ps 37:38

¹⁸Surely you place them on
    slippery ground; Ps 35:6
  you cast them down to ruin.

ᵃ 4 With a different word division of the Hebrew; Masoretic Text *struggles at their death; /
their bodies are healthy*   ᵇ 7 Syriac (see also Septuagint); Hebrew *Their eyes bulge with fat*
ᶜ 10 The meaning of the Hebrew for this verse is uncertain.

19 How suddenly are they
  destroyed,   Isa 47:11
  completely swept away by
  terrors!
20 They are like a dream when
  one awakes;   Job 20:8
  when you arise, Lord,
  you will despise them as
  fantasies.

21 When my heart was grieved
  and my spirit embittered,
22 I was senseless and ignorant;
  I was a brute beast before
  you.   Ecc 3:18

23 Yet I am always with you;
  you hold me by my right
  hand.
24 You guide me with your
  counsel,   Ps 32:8; 48:14
  and afterward you will take
  me into glory.
25 Whom have I in heaven but
  you?
  And earth has nothing I
  desire besides you.   Php 3:8
26 My flesh and my heart may
  fail,   Ps 84:2
  but God is the strength of
  my heart
  and my portion forever.

27 Those who are far from you
  will perish;   Ps 119:155
  you destroy all who are
  unfaithful to you.
28 But as for me, it is good to be
  near God.   Heb 10:22; Jas 4:8
  I have made the Sovereign
  LORD my refuge;
  I will tell of all your deeds.

a Title: Probably a literary or musical term

They burned every place
  where God was
  worshiped in the land.
⁹We are given no signs from
  God;
  no prophets are left,   1Sa 3:1
  and none of us knows how
  long this will be.
¹⁰How long will the enemy
  mock you, God?
  Will the foe revile your
  name forever?   Ps 44:16
¹¹Why do you hold back your
  hand, your right
  hand?
  Take it from the folds of
  your garment and
  destroy them!

¹²But God is my King from long
  ago;   Ps 44:4
  he brings salvation on the
  earth.
¹³It was you who split open the
  sea by your power;
  you broke the heads of the
  monster in the waters.
¹⁴It was you who crushed the
  heads of Leviathan
  and gave it as food to the
  creatures of the desert.
¹⁵It was you who opened up
  springs and streams;
  you dried up the ever-
  flowing rivers.   Jos 43:13
¹⁶The day is yours, and yours
  also the night;
  you established the sun and
  moon.   Ge 1:16; Ps 136:7-9

¹⁷It was you who set all the
  boundaries of the
  earth;
  you made both summer
  and winter.   Ge 8:22
¹⁸Remember how the enemy
  has mocked you, Lord,
  how foolish people have
  reviled your name.   Ps 39:8
¹⁹Do not hand over the life of
  your dove to wild beasts;
  do not forget the lives of
  your afflicted people
  forever.   Ps 9:18
²⁰Have regard for your
  covenant,   Ge 17:7; Ps 106:45
  because haunts of violence
  fill the dark places of
  the land.
²¹Do not let the oppressed
  retreat in disgrace;
  may the poor and needy
  praise your name.   Ps 35:10
²²Rise up, O God, and defend
  your cause;
  remember how fools mock
  you all day long.   Ps 53:1
²³Do not ignore the clamor of
  your adversaries,   Ps 65:7
  the uproar of your enemies,
  which rises continually.

Psalm 75ᵃ

For the director of music.
To the tune of "Do Not Destroy."
A psalm of Asaph. A song.

¹We praise you, God,
  we praise you, for your
  Name is near;   Ps 145:18

ᵃ In Hebrew texts 75:1-10 is numbered 75:2-11.

people tell of your
wonderful deeds.   Ps 44:1

²You say, "I choose the
appointed time;
it is I who judge with
equity.   Ps 7:11
³When the earth and all its
people quake,   Isa 24:19
it is I who hold its pillars
firm.ᵃ   1Sa 2:8
⁴To the arrogant I say, 'Boast
no more,'
and to the wicked, 'Do not
lift up your horns.ᵇ
⁵Do not lift your horns against
heaven;
do not speak so defiantly.'"

⁶No one from the east or the
west
or from the desert can exalt
themselves.
⁷It is God who judges: Ps 50:6
He brings one down, he
exalts another.   1Sa 2:7
⁸In the hand of the LORD is a cup
full of foaming wine mixed
with spices;   Pr 23:30
he pours it out, and all the
wicked of the earth
drink it down to its very
dregs.   Jer 25:15

⁹As for me, I will declare this
forever;   Ps 40:10
I will sing praise to the God
of Jacob,
¹⁰who says, "I will cut off the
horns of all the wicked,

but the horns of the righteous
will be lifted up."   Ps 89:17

Psalm 76ᶜ

For the director of music.
With stringed instruments.
A psalm of Asaph. A song.

¹God is renowned in Judah;
in Israel his name is great.
²His tent is in Salem,   Ge 14:18
his dwelling place in Zion.
³There he broke the flashing
arrows,
the shields and the swords,
the weapons of war.ᵈ

⁴You are radiant with light,
more majestic than
mountains rich with
game.
⁵The valiant lie plundered,
they sleep their last
sleep;   Ps 13:3
not one of the warriors
can lift his hands.
⁶At your rebuke, God of Jacob,
both horse and chariot lie
still.   Ex 15:1

⁷It is you alone who are to be
feared.
Who can stand before you
when you are angry?
⁸From heaven you pronounced
judgment,
and the land feared and was
quiet—   2Ch 20:29-30
⁹when you, God, rose up to
judge,   Ps 9:8

ᵃ 3 The Hebrew has *Selah* (a word of uncertain meaning) here.   ᵇ 4 *Horns* here symbolize
strength; also in verses 5 and 10.   ᶜ In Hebrew texts 76:1-12 is numbered 76:2-13.
ᵈ 3 The Hebrew has *Selah* (a word of uncertain meaning) here and at the end of verse 9.

to save all the afflicted of
the land.
¹⁰ Surely your wrath against
mankind brings you
praise,   Ex 9:16; Ro 9:17
and the survivors of your
wrath are restrained.ᵃ

¹¹ Make vows to the LORD your
God and fulfill them;
let all the neighboring lands
bring gifts to the One to be
feared.   Ps 68:29
¹² He breaks the spirit of rulers;
he is feared by the kings of
the earth.

Psalm 77ᵇ

For the director of music.
For Jeduthun. Of Asaph. A psalm.

¹ I cried out to God for help; Ps 3:4
I cried out to God to hear me.
² When I was in distress, I
sought the Lord;   Ps 50:15
at night I stretched out
untiring hands,   Job 11:13
and I would not be
comforted.   Ge 37:35

³ I remembered you, God, and I
groaned;
I meditated, and my spirit
grew faint.ᶜ   Ps 143:4
⁴ You kept my eyes from closing;
I was too troubled to speak.
⁵ I thought about the former days,
the years of long ago;
⁶ I remembered my songs in the
night.

My heart meditated and my
spirit asked:

⁷ "Will the Lord reject forever?
Will he never show his favor
again?   Ps 85:1
⁸ Has his unfailing love
vanished forever?
Has his promise failed for
all time?   2Pe 3:9
⁹ Has God forgotten to be
merciful?
Has he in anger withheld
his compassion?"   Isa 49:15

¹⁰ Then I thought, "To this I will
appeal:
the years when the Most
High stretched out his
right hand.   Ps 31:22
¹¹ I will remember the deeds of
the LORD;
yes, I will remember your
miracles of long ago.
¹² I will consider all your works
and meditate on all your
mighty deeds."

¹³ Your ways, God, are holy.
What god is as great as our
God?   Ex 15:11
¹⁴ You are the God who
performs miracles;
you display your power
among the peoples.
¹⁵ With your mighty arm you
redeemed your
people,   Ex 6:6; Dt 9:29
the descendants of Jacob
and Joseph.

ᵃ 10 Or *Surely the wrath of mankind brings you praise, / and with the remainder of wrath you arm yourself*   ᵇ In Hebrew texts 77:1-20 is numbered 77:2-21.   ᶜ 3 The Hebrew has *Selah* (a word of uncertain meaning) here and at the end of verses 9 and 15.

¹⁶The waters saw you, God,
  the waters saw you and
    writhed; Ps 114:4
  the very depths were
    convulsed.
¹⁷The clouds poured down
    water, Jdg 5:4
  the heavens resounded with
    thunder;
  your arrows flashed back
    and forth.
¹⁸Your thunder was heard in the
    whirlwind,
  your lightning lit up the
    world;
  the earth trembled and
    quaked. Jdg 5:4
¹⁹Your path led through the sea,
  your way through the
    mighty waters,
  though your footprints were
    not seen.

²⁰You led your people like a flock
  by the hand of Moses and
    Aaron.

Psalm 78

A *maskil*^a of Asaph.

¹My people, hear my teaching;
  listen to the words of my
    mouth.
²I will open my mouth with a
    parable;
  I will utter hidden things, Mt 13:35
    things from of old —
³things we have heard and
    known,
  things our ancestors have
    told us. Ps 44:1

⁴We will not hide them from
  their descendants; Dt 11:19
  we will tell the next
    generation
  the praiseworthy deeds of the
    LORD, Ps 26:7; 71:17
  his power, and the wonders
    he has done.
⁵He decreed statutes for
    Jacob Ps 147:19
  and established the law in
    Israel,
  which he commanded our
    ancestors
  to teach their children,
⁶so the next generation would
    know them,
  even the children yet to be
    born, Ps 102:18
  and they in turn would tell
    their children.
⁷Then they would put their
    trust in God
  and would not forget his
    deeds
  but would keep his
    commands.
⁸They would not be like their
    ancestors —
  a stubborn and rebellious
    generation, Ex 32:9
  whose hearts were not loyal to
    God,
  whose spirits were not
    faithful to him.

⁹The men of Ephraim, though
    armed with bows,
  turned back on the day of
    battle; Jdg 20:39

^a Title: Probably a literary or musical term

¹⁰they did not keep God's
covenant   2Ki 17:15
and refused to live by his
law.
¹¹They forgot what he had done,
the wonders he had shown
them.
¹²He did miracles in the sight of
their ancestors
in the land of Egypt, in the
region of Zoan.   Nu 13:22
¹³He divided the sea and led
them through;   Ex 14:21
he made the water stand up
like a wall.   Ex 15:8
¹⁴He guided them with the
cloud by day
and with light from the fire
all night.   Ex 13:21
¹⁵He split the rocks in the
wilderness   Nu 20:11
and gave them water as
abundant as the seas;
¹⁶he brought streams out of a
rocky crag
and made water flow down
like rivers.
¹⁷But they continued to sin
against him,   Heb 3:16
rebelling in the wilderness
against the Most High.
¹⁸They willfully put God to the
test   1Co 10:9
by demanding the food they
craved.   Nu 11:4
¹⁹They spoke against God; Nu 21:5
they said, "Can God really
spread a table in the
wilderness?
²⁰True, he struck the rock,

and water gushed out, Nu 20:11
streams flowed abundantly,
but can he also give us bread?
Can he supply meat for his
people?"   Nu 11:18
²¹When the LORD heard them,
he was furious;
his fire broke out against
Jacob,   Nu 11:1
and his wrath rose against
Israel,
²²for they did not believe in God
or trust in his deliverance.
²³Yet he gave a command to the
skies above
and opened the doors of the
heavens;   Ge 7:11; Mal 3:10
²⁴he rained down manna for
the people to eat,   Jn 6:31
he gave them the grain of
heaven.
²⁵Human beings ate the bread
of angels;
he sent them all the food
they could eat.
²⁶He let loose the east wind
from the heavens Nu 11:31
and by his power made the
south wind blow.
²⁷He rained meat down on
them like dust,
birds like sand on the
seashore.
²⁸He made them come down
inside their camp,
all around their tents.
²⁹They ate till they were gorged—
he had given them what
they craved.
³⁰But before they turned from
what they craved,

even while the food was still
in their mouths, Nu 11:33
31 God's anger rose against
them;
he put to death the sturdiest
among them, Isa 10:16
cutting down the young
men of Israel.
32 In spite of all this, they kept
on sinning;
in spite of his wonders, they
did not believe. ver 11,22
33 So he ended their days in
futility Nu 14:29,35
and their years in terror.
34 Whenever God slew them,
they would seek him;
they eagerly turned to him
again.
35 They remembered that God
was their Rock, Dt 32:4
that God Most High was
their Redeemer. Dt 9:26
36 But then they would flatter
him with their
mouths,
lying to him with their Eze 33:31
tongues;
37 their hearts were not loyal to
him,
they were not faithful to his
covenant. Ac 8:21
38 Yet he was merciful; Ex 34:6
he forgave their iniquities
and did not destroy them.
Time after time he restrained
his anger
and did not stir up his full
wrath.
39 He remembered that they
were but flesh, Ps 103:14

a passing breeze that does
not return. Job 7:7
40 How often they rebelled
against him in the
wilderness
and grieved him in the
wasteland! Ps 95:8
41 Again and again they put God
to the test; Nu 14:22
they vexed the Holy One of
Israel. Ps 89:18
42 They did not remember his
power —
the day he redeemed them
from the oppressor,
43 the day he displayed his signs
in Egypt,
his wonders in the region of
Zoan.
44 He turned their river into
blood; Ex 7:20-21
they could not drink from
their streams.
45 He sent swarms of flies that
devoured them, Ex 8:24
and frogs that devastated
them. Ex 8:2,6
46 He gave their crops to the
grasshopper,
their produce to the
locust.
47 He destroyed their vines with
hail Ex 9:23
and their sycamore-figs
with sleet.
48 He gave over their cattle to
the hail,
their livestock to bolts of
lightning.
49 He unleashed against them
his hot anger, Ex 15:7

his wrath, indignation and
hostility —
a band of destroying angels.
⁵⁰He prepared a path for his
anger;
he did not spare them from
death
but gave them over to the
plague.
⁵¹He struck down all the
firstborn of Egypt, Ex 12:29
the firstfruits of manhood
in the tents of Ham.
⁵²But he brought his people out
like a flock; Ps 77:20
he led them like sheep
through the wilderness.
⁵³He guided them safely, so
they were unafraid;
but the sea engulfed their
enemies. Ex 14:28
⁵⁴And so he brought them to the
border of his holy land,
to the hill country his right
hand had taken. Ps 44:3
⁵⁵He drove out nations before
them Ps 44:2
and allotted their lands to
them as an inheritance;
he settled the tribes of Israel
in their homes.

⁵⁶But they put God to the test
and rebelled against the
Most High;
they did not keep his
statutes.
⁵⁷Like their ancestors they were
disloyal and faithless,
as unreliable as a faulty
bow.

⁵⁸They angered him with their
high places; Lev 26:30
they aroused his jealousy
with their idols. Dt 32:21
⁵⁹When God heard them, he
was furious;
he rejected Israel
completely. Dt 32:19
⁶⁰He abandoned the tabernacle
of Shiloh, Jos 18:1
the tent he had set up
among humans.
⁶¹He sent the ark of his might
into captivity, Ps 132:8
his splendor into the hands
of the enemy.
⁶²He gave his people over to the
sword;
he was furious with his
inheritance.
⁶³Fire consumed their young
men, Nu 11:1
and their young women had
no wedding songs;Jer 7:34
⁶⁴their priests were put to the
sword, 1Sa 22:18
and their widows could not
weep.

⁶⁵Then the Lord awoke as from
sleep,
as a warrior wakes from the
stupor of wine.
⁶⁶He beat back his enemies;
he put them to everlasting
shame. 1Sa 5:6
⁶⁷Then he rejected the tents of
Joseph,
he did not choose the tribe
of Ephraim;
⁶⁸but he chose the tribe of Judah,

Mount Zion, which he
loved.   Ps 87:2
⁶⁹ He built his sanctuary like the
heights,
like the earth that he
established forever.
⁷⁰ He chose David his servant
and took him from the
sheep pens;
⁷¹ from tending the sheep he
brought him
to be the shepherd of his
people Jacob,   2Sa 5:2
of Israel his inheritance.
⁷² And David shepherded them
with integrity of heart;
with skillful hands he led
them.

Psalm 79

A psalm of Asaph.

¹ O God, the nations have
invaded your
inheritance;   Ps 74:2
they have defiled your holy
temple,
they have reduced
Jerusalem to rubble.
² They have left the dead bodies
of your servants
as food for the birds of the
sky,
the flesh of your own people
for the animals of the
wild.   Jer 7:33
³ They have poured out blood
like water
all around Jerusalem,
and there is no one to bury
the dead.   Jer 16:4

⁴ We are objects of contempt to
our neighbors,
of scorn and derision to
those around us.   Ps 44:13

⁵ How long, LORD? Will you be
angry forever?   Ps 74:1,10
How long will your jealousy
burn like fire?   Zep 3:8
⁶ Pour out your wrath on the
nations
that do not acknowledge you,
on the kingdoms
that do not call on your
name;   Ps 14:4
⁷ for they have devoured Jacob
and devastated his
homeland.

⁸ Do not hold against us the
sins of past generations;
may your mercy come
quickly to meet us,
for we are in desperate need.
⁹ Help us, God our Savior,
for the glory of your name;
deliver us and forgive our sins
for your name's sake.   Jer 14:7
¹⁰ Why should the nations say,
"Where is their God?"   Ps 42:10

Before our eyes, make known
among the nations
that you avenge the
outpoured blood of
your servants.   Ps 94:1
¹¹ May the groans of the
prisoners come before
you;
with your strong arm
preserve those
condemned to die.

¹²Pay back into the laps of our
    neighbors seven times
  the contempt they have
    hurled at you, Lord.
¹³Then we your people, the
    sheep of your pasture,
  will praise you forever;
  from generation to generation
    we will proclaim your
    praise.

Psalm 80ᵃ

For the director of music.
To the tune of "The Lilies of the
Covenant." Of Asaph. A psalm.

¹Hear us, Shepherd of Israel,
  you who lead Joseph like a
    flock.   Ps 77:20
  You who sit enthroned
    between the cherubim,
  shine forth ²before
    Ephraim, Benjamin
    and Manasseh.   Nu 2:18-24
  Awaken your might;
  come and save us.

³Restore us, O God; Nu 6:25; La 5:21
  make your face shine on us,
  that we may be saved.

⁴How long, LORD God
    Almighty,
  will your anger smolder
  against the prayers of your
    people?
⁵You have fed them with the
    bread of tears;
  you have made them drink
    tears by the bowlful.

⁶You have made us an object
    of derisionᵇ to our
    neighbors,
  and our enemies mock us.

⁷Restore us, God Almighty;
  make your face shine on us,
  that we may be saved.

⁸You transplanted a vine from
    Egypt;   Isa 5:1-2
  you drove out the nations
    and planted it.   Jos 13:6
⁹You cleared the ground for it,
  and it took root and filled
    the land.
¹⁰The mountains were covered
    with its shade,
  the mighty cedars with its
    branches.
¹¹Its branches reached as far as
    the Sea,ᶜ
  its shoots as far as the
    River.ᵈ   Ps 72:8

¹²Why have you broken down
    its walls
  so that all who pass by pick
    its grapes?
¹³Boars from the forest ravage it,
  and insects from the fields
    feed on it.
¹⁴Return to us, God Almighty!
  Look down from heaven
    and see!   Isa 63:15
  Watch over this vine,
¹⁵ the root your right hand has
    planted,
  the sonᵉ you have raised up
    for yourself.

ᵃ In Hebrew texts 80:1-19 is numbered 80:2-20.   ᵇ 6 Probable reading of the original
Hebrew text; Masoretic Text *contention*   ᶜ 11 Probably the Mediterranean   ᵈ 11 That is,
the Euphrates   ᵉ 15 Or *branch*

¹⁶Your vine is cut down, it is
burned with fire;
at your rebuke your people
perish.   Ps 39:11; 76:6
¹⁷Let your hand rest on the man
at your right hand,
the son of man you have
raised up for yourself.
¹⁸Then we will not turn away
from you;
revive us, and we will call on
your name.   Ps 5:6; Isa 57:15

¹⁹Restore us, LORD God
Almighty;
make your face shine on us,
that we may be saved.

Psalm 81 [a]

For the director of music.
According to *gittith*. [b] Of Asaph.

¹Sing for joy to God our strength;
shout aloud to the God of
Jacob!   Ps 66:1
²Begin the music, strike the
timbrel,
play the melodious harp
and lyre.   Ps 92:3

³Sound the ram's horn at the
New Moon,
and when the moon is
full, on the day of our
festival;
⁴this is a decree for Israel,
an ordinance of the God of
Jacob.
⁵When God went out against
Egypt,   Ex 11:4

he established it as a statute
for Joseph.

I heard an unknown voice say:

⁶"I removed the burden from
their shoulders;   Isa 9:4
their hands were set free
from the basket.
⁷In your distress you called
and I rescued you,   Ex 2:23
I answered you out of a
thundercloud;   Ex 19:19
I tested you at the waters of
Meribah. [c]   Ex 17:7
⁸Hear me, my people, and I
will warn you —   Ps 50:7
if you would only listen to
me, Israel!
⁹You shall have no foreign god
among you;   Ex 20:3; Dt 32:12
you shall not worship any
god other than me.
¹⁰I am the LORD your God,
who brought you up out of
Egypt.   Ex 20:2
Open wide your mouth and I
will fill it.   Ps 107:9

¹¹"But my people would not
listen to me;
Israel would not submit
to me.
¹²So I gave them over to their
stubborn hearts   Ac 7:42
to follow their own devices.

¹³"If my people would only
listen to me,   Dt 5:29
if Israel would only follow
my ways,

^a In Hebrew texts 81:1-16 is numbered 81:2-17.   ^b Title: Probably a musical term   ^c 7 The
Hebrew has *Selah* (a word of uncertain meaning) here.

¹⁴how quickly I would subdue
    their enemies   Ps 47:3
  and turn my hand against
    their foes!   Am 1:8
¹⁵Those who hate the LORD
    would cringe before him,
  and their punishment
    would last forever.
¹⁶But you would be fed with the
    finest of wheat;   Dt 32:14
  with honey from the rock I
    would satisfy you."

Psalm 82

A psalm of Asaph.

¹God presides in the great
    assembly;
  he renders judgment among
    the "gods":   Ps 58:11; Isa 3:13

²"How long will you^a defend
    the unjust
  and show partiality to the
    wicked?^b   Dt 1:17
³Defend the weak and the
    fatherless;   Dt 24:17
  uphold the cause of the
    poor and the oppressed.
⁴Rescue the weak and the needy;
  deliver them from the hand
    of the wicked.

⁵"The 'gods' know nothing,
    they understand
    nothing.   Mic 3:1
  They walk about in
    darkness;
  all the foundations of the
    earth are shaken.   Ps 11:3

⁶"I said, 'You are "gods";   Jn 10:34
  you are all sons of the Most
    High.'
⁷But you will die like mere
    mortals;   Ps 49:12
  you will fall like every other
    ruler."

⁸Rise up, O God, judge the
    earth,
  for all the nations are your
    inheritance.   Ps 2:8; Rev 11:15

Psalm 83^c

A song. A psalm of Asaph.

¹O God, do not remain silent;
  do not turn a deaf ear,
  do not stand aloof, O God.
²See how your enemies
    growl,   Ps 2:1
  how your foes rear their
    heads.   Ps 81:15
³With cunning they conspire
    against your people;
  they plot against those you
    cherish.
⁴"Come," they say, "let us destroy
    them as a nation,   Est 3:6
  so that Israel's name is
    remembered no more."

⁵With one mind they plot
    together;   Ps 2:2
  they form an alliance
    against you—
⁶the tents of Edom and the
    Ishmaelites,
  of Moab and the Hagrites,
⁷Byblos, Ammon and Amalek,

^a 2 The Hebrew is plural.   ^b 2 The Hebrew has *Selah* (a word of uncertain meaning) here.
^c In Hebrew texts 83:1-18 is numbered 83:2-19.

Philistia, with the people of
Tyre.
⁸Even Assyria has joined them
to reinforce Lot's
descendants.ᵃ   Dt 2:9

⁹Do to them as you did to
Midian,   Jdg 7:1-23
as you did to Sisera and
Jabin at the river
Kishon,   Jdg 4:23-24
¹⁰who perished at Endor
and became like dung on
the ground.   Zep 1:17
¹¹Make their nobles like Oreb
and Zeeb,
all their princes like Zebah
and Zalmunna,   Jdg 8:12,21
¹²who said, "Let us take
possession
of the pasturelands of God."

¹³Make them like tumbleweed,
my God,
like chaff before the wind.
¹⁴As fire consumes the forest
or a flame sets the
mountains ablaze,
¹⁵so pursue them with your
tempest
and terrify them with your
storm.
¹⁶Cover their faces with shame,
LORD,   Ps 109:29; 132:18
so that they will seek your
name.

¹⁷May they ever be ashamed
and dismayed;
may they perish in disgrace.

¹⁸Let them know that you,
whose name is the
LORD —
that you alone are the Most
High over all the earth.

Psalm 84ᵇ

For the director of music.
According to *gittith*.ᶜ
Of the Sons of Korah. A psalm.

¹How lovely is your dwelling
place,   Ps 27:4
LORD Almighty!
²My soul yearns, even faints,
for the courts of the LORD;
my heart and my flesh cry out
for the living God.   Jos 3:10
³Even the sparrow has found a
home,
and the swallow a nest for
herself,
where she may have her
young —
a place near your altar,   Ps 43:4
LORD Almighty, my King
and my God.   Ps 5:2
⁴Blessed are those who dwell
in your house;
they are ever praising you.ᵈ

⁵Blessed are those whose
strength is in you,   Ps 81:1
whose hearts are set on
pilgrimage.   Jer 31:6
⁶As they pass through the
Valley of Baka,
they make it a place of
springs;

ᵃ 8 The Hebrew has *Selah* (a word of uncertain meaning) here.   ᵇ In Hebrew texts 84:1-12
is numbered 84:2-13.   ᶜ Title: Probably a musical term   ᵈ 4 The Hebrew has *Selah* (a
word of uncertain meaning) here and at the end of verse 8.

the autumn rains also cover
   it with pools.*a*   Joel 2:23
⁷They go from strength to
   strength,   Pr 4:18
 till each appears before God
   in Zion.   Dt 16:16

⁸Hear my prayer, Lᴏʀᴅ God
   Almighty;
 listen to me, God of Jacob.
⁹Look on our shield,*b* O God;
 look with favor on your
   anointed one.   1Sa 16:6

¹⁰Better is one day in your courts
   than a thousand elsewhere;
 I would rather be a doorkeeper
   in the house of my God
 than dwell in the tents of
   the wicked.
¹¹For the Lᴏʀᴅ God is a sun and
   shield;   Isa 60:19
 the Lᴏʀᴅ bestows favor and
   honor;
 no good thing does he
   withhold   Ps 34:10
 from those whose walk is
   blameless.

¹²Lᴏʀᴅ Almighty,
 blessed is the one who
   trusts in you.   Ps 2:12

Psalm 85*c*

For the director of music.
Of the Sons of Korah. A psalm.

¹You, Lᴏʀᴅ, showed favor to
   your land;
 you restored the fortunes of
   Jacob.   Jer 30:18; Eze 39:25

²You forgave the iniquity of
   your people   Nu 14:19
 and covered all their sins.*d*
³You set aside all your wrath
 and turned from your fierce
   anger.   Dt 13:17

⁴Restore us again, God our
   Savior,   Ps 80:3,7
 and put away your
   displeasure toward us.
⁵Will you be angry with us
   forever?   Ps 79:5
 Will you prolong your
   anger through all
   generations?
⁶Will you not revive us again,
 that your people may
   rejoice in you?
⁷Show us your unfailing love,
   Lᴏʀᴅ,
 and grant us your salvation.

⁸I will listen to what God the
   Lᴏʀᴅ says;
 he promises peace to his
   people, his faithful
   servants —   Zec 9:10
 but let them not turn to folly.
⁹Surely his salvation is near
   those who fear him,
 that his glory may dwell in
   our land.   Zec 2:5

¹⁰Love and faithfulness meet
   together;
 righteousness and peace
   kiss each other.   Ps 72:2-3
¹¹Faithfulness springs forth
   from the earth,

---

a 6 Or *blessings*   *b* 9 Or *sovereign*   *c* In Hebrew texts 85:1-13 is numbered 85:2-14.
d 2 The Hebrew has *Selah* (a word of uncertain meaning) here.

and righteousness looks
down from heaven.
¹²The LORD will indeed give
what is good,   Ps 84:11
and our land will yield its
harvest.   Ps 67:6; Zec 8:12
¹³Righteousness goes before him
and prepares the way for his
steps.

Psalm 86

A prayer of David.

¹Hear me, LORD, and
answer me,   Ps 17:6
for I am poor and needy.
²Guard my life, for I am
faithful to you;
save your servant who
trusts in you.
You are my God; ³have mercy
on me, Lord,   Ps 57:1
for I call to you all day long.
⁴Bring joy to your servant,
Lord,
for I put my trust in you.

⁵You, Lord, are forgiving and
good,
abounding in love to all
who call to you.   Ps 145:8
⁶Hear my prayer, LORD;
listen to my cry for mercy.
⁷When I am in distress, I call to
you,   Ps 50:15
because you answer me.

⁸Among the gods there is none
like you, Lord;   Ex 15:11
no deeds can compare with
yours.
⁹All the nations you have made

will come and worship
before you, Lord;   Rev 15:4
they will bring glory to your
name.
¹⁰For you are great and do
marvelous deeds;   Ps 72:18
you alone are God.   Dt 6:4

¹¹Teach me your way, LORD,
that I may rely on your
faithfulness;
give me an undivided heart,
that I may fear your name.
¹²I will praise you, Lord my
God, with all my heart;
I will glorify your name
forever.
¹³For great is your love
toward me;
you have delivered me from
the depths,
from the realm of the dead.

¹⁴Arrogant foes are attacking
me, O God;
ruthless people are trying to
kill me —
they have no regard for
you.   Ps 54:3
¹⁵But you, Lord, are a
compassionate and
gracious God,   Ps 103:8
slow to anger, abounding in
love and faithfulness.
¹⁶Turn to me and have mercy
on me;
show your strength in
behalf of your servant;
save me, because I serve you
just as my mother did.
¹⁷Give me a sign of your
goodness,

that my enemies may see it
and be put to shame,
for you, LORD, have helped
me and comforted me.

Psalm 87

Of the Sons of Korah.
A psalm. A song.

¹ He has founded his city on the
holy mountain.   Ps 48:1
² The LORD loves the gates of
Zion   Ps 78:68
more than all the other
dwellings of Jacob.

³ Glorious things are said of you,
city of God:*ᵃ*   Isa 60:1
⁴ "I will record Rahab*ᵇ* and
Babylon   Job 9:13
among those who
acknowledge me —
Philistia too, and Tyre, along
with Cush*ᶜ* —
and will say, 'This one was
born in Zion.'"*ᵈ*   Isa 19:25
⁵ Indeed, of Zion it will be said,
"This one and that one were
born in her,
and the Most High himself
will establish her."
⁶ The LORD will write in the
register of the peoples:
"This one was born in Zion."

⁷ As they make music they will
sing,

"All my fountains are in
you."

Psalm 88*ᵉ*

A song. A psalm of the Sons of Korah.
For the director of music. According
to *mahalath leannoth.ᶠ* A *maskilᵍ* of
Heman the Ezrahite.

¹ LORD, you are the God who
saves me;   Ps 51:14
day and night I cry out to you.
² May my prayer come before
you;
turn your ear to my cry.

³ I am overwhelmed with
troubles
and my life draws near to
death.   Ps 107:18,26
⁴ I am counted among those
who go down to the pit;
I am like one without
strength.
⁵ I am set apart with the dead,
like the slain who lie in the
grave,
whom you remember no more,
who are cut off from your
care.   Isa 53:8
⁶ You have put me in the lowest
pit,
in the darkest depths. Ps 69:15
⁷ Your wrath lies heavily on me;
you have overwhelmed me
with all your waves.*ʰ*

ᵃ 3 The Hebrew has *Selah* (a word of uncertain meaning) here and at the end of verse 6.
ᵇ 4 A poetic name for Egypt   *ᶜ 4* That is, the upper Nile region   *ᵈ 4* Or *"I will record
concerning those who acknowledge me: / 'This one was born in Zion.' / Hear this, Rahab and
Babylon, / and you too, Philistia, Tyre and Cush."*   *ᵉ* In Hebrew texts 88:1-18 is numbered
88:2-19.   *ᶠ* Title: Possibly a tune, "The Suffering of Affliction"   *ᵍ* Title: Probably a literary
or musical term   *ʰ 7* The Hebrew has *Selah* (a word of uncertain meaning) here and at the
end of verse 10.

⁸You have taken from me my
    closest friends   Job 19:13
  and have made me
    repulsive to them.
  I am confined and cannot
    escape;
⁹ my eyes are dim with grief.

  I call to you, LORD, every day;
    I spread out my hands to you.
¹⁰Do you show your wonders to
    the dead?
  Do their spirits rise up and
    praise you?   Ps 6:5
¹¹Is your love declared in the
    grave,
  your faithfulness in
    Destructionᵃ?   Ps 30:9
¹²Are your wonders known in
    the place of darkness,
  or your righteous deeds in
    the land of oblivion?

¹³But I cry to you for help, LORD;
  in the morning my prayer
    comes before you.   Ps 5:3
¹⁴Why, LORD, do you reject me
  and hide your face from me?

¹⁵From my youth I have
    suffered and been close
    to death;
  I have borne your terrors
    and am in despair.   Job 6:4
¹⁶Your wrath has swept over me;
  your terrors have
    destroyed me.
¹⁷All day long they surround me
    like a flood;   Ps 22:16

they have completely
    engulfed me.
¹⁸You have taken from me
    friend and neighbor —
  darkness is my closest
    friend.   Job 19:13

Psalm 89ᵇ

A *maskil*ᶜ of Ethan the Ezrahite.

¹I will sing of the LORD's great
    love forever;   Ps 101:1
  with my mouth I will make
    your faithfulness known
    through all generations.
²I will declare that your love
    stands firm forever,
  that you have established
    your faithfulness in
    heaven itself.   Ps 36:5
³You said, "I have made a
    covenant with my
    chosen one,
  I have sworn to David my
    servant,
⁴'I will establish your line
    forever
  and make your throne
    firm through all
    generations.'"ᵈ   2Sa 7:12-16

⁵The heavens praise your
    wonders, LORD,   Ps 19:1
  your faithfulness too, in the
    assembly of the holy
    ones.
⁶For who in the skies above
    can compare with the
    LORD?

ᵃ 11 Hebrew *Abaddon*   ᵇ In Hebrew texts 89:1-52 is numbered 89:2-53.   ᶜ Title: Probably
a literary or musical term   ᵈ 4 The Hebrew has *Selah* (a word of uncertain meaning) here
and at the end of verses 37, 45 and 48.

Who is like the LORD among
the heavenly beings?
⁷In the council of the holy ones
God is greatly feared;
he is more awesome than
all who surround him.
⁸Who is like you, LORD God
Almighty?   Ps 71:19
You, LORD, are mighty,
and your faithfulness
surrounds you.

⁹You rule over the surging sea;
when its waves mount up,
you still them.   Ps 65:7
¹⁰You crushed Rahab like one of
the slain;   Ps 87:4
with your strong arm you
scattered your enemies.
¹¹The heavens are yours, and
yours also the earth;
you founded the world and
all that is in it.   Ge 1:1
¹²You created the north and the
south;
Tabor and Hermon sing for
joy at your name.   Jos 12:1
¹³Your arm is endowed with
power;
your hand is strong, your
right hand exalted.

¹⁴Righteousness and justice are
the foundation of your
throne;
love and faithfulness go
before you.   Ps 97:2
¹⁵Blessed are those who have
learned to acclaim you,
who walk in the light of
your presence, LORD.

¹⁶They rejoice in your name all
day long;
they celebrate your
righteousness.
¹⁷For you are their glory and
strength,
and by your favor you exalt
our horn.ᵃ   Ps 75:10; 148:14
¹⁸Indeed, our shieldᵇ belongs to
the LORD,
our king to the Holy One of
Israel.   Ps 47:9

¹⁹Once you spoke in a vision,
to your faithful people you
said:
"I have bestowed strength on
a warrior;
I have raised up a young man
from among the people.
²⁰I have found David my
servant;   Ac 13:22
with my sacred oil I have
anointed him.   1Sa 16:1,12
²¹My hand will sustain him;
surely my arm will
strengthen him.   Ps 18:35
²²The enemy will not get the
better of him;
the wicked will not oppress
him.   2Sa 7:10
²³I will crush his foes before him
and strike down his
adversaries.   2Sa 7:9
²⁴My faithful love will be with
him,
and through my name his
hornᶜ will be exalted.
²⁵I will set his hand over the
sea,

ᵃ 17 *Horn* here symbolizes strong one.   ᵇ 18 Or *sovereign*   ᶜ 24 *Horn* here symbolizes
strength.

his right hand over the
  rivers.   Ps 72:8
26 He will call out to me, 'You are
  my Father,
  my God, the Rock my
  Savior.'   2Sa 22:47
27 And I will appoint him to be
  my firstborn,
  the most exalted of the kings
  of the earth.   Nu 24:7
28 I will maintain my love to him
  forever,
  and my covenant with him
  will never fail.   ver 33-34
29 I will establish his line forever,
  his throne as long as the
  heavens endure.   Dt 11:21
30 "If his sons forsake my law
  and do not follow my statutes,
31 if they violate my decrees
  and fail to keep my
  commands,
32 I will punish their sin with the
  rod,
  their iniquity with flogging;
33 but I will not take my love
  from him,   2Sa 7:15
  nor will I ever betray my
  faithfulness.
34 I will not violate my covenant
  or alter what my lips have
  uttered.   Nu 23:19
35 Once for all, I have sworn by
  my holiness —
  and I will not lie to David —
36 that his line will continue
  forever
  and his throne endure
  before me like the sun;
37 it will be established forever
  like the moon,

the faithful witness in the
  sky."
38 But you have rejected, you
  have spurned,   Dt 32:19
  you have been very angry
  with your anointed one.
39 You have renounced the
  covenant with your
  servant
  and have defiled his crown
  in the dust.   La 5:16
40 You have broken through all
  his walls
  and reduced his strongholds
  to ruins.   La 2:2
41 All who pass by have
  plundered him;
  he has become the scorn of
  his neighbors.   Ps 44:13
42 You have exalted the right
  hand of his foes;
  you have made all his
  enemies rejoice.   Ps 13:2
43 Indeed, you have turned back
  the edge of his sword
  and have not supported
  him in battle.   Ps 44:10
44 You have put an end to his
  splendor
  and cast his throne to the
  ground.
45 You have cut short the days of
  his youth;
  you have covered him with a
  mantle of shame.   Ps 44:15
46 How long, LORD? Will you
  hide yourself forever?
  How long will your wrath
  burn like fire?   Ps 79:5
47 Remember how fleeting is my
  life.   Job 7:7

For what futility you have
    created all humanity!
⁴⁸Who can live and not see
        death,
    or who can escape the
        power of the grave? Ps 49:9
⁴⁹Lord, where is your former
        great love,
    which in your faithfulness
        you swore to David?
⁵⁰Remember, Lord, how your
        servant has^a been
        mocked,   Ps 69:19
    how I bear in my heart the
        taunts of all the nations,
⁵¹the taunts with which your
        enemies, LORD, have
        mocked,
    with which they have
        mocked every step of
        your anointed one. Ps 74:10

⁵²Praise be to the LORD forever!
    Amen and Amen.

BOOK IV

Psalms 90–106

Psalm 90

A prayer of Moses the man of God.

¹Lord, you have been our
        dwelling place   Eze 11:16
    throughout all generations.
²Before the mountains were
        born   Pr 8:25
    or you brought forth the
        whole world,

from everlasting to
        everlasting you are God.
³You turn people back to dust,
    saying, "Return to dust, you
        mortals."   Ge 3:19
⁴A thousand years in your sight
    are like a day that has just
        gone by,
    or like a watch in the night.
⁵Yet you sweep people away in
        the sleep of death —
    they are like the new grass
        of the morning:
⁶In the morning it springs up
        new,
    but by evening it is dry and
        withered.   Mt 6:30; Jas 1:10
⁷We are consumed by your
        anger
    and terrified by your
        indignation.
⁸You have set our iniquities
        before you,
    our secret sins in the light of
        your presence.   Ps 19:12
⁹All our days pass away under
        your wrath;
    we finish our years with a
        moan.   Ps 78:33
¹⁰Our days may come to
        seventy years,
    or eighty, if our strength
        endures;
    yet the best of them are but
        trouble and sorrow,
    for they quickly pass, and
        we fly away.   Job 20:8
¹¹If only we knew the power of
        your anger!

---

^a 50 Or *your servants have*

Your wrath is as great as the fear that is your due.

12 Teach us to number our days, that we may gain a heart of wisdom.

13 Relent, Lord! How long will it be? Have compassion on your servants. Dt 32:36

14 Satisfy us in the morning with your unfailing love, that we may sing for joy and be glad all our days.

15 Make us glad for as many days as you have afflicted us, for as many years as we have seen trouble.

16 May your deeds be shown to your servants, your splendor to their children. Hab 3:2

17 May the favor*a* of the Lord our God rest on us; Isa 26:12 establish the work of our hands for us — yes, establish the work of our hands.

Psalm 91

1 Whoever dwells in the shelter of the Most High Ps 31:20 will rest in the shadow of the Almighty.*b* Ps 17:8

2 I will say of the Lord, "He is my refuge and my fortress, Ps 142:5 my God, in whom I trust."

3 Surely he will save you from the fowler's snare and from the deadly pestilence. 1Ki 8:37

4 He will cover you with his feathers, and under his wings you will find refuge; Ps 17:8 his faithfulness will be your shield and rampart.

5 You will not fear the terror of night, Job 5:21 nor the arrow that flies by day,

6 nor the pestilence that stalks in the darkness, nor the plague that destroys at midday.

7 A thousand may fall at your side, ten thousand at your right hand, but it will not come near you.

8 You will only observe with your eyes and see the punishment of the wicked. Mal 1:5

9 If you say, "The Lord is my refuge," and you make the Most High your dwelling,

10 no harm will overtake you, no disaster will come near your tent.

11 For he will command his angels concerning you to guard you in all your ways; Ps 34:7

12 they will lift you up in their hands,

a 17 Or *beauty*   *b* 1 Hebrew *Shaddai*

so that you will not strike
    your foot against a stone.
¹³You will tread on the lion and
    the cobra;
  you will trample the great
    lion and the serpent.

¹⁴"Because he*ᵃ* loves me," says
    the Lᴏʀᴅ, "I will rescue
    him;
  I will protect him, for he
    acknowledges my name.
¹⁵He will call on me, and I will
    answer him;
  I will be with him in trouble,
  I will deliver him and honor
    him.   1Sa 2:30; Ps 50:15
¹⁶With long life I will satisfy
    him   Dt 6:2; Ps 21:4
  and show him my
    salvation."   Ps 50:23

Psalm 92*ᵇ*

A psalm. A song. For the Sabbath day.

¹It is good to praise the Lᴏʀᴅ
  and make music to your
    name, O Most High,
²proclaiming your love in the
    morning
  and your faithfulness at
    night,   Ps 89:1
³to the music of the ten-
    stringed lyre
  and the melody of the harp.

⁴For you make me glad by your
    deeds, Lᴏʀᴅ;
  I sing for joy at what your
    hands have done.   Ps 8:6

⁵How great are your works,
    Lᴏʀᴅ,
  how profound your thoughts!
⁶Senseless people do not know,
    fools do not understand,
⁷that though the wicked spring
    up like grass
  and all evildoers flourish,
  they will be destroyed
    forever.   Ps 37:2

⁸But you, Lᴏʀᴅ, are forever
    exalted.

⁹For surely your enemies, Lᴏʀᴅ,
  surely your enemies will
    perish;
  all evildoers will be
    scattered.   Ps 68:1
¹⁰You have exalted my horn*ᶜ*
    like that of a wild ox;
  fine oils have been poured
    on me.   Ps 23:5
¹¹My eyes have seen the defeat
    of my adversaries;
  my ears have heard the rout
    of my wicked foes. Ps 54:7

¹²The righteous will flourish
    like a palm tree,
  they will grow like a cedar
    of Lebanon;   Ps 52:8
¹³planted in the house of the
    Lᴏʀᴅ,
  they will flourish in the
    courts of our God. Ps 100:4
¹⁴They will still bear fruit in old
    age,   Jn 15:2
  they will stay fresh and
    green,

ᵃ 14 That is, probably the king   *ᵇ* In Hebrew texts 92:1-15 is numbered 92:2-16.
ᶜ 10 Horn here symbolizes strength.

¹⁵proclaiming, "The LORD is
upright;
he is my Rock, and there is
no wickedness in him."

Psalm 93

¹The LORD reigns, he is robed
in majesty; Ps 97:1; 104:1
the LORD is robed in
majesty and armed
with strength; Ps 65:6
indeed, the world is
established, firm and
secure. Ps 96:10
²Your throne was established
long ago;
you are from all eternity.

³The seas have lifted up,
LORD, Ps 96:11
the seas have lifted up their
voice;
the seas have lifted up their
pounding waves.
⁴Mightier than the thunder of
the great waters, Ps 65:7
mightier than the breakers
of the sea —
the LORD on high is mighty.

⁵Your statutes, LORD, stand
firm;
holiness adorns your house
for endless days.

Psalm 94

¹The LORD is a God who
avenges. Na 1:2
O God who avenges, shine
forth.
²Rise up, Judge of the earth;

pay back to the proud what
they deserve. Ps 31:23
³How long, LORD, will the
wicked,
how long will the wicked be
jubilant? Ps 13:2

⁴They pour out arrogant words;
all the evildoers are full of
boasting.
⁵They crush your people, LORD;
they oppress your
inheritance.
⁶They slay the widow and the
foreigner;
they murder the fatherless.
⁷They say, "The LORD does not
see; Ps 10:11
the God of Jacob takes no
notice."

⁸Take notice, you senseless
ones among the people;
you fools, when will you
become wise?
⁹Does he who fashioned the
ear not hear?
Does he who formed the
eye not see? Ex 4:11
¹⁰Does he who disciplines
nations not punish?
Does he who teaches
mankind lack
knowledge? Job 35:11
¹¹The LORD knows all human
plans;
he knows that they are futile.

¹²Blessed is the one you
discipline, LORD, Job 5:17
the one you teach from your
law;

¹³you grant them relief from
     days of trouble,
   till a pit is dug for the
     wicked.   Ps 55:23
¹⁴For the LORD will not reject
     his people; 1Sa 12:22; Ro 11:2
   he will never forsake his
     inheritance.
¹⁵Judgment will again
     be founded on
     righteousness,   Ps 97:2
   and all the upright in heart
     will follow it.

¹⁶Who will rise up for me against
     the wicked?   Nu 10:35
   Who will take a stand for
     me against evildoers?
¹⁷Unless the LORD had given me
     help,   Ps 124:2
   I would soon have dwelt in
     the silence of death.
¹⁸When I said, "My foot is
     slipping,"   Ps 38:16
   your unfailing love, LORD,
     supported me.
¹⁹When anxiety was great
     within me,   Ecc 11:10
   your consolation brought
     me joy.

²⁰Can a corrupt throne be allied
     with you —
   a throne that brings on
     misery by its decrees?
²¹The wicked band together
     against the righteous
   and condemn the innocent
     to death.   Pr 17:15,26
²²But the LORD has become my
     fortress,

and my God the rock in
     whom I take refuge.
²³He will repay them for their sins
   and destroy them for their
     wickedness;
   the LORD our God will
     destroy them.

Psalm 95

¹Come, let us sing for joy to the
     LORD;   Ps 5:11
   let us shout aloud to the
     Rock of our salvation.
²Let us come before him with
     thanksgiving   Mic 6:6
   and extol him with music
     and song.   Ps 81:2; Eph 5:19

³For the LORD is the great God,
   the great King above all gods.
⁴In his hand are the depths of
     the earth,
   and the mountain peaks
     belong to him.
⁵The sea is his, for he made it,
   and his hands formed the
     dry land.   Ge 1:9; Ps 146:6

⁶Come, let us bow down in
     worship,   Php 2:10
   let us kneel before the LORD
     our Maker;   Ps 100:3; 149:2
⁷for he is our God
   and we are the people of his
     pasture,   Ps 79:13
   the flock under his care.

Today, if only you would hear
     his voice,
⁸"Do not harden your hearts as
     you did at Meribah,ᵃ

ᵃ 8 Meribah means quarreling.

as you did that day at
Massah[a] in the
wilderness,
⁹where your ancestors
tested me; Ps 78:18; 1Co 10:9
they tried me, though they
had seen what I did.
¹⁰For forty years I was angry
with that generation;
I said, 'They are a people
whose hearts go astray,
and they have not known
my ways.' Dt 8:6
¹¹So I declared on oath in my
anger,
'They shall never enter my
rest.'" Heb 4:3

Psalm 96

96:1-13pp — 1Ch 16:23-33

¹Sing to the LORD a new song;
sing to the LORD, all the
earth.
²Sing to the LORD, praise his
name;
proclaim his salvation day
after day. Ps 71:15
³Declare his glory among the
nations, Ps 8:1
his marvelous deeds among
all peoples. Ps 71:17

⁴For great is the LORD and
most worthy of praise;
he is to be feared above all
gods. Ps 95:3
⁵For all the gods of the nations
are idols,
but the LORD made the
heavens. Ps 115:15

⁶Splendor and majesty are
before him;
strength and glory are in his
sanctuary. Ps 29:1
⁷Ascribe to the LORD, all you
families of nations,
ascribe to the LORD glory
and strength.
⁸Ascribe to the LORD the glory
due his name;
bring an offering and come
into his courts. Ps 45:12
⁹Worship the LORD in the
splendor of his[b]
holiness;
tremble before him, all the
earth.
¹⁰Say among the nations, "The
LORD reigns." Ps 97:1
The world is firmly
established, it cannot
be moved; Ps 93:1
he will judge the peoples
with equity. Ps 67:4

¹¹Let the heavens rejoice, let the
earth be glad;
let the sea resound, and all
that is in it.
¹²Let the fields be jubilant, and
everything in them;
let all the trees of the forest
sing for joy. Ps 65:13
¹³Let all creation rejoice before
the LORD, for he comes,
he comes to judge the earth.
He will judge the world in
righteousness
and the peoples in his
faithfulness. Ps 86:11

---

[a] 8 Massah means testing. [b] 9 Or LORD with the splendor of

Psalm 97

[1] The LORD reigns, let the earth
be glad;   Ps 96:10
 let the distant shores rejoice.
[2] Clouds and thick darkness
surround him;   Ps 18:11
 righteousness and justice
are the foundation of
his throne.   Ps 89:14
[3] Fire goes before him
and consumes his foes on
every side.   Ps 18:8
[4] His lightning lights up the
world;
 the earth sees and trembles.
[5] The mountains melt like wax
before the LORD,   Mic 1:4
 before the Lord of all the
earth.
[6] The heavens proclaim his
righteousness,   Ps 50:6
 and all peoples see his glory.

[7] All who worship images are
put to shame,
 those who boast in idols —
 worship him, all you gods!

[8] Zion hears and rejoices
and the villages of Judah
are glad
 because of your judgments,
LORD.   Ps 48:11
[9] For you, LORD, are the Most
High over all the earth;
 you are exalted far above all
gods.   Ex 18:11
[10] Let those who love the LORD
hate evil,   Ps 34:14; Am 5:15

for he guards the lives of his
faithful ones
 and delivers them from the
hand of the wicked.
[11] Light shines[a] on the righteous
and joy on the upright in
heart.
[12] Rejoice in the LORD, you who
are righteous,
 and praise his holy name.

Psalm 98

A psalm.

[1] Sing to the LORD a new song,
for he has done marvelous
things;
 his right hand and his holy
arm   Ex 15:6; Isa 52:10
 have worked salvation for
him.
[2] The LORD has made his
salvation known   Isa 52:10
 and revealed his
righteousness to the
nations.
[3] He has remembered his love
and his faithfulness to
Israel;
 all the ends of the earth have
seen
 the salvation of our God.

[4] Shout for joy to the LORD, all
the earth,   Isa 44:23
 burst into jubilant song
with music;
[5] make music to the LORD with
the harp,   Ps 92:3

[a] 11 One Hebrew manuscript and ancient versions (see also 112:4); most Hebrew
manuscripts *Light is sown*

with the harp and the
    sound of singing,
⁶with trumpets and the blast of
    the ram's horn — Nu 10:10
shout for joy before the
    LORD, the King.   Ps 47:7

⁷Let the sea resound, and
    everything in it,
    the world, and all who live
    in it.   Ps 24:1
⁸Let the rivers clap their hands,
    let the mountains sing
    together for joy;   Isa 55:12
⁹let them sing before the LORD,
    for he comes to judge the
    earth.
He will judge the world in
    righteousness
    and the peoples with equity.

Psalm 99

¹The LORD reigns,   Ps 97:1
    let the nations tremble;
he sits enthroned between the
    cherubim,   Ex 25:22
    let the earth shake.
²Great is the LORD in Zion;
    he is exalted over all the
    nations.   Ps 97:9
³Let them praise your great
    and awesome name —
    he is holy.

⁴The King is mighty, he loves
    justice —   Ps 11:7
you have established
    equity;   Ps 98:9
in Jacob you have done
    what is just and right.

⁵Exalt the LORD our God   Ps 132:7
    and worship at his footstool;
    he is holy.

⁶Moses and Aaron were among
    his priests,
    Samuel was among those
    who called on his name;
they called on the LORD
    and he answered them.
⁷He spoke to them from the
    pillar of cloud;   Ex 33:9
    they kept his statutes and
    the decrees he gave
    them.

⁸LORD our God,
    you answered them;
you were to Israel a forgiving
    God,   Nu 14:20
    though you punished their
    misdeeds.^a
⁹Exalt the LORD our God
    and worship at his holy
    mountain,
    for the LORD our God is holy.

Psalm 100

A psalm. For giving grateful praise.

¹Shout for joy to the LORD, all
    the earth.   Ps 98:4
² Worship the LORD with
    gladness;
    come before him with
    joyful songs.   Ps 95:2
³Know that the LORD is God.
    It is he who made us, and
    we are his^b;
    we are his people, the sheep
    of his pasture.   Ps 74:1

---

^a 8 Or *God, / an avenger of the wrongs done to them*   ^b 3 Or *and not we ourselves*

⁴Enter his gates with
   thanksgiving
   and his courts with praise;
   give thanks to him and
      praise his name.   Ps 116:17
⁵For the Lᴏʀᴅ is good and his
      love endures forever;
   his faithfulness continues
      through all generations.

Psalm 101

Of David. A psalm.

¹I will sing of your love and
      justice;   Ps 89:1
   to you, Lᴏʀᴅ, I will sing
      praise.
²I will be careful to lead a
      blameless life —   Ge 17:1
   when will you come to me?

   I will conduct the affairs of my
      house
   with a blameless heart.
³I will not look with approval
   on anything that is vile.

   I hate what faithless
      people do;   Ps 40:4
   I will have no part in it.
⁴The perverse of heart shall be
      far from me;   Pr 11:20
   I will have nothing to do
      with what is evil.

⁵Whoever slanders their
      neighbor in secret,
   I will put to silence;
   whoever has haughty eyes
      and a proud heart, Pr 6:17
   I will not tolerate.

⁶My eyes will be on the faithful
      in the land,
   that they may dwell with me;
   the one whose walk is
      blameless   Ps 119:1
   will minister to me.

⁷No one who practices deceit
   will dwell in my house;
   no one who speaks falsely
   will stand in my presence.

⁸Every morning I will put to
      silence   Jer 21:12
   all the wicked in the land;
   I will cut off every evildoer
   from the city of the Lᴏʀᴅ.

Psalm 102 ᵃ

A prayer of an afflicted person who
   has grown weak and pours out
   a lament before the Lᴏʀᴅ.

¹Hear my prayer, Lᴏʀᴅ;
   let my cry for help come to
      you.   Ex 2:23
²Do not hide your face from me
   when I am in distress.
   Turn your ear to me;   2Ki 19:16
   when I call, answer me
      quickly.

³For my days vanish like smoke;
   my bones burn like glowing
      embers.
⁴My heart is blighted and
      withered like grass;
   I forget to eat my food.
⁵In my distress I groan aloud
   and am reduced to skin and
      bones.
⁶I am like a desert owl,   Isa 34:11

ᵃ In Hebrew texts 102:1-28 is numbered 102:2-29.

like an owl among the ruins.
⁷I lie awake; I have become
like a bird alone on a roof.
⁸All day long my enemies
taunt me;   Ps 42:10
those who rail against me
use my name as a curse.
⁹For I eat ashes as my food
and mingle my drink with
tears   Ps 42:3
¹⁰because of your great wrath,
for you have taken me up
and thrown me aside.
¹¹My days are like the evening
shadow;   Job 14:2
I wither away like grass.
¹²But you, LORD, sit enthroned
forever;   Ps 9:7
your renown endures
through all generations.
¹³You will arise and have
compassion on Zion,
for it is time to show favor to
her;
the appointed time has
come.   Ex 13:10
¹⁴For her stones are dear to your
servants;
her very dust moves them to
pity.
¹⁵The nations will fear the
name of the LORD,
all the kings of the earth
will revere your glory.
¹⁶For the LORD will rebuild Zion
and appear in his glory.
¹⁷He will respond to the prayer
of the destitute;
he will not despise their plea.

¹⁸Let this be written for a future
generation,   Ro 15:4
that a people not yet created
may praise the LORD:
¹⁹"The LORD looked down from
his sanctuary on high,
from heaven he viewed the
earth,
²⁰to hear the groans of the
prisoners
and release those
condemned to death."
²¹So the name of the LORD will
be declared in Zion
and his praise in Jerusalem
²²when the peoples and the
kingdoms
assemble to worship the
LORD.   Ps 22:27
²³In the course of my life[a] he
broke my strength;
he cut short my days.   Ps 39:5
²⁴So I said:
"Do not take me away, my
God, in the midst of my
days;
your years go on through all
generations.   Ps 90:2
²⁵In the beginning you laid
the foundations of the
earth,   Heb 1:10-12
and the heavens are the
work of your hands.
²⁶They will perish, but you
remain;   Isa 34:4
they will all wear out like a
garment.
Like clothing you will change
them

[a] 23 Or By his power

and they will be discarded.
27 But you remain the same,
and your years will never
end.
28 The children of your servants
will live in your
presence;   Ps 69:36
their descendants will be
established before you."

Psalm 103

Of David.

1 Praise the LORD, my soul;
all my inmost being, praise
his holy name.   Ps 30:4
2 Praise the LORD, my soul,
and forget not all his
benefits —
3 who forgives all your sins
and heals all your diseases,
4 who redeems your life from
the pit   Ps 34:22
and crowns you with love
and compassion,   Ps 8:5
5 who satisfies your desires
with good things   Ps 90:14
so that your youth is
renewed like the eagle's.

6 The LORD works righteousness
and justice for all the
oppressed.   Ps 74:21

7 He made known his ways to
Moses,   Ex 33:13
his deeds to the people of
Israel: Ps 106:22
8 The LORD is compassionate
and gracious,   Ex 34:6
slow to anger, abounding in
love.

9 He will not always accuse,
nor will he harbor his anger
forever;   Ps 30:5
10 he does not treat us as our
sins deserve   Ezr 9:13
or repay us according to our
iniquities.
11 For as high as the heavens are
above the earth,
so great is his love for those
who fear him;   Ps 57:10
12 as far as the east is from the
west,
so far has he removed our
transgressions from us.

13 As a father has compassion on
his children,   Mal 3:17
so the LORD has
compassion on those
who fear him;
14 for he knows how we are
formed,   Isa 29:16
he remembers that we are
dust.
15 The life of mortals is like grass,
they flourish like a flower of
the field;   Job 14:2; 1Pe 1:24
16 the wind blows over it and it is
gone,   Isa 40:7
and its place remembers it
no more.   Job 7:10
17 But from everlasting to
everlasting
the LORD's love is with those
who fear him,
and his righteousness
with their children's
children —   Ge 48:11
18 with those who keep his
covenant   Dt 29:9

and remember to obey his
precepts. Dt 7:9

¹⁹The LORD has established his
throne in heaven,
and his kingdom rules over
all. Ps 47:2

²⁰Praise the LORD, you his
angels, Ps 148:2; Heb 1:14
you mighty ones who do his
bidding,
who obey his word.

²¹Praise the LORD, all his
heavenly hosts, 1Ki 22:19
you his servants who do his
will.

²²Praise the LORD, all his
works Ps 145:10
everywhere in his dominion.

Praise the LORD, my soul. ver 1

Psalm 104

¹Praise the LORD, my soul.

LORD my God, you are very
great;
you are clothed with
splendor and majesty.

²The LORD wraps himself in
light as with a garment;
he stretches out the heavens
like a tent Isa 40:22

³ and lays the beams of his
upper chambers on
their waters. Am 9:6
He makes the clouds his
chariot Isa 19:1
and rides on the wings of
the wind. Ps 18:10

⁴He makes winds his
messengers,ᵃ Heb 1:7
flames of fire his servants.

⁵He set the earth on its
foundations; Job 26:7
it can never be moved.

⁶You covered it with the
watery depths as with a
garment; Ge 1:2; 7:19
the waters stood above the
mountains.

⁷But at your rebuke the waters
fled, Ps 18:15
at the sound of your thunder
they took to flight; Ex 9:23

⁸they flowed over the
mountains,
they went down into the
valleys,
to the place you assigned for
them. Ps 33:7

⁹You set a boundary they
cannot cross;
never again will they cover
the earth.

¹⁰He makes springs pour water
into the ravines; Ps 107:33
it flows between the
mountains.

¹¹They give water to all the
beasts of the field;
the wild donkeys quench
their thirst. Ge 16:12

¹²The birds of the sky nest by
the waters; Mt 8:20
they sing among the
branches.

¹³He waters the mountains from
his upper chambers;

ᵃ 4 Or angels

the land is satisfied by the fruit of his work.

¹⁴He makes grass grow for the cattle,   Job 38:27; Ps 147:8

and plants for people to cultivate —

bringing forth food from the earth: Ge 1:30; Job 28:5

¹⁵wine that gladdens human hearts,   Jdg 9:13

oil to make their faces shine,   Ps 23:5; 92:10; Lk 7:46

and bread that sustains their hearts.

¹⁶The trees of the LORD are well watered,

the cedars of Lebanon that he planted.   Ps 72:16

¹⁷There the birds make their nests;   ver 12

the stork has its home in the junipers.

¹⁸The high mountains belong to the wild goats;

the crags are a refuge for the hyrax.   Pr 30:26

¹⁹He made the moon to mark the seasons,   Ge 1:14

and the sun knows when to go down.

²⁰You bring darkness, it becomes night,   Isa 45:7

and all the beasts of the forest prowl.

²¹The lions roar for their prey and seek their food from God.   Job 38:39

²²The sun rises, and they steal away;

they return and lie down in their dens.

²³Then people go out to their work,   Ge 3:19

to their labor until evening.

²⁴How many are your works, LORD!

In wisdom you made them all;   Pr 3:19

the earth is full of your creatures.

²⁵There is the sea, vast and spacious,   Ps 69:34

teeming with creatures beyond number —

living things both large and small.

²⁶There the ships go to and fro, and Leviathan, which you formed to frolic there.

²⁷All creatures look to you to give them their food at the proper time.   Ps 136:25

²⁸When you give it to them, they gather it up;

when you open your hand, they are satisfied with good things.   Ps 145:16

²⁹When you hide your face, they are terrified;   Dt 31:17

when you take away their breath,

they die and return to the dust.   Job 34:14; Ecc 12:7

³⁰When you send your Spirit, they are created,

and you renew the face of the ground.

³¹May the glory of the LORD endure forever;

may the LORD rejoice in his works —   Ge 1:31

³²he who looks at the earth, and
    it trembles,
    who touches the mountains,
    and they smoke.   Ps 144:5
³³I will sing to the Lord all my
    life;   Ps 63:4
    I will sing praise to my God
    as long as I live.
³⁴May my meditation be
    pleasing to him,   Ps 9:2
    as I rejoice in the Lord.
³⁵But may sinners vanish from
    the earth   Ps 37:38
    and the wicked be no more.

Praise the Lord, my soul.

Praise the Lord.[a] Ps 105:45; 106:48

Psalm 105

105:1-15pp — 1Ch 16:8-22

¹Give praise to the Lord,
    proclaim his name;
    make known among the
    nations what he has
    done.
²Sing to him, sing praise to
    him;   Ps 96:1
    tell of all his wonderful acts.
³Glory in his holy name;
    let the hearts of those who
    seek the Lord rejoice.
⁴Look to the Lord and his
    strength;
    seek his face always.   Ps 27:8
⁵Remember the wonders he
    has done,   Ps 40:5
    his miracles, and the
    judgments he
    pronounced,   Ps 77:11

⁶you his servants, the
    descendants of
    Abraham,
    his chosen ones, the
    children of Jacob. Ps 106:5
⁷He is the Lord our God;
    his judgments are in all the
    earth.
⁸He remembers his covenant
    forever,   Lk 1:72
    the promise he made, for a
    thousand generations,
⁹the covenant he made with
    Abraham, Ge 17:2; 22:16-18
    the oath he swore to
    Isaac.
¹⁰He confirmed it to Jacob as a
    decree,   Ge 28:13-15
    to Israel as an everlasting
    covenant:
¹¹"To you I will give the land of
    Canaan   Ge 13:15; 15:18
    as the portion you will
    inherit."   Nu 34:2
¹²When they were but few in
    number, Ge 34:30; Dt 7:7
    few indeed, and strangers
    in it,   Heb 11:9
¹³they wandered from nation to
    nation,
    from one kingdom to
    another.
¹⁴He allowed no one to oppress
    them;   Ge 35:5
    for their sake he rebuked
    kings: Ge 12:17-20
¹⁵"Do not touch my anointed
    ones;
    do my prophets no harm."

a 35 Hebrew Hallelu Yah; in the Septuagint this line stands at the beginning of Psalm 105.

¹⁶He called down famine on the
    land   Lev 26:26; Isa 3:1
and destroyed all their
    supplies of food;
¹⁷and he sent a man before
    them—
Joseph, sold as a slave.
¹⁸They bruised his feet with
    shackles,
his neck was put in irons,
¹⁹till what he foretold came to
    pass,   Ge 40:20-22
till the word of the Lord
    proved him true.
²⁰The king sent and released him,
the ruler of peoples set him
    free.   Ge 41:14
²¹He made him master of his
    household,
ruler over all he possessed,
²²to instruct his princes as he
    pleased   Ge 41:43-44
and teach his elders wisdom.

²³Then Israel entered Egypt;
Jacob resided as a foreigner
    in the land of Ham.
²⁴The Lord made his people
    very fruitful;
he made them too
    numerous for their foes,
²⁵whose hearts he turned to
    hate his people,
to conspire against his
    servants.
²⁶He sent Moses his servant,
and Aaron, whom he had
    chosen.
²⁷They performed his signs
    among them,   Ex 7:8–12:51
his wonders in the land of
    Ham.

²⁸He sent darkness and made
    the land dark—   Ex 10:22
for had they not rebelled
    against his words?
²⁹He turned their waters into
    blood,
causing their fish to die.
³⁰Their land teemed with frogs,
which went up into the
    bedrooms of their
    rulers.
³¹He spoke, and there came
    swarms of flies,
and gnats throughout their
    country.   Ex 8:16-18
³²He turned their rain into hail,
with lightning throughout
    their land;
³³he struck down their vines
    and fig trees   Ps 78:47
and shattered the trees of
    their country.
³⁴He spoke, and the locusts
    came,   Ex 10:4,12-15
grasshoppers without
    number;
³⁵they ate up every green thing
    in their land,
ate up the produce of their
    soil.
³⁶Then he struck down all the
    firstborn in their land,
the firstfruits of all their
    manhood.
³⁷He brought out Israel, laden
    with silver and gold,
and from among their tribes
    no one faltered.
³⁸Egypt was glad when they left,
because dread of Israel had
    fallen on them.   Ex 15:16

³⁹ He spread out a cloud as a
    covering,   Ex 13:21
  and a fire to give light at
    night.
⁴⁰ They asked, and he brought
    them quail;   Ex 16:13
  he fed them well with the
    bread of heaven.
⁴¹ He opened the rock, and
    water gushed out;
  it flowed like a river in the
    desert.

⁴² For he remembered his holy
    promise   Ge 15:13-16
  given to his servant
    Abraham.
⁴³ He brought out his people
    with rejoicing,   Ex 15:1-18
  his chosen ones with shouts
    of joy;
⁴⁴ he gave them the lands of the
    nations,   Jos 13:6-7
  and they fell heir to what
    others had toiled for —
⁴⁵ that they might keep his
    precepts
  and observe his laws.   Dt 4:40

Praise the LORD.ᵃ   Ps 104:35

Psalm 106

106:1,47-48pp — 1Ch 16:34-36

¹ Praise the LORD.ᵇ   Ps 22:23

Give thanks to the LORD, for
    he is good;   Ps 100:5; 105:1
  his love endures forever.

² Who can proclaim the mighty
    acts of the LORD   Ps 145:4,12

or fully declare his praise?
³ Blessed are those who act
    justly,
  who always do what is
    right.   Ps 15:2

⁴ Remember me, LORD, when
    you show favor to your
    people,   Ps 119:132
  come to my aid when you
    save them,
⁵ that I may enjoy the
    prosperity of your
    chosen ones,   Ps 1:3
  that I may share in the joy
    of your nation   Ps 118:15
  and join your inheritance in
    giving praise.

⁶ We have sinned, even as our
    ancestors did;   Da 9:5
  we have done wrong and
    acted wickedly.
⁷ When our ancestors were in
    Egypt,
  they gave no thought to
    your miracles;
  they did not remember your
    many kindnesses,   Ps 78:11
  and they rebelled by the
    sea, the Red Sea.ᶜ   Ex 14:11
⁸ Yet he saved them for his
    name's sake,   Ex 9:16
  to make his mighty power
    known.
⁹ He rebuked the Red Sea, and
    it dried up;   Ex 14:21; Ps 18:15
  he led them through the
    depths as through a
    desert.   Isa 63:11-14

ᵃ 45 Hebrew *Hallelu Yah*   ᵇ 1 Hebrew *Hallelu Yah*; also in verse 48   ᶜ 7 Or *the Sea of Reeds*; also in verses 9 and 22

¹⁰He saved them from the hand
     of the foe;   Ex 14:30
  from the hand of the enemy
     he redeemed them.
¹¹The waters covered their
     adversaries;   Ex 14:28; 15:5
  not one of them survived.
¹²Then they believed his
     promises
  and sang his praise.

¹³But they soon forgot what he
     had done   Ex 15:24
  and did not wait for his plan
     to unfold.
¹⁴In the desert they gave in to
     their craving;
  in the wilderness they put
     God to the test.   1Co 10:9
¹⁵So he gave them what they
     asked for,   Nu 11:31
  but sent a wasting disease
     among them.   Isa 10:16

¹⁶In the camp they grew
     envious of Moses   Nu 16:1-3
  and of Aaron, who was
     consecrated to the
     LORD.
¹⁷The earth opened up and
     swallowed Dathan;
  it buried the company of
     Abiram.
¹⁸Fire blazed among their
     followers;
  a flame consumed the
     wicked.   Nu 16:35
¹⁹At Horeb they made a calf
  and worshiped an idol cast
     from metal.
²⁰They exchanged their glorious
     God   Jer 2:11; Ro 1:23
  for an image of a bull, which
     eats grass.
²¹They forgot the God who
     saved them,   Ps 78:11
  who had done great things
     in Egypt,
²²miracles in the land of Ham
  and awesome deeds by the
     Red Sea.
²³So he said he would destroy
     them—   Ex 32:10
  had not Moses, his chosen
     one,
  stood in the breach before him
     to keep his wrath from
     destroying them.

²⁴Then they despised the
     pleasant land;   Dt 8:7
  they did not believe his
     promise.   Heb 3:18-19
²⁵They grumbled in their tents
  and did not obey the LORD.
²⁶So he swore to them with
     uplifted hand   Eze 20:15
  that he would make them
     fall in the wilderness,
²⁷make their descendants fall
     among the nations
  and scatter them
     throughout the lands.

²⁸They yoked themselves to the
     Baal of Peor   Nu 25:2-3
  and ate sacrifices offered to
     lifeless gods;
²⁹they aroused the LORD's anger
     by their wicked deeds,
  and a plague broke out
     among them.
³⁰But Phinehas stood up and
     intervened,

and the plague was
checked.   Nu 25:8
³¹ This was credited to him as
righteousness   Nu 25:11-13
for endless generations to
come.
³² By the waters of Meribah they
angered the LORD,
and trouble came to Moses
because of them;
³³ for they rebelled against the
Spirit of God,   Ex 23:21
and rash words came from
Moses' lips.^a   Nu 20:8-12
³⁴ They did not destroy the
peoples   Jdg 1:21
as the LORD had
commanded them,
³⁵ but they mingled with the
nations   Jdg 3:5-6
and adopted their customs.
³⁶ They worshiped their idols,
which became a snare to
them.
³⁷ They sacrificed their sons
and their daughters to false
gods.
³⁸ They shed innocent blood,
the blood of their sons and
daughters,   Nu 35:33
whom they sacrificed to the
idols of Canaan,
and the land was
desecrated by their
blood.
³⁹ They defiled themselves by
what they did;   Eze 20:18
by their deeds they
prostituted themselves.

⁴⁰ Therefore the LORD was angry
with his people
and abhorred his
inheritance.
⁴¹ He gave them into the hands
of the nations,   Jdg 2:14
and their foes ruled over
them.
⁴² Their enemies oppressed them
and subjected them to their
power.
⁴³ Many times he delivered them,
but they were bent on
rebellion   Jdg 2:16-19
and they wasted away in
their sin.
⁴⁴ Yet he took note of their distress
when he heard their cry;
⁴⁵ for their sake he remembered
his covenant   Lev 26:42
and out of his great love he
relented.   Jdg 2:18
⁴⁶ He caused all who held them
captive
to show them mercy.   Ezr 9:9

⁴⁷ Save us, LORD our God,
and gather us from the
nations,   Ps 147:2
that we may give thanks to
your holy name
and glory in your praise.

⁴⁸ Praise be to the LORD, the
God of Israel,
from everlasting to
everlasting.

Let all the people say,
"Amen!"   Ps 41:13

Praise the LORD.

^a 33 Or *against his spirit, / and rash words came from his lips*

BOOK V

Psalms 107 – 150

Psalm 107

¹Give thanks to the LORD, for
  he is good;   Ps 106:1
  his love endures forever.
²Let the redeemed of the LORD
    tell their story — Ps 106:10
  those he redeemed from the
    hand of the foe,
³those he gathered from the
    lands,   Ps 106:47
  from east and west, from
    north and south.^{*a*}

⁴Some wandered in desert
    wastelands, Nu 14:33; 32:13
  finding no way to a city
    where they could settle.
⁵They were hungry and
    thirsty,   Ex 15:22
  and their lives ebbed away.
⁶Then they cried out to the
    LORD in their trouble,
  and he delivered them from
    their distress.
⁷He led them by a straight way
  to a city where they could
    settle.
⁸Let them give thanks to the
    LORD for his unfailing
    love   Ps 6:4
  and his wonderful deeds for
    mankind,   Ps 75:1
⁹for he satisfies the thirsty Lk 1:53
  and fills the hungry with
    good things.   Ps 34:10

¹⁰Some sat in darkness, in utter
    darkness,   Lk 1:79
  prisoners suffering in iron
    chains,   Job 36:8
¹¹because they rebelled against
    God's commands
  and despised the plans of
    the Most High.   2Ch 36:16
¹²So he subjected them to bitter
    labor;
  they stumbled, and there
    was no one to help.
¹³Then they cried to the LORD
    in their trouble,
  and he saved them from
    their distress.
¹⁴He brought them out of
    darkness, the utter
    darkness,
  and broke away their
    chains.   Ac 12:7
¹⁵Let them give thanks to the
    LORD for his unfailing
    love   Ps 105:1
  and his wonderful deeds for
    mankind,   Ps 75:1
¹⁶for he breaks down gates of
    bronze
  and cuts through bars of iron.

¹⁷Some became fools through
    their rebellious ways
  and suffered affliction
    because of their
    iniquities. Isa 65:6-7; La 3:39
¹⁸They loathed all food
  and drew near the gates of
    death.   Ps 9:13
¹⁹Then they cried to the LORD
    in their trouble,

---

^{*a*} 3 Hebrew *north and the sea*

and he saved them from their distress.

20 He sent out his word and healed them; Ps 103:3
he rescued them from the grave. Ps 30:3

21 Let them give thanks to the LORD for his unfailing love
and his wonderful deeds for mankind.

22 Let them sacrifice thank offerings Lev 7:12
and tell of his works with songs of joy. Ps 9:11; 73:28

23 Some went out on the sea in ships;
they were merchants on the mighty waters.

24 They saw the works of the LORD, Ps 64:9
his wonderful deeds in the deep.

25 For he spoke and stirred up a tempest Jnh 1:4
that lifted high the waves.

26 They mounted up to the heavens and went down to the depths;
in their peril their courage melted away. Ps 22:14

27 They reeled and staggered like drunkards;
they were at their wits' end.

28 Then they cried out to the LORD in their trouble,
and he brought them out of their distress. Jnh 1:6

29 He stilled the storm to a whisper; Mt 8:26

the waves of the sea[a] were hushed. Ps 89:9

30 They were glad when it grew calm,
and he guided them to their desired haven.

31 Let them give thanks to the LORD for his unfailing love Ps 6:4
and his wonderful deeds for mankind.

32 Let them exalt him in the assembly of the people
and praise him in the council of the elders.

33 He turned rivers into a desert, flowing springs into thirsty ground,

34 and fruitful land into a salt waste, Ge 13:10
because of the wickedness of those who lived there.

35 He turned the desert into pools of water Ps 114:8
and the parched ground into flowing springs;

36 there he brought the hungry to live,
and they founded a city where they could settle.

37 They sowed fields and planted vineyards Isa 65:21
that yielded a fruitful harvest;

38 he blessed them, and their numbers greatly increased, Ge 12:2
and he did not let their herds diminish.

---

a 29 Dead Sea Scrolls; Masoretic Text / *their waves*

³⁹Then their numbers
    decreased, and they
    were humbled   2Ki 10:32
  by oppression, calamity and
    sorrow;
⁴⁰he who pours contempt on
    nobles   Job 12:21
  made them wander in a
    trackless waste.   Job 12:24
⁴¹But he lifted the needy out of
    their affliction   1Sa 2:8
  and increased their families
    like flocks.
⁴²The upright see and rejoice,
  but all the wicked shut their
    mouths.   Job 5:16; Ro 3:19

⁴³Let the one who is wise heed
    these things   Jer 9:12
  and ponder the loving
    deeds of the LORD. Ps 64:9

Psalm 108ᵃ

108:1-5pp — Ps 57:7-11
108:6-13pp — Ps 60:5-12

A song. A psalm of David.

¹My heart, O God, is steadfast;
  I will sing and make music
    with all my soul.   Ps 18:49
²Awake, harp and lyre!   Job 21:12
  I will awaken the dawn.
³I will praise you, LORD, among
    the nations;
  I will sing of you among the
    peoples.
⁴For great is your love, higher
    than the heavens;
  your faithfulness reaches to
    the skies.   Ps 36:5

⁵Be exalted, O God, above the
    heavens;   Ps 8:1
  let your glory be over all the
    earth.   Ps 57:5
⁶Save us and help us with your
    right hand,   Job 40:14
  that those you love may be
    delivered.
⁷God has spoken from his
    sanctuary: Ps 68:35
  "In triumph I will parcel out
    Shechem   Ge 12:6
  and measure off the Valley
    of Sukkoth.   Ge 33:17
⁸Gilead is mine, Manasseh is
    mine;
  Ephraim is my helmet,
  Judah is my scepter.   Ge 49:10
⁹Moab is my washbasin,
  on Edom I toss my
    sandal;   2Sa 8:13-14
  over Philistia I shout in
    triumph."   2Sa 8:1

¹⁰Who will bring me to the
    fortified city?
  Who will lead me to
    Edom?
¹¹Is it not you, God, you who
    have rejected us
  and no longer go out with
    our armies?   Ps 44:9
¹²Give us aid against the enemy,
  for human help is
    worthless.   Ps 118:8
¹³With God we will gain the
    victory,
  and he will trample down
    our enemies.   Ps 44:5

ᵃ In Hebrew texts 108:1-13 is numbered 108:2-14.

Psalm 109

For the director of music.
Of David. A psalm.

[1] My God, whom I praise,
do not remain silent,   Ps 83:1
[2] for people who are wicked
and deceitful   Ps 43:1
have opened their mouths
against me;
they have spoken against
me with lying tongues.
[3] With words of hatred they
surround me;   Ps 69:4
they attack me without
cause.
[4] In return for my friendship
they accuse me,
but I am a man of prayer.
[5] They repay me evil for good,
and hatred for my
friendship.

[6] Appoint someone evil to
oppose my enemy;
let an accuser stand at his
right hand.   Zec 3:1
[7] When he is tried, let him be
found guilty,
and may his prayers
condemn him.   Pr 28:9
[8] May his days be few;
may another take his place
of leadership.   Ac 1:20
[9] May his children be fatherless
and his wife a widow.   Ex 22:24
[10] May his children be
wandering beggars;
may they be driven[a] from
their ruined homes.

[11] May a creditor seize all he has;
may strangers plunder the
fruits of his labor.   Job 5:5
[12] May no one extend kindness
to him
or take pity on his fatherless
children.
[13] May his descendants be cut
off,   Ps 37:28
their names blotted out from
the next generation.
[14] May the iniquity of his fathers
be remembered before
the LORD;   Ex 20:5; Ne 4:5
may the sin of his mother
never be blotted out.
[15] May their sins always remain
before the LORD,
that he may blot out their
name from the earth.

[16] For he never thought of doing
a kindness,
but hounded to death the
poor
and the needy and the
brokenhearted.   Ps 34:18
[17] He loved to pronounce a
curse—
may it come back on him.
He found no pleasure in
blessing—
may it be far from him.
[18] He wore cursing as his
garment;
it entered into his body like
water,   Nu 5:22
into his bones like oil.
[19] May it be like a cloak wrapped
about him,

[a] 10 Septuagint; Hebrew sought

like a belt tied forever
around him.
20 May this be the LORD's
payment to my
accusers,   Ps 94:23; 2Ti 4:14
to those who speak evil
of me.   Ps 71:10

21 But you, Sovereign LORD,
help me for your name's
sake;   Ps 79:9
out of the goodness of your
love, deliver me.   Ps 69:16
22 For I am poor and needy,
and my heart is wounded
within me.
23 I fade away like an evening
shadow;   Ps 102:11
I am shaken off like a locust.
24 My knees give way from
fasting;   Heb 12:12
my body is thin and gaunt.
25 I am an object of scorn to my
accusers;   Ps 22:6
when they see me, they
shake their heads.

26 Help me, LORD my God;
save me according to your
unfailing love.
27 Let them know that it is your
hand,   Job 37:7
that you, LORD, have done it.
28 While they curse, may you
bless;   2Sa 16:12
may those who attack me be
put to shame,
but may your servant
rejoice.   Isa 65:14
29 May my accusers be clothed
with disgrace

and wrapped in shame as in
a cloak.   Ps 35:26
30 With my mouth I will greatly
extol the LORD;
in the great throng of
worshipers I will praise
him.
31 For he stands at the right
hand of the needy,   Ps 16:8
to save their lives from
those who would
condemn them.

Psalm 110

Of David. A psalm.

1 The LORD says to my lord:[a]

"Sit at my right hand
until I make your enemies
a footstool for your feet."

2 The LORD will extend your
mighty scepter from
Zion, saying,   Ps 45:6
"Rule in the midst of your
enemies!"
3 Your troops will be willing
on your day of battle.
Arrayed in holy splendor,   Jdg 5:2
your young men will come
to you
like dew from the morning's
womb.[b]   Mic 5:7

4 The LORD has sworn
and will not change his
mind: Nu 23:19
"You are a priest forever,
in the order of
Melchizedek."   Heb 7:15-17

---

a 1 Or *Lord*   *b 3* The meaning of the Hebrew for this sentence is uncertain.

⁵The Lord is at your right hand*ᵃ*;
  he will crush kings on the
    day of his wrath. Ps 2:5,12
⁶He will judge the nations,
  heaping up the dead
  and crushing the rulers of
    the whole earth. Ps 68:21
⁷He will drink from a brook
    along the way,*ᵇ*
  and so he will lift his head
    high. Ps 27:6

Psalm 111*ᶜ*

¹Praise the Lord.*ᵈ*

I will extol the Lord with all
    my heart Ps 34:1
  in the council of the upright
    and in the assembly.

²Great are the works of the
    Lord; Ps 92:5
  they are pondered by all
    who delight in them.
³Glorious and majestic are his
    deeds,
  and his righteousness
    endures forever. Ps 112:3,9
⁴He has caused his wonders to
    be remembered;
  the Lord is gracious and
    compassionate. Ps 103:8
⁵He provides food for those
    who fear him; Mt 6:26,31-33
  he remembers his covenant
    forever.

⁶He has shown his people the
    power of his works,

giving them the lands of
    other nations. Ps 105:44
⁷The works of his hands are
    faithful and just;
  all his precepts are
    trustworthy. Ps 19:7
⁸They are established for ever
    and ever,
  enacted in faithfulness and
    uprightness.
⁹He provided redemption for
    his people; Lk 1:68
  he ordained his covenant
    forever —
  holy and awesome is his
    name. Ps 99:3

¹⁰The fear of the Lord is the
    beginning of wisdom;
  all who follow his
    precepts have good
    understanding. Ecc 12:13
  To him belongs eternal
    praise. Ps 145:2

Psalm 112*ᶜ*

¹Praise the Lord.*ᵈ* Ps 33:2

Blessed are those who fear the
    Lord, Ps 128:1
  who find great delight in his
    commands.

²Their children will be mighty
    in the land; Ps 25:13
  the generation of the
    upright will be blessed.
³Wealth and riches are in their
    houses, Dt 8:18

ᵃ 5 Or *My lord is at your right hand,* Lord   *ᵇ 7* The meaning of the Hebrew for this
clause is uncertain.   *ᶜ* This psalm is an acrostic poem, the lines of which begin with the
successive letters of the Hebrew alphabet.   *ᵈ 1* Hebrew *Hallelu Yah*

and their righteousness
   endures forever.   Ps 37:6
⁴Even in darkness light dawns
   for the upright,   Job 11:17
for those who are gracious
   and compassionate and
   righteous.   Ps 97:11
⁵Good will come to those who
   are generous and lend
   freely,   Ps 37:21,26
who conduct their affairs
   with justice.

⁶Surely the righteous will
   never be shaken;
they will be remembered
   forever.   Pr 10:7
⁷They will have no fear of bad
   news;
their hearts are steadfast,
   trusting in the LORD.
⁸Their hearts are secure, they
   will have no fear;
in the end they will look in
   triumph on their foes.
⁹They have freely scattered
   their gifts to the poor,
their righteousness endures
   forever;
their horn*a* will be lifted
   high in honor.   Ps 75:10
¹⁰The wicked will see and be
   vexed,
they will gnash their teeth
   and waste away;   Ps 37:12
the longings of the wicked
   will come to nothing.

Psalm 113

¹Praise the LORD.*b*

Praise the LORD, you his
   servants;   Ps 135:1
praise the name of the
   LORD.
²Let the name of the LORD be
   praised,
both now and forevermore.
³From the rising of the sun to
   the place where it sets,
the name of the LORD is to
   be praised.

⁴The LORD is exalted over all
   the nations,   Ps 99:2
his glory above the heavens.
⁵Who is like the LORD our God,
   the One who sits enthroned
   on high,
⁶who stoops down to look   Ps 11:4
on the heavens and the
   earth?

⁷He raises the poor from the
   dust   1Sa 2:8
and lifts the needy from the
   ash heap;   Ps 107:41
⁸he seats them with princes,
   with the princes of his
   people.
⁹He settles the childless
   woman in her home
as a happy mother of
   children.
Praise the LORD.

Psalm 114

¹When Israel came out of
   Egypt,   Ex 13:3
Jacob from a people of
   foreign tongue,

---

a 9 *Horn* here symbolizes dignity.   *b 1* Hebrew *Hallelu Yah*; also in verse 9

²Judah became God's sanctuary,
Israel his dominion.

³The sea looked and fled, Ex 14:21
the Jordan turned back;
⁴the mountains leaped like
rams,
the hills like lambs.

⁵Why was it, sea, that you
fled? Ex 14:21
Why, Jordan, did you turn
back?
⁶Why, mountains, did you leap
like rams,
you hills, like lambs?

⁷Tremble, earth, at the
presence of the Lord,
at the presence of the God
of Jacob,
⁸who turned the rock into a
pool,
the hard rock into springs of
water. Ex 17:6; Nu 20:11

Psalm 115

115:4-11pp — Ps 135:15-20

¹Not to us, LORD, not to us
but to your name be the
glory, Ps 96:8
because of your love and
faithfulness. Ex 34:6

²Why do the nations say,
"Where is their God?" Ps 42:3
³Our God is in heaven; Ps 103:19
he does whatever pleases
him. Ps 135:6
⁴But their idols are silver and
gold,
made by human hands.

⁵They have mouths, but cannot
speak, Jer 10:5
eyes, but cannot see.
⁶They have ears, but cannot
hear,
noses, but cannot smell.
⁷They have hands, but cannot
feel,
feet, but cannot walk,
nor can they utter a sound
with their throats.
⁸Those who make them will be
like them,
and so will all who trust in
them.

⁹All you Israelites, trust in the
LORD— Ps 37:3
he is their help and shield.
¹⁰House of Aaron, trust in the
LORD— Ps 118:3
he is their help and shield.
¹¹You who fear him, trust in the
LORD— Ps 22:23
he is their help and shield.

¹²The LORD remembers us and
will bless us:
He will bless his people
Israel,
he will bless the house of
Aaron,
¹³he will bless those who fear
the LORD— Ps 128:1,4
small and great alike.

¹⁴May the LORD cause you to
flourish,
both you and your children.
¹⁵May you be blessed by the
LORD,
the Maker of heaven and
earth. Ps 96:5

¹⁶The highest heavens belong to
the LORD, Ps 89:11
but the earth he has given
to mankind.
¹⁷It is not the dead who praise
the LORD, Ps 6:5
those who go down to the
place of silence;
¹⁸it is we who extol the LORD,
both now and forevermore.

Praise the LORD.^a Ps 28:6

Psalm 116

¹I love the LORD, for he heard
my voice; Ps 18:1
he heard my cry for mercy.
²Because he turned his ear
to me, Ps 40:1
I will call on him as long as
I live.

³The cords of death
entangled me, Ps 18:4-5
the anguish of the grave
came over me;
I was overcome by distress
and sorrow.
⁴Then I called on the name of
the LORD: Ps 118:5
"LORD, save me!" Ps 22:20

⁵The LORD is gracious and
righteous; Ezr 9:15; Ps 103:8
our God is full of
compassion.
⁶The LORD protects the
unwary;
when I was brought low, he
saved me. Ps 19:7; 79:8

⁷Return to your rest, my soul,

for the LORD has been good
to you. Ps 13:6
⁸For you, LORD, have delivered
me from death, Ps 56:13
my eyes from tears,
my feet from stumbling,
⁹that I may walk before the
LORD
in the land of the living.

¹⁰I trusted in the LORD when I
said, 2Co 4:13
"I am greatly afflicted";
¹¹in my alarm I said,
"Everyone is a liar." Ro 3:4

¹²What shall I return to the
LORD
for all his goodness to me?

¹³I will lift up the cup of
salvation
and call on the name of the
LORD.
¹⁴I will fulfill my vows to the
LORD Ps 22:25
in the presence of all his
people.

¹⁵Precious in the sight of the
LORD Ps 72:14
is the death of his faithful
servants.
¹⁶Truly I am your servant,
LORD; Ps 119:125; 143:12
I serve you just as my
mother did; Ps 86:16
you have freed me from my
chains.
¹⁷I will sacrifice a thank
offering to you Ps 50:14

---

^a 18 Hebrew *Hallelu Yah*

and call on the name of the
LORD.
[18] I will fulfill my vows to the
LORD
in the presence of all his
people,
[19] in the courts of the house of
the LORD —   Ps 96:8
in your midst, Jerusalem.

Praise the LORD.[a]

Psalm 117

[1] Praise the LORD, all you
nations;   Ro 15:11
extol him, all you peoples.
[2] For great is his love toward us,
and the faithfulness of the
LORD endures forever.

Praise the LORD.[a]

Psalm 118

[1] Give thanks to the LORD, for
he is good;   1Ch 16:8
his love endures forever.

[2] Let Israel say: Ps 115:9
"His love endures forever."
[3] Let the house of Aaron say:
"His love endures forever."
[4] Let those who fear the LORD
say: Ps 115:11
"His love endures forever."

[5] When hard pressed, I cried to
the LORD;   Ps 120:1
he brought me into a
spacious place.
[6] The LORD is with me; I will
not be afraid.   Heb 13:6

What can mere mortals do
to me?   Ps 56:4
[7] The LORD is with me; he is my
helper.
I look in triumph on my
enemies.   Ps 59:10

[8] It is better to take refuge in
the LORD
than to trust in humans.
[9] It is better to take refuge in
the LORD
than to trust in princes.
[10] All the nations surrounded me,
but in the name of the LORD
I cut them down.
[11] They surrounded me on every
side,   Ps 3:6; 88:17
but in the name of the LORD
I cut them down.
[12] They swarmed around me
like bees,   Dt 1:44
but they were consumed
as quickly as burning
thorns;
in the name of the LORD I
cut them down.
[13] I was pushed back and about
to fall,
but the LORD helped me.
[14] The LORD is my strength and
my defense[b];   Ex 15:2
he has become my
salvation.   Isa 12:2

[15] Shouts of joy and victory
resound in the tents of the
righteous:
"The LORD's right hand
has done mighty
things!   Ps 89:13

[a] 19,2 Hebrew *Hallelu Yah*   [b] 14 Or *song*

¹⁶ The LORD's right hand is
    lifted high;
  the LORD's right hand has
    done mighty things!"
¹⁷ I will not die but live,   Hab 1:12
  and will proclaim what the
    LORD has done.   Ps 73:28
¹⁸ The LORD has chastened me
    severely,
  but he has not given me
    over to death.   2Co 6:9
¹⁹ Open for me the gates of the
    righteous;   Isa 26:2
  I will enter and give thanks
    to the LORD.
²⁰ This is the gate of the LORD
  through which the
    righteous may enter.
²¹ I will give you thanks, for you
    answered me;   Ps 116:1
  you have become my
    salvation.

²² The stone the builders
    rejected
  has become the cornerstone;
²³ the LORD has done this,
  and it is marvelous in our
    eyes.   Mt 21:42
²⁴ The LORD has done it this very
    day;
  let us rejoice today and be
    glad.   Ps 70:4
²⁵ LORD, save us!
  LORD, grant us success!
²⁶ Blessed is he who comes in
    the name of the LORD.

From the house of the LORD
  we bless you.^a
²⁷ The LORD is God,
  and he has made his light
    shine on us.   1Pe 2:9
With boughs in hand, join in
  the festal procession
  up^b to the horns of the
    altar.   Ex 27:2

²⁸ You are my God, and I will
    praise you;
  you are my God, and I will
    exalt you.   Ex 15:2; Isa 25:1

²⁹ Give thanks to the LORD, for
    he is good;
  his love endures forever.

Psalm 119^c

א Aleph

¹ Blessed are those whose ways
    are blameless,   Ge 17:1
  who walk according to the
    law of the LORD.   Ps 128:1
² Blessed are those who keep
    his statutes
  and seek him with all their
    heart —   Dt 6:5
³ they do no wrong   Jn 3:9; 5:18
  but follow his ways.   Ps 128:1
⁴ You have laid down precepts
  that are to be fully obeyed.
⁵ Oh, that my ways were
    steadfast
  in obeying your decrees!
⁶ Then I would not be put to
    shame

---

^a 26 The Hebrew is plural.   ^b 27 Or *Bind the festal sacrifice with ropes / and take it*
^c This psalm is an acrostic poem, the stanzas of which begin with successive letters of the
Hebrew alphabet; moreover, the verses of each stanza begin with the same letter of the
Hebrew alphabet.

when I consider all your
    commands.   ver 117
[7] I will praise you with an
    upright heart
  as I learn your righteous
    laws.   Dt 4:8
[8] I will obey your decrees;
  do not utterly forsake me.

ב Beth

[9] How can a young person stay
    on the path of purity?
  By living according to your
    word.   2Ch 6:16
[10] I seek you with all my heart;
                 2Ch 15:15
  do not let me stray from
    your commands.
[11] I have hidden your word in
    my heart   Ps 37:31; Lk 2:19,51
  that I might not sin against
    you.
[12] Praise be to you, LORD;
  teach me your decrees.
[13] With my lips I recount
  all the laws that come from
    your mouth.   Ps 40:9
[14] I rejoice in following your
    statutes
  as one rejoices in great
    riches.
[15] I meditate on your precepts
  and consider your ways.
[16] I delight in your decrees;   Ps 1:2
  I will not neglect your word.

ג Gimel

[17] Be good to your servant while
    I live,   Ps 13:6; 116:7
  that I may obey your word.

[18] Open my eyes that I may see
  wonderful things in your law.
[19] I am a stranger on earth;
  do not hide your commands
    from me.
[20] My soul is consumed with
    longing   Ps 42:2; 84:2
  for your laws at all times.
[21] You rebuke the arrogant, who
    are accursed,   Job 30:1
  those who stray from your
    commands.   ver 10
[22] Remove from me their scorn
    and contempt,   Ps 39:8
  for I keep your statutes.
[23] Though rulers sit together and
    slander me,
  your servant will meditate
    on your decrees.
[24] Your statutes are my delight;
  they are my counselors.

ד Daleth

[25] I am laid low in the dust;
  preserve my life according
    to your word.   Ps 143:11
[26] I gave an account of my ways
    and you answered me;
  teach me your decrees. Ps 25:4
[27] Cause me to understand the
    way of your precepts,
  that I may meditate on your
    wonderful deeds. Ps 145:5
[28] My soul is weary with sorrow;
  strengthen me according to
    your word.   Ps 20:2; 1Pe 5:10
[29] Keep me from deceitful ways;
  be gracious to me and teach
    me your law.   Nu 6:25
[30] I have chosen the way of
  faithfulness;   Ps 26:3

I have set my heart on your
laws.   Ps 108:1
³¹I hold fast to your statutes,
LORD;   Dt 10:20; 11:22
do not let me be put to
shame.
³²I run in the path of your
commands,
for you have broadened my
understanding.

ח He

³³Teach me, LORD, the way of
your decrees,   ver 12
that I may follow it to the
end.*a*
³⁴Give me understanding, so
that I may keep your law
and obey it with all my
heart.
³⁵Direct me in the path of your
commands,
for there I find delight.   Ps 1:2
³⁶Turn my heart toward your
statutes
and not toward selfish gain.
³⁷Turn my eyes away from
worthless things;
preserve my life according
to your word.*b*   Ps 71:20
³⁸Fulfill your promise to your
servant,   2Sa 7:25
so that you may be feared.
³⁹Take away the disgrace I
dread,   Ps 69:9
for your laws are good.
⁴⁰How I long for your precepts!
In your righteousness
preserve my life.

ו Waw

⁴¹May your unfailing love come
to me, LORD,   Ps 6:4
your salvation, according to
your promise;   ver 76,116
⁴²then I can answer anyone
who taunts me,   Pr 27:11
for I trust in your word.
⁴³Never take your word of truth
from my mouth,
for I have put my hope in
your laws.   ver 74,81,114,147
⁴⁴I will always obey your law,
for ever and ever.
⁴⁵I will walk about in freedom,
for I have sought out your
precepts.   ver 94,155
⁴⁶I will speak of your statutes
before kings   Mt 10:18
and will not be put to shame,
⁴⁷for I delight in your
commands
because I love them.
⁴⁸I reach out for your commands,
which I love,
that I may meditate on your
decrees.   Ge 24:63

ז Zayin

⁴⁹Remember your word to your
servant,
for you have given me hope.
⁵⁰My comfort in my suffering is
this:
Your promise preserves my
life.   Ro 15:4
⁵¹The arrogant mock me
unmercifully,   Jer 20:7

---

a 33 Or *follow it for its reward*   *b* 37 Two manuscripts of the Masoretic Text and Dead Sea
Scrolls; most manuscripts of the Masoretic Text *life in your way*

but I do not turn from your
law.   Job 23:11
⁵²I remember, LORD, your
ancient laws,   Ps 103:18
and I find comfort in them.
⁵³Indignation grips me because
of the wicked,   Ezr 9:3
who have forsaken your
law.   Ps 89:30
⁵⁴Your decrees are the theme of
my song
wherever I lodge.
⁵⁵In the night, LORD, I
remember your name,
that I may keep your law.
⁵⁶This has been my practice:
I obey your precepts.   Nu 15:40

ח Heth

⁵⁷You are my portion, LORD;
I have promised to obey
your words.
⁵⁸I have sought your face with
all my heart;
be gracious to me according
to your promise.   1Ki 13:6
⁵⁹I have considered my ways
and have turned my steps to
your statutes.
⁶⁰I will hasten and not delay
to obey your commands.
⁶¹Though the wicked bind me
with ropes,
I will not forget your law.
⁶²At midnight I rise to give you
thanks   Ac 16:25
for your righteous laws.
⁶³I am a friend to all who fear
you,   Ps 101:6-7
to all who follow your
precepts.

⁶⁴The earth is filled with your
love, LORD;   Ps 33:5
teach me your decrees.

ט Teth

⁶⁵Do good to your servant
according to your word,
LORD.   Ps 125:4; Mic 2:7
⁶⁶Teach me knowledge and
good judgment,   Ps 51:6
for I trust your commands.
⁶⁷Before I was afflicted I went
astray,   Jer 31:18-19; Heb 12:11
but now I obey your word.
⁶⁸You are good, and what you
do is good;   Ps 106:1; 107:1
teach me your decrees.
⁶⁹Though the arrogant have
smeared me with lies,
I keep your precepts with
all my heart.
⁷⁰Their hearts are callous and
unfeeling,   Ps 17:10; Ac 28:27
but I delight in your law.
⁷¹It was good for me to be
afflicted   ver 67,75
so that I might learn your
decrees.
⁷²The law from your mouth is
more precious to me
than thousands of pieces of
silver and gold.   Ps 19:10

י Yodh

⁷³Your hands made me and
formed me;   Job 10:8
give me understanding to
learn your commands.
⁷⁴May those who fear you rejoice
when they see me,   Ps 34:2

for I have put my hope in
   your word.
75 I know, LORD, that your laws
   are righteous,
   and that in faithfulness you
    have afflicted me.
76 May your unfailing love be my
   comfort,
   according to your promise
    to your servant.   ver 41
77 Let your compassion come to
   me that I may live,   ver 41
   for your law is my delight.
78 May the arrogant be put to
   shame for wronging me
   without cause;   ver 86,161
   but I will meditate on your
    precepts.
79 May those who fear you turn
   to me,
   those who understand your
    statutes.   ver 27,125
80 May I wholeheartedly follow
   your decrees,   Ge 26:5
   that I may not be put to
    shame.

כ Kaph

81 My soul faints with longing
   for your salvation,   Ps 84:2
   but I have put my hope in
    your word.
82 My eyes fail, looking for your
   promise;   Ps 69:3; La 2:11
   I say, "When will you
    comfort me?"
83 Though I am like a wineskin
   in the smoke,
   I do not forget your decrees.
84 How long must your servant
   wait?   Ps 39:4; Rev 6:10

When will you punish my
   persecutors?
85 The arrogant dig pits to
   trap me,   Ps 35:7; Jer 18:20,22
   contrary to your law.
86 All your commands are
   trustworthy;   Ps 35:19
   help me, for I am being
    persecuted without
    cause.   Ps 109:26
87 They almost wiped me from
   the earth,
   but I have not forsaken your
    precepts.   Isa 58:2
88 In your unfailing love
   preserve my life,
   that I may obey the statutes
    of your mouth.   ver 2,100

ל Lamedh

89 Your word, LORD, is eternal;
   it stands firm in the heavens.
90 Your faithfulness continues
   through all generations;
   you established the earth,
    and it endures.   Ps 148:6
91 Your laws endure to this day,
   for all things serve you.
92 If your law had not been my
   delight,   Ps 37:4
   I would have perished in my
    affliction.
93 I will never forget your
   precepts,
   for by them you have
    preserved my life.   Ps 103:5
94 Save me, for I am yours;
   I have sought out your
    precepts.
95 The wicked are waiting to
   destroy me,   Ps 69:4

but I will ponder your
    statutes.
⁹⁶To all perfection I see a limit,
    but your commands are
      boundless.   Ps 19:7

 מ Mem

⁹⁷Oh, how I love your law!
    I meditate on it all day long.
⁹⁸Your commands are always
    with me   Dt 4:6
  and make me wiser than
    my enemies.
⁹⁹I have more insight than all
    my teachers,
  for I meditate on your
    statutes.   ver 15
¹⁰⁰I have more understanding
    than the elders,
  for I obey your precepts.
¹⁰¹I have kept my feet from
    every evil path   Pr 1:15
  so that I might obey your
    word.
¹⁰²I have not departed from your
    laws,
  for you yourself have
    taught me.
¹⁰³How sweet are your words to
    my taste,
  sweeter than honey to my
    mouth!   Ps 19:10; Pr 8:11
¹⁰⁴I gain understanding from
    your precepts;
  therefore I hate every wrong
    path.   ver 128

נ Nun

¹⁰⁵Your word is a lamp for my
    feet,

a light on my path.   Pr 6:23
¹⁰⁶I have taken an oath and
    confirmed it,   Ne 10:29
  that I will follow your
    righteous laws.
¹⁰⁷I have suffered much;
  preserve my life, LORD,
    according to your word.
¹⁰⁸Accept, LORD, the willing
    praise of my mouth,
  and teach me your laws.
¹⁰⁹Though I constantly take my
    life in my hands,   Jdg 12:3
  I will not forget your law.
¹¹⁰The wicked have set a snare
    for me,   Ps 140:5; 141:9
  but I have not strayed from
    your precepts.
¹¹¹Your statutes are my heritage
    forever;
  they are the joy of my heart.
¹¹²My heart is set on keeping
    your decrees   Ps 108:1
  to the very end.ᵃ

ס Samekh

¹¹³I hate double-minded people,
  but I love your law.
¹¹⁴You are my refuge and my
    shield;   Ps 32:7; 91:1
  I have put my hope in your
    word.
¹¹⁵Away from me, you evildoers,
  that I may keep the
    commands of my God!
¹¹⁶Sustain me, my God,
    according to your
    promise, and I will live;
  do not let my hopes be
    dashed.   Ps 25:2; Ro 5:5

ᵃ 112 Or *decrees / for their enduring reward*

117Uphold me, and I will be
 delivered; Isa 41:10
 I will always have regard for
 your decrees.
118You reject all who stray from
 your decrees,
 for their delusions come to
 nothing.
119All the wicked of the earth
 you discard like dross;
 therefore I love your
 statutes.
120My flesh trembles in fear of
 you; Hab 3:16
 I stand in awe of your laws.

ע Ayin

121I have done what is righteous
 and just; 2Sa 8:15
 do not leave me to my
 oppressors.
122Ensure your servant's well-
 being; Job 17:3
 do not let the arrogant
 oppress me.
123My eyes fail, looking for your
 salvation,
 looking for your righteous
 promise. ver 82
124Deal with your servant
 according to your love
 and teach me your
 decrees. ver 12
125I am your servant; give me
 discernment Ps 116:16
 that I may understand your
 statutes.
126It is time for you to act, LORD;
 your law is being broken.
127Because I love your
 commands

more than gold, more than
 pure gold, Ps 19:10
128and because I consider all
 your precepts right,
 I hate every wrong path.

פ Pe

129Your statutes are wonderful;
 therefore I obey them.
130The unfolding of your words
 gives light; Pr 6:23
 it gives understanding to
 the simple. Ps 19:7
131I open my mouth and pant,
 longing for your commands.
132Turn to me and have mercy
 on me, Ps 25:16; 106:4
 as you always do to those
 who love your name.
133Direct my footsteps
 according to your word;
 let no sin rule over me.
134Redeem me from human
 oppression, Ps 142:6; Lk 1:74
 that I may obey your
 precepts.
135Make your face shine on your
 servant Ps 4:6
 and teach me your decrees.
136Streams of tears flow from
 my eyes, Jer 9:1,18
 for your law is not obeyed.

צ Tsadhe

137You are righteous, LORD,
 and your laws are right.
138The statutes you have laid
 down are righteous;
 they are fully trustworthy.
139My zeal wears me out, Ps 69:9

for my enemies ignore your
words.
¹⁴⁰Your promises have been
thoroughly tested, Ps 12:6
and your servant loves them.
¹⁴¹Though I am lowly and
despised, Ps 22:6
I do not forget your precepts.
¹⁴²Your righteousness is
everlasting
and your law is true. Ps 19:7
¹⁴³Trouble and distress have
come upon me,
but your commands give
me delight.
¹⁴⁴Your statutes are always
righteous;
give me understanding that
I may live. Ps 19:9

ק Qoph

¹⁴⁵I call with all my heart;
answer me, Lord,
and I will obey your decrees.
¹⁴⁶I call out to you; save me
and I will keep your statutes.
¹⁴⁷I rise before dawn and cry for
help; Ps 5:3; 57:8; 108:2
I have put my hope in your
word.
¹⁴⁸My eyes stay open through
the watches of the
night, Ps 63:6
that I may meditate on your
promises.
¹⁴⁹Hear my voice in accordance
with your love; Ps 27:7
preserve my life, Lord,
according to your laws.
¹⁵⁰Those who devise wicked
schemes are near,

but they are far from your
law.
¹⁵¹Yet you are near, Lord, Ps 145:18
and all your commands are
true. ver 142
¹⁵²Long ago I learned from your
statutes
that you established them
to last forever. Lk 21:33

ר Resh

¹⁵³Look on my suffering and
deliver me, La 5:1
for I have not forgotten your
law. Pr 3:1
¹⁵⁴Defend my cause and
redeem me; 1Sa 24:15
preserve my life according
to your promise.
¹⁵⁵Salvation is far from the
wicked,
for they do not seek out your
decrees. Job 5:4
¹⁵⁶Your compassion, Lord, is
great;
preserve my life according
to your laws. 2Sa 24:14
¹⁵⁷Many are the foes who
persecute me, Ps 7:1
but I have not turned from
your statutes.
¹⁵⁸I look on the faithless with
loathing, Ps 139:21
for they do not obey your
word.
¹⁵⁹See how I love your
precepts;
preserve my life, Lord, in
accordance with your
love. Ps 41:2
¹⁶⁰All your words are true;

all your righteous laws are
eternal. ver 89; Ps 111:8

שׂ Sin and Shin

161 Rulers persecute me without
cause, 1Sa 24:11
but my heart trembles at
your word.
162 I rejoice in your promise
like one who finds great
spoil. 1Sa 30:16
163 I hate and detest falsehood
but I love your law. ver 47
164 Seven times a day I praise you
for your righteous laws.
165 Great peace have those who
love your law, Pr 3:2
and nothing can make
them stumble.
166 I wait for your salvation,
LORD, Ge 49:18
and I follow your commands.
167 I obey your statutes,
for I love them greatly.
168 I obey your precepts and your
statutes,
for all my ways are known
to you. Pr 5:21

ת Taw

169 May my cry come before you,
LORD; Ps 18:6
give me understanding
according to your word.
170 May my supplication come
before you; Ps 28:2
deliver me according to
your promise. Ps 31:2
171 May my lips overflow with
praise, Ps 51:15

for you teach me your
decrees.
172 May my tongue sing of your
word,
for all your commands are
righteous.
173 May your hand be ready to
help me, Ps 37:24
for I have chosen your
precepts. Jos 24:22
174 I long for your salvation,
LORD,
and your law gives me
delight.
175 Let me live that I may praise
you, Isa 55:3
and may your laws
sustain me.
176 I have strayed like a lost
sheep. Isa 53:6
Seek your servant,
for I have not forgotten your
commands. Ps 44:17

Psalm 120

A song of ascents.

1 I call on the LORD in my
distress, Jnh 2:2
and he answers me.
2 Save me, LORD,
from lying lips Pr 12:22
and from deceitful
tongues. Ps 52:4
3 What will he do to you,
and what more besides,
you deceitful tongue?
4 He will punish you with a
warrior's sharp arrows,
with burning coals of the
broom bush.

5Woe to me that I dwell in
   Meshek,
   that I live among the tents
     of Kedar!   Ge 25:13; Jer 49:28
6Too long have I lived
   among those who hate
     peace.
7I am for peace;
   but when I speak, they are
     for war.

Psalm 121

A song of ascents.

1I lift up my eyes to the
   mountains—
   where does my help come
     from?
2My help comes from the
   LORD,
   the Maker of heaven and
     earth.   Ps 124:8
3He will not let your foot
   slip—
   he who watches over you
     will not slumber;
4indeed, he who watches over
   Israel   Ps 127:1
   will neither slumber nor
     sleep.
5The LORD watches over
   you—   Isa 25:4
   the LORD is your shade at
     your right hand;
6the sun will not harm you by
   day,   Ps 91:5; Isa 49:10
   nor the moon by night.
7The LORD will keep you from
   all harm—   Ps 41:2; 91:10-12
   he will watch over your life;

8the LORD will watch over your
   coming and going
   both now and
     forevermore.   Dt 28:6

Psalm 122

A song of ascents. Of David.

1I rejoiced with those who said
   to me,
   "Let us go to the house of
     the LORD."
2Our feet are standing
   in your gates, Jerusalem.

3Jerusalem is built like a city
   that is closely compacted
     together.
4That is where the tribes
   go up—
   the tribes of the LORD—
to praise the name of the
   LORD
   according to the statute
     given to Israel.
5There stand the thrones for
   judgment,
   the thrones of the house
     of David.

6Pray for the peace of
   Jerusalem:
   "May those who love you be
     secure.   Ps 51:18
7May there be peace within
   your walls   1Sa 25:6
   and security within your
     citadels."   Ps 48:3
8For the sake of my family and
   friends,
   I will say, "Peace be within
     you."

⁹For the sake of the house of
    the Lord our God,
  I will seek your prosperity.

Psalm 123

A song of ascents.

¹I lift up my eyes to you,
    to you who sit enthroned in
        heaven.   Ps 11:4; 121:1; 141:8
²As the eyes of slaves look to the
        hand of their master,
  as the eyes of a female slave
        look to the hand of her
        mistress,
  so our eyes look to the Lord
        our God,   Ps 25:15
  till he shows us his mercy.

³Have mercy on us, Lord, have
        mercy on us,
  for we have endured no end
        of contempt.
⁴We have endured no end
  of ridicule from the
        arrogant,
  of contempt from the proud.

Psalm 124

A song of ascents. Of David.

¹If the Lord had not been on
        our side —
  let Israel say —   Ps 129:1
²if the Lord had not been on
        our side
  when people attacked us,
³they would have swallowed us
        alive
  when their anger flared
        against us;
⁴the flood would have
        engulfed us,

  the torrent would have
        swept over us,
⁵the raging waters
  would have swept us
        away.

⁶Praise be to the Lord,
  who has not let us be torn
        by their teeth.
⁷We have escaped like a bird
  from the fowler's snare;
  the snare has been broken,
        and we have escaped.
⁸Our help is in the name of the
        Lord,
  the Maker of heaven and
        earth.   Ge 1:1; Ps 121:2

Psalm 125

A song of ascents.

¹Those who trust in the Lord
  are like Mount Zion,
  which cannot be shaken but
        endures forever.
²As the mountains surround
        Jerusalem,
  so the Lord surrounds his
        people   Ps 121:8; Zec 2:4-5
  both now and forevermore.

³The scepter of the wicked will
        not remain   Pr 22:8; Isa 14:5
  over the land allotted to the
        righteous,
  for then the righteous might
        use
  their hands to do evil.

⁴Lord, do good to those who
        are good,   Ps 119:68
  to those who are upright in
        heart.   Ps 7:10; 94:15

[5] But those who turn to crooked ways Pr 2:15; Isa 59:8
the LORD will banish with the evildoers.

Peace be on Israel. Ps 128:6

Psalm 126

A song of ascents.

[1] When the LORD restored the fortunes of[a] Zion, Ps 85:1
we were like those who dreamed.[b]
[2] Our mouths were filled with laughter,
our tongues with songs of joy. Ps 51:14
Then it was said among the nations,
"The LORD has done great things for them." Ps 71:19
[3] The LORD has done great things for us,
and we are filled with joy.

[4] Restore our fortunes,[c] LORD,
like streams in the Negev.
[5] Those who sow with tears
will reap with songs of joy.
[6] Those who go out weeping,
carrying seed to sow,
will return with songs of joy,
carrying sheaves with them.

Psalm 127

A song of ascents. Of Solomon.

[1] Unless the LORD builds the house, Ps 78:69
the builders labor in vain.

Unless the LORD watches over the city, Ps 121:4
the guards stand watch in vain.
[2] In vain you rise early
and stay up late,
toiling for food to eat — Ge 3:17
for he grants sleep to[d] those he loves. Job 11:18

[3] Children are a heritage from the LORD,
offspring a reward from him. Ge 33:5
[4] Like arrows in the hands of a warrior Ps 112:2
are children born in one's youth.
[5] Blessed is the man
whose quiver is full of them. Ps 128:2-3
They will not be put to shame
when they contend with their opponents in court. Pr 27:11

Psalm 128

A song of ascents.

[1] Blessed are all who fear the LORD, Ps 112:1
who walk in obedience to him. Ps 119:1-3
[2] You will eat the fruit of your labor; Isa 3:10
blessings and prosperity will be yours. Ecc 8:12
[3] Your wife will be like a fruitful vine
within your house; Eze 19:10

---

[a] 1 Or LORD *brought back the captives to*   [b] 1 Or *those restored to health*   [c] 4 Or *Bring back our captives*   [d] 2 Or *eat — / for while they sleep he provides for*

your children will be like olive
    shoots
    around your table.   Ps 52:8
⁴Yes, this will be the blessing
    for the man who fears the
    LORD.

⁵May the LORD bless you from
    Zion;   Ps 134:3
    may you see the prosperity
    of Jerusalem
    all the days of your life.
⁶May you live to see your
    children's children —
    peace be on Israel.   Ps 125:5

Psalm 129

A song of ascents.

¹ "They have greatly oppressed
    me from my youth,"
    let Israel say;   Ps 124:1
² "they have greatly oppressed
    me from my youth,
    but they have not gained
    the victory over me.
³Plowmen have plowed my
    back
    and made their furrows
    long.
⁴But the LORD is righteous;
    he has cut me free from the
    cords of the wicked."

⁵May all who hate Zion   Mic 4:11
    be turned back in shame.
⁶May they be like grass on the
    roof,
    which withers before it can
    grow;   Ps 37:2
⁷a reaper cannot fill his hands
    with it,   Dt 28:38

nor one who gathers fill his
    arms.
⁸May those who pass by not
    say to them,
    "The blessing of the LORD
    be on you;
    we bless you in the name of
    the LORD."   Ru 2:4; Ps 118:26

Psalm 130

A song of ascents.

¹Out of the depths I cry to you,
    LORD;   Ps 42:7; 69:2; La 3:55
²   Lord, hear my voice.   Ps 28:2
  Let your ears be attentive   Ps 64:1
  to my cry for mercy.

³If you, LORD, kept a record of
    sins,
    Lord, who could stand?
⁴But with you there is
    forgiveness,   Ex 34:7; Jer 33:8
    so that we can, with
    reverence, serve you.

⁵I wait for the LORD, my whole
    being waits,   Ps 27:14; 33:20
    and in his word I put my
    hope.   Ps 119:81
⁶I wait for the Lord
    more than watchmen wait
    for the morning,
    more than watchmen wait
    for the morning.   Ps 119:147

⁷Israel, put your hope in the
    LORD,   Ps 131:3
    for with the LORD is
    unfailing love
    and with him is full
    redemption.

[8] He himself will redeem
    Israel   Lk 1:68
from all their sins.

Psalm 131

A song of ascents. Of David.

[1] My heart is not proud, LORD,
    my eyes are not haughty;
I do not concern myself with
    great matters   Jer 45:5
or things too wonderful
    for me.
[2] But I have calmed and
    quieted myself,   Ps 116:7
I am like a weaned child
    with its mother;
like a weaned child I am
    content.   Mt 18:3; 1Co 14:20

[3] Israel, put your hope in the
    LORD   Ps 130:7
both now and forevermore.

Psalm 132

132:8-10pp — 2Ch 6:41-42

A song of ascents.

[1] LORD, remember David
    and all his self-denial.

[2] He swore an oath to the LORD,
    he made a vow to the
    Mighty One of Jacob:
[3] "I will not enter my house
    or go to my bed,
[4] I will allow no sleep to my
    eyes
    or slumber to my eyelids,
[5] till I find a place for the LORD,

    a dwelling for the Mighty
    One of Jacob."

[6] We heard it in Ephrathah,
    we came upon it in the
    fields of Jaar:[a]   1Sa 7:2
[7] "Let us go to his dwelling
    place,   Ps 5:7
    let us worship at his
    footstool, saying,   Ps 99:5
[8] 'Arise, LORD, and come to
    your resting place,
    you and the ark of your
    might.
[9] May your priests be
    clothed with your
    righteousness;   Job 29:14
    may your faithful people
    sing for joy.'"

[10] For the sake of your servant
    David,
    do not reject your anointed
    one.

[11] The LORD swore an oath to
    David,   Ps 89:3-4,35
    a sure oath he will not
    revoke:
"One of your own descendants
    I will place on your throne.
[12] If your sons keep my covenant
    and the statutes I teach them,
then their sons will sit
    on your throne for ever and
    ever."

[13] For the LORD has chosen
    Zion,   Ps 48:1-2
    he has desired it for his
    dwelling, saying,

---

[a] 6 Or *heard of it in Ephrathah, / we found it in the fields of Jearim.* (See 1 Chron. 13:5,6) (And no quotation marks around verses 7-9)

14 "This is my resting place for
ever and ever;   Ps 68:16
here I will sit enthroned, for
I have desired it.
15 I will bless her with abundant
provisions;
her poor I will satisfy with
food.   Ps 147:14
16 I will clothe her priests with
salvation,
and her faithful people will
ever sing for joy.

17 "Here I will make a horn*a*
grow for David   Eze 29:21
and set up a lamp for my
anointed one.
18 I will clothe his enemies with
shame,   Ps 35:26; 109:29
but his head will be
adorned with a radiant
crown."

Psalm 133

A song of ascents. Of David.

1 How good and pleasant it is
when God's people live
together in unity!   Ge 13:8

2 It is like precious oil poured
on the head,   Ex 30:25
running down on the
beard,
running down on Aaron's
beard,
down on the collar of his
robe.
3 It is as if the dew of Hermon
were falling on Mount Zion.

For there the Lord bestows
his blessing,   Lev 25:21
even life forevermore.   Ps 42:8

Psalm 134

A song of ascents.

1 Praise the Lord, all you
servants of the Lord
who minister by night in
the house of the Lord.
2 Lift up your hands in the
sanctuary   1Ti 2:8
and praise the Lord.

3 May the Lord bless you from
Zion,   Ps 128:5
he who is the Maker of
heaven and earth.   Ps 124:8

Psalm 135

135:15-20pp — Ps 115:4-11

1 Praise the Lord.*b*

Praise the name of the Lord;
praise him, you servants of
the Lord,   Ps 113:1; 134:1
2 you who minister in the house
of the Lord,   Lk 2:37
in the courts of the house of
our God.   Ps 116:19
3 Praise the Lord, for the Lord
is good;   Ps 119:68
sing praise to his name, for
that is pleasant.   Ps 147:1
4 For the Lord has chosen
Jacob to be his own,
Israel to be his treasured
possession.   Ex 19:5; Dt 7:6

---

a 17 *Horn* here symbolizes strong one, that is, king.
verses 3 and 21   *b* 1 Hebrew *Hallelu Yah*; also in

⁵I know that the LORD is
    great,   Ps 48:1
    that our Lord is greater than
    all gods.
⁶The LORD does whatever
    pleases him,   Ps 115:3
    in the heavens and on the
    earth,
    in the seas and all their
    depths.
⁷He makes clouds rise from the
    ends of the earth;
    he sends lightning with the
    rain   Jer 10:13; Zec 10:1
    and brings out the wind
    from his storehouses.
⁸He struck down the firstborn
    of Egypt,   Ex 12:12
    the firstborn of people and
    animals.
⁹He sent his signs and wonders
    into your midst, Egypt,
    against Pharaoh and all his
    servants.   Ps 136:10-15
¹⁰He struck down many nations
    and killed mighty kings —
¹¹Sihon king of the Amorites,
    Og king of Bashan,
    and all the kings of
    Canaan —   Jos 12:7-24
¹²and he gave their land as an
    inheritance,
    an inheritance to his people
    Israel.

¹³Your name, LORD, endures
    forever,   Ex 3:15
    your renown, LORD,
    through all generations.
¹⁴For the LORD will vindicate
    his people   Heb 10:30
    and have compassion on his
    servants.   Dt 32:36

¹⁵The idols of the nations are
    silver and gold,   Ps 96:5
    made by human hands.
¹⁶They have mouths, but cannot
    speak,   1Ki 18:26
    eyes, but cannot see.
¹⁷They have ears, but cannot
    hear,
    nor is there breath in their
    mouths.   Jer 10:14
¹⁸Those who make them will be
    like them,
    and so will all who trust in
    them.

¹⁹All you Israelites, praise the
    LORD;   Ps 22:23
    house of Aaron, praise the
    LORD;
²⁰house of Levi, praise the LORD;
    you who fear him, praise
    the LORD.
²¹Praise be to the LORD from
    Zion,   Ps 134:3
    to him who dwells in
    Jerusalem.

Praise the LORD.

Psalm 136

¹Give thanks to the LORD, for
    he is good.   Ps 106:1
    His love endures forever.
²Give thanks to the God of
    gods.   Dt 10:17
    His love endures forever.
³Give thanks to the Lord of
    lords:
    His love endures forever.

⁴to him who alone does great
wonders,   Ps 72:18
His love endures forever.
⁵who by his understanding
made the heavens, Ge 1:1
His love endures forever.
⁶who spread out the earth
upon the waters, Jer 10:12
His love endures forever.
⁷who made the great
lights —   Ge 1:14,16
His love endures forever.
⁸the sun to govern the day,
His love endures forever.
⁹the moon and stars to govern
the night;
His love endures forever.

¹⁰to him who struck down the
firstborn of Egypt Ex 12:29
His love endures forever.
¹¹and brought Israel out from
among them Ex 6:6; 12:51
His love endures forever.
¹²with a mighty hand and
outstretched arm; Dt 4:34
His love endures forever.

¹³to him who divided the Red
Sea^a asunder   Ex 14:21
His love endures forever.
¹⁴and brought Israel through
the midst of it,
His love endures forever.
¹⁵but swept Pharaoh and his
army into the Red Sea;
His love endures forever.

¹⁶to him who led his people
through the wilderness;
His love endures forever.

¹⁷to him who struck down great
kings,   Ps 135:9-12
His love endures forever.
¹⁸and killed mighty kings —
His love endures forever.
¹⁹Sihon king of the Amorites
His love endures forever.
²⁰and Og king of Bashan —
His love endures forever.
²¹and gave their land as an
inheritance,   Jos 12:1
His love endures forever.
²²an inheritance to his servant
Israel.
His love endures forever.

²³He remembered us in our low
estate   Ps 113:7
His love endures forever.
²⁴and freed us from our enemies.
His love endures forever.
²⁵He gives food to every creature.
His love endures forever.

²⁶Give thanks to the God of
heaven.   Ps 115:3
His love endures forever.

Psalm 137

¹By the rivers of Babylon we sat
and wept   Eze 1:1,3; Ne 1:4
when we remembered Zion.
²There on the poplars
we hung our harps, Job 30:31
³for there our captors asked us
for songs,
our tormentors demanded
songs of joy;   Ps 80:6
they said, "Sing us one of
the songs of Zion!"

---

^a 13 Or *the Sea of Reeds*; also in verse 15

⁴How can we sing the songs of
the Lord   Ne 12:46
while in a foreign land?
⁵If I forget you, Jerusalem,
may my right hand forget its
skill.
⁶May my tongue cling to the
roof of my mouth   Eze 3:26
if I do not remember you,
if I do not consider Jerusalem
my highest joy.

⁷Remember, Lord, what the
Edomites did   Jer 49:7
on the day Jerusalem
fell.   Ob 11
"Tear it down," they cried,
"tear it down to its
foundations!"
⁸Daughter Babylon, doomed to
destruction,   Isa 13:1,19
happy is the one who repays
you
according to what you have
done to us.
⁹Happy is the one who seizes
your infants
and dashes them against
the rocks.   2Ki 8:12; Isa 13:16

Psalm 138

Of David.

¹I will praise you, Lord, with
all my heart;
before the "gods" I will sing
your praise.   Ps 95:3; 96:4
²I will bow down toward your
holy temple   1Ki 8:29; Ps 5:7
and will praise your name
for your unfailing love and
your faithfulness,

for you have so exalted your
solemn decree
that it surpasses your fame.
³When I called, you
answered me;
you greatly emboldened me.

⁴May all the kings of the earth
praise you, Lord, Ps 102:15
when they hear what you
have decreed.
⁵May they sing of the ways of
the Lord,
for the glory of the Lord is
great.

⁶Though the Lord is exalted,
he looks kindly on the
lowly;   Ps 113:6; Isa 57:15
though lofty, he sees them
from afar.   Pr 3:34; Jas 4:6
⁷Though I walk in the midst of
trouble,   Ps 23:4
you preserve my life.
You stretch out your hand
against the anger of my
foes;   Jer 51:25
with your right hand you
save me.   Ps 71:20
⁸The Lord will
vindicate me;   Ps 57:2
your love, Lord, endures
forever —
do not abandon the works
of your hands.   Job 10:3,8

Psalm 139

For the director of music.
Of David. A psalm.

¹You have searched me, Lord,
and you know me.   Jer 12:3

²You know when I sit and when
I rise;   2Ki 19:27
    you perceive my thoughts
        from afar.   Mt 9:4; Jn 2:24
³You discern my going out and
    my lying down;
    you are familiar with all my
        ways.   Job 31:4
⁴Before a word is on my tongue
    you, LORD, know it
        completely.   Heb 4:13
⁵You hem me in behind and
    before,   Ps 34:7
    and you lay your hand
        upon me.
⁶Such knowledge is too
    wonderful for me,
    too lofty for me to attain.

⁷Where can I go from your
    Spirit?
    Where can I flee from your
        presence?   Jer 23:24; Jnh 1:3
⁸If I go up to the heavens, you
    are there;   Am 9:2-3
    if I make my bed in the
        depths, you are
        there.   Pr 15:11
⁹If I rise on the wings of the
    dawn,
    if I settle on the far side of
        the sea,
¹⁰even there your hand will
    guide me,   Ps 23:3
    your right hand will hold
        me fast.
¹¹If I say, "Surely the darkness
    will hide me
    and the light become night
        around me,"

¹²even the darkness will not be
    dark to you;   Job 34:22
    the night will shine like the
        day,
    for darkness is as light to you.

¹³For you created my inmost
    being;   Ps 119:73
    you knit me together in my
        mother's womb.   Job 10:11
¹⁴I praise you because I
    am fearfully and
        wonderfully made;
    your works are wonderful,
    I know that full well.
¹⁵My frame was not hidden
    from you
    when I was made in the
        secret place,
    when I was woven together
        in the depths of the
        earth.   Job 10:11
¹⁶Your eyes saw my unformed
    body;
    all the days ordained for me
        were written in your
        book
    before one of them came
        to be.
¹⁷How precious to me are your
    thoughts,ᵃ God!   Ps 40:5
    How vast is the sum of
        them!
¹⁸Were I to count them,
    they would outnumber the
        grains of sand —
    when I awake, I am still
        with you.   Ps 3:5
¹⁹If only you, God, would slay
    the wicked!   Isa 11:4

ᵃ 17 Or *How amazing are your thoughts concerning me*

Away from me, you who are
    bloodthirsty!   Ps 119:115
²⁰They speak of you with evil
    intent;
    your adversaries misuse
        your name.   Jude 15
²¹Do I not hate those who hate
    you, Lord,   Ps 119:158
    and abhor those who are in
        rebellion against you?
²²I have nothing but hatred for
    them;
    I count them my enemies.
²³Search me, God, and know
    my heart;   Job 31:6; Ps 26:2
    test me and know my
        anxious thoughts.
²⁴See if there is any offensive
    way in me,
    and lead me in the way
        everlasting.   Ps 5:8; 143:10

Psalm 140^a

For the director of music.
A psalm of David.

¹Rescue me, Lord, from
    evildoers;   Ps 17:13
    protect me from the
        violent,   Ps 18:48
²who devise evil plans in their
    hearts   Ps 56:6
    and stir up war every day.
³They make their tongues as
    sharp as a serpent's;
    the poison of vipers is on
        their lips.^b   Ps 58:4; Jas 3:8

⁴Keep me safe, Lord, from the
    hands of the wicked;

protect me from the violent,
    who devise ways to trip my
        feet.
⁵The arrogant have hidden a
    snare for me;   Job 34:30
    they have spread out the
        cords of their net   Job 18:8
    and have set traps for me
        along my path.   Ps 31:4; 35:7

⁶I say to the Lord, "You are my
    God."   Ps 16:2
    Hear, Lord, my cry for mercy.
⁷Sovereign Lord, my strong
    deliverer,   Ps 28:8
    you shield my head in the
        day of battle.
⁸Do not grant the wicked their
    desires, Lord;   Ps 10:2-3
    do not let their plans
        succeed.

⁹Those who surround me
    proudly rear their heads;
    may the mischief of their
        lips engulf them.   Ps 7:16
¹⁰May burning coals fall on
    them;
    may they be thrown into
        the fire,   Ps 11:6; 21:9
    into miry pits, never to rise.
¹¹May slanderers not be
    established in the land;
    may disaster hunt down the
        violent.   Ps 34:21

¹²I know that the Lord secures
    justice for the poor
    and upholds the cause of
        the needy.   Ps 9:4; 35:10

^a In Hebrew texts 140:1-13 is numbered 140:2-14.   ^b 3 The Hebrew has *Selah* (a word of uncertain meaning) here and at the end of verses 5 and 8.

¹³Surely the righteous will
     praise your name,   Ps 97:12
  and the upright will live in
     your presence.   Ps 11:7

Psalm 141

A psalm of David.

¹I call to you, LORD, come
     quickly to me;   Ps 70:5
  hear me when I call to you.
²May my prayer be set before
     you like incense;   Rev 5:8
  may the lifting up of my
     hands be like the
     evening sacrifice.   Ex 29:39

³Set a guard over my mouth,
     LORD;   Ps 34:13
  keep watch over the door of
     my lips.   Ps 12:2
⁴Do not let my heart be drawn
     to what is evil   Jos 24:23
  so that I take part in wicked
     deeds
  along with those who are
     evildoers;
  do not let me eat their
     delicacies.   Pr 23:6

⁵Let a righteous man strike
     me — that is a kindness;
  let him rebuke me — that is
     oil on my head.   Ps 23:5
  My head will not refuse it,
     for my prayer will still be
     against the deeds of
     evildoers.

⁶Their rulers will be thrown
     down from the cliffs,
  and the wicked will learn
     that my words were
     well spoken.
⁷They will say, "As one plows
     and breaks up the earth,
  so our bones have been
     scattered at the mouth
     of the grave."   Ps 53:5

⁸But my eyes are fixed on you,
     Sovereign LORD;   Ps 25:15
  in you I take refuge — do not
     give me over to death.
⁹Keep me safe from the traps
     set by evildoers,   Ps 140:4
  from the snares they have
     laid for me.   Ps 38:12
¹⁰Let the wicked fall into their
     own nets,   Ps 35:8
  while I pass by in safety.

Psalm 142^a

A *maskil*^b of David.
When he was in the cave. A prayer.

¹I cry aloud to the LORD;
  I lift up my voice to the
     LORD for mercy.   Ps 30:8
²I pour out before him my
     complaint;   Isa 26:16
  before him I tell my trouble.

³When my spirit grows faint
     within me,   Ps 140:5; 143:4,7
  it is you who watch over my
     way.
  In the path where I walk
  people have hidden a snare
     for me.
⁴Look and see, there is no one
     at my right hand;

^a In Hebrew texts 142:1-7 is numbered 142:2-8.   ^b Title: Probably a literary or musical term

no one is concerned for me.
I have no refuge;
  no one cares for my life.

⁵I cry to you, LORD;
  I say, "You are my refuge,
  my portion in the land of
    the living." Ps 27:13

⁶Listen to my cry, Ps 17:1
  for I am in desperate need;
rescue me from those who
    pursue me, Ps 25:20
  for they are too strong for me.
⁷Set me free from my prison,
  that I may praise your name.
Then the righteous will gather
    about me
  because of your goodness
    to me. Ps 13:6

Psalm 143

A psalm of David.

¹LORD, hear my prayer,
  listen to my cry for mercy;
in your faithfulness and
    righteousness Ps 71:2; 89:1
  come to my relief.
²Do not bring your servant into
    judgment,
  for no one living is
    righteous before you.
³The enemy pursues me,
  he crushes me to the
    ground;
he makes me dwell in the
    darkness Ps 107:10
  like those long dead.
⁴So my spirit grows faint
  within me;

my heart within me is
    dismayed. Ps 142:3
⁵I remember the days of long
    ago; Ps 77:6
  I meditate on all your works
and consider what your
    hands have done.
⁶I spread out my hands to
    you; Ps 63:1; 88:9
  I thirst for you like a
    parched land.ᵃ

⁷Answer me quickly, LORD;
  my spirit fails.
Do not hide your face from me
  or I will be like those who
    go down to the pit.
⁸Let the morning bring me
    word of your unfailing
    love, Ps 46:5
  for I have put my trust in
    you.
Show me the way I
    should go, Ps 27:11
  for to you I entrust my life.
⁹Rescue me from my enemies,
    LORD, Ps 31:15
  for I hide myself in you.
¹⁰Teach me to do your will,
  for you are my God;
may your good Spirit
  lead me on level ground.

¹¹For your name's sake, LORD,
    preserve my life; Ps 119:25
  in your righteousness, bring
    me out of trouble. Ps 31:1
¹²In your unfailing love, silence
    my enemies;
  destroy all my foes, Ps 54:5
  for I am your servant. Ps 116:16

ᵃ 6 The Hebrew has *Selah* (a word of uncertain meaning) here.

Psalm 144

Of David.

¹ Praise be to the LORD my
Rock,   Ps 18:2,34
who trains my hands for war,
my fingers for battle.
² He is my loving God and my
fortress,   Ps 59:9; 91:2
my stronghold and my
deliverer,
my shield, in whom I take
refuge,   Ps 84:9
who subdues peoples*a*
under me.

³ LORD, what are human beings
that you care for
them,   Ps 8:4; Heb 2:6
mere mortals that you think
of them?
⁴ They are like a breath;
their days are like a fleeting
shadow.   Ps 102:11

⁵ Part your heavens, LORD, and
come down; Ps 18:9; Isa 64:1
touch the mountains, so
that they smoke. Ps 104:32
⁶ Send forth lightning and
scatter the enemy;
shoot your arrows and rout
them.   Ps 18:14
⁷ Reach down your hand from
on high;
deliver me and rescue me
from the mighty waters,
from the hands of foreigners
⁸ whose mouths are full of lies,

whose right hands are
deceitful.

⁹ I will sing a new song to you,
my God;
on the ten-stringed lyre I
will make music to
you,   Ps 33:2-3
¹⁰ to the One who gives victory
to kings,
who delivers his servant
David.   Ps 18:50

From the deadly sword
¹¹ deliver me;
rescue me from the hands
of foreigners
whose mouths are full of lies,
whose right hands are
deceitful.   Ps 12:2; Isa 44:20

¹² Then our sons in their youth
will be like well-nurtured
plants,   Ps 128:3
and our daughters will be like
pillars   SS 4:4
carved to adorn a palace.
¹³ Our barns will be filled   Pr 3:10
with every kind of
provision.
Our sheep will increase by
thousands,
by tens of thousands in our
fields;
¹⁴ our oxen will draw heavy
loads.*b*   Pr 14:4
There will be no breaching of
walls,   2Ki 25:11
no going into captivity,

---

a 2 Many manuscripts of the Masoretic Text, Dead Sea Scrolls, Aquila, Jerome and Syriac;
most manuscripts of the Masoretic Text *subdues my people*   *b 14* Or *our chieftains will be
firmly established*

no cry of distress in our
streets. Isa 24:11
15 Blessed is the people of whom
this is true; Ps 33:12
blessed is the people whose
God is the LORD.

Psalm 145[a]

A psalm of praise. Of David.

1 I will exalt you, my God the
King; Ps 30:1; 34:1
I will praise your name for
ever and ever.
2 Every day I will praise you
and extol your name for
ever and ever.

3 Great is the LORD and most
worthy of praise;
his greatness no one can
fathom. Job 5:9; Ro 11:33
4 One generation commends
your works to
another; Isa 38:19
they tell of your mighty acts.
5 They speak of the glorious
splendor of your
majesty—
and I will meditate on your
wonderful works.[b]
6 They tell of the power of your
awesome works— Ps 66:3
and I will proclaim your
great deeds. Dt 32:3
7 They celebrate your abundant
goodness Isa 63:7

and joyfully sing of your
righteousness. Ps 51:14

8 The LORD is gracious and
compassionate, Ps 86:15
slow to anger and rich in
love.
9 The LORD is good to all; Ps 100:5
he has compassion on all he
has made.
10 All your works praise you,
LORD; Ps 19:1
your faithful people extol
you. Ps 68:26
11 They tell of the glory of your
kingdom
and speak of your might,
12 so that all people may know of
your mighty acts Ps 105:1
and the glorious splendor of
your kingdom.
13 Your kingdom is an
everlasting kingdom,
and your dominion endures
through all generations.

The LORD is trustworthy in all
he promises Dt 7:9
and faithful in all he does.[c]
14 The LORD upholds all who
fall Ps 37:24
and lifts up all who are
bowed down. Ps 146:8
15 The eyes of all look to you,
and you give them their
food at the proper time.

---

[a] This psalm is an acrostic poem, the verses of which (including verse 13b) begin with the successive letters of the Hebrew alphabet. [b] 5 Dead Sea Scrolls and Syriac (see also Septuagint); Masoretic Text *On the glorious splendor of your majesty / and on your wonderful works I will meditate* [c] 13 One manuscript of the Masoretic Text, Dead Sea Scrolls and Syriac (see also Septuagint); most manuscripts of the Masoretic Text do not have the last two lines of verse 13.

¹⁶You open your hand
and satisfy the desires of
every living thing.
¹⁷The LORD is righteous in all
his ways
and faithful in all he does.
¹⁸The LORD is near to all who
call on him,   Dt 4:7; Jn 4:24
to all who call on him in
truth.
¹⁹He fulfills the desires of those
who fear him;   Ps 37:4
he hears their cry and saves
them.   Pr 15:29
²⁰The LORD watches over all
who love him,   Ps 31:23
but all the wicked he will
destroy.   Ps 9:5

²¹My mouth will speak in praise
of the LORD.   Ps 71:8
Let every creature praise his
holy name
for ever and ever.

Psalm 146

¹Praise the LORD.^a

Praise the LORD, my soul.

²I will praise the LORD all my
life;   Ps 104:33
I will sing praise to my God
as long as I live.
³Do not put your trust in
princes,   Ps 118:9
in human beings, who
cannot save.   Isa 2:22
⁴When their spirit departs,
they return to the
ground;   Ecc 12:7

on that very day their plans
come to nothing.   Ps 33:10
⁵Blessed are those whose help
is the God of Jacob,
whose hope is in the LORD
their God.

⁶He is the Maker of heaven and
earth,   Rev 14:7
the sea, and everything in
them —
he remains faithful
forever.
⁷He upholds the cause of the
oppressed   Ps 103:6
and gives food to the
hungry.   Ps 107:9
The LORD sets prisoners free,
⁸   the LORD gives sight to the
blind,   Mt 9:30
the LORD lifts up those who
are bowed down,
the LORD loves the
righteous.
⁹The LORD watches over the
foreigner
and sustains the fatherless
and the widow,   Dt 10:18
but he frustrates the ways of
the wicked.

¹⁰The LORD reigns forever,
your God, O Zion, for all
generations.

Praise the LORD.

Psalm 147

¹Praise the LORD.^b

How good it is to sing praises
to our God,

---

^a 1 Hebrew *Hallelu Yah*; also in verse 10   ^b 1 Hebrew *Hallelu Yah*; also in verse 20

how pleasant and fitting to
  praise him! Ps 33:1; 135:3
²The Lord builds up
  Jerusalem; Ps 102:16
he gathers the exiles of
  Israel. Dt 30:3
³He heals the brokenhearted
  and binds up their wounds.
⁴He determines the number of
  the stars Isa 40:26
and calls them each by
  name.
⁵Great is our Lord and mighty
  in power; Ps 48:1
his understanding has no
  limit. Isa 40:28
⁶The Lord sustains the
  humble Ps 146:8-9
but casts the wicked to the
  ground.
⁷Sing to the Lord with grateful
  praise; Ps 33:3
make music to our God on
  the harp.
⁸He covers the sky with clouds;
he supplies the earth with
  rain Job 38:26
and makes grass grow on
  the hills. Ps 104:14
⁹He provides food for the
  cattle Ps 104:27-28
and for the young ravens
  when they call. Job 38:41
¹⁰His pleasure is not in the
  strength of the horse,
  nor his delight in the legs of
  the warrior;

¹¹the Lord delights in those
  who fear him, Ps 33:18
who put their hope in his
  unfailing love. Ps 119:43
¹²Extol the Lord, Jerusalem;
  praise your God, Zion.
¹³He strengthens the bars of
  your gates Dt 33:25
and blesses your people
  within you. Lev 25:21
¹⁴He grants peace to your
  borders Isa 60:17-18
and satisfies you with the
  finest of wheat. Ps 132:15
¹⁵He sends his command to the
  earth;
  his word runs swiftly.
¹⁶He spreads the snow like wool
  and scatters the frost like
  ashes.
¹⁷He hurls down his hail like
  pebbles.
  Who can withstand his icy
  blast?
¹⁸He sends his word and melts
  them; Ps 33:9
he stirs up his breezes, and
  the waters flow.
¹⁹He has revealed his word to
  Jacob,
  his laws and decrees to
  Israel. Mal 4:4
²⁰He has done this for no other
  nation; Dt 4:7-8,32-34
they do not know his laws.ᵃ

Praise the Lord.

ᵃ 20 Masoretic Text; Dead Sea Scrolls and Septuagint *nation; / he has not made his laws
known to them*

Psalm 148

[1] Praise the LORD.[a]   Ps 33:2; 103:1

Praise the LORD from the
heavens;
praise him in the heights
above.
[2] Praise him, all his angels;
praise him, all his heavenly
hosts.
[3] Praise him, sun and moon;
praise him, all you shining
stars.
[4] Praise him, you highest
heavens
and you waters above the
skies.   Ge 1:7

[5] Let them praise the name of
the LORD,
for at his command they
were created,   Ge 1:1,6
[6] and he established them for
ever and ever —
he issued a decree that will
never pass away.   Ps 89:37

[7] Praise the LORD from the
earth,
you great sea creatures and
all ocean depths,   Ps 74:13
[8] lightning and hail, snow and
clouds,
stormy winds that do his
bidding,   Ps 147:15-18
[9] you mountains and all hills,
fruit trees and all cedars,
[10] wild animals and all cattle,
small creatures and flying
birds,

[11] kings of the earth and all
nations,
you princes and all rulers
on earth,
[12] young men and women,
old men and children.

[13] Let them praise the name of
the LORD,   Isa 12:4
for his name alone is
exalted;
his splendor is above the
earth and the heavens.
Ps 113:4
[14] And he has raised up for his
people a horn,[b]   Ps 75:10
the praise of all his faithful
servants,
of Israel, the people close to
his heart.   Dt 26:19

Praise the LORD.

Psalm 149

[1] Praise the LORD.[c]   Ps 33:2

Sing to the LORD a new song,
his praise in the assembly of
his faithful people.

[2] Let Israel rejoice in their
Maker;   Ps 95:6
let the people of Zion be
glad in their King.   Ps 47:6
[3] Let them praise his name
with dancing
and make music to him
with timbrel and
harp.   Ps 81:2; 150:4
[4] For the LORD takes delight in
his people;   Ps 35:27

---

a 1 Hebrew *Hallelu Yah*; also in verse 14   *b 14* *Horn* here symbolizes strength.
c 1 Hebrew *Hallelu Yah*; also in verse 9

he crowns the humble with
  victory. Ps 132:16
⁵Let his faithful people rejoice
  in this honor
and sing for joy on their
  beds. Job 35:10

⁶May the praise of God be in
  their mouths
and a double-edged sword
  in their hands, Heb 4:12
⁷to inflict vengeance on the
  nations Nu 31:3
and punishment on the
  peoples, Ps 81:15
⁸to bind their kings with
  fetters, 2Sa 3:34
their nobles with shackles
  of iron, 2Ch 33:11
⁹to carry out the sentence
  written against
  them — Dt 7:1; Eze 28:26
this is the glory of all his
  faithful people. Ps 148:14

Praise the LORD.

Psalm 150

¹Praise the LORD.ᵃ

Praise God in his sanctuary;
  praise him in his mighty
  heavens.
²Praise him for his acts of
  power; Dt 3:24
praise him for his
  surpassing greatness.
³Praise him with the sounding
  of the trumpet,
praise him with the harp
  and lyre, Ps 149:3
⁴praise him with timbrel and
  dancing, Ex 15:20
praise him with the strings
  and pipe, Isa 38:20
⁵praise him with the clash of
  cymbals, 1Ch 15:16
praise him with resounding
  cymbals.

⁶Let everything that has breath
  praise the LORD. Ps 145:21

Praise the LORD.

ᵃ 1 Hebrew *Hallelu Yah*; also in verse 6

Proverbs

Purpose and Theme

1 The proverbs of Solomon son of David, king of Israel: 1Ki 4:29

[2] for gaining wisdom and instruction;
for understanding words of insight;

[3] for receiving instruction in prudent behavior,
doing what is right and just and fair;

[4] for giving prudence to those who are simple,[a]   Pr 8:5
knowledge and discretion to the young—   Pr 8:12

[5] let the wise listen and add to their learning,   Pr 9:9
and let the discerning get guidance—

[6] for understanding proverbs and parables,   Ps 78:2
the sayings and riddles of the wise.[b]

[7] The fear of the LORD is the beginning of knowledge,
but fools[c] despise wisdom and instruction. Pr 8:33-36

Prologue: Exhortations to Embrace Wisdom

Warning Against the Invitation of Sinful Men

[8] Listen, my son, to your father's instruction   Pr 4:1
and do not forsake your mother's teaching. Pr 6:20

[9] They are a garland to grace your head
and a chain to adorn your neck.   Pr 4:1-9

[10] My son, if sinful men entice you,   Ge 39:7
do not give in to them. Dt 13:8

[11] If they say, "Come along with us;
let's lie in wait for innocent blood,
let's ambush some harmless soul;

[12] let's swallow them alive, like the grave,

---

[a] 4 The Hebrew word rendered *simple* in Proverbs denotes a person who is gullible, without moral direction and inclined to evil.   [b] 6 Or *understanding a proverb, namely, a parable, / and the sayings of the wise, their riddles*   [c] 7 The Hebrew words rendered *fool* in Proverbs, and often elsewhere in the Old Testament, denote a person who is morally deficient.

and whole, like those who
    go down to the pit; Ps 28:1
¹³we will get all sorts of valuable
    things
    and fill our houses with
        plunder;
¹⁴cast lots with us;
    we will all share the loot" —
¹⁵my son, do not go along with
        them,
    do not set foot on their
        paths; Ps 1:1; 119:101
¹⁶for their feet rush into evil,
    they are swift to shed blood.
¹⁷How useless to spread a net
    where every bird can see it!
¹⁸These men lie in wait for their
        own blood; Ps 71:10
    they ambush only
        themselves!
¹⁹Such are the paths of all who
    go after ill-gotten gain;
    it takes away the life of
        those who get it. Pr 15:27

Wisdom's Rebuke

²⁰Out in the open wisdom calls
    aloud, Pr 8:1
    she raises her voice in the
        public square;
²¹on top of the wallᵃ she cries
        out,
    at the city gate she makes
        her speech:

²²"How long will you who are
    simple love your simple
    ways? Pr 8:5
    How long will mockers
        delight in mockery

and fools hate knowledge?
²³Repent at my rebuke!
    Then I will pour out my
        thoughts to you,
    I will make known to you
        my teachings.
²⁴But since you refuse to listen
        when I call Isa 65:12; 66:4
    and no one pays attention
        when I stretch out my
        hand, 1Sa 8:19
²⁵since you disregard all my
        advice
    and do not accept my
        rebuke,
²⁶I in turn will laugh when
        disaster strikes you; Ps 2:4
    I will mock when calamity
        overtakes you — Pr 10:24
²⁷when calamity overtakes you
        like a storm,
    when disaster sweeps over
        you like a whirlwind,
    when distress and trouble
        overwhelm you.

²⁸"Then they will call to me but
        I will not answer; Isa 1:15
    they will look for me but
        will not find me, Eze 8:18
²⁹since they hated knowledge
    and did not choose to fear
        the LORD. Job 21:14
³⁰Since they would not accept
        my advice
    and spurned my rebuke,
³¹they will eat the fruit of their
        ways
    and be filled with the fruit
        of their schemes. Isa 3:11

ᵃ 21 Septuagint; Hebrew / at noisy street corners

³²For the waywardness of the
simple will kill them,
and the complacency of
fools will destroy them;
³³but whoever listens to me will
live in safety   Ps 25:12
and be at ease, without fear
of harm."   Ps 112:8

Moral Benefits of Wisdom

2 My son, if you accept my
words
and store up my commands
within you,
²turning your ear to wisdom
and applying your heart to
understanding —   Pr 22:17
³indeed, if you call out for
insight
and cry aloud for
understanding,
⁴and if you look for it as for silver
and search for it as for
hidden treasure,   Pr 3:14
⁵then you will understand the
fear of the LORD
and find the knowledge of
God.   Pr 1:7
⁶For the LORD gives wisdom;
from his mouth come
knowledge and
understanding.
⁷He holds success in store for
the upright,
he is a shield to those whose
walk is blameless,   Ps 84:11
⁸for he guards the course of the
just
and protects the way of his
faithful ones.   1Sa 2:9

⁹Then you will understand
what is right and just
and fair — every good path.
¹⁰For wisdom will enter your
heart,   Pr 14:33
and knowledge will be
pleasant to your soul.
¹¹Discretion will protect you,
and understanding will
guard you.   Pr 6:22
¹²Wisdom will save you from
the ways of wicked men,
from men whose words are
perverse,
¹³who have left the straight
paths
to walk in dark ways,   Jn 3:19
¹⁴who delight in doing wrong
and rejoice in the
perverseness of evil,
¹⁵whose paths are crooked
and who are devious in
their ways.   Pr 21:8
¹⁶Wisdom will save you also
from the adulterous
woman,
from the wayward woman
with her seductive
words,
¹⁷who has left the partner of her
youth
and ignored the covenant
she made before God.ᵃ
¹⁸Surely her house leads down
to death
and her paths to the spirits
of the dead.   Pr 7:27
¹⁹None who go to her return
or attain the paths of life.

ᵃ 17 Or *covenant of her God*

PROVERBS 3:15 | 1007

²⁰Thus you will walk in the
ways of the good
and keep to the paths of the
righteous.
²¹For the upright will live in the
land,   Ps 37:29
and the blameless will
remain in it;
²²but the wicked will be cut off
from the land,   Job 18:17
and the unfaithful will be
torn from it.   Dt 28:63

Wisdom Bestows Well-Being

3 My son, do not forget my
teaching,   Pr 4:5
but keep my commands in
your heart,
²for they will prolong your life
many years   Pr 4:10
and bring you peace and
prosperity.

³Let love and faithfulness
never leave you;
bind them around your
neck,
write them on the tablet of
your heart.   Pr 6:21; 2Co 3:3
⁴Then you will win favor and a
good name
in the sight of God and
man.   1Sa 2:26; Lk 2:52

⁵Trust in the LORD with all
your heart   Ps 37:3,5
and lean not on your own
understanding;
⁶in all your ways submit to
him,

and he will make your
paths straight.ᵃ   1Ch 28:9
⁷Do not be wise in your own
eyes;   Ro 12:16
fear the LORD and shun
evil.   Pr 16:6
⁸This will bring health to your
body   Pr 4:22
and nourishment to your
bones.   Job 21:24

⁹Honor the LORD with your
wealth,
with the firstfruits of all
your crops;   Ex 22:29
¹⁰then your barns will be filled
to overflowing,   Dt 28:8
and your vats will brim over
with new wine.   Joel 2:24

¹¹My son, do not despise the
LORD's discipline,   Job 5:17
and do not resent his rebuke,
¹²because the LORD disciplines
those he loves,   Pr 13:24
as a father the son he
delights in.ᵇ   Dt 8:5

¹³Blessed are those who find
wisdom,
those who gain
understanding,
¹⁴for she is more profitable than
silver
and yields better returns
than gold.   Job 28:15; Pr 8:19
¹⁵She is more precious than
rubies;   Job 28:18
nothing you desire can
compare with her.   Pr 8:11

ᵃ 6 Or *will direct your paths*   ᵇ 12 Hebrew; Septuagint *loves, / and he chastens everyone he*
accepts as his child

¹⁶Long life is in her right hand;
  in her left hand are riches
    and honor. Pr 8:18
¹⁷Her ways are pleasant ways,
  and all her paths are
    peace. Pr 16:7; Mt 11:28-30
¹⁸She is a tree of life to those
  who take hold of her;
  those who hold her fast will
    be blessed.

¹⁹By wisdom the LORD laid the
  earth's foundations,
  by understanding he set the
    heavens in place; Pr 8:27
²⁰by his knowledge the watery
  depths were divided,
  and the clouds let drop the
    dew.

²¹My son, do not let wisdom
  and understanding out
  of your sight,
  preserve sound judgment
    and discretion; Pr 4:20-22
²²they will be life for you,
  an ornament to grace your
    neck. Pr 1:8-9
²³Then you will go on your way
  in safety,
  and your foot will not
    stumble. Pr 4:12
²⁴When you lie down, you will
  not be afraid; Ps 3:5
  when you lie down, your
    sleep will be sweet.
²⁵Have no fear of sudden
  disaster
  or of the ruin that overtakes
    the wicked,
²⁶for the LORD will be at your
  side

and will keep your foot from
  being snared. 1Sa 2:9
²⁷Do not withhold good from
  those to whom it is due,
  when it is in your power to
    act.
²⁸Do not say to your neighbor,
  "Come back tomorrow and
  I'll give it to you" —
  when you already have it
    with you. Lev 19:13
²⁹Do not plot harm against your
  neighbor,
  who lives trustfully near you.
³⁰Do not accuse anyone for no
  reason —
  when they have done you
    no harm.

³¹Do not envy the violent Ps 37:1
  or choose any of their ways.

³²For the LORD detests the
  perverse Pr 11:20
  but takes the upright into
    his confidence. Ps 25:14
³³The LORD's curse is on the
  house of the wicked,
  but he blesses the home of
    the righteous. Ps 1:3
³⁴He mocks proud mockers
  but shows favor to the
    humble and oppressed.
³⁵The wise inherit honor,
  but fools get only shame.

Get Wisdom at Any Cost

4 Listen, my sons, to a father's
  instruction; Pr 1:8
  pay attention and gain
    understanding.

²I give you sound learning,
so do not forsake my
teaching.
³For I too was a son to my
father,
still tender, and cherished
by my mother.
⁴Then he taught me, and he
said to me,
"Take hold of my words
with all your heart;
keep my commands, and
you will live.   Pr 7:2
⁵Get wisdom, get
understanding;   Pr 16:16
do not forget my words or
turn away from them.
⁶Do not forsake wisdom, and
she will protect you;
love her, and she will watch
over you.
⁷The beginning of wisdom is
this: Get*ᵃ* wisdom.
Though it cost all you have,*ᵇ*
get understanding.
⁸Cherish her, and she will exalt
you;
embrace her, and she will
honor you.   1Sa 2:30; Pr 3:18
⁹She will give you a garland to
grace your head
and present you with a
glorious crown."   Pr 1:8-9

¹⁰Listen, my son, accept what I
say,
and the years of your life
will be many.   Pr 3:2
¹¹I instruct you in the way of
wisdom   1Sa 12:23

and lead you along straight
paths.
¹²When you walk, your steps
will not be hampered;
when you run, you will not
stumble.   Job 18:7; Pr 3:23
¹³Hold on to instruction, do not
let it go;
guard it well, for it is your
life.   Pr 3:22
¹⁴Do not set foot on the path of
the wicked
or walk in the way of
evildoers.   Ps 1:1; Pr 1:15
¹⁵Avoid it, do not travel on it;
turn from it and go on your
way.
¹⁶For they cannot rest until they
do evil;   Ps 36:4; Mic 2:1
they are robbed of sleep till
they make someone
stumble.
¹⁷They eat the bread of
wickedness
and drink the wine of
violence.   Pr 1:10-19

¹⁸The path of the righteous is
like the morning sun,
shining ever brighter till the
full light of day.   2Sa 23:4
¹⁹But the way of the wicked is
like deep darkness;
they do not know what
makes them stumble.

²⁰My son, pay attention to what
I say;
turn your ear to my words.
²¹Do not let them out of your
sight,   Pr 3:21

ᵃ 7 Or *Wisdom is supreme; therefore get*   *ᵇ* 7 Or *wisdom. / Whatever else you get*

keep them within your
heart;

[22] for they are life to those who
find them
and health to one's whole
body.   Pr 3:8; 12:18

[23] Above all else, guard your
heart,
for everything you do flows
from it.   Mt 12:34; Lk 6:45

[24] Keep your mouth free of
perversity;
keep corrupt talk far from
your lips.

[25] Let your eyes look straight
ahead;
fix your gaze directly before
you.

[26] Give careful thought to the[a]
paths for your feet
and be steadfast in all your
ways.

[27] Do not turn to the right or the
left;   Dt 5:32; 28:14
keep your foot from evil.

Warning Against Adultery

5 My son, pay attention to my
wisdom,
turn your ear to my words
of insight,   Pr 4:20

[2] that you may maintain
discretion
and your lips may preserve
knowledge.

[3] For the lips of the adulterous
woman drip honey,
and her speech is smoother
than oil;   Ps 55:21; Pr 2:16

[4] but in the end she is bitter as
gall,   Ecc 7:26
sharp as a double-edged
sword.

[5] Her feet go down to death;
her steps lead straight to the
grave.   Pr 7:26-27

[6] She gives no thought to the
way of life;
her paths wander aimlessly,
but she does not know it.

[7] Now then, my sons, listen
to me;   Pr 7:24
do not turn aside from what
I say.

[8] Keep to a path far from her,
do not go near the door of
her house,

[9] lest you lose your honor to
others
and your dignity[b] to one
who is cruel,

[10] lest strangers feast on your
wealth
and your toil enrich the
house of another.   Pr 29:3

[11] At the end of your life you will
groan,
when your flesh and body
are spent.

[12] You will say, "How I hated
discipline!
How my heart spurned
correction!   Pr 1:29; 12:1

[13] I would not obey my teachers
or turn my ear to my
instructors.

[14] And I was soon in serious
trouble   Pr 1:24-27

[a] 26 Or Make level   [b] 9 Or years

in the assembly of God's
people."

¹⁵Drink water from your own
cistern,
running water from your
own well.
¹⁶Should your springs overflow
in the streets,
your streams of water in the
public squares?
¹⁷Let them be yours alone,
never to be shared with
strangers.
¹⁸May your fountain be blessed,
and may you rejoice in the
wife of your youth.
¹⁹A loving doe, a graceful
deer —   SS 2:9; 4:5
may her breasts satisfy you
always,
may you ever be intoxicated
with her love.
²⁰Why, my son, be intoxicated
with another man's
wife?
Why embrace the bosom of
a wayward woman?
²¹For your ways are in full view
of the LORD,   Hos 7:2
and he examines all your
paths.   Job 31:4; 34:21; Pr 15:3
²²The evil deeds of the wicked
ensnare them;   Ps 9:16
the cords of their sins hold
them fast.   Nu 32:23; Ps 7:15
²³For lack of discipline they will
die,   Job 4:21; 36:12
led astray by their own
great folly.

Warnings Against Folly

6 My son, if you have put
up security for your
neighbor,   Pr 17:18
if you have shaken hands in
pledge for a stranger,
²you have been trapped by
what you said,
ensnared by the words of
your mouth.
³So do this, my son, to free
yourself,
since you have fallen into
your neighbor's hands:
Go — to the point of
exhaustion — ^a
and give your neighbor no
rest!
⁴Allow no sleep to your eyes,
no slumber to your eyelids.
⁵Free yourself, like a gazelle
from the hand of the
hunter,
like a bird from the snare of
the fowler.   Ps 91:3

⁶Go to the ant, you sluggard;
consider its ways and be
wise!
⁷It has no commander,
no overseer or ruler,
⁸yet it stores its provisions in
summer
and gathers its food at
harvest.   Pr 10:4
⁹How long will you lie there,
you sluggard?   Pr 24:30-34
When will you get up from
your sleep?

^a 3 Or *Go and humble yourself,*

¹⁰A little sleep, a little slumber,
a little folding of the hands
to rest — Pr 24:33
¹¹and poverty will come on you
like a thief Pr 24:30-34
and scarcity like an armed
man.

¹²A troublemaker and a villain,
who goes about with a
corrupt mouth,
¹³ who winks maliciously with
his eye, Ps 35:19
signals with his feet
and motions with his fingers,
¹⁴ who plots evil with deceit in
his heart — Mic 2:1
he always stirs up conflict.
¹⁵Therefore disaster will
overtake him in an
instant;
he will suddenly be
destroyed — without
remedy. 2Ch 36:16

¹⁶There are six things the LORD
hates,
seven that are detestable to
him:
¹⁷ haughty eyes,
a lying tongue, Ps 120:2
hands that shed innocent
blood, Isa 1:15
¹⁸ a heart that devises
wicked schemes,
feet that are quick to rush
into evil, Ge 6:5
¹⁹ a false witness who pours
out lies Ps 27:12
and a person who stirs
up conflict in the
community. ver 12-15

Warning Against Adultery

²⁰My son, keep your father's
command
and do not forsake your
mother's teaching. Pr 1:8
²¹Bind them always on your
heart;
fasten them around your
neck. Pr 3:3; 7:1-3
²²When you walk, they will
guide you;
when you sleep, they will
watch over you;
when you awake, they will
speak to you.
²³For this command is a lamp,
this teaching is a light, Ps 19:8
and correction and instruction
are the way to life,
²⁴keeping you from your
neighbor's wife,
from the smooth talk of a
wayward woman. Pr 2:16

²⁵Do not lust in your heart after
her beauty
or let her captivate you with
her eyes.

²⁶For a prostitute can be had for
a loaf of bread,
but another man's wife
preys on your very life.
²⁷Can a man scoop fire into his
lap
without his clothes being
burned?
²⁸Can a man walk on hot coals
without his feet being
scorched?
²⁹So is he who sleeps with
another man's wife;

no one who touches her will
go unpunished.

30 People do not despise a thief if
he steals
to satisfy his hunger when
he is starving.
31 Yet if he is caught, he must
pay sevenfold,   Ex 22:1-14
though it costs him all the
wealth of his house.
32 But a man who commits
adultery has no sense;
whoever does so destroys
himself.
33 Blows and disgrace are his lot,
and his shame will never be
wiped away.   Pr 5:9-14

34 For jealousy arouses a
husband's fury,   Ge 34:7
and he will show no mercy
when he takes revenge.
35 He will not accept any
compensation;
he will refuse a bribe,
however great it is.

Warning Against the Adulterous Woman

7 My son, keep my words   Pr 2:1
and store up my commands
within you.
2 Keep my commands and you
will live;   Pr 4:4
guard my teachings as the
apple of your eye.
3 Bind them on your fingers;
write them on the tablet of
your heart.   Dt 6:8; Pr 3:3
4 Say to wisdom, "You are my
sister,"

and to insight, "You are my
relative."
5 They will keep you from the
adulterous woman,
from the wayward woman
with her seductive
words.   Pr 2:16; 6:24

6 At the window of my house
I looked down through the
lattice.
7 I saw among the simple,
I noticed among the young
men,
a youth who had no sense.
8 He was going down the street
near her corner,
walking along in the
direction of her house
9 at twilight, as the day was
fading,   Job 24:15
as the dark of night set in.

10 Then out came a woman to
meet him,
dressed like a prostitute
and with crafty intent.
11 (She is unruly and defiant,
her feet never stay at home;
12 now in the street, now in the
squares,
at every corner she lurks.)
13 She took hold of him and
kissed him   Ge 39:12
and with a brazen face she
said:
14 "Today I fulfilled my vows,
and I have food from my
fellowship offering at
home.   Lev 7:11-18
15 So I came out to meet you;

I looked for you and have
found you!
¹⁶I have covered my bed
with colored linens from
Egypt.
¹⁷I have perfumed my bed   Est 1:6
with myrrh, aloes and
cinnamon.   Ge 37:25
¹⁸Come, let's drink deeply of
love till morning;
let's enjoy ourselves with
love!   Ge 39:7
¹⁹My husband is not at home;
he has gone on a long
journey.
²⁰He took his purse filled with
money
and will not be home till
full moon."
²¹With persuasive words she led
him astray;
she seduced him with her
smooth talk.   Pr 5:3
²²All at once he followed her
like an ox going to the
slaughter,
like a deer^a stepping into a
noose^b   Job 18:10
²³   till an arrow pierces his liver,
like a bird darting into a snare,
little knowing it will cost
him his life.   Ecc 9:12
²⁴Now then, my sons, listen
to me;   Pr 1:8-9
pay attention to what I say.
²⁵Do not let your heart turn to
her ways
or stray into her paths. Pr 5:7-8

²⁶Many are the victims she has
brought down;
her slain are a mighty
throng.
²⁷Her house is a highway to the
grave,
leading down to the
chambers of death.

Wisdom's Call

8 Does not wisdom call out?
Does not understanding
raise her voice?
²At the highest point along the
way,
where the paths meet, she
takes her stand;
³beside the gate leading into
the city,
at the entrance, she cries
aloud: Job 29:7
⁴"To you, O people, I call out;
I raise my voice to all
mankind.
⁵You who are simple, gain
prudence;   Pr 1:4,22
you who are foolish, set
your hearts on it.^c
⁶Listen, for I have trustworthy
things to say;
I open my lips to speak what
is right.
⁷My mouth speaks what is
true,   Ps 37:30; Jn 8:14
for my lips detest
wickedness.
⁸All the words of my mouth are
just;
none of them is crooked or
perverse.

---

^a 22 Syriac (see also Septuagint); Hebrew *fool*   ^b 22 The meaning of the Hebrew for this
line is uncertain.   ^c 5 Septuagint; Hebrew *foolish, instruct your minds*

⁹To the discerning all of them
are right;
they are upright to those
who have found
knowledge.
¹⁰Choose my instruction
instead of silver,
knowledge rather than
choice gold,   Pr 3:14-15
¹¹for wisdom is more precious
than rubies,   Job 28:17-19
and nothing you desire can
compare with her. Pr 3:13

¹²"I, wisdom, dwell together
with prudence;
I possess knowledge and
discretion.   Pr 1:4
¹³To fear the LORD is to hate evil;
I hate pride and arrogance,
evil behavior and perverse
speech.
¹⁴Counsel and sound judgment
are mine;
I have insight, I have power.
¹⁵By me kings reign
and rulers issue decrees
that are just;   Da 2:21
¹⁶by me princes govern,
and nobles — all who rule
on earth.ᵃ
¹⁷I love those who love me,
and those who seek me
find me.   Pr 1:28; Jas 1:5
¹⁸With me are riches and honor,
enduring wealth and
prosperity.   Mt 6:33
¹⁹My fruit is better than fine
gold;

what I yield surpasses
choice silver.   Pr 3:13-14
²⁰I walk in the way of
righteousness,
along the paths of justice,
²¹bestowing a rich inheritance
on those who love me
and making their treasuries
full.   Pr 15:6; 24:4

²²"The LORD brought me forth as
the first of his works,ᵇ,ᶜ
before his deeds of old;
²³I was formed long ages ago,
at the very beginning, when
the world came to be.
²⁴When there were no watery
depths, I was given
birth,
when there were no springs
overflowing with
water;   Ge 7:11
²⁵before the mountains were
settled in place,
before the hills, I was given
birth,   Job 15:7
²⁶before he made the world or
its fields
or any of the dust of the
earth.   Ps 90:2
²⁷I was there when he set the
heavens in place, Pr 3:19
when he marked out the
horizon on the face of
the deep,
²⁸when he established the
clouds above
and fixed securely the
fountains of the deep,

ᵃ 16 Some Hebrew manuscripts and Septuagint; other Hebrew manuscripts *all righteous rulers*   ᵇ 22 Or *way*; or *dominion*   ᶜ 22 Or *The LORD possessed me at the beginning of his work*; or *The LORD brought me forth at the beginning of his work*

²⁹when he gave the sea its
boundary   Ge 1:9; Job 38:10
so the waters would not
overstep his command,
and when he marked out
the foundations of the
earth.   Job 38:5
³⁰ Then I was constantly[a] at
his side.   Jn 1:1-3
I was filled with delight day
after day,
rejoicing always in his
presence,
³¹rejoicing in his whole world
and delighting in mankind.

³²"Now then, my children,
listen to me;
blessed are those who keep
my ways.   Ps 119:1-2; Lk 11:28
³³Listen to my instruction and
be wise;
do not disregard it.
³⁴Blessed are those who listen
to me,   Pr 3:13,18
watching daily at my doors,
waiting at my doorway.
³⁵For those who find me find
life   Pr 3:13-18
and receive favor from the
LORD.   Pr 12:2
³⁶But those who fail to find me
harm themselves; Pr 15:32
all who hate me love death."

Invitations of Wisdom and Folly

9 Wisdom has built her house;
she has set up[b] its seven
pillars.

²She has prepared her meat
and mixed her wine;
she has also set her table.
³She has sent out her servants,
and she calls   Pr 8:1-3
from the highest point of
the city,
⁴ "Let all who are simple
come to my house!"
To those who have no sense
she says,   Pr 6:32
⁵ "Come, eat my food
and drink the wine I have
mixed.   Isa 55:1
⁶Leave your simple ways and
you will live;   Pr 8:35
walk in the way of insight."

⁷Whoever corrects a mocker
invites insults;
whoever rebukes the
wicked incurs abuse.
⁸Do not rebuke mockers or
they will hate you;
rebuke the wise and they
will love you.   Ps 141:5
⁹Instruct the wise and they
will be wiser still;
teach the righteous and they
will add to their learning.

¹⁰The fear of the LORD is the
beginning of
wisdom,   Job 28:28; Pr 1:7
and knowledge of the Holy
One is understanding.
¹¹For through wisdom[c] your
days will be many,
and years will be added to
your life.   Pr 3:16

---

[a] 30 Or *was the artisan; or was a little child*   [b] 1 Septuagint, Syriac and Targum; Hebrew
has hewn out   [c] 11 Septuagint, Syriac and Targum; Hebrew *me*

¹²If you are wise, your wisdom
  will reward you;
  if you are a mocker, you
    alone will suffer.
¹³Folly is an unruly woman;
  she is simple and knows
    nothing.   Pr 5:6
¹⁴She sits at the door of her house,
  on a seat at the highest
    point of the city,   ver 3
¹⁵calling out to those who
    pass by,
  who go straight on their way,
¹⁶ "Let all who are simple
      come to my house!"
  To those who have no sense
    she says,   Pr 1:22
¹⁷ "Stolen water is sweet;
    food eaten in secret is
      delicious!"   Pr 20:17
¹⁸But little do they know that
    the dead are there,
  that her guests are deep in
    the realm of the dead.

Proverbs of Solomon

10 The proverbs of Solomon:

A wise son brings joy to his
    father,   Pr 15:20
  but a foolish son brings grief
    to his mother.
²Ill-gotten treasures have no
    lasting value,   Pr 21:6
  but righteousness delivers
    from death.
³The Lord does not let the
    righteous go hungry,

but he thwarts the craving
    of the wicked.
⁴Lazy hands make for poverty,
  but diligent hands bring
    wealth.   Pr 13:4
⁵He who gathers crops in
    summer is a prudent
    son,
  but he who sleeps during
    harvest is a disgraceful
    son.
⁶Blessings crown the head of
    the righteous,
  but violence overwhelms the
    mouth of the wicked.ᵃ
⁷The name of the righteous is
    used in blessings,ᵇ Ps 112:6
  but the name of the wicked
    will rot.   Ps 109:13
⁸The wise in heart accept
    commands,
  but a chattering fool comes
    to ruin.   Mt 7:24-27
⁹Whoever walks in integrity
    walks securely,   Ps 23:4
  but whoever takes crooked
    paths will be found
    out.   Pr 28:18
¹⁰Whoever winks maliciously
    causes grief,
  and a chattering fool comes
    to ruin.
¹¹The mouth of the righteous is
    a fountain of life,   Ps 37:30
  but the mouth of the wicked
    conceals violence.

ᵃ 6 Or *righteous, / but the mouth of the wicked conceals violence*   ᵇ 7 See Gen. 48:20.

¹²Hatred stirs up conflict,
  but love covers over all
    wrongs.   1Pe 4:8

¹³Wisdom is found on the lips of
    the discerning,
  but a rod is for the back of
    one who has no sense.

¹⁴The wise store up knowledge,
  but the mouth of a fool
    invites ruin.   Pr 18:6-7

¹⁵The wealth of the rich is their
    fortified city,   Pr 18:11
  but poverty is the ruin of
    the poor.   Pr 19:7

¹⁶The wages of the righteous is
    life,
  but the earnings of the
    wicked are sin and
    death.   Pr 11:18-19

¹⁷Whoever heeds discipline
    shows the way to life,
  but whoever ignores
    correction leads others
    astray.

¹⁸Whoever conceals hatred
    with lying lips   Ps 31:18
  and spreads slander is a fool.

¹⁹Sin is not ended by
    multiplying words,
  but the prudent hold their
    tongues.   Pr 17:28; Ecc 5:3

²⁰The tongue of the righteous is
    choice silver,
  but the heart of the wicked
    is of little value.

²¹The lips of the righteous
    nourish many,
  but fools die for lack of
    sense.   Hos 4:1,6,14

²²The blessing of the Lord
    brings wealth,   Ge 24:35
  without painful toil for it.

²³A fool finds pleasure in
    wicked schemes,   Pr 15:21
  but a person of
    understanding delights
    in wisdom.

²⁴What the wicked dread will
    overtake them;   Isa 66:4
  what the righteous desire
    will be granted.   Ps 145:17

²⁵When the storm has swept by,
    the wicked are gone,
  but the righteous stand firm
    forever.   Ps 15:5

²⁶As vinegar to the teeth and
    smoke to the eyes,
  so are sluggards to those
    who send them.   Pr 26:6

²⁷The fear of the Lord adds
    length to life,   Pr 9:10-11
  but the years of the wicked
    are cut short.   Job 15:32

²⁸The prospect of the righteous
    is joy,
  but the hopes of the wicked
    come to nothing.   Job 8:13

²⁹The way of the Lord is
    a refuge for the
    blameless,
  but it is the ruin of those
    who do evil.   Pr 21:15

³⁰The righteous will never be
    uprooted,

but the wicked will not
remain in the land.

31 From the mouth of the
righteous comes the
fruit of wisdom, Ps 37:30
but a perverse tongue will
be silenced.

32 The lips of the righteous know
what finds favor, Ecc 10:12
but the mouth of the wicked
only what is perverse.

11 The LORD detests
dishonest scales, Lev 19:36
but accurate weights find
favor with him. Pr 16:11

2 When pride comes, then
comes disgrace, Pr 16:18
but with humility comes
wisdom. Pr 18:12

3 The integrity of the upright
guides them,
but the unfaithful are
destroyed by their
duplicity. Pr 13:6

4 Wealth is worthless in the day
of wrath, Eze 7:19; Zep 1:18
but righteousness delivers
from death. Ge 7:1

5 The righteousness of the
blameless makes their
paths straight,
but the wicked are brought
down by their own
wickedness. Pr 5:21-23

6 The righteousness of the
upright delivers them,

but the unfaithful are
trapped by evil desires.

7 Hopes placed in mortals die
with them;
all the promise of[a] their
power comes to
nothing. Pr 10:28

8 The righteous person is
rescued from trouble,
and it falls on the wicked
instead. Pr 21:18

9 With their mouths the godless
destroy their neighbors,
but through knowledge the
righteous escape. Jer 45:5

10 When the righteous prosper,
the city rejoices; Pr 28:12
when the wicked perish,
there are shouts of joy.

11 Through the blessing of the
upright a city is exalted,
but by the mouth of the
wicked it is destroyed.

12 Whoever derides their
neighbor has no
sense, Pr 14:21
but the one who has
understanding holds
their tongue.

13 A gossip betrays a confidence,
but a trustworthy person
keeps a secret.

14 For lack of guidance a nation
falls,
but victory is won through
many advisers. Pr 15:22

---

a 7 Two Hebrew manuscripts; most Hebrew manuscripts, Vulgate, Syriac and Targum *When the wicked die, their hope perishes; / all they expected from*

15 Whoever puts up security for
   a stranger will surely
   suffer,   Pr 6:1
   but whoever refuses to
   shake hands in pledge
   is safe.

16 A kindhearted woman gains
   honor,
   but ruthless men gain only   Pr 31:31
   wealth.

17 Those who are kind benefit
   themselves,
   but the cruel bring ruin on
   themselves.

18 A wicked person earns
   deceptive wages,
   but the one who sows
   righteousness reaps a
   sure reward.   Hos 10:12-13

19 Truly the righteous attain life,
   but whoever pursues evil
   finds death.   Pr 1:18-19

20 The LORD detests those whose
   hearts are perverse,
   but he delights in those
   whose ways are
   blameless.   Ps 119:1; Pr 12:2

21 Be sure of this: The wicked
   will not go unpunished,
   but those who are righteous
   will go free.   Pr 16:5

22 Like a gold ring in a pig's
   snout
   is a beautiful woman who
   shows no discretion.

23 The desire of the righteous
   ends only in good,

but the hope of the wicked
   only in wrath.

24 One person gives freely, yet
   gains even more;
   another withholds unduly,
   but comes to poverty.

25 A generous person will
   prosper;
   whoever refreshes others
   will be refreshed.   Mt 5:7

26 People curse the one who
   hoards grain,
   but they pray God's blessing
   on the one who is
   willing to sell.

27 Whoever seeks good finds
   favor,
   but evil comes to one who
   searches for it.   Est 7:10

28 Those who trust in their
   riches will fall,   Mk 10:25;
   but the righteous will
   thrive like a green
   leaf.   Ps 1:3; Jer 17:8

29 Whoever brings ruin on their
   family will inherit only
   wind,
   and the fool will be servant
   to the wise.   Pr 14:19

30 The fruit of the righteous is a
   tree of life,   Jas 5:20
   and the one who is wise
   saves lives.

31 If the righteous receive their
   due on earth,   Pr 13:21
   how much more the
   ungodly and the sinner!

12

Whoever loves discipline
loves knowledge,
but whoever hates
correction is stupid.

² Good people obtain favor
from the LORD,   Ps 84:11
but he condemns those who
devise wicked schemes.

³ No one can be established
through wickedness,
but the righteous cannot be
uprooted.   Pr 10:25

⁴ A wife of noble character is
her husband's crown,
but a disgraceful wife is like
decay in his bones.

⁵ The plans of the righteous are
just,
but the advice of the wicked
is deceitful.

⁶ The words of the wicked lie in
wait for blood,
but the speech of the
upright rescues them.

⁷ The wicked are overthrown
and are no more,   Ps 37:36
but the house of the
righteous stands firm.

⁸ A person is praised according
to their prudence,
and one with a warped
mind is despised.

⁹ Better to be a nobody and yet
have a servant
than pretend to be
somebody and have no
food.

¹⁰ The righteous care for the
needs of their
animals,   Nu 22:29
but the kindest acts of the
wicked are cruel.

¹¹ Those who work their land will
have abundant food,
but those who chase
fantasies have no sense.

¹² The wicked desire the
stronghold of evildoers,
but the root of the righteous
endures.

¹³ Evildoers are trapped by their
sinful talk,   Pr 18:7
and so the innocent escape
trouble.   2Pe 2:9

¹⁴ From the fruit of their lips
people are filled with
good things,   Pr 13:2
and the work of their hands
brings them reward.

¹⁵ The way of fools seems right
to them,   Pr 14:12; 16:2,25
but the wise listen to advice.

¹⁶ Fools show their annoyance
at once,
but the prudent overlook an
insult.   Pr 29:11

¹⁷ An honest witness tells the
truth,
but a false witness tells
lies.   Pr 14:5,25

¹⁸ The words of the reckless
pierce like swords,   Ps 57:4
but the tongue of the wise
brings healing.   Pr 15:4

¹⁹ Truthful lips endure forever,
  but a lying tongue lasts only
    a moment.

²⁰ Deceit is in the hearts of those
    who plot evil,
  but those who promote
    peace have joy.

²¹ No harm overtakes the
    righteous,   Ps 91:10
  but the wicked have their
    fill of trouble.

²² The LORD detests lying lips,
  but he delights in people
    who are trustworthy.

²³ The prudent keep their
    knowledge to
    themselves,   Pr 13:16
  but a fool's heart blurts out
    folly.

²⁴ Diligent hands will rule,
  but laziness ends in forced
    labor.   Pr 10:4

²⁵ Anxiety weighs down the
    heart,   Pr 15:13; Isa 50:4
  but a kind word cheers it up.

²⁶ The righteous choose their
    friends carefully,
  but the way of the wicked
    leads them astray.

²⁷ The lazy do not roast*ª* any
    game,
  but the diligent feed on the
    riches of the hunt.

²⁸ In the way of righteousness
    there is life;   Dt 30:15

along that path is
  immortality.

13 A wise son heeds his
    father's instruction,
  but a mocker does not
    respond to rebukes.

² From the fruit of their lips
    people enjoy good
    things,   Pr 12:14
  but the unfaithful have an
    appetite for violence.

³ Those who guard their lips
    preserve their lives,
  but those who speak rashly
    will come to ruin.   Pr 18:7

⁴ A sluggard's appetite is never
    filled,   Pr 21:25-26
  but the desires of the diligent
    are fully satisfied.

⁵ The righteous hate what is
    false,   Ps 119:128
  but the wicked make
    themselves a stench
  and bring shame on
    themselves.

⁶ Righteousness guards the
    person of integrity,
  but wickedness overthrows
    the sinner.   Pr 11:3,5

⁷ One person pretends to be
    rich, yet has nothing;
  another pretends to be
    poor, yet has great
    wealth.

⁸ A person's riches may ransom
    their life,

ª 27 The meaning of the Hebrew for this word is uncertain.

but the poor cannot respond to threatening rebukes.

⁹The light of the righteous shines brightly,
but the lamp of the wicked is snuffed out. Job 18:5

¹⁰Where there is strife, there is pride,
but wisdom is found in those who take advice.

¹¹Dishonest money dwindles away, Pr 10:2
but whoever gathers money little by little makes it grow.

¹²Hope deferred makes the heart sick,
but a longing fulfilled is a tree of life.

¹³Whoever scorns instruction will pay for it, Nu 15:31
but whoever respects a command is rewarded.

¹⁴The teaching of the wise is a fountain of life, Pr 10:11
turning a person from the snares of death. Pr 14:27

¹⁵Good judgment wins favor,
but the way of the unfaithful leads to their destruction.ᵃ

¹⁶All who are prudent act withᵇ knowledge,
but fools expose their folly.

¹⁷A wicked messenger falls into trouble,
but a trustworthy envoy brings healing. Pr 25:13

¹⁸Whoever disregards discipline comes to poverty and shame,
but whoever heeds correction is honored.

¹⁹A longing fulfilled is sweet to the soul,
but fools detest turning from evil.

²⁰Walk with the wise and become wise,
for a companion of fools suffers harm. Pr 15:31

²¹Trouble pursues the sinner,
but the righteous are rewarded with good things. Ps 32:10

²²A good person leaves an inheritance for their children's children,
but a sinner's wealth is stored up for the righteous. Job 27:17; Ecc 2:26

²³An unplowed field produces food for the poor,
but injustice sweeps it away.

²⁴Whoever spares the rod hates their children,
but the one who loves their children is careful to discipline them. Pr 19:18

ᵃ 15 Septuagint and Syriac; the meaning of the Hebrew for this phrase is uncertain.
ᵇ 16 Or *prudent protect themselves through*

²⁵The righteous eat to their
    hearts' content,
but the stomach of the
    wicked goes hungry.

14 The wise woman builds
    her house,   Pr 24:3
but with her own hands the
    foolish one tears hers
    down.

²Whoever fears the LORD
    walks uprightly,
but those who despise him
    are devious in their
    ways.

³A fool's mouth lashes out with
    pride,   Pr 10:14; Ecc 10:12
but the lips of the wise
    protect them.   Pr 12:6

⁴Where there are no oxen, the
    manger is empty,
but from the strength of
    an ox come abundant
    harvests.

⁵An honest witness does not
    deceive,
but a false witness pours
    out lies.   Pr 6:19; 12:17

⁶The mocker seeks wisdom
    and finds none,
but knowledge comes easily
    to the discerning.   Pr 9:9

⁷Stay away from a fool,
for you will not find
    knowledge on their lips.

⁸The wisdom of the prudent is
    to give thought to their
    ways,   Pr 15:28

but the folly of fools is
    deception.   ver 24

⁹Fools mock at making
    amends for sin,
but goodwill is found
    among the upright.

¹⁰Each heart knows its own
    bitterness,
and no one else can share
    its joy.

¹¹The house of the wicked will
    be destroyed,
but the tent of the upright
    will flourish.   Pr 3:33; 12:7

¹²There is a way that appears to
    be right,   Pr 12:15
but in the end it leads to
    death.   Pr 16:25

¹³Even in laughter the heart
    may ache,   Ecc 2:2
and rejoicing may end in
    grief.

¹⁴The faithless will be fully
    repaid for their
    ways,   Pr 1:31
and the good rewarded for
    theirs.   Pr 12:14

¹⁵The simple believe anything,
but the prudent give
    thought to their steps.

¹⁶The wise fear the LORD and
    shun evil,   Pr 22:3
but a fool is hotheaded and
    yet feels secure.   1Sa 25:25

¹⁷A quick-tempered person
    does foolish things,   ver 29

and the one who devises
   evil schemes is hated.

¹⁸The simple inherit folly,
   but the prudent are
      crowned with
      knowledge.

¹⁹Evildoers will bow down in
      the presence of the
      good,
   and the wicked at the gates
      of the righteous.   Pr 11:29

²⁰The poor are shunned even by
      their neighbors,
   but the rich have many
      friends.   Pr 19:4,7

²¹It is a sin to despise one's
      neighbor,   Pr 11:12
   but blessed is the one
      who is kind to the
      needy.   Ps 41:1; Pr 19:17

²²Do not those who plot evil go
      astray?   Pr 4:16-17
   But those who plan what
      is good find*ᵃ* love and
      faithfulness.

²³All hard work brings a profit,
   but mere talk leads only to
      poverty.

²⁴The wealth of the wise is their
      crown,
   but the folly of fools yields
      folly.   ver 8

²⁵A truthful witness saves lives,
   but a false witness is
      deceitful.   ver 5

²⁶Whoever fears the LORD has a
      secure fortress,   Pr 18:10
   and for their children it will
      be a refuge.

²⁷The fear of the LORD is a
      fountain of life,   Pr 10:11
   turning a person from the
      snares of death.   Pr 13:14

²⁸A large population is a king's
      glory,
   but without subjects a
      prince is ruined.   2Sa 19:7

²⁹Whoever is patient has great
      understanding,   Pr 17:27
   but one who is quick-
      tempered displays folly.

³⁰A heart at peace gives life to
      the body,
   but envy rots the bones. Pr 12:4

³¹Whoever oppresses the poor
      shows contempt for
      their Maker,   Pr 17:5
   but whoever is kind to the
      needy honors God.

³²When calamity comes, the
      wicked are brought
      down,   Pr 6:15
   but even in death the
      righteous seek refuge in
      God.   Job 13:15; 2Ti 4:18

³³Wisdom reposes in the heart
      of the discerning Pr 2:6-10
   and even among fools she
      lets herself be known.*ᵇ*

³⁴Righteousness exalts a nation,

ᵃ 22 Or *show
is not known*   *ᵇ 33* Hebrew; Septuagint and Syriac *discerning / but in the heart of fools she*

but sin condemns any
people.

³⁵ A king delights in a wise
servant,
but a shameful servant
arouses his fury. Mt 24:45

15 A gentle answer turns
away wrath, Pr 25:15
but a harsh word stirs up
anger.

² The tongue of the wise adorns
knowledge, Pr 10:31
but the mouth of the fool
gushes folly. Pr 12:23

³ The eyes of the LORD are
everywhere, 2Ch 16:9
keeping watch on the
wicked and the good.

⁴ The soothing tongue is a tree
of life, Ps 5:9
but a perverse tongue
crushes the spirit. Pr 12:18

⁵ A fool spurns a parent's
discipline,
but whoever heeds
correction shows
prudence. Pr 13:1

⁶ The house of the righteous
contains great
treasure, Pr 8:21
but the income of the
wicked brings ruin.

⁷ The lips of the wise spread
knowledge, Pr 10:13
but the hearts of fools are
not upright.

⁸ The LORD detests the sacrifice
of the wicked, Pr 21:27
but the prayer of the upright
pleases him. ver 29

⁹ The LORD detests the way of
the wicked, Pr 6:16
but he loves those who
pursue righteousness.

¹⁰ Stern discipline awaits
anyone who leaves the
path;
the one who hates
correction will die. Pr 1:31

¹¹ Death and Destruction^a lie
open before the
LORD — Job 26:6; Ps 139:8
how much more do human
hearts! 2Ch 6:30; Ps 44:21

¹² Mockers resent correction,
so they avoid the wise.

¹³ A happy heart makes the face
cheerful,
but heartache crushes the
spirit. Pr 12:25; 17:22

¹⁴ The discerning heart seeks
knowledge, Pr 18:15
but the mouth of a fool
feeds on folly.

¹⁵ All the days of the oppressed
are wretched,
but the cheerful heart has a
continual feast. ver 13

¹⁶ Better a little with the fear of
the LORD
than great wealth with
turmoil. Ps 37:16-17; 1Ti 6:6

^a 11 Hebrew *Abaddon*

17 Better a small serving of
  vegetables with love
than a fattened calf with
  hatred. Pr 17:1

18 A hot-tempered person stirs
  up conflict, Pr 26:21
but the one who is patient
  calms a quarrel. Ge 13:8

19 The way of the sluggard is
  blocked with thorns,
but the path of the upright
  is a highway.

20 A wise son brings joy to his
  father, Pr 10:1
but a foolish man despises
  his mother.

21 Folly brings joy to one who
  has no sense, Pr 10:23
but whoever has
  understanding keeps a
  straight course.

22 Plans fail for lack of counsel,
but with many advisers they
  succeed. Pr 11:14

23 A person finds joy in giving an
  apt reply— Pr 12:14
and how good is a timely
  word! Pr 25:11

24 The path of life leads upward
  for the prudent
to keep them from going
  down to the realm of
  the dead.

25 The LORD tears down the
  house of the proud,
but he sets the widow's
  boundary stones in
  place. Ps 68:5-6

26 The LORD detests the
  thoughts of the wicked,
but gracious words are pure
  in his sight.

27 The greedy bring ruin to their
  households,
but the one who hates
  bribes will live. Ex 23:8

28 The heart of the righteous
  weighs its answers,
but the mouth of the wicked
  gushes evil.

29 The LORD is far from the
  wicked,
but he hears the prayer of
  the righteous. Ps 145:18-19

30 Light in a messenger's eyes
  brings joy to the heart,
and good news gives health
  to the bones. Pr 25:25

31 Whoever heeds life-giving
  correction
will be at home among the
  wise. ver 5

32 Those who disregard discipline
  despise themselves, Pr 1:7
but the one who heeds
  correction gains
  understanding. Pr 9:7-9

33 Wisdom's instruction is to fear
  the LORD, Pr 1:7
and humility comes before
  honor. Pr 18:12

16 To humans belong the
  plans of the heart,
but from the LORD comes
  the proper answer of
  the tongue. Pr 19:21

²All a person's ways seem pure
   to them,   Pr 12:15
   but motives are weighed by
      the LORD.   Pr 21:2

³Commit to the LORD whatever
      you do,
   and he will establish your
      plans.   Ps 37:5-6; Pr 3:5-6

⁴The LORD works out everything
   to its proper end —   Isa 43:7
   even the wicked for a day of
      disaster.   Ro 9:22

⁵The LORD detests all the
      proud of heart.   Pr 6:16
   Be sure of this: They will
      not go unpunished.

⁶Through love and faithfulness
      sin is atoned for;
   through the fear of the
      LORD evil is avoided.

⁷When the LORD takes pleasure
   in anyone's way,
   he causes their enemies to
      make peace with them.

⁸Better a little with
      righteousness
   than much gain with
      injustice.   Ps 37:16

⁹In their hearts humans plan
      their course,
   but the LORD establishes
      their steps.   Jer 10:23

¹⁰The lips of a king speak as an
      oracle,
   and his mouth does not
      betray justice.   Pr 17:7

¹¹Honest scales and balances
      belong to the LORD;
   all the weights in the bag
      are of his making.   Pr 11:1

¹²Kings detest wrongdoing,
   for a throne is established
      through righteousness.

¹³Kings take pleasure in honest
      lips;
   they value the one who
      speaks what is right.

¹⁴A king's wrath is a messenger
      of death,   Pr 19:12
   but the wise will appease it.

¹⁵When a king's face brightens,
      it means life;   Job 29:24
   his favor is like a rain cloud
      in spring.   Pr 19:12

¹⁶How much better to get
      wisdom than gold,
   to get insight rather than
      silver!   Ps 49:20; Pr 8:10,19

¹⁷The highway of the upright
      avoids evil;
   those who guard their ways
      preserve their lives.

¹⁸Pride goes before
      destruction,   1Sa 17:42
   a haughty spirit before a fall.

¹⁹Better to be lowly in spirit
      along with the
      oppressed
   than to share plunder with
      the proud.

²⁰Whoever gives heed to
      instruction prospers,ᵃ

ᵃ 20 Or *whoever speaks prudently finds what is good*

and blessed is the one who
trusts in the LORD. Ps 34:8

²¹ The wise in heart are called
discerning,
and gracious words
promote instruction.^a

²² Prudence is a fountain of life
to the prudent,   Pr 13:14
but folly brings punishment
to fools.

²³ The hearts of the wise make
their mouths
prudent,   Job 15:5
and their lips promote
instruction.^b   ver 21

²⁴ Gracious words are a
honeycomb,   1Sa 14:27
sweet to the soul and
healing to the bones.

²⁵ There is a way that appears to
be right,   Pr 12:15
but in the end it leads to
death.   Pr 14:12

²⁶ The appetite of laborers works
for them;
their hunger drives them on.

²⁷ A scoundrel plots evil,   Ps 140:2
and on their lips it is like a
scorching fire.   Jas 3:6

²⁸ A perverse person stirs up
conflict,   Pr 15:18
and a gossip separates close
friends.   Pr 17:9

²⁹ A violent person entices their
neighbor

and leads them down a path
that is not good.   Pr 1:10

³⁰ Whoever winks with their eye
is plotting perversity;
whoever purses their lips is
bent on evil.

³¹ Gray hair is a crown of splendor;
it is attained in the way of
righteousness.

³² Better a patient person than a
warrior,
one with self-control than
one who takes a city.

³³ The lot is cast into the lap,
but its every decision is
from the LORD.   Pr 18:18

17 Better a dry crust with
peace and quiet
than a house full of
feasting, with strife.

² A prudent servant will rule
over a disgraceful son
and will share the
inheritance as one of
the family.

³ The crucible for silver and the
furnace for gold,   Pr 27:21
but the LORD tests the heart.

⁴ A wicked person listens to
deceitful lips;
a liar pays attention to a
destructive tongue.

⁵ Whoever mocks the poor
shows contempt for
their Maker;   Pr 14:31

^a 21 Or *words make a person persuasive*   ^b 23 Or *prudent / and make their lips persuasive*

whoever gloats over disaster
will not go unpunished.

⁶Children's children are a
crown to the aged,
and parents are the pride of
their children.

⁷Eloquent lips are unsuited to
a godless fool—
how much worse lying lips
to a ruler!   Pr 16:10

⁸A bribe is seen as a charm by
the one who gives it;
they think success will
come at every turn.

⁹Whoever would foster love
covers over an offense,
but whoever repeats the
matter separates close
friends.   Pr 16:28

¹⁰A rebuke impresses a
discerning person
more than a hundred lashes
a fool.

¹¹Evildoers foster rebellion
against God;
the messenger of death will
be sent against them.

¹²Better to meet a bear robbed
of her cubs
than a fool bent on folly.

¹³Evil will never leave the house
of one who pays back evil
for good.   Ps 109:4-5; Jer 18:20

¹⁴Starting a quarrel is like
breaching a dam;
so drop the matter before a
dispute breaks out.

¹⁵Acquitting the guilty and
condemning the
innocent—   Pr 18:5
the LORD detests them
both.   Ex 23:6-7; Isa 5:23

¹⁶Why should fools have money
in hand to buy wisdom,
when they are not able to
understand it?   Pr 23:23

¹⁷A friend loves at all times,
and a brother is born for a
time of adversity.   Pr 27:10

¹⁸One who has no sense shakes
hands in pledge
and puts up security for a
neighbor.   Pr 6:1-5; 11:15

¹⁹Whoever loves a quarrel loves
sin;
whoever builds a high gate
invites destruction.

²⁰One whose heart is corrupt
does not prosper;
one whose tongue is
perverse falls into
trouble.

²¹To have a fool for a child
brings grief;
there is no joy for the parent
of a godless fool.   Pr 10:1

²²A cheerful heart is good
medicine,
but a crushed spirit dries up
the bones.   Ps 22:15; Pr 15:13

²³The wicked accept bribes in
secret   Ex 23:8
to pervert the course of
justice.   Job 34:33

²⁴A discerning person keeps wisdom in view,
  but a fool's eyes wander to the ends of the earth.

²⁵A foolish son brings grief to his father
  and bitterness to the mother who bore him. Pr 10:1

²⁶If imposing a fine on the innocent is not good,
  surely to flog honest officials is not right.

²⁷The one who has knowledge uses words with restraint, Job 6:24
  and whoever has understanding is even-tempered. Pr 14:29; Jas 1:19

²⁸Even fools are thought wise if they keep silent,
  and discerning if they hold their tongues. Job 13:5

18 An unfriendly person pursues selfish ends
  and against all sound judgment starts quarrels.

²Fools find no pleasure in understanding
  but delight in airing their own opinions. Pr 12:23

³When wickedness comes, so does contempt,
  and with shame comes reproach.

⁴The words of the mouth are deep waters, Ps 18:16
  but the fountain of wisdom is a rushing stream.

⁵It is not good to be partial to the wicked Lev 19:15
  and so deprive the innocent of justice. Pr 17:15

⁶The lips of fools bring them strife,
  and their mouths invite a beating.

⁷The mouths of fools are their undoing,
  and their lips are a snare to their very lives. Ps 140:9

⁸The words of a gossip are like choice morsels;
  they go down to the inmost parts. Pr 26:22

⁹One who is slack in his work is brother to one who destroys. Pr 28:24

¹⁰The name of the LORD is a fortified tower; 2Sa 22:3
  the righteous run to it and are safe. Pr 14:26

¹¹The wealth of the rich is their fortified city; Pr 10:15
  they imagine it a wall too high to scale.

¹²Before a downfall the heart is haughty,
  but humility comes before honor. Pr 11:2; 16:18

¹³To answer before listening—
  that is folly and shame.

¹⁴The human spirit can endure in sickness,

but a crushed spirit who
   can bear?   Pr 15:13; 17:22

¹⁵ The heart of the discerning
   acquires knowledge,
for the ears of the wise seek
   it out.

¹⁶ A gift opens the way   Ge 32:20
   and ushers the giver into the
   presence of the great.

¹⁷ In a lawsuit the first to speak
   seems right,
until someone comes
   forward and cross-
   examines.

¹⁸ Casting the lot settles disputes
   and keeps strong opponents
   apart.

¹⁹ A brother wronged is more
   unyielding than a
   fortified city;   1Sa 17:28
disputes are like the barred
   gates of a citadel.

²⁰ From the fruit of their mouth
   a person's stomach is
   filled;
with the harvest of their lips
   they are satisfied.   Pr 12:14

²¹ The tongue has the power of
   life and death,   Ps 12:4
and those who love it will
   eat its fruit.   Mt 12:37

²² He who finds a wife finds
   what is good   Pr 12:4
and receives favor from the
   Lord.   Pr 19:14

²³ The poor plead for mercy,
   but the rich answer harshly.

²⁴ One who has unreliable
   friends soon comes to
   ruin,
but there is a friend who
   sticks closer than a
   brother.   Pr 17:17; Jn 15:13-15

19 Better the poor whose
   walk is blameless
than a fool whose lips are
   perverse.   Pr 28:6

² Desire without knowledge is
   not good —
how much more will hasty
   feet miss the way! Pr 29:20

³ A person's own folly leads to
   their ruin,   Ps 14:1
yet their heart rages against
   the Lord.   Jas 1:13-15

⁴ Wealth attracts many friends,
but even the closest friend
   of the poor person
   deserts them.   Pr 14:20

⁵ A false witness will not go
   unpunished,   Ex 23:1
and whoever pours out lies
   will not go free.   Dt 19:19

⁶ Many curry favor with a
   ruler,   Pr 29:26
and everyone is the friend
   of one who gives
   gifts.   Pr 17:8

⁷ The poor are shunned by all
   their relatives —
how much more do
   their friends avoid
   them!   Pr 10:15
Though the poor pursue them
   with pleading,

they are nowhere to be
    found.^a   Ps 38:11

⁸The one who gets wisdom
    loves life;
  the one who cherishes
    understanding will
    soon prosper.   Pr 16:20

⁹A false witness will not go
    unpunished,
  and whoever pours out lies
    will perish.   ver 5

¹⁰It is not fitting for a fool to live
    in luxury —   Pr 26:1
  how much worse for a slave
    to rule over princes!

¹¹A person's wisdom yields
    patience;   Pr 16:32
  it is to one's glory to
    overlook an offense.

¹²A king's rage is like the roar of
    a lion,   Pr 20:2
  but his favor is like dew on
    the grass.   Pr 16:14-15

¹³A foolish child is a father's
    ruin,   Pr 10:1
  and a quarrelsome wife is
    like
  the constant dripping of a
    leaky roof.   Pr 21:9

¹⁴Houses and wealth are
    inherited from parents,
  but a prudent wife is from
    the LORD.   Pr 18:22

¹⁵Laziness brings on deep sleep,
  and the shiftless go hungry.

¹⁶Whoever keeps
    commandments keeps
    their life,
  but whoever shows
    contempt for their ways
    will die.   Lk 10:28

¹⁷Whoever is kind to the poor
    lends to the LORD,
  and he will reward them for
    what they have done.

¹⁸Discipline your children, for
    in that there is hope;
  do not be a willing party to
    their death.   Pr 13:24

¹⁹A hot-tempered person must
    pay the penalty;
  rescue them, and you will
    have to do it again.

²⁰Listen to advice and accept
    discipline,   Pr 4:1
  and at the end you will be
    counted among the wise.

²¹Many are the plans in a
    person's heart,
  but it is the LORD's purpose
    that prevails.   Ps 33:11

²²What a person desires is
    unfailing love^b;
  better to be poor than a liar.

²³The fear of the LORD leads to
    life;
  then one rests content,
    untouched by trouble.

²⁴A sluggard buries his hand in
    the dish;

---

^a 7 The meaning of the Hebrew for this sentence is uncertain.   ^b 22 Or *Greed is a person's shame*

he will not even bring it
    back to his mouth!

25 Flog a mocker, and the simple
        will learn prudence;
    rebuke the discerning,
        and they will gain
        knowledge.   Pr 9:9

26 Whoever robs their father and
        drives out their mother
    is a child who brings shame
        and disgrace.

27 Stop listening to instruction,
        my son,   Pr 1:8
    and you will stray from the
        words of knowledge.

28 A corrupt witness mocks at
        justice,
    and the mouth of the wicked
        gulps down evil.   Job 15:16

29 Penalties are prepared for
        mockers,
    and beatings for the backs
        of fools.   Pr 26:3

20 Wine is a mocker and
      beer a brawler;   1Sa 25:36
    whoever is led astray by
        them is not wise.   Pr 31:4

2 A king's wrath strikes terror
        like the roar of a lion;
    those who anger him forfeit
        their lives.   Pr 8:36

3 It is to one's honor to avoid
        strife,
    but every fool is quick to
        quarrel.   Pr 17:14

4 Sluggards do not plow in
        season;   Pr 6:6

so at harvest time they look
    but find nothing.   Ecc 10:18

5 The purposes of a person's
        heart are deep waters,
    but one who has insight
        draws them out.

6 Many claim to have unfailing
        love,
    but a faithful person who
        can find?   Ps 12:1

7 The righteous lead blameless
        lives;   Ps 26:1
    blessed are their children
        after them.   Ps 37:25-26

8 When a king sits on his throne
        to judge,   1Ki 7:7
    he winnows out all evil with
        his eyes.   ver 26; Pr 25:4-5

9 Who can say, "I have kept my
        heart pure;   Job 15:14
    I am clean and without
        sin"?   1Ki 8:46

10 Differing weights and
        differing measures —
    the LORD detests them both.

11 Even small children are
        known by their actions,
    so is their conduct really
        pure and upright?   Mt 7:16

12 Ears that hear and eyes that
        see —
    the LORD has made them
        both.   Ps 94:9

13 Do not love sleep or you will
        grow poor;   Pr 6:11; 19:15
    stay awake and you will
        have food to spare.

14 "It's no good, it's no good!"
   says the buyer —
   then goes off and boasts
      about the purchase.

15 Gold there is, and rubies in
      abundance,
   but lips that speak
      knowledge are a rare
      jewel.

16 Take the garment of one who
      puts up security for a
      stranger;
   hold it in pledge if it is done
      for an outsider. Ex 22:26

17 Food gained by fraud tastes
      sweet,   Pr 9:17
   but one ends up with a
      mouth full of gravel.

18 Plans are established by
      seeking advice;
   so if you wage war, obtain
      guidance.   Pr 24:6

19 A gossip betrays a confidence;
   so avoid anyone who talks
      too much.   Pr 11:13

20 If someone curses their father
      or mother,   Pr 30:11
   their lamp will be snuffed
      out in pitch darkness.

21 An inheritance claimed too
      soon
   will not be blessed at the
      end.

22 Do not say, "I'll pay you back
      for this wrong!"   Pr 24:29

Wait for the LORD, and he
   will avenge you.   Ro 12:19

23 The LORD detests differing
      weights,
   and dishonest scales do not
      please him.   ver 10

24 A person's steps are directed
      by the LORD.   Ps 90:12
   How then can anyone
      understand their own
      way?   Jer 10:23

25 It is a trap to dedicate
      something rashly
   and only later to consider
      one's vows.   Ecc 5:2,4-5

26 A wise king winnows out the
      wicked;
   he drives the threshing
      wheel over them.   ver 8

27 The human spirit is[a] the lamp
      of the LORD   Ps 119:105
   that sheds light on one's
      inmost being.   Pr 16:2

28 Love and faithfulness keep a
      king safe;
   through love his throne is
      made secure.   Pr 29:14

29 The glory of young men is
      their strength,
   gray hair the splendor of the
      old.   Pr 16:31

30 Blows and wounds scrub
      away evil,   Pr 22:15
   and beatings purge the
      inmost being.   Isa 1:5

a 27 Or *A person's words are*

21

In the LORD's hand the king's heart is a stream of water
that he channels toward all who please him. Est 5:1

2 A person may think their own ways are right,
but the LORD weighs the heart. Pr 16:2; 24:12; Lk 16:15

3 To do what is right and just is more acceptable to the LORD than sacrifice.

4 Haughty eyes and a proud heart — Pr 6:17
the unplowed field of the wicked — produce sin.

5 The plans of the diligent lead to profit Pr 10:4
as surely as haste leads to poverty.

6 A fortune made by a lying tongue
is a fleeting vapor and a deadly snare.[a] 2Pe 2:3

7 The violence of the wicked will drag them away,
for they refuse to do what is right.

8 The way of the guilty is devious, Pr 2:15
but the conduct of the innocent is upright.

9 Better to live on a corner of the roof

than share a house with a quarrelsome wife. Pr 25:24

10 The wicked crave evil;
their neighbors get no mercy from them.

11 When a mocker is punished, the simple gain wisdom;
by paying attention to the wise they get knowledge. Pr 19:25

12 The Righteous One[b] takes note of the house of the wicked
and brings the wicked to ruin. Pr 14:11

13 Whoever shuts their ears to the cry of the poor
will also cry out and not be answered. Mt 18:30-34

14 A gift given in secret soothes anger,
and a bribe concealed in the cloak pacifies great wrath. Pr 18:16; 19:6

15 When justice is done, it brings joy to the righteous
but terror to evildoers. Pr 10:29

16 Whoever strays from the path of prudence
comes to rest in the company of the dead.

17 Whoever loves pleasure will become poor;

---

a 6 Some Hebrew manuscripts, Septuagint and Vulgate; most Hebrew manuscripts *vapor for those who seek death*   *b* 12 Or *The righteous person*

whoever loves wine and
   olive oil will never be
   rich.   Pr 23:20-21,29-35

¹⁸ The wicked become a ransom
   for the righteous,   Pr 11:8
   and the unfaithful for the
   upright.

¹⁹ Better to live in a desert
   than with a quarrelsome
   and nagging wife.   ver 9

²⁰ The wise store up choice food
   and olive oil,
   but fools gulp theirs down.

²¹ Whoever pursues
   righteousness and love
   finds life, prosperity*ᵃ* and
   honor.   Mt 5:6

²² One who is wise can go up
   against the city of the
   mighty   Ecc 9:15-16
   and pull down the
   stronghold in which
   they trust.

²³ Those who guard their
   mouths and their
   tongues   Jas 3:2
   keep themselves from
   calamity.   Pr 12:13

²⁴ The proud and arrogant
   person — "Mocker" is
   his name —   Ps 1:1
   behaves with insolent fury.

²⁵ The craving of a sluggard will
   be the death of him,
   because his hands refuse to
   work.

²⁶ All day long he craves for
   more,
   but the righteous give
   without sparing.   Ps 37:26

²⁷ The sacrifice of the wicked is
   detestable —   Jer 6:20
   how much more so when
   brought with evil
   intent!   Pr 15:8

²⁸ A false witness will perish,
   but a careful listener will
   testify successfully.

²⁹ The wicked put up a bold front,
   but the upright give thought
   to their ways.   Pr 14:8

³⁰ There is no wisdom, no
   insight, no plan   Jer 9:23
   that can succeed against
   the LORD.   Isa 8:10; Ac 5:39

³¹ The horse is made ready for
   the day of battle,
   but victory rests with the
   LORD.   Ps 3:8

22

A good name is more
   desirable than great
   riches;
   to be esteemed is better
   than silver or gold. Ecc 7:1

² Rich and poor have this in
   common:
   The LORD is the Maker of
   them all.   Job 31:15

³ The prudent see danger and
   take refuge,   Pr 14:16
   but the simple keep going
   and pay the penalty.

ᵃ 21 Or *righteousness*

⁴Humility is the fear of the
    LORD;
  its wages are riches and
    honor and life.   Pr 10:27

⁵In the paths of the wicked are
    snares and pitfalls,
  but those who would
    preserve their life stay
    far from them.

⁶Start children off on the way
    they should go,   Eph 6:4
  and even when they are old
    they will not turn from it.

⁷The rich rule over the poor,
  and the borrower is slave to
    the lender.

⁸Whoever sows injustice reaps
    calamity,   Job 4:8
  and the rod they wield in
    fury will be broken.

⁹The generous will themselves
    be blessed,   2Co 9:6
  for they share their food
    with the poor.   Pr 19:17

¹⁰Drive out the mocker, and out
    goes strife;
  quarrels and insults are
    ended.   Pr 26:20

¹¹One who loves a pure heart
    and who speaks with
    grace
  will have the king for a
    friend.   Mt 5:8

¹²The eyes of the LORD keep
    watch over knowledge,
  but he frustrates the words
    of the unfaithful.

¹³The sluggard says, "There's a
    lion outside!   Pr 26:13
  I'll be killed in the public
    square!"

¹⁴The mouth of an adulterous
    woman is a deep pit;
  a man who is under the
    LORD's wrath falls
    into it.   Ecc 7:26

¹⁵Folly is bound up in the heart
    of a child,
  but the rod of discipline will
    drive it far away.   Pr 13:24

¹⁶One who oppresses the poor
    to increase his wealth
  and one who gives gifts to
    the rich — both come to
    poverty.

Thirty Sayings of the Wise

Saying 1

¹⁷Pay attention and turn your
    ear to the sayings of the
    wise;   Pr 5:1
  apply your heart to what I
    teach,   Pr 2:2

¹⁸for it is pleasing when you
    keep them in your heart
  and have all of them ready
    on your lips.

¹⁹So that your trust may be in
    the LORD,
  I teach you today, even you.

²⁰Have I not written thirty
    sayings for you,
  sayings of counsel and
    knowledge,

²¹teaching you to be honest and
    to speak the truth,

so that you bring back
truthful reports
to those you serve?

Saying 2

²²Do not exploit the poor
because they are poor
and do not crush the needy
in court,   Ex 23:6; Mal 3:5

²³for the LORD will take up their
case   Ps 12:5
and will exact life for life.

Saying 3

²⁴Do not make friends with a
hot-tempered person,
do not associate with one
easily angered,

²⁵or you may learn their ways
and get yourself ensnared.

Saying 4

²⁶Do not be one who shakes
hands in pledge   Pr 11:15
or puts up security for
debts;

²⁷if you lack the means to pay,
your very bed will be
snatched from under
you.   Pr 17:18

Saying 5

²⁸Do not move an ancient
boundary stone   Dt 19:14
set up by your ancestors.

Saying 6

²⁹Do you see someone skilled in
their work?

They will serve before
kings;   Ge 41:46
they will not serve before
officials of low rank.

Saying 7

23

When you sit to dine
with a ruler,
note well what[a] is before
you,

²and put a knife to your throat
if you are given to gluttony.

³Do not crave his delicacies,
for that food is deceptive.

Saying 8

⁴Do not wear yourself out to
get rich;
do not trust your own
cleverness.

⁵Cast but a glance at riches,
and they are gone,   Mt 6:19
for they will surely sprout
wings
and fly off to the sky like an
eagle.   Pr 27:24

Saying 9

⁶Do not eat the food of a
begrudging host,
do not crave his
delicacies;   Ps 141:4

⁷for he is the kind of person
who is always thinking
about the cost.[b]
"Eat and drink," he says to
you,
but his heart is not with
you.

---

[a] 1 Or *who*   [b] 7 Or *for as he thinks within himself, / so he is*; or *for as he puts on a feast, / so he is*

8 You will vomit up the little
    you have eaten
    and will have wasted your
    compliments.

Saying 10

9 Do not speak to fools,
    for they will scorn your
    prudent words.   Pr 9:7

Saying 11

10 Do not move an ancient
    boundary stone   Dt 19:14
    or encroach on the fields of
    the fatherless,
11 for their Defender is strong;
    he will take up their case
    against you.   Pr 22:22-23

Saying 12

12 Apply your heart to
    instruction   Pr 2:2
    and your ears to words of
    knowledge.

Saying 13

13 Do not withhold discipline
    from a child;
    if you punish them with the
    rod, they will not die.
14 Punish them with the rod
    and save them from
    death.   Pr 13:24

Saying 14

15 My son, if your heart is wise,
    then my heart will be glad
    indeed;
16 my inmost being will rejoice
    when your lips speak what
    is right.   ver 24; Pr 27:11

Saying 15

17 Do not let your heart envy
    sinners,   Ps 37:1; Pr 28:14
    but always be zealous for
    the fear of the LORD.
18 There is surely a future hope
    for you,
    and your hope will not be
    cut off.   Pr 24:14,19-20

Saying 16

19 Listen, my son, and be wise,
    and set your heart on the
    right path:
20 Do not join those who drink
    too much wine   Isa 5:11,22
    or gorge themselves on
    meat,
21 for drunkards and gluttons
    become poor,   Pr 21:17
    and drowsiness clothes
    them in rags.

Saying 17

22 Listen to your father, who
    gave you life,
    and do not despise your
    mother when she is
    old.   Pr 1:8; Eph 6:1-2
23 Buy the truth and do not
    sell it —
    wisdom, instruction and
    insight as well.   Pr 4:7
24 The father of a righteous child
    has great joy;
    a man who fathers a wise
    son rejoices in him.
25 May your father and mother
    rejoice;
    may she who gave you birth
    be joyful!   Pr 10:1

Saying 18

²⁶My son, give me your heart
and let your eyes delight in
my ways,   Ps 18:21
²⁷for an adulterous woman is a
deep pit,   Pr 22:14
and a wayward wife is a
narrow well.
²⁸Like a bandit she lies in wait
and multiplies the
unfaithful among men.

Saying 19

²⁹Who has woe? Who has
sorrow?
Who has strife? Who has
complaints?
Who has needless bruises?
Who has bloodshot
eyes?   Pr 8:21
³⁰Those who linger over wine,
who go to sample bowls of
mixed wine.
³¹Do not gaze at wine when it is
red,
when it sparkles in the cup,
when it goes down
smoothly!
³²In the end it bites like a snake
and poisons like a viper.
³³Your eyes will see strange
sights,
and your mind will imagine
confusing things.
³⁴You will be like one sleeping
on the high seas,
lying on top of the rigging.
³⁵"They hit me," you will say,
"but I'm not hurt!
They beat me, but I don't
feel it!

When will I wake up
so I can find another
drink?"   Pr 20:1

Saying 20

24 Do not envy the wicked,
do not desire their
company;
²for their hearts plot violence,
and their lips talk about
making trouble.   Ps 10:7

Saying 21

³By wisdom a house is built,
and through understanding
it is established;
⁴through knowledge its rooms
are filled
with rare and beautiful
treasures.   Pr 8:21

Saying 22

⁵The wise prevail through
great power,
and those who have
knowledge muster their
strength.
⁶Surely you need guidance to
wage war,
and victory is won through
many advisers.   Pr 11:14

Saying 23

⁷Wisdom is too high for fools;
in the assembly at the gate
they must not open
their mouths.

Saying 24

⁸Whoever plots evil
will be known as a schemer.

⁹The schemes of folly are sin,
and people detest a mocker.

Saying 25

¹⁰If you falter in a time of trouble,
how small is your strength!
¹¹Rescue those being led away
to death;
hold back those staggering
toward slaughter. Ps 82:4
¹²If you say, "But we knew
nothing about this,"
does not he who weighs the
heart perceive it? Pr 21:2
Does not he who guards your
life know it?
Will he not repay everyone
according to what they
have done? Ro 2:6

Saying 26

¹³Eat honey, my son, for it is
good;
honey from the comb is
sweet to your taste.
¹⁴Know also that wisdom is like
honey for you:
If you find it, there is a
future hope for you,
and your hope will not be
cut off. Ps 119:103; Pr 16:24

Saying 27

¹⁵Do not lurk like a thief near
the house of the
righteous,
do not plunder their
dwelling place;
¹⁶for though the righteous fall
seven times, they rise
again,

but the wicked stumble
when calamity strikes.

Saying 28

¹⁷Do not gloat when your
enemy falls; Ob 12
when they stumble, do not
let your heart rejoice,
¹⁸or the LORD will see and
disapprove
and turn his wrath away
from them. Job 31:29

Saying 29

¹⁹Do not fret because of
evildoers Ps 37:1
or be envious of the wicked,
²⁰for the evildoer has no future
hope,
and the lamp of the wicked
will be snuffed out.

Saying 30

²¹Fear the LORD and the king,
my son, Ro 13:1-5; 1Pe 2:17
and do not join with
rebellious officials,
²²for those two will send sudden
destruction on them,
and who knows what
calamities they can
bring?

Further Sayings of the Wise

²³These also are sayings of the
wise: Pr 1:6

To show partiality in judging
is not good: Lev 19:15
²⁴Whoever says to the guilty,
"You are innocent,"

will be cursed by peoples
and denounced by
nations.
²⁵ But it will go well with those
who convict the
guilty,
and rich blessing will come
on them.

²⁶ An honest answer
is like a kiss on the lips.

²⁷ Put your outdoor work in
order
and get your fields ready;
after that, build your house.

²⁸ Do not testify against your
neighbor without
cause —   Eph 4:25
would you use your lips to
mislead?
²⁹ Do not say, "I'll do to them as
they have done to me;
I'll pay them back for what
they did."   Pr 20:22; Mt 5:38

³⁰ I went past the field of a
sluggard,   Pr 6:6-11
past the vineyard of
someone who has no
sense;
³¹ thorns had come up
everywhere,
the ground was covered
with weeds,
and the stone wall was in
ruins.
³² I applied my heart to what I
observed
and learned a lesson from
what I saw:
³³ A little sleep, a little slumber,

a little folding of the hands
to rest —   Pr 6:10
³⁴ and poverty will come on you
like a thief
and scarcity like an armed
man.   Pr 10:4; Ecc 10:18

More Proverbs of Solomon

25 These are more proverbs
of Solomon, compiled by
the men of Hezekiah king of Judah: 1Ki 4:32; Pr 1:1

² It is the glory of God to
conceal a matter;
to search out a matter is the
glory of kings.   Pr 16:10-15
³ As the heavens are high and
the earth is deep,
so the hearts of kings are
unsearchable.

⁴ Remove the dross from the
silver,
and a silversmith can
produce a vessel;
⁵ remove wicked officials from
the king's presence,
and his throne will be
established through
righteousness.   Pr 16:12

⁶ Do not exalt yourself in the
king's presence,
and do not claim a place
among his great men;
⁷ it is better for him to say to
you, "Come up here,"
than for him to humiliate
you before his nobles.

What you have seen with your
eyes

⁸ do not bring[a] hastily to
court,
for what will you do in the end
if your neighbor puts you to
shame?   Mt 5:25-26

⁹ If you take your neighbor to
court,
do not betray another's
confidence,
¹⁰ or the one who hears it may
shame you
and the charge against you
will stand.

¹¹ Like apples[b] of gold in settings
of silver   Pr 15:23
is a ruling rightly given.
¹² Like an earring of gold or an
ornament of fine gold
is the rebuke of a wise judge
to a listening ear. Pr 15:31

¹³ Like a snow-cooled drink at
harvest time
is a trustworthy messenger
to the one who sends
him;
he refreshes the spirit of his
master.   Pr 13:17
¹⁴ Like clouds and wind without
rain
is one who boasts of gifts
never given.

¹⁵ Through patience a ruler can
be persuaded,   Ecc 10:4
and a gentle tongue can
break a bone.   Pr 15:1

¹⁶ If you find honey, eat just
enough —

too much of it, and you will
vomit.   ver 27
¹⁷ Seldom set foot in your
neighbor's house —
too much of you, and they
will hate you.

¹⁸ Like a club or a sword or a
sharp arrow
is one who gives false
testimony against a
neighbor.   Pr 12:18
¹⁹ Like a broken tooth or a lame
foot
is reliance on the unfaithful
in a time of trouble.
²⁰ Like one who takes away a
garment on a cold day,
or like vinegar poured on a
wound,
is one who sings songs to a
heavy heart.

²¹ If your enemy is hungry, give
him food to eat;
if he is thirsty, give him
water to drink.
²² In doing this, you will heap
burning coals on his
head,   Ps 18:8
and the LORD will reward
you.   2Sa 16:12; Ro 12:20

²³ Like a north wind that brings
unexpected rain
is a sly tongue — which
provokes a horrified
look.

²⁴ Better to live on a corner of
the roof

---

than share a house with a
quarrelsome wife. Pr 21:9

²⁵Like cold water to a weary
soul
is good news from a distant
land. Pr 15:30

²⁶Like a muddied spring or a
polluted well
are the righteous who give
way to the wicked.

²⁷It is not good to eat too much
honey, ver 16
nor is it honorable to search
out matters that are too
deep. Pr 27:2

²⁸Like a city whose walls are
broken through
is a person who lacks self-
control.

26 Like snow in summer or
rain in harvest, 1Sa 12:17
honor is not fitting for a
fool. Pr 19:10

²Like a fluttering sparrow or a
darting swallow,
an undeserved curse does
not come to rest. Dt 23:5

³A whip for the horse, a bridle
for the donkey, Ps 32:9
and a rod for the backs of
fools! Pr 10:13

⁴Do not answer a fool
according to his folly,
or you yourself will be just
like him. ver 5; Isa 36:21

⁵Answer a fool according to his
folly,
or he will be wise in his own
eyes. ver 4; Pr 3:7

⁶Sending a message by the
hands of a fool Pr 10:26
is like cutting off one's feet
or drinking poison.

⁷Like the useless legs of one
who is lame
is a proverb in the mouth of
a fool. ver 9

⁸Like tying a stone in a sling
is the giving of honor to a
fool. ver 1

⁹Like a thornbush in a
drunkard's hand
is a proverb in the mouth of
a fool. ver 7

¹⁰Like an archer who wounds at
random
is one who hires a fool or
any passer-by.

¹¹As a dog returns to its vomit,
so fools repeat their folly.

¹²Do you see a person wise in
their own eyes? Pr 3:7
There is more hope for a
fool than for them.

¹³A sluggard says, "There's a
lion in the road, Pr 6:6-11
a fierce lion roaming the
streets!" Pr 22:13

¹⁴As a door turns on its hinges,
so a sluggard turns on his
bed. Pr 6:9

¹⁵A sluggard buries his hand in
the dish;
he is too lazy to bring it back
to his mouth. Pr 19:24

¹⁶A sluggard is wiser in his own
eyes
than seven people who
answer discreetly.

¹⁷Like one who grabs a stray
    dog by the ears
      is someone who rushes into
        a quarrel not their own.

¹⁸Like a maniac shooting
    flaming arrows of death
¹⁹is one who deceives their
    neighbor
      and says, "I was only joking!"

²⁰Without wood a fire goes out;
    without a gossip a quarrel
      dies down.   Pr 22:10
²¹As charcoal to embers and as
    wood to fire,
      so is a quarrelsome person
        for kindling strife. Pr 15:18
²²The words of a gossip are like
    choice morsels;
      they go down to the inmost
        parts.   Pr 18:8

²³Like a coating of silver dross
    on earthenware
      are fervent*a* lips with an evil
        heart.
²⁴Enemies disguise themselves
    with their lips,   Ps 31:18
      but in their hearts they
        harbor deceit.   Ps 41:6
²⁵Though their speech is
    charming, do not
      believe them,   Ps 28:3
    for seven abominations fill
      their hearts.   Jer 9:4-8
²⁶Their malice may be
    concealed by deception,
      but their wickedness will
        be exposed in the
        assembly.

²⁷Whoever digs a pit will fall
    into it;   Ps 7:15; Est 6:13
    if someone rolls a stone, it
      will roll back on them.
²⁸A lying tongue hates those it
    hurts,
      and a flattering mouth
        works ruin.   Pr 29:5

27 Do not boast about
    tomorrow,   1Ki 20:11
    for you do not know what a
      day may bring. Lk 12:19-20

²Let someone else praise you,
    and not your own
      mouth;
    an outsider, and not your
      own lips.   Pr 25:27

³Stone is heavy and sand a
    burden,   Job 6:3
    but a fool's provocation is
      heavier than both.

⁴Anger is cruel and fury
    overwhelming,
      but who can stand before
        jealousy?   Nu 5:14

⁵Better is open rebuke
    than hidden love.

⁶Wounds from a friend can be
    trusted,
      but an enemy multiplies
        kisses.   Ps 141:5

⁷One who is full loathes honey
    from the comb,
      but to the hungry even what
      is bitter tastes sweet.

⁸Like a bird that flees its nest

a 23 Hebrew; Septuagint *smooth*

is anyone who flees from
   home.

⁹Perfume and incense bring
   joy to the heart,   Est 2:12
and the pleasantness of a
   friend
springs from their heartfelt
   advice.

¹⁰Do not forsake your friend or
   a friend of your family,
and do not go to your
   relative's house when
   disaster strikes you—
better a neighbor nearby
   than a relative far away.

¹¹Be wise, my son, and bring joy
   to my heart;   Pr 10:1; 23:15-16
then I can answer anyone
   who treats me with
   contempt.   Ge 24:60

¹²The prudent see danger and
   take refuge,
but the simple keep going
   and pay the penalty.

¹³Take the garment of one who
   puts up security for a
   stranger;
hold it in pledge if it is done
   for an outsider.   Pr 20:16

¹⁴If anyone loudly blesses their
   neighbor early in the
   morning,
it will be taken as a curse.

¹⁵A quarrelsome wife is like the
   dripping
of a leaky roof in a rainstorm;

¹⁶restraining her is like
   restraining the wind
or grasping oil with the hand.

¹⁷As iron sharpens iron,
   so one person sharpens
   another.

¹⁸The one who guards a fig tree
   will eat its fruit,   1Co 9:7
and whoever protects their
   master will be honored.

¹⁹As water reflects the face,
   so one's life reflects the
   heart.ᵃ

²⁰Death and Destructionᵇ are
   never satisfied,   Hab 2:5
and neither are human eyes.

²¹The crucible for silver and the
   furnace for gold,   Pr 17:3
but people are tested by
   their praise.

²²Though you grind a fool in a
   mortar,
grinding them like grain
   with a pestle,
you will not remove their
   folly from them.

²³Be sure you know the
   condition of your flocks,
give careful attention to
   your herds;
²⁴for riches do not endure
   forever,   Pr 23:5
and a crown is not secure
   for all generations.
²⁵When the hay is removed and
   new growth appears

ᵃ 19 Or *so others reflect your heart back to you*   ᵇ 20 Hebrew *Abaddon*

and the grass from the hills
is gathered in,
26 the lambs will provide you
with clothing,
and the goats with the price
of a field.
27 You will have plenty of goats'
milk to feed your family
and to nourish your female
servants.

28 The wicked flee though
no one pursues, Lev 26:17
but the righteous are as
bold as a lion. Ps 138:3

2 When a country is rebellious,
it has many rulers,
but a ruler with
discernment and
knowledge maintains
order.

3 A ruler*a* who oppresses the
poor
is like a driving rain that
leaves no crops.

4 Those who forsake instruction
praise the wicked,
but those who heed it resist
them.

5 Evildoers do not understand
what is right,
but those who seek the
LORD understand it
fully.

6 Better the poor whose walk is
blameless
than the rich whose ways
are perverse. Pr 19:1

7 A discerning son heeds
instruction,
but a companion of gluttons
disgraces his father.

8 Whoever increases wealth by
taking interest or profit
from the poor Ex 18:21
amasses it for another,
who will be kind to the
poor. Pr 13:22; Lk 14:12-14

9 If anyone turns a deaf ear to
my instruction,
even their prayers are
detestable. Ps 66:18; 109:7

10 Whoever leads the upright
along an evil path
will fall into their own trap,
but the blameless will receive
a good inheritance.

11 The rich are wise in their own
eyes;
one who is poor and
discerning sees how
deluded they are.

12 When the righteous triumph,
there is great elation;
but when the wicked rise to
power, people go into
hiding. Pr 11:10

13 Whoever conceals their sins
does not prosper, Job 31:33
but the one who confesses
and renounces them
finds mercy. Ps 32:1-5

14 Blessed is the one who always
trembles before God,

---

a 3 Or *A poor person*

but whoever hardens their
   heart falls into trouble.

15 Like a roaring lion or a
   charging bear
is a wicked ruler over a
   helpless people.

16 A tyrannical ruler practices
   extortion,
but one who hates ill-gotten
   gain will enjoy a long
   reign.

17 Anyone tormented by the
   guilt of murder
will seek refuge in the
   grave;   Ge 9:6
let no one hold them back.

18 The one whose walk is
   blameless is kept safe,
but the one whose ways are
   perverse will fall into
   the pit.*a*   Pr 10:9

19 Those who work their land will
   have abundant food,
but those who chase
   fantasies will have their
   fill of poverty.   Pr 12:11

20 A faithful person will be richly
   blessed,
but one eager to get rich will
   not go unpunished.

21 To show partiality is not
   good —   Pr 18:5
yet a person will do wrong
   for a piece of bread.

22 The stingy are eager to get
   rich

and are unaware that
   poverty awaits them.

23 Whoever rebukes a person
   will in the end gain
   favor
rather than one who has a
   flattering tongue. Pr 27:5-6

24 Whoever robs their father or
   mother   Pr 19:26
and says, "It's not wrong,"
is partner to one who
   destroys.   Pr 18:9

25 The greedy stir up conflict,
but those who trust in the
   Lord will prosper.

26 Those who trust in
   themselves are fools,
but those who walk in
   wisdom are kept
   safe.   1Co 3:18

27 Those who give to the poor
   will lack nothing,   Dt 24:19
but those who close their
   eyes to them receive
   many curses.   Ps 109:17

28 When the wicked rise to
   power, people go into
   hiding;   ver 12
but when the wicked perish,
   the righteous thrive.

29 Whoever remains stiff-
   necked after many
   rebukes   Ex 32:9
will suddenly be
   destroyed — without
   remedy.   2Ch 36:16; Pr 6:15

a 18 Syriac (see Septuagint); Hebrew *into one*

²When the righteous thrive,
 the people rejoice; Est 8:15
 when the wicked rule, the
 people groan. Pr 28:12

³A man who loves wisdom
 brings joy to his
 father, Pr 10:1
 but a companion of
 prostitutes squanders
 his wealth. Pr 5:8-10; Lk 15:11

⁴By justice a king gives a
 country stability, Pr 8:15-16
 but those who are greedy
 for*ᵃ* bribes tear it down.

⁵Those who flatter their
 neighbors
 are spreading nets for their
 feet. Pr 26:28

⁶Evildoers are snared by their
 own sin, Ecc 9:12
 but the righteous shout for
 joy and are glad.

⁷The righteous care about
 justice for the poor,
 but the wicked have no such
 concern.

⁸Mockers stir up a city,
 but the wise turn away
 anger. Pr 11:11; 16:14

⁹If a wise person goes to court
 with a fool,
 the fool rages and scoffs,
 and there is no peace.

¹⁰The bloodthirsty hate a
 person of integrity
 and seek to kill the upright.

¹¹Fools give full vent to their
 rage, Job 15:13
 but the wise bring calm in
 the end. Pr 12:16

¹²If a ruler listens to lies, 2Ki 21:9
 all his officials become
 wicked. Job 34:30

¹³The poor and the oppressor
 have this in common:
 The Lᴏʀᴅ gives sight to the
 eyes of both. Pr 22:2; Mt 5:45

¹⁴If a king judges the poor with
 fairness,
 his throne will be
 established forever.

¹⁵A rod and a reprimand impart
 wisdom,
 but a child left
 undisciplined disgraces
 its mother. Pr 13:24

¹⁶When the wicked thrive, so
 does sin,
 but the righteous will see
 their downfall. Ps 37:35

¹⁷Discipline your children,
 and they will give you
 peace;
 they will bring you the
 delights you desire.

¹⁸Where there is no revelation,
 people cast off restraint;
 but blessed is the one
 who heeds wisdom's
 instruction. Ps 1:1-2; 119:1-2

¹⁹Servants cannot be corrected
 by mere words;

ᵃ 4 Or *who give*

though they understand,
    they will not
    respond.

²⁰Do you see someone who
    speaks in haste?
    There is more hope for a
    fool than for them.

²¹A servant pampered from
    youth
    will turn out to be
    insolent.

²²An angry person stirs up
    conflict,
    and a hot-tempered person
    commits many sins.

²³Pride brings a person low,
    but the lowly in spirit gain
    honor.   Pr 11:2; Isa 66:2

²⁴The accomplices of thieves
    are their own
    enemies;
    they are put under oath and
    dare not testify.   Lev 5:1

²⁵Fear of man will prove to be a
    snare,   1Sa 15:24
    but whoever trusts in the
    Lord is kept safe.   Pr 28:25

²⁶Many seek an audience with a
    ruler,   Pr 19:6
    but it is from the Lord that
    one gets justice.   Pr 16:33

²⁷The righteous detest the
    dishonest;
    the wicked detest the
    upright.   ver 10

Sayings of Agur

30 The sayings of Agur son
    of Jakeh — an inspired ut-
terance.   Pr 22:17

This man's utterance to Ithiel:

"I am weary, God,
    but I can prevail.ᵃ
²Surely I am only a brute, not a
    man;
    I do not have human
    understanding.
³I have not learned wisdom,
    nor have I attained to the
    knowledge of the Holy
    One.   Pr 9:10
⁴Who has gone up to heaven
    and come down?   Ps 24:1-2
    Whose hands have gathered
    up the wind?   Isa 40:12
Who has wrapped up the
    waters in a cloak?   Ge 1:2
Who has established all the
    ends of the earth?
What is his name, and what
    is the name of his
    son?   Rev 19:12
    Surely you know!

⁵"Every word of God is
    flawless;   Ps 12:6; 18:30
    he is a shield to those who
    take refuge in him.
⁶Do not add to his words,   Dt 4:2
    or he will rebuke you and
    prove you a liar.

⁷"Two things I ask of you,
    Lord;

ᵃ 1 With a different word division of the Hebrew; Masoretic Text *utterance to Ithiel, / to Ithiel and Ukal:*

do not refuse me before I die:

⁸Keep falsehood and lies far
from me;
give me neither poverty nor
riches,
but give me only my daily
bread.   Mt 6:11
⁹Otherwise, I may have too
much and disown you
and say, 'Who is the LORD?'
Or I may become poor and
steal,
and so dishonor the name
of my God.   Dt 8:12

¹⁰"Do not slander a servant to
their master,
or they will curse you, and
you will pay for it.

¹¹"There are those who curse
their fathers
and do not bless their
mothers;   Pr 20:20
¹²those who are pure in their
own eyes   Lk 18:11
and yet are not cleansed of
their filth;   Jer 2:23,35
¹³those whose eyes are ever so
haughty,   Pr 6:17
whose glances are so
disdainful;
¹⁴those whose teeth are swords
and whose jaws are set with
knives   Ps 57:4
to devour the poor from the
earth   Ps 14:4; Am 8:4
and the needy from among
mankind.   Job 19:22

¹⁵"The leech has two daughters.
'Give! Give!' they cry.

"There are three things that
are never satisfied,
four that never say,
'Enough!':
¹⁶the grave, the barren womb,
land, which is never
satisfied with water,
and fire, which never says,
'Enough!'

¹⁷"The eye that mocks a father,
that scorns an aged mother,
will be pecked out by the
ravens of the valley,
will be eaten by the
vultures.   Job 15:23

¹⁸"There are three things that
are too amazing for me,
four that I do not
understand:
¹⁹the way of an eagle in the sky,
the way of a snake on a rock,
the way of a ship on the high
seas,
and the way of a man with a
young woman.

²⁰"This is the way of an
adulterous woman:
She eats and wipes her
mouth
and says, 'I've done nothing
wrong.'   Pr 5:6

²¹"Under three things the earth
trembles,
under four it cannot bear up:
²²a servant who becomes king,
a godless fool who gets
plenty to eat,
²³a contemptible woman who
gets married,

and a servant who displaces
  her mistress.
²⁴"Four things on earth are
  small,
  yet they are extremely wise:
²⁵Ants are creatures of little
  strength,
  yet they store up their food
  in the summer; Pr 6:6-8
²⁶hyraxes are creatures of little
  power, Ps 104:18
  yet they make their home in
  the crags;
²⁷locusts have no king, Ex 10:4
  yet they advance together in
  ranks;
²⁸a lizard can be caught with
  the hand,
  yet it is found in kings'
  palaces.
²⁹"There are three things that
  are stately in their
  stride,
  four that move with stately
  bearing:
³⁰a lion, mighty among beasts,
  who retreats before
  nothing;
³¹a strutting rooster, a he-goat,
  and a king secure against
  revolt.ᵃ
³²"If you play the fool and exalt
  yourself,
  or if you plan evil,
  clap your hand over your
  mouth! Job 21:5
³³For as churning cream
  produces butter,

and as twisting the nose
  produces blood,
  so stirring up anger
  produces strife."

Sayings of King Lemuel

31 The sayings of King Lemuel—an inspired utter-
ance his mother taught him.

²Listen, my son! Listen, son of
  my womb!
  Listen, my son, the answer
  to my prayers! Isa 49:15
³Do not spend your strengthᵇ
  on women,
  your vigor on those who ruin
  kings. Dt 17:17; Ne 13:26

⁴It is not for kings, Lemuel—
  it is not for kings to drink
  wine, Pr 20:1; Ecc 10:16-17
  not for rulers to crave beer,
⁵lest they drink and forget
  what has been
  decreed, 1Ki 16:9; Pr 16:12
  and deprive all the
  oppressed of their
  rights.
⁶Let beer be for those who are
  perishing,
  wine for those who are in
  anguish! Ge 14:18
⁷Let them drink and forget
  their poverty Est 1:10
  and remember their misery
  no more.
⁸Speak up for those who
  cannot speak for
  themselves, Job 29:12-17

ᵃ 31 The meaning of the Hebrew for this phrase is uncertain. ᵇ 3 Or *wealth*

for the rights of all who are
destitute.
⁹Speak up and judge fairly;
defend the rights of the poor
and needy. Lev 19:15; Isa 1:17

Epilogue: The Wife of Noble Character

¹⁰ᵃA wife of noble character
who can find? Ru 3:11
She is worth far more than
rubies.
¹¹Her husband has full
confidence in her Ge 2:18
and lacks nothing of value.
¹²She brings him good, not
harm,
all the days of her life.
¹³She selects wool and flax
and works with eager hands.
¹⁴She is like the merchant ships,
bringing her food from afar.
¹⁵She gets up while it is still
night;
she provides food for her
family
and portions for her female
servants.
¹⁶She considers a field and
buys it;
out of her earnings she
plants a vineyard.
¹⁷She sets about her work
vigorously;
her arms are strong for her
tasks.
¹⁸She sees that her trading is
profitable,

and her lamp does not go
out at night.
¹⁹In her hand she holds the
distaff
and grasps the spindle with
her fingers.
²⁰She opens her arms to the
poor
and extends her hands to
the needy. Dt 15:11; Eph 4:28
²¹When it snows, she has no
fear for her household;
for all of them are clothed in
scarlet.
²²She makes coverings for her
bed;
she is clothed in fine linen
and purple.
²³Her husband is respected at
the city gate,
where he takes his seat
among the elders of the
land. Ru 4:1,11; Pr 12:4
²⁴She makes linen garments
and sells them,
and supplies the merchants
with sashes.
²⁵She is clothed with strength
and dignity;
she can laugh at the days to
come.
²⁶She speaks with wisdom,
and faithful instruction is
on her tongue. Pr 10:31
²⁷She watches over the affairs of
her household
and does not eat the bread
of idleness.

ᵃ 10 Verses 10-31 are an acrostic poem, the verses of which begin with the successive letters of the Hebrew alphabet.

28 Her children arise and call
    her blessed;
  her husband also, and he
    praises her:
29 "Many women do noble
    things,
  but you surpass them
    all."

30 Charm is deceptive, and
    beauty is fleeting;
  but a woman who fears the
    LORD is to be praised.
31 Honor her for all that her
    hands have done,
  and let her works bring her
    praise at the city gate.

Ecclesiastes

Everything Is Meaningless

1 The words of the Teacher,^a son of David, king in Jerusalem: Pr 1:1; Ecc 7:27

²"Meaningless! Meaningless!"
says the Teacher.
"Utterly meaningless!
Everything is meaningless."

³What do people gain from all
their labors
at which they toil under the
sun? Ecc 2:11,22
⁴Generations come and
generations go,
but the earth remains
forever. Ps 104:5; 119:90
⁵The sun rises and the sun sets,
and hurries back to where it
rises. Ps 19:5-6
⁶The wind blows to the south
and turns to the north;
round and round it goes,
ever returning on its course.
⁷All streams flow into the sea,
yet the sea is never full.
To the place the streams come
from,

there they return again.
⁸All things are wearisome,
more than one can say.
The eye never has enough of
seeing, Pr 27:20
nor the ear its fill of hearing.
⁹What has been will be again,
what has been done will be
done again; Ecc 3:15
there is nothing new under
the sun.
¹⁰Is there anything of which
one can say,
"Look! This is something
new"?
It was here already, long ago;
it was here before our time.
¹¹No one remembers the former
generations,
and even those yet to come
will not be remembered
by those who follow
them. Ecc 2:16

Wisdom Is Meaningless

¹²I, the Teacher, was king over
Israel in Jerusalem. ¹³I applied
my mind to study and to explore

^a 1 Or *the leader of the assembly*; also in verses 2 and 12

by wisdom all that is done under the heavens. What a heavy burden God has laid on mankind! ¹⁴I have seen all the things that are done under the sun; all of them are meaningless, a chasing after the wind. Ecc 3:10; 4:4

¹⁵What is crooked cannot be
straightened; Ecc 7:13
  what is lacking cannot be
  counted.

¹⁶I said to myself, "Look, I have increased in wisdom more than anyone who has ruled over Jerusalem before me; I have experienced much of wisdom and knowledge." ¹⁷Then I applied myself to the understanding of wisdom, and also of madness and folly, but I learned that this, too, is a chasing after the wind.

¹⁸For with much wisdom comes
much sorrow;
  the more knowledge, the
  more grief. Ecc 12:12

Pleasures Are Meaningless

2 I said to myself, "Come now, I will test you with pleasure to find out what is good." But that also proved to be meaningless. ²"Laughter," I said, "is madness. And what does pleasure accomplish?" ³I tried cheering myself with wine, and embracing folly — my mind still guiding me with wisdom. I wanted to see what was good for people to do

under the heavens during the few days of their lives. Ecc 1:17; 7:6

⁴I undertook great projects: I built houses for myself and planted vineyards. ⁵I made gardens and parks and planted all kinds of fruit trees in them. ⁶I made reservoirs to water groves of flourishing trees. ⁷I bought male and female slaves and had other slaves who were born in my house. I also owned more herds and flocks than anyone in Jerusalem before me. ⁸I amassed silver and gold for myself, and the treasure of kings and provinces. I acquired male and female singers, and a harem*ᵃ* as well — the delights of a man's heart. ⁹I became greater by far than anyone in Jerusalem before me. In all this my wisdom stayed with me. 1Ki 9:28; 10:10,14,21

¹⁰I denied myself nothing my
eyes desired;
  I refused my heart no
  pleasure.
My heart took delight in all
  my labor,
  and this was the reward for
  all my toil.
¹¹Yet when I surveyed all that
  my hands had done
and what I had toiled to
  achieve,
everything was meaningless,
  a chasing after the
  wind; Ecc 1:14
nothing was gained under
  the sun. Ecc 1:3

ᵃ 8 The meaning of the Hebrew for this phrase is uncertain.

Wisdom and Folly Are Meaningless

[12] Then I turned my thoughts to
   consider wisdom,
   and also madness and
   folly.   Ecc 1:17
What more can the king's
   successor do
than what has already been
   done?   Ecc 1:9
[13] I saw that wisdom is better
   than folly,   Ecc 7:11-12
just as light is better than
   darkness.
[14] The wise have eyes in their
   heads,
while the fool walks in the
   darkness;
but I came to realize
   that the same fate overtakes
   them both.   Ps 49:10; Ecc 9:3

[15] Then I said to myself,

"The fate of the fool will
   overtake me also.
What then do I gain by
   being wise?"   Ecc 6:8
I said to myself,
   "This too is meaningless."
[16] For the wise, like the fool,
   will not be long
   remembered;
the days have already come
   when both have been
   forgotten.   Ecc 1:11
Like the fool, the wise too
   must die!   Ps 49:10

Toil Is Meaningless

[17] So I hated life, because the
work that is done under the sun
was grievous to me. All of it is
meaningless, a chasing after the
wind. [18] I hated all the things I
had toiled for under the sun, because I must leave them to the
one who comes after me. [19] And
who knows whether that person
will be wise or foolish? Yet they
will have control over all the
fruit of my toil into which I have
poured my effort and skill under
the sun. This too is meaningless.
[20] So my heart began to despair
over all my toilsome labor under the sun. [21] For a person may
labor with wisdom, knowledge
and skill, and then they must
leave all they own to another
who has not toiled for it. This too
is meaningless and a great misfortune. [22] What do people get for
all the toil and anxious striving
with which they labor under the
sun? [23] All their days their work
is grief and pain; even at night
their minds do not rest. This too
is meaningless.   Job 5:7; Ecc 1:3,18

[24] A person can do nothing better than to eat and drink and find
satisfaction in their own toil. This
too, I see, is from the hand of God,
[25] for without him, who can eat
or find enjoyment? [26] To the person who pleases him, God gives
wisdom, knowledge and happiness, but to the sinner he gives
the task of gathering and storing
up wealth to hand it over to the
one who pleases God. This too is
meaningless, a chasing after the
wind.   Job 27:17; Pr 13:22; Ecc 3:12-13

A Time for Everything

3 There is a time for everything, ver 11,17; Ecc 8:6 and a season for every activity under the heavens:

2 a time to be born and a time to die,
  a time to plant and a time to uproot, Isa 28:24
3 a time to kill and a time to heal, Dt 5:17
  a time to tear down and a time to build,
4 a time to weep and a time to laugh,
  a time to mourn and a time to dance,
5 a time to scatter stones and a time to gather them,
  a time to embrace and a time to refrain from embracing,
6 a time to search and a time to give up,
  a time to keep and a time to throw away,
7 a time to tear and a time to mend,
  a time to be silent and a time to speak, Am 5:13
8 a time to love and a time to hate,
  a time for war and a time for peace.

9 What do workers gain from their toil? 10 I have seen the burden God has laid on the human race. 11 He has made everything beau-tiful in its time. He has also set eternity in the human heart; yet[a] no one can fathom what God has done from beginning to end. 12 I know that there is nothing better for people than to be happy and to do good while they live. 13 That each of them may eat and drink, and find satisfaction in all their toil—this is the gift of God. 14 I know that everything God does will endure forever; nothing can be added to it and nothing taken from it. God does it so that people will fear him. Ro 11:33; Jas 1:17; Ecc 2:24

15 Whatever is has already been, and what will be has been before; Ecc 1:9
  and God will call the past to account.[b]

16 And I saw something else under the sun:

In the place of judgment—wickedness was there,
in the place of justice—wickedness was there.

17 I said to myself,

"God will bring into judgment both the righteous and the wicked,
for there will be a time for every activity,
  a time to judge every deed."

18 I also said to myself, "As for humans, God tests them so that they may see that they are like the animals. 19 Surely the fate of

---

a 11 Or *also placed ignorance in the human heart, so that*   b 15 Or *God calls back the past* human beings is like that of the animals; the same fate awaits them both: As one dies, so dies the other. All have the same breath*a*; humans have no advantage over animals. Everything is meaningless. 20All go to the same place; all come from dust, and to dust all return. 21Who knows if the human spirit rises upward and if the spirit of the animal goes down into the earth?"   Ps 73:22; Ge 3:19; Ecc 12:7

22So I saw that there is nothing better for a person than to enjoy their work, because that is their lot. For who can bring them to see what will happen after them?   Job 31:2; Ecc 2:24; 5:18

Oppression, Toil, Friendlessness

4 Again I looked and saw all the oppression that was taking place under the sun: Ps 12:5

I saw the tears of the
    oppressed—
and they have no comforter;
power was on the side of their
    oppressors—
and they have no comforter.
2And I declared that the
    dead,   Jer 20:17-18; 22:10
who had already died,
are happier than the living,
    who are still alive.   Job 3:17
3But better than both
    is the one who has never
        been born,   Job 3:16; Ecc 6:3
who has not seen the evil
    that is done under the sun.

4And I saw that all toil and all achievement spring from one person's envy of another. This too is meaningless, a chasing after the wind.   Ecc 1:14

5Fools fold their hands   Pr 6:10
    and ruin themselves.
6Better one handful with
    tranquillity
    than two handfuls with
        toil   Pr 15:16-17; 16:8
    and chasing after the wind.

7Again I saw something meaningless under the sun:

8There was a man all alone;
    he had neither son nor
        brother.
There was no end to his toil,
    yet his eyes were not
        content with his wealth.
"For whom am I toiling," he
    asked,
"and why am I depriving
    myself of enjoyment?"
This too is meaningless—
    a miserable business!

9Two are better than one,
    because they have a good
        return for their labor:
10If either of them falls down,
    one can help the other up.
But pity anyone who falls
    and has no one to help
        them up.
11Also, if two lie down together,
    they will keep warm.
But how can one keep warm
    alone?

---

a 19 Or *spirit*

¹²Though one may be
overpowered,
two can defend themselves.
A cord of three strands is not
quickly broken.

Advancement Is Meaningless

¹³Better a poor but wise youth
than an old but foolish king who
no longer knows how to heed a
warning. ¹⁴The youth may have
come from prison to the kingship,
or he may have been born in poverty within his kingdom. ¹⁵I saw
that all who lived and walked under the sun followed the youth,
the king's successor. ¹⁶There was
no end to all the people who were
before them. But those who came
later were not pleased with the
successor. This too is meaningless, a chasing after the wind.

Fulfill Your Vow to God

5^a Guard your steps when you
go to the house of God. Go
near to listen rather than to offer
the sacrifice of fools, who do not
know that they do wrong.

²Do not be quick with your
mouth,
do not be hasty in your
heart
to utter anything before
God.   Jdg 11:35
God is in heaven
and you are on earth,
so let your words be
few.   Pr 10:19; 20:25

³A dream comes when there
are many cares,   Job 20:8
and many words mark the
speech of a fool.   Ecc 10:14

⁴When you make a vow to God,
do not delay to fulfill it. He has
no pleasure in fools; fulfill your
vow. ⁵It is better not to make a
vow than to make one and not
fulfill it. ⁶Do not let your mouth
lead you into sin. And do not protest to the temple messenger, "My
vow was a mistake." Why should
God be angry at what you say and
destroy the work of your hands?
⁷Much dreaming and many
words are meaningless. Therefore fear God.   Pr 20:25; Ac 5:4

Riches Are Meaningless

⁸If you see the poor oppressed
in a district, and justice and rights
denied, do not be surprised at
such things; for one official is eyed
by a higher one, and over them
both are others higher still. ⁹The
increase from the land is taken by
all; the king himself profits from
the fields.   Ps 12:5; Ecc 4:1

¹⁰Whoever loves money never
has enough;
whoever loves wealth is
never satisfied with
their income.
This too is meaningless.
¹¹As goods increase,
so do those who consume
them.

^a In Hebrew texts 5:1 is numbered 4:17, and 5:2-20 is numbered 5:1-19.

And what benefit are they to
   the owners
     except to feast their eyes on
     them?

[12] The sleep of a laborer is sweet,
   whether they eat little or
     much,
but as for the rich, their
   abundance
     permits them no sleep.

[13] I have seen a grievous evil
under the sun: Ecc 6:1-2

   wealth hoarded to the harm
     of its owners,
[14] or wealth lost through some
     misfortune,
so that when they have
   children
     there is nothing left for
     them to inherit.
[15] Everyone comes naked from
     their mother's womb,
   and as everyone comes, so
     they depart.   Job 1:21
They take nothing from their
   toil   Ps 49:17; 1Ti 6:7
   that they can carry in their
     hands.   Ecc 1:3

[16] This too is a grievous evil:

As everyone comes, so they
   depart,
   and what do they gain,
   since they toil for the
     wind?   Pr 11:29; Ecc 1:3
[17] All their days they eat in
   darkness,
   with great frustration,
     affliction and anger.

[18] This is what I have observed to be good: that it is appropriate for a person to eat, to drink and to find satisfaction in their toilsome labor under the sun during the few days of life God has given them—for this is their lot. [19] Moreover, when God gives someone wealth and possessions, and the ability to enjoy them, to accept their lot and be happy in their toil—this is a gift of God. [20] They seldom reflect on the days of their life, because God keeps them occupied with gladness of heart.   Dt 12:7,18; Ecc 2:24; 3:13

6 I have seen another evil under the sun, and it weighs heavily on mankind: [2] God gives some people wealth, possessions and honor, so that they lack nothing their hearts desire, but God does not grant them the ability to enjoy them, and strangers enjoy them instead. This is meaningless, a grievous evil.   Ps 17:14; Ecc 5:13,19

[3] A man may have a hundred children and live many years; yet no matter how long he lives, if he cannot enjoy his prosperity and does not receive proper burial, I say that a stillborn child is better off than he. [4] It comes without meaning, it departs in darkness, and in darkness its name is shrouded. [5] Though it never saw the sun or knew anything, it has more rest than does that man— [6] even if he lives a thousand years twice over but fails to enjoy his

prosperity. Do not all go to the same place? Job 3:16; Ecc 4:3

⁷Everyone's toil is for their
   mouth,
   yet their appetite is never
      satisfied. Pr 16:26; 27:20
⁸What advantage have the wise
      over fools? Ecc 2:15
What do the poor gain
   by knowing how to conduct
      themselves before
      others?
⁹Better what the eye sees
   than the roving of the
      appetite.
This too is meaningless,
   a chasing after the wind.

¹⁰Whatever exists has already
      been named, Ecc 3:15
   and what humanity is has
      been known;
no one can contend
   with someone who is
      stronger.
¹¹The more the words,
   the less the meaning,
   and how does that profit
      anyone?

¹²For who knows what is good
for a person in life, during the few
and meaningless days they pass
through like a shadow? Who can
tell them what will happen under
the sun after they are gone? Ps 39:6

Wisdom

7 A good name is better than
   fine perfume, Ps 22:1; SS 1:3
   and the day of death better
      than the day of birth.

²It is better to go to a house of
      mourning
   than to go to a house of
      feasting,
   for death is the destiny of
      everyone; Ps 90:12; Pr 11:19
   the living should take this
      to heart.
³Frustration is better than
      laughter, Pr 14:13
   because a sad face is good
      for the heart.
⁴The heart of the wise is in the
      house of mourning,
   but the heart of fools is in
      the house of pleasure.
⁵It is better to heed the rebuke
      of a wise person Ps 141:5
   than to listen to the song of
      fools.
⁶Like the crackling of thorns
      under the pot, Ps 58:9
   so is the laughter of fools.
   This too is meaningless.

⁷Extortion turns a wise person
      into a fool,
   and a bribe corrupts the
      heart. Ex 23:8; Dt 16:19
⁸The end of a matter is better
      than its beginning,
   and patience is better than
      pride. Pr 14:29; Gal 5:22
⁹Do not be quickly provoked in
      your spirit, Pr 14:17; Jas 1:19
   for anger resides in the lap
      of fools. Pr 14:29

¹⁰Do not say, "Why were the old
      days better than these?"
   For it is not wise to ask such
      questions.

[11] Wisdom, like an inheritance,
 is a good thing   Pr 8:10-11
 and benefits those who see
 the sun.   Ecc 11:7
[12] Wisdom is a shelter
 as money is a shelter,
 but the advantage of
 knowledge is this:
 Wisdom preserves those
 who have it.

[13] Consider what God has done:

Who can straighten
 what he has made crooked?
[14] When times are good, be
 happy;
 but when times are bad,
 consider this:
God has made the one
 as well as the other.   Job 1:21
Therefore, no one can
 discover
 anything about their future.

[15] In this meaningless life of
mine I have seen both of these:

the righteous perishing in
 their righteousness,
 and the wicked living long
 in their wickedness.
[16] Do not be overrighteous,
 neither be overwise —
 why destroy yourself?
[17] Do not be overwicked,
 and do not be a fool —
 why die before your time?
[18] It is good to grasp the one
 and not let go of the other.
 Whoever fears God will
 avoid all extremes.[a]

[19] Wisdom makes one wise
 person more powerful
 than ten rulers in a city.

[20] Indeed, there is no one on
 earth who is righteous,
 no one who does what is
 right and never sins.

[21] Do not pay attention to every
 word people say,
 or you may hear your
 servant cursing you —
[22] for you know in your heart
 that many times you
 yourself have cursed
 others.

[23] All this I tested by wisdom
and I said,

"I am determined to be
 wise" —   Ecc 1:17; Ro 1:22
 but this was beyond me.
[24] Whatever exists is far off and
 most profound —
 who can discover it?   Job 28:12
[25] So I turned my mind to
 understand,
 to investigate and to search
 out wisdom and the
 scheme of things   Job 28:3
and to understand the
 stupidity of wickedness
 and the madness of folly.

[26] I find more bitter than death
 the woman who is a snare,
 whose heart is a trap
 and whose hands are chains.
The man who pleases God
 will escape her,

---

[a] 18 Or *will follow them both*

but the sinner she will
ensnare. Pr 5:3-5; 7:23; 22:14

²⁷ "Look," says the Teacher,ᵃ
"this is what I have discovered:

"Adding one thing to another
  to discover the scheme
  of things —
²⁸ while I was still searching
  but not finding —
I found one upright man
  among a thousand,
  but not one upright woman
  among them all. 1Ki 11:3
²⁹ This only have I found:
God created mankind
  upright,
  but they have gone in
  search of many
  schemes."

8 Who is like the wise?
  Who knows the explanation
    of things?
  A person's wisdom brightens
    their face
  and changes its hard
    appearance.

Obey the King

²Obey the king's command,
I say, because you took an oath
before God. ³Do not be in a hurry
to leave the king's presence. Do
not stand up for a bad cause, for
he will do whatever he pleases.
⁴Since a king's word is supreme,
who can say to him, "What are
you doing?" Job 9:12; Est 1:19; Da 4:35

⁵Whoever obeys his command
  will come to no harm,
  and the wise heart will
    know the proper time
    and procedure.
⁶For there is a proper time and
  procedure for every
  matter, Ecc 3:1
  though a person may be
  weighed down by
  misery.
⁷Since no one knows the future,
  who can tell someone else
    what is to come?
⁸As no one has power over the
    wind to contain it,
  soᵇ no one has power over
    the time of their death.
As no one is discharged in
    time of war,
  so wickedness will not
    release those who
    practice it.

⁹All this I saw, as I applied my
mind to everything done under
the sun. There is a time when a
man lords it over others to his
ownᶜ hurt. ¹⁰Then too, I saw the
wicked buried — those who used
to come and go from the holy
place and receive praiseᵈ in the
city where they did this. This too
is meaningless. Ecc 1:11
¹¹When the sentence for a
crime is not quickly carried out,
people's hearts are filled with
schemes to do wrong. ¹²Although

ᵃ 27 Or the leader of the assembly   ᵇ 8 Or over the human spirit to retain it, / and so
ᶜ 9 Or to their   ᵈ 10 Some Hebrew manuscripts and Septuagint (Aquila); most Hebrew
manuscripts and are forgotten

a wicked person who commits a hundred crimes may live a long time, I know that it will go better with those who fear God, who are reverent before him. [13] Yet because the wicked do not fear God, it will not go well with them, and their days will not lengthen like a shadow. Dt 4:40; Isa 3:11

[14] There is something else meaningless that occurs on earth: the righteous who get what the wicked deserve, and the wicked who get what the righteous deserve. This too, I say, is meaningless. [15] So I commend the enjoyment of life, because there is nothing better for a person under the sun than to eat and drink and be glad. Then joy will accompany them in their toil all the days of the life God has given them under the sun. Ecc 2:24

[16] When I applied my mind to know wisdom and to observe the labor that is done on earth— people getting no sleep day or night— [17] then I saw all that God has done. No one can comprehend what goes on under the sun. Despite all their efforts to search it out, no one can discover its meaning. Even if the wise claim they know, they cannot really comprehend it. Ecc 3:11; Ro 11:33

A Common Destiny for All

9 So I reflected on all this and concluded that the righteous and the wise and what they do are in God's hands, but no one knows whether love or hate awaits them. [2] All share a common destiny—the righteous and the wicked, the good and the bad,[a] the clean and the unclean, those who offer sacrifices and those who do not. Dt 33:3; Ecc 10:14

As it is with the good,
　so with the sinful;
as it is with those who take
　　oaths,
　so with those who are afraid
　　to take them. Job 9:22

[3] This is the evil in everything that happens under the sun: The same destiny overtakes all. The hearts of people, moreover, are full of evil and there is madness in their hearts while they live, and afterward they join the dead. [4] Anyone who is among the living has hope[b]—even a live dog is better off than a dead lion! Job 21:26

[5] For the living know that they
　　will die,
　but the dead know nothing;
they have no further reward,
　and even their name is
　　forgotten. Ps 9:6; Ecc 1:11
[6] Their love, their hate
　and their jealousy have long
　　since vanished;
never again will they have a
　　part
　in anything that happens
　　under the sun. Job 21:21

---

[a] 2 Septuagint (Aquila), Vulgate and Syriac; Hebrew does not have *and the bad.*
[b] 4 Or *What then is to be chosen? With all who live, there is hope*

⁷Go, eat your food with gladness, and drink your wine with a joyful heart, for God has already approved what you do. ⁸Always be clothed in white, and always anoint your head with oil. ⁹Enjoy life with your wife, whom you love, all the days of this meaningless life that God has given you under the sun — all your meaningless days. For this is your lot in life and in your toilsome labor under the sun. ¹⁰Whatever your hand finds to do, do it with all your might, for in the realm of the dead, where you are going, there is neither working nor planning nor knowledge nor wisdom. 1Sa 10:7; Ecc 2:24; Ro 12:11

¹¹I have seen something else under the sun:

The race is not to the swift
or the battle to the strong,
nor does food come to the
wise Job 32:13; Jer 9:23
or wealth to the brilliant
or favor to the learned;
but time and chance happen
to them all. Dt 8:18; Ecc 2:14

¹²Moreover, no one knows when their hour will come:

As fish are caught in a cruel
net,
or birds are taken in a
snare,
so people are trapped by evil
times Pr 29:6
that fall unexpectedly upon
them. Ps 73:22; Ecc 8:7

Wisdom Better Than Folly

¹³I also saw under the sun this example of wisdom that greatly impressed me: ¹⁴There was once a small city with only a few people in it. And a powerful king came against it, surrounded it and built huge siege works against it. ¹⁵Now there lived in that city a man poor but wise, and he saved the city by his wisdom. But nobody remembered that poor man. ¹⁶So I said, "Wisdom is better than strength." But the poor man's wisdom is despised, and his words are no longer heeded. Pr 21:22; Ecc 7:19

¹⁷The quiet words of the wise
    are more to be heeded
    than the shouts of a ruler of
        fools.
¹⁸Wisdom is better than
    weapons of war, ver 16
but one sinner destroys
    much good.

10

As dead flies give
    perfume a bad smell,
so a little folly outweighs
    wisdom and honor.
²The heart of the wise inclines
    to the right,
but the heart of the fool to
    the left.
³Even as fools walk along the
    road,
    they lack sense
    and show everyone how
        stupid they are. Pr 13:16
⁴If a ruler's anger rises against
    you,

do not leave your post; Ecc 8:3
calmness can lay great
offenses to rest. Pr 25:15

5 There is an evil I have seen
     under the sun,
   the sort of error that arises
     from a ruler:
6 Fools are put in many high
     positions, Pr 29:2
   while the rich occupy the
     low ones.
7 I have seen slaves on
     horseback,
   while princes go on foot like
     slaves. Pr 19:10
8 Whoever digs a pit may fall
     into it; Ps 7:15; Pr 26:27
   whoever breaks through a
     wall may be bitten by a
     snake. Est 2:23; Ps 9:16
9 Whoever quarries stones may
     be injured by them;
   whoever splits logs may be
     endangered by them.

10 If the ax is dull
   and its edge unsharpened,
   more strength is needed,
   but skill will bring success.

11 If a snake bites before it is
     charmed,
   the charmer receives no fee.

12 Words from the mouth of the
     wise are gracious, Pr 10:32
   but fools are consumed by
     their own lips. Pr 10:14; 14:3
13 At the beginning their words
     are folly;

at the end they are wicked
     madness—
14 and fools multiply words.

   No one knows what is
     coming—
   who can tell someone else
     what will happen after
     them? Ecc 9:1
15 The toil of fools wearies them;
   they do not know the way to
     town.

16 Woe to the land whose king
     was a servant[a] Isa 3:4-5,12
   and whose princes feast in
     the morning.
17 Blessed is the land whose king
     is of noble birth
   and whose princes eat at a
     proper time—
   for strength and not for
     drunkenness. 1Sa 25:36
18 Through laziness, the rafters
     sag;
   because of idle hands, the
     house leaks. Pr 20:4; 24:30

19 A feast is made for laughter,
   wine makes life merry,
   and money is the answer for
     everything.

20 Do not revile the king even in
     your thoughts, Ex 22:28
   or curse the rich in your
     bedroom,
   because a bird in the sky may
     carry your words,
   and a bird on the wing may
     report what you say.

---

a 16 Or *king is a child*

Invest in Many Ventures

11 Ship your grain across the sea; ver 6; Isa 32:20
after many days you may receive a return. Pr 19:17; Mt 10:42
[2] Invest in seven ventures, yes, in eight;
you do not know what disaster may come upon the land.

[3] If clouds are full of water, they pour rain on the earth.
Whether a tree falls to the south or to the north,
in the place where it falls, there it will lie.
[4] Whoever watches the wind will not plant;
whoever looks at the clouds will not reap.

[5] As you do not know the path of the wind, Jn 3:8-10
or how the body is formed[a] in a mother's womb, Ps 139:14-16
so you cannot understand the work of God,
the Maker of all things.

[6] Sow your seed in the morning,
and at evening let your hands not be idle, Ecc 9:10
for you do not know which will succeed,
whether this or that,
or whether both will do equally well.

Remember Your Creator While Young

[7] Light is sweet,
and it pleases the eyes to see the sun. Ecc 7:11
[8] However many years anyone may live,
let them enjoy them all.
But let them remember the days of darkness, Ecc 12:1
for there will be many.
Everything to come is meaningless.

[9] You who are young, be happy while you are young,
and let your heart give you joy in the days of your youth.
Follow the ways of your heart and whatever your eyes see,
but know that for all these things
God will bring you into judgment. Ecc 12:14; Ro 14:10
[10] So then, banish anxiety from your heart Ps 94:19
and cast off the troubles of your body,
for youth and vigor are meaningless. Ecc 2:24

12 Remember your Creator in the days of your youth,
before the days of trouble come
and the years approach
when you will say,
"I find no pleasure in them" —
[2] before the sun and the light

---

[a] 5 Or *know how life* (or *the spirit*) / *enters the body being formed*

and the moon and the stars
grow dark,
and the clouds return after
the rain;
³when the keepers of the house
tremble,
and the strong men stoop,
when the grinders cease
because they are few,
and those looking through
the windows grow dim;
⁴when the doors to the street
are closed
and the sound of grinding
fades;
when people rise up at the
sound of birds,
but all their songs grow faint;
⁵when people are afraid of
heights
and of dangers in the streets;
when the almond tree
blossoms
and the grasshopper drags
itself along
and desire no longer is
stirred.
Then people go to their
eternal home   Job 17:13
and mourners go about the
streets.   Jer 9:17; Am 5:16

⁶Remember him — before the
silver cord is severed,
and the golden bowl is
broken;
before the pitcher is shattered
at the spring,
and the wheel broken at the
well,

⁷and the dust returns to the
ground it came from,
and the spirit returns to
God who gave it.   Ecc 3:21

⁸"Meaningless! Meaningless!"
says the Teacher.ᵃ
"Everything is meaningless!"

The Conclusion of the Matter

⁹Not only was the Teacher wise,
but he also imparted knowledge
to the people. He pondered and
searched out and set in order
many proverbs. ¹⁰The Teacher searched to find just the right
words, and what he wrote was
upright and true. 1Ki 4:32; Pr 22:20-21
¹¹The words of the wise are like
goads, their collected sayings like
firmly embedded nails — given
by one shepherd.ᵇ ¹²Be warned,
my son, of anything in addition
to them.   Ezr 9:8
Of making many books there
is no end, and much study wearies the body.   Ecc 1:18

¹³Now all has been heard;
here is the conclusion of the
matter:
Fear God and keep his
commandments,   Dt 4:2
for this is the duty of all
mankind.   Mic 6:8
¹⁴For God will bring every deed
into judgment,   Ecc 3:17
including every hidden
thing,   Mt 10:26; 1Co 4:5
whether it is good or evil.

ᵃ 8 Or the leader of the assembly; also in verses 9 and 10   ᵇ 11 Or Shepherd

Song of Songs

1 Solomon's Song of Songs.

She[a]

² Let him kiss me with the
  kisses of his mouth —
for your love is more
  delightful than wine.
³ Pleasing is the fragrance of
  your perfumes;   SS 4:10
your name is like perfume
  poured out.   Ecc 7:1
No wonder the young
  women love you!   Ps 45:14
⁴ Take me away with you — let
  us hurry!
Let the king bring me into
  his chambers.   Ps 45:15

Friends

We rejoice and delight in
  you[b];   SS 2:3
we will praise your love
  more than wine.   ver 2

She

How right they are to adore
  you!

⁵ Dark am I, yet lovely,   SS 2:14; 4:3
  daughters of Jerusalem, SS 2:7
dark like the tents of Kedar,
  like the tent curtains of
  Solomon.[c]
⁶ Do not stare at me because I
  am dark,
because I am darkened by
  the sun.
My mother's sons were angry
  with me
and made me take care of
  the vineyards;   Ps 69:8
my own vineyard I had to
  neglect.
⁷ Tell me, you whom I love,
where you graze your flock
and where you rest your
  sheep at midday.   SS 3:1-4
Why should I be like a veiled
  woman   Ge 24:65
beside the flocks of your
  friends?

Friends

⁸ If you do not know, most
  beautiful of women,

---

[a] The main male and female speakers (identified primarily on the basis of the gender of the relevant Hebrew forms) are indicated by the captions *He* and *She* respectively. The words of others are marked *Friends*. In some instances the divisions and their captions are debatable.
[b] 4 The Hebrew is masculine singular.   [c] 5 Or *Salma*

follow the tracks of the
sheep
and graze your young goats
by the tents of the shepherds.

He

⁹I liken you, my darling, to a
mare
among Pharaoh's chariot
horses.   2Ch 1:17
¹⁰Your cheeks are beautiful
with earrings,   SS 5:13
your neck with strings of
jewels.   Isa 61:10
¹¹We will make you earrings of
gold,
studded with silver.

She

¹²While the king was at his table,
my perfume spread its
fragrance.   SS 4:11-14
¹³My beloved is to me a sachet
of myrrh   Ge 37:25
resting between my breasts.
¹⁴My beloved is to me a cluster
of henna blossoms   SS 2:3
from the vineyards of En
Gedi.   1Sa 23:29

He

¹⁵How beautiful you are, my
darling!   SS 4:7; 7:6
Oh, how beautiful!
Your eyes are doves. SS 14:1; 5:2

She

¹⁶How handsome you are, my
beloved!

Oh, how charming!
And our bed is verdant.

He

¹⁷The beams of our house are
cedars;   1Ki 6:9
our rafters are firs.

*She*ᵃ

2 I am a roseᵇ of Sharon, Isa 35:1
  a lily of the valleys.   SS 5:13

He

²Like a lily among thorns
is my darling among the
young women.

She

³Like an appleᶜ tree among the
trees of the forest
is my beloved among the
young men.   SS 1:14
I delight to sit in his shade,
and his fruit is sweet to my
taste.   SS 4:16
⁴Let him lead me to the
banquet hall,   Est 1:11
and let his banner over me
be love.   Nu 1:52
⁵Strengthen me with raisins,
refresh me with apples, SS 7:8
for I am faint with love. SS 5:8
⁶His left arm is under my head,
and his right arm
embraces me.   SS 8:3
⁷Daughters of Jerusalem, I
charge you   SS 5:8
by the gazelles and by the
does of the field:

ᵃ Or *He*   ᵇ 1 Probably a member of the crocus family   ᶜ 3 Or possibly *apricot*; here and
elsewhere in Song of Songs

Do not arouse or awaken love
until it so desires.   SS 3:5; 8:4

8 Listen! My beloved!
Look! Here he comes,
leaping across the mountains,
bounding over the hills.
9 My beloved is like a gazelle or
a young stag.   ver 17; SS 8:14
Look! There he stands
behind our wall,
gazing through the windows,
peering through the
lattice.
10 My beloved spoke and said
to me,
"Arise, my darling,
my beautiful one, come
with me.
11 See! The winter is past;
the rains are over and
gone.
12 Flowers appear on the earth;
the season of singing has
come,
the cooing of doves
is heard in our land.
13 The fig tree forms its early
fruit;   Isa 28:4; Jer 24:2
the blossoming vines
spread their fragrance.
Arise, come, my darling;
my beautiful one, come
with me."

He
14 My dove in the clefts of the
rock,   Ge 8:8; SS 1:15
in the hiding places on the
mountainside,

show me your face,
let me hear your voice;
for your voice is sweet,
and your face is lovely.   SS 1:5
15 Catch for us the foxes,   Jdg 15:4
the little foxes
that ruin the vineyards,   SS 1:6
our vineyards that are in
bloom.   SS 7:12

She
16 My beloved is mine and I am
his;   SS 7:10
he browses among the
lilies.   SS 6:3
17 Until the day breaks
and the shadows flee,   SS 4:6
turn, my beloved,   SS 1:14
and be like a gazelle
or like a young stag   ver 9
on the rugged hills.ᵃ   ver 8

3 All night long on my bed
I looked for the one my
heart loves;   SS 5:6; Isa 26:9
I looked for him but did not
find him.
2 I will get up now and go about
the city,
through its streets and
squares;
I will search for the one my
heart loves.
So I looked for him but did
not find him.
3 The watchmen found me
as they made their rounds
in the city.   SS 5:7
"Have you seen the one my
heart loves?"

⁴Scarcely had I passed them
    when I found the one my
    heart loves.
I held him and would not let
    him go
    till I had brought him to my
    mother's house,   SS 8:2
    to the room of the one who
    conceived me.   SS 6:9
⁵Daughters of Jerusalem, I
    charge you   SS 2:7
by the gazelles and by the
    does of the field:
Do not arouse or awaken
    love
    until it so desires.   SS 8:4

⁶Who is this coming up from
    the wilderness   SS 8:5
like a column of smoke,
perfumed with myrrh and
    incense   SS 1:13; 4:6,14
made from all the spices of
    the merchant?   Ex 30:34
⁷Look! It is Solomon's carriage,
    escorted by sixty warriors,
    the noblest of Israel,
⁸all of them wearing the
    sword,
    all experienced in battle,
each with his sword at his side,
    prepared for the terrors of
    the night.   Job 15:22; Ps 91:5
⁹King Solomon made for
    himself the carriage;
    he made it of wood from
    Lebanon.
¹⁰Its posts he made of silver,
    its base of gold.

Its seat was upholstered with
    purple,
    its interior inlaid with love.
Daughters of Jerusalem,
    ¹¹come out,
    and look, you daughters of
    Zion.   Isa 4:4
Look*a* on King Solomon
    wearing a crown,
    the crown with which his
    mother crowned him
on the day of his wedding,
    the day his heart rejoiced.

He

4

How beautiful you are, my
    darling!
Oh, how beautiful!
Your eyes behind your veil
    are doves.   SS 1:15; 5:12
Your hair is like a flock of
    goats
    descending from the hills of
    Gilead.   Mic 7:14
²Your teeth are like a flock of
    sheep just shorn,
    coming up from the
    washing.
Each has its twin;
    not one of them is alone.
³Your lips are like a scarlet
    ribbon;
    your mouth is lovely.   SS 5:16
Your temples behind your veil
    are like the halves of a
    pomegranate.   SS 6:7
⁴Your neck is like the tower of
    David,   SS 7:4
    built with courses of stone*b*;

---

a 10,11 Or *interior lovingly inlaid / by the daughters of Jerusalem. / *¹¹Come out, you daughters
of Zion, / and look*   *b* 4 The meaning of the Hebrew for this phrase is uncertain.

on it hang a thousand
   shields,   Eze 27:10
all of them shields of
   warriors.
⁵Your breasts are like two
   fawns,   SS 7:3
   like twin fawns of a gazelle
   that browse among the
      lilies.   SS 2:16
⁶Until the day breaks
   and the shadows flee,   SS 2:17
I will go to the mountain of
   myrrh
   and to the hill of incense.
⁷You are altogether beautiful,
   my darling;   SS 1:15
   there is no flaw in you.
⁸Come with me from Lebanon,
   my bride,   SS 5:1
   come with me from
      Lebanon.
Descend from the crest of
   Amana,
   from the top of Senir, the
      summit of Hermon,
from the lions' dens
   and the mountain haunts of
      leopards.
⁹You have stolen my heart, my
   sister, my bride;
   you have stolen my heart
with one glance of your
   eyes,
   with one jewel of your
      necklace.   Ge 41:42
¹⁰How delightful is your love,
   my sister, my bride!   SS 1:2
   How much more pleasing is
   your love than wine,

and the fragrance of your
   perfume   Ps 45:8
   more than any spice!
¹¹Your lips drop sweetness as
   the honeycomb, my
      bride;
   milk and honey are under
      your tongue. Ps 19:10; SS 5:1
The fragrance of your
   garments
   is like the fragrance of
      Lebanon.   Hos 14:6
¹²You are a garden locked up,
   my sister, my bride;
   you are a spring enclosed, a
      sealed fountain.   Pr 5:15-18
¹³Your plants are an orchard of
   pomegranates SS 6:11; 7:12
   with choice fruits,
   with henna and nard,   SS 1:14
¹⁴   nard and saffron,
   calamus and cinnamon,
   with every kind of incense
      tree,
   with myrrh and aloes   SS 3:6
   and all the finest spices.
¹⁵You are ᵃ a garden fountain,
   a well of flowing water
   streaming down from
      Lebanon.

She

¹⁶Awake, north wind,
   and come, south wind!
Blow on my garden,
   that its fragrance may
      spread everywhere.
Let my beloved come into his
   garden
   and taste its choice fruits.

ᵃ 15 Or *I am* (spoken by *She*)

He

5 I have come into my garden,
　　my sister, my bride; SS 4:8
　I have gathered my myrrh
　　with my spice.
　I have eaten my honeycomb
　　and my honey;
　I have drunk my wine and
　　my milk. SS 4:11; Isa 55:1

Friends

　Eat, friends, and drink;
　　drink your fill of love.

She

²I slept but my heart was
　　awake.
　Listen! My beloved is
　　knocking:
　"Open to me, my sister, my
　　darling,
　my dove, my flawless one.
　My head is drenched with
　　dew,
　　my hair with the dampness
　　of the night."
³I have taken off my robe —
　　must I put it on again?
　I have washed my feet —
　　must I soil them again?
⁴My beloved thrust his hand
　　through the latch-
　　opening;
　my heart began to pound
　　for him.
⁵I arose to open for my
　　beloved,
　　and my hands dripped with
　　myrrh,

my fingers with flowing myrrh,
　　on the handles of the bolt.
⁶I opened for my beloved, SS 6:1
　but my beloved had left; he
　　was gone. SS 6:2
　My heart sank at his
　　departure.ᵃ
　I looked for him but did not
　　find him. SS 3:1
　I called him but he did not
　　answer.
⁷The watchmen found me
　as they made their rounds
　　in the city. SS 3:3
　They beat me, they
　　bruised me;
　they took away my cloak,
　　those watchmen of the walls!
⁸Daughters of Jerusalem, I
　　charge you — SS 2:7; 3:5
　if you find my beloved,
what will you tell him?
　Tell him I am faint with love.

Friends

⁹How is your beloved better
　　than others,
　most beautiful of women?
　How is your beloved better
　　than others,
　that you so charge us?

She

¹⁰My beloved is radiant and
　　ruddy,
　outstanding among ten
　　thousand. Ps 45:2
¹¹His head is purest gold;
　his hair is wavy
　and black as a raven.

ᵃ 6 Or *heart had gone out to him when he spoke*

12His eyes are like doves   SS 1:15
     by the water streams,
     washed in milk,   Ge 49:12
     mounted like jewels.
13His cheeks are like beds of
     spice   SS 1:10; 6:2
     yielding perfume.
   His lips are like lilies   SS 2:1
     dripping with myrrh.
14His arms are rods of gold
     set with topaz.
   His body is like polished ivory
     decorated with lapis lazuli.
15His legs are pillars of marble
     set on bases of pure gold.
   His appearance is like
     Lebanon,   1Ki 4:33; SS 7:4
     choice as its cedars.
16His mouth is sweetness itself;
     he is altogether lovely.
   This is my beloved, this is my
     friend,   SS 7:9
     daughters of Jerusalem.   SS 1:5

Friends

6 Where has your beloved
     gone,   SS 5:6
   most beautiful of women?
   Which way did your beloved
     turn,
     that we may look for him
       with you?

She

2My beloved has gone down to
     his garden,   SS 4:12; 5:6
     to the beds of spices,   SS 5:13
   to browse in the gardens
     and to gather lilies.
3I am my beloved's and my
     beloved is mine;   SS 7:10
   he browses among the lilies.

He

4You are as beautiful as Tirzah,
     my darling,   Jos 12:24
   as lovely as Jerusalem,   Ps 48:2
   as majestic as troops with
     banners.   ver 10
5Turn your eyes from me;
     they overwhelm me.
   Your hair is like a flock of
     goats
     descending from Gilead.
6Your teeth are like a flock of
     sheep
     coming up from the
       washing.
   Each has its twin,
     not one of them is missing.
7Your temples behind your veil
     are like the halves of a
       pomegranate.   SS 4:3
8Sixty queens there may be,
     and eighty concubines,
     and virgins beyond number;
9but my dove, my perfect one,
     is unique,   SS 1:15; 5:2
   the only daughter of her
     mother,
   the favorite of the one who
     bore her.   SS 3:4
   The young women saw her
     and called her blessed;
   the queens and concubines
     praised her.

Friends

10Who is this that appears like
     the dawn,
   fair as the moon, bright as
     the sun,
   majestic as the stars in
     procession?

He

11 I went down to the grove of
    nut trees
    to look at the new growth in
        the valley,
    to see if the vines had budded
        or the pomegranates were
        in bloom.   SS 7:12
12 Before I realized it,
    my desire set me among
        the royal chariots of
        my people.[a]

Friends

13 Come back, come back,
    O Shulammite;
    come back, come back, that
        we may gaze on you!

He

    Why would you gaze on the
        Shulammite
    as on the dance of
        Mahanaim?[b]   Ex 15:20

7[c] How beautiful your
        sandaled feet,
    O prince's daughter!   Ps 45:13
    Your graceful legs are like
        jewels,
        the work of an artist's hands.
2 Your navel is a rounded goblet
    that never lacks blended
        wine.
    Your waist is a mound of wheat
        encircled by lilies.
3 Your breasts are like two
        fawns,   SS 4:5
    like twin fawns of a gazelle.

4 Your neck is like an ivory
        tower.   Ps 144:12; SS 4:4
    Your eyes are the pools of
        Heshbon   Nu 21:26
    by the gate of Bath Rabbim.
    Your nose is like the tower of
        Lebanon   SS 5:15
    looking toward Damascus.
5 Your head crowns you like
        Mount Carmel.   Isa 35:2
    Your hair is like royal
        tapestry;
    the king is held captive by
        its tresses.
6 How beautiful you are and
        how pleasing,   SS 1:15
    my love, with your
        delights!   SS 4:10
7 Your stature is like that of the
        palm,
    and your breasts like
        clusters of fruit.   SS 4:5
8 I said, "I will climb the palm
        tree;
    I will take hold of its fruit."
    May your breasts be like
        clusters of grapes on
        the vine,
    the fragrance of your breath
        like apples,   SS 2:5
9   and your mouth like the
        best wine.

She

    May the wine go straight to
        my beloved,   SS 5:16
    flowing gently over lips and
        teeth.[d]

---

[a] 12 Or *among the chariots of Amminadab*; or *among the chariots of the people of the prince*
[b] 13 In Hebrew texts this verse (6:13) is numbered 7:1.   [c] In Hebrew texts 7:1-13 is
numbered 7:2-14.   [d] 9 Septuagint, Aquila, Vulgate and Syriac; Hebrew *lips of sleepers*

¹⁰I belong to my beloved,
    and his desire is for me.
¹¹Come, my beloved, let us go to
        the countryside,
    let us spend the night in the
        villages.ᵃ
¹²Let us go early to the
        vineyards   SS 1:6
    to see if the vines have
        budded,   SS 2:15
    if their blossoms have
        opened,   SS 2:13
    and if the pomegranates are
        in bloom —   SS 4:13; 6:11
    there I will give you my
        love.
¹³The mandrakes send out their
        fragrance,   Ge 30:14
    and at our door is every
        delicacy,
    both new and old,
    that I have stored up for
        you, my beloved.   SS 4:16

8 If only you were to me like a
        brother,
    who was nursed at my
        mother's breasts!
Then, if I found you outside,
    I would kiss you,
    and no one would
        despise me.
²I would lead you
    and bring you to my
        mother's house —   SS 3:4
    she who has taught me.
I would give you spiced wine
        to drink,
    the nectar of my
        pomegranates.

³His left arm is under my head
    and his right arm
        embraces me.
⁴Daughters of Jerusalem, I
        charge you:
Do not arouse or awaken
        love
    until it so desires.   SS 2:7; 3:5

Friends

⁵Who is this coming up from
        the wilderness   SS 3:6
    leaning on her beloved?

She

Under the apple tree I roused
        you;
    there your mother
        conceived you,   SS 3:4
    there she who was in labor
        gave you birth.
⁶Place me like a seal over your
        heart,
    like a seal on your arm;
    for love is as strong as death,
    its jealousyᵇ unyielding as
        the grave.
It burns like blazing fire,
    like a mighty flame.ᶜ   Nu 5:14
⁷Many waters cannot quench
        love;
    rivers cannot sweep it away.
If one were to give
    all the wealth of one's house
        for love,
    itᵈ would be utterly scorned.

Friends

⁸We have a little sister,

ᵃ 11 Or *the henna bushes*   ᵇ 6 Or *ardor*   ᶜ 6 Or *fire, / like the very flame of the* LORD
ᵈ 7 Or *he*

and her breasts are not yet
grown.
What shall we do for our sister
on the day she is spoken for?
⁹If she is a wall,
we will build towers of
silver on her.
If she is a door,
we will enclose her with
panels of cedar.

She

¹⁰I am a wall,
and my breasts are like
towers.
Thus I have become in his eyes
like one bringing
contentment.
¹¹Solomon had a vineyard in
Baal Hamon;   Ecc 2:4
he let out his vineyard to
tenants.

Each was to bring for its fruit
a thousand shekels*ᵃ* of
silver.   Isa 7:23
¹²But my own vineyard is mine
to give;   SS 1:6
the thousand shekels are for
you, Solomon,
and two hundred*ᵇ* are for
those who tend its
fruit.

He

¹³You who dwell in the gardens
with friends in attendance,
let me hear your voice!

She

¹⁴Come away, my beloved,
and be like a gazelle   Pr 5:19
or like a young stag   SS 2:9
on the spice-laden
mountains.   SS 2:8,17

ᵃ 11 That is, about 25 pounds or about 12 kilograms; also in verse 12   *ᵇ 12* That is, about 5
pounds or about 2.3 kilograms

Isaiah

1 The vision concerning Judah
and Jerusalem that Isaiah son
of Amoz saw during the reigns of
Uzziah, Jotham, Ahaz and Hezekiah, kings of Judah.   Isa 2:1

A Rebellious Nation

²Hear me, you heavens! Listen,
     earth!
   For the LORD has spoken:
"I reared children and
     brought them up,
   but they have rebelled
     against me.   Isa 30:1,9; 65:2
³The ox knows its master,
   the donkey its owner's
     manger,
   but Israel does not know,   Jer 9:3
   my people do not
     understand."   Dt 32:28

⁴Woe to the sinful nation,
   a people whose guilt is
     great,   Isa 5:18
   a brood of evildoers,   Isa 14:20
   children given to
     corruption!   Ps 14:3
   They have forsaken the LORD;

they have spurned the Holy
     One of Israel   Isa 5:19,24
   and turned their backs on
     him.   Pr 30:9

⁵Why should you be beaten
     anymore?   Pr 20:30
   Why do you persist in
     rebellion?   Isa 31:6; Heb 3:16
   Your whole head is injured,
   your whole heart afflicted.
⁶From the sole of your foot to
     the top of your head
   there is no soundness —
   only wounds and welts
     and open sores,
   not cleansed or bandaged
     or soothed with olive oil.

⁷Your country is desolate,
   your cities burned with fire;
   your fields are being stripped
     by foreigners   Lev 26:16
   right before you,
   laid waste as when
     overthrown by strangers.
⁸Daughter Zion is left   Ps 9:14
   like a shelter in a vineyard,

like a hut in a cucumber field,
like a city under siege.
⁹Unless the LORD Almighty
had left us some survivors,
we would have become like
Sodom,
we would have been like
Gomorrah. Ge 19:24

¹⁰Hear the word of the LORD,
you rulers of Sodom; Eze 16:49
listen to the instruction of our
God, Isa 8:20
you people of Gomorrah!
¹¹ "The multitude of your
sacrifices—
what are they to me?" says
the LORD.
"I have more than enough of
burnt offerings,
of rams and the fat of
fattened animals; Ps 50:8
I have no pleasure
in the blood of bulls and
lambs and goats. 1Sa 15:22
¹²When you come to appear
before me,
who has asked this of you,
this trampling of my courts?
¹³Stop bringing meaningless
offerings! Isa 66:3
Your incense is detestable
to me. Jer 7:9
New Moons, Sabbaths and
convocations— 1Ch 23:31
I cannot bear your
worthless assemblies.
¹⁴Your New Moon feasts and
your appointed festivals
I hate with all my being.

They have become a burden
to me;
I am weary of bearing them.
¹⁵When you spread out your
hands in prayer,
I hide my eyes from you;
even when you offer many
prayers,
I am not listening. Isa 59:3

Your hands are full of blood!

¹⁶Wash and make yourselves
clean. Mt 27:24; Jas 4:8
Take your evil deeds out of
my sight; Isa 52:11
stop doing wrong. Isa 55:7
¹⁷Learn to do right; seek justice.
Defend the oppressed.ᵃ
Take up the cause of the
fatherless; Ps 82:3; 94:6
plead the case of the widow.

¹⁸ "Come now, let us settle the
matter," Isa 41:1; 43:9,26
says the LORD.
"Though your sins are like
scarlet,
they shall be as white as
snow; Ps 51:7; Rev 7:14
though they are red as
crimson,
they shall be like wool.
¹⁹If you are willing and obedient,
you will eat the good things
of the land; Dt 30:15-16
²⁰but if you resist and rebel,
you will be devoured by the
sword." Isa 3:25; 65:12
For the mouth of the
LORD has spoken.

ᵃ 17 Or justice. / Correct the oppressor

²¹See how the faithful city
 has become a prostitute!
 She once was full of justice;
  righteousness used to dwell
   in her — Isa 5:7; 46:13
  but now murderers! Pr 6:17
²²Your silver has become dross,
  your choice wine is diluted
   with water.
²³Your rulers are rebels,
  partners with thieves; Dt 19:14
 they all love bribes Ex 23:8
  and chase after gifts.
 They do not defend the cause
   of the fatherless;
  the widow's case does not
   come before them. Jer 5:28

²⁴Therefore the Lord, the LORD
   Almighty,
  the Mighty One of Israel,
   declares: Ge 49:24
 "Ah! I will vent my wrath on
   my foes
  and avenge myself on my
   enemies. Isa 35:4; 59:17; 61:2
²⁵I will turn my hand against
   you;ᵃ Dt 28:63
 I will thoroughly purge
   away your dross
  and remove all your
   impurities. Eze 22:22
²⁶I will restore your leaders as
   in days of old, Jer 33:7,11
  your rulers as at the
   beginning.
 Afterward you will be called
   the City of Righteousness,
   the Faithful City." Isa 60:14; 62:2

²⁷Zion will be delivered with
   justice,

her penitent ones with
  righteousness. Isa 35:10
²⁸But rebels and sinners will
   both be broken,
  and those who forsake the
   LORD will perish. Ps 9:5

²⁹"You will be ashamed because
   of the sacred oaks
  in which you have
   delighted;
 you will be disgraced because
   of the gardens Isa 65:3
  that you have chosen.
³⁰You will be like an oak with
   fading leaves,
  like a garden without water.
³¹The mighty man will become
   tinder
  and his work a spark;
 both will burn together,
  with no one to quench the
   fire." Isa 5:24; 9:18-19; 26:11

The Mountain of the LORD
2:1-4pp — Mic 4:1-3

2 This is what Isaiah son of
  Amoz saw concerning Judah
and Jerusalem: Isa 1:1

²In the last days

the mountain of the LORD's
  temple will be
  established Mic 4:7
 as the highest of the
  mountains;
 it will be exalted above the
  hills, Zec 14:10
 and all nations will stream
  to it. Ps 102:15

ᵃ 25 That is, against Jerusalem

³Many peoples will come and say,

"Come, let us go up to the
mountain of the LORD,
to the temple of the God of
Jacob.
He will teach us his ways,
so that we may walk in his
paths."
The law will go out from Zion,
the word of the LORD from
Jerusalem.   Lk 24:47
⁴He will judge between the
nations   Isa 1:27; Joel 3:14
and will settle disputes for
many peoples.   Ge 49:10
They will beat their swords
into plowshares
and their spears into
pruning hooks.   Joel 3:10
Nation will not take up sword
against nation,   Isa 32:18
nor will they train for war
anymore.   Mic 4:1-3

⁵Come, descendants of Jacob,
let us walk in the light of the
LORD.   Isa 60:1,19-20; 1Jn 1:5,7

The Day of the LORD

⁶You, LORD, have abandoned
your people,   Dt 31:17
the descendants of Jacob.
They are full of superstitions
from the East;
they practice divination like
the Philistines   2Ki 1:2
and embrace pagan customs.
⁷Their land is full of silver and
gold;   Dt 17:17

there is no end to their
treasures.   Ps 17:14
Their land is full of horses;
there is no end to their
chariots.   Isa 31:1; Mic 5:10
⁸Their land is full of idols;
they bow down to the work
of their hands,   Ps 135:15
to what their fingers have
made.   Isa 17:8
⁹So people will be brought low
and everyone humbled—
do not forgive them.ᵃ   Ne 4:5
¹⁰Go into the rocks, hide in the
ground
from the fearful presence of
the LORD
and the splendor of his
majesty!   2Th 1:9; Rev 6:15-16
¹¹The eyes of the arrogant will
be humbled   Ne 9:29
and human pride brought
low;   Isa 5:15; 37:23
the LORD alone will be exalted
in that day.   Ps 46:10

¹²The LORD Almighty has a day
in store   Am 5:18; Zep 1:14
for all the proud and lofty,
for all that is exalted   Isa 24:4,21
(and they will be humbled),
¹³for all the cedars of Lebanon,
tall and lofty,
and all the oaks of Bashan,
¹⁴for all the towering mountains
and all the high hills,   Isa 30:25
¹⁵for every lofty tower   Isa 30:25
and every fortified wall,
¹⁶for every trading shipᵇ   1Ki 10:22
and every stately vessel.

ᵃ 9 Or *not raise them up*   ᵇ 16 Hebrew *every ship of Tarshish*

17The arrogance of man will be
      brought low
   and human pride humbled;
   the LORD alone will be exalted
      in that day,   ver 11
18   and the idols will totally
      disappear.   Isa 21:9

19People will flee to caves in the
      rocks   Isa 7:19
   and to holes in the ground
   from the fearful presence of
      the LORD   Dt 2:25
   and the splendor of his
      majesty,   Ps 145:12
   when he rises to shake the
      earth.   Heb 12:26
20In that day people will throw
      away
   to the moles and bats Lev 11:19
   their idols of silver and idols of
      gold,   Rev 9:20
   which they made to worship.
21They will flee to caverns in
      the rocks
   and to the overhanging crags
   from the fearful presence of
      the LORD
   and the splendor of his
      majesty,   Ps 145:12
   when he rises to shake the
      earth.   ver 19; Isa 33:10
22Stop trusting in mere
      humans,   Ps 146:3
   who have but a breath in
      their nostrils.
   Why hold them in esteem?

Judgment on Jerusalem and Judah

3 See now, the Lord,
   the LORD Almighty,

is about to take from
      Jerusalem and Judah
   both supply and support:
   all supplies of food and all
      supplies of water,   Lev 26:26
2   the hero and the warrior,
   the judge and the prophet,
      the diviner and the elder,
3the captain of fifty and the
      man of rank,
   the counselor, skilled
      craftsman and clever
      enchanter.   2Ki 24:14

4"I will make mere youths their
      officials;
   children will rule over
      them."   Ecc 10:16 fn

5People will oppress each
      other—
   man against man, neighbor
      against neighbor.Mic 7:2,6
   The young will rise up against
      the old,
   the nobody against the
      honored.

6A man will seize one of his
      brothers
   in his father's house, and
      say,
   "You have a cloak, you be our
      leader;
   take charge of this heap of
      ruins!"
7But in that day he will cry out,
   "I have no remedy.   Eze 34:4
   I have no food or clothing in
      my house;
   do not make me the leader
      of the people."   Isa 24:2

⁸Jerusalem staggers,
  Judah is falling;   Isa 1:7
their words and deeds are
  against the LORD,   Isa 9:15
defying his glorious
  presence.   Ps 73:9,11
⁹The look on their faces
  testifies against them;
they parade their sin like
  Sodom;   Ge 13:13
they do not hide it.
Woe to them!
  They have brought disaster
  upon themselves.   Pr 8:36

¹⁰Tell the righteous it will be
  well with them,   Dt 28:1-14
for they will enjoy the fruit
  of their deeds.   Ps 128:2
¹¹Woe to the wicked!
  Disaster is upon them!
They will be paid back
  for what their hands have
  done.   2Ch 6:23
¹²Youths oppress my people, ver 4
  women rule over them.
My people, your guides lead
  you astray;   Isa 9:16
they turn you from the path.

¹³The LORD takes his place in
  court;
he rises to judge the people.
¹⁴The LORD enters into
  judgment   Job 22:4
against the elders and
  leaders of his people:
"It is you who have ruined my
  vineyard;
the plunder from the poor is
  in your houses.   Jas 2:6

¹⁵What do you mean by
  crushing my people
and grinding the faces of
  the poor?"   Isa 10:6; 11:4
declares the Lord,
  the LORD Almighty.

¹⁶The LORD says,
  "The women of Zion are
  haughty,   SS 3:11
walking along with
  outstretched necks,
flirting with their eyes,
strutting along with swaying
  hips,
with ornaments jingling on
  their ankles.
¹⁷Therefore the Lord will bring
  sores on the heads of
  the women of Zion;
the LORD will make their
  scalps bald."

¹⁸In that day the Lord will
snatch away their finery: the
bangles and headbands and
crescent necklaces, ¹⁹the earrings and bracelets and veils,
²⁰the headdresses and anklets
and sashes, the perfume bottles
and charms, ²¹the signet rings
and nose rings, ²²the fine robes
and the capes and cloaks, the
purses ²³and mirrors, and the
linen garments and tiaras and
shawls.   Isa 2:11; Eze 16:10

²⁴Instead of fragrance there will
  be a stench;   Est 2:12
instead of a sash, a rope;
instead of well-dressed hair,
  baldness;   Isa 22:12

instead of fine clothing,
　　sackcloth;　　　　La 2:10
instead of beauty,
　　branding.　　　　1Pe 3:3
[25] Your men will fall by the
　　sword,　　　　　Isa 1:20
　　your warriors in battle.
[26] The gates of Zion will lament
　　and mourn;　　　Jer 14:2
　　destitute, she will sit on the
　　　ground.　　　　La 2:10

4 [1] In that day seven women
　will take hold of one
　　man　　　　　　Isa 13:12
and say, "We will eat our own
　food　　　　　　2Th 3:12
and provide our own
　　clothes;
only let us be called by your
　　name.
Take away our disgrace!"

The Branch of the LORD

[2] In that day the Branch of the
LORD will be beautiful and glorious, and the fruit of the land will
be the pride and glory of the survivors in Israel. [3] Those who are
left in Zion, who remain in Jerusalem, will be called holy, all who
are recorded among the living in
Jerusalem. [4] The Lord will wash
away the filth of the women of
Zion; he will cleanse the bloodstains from Jerusalem by a spirit[a]
of judgment and a spirit[a] of fire.
[5] Then the LORD will create over
all of Mount Zion and over those
who assemble there a cloud of
smoke by day and a glow of flam-

ing fire by night; over everything
the glory[b] will be a canopy. [6] It
will be a shelter and shade from
the heat of the day, and a refuge
and hiding place from the storm
and rain.　　　Jer 23:5-6; Isa 25:4

The Song of the Vineyard

5 I will sing for the one I love
　a song about his
　　vineyard:　　　Ps 80:8-9
My loved one had a vineyard
　on a fertile hillside.
[2] He dug it up and cleared it of
　　stones
　and planted it with the
　　choicest vines.　　Jer 2:21
He built a watchtower in it
　and cut out a winepress as
　　well.
Then he looked for a crop of
　　good grapes,
　but it yielded only bad fruit.
[3] "Now you dwellers in
　　Jerusalem and people
　　of Judah,
　judge between me and my
　　vineyard.　　　Mt 21:40
[4] What more could have been
　　done for my vineyard
　than I have done for it?
When I looked for good
　　grapes,
　why did it yield only bad?
[5] Now I will tell you
　what I am going to do to my
　　vineyard:
I will take away its hedge,
　and it will be destroyed;

---

[a] 4 Or the Spirit　　[b] 5 Or over all the glory there

I will break down its wall,
and it will be trampled.
⁶I will make it a wasteland,
neither pruned nor
cultivated,
and briers and thorns will
grow there.   Isa 7:23-24
I will command the clouds
not to rain on it."

⁷The vineyard of the LORD
Almighty
is the nation of Israel, Ps 80:8
and the people of Judah
are the vines he delighted in.
And he looked for justice, but
saw bloodshed;   Isa 59:15
for righteousness, but heard
cries of distress.

Woes and Judgments

⁸Woe to you who add house to
house   Jer 22:13
and join field to field Mic 2:2
till no space is left
and you live alone in the
land.

⁹The LORD Almighty has declared in my hearing: Isa 22:14

"Surely the great houses will
become desolate, Isa 6:11
the fine mansions left
without occupants.
¹⁰A ten-acre vineyard will
produce only a bath^a of
wine;
a homer^b of seed will yield
only an ephah^c of grain."

¹¹Woe to those who rise early in
the morning
to run after their drinks,
who stay up late at night
till they are inflamed with
wine.   Pr 23:29-30
¹²They have harps and lyres at
their banquets,
pipes and timbrels and wine,
but they have no regard for
the deeds of the LORD,
no respect for the work of
his hands. Ps 28:5; Am 6:5-6
¹³Therefore my people will go
into exile
for lack of understanding;
those of high rank will die of
hunger
and the common people
will be parched with
thirst.
¹⁴Therefore Death expands its
jaws,   Pr 30:16
opening wide its mouth;
into it will descend their
nobles and masses
with all their brawlers and
revelers.
¹⁵So people will be brought low
and everyone humbled,
the eyes of the arrogant
humbled.   Isa 2:11
¹⁶But the LORD Almighty will be
exalted by his justice,
and the holy God will be
proved holy by his
righteous acts.   Isa 29:23
¹⁷Then sheep will graze as in
their own pasture; Isa 7:25

---

^a 10 That is, about 6 gallons or about 22 liters
about 160 kilograms   ^c 10 That is, probably about 36 pounds or about 16 kilograms
^b 10 That is, probably about 360 pounds or

lambs will feed*a* among the
ruins of the rich.

¹⁸Woe to those who draw sin
along with cords of
deceit,
and wickedness as with cart
ropes,   Isa 59:4-8; Jer 23:14
¹⁹to those who say, "Let God
hurry;
let him hasten his work
so we may see it.
The plan of the Holy One of
Israel —
let it approach, let it come
into view,
so we may know it."   Jer 17:15

²⁰Woe to those who call evil
good
and good evil,
who put darkness for light
and light for darkness,
who put bitter for sweet
and sweet for bitter.   Am 5:7

²¹Woe to those who are wise in
their own eyes   Ro 12:16
and clever in their own sight.

²²Woe to those who are heroes
at drinking wine   Pr 23:20
and champions at mixing
drinks,
²³who acquit the guilty for a
bribe,   Ex 23:8
but deny justice to the
innocent.   Ps 94:21; Jas 5:6
²⁴Therefore, as tongues of fire
lick up straw
and as dry grass sinks down
in the flames,

so their roots will decay
and their flowers blow away
like dust;   Job 18:16
for they have rejected the law
of the Lord Almighty
and spurned the word of the
Holy One of Israel. Isa 8:6
²⁵Therefore the Lord's anger
burns against his
people;   2Ki 22:13
his hand is raised and he
strikes them down.
The mountains shake,
and the dead bodies are like
refuse in the streets.

Yet for all this, his anger is not
turned away, Jer 4:8; Da 9:16
his hand is still upraised.

²⁶He lifts up a banner for the
distant nations,
he whistles for those at the
ends of the earth.   Isa 7:18
Here they come,
swiftly and speedily!
²⁷Not one of them grows tired
or stumbles,
not one slumbers or sleeps;
not a belt is loosened at the
waist,   Job 12:18
not a sandal strap is broken.
²⁸Their arrows are sharp, Ps 45:5
all their bows are strung;
their horses' hooves seem like
flint,
their chariot wheels like a
whirlwind.
²⁹Their roar is like that of the
lion,   Jer 51:38; Zep 3:3
they roar like young lions;

^a 17 Septuagint; Hebrew / *strangers will eat*

they growl as they seize their
    prey   Isa 10:6; 49:24-25
and carry it off with no one
    to rescue.   Isa 42:22; Mic 5:8
³⁰In that day they will roar over it
    like the roaring of the sea.
And if one looks at the land,
    there is only darkness and
        distress;   Isa 8:22; Jer 4:23-28
even the sun will be
    darkened by clouds.

Isaiah's Commission

6 In the year that King Uzziah died, I saw the Lord, high and exalted, seated on a throne; and the train of his robe filled the temple. ²Above him were seraphim, each with six wings: With two wings they covered their faces, with two they covered their feet, and with two they were flying. ³And they were calling to one another: 2Ch 6:22-23

"Holy, holy, holy is the LORD
    Almighty;   Ex 15:11; Ps 89:8
the whole earth is full of his
    glory."   Ps 72:19; Rev 4:8

⁴At the sound of their voices the doorposts and thresholds shook and the temple was filled with smoke.

⁵"Woe to me!" I cried. "I am ruined! For I am a man of unclean lips, and I live among a people of unclean lips, and my eyes have seen the King, the LORD Almighty."

⁶Then one of the seraphim flew to me with a live coal in his hand, which he had taken with tongs from the altar. ⁷With it he touched my mouth and said, "See, this has touched your lips; your guilt is taken away and your sin atoned for."   Jer 1:9; 1Jn 1:7

⁸Then I heard the voice of the Lord saying, "Whom shall I send? And who will go for us?"

And I said, "Here am I. Send me!"   Ge 22:1; Ex 3:4

⁹He said, "Go and tell this people: Eze 3:11

" 'Be ever hearing, but never
    understanding;
be ever seeing, but never
    perceiving.'   Mt 13:15
¹⁰Make the heart of this people
    calloused;   Ps 119:70
    make their ears dull
    and close their eyes.ᵃ
Otherwise they might see
    with their eyes,
    hear with their ears,   Jer 5:21
    understand with their hearts,
and turn and be healed."   Mk 4:12

¹¹Then I said, "For how long, Lord?"   Ps 79:5

And he answered:

"Until the cities lie ruined
    and without inhabitant,
until the houses are left
    deserted
    and the fields ruined and
        ravaged,   Ps 79:1; 109:11

ᵃ 9,10 Hebrew; Septuagint *'You will be ever hearing, but never understanding; / you will be ever seeing, but never perceiving.' / ¹⁰This people's heart has become calloused; / they hardly hear with their ears, / and they have closed their eyes*

¹²until the LORD has sent
everyone far away Dt 28:64
and the land is utterly
forsaken. Jer 4:29; 30:17
¹³And though a tenth remains
in the land, Isa 1:9
it will again be laid waste.
But as the terebinth and oak
leave stumps when they are
cut down,
so the holy seed will be the
stump in the land." Dt 14:2

The Sign of Immanuel

7 When Ahaz son of Jotham,
the son of Uzziah, was king
of Judah, King Rezin of Aram and
Pekah son of Remaliah king of Israel marched up to fight against
Jerusalem, but they could not
overpower it. 2Ki 15:25,37; 2Ch 28:5

²Now the house of David was
told, "Aram has allied itself with[a]
Ephraim"; so the hearts of Ahaz
and his people were shaken, as
the trees of the forest are shaken
by the wind. ver 13; Isa 9:9; 22:22

³Then the LORD said to Isaiah, "Go out, you and your son
Shear-Jashub,[b] to meet Ahaz at
the end of the aqueduct of the
Upper Pool, on the road to the
Launderer's Field. ⁴Say to him, 'Be
careful, keep calm and don't be
afraid. Do not lose heart because
of these two smoldering stubs of
firewood — because of the fierce
anger of Rezin and Aram and
of the son of Remaliah. ⁵Aram,

Ephraim and Remaliah's son have
plotted your ruin, saying, ⁶"Let us
invade Judah; let us tear it apart
and divide it among ourselves,
and make the son of Tabeel king
over it." ⁷Yet this is what the Sovereign LORD says: Isa 10:24; 30:15

" 'It will not take place,
it will not happen, Isa 8:10
⁸for the head of Aram is
Damascus, Ge 14:15
and the head of Damascus
is only Rezin.
Within sixty-five years
Ephraim will be too
shattered to be a people.
⁹The head of Ephraim is
Samaria,
and the head of Samaria is
only Remaliah's son.
If you do not stand firm in
your faith, 2Ch 20:20
you will not stand at all.' "

¹⁰Again the LORD spoke to
Ahaz, ¹¹"Ask the LORD your God
for a sign, whether in the deepest depths or in the highest
heights." Ex 7:9; Dt 13:2

¹²But Ahaz said, "I will not ask;
I will not put the LORD to the
test." Dt 6:16; Mt 4:7

¹³Then Isaiah said, "Hear
now, you house of David! Is it not
enough to try the patience of humans? Will you try the patience
of my God also? ¹⁴Therefore the
Lord himself will give you[c] a
sign: The virgin[d] will conceive

---

[a] 2 Or has set up camp in   [b] 3 Shear-Jashub means a remnant will return.
[c] 14 The Hebrew is plural.   [d] 14 Or young woman

and give birth to a son, and[a] will call him Immanuel.[b] [15]He will be eating curds and honey when he knows enough to reject the wrong and choose the right, [16]for before the boy knows enough to reject the wrong and choose the right, the land of the two kings you dread will be laid waste. [17]The LORD will bring on you and on your people and on the house of your father a time unlike any since Ephraim broke away from Judah—he will bring the king of Assyria." Isa 8:8,10; Mt 1:23

Assyria, the LORD's Instrument

[18]In that day the LORD will whistle for flies from the Nile delta in Egypt and for bees from the land of Assyria. [19]They will all come and settle in the steep ravines and in the crevices in the rocks, on all the thornbushes and at all the water holes. [20]In that day the Lord will use a razor hired from beyond the Euphrates River—the king of Assyria—to shave your head and private parts, and to cut off your beard also. [21]In that day, a person will keep alive a young cow and two goats. [22]And because of the abundance of the milk they give, there will be curds to eat. All who remain in the land will eat curds and honey. [23]In that day, in every place where there were

a thousand vines worth a thousand silver shekels,[c] there will be only briers and thorns. [24]Hunters will go there with bow and arrow, for the land will be covered with briers and thorns. [25]As for all the hills once cultivated by the hoe, you will no longer go there for fear of the briers and thorns; they will become places where cattle are turned loose and where sheep run. Isa 5:6,17; 10:15

Isaiah and His Children as Signs

8 The LORD said to me, "Take a large scroll and write on it with an ordinary pen: Maher-Shalal-Hash-Baz."[d] [2]So I called in Uriah the priest and Zechariah son of Jeberekiah as reliable witnesses for me. [3]Then I made love to the prophetess, and she conceived and gave birth to a son. And the LORD said to me, "Name him Maher-Shalal-Hash-Baz. [4]For before the boy knows how to say 'My father' or 'My mother,' the wealth of Damascus and the plunder of Samaria will be carried off by the king of Assyria." Isa 7:8,16; 30:8; Hab 2:2
[5]The LORD spoke to me again:

[6]"Because this people has
    rejected   Isa 5:24
  the gently flowing waters of
    Shiloah   Jn 9:7
and rejoices over Rezin
  and the son of Remaliah,

---

[a] 14 Masoretic Text; Dead Sea Scrolls *son, and he* or *son, and they*   [b] 14 *Immanuel* means *God with us.*   [c] 23 That is, about 25 pounds or about 12 kilograms   [d] 1 *Maher-Shalal-Hash-Baz* means *quick to the plunder, swift to the spoil*; also in verse 3.

⁷therefore the Lord is about to
    bring against them
    the mighty floodwaters of
        the Euphrates —
    the king of Assyria with all
        his pomp.   Isa 7:20
    It will overflow all its
        channels,
    run over all its banks
⁸and sweep on into Judah,
    swirling over it,
    passing through it and
        reaching up to the neck.
    Its outspread wings will cover
        the breadth of your land,
        Immanuel[a]!"   Isa 7:14

⁹Raise the war cry,[b] you
    nations, and be
        shattered!   Isa 17:12-13
    Listen, all you distant lands.
    Prepare for battle, and be
        shattered!   Joel 3:9
    Prepare for battle, and be
        shattered!
¹⁰Devise your strategy, but it
    will be thwarted;   Job 5:12
    propose your plan, but it
        will not stand,   Isa 7:7
    for God is with us.[c] Ro 8:31

¹¹This is what the LORD says
to me with his strong hand upon
me, warning me not to follow the
way of this people: Eze 2:8; 3:14

¹²"Do not call conspiracy   Isa 7:2
    everything this people calls
        a conspiracy;
    do not fear what they fear,
    and do not dread it.   1Pe 3:14

¹³The LORD Almighty is the one
    you are to regard as
        holy,   Nu 20:12
    he is the one you are to fear,
    he is the one you are to dread.
¹⁴He will be a holy place;   Isa 4:6
    for both Israel and Judah he
        will be
    a stone that causes people to
        stumble   Lk 2:34; Ro 9:33
    and a rock that makes them
        fall.   Isa 24:17-18
    And for the people of
        Jerusalem he will be
    a trap and a snare.
¹⁵Many of them will stumble;
    they will fall and be broken,
    they will be snared and
        captured."

¹⁶Bind up this testimony of
    warning
    and seal up God's
        instruction among my
        disciples.   Isa 29:11-12
¹⁷I will wait for the LORD,   Hab 2:3
    who is hiding his face from
        the descendants of Jacob.
    I will put my trust in him.

¹⁸Here am I, and the children
the LORD has given me. We are
signs and symbols in Israel from
the LORD Almighty, who dwells
on Mount Zion.   Heb 2:13; Ps 9:11

The Darkness Turns to Light

¹⁹When someone tells you to
consult mediums and spiritists,
who whisper and mutter, should
not a people inquire of their

---

[a] 8 *Immanuel* means *God with us.*   [b] 9 Or *Do your worst*   [c] 10 Hebrew *Immanuel*

God? Why consult the dead on behalf of the living? [20]Consult God's instruction and the testimony of warning. If anyone does not speak according to this word, they have no light of dawn. [21]Distressed and hungry, they will roam through the land; when they are famished, they will become enraged and, looking upward, will curse their king and their God. [22]Then they will look toward the earth and see only distress and darkness and fearful gloom, and they will be thrust into utter darkness. Mic 3:6; Lk 16:29

9[a] Nevertheless, there will be no more gloom for those who were in distress. In the past he humbled the land of Zebulun and the land of Naphtali, but in the future he will honor Galilee of the nations, by the Way of the Sea, beyond the Jordan — 2Ki 15:29

[2]The people walking in
  darkness   Isa 8:20
have seen a great light; Eph 5:8
on those living in the land of
  deep darkness   Lk 1:79
  a light has dawned.   Mt 4:15-16
[3]You have enlarged the nation
  and increased their joy; Isa 25:9
they rejoice before you
  as people rejoice at the
    harvest,
as warriors rejoice
  when dividing the plunder.
[4]For as in the day of Midian's
    defeat,   Jdg 7:25

you have shattered   Job 34:24
the yoke that burdens them,
  the bar across their
    shoulders,   Isa 10:27
  the rod of their oppressor.
[5]Every warrior's boot used in
    battle
  and every garment rolled in
    blood
will be destined for burning,
  will be fuel for the fire.
[6]For to us a child is born, Lk 2:11
  to us a son is given,   Jn 3:16
  and the government will be
    on his shoulders.   Mt 28:18
And he will be called
  Wonderful Counselor,
    Mighty God,   Isa 10:21; 11:2
  Everlasting Father, Prince of
    Peace.   Lk 2:14; Jn 14:9-10
[7]Of the greatness of his
    government and peace
  there will be no end.   Da 2:44
He will reign on David's
    throne
  and over his kingdom,
establishing and upholding it
  with justice and
    righteousness   Isa 11:4; 16:5
from that time on and
    forever.
The zeal of the LORD
    Almighty
  will accomplish this.   Isa 37:32

The LORD's Anger Against Israel

[8]The Lord has sent a message
    against Jacob;
  it will fall on Israel.
[9]All the people will know it —

---

[a] In Hebrew texts 9:1 is numbered 8:23, and 9:2-21 is numbered 9:1-20.

Ephraim and the inhabitants
of Samaria — Isa 7:9
who say with pride
and arrogance of heart, Isa 46:12
10 "The bricks have fallen down,
but we will rebuild with
dressed stone;
the fig trees have been felled,
but we will replace them
with cedars." 1Ki 7:2-3
11 But the LORD has
strengthened Rezin's
foes against them Isa 7:8
and has spurred their
enemies on.
12 Arameans from the east and
Philistines from the
west 2Ch 28:18
have devoured Israel with
open mouth. Ps 79:7

Yet for all this, his anger is not
turned away,
his hand is still upraised.

13 But the people have not
returned to him who
struck them, Jer 5:3
nor have they sought the
LORD Almighty. Isa 31:1
14 So the LORD will cut off from
Israel both head and
tail,
both palm branch and reed
in a single day; Isa 19:15
15 the elders and dignitaries are
the head, Isa 3:2-3
the prophets who teach lies
are the tail. Eze 13:22
16 Those who guide this people
mislead them, Mt 15:14

and those who are guided
are led astray. Isa 3:12
17 Therefore the Lord will take
no pleasure in the
young men, Jer 18:21
nor will he pity the
fatherless and widows,
for everyone is ungodly and
wicked, Isa 1:4; 10:6
every mouth speaks folly.

Yet for all this, his anger is not
turned away,
his hand is still upraised.

18 Surely wickedness burns like
a fire; Mal 4:1
it consumes briers and
thorns,
it sets the forest thickets
ablaze, Ps 83:14
so that it rolls upward in a
column of smoke.
19 By the wrath of the LORD
Almighty Isa 13:9,13
the land will be scorched
and the people will be fuel for
the fire; Isa 1:31
they will not spare one
another. Mic 7:2,6
20 On the right they will devour,
but still be hungry; Lev 26:26
on the left they will eat, Isa 49:26
but not be satisfied.
Each will feed on the flesh of
their own offspring[a]:
21 Manasseh will feed on
Ephraim, and Ephraim
on Manasseh;
together they will turn
against Judah. 2Ch 28:6

a 20 Or arm

Yet for all this, his anger is not
turned away,
his hand is still upraised.

10 Woe to those who make
unjust laws,
to those who issue
oppressive decrees, Ps 58:2
2 to deprive the poor of their
rights
and withhold justice from
the oppressed of my
people, Isa 5:23
making widows their prey
and robbing the fatherless.
3 What will you do on the day of
reckoning, Job 31:14; Hos 9:7
when disaster comes from
afar? Lk 19:44
To whom will you run for
help? Isa 20:6
Where will you leave your
riches?
4 Nothing will remain but
to cringe among the
captives Isa 24:22
or fall among the slain. Isa 22:2

Yet for all this, his anger is not
turned away, Isa 5:25
his hand is still upraised.

God's Judgment on Assyria

5 "Woe to the Assyrian, the rod
of my anger, Isa 14:25
in whose hand is the club of
my wrath! Isa 30:30; 66:14
6 I send him against a godless
nation, Isa 9:17
I dispatch him against a
people who anger me,

to seize loot and snatch
plunder, Isa 5:29
and to trample them down
like mud in the streets.
7 But this is not what he
intends, Ge 50:20; Ac 4:23-28
this is not what he has in
mind;
his purpose is to destroy,
to put an end to many
nations.
8 'Are not my commanders all
kings?' he says. 2Ki 18:24
9 'Has not Kalno fared like
Carchemish? 2Ch 35:20
Is not Hamath like Arpad,
and Samaria like
Damascus? 2Ki 16:9; 17:6
10 As my hand seized the
kingdoms of the idols,
kingdoms whose images
excelled those of
Jerusalem and Samaria—
11 shall I not deal with Jerusalem
and her images
as I dealt with Samaria and
her idols?' " 2Ki 19:13; Isa 2:8

12 When the Lord has finished
all his work against Mount Zion
and Jerusalem, he will say, "I will
punish the king of Assyria for the
willful pride of his heart and the
haughty look in his eyes. 13 For he
says: 2Ki 19:31; Jer 50:18

" 'By the strength of my hand I
have done this, Isa 37:24
and by my wisdom, because
I have understanding.
I removed the boundaries of
nations,

I plundered their treasures;
  like a mighty one I
    subdued*a* their kings.
¹⁴As one reaches into a nest,
  so my hand reached for the
    wealth of the nations;
  as people gather abandoned
    eggs,
  so I gathered all the
    countries;
  not one flapped a wing,
    or opened its mouth to
      chirp.' "

¹⁵Does the ax raise itself above
  the person who
    swings it,
  or the saw boast against the
    one who uses it? Ro 9:20-21
As if a rod were to wield the
    person who lifts it up,
  or a club brandish the one
    who is not wood! ver 5
¹⁶Therefore, the Lord, the LORD
    Almighty,
  will send a wasting disease
    upon his sturdy
      warriors; ver 18; Isa 17:4
  under his pomp a fire will be
    kindled Isa 8:7
  like a blazing flame.
¹⁷The Light of Israel will
    become a fire, Isa 31:9
  their Holy One a flame;
  in a single day it will burn and
    consume
  his thorns and his briers.
¹⁸The splendor of his forests
    and fertile fields 2Ki 19:23

it will completely destroy,
  as when a sick person
    wastes away.
¹⁹And the remaining trees of his
    forests will be so few
  that a child could write
    them down.

The Remnant of Israel

²⁰In that day the remnant of
    Israel, Isa 11:10-11
  the survivors of Jacob,
  will no longer rely on him 2Ki 16:7
  who struck them down
  but will truly rely on the
    LORD, Isa 17:7
  the Holy One of Israel.
²¹A remnant will return,*b* a
    remnant of Jacob Isa 6:13
  will return to the Mighty
    God. Isa 9:6
²²Though your people be like
    the sand by the sea,
  Israel, Ge 12:2; Isa 48:19
  only a remnant will return.
Destruction has been
    decreed, Isa 28:22; Da 9:27
  overwhelming and
    righteous.
²³The Lord, the LORD Almighty,
    will carry out
  the destruction decreed
  upon the whole land.

²⁴Therefore this is what the
Lord, the LORD Almighty, says:

"My people who live in Zion,
  do not be afraid of the
    Assyrians,

---

a 13 Or *treasures; / I subdued the mighty,*
also in verse 22   *b 21* Hebrew *shear-jashub* (see 7:3 and note);

who beat you with a rod   Ex 5:14
  and lift up a club against
    you, as Egypt did.
25 Very soon my anger against
    you will end   Isa 17:14
  and my wrath will be
    directed to their
    destruction."   Da 11:36

26 The LORD Almighty will lash
    them with a whip,
  as when he struck down
    Midian at the rock of
    Oreb;   Isa 9:4
  and he will raise his staff over
    the waters,   Ex 14:16
  as he did in Egypt.
27 In that day their burden will
    be lifted from your
    shoulders,
  their yoke from your neck;
  the yoke will be broken
    because you have grown so
    fat.*a*

28 They enter Aiath;
  they pass through Migron;
  they store supplies at
    Mikmash.   1Sa 13:2
29 They go over the pass, and say,
    "We will camp overnight at
    Geba."
  Ramah trembles;   Jos 18:25
  Gibeah of Saul flees.   Jdg 19:14
30 Cry out, Daughter Gallim!
  Listen, Laishah!
  Poor Anathoth!   Ne 11:32
31 Madmenah is in flight;
  the people of Gebim take
    cover.
32 This day they will halt at Nob;

they will shake their fist
  at the mount of Daughter Zion,
  at the hill of Jerusalem.

33 See, the Lord, the LORD
    Almighty,
  will lop off the boughs with
    great power.
  The lofty trees will be felled,
  the tall ones will be brought
    low.   Am 2:9
34 He will cut down the forest
    thickets with an ax;
  Lebanon will fall before the
    Mighty One.   2Ki 19:23

The Branch From Jesse

11 A shoot will come up
    from the stump of Jesse;
  from his roots a Branch will
    bear fruit.   Isa 4:2
2 The Spirit of the LORD will
    rest on him —   Mt 3:16
  the Spirit of wisdom and of
    understanding,   Eph 1:17
  the Spirit of counsel and of
    might,   2Ti 1:7
  the Spirit of the knowledge
    and fear of the LORD —
3 and he will delight in the fear
    of the LORD.

He will not judge by what he
    sees with his eyes,   Jn 7:24
  or decide by what he hears
    with his ears;   Jn 2:25
4 but with righteousness he will
    judge the needy,   Ps 72:2
  with justice he will give
    decisions for the poor of
    the earth.   Isa 3:14; 9:7

---

a 27 Hebrew; Septuagint *broken / from your shoulders*

He will strike the earth with
    the rod of his mouth;
  with the breath of his lips
    he will slay the wicked.
⁵Righteousness will be his belt
  and faithfulness the sash
    around his waist.   Isa 25:1

⁶The wolf will live with the
    lamb,   Isa 65:25
  the leopard will lie down
    with the goat,
  the calf and the lion and the
    yearling*a* together;
  and a little child will lead
    them.
⁷The cow will feed with the
    bear,
  their young will lie down
    together,
  and the lion will eat straw
    like the ox.
⁸The infant will play near the
    cobra's den,   Isa 65:20
  the young child will put its
    hand into the viper's
    nest.   Isa 14:29
⁹They will neither harm nor
    destroy   Job 5:23
  on all my holy mountain,
  for the earth will be filled
    with the knowledge of
    the Lord   Hab 2:14; Ps 98:2-3
  as the waters cover the sea.

¹⁰In that day the Root of Jesse
will stand as a banner for the peoples; the nations will rally to him,
and his resting place will be glorious. ¹¹In that day the Lord will
reach out his hand a second time
to reclaim the surviving remnant
of his people from Assyria, from
Lower Egypt, from Upper Egypt,
from Cush,*b* from Elam, from
Babylonia,*c* from Hamath and
from the islands of the Mediterranean.   Ro 15:12; Mic 7:12

¹²He will raise a banner for the
    nations   Ps 20:5
  and gather the exiles of
    Israel;   Ps 106:47; Isa 14:1
  he will assemble the scattered
    people of Judah   Zep 3:10
  from the four quarters of
    the earth.   Ps 48:10; Rev 7:1
¹³Ephraim's jealousy will
    vanish,
  and Judah's enemies*d* will
    be destroyed;
  Ephraim will not be jealous of
    Judah,
  nor Judah hostile toward
    Ephraim.   Jer 3:18; Eze 37:16
¹⁴They will swoop down on the
    slopes of Philistia to the
    west;
  together they will plunder
    the people to the east.
  They will subdue Edom and
    Moab,   Da 11:41; Joel 3:19
  and the Ammonites will be
    subject to them.
¹⁵The Lord will dry up
    the gulf of the Egyptian sea;
  with a scorching wind he will
    sweep his hand   Isa 19:16
  over the Euphrates River.

---

a 6 Hebrew; Septuagint *lion will feed*   *b* 11 That is, the upper Nile region   *c* 11 Hebrew
Shinar   *d* 13 Or *hostility*

He will break it up into seven
  streams
  so that anyone can cross
    over in sandals.
¹⁶There will be a highway for
    the remnant of his
    people   Isa 19:23; 62:10
  that is left from Assyria,
as there was for Israel
  when they came up from
    Egypt.   Ex 14:26-31

Songs of Praise

12 In that day you will say:

"I will praise you, LORD. Isa 25:1
  Although you were angry
    with me,
  your anger has turned away
    and you have comforted me.
²Surely God is my salvation;
  I will trust and not be afraid.
The LORD, the LORD himself,
  is my strength and my
    defense*a*;   Ps 18:1
  he has become my
    salvation." Ex 15:2; Ps 118:14
³With joy you will draw water
  from the wells of salvation.

⁴In that day you will say:

"Give praise to the LORD,
    proclaim his name;
  make known among the
    nations what he has
    done,   Isa 54:5; 60:3
  and proclaim that his name
    is exalted.   Ps 113:2
⁵Sing to the LORD, for he has
    done glorious things;

let this be known to all the
    world.
⁶Shout aloud and sing for joy,
    people of Zion,
  for great is the Holy One of
    Israel among you."Isa 49:26

A Prophecy Against Babylon

13 A prophecy against Bab-
    ylon that Isaiah son of
Amoz saw: Ge 10:10; Isa 14:4; 20:2

²Raise a banner on a bare hilltop,
    shout to them;
  beckon to them
    to enter the gates of the
      nobles.
³I have commanded those I
    prepared for battle;
  I have summoned my
    warriors to carry out
      my wrath —   Joel 3:11
  those who rejoice in my
    triumph.   Ps 149:2

⁴Listen, a noise on the
    mountains,
  like that of a great
    multitude!   Joel 3:14
Listen, an uproar among the
    kingdoms,   Ps 46:6
  like nations massing
    together!
The LORD Almighty is
    mustering
  an army for war.   Isa 47:4
⁵They come from faraway lands,
  from the ends of the
    heavens —   Isa 5:26
  the LORD and the weapons of
    his wrath —   Isa 10:25

---

a 2 Or *song*

to destroy the whole
country.   Isa 24:1

⁶Wail, for the day of the LORD
   is near;   Eze 30:2; Joel 1:15
it will come like destruction
   from the Almighty.ᵃ
⁷Because of this, all hands will
   go limp,   2Ki 19:26
every heart will melt with
   fear.   Eze 21:7
⁸Terror will seize them,   Isa 21:4
pain and anguish will grip
   them;   Ex 15:14
they will writhe like a
   woman in labor.   Jn 16:21
They will look aghast at each
   other,
their faces aflame.   Na 2:10

⁹See, the day of the LORD is
   coming   Isa 2:12; Jer 51:2
—a cruel day, with wrath
   and fierce anger—   Isa 9:19
to make the land desolate
and destroy the sinners
   within it.
¹⁰The stars of heaven and their
   constellations
will not show their light.
The rising sun will be darkened
and the moon will not give
   its light.   Eze 32:7; Mt 24:29
¹¹I will punish the world for its
   evil,   Isa 3:11
the wicked for their sins.
I will put an end to the
   arrogance of the
   haughty   Ps 10:5; Pr 16:18
and will humble the pride
   of the ruthless.   Isa 25:3,5

¹²I will make people scarcer
   than pure gold,   Isa 4:1
more rare than the gold of
   Ophir.   Ge 10:29
¹³Therefore I will make the
   heavens tremble;   Isa 34:4
and the earth will shake
   from its place   Isa 14:16
at the wrath of the LORD
   Almighty,   Isa 9:19
in the day of his burning
   anger.   Job 9:5

¹⁴Like a hunted gazelle,
like sheep without a
   shepherd,   1Ki 22:17
they will all return to their
   own people,
they will flee to their native
   land.   Jer 50:16
¹⁵Whoever is captured will be
   thrust through;
all who are caught will fall
   by the sword.   Isa 14:19
¹⁶Their infants will be dashed
   to pieces before their
   eyes;   Ps 137:9
their houses will be looted
   and their wives
   violated.   Ge 34:29; Hos 13:16

¹⁷See, I will stir up against them
   the Medes,   Jer 51:1
who do not care for silver
and have no delight in gold.
¹⁸Their bows will strike down
   the young men;   Ps 7:12
they will have no mercy on
   infants,   Isa 47:6
nor will they look with
   compassion on children.

ᵃ 6 Hebrew *Shaddai*

¹⁹Babylon, the jewel of
kingdoms,
the pride and glory of the
Babylonians,ᵃ   Da 4:30
will be overthrown by God
like Sodom and Gomorrah.
²⁰She will never be inhabited
or lived in through all
generations;
there no nomads will pitch
their tents,   2Ch 17:11
there no shepherds will rest
their flocks.
²¹But desert creatures will lie
there,   Rev 18:2
jackals will fill her houses;
there the owls will dwell,
and there the wild goats
will leap about.
²²Hyenas will inhabit her
strongholds,   Isa 25:2
jackals her luxurious
palaces.   Isa 34:13
Her time is at hand,   Jer 51:33
and her days will not be
prolonged.

14 The Lord will have
compassion on Jacob;
once again he will choose
Israel   Zec 1:17; 2:12
and will settle them in their
own land.
Foreigners will join them
and unite with the
descendants of Jacob.
²Nations will take them
and bring them to their own
place.   Isa 60:9

And Israel will take possession
of the nations
and make them male and
female servants in the
Lord's land.
They will make captives of
their captors   Isa 45:14
and rule over their
oppressors.   Isa 60:14

³On the day the Lord gives
you relief from your suffering
and turmoil and from the harsh
labor forced on you, ⁴you will
take up this taunt against the
king of Babylon: Hab 2:6; Isa 11:10

How the oppressor has come
to an end!   Isa 9:4
How his furyᵇ has ended!
⁵The Lord has broken the rod
of the wicked,   Ps 125:3
the scepter of the rulers,
⁶which in anger struck down
peoples   Isa 10:14
with unceasing blows,
and in fury subdued nations
with relentless aggression.
⁷All the lands are at rest and at
peace;   Ps 98:1; 126:1-3
they break into singing.
⁸Even the junipers and the
cedars of Lebanon
gloat over you and say,
"Now that you have been laid
low,
no one comes to cut us
down."

⁹The realm of the dead below
is all astir   Eze 32:21

ᵃ 19 Or *Chaldeans*   ᵇ 4 Dead Sea Scrolls, Septuagint and Syriac; the meaning of the word
in the Masoretic Text is uncertain.

to meet you at your coming;
it rouses the spirits of the
    departed to greet you —
all those who were leaders
    in the world;   Zec 10:3
it makes them rise from their
    thrones —
all those who were kings
    over the nations.   Job 3:14

10 They will all respond,
    they will say to you,
"You also have become weak,
    as we are;
    you have become like us."

11 All your pomp has been
    brought down to the
    grave,
along with the noise of your
    harps;
maggots are spread out
    beneath you
    and worms cover you.   Isa 51:8

12 How you have fallen from
    heaven,   Isa 34:4; Lk 10:18
    morning star, son of the
    dawn!   2Pe 1:19; Rev 2:28; 8:10
You have been cast down to
    the earth,
you who once laid low the
    nations!

13 You said in your heart,
    "I will ascend to the
    heavens;   Da 8:10; Mt 11:23
I will raise my throne   Eze 28:2
    above the stars of God;
I will sit enthroned on the
    mount of assembly,
    on the utmost heights of
    Mount Zaphon.[a]

14 I will ascend above the tops of
    the clouds;
    I will make myself like the
    Most High."   Isa 47:8; 2Th 2:4

15 But you are brought down to
    the realm of the dead,
    to the depths of the pit.

16 Those who see you stare at you,
    they ponder your fate: Jer 50:23
"Is this the man who shook
    the earth
    and made kingdoms
    tremble,

17 the man who made the world
    a wilderness,   Joel 2:3
who overthrew its cities
    and would not let his
    captives go home?"

18 All the kings of the nations lie
    in state,
    each in his own tomb.

19 But you are cast out of your
    tomb   Isa 22:16-18
    like a rejected branch;
you are covered with the slain,
    with those pierced by the
    sword,
    those who descend to the
    stones of the pit.   Jer 41:7-9
Like a corpse trampled
    underfoot,

20   you will not join them in
    burial,
for you have destroyed your
    land
    and killed your people.

Let the offspring of the wicked
    never be mentioned again.

---

[a] 13 Or *of the north*; Zaphon was the most sacred mountain of the Canaanites.

²¹ Prepare a place to slaughter
   his children
for the sins of their
   ancestors; Ex 20:5; Lev 26:39
they are not to rise to inherit
   the land
and cover the earth with
   their cities.

²² "I will rise up against them,"
   declares the LORD
   Almighty.
"I will wipe out Babylon's
   name and survivors,
her offspring and
   descendants," 1Ki 14:10
      declares the LORD.
²³ "I will turn her into a place for
   owls Isa 34:11-15; Zep 2:14
and into swampland;
I will sweep her with the
   broom of destruction,"
declares the LORD
   Almighty.

²⁴ The LORD Almighty has
sworn, Isa 45:23

"Surely, as I have planned, so
   it will be,
and as I have purposed, so
   it will happen. Ac 4:28
²⁵ I will crush the Assyrian in
   my land; Isa 10:5,12
on my mountains I will
   trample him down.
His yoke will be taken from
   my people, Isa 9:4
and his burden removed
   from their shoulders."

²⁶ This is the plan determined
   for the whole world;

this is the hand stretched
   out over all nations.
²⁷ For the LORD Almighty has
   purposed, and who can
   thwart him?
His hand is stretched out,
   and who can turn it back?

A Prophecy Against the Philistines

²⁸ This prophecy came in the
year King Ahaz died: 2Ki 16:20

²⁹ Do not rejoice, all you
   Philistines, 2Ch 26:6
that the rod that struck you
   is broken;
from the root of that snake
   will spring up a viper,
its fruit will be a darting,
   venomous serpent.
³⁰ The poorest of the poor will
   find pasture,
and the needy will lie down
   in safety. Isa 3:15; 7:21-22
But your root I will destroy by
   famine; Isa 8:21; 9:20
it will slay your survivors.

³¹ Wail, you gate! Howl, you city!
   Melt away, all you
   Philistines!
A cloud of smoke comes from
   the north, Jer 1:14
and there is not a straggler
   in its ranks.
³² What answer shall be given
   to the envoys of that nation?
"The LORD has established
   Zion, Ps 87:2,5; Isa 44:28
and in her his afflicted
   people will find refuge."

A Prophecy Against Moab

16:6-12pp — Jer 48:29-36

15 A prophecy against Moab:

Ar in Moab is ruined, Jer 48:24,41
destroyed in a night!
Kir in Moab is ruined, 2Ki 3:25
destroyed in a night!
²Dibon goes up to its temple,
to its high places to weep;
Moab wails over Nebo and
Medeba.
Every head is shaved Lev 21:5
and every beard cut off.
³In the streets they wear
sackcloth;
on the roofs and in the
public squares Jer 48:38
they all wail,
prostrate with weeping.
⁴Heshbon and Elealeh cry
out,
their voices are heard all
the way to Jahaz.
Therefore the armed men of
Moab cry out,
and their hearts are faint.

⁵My heart cries out over Moab;
her fugitives flee as far as
Zoar,
as far as Eglath Shelishiyah.
They go up the hill to Luhith,
weeping as they go;
on the road to Horonaim
they lament their
destruction. Jer 48:5
⁶The waters of Nimrim are
dried up Isa 19:5-7; Jer 48:34
and the grass is withered;

the vegetation is gone
and nothing green is left.
⁷So the wealth they have
acquired and stored up
they carry away over the
Ravine of the Poplars.
⁸Their outcry echoes along the
border of Moab;
their wailing reaches as far
as Eglaim,
their lamentation as far as
Beer Elim. Nu 21:16
⁹The waters of Dimon^a are full
of blood,
but I will bring still more
upon Dimon^a —
a lion upon the fugitives of
Moab 2Ki 17:25
and upon those who remain
in the land.

16 Send lambs as tribute
to the ruler of the land,
from Sela, across the desert,
to the mount of Daughter
Zion. Isa 10:32
²Like fluttering birds
pushed from the nest, Pr 27:8
so are the women of Moab
at the fords of the Arnon.

³"Make up your mind," Moab
says.
"Render a decision.
Make your shadow like night —
at high noon.
Hide the fugitives, 1Ki 18:4
do not betray the refugees.
⁴Let the Moabite fugitives stay
with you;

---

^a 9 *Dimon*, a wordplay on *Dibon* (see verse 2), sounds like the Hebrew for *blood*.

be their shelter from the
destroyer."

The oppressor will come to an
end,   Isa 9:4
and destruction will cease;
the aggressor will vanish
from the land.
[5]In love a throne will be
established; Da 7:14; Mic 4:7
in faithfulness a man will
sit on it —
one from the house[a] of
David —   Lk 1:32
one who in judging seeks
justice   Isa 9:7
and speeds the cause of
righteousness.

[6]We have heard of Moab's
pride —   Am 2:1; Ob 3
how great is her
arrogance! —
of her conceit, her pride and
her insolence;
but her boasts are empty.
[7]Therefore the Moabites wail,
they wail together for Moab.
Lament and grieve
for the raisin cakes of Kir
Hareseth.   2Ki 3:25; 1Ch 16:3
[8]The fields of Heshbon wither,
the vines of Sibmah also.
The rulers of the nations
have trampled down the
choicest vines,   Isa 5:2
which once reached Jazer
and spread toward the
desert.
Their shoots spread out   Job 8:16
and went as far as the sea.[b]

[9]So I weep, as Jazer weeps,
for the vines of Sibmah.
Heshbon and Elealeh,
I drench you with tears!
The shouts of joy over your
ripened fruit
and over your harvests have
been stilled.   Jer 40:12
[10]Joy and gladness are taken
away from the orchards;
no one sings or shouts in
the vineyards;
no one treads out wine at the
presses,   Jdg 9:27; Job 24:11
for I have put an end to the
shouting.
[11]My heart laments for Moab
like a harp,   Isa 15:5
my inmost being for Kir
Hareseth.   Isa 63:15; Hos 11:8
[12]When Moab appears at her
high place,
she only wears herself out;
when she goes to her shrine to
pray,   Isa 15:2
it is to no avail.   Jer 48:29-36

[13]This is the word the LORD
has already spoken concerning
Moab. [14]But now the LORD says:
"Within three years, as a servant
bound by contract would count
them, Moab's splendor and all
her many people will be despised, and her survivors will be
very few and feeble."   Isa 21:17; 25:10

A Prophecy Against Damascus

17 A prophecy against Damascus:
Jer 49:23; Ac 9:2

---

[a] 5 Hebrew *tent*   [b] 8 Probably the Dead Sea

"See, Damascus will no longer
be a city
but will become a heap of
ruins.   Am 1:3; Zec 9:1
2 The cities of Aroer will be
deserted
and left to flocks, which will
lie down,   Isa 7:21; Eze 25:5
with no one to make them
afraid.   Jer 7:33; Mic 4:4
3 The fortified city will
disappear from
Ephraim,
and royal power from
Damascus;
the remnant of Aram will be
like the glory of the
Israelites,"   ver 4; Isa 7:8,16
declares the LORD
Almighty.
4 "In that day the glory of Jacob
will fade;
the fat of his body will waste
away.   Isa 10:16
5 It will be as when reapers
harvest the standing
grain,
gathering the grain in their
arms —   Jer 51:33; Joel 3:13
as when someone gleans
heads of grain
in the Valley of
Rephaim.   1Ch 11:15
6 Yet some gleanings will
remain,   Isa 24:13
as when an olive tree is
beaten,   Isa 27:12
leaving two or three olives on
the topmost branches,

four or five on the fruitful
boughs,"
declares the LORD,
the God of Israel.
7 In that day people will look to
their Maker   Isa 10:20
and turn their eyes to the
Holy One of Israel. Mic 7:7
8 They will not look to the
altars,
the work of their hands,
and they will have no regard
for the Asherah poles[a]
and the incense altars their
fingers have made. Isa 2:8
9 In that day their strong cities, which they left because of
the Israelites, will be like places
abandoned to thickets and un-
dergrowth. And all will be desolation.   Isa 7:19
10 You have forgotten God your
Savior;   Ps 68:19; Isa 12:2
you have not remembered
the Rock, your fortress.
Therefore, though you set out
the finest plants
and plant imported vines,
11 though on the day you set
them out, you make
them grow,
and on the morning when
you plant them, you
bring them to bud, Ps 90:6
yet the harvest will be as
nothing   Hos 8:7
in the day of disease and
incurable pain.   Job 4:8

a 8 That is, wooden symbols of the goddess Asherah

¹²Woe to the many nations that
    rage —
  they rage like the raging
    sea!   Ps 18:4; Jer 6:23; Lk 21:25
Woe to the peoples who
    roar —
  they roar like the roaring of
    great waters!
¹³Although the peoples roar
    like the roar of surging
    waters,
  when he rebukes them they
    flee far away,   Ps 9:5
  driven before the wind like
    chaff on the hills,   Isa 41:2
  like tumbleweed before a
    gale.   Job 21:18
¹⁴In the evening, sudden terror!
  Before the morning, they
    are gone!   2Ki 19:35
  This is the portion of those
    who loot us,
  the lot of those who
    plunder us.

A Prophecy Against Cush

18 Woe to the land of
    whirring wings[a]
  along the rivers of Cush,[b]
²which sends envoys by sea
  in papyrus boats over the
    water.   Ex 2:3

Go, swift messengers,
to a people tall and smooth-
    skinned,
  to a people feared far and
    wide,
an aggressive nation of
    strange speech,   Ge 10:8-9

whose land is divided by
    rivers.   ver 7

³All you people of the world,
  you who live on the earth,
when a banner is raised on
    the mountains,   Isa 5:26
  you will see it,
and when a trumpet sounds,
    you will hear it.
⁴This is what the LORD says
    to me:
"I will remain quiet and
  will look on from my
    dwelling place,   Isa 26:21
like shimmering heat in the
    sunshine,
  like a cloud of dew in the
    heat of harvest."   Isa 26:19
⁵For, before the harvest, when
    the blossom is gone
  and the flower becomes a
    ripening grape,
he will cut off the shoots with
    pruning knives,
  and cut down and take away
    the spreading branches.
⁶They will all be left to the
    mountain birds of prey
  and to the wild animals;
the birds will feed on them all
    summer,
  the wild animals all winter.

⁷At that time gifts will be
brought to the LORD Almighty

from a people tall and
    smooth-skinned,   Ge 41:14
from a people feared far and
    wide,   Hab 1:7

---

a 1 Or *of locusts*   *b* 1 That is, the upper Nile region

an aggressive nation of
    strange speech,
  whose land is divided by
    rivers —

the gifts will be brought to Mount
Zion, the place of the Name of
the LORD Almighty.   Ps 68:31

A Prophecy Against Egypt

19 A prophecy against Egypt:

See, the LORD rides on a swift
  cloud   Ps 18:10; 104:3; Rev 1:7
and is coming to Egypt.
The idols of Egypt tremble
    before him,
  and the hearts of the
    Egyptians melt with
    fear.   Jos 2:11

2 "I will stir up Egyptian
    against Egyptian —
  brother will fight against
    brother,   Jdg 7:22; Mt 10:21,36
  neighbor against neighbor,
  city against city,
  kingdom against kingdom.
3 The Egyptians will lose heart,
  and I will bring their plans
    to nothing;   1Ch 10:13
they will consult the idols and
    the spirits of the dead,
  the mediums and the
    spiritists.   Isa 8:19; 47:13
4 I will hand the Egyptians over
  to the power of a cruel
    master,
  and a fierce king will rule over
    them,"   Isa 20:4; Jer 46:26
declares the Lord, the LORD
  Almighty.

5 The waters of the river will
    dry up,   Jer 51:36
  and the riverbed will be
    parched and dry.
6 The canals will stink;   Ex 7:18
  the streams of Egypt will
    dwindle and dry up.
The reeds and rushes will
    wither,   Isa 15:6
7   also the plants along the
    Nile,   Isa 23:3
  at the mouth of the river.
Every sown field along the Nile
  will become parched, will
    blow away and be no
    more.
8 The fishermen will groan and
    lament,   Eze 47:10
  all who cast hooks into the
    Nile;   Hab 1:15
those who throw nets on the
    water
  will pine away.
9 Those who work with combed
    flax will despair,
  the weavers of fine linen
    will lose hope.   Pr 7:16
10 The workers in cloth will be
    dejected,
  and all the wage earners
    will be sick at heart.

11 The officials of Zoan are
    nothing but fools;   Nu 13:22
  the wise counselors of
    Pharaoh give senseless
    advice.   Ge 41:37
How can you say to Pharaoh,
  "I am one of the wise men,
  a disciple of the ancient
    kings"?

¹²Where are your wise men now?
    Let them show you and
        make known
    what the Lord Almighty
        has planned against Egypt.
¹³The officials of Zoan have
        become fools,
    the leaders of Memphis are
        deceived;   Jer 2:16
    the cornerstones of her peoples
        have led Egypt astray.
¹⁴The Lord has poured into them
        a spirit of dizziness;   Mt 17:17
    they make Egypt stagger in all
        that she does,
    as a drunkard staggers
        around in his vomit.
¹⁵There is nothing Egypt can do—
    head or tail, palm branch or
        reed.   Isa 9:14

¹⁶In that day the Egyptians will become weaklings. They will shudder with fear at the uplifted hand that the Lord Almighty raises against them. ¹⁷And the land of Judah will bring terror to the Egyptians; everyone to whom Judah is mentioned will be terrified, because of what the Lord Almighty is planning against them.   Isa 11:15; 14:24
¹⁸In that day five cities in Egypt will speak the language of Canaan and swear allegiance to the Lord Almighty. One of them will be called the City of the Sun.ᵃ
¹⁹In that day there will be an altar to the Lord in the heart of Egypt, and a monument to the Lord at its border. ²⁰It will be a sign and witness to the Lord Almighty in the land of Egypt. When they cry out to the Lord because of their oppressors, he will send them a savior and defender, and he will rescue them. ²¹So the Lord will make himself known to the Egyptians, and in that day they will acknowledge the Lord. They will worship with sacrifices and grain offerings; they will make vows to the Lord and keep them. ²²The Lord will strike Egypt with a plague; he will strike them and heal them. They will turn to the Lord, and he will respond to their pleas and heal them.   Isa 45:14; 49:24-26
²³In that day there will be a highway from Egypt to Assyria. The Assyrians will go to Egypt and the Egyptians to Assyria. The Egyptians and Assyrians will worship together. ²⁴In that day Israel will be the third, along with Egypt and Assyria, a blessingᵇ on the earth. ²⁵The Lord Almighty will bless them, saying, "Blessed be Egypt my people, Assyria my handiwork, and Israel my inheritance."

A Prophecy Against Egypt and Cush

20 In the year that the supreme commander, sent

ᵃ 18 Some manuscripts of the Masoretic Text, Dead Sea Scrolls, Symmachus and Vulgate; most manuscripts of the Masoretic Text *City of Destruction*   ᵇ 24 Or *Assyria, whose names will be used in blessings* (see Gen. 48:20); or *Assyria, who will be seen by others as blessed* by Sargon king of Assyria, came to Ashdod and attacked and captured it — ²at that time the LORD spoke through Isaiah son of Amoz. He said to him, "Take off the sackcloth from your body and the sandals from your feet." And he did so, going around stripped and barefoot. 1Sa 19:24

³Then the LORD said, "Just as my servant Isaiah has gone stripped and barefoot for three years, as a sign and portent against Egypt and Cush,ᵃ ⁴so the king of Assyria will lead away stripped and barefoot the Egyptian captives and Cushite exiles, young and old, with buttocks bared — to Egypt's shame. ⁵Those who trusted in Cush and boasted in Egypt will be dismayed and put to shame. ⁶In that day the people who live on this coast will say, 'See what has happened to those we relied on, those we fled to for help and deliverance from the king of Assyria! How then can we escape?' "

A Prophecy Against Babylon

21 A prophecy against the Desert by the Sea: Isa 13:21

Like whirlwinds sweeping
      through the southland,
   an invader comes from the
      desert,
   from a land of terror.

²A dire vision has been shown
      to me: Ps 60:3

The traitor betrays, the
      looter takes loot. Isa 33:1
Elam, attack! Media, lay siege!
   I will bring to an end all the
      groaning she caused.

³At this my body is racked with
      pain,
   pangs seize me, like those
      of a woman in labor;
I am staggered by what I hear,
   I am bewildered by what I
      see.
⁴My heart falters,
   fear makes me tremble;
the twilight I longed for
   has become a horror to me.

⁵They set the tables,
   they spread the rugs,
   they eat, they drink! Jer 51:39,57
Get up, you officers,
   oil the shields! 2Sa 1:21

⁶This is what the Lord says
to me:

"Go, post a lookout 2Ki 9:17
   and have him report what
      he sees.
⁷When he sees chariots ver 9
   with teams of horses,
riders on donkeys
   or riders on camels,
let him be alert,
   fully alert."

⁸And the lookoutᵇ shouted,

"Day after day, my lord,
   I stand on the
      watchtower;

ᵃ 3 That is, the upper Nile region; also in verse 5 Masoretic Text *A lion*   ᵇ 8 Dead Sea Scrolls and Syriac;

every night I stay at my post.
⁹Look, here comes a man in a
    chariot
with a team of horses.
And he gives back the answer:
    'Babylon has fallen, has
        fallen! Jer 51:8; Rev 14:8; 18:2
All the images of its gods
    lie shattered on the
        ground!' " Isa 46:1

¹⁰My people who are crushed
    on the threshing floor,
I tell you what I have heard
from the LORD Almighty,
    from the God of Israel.

A Prophecy Against Edom

¹¹A prophecy against Dumah[a]:

Someone calls to me from
    Seir, Ge 32:3
"Watchman, what is left of
    the night?
Watchman, what is left of
    the night?"
¹²The watchman replies,
"Morning is coming, but
    also the night.
If you would ask, then ask;
    and come back yet again."

A Prophecy Against Arabia

¹³A prophecy against Arabia:

You caravans of Dedanites,
    who camp in the thickets of
        Arabia,
¹⁴   bring water for the thirsty;
you who live in Tema, Ge 25:15
    bring food for the fugitives.

¹⁵They flee from the sword,
    from the drawn sword,
from the bent bow
    and from the heat of battle.

¹⁶This is what the Lord says to
me: "Within one year, as a servant bound by contract would
count it, all the splendor of Kedar
will come to an end. ¹⁷The survivors of the archers, the warriors
of Kedar, will be few." The LORD,
the God of Israel, has spoken.

A Prophecy About Jerusalem

22 A prophecy against the
    Valley of Vision: Isa 13:1

What troubles you now,
    that you have all gone up on
        the roofs,
²you town so full of
    commotion,
    you city of tumult and
        revelry? Isa 32:13
Your slain were not killed by
    the sword, 2Ki 25:3; Isa 10:4
    nor did they die in battle.
³All your leaders have fled
    together;
    they have been captured
        without using the bow.
All you who were caught
    were taken prisoner
        together,
    having fled while the enemy
        was still far away.
⁴Therefore I said, "Turn away
    from me;
    let me weep bitterly. Isa 15:3
Do not try to console me

---

a 11 *Dumah*, a wordplay on *Edom*, means *silence* or *stillness*.

over the destruction of my
    people." Jer 9:1

⁵The Lord, the LORD Almighty,
    has a day Isa 2:12
of tumult and trampling
    and terror La 1:5; Zep 1:15
in the Valley of Vision,
a day of battering down walls
    and of crying out to the
    mountains.
⁶Elam takes up the quiver, Isa 21:2
    with her charioteers and
    horses;
Kir uncovers the shield.
⁷Your choicest valleys are full
    of chariots,
    and horsemen are posted at
    the city gates. 2Ch 32:1-2

⁸The Lord stripped away the
    defenses of Judah,
and you looked in that day
    to the weapons in the
    Palace of the Forest.
⁹You saw that the walls of the
    City of David
were broken through in
    many places;
you stored up water
    in the Lower Pool. 2Ch 32:4
¹⁰You counted the buildings in
    Jerusalem
and tore down houses to
    strengthen the wall.
¹¹You built a reservoir between
    the two walls 2Ki 25:4
    for the water of the Old Pool,
but you did not look to the
    One who made it,
or have regard for the One
    who planned it long ago.

¹²The Lord, the LORD Almighty,
    called you on that day
to weep and to wail, Joel 2:17
    to tear out your hair and put
    on sackcloth. Joel 1:13
¹³But see, there is joy and
    revelry,
    slaughtering of cattle and
    killing of sheep,
    eating of meat and drinking
    of wine! Isa 56:12; Lk 17:26-29
"Let us eat and drink," you
    say,
    "for tomorrow we die!"

¹⁴The LORD Almighty has revealed this in my hearing: "Till
your dying day this sin will not
be atoned for," says the Lord, the
LORD Almighty. Isa 5:9; 13:11; 26:21

¹⁵This is what the Lord, the
LORD Almighty, says:

"Go, say to this steward,
    to Shebna the palace
    administrator: 2Ki 18:18
¹⁶What are you doing here
    and who gave you
    permission
    to cut out a grave for
    yourself here, Mt 27:60
hewing your grave on the
    height
    and chiseling your resting
    place in the rock?
¹⁷"Beware, the LORD is about to
    take firm hold of you
    and hurl you away, you
    mighty man.
¹⁸He will roll you up tightly like
    a ball

and throw you into a large
country. Isa 17:13
There you will die
and there the chariots you
were so proud of
will become a disgrace to
your master's house.
¹⁹I will depose you from your
office,
and you will be ousted from
your position. 1Sa 2:7

²⁰"In that day I will summon my servant, Eliakim son of Hilkiah. ²¹I will clothe him with your robe and fasten your sash around him and hand your authority over to him. He will be a father to those who live in Jerusalem and to the people of Judah. ²²I will place on his shoulder the key to the house of David; what he opens no one can shut, and what he shuts no one can open. ²³I will drive him like a peg into a firm place; he will become a seat*a* of honor for the house of his father. ²⁴All the glory of his family will hang on him: its offspring and offshoots — all its lesser vessels, from the bowls to all the jars. Job 36:7; Ezr 9:8; Rev 3:7

²⁵"In that day," declares the LORD Almighty, "the peg driven into the firm place will give way; it will be sheared off and will fall, and the load hanging on it will be cut down." The LORD has spoken. ver 23; Isa 46:11; Mic 4:4

A Prophecy Against Tyre

23 A prophecy against Tyre:

Wail, you ships of Tarshish!
For Tyre is destroyed
and left without house or
harbor.
From the land of Cyprus
word has come to them.

²Be silent, you people of the
island
and you merchants of Sidon,
whom the seafarers have
enriched.
³On the great waters
came the grain of the Shihor;
the harvest of the Nile*b* was
the revenue of Tyre,
and she became the
marketplace of the
nations.

⁴Be ashamed, Sidon, and you
fortress of the sea,
for the sea has spoken:
"I have neither been in labor
nor given birth;
I have neither reared
sons nor brought up
daughters."
⁵When word comes to Egypt,
they will be in anguish at
the report from Tyre.

⁶Cross over to Tarshish;
wail, you people of the island.
⁷Is this your city of revelry,
the old, old city,
whose feet have taken her

---

a 23 Or *throne*   *b 2,3* Masoretic Text; Dead Sea Scrolls *Sidon, / who cross over the sea; / your envoys* ³*are on the great waters. / The grain of the Shihor, / the harvest of the Nile,*

to settle in far-off lands?
⁸Who planned this against Tyre,
 the bestower of crowns,
 whose merchants are princes,
 whose traders are
  renowned in the earth?
⁹The Lord Almighty planned it,
 to bring down her pride in
  all her splendor   Job 40:11
 and to humble all who are
  renowned on the earth.

¹⁰Till*a* your land as they do
  along the Nile,
 Daughter Tarshish,
 for you no longer have a
  harbor.
¹¹The Lord has stretched out
  his hand over the sea
 and made its kingdoms
  tremble.   Ps 46:6
 He has given an order
  concerning Phoenicia
 that her fortresses be
  destroyed. Isa 25:2; Zec 9:3-4
¹²He said, "No more of your
  reveling,   Rev 18:22
 Virgin Daughter Sidon, now
  crushed!   Isa 47:1

"Up, cross over to Cyprus;
 even there you will find no
  rest."
¹³Look at the land of the
  Babylonians,*b*
 this people that is now of no
  account!
 The Assyrians have made it
  a place for desert creatures;

they raised up their siege
  towers,
 they stripped its fortresses
  bare
 and turned it into a ruin.

¹⁴Wail, you ships of Tarshish;
 your fortress is destroyed!

¹⁵At that time Tyre will be forgotten for seventy years, the span of a king's life. But at the end of these seventy years, it will happen to Tyre as in the song of the prostitute: Jer 25:22

¹⁶"Take up a harp, walk through
  the city,
 you forgotten prostitute;
 play the harp well, sing many
  a song,
 so that you will be
  remembered."

¹⁷At the end of seventy years, the Lord will deal with Tyre. She will return to her lucrative prostitution and will ply her trade with all the kingdoms on the face of the earth. ¹⁸Yet her profit and her earnings will be set apart for the Lord; they will not be stored up or hoarded. Her profits will go to those who live before the Lord, for abundant food and fine clothes.   Isa 60:5-9; Eze 16:26; Rev 17:1

The Lord's Devastation of the Earth

24 See, the Lord is going to lay waste the earth

---

a 10 Dead Sea Scrolls and some Septuagint manuscripts; Masoretic Text *Go through*
b 13 Or *Chaldeans*

and devastate it;
he will ruin its face
and scatter its
    inhabitants —
²it will be the same
    for priest as for people, Hos 4:9
    for the master as for his
        servant,
    for the mistress as for her
        servant,
    for seller as for buyer, Eze 7:12
    for borrower as for lender,
    for debtor as for creditor.
³The earth will be completely
        laid waste
    and totally plundered.
            The LORD has spoken
                this word.

⁴The earth dries up and
        withers,
    the world languishes and
        withers,
    the heavens languish with
        the earth.   Isa 2:12
⁵The earth is defiled by its
        people;   Ge 3:17; Nu 35:33
    they have disobeyed the
        laws,   Isa 10:6; 59:12
    violated the statutes
    and broken the everlasting
        covenant.
⁶Therefore a curse consumes
        the earth;
    its people must bear their
        guilt.
    Therefore earth's inhabitants
        are burned up,   Isa 1:31
    and very few are left.
⁷The new wine dries up and
        the vine withers;

all the merrymakers groan.
⁸The joyful timbrels are stilled,
    the noise of the revelers has
        stopped,   Hos 2:11
    the joyful harp is silent.
⁹No longer do they drink wine
        with a song;   Isa 5:11,22
    the beer is bitter to its
        drinkers.   Isa 5:20
¹⁰The ruined city lies desolate;
    the entrance to every house
        is barred.
¹¹In the streets they cry out for
        wine;
    all joy turns to gloom, Isa 16:10
    all joyful sounds are
        banished from the earth.
¹²The city is left in ruins, Isa 19:18
    its gate is battered to pieces.
¹³So will it be on the earth
    and among the nations,
    as when an olive tree is beaten,
    or as when gleanings are
        left after the grape
        harvest.

¹⁴They raise their voices, they
        shout for joy;   Isa 12:6
    from the west they acclaim
        the LORD's majesty.
¹⁵Therefore in the east give
        glory to the LORD; Isa 66:19
    exalt the name of the LORD,
        the God of Israel, Mal 1:11
    in the islands of the sea.
¹⁶From the ends of the earth we
        hear singing: Ps 48:10; 65:8
    "Glory to the Righteous
        One."   Isa 28:5

But I said, "I waste away, I
        waste away!

Woe to me!
The treacherous betray!
  With treachery the
    treacherous betray!"
[17] Terror and pit and snare await
    you,   Jer 48:43
  people of the earth.   Lk 21:35
[18] Whoever flees at the sound of
    terror   Job 20:24
  will fall into a pit;
whoever climbs out of the pit
  will be caught in a snare.

The floodgates of the heavens
    are opened,   Ge 7:11
  the foundations of the earth
    shake.   Ps 18:7
[19] The earth is broken up,
  the earth is split asunder,
  the earth is violently shaken.
[20] The earth reels like a drunkard,
  it sways like a hut in the
    wind;
so heavy upon it is the guilt of
    its rebellion   Isa 1:2,28; 43:27
  that it falls — never to rise
    again.   Ps 46:2

[21] In that day the LORD will
    punish   Isa 10:12
  the powers in the heavens
    above
  and the kings on the earth
    below.   Isa 2:12
[22] They will be herded together
  like prisoners bound in a
    dungeon;   Isa 10:4; 42:7,22
  they will be shut up in prison
  and be punished[a] after
    many days.   Eze 38:8
[23] The moon will be dismayed,

  the sun ashamed;   Isa 13:10
for the LORD Almighty will
    reign   Rev 22:5
on Mount Zion and in
    Jerusalem,   Heb 12:22
and before its elders — with
    great glory.   Isa 60:19

Praise to the LORD

25 LORD, you are my God;
  I will exalt you and
    praise your name, Ps 145:2
for in perfect faithfulness
  you have done wonderful
    things,   Ps 98:1
  things planned long ago.
[2] You have made the city a heap
    of rubble,   Isa 17:1
  the fortified town a ruin,
the foreigners' stronghold a
    city no more;   Isa 13:22
  it will never be rebuilt.
[3] Therefore strong peoples will
    honor you;   Ex 6:2; Ps 22:23
  cities of ruthless nations
    will revere you.   Isa 13:11
[4] You have been a refuge for the
    poor,   Isa 4:6; 17:10
  a refuge for the needy in
    their distress,   Isa 14:30
  a shelter from the storm Ps 55:8
  and a shade from the heat.
For the breath of the ruthless
  is like a storm driving
    against a wall
[5]   and like the heat of the desert.
You silence the uproar of
    foreigners;   Jer 51:55
  as heat is reduced by the
    shadow of a cloud,

[a] 22 Or *released*

so the song of the ruthless is
	stilled.

6 On this mountain the Lord
		Almighty will prepare
	a feast of rich food for all
		peoples, Mt 8:11; 22:4
	a banquet of aged wine —
		the best of meats and the
		finest of wines. Pr 9:2
7 On this mountain he will
		destroy
	the shroud that enfolds all
		peoples, 2Co 3:15-16; Eph 4:18
	the sheet that covers all
		nations;
8   he will swallow up death
		forever. Hos 13:14
	The Sovereign Lord will wipe
		away the tears Rev 7:17; 21:4
	from all faces;
	he will remove his people's
		disgrace Mt 5:11; 1Pe 4:14
	from all the earth.
		The Lord has spoken.

9 In that day they will say,

	"Surely this is our God; Isa 40:9
		we trusted in him, and he
		saved us. Ps 20:5; Isa 33:22
	This is the Lord, we trusted
		in him;
		let us rejoice and be glad in
		his salvation." Isa 35:2,10

10 The hand of the Lord will rest
		on this mountain; Isa 2:2
	but Moab will be trampled
		in their land Am 2:1-3
	as straw is trampled down
		in the manure.

11 They will stretch out their
		hands in it,
	as swimmers stretch out
		their hands to swim.
	God will bring down their
		pride Job 40:12; Isa 5:25
	despite the cleverness[a] of
		their hands.
12 He will bring down your high
		fortified walls
	and lay them low; Isa 15:1
	he will bring them down to
		the ground,
	to the very dust.

A Song of Praise

26 In that day this song will
	be sung in the land of Ju-
dah:

	We have a strong city; Isa 14:32
		God makes salvation
		its walls and ramparts.
2 Open the gates
	that the righteous nation
		may enter, Isa 54:14; 58:8
	the nation that keeps faith.
3 You will keep in perfect peace
		those whose minds are
		steadfast,
	because they trust in you.
4 Trust in the Lord forever,
	for the Lord, the Lord
		himself, is the Rock
		eternal. Ge 49:24
5 He humbles those who dwell
		on high,
	he lays the lofty city low;
	he levels it to the ground
		and casts it down to the dust.

---

a 11 The meaning of the Hebrew for this word is uncertain.

⁶Feet trample it down —
   the feet of the oppressed,
   the footsteps of the poor.

⁷The path of the righteous is
      level;
   you, the Upright One, make
      the way of the righteous
      smooth.   Isa 42:16
⁸Yes, LORD, walking in the way
      of your laws,ᵃ   Isa 56:1
   we wait for you;   Ps 37:9
   your name and renown   Isa 12:4
   are the desire of our hearts.
⁹My soul yearns for you in the
      night;
   in the morning my spirit
      longs for you.   Ps 63:1; 78:34
   When your judgments come
      upon the earth,
   the people of the world
      learn righteousness.
¹⁰But when grace is shown to
      the wicked,
   they do not learn
      righteousness;
   even in a land of uprightness
      they go on doing evil
   and do not regard the
      majesty of the LORD.
¹¹LORD, your hand is lifted high,
   but they do not see it.   Isa 44:9
   Let them see your zeal for
      your people and be put
      to shame;
   let the fire reserved for
      your enemies consume
      them.   Heb 10:27

¹²LORD, you establish peace
      for us;   Ps 119:165; Isa 9:6

all that we have
      accomplished you have
      done for us.   Ps 68:28
¹³LORD our God, other lords
      besides you have ruled
      over us,   Isa 2:8; 10:5,11
   but your name alone do we
      honor.   Isa 63:7
¹⁴They are now dead, they live
      no more;   Dt 4:28
   their spirits do not rise.
   You punished them and
      brought them to ruin;
   you wiped out all memory
      of them.
¹⁵You have enlarged the nation,
      LORD;
   you have enlarged the
      nation.   Isa 14:2
   You have gained glory for
      yourself;
   you have extended all the
      borders of the land.

¹⁶LORD, they came to you in
      their distress;   Hos 5:15
   when you disciplined them,
      they could barely whisper a
      prayer.ᵇ
¹⁷As a pregnant woman about
      to give birth   Jn 16:21
   writhes and cries out in her
      pain,
   so were we in your
      presence, LORD.
¹⁸We were with child, we
      writhed in labor,
   but we gave birth to wind.
   We have not brought salvation
      to the earth,   Ps 17:14

ᵃ 8 Or judgments   ᵇ 16 The meaning of the Hebrew for this clause is uncertain.

and the people of the world
  have not come to life.

19 But your dead will live, LORD;
  their bodies will rise —
let those who dwell in the
  dust
  wake up and shout for joy —
your dew is like the dew of the
  morning;
  the earth will give birth to
  her dead. Eze 37:1-14; Da 12:2

20 Go, my people, enter your
  rooms
  and shut the doors behind
  you; Ex 12:23
hide yourselves for a little
  while Ps 91:1,4
  until his wrath has passed by.
21 See, the LORD is coming out of
  his dwelling Mic 1:3
  to punish the people of the
  earth for their sins.
The earth will disclose the
  blood shed on it; Job 16:18
  the earth will conceal its
  slain no longer.

Deliverance of Israel

27 In that day,
  the LORD will punish with his
  sword — Isa 34:6; 66:16
  his fierce, great and
  powerful sword —
Leviathan the gliding serpent,
Leviathan the coiling
  serpent;
he will slay the monster of the
  sea. Ps 74:13; Rev 12:9

2 In that day —

"Sing about a fruitful
  vineyard: Jer 2:21
3   I, the LORD, watch over it;
  I water it continually. Isa 58:11
I guard it day and night Ps 91:4
  so that no one may harm it.
4   I am not angry.
If only there were briers and
  thorns confronting me!
  I would march against them
  in battle;
  I would set them all on fire.
5 Or else let them come to me
  for refuge; Isa 25:4
  let them make peace with
  me, Job 22:21; Ro 5:1; 2Co 5:20
yes, let them make peace
  with me."

6 In days to come Jacob will
  take root, Isa 11:10
  Israel will bud and blossom
and fill all the world with
  fruit. Isa 37:31

7 Has the LORD struck her
  as he struck down those
  who struck her? Isa 37:36
Has she been killed
  as those were killed who
  killed her?
8 By warfare[a] and exile you
  contend with her —
with his fierce blast he
  drives her out,
  as on a day the east wind
  blows.
9 By this, then, will Jacob's guilt
  be atoned for, Ps 78:38

---

[a] 8 See Septuagint; the meaning of the Hebrew for this word is uncertain.

and this will be the full fruit
of the removal of his
sin: Ro 11:27
When he makes all the altar
stones
to be like limestone crushed
to pieces,
no Asherah poles*a* or incense
altars   Ex 34:13
will be left standing.
¹⁰The fortified city stands
desolate,   Isa 32:14; Jer 26:6
an abandoned settlement,
forsaken like the
wilderness;   Isa 5:5
there the calves graze,
there they lie down;   Isa 17:2
they strip its branches bare.
¹¹When its twigs are dry, they
are broken off
and women come and make
fires with them.
For this is a people without
understanding;   Dt 32:28
so their Maker has no
compassion on them,
and their Creator shows
them no favor.   Dt 32:18

¹²In that day the LORD will
thresh from the flowing Euphrates to the Wadi of Egypt, and you,
Israel, will be gathered up one
by one. ¹³And in that day a great
trumpet will sound. Those who
were perishing in Assyria and
those who were exiled in Egypt
will come and worship the LORD
on the holy mountain in Jerusa-
lem.   Isa 2:2; Lev 25:9; Mt 24:31

Woe to the Leaders of Ephraim and Judah

28 Woe to that wreath, the
pride of Ephraim's
drunkards,   ver 3; Isa 9:9
to the fading flower, his
glorious beauty,
set on the head of a fertile
valley —   ver 4
to that city, the pride of
those laid low by wine!
²See, the Lord has one who is
powerful and strong.
Like a hailstorm and a
destructive wind,   Isa 29:6
like a driving rain and a
flooding downpour,   Isa 8:7
he will throw it forcefully to
the ground.
³That wreath, the pride of
Ephraim's drunkards,
will be trampled underfoot.
⁴That fading flower, his
glorious beauty,
set on the head of a fertile
valley,
will be like figs ripe before
harvest —   Hos 9:10; Na 3:12
as soon as people see them
and take them in hand,
they swallow them.

⁵In that day the LORD Almighty
will be a glorious crown,
a beautiful wreath
for the remnant of his
people.   Isa 1:9
⁶He will be a spirit of justice
to the one who sits in
judgment,   Jn 5:30

---

a 9 That is, wooden symbols of the goddess Asherah

a source of strength
  to those who turn back the
    battle at the gate. 2Ch 32:8

⁷And these also stagger from
  wine   Isa 22:13
  and reel from beer: Isa 56:10-12
Priests and prophets stagger
  from beer   Isa 9:15; 24:2
  and are befuddled with
    wine;
they reel from beer,
  they stagger when seeing
    visions,   Isa 29:11; Hos 4:11
  they stumble when
    rendering decisions.
⁸All the tables are covered with
  vomit   Jer 48:26
  and there is not a spot
    without filth.

⁹"Who is it he is trying to
  teach?   ver 26; Isa 30:20
  To whom is he explaining
    his message?   Isa 53:1
To children weaned from
  their milk,   Ps 131:2
  to those just taken from the
    breast?
¹⁰For it is:
  Do this, do that,
  a rule for this, a rule for thatᵃ;
  a little here, a little there."

¹¹Very well then, with foreign
  lips and strange
    tongues   Isa 33:19
  God will speak to this
    people,   1Co 14:21
¹²to whom he said,

"This is the resting place, let
  the weary rest";Mt 11:28-29
and, "This is the place of
  repose" —
  but they would not listen.
¹³So then, the word of the Lord
  to them will become:
  Do this, do that,
  a rule for this, a rule for that;
  a little here, a little there —
so that as they go they will fall
  backward;
  they will be injured and
    snared and captured.

¹⁴Therefore hear the word of the
  Lord, you scoffers Isa 1:10
  who rule this people in
    Jerusalem.
¹⁵You boast, "We have entered
  into a covenant with
    death,
  with the realm of the dead
    we have made an
      agreement.
When an overwhelming
  scourge sweeps by,
  it cannot touch us,
for we have made a lie our
  refuge   Isa 9:15
  and falsehoodᵇ our hiding
    place."   Isa 29:15

¹⁶So this is what the Sovereign
Lord says:

"See, I lay a stone in Zion, a
  tested stone,   Ps 118:22
  a precious cornerstone for a
    sure foundation; Jer 51:26

ᵃ 10 Hebrew / sav lasav sav lasav / kav lakav kav lakav (probably meaningless sounds
mimicking the prophet's words); also in verse 13   ᵇ 15 Or false gods

the one who relies on it
  will never be stricken with
    panic.   Ro 9:33; 10:11
[17]I will make justice the
    measuring line   Isa 5:16
  and righteousness the
    plumb line;   2Ki 21:13
hail will sweep away your
    refuge, the lie,
  and water will overflow
    your hiding place.
[18]Your covenant with death will
    be annulled;
  your agreement with the
    realm of the dead will
    not stand.   Isa 7:7
When the overwhelming
    scourge sweeps by,   ver 15
  you will be beaten down
    by it.   Da 8:13
[19]As often as it comes it will
    carry you away;   2Ki 24:2
  morning after morning, by
    day and by night,
  it will sweep through."

The understanding of this
    message
  will bring sheer terror.Job 18:11
[20]The bed is too short to stretch
    out on,
  the blanket too narrow to
    wrap around you.   Isa 59:6
[21]The LORD will rise up as he
    did at Mount Perazim,
  he will rouse himself as in
    the Valley of Gibeon —
to do his work, his strange work,
  and perform his task, his
    alien task.

[22]Now stop your mocking,
  or your chains will become
    heavier;
  the Lord, the LORD Almighty,
    has told me
  of the destruction decreed
    against the whole land.

[23]Listen and hear my voice;
  pay attention and hear what
    I say.
[24]When a farmer plows for
    planting, does he plow
    continually?   Ecc 3:2
  Does he keep on breaking
    up and working the soil?
[25]When he has leveled the
    surface,
  does he not sow caraway
    and scatter cumin?
Does he not plant wheat in its
    place,[a]
  barley in its plot,[a]
  and spelt in its field?   Ex 9:32
[26]His God instructs him
  and teaches him the right
    way.   Ps 94:10
[27]Caraway is not threshed with
    a sledge,   Job 41:30
  nor is the wheel of a cart
    rolled over cumin;
  caraway is beaten out with a
    rod,   Isa 10:5
  and cumin with a stick.
[28]Grain must be ground to
    make bread;
  so one does not go on
    threshing it forever.
The wheels of a threshing cart
  may be rolled over it,

---

[a] 25 The meaning of the Hebrew for this word is uncertain.

but one does not use horses
    to grind grain.
29 All this also comes from the
    LORD Almighty,
  whose plan is wonderful,
  whose wisdom is
    magnificent.   Isa 9:6

Woe to David's City

29 Woe to you, Ariel, Ariel,
    the city where David
    settled!   2Sa 5:7
  Add year to year
    and let your cycle of
    festivals go on.   Isa 1:14
2 Yet I will besiege Ariel;
  she will mourn and lament,
  she will be to me like an
    altar hearth.ᵃ
3 I will encamp against you on
    all sides;
  I will encircle you with
    towers   Lk 19:43-44
  and set up my siege works
    against you.   2Ki 25:1
4 Brought low, you will speak
    from the ground;
  your speech will mumble
    out of the dust.   Isa 8:19
  Your voice will come ghostlike
    from the earth;
  out of the dust your speech
    will whisper.   Isa 26:16

5 But your many enemies will
    become like fine dust,
  the ruthless hordes like
    blown chaff.   Isa 17:13
  Suddenly, in an instant,   Isa 17:14
6   the LORD Almighty will come

  with thunder and earthquake
    and great noise,   Mt 24:7
  with windstorm and
    tempest and flames of a
    devouring fire.   Ps 83:13-15
7 Then the hordes of all the
    nations that fight
    against Ariel,   Mic 4:11-12
  that attack her and her
    fortress and besiege her,
  will be as it is with a dream,
  with a vision in the night —
8 as when a hungry person
    dreams of eating,
  but awakens hungry still;
  as when a thirsty person
    dreams of drinking,
  but awakens faint and
    thirsty still.
  So will it be with the hordes of
    all the nations
  that fight against Mount
    Zion.   Isa 17:12-14; 54:17

9 Be stunned and amazed,   Jer 4:9
  blind yourselves and be
    sightless;   Isa 6:10
  be drunk, but not from wine,
  stagger, but not from beer.
10 The LORD has brought over
    you a deep sleep:
  He has sealed your eyes (the
    prophets);   Ps 69:23
  he has covered your heads
    (the seers).   1Sa 9:9

11 For you this whole vision is
nothing but words sealed in a
scroll. And if you give the scroll
to someone who can read, and
say, "Read this, please," they will

ᵃ 2 The Hebrew for *altar hearth* sounds like the Hebrew for *Ariel*.

answer, "I can't; it is sealed." ¹²Or
if you give the scroll to someone
who cannot read, and say, "Read
this, please," they will answer, "I
don't know how to read." Isa 8:16

¹³The Lord says:

"These people come near to
    me with their mouth
and honor me with their
    lips,
but their hearts are far
    from me.   Eze 33:31
Their worship of me
is based on merely human
    rules they have been
    taught.^a   Mt 15:8-9; Col 2:22
¹⁴Therefore once more I will
    astound these people
with wonder upon wonder;
the wisdom of the wise will
    perish,   Jer 49:7
the intelligence of the
    intelligent will vanish."
¹⁵Woe to those who go to great
    depths
to hide their plans from the
    LORD,   Isa 28:15
who do their work in darkness
    and think,
"Who sees us? Who will
    know?"   Job 22:13; Ps 94:7
¹⁶You turn things upside down,
as if the potter were thought
    to be like the clay! Job 10:9
Shall what is formed say to the
    one who formed it, Ge 2:7
"You did not make me"?
Can the pot say to the potter,
"You know nothing"? Job 9:12

¹⁷In a very short time, will not
    Lebanon be turned into
    a fertile field   Ps 84:6
and the fertile field seem
    like a forest?   Isa 32:15
¹⁸In that day the deaf will hear
    the words of the scroll,
and out of gloom and
    darkness
the eyes of the blind will see.
¹⁹Once more the humble will
    rejoice in the LORD; Isa 61:1
the needy will rejoice in the
    Holy One of Israel. Jas 2:5
²⁰The ruthless will vanish,
the mockers will disappear,
and all who have an eye for
    evil will be cut down —
²¹those who with a word make
    someone out to be guilty,
who ensnare the defender
    in court   Am 5:10,15
and with false testimony
    deprive the innocent of
    justice.   Isa 32:7

²²Therefore this is what the
LORD, who redeemed Abraham,
says to the descendants of Jacob:

"No longer will Jacob be
    ashamed;   Isa 49:23
no longer will their faces
    grow pale.   Jer 30:6,10
²³When they see among them
    their children, Isa 49:20-26
the work of my hands,
they will keep my name holy;
they will acknowledge the
    holiness of the Holy
    One of Jacob,   Isa 5:19

---

^a 13 Hebrew; Septuagint *They worship me in vain; / their teachings are merely human rules*

and will stand in awe of the
God of Israel.
²⁴Those who are wayward
in spirit will gain
understanding;   Isa 28:7
those who complain will
accept instruction."

Woe to the Obstinate Nation

30 "Woe to the obstinate
children,"   Isa 29:15
declares the LORD,
"to those who carry out plans
that are not mine,
forming an alliance, but not
by my Spirit,   Isa 8:12
heaping sin upon sin;
²who go down to Egypt   Isa 31:1
without consulting me;
who look for help to Pharaoh's
protection,   Isa 36:9
to Egypt's shade for refuge.
³But Pharaoh's protection will
be to your shame,
Egypt's shade will bring you
disgrace.   Isa 20:4-5; 36:6
⁴Though they have officials in
Zoan   Isa 19:11
and their envoys have
arrived in Hanes,
⁵everyone will be put to shame
because of a people useless
to them,   ver 7; 2Ki 18:21
who bring neither help nor
advantage,   Jer 37:3-5
but only shame and disgrace."

⁶A prophecy concerning the
animals of the Negev: Isa 13:1

Through a land of hardship
and distress,   Ex 5:10,21

of lions and lionesses,
of adders and darting
snakes,   Dt 8:15
the envoys carry their riches
on donkeys' backs,
their treasures on the
humps of camels,   Isa 15:7
to that unprofitable nation,
⁷ to Egypt, whose help is
utterly useless.   2Ki 18:21
Therefore I call her
Rahab the Do-Nothing.

⁸Go now, write it on a tablet for
them,   Dt 27:8
inscribe it on a scroll,   Isa 8:1
that for the days to come
it may be an everlasting
witness.   Jos 24:26-27
⁹For these are rebellious
people, deceitful
children,   Isa 28:15; 59:3-4
children unwilling to
listen to the LORD's
instruction.   Isa 1:10
¹⁰They say to the seers,
"See no more visions!"   Jer 11:21
and to the prophets,
"Give us no more visions of
what is right!
Tell us pleasant things,   1Ki 22:8
prophesy illusions.   Eze 13:7
¹¹Leave this way,   ver 21; Pr 3:6
get off this path,
and stop confronting us   Job 21:14
with the Holy One of Israel!"

¹²Therefore this is what the
Holy One of Israel says: Isa 5:19

"Because you have rejected
this message,   Isa 5:24

relied on oppression   Isa 5:7
and depended on deceit,
¹³ this sin will become for you
    like a high wall, cracked
        and bulging,   Ps 62:3
    that collapses suddenly, in
        an instant. 1Ki 20:30; Isa 29:5
¹⁴ It will break in pieces like
        pottery,   Ps 2:9; Jer 19:10-11
    shattered so mercilessly
    that among its pieces not a
        fragment will be found
    for taking coals from a
        hearth
    or scooping water out of a
        cistern."

¹⁵ This is what the Sovereign
LORD, the Holy One of Israel,
says:

"In repentance and rest is
        your salvation,   Ex 14:14
    in quietness and trust is
        your strength,   Isa 32:17
    but you would have none
        of it.   Isa 8:6; 42:24
¹⁶ You said, 'No, we will flee on
        horses.'   Isa 31:1,3
    Therefore you will flee!
You said, 'We will ride off on
        swift horses.'
    Therefore your pursuers
        will be swift!
¹⁷ A thousand will flee
    at the threat of one;
    at the threat of five   Lev 26:8
    you will all flee away,   Dt 28:25
    till you are left   Isa 1:8
    like a flagstaff on a
        mountaintop,
    like a banner on a hill."

¹⁸ Yet the LORD longs to be
    gracious to you;   Isa 42:14
    therefore he will rise up to
        show you compassion.
For the LORD is a God of
    justice.   Isa 5:16
    Blessed are all who wait for
        him!   Isa 25:9; La 3:25

¹⁹ People of Zion, who live in
Jerusalem, you will weep no
more. How gracious he will be
when you cry for help! As soon
as he hears, he will answer you.
²⁰ Although the Lord gives you
the bread of adversity and the
water of affliction, your teachers will be hidden no more; with
your own eyes you will see them.
²¹ Whether you turn to the right
or to the left, your ears will hear
a voice behind you, saying, "This
is the way; walk in it." ²² Then
you will desecrate your idols
overlaid with silver and your images covered with gold; you will
throw them away like a menstru-
al cloth and say to them, "Away
with you!"   Ps 74:9; Isa 29:24; Am 8:11

²³ He will also send you rain for
the seed you sow in the ground,
and the food that comes from the
land will be rich and plentiful. In
that day your cattle will graze in
broad meadows. ²⁴ The oxen and
donkeys that work the soil will eat
fodder and mash, spread out with
fork and shovel. ²⁵ In the day of
great slaughter, when the towers
fall, streams of water will flow on
every high mountain and every

lofty hill. [26] The moon will shine like the sun, and the sunlight will be seven times brighter, like the light of seven full days, when the LORD binds up the bruises of his people and heals the wounds he inflicted. Isa 1:5; 60:19-20; Rev 21:23

[27] See, the Name of the LORD
    comes from afar, Isa 59:19
  with burning anger and
    dense clouds of smoke;
his lips are full of wrath, Isa 10:5
  and his tongue is a
    consuming fire. Job 41:21
[28] His breath is like a rushing
    torrent, Isa 11:4
  rising up to the neck. Isa 8:8
He shakes the nations in the
    sieve of destruction;
he places in the jaws of the
    peoples
  a bit that leads them astray.
[29] And you will sing
  as on the night you
    celebrate a holy festival;
your hearts will rejoice Isa 12:1
  as when people playing
    pipes go up
to the mountain of the LORD,
  to the Rock of Israel. Ge 49:24
[30] The LORD will cause people to
    hear his majestic voice
  and will make them see his
    arm coming down Isa 9:12
with raging anger and
    consuming fire, Isa 10:25
  with cloudburst,
    thunderstorm and hail.
[31] The voice of the LORD will
    shatter Assyria; Isa 10:5,12

with his rod he will strike
    them down. Isa 11:4
[32] Every stroke the LORD lays on
    them
  with his punishing club
will be to the music of
    timbrels and harps,
  as he fights them in battle
    with the blows of his
    arm. Isa 11:15; Eze 32:10
[33] Topheth has long been
    prepared;
  it has been made ready for
    the king.
Its fire pit has been made
    deep and wide,
  with an abundance of fire
    and wood;
the breath of the LORD,
  like a stream of burning
    sulfur, Ge 19:24; Rev 9:17
  sets it ablaze. Isa 1:31

Woe to Those Who Rely on Egypt

31   Woe to those who go
    down to Egypt for help,
who rely on horses,
who trust in the multitude of
    their chariots Isa 2:7
and in the great strength of
    their horsemen,
but do not look to the Holy
    One of Israel,
  or seek help from the LORD.
[2] Yet he too is wise and can
    bring disaster; Isa 45:7
  he does not take back his
    words. Nu 23:19
He will rise up against that
    wicked nation, Isa 32:6

against those who help
evildoers.
³But the Egyptians are mere
    mortals and not God;
their horses are flesh and
    not spirit.   Isa 30:16
When the LORD stretches out
    his hand,   Isa 9:17,21
those who help will stumble,
those who are helped will
    fall;   Isa 30:5-7
all will perish together.

⁴This is what the LORD says
to me:

"As a lion growls,   Am 3:8
    a great lion over its prey —
and though a whole band of
    shepherds
is called together against it,
it is not frightened by their
    shouts
or disturbed by their
    clamor —
so the LORD Almighty will
    come down   Isa 42:13
to do battle on Mount Zion
    and on its heights.
⁵Like birds hovering overhead,
    the LORD Almighty will
    shield Jerusalem;   Ps 91:4
he will shield it and deliver it,
    he will 'pass over' it and will
    rescue it."   Ex 12:23

⁶Return, you Israelites, to the
One you have so greatly revolted against. ⁷For in that day every
one of you will reject the idols of
silver and gold your sinful hands
have made.   Isa 2:20; 30:22

⁸"Assyria will fall by no human
    sword;   Isa 10:12
a sword, not of mortals, will
    devour them. Isa 14:25; 37:7
They will flee before the
    sword
and their young men will be
    put to forced labor.
⁹Their stronghold will fall
    because of terror;   Dt 32:31
at the sight of the battle
    standard their
    commanders will
    panic,"   Isa 18:3; Jer 51:9
declares the LORD,
    whose fire is in Zion,   Isa 10:17
    whose furnace is in
    Jerusalem.   Mal 4:1

The Kingdom of Righteousness

32 See, a king will reign in
    righteousness   Eze 37:24
and rulers will rule with
    justice.   Isa 9:7
²Each one will be like a shelter
    from the wind   Isa 4:6
and a refuge from the storm,
like streams of water in the
    desert Ps 23:2; 107:35; Jer 31:9
and the shadow of a great
    rock in a thirsty land.

³Then the eyes of those who
    see will no longer be
    closed,   Isa 29:18
and the ears of those who
    hear will listen.   Dt 29:4
⁴The fearful heart will know
    and understand,   Isa 29:24
and the stammering tongue
    will be fluent and clear.

⁵No longer will the fool be
    called noble   1Sa 25:25
  nor the scoundrel be highly
    respected.
⁶For fools speak folly,   Pr 19:3
  their hearts are bent on evil:
They practice ungodliness
  and spread error
    concerning the Lord;
  the hungry they leave empty
  and from the thirsty they
    withhold water.
⁷Scoundrels use wicked
    methods,   Jer 5:26-28
  they make up evil schemes
to destroy the poor with lies,
  even when the plea of the
    needy is just.   Isa 61:1
⁸But the noble make noble
    plans,
  and by noble deeds they
    stand.   Pr 11:25

The Women of Jerusalem

⁹You women who are so
    complacent,
  rise up and listen to me;
you daughters who feel
    secure,   Isa 47:8; Am 6:1
  hear what I have to say!
¹⁰In little more than a year
  you who feel secure will
    tremble;
  the grape harvest will fail,
  and the harvest of fruit will
    not come.
¹¹Tremble, you complacent
    women;
  shudder, you daughters who
    feel secure!
Strip off your fine clothes

and wrap yourselves in rags.
¹²Beat your breasts for the
    pleasant fields,   Na 2:7
  for the fruitful vines   Isa 16:9
¹³and for the land of my people,
  a land overgrown with
    thorns and briers —   Isa 5:6
yes, mourn for all houses of
    merriment
  and for this city of revelry.
¹⁴The fortress will be
    abandoned,   Isa 13:22
  the noisy city deserted;   Isa 6:11
citadel and watchtower will
    become a wasteland
    forever,   Isa 34:13
  the delight of donkeys, a
    pasture for flocks,   Ps 104:11
¹⁵till the Spirit is poured on us
    from on high,   Joel 2:28
  and the desert becomes a
    fertile field,   Ps 107:35
  and the fertile field seems
    like a forest.   Isa 29:17
¹⁶The Lord's justice will dwell
    in the desert,   Isa 9:7; 35:1,6
  his righteousness live in the
    fertile field.   Ps 48:1
¹⁷The fruit of that righteousness
    will be peace;   Ps 119:165
  its effect will be quietness
    and confidence forever.
¹⁸My people will live in
    peaceful dwelling
    places,   Isa 2:4
  in secure homes,   Isa 26:1
  in undisturbed places of
    rest.   Hos 2:18-23
¹⁹Though hail flattens the forest
  and the city is leveled
    completely,   Isa 24:10; 27:10

²⁰ how blessed you will be,
    sowing your seed by every
        stream,   Ecc 11:1
    and letting your cattle and
        donkeys range free.

Distress and Help

33 Woe to you, destroyer,
        you who have not been
        destroyed!
    Woe to you, betrayer,
        you who have not been
            betrayed!
    When you stop destroying,
        you will be destroyed; Hab 2:8
    when you stop betraying,
        you will be betrayed.   Isa 21:2

² Lord, be gracious to us;
    we long for you.
    Be our strength every
        morning,   Isa 40:10; 51:9
    our salvation in time of
        distress.   Isa 5:30; 25:9
³ At the uproar of your army,
        the peoples flee;   Ps 68:1
    when you rise up, the
        nations scatter. Isa 59:16-18
⁴ Your plunder, O nations, is
        harvested as by young
            locusts;   Joel 1:4
    like a swarm of locusts
        people pounce on it.

⁵ The Lord is exalted, for he
        dwells on high;   Ps 97:9
    he will fill Zion with
        his justice and
        righteousness. Isa 1:26; 28:6
⁶ He will be the sure foundation
        for your times,

a rich store of salvation
    and wisdom and
    knowledge;   Isa 51:6
the fear of the Lord is the
    key to this treasure. ᵃ

⁷ Look, their brave men cry
        aloud in the streets;
    the envoys of peace weep
        bitterly.   2Ki 18:37
⁸ The highways are deserted,
    no travelers are on the
        roads.   Jdg 5:6; Isa 35:8
    The treaty is broken,
        its witnesses ᵇ are despised,
    no one is respected.
⁹ The land dries up and wastes
        away,   Isa 3:26
    Lebanon is ashamed and
        withers;   Isa 2:13; 24:4
    Sharon is like the Arabah,
        and Bashan and Carmel
        drop their leaves. 1Ki 18:19

¹⁰ "Now will I arise," says the
        Lord.   Ps 12:5; Isa 2:21
    "Now will I be exalted; Isa 5:16
    now will I be lifted up.
¹¹ You conceive chaff,   Ps 7:14
    you give birth to straw; Isa 26:18
    your breath is a fire that
        consumes you.   Isa 1:31
¹² The peoples will be burned to
        ashes;
    like cut thornbushes they
        will be set ablaze."

¹³ You who are far away, hear
        what I have done;   Ps 49:1
    you who are near,
        acknowledge my power!

ᵃ 6 Or *is a treasure from him*   ᵇ 8 Dead Sea Scrolls; Masoretic Text / *the cities*

¹⁴The sinners in Zion are
    terrified;
    trembling grips the godless:
  "Who of us can dwell with the
    consuming fire?   Isa 30:30
  Who of us can dwell with
    everlasting burning?"
¹⁵Those who walk righteously
    and speak what is right,
  who reject gain from extortion
    and keep their hands from
    accepting bribes,   Pr 15:27
  who stop their ears against
    plots of murder
    and shut their eyes against
    contemplating evil —
¹⁶they are the ones who will
    dwell on the heights,
  whose refuge will be the
    mountain fortress.
  Their bread will be supplied,
    and water will not fail them.

¹⁷Your eyes will see the king in
    his beauty   Isa 6:5
  and view a land that
    stretches afar.   Isa 26:15
¹⁸In your thoughts you will
    ponder the former
    terror: Isa 17:14
  "Where is that chief officer?
  Where is the one who took the
    revenue?
  Where is the officer in
    charge of the towers?"
¹⁹You will see those arrogant
    people no more,
  people whose speech is
    obscure,
  whose language is strange
    and incomprehensible.

²⁰Look on Zion, the city of our
    festivals;
  your eyes will see
    Jerusalem,
  a peaceful abode, a tent that
    will not be moved;   Ps 46:5
  its stakes will never be
    pulled up,
  nor any of its ropes broken.
²¹There the LORD will be our
    Mighty One.
  It will be like a place of
    broad rivers and
    streams.   Isa 41:18; 48:18
  No galley with oars will ride
    them,
  no mighty ship will sail them.
²²For the LORD is our judge, Isa 11:4
  the LORD is our lawgiver,
  the LORD is our king;   Ps 89:18
  it is he who will save us.

²³Your rigging hangs loose:
  The mast is not held secure,
  the sail is not spread.
  Then an abundance of spoils
    will be divided
  and even the lame will
    carry off plunder.
²⁴No one living in Zion will say,
    "I am ill";   Isa 30:26
  and the sins of those who
    dwell there will be
    forgiven.   Jer 50:20; 1Jn 1:7-9

Judgment Against the Nations

34 Come near, you nations,
    and listen;
  pay attention, you peoples!
  Let the earth hear, and all that
    is in it,   Ps 49:1

the world, and all that
comes out of it! Dt 32:1
2 The LORD is angry with all
nations;
his wrath is on all their
armies.
He will totally destroy[a] them,
he will give them over to
slaughter. Isa 30:25
3 Their slain will be thrown out,
their dead bodies will stink;
the mountains will be
soaked with their
blood. Eze 14:19; 35:6; 38:22
4 All the stars in the sky will be
dissolved Isa 13:13; 2Pe 3:10
and the heavens rolled up
like a scroll; Eze 32:7-8
all the starry host will fall
like withered leaves from
the vine, Isa 15:6; Mt 21:19
like shriveled figs from the
fig tree.
5 My sword has drunk its fill in
the heavens; Jer 46:10
see, it descends in judgment
on Edom, Am 1:11-12
the people I have totally
destroyed. Mal 1:4; Isa 24:6
6 The sword of the LORD is
bathed in blood, Dt 32:41
it is covered with fat —
the blood of lambs and goats,
fat from the kidneys of rams.
For the LORD has a sacrifice in
Bozrah Ge 36:33
and a great slaughter in the
land of Edom. Isa 30:25

7 And the wild oxen will fall
with them,
the bull calves and the great
bulls. Ps 68:30
Their land will be drenched
with blood,
and the dust will be soaked
with fat.
8 For the LORD has a day of
vengeance, Isa 63:4
a year of retribution, to
uphold Zion's cause.
9 Edom's streams will be turned
into pitch,
her dust into burning sulfur;
her land will become
blazing pitch!
10 It will not be quenched night
or day;
its smoke will rise forever.
From generation to generation
it will lie desolate;
no one will ever pass
through it again.
11 The desert owl[b] and screech
owl[b] will possess it;
the great owl[b] and the raven
will nest there.
God will stretch out over
Edom Isa 21:11; Eze 35:15
the measuring line of chaos
and the plumb line of
desolation. 2Ki 21:13; La 2:8
12 Her nobles will have nothing
there to be called a
kingdom,
all her princes will vanish
away. Isa 41:11-12; Jer 27:20

¹³Thorns will overrun her
  citadels,
  nettles and brambles her
  strongholds. Isa 13:22; 32:13
She will become a haunt for
  jackals, Ps 44:19; Jer 9:11
a home for owls.
¹⁴Desert creatures will meet
  with hyenas, Isa 13:22
  and wild goats will bleat to
  each other;
there the night creatures will
  also lie down Rev 18:2
  and find for themselves
  places of rest.
¹⁵The owl will nest there and
  lay eggs,
  she will hatch them, and
  care for her young
  under the shadow of her
  wings;
there also the falcons will
  gather, Dt 14:13
  each with its mate.

¹⁶Look in the scroll of the LORD
and read: Isa 30:8

None of these will be
  missing,
  not one will lack her mate.
For it is his mouth that has
  given the order, Isa 1:20
  and his Spirit will gather
  them together.
¹⁷He allots their portions; Isa 17:14
  his hand distributes them
  by measure.
They will possess it forever
  and dwell there from
  generation to
  generation. ver 10

Joy of the Redeemed

35 The desert and the
  parched land will be
  glad; Isa 27:10; 41:18-19
the wilderness will rejoice
  and blossom. Isa 51:3
Like the crocus, ²it will burst
  into bloom; SS 2:1
  it will rejoice greatly and
  shout for joy. Isa 25:9; 55:12
The glory of Lebanon will be
  given to it, Isa 32:15
  the splendor of Carmel and
  Sharon; SS 7:5
they will see the glory of the
  LORD, Ex 16:7; Isa 4:5
  the splendor of our God.

³Strengthen the feeble hands,
  steady the knees that give
  way; Job 4:4; Heb 12:12
⁴say to those with fearful
  hearts, Isa 40:2; Zec 1:13
  "Be strong, do not fear; Isa 7:4
your God will come, Isa 62:11
  he will come with vengeance;
with divine retribution
  he will come to save you."

⁵Then will the eyes of the blind
  be opened Mt 11:5; Jn 9:6-7
  and the ears of the deaf
  unstopped. Isa 29:18
⁶Then will the lame leap like a
  deer, Mt 15:30; Jn 5:8-9
  and the mute tongue shout
  for joy. Mt 9:32-33
Water will gush forth in the
  wilderness
  and streams in the desert.
⁷The burning sand will
  become a pool,

the thirsty ground bubbling
springs.   Isa 49:10
In the haunts where jackals
once lay,   Isa 13:22
grass and reeds and
papyrus will grow. Job 8:11
8 And a highway will be there;
it will be called the Way of
Holiness;   Isa 4:3; 1Pe 1:15
it will be for those who walk
on that Way.
The unclean will not journey
on it;   Isa 52:1
wicked fools will not go
about on it.
9 No lion will be there,   Isa 30:6
nor any ravenous beast;
they will not be found there.
But only the redeemed will
walk there,   Isa 51:11; 62:12
10 and those the LORD has
rescued will return.
They will enter Zion with
singing;
everlasting joy will crown
their heads.   Isa 25:9
Gladness and joy will
overtake them,   Ps 51:8
and sorrow and sighing will
flee away.   Isa 51:11; Rev 7:17

Sennacherib Threatens Jerusalem
36:1-22pp — 2Ki 18:13,17-37; 2Ch 32:9-19

36 In the fourteenth year of
King Hezekiah's reign,
Sennacherib king of Assyria attacked all the fortified cities of
Judah and captured them. **2** Then
the king of Assyria sent his field
commander with a large army

from Lachish to King Hezekiah at
Jerusalem. When the commander stopped at the aqueduct of the
Upper Pool, on the road to the
Launderer's Field, **3** Eliakim son
of Hilkiah the palace administrator, Shebna the secretary, and
Joah son of Asaph the recorder
went out to him. 2Ch 32:1; Isa 22:20-21

4 The field commander said to
them, "Tell Hezekiah:

"'This is what the great
king, the king of Assyria,
says: On what are you basing this confidence of yours?
5 You say you have counsel
and might for war — but you
speak only empty words.
On whom are you depend-
ing, that you rebel against
me? **6** Look, I know you are
depending on Egypt, that
splintered reed of a staff,
which pierces the hand of
anyone who leans on it! Such
is Pharaoh king of Egypt
to all who depend on him.
7 But if you say to me, "We
are depending on the LORD
our God" — isn't he the one
whose high places and altars
Hezekiah removed, saying to
Judah and Jerusalem, "You
must worship before this al-
tar"?   2Ki 18:4; Isa 30:2,5; Eze 29:6-7
8 "'Come now, make a bar-
gain with my master, the
king of Assyria: I will give
you two thousand horses —
if you can put riders on

them! [9] How then can you repulse one officer of the least of my master's officials, even though you are depending on Egypt for chariots and horsemen[a]? [10] Furthermore, have I come to attack and destroy this land without the LORD? The LORD himself told me to march against this country and destroy it.'"

[11] Then Eliakim, Shebna and Joah said to the field commander, "Please speak to your servants in Aramaic, since we understand it. Don't speak to us in Hebrew in the hearing of the people on the wall." Ezr 4:7

[12] But the commander replied, "Was it only to your master and you that my master sent me to say these things, and not to the people sitting on the wall — who, like you, will have to eat their own excrement and drink their own urine?"

[13] Then the commander stood and called out in Hebrew, "Hear the words of the great king, the king of Assyria! [14] This is what the king says: Do not let Hezekiah deceive you. He cannot deliver you! [15] Do not let Hezekiah persuade you to trust in the LORD when he says, 'The LORD will surely deliver us; this city will not be given into the hand of the king of Assyria.' 2Ch 32:18; Isa 37:10

[16] "Do not listen to Hezekiah. This is what the king of Assyria says: Make peace with me and come out to me. Then each of you will eat fruit from your own vine and fig tree and drink water from your own cistern, [17] until I come and take you to a land like your own — a land of grain and new wine, a land of bread and vineyards. Pr 5:15; Zec 3:10

[18] "Do not let Hezekiah mislead you when he says, 'The LORD will deliver us.' Have the gods of any nations ever delivered their lands from the hand of the king of Assyria? [19] Where are the gods of Hamath and Arpad? Where are the gods of Sepharvaim? Have they rescued Samaria from my hand? [20] Who of all the gods of these countries have been able to save their lands from me? How then can the LORD deliver Jerusalem from my hand?" 1Ki 20:23

[21] But the people remained silent and said nothing in reply, because the king had commanded, "Do not answer him." Pr 9:7-8

[22] Then Eliakim son of Hilkiah the palace administrator, Shebna the secretary and Joah son of Asaph the recorder went to Hezekiah, with their clothes torn, and told him what the field commander had said. 2Ki 18:17-37

Jerusalem's Deliverance Foretold

37:1-13pp — 2Ki 19:1-13

37 When King Hezekiah heard this, he tore his

---

[a] 9 Or *charioteers*

clothes and put on sackcloth and went into the temple of the LORD. ²He sent Eliakim the palace administrator, Shebna the secretary, and the leading priests, all wearing sackcloth, to the prophet Isaiah son of Amoz. ³They told him, "This is what Hezekiah says: This day is a day of distress and rebuke and disgrace, as when children come to the moment of birth and there is no strength to deliver them. ⁴It may be that the LORD your God will hear the words of the field commander, whom his master, the king of Assyria, has sent to ridicule the living God, and that he will rebuke him for the words the LORD your God has heard. Therefore pray for the remnant that still survives." 1Sa 7:8; Isa 36:13,18-20

⁵When King Hezekiah's officials came to Isaiah, ⁶Isaiah said to them, "Tell your master, 'This is what the LORD says: Do not be afraid of what you have heard — those words with which the underlings of the king of Assyria have blasphemed me. ⁷Listen! When he hears a certain report, I will make him want to return to his own country, and there I will have him cut down with the sword.'" Isa 7:4

⁸When the field commander heard that the king of Assyria had left Lachish, he withdrew and found the king fighting against Libnah. Nu 33:20

⁹Now Sennacherib received a report that Tirhakah, the king of Cush,ᵃ was marching out to fight against him. When he heard it, he sent messengers to Hezekiah with this word: ¹⁰"Say to Hezekiah king of Judah: Do not let the god you depend on deceive you when he says, 'Jerusalem will not be given into the hands of the king of Assyria.' ¹¹Surely you have heard what the kings of Assyria have done to all the countries, destroying them completely. And will you be delivered? ¹²Did the gods of the nations that were destroyed by my predecessors deliver them — the gods of Gozan, Harran, Rezeph and the people of Eden who were in Tel Assar? ¹³Where is the king of Hamath or the king of Arpad? Where are the kings of Lair, Sepharvaim, Hena and Ivvah?" 2Ki 19:1-13

Hezekiah's Prayer

37:14-20pp — 2Ki 19:14-19

¹⁴Hezekiah received the letter from the messengers and read it. Then he went up to the temple of the LORD and spread it out before the LORD. ¹⁵And Hezekiah prayed to the LORD: ¹⁶"LORD Almighty, the God of Israel, enthroned between the cherubim, you alone are God over all the kingdoms of the earth. You have made heaven and earth. ¹⁷Give ear, LORD, and hear; open your eyes, LORD, and see; lis-

ᵃ 9 That is, the upper Nile region

ten to all the words Sennacherib has sent to ridicule the living God. Dt 10:17; Ps 86:10

18 "It is true, LORD, that the Assyrian kings have laid waste all these peoples and their lands. 19 They have thrown their gods into the fire and destroyed them, for they were not gods but only wood and stone, fashioned by human hands. 20 Now, LORD our God, deliver us from his hand, so that all the kingdoms of the earth may know that you, LORD, are the only God.*a*" 2Ki 19:14-19; Ps 46:10

Sennacherib's Fall

37:21-38pp — 2Ki 19:20-37; 2Ch 32:20-21

21 Then Isaiah son of Amoz sent a message to Hezekiah: "This is what the LORD, the God of Israel, says: Because you have prayed to me concerning Sennacherib king of Assyria, 22 this is the word the LORD has spoken against him:

"Virgin Daughter Zion
  despises and mocks you.
Daughter Jerusalem
  tosses her head as you flee.
23 Who is it you have ridiculed
  and blasphemed?
Against whom have you
  raised your voice
and lifted your eyes in
  pride? Isa 2:11
Against the Holy One of
  Israel! Isa 1:4; 12:6

24 By your messengers
  you have ridiculed the Lord.
And you have said,
  'With my many chariots
I have ascended the heights of
  the mountains,
  the utmost heights of
  Lebanon. Isa 14:8
I have cut down its tallest
  cedars,
  the choicest of its
  junipers. 1Ki 5:8-10; Isa 41:19
I have reached its remotest
  heights,
  the finest of its forests.
25 I have dug wells in foreign
  lands*b*
and drunk the water there.
With the soles of my feet
I have dried up all the
  streams of Egypt.' Dt 11:10

26 "Have you not heard?
  Long ago I ordained it.
In days of old I planned it;
  now I have brought it to
  pass,
that you have turned fortified
  cities
into piles of stone. Isa 25:2
27 Their people, drained of
  power,
  are dismayed and put to
  shame.
They are like plants in the
  field,
  like tender green shoots,
like grass sprouting on the
  roof, Ps 129:6

a 20 Dead Sea Scrolls (see also 2 Kings 19:19); Masoretic Text *you alone are the LORD*
b 25 Dead Sea Scrolls (see also 2 Kings 19:24); Masoretic Text does not have *in foreign lands.*

scorched[a] before it
grows up.

28 "But I know where you are
and when you come and go
and how you rage against me.
29 Because you rage against me
and because your insolence
has reached my ears,
I will put my hook in your
nose   Isa 30:28; Eze 38:4
and my bit in your mouth,
and I will make you return
by the way you came.   ver 34

30 "This will be the sign for you,
Hezekiah: Isa 20:3

"This year you will eat what
grows by itself,
and the second year what
springs from that.
But in the third year sow and
reap,   Isa 16:14
plant vineyards and eat
their fruit.   Ps 107:37
31 Once more a remnant of the
kingdom of Judah
will take root below and
bear fruit above.   Isa 27:6
32 For out of Jerusalem will come
a remnant,
and out of Mount Zion a
band of survivors.
The zeal of the LORD Almighty
will accomplish this.   Isa 9:7

33 "Therefore this is what the
LORD says concerning the king
of Assyria:

"He will not enter this city
or shoot an arrow here.
He will not come before it
with shield
or build a siege ramp
against it.
34 By the way that he came he
will return;   ver 29
he will not enter this city,"
declares the LORD.
35 "I will defend this city and
save it,   Isa 38:6
for my sake and for the sake
of David my servant!"

36 Then the angel of the LORD
went out and put to death a hundred and eighty-five thousand
in the Assyrian camp. When the
people got up the next morning—there were all the dead
bodies! 37 So Sennacherib king
of Assyria broke camp and withdrew. He returned to Nineveh
and stayed there.   Ge 10:11; Isa 10:12
38 One day, while he was wor-
shiping in the temple of his god
Nisrok, his sons Adrammelek
and Sharezer killed him with the
sword, and they escaped to the
land of Ararat. And Esarhaddon
his son succeeded him as king.

Hezekiah's Illness
38:1-8pp — 2Ki 20:1-11; 2Ch 32:24-26

38 In those days Hezekiah
became ill and was at the
point of death. The prophet Isaiah son of Amoz went to him and

[a] 27 Some manuscripts of the Masoretic Text, Dead Sea Scrolls and some Septuagint manuscripts (see also 2 Kings 19:26); most manuscripts of the Masoretic Text roof / and terraced fields

said, "This is what the LORD says: Put your house in order, because you are going to die; you will not recover." 2Sa 17:23; 2Ki 8:10; Isa 37:2

²Hezekiah turned his face to the wall and prayed to the LORD, ³"Remember, LORD, how I have walked before you faithfully and with wholehearted devotion and have done what is good in your eyes." And Hezekiah wept bitterly.

⁴Then the word of the LORD came to Isaiah: ⁵"Go and tell Hezekiah, 'This is what the LORD, the God of your father David, says: I have heard your prayer and seen your tears; I will add fifteen years to your life. ⁶And I will deliver you and this city from the hand of the king of Assyria. I will defend this city. 2Ki 18:2; Isa 37:35

⁷"'This is the LORD's sign to you that the LORD will do what he has promised: ⁸I will make the shadow cast by the sun go back the ten steps it has gone down on the stairway of Ahaz.'" So the sunlight went back the ten steps it had gone down. 2Ki 20:1-11

⁹A writing of Hezekiah king of Judah after his illness and recovery:

¹⁰I said, "In the prime of my life
    must I go through the gates
        of death   Ps 107:18; 2Co 1:9
    and be robbed of the rest of
        my years?"   Job 17:11
¹¹I said, "I will not again see the
        LORD himself
    in the land of the living;

no longer will I look on my
        fellow man,
    or be with those who now
        dwell in this world.
¹²Like a shepherd's tent my
        house   2Co 5:1,4; 2Pe 1:13-14
    has been pulled down and
        taken from me.   Job 4:21
Like a weaver I have rolled up
        my life,   Heb 1:12
    and he has cut me off from
        the loom;   Job 7:6
    day and night you made an
        end of me.   Ps 73:14
¹³I waited patiently till dawn,
    but like a lion he broke all
        my bones;   Job 10:16; Ps 51:8
    day and night you made an
        end of me.
¹⁴I cried like a swift or thrush,
    I moaned like a mourning
        dove.   Isa 59:11
My eyes grew weak as I looked
        to the heavens.   Ps 6:7
    I am being threatened;
        Lord, come to my aid!"

¹⁵But what can I say?
    He has spoken to me, and
        he himself has done
        this.
I will walk humbly all my
        years   1Ki 21:27
    because of this anguish of
        my soul.   Job 7:11
¹⁶Lord, by such things people
        live;
    and my spirit finds life in
        them too.
You restored me to health
    and let me live.   Ps 119:25

¹⁷Surely it was for my benefit
that I suffered such anguish.
In your love you kept me
from the pit of destruction;
you have put all my sins Jer 31:34
behind your back.   Isa 43:25
¹⁸For the grave cannot praise
you,   Ecc 9:10
death cannot sing your
praise;   Ps 6:5; 88:10-11
those who go down to the pit
cannot hope for your
faithfulness.
¹⁹The living, the living — they
praise you,   Dt 6:7; Ps 118:17
as I am doing today;
parents tell their children
about your faithfulness.

²⁰The Lord will save me,
and we will sing with
stringed instruments
all the days of our lives Ps 116:2
in the temple of the Lord.

²¹Isaiah had said, "Prepare a
poultice of figs and apply it to the
boil, and he will recover."
²²Hezekiah had asked, "What
will be the sign that I will go up
to the temple of the Lord?"

Envoys From Babylon
39:1-8pp — 2Ki 20:12-19

39 At that time Marduk-Baladan son of Baladan king
of Babylon sent Hezekiah letters
and a gift, because he had heard
of his illness and recovery. ²Hezekiah received the envoys gladly
and showed them what was in his
storehouses — the silver, the gold,
the spices, the fine olive oil — his

entire armory and everything
found among his treasures. There
was nothing in his palace or in all
his kingdom that Hezekiah did
not show them.   2Ki 18:15; 2Ch 32:31
³Then Isaiah the prophet went
to King Hezekiah and asked,
"What did those men say, and
where did they come from?"

"From a distant land," Hezekiah replied. "They came to me
from Babylon."   Dt 28:49
⁴The prophet asked, "What did
they see in your palace?"

"They saw everything in my
palace," Hezekiah said. "There
is nothing among my treasures
that I did not show them."

⁵Then Isaiah said to Hezekiah, "Hear the word of the Lord
Almighty: ⁶The time will surely
come when everything in your
palace, and all that your predecessors have stored up until this
day, will be carried off to Babylon. Nothing will be left, says
the Lord. ⁷And some of your descendants, your own flesh and
blood who will be born to you,
will be taken away, and they will
become eunuchs in the palace of
the king of Babylon."Jer 20:5; Da 1:1-7
⁸"The word of the Lord you
have spoken is good," Hezekiah
replied. For he thought, "There
will be peace and security in my
lifetime."   2Ki 20:12-19; 2Ch 32:26

Comfort for God's People

40 Comfort, comfort my
people,   Isa 12:1; 49:13
says your God.

²Speak tenderly to Jerusalem,
and proclaim to her
that her hard service has been
completed,   Isa 41:11-13
that her sin has been paid
for,
that she has received from the
LORD's hand
double for all her sins.   Isa 61:7

³A voice of one calling:
"In the wilderness prepare
the way for the LORD[a];   Mal 3:1
make straight in the desert
a highway for our God.[b]
⁴Every valley shall be
raised up,
every mountain and hill
made low;
the rough ground shall
become level,   Isa 45:2,13
the rugged places a plain.
⁵And the glory of the LORD will
be revealed,
and all people will see it
together.
For the mouth of the
LORD has spoken."

⁶A voice says, "Cry out."
And I said, "What shall I cry?"

"All people are like grass,   Job 14:2
and all their faithfulness is
like the flowers of the
field.
⁷The grass withers and the
flowers fall,   Isa 15:6
because the breath of the
LORD blows on them.

Surely the people are grass.
⁸The grass withers and the
flowers fall,
but the word of our God
endures forever."   Isa 55:11

⁹You who bring good news to
Zion,   Isa 52:7-10; Ro 10:15
go up on a high mountain.
You who bring good news to
Jerusalem,[c]
lift up your voice with a shout,
lift it up, do not be afraid;
say to the towns of Judah,
"Here is your God!"   Isa 25:9
¹⁰See, the Sovereign LORD
comes with power,
and he rules with a mighty
arm.   Isa 9:6-7; 59:16
See, his reward is with him,
and his recompense
accompanies him.
¹¹He tends his flock like a
shepherd: Eze 34:23; Mic 5:4
He gathers the lambs in his
arms   Nu 11:12
and carries them close to his
heart;   Dt 26:19
he gently leads those that
have young.   Ge 33:13

¹²Who has measured the waters
in the hollow of his
hand,   Job 38:10; Pr 30:4
or with the breadth of his
hand marked off the
heavens?   Heb 1:10-12
Who has held the dust of the
earth in a basket,

---

[a] 3 Or *A voice of one calling in the wilderness:* / *"Prepare the way for the LORD*   [b] 3 Hebrew;
Septuagint *make straight the paths of our God*   [c] 9 Or *Zion, bringer of good news,* / *go up on
a high mountain.* / *Jerusalem, bringer of good news*

or weighed the mountains
on the scales
and the hills in a balance?
¹³Who can fathom the Spirit*ᵃ* of
the Lᴏʀᴅ,
or instruct the Lᴏʀᴅ as his
counselor? Ro 11:34
¹⁴Whom did the Lᴏʀᴅ consult
to enlighten him,
and who taught him the
right way?
Who was it that taught him
knowledge, Job 21:22
or showed him the path of
understanding? Job 12:13
¹⁵Surely the nations are like a
drop in a bucket;
they are regarded as dust on
the scales; Ps 62:9
he weighs the islands as
though they were fine
dust. Dt 9:21
¹⁶Lebanon is not sufficient for
altar fires,
nor its animals enough for
burnt offerings. Ps 50:9-11
¹⁷Before him all the nations are
as nothing; Isa 29:7; 30:28
they are regarded by him as
worthless
and less than nothing. Da 4:35
¹⁸With whom, then, will you
compare God? Ex 8:10
To what image will you
liken him? Ac 17:29
¹⁹As for an idol, a metalworker
casts it, Ps 115:4
and a goldsmith overlays it
with gold Isa 2:20; 41:7

and fashions silver chains
for it.
²⁰A person too poor to present
such an offering
selects wood that will not
rot;
they look for a skilled worker
to set up an idol that will
not topple. 1Sa 5:3
²¹Do you not know?
Have you not heard?
Has it not been told you from
the beginning? Ps 19:1
Have you not understood
since the earth was
founded? Ro 1:19; Isa 48:13
²²He sits enthroned above the
circle of the earth,
and its people are like
grasshoppers. Ps 104:2
He stretches out the heavens
like a canopy, Job 22:14
and spreads them out like a
tent to live in. Job 36:29
²³He brings princes to naught
and reduces the rulers of
this world to nothing.
²⁴No sooner are they planted,
no sooner are they sown,
no sooner do they take root
in the ground,
than he blows on them and
they wither, Isa 41:16
and a whirlwind sweeps
them away like chaff.
²⁵"To whom will you compare
me? ver 18; 1Ch 16:25
Or who is my equal?" says
the Holy One. Isa 1:4

26 Lift up your eyes and look to
the heavens: Isa 51:6
Who created all these?
He who brings out the starry
host one by one   Ps 147:4
and calls forth each of them
by name.
Because of his great power
and mighty strength,
not one of them is missing.

27 Why do you complain, Jacob?
Why do you say, Israel,
"My way is hidden from the
LORD;
my cause is disregarded by
my God"?   Job 27:2; Lk 18:7-8
28 Do you not know?
Have you not heard?
The LORD is the everlasting
God,   Ps 90:2
the Creator of the ends of
the earth.   Isa 37:16
He will not grow tired or weary,
and his understanding no
one can fathom.   Ps 147:5
29 He gives strength to the weary
and increases the power of
the weak.
30 Even youths grow tired and
weary,
and young men stumble
and fall;   Isa 9:17; Jer 6:11; 9:21
31 but those who hope in the
LORD
                 Lk 18:1
will renew their strength.
They will soar on wings like
eagles;   Ps 103:5
they will run and not grow
weary,

they will walk and not be
faint.   2Co 4:1; Heb 12:1-3

The Helper of Israel

41 "Be silent before me, you
islands!
                 Zec 2:13
Let the nations renew their
strength!
Let them come forward and
speak;   Isa 48:16
let us meet together at the
place of judgment. Isa 34:1

2 "Who has stirred up one from
the east,   Ezr 1:2; Isa 45:1,13
calling him in righteousness
to his service[a]?
He hands nations over to him
and subdues kings before
him.
He turns them to dust with
his sword,   2Sa 22:43
to windblown chaff with his
bow.   Isa 40:24
3 He pursues them and moves
on unscathed,
by a path his feet have not
traveled before.
4 Who has done this and
carried it through,
calling forth the generations
from the beginning?
I, the LORD — with the first of
them
and with the last — I am he."
5 The islands have seen it and
fear;   Eze 26:17-18
the ends of the earth tremble.
They approach and come
forward;

___
a 2 Or east, / whom victory meets at every step

6
they help each other
    and say to their companions,
        "Be strong!"
7 The metalworker encourages
    the goldsmith,   Isa 40:19
    and the one who smooths
        with the hammer
    spurs on the one who
        strikes the anvil.
    One says of the welding, "It is
        good."
    The other nails down the
        idol so it will not topple.

8 "But you, Israel, my servant,
    Jacob, whom I have chosen,
    you descendants of
        Abraham my friend,
9 I took you from the ends of the
        earth,   Isa 11:12
    from its farthest corners I
        called you.
    I said, 'You are my servant';
    I have chosen you and have
        not rejected you.   Dt 7:6
10 So do not fear, for I am with
        you;   Isa 43:2,5; Ro 8:31
    do not be dismayed, for I
        am your God.
    I will strengthen you and help
        you;   ver 13-14; Isa 44:2
    I will uphold you with my
        righteous right hand.

11 "All who rage against you
    will surely be ashamed and
        disgraced;   Isa 45:24
    those who oppose you   Ex 23:22
    will be as nothing and perish.
12 Though you search for your
        enemies,
    you will not find them.

Those who wage war against
        you
    will be as nothing at all.
13 For I am the LORD your God
    who takes hold of your right
        hand   Isa 42:6; 45:1
    and says to you, Do not fear;
    I will help you.   ver 10
14 Do not be afraid, you worm
        Jacob,   Ge 15:1; Job 4:19
    little Israel, do not fear,
    for I myself will help you,"
        declares the LORD,
    your Redeemer, the Holy
        One of Israel.   Ex 15:13
15 "See, I will make you into a
        threshing sledge,   Mic 4:13
    new and sharp, with many
        teeth.
    You will thresh the mountains
        and crush them,   Ex 19:18
    and reduce the hills to
        chaff.
16 You will winnow them, the
        wind will pick them up,
    and a gale will blow them
        away.   Isa 40:24
    But you will rejoice in the
        LORD   Isa 25:9
    and glory in the Holy One of
        Israel.   Isa 45:25; Mi 1:24

17 "The poor and needy search
        for water,   Isa 43:20
    but there is none;
    their tongues are parched
        with thirst.
    But I the LORD will answer
        them;   Isa 30:19
    I, the God of Israel, will not
        forsake them.   Dt 31:6

18 I will make rivers flow on
    barren heights,   Isa 30:25
  and springs within the
    valleys.
  I will turn the desert into
    pools of water,   Isa 43:19
  and the parched ground
    into springs.   Isa 35:7
19 I will put in the desert   Isa 35:1
  the cedar and the acacia,
    the myrtle and the olive.
  I will set junipers in the
    wasteland,
  the fir and the cypress
    together,   Isa 60:13
20 so that people may see and
    know,   Ex 6:7
  may consider and
    understand,   Isa 29:24
  that the hand of the LORD has
    done this,   Ezr 7:6; 8:31
  that the Holy One of Israel
    has created it.   Job 12:9

21 "Present your case," says the
    LORD.
  "Set forth your arguments,"
    says Jacob's King.   Isa 43:15
22 "Tell us, you idols,
  what is going to happen.
  Tell us what the former things
    were,
  so that we may consider
    them
  and know their final
    outcome.
  Or declare to us the things to
    come,   Isa 46:10; Jn 13:19
23   tell us what the future holds,
  so we may know that you
    are gods.   Isa 42:9; 44:7-8; 45:3

  Do something, whether good
    or bad,   Jer 10:5
  so that we will be dismayed
    and filled with fear.
24 But you are less than nothing
  and your works are utterly
    worthless;
  whoever chooses you is
    detestable.   Ps 115:8

25 "I have stirred up one from the
    north, and he comes —
  one from the rising sun who
    calls on my name.
  He treads on rulers as if they
    were mortar,   2Sa 22:43
  as if he were a potter
    treading the clay.
26 Who told of this from the
    beginning, so we could
    know,
  or beforehand, so we could
    say, 'He was right'?
  No one told of this,
  no one foretold it,
  no one heard any words
    from you.   Hab 2:18-19
27 I was the first to tell Zion,
    'Look, here they are!'
  I gave to Jerusalem a
    messenger of good news.
28 I look but there is no one —
  no one among the gods to
    give counsel,   Isa 40:13-14
  no one to give answer when
    I ask them.
29 See, they are all false!
  Their deeds amount to
    nothing;   ver 24
  their images are but wind
    and confusion.   Jer 5:13

The Servant of the LORD

42 "Here is my servant,
    whom I uphold,   Isa 20:3
my chosen one in whom I
    delight;   Isa 43:10; 1Pe 2:4,6
I will put my Spirit on him,
    and he will bring justice to
    the nations. Ge 49:10; Isa 9:7
² He will not shout or cry out,
    or raise his voice in the streets.
³ A bruised reed he will not
    break,   Isa 36:6
and a smoldering wick he
    will not snuff out.
In faithfulness he will bring
    forth justice; Ps 72:2; 96:13
⁴ he will not falter or be
    discouraged
till he establishes justice on
    earth.   Isa 2:4
In his teaching the islands
    will put their hope."

⁵ This is what God the LORD
    says —
the Creator of the heavens,
    who stretches them out,
who spreads out the earth
    with all that springs
    from it,   Ps 24:2
who gives breath to its
    people,   Ac 17:25
and life to those who walk
    on it:
⁶ "I, the LORD, have called you
    in righteousness; Isa 43:1
I will take hold of your hand.
I will keep you and will make
    you   Isa 26:3
to be a covenant for the
    people   Isa 49:8
and a light for the Gentiles,
⁷ to open eyes that are blind,
to free captives from prison
and to release from the
    dungeon those who sit
    in darkness. Ps 107:10,14

⁸ "I am the LORD; that is my
    name!   Ex 3:15
I will not yield my glory to
    another   Isa 48:11
or my praise to idols. Ex 8:10
⁹ See, the former things have
    taken place, Isa 41:22
and new things I declare;
before they spring into being
    I announce them to you."

Song of Praise to the LORD

¹⁰ Sing to the LORD a new song,
    his praise from the ends of
    the earth,   Isa 49:6
you who go down to the sea,
    and all that is in it,
you islands, and all who live
    in them.   Isa 11:11
¹¹ Let the wilderness and its
    towns raise their voices;
let the settlements where
    Kedar lives rejoice. Isa 60:7
Let the people of Sela sing for
    joy;
let them shout from the
    mountaintops. Isa 52:7
¹² Let them give glory to the LORD
    and proclaim his praise in
    the islands. Ps 26:7; 66:2
¹³ The LORD will march out like
    a champion, Isa 9:6
like a warrior he will stir up
    his zeal;   Isa 26:11

with a shout he will raise the
battle cry   Hos 11:10
and will triumph over his
enemies.   Isa 66:14
14 "For a long time I have kept
silent,   Ps 50:21
I have been quiet and held
myself back.   Ge 43:31
But now, like a woman in
childbirth,
I cry out, I gasp and pant.
15 I will lay waste the mountains
and hills   Eze 38:20
and dry up all their
vegetation;
I will turn rivers into islands
and dry up the pools.   Isa 50:2
16 I will lead the blind by ways
they have not known,
along unfamiliar paths I
will guide them;
I will turn the darkness into
light before them
and make the rough places
smooth.   Lk 3:5
These are the things I will do;
I will not forsake them.
17 But those who trust in idols,
who say to images, 'You are
our gods,'
will be turned back in utter
shame. Ps 97:7; Isa 1:29; 44:11

Israel Blind and Deaf

18 "Hear, you deaf;   Isa 35:5
look, you blind, and see!
19 Who is blind but my
servant,   Isa 43:8; Eze 12:2
and deaf like the messenger
I send?   Isa 44:26

Who is blind like the one in
covenant with me,   Isa 26:3
blind like the servant of the
LORD?
20 You have seen many things,
but you pay no
attention;
your ears are open, but you
do not listen."   Jer 6:10
21 It pleased the LORD
for the sake of his
righteousness
to make his law great and
glorious.   ver 4; 2Co 3:7
22 But this is a people plundered
and looted,   2Ki 24:13
all of them trapped in pits
or hidden away in prisons.
They have become plunder,
with no one to rescue them;
they have been made loot,
with no one to say, "Send
them back."
23 Which of you will listen to this
or pay close attention in
time to come?   Isa 48:18
24 Who handed Jacob over to
become loot,
and Israel to the
plunderers?   2Ki 17:6
Was it not the LORD,
against whom we have
sinned?
For they would not follow his
ways;   Isa 30:15
they did not obey his
law.   Ps 119:136
25 So he poured out on them his
burning anger,   2Ki 22:13
the violence of war.

It enveloped them in flames,
  yet they did not
  understand;   2Ki 25:9
  it consumed them, but they
  did not take it to heart.

Israel's Only Savior

43 But now, this is what the
  LORD says —
he who created you, Jacob,
he who formed you, Israel:
"Do not fear, for I have
  redeemed you;   Isa 44:2,6
I have summoned you by
  name; you are mine.
²When you pass through the
  waters,   Isa 8:7
I will be with you;   Dt 31:6,8
and when you pass through
  the rivers,
  they will not sweep over you.
When you walk through the
  fire,   Isa 29:6; 30:27
  you will not be burned;
  the flames will not set you
  ablaze.   Ps 66:12; Da 3:25-27
³For I am the LORD your God,
  the Holy One of Israel, your
  Savior;   Ps 3:8; Isa 41:20
I give Egypt for your ransom,
  Cush*a* and Seba in your stead.
⁴Since you are precious and
  honored in my sight,
  and because I love you,
I will give people in exchange
  for you,
  nations in exchange for
  your life.
⁵Do not be afraid, for I am with
  you;   Isa 44:2; Jer 30:10-11

I will bring your children
  from the east   Isa 41:8
  and gather you from the
  west.   Isa 24:14; Zec 8:7
⁶I will say to the north, 'Give
  them up!'
  and to the south, 'Do not
  hold them back.'   Ps 107:3
Bring my sons from afar
  and my daughters from the
  ends of the earth —
⁷everyone who is called by my
  name,   Isa 56:5; Jas 2:7
  whom I created for my
  glory,
  whom I formed and made."

⁸Lead out those who have eyes
  but are blind,   Isa 6:9-10
  who have ears but are deaf.
⁹All the nations gather together
  and the peoples assemble.
Which of their gods foretold
  this
  and proclaimed to us the
  former things?   Isa 41:26
Let them bring in their
  witnesses to prove they
  were right,
  so that others may hear and
  say, "It is true."
¹⁰"You are my witnesses,"
  declares the LORD,
  "and my servant whom I
  have chosen,   Isa 41:8-9
so that you may know and
  believe me   Ex 6:7
  and understand that I am he.
Before me no god was formed,
  nor will there be one after me.

---

a 3 That is, the upper Nile region

¹¹I, even I, am the LORD,
  and apart from me there is
    no savior. Isa 45:21
¹²I have revealed and saved and
    proclaimed —
  I, and not some foreign god
    among you. Dt 32:12; Ps 81:9
You are my witnesses,"
  declares the LORD, "that
    I am God. Isa 44:8
¹³ Yes, and from ancient days I
    am he. Ps 90:2
No one can deliver out of my
    hand.
  When I act, who can
    reverse it?" Isa 14:27

God's Mercy and Israel's Unfaithfulness

¹⁴This is what the LORD says —
  your Redeemer, the Holy
    One of Israel: Ex 15:13
"For your sake I will send to
    Babylon
  and bring down as fugitives
    all the Babylonians,ᵃ
in the ships in which they
    took pride.
¹⁵I am the LORD, your Holy One,
  Israel's Creator, your King."

¹⁶This is what the LORD says —
  he who made a way through
    the sea,
  a path through the mighty
    waters, Isa 51:10
¹⁷who drew out the chariots
    and horses, Ps 118:12
  the army and reinforcements
    together, Ex 14:9

and they lay there, never to
    rise again,
  extinguished, snuffed out
    like a wick: Job 13:25
¹⁸"Forget the former things;
  do not dwell on the past.
¹⁹See, I am doing a new thing!
  Now it springs up; do you
    not perceive it?
I am making a way in the
    wilderness Ex 17:6; Nu 20:11
  and streams in the wasteland.
²⁰The wild animals honor me,
  the jackals and the owls,
because I provide water in the
    wilderness Isa 48:21
  and streams in the wasteland,
to give drink to my people, my
    chosen,
²¹ the people I formed for
    myself Mal 3:17
  that they may proclaim my
    praise. Ps 102:18; 1Pe 2:9
²²"Yet you have not called on
    me, Jacob,
  you have not wearied
    yourselves forᵇ me,
    Israel. Isa 30:11
²³You have not brought me
    sheep for burnt
    offerings,
  nor honored me with your
    sacrifices. Am 5:25; Zec 7:5-6
I have not burdened you with
    grain offerings
  nor wearied you with
    demands for incense.
²⁴You have not bought any
    fragrant calamus for me,

ᵃ 14 Or *Chaldeans*   ᵇ 22 Or *Jacob; / surely you have grown weary of*

or lavished on me the fat of
  your sacrifices.
But you have burdened me
  with your sins
and wearied me with your
  offenses.   Isa 1:14; Mal 2:17

25 "I, even I, am he who blots out
  your transgressions, for my
  own sake,   Ac 3:19; Eze 36:22
and remembers your sins
  no more.   Jer 31:34
26 Review the past for me,
  let us argue the matter
  together;   Isa 1:18
  state the case for your
  innocence.   Isa 41:1; 50:8
27 Your first father sinned;
  those I sent to teach you
  rebelled against me.
28 So I disgraced the dignitaries
  of your temple;
  I consigned Jacob to
  destruction[a]
  and Israel to scorn.   Jer 24:9

Israel the Chosen

44 "But now listen, Jacob,
  my servant,   Jer 30:10
Israel, whom I have chosen.
2 This is what the LORD says —
  he who made you, who
  formed you in the
  womb,   Ps 139:13; 149:2
  and who will help you:
Do not be afraid, Jacob, my
  servant,
Jeshurun,[b] whom I have
  chosen.   Dt 32:15

3 For I will pour water on the
  thirsty land,   Joel 3:18
and streams on the dry
  ground;   Isa 32:2
I will pour out my Spirit on
  your offspring,   Joel 2:28
and my blessing on your
  descendants. Isa 61:9; 65:23
4 They will spring up like grass
  in a meadow,
like poplar trees by flowing
  streams. Lev 23:40; Job 40:22
5 Some will say, 'I belong to the
  LORD';   Ps 116:16
others will call themselves
  by the name of Jacob;
still others will write on their
  hand, 'The LORD's,'
  and will take the name
  Israel.

The LORD, Not Idols

6 "This is what the LORD says —
  Israel's King and Redeemer,
  the LORD Almighty:
I am the first and I am the
  last; Isa 41:4; Rev 1:8,17; 22:13
apart from me there is no
  God.   Dt 6:4; 1Ch 17:20
7 Who then is like me? Let him
  proclaim it.
Let him declare and lay out
  before me
what has happened since I
  established my ancient
  people,
  and what is yet to come —
yes, let them foretell what
  will come.   Isa 41:22,26

---

[a] 28 The Hebrew term refers to the irrevocable giving over of things or persons to the LORD, often by totally destroying them.   [b] 2 Jeshurun means the upright one, that is, Israel.

⁸Do not tremble, do not be
   afraid.
   Did I not proclaim this and
      foretell it long ago?
   You are my witnesses. Is there
      any God besides me?
   No, there is no other Rock; I
      know not one." Dt 4:35

⁹All who make idols are
      nothing,
   and the things they treasure
      are worthless. Isa 41:24
   Those who would speak up for
      them are blind;
   they are ignorant, to their
      own shame. Isa 1:29
¹⁰Who shapes a god and casts
      an idol,
   which can profit nothing?
¹¹People who do that will be put
      to shame; Isa 1:29
   such craftsmen are only
      human beings.
   Let them all come together
      and take their stand;
   they will be brought down
      to terror and shame.

¹²The blacksmith takes a tool
      and works with it in the
      coals;
   he shapes an idol with
      hammers,
   he forges it with the might
      of his arm. Ac 17:29
   He gets hungry and loses his
      strength;
   he drinks no water and
      grows faint. Isa 40:28
¹³The carpenter measures with
      a line Isa 41:7

   and makes an outline with
      a marker;
   he roughs it out with chisels
      and marks it with
      compasses.
   He shapes it in human form,
      human form in all its glory,
   that it may dwell in a
      shrine. Jdg 17:4-5
¹⁴He cut down cedars,
   or perhaps took a cypress or
      oak.
   He let it grow among the trees
      of the forest,
   or planted a pine, and the
      rain made it grow.
¹⁵It is used as fuel for burning;
   some of it he takes and
      warms himself,
   he kindles a fire and bakes
      bread.
   But he also fashions a god and
      worships it;
   he makes an idol and bows
      down to it. 2Ch 25:14
¹⁶Half of the wood he burns in
      the fire;
   over it he prepares his meal,
   he roasts his meat and eats
      his fill.
   He also warms himself and says,
   "Ah! I am warm; I see the
      fire."
¹⁷From the rest he makes a god,
      his idol;
   he bows down to it and
      worships.
   He prays to it and says, 1Ki 18:26
   "Save me! You are my god!"
¹⁸They know nothing, they
      understand nothing;

their eyes are plastered over
　　so they cannot see,
and their minds closed
　　so they cannot
　　understand.
¹⁹No one stops to think,
　　no one has the knowledge
　　　or understanding to say,
"Half of it I used for fuel;
　　I even baked bread over its
　　　coals,
　　I roasted meat and I ate.
Shall I make a detestable
　　thing from what is left?
　　Shall I bow down to a block
　　　of wood?"
²⁰Such a person feeds on
　　ashes; a deluded heart
　　misleads him;　　　Ps 102:9
he cannot save himself, or
　　say,
"Is not this thing in my right
　　hand a lie?"　　Isa 59:3-4,13

²¹"Remember these things,
　　Jacob,　　Isa 46:8; Zec 10:9
for you, Israel, are my
　　servant.
I have made you, you are my
　　servant;
Israel, I will not forget you.
²²I have swept away your
　　offenses like a cloud,
　　your sins like the morning
　　mist.
Return to me,　　Isa 55:7
　　for I have redeemed you."

²³Sing for joy, you heavens, for
　　the LORD has done this;
　　shout aloud, you earth
　　beneath.　　Ps 148:7

Burst into song, you
　　mountains,　　Ps 98:8
you forests and all your
　　trees,
for the LORD has redeemed
　　Jacob,
he displays his glory in
　　Israel.　　Isa 61:3

Jerusalem to Be Inhabited

²⁴"This is what the LORD says —
　　your Redeemer, who formed
　　you in the womb:Ps 139:13

I am the LORD,
　　the Maker of all things,
　　who stretches out the
　　　heavens,　　Isa 42:5
　　who spreads out the earth
　　　by myself,
²⁵who foils the signs of false
　　prophets　　Ps 33:10
　　and makes fools of diviners,
who overthrows the learning
　　of the wise　　1Co 1:27
　　and turns it into nonsense,
²⁶who carries out the words of
　　his servants　　Zec 1:6
　　and fulfills the predictions
　　　of his messengers,

who says of Jerusalem, 'It
　　shall be inhabited,'
　　of the towns of Judah, 'They
　　　shall be rebuilt,'
　　and of their ruins, 'I will
　　　restore them,'　　Isa 49:8-21
²⁷who says to the watery deep,
　　'Be dry,
　　and I will dry up your
　　　streams,'　　Isa 11:15

28who says of Cyrus, 'He is my
    shepherd   2Ch 36:22
and will accomplish all that
    I please;
he will say of Jerusalem, "Let
    it be rebuilt,"   Isa 14:32
and of the temple, "Let its
    foundations be laid." '

45

"This is what the LORD
    says to his anointed,
to Cyrus, whose right hand
    I take hold of   Ps 73:23
to subdue nations before him
    and to strip kings of their
    armor,
to open doors before him
    so that gates will not be
    shut:
2I will go before you   Ex 23:20
    and will level the
    mountains^a;   Isa 40:4
I will break down gates of
    bronze
    and cut through bars of iron.
3I will give you hidden
    treasures,   Jer 50:37
    riches stored in secret
    places,   Jer 41:8
so that you may know that I
    am the LORD,   Isa 41:23
    the God of Israel, who
    summons you by name.
4For the sake of Jacob my
    servant,   Isa 41:8-9
    of Israel my chosen,
I summon you by name
    and bestow on you a title of
    honor,

though you do not
    acknowledge me.   Ac 17:23
5I am the LORD, and there is no
    other;   Isa 44:8
apart from me there is no
    God.   Ps 18:31
I will strengthen you,   Ps 18:39
    though you have not
    acknowledged me,
6so that from the rising of the
    sun
to the place of its setting
people may know there is
    none besides me.   Isa 11:9
I am the LORD, and there is
    no other.
7I form the light and create
    darkness,
I bring prosperity and
    create disaster;   Isa 31:2
I, the LORD, do all these
    things.

8"You heavens above,
    rain down my
    righteousness;   Ps 72:6
    let the clouds shower it down.
Let the earth open wide,
    let salvation spring up,   Isa 12:3
let righteousness flourish
    with it;
    I, the LORD, have created it.

9"Woe to those who quarrel
    with their Maker,Job 15:25
    those who are nothing but
    potsherds
among the potsherds on the
    ground.
Does the clay say to the potter,

_a 2 Dead Sea Scrolls and Septuagint; the meaning of the word in the Masoretic Text is
uncertain.

'What are you making?'
Does your work say,
    'The potter has no hands'?
[10] Woe to the one who says to a
    father,
    'What have you begotten?'
or to a mother,
    'What have you brought to
        birth?'

[11] "This is what the LORD says —
    the Holy One of Israel, and
    its Maker: Isa 1:4; 51:13
Concerning things to come,
    do you question me about
        my children,
    or give me orders about the
        work of my hands?
[12] It is I who made the earth
    and created mankind on it.
My own hands stretched out
        the heavens;   Ge 2:1; Isa 42:5
    I marshaled their starry
        hosts.   Ne 9:6
[13] I will raise up Cyrus[a] in my
        righteousness: Isa 41:2
    I will make all his ways
        straight.   Ps 26:12; Isa 40:4
He will rebuild my city
    and set my exiles free,
but not for a price or reward,
    says the LORD Almighty."

[14] This is what the LORD says:

"The products of Egypt and
        the merchandise of
        Cush,[b]   2Sa 8:2
    and those tall Sabeans —
they will come over to you
    and will be yours;

they will trudge behind you,
    coming over to you in
        chains.   Isa 14:1-2
They will bow down before
        you
    and plead with you, saying,
'Surely God is with you, and
    there is no other;   1Co 14:25
    there is no other god.'" Ps 18:31

[15] Truly you are a God who has
        been hiding himself,
    the God and Savior of Israel.
[16] All the makers of idols will
        be put to shame and
        disgraced;   Isa 44:9,11
    they will go off into disgrace
        together.
[17] But Israel will be saved by the
        LORD   Ro 11:26
    with an everlasting
        salvation;   Isa 26:4
you will never be put to
        shame or disgraced,
    to ages everlasting.

[18] For this is what the LORD
        says —
he who created the heavens,
    he is God;
he who fashioned and made
        the earth,
    he founded it;
he did not create it to be
        empty,   Ge 1:2
    but formed it to be
        inhabited —   Ge 1:26
he says:
"I am the LORD,
    and there is no other.   ver 5
[19] I have not spoken in secret,

from somewhere in a land
of darkness;
I have not said to Jacob's
descendants,   Isa 41:8
'Seek me in vain.'   2Ch 15:2
I, the LORD, speak the truth;
I declare what is right. Dt 30:11

²⁰ "Gather together and come;
assemble, you fugitives
from the nations.
Ignorant are those who carry
about idols of wood,
who pray to gods that
cannot save.   Isa 46:6-7

²¹ Declare what is to be,
present it —
let them take counsel
together.
Who foretold this long ago,
who declared it from the
distant past?
Was it not I, the LORD?
And there is no God apart
from me,   ver 5; Ps 46:10
a righteous God and a Savior;
there is none but me.

²² "Turn to me and be saved,
all you ends of the earth;
for I am God, and there is
no other.   Hos 13:4

²³ By myself I have sworn, Ge 22:16
my mouth has uttered in all
integrity   Heb 6:13
a word that will not be
revoked: Isa 55:11
Before me every knee will
bow;
by me every tongue will
swear.   Ro 14:11; Php 2:10-11

²⁴ They will say of me, 'In the
LORD alone
are deliverance and
strength.' "   Jer 33:16
All who have raged against
him
will come to him and be put
to shame.   Isa 41:11

²⁵ But all the descendants of
Israel
will find deliverance in the
LORD
and will make their boast in
him.   Isa 41:16

Gods of Babylon

46 Bel bows down, Nebo
stoops low;   Isa 21:9; Jer 50:2
their idols are borne by
beasts of burden.^a 1Sa 5:2
The images that are carried
about are burdensome,
a burden for the weary.

² They stoop and bow down
together;
unable to rescue the
burden,
they themselves go off into
captivity.   Jdg 18:17-18

³ "Listen to me, you
descendants of Jacob,
all the remnant of the
people of Israel,   Isa 1:9
you whom I have upheld since
your birth,   Ps 139:13
and have carried since you
were born.   Ps 22:10

⁴ Even to your old age and gray
hairs   Ps 71:18

---

^a 1 Or *are but beasts and cattle*

I am he, I am he who will
  sustain you.   Isa 43:13
I have made you and I will
  carry you;
I will sustain you and I will
  rescue you.   Ps 18:35
[5] "With whom will you
       compare me or count
       me equal?
To whom will you liken
   me that we may be
   compared?   Isa 40:18,25
[6] Some pour out gold from their
    bags
  and weigh out silver on the
    scales;
they hire a goldsmith to make
   it into a god,   Isa 40:19
  and they bow down and
    worship it.   Isa 44:17
[7] They lift it to their shoulders
     and carry it;   ver 1
  they set it up in its place,
    and there it stands.
From that spot it cannot move.
Even though someone cries
   out to it, it cannot
   answer;   1Ki 18:26
  it cannot save them from
    their troubles.   Isa 44:17
[8] "Remember this, keep it in
     mind,   Isa 44:21
  take it to heart, you rebels.
[9] Remember the former things,
     those of long ago;   Dt 32:7
I am God, and there is no
   other;
I am God, and there is none
   like me.   Isa 45:5,21

[10] I make known the end from
      the beginning,
  from ancient times, what is
    still to come.   Isa 45:21
I say, 'My purpose will stand,
   and I will do all that I please.'
[11] From the east I summon a
      bird of prey;
  from a far-off land, a man to
    fulfill my purpose.
What I have said, that I will
   bring about;
  what I have planned, that I
    will do.   Isa 25:1; Jer 44:28
[12] Listen to me, you stubborn-
      hearted,   ver 3; Isa 9:9
  you who are now far from
    my righteousness.   Jer 2:5
[13] I am bringing my
      righteousness near, Isa 1:26
  it is not far away;
  and my salvation will not be
    delayed.   Ps 85:9
I will grant salvation to Zion,
   my splendor to Israel. Isa 44:23

The Fall of Babylon

47 "Go down, sit in the dust,
     Virgin Daughter Babylon;
sit on the ground without a
   throne,
  queen city of the
    Babylonians.[a]   Jer 51:33
No more will you be called
   tender or delicate.   Dt 28:56
[2] Take millstones and grind
     flour;   Ex 11:5; Mt 24:41
  take off your veil.   Ge 24:65
Lift up your skirts, bare your
   legs,   Isa 32:11

[a] 1 Or Chaldeans; also in verse 5

and wade through the
  streams.
³Your nakedness will be
  exposed   Eze 16:37; Na 3:5
and your shame uncovered.
I will take vengeance;   Isa 34:8
I will spare no one."

⁴Our Redeemer — the Lord
  Almighty is his name —
is the Holy One of Israel.

⁵"Sit in silence, go into
  darkness,   Isa 13:10
  queen city of the
  Babylonians;   Isa 21:9
no more will you be called
  queen of kingdoms.   Isa 13:19
⁶I was angry with my people
  and desecrated my
  inheritance;   Dt 13:15
I gave them into your hand,
  and you showed them no
  mercy.   Isa 14:6
Even on the aged
  you laid a very heavy yoke.
⁷You said, 'I am forever —
  the eternal queen!'   ver 5
But you did not consider these
  things
  or reflect on what might
  happen. Dt 32:29; Isa 42:23,25

⁸"Now then, listen, you lover of
  pleasure,
  lounging in your security
and saying to yourself,
  'I am, and there is none
  besides me.   Isa 45:6
I will never be a widow   Rev 18:7
  or suffer the loss of children.'
⁹Both of these will overtake you

in a moment, on a single
  day: 1Th 5:3; Rev 18:8-10
loss of children and
  widowhood.   Isa 13:18
They will come upon you in
  full measure,
  in spite of your many
  sorceries   Na 3:4
and all your potent spells.
¹⁰You have trusted in your
  wickedness   Ps 52:7; 62:10
and have said, 'No one
  sees me.'   Isa 29:15
Your wisdom and knowledge
  mislead you   Isa 5:21; 44:20
when you say to yourself,
  'I am, and there is none
  besides me.'
¹¹Disaster will come upon you,
  and you will not know how
  to conjure it away.
A calamity will fall upon you
  that you cannot ward off
  with a ransom;
a catastrophe you cannot
  foresee
  will suddenly come upon
  you.   1Th 5:3

¹²"Keep on, then, with your
  magic spells
  and with your many
  sorceries,   ver 9; Ex 7:11
  which you have labored at
  since childhood.
Perhaps you will succeed,
  perhaps you will cause
  terror.
¹³All the counsel you have
  received has only worn
  you out!   Isa 57:10; Jer 51:58

Let your astrologers come
forward,   Isa 44:25
those stargazers who make
predictions month by
month,
let them save you from what
is coming upon you.
¹⁴ Surely they are like stubble;
the fire will burn them up.
They cannot even save
themselves
from the power of the
flame. Isa 10:17; Jer 51:30,32,58
These are not coals for
warmth;
this is not a fire to sit by.
¹⁵ That is all they are to you —
these you have dealt with
and labored with since
childhood.   Rev 18:11
All of them go on in their error;
there is not one that can
save you.   ver 13; Isa 44:17

Stubborn Israel

48 "Listen to this, you
descendants of Jacob,
you who are called by the
name of Israel   Ge 17:5
and come from the line of
Judah,
you who take oaths in the
name of the LORD
and invoke the God of
Israel —   Isa 58:2
but not in truth or
righteousness —   Jer 4:2
² you who call yourselves
citizens of the holy city
and claim to rely on the
God of Israel —   Mic 3:11

the LORD Almighty is his
name: Isa 47:4
³ I foretold the former things
long ago,   Isa 41:22
my mouth announced
them and I made them
known;   Isa 45:21
then suddenly I acted, and
they came to pass.
⁴ For I knew how stubborn you
were;   Dt 31:27
your neck muscles were iron,
your forehead was bronze.
⁵ Therefore I told you these
things long ago;
before they happened I
announced them to you
so that you could not say,
'My images brought them
about;   Jer 44:15-18
my wooden image and
metal god ordained
them.'
⁶ You have heard these things;
look at them all.
Will you not admit them?

"From now on I will tell you of
new things,   Isa 41:22
of hidden things unknown
to you.
⁷ They are created now, and not
long ago;   Isa 45:21
you have not heard of them
before today.
So you cannot say,
'Yes, I knew of them.'   Ex 6:7
⁸ You have neither heard nor
understood;   Isa 1:3
from of old your ears have
not been open.   Dt 29:4

Well do I know how
    treacherous you are;
you were called a rebel from
    birth.   Dt 9:7,24; Ps 58:3
⁹ For my own name's sake I
    delay my wrath;   Ps 78:38
for the sake of my praise I
    hold it back from you,
so as not to destroy you
    completely.   Ne 9:31
¹⁰ See, I have refined you,
    though not as silver;
I have tested you in the
    furnace of affliction.
¹¹ For my own sake, for my own
    sake, I do this.   1Sa 12:22
How can I let myself be
    defamed?   Dt 32:27
I will not yield my glory to
    another.   Isa 42:8

Israel Freed

¹² "Listen to me, Jacob,   Isa 46:3
    Israel, whom I have called:
I am he;   Isa 43:13
I am the first and I am the
    last.   Isa 41:4; Rev 1:17; 22:13
¹³ My own hand laid the
    foundations of the
    earth,   Heb 1:10-12
and my right hand spread
    out the heavens;   Ex 20:11
when I summon them,
    they all stand up together.

¹⁴ "Come together, all of you,
    and listen: Isa 43:9
Which of the idols has
    foretold these things?
The LORD's chosen ally

will carry out his purpose
    against Babylon;
his arm will be against the
    Babylonians.ᵃ
¹⁵ I, even I, have spoken;
    yes, I have called him.   Isa 45:1
I will bring him,
    and he will succeed in his
    mission.

¹⁶ "Come near me and listen to
this: Isa 41:1

"From the first announcement I
    have not spoken in secret;
at the time it happens, I am
    there."

And now the Sovereign LORD
    has sent me,   Zec 2:9,11
endowed with his Spirit.

¹⁷ This is what the LORD says —
    your Redeemer, the Holy
    One of Israel: Isa 43:14; 49:7
"I am the LORD your God,
    who teaches you what is
    best for you, Isa 28:9; Jer 7:13
who directs you in the way
    you should go.   Ps 32:8
¹⁸ If only you had paid attention
    to my commands,
your peace would have
    been like a river, Ps 119:165
your well-being like the
    waves of the sea.   Isa 45:8
¹⁹ Your descendants would have
    been like the sand,
your children like its
    numberless grains;
their name would never be
    blotted out   Isa 56:5; 66:22

ᵃ 14 Or Chaldeans; also in verse 20

nor destroyed from
before me."

²⁰ Leave Babylon,
flee from the Babylonians!
Announce this with shouts of
joy   Isa 49:13
and proclaim it.
Send it out to the ends of the
earth;
say, "The LORD has redeemed
his servant Jacob."
²¹ They did not thirst when he
led them through the
deserts;   Isa 41:17
he made water flow for
them from the rock;
he split the rock
and water gushed out. Ex 17:6
²² "There is no peace," says the
LORD, "for the wicked."

The Servant of the LORD

49 Listen to me, you islands;
hear this, you distant
nations:
Before I was born the LORD
called me;   Isa 44:24; 46:3
from my mother's womb he
has spoken my name.
² He made my mouth like a
sharpened sword, Isa 11:4
in the shadow of his hand
he hid me;   Ps 91:1
he made me into a polished
arrow   Dt 32:23; Zec 9:13
and concealed me in his
quiver.
³ He said to me, "You are my
servant,   Zec 3:8

Israel, in whom I will
display my splendor."
⁴ But I said, "I have labored in
vain;
I have spent my strength for
nothing at all.   Isa 65:23
Yet what is due me is in the
LORD's hand,
and my reward is with my
God."   Isa 35:4
⁵ And now the LORD says —
he who formed me in the
womb to be his servant
to bring Jacob back to him
and gather Israel to himself,
for I am ᵃ honored in the eyes
of the LORD   Isa 43:4
and my God has been my
strength —   Ps 18:1
⁶ he says:
"It is too small a thing for you
to be my servant
to restore the tribes of Jacob
and bring back those of
Israel I have kept.   Isa 1:9
I will also make you a light for
the Gentiles,   Lk 2:32; Jn 1:9
that my salvation may reach
to the ends of the earth."
⁷ This is what the LORD says —
the Redeemer and Holy One
of Israel —   Isa 48:17
to him who was despised and
abhorred by the nation,
to the servant of rulers:
"Kings will see you and
stand up,   Isa 52:15
princes will see and bow
down,

ᵃ 5 Or him, / but Israel would not be gathered; / yet I will be

because of the LORD, who is
  faithful,   1Co 1:9
the Holy One of Israel, who
  has chosen you."   Isa 14:1

Restoration of Israel

⁸ This is what the LORD says:

"In the time of my favor I will
  answer you,   Ps 69:13
and in the day of salvation I
  will help you;   2Co 6:2
I will keep you and will make
  you   Isa 26:3
to be a covenant for the
  people,   Isa 42:6
to restore the land   Isa 44:26
and to reassign its desolate
  inheritances,   Isa 60:21
⁹ to say to the captives, 'Come
  out,'   Isa 42:7; Lk 4:19
and to those in darkness,
  'Be free!'

"They will feed beside the
  roads
and find pasture on every
  barren hill.   Isa 41:18
¹⁰ They will neither hunger nor
  thirst,   Isa 33:16
nor will the desert heat or
  the sun beat down on
  them.   Ps 121:6; Rev 7:16
He who has compassion on
  them will guide them
and lead them beside
  springs of water.   Isa 35:7
¹¹ I will turn all my mountains
  into roads,
and my highways will be
  raised up.   Isa 11:16; 40:4

¹² See, they will come from afar—
  some from the north, some
    from the west,
  some from the region of
    Aswan.ᵃ"
¹³ Shout for joy, you heavens;
  rejoice, you earth;
  burst into song, you
    mountains!   Isa 44:23
For the LORD comforts his
  people   Isa 40:1; 2Co 1:4
and will have compassion
  on his afflicted ones.

¹⁴ But Zion said, "The LORD has
  forsaken me,   Ps 9:10; 71:11
the Lord has forgotten me."

¹⁵ "Can a mother forget the baby
  at her breast
and have no compassion on
  the child she has borne?
Though she may forget,
  I will not forget you!   Isa 44:21
¹⁶ See, I have engraved you on
  the palms of my hands;
  your walls are ever before me.
¹⁷ Your children hasten back,
  and those who laid you
    waste depart from you.
¹⁸ Lift up your eyes and look
  around;
  all your children gather and
    come to you.   Isa 60:4; 43:5
As surely as I live," declares
  the LORD,   Ro 14:11
"you will wear them all as
  ornaments;   Isa 52:1
you will put them on, like a
  bride.

ᵃ 12 Dead Sea Scrolls; Masoretic Text *Sinim*

19 "Though you were ruined and
    made desolate   Isa 54:1,3
and your land laid waste,
now you will be too small for
    your people,   Zec 10:10
and those who devoured
    you will be far away.
20 The children born during
    your bereavement
will yet say in your hearing,
'This place is too small for us;
give us more space to
    live in.'   Isa 54:1-3
21 Then you will say in your heart,
'Who bore me these?
I was bereaved and barren;
I was exiled and rejected.
Who brought these up?
I was left all alone,   Isa 1:8
but these — where have
    they come from?' "

22 This is what the Sovereign
Lord says: Ge 15:2

"See, I will beckon to the
    nations,
I will lift up my banner to
    the peoples;   Isa 11:10
they will bring your sons in
    their arms   Isa 11:12
and carry your daughters
    on their hips.   Isa 60:4
23 Kings will be your foster
    fathers,   Isa 60:3,10-11
and their queens your
    nursing mothers.   Isa 60:16
They will bow down before
    you with their faces to
    the ground;

they will lick the dust at
    your feet.   Ps 72:9
Then you will know that I am
    the Lord;   Mic 7:17
those who hope in me will
    not be disappointed."

24 Can plunder be taken from
    warriors,   Mt 12:29; Lk 11:21
or captives be rescued from
    the fierce[a]?
25 But this is what the Lord
says:

"Yes, captives will be taken
    from warriors,   Isa 14:2
and plunder retrieved from
    the fierce;
I will contend with those who
    contend with you,
and your children I will
    save.   Isa 25:9; 35:4
26 I will make your oppressors
    eat their own flesh;
they will be drunk on their
    own blood, as with
    wine.   Rev 16:6
Then all mankind will know
    that I, the Lord, am your
    Savior,   Isa 25:9
your Redeemer, the Mighty
    One of Jacob."   Isa 48:17

Israel's Sin and the Servant's Obedience

50 This is what the Lord
    says:

"Where is your mother's
    certificate of divorce

---

[a] 24 Dead Sea Scrolls, Vulgate and Syriac (see also Septuagint and verse 25); Masoretic Text *righteous*

with which I sent her away?
Or to which of my creditors
    did I sell you? Ne 5:5; Mt 18:25
Because of your sins you were
    sold; Dt 32:30; Isa 52:3
because of your
    transgressions your
    mother was sent away.
²When I came, why was there
    no one?
When I called, why was
    there no one to answer?
Was my arm too short to
    deliver you? Nu 11:23
Do I lack the strength to
    rescue you? Ge 18:14
By a mere rebuke I dry up the
    sea, Ex 14:22; Jos 3:16
I turn rivers into a desert;
their fish rot for lack of water
    and die of thirst.
³I clothe the heavens with
    darkness
and make sackcloth its
    covering." Rev 6:12

⁴The Sovereign Lᴏʀᴅ has given
    me a well-instructed
    tongue, Ex 4:12
to know the word that
    sustains the weary.
He wakens me morning by
    morning, Ps 5:3; 119:147
wakens my ear to listen like
    one being instructed.
⁵The Sovereign Lᴏʀᴅ has
    opened my ears; Isa 35:5
I have not been rebellious,
I have not turned away.
⁶I offered my back to those
    who beat me, Isa 53:5

my cheeks to those who
    pulled out my beard;
I did not hide my face
    from mocking and spitting.
⁷Because the Sovereign Lᴏʀᴅ
    helps me, Isa 42:1
I will not be disgraced.
Therefore have I set my face
    like flint, Eze 3:8-9
and I know I will not be put
    to shame. Isa 28:16
⁸He who vindicates me is near.
Who then will bring
    charges against me?
Let us face each other! Isa 41:1
Who is my accuser?
Let him confront me!
⁹It is the Sovereign Lᴏʀᴅ who
    helps me. Isa 41:10
Who will condemn me?
They will all wear out like a
    garment;
the moths will eat them up.

¹⁰Who among you fears the
    Lᴏʀᴅ
and obeys the word of his
    servant? Isa 49:3
Let the one who walks in the
    dark,
who has no light, Ps 107:14
trust in the name of the Lᴏʀᴅ
    and rely on their God.
¹¹But now, all you who light
    fires
and provide yourselves with
    flaming torches, Pr 26:18
go, walk in the light of your
    fires Jas 3:6
and of the torches you have
    set ablaze.

This is what you shall receive
    from my hand: Pr 26:27
    You will lie down in
        torment.   Isa 65:13-15

Everlasting Salvation for Zion

51 "Listen to me, you who
        pursue righteousness
    and who seek the Lord:
    Look to the rock from which
        you were cut   Isa 17:10
    and to the quarry from
        which you were hewn;
² look to Abraham, your father,
    and to Sarah, who gave you
        birth.
    When I called him he was
        only one man,
    and I blessed him and made
        him many.   Ge 12:2
³ The Lord will surely comfort
    Zion   Isa 40:1
    and will look with
        compassion on all her
        ruins;   Isa 52:9
    he will make her deserts like
        Eden,   Ge 2:8
    her wastelands like the
        garden of the Lord.
    Joy and gladness will be
        found in her, Isa 25:9; 66:10
    thanksgiving and the sound
        of singing.   Jer 17:26

⁴ "Listen to me, my people;
    hear me, my nation:
    Instruction will go out from me;
    my justice will become a
        light to the nations.
⁵ My righteousness draws near
        speedily,

my salvation is on the way,
    and my arm will bring
        justice to the nations.
    The islands will look to me
        and wait in hope for my
        arm.   Ge 49:10; Ps 37:9
⁶ Lift up your eyes to the
        heavens,
    look at the earth beneath;
    the heavens will vanish like
        smoke,   Mt 24:35; 2Pe 3:10
    the earth will wear out like
        a garment   Ps 102:25-26
    and its inhabitants die like
        flies.
    But my salvation will last
        forever,   Ps 119:89
    my righteousness will never
        fail.   Ps 89:33

⁷ "Hear me, you who know
        what is right,
    you people who have taken
        my instruction to heart:
    Do not fear the reproach of
        mere mortals
    or be terrified by their
        insults.   Mt 5:11; Ac 5:41
⁸ For the moth will eat them up
        like a garment;   Isa 50:9
    the worm will devour them
        like wool.   Isa 14:11
    But my righteousness will last
        forever,   ver 6
    my salvation through all
        generations."

⁹ Awake, awake, arm of the Lord,
    clothe yourself with
        strength!   Isa 52:1
    Awake, as in days gone by,
    as in generations of old.

Was it not you who cut Rahab
  to pieces,   Job 9:13
who pierced that monster
  through?   Ps 74:13
¹⁰Was it not you who dried up
  the sea,   Ex 14:22
  the waters of the great deep,
who made a road in the
  depths of the sea Job 36:30
so that the redeemed might
  cross over?   Ex 15:13
¹¹Those the LORD has rescued
  will return.   Isa 35:9
  They will enter Zion with
    singing;   Ps 109:28
  everlasting joy will crown
    their heads.
  Gladness and joy will
    overtake them,   Jer 33:11
  and sorrow and sighing will
    flee away.   Rev 7:17

¹²"I, even I, am he who comforts
  you.   2Co 1:4
  Who are you that you fear
    mere mortals,   Ps 118:6
  human beings who are but
    grass,   1Pe 1:24
¹³that you forget the LORD your
  Maker,   Isa 17:10; 45:11
  who stretches out the
    heavens   Ps 104:2; Isa 48:13
  and who lays the foundations
    of the earth,
  that you live in constant terror
    every day   Isa 7:4
  because of the wrath of the
    oppressor,
  who is bent on destruction?
For where is the wrath of the
  oppressor?   Isa 9:4

¹⁴ The cowering prisoners will
  soon be set free;
  they will not die in their
    dungeon,
  nor will they lack bread.
¹⁵For I am the LORD your God,
  who stirs up the sea so that
    its waves roar —   Jer 31:35
  the LORD Almighty is his
    name.   Isa 13:4
¹⁶I have put my words in your
  mouth   Dt 18:18; Isa 59:21
  and covered you with the
    shadow of my hand —
I who set the heavens in place,
  who laid the foundations of
    the earth,   Isa 48:13
  and who say to Zion, 'You
    are my people.'"   Jer 7:23

The Cup of the LORD's Wrath

¹⁷Awake, awake!   Isa 52:1
  Rise up, Jerusalem,
you who have drunk from the
  hand of the LORD
  the cup of his wrath,   Job 21:20
you who have drained to its
  dregs   Ps 75:8
  the goblet that makes
    people stagger.   Ps 60:3
¹⁸Among all the children she
  bore   Ps 88:18
  there was none to guide
    her;
  among all the children she
    reared
  there was none to take her
    by the hand.
¹⁹These double calamities have
  come upon you —   Isa 47:9
  who can comfort you? —

ruin and destruction, famine
and sword —   Isa 14:30
who can*a* console you?
20 Your children have fainted;
they lie at every street
corner,   Isa 5:25; Jer 14:16
like antelope caught in a net.
They are filled with the wrath
of the LORD,   Job 40:11
with the rebuke of your God.

21 Therefore hear this, you
afflicted one,   Isa 14:32
made drunk, but not with
wine.   Isa 29:9
22 This is what your Sovereign
LORD says,
your God, who defends his
people: Isa 49:25
"See, I have taken out of your
hand
the cup that made you stagger;
from that cup, the goblet of
my wrath,
you will never drink again.
23 I will put it into the hands of
your tormentors,   Jer 25:15
who said to you,
'Fall prostrate that we may
walk on you.'   Zec 12:2
And you made your back like
the ground,
like a street to be walked on."

52 Awake, awake, Zion,
clothe yourself with
strength!   Isa 51:9
Put on your garments of
splendor,   Ps 110:3

Jerusalem, the holy city.
The uncircumcised and
defiled
will not enter you again.
2 Shake off your dust;   Isa 29:4
rise up, sit enthroned,
Jerusalem.
Free yourself from the chains
on your neck,   Ps 81:6
Daughter Zion, now a captive.

3 For this is what the LORD says:

"You were sold for nothing,
and without money you will
be redeemed."   Isa 45:13

4 For this is what the Sovereign
LORD says:

"At first my people went down
to Egypt to live;   Ge 46:6
lately, Assyria has
oppressed them.

5 "And now what do I have
here?" declares the LORD.

"For my people have been
taken away for nothing,
and those who rule them
mock,*b*"
declares the LORD.
"And all day long
my name is constantly
blasphemed.   Eze 36:20
6 Therefore my people will
know my name;   Isa 49:23
therefore in that day they
will know   Isa 10:20
that it is I who foretold it.
Yes, it is I."

---

a 19 Dead Sea Scrolls, Septuagint, Vulgate and Syriac; Masoretic Text / *how can I*
b 5 Dead Sea Scrolls and Vulgate; Masoretic Text *wail*

⁷How beautiful on the
mountains
are the feet of those who
bring good news,   Ro 10:15
who proclaim peace,   Eph 6:15
who bring good tidings,
who proclaim salvation,
who say to Zion,
"Your God reigns!"   Ps 93:1
⁸Listen! Your watchmen lift up
their voices;   Isa 62:6
together they shout for joy.
When the LORD returns to
Zion,   Isa 59:20
they will see it with their
own eyes.
⁹Burst into songs of joy
together,   Ps 98:4
you ruins of Jerusalem,
for the LORD has comforted
his people,   Lk 2:25
he has redeemed Jerusalem.
¹⁰The LORD will lay bare his
holy arm   Ps 44:3
in the sight of all the
nations,   Isa 66:18
and all the ends of the earth
will see   Isa 11:9
the salvation of our God.

¹¹Depart, depart, go out from
there!   Isa 48:20
Touch no unclean thing!
Come out from it and be pure,
you who carry the articles
of the LORD's house.
¹²But you will not leave in haste
or go in flight;
for the LORD will go before you,

the God of Israel will be
your rear guard.   Ex 14:19

The Suffering and Glory of the Servant

¹³See, my servant will act
wisely[a];   Isa 42:1
he will be raised and lifted
up and highly exalted.
¹⁴Just as there were many who
were appalled at him[b] —
his appearance was so
disfigured beyond that
of any human being
and his form marred beyond
human likeness—
¹⁵so he will sprinkle many
nations,[c]   Lev 14:7; 16:14-15
and kings will shut their
mouths because of him.
For what they were not told,
they will see,
and what they have not heard,
they will understand.

53 Who has believed our
message   Ro 10:16
and to whom has the arm
of the LORD been
revealed?   Jn 12:38
²He grew up before him like a
tender shoot,   2Ki 19:26
and like a root out of dry
ground.   Isa 11:10
He had no beauty or majesty
to attract us to him,
nothing in his appearance
that we should desire
him.   Isa 52:14

---

a 13 Or *will prosper*   *b* 14 Hebrew *you*   *c* 15 Or *so will many nations be amazed at him*
(see also Septuagint)

³He was despised and rejected
    by mankind,
a man of suffering, and
    familiar with pain.
Like one from whom people
    hide their faces   Dt 31:17
he was despised, and we
    held him in low esteem.

⁴Surely he took up our pain
    and bore our suffering,
yet we considered him
    punished by God,   Jn 19:7
stricken by him, and
    afflicted.   Ge 12:17; Ru 1:21
⁵But he was pierced for our
    transgressions,   Ro 4:25
he was crushed for our
    iniquities;   Ps 34:18
the punishment that brought
    us peace was on him,
and by his wounds we are
    healed.   1Pe 2:24-25
⁶We all, like sheep, have gone
    astray,   Ps 95:10; 1Pe 2:24-25
each of us has turned to our
    own way;   1Sa 8:3
and the Lᴏʀᴅ has laid on him
    the iniquity of us all.   Ex 28:38

⁷He was oppressed and
    afflicted,   Isa 49:26
yet he did not open his
    mouth;   Mk 14:61
he was led like a lamb to the
    slaughter,   Ps 44:22
and as a sheep before its
    shearers is silent,

so he did not open his
    mouth.
⁸By oppressionᵃ and judgment
    he was taken away.
Yet who of his generation
    protested?
For he was cut off from the
    land of the living;   Da 9:26
for the transgression of
    my people he was
    punished.ᵇ   Ps 39:8
⁹He was assigned a grave with
    the wicked,
and with the rich in his
    death,   Mt 27:57-60
though he had done no
    violence,   Isa 42:1-3
nor was any deceit in his
    mouth.   1Pe 2:22

¹⁰Yet it was the Lᴏʀᴅ's will to
    crush him and cause
    him to suffer,   Isa 46:10
and though the Lᴏʀᴅ
    makesᶜ his life an
    offering for sin,   Lev 5:15
he will see his offspring and
    prolong his days,   Ps 22:30
and the will of the Lᴏʀᴅ
    will prosper in his
    hand.   Isa 49:4
¹¹After he has suffered,   Jn 10:14-18
    he will see the light of lifeᵈ
    and be satisfiedᵉ;   Job 33:30
by his knowledgeᶠ my
    righteous servant will
    justify many,   Ro 5:18-19

ᵃ 8 Or *From arrest*   ᵇ 8 Or *generation considered / that he was cut off from the land of the living, / that he was punished for the transgression of my people?*   ᶜ 10 Hebrew *though you make*   ᵈ 11 Dead Sea Scrolls (see also Septuagint); Masoretic Text does not have *the light of life.*   ᵉ 11 Or (with Masoretic Text) ¹¹*He will see the fruit of his suffering / and will be satisfied*   ᶠ 11 Or *by knowledge of him*

and he will bear their
  iniquities.   Ex 28:38
¹²Therefore I will give him a
  portion among the
  great,ᵃ   Php 2:9
and he will divide the spoils
  with the strong,ᵇ   Lk 11:22
because he poured out his life
  unto death,   Mt 26:28,38-39
and was numbered with the
  transgressors.   Lk 22:37
For he bore the sin of many,
  and made intercession for
  the transgressors.   Ro 8:34

The Future Glory of Zion

54 "Sing, barren woman,
  you who never bore a
  child;
burst into song, shout for joy,
  you who were never in labor;
because more are the children
  of the desolate woman
than of her who has a
  husband,"   Gal 4:27
    says the LORD.
² "Enlarge the place of your tent,
  stretch your tent curtains
  wide,
  do not hold back;
lengthen your cords,
  strengthen your stakes.
³ For you will spread out to the
  right and to the left;
your descendants will
  dispossess nations
and settle in their desolate
  cities.   Isa 49:19

⁴ "Do not be afraid; you will not
  be put to shame.   Isa 28:16

Do not fear disgrace; you
  will not be humiliated.
You will forget the shame of
  your youth   Jer 2:2
and remember no more
  the reproach of your
  widowhood.   Isa 51:7
⁵ For your Maker is your
  husband —   Jer 3:14
  the LORD Almighty is his
  name —
  the Holy One of Israel is your
  Redeemer;   Isa 48:17
he is called the God of all
  the earth.   Isa 6:3
⁶ The LORD will call you back
  as if you were a wife
  deserted and distressed
  in spirit —   Isa 62:4,12
a wife who married young,
  only to be rejected," says
  your God.
⁷ "For a brief moment I
  abandoned you,   Isa 26:20
but with deep compassion I
  will bring you back.
⁸ In a surge of anger   Isa 60:10
I hid my face from you for a
  moment,   Isa 1:15
but with everlasting kindness
  I will have compassion on
  you,"   Ps 102:13; Isa 14:1
  says the LORD your
  Redeemer.

⁹ "To me this is like the days of
  Noah,
when I swore that the waters
  of Noah would never
  again cover the earth.

ᵃ 12 Or *many*   ᵇ 12 Or *numerous*

So now I have sworn not to be
    angry with you,   Isa 12:1
    never to rebuke you again.
¹⁰Though the mountains be
    shaken   Ps 46:2; Rev 6:14
    and the hills be removed,
yet my unfailing love for you
    will not be shaken Isa 51:6
nor my covenant of peace
    be removed,"   Ps 89:34
says the Lord, who has
    compassion on you. ver 8

¹¹ "Afflicted city, lashed by
    storms and not
    comforted,   Isa 14:32; 28:2
    I will rebuild you with
    stones of turquoise,*ᵃ*
    your foundations with lapis
    lazuli.   Isa 28:16; Rev 21:19-20
¹²I will make your battlements
    of rubies,
    your gates of sparkling
    jewels,
    and all your walls of
    precious stones.
¹³All your children will be
    taught by the Lord,
    and great will be their
    peace.   Isa 48:18
¹⁴In righteousness you will be
    established: Isa 26:2
Tyranny will be far from you;
    you will have nothing to fear.
Terror will be far removed;
    it will not come near you.
¹⁵If anyone does attack you, it
    will not be my doing;
    whoever attacks you will
    surrender to you.

¹⁶ "See, it is I who created the
    blacksmith   Isa 44:12
    who fans the coals into
    flame
    and forges a weapon fit for
    its work.   Isa 10:5
And it is I who have created
    the destroyer to wreak
    havoc;   Isa 13:5
¹⁷ no weapon forged against
    you will prevail,   Isa 29:8
    and you will refute every
    tongue that accuses you.
This is the heritage of the
    servants of the Lord,
    and this is their vindication
    from me,"   Ps 17:2
        declares the Lord.

Invitation to the Thirsty

55 "Come, all you who are
    thirsty,   Jn 4:14; 7:37
    come to the waters; Jer 2:13
and you who have no money,
    come, buy and eat! Rev 3:18
Come, buy wine and milk SS 5:1
    without money and without
    cost.   Hos 14:4; Mt 10:8
²Why spend money on what is
    not bread,
    and your labor on what
    does not satisfy? Ps 22:26
Listen, listen to me, and eat
    what is good,   Isa 1:19
    and you will delight in the
    richest of fare. Isa 30:23
³Give ear and come to me;
    listen, that you may live.
I will make an everlasting
    covenant with you,

ᵃ 11 The meaning of the Hebrew for this word is uncertain.

my faithful love promised
    to David.   Ac 13:34; Isa 54:8
⁴See, I have made him a
    witness to the peoples,
a ruler and commander of
    the peoples.
⁵Surely you will summon
    nations you know not,
and nations you do not
    know will come
    running to you,   Isa 2:3
because of the LORD your God,
    the Holy One of Israel,   Isa 12:6
for he has endowed you
    with splendor."   Isa 60:9

⁶Seek the LORD while he may
    be found;   Ps 32:6; 2Co 6:1-2
call on him while he is near.
⁷Let the wicked forsake their
    ways   2Ch 7:14
    and the unrighteous their
    thoughts.   Isa 32:7; 59:7
Let them turn to the LORD,
    and he will have mercy
    on them,   Isa 44:22; 54:10
and to our God, for he will
    freely pardon.   Isa 1:18; 40:2

⁸"For my thoughts are not your
    thoughts,   Php 2:5; 4:8
neither are your ways my
    ways,"   Isa 53:6; Mic 4:12
    declares the LORD.
⁹"As the heavens are higher
    than the earth,   Ps 103:11
so are my ways higher than
    your ways
and my thoughts than your
    thoughts.   Isa 40:13-14
¹⁰As the rain and the snow
    come down from heaven,

and do not return to it
    without watering the earth
and making it bud and
    flourish,   Ps 67:6
so that it yields seed for the
    sower and bread for the
    eater,   2Co 9:10
¹¹so is my word that goes out
    from my mouth: Dt 32:2
It will not return to me
    empty,   Isa 45:23
but will accomplish what I
    desire
and achieve the purpose for
    which I sent it.   Isa 44:26
¹²You will go out in joy   Ps 98:4
    and be led forth in peace;
the mountains and hills
    will burst into song before
    you,   Ps 65:12-13
and all the trees of the field
    will clap their hands.   Ps 98:8
¹³Instead of the thornbush will
    grow the juniper,
and instead of briers the
    myrtle will grow.   Isa 5:6
This will be for the LORD's
    renown,   Isa 63:12
for an everlasting sign,
    that will endure forever."

Salvation for Others

56 This is what the LORD
        says:

"Maintain justice   Isa 1:17
    and do what is right,   Isa 26:8
for my salvation is close at
    hand   Ps 85:9
and my righteousness will
    soon be revealed.   Jer 23:6

2 Blessed is the one who does
   this — Ps 119:2
   the person who holds it fast,
who keeps the Sabbath
      without desecrating it,
   and keeps their hands from
      doing any evil."

3 Let no foreigner who is bound
      to the LORD say,   Ex 12:43
   "The LORD will surely
      exclude me from his
      people."   Dt 23:3
And let no eunuch complain,
   "I am only a dry tree."

4 For this is what the LORD says:

"To the eunuchs who keep my
      Sabbaths,
   who choose what pleases me
   and hold fast to my
      covenant —   Ex 31:13
5 to them I will give within my
      temple and its walls
   a memorial and a name
   better than sons and
      daughters;
   I will give them an everlasting
      name
   that will endure forever.
6 And foreigners who bind
      themselves to the LORD
   to minister to him,   Isa 60:7,10
   to love the name of the LORD,
   and to be his servants,
   all who keep the Sabbath
      without desecrating it
   and who hold fast to my
      covenant —
7 these I will bring to my holy
      mountain   Isa 2:2

and give them joy in my
   house of prayer.
Their burnt offerings and
   sacrifices   Ro 12:1; Heb 13:15
will be accepted on my
   altar;
for my house will be called
   a house of prayer for all
   nations."   Mt 21:13; Mk 11:17
8 The Sovereign LORD
   declares —
he who gathers the exiles of
   Israel:
"I will gather still others to
   them   Isa 11:12; Jn 10:16
   besides those already
      gathered."

God's Accusation Against the Wicked

9 Come, all you beasts of the
   field,   Jer 12:9
   come and devour, all you
   beasts of the forest!
10 Israel's watchmen are blind,
   they all lack knowledge; Jer 2:8
they are all mute dogs,
   they cannot bark;
they lie around and dream,
   they love to sleep.   Na 3:18
11 They are dogs with mighty
   appetites;
   they never have enough.
They are shepherds who lack
   understanding;   Isa 1:3
they all turn to their own
   way,   Isa 53:6
   they seek their own gain.
12 "Come," each one cries, "let
   me get wine!   Lev 10:9
Let us drink our fill of beer!

And tomorrow will be like
today,
or even far better." Lk 12:18-19

57 The righteous perish,
and no one takes it to
heart; Isa 42:25
the devout are taken away,
and no one understands
that the righteous are taken
away
to be spared from evil.
2 Those who walk uprightly
enter into peace;
they find rest as they lie in
death. Da 12:13

3 "But you — come here, you
children of a sorceress,
you offspring of adulterers
and prostitutes! Isa 1:21
4 Who are you mocking?
At whom do you sneer
and stick out your tongue?
Are you not a brood of rebels,
the offspring of liars?
5 You burn with lust among the
oaks
and under every spreading
tree; 2Ki 16:4
you sacrifice your children in
the ravines Lev 18:21
and under the overhanging
crags.
6 The idols among the smooth
stones of the ravines are
your portion; Jer 3:9
indeed, they are your lot.
Yes, to them you have poured
out drink offerings

and offered grain offerings.
In view of all this, should I
relent? Jer 5:9,29; 9:9
7 You have made your bed on a
high and lofty hill; Jer 3:6
there you went up to offer
your sacrifices. Jer 13:27
8 Behind your doors and your
doorposts
you have put your pagan
symbols.
Forsaking me, you uncovered
your bed,
you climbed into it and
opened it wide;
you made a pact with those
whose beds you love,
and you looked with lust on
their naked bodies.
9 You went to Molek[a] with olive
oil 1Ki 11:5
and increased your perfumes.
You sent your ambassadors[b]
far away; Eze 23:16,40
you descended to the very
realm of the dead! Isa 8:19
10 You wearied yourself by such
going about,
but you would not say, 'It is
hopeless.' Jer 2:25; 18:12
You found renewal of your
strength,
and so you did not faint.
11 "Whom have you so dreaded
and feared Pr 29:25
that you have not been true
to me,
and have neither
remembered me Jer 2:32

---

a 9 Or *to the king*   *b* 9 Or *idols*

nor taken this to heart?
Is it not because I have long
    been silent   Ps 50:21
    that you do not fear me?
[12] I will expose your
    righteousness and your
    works,   Isa 29:15; Mic 3:2-4,8
    and they will not benefit you.
[13] When you cry out for help,
    let your collection of idols
        save you!
The wind will carry all of
    them off,
    a mere breath will blow
        them away.   Is 40:7,24
But whoever takes refuge in me
    will inherit the land   Ps 37:9
    and possess my holy
        mountain."   Isa 65:9-11

Comfort for the Contrite

[14] And it will be said:

"Build up, build up, prepare
    the road!
    Remove the obstacles out of
        the way of my people."
[15] For this is what the high and
    exalted One says —
    he who lives forever, whose
        name is holy: Dt 33:27
"I live in a high and holy
    place,   Job 16:19
    but also with the one who
        is contrite and lowly in
        spirit,   Ps 34:18; 51:17; 147:3
    to revive the spirit of the lowly
    and to revive the heart of
        the contrite.   Isa 61:1
[16] I will not accuse them forever,
    nor will I always be angry,

for then they would faint away
    because of me —
    the very people I have
        created.   Ge 2:7; Zec 12:1
[17] I was enraged by their sinful
    greed;   Isa 56:11
    I punished them, and hid
        my face in anger,   Isa 1:15
    yet they kept on in their
        willful ways.   Isa 1:4
[18] I have seen their ways, but I
    will heal them;   Isa 30:26
    I will guide them and
        restore comfort to
        Israel's mourners,
[19]   creating praise on their lips.
Peace, peace, to those far and
        near,"   Ac 2:39; Eph 2:17
    says the LORD. "And I will
        heal them."
[20] But the wicked are like the
    tossing sea,   Job 18:5-21
    which cannot rest,
    whose waves cast up mire
        and mud.   Ps 69:14
[21] "There is no peace," says my
    God, "for the wicked."

True Fasting

58 "Shout it aloud, do not
    hold back.   Isa 40:6
    Raise your voice like a
        trumpet.   Ex 20:18
Declare to my people their
    rebellion   Isa 48:8
    and to the descendants of
        Jacob their sins.   Isa 57:12
[2] For day after day they seek me
    out;   Isa 48:1; Tit 1:16; Jas 4:8
    they seem eager to know my
        ways,

as if they were a nation that
  does what is right
and has not forsaken the
  commands of its God.
They ask me for just decisions
and seem eager for God to
  come near them. Isa 29:13
[3]'Why have we fasted,' they say,
  'and you have not seen it?
Why have we humbled
  ourselves, Ex 10:3
and you have not noticed?'

"Yet on the day of your
  fasting, you do as you
  please Isa 22:13; Zec 7:5-6
and exploit all your workers.
[4]Your fasting ends in
  quarreling and strife,
and in striking each other
  with wicked fists.
You cannot fast as you do today
and expect your voice to be
  heard on high. Isa 59:2
[5]Is this the kind of fast I have
  chosen, Zec 7:5
only a day for people to
  humble themselves?
Is it only for bowing one's
  head like a reed
and for lying in sackcloth
  and ashes? Job 2:8
Is that what you call a fast,
  a day acceptable to the LORD?

[6]"Is not this the kind of fasting
  I have chosen: Joel 2:12-14
to loose the chains of injustice
  and untie the cords of the
  yoke,
to set the oppressed free Jer 34:9

and break every yoke? Isa 9:4
[7]Is it not to share your food
  with the hungry Eze 18:16
and to provide the poor
  wanderer with
  shelter — Isa 16:4; Heb 13:2
when you see the naked, to
  clothe them, Job 31:19-20
and not to turn away from
  your own flesh and
  blood? Ge 29:14; Lk 10:31-32
[8]Then your light will break
  forth like the dawn,
and your healing will
  quickly appear; Isa 30:26
then your righteousness[a] will
  go before you, Isa 26:2
and the glory of the LORD
  will be your rear guard.
[9]Then you will call, and the
  LORD will answer;Ps 50:15
you will cry for help, and he
  will say: Here am I.

"If you do away with the yoke
  of oppression,
  with the pointing finger and
  malicious talk, Ps 12:2
[10]and if you spend yourselves in
  behalf of the hungry
and satisfy the needs of the
  oppressed, Dt 15:7-8
then your light will rise in the
  darkness, Isa 42:16
and your night will become
  like the noonday. Job 11:17
[11]The LORD will guide you
  always; Ps 48:14
he will satisfy your needs in
  a sun-scorched land

---

[a] 8 Or *your righteous One*

and will strengthen your
frame.   Ps 72:16
You will be like a well-watered
garden,   SS 4:15
like a spring whose waters
never fail.   Jn 4:14
¹²Your people will rebuild the
ancient ruins   Isa 49:8
and will raise up the age-
old foundations;   Isa 44:28
you will be called Repairer of
Broken Walls,   Ne 2:17
Restorer of Streets with
Dwellings.

¹³"If you keep your feet from
breaking the Sabbath
and from doing as you
please on my holy day,
if you call the Sabbath a
delight   Ps 84:2,10
and the LORD's holy day
honorable,
and if you honor it by not
going your own way
and not doing as you please
or speaking idle words,
¹⁴then you will find your joy in
the LORD,   Job 22:26
and I will cause you to
ride in triumph on the
heights of the land
and to feast on the inheritance
of your father Jacob."
          For the mouth of the
          LORD has spoken.

Sin, Confession and Redemption

59 Surely the arm of the
LORD is not too short to
save,   Nu 11:23; Isa 50:2

nor his ear too dull to hear.
²But your iniquities have
separated
you from your God;
your sins have hidden his face
from you,
so that he will not hear.
³For your hands are stained
with blood,   Isa 1:15
your fingers with guilt.   Ps 7:3
Your lips have spoken falsely,
and your tongue mutters
wicked things.
⁴No one calls for justice;   Isa 5:23
no one pleads a case with
integrity.
They rely on empty arguments,
they utter lies;   Isa 44:20
they conceive trouble and
give birth to evil.   Job 15:35
⁵They hatch the eggs of vipers
and spin a spider's web.
Whoever eats their eggs will die,
and when one is broken, an
adder is hatched.
⁶Their cobwebs are useless for
clothing;
they cannot cover
themselves with what
they make.   Isa 28:20
Their deeds are evil deeds,
and acts of violence are in
their hands.   Isa 58:4
⁷Their feet rush into sin;
they are swift to shed
innocent blood.   Pr 6:17
They pursue evil schemes;
acts of violence mark their
ways.   Ro 3:15-17
⁸The way of peace they do not
know;   Ro 3:15-17

there is no justice in their
  paths.
They have turned them into
  crooked roads;
no one who walks along
  them will know peace.
⁹So justice is far from us,
  and righteousness does not
  reach us.
We look for light, but all is
  darkness;   Isa 5:30
for brightness, but we walk
  in deep shadows.
¹⁰Like the blind we grope along
  the wall,   Dt 28:29
feeling our way like people
  without eyes.
At midday we stumble as if it
  were twilight;   Isa 8:15
among the strong, we are
  like the dead.   La 3:6
¹¹We all growl like bears;
  we moan mournfully like
  doves.   Isa 38:14; Eze 7:16
We look for justice, but find
  none;
for deliverance, but it is far
  away.
¹²For our offenses are many in
  your sight,   Ezr 9:6
  and our sins testify
  against us.   Isa 3:9
Our offenses are ever with us,
  and we acknowledge our
  iniquities: Ps 51:3
¹³rebellion and treachery
  against the Lord, Isa 46:8
turning our backs on our
  God,   Tit 1:16
inciting revolt and oppression,

uttering lies our hearts have
  conceived.   Mk 7:21-22
¹⁴So justice is driven back, Isa 29:21
  and righteousness stands at
  a distance;   Isa 1:21
truth has stumbled in the
  streets,   Isa 48:1
honesty cannot enter.
¹⁵Truth is nowhere to be found,
  and whoever shuns evil
  becomes a prey.

The Lord looked and was
  displeased
that there was no justice.
¹⁶He saw that there was no one,
  he was appalled that
  there was no one to
  intervene;   Isa 53:12
so his own arm achieved
  salvation for him, Ps 98:1
and his own righteousness
  sustained him.   Isa 45:8,13
¹⁷He put on righteousness as
  his breastplate,   Eph 6:14
and the helmet of salvation
  on his head;   1Th 5:8
he put on the garments of
  vengeance   Isa 63:3
and wrapped himself in
  zeal as in a cloak. Isa 9:7
¹⁸According to what they have
  done,
so will he repay   Mt 16:27
wrath to his enemies
  and retribution to his foes;
he will repay the islands
  their due.
¹⁹From the west, people will
  fear the name of the
  Lord,   Isa 49:12

and from the rising of the
sun, they will revere his
glory.   Ps 113:3
For he will come like a
pent-up flood
that the breath of the LORD
drives along.*   Isa 11:4

20 "The Redeemer will come to
Zion,   Job 19:25; Isa 52:8
to those in Jacob who repent
of their sins,"   Ro 11:26-27
declares the LORD.

21 "As for me, this is my covenant with them," says the LORD.
"My Spirit, who is on you, will not
depart from you, and my words
that I have put in your mouth
will always be on your lips, on
the lips of your children and on
the lips of their descendants —
from this time on and forever,"
says the LORD.   Isa 11:2

The Glory of Zion

60 "Arise, shine, for your
light has come,   Eph 5:14
and the glory of the LORD
rises upon you.   Isa 4:5
2 See, darkness covers the earth
and thick darkness is over
the peoples,   Col 1:13
but the LORD rises upon you
and his glory appears over
you.
3 Nations will come to your
light,   Isa 45:14; Rev 21:24
and kings to the brightness
of your dawn.   Isa 49:23

4 "Lift up your eyes and look
about you:
All assemble and come to
you;   Isa 11:12
your sons come from afar,
and your daughters are
carried on the hip. Isa 43:6
5 Then you will look and be
radiant,   Ex 34:29
your heart will throb and
swell with joy;   Isa 35:2
the wealth on the seas will be
brought to you,   Dt 33:19
to you the riches of the
nations will come.
6 Herds of camels will cover
your land,
young camels of Midian
and Ephah.   Ge 25:2,4
And all from Sheba will
come,
bearing gold and incense
and proclaiming the praise
of the LORD.   Isa 42:10
7 All Kedar's flocks will be
gathered to you,   Ge 25:13
the rams of Nebaioth will
serve you;
they will be accepted as
offerings on my altar,
and I will adorn my glorious
temple.   Hag 2:3,7,9

8 "Who are these that fly along
like clouds,   Isa 49:21
like doves to their nests?
9 Surely the islands look to me;
in the lead are the ships of
Tarshish,ᵇ   Isa 2:16 fn

ᵃ 19 Or *When enemies come in like a flood, / the Spirit of the LORD will put them to flight*
ᵇ 9 Or *the trading ships*

bringing your children from
    afar,   Isa 14:2; 43:6
with their silver and gold,
to the honor of the LORD your
    God,   Ps 22:23
    the Holy One of Israel,
for he has endowed you
    with splendor.   Isa 55:5

10 "Foreigners will rebuild your
    walls,   Isa 14:1-2
    and their kings will serve
    you.   Isa 49:23; Rev 21:24
Though in anger I struck
    you,
    in favor I will show you
    compassion.   Isa 54:8
11 Your gates will always stand
    open,   Isa 62:10; Rev 21:25
    they will never be shut, day
    or night,
so that people may bring
    you the wealth of the
    nations—   Rev 21:26
    their kings led in triumphal
    procession.   Ps 149:8
12 For the nation or kingdom
    that will not serve you
    will perish;   Isa 14:2
    it will be utterly ruined.

13 "The glory of Lebanon will
    come to you,   Isa 35:2
    the juniper, the fir and the
    cypress together,   Isa 41:19
to adorn my sanctuary;
    and I will glorify the place
    for my feet.   1Ch 28:2
14 The children of your
    oppressors will come
    bowing before you;

all who despise you will
    bow down at your feet
and will call you the City of
    the LORD,   Isa 1:26
    Zion of the Holy One of
    Israel.   Heb 12:22
15 "Although you have been
    forsaken and hated,
    with no one traveling
    through,   Isa 33:8
I will make you the
    everlasting pride   Isa 4:2
    and the joy of all
    generations.   Isa 65:18
16 You will drink the milk of
    nations
    and be nursed at royal
    breasts.   Isa 49:23; 66:11-12
Then you will know that I, the
    LORD, am your Savior,
    your Redeemer, the Mighty
    One of Jacob.   Isa 59:20
17 Instead of bronze I will bring
    you gold,
    and silver in place of iron.
Instead of wood I will bring
    you bronze,
    and iron in place of stones.
I will make peace your
    governor   Ps 85:8; Isa 66:12
    and well-being your ruler.
18 No longer will violence be
    heard in your land,   Isa 9:4
    nor ruin or destruction
    within your borders,
but you will call your walls
    Salvation   Isa 26:1
    and your gates Praise.   Isa 61:11
19 The sun will no more be your
    light by day,

nor will the brightness of
the moon shine on you,
for the LORD will be your
everlasting light, Rev 22:5
and your God will be your
glory. Zec 2:5; Rev 21:23
²⁰ Your sun will never set again,
and your moon will wane
no more;
the LORD will be your
everlasting light,
and your days of sorrow will
end. Isa 35:10
²¹ Then all your people will be
righteous Rev 21:27
and they will possess the
land forever. Ps 37:11
They are the shoot I have
planted, Mt 15:13
the work of my hands, Isa 29:23
for the display of my
splendor. Isa 52:1
²² The least of you will become a
thousand,
the smallest a mighty nation.
I am the LORD;
in its time I will do this
swiftly." Isa 5:19

The Year of the LORD's Favor

61 The Spirit of the Sovereign
LORD is on me, Isa 11:2
because the LORD has
anointed me Ps 45:7
to proclaim good news to
the poor. Mt 11:5; Lk 7:22
He has sent me to bind up the
brokenhearted, Isa 57:15
to proclaim freedom for the
captives Isa 42:7; 49:9

and release from darkness
for the prisoners,ᵃ
² to proclaim the year of the
LORD's favor Lk 4:18-19
and the day of vengeance of
our God, Isa 34:8
to comfort all who mourn,
³ and provide for those who
grieve in Zion —
to bestow on them a crown of
beauty Isa 3:23
instead of ashes,
the oil of joy Isa 1:6
instead of mourning,
and a garment of praise
instead of a spirit of despair.
They will be called oaks of
righteousness,
a planting of the LORD Ps 1:3
for the display of his
splendor. Isa 60:20-21

⁴ They will rebuild the ancient
ruins Isa 49:8; Eze 36:33
and restore the places long
devastated;
they will renew the ruined
cities
that have been devastated
for generations.
⁵ Strangers will shepherd your
flocks; Isa 14:1-2
foreigners will work your
fields and vineyards.
⁶ And you will be called priests
of the LORD, Ex 19:6; 1Pe 2:5
you will be named
ministers of our God.
You will feed on the wealth of
nations, Isa 60:11

ᵃ 1 Hebrew; Septuagint *the blind*

and in their riches you will
    boast.

⁷Instead of your shame
    you will receive a double
        portion,   Isa 40:2; Zec 9:12
and instead of disgrace
    you will rejoice in your
        inheritance.
And so you will inherit a double
    portion in your land,
    and everlasting joy will be
        yours.   Isa 25:9

⁸"For I, the LORD, love justice;
    I hate robbery and
        wrongdoing.
In my faithfulness I will
    reward my people
    and make an everlasting
        covenant with them.
⁹Their descendants will be
    known among the
        nations   Isa 43:5
and their offspring among
    the peoples.
All who see them will
    acknowledge
    that they are a people the
        LORD has blessed."

¹⁰I delight greatly in the LORD;
    my soul rejoices in my God.
For he has clothed me with
    garments of salvation
    and arrayed me in a robe of
        his righteousness, Ps 132:9
as a bridegroom adorns his
    head like a priest,
    and as a bride adorns
        herself with her jewels.

¹¹For as the soil makes the
    sprout come up
    and a garden causes seeds
        to grow,
so the Sovereign LORD will
    make righteousness
    and praise spring up before
        all nations.

Zion's New Name

62 For Zion's sake I will not
    keep silent,   Ps 50:21
for Jerusalem's sake I will
    not remain quiet,
till her vindication shines out
    like the dawn,   Isa 1:26
    her salvation like a blazing
        torch.   Ps 67:2
²The nations will see your
    vindication,   Isa 52:10; 60:3
    and all kings your glory;
you will be called by a new
    name   ver 4,12; Isa 1:26
    that the mouth of the LORD
        will bestow.
³You will be a crown of
    splendor in the LORD's
        hand,   Zec 9:16; 1Th 2:19
    a royal diadem in the hand
        of your God.
⁴No longer will they call you
    Deserted,   Isa 54:6
or name your land Desolate.
But you will be called
    Hephzibah,ᵃ
    and your land Beulahᵇ;
for the LORD will take delight
    in you,   Jer 32:41; Zep 3:17
    and your land will be
        married.   Jer 3:14; Hos 2:19

ᵃ 4 *Hephzibah* means *my delight is in her.*   ᵇ 4 *Beulah* means *married.*

⁵As a young man marries a
young woman,
so will your Builder marry
you;
as a bridegroom rejoices over
his bride,
so will your God rejoice
over you. Isa 65:19; Zep 3:17

⁶I have posted watchmen on
your walls, Jerusalem;
they will never be silent day
or night.
You who call on the LORD,
give yourselves no rest,
⁷and give him no rest till he
establishes Jerusalem
and makes her the praise of
the earth. Dt 26:19

⁸The LORD has sworn by his
right hand
and by his mighty arm:
"Never again will I give your
grain
as food for your enemies,
and never again will
foreigners drink the
new wine
for which you have toiled;
⁹but those who harvest it will
eat it Isa 1:19
and praise the LORD, Dt 12:7
and those who gather the
grapes will drink it
in the courts of my
sanctuary." Lev 23:39

¹⁰Pass through, pass through
the gates! Isa 60:11
Prepare the way for the
people.

Build up, build up the
highway! Isa 11:16; 57:14
Remove the stones.
Raise a banner for the
nations. Isa 11:10

¹¹The LORD has made
proclamation
to the ends of the earth: Dt 30:4
"Say to Daughter Zion, Zec 9:9
'See, your Savior comes!
See, his reward is with him,
and his recompense
accompanies him.'"
¹²They will be called the Holy
People, ver 4; Ge 32:28
the Redeemed of the LORD;
and you will be called Sought
After,
the City No Longer Deserted.

God's Day of Vengeance and Redemption

63 Who is this coming from
Edom, 2Ch 28:17
from Bozrah, with his
garments stained
crimson? Am 1:12
Who is this, robed in splendor,
striding forward in the
greatness of his
strength? Isa 45:24

"It is I, proclaiming victory,
mighty to save." Isa 46:13

²Why are your garments red,
like those of one treading
the winepress? Ge 49:11

³"I have trodden the winepress
alone; Rev 14:20; 19:15

from the nations no one was
  with me.
I trampled them in my anger
  and trod them down in my
  wrath;   Isa 22:5
their blood spattered my
  garments,   Rev 19:13
  and I stained all my clothing.
[4] It was for me the day of
  vengeance;   Jer 50:15
the year for me to redeem
  had come.
[5] I looked, but there was no one
  to help,   Isa 41:28
I was appalled that no one
  gave support;
so my own arm achieved
  salvation for me,   Ps 44:3
and my own wrath
  sustained me.   Isa 59:16
[6] I trampled the nations in my
  anger;   Ps 108:13
in my wrath I made them
  drunk   Isa 29:9
and poured their blood on
  the ground."   Isa 34:3

Praise and Prayer

[7] I will tell of the kindnesses of
  the LORD,   Isa 54:8
the deeds for which he is to
  be praised,
according to all the LORD
  has done for us —
yes, the many good things
  he has done for Israel,   Ex 18:9
according to his
  compassion and many
  kindnesses.   Ps 51:1; Eph 2:4

[8] He said, "Surely they are my
  people,   Isa 51:4
children who will be true
  to me";
and so he became their
  Savior.   Isa 25:9
[9] In all their distress he too was
  distressed,
and the angel of his
  presence saved them. [a]
In his love and mercy he
  redeemed them;   Dt 7:7-8
he lifted them up and
  carried them   Dt 1:31
all the days of old.   Dt 32:7
[10] Yet they rebelled   Ps 78:40
  and grieved his Holy Spirit.
So he turned and became
  their enemy   Ps 106:40
and he himself fought
  against them.   Jos 10:14

[11] Then his people recalled [b] the
  days of old,
the days of Moses and his
  people —
where is he who brought them
  through the sea,   Ex 14:22
with the shepherd of his
  flock?
Where is he who set
  his Holy Spirit among them,
[12] who sent his glorious arm of
  power
to be at Moses' right hand,
who divided the waters before
  them,   Ex 14:21-22; Isa 11:15
to gain for himself
  everlasting renown,

[a] 9 Or *Savior* [9] *in their distress. / It was no envoy or angel / but his own presence that saved them*   [b] 11 Or *But may he recall*

¹³who led them through the
depths?   Dt 32:12
Like a horse in open country,
they did not stumble;   Jer 31:9
¹⁴like cattle that go down to the
plain,
they were given rest by the
Spirit of the LORD. Dt 12:9
This is how you guided your
people
to make for yourself a
glorious name.

¹⁵Look down from heaven and
see,   Dt 26:15; Ps 80:14
from your lofty throne, holy
and glorious.   Ps 123:1
Where are your zeal and your
might?   Isa 9:7
Your tenderness and
compassion are
withheld from us.Jer 31:20
¹⁶But you are our Father,   Ex 4:22
though Abraham does not
know us
or Israel acknowledge us;
you, LORD, are our Father,
our Redeemer from of old is
your name.   Isa 41:14; 44:6
¹⁷Why, LORD, do you make us
wander from your ways
and harden our hearts so
we do not revere you?
Return for the sake of your
servants,   Nu 10:36
the tribes that are your
inheritance.   Ex 34:9
¹⁸For a little while your people
possessed your holy place,

but now our enemies have
trampled down your
sanctuary.   Ps 74:3-8
¹⁹We are yours from of old;
but you have not ruled over
them,
they have not been called[a]
by your name.   Isa 43:7

64 [b] Oh, that you would rend
the heavens and come
down,   Ps 144:5; Mic 1:3
that the mountains would
tremble before you!
²As when fire sets twigs ablaze
and causes water to boil,
come down to make your
name known to your
enemies
and cause the nations to
quake before you! Ps 99:1
³For when you did awesome
things that we did not
expect,   Ps 65:5
you came down, and the
mountains trembled
before you.
⁴Since ancient times no one
has heard,
no ear has perceived,
no eye has seen any God
besides you,   Isa 43:10-11
who acts on behalf of those
who wait for him. Isa 30:18
⁵You come to the help of those
who gladly do right,
who remember your ways.
But when we continued to sin
against them,

---

a 19 Or *We are like those you have never ruled, / like those never called*   *b* In Hebrew texts
64:1 is numbered 63:19b, and 64:2-12 is numbered 64:1-11.

you were angry. Isa 10:4
How then can we be saved?
⁶All of us have become like one
who is unclean, Lev 5:2
and all our righteous acts
are like filthy rags;
we all shrivel up like a leaf,
and like the wind our sins
sweep us away. Jer 4:12
⁷No one calls on your name
or strives to lay hold of you;
for you have hidden your face
from us Dt 31:18; Isa 1:15; 54:8
and have given us over to*a*
our sins. Isa 9:18

⁸Yet you, LORD, are our Father.
We are the clay, you are the
potter; Isa 29:16
we are all the work of your
hand. Isa 19:25
⁹Do not be angry beyond
measure, LORD; Isa 57:17
do not remember our sins
forever. Isa 43:25
Oh, look on us, we pray,
for we are all your people.
¹⁰Your sacred cities have
become a wasteland;
even Zion is a wasteland,
Jerusalem a desolation.
¹¹Our holy and glorious temple,
where our ancestors
praised you, Ps 74:3-7
has been burned with fire,
and all that we treasured
lies in ruins. La 1:7,10
¹²After all this, LORD, will
you hold yourself
back? Ps 74:10-11; Isa 42:14

Will you keep silent and
punish us beyond
measure? Ps 83:1

Judgment and Salvation

65 "I revealed myself to
those who did not ask
for me;
I was found by those who
did not seek me. Ro 10:20
To a nation that did not call
on my name, Eph 2:12
I said, 'Here am I, here am I.'
²All day long I have held out
my hands
to an obstinate people,
who walk in ways not good,
pursuing their own
imaginations — Ps 81:11-12
³a people who continually
provoke me
to my very face, Job 1:11
offering sacrifices in gardens
and burning incense on
altars of brick;
⁴who sit among the graves
and spend their nights
keeping secret vigil;
who eat the flesh of pigs, Lev 11:7
and whose pots hold broth
of impure meat;
⁵who say, 'Keep away; don't
come near me,
for I am too sacred for you!'
Such people are smoke in my
nostrils,
a fire that keeps burning all
day.

⁶"See, it stands written
before me:

---

a 7 Septuagint, Syriac and Targum; Hebrew *have made us melt because of*

I will not keep silent but will
    pay back in full;   Ps 50:3
I will pay it back into their
    laps —   Ps 79:12
⁷both your sins and the sins of
    your ancestors,"   Ex 20:5
says the LORD.
"Because they burned
    sacrifices on the
    mountains
and defied me on the hills,
I will measure into their laps
    the full payment for their
    former deeds."   Pr 10:24

⁸This is what the LORD says:

"As when juice is still found in
    a cluster of grapes
and people say, 'Don't
    destroy it,
    there is still a blessing in it,'
so will I do in behalf of my
    servants;   Isa 54:17
I will not destroy them all.
⁹I will bring forth descendants
    from Jacob,   Isa 45:19
    and from Judah those
    who will possess my
    mountains;   Am 9:11-15
my chosen people will inherit
    them,   Isa 14:1
    and there will my servants
    live.   Isa 32:18
¹⁰Sharon will become a pasture
    for flocks,   Isa 35:2
and the Valley of Achor a
    resting place for herds,
for my people who seek me.

¹¹"But as for you who forsake
    the LORD   Dt 29:24-25; Isa 1:28

and forget my holy
    mountain,   Ps 137:5
who spread a table for Fortune
and fill bowls of mixed wine
    for Destiny,   Isa 5:22
¹²I will destine you for the
    sword,   Isa 27:1
and all of you will fall in the
    slaughter;
for I called but you did not
    answer,   Pr 1:24-25; Isa 41:28
I spoke but you did not
    listen.   2Ch 36:15-16; Jer 7:13
You did evil in my sight
and chose what
    displeases me."   Isa 1:24

¹³Therefore this is what the
Sovereign LORD says:

"My servants will eat,   Isa 1:19
    but you will go hungry;
my servants will drink,   Isa 33:16
    but you will go thirsty;
my servants will rejoice,   Isa 60:5
    but you will be put to
    shame.   Isa 44:9
¹⁴My servants will sing
    out of the joy of their hearts,
but you will cry out   Mt 8:12
    from anguish of heart
    and wail in brokenness of
    spirit.
¹⁵You will leave your name
    for my chosen ones to use in
    their curses;   Zec 8:13
the Sovereign LORD will put
    you to death,
but to his servants he will
    give another name.
¹⁶Whoever invokes a blessing in
    the land   Dt 29:19

will do so by the one true
God; Ps 31:5
whoever takes an oath in the
land
will swear by the one true
God. Isa 19:18
For the past troubles will be
forgotten Job 11:16
and hidden from my eyes.

New Heavens and a New Earth

[17] "See, I will create
new heavens and a new
earth. Isa 66:22; 2Pe 3:13
The former things will not be
remembered, Isa 43:18
nor will they come to mind.
[18] But be glad and rejoice forever
in what I will create,
for I will create Jerusalem to
be a delight
and its people a joy.
[19] I will rejoice over Jerusalem
and take delight in my
people;
the sound of weeping and of
crying Isa 25:8; Rev 7:17
will be heard in it no more.

[20] "Never again will there be in it
an infant who lives but a
few days,
or an old man who does not
live out his years; Ecc 8:13
the one who dies at a hundred
will be thought a mere
child;
the one who fails to reach[a] a
hundred
will be considered accursed.

[21] They will build houses and
dwell in them; Isa 32:18
they will plant vineyards
and eat their fruit.
[22] No longer will they build
houses and others live
in them, Dt 28:30
or plant and others eat.
For as the days of a tree,
so will be the days of my
people; Ps 21:4; 91:16
my chosen ones will long
enjoy Isa 14:1
the work of their hands.
[23] They will not labor in vain,
nor will they bear children
doomed to misfortune;
for they will be a people
blessed by the LORD,
they and their descendants
with them. Ac 2:39
[24] Before they call I will answer;
while they are still speaking
I will hear. Da 9:20-23; 10:12
[25] The wolf and the lamb will
feed together, Isa 11:6
and the lion will eat straw
like the ox,
and dust will be the
serpent's food. Ge 3:14
They will neither harm nor
destroy
on all my holy mountain,"
says the LORD.

Judgment and Hope

66 This is what the LORD
says:

"Heaven is my throne, Mt 23:22

---

[a] 20 Or the sinner who reaches

and the earth is my
footstool. 1Ki 8:27; Mt 5:34-35
Where is the house you will
build for me? 2Sa 7:7
Where will my resting
place be?
²Has not my hand made all
these things, Ac 7:50
and so they came into
being?"
declares the LORD.

"These are the ones I look on
with favor:
those who are humble and
contrite in spirit, Isa 57:15
and who tremble at my
word. Ezr 9:4
³But whoever sacrifices a bull
is like one who kills a
person,
and whoever offers a lamb
is like one who breaks a
dog's neck;
whoever makes a grain offering
is like one who presents
pig's blood,
and whoever burns memorial
incense Lev 2:2
is like one who worships an
idol.
They have chosen their own
ways, Isa 57:17
and they delight in their
abominations; Dt 27:15
⁴so I also will choose harsh
treatment for them
and will bring on them
what they dread. Pr 10:24
For when I called, no one
answered, Pr 1:24; Jer 7:13

when I spoke, no one
listened.
They did evil in my sight
and chose what
displeases me." Isa 65:12

⁵Hear the word of the LORD,
you who tremble at his
word:
"Your own people who hate
you, Ps 38:20
and exclude you because of
my name, have said,
'Let the LORD be glorified,
that we may see your joy!'
Yet they will be put to
shame. Lk 13:17
⁶Hear that uproar from the
city,
hear that noise from the
temple!
It is the sound of the LORD
repaying his enemies all
they deserve. Isa 65:6

⁷"Before she goes into labor,
she gives birth;
before the pains come upon
her,
she delivers a son. Rev 12:5
⁸Who has ever heard of such
things?
Who has ever seen things
like this? Isa 64:4
Can a country be born in a
day
or a nation be brought forth
in a moment?
Yet no sooner is Zion in labor
than she gives birth to her
children. Isa 49:21

⁹Do I bring to the moment of
    birth   Isa 37:3
  and not give delivery?" says
    the LORD.
  "Do I close up the womb
    when I bring to delivery?"
  says your God.
¹⁰"Rejoice with Jerusalem and
    be glad for her,   Dt 32:43
  all you who love her;   Ps 26:8
rejoice greatly with her,
  all you who mourn over
    her.
¹¹For you will nurse and be
    satisfied   Isa 60:16
  at her comforting breasts;
you will drink deeply
  and delight in her
    overflowing abundance."

¹²For this is what the LORD
says:

"I will extend peace to her like
    a river,   Isa 48:18
  and the wealth of nations
    like a flooding stream;
you will nurse and be carried
    on her arm   Isa 60:4
  and dandled on her knees.
¹³As a mother comforts her
    child,
  so will I comfort you;   Isa 40:1
and you will be comforted
    over Jerusalem."

¹⁴When you see this, your heart
    will rejoice   Joel 2:23
  and you will flourish like
    grass;

the hand of the LORD will
    be made known to his
    servants,   Isa 54:17
  but his fury will be shown
    to his foes.   Isa 10:5
¹⁵See, the LORD is coming with
    fire,   Isa 1:31
  and his chariots are like a
    whirlwind;   Ps 68:17
he will bring down his anger
    with fury,
  and his rebuke with flames
    of fire.   Ps 9:5
¹⁶For with fire and with his sword
  the LORD will execute
    judgment on all people,
  and many will be those
    slain by the LORD.   Isa 10:4

¹⁷"Those who consecrate and
purify themselves to go into the
gardens, following one who is
among those who eat the flesh
of pigs, rats and other unclean
things—they will meet their end
together with the one they follow,"
declares the LORD.   Ps 37:20; Isa 1:28

¹⁸"And I, because of what they
have planned and done, am
about to come[a] and gather the
people of all nations and languages, and they will come and
see my glory.   Isa 59:19
¹⁹"I will set a sign among them,
and I will send some of those who
survive to the nations—to Tarshish, to the Libyans[b] and Lydians
(famous as archers), to Tubal and
Greece, and to the distant islands

---

[a] 18 The meaning of the Hebrew for this clause is uncertain.   [b] 19 Some Septuagint
manuscripts Put (Libyans); Hebrew Pul

that have not heard of my fame or seen my glory. They will proclaim my glory among the nations. ²⁰And they will bring all your people, from all the nations, to my holy mountain in Jerusalem as an offering to the LORD — on horses, in chariots and wagons, and on mules and camels," says the LORD. "They will bring them, as the Israelites bring their grain offerings, to the temple of the LORD in ceremonially clean vessels. ²¹And I will select some of them also to be priests and Levites," says the LORD.

Ex 19:6; Isa 61:6; 1Pe 2:5,9

²²"As the new heavens and the new earth that I make will endure before me," declares the LORD, "so will your name and descendants endure. ²³From one New Moon to another and from one Sabbath to another, all mankind will come and bow down before me," says the LORD. ²⁴"And they will go out and look on the dead bodies of those who rebelled against me; the worms that eat them will not die, the fire that burns them will not be quenched, and they will be loathsome to all mankind."

Isa 1:31

Jeremiah

1 The words of Jeremiah son of Hilkiah, one of the priests at Anathoth in the territory of Benjamin. ²The word of the LORD came to him in the thirteenth year of the reign of Josiah son of Amon king of Judah, ³and through the reign of Jehoiakim son of Josiah king of Judah, down to the fifth month of the eleventh year of Zedekiah son of Josiah king of Judah, when the people of Jerusalem went into exile.   Jos 21:18; 1Ch 6:60; Jer 52:15

The Call of Jeremiah

⁴The word of the LORD came to me, saying,

⁵"Before I formed you in the
    womb I knew*ᵃ* you,
  before you were born I set
    you apart;   Isa 49:1
  I appointed you as a
    prophet to the nations."

⁶"Alas, Sovereign LORD," I said, "I do not know how to speak; I am too young."   Ex 4:10; 1Ki 3:7

⁷But the LORD said to me, "Do not say, 'I am too young.' You must go to everyone I send you to and say whatever I command you. ⁸Do not be afraid of them, for I am with you and will rescue you," declares the LORD.   Jer 15:20; Eze 2:6

⁹Then the LORD reached out his hand and touched my mouth and said to me, "I have put my words in your mouth. ¹⁰See, today I appoint you over nations and kingdoms to uproot and tear down, to destroy and overthrow, to build and to plant."   Jer 18:7-10; Isa 6:7

¹¹The word of the LORD came to me: "What do you see, Jeremiah?"   Jer 24:3; Am 7:8

"I see the branch of an almond tree," I replied.

¹²The LORD said to me, "You have seen correctly, for I am watching*ᵇ* to see that my word is fulfilled."   Jer 44:27

¹³The word of the LORD came to me again: "What do you see?"

"I see a pot that is boiling," I answered. "It is tilting toward us from the north."

¹⁴The LORD said to me, "From

ᵃ 5 Or *chose*   *ᵇ* 12 The Hebrew for *watching* sounds like the Hebrew for *almond tree*.

the north disaster will be poured out on all who live in the land. ¹⁵I am about to summon all the peoples of the northern kingdoms," declares the LORD. Isa 14:31

"Their kings will come and set up their thrones
in the entrance of the gates of Jerusalem;
they will come against all her surrounding walls
and against all the towns of Judah. Jer 4:16; 9:11
¹⁶I will pronounce my judgments on my people because of their wickedness in forsaking me, Dt 28:20
in burning incense to other gods Jer 7:9
and in worshiping what their hands have made.

¹⁷ "Get yourself ready! Stand up and say to them whatever I command you. Do not be terrified by them, or I will terrify you before them. ¹⁸Today I have made you a fortified city, an iron pillar and a bronze wall to stand against the whole land — against the kings of Judah, its officials, its priests and the people of the land. ¹⁹They will fight against you but will not overcome you, for I am with you and will rescue you," declares the LORD. Isa 50:7; Jer 20:11; Eze 2:6

Israel Forsakes God

2 The word of the LORD came to me: ²"Go and proclaim in the hearing of Jerusalem: Isa 38:4

"This is what the LORD says:

" 'I remember the devotion of your youth, Eze 16:8-14,60
how as a bride you loved me
and followed me through the wilderness, Dt 2:7
through a land not sown.
³Israel was holy to the LORD,
the firstfruits of his harvest; Jas 1:18; Rev 14:4
all who devoured her were held guilty, Isa 41:11; Jer 50:7
and disaster overtook them,' "
declares the LORD.

⁴Hear the word of the LORD, you descendants of Jacob,
all you clans of Israel.

⁵This is what the LORD says:

"What fault did your ancestors find in me,
that they strayed so far from me?
They followed worthless idols
and became worthless themselves. 2Ki 17:15
⁶They did not ask, 'Where is the LORD,
who brought us up out of Egypt Hos 13:4
and led us through the barren wilderness,
through a land of deserts and ravines, Dt 8:15; 32:10
a land of drought and utter darkness,
a land where no one travels and no one lives?' Jer 51:43

⁷I brought you into a fertile
  land
  to eat its fruit and rich
    produce.   Nu 13:27; Dt 8:7-9
But you came and defiled my
  land
  and made my inheritance
    detestable.   Ps 106:34-39
⁸The priests did not ask,
  'Where is the LORD?'
Those who deal with the law
  did not know me;   Jer 4:22
  the leaders rebelled
    against me.
The prophets prophesied by
  Baal,   Jer 23:13
  following worthless idols.

⁹"Therefore I bring charges
  against you again,"
    declares the LORD.
"And I will bring charges
  against your children's
  children.
¹⁰Cross over to the coasts of
  Cyprus and look,   Ge 10:4
  send to Kedar^a and observe
    closely;   Ge 25:13
  see if there has ever been
  anything like this:
¹¹Has a nation ever changed its
  gods?
  (Yet they are not gods at
    all.)   Isa 37:19; Jer 16:20
But my people have
  exchanged their
  glorious God   Ps 106:20
  for worthless idols.
¹²Be appalled at this, you
  heavens,

and shudder with great
  horror,"
    declares the LORD.
¹³"My people have committed
  two sins:
They have forsaken me,
  the spring of living
    water,   Ps 36:9; Jn 4:14
and have dug their own
  cisterns,
  broken cisterns that cannot
  hold water.
¹⁴Is Israel a servant, a slave by
  birth?   Ex 4:22
  Why then has he become
  plunder?
¹⁵Lions have roared;   Jer 4:7; 50:17
  they have growled at him.
They have laid waste his
  land;   Isa 1:7
  his towns are burned and
  deserted.   2Ki 25:9
¹⁶Also, the men of Memphis
  and Tahpanhes   Isa 19:13
  have cracked your skull.
¹⁷Have you not brought this on
  yourselves   Jer 4:18
  by forsaking the LORD your
  God   Isa 1:28; Jer 17:13
  when he led you in the way?
¹⁸Now why go to Egypt   Isa 30:2
  to drink water from the
    Nile^b?   Jos 13:3
And why go to Assyria   Hos 5:13
  to drink water from the
    Euphrates?   Isa 7:20
¹⁹Your wickedness will punish
  you;
  your backsliding will
  rebuke you.   Jer 3:11,22

^{a} 10 In the Syro-Arabian desert ^{b} 18 Hebrew *Shihor*; that is, a branch of the Nile

Consider then and realize
　how evil and bitter it is for
　you   Job 20:14
when you forsake the LORD
　your God   Jer 19:4
and have no awe of me,"
　　declares the Lord,
　　the LORD Almighty.

20 "Long ago you broke off your
　yoke   Lev 26:13
　and tore off your bonds;
you said, 'I will not serve you!'
Indeed, on every high hill
　and under every spreading
　tree   Dt 12:2
you lay down as a
　prostitute.   Isa 1:21
21 I had planted you like a choice
　vine   Ex 15:17; Ps 80:8
of sound and reliable stock.
How then did you turn
　against me
into a corrupt, wild vine?
22 Although you wash yourself
　with soap   Ps 51:2
and use an abundance of
　cleansing powder,
the stain of your guilt is still
　before me,"
　　declares the Sovereign
　　LORD.
23 "How can you say, 'I am not
　defiled;   Pr 30:12
I have not run after the
　Baals'?   Jer 9:14
See how you behaved in the
　valley;   Jer 7:31
consider what you have
　done.
You are a swift she-camel

running here and there,
24 a wild donkey accustomed to
　the desert,   Jer 14:6
sniffing the wind in her
　craving—
in her heat who can restrain
　her?
Any males that pursue her
　need not tire themselves;
at mating time they will
　find her.
25 Do not run until your feet are
　bare
and your throat is dry.
But you said, 'It's no use!
I love foreign gods,   Dt 32:16
and I must go after them.'
26 "As a thief is disgraced when
　he is caught,   Jer 48:27
so the people of Israel are
　disgraced—
they, their kings and their
　officials,
their priests and their
　prophets.   Jer 32:32
27 They say to wood, 'You are my
　father,'
and to stone, 'You gave me
　birth.'   Jer 3:9
They have turned their backs
　to me   Ps 14:3
and not their faces;   Jer 18:17
yet when they are in trouble,
　they say,   Isa 26:16
'Come and save us!'   Hos 5:15
28 Where then are the gods you
　made for yourselves?
Let them come if they can
　save you
when you are in trouble!

For you, Judah, have as many
gods
as you have towns.   Jer 11:13

29 "Why do you bring charges
against me?
You have all rebelled
against me,"   Jer 5:1; 6:13
declares the LORD.
30 "In vain I punished your
people;
they did not respond to
correction.
Your sword has devoured
your prophets   Ac 7:52
like a ravenous lion.

31 "You of this generation, consider the word of the LORD:

"Have I been a desert to Israel
or a land of great darkness?
Why do my people say, 'We
are free to roam;
we will come to you no
more'?
32 Does a young woman forget
her jewelry,
a bride her wedding
ornaments?
Yet my people have
forgotten me,   Isa 57:11
days without number.
33 How skilled you are at
pursuing love!
Even the worst of women
can learn from your ways.
34 On your clothes is found
the lifeblood of the innocent
poor,   2Ki 21:16
though you did not catch
them breaking in.   Ex 22:2

Yet in spite of all this
35 you say, 'I am innocent;
he is not angry with me.'
But I will pass judgment on
you   Jer 25:31
because you say, 'I have not
sinned.'   1Jn 1:8,10
36 Why do you go about so
much,
changing your ways?   Jer 31:22
You will be disappointed by
Egypt   Isa 30:2-3,7
as you were by Assyria.
37 You will also leave that place
with your hands on your
head,   2Sa 13:19
for the LORD has rejected
those you trust;
you will not be helped by
them.   Jer 37:7

3 "If a man divorces his wife
and she leaves him and
marries another man,
should he return to her again?
Would not the land be
completely defiled?
But you have lived as a
prostitute with many
lovers —   Jer 2:20,25
would you now return
to me?"
declares the LORD.
2 "Look up to the barren
heights and see.
Is there any place where you
have not been ravished?
By the roadside you sat
waiting for lovers,   Ge 38:14
sat like a nomad in the
desert.

You have defiled the land Jer 2:7
with your prostitution and
wickedness. Isa 1:21
³Therefore the showers have
been withheld, Lev 26:19
and no spring rains have
fallen. Jer 14:4
Yet you have the brazen look
of a prostitute;
you refuse to blush with
shame. Jer 6:15; 8:12
⁴Have you not just called to me:
'My Father, my friend from
my youth, ver 19; Jer 2:2
⁵will you always be angry?
Will your wrath continue
forever?'
This is how you talk,
but you do all the evil you
can."

Unfaithful Israel

⁶During the reign of King Josiah, the LORD said to me, "Have you seen what faithless Israel has done? She has gone up on every high hill and under every spreading tree and has committed adultery there. ⁷I thought that after she had done all this she would return to me but she did not, and her unfaithful sister Judah saw it. ⁸I gave faithless Israel her certificate of divorce and sent her away because of all her adulteries. Yet I saw that her unfaithful sister Judah had no fear; she also went out and committed adultery. ⁹Because Israel's immorality mattered so little to her, she defiled the land and committed adultery with stone and wood. ¹⁰In spite of all this, her unfaithful sister Judah did not return to me with all her heart, but only in pretense," declares the LORD. Jer 12:2; Eze 33:31

¹¹The LORD said to me, "Faithless Israel is more righteous than unfaithful Judah. ¹²Go, proclaim this message toward the north:

" 'Return, faithless Israel,'
declares the LORD,
'I will frown on you no
longer,
for I am faithful,' declares the
LORD, Ps 6:2
'I will not be angry forever.
¹³Only acknowledge your guilt—
you have rebelled against
the LORD your God,
you have scattered your favors
to foreign gods Jer 2:25
under every spreading tree,
and have not obeyed me,' "
declares the LORD.

¹⁴"Return, faithless people," declares the LORD, "for I am your husband. I will choose you—one from a town and two from a clan—and bring you to Zion. ¹⁵Then I will give you shepherds after my own heart, who will lead you with knowledge and understanding. ¹⁶In those days, when your numbers have increased greatly in the land," declares the LORD, "people will no longer say, 'The ark of the covenant of the LORD.' It will never enter their minds or be remembered; it will

not be missed, nor will another one be made. ¹⁷At that time they will call Jerusalem The Throne of the LORD, and all nations will gather in Jerusalem to honor the name of the LORD. No longer will they follow the stubbornness of their evil hearts. ¹⁸In those days the people of Judah will join the people of Israel, and together they will come from a northern land to the land I gave your ancestors as an inheritance. Hos 2:19

¹⁹"I myself said,

"'How gladly would I treat
          you like my children
    and give you a pleasant land,
    the most beautiful
          inheritance of any
          nation.'
I thought you would call me
          'Father'   Isa 63:16
    and not turn away from
          following me.
²⁰But like a woman unfaithful
          to her husband,
    so you, Israel, have been
          unfaithful to me,"
          declares the LORD.

²¹A cry is heard on the barren
          heights,
    the weeping and pleading
          of the people of Israel,
because they have perverted
          their ways
    and have forgotten the
          LORD their God.   Isa 57:11

²²"Return, faithless people;
    I will cure you of backsliding."

"Yes, we will come to you,
    for you are the LORD our God.
²³Surely the idolatrous
          commotion on the hills
    and mountains is a
          deception;
surely in the LORD our God
    is the salvation of Israel.Ps 3:8
²⁴From our youth shameful
          gods have consumed
    the fruits of our ancestors'
          labor—
their flocks and herds,
    their sons and daughters.
²⁵Let us lie down in our shame,
    and let our disgrace cover us.
We have sinned against the
          LORD our God,   Jdg 10:10
    both we and our ancestors;
from our youth till this day
    we have not obeyed the
          LORD our God."   Eze 2:3

4 "If you, Israel, will return,
    then return to me,"
          declares the LORD.
"If you put your detestable
          idols out of my sight
    and no longer go astray,
²and if in a truthful, just and
          righteous way
    you swear, 'As surely as the
          LORD lives,'   Dt 10:20
then the nations will invoke
          blessings by him Ge 22:18
    and in him they will boast."

³This is what the LORD says to the people of Judah and to Jerusalem:

"Break up your unplowed
          ground   Hos 10:12

and do not sow among
thorns. Mk 4:18
⁴Circumcise yourselves to the
Lord,
circumcise your hearts,
you people of Judah
and inhabitants of
Jerusalem,
or my wrath will flare up and
burn like fire Zep 2:2
because of the evil you have
done — Ex 32:22
burn with no one to
quench it. Am 5:6

Disaster From the North

⁵"Announce in Judah and
proclaim in Jerusalem
and say: Jer 5:20
'Sound the trumpet
throughout the land!'
Cry aloud and say:
'Gather together!
Let us flee to the fortified
cities!' Jos 10:20; Jer 8:14
⁶Raise the signal to go to Zion!
Flee for safety without
delay!
For I am bringing disaster
from the north, Jer 1:13-15
even terrible destruction."

⁷A lion has come out of his lair;
a destroyer of nations has
set out. Jer 6:26
He has left his place
to lay waste your land. Isa 1:7
Your towns will lie in ruins
without inhabitant.
⁸So put on sackcloth, Isa 22:12
lament and wail, Jer 7:29

for the fierce anger of the
Lord
has not turned away from us.

⁹"In that day," declares the
Lord,
"the king and the officials
will lose heart, 1Sa 17:32
the priests will be horrified,
and the prophets will be
appalled." Isa 29:9

¹⁰Then I said, "Alas, Sovereign
Lord! How completely you have
deceived this people and Jerusalem by saying, 'You will have
peace,' when the sword is at our
throats!" 2Th 2:11; Jer 14:13
¹¹At that time this people and
Jerusalem will be told, "A scorching wind from the barren heights
in the desert blows toward my
people, but not to winnow or
cleanse; ¹²a wind too strong for
that comes from me. Now I pronounce my judgments against
them." Jer 1:16; Eze 17:10; Hos 13:15

¹³Look! He advances like the
clouds, Isa 19:1
his chariots come like a
whirlwind, Isa 5:28
his horses are swifter than
eagles. Dt 28:49; Hab 1:8
Woe to us! We are ruined!
¹⁴Jerusalem, wash the evil
from your heart and be
saved. Jas 4:8
How long will you harbor
wicked thoughts? Ps 6:3
¹⁵A voice is announcing from
Dan, Jer 8:16

proclaiming disaster from
the hills of Ephraim.

¹⁶ "Tell this to the nations,
proclaim concerning
Jerusalem:
'A besieging army is coming
from a distant land,
raising a war cry against the
cities of Judah. Eze 21:22

¹⁷ They surround her like men
guarding a field, 2Ki 25:1,4
because she has rebelled
against me,' "
declares the LORD. Jer 5:23

¹⁸ "Your own conduct and actions
have brought this on you.
This is your punishment.
How bitter it is!
How it pierces to the heart!" Jer 2:19

¹⁹ Oh, my anguish, my anguish!
I writhe in pain.
Oh, the agony of my heart!
My heart pounds within me,
I cannot keep silent. Jer 20:9
For I have heard the sound of
the trumpet; Nu 10:2
I have heard the battle cry.

²⁰ Disaster follows disaster; Ps 42:7
the whole land lies in ruins.
In an instant my tents are
destroyed, Jer 10:20
my shelter in a moment.

²¹ How long must I see the battle
standard Nu 2:2
and hear the sound of the
trumpet? Jos 6:20; Jer 6:1

²² "My people are fools; Jer 10:8
they do not know me. Jer 2:8
They are senseless children;
they have no understanding.

They are skilled in doing evil;
they know not how to do
good." Ro 16:19

²³ I looked at the earth,
and it was formless and
empty; Ge 1:2
and at the heavens,
and their light was gone.

²⁴ I looked at the mountains,
and they were quaking;
all the hills were swaying.

²⁵ I looked, and there were no
people;
every bird in the sky had
flown away. Jer 9:10; Zep 1:3

²⁶ I looked, and the fruitful land
was a desert; Jer 12:4
all its towns lay in ruins
before the LORD, before his
fierce anger. Jer 12:13

²⁷ This is what the LORD says:

"The whole land will be ruined,
though I will not destroy it
completely. Jer 5:10,18; 30:11

²⁸ Therefore the earth will mourn
and the heavens above
grow dark, Isa 5:30; 50:3
because I have spoken and
will not relent, Nu 23:19
I have decided and will not
turn back." Jer 23:20; 30:24

²⁹ At the sound of horsemen and
archers Jer 6:23
every town takes to flight.
Some go into the thickets;
some climb up among the
rocks. 1Sa 26:20
All the towns are deserted;
no one lives in them.

³⁰What are you doing, you
    devastated one? Isa 10:3-4
  Why dress yourself in scarlet
  and put on jewels of gold?
  Why highlight your eyes with
    makeup? 2Ki 9:30
  You adorn yourself in vain.
  Your lovers despise you; La 1:2
  they want to kill you. Ps 35:4

³¹I hear a cry as of a woman in
    labor, Jer 13:21
  a groan as of one bearing
    her first child —
  the cry of Daughter Zion
    gasping for breath, Isa 42:14
  stretching out her hands
    and saying, Isa 1:15; La 1:17
  "Alas! I am fainting;
  my life is given over to
    murderers." La 2:21

Not One Is Upright

5 "Go up and down the
    streets of Jerusalem,
  look around and consider,
  search through her squares.
  If you can find but one person
  who deals honestly and
    seeks the truth, Jer 14:14
  I will forgive this city. Ge 18:24
²Although they say, 'As surely
  as the LORD lives,' Jer 4:2
  still they are swearing
    falsely." Lev 19:12

³LORD, do not your eyes look
    for truth? 2Ch 16:9
  You struck them, but they
    felt no pain; Isa 9:13
  you crushed them, but they
    refused correction. Jer 2:30

They made their faces harder
    than stone Jer 7:26; 19:15
  and refused to repent.
⁴I thought, "These are only the
    poor;
  they are foolish, Jer 4:22
  for they do not know the way
    of the LORD, Pr 10:21; Jer 8:7
  the requirements of their
    God.
⁵So I will go to the leaders
  and speak to them;
  surely they know the way of
    the LORD,
  the requirements of their
    God."
But with one accord they too
    had broken off the yoke
  and torn off the bonds. Ps 2:3
⁶Therefore a lion from the
    forest will attack them,
  a wolf from the desert will
    ravage them,
  a leopard will lie in wait near
    their towns Hos 13:7
  to tear to pieces any who
    venture out,
  for their rebellion is great
  and their backslidings
    many. Jer 30:14

⁷"Why should I forgive you?
  Your children have
    forsaken me
  and sworn by gods that are
    not gods. Dt 32:21; Jos 23:7
I supplied all their needs,
  yet they committed adultery
  and thronged to the houses
    of prostitutes. Jer 13:27
⁸They are well-fed, lusty stallions,

each neighing for another
man's wife. Eze 22:11
⁹Should I not punish them for
this?" Jer 9:9
declares the LORD.
"Should I not avenge myself
on such a nation as this?

¹⁰"Go through her vineyards
and ravage them,
but do not destroy them
completely. Jer 4:27; Am 9:8
Strip off her branches,
for these people do not
belong to the LORD.
¹¹The people of Israel and the
people of Judah
have been utterly unfaithful
to me," Jer 3:20
declares the LORD.

¹²They have lied about the LORD;
they said, "He will do
nothing!
No harm will come to us;
we will never see sword or
famine. Jer 14:13
¹³The prophets are but wind
and the word is not in them;
so let what they say be done
to them."

¹⁴Therefore this is what the
LORD God Almighty says:

"Because the people have
spoken these words,
I will make my words in
your mouth a fire Jer 1:9
and these people the wood
it consumes.
¹⁵People of Israel," declares the
LORD,

"I am bringing a distant
nation against you—
an ancient and enduring
nation,
a people whose language
you do not know, Isa 28:11
whose speech you do not
understand.
¹⁶Their quivers are like an open
grave;
all of them are mighty
warriors.
¹⁷They will devour your
harvests and food,
devour your sons and
daughters; Dt 28:32
they will devour your flocks
and herds, Dt 28:31
devour your vines and fig
trees. Nu 16:14
With the sword they will
destroy Lev 26:25
the fortified cities in which
you trust. Dt 28:33

¹⁸"Yet even in those days," declares the LORD, "I will not destroy you completely. ¹⁹And when the people ask, 'Why has the LORD our God done all this to us?' you will tell them, 'As you have forsaken me and served foreign gods in your own land, so now you will serve foreigners in a land not your own.' Dt 28:48; Jer 4:27

²⁰"Announce this to the
descendants of Jacob
and proclaim it in Judah:
²¹Hear this, you foolish and
senseless people, Jer 4:22
who have eyes but do not see,

who have ears but do not
    hear: Mt 13:15; Mk 8:18
22 Should you not fear me?"
    declares the LORD. Dt 28:58
"Should you not tremble in
    my presence?   Isa 64:2
I made the sand a boundary
    for the sea,   Ge 1:9
an everlasting barrier it
    cannot cross.
The waves may roll, but they
    cannot prevail;
they may roar, but they
    cannot cross it.   Ps 46:3
23 But these people have
    stubborn and rebellious
    hearts;   Dt 21:18
they have turned aside and
    gone away.   Ps 14:3
24 They do not say to themselves,
    'Let us fear the LORD our
    God,
who gives autumn and spring
    rains in season,   Ps 147:8
who assures us of the
    regular weeks of
    harvest.'   Ge 8:22; Ac 14:17
25 Your wrongdoings have kept
    these away;
your sins have deprived you
    of good.

26 "Among my people are the
    wicked
who lie in wait like men
    who snare birds   Ps 10:8
and like those who set traps
    to catch people.   Mic 7:2
27 Like cages full of birds,
    their houses are full of
    deceit;   Jer 9:6

they have become rich and
    powerful   Jer 12:1
28 and have grown fat and
    sleek.   Dt 32:15
Their evil deeds have no limit;
    they do not seek justice.
They do not promote the case
    of the fatherless;   Zec 7:10
they do not defend the just
    cause of the poor.   Isa 1:23
29 Should I not punish them for
    this?"
    declares the LORD.
"Should I not avenge myself
    on such a nation as this?

30 "A horrible and shocking thing
    has happened in the land:
31 The prophets prophesy lies,
    the priests rule by their own
    authority,   La 4:13
and my people love it this way.
    But what will you do in the
    end?

Jerusalem Under Siege

6 "Flee for safety, people of
    Benjamin!
Flee from Jerusalem!
Sound the trumpet in Tekoa!
Raise the signal over Beth
    Hakkerem!   Ne 3:14
For disaster looms out of the
    north,   Jer 4:6
even terrible destruction.
2 I will destroy Daughter Zion,
    so beautiful and delicate.
3 Shepherds with their flocks
    will come against her;
they will pitch their tents
    around her,   2Ki 25:4

each tending his own portion."

4 "Prepare for battle against her!
    Arise, let us attack at noon!
But, alas, the daylight is fading,
    and the shadows of evening
        grow long.
5 So arise, let us attack at night
    and destroy her fortresses!"

6 This is what the LORD Almighty says:

"Cut down the trees   Dt 20:19-20
    and build siege ramps
        against Jerusalem. Jer 32:24
This city must be punished;
    it is filled with oppression.
7 As a well pours out its water,
    so she pours out her
        wickedness.
Violence and destruction
    resound in her;   Ps 55:9
    her sickness and wounds
        are ever before me.
8 Take warning, Jerusalem,
    or I will turn away from you
and make your land desolate
    so no one can live in it."

9 This is what the LORD Almighty says:

"Let them glean the remnant
    of Israel
    as thoroughly as a vine;
pass your hand over the
        branches again,
    like one gathering grapes."

10 To whom can I speak and give
        warning?

Who will listen to me?
Their ears are closed[a]   Ac 7:51
    so they cannot hear.   Isa 42:20
The word of the LORD is
        offensive to them;   Jer 20:8
    they find no pleasure in it.
11 But I am full of the wrath of
        the LORD,   Jer 7:20
    and I cannot hold it in. Job 32:20

"Pour it out on the children in
        the street
    and on the young men
        gathered together; Jer 9:21
both husband and wife will
        be caught in it,
    and the old, those weighed
        down with years.   La 2:21
12 Their houses will be turned
        over to others,   Dt 28:30
    together with their fields
        and their wives,   Jer 8:10
when I stretch out my hand
    against those who live in
        the land,"
            declares the LORD.
13 "From the least to the
        greatest,
    all are greedy for gain; Isa 56:11
prophets and priests alike,
    all practice deceit.   Jer 8:10
14 They dress the wound of my
        people
    as though it were not serious.
'Peace, peace,' they say,
    when there is no peace. Jer 4:10
15 Are they ashamed of their
        detestable conduct?
    No, they have no shame at
        all;

---

a 10 Hebrew uncircumcised

they do not even know how
to blush. Jer 3:3; 8:10-12
So they will fall among the
fallen;
they will be brought down
when I punish them,"
says the LORD.

¹⁶ This is what the LORD says:

"Stand at the crossroads and
look;
ask for the ancient paths,
ask where the good way is,
and walk in it, Ps 119:3
and you will find rest for
your souls. Mt 11:29
But you said, 'We will not
walk in it.'
¹⁷ I appointed watchmen over
you and said, Eze 3:17
'Listen to the sound of the
trumpet!'
But you said, 'We will not
listen.'
Jer 11:7-8; 25:4
¹⁸ Therefore hear, you nations;
you who are witnesses,
observe what will happen to
them.
¹⁹ Hear, you earth: Isa 1:2; Jer 22:29
I am bringing disaster on
this people,
Jos 23:15
the fruit of their schemes,
because they have not
listened to my words
and have rejected my law.
²⁰ What do I care about incense
from Sheba
or sweet calamus from a
distant land? Ex 30:23
Your burnt offerings are not
acceptable; Am 5:22

your sacrifices do not please
me." Isa 1:11; Mic 6:7-8
²¹ Therefore this is what the
LORD says:

"I will put obstacles before
this people.
Parents and children alike
will stumble over them;
neighbors and friends will
perish."

²² This is what the LORD says:

"Look, an army is coming
from the land of the north;
a great nation is being stirred up
from the ends of the earth.
²³ They are armed with bow and
spear;
they are cruel and show no
mercy. Isa 13:18
They sound like the roaring sea
as they ride on their horses;
they come like men in battle
formation
to attack you, Daughter Zion."

²⁴ We have heard reports about
them,
and our hands hang limp.
Anguish has gripped us, Jer 4:19
pain like that of a woman in
labor. Jer 4:31; 50:41-43
²⁵ Do not go out to the fields
or walk on the roads,
for the enemy has a sword,
and there is terror on every
side. Jer 49:29
²⁶ Put on sackcloth, my people,
and roll in ashes; Jer 25:34
mourn with bitter wailing

as for an only son,   Zec 12:10
for suddenly the destroyer
    will come upon us.

27 "I have made you a tester of
        metals   Jer 9:7
    and my people the ore,
that you may observe
    and test their ways.
28 They are all hardened rebels,
    going about to slander.   Jer 9:4
They are bronze and iron;
    they all act corruptly.
29 The bellows blow fiercely
    to burn away the lead with
        fire,
but the refining goes on in vain;
    the wicked are not purged
        out.
30 They are called rejected silver,
    because the LORD has
        rejected them."   Ps 119:119

False Religion Worthless

7 This is the word that came
    to Jeremiah from the LORD:
2 "Stand at the gate of the LORD's
house and there proclaim this
message: Jer 17:19
    " 'Hear the word of the LORD,
all you people of Judah who come
through these gates to worship
the LORD. 3 This is what the LORD
Almighty, the God of Israel, says:
Reform your ways and your actions, and I will let you live in this
place. 4 Do not trust in deceptive
words and say, "This is the temple of the LORD, the temple of the
LORD, the temple of the LORD!"

5 If you really change your ways
and your actions and deal with
each other justly, 6 if you do not
oppress the foreigner, the fatherless or the widow and do not shed
innocent blood in this place, and
if you do not follow other gods to
your own harm, 7 then I will let
you live in this place, in the land
I gave your ancestors for ever and
ever. 8 But look, you are trusting in deceptive words that are
worthless.   Jer 18:11; 26:13; Mic 3:11

9 " 'Will you steal and murder,
commit adultery and perjury,[a]
burn incense to Baal and follow
other gods you have not known,
10 and then come and stand before me in this house, which
bears my Name, and say, "We
are safe" — safe to do all these
detestable things? 11 Has this
house, which bears my Name,
become a den of robbers to you?
But I have been watching! declares the LORD.   Mk 11:17; Jer 29:23

12 " 'Go now to the place in Shiloh where I first made a dwelling
for my Name, and see what I did
to it because of the wickedness
of my people Israel. 13 While you
were doing all these things, declares the LORD, I spoke to you
again and again, but you did not
listen; I called you, but you did
not answer. 14 Therefore, what I
did to Shiloh I will now do to the
house that bears my Name, the
temple you trust in, the place I
gave to you and your ancestors.

a 9 Or and swear by false gods

¹⁵ I will thrust you from my presence, just as I did all your fellow Israelites, the people of Ephraim.' Ps 78:67; Isa 65:12

¹⁶ "So do not pray for this people nor offer any plea or petition for them; do not plead with me, for I will not listen to you. ¹⁷ Do you not see what they are doing in the towns of Judah and in the streets of Jerusalem? ¹⁸ The children gather wood, the fathers light the fire, and the women knead the dough and make cakes to offer to the Queen of Heaven. They pour out drink offerings to other gods to arouse my anger. ¹⁹ But am I the one they are provoking? declares the LORD. Are they not rather harming themselves, to their own shame? Ex 32:10; Jer 9:19

²⁰ "Therefore this is what the Sovereign LORD says: My anger and my wrath will be poured out on this place — on man and beast, on the trees of the field and on the crops of your land — and it will burn and not be quenched.

²¹ "'This is what the LORD Almighty, the God of Israel, says: Go ahead, add your burnt offerings to your other sacrifices and eat the meat yourselves! ²² For when I brought your ancestors out of Egypt and spoke to them, I did not just give them commands about burnt offerings and sacrifices, ²³ but I gave them this command: Obey me, and I will be your God and you will be my people. Walk in obedience to all I command you, that it may go well with you. ²⁴ But they did not listen or pay attention; instead, they followed the stubborn inclinations of their evil hearts. They went backward and not forward. ²⁵ From the time your ancestors left Egypt until now, day after day, again and again I sent you my servants the prophets. ²⁶ But they did not listen to me or pay attention. They were stiff-necked and did more evil than their ancestors.' Ex 19:5; Jer 16:12

²⁷ "When you tell them all this, they will not listen to you; when you call to them, they will not answer. ²⁸ Therefore say to them, 'This is the nation that has not obeyed the LORD its God or responded to correction. Truth has perished; it has vanished from their lips.

²⁹ "'Cut off your hair and throw it away; take up a lament on the barren heights, for the LORD has rejected and abandoned this generation that is under his wrath. Jer 6:30; Eze 3:7

The Valley of Slaughter

³⁰ "'The people of Judah have done evil in my eyes, declares the LORD. They have set up their detestable idols in the house that bears my Name and have defiled it. ³¹ They have built the high places of Topheth in the Valley of Ben Hinnom to burn their sons and daughters in the fire — something I did not com-

mand, nor did it enter my mind. ³²So beware, the days are coming, declares the LORD, when people will no longer call it Topheth or the Valley of Ben Hinnom, but the Valley of Slaughter, for they will bury the dead in Topheth until there is no more room. ³³Then the carcasses of this people will become food for the birds and the wild animals, and there will be no one to frighten them away. ³⁴I will bring an end to the sounds of joy and gladness and to the voices of bride and bridegroom in the towns of Judah and the streets of Jerusalem, for the land will become desolate. Isa 24:8; Rev 18:23

8 "'At that time, declares the LORD, the bones of the kings and officials of Judah, the bones of the priests and prophets, and the bones of the people of Jerusalem will be removed from their graves. ²They will be exposed to the sun and the moon and all the stars of the heavens, which they have loved and served and which they have followed and consulted and worshiped. They will not be gathered up or buried, but will be like dung lying on the ground. ³Wherever I banish them, all the survivors of this evil nation will prefer death to life, declares the LORD Almighty.' Job 3:22; Rev 9:6

Sin and Punishment

⁴"Say to them, 'This is what the LORD says:

" 'When people fall down, do
    they not get up? Pr 24:16
When someone turns away,
    do they not return?
⁵Why then have these people
    turned away?
Why does Jerusalem always
    turn away?
They cling to deceit; Jer 5:27
    they refuse to return. Jer 7:24
⁶I have listened attentively,
    but they do not say what is
        right.
None of them repent of their
    wickedness, Rev 9:20
    saying, "What have I done?"
Each pursues their own
    course Ps 14:1-3
    like a horse charging into
        battle.
⁷Even the stork in the sky
    knows her appointed seasons,
and the dove, the swift and
    the thrush
    observe the time of their
        migration.
But my people do not know
    the requirements of the LORD.

⁸" 'How can you say, "We are
    wise,
    for we have the law of the
        LORD," Ro 2:17
when actually the lying pen of
    the scribes
    has handled it falsely?
⁹The wise will be put to shame;
    they will be dismayed and
        trapped. Job 5:13
Since they have rejected the
    word of the LORD, Jer 6:19

what kind of wisdom do
they have? *Pr 1:7*
10 Therefore I will give their
wives to other men
and their fields to new
owners. *Jer 6:12*
From the least to the greatest,
all are greedy for gain;
prophets and priests alike,
all practice deceit. *Jer 23:11,15*
11 They dress the wound of my
people
as though it were not serious.
"Peace, peace," they say,
when there is no peace. *Jer 6:14*
12 Are they ashamed of their
detestable conduct?
No, they have no shame at
all; *Jer 3:3*
they do not even know how
to blush.
So they will fall among the
fallen;
they will be brought down
when they are punished,
says the LORD.

13 " 'I will take away their harvest,
declares the LORD.
There will be no grapes on
the vine. *Joel 1:7*
There will be no figs on the
tree, *Lk 13:6*
and their leaves will wither.
Mt 21:19
What I have given them
will be taken from them.*ᵃ* ' "

14 Why are we sitting here?
Gather together!

Let us flee to the fortified
cities *Jer 4:5; 35:11*
and perish there!
For the LORD our God has
doomed us to perish
and given us poisoned
water to drink, *Jer 9:15*
because we have sinned
against him. *Jer 14:7,20*
15 We hoped for peace *ver 11*
but no good has come,
for a time of healing
but there is only terror. *Jer 14:19*
16 The snorting of the enemy's
horses
is heard from Dan; *Jer 4:15*
at the neighing of their stallions
the whole land trembles.
They have come to devour
the land and everything in it,
the city and all who live
there.
17 "See, I will send venomous
snakes among you,
vipers that cannot be
charmed, *Ps 58:5*
and they will bite you,"
declares the LORD.

18 You who are my Comforter*ᵇ* in
sorrow,
my heart is faint within me.
19 Listen to the cry of my people
from a land far away: *Jer 9:16*
"Is the LORD not in Zion?
Is her King no longer there?"

"Why have they aroused my
anger with their images,

ᵃ 13 The meaning of the Hebrew for this sentence is uncertain.   *ᵇ 18* The meaning of the
Hebrew for this word is uncertain.

with their worthless foreign idols?" Dt 32:21

20 "The harvest is past,
the summer has ended,
and we are not saved."

21 Since my people are crushed,
I am crushed; Ps 94:5
I mourn, and horror
grips me. Jer 14:17
22 Is there no balm in Gilead?
Is there no physician there?
Why then is there no healing
for the wound of my people?

9 ^a 1 Oh, that my head were a
spring of water
and my eyes a fountain of
tears! Ps 119:136
I would weep day and night
for the slain of my people.
2 Oh, that I had in the desert
a lodging place for travelers,
so that I might leave my people
and go away from them;
for they are all adulterers,
a crowd of unfaithful
people. 1Ki 19:10

3 "They make ready their
tongue
like a bow, to shoot lies; Ps 64:3
it is not by truth
that they triumph^b in the
land.
They go from one sin to
another;
they do not acknowledge me,"
declares the LORD.
4 "Beware of your friends;

do not trust anyone in your
clan. Mic 7:5-6
For every one of them is a
deceiver,^c Ge 27:35
and every friend a
slanderer. Ex 20:16
5 Friend deceives friend, Lev 6:2
and no one speaks the
truth. Ps 15:2
They have taught their
tongues to lie; Ps 52:3
they weary themselves with
sinning.
6 You^d live in the midst of
deception; Jer 5:27
in their deceit they refuse to
acknowledge me,"
declares the LORD.

7 Therefore this is what the
LORD Almighty says:

"See, I will refine and test them,
for what else can I do
because of the sin of my
people?
8 Their tongue is a deadly
arrow; ver 3; Ps 35:20
it speaks deceitfully.
With their mouths they all
speak cordially to their
neighbors, Isa 3:5
but in their hearts they set
traps for them. Jer 5:26
9 Should I not punish them for
this?"
declares the LORD.
"Should I not avenge myself
on such a nation as this?"

^a In Hebrew texts 9:1 is numbered 8:23, and 9:2-26 is numbered 9:1-25. ^b 3 Or lies; / they
are not valiant for truth ^c 4 Or a deceiving Jacob ^d 6 That is, Jeremiah (the Hebrew is
singular)

¹⁰I will weep and wail for the
  mountains
    and take up a lament
    concerning the
    wilderness grasslands.
They are desolate and
  untraveled,
    and the lowing of cattle is
    not heard.
The birds have all fled
  and the animals are gone.

¹¹"I will make Jerusalem a heap
  of ruins,
    a haunt of jackals;   Isa 34:13
and I will lay waste the towns
  of Judah   Jer 1:15
    so no one can live there."

¹²Who is wise enough to understand this? Who has been instructed by the LORD and can explain it? Why has the land been ruined and laid waste like a desert that no one can cross? Ps 107:43 ¹³The LORD said, "It is because they have forsaken my law, which I set before them; they have not obeyed me or followed my law. ¹⁴Instead, they have followed the stubbornness of their hearts; they have followed the Baals, as their ancestors taught them." ¹⁵Therefore this is what the LORD Almighty, the God of Israel, says: "See, I will make this people eat bitter food and drink poisoned water. ¹⁶I will scatter them among nations that neither they nor their ancestors have known, and I will pursue them with the sword until I have made an end of them."

¹⁷This is what the LORD Almighty says:

"Consider now! Call for the
  wailing women to come;
    send for the most skillful of
    them.
¹⁸Let them come quickly
  and wail over us
till our eyes overflow with tears
  and water streams from our
  eyelids.   Jer 14:17
¹⁹The sound of wailing is heard
  from Zion:
    'How ruined we are!   Jer 4:13
    How great is our shame!
We must leave our land
  because our houses are in
  ruins.'"

²⁰Now, you women, hear the
  word of the LORD;
    open your ears to the words
    of his mouth.
Teach your daughters how to
  wail;
    teach one another a lament.
²¹Death has climbed in through
  our windows
    and has entered our
    fortresses;
it has removed the children
  from the streets
    and the young men from
    the public squares.

²²Say, "This is what the LORD
declares:

"'Dead bodies will lie
  like dung on the open field,
like cut grain behind the
  reaper,

with no one to gather
  them.'"

²³This is what the LORD says:

"Let not the wise boast of their
  wisdom   Ecc 9:11
or the strong boast of their
  strength   1Ki 20:11
or the rich boast of their
  riches,   Eze 28:4-5
²⁴but let the one who boasts
  boast about this: 1Co 1:31
that they have the
  understanding to
  know me,   Ps 36:10
that I am the LORD, who
  exercises kindness, Ps 51:1
justice and righteousness
  on earth,   Ps 36:6
for in these I delight,"
      declares the LORD.

²⁵"The days are coming," declares the LORD, "when I will punish all who are circumcised only in the flesh — ²⁶Egypt, Judah, Edom, Ammon, Moab and all who live in the wilderness in distant places.ᵃ For all these nations are really uncircumcised, and even the whole house of Israel is uncircumcised in heart."

God and Idols

10:12-16pp — Jer 51:15-19

10 Hear what the LORD says to you, people of Israel. ²This is what the LORD says:

"Do not learn the ways of the
  nations   Lev 20:23

or be terrified by signs in
  the heavens,
though the nations are
  terrified by them.
³For the practices of the
  peoples are worthless;
they cut a tree out of the forest,
and a craftsman shapes it
  with his chisel.   Isa 40:19
⁴They adorn it with silver and
  gold;   Hos 13:2
they fasten it with hammer
  and nails
so it will not totter.   Isa 41:7
⁵Like a scarecrow in a
  cucumber field,
their idols cannot speak;
they must be carried
  because they cannot walk.
Do not fear them;
  they can do no harm
nor can they do any good."

⁶No one is like you, LORD;
  you are great,   Ps 48:1
and your name is mighty in
  power.
⁷Who should not fear you,
  King of the nations?   Ps 22:28
This is your due.
Among all the wise leaders of
  the nations
and in all their kingdoms,
  there is no one like you.

⁸They are all senseless and
  foolish;   Isa 40:19; Jer 4:22
they are taught by worthless
  wooden idols.   Dt 32:21
⁹Hammered silver is brought
  from Tarshish

ᵃ 26 Or *wilderness and who clip the hair by their foreheads*

and gold from Uphaz.
What the craftsman and
  goldsmith have made
is then dressed in blue and
  purple —
all made by skilled workers.
¹⁰ But the LORD is the true God;
  he is the living God, the
  eternal King.   Ge 21:33
When he is angry, the earth
  trembles;   Ps 29:8
  the nations cannot endure
  his wrath.   Ps 76:7

¹¹ "Tell them this: 'These gods,
who did not make the heavens
and the earth, will perish from
the earth and from under the
heavens.'"*ᵃ*   Ps 96:5; Isa 2:18

¹² But God made the earth by
  his power;
he founded the world by his
  wisdom
and stretched out the heavens
  by his understanding.
¹³ When he thunders, the waters
  in the heavens roar;
he makes clouds rise from
  the ends of the earth.
He sends lightning with the
  rain   Ps 135:7
and brings out the wind
  from his storehouses.

¹⁴ Everyone is senseless and
  without knowledge;
  every goldsmith is shamed
  by his idols.   Isa 1:29
The images he makes are a
  fraud;   Isa 44:20

they have no breath in
  them.
¹⁵ They are worthless, the
  objects of mockery;
when their judgment
  comes, they will perish.
¹⁶ He who is the Portion of Jacob
  is not like these,   Dt 32:9
for he is the Maker of all
  things,   ver 12; Jer 32:17
including Israel, the people of
  his inheritance —   Ps 74:2
the LORD Almighty is his
  name.   Jer 51:15-19

Coming Destruction

¹⁷ Gather up your belongings to
  leave the land,   Eze 12:3-12
  you who live under siege.
¹⁸ For this is what the LORD says:
  "At this time I will hurl out
  those who live in this land;
I will bring distress on them
  so that they may be
  captured."

¹⁹ Woe to me because of my
  injury!
  My wound is incurable!
Yet I said to myself,
  "This is my sickness, and I
  must endure it."   Mic 7:9
²⁰ My tent is destroyed;   Jer 4:20
  all its ropes are snapped.
My children are gone from me
  and are no more;   Jer 31:15
no one is left now to pitch
  my tent
or to set up my shelter.
²¹ The shepherds are senseless

ᵃ 11 The text of this verse is in Aramaic.

and do not inquire of the
LORD;   Isa 56:10
so they do not prosper
and all their flock is
scattered.   Jer 23:2
22 Listen! The report is
coming —
a great commotion from the
land of the north!
It will make the towns of
Judah desolate,
a haunt of jackals.   Jer 9:11

Jeremiah's Prayer

23 LORD, I know that people's
lives are not their own;
it is not for them to direct
their steps.   Pr 20:24
24 Discipline me, LORD, but only
in due measure —
not in your anger,   Ps 6:1; 38:1
or you will reduce me to
nothing.   Jer 30:11
25 Pour out your wrath on the
nations   Zep 3:8
that do not acknowledge
you,
on the peoples who do not
call on your name.
For they have devoured Jacob;
they have devoured him
completely
and destroyed his homeland.

The Covenant Is Broken

11 This is the word that
came to Jeremiah from
the LORD: 2 "Listen to the terms
of this covenant and tell them to
the people of Judah and to those
who live in Jerusalem. 3 Tell them

that this is what the LORD, the
God of Israel, says: 'Cursed is
the one who does not obey the
terms of this covenant — 4 the
terms I commanded your ancestors when I brought them out of
Egypt, out of the iron-smelting
furnace.' I said, 'Obey me and do
everything I command you, and
you will be my people, and I will
be your God. 5 Then I will fulfill
the oath I swore to your ancestors, to give them a land flowing
with milk and honey' — the land
you possess today."   Ex 24:8; Jer 7:23
I answered, "Amen, LORD."

6 The LORD said to me, "Proclaim all these words in the
towns of Judah and in the streets
of Jerusalem: 'Listen to the terms
of this covenant and follow them.
7 From the time I brought your ancestors up from Egypt until today,
I warned them again and again,
saying, "Obey me." 8 But they
did not listen or pay attention;
instead, they followed the stubbornness of their evil hearts. So I
brought on them all the curses of
the covenant I had commanded
them to follow but that they did
not keep.' "   Dt 15:5; Ro 2:13; Jas 1:22

9 Then the LORD said to me,
"There is a conspiracy among the
people of Judah and those who
live in Jerusalem. 10 They have returned to the sins of their ancestors, who refused to listen to my
words. They have followed other
gods to serve them. Both Israel
and Judah have broken the cov-

enant I made with their ancestors. **11**Therefore this is what the LORD says: 'I will bring on them a disaster they cannot escape. Although they cry out to me, I will not listen to them. **12**The towns of Judah and the people of Jerusalem will go and cry out to the gods to whom they burn incense, but they will not help them at all when disaster strikes. **13**You, Judah, have as many gods as you have towns; and the altars you have set up to burn incense to that shameful god Baal are as many as the streets of Jerusalem.' Eze 22:25; Jdg 2:12-13

14"Do not pray for this people or offer any plea or petition for them, because I will not listen when they call to me in the time of their distress. Ex 32:10

15"What is my beloved doing in my temple
as she, with many others, works out her evil schemes?
Can consecrated meat avert your punishment?
When you engage in your wickedness, then you rejoice.*a*" Jer 7:9-10

16The LORD called you a thriving olive tree Ps 1:3
with fruit beautiful in form.
But with the roar of a mighty storm
he will set it on fire, Jer 21:14
and its branches will be broken. Isa 27:11; Ro 11:17-24

17The LORD Almighty, who planted you, has decreed disaster for you, because the people of both Israel and Judah have done evil and aroused my anger by burning incense to Baal. Isa 5:2; Jer 12:2

Plot Against Jeremiah

18Because the LORD revealed their plot to me, I knew it, for at that time he showed me what they were doing. **19**I had been like a gentle lamb led to the slaughter; I did not realize that they had plotted against me, saying, Jer 18:18

"Let us destroy the tree and its fruit;
let us cut him off from the land of the living, Isa 53:8
that his name be remembered no more."
20But you, LORD Almighty, who judge righteously Ps 7:11
and test the heart and mind,
let me see your vengeance on them, Ps 58:10
for to you I have committed my cause.

21Therefore this is what the LORD says about the people of Anathoth who are threatening to kill you, saying, "Do not prophesy in the name of the LORD or you will die by our hands" — **22**therefore this is what the LORD Almighty says: "I will punish them. Their young men will die by the sword, their sons and daughters by famine. **23**Not even a remnant

a 15 Or *Could consecrated meat avert your punishment? / Then you would rejoice* will be left to them, because I will bring disaster on the people of Anathoth in the year of their punishment." Jer 6:9; 23:12

Jeremiah's Complaint

12 You are always righteous, LORD,
                    Ezr 9:15
  when I bring a case before
    you.
Yet I would speak with you
    about your justice:
Why does the way of the
    wicked prosper? Jer 5:27-28
Why do all the faithless live
    at ease?
2 You have planted them, and
    they have taken root;
  they grow and bear fruit.
You are always on their lips
  but far from their hearts.
3 Yet you know me, LORD;
  you see me and test my
    thoughts about you.
Drag them off like sheep to be
    butchered!
  Set them apart for the day of
    slaughter! Jer 17:18
4 How long will the land lie
    parched Jer 4:28
  and the grass in every field
    be withered? Joel 1:10-12
Because those who live in it
    are wicked,
  the animals and birds have
    perished. Jer 4:25
Moreover, the people are
    saying,
  "He will not see what
    happens to us."

God's Answer

5 "If you have raced with men
    on foot
  and they have worn you out,
    how can you compete with
      horses?
If you stumble^a in safe
    country,
  how will you manage in the
    thickets by^b the Jordan?
6 Your relatives, members of
    your own family —
  even they have betrayed
    you;
  they have raised a loud cry
    against you. Pr 26:24-25
Do not trust them,
  though they speak well of
    you. Ps 12:2

7 "I will forsake my house, 2Ki 21:14
  abandon my inheritance;
I will give the one I love Isa 5:1
  into the hands of her enemies.
8 My inheritance has become
    to me
  like a lion in the forest.
She roars at me;
  therefore I hate her. Hos 9:15
9 Has not my inheritance
    become to me
  like a speckled bird of prey
  that other birds of prey
    surround and attack?
Go and gather all the wild
    beasts;
  bring them to devour. Isa 56:9
10 Many shepherds will ruin my
    vineyard Jer 23:1
  and trample down my field;

^a 5 Or *you feel secure only*   ^b 5 Or *the flooding of*

they will turn my pleasant
    field
into a desolate wasteland.
¹¹It will be made a wasteland,
    parched and desolate before
    me;   Isa 42:25; Jer 23:10
the whole land will be laid
    waste
because there is no one who
    cares.
¹²Over all the barren heights in
    the desert
destroyers will swarm,
for the sword of the LORD will
    devour   Jer 47:6
from one end of the land to
    the other;   Jer 3:2
no one will be safe.   Jer 7:10
¹³They will sow wheat but reap
    thorns;
they will wear themselves
    out but gain nothing.
They will bear the shame of
    their harvest
because of the LORD's fierce
    anger."   Jer 4:26

¹⁴This is what the LORD says:
"As for all my wicked neighbors
who seize the inheritance I gave
my people Israel, I will uproot
them from their lands and I will
uproot the people of Judah from
among them. ¹⁵But after I uproot
them, I will again have compassion and will bring each of them
back to their own inheritance and
their own country. ¹⁶And if they
learn well the ways of my people
and swear by my name, saying,

'As surely as the LORD lives' —
even as they once taught my people to swear by Baal — then they
will be established among my
people. ¹⁷But if any nation does
not listen, I will completely uproot and destroy it," declares the
LORD.   Isa 60:12; Jer 4:2; Zec 2:7-9

A Linen Belt

13 This is what the LORD said
to me: "Go and buy a linen belt and put it around your
waist, but do not let it touch water." ²So I bought a belt, as the
LORD directed, and put it around
my waist.

³Then the word of the LORD
came to me a second time: ⁴"Take the belt you bought and
are wearing around your waist,
and go now to Perath^a and hide
it there in a crevice in the rocks."
⁵So I went and hid it at Perath, as
the LORD told me.   Ex 40:16

⁶Many days later the LORD
said to me, "Go now to Perath
and get the belt I told you to hide
there." ⁷So I went to Perath and
dug up the belt and took it from
the place where I had hidden it,
but now it was ruined and completely useless.

⁸Then the word of the LORD
came to me: ⁹"This is what the
LORD says: 'In the same way I will
ruin the pride of Judah and the
great pride of Jerusalem. ¹⁰These
wicked people, who refuse to listen to my words, who follow the

---

^a 4 Or possibly to the Euphrates; similarly in verses 5-7

stubbornness of their hearts and go after other gods to serve and worship them, will be like this belt — completely useless! **11** For as a belt is bound around the waist, so I bound all the people of Israel and all the people of Judah to me,' declares the LORD, 'to be my people for my renown and praise and honor. But they have not listened.' Lev 26:19; Jer 7:26; 32:20

Wineskins

12 "Say to them: 'This is what the LORD, the God of Israel, says: Every wineskin should be filled with wine.' And if they say to you, 'Don't we know that every wineskin should be filled with wine?' **13** then tell them, 'This is what the LORD says: I am going to fill with drunkenness all who live in this land, including the kings who sit on David's throne, the priests, the prophets and all those living in Jerusalem. **14** I will smash them one against the other, parents and children alike, declares the LORD. I will allow no pity or mercy or compassion to keep me from destroying them.' " Isa 51:17; Jer 16:5

Threat of Captivity

15 Hear and pay attention,
  do not be arrogant,
  for the LORD has spoken.
16 Give glory to the LORD your
      God Jos 7:19
  before he brings the
      darkness,
  before your feet stumble Jer 23:12
on the darkening hills.
You hope for light,
  but he will turn it to utter
      darkness
  and change it to deep
      gloom. Isa 59:9
17 If you do not listen, Mal 2:2
  I will weep in secret
  because of your pride;
my eyes will weep bitterly,
  overflowing with tears, Jer 9:1
  because the LORD's flock
      will be taken captive.

18 Say to the king and to the
      queen mother, Isa 22:17
  "Come down from your
      thrones,
  for your glorious crowns
      will fall from your heads."
19 The cities in the Negev will be
      shut up,
  and there will be no one to
      open them.
All Judah will be carried into
      exile, Jer 20:4; 52:30
  carried completely away.

20 Look up and see
  those who are coming from
      the north. Jer 6:22; Hab 1:6
Where is the flock that was
      entrusted to you, Jer 23:2
  the sheep of which you
      boasted?
21 What will you say when the
      LORD sets over you
  those you cultivated as your
      special allies? Jer 38:22
Will not pain grip you
  like that of a woman in
      labor? Jer 4:31

22 And if you ask yourself,
  "Why has this happened to
      me?" —
  it is because of your many sins
    that your skirts have been
      torn off   Isa 20:4
    and your body mistreated.
23 Can an Ethiopian[a] change his
      skin
  or a leopard its spots?
  Neither can you do good
    who are accustomed to
      doing evil.   2Ch 6:36

24 "I will scatter you like chaff
    driven by the desert wind.
25 This is your lot,
    the portion I have decreed
      for you,"   Job 20:29; Mt 24:51
        declares the LORD,
  "because you have
      forgotten me   Isa 17:10
    and trusted in false gods.
26 I will pull up your skirts over
      your face
    that your shame may be
      seen —   La 1:8; Eze 16:37
27 your adulteries and lustful
      neighings,
  your shameless prostitution!
  I have seen your detestable acts
    on the hills and in the fields.
  Woe to you, Jerusalem!
    How long will you be
      unclean?"   Hos 8:5

Drought, Famine, Sword

14 This is the word of the
LORD that came to Jere-
miah concerning the drought:

2 "Judah mourns,   Isa 3:26; Jer 8:21
    her cities languish;
  they wail for the land,
    and a cry goes up from
      Jerusalem.
3 The nobles send their
      servants for water;
  they go to the cisterns
    but find no water.   2Ki 18:31
  They return with their jars
      unfilled;
  dismayed and despairing,
    they cover their heads.
4 The ground is cracked
    because there is no rain in
      the land;   Jer 3:3
  the farmers are dismayed
    and cover their heads.
5 Even the doe in the field
    deserts her newborn fawn
    because there is no grass.
6 Wild donkeys stand on the
      barren heights   Job 39:5-6
    and pant like jackals;
  their eyes fail
    for lack of food."

7 Although our sins testify
      against us,   Hos 5:5
  do something, LORD, for the
    sake of your name. Ps 79:9
  For we have often rebelled;
    we have sinned against you.
8 You who are the hope of Israel,
    its Savior in times of
      distress,   Ps 46:1
  why are you like a stranger in
      the land,
  like a traveler who stays
    only a night?

_a_ 23 Hebrew _Cushite_ (probably a person from the upper Nile region)

⁹Why are you like a man taken
   by surprise,
like a warrior powerless to
   save?   Isa 50:2
You are among us, Lord,   Jer 8:19
and we bear your name;
   do not forsake us!   Ps 27:9

¹⁰This is what the Lord says
about this people:

"They greatly love to wander;
   they do not restrain their
   feet.   Ps 119:101; Jer 2:25
So the Lord does not accept
   them;   Jer 6:20; Am 5:22
he will now remember their
   wickedness   Hos 9:9
and punish them for their
   sins."   Hos 8:13

¹¹Then the Lord said to me,
"Do not pray for the well-being
of this people. ¹²Although they
fast, I will not listen to their cry;
though they offer burnt offerings
and grain offerings, I will not accept them. Instead, I will destroy
them with the sword, famine
and plague."   Ex 32:10; Isa 1:15; Jer 7:21
¹³But I said, "Alas, Sovereign
Lord! The prophets keep telling them, 'You will not see the
sword or suffer famine. Indeed, I
will give you lasting peace in this
place.'"   Jer 5:12
¹⁴Then the Lord said to me,
"The prophets are prophesying
lies in my name. I have not sent
them or appointed them or spoken to them. They are prophe-

sying to you false visions, divinations, idolatries[a] and the
delusions of their own minds.
¹⁵Therefore this is what the Lord
says about the prophets who are
prophesying in my name: I did
not send them, yet they are saying, 'No sword or famine will
touch this land.' Those same
prophets will perish by sword
and famine. ¹⁶And the people
they are prophesying to will be
thrown out into the streets of Jerusalem because of the famine
and sword. There will be no one
to bury them, their wives, their
sons and their daughters. I will
pour out on them the calamity
they deserve.   Jer 5:12-13; 27:14

¹⁷"Speak this word to them:

"'Let my eyes overflow with
   tears   Jer 9:1
night and day without
   ceasing;
for the Virgin Daughter, my
   people,   2Ki 19:21
has suffered a grievous
   wound,
a crushing blow.   Jer 8:21
¹⁸If I go into the country,
   I see those slain by the sword;
if I go into the city,
   I see the ravages of famine.
Both prophet and priest
   have gone to a land they
   know not.'"   2Ch 36:10
¹⁹Have you rejected Judah
   completely?   Jer 7:29

---

[a] 14 Or visions, worthless divinations

Do you despise Zion?
Why have you afflicted us
    so that we cannot be
        healed? Jer 30:12-13
We hoped for peace
    but no good has come,
for a time of healing
    but there is only terror. Jer 8:15
²⁰We acknowledge our
        wickedness, LORD, Jer 3:13
    and the guilt of our
        ancestors; 1Ki 8:47
    we have indeed sinned
        against you. Da 9:7-8
²¹For the sake of your name do
        not despise us; Jos 7:9
    do not dishonor your
        glorious throne. Jer 3:17
Remember your covenant
        with us
    and do not break it. Ex 2:24
²²Do any of the worthless idols
        of the nations bring
        rain? Ps 135:7
    Do the skies themselves
        send down showers?
No, it is you, LORD our God.
    Therefore our hope is in
        you,
    for you are the one who
        does all this. Isa 43:10

15 Then the LORD said to me:
"Even if Moses and Samuel were to stand before me, my heart would not go out to this people. Send them away from my presence! Let them go! ²And if they ask you, 'Where shall we go?' tell them, 'This is what the LORD says: Jer 7:16; Eze 14:14,20

" 'Those destined for death, to
        death;
those for the sword, to the
        sword; Jer 43:11
those for starvation, to
        starvation; Jer 14:12
those for captivity, to
        captivity.' Rev 13:10

³"I will send four kinds of destroyers against them," declares the LORD, "the sword to kill and the dogs to drag away and the birds and the wild animals to devour and destroy. ⁴I will make them abhorrent to all the kingdoms of the earth because of what Manasseh son of Hezekiah king of Judah did in Jerusalem. Dt 28:25

⁵"Who will have pity on you,
        Jerusalem? Isa 51:19; Jer 13:14
    Who will mourn for you?
    Who will stop to ask how
        you are?
⁶You have rejected me,"
        declares the LORD. Jer 6:19
    "You keep on backsliding.
So I will reach out and destroy
        you; Zep 1:4
    I am tired of holding back.
⁷I will winnow them with a
        winnowing fork
    at the city gates of the land.
I will bring bereavement and
        destruction on my
        people, Jer 18:21
    for they have not changed
        their ways. 2Ch 28:22
⁸I will make their widows more
        numerous Isa 47:9
    than the sand of the sea.

At midday I will bring a
    destroyer   Jer 6:4
  against the mothers of their
    young men;
  suddenly I will bring down on
    them
  anguish and terror.   Job 18:11
⁹The mother of seven will grow
    faint   1Sa 2:5
  and breathe her last.
  Her sun will set while it is still
    day;
  she will be disgraced and
    humiliated.   Jer 7:19
  I will put the survivors to the
    sword   Jer 21:7
  before their enemies,"   2Ki 25:7
    declares the LORD.

¹⁰Alas, my mother, that you
    gave me birth,   Job 3:1
  a man with whom the
    whole land strives and
    contends!   Jer 1:19
  I have neither lent nor
    borrowed,   Lev 25:36
  yet everyone curses me.

¹¹The LORD said,

"Surely I will deliver you for a
    good purpose;   Jer 40:4
  surely I will make your
    enemies plead with
    you   Jer 21:1-2; 37:3; 42:1-3
  in times of disaster and
    times of distress.

¹²"Can a man break iron —
  iron from the north — or
    bronze?   Jer 28:14

¹³"Your wealth and your
    treasures   2Ki 25:15
  I will give as plunder,
    without charge,   Ps 44:12
  because of all your sins
    throughout your country.
¹⁴I will enslave you to your
    enemies
  in*a* a land you do not know,
  for my anger will kindle a fire
    that will burn against you."

¹⁵LORD, you understand;
  remember me and care
    for me.
  Avenge me on my
    persecutors.   Jer 12:3
  You are long-suffering — do
    not take me away;   Ex 34:6
  think of how I suffer
    reproach for your sake.
¹⁶When your words came, I ate
    them;   Eze 3:3; Rev 10:10
  they were my joy and my
    heart's delight,   Ps 119:72
  for I bear your name,   Jer 14:9
    LORD God Almighty.
¹⁷I never sat in the company of
    revelers, Ps 1:1; 26:4-5; Jer 16:8
  never made merry with them;
  I sat alone because your hand
    was on me   2Ki 3:15
  and you had filled me with
    indignation.
¹⁸Why is my pain unending
  and my wound grievous
    and incurable?   Jer 30:15
  You are to me like a deceptive
    brook,
  like a spring that fails.   Job 6:15

a 14 Some Hebrew manuscripts, Septuagint and Syriac (see also 17:4); most Hebrew
manuscripts *I will cause your enemies to bring you / into*

¹⁹Therefore this is what the LORD says:

"If you repent, I will restore you
    that you may serve me; Zec 3:7
if you utter worthy, not
        worthless, words,
    you will be my spokesman.
Let this people turn to you,
    but you must not turn to
        them.
²⁰I will make you a wall to this
        people,
    a fortified wall of bronze;
they will fight against you
    but will not overcome you,
for I am with you
    to rescue and save you,"
                declares the LORD.
²¹"I will save you from the
        hands of the wicked Jer 1:8
    and deliver you from the
        grasp of the cruel."

Day of Disaster

16 Then the word of the LORD came to me: ²"You must not marry and have sons or daughters in this place." ³For this is what the LORD says about the sons and daughters born in this land and about the women who are their mothers and the men who are their fathers: ⁴"They will die of deadly diseases. They will not be mourned or buried but will be like dung lying on the ground. They will perish by sword and famine, and their dead bodies will become food for the birds and the wild animals."

⁵For this is what the LORD says: "Do not enter a house where there is a funeral meal; do not go to mourn or show sympathy, because I have withdrawn my blessing, my love and my pity from this people," declares the LORD. ⁶"Both high and low will die in this land. They will not be buried or mourned, and no one will cut themselves or shave their head for the dead. ⁷No one will offer food to comfort those who mourn for the dead—not even for a father or a mother—nor will anyone give them a drink to console them. Jer 15:5; Eze 9:5-6

⁸"And do not enter a house where there is feasting and sit down to eat and drink. ⁹For this is what the LORD Almighty, the God of Israel, says: Before your eyes and in your days I will bring an end to the sounds of joy and gladness and to the voices of bride and bridegroom in this place. Rev 18:23; Hos 2:11

¹⁰"When you tell these people all this and they ask you, 'Why has the LORD decreed such a great disaster against us? What wrong have we done? What sin have we committed against the LORD our God?' ¹¹then say to them, 'It is because your ancestors forsook me,' declares the LORD, 'and followed other gods and served and worshiped them. They forsook me and did not keep my law. ¹²But you have behaved more wickedly than your ancestors. See how

all of you are following the stubbornness of your evil hearts instead of obeying me. ¹³So I will throw you out of this land into a land neither you nor your ancestors have known, and there you will serve other gods day and night, for I will show you no favor.' Dt 29:24; Jer 5:19; 13:10

¹⁴ "However, the days are coming," declares the LORD, "when it will no longer be said, 'As surely as the LORD lives, who brought the Israelites up out of Egypt,' ¹⁵but it will be said, 'As surely as the LORD lives, who brought the Israelites up out of the land of the north and out of all the countries where he had banished them.' For I will restore them to the land I gave their ancestors. Jer 23:7-8; 24:6

¹⁶ "But now I will send for many fishermen," declares the LORD, "and they will catch them. After that I will send for many hunters, and they will hunt them down on every mountain and hill and from the crevices of the rocks. ¹⁷My eyes are on all their ways; they are not hidden from me, nor is their sin concealed from my eyes. ¹⁸I will repay them double for their wickedness and their sin, because they have defiled my land with the lifeless forms of their vile images and have filled my inheritance with their detestable idols." Pr 15:3; 1Co 4:5; Heb 4:13

¹⁹LORD, my strength and my fortress,
    my refuge in time of distress,
to you the nations will come
    from the ends of the earth
    and say,
"Our ancestors possessed
    nothing but false gods,
    worthless idols that did
    them no good. Isa 40:19
²⁰Do people make their own
    gods?
    Yes, but they are not gods!"

²¹ "Therefore I will teach
    them—
    this time I will teach them
    my power and might.
Then they will know
    that my name is the LORD.

17 "Judah's sin is engraved
    with an iron tool, Job 19:24
inscribed with a flint point,
on the tablets of their hearts
    and on the horns of their
    altars. Ex 27:2
²Even their children remember
    their altars and Asherah
    poles*ᵃ* 2Ch 24:18
beside the spreading trees
    and on the high hills. Jer 2:20
³My mountain in the land
    and your*ᵇ* wealth and all
    your treasures
I will give away as plunder,
    together with your high
    places, Jer 26:18; Mic 3:12
because of sin throughout
    your country. Jer 15:13

ᵃ 2 That is, wooden symbols of the goddess Asherah   *ᵇ 2,3* Or *hills / ³and the mountains of the land. / Your*

⁴Through your own fault you
will lose
the inheritance I gave you.
I will enslave you to your
enemies   Dt 28:48; Jer 12:7
in a land you do not know,
for you have kindled my anger,
and it will burn forever."

⁵This is what the LORD says:

"Cursed is the one who trusts
in man,   Isa 2:22; 30:1-3
who draws strength from
mere flesh
and whose heart turns away
from the LORD.   2Co 1:9
⁶That person will be like a
bush in the wastelands;
they will not see prosperity
when it comes.
They will dwell in the parched
places of the desert,
in a salt land where no one
lives.   Dt 29:23; Job 39:6

⁷"But blessed is the one who
trusts in the LORD, Ps 34:8
whose confidence is in him.
⁸They will be like a tree
planted by the water
that sends out its roots by
the stream.
It does not fear when heat
comes;
its leaves are always green.
It has no worries in a year of
drought   Jer 14:1-6
and never fails to bear
fruit."   Ps 1:3; 92:12-14

⁹The heart is deceitful above
all things   Ecc 9:3; Mt 13:15

and beyond cure.
Who can understand it?

¹⁰"I the LORD search the heart
and examine the mind,
to reward each person
according to their
conduct,   Jer 32:19
according to what their
deeds deserve."   Ro 2:6

¹¹Like a partridge that hatches
eggs it did not lay
are those who gain riches
by unjust means.
When their lives are half
gone, their riches will
desert them,
and in the end they will
prove to be fools. Lk 12:20

¹²A glorious throne, exalted
from the beginning,
is the place of our
sanctuary.
¹³LORD, you are the hope of
Israel;   Jer 14:8
all who forsake you will be
put to shame.   Isa 1:28
Those who turn away from
you will be written in
the dust   Ps 69:28
because they have forsaken
the LORD,
the spring of living water.

¹⁴Heal me, LORD, and I will be
healed;   Isa 30:26
save me and I will be saved,
for you are the one I praise.
¹⁵They keep saying to me,
"Where is the word of the
LORD?

Let it now be fulfilled!" Isa 5:19

¹⁶I have not run away from
  being your shepherd;
you know I have not desired
  the day of despair.
What passes my lips is open
  before you.
¹⁷Do not be a terror to me; Ps 88:15
you are my refuge in the day
  of disaster. Jer 16:19; Na 1:7
¹⁸Let my persecutors be put to
  shame,
but keep me from shame;
let them be terrified,
  but keep me from terror.
Bring on them the day of
  disaster;
destroy them with double
  destruction. Ps 35:1-8

Keeping the Sabbath Day Holy

¹⁹This is what the LORD said to me: "Go and stand at the Gate of the People,ᵃ through which the kings of Judah go in and out; stand also at all the other gates of Jerusalem. ²⁰Say to them, 'Hear the word of the LORD, you kings of Judah and all people of Judah and everyone living in Jerusalem who come through these gates. ²¹This is what the LORD says: Be careful not to carry a load on the Sabbath day or bring it through the gates of Jerusalem. ²²Do not bring a load out of your houses or do any work on the Sabbath, but keep the Sabbath day holy, as I commanded your ancestors. ²³Yet they did not listen or pay attention; they were stiff-necked and would not listen or respond to discipline. ²⁴But if you are careful to obey me, declares the LORD, and bring no load through the gates of this city on the Sabbath, but keep the Sabbath day holy by not doing any work on it, ²⁵then kings who sit on David's throne will come through the gates of this city with their officials. They and their officials will come riding in chariots and on horses, accompanied by the men of Judah and those living in Jerusalem, and this city will be inhabited forever. ²⁶People will come from the towns of Judah and the villages around Jerusalem, from the territory of Benjamin and the western foothills, from the hill country and the Negev, bringing burnt offerings and sacrifices, grain offerings and incense, and bringing thank offerings to the house of the LORD. ²⁷But if you do not obey me to keep the Sabbath day holy by not carrying any load as you come through the gates of Jerusalem on the Sabbath day, then I will kindle an unquenchable fire in the gates of Jerusalem that will consume her fortresses.'" 2Ki 25:9; Jer 22:5; Am 2:5

At the Potter's House

18 This is the word that came to Jeremiah from the LORD: ²"Go down to the potter's house, and there I will give you

ᵃ 19 Or *Army*

my message." ³So I went down to the potter's house, and I saw him working at the wheel. ⁴But the pot he was shaping from the clay was marred in his hands; so the potter formed it into another pot, shaping it as seemed best to him.

⁵Then the word of the LORD came to me. ⁶He said, "Can I not do with you, Israel, as this potter does?" declares the LORD. "Like clay in the hand of the potter, so are you in my hand, Israel. ⁷If at any time I announce that a nation or kingdom is to be uprooted, torn down and destroyed, ⁸and if that nation I warned repents of its evil, then I will relent and not inflict on it the disaster I had planned. ⁹And if at another time I announce that a nation or kingdom is to be built up and planted, ¹⁰and if it does evil in my sight and does not obey me, then I will reconsider the good I had intended to do for it.   Isa 45:9; Ro 9:20-21

¹¹ "Now therefore say to the people of Judah and those living in Jerusalem, 'This is what the LORD says: Look! I am preparing a disaster for you and devising a plan against you. So turn from your evil ways, each one of you, and reform your ways and your actions.' ¹²But they will reply, 'It's no use. We will continue with our own plans; we will all follow the stubbornness of our evil hearts.' "   2Ki 17:13; Isa 57:10

¹³Therefore this is what the LORD says:

"Inquire among the nations:
    Who has ever heard
        anything like this? Isa 66:8
A most horrible thing has
        been done   Jer 5:30
    by Virgin Israel.   2Ki 19:21
¹⁴Does the snow of Lebanon
    ever vanish from its rocky
        slopes?
Do its cool waters from
        distant sources
    ever stop flowing?ᵃ
¹⁵Yet my people have forgotten
        me;   Isa 17:10
    they burn incense to
        worthless idols,   Jer 10:15
which made them stumble in
        their ways,
    in the ancient paths.   Jer 6:16
They made them walk in
        byways,
    on roads not built up. Isa 57:14
¹⁶Their land will be an object of
        horror   Jer 25:9
    and of lasting scorn;   Jer 19:8
all who pass by will be
        appalled
    and will shake their heads.
¹⁷Like a wind from the east,
    I will scatter them before
        their enemies;
I will show them my back and
        not my face   Jer 2:27
    in the day of their disaster."

¹⁸They said, "Come, let's make plans against Jeremiah; for the teaching of the law by the priest

---

ᵃ 14 The meaning of the Hebrew for this sentence is uncertain.

will not cease, nor will counsel
from the wise, nor the word from
the prophets. So come, let's attack him with our tongues and
pay no attention to anything he
says." Jer 11:19; Mal 2:7

¹⁹Listen to me, LORD;
hear what my accusers are
saying! Ps 71:13
²⁰Should good be repaid with
evil? Ge 44:4
Yet they have dug a pit for me.
Remember that I stood before
you Jer 15:1
and spoke in their behalf
to turn your wrath away
from them.
²¹So give their children over to
famine; Jer 11:22
hand them over to the
power of the sword.
Let their wives be made
childless and widows;
let their men be put to death,
their young men slain by
the sword in battle. Isa 9:17
²²Let a cry be heard from their
houses Jer 6:26
when you suddenly bring
invaders against them,
for they have dug a pit to
capture me
and have hidden snares for
my feet. Ps 140:5
²³But you, LORD, know
all their plots to kill me.
Do not forgive their crimes
or blot out their sins from
your sight.

Let them be overthrown
before you;
deal with them in the time
of your anger. Jer 10:24

19 This is what the LORD
says: "Go and buy a clay
jar from a potter. Take along
some of the elders of the people
and of the priests ²and go out to
the Valley of Ben Hinnom, near
the entrance of the Potsherd
Gate. There proclaim the words I
tell you, ³and say, 'Hear the word
of the LORD, you kings of Judah
and people of Jerusalem. This
is what the LORD Almighty, the
God of Israel, says: Listen! I am
going to bring a disaster on this
place that will make the ears of
everyone who hears of it tingle.
⁴For they have forsaken me and
made this a place of foreign gods;
they have burned incense in it to
gods that neither they nor their
ancestors nor the kings of Judah
ever knew, and they have filled
this place with the blood of the
innocent. ⁵They have built the
high places of Baal to burn their
children in the fire as offerings to
Baal—something I did not command or mention, nor did it enter
my mind. ⁶So beware, the days
are coming, declares the LORD,
when people will no longer call
this place Topheth or the Valley
of Ben Hinnom, but the Valley of
Slaughter. 1Sa 3:11; 2Ki 21:16; Jer 6:19
⁷"'In this place I will ruin*ᵃ the

ᵃ 7 The Hebrew for *ruin* sounds like the Hebrew for *jar* (see verses 1 and 10).

plans of Judah and Jerusalem. I will make them fall by the sword before their enemies, at the hands of those who want to kill them, and I will give their carcasses as food to the birds and the wild animals. [8] I will devastate this city and make it an object of horror and scorn; all who pass by will be appalled and will scoff because of all its wounds. [9] I will make them eat the flesh of their sons and daughters, and they will eat one another's flesh because their enemies will press the siege so hard against them to destroy them.' Dt 28:49-57; Jer 18:16

[10] "Then break the jar while those who go with you are watching, [11] and say to them, 'This is what the LORD Almighty says: I will smash this nation and this city just as this potter's jar is smashed and cannot be repaired. They will bury the dead in Topheth until there is no more room. [12] This is what I will do to this place and to those who live here, declares the LORD. I will make this city like Topheth. [13] The houses in Jerusalem and those of the kings of Judah will be defiled like this place, Topheth — all the houses where they burned incense on the roofs to all the starry hosts and poured out drink offerings to other gods.'" Ps 2:9; Jer 7:32

[14] Jeremiah then returned from Topheth, where the LORD had sent him to prophesy, and stood in the court of the LORD's temple and said to all the people, [15] "This is what the LORD Almighty, the God of Israel, says: 'Listen! I am going to bring on this city and all the villages around it every disaster I pronounced against them, because they were stiff-necked and would not listen to my words.'" Jer 7:26; 17:23

Jeremiah and Pashhur

20 When the priest Pashhur son of Immer, the official in charge of the temple of the LORD, heard Jeremiah prophesying these things, [2] he had Jeremiah the prophet beaten and put in the stocks at the Upper Gate of Benjamin at the LORD's temple. [3] The next day, when Pashhur released him from the stocks, Jeremiah said to him, "The LORD's name for you is not Pashhur, but Terror on Every Side. [4] For this is what the LORD says: 'I will make you a terror to yourself and to all your friends; with your own eyes you will see them fall by the sword of their enemies. I will give all Judah into the hands of the king of Babylon, who will carry them away to Babylon or put them to the sword. [5] I will deliver all the wealth of this city into the hands of their enemies — all its products, all its valuables and all the treasures of the kings of Judah. They will take it away as plunder and carry it off to Babylon. [6] And you, Pashhur, and all

who live in your house will go into exile to Babylon. There you will die and be buried, you and all your friends to whom you have prophesied lies.' " 2Ki 20:17; Jer 52:27

Jeremiah's Complaint

7 You deceived[a] me, LORD, and
    I was deceived[a];   Ex 5:23
you overpowered me and
    prevailed.   Isa 8:11
I am ridiculed all day long;
    everyone mocks me.   Job 17:2
8 Whenever I speak, I cry out
    proclaiming violence and
    destruction.   Jer 6:7
So the word of the LORD has
    brought me
insult and reproach all day
    long.   2Ch 36:16; Jer 6:10
9 But if I say, "I will not mention
    his word
or speak anymore in his
    name,"
his word is in my heart like a
    fire,   Ps 39:3
a fire shut up in my bones.
I am weary of holding it in;
    indeed, I cannot.
10 I hear many whispering,
    "Terror on every side!   Jer 6:25
Denounce him! Let's
    denounce him!"   Isa 29:21
All my friends   Ps 41:9
    are waiting for me to slip,
    saying,   Lk 11:53-54
"Perhaps he will be deceived;
    then we will prevail over
    him   1Ki 19:2
and take our revenge on him."

11 But the LORD is with me like a
    mighty warrior;   Jer 1:8
so my persecutors will
    stumble and not prevail.
They will fail and be
    thoroughly disgraced;
    their dishonor will never be
    forgotten.
12 LORD Almighty, you who
    examine the righteous
and probe the heart and
    mind,   Jer 17:10
let me see your vengeance on
    them,   Ps 54:7; 59:10
for to you I have committed
    my cause.   Jer 11:20

13 Sing to the LORD!   Isa 12:6
    Give praise to the LORD!
He rescues the life of the needy
    from the hands of the wicked.

14 Cursed be the day I was born!
    May the day my mother
    bore me not be blessed!
15 Cursed be the man who
    brought my father the
    news,
who made him very glad,
    saying,
    "A child is born to you — a
    son!"
16 May that man be like the
    towns   Ge 19:25
the LORD overthrew
    without pity.
May he hear wailing in the
    morning,
a battle cry at noon.
17 For he did not kill me in the
    womb,   Job 10:18-19

---

a 7 Or *persuaded*

with my mother as my
grave,
her womb enlarged forever.
¹⁸Why did I ever come out of
the womb   Job 3:10-11
to see trouble and sorrow
and to end my days in
shame?   Ps 90:9

God Rejects Zedekiah's Request

21 The word came to Jeremiah from the LORD when King Zedekiah sent to him Pashhur son of Malkijah and the priest Zephaniah son of Maaseiah. They said: ²"Inquire now of the LORD for us because Nebuchadnezzar*^a* king of Babylon is attacking us. Perhaps the LORD will perform wonders for us as in times past so that he will withdraw from us."   2Ki 24:18; 25:18

³But Jeremiah answered them, "Tell Zedekiah, ⁴'This is what the LORD, the God of Israel, says: I am about to turn against you the weapons of war that are in your hands, which you are using to fight the king of Babylon and the Babylonians*^b* who are outside the wall besieging you. And I will gather them inside this city. ⁵I myself will fight against you with an outstretched hand and a mighty arm in furious anger and in great wrath. ⁶I will strike down those who live in this city—both man and beast— and they will die of a terrible plague. ⁷After that, declares the LORD, I will give Zedekiah king of Judah, his officials and the people in this city who survive the plague, sword and famine, into the hands of Nebuchadnezzar king of Babylon and to their enemies who want to kill them. He will put them to the sword; he will show them no mercy or pity or compassion.'   2Ch 36:17; Jer 37:17

⁸"Furthermore, tell the people, 'This is what the LORD says: See, I am setting before you the way of life and the way of death. ⁹Whoever stays in this city will die by the sword, famine or plague. But whoever goes out and surrenders to the Babylonians who are besieging you will live; they will escape with their lives. ¹⁰I have determined to do this city harm and not good, declares the LORD. It will be given into the hands of the king of Babylon, and he will destroy it with fire.' Jer 44:11,27; 52:13

¹¹"Moreover, say to the royal house of Judah, 'Hear the word of the LORD. ¹²This is what the LORD says to you, house of David: Jer 13:18

"'Administer justice every
morning;   Jer 22:3
rescue from the hand of the
oppressor   Ps 27:11
the one who has been robbed,
or my wrath will break out
and burn like fire Jer 10:10

---

^a 2 Hebrew *Nebuchadrezzar,* of which *Nebuchadnezzar* is a variant; here and often in Jeremiah and Ezekiel   *^b* 4 Or *Chaldeans;* also in verse 9

because of the evil you have
done —   Jer 23:2
burn with no one to
quench it.   Isa 1:31
¹³I am against you, Jerusalem,
you who live above this
valley   Ps 125:2
on the rocky plateau,
declares the LORD —
you who say, "Who can come
against us?
Who can enter our refuge?"
¹⁴I will punish you as your
deeds deserve,   Isa 3:10-11
declares the LORD.
I will kindle a fire in your
forests   2Ch 36:19; Eze 20:47
that will consume
everything around you.' "

Judgment Against Wicked Kings

22 This is what the LORD
says: "Go down to the palace of the king of Judah and proclaim this message there: ²'Hear
the word of the LORD to you, king
of Judah, you who sit on David's
throne — you, your officials and
your people who come through
these gates. ³This is what the
LORD says: Do what is just and
right. Rescue from the hand of the
oppressor the one who has been
robbed. Do no wrong or violence
to the foreigner, the fatherless or
the widow, and do not shed innocent blood in this place. ⁴For if
you are careful to carry out these
commands, then kings who sit
on David's throne will come
through the gates of this palace,

riding in chariots and on horses,
accompanied by their officials
and their people. ⁵But if you do
not obey these commands, declares the LORD, I swear by myself that this palace will become
a ruin.' "   Jer 17:27; Mic 6:8; Heb 6:13

⁶For this is what the LORD says
about the palace of the king of
Judah:

"Though you are like Gilead
to me,   Ge 31:21
like the summit of Lebanon,
I will surely make you like a
wasteland,   Mic 3:12
like towns not inhabited.
⁷I will send destroyers against
you,   Jer 4:7
each man with his
weapons,
and they will cut up your fine
cedar beams   Isa 10:34
and throw them into the fire.

⁸"People from many nations
will pass by this city and will ask
one another, 'Why has the LORD
done such a thing to this great
city?' ⁹And the answer will be:
'Because they have forsaken the
covenant of the LORD their God
and have worshiped and served
other gods.' "   2Ki 22:17; 2Ch 34:25

¹⁰Do not weep for the dead king
or mourn his loss;   Ecc 4:2
rather, weep bitterly for him
who is exiled,
because he will never return
nor see his native land
again.

¹¹For this is what the LORD says about Shallum[a] son of Josiah, who succeeded his father as king of Judah but has gone from this place: "He will never return. ¹²He will die in the place where they have led him captive; he will not see this land again." 2Ki 23:31,34

¹³"Woe to him who builds
    his palace by
    unrighteousness, Mic 3:10
his upper rooms by
    injustice,
making his own people work
    for nothing,
not paying them for their
    labor. Jas 5:4
¹⁴He says, 'I will build myself a
    great palace Isa 5:8-9
with spacious upper rooms.'
So he makes large windows
    in it,
panels it with cedar 2Sa 7:2
and decorates it in red.

¹⁵"Does it make you a king
    to have more and more
    cedar?
Did not your father have food
    and drink?
He did what was right and
    just, 2Ki 23:25
so all went well with him.
¹⁶He defended the cause of the
    poor and needy, Ps 72:1-4
    and so all went well.
Is that not what it means to
    know me?" Ps 36:10
    declares the LORD.
¹⁷"But your eyes and your heart

are set only on dishonest
    gain, Isa 56:11
on shedding innocent blood
and on oppression and
    extortion." Dt 28:33

¹⁸Therefore this is what the LORD says about Jehoiakim son of Josiah king of Judah:

"They will not mourn for him:
    'Alas, my brother! Alas, my
    sister!'
They will not mourn for him:
    'Alas, my master! Alas, his
    splendor!'
¹⁹He will have the burial of a
    donkey—
    dragged away and thrown
    outside the gates of
    Jerusalem."

²⁰"Go up to Lebanon and cry out,
    let your voice be heard in
    Bashan, Ps 68:15
cry out from Abarim, Nu 27:12
    for all your allies are crushed.
²¹I warned you when you felt
    secure,
    but you said, 'I will not listen!'
This has been your way from
    your youth; Jer 3:25; 32:30
    you have not obeyed me.
²²The wind will drive all your
    shepherds away, Dt 28:64
and your allies will go into
    exile. ver 20
Then you will be ashamed
    and disgraced Jer 7:19
because of all your
    wickedness.

ᵃ 11 Also called *Jehoahaz*

23 You who live in 'Lebanon,^{a}'
    who are nestled in cedar
        buildings,
how you will groan when
        pangs come upon you,
    pain like that of a woman in
        labor!   Jer 4:31

24 "As surely as I live," declares the LORD, "even if you, Jehoiachin^b son of Jehoiakim king of Judah, were a signet ring on my right hand, I would still pull you off. 25 I will deliver you into the hands of those who want to kill you, those you fear — Nebuchadnezzar king of Babylon and the Babylonians.^{c} 26 I will hurl you and the mother who gave you birth into another country, where neither of you was born, and there you both will die. 27 You will never come back to the land you long to return to."   2Ki 24:8

28 Is this man Jehoiachin a
        despised, broken pot,
    an object no one wants?
Why will he and his children
        be hurled out,   Jer 15:1
    cast into a land they do not
        know?   Jer 17:4
29 O land, land, land,   Jer 6:19; Mic 1:2
    hear the word of the LORD!
30 This is what the LORD says:
    "Record this man as if childless,
    a man who will not prosper
        in his lifetime,   Jer 10:21
    for none of his offspring will
        prosper,   Job 18:19

    none will sit on the throne
        of David   Ps 94:20
    or rule anymore in Judah."

The Righteous Branch

23 "Woe to the shepherds who are destroying and scattering the sheep of my pasture!" declares the LORD. 2 Therefore this is what the LORD, the God of Israel, says to the shepherds who tend my people: "Because you have scattered my flock and driven them away and have not bestowed care on them, I will bestow punishment on you for the evil you have done," declares the LORD. 3 "I myself will gather the remnant of my flock out of all the countries where I have driven them and will bring them back to their pasture, where they will be fruitful and increase in number. 4 I will place shepherds over them who will tend them, and they will no longer be afraid or terrified, nor will any be missing," declares the LORD.   Jer 3:15; 30:10; Eze 34:23

5 "The days are coming,"
        declares the LORD,
    "when I will raise up for
        David^d a righteous
        Branch,   Isa 4:2
    a King who will reign wisely
    and do what is just and right
        in the land. Isa 11:1; Zec 6:12
6 In his days Judah will be saved

---

^{a} 23 That is, the palace in Jerusalem (see 1 Kings 7:2) ^{b} 24 Hebrew *Koniah*, a variant of *Jehoiachin*; also in verse 28 ^{c} 25 Or *Chaldeans* ^{d} 5 Or *up from David's line*

and Israel will live in safety.
This is the name by which he
will be called: Jer 33:16
The LORD Our Righteous
Savior.   Ro 3:21-22; 1Co 1:30

[7] "So then, the days are coming," declares the LORD, "when people will no longer say, 'As surely as the LORD lives, who brought the Israelites up out of Egypt,' [8]but they will say, 'As surely as the LORD lives, who brought the descendants of Israel up out of the land of the north and out of all the countries where he had banished them.' Then they will live in their own land."   Isa 43:5-6; Am 9:14-15

Lying Prophets

[9]Concerning the prophets:

My heart is broken within me;
    all my bones tremble.
I am like a drunken man,
    like a strong man overcome
        by wine,
because of the LORD
    and his holy words.   Jer 20:8-9
[10]The land is full of adulterers;
    because of the curse[a] the
        land lies parched   Dt 28:23
and the pastures in
    the wilderness are
        withered.   Jer 9:10; Hos 4:2-3
The prophets follow an evil
    course
and use their power unjustly.

[11] "Both prophet and priest are
    godless;   Jer 6:13; Zep 3:4

even in my temple I find
    their wickedness,"   Jer 7:10
        declares the LORD.
[12] "Therefore their path will
    become slippery;   Jer 13:16
they will be banished to
    darkness
and there they will fall.
I will bring disaster on them
    in the year they are
        punished,"   Jer 11:23
        declares the LORD.

[13] "Among the prophets of
    Samaria
I saw this repulsive thing:
They prophesied by Baal   Jer 2:8
    and led my people Israel
        astray.   Eze 13:10
[14]And among the prophets of
    Jerusalem
I have seen something
    horrible: Jer 5:30
They commit adultery and
    live a lie.   Jer 29:23
They strengthen the hands of
    evildoers,   Eze 13:22
so that not one of them
    turns from their
        wickedness.
They are all like Sodom to me;
    the people of Jerusalem are
        like Gomorrah."   Jer 20:16

[15]Therefore this is what the LORD Almighty says concerning the prophets:

"I will make them eat bitter
    food
and drink poisoned water,

---

[a] 10 Or *because of these things*

because from the prophets of
Jerusalem
ungodliness has spread
throughout the land."

16 This is what the LORD Almighty says:

"Do not listen to what
the prophets are
prophesying to you;
they fill you with false hopes.
They speak visions from their
own minds,   Jer 14:14
not from the mouth of the
LORD.   Jer 9:20
17 They keep saying to those
who despise me,
'The LORD says: You will
have peace.'   Jer 8:11
And to all who follow the
stubbornness of their
hearts   Jer 13:10
they say, 'No harm will
come to you.'   Jer 5:12
18 But which of them has stood
in the council of the
LORD   Ro 11:34
to see or to hear his word?
Who has listened and heard
his word?
19 See, the storm of the LORD
will burst out in wrath,
a whirlwind swirling down
on the heads of the wicked.
20 The anger of the LORD will not
turn back   2Ki 23:26; Jer 30:24
until he fully accomplishes
the purposes of his heart.
In days to come
you will understand it
clearly.

21 I did not send these prophets,
yet they have run with their
message;
I did not speak to them,
yet they have prophesied.
22 But if they had stood in my
council,   1Ki 22:19
they would have proclaimed
my words to my people
and would have turned them
from their evil ways
and from their evil deeds.

23 "Am I only a God nearby,"
declares the LORD,
"and not a God far away?
24 Who can hide in secret places
so that I cannot see them?"
declares the LORD.
"Do not I fill heaven and
earth?"   1Ki 8:27
declares the LORD.

25 "I have heard what the
prophets say who prophesy lies
in my name. They say, 'I had a
dream! I had a dream!' 26 How
long will this continue in the
hearts of these lying prophets,
who prophesy the delusions of
their own minds? 27 They think
the dreams they tell one another will make my people forget
my name, just as their ancestors
forgot my name through Baal
worship. 28 Let the prophet who
has a dream recount the dream,
but let the one who has my word
speak it faithfully. For what has
straw to do with grain?" declares
the LORD. 29 "Is not my word like
fire," declares the LORD, "and

like a hammer that breaks a rock in pieces? Jdg 3:7; Jer 14:14

³⁰ "Therefore," declares the LORD, "I am against the prophets who steal from one another words supposedly from me. ³¹ Yes," declares the LORD, "I am against the prophets who wag their own tongues and yet declare, 'The LORD declares.' ³² Indeed, I am against those who prophesy false dreams," declares the LORD. "They tell them and lead my people astray with their reckless lies, yet I did not send or appoint them. They do not benefit these people in the least," declares the LORD. Dt 18:20; Ps 34:16

False Prophecy

³³ "When these people, or a prophet or a priest, ask you, 'What is the message from the LORD?' say to them, 'What message? I will forsake you, declares the LORD.' ³⁴ If a prophet or a priest or anyone else claims, 'This is a message from the LORD,' I will punish them and their household. ³⁵ This is what each of you keeps saying to your friends and other Israelites: 'What is the LORD's answer?' or 'What has the LORD spoken?' ³⁶ But you must not mention 'a message from the LORD' again, because each one's word becomes their own message. So you distort the words of the living God, the LORD Almighty, our God.

³⁷ This is what you keep saying to a prophet: 'What is the LORD's answer to you?' or 'What has the LORD spoken?' ³⁸ Although you claim, 'This is a message from the LORD,' this is what the LORD says: You used the words, 'This is a message from the LORD,' even though I told you that you must not claim, 'This is a message from the LORD.' ³⁹ Therefore, I will surely forget you and cast you out of my presence along with the city I gave to you and your ancestors. ⁴⁰ I will bring on you everlasting disgrace — everlasting shame that will not be forgotten." Jer 20:11; Eze 5:14-15

Two Baskets of Figs

24 After Jehoiachin[a] son of Jehoiakim king of Judah and the officials, the skilled workers and the artisans of Judah were carried into exile from Jerusalem to Babylon by Nebuchadnezzar king of Babylon, the LORD showed me two baskets of figs placed in front of the temple of the LORD. ² One basket had very good figs, like those that ripen early; the other basket had very bad figs, so bad they could not be eaten. Isa 5:4; Am 8:1-2

³ Then the LORD asked me, "What do you see, Jeremiah?"

"Figs," I answered. "The good ones are very good, but the bad ones are so bad they cannot be eaten."

ᵃ 1 Hebrew *Jeconiah,* a variant of *Jehoiachin*

[4] Then the word of the LORD came to me: [5] "This is what the LORD, the God of Israel, says: 'Like these good figs, I regard as good the exiles from Judah, whom I sent away from this place to the land of the Babylonians.[a] [6] My eyes will watch over them for their good, and I will bring them back to this land. I will build them up and not tear them down; I will plant them and not uproot them. [7] I will give them a heart to know me, that I am the LORD. They will be my people, and I will be their God, for they will return to me with all their heart.   Jer 31:33; 32:40

[8] "'But like the bad figs, which are so bad they cannot be eaten,' says the LORD, 'so will I deal with Zedekiah king of Judah, his officials and the survivors from Jerusalem, whether they remain in this land or live in Egypt. [9] I will make them abhorrent and an offense to all the kingdoms of the earth, a reproach and a byword, a curse[b] and an object of ridicule, wherever I banish them. [10] I will send the sword, famine and plague against them until they are destroyed from the land I gave to them and their ancestors.'"   Jer 15:4; 32:4-5

Seventy Years of Captivity

25 The word came to Jeremiah concerning all the people of Judah in the fourth year of Jehoiakim son of Josiah king of Judah, which was the first year of Nebuchadnezzar king of Babylon. [2] So Jeremiah the prophet said to all the people of Judah and to all those living in Jerusalem: [3] For twenty-three years—from the thirteenth year of Josiah son of Amon king of Judah until this very day—the word of the LORD has come to me and I have spoken to you again and again, but you have not listened.   Jer 1:2; 7:26; 36:1

[4] And though the LORD has sent all his servants the prophets to you again and again, you have not listened or paid any attention. [5] They said, "Turn now, each of you, from your evil ways and your evil practices, and you can stay in the land the LORD gave to you and your ancestors for ever and ever. [6] Do not follow other gods to serve and worship them; do not arouse my anger with what your hands have made. Then I will not harm you."   Dt 8:19; Jer 7:25

[7] "But you did not listen to me," declares the LORD, "and you have aroused my anger with what your hands have made, and you have brought harm to yourselves."   Dt 32:21; 2Ki 21:15

[8] Therefore the LORD Almighty says this: "Because you have not listened to my words, [9] I will summon all the peoples of the

---

[a] 5 Or *Chaldeans*   [b] 9 That is, their names will be used in cursing (see 29:22); or, others will see that they are cursed.

north and my servant Nebuchadnezzar king of Babylon," declares the LORD, "and I will bring them against this land and its inhabitants and against all the surrounding nations. I will completely destroy*a* them and make them an object of horror and scorn, and an everlasting ruin. [10] I will banish from them the sounds of joy and gladness, the voices of bride and bridegroom, the sound of millstones and the light of the lamp. [11] This whole country will become a desolate wasteland, and these nations will serve the king of Babylon seventy years. Jer 18:16; 27:6; Rev 18:22-23

[12] "But when the seventy years are fulfilled, I will punish the king of Babylon and his nation, the land of the Babylonians,*b* for their guilt," declares the LORD, "and will make it desolate forever. [13] I will bring on that land all the things I have spoken against it, all that are written in this book and prophesied by Jeremiah against all the nations. [14] They themselves will be enslaved by many nations and great kings; I will repay them according to their deeds and the work of their hands." Jer 50:9; 51:6

The Cup of God's Wrath

[15] This is what the LORD, the God of Israel, said to me: "Take from my hand this cup filled with the wine of my wrath and make all the nations to whom I send you drink it. [16] When they drink it, they will stagger and go mad because of the sword I will send among them." Isa 51:17; Na 3:11

[17] So I took the cup from the LORD's hand and made all the nations to whom he sent me drink it: [18] Jerusalem and the towns of Judah, its kings and officials, to make them a ruin and an object of horror and scorn, a curse*c* — as they are today; [19] Pharaoh king of Egypt, his attendants, his officials and all his people, [20] and all the foreign people there; all the kings of Uz; all the kings of the Philistines (those of Ashkelon, Gaza, Ekron, and the people left at Ashdod); [21] Edom, Moab and Ammon; [22] all the kings of Tyre and Sidon; the kings of the coastlands across the sea; [23] Dedan, Tema, Buz and all who are in distant places*d*; [24] all the kings of Arabia and all the kings of the foreign people who live in the wilderness; [25] all the kings of Zimri, Elam and Media; [26] and all the kings of the north, near and far, one after the other — all the kingdoms on the face of the earth. And after all of them, the king of Sheshak*e* will drink it too. Jer 1:10; 44:22

[27] "Then tell them, 'This is what

---

a 9 The Hebrew term refers to the irrevocable giving over of things or persons to the LORD, often by totally destroying them.   *b 12* Or *Chaldeans*   *c 18* That is, their names to be used in cursing (see 29:22); or, to be seen by others as cursed   *d 23* Or *who clip the hair by their foreheads*   *e 26* *Sheshak* is a cryptogram for Babylon.

the Lord Almighty, the God of Israel, says: Drink, get drunk and vomit, and fall to rise no more because of the sword I will send among you.' ²⁸But if they refuse to take the cup from your hand and drink, tell them, 'This is what the Lord Almighty says: You must drink it! ²⁹See, I am beginning to bring disaster on the city that bears my Name, and will you indeed go unpunished? You will not go unpunished, for I am calling down a sword on all who live on the earth, declares the Lord Almighty.' Eze 21:4; 1Pe 4:17

³⁰"Now prophesy all these words against them and say to them:

" 'The Lord will roar from on high; Isa 16:10; 42:13
he will thunder from his holy dwelling Joel 3:16
and roar mightily against his land.
He will shout like those who tread the grapes, Rev 14:19
shout against all who live on the earth.
³¹The tumult will resound to the ends of the earth,
for the Lord will bring charges against the nations; Hos 4:1; Joel 3:2
he will bring judgment on all mankind Jer 2:35
and put the wicked to the sword,' " Jer 15:9
declares the Lord.

³²This is what the Lord Almighty says:

"Look! Disaster is spreading from nation to nation; Isa 34:2
a mighty storm is rising Jer 23:19
from the ends of the earth."

³³At that time those slain by the Lord will be everywhere—from one end of the earth to the other. They will not be mourned or gathered up or buried, but will be like dung lying on the ground.

³⁴Weep and wail, you shepherds;
roll in the dust, you leaders of the flock. Jer 6:26
For your time to be slaughtered has come;
you will fall like the best of the rams.^a Jer 22:28
³⁵The shepherds will have nowhere to flee,
the leaders of the flock no place to escape. Job 11:20
³⁶Hear the cry of the shepherds, Jer 23:1; Zec 11:3
the wailing of the leaders of the flock,
for the Lord is destroying their pasture.
³⁷The peaceful meadows will be laid waste
because of the fierce anger of the Lord.
³⁸Like a lion he will leave his lair, Jer 4:7
and their land will become desolate Jer 44:22

^a 34 Septuagint; Hebrew *fall and be shattered like fine pottery*

because of the sword*ᵃ* of the
oppressor Jer 46:16
and because of the LORD's
fierce anger. Ex 15:7

Jeremiah Threatened With Death

26 Early in the reign of Jehoiakim son of Josiah king of
Judah, this word came from the
LORD: ²"This is what the LORD
says: Stand in the courtyard of
the LORD's house and speak to
all the people of the towns of Judah who come to worship in the
house of the LORD. Tell them everything I command you; do not
omit a word. ³Perhaps they will
listen and each will turn from
their evil ways. Then I will relent
and not inflict on them the disaster I was planning because of the
evil they have done. ⁴Say to them,
'This is what the LORD says: If you
do not listen to me and follow my
law, which I have set before you,
⁵and if you do not listen to the
words of my servants the prophets, whom I have sent to you again
and again (though you have not
listened), ⁶then I will make this
house like Shiloh and this city a
curse*ᵇ* among all the nations of
the earth.'" Lev 26:14; Jer 25:4

⁷The priests, the prophets
and all the people heard Jeremiah speak these words in the
house of the LORD. ⁸But as soon
as Jeremiah finished telling all
the people everything the LORD
had commanded him to say, the
priests, the prophets and all the
people seized him and said, "You
must die! ⁹Why do you prophesy in the LORD's name that this
house will be like Shiloh and this
city will be desolate and deserted?" And all the people crowded
around Jeremiah in the house of
the LORD. Jer 9:11

¹⁰When the officials of Judah
heard about these things, they
went up from the royal palace
to the house of the LORD and
took their places at the entrance
of the New Gate of the LORD's
house. ¹¹Then the priests and the
prophets said to the officials and
all the people, "This man should
be sentenced to death because
he has prophesied against this
city. You have heard it with your
own ears!" Jer 38:4; Mt 26:66; Ac 6:11

¹²Then Jeremiah said to all the
officials and all the people: "The
LORD sent me to prophesy against
this house and this city all the
things you have heard. ¹³Now
reform your ways and your actions and obey the LORD your
God. Then the LORD will relent
and not bring the disaster he has
pronounced against you. ¹⁴As for
me, I am in your hands; do with
me whatever you think is good
and right. ¹⁵Be assured, however,
that if you put me to death, you

ᵃ 38 Some Hebrew manuscripts and Septuagint (see also 46:16 and 50:16); most Hebrew
manuscripts *anger*   *ᵇ 6* That is, its name will be used in cursing (see 29:22); or, others will
see that it is cursed.

will bring the guilt of innocent blood on yourselves and on this city and on those who live in it, for in truth the LORD has sent me to you to speak all these words in your hearing." Jer 7:5; 38:5

[16] Then the officials and all the people said to the priests and the prophets, "This man should not be sentenced to death! He has spoken to us in the name of the LORD our God." Ac 5:34-39; 23:9,29

[17] Some of the elders of the land stepped forward and said to the entire assembly of people, [18] "Micah of Moresheth prophesied in the days of Hezekiah king of Judah. He told all the people of Judah, 'This is what the LORD Almighty says: Mic 1:1

" 'Zion will be plowed like a
    field, Isa 2:3
Jerusalem will become a
    heap of rubble, Ne 4:2
the temple hill a mound
    overgrown with
    thickets.'[a] Jer 17:3; Zec 8:3

[19] "Did Hezekiah king of Judah or anyone else in Judah put him to death? Did not Hezekiah fear the LORD and seek his favor? And did not the LORD relent, so that he did not bring the disaster he pronounced against them? We are about to bring a terrible disaster on ourselves!" 2Sa 24:16

[20] (Now Uriah son of Shemaiah from Kiriath Jearim was another man who prophesied in the name of the LORD; he prophesied the same things against this city and this land as Jeremiah did. [21] When King Jehoiakim and all his officers and officials heard his words, the king was determined to put him to death. But Uriah heard of it and fled in fear to Egypt. [22] King Jehoiakim, however, sent Elnathan son of Akbor to Egypt, along with some other men. [23] They brought Uriah out of Egypt and took him to King Jehoiakim, who had him struck down with a sword and his body thrown into the burial place of the common people.) Jer 36:12,25

[24] Furthermore, Ahikam son of Shaphan supported Jeremiah, and so he was not handed over to the people to be put to death.

Judah to Serve Nebuchadnezzar

27 Early in the reign of Zedekiah[b] son of Josiah king of Judah, this word came to Jeremiah from the LORD: [2] This is what the LORD said to me: "Make a yoke out of straps and crossbars and put it on your neck. [3] Then send word to the kings of Edom, Moab, Ammon, Tyre and Sidon through the envoys who have come to Jerusalem to Zedekiah king of Judah. [4] Give them a message for their masters and say, 'This is what the LORD Almighty, the God of Israel, says: "Tell this

---

[a] 18 Micah 3:12   [b] 1 A few Hebrew manuscripts and Syriac (see also 27:3,12 and 28:1); most Hebrew manuscripts *Jehoiakim* (Most Septuagint manuscripts do not have this verse.)

to your masters: ⁵With my great power and outstretched arm I made the earth and its people and the animals that are on it, and I give it to anyone I please. ⁶Now I will give all your countries into the hands of my servant Nebuchadnezzar king of Babylon; I will make even the wild animals subject to him. ⁷All nations will serve him and his son and his grandson until the time for his land comes; then many nations and great kings will subjugate him. *Jer 25:12,14; 28:10,13*

⁸" ' "If, however, any nation or kingdom will not serve Nebuchadnezzar king of Babylon or bow its neck under his yoke, I will punish that nation with the sword, famine and plague, declares the LORD, until I destroy it by his hand. ⁹So do not listen to your prophets, your diviners, your interpreters of dreams, your mediums or your sorcerers who tell you, 'You will not serve the king of Babylon.' ¹⁰They prophesy lies to you that will only serve to remove you far from your lands; I will banish you and you will perish. ¹¹But if any nation will bow its neck under the yoke of the king of Babylon and serve him, I will let that nation remain in its own land to till it and to live there, declares the LORD.' " *Jer 21:9; 23:25*

¹²I gave the same message to Zedekiah king of Judah. I said, "Bow your neck under the yoke of the king of Babylon; serve him and his people, and you will live. ¹³Why will you and your people die by the sword, famine and plague with which the LORD has threatened any nation that will not serve the king of Babylon? ¹⁴Do not listen to the words of the prophets who say to you, 'You will not serve the king of Babylon,' for they are prophesying lies to you. ¹⁵'I have not sent them,' declares the LORD. 'They are prophesying lies in my name. Therefore, I will banish you and you will perish, both you and the prophets who prophesy to you.' " *Jer 6:15; 14:14; 23:21*

¹⁶Then I said to the priests and all these people, "This is what the LORD says: Do not listen to the prophets who say, 'Very soon now the articles from the LORD's house will be brought back from Babylon.' They are prophesying lies to you. ¹⁷Do not listen to them. Serve the king of Babylon, and you will live. Why should this city become a ruin? ¹⁸If they are prophets and have the word of the LORD, let them plead with the LORD Almighty that the articles remaining in the house of the LORD and in the palace of the king of Judah and in Jerusalem not be taken to Babylon. ¹⁹For this is what the LORD Almighty says about the pillars, the bronze Sea, the movable stands and the other articles that are left in this city, ²⁰which Nebuchadnezzar king of Babylon did not take away when he carried

Jehoiachin[a] son of Jehoiakim king of Judah into exile from Jerusalem to Babylon, along with all the nobles of Judah and Jerusalem — [21]yes, this is what the LORD Almighty, the God of Israel, says about the things that are left in the house of the LORD and in the palace of the king of Judah and in Jerusalem: [22]'They will be taken to Babylon and there they will remain until the day I come for them,' declares the LORD. 'Then I will bring them back and restore them to this place.'" Ezr 1:7

The False Prophet Hananiah

28 In the fifth month of that same year, the fourth year, early in the reign of Zedekiah king of Judah, the prophet Hananiah son of Azzur, who was from Gibeon, said to me in the house of the LORD in the presence of the priests and all the people: [2]"This is what the LORD Almighty, the God of Israel, says: 'I will break the yoke of the king of Babylon. [3]Within two years I will bring back to this place all the articles of the LORD's house that Nebuchadnezzar king of Babylon removed from here and took to Babylon. [4]I will also bring back to this place Jehoiachin[a] son of Jehoiakim king of Judah and all the other exiles from Judah who went to Babylon,' declares the LORD, 'for I will break the yoke of the king of Babylon.'" 2Ki 24:13

[5]Then the prophet Jeremiah replied to the prophet Hananiah before the priests and all the people who were standing in the house of the LORD. [6]He said, "Amen! May the LORD do so! May the LORD fulfill the words you have prophesied by bringing the articles of the LORD's house and all the exiles back to this place from Babylon. [7]Nevertheless, listen to what I have to say in your hearing and in the hearing of all the people: [8]From early times the prophets who preceded you and me have prophesied war, disaster and plague against many countries and great kingdoms. [9]But the prophet who prophesies peace will be recognized as one truly sent by the LORD only if his prediction comes true." Lev 26:14-17

[10]Then the prophet Hananiah took the yoke off the neck of the prophet Jeremiah and broke it, [11]and he said before all the people, "This is what the LORD says: 'In the same way I will break the yoke of Nebuchadnezzar king of Babylon off the neck of all the nations within two years.'" At this, the prophet Jeremiah went on his way. Jer 14:14; 27:2,10

[12]After the prophet Hananiah had broken the yoke off the neck of the prophet Jeremiah, the word of the LORD came to Jeremiah: [13]"Go and tell Hananiah, 'This is what the LORD says: You have broken a wooden

[a] 20 Hebrew *Jeconiah*, a variant of *Jehoiachin*

yoke, but in its place you will get a yoke of iron. [14] This is what the LORD Almighty, the God of Israel, says: I will put an iron yoke on the necks of all these nations to make them serve Nebuchadnezzar king of Babylon, and they will serve him. I will even give him control over the wild animals.'" Dt 28:48; Jer 27:6

[15] Then the prophet Jeremiah said to Hananiah the prophet, "Listen, Hananiah! The LORD has not sent you, yet you have persuaded this nation to trust in lies. [16] Therefore this is what the LORD says: 'I am about to remove you from the face of the earth. This very year you are going to die, because you have preached rebellion against the LORD.'" Dt 13:5

[17] In the seventh month of that same year, Hananiah the prophet died. 2Ki 1:17

A Letter to the Exiles

29 This is the text of the letter that the prophet Jeremiah sent from Jerusalem to the surviving elders among the exiles and to the priests, the prophets and all the other people Nebuchadnezzar had carried into exile from Jerusalem to Babylon. [2] (This was after King Jehoiachin[a] and the queen mother, the court officials and the leaders of Judah and Jerusalem, the skilled workers and the artisans had gone into exile from Jeru-

salem.) [3] He entrusted the letter to Elasah son of Shaphan and to Gemariah son of Hilkiah, whom Zedekiah king of Judah sent to King Nebuchadnezzar in Babylon. It said: 2Ki 24:12

[4] This is what the LORD Almighty, the God of Israel, says to all those I carried into exile from Jerusalem to Babylon: [5] "Build houses and settle down; plant gardens and eat what they produce. [6] Marry and have sons and daughters; find wives for your sons and give your daughters in marriage, so that they too may have sons and daughters. Increase in number there; do not decrease. [7] Also, seek the peace and prosperity of the city to which I have carried you into exile. Pray to the LORD for it, because if it prospers, you too will prosper." [8] Yes, this is what the LORD Almighty, the God of Israel, says: "Do not let the prophets and diviners among you deceive you. Do not listen to the dreams you encourage them to have. [9] They are prophesying lies to you in my name. I have not sent them," declares the LORD. Jer 14:14; 1Ti 2:1-2

[10] This is what the LORD says: "When seventy years are completed for Babylon, I will come to you and fulfill

---

[a] 2 Hebrew *Jeconiah*, a variant of *Jehoiachin*

my good promise to bring you back to this place. [11] For I know the plans I have for you," declares the LORD, "plans to prosper you and not to harm you, plans to give you hope and a future. [12] Then you will call on me and come and pray to me, and I will listen to you. [13] You will seek me and find me when you seek me with all your heart. [14] I will be found by you," declares the LORD, "and will bring you back from captivity.[a] I will gather you from all the nations and places where I have banished you," declares the LORD, "and will bring you back to the place from which I carried you into exile."   Jer 24:7; 25:12

[15] You may say, "The LORD has raised up prophets for us in Babylon," [16] but this is what the LORD says about the king who sits on David's throne and all the people who remain in this city, your fellow citizens who did not go with you into exile — [17] yes, this is what the LORD Almighty says: "I will send the sword, famine and plague against them and I will make them like figs that are so bad they cannot be eaten. [18] I will pursue them with the sword, famine and plague and will make them abhorrent to all the kingdoms of the earth, a curse[b] and an object of horror, of scorn and reproach, among all the nations where I drive them. [19] For they have not listened to my words," declares the LORD, "words that I sent to them again and again by my servants the prophets. And you exiles have not listened either," declares the LORD.   Jer 6:19; 25:4

[20] Therefore, hear the word of the LORD, all you exiles whom I have sent away from Jerusalem to Babylon. [21] This is what the LORD Almighty, the God of Israel, says about Ahab son of Kolaiah and Zedekiah son of Maaseiah, who are prophesying lies to you in my name: "I will deliver them into the hands of Nebuchadnezzar king of Babylon, and he will put them to death before your very eyes. [22] Because of them, all the exiles from Judah who are in Babylon will use this curse: 'May the LORD treat you like Zedekiah and Ahab, whom the king of Babylon burned in the fire.' [23] For they have done outrageous things in Israel; they have committed adultery with their neighbors' wives,

---

[a] 14 Or *will restore your fortunes*   [b] 18 That is, their names will be used in cursing (see verse 22); or, others will see that they are cursed.

and in my name they have uttered lies — which I did not authorize. I know it and am a witness to it," declares the LORD.   Jer 23:14; Heb 4:13

Message to Shemaiah

²⁴Tell Shemaiah the Nehelamite, ²⁵"This is what the LORD Almighty, the God of Israel, says: You sent letters in your own name to all the people in Jerusalem, to the priest Zephaniah son of Maaseiah, and to all the other priests. You said to Zephaniah, ²⁶'The LORD has appointed you priest in place of Jehoiada to be in charge of the house of the LORD; you should put any maniac who acts like a prophet into the stocks and neck-irons. ²⁷So why have you not reprimanded Jeremiah from Anathoth, who poses as a prophet among you? ²⁸He has sent this message to us in Babylon: It will be a long time. Therefore build houses and settle down; plant gardens and eat what they produce.'"   2Ki 25:18; Jer 21:1

²⁹Zephaniah the priest, however, read the letter to Jeremiah the prophet. ³⁰Then the word of the LORD came to Jeremiah: ³¹"Send this message to all the exiles: 'This is what the LORD says about Shemaiah the Nehelamite: Because Shemaiah has prophesied to you, even though I did not send him, and has persuaded you to trust in lies, ³²this is what the

LORD says: I will surely punish Shemaiah the Nehelamite and his descendants. He will have no one left among this people, nor will he see the good things I will do for my people, declares the LORD, because he has preached rebellion against me.'"   Jer 14:14

Restoration of Israel

30 This is the word that came to Jeremiah from the LORD: ²"This is what the LORD, the God of Israel, says: 'Write in a book all the words I have spoken to you. ³The days are coming,' declares the LORD, 'when I will bring my people Israel and Judah back from captivityᵃ and restore them to the land I gave their ancestors to possess,' says the LORD."   Isa 30:8; Jer 16:15; 29:14

⁴These are the words the LORD spoke concerning Israel and Judah: ⁵"This is what the LORD says:

" 'Cries of fear are heard —
    terror, not peace.
⁶Ask and see:
    Can a man bear children?
Then why do I see every
        strong man
    with his hands on his
        stomach like a woman
        in labor,   Jer 4:31
    every face turned deathly
        pale?   Isa 29:22
⁷How awful that day will be!
    No other will be like it.

ᵃ 3 Or *will restore the fortunes of my people Israel and Judah*

It will be a time of trouble for
Jacob,   Zep 1:15
but he will be saved out of it.

8 " 'In that day,' declares the
LORD Almighty,
'I will break the yoke off
their necks   Isa 9:4
and will tear off their bonds;
no longer will foreigners
enslave them.   Eze 34:27
9 Instead, they will serve the
LORD their God
and David their king,
whom I will raise up for them.

10 " 'So do not be afraid, Jacob
my servant;   Isa 43:5; 44:2
do not be dismayed, Israel,'
declares the LORD.
'I will surely save you out of a
distant place,   Jer 29:14
your descendants from the
land of their exile.
Jacob will again have peace
and security,   Isa 35:9
and no one will make him
afraid.
11 I am with you and will save
you,'
declares the LORD.
'Though I completely destroy
all the nations
among which I scatter you,
I will not completely destroy
you.   Jer 4:27; 46:28
I will discipline you but only
in due measure;   Jer 10:24
I will not let you go entirely
unpunished.'   Am 9:8

12 "This is what the LORD says:

" 'Your wound is incurable,
your injury beyond healing.
13 There is no one to plead your
cause,
no remedy for your sore,
no healing for you.   Jer 8:22
14 All your allies have forgotten
you;   La 1:2
they care nothing for you.
I have struck you as an enemy
would   Job 13:24
and punished you as would
the cruel,   Job 30:21
because your guilt is so great
and your sins so many.   Jer 5:6
15 Why do you cry out over your
wound,
your pain that has no cure?
Because of your great guilt
and many sins
I have done these things to
you.   Pr 1:31

16 " 'But all who devour you will
be devoured;   Isa 33:1
all your enemies will go into
exile.   Isa 14:2; Joel 3:4-8
Those who plunder you will
be plundered;   Jer 50:10
all who make spoil of you I
will despoil.
17 But I will restore you to health
and heal your wounds,'   Isa 1:5
declares the LORD,
'because you are called an
outcast,   Jer 33:24
Zion for whom no one cares.'

18 "This is what the LORD says:

" 'I will restore the fortunes of
Jacob's tents   Jer 31:23

and have compassion on his
dwellings; Ps 102:13
the city will be rebuilt on her
ruins, Jer 31:4,24,38
and the palace will stand in
its proper place.
19 From them will come songs of
thanksgiving Isa 35:10; 51:3
and the sound of rejoicing.
I will add to their numbers,
and they will not be
decreased;
I will bring them honor, Isa 60:9
and they will not be
disdained.
20 Their children will be as in
days of old, Isa 54:13
and their community will be
established before me;
I will punish all who
oppress them. Ex 23:22
21 Their leader will be one of
their own; Jer 23:5-6
their ruler will arise from
among them. Dt 17:15
I will bring him near and he
will come close to me —
for who is he who will
devote himself
to be close to me?'
declares the LORD.
22 " 'So you will be my people,
and I will be your God.' "
23 See, the storm of the LORD
will burst out in wrath,
a driving wind swirling down
on the heads of the wicked.
24 The fierce anger of the LORD
will not turn back Jer 4:8

until he fully accomplishes
the purposes of his heart.
In days to come
you will understand this.

31 "At that time," declares
the LORD, "I will be the
God of all the families of Israel,
and they will be my people."

2 This is what the LORD says:

"The people who survive the
sword
will find favor in the
wilderness; Nu 14:20
I will come to give rest to
Israel." Ex 33:14

3 The LORD appeared to us in
the past,ᵃ saying:

"I have loved you with an
everlasting love; Dt 4:37
I have drawn you with
unfailing kindness.
4 I will build you up again,
and you, Virgin Israel, will
be rebuilt. 2Ki 19:21; Jer 1:10
Again you will take up your
timbrels Ge 31:27
and go out to dance with
the joyful. Jer 30:19
5 Again you will plant vineyards
on the hills of Samaria;
the farmers will plant them
and enjoy their fruit. Isa 65:21
6 There will be a day when
watchmen cry out
on the hills of Ephraim,
'Come, let us go up to Zion,
to the LORD our God.' " Isa 2:3

ᵃ 3 Or LORD has appeared to us from afar

⁷This is what the LORD says:

"Sing with joy for Jacob;
  shout for the foremost of the
    nations.   Dt 28:13; Isa 61:9
Make your praises heard, and
  say,
  'LORD, save your people,
  the remnant of Israel.' Isa 37:31
⁸See, I will bring them from
    the land of the north
  and gather them from the
    ends of the earth. Dt 30:4
Among them will be the blind
    and the lame,   Isa 42:16
  expectant mothers and
    women in labor;
  a great throng will return.
⁹They will come with weeping;
  they will pray as I bring
    them back.
I will lead them beside
    streams of water Isa 63:13
  on a level path where they
    will not stumble, Isa 49:11
because I am Israel's father,
  and Ephraim is my firstborn
    son.

¹⁰"Hear the word of the LORD,
    you nations;
  proclaim it in distant
    coastlands: Isa 66:19
  'He who scattered Israel will
    gather them   Jer 50:19
  and will watch over his
    flock like a shepherd.'
¹¹For the LORD will deliver
    Jacob
  and redeem them from the
    hand of those stronger
    than they. Ps 142:6; Isa 44:23

¹²They will come and shout for
    joy on the heights of
    Zion;   Eze 17:23; Mic 4:1
  they will rejoice in the
    bounty of the LORD —
  the grain, the new wine and
    the olive oil,   Hos 2:21-22
  the young of the flocks and
    herds.
They will be like a well-
    watered garden, Isa 58:11
  and they will sorrow no
    more.   Isa 65:19; Jn 16:22
¹³Then young women will
    dance and be glad,
  young men and old as well.
I will turn their mourning
    into gladness;   Isa 61:3
  I will give them comfort and
    joy instead of sorrow.
¹⁴I will satisfy the priests with
    abundance,   Lev 7:35-36
  and my people will be filled
    with my bounty," Isa 30:23
    declares the LORD.

¹⁵This is what the LORD says:

"A voice is heard in Ramah,
  mourning and great
    weeping,
Rachel weeping for her
    children
  and refusing to be comforted,
  because they are no more."

¹⁶This is what the LORD says:

"Restrain your voice from
    weeping
  and your eyes from tears,
for your work will be rewarded,"
    declares the LORD.

"They will return from the
land of the enemy. Eze 11:17
¹⁷So there is hope for your
descendants," Job 8:7
declares the LORD.
"Your children will return
to their own land.

¹⁸"I have surely heard
Ephraim's moaning:
'You disciplined me like an
unruly calf, Job 5:17
and I have been disciplined.
Restore me, and I will return,
because you are the LORD
my God.
¹⁹After I strayed, Eze 36:31
I repented;
after I came to understand,
I beat my breast. Eze 21:12
I was ashamed and
humiliated Ezr 9:6
because I bore the disgrace
of my youth.' Jer 22:21
²⁰Is not Ephraim my dear son,
the child in whom I delight?
Though I often speak against
him,
I still remember him. Hos 4:4
Therefore my heart yearns for
him;
I have great compassion for
him," Isa 63:15; Mic 7:18
declares the LORD.

²¹"Set up road signs;
put up guideposts.
Take note of the highway, Jer 50:5
the road that you take.
Return, Virgin Israel, Isa 52:11
return to your towns.

²²How long will you wander,
unfaithful Daughter Israel? Jer 3:6
The LORD will create a new
thing on earth — Isa 43:19
the woman will return to[a]
the man." Dt 32:10

²³This is what the LORD Almighty, the God of Israel, says: "When I bring them back from captivity,[b] the people in the land of Judah and in its towns will once again use these words: 'The LORD bless you, you prosperous city, you sacred mountain.' ²⁴People will live together in Judah and all its towns — farmers and those who move about with their flocks. ²⁵I will refresh the weary and satisfy the faint."Jn 4:14 ²⁶At this I awoke and looked around. My sleep had been pleasant to me. Zec 4:1

²⁷"The days are coming," declares the LORD, "when I will plant the kingdoms of Israel and Judah with the offspring of people and of animals. ²⁸Just as I watched over them to uproot and tear down, and to overthrow, destroy and bring disaster, so I will watch over them to build and to plant," declares the LORD. ²⁹"In those days people will no longer say, Jer 1:10; 18:8; 44:27

'The parents have eaten sour
grapes, La 5:7
and the children's teeth are
set on edge.' Eze 18:2

ᵃ 22 Or *will protect*   ᵇ 23 Or *I restore their fortunes*

³⁰Instead, everyone will die for their own sin; whoever eats sour grapes — their own teeth will be set on edge. Isa 3:11; Gal 6:7

³¹ "The days are coming," declares the LORD, "when I will make a new covenant Heb 8:8-12 with the people of Israel and with the people of Judah. ³²It will not be like the covenant I made with their ancestors when I took them by the hand to lead them out of Egypt, because they broke my covenant, though I was a husband to[a] them,[b]" Isa 54:5 declares the LORD. ³³ "This is the covenant I will make with the people of Israel after that time," declares the LORD. "I will put my law in their minds and write it on their hearts. I will be their God, and they will be my people. ³⁴No longer will they teach their neighbor, 1Jn 2:27 or say to one another, 'Know the LORD,' because they will all know me, from the least of them to the greatest," declares the LORD. "For I will forgive their wickedness Isa 54:13

and will remember their sins no more." Mic 7:19

³⁵This is what the LORD says,

he who appoints the sun
    to shine by day,
who decrees the moon and
        stars
    to shine by night, Ge 1:16
who stirs up the sea Ex 14:21
    so that its waves roar — Ps 93:3
the LORD Almighty is his
        name: Jer 10:16
³⁶ "Only if these decrees vanish
        from my sight," Jer 33:20-26
declares the LORD,
"will Israel ever cease Ps 89:36-37
    being a nation before me."

³⁷This is what the LORD says:

"Only if the heavens above
    can be measured Jer 33:22
and the foundations of
        the earth below be
        searched out
will I reject all the
        descendants of Israel
because of all they have
        done,"
            declares the LORD.

³⁸ "The days are coming," declares the LORD, "when this city will be rebuilt for me from the Tower of Hananel to the Corner Gate. ³⁹The measuring line will stretch from there straight to the hill of Gareb and then turn to Goah. ⁴⁰The whole valley where dead bodies and ashes are

---

[a] 32 Hebrew; Septuagint and Syriac / *and I turned away from*   [b] 32 Or *was their master*

thrown, and all the terraces out to the Kidron Valley on the east as far as the corner of the Horse Gate, will be holy to the LORD. The city will never again be uprooted or demolished." Joel 3:17; Zec 14:21

Jeremiah Buys a Field

32 This is the word that came to Jeremiah from the LORD in the tenth year of Zedekiah king of Judah, which was the eighteenth year of Nebuchadnezzar. [2] The army of the king of Babylon was then besieging Jerusalem, and Jeremiah the prophet was confined in the courtyard of the guard in the royal palace of Judah. 2Ki 25:1; Ne 3:25

[3] Now Zedekiah king of Judah had imprisoned him there, saying, "Why do you prophesy as you do? You say, 'This is what the LORD says: I am about to give this city into the hands of the king of Babylon, and he will capture it. [4] Zedekiah king of Judah will not escape the Babylonians[a] but will certainly be given into the hands of the king of Babylon, and will speak with him face to face and see him with his own eyes. [5] He will take Zedekiah to Babylon, where he will remain until I deal with him, declares the LORD. If you fight against the Babylonians, you will not succeed.'" Jer 34:2-3

[6] Jeremiah said, "The word of the LORD came to me: [7] Hanamel son of Shallum your uncle is going to come to you and say, 'Buy my field at Anathoth, because as nearest relative it is your right and duty to buy it.' Lev 25:24-25

[8] "Then, just as the LORD had said, my cousin Hanamel came to me in the courtyard of the guard and said, 'Buy my field at Anathoth in the territory of Benjamin. Since it is your right to redeem it and possess it, buy it for yourself.'

"I knew that this was the word of the LORD; [9] so I bought the field at Anathoth from my cousin Hanamel and weighed out for him seventeen shekels[b] of silver. [10] I signed and sealed the deed, had it witnessed, and weighed out the silver on the scales. [11] I took the deed of purchase — the sealed copy containing the terms and conditions, as well as the unsealed copy — [12] and I gave this deed to Baruch son of Neriah, the son of Mahseiah, in the presence of my cousin Hanamel and of the witnesses who had signed the deed and of all the Jews sitting in the courtyard of the guard. Jer 36:4; 51:59

[13] "In their presence I gave Baruch these instructions: [14] 'This is what the LORD Almighty, the God of Israel, says: Take these documents, both the sealed and unsealed copies of the deed of purchase, and put them in a clay jar

---

[a] 4 Or Chaldeans; also in verses 5, 24, 25, 28, 29 and 43 about 200 grams   [b] 9 That is, about 7 ounces or

so they will last a long time. ¹⁵For this is what the LORD Almighty, the God of Israel, says: Houses, fields and vineyards will again be bought in this land.' Jer 30:18

¹⁶"After I had given the deed of purchase to Baruch son of Neriah, I prayed to the LORD:

¹⁷"Ah, Sovereign LORD, you have made the heavens and the earth by your great power and outstretched arm. Nothing is too hard for you. ¹⁸You show love to thousands but bring the punishment for the parents' sins into the laps of their children after them. Great and mighty God, whose name is the LORD Almighty, ¹⁹great are your purposes and mighty are your deeds. Your eyes are open to the ways of all mankind; you reward each person according to their conduct and as their deeds deserve. ²⁰You performed signs and wonders in Egypt and have continued them to this day, in Israel and among all mankind, and have gained the renown that is still yours. ²¹You brought your people Israel out of Egypt with signs and wonders, by a mighty hand and an outstretched arm and with great terror. ²²You gave them this land you had sworn to give their ancestors, a land flowing with milk and honey. ²³They came in and took possession of it, but they did not obey you or follow your law; they did not do what you commanded them to do. So you brought all this disaster on them. Ps 44:2; Jer 11:8; Da 9:14

²⁴"See how the siege ramps are built up to take the city. Because of the sword, famine and plague, the city will be given into the hands of the Babylonians who are attacking it. What you said has happened, as you now see. ²⁵And though the city will be given into the hands of the Babylonians, you, Sovereign LORD, say to me, 'Buy the field with silver and have the transaction witnessed.'"

²⁶Then the word of the LORD came to Jeremiah: ²⁷"I am the LORD, the God of all mankind. Is anything too hard for me? ²⁸Therefore this is what the LORD says: I am about to give this city into the hands of the Babylonians and to Nebuchadnezzar king of Babylon, who will capture it. ²⁹The Babylonians who are attacking this city will come in and set it on fire; they will burn it down, along with the houses where the people aroused my anger by burning incense on the roofs to Baal and by pouring out drink offerings to other gods. Ge 18:14

³⁰"The people of Israel and Judah have done nothing but evil

in my sight from their youth; indeed, the people of Israel have done nothing but arouse my anger with what their hands have made, declares the LORD. ³¹From the day it was built until now, this city has so aroused my anger and wrath that I must remove it from my sight. ³²The people of Israel and Judah have provoked me by all the evil they have done — they, their kings and officials, their priests and prophets, the people of Judah and those living in Jerusalem. ³³They turned their backs to me and not their faces; though I taught them again and again, they would not listen or respond to discipline. ³⁴They set up their vile images in the house that bears my Name and defiled it. ³⁵They built high places for Baal in the Valley of Ben Hinnom to sacrifice their sons and daughters to Molek, though I never commanded — nor did it enter my mind — that they should do such a detestable thing and so make Judah sin. Lev 18:21; Jer 19:5

³⁶"You are saying about this city, 'By the sword, famine and plague it will be given into the hands of the king of Babylon'; but this is what the LORD, the God of Israel, says: ³⁷I will surely gather them from all the lands where I banish them in my furious anger and great wrath; I will bring them back to this place and let them live in safety. ³⁸They will be my people, and I will be their God. ³⁹I will give them singleness of heart and action, so that they will always fear me and that all will then go well for them and for their children after them. ⁴⁰I will make an everlasting covenant with them: I will never stop doing good to them, and I will inspire them to fear me, so that they will never turn away from me. ⁴¹I will rejoice in doing them good and will assuredly plant them in this land with all my heart and soul. Dt 30:9; Am 9:15

⁴²"This is what the LORD says: As I have brought all this great calamity on this people, so I will give them all the prosperity I have promised them. ⁴³Once more fields will be bought in this land of which you say, 'It is a desolate waste, without people or animals, for it has been given into the hands of the Babylonians.' ⁴⁴Fields will be bought for silver, and deeds will be signed, sealed and witnessed in the territory of Benjamin, in the villages around Jerusalem, in the towns of Judah and in the towns of the hill country, of the western foothills and of the Negev, because I will restore their fortunes,ᵃ declares the LORD." Jer 17:26; 33:7,11,26

Promise of Restoration

33 While Jeremiah was still confined in the courtyard of the guard, the word of

ᵃ 44 Or *will bring them back from captivity*

the LORD came to him a second time: ²"This is what the LORD says, he who made the earth, the LORD who formed it and established it—the LORD is his name: ³'Call to me and I will answer you and tell you great and unsearchable things you do not know.' ⁴For this is what the LORD, the God of Israel, says about the houses in this city and the royal palaces of Judah that have been torn down to be used against the siege ramps and the sword ⁵in the fight with the Babylonians*: 'They will be filled with the dead bodies of the people I will slay in my anger and wrath. I will hide my face from this city because of all its wickedness. Isa 55:6; Jer 29:12

⁶"'Nevertheless, I will bring health and healing to it; I will heal my people and will let them enjoy abundant peace and security. ⁷I will bring Judah and Israel back from captivity*b and will rebuild them as they were before. ⁸I will cleanse them from all the sin they have committed against me and will forgive all their sins of rebellion against me. ⁹Then this city will bring me renown, joy, praise and honor before all nations on earth that hear of all the good things I do for it; and they will be in awe and will tremble at the abundant prosperity and peace I provide for it.' Heb 9:13-14; Jer 3:17

¹⁰"This is what the LORD says: 'You say about this place, "It is a desolate waste, without people or animals." Yet in the towns of Judah and the streets of Jerusalem that are deserted, inhabited by neither people nor animals, there will be heard once more ¹¹the sounds of joy and gladness, the voices of bride and bridegroom, and the voices of those who bring thank offerings to the house of the LORD, saying, Lev 7:12; Jer 32:43

"Give thanks to the LORD
    Almighty,
for the LORD is good; Ps 136:1
    his love endures forever."

For I will restore the fortunes of the land as they were before,' says the LORD. Ps 14:7; Isa 1:26

¹²"This is what the LORD Almighty says: 'In this place, desolate and without people or animals—in all its towns there will again be pastures for shepherds to rest their flocks. ¹³In the towns of the hill country, of the western foothills and of the Negev, in the territory of Benjamin, in the villages around Jerusalem and in the towns of Judah, flocks will again pass under the hand of the one who counts them,' says the LORD. Lev 27:32; Isa 65:10; Jer 17:26

¹⁴"'The days are coming,' declares the LORD, 'when I will fulfill the good promise I made to the people of Israel and Judah.

¹⁵"'In those days and at that time

---

a 5 Or *Chaldeans*   *b* 7 Or *will restore the fortunes of Judah and Israel*

I will make a righteous
 Branch sprout from
 David's line; Ps 72:2; Isa 4:2
he will do what is just and
 right in the land.
[16]In those days Judah will be
 saved Isa 45:17
and Jerusalem will live in
 safety.
This is the name by which it[a]
 will be called: Isa 59:14
The LORD Our Righteous
 Savior.' 1Co 1:30

[17]For this is what the LORD says: 'David will never fail to have a man to sit on the throne of Israel, [18]nor will the Levitical priests ever fail to have a man to stand before me continually to offer burnt offerings, to burn grain offerings and to present sacrifices.'" 2Sa 7:13; 1Ki 2:4; Lk 1:33

[19]The word of the LORD came to Jeremiah: [20]"This is what the LORD says: 'If you can break my covenant with the day and my covenant with the night, so that day and night no longer come at their appointed time, [21]then my covenant with David my servant—and my covenant with the Levites who are priests ministering before me—can be broken and David will no longer have a descendant to reign on his throne. [22]I will make the descendants of David my servant and the Levites who minister before me as countless as the stars in the sky and as measureless as the sand on the seashore.'" Ge 15:5; Ps 89:34

[23]The word of the LORD came to Jeremiah: [24]"Have you not noticed that these people are saying, 'The LORD has rejected the two kingdoms[b] he chose'? So they despise my people and no longer regard them as a nation. [25]This is what the LORD says: 'If I have not made my covenant with day and night and established the laws of heaven and earth, [26]then I will reject the descendants of Jacob and David my servant and will not choose one of his sons to rule over the descendants of Abraham, Isaac and Jacob. For I will restore their fortunes[c] and have compassion on them.'" Ps 74:16-17; Jer 31:35-37

Warning to Zedekiah

34 While Nebuchadnezzar king of Babylon and all his army and all the kingdoms and peoples in the empire he ruled were fighting against Jerusalem and all its surrounding towns, this word came to Jeremiah from the LORD: [2]"This is what the LORD, the God of Israel, says: Go to Zedekiah king of Judah and tell him, 'This is what the LORD says: I am about to give this city into the hands of the king of Babylon, and he will burn it down. [3]You will not escape from his grasp but will surely be captured and given into his hands. You will

---

[a] 16 Or he   [b] 24 Or families   [c] 26 Or will bring them back from captivity

see the king of Babylon with your own eyes, and he will speak with you face to face. And you will go to Babylon. 2Ki 25:1; Jer 32:4,29

4 " 'Yet hear the LORD's promise to you, Zedekiah king of Judah. This is what the LORD says concerning you: You will not die by the sword; 5you will die peacefully. As people made a funeral fire in honor of your predecessors, the kings who ruled before you, so they will make a fire in your honor and lament, "Alas, master!" I myself make this promise, declares the LORD.' " 2Ch 16:14; Jer 22:18

6Then Jeremiah the prophet told all this to Zedekiah king of Judah, in Jerusalem, 7while the army of the king of Babylon was fighting against Jerusalem and the other cities of Judah that were still holding out — Lachish and Azekah. These were the only fortified cities left in Judah. Jos 10:3

Freedom for Slaves

8The word came to Jeremiah from the LORD after King Zedekiah had made a covenant with all the people in Jerusalem to proclaim freedom for the slaves. 9Everyone was to free their Hebrew slaves, both male and female; no one was to hold a fellow Hebrew in bondage. 10So all the officials and people who entered into this covenant agreed that they would free their male and female slaves and no longer hold them in bondage. They agreed, and set them free. 11But afterward they changed their minds and took back the slaves they had freed and enslaved them again. Ex 21:2; Lev 25:39-46

12Then the word of the LORD came to Jeremiah: 13"This is what the LORD, the God of Israel, says: I made a covenant with your ancestors when I brought them out of Egypt, out of the land of slavery. I said, 14'Every seventh year each of you must free any fellow Hebrews who have sold themselves to you. After they have served you six years, you must let them go free.'ª Your ancestors, however, did not listen to me or pay attention to me. 15Recently you repented and did what is right in my sight: Each of you proclaimed freedom to your own people. You even made a covenant before me in the house that bears my Name. 16But now you have turned around and profaned my name; each of you has taken back the male and female slaves you had set free to go where they wished. You have forced them to become your slaves again. Ex 20:7; Lev 19:12

17"Therefore this is what the LORD says: You have not obeyed me; you have not proclaimed freedom to your own people. So I now proclaim 'freedom' for you, declares the LORD — 'freedom' to fall by the sword, plague and fam-

ª 14 Deut. 15:12

ine. I will make you abhorrent to all the kingdoms of the earth. ¹⁸Those who have violated my covenant and have not fulfilled the terms of the covenant they made before me, I will treat like the calf they cut in two and then walked between its pieces. ¹⁹The leaders of Judah and Jerusalem, the court officials, the priests and all the people of the land who walked between the pieces of the calf, ²⁰I will deliver into the hands of their enemies who want to kill them. Their dead bodies will become food for the birds and the wild animals.   Dt 28:26; Jer 7:33; 19:7

²¹"I will deliver Zedekiah king of Judah and his officials into the hands of their enemies who want to kill them, to the army of the king of Babylon, which has withdrawn from you. ²²I am going to give the order, declares the LORD, and I will bring them back to this city. They will fight against it, take it and burn it down. And I will lay waste the towns of Judah so no one can live there."   Jer 37:5

The Rekabites

35 This is the word that came to Jeremiah from the LORD during the reign of Jehoiakim son of Josiah king of Judah: ²"Go to the Rekabite family and invite them to come to one of the side rooms of the house of the LORD and give them wine to drink."   1Ki 6:5; 2Ki 10:15; 1Ch 2:55

³So I went to get Jaazaniah son of Jeremiah, the son of Habazziniah, and his brothers and all his sons — the whole family of the Rekabites. ⁴I brought them into the house of the LORD, into the room of the sons of Hanan son of Igdaliah the man of God. It was next to the room of the officials, which was over that of Maaseiah son of Shallum the doorkeeper. ⁵Then I set bowls full of wine and some cups before the Rekabites and said to them, "Drink some wine."   Dt 33:1; 1Ch 9:19

⁶But they replied, "We do not drink wine, because our forefather Jehonadab^a son of Rekab gave us this command: 'Neither you nor your descendants must ever drink wine. ⁷Also you must never build houses, sow seed or plant vineyards; you must never have any of these things, but must always live in tents. Then you will live a long time in the land where you are nomads.' ⁸We have obeyed everything our forefather Jehonadab son of Rekab commanded us. Neither we nor our wives nor our sons and daughters have ever drunk wine ⁹or built houses to live in or had vineyards, fields or crops. ¹⁰We have lived in tents and have fully obeyed everything our forefather Jehonadab commanded us. ¹¹But when Nebuchadnezzar king of Babylon invaded this land, we said, 'Come, we must go

^a 6 Hebrew *Jonadab*, a variant of *Jehonadab*; here and often in this chapter

to Jerusalem to escape the Babylonian*a* and Aramean armies.' So we have remained in Jerusalem." 2Ki 10:15; Jer 8:14

¹²Then the word of the LORD came to Jeremiah, saying: ¹³"This is what the LORD Almighty, the God of Israel, says: Go and tell the people of Judah and those living in Jerusalem, 'Will you not learn a lesson and obey my words?' declares the LORD. ¹⁴'Jehonadab son of Rekab ordered his descendants not to drink wine and this command has been kept. To this day they do not drink wine, because they obey their forefather's command. But I have spoken to you again and again, yet you have not obeyed me. ¹⁵Again and again I sent all my servants the prophets to you. They said, "Each of you must turn from your wicked ways and reform your actions; do not follow other gods to serve them. Then you will live in the land I have given to you and your ancestors." But you have not paid attention or listened to me. ¹⁶The descendants of Jehonadab son of Rekab have carried out the command their forefather gave them, but these people have not obeyed me.' Jer 7:13; 18:11; 32:33

¹⁷"Therefore this is what the LORD God Almighty, the God of Israel, says: 'Listen! I am going to bring on Judah and on everyone living in Jerusalem every disaster I pronounced against them. I spoke to them, but they did not listen; I called to them, but they did not answer.'" Isa 65:12; Jer 7:13

¹⁸Then Jeremiah said to the family of the Rekabites, "This is what the LORD Almighty, the God of Israel, says: 'You have obeyed the command of your forefather Jehonadab and have followed all his instructions and have done everything he ordered.' ¹⁹Therefore this is what the LORD Almighty, the God of Israel, says: 'Jehonadab son of Rekab will never fail to have a descendant to serve me.'" Jer 15:19; 33:17

Jehoiakim Burns Jeremiah's Scroll

36 In the fourth year of Jehoiakim son of Josiah king of Judah, this word came to Jeremiah from the LORD: ²"Take a scroll and write on it all the words I have spoken to you concerning Israel, Judah and all the other nations from the time I began speaking to you in the reign of Josiah till now. ³Perhaps when the people of Judah hear about every disaster I plan to inflict on them, they will each turn from their wicked ways; then I will forgive their wickedness and their sin." Jer 18:8; 26:3; Jnh 3:8

⁴So Jeremiah called Baruch son of Neriah, and while Jeremiah dictated all the words the LORD had spoken to him, Baruch wrote

^a *11* Or *Chaldean*

them on the scroll. ⁵Then Jeremiah told Baruch, "I am restricted; I am not allowed to go to the Lord's temple. ⁶So you go to the house of the Lord on a day of fasting and read to the people from the scroll the words of the Lord that you wrote as I dictated. Read them to all the people of Judah who come in from their towns. ⁷Perhaps they will bring their petition before the Lord and will each turn from their wicked ways, for the anger and wrath pronounced against this people by the Lord are great." Jer 32:12; Eze 2:9

⁸Baruch son of Neriah did everything Jeremiah the prophet told him to do; at the Lord's temple he read the words of the Lord from the scroll. ⁹In the ninth month of the fifth year of Jehoiakim son of Josiah king of Judah, a time of fasting before the Lord was proclaimed for all the people in Jerusalem and those who had come from the towns of Judah. ¹⁰From the room of Gemariah son of Shaphan the secretary, which was in the upper courtyard at the entrance of the New Gate of the temple, Baruch read to all the people at the Lord's temple the words of Jeremiah from the scroll. 2Ch 20:3; Jer 26:10

¹¹When Micaiah son of Gemariah, the son of Shaphan, heard all the words of the Lord from the scroll, ¹²he went down to the secretary's room in the royal palace, where all the officials were sitting: Elishama the secretary, Delaiah son of Shemaiah, Elnathan son of Akbor, Gemariah son of Shaphan, Zedekiah son of Hananiah, and all the other officials. ¹³After Micaiah told them everything he had heard Baruch read to the people from the scroll, ¹⁴all the officials sent Jehudi son of Nethaniah, the son of Shelemiah, the son of Cushi, to say to Baruch, "Bring the scroll from which you have read to the people and come." So Baruch son of Neriah went to them with the scroll in his hand. ¹⁵They said to him, "Sit down, please, and read it to us." Jer 26:22

So Baruch read it to them. ¹⁶When they heard all these words, they looked at each other in fear and said to Baruch, "We must report all these words to the king." ¹⁷Then they asked Baruch, "Tell us, how did you come to write all this? Did Jeremiah dictate it?" Jer 30:2

¹⁸"Yes," Baruch replied, "he dictated all these words to me, and I wrote them in ink on the scroll." ver 4

¹⁹Then the officials said to Baruch, "You and Jeremiah, go and hide. Don't let anyone know where you are." 1Ki 17:3

²⁰After they put the scroll in the room of Elishama the secretary, they went to the king in the courtyard and reported everything to him. ²¹The king sent Jehudi to get the scroll, and Jehudi

brought it from the room of Elishama the secretary and read it to the king and all the officials standing beside him. ²²It was the ninth month and the king was sitting in the winter apartment, with a fire burning in the firepot in front of him. ²³Whenever Jehudi had read three or four columns of the scroll, the king cut them off with a scribe's knife and threw them into the firepot, until the entire scroll was burned in the fire. ²⁴The king and all his attendants who heard all these words showed no fear, nor did they tear their clothes. ²⁵Even though Elnathan, Delaiah and Gemariah urged the king not to burn the scroll, he would not listen to them. ²⁶Instead, the king commanded Jerahmeel, a son of the king, Seraiah son of Azriel and Shelemiah son of Abdeel to arrest Baruch the scribe and Jeremiah the prophet. But the LORD had hidden them. 1Ki 22:8; Jer 15:21

²⁷After the king burned the scroll containing the words that Baruch had written at Jeremiah's dictation, the word of the LORD came to Jeremiah: ²⁸"Take another scroll and write on it all the words that were on the first scroll, which Jehoiakim king of Judah burned up. ²⁹Also tell Jehoiakim king of Judah, 'This is what the LORD says: You burned that scroll and said, "Why did you write on it that the king of

Babylon would certainly come and destroy this land and wipe from it both man and beast?" ³⁰Therefore this is what the LORD says about Jehoiakim king of Judah: He will have no one to sit on the throne of David; his body will be thrown out and exposed to the heat by day and the frost by night. ³¹I will punish him and his children and his attendants for their wickedness; I will bring on them and those living in Jerusalem and the people of Judah every disaster I pronounced against them, because they have not listened.'" Isa 30:10; Jer 22:19

³²So Jeremiah took another scroll and gave it to the scribe Baruch son of Neriah, and as Jeremiah dictated, Baruch wrote on it all the words of the scroll that Jehoiakim king of Judah had burned in the fire. And many similar words were added to them. ver 4; Ex 34:1

Jeremiah in Prison

37 Zedekiah son of Josiah was made king of Judah by Nebuchadnezzar king of Babylon; he reigned in place of Jehoiachin[a] son of Jehoiakim. ²Neither he nor his attendants nor the people of the land paid any attention to the words the LORD had spoken through Jeremiah the prophet. 2Ch 36:12,14; Jer 22:24

³King Zedekiah, however, sent Jehukal son of Shelemiah with

---

a 1 Hebrew *Koniah,* a variant of *Jehoiachin*

the priest Zephaniah son of Maaseiah to Jeremiah the prophet with this message: "Please pray to the LORD our God for us." Jer 21:1-2

⁴Now Jeremiah was free to come and go among the people, for he had not yet been put in prison. ⁵Pharaoh's army had marched out of Egypt, and when the Babylonians*a* who were besieging Jerusalem heard the report about them, they withdrew from Jerusalem. 2Ki 24:7; Eze 17:15

⁶Then the word of the LORD came to Jeremiah the prophet: ⁷"This is what the LORD, the God of Israel, says: Tell the king of Judah, who sent you to inquire of me, 'Pharaoh's army, which has marched out to support you, will go back to its own land, to Egypt. ⁸Then the Babylonians will return and attack this city; they will capture it and burn it down.' ⁹"This is what the LORD says: Do not deceive yourselves, thinking, 'The Babylonians will surely leave us.' They will not! ¹⁰Even if you were to defeat the entire Babylonian*b* army that is attacking you and only wounded men were left in their tents, they would come out and burn this city down." Jer 34:22

¹¹After the Babylonian army had withdrawn from Jerusalem because of Pharaoh's army, ¹²Jeremiah started to leave the city to go to the territory of Benjamin to get his share of the property among the people there. ¹³But when he reached the Benjamin Gate, the captain of the guard, whose name was Irijah son of Shelemiah, the son of Hananiah, arrested him and said, "You are deserting to the Babylonians!" Jer 32:9

¹⁴"That's not true!" Jeremiah said. "I am not deserting to the Babylonians." But Irijah would not listen to him; instead, he arrested Jeremiah and brought him to the officials. ¹⁵They were angry with Jeremiah and had him beaten and imprisoned in the house of Jonathan the secretary, which they had made into a prison. Jer 38:26; 40:4

¹⁶Jeremiah was put into a vaulted cell in a dungeon, where he remained a long time. ¹⁷Then King Zedekiah sent for him and had him brought to the palace, where he asked him privately, "Is there any word from the LORD?" Jer 15:11; 38:16

"Yes," Jeremiah replied, "you will be delivered into the hands of the king of Babylon." Jer 21:7

¹⁸Then Jeremiah said to King Zedekiah, "What crime have I committed against you or your attendants or this people, that you have put me in prison? ¹⁹Where are your prophets who prophesied to you, 'The king of Babylon will not attack you or this land'? ²⁰But now, my lord the king, please listen. Let me bring my petition before you: Do

---

a 5 Or *Chaldeans*; also in verses 8, 9, 13 and 14   *b* 10 Or *Chaldean*; also in verse 11 not send me back to the house of Jonathan the secretary, or I will die there." 1Sa 26:18; Jn 10:32

²¹ King Zedekiah then gave orders for Jeremiah to be placed in the courtyard of the guard and given a loaf of bread from the street of the bakers each day until all the bread in the city was gone. So Jeremiah remained in the courtyard of the guard. Jer 32:2

Jeremiah Thrown Into a Cistern

38 Shephatiah son of Mattan, Gedaliah son of Pashhur, Jehukal[a] son of Shelemiah, and Pashhur son of Malkijah heard what Jeremiah was telling all the people when he said, ² "This is what the LORD says: 'Whoever stays in this city will die by the sword, famine or plague, but whoever goes over to the Babylonians[b] will live. They will escape with their lives; they will live.' ³ And this is what the LORD says: 'This city will certainly be given into the hands of the army of the king of Babylon, who will capture it.'" Jer 21:4,10; 32:3; 37:3

⁴ Then the officials said to the king, "This man should be put to death. He is discouraging the soldiers who are left in this city, as well as all the people, by the things he is saying to them. This man is not seeking the good of these people but their ruin."

⁵ "He is in your hands," King Zedekiah answered. "The king can do nothing to oppose you."

⁶ So they took Jeremiah and put him into the cistern of Malkijah, the king's son, which was in the courtyard of the guard. They lowered Jeremiah by ropes into the cistern; it had no water in it, only mud, and Jeremiah sank down into the mud. Jer 37:21; La 3:53

⁷ But Ebed-Melek, a Cushite,[c] an official[d] in the royal palace, heard that they had put Jeremiah into the cistern. While the king was sitting in the Benjamin Gate, ⁸ Ebed-Melek went out of the palace and said to him, ⁹ "My lord the king, these men have acted wickedly in all they have done to Jeremiah the prophet. They have thrown him into a cistern, where he will starve to death when there is no longer any bread in the city." Jer 37:21; Ac 8:27

¹⁰ Then the king commanded Ebed-Melek the Cushite, "Take thirty men from here with you and lift Jeremiah the prophet out of the cistern before he dies."

¹¹ So Ebed-Melek took the men with him and went to a room under the treasury in the palace. He took some old rags and worn-out clothes from there and let them down with ropes to Jeremiah in the cistern. ¹² Ebed-Melek the Cushite said to Jeremiah, "Put these old rags and worn-out clothes under your

---

[a] 1 Hebrew *Jukal*, a variant of *Jehukal*   [b] 2 Or *Chaldeans*; also in verses 18, 19 and 23
[c] 7 Probably from the upper Nile region   [d] 7 Or *a eunuch*

arms to pad the ropes." Jeremiah did so, ¹³ and they pulled him up with the ropes and lifted him out of the cistern. And Jeremiah remained in the courtyard of the guard.   Jer 37:21

Zedekiah Questions Jeremiah Again

¹⁴ Then King Zedekiah sent for Jeremiah the prophet and had him brought to the third entrance to the temple of the LORD. "I am going to ask you something," the king said to Jeremiah. "Do not hide anything from me."   1Sa 3:17; Jer 37:3

¹⁵ Jeremiah said to Zedekiah, "If I give you an answer, will you not kill me? Even if I did give you counsel, you would not listen to me."

¹⁶ But King Zedekiah swore this oath secretly to Jeremiah: "As surely as the LORD lives, who has given us breath, I will neither kill you nor hand you over to those who want to kill you."   Isa 57:16

¹⁷ Then Jeremiah said to Zedekiah, "This is what the LORD God Almighty, the God of Israel, says: 'If you surrender to the officers of the king of Babylon, your life will be spared and this city will not be burned down; you and your family will live. ¹⁸ But if you will not surrender to the officers of the king of Babylon, this city will be given into the hands of the Babylonians and they will burn

it down; you yourself will not escape from them.'"   Jer 32:4; 34:3

¹⁹ King Zedekiah said to Jeremiah, "I am afraid of the Jews who have gone over to the Babylonians, for the Babylonians may hand me over to them and they will mistreat me."   Isa 51:12; Jn 12:42

²⁰ "They will not hand you over," Jeremiah replied. "Obey the LORD by doing what I tell you. Then it will go well with you, and your life will be spared. ²¹ But if you refuse to surrender, this is what the LORD has revealed to me: ²² All the women left in the palace of the king of Judah will be brought out to the officials of the king of Babylon. Those women will say to you: Jer 6:12; 11:4

"'They misled you and
    overcame you —
those trusted friends of
    yours.   Jer 13:21
Your feet are sunk in the mud;
    your friends have deserted
    you.'

²³ "All your wives and children will be brought out to the Babylonians. You yourself will not escape from their hands but will be captured by the king of Babylon; and this city will^a be burned down."   2Ki 25:6; Jer 41:10

²⁴ Then Zedekiah said to Jeremiah, "Do not let anyone know about this conversation, or you may die. ²⁵ If the officials hear that I talked with you, and they

^a 23 Or and you will cause this city to

come to you and say, 'Tell us what you said to the king and what the king said to you; do not hide it from us or we will kill you,' [26] then tell them, 'I was pleading with the king not to send me back to Jonathan's house to die there.'" *Jer 37:15*

[27] All the officials did come to Jeremiah and question him, and he told them everything the king had ordered him to say. So they said no more to him, for no one had heard his conversation with the king.

[28] And Jeremiah remained in the courtyard of the guard until the day Jerusalem was captured.

The Fall of Jerusalem

39:1-10pp — 2Ki 25:1-12; Jer 52:4-16

39 This is how Jerusalem was taken: [1] In the ninth year of Zedekiah king of Judah, in the tenth month, Nebuchadnezzar king of Babylon marched against Jerusalem with his whole army and laid siege to it. [2] And on the ninth day of the fourth month of Zedekiah's eleventh year, the city wall was broken through. [3] Then all the officials of the king of Babylon came and took seats in the Middle Gate: Nergal-Sharezer of Samgar, Nebo-Sarsekim a chief officer, Nergal-Sharezer a high official and all the other officials of the king of Babylon. [4] When Zedekiah king of Judah and all the soldiers saw them,

they fled; they left the city at night by way of the king's garden, through the gate between the two walls, and headed toward the Arabah.[a] *Jer 25:29; 2Ch 36:11*

[5] But the Babylonian[b] army pursued them and overtook Zedekiah in the plains of Jericho. They captured him and took him to Nebuchadnezzar king of Babylon at Riblah in the land of Hamath, where he pronounced sentence on him. [6] There at Riblah the king of Babylon slaughtered the sons of Zedekiah before his eyes and also killed all the nobles of Judah. [7] Then he put out Zedekiah's eyes and bound him with bronze shackles to take him to Babylon. *2Ki 23:33; Jer 32:5; Eze 12:13*

[8] The Babylonians[c] set fire to the royal palace and the houses of the people and broke down the walls of Jerusalem. [9] Nebuzaradan commander of the imperial guard carried into exile to Babylon the people who remained in the city, along with those who had gone over to him, and the rest of the people. [10] But Nebuzaradan the commander of the guard left behind in the land of Judah some of the poor people, who owned nothing; and at that time he gave them vineyards and fields. *2Ki 25:1-12; Jer 52:4-16*

[11] Now Nebuchadnezzar king of Babylon had given these orders about Jeremiah through Nebuzaradan commander of

[a] 4 Or *the Jordan Valley*   [b] 5 Or *Chaldean*   [c] 8 Or *Chaldeans*

the imperial guard: [12] "Take him and look after him; don't harm him but do for him whatever he asks." [13] So Nebuzaradan the commander of the guard, Nebushazban a chief officer, Nergal-Sharezer a high official and all the other officers of the king of Babylon [14] sent and had Jeremiah taken out of the courtyard of the guard. They turned him over to Gedaliah son of Ahikam, the son of Shaphan, to take him back to his home. So he remained among his own people.   Jer 38:28; 1Pe 3:13

[15] While Jeremiah had been confined in the courtyard of the guard, the word of the LORD came to him: [16] "Go and tell Ebed-Melek the Cushite, 'This is what the LORD Almighty, the God of Israel, says: I am about to fulfill my words against this city—words concerning disaster, not prosperity. At that time they will be fulfilled before your eyes. [17] But I will rescue you on that day, declares the LORD; you will not be given into the hands of those you fear. [18] I will save you; you will not fall by the sword but will escape with your life, because you trust in me, declares the LORD.'"   Jer 21:9

Jeremiah Freed

40 The word came to Jeremiah from the LORD after Nebuzaradan commander of the imperial guard had released him at Ramah. He had found Jeremiah bound in chains among all the captives from Jerusalem and Judah who were being carried into exile to Babylon. [2] When the commander of the guard found Jeremiah, he said to him, "The LORD your God decreed this disaster for this place. [3] And now the LORD has brought it about; he has done just as he said he would. All this happened because you people sinned against the LORD and did not obey him. [4] But today I am freeing you from the chains on your wrists. Come with me to Babylon, if you like, and I will look after you; but if you do not want to, then don't come. Look, the whole country lies before you; go wherever you please." [5] However, before Jeremiah turned to go,[a] Nebuzaradan added, "Go back to Gedaliah son of Ahikam, the son of Shaphan, whom the king of Babylon has appointed over the towns of Judah, and live with him among the people, or go anywhere else you please."   Jer 39:11-12; Da 9:11

Then the commander gave him provisions and a present and let him go. [6] So Jeremiah went to Gedaliah son of Ahikam at Mizpah and stayed with him among the people who were left behind in the land.   Jdg 20:1; 1Sa 7:5-17

Gedaliah Assassinated

40:7-9; 41:1-3pp — 2Ki 25:22-26

[7] When all the army officers

---

[a] 5 Or *Jeremiah answered*

and their men who were still in the open country heard that the king of Babylon had appointed Gedaliah son of Ahikam as governor over the land and had put him in charge of the men, women and children who were the poorest in the land and who had not been carried into exile to Babylon, ⁸ they came to Gedaliah at Mizpah — Ishmael son of Nethaniah, Johanan and Jonathan the sons of Kareah, Seraiah son of Tanhumeth, the sons of Ephai the Netophathite, and Jaazaniah^a the son of the Maakathite, and their men. ⁹ Gedaliah son of Ahikam, the son of Shaphan, took an oath to reassure them and their men. "Do not be afraid to serve the Babylonians,^b" he said. "Settle down in the land and serve the king of Babylon, and it will go well with you. ¹⁰ I myself will stay at Mizpah to represent you before the Babylonians who come to us, but you are to harvest the wine, summer fruit and olive oil, and put them in your storage jars, and live in the towns you have taken over." Dt 1:39; Jer 38:20

¹¹ When all the Jews in Moab, Ammon, Edom and all the other countries heard that the king of Babylon had left a remnant in Judah and had appointed Gedaliah son of Ahikam, the son of Shaphan, as governor over them, ¹² they all came back to the land of Judah, to Gedaliah at Mizpah, from all the countries where they had been scattered. And they harvested an abundance of wine and summer fruit. Jer 43:5

¹³ Johanan son of Kareah and all the army officers still in the open country came to Gedaliah at Mizpah ¹⁴ and said to him, "Don't you know that Baalis king of the Ammonites has sent Ishmael son of Nethaniah to take your life?" But Gedaliah son of Ahikam did not believe them. Jer 41:10

¹⁵ Then Johanan son of Kareah said privately to Gedaliah in Mizpah, "Let me go and kill Ishmael son of Nethaniah, and no one will know it. Why should he take your life and cause all the Jews who are gathered around you to be scattered and the remnant of Judah to perish?" 2Ki 21:14

¹⁶ But Gedaliah son of Ahikam said to Johanan son of Kareah, "Don't do such a thing! What you are saying about Ishmael is not true."

41 In the seventh month Ishmael son of Nethaniah, the son of Elishama, who was of royal blood and had been one of the king's officers, came with ten men to Gedaliah son of Ahikam at Mizpah. While they were eating together there, ² Ishmael son of Nethaniah and the ten men who were with him got up and struck down Gedaliah son of Ahikam, the son of Shaphan,

^a 8 Hebrew *Jezaniah*, a variant of *Jaazaniah*   ^b 9 Or *Chaldeans*; also in verse 10

with the sword, killing the one whom the king of Babylon had appointed as governor over the land. [3]Ishmael also killed all the men of Judah who were with Gedaliah at Mizpah, as well as the Babylonian[a] soldiers who were there. 2Ki 25:22-26; Jer 40:5,8

[4]The day after Gedaliah's assassination, before anyone knew about it, [5]eighty men who had shaved off their beards, torn their clothes and cut themselves came from Shechem, Shiloh and Samaria, bringing grain offerings and incense with them to the house of the LORD. [6]Ishmael son of Nethaniah went out from Mizpah to meet them, weeping as he went. When he met them, he said, "Come to Gedaliah son of Ahikam." [7]When they went into the city, Ishmael son of Nethaniah and the men who were with him slaughtered them and threw them into a cistern. [8]But ten of them said to Ishmael, "Don't kill us! We have wheat and barley, olive oil and honey, hidden in a field." So he let them alone and did not kill them with the others. [9]Now the cistern where he threw all the bodies of the men he had killed along with Gedaliah was the one King Asa had made as part of his defense against Baasha king of Israel. Ishmael son of Nethaniah filled it with the dead. 1Ki 15:22; 2Ch 16:1,6

[10]Ishmael made captives of all the rest of the people who were in Mizpah—the king's daughters along with all the others who were left there, over whom Nebuzaradan commander of the imperial guard had appointed Gedaliah son of Ahikam. Ishmael son of Nethaniah took them captive and set out to cross over to the Ammonites. Jer 40:14

[11]When Johanan son of Kareah and all the army officers who were with him heard about all the crimes Ishmael son of Nethaniah had committed, [12]they took all their men and went to fight Ishmael son of Nethaniah. They caught up with him near the great pool in Gibeon. [13]When all the people Ishmael had with him saw Johanan son of Kareah and the army officers who were with him, they were glad. [14]All the people Ishmael had taken captive at Mizpah turned and went over to Johanan son of Kareah. [15]But Ishmael son of Nethaniah and eight of his men escaped from Johanan and fled to the Ammonites. 2Sa 2:13; Pr 28:17

Flight to Egypt

[16]Then Johanan son of Kareah and all the army officers who were with him led away all the people of Mizpah who had survived, whom Johanan had recovered from Ishmael son of Nethaniah after Ishmael had assassinated Gedaliah son of Ahikam—

[a] 3 Or Chaldean

the soldiers, women, children and court officials he had recovered from Gibeon. [17]And they went on, stopping at Geruth Kimham near Bethlehem on their way to Egypt [18]to escape the Babylonians.[a] They were afraid of them because Ishmael son of Nethaniah had killed Gedaliah son of Ahikam, whom the king of Babylon had appointed as governor over the land.

42 Then all the army officers, including Johanan son of Kareah and Jezaniah[b] son of Hoshaiah, and all the people from the least to the greatest approached [2]Jeremiah the prophet and said to him, "Please hear our petition and pray to the LORD your God for this entire remnant. For as you now see, though we were once many, now only a few are left. [3]Pray that the LORD your God will tell us where we should go and what we should do." Ps 86:11

[4]"I have heard you," replied Jeremiah the prophet. "I will certainly pray to the LORD your God as you have requested; I will tell you everything the LORD says and will keep nothing back from you." 1Ki 22:14; 1Sa 3:17

[5]Then they said to Jeremiah, "May the LORD be a true and faithful witness against us if we do not act in accordance with everything the LORD your God sends you to tell us. [6]Whether it is favorable or unfavorable, we will obey the LORD our God, to whom we are sending you, so that it will go well with us, for we will obey the LORD our God." Dt 6:3

[7]Ten days later the word of the LORD came to Jeremiah. [8]So he called together Johanan son of Kareah and all the army officers who were with him and all the people from the least to the greatest. [9]He said to them, "This is what the LORD, the God of Israel, to whom you sent me to present your petition, says: [10]'If you stay in this land, I will build you up and not tear you down; I will plant you and not uproot you, for I have relented concerning the disaster I have inflicted on you. [11]Do not be afraid of the king of Babylon, whom you now fear. Do not be afraid of him, declares the LORD, for I am with you and will save you and deliver you from his hands. [12]I will show you compassion so that he will have compassion on you and restore you to your land.' Ps 106:44-46

[13]"However, if you say, 'We will not stay in this land,' and so disobey the LORD your God, [14]and if you say, 'No, we will go and live in Egypt, where we will not see war or hear the trumpet or be hungry for bread,' [15]then hear the word of the LORD, you remnant of Judah. This is what the LORD Almighty, the God of Israel, says: 'If you are determined to go to Egypt and you do go to

[a] 18 Or *Chaldeans*   [b] 1 Hebrew; Septuagint (see also 43:2) *Azariah*

settle there, ¹⁶then the sword you fear will overtake you there, and the famine you dread will follow you into Egypt, and there you will die. ¹⁷Indeed, all who are determined to go to Egypt to settle there will die by the sword, famine and plague; not one of them will survive or escape the disaster I will bring on them.' ¹⁸This is what the LORD Almighty, the God of Israel, says: 'As my anger and wrath have been poured out on those who lived in Jerusalem, so will my wrath be poured out on you when you go to Egypt. You will be a curse[a] and an object of horror, a curse[a] and an object of reproach; you will never see this place again.'   Jer 7:20; 29:18; 44:13

¹⁹"Remnant of Judah, the LORD has told you, 'Do not go to Egypt.' Be sure of this: I warn you today ²⁰that you made a fatal mistake when you sent me to the LORD your God and said, 'Pray to the LORD our God for us; tell us everything he says and we will do it.' ²¹I have told you today, but you still have not obeyed the LORD your God in all he sent me to tell you. ²²So now, be sure of this: You will die by the sword, famine and plague in the place where you want to go to settle."   Eze 6:11; Hos 9:6

43 When Jeremiah had finished telling the people all the words of the LORD their God—everything the LORD had sent him to tell them— ²Azariah son of Hoshaiah and Johanan son of Kareah and all the arrogant men said to Jeremiah, "You are lying! The LORD our God has not sent you to say, 'You must not go to Egypt to settle there.' ³But Baruch son of Neriah is inciting you against us to hand us over to the Babylonians,[b] so they may kill us or carry us into exile to Babylon."   Jer 26:8; 42:1

⁴So Johanan son of Kareah and all the army officers and all the people disobeyed the LORD's command to stay in the land of Judah. ⁵Instead, Johanan son of Kareah and all the army officers led away all the remnant of Judah who had come back to live in the land of Judah from all the nations where they had been scattered. ⁶They also led away all those whom Nebuzaradan commander of the imperial guard had left with Gedaliah son of Ahikam, the son of Shaphan—the men, the women, the children and the king's daughters. And they took Jeremiah the prophet and Baruch son of Neriah along with them. ⁷So they entered Egypt in disobedience to the LORD and went as far as Tahpanhes.   Jer 40:12; 44:1

⁸In Tahpanhes the word of the LORD came to Jeremiah: ⁹"While the Jews are watching, take some large stones with you and bury

---

[a] 18 That is, your name will be used in cursing (see 29:22); or, others will see that you are cursed.   [b] 3 Or *Chaldeans*

them in clay in the brick pavement at the entrance to Pharaoh's palace in Tahpanhes. ¹⁰Then say to them, 'This is what the LORD Almighty, the God of Israel, says: I will send for my servant Nebuchadnezzar king of Babylon, and I will set his throne over these stones I have buried here; he will spread his royal canopy above them. ¹¹He will come and attack Egypt, bringing death to those destined for death, captivity to those destined for captivity, and the sword to those destined for the sword. ¹²He will set fire to the temples of the gods of Egypt; he will burn their temples and take their gods captive. As a shepherd picks his garment clean of lice, so he will pick Egypt clean and depart. ¹³There in the temple of the sun*a* in Egypt he will demolish the sacred pillars and will burn down the temples of the gods of Egypt.'"   Jer 15:2; 44:13; 46:13-26

Disaster Because of Idolatry

44 This word came to Jeremiah concerning all the Jews living in Lower Egypt — in Migdol, Tahpanhes and Memphis — and in Upper Egypt: ²"This is what the LORD Almighty, the God of Israel, says: You saw the great disaster I brought on Jerusalem and on all the towns of Judah. Today they lie deserted and in ruins ³because of the evil they have done. They aroused my anger by burning incense to and worshiping other gods that neither they nor you nor your ancestors ever knew. ⁴Again and again I sent my servants the prophets, who said, 'Do not do this detestable thing that I hate!' ⁵But they did not listen or pay attention; they did not turn from their wickedness or stop burning incense to other gods. ⁶Therefore, my fierce anger was poured out; it raged against the towns of Judah and the streets of Jerusalem and made them the desolate ruins they are today.   Jer 7:25; 25:4; 26:5

⁷"Now this is what the LORD God Almighty, the God of Israel, says: Why bring such great disaster on yourselves by cutting off from Judah the men and women, the children and infants, and so leave yourselves without a remnant? ⁸Why arouse my anger with what your hands have made, burning incense to other gods in Egypt, where you have come to live? You will destroy yourselves and make yourselves a curse*b* and an object of reproach among all the nations on earth. ⁹Have you forgotten the wickedness committed by your ancestors and by the kings and queens of Judah and the wickedness committed by you and your wives in the land of Judah and the streets of Jerusalem? ¹⁰To

---

a 13 Or *in Heliopolis*   *b 8* That is, your name will be used in cursing (see 29:22); or, others will see that you are cursed; also in verse 12; similarly in verse 22.

this day they have not humbled themselves or shown reverence, nor have they followed my law and the decrees I set before you and your ancestors. 1Ki 9:6-9

¹¹ "Therefore this is what the LORD Almighty, the God of Israel, says: I am determined to bring disaster on you and to destroy all Judah. ¹²I will take away the remnant of Judah who were determined to go to Egypt to settle there. They will all perish in Egypt; they will fall by the sword or die from famine. From the least to the greatest, they will die by sword or famine. They will become a curse and an object of horror, a curse and an object of reproach. ¹³I will punish those who live in Egypt with the sword, famine and plague, as I punished Jerusalem. ¹⁴None of the remnant of Judah who have gone to live in Egypt will escape or survive to return to the land of Judah, to which they long to return and live; none will return except a few fugitives." Jer 21:10; 22:24-27

¹⁵Then all the men who knew that their wives were burning incense to other gods, along with all the women who were present — a large assembly — and all the people living in Lower and Upper Egypt, said to Jeremiah, ¹⁶"We will not listen to the message you have spoken to us in the name of the LORD! ¹⁷We will certainly do everything we said we would: We will burn incense to the Queen of Heaven and will pour out drink offerings to her just as we and our ancestors, our kings and our officials did in the towns of Judah and in the streets of Jerusalem. At that time we had plenty of food and were well off and suffered no harm. ¹⁸But ever since we stopped burning incense to the Queen of Heaven and pouring out drink offerings to her, we have had nothing and have been perishing by sword and famine." Dt 23:23; Jer 7:18

¹⁹The women added, "When we burned incense to the Queen of Heaven and poured out drink offerings to her, did not our husbands know that we were making cakes impressed with her image and pouring out drink offerings to her?" Jer 7:18

²⁰Then Jeremiah said to all the people, both men and women, who were answering him, ²¹"Did not the LORD remember and call to mind the incense burned in the towns of Judah and the streets of Jerusalem by you and your ancestors, your kings and your officials and the people of the land? ²²When the LORD could no longer endure your wicked actions and the detestable things you did, your land became a curse and a desolate waste without inhabitants, as it is today. ²³Because you have burned incense and have sinned against the LORD and have not obeyed him or followed his law or his decrees

or his stipulations, this disaster has come upon you, as you now see." 1Ki 9:9; Da 9:11-12; Jer 40:2

²⁴Then Jeremiah said to all the people, including the women, "Hear the word of the Lord, all you people of Judah in Egypt. ²⁵This is what the Lord Almighty, the God of Israel, says: You and your wives have done what you said you would do when you promised, 'We will certainly carry out the vows we made to burn incense and pour out drink offerings to the Queen of Heaven.' Jer 43:7

"Go ahead then, do what you promised! Keep your vows! ²⁶But hear the word of the Lord, all you Jews living in Egypt: 'I swear by my great name,' says the Lord, 'that no one from Judah living anywhere in Egypt will ever again invoke my name or swear, "As surely as the Sovereign Lord lives." ²⁷For I am watching over them for harm, not for good; the Jews in Egypt will perish by sword and famine until they are all destroyed. ²⁸Those who escape the sword and return to the land of Judah from Egypt will be very few. Then the whole remnant of Judah who came to live in Egypt will know whose word will stand—mine or theirs. Jer 31:28; Eze 20:39

²⁹ "'This will be the sign to you that I will punish you in this place,' declares the Lord, 'so that you will know that my threats of harm against you will surely stand.' ³⁰This is what the Lord says: 'I am going to deliver Pharaoh Hophra king of Egypt into the hands of his enemies who want to kill him, just as I gave Zedekiah king of Judah into the hands of Nebuchadnezzar king of Babylon, the enemy who wanted to kill him.'" Jer 39:5; 46:26

A Message to Baruch

45 When Baruch son of Neriah wrote on a scroll the words Jeremiah the prophet dictated in the fourth year of Jehoiakim son of Josiah king of Judah, Jeremiah said this to Baruch: ²"This is what the Lord, the God of Israel, says to you, Baruch: ³You said, 'Woe to me! The Lord has added sorrow to my pain; I am worn out with groaning and find no rest.' ⁴But the Lord has told me to say to you, 'This is what the Lord says: I will overthrow what I have built and uproot what I have planted, throughout the earth. ⁵Should you then seek great things for yourself? Do not seek them. For I will bring disaster on all people, declares the Lord, but wherever you go I will let you escape with your life.'" Jer 21:9; 36:4,18,32; 38:2; 39:18

A Message About Egypt

46 This is the word of the Lord that came to Jeremiah the prophet concerning the nations: Jer 25:15-38

²Concerning Egypt:

This is the message against the army of Pharaoh Necho king of Egypt, which was defeated at Carchemish on the Euphrates River by Nebuchadnezzar king of Babylon in the fourth year of Jehoiakim son of Josiah king of Judah: 2Ki 23:29; 2Ch 35:20

³ "Prepare your shields, both
    large and small, Isa 21:5
  and march out for battle!
⁴ Harness the horses,
    mount the steeds!
  Take your positions
    with helmets on!
  Polish your spears, Eze 21:9-11
    put on your armor! 1Sa 17:5,38
⁵ What do I see?
  They are terrified,
  they are retreating,
    their warriors are defeated.
  They flee in haste Jer 48:44
    without looking back,
    and there is terror on every
      side," Jer 49:29
  declares the LORD.
⁶ "The swift cannot flee Isa 30:16
    nor the strong escape.
  In the north by the River
    Euphrates
    they stumble and fall. Da 11:19

⁷ "Who is this that rises like the
    Nile,
  like rivers of surging
    waters?
⁸ Egypt rises like the Nile, Eze 29:3
    like rivers of surging waters.
  She says, 'I will rise and cover
    the earth;

  I will destroy cities and
    their people.' Da 11:10
⁹ Charge, you horses!
  Drive furiously, you
    charioteers! Jer 47:3
  March on, you warriors —
    men of Cush[a] and Put
    who carry shields,
    men of Lydia who draw the
      bow. Isa 66:19
¹⁰ But that day belongs to the Lord,
    the LORD Almighty —
  a day of vengeance, for
    vengeance on his foes.
  The sword will devour till it is
    satisfied, Dt 32:42
    till it has quenched its thirst
      with blood. Dt 32:42
  For the Lord, the LORD
    Almighty, will offer
    sacrifice Zep 1:7
  in the land of the north by
    the River Euphrates.

¹¹ "Go up to Gilead and get balm,
  Virgin Daughter Egypt.
  But you try many medicines
    in vain;
    there is no healing for you.
¹² The nations will hear of your
    shame;
    your cries will fill the earth.
  One warrior will stumble over
    another;
    both will fall down together."

¹³ This is the message the LORD spoke to Jeremiah the prophet about the coming of Nebuchadnezzar king of Babylon to attack Egypt: Isa 19:1

ᵃ 9 That is, the upper Nile region

¹⁴ "Announce this in Egypt, and
          proclaim it in Migdol;
    proclaim it also in Memphis
          and Tahpanhes: Jer 43:8
    'Take your positions and get
          ready,
    for the sword devours those
          around you.' Jer 24:8
¹⁵ Why will your warriors be laid
          low?
    They cannot stand, for the
          LORD will push them
          down. Isa 66:15-16
¹⁶ They will stumble repeatedly;
    they will fall over each other.
    They will say, 'Get up, let us
          go back
    to our own people and our
          native lands, Isa 13:14
    away from the sword of the
          oppressor.' Jer 25:38
¹⁷ There they will exclaim,
    'Pharaoh king of Egypt is
          only a loud noise; 1Ki 20:10
    he has missed his
          opportunity.' Isa 19:11-16

¹⁸ "As surely as I live," declares
          the King, Jer 48:15
    whose name is the LORD
          Almighty,
    "one will come who is like
          Tabor among the
          mountains, Jos 19:22
    like Carmel by the sea.
¹⁹ Pack your belongings for exile,
    you who live in Egypt,
    for Memphis will be laid
          waste Eze 29:10,12
    and lie in ruins without
          inhabitant.

²⁰ "Egypt is a beautiful heifer,
    but a gadfly is coming
          against her from the north.
²¹ The mercenaries in her ranks
    are like fattened calves.
    They too will turn and flee
          together,
    they will not stand their
          ground,
    for the day of disaster is
          coming upon them,
    the time for them to be
          punished. Job 18:20
²² Egypt will hiss like a fleeing
          serpent
    as the enemy advances in
          force;
    they will come against her
          with axes,
    like men who cut down trees.
²³ They will chop down her
          forest,"
          declares the LORD,
    "dense though it be.
    They are more numerous
          than locusts, Jdg 7:12
    they cannot be counted.
²⁴ Daughter Egypt will be put to
          shame,
    given into the hands of the
          people of the north."

²⁵ The LORD Almighty, the God
of Israel, says: "I am about to
bring punishment on Amon god
of Thebes, on Pharaoh, on Egypt
and her gods and her kings,
and on those who rely on Pharaoh. ²⁶ I will give them into the
hands of those who want to kill
them — Nebuchadnezzar king of

Babylon and his officers. Later, however, Egypt will be inhabited as in times past," declares the LORD.   Eze 29:11-16; 32:11

27 "Do not be afraid, Jacob my
        servant;   Isa 41:13; 43:5
    do not be dismayed, Israel.
I will surely save you out of a
        distant place,
    your descendants from the
        land of their exile. Isa 11:11
Jacob will again have peace
        and security,
    and no one will make him
        afraid.
28 Do not be afraid, Jacob my
        servant,
    for I am with you," declares
        the LORD.   Isa 8:9-10
"Though I completely destroy
        all the nations   Jer 4:27
    among which I scatter you,
I will not completely destroy
        you.
I will discipline you but only
        in due measure;
    I will not let you go entirely
        unpunished."

A Message About the Philistines

47 This is the word of the
    LORD that came to Jeremiah the prophet concerning the Philistines before Pharaoh attacked Gaza: Am 1:6; Zec 9:5-7

2 This is what the LORD says:

"See how the waters are rising
        in the north;   Isa 8:7; 14:31

    they will become an
        overflowing torrent.
They will overflow the land
        and everything in it,
    the towns and those who
        live in them.
The people will cry out;
    all who dwell in the land
        will wail   Isa 15:3
3 at the sound of the hooves of
        galloping steeds,
    at the noise of enemy chariots
        and the rumble of their
        wheels.
Parents will not turn to help
        their children;
    their hands will hang limp.
4 For the day has come
    to destroy all the Philistines
and to remove all survivors
    who could help Tyre and
        Sidon.   Am 1:9-10; Zec 9:2-4
The LORD is about to destroy
        the Philistines,   Ge 10:14
    the remnant from the
        coasts of Caphtor.ᵃ
5 Gaza will shave her head in
        mourning;   Jer 41:5; Mic 1:16
    Ashkelon will be silenced.
You remnant on the plain,
    how long will you cut
        yourselves?

6 " 'Alas, sword of the LORD,
    how long till you rest?
Return to your sheath;
    cease and be still.'   Eze 21:30
7 But how can it rest
    when the LORD has
        commanded it,

ᵃ 4 That is, Crete

when he has ordered it
  to attack Ashkelon and the
  coast?"   *Eze 25:15-17*

A Message About Moab
48:29-36pp — Isa 16:6-12

48   Concerning Moab: *Ge 19:37*

This is what the LORD Al-
mighty, the God of Israel, says:

"Woe to Nebo, for it will be
  ruined.   *Nu 32:38*
  Kiriathaim will be
    disgraced and
    captured;   *Nu 32:37*
  the stronghold*a* will be
    disgraced and shattered.
2 Moab will be praised no more;
  in Heshbon*b* people will
    plot her downfall:
  'Come, let us put an end to
    that nation.'
  You, the people of Madmen,*c*
    will also be silenced;
  the sword will pursue you.
3 Cries of anguish arise from
  Horonaim,   *Isa 15:5*
  cries of great havoc and
    destruction.
4 Moab will be broken;
  her little ones will cry out.*d*
5 They go up the hill to Luhith,
  weeping bitterly as they go;
  on the road down to
    Horonaim
  anguished cries over the
    destruction are heard.

6 Flee! Run for your lives;
  become like a bush*e* in the
    desert.   *Jer 17:6*
7 Since you trust in your deeds
  and riches,   *Ps 49:6*
  you too will be taken
    captive,
  and Chemosh will go into
    exile,   *Nu 21:29; Isa 46:1-2*
  together with his priests
    and officials.   *Am 2:3*
8 The destroyer will come
    against every town,
  and not a town will escape.
  The valley will be ruined
  and the plateau destroyed,
    because the LORD has
    spoken.
9 Put salt on Moab,   *Jdg 9:45*
  for she will be laid waste*f*;
  her towns will become
    desolate,
  with no one to live in them.

10 "A curse on anyone who is lax
  in doing the LORD's work!
  A curse on anyone who
    keeps their sword from
    bloodshed!   *1Ki 20:42*

11 "Moab has been at rest from
  youth,   *Zec 1:15*
  like wine left on its dregs,
  not poured from one jar to
    another —
  she has not gone into exile.
  So she tastes as she did,
  and her aroma is unchanged.

---

a 1 Or *captured; / Misgab*   *b 2* The Hebrew for *Heshbon* sounds like the Hebrew for *plot.*
c 2 The name of the Moabite town Madmen sounds like the Hebrew for *be silenced.*
d 4 Hebrew; Septuagint / *proclaim it to Zoar*   *e 6* Or *like Aroer*   *f 9* Or *Give wings to Moab, / for she will fly away*

¹²But days are coming,"
    declares the LORD,
  "when I will send men who
    pour from pitchers,
  and they will pour her out;
  they will empty her pitchers
    and smash her jars.
¹³Then Moab will be ashamed
    of Chemosh,   Hos 10:6
  as Israel was ashamed
    when they trusted in Bethel.

¹⁴"How can you say, 'We are
    warriors,   Ps 33:16
  men valiant in battle'?
¹⁵Moab will be destroyed and
    her towns invaded;
  her finest young men will go
    down in the slaughter,"
    declares the King, whose
      name is the LORD
      Almighty.   Jer 46:18; 51:57
¹⁶"The fall of Moab is at hand;
  her calamity will come
    quickly.
¹⁷Mourn for her, all who live
    around her,
  all who know her fame;
  say, 'How broken is the
    mighty scepter, Ps 110:2
  how broken the glorious
    staff!'
¹⁸"Come down from your glory
  and sit on the parched
    ground,   Isa 47:1
  you inhabitants of Daughter
    Dibon,   Nu 21:30; Jos 13:9
  for the one who destroys
    Moab
  will come up against you

  and ruin your fortified
    cities.
¹⁹Stand by the road and watch,
  you who live in Aroer. Dt 2:36
Ask the man fleeing and the
    woman escaping,
  ask them, 'What has
    happened?'
²⁰Moab is disgraced, for she is
    shattered.
  Wail and cry out!   Isa 16:7
Announce by the Arnon Nu 21:13
  that Moab is destroyed.
²¹Judgment has come to the
    plateau —
  to Holon, Jahzah and
    Mephaath,   Nu 21:23
²² to Dibon, Nebo and Beth
      Diblathaim,   Jos 13:9,17
²³ to Kiriathaim, Beth Gamul
      and Beth Meon,   Jos 13:17
²⁴ to Kerioth and Bozrah —
  to all the towns of Moab, far
      and near.   Isa 15:1
²⁵Moab's hornᵃ is cut off;   Ps 75:10
  her arm is broken,"   Ps 10:15
      declares the LORD.

²⁶"Make her drunk,   Jer 25:16,27
  for she has defied the LORD.
Let Moab wallow in her vomit;
  let her be an object of
    ridicule.
²⁷Was not Israel the object of
    your ridicule?   Jer 2:26
Was she caught among
    thieves,   2Ki 17:3-6
  that you shake your head in
    scorn   Jer 18:16; Mic 7:8-10
  whenever you speak of her?

ᵃ 25 Horn here symbolizes strength.

28 Abandon your towns and
 dwell among the rocks,
you who live in Moab.
Be like a dove that makes its
 nest   Ps 55:6-7
 at the mouth of a cave.   Jdg 6:2

29 "We have heard of Moab's
 pride —   Isa 16:6
 how great is her
 arrogance! —
of her insolence, her pride, her
 conceit
 and the haughtiness of her
 heart.   Pr 16:18
30 I know her insolence but it is
 futile,"
  declares the LORD,
 "and her boasts accomplish
 nothing.   Ps 10:3
31 Therefore I wail over Moab,
 for all Moab I cry out,
 I moan for the people of Kir
 Haresheth.   2Ki 3:25
32 I weep for you, as Jazer weeps,
 you vines of Sibmah.   Isa 16:8-9
Your branches spread as far as
 the sea[a];
 they reached as far as[b] Jazer.
The destroyer has fallen
 on your ripened fruit and
 grapes.
33 Joy and gladness are gone
 from the orchards and
 fields of Moab.
I have stopped the flow of
 wine from the presses;
 no one treads them with
 shouts of joy.   Joel 1:12

Although there are shouts,
 they are not shouts of joy.

34 "The sound of their cry rises
 from Heshbon to Elealeh
 and Jahaz,   Isa 15:4
 from Zoar as far as Horonaim
 and Eglath Shelishiyah,
 for even the waters of
 Nimrim are dried up.
35 In Moab I will put an end
 to those who make offerings
 on the high places   Isa 15:2
 and burn incense to their
 gods,"   Jer 11:13
  declares the LORD.
36 "So my heart laments for Moab
 like the music of a pipe;
 it laments like a pipe for the
 people of Kir Haresheth.
The wealth they acquired is
 gone.   Isa 16:6-12
37 Every head is shaved   Isa 15:2
 and every beard cut off;
 every hand is slashed
 and every waist is covered
 with sackcloth.   Ge 37:34
38 On all the roofs in Moab
 and in the public squares
 there is nothing but mourning,
 for I have broken Moab
 like a jar that no one wants,"
  declares the LORD.
39 "How shattered she is! How
 they wail!
How Moab turns her back
 in shame!
Moab has become an object of
 ridicule,

---

[a] 32 Probably the Dead Sea   [b] 32 Two Hebrew manuscripts and Septuagint; most Hebrew
manuscripts *as far as the Sea of*

an object of horror to all
those around her."

⁴⁰This is what the LORD says:

"Look! An eagle is swooping
down,   Dt 28:49; Hab 1:8
spreading its wings over
Moab.   Isa 8:8
⁴¹Kerioth*a* will be captured Isa 15:1
and the strongholds taken.
In that day the hearts of
Moab's warriors
will be like the heart of a
woman in labor.   Isa 21:3
⁴²Moab will be destroyed as a
nation   Ps 83:4; Isa 16:14
because she defied the
LORD.   ver 26
⁴³Terror and pit and snare await
you,   Isa 24:17
you people of Moab,"
declares the LORD.
⁴⁴"Whoever flees from the terror
will fall into a pit,
whoever climbs out of the pit
will be caught in a snare;
for I will bring on Moab
the year of her punishment,"
declares the LORD.

⁴⁵"In the shadow of Heshbon
the fugitives stand helpless,
for a fire has gone out from
Heshbon,
a blaze from the midst of
Sihon;   Nu 21:21,26-28
it burns the foreheads of Moab,
the skulls of the noisy
boasters.   Nu 24:17
⁴⁶Woe to you, Moab!   Nu 21:29

The people of Chemosh are
destroyed;
your sons are taken into exile
and your daughters into
captivity.

⁴⁷"Yet I will restore the fortunes
of Moab   Jer 49:6,39
in days to come,"
declares the LORD.

Here ends the judgment on
Moab.

A Message About Ammon

49 Concerning the Ammon-
ites: Am 1:13; Zep 2:8-9

This is what the LORD says:

"Has Israel no sons?
Has Israel no heir?
Why then has Molek*b* taken
possession of Gad?
Why do his people live in its
towns?
²But the days are coming,"
declares the LORD,
"when I will sound the battle
cry   Jer 4:19
against Rabbah of the
Ammonites;   Dt 3:11
it will become a mound of
ruins,   Dt 13:16
and its surrounding villages
will be set on fire.
Then Israel will drive out
those who drove her out,"
says the LORD.
³"Wail, Heshbon, for Ai is
destroyed!   Jos 8:28

---

a 41 Or *The cities*   *b* 1 Or *their king*; also in verse 3

Cry out, you inhabitants of
Rabbah!
Put on sackcloth and mourn;
rush here and there inside
the walls,
for Molek will go into exile,
together with his priests
and officials.
⁴Why do you boast of your
valleys,
boast of your valleys so
fruitful?
Unfaithful Daughter Ammon,
you trust in your riches and
say,   Jer 9:23; 1Ti 6:17
'Who will attack me?'   Jer 21:13
⁵I will bring terror on you
from all those around
you,"
declares the Lord,
the LORD Almighty.
"Every one of you will be
driven away,
and no one will gather the
fugitives.

⁶"Yet afterward, I will restore
the fortunes of the
Ammonites,"   ver 39
declares the LORD.

A Message About Edom
49:9-10pp — Ob 5-6
49:14-16pp — Ob 1-4

⁷Concerning Edom: Eze 25:12

This is what the LORD Al-
mighty says:

"Is there no longer wisdom in
Teman?   Ge 36:11,15,34

Has counsel perished from
the prudent?
Has their wisdom decayed?
⁸Turn and flee, hide in deep
caves,
you who live in Dedan,
for I will bring disaster on Esau
at the time when I punish
him.
⁹If grape pickers came to you,
would they not leave a few
grapes?
If thieves came during the
night,
would they not steal only as
much as they wanted?
¹⁰But I will strip Esau bare;
I will uncover his hiding
places,
so that he cannot conceal
himself.
His armed men are destroyed,
also his allies and
neighbors,
so there is no one to say,
¹¹'Leave your fatherless
children; I will keep
them alive.   Hos 14:3
Your widows too can
depend on me.' "   Dt 10:18

¹²This is what the LORD says:
"If those who do not deserve to
drink the cup must drink it, why
should you go unpunished? You
will not go unpunished, but must
drink it. ¹³I swear by myself," declares the LORD, "that Bozrah
will become a ruin and a curse,ᵃ
an object of horror and reproach;

ᵃ 13 That is, its name will be used in cursing (see 29:22); or, others will see that it is cursed.

and all its towns will be in ruins
forever." Isa 34:6; Jer 25:28-29

[14] I have heard a message from
the LORD;
an envoy was sent to the
nations to say,
"Assemble yourselves to
attack it!
Rise up for battle!"

[15] "Now I will make you small
among the nations,
despised by mankind.
[16] The terror you inspire
and the pride of your heart
have deceived you,
you who live in the clefts of
the rocks,
who occupy the heights of
the hill.
Though you build your nest as
high as the eagle's,
from there I will bring you
down,"
declares the LORD.
[17] "Edom will become an object
of horror;
all who pass by will be
appalled and will scoff
because of all its wounds.
[18] As Sodom and Gomorrah
were overthrown,
along with their
neighboring towns,"
says the LORD,
"so no one will live there;
no people will dwell in it.
[19] "Like a lion coming up from
Jordan's thickets Jer 12:5

to a rich pastureland,
I will chase Edom from its
land in an instant.
Who is the chosen one I will
appoint for this?
Who is like me and who can
challenge me? Jer 50:44
And what shepherd can
stand against me?"

[20] Therefore, hear what the
LORD has planned
against Edom, Isa 34:5
what he has purposed
against those who live
in Teman: Isa 14:27
The young of the flock will be
dragged away; Jer 50:45
their pasture will be
appalled at their fate.
[21] At the sound of their fall the
earth will tremble;
their cry will resound to the
Red Sea.[a] Jer 50:46; Eze 26:18
[22] Look! An eagle will soar and
swoop down, Hos 8:1
spreading its wings over
Bozrah. Ge 36:33
In that day the hearts of
Edom's warriors Jer 50:36
will be like the heart of a
woman in labor. Isa 13:8

A Message About Damascus

[23] Concerning Damascus:

"Hamath and Arpad are
dismayed, Isa 10:9
for they have heard bad
news.
They are disheartened,

[a] 21 Or the Sea of Reeds

troubled like*a* the restless
    sea.   Isa 57:20
²⁴Damascus has become feeble,
  she has turned to flee
  and panic has gripped her;
anguish and pain have seized
    her,
  pain like that of a woman in
    labor.
²⁵Why has the city of renown
    not been abandoned,
  the town in which I delight?
²⁶Surely, her young men will fall
    in the streets;
  all her soldiers will be
    silenced in that day,"
      declares the LORD
      Almighty.
²⁷"I will set fire to the walls of
    Damascus;   Am 1:4
  it will consume the
    fortresses of Ben-Hadad."

A Message About Kedar and Hazor

²⁸Concerning Kedar and the kingdoms of Hazor, which Nebuchadnezzar king of Babylon attacked: Ge 25:13

This is what the LORD says:

"Arise, and attack Kedar
  and destroy the people of
    the East.   Jdg 6:3
²⁹Their tents and their flocks
    will be taken;
  their shelters will be carried
    off
  with all their goods and
    camels.

People will shout to them,
  'Terror on every side!'   Jer 6:25

³⁰"Flee quickly away!
  Stay in deep caves, you who
    live in Hazor,"   Jdg 6:2
      declares the LORD.
"Nebuchadnezzar king of
    Babylon has plotted
    against you;   Jer 10:22
  he has devised a plan
    against you.

³¹"Arise and attack a nation at
    ease,
  which lives in confidence,"
      declares the LORD,
"a nation that has neither
    gates nor bars;   Eze 38:11
  its people live far from danger.
³²Their camels will become
    plunder,   Jdg 6:5
  and their large herds will be
    spoils of war.
I will scatter to the winds
  those who are in distant
    places*b*   Jer 9:26
  and will bring disaster on
    them from every side,"
      declares the LORD.
³³"Hazor will become a haunt of
    jackals,   Isa 13:22
  a desolate place forever.
No one will live there;
  no people will dwell in it."

A Message About Elam

³⁴This is the word of the LORD that came to Jeremiah the prophet concerning Elam, early in the reign of Zedekiah king of Judah:

a 23 Hebrew *on* or *by*   *b 32* Or *who clip the hair by their foreheads*

³⁵This is what the LORD Almighty says:

"See, I will break the bow of
    Elam,   Isa 22:6
  the mainstay of their might.
³⁶I will bring against Elam the
    four winds   ver 32
  from the four quarters of
    heaven;   Da 11:4
I will scatter them to the four
    winds,
  and there will not be a nation
  where Elam's exiles do
    not go.
³⁷I will shatter Elam before
    their foes,
  before those who want to
    kill them;
I will bring disaster on them,
  even my fierce anger,"
            declares the LORD.
"I will pursue them with the
    sword   Jer 9:16
  until I have made an end of
    them.
³⁸I will set my throne in Elam
  and destroy her king and
    officials,"
            declares the LORD.
³⁹"Yet I will restore the fortunes
    of Elam   Jer 48:47
  in days to come,"
            declares the LORD.

A Message About Babylon
51:15-19pp — Jer 10:12-16

50 This is the word the LORD
spoke through Jeremiah
the prophet concerning Babylon

and the land of the Babylonians[a]:
            Ge 10:10; Isa 13:1

²"Announce and proclaim
    among the nations,
  lift up a banner and
    proclaim it;   Ps 20:5
  keep nothing back, but say,
'Babylon will be captured;
  Bel will be put to shame,
  Marduk filled with terror.
Her images will be put to
    shame
  and her idols filled with
    terror.'   Lev 26:30
³A nation from the north will
    attack her   Isa 41:25
  and lay waste her land.
No one will live in it;   Isa 14:22-23
  both people and animals
    will flee away.   Zep 1:3

⁴"In those days, at that time,"
    declares the LORD,
  "the people of Israel and
    the people of Judah
      together   Hos 1:11
  will go in tears to seek the
    LORD their God.   Ezr 3:12
⁵They will ask the way to Zion
  and turn their faces
    toward it.
They will come and bind
    themselves to the LORD
  in an everlasting covenant
    that will not be forgotten.

⁶"My people have been lost
    sheep;   Isa 53:6; Mt 9:36; 10:6
  their shepherds have led
    them astray   Jer 23:32

ᵃ 1 Or *Chaldeans*; also in verses 8, 25, 35 and 45

and caused them to roam
on the mountains.
They wandered over
mountain and hill   Jer 3:6
and forgot their own resting
place.
⁷ Whoever found them
devoured them;
their enemies said, 'We are
not guilty,   Jer 2:3
for they sinned against the
LORD, their verdant
pasture,
the LORD, the hope of their
ancestors.'   Jer 14:8

⁸ "Flee out of Babylon;   Isa 48:20
leave the land of the
Babylonians,
and be like the goats that
lead the flock.
⁹ For I will stir up and bring
against Babylon   Isa 13:17
an alliance of great nations
from the land of the
north.   Isa 41:25; Jer 25:26
They will take up their
positions against her,
and from the north she will
be captured.
Their arrows will be like
skilled warriors   Isa 13:18
who do not return empty-
handed.
¹⁰ So Babylonia^a will be
plundered;   Jer 30:16
all who plunder her will
have their fill,"
declares the LORD.

¹¹ "Because you rejoice and are
glad,

you who pillage my
inheritance,   Isa 47:6
because you frolic like a heifer
threshing grain   Jer 31:18
and neigh like stallions,
¹² your mother will be greatly
ashamed;
she who gave you birth will
be disgraced.
She will be the least of the
nations —
a wilderness, a dry land, a
desert.   Isa 21:1; Jer 25:12
¹³ Because of the LORD's
anger she will not be
inhabited
but will be completely
desolate.   Jer 9:11
All who pass Babylon will be
appalled;
they will scoff because of all
her wounds.   Jer 18:16; 49:17

¹⁴ "Take up your positions
around Babylon,
all you who draw the bow.
Shoot at her! Spare no arrows,
for she has sinned against
the LORD.
¹⁵ Shout against her on every
side!   Jer 51:14
She surrenders, her towers
fall,
her walls are torn down.
Since this is the vengeance of
the LORD,   Jer 51:6
take vengeance on her;
do to her as she has done to
others.   Ps 137:8; Rev 18:6
¹⁶ Cut off from Babylon the sower,

^a 10 Or Chaldea

and the reaper with his
sickle at harvest.
Because of the sword of the
oppressor   Jer 25:38
let everyone return to their
own people,   Isa 13:14
let everyone flee to their
own land.   Jer 51:9

¹⁷ "Israel is a scattered flock
that lions have chased
away.   Jer 2:15
The first to devour them
was the king of Assyria;
the last to crush their bones
was Nebuchadnezzar king
of Babylon."   2Ki 24:10,14

¹⁸ Therefore this is what the
LORD Almighty, the God of Israel, says:

"I will punish the king of
Babylon and his land
as I punished the king of
Assyria.   Isa 10:12; Eze 31:3
¹⁹ But I will bring Israel back to
their own pasture,
and they will graze on
Carmel and Bashan;
their appetite will be satisfied
on the hills of Ephraim and
Gilead.   Jer 10:12-16; 33:12
²⁰ In those days, at that time,"
declares the LORD,
"search will be made for
Israel's guilt,
but there will be none,
and for the sins of Judah,
but none will be found,

for I will forgive the
remnant I spare.   Isa 1:9

²¹ "Attack the land of Merathaim
and those who live in
Pekod.   Eze 23:23
Pursue, kill and completely
destroy^a them,"
declares the LORD.
"Do everything I have
commanded you.
²² The noise of battle is in the
land,   Jer 4:19-21; 51:54
the noise of great
destruction!
²³ How broken and shattered
is the hammer of the whole
earth!   Isa 10:5
How desolate is Babylon Isa 14:16
among the nations!
²⁴ I set a trap for you, Babylon,
and you were caught before
you knew it;
you were found and captured
because you opposed the
LORD.   Job 9:4
²⁵ The LORD has opened his
arsenal
and brought out the
weapons of his wrath,
for the Sovereign LORD
Almighty has work to do
in the land of the
Babylonians.   Jer 51:25,55
²⁶ Come against her from afar.
Break open her granaries;
pile her up like heaps of
grain.
Completely destroy her

---

^a 21 The Hebrew term refers to the irrevocable giving over of things or persons to the LORD, often by totally destroying them; also in verse 26.

and leave her no remnant.
²⁷Kill all her young bulls; Ps 68:30
let them go down to the
slaughter! Isa 30:25
Woe to them! For their day
has come, Job 18:20
the time for them to be
punished. Jer 51:6
²⁸Listen to the fugitives and
refugees from Babylon
declaring in Zion Isa 48:20
how the LORD our God has
taken vengeance, ver 15
vengeance for his temple.

²⁹"Summon archers against
Babylon,
all those who draw the bow.
Encamp all around her;
let no one escape. Isa 13:18
Repay her for her deeds; Jer 51:56
do to her as she has done.
For she has defied the LORD,
the Holy One of Israel. Ps 78:41
³⁰Therefore, her young men will
fall in the streets; Isa 13:18
all her soldiers will be
silenced in that day,"
declares the LORD.
³¹"See, I am against you, you
arrogant one," Jer 21:13
declares the Lord, the LORD
Almighty,
"for your day has come,
the time for you to be
punished.
³²The arrogant one will stumble
and fall Ps 119:21
and no one will help her up;
I will kindle a fire in her
towns Jer 21:14; 49:27

that will consume all who
are around her."

³³This is what the LORD Almighty says:

"The people of Israel are
oppressed, Isa 58:6
and the people of Judah as
well.
All their captors hold them
fast,
refusing to let them go. Isa 14:17
³⁴Yet their Redeemer is strong;
the LORD Almighty is his
name. Jer 51:19
He will vigorously defend
their cause Jer 15:21; 51:36
so that he may bring rest to
their land, Isa 14:7
but unrest to those who live
in Babylon.

³⁵"A sword against the
Babylonians!" Jer 47:6
declares the LORD —
"against those who live in
Babylon
and against her officials
and wise men! Da 5:7
³⁶A sword against her false
prophets!
They will become fools.
A sword against her warriors!
They will be filled with
terror.
³⁷A sword against her horses
and chariots Jer 51:21
and all the foreigners in her
ranks!
They will become
weaklings. Jer 51:30; Na 3:13

A sword against her treasures!
They will be plundered.
³⁸ A drought on*ᵃ* her waters!
They will dry up.   Ps 137:1
For it is a land of idols,   Jer 51:36
idols that will go mad with
terror.

³⁹ "So desert creatures and
hyenas will live there,
and there the owl will
dwell.
It will never again be
inhabited
or lived in from generation
to generation.   Isa 13:19-22
⁴⁰ As I overthrew Sodom and
Gomorrah   Ge 19:24
along with their
neighboring towns,"
declares the LORD,
"so no one will live there;
no people will dwell in it.

⁴¹ "Look! An army is coming
from the north;   Jer 6:22
a great nation and many
kings
are being stirred up from
the ends of the earth.
⁴² They are armed with bows
and spears;
they are cruel and without
mercy.   Isa 13:18
They sound like the roaring
sea   Isa 5:30
as they ride on their horses;
they come like men in battle
formation
to attack you, Daughter
Babylon.   Jer 6:23

⁴³ The king of Babylon has heard
reports about them,
and his hands hang limp.
Anguish has gripped him,
pain like that of a woman in
labor.   Jer 6:22-24
⁴⁴ Like a lion coming up from
Jordan's thickets
to a rich pastureland,
I will chase Babylon from its
land in an instant.
Who is the chosen one I will
appoint for this?   Nu 16:5
Who is like me and who can
challenge me?   Job 41:10
And what shepherd can
stand against me?"

⁴⁵ Therefore, hear what the
LORD has planned
against Babylon,
what he has purposed
against the land of the
Babylonians: Isa 14:24
The young of the flock will be
dragged away;
their pasture will be
appalled at their fate.
⁴⁶ At the sound of Babylon's
capture the earth will
tremble;   Jer 49:21
its cry will resound among
the nations.   Rev 18:9-10

51 This is what the LORD
says:

"See, I will stir up the spirit of
a destroyer   Isa 13:17
against Babylon and the
people of Leb Kamai.*ᵇ*

ᵃ 38 Or *A sword against*   *ᵇ 1 Leb Kamai* is a cryptogram for Chaldea, that is, Babylonia.

² I will send foreigners to Babylon
to winnow her and to devastate her land; Jer 15:7
they will oppose her on every side
in the day of her disaster.
³ Let not the archer string his bow, Jer 50:29
nor let him put on his armor. Jer 46:4
Do not spare her young men;
completely destroy^a her army.
⁴ They will fall down slain in Babylon,^b Isa 13:15
fatally wounded in her streets. Jer 49:26; 50:30
⁵ For Israel and Judah have not been forsaken Isa 54:6-8
by their God, the LORD Almighty,
though their land^c is full of guilt Hos 4:1
before the Holy One of Israel.

⁶ "Flee from Babylon! Jer 50:8
Run for your lives!
Do not be destroyed because of her sins.
It is time for the LORD's vengeance; Jer 50:15
he will repay her what she deserves. Jer 25:14
⁷ Babylon was a gold cup in the LORD's hand; Jer 25:15-16
she made the whole earth drunk.

The nations drank her wine;
therefore they have now gone mad.
⁸ Babylon will suddenly fall and be broken. Isa 21:9; Rev 14:8
Wail over her!
Get balm for her pain; Jer 46:11
perhaps she can be healed.

⁹ " 'We would have healed Babylon,
but she cannot be healed;
let us leave her and each go to our own land, Isa 13:14
for her judgment reaches to the skies, Rev 18:4-5
it rises as high as the heavens.'

¹⁰ " 'The LORD has vindicated us;
come, let us tell in Zion
what the LORD our God has done.' Jer 50:28

¹¹ "Sharpen the arrows, Jer 50:9
take up the shields! Jer 46:4
The LORD has stirred up the kings of the Medes, Isa 41:2
because his purpose is to destroy Babylon. Jer 50:45
The LORD will take vengeance,
vengeance for his temple.
¹² Lift up a banner against the walls of Babylon! Ps 20:5
Reinforce the guard,
station the watchmen, 2Sa 18:24
prepare an ambush! Jer 50:24
The LORD will carry out his purpose, Ps 33:11

---

^a 3 The Hebrew term refers to the irrevocable giving over of things or persons to the LORD, often by totally destroying them. ^b 4 Or *Chaldea* ^c 5 Or *Almighty, / and the land of the Babylonians*

his decree against the
people of Babylon.
¹³You who live by many waters
and are rich in treasures,
your end has come,
the time for you to be
destroyed. Jer 50:3
¹⁴The LORD Almighty has
sworn by himself: Am 6:8
I will surely fill you with
troops, as with a swarm
of locusts, Na 3:15
and they will shout in
triumph over you. Jer 50:15

¹⁵"He made the earth by his
power;
he founded the world by his
wisdom
and stretched out the
heavens by his
understanding. Ge 1:1
¹⁶When he thunders, the waters
in the heavens roar;
he makes clouds rise from
the ends of the earth.
He sends lightning with the
rain
and brings out the wind
from his storehouses.

¹⁷"Everyone is senseless and
without knowledge;
every goldsmith is shamed
by his idols.
The images he makes are a
fraud; Isa 44:20; Hab 2:18-19
they have no breath in
them.
¹⁸They are worthless, the
objects of mockery;

when their judgment
comes, they will perish.
¹⁹He who is the Portion of Jacob
is not like these, Ps 119:57
for he is the Maker of all
things,
including the people of his
inheritance — Ex 34:9
the LORD Almighty is his
name.

²⁰"You are my war club, Isa 10:5
my weapon for battle —
with you I shatter nations,
with you I destroy
kingdoms,
²¹with you I shatter horse and
rider, Ex 15:1
with you I shatter chariot
and driver, Jer 50:37
²²with you I shatter man and
woman,
with you I shatter old man
and youth,
with you I shatter young
man and young woman,
²³with you I shatter shepherd
and flock,
with you I shatter farmer
and oxen,
with you I shatter governors
and officials.

²⁴"Before your eyes I will repay Babylon and all who live in
Babylonia*a* for all the wrong they
have done in Zion," declares the
LORD. Jer 50:15

²⁵"I am against you, you
destroying mountain,

a 24 Or *Chaldea*; also in verse 35

you who destroy the whole
earth,"
      declares the LORD.
"I will stretch out my hand
    against you,
roll you off the cliffs,
and make you a burned-out
    mountain.   Zec 4:7
26 No rock will be taken from
    you for a cornerstone,
nor any stone for a
    foundation,
for you will be desolate
    forever,"
      declares the LORD.

27 "Lift up a banner in the land!
Blow the trumpet among
    the nations!
Prepare the nations for battle
    against her;
summon against her these
    kingdoms: Jer 25:14
Ararat, Minni and
    Ashkenaz.   Ge 8:4; 10:3
Appoint a commander against
    her;
send up horses like a swarm
    of locusts.
28 Prepare the nations for battle
    against her —
the kings of the Medes,   ver 11
their governors and all their
    officials,
and all the countries they
    rule.
29 The land trembles and
    writhes,   Jer 49:21
for the LORD's purposes
    against Babylon stand —
to lay waste the land of Babylon

so that no one will live there.
30 Babylon's warriors have
    stopped fighting;   Jer 50:36
they remain in their
    strongholds.
Their strength is exhausted;
    they have become weaklings.
Her dwellings are set on fire;
    the bars of her gates are
    broken.   La 2:9; Na 3:13
31 One courier follows another
    and messenger follows
    messenger
to announce to the king of
    Babylon
that his entire city is
    captured,   Jer 50:2
32 the river crossings seized,
    the marshes set on fire,
    and the soldiers terrified."

33 This is what the LORD Almighty, the God of Israel, says:

"Daughter Babylon is like a
    threshing floor   Isa 21:10
at the time it is trampled;
the time to harvest her will
    soon come."   Isa 17:5

34 "Nebuchadnezzar king of
    Babylon has devoured us,
he has thrown us into
    confusion,
he has made us an empty
    jar.
Like a serpent he has
    swallowed us
and filled his stomach with
    our delicacies,
and then has spewed us
    out.   Lev 18:25

35 May the violence done to our
    flesh[a] be on Babylon,"
  say the inhabitants of Zion.
"May our blood be on those
    who live in Babylonia,"
  says Jerusalem.   Ps 137:8

36 Therefore this is what the
  LORD says:

"See, I will defend your cause
    and avenge you;   Ro 12:19
I will dry up her sea   Jer 50:38
  and make her springs dry.
37 Babylon will be a heap of
    ruins,
  a haunt of jackals,   Isa 13:22
an object of horror and scorn,
  a place where no one lives.
38 Her people all roar like young
    lions,
  they growl like lion cubs.
39 But while they are aroused,
  I will set out a feast for them
    and make them drunk, Isa 21:5
so that they shout with
    laughter—
  then sleep forever and not
    awake,"   Ps 13:3
          declares the LORD.
40 "I will bring them down
  like lambs to the slaughter,
  like rams and goats.   Eze 39:18

41 "How Sheshak[b] will be
    captured,   Isa 13:19; Jer 25:26
  the boast of the whole earth
    seized!
How desolate Babylon will be
  among the nations!
42 The sea will rise over Babylon;

  its roaring waves will cover
    her.   Isa 8:7
43 Her towns will be desolate,
  a dry and desert land,
a land where no one lives,
  through which no one
    travels.   Isa 13:20; Jer 2:6
44 I will punish Bel in Babylon
  and make him spew out
    what he has swallowed.
The nations will no longer
    stream to him.
  And the wall of Babylon will
    fall.   Jer 50:15
45 "Come out of her, my people!
  Run for your lives!   Jer 50:8
  Run from the fierce anger of
    the LORD.   Ps 76:10
46 Do not lose heart or be afraid
  when rumors are heard in
    the land;   2Ki 19:7
one rumor comes this year,
    another the next,
  rumors of violence in the
    land
  and of ruler against ruler.
47 For the time will surely come
  when I will punish the idols
    of Babylon;   Isa 46:1-2
her whole land will be
    disgraced   Jer 50:12
  and her slain will all lie
    fallen within her.
48 Then heaven and earth and
    all that is in them
  will shout for joy over
    Babylon,   Isa 44:23; Rev 18:20
for out of the north   Isa 41:25
  destroyers will attack her,"
          declares the LORD.

---

[a] 35 Or *done to us and to our children*   [b] 41 *Sheshak* is a cryptogram for Babylon.

49 "Babylon must fall because of
    Israel's slain,
    just as the slain in all the
      earth
    have fallen because of
      Babylon.   Jer 50:29
50 You who have escaped the
      sword,
    leave and do not linger!   ver 45
Remember the LORD in a
      distant land,   Ps 137:6
    and call to mind
      Jerusalem."

51 "We are disgraced,   Ps 44:13-16
    for we have been insulted
    and shame covers our
      faces,
  because foreigners have
      entered
    the holy places of the LORD's
      house."   La 1:10

52 "But days are coming,"
    declares the LORD,
   "when I will punish her
      idols,
  and throughout her land
    the wounded will groan.
53 Even if Babylon ascends to the
      heavens   Isa 14:13-14
    and fortifies her lofty
      stronghold,
    I will send destroyers
      against her,"   Jer 49:16
      declares the LORD.

54 "The sound of a cry comes
    from Babylon,
    the sound of great
      destruction   Jer 50:22

from the land of the
    Babylonians.*a*
55 The LORD will destroy
    Babylon;
    he will silence her noisy din.
Waves of enemies will rage
    like great waters;   Ps 18:4
    the roar of their voices will
      resound.
56 A destroyer will come against
    Babylon;
    her warriors will be
      captured,
    and their bows will be
      broken.   Ps 46:9
For the LORD is a God of
    retribution;
    he will repay in full.   Ps 94:1-2
57 I will make her officials and
    wise men drunk,
    her governors, officers and
      warriors as well;
  they will sleep forever and not
      awake,"   Ps 76:5; Jer 25:27
    declares the King, whose
      name is the LORD
      Almighty.   Jer 46:18; 48:15

58 This is what the LORD Almighty says:

"Babylon's thick wall will be
    leveled   Isa 15:1
    and her high gates set on fire;
  the peoples exhaust
      themselves for nothing,
    the nations' labor is only
      fuel for the flames."

59 This is the message Jeremiah the prophet gave to the staff

a 54 Or Chaldeans

officer Seraiah son of Neriah, the son of Mahseiah, when he went to Babylon with Zedekiah king of Judah in the fourth year of his reign. ⁶⁰Jeremiah had written on a scroll about all the disasters that would come upon Babylon — all that had been recorded concerning Babylon. ⁶¹He said to Seraiah, "When you get to Babylon, see that you read all these words aloud. ⁶²Then say, 'LORD, you have said you will destroy this place, so that neither people nor animals will live in it; it will be desolate forever.' ⁶³When you finish reading this scroll, tie a stone to it and throw it into the Euphrates. ⁶⁴Then say, 'So will Babylon sink to rise no more because of the disaster I will bring on her. And her people will fall.' " Rev 18:21; Jer 50:13,39

The words of Jeremiah end here.

The Fall of Jerusalem
52:1-3pp — 2Ki 24:18-20; 2Ch 36:11-16
52:4-16pp — Jer 39:1-10
52:4-21pp — 2Ki 25:1-21; 2Ch 36:17-20

52 Zedekiah was twenty-one years old when he became king, and he reigned in Jerusalem eleven years. His mother's name was Hamutal daughter of Jeremiah; she was from Libnah. ²He did evil in the eyes of the LORD, just as Jehoiakim had done. ³It was because

of the LORD's anger that all this happened to Jerusalem and Judah, and in the end he thrust them from his presence. 2Ki 24:17

Now Zedekiah rebelled against the king of Babylon. 2Ki 24:18-20

⁴So in the ninth year of Zedekiah's reign, on the tenth day of the tenth month, Nebuchadnezzar king of Babylon marched against Jerusalem with his whole army. They encamped outside the city and built siege works all around it. ⁵The city was kept under siege until the eleventh year of King Zedekiah. 2Ki 25:1-7; Jer 39:1

⁶By the ninth day of the fourth month the famine in the city had become so severe that there was no food for the people to eat. ⁷Then the city wall was broken through, and the whole army fled. They left the city at night through the gate between the two walls near the king's garden, though the Babylonians[a] were surrounding the city. They fled toward the Arabah,[b] ⁸but the Babylonian[c] army pursued King Zedekiah and overtook him in the plains of Jericho. All his soldiers were separated from him and scattered, ⁹and he was captured. Jer 32:4

He was taken to the king of Babylon at Riblah in the land of Hamath, where he pronounced sentence on him. ¹⁰There at Riblah the king of Babylon killed the

---

[a] 7 Or Chaldeans; also in verse 17   [b] 7 Or the Jordan Valley   [c] 8 Or Chaldean; also in verse 14

sons of Zedekiah before his eyes; he also killed all the officials of Judah. ¹¹ Then he put out Zedekiah's eyes, bound him with bronze shackles and took him to Babylon, where he put him in prison till the day of his death. Jer 22:30

¹² On the tenth day of the fifth month, in the nineteenth year of Nebuchadnezzar king of Babylon, Nebuzaradan commander of the imperial guard, who served the king of Babylon, came to Jerusalem. ¹³ He set fire to the temple of the LORD, the royal palace and all the houses of Jerusalem. Every important building he burned down. ¹⁴ The whole Babylonian army, under the commander of the imperial guard, broke down all the walls around Jerusalem. ¹⁵ Nebuzaradan the commander of the guard carried into exile some of the poorest people and those who remained in the city, along with the rest of the craftsmen[a] and those who had deserted to the king of Babylon. ¹⁶ But Nebuzaradan left behind the rest of the poorest people of the land to work the vineyards and fields. Jer 39:1-10

¹⁷ The Babylonians broke up the bronze pillars, the movable stands and the bronze Sea that were at the temple of the LORD and they carried all the bronze to Babylon. ¹⁸ They also took away the pots, shovels, wick trimmers, sprinkling bowls, dishes and all the bronze articles used in the temple service. ¹⁹ The commander of the imperial guard took away the basins, censers, sprinkling bowls, pots, lampstands, dishes and bowls used for drink offerings — all that were made of pure gold or silver. Jer 27:19-22

²⁰ The bronze from the two pillars, the Sea and the twelve bronze bulls under it, and the movable stands, which King Solomon had made for the temple of the LORD, was more than could be weighed. ²¹ Each pillar was eighteen cubits high and twelve cubits in circumference[b]; each was four fingers thick, and hollow. ²² The bronze capital on top of one pillar was five cubits[c] high and was decorated with a network and pomegranates of bronze all around. The other pillar, with its pomegranates, was similar. ²³ There were ninety-six pomegranates on the sides; the total number of pomegranates above the surrounding network was a hundred. 2Ki 25:1-21

²⁴ The commander of the guard took as prisoners Seraiah the chief priest, Zephaniah the priest next in rank and the three doorkeepers. ²⁵ Of those still in the city, he took the officer in charge of the fighting men,

---

[a] 15 Or the populace   [b] 21 That is, about 27 feet high and 18 feet in circumference or about 8.1 meters high and 5.4 meters in circumference   [c] 22 That is, about 7 1/2 feet or about 2.3 meters

and seven royal advisers. He also took the secretary who was chief officer in charge of conscripting the people of the land, sixty of whom were found in the city. ²⁶Nebuzaradan the commander took them all and brought them to the king of Babylon at Riblah. ²⁷There at Riblah, in the land of Hamath, the king had them executed. 2Ki 25:18; Jer 21:1; 37:3

So Judah went into captivity, away from her land. ²⁸This is the number of the people Nebuchadnezzar carried into exile: 2Ki 24:14-16; 2Ch 36:20

in the seventh year, 3,023 Jews;
²⁹in Nebuchadnezzar's eighteen year,
832 people from Jerusalem;
³⁰in his twenty-third year,
745 Jews taken into exile by Nebuzaradan the commander of the imperial guard. Jer 43:3
There were 4,600 people in all. Jer 13:19

Jehoiachin Released
52:31-34pp — 2Ki 25:27-30

³¹In the thirty-seventh year of the exile of Jehoiachin king of Judah, in the year Awel-Marduk became king of Babylon, on the twenty-fifth day of the twelfth month, he released Jehoiachin king of Judah and freed him from prison. ³²He spoke kindly to him and gave him a seat of honor higher than those of the other kings who were with him in Babylon. ³³So Jehoiachin put aside his prison clothes and for the rest of his life ate regularly at the king's table. ³⁴Day by day the king of Babylon gave Jehoiachin a regular allowance as long as he lived, till the day of his death. 2Ki 25:27-30

Lamentations

1 ^a How deserted lies the city,
    once so full of people! Jer 42:2
How like a widow is she, Isa 47:8
    who once was great among
        the nations! 1Ki 4:21
She who was queen among
        the provinces
    has now become a slave.

² Bitterly she weeps at night,
    tears are on her cheeks.
Among all her lovers Jer 3:1
    there is no one to comfort
    her.
All her friends have betrayed
    her; Jer 4:30; Mic 7:5
    they have become her
    enemies. Jer 30:14

³ After affliction and harsh
    labor,
    Judah has gone into exile.
She dwells among the nations;
    she finds no resting
        place. Dt 28:65
All who pursue her have
    overtaken her
    in the midst of her distress.

⁴ The roads to Zion mourn,
    for no one comes to her
        appointed festivals.
All her gateways are desolate,
    her priests groan,
her young women grieve,
    and she is in bitter anguish.

⁵ Her foes have become her
        masters;
    her enemies are at ease.
The LORD has brought her grief
    because of her many sins.
Her children have gone into
        exile, Jer 52:28-30
    captive before the foe. Ps 137:3

⁶ All the splendor has departed
    from Daughter Zion. Jer 13:18
Her princes are like deer
    that find no pasture;
in weakness they have fled
    before the pursuer.

⁷ In the days of her affliction
    and wandering
Jerusalem remembers all
    the treasures
that were hers in days of old.

^a This chapter is an acrostic poem, the verses of which begin with the successive letters of the Hebrew alphabet.

When her people fell into
enemy hands,
there was no one to help
her.   Jer 37:7; La 4:17
Her enemies looked at her
and laughed at her
destruction.

⁸Jerusalem has sinned greatly
and so has become unclean.
All who honored her despise
her,
for they have all seen her
naked;   Jer 13:22,26
she herself groans   Ps 6:6
and turns away.

⁹Her filthiness clung to her
skirts;
she did not consider her
future.   Dt 32:28-29; Isa 47:7
Her fall was astounding;Jer 13:18
there was none to comfort
her.   Ecc 4:1; Jer 16:7
"Look, LORD, on my affliction,
for the enemy has triumphed."

¹⁰The enemy laid hands
on all her treasures;   Isa 64:11
she saw pagan nations
enter her sanctuary— Ps 74:7-8
those you had forbidden Dt 23:3
to enter your assembly.

¹¹All her people groan   Ps 38:8
as they search for bread;
they barter their treasures for
food
to keep themselves alive.
"Look, LORD, and consider,
for I am despised."

¹²"Is it nothing to you, all you
who pass by?   Jer 18:16
Look around and see.
Is any suffering like my
suffering
that was inflicted on me,
that the LORD brought me
in the day of his fierce
anger?   Jer 30:24

¹³"From on high he sent fire,
sent it down into my bones.
He spread a net for my feet
and turned me back.
He made me desolate,   Jer 44:6
faint all the day long. Hab 3:16

¹⁴"My sins have been bound
into a yoke^a;   Dt 28:48
by his hands they were
woven together.
They have been hung on my
neck,
and the Lord has sapped my
strength.
He has given me into the hands
of those I cannot withstand.

¹⁵"The Lord has rejected
all the warriors in my midst;
he has summoned an army
against me   Isa 41:2
to^b crush my young men.
In his winepress the Lord has
trampled   Jdg 6:11
Virgin Daughter Judah.

¹⁶"This is why I weep
and my eyes overflow with
tears.   La 2:11,18; 3:48-49
No one is near to comfort me,

---

^{a} 14 Most Hebrew manuscripts; many Hebrew manuscripts and Septuagint *He kept watch
over my sins* ^{b} 15 Or *has set a time for me / when he will*

no one to restore my spirit.
My children are destitute
  because the enemy has
    prevailed." Jer 13:17; 14:17

¹⁷Zion stretches out her hands,
  but there is no one to
    comfort her.
The LORD has decreed for Jacob
  that his neighbors become
    his foes; Ex 23:21
Jerusalem has become
  an unclean thing among
    them. Lev 18:25-28

¹⁸"The LORD is righteous, Ex 9:27
  yet I rebelled against his
    command. 1Sa 12:14
Listen, all you peoples;
  look on my suffering.
My young men and young
    women
  have gone into exile. Dt 28:32

¹⁹"I called to my allies
  but they betrayed me.
My priests and my elders
  perished in the city Jer 14:15
while they searched for food
  to keep themselves alive.

²⁰"See, LORD, how distressed
    I am! Jer 4:19
I am in torment within,
and in my heart I am
    disturbed,
  for I have been most
    rebellious.
Outside, the sword bereaves;
  inside, there is only death.

²¹"People have heard my
    groaning, ver 8; Ps 6:6
  but there is no one to
    comfort me. ver 4
All my enemies have heard of
    my distress;
  they rejoice at what you
    have done. La 2:15
May you bring the day you
  have announced Jer 30:16
so they may become like me.

²²"Let all their wickedness
    come before you;
  deal with them
as you have dealt with me
  because of all my sins. Ne 4:5
My groans are many Ps 6:6
  and my heart is faint."

2ᵃ How the Lord has covered
    Daughter Zion
  with the cloud of his angerᵇ!
He has hurled down the
    splendor of Israel
  from heaven to earth;
he has not remembered his
    footstool Ps 99:5; 132:7
  in the day of his anger. Jer 12:7

²Without pity the Lord has
    swallowed up Ps 21:9
  all the dwellings of Jacob;
in his wrath he has torn down
  the strongholds of Daughter
    Judah. Ps 89:39-40; Mic 5:11
He has brought her kingdom
    and its princes
  down to the ground in
    dishonor. Isa 25:12

ᵃ This chapter is an acrostic poem, the verses of which begin with the successive letters of the Hebrew alphabet. ᵇ 1 Or *How the Lord in his anger / has treated Daughter Zion with contempt*

³In fierce anger he has cut off
  every horn[a,b] of Israel.   Ps 75:5
He has withdrawn his right
  hand   Ps 74:11
  at the approach of the enemy.
He has burned in Jacob like a
  flaming fire
  that consumes everything
  around it.   Isa 42:25

⁴Like an enemy he has strung
  his bow;   La 3:12-13
  his right hand is ready.
Like a foe he has slain
  all who were pleasing to the
  eye;   Eze 24:16,25
he has poured out his wrath
  like fire   Jer 7:20
  on the tent of Daughter Zion.

⁵The Lord is like an enemy;
  he has swallowed up Israel.
He has swallowed up all her
  palaces
  and destroyed her
  strongholds.   ver 2
He has multiplied mourning
  and lamentation
  for Daughter Judah.   Jer 9:17-20

⁶He has laid waste his dwelling
  like a garden;
  he has destroyed his place
  of meeting.   Jer 52:13
The LORD has made Zion
  forget
  her appointed festivals and
  her Sabbaths;   Zep 3:18
in his fierce anger he has
  spurned
  both king and priest.   La 4:16

⁷The Lord has rejected his altar
  and abandoned his
  sanctuary.   Eze 7:24
He has given the walls of her
  palaces
  into the hands of the
  enemy;   Ps 74:7-8; Isa 64:11
they have raised a shout in the
  house of the LORD
  as on the day of an
  appointed festival.

⁸The LORD determined to tear
  down
  the wall around Daughter
  Zion.
He stretched out a measuring
  line   2Ki 21:13; Isa 34:11
  and did not withhold his
  hand from destroying.
He made ramparts and walls
  lament;   Ps 48:13
  together they wasted away.

⁹Her gates have sunk into the
  ground;   Ne 1:3
  their bars he has broken
  and destroyed.
Her king and her princes
  are exiled among the
  nations,   Dt 28:36
  the law is no more,   2Ch 15:3
and her prophets no longer
  find
  visions from the LORD.

¹⁰The elders of Daughter Zion
  sit on the ground in silence;
they have sprinkled dust on
  their heads   Job 2:12
  and put on sackcloth.   Isa 15:3

---

[a] 3 Or off / all the strength; or every king   [b] 3 Horn here symbolizes strength.

The young women of
   Jerusalem
   have bowed their heads to
      the ground. Job 2:13; Isa 3:26

11 My eyes fail from weeping,
   I am in torment within;
my heart is poured out on the
   ground   ver 19; Ps 22:14
because my people are
   destroyed,
because children and infants
   faint   La 4:4
   in the streets of the city.

12 They say to their mothers,
   "Where is bread and wine?"
as they faint like the wounded
   in the streets of the city,
as their lives ebb away
   in their mothers' arms. La 4:4

13 What can I say for you?
   With what can I compare
      you,
   Daughter Jerusalem?
To what can I liken you,
   that I may comfort you,
   Virgin Daughter Zion?
Your wound is as deep as the
      sea.   Jer 14:17; La 1:12
   Who can heal you?

14 The visions of your prophets
      were false and worthless;
   they did not expose your sin
      to ward off your captivity.
   The prophecies they gave you
      were false and misleading.

15 All who pass your way
   clap their hands at you;

they scoff and shake their
      heads   Jer 19:8
   at Daughter Jerusalem: La 1:21
"Is this the city that was
      called
   the perfection of beauty,
   the joy of the whole earth?"

16 All your enemies open their
      mouths
   wide against you;   Ps 56:2
they scoff and gnash their
      teeth   Job 16:9
   and say, "We have
      swallowed her up.
This is the day we have waited
      for;
   we have lived to see it."

17 The LORD has done what he
      planned;
   he has fulfilled his word,
   which he decreed long ago.
He has overthrown you
      without pity,   ver 2; Eze 5:11
   he has let the enemy gloat
      over you,   Ps 22:17
   he has exalted the horn[a] of
      your foes.   Ps 89:42

18 The hearts of the people
   cry out to the Lord.   Ps 119:145
You walls of Daughter Zion,
   let your tears flow like a
      river   La 1:16
   day and night;   Jer 9:1
give yourself no relief,
   your eyes no rest.   La 3:49

19 Arise, cry out in the night,
   as the watches of the night
      begin;

a 17 Horn here symbolizes strength.

pour out your heart like water
  in the presence of the Lord.
Lift up your hands to him
  for the lives of your
    children,
who faint from hunger   Isa 51:20
  at every street corner.

²⁰ "Look, LORD, and consider:
  Whom have you ever
    treated like this?
Should women eat their
  offspring,   Jer 19:9
the children they have
  cared for?   La 4:10
Should priest and prophet be
  killed   Ps 78:64; Jer 14:15
in the sanctuary of the Lord?

²¹ "Young and old lie together
  in the dust of the streets;
my young men and young
  women
have fallen by the sword.
You have slain them in the
  day of your anger;
you have slaughtered them
  without pity.   Jer 13:14

²² "As you summon to a feast day,
  so you summoned against
    me terrors on every side.
In the day of the LORD's anger
  no one escaped or survived;
those I cared for and reared
  my enemy has destroyed."

3 ^{*a*} I am the man who has seen
    affliction
  by the rod of the LORD's
    wrath.   Job 19:21; Ps 88:7

² He has driven me away and
  made me walk
  in darkness rather than light;
³ indeed, he has turned his
  hand against me   Isa 5:25
again and again, all day long.

⁴ He has made my skin and my
  flesh grow old
  and has broken my bones.
⁵ He has besieged me and
  surrounded me
with bitterness and
  hardship.   ver 19; Jer 23:15
⁶ He has made me dwell in
  darkness
  like those long dead.   Ps 88:5-6

⁷ He has walled me in so I
  cannot escape;   Job 3:23
he has weighed me down
  with chains.   Jer 40:4
⁸ Even when I call out or cry for
  help,
  he shuts out my prayer.
⁹ He has barred my way with
  blocks of stone;
he has made my paths
  crooked.   Isa 63:17; Hos 2:6

¹⁰ Like a bear lying in wait,
  like a lion in hiding,   Hos 13:8
¹¹ he dragged me from the path
  and mangled me   Hos 6:1
  and left me without help.
¹² He drew his bow   La 2:4
  and made me the target for
  his arrows.   Job 7:20

¹³ He pierced my heart
  with arrows from his quiver.

a This chapter is an acrostic poem; the verses of each stanza begin with the successive letters of the Hebrew alphabet, and the verses within each stanza begin with the same letter.

14 I became the laughingstock of
    all my people;   Jer 20:7
  they mock me in song all
    day long.   Job 30:9
15 He has filled me with bitter
    herbs
  and given me gall to drink.
16 He has broken my teeth with
    gravel;   Pr 20:17
  he has trampled me in the
    dust.   Ps 7:5
17 I have been deprived of peace;
  I have forgotten what
    prosperity is.
18 So I say, "My splendor is gone
  and all that I had hoped
    from the LORD."   Job 17:15

19 I remember my affliction and
    my wandering,
  the bitterness and the gall.
20 I well remember them,
  and my soul is downcast
    within me.   Ps 42:5,11
21 Yet this I call to mind
  and therefore I have hope:

22 Because of the LORD's
    great love we are not
    consumed,   Ps 103:11
  for his compassions never
    fail.   Ps 78:38; Mal 3:6
23 They are new every morning;
  great is your faithfulness.
24 I say to myself, "The LORD is
    my portion;   Ps 16:5
  therefore I will wait for him."

25 The LORD is good to those
    whose hope is in him,
  to the one who seeks him;
26 it is good to wait quietly   Isa 30:15

for the salvation of the
    LORD.   Ps 37:7; 40:1
27 It is good for a man to bear the
    yoke
  while he is young.

28 Let him sit alone in silence,
  for the LORD has laid it on
    him.
29 Let him bury his face in the
    dust —
  there may yet be hope. Jer 31:17
30 Let him offer his cheek to one
    who would strike him,
  and let him be filled with
    disgrace.

31 For no one is cast off
  by the Lord forever.   Ps 94:14
32 Though he brings grief, he
    will show compassion,
  so great is his unfailing love.
33 For he does not willingly
    bring affliction
  or grief to anyone.   Eze 33:11

34 To crush underfoot
  all prisoners in the land,
35 to deny people their rights
  before the Most High,
36 to deprive them of justice —
  would not the Lord see such
    things?   Jer 22:3; Hab 1:13
37 Who can speak and have it
    happen
  if the Lord has not decreed it?
38 Is it not from the mouth of the
    Most High
  that both calamities and
    good things come?   Job 2:10
39 Why should the living
  complain

when punished for their
sins? Jer 30:15; Mic 7:9
40 Let us examine our ways and
test them, 2Co 13:5
and let us return to the LORD.
41 Let us lift up our hearts and
our hands
to God in heaven, and say:
42 "We have sinned and rebelled
and you have not forgiven.

43 "You have covered yourself
with anger and
pursued us;
you have slain without pity.
44 You have covered yourself
with a cloud Ps 97:2
so that no prayer can get
through. Zec 7:13
45 You have made us scum and
refuse 1Co 4:13
among the nations.

46 "All our enemies have opened
their mouths
wide against us. La 2:16
47 We have suffered terror and
pitfalls, Jer 48:43
ruin and destruction."
48 Streams of tears flow from my
eyes La 1:16
because my people are
destroyed. La 2:11

49 My eyes will flow unceasingly,
without relief, Jer 14:17
50 until the LORD looks down
from heaven and sees.
51 What I see brings grief to my
soul
because of all the women of
my city.

52 Those who were my enemies
without cause
hunted me like a bird. Ps 35:7
53 They tried to end my life in a
pit Jer 37:16
and threw stones at me;
54 the waters closed over my head,
and I thought I was about to
perish. Ps 88:5

55 I called on your name, LORD,
from the depths of the pit.
56 You heard my plea: "Do not
close your ears Ps 55:1
to my cry for relief."
57 You came near when I called
you, Ps 46:1
and you said, "Do not fear."

58 You, Lord, took up my case;
you redeemed my life. Ps 34:22
59 LORD, you have seen the
wrong done to me.
Uphold my cause!
60 You have seen the depth of
their vengeance,
all their plots against me.

61 LORD, you have heard their
insults, Ps 89:50
all their plots against me —
62 what my enemies whisper
and mutter
against me all day long.
63 Look at them! Sitting or
standing,
they mock me in their
songs.

64 Pay them back what they
deserve, LORD,
for what their hands have
done. Ps 28:4

65 Put a veil over their hearts,
    and may your curse be on
        them!
66 Pursue them in anger and
        destroy them
    from under the heavens of
        the LORD.

4 *a* How the gold has lost its
        luster,
    the fine gold become dull!
The sacred gems are scattered
    at every street corner. Eze 7:19

2 How the precious children of
        Zion,   Isa 51:18
    once worth their weight in
        gold,
are now considered as pots of
        clay,
    the work of a potter's hands!

3 Even jackals offer their breasts
        to nurse their young,
    but my people have become
        heartless
    like ostriches in the desert.

4 Because of thirst the infant's
        tongue
    sticks to the roof of its
        mouth;   Ps 22:15
the children beg for bread,
    but no one gives it to
        them.   La 2:11-12

5 Those who once ate delicacies
    are destitute in the streets.
Those brought up in royal
        purple   Jer 6:2
    now lie on ash heaps. Am 6:3-7

6 The punishment of my people
    is greater than that of
        Sodom,   Ge 19:25
which was overthrown in a
        moment
    without a hand turned to
        help her.

7 Their princes were brighter
        than snow
    and whiter than milk,
their bodies more ruddy than
        rubies,
    their appearance like lapis
        lazuli.

8 But now they are blacker than
        soot;   Job 30:28
    they are not recognized in
        the streets.
Their skin has shriveled on
        their bones;   Ps 102:3-5
    it has become as dry as a stick.

9 Those killed by the sword are
        better off
    than those who die of famine;
racked with hunger, they
        waste away
    for lack of food from the field.

10 With their own hands
        compassionate women
have cooked their own
        children, Dt 28:53-57; La 2:20
who became their food
    when my people were
        destroyed.

11 The LORD has given full vent
    to his wrath;   Job 20:23

---

a This chapter is an acrostic poem, the verses of which begin with the successive letters of
the Hebrew alphabet.

he has poured out his fierce
anger. Zep 2:2; 3:8
He kindled a fire in Zion Jer 17:27
that consumed her
foundations. Dt 32:22

¹²The kings of the earth did not
believe,
nor did any of the peoples of
the world,
that enemies and foes could
enter
the gates of Jerusalem. 1Ki 9:9

¹³But it happened because of
the sins of her prophets
and the iniquities of her
priests, Jer 6:13; Eze 22:28
who shed within her
the blood of the righteous.

¹⁴Now they grope through the
streets
as if they were blind. Isa 59:10
They are so defiled with blood
that no one dares to touch
their garments.

¹⁵"Go away! You are unclean!"
people cry to them.
"Away! Away! Don't touch
us!"
When they flee and wander
about,
people among the nations
say,
"They can stay here no
longer." Lev 13:46

¹⁶The Lord himself has
scattered them;
he no longer watches over
them. Isa 9:14-16

The priests are shown no
honor,
the elders no favor. La 5:12

¹⁷Moreover, our eyes failed,
looking in vain for help;
from our towers we watched
for a nation that could not
save us. Jer 37:7

¹⁸People stalked us at every step,
so we could not walk in our
streets.
Our end was near, our days
were numbered,
for our end had come.

¹⁹Our pursuers were swifter
than eagles in the sky;
they chased us over the
mountains Isa 5:26-28
and lay in wait for us in the
desert. Jer 52:7

²⁰The Lord's anointed, our very
life breath, 2Sa 19:21
was caught in their traps.
We thought that under his
shadow
we would live among the
nations.

²¹Rejoice and be glad, Daughter
Edom,
you who live in the land of Uz.
But to you also the cup will be
passed; Jer 25:15
you will be drunk and
stripped naked. Am 1:11-12

²²Your punishment will end,
Daughter Zion; Isa 40:2
he will not prolong your
exile.

But he will punish your sin,
Daughter Edom,
and expose your
wickedness.   Ps 137:7

5 Remember, Lord, what has
happened to us;
look, and see our disgrace.
²Our inheritance has been
turned over to strangers,
our homes to foreigners.
³We have become fatherless,
our mothers are widows.
⁴We must buy the water we
drink;
our wood can be had only at
a price.   Isa 3:1
⁵Those who pursue us are at
our heels;
we are weary and find no
rest.   Jos 1:13; Ne 9:37
⁶We submitted to Egypt and
Assyria   Hos 9:3
to get enough bread.
⁷Our ancestors sinned and are
no more,
and we bear their
punishment. Jer 14:20; 16:12
⁸Slaves rule over us,   Ne 5:15
and there is no one to free
us from their hands.
⁹We get our bread at the risk of
our lives
because of the sword in the
desert.
¹⁰Our skin is hot as an oven,
feverish from hunger. La 4:8-9
¹¹Women have been violated in
Zion,   Zec 14:2
and virgins in the towns of
Judah.

¹²Princes have been hung up by
their hands;
elders are shown no
respect.   La 4:16
¹³Young men toil at the
millstones;
boys stagger under loads of
wood.
¹⁴The elders are gone from the
city gate;
the young men have
stopped their music.
¹⁵Joy is gone from our hearts;
our dancing has turned to
mourning.   Jer 25:10
¹⁶The crown has fallen from our
head.   Ps 89:39
Woe to us, for we have
sinned!   Isa 3:11
¹⁷Because of this our hearts are
faint,   Isa 1:5
because of these things our
eyes grow dim   Ps 6:7
¹⁸for Mount Zion, which lies
desolate,   Mic 3:12
with jackals prowling over it.

¹⁹You, Lord, reign forever;
your throne endures
from generation to
generation.   Ps 45:6
²⁰Why do you always forget us?
Why do you forsake us so
long?
²¹Restore us to yourself, Lord,
that we may return;
renew our days as of old
²²unless you have utterly
rejected us   Ps 53:5; 60:1-2
and are angry with us
beyond measure.   Isa 64:9

Ezekiel

Ezekiel's Inaugural Vision

1 In my thirtieth year, in the fourth month on the fifth day, while I was among the exiles by the Kebar River, the heavens were opened and I saw visions of God. Mt 3:16; Ac 7:56; Ex 24:10

²On the fifth of the month — it was the fifth year of the exile of King Jehoiachin — ³the word of the LORD came to Ezekiel the priest, the son of Buzi, by the Kebar River in the land of the Babylonians.ᵃ There the hand of the LORD was on him. 2Ki 3:15; Eze 3:14,22

⁴I looked, and I saw a windstorm coming out of the north — an immense cloud with flashing lightning and surrounded by brilliant light. The center of the fire looked like glowing metal, ⁵and in the fire was what looked like four living creatures. In appearance their form was human, ⁶but each of them had four faces and four wings. ⁷Their legs were straight; their feet were like those of a calf and gleamed like burnished bronze. ⁸Under their wings on their four sides they had human hands. All four of them had faces and wings, ⁹and the wings of one touched the wings of another. Each one went straight ahead; they did not turn as they moved. Rev 4:6; Eze 10:8

¹⁰Their faces looked like this: Each of the four had the face of a human being, and on the right side each had the face of a lion, and on the left the face of an ox; each also had the face of an eagle. ¹¹Such were their faces. They each had two wings spreading out upward, each wing touching that of the creature on either side; and each had two other wings covering its body. ¹²Each one went straight ahead. Wherever the spirit would go, they would go, without turning as they went. ¹³The appearance of the living creatures was like burning coals of fire or like torches. Fire moved back and forth among the creatures; it was bright, and lightning

ᵃ 3 Or Chaldeans

flashed out of it. [14]The creatures sped back and forth like flashes of lightning.　　Isa 6:2; Rev 4:5,7

[15]As I looked at the living creatures, I saw a wheel on the ground beside each creature with its four faces. [16]This was the appearance and structure of the wheels: They sparkled like topaz, and all four looked alike. Each appeared to be made like a wheel intersecting a wheel. [17]As they moved, they would go in any one of the four directions the creatures faced; the wheels did not change direction as the creatures went. [18]Their rims were high and awesome, and all four rims were full of eyes all around.　　Eze 10:12; Rev 4:6

[19]When the living creatures moved, the wheels beside them moved; and when the living creatures rose from the ground, the wheels also rose. [20]Wherever the spirit would go, they would go, and the wheels would rise along with them, because the spirit of the living creatures was in the wheels. [21]When the creatures moved, they also moved; when the creatures stood still, they also stood still; and when the creatures rose from the ground, the wheels rose along with them, because the spirit of the living creatures was in the wheels.　　ver 12; Eze 10:17

[22]Spread out above the heads of the living creatures was what looked something like a vault, sparkling like crystal, and awesome. [23]Under the vault their wings were stretched out one toward the other, and each had two wings covering its body. [24]When the creatures moved, I heard the sound of their wings, like the roar of rushing waters, like the voice of the Almighty,[a] like the tumult of an army. When they stood still, they lowered their wings.　　Eze 10:5

[25]Then there came a voice from above the vault over their heads as they stood with lowered wings. [26]Above the vault over their heads was what looked like a throne of lapis lazuli, and high above on the throne was a figure like that of a man. [27]I saw that from what appeared to be his waist up he looked like glowing metal, as if full of fire, and that from there down he looked like fire; and brilliant light surrounded him. [28]Like the appearance of a rainbow in the clouds on a rainy day, so was the radiance around him.　　Rev 4:2; 10:1

This was the appearance of the likeness of the glory of the LORD. When I saw it, I fell facedown, and I heard the voice of one speaking.　　Eze 3:23; 8:4

Ezekiel's Call to Be a Prophet

2 He said to me, "Son of man,[b] stand up on your feet and I will speak to you." [2]As he spoke, the Spirit came into me and

---

[a] 24 Hebrew *Shaddai*　　[b] 1 The Hebrew phrase *ben adam* means *human being*. The phrase *son of man* is retained as a form of address here and throughout Ezekiel because of its possible association with "Son of Man" in the New Testament.

raised me to my feet, and I heard him speaking to me. Eze 3:24; Da 8:18

³He said: "Son of man, I am sending you to the Israelites, to a rebellious nation that has rebelled against me; they and their ancestors have been in revolt against me to this very day. ⁴The people to whom I am sending you are obstinate and stubborn. Say to them, 'This is what the Sovereign LORD says.' ⁵And whether they listen or fail to listen — for they are a rebellious people — they will know that a prophet has been among them. ⁶And you, son of man, do not be afraid of them or their words. Do not be afraid, though briers and thorns are all around you and you live among scorpions. Do not be afraid of what they say or be terrified by them, though they are a rebellious people. ⁷You must speak my words to them, whether they listen or fail to listen, for they are rebellious. ⁸But you, son of man, listen to what I say to you. Do not rebel like that rebellious people; open your mouth and eat what I give you." Jer 3:25; Rev 10:9

⁹Then I looked, and I saw a hand stretched out to me. In it was a scroll, ¹⁰which he unrolled before me. On both sides of it were written words of lament and mourning and woe. Eze 8:3; Rev 8:13

3 And he said to me, "Son of man, eat what is before you, eat this scroll; then go and speak to the people of Israel." ²So I opened my mouth, and he gave me the scroll to eat.

³Then he said to me, "Son of man, eat this scroll I am giving you and fill your stomach with it." So I ate it, and it tasted as sweet as honey in my mouth. Ps 19:10; Rev 10:9

⁴He then said to me: "Son of man, go now to the people of Israel and speak my words to them. ⁵You are not being sent to a people of obscure speech and strange language, but to the people of Israel — ⁶not to many peoples of obscure speech and strange language, whose words you cannot understand. Surely if I had sent you to them, they would have listened to you. ⁷But the people of Israel are not willing to listen to you because they are not willing to listen to me, for all the Israelites are hardened and obstinate. ⁸But I will make you as unyielding and hardened as they are. ⁹I will make your forehead like the hardest stone, harder than flint. Do not be afraid of them or terrified by them, though they are a rebellious people." Isa 50:7; Eze 2:6; Mic 3:8

¹⁰And he said to me, "Son of man, listen carefully and take to heart all the words I speak to you. ¹¹Go now to your people in exile and speak to them. Say to them, 'This is what the Sovereign LORD says,' whether they listen or fail to listen." Eze 2:4-5,7

¹²Then the Spirit lifted me up, and I heard behind me a loud

rumbling sound as the glory of the LORD rose from the place where it was standing.*a* [13] It was the sound of the wings of the living creatures brushing against each other and the sound of the wheels beside them, a loud rumbling sound. [14] The Spirit then lifted me up and took me away, and I went in bitterness and in the anger of my spirit, with the strong hand of the LORD on me. [15] I came to the exiles who lived at Tel Aviv near the Kebar River. And there, where they were living, I sat among them for seven days — deeply distressed.   Eze 8:3; 1Ki 18:12; Ac 8:39

Ezekiel's Task as Watchman

[16] At the end of seven days the word of the LORD came to me: [17] "Son of man, I have made you a watchman for the people of Israel; so hear the word I speak and give them warning from me. [18] When I say to a wicked person, 'You will surely die,' and you do not warn them or speak out to dissuade them from their evil ways in order to save their life, that wicked person will die for*b* their sin, and I will hold you accountable for their blood. [19] But if you do warn the wicked person and they do not turn from their wickedness or from their evil ways, they will die for their sin; but you will have saved yourself.   Isa 52:8; Jer 6:17

[20] "Again, when a righteous person turns from their righteousness and does evil, and I put a stumbling block before them, they will die. Since you did not warn them, they will die for their sin. The righteous things that person did will not be remembered, and I will hold you accountable for their blood. [21] But if you do warn the righteous person not to sin and they do not sin, they will surely live because they took warning, and you will have saved yourself."   Eze 18:24; Ac 20:31

[22] The hand of the LORD was on me there, and he said to me, "Get up and go out to the plain, and there I will speak to you." [23] So I got up and went out to the plain. And the glory of the LORD was standing there, like the glory I had seen by the Kebar River, and I fell facedown.   Eze 1:1; 8:4; Ac 9:6

[24] Then the Spirit came into me and raised me to my feet. He spoke to me and said: "Go, shut yourself inside your house. [25] And you, son of man, they will tie with ropes; you will be bound so that you cannot go out among the people. [26] I will make your tongue stick to the roof of your mouth so that you will be silent and unable to rebuke them, for they are a rebellious people. [27] But when I speak to you, I will open your mouth and you shall say to them, 'This is what the Sovereign LORD says.' Who-

---

a 12 Probable reading of the original Hebrew text; Masoretic Text *sound — may the glory of the LORD be praised from his place*   *b* 18 Or *in*; also in verses 19 and 20 ever will listen let them listen, and whoever will refuse let them refuse; for they are a rebellious people. Eze 24:27; 33:22

Siege of Jerusalem Symbolized

4 "Now, son of man, take a block of clay, put it in front of you and draw the city of Jerusalem on it. ²Then lay siege to it: Erect siege works against it, build a ramp up to it, set up camps against it and put battering rams around it. ³Then take an iron pan, place it as an iron wall between you and the city and turn your face toward it. It will be under siege, and you shall besiege it. This will be a sign to the people of Israel. Eze 12:3-6; 24:24,27; Jer 39:1

⁴"Then lie on your left side and put the sin of the people of Israel upon yourself.ᵃ You are to bear their sin for the number of days you lie on your side. ⁵I have assigned you the same number of days as the years of their sin. So for 390 days you will bear the sin of the people of Israel.

⁶"After you have finished this, lie down again, this time on your right side, and bear the sin of the people of Judah. I have assigned you 40 days, a day for each year. ⁷Turn your face toward the siege of Jerusalem and with bared arm prophesy against her. ⁸I will tie you up with ropes so that you cannot turn from one side to the other until you have finished the days of your siege. Nu 14:34; Eze 3:25

⁹"Take wheat and barley, beans and lentils, millet and spelt; put them in a storage jar and use them to make bread for yourself. You are to eat it during the 390 days you lie on your side. ¹⁰Weigh out twenty shekelsᵇ of food to eat each day and eat it at set times. ¹¹Also measure out a sixth of a hinᶜ of water and drink it at set times. ¹²Eat the food as you would a loaf of barley bread; bake it in the sight of the people, using human excrement for fuel." ¹³The LORD said, "In this way the people of Israel will eat defiled food among the nations where I will drive them." Hos 9:3; Am 7:17

¹⁴Then I said, "Not so, Sovereign LORD! I have never defiled myself. From my youth until now I have never eaten anything found dead or torn by wild animals. No impure meat has ever entered my mouth." Ex 22:31; Ac 10:14

¹⁵"Very well," he said, "I will let you bake your bread over cow dung instead of human excrement."

¹⁶He then said to me: "Son of man, I am about to cut off the food supply in Jerusalem. The people will eat rationed food in anxiety and drink rationed water in despair, ¹⁷for food and water will be scarce. They will be appalled at the sight of each other

ᵃ 4 Or upon your side   ᵇ 10 That is, about 8 ounces or about 230 grams   ᶜ 11 That is, about 2/3 quart or about 0.6 liter and will waste away because of[a] their sin.   Lev 26:39; Eze 24:23; 33:10

God's Razor of Judgment

5 "Now, son of man, take a sharp sword and use it as a barber's razor to shave your head and your beard. Then take a set of scales and divide up the hair. ²When the days of your siege come to an end, burn a third of the hair inside the city. Take a third and strike it with the sword all around the city. And scatter a third to the wind. For I will pursue them with drawn sword. ³But take a few hairs and tuck them away in the folds of your garment. ⁴Again, take a few of these and throw them into the fire and burn them up. A fire will spread from there to all Israel.   Lev 26:33

⁵"This is what the Sovereign LORD says: This is Jerusalem, which I have set in the center of the nations, with countries all around her. ⁶Yet in her wickedness she has rebelled against my laws and decrees more than the nations and countries around her. She has rejected my laws and has not followed my decrees.   Jer 11:10; Zec 7:11

⁷"Therefore this is what the Sovereign LORD says: You have been more unruly than the nations around you and have not followed my decrees or kept my laws. You have not even[b] conformed to the standards of the nations around you.   2Ch 33:9; Eze 16:47

⁸"Therefore this is what the Sovereign LORD says: I myself am against you, Jerusalem, and I will inflict punishment on you in the sight of the nations. ⁹Because of all your detestable idols, I will do to you what I have never done before and will never do again. ¹⁰Therefore in your midst parents will eat their children, and children will eat their parents. I will inflict punishment on you and will scatter all your survivors to the winds. ¹¹Therefore as surely as I live, declares the Sovereign LORD, because you have defiled my sanctuary with all your vile images and detestable practices, I myself will shave you; I will not look on you with pity or spare you. ¹²A third of your people will die of the plague or perish by famine inside you; a third will fall by the sword outside your walls; and a third I will scatter to the winds and pursue with drawn sword.   Da 9:12; Zec 2:6

¹³"Then my anger will cease and my wrath against them will subside, and I will be avenged. And when I have spent my wrath on them, they will know that I the LORD have spoken in my zeal.   Isa 1:24; Eze 21:17

¹⁴"I will make you a ruin and a reproach among the nations around you, in the sight of all

---

[a] 17 Or *away in*   [b] 7 Most Hebrew manuscripts; some Hebrew manuscripts and Syriac *You have*

who pass by. ¹⁵You will be a reproach and a taunt, a warning and an object of horror to the nations around you when I inflict punishment on you in anger and in wrath and with stinging rebuke. I the LORD have spoken. ¹⁶When I shoot at you with my deadly and destructive arrows of famine, I will shoot to destroy you. I will bring more and more famine upon you and cut off your supply of food. ¹⁷I will send famine and wild beasts against you, and they will leave you childless. Plague and bloodshed will sweep through you, and I will bring the sword against you. I the LORD have spoken." Ne 2:17; Eze 25:17

Doom for the Mountains of Israel

6 The word of the LORD came to me: ²"Son of man, set your face against the mountains of Israel; prophesy against them ³and say: 'You mountains of Israel, hear the word of the Sovereign LORD. This is what the Sovereign LORD says to the mountains and hills, to the ravines and valleys: I am about to bring a sword against you, and I will destroy your high places. ⁴Your altars will be demolished and your incense altars will be smashed; and I will slay your people in front of your idols. ⁵I will lay the dead bodies of the Israelites in front of their idols, and I will scatter your bones around your altars. ⁶Wherever you live, the towns will be laid waste and the high places demolished, so that your altars will be laid waste and devastated, your idols smashed and ruined, your incense altars broken down, and what you have made wiped out. ⁷Your people will fall slain among you, and you will know that I am the LORD. Lev 26:30; Eze 36:1

⁸"'But I will spare some, for some of you will escape the sword when you are scattered among the lands and nations. ⁹Then in the nations where they have been carried captive, those who escape will remember me—how I have been grieved by their adulterous hearts, which have turned away from me, and by their eyes, which have lusted after their idols. They will loathe themselves for the evil they have done and for all their detestable practices. ¹⁰And they will know that I am the LORD; I did not threaten in vain to bring this calamity on them. Isa 7:13; Jer 44:28; Eze 14:22

¹¹"'This is what the Sovereign LORD says: Strike your hands together and stamp your feet and cry out "Alas!" because of all the wicked and detestable practices of the people of Israel, for they will fall by the sword, famine and plague. ¹²One who is far away will die of the plague, and one who is near will fall by the sword, and anyone who survives and is spared will die of famine.

So will I pour out my wrath on them. [13] And they will know that I am the LORD, when their people lie slain among their idols around their altars, on every high hill and on all the mountaintops, under every spreading tree and every leafy oak—places where they offered fragrant incense to all their idols. [14] And I will stretch out my hand against them and make the land a desolate waste from the desert to Diblah[a]—wherever they live. Then they will know that I am the LORD.' "   Eze 21:14,17; Jer 2:20; Hos 4:13

The End Has Come

7 The word of the LORD came to me: [2] "Son of man, this is what the Sovereign LORD says to the land of Israel:

" 'The end! The end has come
    upon the four corners of the
    land!
[3] The end is now upon you,
    and I will unleash my anger
        against you.
I will judge you according to
    your conduct
    and repay you for all your
        detestable practices.
[4] I will not look on you with pity;
    I will not spare you.
I will surely repay you for your
    conduct
    and for the detestable
        practices among you.

" 'Then you will know that I am
the LORD.'   Eze 5:11; Am 8:2,10

[5] "This is what the Sovereign
LORD says:

" 'Disaster! Unheard-of[b]
    disaster!
    See, it comes!
[6] The end has come!
    The end has come!
It has roused itself against you.
    See, it comes!
[7] Doom has come upon you,
    upon you who dwell in the
        land.
The time has come! The day is
    near!
There is panic, not joy, on
    the mountains.
[8] I am about to pour out my
    wrath on you
    and spend my anger against
        you.
I will judge you according to
    your conduct
    and repay you for all your
        detestable practices.
[9] I will not look on you with pity;
    I will not spare you.
I will repay you for your
    conduct
    and for the detestable
        practices among you.

" 'Then you will know that it is I
the LORD who strikes you.   2Ki 21:12

[10] " 'See, the day!
    See, it comes!
Doom has burst forth,

---

[a] 14 Most Hebrew manuscripts; a few Hebrew manuscripts *Riblah*   [b] 5 Most Hebrew manuscripts; some Hebrew manuscripts and Syriac *Disaster after*

the rod has budded,
  arrogance has blossomed!
11 Violence has arisen,[a]
  a rod to punish the wicked.
None of the people will be left,
  none of that crowd—
none of their wealth,
  nothing of value.
12 The time has come!
  The day has arrived!
Let not the buyer rejoice
  nor the seller grieve,
  for my wrath is on the whole
    crowd.
13 The seller will not recover
  the property that was sold—
  as long as both buyer and
    seller live.
For the vision concerning the
    whole crowd
  will not be reversed.
Because of their sins, not one
    of them
  will preserve their life.

14 " 'They have blown the
    trumpet,
  they have made all things
    ready,
but no one will go into battle,
  for my wrath is on the whole
    crowd. Lev 25:24-28; Jer 16:6
15 Outside is the sword;
  inside are plague and
    famine.
Those in the country
  will die by the sword;
those in the city
  will be devoured by famine
    and plague.

16 The fugitives who escape
  will flee to the mountains.
Like doves of the valleys,
  they will all moan,
  each for their own sins.
17 Every hand will go limp;
  every leg will be wet with
    urine.
18 They will put on sackcloth
  and be clothed with terror.
Every face will be covered
    with shame,
  and every head will be
    shaved.

19 " 'They will throw their silver
    into the streets,
  and their gold will be
    treated as a thing
    unclean.
Their silver and gold
  will not be able to deliver
    them
  in the day of the Lord's
    wrath.
It will not satisfy their hunger
  or fill their stomachs,
  for it has caused them to
    stumble into sin.
20 They took pride in their
    beautiful jewelry
  and used it to make their
    detestable idols.
They made it into vile images;
  therefore I will make it a
    thing unclean for them.
21 I will give their wealth as
    plunder to foreigners
  and as loot to the wicked of
    the earth,

a 11 Or *The violent one has become*

who will defile it.
²²I will turn my face away from
the people,
and robbers will desecrate
the place I treasure.
They will enter it
and will defile it.   Dt 32:25

²³" 'Prepare chains!
For the land is full of
bloodshed,
and the city is full of
violence.
²⁴I will bring the most wicked of
nations
to take possession of their
houses.
I will put an end to the pride
of the mighty,
and their sanctuaries will
be desecrated.
²⁵When terror comes,
they will seek peace in vain.
²⁶Calamity upon calamity will
come,
and rumor upon rumor.
They will go searching for a
vision from the prophet,
priestly instruction in the
law will cease,
the counsel of the elders
will come to an end.
²⁷The king will mourn,
the prince will be clothed
with despair,
and the hands of the people
of the land will tremble.
I will deal with them
according to their
conduct,

and by their own standards
I will judge them.

" 'Then they will know that I am
the Lord.' "   Eze 24:21; 26:16

Idolatry in the Temple

8 In the sixth year, in the sixth
month on the fifth day, while
I was sitting in my house and
the elders of Judah were sitting
before me, the hand of the Sovereign Lord came on me there.
²I looked, and I saw a figure like
that of a man.^a From what appeared to be his waist down he
was like fire, and from there up
his appearance was as bright as
glowing metal. ³He stretched out
what looked like a hand and took
me by the hair of my head. The
Spirit lifted me up between earth
and heaven and in visions of God
he took me to Jerusalem, to the
entrance of the north gate of the
inner court, where the idol that
provokes to jealousy stood. ⁴And
there before me was the glory of
the God of Israel, as in the vision
I had seen in the plain.Eze 1:28; 3:22
⁵Then he said to me, "Son of
man, look toward the north."
So I looked, and in the entrance
north of the gate of the altar I saw
this idol of jealousy.   Jer 32:34
⁶And he said to me, "Son of
man, do you see what they are
doing—the utterly detestable
things the Israelites are doing
here, things that will drive me far

---

^a 2 Or saw a fiery figure

from my sanctuary? But you will see things that are even more detestable." Eze 5:11; Hos 5:6

⁷Then he brought me to the entrance to the court. I looked, and I saw a hole in the wall. ⁸He said to me, "Son of man, now dig into the wall." So I dug into the wall and saw a doorway there.

⁹And he said to me, "Go in and see the wicked and detestable things they are doing here." ¹⁰So I went in and looked, and I saw portrayed all over the walls all kinds of crawling things and unclean animals and all the idols of Israel. ¹¹In front of them stood seventy elders of Israel, and Jaazaniah son of Shaphan was standing among them. Each had a censer in his hand, and a fragrant cloud of incense was rising. Ex 3:16; 20:4

¹²He said to me, "Son of man, have you seen what the elders of Israel are doing in the darkness, each at the shrine of his own idol? They say, 'The LORD does not see us; the LORD has forsaken the land.' " ¹³Again, he said, "You will see them doing things that are even more detestable." Ps 10:11

¹⁴Then he brought me to the entrance of the north gate of the house of the LORD, and I saw women sitting there, mourning the god Tammuz. ¹⁵He said to me, "Do you see this, son of man? You will see things that are even more detestable than this." Eze 11:12

¹⁶He then brought me into the inner court of the house of the LORD, and there at the entrance to the temple, between the portico and the altar, were about twenty-five men. With their backs toward the temple of the LORD and their faces toward the east, they were bowing down to the sun in the east. Dt 4:19; Jer 2:27

¹⁷He said to me, "Have you seen this, son of man? Is it a trivial matter for the people of Judah to do the detestable things they are doing here? Must they also fill the land with violence and continually arouse my anger? Look at them putting the branch to their nose! ¹⁸Therefore I will deal with them in anger; I will not look on them with pity or spare them. Although they shout in my ears, I will not listen to them." Isa 1:15; Jer 11:11; Mic 3:4

Judgment on the Idolaters

9 Then I heard him call out in a loud voice, "Bring near those who are appointed to execute judgment on the city, each with a weapon in his hand." ²And I saw six men coming from the direction of the upper gate, which faces north, each with a deadly weapon in his hand. With them was a man clothed in linen who had a writing kit at his side. They came in and stood beside the bronze altar. Lev 16:4; Eze 10:2

³Now the glory of the God of Israel went up from above the cherubim, where it had been,

and moved to the threshold of the temple. Then the LORD called to the man clothed in linen who had the writing kit at his side [4] and said to him, "Go throughout the city of Jerusalem and put a mark on the foreheads of those who grieve and lament over all the detestable things that are done in it." Ex 12:7; Rev 7:3; 9:4

[5] As I listened, he said to the others, "Follow him through the city and kill, without showing pity or compassion. [6] Slaughter the old men, the young men and women, the mothers and children, but do not touch anyone who has the mark. Begin at my sanctuary." So they began with the old men who were in front of the temple. 2Ch 36:17; 1Pe 4:17

[7] Then he said to them, "Defile the temple and fill the courts with the slain. Go!" So they went out and began killing throughout the city. [8] While they were killing and I was left alone, I fell facedown, crying out, "Alas, Sovereign LORD! Are you going to destroy the entire remnant of Israel in this outpouring of your wrath on Jerusalem?" Eze 11:13; Am 7:1-6

[9] He answered me, "The sin of the people of Israel and Judah is exceedingly great; the land is full of bloodshed and the city is full of injustice. They say, 'The LORD has forsaken the land; the LORD does not see.' [10] So I will not look on them with pity or spare

them, but I will bring down on their own heads what they have done." Eze 8:18; 11:21

[11] Then the man in linen with the writing kit at his side brought back word, saying, "I have done as you commanded."

God's Glory Departs From the Temple

10 I looked, and I saw the likeness of a throne of lapis lazuli above the vault that was over the heads of the cherubim. [2] The LORD said to the man clothed in linen, "Go in among the wheels beneath the cherubim. Fill your hands with burning coals from among the cherubim and scatter them over the city." And as I watched, he went in. Eze 1:22; Rev 8:5

[3] Now the cherubim were standing on the south side of the temple when the man went in, and a cloud filled the inner court. [4] Then the glory of the LORD rose from above the cherubim and moved to the threshold of the temple. The cloud filled the temple, and the court was full of the radiance of the glory of the LORD. [5] The sound of the wings of the cherubim could be heard as far away as the outer court, like the voice of God Almighty[a] when he speaks. Eze 1:24,28; 9:3

[6] When the LORD commanded the man in linen, "Take fire from among the wheels, from among

[a] 5 Hebrew *El-Shaddai*

the cherubim," the man went in and stood beside a wheel. ⁷Then one of the cherubim reached out his hand to the fire that was among them. He took up some of it and put it into the hands of the man in linen, who took it and went out. ⁸(Under the wings of the cherubim could be seen what looked like human hands.) Eze 1:8

⁹I looked, and I saw beside the cherubim four wheels, one beside each of the cherubim; the wheels sparkled like topaz. ¹⁰As for their appearance, the four of them looked alike; each was like a wheel intersecting a wheel. ¹¹As they moved, they would go in any one of the four directions the cherubim faced; the wheels did not turn about*a* as the cherubim went. The cherubim went in whatever direction the head faced, without turning as they went. ¹²Their entire bodies, including their backs, their hands and their wings, were completely full of eyes, as were their four wheels. ¹³I heard the wheels being called "the whirling wheels." ¹⁴Each of the cherubim had four faces: One face was that of a cherub, the second the face of a human being, the third the face of a lion, and the fourth the face of an eagle. Eze 1:10; Rev 4:7

¹⁵Then the cherubim rose upward. These were the living creatures I had seen by the Kebar River. ¹⁶When the cherubim

moved, the wheels beside them moved; and when the cherubim spread their wings to rise from the ground, the wheels did not leave their side. ¹⁷When the cherubim stood still, they also stood still; and when the cherubim rose, they rose with them, because the spirit of the living creatures was in them. Eze 1:20-21

¹⁸Then the glory of the LORD departed from over the threshold of the temple and stopped above the cherubim. ¹⁹While I watched, the cherubim spread their wings and rose from the ground, and as they went, the wheels went with them. They stopped at the entrance of the east gate of the LORD's house, and the glory of the God of Israel was above them. Ps 18:10; Eze 11:1,22

²⁰These were the living creatures I had seen beneath the God of Israel by the Kebar River, and I realized that they were cherubim. ²¹Each had four faces and four wings, and under their wings was what looked like human hands. ²²Their faces had the same appearance as those I had seen by the Kebar River. Each one went straight ahead. Eze 1:6

God's Sure Judgment on Jerusalem

11 Then the Spirit lifted me up and brought me to the gate of the house of the LORD that faces east. There at the entrance

a 11 Or *aside*

of the gate were twenty-five men, and I saw among them Jaazaniah son of Azzur and Pelatiah son of Benaiah, leaders of the people. [2] The LORD said to me, "Son of man, these are the men who are plotting evil and giving wicked advice in this city. [3] They say, 'Haven't our houses been recently rebuilt? This city is a pot, and we are the meat in it.' [4] Therefore prophesy against them; prophesy, son of man." Eze 3:4,17; 8:16

[5] Then the Spirit of the LORD came on me, and he told me to say: "This is what the LORD says: That is what you are saying, you leaders in Israel, but I know what is going through your mind. [6] You have killed many people in this city and filled its streets with the dead. Jer 17:10; Eze 7:23

[7] "Therefore this is what the Sovereign LORD says: The bodies you have thrown there are the meat and this city is the pot, but I will drive you out of it. [8] You fear the sword, and the sword is what I will bring against you, declares the Sovereign LORD. [9] I will drive you out of the city and deliver you into the hands of foreigners and inflict punishment on you. [10] You will fall by the sword, and I will execute judgment on you at the borders of Israel. Then you will know that I am the LORD. [11] This city will not be a pot for you, nor will you be the meat in it; I will execute judgment on you at the borders of Israel. [12] And you will know that I am the LORD, for you have not followed my decrees or kept my laws but have conformed to the standards of the nations around you." Lev 18:4; Eze 8:10

[13] Now as I was prophesying, Pelatiah son of Benaiah died. Then I fell facedown and cried out in a loud voice, "Alas, Sovereign LORD! Will you completely destroy the remnant of Israel?" Eze 9:8; Am 7:2

The Promise of Israel's Return

[14] The word of the LORD came to me: [15] "Son of man, the people of Jerusalem have said of your fellow exiles and all the other Israelites, 'They are far away from the LORD; this land was given to us as our possession.' Eze 33:24

[16] "Therefore say: 'This is what the Sovereign LORD says: Although I sent them far away among the nations and scattered them among the countries, yet for a little while I have been a sanctuary for them in the countries where they have gone.' Ps 90:1

[17] "Therefore say: 'This is what the Sovereign LORD says: I will gather you from the nations and bring you back from the countries where you have been scattered, and I will give you back the land of Israel again.' Jer 24:5-6

[18] "They will return to it and remove all its vile images and detestable idols. [19] I will give them an undivided heart and put a new spirit in them; I will remove from them their heart of stone

and give them a heart of flesh. ²⁰Then they will follow my decrees and be careful to keep my laws. They will be my people, and I will be their God. ²¹But as for those whose hearts are devoted to their vile images and detestable idols, I will bring down on their own heads what they have done, declares the Sovereign LORD." Jer 32:39; Eze 18:31; 36:26

²²Then the cherubim, with the wheels beside them, spread their wings, and the glory of the God of Israel was above them. ²³The glory of the LORD went up from within the city and stopped above the mountain east of it. ²⁴The Spirit lifted me up and brought me to the exiles in Babylonia[a] in the vision given by the Spirit of God. Zec 14:4; 2Co 12:2-4

Then the vision I had seen went up from me, ²⁵and I told the exiles everything the LORD had shown me. Eze 3:4,11

The Exile Symbolized

12 The word of the LORD came to me: ²"Son of man, you are living among a rebellious people. They have eyes to see but do not see and ears to hear but do not hear, for they are a rebellious people.

³"Therefore, son of man, pack your belongings for exile and in the daytime, as they watch, set out and go from where you are to another place. Perhaps they will understand, though they are a rebellious people. ⁴During the daytime, while they watch, bring out your belongings packed for exile. Then in the evening, while they are watching, go out like those who go into exile. ⁵While they watch, dig through the wall and take your belongings out through it. ⁶Put them on your shoulder as they are watching and carry them out at dusk. Cover your face so that you cannot see the land, for I have made you a sign to the Israelites." Isa 8:18; Eze 4:3; 24:24

⁷So I did as I was commanded. During the day I brought out my things packed for exile. Then in the evening I dug through the wall with my hands. I took my belongings out at dusk, carrying them on my shoulders while they watched. Eze 24:18; 37:10

⁸In the morning the word of the LORD came to me: ⁹"Son of man, did not the Israelites, that rebellious people, ask you, 'What are you doing?' Eze 17:12; 24:19

¹⁰"Say to them, 'This is what the Sovereign LORD says: This prophecy concerns the prince in Jerusalem and all the Israelites who are there.' ¹¹Say to them, 'I am a sign to you.' Zec 3:8

"As I have done, so it will be done to them. They will go into exile as captives. Jer 15:2; 52:15

¹²"The prince among them will put his things on his shoulder at dusk and leave, and a hole

^a 24 Or *Chaldea*

will be dug in the wall for him to go through. He will cover his face so that he cannot see the land. [13] I will spread my net for him, and he will be caught in my snare; I will bring him to Babylonia, the land of the Chaldeans, but he will not see it, and there he will die. [14] I will scatter to the winds all those around him — his staff and all his troops — and I will pursue them with drawn sword. 2Ki 25:5; Eze 5:10,12

[15] "They will know that I am the LORD, when I disperse them among the nations and scatter them through the countries. [16] But I will spare a few of them from the sword, famine and plague, so that in the nations where they go they may acknowledge all their detestable practices. Then they will know that I am the LORD." Jer 22:8-9; Eze 6:8-10; 14:22

[17] The word of the LORD came to me: [18] "Son of man, tremble as you eat your food, and shudder in fear as you drink your water. [19] Say to the people of the land: 'This is what the Sovereign LORD says about those living in Jerusalem and in the land of Israel: They will eat their food in anxiety and drink their water in despair, for their land will be stripped of everything in it because of the violence of all who live there. [20] The inhabited towns will be laid waste and the land will be desolate. Then you will know that I am the LORD.'" Isa 7:23-24; Jer 4:7

There Will Be No Delay

[21] The word of the LORD came to me: [22] "Son of man, what is this proverb you have in the land of Israel: 'The days go by and every vision comes to nothing'? [23] Say to them, 'This is what the Sovereign LORD says: I am going to put an end to this proverb, and they will no longer quote it in Israel.' Say to them, 'The days are near when every vision will be fulfilled. [24] For there will be no more false visions or flattering divinations among the people of Israel. [25] But I the LORD will speak what I will, and it shall be fulfilled without delay. For in your days, you rebellious people, I will fulfill whatever I say, declares the Sovereign LORD.'" Eze 13:23; Zec 13:2-4

[26] The word of the LORD came to me: [27] "Son of man, the Israelites are saying, 'The vision he sees is for many years from now, and he prophesies about the distant future.' Da 10:14

[28] "Therefore say to them, 'This is what the Sovereign LORD says: None of my words will be delayed any longer; whatever I say will be fulfilled, declares the Sovereign LORD.'"

False Prophets Condemned

13 The word of the LORD came to me: [2] "Son of man, prophesy against the prophets of Israel who are now prophesying. Say to those who prophesy out of their own imagination: 'Hear the

word of the LORD! ³This is what the Sovereign LORD says: Woe to the foolish[a] prophets who follow their own spirit and have seen nothing! ⁴Your prophets, Israel, are like jackals among ruins. ⁵You have not gone up to the breaches in the wall to repair it for the people of Israel so that it will stand firm in the battle on the day of the LORD. ⁶Their visions are false and their divinations a lie. Even though the LORD has not sent them, they say, "The LORD declares," and expect him to fulfill their words. ⁷Have you not seen false visions and uttered lying divinations when you say, "The LORD declares," though I have not spoken? Eze 22:28,30; Jer 23:16

⁸" 'Therefore this is what the Sovereign LORD says: Because of your false words and lying visions, I am against you, declares the Sovereign LORD. ⁹My hand will be against the prophets who see false visions and utter lying divinations. They will not belong to the council of my people or be listed in the records of Israel, nor will they enter the land of Israel. Then you will know that I am the Sovereign LORD. Jer 17:13; Eze 20:38

¹⁰" 'Because they lead my people astray, saying, "Peace," when there is no peace, and because, when a flimsy wall is built, they cover it with whitewash, ¹¹therefore tell those who cover it with whitewash that it is going to fall.

Rain will come in torrents, and I will send hailstones hurtling down, and violent winds will burst forth. ¹²When the wall collapses, will people not ask you, "Where is the whitewash you covered it with?" Eze 22:28; 38:22

¹³" 'Therefore this is what the Sovereign LORD says: In my wrath I will unleash a violent wind, and in my anger hailstones and torrents of rain will fall with destructive fury. ¹⁴I will tear down the wall you have covered with whitewash and will level it to the ground so that its foundation will be laid bare. When it[b] falls, you will be destroyed in it; and you will know that I am the LORD. ¹⁵So I will pour out my wrath against the wall and against those who covered it with whitewash. I will say to you, "The wall is gone and so are those who whitewashed it, ¹⁶those prophets of Israel who prophesied to Jerusalem and saw visions of peace for her when there was no peace, declares the Sovereign LORD." ' Isa 57:21; Jer 6:14

¹⁷"Now, son of man, set your face against the daughters of your people who prophesy out of their own imagination. Prophesy against them ¹⁸and say, 'This is what the Sovereign LORD says: Woe to the women who sew magic charms on all their wrists and make veils of various lengths for their heads in order to ensnare

a 3 Or wicked   b 14 Or the city

people. Will you ensnare the lives of my people but preserve your own? ¹⁹You have profaned me among my people for a few handfuls of barley and scraps of bread. By lying to my people, who listen to lies, you have killed those who should not have died and have spared those who should not live. Pr 28:21; Rev 2:20

²⁰"'Therefore this is what the Sovereign Lord says: I am against your magic charms with which you ensnare people like birds and I will tear them from your arms; I will set free the people that you ensnare like birds. ²¹I will tear off your veils and save my people from your hands, and they will no longer fall prey to your power. Then you will know that I am the Lord. ²²Because you disheartened the righteous with your lies, when I had brought them no grief, and because you encouraged the wicked not to turn from their evil ways and so save their lives, ²³therefore you will no longer see false visions or practice divination. I will save my people from your hands. And then you will know that I am the Lord.'" Eze 12:24; Mic 3:6

Idolaters Condemned

14 Some of the elders of Israel came to me and sat down in front of me. ²Then the word of the Lord came to me: ³"Son of man, these men have set up idols in their hearts and put wicked

stumbling blocks before their faces. Should I let them inquire of me at all? ⁴Therefore speak to them and tell them, 'This is what the Sovereign Lord says: When any of the Israelites set up idols in their hearts and put a wicked stumbling block before their faces and then go to a prophet, I the Lord will answer them myself in keeping with their great idolatry. ⁵I will do this to recapture the hearts of the people of Israel, who have all deserted me for their idols.' Eze 7:19; Zec 11:8

⁶"Therefore say to the people of Israel, 'This is what the Sovereign Lord says: Repent! Turn from your idols and renounce all your detestable practices! Isa 2:20

⁷"'When any of the Israelites or any foreigner residing in Israel separate themselves from me and set up idols in their hearts and put a wicked stumbling block before their faces and then go to a prophet to inquire of me, I the Lord will answer them myself. ⁸I will set my face against them and make them an example and a byword. I will remove them from my people. Then you will know that I am the Lord. Eze 5:15; 15:7

⁹"'And if the prophet is enticed to utter a prophecy, I the Lord have enticed that prophet, and I will stretch out my hand against him and destroy him from among my people Israel. ¹⁰They will bear their guilt—the prophet will be as guilty as the one who

consults him. ¹¹Then the people of Israel will no longer stray from me, nor will they defile themselves anymore with all their sins. They will be my people, and I will be their God, declares the Sovereign LORD.'" Eze 11:19-20; 48:11

Jerusalem's Judgment Inescapable

¹²The word of the LORD came to me: ¹³"Son of man, if a country sins against me by being unfaithful and I stretch out my hand against it to cut off its food supply and send famine upon it and kill its people and their animals, ¹⁴even if these three men — Noah, Daniel*a* and Job — were in it, they could save only themselves by their righteousness, declares the Sovereign LORD. Jer 15:1; Eze 18:20

¹⁵"Or if I send wild beasts through that country and they leave it childless and it becomes desolate so that no one can pass through it because of the beasts, ¹⁶as surely as I live, declares the Sovereign LORD, even if these three men were in it, they could not save their own sons or daughters. They alone would be saved, but the land would be desolate.

¹⁷"Or if I bring a sword against that country and say, 'Let the sword pass throughout the land,' and I kill its people and their animals, ¹⁸as surely as I live, declares the Sovereign LORD, even

if these three men were in it, they could not save their own sons or daughters. They alone would be saved. Eze 5:12; 21:3-4; 25:13

¹⁹"Or if I send a plague into that land and pour out my wrath on it through bloodshed, killing its people and their animals, ²⁰as surely as I live, declares the Sovereign LORD, even if Noah, Daniel and Job were in it, they could save neither son nor daughter. They would save only themselves by their righteousness. ver 14

²¹"For this is what the Sovereign LORD says: How much worse will it be when I send against Jerusalem my four dreadful judgments — sword and famine and wild beasts and plague — to kill its men and their animals! ²²Yet there will be some survivors — sons and daughters who will be brought out of it. They will come to you, and when you see their conduct and their actions, you will be consoled regarding the disaster I have brought on Jerusalem — every disaster I have brought on it. ²³You will be consoled when you see their conduct and their actions, for you will know that I have done nothing in it without cause, declares the Sovereign LORD." Jer 22:8-9

Jerusalem as a Useless Vine

15 The word of the LORD came to me: ²"Son of man, how is the wood of a vine different

---

a 14 Or *Danel*, a man of renown in ancient literature; also in verse 20 from that of a branch from any of the trees in the forest? ³Is wood ever taken from it to make anything useful? Do they make pegs from it to hang things on? ⁴And after it is thrown on the fire as fuel and the fire burns both ends and chars the middle, is it then useful for anything? ⁵If it was not useful for anything when it was whole, how much less can it be made into something useful when the fire has burned it and it is charred? Jn 15:6; Hos 10:1

⁶"Therefore this is what the Sovereign LORD says: As I have given the wood of the vine among the trees of the forest as fuel for the fire, so will I treat the people living in Jerusalem. ⁷I will set my face against them. Although they have come out of the fire, the fire will yet consume them. And when I set my face against them, you will know that I am the LORD. ⁸I will make the land desolate because they have been unfaithful, declares the Sovereign LORD." Isa 24:18; Am 9:1-4

Jerusalem as an Adulterous Wife

16 The word of the LORD came to me: ²"Son of man, confront Jerusalem with her detestable practices ³and say, 'This is what the Sovereign LORD says to Jerusalem: Your ancestry and birth were in the land of the Canaanites; your father was an Am-orite and your mother a Hittite. ⁴On the day you were born your cord was not cut, nor were you washed with water to make you clean, nor were you rubbed with salt or wrapped in cloths. ⁵No one looked on you with pity or had compassion enough to do any of these things for you. Rather, you were thrown out into the open field, for on the day you were born you were despised. Eze 20:4; 22:2

⁶"'Then I passed by and saw you kicking about in your blood, and as you lay there in your blood I said to you, "Live!"ᵃ ⁷I made you grow like a plant of the field. You grew and developed and entered puberty. Your breasts had formed and your hair had grown, yet you were stark naked. Ex 19:4

⁸"'Later I passed by, and when I looked at you and saw that you were old enough for love, I spread the corner of my garment over you and covered your naked body. I gave you my solemn oath and entered into a covenant with you, declares the Sovereign LORD, and you became mine. Jer 2:2

⁹"'I bathed you with water and washed the blood from you and put ointments on you. ¹⁰I clothed you with an embroidered dress and put sandals of fine leather on you. I dressed you in fine linen and covered you with costly garments. ¹¹I adorned you with jewelry: I put bracelets on your

---

ᵃ 6 A few Hebrew manuscripts, Septuagint and Syriac; most Hebrew manuscripts repeat *and as you lay there in your blood I said to you, "Live!"*

arms and a necklace around your neck, ¹²and I put a ring on your nose, earrings on your ears and a beautiful crown on your head. ¹³So you were adorned with gold and silver; your clothes were of fine linen and costly fabric and embroidered cloth. Your food was honey, olive oil and the finest flour. You became very beautiful and rose to be a queen. ¹⁴And your fame spread among the nations on account of your beauty, because the splendor I had given you made your beauty perfect, declares the Sovereign LORD. 1Ki 10:24; La 2:15

¹⁵ " 'But you trusted in your beauty and used your fame to become a prostitute. You lavished your favors on anyone who passed by and your beauty became his. ¹⁶You took some of your garments to make gaudy high places, where you carried on your prostitution. You went to him, and he possessed your beauty.ᵃ ¹⁷You also took the fine jewelry I gave you, the jewelry made of my gold and silver, and you made for yourself male idols and engaged in prostitution with them. ¹⁸And you took your embroidered clothes to put on them, and you offered my oil and incense before them. ¹⁹Also the food I provided for you — the flour, olive oil and honey I gave you to eat — you offered as fragrant incense before them. That is what hap-

pened, declares the Sovereign LORD. Isa 57:8; Jer 2:20; Eze 23:3

²⁰ " 'And you took your sons and daughters whom you bore to me and sacrificed them as food to the idols. Was your prostitution not enough? ²¹You slaughtered my children and sacrificed them to the idols. ²²In all your detestable practices and your prostitution you did not remember the days of your youth, when you were naked and bare, kicking about in your blood. Ps 106:37-38

²³ " 'Woe! Woe to you, declares the Sovereign LORD. In addition to all your other wickedness, ²⁴you built a mound for yourself and made a lofty shrine in every public square. ²⁵At every street corner you built your lofty shrines and degraded your beauty, spreading your legs with increasing promiscuity to anyone who passed by. ²⁶You engaged in prostitution with the Egyptians, your neighbors with large genitals, and aroused my anger with your increasing promiscuity. ²⁷So I stretched out my hand against you and reduced your territory; I gave you over to the greed of your enemies, the daughters of the Philistines, who were shocked by your lewd conduct. ²⁸You engaged in prostitution with the Assyrians too, because you were insatiable; and even after that, you still were not satisfied. ²⁹Then you increased

---

ᵃ 16 The meaning of the Hebrew for this sentence is uncertain.

your promiscuity to include Babylonia,[a] a land of merchants, but even with this you were not satisfied.   Isa 57:7; Jer 2:20; Eze 20:28

30 "'I am filled with fury against you,[b] declares the Sovereign LORD, when you do all these things, acting like a brazen prostitute! 31 When you built your mounds at every street corner and made your lofty shrines in every public square, you were unlike a prostitute, because you scorned payment.   Jer 3:3

32 "'You adulterous wife! You prefer strangers to your own husband! 33 All prostitutes receive gifts, but you give gifts to all your lovers, bribing them to come to you from everywhere for your illicit favors. 34 So in your prostitution you are the opposite of others; no one runs after you for your favors. You are the very opposite, for you give payment and none is given to you.   Hos 8:9-10

35 "'Therefore, you prostitute, hear the word of the LORD! 36 This is what the Sovereign LORD says: Because you poured out your lust and exposed your naked body in your promiscuity with your lovers, and because of all your detestable idols, and because you gave them your children's blood, 37 therefore I am going to gather all your lovers, with whom you found pleasure, those you loved as well as those you hated. I will gather them against you from all

around and will strip you in front of them, and they will see you stark naked. 38 I will sentence you to the punishment of women who commit adultery and who shed blood; I will bring on you the blood vengeance of my wrath and jealous anger. 39 Then I will deliver you into the hands of your lovers, and they will tear down your mounds and destroy your lofty shrines. They will strip you of your clothes and take your fine jewelry and leave you stark naked. 40 They will bring a mob against you, who will stone you and hack you to pieces with their swords. 41 They will burn down your houses and inflict punishment on you in the sight of many women. I will put a stop to your prostitution, and you will no longer pay your lovers. 42 Then my wrath against you will subside and my jealous anger will turn away from you; I will be calm and no longer angry.   Eze 5:13; 39:29

43 "'Because you did not remember the days of your youth but enraged me with all these things, I will surely bring down on your head what you have done, declares the Sovereign LORD. Did you not add lewdness to all your other detestable practices?   Ps 78:42; Eze 11:21; 22:31

44 "'Everyone who quotes proverbs will quote this proverb about you: "Like mother, like daughter." 45 You are a true daughter

of your mother, who despised her husband and her children; and you are a true sister of your sisters, who despised their husbands and their children. Your mother was a Hittite and your father an Amorite. ⁴⁶ Your older sister was Samaria, who lived to the north of you with her daughters; and your younger sister, who lived to the south of you with her daughters, was Sodom. ⁴⁷ You not only followed their ways and copied their detestable practices, but in all your ways you soon became more depraved than they. ⁴⁸ As surely as I live, declares the Sovereign LORD, your sister Sodom and her daughters never did what you and your daughters have done. Mt 10:15; 11:23-24

⁴⁹ " 'Now this was the sin of your sister Sodom: She and her daughters were arrogant, overfed and unconcerned; they did not help the poor and needy. ⁵⁰ They were haughty and did detestable things before me. Therefore I did away with them as you have seen. ⁵¹ Samaria did not commit half the sins you did. You have done more detestable things than they, and have made your sisters seem righteous by all these things you have done. ⁵² Bear your disgrace, for you have furnished some justification for your sisters. Because your sins were more vile than theirs,

they appear more righteous than you. So then, be ashamed and bear your disgrace, for you have made your sisters appear righteous. Ge 13:13; Lk 12:16-20

⁵³ " 'However, I will restore the fortunes of Sodom and her daughters and of Samaria and her daughters, and your fortunes along with them, ⁵⁴ so that you may bear your disgrace and be ashamed of all you have done in giving them comfort. ⁵⁵ And your sisters, Sodom with her daughters and Samaria with her daughters, will return to what they were before; and you and your daughters will return to what you were before. ⁵⁶ You would not even mention your sister Sodom in the day of your pride, ⁵⁷ before your wickedness was uncovered. Even so, you are now scorned by the daughters of Edom[a] and all her neighbors and the daughters of the Philistines — all those around you who despise you. ⁵⁸ You will bear the consequences of your lewdness and your detestable practices, declares the LORD. 2Ki 16:6; Eze 23:49

⁵⁹ " 'This is what the Sovereign LORD says: I will deal with you as you deserve, because you have despised my oath by breaking the covenant. ⁶⁰ Yet I will remember the covenant I made with you in the days of your youth, and I will establish an everlasting

---

[a] 57 Many Hebrew manuscripts and Syriac; most Hebrew manuscripts, Septuagint and Vulgate *Aram*

covenant with you. ⁶¹ Then you will remember your ways and be ashamed when you receive your sisters, both those who are older than you and those who are younger. I will give them to you as daughters, but not on the basis of my covenant with you. ⁶² So I will establish my covenant with you, and you will know that I am the LORD. ⁶³ Then, when I make atonement for you for all you have done, you will remember and be ashamed and never again open your mouth because of your humiliation, declares the Sovereign LORD.' " Jer 32:40; Ro 3:19

Two Eagles and a Vine

17 The word of the LORD came to me: ² "Son of man, set forth an allegory and tell it to the Israelites as a parable. ³ Say to them, 'This is what the Sovereign LORD says: A great eagle with powerful wings, long feathers and full plumage of varied colors came to Lebanon. Taking hold of the top of a cedar, ⁴ he broke off its topmost shoot and carried it away to a land of merchants, where he planted it in a city of traders. Jer 22:23; Eze 20:49

⁵ " 'He took one of the seedlings of the land and put it in fertile soil. He planted it like a willow by abundant water, ⁶ and it sprouted and became a low, spreading vine. Its branches turned toward him, but its roots remained under it. So it became a vine and produced branches and put out leafy boughs. Dt 8:7-9; Isa 44:4

⁷ " 'But there was another great eagle with powerful wings and full plumage. The vine now sent out its roots toward him from the plot where it was planted and stretched out its branches to him for water. ⁸ It had been planted in good soil by abundant water so that it would produce branches, bear fruit and become a splendid vine.' Eze 31:4

⁹ "Say to them, 'This is what the Sovereign LORD says: Will it thrive? Will it not be uprooted and stripped of its fruit so that it withers? All its new growth will wither. It will not take a strong arm or many people to pull it up by the roots. ¹⁰ It has been planted, but will it thrive? Will it not wither completely when the east wind strikes it — wither away in the plot where it grew?' " Hos 13:15

¹¹ Then the word of the LORD came to me: ¹² "Say to this rebellious people, 'Do you not know what these things mean?' Say to them: 'The king of Babylon went to Jerusalem and carried off her king and her nobles, bringing them back with him to Babylon. ¹³ Then he took a member of the royal family and made a treaty with him, putting him under oath. He also carried away the leading men of the land, ¹⁴ so that the kingdom would be brought low, unable to rise again, surviving only by keeping his treaty.

¹⁵But the king rebelled against him by sending his envoys to Egypt to get horses and a large army. Will he succeed? Will he who does such things escape? Will he break the treaty and yet escape? 2Ch 36:13; Eze 12:9; 29:14

¹⁶" 'As surely as I live, declares the Sovereign LORD, he shall die in Babylon, in the land of the king who put him on the throne, whose oath he despised and whose treaty he broke. ¹⁷Pharaoh with his mighty army and great horde will be of no help to him in war, when ramps are built and siege works erected to destroy many lives. ¹⁸He despised the oath by breaking the covenant. Because he had given his hand in pledge and yet did all these things, he shall not escape. 1Ch 29:24; Eze 29:6-7

¹⁹" 'Therefore this is what the Sovereign LORD says: As surely as I live, I will repay him for despising my oath and breaking my covenant. ²⁰I will spread my net for him, and he will be caught in my snare. I will bring him to Babylon and execute judgment on him there because he was unfaithful to me. ²¹All his choice troops will fall by the sword, and the survivors will be scattered to the winds. Then you will know that I the LORD have spoken. Eze 12:13-14

²²" 'This is what the Sovereign LORD says: I myself will take a shoot from the very top of a cedar and plant it; I will break off a tender sprig from its topmost shoots and plant it on a high and lofty mountain. ²³On the mountain heights of Israel I will plant it; it will produce branches and bear fruit and become a splendid cedar. Birds of every kind will nest in it; they will find shelter in the shade of its branches. ²⁴All the trees of the forest will know that I the LORD bring down the tall tree and make the low tree grow tall. I dry up the green tree and make the dry tree flourish. Ps 96:12; Jer 23:5

" 'I the LORD have spoken, and I will do it.' " Eze 19:12; Am 9:11

The One Who Sins Will Die

18 The word of the LORD came to me: ²"What do you people mean by quoting this proverb about the land of Israel:

" 'The parents eat sour grapes,
    and the children's teeth are
        set on edge'? Isa 3:15

³"As surely as I live, declares the Sovereign LORD, you will no longer quote this proverb in Israel. ⁴For everyone belongs to me, the parent as well as the child — both alike belong to me. The one who sins is the one who will die. Ro 6:23; Isa 42:5

⁵"Suppose there is a righteous man
    who does what is just and
        right.
⁶He does not eat at the
        mountain shrines Eze 22:9
    or look to the idols of Israel.

He does not defile his
neighbor's wife
or have sexual relations
with a woman during
her period. Lev 12:2
⁷He does not oppress anyone,
but returns what he took in
pledge for a loan. Dt 24:12
He does not commit robbery
but gives his food to the
hungry Job 22:7
and provides clothing for
the naked. Dt 15:11; Mt 25:36
⁸He does not lend to them at
interest
or take a profit from them.
He withholds his hand from
doing wrong
and judges fairly between
two parties. Zec 8:16
⁹He follows my decrees Lev 19:37
and faithfully keeps my laws.
That man is righteous; Hab 2:4
he will surely live, Lev 18:5
declares the Sovereign
Lᴏʀᴅ.

¹⁰"Suppose he has a violent
son, who sheds blood or does any
of these other things[a] ¹¹(though
the father has done none of
them): Ex 21:12

"He eats at the mountain
shrines.
He defiles his neighbor's wife.
¹²He oppresses the poor and
needy. Am 4:1
He commits robbery.
He does not return what he
took in pledge.

He looks to the idols.
He does detestable things.
¹³He lends at interest and takes
a profit. Ex 22:25

Will such a man live? He will not!
Because he has done all these
detestable things, he is to be put
to death; his blood will be on his
own head. Eze 33:4-5
¹⁴"But suppose this son has a
son who sees all the sins his father commits, and though he
sees them, he does not do such
things: 2Ch 34:21; Pr 23:24

¹⁵"He does not eat at the
mountain shrines
or look to the idols of Israel.
He does not defile his
neighbor's wife.
¹⁶He does not oppress anyone
or require a pledge for a loan.
He does not commit robbery
but gives his food to the
hungry
and provides clothing for
the naked. Ps 41:1; Isa 58:10
¹⁷He withholds his hand from
mistreating the poor
and takes no interest or
profit from them.
He keeps my laws and follows
my decrees.

He will not die for his father's
sin; he will surely live. ¹⁸But his
father will die for his own sin,
because he practiced extortion,
robbed his brother and did what
was wrong among his people.

a 10 Or things to a brother

19 "Yet you ask, 'Why does the son not share the guilt of his father?' Since the son has done what is just and right and has been careful to keep all my decrees, he will surely live. 20 The one who sins is the one who will die. The child will not share the guilt of the parent, nor will the parent share the guilt of the child. The righteousness of the righteous will be credited to them, and the wickedness of the wicked will be charged against them. Dt 24:16; Isa 3:11; Ro 2:9

21 "But if a wicked person turns away from all the sins they have committed and keeps all my decrees and does what is just and right, that person will surely live; they will not die. 22 None of the offenses they have committed will be remembered against them. Because of the righteous things they have done, they will live. 23 Do I take any pleasure in the death of the wicked? declares the Sovereign LORD. Rather, am I not pleased when they turn from their ways and live? Eze 33:11; 1Ti 2:4

24 "But if a righteous person turns from their righteousness and commits sin and does the same detestable things the wicked person does, will they live? None of the righteous things that person has done will be remembered. Because of the unfaithfulness they are guilty of and because of the sins they have committed, they will die. Eze 3:20

25 "Yet you say, 'The way of the Lord is not just.' Hear, you Israelites: Is my way unjust? Is it not your ways that are unjust? 26 If a righteous person turns from their righteousness and commits sin, they will die for it; because of the sin they have committed they will die. 27 But if a wicked person turns away from the wickedness they have committed and does what is just and right, they will save their life. 28 Because they consider all the offenses they have committed and turn away from them, that person will surely live; they will not die. 29 Yet the Israelites say, 'The way of the Lord is not just.' Are my ways unjust, people of Israel? Is it not your ways that are unjust? Eze 33:17; Zep 3:5; Mal 2:17

30 "Therefore, you Israelites, I will judge each of you according to your own ways, declares the Sovereign LORD. Repent! Turn away from all your offenses; then sin will not be your downfall. 31 Rid yourselves of all the offenses you have committed, and get a new heart and a new spirit. Why will you die, people of Israel? 32 For I take no pleasure in the death of anyone, declares the Sovereign LORD. Repent and live! Eze 7:3; 11:19

A Lament Over Israel's Princes

19 "Take up a lament concerning the princes of Israel 2 and say: 2Ki 24:6; Eze 26:17

" 'What a lioness was your
  mother
among the lions!
She lay down among them
  and reared her cubs.
3 She brought up one of her
  cubs,
and he became a strong
  lion.
He learned to tear the prey
  and he became a man-
    eater.
4 The nations heard about him,
  and he was trapped in their
    pit.
They led him with hooks
  to the land of Egypt.

5 " 'When she saw her hope
  unfulfilled,
her expectation gone,
she took another of her cubs
  and made him a strong lion.
6 He prowled among the lions,
  for he was now a strong lion.
He learned to tear the prey
  and he became a man-
    eater. 2Ki 24:9; 2Ch 36:9
7 He broke down[a] their
  strongholds
  and devastated their towns.
The land and all who were in it
  were terrified by his
    roaring.
8 Then the nations came
  against him, 2Ki 24:2
  those from regions round
    about.
They spread their net for him,

and he was trapped in their
  pit. 2Ki 24:11
9 With hooks they pulled him
  into a cage
  and brought him to the king
    of Babylon. 2Ch 36:6
They put him in prison,
  so his roar was heard no
    longer
  on the mountains of Israel.

10 " 'Your mother was like a vine
  in your vineyard[b]
planted by the water; Ps 80:8-11
it was fruitful and full of
  branches
  because of abundant water.
11 Its branches were strong,
  fit for a ruler's scepter.
It towered high
  above the thick foliage,
conspicuous for its height
  and for its many branches.
12 But it was uprooted in fury
  and thrown to the ground.
The east wind made it shrivel,
  it was stripped of its fruit;
its strong branches withered
  and fire consumed them.
13 Now it is planted in the
  desert, Eze 20:35
  in a dry and thirsty land.
14 Fire spread from one of its
  main[c] branches
  and consumed its fruit.
No strong branch is left on it
  fit for a ruler's scepter.'

"This is a lament and is to be
used as a lament."

---

[a] 7 Targum (see Septuagint); Hebrew *He knew*
Hebrew manuscripts *your blood*   [c] 14 Or *from under its*
[b] 10 Two Hebrew manuscripts; most

Rebellious Israel Purged

20 In the seventh year, in the fifth month on the tenth day, some of the elders of Israel came to inquire of the LORD, and they sat down in front of me. Eze 8:1

[2] Then the word of the LORD came to me: [3] "Son of man, speak to the elders of Israel and say to them, 'This is what the Sovereign LORD says: Have you come to inquire of me? As surely as I live, I will not let you inquire of me, declares the Sovereign LORD.' Eze 14:3

[4] "Will you judge them? Will you judge them, son of man? Then confront them with the detestable practices of their ancestors [5] and say to them: 'This is what the Sovereign LORD says: On the day I chose Israel, I swore with uplifted hand to the descendants of Jacob and revealed myself to them in Egypt. With uplifted hand I said to them, "I am the LORD your God." [6] On that day I swore to them that I would bring them out of Egypt into a land I had searched out for them, a land flowing with milk and honey, the most beautiful of all lands. [7] And I said to them, "Each of you, get rid of the vile images you have set your eyes on, and do not defile yourselves with the idols of Egypt. I am the LORD your God." Ex 6:7; Dt 8:7; Ps 48:2

[8] "'But they rebelled against me and would not listen to me; they did not get rid of the vile images they had set their eyes on, nor did they forsake the idols of Egypt. So I said I would pour out my wrath on them and spend my anger against them in Egypt. [9] But for the sake of my name, I brought them out of Egypt. I did it to keep my name from being profaned in the eyes of the nations among whom they lived and in whose sight I had revealed myself to the Israelites. [10] Therefore I led them out of Egypt and brought them into the wilderness. [11] I gave them my decrees and made known to them my laws, by which the person who obeys them will live. [12] Also I gave them my Sabbaths as a sign between us, so they would know that I the LORD made them holy. Lev 18:5; Dt 4:7-8; Ro 10:5

[13] "'Yet the people of Israel rebelled against me in the wilderness. They did not follow my decrees but rejected my laws — by which the person who obeys them will live — and they utterly desecrated my Sabbaths. So I said I would pour out my wrath on them and destroy them in the wilderness. [14] But for the sake of my name I did what would keep it from being profaned in the eyes of the nations in whose sight I had brought them out. [15] Also with uplifted hand I swore to them in the wilderness that I would not bring them into the land I had given them — a land flowing with milk and honey, the most beautiful of all lands — [16] because they rejected my laws and did not

follow my decrees and desecrated my Sabbaths. For their hearts were devoted to their idols. [17]Yet I looked on them with pity and did not destroy them or put an end to them in the wilderness. [18]I said to their children in the wilderness, "Do not follow the statutes of your parents or keep their laws or defile yourselves with their idols. [19]I am the LORD your God; follow my decrees and be careful to keep my laws. [20]Keep my Sabbaths holy, that they may be a sign between us. Then you will know that I am the LORD your God."   Dt 5:32-33; Am 5:26

[21]"'But the children rebelled against me: They did not follow my decrees, they were not careful to keep my laws, of which I said, "The person who obeys them will live by them," and they desecrated my Sabbaths. So I said I would pour out my wrath on them and spend my anger against them in the wilderness. [22]But I withheld my hand, and for the sake of my name I did what would keep it from being profaned in the eyes of the nations in whose sight I had brought them out. [23]Also with uplifted hand I swore to them in the wilderness that I would disperse them among the nations and scatter them through the countries, [24]because they had not obeyed my laws but had rejected my decrees and desecrated my Sabbaths, and their eyes lusted after their parents' idols. [25]So I gave them other statutes that were not good and laws through which they could not live; [26]I defiled them through their gifts—the sacrifice of every firstborn—that I might fill them with horror so they would know that I am the LORD.'   Lev 26:33; Dt 28:64; Ps 81:12

[27]"Therefore, son of man, speak to the people of Israel and say to them, 'This is what the Sovereign LORD says: In this also your ancestors blasphemed me by being unfaithful to me: [28]When I brought them into the land I had sworn to give them and they saw any high hill or any leafy tree, there they offered their sacrifices, made offerings that aroused my anger, presented their fragrant incense and poured out their drink offerings. [29]Then I said to them: What is this high place you go to?'" (It is called Bamah[a] to this day.)   Eze 6:13; Ro 2:24

Rebellious Israel Renewed

[30]"Therefore say to the Israelites: 'This is what the Sovereign LORD says: Will you defile yourselves the way your ancestors did and lust after their vile images? [31]When you offer your gifts—the sacrifice of your children in the fire—you continue to defile yourselves with all your idols to this day. Am I to let you inquire of me, you Israelites? As surely as I live, declares the Sovereign

---

[a] 29 Bamah means high place.

LORD, I will not let you inquire of me. Ps 106:37-39; Jer 16:12; Eze 16:20 [32] " 'You say, "We want to be like the nations, like the peoples of the world, who serve wood and stone." But what you have in mind will never happen. [33] As surely as I live, declares the Sovereign LORD, I will reign over you with a mighty hand and an outstretched arm and with outpoured wrath. [34] I will bring you from the nations and gather you from the countries where you have been scattered — with a mighty hand and an outstretched arm and with outpoured wrath. [35] I will bring you into the wilderness of the nations and there, face to face, I will execute judgment upon you. [36] As I judged your ancestors in the wilderness of the land of Egypt, so I will judge you, declares the Sovereign LORD. [37] I will take note of you as you pass under my rod, and I will bring you into the bond of the covenant. [38] I will purge you of those who revolt and rebel against me. Although I will bring them out of the land where they are living, yet they will not enter the land of Israel. Then you will know that I am the LORD. Lev 27:32; Jer 33:13; Eze 16:62

[39] " 'As for you, people of Israel, this is what the Sovereign LORD says: Go and serve your idols, every one of you! But afterward you will surely listen to me and no longer profane my holy name with your gifts and idols. [40] For on my holy mountain, the high mountain of Israel, declares the Sovereign LORD, there in the land all the people of Israel will serve me, and there I will accept them. There I will require your offerings and your choice gifts,[a] along with all your holy sacrifices. [41] I will accept you as fragrant incense when I bring you out from the nations and gather you from the countries where you have been scattered, and I will be proved holy through you in the sight of the nations. [42] Then you will know that I am the LORD, when I bring you into the land of Israel, the land I had sworn with uplifted hand to give to your ancestors. [43] There you will remember your conduct and all the actions by which you have defiled yourselves, and you will loathe yourselves for all the evil you have done. [44] You will know that I am the LORD, when I deal with you for my name's sake and not according to your evil ways and your corrupt practices, you people of Israel, declares the Sovereign LORD.' " Eze 16:61; Hos 5:15

Prophecy Against the South

[45] The word of the LORD came to me: [46] "Son of man, set your face toward the south; preach against the south and prophesy against the forest of the southland. [47] Say to the southern forest:

---

[a] 40 Or *and the gifts of your firstfruits*

'Hear the word of the LORD. This is what the Sovereign LORD says: I am about to set fire to you, and it will consume all your trees, both green and dry. The blazing flame will not be quenched, and every face from south to north will be scorched by it. [48]Everyone will see that I the LORD have kindled it; it will not be quenched.' " Jer 7:20

[49]Then I said, "Sovereign LORD, they are saying of me, 'Isn't he just telling parables?' "[a] Mt 13:13

Babylon as God's Sword of Judgment

21[b] The word of the LORD came to me: [2]"Son of man, set your face against Jerusalem and preach against the sanctuary. Prophesy against the land of Israel [3]and say to her: 'This is what the LORD says: I am against you. I will draw my sword from its sheath and cut off from you both the righteous and the wicked. [4]Because I am going to cut off the righteous and the wicked, my sword will be unsheathed against everyone from south to north. [5]Then all people will know that I the LORD have drawn my sword from its sheath; it will not return again.' Eze 20:46-47; Na 1:9

[6]"Therefore groan, son of man! Groan before them with broken heart and bitter grief. [7]And when they ask you, 'Why are you groaning?' you shall say, 'Be-cause of the news that is coming. Every heart will melt with fear and every hand go limp; every spirit will become faint and every leg will be wet with urine.' It is coming! It will surely take place, declares the Sovereign LORD." Isa 22:4; Eze 7:17

[8]The word of the LORD came to me: [9]"Son of man, prophesy and say, 'This is what the Lord says:

" 'A sword, a sword,
    sharpened and polished —
[10]sharpened for the slaughter,
    polished to flash like
        lightning!

" 'Shall we rejoice in the scepter of my royal son? The sword despises every such stick.

[11]" 'The sword is appointed to
        be polished, Jer 46:4
    to be grasped with the hand;
it is sharpened and polished,
    made ready for the hand of
        the slayer.
[12]Cry out and wail, son of man,
    for it is against my people;
    it is against all the princes
        of Israel.
They are thrown to the sword
    along with my people.
    Therefore beat your breast.

[13]" 'Testing will surely come. And what if even the scepter, which the sword despises, does not continue? declares the Sovereign LORD.'

¹⁴"So then, son of man, prophesy
and strike your hands
together.   Nu 24:10
Let the sword strike twice,
even three times.
It is a sword for slaughter —
a sword for great slaughter,
closing in on them from
every side.   Eze 6:11; 30:24
¹⁵So that hearts may melt with
fear   2Sa 17:10
and the fallen be many,
I have stationed the sword for
slaughter*ᵃ*   Ps 22:14
at all their gates.
Look! It is forged to strike like
lightning,
it is grasped for slaughter.
¹⁶Slash to the right, you sword,
then to the left,
wherever your blade is
turned.
¹⁷I too will strike my hands
together,   Eze 22:13
and my wrath will subside.
I the LORD have spoken."

¹⁸The word of the LORD came
to me: ¹⁹"Son of man, mark out
two roads for the sword of the
king of Babylon to take, both
starting from the same country.
Make a signpost where the road
branches off to the city. ²⁰Mark
out one road for the sword to
come against Rabbah of the Ammonites and another against
Judah and fortified Jerusalem.
²¹For the king of Babylon will
stop at the fork in the road, at the
junction of the two roads, to seek
an omen: He will cast lots with
arrows, he will consult his idols,
he will examine the liver. ²²Into
his right hand will come the lot
for Jerusalem, where he is to set
up battering rams, to give the
command to slaughter, to sound
the battle cry, to set battering
rams against the gates, to build
a ramp and to erect siege works.
²³It will seem like a false omen to
those who have sworn allegiance
to him, but he will remind them
of their guilt and take them captive.   Nu 23:23; Eze 4:2
²⁴"Therefore this is what the
Sovereign LORD says: 'Because
you people have brought to mind
your guilt by your open rebellion, revealing your sins in all
that you do — because you have
done this, you will be taken captive.
²⁵"'You profane and wick-
ed prince of Israel, whose day
has come, whose time of punishment has reached its climax,
²⁶this is what the Sovereign LORD
says: Take off the turban, remove
the crown. It will not be as it was:
The lowly will be exalted and the
exalted will be brought low. ²⁷A
ruin! A ruin! I will make it a ruin!
The crown will not be restored
until he to whom it rightfully belongs shall come; to him I will
give it.'   Ps 2:6; Eze 37:24; Hag 2:21-22
²⁸"And you, son of man, proph-
esy and say, 'This is what the

ᵃ 15 Septuagint; the meaning of the Hebrew for this word is uncertain.

Sovereign Lord says about the Ammonites and their insults:

"'A sword, a sword,   Jer 12:12
   drawn for the slaughter,
polished to consume
   and to flash like lightning!
29 Despite false visions
      concerning you
   and lying divinations about
      you,
it will be laid on the necks
   of the wicked who are to be
      slain,
whose day has come,
   whose time of punishment
      has reached its climax.

30 "'Let the sword return to its
      sheath.   Jer 47:6
In the place where you were
      created,
in the land of your ancestry,
   I will judge you.
31 I will pour out my wrath on
      you
   and breathe out my fiery
      anger against you;
I will deliver you into the
      hands of brutal men,
   men skilled in destruction.
32 You will be fuel for the fire,
   your blood will be shed in
      your land,
you will be remembered no
      more;   Eze 25:10
   for I the Lord have
      spoken.'"

Judgment on Jerusalem's Sins

22 The word of the Lord came to me:

2 "Son of man, will you judge her? Will you judge this city of bloodshed? Then confront her with all her detestable practices 3 and say: 'This is what the Sovereign Lord says: You city that brings on herself doom by shedding blood in her midst and defiles herself by making idols, 4 you have become guilty because of the blood you have shed and have become defiled by the idols you have made. You have brought your days to a close, and the end of your years has come. Therefore I will make you an object of scorn to the nations and a laughingstock to all the countries. 5 Those who are near and those who are far away will mock you, you infamous city, full of turmoil.   2Ki 21:16; Eze 5:14; Na 3:1

6 "'See how each of the princes of Israel who are in you uses his power to shed blood. 7 In you they have treated father and mother with contempt; in you they have oppressed the foreigner and mistreated the fatherless and the widow. 8 You have despised my holy things and desecrated my Sabbaths. 9 In you are slanderers who are bent on shedding blood; in you are those who eat at the mountain shrines and commit lewd acts. 10 In you are those who dishonor their father's bed; in you are those who violate women during their period, when they are ceremonially unclean. 11 In you one man com-

mits a detestable offense with his neighbor's wife, another shamefully defiles his daughter-in-law, and another violates his sister, his own father's daughter. [12] In you are people who accept bribes to shed blood; you take interest and make a profit from the poor. You extort unjust gain from your neighbors. And you have forgotten me, declares the Sovereign LORD.   Lev 18:15; Dt 27:25; Mic 7:3

[13] "'I will surely strike my hands together at the unjust gain you have made and at the blood you have shed in your midst. [14] Will your courage endure or your hands be strong in the day I deal with you? I the LORD have spoken, and I will do it. [15] I will disperse you among the nations and scatter you through the countries; and I will put an end to your uncleanness. [16] When you have been defiled[a] in the eyes of the nations, you will know that I am the LORD.'"   Dt 4:27; Eze 21:7; 23:27

[17] Then the word of the LORD came to me: [18] "Son of man, the people of Israel have become dross to me; all of them are the copper, tin, iron and lead left inside a furnace. They are but the dross of silver. [19] Therefore this is what the Sovereign LORD says: 'Because you have all become dross, I will gather you into Jerusalem. [20] As silver, copper, iron, lead and tin are gathered into a furnace to be melted with a fiery blast, so will I gather you in my anger and my wrath and put you inside the city and melt you. [21] I will gather you and I will blow on you with my fiery wrath, and you will be melted inside her. [22] As silver is melted in a furnace, so you will be melted inside her, and you will know that I the LORD have poured out my wrath on you.'"   Jer 6:28-30; Eze 20:8,33; Mal 3:2

[23] Again the word of the LORD came to me: [24] "Son of man, say to the land, 'You are a land that has not been cleansed or rained on in the day of wrath.' [25] There is a conspiracy of her princes[b] within her like a roaring lion tearing its prey; they devour people, take treasures and precious things and make many widows within her. [26] Her priests do violence to my law and profane my holy things; they do not distinguish between the holy and the common; they teach that there is no difference between the unclean and the clean; and they shut their eyes to the keeping of my Sabbaths, so that I am profaned among them. [27] Her officials within her are like wolves tearing their prey; they shed blood and kill people to make unjust gain. [28] Her prophets whitewash these deeds for them by false visions and lying divinations. They say, 'This is what the Sovereign LORD says' — when the LORD has not spoken. [29] The people of

---

[a] 16 Or *When I have allotted you your inheritance*   [b] 25 Septuagint; Hebrew *prophets*

the land practice extortion and commit robbery; they oppress the poor and needy and mistreat the foreigner, denying them justice. Ex 23:9; Eze 13:2,6-7

30 "I looked for someone among them who would build up the wall and stand before me in the gap on behalf of the land so I would not have to destroy it, but I found no one. 31 So I will pour out my wrath on them and consume them with my fiery anger, bringing down on their own heads all they have done, declares the Sovereign Lord." Jer 5:1; Eze 13:5

Two Adulterous Sisters

23 The word of the Lord came to me: 2 "Son of man, there were two women, daughters of the same mother. 3 They became prostitutes in Egypt, engaging in prostitution from their youth. In that land their breasts were fondled and their virgin bosoms caressed. 4 The older was named Oholah, and her sister was Oholibah. They were mine and gave birth to sons and daughters. Oholah is Samaria, and Oholibah is Jerusalem. Jer 3:7; Eze 16:45

5 "Oholah engaged in prostitution while she was still mine; and she lusted after her lovers, the Assyrians—warriors 6 clothed in blue, governors and commanders, all of them handsome young men, and mounted horsemen. 7 She gave herself as a prostitute to all the elite of the Assyrians and defiled herself with all the idols of everyone she lusted after. 8 She did not give up the prostitution she began in Egypt, when during her youth men slept with her, caressed her virgin bosom and poured out their lust on her. 2Ki 16:7; Hos 8:9

9 "Therefore I delivered her into the hands of her lovers, the Assyrians, for whom she lusted. 10 They stripped her naked, took away her sons and daughters and killed her with the sword. She became a byword among women, and punishment was inflicted on her. Eze 16:36; Hos 11:5

11 "Her sister Oholibah saw this, yet in her lust and prostitution she was more depraved than her sister. 12 She too lusted after the Assyrians—governors and commanders, warriors in full dress, mounted horsemen, all handsome young men. 13 I saw that she too defiled herself; both of them went the same way. 2Ki 16:7-15

14 "But she carried her prostitution still further. She saw men portrayed on a wall, figures of Chaldeans[a] portrayed in red, 15 with belts around their waists and flowing turbans on their heads; all of them looked like Babylonian chariot officers, natives of Chaldea.[b] 16 As soon as she saw them, she lusted after them and sent messengers to them

---

[a] 14 Or Babylonians   [b] 15 Or Babylonia; also in verse 16

in Chaldea. [17] Then the Babylonians came to her, to the bed of love, and in their lust they defiled her. After she had been defiled by them, she turned away from them in disgust. [18] When she carried on her prostitution openly and exposed her naked body, I turned away from her in disgust, just as I had turned away from her sister. [19] Yet she became more and more promiscuous as she recalled the days of her youth, when she was a prostitute in Egypt. [20] There she lusted after her lovers, whose genitals were like those of donkeys and whose emission was like that of horses. [21] So you longed for the lewdness of your youth, when in Egypt your bosom was caressed and your young breasts fondled.[a]

Jer 40:9; Eze 16:29

[22] "Therefore, Oholibah, this is what the Sovereign LORD says: I will stir up your lovers against you, those you turned away from in disgust, and I will bring them against you from every side — [23] the Babylonians and all the Chaldeans, the men of Pekod and Shoa and Koa, and all the Assyrians with them, handsome young men, all of them governors and commanders, chariot officers and men of high rank, all mounted on horses. [24] They will come against you with weapons,[b] chariots and wagons and with a throng of people; they will take up positions against you on every side with large and small shields and with helmets. I will turn you over to them for punishment, and they will punish you according to their standards. [25] I will direct my jealous anger against you, and they will deal with you in fury. They will cut off your noses and your ears, and those of you who are left will fall by the sword. They will take away your sons and daughters, and those of you who are left will be consumed by fire. [26] They will also strip you of your clothes and take your fine jewelry. [27] So I will put a stop to the lewdness and prostitution you began in Egypt. You will not look on these things with longing or remember Egypt anymore.

Eze 16:37,39,41

[28] "For this is what the Sovereign LORD says: I am about to deliver you into the hands of those you hate, to those you turned away from in disgust. [29] They will deal with you in hatred and take away everything you have worked for. They will leave you stark naked, and the shame of your prostitution will be exposed. Your lewdness and promiscuity [30] have brought this on you, because you lusted after the nations and defiled yourself with their idols. [31] You have gone the way of your sister; so I will put her cup into your hand. Jer 34:20; Eze 6:9

---

[a] 21 Syriac (see also verse 3); Hebrew *caressed because of your young breasts*
[b] 24 The meaning of the Hebrew for this word is uncertain.

³² "This is what the Sovereign LORD says:

"You will drink your sister's
    cup,
  a cup large and deep;
it will bring scorn and
    derision,
  for it holds so much.   Ps 60:3

³³ You will be filled with
    drunkenness and
    sorrow,
  the cup of ruin and
    desolation,
  the cup of your sister
    Samaria.   Jer 25:15-16

³⁴ You will drink it and drain it
    dry   Ps 75:8; Isa 51:17
  and chew on its pieces —
  and you will tear your
    breasts.

I have spoken, declares the Sovereign LORD.

³⁵ "Therefore this is what the Sovereign LORD says: Since you have forgotten me and turned your back on me, you must bear the consequences of your lewdness and prostitution."   1Ki 14:9

³⁶ The LORD said to me: "Son of man, will you judge Oholah and Oholibah? Then confront them with their detestable practices, ³⁷ for they have committed adultery and blood is on their hands. They committed adultery with their idols; they even sacrificed their children, whom they bore to me, as food for them. ³⁸ They have also done this to me: At that same time they defiled my sanctuary and desecrated my Sabbaths. ³⁹ On the very day they sacrificed their children to their idols, they entered my sanctuary and desecrated it. That is what they did in my house.   2Ki 21:4; Jer 7:10

⁴⁰ "They even sent messengers for men who came from far away, and when they arrived you bathed yourself for them, applied eye makeup and put on your jewelry. ⁴¹ You sat on an elegant couch, with a table spread before it on which you had placed the incense and olive oil that belonged to me.   Isa 57:9; Am 6:4

⁴² "The noise of a carefree crowd was around her; drunkards were brought from the desert along with men from the rabble, and they put bracelets on the wrists of the woman and her sister and beautiful crowns on their heads. ⁴³ Then I said about the one worn out by adultery, 'Now let them use her as a prostitute, for that is all she is.' ⁴⁴ And they slept with her. As men sleep with a prostitute, so they slept with those lewd women, Oholah and Oholibah. ⁴⁵ But righteous judges will sentence them to the punishment of women who commit adultery and shed blood, because they are adulterous and blood is on their hands.   Eze 16:38; Hos 6:5

⁴⁶ "This is what the Sovereign LORD says: Bring a mob against them and give them over to terror and plunder. ⁴⁷ The mob will

stone them and cut them down with their swords; they will kill their sons and daughters and burn down their houses. 2Ch 36:19

⁴⁸ "So I will put an end to lewdness in the land, that all women may take warning and not imitate you. ⁴⁹ You will suffer the penalty for your lewdness and bear the consequences of your sins of idolatry. Then you will know that I am the Sovereign LORD." Eze 7:4; 2Pe 2:6

Jerusalem as a Cooking Pot

24 In the ninth year, in the tenth month on the tenth day, the word of the LORD came to me: ² "Son of man, record this date, this very date, because the king of Babylon has laid siege to Jerusalem this very day. ³ Tell this rebellious people a parable and say to them: 'This is what the Sovereign LORD says: Jer 39:1

" 'Put on the cooking pot; put it on
    and pour water into it. Jer 1:13
⁴ Put into it the pieces of meat,
    all the choice pieces — the
    leg and the shoulder.
Fill it with the best of these
    bones;
⁵   take the pick of the flock.
Pile wood beneath it for the
    bones;
    bring it to a boil
    and cook the bones in it.

⁶ " 'For this is what the Sovereign LORD says:

" 'Woe to the city of
    bloodshed, Eze 22:2
to the pot now encrusted,
    whose deposit will not go
    away!
Take the meat out piece by
    piece
    in whatever order it comes.

⁷ " 'For the blood she shed is in
    her midst:
    She poured it on the bare
    rock;
she did not pour it on the
    ground,
    where the dust would
    cover it. Lev 17:13
⁸ To stir up wrath and take
    revenge
    I put her blood on the bare
    rock,
    so that it would not be
    covered.

⁹ " 'Therefore this is what the Sovereign LORD says:

" 'Woe to the city of
    bloodshed!
    I, too, will pile the wood high.
¹⁰ So heap on the wood
    and kindle the fire.
Cook the meat well,
    mixing in the spices;
    and let the bones be
    charred.
¹¹ Then set the empty pot on the
    coals
    till it becomes hot and its
    copper glows,
so that its impurities may be
    melted

and its deposit burned
away. Jer 21:10; Eze 22:15

¹²It has frustrated all efforts;
its heavy deposit has not
been removed,
not even by fire.

¹³ " 'Now your impurity is lewdness. Because I tried to cleanse you but you would not be cleansed from your impurity, you will not be clean again until my wrath against you has subsided. Jer 6:28-30; Eze 16:42; 22:24

¹⁴ " 'I the LORD have spoken. The time has come for me to act. I will not hold back; I will not have pity, nor will I relent. You will be judged according to your conduct and your actions, declares the Sovereign LORD.' " Eze 18:30

Ezekiel's Wife Dies

¹⁵The word of the LORD came to me: ¹⁶ "Son of man, with one blow I am about to take away from you the delight of your eyes. Yet do not lament or weep or shed any tears. ¹⁷Groan quietly; do not mourn for the dead. Keep your turban fastened and your sandals on your feet; do not cover your mustache and beard or eat the customary food of mourners." Jer 13:17; 16:7

¹⁸So I spoke to the people in the morning, and in the evening my wife died. The next morning I did as I had been commanded.

¹⁹Then the people asked me,

"Won't you tell us what these things have to do with us? Why are you acting like this?" Eze 12:9

²⁰So I said to them, "The word of the LORD came to me: ²¹Say to the people of Israel, 'This is what the Sovereign LORD says: I am about to desecrate my sanctuary—the stronghold in which you take pride, the delight of your eyes, the object of your affection. The sons and daughters you left behind will fall by the sword. ²²And you will do as I have done. You will not cover your mustache and beard or eat the customary food of mourners. ²³You will keep your turbans on your heads and your sandals on your feet. You will not mourn or weep but will waste away because of*a* your sins and groan among yourselves. ²⁴Ezekiel will be a sign to you; you will do just as he has done. When this happens, you will know that I am the Sovereign LORD.' Eze 4:3; 12:11

²⁵ "And you, son of man, on the day I take away their stronghold, their joy and glory, the delight of their eyes, their heart's desire, and their sons and daughters as well— ²⁶on that day a fugitive will come to tell you the news. ²⁷At that time your mouth will be opened; you will speak with him and will no longer be silent. So you will be a sign to them, and they will know that I am the LORD." Jer 11:22; Eze 3:26

a 23 Or *away in*

A Prophecy Against Ammon

25 The word of the LORD came to me: ² "Son of man, set your face against the Ammonites and prophesy against them. ³ Say to them, 'Hear the word of the Sovereign LORD. This is what the Sovereign LORD says: Because you said "Aha!" over my sanctuary when it was desecrated and over the land of Israel when it was laid waste and over the people of Judah when they went into exile, ⁴ therefore I am going to give you to the people of the East as a possession. They will set up their camps and pitch their tents among you; they will eat your fruit and drink your milk. ⁵ I will turn Rabbah into a pasture for camels and Ammon into a resting place for sheep. Then you will know that I am the LORD. ⁶ For this is what the Sovereign LORD says: Because you have clapped your hands and stamped your feet, rejoicing with all the malice of your heart against the land of Israel, ⁷ therefore I will stretch out my hand against you and give you as plunder to the nations. I will wipe you out from among the nations and exterminate you from the countries. I will destroy you, and you will know that I am the LORD.' "   Zep 2:8-9; Eze 21:31

A Prophecy Against Moab

⁸ "This is what the Sovereign LORD says: 'Because Moab and Seir said, "Look, Judah has become like all the other nations," ⁹ therefore I will expose the flank of Moab, beginning at its frontier towns — Beth Jeshimoth, Baal Meon and Kiriathaim — the glory of that land. ¹⁰ I will give Moab along with the Ammonites to the people of the East as a possession, so that the Ammonites will not be remembered among the nations; ¹¹ and I will inflict punishment on Moab. Then they will know that I am the LORD.' "   Jer 48:1; Am 2:1

A Prophecy Against Edom

¹² "This is what the Sovereign LORD says: 'Because Edom took revenge on Judah and became very guilty by doing so, ¹³ therefore this is what the Sovereign LORD says: I will stretch out my hand against Edom and kill both man and beast. I will lay it waste, and from Teman to Dedan they will fall by the sword. ¹⁴ I will take vengeance on Edom by the hand of my people Israel, and they will deal with Edom in accordance with my anger and my wrath; they will know my vengeance, declares the Sovereign LORD.' "   2Ch 28:17; Eze 35:11

A Prophecy Against Philistia

¹⁵ "This is what the Sovereign LORD says: 'Because the Philistines acted in vengeance and took revenge with malice in their hearts, and with ancient hostility sought to destroy Judah, ¹⁶ therefore this is what the

Sovereign LORD says: I am about to stretch out my hand against the Philistines, and I will wipe out the Kerethites and destroy those remaining along the coast. [17] I will carry out great vengeance on them and punish them in my wrath. Then they will know that I am the LORD, when I take vengeance on them.'" 2Ch 28:18; Jer 47:1-7

A Prophecy Against Tyre

26 In the eleventh month of the twelfth[a] year, on the first day of the month, the word of the LORD came to me: [2] "Son of man, because Tyre has said of Jerusalem, 'Aha! The gate to the nations is broken, and its doors have swung open to me; now that she lies in ruins I will prosper,' [3] therefore this is what the Sovereign LORD says: I am against you, Tyre, and I will bring many nations against you, like the sea casting up its waves. [4] They will destroy the walls of Tyre and pull down her towers; I will scrape away her rubble and make her a bare rock. [5] Out in the sea she will become a place to spread fishnets, for I have spoken, declares the Sovereign LORD. She will become plunder for the nations, [6] and her settlements on the mainland will be ravaged by the sword. Then they will know that I am the LORD. Isa 23; Eze 27:32

[7] "For this is what the Sovereign LORD says: From the north I am going to bring against Tyre Nebuchadnezzar[b] king of Babylon, king of kings, with horses and chariots, with horsemen and a great army. [8] He will ravage your settlements on the mainland with the sword; he will set up siege works against you, build a ramp up to your walls and raise his shields against you. [9] He will direct the blows of his battering rams against your walls and demolish your towers with his weapons. [10] His horses will be so many that they will cover you with dust. Your walls will tremble at the noise of the warhorses, wagons and chariots when he enters your gates as men enter a city whose walls have been broken through. [11] The hooves of his horses will trample all your streets; he will kill your people with the sword, and your strong pillars will fall to the ground. [12] They will plunder your wealth and loot your merchandise; they will break down your walls and demolish your fine houses and throw your stones, timber and rubble into the sea. [13] I will put an end to your noisy songs, and the music of your harps will be heard no more. [14] I will make you a bare rock, and you will become a place to spread fishnets.

---

[a] 1 Probable reading of the original Hebrew text; Masoretic Text does not have *month of the twelfth*.   [b] 7 Hebrew *Nebuchadrezzar*, of which *Nebuchadnezzar* is a variant; here and often in Ezekiel and Jeremiah

You will never be rebuilt, for I the LORD have spoken, declares the Sovereign LORD. Jer 27:6; Mal 1:4

15 "This is what the Sovereign LORD says to Tyre: Will not the coastlands tremble at the sound of your fall, when the wounded groan and the slaughter takes place in you? 16 Then all the princes of the coast will step down from their thrones and lay aside their robes and take off their embroidered garments. Clothed with terror, they will sit on the ground, trembling every moment, appalled at you. 17 Then they will take up a lament concerning you and say to you: Eze 27:32

" 'How you are destroyed, city of renown,
    peopled by men of the sea!
You were a power on the seas,
    you and your citizens;
you put your terror
    on all who lived there. Isa 14:12
18 Now the coastlands tremble
    on the day of your fall;
the islands in the sea
    are terrified at your
        collapse.' Isa 23:5; 41:5

19 "This is what the Sovereign LORD says: When I make you a desolate city, like cities no longer inhabited, and when I bring the ocean depths over you and its vast waters cover you, 20 then I will bring you down with those who go down to the pit, to the people of long ago. I will make you dwell in the earth below, as in ancient ruins, with those who go down to the pit, and you will not return or take your place[a] in the land of the living. 21 I will bring you to a horrible end and you will be no more. You will be sought, but you will never again be found, declares the Sovereign LORD." Eze 27:36; 28:19; Rev 18:21

A Lament Over Tyre

27 The word of the LORD came to me: 2 "Son of man, take up a lament concerning Tyre. 3 Say to Tyre, situated at the gateway to the sea, merchant of peoples on many coasts, 'This is what the Sovereign LORD says: Eze 19:1

" 'You say, Tyre,
    "I am perfect in beauty."
4 Your domain was on the high
        seas;
    your builders brought
        your beauty to
        perfection.
5 They made all your timbers
    of juniper from Senir[b]; Dt 3:9
they took a cedar from
        Lebanon Isa 2:13
    to make a mast for you.
6 Of oaks from Bashan Nu 21:33
    they made your oars;
of cypress wood[c] from the
        coasts of Cyprus Ge 10:4
    they made your deck,
        adorned with ivory.

⁷Fine embroidered linen from
  Egypt was your sail
  and served as your banner;
  your awnings were of blue
  and purple Ex 25:4; Jer 10:9
  from the coasts of Elishah.
⁸Men of Sidon and Arvad were
  your oarsmen; Ge 10:18
  your skilled men, Tyre, were
  aboard as your sailors.
⁹Veteran craftsmen of Byblos
  were on board Jos 13:5
  as shipwrights to caulk your
  seams.
All the ships of the sea and
  their sailors
  came alongside to trade for
  your wares.

¹⁰ " 'Men of Persia, Lydia and Put
  served as soldiers in your
  army.
They hung their shields and
  helmets on your walls,
  bringing you splendor.
¹¹Men of Arvad and Helek
  guarded your walls on every
  side;
men of Gammad
  were in your towers.
They hung their shields
  around your walls;
  they brought your beauty to
  perfection.

¹² " 'Tarshish did business with
you because of your great wealth
of goods; they exchanged silver,
iron, tin and lead for your merchandise. Ge 10:4

¹³ " 'Greece, Tubal and Meshek
did business with you; they traded human beings and articles of
bronze for your wares. Ge 10:2
¹⁴ " 'Men of Beth Togarmah exchanged chariot horses, cavalry
horses and mules for your merchandise. Ge 10:3; Eze 38:6
¹⁵ " 'The men of Rhodesᵃ traded with you, and many coastlands were your customers; they
paid you with ivory tusks and
ebony. Ge 10:7; Rev 18:12
¹⁶ " 'Aramᵇ did business with
you because of your many products; they exchanged turquoise,
purple fabric, embroidered work,
fine linen, coral and rubies for
your merchandise. Jdg 10:6; Eze 28:13
¹⁷ " 'Judah and Israel traded
with you; they exchanged wheat
from Minnith and confections,ᶜ
honey, olive oil and balm for
your wares. Jdg 11:33
¹⁸ " 'Damascus did business
with you because of your many
products and great wealth of
goods. They offered wine from
Helbon, wool from Zahar ¹⁹and
casks of wine from Izal in exchange for your wares: wrought
iron, cassia and calamus. Ge 10:2
²⁰ " 'Dedan traded in saddle
blankets with you.
²¹ " 'Arabia and all the princes of
Kedar were your customers; they
did business with you in lambs,
rams and goats. Ge 25:13; Isa 60:7
²² " 'The merchants of Sheba

ᵃ 15 Septuagint; Hebrew *Dedan*   ᵇ 16 Most Hebrew manuscripts; some Hebrew
manuscripts and Syriac *Edom*   ᶜ 17 The meaning of the Hebrew for this word is uncertain.

and Raamah traded with you;
for your merchandise they exchanged the finest of all kinds of
spices and precious stones, and
gold. Ge 10:7,28; 1Ki 10:1-2; Isa 60:6

[23] " 'Harran, Kanneh and Eden
and merchants of Sheba, Ashur and Kilmad traded with you.
[24] In your marketplace they traded with you beautiful garments,
blue fabric, embroidered work
and multicolored rugs with cords
twisted and tightly knotted.

[25] " 'The ships of Tarshish serve
    as carriers for your wares.
  You are filled with heavy cargo
    as you sail the sea.
[26] Your oarsmen take you
    out to the high seas.
  But the east wind will break
      you to pieces Ps 48:7
    far out at sea.
[27] Your wealth, merchandise
      and wares, Pr 11:4
    your mariners, sailors and
      shipwrights,
  your merchants and all your
      soldiers,
    and everyone else on board
  will sink into the heart of the
      sea Eze 28:8
    on the day of your shipwreck.
[28] The shorelands will quake
    when your sailors cry out.
[29] All who handle the oars
    will abandon their ships;
  the mariners and all the
      sailors
    will stand on the shore.
[30] They will raise their voice
    and cry bitterly over you;
  they will sprinkle dust on
      their heads 2Sa 1:2
    and roll in ashes. Jer 6:26
[31] They will shave their heads
      because of you
    and will put on sackcloth.
  They will weep over you with
      anguish of soul Isa 16:9
    and with bitter mourning.
[32] As they wail and mourn over
      you,
    they will take up a lament
      concerning you: Eze 26:17
  "Who was ever silenced like
      Tyre,
    surrounded by the sea?"
[33] When your merchandise went
      out on the seas,
    you satisfied many nations;
  with your great wealth and
      your wares ver 12; Eze 28:4-5
    you enriched the kings of
      the earth.
[34] Now you are shattered by the
      sea
    in the depths of the waters;
  your wares and all your
      company
    have gone down with you.
[35] All who live in the coastlands
    are appalled at you; Lev 26:32
  their kings shudder with
      horror
    and their faces are distorted
      with fear. Eze 26:17-18
[36] The merchants among the
      nations scoff at you;
  you have come to a horrible
      end
    and will be no more.' " Ps 37:10

A Prophecy Against the King of Tyre

28 The word of the LORD came to me: [2] "Son of man, say to the ruler of Tyre, 'This is what the Sovereign LORD says: Isa 13:11

" 'In the pride of your heart
    you say, "I am a god;
I sit on the throne of a god
    in the heart of the seas."
But you are a mere mortal and
        not a god,
    though you think you are as
        wise as a god.   Ps 9:20
[3] Are you wiser than Daniel[a]?
    Is no secret hidden from you?
[4] By your wisdom and
        understanding
    you have gained wealth for
        yourself
and amassed gold and silver
    in your treasuries.   Zec 9:3
[5] By your great skill in trading
    you have increased your
        wealth,   Eze 27:33
and because of your wealth
    your heart has grown
        proud. Ps 52:7; 62:10; Hos 12:8

[6] " 'Therefore this is what the
Sovereign LORD says:

" 'Because you think you are
        wise,
    as wise as a god,
[7] I am going to bring foreigners
        against you,
    the most ruthless of
        nations; Eze 30:11; 31:12; 32:12

they will draw their swords
    against your beauty and
        wisdom   Jer 9:23
and pierce your shining
        splendor.
[8] They will bring you down to
        the pit,   Eze 32:30
    and you will die a violent
        death
    in the heart of the seas.
[9] Will you then say, "I am a god,"
    in the presence of those
        who kill you?
You will be but a mortal, not a
        god,   Isa 31:3
    in the hands of those who
        slay you.   Eze 16:49
[10] You will die the death of the
        uncircumcised   Eze 31:18
    at the hands of foreigners.

I have spoken, declares the Sovereign LORD.' "

[11] The word of the LORD came to me: [12] "Son of man, take up a lament concerning the king of Tyre and say to him: 'This is what the Sovereign LORD says: Eze 19:1

" 'You were the seal of
        perfection,
    full of wisdom and perfect
        in beauty.   Eze 27:2-4
[13] You were in Eden,   Ge 2:8
    the garden of God;   Eze 31:8-9
every precious stone adorned
        you:
    carnelian, chrysolite and
        emerald,
    topaz, onyx and jasper,

---

[a] 3 Or *Danel*, a man of renown in ancient literature

lapis lazuli, turquoise and
beryl.*a*   Eze 27:16
Your settings and mountings*b*
were made of gold;
on the day you were created
they were prepared.
¹⁴You were anointed as a
guardian cherub,   Ex 25:17
for so I ordained you.
You were on the holy mount of
God;
you walked among the fiery
stones.
¹⁵You were blameless in your
ways
from the day you were
created
till wickedness was found in
you.
¹⁶Through your widespread
trade
you were filled with
violence,   Hab 2:17
and you sinned.
So I drove you in disgrace
from the mount of God,
and I expelled you,
guardian cherub,   Ge 3:24
from among the fiery stones.
¹⁷Your heart became proud
on account of your beauty,
and you corrupted your
wisdom
because of your splendor.
So I threw you to the earth;
I made a spectacle of you
before kings.   Eze 19:12
¹⁸By your many sins and
dishonest trade

you have desecrated your
sanctuaries.
So I made a fire come out
from you,
and it consumed you,
and I reduced you to ashes on
the ground   Mal 4:3
in the sight of all who were
watching.
¹⁹All the nations who knew you
are appalled at you;
you have come to a horrible
end
and will be no more.' "

A Prophecy Against Sidon

²⁰The word of the LORD came to
me: ²¹"Son of man, set your face
against Sidon; prophesy against
her ²²and say: 'This is what the
Sovereign LORD says: Jer 25:22

" 'I am against you, Sidon,
and among you I will
display my glory. Eze 39:13
You will know that I am the
LORD,
when I inflict punishment
on you   Eze 30:19
and within you am proved
to be holy.   Lev 10:3
²³I will send a plague upon you
and make blood flow in
your streets.
The slain will fall within you,
with the sword against you
on every side.
Then you will know that I am
the LORD.   Eze 38:22

---

a 13 The precise identification of some of these precious stones is uncertain.
b 13 The meaning of the Hebrew for this phrase is uncertain.

²⁴ " 'No longer will the people of Israel have malicious neighbors who are painful briers and sharp thorns. Then they will know that I am the Sovereign LORD. Nu 33:55

²⁵ " 'This is what the Sovereign LORD says: When I gather the people of Israel from the nations where they have been scattered, I will be proved holy through them in the sight of the nations. Then they will live in their own land, which I gave to my servant Jacob. ²⁶ They will live there in safety and will build houses and plant vineyards; they will live in safety when I inflict punishment on all their neighbors who maligned them. Then they will know that I am the LORD their God.' " Isa 11:12; Jer 23:6; Am 9:14-15

A Prophecy Against Egypt

Judgment on Pharaoh

29 In the tenth year, in the tenth month on the twelfth day, the word of the LORD came to me: ² "Son of man, set your face against Pharaoh king of Egypt and prophesy against him and against all Egypt. ³ Speak to him and say: 'This is what the Sovereign LORD says: Isa 19:1-17

" 'I am against you, Pharaoh
   king of Egypt, Jer 44:30
you great monster lying
   among your streams.
You say, "The Nile belongs
   to me;

I made it for myself."
⁴ But I will put hooks in your
   jaws 2Ki 19:28
and make the fish of your
   streams stick to your
   scales.
I will pull you out from among
   your streams,
with all the fish sticking to
   your scales. Eze 38:4
⁵ I will leave you in the desert,
you and all the fish of your
   streams.
You will fall on the open field
and not be gathered or
   picked up.
I will give you as food
to the beasts of the earth
   and the birds of the sky.

⁶ Then all who live in Egypt will know that I am the LORD.

" 'You have been a staff of reed for the people of Israel. ⁷ When they grasped you with their hands, you splintered and you tore open their shoulders; when they leaned on you, you broke and their backs were wrenched.ᵃ Isa 36:6; Eze 17:15-17

⁸ " 'Therefore this is what the Sovereign LORD says: I will bring a sword against you and kill both man and beast. ⁹ Egypt will become a desolate wasteland. Then they will know that I am the LORD. Eze 14:17; 32:11-13

" 'Because you said, "The Nile is mine; I made it," ¹⁰ therefore I am against you and against

---

ᵃ 7 Syriac (see also Septuagint and Vulgate); Hebrew *and you caused their backs to stand* your streams, and I will make the land of Egypt a ruin and a desolate waste from Migdol to Aswan, as far as the border of Cush.*a* **11** The foot of neither man nor beast will pass through it; no one will live there for forty years. **12** I will make the land of Egypt desolate among devastated lands, and her cities will lie desolate forty years among ruined cities. And I will disperse the Egyptians among the nations and scatter them through the countries.   Eze 30:7,23,26

13 "'Yet this is what the Sovereign Lord says: At the end of forty years I will gather the Egyptians from the nations where they were scattered. **14** I will bring them back from captivity and return them to Upper Egypt, the land of their ancestry. There they will be a lowly kingdom. **15** It will be the lowliest of kingdoms and will never again exalt itself above the other nations. I will make it so weak that it will never again rule over the nations. **16** Egypt will no longer be a source of confidence for the people of Israel but will be a reminder of their sin in turning to her for help. Then they will know that I am the Sovereign Lord.'"   Isa 30:2; Hos 8:13

Nebuchadnezzar's Reward

17 In the twenty-seventh year, in the first month on the first day, the word of the Lord came to me: **18** "Son of man, Nebuchadnezzar king of Babylon drove his army in a hard campaign against Tyre; every head was rubbed bare and every shoulder made raw. Yet he and his army got no reward from the campaign he led against Tyre. **19** Therefore this is what the Sovereign Lord says: I am going to give Egypt to Nebuchadnezzar king of Babylon, and he will carry off its wealth. He will loot and plunder the land as pay for his army. **20** I have given him Egypt as a reward for his efforts because he and his army did it for me, declares the Sovereign Lord.   Isa 10:6-7; Jer 25:9

21 "On that day I will make a horn*b* grow for the Israelites, and I will open your mouth among them. Then they will know that I am the Lord."   Ps 132:17; Eze 24:27

A Lament Over Egypt

30 The word of the Lord came to me: **2** "Son of man, prophesy and say: 'This is what the Sovereign Lord says:

"'Wail and say,   Isa 13:6
"Alas for that day!"
3 For the day is near,   Joel 2:1,11
the day of the Lord is
near —   Eze 7:12,19
a day of clouds,
a time of doom for the
nations.
4 A sword will come against
Egypt,   Da 11:43

---

a 10 That is, the upper Nile region   *b 21 Horn* here symbolizes strength.

and anguish will come
    upon Cush.[a]   Eze 29:10
When the slain fall in Egypt,
    her wealth will be carried
        away
    and her foundations torn
        down.   Eze 29:19

5 Cush and Libya, Lydia and all
Arabia, Kub and the people of
the covenant land will fall by the
sword along with Egypt.   Jer 25:20

6 " 'This is what the LORD says:

" 'The allies of Egypt will fall
    and her proud strength will
        fail.
From Migdol to Aswan   Eze 29:10
    they will fall by the sword
        within her,
            declares the Sovereign
                LORD.

7 " 'They will be desolate
    among desolate lands,
    and their cities will lie
        among ruined cities. Eze 29:12

8 Then they will know that I am
    the LORD,
    when I set fire to Egypt
    and all her helpers are
        crushed.   Eze 29:9

9 " 'On that day messengers will
go out from me in ships to fright-
en Cush out of her complacency.
Anguish will take hold of them
on the day of Egypt's doom, for it
is sure to come. Isa 18:1-2; Eze 32:9-10

10 " 'This is what the Sovereign
LORD says:

" 'I will put an end to the
    hordes of Egypt

by the hand of
    Nebuchadnezzar king
    of Babylon.   Eze 29:19

11 He and his army — the most
    ruthless of nations —
    will be brought in to destroy
        the land.
They will draw their swords
    against Egypt
    and fill the land with the
        slain.

12 I will dry up the waters of the
    Nile   Isa 19:6; Eze 29:9
    and sell the land to an evil
        nation;
by the hand of foreigners
    I will lay waste the land and
        everything in it.   Eze 19:7

I the LORD have spoken.

13 " 'This is what the Sovereign
LORD says:

" 'I will destroy the idols Jer 43:12
    and put an end to the
        images in Memphis.
No longer will there be a
    prince in Egypt,   Zec 10:11
    and I will spread fear
        throughout the land.

14 I will lay waste Upper Egypt,
    set fire to Zoan   Ps 78:12,43
    and inflict punishment on
        Thebes.   Jer 46:25

15 I will pour out my wrath on
    Pelusium,
    the stronghold of Egypt,
    and wipe out the hordes of
        Thebes.

16 I will set fire to Egypt;   Jos 7:15

[a] 4 That is, the upper Nile region; also in verses 5 and 9

Pelusium will writhe in
agony.
Thebes will be taken by
storm;
Memphis will be in
constant distress. Isa 19:13
¹⁷ The young men of Heliopolis
and Bubastis Ge 41:45
will fall by the sword,
and the cities themselves
will go into captivity.
¹⁸ Dark will be the day at
Tahpanhes
when I break the yoke of
Egypt; Lev 26:13; Isa 9:4
there her proud strength
will come to an end.
She will be covered with
clouds,
and her villages will go into
captivity.
¹⁹ So I will inflict punishment
on Egypt, Eze 28:22
and they will know that I
am the LORD.' "

Pharaoh's Arms Are Broken

²⁰ In the eleventh year, in the
first month on the seventh day,
the word of the LORD came to me:
²¹ "Son of man, I have broken the
arm of Pharaoh king of Egypt.
It has not been bound up to be
healed or put in a splint so that
it may become strong enough to
hold a sword. ²² Therefore this is
what the Sovereign LORD says:
I am against Pharaoh king of
Egypt. I will break both his arms,
the good arm as well as the broken one, and make the sword fall

from his hand. ²³ I will disperse
the Egyptians among the nations
and scatter them through the
countries. ²⁴ I will strengthen the
arms of the king of Babylon and
put my sword in his hand, but I
will break the arms of Pharaoh,
and he will groan before him like
a mortally wounded man. ²⁵ I
will strengthen the arms of the
king of Babylon, but the arms of
Pharaoh will fall limp. Then they
will know that I am the LORD,
when I put my sword into the
hand of the king of Babylon and
he brandishes it against Egypt.
²⁶ I will disperse the Egyptians
among the nations and scatter them through the countries.
Then they will know that I am
the LORD." Zep 2:12; Zec 10:6,12

Pharaoh as a Felled Cedar of Lebanon

31 In the eleventh year, in
the third month on the
first day, the word of the LORD
came to me: ² "Son of man, say to
Pharaoh king of Egypt and to his
hordes: Jer 52:5; Eze 30:20

" 'Who can be compared with
you in majesty?
³ Consider Assyria, once a
cedar in Lebanon,
with beautiful branches
overshadowing the
forest;
it towered on high,
its top above the thick
foliage. Isa 10:34

⁴The waters nourished it, Eze 17:7
deep springs made it grow
tall;
their streams flowed
all around its base
and sent their channels
to all the trees of the field.
⁵So it towered higher
than all the trees of the field;
its boughs increased
and its branches grew long,
spreading because of
abundant waters. Eze 17:5
⁶All the birds of the sky
nested in its boughs,
all the animals of the wild
gave birth under its branches;
all the great nations
lived in its shade. Eze 17:23
⁷It was majestic in beauty,
with its spreading boughs,
for its roots went down
to abundant waters.
⁸The cedars in the garden of
God Ps 80:10
could not rival it,
nor could the junipers
equal its boughs,
nor could the plane trees
compare with its branches—
no tree in the garden of God
could match its beauty.
⁹I made it beautiful
with abundant branches,
the envy of all the trees of
Eden Ge 2:8
in the garden of God. Ge 13:10

¹⁰ "'Therefore this is what the
Sovereign Lord says: Because
the great cedar towered over the
thick foliage, and because it was
proud of its height, ¹¹I gave it into
the hands of the ruler of the nations, for him to deal with according to its wickedness. I cast
it aside, ¹²and the most ruthless
of foreign nations cut it down and
left it. Its boughs fell on the mountains and in all the valleys; its
branches lay broken in all the ravines of the land. All the nations
of the earth came out from under
its shade and left it. ¹³All the birds
settled on the fallen tree, and all
the wild animals lived among its
branches. ¹⁴Therefore no other
trees by the waters are ever to
tower proudly on high, lifting
their tops above the thick foliage.
No other trees so well-watered
are ever to reach such a height;
they are all destined for death, for
the earth below, among mortals
who go down to the realm of the
dead. Eze 28:7; Da 5:20

¹⁵ "'This is what the Sovereign
Lord says: On the day it was
brought down to the realm of the
dead I covered the deep springs
with mourning for it; I held back
its streams, and its abundant waters were restrained. Because of
it I clothed Lebanon with gloom,
and all the trees of the field withered away. ¹⁶I made the nations
tremble at the sound of its fall
when I brought it down to the
realm of the dead to be with those
who go down to the pit. Then all
the trees of Eden, the choicest
and best of Lebanon, the well-

watered trees, were consoled in the earth below. ¹⁷ They too, like the great cedar, had gone down to the realm of the dead, to those killed by the sword, along with the armed men who lived in its shade among the nations.   Ps 9:17

¹⁸ " 'Which of the trees of Eden can be compared with you in splendor and majesty? Yet you, too, will be brought down with the trees of Eden to the earth below; you will lie among the uncircumcised, with those killed by the sword.   Eze 32:19,21

" 'This is Pharaoh and all his hordes, declares the Sovereign Lord.' "

A Lament Over Pharaoh

32 In the twelfth year, in the twelfth month on the first day, the word of the Lord came to me: ² "Son of man, take up a lament concerning Pharaoh king of Egypt and say to him: Eze 27:2

" 'You are like a lion among
　　the nations;   Eze 19:3,6
you are like a monster in
　　the seas
thrashing about in your
　　streams,
churning the water with
　　your feet
and muddying the streams.

³ " 'This is what the Sovereign Lord says:

" 'With a great throng of
　　people

I will cast my net over you,
　　and they will haul you up in
　　　my net.   Eze 12:13
⁴ I will throw you on the land
　　and hurl you on the open
　　　field.
I will let all the birds of the
　　sky settle on you
and all the animals of the
　　wild gorge themselves
　　　on you.   Isa 18:6; Eze 31:12-13
⁵ I will spread your flesh on the
　　mountains
and fill the valleys with
　　your remains.   Eze 31:12
⁶ I will drench the land with
　　your flowing blood
all the way to the
　　mountains,
and the ravines will be
　　filled with your
　　　flesh.
⁷ When I snuff you out, I will
　　cover the heavens
and darken their stars;
I will cover the sun with a
　　cloud,
and the moon will not give
　　its light.   Joel 2:2,31; 3:15
⁸ All the shining lights in the
　　heavens
I will darken over you;
I will bring darkness over
　　your land,   Joel 2:10
　　declares the Sovereign
　　　Lord.
⁹ I will trouble the hearts of
　　many peoples
when I bring about your
　　destruction among the
　　　nations,

among[a] lands you have not
  known.
[10] I will cause many peoples to
    be appalled at you,
  and their kings will shudder
    with horror because of
    you
  when I brandish my sword
    before them.
On the day of your downfall
  each of them will tremble
  every moment for his life.

[11] " 'For this is what the Sovereign LORD says:

" 'The sword of the king of
    Babylon   Jer 46:26
  will come against you.
[12] I will cause your hordes to fall
    by the swords of mighty
    men —
  the most ruthless of all
    nations.   Eze 28:7
They will shatter the pride of
  Egypt,
  and all her hordes will be
    overthrown.   Eze 31:11-12
[13] I will destroy all her cattle
    from beside abundant
    waters
  no longer to be stirred by the
    foot of man
  or muddied by the hooves
    of cattle.   Eze 29:8,11
[14] Then I will let her waters
    settle
  and make her streams flow
    like oil,
        declares the Sovereign
        LORD.

[15] When I make Egypt desolate
  and strip the land of
    everything in it,
  when I strike down all who
    live there,
  then they will know that I
    am the LORD.'   Ex 7:5

[16] "This is the lament they
will chant for her. The daughters of the nations will chant it;
for Egypt and all her hordes they
will chant it, declares the Sovereign LORD."   2Ch 35:25; Eze 26:17

*Egypt's Descent Into the Realm
of the Dead*

[17] In the twelfth year, on the fifteenth day of the month, the word
of the LORD came to me: [18] "Son of
man, wail for the hordes of Egypt
and consign to the earth below
both her and the daughters of
mighty nations, along with those
who go down to the pit. [19] Say
to them, 'Are you more favored
than others? Go down and be
laid among the uncircumcised.'
[20] They will fall among those
killed by the sword. The sword
is drawn; let her be dragged
off with all her hordes. [21] From
within the realm of the dead the
mighty leaders will say of Egypt
and her allies, 'They have come
down and they lie with the uncircumcised, with those killed by
the sword.'   Isa 14:9; Eze 28:10
[22] "Assyria is there with her
whole army; she is surrounded by

---

[a] 9 Hebrew; Septuagint *bring you into captivity among the nations, / to*

the graves of all her slain, all who have fallen by the sword. [23] Their graves are in the depths of the pit and her army lies around her grave. All who had spread terror in the land of the living are slain, fallen by the sword. Isa 14:15

[24] "Elam is there, with all her hordes around her grave. All of them are slain, fallen by the sword. All who had spread terror in the land of the living went down uncircumcised to the earth below. They bear their shame with those who go down to the pit. [25] A bed is made for her among the slain, with all her hordes around her grave. All of them are uncircumcised, killed by the sword. Because their terror had spread in the land of the living, they bear their shame with those who go down to the pit; they are laid among the slain. Jer 49:37

[26] "Meshek and Tubal are there, with all their hordes around their graves. All of them are uncircumcised, killed by the sword because they spread their terror in the land of the living. [27] But they do not lie with the fallen warriors of old,[a] who went down to the realm of the dead with their weapons of war — their swords placed under their heads and their shields[b] resting on their bones — though these warriors also had terrorized the land of the living. Eze 27:13

[28] "You too, Pharaoh, will be broken and will lie among the uncircumcised, with those killed by the sword.

[29] "Edom is there, her kings and all her princes; despite their power, they are laid with those killed by the sword. They lie with the uncircumcised, with those who go down to the pit. Isa 34:5-15

[30] "All the princes of the north and all the Sidonians are there; they went down with the slain in disgrace despite the terror caused by their power. They lie uncircumcised with those killed by the sword and bear their shame with those who go down to the pit. Eze 38:6; 39:2

[31] "Pharaoh — he and all his army — will see them and he will be consoled for all his hordes that were killed by the sword, declares the Sovereign LORD. [32] Although I had him spread terror in the land of the living, Pharaoh and all his hordes will be laid among the uncircumcised, with those killed by the sword, declares the Sovereign LORD." Eze 31:16

Renewal of Ezekiel's Call as Watchman

33 The word of the LORD came to me: [2] "Son of man, speak to your people and say to them: 'When I bring the sword against a land, and the people of the land choose one

---

[a] 27 Septuagint; Hebrew *warriors who were uncircumcised* [b] 27 Probable reading of the original Hebrew text; Masoretic Text *punishment*

of their men and make him their watchman, ³ and he sees the sword coming against the land and blows the trumpet to warn the people, ⁴ then if anyone hears the trumpet but does not heed the warning and the sword comes and takes their life, their blood will be on their own head. ⁵ Since they heard the sound of the trumpet but did not heed the warning, their blood will be on their own head. If they had heeded the warning, they would have saved themselves. ⁶ But if the watchman sees the sword coming and does not blow the trumpet to warn the people and the sword comes and takes someone's life, that person's life will be taken because of their sin, but I will hold the watchman accountable for their blood.' Eze 3:11,18

⁷ "Son of man, I have made you a watchman for the people of Israel; so hear the word I speak and give them warning from me. ⁸ When I say to the wicked, 'You wicked person, you will surely die,' and you do not speak out to dissuade them from their ways, that wicked person will die for^a their sin, and I will hold you accountable for their blood. ⁹ But if you do warn the wicked person to turn from their ways and they do not do so, they will die for their sin, though you yourself will be saved. Eze 3:17-19

¹⁰ "Son of man, say to the Israel-ites, 'This is what you are saying: "Our offenses and sins weigh us down, and we are wasting away because of^b them. How then can we live?"' ¹¹ Say to them, 'As surely as I live, declares the Sovereign LORD, I take no pleasure in the death of the wicked, but rather that they turn from their ways and live. Turn! Turn from your evil ways! Why will you die, people of Israel?' Eze 18:32; 2Pe 3:9

¹² "Therefore, son of man, say to your people, 'If someone who is righteous disobeys, that person's former righteousness will count for nothing. And if someone who is wicked repents, that person's former wickedness will not bring condemnation. The righteous person who sins will not be allowed to live even though they were formerly righteous.' ¹³ If I tell a righteous person that they will surely live, but then they trust in their righteousness and do evil, none of the righteous things that person has done will be remembered; they will die for the evil they have done. ¹⁴ And if I say to a wicked person, 'You will surely die,' but they then turn away from their sin and do what is just and right— ¹⁵ if they give back what they took in pledge for a loan, return what they have stolen, follow the decrees that give life, and do no evil—that person will surely live; they will not die. ¹⁶ None of the sins that

^a 8 Or *in*; also in verse 9   ^b 10 Or *away in*

person has committed will be remembered against them. They have done what is just and right; they will surely live. Eze 18:22; 20:11

17 "Yet your people say, 'The way of the Lord is not just.' But it is their way that is not just. 18 If a righteous person turns from their righteousness and does evil, they will die for it. 19 And if a wicked person turns away from their wickedness and does what is just and right, they will live by doing so. 20 Yet you Israelites say, 'The way of the Lord is not just.' But I will judge each of you according to your own ways." Eze 3:20; 18:26

Jerusalem's Fall Explained

21 In the twelfth year of our exile, in the tenth month on the fifth day, a man who had escaped from Jerusalem came to me and said, "The city has fallen!" 22 Now the evening before the man arrived, the hand of the LORD was on me, and he opened my mouth before the man came to me in the morning. So my mouth was opened and I was no longer silent. Eze 24:27

23 Then the word of the LORD came to me: 24 "Son of man, the people living in those ruins in the land of Israel are saying, 'Abraham was only one man, yet he possessed the land. But we are many; surely the land has been given to us as our possession.' 25 Therefore say to them, 'This is what the Sovereign LORD says: Since you eat meat with the blood still in it and look to your idols and shed blood, should you then possess the land? 26 You rely on your sword, you do detestable things, and each of you defiles his neighbor's wife. Should you then possess the land?' Eze 22:6,11,27

27 "Say this to them: 'This is what the Sovereign LORD says: As surely as I live, those who are left in the ruins will fall by the sword, those out in the country I will give to the wild animals to be devoured, and those in strongholds and caves will die of a plague. 28 I will make the land a desolate waste, and her proud strength will come to an end, and the mountains of Israel will become desolate so that no one will cross them. 29 Then they will know that I am the LORD, when I have made the land a desolate waste because of all the detestable things they have done.' 1Sa 13:6; Isa 2:19

30 "As for you, son of man, your people are talking together about you by the walls and at the doors of the houses, saying to each other, 'Come and hear the message that has come from the LORD.' 31 My people come to you, as they usually do, and sit before you to hear your words, but they do not put them into practice. Their mouths speak of love, but their hearts are greedy for unjust gain. 32 Indeed, to them you are nothing more than one who sings love songs with a beautiful voice

and plays an instrument well, for they hear your words but do not put them into practice. Mk 6:20

[33] "When all this comes true — and it surely will — then they will know that a prophet has been among them." 1Sa 3:20; Eze 2:5

The LORD Will Be Israel's Shepherd

34 The word of the LORD came to me: [2] "Son of man, prophesy against the shepherds of Israel; prophesy and say to them: 'This is what the Sovereign LORD says: Woe to you shepherds of Israel who only take care of yourselves! Should not shepherds take care of the flock? [3] You eat the curds, clothe yourselves with the wool and slaughter the choice animals, but you do not take care of the flock. [4] You have not strengthened the weak or healed the sick or bound up the injured. You have not brought back the strays or searched for the lost. You have ruled them harshly and brutally. [5] So they were scattered because there was no shepherd, and when they were scattered they became food for all the wild animals. [6] My sheep wandered over all the mountains and on every high hill. They were scattered over the whole earth, and no one searched or looked for them. Jer 23:1; Jn 10:11

[7] " 'Therefore, you shepherds, hear the word of the LORD: [8] As surely as I live, declares the Sovereign LORD, because my flock lacks a shepherd and so has been plundered and has become food for all the wild animals, and because my shepherds did not search for my flock but cared for themselves rather than for my flock, [9] therefore, you shepherds, hear the word of the LORD: [10] This is what the Sovereign LORD says: I am against the shepherds and will hold them accountable for my flock. I will remove them from tending the flock so that the shepherds can no longer feed themselves. I will rescue my flock from their mouths, and it will no longer be food for them. Jer 21:13

[11] " 'For this is what the Sovereign LORD says: I myself will search for my sheep and look after them. [12] As a shepherd looks after his scattered flock when he is with them, so will I look after my sheep. I will rescue them from all the places where they were scattered on a day of clouds and darkness. [13] I will bring them out from the nations and gather them from the countries, and I will bring them into their own land. I will pasture them on the mountains of Israel, in the ravines and in all the settlements in the land. [14] I will tend them in a good pasture, and the mountain heights of Israel will be their grazing land. There they will lie down in good grazing land, and there they will feed in a rich pasture on the mountains of Israel.

15 I myself will tend my sheep and have them lie down, declares the Sovereign LORD. 16 I will search for the lost and bring back the strays. I will bind up the injured and strengthen the weak, but the sleek and the strong I will destroy. I will shepherd the flock with justice. Isa 10:16; Lk 5:32

17 "'As for you, my flock, this is what the Sovereign LORD says: I will judge between one sheep and another, and between rams and goats. 18 Is it not enough for you to feed on the good pasture? Must you also trample the rest of your pasture with your feet? Is it not enough for you to drink clear water? Must you also muddy the rest with your feet? 19 Must my flock feed on what you have trampled and drink what you have muddied with your feet? Mt 25:32-33

20 "'Therefore this is what the Sovereign LORD says to them: See, I myself will judge between the fat sheep and the lean sheep. 21 Because you shove with flank and shoulder, butting all the weak sheep with your horns until you have driven them away, 22 I will save my flock, and they will no longer be plundered. I will judge between one sheep and another. 23 I will place over them one shepherd, my servant David, and he will tend them; he will tend them and be their

shepherd. 24 I the LORD will be their God, and my servant David will be prince among them. I the LORD have spoken. Isa 40:11; Eze 36:28

25 "'I will make a covenant of peace with them and rid the land of savage beasts so that they may live in the wilderness and sleep in the forests in safety. 26 I will make them and the places surrounding my hill a blessing.ᵃ I will send down showers in season; there will be showers of blessing. 27 The trees will yield their fruit and the ground will yield its crops; the people will be secure in their land. They will know that I am the LORD, when I break the bars of their yoke and rescue them from the hands of those who enslaved them. 28 They will no longer be plundered by the nations, nor will wild animals devour them. They will live in safety, and no one will make them afraid. 29 I will provide for them a land renowned for its crops, and they will no longer be victims of famine in the land or bear the scorn of the nations. 30 Then they will know that I, the LORD their God, am with them and that they, the Israelites, are my people, declares the Sovereign LORD. 31 You are my sheep, the sheep of my pasture, and I am your God, declares the Sovereign LORD.'" Ps 100:3; Jer 23:1

ᵃ 26 Or *I will cause them and the places surrounding my hill to be named in blessings* (see Gen. 48:20); or *I will cause them and the places surrounding my hill to be seen as blessed*

A Prophecy Against Edom

35 The word of the Lord came to me: [2] "Son of man, set your face against Mount Seir; prophesy against it [3] and say: 'This is what the Sovereign Lord says: I am against you, Mount Seir, and I will stretch out my hand against you and make you a desolate waste. [4] I will turn your towns into ruins and you will be desolate. Then you will know that I am the Lord. Jer 6:12; Eze 25:12-14

[5] "'Because you harbored an ancient hostility and delivered the Israelites over to the sword at the time of their calamity, the time their punishment reached its climax, [6] therefore as surely as I live, declares the Sovereign Lord, I will give you over to bloodshed and it will pursue you. Since you did not hate bloodshed, bloodshed will pursue you. [7] I will make Mount Seir a desolate waste and cut off from it all who come and go. [8] I will fill your mountains with the slain; those killed by the sword will fall on your hills and in your valleys and in all your ravines. [9] I will make you desolate forever; your towns will not be inhabited. Then you will know that I am the Lord.

[10] "'Because you have said, "These two nations and countries will be ours and we will take possession of them," even though I the Lord was there, [11] therefore as surely as I live, declares the Sovereign Lord, I will treat you in accordance with the anger and jealousy you showed in your hatred of them and I will make myself known among them when I judge you. [12] Then you will know that I the Lord have heard all the contemptible things you have said against the mountains of Israel. You said, "They have been laid waste and have been given over to us to devour." [13] You boasted against me and spoke against me without restraint, and I heard it. [14] This is what the Sovereign Lord says: While the whole earth rejoices, I will make you desolate. [15] Because you rejoiced when the inheritance of Israel became desolate, that is how I will treat you. You will be desolate, Mount Seir, you and all of Edom. Then they will know that I am the Lord.'" Jer 50:11-13; La 4:21; Ob 12

Hope for the Mountains of Israel

36 "Son of man, prophesy to the mountains of Israel and say, 'Mountains of Israel, hear the word of the Lord. [2] This is what the Sovereign Lord says: The enemy said of you, "Aha! The ancient heights have become our possession."' [3] Therefore prophesy and say, 'This is what the Sovereign Lord says: Because they ravaged and crushed you from every side so that you became the possession of the rest of the nations and the object of people's malicious talk and slander,

[4] therefore, mountains of Israel, hear the word of the Sovereign LORD: This is what the Sovereign LORD says to the mountains and hills, to the ravines and valleys, to the desolate ruins and the deserted towns that have been plundered and ridiculed by the rest of the nations around you— [5] this is what the Sovereign LORD says: In my burning zeal I have spoken against the rest of the nations, and against all Edom, for with glee and with malice in their hearts they made my land their own possession so that they might plunder its pastureland.' [6] Therefore prophesy concerning the land of Israel and say to the mountains and hills, to the ravines and valleys: 'This is what the Sovereign LORD says: I speak in my jealous wrath because you have suffered the scorn of the nations. [7] Therefore this is what the Sovereign LORD says: I swear with uplifted hand that the nations around you will also suffer scorn. Ps 123:3-4; Eze 34:29; 35:10,15

[8] " 'But you, mountains of Israel, will produce branches and fruit for my people Israel, for they will soon come home. [9] I am concerned for you and will look on you with favor; you will be plowed and sown, [10] and I will cause many people to live on you—yes, all of Israel. The towns will be inhabited and the ruins rebuilt. [11] I will increase the number of people and animals living on you, and they will be fruitful and become numerous. I will settle people on you as in the past and will make you prosper more than before. Then you will know that I am the LORD. [12] I will cause people, my people Israel, to live on you. They will possess you, and you will be their inheritance; you will never again deprive them of their children. Eze 47:14,22

[13] " 'This is what the Sovereign LORD says: Because some say to you, "You devour people and deprive your nation of its children," [14] therefore you will no longer devour people or make your nation childless, declares the Sovereign LORD. [15] No longer will I make you hear the taunts of the nations, and no longer will you suffer the scorn of the peoples or cause your nation to fall, declares the Sovereign LORD.' " Nu 13:32

Israel's Restoration Assured

[16] Again the word of the LORD came to me: [17] "Son of man, when the people of Israel were living in their own land, they defiled it by their conduct and their actions. Their conduct was like a woman's monthly uncleanness in my sight. [18] So I poured out my wrath on them because they had shed blood in the land and because they had defiled it with their idols. [19] I dispersed them among the nations, and they were scattered through the countries; I judged them according to their conduct

and their actions. [20] And wherever they went among the nations they profaned my holy name, for it was said of them, 'These are the LORD's people, and yet they had to leave his land.' [21] I had concern for my holy name, which the people of Israel profaned among the nations where they had gone.

[22] "Therefore say to the Israelites, 'This is what the Sovereign LORD says: It is not for your sake, people of Israel, that I am going to do these things, but for the sake of my holy name, which you have profaned among the nations where you have gone. [23] I will show the holiness of my great name, which has been profaned among the nations, the name you have profaned among them. Then the nations will know that I am the LORD, declares the Sovereign LORD, when I am proved holy through you before their eyes. Ps 126:2; Isa 5:16

[24] "'For I will take you out of the nations; I will gather you from all the countries and bring you back into your own land. [25] I will sprinkle clean water on you, and you will be clean; I will cleanse you from all your impurities and from all your idols. [26] I will give you a new heart and put a new spirit in you; I will remove from you your heart of stone and give you a heart of flesh. [27] And I will put my Spirit in you and move you to follow my decrees and be careful to keep my laws. [28] Then you will live in the land I gave your ancestors; you will be my people, and I will be your God. [29] I will save you from all your uncleanness. I will call for the grain and make it plentiful and will not bring famine upon you. [30] I will increase the fruit of the trees and the crops of the field, so that you will no longer suffer disgrace among the nations because of famine. [31] Then you will remember your evil ways and wicked deeds, and you will loathe yourselves for your sins and detestable practices. [32] I want you to know that I am not doing this for your sake, declares the Sovereign LORD. Be ashamed and disgraced for your conduct, people of Israel! Jer 24:7; Eze 11:19

[33] "'This is what the Sovereign LORD says: On the day I cleanse you from all your sins, I will resettle your towns, and the ruins will be rebuilt. [34] The desolate land will be cultivated instead of lying desolate in the sight of all who pass through it. [35] They will say, "This land that was laid waste has become like the garden of Eden; the cities that were lying in ruins, desolate and destroyed, are now fortified and inhabited." [36] Then the nations around you that remain will know that I the LORD have rebuilt what was destroyed and have replanted what was desolate. I the LORD have spoken, and I will do it.' Eze 22:14; 37:14

[37] "This is what the Sovereign

LORD says: Once again I will yield to Israel's plea and do this for them: I will make their people as numerous as sheep, [38] as numerous as the flocks for offerings at Jerusalem during her appointed festivals. So will the ruined cities be filled with flocks of people. Then they will know that I am the LORD." 1Ki 8:63; 2Ch 35:7-9

The Valley of Dry Bones

37 The hand of the LORD was on me, and he brought me out by the Spirit of the LORD and set me in the middle of a valley; it was full of bones. [2] He led me back and forth among them, and I saw a great many bones on the floor of the valley, bones that were very dry. [3] He asked me, "Son of man, can these bones live?" Eze 1:3; 8:3

I said, "Sovereign LORD, you alone know." Dt 32:39; 1Sa 2:6

[4] Then he said to me, "Prophesy to these bones and say to them, 'Dry bones, hear the word of the LORD! [5] This is what the Sovereign LORD says to these bones: I will make breath[a] enter you, and you will come to life. [6] I will attach tendons to you and make flesh come upon you and cover you with skin; I will put breath in you, and you will come to life. Then you will know that I am the LORD.'" Ps 104:29-30; Joel 2:27; 3:17

[7] So I prophesied as I was commanded. And as I was prophesying, there was a noise, a rattling sound, and the bones came together, bone to bone. [8] I looked, and tendons and flesh appeared on them and skin covered them, but there was no breath in them.

[9] Then he said to me, "Prophesy to the breath; prophesy, son of man, and say to it, 'This is what the Sovereign LORD says: Come, breath, from the four winds and breathe into these slain, that they may live.'" [10] So I prophesied as he commanded me, and breath entered them; they came to life and stood up on their feet—a vast army. Ps 104:30; Rev 11:11

[11] Then he said to me: "Son of man, these bones are the people of Israel. They say, 'Our bones are dried up and our hope is gone; we are cut off.' [12] Therefore prophesy and say to them: 'This is what the Sovereign LORD says: My people, I am going to open your graves and bring you up from them; I will bring you back to the land of Israel. [13] Then you, my people, will know that I am the LORD, when I open your graves and bring you up from them. [14] I will put my Spirit in you and you will live, and I will settle you in your own land. Then you will know that I the LORD have spoken, and I have done it, declares the LORD.'" Hos 13:14; Joel 2:28-29

One Nation Under One King

[15] The word of the LORD came to me: [16] "Son of man, take a stick

---

[a] 5 The Hebrew for this word can also mean *wind* or *spirit* (see verses 6-14).

of wood and write on it, 'Belonging to Judah and the Israelites associated with him.' Then take another stick of wood, and write on it, 'Belonging to Joseph (that is, to Ephraim) and all the Israelites associated with him.' [17] Join them together into one stick so that they will become one in your hand. Nu 17:2-3; 2Ch 15:9

[18] "When your people ask you, 'Won't you tell us what you mean by this?' [19] say to them, 'This is what the Sovereign LORD says: I am going to take the stick of Joseph—which is in Ephraim's hand—and of the Israelite tribes associated with him, and join it to Judah's stick. I will make them into a single stick of wood, and they will become one in my hand.' [20] Hold before their eyes the sticks you have written on [21] and say to them, 'This is what the Sovereign LORD says: I will take the Israelites out of the nations where they have gone. I will gather them from all around and bring them back into their own land. [22] I will make them one nation in the land, on the mountains of Israel. There will be one king over all of them and they will never again be two nations or be divided into two kingdoms. [23] They will no longer defile themselves with their idols and vile images or with any of their offenses, for I will save them from all their sinful backsliding, [a] and I will cleanse them. They will be my people, and I will be their God. Eze 36:25,28

[24] "'My servant David will be king over them, and they will all have one shepherd. They will follow my laws and be careful to keep my decrees. [25] They will live in the land I gave to my servant Jacob, the land where your ancestors lived. They and their children and their children's children will live there forever, and David my servant will be their prince forever. [26] I will make a covenant of peace with them; it will be an everlasting covenant. I will establish them and increase their numbers, and I will put my sanctuary among them forever. [27] My dwelling place will be with them; I will be their God, and they will be my people. [28] Then the nations will know that I the LORD make Israel holy, when my sanctuary is among them forever.'" Eze 20:12; 2Co 6:16

The LORD's Great Victory Over the Nations

38 The word of the LORD came to me: [2] "Son of man, set your face against Gog, of the land of Magog, the chief prince of[b] Meshek and Tubal; prophesy against him [3] and say: 'This is what the Sovereign LORD says: I am against you, Gog, chief prince

---

[a] 23 Many Hebrew manuscripts (see also Septuagint); most Hebrew manuscripts *all their dwelling places where they sinned*   [b] 2 Or *the prince of Rosh,*

of[a] Meshek and Tubal. [4] I will turn you around, put hooks in your jaws and bring you out with your whole army—your horses, your horsemen fully armed, and a great horde with large and small shields, all of them brandishing their swords. [5] Persia, Cush[b] and Put will be with them, all with shields and helmets, [6] also Gomer with all its troops, and Beth Togarmah from the far north with all its troops—the many nations with you. Ge 10:2; Eze 39:11

[7] " 'Get ready; be prepared, you and all the hordes gathered about you, and take command of them. [8] After many days you will be called to arms. In future years you will invade a land that has recovered from war, whose people were gathered from many nations to the mountains of Israel, which had long been desolate. They had been brought out from the nations, and now all of them live in safety. [9] You and all your troops and the many nations with you will go up, advancing like a storm; you will be like a cloud covering the land. Isa 28:2

[10] " 'This is what the Sovereign LORD says: On that day thoughts will come into your mind and you will devise an evil scheme. [11] You will say, "I will invade a land of unwalled villages; I will attack a peaceful and unsuspecting people—all of them living without walls and without gates and bars. [12] I will plunder and loot and turn my hand against the resettled ruins and the people gathered from the nations, rich in livestock and goods, living at the center of the land.[c]" [13] Sheba and Dedan and the merchants of Tarshish and all her villages[d] will say to you, "Have you come to plunder? Have you gathered your hordes to loot, to carry off silver and gold, to take away livestock and goods and to seize much plunder?" ' Eze 27:22; Jer 15:13

[14] "Therefore, son of man, prophesy and say to Gog: 'This is what the Sovereign LORD says: In that day, when my people Israel are living in safety, will you not take notice of it? [15] You will come from your place in the far north, you and many nations with you, all of them riding on horses, a great horde, a mighty army. [16] You will advance against my people Israel like a cloud that covers the land. In days to come, Gog, I will bring you against my land, so that the nations may know me when I am proved holy through you before their eyes. Isa 29:23; Eze 39:21

[17] " 'This is what the Sovereign LORD says: You are the one I spoke of in former days by my servants the prophets of Israel. At that time they prophesied for years that I would bring you against them. [18] This is what will

---

[a] 3 Or *Gog, prince of Rosh,*   [b] 5 That is, the upper Nile region   [c] 12 The Hebrew for this phrase means *the navel of the earth.*   [d] 13 Or *her strong lions*

happen in that day: When Gog attacks the land of Israel, my hot anger will be aroused, declares the Sovereign LORD. [19] In my zeal and fiery wrath I declare that at that time there shall be a great earthquake in the land of Israel. [20] The fish in the sea, the birds in the sky, the beasts of the field, every creature that moves along the ground, and all the people on the face of the earth will tremble at my presence. The mountains will be overturned, the cliffs will crumble and every wall will fall to the ground. [21] I will summon a sword against Gog on all my mountains, declares the Sovereign LORD. Every man's sword will be against his brother. [22] I will execute judgment on him with plague and bloodshed; I will pour down torrents of rain, hailstones and burning sulfur on him and on his troops and on the many nations with him. [23] And so I will show my greatness and my holiness, and I will make myself known in the sight of many nations. Then they will know that I am the LORD.'   1Sa 14:20; Hag 2:6,21

39 "Son of man, prophesy against Gog and say: 'This is what the Sovereign LORD says: I am against you, Gog, chief prince of[a] Meshek and Tubal. [2] I will turn you around and drag you along. I will bring you from the far north and send you against the mountains of Israel.

[3] Then I will strike your bow from your left hand and make your arrows drop from your right hand. [4] On the mountains of Israel you will fall, you and all your troops and the nations with you. I will give you as food to all kinds of carrion birds and to the wild animals. [5] You will fall in the open field, for I have spoken, declares the Sovereign LORD. [6] I will send fire on Magog and on those who live in safety in the coastlands, and they will know that I am the LORD.   Jer 25:22; Am 1:4

[7] "'I will make known my holy name among my people Israel. I will no longer let my holy name be profaned, and the nations will know that I the LORD am the Holy One in Israel. [8] It is coming! It will surely take place, declares the Sovereign LORD. This is the day I have spoken of.   Ex 20:7; Eze 36:16,23

[9] "'Then those who live in the towns of Israel will go out and use the weapons for fuel and burn them up — the small and large shields, the bows and arrows, the war clubs and spears. For seven years they will use them for fuel. [10] They will not need to gather wood from the fields or cut it from the forests, because they will use the weapons for fuel. And they will plunder those who plundered them and loot those who looted them, declares the Sovereign LORD. Isa 14:2; 33:1; Hab 2:8

[11] "'On that day I will give Gog

---

[a] 1 Or Gog, prince of Rosh,

a burial place in Israel, in the valley of those who travel east of the Sea. It will block the way of travelers, because Gog and all his hordes will be buried there. So it will be called the Valley of Hamon Gog.[a]   Eze 38:2

[12] " 'For seven months the Israelites will be burying them in order to cleanse the land. [13] All the people of the land will bury them, and the day I display my glory will be a memorable day for them, declares the Sovereign LORD. [14] People will be continually employed in cleansing the land. They will spread out across the land and, along with others, they will bury any bodies that are lying on the ground.   Dt 21:23; Eze 28:22

" 'After the seven months they will carry out a more detailed search. [15] As they go through the land, anyone who sees a human bone will leave a marker beside it until the gravediggers bury it in the Valley of Hamon Gog, [16] near a town called Hamonah.[b] And so they will cleanse the land.'

[17] "Son of man, this is what the Sovereign LORD says: Call out to every kind of bird and all the wild animals: 'Assemble and come together from all around to the sacrifice I am preparing for you, the great sacrifice on the mountains of Israel. There you will eat flesh and drink blood. [18] You will eat the flesh of mighty men and

drink the blood of the princes of the earth as if they were rams and lambs, goats and bulls—all of them fattened animals from Bashan. [19] At the sacrifice I am preparing for you, you will eat fat till you are glutted and drink blood till you are drunk. [20] At my table you will eat your fill of horses and riders, mighty men and soldiers of every kind,' declares the Sovereign LORD.   Ps 22:12; Rev 19:17-18

[21] "I will display my glory among the nations, and all the nations will see the punishment I inflict and the hand I lay on them. [22] From that day forward the people of Israel will know that I am the LORD their God. [23] And the nations will know that the people of Israel went into exile for their sin, because they were unfaithful to me. So I hid my face from them and handed them over to their enemies, and they all fell by the sword. [24] I dealt with them according to their uncleanness and their offenses, and I hid my face from them.   Eze 36:19

[25] "Therefore this is what the Sovereign LORD says: I will now restore the fortunes of Jacob[c] and will have compassion on all the people of Israel, and I will be zealous for my holy name. [26] They will forget their shame and all the unfaithfulness they showed toward me when they lived in

[a] 11 *Hamon Gog* means *hordes of Gog.*   [b] 16 *Hamonah* means *horde.*   [c] 25 Or *now bring Jacob back from captivity*

safety in their land with no one to make them afraid. **27**When I have brought them back from the nations and have gathered them from the countries of their enemies, I will be proved holy through them in the sight of many nations. **28**Then they will know that I am the LORD their God, for though I sent them into exile among the nations, I will gather them to their own land, not leaving any behind. **29**I will no longer hide my face from them, for I will pour out my Spirit on the people of Israel, declares the Sovereign LORD." Joel 2:28; Ac 2:17

The Temple Area Restored

40 In the twenty-fifth year of our exile, at the beginning of the year, on the tenth of the month, in the fourteenth year after the fall of the city— on that very day the hand of the LORD was on me and he took me there. **2**In visions of God he took me to the land of Israel and set me on a very high mountain, on whose south side were some buildings that looked like a city. **3**He took me there, and I saw a man whose appearance was like bronze; he was standing in the gateway with a linen cord and a measuring rod in his hand. **4**The man said to me, "Son of man, look carefully and listen closely and pay attention to everything I am going to show you, for that is why you have been brought here. Tell the people of Israel everything you see." Jer 26:2; Eze 44:5

The East Gate to the Outer Court

5I saw a wall completely surrounding the temple area. The length of the measuring rod in the man's hand was six long cubits,*a* each of which was a cubit and a handbreadth. He measured the wall; it was one measuring rod thick and one rod high.

6Then he went to the east gate. He climbed its steps and measured the threshold of the gate; it was one rod deep. **7**The alcoves for the guards were one rod long and one rod wide, and the projecting walls between the alcoves were five cubits*b* thick. And the threshold of the gate next to the portico facing the temple was one rod deep. ver 36; Eze 8:16

8Then he measured the portico of the gateway; **9**it*c* was eight cubits*d* deep and its jambs were two cubits*e* thick. The portico of the gateway faced the temple.

10Inside the east gate were

---

a 5 That is, about 11 feet or about 3.2 meters; also in verse 12. The long cubit of about 21 inches or about 53 centimeters is the basic unit of measurement of length throughout chapters 40–48. *b* 7 That is, about 8 3/4 feet or about 2.7 meters; also in verse 48 *c* 8,9 Many Hebrew manuscripts, Septuagint, Vulgate and Syriac; most Hebrew manuscripts *gateway facing the temple; it was one rod deep.* *9Then he measured the portico of the gateway; it* *d* 9 That is, about 14 feet or about 4.2 meters *e* 9 That is, about 3 1/2 feet or about 1 meter three alcoves on each side; the three had the same measurements, and the faces of the projecting walls on each side had the same measurements. ¹¹ Then he measured the width of the entrance of the gateway; it was ten cubits and its length was thirteen cubits.ᵃ ¹² In front of each alcove was a wall one cubit high, and the alcoves were six cubits square. ¹³ Then he measured the gateway from the top of the rear wall of one alcove to the top of the opposite one; the distance was twenty-five cubitsᵇ from one parapet opening to the opposite one. ¹⁴ He measured along the faces of the projecting walls all around the inside of the gateway — sixty cubits.ᶜ The measurement was up to the porticoᵈ facing the courtyard.ᵉ ¹⁵ The distance from the entrance of the gateway to the far end of its portico was fifty cubits.ᶠ ¹⁶ The alcoves and the projecting walls inside the gateway were surmounted by narrow parapet openings all around, as was the portico; the openings all around faced inward. The faces of the projecting walls were decorated with palm trees.   Ex 27:9; 2Ch 3:5

The Outer Court

¹⁷ Then he brought me into the outer court. There I saw some rooms and a pavement that had been constructed all around the court; there were thirty rooms along the pavement. ¹⁸ It abutted the sides of the gateways and was as wide as they were long; this was the lower pavement. ¹⁹ Then he measured the distance from the inside of the lower gateway to the outside of the inner court; it was a hundred cubitsᵍ on the east side as well as on the north.   Eze 41:6; 46:1

The North Gate

²⁰ Then he measured the length and width of the north gate, leading into the outer court. ²¹ Its alcoves — three on each side — its projecting walls and its portico had the same measurements as those of the first gateway. It was fifty cubits long and twenty-five cubits wide. ²² Its openings, its portico and its palm tree decorations had the same measurements as those of the gate facing east. Seven steps led up to it, with its portico opposite them. ²³ There was a gate to the inner court facing the north gate, just as there was on the east. He measured from one gate to the opposite one; it was a hundred cubits.   ver 49

ᵃ *11* That is, about 18 feet wide and 23 feet long or about 5.3 meters wide and 6.9 meters long   ᵇ *13* That is, about 44 feet or about 13 meters; also in verses 21, 25, 29, 30, 33 and 36   ᶜ *14* That is, about 105 feet or about 32 meters   ᵈ *14* Septuagint; Hebrew *projecting wall*   ᵉ *14* The meaning of the Hebrew for this verse is uncertain.   ᶠ *15* That is, about 88 feet or about 27 meters; also in verses 21, 25, 29, 33 and 36   ᵍ *19* That is, about 175 feet or about 53 meters; also in verses 23, 27 and 47

The South Gate

²⁴Then he led me to the south side and I saw the south gate. He measured its jambs and its portico, and they had the same measurements as the others. ²⁵The gateway and its portico had narrow openings all around, like the openings of the others. It was fifty cubits long and twenty-five cubits wide. ²⁶Seven steps led up to it, with its portico opposite them; it had palm tree decorations on the faces of the projecting walls on each side. ²⁷The inner court also had a gate facing south, and he measured from this gate to the outer gate on the south side; it was a hundred cubits. ver 22,32

The Gates to the Inner Court

²⁸Then he brought me into the inner court through the south gate, and he measured the south gate; it had the same measurements as the others. ²⁹Its alcoves, its projecting walls and its portico had the same measurements as the others. The gateway and its portico had openings all around. It was fifty cubits long and twenty-five cubits wide. ³⁰(The porticoes of the gateways around the inner court were twenty-five cubits wide and five cubits deep.) ³¹Its portico faced the outer court; palm trees decorated its jambs, and eight steps led up to it. ver 21-22

³²Then he brought me to the inner court on the east side, and he measured the gateway; it had the same measurements as the others. ³³Its alcoves, its projecting walls and its portico had the same measurements as the others. The gateway and its portico had openings all around. It was fifty cubits long and twenty-five cubits wide. ³⁴Its portico faced the outer court; palm trees decorated the jambs on either side, and eight steps led up to it. ver 22

³⁵Then he brought me to the north gate and measured it. It had the same measurements as the others, ³⁶as did its alcoves, its projecting walls and its portico, and it had openings all around. It was fifty cubits long and twenty-five cubits wide. ³⁷Its porticoᵃ faced the outer court; palm trees decorated the jambs on either side, and eight steps led up to it. Eze 44:4; 47:2

The Rooms for Preparing Sacrifices

³⁸A room with a doorway was by the portico in each of the inner gateways, where the burnt offerings were washed. ³⁹In the portico of the gateway were two tables on each side, on which the burnt offerings, sin offeringsᵇ and guilt offerings were slaughtered. ⁴⁰By the outside wall of the portico of the gateway, near the steps at the entrance of the north gateway were two tables, and on the oth-

---

ᵃ 37 Septuagint (see also verses 31 and 34); Hebrew *jambs*   ᵇ 39 Or *purification offerings* er side of the steps were two tables. ⁴¹So there were four tables on one side of the gateway and four on the other—eight tables in all—on which the sacrifices were slaughtered. ⁴²There were also four tables of dressed stone for the burnt offerings, each a cubit and a half long, a cubit and a half wide and a cubit high.ᵃ On them were placed the utensils for slaughtering the burnt offerings and the other sacrifices. ⁴³And double-pronged hooks, each a handbreadthᵇ long, were attached to the wall all around. The tables were for the flesh of the offerings.   Lev 4:3,28; 7:1

The Rooms for the Priests

⁴⁴Outside the inner gate, within the inner court, were two rooms, oneᶜ at the side of the north gate and facing south, and another at the side of the southᵈ gate and facing north. ⁴⁵He said to me, "The room facing south is for the priests who guard the temple, ⁴⁶and the room facing north is for the priests who guard the altar. These are the sons of Zadok, who are the only Levites who may draw near to the LORD to minister before him."   1Ki 2:35; Eze 43:19; 44:15

⁴⁷Then he measured the court: It was square—a hundred cubits long and a hundred cubits wide. And the altar was in front of the temple.   Eze 41:13-14

The New Temple

⁴⁸He brought me to the portico of the temple and measured the jambs of the portico; they were five cubits wide on either side. The width of the entrance was fourteen cubitsᵉ and its projecting walls wereᶠ three cubitsᵍ wide on either side. ⁴⁹The portico was twenty cubitsʰ wide, and twelveⁱ cubitsʲ from front to back. It was reached by a flight of stairs,ᵏ and there were pillars on each side of the jambs.   1Ki 6:3; 7:15

41 Then the man brought me to the main hall and measured the jambs; the width of the jambs was six cubitsˡ on each side.ᵐ ²The entrance was ten cubitsⁿ wide, and the projecting walls on each side of it were five cubitsᵒ wide. He also measured the main hall; it was forty cubits long and twenty cubits wide.ᵖ   ver 23; 2Ch 3:3

ᵃ 42 That is, about 2 2/3 feet long and wide and 21 inches high or about 80 centimeters long and wide and 53 centimeters high   ᵇ 43 That is, about 3 1/2 inches or about 9 centimeters   ᶜ 44 Septuagint; Hebrew *were rooms for singers, which were*   ᵈ 44 Septuagint; Hebrew *east*   ᵉ 48 That is, about 25 feet or about 7.4 meters   ᶠ 48 Septuagint; Hebrew *entrance was*   ᵍ 48 That is, about 5 1/4 feet or about 1.6 meters   ʰ 49 That is, about 35 feet or about 11 meters   ⁱ 49 Septuagint; Hebrew *eleven*   ʲ 49 That is, about 21 feet or about 6.4 meters   ᵏ 49 Hebrew; Septuagint *Ten steps led up to it*   ˡ 1 That is, about 11 feet or about 3.2 meters; also in verses 3, 5 and 8   ᵐ 1 One Hebrew manuscript and Septuagint; most Hebrew manuscripts *side, the width of the tent*   ⁿ 2 That is, about 18 feet or about 5.3 meters   ᵒ 2 That is, about 8 3/4 feet or about 2.7 meters; also in verses 9, 11 and 12   ᵖ 2 That is, about 70 feet long and 35 feet wide or about 21 meters long and 11 meters wide

³Then he went into the inner sanctuary and measured the jambs of the entrance; each was two cubits*a* wide. The entrance was six cubits wide, and the projecting walls on each side of it were seven cubits*b* wide. ⁴And he measured the length of the inner sanctuary; it was twenty cubits, and its width was twenty cubits across the end of the main hall. He said to me, "This is the Most Holy Place."   1Ki 6:20; Heb 9:3-8

⁵Then he measured the wall of the temple; it was six cubits thick, and each side room around the temple was four cubits*c* wide. ⁶The side rooms were on three levels, one above another, thirty on each level. There were ledges all around the wall of the temple to serve as supports for the side rooms, so that the supports were not inserted into the wall of the temple. ⁷The side rooms all around the temple were wider at each successive level. The structure surrounding the temple was built in ascending stages, so that the rooms widened as one went upward. A stairway went up from the lowest floor to the top floor through the middle floor.   1Ki 6:5,8

⁸I saw that the temple had a raised base all around it, forming the foundation of the side rooms. It was the length of the rod, six long cubits. ⁹The outer wall of the side rooms was five cubits thick. The open area between the side rooms of the temple ¹⁰and the priests' rooms was twenty cubits wide all around the temple. ¹¹There were entrances to the side rooms from the open area, one on the north and another on the south; and the base adjoining the open area was five cubits wide all around.

¹²The building facing the temple courtyard on the west side was seventy cubits*d* wide. The wall of the building was five cubits thick all around, and its length was ninety cubits.*e*

¹³Then he measured the temple; it was a hundred cubits*f* long, and the temple courtyard and the building with its walls were also a hundred cubits long. ¹⁴The width of the temple courtyard on the east, including the front of the temple, was a hundred cubits.   Eze 40:47

¹⁵Then he measured the length of the building facing the courtyard at the rear of the temple, including its galleries on each side; it was a hundred cubits.   Eze 42:3

The main hall, the inner sanctuary and the portico facing the court, ¹⁶as well as the thresholds and the narrow windows and galleries around the three of

---

a 3 That is, about 3 1/2 feet or about 1.1 meters; also in verse 22   *b 3* That is, about 12 feet or about 3.7 meters   *c 5* That is, about 7 feet or about 2.1 meters   *d 12* That is, about 123 feet or about 37 meters   *e 12* That is, about 158 feet or about 48 meters   *f 13* That is, about 175 feet or about 53 meters; also in verses 14 and 15 them—everything beyond and including the threshold was covered with wood. The floor, the wall up to the windows, and the windows were covered. [17] In the space above the outside of the entrance to the inner sanctuary and on the walls at regular intervals all around the inner and outer sanctuary [18] were carved cherubim and palm trees. Palm trees alternated with cherubim. Each cherub had two faces: [19] the face of a human being toward the palm tree on one side and the face of a lion toward the palm tree on the other. They were carved all around the whole temple. [20] From the floor to the area above the entrance, cherubim and palm trees were carved on the wall of the main hall.

[21] The main hall had a rectangular doorframe, and the one at the front of the Most Holy Place was similar. [22] There was a wooden altar three cubits[a] high and two cubits square[b]; its corners, its base[c] and its sides were of wood. The man said to me, "This is the table that is before the LORD." [23] Both the main hall and the Most Holy Place had double doors. [24] Each door had two leaves—two hinged leaves for each door. [25] And on the doors of the main hall were carved cherubim and palm trees like those carved on the walls, and there was a wooden overhang on the front of the portico. [26] On the sidewalls of the portico were narrow windows with palm trees carved on each side. The side rooms of the temple also had overhangs. Eze 44:16; Mal 1:7,12

The Rooms for the Priests

42 Then the man led me northward into the outer court and brought me to the rooms opposite the temple courtyard and opposite the outer wall on the north side. [2] The building whose door faced north was a hundred cubits long and fifty cubits wide.[d] [3] Both in the section twenty cubits[e] from the inner court and in the section opposite the pavement of the outer court, gallery faced gallery at the three levels. [4] In front of the rooms was an inner passageway ten cubits wide and a hundred cubits[f] long.[g] Their doors were on the north. [5] Now the upper rooms were narrower, for the galleries took more space from them than from the rooms on the lower and middle floors of the building. [6] The rooms on the top floor had no pillars, as the courts had; so they were smaller in floor space than those on the lower and middle

---

[a] 22 That is, about 5 1/4 feet or about 1.5 meters   [b] 22 Septuagint; Hebrew *long*
[c] 22 Septuagint; Hebrew *length*   [d] 2 That is, about 175 feet long and 88 feet wide or about 53 meters long and 27 meters wide   [e] 3 That is, about 35 feet or about 11 meters
[f] 4 Septuagint and Syriac; Hebrew *and one cubit*   [g] 4 That is, about 18 feet wide and 175 feet long or about 5.3 meters wide and 53 meters long

floors. [7] There was an outer wall parallel to the rooms and the outer court; it extended in front of the rooms for fifty cubits. [8] While the row of rooms on the side next to the outer court was fifty cubits long, the row on the side nearest the sanctuary was a hundred cubits long. [9] The lower rooms had an entrance on the east side as one enters them from the outer court. Eze 41:12-14; 44:5

[10] On the south side[a] along the length of the wall of the outer court, adjoining the temple courtyard and opposite the outer wall, were rooms [11] with a passageway in front of them. These were like the rooms on the north; they had the same length and width, with similar exits and dimensions. Similar to the doorways on the north [12] were the doorways of the rooms on the south. There was a doorway at the beginning of the passageway that was parallel to the corresponding wall extending eastward, by which one enters the rooms. Eze 41:12-14

[13] Then he said to me, "The north and south rooms facing the temple courtyard are the priests' rooms, where the priests who approach the LORD will eat the most holy offerings. There they will put the most holy offerings — the grain offerings, the sin offerings[b] and the guilt offerings —

for the place is holy. [14] Once the priests enter the holy precincts, they are not to go into the outer court until they leave behind the garments in which they minister, for these are holy. They are to put on other clothes before they go near the places that are for the people." Ex 29:9; Lev 8:7-9

[15] When he had finished measuring what was inside the temple area, he led me out by the east gate and measured the area all around: [16] He measured the east side with the measuring rod; it was five hundred cubits.[c,d] [17] He measured the north side; it was five hundred cubits[e] by the measuring rod. [18] He measured the south side; it was five hundred cubits by the measuring rod. [19] Then he turned to the west side and measured; it was five hundred cubits by the measuring rod. [20] So he measured the area on all four sides. It had a wall around it, five hundred cubits long and five hundred cubits wide, to separate the holy from the common. Eze 45:2; Rev 21:16

God's Glory Returns to the Temple

43 Then the man brought me to the gate facing east, [2] and I saw the glory of the God of Israel coming from the east. His voice was like the roar

---

[a] 10 Septuagint; Hebrew *Eastward*   [b] 13 Or *purification offerings*   [c] 16 See Septuagint of verse 17; Hebrew *rods*; also in verses 18 and 19.   [d] 16 Five hundred cubits equal about 875 feet or about 265 meters; also in verses 17, 18 and 19.   [e] 17 Septuagint; Hebrew *rods*

of rushing waters, and the land was radiant with his glory. ³The vision I saw was like the vision I had seen when he[a] came to destroy the city and like the visions I had seen by the Kebar River, and I fell facedown. ⁴The glory of the LORD entered the temple through the gate facing east. ⁵Then the Spirit lifted me up and brought me into the inner court, and the glory of the LORD filled the temple.   Eze 11:24; 8:3

⁶While the man was standing beside me, I heard someone speaking to me from inside the temple. ⁷He said: "Son of man, this is the place of my throne and the place for the soles of my feet. This is where I will live among the Israelites forever. The people of Israel will never again defile my holy name — neither they nor their kings — by their prostitution and the funeral offerings[b] for their kings at their death.[c] ⁸When they placed their threshold next to my threshold and their doorposts beside my doorposts, with only a wall between me and them, they defiled my holy name by their detestable practices. So I destroyed them in my anger. ⁹Now let them put away from me their prostitu-

tion and the funeral offerings for their kings, and I will live among them forever.   Eze 37:26-28

¹⁰"Son of man, describe the temple to the people of Israel, that they may be ashamed of their sins. Let them consider its perfection, ¹¹and if they are ashamed of all they have done, make known to them the design of the temple — its arrangement, its exits and entrances — its whole design and all its regulations[d] and laws. Write these down before them so that they may be faithful to its design and follow all its regulations.   Eze 16:61; 44:5

¹²"This is the law of the temple: All the surrounding area on top of the mountain will be most holy. Such is the law of the temple.

The Great Altar Restored

¹³"These are the measurements of the altar in long cubits,[e] that cubit being a cubit and a handbreadth: Its gutter is a cubit deep and a cubit wide, with a rim of one span[f] around the edge. And this is the height of the altar: ¹⁴From the gutter on the ground up to the lower ledge that goes around the altar it is two cubits high, and the ledge is a cubit wide.[g] From this lower

---

[a] 3 Some Hebrew manuscripts and Vulgate; most Hebrew manuscripts *I*   [b] 7 Or *the memorial monuments*; also in verse 9   [c] 7 Or *their high places*   [d] 11 Some Hebrew manuscripts and Septuagint; most Hebrew manuscripts *regulations and its whole design*   [e] 13 That is, about 21 inches or about 53 centimeters; also in verses 14 and 17. The long cubit is the basic unit for linear measurement throughout Ezekiel 40–48.   [f] 13 That is, about 11 inches or about 27 centimeters   [g] 14 That is, about 3 1/2 feet high and 1 3/4 feet wide or about 105 centimeters high and 53 centimeters wide

ledge to the upper ledge that goes around the altar it is four cubits high, and that ledge is also a cubit wide.*a* ¹⁵Above that, the altar hearth is four cubits high, and four horns project upward from the hearth. ¹⁶The altar hearth is square, twelve cubits*b* long and twelve cubits wide. ¹⁷The upper ledge also is square, fourteen cubits*c* long and fourteen cubits wide. All around the altar is a gutter of one cubit with a rim of half a cubit.*d* The steps of the altar face east." Ex 20:26; 2Ch 4:1

¹⁸Then he said to me, "Son of man, this is what the Sovereign LORD says: These will be the regulations for sacrificing burnt offerings and splashing blood against the altar when it is built: ¹⁹You are to give a young bull as a sin offering*e* to the Levitical priests of the family of Zadok, who come near to minister before me, declares the Sovereign LORD. ²⁰You are to take some of its blood and put it on the four horns of the altar and on the four corners of the upper ledge and all around the rim, and so purify the altar and make atonement for it. ²¹You are to take the bull for the sin offering and burn it in the designated part of the temple area outside the sanctuary. Ex 29:14; Heb 13:11

²²"On the second day you are to offer a male goat without defect for a sin offering, and the altar is to be purified as it was purified with the bull. ²³When you have finished purifying it, you are to offer a young bull and a ram from the flock, both without defect. ²⁴You are to offer them before the LORD, and the priests are to sprinkle salt on them and sacrifice them as a burnt offering to the LORD. Lev 2:13; Mk 9:49-50

²⁵"For seven days you are to provide a male goat daily for a sin offering; you are also to provide a young bull and a ram from the flock, both without defect. ²⁶For seven days they are to make atonement for the altar and cleanse it; thus they will dedicate it. ²⁷At the end of these days, from the eighth day on, the priests are to present your burnt offerings and fellowship offerings on the altar. Then I will accept you, declares the Sovereign LORD." Lev 8:33; 17:5

The Priesthood Restored

44 Then the man brought me back to the outer gate of the sanctuary, the one facing east, and it was shut. ²The LORD said to me, "This gate is to remain shut. It must not be opened; no one may enter through it. It is to remain shut because the

---

a 14 That is, about 7 feet high and 1 3/4 feet wide or about 2.1 meters high and 53 centimeters wide   *b 16* That is, about 21 feet or about 6.4 meters   *c 17* That is, about 25 feet or about 7.4 meters   *d 17* That is, about 11 inches or about 27 centimeters   *e 19* Or *purification offering*; also in verses 21, 22 and 25

LORD, the God of Israel, has entered through it. ³The prince himself is the only one who may sit inside the gateway to eat in the presence of the LORD. He is to enter by way of the portico of the gateway and go out the same way." Eze 46:2,8

⁴Then the man brought me by way of the north gate to the front of the temple. I looked and saw the glory of the LORD filling the temple of the LORD, and I fell facedown. Eze 1:28; 3:23

⁵The LORD said to me, "Son of man, look carefully, listen closely and give attention to everything I tell you concerning all the regulations and instructions regarding the temple of the LORD. Give attention to the entrance to the temple and all the exits of the sanctuary. ⁶Say to rebellious Israel, 'This is what the Sovereign LORD says: Enough of your detestable practices, people of Israel! ⁷In addition to all your other detestable practices, you brought foreigners uncircumcised in heart and flesh into my sanctuary, desecrating my temple while you offered me food, fat and blood, and you broke my covenant. ⁸Instead of carrying out your duty in regard to my holy things, you put others in charge of my sanctuary. ⁹This is what the Sovereign LORD says: No foreigner uncircumcised in heart and flesh is to enter my sanctuary, not even the foreigners who live among the Israelites. Lev 26:41; Joel 3:17

¹⁰"'The Levites who went far from me when Israel went astray and who wandered from me after their idols must bear the consequences of their sin. ¹¹They may serve in my sanctuary, having charge of the gates of the temple and serving in it; they may slaughter the burnt offerings and sacrifices for the people and stand before the people and serve them. ¹²But because they served them in the presence of their idols and made the people of Israel fall into sin, therefore I have sworn with uplifted hand that they must bear the consequences of their sin, declares the Sovereign LORD. ¹³They are not to come near to serve me as priests or come near any of my holy things or my most holy offerings; they must bear the shame of their detestable practices. ¹⁴And I will appoint them to guard the temple for all the work that is to be done in it. 2Ki 23:8

¹⁵"'But the Levitical priests, who are descendants of Zadok and who guarded my sanctuary when the Israelites went astray from me, are to come near to minister before me; they are to stand before me to offer sacrifices of fat and blood, declares the Sovereign LORD. ¹⁶They alone are to enter my sanctuary; they alone are to come near my table to minister before me and serve me as guards. Nu 18:5; Eze 40:46

¹⁷"'When they enter the gates

of the inner court, they are to wear linen clothes; they must not wear any woolen garment while ministering at the gates of the inner court or inside the temple. ¹⁸They are to wear linen turbans on their heads and linen undergarments around their waists. They must not wear anything that makes them perspire. ¹⁹When they go out into the outer court where the people are, they are to take off the clothes they have been ministering in and are to leave them in the sacred rooms, and put on other clothes, so that the people are not consecrated through contact with their garments. Eze 42:14; 46:20

²⁰ "'They must not shave their heads or let their hair grow long, but they are to keep the hair of their heads trimmed. ²¹No priest is to drink wine when he enters the inner court. ²²They must not marry widows or divorced women; they may marry only virgins of Israelite descent or widows of priests. ²³They are to teach my people the difference between the holy and the common and show them how to distinguish between the unclean and the clean. Eze 22:26; Mal 2:7

²⁴ "'In any dispute, the priests are to serve as judges and decide it according to my ordinances. They are to keep my laws and my decrees for all my appointed festivals, and they are to keep my Sabbaths holy. Dt 17:8-9; 2Ch 19:8

²⁵ "'A priest must not defile himself by going near a dead person; however, if the dead person was his father or mother, son or daughter, brother or unmarried sister, then he may defile himself. ²⁶After he is cleansed, he must wait seven days. ²⁷On the day he goes into the inner court of the sanctuary to minister in the sanctuary, he is to offer a sin offering^a for himself, declares the Sovereign LORD. Lev 21:1-4; Nu 19:14

²⁸ "'I am to be the only inheritance the priests have. You are to give them no possession in Israel; I will be their possession. ²⁹They will eat the grain offerings, the sin offerings and the guilt offerings; and everything in Israel devoted^b to the LORD will belong to them. ³⁰The best of all the firstfruits and of all your special gifts will belong to the priests. You are to give them the first portion of your ground meal so that a blessing may rest on your household. ³¹The priests must not eat anything, whether bird or animal, found dead or torn by wild animals. Nu 18:20; Dt 10:9; 18:1-2

Israel Fully Restored

45 "'When you allot the land as an inheritance, you are to present to the LORD a portion of the land as a sacred

---

^a 27 Or *purification offering*; also in verse 29   ^b 29 The Hebrew term refers to the irrevocable giving over of things or persons to the LORD.

district, 25,000 cubits[a] long and 20,000[b] cubits[c] wide; the entire area will be holy. [2]Of this, a section 500 cubits[d] square is to be for the sanctuary, with 50 cubits[e] around it for open land. [3]In the sacred district, measure off a section 25,000 cubits long and 10,000 cubits[f] wide. In it will be the sanctuary, the Most Holy Place. [4]It will be the sacred portion of the land for the priests, who minister in the sanctuary and who draw near to minister before the LORD. It will be a place for their houses as well as a holy place for the sanctuary. [5]An area 25,000 cubits long and 10,000 cubits wide will belong to the Levites, who serve in the temple, as their possession for towns to live in.[g]   Eze 47:21-22; 48:13

[6]"'You are to give the city as its property an area 5,000 cubits[h] wide and 25,000 cubits long, adjoining the sacred portion; it will belong to all Israel.   Eze 48:15-18

[7]"'The prince will have the land bordering each side of the area formed by the sacred district and the property of the city. It will extend westward from the west side and eastward from the east side, running lengthwise from the western to the eastern border parallel to one of the tribal portions. [8]This land will be his possession in Israel. And my princes will no longer oppress my people but will allow the people of Israel to possess the land according to their tribes. Eze 46:18

[9]"'This is what the Sovereign LORD says: You have gone far enough, princes of Israel! Give up your violence and oppression and do what is just and right. Stop dispossessing my people, declares the Sovereign LORD. [10]You are to use accurate scales, an accurate ephah[i] and an accurate bath.[j] [11]The ephah and the bath are to be the same size, the bath containing a tenth of a homer and the ephah a tenth of a homer; the homer is to be the standard measure for both. [12]The shekel[k] is to consist of twenty gerahs. Twenty shekels plus twenty-five shekels plus fifteen shekels equal one mina.[l]   Jer 22:3; Zec 7:9-10; 8:16

[13]"'This is the special gift you are to offer: a sixth of an ephah[m] from each homer of wheat and a

[a] 1 That is, about 8 miles or about 13 kilometers; also in verses 3, 5 and 6   [b] 1 Septuagint (see also verses 3 and 5 and 48:9); Hebrew 10,000   [c] 1 That is, about 6 1/2 miles or about 11 kilometers   [d] 2 That is, about 875 feet or about 265 meters   [e] 2 That is, about 88 feet or about 27 meters   [f] 3 That is, about 3 1/3 miles or about 5.3 kilometers; also in verse 5   [g] 5 Septuagint; Hebrew temple; they will have as their possession 20 rooms   [h] 6 That is, about 1 2/3 miles or about 2.7 kilometers   [i] 10 An ephah was a dry measure having the capacity of about 3/5 bushel or about 22 liters.   [j] 10 A bath was a liquid measure equaling about 6 gallons or about 22 liters.   [k] 12 A shekel weighed about 2/5 ounce or about 12 grams.   [l] 12 That is, 60 shekels; the common mina was 50 shekels. Sixty shekels were about 1 1/2 pounds or about 690 grams.   [m] 13 That is, probably about 6 pounds or about 2.7 kilograms

sixth of an ephah[a] from each homer of barley. [14] The prescribed portion of olive oil, measured by the bath, is a tenth of a bath[b] from each cor (which consists of ten baths or one homer, for ten baths are equivalent to a homer). [15] Also one sheep is to be taken from every flock of two hundred from the well-watered pastures of Israel. These will be used for the grain offerings, burnt offerings and fellowship offerings to make atonement for the people, declares the Sovereign LORD. [16] All the people of the land will be required to give this special offering to the prince in Israel. [17] It will be the duty of the prince to provide the burnt offerings, grain offerings and drink offerings at the festivals, the New Moons and the Sabbaths — at all the appointed festivals of Israel. He will provide the sin offerings,[c] grain offerings, burnt offerings and fellowship offerings to make atonement for the Israelites. 1Ki 8:62; 2Ch 31:3

[18] "'This is what the Sovereign LORD says: In the first month on the first day you are to take a young bull without defect and purify the sanctuary. [19] The priest is to take some of the blood of the sin offering and put it on the doorposts of the temple, on the four corners of the upper ledge of the altar and on the gateposts of the inner court. [20] You are to do the same on the seventh day of the month for anyone who sins unintentionally or through ignorance; so you are to make atonement for the temple. Lev 4:27; Eze 43:20

[21] "'In the first month on the fourteenth day you are to observe the Passover, a festival lasting seven days, during which you shall eat bread made without yeast. [22] On that day the prince is to provide a bull as a sin offering for himself and for all the people of the land. [23] Every day during the seven days of the festival he is to provide seven bulls and seven rams without defect as a burnt offering to the LORD, and a male goat for a sin offering. [24] He is to provide as a grain offering an ephah for each bull and an ephah for each ram, along with a hin[d] of olive oil for each ephah. Ex 12:11

[25] "'During the seven days of the festival, which begins in the seventh month on the fifteenth day, he is to make the same provision for sin offerings, burnt offerings, grain offerings and oil.

46 "'This is what the Sovereign LORD says: The gate of the inner court facing east is to be shut on the six working days, but on the Sabbath day and on the day of the New Moon it is to be opened. [2] The prince is to enter from the outside through the

---

[a] 13 That is, probably about 5 pounds or about 2.3 kilograms   [b] 14 That is, about 2 1/2 quarts or about 2.2 liters   [c] 17 Or purification offerings; also in verses 19, 22, 23 and 25   [d] 24 That is, about 1 gallon or about 3.8 liters

portico of the gateway and stand by the gatepost. The priests are to sacrifice his burnt offering and his fellowship offerings. He is to bow down in worship at the threshold of the gateway and then go out, but the gate will not be shut until evening. ³On the Sabbaths and New Moons the people of the land are to worship in the presence of the LORD at the entrance of that gateway. ⁴The burnt offering the prince brings to the LORD on the Sabbath day is to be six male lambs and a ram, all without defect. ⁵The grain offering given with the ram is to be an ephah,ᵃ and the grain offering with the lambs is to be as much as he pleases, along with a hinᵇ of olive oil for each ephah. ⁶On the day of the New Moon he is to offer a young bull, six lambs and a ram, all without defect. ⁷He is to provide as a grain offering one ephah with the bull, one ephah with the ram, and with the lambs as much as he wants to give, along with a hin of oil for each ephah. ⁸When the prince enters, he is to go in through the portico of the gateway, and he is to come out the same way.   Eze 40:19; 44:3

⁹"'When the people of the land come before the LORD at the appointed festivals, whoever enters by the north gate to worship is to go out the south gate; and who-ever enters by the south gate is to go out the north gate. No one is to return through the gate by which they entered, but each is to go out the opposite gate. ¹⁰The prince is to be among them, going in when they go in and going out when they go out. ¹¹At the feasts and the appointed festivals, the grain offering is to be an ephah with a bull, an ephah with a ram, and with the lambs as much as he pleases, along with a hin of oil for each ephah.   Ex 23:14; Ps 42:4

¹²"'When the prince provides a freewill offering to the LORD — whether a burnt offering or fellowship offerings — the gate facing east is to be opened for him. He shall offer his burnt offering or his fellowship offerings as he does on the Sabbath day. Then he shall go out, and after he has gone out, the gate will be shut.   Eze 45:17

¹³"'Every day you are to provide a year-old lamb without defect for a burnt offering to the LORD; morning by morning you shall provide it. ¹⁴You are also to provide with it morning by morning a grain offering, consisting of a sixth of an ephahᶜ with a third of a hinᵈ of oil to moisten the flour. The presenting of this grain offering to the LORD is a lasting ordinance. ¹⁵So the lamb and the grain offering and the oil shall be provided morning by

---

ᵃ 5 That is, probably about 35 pounds or about 16 kilograms; also in verses 7 and 11
ᵇ 5 That is, about 1 gallon or about 3.8 liters; also in verses 7 and 11   ᶜ 14 That is, probably about 6 pounds or about 2.7 kilograms   ᵈ 14 That is, about 1 1/2 quarts or about 1.3 liters

morning for a regular burnt offering. Nu 28:5-6; Ex 29:38,42

16 "'This is what the Sovereign LORD says: If the prince makes a gift from his inheritance to one of his sons, it will also belong to his descendants; it is to be their property by inheritance. 17 If, however, he makes a gift from his inheritance to one of his servants, the servant may keep it until the year of freedom; then it will revert to the prince. His inheritance belongs to his sons only; it is theirs. 18 The prince must not take any of the inheritance of the people, driving them off their property. He is to give his sons their inheritance out of his own property, so that not one of my people will be separated from their property.'" Eze 45:8; Mic 2:1-2

19 Then the man brought me through the entrance at the side of the gate to the sacred rooms facing north, which belonged to the priests, and showed me a place at the western end. 20 He said to me, "This is the place where the priests are to cook the guilt offering and the sin offering[a] and bake the grain offering, to avoid bringing them into the outer court and consecrating the people." Zec 14:20

21 He then brought me to the outer court and led me around to its four corners, and I saw in each corner another court. 22 In the four corners of the outer court were enclosed[b] courts, forty cubits long and thirty cubits wide;[c] each of the courts in the four corners was the same size. 23 Around the inside of each of the four courts was a ledge of stone, with places for fire built all around under the ledge. 24 He said to me, "These are the kitchens where those who minister at the temple are to cook the sacrifices of the people."

The River From the Temple

47 The man brought me back to the entrance to the temple, and I saw water coming out from under the threshold of the temple toward the east (for the temple faced east). The water was coming down from under the south side of the temple, south of the altar. 2 He then brought me out through the north gate and led me around the outside to the outer gate facing east, and the water was trickling from the south side. Joel 3:18; Rev 22:1

3 As the man went eastward with a measuring line in his hand, he measured off a thousand cubits[d] and then led me through water that was ankle-deep. 4 He measured off another thousand cubits and led me through water that was knee-

---

[a] 20 Or purification offering   [b] 22 The meaning of the Hebrew for this word is uncertain.
[c] 22 That is, about 70 feet long and 53 feet wide or about 21 meters long and 16 meters wide
[d] 3 That is, about 1,700 feet or about 530 meters

deep. He measured off another thousand and led me through water that was up to the waist. ⁵He measured off another thousand, but now it was a river that I could not cross, because the water had risen and was deep enough to swim in — a river that no one could cross. ⁶He asked me, "Son of man, do you see this?" Isa 11:9; Eze 40:3

Then he led me back to the bank of the river. ⁷When I arrived there, I saw a great number of trees on each side of the river. ⁸He said to me, "This water flows toward the eastern region and goes down into the Arabah,ᵃ where it enters the Dead Sea. When it empties into the sea, the salty water there becomes fresh. ⁹Swarms of living creatures will live wherever the river flows. There will be large numbers of fish, because this water flows there and makes the salt water fresh; so where the river flows everything will live. ¹⁰Fishermen will stand along the shore; from En Gedi to En Eglaim there will be places for spreading nets. The fish will be of many kinds — like the fish of the Mediterranean Sea. ¹¹But the swamps and marshes will not become fresh; they will be left for salt. ¹²Fruit trees of all kinds will grow on both banks of the river. Their leaves will not wither, nor will their fruit fail. Every month they will bear fruit, because the water from the sanctuary flows to them. Their fruit will serve for food and their leaves for healing." Ps 1:3; Jer 17:8

The Boundaries of the Land

¹³This is what the Sovereign Lord says: "These are the boundaries of the land that you will divide among the twelve tribes of Israel as their inheritance, with two portions for Joseph. ¹⁴You are to divide it equally among them. Because I swore with uplifted hand to give it to your ancestors, this land will become your inheritance. Dt 1:8; Eze 20:5-6

¹⁵"This is to be the boundary of the land:

"On the north side it will run from the Mediterranean Sea by the Hethlon road past Lebo Hamath to Zedad, ¹⁶Berothahᵇ and Sibraim (which lies on the border between Damascus and Hamath), as far as Hazer Hattikon, which is on the border of Hauran. ¹⁷The boundary will extend from the sea to Hazar Enan,ᶜ along the northern border of Damascus, with the border of Hamath to the north. This will be the northern boundary. Eze 48:1

ᵃ 8 Or *the Jordan Valley* ᵇ 15,16 See Septuagint and 48:1; Hebrew *road to go into Zedad,* ¹⁶Hamath, Berothah. ᶜ 17 Hebrew *Enon,* a variant of *Enan*

¹⁸"On the east side the boundary will run between Hauran and Damascus, along the Jordan between Gilead and the land of Israel, to the Dead Sea and as far as Tamar.*ᵃ* This will be the eastern boundary. Eze 27:18

¹⁹"On the south side it will run from Tamar as far as the waters of Meribah Kadesh, then along the Wadi of Egypt to the Mediterranean Sea. This will be the southern boundary.

²⁰"On the west side, the Mediterranean Sea will be the boundary to a point opposite Lebo Hamath. This will be the western boundary.

²¹"You are to distribute this land among yourselves according to the tribes of Israel. ²²You are to allot it as an inheritance for yourselves and for the foreigners residing among you and who have children. You are to consider them as native-born Israelites; along with you they are to be allotted an inheritance among the tribes of Israel. ²³In whatever tribe a foreigner resides, there you are to give them their inheritance," declares the Sovereign LORD. Eph 3:6; Col 3:11

The Division of the Land

48 "These are the tribes, listed by name: At the northern frontier, Dan will have one portion; it will follow the Hethlon road to Lebo Hamath; Hazar Enan and the northern border of Damascus next to Hamath will be part of its border from the east side to the west side. Ge 30:6; Eze 47:20

²"Asher will have one portion; it will border the territory of Dan from east to west. Jos 19:24-31

³"Naphtali will have one portion; it will border the territory of Asher from east to west. Jos 19:32-39

⁴"Manasseh will have one portion; it will border the territory of Naphtali from east to west.

⁵"Ephraim will have one portion; it will border the territory of Manasseh from east to west.

⁶"Reuben will have one portion; it will border the territory of Ephraim from east to west.

⁷"Judah will have one portion; it will border the territory of Reuben from east to west. Jos 15:1-63

⁸"Bordering the territory of Judah from east to west will be the portion you are to present as a special gift. It will be 25,000 cubits*ᵇ* wide, and its length from east to west will equal one of the tribal portions; the sanctuary will be in the center of it. ver 21

⁹"The special portion you are to offer to the LORD will be 25,000 cubits long and 10,000 cubits*ᶜ* wide. ¹⁰This will be the

ᵃ 18 See Syriac; Hebrew *Israel. You will measure to the Dead Sea.*   *ᵇ 8* That is, about 8 miles or about 13 kilometers; also in verses 9, 10, 13, 15, 20 and 21   *ᶜ 9* That is, about 3 1/3 miles or about 5.3 kilometers; also in verses 10, 13 and 18

sacred portion for the priests. It will be 25,000 cubits long on the north side, 10,000 cubits wide on the west side, 10,000 cubits wide on the east side and 25,000 cubits long on the south side. In the center of it will be the sanctuary of the LORD. ¹¹ This will be for the consecrated priests, the Zadokites, who were faithful in serving me and did not go astray as the Levites did when the Israelites went astray. ¹² It will be a special gift to them from the sacred portion of the land, a most holy portion, bordering the territory of the Levites. Eze 44:15

¹³ "Alongside the territory of the priests, the Levites will have an allotment 25,000 cubits long and 10,000 cubits wide. Its total length will be 25,000 cubits and its width 10,000 cubits. ¹⁴ They must not sell or exchange any of it. This is the best of the land and must not pass into other hands, because it is holy to the LORD. Lev 25:34; 27:10,28

¹⁵ "The remaining area, 5,000 cubits^a wide and 25,000 cubits long, will be for the common use of the city, for houses and for pastureland. The city will be in the center of it ¹⁶ and will have these measurements: the north side 4,500 cubits,^{b} the south side 4,500 cubits, the east side 4,500 cubits, and the west side 4,500 cubits.

¹⁷ The pastureland for the city will be 250 cubits^c on the north, 250 cubits on the south, 250 cubits on the east, and 250 cubits on the west. ¹⁸ What remains of the area, bordering on the sacred portion and running the length of it, will be 10,000 cubits on the east side and 10,000 cubits on the west side. Its produce will supply food for the workers of the city. ¹⁹ The workers from the city who farm it will come from all the tribes of Israel. ²⁰ The entire portion will be a square, 25,000 cubits on each side. As a special gift you will set aside the sacred portion, along with the property of the city. Rev 21:16

²¹ "What remains on both sides of the area formed by the sacred portion and the property of the city will belong to the prince. It will extend eastward from the 25,000 cubits of the sacred portion to the eastern border, and westward from the 25,000 cubits to the western border. Both these areas running the length of the tribal portions will belong to the prince, and the sacred portion with the temple sanctuary will be in the center of them. ²² So the property of the Levites and the property of the city will lie in the center of the area that belongs to the prince. The area belonging to the prince will lie

between the border of Judah and the border of Benjamin.   Eze 45:7

²³ "As for the rest of the tribes: Benjamin will have one portion; it will extend from the east side to the west side.   Jos 18:11-28

²⁴ "Simeon will have one portion; it will border the territory of Benjamin from east to west.

²⁵ "Issachar will have one portion; it will border the territory of Simeon from east to west.

²⁶ "Zebulun will have one portion; it will border the territory of Issachar from east to west.

²⁷ "Gad will have one portion; it will border the territory of Zebulun from east to west.   Jos 13:24-28

²⁸ "The southern boundary of Gad will run south from Tamar to the waters of Meribah Kadesh, then along the Wadi of Egypt to the Mediterranean Sea.   Eze 47:19

²⁹ "This is the land you are to allot as an inheritance to the tribes of Israel, and these will be their portions," declares the Sovereign LORD.   Eze 45:1

The Gates of the New City

³⁰ "These will be the exits of the city: Beginning on the north side, which is 4,500 cubits long, ³¹ the gates of the city will be named after the tribes of Israel. The three gates on the north side will be the gate of Reuben, the gate of Judah and the gate of Levi.

³² "On the east side, which is 4,500 cubits long, will be three gates: the gate of Joseph, the gate of Benjamin and the gate of Dan.

³³ "On the south side, which measures 4,500 cubits, will be three gates: the gate of Simeon, the gate of Issachar and the gate of Zebulun.

³⁴ "On the west side, which is 4,500 cubits long, will be three gates: the gate of Gad, the gate of Asher and the gate of Naphtali.

³⁵ "The distance all around will be 18,000 cubits.ᵃ

"And the name of the city from that time on will be:

THE LORD IS THERE."

ᵃ 35 That is, about 6 miles or about 9.5 kilometers

Daniel

Daniel's Training in Babylon

1 In the third year of the reign of Jehoiakim king of Judah, Nebuchadnezzar king of Babylon came to Jerusalem and besieged it. ²And the Lord delivered Jehoiakim king of Judah into his hand, along with some of the articles from the temple of God. These he carried off to the temple of his god in Babylonia*a* and put in the treasure house of his god. 2Ch 36:6; Jer 27:19-20; Zec 5:5-11

³Then the king ordered Ashpenaz, chief of his court officials, to bring into the king's service some of the Israelites from the royal family and the nobility — ⁴young men without any physical defect, handsome, showing aptitude for every kind of learning, well informed, quick to understand, and qualified to serve in the king's palace. He was to teach them the language and literature of the Babylonians.*b*

⁵The king assigned them a daily amount of food and wine from the king's table. They were to be trained for three years, and after that they were to enter the king's service. Isa 39:7

⁶Among those who were chosen were some from Judah: Daniel, Hananiah, Mishael and Azariah. ⁷The chief official gave them new names: to Daniel, the name Belteshazzar; to Hananiah, Shadrach; to Mishael, Meshach; and to Azariah, Abednego. Da 4:8; 5:12

⁸But Daniel resolved not to defile himself with the royal food and wine, and he asked the chief official for permission not to defile himself this way. ⁹Now God had caused the official to show favor and compassion to Daniel, ¹⁰but the official told Daniel, "I am afraid of my lord the king, who has assigned your*c* food and drink. Why should he see

---

a 2 Hebrew *Shinar*   *b 4* Or *Chaldeans*   *c 10* The Hebrew for *your* and *you* in this verse is plural.

you looking worse than the other young men your age? The king would then have my head because of you." Ge 39:21; 1Ki 8:50

[11] Daniel then said to the guard whom the chief official had appointed over Daniel, Hananiah, Mishael and Azariah, [12] "Please test your servants for ten days: Give us nothing but vegetables to eat and water to drink. [13] Then compare our appearance with that of the young men who eat the royal food, and treat your servants in accordance with what you see." [14] So he agreed to this and tested them for ten days. Rev 2:10

[15] At the end of the ten days they looked healthier and better nourished than any of the young men who ate the royal food. [16] So the guard took away their choice food and the wine they were to drink and gave them vegetables instead. Ex 23:25

[17] To these four young men God gave knowledge and understanding of all kinds of literature and learning. And Daniel could understand visions and dreams of all kinds. Da 2:19,30; 7:1; 8:1

[18] At the end of the time set by the king to bring them into his service, the chief official presented them to Nebuchadnezzar. [19] The king talked with them, and he found none equal to Daniel, Hananiah, Mishael and Azariah;

so they entered the king's service. [20] In every matter of wisdom and understanding about which the king questioned them, he found them ten times better than all the magicians and enchanters in his whole kingdom. 1Ki 4:30; Da 2:13,28

[21] And Daniel remained there until the first year of King Cyrus. Da 6:28; 10:1

Nebuchadnezzar's Dream

2 In the second year of his reign, Nebuchadnezzar had dreams; his mind was troubled and he could not sleep. [2] So the king summoned the magicians, enchanters, sorcerers and astrologers[a] to tell him what he had dreamed. When they came in and stood before the king, [3] he said to them, "I have had a dream that troubles me and I want to know what it means.[b]" Da 4:5-6

[4] Then the astrologers answered the king,[c] "May the king live forever! Tell your servants the dream, and we will interpret it." Ezr 4:7; Da 3:9; 5:10

[5] The king replied to the astrologers, "This is what I have firmly decided: If you do not tell me what my dream was and interpret it, I will have you cut into pieces and your houses turned into piles of rubble. [6] But if you tell me the dream and explain it, you will receive from me gifts

---

[a] 2 Or Chaldeans; also in verses 4, 5 and 10 [b] 3 Or was [c] 4 At this point the Hebrew text has in Aramaic, indicating that the text from here through the end of chapter 7 is in Aramaic.

and rewards and great honor. So tell me the dream and interpret it for me." Da 5:7,16

⁷Once more they replied, "Let the king tell his servants the dream, and we will interpret it."

⁸Then the king answered, "I am certain that you are trying to gain time, because you realize that this is what I have firmly decided: ⁹If you do not tell me the dream, there is only one penalty for you. You have conspired to tell me misleading and wicked things, hoping the situation will change. So then, tell me the dream, and I will know that you can interpret it for me." Est 4:11

¹⁰The astrologers answered the king, "There is no one on earth who can do what the king asks! No king, however great and mighty, has ever asked such a thing of any magician or enchanter or astrologer. ¹¹What the king asks is too difficult. No one can reveal it to the king except the gods, and they do not live among humans." Da 5:8,11

¹²This made the king so angry and furious that he ordered the execution of all the wise men of Babylon. ¹³So the decree was issued to put the wise men to death, and men were sent to look for Daniel and his friends to put them to death. Da 1:20; 3:13,19

¹⁴When Arioch, the commander of the king's guard, had gone out to put to death the wise men of Babylon, Daniel spoke to

him with wisdom and tact. ¹⁵He asked the king's officer, "Why did the king issue such a harsh decree?" Arioch then explained the matter to Daniel. ¹⁶At this, Daniel went in to the king and asked for time, so that he might interpret the dream for him.

¹⁷Then Daniel returned to his house and explained the matter to his friends Hananiah, Mishael and Azariah. ¹⁸He urged them to plead for mercy from the God of heaven concerning this mystery, so that he and his friends might not be executed with the rest of the wise men of Babylon. ¹⁹During the night the mystery was revealed to Daniel in a vision. Then Daniel praised the God of heaven ²⁰and said: Job 33:15; Da 1:17

"Praise be to the name of God
    for ever and ever; Ps 113:2
    wisdom and power are his.
²¹He changes times and
        seasons; Da 7:25
    he deposes kings and raises
        up others. Ps 75:6-7
He gives wisdom to the wise
    and knowledge to the
        discerning. 2Sa 14:17
²²He reveals deep and hidden
        things; Da 5:11
    he knows what lies in
        darkness, Ps 139:11-12
    and light dwells with him.
²³I thank and praise you, God of
    my ancestors: Ex 3:15
    You have given me wisdom
        and power, Da 1:17

you have made known to me what we asked of you, you have made known to us the dream of the king."

Daniel Interprets the Dream

²⁴Then Daniel went to Arioch, whom the king had appointed to execute the wise men of Babylon, and said to him, "Do not execute the wise men of Babylon. Take me to the king, and I will interpret his dream for him."   ver 14

²⁵Arioch took Daniel to the king at once and said, "I have found a man among the exiles from Judah who can tell the king what his dream means."   Da 1:6

²⁶The king asked Daniel (also called Belteshazzar), "Are you able to tell me what I saw in my dream and interpret it?"   Da 1:7

²⁷Daniel replied, "No wise man, enchanter, magician or diviner can explain to the king the mystery he has asked about, ²⁸but there is a God in heaven who reveals mysteries. He has shown King Nebuchadnezzar what will happen in days to come. Your dream and the visions that passed through your mind as you were lying in bed are these: Da 4:5; Am 4:13

²⁹"As Your Majesty was lying there, your mind turned to things to come, and the revealer of mysteries showed you what is going to happen. ³⁰As for me, this mystery has been revealed to me, not because I have greater wisdom than anyone else alive, but so that Your Majesty may know the interpretation and that you may understand what went through your mind.   Isa 45:3; Da 1:17; Am 4:13

³¹"Your Majesty looked, and there before you stood a large statue — an enormous, dazzling statue, awesome in appearance. ³²The head of the statue was made of pure gold, its chest and arms of silver, its belly and thighs of bronze, ³³its legs of iron, its feet partly of iron and partly of baked clay. ³⁴While you were watching, a rock was cut out, but not by human hands. It struck the statue on its feet of iron and clay and smashed them. ³⁵Then the iron, the clay, the bronze, the silver and the gold were all broken to pieces and became like chaff on a threshing floor in the summer. The wind swept them away without leaving a trace. But the rock that struck the statue became a huge mountain and filled the whole earth.   Hab 1:7; Zec 4:6

³⁶"This was the dream, and now we will interpret it to the king. ³⁷Your Majesty, you are the king of kings. The God of heaven has given you dominion and power and might and glory; ³⁸in your hands he has placed all mankind and the beasts of the field and the birds in the sky. Wherever they live, he has made you ruler over them all. You are that head of gold.   Da 4:21-22

³⁹"After you, another kingdom

will arise, inferior to yours. Next, a third kingdom, one of bronze, will rule over the whole earth. [40] Finally, there will be a fourth kingdom, strong as iron — for iron breaks and smashes everything — and as iron breaks things to pieces, so it will crush and break all the others. [41] Just as you saw that the feet and toes were partly of baked clay and partly of iron, so this will be a divided kingdom; yet it will have some of the strength of iron in it, even as you saw iron mixed with clay. [42] As the toes were partly iron and partly clay, so this kingdom will be partly strong and partly brittle. [43] And just as you saw the iron mixed with baked clay, so the people will be a mixture and will not remain united, any more than iron mixes with clay. Da 7:7,23

[44] "In the time of those kings, the God of heaven will set up a kingdom that will never be destroyed, nor will it be left to another people. It will crush all those kingdoms and bring them to an end, but it will itself endure forever. [45] This is the meaning of the vision of the rock cut out of a mountain, but not by human hands — a rock that broke the iron, the bronze, the clay, the silver and the gold to pieces. Isa 9:7

"The great God has shown the king what will take place in the future. The dream is true and its interpretation is trustworthy."

[46] Then King Nebuchadnezzar fell prostrate before Daniel and paid him honor and ordered that an offering and incense be presented to him. [47] The king said to Daniel, "Surely your God is the God of gods and the Lord of kings and a revealer of mysteries, for you were able to reveal this mystery." Da 11:36; Ac 10:25

[48] Then the king placed Daniel in a high position and lavished many gifts on him. He made him ruler over the entire province of Babylon and placed him in charge of all its wise men. [49] Moreover, at Daniel's request the king appointed Shadrach, Meshach and Abednego administrators over the province of Babylon, while Daniel himself remained at the royal court. Da 4:9; 5:11

The Image of Gold and the Blazing Furnace

3 King Nebuchadnezzar made an image of gold, sixty cubits high and six cubits wide,[a] and set it up on the plain of Dura in the province of Babylon. [2] He then summoned the satraps, prefects, governors, advisers, treasurers, judges, magistrates and all the other provincial officials to come to the dedication of the image he had set up. [3] So the satraps, prefects, governors, advisers, treasurers, judges, magistrates and all the other provincial officials assembled for the dedication of

---

[a] 1 That is, about 90 feet high and 9 feet wide or about 27 meters high and 2.7 meters wide

the image that King Nebuchadnezzar had set up, and they stood before it. Isa 46:6; Hab 2:19

⁴Then the herald loudly proclaimed, "Nations and peoples of every language, this is what you are commanded to do: ⁵As soon as you hear the sound of the horn, flute, zither, lyre, harp, pipe and all kinds of music, you must fall down and worship the image of gold that King Nebuchadnezzar has set up. ⁶Whoever does not fall down and worship will immediately be thrown into a blazing furnace." Jer 29:22; Da 6:7

⁷Therefore, as soon as they heard the sound of the horn, flute, zither, lyre, harp and all kinds of music, all the nations and peoples of every language fell down and worshiped the image of gold that King Nebuchadnezzar had set up.

⁸At this time some astrologersᵃ came forward and denounced the Jews. ⁹They said to King Nebuchadnezzar, "May the king live forever! ¹⁰Your Majesty has issued a decree that everyone who hears the sound of the horn, flute, zither, lyre, harp, pipe and all kinds of music must fall down and worship the image of gold, ¹¹and that whoever does not fall down and worship will be thrown into a blazing furnace. ¹²But there are some Jews whom you have set over the affairs of the province of Babylon — Shadrach, Meshach and Abednego — who pay no attention to you, Your Majesty. They neither serve your gods nor worship the image of gold you have set up." Da 2:49; 6:13

¹³Furious with rage, Nebuchadnezzar summoned Shadrach, Meshach and Abednego. So these men were brought before the king, ¹⁴and Nebuchadnezzar said to them, "Is it true, Shadrach, Meshach and Abednego, that you do not serve my gods or worship the image of gold I have set up? ¹⁵Now when you hear the sound of the horn, flute, zither, lyre, harp, pipe and all kinds of music, if you are ready to fall down and worship the image I made, very good. But if you do not worship it, you will be thrown immediately into a blazing furnace. Then what god will be able to rescue you from my hand?" Isa 36:18-20

¹⁶Shadrach, Meshach and Abednego replied to him, "King Nebuchadnezzar, we do not need to defend ourselves before you in this matter. ¹⁷If we are thrown into the blazing furnace, the God we serve is able to deliver us from it, and he will deliver usᵇ from Your Majesty's hand. ¹⁸But even if he does not, we want you to know, Your Majesty, that we will not serve your gods

ᵃ 8 Or Chaldeans   ᵇ 17 Or If the God we serve is able to deliver us, then he will deliver us from the blazing furnace and or worship the image of gold you have set up." Ps 27:1-2

[19] Then Nebuchadnezzar was furious with Shadrach, Meshach and Abednego, and his attitude toward them changed. He ordered the furnace heated seven times hotter than usual [20] and commanded some of the strongest soldiers in his army to tie up Shadrach, Meshach and Abednego and throw them into the blazing furnace. [21] So these men, wearing their robes, trousers, turbans and other clothes, were bound and thrown into the blazing furnace. [22] The king's command was so urgent and the furnace so hot that the flames of the fire killed the soldiers who took up Shadrach, Meshach and Abednego, [23] and these three men, firmly tied, fell into the blazing furnace. Lev 26:18-28; Da 1:7

[24] Then King Nebuchadnezzar leaped to his feet in amazement and asked his advisers, "Weren't there three men that we tied up and threw into the fire?"

They replied, "Certainly, Your Majesty."

[25] He said, "Look! I see four men walking around in the fire, unbound and unharmed, and the fourth looks like a son of the gods."

[26] Nebuchadnezzar then approached the opening of the blazing furnace and shouted, "Shadrach, Meshach and Abednego, servants of the Most High God, come out! Come here!" Da 4:2,34

So Shadrach, Meshach and Abednego came out of the fire, [27] and the satraps, prefects, governors and royal advisers crowded around them. They saw that the fire had not harmed their bodies, nor was a hair of their heads singed; their robes were not scorched, and there was no smell of fire on them. Heb 11:32-34

[28] Then Nebuchadnezzar said, "Praise be to the God of Shadrach, Meshach and Abednego, who has sent his angel and rescued his servants! They trusted in him and defied the king's command and were willing to give up their lives rather than serve or worship any god except their own God. [29] Therefore I decree that the people of any nation or language who say anything against the God of Shadrach, Meshach and Abednego be cut into pieces and their houses be turned into piles of rubble, for no other god can save in this way." Da 6:27

[30] Then the king promoted Shadrach, Meshach and Abednego in the province of Babylon.

Nebuchadnezzar's Dream of a Tree

4 [a] King Nebuchadnezzar,

To the nations and peoples of every language, who live in all the earth: Da 3:4

---

[a] In Aramaic texts 4:1-3 is numbered 3:31-33, and 4:4-37 is numbered 4:1-34.

May you prosper greatly!

² It is my pleasure to tell you about the miraculous signs and wonders that the Most High God has performed for me. Ps 74:9; Da 3:26

³ How great are his signs,
    how mighty his
    wonders! Da 6:27
His kingdom is an eternal
    kingdom;
his dominion endures
    from generation to
    generation. Da 2:44

⁴ I, Nebuchadnezzar, was at home in my palace, contented and prosperous. ⁵ I had a dream that made me afraid. As I was lying in bed, the images and visions that passed through my mind terrified me. ⁶ So I commanded that all the wise men of Babylon be brought before me to interpret the dream for me. ⁷ When the magicians, enchanters, astrologers*a* and diviners came, I told them the dream, but they could not interpret it for me. ⁸ Finally, Daniel came into my presence and I told him the dream. (He is called Belteshazzar, after the name of my god, and the spirit of the holy gods is in him.) Da 2:1; 5:11,14
⁹ I said, "Belteshazzar, chief of the magicians, I know that the spirit of the holy gods is in you, and no mystery is too difficult for you. Here is my dream; interpret it for me. ¹⁰ These are the visions I saw while lying in bed: I looked, and there before me stood a tree in the middle of the land. Its height was enormous. ¹¹ The tree grew large and strong and its top touched the sky; it was visible to the ends of the earth. ¹² Its leaves were beautiful, its fruit abundant, and on it was food for all. Under it the wild animals found shelter, and the birds lived in its branches; from it every creature was fed. Da 2:48; 5:11-12
¹³ "In the visions I saw while lying in bed, I looked, and there before me was a holy one, a messenger,*b* coming down from heaven. ¹⁴ He called in a loud voice: 'Cut down the tree and trim off its branches; strip off its leaves and scatter its fruit. Let the animals flee from under it and the birds from its branches. ¹⁵ But let the stump and its roots, bound with iron and bronze, remain in the ground, in the grass of the field. Eze 31:12; Mt 3:10
"'Let him be drenched with the dew of heaven, and let him live with the animals among the plants of the earth.

---

a 7 Or *Chaldeans*   *b* 13 Or *watchman*; also in verses 17 and 23

¹⁶Let his mind be changed from that of a man and let him be given the mind of an animal, till seven times*a* pass by for him.   ver 23,32

¹⁷ "'The decision is announced by messengers, the holy ones declare the verdict, so that the living may know that the Most High is sovereign over all kingdoms on earth and gives them to anyone he wishes and sets over them the lowliest of people.'   Da 5:18-21; Mt 23:12

¹⁸"This is the dream that I, King Nebuchadnezzar, had. Now, Belteshazzar, tell me what it means, for none of the wise men in my kingdom can interpret it for me. But you can, because the spirit of the holy gods is in you."   Ge 41:8; Da 1:20

Daniel Interprets the Dream

¹⁹Then Daniel (also called Belteshazzar) was greatly perplexed for a time, and his thoughts terrified him. So the king said, "Belteshazzar, do not let the dream or its meaning alarm you." Da 7:15,28

Belteshazzar answered, "My lord, if only the dream applied to your enemies and its meaning to your adversaries! ²⁰The tree you saw, which grew large and strong, with its top touching the sky, visible to the whole earth, ²¹with beautiful leaves and abundant fruit, providing food for all, giving shelter to the wild animals, and having nesting places in its branches for the birds — ²²Your Majesty, you are that tree! You have become great and strong; your greatness has grown until it reaches the sky, and your dominion extends to distant parts of the earth.   Jer 27:7; Da 5:18-19

²³"Your Majesty saw a holy one, a messenger, coming down from heaven and saying, 'Cut down the tree and destroy it, but leave the stump, bound with iron and bronze, in the grass of the field, while its roots remain in the ground. Let him be drenched with the dew of heaven; let him live with the wild animals, until seven times pass by for him.' Da 5:21

²⁴"This is the interpretation, Your Majesty, and this is the decree the Most High has issued against my lord the king: ²⁵You will be driven away from people and will live with the wild animals; you will eat grass like the ox and be drenched with the dew of heaven. Seven times will pass by for you until you acknowledge that the Most High is sovereign over all

a 16 Or *years*; also in verses 23, 25 and 32

kingdoms on earth and gives them to anyone he wishes. [26]The command to leave the stump of the tree with its roots means that your kingdom will be restored to you when you acknowledge that Heaven rules. [27]Therefore, Your Majesty, be pleased to accept my advice: Renounce your sins by doing what is right, and your wickedness by being kind to the oppressed. It may be that then your prosperity will continue." Isa 55:6-7; Eze 18:22

The Dream Is Fulfilled

[28]All this happened to King Nebuchadnezzar. [29]Twelve months later, as the king was walking on the roof of the royal palace of Babylon, [30]he said, "Is not this the great Babylon I have built as the royal residence, by my mighty power and for the glory of my majesty?" Da 5:20; Hab 2:4

[31]Even as the words were on his lips, a voice came from heaven, "This is what is decreed for you, King Nebuchadnezzar: Your royal authority has been taken from you. [32]You will be driven away from people and will live with the wild animals; you will eat grass like the ox. Seven times will pass by for you until you acknowledge that the Most High is sover-

eign over all kingdoms on earth and gives them to anyone he wishes." 2Sa 22:28; Job 9:12

[33]Immediately what had been said about Nebuchadnezzar was fulfilled. He was driven away from people and ate grass like the ox. His body was drenched with the dew of heaven until his hair grew like the feathers of an eagle and his nails like the claws of a bird. Da 5:20-21

[34]At the end of that time, I, Nebuchadnezzar, raised my eyes toward heaven, and my sanity was restored. Then I praised the Most High; I honored and glorified him who lives forever. Da 12:7; Rev 4:10

His dominion is an eternal
  dominion;
 his kingdom endures
   from generation to
    generation. Lk 1:33
[35]All the peoples of the earth
 are regarded as nothing.
He does as he pleases Ps 115:3
 with the powers of heaven
 and the peoples of the earth.
No one can hold back his hand
 or say to him: "What have
  you done?" Isa 45:9; Ro 9:20

[36]At the same time that my sanity was restored, my honor and splendor were returned to me for the glory of my kingdom. My advisers and nobles sought me

out, and I was restored to my throne and became even greater than before. [37] Now I, Nebuchadnezzar, praise and exalt and glorify the King of heaven, because everything he does is right and all his ways are just. And those who walk in pride he is able to humble. Da 5:20,23

The Writing on the Wall

5 King Belshazzar gave a great banquet for a thousand of his nobles and drank wine with them. [2] While Belshazzar was drinking his wine, he gave orders to bring in the gold and silver goblets that Nebuchadnezzar his father[a] had taken from the temple in Jerusalem, so that the king and his nobles, his wives and his concubines might drink from them. [3] So they brought in the gold goblets that had been taken from the temple of God in Jerusalem, and the king and his nobles, his wives and his concubines drank from them. [4] As they drank the wine, they praised the gods of gold and silver, of bronze, iron, wood and stone. Da 1:2; Rev 9:20

[5] Suddenly the fingers of a human hand appeared and wrote on the plaster of the wall, near the lampstand in the royal palace. The king watched the hand as it wrote. [6] His face turned pale and he was so frightened that his legs became weak and his knees were knocking. Eze 7:17; Da 4:5

[7] The king summoned the enchanters, astrologers[b] and diviners. Then he said to these wise men of Babylon, "Whoever reads this writing and tells me what it means will be clothed in purple and have a gold chain placed around his neck, and he will be made the third highest ruler in the kingdom." Da 2:5-6,48

[8] Then all the king's wise men came in, but they could not read the writing or tell the king what it meant. [9] So King Belshazzar became even more terrified and his face grew more pale. His nobles were baffled. Isa 21:4

[10] The queen,[c] hearing the voices of the king and his nobles, came into the banquet hall. "May the king live forever!" she said. "Don't be alarmed! Don't look so pale! [11] There is a man in your kingdom who has the spirit of the holy gods in him. In the time of your father he was found to have insight and intelligence and wisdom like that of the gods. Your father, King Nebuchadnezzar, appointed him chief of the magicians, enchanters, astrologers and diviners. [12] He did this because Daniel, whom the king called Belteshazzar, was found to have a keen mind and knowledge and understanding, and also the ability to interpret

---

[a] 2 Or *ancestor*; or *predecessor*; also in verses 11, 13 and 18   [b] 7 Or *Chaldeans*; also in verse 11   [c] 10 Or *queen mother*

dreams, explain riddles and solve difficult problems. Call for Daniel, and he will tell you what the writing means." Da 1:7; 6:3 ¹³So Daniel was brought before the king, and the king said to him, "Are you Daniel, one of the exiles my father the king brought from Judah? ¹⁴I have heard that the spirit of the gods is in you and that you have insight, intelligence and outstanding wisdom. ¹⁵The wise men and enchanters were brought before me to read this writing and tell me what it means, but they could not explain it. ¹⁶Now I have heard that you are able to give interpretations and to solve difficult problems. If you can read this writing and tell me what it means, you will be clothed in purple and have a gold chain placed around your neck, and you will be made the third highest ruler in the kingdom." Da 6:13

¹⁷Then Daniel answered the king, "You may keep your gifts for yourself and give your rewards to someone else. Nevertheless, I will read the writing for the king and tell him what it means. 2Ki 5:16

¹⁸"Your Majesty, the Most High God gave your father Nebuchadnezzar sovereignty and greatness and glory and splendor. ¹⁹Because of the high position he gave him, all the nations and peoples of every language dreaded and feared him. Those the king wanted to put to death, he put to death; those he wanted to spare, he spared; those he wanted to promote, he promoted; and those he wanted to humble, he humbled. ²⁰But when his heart became arrogant and hardened with pride, he was deposed from his royal throne and stripped of his glory. ²¹He was driven away from people and given the mind of an animal; he lived with the wild donkeys and ate grass like the ox; and his body was drenched with the dew of heaven, until he acknowledged that the Most High God is sovereign over all kingdoms on earth and sets over them anyone he wishes. Da 4:16-17,35; Eze 17:24

²²"But you, Belshazzar, his son,ᵃ have not humbled yourself, though you knew all this. ²³Instead, you have set yourself up against the Lord of heaven. You had the goblets from his temple brought to you, and you and your nobles, your wives and your concubines drank wine from them. You praised the gods of silver and gold, of bronze, iron, wood and stone, which cannot see or hear or understand. But you did not honor the God who holds in his hand your life and all your ways. ²⁴Therefore he sent the hand that wrote the inscription. Ps 115:4-8; Jer 10:23

²⁵"This is the inscription that was written:

ᵃ 22 Or *descendant*; or *successor*

MENE, MENE, TEKEL, PARSIN

26 "Here is what these words mean:

Mene[a]: God has numbered the days of your reign and brought it to an end.

27 Tekel[b]: You have been weighed on the scales and found wanting. Ps 62:9

28 Peres[c]: Your kingdom is divided and given to the Medes and Persians." Da 6:28

29 Then at Belshazzar's command, Daniel was clothed in purple, a gold chain was placed around his neck, and he was proclaimed the third highest ruler in the kingdom. Da 2:6

30 That very night Belshazzar, king of the Babylonians,[d] was slain, 31 and Darius the Mede took over the kingdom, at the age of sixty-two.[e] Da 6:1; 9:1

Daniel in the Den of Lions

6 [f] It pleased Darius to appoint 120 satraps to rule throughout the kingdom, 2 with three administrators over them, one of whom was Daniel. The satraps were made accountable to them so that the king might not suffer loss. 3 Now Daniel so distinguished himself among the administrators and the satraps by his exceptional qualities that the king planned to set him over the whole kingdom. 4 At this, the administrators and the satraps tried to find grounds for charges against Daniel in his conduct of government affairs, but they were unable to do so. They could find no corruption in him, because he was trustworthy and neither corrupt nor negligent. 5 Finally these men said, "We will never find any basis for charges against this man Daniel unless it has something to do with the law of his God." Est 10:3; Da 5:12-14

6 So these administrators and satraps went as a group to the king and said: "May King Darius live forever! 7 The royal administrators, prefects, satraps, advisers and governors have all agreed that the king should issue an edict and enforce the decree that anyone who prays to any god or human being during the next thirty days, except to you, Your Majesty, shall be thrown into the lions' den. 8 Now, Your Majesty, issue the decree and put it in writing so that it cannot be altered—in accordance with the law of the Medes and Persians, which cannot be repealed." 9 So King Darius put the decree in writing. Ps 59:3; Da 3:6

---

[a] 26 Mene can mean numbered or mina (a unit of money).   [b] 27 Tekel can mean weighed or shekel.   [c] 28 Peres (the singular of Parsin) can mean divided or Persia or a half mina or a half shekel.   [d] 30 Or Chaldeans   [e] 31 In Aramaic texts this verse (5:31) is numbered 6:1.   [f] In Aramaic texts 6:1-28 is numbered 6:2-29.

10 Now when Daniel learned that the decree had been published, he went home to his upstairs room where the windows opened toward Jerusalem. Three times a day he got down on his knees and prayed, giving thanks to his God, just as he had done before. 11 Then these men went as a group and found Daniel praying and asking God for help. 12 So they went to the king and spoke to him about his royal decree: "Did you not publish a decree that during the next thirty days anyone who prays to any god or human being except to you, Your Majesty, would be thrown into the lions' den?" Ps 95:6; Ac 5:29

The king answered, "The decree stands — in accordance with the law of the Medes and Persians, which cannot be repealed." Da 3:8-12

13 Then they said to the king, "Daniel, who is one of the exiles from Judah, pays no attention to you, Your Majesty, or to the decree you put in writing. He still prays three times a day." 14 When the king heard this, he was greatly distressed; he was determined to rescue Daniel and made every effort until sundown to save him.

15 Then the men went as a group to King Darius and said to him, "Remember, Your Majesty, that according to the law of the Medes and Persians no decree or edict that the king issues can be changed." Est 8:8

16 So the king gave the order, and they brought Daniel and threw him into the lions' den. The king said to Daniel, "May your God, whom you serve continually, rescue you!" Ps 37:39-40

17 A stone was brought and placed over the mouth of the den, and the king sealed it with his own signet ring and with the rings of his nobles, so that Daniel's situation might not be changed. 18 Then the king returned to his palace and spent the night without eating and without any entertainment being brought to him. And he could not sleep. Mt 27:66

19 At the first light of dawn, the king got up and hurried to the lions' den. 20 When he came near the den, he called to Daniel in an anguished voice, "Daniel, servant of the living God, has your God, whom you serve continually, been able to rescue you from the lions?" Da 3:17

21 Daniel answered, "May the king live forever! 22 My God sent his angel, and he shut the mouths of the lions. They have not hurt me, because I was found innocent in his sight. Nor have I ever done any wrong before you, Your Majesty." Heb 11:33; 2Ti 4:17

23 The king was overjoyed and gave orders to lift Daniel out of the den. And when Daniel was lifted from the den, no wound was found on him, because he had trusted in his God. 1Ch 5:20

²⁴At the king's command, the men who had falsely accused Daniel were brought in and thrown into the lions' den, along with their wives and children. And before they reached the floor of the den, the lions overpowered them and crushed all their bones. Dt 24:16; 2Ki 14:6

²⁵Then King Darius wrote to all the nations and peoples of every language in all the earth:

"May you prosper greatly!

²⁶"I issue a decree that in every part of my kingdom people must fear and reverence the God of Daniel.

"For he is the living God Jos 2:11
  and he endures forever;
his kingdom will not be
    destroyed,
  his dominion will never
    end. Da 2:44
²⁷He rescues and he saves;
  he performs signs and
    wonders Da 4:3
in the heavens and on the
    earth.
He has rescued Daniel
  from the power of the lions."

²⁸So Daniel prospered during the reign of Darius and the reign of Cyrus*ᵃ the Persian. Da 1:21

Daniel's Dream of Four Beasts

7 In the first year of Belshazzar king of Babylon, Daniel had a dream, and visions passed through his mind as he was lying in bed. He wrote down the substance of his dream. Da 1:17; 5:1

²Daniel said: "In my vision at night I looked, and there before me were the four winds of heaven churning up the great sea. ³Four great beasts, each different from the others, came up out of the sea. Rev 13:1

⁴"The first was like a lion, and it had the wings of an eagle. I watched until its wings were torn off and it was lifted from the ground so that it stood on two feet like a human being, and the mind of a human was given to it. Jer 4:7; Eze 17:3

⁵"And there before me was a second beast, which looked like a bear. It was raised up on one of its sides, and it had three ribs in its mouth between its teeth. It was told, 'Get up and eat your fill of flesh!' Da 2:39

⁶"After that, I looked, and there before me was another beast, one that looked like a leopard. And on its back it had four wings like those of a bird. This beast had four heads, and it was given authority to rule. Rev 13:2

⁷"After that, in my vision at night I looked, and there before me was a fourth beast — terrifying and frightening and very powerful. It had large iron teeth; it crushed and devoured its victims and trampled underfoot whatever was left. It was different

ᵃ 28 Or *Darius, that is, the reign of Cyrus*

from all the former beasts, and it had ten horns. Da 2:40; Rev 12:3

8 "While I was thinking about the horns, there before me was another horn, a little one, which came up among them; and three of the first horns were uprooted before it. This horn had eyes like the eyes of a human being and a mouth that spoke boastfully.

9 "As I looked,

"thrones were set in place,
  and the Ancient of Days
    took his seat. Mt 19:28
His clothing was as white as
  snow; Mt 28:3
the hair of his head was
  white like wool. Rev 1:14
His throne was flaming with
  fire,
and its wheels were all
  ablaze. Eze 1:15
10 A river of fire was flowing,
  coming out from before him.
Thousands upon thousands
  attended him;
ten thousand times ten
  thousand stood before
  him.
The court was seated,
  and the books were opened.

11 "Then I continued to watch because of the boastful words the horn was speaking. I kept looking until the beast was slain and its body destroyed and thrown into the blazing fire. 12 (The other beasts had been stripped of their authority, but were allowed to live for a period of time.) Rev 19:20

13 "In my vision at night I looked, and there before me was one like a son of man,[a] coming with the clouds of heaven. He approached the Ancient of Days and was led into his presence. 14 He was given authority, glory and sovereign power; all nations and peoples of every language worshiped him. His dominion is an everlasting dominion that will not pass away, and his kingdom is one that will never be destroyed. Heb 12:28; Rev 11:15

The Interpretation of the Dream

15 "I, Daniel, was troubled in spirit, and the visions that passed through my mind disturbed me. 16 I approached one of those standing there and asked him the meaning of all this. Da 4:19

"So he told me and gave me the interpretation of these things: 17 'The four great beasts are four kings that will rise from the earth. 18 But the holy people of the Most High will receive the kingdom and will possess it forever—yes, for ever and ever.' Isa 60:12-14

19 "Then I wanted to know the meaning of the fourth beast, which was different from all the others and most terrifying, with its iron teeth and bronze claws—

---

[a] 13 The Aramaic phrase *bar enash* means *human being*. The phrase *son of man* is retained here because of its use in the New Testament as a title of Jesus, probably based largely on this verse.

the beast that crushed and devoured its victims and trampled underfoot whatever was left. ²⁰I also wanted to know about the ten horns on its head and about the other horn that came up, before which three of them fell — the horn that looked more imposing than the others and that had eyes and a mouth that spoke boastfully. ²¹As I watched, this horn was waging war against the holy people and defeating them, ²²until the Ancient of Days came and pronounced judgment in favor of the holy people of the Most High, and the time came when they possessed the kingdom. Rev 13:7

²³"He gave me this explanation: 'The fourth beast is a fourth kingdom that will appear on earth. It will be different from all the other kingdoms and will devour the whole earth, trampling it down and crushing it. ²⁴The ten horns are ten kings who will come from this kingdom. After them another king will arise, different from the earlier ones; he will subdue three kings. ²⁵He will speak against the Most High and oppress his holy people and try to change the set times and the laws. The holy people will be delivered into his hands for a time, times and half a time.ᵃ Da 2:21; Rev 17:12

²⁶"'But the court will sit, and his power will be taken away and completely destroyed forever. ²⁷Then the sovereignty, power and greatness of all the kingdoms under heaven will be handed over to the holy people of the Most High. His kingdom will be an everlasting kingdom, and all rulers will worship and obey him.' Ps 22:27; 72:11

²⁸"This is the end of the matter. I, Daniel, was deeply troubled by my thoughts, and my face turned pale, but I kept the matter to myself." Da 4:19

Daniel's Vision of a Ram and a Goat

8 In the third year of King Belshazzar's reign, I, Daniel, had a vision, after the one that had already appeared to me. ²In my vision I saw myself in the citadel of Susa in the province of Elam; in the vision I was beside the Ulai Canal. ³I looked up, and there before me was a ram with two horns, standing beside the canal, and the horns were long. One of the horns was longer than the other but grew up later. ⁴I watched the ram as it charged toward the west and the north and the south. No animal could stand against it, and none could rescue from its power. It did as it pleased and became great. Da 11:3,16

⁵As I was thinking about this, suddenly a goat with a prominent horn between its eyes came from the west, crossing the whole earth without touching the ground. ⁶It came toward

ᵃ 25 Or *for a year, two years and half a year*

the two-horned ram I had seen standing beside the canal and charged at it in great rage. [7]I saw it attack the ram furiously, striking the ram and shattering its two horns. The ram was powerless to stand against it; the goat knocked it to the ground and trampled on it, and none could rescue the ram from its power. [8]The goat became very great, but at the height of its power the large horn was broken off, and in its place four prominent horns grew up toward the four winds of heaven. 2Ch 26:16-21; Rev 7:1

[9]Out of one of them came another horn, which started small but grew in power to the south and to the east and toward the Beautiful Land. [10]It grew until it reached the host of the heavens, and it threw some of the starry host down to the earth and trampled on them. [11]It set itself up to be as great as the commander of the army of the LORD; it took away the daily sacrifice from the LORD, and his sanctuary was thrown down. [12]Because of rebellion, the LORD's people[a] and the daily sacrifice were given over to it. It prospered in everything it did, and truth was thrown to the ground. Da 11:16,31; 12:11

[13]Then I heard a holy one speaking, and another holy one said to him, "How long will it take for the vision to be fulfilled — the vision concerning the daily sacrifice, the rebellion that causes desolation, the surrender of the sanctuary and the trampling underfoot of the LORD's people?"

[14]He said to me, "It will take 2,300 evenings and mornings; then the sanctuary will be reconsecrated." Da 12:11-12

The Interpretation of the Vision

[15]While I, Daniel, was watching the vision and trying to understand it, there before me stood one who looked like a man. [16]And I heard a man's voice from the Ulai calling, "Gabriel, tell this man the meaning of the vision." Da 10:16-18; Lk 1:19

[17]As he came near the place where I was standing, I was terrified and fell prostrate. "Son of man,"[b] he said to me, "understand that the vision concerns the time of the end." Eze 1:28; Rev 1:17

[18]While he was speaking to me, I was in a deep sleep, with my face to the ground. Then he touched me and raised me to my feet. Eze 2:2; Da 10:16-18

[19]He said: "I am going to tell you what will happen later in the time of wrath, because the vision concerns the appointed time of the end.[c] [20]The two-horned ram

***

[a] 12 Or rebellion, the armies   [b] 17 The Hebrew phrase ben adam means human being. The phrase son of man is retained as a form of address here because of its possible association with "Son of Man" in the New Testament.   [c] 19 Or because the end will be at the appointed time

that you saw represents the kings of Media and Persia. ²¹The shaggy goat is the king of Greece, and the large horn between its eyes is the first king. ²²The four horns that replaced the one that was broken off represent four kingdoms that will emerge from his nation but will not have the same power.   Hab 2:3

²³"In the latter part of their reign, when rebels have become completely wicked, a fierce-looking king, a master of intrigue, will arise. ²⁴He will become very strong, but not by his own power. He will cause astounding devastation and will succeed in whatever he does. He will destroy those who are mighty, the holy people. ²⁵He will cause deceit to prosper, and he will consider himself superior. When they feel secure, he will destroy many and take his stand against the Prince of princes. Yet he will be destroyed, but not by human power.   Da 2:34; 11:21,36

²⁶"The vision of the evenings and mornings that has been given you is true, but seal up the vision, for it concerns the distant future."   Da 10:1,14

²⁷I, Daniel, was worn out. I lay exhausted for several days. Then I got up and went about the king's business. I was appalled by the vision; it was beyond understanding.   Da 7:28

Daniel's Prayer

9 In the first year of Darius son of Xerxes[a] (a Mede by descent), who was made ruler over the Babylonian[b] kingdom — ²in the first year of his reign, I, Daniel, understood from the Scriptures, according to the word of the LORD given to Jeremiah the prophet, that the desolation of Jerusalem would last seventy years. ³So I turned to the Lord God and pleaded with him in prayer and petition, in fasting, and in sackcloth and ashes.   2Ch 36:21

⁴I prayed to the LORD my God and confessed: 1Ki 8:30

"Lord, the great and awesome God, who keeps his covenant of love with those who love him and keep his commandments, ⁵we have sinned and done wrong. We have been wicked and have rebelled; we have turned away from your commands and laws. ⁶We have not listened to your servants the prophets, who spoke in your name to our kings, our princes and our ancestors, and to all the people of the land.   2Ch 36:16; Ps 106:6

⁷"Lord, you are righteous, but this day we are covered with shame — the people of Judah and the inhabitants of Jerusalem and all Israel, both near and far, in all the

---

^a 1 Hebrew *Ahasuerus*   ^b 1 Or *Chaldean*

countries where you have scattered us because of our unfaithfulness to you. [8]We and our kings, our princes and our ancestors are covered with shame, LORD, because we have sinned against you. [9]The Lord our God is merciful and forgiving, even though we have rebelled against him; [10]we have not obeyed the LORD our God or kept the laws he gave us through his servants the prophets. [11]All Israel has transgressed your law and turned away, refusing to obey you.   2Ki 17:13-15; Ne 9:17

"Therefore the curses and sworn judgments written in the Law of Moses, the servant of God, have been poured out on us, because we have sinned against you. [12]You have fulfilled the words spoken against us and against our rulers by bringing on us great disaster. Under the whole heaven nothing has ever been done like what has been done to Jerusalem. [13]Just as it is written in the Law of Moses, all this disaster has come on us, yet we have not sought the favor of the LORD our God by turning from our sins and giving attention to your truth. [14]The LORD did not hesitate to bring the disaster on us, for the LORD our God is righteous in everything he does; yet we have not obeyed him.   Isa 1:4-6; Eze 5:9

[15]"Now, Lord our God, who brought your people out of Egypt with a mighty hand and who made for yourself a name that endures to this day, we have sinned, we have done wrong. [16]Lord, in keeping with all your righteous acts, turn away your anger and your wrath from Jerusalem, your city, your holy hill. Our sins and the iniquities of our ancestors have made Jerusalem and your people an object of scorn to all those around us. Ps 31:1; Zec 8:3

[17]"Now, our God, hear the prayers and petitions of your servant. For your sake, Lord, look with favor on your desolate sanctuary. [18]Give ear, our God, and hear; open your eyes and see the desolation of the city that bears your Name. We do not make requests of you because we are righteous, but because of your great mercy. [19]Lord, listen! Lord, forgive! Lord, hear and act! For your sake, my God, do not delay, because your city and your people bear your Name."   Isa 37:17; Jer 7:10-12; 25:29

The Seventy "Sevens"

[20]While I was speaking and praying, confessing my sin and

the sin of my people Israel and making my request to the LORD my God for his holy hill — [21]while I was still in prayer, Gabriel, the man I had seen in the earlier vision, came to me in swift flight about the time of the evening sacrifice. [22]He instructed me and said to me, "Daniel, I have now come to give you insight and understanding. [23]As soon as you began to pray, a word went out, which I have come to tell you, for you are highly esteemed. Therefore, consider the word and understand the vision: Mt 24:15

[24]"Seventy 'sevens'[a] are decreed for your people and your holy city to finish[b] transgression, to put an end to sin, to atone for wickedness, to bring in everlasting righteousness, to seal up vision and prophecy and to anoint the Most Holy Place.[c] Isa 53:10; 56:1

[25]"Know and understand this: From the time the word goes out to restore and rebuild Jerusalem until the Anointed One,[d] the ruler, comes, there will be seven 'sevens,' and sixty-two 'sevens.' It will be rebuilt with streets and a trench, but in times of trouble. [26]After the sixty-two 'sevens,' the Anointed One will be put to death and will have nothing.[e] The people of the ruler who will come will destroy the city and the sanctuary. The end will come like a flood: War will continue until the end, and desolations have been decreed. [27]He will confirm a covenant with many for one 'seven.'[f] In the middle of the 'seven'[f] he will put an end to sacrifice and offering. And at the temple[g] he will set up an abomination that causes desolation, until the end that is decreed is poured out on him.[h]"[i] Isa 10:22; 53:8

Daniel's Vision of a Man

10 In the third year of Cyrus king of Persia, a revelation was given to Daniel (who was called Belteshazzar). Its message was true and it concerned a great war.[j] The understanding of the message came to him in a vision. Da 8:26

[2]At that time I, Daniel, mourned for three weeks. [3]I ate no choice food; no meat or wine touched my lips; and I used no lotions at all until the three weeks were over. Ezr 9:4

[4]On the twenty-fourth day of the first month, as I was standing on the bank of the great river, the Tigris, [5]I looked up and there before me was a man dressed in linen, with a belt of fine gold from Uphaz around his waist. [6]His

---

[a] 24 Or 'weeks'; also in verses 25 and 26   [b] 24 Or restrain   [c] 24 Or the most holy One
[d] 25 Or an anointed one; also in verse 26   [e] 26 Or death and will have no one; or
death, but not for himself   [f] 27 Or 'week'   [g] 27 Septuagint and Theodotion; Hebrew
wing   [h] 27 Or it   [i] 27 Or And one who causes desolation will come upon the wing of
the abominable temple, until the end that is decreed is poured out on the desolated city
[j] 1 Or true and burdensome

body was like topaz, his face like lightning, his eyes like flaming torches, his arms and legs like the gleam of burnished bronze, and his voice like the sound of a multitude. Rev 1:15; 19:12

⁷I, Daniel, was the only one who saw the vision; those who were with me did not see it, but such terror overwhelmed them that they fled and hid themselves. ⁸So I was left alone, gazing at this great vision; I had no strength left, my face turned deathly pale and I was helpless. ⁹Then I heard him speaking, and as I listened to him, I fell into a deep sleep, my face to the ground. 2Ki 6:17-20; Da 8:18,27

¹⁰A hand touched me and set me trembling on my hands and knees. ¹¹He said, "Daniel, you who are highly esteemed, consider carefully the words I am about to speak to you, and stand up, for I have now been sent to you." And when he said this to me, I stood up trembling. Da 9:23; Eze 2:1

¹²Then he continued, "Do not be afraid, Daniel. Since the first day that you set your mind to gain understanding and to humble yourself before your God, your words were heard, and I have come in response to them. ¹³But the prince of the Persian kingdom resisted me twenty-one days. Then Michael, one of the chief princes, came to help me,

because I was detained there with the king of Persia. ¹⁴Now I have come to explain to you what will happen to your people in the future, for the vision concerns a time yet to come." Da 2:28; 8:26

¹⁵While he was saying this to me, I bowed with my face toward the ground and was speechless. ¹⁶Then one who looked like a manᵃ touched my lips, and I opened my mouth and began to speak. I said to the one standing before me, "I am overcome with anguish because of the vision, my lord, and I feel very weak. ¹⁷How can I, your servant, talk with you, my lord? My strength is gone and I can hardly breathe." Jer 1:9; Da 4:19

¹⁸Again the one who looked like a man touched me and gave me strength. ¹⁹"Do not be afraid, you who are highly esteemed," he said. "Peace! Be strong now; be strong." Jdg 6:23; Isa 35:4

When he spoke to me, I was strengthened and said, "Speak, my lord, since you have given me strength." Isa 6:1-8

²⁰So he said, "Do you know why I have come to you? Soon I will return to fight against the prince of Persia, and when I go, the prince of Greece will come; ²¹but first I will tell you what is written in the Book of Truth. (No one supports me against them except Michael, your prince.

ᵃ 16 Most manuscripts of the Masoretic Text; one manuscript of the Masoretic Text, Dead Sea Scrolls and Septuagint *Then something that looked like a human hand*

11

¹And in the first year of Darius the Mede, I took my stand to support and protect him.) Da 11:2; Jude 9

The Kings of the South and the North

²"Now then, I tell you the truth: Three more kings will arise in Persia, and then a fourth, who will be far richer than all the others. When he has gained power by his wealth, he will stir up everyone against the kingdom of Greece. ³Then a mighty king will arise, who will rule with great power and do as he pleases. ⁴After he has arisen, his empire will be broken up and parceled out toward the four winds of heaven. It will not go to his descendants, nor will it have the power he exercised, because his empire will be uprooted and given to others. Da 8:4,21-22

⁵"The king of the South will become strong, but one of his commanders will become even stronger than he and will rule his own kingdom with great power. ⁶After some years, they will become allies. The daughter of the king of the South will go to the king of the North to make an alliance, but she will not retain her power, and he and his power[a] will not last. In those days she will be betrayed, together with her royal escort and her father[b] and the one who supported her. ⁷"One from her family line

will arise to take her place. He will attack the forces of the king of the North and enter his fortress; he will fight against them and be victorious. ⁸He will also seize their gods, their metal images and their valuable articles of silver and gold and carry them off to Egypt. For some years he will leave the king of the North alone. ⁹Then the king of the North will invade the realm of the king of the South but will retreat to his own country. ¹⁰His sons will prepare for war and assemble a great army, which will sweep on like an irresistible flood and carry the battle as far as his fortress. Isa 8:8; Da 9:26

¹¹"Then the king of the South will march out in a rage and fight against the king of the North, who will raise a large army, but it will be defeated. ¹²When the army is carried off, the king of the South will be filled with pride and will slaughter many thousands, yet he will not remain triumphant. ¹³For the king of the North will muster another army, larger than the first; and after several years, he will advance with a huge army fully equipped. Da 8:7-8

¹⁴"In those times many will rise against the king of the South. Those who are violent among your own people will rebel in fulfillment of the vision, but without success. ¹⁵Then the king of

---

[a] 6 Or *offspring*   [b] 6 Or *child* (see Vulgate and Syriac)

the North will come and build up siege ramps and will capture a fortified city. The forces of the South will be powerless to resist; even their best troops will not have the strength to stand. [16] The invader will do as he pleases; no one will be able to stand against him. He will establish himself in the Beautiful Land and will have the power to destroy it. [17] He will determine to come with the might of his entire kingdom and will make an alliance with the king of the South. And he will give him a daughter in marriage in order to overthrow the kingdom, but his plans[a] will not succeed or help him. [18] Then he will turn his attention to the coastlands and will take many of them, but a commander will put an end to his insolence and will turn his insolence back on him. [19] After this, he will turn back toward the fortresses of his own country but will stumble and fall, to be seen no more. Ps 27:2; Eze 26:21

[20] "His successor will send out a tax collector to maintain the royal splendor. In a few years, however, he will be destroyed, yet not in anger or in battle. Isa 60:17

[21] "He will be succeeded by a contemptible person who has not been given the honor of royalty. He will invade the kingdom when its people feel secure, and he will seize it through intrigue. [22] Then an overwhelming army will be swept away before him; both it and a prince of the covenant will be destroyed. [23] After coming to an agreement with him, he will act deceitfully, and with only a few people he will rise to power. [24] When the richest provinces feel secure, he will invade them and will achieve what neither his fathers nor his forefathers did. He will distribute plunder, loot and wealth among his followers. He will plot the overthrow of fortresses — but only for a time. Ne 9:25; Da 8:25

[25] "With a large army he will stir up his strength and courage against the king of the South. The king of the South will wage war with a large and very powerful army, but he will not be able to stand because of the plots devised against him. [26] Those who eat from the king's provisions will try to destroy him; his army will be swept away, and many will fall in battle. [27] The two kings, with their hearts bent on evil, will sit at the same table and lie to each other, but to no avail, because an end will still come at the appointed time. [28] The king of the North will return to his own country with great wealth, but his heart will be set against the holy covenant. He will take action against it and then return to his own country. Ps 64:6; Hab 2:3

[29] "At the appointed time he will invade the South again, but

---

[a] 17 Or but she

this time the outcome will be different from what it was before. ³⁰Ships of the western coastlands will oppose him, and he will lose heart. Then he will turn back and vent his fury against the holy covenant. He will return and show favor to those who forsake the holy covenant. Ge 10:4

³¹ "His armed forces will rise up to desecrate the temple fortress and will abolish the daily sacrifice. Then they will set up the abomination that causes desolation. ³²With flattery he will corrupt those who have violated the covenant, but the people who know their God will firmly resist him. Mt 24:15; Mic 5:7-9

³³ "Those who are wise will instruct many, though for a time they will fall by the sword or be burned or captured or plundered. ³⁴When they fall, they will receive a little help, and many who are not sincere will join them. ³⁵Some of the wise will stumble, so that they may be refined, purified and made spotless until the time of the end, for it will still come at the appointed time. Da 12:10; Zec 13:9; Jn 15:2

The King Who Exalts Himself

³⁶ "The king will do as he pleases. He will exalt and magnify himself above every god and will say unheard-of things against the God of gods. He will be successful until the time of wrath is completed, for what has been determined must take place. ³⁷He will show no regard for the gods of his ancestors or for the one desired by women, nor will he regard any god, but will exalt himself above them all. ³⁸Instead of them, he will honor a god of fortresses; a god unknown to his ancestors he will honor with gold and silver, with precious stones and costly gifts. ³⁹He will attack the mightiest fortresses with the help of a foreign god and will greatly honor those who acknowledge him. He will make them rulers over many people and will distribute the land at a price.ᵃ Da 7:25; Rev 13:5-6

⁴⁰ "At the time of the end the king of the South will engage him in battle, and the king of the North will storm out against him with chariots and cavalry and a great fleet of ships. He will invade many countries and sweep through them like a flood. ⁴¹He will also invade the Beautiful Land. Many countries will fall, but Edom, Moab and the leaders of Ammon will be delivered from his hand. ⁴²He will extend his power over many countries; Egypt will not escape. ⁴³He will gain control of the treasures of gold and silver and all the riches of Egypt, with the Libyans and Cushitesᵇ in submission. ⁴⁴But reports from the east and the north will alarm him, and he will

ᵃ 39 Or *land for a reward*   ᵇ 43 That is, people from the upper Nile region set out in a great rage to destroy and annihilate many. ⁴⁵He will pitch his royal tents between the seas at[a] the beautiful holy mountain. Yet he will come to his end, and no one will help him. Isa 5:28

The End Times

12 "At that time Michael, the great prince who protects your people, will arise. There will be a time of distress such as has not happened from the beginning of nations until then. But at that time your people—everyone whose name is found written in the book—will be delivered. ²Multitudes who sleep in the dust of the earth will awake: some to everlasting life, others to shame and everlasting contempt. ³Those who are wise[b] will shine like the brightness of the heavens, and those who lead many to righteousness, like the stars for ever and ever. ⁴But you, Daniel, roll up and seal the words of the scroll until the time of the end. Many will go here and there to increase knowledge." Isa 8:16; Rev 22:10

⁵Then I, Daniel, looked, and there before me stood two others, one on this bank of the river and one on the opposite bank. ⁶One of them said to the man clothed in linen, who was above the waters of the river, "How long will it be before these astonishing things are fulfilled?" Da 8:13; 10:4

⁷The man clothed in linen, who was above the waters of the river, lifted his right hand and his left hand toward heaven, and I heard him swear by him who lives forever, saying, "It will be for a time, times and half a time.[c] When the power of the holy people has been finally broken, all these things will be completed."

⁸I heard, but I did not understand. So I asked, "My lord, what will the outcome of all this be?"

⁹He replied, "Go your way, Daniel, because the words are rolled up and sealed until the time of the end. ¹⁰Many will be purified, made spotless and refined, but the wicked will continue to be wicked. None of the wicked will understand, but those who are wise will understand. Isa 32:7; Rev 22:11

¹¹"From the time that the daily sacrifice is abolished and the abomination that causes desolation is set up, there will be 1,290 days. ¹²Blessed is the one who waits for and reaches the end of the 1,335 days. Isa 30:18; Da 8:14

¹³"As for you, go your way till the end. You will rest, and then at the end of the days you will rise to receive your allotted inheritance." Rev 14:13

---

a 45 Or *the sea and*   *b* 3 Or *who impart wisdom*   *c* 7 Or *a year, two years and half a year*

Hosea

1 The word of the LORD that came to Hosea son of Beeri during the reigns of Uzziah, Jotham, Ahaz and Hezekiah, kings of Judah, and during the reign of Jeroboam son of Jehoash[a] king of Israel: Jer 1:2; 2Ki 13:13

Hosea's Wife and Children

²When the LORD began to speak through Hosea, the LORD said to him, "Go, marry a promiscuous woman and have children with her, for like an adulterous wife this land is guilty of unfaithfulness to the LORD." ³So he married Gomer daughter of Diblaim, and she conceived and bore him a son.   Dt 31:16; Hos 5:3

⁴Then the LORD said to Hosea, "Call him Jezreel, because I will soon punish the house of Jehu for the massacre at Jezreel, and I will put an end to the kingdom of Israel. ⁵In that day I will break Israel's bow in the Valley of Jezreel."

⁶Gomer conceived again and gave birth to a daughter. Then the LORD said to Hosea, "Call her Lo-Ruhamah (which means "not loved"), for I will no longer show love to Israel, that I should at all forgive them. ⁷Yet I will show love to Judah; and I will save them — not by bow, sword or battle, or by horses and horsemen, but I, the LORD their God, will save them."   Ps 44:6; Zec 4:6

⁸After she had weaned Lo-Ruhamah, Gomer had another son. ⁹Then the LORD said, "Call him Lo-Ammi (which means "not my people"), for you are not my people, and I am not your God.[b]

¹⁰"Yet the Israelites will be like the sand on the seashore, which cannot be measured or counted. In the place where it was said to them, 'You are not my people,' they will be called 'children of the living God.' ¹¹The people of Judah and the people of Israel will come together; they will appoint one leader and will come up out of the land, for great will be the day of Jezreel.[c]   Ro 9:26

---

a 1 Hebrew *Joash*, a variant of *Jehoash*   *b* 9 Or *your I* AM   *c* 11 In Hebrew texts 1:10,11 is numbered 2:1,2.

2

a "Say of your brothers, 'My people,' and of your sisters, 'My loved one.' 1Pe 2:10

Israel Punished and Restored

2 "Rebuke your mother, rebuke her, Isa 50:1; Hos 1:2
for she is not my wife,
and I am not her husband.
Let her remove the adulterous look from her face
and the unfaithfulness from between her breasts.

3 Otherwise I will strip her naked
and make her as bare as on the day she was born;
I will make her like a desert,
turn her into a parched land,
and slay her with thirst.

4 I will not show my love to her children, Eze 8:18
because they are the children of adultery.

5 Their mother has been unfaithful
and has conceived them in disgrace.
She said, 'I will go after my lovers, Jer 3:6
who give me my food and my water,
my wool and my linen, my olive oil and my drink.'

6 Therefore I will block her path with thornbushes;
I will wall her in so that she cannot find her way.

7 She will chase after her lovers but not catch them;
she will look for them but not find them. Hos 5:13
Then she will say,
'I will go back to my husband as at first, Jer 2:2
for then I was better off than now.' Eze 16:8

8 She has not acknowledged that I was the one Isa 1:3
who gave her the grain, the new wine and oil,
who lavished on her the silver and gold —
which they used for Baal.

9 "Therefore I will take away my grain when it ripens,
and my new wine when it is ready. Hos 9:2
I will take back my wool and my linen,
intended to cover her naked body.

10 So now I will expose her lewdness
before the eyes of her lovers;
no one will take her out of my hands. Eze 16:37

11 I will stop all her celebrations:
her yearly festivals, her New Moons,
her Sabbath days — all her appointed festivals.

12 I will ruin her vines and her fig trees, Isa 7:23; Jer 8:13
which she said were her pay from her lovers;
I will make them a thicket,
and wild animals will devour them. Hos 13:8

a In Hebrew texts 2:1-23 is numbered 2:3-25.

¹³I will punish her for the days
  she burned incense to the
  Baals; Hos 11:2
she decked herself with rings
  and jewelry, Eze 16:17
and went after her lovers,
but me she forgot," Hos 4:6; 8:14
  declares the LORD.

¹⁴"Therefore I am now going to
  allure her;
I will lead her into the
  wilderness
and speak tenderly to her.
¹⁵There I will give her back her
  vineyards,
and will make the Valley of
  Achorᵃ a door of hope.
There she will respondᵇ as in
  the days of her youth,
as in the day she came up
  out of Egypt. Hos 12:9

¹⁶"In that day," declares the LORD,
  "you will call me 'my
  husband'; Isa 54:5
you will no longer call me
  'my master.ᶜ'
¹⁷I will remove the names of the
  Baals from her lips;
no longer will their names
  be invoked. Jos 23:7
¹⁸In that day I will make a
  covenant for them
with the beasts of the field,
  the birds in the sky
and the creatures that move
  along the ground. Job 5:22
Bow and sword and battle

I will abolish from the land,
  so that all may lie down in
  safety. Eze 34:25
¹⁹I will betroth you to me forever;
I will betroth you inᵈ
  righteousness and
  justice, Isa 1:27
inᵈ love and compassion.
²⁰I will betroth you inᵈ
  faithfulness,
and you will acknowledge
  the LORD. Jer 31:34; Hos 6:6

²¹"In that day I will respond,"
  declares the LORD —
"I will respond to the skies,
  and they will respond to the
  earth;
²²and the earth will respond to
  the grain,
the new wine and the olive
  oil, Jer 31:12; Joel 2:19
and they will respond to
  Jezreel. ᵉ Hos 1:4
²³I will plant her for myself in
  the land; Jer 31:27
I will show my love to the
  one I called 'Not my
  loved one.ᶠ' Hos 1:6
I will say to those called 'Not
  my people,ᵍ' 'You are
  my people'; Hos 1:10
and they will say, 'You are
  my God.'" Ro 9:25; 1Pe 2:10

Hosea's Reconciliation With His Wife

3 The LORD said to me, "Go,
  show your love to your wife

ᵃ 15 Achor means trouble.   ᵇ 15 Or sing   ᶜ 16 Hebrew baal   ᵈ 19,20 Or with
ᵉ 22 Jezreel means God plants.   ᶠ 23 Hebrew Lo-Ruhamah (see 1:6)   ᵍ 23 Hebrew Lo-
Ammi (see 1:9)

again, though she is loved by another man and is an adulteress. Love her as the LORD loves the Israelites, though they turn to other gods and love the sacred raisin cakes." 2Sa 6:19; Hos 1:2

²So I bought her for fifteen shekels^a of silver and about a homer and a lethek^b of barley. ³Then I told her, "You are to live with me many days; you must not be a prostitute or be intimate with any man, and I will behave the same way toward you."

⁴For the Israelites will live many days without king or prince, without sacrifice or sacred stones, without ephod or household gods. ⁵Afterward the Israelites will return and seek the LORD their God and David their king. They will come trembling to the LORD and to his blessings in the last days. Jer 50:4-5; Eze 34:23-24

The Charge Against Israel

4 Hear the word of the LORD,
  you Israelites,
 because the LORD has a
  charge to bring Jer 2:9
 against you who live in the
  land: Joel 1:2,14
 "There is no faithfulness, no
  love, Pr 24:2
 no acknowledgment of God
  in the land. Jer 7:28
²There is only cursing,^c lying
  and murder, Hos 6:9; 7:3

stealing and adultery; Hos 7:1
 they break all bounds,
  and bloodshed follows
   bloodshed. 2Ki 21:16
³Because of this the land
  dries up, Jer 4:28
 and all who live in it waste
  away; Isa 33:9
 the beasts of the field, the
  birds in the sky
 and the fish in the sea are
  swept away. Jer 4:25; Zep 1:3

⁴"But let no one bring a
  charge,
 let no one accuse another,
 for your people are like those
  who bring charges against a
   priest. Dt 17:12; Eze 3:26
⁵You stumble day and
  night, Eze 14:7
 and the prophets stumble
  with you.
 So I will destroy your
  mother— Hos 2:2
⁶ my people are destroyed
  from lack of
   knowledge. Hos 2:13

 "Because you have rejected
  knowledge,
 I also reject you as my
  priests;
 because you have ignored the
  law of your God, Hos 8:1,12
 I also will ignore your
  children.
⁷The more priests there were,
  the more they sinned
   against me;

---

^a 2 That is, about 6 ounces or about 170 grams   ^b 2 A homer and a lethek possibly weighed
about 430 pounds or about 195 kilograms.   ^c 2 That is, to pronounce a curse on

they exchanged their
glorious God[a] for
something disgraceful.
⁸They feed on the sins of my
people
and relish their wickedness.
⁹And it will be: Like people,
like priests.   Isa 24:2
I will punish both of them
for their ways
and repay them for their
deeds.   Jer 5:31; Hos 9:9,15

¹⁰"They will eat but not have
enough;   Lev 26:26; Mic 6:14
they will engage in
prostitution but not
flourish,
because they have deserted
the LORD   Hos 7:14; 9:17
to give themselves ¹¹to
prostitution;   Hos 5:4
old wine and new wine
take away their
understanding.   Pr 20:1
¹²My people consult a wooden
idol,   Jer 2:27
and a diviner's rod speaks
to them.   Hab 2:19
A spirit of prostitution leads
them astray;   Isa 44:20
they are unfaithful to their
God.   Ps 73:27
¹³They sacrifice on the
mountaintops
and burn offerings on the
hills,
under oak, poplar and
terebinth,   Isa 1:29

where the shade is pleasant.
Therefore your daughters turn
to prostitution   Jer 2:20
and your daughters-in-law
to adultery.   Hos 2:13
¹⁴"I will not punish your
daughters
when they turn to
prostitution,
nor your daughters-in-law
when they commit adultery,
because the men themselves
consort with harlots
and sacrifice with shrine
prostitutes—   Hos 9:10
a people without
understanding will
come to ruin!   Pr 10:21

¹⁵"Though you, Israel, commit
adultery,
do not let Judah become
guilty.

"Do not go to Gilgal;   Hos 9:15
do not go up to Beth Aven.[b]
And do not swear, 'As surely
as the LORD lives!'   Jer 4:2
¹⁶The Israelites are stubborn,
like a stubborn heifer.   Jer 31:18
How then can the LORD
pasture them
like lambs in a meadow?
¹⁷Ephraim is joined to idols;
leave him alone!
¹⁸Even when their drinks are
gone,
they continue their
prostitution;

[a] 7 Syriac (see also an ancient Hebrew scribal tradition); Masoretic Text *me; / I will exchange their glory*   [b] 15 *Beth Aven* means *house of wickedness* (a derogatory name for Bethel, which means *house of God*).

their rulers dearly love
shameful ways.
¹⁹A whirlwind will sweep them
away,   Hos 12:1; 13:15
and their sacrifices will
bring them shame.

Judgment Against Israel

5 "Hear this, you priests!
Pay attention, you Israelites!
Listen, royal house!
This judgment is against
you: Job 10:2
You have been a snare at
Mizpah,   Hos 6:9; 9:8
a net spread out on Tabor.
²The rebels are knee-deep in
slaughter.   Hos 4:2
I will discipline all of them.
³I know all about Ephraim;
Israel is not hidden from me.
Ephraim, you have now
turned to prostitution;
Israel is corrupt.   Hos 6:10

⁴"Their deeds do not permit
them
to return to their God.
A spirit of prostitution is in
their heart;   Hos 4:11
they do not acknowledge
the LORD.   Hos 4:6
⁵Israel's arrogance testifies
against them;   Hos 7:10
the Israelites, even
Ephraim, stumble in
their sin;   Eze 14:7
Judah also stumbles with
them.   Hos 14:1

⁶When they go with their
flocks and herds
to seek the LORD,   Mic 6:6-7
they will not find him;
he has withdrawn himself
from them.   Pr 1:28; Isa 1:15
⁷They are unfaithful to the
LORD;   Hos 6:7
they give birth to
illegitimate children.
When they celebrate their
New Moon feasts,   Isa 1:14
he will devour^a their
fields.

⁸"Sound the trumpet in Gibeah,
the horn in Ramah.   Isa 10:29
Raise the battle cry in Beth
Aven^b;   Hos 4:15
lead on, Benjamin.
⁹Ephraim will be laid waste
on the day of reckoning.
Among the tribes of Israel
I proclaim what is certain.
¹⁰Judah's leaders are like those
who move boundary stones.
I will pour out my wrath on
them
like a flood of water.   Eze 7:8
¹¹Ephraim is oppressed,
trampled in judgment,
intent on pursuing idols.^c
¹²I am like a moth to Ephraim,
like rot to the people of
Judah.
¹³"When Ephraim saw his
sickness,   Isa 7:16
and Judah his sores,

---

^a 7 Or Now their New Moon feasts / will devour them and   ^b 8 Beth Aven means house of
wickedness (a derogatory name for Bethel, which means house of God).   ^c 11 The meaning
of the Hebrew for this word is uncertain.

then Ephraim turned to
  Assyria,   Hos 7:11; 8:9
  and sent to the great king
    for help.   Hos 10:6
But he is not able to cure you,
  not able to heal your sores.
¹⁴For I will be like a lion to
  Ephraim,   Am 3:4
  like a great lion to Judah.
I will tear them to pieces and
  go away;   Hos 6:1
I will carry them off, with
  no one to rescue them.
¹⁵Then I will return to my lair
  until they have borne their
    guilt
  and seek my face —   Hos 3:5
in their misery
  they will earnestly seek me."

Israel Unrepentant

6 "Come, let us return to the
    LORD.   Isa 10:20
He has torn us to pieces   Hos 5:14
  but he will heal us;   Jer 3:22
he has injured us
  but he will bind up our
    wounds.   Dt 32:39; Jer 30:17
²After two days he will
    revive us;   Ps 30:5
  on the third day he will
    restore us,   Ps 71:20
  that we may live in his
    presence.
³Let us acknowledge the LORD;
  let us press on to
    acknowledge him.
As surely as the sun rises,
  he will appear;

he will come to us like the
    winter rains,   Joel 2:23
  like the spring rains that
    water the earth."   Ps 72:6

⁴"What can I do with you,
  Ephraim?   Hos 11:8
What can I do with you,
  Judah?
Your love is like the morning
    mist,
  like the early dew that
    disappears.   Hos 7:1; 13:3
⁵Therefore I cut you in
    pieces with my
    prophets,
  I killed you with the words
    of my mouth —   Jer 1:9-10
  then my judgments go forth
    like the sun.ᵃ   Heb 4:12
⁶For I desire mercy, not
    sacrifice,   Isa 1:11; Mt 9:13
  and acknowledgment of
    God rather than burnt
    offerings.   Hos 2:20
⁷As at Adam,ᵇ they have
    broken the covenant;
  they were unfaithful to me
    there.   Hos 5:7
⁸Gilead is a city of evildoers,
  stained with footprints of
    blood.
⁹As marauders lie in ambush
    for a victim,   Ps 10:8
  so do bands of priests;
they murder on the road to
    Shechem,
  carrying out their wicked
    schemes.   Jer 7:9-10; Eze 22:9

ᵃ 5 The meaning of the Hebrew for this line is uncertain.   ᵇ 7 Or *Like Adam*; or *Like human beings*

¹⁰I have seen a horrible thing in
  Israel: Jer 5:30
    There Ephraim is given to
      prostitution,
    Israel is defiled.   Hos 5:3

¹¹ "Also for you, Judah,
    a harvest is appointed.

  "Whenever I would restore
      the fortunes of my
      people,   Ps 126:1; Zep 2:7
7 ¹whenever I would heal
      Israel,
    the sins of Ephraim are
      exposed
    and the crimes of Samaria
      revealed.   Hos 6:4
    They practice deceit,
      thieves break into houses,
      bandits rob in the streets;
  ²but they do not realize
      that I remember all their
      evil deeds. Jer 14:10; Hos 8:13
    Their sins engulf them;   Jer 2:19
      they are always before me.

³ "They delight the king with
      their wickedness,
    the princes with their lies.
⁴They are all adulterers,   Jer 9:2
    burning like an oven
    whose fire the baker need not
      stir
    from the kneading of the
      dough till it rises.
⁵On the day of the festival of
      our king
    the princes become
      inflamed with wine,
    and he joins hands with the
      mockers.   Ps 1:1

⁶Their hearts are like an oven;
    they approach him with
      intrigue.
    Their passion smolders all
      night;
    in the morning it blazes like
      a flaming fire.
⁷All of them are hot as an oven;
    they devour their rulers.
    All their kings fall,   Hos 13:10
    and none of them calls on me.

⁸ "Ephraim mixes with the
      nations;   Ps 106:35; Hos 5:13
    Ephraim is a flat loaf not
      turned over.
⁹Foreigners sap his strength,
    but he does not realize it.
    His hair is sprinkled with gray,
    but he does not notice.
¹⁰Israel's arrogance testifies
      against him,   Hos 5:5
    but despite all this
    he does not return to the
      LORD his God
    or search for him.   Isa 9:13

¹¹ "Ephraim is like a dove,
    easily deceived and
      senseless —
    now calling to Egypt,   Hos 9:6
    now turning to Assyria.
¹²When they go, I will throw my
      net over them;   Eze 12:13
    I will pull them down like
      the birds in the sky.
    When I hear them flocking
      together,
    I will catch them.
¹³Woe to them,   Hos 9:12
    because they have strayed
      from me! Jer 14:10; Eze 34:4-6

Destruction to them,
    because they have rebelled
        against me!
I long to redeem them
    but they speak about me
        falsely. Mt 23:37
[14] They do not cry out to me
        from their hearts Jer 3:10
    but wail on their beds.
They slash themselves,[a]
    appealing to their gods
    for grain and new wine,
    but they turn away from me.
[15] I trained them and
        strengthened their
        arms,
    but they plot evil against me.
[16] They do not turn to the Most
        High;
    they are like a faulty bow.
Their leaders will fall by the
        sword
    because of their insolent
        words.
For this they will be ridiculed
    in the land of Egypt. Hos 9:3

Israel to Reap the Whirlwind

8 "Put the trumpet to your
        lips!
    An eagle is over the house
        of the LORD Jer 4:13
because the people have
        broken my covenant
    and rebelled against my
        law. Hos 4:6; 6:7
[2] Israel cries out to me,
    'Our God, we acknowledge
        you!'

[3] But Israel has rejected what is
        good;
    an enemy will pursue him.
[4] They set up kings without my
        consent;
    they choose princes without
        my approval. Hos 13:10
With their silver and gold
    they make idols for
        themselves Hos 2:8
    to their own destruction.
[5] Samaria, throw out your calf-
        idol! Hos 10:5
    My anger burns against
        them.
How long will they be
    incapable of purity?
[6] They are from Israel!
This calf — a metalworker has
        made it;
    it is not God. Hos 14:3
It will be broken in pieces,
    that calf of Samaria. Ex 32:4

[7] "They sow the wind
    and reap the whirlwind.
The stalk has no head;
    it will produce no flour.
Were it to yield grain,
    foreigners would swallow
        it up. Hos 2:9
[8] Israel is swallowed up; Jer 51:34
    now she is among the nations
    like something no one wants.
[9] For they have gone up to Assyria
    like a wild donkey
        wandering alone.
    Ephraim has sold herself to
        lovers. Eze 23:5; Hos 5:13

---

[a] 14 Some Hebrew manuscripts and Septuagint; most Hebrew manuscripts *They gather together*

¹⁰Although they have sold
themselves among the
nations,
I will now gather them
together. Eze 16:37; 22:20
They will begin to waste away
under the oppression of the
mighty king.

¹¹"Though Ephraim built many
altars for sin offerings,
these have become altars
for sinning. Hos 10:1; 12:11
¹²I wrote for them the many
things of my law,
but they regarded them as
something foreign.
¹³Though they offer sacrifices
as gifts to me,
and though they eat the
meat, Jer 7:21
the LORD is not pleased
with them.
Now he will remember their
wickedness Hos 7:2
and punish their sins: Hos 4:9
They will return to Egypt.
¹⁴Israel has forgotten their
Maker Dt 32:18; Hos 2:13
and built palaces;
Judah has fortified many
towns.
But I will send fire on their
cities
that will consume their
fortresses." Jer 17:27

Punishment for Israel

9 Do not rejoice, Israel;
do not be jubilant like the
other nations.

For you have been unfaithful
to your God; Hos 10:5
you love the wages of a
prostitute Ge 30:15
at every threshing floor.
²Threshing floors and
winepresses will not
feed the people;
the new wine will fail them.
³They will not remain in the
LORD's land; Lev 25:23
Ephraim will return to
Egypt Hos 8:13
and eat unclean food in
Assyria. Eze 4:13; Hos 7:11
⁴They will not pour out wine
offerings to the LORD,
nor will their sacrifices
please him. Hos 8:13
Such sacrifices will be to
them like the bread of
mourners; Jer 16:7
all who eat them will be
unclean. Hag 2:13-14
This food will be for
themselves;
it will not come into the
temple of the LORD.

⁵What will you do on the day
of your appointed
festivals, Isa 10:3; Jer 5:31
on the feast days of the
LORD?
⁶Even if they escape from
destruction,
Egypt will gather them,
and Memphis will bury
them. Isa 19:13
Their treasures of silver will
be taken over by briers,

and thorns will overrun
    their tents. Isa 5:6; Hos 10:8
⁷The days of punishment are
    coming, Isa 34:8; Jer 10:15
the days of reckoning are at
    hand.
Let Israel know this.
Because your sins are so many
    and your hostility so great,
the prophet is considered a
    fool, Isa 44:25; La 2:14
the inspired person a
    maniac. Hos 14:1
⁸The prophet, along with my
    God,
is the watchman over
    Ephraim,ᵃ
yet snares await him on all his
    paths, Hos 5:1
and hostility in the house of
    his God.
⁹They have sunk deep into
    corruption,
    as in the days of Gibeah.
God will remember their
    wickedness Hos 8:13
and punish them for their
    sins. Hos 4:9

¹⁰"When I found Israel,
    it was like finding grapes in
    the desert;
when I saw your ancestors,
    it was like seeing the early
    fruit on the fig tree.
But when they came to Baal
    Peor, Nu 25:1-5; Ps 106:28-29
they consecrated
    themselves to that
    shameful idol Jer 11:13

and became as vile as the
    thing they loved.
¹¹Ephraim's glory will fly away
    like a bird — Hos 4:7; 10:5
no birth, no pregnancy, no
    conception.
¹²Even if they rear children,
    I will bereave them of every
    one. Eze 24:21
Woe to them Hos 7:13
when I turn away from
    them! Dt 31:17
¹³I have seen Ephraim, like Tyre,
    planted in a pleasant place.
But Ephraim will bring out
    their children to the slayer."

¹⁴Give them, LORD —
    what will you give them?
Give them wombs that miscarry
    and breasts that are dry.

¹⁵"Because of all their
    wickedness in Gilgal,
I hated them there.
Because of their sinful deeds,
    I will drive them out of my
    house.
I will no longer love them;
    all their leaders are
    rebellious. Isa 1:23; Hos 4:9
¹⁶Ephraim is blighted, Hos 5:11
    their root is withered,
    they yield no fruit. Hos 8:7
Even if they bear children,
    I will slay their cherished
    offspring." ver 12

¹⁷My God will reject them
    because they have not
    obeyed him; Hos 4:10

ᵃ 8 Or The prophet is the watchman over Ephraim, / the people of my God

they will be wanderers
  among the nations.

10 Israel was a spreading
    vine;   *Eze 15:2*
  he brought forth fruit for
    himself.
As his fruit increased,
  he built more altars; *1Ki 14:23*
as his land prospered,
  he adorned his sacred
    stones.   *Hos 8:11; 12:11*
²Their heart is deceitful, *1Ki 18:21*
  and now they must bear
    their guilt.   *Hos 13:16*
The LORD will demolish their
    altars   *ver 8*
  and destroy their sacred
    stones.   *Mic 5:13*

³Then they will say, "We have
    no king
  because we did not revere
    the LORD.
But even if we had a king,
  what could he do for us?"
⁴They make many promises,
  take false oaths   *Hos 4:2*
  and make agreements;
therefore lawsuits spring up
  like poisonous weeds in a
    plowed field.   *Am 6:12*
⁵The people who live in
    Samaria fear
  for the calf-idol of Beth
    Aven.*ᵃ*   *Hos 5:8*
Its people will mourn over it,
  and so will its idolatrous
    priests,   *2Ki 23:5*

those who had rejoiced over
    its splendor,
  because it is taken from
    them into exile.   *Hos 8:5*
⁶It will be carried to Assyria
  as tribute for the great king.
Ephraim will be disgraced;
  Israel will be ashamed of its
    foreign alliances. *Jer 48:13*
⁷Samaria's king will be
    destroyed,   *Hos 13:11*
  swept away like a twig
    on the surface of the
    waters.
⁸The high places of
    wickedness*ᵇ* will be
    destroyed —   *1Ki 12:28-30*
  it is the sin of Israel.
Thorns and thistles will
    grow up
  and cover their altars. *Isa 32:13*
Then they will say to the
    mountains, "Cover us!"
  and to the hills, "Fall on us!"
⁹"Since the days of Gibeah, you
    have sinned, Israel,
  and there you have
    remained.*ᶜ*
Will not war again overtake
    the evildoers in Gibeah?
¹⁰When I please, I will punish
    them;   *Eze 5:13; Hos 4:9*
  nations will be gathered
    against them
  to put them in bonds for
    their double sin.
¹¹Ephraim is a trained heifer
  that loves to thresh;

ᵃ 5 Beth Aven means house of wickedness (a derogatory name for Bethel, which means house of God).   *ᵇ 8 Hebrew aven, a reference to Beth Aven (a derogatory name for Bethel); see verse 5.*   *ᶜ 9 Or there a stand was taken*

so I will put a yoke
on her fair neck.
I will drive Ephraim,
Judah must plow,
and Jacob must break up
the ground.
[12] Sow righteousness for
yourselves,   Pr 11:18
reap the fruit of unfailing
love,
and break up your unplowed
ground;   Jer 4:3
for it is time to seek the
LORD,   Hos 12:6
until he comes
and showers his
righteousness on you.
[13] But you have planted
wickedness,
you have reaped evil,   Job 4:8
you have eaten the fruit of
deception.
Because you have depended
on your own strength
and on your many
warriors,
[14] the roar of battle will rise
against your people,
so that all your fortresses
will be devastated —
as Shalman devastated Beth
Arbel on the day of
battle,   2Ki 17:3
when mothers were dashed
to the ground with their
children.   Hos 13:16
[15] So will it happen to you,
Bethel,
because your wickedness is
great.

When that day dawns,
the king of Israel will be
completely destroyed.

God's Love for Israel

11 "When Israel was a child,
I loved him,   Jer 2:2
and out of Egypt I called my
son.   Hos 12:9,13; Mt 2:15
[2] But the more they were called,
the more they went away
from me.[a]
They sacrificed to the Baals
and they burned incense to
images.   2Ki 17:15; Jer 18:15
[3] It was I who taught Ephraim
to walk,
taking them by the arms;
but they did not realize
it was I who healed them.
[4] I led them with cords of
human kindness,
with ties of love.   Jer 31:2-3
To them I was like one who
lifts
a little child to the cheek,
and I bent down to feed
them.   Ps 78:25

[5] "Will they not return to Egypt
and will not Assyria rule
over them   Hos 10:6
because they refuse to
repent?
[6] A sword will flash in their
cities;   Hos 13:16
it will devour their false
prophets
and put an end to their
plans.

---

a 2 Septuagint; Hebrew *them*

7My people are determined to
   turn from me. Jer 3:6-7; 8:5
Even though they call me
   God Most High,
I will by no means exalt
   them.

8"How can I give you up,
   Ephraim? Hos 6:4
How can I hand you over,
   Israel?
How can I treat you like Admah?
How can I make you like
   Zeboyim? Ge 14:8
My heart is changed within
   me;
all my compassion is
   aroused. 1Ki 3:26; Ps 25:6
9I will not carry out my fierce
   anger, Dt 13:17; Jer 30:11
nor will I devastate
   Ephraim again. Mal 3:6
For I am God, and not a
   man—
the Holy One among you.
I will not come against their
   cities.
10They will follow the LORD;
   he will roar like a lion.
When he roars,
   his children will come
      trembling from the west.
11They will come from Egypt,
   trembling like sparrows,
   from Assyria, fluttering like
      doves. Isa 11:11
I will settle them in their
   homes,"
      Eze 28:26
declares the LORD.

Israel's Sin

12Ephraim has surrounded me
   with lies, Hos 4:2
   Israel with deceit.
And Judah is unruly against
   God,
   even against the faithful
      Holy One.a Hos 10:13

12 b 1Ephraim feeds on the
      wind; Eze 17:10
he pursues the east wind all
   day
and multiplies lies and
   violence. Hos 4:19
He makes a treaty with
   Assyria
and sends olive oil to Egypt.
2The LORD has a charge to
   bring against Judah;
he will punish Jacobc
   according to his ways
and repay him according to
   his deeds. Hos 4:9
3In the womb he grasped his
   brother's heel; Ge 25:26
as a man he struggled with
   God. Ge 32:24-29
4He struggled with the angel
   and overcame him;
he wept and begged for his
   favor.
He found him at Bethel
   and talked with him there—
5the LORD God Almighty,
   the LORD is his name! Ex 3:15
6But you must return to your
   God; Isa 19:22
maintain love and justice,

---

a 12 In Hebrew texts this verse (11:12) is numbered 12:1.   b In Hebrew texts 12:1-14 is
numbered 12:2-15.   c 2 Jacob means he grasps the heel, a Hebrew idiom for he takes
advantage of or he deceives.

and wait for your God
always.   Hos 6:1-3; 10:12

⁷The merchant uses dishonest
    scales   Am 8:5
  and loves to defraud.
⁸Ephraim boasts,
  "I am very rich; I have
      become wealthy.   Ps 62:10
  With all my wealth they will
      not find in me
    any iniquity or sin."

⁹"I have been the LORD your
    God
  ever since you came out of
      Egypt;   Lev 23:43; Hos 11:1
  I will make you live in tents
      again,   Ne 8:17
  as in the days of your
      appointed festivals.
¹⁰I spoke to the prophets,
  gave them many visions
  and told parables through
      them."   2Ki 17:13; Eze 20:49

¹¹Is Gilead wicked?   Hos 6:8
  Its people are worthless!
  Do they sacrifice bulls in
      Gilgal?   Hos 4:15
  Their altars will be like piles
      of stones
  on a plowed field.   Hos 8:11
¹²Jacob fled to the country of
      Aramᵃ;   Ge 28:5
  Israel served to get a wife,
  and to pay for her he tended
      sheep.   Ge 29:18
¹³The LORD used a prophet to
    bring Israel up from
      Egypt,   Hos 11:1
  by a prophet he cared for him.

¹⁴But Ephraim has aroused his
    bitter anger;
  his Lord will leave on him the
      guilt of his bloodshed
  and will repay him for his
      contempt.   Da 11:18

The LORD's Anger Against Israel

13 When Ephraim spoke,
    people trembled;   Jdg 12:1
  he was exalted in Israel.
  But he became guilty of
      Baal worship and died.
²Now they sin more and
    more;
  they make idols for
      themselves from their
      silver,   Isa 46:6; Jer 10:4
  cleverly fashioned images,
    all of them the work of
      craftsmen.
  It is said of these people,
  "They offer human sacrifices!
  They kissᵇ calf-idols!"
³Therefore they will be like the
    morning mist,
  like the early dew that
      disappears,   Hos 6:4
  like chaff swirling from a
      threshing floor,   Isa 17:13
  like smoke escaping
      through a window.

⁴"But I have been the LORD
    your God
  ever since you came out of
      Egypt.   Hos 12:9
  You shall acknowledge no
      God but me,   Ex 20:3
  no Savior except me.   Isa 43:11

ᵃ 12 That is, Northwest Mesopotamia   ᵇ 2 Or *"Men who sacrifice / kiss"*

⁵I cared for you in the
  wilderness,   Dt 1:19
  in the land of burning heat.
⁶When I fed them, they were
    satisfied;
  when they were satisfied,
    they became proud;
  then they forgot me.
⁷So I will be like a lion to them,
  like a leopard I will lurk by
    the path.
⁸Like a bear robbed of her
    cubs,   2Sa 17:8
  I will attack them and rip
    them open;
  like a lion I will devour
    them—   Ps 17:12
  a wild animal will tear
    them apart.   Ps 50:22

⁹"You are destroyed, Israel,
  because you are against me,
    against your helper.
¹⁰Where is your king, that he
    may save you?   2Ki 17:4
  Where are your rulers in all
    your towns,
  of whom you said,
    'Give me a king and
      princes'?   Hos 8:4
¹¹So in my anger I gave you a
    king,
  and in my wrath I took him
    away.   1Ki 14:10; Hos 10:7
¹²The guilt of Ephraim is
    stored up,
  his sins are kept on record.
¹³Pains as of a woman in
    childbirth come to him,

but he is a child without
    wisdom;
  when the time arrives,   2Ki 19:3
  he doesn't have the sense to
    come out of the womb.

¹⁴"I will deliver this people
    from the power of the
    grave;   Eze 37:12-13
  I will redeem them from
    death.   Isa 25:8
  Where, O death, are your
    plagues?
  Where, O grave, is your
    destruction?   1Co 15:55

  "I will have no compassion,
¹⁵ even though he thrives
    among his brothers.
  An east wind from the LORD
    will come,   Eze 19:12
  blowing in from the desert;
  his spring will fail
    and his well dry up.   Jer 51:36
  His storehouse will be
    plundered   Jer 20:5
    of all its treasures.
¹⁶The people of Samaria must
    bear their guilt,   Hos 10:2
  because they have rebelled
    against their God.
  They will fall by the sword;
    their little ones will be
      dashed to the ground,
    their pregnant women
      ripped open."ᵃ   2Ki 15:16

Repentance to Bring Blessing

14ᵇ Return, Israel, to the
      LORD your God.   Jer 3:12

ᵃ 16 In Hebrew texts this verse (13:16) is numbered 14:1.   ᵇ In Hebrew texts 14:1-9 is
numbered 14:2-10.

Your sins have been your
downfall! Hos 5:5
²Take words with you
and return to the LORD.
Say to him:
"Forgive all our sins
and receive us graciously,
that we may offer the fruit
of our lips.ᵃ Heb 13:15
³Assyria cannot save us;
we will not mount warhorses.
We will never again say 'Our
gods' Hos 8:6
to what our own hands have
made,
for in you the fatherless find
compassion." Ps 10:14; 68:5

⁴"I will heal their waywardness
and love them freely, Zep 3:17
for my anger has turned
away from them. Job 13:16
⁵I will be like the dew to Israel;
he will blossom like a lily.
Like a cedar of Lebanon Isa 35:2
he will send down his roots;
⁶ his young shoots will grow.
His splendor will be like an
olive tree, Ps 52:8; Jer 11:16

his fragrance like a cedar of
Lebanon. SS 4:11
⁷People will dwell again in his
shade; Ps 91:1-4
they will flourish like the
grain,
they will blossom like the
vine —
Israel's fame will be like the
wine of Lebanon.
⁸Ephraim, what more have Iᵇ
to do with idols?
I will answer him and care
for him.
I am like a flourishing
juniper; Isa 37:24
your fruitfulness comes
from me."

⁹Who is wise? Let them realize
these things. Ps 107:43
Who is discerning? Let
them understand.
The ways of the LORD are
right; Ps 111:7-8; Zep 3:5
the righteous walk in
them,
but the rebellious stumble
in them.

ᵃ 2 Or offer our lips as sacrifices of bulls   ᵇ 8 Or Hebrew; Septuagint What more has
Ephraim

Joel

1

The word of the LORD that came to Joel son of Pethuel.

An Invasion of Locusts

[2] Hear this, you elders;   Hos 5:1
listen, all who live in the land.
Has anything like this ever
happened in your days
or in the days of your
ancestors?   Joel 2:2
[3] Tell it to your children,   Ex 10:2
and let your children tell it
to their children,
and their children to the
next generation.
[4] What the locust swarm has
left   Ex 10:14
the great locusts have eaten;
what the great locusts have
left
the young locusts have
eaten;
what the young locusts have
left   Ex 10:5
other locusts[a] have eaten.

[5] Wake up, you drunkards, and
weep!
Wail, all you drinkers of wine;
wail because of the new wine,
for it has been snatched
from your lips.
[6] A nation has invaded my land,
a mighty army without
number;   Joel 2:2,11,25
it has the teeth of a lion,   Rev 9:8
the fangs of a lioness.
[7] It has laid waste my vines Isa 5:6
and ruined my fig trees.
It has stripped off their bark
and thrown it away,
leaving their branches white.

[8] Mourn like a virgin in
sackcloth   Isa 22:12; Am 8:10
grieving for the betrothed of
her youth.
[9] Grain offerings and drink
offerings   Hos 9:4; Joel 2:14,17
are cut off from the house of
the LORD.
The priests are in mourning,
those who minister before
the LORD.
[10] The fields are ruined,
the ground is dried up; Isa 24:4

---

[a] 4 The precise meaning of the four Hebrew words used here for locusts is uncertain.

the grain is destroyed,
  the new wine is dried up,
  the olive oil fails.

¹¹ Despair, you farmers,   Jer 14:3-4
  wail, you vine growers;
grieve for the wheat and the
    barley,
  because the harvest of the
    field is destroyed.   Isa 17:11
¹² The vine is dried up
  and the fig tree is withered;
the pomegranate, the palm
    and the apple*ᵃ* tree —
  all the trees of the field —
  are dried up.   Hag 2:19
Surely the people's joy
  is withered away.

A Call to Lamentation

¹³ Put on sackcloth, you priests,
    and mourn;   Jer 4:8
  wail, you who minister
    before the altar.   Joel 2:17
Come, spend the night in
    sackcloth,
  you who minister before my
    God;
for the grain offerings and
    drink offerings
  are withheld from the
    house of your God.
¹⁴ Declare a holy fast;   2Ch 20:3
  call a sacred assembly.
Summon the elders
  and all who live in the land
to the house of the Lᴏʀᴅ your
    God,
  and cry out to the Lᴏʀᴅ.

¹⁵ Alas for that day!   Jer 30:7
  For the day of the Lᴏʀᴅ is
    near;   Joel 2:1,11,31
  it will come like destruction
    from the Almighty.*ᵇ*

¹⁶ Has not the food been cut off
    before our very eyes —
joy and gladness
  from the house of our God?
¹⁷ The seeds are shriveled
  beneath the clods.*ᶜ*   Isa 17:10-11
The storehouses are in ruins,
  the granaries have been
    broken down,
  for the grain has dried up.
¹⁸ How the cattle moan!
  The herds mill about
because they have no pasture;
  even the flocks of sheep are
    suffering.   Jer 9:10

¹⁹ To you, Lᴏʀᴅ, I call,   Ps 50:15
  for fire has devoured
    the pastures in the
      wilderness   Jer 9:10; Am 7:4
  and flames have burned up
    all the trees of the field.
²⁰ Even the wild animals pant
    for you;   Ps 104:21
  the streams of water have
    dried up   1Ki 17:7
  and fire has devoured
    the pastures in the
      wilderness.

An Army of Locusts

2 Blow the trumpet in Zion;
  sound the alarm on my holy
    hill.   Ex 15:17

ᵃ 12 Or possibly *apricot*   *ᵇ 15* Hebrew *Shaddai*   *ᶜ 17* The meaning of the Hebrew for this word is uncertain.

Let all who live in the land
　　tremble,
　for the day of the Lord is
　　coming.　　　Zep 1:14-16
It is close at hand —　　Ob 15
2　a day of darkness and
　　　gloom,　　Da 9:12; Am 5:18
　a day of clouds and
　　　blackness.　　Rev 9:2
Like dawn spreading across
　　the mountains
　a large and mighty army
　　comes,　　Joel 1:6
such as never was in ancient
　　times　　Joel 1:2
nor ever will be in ages to
　　come.

3 Before them fire devours,
　behind them a flame
　　blazes.
　Before them the land is like
　　the garden of Eden,
　behind them, a desert
　　waste —　　Ps 105:34-35
　nothing escapes them.
4 They have the appearance of
　　horses;　　Rev 9:7
　they gallop along like
　　cavalry.
5 With a noise like that of
　　chariots　　Rev 9:9
　they leap over the
　　mountaintops,
　like a crackling fire
　　consuming stubble,
　like a mighty army drawn
　　up for battle.
6 At the sight of them, nations
　　are in anguish;　　Isa 13:8
　every face turns pale.　　Na 2:10

7 They charge like warriors;
　they scale walls like
　　soldiers.
　They all march in line,
　　not swerving from their
　　course.　　Isa 5:27
8 They do not jostle each other;
　each marches straight
　　ahead.
　They plunge through defenses
　　without breaking ranks.
9 They rush upon the city;
　they run along the wall.
　They climb into the houses;
　like thieves they enter
　　through the windows.

10 Before them the earth shakes,
　the heavens tremble,
　the sun and moon are
　　darkened,　　Mt 24:29
　and the stars no longer
　　shine.　　Isa 13:10; Eze 32:8
11 The Lord thunders　　Joel 1:15
　at the head of his army;
　his forces are beyond number,
　　and mighty is the army that
　　obeys his command.
　The day of the Lord is great;
　it is dreadful.
　Who can endure it?　　Eze 22:14

Rend Your Heart

12 "Even now," declares the Lord,
　"return to me with all your
　　heart,　　Jer 4:1; Hos 12:6
　with fasting and weeping
　　and mourning."

13 Rend your heart　　Isa 57:15
　and not your garments.
　Return to the Lord your God,

for he is gracious and
compassionate,   Dt 4:31
slow to anger and abounding
in love,   Ex 34:6
and he relents from sending
calamity.   Jer 18:8
¹⁴Who knows? He may turn and
relent   Jer 26:3
and leave behind a
blessing —   Hag 2:19
grain offerings and drink
offerings   Joel 1:13
for the LORD your God.

¹⁵Blow the trumpet in Zion,
declare a holy fast,   Jer 36:9
call a sacred assembly.
¹⁶Gather the people,
consecrate the assembly;
bring together the
elders,   Joel 1:2
gather the children,
those nursing at the breast.
Let the bridegroom leave his
room   Ps 19:5
and the bride her chamber.
¹⁷Let the priests, who minister
before the LORD,
weep between the portico
and the altar.   Eze 8:16
Let them say, "Spare your
people, LORD.
Do not make your
inheritance an object of
scorn,   Ps 44:13
a byword among the
nations.   1Ki 9:7
Why should they say among
the peoples,
'Where is their God?'"   Ps 42:3

The LORD's Answer

¹⁸Then the LORD was jealous for
his land   Zec 1:14
and took pity on his
people.   Ps 72:13

¹⁹The LORD repliedᵃ to them:

"I am sending you grain, new
wine and olive oil,
enough to satisfy you fully;
never again will I make you
an object of scorn to the
nations.   Eze 34:29

²⁰"I will drive the northern
horde far from you,
pushing it into a parched
and barren land;
its eastern ranks will drown
in the Dead Sea   Zec 14:8
and its western ranks in the
Mediterranean Sea.
And its stench will go up;
its smell will rise."

Surely he has done great things!
²¹ Do not be afraid, land of
Judah;   Isa 54:4; Zep 3:16-17
be glad and rejoice.   Ps 9:2
Surely the LORD has done
great things!   Ps 126:3
²² Do not be afraid, you wild
animals,
for the pastures in the
wilderness are
becoming green.   Ps 65:12
The trees are bearing their
fruit;
the fig tree and the vine
yield their riches.

ᵃ 18,19 Or LORD will be jealous . . . / and take pity . . . / ¹⁹The LORD will reply

²³Be glad, people of Zion,
  rejoice in the LORD your
  God,   Isa 41:16; Hab 3:18
for he has given you the
  autumn rains
because he is faithful.
He sends you abundant
  showers,   Eze 34:26
both autumn and spring
  rains, as before.   Lev 26:4
²⁴The threshing floors will be
  filled with grain;
the vats will overflow with
  new wine and oil.   Am 9:13
²⁵"I will repay you for the
  years the locusts have
  eaten —   Dt 28:39
the great locust and the
  young locust,
the other locusts and the
  locust swarm*ᵃ —
my great army that I sent
  among you.   Joel 1:6
²⁶You will have plenty to eat,
  until you are full, Lev 26:5
and you will praise the
  name of the LORD your
  God,   Isa 62:9
who has worked wonders
  for you;   Isa 25:1
never again will my people be
  shamed.   Isa 29:22
²⁷Then you will know that I am
  in Israel,   Ex 6:7
that I am the LORD your God,
  and that there is no other;
never again will my people be
  shamed.   Zep 3:11

The Day of the LORD

²⁸"And afterward,
  I will pour out my Spirit on
  all people.   Eze 39:29
Your sons and daughters will
  prophesy,   1Sa 19:20
your old men will dream
  dreams,   Jer 23:25
your young men will see
  visions.
²⁹Even on my servants, both
  men and women, 1Co 12:13
I will pour out my Spirit in
  those days.   Eze 36:27
³⁰I will show wonders in the
  heavens   Lk 21:11
and on the earth,   Mk 13:24-25
blood and fire and billows
  of smoke.
³¹The sun will be turned to
  darkness   Mt 24:29
and the moon to blood
before the coming of the
  great and dreadful day
  of the LORD.   Isa 13:9-10
³²And everyone who calls
  on the name of the LORD
  will be saved;   Ro 10:13
for on Mount Zion and in
  Jerusalem   Isa 46:13
there will be deliverance,
  as the LORD has said,
even among the survivors
  whom the LORD
  calls.ᵇ   Ac 2:39

The Nations Judged

3ᶜ "In those days and at that
  time,

ᵃ 25 The precise meaning of the four Hebrew words used here for locusts is uncertain.
ᵇ 32 In Hebrew texts 2:28-32 is numbered 3:1-5.   ᶜ In Hebrew texts 3:1-21 is numbered 4:1-21.

when I restore the fortunes
  of Judah and Jerusalem,
²I will gather all nations   Zep 3:8
  and bring them down to the
    Valley of Jehoshaphat.ᵃ
There I will put them on trial
  for what they did to my
    inheritance, my people
    Israel,
because they scattered my
  people among the
    nations   Lev 26:33
and divided up my land.
³They cast lots for my people
  and traded boys for
    prostitutes;
they sold girls for wine to
  drink.   Am 2:6

⁴"Now what have you against
me, Tyre and Sidon and all you
regions of Philistia? Are you repaying me for something I have
done? If you are paying me back,
I will swiftly and speedily return
on your own heads what you
have done. ⁵For you took my silver and my gold and carried off
my finest treasures to your tem-
ples.ᵇ ⁶You sold the people of Judah and Jerusalem to the Greeks,
that you might send them far
from their homeland.   2Ch 21:16-17

⁷"See, I am going to rouse
them out of the places to which
you sold them, and I will return
on your own heads what you
have done. ⁸I will sell your sons
and daughters to the people of
Judah, and they will sell them to

the Sabeans, a nation far away."
The LORD has spoken.   Isa 43:5-6

⁹Proclaim this among the
  nations:
  Prepare for war!   Isa 8:9
  Rouse the warriors!   Jer 46:4
  Let all the fighting men
    draw near and attack.
¹⁰Beat your plowshares into
  swords
  and your pruning hooks
    into spears.   Isa 2:4; Mic 4:3
  Let the weakling say,   Zec 12:8
  "I am strong!"   Jos 1:6
¹¹Come quickly, all you nations
  from every side,
  and assemble there.

  Bring down your warriors,
    LORD!   Isa 13:3

¹²"Let the nations be roused;
  let them advance into the
    Valley of Jehoshaphat,
  for there I will sit
    to judge all the nations on
      every side.   Isa 2:4
¹³Swing the sickle,   Mk 4:29
  for the harvest is ripe.   Hos 6:11
  Come, trample the grapes,
    for the winepress is full
    and the vats overflow—
  so great is their wickedness!"

¹⁴Multitudes, multitudes
  in the valley of decision!
For the day of the LORD is
  near   Isa 34:2-8; Joel 1:15
  in the valley of decision.
¹⁵The sun and moon will be
  darkened,

ᵃ 2 *Jehoshaphat* means *the LORD judges*; also in verse 12.   ᵇ 5 Or *palaces*

and the stars no longer
   shine.   Eze 32:7
¹⁶The LORD will roar from Zion
   and thunder from
      Jerusalem;   Am 1:2
the earth and the heavens
   will tremble.   Eze 38:19
But the LORD will be a refuge
   for his people,   Ps 46:1
a stronghold for the people
   of Israel.   Jer 16:19

Blessings for God's People

¹⁷"Then you will know that I,
   the LORD your God,
   dwell in Zion, my holy hill.
Jerusalem will be holy;   Jer 31:40
never again will foreigners
   invade her.   Isa 52:1

¹⁸"In that day the mountains
   will drip new wine,

and the hills will flow with
   milk;   Ex 3:8
all the ravines of Judah will
   run with water.   Isa 30:25
A fountain will flow out of the
   LORD's house   Rev 22:1-2
and will water the valley of
   acacias.ᵃ   Eze 47:1; Am 9:13
¹⁹But Egypt will be desolate,
   Edom a desert waste,   Isa 11:14
because of violence done to
      the people of Judah,
   in whose land they shed
      innocent blood.
²⁰Judah will be inhabited forever
   and Jerusalem through all
      generations.
²¹Shall I leave their innocent
      blood unavenged?   Isa 1:15
   No, I will not."   Eze 36:25
The LORD dwells in Zion!

ᵃ 18 Or *Valley of Shittim*

Amos

1 The words of Amos, one of the shepherds of Tekoa — the vision he saw concerning Israel two years before the earthquake, when Uzziah was king of Judah and Jeroboam son of Jehoash[a] was king of Israel. 2Sa 14:2

2 He said:

"The LORD roars from Zion
　and thunders from
　　Jerusalem; Joel 3:16
the pastures of the shepherds
　dry up,
　and the top of Carmel
　　withers." Jer 12:4; Am 9:3

Judgment on Israel's Neighbors

3 This is what the LORD says:

"For three sins of Damascus,
　even for four, I will not
　　relent. Am 2:6
Because she threshed Gilead
　with sledges having iron
　　teeth,
4 I will send fire on the house of
　Hazah Jer 49:27

that will consume the
　fortresses of Ben-
　　Hadad. 2Ki 6:24; Jer 17:27
5 I will break down the gate of
　Damascus; Jer 51:30
I will destroy the king who
　is in[b] the Valley of
　　Aven[c]
and the one who holds the
　scepter in Beth Eden.
The people of Aram will go
　into exile to Kir," 2Ki 16:9
　　says the LORD.

6 This is what the LORD says:

"For three sins of Gaza, 1Sa 6:17
　even for four, I will not
　　relent.
Because she took captive
　whole communities
　and sold them to Edom,
7 I will send fire on the walls of
　Gaza
that will consume her
　fortresses.
8 I will destroy the king[d] of
　Ashdod 2Ch 26:6

---

a 1 Hebrew *Joash*, a variant of *Jehoash*   b 5 Or *the inhabitants of*   c 5 *Aven* means *wickedness.*   d 8 Or *inhabitants*

and the one who holds the
scepter in Ashkelon.
I will turn my hand against
Ekron,   Ps 81:14
till the last of the Philistines
are dead,"   Eze 25:16
says the Sovereign
Lord.

9 This is what the Lord says:

"For three sins of Tyre, Isa 23:1-18
even for four, I will not relent.
Because she sold whole
communities of
captives to Edom,
disregarding a treaty of
brotherhood,   1Ki 5:12
10 I will send fire on the walls of
Tyre
that will consume her
fortresses."   Zec 9:1-4

11 This is what the Lord says:

"For three sins of Edom,
even for four, I will not relent.
Because he pursued his
brother with a sword
and slaughtered the women
of the land,
because his anger raged
continually
and his fury flamed
unchecked,   Eze 25:12-14
12 I will send fire on Teman
that will consume the
fortresses of Bozrah."

13 This is what the Lord says:

"For three sins of Ammon,
even for four, I will not
relent.

Because he ripped open the
pregnant women of
Gilead   Hos 13:16
in order to extend his
borders,
14 I will set fire to the walls of
Rabbah   Dt 3:11
that will consume her
fortresses
amid war cries on the day of
battle,   Am 2:2
amid violent winds on a
stormy day.
15 Her king[a] will go into exile,
he and his officials
together,"   Jer 25:21
says the Lord.

2 This is what the Lord says:

"For three sins of Moab,
even for four, I will not relent.
Because he burned to ashes
the bones of Edom's king,
2 I will send fire on Moab
that will consume the
fortresses of Kerioth.[b]
Moab will go down in great
tumult
amid war cries and the blast
of the trumpet.   Jos 6:20
3 I will destroy her ruler   Ps 2:10
and kill all her officials with
him,"   Isa 40:23
says the Lord.

4 This is what the Lord says:

"For three sins of Judah,
even for four, I will not relent.
Because they have rejected
the law of the Lord

---

^a 15 Or / Molek   ^b 2 Or of her cities

and have not kept his
decrees,   Eze 20:24
because they have been led
astray by false gods,[a]
the gods[b] their ancestors
followed,   2Ki 22:13; Jer 16:12
[5] I will send fire on Judah
that will consume the
fortresses of Jerusalem."

Judgment on Israel

[6] This is what the LORD says:

"For three sins of Israel,
even for four, I will not relent.
They sell the innocent for
silver,
and the needy for a pair of
sandals.   Joel 3:3; Am 8:6
[7] They trample on the heads of
the poor
as on the dust of the ground
and deny justice to the
oppressed.
Father and son use the same
girl
and so profane my holy
name.   Am 5:11-12; 8:4
[8] They lie down beside every
altar
on garments taken in pledge.
In the house of their god
they drink wine taken as
fines.   Am 4:1; 6:6

[9] "Yet I destroyed the Amorites
before them,   Nu 21:23-26
though they were tall as the
cedars
and strong as the oaks. Ps 29:9
I destroyed their fruit above

and their roots below. Eze 17:9
[10] I brought you up out of Egypt
and led you forty years in
the wilderness   Dt 2:7
to give you the land of the
Amorites.   Ex 3:8; Am 9:7

[11] "I also raised up prophets
from among your
children   Dt 18:18; Jer 7:25
and Nazirites from among
your youths.   Nu 6:2-3
Is this not true, people of Israel?"
declares the LORD.
[12] "But you made the Nazirites
drink wine
and commanded the
prophets not to prophesy.

[13] "Now then, I will crush you
as a cart crushes when
loaded with grain.
[14] The swift will not escape,
the strong will not muster
their strength,   Jer 9:23
and the warrior will not
save his life.   Ps 33:16
[15] The archer will not stand his
ground,   Eze 39:3
the fleet-footed soldier will
not get away,
and the horseman will not
save his life.   Ecc 9:11
[16] Even the bravest warriors
will flee naked on that day,"
declares the LORD.

Witnesses Summoned Against Israel

3 Hear this word, people of Israel, the word the LORD has

[a] 4 Or *by lies*   [b] 4 Or *lies*

spoken against you — against the whole family I brought up out of Egypt: Am 2:10

2 "You only have I chosen Dt 7:6
    of all the families of the earth;
  therefore I will punish you
    for all your sins." Jer 14:10

3 Do two walk together
    unless they have agreed to
      do so?
4 Does a lion roar in the thicket
    when it has no prey? Ps 104:21
  Does it growl in its den
    when it has caught nothing?
5 Does a bird swoop down to a
      trap on the ground
    when no bait is there?
  Does a trap spring up from
      the ground
    if it has not caught anything?
6 When a trumpet sounds in a
      city,
    do not the people tremble?
  When disaster comes to a city,
    has not the LORD caused it?

7 Surely the Sovereign LORD
      does nothing
    without revealing his plan
    to his servants the prophets.

8 The lion has roared —
    who will not fear?
  The Sovereign LORD has
      spoken —
    who can but prophesy?

9 Proclaim to the fortresses of
    Ashdod

and to the fortresses of
  Egypt:
"Assemble yourselves on the
    mountains of Samaria;
  see the great unrest within
    her
  and the oppression among
    her people."

10 "They do not know how to
    do right," declares the
      LORD, Jer 4:22; Am 5:7; 6:12
  "who store up in their
    fortresses
  what they have plundered
    and looted." Hab 2:8

11 Therefore this is what the Sovereign LORD says:

"An enemy will overrun your
    land,
  pull down your strongholds
  and plunder your
    fortresses." Am 2:5; 6:14

12 This is what the LORD says:

"As a shepherd rescues from
    the lion's mouth 1Sa 17:34
  only two leg bones or a
    piece of an ear,
  so will the Israelites living in
    Samaria be rescued,
  with only the head of a bed
  and a piece of fabric[a] from a
    couch.[b]" Am 6:4

13 "Hear this and testify against the descendants of Jacob," declares the Lord, the LORD God Almighty. Eze 2:7

---

[a] 12 The meaning of the Hebrew for this phrase is uncertain. [b] 12 Or *Israelites be rescued,* / *those who sit in Samaria* / *on the edge of their beds* / *and in Damascus on their couches.*

14 "On the day I punish Israel for
her sins,
I will destroy the altars of
Bethel;   Am 5:5-6
the horns of the altar will be
cut off
and fall to the ground.
15 I will tear down the winter
house   Jer 36:22
along with the summer
house;   Jdg 3:20
the houses adorned with ivory
will be destroyed 1Ki 22:39
and the mansions will be
demolished,"   Isa 34:5
declares the LORD.

Israel Has Not Returned to God

4 Hear this word, you cows
of Bashan on Mount
Samaria,   Ps 22:12; Am 3:9
you women who oppress
the poor and crush the
needy   Dt 24:14
and say to your husbands,
"Bring us some drinks!"
2 The Sovereign LORD has
sworn by his holiness:
"The time will surely come
when you will be taken away
with hooks,   Am 6:8
the last of you with
fishhooks.[a]
3 You will each go straight out
through breaches in the
wall,   Eze 12:5
and you will be cast out
toward Harmon,[b]"
declares the LORD.

4 "Go to Bethel and sin;
go to Gilgal and sin yet more.
Bring your sacrifices every
morning,   Nu 28:3
your tithes every three
years.[c]   Dt 14:28; Eze 20:39
5 Burn leavened bread as a
thank offering   Lev 7:13
and brag about your
freewill offerings —
boast about them, you
Israelites,
for this is what you love to do,"
declares the Sovereign
LORD.

6 "I gave you empty stomachs
in every city
and lack of bread in every
town,
yet you have not returned
to me,"
declares the LORD.

7 "I also withheld rain from you
when the harvest was still
three months away.
I sent rain on one town,
but withheld it from
another.   Dt 11:17; 2Ch 7:13
One field had rain;
another had none and
dried up.
8 People staggered from town to
town for water   Eze 4:16-17
but did not get enough to
drink,
yet you have not returned
to me,"   Jer 3:7
declares the LORD.

a 2 Or *away in baskets, / the last of you in fish baskets*   b 3 Masoretic Text; with a different
word division of the Hebrew (see Septuagint) *out, you mountain of oppression*   c 4 Or *days*

⁹ "Many times I struck your
    gardens and vineyards,
    destroying them with blight
    and mildew.   Dt 28:22
Locusts devoured your fig and
    olive trees,   Joel 1:7
yet you have not returned
    to me,"   Jer 3:10; Hag 2:17
    declares the LORD.

¹⁰ "I sent plagues among you
    as I did to Egypt.   Ex 11:5
I killed your young men with
    the sword,   Isa 9:17
    along with your captured
    horses.
I filled your nostrils with the
    stench of your camps,
yet you have not returned
    to me,"   Dt 28:21
    declares the LORD.

¹¹ "I overthrew some of you
    as I overthrew Sodom and
    Gomorrah.   Ge 19:24
You were like a burning stick
    snatched from the fire,
yet you have not returned
    to me,"
    declares the LORD.

¹² "Therefore this is what I will
    do to you, Israel,
and because I will do this to
    you, Israel,
    prepare to meet your God."

¹³ He who forms the mountains,
    who creates the wind,
    and who reveals his
    thoughts to mankind,
    who turns dawn to darkness,

and treads on the heights of
    the earth —   Mic 1:3
the LORD God Almighty is
    his name.   Isa 47:4; Am 5:8,27

A Lament and Call to Repentance

5 Hear this word, Israel, this
    lament I take up concerning
you: Eze 19:1

² "Fallen is Virgin Israel,   Jer 14:17
    never to rise again,
deserted in her own land,
    with no one to lift her up."

³ This is what the Sovereign
LORD says to Israel:

"Your city that marches out a
    thousand strong
    will have only a hundred left;
your town that marches out a
    hundred strong
    will have only ten left."   Isa 6:13

⁴ This is what the LORD says to
Israel:

"Seek me and live;   Isa 55:3
⁵   do not seek Bethel,
do not go to Gilgal,   Am 4:4
    do not journey to
    Beersheba.   Am 8:14
For Gilgal will surely go into
    exile,
    and Bethel will be reduced
    to nothing.ᵃ"   1Sa 7:16
⁶ Seek the LORD and live,   Isa 55:6
    or he will sweep through
    the tribes of Joseph like
    a fire;   Dt 4:24

ᵃ 5 Hebrew *aven*, a reference to Beth Aven (a derogatory name for Bethel); see Hosea 4:15.

it will devour them,
    and Bethel will have no one
      to quench it.   Am 3:14

7 There are those who turn
    justice into bitterness
  and cast righteousness to
      the ground.   Hos 10:4

8 He who made the Pleiades
    and Orion,   Job 9:9
  who turns midnight into
    dawn   Isa 42:16
  and darkens day into night,
  who calls for the waters of the
    sea
  and pours them out over
    the face of the land —
  the LORD is his name.
9 With a blinding flash he
    destroys the stronghold
  and brings the fortified city
    to ruin.   Mic 5:11

10 There are those who hate
    the one who upholds
    justice in court   Isa 29:21
  and detest the one who tells
    the truth.   1Ki 22:8

11 You levy a straw tax on the
    poor   Am 8:6
  and impose a tax on their
    grain.
  Therefore, though you have
    built stone mansions,
  you will not live in them;
  though you have planted lush
    vineyards,
  you will not drink their wine.
12 For I know how many are your
    offenses
  and how great your sins.

There are those who oppress
    the innocent and take
    bribes
  and deprive the poor of
    justice in the courts.
13 Therefore the prudent keep
    quiet in such times,
  for the times are evil.   Mic 2:3

14 Seek good, not evil,
    that you may live.   ver 6
  Then the LORD God Almighty
    will be with you,
    just as you say he is.
15 Hate evil, love good;   Ro 12:9
    maintain justice in the
    courts.   Isa 1:17
  Perhaps the LORD God
    Almighty will have mercy
    on the remnant of
    Joseph.   Mic 5:7-8

16 Therefore this is what the
Lord, the LORD God Almighty,
says:

  "There will be wailing in all
    the streets   Jer 9:17
  and cries of anguish in
    every public square.
  The farmers will be
    summoned to weep
  and the mourners to wail.
17 There will be wailing in all
    the vineyards,
  for I will pass through your
    midst,"   Ex 12:12
      says the LORD.

The Day of the LORD

18 Woe to you who long
    for the day of the LORD!

Why do you long for the day of
the LORD?
That day will be darkness,
not light. Isa 5:19,30; Joel 2:2
[19] It will be as though a man fled
from a lion
only to meet a bear,
as though he entered his house
and rested his hand on the
wall
only to have a snake bite
him. Job 20:24; Jer 48:44
[20] Will not the day of the LORD
be darkness, not light —
pitch-dark, without a ray of
brightness? Isa 13:10

[21] "I hate, I despise your
religious festivals;
your assemblies are a
stench to me. Isa 1:11-16
[22] Even though you bring me
burnt offerings and
grain offerings,
I will not accept them. Ps 40:6
Though you bring choice
fellowship offerings,
I will have no regard for
them. Isa 66:3; Mic 6:6-7
[23] Away with the noise of your
songs!
I will not listen to the music
of your harps. Am 6:5
[24] But let justice roll on like a
river, Jer 22:3
righteousness like a never-
failing stream! Mic 6:8

[25] "Did you bring me sacrifices
and offerings Isa 43:23

forty years in the wilderness,
people of Israel?
[26] You have lifted up the shrine
of your king,
the pedestal of your idols,
the star of your god[a] —
which you made for
yourselves.
[27] Therefore I will send you
into exile beyond
Damascus,"
says the LORD, whose name
is God Almighty. Am 4:13

Woe to the Complacent

6 Woe to you who are
complacent in Zion,
and to you who feel secure
on Mount Samaria,
you notable men of the
foremost nation,
to whom the people of Israel
come! Isa 32:9-11
[2] Go to Kalneh and look at it;
go from there to great
Hamath, 2Ki 18:34
and then go down to Gath
in Philistia. 2Ch 26:6
Are they better off than your
two kingdoms? Na 3:8
Is their land larger than
yours?
[3] You put off the day of disaster
and bring near a reign of
terror. Isa 56:12; Am 9:10
[4] You lie on beds adorned with
ivory
and lounge on your couches.
You dine on choice lambs

---

[a] 26 Or *lifted up Sakkuth your king / and Kaiwan your idols, / your star-gods*; Septuagint
lifted up the shrine of Molek / and the star of your god Rephan, / their idols

and fattened calves. Eze 34:2-3
⁵You strum away on your
    harps like David Isa 5:12
and improvise on musical
    instruments. 1Ch 15:16
⁶You drink wine by the bowlful
    and use the finest lotions,
but you do not grieve over
    the ruin of Joseph. Eze 9:4
⁷Therefore you will be among
    the first to go into exile;
your feasting and lounging
    will end. Jer 16:9

The LORD Abhors the Pride of Israel

⁸The Sovereign LORD has sworn by himself—the LORD God Almighty declares: Ge 22:16

"I abhor the pride of Jacob
    and detest his fortresses;
I will deliver up the city Am 4:2
    and everything in it." Dt 32:19

⁹If ten people are left in one house, they too will die. ¹⁰And if the relative who comes to carry the bodies out of the house to burn them*ᵃ* asks anyone who might be hiding there, "Is anyone else with you?" and he says, "No," then he will go on to say, "Hush! We must not mention the name of the LORD." Am 5:3; 8:3

¹¹For the LORD has given the command,
    and he will smash the great house into pieces Am 3:15
and the small house into
    bits. Isa 55:11

¹²Do horses run on the rocky
    crags?
Does one plow the sea*ᵇ* with
    oxen?
But you have turned justice
    into poison Hos 10:4
and the fruit of
    righteousness into
    bitterness— Am 5:7
¹³you who rejoice in the
    conquest of Lo Debar*ᶜ*
and say, "Did we not take
    Karnaim*ᵈ* by our own
    strength?" Job 8:15
¹⁴For the LORD God Almighty
    declares,
"I will stir up a nation
    against you, Israel, Jer 5:15
that will oppress you all the
    way
    from Lebo Hamath to the
    valley of the Arabah."

Locusts, Fire and a Plumb Line

7 This is what the Sovereign LORD showed me: He was preparing swarms of locusts after the king's share had been harvested and just as the late crops were coming up. ²When they had stripped the land clean, I cried out, "Sovereign LORD, forgive! How can Jacob survive? He is so small!" Isa 37:4; Eze 11:13

³So the LORD relented.

ᵃ 10 Or *to make a funeral fire in honor of the dead*   *ᵇ 12* With a different word division of the Hebrew; Masoretic Text *plow there* *ᶜ 13* *Lo Debar* means *nothing.* *ᵈ 13* *Karnaim* means *horns; horn* here symbolizes strength.

"This will not happen," the LORD said.   Hos 11:8

⁴This is what the Sovereign LORD showed me: The Sovereign LORD was calling for judgment by fire; it dried up the great deep and devoured the land. ⁵Then I cried out, "Sovereign LORD, I beg you, stop! How can Jacob survive? He is so small!"   Joel 2:17

⁶So the LORD relented.   Jnh 3:10 "This will not happen either," the Sovereign LORD said.   Eze 9:8

⁷This is what he showed me: The Lord was standing by a wall that had been built true to plumb,ᵃ with a plumb lineᵇ in his hand. ⁸And the LORD asked me, "What do you see, Amos?"

"A plumb line," I replied.

Then the Lord said, "Look, I am setting a plumb line among my people Israel; I will spare them no longer.   Jer 15:6; Eze 7:2-9

⁹ "The high places of Isaac will
    be destroyed
and the sanctuaries of Israel
    will be ruined;   Lev 26:31
with my sword I will rise
    against the house of
    Jeroboam."   2Ki 15:9

Amos and Amaziah

¹⁰Then Amaziah the priest of Bethel sent a message to Jeroboam king of Israel: "Amos is raising a conspiracy against you in the very heart of Israel. The land cannot bear all his words. ¹¹For this is what Amos is saying: 1Ki 12:32

" 'Jeroboam will die by the
    sword,
  and Israel will surely go into
    exile,   Am 5:27
  away from their native land.' "

¹²Then Amaziah said to Amos, "Get out, you seer! Go back to the land of Judah. Earn your bread there and do your prophesying there. ¹³Don't prophesy anymore at Bethel, because this is the king's sanctuary and the temple of the kingdom."   Am 2:12; Ac 4:18

¹⁴Amos answered Amaziah, "I was neither a prophet nor the son of a prophet, but I was a shepherd, and I also took care of sycamore-fig trees. ¹⁵But the LORD took me from tending the flock and said to me, 'Go, prophesy to my people Israel.' ¹⁶Now then, hear the word of the LORD. You say,   2Ki 2:5; Eze 2:3-4

" 'Do not prophesy against
    Israel,   Eze 20:46; Mic 2:6
  and stop preaching against
    the descendants of
    Isaac.'

¹⁷"Therefore this is what the LORD says:

" 'Your wife will become a
    prostitute in the city,
  and your sons and daughters
    will fall by the sword.

ᵃ 7 The meaning of the Hebrew for this phrase is uncertain.   ᵇ 7 The meaning of the Hebrew for this phrase is uncertain; also in verse 8.

Your land will be measured
    and divided up,
and you yourself will die in
    a pagan*a* country.
And Israel will surely go into
    exile,
    away from their native
    land.'" Eze 4:13; Hos 9:3

A Basket of Ripe Fruit

8 This is what the Sovereign
LORD showed me: a basket
of ripe fruit. 2 "What do you see,
Amos?" he asked. Am 7:8

"A basket of ripe fruit," I answered. Ge 40:16

Then the LORD said to me,
"The time is ripe for my people
Israel; I will spare them no longer. Eze 7:2-9
3 "In that day," declares the
Sovereign LORD, "the songs in
the temple will turn to wailing.*b*
Many, many bodies—flung everywhere! Silence!" Am 5:16; 6:10

4 Hear this, you who trample
    the needy
    and do away with the poor
    of the land, Ps 14:4; Pr 30:14

5 saying,

"When will the New Moon be
    over
that we may sell grain,
and the Sabbath be ended
    that we may market
    wheat?" —
skimping on the measure,
    boosting the price

and cheating with
    dishonest scales,
6 buying the poor with silver
and the needy for a pair of
    sandals,
selling even the sweepings
    with the wheat. Am 2:6

7 The LORD has sworn by himself, the Pride of Jacob: "I will
never forget anything they have
done. Hos 8:13; Am 6:8

8 "Will not the land tremble for
    this, Hos 4:3
    and all who live in it
    mourn?
The whole land will rise like
    the Nile;
it will be stirred up and
    then sink
    like the river of Egypt. Jer 46:8

9 "In that day," declares the
Sovereign LORD,

"I will make the sun go down
    at noon
    and darken the earth in
    broad daylight. Jer 15:9
10 I will turn your religious
    festivals into mourning
    and all your singing into
    weeping.
I will make all of you wear
    sackcloth Jer 48:37
and shave your heads.
I will make that time like
    mourning for an only
    son Jer 6:26; Zec 12:10
and the end of it like a bitter
    day. Eze 7:18

a 17 Hebrew *an unclean*   *b* 3 Or *"the temple singers will wail*

[11] "The days are coming,"
        declares the Sovereign
        LORD,   1Sa 3:1; 2Ch 15:3
"when I will send a famine
        through the land —
not a famine of food or a thirst
        for water,
    but a famine of hearing the
        words of the LORD.
[12] People will stagger from sea to
        sea
    and wander from north to
        east,
searching for the word of the
        LORD,
    but they will not find it.

[13] "In that day

"the lovely young women and
        strong young men
    will faint because of thirst.
[14] Those who swear by the sin of
        Samaria —
who say, 'As surely as your
        god lives, Dan,'   1Ki 12:29
or, 'As surely as the god[a] of
        Beersheba lives' —
they will fall, never to rise
        again."   Am 5:2

Israel to Be Destroyed

9 I saw the Lord standing by
    the altar, and he said:

"Strike the tops of the pillars
        so that the thresholds
        shake.
Bring them down on the
        heads of all the people;

those who are left I will kill
        with the sword.
Not one will get away,
        none will escape.
[2] Though they dig down to the
        depths below,   Ps 139:8
    from there my hand will
        take them.
Though they climb up to the
        heavens above,   Jer 51:53
    from there I will bring them
        down.   Ob 4
[3] Though they hide themselves
        on the top of Carmel,
there I will hunt them down
        and seize them. Ps 139:8-10
Though they hide from my
        eyes at the bottom of
        the sea,
there I will command the
        serpent to bite them.
[4] Though they are driven into
        exile by their enemies,
there I will command the
        sword to slay them.

"I will keep my eye on them
        for harm and not for good."

[5] The Lord, the LORD Almighty —
he touches the earth and it
        melts,   Ps 46:2; Mic 1:4
    and all who live in it mourn;
the whole land rises like the Nile,
    then sinks like the river of
        Egypt;   Am 8:8
[6] he builds his lofty palace[b] in
        the heavens
    and sets its foundation[c] on
        the earth;

---

[a] 14 Hebrew *the way*   [b] 6 The meaning of the Hebrew for this phrase is uncertain.
[c] 6 The meaning of the Hebrew for this word is uncertain.

he calls for the waters of the
    sea
  and pours them out over
    the face of the land —
  the LORD is his name.

7 "Are not you Israelites
  the same to me as the
    Cushites*a*?"   Isa 20:4; 43:3
        declares the LORD.
"Did I not bring Israel up from
    Egypt,
  the Philistines from Caphtor*b*
  and the Arameans from Kir?

8 "Surely the eyes of the
    Sovereign LORD
  are on the sinful kingdom.
I will destroy it
  from the face of the earth.
Yet I will not totally destroy
  the descendants of Jacob,"
        declares the LORD.
9 "For I will give the command,
  and I will shake the people
    of Israel
  among all the nations
as grain is shaken in a sieve,
  and not a pebble will reach
    the ground.
10 All the sinners among my
    people
  will die by the sword,
all those who say,
  'Disaster will not overtake
    or meet us.'   Am 6:3

Israel's Restoration

11 "In that day

"I will restore David's fallen
    shelter —   Isa 7:2
I will repair its broken walls
  and restore its ruins — Ps 53:6
  and will rebuild it as it used
    to be,   Ps 80:12
12 so that they may possess the
  remnant of Edom Nu 24:18
  and all the nations that bear
    my name,*c*"   Isa 43:7
        declares the LORD,
  who will do these things.

13 "The days are coming," declares the LORD,

"when the reaper will be
  overtaken by the
    plowman   Lev 26:5
  and the planter by the one
    treading grapes.
New wine will drip from the
    mountains
  and flow from all the hills,
14 and I will bring my people
    Israel back from exile.*d*

"They will rebuild the ruined
  cities and live in them.
They will plant vineyards
  and drink their wine;
  they will make gardens and
    eat their fruit.   Jer 30:18
15 I will plant Israel in their own
    land,   Isa 60:21
  never again to be uprooted
  from the land I have given
    them,"   Isa 65:9
  says the LORD your God.

a 7 That is, people from the upper Nile region   *b* 7 That is, Crete   *c* 12 Hebrew;
Septuagint *so that the remnant of people / and all the nations that bear my name may seek me*
d 14 Or *will restore the fortunes of my people Israel*

Obadiah

Obadiah's Vision

1-4pp — Jer 49:14-16
5-6pp — Jer 49:9-10

¹ The vision of Obadiah.

This is what the Sovereign
LORD says about Edom — Jer 49:7-22

We have heard a message
from the LORD:
An envoy was sent to the
nations to say,   Isa 18:2
"Rise, let us go against her for
battle" —   Jer 6:4-5

² "See, I will make you small
among the nations;
you will be utterly despised.
³ The pride of your heart has
deceived you,   Isa 16:6
you who live in the clefts of
the rocks*a*
and make your home on the
heights,
you who say to yourself,
'Who can bring me down to
the ground?'   Isa 14:13-15
⁴ Though you soar like the eagle
and make your nest among
the stars,   Hab 2:9

from there I will bring you
down,"   Jer 49:14-16; Isa 14:13
declares the LORD.
⁵ "If thieves came to you,
if robbers in the night —
oh, what a disaster awaits
you! —
would they not steal only
as much as they
wanted?
If grape pickers came to you,
would they not leave a few
grapes?   Jer 49:9-10
⁶ But how Esau will be
ransacked,
his hidden treasures
pillaged!
⁷ All your allies will force you to
the border;   Jer 30:14
your friends will deceive
and overpower you;
those who eat your bread will
set a trap for you,*b* Ps 41:9
but you will not detect it.

⁸ "In that day," declares the
LORD,
"will I not destroy the wise
men of Edom,   Job 5:12

---

a 3 Or *of Sela*   *b* 7 The meaning of the Hebrew for this clause is uncertain.

those of understanding in the mountains of Esau?

⁹Your warriors, Teman, will be terrified,   Ge 36:11,34

and everyone in Esau's mountains

will be cut down in the slaughter.

¹⁰Because of the violence against your brother Jacob,   Joel 3:19; Am 1:11-12

you will be covered with shame;

you will be destroyed forever.   Eze 35:9

¹¹On the day you stood aloof while strangers carried off his wealth

and foreigners entered his gates

and cast lots for Jerusalem,   Na 3:10

you were like one of them.

¹²You should not gloat over your brother   Pr 24:17

in the day of his misfortune,   Job 31:29

nor rejoice over the people of Judah   Eze 35:15

in the day of their destruction,   Pr 17:5

nor boast so much   Ps 137:7

in the day of their trouble.   Mic 4:11

¹³You should not march through the gates of my people

in the day of their disaster,

nor gloat over them in their calamity   Eze 35:5

in the day of their disaster,

nor seize their wealth

in the day of their disaster.

¹⁴You should not wait at the crossroads

to cut down their fugitives,

nor hand over their survivors

in the day of their trouble.

¹⁵"The day of the LORD is near   Eze 30:3

for all nations.

As you have done, it will be done to you;

your deeds will return upon your own head.   Jer 50:29

¹⁶Just as you drank on my holy hill,

so all the nations will drink continually;   Jer 25:15; 49:12

they will drink and drink

and be as if they had never been.

¹⁷But on Mount Zion will be deliverance;   Am 9:11-15

it will be holy,   Isa 4:3

and Jacob will possess his inheritance.   Zec 8:12

¹⁸Jacob will be a fire

and Joseph a flame;

Esau will be stubble,

and they will set him on fire and destroy him.   Zec 12:6

There will be no survivors from Esau."

The LORD has spoken.

¹⁹People from the Negev will occupy

the mountains of Esau,

and people from the foothills will possess

the land of the Philistines.

They will occupy the fields
of Ephraim and
Samaria,   Jer 31:5
and Benjamin will possess
Gilead.
²⁰This company of Israelite
exiles who are in
Canaan
will possess the land as far
as Zarephath;   1Ki 17:9-10

the exiles from Jerusalem who
are in Sepharad
will possess the towns of
the Negev.   Jer 33:13
²¹Deliverers will go up on^a
Mount Zion
to govern the mountains of
Esau.
And the kingdom will be
the LORD's.   Zec 14:9,16

^a 21 Or *from*

Jonah

Jonah Flees From the LORD

1 The word of the LORD came to Jonah son of Amittai: ² "Go to the great city of Nineveh and preach against it, because its wickedness has come up before me." Ge 10:11; Mt 12:39-41

³ But Jonah ran away from the LORD and headed for Tarshish. He went down to Joppa, where he found a ship bound for that port. After paying the fare, he went aboard and sailed for Tarshish to flee from the LORD. Jos 19:46

⁴ Then the LORD sent a great wind on the sea, and such a violent storm arose that the ship threatened to break up. ⁵ All the sailors were afraid and each cried out to his own god. And they threw the cargo into the sea to lighten the ship. Ps 107:23-26

But Jonah had gone below deck, where he lay down and fell into a deep sleep. ⁶ The captain went to him and said, "How can you sleep? Get up and call on your god! Maybe he will take notice of us so that we will not perish." Jnh 3:8; Ps 107:28

⁷ Then the sailors said to each other, "Come, let us cast lots to find out who is responsible for this calamity." They cast lots and the lot fell on Jonah. ⁸ So they asked him, "Tell us, who is responsible for making all this trouble for us? What kind of work do you do? Where do you come from? What is your country? From what people are you?" Jos 7:10-18

⁹ He answered, "I am a Hebrew and I worship the LORD, the God of heaven, who made the sea and the dry land." Ps 146:6; Ac 17:24

¹⁰ This terrified them and they asked, "What have you done?" (They knew he was running away from the LORD, because he had already told them so.)

¹¹ The sea was getting rougher and rougher. So they asked him, "What should we do to you to make the sea calm down for us?"

¹² "Pick me up and throw me into the sea," he replied, "and it

will become calm. I know that it is my fault that this great storm has come upon you." 2Sa 24:17

13 Instead, the men did their best to row back to land. But they could not, for the sea grew even wilder than before. 14 Then they cried out to the LORD, "Please, LORD, do not let us die for taking this man's life. Do not hold us accountable for killing an innocent man, for you, LORD, have done as you pleased." 15 Then they took Jonah and threw him overboard, and the raging sea grew calm. 16 At this the men greatly feared the LORD, and they offered a sacrifice to the LORD and made vows to him. Lk 8:24; Dt 21:8

Jonah's Prayer

17 Now the LORD provided a huge fish to swallow Jonah, and Jonah was in the belly of the fish three days and three nights.

2 a 1 From inside the fish Jonah prayed to the LORD his God. 2 He said:

"In my distress I called to the
    LORD, Ps 18:6; 120:1
and he answered me.
From deep in the realm of the
    dead I called for help,
    and you listened to my cry.
3 You hurled me into the
    depths, Ps 88:6
into the very heart of the
    seas,

and the currents swirled
    about me;
all your waves and breakers
    swept over me. Ps 42:7
4 I said, 'I have been banished
    from your sight; Ps 31:22
yet I will look again
    toward your holy temple.'
5 The engulfing waters
    threatened me,b
the deep surrounded me;
seaweed was wrapped
    around my head. Ps 69:1-2
6 To the roots of the mountains
    I sank down;
the earth beneath barred
    me in forever.
But you, LORD my God,
    brought my life up from the
    pit. Ps 30:3
7 "When my life was ebbing
    away,
    I remembered you, LORD,
and my prayer rose to you,
    to your holy temple. Ps 18:6
8 "Those who cling to worthless
    idols 2Ki 17:15; Jer 10:8
    turn away from God's love
    for them.
9 But I, with shouts of grateful
    praise,
    will sacrifice to you. Ps 50:14,23
What I have vowed I will
    make good. Ecc 5:4-5
I will say, 'Salvation comes
    from the LORD.'" Ps 3:8
10 And the LORD commanded

a In Hebrew texts 2:1 is numbered 1:17, and 2:1-10 is numbered 2:2-11.   b 5 Or waters were at my throat the fish, and it vomited Jonah onto dry land.

Jonah Goes to Nineveh

3 Then the word of the LORD came to Jonah a second time: ² "Go to the great city of Nineveh and proclaim to it the message I give you." Jnh 1:1

³ Jonah obeyed the word of the LORD and went to Nineveh. Now Nineveh was a very large city; it took three days to go through it. ⁴ Jonah began by going a day's journey into the city, proclaiming, "Forty more days and Nineveh will be overthrown." ⁵ The Ninevites believed God. A fast was proclaimed, and all of them, from the greatest to the least, put on sackcloth. Da 9:3; Lk 11:32

⁶ When Jonah's warning reached the king of Nineveh, he rose from his throne, took off his royal robes, covered himself with sackcloth and sat down in the dust. ⁷ This is the proclamation he issued in Nineveh: Job 2:8,13

"By the decree of the king and his nobles:

Do not let people or animals, herds or flocks, taste anything; do not let them eat or drink. ⁸ But let people and animals be covered with sackcloth. Let everyone call urgently on God. Let them give up their evil ways and their violence. ⁹ Who knows?

God may yet relent and with compassion turn from his fierce anger so that we will not perish." Joel 2:14; Jnh 1:6

¹⁰ When God saw what they did and how they turned from their evil ways, he relented and did not bring on them the destruction he had threatened. Jer 18:8

Jonah's Anger at the LORD's Compassion

4 But to Jonah this seemed very wrong, and he became angry. ² He prayed to the LORD, "Isn't this what I said, LORD, when I was still at home? That is what I tried to forestall by fleeing to Tarshish. I knew that you are a gracious and compassionate God, slow to anger and abounding in love, a God who relents from sending calamity. ³ Now, LORD, take away my life, for it is better for me to die than to live." 1Ki 19:4; Ps 86:5,15

⁴ But the LORD replied, "Is it right for you to be angry?"

⁵ Jonah had gone out and sat down at a place east of the city. There he made himself a shelter, sat in its shade and waited to see what would happen to the city. ⁶ Then the LORD God provided a leafy plant*a* and made it grow up over Jonah to give shade for his head to ease his discomfort, and Jonah was very happy about the plant. ⁷ But at dawn the next day God provided a worm, which

---

a 6 The precise identification of this plant is uncertain; also in verses 7, 9 and 10.

chewed the plant so that it withered. ⁸When the sun rose, God provided a scorching east wind, and the sun blazed on Jonah's head so that he grew faint. He wanted to die, and said, "It would be better for me to die than to live."

⁹But God said to Jonah, "Is it right for you to be angry about the plant?"

"It is," he said. "And I'm so angry I wish I were dead."

¹⁰But the LORD said, "You have been concerned about this plant, though you did not tend it or make it grow. It sprang up overnight and died overnight. ¹¹And should I not have concern for the great city of Nineveh, in which there are more than a hundred and twenty thousand people who cannot tell their right hand from their left — and also many animals?"

Jnh 1:2; 3:10

Micah

1 The word of the LORD that came to Micah of Moresheth during the reigns of Jotham, Ahaz and Hezekiah, kings of Judah — the vision he saw concerning Samaria and Jerusalem.

² Hear, you peoples, all of you,
    listen, earth and all who
        live in it,   Jer 6:19
    that the Sovereign LORD may
        bear witness against
        you,   Dt 4:26
    the Lord from his holy temple.

Judgment Against Samaria and Jerusalem

³ Look! The LORD is coming
        from his dwelling place;
    he comes down and treads
        on the heights of the
        earth.   Am 4:13
⁴ The mountains melt beneath
        him   Ps 46:2,6
    and the valleys split apart,
    like wax before the fire,
        like water rushing down a
        slope.
⁵ All this is because of Jacob's
        transgression,
    because of the sins of the
        people of Israel.
    What is Jacob's transgression?
        Is it not Samaria?   Am 8:14
    What is Judah's high place?
        Is it not Jerusalem?

⁶ "Therefore I will make Samaria
        a heap of rubble,
    a place for planting
        vineyards.
    I will pour her stones into the
        valley   Am 5:11
    and lay bare her
        foundations.   Eze 13:14
⁷ All her idols will be broken to
        pieces;   Eze 6:6
    all her temple gifts will be
        burned with fire;
    I will destroy all her images.
    Since she gathered her gifts
        from the wages of
        prostitutes,   Dt 23:17-18
    as the wages of prostitutes
        they will again be
        used."

Weeping and Mourning

⁸ Because of this I will weep
        and wail;   Isa 15:3

I will go about barefoot and
 naked.
I will howl like a jackal
 and moan like an owl.
⁹For Samaria's plague is
 incurable;   Jer 46:11
 it has spread to Judah.
It has reached the very gate of
 my people,   Isa 3:26
 even to Jerusalem itself.
¹⁰Tell it not in Gath*a*;
 weep not at all.
In Beth Ophrah*b*
 roll in the dust.
¹¹Pass by naked and in shame,
 you who live in Shaphir.*c*
Those who live in Zaanan*d*
 will not come out.
Beth Ezel is in mourning;
 it no longer protects you.
¹²Those who live in Maroth*e*
 writhe in pain,
 waiting for relief,   Jer 14:19
because disaster has come
 from the LORD,   Jer 40:2
 even to the gate of
 Jerusalem.
¹³You who live in Lachish, Jos 10:3
 harness fast horses to the
 chariot.
You are where the sin of
 Daughter Zion began,
 for the transgressions of
 Israel were found in
 you.
¹⁴Therefore you will give
 parting gifts   2Ki 16:8

to Moresheth Gath.
The town of Akzib*f* will prove
 deceptive Jos 15:44; Jer 15:18
 to the kings of Israel.
¹⁵I will bring a conqueror
 against you
 who live in Mareshah.*g*
The nobles of Israel
 will flee to Adullam. Jos 12:15
¹⁶Shave your head in mourning
 for the children in whom
 you delight;
make yourself as bald as the
 vulture,
 for they will go from you
 into exile.   Am 5:27

Human Plans and God's Plans

2 Woe to those who plan
 iniquity,
 to those who plot evil on
 their beds!   Ps 36:4
At morning's light they carry
 it out
 because it is in their power
 to do it.
²They covet fields and seize
 them,   Isa 5:8
 and houses, and take them.
They defraud people of their
 homes,   Jer 22:17
 they rob them of their
 inheritance.   Eze 46:18

³Therefore, the LORD says:

"I am planning disaster
 against this people,

---

a 10 Gath sounds like the Hebrew for *tell.*   *b 10 Beth Ophrah* means *house of dust.*
c 11 Shaphir means *pleasant.*   *d 11 Zaanan* sounds like the Hebrew for *come out.*
e 12 Maroth sounds like the Hebrew for *bitter.*   *f 14 Akzib* means *deception.*
g 15 Mareshah sounds like the Hebrew for *conqueror.*

from which you cannot save
yourselves.
You will no longer walk
proudly, Isa 2:12
for it will be a time of
calamity.
⁴In that day people will
ridicule you;
they will taunt you with this
mournful song:
'We are utterly ruined; Jer 4:13
my people's possession is
divided up.
He takes it from me!
He assigns our fields to
traitors.'"

⁵Therefore you will have no
one in the assembly of
the LORD
to divide the land by lot.

False Prophets

⁶"Do not prophesy," their
prophets say.
"Do not prophesy about
these things;
disgrace will not overtake
us." Am 2:12; Mic 6:16
⁷You descendants of Jacob,
should it be said,
"Does the LORD becomeᵃ
impatient?
Does he do such things?"

"Do not my words do good
to the one whose ways are
upright? Ps 15:2; 84:11
⁸Lately my people have
risen up
like an enemy.

You strip off the rich robe
from those who pass by
without a care,
like men returning from
battle.
⁹You drive the women of my
people
from their pleasant
homes. Jer 10:20
You take away my blessing
from their children forever.
¹⁰Get up, go away!
For this is not your resting
place, Dt 12:9
because it is defiled, Lev 18:25-29
it is ruined, beyond all
remedy.
¹¹If a liar and deceiver comes
and says, Jer 5:31
'I will prophesy for you
plenty of wine and beer,'
that would be just the
prophet for this people!

Deliverance Promised

¹²"I will surely gather all of you,
Jacob;
I will surely bring together
the remnant of
Israel. Mic 4:7; 5:7; 7:18
I will bring them together like
sheep in a pen,
like a flock in its pasture;
the place will throng with
people.
¹³The One who breaks open the
way will go up before
them; Isa 52:12
they will break through the
gate and go out.

ᵃ 7 Or *Is the Spirit of the LORD*

Their King will pass through
  before them,
    the LORD at their head."

Leaders and Prophets Rebuked

3 Then I said,

"Listen, you leaders of Jacob,
    you rulers of Israel.
  Should you not embrace
      justice,
2   you who hate good and love
        evil;
  who tear the skin from my
      people
    and the flesh from their
        bones;   Ps 53:4; Eze 22:27
3 who eat my people's flesh,
    strip off their skin
    and break their bones in
        pieces;   Zep 3:3
  who chop them up like meat
      for the pan,   Job 24:14
    like flesh for the pot?" Eze 11:7

4 Then they will cry out to the
      LORD,
    but he will not answer
        them.   Ps 18:41; Isa 1:15
  At that time he will hide his
      face from them   Dt 31:17
    because of the evil they
        have done.   Eze 8:18

5 This is what the LORD says:

"As for the prophets
    who lead my people
        astray,
  they proclaim 'peace'   Jer 4:10
    if they have something to
        eat,

but prepare to wage war
    against anyone
  who refuses to feed them.
6 Therefore night will come
    over you, without
        visions,
  and darkness, without
      divination.   Isa 8:19-22
The sun will set for the
    prophets,   Isa 29:10
  and the day will go dark for
      them.   Eze 7:26
7 The seers will be ashamed
    and the diviners disgraced.
  They will all cover their faces
    because there is no answer
        from God."   Eze 20:3
8 But as for me, I am filled with
      power,
  with the Spirit of the LORD,
    and with justice and might,
  to declare to Jacob his
      transgression,
    to Israel his sin.   Isa 58:1

9 Hear this, you leaders of
      Jacob,
    you rulers of Israel,
  who despise justice
    and distort all that is right;
10 who build Zion with
      bloodshed,   Jer 22:13
    and Jerusalem with
        wickedness.   Eze 22:27
11 Her leaders judge for a bribe,
    her priests teach for a price,
    and her prophets tell
        fortunes for money.
  Yet they look for the LORD's
      support and say,
    "Is not the LORD among us?

No disaster will come
upon us." Jer 7:4
¹²Therefore because of you,
Zion will be plowed like a
field,
Jerusalem will become a heap
of rubble, Jer 26:18
the temple hill a mound
overgrown with thickets.

The Mountain of the LORD

4:1-3pp — Isa 2:1-4

4 In the last days

the mountain of the LORD's
temple will be
established Zec 8:3
as the highest of the
mountains;
it will be exalted above the hills,
and peoples will stream to it.

²Many nations will come and
say,

"Come, let us go up to the
mountain of the LORD,
to the temple of the God of
Jacob. Zec 2:11; 14:16
He will teach us his ways,
so that we may walk in his
paths."
The law will go out from Zion,
the word of the LORD from
Jerusalem.
³He will judge between many
peoples
and will settle disputes for
strong nations far and
wide. Isa 11:4
They will beat their swords
into plowshares

and their spears into
pruning hooks. Joel 3:10
Nation will not take up sword
against nation,
nor will they train for war
anymore. Isa 2:1-4
⁴Everyone will sit under their
own vine
and under their own fig tree,
and no one will make them
afraid, Lev 26:6
for the LORD Almighty has
spoken. Isa 1:20; Zec 3:10
⁵All the nations may walk
in the name of their gods,
but we will walk in the name
of the LORD
our God for ever and ever.

The LORD's Plan

⁶"In that day," declares the
LORD,

"I will gather the lame;
I will assemble the exiles
and those I have brought to
grief. Eze 34:13,16; 37:21
⁷I will make the lame my
remnant, Mic 2:12
those driven away a strong
nation.
The LORD will rule over them
in Mount Zion
from that day and forever.
⁸As for you, watchtower of the
flock,
stronghold*a* of Daughter
Zion,
the former dominion will be
restored to you; Isa 1:26

a 8 Or hill

kingship will come to
  Daughter Jerusalem."

9 Why do you now cry aloud—
  have you no king[a]?   Jer 8:19
Has your ruler[b] perished,
  that pain seizes you like
    that of a woman in
    labor?   Jer 30:6
10 Writhe in agony, Daughter
  Zion,
  like a woman in labor,
for now you must leave the city
  to camp in the open field.
You will go to Babylon;   2Ki 20:18
  there you will be rescued.
There the LORD will redeem
  you   Isa 48:20
  out of the hand of your
    enemies.

11 But now many nations
  are gathered against you.
They say, "Let her be defiled,
  let our eyes gloat over Zion!"
12 But they do not know
  the thoughts of the LORD;
they do not understand his
  plan,   Isa 55:8; Ro 11:33-34
  that he has gathered them
    like sheaves to the
    threshing floor.
13 "Rise and thresh, Daughter
  Zion,
  for I will give you horns of
    iron;
I will give you hooves of
  bronze,
  and you will break to pieces
    many nations."   Da 2:44

You will devote their ill-gotten
  gains to the LORD,
  their wealth to the Lord of
    all the earth.

A Promised Ruler From Bethlehem

5 [c] Marshal your troops now,
    city of troops,
  for a siege is laid against us.
They will strike Israel's ruler
  on the cheek with a rod.

2 "But you, Bethlehem
    Ephrathah,   Jn 7:42; Ge 48:7
  though you are small
    among the clans[d] of
    Judah,
  out of you will come for me
    one who will be ruler over
    Israel,   1Sa 13:14
  whose origins are from of old,
    from ancient times."   Mt 2:6

3 Therefore Israel will be
    abandoned
  until the time when she
    who is in labor bears a
    son,
  and the rest of his brothers
    return
    to join the Israelites.

4 He will stand and shepherd
    his flock   Isa 40:11
  in the strength of the LORD,
  in the majesty of the name
    of the LORD his God.
And they will live securely, for
  then his greatness

---

[a] 9 Or *King*   [b] 9 Or *Ruler*   [c] In Hebrew texts 5:1 is numbered 4:14, and 5:2-15 is numbered 5:1-14.   [d] 2 Or *rulers*

will reach to the ends of the
earth.

⁵And he will be our peace   Isa 9:6
    when the Assyrians invade
        our land   Isa 8:7
    and march through our
        fortresses.
We will raise against them
        seven shepherds,
    even eight commanders,
⁶who will rule*ᵃ* the land of
        Assyria with the sword,
    the land of Nimrod with
        drawn sword.*ᵇ*   Ge 10:8
He will deliver us from the
        Assyrians
    when they invade our land
    and march across our
        borders.   Na 2:11-13

⁷The remnant of Jacob will be
    in the midst of many peoples
like dew from the LORD,   Ps 133:3
    like showers on the grass,
which do not wait for anyone
    or depend on man.
⁸The remnant of Jacob will be
        among the nations,
    in the midst of many peoples,
    like a lion among the beasts of
        the forest,   Ge 49:9
    like a young lion among
        flocks of sheep,
which mauls and mangles as
    it goes,   Mic 4:13; Zec 10:5
    and no one can rescue.
⁹Your hand will be lifted up
    in triumph over your
        enemies,   Ps 10:12

and all your foes will be
    destroyed.

¹⁰"In that day," declares the
LORD,
"I will destroy your horses
    from among you
    and demolish your chariots.
¹¹I will destroy the cities of your
        land   Isa 6:11
    and tear down all your
        strongholds.   Hos 10:14
¹²I will destroy your witchcraft
    and you will no longer cast
        spells.   Dt 18:10-12; Isa 2:6
¹³I will destroy your idols
    and your sacred stones from
        among you;
you will no longer bow down
    to the work of your hands.
¹⁴I will uproot from among you
        your Asherah poles*ᶜ*
    when I demolish your cities.
¹⁵I will take vengeance in anger
        and wrath   Isa 65:12
    on the nations that have not
        obeyed me."

The LORD's Case Against Israel

6 Listen to what the LORD says:

"Stand up, plead my case
        before the mountains;
    let the hills hear what you
        have to say.
²"Hear, you mountains,
        the LORD's
        accusation; Dt 32:1; Hos 12:2

ᵃ 6 Or *crush*   *ᵇ* 6 Or *Nimrod in its gates*   *ᶜ* 14 That is, wooden symbols of the goddess Asherah

listen, you everlasting
foundations of the
earth.
For the LORD has a case
against his people;
he is lodging a charge
against Israel.   Ps 50:7

3 "My people, what have I done
to you?
How have I burdened you?
Answer me.   Jer 2:5
4 I brought you up out of Egypt
and redeemed you from the
land of slavery.   Dt 7:8
I sent Moses to lead you, Ex 4:16
also Aaron and Miriam.
5 My people, remember
what Balak king of Moab
plotted   Nu 22:5-6
and what Balaam son of
Beor answered.
Remember your journey from
Shittim to Gilgal, Nu 25:1
that you may know the
righteous acts of the
LORD."   Jdg 5:11; 1Sa 12:7

6 With what shall I come before
the LORD
and bow down before the
exalted God?
Shall I come before him with
burnt offerings,
with calves a year old?
7 Will the LORD be pleased with
thousands of rams,
with ten thousand rivers of
olive oil?   Ps 50:8-10

Shall I offer my firstborn for
my transgression,
the fruit of my body for the
sin of my soul?   2Ki 16:3
8 He has shown you, O mortal,
what is good.
And what does the LORD
require of you?
To act justly and to love mercy
and to walk humbly[a] with
your God.   Dt 10:12-13

Israel's Guilt and Punishment

9 Listen! The LORD is calling to
the city—
and to fear your name is
wisdom—
"Heed the rod and the One
who appointed it.[b] Isa 11:4
10 Am I still to forget your ill-
gotten treasures, you
wicked house,
and the short ephah,[c] which
is accursed?   Eze 45:9-10
11 Shall I acquit someone with
dishonest scales, Lev 19:36
with a bag of false weights?
12 Your rich people are violent;
your inhabitants are liars
and their tongues speak
deceitfully.   Jer 9:3
13 Therefore, I have begun to
destroy you,   Isa 1:7; 6:11
to ruin[d] you because of your
sins.
14 You will eat but not be satisfied;
your stomach will still be
empty.[e]

a 8 Or *prudently*   b 9 The meaning of the Hebrew for this line is uncertain.
c 10 An ephah was a dry measure.   d 13 Or *Therefore, I will make you ill and destroy you; / I will ruin*   e 14 The meaning of the Hebrew for this word is uncertain.

You will store up but save
    nothing,   Isa 30:6
    because what you save*a* I
    will give to the sword.
15 You will plant but not harvest;
    you will press olives but not
    use the oil,
    you will crush grapes but
    not drink the wine.
16 You have observed the
    statutes of Omri   1Ki 16:25
    and all the practices of
    Ahab's house;   1Ki 16:29-33
    you have followed their
    traditions.   Jer 7:24
Therefore I will give you over
    to ruin   Jer 25:9
    and your people to derision;
    you will bear the scorn of
    the nations.*b"*   Jer 51:51

Israel's Misery

7 What misery is mine!
    I am like one who gathers
    summer fruit
    at the gleaning of the
    vineyard;
    there is no cluster of grapes to
    eat,
    none of the early figs that I
    crave.
2 The faithful have been swept
    from the land;   Ps 12:1
    not one upright person
    remains.   Jer 2:29
Everyone lies in wait to shed
    blood;   Mic 3:10
    they hunt each other with
    nets.   Jer 5:26

3 Both hands are skilled in
    doing evil;   Pr 4:16
    the ruler demands gifts,
    the judge accepts bribes,
    the powerful dictate what
    they desire —
    they all conspire together.
4 The best of them is like a brier,
    the most upright worse than
    a thorn hedge.   2Sa 23:6
The day God visits you has
    come,
    the day your watchmen
    sound the alarm.
Now is the time of your
    confusion.   Isa 22:5; Hos 9:7
5 Do not trust a neighbor;
    put no confidence in a
    friend.   Jer 9:4
Even with the woman who
    lies in your embrace
    guard the words of your lips.
6 For a son dishonors his father,
    a daughter rises up against
    her mother,   Eze 22:7
    a daughter-in-law against her
    mother-in-law —
    a man's enemies are the
    members of his own
    household.   Mt 10:35-36

7 But as for me, I watch in hope
    for the LORD,   Ps 130:5
    I wait for God my Savior;
    my God will hear me.   Ps 4:3

Israel Will Rise

8 Do not gloat over me, my
    enemy!   Pr 24:17

---

a 14 Or *You will press toward birth but not give birth, / and what you bring to birth*
b 16 Septuagint; Hebrew *scorn due my people*

Though I have fallen, I will
rise. Ps 37:24; Am 9:11
Though I sit in darkness,
the LORD will be my light.
⁹Because I have sinned against
him,
I will bear the LORD's wrath,
until he pleads my case
and upholds my cause.
He will bring me out into the
light;
I will see his righteousness.
¹⁰Then my enemy will see it
and will be covered with
shame, Ps 35:26
she who said to me,
"Where is the LORD your
God?"
My eyes will see her downfall;
even now she will be
trampled underfoot
like mire in the streets.

¹¹The day for building your
walls will come, Isa 54:11
the day for extending your
boundaries.
¹²In that day people will come
to you
from Assyria and the cities
of Egypt,
even from Egypt to the
Euphrates
and from sea to sea
and from mountain to
mountain. Isa 19:23-25
¹³The earth will become
desolate because of its
inhabitants,
as the result of their deeds.

Prayer and Praise

¹⁴Shepherd your people with
your staff, Ps 23:4; Mic 5:4
the flock of your
inheritance,
which lives by itself in a forest,
in fertile pasturelands.ᵃ
Let them feed in Bashan and
Gilead Jer 50:19
as in days long ago.

¹⁵"As in the days when you
came out of Egypt,
I will show them my
wonders." Ex 3:20; Ps 78:12

¹⁶Nations will see and be
ashamed, Isa 26:11
deprived of all their power.
They will put their hands over
their mouths
and their ears will become
deaf.
¹⁷They will lick dust like a snake,
like creatures that crawl on
the ground.
They will come trembling out
of their dens;
they will turn in fear to the
LORD our God Isa 49:23
and will be afraid of you.
¹⁸Who is a God like you,
who pardons sin and forgives
the transgression
of the remnant of his
inheritance? Ex 34:9
You do not stay angry forever
but delight to show mercy.
¹⁹You will again have
compassion on us;

ᵃ 14 Or in the middle of Carmel

you will tread our sins
    underfoot
and hurl all our iniquities
    into the depths of the
    sea.   Isa 43:25; Jer 31:34

20 You will be faithful to Jacob,
    and show love to Abraham,
as you pledged on oath to our
    ancestors   Dt 7:8; Lk 1:72
in days long ago.   Ps 108:4

MICAH 7:20 | 1475

²⁰You will be faithful to Jacob,
and show love to Abraham,
as you pledged on oath to our

in days long ago.

you will tread our sins
underfoot
and hurl all our iniquities
into the depths of the
sea
Isa 43:25; Jer 31:34

Nahum

1 A prophecy concerning Nineveh. The book of the vision
of Nahum the Elkoshite.   Jnh 1:2

The LORD's Anger Against Nineveh

²The LORD is a jealous and
avenging God;   Ex 20:5
the LORD takes vengeance
and is filled with wrath.
The LORD takes vengeance on
his foes
and vents his wrath against
his enemies.
³The LORD is slow to anger but
great in power;   Ne 9:17
the LORD will not leave the
guilty unpunished.
His way is in the whirlwind
and the storm,
and clouds are the dust of
his feet.   Ps 104:3
⁴He rebukes the sea and dries
it up;   Ex 14:22
he makes all the rivers run
dry.
Bashan and Carmel wither
and the blossoms of
Lebanon fade.

⁵The mountains quake before
him   Ex 19:18
and the hills melt away.
The earth trembles at his
presence,
the world and all who live
in it.   Eze 38:20
⁶Who can withstand his
indignation?   Ps 130:3
Who can endure his fierce
anger?   Mal 3:2
His wrath is poured out like
fire;   Jer 10:10
the rocks are shattered
before him.   1Ki 19:11

⁷The LORD is good,   Jer 33:11
a refuge in times of
trouble.
He cares for those who trust
in him,   Ps 1:6
⁸ but with an overwhelming
flood
he will make an end of
Nineveh;
he will pursue his foes into
the realm of darkness.

⁹Whatever they plot against
the LORD

he will bring[a] to an end;
  trouble will not come a
    second time.
10They will be entangled among
  thorns   2Sa 23:6
  and drunk from their wine;
  they will be consumed like
    dry stubble.[b]   Isa 5:24
11From you, Nineveh, has one
  come forth
  who plots evil against the
    Lord
  and devises wicked plans.

12This is what the Lord says:

"Although they have allies
  and are numerous,
  they will be destroyed and
    pass away.   Isa 10:34
Although I have afflicted you,
  Judah,
  I will afflict you no more.
13Now I will break their yoke
  from your neck   Isa 9:4
  and tear your shackles away."

14The Lord has given a
  command concerning
    you, Nineveh:
"You will have no
  descendants to bear
    your name.   Isa 14:22
I will destroy the images and
  idols   Mic 5:13
that are in the temple of
  your gods.
I will prepare your grave,
  for you are vile."

15Look, there on the mountains,
  the feet of one who brings
    good news,   Ro 10:15
  who proclaims peace! Isa 52:7
Celebrate your festivals, Judah,
  and fulfill your vows.
No more will the wicked
  invade you;   Isa 52:1
  they will be completely
    destroyed.[c]

Nineveh to Fall

2[d] An attacker advances
  against you, Nineveh.
Guard the fortress,
  watch the road,
  brace yourselves,
  marshal all your strength!

2The Lord will restore the
  splendor of Jacob Isa 60:15
  like the splendor of Israel,
though destroyers have laid
    them waste
  and have ruined their vines.

3The shields of the soldiers are
  red;
  the warriors are clad in
    scarlet.   Eze 23:14-15
The metal on the chariots
  flashes
  on the day they are made
    ready;
  the spears of juniper are
    brandished.[e]
4The chariots storm through
  the streets,   Jer 4:13

---

[a] 9 Or *What do you foes plot against the Lord? / He will bring it*   [b] 10 The meaning of the Hebrew for this verse is uncertain.   [c] 15 In Hebrew texts this verse (1:15) is numbered 2:1. [d] In Hebrew texts 2:1-13 is numbered 2:2-14.   [e] 3 Hebrew; Septuagint and Syriac *ready; / the horsemen rush to and fro.*

rushing back and forth
    through the squares.
They look like flaming
    torches;
they dart about like
    lightning.

⁵ Nineveh summons her picked
    troops,
    yet they stumble on their
      way.   Jer 46:12
They dash to the city wall;
    the protective shield is put
      in place.
⁶ The river gates are thrown
    open   Na 3:13
    and the palace collapses.
⁷ It is decreed*ᵃ* that Nineveh
    be exiled and carried away.
Her female slaves moan like
    doves   Isa 59:11
    and beat on their breasts.
⁸ Nineveh is like a pool
    whose water is draining
      away.
"Stop! Stop!" they cry,
    but no one turns back.
⁹ Plunder the silver!
    Plunder the gold!
The supply is endless,
    the wealth from all its
      treasures!
¹⁰ She is pillaged, plundered,
    stripped!
Hearts melt, knees give way,
    bodies tremble, every face
      grows pale.   Isa 29:22

¹¹ Where now is the lions' den,
    the place where they fed
      their young,
where the lion and lioness
    went,
    and the cubs, with nothing
      to fear?
¹² The lion killed enough for his
    cubs   Jer 51:34
    and strangled the prey for
      his mate,
filling his lairs with the kill
    and his dens with the prey.

¹³ "I am against you,"   Jer 21:13
    declares the Lᴏʀᴅ
    Almighty.
"I will burn up your chariots
    in smoke,   Ps 46:9
    and the sword will devour
      your young lions.
I will leave you no prey on
    the earth.
The voices of your messengers
    will no longer be heard."

Woe to Nineveh

3 Woe to the city of blood,
    full of lies,   Ps 12:2
    full of plunder,
    never without victims!
² The crack of whips,
    the clatter of wheels,
galloping horses
    and jolting chariots!
³ Charging cavalry,
    flashing swords
    and glittering spears!
Many casualties,
    piles of dead,
bodies without number,
    people stumbling over the
      corpses — 2Ki 19:35; Isa 34:3

ᵃ 7 The meaning of the Hebrew for this word is uncertain.

4all because of the wanton lust
  of a prostitute,
  alluring, the mistress of
  sorceries,   Isa 47:9
who enslaved nations by her
  prostitution   Isa 23:17
and peoples by her
  witchcraft.

5"I am against you," declares
  the LORD Almighty.
"I will lift your skirts over
  your face.   Jer 13:22
I will show the nations your
  nakedness   Isa 47:3
and the kingdoms your
  shame.
6I will pelt you with filth, Job 9:31
  I will treat you with
  contempt   Jer 51:37
and make you a spectacle.
7All who see you will flee from
  you and say,   Isa 13:14
  'Nineveh is in ruins — who
  will mourn for her?'
Where can I find anyone to
  comfort you?"   Isa 51:19

8Are you better than Thebes,
  situated on the Nile, Isa 19:6-9
  with water around her?
The river was her defense,
  the waters her wall.
9Cush*a* and Egypt were her
  boundless strength;
Put and Libya were among
  her allies.   Eze 27:10; 30:5
10Yet she was taken captive
  and went into exile.
Her infants were dashed to
  pieces   Isa 13:16; Hos 13:16

at every street corner.
Lots were cast for her
  nobles,   Job 6:27
and all her great men were
  put in chains.   Jer 40:1
11You too will become drunk;
  you will go into hiding Isa 2:10
and seek refuge from the
  enemy.

12All your fortresses are like fig
  trees
with their first ripe fruit;
  when they are shaken,
  the figs fall into the mouth
  of the eater.   Isa 28:4
13Look at your troops —
  they are all weaklings.
The gates of your land   Na 2:6
  are wide open to your
  enemies;
  fire has consumed the bars
  of your gates.   Isa 45:2

14Draw water for the siege,
  strengthen your
  defenses!   Na 2:1
Work the clay,
  tread the mortar,
  repair the brickwork!
15There the fire will consume
  you;
  the sword will cut you
  down —
  they will devour you like a
  swarm of locusts.
Multiply like grasshoppers,
  multiply like locusts! Joel 1:4
16You have increased the
  number of your
  merchants

---

a 9 That is, the upper Nile region

till they are more numerous
than the stars in the
sky,
but like locusts they strip the
land   Ex 10:13
and then fly away.
¹⁷Your guards are like locusts,
your officials like swarms of
locusts
that settle in the walls on a
cold day —
but when the sun appears
they fly away,
and no one knows where.

¹⁸King of Assyria, your
shepherds^a slumber;
your nobles lie down to
rest.
Your people are scattered on
the mountains   1Ki 22:17
with no one to gather them.
¹⁹Nothing can heal you;   Mic 1:9
your wound is fatal.
All who hear the news about
you
clap their hands at your fall,
for who has not felt
your endless cruelty?   Isa 37:18

^a 18 That is, rulers

Habakkuk

1 The prophecy that Habakkuk the prophet received.

Habakkuk's Complaint

²How long, LORD, must I call
  for help,
  but you do not listen? Ps 13:1-2
Or cry out to you, "Violence!"
  but you do not save?   Jer 14:9
³Why do you make me look at
  injustice?
Why do you tolerate
  wrongdoing?   Job 9:23
Destruction and violence are
  before me;   Jer 20:8
there is strife, and conflict
  abounds.   Ps 55:9
⁴Therefore the law is
  paralyzed,   Ps 119:126
and justice never prevails.
The wicked hem in the
  righteous,
  so that justice is perverted.

The LORD's Answer

⁵"Look at the nations and
  watch —
  and be utterly amazed.
For I am going to do
  something in your days
that you would not believe,
  even if you were told.   Ac 13:41
⁶I am raising up the
  Babylonians,ᵃ   2Ki 24:2
that ruthless and
  impetuous people,
who sweep across the whole
  earth
to seize dwellings not their
  own.   Jer 13:20
⁷They are a feared and dreaded
  people;   Isa 18:7; Jer 39:5-9
they are a law to themselves
and promote their own
  honor.
⁸Their horses are swifter than
  leopards,   Jer 4:13
fiercer than wolves at dusk.
Their cavalry gallops
  headlong;
their horsemen come from
  afar.
They fly like an eagle
  swooping to devour;
⁹ they all come intent on
  violence.

ᵃ 6 Or *Chaldeans*

Their hordes[a] advance like a
    desert wind
  and gather prisoners like
    sand.   Hab 2:5
10 They mock kings
  and scoff at rulers.   2Ch 36:6
  They laugh at all fortified cities;
  by building earthen ramps
    they capture them.
11 Then they sweep past like the
    wind and go on —
  guilty people, whose own
    strength is their god."

Habakkuk's Second Complaint

12 Lord, are you not from
    everlasting?   Ge 21:33
  My God, my Holy One, you[b]
    will never die.   Isa 31:1
  You, Lord, have appointed
    them to execute
    judgment;   Isa 10:6
  you, my Rock, have
    ordained them to
    punish.   Ex 33:22
13 Your eyes are too pure to look
    on evil;   Ps 18:26
  you cannot tolerate
    wrongdoing.   La 3:34-36
  Why then do you tolerate the
    treacherous?   Ps 25:3
  Why are you silent while the
    wicked
  swallow up those more
    righteous than
    themselves?   Job 21:7
14 You have made people like the
    fish in the sea,

like the sea creatures that
    have no ruler.
15 The wicked foe pulls all of
    them up with hooks,
  he catches them in his net,
  he gathers them up in his
    dragnet;
  and so he rejoices and is
    glad.
16 Therefore he sacrifices to his
    net
  and burns incense to his
    dragnet,   Jer 44:8
  for by his net he lives in
    luxury
  and enjoys the choicest
    food.
17 Is he to keep on emptying his
    net,
  destroying nations without
    mercy?   Isa 14:6; 19:8

2 I will stand at my watch
  and station myself on the
    ramparts;   Ps 48:13
  I will look to see what he will
    say to me,   Ps 85:8
  and what answer I am to
    give to this complaint.[c]

The Lord's Answer

2 Then the Lord replied:

"Write down the revelation
  and make it plain on tablets
  so that a herald[d] may run
    with it.
3 For the revelation awaits an
    appointed time;   Da 11:27

---

a 9 The meaning of the Hebrew for this word is uncertain.   b 12 An ancient Hebrew
scribal tradition; Masoretic Text we   c 1 Or and what to answer when I am rebuked
d 2 Or so that whoever reads it

it speaks of the end   Da 8:17
and will not prove false.
Though it linger, wait for it;
   it[a] will certainly come
and will not delay.   Eze 12:25

4 "See, the enemy is puffed up;
   his desires are not
      upright —
but the righteous person
   will live by his
   faithfulness[b] —   Ro 1:17
5 indeed, wine betrays him;
   he is arrogant and never at
      rest.   Isa 2:11
Because he is as greedy as the
      grave
and like death is never
      satisfied,   Pr 27:20; 30:15-16
he gathers to himself all the
      nations
and takes captive all the
      peoples.   Hab 1:9

6 "Will not all of them taunt
him with ridicule and scorn, saying,   Isa 14:4

" 'Woe to him who piles up
      stolen goods
and makes himself wealthy
   by extortion!   Am 2:8
How long must this go on?'
7 Will not your creditors
   suddenly arise?
Will they not wake up and
   make you tremble?
Then you will become their
   prey.   Pr 29:1
8 Because you have plundered
   many nations,

the peoples who are left will
   plunder you.   Isa 33:1
For you have shed human
   blood;
you have destroyed lands
   and cities and everyone
   in them.   Eze 39:10

9 "Woe to him who builds his
   house by unjust gain,
setting his nest on high
   to escape the clutches of ruin!
10 You have plotted the ruin of
   many peoples,   Jer 26:19
shaming your own house
   and forfeiting your life.
11 The stones of the wall will cry
   out,   Jos 24:27; Lk 19:40
and the beams of the
   woodwork will echo it.

12 "Woe to him who builds a city
   with bloodshed   Mic 3:10
and establishes a town by
   injustice!
13 Has not the LORD Almighty
   determined
that the people's labor is
   only fuel for the fire,
that the nations exhaust
   themselves for nothing?
14 For the earth will be filled
   with the knowledge of
   the glory of the LORD
as the waters cover the sea.

15 "Woe to him who gives drink
   to his neighbors,
pouring it from the
   wineskin till they are
   drunk,

so that he can gaze on their
    naked bodies!
[16] You will be filled with shame
    instead of glory.
Now it is your turn! Drink
    and let your nakedness
    be exposed[a]!   La 4:21
The cup from the Lord's right
    hand is coming around
    to you,   Isa 51:22
and disgrace will cover your
    glory.
[17] The violence you have
    done to Lebanon will
    overwhelm you,   Jer 51:35
and your destruction of
    animals will terrify you.
For you have shed human
    blood;
you have destroyed lands
    and cities and everyone
    in them.

[18] "Of what value is an idol
    carved by a craftsman?
Or an image that teaches
    lies?
For the one who makes
    it trusts in his own
    creation;
he makes idols that cannot
    speak.   Ps 115:4-5; Jer 10:14
[19] Woe to him who says to wood,
    'Come to life!'
Or to lifeless stone, 'Wake up!'
Can it give guidance?
It is covered with gold and
    silver;
there is no breath in it." Jer 10:4

[20] The Lord is in his holy
    temple;   Ps 11:4
let all the earth be silent
    before him.   Isa 41:1

Habakkuk's Prayer

3 A prayer of Habakkuk the
    prophet. On *shigionoth*.[b]

[2] Lord, I have heard of your
    fame;   Ps 44:1
I stand in awe of your
    deeds, Lord.   Ps 119:120
Repeat them in our day,   Ps 85:6
in our time make them
    known;
in wrath remember mercy.

[3] God came from Teman,
    the Holy One from Mount
    Paran.[c]
His glory covered the heavens
    and his praise filled the
    earth.   Ps 48:10
[4] His splendor was like the
    sunrise;   Isa 18:4
rays flashed from his hand,
    where his power was
    hidden.   Job 9:6
[5] Plague went before him;
    pestilence followed his steps.
[6] He stood, and shook the
    earth;
he looked, and made the
    nations tremble.
The ancient mountains
    crumbled   Ps 46:2
    and the age-old hills
    collapsed —   Ps 114:1-6

---

a 16 Masoretic Text; Dead Sea Scrolls, Aquila, Vulgate and Syriac (see also Septuagint) *and
stagger*   *b 1* Probably a literary or musical term   *c 3* The Hebrew has *Selah* (a word of
uncertain meaning) here and at the middle of verse 9 and at the end of verse 13.

but he marches on forever.
⁷I saw the tents of Cushan in
distress,
the dwellings of Midian in
anguish. Ex 15:14; Jdg 7:24-25

⁸Were you angry with the
rivers, Lᴏʀᴅ? Ex 7:20
Was your wrath against the
streams?
Did you rage against the sea
when you rode your horses
and your chariots to
victory? Ps 68:17
⁹You uncovered your bow,
you called for many arrows.
You split the earth with rivers;
¹⁰ the mountains saw you and
writhed.
Torrents of water swept by;
the deep roared Ps 98:7
and lifted its waves on high.

¹¹Sun and moon stood still in
the heavens Jos 10:13
at the glint of your flying
arrows, Ps 18:14
at the lightning of your
flashing spear. Zec 9:14
¹²In wrath you strode through
the earth
and in anger you threshed
the nations. Isa 41:15
¹³You came out to deliver your
people, Ps 20:6; 28:8
to save your anointed one.
You crushed the leader of the
land of wickedness,
you stripped him from head
to foot.
¹⁴With his own spear you
pierced his head

when his warriors stormed
out to scatter us, Jdg 7:22
gloating as though about to
devour
the wretched who were in
hiding. Ps 64:2-5
¹⁵You trampled the sea with
your horses,
churning the great waters.

¹⁶I heard and my heart pounded,
my lips quivered at the
sound;
decay crept into my bones,
and my legs trembled.
Yet I will wait patiently for the
day of calamity Ps 37:7
to come on the nation
invading us.
¹⁷Though the fig tree does not bud
and there are no grapes on
the vines,
though the olive crop fails
and the fields produce no
food, Joel 1:10-12,18
though there are no sheep in
the pen
and no cattle in the stalls,
¹⁸yet I will rejoice in the Lᴏʀᴅ,
I will be joyful in God my
Savior. Lk 1:47

¹⁹The Sovereign Lᴏʀᴅ is my
strength; Dt 33:29; Ps 46:1-5
he makes my feet like the
feet of a deer,
he enables me to tread on
the heights. 2Sa 22:34

For the director of music.
On my stringed
instruments.

Zephaniah

1 The word of the LORD that came to Zephaniah son of Cushi, the son of Gedaliah, the son of Amariah, the son of Hezekiah, during the reign of Josiah son of Amon king of Judah: 2Ki 22:1

Judgment on the Whole Earth in the Day of the LORD

² "I will sweep away everything
from the face of the
earth," Ge 6:7
declares the LORD.
³ "I will sweep away both man
and beast; Jer 50:3
I will sweep away the birds
in the sky Jer 4:25
and the fish in the sea —
and the idols that cause the
wicked to stumble."ᵃ

"When I destroy all mankind
on the face of the earth,"
declares the LORD,
⁴ "I will stretch out my hand
against Judah Jer 6:12
and against all who live in
Jerusalem.

I will destroy every remnant
of Baal worship in this
place, Mic 5:13
the very names of the
idolatrous priests —
⁵ those who bow down on the
roofs
to worship the starry host,
those who bow down and
swear by the LORD
and who also swear by
Molek,ᵇ Jer 5:7
⁶ those who turn back from
following the LORD Isa 1:4
and neither seek the LORD
nor inquire of him."

⁷ Be silent before the Sovereign
LORD, Hab 2:20; Zec 2:13
for the day of the LORD is
near. Isa 13:6
The LORD has prepared a
sacrifice; Jer 46:10
he has consecrated those he
has invited.
⁸ "On the day of the LORD's
sacrifice

ᵃ 3 The meaning of the Hebrew for this line is uncertain.   ᵇ 5 Hebrew *Malkam*

I will punish the officials
and the king's sons   Jer 39:6
and all those clad
in foreign clothes.
⁹On that day I will punish
all who avoid stepping on
the threshold,ᵃ
who fill the temple of their
gods
with violence and deceit.

¹⁰"On that day,"
declares the Lord,   Isa 22:5
"a cry will go up from the Fish
Gate,   2Ch 33:14
wailing from the New
Quarter,
and a loud crash from the
hills.
¹¹Wail, you who live in the
market districtᵇ;   Jas 5:1
all your merchants will be
wiped out,
all who trade withᶜ silver
will be destroyed.   Hos 9:6
¹²At that time I will search
Jerusalem with lamps
and punish those who are
complacent,   Am 6:1
who are like wine left on its
dregs,   Jer 48:11
who think, 'The Lord will do
nothing,   Eze 8:12
either good or bad.'
¹³Their wealth will be
plundered,   Jer 15:13
their houses demolished.
Though they build houses,
they will not live in them;
though they plant vineyards,

they will not drink the
wine."   Am 5:11; Mic 6:15
¹⁴The great day of the Lord is
near —   Eze 7:7; Joel 1:15
near and coming quickly.
The cry on the day of the
Lord is bitter;
the Mighty Warrior shouts
his battle cry.
¹⁵That day will be a day of
wrath —
a day of distress and
anguish,
a day of trouble and ruin,
a day of darkness and
gloom,
a day of clouds and
blackness — Isa 22:5; Joel 2:2
¹⁶   a day of trumpet and battle
cry   Jer 4:19
against the fortified cities
and against the corner
towers.   Isa 2:15
¹⁷"I will bring such distress on
all people   Dt 28:52
that they will grope about
like those who are
blind,   Isa 59:10
because they have sinned
against the Lord.
Their blood will be poured
out like dust   Ps 79:3
and their entrails like
dung.   Jer 9:22
¹⁸Neither their silver nor their
gold
will be able to save them
on the day of the Lord's
wrath."   Eze 7:19

ᵃ 9 See 1 Samuel 5:5.   ᵇ 11 Or the Mortar   ᶜ 11 Or in

In the fire of his jealousy Dt 29:20
  the whole earth will be
      consumed, Zep 3:8
for he will make a sudden end
  of all who live on the
      earth. Ge 6:7

Judah and Jerusalem Judged Along With the Nations

Judah Summoned to Repent

2 Gather together, gather
    yourselves together,
  you shameful nation, Jer 3:3
²before the decree takes effect
  and that day passes
    like windblown
      chaff, Isa 17:13; Hos 13:3
before the LORD's fierce anger
  comes upon you, La 4:11
before the day of the LORD's
  wrath
  comes upon you. Eze 7:19
³Seek the LORD, all you humble
  of the land, Am 5:6
  you who do what he
    commands.
Seek righteousness, seek
    humility; Ps 45:4; Am 5:14-15
perhaps you will be
    sheltered Ps 57:1
on the day of the LORD's
  anger.

Philistia

⁴Gaza will be abandoned Am 1:6
  and Ashkelon left in
    ruins.
At midday Ashdod will be
    emptied
  and Ekron uprooted.

⁵Woe to you who live by the
    sea,
  you Kerethite people; Eze 25:16
the word of the LORD is
  against you, Am 3:1
Canaan, land of the
    Philistines.
He says, "I will destroy you,
  and none will be left." Isa 14:30
⁶The land by the sea will
    become pastures
having wells for shepherds
  and pens for flocks. Isa 5:17
⁷That land will belong
  to the remnant of the
    people of Judah; Ge 45:7
there they will find
    pasture.
In the evening they will lie
    down
  in the houses of Ashkelon.
The LORD their God will care
  for them;
  he will restore their
    fortunes.ᵃ Ps 126:4; Jer 32:44

Moab and Ammon

⁸"I have heard the insults of
    Moab Jer 48:27
  and the taunts of the
    Ammonites, Eze 21:28
who insulted my people Eze 25:3
  and made threats against
    their land. La 3:61
⁹Therefore, as surely as I live,"
  declares the LORD
    Almighty,
  the God of Israel,
"surely Moab will become like
    Sodom, Dt 29:23

ᵃ 7 Or *will bring back their captives*

the Ammonites like
  Gomorrah —   Jer 49:1-6
a place of weeds and salt pits,
  a wasteland forever.
The remnant of my people will
  plunder them;   Isa 11:14
  the survivors of my nation
  will inherit their
  land."   Am 2:1-3

¹⁰This is what they will get
  in return for their
  pride,   Isa 16:6
  for insulting and mocking
  the people of the LORD
  Almighty.   Jer 48:27
¹¹The LORD will be awesome to
  them   Joel 2:11
  when he destroys all the
  gods of the earth.   Zep 1:4
Distant nations will bow
  down to him,   Zep 3:9
  all of them in their own
  lands.

Cush

¹²"You Cushites,ᵃ too,   Isa 18:1; 20:4
  will be slain by my
  sword."   Jer 46:10

Assyria

¹³He will stretch out his hand
  against the north
  and destroy Assyria,
leaving Nineveh utterly
  desolate
  and dry as the desert.   Na 1:1
¹⁴Flocks and herds will lie down
  there,   Isa 5:17
  creatures of every kind.

The desert owl and the screech
  owl   Ps 102:6; Isa 14:23
  will roost on her columns.
Their hooting will echo
  through the windows,
  rubble will fill the
  doorways,
  the beams of cedar will be
  exposed.
¹⁵This is the city of revelry   Isa 32:9
  that lived in safety.   Isa 47:8
She said to herself,
  "I am the one! And there is
  none besides me."   Eze 28:2
What a ruin she has become,
  a lair for wild beasts!
All who pass by her scoff   Na 3:19
  and shake their fists.

Jerusalem

3 Woe to the city of
  oppressors,
  rebellious and defiled!   Jer 6:6
²She obeys no one,   Jer 22:21
  she accepts no
  correction.   Jer 7:28
She does not trust in the
  LORD,   Dt 1:32
  she does not draw near to
  her God.   Ps 73:28; Jer 5:3
³Her officials within her
  are roaring lions;
her rulers are evening
  wolves,   Eze 22:27
who leave nothing for the
  morning.
⁴Her prophets are
  unprincipled;
  they are treacherous
  people.   Jer 9:4

ᵃ 12 That is, people from the upper Nile region

Her priests profane the
   sanctuary
   and do violence to the
      law.   Eze 22:26
5 The LORD within her is
   righteous;   Ezr 9:15
   he does no wrong.   Dt 32:4
Morning by morning he
   dispenses his justice,
   and every new day he does
      not fail,   La 3:23
yet the unrighteous know
   no shame.   Eze 18:25

Jerusalem Remains Unrepentant

6 "I have destroyed nations;
   their strongholds are
      demolished.
I have left their streets
      deserted,
   with no one passing
      through.
Their cities are laid waste;
   they are deserted and
      empty.
7 Of Jerusalem I thought,
   'Surely you will fear me
   and accept correction!'   Jer 7:28
Then her place of refuge^a
   would not be destroyed,
   nor all my punishments
      come upon^b her.
But they were still eager
   to act corruptly in all they
      did.   Hos 9:9
8 Therefore wait for me,"
   declares the LORD,   Ps 27:14
   "for the day I will stand up
      to testify.^c

I have decided to assemble
   the nations,   Joel 3:2
   to gather the kingdoms
   and to pour out my wrath on
      them —
   all my fierce anger.   Jer 10:25
The whole world will be
   consumed   Zep 1:18
   by the fire of my jealous
      anger.

Restoration of Israel's Remnant

9 "Then I will purify the lips of
   the peoples,
   that all of them may call
   on the name of the
      LORD   Zep 2:11
   and serve him shoulder to
      shoulder.   Isa 19:18
10 From beyond the rivers of
   Cush^d   Ps 68:31
   my worshipers, my
      scattered people,
   will bring me offerings.   Isa 60:7
11 On that day you, Jerusalem,
   will not be put to
      shame   Joel 2:26-27
   for all the wrongs you have
      done to me,   Ge 50:15
   because I will remove from
      you
   your arrogant boasters.
Never again will you be
   haughty
   on my holy hill.   Ex 15:17
12 But I will leave within you
   the meek and humble.
The remnant of Israel

---

^a 7 Or *her sanctuary*   ^b 7 Or *all those I appointed over*   ^c 8 Septuagint and Syriac;
Hebrew *will rise up to plunder*   ^d 10 That is, the upper Nile region

will trust in the name of the
LORD.   Na 1:7
¹³They will do no wrong; Isa 10:21;
they will tell no lies.   Rev 14:5
A deceitful tongue
will not be found in their
mouths.
They will eat and lie down
and no one will make them
afraid."   Eze 34:25-28

¹⁴Sing, Daughter Zion;   Zec 2:10
shout aloud, Israel!   Isa 12:6
Be glad and rejoice with all
your heart,   Isa 51:11
Daughter Jerusalem!
¹⁵The LORD has taken away
your punishment,
he has turned back your
enemy.
The LORD, the King of Israel,
is with you;   Eze 37:26-28
never again will you fear
any harm.   Isa 54:14
¹⁶On that day
they will say to Jerusalem,
"Do not fear, Zion;
do not let your hands hang
limp.   Isa 35:3-4; Heb 12:12
¹⁷The LORD your God is with
you,
the Mighty Warrior who
saves.   Isa 63:1

He will take great delight in
you;   Isa 62:4
in his love he will no longer
rebuke you,   Hos 14:4
but will rejoice over you
with singing."   Isa 40:1

¹⁸"I will remove from you
all who mourn over the
loss of your appointed
festivals,
which is a burden and
reproach for you.
¹⁹At that time I will deal
with all who oppressed
you.
I will rescue the lame;
I will gather the exiles.
I will give them praise and
honor   Isa 60:18
in every land where they
have suffered shame.
²⁰At that time I will gather you;
at that time I will bring you
home.   Jer 29:14; Eze 37:12
I will give you honor and
praise   Isa 56:5
among all the peoples of the
earth
when I restore your
fortunes^a   Joel 3:1
before your very eyes,"
says the LORD.

---

^a 20 Or *I bring back your captives*

Haggai

A Call to Build the House of the LORD

1 In the second year of King Darius, on the first day of the sixth month, the word of the LORD came through the prophet Haggai to Zerubbabel son of Shealtiel, governor of Judah, and to Joshua*a* son of Jozadak,*b* the high priest: 	Ezr 4:24; 5:3; Mt 1:12-13

²This is what the LORD Almighty says: "These people say, 'The time has not yet come to rebuild the LORD's house.'" 	Ezr 1:2

³Then the word of the LORD came through the prophet Haggai: ⁴"Is it a time for you yourselves to be living in your paneled houses, while this house remains a ruin?" 	2Sa 7:2; Ezr 5:1; Jer 33:12

⁵Now this is what the LORD Almighty says: "Give careful thought to your ways. ⁶You have planted much, but harvested little. You eat, but never have enough. You drink, but never have your fill. You put on clothes, but are not warm. You earn wages, only to put them in a purse with holes in it." 	La 3:40; Hag 2:15,18

⁷This is what the LORD Almighty says: "Give careful thought to your ways. ⁸Go up into the mountains and bring down timber and build my house, so that I may take pleasure in it and be honored," says the LORD. ⁹"You expected much, but see, it turned out to be little. What you brought home, I blew away. Why?" declares the LORD Almighty. "Because of my house, which remains a ruin, while each of you is busy with your own house. ¹⁰Therefore, because of you the heavens have withheld their dew and the earth its crops. ¹¹I called for a drought on the fields and the mountains, on the grain, the new wine, the olive oil and everything else the ground produces, on people and livestock, and on all the labor of your hands." 	Ps 132:13-14; Hag 2:17

¹²Then Zerubbabel son of Shealtiel, Joshua son of Jozadak, the

---

a 1 A variant of *Jeshua*; here and elsewhere in Haggai *Jozadak*; also in verses 12 and 14   *b* 1 Hebrew *Jehozadak*, a variant of *Jozadak* high priest, and the whole remnant of the people obeyed the voice of the LORD their God and the message of the prophet Haggai, because the LORD their God had sent him. And the people feared the LORD. _{Dt 31:12; Isa 50:10}

13 Then Haggai, the LORD's messenger, gave this message of the LORD to the people: "I am with you," declares the LORD. **14** So the LORD stirred up the spirit of Zerubbabel son of Shealtiel, governor of Judah, and the spirit of Joshua son of Jozadak, the high priest, and the spirit of the whole remnant of the people. They came and began to work on the house of the LORD Almighty, their God, **15** on the twenty-fourth day of the sixth month. _{Ezr 5:2; Ro 8:31}

The Promised Glory of the New House

In the second year of King **2** Darius, **1** on the twenty-first day of the seventh month, the word of the LORD came through the prophet Haggai: **2** "Speak to Zerubbabel son of Shealtiel, governor of Judah, to Joshua son of Jozadak,*a* the high priest, and to the remnant of the people. Ask them, **3** 'Who of you is left who saw this house in its former glory? How does it look to you now? Does it not seem to you like nothing? **4** But now be strong, Zerubbabel,' declares the LORD. 'Be strong, Joshua son of Jozadak,

the high priest. Be strong, all you people of the land,' declares the LORD, 'and work. For I am with you,' declares the LORD Almighty. **5** 'This is what I covenanted with you when you came out of Egypt. And my Spirit remains among you. Do not fear.' _{1Ch 28:20; Isa 63:11}

6 "This is what the LORD Almighty says: 'In a little while I will once more shake the heavens and the earth, the sea and the dry land. **7** I will shake all nations, and what is desired by all nations will come, and I will fill this house with glory,' says the LORD Almighty. **8** 'The silver is mine and the gold is mine,' declares the LORD Almighty. **9** 'The glory of this present house will be greater than the glory of the former house,' says the LORD Almighty. 'And in this place I will grant peace,' declares the LORD Almighty." _{Heb 12:26}

Blessings for a Defiled People

10 On the twenty-fourth day of the ninth month, in the second year of Darius, the word of the LORD came to the prophet Haggai: **11** "This is what the LORD Almighty says: 'Ask the priests what the law says: **12** If someone carries consecrated meat in the fold of their garment, and that fold touches some bread or stew, some wine, olive oil or other food, does it become consecrated?' " _{Lev 10:10-11; Mt 23:19}

---

a 2 Hebrew *Jehozadak,* a variant of *Jozadak*; also in verse 4

The priests answered, "No."

[13] Then Haggai said, "If a person defiled by contact with a dead body touches one of these things, does it become defiled?"

"Yes," the priests replied, "it becomes defiled." Lev 22:4-6

[14] Then Haggai said, "'So it is with this people and this nation in my sight,' declares the LORD. 'Whatever they do and whatever they offer there is defiled. Isa 1:13

[15] "'Now give careful thought to this from this day on[a] — consider how things were before one stone was laid on another in the LORD's temple. [16] When anyone came to a heap of twenty measures, there were only ten. When anyone went to a wine vat to draw fifty measures, there were only twenty. [17] I struck all the work of your hands with blight, mildew and hail, yet you did not return to me,' declares the LORD. [18] 'From this day on, from this twenty-fourth day of the ninth month, give careful thought to the day when the foundation of the LORD's temple was laid. Give careful thought: [19] Is there yet any seed left in the barn? Until now, the vine and the fig tree, the pomegranate and the olive tree have not borne fruit. Hag 1:5-6; Zec 8:9

"'From this day on I will bless you.'" Joel 2:14

Zerubbabel the LORD's Signet Ring

[20] The word of the LORD came to Haggai a second time on the twenty-fourth day of the month: [21] "Tell Zerubbabel governor of Judah that I am going to shake the heavens and the earth. [22] I will overturn royal thrones and shatter the power of the foreign kingdoms. I will overthrow chariots and their drivers; horses and their riders will fall, each by the sword of his brother. Jdg 7:22; Da 2:44; Mic 5:10

[23] "'On that day,' declares the LORD Almighty, 'I will take you, my servant Zerubbabel son of Shealtiel,' declares the LORD, 'and I will make you like my signet ring, for I have chosen you,' declares the LORD Almighty." Isa 43:10

---

[a] 15 Or to the days past

Zechariah

A Call to Return to the LORD

1 In the eighth month of the second year of Darius, the word of the LORD came to the prophet Zechariah son of Berekiah, the son of Iddo: Ezr 4:24; Ne 12:4

²"The LORD was very angry with your ancestors. ³Therefore tell the people: This is what the LORD Almighty says: 'Return to me,' declares the LORD Almighty, 'and I will return to you,' says the LORD Almighty. ⁴Do not be like your ancestors, to whom the earlier prophets proclaimed: This is what the LORD Almighty says: 'Turn from your evil ways and your evil practices.' But they would not listen or pay attention to me, declares the LORD. ⁵Where are your ancestors now? And the prophets, do they live forever? ⁶But did not my words and my decrees, which I commanded my servants the prophets, overtake your ancestors?   Mal 3:7; Jas 4:8

"Then they repented and said, 'The LORD Almighty has done to us what our ways and practices deserve, just as he determined to do.'"   Jer 12:14-17; La 2:17

The Man Among the Myrtle Trees

⁷On the twenty-fourth day of the eleventh month, the month of Shebat, in the second year of Darius, the word of the LORD came to the prophet Zechariah son of Berekiah, the son of Iddo.

⁸During the night I had a vision, and there before me was a man mounted on a red horse. He was standing among the myrtle trees in a ravine. Behind him were red, brown and white horses.   Zec 6:2-7; Rev 6:4

⁹I asked, "What are these, my lord?"

The angel who was talking with me answered, "I will show you what they are."   Zec 4:1,4-5

¹⁰Then the man standing among the myrtle trees explained, "They are the ones the LORD has sent to go throughout the earth."   Zec 6:5-8

¹¹And they reported to the angel of the LORD who was standing among the myrtle trees, "We

have gone throughout the earth and found the whole world at rest and in peace." Isa 14:7

¹²Then the angel of the LORD said, "LORD Almighty, how long will you withhold mercy from Jerusalem and from the towns of Judah, which you have been angry with these seventy years?" ¹³So the LORD spoke kind and comforting words to the angel who talked with me. Da 9:2; Zec 4:1

¹⁴Then the angel who was speaking to me said, "Proclaim this word: This is what the LORD Almighty says: 'I am very jealous for Jerusalem and Zion, ¹⁵and I am very angry with the nations that feel secure. I was only a little angry, but they went too far with the punishment.' Am 1:11; Zec 8:2

¹⁶"Therefore this is what the LORD says: 'I will return to Jerusalem with mercy, and there my house will be rebuilt. And the measuring line will be stretched out over Jerusalem,' declares the LORD Almighty. Zec 2:1-2

¹⁷"Proclaim further: This is what the LORD Almighty says: 'My towns will again overflow with prosperity, and the LORD will again comfort Zion and choose Jerusalem.' " Isa 51:3; Zec 2:12

Four Horns and Four Craftsmen

¹⁸Then I looked up, and there before me were four horns. ¹⁹I asked the angel who was speaking to me, "What are these?"

He answered me, "These are the horns that scattered Judah, Israel and Jerusalem." Am 6:13

²⁰Then the LORD showed me four craftsmen. ²¹I asked, "What are these coming to do?"

He answered, "These are the horns that scattered Judah so that no one could raise their head, but the craftsmen have come to terrify them and throw down these horns of the nations who lifted up their horns against the land of Judah to scatter its people."ᵃ Ps 75:4,10

A Man With a Measuring Line

2ᵇ Then I looked up, and there before me was a man with a measuring line in his hand. ²I asked, "Where are you going?"

He answered me, "To measure Jerusalem, to find out how wide and how long it is." Rev 21:15

³While the angel who was speaking to me was leaving, another angel came to meet him ⁴and said to him: "Run, tell that young man, 'Jerusalem will be a city without walls because of the great number of people and animals in it. ⁵And I myself will be a wall of fire around it,' declares the LORD, 'and I will be its glory within.' Ps 46:5; Rev 21:23

⁶"Come! Come! Flee from the land of the north," declares the

ᵃ 21 In Hebrew texts 1:18-21 is numbered 2:1-4. 2:5-17.   ᵇ In Hebrew texts 2:1-13 is numbered

LORD, "for I have scattered you to the four winds of heaven," declares the LORD. Eze 17:21

⁷ "Come, Zion! Escape, you who live in Daughter Babylon!" ⁸ For this is what the LORD Almighty says: "After the Glorious One has sent me against the nations that have plundered you — for whoever touches you touches the apple of his eye — ⁹ I will surely raise my hand against them so that their slaves will plunder them.ᵃ Then you will know that the LORD Almighty has sent me. Dt 32:10; Zec 4:9

¹⁰ "Shout and be glad, Daughter Zion. For I am coming, and I will live among you," declares the LORD. ¹¹ "Many nations will be joined with the LORD in that day and will become my people. I will live among you and you will know that the LORD Almighty has sent me to you. ¹² The LORD will inherit Judah as his portion in the holy land and will again choose Jerusalem. ¹³ Be still before the LORD, all mankind, because he has roused himself from his holy dwelling." Hab 2:20; Zec 1:17

Clean Garments for the High Priest

3 Then he showed me Joshuaᵇ the high priest standing before the angel of the LORD, and Satanᶜ standing at his right side to accuse him. ² The LORD said to Satan, "The LORD rebuke you, Sa-

tan! The LORD, who has chosen Jerusalem, rebuke you! Is not this man a burning stick snatched from the fire?" Ps 109:6; Jude 9,23

³ Now Joshua was dressed in filthy clothes as he stood before the angel. ⁴ The angel said to those who were standing before him, "Take off his filthy clothes."

Then he said to Joshua, "See, I have taken away your sin, and I will put fine garments on you." Isa 52:1; Mic 7:18

⁵ Then I said, "Put a clean turban on his head." So they put a clean turban on his head and clothed him, while the angel of the LORD stood by. Ex 29:6

⁶ The angel of the LORD gave this charge to Joshua: ⁷ "This is what the LORD Almighty says: 'If you will walk in obedience to me and keep my requirements, then you will govern my house and have charge of my courts, and I will give you a place among these standing here. Dt 17:8-11; Eze 44:15-16

⁸ " 'Listen, High Priest Joshua, you and your associates seated before you, who are men symbolic of things to come: I am going to bring my servant, the Branch. ⁹ See, the stone I have set in front of Joshua! There are seven eyesᵈ on that one stone, and I will engrave an inscription on it,' says the LORD Almighty, 'and I will remove the sin of this land in a single day. Isa 28:16; Eze 12:11

ᵃ 8,9 Or says after . . . eye: ⁹ "I . . . plunder them."   ᵇ 1 A variant of Jeshua; here and elsewhere in Zechariah   ᶜ 1 Hebrew satan means adversary.   ᵈ 9 Or facets

10 " 'In that day each of you will invite your neighbor to sit under your vine and fig tree,' declares the LORD Almighty." 1Ki 4:25; Mic 4:4

The Gold Lampstand and the Two Olive Trees

4 Then the angel who talked with me returned and woke me up, like someone awakened from sleep. 2 He asked me, "What do you see?" Jer 1:13; Da 8:18

I answered, "I see a solid gold lampstand with a bowl at the top and seven lamps on it, with seven channels to the lamps. 3 Also there are two olive trees by it, one on the right of the bowl and the other on its left." Rev 4:5; 11:4

4 I asked the angel who talked with me, "What are these, my lord?"

5 He answered, "Do you not know what these are?"

"No, my lord," I replied. Zec 1:9

6 So he said to me, "This is the word of the LORD to Zerubbabel: 'Not by might nor by power, but by my Spirit,' says the LORD Almighty. Isa 11:2-4; Hos 1:7

7 "What are you, mighty mountain? Before Zerubbabel you will become level ground. Then he will bring out the capstone to shouts of 'God bless it! God bless it!' " Ps 118:22; Jer 51:25

8 Then the word of the LORD came to me: 9 "The hands of Zerubbabel have laid the founda-

tion of this temple; his hands will also complete it. Then you will know that the LORD Almighty has sent me to you. Zec 2:9; 6:12

10 "Who dares despise the day of small things, since the seven eyes of the LORD that range throughout the earth will rejoice when they see the chosen capstone[a] in the hand of Zerubbabel?" Hag 2:3; Zec 3:9; Rev 5:6

11 Then I asked the angel, "What are these two olive trees on the right and the left of the lampstand?" Rev 11:4

12 Again I asked him, "What are these two olive branches beside the two gold pipes that pour out golden oil?"

13 He replied, "Do you not know what these are?"

"No, my lord," I said.

14 So he said, "These are the two who are anointed to[b] serve the Lord of all the earth." Ex 29:7; Da 9:24

The Flying Scroll

5 I looked again, and there before me was a flying scroll. Eze 2:9; Rev 5:1

2 He asked me, "What do you see?"

I answered, "I see a flying scroll, twenty cubits long and ten cubits wide.[c]"

3 And he said to me, "This is the curse that is going out over the whole land; for according to what it says on one side, every thief will

---

[a] 10 Or the plumb line   [b] 14 Or two who bring oil and   [c] 2 That is, about 30 feet long and 15 feet wide or about 9 meters long and 4.5 meters wide

be banished, and according to what it says on the other, everyone who swears falsely will be banished. ⁴The LORD Almighty declares, 'I will send it out, and it will enter the house of the thief and the house of anyone who swears falsely by my name. It will remain in that house and destroy it completely, both its timbers and its stones.'" Lev 14:34-45; Mal 3:5

The Woman in a Basket

⁵Then the angel who was speaking to me came forward and said to me, "Look up and see what is appearing."

⁶I asked, "What is it?"

He replied, "It is a basket." And he added, "This is the iniquity*a* of the people throughout the land."

⁷Then the cover of lead was raised, and there in the basket sat a woman! ⁸He said, "This is wickedness," and he pushed her back into the basket and pushed its lead cover down on it. Mic 6:11

⁹Then I looked up — and there before me were two women, with the wind in their wings! They had wings like those of a stork, and they lifted up the basket between heaven and earth. Lev 11:19

¹⁰"Where are they taking the basket?" I asked the angel who was speaking to me.

¹¹He replied, "To the country of Babylonia*b* to build a house for it. When the house is ready,

the basket will be set there in its place." Ge 10:10; Jer 29:5,28; Da 1:2

Four Chariots

6 I looked up again, and there before me were four chariots coming out from between two mountains — mountains of bronze. ²The first chariot had red horses, the second black, ³the third white, and the fourth dappled — all of them powerful. ⁴I asked the angel who was speaking to me, "What are these, my lord?" Rev 6:2,5

⁵The angel answered me, "These are the four spirits*c* of heaven, going out from standing in the presence of the Lord of the whole world. ⁶The one with the black horses is going toward the north country, the one with the white horses toward the west,*d* and the one with the dappled horses toward the south." Eze 37:9; Mt 24:31; Rev 7:1

⁷When the powerful horses went out, they were straining to go throughout the earth. And he said, "Go throughout the earth!" So they went throughout the earth. Zec 1:10

⁸Then he called to me, "Look, those going toward the north country have given my Spirit*e* rest in the land of the north." Eze 5:13

A Crown for Joshua

⁹The word of the LORD came to

---

a 6 Or *appearance*   *b* 11 Hebrew *Shinar*   *c* 5 Or *winds*   *d* 6 Or *horses after them*
e 8 Or *spirit*

me: [10] "Take silver and gold from the exiles Heldai, Tobijah and Jedaiah, who have arrived from Babylon. Go the same day to the house of Josiah son of Zephaniah. [11] Take the silver and gold and make a crown, and set it on the head of the high priest, Joshua son of Jozadak.[a] [12] Tell him this is what the LORD Almighty says: 'Here is the man whose name is the Branch, and he will branch out from his place and build the temple of the LORD. [13] It is he who will build the temple of the LORD, and he will be clothed with majesty and will sit and rule on his throne. And he[b] will be a priest on his throne. And there will be harmony between the two.' [14] The crown will be given to Heldai,[c] Tobijah, Jedaiah and Hen[d] son of Zephaniah as a memorial in the temple of the LORD. [15] Those who are far away will come and help to build the temple of the LORD, and you will know that the LORD Almighty has sent me to you. This will happen if you diligently obey the LORD your God." *Isa 60:10; Zec 2:9-11*

Justice and Mercy, Not Fasting

7 In the fourth year of King Darius, the word of the LORD came to Zechariah on the fourth day of the ninth month, the month of Kislev. [2] The people of Bethel had sent Sharezer and Regem-Melek, together with their men, to entreat the LORD [3] by asking the priests of the house of the LORD Almighty and the prophets, "Should I mourn and fast in the fifth month, as I have done for so many years?" *Jer 52:12-14; Zec 8:19*

[4] Then the word of the LORD Almighty came to me: [5] "Ask all the people of the land and the priests, 'When you fasted and mourned in the fifth and seventh months for the past seventy years, was it really for me that you fasted? [6] And when you were eating and drinking, were you not just feasting for yourselves? [7] Are these not the words the LORD proclaimed through the earlier prophets when Jerusalem and its surrounding towns were at rest and prosperous, and the Negev and the western foothills were settled?' " *Jer 22:21; Zec 1:4*

[8] And the word of the LORD came again to Zechariah: [9] "This is what the LORD Almighty said: 'Administer true justice; show mercy and compassion to one another. [10] Do not oppress the widow or the fatherless, the foreigner or the poor. Do not plot evil against each other.' *Isa 1:17; Zec 8:16*

[11] "But they refused to pay attention; stubbornly they turned their backs and covered their ears. [12] They made their hearts as hard as flint and would not listen to the law or to the words that the LORD Almighty had sent by his

---

[a] 11 Hebrew *Jehozadak*, a variant of *Jozadak*
[d] 14 Or *and the gracious one, the*
[b] 13 Or *there*   [c] 14 Syriac; Hebrew *Helem*

Spirit through the earlier prophets. So the LORD Almighty was very angry. Ne 9:29; Eze 11:19; Da 9:12

¹³ " 'When I called, they did not listen; so when they called, I would not listen,' says the LORD Almighty. ¹⁴ 'I scattered them with a whirlwind among all the nations, where they were strangers. The land they left behind them was so desolate that no one traveled through it. This is how they made the pleasant land desolate.' " Isa 1:15; Jer 44:6

The LORD Promises to Bless Jerusalem

8 The word of the LORD Almighty came to me. ²This is what the LORD Almighty says: "I am very jealous for Zion; I am burning with jealousy for her." Joel 2:18

³This is what the LORD says: "I will return to Zion and dwell in Jerusalem. Then Jerusalem will be called the Faithful City, and the mountain of the LORD Almighty will be called the Holy Mountain." Zec 1:16; 2:10

⁴This is what the LORD Almighty says: "Once again men and women of ripe old age will sit in the streets of Jerusalem, each of them with cane in hand because of their age. ⁵The city streets will be filled with boys and girls playing there." Isa 65:20; Jer 30:20

⁶This is what the LORD Almighty says: "It may seem marvelous to the remnant of this people at that time, but will it seem marvelous to me?" declares the LORD Almighty. Ps 118:23; 126:1-3

⁷This is what the LORD Almighty says: "I will save my people from the countries of the east and the west. ⁸I will bring them back to live in Jerusalem; they will be my people, and I will be faithful and righteous to them as their God." Zec 2:11; 10:6

⁹This is what the LORD Almighty says: "Now hear these words, 'Let your hands be strong so that the temple may be built.' This is also what the prophets said who were present when the foundation was laid for the house of the LORD Almighty. ¹⁰Before that time there were no wages for people or hire for animals. No one could go about their business safely because of their enemies, since I had turned everyone against their neighbor. ¹¹But now I will not deal with the remnant of this people as I did in the past," declares the LORD Almighty. Isa 12:1; Hag 2:4

¹² "The seed will grow well, the vine will yield its fruit, the ground will produce its crops, and the heavens will drop their dew. I will give all these things as an inheritance to the remnant of this people. ¹³Just as you, Judah and Israel, have been a curse[a] among

---

[a] 13 That is, your name has been used in cursing (see Jer. 29:22); or, you have been regarded as under a curse.

the nations, so I will save you, and you will be a blessing.[a] Do not be afraid, but let your hands be strong." Ge 12:2; Jer 42:18; Joel 2:22 [14]This is what the LORD Almighty says: "Just as I had determined to bring disaster on you and showed no pity when your ancestors angered me," says the LORD Almighty, [15]"so now I have determined to do good again to Jerusalem and Judah. Do not be afraid. [16]These are the things you are to do: Speak the truth to each other, and render true and sound judgment in your courts; [17]do not plot evil against each other, and do not love to swear falsely. I hate all this," declares the LORD. Pr 3:29; Zec 7:9; Eph 4:25

[18]The word of the LORD Almighty came to me. [19]This is what the LORD Almighty says: "The fasts of the fourth, fifth, seventh and tenth months will become joyful and glad occasions and happy festivals for Judah. Therefore love truth and peace." Ps 30:11

[20]This is what the LORD Almighty says: "Many peoples and the inhabitants of many cities will yet come, [21]and the inhabitants of one city will go to another and say, 'Let us go at once to entreat the LORD and seek the LORD Almighty. I myself am going.' [22]And many peoples and power-ful nations will come to Jerusalem to seek the LORD Almighty and to entreat him." Ps 117:1; Zec 2:11 [23]This is what the LORD Almighty says: "In those days ten people from all languages and nations will take firm hold of one Jew by the hem of his robe and say, 'Let us go with you, because we have heard that God is with you.'" Isa 45:14; 1Co 14:25

Judgment on Israel's Enemies

9 A prophecy:

The word of the LORD is
    against the land of
    Hadrak
and will come to rest on
    Damascus— Isa 17:1
for the eyes of all people and
    all the tribes of Israel
are on the LORD— [b]
[2]and on Hamath too, which
    borders on it, Jer 49:23
and on Tyre and Sidon,
    though they are very
    skillful. Eze 28:1-19
[3]Tyre has built herself a
    stronghold;
she has heaped up silver
    like dust,
and gold like the dirt of the
    streets. Job 27:16; Eze 28:4
[4]But the Lord will take away
    her possessions
and destroy her power on
    the sea,

---

[a] 13 Or *and your name will be used in blessings* (see Gen. 48:20); or *and you will be seen as blessed* [b] 1 Or *Damascus. / For the eye of the LORD is on all people, / as well as on the tribes of Israel,*

and she will be consumed
    by fire.   Isa 23:1; Eze 26:3-5
⁵Ashkelon will see it and
    fear;   Jer 47:5
  Gaza will writhe in agony,
    and Ekron too, for her hope
    will wither.
  Gaza will lose her king
    and Ashkelon will be
    deserted.
⁶A mongrel people will occupy
    Ashdod,
  and I will put an end to
    the pride of the
    Philistines.   Isa 14:30
⁷I will take the blood from
    their mouths,
  the forbidden food from
    between their teeth.
  Those who are left will belong
    to our God   Job 25:2
  and become a clan in
    Judah,
  and Ekron will be like the
    Jebusites.   Jer 47:1
⁸But I will encamp at my
    temple
  to guard it against
    marauding forces.
  Never again will an oppressor
    overrun my people,
  for now I am keeping
    watch.   Isa 52:1; 54:14

The Coming of Zion's King

⁹Rejoice greatly, Daughter
    Zion!   Isa 62:11
  Shout, Daughter Jerusalem!
  See, your king comes to you,

    righteous and
    victorious, Isa 9:6-7; Zep 3:14
  lowly and riding on a donkey,
    on a colt, the foal of a
    donkey.   Mt 21:5; Jn 12:15
¹⁰I will take away the chariots
    from Ephraim
  and the warhorses from
    Jerusalem,
  and the battle bow will be
    broken.   Hos 1:7; 2:18
  He will proclaim peace to the
    nations.   Isa 2:4
  His rule will extend from
    sea to sea
  and from the River*a* to the
    ends of the earth.   Ps 72:8
¹¹As for you, because of the
    blood of my covenant
    with you,   Ex 24:8
  I will free your prisoners
    from the waterless
    pit.   Isa 42:7
¹²Return to your fortress, you
    prisoners of hope; Joel 3:16
  even now I announce that
    I will restore twice as
    much to you.   Isa 40:2
¹³I will bend Judah as I bend my
    bow
  and fill it with Ephraim.
  I will rouse your sons, Zion,
    against your sons,
    Greece,   Joel 3:6
  and make you like a
    warrior's sword.   Jer 51:20

The Lord Will Appear

¹⁴Then the Lord will appear
    over them;   Isa 31:5

---

a 10 That is, the Euphrates

his arrow will flash like
lightning. Ps 18:14; Hab 3:11
The Sovereign LORD will
sound the trumpet;
he will march in the storms
of the south, Isa 21:1; 66:15
15 and the LORD Almighty will
shield them. Isa 37:35
They will destroy
and overcome with
slingstones.
They will drink and roar as
with wine;
they will be full like a bowl
used for sprinkling[a] the
corners of the altar. Ex 27:2
16 The LORD their God will save
his people on that day
as a shepherd saves his
flock.
They will sparkle in his land
like jewels in a crown. Isa 62:3
17 How attractive and beautiful
they will be!
Grain will make the young
men thrive,
and new wine the young
women.

The LORD Will Care for Judah

10 Ask the LORD for rain in
the springtime;
it is the LORD who sends the
thunderstorms.
He gives showers of rain to all
people, Lev 26:4
and plants of the field to
everyone. Job 14:9
2 The idols speak deceitfully,

diviners see visions that
lie; Isa 44:25
they tell dreams that are false,
they give comfort in
vain. Isa 40:19
Therefore the people wander
like sheep
oppressed for lack of a
shepherd. Eze 34:5; Hos 3:4

3 "My anger burns against the
shepherds,
and I will punish the
leaders; Jer 25:34
for the LORD Almighty will
care
for his flock, the people of
Judah,
and make them like a proud
horse in battle. Eze 34:8-10
4 From Judah will come the
cornerstone, Ps 118:22
from him the tent peg, Isa 22:23
from him the battle bow, Zec 9:10
from him every ruler.
5 Together they[b] will be like
warriors in battle
trampling their enemy
into the mud of the
streets. 2Sa 22:43
They will fight because the
LORD is with them,
and they will put the
enemy horsemen to
shame. Am 2:15; Hag 2:22
6 "I will strengthen Judah
and save the tribes of
Joseph.
I will restore them

---

[a] 15 Or bowl, / like   [b] 4,5 Or ruler, all of them together. / 5They

because I have compassion
on them.   Zec 8:7-8
They will be as though
   I had not rejected them,
for I am the Lord their God
   and I will answer them.
⁷The Ephraimites will become
   like warriors,
   and their hearts will be glad
      as with wine.   Zec 9:15
Their children will see it and
   be joyful;
   their hearts will rejoice in
      the Lord.
⁸I will signal for them   Isa 5:26
   and gather them in.
Surely I will redeem them;
   they will be as numerous as
      before.   Eze 36:11
⁹Though I scatter them among
   the peoples,
   yet in distant lands they will
      remember me.   Eze 6:9
They and their children will
   survive,
   and they will return.
¹⁰I will bring them back from
   Egypt
   and gather them from
      Assyria.   Isa 11:11
I will bring them to Gilead
   and Lebanon,   Jer 50:19
   and there will not be room
      enough for them. Isa 49:19
¹¹They will pass through the
   sea of trouble;
   the surging sea will be
      subdued
   and all the depths of the
      Nile will dry up. Isa 19:5-7

Assyria's pride will be brought
   down   Zep 2:13
and Egypt's scepter will
   pass away.   Eze 30:13
¹²I will strengthen them in the
   Lord
   and in his name they will
      live securely,"   Mic 4:5
   declares the Lord.

11 Open your doors,
         Lebanon,   Eze 31:3
   so that fire may devour your
      cedars!   Zec 12:6
²Wail, you juniper, for the
      cedar has fallen;
   the stately trees are ruined!
Wail, oaks of Bashan;   Isa 2:13
   the dense forest has been
      cut down!   Isa 32:19
³Listen to the wail of the
      shepherds;
   their rich pastures are
      destroyed!
Listen to the roar of the lions;
   the lush thicket of the
      Jordan is ruined!   Jer 2:15

Two Shepherds

⁴This is what the Lord my
God says: "Shepherd the flock
marked for slaughter. ⁵Their
buyers slaughter them and go
unpunished. Those who sell
them say, 'Praise the Lord, I am
rich!' Their own shepherds do
not spare them. ⁶For I will no
longer have pity on the people of
the land," declares the Lord. "I
will give everyone into the hands
of their neighbors and their king.

They will devastate the land, and I will not rescue anyone from their hands." Mic 5:8; 7:2-6

⁷So I shepherded the flock marked for slaughter, particularly the oppressed of the flock. Then I took two staffs and called one Favor and the other Union, and I shepherded the flock. ⁸In one month I got rid of the three shepherds. Jer 25:34

The flock detested me, and I grew weary of them ⁹and said, "I will not be your shepherd. Let the dying die, and the perishing perish. Let those who are left eat one another's flesh." Jer 15:2; 43:11

¹⁰Then I took my staff called Favor and broke it, revoking the covenant I had made with all the nations. ¹¹It was revoked on that day, and so the oppressed of the flock who were watching me knew it was the word of the LORD. Jer 14:21

¹²I told them, "If you think it best, give me my pay; but if not, keep it." So they paid me thirty pieces of silver. Ex 21:32; Mt 26:15

¹³And the LORD said to me, "Throw it to the potter"—the handsome price at which they valued me! So I took the thirty pieces of silver and threw them to the potter at the house of the LORD. Mt 27:9-10; Ac 1:18-19

¹⁴Then I broke my second staff called Union, breaking the family bond between Judah and Israel.

¹⁵Then the LORD said to me,

"Take again the equipment of a foolish shepherd. ¹⁶For I am going to raise up a shepherd over the land who will not care for the lost, or seek the young, or heal the injured, or feed the healthy, but will eat the meat of the choice sheep, tearing off their hooves.

¹⁷"Woe to the worthless
　　shepherd, Jer 23:1
who deserts the flock!
May the sword strike his arm
　　and his right eye!
May his arm be completely
　　withered,
his right eye totally
　　blinded!" Isa 13:1; Jer 23:1

Jerusalem's Enemies to Be Destroyed

12 A prophecy: The word of the LORD concerning Israel.

The LORD, who stretches out the heavens, who lays the foundation of the earth, and who forms the human spirit within a person, declares: ²"I am going to make Jerusalem a cup that sends all the surrounding peoples reeling. Judah will be besieged as well as Jerusalem. ³On that day, when all the nations of the earth are gathered against her, I will make Jerusalem an immovable rock for all the nations. All who try to move it will injure themselves. ⁴On that day I will strike every horse with panic and its rider with madness," declares the LORD. "I will keep a watchful eye over Judah, but I will blind all the horses of the nations. ⁵Then the clans of Judah will say in their hearts, 'The people of Jerusalem are strong, because the LORD Almighty is their God.' Ps 75:8; Isa 51:23; Zec 14:14

⁶"On that day I will make the clans of Judah like a firepot in a woodpile, like a flaming torch among sheaves. They will consume all the surrounding peoples right and left, but Jerusalem will remain intact in her place. Isa 10:17-18; Ob 18

⁷"The LORD will save the dwellings of Judah first, so that the honor of the house of David and of Jerusalem's inhabitants may not be greater than that of Judah. ⁸On that day the LORD will shield those who live in Jerusalem, so that the feeblest among them will be like David, and the house of David will be like God, like the angel of the LORD going before them. ⁹On that day I will set out to destroy all the nations that attack Jerusalem. Zec 9:15; 14:2-3

Mourning for the One They Pierced

¹⁰"And I will pour out on the house of David and the inhabitants of Jerusalem a spirit^a of grace and supplication. They will look on^b me, the one they have pierced, and they will mourn for him as one mourns for an

only child, and grieve bitterly for him as one grieves for a firstborn son. ¹¹On that day the weeping in Jerusalem will be as great as the weeping of Hadad Rimmon in the plain of Megiddo. ¹²The land will mourn, each clan by itself, with their wives by themselves: the clan of the house of David and their wives, the clan of the house of Nathan and their wives, ¹³the clan of the house of Levi and their wives, the clan of Shimei and their wives, ¹⁴and all the rest of the clans and their wives. Jn 19:34,37; Rev 1:7

Cleansing From Sin

13 "On that day a fountain will be opened to the house of David and the inhabitants of Jerusalem, to cleanse them from sin and impurity. Ps 51:2; Heb 9:14; Jer 17:13

²"On that day, I will banish the names of the idols from the land, and they will be remembered no more," declares the LORD Almighty. "I will remove both the prophets and the spirit of impurity from the land. ³And if anyone still prophesies, their father and mother, to whom they were born, will say to them, 'You must die, because you have told lies in the LORD's name.' Then their own parents will stab the one who prophesies. Dt 18:20; Jer 23:14-15,34

⁴"On that day every prophet will be ashamed of their prophetic vision. They will not put

---

^a 10 Or *the Spirit*   ^b 10 Or *to*

on a prophet's garment of hair in order to deceive. [5] Each will say, 'I am not a prophet. I am a farmer; the land has been my livelihood since my youth.'[a'] [6] If someone asks, 'What are these wounds on your body[b]?' they will answer, 'The wounds I was given at the house of my friends.' Mic 3:6-7; Mt 3:4

The Shepherd Struck, the Sheep Scattered

[7] "Awake, sword, against my
shepherd,   Isa 40:11; Jer 47:6
against the man who is
close to me!"
declares the LORD
Almighty.
"Strike the shepherd,
and the sheep will be
scattered,   Mt 26:31
and I will turn my hand
against the little ones.
[8] In the whole land," declares
the LORD,
"two-thirds will be struck
down and perish;
yet one-third will be left
in it.   Eze 5:2-4,12
[9] This third I will put into the
fire;   Mal 3:2
I will refine them like
silver   1Pe 1:6-7
and test them like gold.
They will call on my name
and I will answer them;
I will say, 'They are my
people,'   Jer 30:22

and they will say, 'The LORD
is our God.'"   Jer 29:12

The LORD Comes and Reigns

14 A day of the LORD is coming, Jerusalem, when your possessions will be plundered and divided up within your very walls.   Isa 13:9; Mal 4:1
[2] I will gather all the nations to Jerusalem to fight against it; the city will be captured, the houses ransacked, and the women raped. Half of the city will go into exile, but the rest of the people will not be taken from the city. [3] Then the LORD will go out and fight against those nations, as he fights on a day of battle. [4] On that day his feet will stand on the Mount of Olives, east of Jerusalem, and the Mount of Olives will be split in two from east to west, forming a great valley, with half of the mountain moving north and half moving south. [5] You will flee by my mountain valley, for it will extend to Azel. You will flee as you fled from the earthquake[c] in the days of Uzziah king of Judah. Then the LORD my God will come, and all the holy ones with him.   Eze 11:23; Am 1:1; Mt 16:27
[6] On that day there will be neither sunlight nor cold, frosty darkness. [7] It will be a unique day — a day known only to the LORD — with no distinction be-

---

[a] 5 Or *farmer; a man sold me in my youth*   [b] 6 Or *wounds between your hands*
[c] 5 Or *⁵My mountain valley will be blocked and will extend to Azel. It will be blocked as it was blocked because of the earthquake*

tween day and night. When evening comes, there will be light. Rev 21:23-25; 22:5

⁸On that day living water will flow out from Jerusalem, half of it east to the Dead Sea and half of it west to the Mediterranean Sea, in summer and in winter. Eze 47:1-12

⁹The Lord will be king over the whole earth. On that day there will be one Lord, and his name the only name. Eph 4:5-6; Rev 11:15

¹⁰The whole land, from Geba to Rimmon, south of Jerusalem, will become like the Arabah. But Jerusalem will be raised up high from the Benjamin Gate to the site of the First Gate, to the Corner Gate, and from the Tower of Hananel to the royal winepresses, and will remain in its place. ¹¹It will be inhabited; never again will it be destroyed. Jerusalem will be secure. Am 9:11; Zec 12:6

¹²This is the plague with which the Lord will strike all the nations that fought against Jerusalem: Their flesh will rot while they are still standing on their feet, their eyes will rot in their sockets, and their tongues will rot in their mouths. ¹³On that day people will be stricken by the Lord with great panic. They will seize each other by the hand and attack one another. ¹⁴Judah too will fight at Jerusalem. The wealth of all the surrounding nations will be collected—great quantities of gold

and silver and clothing. ¹⁵A similar plague will strike the horses and mules, the camels and donkeys, and all the animals in those camps. Dt 28:22; Zec 11:6

¹⁶Then the survivors from all the nations that have attacked Jerusalem will go up year after year to worship the King, the Lord Almighty, and to celebrate the Festival of Tabernacles. ¹⁷If any of the peoples of the earth do not go up to Jerusalem to worship the King, the Lord Almighty, they will have no rain. ¹⁸If the Egyptian people do not go up and take part, they will have no rain. The Lord[a] will bring on them the plague he inflicts on the nations that do not go up to celebrate the Festival of Tabernacles. ¹⁹This will be the punishment of Egypt and the punishment of all the nations that do not go up to celebrate the Festival of Tabernacles. Isa 60:6-9; Am 4:7

²⁰On that day HOLY TO THE LORD will be inscribed on the bells of the horses, and the cooking pots in the Lord's house will be like the sacred bowls in front of the altar. ²¹Every pot in Jerusalem and Judah will be holy to the Lord Almighty, and all who come to sacrifice will take some of the pots and cook in them. And on that day there will no longer be a Canaanite[b] in the house of the Lord Almighty. 1Co 10:31; Eze 44:9

---

[a] 18 Or part, then the Lord   [b] 21 Or merchant

Malachi

1

A prophecy: The word of the LORD to Israel through Malachi.[a]

Na 1:1; 1Pe 4:11

Israel Doubts God's Love

[2] "I have loved you," says the LORD.

Dt 4:37

"But you ask, 'How have you loved us?'

Mal 2:14,17

"Was not Esau Jacob's brother?" declares the LORD. "Yet I have loved Jacob, [3]but Esau I have hated, and I have turned his hill country into a wasteland and left his inheritance to the desert jackals."

Ro 9:13; Isa 34:10; Eze 35:3-9

[4]Edom may say, "Though we have been crushed, we will rebuild the ruins."

Isa 9:10

But this is what the LORD Almighty says: "They may build, but I will demolish. They will be called the Wicked Land, a people always under the wrath of the LORD. [5]You will see it with your own eyes and say, 'Great is the LORD — even beyond the borders of Israel!'

Ps 35:27; Am 1:11-12

Breaking Covenant Through Blemished Sacrifices

[6] "A son honors his father, and a slave his master. If I am a father, where is the honor due me? If I am a master, where is the respect due me?" says the LORD Almighty.

Isa 1:2; Mt 15:4

"It is you priests who show contempt for my name.

"But you ask, 'How have we shown contempt for your name?'

[7] "By offering defiled food on my altar.

Lev 21:6

"But you ask, 'How have we defiled you?'

"By saying that the LORD's table is contemptible. [8]When you offer blind animals for sacrifice, is that not wrong? When you sacrifice lame or diseased animals, is that not wrong? Try offering them to your governor! Would he be pleased with you? Would he accept you?" says the LORD Almighty.

Lev 22:22; Dt 15:21; Isa 43:23

[9] "Now plead with God to be gracious to us. With such offer-

---

[a] 1 Malachi means my messenger.

ings from your hands, will he accept you?" — says the LORD Almighty. Lev 23:33-44

10 "Oh, that one of you would shut the temple doors, so that you would not light useless fires on my altar! I am not pleased with you," says the LORD Almighty, "and I will accept no offering from your hands. 11 My name will be great among the nations, from where the sun rises to where it sets. In every place incense and pure offerings will be brought to me, because my name will be great among the nations," says the LORD Almighty. Isa 1:11-14

12 "But you profane it by saying, 'The Lord's table is defiled,' and, 'Its food is contemptible.' 13 And you say, 'What a burden!' and you sniff at it contemptuously," says the LORD Almighty. Isa 43:22-24

"When you bring injured, lame or diseased animals and offer them as sacrifices, should I accept them from your hands?" says the LORD. 14 "Cursed is the cheat who has an acceptable male in his flock and vows to give it, but then sacrifices a blemished animal to the Lord. For I am a great king," says the LORD Almighty, "and my name is to be feared among the nations. Lev 22:18-21; 1Ti 6:15

Additional Warning to the Priests

2 "And now, you priests, this warning is for you. 2 If you do not listen, and if you do not re-

solve to honor my name," says the LORD Almighty, "I will send a curse on you, and I will curse your blessings. Yes, I have already cursed them, because you have not resolved to honor me. Dt 28:20

3 "Because of you I will rebuke your descendants[a]; I will smear on your faces the dung from your festival sacrifices, and you will be carried off with it. 4 And you will know that I have sent you this warning so that my covenant with Levi may continue," says the LORD Almighty. 5 "My covenant was with him, a covenant of life and peace, and I gave them to him; this called for reverence and he revered me and stood in awe of my name. 6 True instruction was in his mouth and nothing false was found on his lips. He walked with me in peace and uprightness, and turned many from sin. Nu 25:12; Jer 23:22

7 "For the lips of a priest ought to preserve knowledge, because he is the messenger of the LORD Almighty and people seek instruction from his mouth. 8 But you have turned from the way and by your teaching have caused many to stumble; you have violated the covenant with Levi," says the LORD Almighty. 9 "So I have caused you to be despised and humiliated before all the people, because you have not followed my ways but have

a 3 Or will blight your grain

shown partiality in matters of the law." 1Sa 2:30; Jer 18:15

Breaking Covenant Through Divorce

¹⁰Do we not all have one Father*a*? Did not one God create us? Why do we profane the covenant of our ancestors by being unfaithful to one another? Ex 19:5; 1Co 8:6

¹¹Judah has been unfaithful. A detestable thing has been committed in Israel and in Jerusalem: Judah has desecrated the sanctuary the LORD loves by marrying women who worship a foreign god. ¹²As for the man who does this, whoever he may be, may the LORD remove him from the tents of Jacob*b* — even though he brings an offering to the LORD Almighty. Mal 1:10

¹³Another thing you do: You flood the LORD's altar with tears. You weep and wail because he no longer looks with favor on your offerings or accepts them with pleasure from your hands. ¹⁴You ask, "Why?" It is because the LORD is the witness between you and the wife of your youth. You have been unfaithful to her, though she is your partner, the wife of your marriage covenant. Pr 5:18; Heb 13:4

¹⁵Has not the one God made you? You belong to him in body and spirit. And what does the one God seek? Godly offspring.*c* So be on your guard, and do not be unfaithful to the wife of your youth. Mt 19:4-6; 1Co 7:14

¹⁶"The man who hates and divorces his wife," says the LORD, the God of Israel, "does violence to the one he should protect,"*d* says the LORD Almighty. Dt 24:1

So be on your guard, and do not be unfaithful. Ps 51:10

Breaking Covenant Through Injustice

¹⁷You have wearied the LORD with your words. Isa 43:24

"How have we wearied him?" you ask. Mal 1:2

By saying, "All who do evil are good in the eyes of the LORD, and he is pleased with them" or "Where is the God of justice?"

3 "I will send my messenger, who will prepare the way before me. Then suddenly the Lord you are seeking will come to his temple; the messenger of the covenant, whom you desire, will come," says the LORD Almighty. Mt 11:10

²But who can endure the day of his coming? Who can stand when he appears? For he will be like a refiner's fire or a launderer's soap. ³He will sit as a refiner and purifier of silver; he will purify the Levites and refine them like

---

a 10 Or *father*   *b* 12 Or *¹²May the LORD remove from the tents of Jacob anyone who gives testimony in behalf of the man who does this*   *c* 15 The meaning of the Hebrew for the first part of this verse is uncertain.   *d* 16 Or *"I hate divorce," says the LORD, the God of Israel, "because the man who divorces his wife covers his garment with violence,"* gold and silver. Then the LORD will have men who will bring offerings in righteousness, [4] and the offerings of Judah and Jerusalem will be acceptable to the LORD, as in days gone by, as in former years. Rev 6:17; Isa 1:25; Mal 1:11

[5] "So I will come to put you on trial. I will be quick to testify against sorcerers, adulterers and perjurers, against those who defraud laborers of their wages, who oppress the widows and the fatherless, and deprive the foreigners among you of justice, but do not fear me," says the LORD Almighty. Lev 19:13; Jer 7:9; Jas 5:4

Breaking Covenant by Withholding Tithes

[6] "I the LORD do not change. So you, the descendants of Jacob, are not destroyed. [7] Ever since the time of your ancestors you have turned away from my decrees and have not kept them. Return to me, and I will return to you," says the LORD Almighty. Ac 7:51; Jas 1:17

"But you ask, 'How are we to return?'

[8] "Will a mere mortal rob God? Yet you rob me.

"But you ask, 'How are we robbing you?'

"In tithes and offerings. [9] You are under a curse — your whole nation — because you are robbing me. [10] Bring the whole tithe into the storehouse, that there may be food in my house. Test me in this,"

says the LORD Almighty, "and see if I will not throw open the floodgates of heaven and pour out so much blessing that there will not be room enough to store it. [11] I will prevent pests from devouring your crops, and the vines in your fields will not drop their fruit before it is ripe," says the LORD Almighty. [12] "Then all the nations will call you blessed, for yours will be a delightful land," says the LORD Almighty. Ne 13:10-12; Isa 62:4

Israel Speaks Arrogantly Against God

[13] "You have spoken arrogantly against me," says the LORD. Mal 2:17

"Yet you ask, 'What have we said against you?'

[14] "You have said, 'It is futile to serve God. What do we gain by carrying out his requirements and going about like mourners before the LORD Almighty? [15] But now we call the arrogant blessed. Certainly evildoers prosper, and even when they put God to the test, they get away with it.'" Isa 58:3; Jer 7:10

The Faithful Remnant

[16] Then those who feared the LORD talked with each other, and the LORD listened and heard. A scroll of remembrance was written in his presence concerning those who feared the LORD and honored his name. Ps 34:15; 56:8

[17] "On the day when I act," says the LORD Almighty, "they

will be my treasured possession. I will spare them, just as a father has compassion and spares his son who serves him. [18] And you will again see the distinction between the righteous and the wicked, between those who serve God and those who do not. Ps 103:13; Mt 25:32-33,41

Judgment and Covenant Renewal

4 [a] "Surely the day is coming; it will burn like a furnace. All the arrogant and every evildoer will be stubble, and the day that is coming will set them on fire," says the LORD Almighty. "Not a root or a branch will be left to them. [2] But for you who revere my name, the sun of righ-

teousness will rise with healing in its rays. And you will go out and frolic like well-fed calves. [3] Then you will trample on the wicked; they will be ashes under the soles of your feet on the day when I act," says the LORD Almighty. Lk 1:78; Eph 5:14

[4] "Remember the law of my servant Moses, the decrees and laws I gave him at Horeb for all Israel. Ex 20:1

[5] "See, I will send the prophet Elijah to you before that great and dreadful day of the LORD comes. [6] He will turn the hearts of the parents to their children, and the hearts of the children to their parents; or else I will come and strike the land with total destruction." Mt 11:14; Lk 1:17

---

[a] In Hebrew texts 4:1-6 is numbered 3:19-24.

The New Testament

Matthew

The Genealogy of Jesus the Messiah

1:1-17pp — Lk 3:23-38
1:3-6pp — Ru 4:18-22
1:7-11pp — 1Ch 3:10-17

1 This is the genealogy*a* of Jesus the Messiah*b* the son of David, the son of Abraham: Ge 22:18

² Abraham was the father of Isaac, Ge 21:3,12
Isaac the father of Jacob,
Jacob the father of Judah and his brothers, Ge 29:35
³ Judah the father of Perez and Zerah, whose mother was Tamar, Ge 38:27-30
Perez the father of Hezron,
Hezron the father of Ram,
⁴ Ram the father of Amminadab,
Amminadab the father of Nahshon,
Nahshon the father of Salmon,
⁵ Salmon the father of Boaz, whose mother was Rahab,
Boaz the father of Obed, whose mother was Ruth,
Obed the father of Jesse,
⁶ and Jesse the father of King David. Ru 4:18-22; 1Sa 16:1

David was the father of Solomon, whose mother had been Uriah's wife, 2Sa 12:24
⁷ Solomon the father of Rehoboam,
Rehoboam the father of Abijah,
Abijah the father of Asa,
⁸ Asa the father of Jehoshaphat,
Jehoshaphat the father of Jehoram,
Jehoram the father of Uzziah,
⁹ Uzziah the father of Jotham,
Jotham the father of Ahaz,
Ahaz the father of Hezekiah,

¹⁰ Hezekiah the father of Manasseh,
Manasseh the father of Amon,
Amon the father of Josiah,
¹¹ and Josiah the father of Jeconiah and his brothers at the time of the exile to Babylon.

¹² After the exile to Babylon:
Jeconiah was the father of Shealtiel,
Shealtiel the father of Zerubbabel,

---

a 1 Or *is an account of the origin*   *b* 1 Or *Jesus Christ. Messiah* (Hebrew) and *Christ* (Greek) both mean *Anointed One*; also in verse 18.

¹⁰Hezekiah the father of Manasseh, 2Ki 20:21

Manasseh the father of Amon,

Amon the father of Josiah,

¹¹and Josiah the father of Jeconiah*ᵃ* and his brothers at the time of the exile to Babylon. 1Ch 3:10-17

¹²After the exile to Babylon:

Jeconiah was the father of Shealtiel, 1Ch 3:17

Shealtiel the father of Zerubbabel, 1Ch 3:19; Ezr 3:2

¹³Zerubbabel the father of Abihud,

Abihud the father of Eliakim,

Eliakim the father of Azor,

¹⁴Azor the father of Zadok,

Zadok the father of Akim,

Akim the father of Elihud,

¹⁵Elihud the father of Eleazar,

Eleazar the father of Matthan,

Matthan the father of Jacob,

¹⁶and Jacob the father of Joseph, the husband of Mary, and Mary was the mother of Jesus who is called the Messiah.

¹⁷Thus there were fourteen generations in all from Abraham to David, fourteen from David to the exile to Babylon, and fourteen from the exile to the Messiah. Lk 3:23-38

Joseph Accepts Jesus as His Son

¹⁸This is how the birth of Jesus the Messiah came about*ᵇ*: His mother Mary was pledged to be married to Joseph, but before they came together, she was found to be pregnant through the Holy Spirit. ¹⁹Because Joseph her husband was faithful to the law, and yet*ᶜ* did not want to expose her to public disgrace, he had in mind to divorce her quietly. Lk 1:35; Dt 24:1

²⁰But after he had considered this, an angel of the Lord appeared to him in a dream and said, "Joseph son of David, do not be afraid to take Mary home as your wife, because what is conceived in her is from the Holy Spirit. ²¹She will give birth to a son, and you are to give him the name Jesus,*ᵈ* because he will save his people from their sins." Lk 2:11; Ac 13:23,28

²²All this took place to fulfill what the Lord had said through the prophet: ²³"The virgin will conceive and give birth to a son, and they will call him Immanuel"*ᵉ* (which means "God with us"). Isa 8:8,10

²⁴When Joseph woke up, he did what the angel of the Lord had commanded him and took

---

ᵃ 11 That is, Jehoiachin; also in verse 12   *ᵇ* 18 Or *The origin of Jesus the Messiah was like this*   *ᶜ* 19 Or *was a righteous man and* means *the LORD saves.*   *ᵈ* 21 *Jesus* is the Greek form of *Joshua,* which   *ᵉ* 23 Isaiah 7:14

Mary home as his wife. ²⁵But he did not consummate their marriage until she gave birth to a son. And he gave him the name Jesus. Lk 1:31

The Magi Visit the Messiah

2 After Jesus was born in Bethlehem in Judea, during the time of King Herod, Magi*ᵃ* from the east came to Jerusalem ²and asked, "Where is the one who has been born king of the Jews? We saw his star when it rose and have come to worship him." Nu 24:17

³When King Herod heard this he was disturbed, and all Jerusalem with him. ⁴When he had called together all the people's chief priests and teachers of the law, he asked them where the Messiah was to be born. ⁵"In Bethlehem in Judea," they replied, "for this is what the prophet has written:

⁶" 'But you, Bethlehem, in the
land of Judah,
    are by no means least
        among the rulers of
        Judah;
for out of you will come a
    ruler
    who will shepherd my
        people Israel.'ᵇ" Jn 7:42

⁷Then Herod called the Magi secretly and found out from them the exact time the star had appeared. ⁸He sent them

to Bethlehem and said, "Go and search carefully for the child. As soon as you find him, report to me, so that I too may go and worship him."

⁹After they had heard the king, they went on their way, and the star they had seen when it rose went ahead of them until it stopped over the place where the child was. ¹⁰When they saw the star, they were overjoyed. ¹¹On coming to the house, they saw the child with his mother Mary, and they bowed down and worshiped him. Then they opened their treasures and presented him with gifts of gold, frankincense and myrrh. ¹²And having been warned in a dream not to go back to Herod, they returned to their country by another route. Ps 72:10; Isa 60:3

The Escape to Egypt

¹³When they had gone, an angel of the Lord appeared to Joseph in a dream. "Get up," he said, "take the child and his mother and escape to Egypt. Stay there until I tell you, for Herod is going to search for the child to kill him." Rev 12:4

¹⁴So he got up, took the child and his mother during the night and left for Egypt, ¹⁵where he stayed until the death of Herod. And so was fulfilled what the Lord had said through the

ᵃ 1 Traditionally *wise men*   ᵇ 6 Micah 5:2,4

prophet: "Out of Egypt I called my son."[a]   Ex 4:22-23

[16]When Herod realized that he had been outwitted by the Magi, he was furious, and he gave orders to kill all the boys in Bethlehem and its vicinity who were two years old and under, in accordance with the time he had learned from the Magi. [17]Then what was said through the prophet Jeremiah was fulfilled: Mt 1:22

[18]"A voice is heard in Ramah,
    weeping and great
        mourning,
    Rachel weeping for her
        children
    and refusing to be
        comforted,
    because they are no more."[b]

The Return to Nazareth

[19]After Herod died, an angel of the Lord appeared in a dream to Joseph in Egypt [20]and said, "Get up, take the child and his mother and go to the land of Israel, for those who were trying to take the child's life are dead."   Ex 4:19

[21]So he got up, took the child and his mother and went to the land of Israel. [22]But when he heard that Archelaus was reigning in Judea in place of his father Herod, he was afraid to go there. Having been warned in a dream, he withdrew to the district of Galilee, [23]and he went and lived in a town called Nazareth. So was fulfilled what was said through the prophets, that he would be called a Nazarene.   Lk 1:26; Jn 1:45-46

John the Baptist Prepares the Way

3:1-12pp — Mk 1:3-8; Lk 3:2-17

3 In those days John the Baptist came, preaching in the wilderness of Judea [2]and saying, "Repent, for the kingdom of heaven has come near." [3]This is he who was spoken of through the prophet Isaiah: Mt 4:17

"A voice of one calling in the
    wilderness,
'Prepare the way for the Lord,
    make straight paths for
        him.' "[c]   Lk 1:76; Jn 1:23

[4]John's clothes were made of camel's hair, and he had a leather belt around his waist. His food was locusts and wild honey. [5]People went out to him from Jerusalem and all Judea and the whole region of the Jordan. [6]Confessing their sins, they were baptized by him in the Jordan River.   Lev 11:22; 2Ki 1:8

[7]But when he saw many of the Pharisees and Sadducees coming to where he was baptizing, he said to them: "You brood of vipers! Who warned you to flee from the coming wrath? [8]Produce fruit in keeping with repentance. [9]And do not think you can say to yourselves, 'We have

---

[a] 15 Hosea 11:1   [b] 18 Jer. 31:15   [c] 3 Isaiah 40:3

Abraham as our father.' I tell you that out of these stones God can raise up children for Abraham. [10]The ax is already at the root of the trees, and every tree that does not produce good fruit will be cut down and thrown into the fire. Mt 7:19; Ac 26:20

[11]"I baptize you with[a] water for repentance. But after me comes one who is more powerful than I, whose sandals I am not worthy to carry. He will baptize you with[a] the Holy Spirit and fire. [12]His winnowing fork is in his hand, and he will clear his threshing floor, gathering his wheat into the barn and burning up the chaff with unquenchable fire." Mk 1:3-8; Lk 3:2-17

The Baptism of Jesus
3:13-17pp — Mk 1:9-11; Lk 3:21,22; Jn 1:31-34

[13]Then Jesus came from Galilee to the Jordan to be baptized by John. [14]But John tried to deter him, saying, "I need to be baptized by you, and do you come to me?" Mk 1:4

[15]Jesus replied, "Let it be so now; it is proper for us to do this to fulfill all righteousness." Then John consented.

[16]As soon as Jesus was baptized, he went up out of the water. At that moment heaven was opened, and he saw the Spirit of God descending like a dove and

alighting on him. [17]And a voice from heaven said, "This is my Son, whom I love; with him I am well pleased." Mk 1:9-11; Lk 3:21-22

Jesus Is Tested in the Wilderness
4:1-11pp — Mk 1:12,13; Lk 4:1-13

4 Then Jesus was led by the Spirit into the wilderness to be tempted[b] by the devil. [2]After fasting forty days and forty nights, he was hungry. [3]The tempter came to him and said, "If you are the Son of God, tell these stones to become bread." 1Ki 19:8; 1Th 3:5

[4]Jesus answered, "It is written: 'Man shall not live on bread alone, but on every word that comes from the mouth of God.'[c]" Jn 4:34

[5]Then the devil took him to the holy city and had him stand on the highest point of the temple. [6]"If you are the Son of God," he said, "throw yourself down. For it is written: Mt 27:53

" 'He will command his angels concerning you,
and they will lift you up in their hands,
so that you will not strike your foot against a stone.'[d]"

[7]Jesus answered him, "It is also written: 'Do not put the Lord your God to the test.'[e]"

[8]Again, the devil took him

---

[a] 11 Or in   [b] 1 The Greek for tempted can also mean tested.   [c] 4 Deut. 8:3
[d] 6 Psalm 91:11,12   [e] 7 Deut. 6:16

to a very high mountain and showed him all the kingdoms of the world and their splendor. [9]"All this I will give you," he said, "if you will bow down and worship me."

[10]Jesus said to him, "Away from me, Satan! For it is written: 'Worship the Lord your God, and serve him only.'[a]"

[11]Then the devil left him, and angels came and attended him.   Mk 1:12-13; Lk 4:1-13

Jesus Begins to Preach

[12]When Jesus heard that John had been put in prison, he withdrew to Galilee. [13]Leaving Nazareth, he went and lived in Capernaum, which was by the lake in the area of Zebulun and Naphtali— [14]to fulfill what was said through the prophet Isaiah: Mt 14:3; Mk 1:21

[15]"Land of Zebulun and land of
        Naphtali,
    the Way of the Sea, beyond
        the Jordan,
    Galilee of the Gentiles—
[16]the people living in
        darkness
    have seen a great light;
    on those living in the land of
        the shadow of death
    a light has dawned."[b]   Lk 2:32

[17]From that time on Jesus began to preach, "Repent, for the kingdom of heaven has come near."   Mt 3:2

Jesus Calls His First Disciples

4:18-22pp — Mk 1:16-20; Lk 5:2-11;
        Jn 1:35-42

[18]As Jesus was walking beside the Sea of Galilee, he saw two brothers, Simon called Peter and his brother Andrew. They were casting a net into the lake, for they were fishermen. [19]"Come, follow me," Jesus said, "and I will send you out to fish for people." [20]At once they left their nets and followed him.   Mk 10:21,28,52

[21]Going on from there, he saw two other brothers, James son of Zebedee and his brother John. They were in a boat with their father Zebedee, preparing their nets. Jesus called them, [22]and immediately they left the boat and their father and followed him.   Mk 1:16-20; Lk 5:2-11; Jn 1:35-42

Jesus Heals the Sick

[23]Jesus went throughout Galilee, teaching in their synagogues, proclaiming the good news of the kingdom, and healing every disease and sickness among the people. [24]News about him spread all over Syria, and people brought to him all who were ill with various diseases, those suffering severe pain, the demon-possessed, those having seizures, and the paralyzed; and he healed them. [25]Large crowds from Galilee, the Decapolis,[c] Jerusalem, Judea and the re-

[a] 10 Deut. 6:13   [b] 16 Isaiah 9:1,2   [c] 25 That is, the Ten Cities

gion across the Jordan followed him. Mk 1:14; Ac 10:38

Introduction to the Sermon on the Mount

5 Now when Jesus saw the crowds, he went up on a mountainside and sat down. His disciples came to him, ²and he began to teach them.

The Beatitudes

5:3-12pp — Lk 6:20-23

He said:

³ "Blessed are the poor in spirit,
   for theirs is the kingdom of
   heaven.   Mt 25:34
⁴ Blessed are those who mourn,
   for they will be
   comforted.   Isa 61:2-3
⁵ Blessed are the meek,
   for they will inherit the
   earth.   Ps 37:11; Ro 4:13
⁶ Blessed are those who
   hunger and thirst for
   righteousness,
   for they will be filled. Isa 55:1-2
⁷ Blessed are the merciful,
   for they will be shown
   mercy.   Jas 2:13
⁸ Blessed are the pure in heart,
   for they will see God. Heb 12:14
⁹ Blessed are the peacemakers,
   for they will be called
   children of God.   Ro 8:14
¹⁰ Blessed are those who
   persecuted because of
   righteousness,   1Pe 3:14
   for theirs is the kingdom of
   heaven.   Mt 25:34

¹¹ "Blessed are you when people insult you, persecute you and falsely say all kinds of evil against you because of me. ¹²Rejoice and be glad, because great is your reward in heaven, for in the same way they persecuted the prophets who were before you.   Ac 7:52; 1Pe 4:14

Salt and Light

¹³ "You are the salt of the earth. But if the salt loses its saltiness, how can it be made salty again? It is no longer good for anything, except to be thrown out and trampled underfoot. Mk 9:50; Lk 14:34-35
¹⁴ "You are the light of the world. A town built on a hill cannot be hidden. ¹⁵Neither do people light a lamp and put it under a bowl. Instead they put it on its stand, and it gives light to everyone in the house. ¹⁶In the same way, let your light shine before others, that they may see your good deeds and glorify your Father in heaven.   Jn 8:12; 1Co 10:31

The Fulfillment of the Law

¹⁷ "Do not think that I have come to abolish the Law or the Prophets; I have not come to abolish them but to fulfill them. ¹⁸For truly I tell you, until heaven and earth disappear, not the smallest letter, not the least stroke of a pen, will by any means disappear from the Law until everything is accomplished. ¹⁹Therefore anyone who sets

1524 | MATTHEW 5:20

aside one of the least of these commands and teaches others accordingly will be called least in the kingdom of heaven, but whoever practices and teaches these commands will be called great in the kingdom of heaven. 20 For I tell you that unless your righteousness surpasses that of the Pharisees and the teachers of the law, you will certainly not enter the kingdom of heaven. Lk 16:17; Jas 2:10

Murder

5:25,26pp — Lk 12:58,59

21 "You have heard that it was said to the people long ago, 'You shall not murder,*a* and anyone who murders will be subject to judgment.' 22 But I tell you that anyone who is angry with a brother or sister*b,c* will be subject to judgment. Again, anyone who says to a brother or sister, 'Raca,'*d* is answerable to the court. And anyone who says, 'You fool!' will be in danger of the fire of hell. 1Jn 3:15

23 "Therefore, if you are offering your gift at the altar and there remember that your brother or sister has something against you, 24 leave your gift there in front of the altar. First go and be reconciled to them; then come and offer your gift.

25 "Settle matters quickly with your adversary who is taking you to court. Do it while you are still together on the way, or your adversary may hand you over to the judge, and the judge may hand you over to the officer, and you may be thrown into prison. 26 Truly I tell you, you will not get out until you have paid the last penny. Lk 12:58-59

Adultery

27 "You have heard that it was said, 'You shall not commit adultery.'*e* 28 But I tell you that anyone who looks at a woman lustfully has already committed adultery with her in his heart. 29 If your right eye causes you to stumble, gouge it out and throw it away. It is better for you to lose one part of your body than for your whole body to be thrown into hell. 30 And if your right hand causes you to stumble, cut it off and throw it away. It is better for you to lose one part of your body than for your whole body to go into hell. Mk 9:42-47; Pr 6:25

Divorce

31 "It has been said, 'Anyone who divorces his wife must give her a certificate of divorce.'*f* 32 But I tell you that anyone who divorces his wife, except for sexual immorality, makes her the

---

a 21 Exodus 20:13   *b 22* The Greek word for *brother or sister* (*adelphos*) refers here to a fellow disciple, whether man or woman; also in verse 23.   *c 22* Some manuscripts *brother or sister without cause*   *d 22* An Aramaic term of contempt   *e 27* Exodus 20:14   *f 31* Deut. 24:1

victim of adultery, and anyone who marries a divorced woman commits adultery. Lk 16:18

Oaths

33 "Again, you have heard that it was said to the people long ago, 'Do not break your oath, but fulfill to the Lord the vows you have made.' 34 But I tell you, do not swear an oath at all: either by heaven, for it is God's throne; 35 or by the earth, for it is his footstool; or by Jerusalem, for it is the city of the Great King. 36 And do not swear by your head, for you cannot make even one hair white or black. 37 All you need to say is simply 'Yes' or 'No'; anything beyond this comes from the evil one.[a] Nu 30:2; Jas 5:12

Eye for Eye

38 "You have heard that it was said, 'Eye for eye, and tooth for tooth.'[b] 39 But I tell you, do not resist an evil person. If anyone slaps you on the right cheek, turn to them the other cheek also. 40 And if anyone wants to sue you and take your shirt, hand over your coat as well. 41 If anyone forces you to go one mile, go with them two miles. 42 Give to the one who asks you, and do not turn away from the one who wants to borrow from you. Lk 6:29-30

Love for Enemies

43 "You have heard that it was said, 'Love your neighbor[c] and hate your enemy.' 44 But I tell you, love your enemies and pray for those who persecute you, 45 that you may be children of your Father in heaven. He causes his sun to rise on the evil and the good, and sends rain on the righteous and the unrighteous. 46 If you love those who love you, what reward will you get? Are not even the tax collectors doing that? 47 And if you greet only your own people, what are you doing more than others? Do not even pagans do that? 48 Be perfect, therefore, as your heavenly Father is perfect. Lev 19:2; Lk 6:27-28

Giving to the Needy

6 "Be careful not to practice your righteousness in front of others to be seen by them. If you do, you will have no reward from your Father in heaven. Mt 23:5

2 "So when you give to the needy, do not announce it with trumpets, as the hypocrites do in the synagogues and on the streets, to be honored by others. Truly I tell you, they have received their reward in full. 3 But when you give to the needy, do not let your left hand know what your right hand is doing, 4 so that your giving may be in secret. Then your Father, who sees what is done in secret, will reward you. Col 3:23-24

---

[a] 37 Or *from evil*   [b] 38 Exodus 21:24; Lev. 24:20; Deut. 19:21   [c] 43 Lev. 19:18

Prayer

6:9-13pp — Lk 11:2-4

5 "And when you pray, do not be like the hypocrites, for they love to pray standing in the synagogues and on the street corners to be seen by others. Truly I tell you, they have received their reward in full. 6 But when you pray, go into your room, close the door and pray to your Father, who is unseen. Then your Father, who sees what is done in secret, will reward you. 7 And when you pray, do not keep on babbling like pagans, for they think they will be heard because of their many words. 8 Do not be like them, for your Father knows what you need before you ask him.   Lk 18:10-14

9 "This, then, is how you should pray:

" 'Our Father in heaven, Mal 2:10
   hallowed be your name,
10 your kingdom come, Mt 3:2
   your will be done, Mt 26:39
      on earth as it is in heaven.
11 Give us today our daily bread.
12 And forgive us our debts,
   as we also have forgiven our
      debtors. Mt 18:21-35
13 And lead us not into
      temptation,[a] Jas 1:13
   but deliver us from the evil
      one.[b]'

14 For if you forgive other people when they sin against you, your heavenly Father will also forgive you. 15 But if you do not forgive others their sins, your Father will not forgive your sins. Mt 18:21-35; Mk 11:25,26; Luke 11:2-4

Fasting

16 "When you fast, do not look somber as the hypocrites do, for they disfigure their faces to show others they are fasting. Truly I tell you, they have received their reward in full. 17 But when you fast, put oil on your head and wash your face, 18 so that it will not be obvious to others that you are fasting, but only to your Father, who is unseen; and your Father, who sees what is done in secret, will reward you.   ver 4,6; Isa 58:5

Treasures in Heaven

6:22,23pp — Lk 11:34-36

19 "Do not store up for yourselves treasures on earth, where moths and vermin destroy, and where thieves break in and steal. 20 But store up for yourselves treasures in heaven, where moths and vermin do not destroy, and where thieves do not break in and steal. 21 For where your treasure is, there your heart will be also.   Lk 12:33-34; Heb 13:5

22 "The eye is the lamp of the body. If your eyes are healthy,[c] your whole body will be full of

---

[a] 13 The Greek for *temptation* can also mean *testing*. [b] 13 Or *from evil*; some late manuscripts *one, / for yours is the kingdom and the power and the glory forever. Amen.*
[c] 22 The Greek for *healthy* here implies *generous*.

light. ²³But if your eyes are un-healthy,ª your whole body will be full of darkness. If then the light within you is darkness, how great is that darkness! Lk 11:34-36

²⁴"No one can serve two mas-ters. Either you will hate the one and love the other, or you will be devoted to the one and despise the other. You cannot serve both God and money. Lk 16:13

Do Not Worry

6:25-33pp — Lk 12:22-31

²⁵"Therefore I tell you, do not worry about your life, what you will eat or drink; or about your body, what you will wear. Is not life more than food, and the body more than clothes? ²⁶Look at the birds of the air; they do not sow or reap or store away in barns, and yet your heavenly Father feeds them. Are you not much more valuable than they? ²⁷Can any one of you by wor-rying add a single hour to your lifeᵇ? Mt 10:29-31; 1Pe 5:7

²⁸"And why do you wor-ry about clothes? See how the flowers of the field grow. They do not labor or spin. ²⁹Yet I tell you that not even Solomon in all his splendor was dressed like one of these. ³⁰If that is how God clothes the grass of the field, which is here today and tomor-row is thrown into the fire, will he not much more clothe you — you of little faith? ³¹So do not worry, saying, 'What shall we eat?' or 'What shall we drink?' or 'What shall we wear?' ³²For the pagans run after all these things, and your heavenly Fa-ther knows that you need them. ³³But seek first his kingdom and his righteousness, and all these things will be given to you as well. ³⁴Therefore do not worry about tomorrow, for tomorrow will worry about itself. Each day has enough trouble of its own. Lk 12:22-31

Judging Others

7:3-5pp — Lk 6:41,42

7 "Do not judge, or you too will be judged. ²For in the same way you judge others, you will be judged, and with the measure you use, it will be measured to you. Mk 4:24; Lk 6:38

³"Why do you look at the speck of sawdust in your brother's eye and pay no attention to the plank in your own eye? ⁴How can you say to your brother, 'Let me take the speck out of your eye,' when all the time there is a plank in your own eye? ⁵You hypocrite, first take the plank out of your own eye, and then you will see clearly to remove the speck from your brother's eye. Lk 6:41-42

⁶"Do not give dogs what is sa-cred; do not throw your pearls to pigs. If you do, they may trample them under their feet, and turn and tear you to pieces.

ª 23 The Greek for *unhealthy* here implies *stingy*.   ᵇ 27 Or *single cubit to your height*

Ask, Seek, Knock

7:7-11pp — Lk 11:9-13

7 "Ask and it will be given to you; seek and you will find; knock and the door will be opened to you. 8 For everyone who asks receives; the one who seeks finds; and to the one who knocks, the door will be opened. Jer 29:12-13; Jn 15:7,16

9 "Which of you, if your son asks for bread, will give him a stone? 10 Or if he asks for a fish, will give him a snake? 11 If you, then, though you are evil, know how to give good gifts to your children, how much more will your Father in heaven give good gifts to those who ask him! 12 So in everything, do to others what you would have them do to you, for this sums up the Law and the Prophets. Lk 11:9-13

The Narrow and Wide Gates

13 "Enter through the narrow gate. For wide is the gate and broad is the road that leads to destruction, and many enter through it. 14 But small is the gate and narrow the road that leads to life, and only a few find it. Lk 13:24; Jn 10:7,9

True and False Prophets

15 "Watch out for false prophets. They come to you in sheep's clothing, but inwardly they are ferocious wolves. 16 By their fruit you will recognize them. Do people pick grapes from thornbushes, or figs from thistles? 17 Like-wise, every good tree bears good fruit, but a bad tree bears bad fruit. 18 A good tree cannot bear bad fruit, and a bad tree cannot bear good fruit. 19 Every tree that does not bear good fruit is cut down and thrown into the fire. 20 Thus, by their fruit you will recognize them. Mk 13:22; Lk 6:44

True and False Disciples

21 "Not everyone who says to me, 'Lord, Lord,' will enter the kingdom of heaven, but only the one who does the will of my Father who is in heaven. 22 Many will say to me on that day, 'Lord, Lord, did we not prophesy in your name and in your name drive out demons and in your name perform many miracles?' 23 Then I will tell them plainly, 'I never knew you. Away from me, you evildoers!' Mt 25:12,41; Lk 13:25-27

The Wise and Foolish Builders

7:24-27pp — Lk 6:47-49

24 "Therefore everyone who hears these words of mine and puts them into practice is like a wise man who built his house on the rock. 25 The rain came down, the streams rose, and the winds blew and beat against that house; yet it did not fall, because it had its foundation on the rock. 26 But everyone who hears these words of mine and does not put them into practice is like a foolish man who built his house on sand. 27 The rain came down, the

streams rose, and the winds blew and beat against that house, and it fell with a great crash." Lk 6:47-49

²⁸When Jesus had finished saying these things, the crowds were amazed at his teaching, ²⁹because he taught as one who had authority, and not as their teachers of the law.   Lk 4:32; Jn 7:46

Jesus Heals a Man With Leprosy
8:2-4pp — Mk 1:40-44; Lk 5:12-14

8 When Jesus came down from the mountainside, large crowds followed him. ²A man with leprosy*ᵃ* came and knelt before him and said, "Lord, if you are willing, you can make me clean."   Mt 15:25

³Jesus reached out his hand and touched the man. "I am willing," he said. "Be clean!" Immediately he was cleansed of his leprosy. ⁴Then Jesus said to him, "See that you don't tell anyone. But go, show yourself to the priest and offer the gift Moses commanded, as a testimony to them."   Mk 1:40-44; Lk 5:12-14

The Faith of the Centurion
8:5-13pp — Lk 7:1-10

⁵When Jesus had entered Capernaum, a centurion came to him, asking for help. ⁶"Lord," he said, "my servant lies at home paralyzed, suffering terribly."   Mt 4:24

⁷Jesus said to him, "Shall I come and heal him?"

⁸The centurion replied, "Lord, I do not deserve to have you come under my roof. But just say the word, and my servant will be healed. ⁹For I myself am a man under authority, with soldiers under me. I tell this one, 'Go,' and he goes; and that one, 'Come,' and he comes. I say to my servant, 'Do this,' and he does it."   Ps 107:20

¹⁰When Jesus heard this, he was amazed and said to those following him, "Truly I tell you, I have not found anyone in Israel with such great faith. ¹¹I say to you that many will come from the east and the west, and will take their places at the feast with Abraham, Isaac and Jacob in the kingdom of heaven. ¹²But the subjects of the kingdom will be thrown outside, into the darkness, where there will be weeping and gnashing of teeth."   Lk 13:28-29

¹³Then Jesus said to the centurion, "Go! Let it be done just as you believed it would." And his servant was healed at that moment.   Lk 7:1-10

Jesus Heals Many
8:14-16pp — Mk 1:29-34; Lk 4:38-41

¹⁴When Jesus came into Peter's house, he saw Peter's mother-in-law lying in bed with a fever. ¹⁵He touched her hand and the fever left her, and she got up and began to wait on him. Mk 1:29-34; Lk 4:38-41

ᵃ 2 The Greek word traditionally translated *leprosy* was used for various diseases affecting the skin.

¹⁶When evening came, many who were demon-possessed were brought to him, and he drove out the spirits with a word and healed all the sick. ¹⁷This was to fulfill what was spoken through the prophet Isaiah: Mt 1:22

"He took up our infirmities
and bore our diseases."ᵃ

The Cost of Following Jesus
8:19-22pp — Lk 9:57-60

¹⁸When Jesus saw the crowd around him, he gave orders to cross to the other side of the lake. ¹⁹Then a teacher of the law came to him and said, "Teacher, I will follow you wherever you go." Mk 4:35

²⁰Jesus replied, "Foxes have dens and birds have nests, but the Son of Man has no place to lay his head." Mk 8:31

²¹Another disciple said to him, "Lord, first let me go and bury my father."

²²But Jesus told him, "Follow me, and let the dead bury their own dead." Lk 9:57-60

Jesus Calms the Storm
8:23-27pp — Mk 4:36-41; Lk 8:22-25
8:23-27Ref — Mt 14:22-33

²³Then he got into the boat and his disciples followed him. ²⁴Suddenly a furious storm came up on the lake, so that the waves swept over the boat. But Jesus was sleeping. ²⁵The disciples went and woke him, saying, "Lord, save us! We're going to drown!" Mk 4:36-41; Lk 8:22-25

²⁶He replied, "You of little faith, why are you so afraid?" Then he got up and rebuked the winds and the waves, and it was completely calm. Ps 65:7; 107:29

²⁷The men were amazed and asked, "What kind of man is this? Even the winds and the waves obey him!" Mt 14:22-33

Jesus Restores Two Demon-Possessed Men
8:28-34pp — Mk 5:1-17; Lk 8:26-37

²⁸When he arrived at the other side in the region of the Gadarenes,ᵇ two demon-possessed men coming from the tombs met him. They were so violent that no one could pass that way. ²⁹"What do you want with us, Son of God?" they shouted. "Have you come here to torture us before the appointed time?" Mk 1:24; Jn 2:4

³⁰Some distance from them a large herd of pigs was feeding. ³¹The demons begged Jesus, "If you drive us out, send us into the herd of pigs."

³²He said to them, "Go!" So they came out and went into the pigs, and the whole herd rushed down the steep bank into the lake and died in the water. ³³Those tending the pigs ran off,

---

ᵃ 17 Isaiah 53:4 (see Septuagint)   ᵇ 28 Some manuscripts *Gergesenes*; other manuscripts *Gerasenes* went into the town and reported all this, including what had happened to the demon-possessed men. ³⁴Then the whole town went out to meet Jesus. And when they saw him, they pleaded with him to leave their region. Mk 5:1-17; Lk 8:26-37

Jesus Forgives and Heals a Paralyzed Man
9:2-8pp — Mk 2:3-12; Lk 5:18-26

9 Jesus stepped into a boat, crossed over and came to his own town. ²Some men brought to him a paralyzed man, lying on a mat. When Jesus saw their faith, he said to the man, "Take heart, son; your sins are forgiven." Lk 7:48; Jn 16:33

³At this, some of the teachers of the law said to themselves, "This fellow is blaspheming!"

⁴Knowing their thoughts, Jesus said, "Why do you entertain evil thoughts in your hearts? ⁵Which is easier: to say, 'Your sins are forgiven,' or to say, 'Get up and walk'? ⁶But I want you to know that the Son of Man has authority on earth to forgive sins." So he said to the paralyzed man, "Get up, take your mat and go home." ⁷Then the man got up and went home. ⁸When the crowd saw this, they were filled with awe; and they praised God, who had given such authority to man. Mk 2:3-12; Lk 5:18-26

The Calling of Matthew
9:9-13pp — Mk 2:14-17; Lk 5:27-32

⁹As Jesus went on from there, he saw a man named Matthew sitting at the tax collector's booth. "Follow me," he told him, and Matthew got up and followed him. Mt 4:19

¹⁰While Jesus was having dinner at Matthew's house, many tax collectors and sinners came and ate with him and his disciples. ¹¹When the Pharisees saw this, they asked his disciples, "Why does your teacher eat with tax collectors and sinners?" Mt 11:19

¹²On hearing this, Jesus said, "It is not the healthy who need a doctor, but the sick. ¹³But go and learn what this means: 'I desire mercy, not sacrifice.'ᵃ For I have not come to call the righteous, but sinners." Mk 2:14-17; Lk 5:27-32

Jesus Questioned About Fasting
9:14-17pp — Mk 2:18-22; Lk 5:33-39

¹⁴Then John's disciples came and asked him, "How is it that we and the Pharisees fast often, but your disciples do not fast?" Lk 18:12

¹⁵Jesus answered, "How can the guests of the bridegroom mourn while he is with them? The time will come when the bridegroom will be taken from them; then they will fast. Jn 3:29; Ac 13:2-3

¹⁶"No one sews a patch of unshrunk cloth on an old garment, for the patch will pull away

ᵃ 13 Hosea 6:6

from the garment, making the tear worse. [17] Neither do people pour new wine into old wineskins. If they do, the skins will burst; the wine will run out and the wineskins will be ruined. No, they pour new wine into new wineskins, and both are preserved." Mk 2:18-22; Lk 5:33-39

Jesus Raises a Dead Girl and Heals a Sick Woman

9:18-26pp — Mk 5:22-43; Lk 8:41-56

[18] While he was saying this, a synagogue leader came and knelt before him and said, "My daughter has just died. But come and put your hand on her, and she will live." [19] Jesus got up and went with him, and so did his disciples. Mt 8:2

[20] Just then a woman who had been subject to bleeding for twelve years came up behind him and touched the edge of his cloak. [21] She said to herself, "If I only touch his cloak, I will be healed." Mt 14:36; Mk 3:10

[22] Jesus turned and saw her. "Take heart, daughter," he said, "your faith has healed you." And the woman was healed at that moment. Lk 7:50; 17:19; 18:42

[23] When Jesus entered the synagogue leader's house and saw the noisy crowd and people playing pipes, [24] he said, "Go away. The girl is not dead but asleep." But they laughed at him. [25] After the crowd had been put outside, he went in and took the girl by the hand, and she got up. [26] News of this spread through all that region. Mk 5:22-43; Lk 8:41-56

Jesus Heals the Blind and the Mute

[27] As Jesus went on from there, two blind men followed him, calling out, "Have mercy on us, Son of David!" Mt 15:22; Mk 10:47

[28] When he had gone indoors, the blind men came to him, and he asked them, "Do you believe that I am able to do this?"

"Yes, Lord," they replied. Ac 14:9

[29] Then he touched their eyes and said, "According to your faith let it be done to you"; [30] and their sight was restored. Jesus warned them sternly, "See that no one knows about this." [31] But they went out and spread the news about him all over that region. Mt 8:4; Mk 7:36

[32] While they were going out, a man who was demon-possessed and could not talk was brought to Jesus. [33] And when the demon was driven out, the man who had been mute spoke. The crowd was amazed and said, "Nothing like this has ever been seen in Israel." Mk 2:12

[34] But the Pharisees said, "It is by the prince of demons that he drives out demons." Mt 12:24; Lk 11:15

The Workers Are Few

[35] Jesus went through all the towns and villages, teaching in their synagogues, proclaiming

the good news of the kingdom and healing every disease and sickness. [36] When he saw the crowds, he had compassion on them, because they were harassed and helpless, like sheep without a shepherd. [37] Then he said to his disciples, "The harvest is plentiful but the workers are few. [38] Ask the Lord of the harvest, therefore, to send out workers into his harvest field."   Lk 10:2; Jn 4:35

Jesus Sends Out the Twelve

10:2-4pp — Mk 3:16-19; Lk 6:14-16; Ac 1:13
10:9-15pp — Mk 6:8-11; Lk 9:3-5; 10:4-12
10:19-22pp — Mk 13:11-13; Lk 21:12-17
10:26-33pp — Lk 12:2-9
10:34,35pp — Lk 12:51-53

10 Jesus called his twelve disciples to him and gave them authority to drive out impure spirits and to heal every disease and sickness.   Mk 3:13-15

[2] These are the names of the twelve apostles: first, Simon (who is called Peter) and his brother Andrew; James son of Zebedee, and his brother John; [3] Philip and Bartholomew; Thomas and Matthew the tax collector; James son of Alphaeus, and Thaddaeus; [4] Simon the Zealot and Judas Iscariot, who betrayed him.   Mk 3:16-19; Lk 6:14-16; Ac 1:13

[5] These twelve Jesus sent out with the following instructions: "Do not go among the Gentiles or enter any town of the Samaritans. [6] Go rather to the lost sheep of Israel. [7] As you go, proclaim this message: 'The kingdom of heaven has come near.' [8] Heal the sick, raise the dead, cleanse those who have leprosy,[a] drive out demons. Freely you have received; freely give.

[9] "Do not get any gold or silver or copper to take with you in your belts — [10] no bag for the journey or extra shirt or sandals or a staff, for the worker is worth his keep. [11] Whatever town or village you enter, search there for some worthy person and stay at their house until you leave. [12] As you enter the home, give it your greeting. [13] If the home is deserving, let your peace rest on it; if it is not, let your peace return to you. [14] If anyone will not welcome you or listen to your words, leave that home or town and shake the dust off your feet. [15] Truly I tell you, it will be more bearable for Sodom and Gomorrah on the day of judgment than for that town.   Mt 3:2; 15:24; 1Ti 5:18

[16] "I am sending you out like sheep among wolves. Therefore be as shrewd as snakes and as innocent as doves. [17] Be on your guard; you will be handed over to the local councils and be flogged in the synagogues. [18] On my account you will be brought before

---

a 8 The Greek word traditionally translated *leprosy* was used for various diseases affecting the skin.

governors and kings as witnesses to them and to the Gentiles. ¹⁹But when they arrest you, do not worry about what to say or how to say it. At that time you will be given what to say, ²⁰for it will not be you speaking, but the Spirit of your Father speaking through you.   Mk 13:9; Ac 5:40

²¹"Brother will betray brother to death, and a father his child; children will rebel against their parents and have them put to death. ²²You will be hated by everyone because of me, but the one who stands firm to the end will be saved. ²³When you are persecuted in one place, flee to another. Truly I tell you, you will not finish going through the towns of Israel before the Son of Man comes.   Mk 13:11-13; Lk 21:12-17

²⁴"The student is not above the teacher, nor a servant above his master. ²⁵It is enough for students to be like their teachers, and servants like their masters. If the head of the house has been called Beelzebul, how much more the members of his household!   Mk 3:22; Lk 6:40

²⁶"So do not be afraid of them, for there is nothing concealed that will not be disclosed, or hidden that will not be made known. ²⁷What I tell you in the dark, speak in the daylight; what is whispered in your ear, proclaim from the roofs. ²⁸Do not be afraid of those who kill the body but cannot kill the soul. Rather, be afraid of the One who can destroy both soul and body in hell. ²⁹Are not two sparrows sold for a penny? Yet not one of them will fall to the ground outside your Father's care.[a] ³⁰And even the very hairs of your head are all numbered. ³¹So don't be afraid; you are worth more than many sparrows.   Mk 4:22; Heb 10:31

³²"Whoever acknowledges me before others, I will also acknowledge before my Father in heaven. ³³But whoever disowns me before others, I will disown before my Father in heaven.   Lk 12:2-9

³⁴"Do not suppose that I have come to bring peace to the earth. I did not come to bring peace, but a sword. ³⁵For I have come to turn

" 'a man against his father,
    a daughter against her
        mother,
    a daughter-in-law against her
        mother-in-law—
³⁶   a man's enemies will be the
        members of his own
        household.'[b]   Mic 7:6

³⁷"Anyone who loves their father or mother more than me is not worthy of me; anyone who loves their son or daughter more than me is not worthy of me. ³⁸Whoever does not take up their cross and follow me is not worthy of me. ³⁹Whoever finds their life will lose it, and whoev-

[a] 29 Or *will*; or *knowledge*   [b] 36 Micah 7:6

er loses their life for my sake will find it. Lk 14:26; Jn 12:25

40 "Anyone who welcomes you welcomes me, and anyone who welcomes me welcomes the one who sent me. **41** Whoever welcomes a prophet as a prophet will receive a prophet's reward, and whoever welcomes a righteous person as a righteous person will receive a righteous person's reward. **42** And if anyone gives even a cup of cold water to one of these little ones who is my disciple, truly I tell you, that person will certainly not lose their reward." Lk 9:48; Jn 12:44; Gal 4:14

Jesus and John the Baptist

11:2-19pp — Lk 7:18-35

11 After Jesus had finished instructing his twelve disciples, he went on from there to teach and preach in the towns of Galilee.[a] Mt 7:28

2 When John, who was in prison, heard about the deeds of the Messiah, he sent his disciples **3** to ask him, "Are you the one who is to come, or should we expect someone else?" Mt 14:3; Jn 11:27

4 Jesus replied, "Go back and report to John what you hear and see: **5** The blind receive sight, the lame walk, those who have leprosy[b] are cleansed, the deaf hear, the dead are raised, and the good news is proclaimed to the poor. **6** Blessed is anyone who

does not stumble on account of me." Isa 35:4-6; Lk 4:18-19

7 As John's disciples were leaving, Jesus began to speak to the crowd about John: "What did you go out into the wilderness to see? A reed swayed by the wind? **8** If not, what did you go out to see? A man dressed in fine clothes? No, those who wear fine clothes are in kings' palaces. **9** Then what did you go out to see? A prophet? Yes, I tell you, and more than a prophet. **10** This is the one about whom it is written: Lk 1:76

" 'I will send my messenger
   ahead of you,
 who will prepare your way
   before you.'[c]

11 Truly I tell you, among those born of women there has not risen anyone greater than John the Baptist; yet whoever is least in the kingdom of heaven is greater than he. **12** From the days of John the Baptist until now, the kingdom of heaven has been subjected to violence,[d] and violent people have been raiding it. **13** For all the Prophets and the Law prophesied until John. **14** And if you are willing to accept it, he is the Elijah who was to come. **15** Whoever has ears, let them hear. Mal 4:5; Lk 1:17

16 "To what can I compare this generation? They are like children sitting in the marketplaces and calling out to others:

---

[a] 1 Greek *in their towns* [b] 5 The Greek word traditionally translated *leprosy* was used for various diseases affecting the skin. [c] 10 Mal. 3:1 [d] 12 Or *been forcefully advancing*

17 " 'We played the pipe for you,
　　and you did not dance;
　we sang a dirge,
　　and you did not mourn.'

18 For John came neither eating nor drinking, and they say, 'He has a demon.' 19 The Son of Man came eating and drinking, and they say, 'Here is a glutton and a drunkard, a friend of tax collectors and sinners.' But wisdom is proved right by her deeds."   Lk 7:18-35

Woe on Unrepentant Towns

11:21-23pp — Lk 10:13-15

20 Then Jesus began to denounce the towns in which most of his miracles had been performed, because they did not repent. 21 "Woe to you, Chorazin! Woe to you, Bethsaida! For if the miracles that were performed in you had been performed in Tyre and Sidon, they would have repented long ago in sackcloth and ashes. 22 But I tell you, it will be more bearable for Tyre and Sidon on the day of judgment than for you. 23 And you, Capernaum, will you be lifted to the heavens? No, you will go down to Hades.[a] For if the miracles that were performed in you had been performed in Sodom, it would have remained to this day. 24 But I tell you that it will be more bearable for Sodom on the day of judgment than for you."   Lk 10:13-15

[a] 23 That is, the realm of the dead

The Father Revealed in the Son

11:25-27pp — Lk 10:21,22

25 At that time Jesus said, "I praise you, Father, Lord of heaven and earth, because you have hidden these things from the wise and learned, and revealed them to little children. 26 Yes, Father, for this is what you were pleased to do.   1Co 1:26-29

27 "All things have been committed to me by my Father. No one knows the Son except the Father, and no one knows the Father except the Son and those to whom the Son chooses to reveal him.   Lk 10:21-22

28 "Come to me, all you who are weary and burdened, and I will give you rest. 29 Take my yoke upon you and learn from me, for I am gentle and humble in heart, and you will find rest for your souls. 30 For my yoke is easy and my burden is light."   Jer 6:16; Jn 13:15

Jesus Is Lord of the Sabbath

12:1-8pp — Mk 2:23-28; Lk 6:1-5
12:9-14pp — Mk 3:1-6; Lk 6:6-11

12 At that time Jesus went through the grainfields on the Sabbath. His disciples were hungry and began to pick some heads of grain and eat them. 2 When the Pharisees saw this, they said to him, "Look! Your disciples are doing what is unlawful on the Sabbath."   Ex 20:10; Lk 13:14

3 He answered, "Haven't you read what David did when he

and his companions were hungry? ⁴He entered the house of God, and he and his companions ate the consecrated bread—which was not lawful for them to do, but only for the priests. ⁵Or haven't you read in the Law that the priests on Sabbath duty in the temple desecrate the Sabbath and yet are innocent? ⁶I tell you that something greater than the temple is here. ⁷If you had known what these words mean, 'I desire mercy, not sacrifice,'ᵃ you would not have condemned the innocent. ⁸For the Son of Man is Lord of the Sabbath." Mk 2:23-28; Lk 6:1-5

⁹Going on from that place, he went into their synagogue, ¹⁰and a man with a shriveled hand was there. Looking for a reason to bring charges against Jesus, they asked him, "Is it lawful to heal on the Sabbath?" Lk 13:14; 14:3

¹¹He said to them, "If any of you has a sheep and it falls into a pit on the Sabbath, will you not take hold of it and lift it out? ¹²How much more valuable is a person than a sheep! Therefore it is lawful to do good on the Sabbath."

¹³Then he said to the man, "Stretch out your hand." So he stretched it out and it was completely restored, just as sound as the other. ¹⁴But the Pharisees went out and plotted how they might kill Jesus. Mk 3:1-6; Lk 6:6-11

God's Chosen Servant

¹⁵Aware of this, Jesus withdrew from that place. A large crowd followed him, and he healed all who were ill. ¹⁶He warned them not to tell others about him. ¹⁷This was to fulfill what was spoken through the prophet Isaiah: Mt 4:23; 8:4

¹⁸"Here is my servant whom I
     have chosen,
  the one I love, in whom I
     delight; Mt 3:17
  I will put my Spirit on
     him, Jn 3:34
  and he will proclaim justice
     to the nations.
¹⁹He will not quarrel or cry out;
  no one will hear his voice in
     the streets.
²⁰A bruised reed he will not
     break,
  and a smoldering wick he
     will not snuff out,
  till he has brought justice
     through to victory.
²¹ In his name the nations will
     put their hope."ᵇ Isa 42:1-4

Jesus and Beelzebul

12:25-29pp — Mk 3:23-27; Lk 11:17-22

²²Then they brought him a demon-possessed man who was blind and mute, and Jesus healed him, so that he could both talk and see. ²³All the people were astonished and said, "Could this be the Son of David?" Mt 4:24; 9:32-33

ᵃ 7 Hosea 6:6 ᵇ 21 Isaiah 42:1-4

24 But when the Pharisees heard this, they said, "It is only by Beelzebul, the prince of demons, that this fellow drives out demons." Mt 9:34; Mk 3:22

25 Jesus knew their thoughts and said to them, "Every kingdom divided against itself will be ruined, and every city or household divided against itself will not stand. 26 If Satan drives out Satan, he is divided against himself. How then can his kingdom stand? 27 And if I drive out demons by Beelzebul, by whom do your people drive them out? So then, they will be your judges. 28 But if it is by the Spirit of God that I drive out demons, then the kingdom of God has come upon you. Mt 9:4; Ac 19:13

29 "Or again, how can anyone enter a strong man's house and carry off his possessions unless he first ties up the strong man? Then he can plunder his house. Mk 3:23-27; Lk 11:17-22

30 "Whoever is not with me is against me, and whoever does not gather with me scatters. 31 And so I tell you, every kind of sin and slander can be forgiven, but blasphemy against the Spirit will not be forgiven. 32 Anyone who speaks a word against the Son of Man will be forgiven, but anyone who speaks against the Holy Spirit will not be forgiven, either in this age or in the age to come. Mk 9:40; Lk 12:10

33 "Make a tree good and its fruit will be good, or make a tree bad and its fruit will be bad, for a tree is recognized by its fruit. 34 You brood of vipers, how can you who are evil say anything good? For the mouth speaks what the heart is full of. 35 A good man brings good things out of the good stored up in him, and an evil man brings evil things out of the evil stored up in him. 36 But I tell you that everyone will have to give account on the day of judgment for every empty word they have spoken. 37 For by your words you will be acquitted, and by your words you will be condemned." Mt 15:18; Lk 6:45

The Sign of Jonah

12:39-42pp — Lk 11:29-32
12:43-45pp — Lk 11:24-26

38 Then some of the Pharisees and teachers of the law said to him, "Teacher, we want to see a sign from you." Mt 16:1; Jn 2:18; 1Co 1:22

39 He answered, "A wicked and adulterous generation asks for a sign! But none will be given it except the sign of the prophet Jonah. 40 For as Jonah was three days and three nights in the belly of a huge fish, so the Son of Man will be three days and three nights in the heart of the earth. 41 The men of Nineveh will stand up at the judgment with this generation and condemn it; for they repented at the preaching of Jonah, and now something greater than Jo-

nah is here. ⁴²The Queen of the South will rise at the judgment with this generation and condemn it; for she came from the ends of the earth to listen to Solomon's wisdom, and now something greater than Solomon is here. Lk 11:29-32

⁴³"When an impure spirit comes out of a person, it goes through arid places seeking rest and does not find it. ⁴⁴Then it says, 'I will return to the house I left.' When it arrives, it finds the house unoccupied, swept clean and put in order. ⁴⁵Then it goes and takes with it seven other spirits more wicked than itself, and they go in and live there. And the final condition of that person is worse than the first. That is how it will be with this wicked generation." Lk 11:24-26; 2Pe 2:20

Jesus' Mother and Brothers

12:46-50pp — Mk 3:31-35; Lk 8:19-21

⁴⁶While Jesus was still talking to the crowd, his mother and brothers stood outside, wanting to speak to him. ⁴⁷Someone told him, "Your mother and brothers are standing outside, wanting to speak to you." Mt 13:55; Jn 2:12

⁴⁸He replied to him, "Who is my mother, and who are my brothers?" ⁴⁹Pointing to his disciples, he said, "Here are my mother and my brothers. ⁵⁰For whoever does the will of my Father in heaven is my brother and sister and mother." Mk 3:31-35; Lk 8:19

The Parable of the Sower

13:1-15pp — Mk 4:1-12; Lk 8:4-10
13:16,17pp — Lk 10:23,24
13:18-23pp — Mk 4:13-20; Lk 8:11-15

13 That same day Jesus went out of the house and sat by the lake. ²Such large crowds gathered around him that he got into a boat and sat in it, while all the people stood on the shore. ³Then he told them many things in parables, saying: "A farmer went out to sow his seed. ⁴As he was scattering the seed, some fell along the path, and the birds came and ate it up. ⁵Some fell on rocky places, where it did not have much soil. It sprang up quickly, because the soil was shallow. ⁶But when the sun came up, the plants were scorched, and they withered because they had no root. ⁷Other seed fell among thorns, which grew up and choked the plants. ⁸Still other seed fell on good soil, where it produced a crop—a hundred, sixty or thirty times what was sown. ⁹Whoever has ears, let them hear." Ge 26:12; Mt 11:15

¹⁰The disciples came to him and asked, "Why do you speak to the people in parables?"

¹¹He replied, "Because the knowledge of the secrets of the kingdom of heaven has been given to you, but not to them. ¹²Whoever has will be given more, and they will have an abundance. Whoever does not have, even what they have will be taken

from them. [13] This is why I speak to them in parables: Lk 19:26

"Though seeing, they do not
see;
though hearing, they do not
hear or understand.

[14] In them is fulfilled the prophecy of Isaiah:

" 'You will be ever hearing but
never understanding;
you will be ever seeing but
never perceiving.
[15] For this people's heart has
become calloused;
they hardly hear with their
ears,
and they have closed their
eyes.
Otherwise they might see
with their eyes,
hear with their ears,
understand with their
hearts
and turn, and I would heal
them.' [a]

[16] But blessed are your eyes because they see, and your ears because they hear. [17] For truly I tell you, many prophets and righteous people longed to see what you see but did not see it, and to hear what you hear but did not hear it. Lk 10:23-24; Heb 11:13

[18] "Listen then to what the parable of the sower means: [19] When anyone hears the message about the kingdom and does not understand it, the evil one comes

and snatches away what was sown in their heart. This is the seed sown along the path. [20] The seed falling on rocky ground refers to someone who hears the word and at once receives it with joy. [21] But since they have no root, they last only a short time. When trouble or persecution comes because of the word, they quickly fall away. [22] The seed falling among the thorns refers to someone who hears the word, but the worries of this life and the deceitfulness of wealth choke the word, making it unfruitful. [23] But the seed falling on good soil refers to someone who hears the word and understands it. This is the one who produces a crop, yielding a hundred, sixty or thirty times what was sown." Mk 4:13-20; Lk 8:11-15

The Parable of the Weeds

[24] Jesus told them another parable: "The kingdom of heaven is like a man who sowed good seed in his field. [25] But while everyone was sleeping, his enemy came and sowed weeds among the wheat, and went away. [26] When the wheat sprouted and formed heads, then the weeds also appeared. Mt 18:23; 20:1

[27] "The owner's servants came to him and said, 'Sir, didn't you sow good seed in your field? Where then did the weeds come from?'

[a] 15 Isaiah 6:9,10 (see Septuagint)

28 " 'An enemy did this,' he replied.

"The servants asked him, 'Do you want us to go and pull them up?'

29 " 'No,' he answered, 'because while you are pulling the weeds, you may uproot the wheat with them. 30 Let both grow together until the harvest. At that time I will tell the harvesters: First collect the weeds and tie them in bundles to be burned; then gather the wheat and bring it into my barn.' " Mt 3:12

The Parables of the Mustard Seed and the Yeast

13:31,32pp — Mk 4:30-32
13:31-33pp — Lk 13:18-21

31 He told them another parable: "The kingdom of heaven is like a mustard seed, which a man took and planted in his field. 32 Though it is the smallest of all seeds, yet when it grows, it is the largest of garden plants and becomes a tree, so that the birds come and perch in its branches." Mk 4:30-32

33 He told them still another parable: "The kingdom of heaven is like yeast that a woman took and mixed into about sixty pounds[a] of flour until it worked all through the dough." Lk 13:18-21

34 Jesus spoke all these things to the crowd in parables; he did not say anything to them without using a parable. 35 So was ful- filled what was spoken through the prophet: Mk 4:33; Jn 16:25

"I will open my mouth in parables,
I will utter things hidden since the creation of the world."[b] Ps 78:2; 1Co 2:7

The Parable of the Weeds Explained

36 Then he left the crowd and went into the house. His disciples came to him and said, "Explain to us the parable of the weeds in the field." Mt 15:15

37 He answered, "The one who sowed the good seed is the Son of Man. 38 The field is the world, and the good seed stands for the people of the kingdom. The weeds are the people of the evil one, 39 and the enemy who sows them is the devil. The harvest is the end of the age, and the harvesters are angels. Mt 24:3; Rev 14:15

40 "As the weeds are pulled up and burned in the fire, so it will be at the end of the age. 41 The Son of Man will send out his angels, and they will weed out of his kingdom everything that causes sin and all who do evil. 42 They will throw them into the blazing furnace, where there will be weeping and gnashing of teeth. 43 Then the righteous will shine like the sun in the kingdom of their Father. Whoever has ears, let them hear. Da 12:3; Mt 8:12; 11:15

---

a 33 Or about 27 kilograms   b 35 Psalm 78:2

The Parables of the Hidden Treasure and the Pearl

⁴⁴ "The kingdom of heaven is like treasure hidden in a field. When a man found it, he hid it again, and then in his joy went and sold all he had and bought that field.   Isa 55:1; Php 3:7-8

⁴⁵ "Again, the kingdom of heaven is like a merchant looking for fine pearls. ⁴⁶ When he found one of great value, he went away and sold everything he had and bought it.   ver 24

The Parable of the Net

⁴⁷ "Once again, the kingdom of heaven is like a net that was let down into the lake and caught all kinds of fish. ⁴⁸ When it was full, the fishermen pulled it up on the shore. Then they sat down and collected the good fish in baskets, but threw the bad away. ⁴⁹ This is how it will be at the end of the age. The angels will come and separate the wicked from the righteous ⁵⁰ and throw them into the blazing furnace, where there will be weeping and gnashing of teeth.   Mt 25:32

⁵¹ "Have you understood all these things?" Jesus asked.

"Yes," they replied.

⁵² He said to them, "Therefore every teacher of the law who has become a disciple in the kingdom of heaven is like the owner of a house who brings out of his storeroom new treasures as well as old."

A Prophet Without Honor
13:54-58pp — Mk 6:1-6

⁵³ When Jesus had finished these parables, he moved on from there. ⁵⁴ Coming to his hometown, he began teaching the people in their synagogue, and they were amazed. "Where did this man get this wisdom and these miraculous powers?" they asked. ⁵⁵ "Isn't this the carpenter's son? Isn't his mother's name Mary, and aren't his brothers James, Joseph, Simon and Judas? ⁵⁶ Aren't all his sisters with us? Where then did this man get all these things?" ⁵⁷ And they took offense at him.   Mt 7:28; Jn 6:42

But Jesus said to them, "A prophet is not without honor except in his own town and in his own home."   Lk 4:24; Jn 4:44

⁵⁸ And he did not do many miracles there because of their lack of faith.   Mk 6:1-6

John the Baptist Beheaded
14:1-12pp — Mk 6:14-29

14 At that time Herod the tetrarch heard the reports about Jesus, ² and he said to his attendants, "This is John the Baptist; he has risen from the dead! That is why miraculous powers are at work in him."   Lk 9:7-9

³ Now Herod had arrested John and bound him and put him in prison because of Herodias, his brother Philip's wife, ⁴ for John had been saying to him: "It is not lawful for you to have her."

⁵Herod wanted to kill John, but he was afraid of the people, because they considered John a prophet. Mt 11:9; Lk 3:19-20

⁶On Herod's birthday the daughter of Herodias danced for the guests and pleased Herod so much ⁷that he promised with an oath to give her whatever she asked. ⁸Prompted by her mother, she said, "Give me here on a platter the head of John the Baptist." ⁹The king was distressed, but because of his oaths and his dinner guests, he ordered that her request be granted ¹⁰and had John beheaded in the prison. ¹¹His head was brought in on a platter and given to the girl, who carried it to her mother. ¹²John's disciples came and took his body and buried it. Then they went and told Jesus. Mk 6:14-29

Jesus Feeds the Five Thousand

14:13-21pp — Mk 6:32-44; Lk 9:10-17; Jn 6:1-13
14:13-21Ref — Mt 15:32-38

¹³When Jesus heard what had happened, he withdrew by boat privately to a solitary place. Hearing of this, the crowds followed him on foot from the towns. ¹⁴When Jesus landed and saw a large crowd, he had compassion on them and healed their sick. Mt 15:32-38

¹⁵As evening approached, the disciples came to him and said, "This is a remote place, and it's already getting late. Send the crowds away, so they can go to the villages and buy themselves some food."

¹⁶Jesus replied, "They do not need to go away. You give them something to eat."

¹⁷"We have here only five loaves of bread and two fish," they answered.

¹⁸"Bring them here to me," he said. ¹⁹And he directed the people to sit down on the grass. Taking the five loaves and the two fish and looking up to heaven, he gave thanks and broke the loaves. Then he gave them to the disciples, and the disciples gave them to the people. ²⁰They all ate and were satisfied, and the disciples picked up twelve basketfuls of broken pieces that were left over. ²¹The number of those who ate was about five thousand men, besides women and children. Mk 6:32-44; Lk 9:10-17; Jn 6:1-13

Jesus Walks on the Water

14:22-33pp — Mk 6:45-51; Jn 6:16-21
14:34-36pp — Mk 6:53-56

²²Immediately Jesus made the disciples get into the boat and go on ahead of him to the other side, while he dismissed the crowd. ²³After he had dismissed them, he went up on a mountainside by himself to pray. Later that night, he was there alone, ²⁴and the boat was already a considerable distance from land, buffeted by the waves because the wind was against it. Lk 3:21

25 Shortly before dawn Jesus went out to them, walking on the lake. 26 When the disciples saw him walking on the lake, they were terrified. "It's a ghost," they said, and cried out in fear.   Lk 24:37

27 But Jesus immediately said to them: "Take courage! It is I. Don't be afraid."   Mt 17:7; Rev 1:17

28 "Lord, if it's you," Peter replied, "tell me to come to you on the water."

29 "Come," he said.

Then Peter got down out of the boat, walked on the water and came toward Jesus. 30 But when he saw the wind, he was afraid and, beginning to sink, cried out, "Lord, save me!"

31 Immediately Jesus reached out his hand and caught him. "You of little faith," he said, "why did you doubt?"   Mt 6:30

32 And when they climbed into the boat, the wind died down. 33 Then those who were in the boat worshiped him, saying, "Truly you are the Son of God."   Mk 6:45-51; Jn 6:15-21

34 When they had crossed over, they landed at Gennesaret. 35 And when the men of that place recognized Jesus, they sent word to all the surrounding country. People brought all their sick to him 36 and begged him to let the sick just touch the edge of his cloak, and all who touched it were healed.   Mk 6:53-56

That Which Defiles

15:1-20pp — Mk 7:1-23

15 Then some Pharisees and teachers of the law came to Jesus from Jerusalem and asked, 2 "Why do your disciples break the tradition of the elders? They don't wash their hands before they eat!"   Lk 11:38

3 Jesus replied, "And why do you break the command of God for the sake of your tradition? 4 For God said, 'Honor your father and mother'ᵃ and 'Anyone who curses their father or mother is to be put to death.'ᵇ 5 But you say that if anyone declares that what might have been used to help their father or mother is 'devoted to God,' 6 they are not to 'honor their father or mother' with it. Thus you nullify the word of God for the sake of your tradition. 7 You hypocrites! Isaiah was right when he prophesied about you:

8 " 'These people honor me with their lips,
    but their hearts are far from me.
9 They worship me in vain;
    their teachings are merely human rules.'ᶜ"   Col 2:20-22

10 Jesus called the crowd to him and said, "Listen and understand. 11 What goes into someone's mouth does not defile them, but what comes out of

---

ᵃ 4 Exodus 20:12; Deut. 5:16   ᵇ 4 Exodus 21:17; Lev. 20:9   ᶜ 9 Isaiah 29:13

their mouth, that is what defiles them." Ac 10:14-15

¹²Then the disciples came to him and asked, "Do you know that the Pharisees were offended when they heard this?"

¹³He replied, "Every plant that my heavenly Father has not planted will be pulled up by the roots. ¹⁴Leave them; they are blind guides.ᵃ If the blind lead the blind, both will fall into a pit." Mt 23:16,24; Lk 6:39

¹⁵Peter said, "Explain the parable to us." Mt 13:36

¹⁶"Are you still so dull?" Jesus asked them. ¹⁷"Don't you see that whatever enters the mouth goes into the stomach and then out of the body? ¹⁸But the things that come out of a person's mouth come from the heart, and these defile them. ¹⁹For out of the heart come evil thoughts—murder, adultery, sexual immorality, theft, false testimony, slander. ²⁰These are what defile a person; but eating with unwashed hands does not defile them." Mk 7:1-23; Gal 5:19-21

The Faith of a Canaanite Woman

15:21-28pp — Mk 7:24-30

²¹Leaving that place, Jesus withdrew to the region of Tyre and Sidon. ²²A Canaanite woman from that vicinity came to him, crying out, "Lord, Son of David, have mercy on me! My daughter is demon-possessed and suffering terribly." Mt 4:24; 9:27

²³Jesus did not answer a word. So his disciples came to him and urged him, "Send her away, for she keeps crying out after us."

²⁴He answered, "I was sent only to the lost sheep of Israel."

²⁵The woman came and knelt before him. "Lord, help me!" she said. Mt 8:2

²⁶He replied, "It is not right to take the children's bread and toss it to the dogs."

²⁷"Yes it is, Lord," she said. "Even the dogs eat the crumbs that fall from their master's table."

²⁸Then Jesus said to her, "Woman, you have great faith! Your request is granted." And her daughter was healed at that moment. Mk 7:24-30

Jesus Feeds the Four Thousand

15:29-31pp — Mk 7:31-37
15:32-39pp — Mk 8:1-10
15:32-39Ref — Mt 14:13-21

²⁹Jesus left there and went along the Sea of Galilee. Then he went up on a mountainside and sat down. ³⁰Great crowds came to him, bringing the lame, the blind, the crippled, the mute and many others, and laid them at his feet; and he healed them. ³¹The people were amazed when they saw the mute speaking, the crippled made well, the lame walking and the blind seeing.

ᵃ 14 Some manuscripts blind guides of the blind

And they praised the God of Israel. Mk 7:31-37

32 Jesus called his disciples to him and said, "I have compassion for these people; they have already been with me three days and have nothing to eat. I do not want to send them away hungry, or they may collapse on the way." Mt 9:36

33 His disciples answered, "Where could we get enough bread in this remote place to feed such a crowd?"

34 "How many loaves do you have?" Jesus asked.

"Seven," they replied, "and a few small fish."

35 He told the crowd to sit down on the ground. 36 Then he took the seven loaves and the fish, and when he had given thanks, he broke them and gave them to the disciples, and they in turn to the people. 37 They all ate and were satisfied. Afterward the disciples picked up seven basketfuls of broken pieces that were left over. 38 The number of those who ate was four thousand men, besides women and children. 39 After Jesus had sent the crowd away, he got into the boat and went to the vicinity of Magadan. Mt 14:13-21; Mk 8:1-10

The Demand for a Sign
16:1-12pp — Mk 8:11-21

16 The Pharisees and Sadducees came to Jesus and tested him by asking him to show them a sign from heaven. Mt 12:38

2 He replied, "When evening comes, you say, 'It will be fair weather, for the sky is red,' 3 and in the morning, 'Today it will be stormy, for the sky is red and overcast.' You know how to interpret the appearance of the sky, but you cannot interpret the signs of the times.[a] 4 A wicked and adulterous generation looks for a sign, but none will be given it except the sign of Jonah." Jesus then left them and went away. Mt 12:39; Lk 12:54-56

The Yeast of the Pharisees and Sadducees

5 When they went across the lake, the disciples forgot to take bread. 6 "Be careful," Jesus said to them. "Be on your guard against the yeast of the Pharisees and Sadducees." Lk 12:1

7 They discussed this among themselves and said, "It is because we didn't bring any bread."

8 Aware of their discussion, Jesus asked, "You of little faith, why are you talking among yourselves about having no bread? 9 Do you still not understand? Don't you remember the five loaves for the five thousand, and how many basketfuls you gathered? 10 Or the seven loaves for the four thousand, and how many basketfuls you gathered? 11 How is it you don't understand

---

a 2,3 Some early manuscripts do not have *When evening comes . . . of the times.*

that I was not talking to you about bread? But be on your guard against the yeast of the Pharisees and Sadducees." [12] Then they understood that he was not telling them to guard against the yeast used in bread, but against the teaching of the Pharisees and Sadducees. Mk 8:11-21

Peter Declares That Jesus Is the Messiah

16:13-16pp — Mk 8:27-29; Lk 9:18-20

[13] When Jesus came to the region of Caesarea Philippi, he asked his disciples, "Who do people say the Son of Man is?" [14] They replied, "Some say John the Baptist; others say Elijah; and still others, Jeremiah or one of the prophets." Mt 14:2; Mk 6:15

[15] "But what about you?" he asked. "Who do you say I am?"

[16] Simon Peter answered, "You are the Messiah, the Son of the living God." Jn 11:27

[17] Jesus replied, "Blessed are you, Simon son of Jonah, for this was not revealed to you by flesh and blood, but by my Father in heaven. [18] And I tell you that you are Peter,[a] and on this rock I will build my church, and the gates of Hades[b] will not overcome it. [19] I will give you the keys of the kingdom of heaven; whatever you bind on earth will be[c] bound in heaven, and whatever you loose on earth will be[c]

loosed in heaven." [20] Then he ordered his disciples not to tell anyone that he was the Messiah. Jn 1:42; Eph 2:20

Jesus Predicts His Death

16:21-28pp — Mk 8:31–9:1; Lk 9:22-27

[21] From that time on Jesus began to explain to his disciples that he must go to Jerusalem and suffer many things at the hands of the elders, the chief priests and the teachers of the law, and that he must be killed and on the third day be raised to life. Mk 9:31; Lk 17:25

[22] Peter took him aside and began to rebuke him. "Never, Lord!" he said. "This shall never happen to you!"

[23] Jesus turned and said to Peter, "Get behind me, Satan! You are a stumbling block to me; you do not have in mind the concerns of God, but merely human concerns." Mt 4:10

[24] Then Jesus said to his disciples, "Whoever wants to be my disciple must deny themselves and take up their cross and follow me. [25] For whoever wants to save their life[d] will lose it, but whoever loses their life for me will find it. [26] What good will it be for someone to gain the whole world, yet forfeit their soul? Or what can anyone give in exchange for their soul? [27] For the Son of Man is going to come in

---

[a] 18 The Greek word for *Peter* means *rock*.   [b] 18 That is, the realm of the dead
[c] 19 Or *will have been*   [d] 25 The Greek word means either *life* or *soul*; also in verse 26.

his Father's glory with his angels, and then he will reward each person according to what they have done.

28 "Truly I tell you, some who are standing here will not taste death before they see the Son of Man coming in his kingdom."

The Transfiguration

17:1-8pp — Lk 9:28-36
17:1-13pp — Mk 9:2-13

17 After six days Jesus took with him Peter, James and John the brother of James, and led them up a high mountain by themselves. ²There he was transfigured before them. His face shone like the sun, and his clothes became as white as the light. ³Just then there appeared before them Moses and Elijah, talking with Jesus.   Mt 4:21

⁴Peter said to Jesus, "Lord, it is good for us to be here. If you wish, I will put up three shelters — one for you, one for Moses and one for Elijah."

⁵While he was still speaking, a bright cloud covered them, and a voice from the cloud said, "This is my Son, whom I love; with him I am well pleased. Listen to him!"   Mt 3:17; 2Pe 1:17

⁶When the disciples heard this, they fell facedown to the ground, terrified. ⁷But Jesus came and touched them. "Get up," he said. "Don't be afraid." ⁸When they looked up, they saw no one except Jesus.   Lk 9:28-36

⁹As they were coming down the mountain, Jesus instructed them, "Don't tell anyone what you have seen, until the Son of Man has been raised from the dead."   Mt 16:21; Mk 8:30

¹⁰The disciples asked him, "Why then do the teachers of the law say that Elijah must come first?"

¹¹Jesus replied, "To be sure, Elijah comes and will restore all things. ¹²But I tell you, Elijah has already come, and they did not recognize him, but have done to him everything they wished. In the same way the Son of Man is going to suffer at their hands." ¹³Then the disciples understood that he was talking to them about John the Baptist.   Mk 9:2-13

Jesus Heals a Demon-Possessed Boy

17:14-19pp — Mk 9:14-28; Lk 9:37-42

¹⁴When they came to the crowd, a man approached Jesus and knelt before him. ¹⁵"Lord, have mercy on my son," he said. "He has seizures and is suffering greatly. He often falls into the fire or into the water. ¹⁶I brought him to your disciples, but they could not heal him."   Mt 4:24

¹⁷"You unbelieving and perverse generation," Jesus replied, "how long shall I stay with you? How long shall I put up with you? Bring the boy here to me." ¹⁸Jesus rebuked the demon, and it came out of the boy, and he was healed at that moment.

¹⁹Then the disciples came to Jesus in private and asked, "Why couldn't we drive it out?" Mk 9:14-28

²⁰He replied, "Because you have so little faith. Truly I tell you, if you have faith as small as a mustard seed, you can say to this mountain, 'Move from here to there,' and it will move. Nothing will be impossible for you." [21] *a*   Mk 11:23; Lk 17:6

Jesus Predicts His Death a Second Time

²²When they came together in Galilee, he said to them, "The Son of Man is going to be delivered into the hands of men. ²³They will kill him, and on the third day he will be raised to life." And the disciples were filled with grief.   Mt 16:21; Ac 2:23; 3:13

The Temple Tax

²⁴After Jesus and his disciples arrived in Capernaum, the collectors of the two-drachma temple tax came to Peter and asked, "Doesn't your teacher pay the temple tax?"   Ex 30:13

²⁵"Yes, he does," he replied.

When Peter came into the house, Jesus was the first to speak. "What do you think, Simon?" he asked. "From whom do the kings of the earth collect duty and taxes—from their own children or from others?"   Mt 22:17-21

²⁶"From others," Peter answered.

"Then the children are exempt," Jesus said to him. ²⁷"But so that we may not cause offense, go to the lake and throw out your line. Take the first fish you catch; open its mouth and you will find a four-drachma coin. Take it and give it to them for my tax and yours."   Jn 6:61

The Greatest in the Kingdom of Heaven

18:1-5pp — Mk 9:33-37; Lk 9:46-48

18 At that time the disciples came to Jesus and asked, "Who, then, is the greatest in the kingdom of heaven?"

²He called a little child to him, and placed the child among them. ³And he said: "Truly I tell you, unless you change and become like little children, you will never enter the kingdom of heaven. ⁴Therefore, whoever takes the lowly position of this child is the greatest in the kingdom of heaven. ⁵And whoever welcomes one such child in my name welcomes me.   Mt 19:14; 1Pe 2:2

Causing to Stumble

⁶"If anyone causes one of these little ones—those who believe in me—to stumble, it would be better for them to have a large millstone hung around their neck and to be drowned in the depths of the sea. ⁷Woe to the world because of the things that cause people to stumble!

a 21 Some manuscripts include here words similar to Mark 9:29.

Such things must come, but woe to the person through whom they come! **8** If your hand or your foot causes you to stumble, cut it off and throw it away. It is better for you to enter life maimed or crippled than to have two hands or two feet and be thrown into eternal fire. **9** And if your eye causes you to stumble, gouge it out and throw it away. It is better for you to enter life with one eye than to have two eyes and be thrown into the fire of hell. Mt 5:29; Mk 9:43,45; Lk 17:1

The Parable of the Wandering Sheep

18:12-14pp — Lk 15:4-7

10 "See that you do not despise one of these little ones. For I tell you that their angels in heaven always see the face of my Father in heaven. [11]*a* Ge 48:16; Ps 34:7; Heb 1:14

12 "What do you think? If a man owns a hundred sheep, and one of them wanders away, will he not leave the ninety-nine on the hills and go to look for the one that wandered off? **13** And if he finds it, truly I tell you, he is happier about that one sheep than about the ninety-nine that did not wander off. **14** In the same way your Father in heaven is not willing that any of these little ones should perish. Lk 15:4-7

Dealing With Sin in the Church

15 "If your brother or sister*b* sins,*c* go and point out their fault, just between the two of you. If they listen to you, you have won them over. **16** But if they will not listen, take one or two others along, so that 'every matter may be established by the testimony of two or three witnesses.'*d* **17** If they still refuse to listen, tell it to the church; and if they refuse to listen even to the church, treat them as you would a pagan or a tax collector. 1Co 6:1-6; Jas 5:19-20

18 "Truly I tell you, whatever you bind on earth will be*e* bound in heaven, and whatever you loose on earth will be*e* loosed in heaven. Mt 16:19; Jn 20:23

19 "Again, truly I tell you that if two of you on earth agree about anything they ask for, it will be done for them by my Father in heaven. **20** For where two or three gather in my name, there am I with them." Mt 7:7

The Parable of the Unmerciful Servant

21 Then Peter came to Jesus and asked, "Lord, how many times shall I forgive my brother or sister who sins against me? Up to seven times?" Lk 17:4

22 Jesus answered, "I tell you, not seven times, but seventy-seven times.*f* Ge 4:24

---

a 11 Some manuscripts include here the words of Luke 19:10.   *b* 15 The Greek word for *brother or sister* (*adelphos*) refers here to a fellow disciple, whether man or woman; also in verses 21 and 35.   *c* 15 Some manuscripts *sins against you*   *d* 16 Deut. 19:15   *e* 18 Or *will have been*   *f* 22 Or *seventy times seven*

²³"Therefore, the kingdom of heaven is like a king who wanted to settle accounts with his servants. ²⁴As he began the settlement, a man who owed him ten thousand bags of gold*ᵃ* was brought to him. ²⁵Since he was not able to pay, the master ordered that he and his wife and his children and all that he had be sold to repay the debt.   2Ki 4:1; Mt 25:19

²⁶"At this the servant fell on his knees before him. 'Be patient with me,' he begged, 'and I will pay back everything.' ²⁷The servant's master took pity on him, canceled the debt and let him go.   Mt 8:2

²⁸"But when that servant went out, he found one of his fellow servants who owed him a hundred silver coins.*ᵇ* He grabbed him and began to choke him. 'Pay back what you owe me!' he demanded.

²⁹"His fellow servant fell to his knees and begged him, 'Be patient with me, and I will pay it back.'

³⁰"But he refused. Instead, he went off and had the man thrown into prison until he could pay the debt. ³¹When the other servants saw what had happened, they were outraged and went and told their master everything that had happened.

³²"Then the master called the servant in. 'You wicked servant,' he said, 'I canceled all that debt of yours because you begged me to. ³³Shouldn't you have had mercy on your fellow servant just as I had on you?' ³⁴In anger his master handed him over to the jailers to be tortured, until he should pay back all he owed.

³⁵"This is how my heavenly Father will treat each of you unless you forgive your brother or sister from your heart."   Mt 6:14; Jas 2:13

Divorce
19:1-9pp — Mk 10:1-12

19 When Jesus had finished saying these things, he left Galilee and went into the region of Judea to the other side of the Jordan. ²Large crowds followed him, and he healed them there.   Mt 4:23; 7:28

³Some Pharisees came to him to test him. They asked, "Is it lawful for a man to divorce his wife for any and every reason?"   Mt 5:31

⁴"Haven't you read," he replied, "that at the beginning the Creator 'made them male and female,'*ᶜ* ⁵and said, 'For this reason a man will leave his father and mother and be united to his wife, and the two will become one flesh'*ᵈ*? ⁶So they are no longer two, but one flesh. Therefore what God has joined together, let no one separate."   Ge 5:2; 1Co 6:16; Eph 5:31

ᵃ 24 Greek *ten thousand talents*; a talent was worth about 20 years of a day laborer's wages.
ᵇ 28 Greek *a hundred denarii*; a denarius was the usual daily wage of a day laborer (see 20:2).
ᶜ 4 Gen. 1:27   *ᵈ 5* Gen. 2:24

7 "Why then," they asked, "did Moses command that a man give his wife a certificate of divorce and send her away?" Dt 24:1-4; Mt 5:31

8 Jesus replied, "Moses permitted you to divorce your wives because your hearts were hard. But it was not this way from the beginning. 9 I tell you that anyone who divorces his wife, except for sexual immorality, and marries another woman commits adultery." Mk 10:1-12; Lk 16:18

10 The disciples said to him, "If this is the situation between a husband and wife, it is better not to marry."

11 Jesus replied, "Not everyone can accept this word, but only those to whom it has been given. 12 For there are eunuchs who were born that way, and there are eunuchs who have been made eunuchs by others — and there are those who choose to live like eunuchs for the sake of the kingdom of heaven. The one who can accept this should accept it." Mt 13:11; 1Co 7:7-9,17

The Little Children and Jesus
19:13-15pp — Mk 10:13-16; Lk 18:15-17

13 Then people brought little children to Jesus for him to place his hands on them and pray for them. But the disciples rebuked them. Mk 5:23

14 Jesus said, "Let the little children come to me, and do not hinder them, for the kingdom of heaven belongs to such as these." 15 When he had placed his hands on them, he went on from there. Mk 10:13-16; Lk 18:15-17

The Rich and the Kingdom of God
19:16-29pp — Mk 10:17-30; Lk 18:18-30

16 Just then a man came up to Jesus and asked, "Teacher, what good thing must I do to get eternal life?" Mt 25:46; Lk 10:25

17 "Why do you ask me about what is good?" Jesus replied. "There is only One who is good. If you want to enter life, keep the commandments." Lev 18:5

18 "Which ones?" he inquired.

Jesus replied, " 'You shall not murder, you shall not commit adultery, you shall not steal, you shall not give false testimony, 19 honor your father and mother,'ᵃ and 'love your neighbor as yourself.'ᵇ" Lev 19:18; Jas 2:11

20 "All these I have kept," the young man said. "What do I still lack?"

21 Jesus answered, "If you want to be perfect, go, sell your possessions and give to the poor, and you will have treasure in heaven. Then come, follow me." Mt 6:20; Lk 12:33; Ac 4:34-35

22 When the young man heard this, he went away sad, because he had great wealth.

23 Then Jesus said to his disciples, "Truly I tell you, it is hard for someone who is rich to enter the

ᵃ 19 Exodus 20:12-16; Deut. 5:16-20   ᵇ 19 Lev. 19:18

kingdom of heaven. ²⁴ Again I tell you, it is easier for a camel to go through the eye of a needle than for someone who is rich to enter the kingdom of God." Mt 13:22

²⁵ When the disciples heard this, they were greatly astonished and asked, "Who then can be saved?"

²⁶ Jesus looked at them and said, "With man this is impossible, but with God all things are possible." Ge 18:14; Lk 1:37; Ro 4:21

²⁷ Peter answered him, "We have left everything to follow you! What then will there be for us?" Mt 4:19

²⁸ Jesus said to them, "Truly I tell you, at the renewal of all things, when the Son of Man sits on his glorious throne, you who have followed me will also sit on twelve thrones, judging the twelve tribes of Israel. ²⁹ And everyone who has left houses or brothers or sisters or father or mother or wife*a* or children or fields for my sake will receive a hundred times as much and will inherit eternal life. ³⁰ But many who are first will be last, and many who are last will be first. Mk 10:17-30; Lk 18:18-30

The Parable of the Workers in the Vineyard

20 "For the kingdom of heaven is like a landowner who went out early in the morning to hire workers for his vineyard. ² He agreed to pay them a denarius*b* for the day and sent them into his vineyard. Mt 21:28,33

³ "About nine in the morning he went out and saw others standing in the marketplace doing nothing. ⁴ He told them, 'You also go and work in my vineyard, and I will pay you whatever is right.' ⁵ So they went.

"He went out again about noon and about three in the afternoon and did the same thing. ⁶ About five in the afternoon he went out and found still others standing around. He asked them, 'Why have you been standing here all day long doing nothing?'

⁷ " 'Because no one has hired us,' they answered.

"He said to them, 'You also go and work in my vineyard.'

⁸ "When evening came, the owner of the vineyard said to his foreman, 'Call the workers and pay them their wages, beginning with the last ones hired and going on to the first.' Lev 19:13; Dt 24:15

⁹ "The workers who were hired about five in the afternoon came and each received a denarius. ¹⁰ So when those came who were hired first, they expected to receive more. But each one of them also received a denarius. ¹¹ When they received it, they began to grumble against the landowner. ¹² 'These who were hired last

---

a 29 Some manuscripts do not have *or wife*. day laborer.   *b* 2 A denarius was the usual daily wage of a worked only one hour,' they said, 'and you have made them equal to us who have borne the burden of the work and the heat of the day.' Jnh 4:8; Jas 1:11 ¹³"But he answered one of them, 'I am not being unfair to you, friend. Didn't you agree to work for a denarius? ¹⁴Take your pay and go. I want to give the one who was hired last the same as I gave you. ¹⁵Don't I have the right to do what I want with my own money? Or are you envious because I am generous?' Dt 15:9 ¹⁶"So the last will be first, and the first will be last." Mt 19:30

Jesus Predicts His Death a Third Time
20:17-19pp — Mk 10:32-34; Lk 18:31-33

¹⁷Now Jesus was going up to Jerusalem. On the way, he took the Twelve aside and said to them, ¹⁸"We are going up to Jerusalem, and the Son of Man will be delivered over to the chief priests and the teachers of the law. They will condemn him to death ¹⁹and will hand him over to the Gentiles to be mocked and flogged and crucified. On the third day he will be raised to life!" Mk 10:32-34; Lk 18:31-33

A Mother's Request
20:20-28pp — Mk 10:35-45

²⁰Then the mother of Zebedee's sons came to Jesus with her sons and, kneeling down, asked a favor of him. Mt 4:21; 8:2

²¹"What is it you want?" he asked.

She said, "Grant that one of these two sons of mine may sit at your right and the other at your left in your kingdom." Mt 19:28 ²²"You don't know what you are asking," Jesus said to them. "Can you drink the cup I am going to drink?" Mt 26:39,42; Lk 22:42

"We can," they answered.

²³Jesus said to them, "You will indeed drink from my cup, but to sit at my right or left is not for me to grant. These places belong to those for whom they have been prepared by my Father." Ac 12:2 ²⁴When the ten heard about this, they were indignant with the two brothers. ²⁵Jesus called them together and said, "You know that the rulers of the Gentiles lord it over them, and their high officials exercise authority over them. ²⁶Not so with you. Instead, whoever wants to become great among you must be your servant, ²⁷and whoever wants to be first must be your slave— ²⁸just as the Son of Man did not come to be served, but to serve, and to give his life as a ransom for many." Mk 10:35-45; Jn 13:13-16

Two Blind Men Receive Sight
20:29-34pp — Mk 10:46-52; Lk 18:35-43

²⁹As Jesus and his disciples were leaving Jericho, a large crowd followed him. ³⁰Two blind men were sitting by the roadside, and when they heard that

Jesus was going by, they shouted, "Lord, Son of David, have mercy on us!" Mt 9:27

31 The crowd rebuked them and told them to be quiet, but they shouted all the louder, "Lord, Son of David, have mercy on us!"

32 Jesus stopped and called them. "What do you want me to do for you?" he asked.

33 "Lord," they answered, "we want our sight."

34 Jesus had compassion on them and touched their eyes. Immediately they received their sight and followed him. Mk 10:46-52

Jesus Comes to Jerusalem as King

21:1-9pp — Mk 11:1-10; Lk 19:29-38
21:4-9pp — Jn 12:12-15

21 As they approached Jerusalem and came to Bethphage on the Mount of Olives, Jesus sent two disciples, **2** saying to them, "Go to the village ahead of you, and at once you will find a donkey tied there, with her colt by her. Untie them and bring them to me. **3** If anyone says anything to you, say that the Lord needs them, and he will send them right away." Mk 11:1-10

4 This took place to fulfill what was spoken through the prophet:

5 "Say to Daughter Zion,
'See, your king comes to you,

gentle and riding on a donkey,
and on a colt, the foal of a
donkey.' "*a* Isa 62:11

6 The disciples went and did as Jesus had instructed them. **7** They brought the donkey and the colt and placed their cloaks on them for Jesus to sit on. **8** A very large crowd spread their cloaks on the road, while others cut branches from the trees and spread them on the road. **9** The crowds that went ahead of him and those that followed shouted, 2Ki 9:13

"Hosanna*b* to the Son of
David!" Mt 9:27

"Blessed is he who comes
in the name of the
Lord!"*c* Lk 19:29-38

"Hosanna*b* in the highest
heaven!" Jn 12:12-15

10 When Jesus entered Jerusalem, the whole city was stirred and asked, "Who is this?"

11 The crowds answered, "This is Jesus, the prophet from Nazareth in Galilee." Jn 6:14; 7:40

Jesus at the Temple

21:12-16pp — Mk 11:15-18; Lk 19:45-47

12 Jesus entered the temple courts and drove out all who were buying and selling there. He overturned the tables of the money changers and the benches

---

a 5 Zech. 9:9   *b* 9 A Hebrew expression meaning "Save!" which became an exclamation of praise; also in verse 15   *c* 9 Psalm 118:25,26 of those selling doves. ¹³"It is written," he said to them, " 'My house will be called a house of prayer,'*ᵃ* but you are making it 'a den of robbers.'*ᵇ*" Ex 30:13; Dt 14:26

¹⁴The blind and the lame came to him at the temple, and he healed them. ¹⁵But when the chief priests and the teachers of the law saw the wonderful things he did and the children shouting in the temple courts, "Hosanna to the Son of David," they were indignant. Mt 9:27; Lk 19:39

¹⁶"Do you hear what these children are saying?" they asked him.

"Yes," replied Jesus, "have you never read,

" 'From the lips of children
and infants
you, Lord, have called forth
your praise'*ᶜ*?" Mk 11:15-18

¹⁷And he left them and went out of the city to Bethany, where he spent the night. Mt 26:6; Mk 11:1

Jesus Curses a Fig Tree
21:18-22pp — Mk 11:12-14,20-24

¹⁸Early in the morning, as Jesus was on his way back to the city, he was hungry. ¹⁹Seeing a fig tree by the road, he went up to it but found nothing on it except leaves. Then he said to it, "May you never bear fruit again!" Immediately the tree withered. Isa 34:4; Jer 8:13

²⁰When the disciples saw this,

they were amazed. "How did the fig tree wither so quickly?" they asked.

²¹Jesus replied, "Truly I tell you, if you have faith and do not doubt, not only can you do what was done to the fig tree, but also you can say to this mountain, 'Go, throw yourself into the sea,' and it will be done. ²²If you believe, you will receive whatever you ask for in prayer." Mk 11:12-14,20-24; Jas 1:6

The Authority of Jesus Questioned
21:23-27pp — Mk 11:27-33; Lk 20:1-8

²³Jesus entered the temple courts, and, while he was teaching, the chief priests and the elders of the people came to him. "By what authority are you doing these things?" they asked. "And who gave you this authority?"

²⁴Jesus replied, "I will also ask you one question. If you answer me, I will tell you by what authority I am doing these things. ²⁵John's baptism—where did it come from? Was it from heaven, or of human origin?"

They discussed it among themselves and said, "If we say, 'From heaven,' he will ask, 'Then why didn't you believe him?' ²⁶But if we say, 'Of human origin'— we are afraid of the people, for they all hold that John was a prophet." Mk 6:20

²⁷So they answered Jesus, "We don't know."

Then he said, "Neither will I tell you by what authority I am doing these things. Mk 11:27-33

The Parable of the Two Sons

28 "What do you think? There was a man who had two sons. He went to the first and said, 'Son, go and work today in the vineyard.' Mt 20:1

29 "'I will not,' he answered, but later he changed his mind and went.

30 "Then the father went to the other son and said the same thing. He answered, 'I will, sir,' but he did not go.

31 "Which of the two did what his father wanted?"

"The first," they answered.

Jesus said to them, "Truly I tell you, the tax collectors and the prostitutes are entering the kingdom of God ahead of you. 32 For John came to you to show you the way of righteousness, and you did not believe him, but the tax collectors and the prostitutes did. And even after you saw this, you did not repent and believe him.

The Parable of the Tenants

21:33-46pp — Mk 12:1-12; Lk 20:9-19

33 "Listen to another parable: There was a landowner who planted a vineyard. He put a wall around it, dug a winepress in it and built a watchtower. Then he rented the vineyard to some farmers and moved to another place. 34 When the harvest time approached, he sent his servants to the tenants to collect his fruit. Ps 80:8; Isa 5:1-7

35 "The tenants seized his servants; they beat one, killed another, and stoned a third. 36 Then he sent other servants to them, more than the first time, and the tenants treated them the same way. 37 Last of all, he sent his son to them. 'They will respect my son,' he said. 2Ch 24:21; Mt 23:34,37

38 "But when the tenants saw the son, they said to each other, 'This is the heir. Come, let's kill him and take his inheritance.' 39 So they took him and threw him out of the vineyard and killed him. Ps 2:8; Mt 12:14; Heb 1:2

40 "Therefore, when the owner of the vineyard comes, what will he do to those tenants?"

41 "He will bring those wretches to a wretched end," they replied, "and he will rent the vineyard to other tenants, who will give him his share of the crop at harvest time." Ac 13:46; 18:6; 28:28

42 Jesus said to them, "Have you never read in the Scriptures:

"'The stone the builders rejected
has become the cornerstone;
the Lord has done this,
and it is marvelous in our eyes'*a*? Ac 4:11; 1Pe 2:7

a 42 Psalm 118:22,23

⁴³"Therefore I tell you that the kingdom of God will be taken away from you and given to a people who will produce its fruit. ⁴⁴Anyone who falls on this stone will be broken to pieces; anyone on whom it falls will be crushed."ᵃ   Mt 8:12; Lk 2:34

⁴⁵When the chief priests and the Pharisees heard Jesus' parables, they knew he was talking about them. ⁴⁶They looked for a way to arrest him, but they were afraid of the crowd because the people held that he was a prophet.   Mk 12:1-12; Lk 20:9-19

The Parable of the Wedding Banquet

22:2-14Ref — Lk 14:16-24

22 Jesus spoke to them again in parables, saying: ²"The kingdom of heaven is like a king who prepared a wedding banquet for his son. ³He sent his servants to those who had been invited to the banquet to tell them to come, but they refused to come.   Mt 21:34

⁴"Then he sent some more servants and said, 'Tell those who have been invited that I have prepared my dinner: My oxen and fattened cattle have been butchered, and everything is ready. Come to the wedding banquet.'   Mt 21:36

⁵"But they paid no attention and went off—one to his field, another to his business. ⁶The rest

seized his servants, mistreated them and killed them. ⁷The king was enraged. He sent his army and destroyed those murderers and burned their city.   Lk 19:27

⁸"Then he said to his servants, 'The wedding banquet is ready, but those I invited did not deserve to come. ⁹So go to the street corners and invite to the banquet anyone you find.' ¹⁰So the servants went out into the streets and gathered all the people they could find, the bad as well as the good, and the wedding hall was filled with guests.   Eze 21:21; Mt 13:47-48

¹¹"But when the king came in to see the guests, he noticed a man there who was not wearing wedding clothes. ¹²He asked, 'How did you get in here without wedding clothes, friend?' The man was speechless.   Mt 20:13; 26:50

¹³"Then the king told the attendants, 'Tie him hand and foot, and throw him outside, into the darkness, where there will be weeping and gnashing of teeth.'   Mt 8:12

¹⁴"For many are invited, but few are chosen."   Lk 14:6-24

Paying the Imperial Tax to Caesar

22:15-22pp — Mk 12:13-17; Lk 20:20-26

¹⁵Then the Pharisees went out and laid plans to trap him in his words. ¹⁶They sent their disciples to him along with the He-

---

ᵃ 44 Some manuscripts do not have verse 44.

rodians. "Teacher," they said, "we know that you are a man of integrity and that you teach the way of God in accordance with the truth. You aren't swayed by others, because you pay no attention to who they are. ¹⁷ Tell us then, what is your opinion? Is it right to pay the imperial tax*a* to Caesar or not?" Mt 17:25; Mk 3:6

¹⁸ But Jesus, knowing their evil intent, said, "You hypocrites, why are you trying to trap me? ¹⁹ Show me the coin used for paying the tax." They brought him a denarius, ²⁰ and he asked them, "Whose image is this? And whose inscription?"

²¹ "Caesar's," they replied.

Then he said to them, "So give back to Caesar what is Caesar's, and to God what is God's." Ro 13:7

²² When they heard this, they were amazed. So they left him and went away. Mk 12:13-17

Marriage at the Resurrection
22:23-33pp — Mk 12:18-27; Lk 20:27-40

²³ That same day the Sadducees, who say there is no resurrection, came to him with a question. ²⁴ "Teacher," they said, "Moses told us that if a man dies without having children, his brother must marry the widow and raise up offspring for him. ²⁵ Now there were seven brothers among us. The first one married and died, and since he had no children, he left his wife to his brother. ²⁶ The same thing happened to the second and third brother, right on down to the seventh. ²⁷ Finally, the woman died. ²⁸ Now then, at the resurrection, whose wife will she be of the seven, since all of them were married to her?" Dt 25:5-6; Ac 23:8

²⁹ Jesus replied, "You are in error because you do not know the Scriptures or the power of God. ³⁰ At the resurrection people will neither marry nor be given in marriage; they will be like the angels in heaven. ³¹ But about the resurrection of the dead — have you not read what God said to you, ³² 'I am the God of Abraham, the God of Isaac, and the God of Jacob'*b*? He is not the God of the dead but of the living." Ex 3:6; Jn 20:9

³³ When the crowds heard this, they were astonished at his teaching. Mk 12:18-27; Lk 20:27-40

The Greatest Commandment
22:34-40pp — Mk 12:28-31

³⁴ Hearing that Jesus had silenced the Sadducees, the Pharisees got together. ³⁵ One of them, an expert in the law, tested him with this question: ³⁶ "Teacher, which is the greatest commandment in the Law?" Lk 7:30; 10:25; 11:45

³⁷ Jesus replied: "'Love the Lord your God with all your heart and with all your soul and with all your mind.'*c* ³⁸ This

a 17 A special tax levied on subject peoples, not on Roman citizens   *b 32* Exodus 3:6
c 37 Deut. 6:5

is the first and greatest commandment. **39**And the second is like it: 'Love your neighbor as yourself.'*a* **40**All the Law and the Prophets hang on these two commandments." Mk 12:28-31

Whose Son Is the Messiah?

22:41-46pp — Mk 12:35-37; Lk 20:41-44

41While the Pharisees were gathered together, Jesus asked them, **42**"What do you think about the Messiah? Whose son is he?"

"The son of David," they replied. Mt 9:27

43He said to them, "How is it then that David, speaking by the Spirit, calls him 'Lord'? For he says,

44" 'The Lord said to my Lord:
    "Sit at my right hand
    until I put your enemies
        under your feet." '*b*

45If then David calls him 'Lord,' how can he be his son?" **46**No one could say a word in reply, and from that day on no one dared to ask him any more questions. Mk 12:35-37; Lk 20:41-44; Heb 1:13

A Warning Against Hypocrisy

23:1-7pp — Mk 12:38,39; Lk 20:45,46
23:37-39pp — Lk 13:34,35

23 Then Jesus said to the crowds and to his disciples: **2**"The teachers of the law and the Pharisees sit in Moses' seat. **3**So you must be careful to do everything they tell you. But do not do what they do, for they do not practice what they preach. **4**They tie up heavy, cumbersome loads and put them on other people's shoulders, but they themselves are not willing to lift a finger to move them. Lk 11:46; Ac 15:10

5"Everything they do is done for people to see: They make their phylacteries*c* wide and the tassels on their garments long; **6**they love the place of honor at banquets and the most important seats in the synagogues; **7**they love to be greeted with respect in the marketplaces and to be called 'Rabbi' by others. Mk 12:38-39; Lk 20:45-46

8"But you are not to be called 'Rabbi,' for you have one Teacher, and you are all brothers. **9**And do not call anyone on earth 'father,' for you have one Father, and he is in heaven. **10**Nor are you to be called instructors, for you have one Instructor, the Messiah. **11**The greatest among you will be your servant. **12**For those who exalt themselves will be humbled, and those who humble themselves will be exalted. Mt 20:26

Seven Woes on the Teachers of the Law and the Pharisees

13"Woe to you, teachers of the law and Pharisees, you hypocrites! You shut the door of the

---

a 39 Lev. 19:18 *b 44* Psalm 110:1 *c 5* That is, boxes containing Scripture verses, worn on forehead and arm kingdom of heaven in people's faces. You yourselves do not enter, nor will you let those enter who are trying to. [14] *a* Lk 11:52

15 "Woe to you, teachers of the law and Pharisees, you hypocrites! You travel over land and sea to win a single convert, and when you have succeeded, you make them twice as much a child of hell as you are. Mt 5:22; Ac 2:11

16 "Woe to you, blind guides! You say, 'If anyone swears by the temple, it means nothing; but anyone who swears by the gold of the temple is bound by that oath.' 17 You blind fools! Which is greater: the gold, or the temple that makes the gold sacred? 18 You also say, 'If anyone swears by the altar, it means nothing; but anyone who swears by the gift on the altar is bound by that oath.' 19 You blind men! Which is greater: the gift, or the altar that makes the gift sacred? 20 Therefore, anyone who swears by the altar swears by it and by everything on it. 21 And anyone who swears by the temple swears by it and by the one who dwells in it. 22 And anyone who swears by heaven swears by God's throne and by the one who sits on it. Ex 29:37; Mt 5:34

23 "Woe to you, teachers of the law and Pharisees, you hypocrites! You give a tenth of your spices—mint, dill and cumin. But you have neglected the more important matters of the law—justice, mercy and faithfulness. You should have practiced the latter, without neglecting the former. 24 You blind guides! You strain out a gnat but swallow a camel. Lev 27:30; Lk 11:42

25 "Woe to you, teachers of the law and Pharisees, you hypocrites! You clean the outside of the cup and dish, but inside they are full of greed and self-indulgence. 26 Blind Pharisee! First clean the inside of the cup and dish, and then the outside also will be clean. Mk 7:4; Lk 11:39

27 "Woe to you, teachers of the law and Pharisees, you hypocrites! You are like whitewashed tombs, which look beautiful on the outside but on the inside are full of the bones of the dead and everything unclean. 28 In the same way, on the outside you appear to people as righteous but on the inside you are full of hypocrisy and wickedness. Lk 11:44

29 "Woe to you, teachers of the law and Pharisees, you hypocrites! You build tombs for the prophets and decorate the graves of the righteous. 30 And you say, 'If we had lived in the days of our ancestors, we would not have taken part with them in shedding the blood of the prophets.' 31 So you testify against yourselves that you are the descendants of those who murdered the prophets. 32 Go ahead, then, and

a 14 Some manuscripts include here words similar to Mark 12:40 and Luke 20:47.

complete what your ancestors started! Lk 11:47-48; Ac 7:51-52

³³ "You snakes! You brood of vipers! How will you escape being condemned to hell? ³⁴ Therefore I am sending you prophets and sages and teachers. Some of them you will kill and crucify; others you will flog in your synagogues and pursue from town to town. ³⁵ And so upon you will come all the righteous blood that has been shed on earth, from the blood of righteous Abel to the blood of Zechariah son of Berekiah, whom you murdered between the temple and the altar. ³⁶ Truly I tell you, all this will come on this generation. Lk 11:49-51

³⁷ "Jerusalem, Jerusalem, you who kill the prophets and stone those sent to you, how often I have longed to gather your children together, as a hen gathers her chicks under her wings, and you were not willing. ³⁸ Look, your house is left to you desolate. ³⁹ For I tell you, you will not see me again until you say, 'Blessed is he who comes in the name of the Lord.'ᵃ" Lk 13:34-35; 2Ch 24:21

The Destruction of the Temple and Signs of the End Times
24:1-51pp — Mk 13:1-37; Lk 21:5-36

24 Jesus left the temple and was walking away when his disciples came up to him to call his attention to its buildings. ² "Do you see all these things?"

he asked. "Truly I tell you, not one stone here will be left on another; every one will be thrown down." Mk 13:1-37; Lk 21:5-36

³ As Jesus was sitting on the Mount of Olives, the disciples came to him privately. "Tell us," they said, "when will this happen, and what will be the sign of your coming and of the end of the age?" Mt 21:1

⁴ Jesus answered: "Watch out that no one deceives you. ⁵ For many will come in my name, claiming, 'I am the Messiah,' and will deceive many. ⁶ You will hear of wars and rumors of wars, but see to it that you are not alarmed. Such things must happen, but the end is still to come. ⁷ Nation will rise against nation, and kingdom against kingdom. There will be famines and earthquakes in various places. ⁸ All these are the beginning of birth pains. Isa 19:2; Ac 11:28

⁹ "Then you will be handed over to be persecuted and put to death, and you will be hated by all nations because of me. ¹⁰ At that time many will turn away from the faith and will betray and hate each other, ¹¹ and many false prophets will appear and deceive many people. ¹² Because of the increase of wickedness, the love of most will grow cold, ¹³ but the one who stands firm to the end will be saved. ¹⁴ And this gospel of the king-

ᵃ 39 Psalm 118:26

dom will be preached in the whole world as a testimony to all nations, and then the end will come.   Ro 10:18; Col 1:6,23

¹⁵ "So when you see standing in the holy place 'the abomination that causes desolation,'ᵃ spoken of through the prophet Daniel — let the reader understand — ¹⁶ then let those who are in Judea flee to the mountains. ¹⁷ Let no one on the housetop go down to take anything out of the house. ¹⁸ Let no one in the field go back to get their cloak. ¹⁹ How dreadful it will be in those days for pregnant women and nursing mothers! ²⁰ Pray that your flight will not take place in winter or on the Sabbath. ²¹ For then there will be great distress, unequaled from the beginning of the world until now — and never to be equaled again.

²² "If those days had not been cut short, no one would survive, but for the sake of the elect those days will be shortened. ²³ At that time if anyone says to you, 'Look, here is the Messiah!' or, 'There he is!' do not believe it. ²⁴ For false messiahs and false prophets will appear and perform great signs and wonders to deceive, if possible, even the elect. ²⁵ See, I have told you ahead of time.   Lk 17:23; 2Th 2:9-11

²⁶ "So if anyone tells you, 'There he is, out in the wilderness,' do not go out; or, 'Here he is, in the inner rooms,' do not believe it. ²⁷ For as lightning that comes from the east is visible even in the west, so will be the coming of the Son of Man. ²⁸ Wherever there is a carcass, there the vultures will gather.   Lk 17:24,30,37

²⁹ "Immediately after the distress of those days

" 'the sun will be darkened,
    and the moon will not give
        its light;
the stars will fall from the sky,
    and the heavenly bodies
        will be shaken.'ᵇ   Eze 32:7

³⁰ "Then will appear the sign of the Son of Man in heaven. And then all the peoples of the earthᶜ will mourn when they see the Son of Man coming on the clouds of heaven, with power and great glory.ᵈ ³¹ And he will send his angels with a loud trumpet call, and they will gather his elect from the four winds, from one end of the heavens to the other.   Da 7:13; Isa 27:13; 1Co 15:52

³² "Now learn this lesson from the fig tree: As soon as its twigs get tender and its leaves come out, you know that summer is near. ³³ Even so, when you see all these things, you know that itᵉ is near, right at the door. ³⁴ Truly I tell you, this generation will certainly not pass away until all these things have happened.

³⁵Heaven and earth will pass away, but my words will never pass away. *Mt 5:18; 16:28*

The Day and Hour Unknown

24:37-39pp — Lk 17:26,27
24:45-51pp — Lk 12:42-46

³⁶"But about that day or hour no one knows, not even the angels in heaven, nor the Son,ᵃ but only the Father. ³⁷As it was in the days of Noah, so it will be at the coming of the Son of Man. ³⁸For in the days before the flood, people were eating and drinking, marrying and giving in marriage, up to the day Noah entered the ark; ³⁹and they knew nothing about what would happen until the flood came and took them all away. That is how it will be at the coming of the Son of Man. ⁴⁰Two men will be in the field; one will be taken and the other left. ⁴¹Two women will be grinding with a hand mill; one will be taken and the other left. *Lk 17:26-27,34-35*

⁴²"Therefore keep watch, because you do not know on what day your Lord will come. ⁴³But understand this: If the owner of the house had known at what time of night the thief was coming, he would have kept watch and would not have let his house be broken into. ⁴⁴So you also must be ready, because the Son of Man will come at an hour when you do not expect him. *Mt 25:13; Lk 12:39-40*

⁴⁵"Who then is the faithful and wise servant, whom the master has put in charge of the servants in his household to give them their food at the proper time? ⁴⁶It will be good for that servant whose master finds him doing so when he returns. ⁴⁷Truly I tell you, he will put him in charge of all his possessions. ⁴⁸But suppose that servant is wicked and says to himself, 'My master is staying away a long time,' ⁴⁹and he then begins to beat his fellow servants and to eat and drink with drunkards. ⁵⁰The master of that servant will come on a day when he does not expect him and at an hour he is not aware of. ⁵¹He will cut him to pieces and assign him a place with the hypocrites, where there will be weeping and gnashing of teeth. *Lk 12:42-46; Rev 16:15*

The Parable of the Ten Virgins

25 "At that time the kingdom of heaven will be like ten virgins who took their lamps and went out to meet the bridegroom. ²Five of them were foolish and five were wise. ³The foolish ones took their lamps but did not take any oil with them. ⁴The wise ones, however, took oil in jars along with their lamps. ⁵The bridegroom was a long time in coming, and they all became drowsy and fell asleep. *1Th 5:6; Rev 19:7*

⁶"At midnight the cry rang out:

ᵃ 36 Some manuscripts do not have *nor the Son*.

'Here's the bridegroom! Come out to meet him!'

7 "Then all the virgins woke up and trimmed their lamps. 8 The foolish ones said to the wise, 'Give us some of your oil; our lamps are going out.' Lk 12:35

9 "'No,' they replied, 'there may not be enough for both us and you. Instead, go to those who sell oil and buy some for yourselves.'

10 "But while they were on their way to buy the oil, the bridegroom arrived. The virgins who were ready went in with him to the wedding banquet. And the door was shut. Rev 19:9

11 "Later the others also came. 'Lord, Lord,' they said, 'open the door for us!'

12 "But he replied, 'Truly I tell you, I don't know you.' Mt 7:23

13 "Therefore keep watch, because you do not know the day or the hour. Mt 24:42,44; Mk 13:35; Lk 12:40

The Parable of the Bags of Gold

25:14-30Ref — Lk 19:12-27

14 "Again, it will be like a man going on a journey, who called his servants and entrusted his wealth to them. 15 To one he gave five bags of gold, to another two bags, and to another one bag,[a] each according to his ability. Then he went on his journey. 16 The man who had received five bags of gold went at once and put his money to work and gained five bags more. 17 So also, the one with two bags of gold gained two more. 18 But the man who had received one bag went off, dug a hole in the ground and hid his master's money. Mt 18:24-25; 21:33

19 "After a long time the master of those servants returned and settled accounts with them. 20 The man who had received five bags of gold brought the other five. 'Master,' he said, 'you entrusted me with five bags of gold. See, I have gained five more.' Mt 18:23

21 "His master replied, 'Well done, good and faithful servant! You have been faithful with a few things; I will put you in charge of many things. Come and share your master's happiness!' Mt 24:45

22 "The man with two bags of gold also came. 'Master,' he said, 'you entrusted me with two bags of gold; see, I have gained two more.'

23 "His master replied, 'Well done, good and faithful servant! You have been faithful with a few things; I will put you in charge of many things. Come and share your master's happiness!' ver 21

24 "Then the man who had received one bag of gold came. 'Master,' he said, 'I knew that you are a hard man, harvesting where you have not sown and gathering where you have not scattered seed. 25 So I was afraid

---

a 15 Greek *five talents . . . two talents . . . one talent*; also throughout this parable; a talent was worth about 20 years of a day laborer's wage.

and went out and hid your gold in the ground. See, here is what belongs to you.'

²⁶ "His master replied, 'You wicked, lazy servant! So you knew that I harvest where I have not sown and gather where I have not scattered seed? ²⁷ Well then, you should have put my money on deposit with the bankers, so that when I returned I would have received it back with interest.

²⁸ " 'So take the bag of gold from him and give it to the one who has ten bags. ²⁹ For whoever has will be given more, and they will have an abundance. Whoever does not have, even what they have will be taken from them. ³⁰ And throw that worthless servant outside, into the darkness, where there will be weeping and gnashing of teeth.'   Lk 19:12-27

The Sheep and the Goats

³¹ "When the Son of Man comes in his glory, and all the angels with him, he will sit on his glorious throne. ³² All the nations will be gathered before him, and he will separate the people one from another as a shepherd separates the sheep from the goats. ³³ He will put the sheep on his right and the goats on his left.   Eze 34:17,20; Mal 3:18

³⁴ "Then the King will say to those on his right, 'Come, you who are blessed by my Father; take your inheritance, the kingdom prepared for you since the creation of the world. ³⁵ For I was hungry and you gave me something to eat, I was thirsty and you gave me something to drink, I was a stranger and you invited me in, ³⁶ I needed clothes and you clothed me, I was sick and you looked after me, I was in prison and you came to visit me.' 1Co 15:50; Jas 2:15-16; Rev 13:8

³⁷ "Then the righteous will answer him, 'Lord, when did we see you hungry and feed you, or thirsty and give you something to drink? ³⁸ When did we see you a stranger and invite you in, or needing clothes and clothe you? ³⁹ When did we see you sick or in prison and go to visit you?'

⁴⁰ "The King will reply, 'Truly I tell you, whatever you did for one of the least of these brothers and sisters of mine, you did for me.'   Pr 19:17; Mt 10:40,42

⁴¹ "Then he will say to those on his left, 'Depart from me, you who are cursed, into the eternal fire prepared for the devil and his angels. ⁴² For I was hungry and you gave me nothing to eat, I was thirsty and you gave me nothing to drink, ⁴³ I was a stranger and you did not invite me in, I needed clothes and you did not clothe me, I was sick and in prison and you did not look after me.'   Mt 7:23; Mk 9:43,48; 2Pe 2:4

⁴⁴ "They also will answer, 'Lord, when did we see you hungry or thirsty or a stranger or

needing clothes or sick or in prison, and did not help you?'

[45] "He will reply, 'Truly I tell you, whatever you did not do for one of the least of these, you did not do for me.' Pr 14:31; 17:5

[46] "Then they will go away to eternal punishment, but the righteous to eternal life." Da 12:2; Jn 5:29

The Plot Against Jesus

26:2-5pp — Mk 14:1,2; Lk 22:1,2

26 When Jesus had finished saying all these things, he said to his disciples, [2] "As you know, the Passover is two days away—and the Son of Man will be handed over to be crucified."

[3] Then the chief priests and the elders of the people assembled in the palace of the high priest, whose name was Caiaphas, [4] and they schemed to arrest Jesus secretly and kill him. [5] "But not during the festival," they said, "or there may be a riot among the people." Mk 14:1-2; Lk 22:1-2

Jesus Anointed at Bethany

26:6-13pp — Mk 14:3-9
26:6-13Ref — Lk 7:37,38; Jn 12:1-8

[6] While Jesus was in Bethany in the home of Simon the Leper, [7] a woman came to him with an alabaster jar of very expensive perfume, which she poured on his head as he was reclining at the table. Mt 21:17

[8] When the disciples saw this, they were indignant. "Why this waste?" they asked. [9] "This perfume could have been sold at a high price and the money given to the poor."

[10] Aware of this, Jesus said to them, "Why are you bothering this woman? She has done a beautiful thing to me. [11] The poor you will always have with you,[a] but you will not always have me. [12] When she poured this perfume on my body, she did it to prepare me for burial. [13] Truly I tell you, wherever this gospel is preached throughout the world, what she has done will also be told, in memory of her." Mk 14:3-9; Lk 7:37-38; Jn 12:1-8

Judas Agrees to Betray Jesus

26:14-16pp — Mk 14:10,11; Lk 22:3-6

[14] Then one of the Twelve—the one called Judas Iscariot—went to the chief priests [15] and asked, "What are you willing to give me if I deliver him over to you?" So they counted out for him thirty pieces of silver. [16] From then on Judas watched for an opportunity to hand him over. Mk 14:10-11; Lk 22:3-6

The Last Supper

26:17-19pp — Mk 14:12-16; Lk 22:7-13
26:20-24pp — Mk 14:17-21
26:26-29pp — Mk 14:22-25; Lk 22:17-20;
1Co 11:23-25

[17] On the first day of the Festival of Unleavened Bread, the disciples came to Jesus and asked,

[a] 11 See Deut. 15:11.

"Where do you want us to make preparations for you to eat the Passover?" Ex 12:18-20

¹⁸He replied, "Go into the city to a certain man and tell him, 'The Teacher says: My appointed time is near. I am going to celebrate the Passover with my disciples at your house.'" ¹⁹So the disciples did as Jesus had directed them and prepared the Passover. Mk 14:12-16; Lk 22:7-13

²⁰When evening came, Jesus was reclining at the table with the Twelve. ²¹And while they were eating, he said, "Truly I tell you, one of you will betray me."

²²They were very sad and began to say to him one after the other, "Surely you don't mean me, Lord?"

²³Jesus replied, "The one who has dipped his hand into the bowl with me will betray me. ²⁴The Son of Man will go just as it is written about him. But woe to that man who betrays the Son of Man! It would be better for him if he had not been born." Mk 14:17-21; Jn 13:18

²⁵Then Judas, the one who would betray him, said, "Surely you don't mean me, Rabbi?" Mt 23:7

Jesus answered, "You have said so."

²⁶While they were eating, Jesus took bread, and when he had given thanks, he broke it and gave it to his disciples, saying, "Take and eat; this is my body." 1Co 10:16

²⁷Then he took a cup, and when he had given thanks, he gave it to them, saying, "Drink from it, all of you. ²⁸This is my blood of the^a covenant, which is poured out for many for the forgiveness of sins. ²⁹I tell you, I will not drink from this fruit of the vine from now on until that day when I drink it new with you in my Father's kingdom." Lk 22:17-20; 1Co 11:23-25

³⁰When they had sung a hymn, they went out to the Mount of Olives. Mk 14:22-26

Jesus Predicts Peter's Denial

26:31-35pp — Mk 14:27-31; Lk 22:31-34

³¹Then Jesus told them, "This very night you will all fall away on account of me, for it is written: Mt 11:6; 13:21

"'I will strike the shepherd,
    and the sheep of the flock
        will be scattered.'^b

³²But after I have risen, I will go ahead of you into Galilee." Mt 28:7

³³Peter replied, "Even if all fall away on account of you, I never will."

³⁴"Truly I tell you," Jesus answered, "this very night, before the rooster crows, you will disown me three times." Jn 13:37-38

³⁵But Peter declared, "Even if I have to die with you, I will never disown you." And all the other disciples said the same. Mk 14:27-31

^a 28 Some manuscripts *the new*   ^b 31 Zech. 13:7

Gethsemane

26:36-46pp — Mk 14:32-42; Lk 22:40-46

36 Then Jesus went with his disciples to a place called Gethsemane, and he said to them, "Sit here while I go over there and pray." **37** He took Peter and the two sons of Zebedee along with him, and he began to be sorrowful and troubled. **38** Then he said to them, "My soul is overwhelmed with sorrow to the point of death. Stay here and keep watch with me."   Mt 4:21; Jn 12:27

39 Going a little farther, he fell with his face to the ground and prayed, "My Father, if it is possible, may this cup be taken from me. Yet not as I will, but as you will."   Mt 20:22; Jn 6:38

40 Then he returned to his disciples and found them sleeping. "Couldn't you men keep watch with me for one hour?" he asked Peter. **41** "Watch and pray so that you will not fall into temptation. The spirit is willing, but the flesh is weak."   Mt 6:13

42 He went away a second time and prayed, "My Father, if it is not possible for this cup to be taken away unless I drink it, may your will be done."

43 When he came back, he again found them sleeping, because their eyes were heavy. **44** So he left them and went away once more and prayed the third time, saying the same thing.

45 Then he returned to the disciples and said to them, "Are you still sleeping and resting? Look, the hour has come, and the Son of Man is delivered into the hands of sinners. **46** Rise! Let us go! Here comes my betrayer!"   Mk 14:32-42; Lk 22:40-46

Jesus Arrested

26:47-56pp — Mk 14:43-50; Lk 22:47-53

47 While he was still speaking, Judas, one of the Twelve, arrived. With him was a large crowd armed with swords and clubs, sent from the chief priests and the elders of the people. **48** Now the betrayer had arranged a signal with them: "The one I kiss is the man; arrest him." **49** Going at once to Jesus, Judas said, "Greetings, Rabbi!" and kissed him.   Mt 23:7

50 Jesus replied, "Do what you came for, friend."[a]   Mt 20:13; 22:12

Then the men stepped forward, seized Jesus and arrested him. **51** With that, one of Jesus' companions reached for his sword, drew it out and struck the servant of the high priest, cutting off his ear.   Lk 22:36,38; Jn 18:10

52 "Put your sword back in its place," Jesus said to him, "for all who draw the sword will die by the sword. **53** Do you think I cannot call on my Father, and he will at once put at my disposal more than twelve legions of angels? **54** But how then would the

---

[a] 50 Or "Why have you come, friend?"

Scriptures be fulfilled that say it must happen in this way?" Ge 9:6

⁵⁵In that hour Jesus said to the crowd, "Am I leading a rebellion, that you have come out with swords and clubs to capture me? Every day I sat in the temple courts teaching, and you did not arrest me. ⁵⁶But this has all taken place that the writings of the prophets might be fulfilled." Then all the disciples deserted him and fled. Mk 14:43-50; Lk 22:47-53

Jesus Before the Sanhedrin
26:57-68pp — Mk 14:53-65;
Jn 18:12,13,19-24

⁵⁷Those who had arrested Jesus took him to Caiaphas the high priest, where the teachers of the law and the elders had assembled. ⁵⁸But Peter followed him at a distance, right up to the courtyard of the high priest. He entered and sat down with the guards to see the outcome. Jn 18:15

⁵⁹The chief priests and the whole Sanhedrin were looking for false evidence against Jesus so that they could put him to death. ⁶⁰But they did not find any, though many false witnesses came forward. Ps 27:12; 35:11; Ac 6:13

Finally two came forward ⁶¹and declared, "This fellow said, 'I am able to destroy the temple of God and rebuild it in three days.'" Dt 19:15; Jn 2:19

⁶²Then the high priest stood up and said to Jesus, "Are you

not going to answer? What is this testimony that these men are bringing against you?" ⁶³But Jesus remained silent. Mt 27:12,14

The high priest said to him, "I charge you under oath by the living God: Tell us if you are the Messiah, the Son of God." Lk 22:67

⁶⁴"You have said so," Jesus replied. "But I say to all of you: From now on you will see the Son of Man sitting at the right hand of the Mighty One and coming on the clouds of heaven."[a] Ps 110:1; Da 7:13; Rev 1:7

⁶⁵Then the high priest tore his clothes and said, "He has spoken blasphemy! Why do we need any more witnesses? Look, now you have heard the blasphemy. ⁶⁶What do you think?" Mk 14:63

"He is worthy of death," they answered. Lev 24:16; Jn 19:7

⁶⁷Then they spit in his face and struck him with their fists. Others slapped him ⁶⁸and said, "Prophesy to us, Messiah. Who hit you?" Mk 14:53-65; Jn 18:12-13,19-24

Peter Disowns Jesus
26:69-75pp — Mk 14:66-72; Lk 22:55-62;
Jn 18:16-18,25-27

⁶⁹Now Peter was sitting out in the courtyard, and a servant girl came to him. "You also were with Jesus of Galilee," she said.

⁷⁰But he denied it before them all. "I don't know what you're talking about," he said.

⁷¹Then he went out to the gate-

---

[a] 64 See Psalm 110:1; Daniel 7:13.

way, where another servant girl saw him and said to the people there, "This fellow was with Jesus of Nazareth."

⁷²He denied it again, with an oath: "I don't know the man!"

⁷³After a little while, those standing there went up to Peter and said, "Surely you are one of them; your accent gives you away."

⁷⁴Then he began to call down curses, and he swore to them, "I don't know the man!"

Immediately a rooster crowed. ⁷⁵Then Peter remembered the word Jesus had spoken: "Before the rooster crows, you will disown me three times." And he went outside and wept bitterly. ver 34

Judas Hangs Himself

27 Early in the morning, all the chief priests and the elders of the people made their plans how to have Jesus executed. ²So they bound him, led him away and handed him over to Pilate the governor. Mt 20:19; Mk 15:1

³When Judas, who had betrayed him, saw that Jesus was condemned, he was seized with remorse and returned the thirty pieces of silver to the chief priests and the elders. ⁴"I have sinned," he said, "for I have betrayed innocent blood." Mt 26:14-15

"What is that to us?" they replied. "That's your responsibility."

⁵So Judas threw the money into the temple and left. Then he went away and hanged himself. Lk 1:9,21; Ac 1:18

⁶The chief priests picked up the coins and said, "It is against the law to put this into the treasury, since it is blood money." ⁷So they decided to use the money to buy the potter's field as a burial place for foreigners. ⁸That is why it has been called the Field of Blood to this day. ⁹Then what was spoken by Jeremiah the prophet was fulfilled: "They took the thirty pieces of silver, the price set on him by the people of Israel, ¹⁰and they used them to buy the potter's field, as the Lord commanded me."ᵃ Mt 1:22; Ac 1:19

Jesus Before Pilate

27:11-26pp — Mk 15:2-15; Lk 23:2,3, 18-25; Jn 18:29-19:16

¹¹Meanwhile Jesus stood before the governor, and the governor asked him, "Are you the king of the Jews?" Mt 2:2

"You have said so," Jesus replied.

¹²When he was accused by the chief priests and the elders, he gave no answer. ¹³Then Pilate asked him, "Don't you hear the testimony they are bringing against you?" ¹⁴But Jesus made no reply, not even to a single charge—to the great amazement of the governor. Mt 26:62-63; Jn 19:9

ᵃ 10 See Zech. 11:12,13; Jer. 19:1-13; 32:6-9.

¹⁵Now it was the governor's custom at the festival to release a prisoner chosen by the crowd. ¹⁶At that time they had a well-known prisoner whose name was Jesus*ᵃ* Barabbas. ¹⁷So when the crowd had gathered, Pilate asked them, "Which one do you want me to release to you: Jesus Barabbas, or Jesus who is called the Messiah?" ¹⁸For he knew it was out of self-interest that they had handed Jesus over to him. Jn 18:39

¹⁹While Pilate was sitting on the judge's seat, his wife sent him this message: "Don't have anything to do with that innocent man, for I have suffered a great deal today in a dream because of him." Mt 1:20; Jn 19:13

²⁰But the chief priests and the elders persuaded the crowd to ask for Barabbas and to have Jesus executed. Ac 3:14

²¹"Which of the two do you want me to release to you?" asked the governor.

"Barabbas," they answered.

²²"What shall I do, then, with Jesus who is called the Messiah?" Pilate asked. Mt 1:16

They all answered, "Crucify him!"

²³"Why? What crime has he committed?" asked Pilate.

But they shouted all the louder, "Crucify him!"

²⁴When Pilate saw that he was getting nowhere, but that instead an uproar was starting, he took water and washed his hands in front of the crowd. "I am innocent of this man's blood," he said. "It is your responsibility!" Dt 21:6-8; Mt 26:5

²⁵All the people answered, "His blood is on us and on our children!" Jos 2:19; Ac 5:28

²⁶Then he released Barabbas to them. But he had Jesus flogged, and handed him over to be crucified. Mk 15:2-15; Lk 23:2-3,18-25

The Soldiers Mock Jesus
27:27-31pp — Mk 15:16-20

²⁷Then the governor's soldiers took Jesus into the Praetorium and gathered the whole company of soldiers around him. ²⁸They stripped him and put a scarlet robe on him, ²⁹and then twisted together a crown of thorns and set it on his head. They put a staff in his right hand. Then they knelt in front of him and mocked him. "Hail, king of the Jews!" they said. ³⁰They spit on him, and took the staff and struck him on the head again and again. ³¹After they had mocked him, they took off the robe and put his own clothes on him. Then they led him away to crucify him. Mk 15:16-20; Isa 53:3,7

The Crucifixion of Jesus
27:33-44pp — Mk 15:22-32; Lk 23:33-43; Jn 19:17-24

³²As they were going out, they met a man from Cyrene, named

ᵃ 16 Many manuscripts do not have *Jesus*; also in verse 17.

Simon, and they forced him to carry the cross. ³³They came to a place called Golgotha (which means "the place of the skull"). ³⁴There they offered Jesus wine to drink, mixed with gall; but after tasting it, he refused to drink it. ³⁵When they had crucified him, they divided up his clothes by casting lots. ³⁶And sitting down, they kept watch over him there. ³⁷Above his head they placed the written charge against him: THIS IS JESUS, THE KING OF THE JEWS.

³⁸Two rebels were crucified with him, one on his right and one on his left. ³⁹Those who passed by hurled insults at him, shaking their heads ⁴⁰and saying, "You who are going to destroy the temple and build it in three days, save yourself! Come down from the cross, if you are the Son of God!" ⁴¹In the same way the chief priests, the teachers of the law and the elders mocked him. ⁴²"He saved others," they said, "but he can't save himself! He's the king of Israel! Let him come down now from the cross, and we will believe in him. ⁴³He trusts in God. Let God rescue him now if he wants him, for he said, 'I am the Son of God.' " ⁴⁴In the same way the rebels who were crucified with him also heaped insults on him. Mk 15:22-32; Lk 23:33-43; Jn 19:17-24

The Death of Jesus
27:45-56pp — Mk 15:33-41; Lk 23:44-49; Jn 19:29-30

⁴⁵From noon until three in the afternoon darkness came over all the land. ⁴⁶About three in the afternoon Jesus cried out in a loud voice, *"Eli, Eli,ᵃ lema sabachthani?"* (which means "My God, my God, why have you forsaken me?").ᵇ   Am 8:9

⁴⁷When some of those standing there heard this, they said, "He's calling Elijah."

⁴⁸Immediately one of them ran and got a sponge. He filled it with wine vinegar, put it on a staff, and offered it to Jesus to drink. ⁴⁹The rest said, "Now leave him alone. Let's see if Elijah comes to save him."   Ps 69:21

⁵⁰And when Jesus had cried out again in a loud voice, he gave up his spirit.   Jn 19:30

⁵¹At that moment the curtain of the temple was torn in two from top to bottom. The earth shook, the rocks split ⁵²and the tombs broke open. The bodies of many holy people who had died were raised to life. ⁵³They came out of the tombs after Jesus' resurrection andᶜ went into the holy city and appeared to many people.   Ex 26:31-33; Mt 4:5

⁵⁴When the centurion and those with him who were guarding Jesus saw the earthquake and all that had happened, they

---

ᵃ 46 Some manuscripts *Eloi, Eloi*   ᵇ 46 Psalm 22:1   ᶜ 53 Or *tombs, and after Jesus' resurrection they* were terrified, and exclaimed, "Surely he was the Son of God!" Mt 4:3; 17:5

55 Many women were there, watching from a distance. They had followed Jesus from Galilee to care for his needs. **56** Among them were Mary Magdalene, Mary the mother of James and Joseph,*a* and the mother of Zebedee's sons. Mk 15:33-41; Lk 23:44-49

The Burial of Jesus

27:57-61pp — Mk 15:42-47; Lk 23:50-56; Jn 19:38-42

57 As evening approached, there came a rich man from Arimathea, named Joseph, who had himself become a disciple of Jesus. **58** Going to Pilate, he asked for Jesus' body, and Pilate ordered that it be given to him. **59** Joseph took the body, wrapped it in a clean linen cloth, **60** and placed it in his own new tomb that he had cut out of the rock. He rolled a big stone in front of the entrance to the tomb and went away. **61** Mary Magdalene and the other Mary were sitting there opposite the tomb. Mk 15:42-47; Lk 23:50-56; Jn 19:38-42

The Guard at the Tomb

62 The next day, the one after Preparation Day, the chief priests and the Pharisees went to Pilate. **63** "Sir," they said, "we remember that while he was still alive that deceiver said, 'After three days I will rise again.' **64** So give the order for the tomb to be made secure until the third day. Otherwise, his disciples may come and steal the body and tell the people that he has been raised from the dead. This last deception will be worse than the first." Mt 16:21; 28:13

65 "Take a guard," Pilate answered. "Go, make the tomb as secure as you know how." **66** So they went and made the tomb secure by putting a seal on the stone and posting the guard. Da 6:17

Jesus Has Risen

28:1-8pp — Mk 16:1-8; Lk 24:1-10; Jn 20:1-8

28 After the Sabbath, at dawn on the first day of the week, Mary Magdalene and the other Mary went to look at the tomb. Mt 27:56

2 There was a violent earthquake, for an angel of the Lord came down from heaven and, going to the tomb, rolled back the stone and sat on it. **3** His appearance was like lightning, and his clothes were white as snow. **4** The guards were so afraid of him that they shook and became like dead men. Da 10:6; Mk 9:3

5 The angel said to the women, "Do not be afraid, for I know that you are looking for Jesus, who was crucified. **6** He is not here; he has risen, just as he said. Come and see the place where he lay. **7** Then go quickly and tell his disciples: 'He has

a 56 Greek Joses, a variant of Joseph

risen from the dead and is going ahead of you into Galilee. There you will see him.' Now I have told you." Mk 16:1-8; Lk 24:1-10

[8] So the women hurried away from the tomb, afraid yet filled with joy, and ran to tell his disciples. [9] Suddenly Jesus met them. "Greetings," he said. They came to him, clasped his feet and worshiped him. [10] Then Jesus said to them, "Do not be afraid. Go and tell my brothers to go to Galilee; there they will see me." Ro 8:29

The Guards' Report

[11] While the women were on their way, some of the guards went into the city and reported to the chief priests everything that had happened. [12] When the chief priests had met with the elders and devised a plan, they gave the soldiers a large sum of money, [13] telling them, "You are to say, 'His disciples came during the night and stole him away while we were asleep.' [14] If this report gets to the governor, we will satisfy him and keep you out of trouble." [15] So the soldiers took the money and did as they were instructed. And this story has been widely circulated among the Jews to this very day. Mt 27:2,65-66

The Great Commission

[16] Then the eleven disciples went to Galilee, to the mountain where Jesus had told them to go. [17] When they saw him, they worshiped him; but some doubted. [18] Then Jesus came to them and said, "All authority in heaven and on earth has been given to me. [19] Therefore go and make disciples of all nations, baptizing them in the name of the Father and of the Son and of the Holy Spirit, [20] and teaching them to obey everything I have commanded you. And surely I am with you always, to the very end of the age." Mk 16:15-16; Php 2:9-10

Mark

John the Baptist Prepares the Way

1:2-8pp — Mt 3:1-11; Lk 3:2-16

1 The beginning of the good news about Jesus the Messiah,*a* the Son of God,*b* 2 as it is written in Isaiah the prophet: Mt 4:3

"I will send my messenger
    ahead of you,
who will prepare your
    way"*c* —   Mal 3:1; Mt 11:10
3 "a voice of one calling in the
    wilderness,
'Prepare the way for the Lord,
    make straight paths for
    him.' "*d*

4 And so John the Baptist appeared in the wilderness, preaching a baptism of repentance for the forgiveness of sins. 5 The whole Judean countryside and all the people of Jerusalem went out to him. Confessing their sins, they were baptized by him in the Jordan River. 6 John wore clothing made of camel's hair, with a leather belt around his waist, and he ate locusts and wild honey. 7 And this was his message: "After me comes the one more powerful than I, the straps of whose sandals I am not worthy to stoop down and untie. 8 I baptize you with*e* water, but he will baptize you with*e* the Holy Spirit."   Mt 3:1-11; Lk 3:2-16

The Baptism and Testing of Jesus

1:9-11pp — Mt 3:13-17; Lk 3:21,22
1:12,13pp — Mt 4:1-11; Lk 4:1-13

9 At that time Jesus came from Nazareth in Galilee and was baptized by John in the Jordan. 10 Just as Jesus was coming up out of the water, he saw heaven being torn open and the Spirit descending on him like a dove. 11 And a voice came from heaven: "You are my Son, whom I love; with you I am well pleased."   Mt 3:13-17; Lk 3:21-22

---

a 1 Or *Jesus Christ. Messiah* (Hebrew) and *Christ* (Greek) both mean *Anointed One.*
b 1 Some manuscripts do not have *the Son of God.*   *c* 2 Mal. 3:1   *d* 3 Isaiah 40:3
e 8 Or *in*

¹²At once the Spirit sent him out into the wilderness, ¹³and he was in the wilderness forty days, being tempted*ᵃ* by Satan. He was with the wild animals, and angels attended him. Mt 4:1-11; Lk 4:1-13

Jesus Announces the Good News

1:16-20pp — Mt 4:18-22; Lk 5:2-11;
 Jn 1:35-42

¹⁴After John was put in prison, Jesus went into Galilee, proclaiming the good news of God. ¹⁵"The time has come," he said. "The kingdom of God has come near. Repent and believe the good news!" Ac 20:21; Gal 4:4; Eph 1:10

Jesus Calls His First Disciples

¹⁶As Jesus walked beside the Sea of Galilee, he saw Simon and his brother Andrew casting a net into the lake, for they were fishermen. ¹⁷"Come, follow me," Jesus said, "and I will send you out to fish for people." ¹⁸At once they left their nets and followed him. Mt 4:19

¹⁹When he had gone a little farther, he saw James son of Zebedee and his brother John in a boat, preparing their nets. ²⁰Without delay he called them, and they left their father Zebedee in the boat with the hired men and followed him. Mt 4:18-22; Lk 5:2-11; Jn 1:35-42

Jesus Drives Out an Impure Spirit

1:21-28pp — Lk 4:31-37

²¹They went to Capernaum, and when the Sabbath came, Jesus went into the synagogue and began to teach. ²²The people were amazed at his teaching, because he taught them as one who had authority, not as the teachers of the law. ²³Just then a man in their synagogue who was possessed by an impure spirit cried out, ²⁴"What do you want with us, Jesus of Nazareth? Have you come to destroy us? I know who you are—the Holy One of God!" Mt 7:28-29; 8:29; Lk 1:35

²⁵"Be quiet!" said Jesus sternly. "Come out of him!" ²⁶The impure spirit shook the man violently and came out of him with a shriek. Mk 9:20

²⁷The people were all so amazed that they asked each other, "What is this? A new teaching—and with authority! He even gives orders to impure spirits and they obey him." ²⁸News about him spread quickly over the whole region of Galilee. Lk 4:31-37

Jesus Heals Many

1:29-31pp — Mt 8:14,15; Lk 4:38,39
1:32-34pp — Mt 8:16,17; Lk 4:40,41

²⁹As soon as they left the synagogue, they went with James and John to the home of Simon and Andrew. ³⁰Simon's mother-in-law was in bed with a fever, and they immediately told Jesus about her. ³¹So he went to her, took her hand and helped her up.

The fever left her and she began to wait on them. Mt 8:14-15; Lk 4:38-39

³²That evening after sunset the people brought to Jesus all the sick and demon-possessed. ³³The whole town gathered at the door, ³⁴and Jesus healed many who had various diseases. He also drove out many demons, but he would not let the demons speak because they knew who he was. Mt 8:16-17; Lk 4:40-41

Jesus Prays in a Solitary Place
1:35-38pp — Lk 4:42,43

³⁵Very early in the morning, while it was still dark, Jesus got up, left the house and went off to a solitary place, where he prayed. ³⁶Simon and his companions went to look for him, ³⁷and when they found him, they exclaimed: "Everyone is looking for you!" Lk 3:21

³⁸Jesus replied, "Let us go somewhere else — to the nearby villages — so I can preach there also. That is why I have come." ³⁹So he traveled throughout Galilee, preaching in their synagogues and driving out demons. Lk 4:42-43

Jesus Heals a Man With Leprosy
1:40-44pp — Mt 8:2-4; Lk 5:12-14

⁴⁰A man with leprosy[a] came to him and begged him on his knees, "If you are willing, you can make me clean." Mk 10:17

⁴¹Jesus was indignant.[b] He reached out his hand and touched the man. "I am willing," he said. "Be clean!" ⁴²Immediately the leprosy left him and he was cleansed.

⁴³Jesus sent him away at once with a strong warning: ⁴⁴"See that you don't tell this to anyone. But go, show yourself to the priest and offer the sacrifices that Moses commanded for your cleansing, as a testimony to them." ⁴⁵Instead he went out and began to talk freely, spreading the news. As a result, Jesus could no longer enter a town openly but stayed outside in lonely places. Yet the people still came to him from everywhere. Mt 8:2-4; Lk 5:12-14

Jesus Forgives and Heals a Paralyzed Man
2:3-12pp — Mt 9:2-8; Lk 5:18-26

2 A few days later, when Jesus again entered Capernaum, the people heard that he had come home. ²They gathered in such large numbers that there was no room left, not even outside the door, and he preached the word to them. ³Some men came, bringing to him a paralyzed man, carried by four of them. ⁴Since they could not get him to Jesus because of the crowd, they made an opening in the roof above Jesus by digging through it and

---

[a] 40 The Greek word traditionally translated *leprosy* was used for various diseases affecting the skin.   [b] 41 Many manuscripts *Jesus was filled with compassion*

then lowered the mat the man was lying on. [5]When Jesus saw their faith, he said to the paralyzed man, "Son, your sins are forgiven." Mt 4:24; Lk 7:48

[6]Now some teachers of the law were sitting there, thinking to themselves, [7]"Why does this fellow talk like that? He's blaspheming! Who can forgive sins but God alone?" Isa 43:25

[8]Immediately Jesus knew in his spirit that this was what they were thinking in their hearts, and he said to them, "Why are you thinking these things? [9]Which is easier: to say to this paralyzed man, 'Your sins are forgiven,' or to say, 'Get up, take your mat and walk'? [10]But I want you to know that the Son of Man has authority on earth to forgive sins." So he said to the man, [11]"I tell you, get up, take your mat and go home." [12]He got up, took his mat and walked out in full view of them all. This amazed everyone and they praised God, saying, "We have never seen anything like this!" Mt 9:2-8; Lk 5:18-26

Jesus Calls Levi and Eats With Sinners

2:14-17pp — Mt 9:9-13; Lk 5:27-32

[13]Once again Jesus went out beside the lake. A large crowd came to him, and he began to teach them. [14]As he walked along, he saw Levi son of Alphaeus sitting at the tax collector's booth. "Follow me," Jesus told him, and Levi got up and followed him. Mt 4:19; Mk 1:45

[15]While Jesus was having dinner at Levi's house, many tax collectors and sinners were eating with him and his disciples, for there were many who followed him. [16]When the teachers of the law who were Pharisees saw him eating with the sinners and tax collectors, they asked his disciples: "Why does he eat with tax collectors and sinners?" Mt 9:11; Ac 23:9

[17]On hearing this, Jesus said to them, "It is not the healthy who need a doctor, but the sick. I have not come to call the righteous, but sinners." Mt 9:9-13; Lk 5:27-32

Jesus Questioned About Fasting

2:18-22pp — Mt 9:14-17; Lk 5:33-38

[18]Now John's disciples and the Pharisees were fasting. Some people came and asked Jesus, "How is it that John's disciples and the disciples of the Pharisees are fasting, but yours are not?" Mt 6:16-18; Ac 13:2

[19]Jesus answered, "How can the guests of the bridegroom fast while he is with them? They cannot, so long as they have him with them. [20]But the time will come when the bridegroom will be taken from them, and on that day they will fast. Lk 17:22

[21]"No one sews a patch of unshrunk cloth on an old garment. Otherwise, the new piece will pull away from the old, making

the tear worse. 22 And no one pours new wine into old wineskins. Otherwise, the wine will burst the skins, and both the wine and the wineskins will be ruined. No, they pour new wine into new wineskins." Mt 9:14-17; Lk 5:33-38

Jesus Is Lord of the Sabbath

2:23-28pp — Mt 12:1-8; Lk 6:1-5
3:1-6pp — Mt 12:9-14; Lk 6:6-11

23 One Sabbath Jesus was going through the grainfields, and as his disciples walked along, they began to pick some heads of grain. 24 The Pharisees said to him, "Look, why are they doing what is unlawful on the Sabbath?" Dt 23:25; Mt 12:2

25 He answered, "Have you never read what David did when he and his companions were hungry and in need? 26 In the days of Abiathar the high priest, he entered the house of God and ate the consecrated bread, which is lawful only for priests to eat. And he also gave some to his companions." Lev 24:5-9; 1Sa 21:1-6; 2Sa 8:17

27 Then he said to them, "The Sabbath was made for man, not man for the Sabbath. 28 So the Son of Man is Lord even of the Sabbath." Mt 12:1-8; Lk 6:1-5

Jesus Heals on the Sabbath

3 Another time Jesus went into the synagogue, and a man with a shriveled hand was there. 2 Some of them were looking for a reason to accuse Jesus, so they watched him closely to see if he would heal him on the Sabbath. 3 Jesus said to the man with the shriveled hand, "Stand up in front of everyone." Mk 1:21; Lk 14:1

4 Then Jesus asked them, "Which is lawful on the Sabbath: to do good or to do evil, to save life or to kill?" But they remained silent.

5 He looked around at them in anger and, deeply distressed at their stubborn hearts, said to the man, "Stretch out your hand." He stretched it out, and his hand was completely restored. 6 Then the Pharisees went out and began to plot with the Herodians how they might kill Jesus. Mt 12:9-14; Lk 6:6-11

Crowds Follow Jesus

3:7-12pp — Mt 12:15,16; Lk 6:17-19

7 Jesus withdrew with his disciples to the lake, and a large crowd from Galilee followed. 8 When they heard about all he was doing, many people came to him from Judea, Jerusalem, Idumea, and the regions across the Jordan and around Tyre and Sidon. 9 Because of the crowd he told his disciples to have a small boat ready for him, to keep the people from crowding him. 10 For he had healed many, so that those with diseases were pushing forward to touch him. 11 Whenever the impure spirits saw him, they fell down before him and cried out, "You are the

Son of God." [12] But he gave them strict orders not to tell others about him. Mt 12:15-16; Lk 6:17-19

Jesus Appoints the Twelve

3:16-19pp — Mt 10:2-4; Lk 6:14-16;
   Ac 1:13

[13] Jesus went up on a mountainside and called to him those he wanted, and they came to him. [14] He appointed twelve[a] that they might be with him and that he might send them out to preach [15] and to have authority to drive out demons. [16] These are the twelve he appointed: Simon (to whom he gave the name Peter), [17] James son of Zebedee and his brother John (to them he gave the name Boanerges, which means "sons of thunder"), [18] Andrew, Philip, Bartholomew, Matthew, Thomas, James son of Alphaeus, Thaddaeus, Simon the Zealot [19] and Judas Iscariot, who betrayed him. Mt 10:2-4; Lk 6:14-16; Ac 1:13

Jesus Accused by His Family and by Teachers of the Law

3:23-27pp — Mt 12:25-29; Lk 11:17-22
3:31-35pp — Mt 12:46-50; Lk 8:19-21

[20] Then Jesus entered a house, and again a crowd gathered, so that he and his disciples were not even able to eat. [21] When his family[b] heard about this, they went to take charge of him, for they said, "He is out of his mind." Jn 10:20; Ac 26:24

[22] And the teachers of the law who came down from Jerusalem said, "He is possessed by Beelzebul! By the prince of demons he is driving out demons." Mt 9:34; 10:25

[23] So Jesus called them over to him and began to speak to them in parables: "How can Satan drive out Satan? [24] If a kingdom is divided against itself, that kingdom cannot stand. [25] If a house is divided against itself, that house cannot stand. [26] And if Satan opposes himself and is divided, he cannot stand; his end has come. [27] In fact, no one can enter a strong man's house without first tying him up. Then he can plunder the strong man's house. [28] Truly I tell you, people can be forgiven all their sins and every slander they utter, [29] but whoever blasphemes against the Holy Spirit will never be forgiven; they are guilty of an eternal sin." Mt 12:25-29; Lk 11:17-22

[30] He said this because they were saying, "He has an impure spirit."

[31] Then Jesus' mother and brothers arrived. Standing outside, they sent someone in to call him. [32] A crowd was sitting around him, and they told him, "Your mother and brothers are outside looking for you." ver 21

[33] "Who are my mother and my brothers?" he asked.

[34] Then he looked at those seated in a circle around him and said, "Here are my mother and

---

[a] 14 Some manuscripts twelve—designating them apostles—   [b] 21 Or his associates

my brothers! [35]Whoever does God's will is my brother and sister and mother."Mt 12:46-50; Lk 8:19-21

The Parable of the Sower

4:1-12pp — Mt 13:1-15; Lk 8:4-10
4:13-20pp — Mt 13:18-23; Lk 8:11-15

4 Again Jesus began to teach by the lake. The crowd that gathered around him was so large that he got into a boat and sat in it out on the lake, while all the people were along the shore at the water's edge. [2]He taught them many things by parables, and in his teaching said: [3]"Listen! A farmer went out to sow his seed. [4]As he was scattering the seed, some fell along the path, and the birds came and ate it up. [5]Some fell on rocky places, where it did not have much soil. It sprang up quickly, because the soil was shallow. [6]But when the sun came up, the plants were scorched, and they withered because they had no root. [7]Other seed fell among thorns, which grew up and choked the plants, so that they did not bear grain. [8]Still other seed fell on good soil. It came up, grew and produced a crop, some multiplying thirty, some sixty, some a hundred times." Mk 3:23; Jn 15:5; Col 1:6

[9]Then Jesus said, "Whoever has ears to hear, let them hear."

[10]When he was alone, the Twelve and the others around him asked him about the parables. [11]He told them, "The secret of the kingdom of God has been given to you. But to those on the outside everything is said in parables [12]so that, 1Co 5:12-13; Col 4:5

" 'they may be ever seeing but
never perceiving,
and ever hearing but never
understanding;
otherwise they might turn and
be forgiven!'[a]" Mt 13:1-15

[13]Then Jesus said to them, "Don't you understand this parable? How then will you understand any parable? [14]The farmer sows the word. [15]Some people are like seed along the path, where the word is sown. As soon as they hear it, Satan comes and takes away the word that was sown in them. [16]Others, like seed sown on rocky places, hear the word and at once receive it with joy. [17]But since they have no root, they last only a short time. When trouble or persecution comes because of the word, they quickly fall away. [18]Still others, like seed sown among thorns, hear the word; [19]but the worries of this life, the deceitfulness of wealth and the desires for other things come in and choke the word, making it unfruitful. [20]Others, like seed sown on good soil, hear the word, accept it, and produce a crop — some thirty, some sixty, some a hundred times what was sown." Mt 13:18-23; Lk 8:11-15

[a] 12 Isaiah 6:9,10

A Lamp on a Stand

[21] He said to them, "Do you bring in a lamp to put it under a bowl or a bed? Instead, don't you put it on its stand? [22] For whatever is hidden is meant to be disclosed, and whatever is concealed is meant to be brought out into the open. [23] If anyone has ears to hear, let them hear." Mt 5:15; 10:26; 11:15

[24] "Consider carefully what you hear," he continued. "With the measure you use, it will be measured to you—and even more. [25] Whoever has will be given more; whoever does not have, even what they have will be taken from them." Mt 25:29; Lk 6:38

The Parable of the Growing Seed

[26] He also said, "This is what the kingdom of God is like. A man scatters seed on the ground. [27] Night and day, whether he sleeps or gets up, the seed sprouts and grows, though he does not know how. [28] All by itself the soil produces grain—first the stalk, then the head, then the full kernel in the head. [29] As soon as the grain is ripe, he puts the sickle to it, because the harvest has come." Mt 13:24; Rev 14:15

The Parable of the Mustard Seed

4:30-32pp — Mt 13:31,32; Lk 13:18,19

[30] Again he said, "What shall we say the kingdom of God is like, or what parable shall we use to describe it? [31] It is like a mustard seed, which is the smallest of all seeds on earth. [32] Yet when planted, it grows and becomes the largest of all garden plants, with such big branches that the birds can perch in its shade." Mt 13:31-32

[33] With many similar parables Jesus spoke the word to them, as much as they could understand. [34] He did not say anything to them without using a parable. But when he was alone with his own disciples, he explained everything. Jn 16:12,25

Jesus Calms the Storm

4:35-41pp — Mt 8:18,23-27; Lk 8:22-25

[35] That day when evening came, he said to his disciples, "Let us go over to the other side." [36] Leaving the crowd behind, they took him along, just as he was, in the boat. There were also other boats with him. [37] A furious squall came up, and the waves broke over the boat, so that it was nearly swamped. [38] Jesus was in the stern, sleeping on a cushion. The disciples woke him and said to him, "Teacher, don't you care if we drown?" Mk 3:9; 5:2,21; 6:32,45

[39] He got up, rebuked the wind and said to the waves, "Quiet! Be still!" Then the wind died down and it was completely calm.

[40] He said to his disciples, "Why are you so afraid? Do you still have no faith?" Mt 14:31; Mk 16:14

[41] They were terrified and

asked each other, "Who is this? Even the wind and the waves obey him!" Mt 8:18,23-27; Lk 8:22-25

Jesus Restores a Demon-Possessed Man

5:1-17pp — Mt 8:28-34; Lk 8:26-37
5:18-20pp — Lk 8:38,39

5 They went across the lake to the region of the Gerasenes.[a] 2 When Jesus got out of the boat, a man with an impure spirit came from the tombs to meet him. 3 This man lived in the tombs, and no one could bind him anymore, not even with a chain. 4 For he had often been chained hand and foot, but he tore the chains apart and broke the irons on his feet. No one was strong enough to subdue him. 5 Night and day among the tombs and in the hills he would cry out and cut himself with stones. Mk 1:23; 4:1

6 When he saw Jesus from a distance, he ran and fell on his knees in front of him. 7 He shouted at the top of his voice, "What do you want with me, Jesus, Son of the Most High God? In God's name don't torture me!" 8 For Jesus had said to him, "Come out of this man, you impure spirit!" Mt 8:29

9 Then Jesus asked him, "What is your name?"

"My name is Legion," he replied, "for we are many." 10 And he begged Jesus again and again not to send them out of the area.

11 A large herd of pigs was feeding on the nearby hillside. 12 The demons begged Jesus, "Send us among the pigs; allow us to go into them." 13 He gave them permission, and the impure spirits came out and went into the pigs. The herd, about two thousand in number, rushed down the steep bank into the lake and were drowned.

14 Those tending the pigs ran off and reported this in the town and countryside, and the people went out to see what had happened. 15 When they came to Jesus, they saw the man who had been possessed by the legion of demons, sitting there, dressed and in his right mind; and they were afraid. 16 Those who had seen it told the people what had happened to the demon-possessed man—and told about the pigs as well. 17 Then the people began to plead with Jesus to leave their region. Mt 8:28-34

18 As Jesus was getting into the boat, the man who had been demon-possessed begged to go with him. 19 Jesus did not let him, but said, "Go home to your own people and tell them how much the Lord has done for you, and how he has had mercy on you." 20 So the man went away and began to tell in the Decapolis[b] how much Jesus had done for him. And all the people were amazed. Lk 8:38-39

[a] 1 Some manuscripts Gadarenes; other manuscripts Gergesenes   [b] 20 That is, the Ten Cities

Jesus Raises a Dead Girl and Heals a Sick Woman

5:22-43pp — Mt 9:18-26; Lk 8:41-56

²¹ When Jesus had again crossed over by boat to the other side of the lake, a large crowd gathered around him while he was by the lake. ²² Then one of the synagogue leaders, named Jairus, came, and when he saw Jesus, he fell at his feet. ²³ He pleaded earnestly with him, "My little daughter is dying. Please come and put your hands on her so that she will be healed and live." ²⁴ So Jesus went with him. Mk 6:5; Lk 13:14

A large crowd followed and pressed around him. ²⁵ And a woman was there who had been subject to bleeding for twelve years. ²⁶ She had suffered a great deal under the care of many doctors and had spent all she had, yet instead of getting better she grew worse. ²⁷ When she heard about Jesus, she came up behind him in the crowd and touched his cloak, ²⁸ because she thought, "If I just touch his clothes, I will be healed." ²⁹ Immediately her bleeding stopped and she felt in her body that she was freed from her suffering. Lev 15:25-30; Mt 9:20

³⁰ At once Jesus realized that power had gone out from him. He turned around in the crowd and asked, "Who touched my clothes?" Lk 5:17; 6:19

³¹ "You see the people crowding against you," his disciples answered, "and yet you can ask, 'Who touched me?'"

³² But Jesus kept looking around to see who had done it. ³³ Then the woman, knowing what had happened to her, came and fell at his feet and, trembling with fear, told him the whole truth. ³⁴ He said to her, "Daughter, your faith has healed you. Go in peace and be freed from your suffering." Mt 9:22; Ac 15:33

³⁵ While Jesus was still speaking, some people came from the house of Jairus, the synagogue leader. "Your daughter is dead," they said. "Why bother the teacher anymore?"

³⁶ Overhearing*a* what they said, Jesus told him, "Don't be afraid; just believe."

³⁷ He did not let anyone follow him except Peter, James and John the brother of James. ³⁸ When they came to the home of the synagogue leader, Jesus saw a commotion, with people crying and wailing loudly. ³⁹ He went in and said to them, "Why all this commotion and wailing? The child is not dead but asleep." ⁴⁰ But they laughed at him. Mt 4:21; 9:24

After he put them all out, he took the child's father and mother and the disciples who were with him, and went in where the child was. ⁴¹ He took her by

---

a 36 Or *Ignoring*

the hand and said to her, *"Talitha koum!"* (which means "Little girl, I say to you, get up!"). ⁴²Immediately the girl stood up and began to walk around (she was twelve years old). At this they were completely astonished. ⁴³He gave strict orders not to let anyone know about this, and told them to give her something to eat. Mt 9:18-26; Lk 8:41-56

A Prophet Without Honor
6:1-6pp — Mt 13:54-58

6 Jesus left there and went to his hometown, accompanied by his disciples. ²When the Sabbath came, he began to teach in the synagogue, and many who heard him were amazed. Mt 4:23

"Where did this man get these things?" they asked. "What's this wisdom that has been given him? What are these remarkable miracles he is performing? ³Isn't this the carpenter? Isn't this Mary's son and the brother of James, Joseph,ᵃ Judas and Simon? Aren't his sisters here with us?" And they took offense at him. Mt 11:6; 12:46

⁴Jesus said to them, "A prophet is not without honor except in his own town, among his relatives and in his own home." ⁵He could not do any miracles there, except lay his hands on a few sick people and heal them. ⁶He was amazed at their lack of faith. Mt 13:54-58

Jesus Sends Out the Twelve
6:7-11pp — Mt 10:1,9-14; Lk 9:1,3-5

Then Jesus went around teaching from village to village. ⁷Calling the Twelve to him, he began to send them out two by two and gave them authority over impure spirits. Mt 10:1; Mk 3:13; Lk 13:22

⁸These were his instructions: "Take nothing for the journey except a staff — no bread, no bag, no money in your belts. ⁹Wear sandals but not an extra shirt. ¹⁰Whenever you enter a house, stay there until you leave that town. ¹¹And if any place will not welcome you or listen to you, leave that place and shake the dust off your feet as a testimony against them." Mt 10:1,9-14; Lk 9:1,3-5

¹²They went out and preached that people should repent. ¹³They drove out many demons and anointed many sick people with oil and healed them. Lk 9:6

John the Baptist Beheaded
6:14-29pp — Mt 14:1-12
6:14-16pp — Lk 9:7-9

¹⁴King Herod heard about this, for Jesus' name had become well known. Some were saying,ᵇ "John the Baptist has been raised from the dead, and that is why miraculous powers are at work in him." Mt 3:1

¹⁵Others said, "He is Elijah."

And still others claimed, "He is a prophet, like one of the prophets of long ago." Mt 16:14; Mk 8:28

ᵃ 3 Greek *Joses*, a variant of *Joseph*   ᵇ 14 Some early manuscripts *He was saying*

¹⁶But when Herod heard this, he said, "John, whom I beheaded, has been raised from the dead!" Lk 9:7-9

¹⁷For Herod himself had given orders to have John arrested, and he had him bound and put in prison. He did this because of Herodias, his brother Philip's wife, whom he had married. ¹⁸For John had been saying to Herod, "It is not lawful for you to have your brother's wife." ¹⁹So Herodias nursed a grudge against John and wanted to kill him. But she was not able to, ²⁰because Herod feared John and protected him, knowing him to be a righteous and holy man. When Herod heard John, he was greatly puzzled[a]; yet he liked to listen to him. Lev 18:16; Mt 21:26

²¹Finally the opportune time came. On his birthday Herod gave a banquet for his high officials and military commanders and the leading men of Galilee. ²²When the daughter of[b] Herodias came in and danced, she pleased Herod and his dinner guests. Est 1:3; Lk 3:1

The king said to the girl, "Ask me for anything you want, and I'll give it to you." ²³And he promised her with an oath, "Whatever you ask I will give you, up to half my kingdom." Est 5:3,6; 7:2

²⁴She went out and said to her mother, "What shall I ask for?"

"The head of John the Baptist," she answered.

²⁵At once the girl hurried in to the king with the request: "I want you to give me right now the head of John the Baptist on a platter."

²⁶The king was greatly distressed, but because of his oaths and his dinner guests, he did not want to refuse her. ²⁷So he immediately sent an executioner with orders to bring John's head. The man went, beheaded John in the prison, ²⁸and brought back his head on a platter. He presented it to the girl, and she gave it to her mother. ²⁹On hearing of this, John's disciples came and took his body and laid it in a tomb. Mt 14:1-12

Jesus Feeds the Five Thousand

6:32-44pp — Mt 14:13-21; Lk 9:10-17;
Jn 6:5-13
6:32-44Ref — Mk 8:2-9

³⁰The apostles gathered around Jesus and reported to him all they had done and taught. ³¹Then, because so many people were coming and going that they did not even have a chance to eat, he said to them, "Come with me by yourselves to a quiet place and get some rest." Lk 9:10; Ac 1:2,26

³²So they went away by themselves in a boat to a solitary place. ³³But many who saw them

---

a 20 Some early manuscripts *he did many things his daughter*   b 22 Some early manuscripts *When* leaving recognized them and ran on foot from all the towns and got there ahead of them. [34]When Jesus landed and saw a large crowd, he had compassion on them, because they were like sheep without a shepherd. So he began teaching them many things.

Mt 14:13-21; Mk 4:36

[35]By this time it was late in the day, so his disciples came to him. "This is a remote place," they said, "and it's already very late. [36]Send the people away so that they can go to the surrounding countryside and villages and buy themselves something to eat."

Mk 8:2-9

[37]But he answered, "You give them something to eat."

They said to him, "That would take more than half a year's wages[a]! Are we to go and spend that much on bread and give it to them to eat?"

2Ki 4:42-44

[38]"How many loaves do you have?" he asked. "Go and see."

When they found out, they said, "Five — and two fish."

Lk 9:10-17

[39]Then Jesus directed them to have all the people sit down in groups on the green grass. [40]So they sat down in groups of hundreds and fifties. [41]Taking the five loaves and the two fish and looking up to heaven, he gave thanks and broke the loaves. Then he gave them to his disciples to distribute to the people. He also divided the two

fish among them all. [42]They all ate and were satisfied, [43]and the disciples picked up twelve basketfuls of broken pieces of bread and fish. [44]The number of the men who had eaten was five thousand.

Jn 6:5-13

Jesus Walks on the Water

6:45-51pp — Mt 14:22-32; Jn 6:15-21
6:53-56pp — Mt 14:34-36

[45]Immediately Jesus made his disciples get into the boat and go on ahead of him to Bethsaida, while he dismissed the crowd. [46]After leaving them, he went up on a mountainside to pray.

Mt 11:21

[47]Later that night, the boat was in the middle of the lake, and he was alone on land. [48]He saw the disciples straining at the oars, because the wind was against them. Shortly before dawn he went out to them, walking on the lake. He was about to pass by them, [49]but when they saw him walking on the lake, they thought he was a ghost. They cried out, [50]because they all saw him and were terrified.

Lk 24:37

Immediately he spoke to them and said, "Take courage! It is I. Don't be afraid." [51]Then he climbed into the boat with them, and the wind died down. They were completely amazed, [52]for they had not understood about the loaves; their hearts were hardened.

Mt 14:22-32; Jn 6:15-21

---

[a] 37 Greek take two hundred denarii

[53] When they had crossed over, they landed at Gennesaret and anchored there. [54] As soon as they got out of the boat, people recognized Jesus. [55] They ran throughout that whole region and carried the sick on mats to wherever they heard he was. [56] And wherever he went — into villages, towns or countryside — they placed the sick in the marketplaces. They begged him to let them touch even the edge of his cloak, and all who touched it were healed. Mt 14:34-36

That Which Defiles

7:1-23pp — Mt 15:1-20

7 The Pharisees and some of the teachers of the law who had come from Jerusalem gathered around Jesus [2] and saw some of his disciples eating food with hands that were defiled, that is, unwashed. [3] (The Pharisees and all the Jews do not eat unless they give their hands a ceremonial washing, holding to the tradition of the elders. [4] When they come from the marketplace they do not eat unless they wash. And they observe many other traditions, such as the washing of cups, pitchers and kettles.[a]) Mt 23:25; Ac 10:14,28

[5] So the Pharisees and teachers of the law asked Jesus, "Why don't your disciples live according to the tradition of the elders instead of eating their food with defiled hands?" Gal 1:14; Col 2:8

[6] He replied, "Isaiah was right when he prophesied about you hypocrites; as it is written:

" 'These people honor me with their lips,
    but their hearts are far from me.
[7] They worship me in vain;
    their teachings are merely human rules.'[b]

[8] You have let go of the commands of God and are holding on to human traditions."

[9] And he continued, "You have a fine way of setting aside the commands of God in order to observe[c] your own traditions! [10] For Moses said, 'Honor your father and mother,'[d] and, 'Anyone who curses their father or mother is to be put to death.'[e] [11] But you say that if anyone declares that what might have been used to help their father or mother is Corban (that is, devoted to God) — [12] then you no longer let them do anything for their father or mother. [13] Thus you nullify the word of God by your tradition that you have handed down. And you do many things like that." Mt 23:16,18; Heb 4:12

[14] Again Jesus called the crowd to him and said, "Listen to me, everyone, and understand this. [15] Nothing outside a person can

[a] 4 Some early manuscripts pitchers, kettles and dining couches   [b] 6,7 Isaiah 29:13   [c] 9 Some manuscripts set up   [d] 10 Exodus 20:12; Deut. 5:16   [e] 10 Exodus 21:17; Lev. 20:9

defile them by going into them. Rather, it is what comes out of a person that defiles them." [16] *a*

¹⁷After he had left the crowd and entered the house, his disciples asked him about this parable. ¹⁸"Are you so dull?" he asked. "Don't you see that nothing that enters a person from the outside can defile them? ¹⁹For it doesn't go into their heart but into their stomach, and then out of the body." (In saying this, Jesus declared all foods clean.) Ac 10:15

²⁰He went on: "What comes out of a person is what defiles them. ²¹For it is from within, out of a person's heart, that evil thoughts come—sexual immorality, theft, murder, ²²adultery, greed, malice, deceit, lewdness, envy, slander, arrogance and folly. ²³All these evils come from inside and defile a person." Mt 15:1-20

Jesus Honors a Syrophoenician Woman's Faith

7:24-30pp — Mt 15:21-28

²⁴Jesus left that place and went to the vicinity of Tyre.*b* He entered a house and did not want anyone to know it; yet he could not keep his presence secret. ²⁵In fact, as soon as she heard about him, a woman whose little daughter was possessed by an impure spirit came and fell at his feet. ²⁶The woman was a Greek, born in Syrian Phoenicia. She

begged Jesus to drive the demon out of her daughter. Mt 4:24; 11:21

²⁷"First let the children eat all they want," he told her, "for it is not right to take the children's bread and toss it to the dogs."

²⁸"Lord," she replied, "even the dogs under the table eat the children's crumbs."

²⁹Then he told her, "For such a reply, you may go; the demon has left your daughter."

³⁰She went home and found her child lying on the bed, and the demon gone. Mt 15:21-28

Jesus Heals a Deaf and Mute Man

7:31-37pp — Mt 15:29-31

³¹Then Jesus left the vicinity of Tyre and went through Sidon, down to the Sea of Galilee and into the region of the Decapolis.*c* ³²There some people brought to him a man who was deaf and could hardly talk, and they begged Jesus to place his hand on him. Mk 5:23; Lk 11:14

³³After he took him aside, away from the crowd, Jesus put his fingers into the man's ears. Then he spit and touched the man's tongue. ³⁴He looked up to heaven and with a deep sigh said to him, *"Ephphatha!"* (which means "Be opened!"). ³⁵At this, the man's ears were opened, his tongue was loosened and he began to speak plainly. Isa 35:5-6

a 16 Some manuscripts include here the words of 4:23.   *b* 24 Many early manuscripts *Tyre and Sidon*   *c* 31 That is, the Ten Cities

³⁶Jesus commanded them not to tell anyone. But the more he did so, the more they kept talking about it. ³⁷People were overwhelmed with amazement. "He has done everything well," they said. "He even makes the deaf hear and the mute speak."

Jesus Feeds the Four Thousand

8:1-9pp — Mt 15:32-39
8:1-9Ref — Mk 6:32-44
8:11-21pp — Mt 16:1-12

8 During those days another large crowd gathered. Since they had nothing to eat, Jesus called his disciples to him and said, ²"I have compassion for these people; they have already been with me three days and have nothing to eat. ³If I send them home hungry, they will collapse on the way, because some of them have come a long distance." Mt 9:36

⁴His disciples answered, "But where in this remote place can anyone get enough bread to feed them?"

⁵"How many loaves do you have?" Jesus asked.

"Seven," they replied.

⁶He told the crowd to sit down on the ground. When he had taken the seven loaves and given thanks, he broke them and gave them to his disciples to distribute to the people, and they did so. ⁷They had a few small fish as well; he gave thanks for them also and told the disciples to distribute them. ⁸The people ate and were satisfied. Afterward the disciples picked up seven basketfuls of broken pieces that were left over. ⁹About four thousand were present. After he had sent them away, ¹⁰he got into the boat with his disciples and went to the region of Dalmanutha. Mt 15:32-39; Mk 6:32-44

¹¹The Pharisees came and began to question Jesus. To test him, they asked him for a sign from heaven. ¹²He sighed deeply and said, "Why does this generation ask for a sign? Truly I tell you, no sign will be given to it." ¹³Then he left them, got back into the boat and crossed to the other side. Mt 12:38; Mk 7:34

The Yeast of the Pharisees and Herod

¹⁴The disciples had forgotten to bring bread, except for one loaf they had with them in the boat. ¹⁵"Be careful," Jesus warned them. "Watch out for the yeast of the Pharisees and that of Herod." Mt 14:1; Lk 12:1; 1Co 5:6-8

¹⁶They discussed this with one another and said, "It is because we have no bread."

¹⁷Aware of their discussion, Jesus asked them: "Why are you talking about having no bread? Do you still not see or understand? Are your hearts hardened? ¹⁸Do you have eyes but fail to see, and ears but fail to hear? And don't you remember?

¹⁹When I broke the five loaves for the five thousand, how many basketfuls of pieces did you pick up?"   Isa 6:9-10; Mk 6:52

"Twelve," they replied.   Mt 14:20

²⁰"And when I broke the seven loaves for the four thousand, how many basketfuls of pieces did you pick up?"

They answered, "Seven."Mt 15:37

²¹He said to them, "Do you still not understand?"   Mk 6:52

Jesus Heals a Blind Man at Bethsaida

²²They came to Bethsaida, and some people brought a blind man and begged Jesus to touch him. ²³He took the blind man by the hand and led him outside the village. When he had spit on the man's eyes and put his hands on him, Jesus asked, "Do you see anything?"   Mk 5:23; 7:33

²⁴He looked up and said, "I see people; they look like trees walking around."

²⁵Once more Jesus put his hands on the man's eyes. Then his eyes were opened, his sight was restored, and he saw everything clearly. ²⁶Jesus sent him home, saying, "Don't even go into[a] the village."

Peter Declares That Jesus Is the Messiah

8:27-29pp — Mt 16:13-16; Lk 9:18-20

²⁷Jesus and his disciples went on to the villages around Caes-

area Philippi. On the way he asked them, "Who do people say I am?"

²⁸They replied, "Some say John the Baptist; others say Elijah; and still others, one of the prophets."   Mt 3:1; Mal 4:5

²⁹"But what about you?" he asked. "Who do you say I am?"

Peter answered, "You are the Messiah."   Mt 16:13-16; Lk 9:18-20

³⁰Jesus warned them not to tell anyone about him. Mt 8:4; 16:20; 17:9

Jesus Predicts His Death

8:31 — 9:1pp — Mt 16:21-28; Lk 9:22-27

³¹He then began to teach them that the Son of Man must suffer many things and be rejected by the elders, the chief priests and the teachers of the law, and that he must be killed and after three days rise again. ³²He spoke plainly about this, and Peter took him aside and began to rebuke him.   Mt 16:21; Jn 18:20

³³But when Jesus turned and looked at his disciples, he rebuked Peter. "Get behind me, Satan!" he said. "You do not have in mind the concerns of God, but merely human concerns." Mt 4:10

The Way of the Cross

³⁴Then he called the crowd to him along with his disciples and said: "Whoever wants to be my disciple must deny themselves and take up their cross and follow me. ³⁵For whoever wants to

[a] 26 Some manuscripts go and tell anyone in

save their life*a* will lose it, but whoever loses their life for me and for the gospel will save it. ³⁶What good is it for someone to gain the whole world, yet forfeit their soul? ³⁷Or what can anyone give in exchange for their soul? ³⁸If anyone is ashamed of me and my words in this adulterous and sinful generation, the Son of Man will be ashamed of them when he comes in his Father's glory with the holy angels." Mt 10:33; Jn 12:25

9 And he said to them, "Truly I tell you, some who are standing here will not taste death before they see that the kingdom of God has come with power." Mt 16:21-28

The Transfiguration

9:2-8pp — Lk 9:28-36
9:2-13pp — Mt 17:1-13

²After six days Jesus took Peter, James and John with him and led them up a high mountain, where they were all alone. There he was transfigured before them. ³His clothes became dazzling white, whiter than anyone in the world could bleach them. ⁴And there appeared before them Elijah and Moses, who were talking with Jesus. Mt 28:3 ⁵Peter said to Jesus, "Rabbi, it is good for us to be here. Let us put up three shelters — one for you, one for Moses and one for Elijah." ⁶(He did not know what to say, they were so frightened.) ⁷Then a cloud appeared and covered them, and a voice came from the cloud: "This is my Son, whom I love. Listen to him!"

⁸Suddenly, when they looked around, they no longer saw anyone with them except Jesus. Lk 9:28

⁹As they were coming down the mountain, Jesus gave them orders not to tell anyone what they had seen until the Son of Man had risen from the dead. ¹⁰They kept the matter to themselves, discussing what "rising from the dead" meant. Mt 8:20

¹¹And they asked him, "Why do the teachers of the law say that Elijah must come first?" ¹²Jesus replied, "To be sure, Elijah does come first, and restores all things. Why then is it written that the Son of Man must suffer much and be rejected? ¹³But I tell you, Elijah has come, and they have done to him everything they wished, just as it is written about him." Mt 17:1-13

Jesus Heals a Boy Possessed by an Impure Spirit

9:14-28; 30-32pp — Mt 17:14-19; 22,23;
Lk 9:37-45

¹⁴When they came to the other disciples, they saw a large crowd around them and the teachers of the law arguing with them. ¹⁵As soon as all the people saw Jesus, they were overwhelmed with wonder and ran to greet him.

¹⁶"What are you arguing with them about?" he asked.

a 35 The Greek word means either *life* or *soul*; also in verses 36 and 37.

[17]A man in the crowd answered, "Teacher, I brought you my son, who is possessed by a spirit that has robbed him of speech. [18]Whenever it seizes him, it throws him to the ground. He foams at the mouth, gnashes his teeth and becomes rigid. I asked your disciples to drive out the spirit, but they could not."

[19]"You unbelieving generation," Jesus replied, "how long shall I stay with you? How long shall I put up with you? Bring the boy to me."

[20]So they brought him. When the spirit saw Jesus, it immediately threw the boy into a convulsion. He fell to the ground and rolled around, foaming at the mouth.   Mk 1:26

[21]Jesus asked the boy's father, "How long has he been like this?"

"From childhood," he answered. [22]"It has often thrown him into fire or water to kill him. But if you can do anything, take pity on us and help us."

[23]"'If you can'?" said Jesus. "Everything is possible for one who believes."   Mk 11:23; Jn 11:40

[24]Immediately the boy's father exclaimed, "I do believe; help me overcome my unbelief!"

[25]When Jesus saw that a crowd was running to the scene, he rebuked the impure spirit. "You deaf and mute spirit," he said, "I command you, come out of him and never enter him again."

[26]The spirit shrieked, convulsed him violently and came out. The boy looked so much like a corpse that many said, "He's dead." [27]But Jesus took him by the hand and lifted him to his feet, and he stood up.

[28]After Jesus had gone indoors, his disciples asked him privately, "Why couldn't we drive it out?"   Mt 17:14-19; Mk 7:17

[29]He replied, "This kind can come out only by prayer.[a]"

Jesus Predicts His Death a Second Time

9:33-37pp — Mt 18:1-5; Lk 9:46-48

[30]They left that place and passed through Galilee. Jesus did not want anyone to know where they were, [31]because he was teaching his disciples. He said to them, "The Son of Man is going to be delivered into the hands of men. They will kill him, and after three days he will rise." [32]But they did not understand what he meant and were afraid to ask him about it.   Lk 9:37-45

[33]They came to Capernaum. When he was in the house, he asked them, "What were you arguing about on the road?" [34]But they kept quiet because on the way they had argued about who was the greatest.   Mt 4:13; Lk 22:24

[35]Sitting down, Jesus called the Twelve and said, "Anyone who wants to be first must be the very last, and the servant of all." Mt 20:26

---

[a] 29 Some manuscripts *prayer and fasting*

³⁶He took a little child whom he placed among them. Taking the child in his arms, he said to them, ³⁷"Whoever welcomes one of these little children in my name welcomes me; and whoever welcomes me does not welcome me but the one who sent me." Mt 18:1-5; Lk 9:46-48

Whoever Is Not Against Us Is for Us

9:38-40pp — Lk 9:49,50

³⁸"Teacher," said John, "we saw someone driving out demons in your name and we told him to stop, because he was not one of us." Nu 11:27-29

³⁹"Do not stop him," Jesus said. "For no one who does a miracle in my name can in the next moment say anything bad about me, ⁴⁰for whoever is not against us is for us. ⁴¹Truly I tell you, anyone who gives you a cup of water in my name because you belong to the Messiah will certainly not lose their reward. Mt 10:42; Mt 12:30

Causing to Stumble

⁴²"If anyone causes one of these little ones — those who believe in me — to stumble, it would be better for them if a large millstone were hung around their neck and they were thrown into the sea. ⁴³If your hand causes you to stumble, cut it off. It is better for you to enter life maimed than with two hands to go into

hell, where the fire never goes out. [44] ᵃ ⁴⁵And if your foot causes you to stumble, cut it off. It is better for you to enter life crippled than to have two feet and be thrown into hell. [46] ᵃ ⁴⁷And if your eye causes you to stumble, pluck it out. It is better for you to enter the kingdom of God with one eye than to have two eyes and be thrown into hell, ⁴⁸where

> " 'the worms that eat them do
> not die,
> and the fire is not
> quenched.'ᵇ

⁴⁹Everyone will be salted with fire. Mt 5:29; 18:9

⁵⁰"Salt is good, but if it loses its saltiness, how can you make it salty again? Have salt among yourselves, and be at peace with each other." Mt 5:13; Ro 12:18

Divorce

10:1-12pp — Mt 19:1-9

10 Jesus then left that place and went into the region of Judea and across the Jordan. Again crowds of people came to him, and as was his custom, he taught them. Jn 10:40; 11:7

²Some Pharisees came and tested him by asking, "Is it lawful for a man to divorce his wife?"

³"What did Moses command you?" he replied.

⁴They said, "Moses permitted a man to write a certificate of divorce and send her away." Dt 24:1-4

ᵃ 44 Some manuscripts include here the words of verse 48.   ᵇ 48 Isaiah 66:24

5 "It was because your hearts were hard that Moses wrote you this law," Jesus replied. 6 "But at the beginning of creation God 'made them male and female.'[a] 7 'For this reason a man will leave his father and mother and be united to his wife,[b] 8 and the two will become one flesh.'[c] So they are no longer two, but one flesh. 9 Therefore what God has joined together, let no one separate." Ge 5:2; 1Co 6:16

10 When they were in the house again, the disciples asked Jesus about this. 11 He answered, "Anyone who divorces his wife and marries another woman commits adultery against her. 12 And if she divorces her husband and marries another man, she commits adultery." Mt 19:1-9; Lk 16:18; Ro 7:3

The Little Children and Jesus

10:13-16pp — Mt 19:13-15; Lk 18:15-17

13 People were bringing little children to Jesus for him to place his hands on them, but the disciples rebuked them. 14 When Jesus saw this, he was indignant. He said to them, "Let the little children come to me, and do not hinder them, for the kingdom of God belongs to such as these. 15 Truly I tell you, anyone who will not receive the kingdom of God like a little child will never enter it." 16 And he took the children in his arms, placed his hands on them and blessed them. Mt 19:13-15; Lk 18:15-17

The Rich and the Kingdom of God

10:17-31pp — Mt 19:16-30; Lk 18:18-30

17 As Jesus started on his way, a man ran up to him and fell on his knees before him. "Good teacher," he asked, "what must I do to inherit eternal life?" Lk 10:25; Ac 20:32

18 "Why do you call me good?" Jesus answered. "No one is good — except God alone. 19 You know the commandments: 'You shall not murder, you shall not commit adultery, you shall not steal, you shall not give false testimony, you shall not defraud, honor your father and mother.'[d] Ex 20:12-16; Dt 5:16-20

20 "Teacher," he declared, "all these I have kept since I was a boy."

21 Jesus looked at him and loved him. "One thing you lack," he said. "Go, sell everything you have and give to the poor, and you will have treasure in heaven. Then come, follow me." Mt 6:20

22 At this the man's face fell. He went away sad, because he had great wealth.

23 Jesus looked around and said to his disciples, "How hard it is for the rich to enter the kingdom of God!" Ps 52:7; 1Ti 6:9-10,17

24 The disciples were amazed at his words. But Jesus said again,

---

[a] 6 Gen. 1:27   [b] 7 Some early manuscripts do not have *and be united to his wife.*
[c] 8 Gen. 2:24   [d] 19 Exodus 20:12-16; Deut. 5:16-20

"Children, how hard it is^a to enter the kingdom of God! ²⁵It is easier for a camel to go through the eye of a needle than for someone who is rich to enter the kingdom of God." Mt 7:13-14; Lk 12:16-20

²⁶The disciples were even more amazed, and said to each other, "Who then can be saved?"

²⁷Jesus looked at them and said, "With man this is impossible, but not with God; all things are possible with God." Mt 19:26

²⁸Then Peter spoke up, "We have left everything to follow you!" Mt 4:19

²⁹"Truly I tell you," Jesus replied, "no one who has left home or brothers or sisters or mother or father or children or fields for me and the gospel ³⁰will fail to receive a hundred times as much in this present age: homes, brothers, sisters, mothers, children and fields—along with persecutions—and in the age to come eternal life. ³¹But many who are first will be last, and the last first." Mt 19:16-30; Lk 18:18-30

Jesus Predicts His Death a Third Time
10:32-34pp — Mt 20:17-19; Lk 18:31-33

³²They were on their way up to Jerusalem, with Jesus leading the way, and the disciples were astonished, while those who followed were afraid. Again he took the Twelve aside and told them what was going to happen to him. ³³"We are going up to Jerusalem," he said, "and the Son of Man will be delivered over to the chief priests and the teachers of the law. They will condemn him to death and will hand him over to the Gentiles, ³⁴who will mock him and spit on him, flog him and kill him. Three days later he will rise." Mt 20:17-19; Lk 18:31-33

The Request of James and John
10:35-45pp — Mt 20:20-28

³⁵Then James and John, the sons of Zebedee, came to him. "Teacher," they said, "we want you to do for us whatever we ask."

³⁶"What do you want me to do for you?" he asked.

³⁷They replied, "Let one of us sit at your right and the other at your left in your glory." Mt 19:28

³⁸"You don't know what you are asking," Jesus said. "Can you drink the cup I drink or be baptized with the baptism I am baptized with?" Mt 20:22; Lk 12:50

³⁹"We can," they answered.

Jesus said to them, "You will drink the cup I drink and be baptized with the baptism I am baptized with, ⁴⁰but to sit at my right or left is not for me to grant. These places belong to those for whom they have been prepared." Ac 12:2; Rev 1:9

⁴¹When the ten heard about this, they became indignant with James and John. ⁴²Jesus

^a 24 Some manuscripts *is for those who trust in riches*

called them together and said, "You know that those who are regarded as rulers of the Gentiles lord it over them, and their high officials exercise authority over them. ⁴³Not so with you. Instead, whoever wants to become great among you must be your servant, ⁴⁴and whoever wants to be first must be slave of all. ⁴⁵For even the Son of Man did not come to be served, but to serve, and to give his life as a ransom for many."

Mt 20:20-28; Mk 9:35

Blind Bartimaeus Receives His Sight

10:46-52pp — Mt 20:29-34; Lk 18:35-43

⁴⁶Then they came to Jericho. As Jesus and his disciples, together with a large crowd, were leaving the city, a blind man, Bartimaeus (which means "son of Timaeus"), was sitting by the roadside begging. ⁴⁷When he heard that it was Jesus of Nazareth, he began to shout, "Jesus, Son of David, have mercy on me!"

Mt 9:27; Mk 1:24

⁴⁸Many rebuked him and told him to be quiet, but he shouted all the more, "Son of David, have mercy on me!"

⁴⁹Jesus stopped and said, "Call him."

So they called to the blind man, "Cheer up! On your feet! He's calling you." ⁵⁰Throwing his cloak aside, he jumped to his feet and came to Jesus.

⁵¹"What do you want me to do for you?" Jesus asked him.

The blind man said, "Rabbi, I want to see."

Mt 23:7

⁵²"Go," said Jesus, "your faith has healed you." Immediately he received his sight and followed Jesus along the road.

Mt 20:29-34

Jesus Comes to Jerusalem as King

11:1-10pp — Mt 21:1-9; Lk 19:29-38
11:7-10pp — Jn 12:12-15

11 As they approached Jerusalem and came to Bethphage and Bethany at the Mount of Olives, Jesus sent two of his disciples, ²saying to them, "Go to the village ahead of you, and just as you enter it, you will find a colt tied there, which no one has ever ridden. Untie it and bring it here. ³If anyone asks you, 'Why are you doing this?' say, 'The Lord needs it and will send it back here shortly.'"

Nu 19:2; Dt 21:3; Mt 21:1

⁴They went and found a colt outside in the street, tied at a doorway. As they untied it, ⁵some people standing there asked, "What are you doing, untying that colt?" ⁶They answered as Jesus had told them to, and the people let them go. ⁷When they brought the colt to Jesus and threw their cloaks over it, he sat on it. ⁸Many people spread their cloaks on the road, while others spread branches they had cut in the fields. ⁹Those who went

ahead and those who followed shouted, Mt 23:39; Mk 14:16

"Hosanna!*a*"

"Blessed is he who comes
in the name of the
Lord!"*b*

[10]"Blessed is the coming
kingdom of our father
David!"

"Hosanna in the highest
heaven!" Mt 21:1-9; Lk 19:29

[11]Jesus entered Jerusalem and went into the temple courts. He looked around at everything, but since it was already late, he went out to Bethany with the Twelve. Mt 21:12,17

Jesus Curses a Fig Tree and Clears the Temple Courts

11:12-14pp — Mt 21:18-22
11:15-18pp — Mt 21:12-16; Lk 19:45-47; Jn 2:13-16
11:20-24pp — Mt 21:19-22

[12]The next day as they were leaving Bethany, Jesus was hungry. [13]Seeing in the distance a fig tree in leaf, he went to find out if it had any fruit. When he reached it, he found nothing but leaves, because it was not the season for figs. [14]Then he said to the tree, "May no one ever eat fruit from you again." And his disciples heard him say it. Mt 21:18-22

[15]On reaching Jerusalem, Jesus entered the temple courts and began driving out those who were buying and selling there. He overturned the tables of the money changers and the benches of those selling doves, [16]and would not allow anyone to carry merchandise through the temple courts. [17]And as he taught them, he said, "Is it not written: 'My house will be called a house of prayer for all nations'*c*? But you have made it 'a den of robbers.'*d*" Mt 21:12-16; Lk 19:45-47

[18]The chief priests and the teachers of the law heard this and began looking for a way to kill him, for they feared him, because the whole crowd was amazed at his teaching. Jn 2:13-16

[19]When evening came, Jesus and his disciples*e* went out of the city. Lk 21:37

[20]In the morning, as they went along, they saw the fig tree withered from the roots. [21]Peter remembered and said to Jesus, "Rabbi, look! The fig tree you cursed has withered!" Mt 23:7

[22]"Have faith in God," Jesus answered. [23]"Truly*f* I tell you, if anyone says to this mountain, 'Go, throw yourself into the sea,' and does not doubt in their heart but believes that what they say will happen, it will be done for them. [24]Therefore I tell you,

a 9 A Hebrew expression meaning "Save!" which became an exclamation of praise; also in verse 10 *b* 9 Psalm 118:25,26 *c* 17 Isaiah 56:7 *d* 17 Jer. 7:11 *e* 19 Some early manuscripts *came, Jesus* *f* 22,23 Some early manuscripts *"If you have faith in God," Jesus answered,* 23*"truly* whatever you ask for in prayer, believe that you have received it, and it will be yours. [25] And when you stand praying, if you hold anything against anyone, forgive them, so that your Father in heaven may forgive you your sins." [26] *a*

Mt 21:19-22

The Authority of Jesus Questioned

11:27-33pp — Mt 21:23-27; Lk 20:1-8

[27] They arrived again in Jerusalem, and while Jesus was walking in the temple courts, the chief priests, the teachers of the law and the elders came to him. [28] "By what authority are you doing these things?" they asked. "And who gave you authority to do this?"

[29] Jesus replied, "I will ask you one question. Answer me, and I will tell you by what authority I am doing these things. [30] John's baptism — was it from heaven, or of human origin? Tell me!"

[31] They discussed it among themselves and said, "If we say, 'From heaven,' he will ask, 'Then why didn't you believe him?' [32] But if we say, 'Of human origin' . . ." (They feared the people, for everyone held that John really was a prophet.)

Mt 11:9

[33] So they answered Jesus, "We don't know."

Jesus said, "Neither will I tell you by what authority I am doing these things." Mt 21:23-27; Lk 20:1-8

The Parable of the Tenants

12:1-12pp — Mt 21:33-46; Lk 20:9-19

12 Jesus then began to speak to them in parables: "A man planted a vineyard. He put a wall around it, dug a pit for the winepress and built a watchtower. Then he rented the vineyard to some farmers and moved to another place. [2] At harvest time he sent a servant to the tenants to collect from them some of the fruit of the vineyard. [3] But they seized him, beat him and sent him away empty-handed. [4] Then he sent another servant to them; they struck this man on the head and treated him shamefully. [5] He sent still another, and that one they killed. He sent many others; some of them they beat, others they killed. Isa 5:1-7

[6] "He had one left to send, a son, whom he loved. He sent him last of all, saying, 'They will respect my son.' Heb 1:1-3

[7] "But the tenants said to one another, 'This is the heir. Come, let's kill him, and the inheritance will be ours.' [8] So they took him and killed him, and threw him out of the vineyard.

[9] "What then will the owner of the vineyard do? He will come and kill those tenants and give the vineyard to others. [10] Haven't you read this passage of Scripture:

" 'The stone the builders rejected

---

a 26 Some manuscripts include here words similar to Matt. 6:15.

has become the
cornerstone;
¹¹the Lord has done this,
and it is marvelous in our
eyes'ᵃ?"   Ac 4:11

¹²Then the chief priests, the teachers of the law and the elders looked for a way to arrest him because they knew he had spoken the parable against them. But they were afraid of the crowd; so they left him and went away.   Mt 21:33-46; Lk 20:9-19

Paying the Imperial Tax to Caesar
12:13-17pp — Mt 22:15-22; Lk 20:20-26

¹³Later they sent some of the Pharisees and Herodians to Jesus to catch him in his words. ¹⁴They came to him and said, "Teacher, we know that you are a man of integrity. You aren't swayed by others, because you pay no attention to who they are; but you teach the way of God in accordance with the truth. Is it right to pay the imperial taxᵇ to Caesar or not? ¹⁵Should we pay or shouldn't we?"   Mt 12:10; 22:16

But Jesus knew their hypocrisy. "Why are you trying to trap me?" he asked. "Bring me a denarius and let me look at it." ¹⁶They brought the coin, and he asked them, "Whose image is this? And whose inscription?"

"Caesar's," they replied.

¹⁷Then Jesus said to them, "Give back to Caesar what is Caesar's and to God what is God's."   Ro 13:7

And they were amazed at him.   Mt 22:15-22; Lk 20:20-26

Marriage at the Resurrection
12:18-27pp — Mt 22:23-33; Lk 20:27-38

¹⁸Then the Sadducees, who say there is no resurrection, came to him with a question. ¹⁹"Teacher," they said, "Moses wrote for us that if a man's brother dies and leaves a wife but no children, the man must marry the widow and raise up offspring for his brother. ²⁰Now there were seven brothers. The first one married and died without leaving any children. ²¹The second one married the widow, but he also died, leaving no child. It was the same with the third. ²²In fact, none of the seven left any children. Last of all, the woman died too. ²³At the resurrectionᶜ whose wife will she be, since the seven were married to her?"   Dt 25:5; Ac 23:8

²⁴Jesus replied, "Are you not in error because you do not know the Scriptures or the power of God? ²⁵When the dead rise, they will neither marry nor be given in marriage; they will be like the angels in heaven. ²⁶Now about the dead rising—have you not read in the Book of Moses, in the account of the burning bush,

---

ᵃ 11 Psalm 118:22,23   ᵇ 14 A special tax levied on subject peoples, not on Roman citizens   ᶜ 23 Some manuscripts resurrection, when people rise from the dead, how God said to him, 'I am the God of Abraham, the God of Isaac, and the God of Jacob'[a]? [27]He is not the God of the dead, but of the living. You are badly mistaken!" Mt 22:23-33; Lk 20:27-38

The Greatest Commandment
12:28-34pp — Mt 22:34-40

[28]One of the teachers of the law came and heard them debating. Noticing that Jesus had given them a good answer, he asked him, "Of all the commandments, which is the most important?" Lk 10:25-28; 20:39
[29]"The most important one," answered Jesus, "is this: 'Hear, O Israel: The Lord our God, the Lord is one.[b] [30]Love the Lord your God with all your heart and with all your soul and with all your mind and with all your strength.'[c] [31]The second is this: 'Love your neighbor as yourself.'[d] There is no commandment greater than these." Mt 5:43
[32]"Well said, teacher," the man replied. "You are right in saying that God is one and there is no other but him. [33]To love him with all your heart, with all your understanding and with all your strength, and to love your neighbor as yourself is more important than all burnt offerings and sacrifices." 1Sa 15:22; Mic 6:6-8
[34]When Jesus saw that he had answered wisely, he said to him, "You are not far from the kingdom of God." And from then on no one dared ask him any more questions. Mt 22:34-40; Lk 20:40

Whose Son Is the Messiah?
12:35-37pp — Mt 22:41-46; Lk 20:41-44
12:38-40pp — Mt 23:1-7; Lk 20:45-47

[35]While Jesus was teaching in the temple courts, he asked, "Why do the teachers of the law say that the Messiah is the son of David? [36]David himself, speaking by the Holy Spirit, declared:

" 'The Lord said to my Lord:
  "Sit at my right hand
until I put your enemies
  under your feet." '[e]

[37]David himself calls him 'Lord.' How then can he be his son?" Mt 22:41-46; Lk 20:41-44
The large crowd listened to him with delight. Mt 9:27; 22:44

Warning Against the Teachers of the Law

[38]As he taught, Jesus said, "Watch out for the teachers of the law. They like to walk around in flowing robes and be greeted with respect in the marketplaces, [39]and have the most important seats in the synagogues and the places of honor at banquets. [40]They devour widows' houses and for a show make lengthy prayers. These men will be punished most severely." Mt 23:1-7

[a] 26 Exodus 3:6   [b] 29 Or The Lord our God is one Lord   [c] 30 Deut. 6:4,5   [d] 31 Lev. 19:18   [e] 36 Psalm 110:1

The Widow's Offering

12:41-44pp — Lk 21:1-4

⁴¹ Jesus sat down opposite the place where the offerings were put and watched the crowd putting their money into the temple treasury. Many rich people threw in large amounts. ⁴²But a poor widow came and put in two very small copper coins, worth only a few cents. 2Ki 12:9; Jn 8:20

⁴³Calling his disciples to him, Jesus said, "Truly I tell you, this poor widow has put more into the treasury than all the others. ⁴⁴They all gave out of their wealth; but she, out of her poverty, put in everything—all she had to live on." 2Co 8:12

The Destruction of the Temple and Signs of the End Times

13:1-37pp — Mt 24:1-51; Lk 21:5-36

13 As Jesus was leaving the temple, one of his disciples said to him, "Look, Teacher! What massive stones! What magnificent buildings!"

² "Do you see all these great buildings?" replied Jesus. "Not one stone here will be left on another; every one will be thrown down." Lk 19:44

³As Jesus was sitting on the Mount of Olives opposite the temple, Peter, James, John and Andrew asked him privately, ⁴ "Tell us, when will these things happen? And what will be the

sign that they are all about to be fulfilled?" Mt 4:21; 21:1

⁵Jesus said to them: "Watch out that no one deceives you. ⁶Many will come in my name, claiming, 'I am he,' and will deceive many. ⁷When you hear of wars and rumors of wars, do not be alarmed. Such things must happen, but the end is still to come. ⁸Nation will rise against nation, and kingdom against kingdom. There will be earthquakes in various places, and famines. These are the beginning of birth pains. Eph 5:6; 2Th 2:3,10-12

⁹ "You must be on your guard. You will be handed over to the local councils and flogged in the synagogues. On account of me you will stand before governors and kings as witnesses to them. ¹⁰And the gospel must first be preached to all nations. ¹¹Whenever you are arrested and brought to trial, do not worry beforehand about what to say. Just say whatever is given you at the time, for it is not you speaking, but the Holy Spirit. Mt 10:19-20; Lk 12:11-12

¹² "Brother will betray brother to death, and a father his child. Children will rebel against their parents and have them put to death. ¹³Everyone will hate you because of me, but the one who stands firm to the end will be saved. Mic 7:6; Mt 10:21-22

¹⁴ "When you see 'the abomination that causes desolation'ᵃ

ᵃ 14 Daniel 9:27; 11:31; 12:11

standing where it[a] does not belong—let the reader understand—then let those who are in Judea flee to the mountains. [15]Let no one on the housetop go down or enter the house to take anything out. [16]Let no one in the field go back to get their cloak. [17]How dreadful it will be in those days for pregnant women and nursing mothers! [18]Pray that this will not take place in winter, [19]because those will be days of distress unequaled from the beginning, when God created the world, until now—and never to be equaled again.

[20]"If the Lord had not cut short those days, no one would survive. But for the sake of the elect, whom he has chosen, he has shortened them. [21]At that time if anyone says to you, 'Look, here is the Messiah!' or, 'Look, there he is!' do not believe it. [22]For false messiahs and false prophets will appear and perform signs and wonders to deceive, if possible, even the elect. [23]So be on your guard; I have told you everything ahead of time.   Jn 4:48; 2Pe 3:17

[24]"But in those days, following that distress,

" 'the sun will be darkened,
    and the moon will not give
        its light;
[25]the stars will fall from the sky,
    and the heavenly bodies
        will be shaken.'[b]   Mt 24:29

[26]"At that time people will see the Son of Man coming in clouds with great power and glory. [27]And he will send his angels and gather his elect from the four winds, from the ends of the earth to the ends of the heavens.   Da 7:13; Zec 2:6; Rev 1:7

[28]"Now learn this lesson from the fig tree: As soon as its twigs get tender and its leaves come out, you know that summer is near. [29]Even so, when you see these things happening, you know that it[a] is near, right at the door. [30]Truly I tell you, this generation will certainly not pass away until all these things have happened. [31]Heaven and earth will pass away, but my words will never pass away.   Mt 5:18; Mk 9:1

The Day and Hour Unknown

[32]"But about that day or hour no one knows, not even the angels in heaven, nor the Son, but only the Father. [33]Be on guard! Be alert[c]! You do not know when that time will come. [34]It's like a man going away: He leaves his house and puts his servants in charge, each with their assigned task, and tells the one at the door to keep watch.   Mt 25:14; Ac 1:7; 1Th 5:6

[35]"Therefore keep watch because you do not know when the owner of the house will come back—whether in the evening, or at midnight, or when the rooster crows, or at dawn. [36]If

[a] 14,29 Or he   [b] 25 Isaiah 13:10; 34:4   [c] 33 Some manuscripts alert and pray

he comes suddenly, do not let him find you sleeping. [37]What I say to you, I say to everyone: 'Watch!'"
Lk 12:35-40

Jesus Anointed at Bethany

14:1-11pp — Mt 26:2-16
14:1,2,10,11pp — Lk 22:1-6
14:3-8Ref — Jn 12:1-8

14 Now the Passover and the Festival of Unleavened Bread were only two days away, and the chief priests and the teachers of the law were scheming to arrest Jesus secretly and kill him. [2]"But not during the festival," they said, "or the people may riot." Mt 12:14; Jn 11:55; 13:1

[3]While he was in Bethany, reclining at the table in the home of Simon the Leper, a woman came with an alabaster jar of very expensive perfume, made of pure nard. She broke the jar and poured the perfume on his head. Mt 21:17; Lk 7:37-39

[4]Some of those present were saying indignantly to one another, "Why this waste of perfume? [5]It could have been sold for more than a year's wages[a] and the money given to the poor." And they rebuked her harshly.

[6]"Leave her alone," said Jesus. "Why are you bothering her? She has done a beautiful thing to me. [7]The poor you will always have with you,[b] and you can help them any time you want. But you will not always have me.

[8]She did what she could. She poured perfume on my body beforehand to prepare for my burial. [9]Truly I tell you, wherever the gospel is preached throughout the world, what she has done will also be told, in memory of her." Jn 12:1-8; Dt 15:11

[10]Then Judas Iscariot, one of the Twelve, went to the chief priests to betray Jesus to them. [11]They were delighted to hear this and promised to give him money. So he watched for an opportunity to hand him over. Mt 26:2-16; Lk 22:1-6

The Last Supper

14:12-26pp — Mt 26:17-30; Lk 22:7-23
14:22-25pp — 1Co 11:23-25

[12]On the first day of the Festival of Unleavened Bread, when it was customary to sacrifice the Passover lamb, Jesus' disciples asked him, "Where do you want us to go and make preparations for you to eat the Passover?" Ex 12:1-11; Dt 16:1-4

[13]So he sent two of his disciples, telling them, "Go into the city, and a man carrying a jar of water will meet you. Follow him. [14]Say to the owner of the house he enters, 'The Teacher asks: Where is my guest room, where I may eat the Passover with my disciples?' [15]He will show you a large room upstairs, furnished and ready. Make preparations for us there." Ac 1:13

[16]The disciples left, went into

---

[a] 5 Greek *than three hundred denarii*   [b] 7 See Deut. 15:11.

the city and found things just as Jesus had told them. So they prepared the Passover.

¹⁷When evening came, Jesus arrived with the Twelve. ¹⁸While they were reclining at the table eating, he said, "Truly I tell you, one of you will betray me — one who is eating with me."

¹⁹They were saddened, and one by one they said to him, "Surely you don't mean me?"

²⁰"It is one of the Twelve," he replied, "one who dips bread into the bowl with me. ²¹The Son of Man will go just as it is written about him. But woe to that man who betrays the Son of Man! It would be better for him if he had not been born." Mt 8:20; Jn 13:18-27

²²While they were eating, Jesus took bread, and when he had given thanks, he broke it and gave it to his disciples, saying, "Take it; this is my body." Mt 14:19

²³Then he took a cup, and when he had given thanks, he gave it to them, and they all drank from it. 1Co 10:16

²⁴"This is my blood of the*a* covenant, which is poured out for many," he said to them. ²⁵"Truly I tell you, I will not drink again from the fruit of the vine until that day when I drink it new in the kingdom of God." 1Co 11:23-25

²⁶When they had sung a hymn, they went out to the Mount of Olives. Mt 26:17-30; Lk 22:7-23

Jesus Predicts Peter's Denial
14:27-31pp — Mt 26:31-35

²⁷"You will all fall away," Jesus told them, "for it is written:

" 'I will strike the shepherd,
   and the sheep will be
      scattered.'*b*

²⁸But after I have risen, I will go ahead of you into Galilee." Mk 16:7

²⁹Peter declared, "Even if all fall away, I will not."

³⁰"Truly I tell you," Jesus answered, "today — yes, tonight — before the rooster crows twice*c* you yourself will disown me three times." Lk 22:34; Jn 13:38

³¹But Peter insisted emphatically, "Even if I have to die with you, I will never disown you." And all the others said the same. Mt 26:31-35

Gethsemane
14:32-42pp — Mt 26:36-46; Lk 22:40-46

³²They went to a place called Gethsemane, and Jesus said to his disciples, "Sit here while I pray." ³³He took Peter, James and John along with him, and he began to be deeply distressed and troubled. ³⁴"My soul is overwhelmed with sorrow to the point of death," he said to them. "Stay here and keep watch." Jn 12:27

³⁵Going a little farther, he fell to the ground and prayed that if possible the hour might pass

a 24 Some manuscripts *the new*   *b 27* Zech. 13:7   *c 30* Some early manuscripts do not have *twice.*

from him. [36] *"Abba,[a]* Father,"
he said, "everything is possible
for you. Take this cup from me.
Yet not what I will, but what you
will."   Mt 26:39; Ro 8:15

[37] Then he returned to his disciples and found them sleeping.
"Simon," he said to Peter, "are you
asleep? Couldn't you keep watch
for one hour? [38] Watch and pray so
that you will not fall into temptation. The spirit is willing, but the
flesh is weak."   Mt 6:13; Ro 7:22-23

[39] Once more he went away
and prayed the same thing.
[40] When he came back, he again
found them sleeping, because
their eyes were heavy. They did
not know what to say to him.

[41] Returning the third time, he
said to them, "Are you still sleeping and resting? Enough! The
hour has come. Look, the Son of
Man is delivered into the hands
of sinners. [42] Rise! Let us go! Here
comes my betrayer!"   Mt 26:36-46

Jesus Arrested
14:43-50pp — Mt 26:47-56; Lk 22:47-50;
    Jn 18:3-11

[43] Just as he was speaking, Judas, one of the Twelve, appeared.
With him was a crowd armed
with swords and clubs, sent from
the chief priests, the teachers of
the law, and the elders.   Mt 10:4

[44] Now the betrayer had arranged a signal with them: "The
one I kiss is the man; arrest him
and lead him away under guard."

[45] Going at once to Jesus, Judas
said, "Rabbi!" and kissed him.
[46] The men seized Jesus and arrested him. [47] Then one of those
standing near drew his sword
and struck the servant of the high
priest, cutting off his ear.   Mt 23:7

[48] "Am I leading a rebellion,"
said Jesus, "that you have come
out with swords and clubs to
capture me? [49] Every day I was
with you, teaching in the temple
courts, and you did not arrest me.
But the Scriptures must be fulfilled." [50] Then everyone deserted
him and fled.   Mt 26:47-56; Lk 22:47-50

[51] A young man, wearing nothing but a linen garment, was following Jesus. When they seized
him, [52] he fled naked, leaving his
garment behind.

Jesus Before the Sanhedrin
14:53-65pp — Mt 26:57-68;
    Jn 18:12,13,19-24
14:61-63pp — Lk 22:67-71

[53] They took Jesus to the high
priest, and all the chief priests,
the elders and the teachers of
the law came together. [54] Peter followed him at a distance,
right into the courtyard of the
high priest. There he sat with the
guards and warmed himself at
the fire.   Mt 26:3; Jn 18:18

[55] The chief priests and the
whole Sanhedrin were looking for evidence against Jesus
so that they could put him to
death, but they did not find any.

---

[a] 36 Aramaic for *father*

⁵⁶Many testified falsely against him, but their statements did not agree. Mt 5:22

⁵⁷Then some stood up and gave this false testimony against him: ⁵⁸"We heard him say, 'I will destroy this temple made with human hands and in three days will build another, not made with hands.'" ⁵⁹Yet even then their testimony did not agree. Mk 15:29; Jn 2:19

⁶⁰Then the high priest stood up before them and asked Jesus, "Are you not going to answer? What is this testimony that these men are bringing against you?" ⁶¹But Jesus remained silent and gave no answer. Isa 53:7; Mt 27:12,14

Again the high priest asked him, "Are you the Messiah, the Son of the Blessed One?" Mt 16:16

⁶²"I am," said Jesus. "And you will see the Son of Man sitting at the right hand of the Mighty One and coming on the clouds of heaven." Rev 1:7

⁶³The high priest tore his clothes. "Why do we need any more witnesses?" he asked. ⁶⁴"You have heard the blasphemy. What do you think?" Lk 22:67-71

They all condemned him as worthy of death. ⁶⁵Then some began to spit at him; they blindfolded him, struck him with their fists, and said, "Prophesy!" And the guards took him and beat him. Mt 26:57-68; Jn 18:12-13,19-24

Peter Disowns Jesus

14:66-72pp — Mt 26:69-75; Lk 22:56-62; Jn 18:16-18,25-27

⁶⁶While Peter was below in the courtyard, one of the servant girls of the high priest came by. ⁶⁷When she saw Peter warming himself, she looked closely at him.

"You also were with that Nazarene, Jesus," she said. Mk 1:24

⁶⁸But he denied it. "I don't know or understand what you're talking about," he said, and went out into the entryway.ᵃ

⁶⁹When the servant girl saw him there, she said again to those standing around, "This fellow is one of them." ⁷⁰Again he denied it.

After a little while, those standing near said to Peter, "Surely you are one of them, for you are a Galilean." Ac 2:7

⁷¹He began to call down curses, and he swore to them, "I don't know this man you're talking about."

⁷²Immediately the rooster crowed the second time.ᵇ Then Peter remembered the word Jesus had spoken to him: "Before the rooster crows twiceᶜ you will disown me three times." And he broke down and wept. Mt 26:69-75

Jesus Before Pilate

15:2-15pp — Mt 27:11-26; Lk 23:2,3, 18-25; Jn 18:29-19:16

15 Very early in the morning, the chief priests, with the elders, the teachers of the law

---

ᵃ 68 Some early manuscripts *entryway and the rooster crowed*   ᵇ 72 Some early manuscripts do not have *the second time.*   ᶜ 72 Some early manuscripts do not have *twice.*

and the whole Sanhedrin, made their plans. So they bound Jesus, led him away and handed him over to Pilate. Mt 27:1-2

² "Are you the king of the Jews?" asked Pilate. Mt 2:2

"You have said so," Jesus replied.

³ The chief priests accused him of many things. ⁴ So again Pilate asked him, "Aren't you going to answer? See how many things they are accusing you of."

⁵ But Jesus still made no reply, and Pilate was amazed. Mk 14:61

⁶ Now it was the custom at the festival to release a prisoner whom the people requested. ⁷ A man called Barabbas was in prison with the insurrectionists who had committed murder in the uprising. ⁸ The crowd came up and asked Pilate to do for them what he usually did.

⁹ "Do you want me to release to you the king of the Jews?" asked Pilate, ¹⁰ knowing it was out of self-interest that the chief priests had handed Jesus over to him. ¹¹ But the chief priests stirred up the crowd to have Pilate release Barabbas instead. Ac 3:14

¹² "What shall I do, then, with the one you call the king of the Jews?" Pilate asked them.

¹³ "Crucify him!" they shouted.

¹⁴ "Why? What crime has he committed?" asked Pilate.

But they shouted all the louder, "Crucify him!"

¹⁵ Wanting to satisfy the crowd, Pilate released Barabbas to them. He had Jesus flogged, and handed him over to be crucified. Mt 27:11-26; Lk 23:2-3,18-25

The Soldiers Mock Jesus
15:16-20pp — Mt 27:27-31

¹⁶ The soldiers led Jesus away into the palace (that is, the Praetorium) and called together the whole company of soldiers. ¹⁷ They put a purple robe on him, then twisted together a crown of thorns and set it on him. ¹⁸ And they began to call out to him, "Hail, king of the Jews!" ¹⁹ Again and again they struck him on the head with a staff and spit on him. Falling on their knees, they paid homage to him. ²⁰ And when they had mocked him, they took off the purple robe and put his own clothes on him. Then they led him out to crucify him. Mt 27:27-31

The Crucifixion of Jesus
15:22-32pp — Mt 27:33-44; Lk 23:33-43; Jn 19:17-24

²¹ A certain man from Cyrene, Simon, the father of Alexander and Rufus, was passing by on his way in from the country, and they forced him to carry the cross. ²² They brought Jesus to the place called Golgotha (which means "the place of the skull"). ²³ Then they offered him wine mixed with myrrh, but he did not take it. ²⁴ And they crucified him. Dividing up his clothes,

they cast lots to see what each would get. Ps 22:18; Lk 23:26

²⁵It was nine in the morning when they crucified him. ²⁶The written notice of the charge against him read: THE KING OF THE JEWS.

²⁷They crucified two rebels with him, one on his right and one on his left. [28]ᵃ ²⁹Those who passed by hurled insults at him, shaking their heads and saying, "So! You who are going to destroy the temple and build it in three days, ³⁰come down from the cross and save yourself!" ³¹In the same way the chief priests and the teachers of the law mocked him among themselves. "He saved others," they said, "but he can't save himself! ³²Let this Messiah, this king of Israel, come down now from the cross, that we may see and believe." Those crucified with him also heaped insults on him. Mt 27:33-44; Lk 23:33-43; Jn 19:17-24

The Death of Jesus

15:33-41pp — Mt 27:45-56; Lk 23:44-49; Jn 19:29-30

³³At noon, darkness came over the whole land until three in the afternoon. ³⁴And at three in the afternoon Jesus cried out in a loud voice, *"Eloi, Eloi, lema sabachthani?"* (which means "My God, my God, why have you forsaken me?").ᵇ Am 8:9

³⁵When some of those standing near heard this, they said, "Listen, he's calling Elijah."

³⁶Someone ran, filled a sponge with wine vinegar, put it on a staff, and offered it to Jesus to drink. "Now leave him alone. Let's see if Elijah comes to take him down," he said. Ps 69:21

³⁷With a loud cry, Jesus breathed his last. Jn 19:30

³⁸The curtain of the temple was torn in two from top to bottom. ³⁹And when the centurion, who stood there in front of Jesus, saw how he died,ᶜ he said, "Surely this man was the Son of God!" Mt 4:3; Heb 10:19-20

⁴⁰Some women were watching from a distance. Among them were Mary Magdalene, Mary the mother of James the younger and of Joseph,ᵈ and Salome. ⁴¹In Galilee these women had followed him and cared for his needs. Many other women who had come up with him to Jerusalem were also there. Mt 27:45-46

The Burial of Jesus

15:42-47pp — Mt 27:57-61; Lk 23:50-56; Jn 19:38-42

⁴²It was Preparation Day (that is, the day before the Sabbath). So as evening approached, ⁴³Joseph of Arimathea, a prominent member of the Council, who was himself waiting for the kingdom

---

ᵃ 28 Some manuscripts include here words similar to Luke 22:37.   ᵇ 34 Psalm 22:1
ᶜ 39 Some manuscripts *saw that he died with such a cry*   ᵈ 40 Greek *Joses,* a variant of *Joseph*; also in verse 47

of God, went boldly to Pilate and asked for Jesus' body. [44]Pilate was surprised to hear that he was already dead. Summoning the centurion, he asked him if Jesus had already died. [45]When he learned from the centurion that it was so, he gave the body to Joseph. [46]So Joseph bought some linen cloth, took down the body, wrapped it in the linen, and placed it in a tomb cut out of rock. Then he rolled a stone against the entrance of the tomb. [47]Mary Magdalene and Mary the mother of Joseph saw where he was laid. Mt 27:57-61; Lk 23:50-56

Jesus Has Risen

16:1-8pp — Mt 28:1-8; Lk 24:1-10

16 When the Sabbath was over, Mary Magdalene, Mary the mother of James, and Salome bought spices so that they might go to anoint Jesus' body. [2]Very early on the first day of the week, just after sunrise, they were on their way to the tomb [3]and they asked each other, "Who will roll the stone away from the entrance of the tomb?" Mk 15:46; Lk 23:56; Jn 19:39-40

[4]But when they looked up, they saw that the stone, which was very large, had been rolled away. [5]As they entered the tomb, they saw a young man dressed in a white robe sitting on the right side, and they were alarmed. Jn 20:12

[6]"Don't be alarmed," he said. "You are looking for Jesus the Nazarene, who was crucified. He has risen! He is not here. See the place where they laid him. [7]But go, tell his disciples and Peter, 'He is going ahead of you into Galilee. There you will see him, just as he told you.'" Mk 1:24; 14:28

[8]Trembling and bewildered, the women went out and fled from the tomb. They said nothing to anyone, because they were afraid.[a] Mt 28:1-8; Lk 24:1-10

[The earliest manuscripts and some other ancient witnesses do not have verses 9–20.]

[9]*When Jesus rose early on the first day of the week, he appeared first to Mary Magdalene, out of whom he had driven seven demons.* [10]*She went and told those who had been with him and who were mourning and weeping.* [11]*When they heard that Jesus was alive and that she had seen him, they did not believe it.* Lk 24:11; Jn 20:11-18

[12]*Afterward Jesus appeared in a different form to two of them while they were walking in the country.* [13]*These returned and reported it to the rest; but they did not believe them either.* Lk 24:13-32

---

[a] 8 Some manuscripts have the following ending between verses 8 and 9, and one manuscript has it after verse 8 (omitting verses 9-20): *Then they quickly reported all these instructions to those around Peter. After this, Jesus himself also sent out through them from east to west the sacred and imperishable proclamation of eternal salvation. Amen.*

[14] Later Jesus appeared to the Eleven as they were eating; he rebuked them for their lack of faith and their stubborn refusal to believe those who had seen him after he had risen. Lk 24:36-43

[15] He said to them, "Go into all the world and preach the gospel to all creation. [16] Whoever believes and is baptized will be saved, but whoever does not believe will be condemned. [17] And these signs will accompany those who believe: In my name they will drive out demons; they will speak in new tongues; [18] they will pick up snakes with their hands; and when they drink deadly poison, it will not hurt them at all; they will place their hands on sick people, and they will get well." Mt 28:18-20; Lk 24:47-48

[19] After the Lord Jesus had spoken to them, he was taken up into heaven and he sat at the right hand of God. [20] Then the disciples went out and preached everywhere, and the Lord worked with them and confirmed his word by the signs that accompanied it. Lk 24:50-51; Ps 110:1

Luke

Introduction

1:1-4Ref — Ac 1:1

1 Many have undertaken to draw up an account of the things that have been fulfilled[a] among us, [2] just as they were handed down to us by those who from the first were eyewitnesses and servants of the word. [3] With this in mind, since I myself have carefully investigated everything from the beginning, I too decided to write an orderly account for you, most excellent Theophilus, [4] so that you may know the certainty of the things you have been taught. Ac 1:1; 11:4; Heb 2:3

The Birth of John the Baptist Foretold

[5] In the time of Herod king of Judea there was a priest named Zechariah, who belonged to the priestly division of Abijah; his wife Elizabeth was also a descendant of Aaron. [6] Both of them were righteous in the sight of God, observing all the Lord's commands and decrees blamelessly. [7] But they were childless because Elizabeth was not able to conceive, and they were both very old. Ge 7:1; 1Ch 24:10

[8] Once when Zechariah's division was on duty and he was serving as priest before God, [9] he was chosen by lot, according to the custom of the priesthood, to go into the temple of the Lord and burn incense. [10] And when the time for the burning of incense came, all the assembled worshipers were praying outside. Ex 30:7-8; Lev 16:17; 1Ch 24:19

[11] Then an angel of the Lord appeared to him, standing at the right side of the altar of incense. [12] When Zechariah saw him, he was startled and was gripped with fear. [13] But the angel said to him: "Do not be afraid, Zechariah; your prayer has been heard. Your wife Elizabeth will bear you a son, and you are to call him John. [14] He will be a joy and delight to you, and many will rejoice

---

[a] 1 Or been surely believed

because of his birth, [15] for he will be great in the sight of the Lord. He is never to take wine or other fermented drink, and he will be filled with the Holy Spirit even before he is born. [16] He will bring back many of the people of Israel to the Lord their God. [17] And he will go on before the Lord, in the spirit and power of Elijah, to turn the hearts of the parents to their children and the disobedient to the wisdom of the righteous — to make ready a people prepared for the Lord."   Jer 1:5; Mt 11:14

[18] Zechariah asked the angel, "How can I be sure of this? I am an old man and my wife is well along in years."   Ge 17:17

[19] The angel said to him, "I am Gabriel. I stand in the presence of God, and I have been sent to speak to you and to tell you this good news. [20] And now you will be silent and not able to speak until the day this happens, because you did not believe my words, which will come true at their appointed time."   Eze 3:26; Da 8:16; 9:21

[21] Meanwhile, the people were waiting for Zechariah and wondering why he stayed so long in the temple. [22] When he came out, he could not speak to them. They realized he had seen a vision in the temple, for he kept making signs to them but remained unable to speak.

[23] When his time of service was completed, he returned home. [24] After this his wife Elizabeth became pregnant and for five months remained in seclusion. [25] "The Lord has done this for me," she said. "In these days he has shown his favor and taken away my disgrace among the people."   Ge 30:23; Isa 4:1

The Birth of Jesus Foretold

[26] In the sixth month of Elizabeth's pregnancy, God sent the angel Gabriel to Nazareth, a town in Galilee, [27] to a virgin pledged to be married to a man named Joseph, a descendant of David. The virgin's name was Mary. [28] The angel went to her and said, "Greetings, you who are highly favored! The Lord is with you."   Mt 1:16,18,20; 2:23

[29] Mary was greatly troubled at his words and wondered what kind of greeting this might be. [30] But the angel said to her, "Do not be afraid, Mary; you have found favor with God. [31] You will conceive and give birth to a son, and you are to call him Jesus. [32] He will be great and will be called the Son of the Most High. The Lord God will give him the throne of his father David, [33] and he will reign over Jacob's descendants forever; his kingdom will never end."   Da 2:44; 7:14,27; Mic 4:7

[34] "How will this be," Mary asked the angel, "since I am a virgin?"

[35] The angel answered, "The Holy Spirit will come on you, and the power of the Most High will

overshadow you. So the holy one to be born will be called*a* the Son of God. **36**Even Elizabeth your relative is going to have a child in her old age, and she who was said to be unable to conceive is in her sixth month. **37**For no word from God will ever fail." Mt 19:26

38"I am the Lord's servant," Mary answered. "May your word to me be fulfilled." Then the angel left her.

Mary Visits Elizabeth

39At that time Mary got ready and hurried to a town in the hill country of Judea, **40**where she entered Zechariah's home and greeted Elizabeth. **41**When Elizabeth heard Mary's greeting, the baby leaped in her womb, and Elizabeth was filled with the Holy Spirit. **42**In a loud voice she exclaimed: "Blessed are you among women, and blessed is the child you will bear! **43**But why am I so favored, that the mother of my Lord should come to me? **44**As soon as the sound of your greeting reached my ears, the baby in my womb leaped for joy. **45**Blessed is she who has believed that the Lord would fulfill his promises to her!" Jdg 5:24; Jn 13:13

Mary's Song

1:46-53pp — 1Sa 2:1-10

46And Mary said:

"My soul glorifies the
    Lord   Ps 34:2-3

47   and my spirit rejoices in
        God my Savior, 1Ti 1:1; 2:3
48for he has been mindful
    of the humble state of his
        servant.   Ps 138:6
From now on all generations
        will call me blessed,
49   for the Mighty One has
        done great things
        for me —   Ps 71:19
    holy is his name.   Ps 111:9
50His mercy extends to those
        who fear him,
    from generation to
        generation. Ex 20:6; Ps 103:17
51He has performed mighty
        deeds with his arm; Ps 98:1
    he has scattered those
        who are proud in their
        inmost thoughts.   Ge 11:8
52He has brought down rulers
        from their thrones
    but has lifted up the
        humble.   Mt 23:12
53He has filled the hungry with
        good things   Ps 107:9
    but has sent the rich away
        empty.   1Sa 2:1-10
54He has helped his servant
        Israel,
    remembering to be
        merciful   Ps 98:3
55to Abraham and his
        descendants forever,
    just as he promised our
        ancestors."

56Mary stayed with Elizabeth for about three months and then returned home.

---

a 35 Or *So the child to be born will be called holy,*

The Birth of John the Baptist

57 When it was time for Elizabeth to have her baby, she gave birth to a son. 58 Her neighbors and relatives heard that the Lord had shown her great mercy, and they shared her joy.

59 On the eighth day they came to circumcise the child, and they were going to name him after his father Zechariah, 60 but his mother spoke up and said, "No! He is to be called John." Ge 17:12; Lk 2:21

61 They said to her, "There is no one among your relatives who has that name."

62 Then they made signs to his father, to find out what he would like to name the child. 63 He asked for a writing tablet, and to everyone's astonishment he wrote, "His name is John." 64 Immediately his mouth was opened and his tongue set free, and he began to speak, praising God. 65 All the neighbors were filled with awe, and throughout the hill country of Judea people were talking about all these things. 66 Everyone who heard this wondered about it, asking, "What then is this child going to be?" For the Lord's hand was with him. Ge 39:2; Ac 11:21

Zechariah's Song

67 His father Zechariah was filled with the Holy Spirit and prophesied: Joel 2:28

68 "Praise be to the Lord, the
 God of Israel, Ps 72:18
because he has come to his
 people and redeemed
 them. Ps 111:9; Lk 7:16
69 He has raised up a horn[a] of
 salvation for us Ps 18:2
in the house of his servant
 David Mt 1:1
70 (as he said through his holy
 prophets of long
 ago), Jer 23:5
71 salvation from our enemies
 and from the hand of all
 who hate us—
72 to show mercy to our
 ancestors Mic 7:20
and to remember his holy
 covenant, Ps 105:8-9; 106:45
73   the oath he swore to our
 father Abraham:
74 to rescue us from the hand of
 our enemies,
 and to enable us to serve
 him without fear Heb 9:14
75   in holiness and
 righteousness before
 him all our days. Eph 4:24

76 And you, my child, will be
 called a prophet of the
 Most High; Mt 11:9
for you will go on before the
 Lord to prepare the way
 for him, Mal 3:1
77 to give his people the
 knowledge of salvation
through the forgiveness of
 their sins, Jer 31:34; Mk 1:4

a 69 Horn here symbolizes a strong king.

78because of the tender mercy
of our God,
by which the rising sun
will come to us from
heaven   Mal 4:2
79to shine on those living in
darkness
and in the shadow of
death,   Isa 9:2; Mt 4:16
to guide our feet into the path
of peace."   Lk 2:14

80And the child grew and became strong in spirit*a*; and he
lived in the wilderness until he
appeared publicly to Israel.Lk 2:40

The Birth of Jesus

2 In those days Caesar Augustus issued a decree that a
census should be taken of the entire Roman world. 2(This was the
first census that took place while*b*
Quirinius was governor of Syria.)
3And everyone went to their own
town to register.   Mt 24:14; Lk 3:1

4So Joseph also went up from
the town of Nazareth in Galilee
to Judea, to Bethlehem the town
of David, because he belonged
to the house and line of David.
5He went there to register with
Mary, who was pledged to be
married to him and was expecting a child. 6While they were
there, the time came for the baby
to be born, 7and she gave birth to
her firstborn, a son. She wrapped
him in cloths and placed him
in a manger, because there was

no guest room available for
them.   Jn 7:42
8And there were shepherds
living out in the fields nearby,
keeping watch over their flocks
at night. 9An angel of the Lord
appeared to them, and the glory of the Lord shone around
them, and they were terrified.
10But the angel said to them,
"Do not be afraid. I bring you
good news that will cause great
joy for all the people. 11Today in
the town of David a Savior has
been born to you; he is the Messiah, the Lord. 12This will be a
sign to you: You will find a baby
wrapped in cloths and lying in a
manger."   Isa 7:14; Mt 1:21
13Suddenly a great company of
the heavenly host appeared with
the angel, praising God and saying,

14"Glory to God in the highest
heaven,
and on earth peace to those
on whom his favor
rests."   Ro 5:1; Eph 2:14,17

15When the angels had left
them and gone into heaven,
the shepherds said to one another, "Let's go to Bethlehem
and see this thing that has happened, which the Lord has told
us about."
16So they hurried off and
found Mary and Joseph, and the
baby, who was lying in the manger. 17When they had seen him,

a 80 Or *in the Spirit*   *b 2* Or *This census took place before* they spread the word concerning what had been told them about this child, [18] and all who heard it were amazed at what the shepherds said to them. [19] But Mary treasured up all these things and pondered them in her heart. [20] The shepherds returned, glorifying and praising God for all the things they had heard and seen, which were just as they had been told. Mt 9:8

[21] On the eighth day, when it was time to circumcise the child, he was named Jesus, the name the angel had given him before he was conceived. Lk 1:31,59

Jesus Presented in the Temple

[22] When the time came for the purification rites required by the Law of Moses, Joseph and Mary took him to Jerusalem to present him to the Lord [23] (as it is written in the Law of the Lord, "Every firstborn male is to be consecrated to the Lord"[a]), [24] and to offer a sacrifice in keeping with what is said in the Law of the Lord: "a pair of doves or two young pigeons."[b] Ex 13:2,12,15; Lev 12:8

[25] Now there was a man in Jerusalem called Simeon, who was righteous and devout. He was waiting for the consolation of Israel, and the Holy Spirit was on him. [26] It had been revealed to him by the Holy Spirit that he would not die before he had seen the Lord's Messiah. [27] Moved by the Spirit, he went into the temple courts. When the parents brought in the child Jesus to do for him what the custom of the Law required, [28] Simeon took him in his arms and praised God, saying: Lk 1:6; 23:51

[29] "Sovereign Lord, as you have
     promised,   ver 26
  you may now dismiss[c] your
     servant in peace. Ac 2:24
[30] For my eyes have seen your
     salvation,   Isa 52:10
[31] which you have prepared in
     the sight of all nations:
[32] a light for revelation to the
     Gentiles,
  and the glory of your people
     Israel." Isa 42:6; 49:6; Ac 13:47

[33] The child's father and mother marveled at what was said about him. [34] Then Simeon blessed them and said to Mary, his mother: "This child is destined to cause the falling and rising of many in Israel, and to be a sign that will be spoken against, [35] so that the thoughts of many hearts will be revealed. And a sword will pierce your own soul too." Mt 21:44; 1Co 1:23

[36] There was also a prophet, Anna, the daughter of Penuel, of the tribe of Asher. She was very old; she had lived with her husband seven years after her marriage, [37] and then was a widow until she was eighty-four.[d] She

---

[a] 23 Exodus 13:2,12   [b] 24 Lev. 12:8   [c] 29 Or promised, / now dismiss   [d] 37 Or then had been a widow for eighty-four years.

never left the temple but worshiped night and day, fasting and praying. ³⁸Coming up to them at that very moment, she gave thanks to God and spoke about the child to all who were looking forward to the redemption of Jerusalem. Lk 1:68; 1Ti 5:5

³⁹When Joseph and Mary had done everything required by the Law of the Lord, they returned to Galilee to their own town of Nazareth. ⁴⁰And the child grew and became strong; he was filled with wisdom, and the grace of God was on him. Mt 2:23; Lk 1:80

The Boy Jesus at the Temple

⁴¹Every year Jesus' parents went to Jerusalem for the Festival of the Passover. ⁴²When he was twelve years old, they went up to the festival, according to the custom. ⁴³After the festival was over, while his parents were returning home, the boy Jesus stayed behind in Jerusalem, but they were unaware of it. ⁴⁴Thinking he was in their company, they traveled on for a day. Then they began looking for him among their relatives and friends. ⁴⁵When they did not find him, they went back to Jerusalem to look for him. ⁴⁶After three days they found him in the temple courts, sitting among the teachers, listening to them and asking them questions. ⁴⁷Everyone who heard him was amazed at his understanding and his answers. ⁴⁸When his parents saw him, they were astonished. His mother said to him, "Son, why have you treated us like this? Your father and I have been anxiously searching for you." Ex 23:15; Dt 16:1-8; Mt 12:46

⁴⁹"Why were you searching for me?" he asked. "Didn't you know I had to be in my Father's house?"ᵃ ⁵⁰But they did not understand what he was saying to them. Mk 9:32; Jn 2:16

⁵¹Then he went down to Nazareth with them and was obedient to them. But his mother treasured all these things in her heart. ⁵²And Jesus grew in wisdom and stature, and in favor with God and man. Mt 2:23; Lk 1:80

John the Baptist Prepares the Way

3:2-10pp — Mt 3:1-10; Mk 1:3-5
3:16,17pp — Mt 3:11,12; Mk 1:7,8

3 In the fifteenth year of the reign of Tiberius Caesar—when Pontius Pilate was governor of Judea, Herod tetrarch of Galilee, his brother Philip tetrarch of Iturea and Traconitis, and Lysanias tetrarch of Abilene— ²during the high-priesthood of Annas and Caiaphas, the word of God came to John son of Zechariah in the wilderness. ³He went into all the country around the Jordan, preaching a baptism of repentance for the forgiveness

ᵃ 49 Or *be about my Father's business*

of sins. ⁴As it is written in the book of the words of Isaiah the prophet: Mk 1:4; Jn 18:13; Ac 4:6

"A voice of one calling in the
    wilderness,
'Prepare the way for the Lord,
    make straight paths for
    him.
⁵Every valley shall be filled in,
    every mountain and hill
    made low.
The crooked roads shall
    become straight,
    the rough ways smooth.
⁶And all people will see God's
    salvation.' "^a   Ps 98:2

⁷John said to the crowds coming out to be baptized by him, "You brood of vipers! Who warned you to flee from the coming wrath? ⁸Produce fruit in keeping with repentance. And do not begin to say to yourselves, 'We have Abraham as our father.' For I tell you that out of these stones God can raise up children for Abraham. ⁹The ax is already at the root of the trees, and every tree that does not produce good fruit will be cut down and thrown into the fire."   Jn 8:33,39; Gal 3:7

¹⁰"What should we do then?" the crowd asked.   Mt 3:1-10; Mk 1:3-5

¹¹John answered, "Anyone who has two shirts should share with the one who has none, and anyone who has food should do the same."   Isa 58:7

¹²Even tax collectors came to be baptized. "Teacher," they asked, "what should we do?"   Lk 7:29

¹³"Don't collect any more than you are required to," he told them.   Lk 19:8

¹⁴Then some soldiers asked him, "And what should we do?" He replied, "Don't extort money and don't accuse people falsely—be content with your pay."   Ex 23:1; Lev 19:11

¹⁵The people were waiting expectantly and were all wondering in their hearts if John might possibly be the Messiah. ¹⁶John answered them all, "I baptize you with^b water. But one who is more powerful than I will come, the straps of whose sandals I am not worthy to untie. He will baptize you with^b the Holy Spirit and fire. ¹⁷His winnowing fork is in his hand to clear his threshing floor and to gather the wheat into his barn, but he will burn up the chaff with unquenchable fire." ¹⁸And with many other words John exhorted the people and proclaimed the good news to them.   Mt 3:11-12; Mk 1:7-8

¹⁹But when John rebuked Herod the tetrarch because of his marriage to Herodias, his brother's wife, and all the other evil things he had done, ²⁰Herod added this to them all: He locked John up in prison. Mt 14:3-4; Mk 6:17

^a 6 Isaiah 40:3-5   ^b 16 Or in

The Baptism and Genealogy of Jesus

3:21,22pp — Mt 3:13-17; Mk 1:9-11
3:23-38pp — Mt 1:1-17

21 When all the people were being baptized, Jesus was baptized too. And as he was praying, heaven was opened **22** and the Holy Spirit descended on him in bodily form like a dove. And a voice came from heaven: "You are my Son, whom I love; with you I am well pleased." *Mt 3:13-17; Mk 1:9-11*

23 Now Jesus himself was about thirty years old when he began his ministry. He was the son, so it was thought, of Joseph, *Mt 4:17*

the son of Heli, **24** the son of Matthat,

the son of Levi, the son of Melki,

the son of Jannai, the son of Joseph,

25 the son of Mattathias, the son of Amos,

the son of Nahum, the son of Esli,

the son of Naggai, **26** the son of Maath,

the son of Mattathias, the son of Semein,

the son of Josek, the son of Joda,

27 the son of Joanan, the son of Rhesa,

the son of Zerubbabel, the son of Shealtiel, *Mt 1:12*

the son of Neri, **28** the son of Melki,

the son of Addi, the son of Cosam,

the son of Elmadam, the son of Er,

29 the son of Joshua, the son of Eliezer,

the son of Jorim, the son of Matthat,

the son of Levi, **30** the son of Simeon,

the son of Judah, the son of Joseph,

the son of Jonam, the son of Eliakim,

31 the son of Melea, the son of Menna,

the son of Mattatha, the son of Nathan, *2Sa 5:14; 1Ch 3:5*

the son of David, **32** the son of Jesse,

the son of Obed, the son of Boaz,

the son of Salmon,*a* the son of Nahshon,

33 the son of Amminadab, the son of Ram,*b*

the son of Hezron, the son of Perez, *Ru 4:18-22; 1Ch 2:10-12*

the son of Judah, **34** the son of Jacob,

the son of Isaac, the son of Abraham,

the son of Terah, the son of Nahor, *Ge 11:24,26*

35 the son of Serug, the son of Reu,

the son of Peleg, the son of Eber,

---

a 32 Some early manuscripts *Sala*   *b 33* Some manuscripts *Amminadab, the son of Admin, the son of Arni*; other manuscripts vary widely.

the son of Shelah, ³⁶the son of Cainan,

the son of Arphaxad, the son of Shem,   Ge 11:12

the son of Noah, the son of Lamech,   Ge 5:28-32

³⁷the son of Methuselah, the son of Enoch,

the son of Jared, the son of Mahalalel,

the son of Kenan, ³⁸the son of Enosh,   Ge 5:12-25

the son of Seth, the son of Adam,

the son of God.   Mt 1:1-17

Jesus Is Tested in the Wilderness

4:1-13pp — Mt 4:1-11; Mk 1:12,13

4 Jesus, full of the Holy Spirit, left the Jordan and was led by the Spirit into the wilderness, ²where for forty days he was tempted[a] by the devil. He ate nothing during those days, and at the end of them he was hungry.   Ex 34:28; Lk 2:27

³The devil said to him, "If you are the Son of God, tell this stone to become bread."   Mt 4:3

⁴Jesus answered, "It is written: 'Man shall not live on bread alone.'[b]"   Dt 8:3

⁵The devil led him up to a high place and showed him in an instant all the kingdoms of the world. ⁶And he said to him, "I will give you all their authority and splendor; it has been given to me,

and I can give it to anyone I want to. ⁷If you worship me, it will all be yours."   Jn 12:31; 14:30; 1Jn 5:19

⁸Jesus answered, "It is written: 'Worship the Lord your God and serve him only.'[c]"   Dt 6:13

⁹The devil led him to Jerusalem and had him stand on the highest point of the temple. "If you are the Son of God," he said, "throw yourself down from here. ¹⁰For it is written:

"'He will command his angels concerning you
to guard you carefully;
¹¹they will lift you up in their hands,
so that you will not strike your foot against a stone.'[d]"   Ps 91:11-12

¹²Jesus answered, "It is said: 'Do not put the Lord your God to the test.'[e]"   Dt 6:16

¹³When the devil had finished all this tempting, he left him until an opportune time.   Mt 4:1-11

Jesus Rejected at Nazareth

¹⁴Jesus returned to Galilee in the power of the Spirit, and news about him spread through the whole countryside. ¹⁵He was teaching in their synagogues, and everyone praised him.   Mt 4:12; 9:26

¹⁶He went to Nazareth, where he had been brought up, and on the Sabbath day he went into the synagogue, as was his custom.

---

[a] 2 The Greek for *tempted* can also mean *tested*.   [b] 4 Deut. 8:3   [c] 8 Deut. 6:13
[d] 11 Psalm 91:11,12   [e] 12 Deut. 6:16

He stood up to read, [17]and the scroll of the prophet Isaiah was handed to him. Unrolling it, he found the place where it is written: Mt 13:54

[18]"The Spirit of the Lord is
        on me,   Jn 3:34
    because he has anointed
        me
    to proclaim good news to
        the poor.   Mk 16:15
He has sent me to proclaim
        freedom for the
        prisoners
    and recovery of sight for the
        blind,
    to set the oppressed free,
[19]   to proclaim the year of the
        Lord's favor."[a]   Lev 25:10

[20]Then he rolled up the scroll, gave it back to the attendant and sat down. The eyes of everyone in the synagogue were fastened on him. [21]He began by saying to them, "Today this scripture is fulfilled in your hearing." Mt 26:55

[22]All spoke well of him and were amazed at the gracious words that came from his lips. "Isn't this Joseph's son?" they asked.   Mt 13:54-55; Jn 6:42; 7:15

[23]Jesus said to them, "Surely you will quote this proverb to me: 'Physician, heal yourself!' And you will tell me, 'Do here in your hometown what we have heard that you did in Capernaum.'"   Mk 1:21-28; 2:1-12

[24]"Truly I tell you," he continued, "no prophet is accepted in his hometown. [25]I assure you that there were many widows in Israel in Elijah's time, when the sky was shut for three and a half years and there was a severe famine throughout the land. [26]Yet Elijah was not sent to any of them, but to a widow in Zarephath in the region of Sidon. [27]And there were many in Israel with leprosy[b] in the time of Elisha the prophet, yet not one of them was cleansed—only Naaman the Syrian."   Mt 13:57; Jn 4:44

[28]All the people in the synagogue were furious when they heard this. [29]They got up, drove him out of the town, and took him to the brow of the hill on which the town was built, in order to throw him off the cliff. [30]But he walked right through the crowd and went on his way.   Jn 8:59; 10:39

Jesus Drives Out an Impure Spirit

4:31-37pp — Mk 1:21-28

[31]Then he went down to Capernaum, a town in Galilee, and on the Sabbath he taught the people. [32]They were amazed at his teaching, because his words had authority.   Mt 7:28-29

[33]In the synagogue there was a man possessed by a demon, an impure spirit. He cried out at the top of his voice, [34]"Go away! What

---

[a] 19 Isaiah 61:1,2 (see Septuagint); Isaiah 58:6 translated *leprosy* was used for various diseases affecting the skin.   [b] 27 The Greek word traditionally

do you want with us, Jesus of Nazareth? Have you come to destroy us? I know who you are—the Holy One of God!" Mk 1:24; Jas 2:19

35 "Be quiet!" Jesus said sternly. "Come out of him!" Then the demon threw the man down before them all and came out without injuring him.

36 All the people were amazed and said to each other, "What words these are! With authority and power he gives orders to impure spirits and they come out!" 37 And the news about him spread throughout the surrounding area. Mk 1:21-28

Jesus Heals Many
4:38-41pp — Mt 8:14-17
4:38-43pp — Mk 1:29-38

38 Jesus left the synagogue and went to the home of Simon. Now Simon's mother-in-law was suffering from a high fever, and they asked Jesus to help her. 39 So he bent over her and rebuked the fever, and it left her. She got up at once and began to wait on them.

40 At sunset, the people brought to Jesus all who had various kinds of sickness, and laying his hands on each one, he healed them. 41 Moreover, demons came out of many people, shouting, "You are the Son of God!" But he rebuked them and would not allow them to speak, because they knew he was the Messiah. Mt 8:14-17; Mk 5:23

42 At daybreak, Jesus went out to a solitary place. The people were looking for him and when they came to where he was, they tried to keep him from leaving them. 43 But he said, "I must proclaim the good news of the kingdom of God to the other towns also, because that is why I was sent." 44 And he kept on preaching in the synagogues of Judea. Mt 3:2; 4:23

Jesus Calls His First Disciples
5:1-11pp — Mt 4:18-22; Mk 1:16-20;
Jn 1:40-42

5 One day as Jesus was standing by the Lake of Gennesaret,*a* the people were crowding around him and listening to the word of God. 2 He saw at the water's edge two boats, left there by the fishermen, who were washing their nets. 3 He got into one of the boats, the one belonging to Simon, and asked him to put out a little from shore. Then he sat down and taught the people from the boat. Mt 13:2; Heb 4:12

4 When he had finished speaking, he said to Simon, "Put out into deep water, and let down the nets for a catch." Jn 21:6

5 Simon answered, "Master, we've worked hard all night and haven't caught anything. But because you say so, I will let down the nets." Lk 8:24,45; 9:33,49; 17:13

6 When they had done so, they caught such a large number of fish that their nets began to break. 7 So they signaled their

---

a 1 That is, the Sea of Galilee

partners in the other boat to come and help them, and they came and filled both boats so full that they began to sink.   Jn 21:11

⁸When Simon Peter saw this, he fell at Jesus' knees and said, "Go away from me, Lord; I am a sinful man!" ⁹For he and all his companions were astonished at the catch of fish they had taken, ¹⁰and so were James and John, the sons of Zebedee, Simon's partners.   Ge 18:27; Job 42:6; Isa 6:5

Then Jesus said to Simon, "Don't be afraid; from now on you will fish for people." ¹¹So they pulled their boats up on shore, left everything and followed him.   Mt 4:18-22; Mk 1:16-20; Jn 1:40-42

Jesus Heals a Man With Leprosy

5:12-14pp — Mt 8:2-4; Mk 1:40-44

¹²While Jesus was in one of the towns, a man came along who was covered with leprosy.ᵃ When he saw Jesus, he fell with his face to the ground and begged him, "Lord, if you are willing, you can make me clean."   Mt 8:2

¹³Jesus reached out his hand and touched the man. "I am willing," he said. "Be clean!" And immediately the leprosy left him.

¹⁴Then Jesus ordered him, "Don't tell anyone, but go, show yourself to the priest and offer the sacrifices that Moses command-ed for your cleansing, as a testimony to them."   Mt 8:2-4; Mk 1:40-44

¹⁵Yet the news about him spread all the more, so that crowds of people came to hear him and to be healed of their sicknesses. ¹⁶But Jesus often withdrew to lonely places and prayed.   Mt 14:23; Lk 3:21

Jesus Forgives and Heals a Paralyzed Man

5:18-26pp — Mt 9:2-8; Mk 2:3-12

¹⁷One day Jesus was teaching, and Pharisees and teachers of the law were sitting there. They had come from every village of Galilee and from Judea and Jerusalem. And the power of the Lord was with Jesus to heal the sick. ¹⁸Some men came carrying a paralyzed man on a mat and tried to take him into the house to lay him before Jesus. ¹⁹When they could not find a way to do this because of the crowd, they went up on the roof and lowered him on his mat through the tiles into the middle of the crowd, right in front of Jesus.   Mk 5:30; Lk 6:19

²⁰When Jesus saw their faith, he said, "Friend, your sins are forgiven."   Lk 7:48-49

²¹The Pharisees and the teachers of the law began thinking to themselves, "Who is this fellow who speaks blasphemy? Who can forgive sins but God alone?"   Isa 43:25

ᵃ 12 The Greek word traditionally translated *leprosy* was used for various diseases affecting the skin.

22 Jesus knew what they were thinking and asked, "Why are you thinking these things in your hearts? 23 Which is easier: to say, 'Your sins are forgiven,' or to say, 'Get up and walk'? 24 But I want you to know that the Son of Man has authority on earth to forgive sins." So he said to the paralyzed man, "I tell you, get up, take your mat and go home." 25 Immediately he stood up in front of them, took what he had been lying on and went home praising God. 26 Everyone was amazed and gave praise to God. They were filled with awe and said, "We have seen remarkable things today."   Mt 9:2-8; Mk 2:3-12

Jesus Calls Levi and Eats With Sinners

5:27-32pp — Mt 9:9-13; Mk 2:14-17

27 After this, Jesus went out and saw a tax collector by the name of Levi sitting at his tax booth. "Follow me," Jesus said to him, 28 and Levi got up, left everything and followed him.   Mt 4:19

29 Then Levi held a great banquet for Jesus at his house, and a large crowd of tax collectors and others were eating with them. 30 But the Pharisees and the teachers of the law who belonged to their sect complained to his disciples, "Why do you eat and drink with tax collectors and sinners?"   Lk 15:1; Ac 23:9

31 Jesus answered them, "It is not the healthy who need a doc-tor, but the sick. 32 I have not come to call the righteous, but sinners to repentance."   Mt 9:9-13; Mk 2:14-17

Jesus Questioned About Fasting

5:33-39pp — Mt 9:14-17; Mk 2:18-22

33 They said to him, "John's disciples often fast and pray, and so do the disciples of the Pharisees, but yours go on eating and drinking."   Lk 7:18; Jn 1:35; 3:25-26

34 Jesus answered, "Can you make the friends of the bridegroom fast while he is with them? 35 But the time will come when the bridegroom will be taken from them; in those days they will fast."   Lk 17:22; Jn 16:5-7

36 He told them this parable: "No one tears a piece out of a new garment to patch an old one. Otherwise, they will have torn the new garment, and the patch from the new will not match the old. 37 And no one pours new wine into old wineskins. Otherwise, the new wine will burst the skins; the wine will run out and the wineskins will be ruined. 38 No, new wine must be poured into new wineskins. 39 And no one after drinking old wine wants the new, for they say, 'The old is better.'"   Mt 9:14-17; Mk 2:18-22

Jesus Is Lord of the Sabbath

6:1-11pp — Mt 12:1-14; Mk 2:23-3:6

6 One Sabbath Jesus was going through the grainfields, and his disciples began to pick some heads of grain, rub them in

their hands and eat the kernels. ²Some of the Pharisees asked, "Why are you doing what is unlawful on the Sabbath?" Dt 23:25

³Jesus answered them, "Have you never read what David did when he and his companions were hungry? ⁴He entered the house of God, and taking the consecrated bread, he ate what is lawful only for priests to eat. And he also gave some to his companions." ⁵Then Jesus said to them, "The Son of Man is Lord of the Sabbath." Lev 24:5,9; 1Sa 21:6

⁶On another Sabbath he went into the synagogue and was teaching, and a man was there whose right hand was shriveled. ⁷The Pharisees and the teachers of the law were looking for a reason to accuse Jesus, so they watched him closely to see if he would heal on the Sabbath. ⁸But Jesus knew what they were thinking and said to the man with the shriveled hand, "Get up and stand in front of everyone." So he got up and stood there. Mt 12:2,10

⁹Then Jesus said to them, "I ask you, which is lawful on the Sabbath: to do good or to do evil, to save life or to destroy it?"

¹⁰He looked around at them all, and then said to the man, "Stretch out your hand." He did so, and his hand was completely restored. ¹¹But the Pharisees and the teachers of the law were fu-

rious and began to discuss with one another what they might do to Jesus. Mt 12:1-14; Mk 2:23-3:6

The Twelve Apostles

6:13-16pp — Mt 10:2-4; Mk 3:16-19; Ac 1:13

¹²One of those days Jesus went out to a mountainside to pray, and spent the night praying to God. ¹³When morning came, he called his disciples to him and chose twelve of them, whom he also designated apostles: ¹⁴Simon (whom he named Peter), his brother Andrew, James, John, Philip, Bartholomew, ¹⁵Matthew, Thomas, James son of Alphaeus, Simon who was called the Zealot, ¹⁶Judas son of James, and Judas Iscariot, who became a traitor. Mt 10:2-4; Mk 3:16-19; Ac 1:13

Blessings and Woes

6:20-23pp — Mt 5:3-12

¹⁷He went down with them and stood on a level place. A large crowd of his disciples was there and a great number of people from all over Judea, from Jerusalem, and from the coastal region around Tyre and Sidon, ¹⁸who had come to hear him and to be healed of their diseases. Those troubled by impure spirits were cured, ¹⁹and the people all tried to touch him, because power was coming from him and healing them all. Mt 14:36; Lk 5:17

²⁰Looking at his disciples, he said:

"Blessed are you who are
poor,
for yours is the kingdom of
God.   Mt 25:34
²¹ Blessed are you who hunger
now,
for you will be
satisfied.   Isa 55:1-2; Mt 5:6
Blessed are you who weep
now,
for you will laugh.   Isa 61:2-3
²² Blessed are you when people
hate you,
when they exclude you and
insult you   Jn 9:22; 16:2
and reject your name as
evil,
because of the Son of
Man.   Jn 15:21

²³ "Rejoice in that day and leap for joy, because great is your reward in heaven. For that is how their ancestors treated the prophets.   Mt 5:12

²⁴ "But woe to you who are
rich,   Jas 5:1
for you have already
received your
comfort.   Lk 16:25
²⁵ Woe to you who are well fed
now,
for you will go hungry. Isa 65:13
Woe to you who laugh now,
for you will mourn and
weep.   Pr 14:13
²⁶ Woe to you when everyone
speaks well of you,
for that is how their
ancestors treated the
false prophets.   Mt 7:15

Love for Enemies
6:29,30pp — Mt 5:39-42

²⁷ "But to you who are listening I say: Love your enemies, do good to those who hate you, ²⁸ bless those who curse you, pray for those who mistreat you. ²⁹ If someone slaps you on one cheek, turn to them the other also. If someone takes your coat, do not withhold your shirt from them. ³⁰ Give to everyone who asks you, and if anyone takes what belongs to you, do not demand it back. ³¹ Do to others as you would have them do to you.   Mt 5:39-42

³² "If you love those who love you, what credit is that to you? Even sinners love those who love them. ³³ And if you do good to those who are good to you, what credit is that to you? Even sinners do that. ³⁴ And if you lend to those from whom you expect repayment, what credit is that to you? Even sinners lend to sinners, expecting to be repaid in full. ³⁵ But love your enemies, do good to them, and lend to them without expecting to get anything back. Then your reward will be great, and you will be children of the Most High, because he is kind to the ungrateful and wicked. ³⁶ Be merciful, just as your Father is merciful.   Jas 2:13; Mt 5:48

Judging Others
6:37-42pp — Mt 7:1-5

³⁷ "Do not judge, and you will not be judged. Do not condemn,

and you will not be condemned. Forgive, and you will be forgiven. [38]Give, and it will be given to you. A good measure, pressed down, shaken together and running over, will be poured into your lap. For with the measure you use, it will be measured to you." Mt 7:1; Mk 4:24

[39]He also told them this parable: "Can the blind lead the blind? Will they not both fall into a pit? [40]The student is not above the teacher, but everyone who is fully trained will be like their teacher. Mt 10:24; Jn 13:16

[41]"Why do you look at the speck of sawdust in your brother's eye and pay no attention to the plank in your own eye? [42]How can you say to your brother, 'Brother, let me take the speck out of your eye,' when you yourself fail to see the plank in your own eye? You hypocrite, first take the plank out of your eye, and then you will see clearly to remove the speck from your brother's eye. Mt 7:1-5

A Tree and Its Fruit
6:43,44pp — Mt 7:16,18,20

[43]"No good tree bears bad fruit, nor does a bad tree bear good fruit. [44]Each tree is recognized by its own fruit. People do not pick figs from thornbushes, or grapes from briers. [45]A good man brings good things out of the good stored up in his heart, and an evil man brings evil things out of the evil stored up in

his heart. For the mouth speaks what the heart is full of. Mt 12:33-35

The Wise and Foolish Builders
6:47-49pp — Mt 7:24-27

[46]"Why do you call me, 'Lord, Lord,' and do not do what I say? [47]As for everyone who comes to me and hears my words and puts them into practice, I will show you what they are like. [48]They are like a man building a house, who dug down deep and laid the foundation on rock. When a flood came, the torrent struck that house but could not shake it, because it was well built. [49]But the one who hears my words and does not put them into practice is like a man who built a house on the ground without a foundation. The moment the torrent struck that house, it collapsed and its destruction was complete." Mt 7:24-27

The Faith of the Centurion
7:1-10pp — Mt 8:5-13

7 When Jesus had finished saying all this to the people who were listening, he entered Capernaum. [2]There a centurion's servant, whom his master valued highly, was sick and about to die. [3]The centurion heard of Jesus and sent some elders of the Jews to him, asking him to come and heal his servant. [4]When they came to Jesus, they pleaded earnestly with him, "This man deserves to have you do this,

[5]because he loves our nation and has built our synagogue." [6]So Jesus went with them.   Mt 7:28

He was not far from the house when the centurion sent friends to say to him: "Lord, don't trouble yourself, for I do not deserve to have you come under my roof. [7]That is why I did not even consider myself worthy to come to you. But say the word, and my servant will be healed. [8]For I myself am a man under authority, with soldiers under me. I tell this one, 'Go,' and he goes; and that one, 'Come,' and he comes. I say to my servant, 'Do this,' and he does it."   Ps 107:20

[9]When Jesus heard this, he was amazed at him, and turning to the crowd following him, he said, "I tell you, I have not found such great faith even in Israel." [10]Then the men who had been sent returned to the house and found the servant well.   Mt 8:5-13

Jesus Raises a Widow's Son

7:11-16Ref — 1Ki 17:17-24; 2Ki 4:32-37; Mk 5:21-24,35-43; Jn 11:1-44

[11]Soon afterward, Jesus went to a town called Nain, and his disciples and a large crowd went along with him. [12]As he approached the town gate, a dead person was being carried out — the only son of his mother, and she was a widow. And a large crowd from the town was with her. [13]When the Lord saw her, his heart went out to her and he said, "Don't cry." Jn 11:1-44

[14]Then he went up and touched the bier they were carrying him on, and the bearers stood still. He said, "Young man, I say to you, get up!" [15]The dead man sat up and began to talk, and Jesus gave him back to his mother.   1Ki 17:17-24

[16]They were all filled with awe and praised God. "A great prophet has appeared among us," they said. "God has come to help his people." [17]This news about Jesus spread throughout Judea and the surrounding country. Mk 5:21-24,35

Jesus and John the Baptist

7:18–35pp — Mt 11:2-19

[18]John's disciples told him about all these things. Calling two of them, [19]he sent them to the Lord to ask, "Are you the one who is to come, or should we expect someone else?"   Mt 3:1; Lk 5:33

[20]When the men came to Jesus, they said, "John the Baptist sent us to you to ask, 'Are you the one who is to come, or should we expect someone else?'"

[21]At that very time Jesus cured many who had diseases, sicknesses and evil spirits, and gave sight to many who were blind. [22]So he replied to the messengers, "Go back and report to John what you have seen and heard: The blind receive sight, the lame walk, those who have leprosy[a]

[a] 22 The Greek word traditionally translated leprosy was used for various diseases affecting the skin.

are cleansed, the deaf hear, the dead are raised, and the good news is proclaimed to the poor. [23] Blessed is anyone who does not stumble on account of me." Isa 29:18-19; Lk 4:18

[24] After John's messengers left, Jesus began to speak to the crowd about John: "What did you go out into the wilderness to see? A reed swayed by the wind? [25] If not, what did you go out to see? A man dressed in fine clothes? No, those who wear expensive clothes and indulge in luxury are in palaces. [26] But what did you go out to see? A prophet? Yes, I tell you, and more than a prophet. [27] This is the one about whom it is written: Mt 11:9

" 'I will send my messenger
      ahead of you,
   who will prepare your way
      before you.'[a]

[28] I tell you, among those born of women there is no one greater than John; yet the one who is least in the kingdom of God is greater than he." Mt 3:2; 11:10; Mk 1:2

[29] (All the people, even the tax collectors, when they heard Jesus' words, acknowledged that God's way was right, because they had been baptized by John. [30] But the Pharisees and the experts in the law rejected God's purpose for themselves, because they had not been baptized by John.) Mt 22:35; Lk 3:12

[31] Jesus went on to say, "To what, then, can I compare the people of this generation? What are they like? [32] They are like children sitting in the marketplace and calling out to each other:

" 'We played the pipe for you,
      and you did not dance;
   we sang a dirge,
      and you did not cry.'

[33] For John the Baptist came neither eating bread nor drinking wine, and you say, 'He has a demon.' [34] The Son of Man came eating and drinking, and you say, 'Here is a glutton and a drunkard, a friend of tax collectors and sinners.' [35] But wisdom is proved right by all her children." Mt 11:2-19

Jesus Anointed by a Sinful Woman

7:37-39Ref — Mt 26:6-13; Mk 14:3-9; Jn 12:1-8
7:41,42Ref — Mt 18:23-34

[36] When one of the Pharisees invited Jesus to have dinner with him, he went to the Pharisee's house and reclined at the table. [37] A woman in that town who lived a sinful life learned that Jesus was eating at the Pharisee's house, so she came there with an alabaster jar of perfume. [38] As she stood behind him at his feet weeping, she began to wet his feet with her tears. Then she wiped them with her hair, kissed

---

[a] 27 Mal. 3:1

them and poured perfume on them.

39 When the Pharisee who had invited him saw this, he said to himself, "If this man were a prophet, he would know who is touching him and what kind of woman she is — that she is a sinner." Mt 21:11

40 Jesus answered him, "Simon, I have something to tell you."

"Tell me, teacher," he said.

41 "Two people owed money to a certain moneylender. One owed him five hundred denarii,[a] and the other fifty. **42** Neither of them had the money to pay him back, so he forgave the debts of both. Now which of them will love him more?"

43 Simon replied, "I suppose the one who had the bigger debt forgiven."

"You have judged correctly," Jesus said.

44 Then he turned toward the woman and said to Simon, "Do you see this woman? I came into your house. You did not give me any water for my feet, but she wet my feet with her tears and wiped them with her hair. **45** You did not give me a kiss, but this woman, from the time I entered, has not stopped kissing my feet. **46** You did not put oil on my head, but she has poured perfume on my feet. **47** Therefore, I tell you, her many sins have been forgiven — as her great love has shown. But

whoever has been forgiven little loves little." Ge 18:4; Ps 23:5; 1Ti 5:10

48 Then Jesus said to her, "Your sins are forgiven." Mt 9:2

49 The other guests began to say among themselves, "Who is this who even forgives sins?"

50 Jesus said to the woman, "Your faith has saved you; go in peace." Mk 5:34; Lk 8:48; Ac 15:33

The Parable of the Sower

8:4-15pp — Mt 13:2-23; Mk 4:1-20

8 After this, Jesus traveled about from one town and village to another, proclaiming the good news of the kingdom of God. The Twelve were with him, **2** and also some women who had been cured of evil spirits and diseases: Mary (called Magdalene) from whom seven demons had come out; **3** Joanna the wife of Chuza, the manager of Herod's household; Susanna; and many others. These women were helping to support them out of their own means. Mt 4:23; 14:1; 27:55-56

4 While a large crowd was gathering and people were coming to Jesus from town after town, he told this parable: **5** "A farmer went out to sow his seed. As he was scattering the seed, some fell along the path; it was trampled on, and the birds ate it up. **6** Some fell on rocky ground, and when it came up, the plants withered because they had no moisture. **7** Other seed fell among

---

[a] 41 A denarius was the usual daily wage of a day laborer (see Matt. 20:2).

thorns, which grew up with it and choked the plants. ⁸ Still other seed fell on good soil. It came up and yielded a crop, a hundred times more than was sown."

When he said this, he called out, "Whoever has ears to hear, let them hear." Mt 11:15

⁹ His disciples asked him what this parable meant. ¹⁰ He said, "The knowledge of the secrets of the kingdom of God has been given to you, but to others I speak in parables, so that, Mt 13:11

" 'though seeing, they may not
    see;
though hearing, they may
    not understand.'ᵃ Isa 6:9

¹¹ "This is the meaning of the parable: The seed is the word of God. ¹² Those along the path are the ones who hear, and then the devil comes and takes away the word from their hearts, so that they may not believe and be saved. ¹³ Those on the rocky ground are the ones who receive the word with joy when they hear it, but they have no root. They believe for a while, but in the time of testing they fall away. ¹⁴ The seed that fell among thorns stands for those who hear, but as they go on their way they are choked by life's worries, riches and pleasures, and they do not mature. ¹⁵ But the seed on good soil stands for those with a noble and good heart, who hear the word, retain

it, and by persevering produce a crop. Mt 13:2-23; Mk 4:1-20

A Lamp on a Stand

¹⁶ "No one lights a lamp and hides it in a clay jar or puts it under a bed. Instead, they put it on a stand, so that those who come in can see the light. ¹⁷ For there is nothing hidden that will not be disclosed, and nothing concealed that will not be known or brought out into the open. ¹⁸ Therefore consider carefully how you listen. Whoever has will be given more; whoever does not have, even what they think they have will be taken from them." Mt 5:15; Mk 4:22; Lk 19:26

Jesus' Mother and Brothers
8:19-21pp — Mt 12:46-50; Mk 3:31-35

¹⁹ Now Jesus' mother and brothers came to see him, but they were not able to get near him because of the crowd. ²⁰ Someone told him, "Your mother and brothers are standing outside, wanting to see you." Jn 7:5

²¹ He replied, "My mother and brothers are those who hear God's word and put it into practice." Mt 12:46-50; Mk 3:31-35

Jesus Calms the Storm
8:22-25pp — Mt 8:23-27; Mk 4:36-41
8:22-25Ref — Mk 6:47-52; Jn 6:16-21

²² One day Jesus said to his disciples, "Let us go over to the other side of the lake." So they got into a boat and set out. ²³ As they

ᵃ 10 Isaiah 6:9

sailed, he fell asleep. A squall came down on the lake, so that the boat was being swamped, and they were in great danger.

²⁴ The disciples went and woke him, saying, "Master, Master, we're going to drown!" Mk 6:47-52

He got up and rebuked the wind and the raging waters; the storm subsided, and all was calm. ²⁵ "Where is your faith?" he asked his disciples. Mt 8:23-27

In fear and amazement they asked one another, "Who is this? He commands even the winds and the water, and they obey him." Mk 4:36-41

Jesus Restores a Demon-Possessed Man

8:26-37pp — Mt 8:28-34
8:26-39pp — Mk 5:1-20

²⁶ They sailed to the region of the Gerasenes,ᵃ which is across the lake from Galilee. ²⁷ When Jesus stepped ashore, he was met by a demon-possessed man from the town. For a long time this man had not worn clothes or lived in a house, but had lived in the tombs. ²⁸ When he saw Jesus, he cried out and fell at his feet, shouting at the top of his voice, "What do you want with me, Jesus, Son of the Most High God? I beg you, don't torture me!" ²⁹ For Jesus had commanded the impure spirit to come out of the man. Many times it had seized him, and though he was chained hand and foot and kept under guard, he had broken his chains and had been driven by the demon into solitary places. Mt 8:29; Mk 5:7

³⁰ Jesus asked him, "What is your name?"

"Legion," he replied, because many demons had gone into him. ³¹ And they begged Jesus repeatedly not to order them to go into the Abyss. Rev 9:1-2,11; 11:7

³² A large herd of pigs was feeding there on the hillside. The demons begged Jesus to let them go into the pigs, and he gave them permission. ³³ When the demons came out of the man, they went into the pigs, and the herd rushed down the steep bank into the lake and was drowned. ver 22-23

³⁴ When those tending the pigs saw what had happened, they ran off and reported this in the town and countryside, ³⁵ and the people went out to see what had happened. When they came to Jesus, they found the man from whom the demons had gone out, sitting at Jesus' feet, dressed and in his right mind; and they were afraid. ³⁶ Those who had seen it told the people how the demon-possessed man had been cured. ³⁷ Then all the people of the region of the Gerasenes asked Jesus to leave them, because they were overcome with fear. So he got into the boat and left. Mt 8:28-34

³⁸ The man from whom the demons had gone out begged to

ᵃ 26 Some manuscripts *Gadarenes*; other manuscripts *Gergesenes*; also in verse 37 go with him, but Jesus sent him away, saying, **39** "Return home and tell how much God has done for you." So the man went away and told all over town how much Jesus had done for him. Mk 5:1-20

Jesus Raises a Dead Girl and Heals a Sick Woman

8:40-56pp — Mt 9:18-26; Mk 5:22-43

40 Now when Jesus returned, a crowd welcomed him, for they were all expecting him. **41** Then a man named Jairus, a synagogue leader, came and fell at Jesus' feet, pleading with him to come to his house **42** because his only daughter, a girl of about twelve, was dying. Mk 5:22

As Jesus was on his way, the crowds almost crushed him. **43** And a woman was there who had been subject to bleeding for twelve years,[a] but no one could heal her. **44** She came up behind him and touched the edge of his cloak, and immediately her bleeding stopped. Lev 15:25-30; Mt 9:20

45 "Who touched me?" Jesus asked.

When they all denied it, Peter said, "Master, the people are crowding and pressing against you." Lk 5:5

46 But Jesus said, "Someone touched me; I know that power has gone out from me." Lk 5:17; 6:19

47 Then the woman, seeing that she could not go unnoticed, came trembling and fell at his feet. In the presence of all the people, she told why she had touched him and how she had been instantly healed. **48** Then he said to her, "Daughter, your faith has healed you. Go in peace." Mt 9:22; Ac 15:33

49 While Jesus was still speaking, someone came from the house of Jairus, the synagogue leader. "Your daughter is dead," he said. "Don't bother the teacher anymore." ver 41

50 Hearing this, Jesus said to Jairus, "Don't be afraid; just believe, and she will be healed."

51 When he arrived at the house of Jairus, he did not let anyone go in with him except Peter, John and James, and the child's father and mother. **52** Meanwhile, all the people were wailing and mourning for her. "Stop wailing," Jesus said. "She is not dead but asleep."

53 They laughed at him, knowing that she was dead. **54** But he took her by the hand and said, "My child, get up!" **55** Her spirit returned, and at once she stood up. Then Jesus told them to give her something to eat. **56** Her parents were astonished, but he ordered them not to tell anyone what had happened. Mt 9:18-26; Mk 5:22-43

Jesus Sends Out the Twelve

9:3-5pp — Mt 10:9-15; Mk 6:8-11
9:7-9pp — Mt 14:1,2; Mk 6:14-16

9 When Jesus had called the Twelve together, he gave them power and authority to

[a] 43 Many manuscripts *years, and she had spent all she had on doctors*

drive out all demons and to cure diseases, ²and he sent them out to proclaim the kingdom of God and to heal the sick. ³He told them: "Take nothing for the journey— no staff, no bag, no bread, no money, no extra shirt. ⁴Whatever house you enter, stay there until you leave that town. ⁵If people do not welcome you, leave their town and shake the dust off your feet as a testimony against them." ⁶So they set out and went from village to village, proclaiming the good news and healing people everywhere.   Mt 10:9-15; Mk 6:8-11

⁷Now Herod the tetrarch heard about all that was going on. And he was perplexed because some were saying that John had been raised from the dead, ⁸others that Elijah had appeared, and still others that one of the prophets of long ago had come back to life. ⁹But Herod said, "I beheaded John. Who, then, is this I hear such things about?" And he tried to see him.   Mt 14:1-2; Mk 6:14-16

Jesus Feeds the Five Thousand

9:10-17pp — Mt 14:13-21; Mk 6:32-44; Jn 6:5-13
9:13-17Ref — 2Ki 4:42-44

¹⁰When the apostles returned, they reported to Jesus what they had done. Then he took them with him and they withdrew by themselves to a town called Bethsaida, ¹¹but the crowds learned about it and followed him. He welcomed them and spoke to them about the kingdom of God, and healed those who needed healing.   Mt 11:21; Mk 6:30

¹²Late in the afternoon the Twelve came to him and said, "Send the crowd away so they can go to the surrounding villages and countryside and find food and lodging, because we are in a remote place here."

¹³He replied, "You give them something to eat."   Mt 14:13-21

They answered, "We have only five loaves of bread and two fish— unless we go and buy food for all this crowd." ¹⁴(About five thousand men were there.)   Jn 6:5-13

But he said to his disciples, "Have them sit down in groups of about fifty each." ¹⁵The disciples did so, and everyone sat down. ¹⁶Taking the five loaves and the two fish and looking up to heaven, he gave thanks and broke them. Then he gave them to the disciples to distribute to the people. ¹⁷They all ate and were satisfied, and the disciples picked up twelve basketfuls of broken pieces that were left over.   2Ki 4:42-44

Peter Declares That Jesus Is the Messiah

9:18-20pp — Mt 16:13-16; Mk 8:27-29
9:22-27pp — Mt 16:21-28; Mk 8:31–9:1

¹⁸Once when Jesus was praying in private and his disciples were with him, he asked them, "Who do the crowds say I am?"   Lk 3:21

¹⁹They replied, "Some say John

the Baptist; others say Elijah; and still others, that one of the prophets of long ago has come back to life." Mt 3:1

20 "But what about you?" he asked. "Who do you say I am?"

Peter answered, "God's Messiah." Mk 8:27-29; Jn 6:66-69

Jesus Predicts His Death

21 Jesus strictly warned them not to tell this to anyone. 22 And he said, "The Son of Man must suffer many things and be rejected by the elders, the chief priests and the teachers of the law, and he must be killed and on the third day be raised to life." Mt 16:20-21; Mk 8:30

23 Then he said to them all: "Whoever wants to be my disciple must deny themselves and take up their cross daily and follow me. 24 For whoever wants to save their life will lose it, but whoever loses their life for me will save it. 25 What good is it for someone to gain the whole world, and yet lose or forfeit their very self? 26 Whoever is ashamed of me and my words, the Son of Man will be ashamed of them when he comes in his glory and in the glory of the Father and of the holy angels.

27 "Truly I tell you, some who are standing here will not taste death before they see the kingdom of God." Mt 16:21-28; Mk 8:31-9:1

The Transfiguration
9:28-36pp — Mt 17:1-8; Mk 9:2-8

28 About eight days after Jesus said this, he took Peter, John and James with him and went up onto a mountain to pray. 29 As he was praying, the appearance of his face changed, and his clothes became as bright as a flash of lightning. 30 Two men, Moses and Elijah, appeared in glorious splendor, talking with Jesus. 31 They spoke about his departure,[a] which he was about to bring to fulfillment at Jerusalem. 32 Peter and his companions were very sleepy, but when they became fully awake, they saw his glory and the two men standing with him. 33 As the men were leaving Jesus, Peter said to him, "Master, it is good for us to be here. Let us put up three shelters — one for you, one for Moses and one for Elijah." (He did not know what he was saying.) Lk 3:21; 2Pe 1:15

34 While he was speaking, a cloud appeared and covered them, and they were afraid as they entered the cloud. 35 A voice came from the cloud, saying, "This is my Son, whom I have chosen; listen to him." 36 When the voice had spoken, they found that Jesus was alone. The disciples kept this to themselves and did not tell anyone at that time what they had seen. Mt 17:1-8; Mk 9:2-8

a 31 Greek *exodus*

Jesus Heals a Demon-Possessed Boy

9:37-42,43-45pp — Mt 17:14-18,22,23;
Mk 9:14-27,30-32

[37] The next day, when they came down from the mountain, a large crowd met him. [38] A man in the crowd called out, "Teacher, I beg you to look at my son, for he is my only child. [39] A spirit seizes him and he suddenly screams; it throws him into convulsions so that he foams at the mouth. It scarcely ever leaves him and is destroying him. [40] I begged your disciples to drive it out, but they could not." Mt 17:14-18,22-23

[41] "You unbelieving and perverse generation," Jesus replied, "how long shall I stay with you and put up with you? Bring your son here." Dt 32:5

[42] Even while the boy was coming, the demon threw him to the ground in a convulsion. But Jesus rebuked the impure spirit, healed the boy and gave him back to his father. [43] And they were all amazed at the greatness of God.

Jesus Predicts His Death a Second Time

While everyone was marveling at all that Jesus did, he said to his disciples, [44] "Listen carefully to what I am about to tell you: The Son of Man is going to be delivered into the hands of men." [45] But they did not understand what this meant. It was hidden from them, so that they did not grasp it, and they were afraid to ask him about it. Mk 9:14-27,30-32

[46] An argument started among the disciples as to which of them would be the greatest. [47] Jesus, knowing their thoughts, took a little child and had him stand beside him. [48] Then he said to them, "Whoever welcomes this little child in my name welcomes me; and whoever welcomes me welcomes the one who sent me. For it is the one who is least among you all who is the greatest." Mt 18:1-5

[49] "Master," said John, "we saw someone driving out demons in your name and we tried to stop him, because he is not one of us."

[50] "Do not stop him," Jesus said, "for whoever is not against you is for you." Mt 12:30; Lk 11:23

Samaritan Opposition

[51] As the time approached for him to be taken up to heaven, Jesus resolutely set out for Jerusalem. [52] And he sent messengers on ahead, who went into a Samaritan village to get things ready for him; [53] but the people there did not welcome him, because he was heading for Jerusalem. [54] When the disciples James and John saw this, they asked, "Lord, do you want us to call fire down from heaven to destroy them[a]?" [55] But Jesus turned and rebuked them. [56] Then he and his disciples went to another village. 2Ki 1:10,12; Mk 16:19; Lk 13:22

[a] 54 Some manuscripts *them, just as Elijah did*

The Cost of Following Jesus

9:57-60pp — Mt 8:19-22

⁵⁷As they were walking along the road, a man said to him, "I will follow you wherever you go."

⁵⁸Jesus replied, "Foxes have dens and birds have nests, but the Son of Man has no place to lay his head."

⁵⁹He said to another man, "Follow me."

But he replied, "Lord, first let me go and bury my father."

⁶⁰Jesus said to him, "Let the dead bury their own dead, but you go and proclaim the kingdom of God." Mt 8:19-22

⁶¹Still another said, "I will follow you, Lord; but first let me go back and say goodbye to my family." 1Ki 19:20

⁶²Jesus replied, "No one who puts a hand to the plow and looks back is fit for service in the kingdom of God."

Jesus Sends Out the Seventy-Two

10:4-12pp — Lk 9:3-5
10:13-15,21,22pp — Mt 11:21-23,25-27
10:23,24pp — Mt 13:16,17

10 After this the Lord appointed seventy-two[a] others and sent them two by two ahead of him to every town and place where he was about to go. ²He told them, "The harvest is plentiful, but the workers are few. Ask the Lord of the harvest, therefore, to send out workers into his harvest field. ³Go! I am sending you out like lambs among wolves. ⁴Do not take a purse or bag or sandals; and do not greet anyone on the road. Mt 9:37-38; 10:16; Jn 4:35

⁵"When you enter a house, first say, 'Peace to this house.' ⁶If someone who promotes peace is there, your peace will rest on them; if not, it will return to you. ⁷Stay there, eating and drinking whatever they give you, for the worker deserves his wages. Do not move around from house to house. Mt 10:10; 1Co 9:14; 1Ti 5:18

⁸"When you enter a town and are welcomed, eat what is offered to you. ⁹Heal the sick who are there and tell them, 'The kingdom of God has come near to you.' ¹⁰But when you enter a town and are not welcomed, go into its streets and say, ¹¹'Even the dust of your town we wipe from our feet as a warning to you. Yet be sure of this: The kingdom of God has come near.' ¹²I tell you, it will be more bearable on that day for Sodom than for that town. Lk 9:3-5; 1Co 10:27

¹³"Woe to you, Chorazin! Woe to you, Bethsaida! For if the miracles that were performed in you had been performed in Tyre and Sidon, they would have repented long ago, sitting in sackcloth and ashes. ¹⁴But it will be more bearable for Tyre and Sidon at the judgment than for you. ¹⁵And you, Capernaum, will you be

_____

[a] 1 Some manuscripts seventy; also in verse 17

lifted to the heavens? No, you will go down to Hades.[a]   Mt 4:13; Rev 11:3

16 "Whoever listens to you listens to me; whoever rejects you rejects me; but whoever rejects me rejects him who sent me."

17 The seventy-two returned with joy and said, "Lord, even the demons submit to us in your name."   Mk 16:17

18 He replied, "I saw Satan fall like lightning from heaven. 19 I have given you authority to trample on snakes and scorpions and to overcome all the power of the enemy; nothing will harm you. 20 However, do not rejoice that the spirits submit to you, but rejoice that your names are written in heaven."Ex 32:32; Heb 12:23; Rev 13:8

21 At that time Jesus, full of joy through the Holy Spirit, said, "I praise you, Father, Lord of heaven and earth, because you have hidden these things from the wise and learned, and revealed them to little children. Yes, Father, for this is what you were pleased to do.   1Co 1:26-29

22 "All things have been committed to me by my Father. No one knows who the Son is except the Father, and no one knows who the Father is except the Son and those to whom the Son chooses to reveal him."   Mt 11:21-23,25-27

23 Then he turned to his disciples and said privately, "Blessed are the eyes that see what you see. 24 For I tell you that many prophets and kings wanted to see what you see but did not see it, and to hear what you hear but did not hear it."   Mt 13:16-17

The Parable of the Good Samaritan

10:25-28pp — Mt 22:34-40; Mk 12:28-31

25 On one occasion an expert in the law stood up to test Jesus. "Teacher," he asked, "what must I do to inherit eternal life?"   Mt 19:16

26 "What is written in the Law?" he replied. "How do you read it?"

27 He answered, " 'Love the Lord your God with all your heart and with all your soul and with all your strength and with all your mind'[b]; and, 'Love your neighbor as yourself.'[c]"   Lev 19:18; Dt 6:5

28 "You have answered correctly," Jesus replied. "Do this and you will live."Mt 22:34-40; Mk 12:28-31

29 But he wanted to justify himself, so he asked Jesus, "And who is my neighbor?"   Lk 16:15

30 In reply Jesus said: "A man was going down from Jerusalem to Jericho, when he was attacked by robbers. They stripped him of his clothes, beat him and went away, leaving him half dead. 31 A priest happened to be going down the same road, and when he saw the man, he passed by on the other side. 32 So too, a Levite, when he came to the place and saw him, passed by on the other side. 33 But a Samaritan, as he traveled, came where the man was; and when

---

[a] 15 That is, the realm of the dead   [b] 27 Deut. 6:5   [c] 27 Lev. 19:18

he saw him, he took pity on him. ³⁴He went to him and bandaged his wounds, pouring on oil and wine. Then he put the man on his own donkey, brought him to an inn and took care of him. ³⁵The next day he took out two denarii*ᵃ* and gave them to the innkeeper. 'Look after him,' he said, 'and when I return, I will reimburse you for any extra expense you may have.' Mt 10:5; Lev 21:1-3

³⁶"Which of these three do you think was a neighbor to the man who fell into the hands of robbers?"

³⁷The expert in the law replied, "The one who had mercy on him."

Jesus told him, "Go and do likewise."

At the Home of Martha and Mary

³⁸As Jesus and his disciples were on their way, he came to a village where a woman named Martha opened her home to him. ³⁹She had a sister called Mary, who sat at the Lord's feet listening to what he said. ⁴⁰But Martha was distracted by all the preparations that had to be made. She came to him and asked, "Lord, don't you care that my sister has left me to do the work by myself? Tell her to help me!" Lk 8:35; Jn 11:1

⁴¹"Martha, Martha," the Lord answered, "you are worried and upset about many things, ⁴²but few things are needed—or indeed only one.*ᵇ* Mary has chosen what is better, and it will not be taken away from her." Ps 27:4

Jesus' Teaching on Prayer

11:2-4pp — Mt 6:9-13
11:9-13pp — Mt 7:7-11

11 One day Jesus was praying in a certain place. When he finished, one of his disciples said to him, "Lord, teach us to pray, just as John taught his disciples." Lk 3:21; Jn 13:13

²He said to them, "When you pray, say:

" 'Father,*ᶜ*
hallowed be your name,
your kingdom come.*ᵈ* Mt 3:2
³Give us each day our daily bread.
⁴Forgive us our sins,
for we also forgive
everyone who sins
against us.*ᵉ* Mt 18:35
And lead us not into
temptation.*ᶠ* '" Mt 6:9-13

⁵Then Jesus said to them, "Suppose you have a friend, and you go to him at midnight and say, 'Friend, lend me three loaves of bread; ⁶a friend of mine on a journey has come to

---

ᵃ 35 A denarius was the usual daily wage of a day laborer (see Matt. 20:2). *ᵇ 42* Some manuscripts *but only one thing is needed* *ᶜ 2* Some manuscripts *Our Father in heaven* *ᵈ 2* Some manuscripts *come. May your will be done on earth as it is in heaven.* *ᵉ 4* Greek *everyone who is indebted to us* *ᶠ 4* Some manuscripts *temptation, but deliver us from the evil one* me, and I have no food to offer him.' ⁷And suppose the one inside answers, 'Don't bother me. The door is already locked, and my children and I are in bed. I can't get up and give you anything.' ⁸I tell you, even though he will not get up and give you the bread because of friendship, yet because of your shameless audacity*ᵃ* he will surely get up and give you as much as you need. Lk 18:1-6

⁹"So I say to you: Ask and it will be given to you; seek and you will find; knock and the door will be opened to you. ¹⁰For everyone who asks receives; the one who seeks finds; and to the one who knocks, the door will be opened. Mt 7:7

¹¹"Which of you fathers, if your son asks for*ᵇ* a fish, will give him a snake instead? ¹²Or if he asks for an egg, will give him a scorpion? ¹³If you then, though you are evil, know how to give good gifts to your children, how much more will your Father in heaven give the Holy Spirit to those who ask him!"

Jesus and Beelzebul

11:14,15,17-22,24-26pp — Mt 12:22, 24-29,43-45
11:17-22pp — Mk 3:23-27

¹⁴Jesus was driving out a demon that was mute. When the demon left, the man who had been mute spoke, and the crowd was amazed. ¹⁵But some of them said, "By Beelzebul, the prince of demons, he is driving out demons." ¹⁶Others tested him by asking for a sign from heaven. Mt 12:22,24

¹⁷Jesus knew their thoughts and said to them: "Any kingdom divided against itself will be ruined, and a house divided against itself will fall. ¹⁸If Satan is divided against himself, how can his kingdom stand? I say this because you claim that I drive out demons by Beelzebul. ¹⁹Now if I drive out demons by Beelzebul, by whom do your followers drive them out? So then, they will be your judges. ²⁰But if I drive out demons by the finger of God, then the kingdom of God has come upon you. Mt 12:25-28

²¹"When a strong man, fully armed, guards his own house, his possessions are safe. ²²But when someone stronger attacks and overpowers him, he takes away the armor in which the man trusted and divides up his plunder. Mk 3:23-27

²³"Whoever is not with me is against me, and whoever does not gather with me scatters. Mt 12:30

²⁴"When an impure spirit comes out of a person, it goes through arid places seeking rest and does not find it. Then it says, 'I will return to the house I left.' ²⁵When it arrives, it finds the

ᵃ 8 Or yet to preserve his good name *ᵇ 11 Some manuscripts for bread, will give him a stone? Or if he asks for* house swept clean and put in order. ²⁶Then it goes and takes seven other spirits more wicked than itself, and they go in and live there. And the final condition of that person is worse than the first." Mt 12:43-45

²⁷As Jesus was saying these things, a woman in the crowd called out, "Blessed is the mother who gave you birth and nursed you." Lk 23:29

²⁸He replied, "Blessed rather are those who hear the word of God and obey it." Lk 8:21; Jn 14:21

The Sign of Jonah
11:29-32pp — Mt 12:39-42

²⁹As the crowds increased, Jesus said, "This is a wicked generation. It asks for a sign, but none will be given it except the sign of Jonah. ³⁰For as Jonah was a sign to the Ninevites, so also will the Son of Man be to this generation. ³¹The Queen of the South will rise at the judgment with the people of this generation and condemn them, for she came from the ends of the earth to listen to Solomon's wisdom; and now something greater than Solomon is here. ³²The men of Nineveh will stand up at the judgment with this generation and condemn it, for they repented at the preaching of Jonah; and now something greater than Jonah is here. Mt 12:39-42

The Lamp of the Body
11:34,35pp — Mt 6:22,23

³³"No one lights a lamp and puts it in a place where it will be hidden, or under a bowl. Instead they put it on its stand, so that those who come in may see the light. ³⁴Your eye is the lamp of your body. When your eyes are healthy,ᵃ your whole body also is full of light. But when they are unhealthy,ᵇ your body also is full of darkness. ³⁵See to it, then, that the light within you is not darkness. ³⁶Therefore, if your whole body is full of light, and no part of it dark, it will be just as full of light as when a lamp shines its light on you." Mt 6:22-23; Mk 4:21; Lk 8:16

Woes on the Pharisees and the Experts in the Law

³⁷When Jesus had finished speaking, a Pharisee invited him to eat with him; so he went in and reclined at the table. ³⁸But the Pharisee was surprised when he noticed that Jesus did not first wash before the meal. Mk 7:3-4

³⁹Then the Lord said to him, "Now then, you Pharisees clean the outside of the cup and dish, but inside you are full of greed and wickedness. ⁴⁰You foolish people! Did not the one who made the outside make the inside also? ⁴¹But now as for what is inside you — be generous to

ᵃ 34 The Greek for *healthy* here implies *generous*. ᵇ 34 The Greek for *unhealthy* here implies *stingy*.

the poor, and everything will be clean for you.   Mt 23:25-26; Lk 12:33

42 "Woe to you Pharisees, because you give God a tenth of your mint, rue and all other kinds of garden herbs, but you neglect justice and the love of God. You should have practiced the latter without leaving the former undone.   Mic 6:8; Mt 23:23

43 "Woe to you Pharisees, because you love the most important seats in the synagogues and respectful greetings in the marketplaces.   Mt 23:6-7; Mk 12:38-39

44 "Woe to you, because you are like unmarked graves, which people walk over without knowing it."   Mt 23:27

45 One of the experts in the law answered him, "Teacher, when you say these things, you insult us also."   Mt 22:35

46 Jesus replied, "And you experts in the law, woe to you, because you load people down with burdens they can hardly carry, and you yourselves will not lift one finger to help them.   Mt 23:4

47 "Woe to you, because you build tombs for the prophets, and it was your ancestors who killed them. 48 So you testify that you approve of what your ancestors did; they killed the prophets, and you build their tombs. 49 Because of this, God in his wisdom said, 'I will send them prophets and apostles, some of whom they will kill and others they will perse-

cute.' 50 Therefore this generation will be held responsible for the blood of all the prophets that has been shed since the beginning of the world, 51 from the blood of Abel to the blood of Zechariah, who was killed between the altar and the sanctuary. Yes, I tell you, this generation will be held responsible for it all.   Mt 23:29-32,34-36

52 "Woe to you experts in the law, because you have taken away the key to knowledge. You yourselves have not entered, and you have hindered those who were entering."   Mt 23:13

53 When Jesus went outside, the Pharisees and the teachers of the law began to oppose him fiercely and to besiege him with questions, 54 waiting to catch him in something he might say.   Mk 12:13

Warnings and Encouragements
12:2-9pp — Mt 10:26-33

12 Meanwhile, when a crowd of many thousands had gathered, so that they were trampling on one another, Jesus began to speak first to his disciples, saying: "Be[a] on your guard against the yeast of the Pharisees, which is hypocrisy. 2 There is nothing concealed that will not be disclosed, or hidden that will not be made known. 3 What you have said in the dark will be heard in the daylight, and what you have whispered in the ear in the in-

a 1 Or *speak to his disciples, saying: "First of all, be*

ner rooms will be proclaimed from the roofs. Mk 4:22; Lk 8:17

4 "I tell you, my friends, do not be afraid of those who kill the body and after that can do no more. 5 But I will show you whom you should fear: Fear him who, after your body has been killed, has authority to throw you into hell. Yes, I tell you, fear him. 6 Are not five sparrows sold for two pennies? Yet not one of them is forgotten by God. 7 Indeed, the very hairs of your head are all numbered. Don't be afraid; you are worth more than many sparrows. Mt 10:30; Jn 15:14,15; Heb 10:31

8 "I tell you, whoever publicly acknowledges me before others, the Son of Man will also acknowledge before the angels of God. 9 But whoever disowns me before others will be disowned before the angels of God. 10 And everyone who speaks a word against the Son of Man will be forgiven, but anyone who blasphemes against the Holy Spirit will not be forgiven. Mt 10:26-33; 1Jn 5:16

11 "When you are brought before synagogues, rulers and authorities, do not worry about how you will defend yourselves or what you will say, 12 for the Holy Spirit will teach you at that time what you should say." Mt 10:20

The Parable of the Rich Fool

13 Someone in the crowd said to him, "Teacher, tell my brother to divide the inheritance with me."

14 Jesus replied, "Man, who appointed me a judge or an arbiter between you?" 15 Then he said to them, "Watch out! Be on your guard against all kinds of greed; life does not consist in an abundance of possessions." Job 20:20

16 And he told them this parable: "The ground of a certain rich man yielded an abundant harvest. 17 He thought to himself, 'What shall I do? I have no place to store my crops.'

18 "Then he said, 'This is what I'll do. I will tear down my barns and build bigger ones, and there I will store my surplus grain. 19 And I'll say to myself, "You have plenty of grain laid up for many years. Take life easy; eat, drink and be merry."'

20 "But God said to him, 'You fool! This very night your life will be demanded from you. Then who will get what you have prepared for yourself?' Ps 39:6; Jer 17:11

21 "This is how it will be with whoever stores up things for themselves but is not rich toward God." ver 33

Do Not Worry

12:22-31pp — Mt 6:25-33

22 Then Jesus said to his disciples: "Therefore I tell you, do not worry about your life, what you will eat; or about your body, what you will wear. 23 For life is more than food, and the body more than clothes. 24 Consider the ravens: They do not sow or

reap, they have no storeroom or barn; yet God feeds them. And how much more valuable you are than birds! ²⁵Who of you by worrying can add a single hour to your life^a? ²⁶Since you cannot do this very little thing, why do you worry about the rest?   Job 38:41; Ps 147:9

²⁷"Consider how the wild flowers grow. They do not labor or spin. Yet I tell you, not even Solomon in all his splendor was dressed like one of these. ²⁸If that is how God clothes the grass of the field, which is here today, and tomorrow is thrown into the fire, how much more will he clothe you—you of little faith! ²⁹And do not set your heart on what you will eat or drink; do not worry about it. ³⁰For the pagan world runs after all such things, and your Father knows that you need them. ³¹But seek his kingdom, and these things will be given to you as well.   Mt 6:25-33

³²"Do not be afraid, little flock, for your Father has been pleased to give you the kingdom. ³³Sell your possessions and give to the poor. Provide purses for yourselves that will not wear out, a treasure in heaven that will never fail, where no thief comes near and no moth destroys. ³⁴For where your treasure is, there your heart will be also.   Mt 6:20-21; 14:27

Watchfulness
12:35,36pp — Mt 25:1-13; Mk 13:33-37
12:39,40; 42-46pp — Mt 24:43-51

³⁵"Be dressed ready for service and keep your lamps burning, ³⁶like servants waiting for their master to return from a wedding banquet, so that when he comes and knocks they can immediately open the door for him. ³⁷It will be good for those servants whose master finds them watching when he comes. Truly I tell you, he will dress himself to serve, will have them recline at the table and will come and wait on them. ³⁸It will be good for those servants whose master finds them ready, even if he comes in the middle of the night or toward daybreak. ³⁹But understand this: If the owner of the house had known at what hour the thief was coming, he would not have let his house be broken into. ⁴⁰You also must be ready, because the Son of Man will come at an hour when you do not expect him."   Mt 25:1-13; Mk 13:33-37

⁴¹Peter asked, "Lord, are you telling this parable to us, or to everyone?"

⁴²The Lord answered, "Who then is the faithful and wise manager, whom the master puts in charge of his servants to give them their food allowance at the proper time? ⁴³It will be good for that servant whom the master finds doing so when he returns.

^a 25 Or *single cubit to your height*

⁴⁴Truly I tell you, he will put him in charge of all his possessions. ⁴⁵But suppose the servant says to himself, 'My master is taking a long time in coming,' and he then begins to beat the other servants, both men and women, and to eat and drink and get drunk. ⁴⁶The master of that servant will come on a day when he does not expect him and at an hour he is not aware of. He will cut him to pieces and assign him a place with the unbelievers. Mt 24:43-51

⁴⁷"The servant who knows the master's will and does not get ready or does not do what the master wants will be beaten with many blows. ⁴⁸But the one who does not know and does things deserving punishment will be beaten with few blows. From everyone who has been given much, much will be demanded; and from the one who has been entrusted with much, much more will be asked. Lev 5:17; Dt 25:2

Not Peace but Division
12:51-53pp — Mt 10:34-36

⁴⁹"I have come to bring fire on the earth, and how I wish it were already kindled! ⁵⁰But I have a baptism to undergo, and what constraint I am under until it is completed! ⁵¹Do you think I came to bring peace on earth? No, I tell you, but division. ⁵²From now on there will be five in one family divided against each other, three against two and two against

three. ⁵³They will be divided, father against son and son against father, mother against daughter and daughter against mother, mother-in-law against daughter-in-law and daughter-in-law against mother-in-law." Mt 10:34-36

Interpreting the Times

⁵⁴He said to the crowd: "When you see a cloud rising in the west, immediately you say, 'It's going to rain,' and it does. ⁵⁵And when the south wind blows, you say, 'It's going to be hot,' and it is. ⁵⁶Hypocrites! You know how to interpret the appearance of the earth and the sky. How is it that you don't know how to interpret this present time? Mt 16:2-3

⁵⁷"Why don't you judge for yourselves what is right? ⁵⁸As you are going with your adversary to the magistrate, try hard to be reconciled on the way, or your adversary may drag you off to the judge, and the judge turn you over to the officer, and the officer throw you into prison. ⁵⁹I tell you, you will not get out until you have paid the last penny." Mt 5:25-26; Mk 12:42

Repent or Perish

13 Now there were some present at that time who told Jesus about the Galileans whose blood Pilate had mixed with their sacrifices. ²Jesus answered, "Do you think that these Galileans were worse sin-

ners than all the other Galileans because they suffered this
way? ³I tell you, no! But unless
you repent, you too will all perish. ⁴Or those eighteen who died
when the tower in Siloam fell on
them — do you think they were
more guilty than all the others
living in Jerusalem? ⁵I tell you,
no! But unless you repent, you
too will all perish." Mt 27:2; Jn 9:2-3,7

⁶Then he told this parable:
"A man had a fig tree growing
in his vineyard, and he went to
look for fruit on it but did not
find any. ⁷So he said to the man
who took care of the vineyard,
'For three years now I've been
coming to look for fruit on this
fig tree and haven't found any.
Cut it down! Why should it use
up the soil?' Mt 3:10; 21:19

⁸"'Sir,' the man replied, 'leave
it alone for one more year, and
I'll dig around it and fertilize it.
⁹If it bears fruit next year, fine! If
not, then cut it down.'"

Jesus Heals a Crippled Woman on the Sabbath

¹⁰On a Sabbath Jesus was
teaching in one of the synagogues, ¹¹and a woman was
there who had been crippled by a
spirit for eighteen years. She was
bent over and could not straight-
en up at all. ¹²When Jesus saw
her, he called her forward and
said to her, "Woman, you are set
free from your infirmity." ¹³Then
he put his hands on her, and immediately she straightened up
and praised God. Mt 4:23; Mk 5:23

¹⁴Indignant because Jesus had
healed on the Sabbath, the synagogue leader said to the people,
"There are six days for work. So
come and be healed on those
days, not on the Sabbath." Ex 20:9

¹⁵The Lord answered him,
"You hypocrites! Doesn't each
of you on the Sabbath untie
your ox or donkey from the stall
and lead it out to give it water?
¹⁶Then should not this woman,
a daughter of Abraham, whom
Satan has kept bound for eighteen long years, be set free on
the Sabbath day from what
bound her?" Lk 14:5; 19:9

¹⁷When he said this, all his opponents were humiliated, but
the people were delighted with
all the wonderful things he was
doing. Isa 66:5

The Parables of the Mustard Seed and the Yeast

13:18,19pp — Mk 4:30-32
13:18-21pp — Mt 13:31-33

¹⁸Then Jesus asked, "What is
the kingdom of God like? What
shall I compare it to? ¹⁹It is like
a mustard seed, which a man
took and planted in his garden.
It grew and became a tree, and
the birds perched in its branches." Mk 4:30-32

²⁰Again he asked, "What shall
I compare the kingdom of God
to? ²¹It is like yeast that a woman
took and mixed into about sixty

pounds[a] of flour until it worked all through the dough." Mt 13:31-33

The Narrow Door

22 Then Jesus went through the towns and villages, teaching as he made his way to Jerusalem. 23 Someone asked him, "Lord, are only a few people going to be saved?" Lk 9:51

He said to them, 24 "Make every effort to enter through the narrow door, because many, I tell you, will try to enter and will not be able to. 25 Once the owner of the house gets up and closes the door, you will stand outside knocking and pleading, 'Sir, open the door for us.' Mt 7:13

"But he will answer, 'I don't know you or where you come from.' Mt 7:23; 25:10-12

26 "Then you will say, 'We ate and drank with you, and you taught in our streets.'

27 "But he will reply, 'I don't know you or where you come from. Away from me, all you evildoers!' Mt 7:23; 25:41

28 "There will be weeping there, and gnashing of teeth, when you see Abraham, Isaac and Jacob and all the prophets in the kingdom of God, but you yourselves thrown out. 29 People will come from east and west and north and south, and will take their places at the feast in the kingdom of God. 30 Indeed there are those who are last who

will be first, and first who will be last." Mt 19:30

Jesus' Sorrow for Jerusalem
13:34,35pp — Mt 23:37-39
13:34,35Ref — Lk 19:41

31 At that time some Pharisees came to Jesus and said to him, "Leave this place and go somewhere else. Herod wants to kill you." Mt 14:1

32 He replied, "Go tell that fox, 'I will keep on driving out demons and healing people today and tomorrow, and on the third day I will reach my goal.' 33 In any case, I must press on today and tomorrow and the next day — for surely no prophet can die outside Jerusalem! Mt 21:11; Heb 2:10

34 "Jerusalem, Jerusalem, you who kill the prophets and stone those sent to you, how often I have longed to gather your children together, as a hen gathers her chicks under her wings, and you were not willing. 35 Look, your house is left to you desolate. I tell you, you will not see me again until you say, 'Blessed is he who comes in the name of the Lord.'[b] Mt 23:37-39; Lk 19:41

Jesus at a Pharisee's House
14:8-10Ref — Pr 25:6,7

14 One Sabbath, when Jesus went to eat in the house of a prominent Pharisee, he was being carefully watched. 2 There in front of him was a man suffering

---

[a] 21 Or about 27 kilograms   [b] 35 Psalm 118:26

from abnormal swelling of his body. ³Jesus asked the Pharisees and experts in the law, "Is it lawful to heal on the Sabbath or not?" ⁴But they remained silent. So taking hold of the man, he healed him and sent him on his way.   Mt 12:2; 22:35

⁵Then he asked them, "If one of you has a child*a* or an ox that falls into a well on the Sabbath day, will you not immediately pull it out?" ⁶And they had nothing to say.   Lk 13:15

⁷When he noticed how the guests picked the places of honor at the table, he told them this parable: ⁸"When someone invites you to a wedding feast, do not take the place of honor, for a person more distinguished than you may have been invited. ⁹If so, the host who invited both of you will come and say to you, 'Give this person your seat.' Then, humiliated, you will have to take the least important place. ¹⁰But when you are invited, take the lowest place, so that when your host comes, he will say to you, 'Friend, move up to a better place.' Then you will be honored in the presence of all the other guests. ¹¹For all those who exalt themselves will be humbled, and those who humble themselves will be exalted."   Pr 25:6-7

¹²Then Jesus said to his host, "When you give a luncheon or dinner, do not invite your friends, your brothers or sisters, your relatives, or your rich neighbors; if you do, they may invite you back and so you will be repaid. ¹³But when you give a banquet, invite the poor, the crippled, the lame, the blind, ¹⁴and you will be blessed. Although they cannot repay you, you will be repaid at the resurrection of the righteous."   Ac 24:15

The Parable of the Great Banquet
14:16-24Ref — Mt 22:2-14

¹⁵When one of those at the table with him heard this, he said to Jesus, "Blessed is the one who will eat at the feast in the kingdom of God."   Rev 19:9

¹⁶Jesus replied: "A certain man was preparing a great banquet and invited many guests. ¹⁷At the time of the banquet he sent his servant to tell those who had been invited, 'Come, for everything is now ready.'

¹⁸"But they all alike began to make excuses. The first said, 'I have just bought a field, and I must go and see it. Please excuse me.'

¹⁹"Another said, 'I have just bought five yoke of oxen, and I'm on my way to try them out. Please excuse me.'

²⁰"Still another said, 'I just got married, so I can't come.'

²¹"The servant came back and reported this to his master. Then

---

a 5 Some manuscripts *donkey*

the owner of the house became angry and ordered his servant, 'Go out quickly into the streets and alleys of the town and bring in the poor, the crippled, the blind and the lame.' ver 13

22 " 'Sir,' the servant said, 'what you ordered has been done, but there is still room.'

23 "Then the master told his servant, 'Go out to the roads and country lanes and compel them to come in, so that my house will be full. 24 I tell you, not one of those who were invited will get a taste of my banquet.' " Mt 22:2-14; Ac 13:46

The Cost of Being a Disciple

25 Large crowds were traveling with Jesus, and turning to them he said: 26 "If anyone comes to me and does not hate father and mother, wife and children, brothers and sisters — yes, even their own life — such a person cannot be my disciple. 27 And whoever does not carry their cross and follow me cannot be my disciple. Mt 10:37-38; Lk 9:23

28 "Suppose one of you wants to build a tower. Won't you first sit down and estimate the cost to see if you have enough money to complete it? 29 For if you lay the foundation and are not able to finish it, everyone who sees it will ridicule you, 30 saying, 'This person began to build and wasn't able to finish.'

31 "Or suppose a king is about to go to war against another king. Won't he first sit down and consider whether he is able with ten thousand men to oppose the one coming against him with twenty thousand? 32 If he is not able, he will send a delegation while the other is still a long way off and will ask for terms of peace. 33 In the same way, those of you who do not give up everything you have cannot be my disciples. Php 3:7-8

34 "Salt is good, but if it loses its saltiness, how can it be made salty again? 35 It is fit neither for the soil nor for the manure pile; it is thrown out. Mt 5:13; Mk 9:50

"Whoever has ears to hear, let them hear." Mt 11:15

The Parable of the Lost Sheep

15:4-7pp — Mt 18:12-14

15 Now the tax collectors and sinners were all gathering around to hear Jesus. 2 But the Pharisees and the teachers of the law muttered, "This man welcomes sinners and eats with them." Mt 9:11; Lk 5:29

3 Then Jesus told them this parable: 4 "Suppose one of you has a hundred sheep and loses one of them. Doesn't he leave the ninety-nine in the open country and go after the lost sheep until he finds it? 5 And when he finds it, he joyfully puts it on his shoulders 6 and goes home. Then he calls his friends and neighbors together and says, 'Rejoice with me; I have found my lost sheep.' 7 I tell you that in the same way

there will be more rejoicing in heaven over one sinner who repents than over ninety-nine righteous persons who do not need to repent. Mt 18:12-14

The Parable of the Lost Coin

8 "Or suppose a woman has ten silver coins[a] and loses one. Doesn't she light a lamp, sweep the house and search carefully until she finds it? 9 And when she finds it, she calls her friends and neighbors together and says, 'Rejoice with me; I have found my lost coin.' 10 In the same way, I tell you, there is rejoicing in the presence of the angels of God over one sinner who repents." ver 6-7

The Parable of the Lost Son

11 Jesus continued: "There was a man who had two sons. 12 The younger one said to his father, 'Father, give me my share of the estate.' So he divided his property between them. Dt 21:17; Mt 21:28

13 "Not long after that, the younger son got together all he had, set off for a distant country and there squandered his wealth in wild living. 14 After he had spent everything, there was a severe famine in that whole country, and he began to be in need. 15 So he went and hired himself out to a citizen of that country, who sent him to his fields to feed pigs. 16 He longed to fill his stomach with the pods that the pigs

were eating, but no one gave him anything. Lev 11:7; Lk 16:1

17 "When he came to his senses, he said, 'How many of my father's hired servants have food to spare, and here I am starving to death! 18 I will set out and go back to my father and say to him: Father, I have sinned against heaven and against you. 19 I am no longer worthy to be called your son; make me like one of your hired servants.' 20 So he got up and went to his father. Lev 26:40; Mt 3:2

"But while he was still a long way off, his father saw him and was filled with compassion for him; he ran to his son, threw his arms around him and kissed him. Ge 45:14-15; Ac 20:37

21 "The son said to him, 'Father, I have sinned against heaven and against you. I am no longer worthy to be called your son.' Ps 51:4

22 "But the father said to his servants, 'Quick! Bring the best robe and put it on him. Put a ring on his finger and sandals on his feet. 23 Bring the fattened calf and kill it. Let's have a feast and celebrate. 24 For this son of mine was dead and is alive again; he was lost and is found.' So they began to celebrate. Eph 2:1,5; 5:14; 1Ti 5:6

25 "Meanwhile, the older son was in the field. When he came near the house, he heard music and dancing. 26 So he called one of the servants and asked

[a] 8 Greek ten drachmas, each worth about a day's wages

him what was going on. ²⁷'Your brother has come,' he replied, 'and your father has killed the fattened calf because he has him back safe and sound.'

²⁸"The older brother became angry and refused to go in. So his father went out and pleaded with him. ²⁹But he answered his father, 'Look! All these years I've been slaving for you and never disobeyed your orders. Yet you never gave me even a young goat so I could celebrate with my friends. ³⁰But when this son of yours who has squandered your property with prostitutes comes home, you kill the fattened calf for him!' Pr 29:3; Jnh 4:1

³¹"'My son,' the father said, 'you are always with me, and everything I have is yours. ³²But we had to celebrate and be glad, because this brother of yours was dead and is alive again; he was lost and is found.'" Mal 3:17

The Parable of the Shrewd Manager

16 Jesus told his disciples: "There was a rich man whose manager was accused of wasting his possessions. ²So he called him in and asked him, 'What is this I hear about you? Give an account of your management, because you cannot be manager any longer.' Lk 15:13,30

³"The manager said to himself, 'What shall I do now? My master is taking away my job. I'm not strong enough to dig, and I'm ashamed to beg— ⁴I know what I'll do so that, when I lose my job here, people will welcome me into their houses.'

⁵"So he called in each one of his master's debtors. He asked the first, 'How much do you owe my master?'

⁶"'Nine hundred gallons*a* of olive oil,' he replied.

"The manager told him, 'Take your bill, sit down quickly, and make it four hundred and fifty.'

⁷"Then he asked the second, 'And how much do you owe?'

"'A thousand bushels*b* of wheat,' he replied.

"He told him, 'Take your bill and make it eight hundred.'

⁸"The master commended the dishonest manager because he had acted shrewdly. For the people of this world are more shrewd in dealing with their own kind than are the people of the light. ⁹I tell you, use worldly wealth to gain friends for yourselves, so that when it is gone, you will be welcomed into eternal dwellings. Mt 19:21; Jn 12:36

¹⁰"Whoever can be trusted with very little can also be trusted with much, and whoever is dishonest with very little will also be dishonest with much. ¹¹So if you have not been trustworthy in handling worldly wealth, who will trust you with true riches?

---

a 6 Or about 3,000 liters   *b* 7 Or about 30 tons

¹²And if you have not been trustworthy with someone else's property, who will give you property of your own? Mt 25:21,23; Lk 19:17

¹³"No one can serve two masters. Either you will hate the one and love the other, or you will be devoted to the one and despise the other. You cannot serve both God and money." Mt 6:24

¹⁴The Pharisees, who loved money, heard all this and were sneering at Jesus. ¹⁵He said to them, "You are the ones who justify yourselves in the eyes of others, but God knows your hearts. What people value highly is detestable in God's sight. 1Sa 16:7

Additional Teachings

¹⁶"The Law and the Prophets were proclaimed until John. Since that time, the good news of the kingdom of God is being preached, and everyone is forcing their way into it. ¹⁷It is easier for heaven and earth to disappear than for the least stroke of a pen to drop out of the Law. Mt 5:18; 11:12-13

¹⁸"Anyone who divorces his wife and marries another woman commits adultery, and the man who marries a divorced woman commits adultery. Mt 5:31-32

The Rich Man and Lazarus

¹⁹"There was a rich man who was dressed in purple and fine linen and lived in luxury every day. ²⁰At his gate was laid a beggar named Lazarus, covered with sores ²¹and longing to eat what fell from the rich man's table. Even the dogs came and licked his sores. Eze 16:49; Ac 3:2

²²"The time came when the beggar died and the angels carried him to Abraham's side. The rich man also died and was buried. ²³In Hades, where he was in torment, he looked up and saw Abraham far away, with Lazarus by his side. ²⁴So he called to him, 'Father Abraham, have pity on me and send Lazarus to dip the tip of his finger in water and cool my tongue, because I am in agony in this fire.' Mt 5:22; Lk 3:8

²⁵"But Abraham replied, 'Son, remember that in your lifetime you received your good things, while Lazarus received bad things, but now he is comforted here and you are in agony. ²⁶And besides all this, between us and you a great chasm has been set in place, so that those who want to go from here to you cannot, nor can anyone cross over from there to us.' Ps 17:14; Lk 6:21,24-25

²⁷"He answered, 'Then I beg you, father, send Lazarus to my family, ²⁸for I have five brothers. Let him warn them, so that they will not also come to this place of torment.' Ac 2:40; 1Th 4:6

²⁹"Abraham replied, 'They have Moses and the Prophets; let them listen to them.' Lk 4:17; Jn 5:45-47

³⁰" 'No, father Abraham,' he said, 'but if someone from the

dead goes to them, they will repent.' Lk 3:8

³¹"He said to him, 'If they do not listen to Moses and the Prophets, they will not be convinced even if someone rises from the dead.'"

Sin, Faith, Duty

17 Jesus said to his disciples: "Things that cause people to stumble are bound to come, but woe to anyone through whom they come. ²It would be better for them to be thrown into the sea with a millstone tied around their neck than to cause one of these little ones to stumble. ³So watch yourselves. Mt 18:7; Mk 10:24

"If your brother or sister*a* sins against you, rebuke them; and if they repent, forgive them. ⁴Even if they sin against you seven times in a day and seven times come back to you saying 'I repent,' you must forgive them." Mt 18:15,21-22

⁵The apostles said to the Lord, "Increase our faith!" Mk 6:30; Lk 7:13

⁶He replied, "If you have faith as small as a mustard seed, you can say to this mulberry tree, 'Be uprooted and planted in the sea,' and it will obey you. Mt 17:20; 21:21

⁷"Suppose one of you has a servant plowing or looking after the sheep. Will he say to the servant when he comes in from the field, 'Come along now and sit down to eat'? ⁸Won't he rather say, 'Prepare my supper, get yourself ready and wait on me while I eat and drink; after that you may eat and drink'? ⁹Will he thank the servant because he did what he was told to do? ¹⁰So you also, when you have done everything you were told to do, should say, 'We are unworthy servants; we have only done our duty.'" Lk 12:37

Jesus Heals Ten Men With Leprosy

¹¹Now on his way to Jerusalem, Jesus traveled along the border between Samaria and Galilee. ¹²As he was going into a village, ten men who had leprosy*b* met him. They stood at a distance ¹³and called out in a loud voice, "Jesus, Master, have pity on us!" Lk 5:5; 9:51; Jn 4:3-4

¹⁴When he saw them, he said, "Go, show yourselves to the priests." And as they went, they were cleansed. Lev 14:2; Mt 8:4

¹⁵One of them, when he saw he was healed, came back, praising God in a loud voice. ¹⁶He threw himself at Jesus' feet and thanked him — and he was a Samaritan. Mt 9:8; 10:5

¹⁷Jesus asked, "Were not all ten cleansed? Where are the other nine? ¹⁸Has no one returned to give praise to God except this foreigner?" ¹⁹Then he said to

a 3 The Greek word for *brother or sister* (*adelphos*) refers here to a fellow disciple, whether man or woman. *b 12* The Greek word traditionally translated *leprosy* was used for various diseases affecting the skin.

him, "Rise and go; your faith has made you well." Mt 9:22

The Coming of the Kingdom of God

17:26,27pp — Mt 24:37-39

²⁰Once, on being asked by the Pharisees when the kingdom of God would come, Jesus replied, "The coming of the kingdom of God is not something that can be observed, ²¹nor will people say, 'Here it is,' or 'There it is,' because the kingdom of God is in your midst."ᵃ ver 23; Mt 3:2

²²Then he said to his disciples, "The time is coming when you will long to see one of the days of the Son of Man, but you will not see it. ²³People will tell you, 'There he is!' or 'Here he is!' Do not go running off after them. ²⁴For the Son of Man in his dayᵇ will be like the lightning, which flashes and lights up the sky from one end to the other. ²⁵But first he must suffer many things and be rejected by this generation. Mt 9:15

²⁶"Just as it was in the days of Noah, so also will it be in the days of the Son of Man. ²⁷People were eating, drinking, marrying and being given in marriage up to the day Noah entered the ark. Then the flood came and destroyed them all. Ge 7:6-24; Mt 24:37-39

²⁸"It was the same in the days of Lot. People were eating and drinking, buying and selling,

planting and building. ²⁹But the day Lot left Sodom, fire and sulfur rained down from heaven and destroyed them all. Ge 19:1-28

³⁰"It will be just like this on the day the Son of Man is revealed. ³¹On that day no one who is on the housetop, with possessions inside, should go down to get them. Likewise, no one in the field should go back for anything. ³²Remember Lot's wife! ³³Whoever tries to keep their life will lose it, and whoever loses their life will preserve it. ³⁴I tell you, on that night two people will be in one bed; one will be taken and the other left. ³⁵Two women will be grinding grain together; one will be taken and the other left." [36]ᶜ Mt 24:41; Mk 13:15-16

³⁷"Where, Lord?" they asked.

He replied, "Where there is a dead body, there the vultures will gather." Mt 24:28

The Parable of the Persistent Widow

18 Then Jesus told his disciples a parable to show them that they should always pray and not give up. ²He said: "In a certain town there was a judge who neither feared God nor cared what people thought. ³And there was a widow in that town who kept coming to him with the plea, 'Grant me justice against my adversary.' Isa 40:31

ᵃ 21 Or *is within you*   ᵇ 24 Some manuscripts do not have *in his day.*   ᶜ 36 Some manuscripts include here words similar to Matt. 24:40.

⁴"For some time he refused. But finally he said to himself, 'Even though I don't fear God or care what people think, ⁵yet because this widow keeps bothering me, I will see that she gets justice, so that she won't eventually come and attack me!' " Lk 11:8

⁶And the Lord said, "Listen to what the unjust judge says. ⁷And will not God bring about justice for his chosen ones, who cry out to him day and night? Will he keep putting them off? ⁸I tell you, he will see that they get justice, and quickly. However, when the Son of Man comes, will he find faith on the earth?" Mt 8:20; Rev 6:10

The Parable of the Pharisee and the Tax Collector

⁹To some who were confident of their own righteousness and looked down on everyone else, Jesus told this parable: ¹⁰"Two men went up to the temple to pray, one a Pharisee and the other a tax collector. ¹¹The Pharisee stood by himself and prayed: 'God, I thank you that I am not like other people—robbers, evildoers, adulterers—or even like this tax collector. ¹²I fast twice a week and give a tenth of all I get.' Isa 65:5; Lk 16:15

¹³"But the tax collector stood at a distance. He would not even look up to heaven, but beat his breast and said, 'God, have mercy on me, a sinner.' Lk 5:32; 23:48

^a 20 Exodus 20:12-16; Deut. 5:16-20

¹⁴"I tell you that this man, rather than the other, went home justified before God. For all those who exalt themselves will be humbled, and those who humble themselves will be exalted." Mt 23:12

The Little Children and Jesus
18:15-17pp — Mt 19:13-15; Mk 10:13-16

¹⁵People were also bringing babies to Jesus for him to place his hands on them. When the disciples saw this, they rebuked them. ¹⁶But Jesus called the children to him and said, "Let the little children come to me, and do not hinder them, for the kingdom of God belongs to such as these. ¹⁷Truly I tell you, anyone who will not receive the kingdom of God like a little child will never enter it." Mt 18:3

The Rich and the Kingdom of God
18:18-30pp — Mt 19:16-29; Mk 10:17-30

¹⁸A certain ruler asked him, "Good teacher, what must I do to inherit eternal life?" Lk 10:25

¹⁹"Why do you call me good?" Jesus answered. "No one is good—except God alone. ²⁰You know the commandments: 'You shall not commit adultery, you shall not murder, you shall not steal, you shall not give false testimony, honor your father and mother.' ^a"Ex 20:12-16; Dt 5:16-20; Ro 13:9

²¹"All these I have kept since I was a boy," he said.

²²When Jesus heard this, he said to him, "You still lack one thing. Sell everything you have and give to the poor, and you will have treasure in heaven. Then come, follow me." Mt 6:20; Ac 2:45

²³When he heard this, he became very sad, because he was very wealthy. ²⁴Jesus looked at him and said, "How hard it is for the rich to enter the kingdom of God! ²⁵Indeed, it is easier for a camel to go through the eye of a needle than for someone who is rich to enter the kingdom of God." Pr 11:28

²⁶Those who heard this asked, "Who then can be saved?"

²⁷Jesus replied, "What is impossible with man is possible with God." Mt 19:26

²⁸Peter said to him, "We have left all we had to follow you!" Mt 4:19

²⁹"Truly I tell you," Jesus said to them, "no one who has left home or wife or brothers or sisters or parents or children for the sake of the kingdom of God ³⁰will fail to receive many times as much in this age, and in the age to come eternal life." Mt 19:16-29; Mk 10:17-30

Jesus Predicts His Death a Third Time

18:31-33pp — Mt 20:17-19; Mk 10:32-34

³¹Jesus took the Twelve aside and told them, "We are going up to Jerusalem, and everything that is written by the prophets about the Son of Man will be fulfilled. ³²He will be delivered over to the Gentiles. They will mock him, insult him and spit on him; ³³they will flog him and kill him. On the third day he will rise again." Mt 20:17-19; Mk 10:32-34

³⁴The disciples did not understand any of this. Its meaning was hidden from them, and they did not know what he was talking about. Mk 9:32; Lk 9:45

A Blind Beggar Receives His Sight

18:35-43pp — Mt 20:29-34; Mk 10:46-52

³⁵As Jesus approached Jericho, a blind man was sitting by the roadside begging. ³⁶When he heard the crowd going by, he asked what was happening. ³⁷They told him, "Jesus of Nazareth is passing by." Lk 19:1,4

³⁸He called out, "Jesus, Son of David, have mercy on me!" Mt 9:27

³⁹Those who led the way rebuked him and told him to be quiet, but he shouted all the more, "Son of David, have mercy on me!"

⁴⁰Jesus stopped and ordered the man to be brought to him. When he came near, Jesus asked him, ⁴¹"What do you want me to do for you?"

"Lord, I want to see," he replied.

⁴²Jesus said to him, "Receive your sight; your faith has healed you." ⁴³Immediately he received his sight and followed Jesus, praising God. When all the people saw it, they also praised God. Mt 20:29-34

Zacchaeus the Tax Collector

19 Jesus entered Jericho and was passing through. ²A man was there by the name of Zacchaeus; he was a chief tax collector and was wealthy. ³He wanted to see who Jesus was, but because he was short he could not see over the crowd. ⁴So he ran ahead and climbed a sycamore-fig tree to see him, since Jesus was coming that way.   1Ki 10:27

⁵When Jesus reached the spot, he looked up and said to him, "Zacchaeus, come down immediately. I must stay at your house today." ⁶So he came down at once and welcomed him gladly.

⁷All the people saw this and began to mutter, "He has gone to be the guest of a sinner."   Mt 9:11

⁸But Zacchaeus stood up and said to the Lord, "Look, Lord! Here and now I give half of my possessions to the poor, and if I have cheated anybody out of anything, I will pay back four times the amount."   Ex 22:1; Lk 7:13

⁹Jesus said to him, "Today salvation has come to this house, because this man, too, is a son of Abraham. ¹⁰For the Son of Man came to seek and to save the lost."   Lk 3:8; Jn 3:17

The Parable of the Ten Minas

19:12-27Ref — Mt 25:14-30

¹¹While they were listening to this, he went on to tell them a parable, because he was near Jerusalem and the people thought that the kingdom of God was going to appear at once. ¹²He said: "A man of noble birth went to a distant country to have himself appointed king and then to return. ¹³So he called ten of his servants and gave them ten minas.^a 'Put this money to work,' he said, 'until I come back.'   Mk 13:34; Lk 17:20

¹⁴"But his subjects hated him and sent a delegation after him to say, 'We don't want this man to be our king.'

¹⁵"He was made king, however, and returned home. Then he sent for the servants to whom he had given the money, in order to find out what they had gained with it.

¹⁶"The first one came and said, 'Sir, your mina has earned ten more.'

¹⁷"'Well done, my good servant!' his master replied. 'Because you have been trustworthy in a very small matter, take charge of ten cities.'   Pr 27:18; Lk 16:10

¹⁸"The second came and said, 'Sir, your mina has earned five more.'

¹⁹"His master answered, 'You take charge of five cities.'

²⁰"Then another servant came and said, 'Sir, here is your mina; I have kept it laid away in a piece of cloth. ²¹I was afraid of you, because you are a hard man. You take out what you did

^a 13 A mina was about three months' wages.

not put in and reap what you did not sow.' Mt 25:24

²² "His master replied, 'I will judge you by your own words, you wicked servant! You knew, did you, that I am a hard man, taking out what I did not put in, and reaping what I did not sow? ²³ Why then didn't you put my money on deposit, so that when I came back, I could have collected it with interest?' 2Sa 1:16; Mt 25:26 ²⁴ "Then he said to those standing by, 'Take his mina away from him and give it to the one who has ten minas.'

²⁵ "'Sir,' they said, 'he already has ten!'

²⁶ "He replied, 'I tell you that to everyone who has, more will be given, but as for the one who has nothing, even what they have will be taken away. ²⁷ But those enemies of mine who did not want me to be king over them — bring them here and kill them in front of me.' " Mt 25:14-30

Jesus Comes to Jerusalem as King

19:29-38pp — Mt 21:1-9; Mk 11:1-10
19:35-38pp — Jn 12:12-15

²⁸ After Jesus had said this, he went on ahead, going up to Jerusalem. ²⁹ As he approached Bethphage and Bethany at the hill called the Mount of Olives, he sent two of his disciples, saying to them, ³⁰ "Go to the village ahead of you, and as you

enter it, you will find a colt tied there, which no one has ever ridden. Untie it and bring it here. ³¹ If anyone asks you, 'Why are you untying it?' say, 'The Lord needs it.' " Mt 21:1-9; Mk 10:32

³² Those who were sent ahead went and found it just as he had told them. ³³ As they were untying the colt, its owners asked them, "Why are you untying the colt?" Lk 22:13

³⁴ They replied, "The Lord needs it."

³⁵ They brought it to Jesus, threw their cloaks on the colt and put Jesus on it. ³⁶ As he went along, people spread their cloaks on the road. Mk 11:1-10; 2Ki 9:13

³⁷ When he came near the place where the road goes down the Mount of Olives, the whole crowd of disciples began joyfully to praise God in loud voices for all the miracles they had seen:

³⁸ "Blessed is the king who comes in the name of the Lord!"[a] Ps 118:26

"Peace in heaven and glory in the highest!" Jn 12:12-15

³⁹ Some of the Pharisees in the crowd said to Jesus, "Teacher, rebuke your disciples!" Mt 21:15-16

⁴⁰ "I tell you," he replied, "if they keep quiet, the stones will cry out." Hab 2:11

⁴¹ As he approached Jerusalem and saw the city, he wept over

---

a 38 Psalm 118:26

it ⁴² and said, "If you, even you, had only known on this day what would bring you peace — but now it is hidden from your eyes. ⁴³The days will come upon you when your enemies will build an embankment against you and encircle you and hem you in on every side. ⁴⁴They will dash you to the ground, you and the children within your walls. They will not leave one stone on another, because you did not recognize the time of God's coming to you."

Jesus at the Temple

19:45,46pp — Mt 21:12-16; Mk 11:15-18; Jn 2:13-16

⁴⁵When Jesus entered the temple courts, he began to drive out those who were selling. ⁴⁶"It is written," he said to them, " 'My house will be a house of prayer'^a; but you have made it 'a den of robbers.'^b" Mt 21:12-16; Isa 56:7; Jer 7:11

⁴⁷Every day he was teaching at the temple. But the chief priests, the teachers of the law and the leaders among the people were trying to kill him. ⁴⁸Yet they could not find any way to do it, because all the people hung on his words. Mt 26:55; Mk 11:18

The Authority of Jesus Questioned

20:1-8pp — Mt 21:23-27; Mk 11:27-33

20 One day as Jesus was teaching the people in the temple courts and proclaiming

the good news, the chief priests and the teachers of the law, together with the elders, came up to him. ²"Tell us by what authority you are doing these things," they said. "Who gave you this authority?" Lk 8:1; Ac 4:7

³He replied, "I will also ask you a question. Tell me: ⁴John's baptism — was it from heaven, or of human origin?" Mk 1:4

⁵They discussed it among themselves and said, "If we say, 'From heaven,' he will ask, 'Why didn't you believe him?' ⁶But if we say, 'Of human origin,' all the people will stone us, because they are persuaded that John was a prophet." Mt 11:9; Lk 7:29

⁷So they answered, "We don't know where it was from."

⁸Jesus said, "Neither will I tell you by what authority I am doing these things." Mt 21:23-27; Mk 11:27-33

The Parable of the Tenants

20:9-19pp — Mt 21:33-46; Mk 12:1-12

⁹He went on to tell the people this parable: "A man planted a vineyard, rented it to some farmers and went away for a long time. ¹⁰At harvest time he sent a servant to the tenants so they would give him some of the fruit of the vineyard. But the tenants beat him and sent him away empty-handed. ¹¹He sent another servant, but that one also they beat and treated shamefully and sent away empty-handed.

^a 46 Isaiah 56:7   ^b 46 Jer. 7:11

¹²He sent still a third, and they wounded him and threw him out. Isa 5:1-7; Mt 25:14

¹³"Then the owner of the vineyard said, 'What shall I do? I will send my son, whom I love; perhaps they will respect him.' Mt 3:17

¹⁴"But when the tenants saw him, they talked the matter over. 'This is the heir,' they said. 'Let's kill him, and the inheritance will be ours.' ¹⁵So they threw him out of the vineyard and killed him.

"What then will the owner of the vineyard do to them? ¹⁶He will come and kill those tenants and give the vineyard to others." Lk 19:27

When the people heard this, they said, "God forbid!"

¹⁷Jesus looked directly at them and asked, "Then what is the meaning of that which is written:

" 'The stone the builders rejected
has become the cornerstone'ᵃ?

¹⁸Everyone who falls on that stone will be broken to pieces; anyone on whom it falls will be crushed." Isa 8:14-15; Ac 4:11

¹⁹The teachers of the law and the chief priests looked for a way to arrest him immediately, because they knew he had spoken this parable against them. But they were afraid of the people. Mt 21:33-46; Mk 12:1-12

Paying Taxes to Caesar

20:20-26pp — Mt 22:15-22; Mk 12:13-17

²⁰Keeping a close watch on him, they sent spies, who pretended to be sincere. They hoped to catch Jesus in something he said, so that they might hand him over to the power and authority of the governor. ²¹So the spies questioned him: "Teacher, we know that you speak and teach what is right, and that you do not show partiality but teach the way of God in accordance with the truth. ²²Is it right for us to pay taxes to Caesar or not?" Mt 12:10; Jn 3:2

²³He saw through their duplicity and said to them, ²⁴"Show me a denarius. Whose image and inscription are on it?"

"Caesar's," they replied.

²⁵He said to them, "Then give back to Caesar what is Caesar's, and to God what is God's." Lk 23:2

²⁶They were unable to trap him in what he had said there in public. And astonished by his answer, they became silent. Mt 22:15-22

The Resurrection and Marriage

20:27-40pp — Mt 22:23-33; Mk 12:18-27

²⁷Some of the Sadducees, who say there is no resurrection, came to Jesus with a question. ²⁸"Teacher," they said, "Moses wrote for us that if a man's brother dies and leaves a wife but no children, the man must marry the widow and raise up offspring for his brother. ²⁹Now there

ᵃ 17 Psalm 118:22

were seven brothers. The first one married a woman and died childless. ³⁰The second ³¹and then the third married her, and in the same way the seven died, leaving no children. ³²Finally, the woman died too. ³³Now then, at the resurrection whose wife will she be, since the seven were married to her?" Dt 25:5; Ac 23:8

³⁴Jesus replied, "The people of this age marry and are given in marriage. ³⁵But those who are considered worthy of taking part in the age to come and in the resurrection from the dead will neither marry nor be given in marriage, ³⁶and they can no longer die; for they are like the angels. They are God's children, since they are children of the resurrection. ³⁷But in the account of the burning bush, even Moses showed that the dead rise, for he calls the Lord 'the God of Abraham, and the God of Isaac, and the God of Jacob.'ᵃ ³⁸He is not the God of the dead, but of the living, for to him all are alive." Ex 3:6

³⁹Some of the teachers of the law responded, "Well said, teacher!" ⁴⁰And no one dared to ask him any more questions. Mt 22:23-33

Whose Son Is the Messiah?
20:41-47pp — Mt 22:41-23:7;
    Mk 12:35-40

⁴¹Then Jesus said to them, "Why is it said that the Messiah is the son of David? ⁴²David

himself declares in the Book of Psalms: Mt 1:1

" 'The Lord said to my Lord:
    "Sit at my right hand
⁴³until I make your enemies
    a footstool for your feet." 'ᵇ

⁴⁴David calls him 'Lord.' How then can he be his son?"

Warning Against the Teachers of the Law

⁴⁵While all the people were listening, Jesus said to his disciples, ⁴⁶"Beware of the teachers of the law. They like to walk around in flowing robes and love to be greeted with respect in the marketplaces and have the most important seats in the synagogues and the places of honor at banquets. ⁴⁷They devour widows' houses and for a show make lengthy prayers. These men will be punished most severely." Mt 22:41-23:7

The Widow's Offering
21:1-4pp — Mk 12:41-44

21 As Jesus looked up, he saw the rich putting their gifts into the temple treasury. ²He also saw a poor widow put in two very small copper coins. ³"Truly I tell you," he said, "this poor widow has put in more than all the others. ⁴All these people gave their gifts out of their wealth; but she out of her poverty put in all she had to live on." Mk 12:41-44

ᵃ 37 Exodus 3:6   ᵇ 43 Psalm 110:1

The Destruction of the Temple and Signs of the End Times

21:5-36pp — Mt 24; Mk 13
21:12-17pp — Mt 10:17-22

⁵Some of his disciples were remarking about how the temple was adorned with beautiful stones and with gifts dedicated to God. But Jesus said, ⁶"As for what you see here, the time will come when not one stone will be left on another; every one of them will be thrown down." Lk 19:44

⁷"Teacher," they asked, "when will these things happen? And what will be the sign that they are about to take place?"

⁸He replied: "Watch out that you are not deceived. For many will come in my name, claiming, 'I am he,' and, 'The time is near.' Do not follow them. ⁹When you hear of wars and uprisings, do not be frightened. These things must happen first, but the end will not come right away." Lk 17:23

¹⁰Then he said to them: "Nation will rise against nation, and kingdom against kingdom. ¹¹There will be great earthquakes, famines and pestilences in various places, and fearful events and great signs from heaven. 2Ch 15:6; Isa 29:6

¹²"But before all this, they will seize you and persecute you. They will hand you over to synagogues and put you in prison, and you will be brought before kings and governors, and all on account of my name. ¹³And so you will bear testimony to me. ¹⁴But make up your mind not to worry beforehand how you will defend yourselves. ¹⁵For I will give you words and wisdom that none of your adversaries will be able to resist or contradict. ¹⁶You will be betrayed even by parents, brothers and sisters, relatives and friends, and they will put some of you to death. ¹⁷Everyone will hate you because of me. ¹⁸But not a hair of your head will perish. ¹⁹Stand firm, and you will win life. Mt 10:17-22

²⁰"When you see Jerusalem being surrounded by armies, you will know that its desolation is near. ²¹Then let those who are in Judea flee to the mountains, let those in the city get out, and let those in the country not enter the city. ²²For this is the time of punishment in fulfillment of all that has been written. ²³How dreadful it will be in those days for pregnant women and nursing mothers! There will be great distress in the land and wrath against this people. ²⁴They will fall by the sword and will be taken as prisoners to all the nations. Jerusalem will be trampled on by the Gentiles until the times of the Gentiles are fulfilled. Isa 63:18; Da 8:13

²⁵"There will be signs in the sun, moon and stars. On the earth, nations will be in anguish and perplexity at the roaring and tossing of the sea. ²⁶People will faint from terror, apprehensive

of what is coming on the world, for the heavenly bodies will be shaken. ²⁷At that time they will see the Son of Man coming in a cloud with power and great glory. ²⁸When these things begin to take place, stand up and lift up your heads, because your redemption is drawing near." Lk 18:7; Rev 1:7

²⁹He told them this parable: "Look at the fig tree and all the trees. ³⁰When they sprout leaves, you can see for yourselves and know that summer is near. ³¹Even so, when you see these things happening, you know that the kingdom of God is near. Mt 3:2

³²"Truly I tell you, this generation will certainly not pass away until all these things have happened. ³³Heaven and earth will pass away, but my words will never pass away. Mt 5:18; Lk 11:50

³⁴"Be careful, or your hearts will be weighed down with carousing, drunkenness and the anxieties of life, and that day will close on you suddenly like a trap. ³⁵For it will come on all those who live on the face of the whole earth. ³⁶Be always on the watch, and pray that you may be able to escape all that is about to happen, and that you may be able to stand before the Son of Man." Mk 4:19

³⁷Each day Jesus was teaching at the temple, and each evening he went out to spend the night on the hill called the Mount of Olives, ³⁸and all the people came early in the morning to hear him at the temple. Mk 11:19; Jn 8:2

Judas Agrees to Betray Jesus
22:1,2pp — Mt 26:2-5; Mk 14:1,2,10,11

22 Now the Festival of Unleavened Bread, called the Passover, was approaching, ²and the chief priests and the teachers of the law were looking for some way to get rid of Jesus, for they were afraid of the people. ³Then Satan entered Judas, called Iscariot, one of the Twelve. ⁴And Judas went to the chief priests and the officers of the temple guard and discussed with them how he might betray Jesus. ⁵They were delighted and agreed to give him money. ⁶He consented, and watched for an opportunity to hand Jesus over to them when no crowd was present. Mt 26:2-5; Mk 14:1-2,10-11

The Last Supper
22:7-13pp — Mt 26:17-19; Mk 14:12-16
22:17-20pp — Mt 26:26-29; Mk 14:22-25; 1Co 11:23-25
22:21-23pp — Mt 26:21-24; Mk 14:18-21; Jn 13:21-30
22:25-27pp — Mt 20:25-28; Mk 10:42-45
22:33,34pp — Mt 26:33-35; Mk 14:29-31; Jn 13:37,38

⁷Then came the day of Unleavened Bread on which the Passover lamb had to be sacrificed. ⁸Jesus sent Peter and John, saying, "Go and make preparations for us to eat the Passover." Dt 16:5-8

⁹"Where do you want us to prepare for it?" they asked.

[10] He replied, "As you enter the city, a man carrying a jar of water will meet you. Follow him to the house that he enters, [11] and say to the owner of the house, 'The Teacher asks: Where is the guest room, where I may eat the Passover with my disciples?' [12] He will show you a large room upstairs, all furnished. Make preparations there."

[13] They left and found things just as Jesus had told them. So they prepared the Passover.

[14] When the hour came, Jesus and his apostles reclined at the table. [15] And he said to them, "I have eagerly desired to eat this Passover with you before I suffer. [16] For I tell you, I will not eat it again until it finds fulfillment in the kingdom of God." Lk 14:15

[17] After taking the cup, he gave thanks and said, "Take this and divide it among you. [18] For I tell you I will not drink again from the fruit of the vine until the kingdom of God comes."

[19] And he took bread, gave thanks and broke it, and gave it to them, saying, "This is my body given for you; do this in remembrance of me." Mt 26:26-29; Mk 14:22-25

[20] In the same way, after the supper he took the cup, saying, "This cup is the new covenant in my blood, which is poured out for you.[a] [21] But the hand of him who is going to betray me is with mine on the table. [22] The Son of Man will go as it has been decreed. But woe to that man who betrays him!" [23] They began to question among themselves which of them it might be who would do this. Mt 26:21-24; Mk 14:18-21

[24] A dispute also arose among them as to which of them was considered to be greatest. [25] Jesus said to them, "The kings of the Gentiles lord it over them; and those who exercise authority over them call themselves Benefactors. [26] But you are not to be like that. Instead, the greatest among you should be like the youngest, and the one who rules like the one who serves. [27] For who is greater, the one who is at the table or the one who serves? Is it not the one who is at the table? But I am among you as one who serves. [28] You are those who have stood by me in my trials. [29] And I confer on you a kingdom, just as my Father conferred one on me, [30] so that you may eat and drink at my table in my kingdom and sit on thrones, judging the twelve tribes of Israel. Mt 20:25-28; Mk 10:42-45

[31] "Simon, Simon, Satan has asked to sift all of you as wheat. [32] But I have prayed for you, Simon, that your faith may not fail. And when you have turned back, strengthen your brothers." Jn 21:15

[33] But he replied, "Lord, I am ready to go with you to prison and to death." Jn 11:16

[a] 19,20 Some manuscripts do not have *given for you . . . poured out for you.*

³⁴Jesus answered, "I tell you, Peter, before the rooster crows today, you will deny three times that you know me."   Mt 26:33-35

³⁵Then Jesus asked them, "When I sent you without purse, bag or sandals, did you lack anything?"   Mt 10:9-10; Lk 9:3; 10:4

"Nothing," they answered.

³⁶He said to them, "But now if you have a purse, take it, and also a bag; and if you don't have a sword, sell your cloak and buy one. ³⁷It is written: 'And he was numbered with the transgressors'ᵃ; and I tell you that this must be fulfilled in me. Yes, what is written about me is reaching its fulfillment."   Isa 53:12

³⁸The disciples said, "See, Lord, here are two swords."

"That's enough!" he replied.

Jesus Prays on the Mount of Olives

22:40-46pp — Mt 26:36-46; Mk 14:32-42

³⁹Jesus went out as usual to the Mount of Olives, and his disciples followed him. ⁴⁰On reaching the place, he said to them, "Pray that you will not fall into temptation." ⁴¹He withdrew about a stone's throw beyond them, knelt down and prayed, ⁴²"Father, if you are willing, take this cup from me; yet not my will, but yours be done." ⁴³An angel from heaven appeared to him and strengthened him. ⁴⁴And being in anguish, he prayed more earnestly, and his sweat was like drops of blood falling to the ground.ᵇ   Mt 4:11; 6:13

⁴⁵When he rose from prayer and went back to the disciples, he found them asleep, exhausted from sorrow. ⁴⁶"Why are you sleeping?" he asked them. "Get up and pray so that you will not fall into temptation."   Mt 26:36-46

Jesus Arrested

22:47-53pp — Mt 26:47-56; Mk 14:43-50; Jn 18:3-11

⁴⁷While he was still speaking a crowd came up, and the man who was called Judas, one of the Twelve, was leading them. He approached Jesus to kiss him, ⁴⁸but Jesus asked him, "Judas, are you betraying the Son of Man with a kiss?"

⁴⁹When Jesus' followers saw what was going to happen, they said, "Lord, should we strike with our swords?" ⁵⁰And one of them struck the servant of the high priest, cutting off his right ear.

⁵¹But Jesus answered, "No more of this!" And he touched the man's ear and healed him.

⁵²Then Jesus said to the chief priests, the officers of the temple guard, and the elders, who had come for him, "Am I leading a rebellion, that you have come with swords and clubs? ⁵³Every day I was with you in

ᵃ 37 Isaiah 53:12   ᵇ 43,44 Many early manuscripts do not have verses 43 and 44.

the temple courts, and you did not lay a hand on me. But this is your hour — when darkness reigns." Mt 26:47-56; Mk 14:43-50

Peter Disowns Jesus

22:55-62pp — Mt 26:69-75; Mk 14:66-72; Jn 18:16-18,25-27

⁵⁴ Then seizing him, they led him away and took him into the house of the high priest. Peter followed at a distance. ⁵⁵ And when some there had kindled a fire in the middle of the courtyard and had sat down together, Peter sat down with them. ⁵⁶ A servant girl saw him seated there in the firelight. She looked closely at him and said, "This man was with him." Mt 26:57-58; Mk 14:53-54

⁵⁷ But he denied it. "Woman, I don't know him," he said.

⁵⁸ A little later someone else saw him and said, "You also are one of them."

"Man, I am not!" Peter replied.

⁵⁹ About an hour later another asserted, "Certainly this fellow was with him, for he is a Galilean." Lk 23:6

⁶⁰ Peter replied, "Man, I don't know what you're talking about!" Just as he was speaking, the rooster crowed. ⁶¹ The Lord turned and looked straight at Peter. Then Peter remembered the word the Lord had spoken to him: "Before the rooster crows today, you will disown me three times." ⁶² And he went outside and wept bitterly. Mt 26:69-75; Mk 14:66-72

The Guards Mock Jesus

22:63-65pp — Mt 26:67,68; Mk 14:65; Jn 18:22,23

⁶³ The men who were guarding Jesus began mocking and beating him. ⁶⁴ They blindfolded him and demanded, "Prophesy! Who hit you?" ⁶⁵ And they said many other insulting things to him. Mt 26:67-68; Mk 14:65; Jn 18:22-23

Jesus Before Pilate and Herod

22:67-71pp — Mt 26:63-66; Mk 14:61-63; Jn 18:19-21
23:2,3pp — Mt 27:11-14; Mk 15:2-5; Jn 18:29-37
23:18-25pp — Mt 27:15-26; Mk 15:6-15; Jn 18:39 – 19:16

⁶⁶ At daybreak the council of the elders of the people, both the chief priests and the teachers of the law, met together, and Jesus was led before them. ⁶⁷ "If you are the Messiah," they said, "tell us." Mt 27:1; Mk 15:1

Jesus answered, "If I tell you, you will not believe me, ⁶⁸ and if I asked you, you would not answer. ⁶⁹ But from now on, the Son of Man will be seated at the right hand of the mighty God." Mk 16:19

⁷⁰ They all asked, "Are you then the Son of God?" Mt 4:3

He replied, "You say that I am." Mt 27:11; Lk 23:3

⁷¹ Then they said, "Why do we need any more testimony? We have heard it from his own lips." Mt 26:63-66; Mk 14:61-63

23 Then the whole assembly rose and led him off to Pilate. ² And they began to accuse him, saying, "We have found this man subverting our nation. He opposes payment of taxes to Caesar and claims to be Messiah, a king." Lk 20:22; Jn 19:12

³So Pilate asked Jesus, "Are you the king of the Jews?"

"You have said so," Jesus replied. Mt 27:11-14; Mk 15:2-5; Jn 18:29-37

⁴Then Pilate announced to the chief priests and the crowd, "I find no basis for a charge against this man." Mt 27:23; 2Co 5:21

⁵But they insisted, "He stirs up the people all over Judea by his teaching. He started in Galilee and has come all the way here." Mk 1:14

⁶On hearing this, Pilate asked if the man was a Galilean. ⁷When he learned that Jesus was under Herod's jurisdiction, he sent him to Herod, who was also in Jerusalem at that time. Mt 14:1; Lk 3:1

⁸When Herod saw Jesus, he was greatly pleased, because for a long time he had been wanting to see him. From what he had heard about him, he hoped to see him perform a sign of some sort. ⁹He plied him with many questions, but Jesus gave him no answer. ¹⁰The chief priests and the teachers of the law were standing there, vehemently accusing him. ¹¹Then Herod and his soldiers ridiculed and mocked him. Dressing him in an elegant robe, they sent him back to Pilate. ¹²That day Herod and Pilate became friends—before this they had been enemies. Mk 15:17-19; Lk 9:9

¹³Pilate called together the chief priests, the rulers and the people, ¹⁴and said to them, "You brought me this man as one who was inciting the people to rebellion. I have examined him in your presence and have found no basis for your charges against him. ¹⁵Neither has Herod, for he sent him back to us; as you can see, he has done nothing to deserve death. ¹⁶Therefore, I will punish him and then release him." [17]ᵃ Mt 27:26; Jn 19:1

¹⁸But the whole crowd shouted, "Away with this man! Release Barabbas to us!" ¹⁹(Barabbas had been thrown into prison for an insurrection in the city, and for murder.) Ac 3:13-14

²⁰Wanting to release Jesus, Pilate appealed to them again. ²¹But they kept shouting, "Crucify him! Crucify him!"

²²For the third time he spoke to them: "Why? What crime has this man committed? I have found in him no grounds for the death penalty. Therefore I will have him punished and then release him." ver 16

²³But with loud shouts they insistently demanded that he be crucified, and their shouts prevailed. ²⁴So Pilate decided to grant their demand. ²⁵He released the man who had been thrown into prison for insurrection

ᵃ 17 Some manuscripts include here words similar to Matt. 27:15 and Mark 15:6.

and murder, the one they asked for, and surrendered Jesus to their will. Mt 27:15-26; Mk 15:6-15

The Crucifixion of Jesus

23:33-43pp — Mt 27:33-44;
Mk 15:22-32; Jn 19:17-24

²⁶ As the soldiers led him away, they seized Simon from Cyrene, who was on his way in from the country, and put the cross on him and made him carry it behind Jesus. ²⁷ A large number of people followed him, including women who mourned and wailed for him. ²⁸ Jesus turned and said to them, "Daughters of Jerusalem, do not weep for me; weep for yourselves and for your children. ²⁹ For the time will come when you will say, 'Blessed are the childless women, the wombs that never bore and the breasts that never nursed!' ³⁰ Then

"'they will say to the
    mountains, "Fall on us!"
and to the hills, "Cover us!"'ᵃ

³¹ For if people do these things when the tree is green, what will happen when it is dry?" Eze 20:47

³² Two other men, both criminals, were also led out with him to be executed. ³³ When they came to the place called the Skull, they crucified him there, along with the criminals — one on his right, the other on his left. ³⁴ Jesus said, "Father, forgive them, for they do not know what they are doing."ᵇ And they divided up his clothes by casting lots. Ps 22:18; Mt 27:38

³⁵ The people stood watching, and the rulers even sneered at him. They said, "He saved others; let him save himself if he is God's Messiah, the Chosen One." Ps 22:17; Isa 42:1

³⁶ The soldiers also came up and mocked him. They offered him wine vinegar ³⁷ and said, "If you are the king of the Jews, save yourself." Mt 27:48; Lk 4:3,9

³⁸ There was a written notice above him, which read: THIS IS THE KING OF THE JEWS. Mt 2:2

³⁹ One of the criminals who hung there hurled insults at him: "Aren't you the Messiah? Save yourself and us!" ver 35,37

⁴⁰ But the other criminal rebuked him. "Don't you fear God," he said, "since you are under the same sentence? ⁴¹ We are punished justly, for we are getting what our deeds deserve. But this man has done nothing wrong."

⁴² Then he said, "Jesus, remember me when you come into your kingdom.ᶜ" Mt 16:27

⁴³ Jesus answered him, "Truly I tell you, today you will be with me in paradise." Mt 27:33-44

The Death of Jesus

23:44-49pp — Mt 27:45-56;
Mk 15:33-41; Jn 19:29-30

⁴⁴ It was now about noon, and

ᵃ 30 Hosea 10:8   ᵇ 34 Some early manuscripts do not have this sentence.   ᶜ 42 Some manuscripts *come with your kingly power*

darkness came over the whole land until three in the afternoon, ⁴⁵for the sun stopped shining. And the curtain of the temple was torn in two. ⁴⁶Jesus called out with a loud voice, "Father, into your hands I commit my spirit."^a When he had said this, he breathed his last. Ps 31:5; Jn 19:30

⁴⁷The centurion, seeing what had happened, praised God and said, "Surely this was a righteous man." ⁴⁸When all the people who had gathered to witness this sight saw what took place, they beat their breasts and went away. ⁴⁹But all those who knew him, including the women who had followed him from Galilee, stood at a distance, watching these things. Mt 27:45-56; Mk 15:33-41

The Burial of Jesus

23:50-56pp — Mt 27:57-61; Mk 15:42-47; Jn 19:38-42

⁵⁰Now there was a man named Joseph, a member of the Council, a good and upright man, ⁵¹who had not consented to their decision and action. He came from the Judean town of Arimathea, and he himself was waiting for the kingdom of God. ⁵²Going to Pilate, he asked for Jesus' body. ⁵³Then he took it down, wrapped it in linen cloth and placed it in a tomb cut in the rock, one in which no one had yet been laid. ⁵⁴It was Preparation Day, and the Sabbath was about to begin. Mt 27:62

⁵⁵The women who had come with Jesus from Galilee followed Joseph and saw the tomb and how his body was laid in it. ⁵⁶Then they went home and prepared spices and perfumes. But they rested on the Sabbath in obedience to the commandment.Mt 27:57-61; Mk 15:42-47; Jn 19:38-42

Jesus Has Risen

24:1-10pp — Mt 28:1-8; Mk 16:1-8; Jn 20:1-8

24 On the first day of the week, very early in the morning, the women took the spices they had prepared and went to the tomb. ²They found the stone rolled away from the tomb, ³but when they entered, they did not find the body of the Lord Jesus. ⁴While they were wondering about this, suddenly two men in clothes that gleamed like lightning stood beside them. ⁵In their fright the women bowed down with their faces to the ground, but the men said to them, "Why do you look for the living among the dead? ⁶He is not here; he has risen! Remember how he told you, while he was still with you in Galilee: ⁷'The Son of Man must be delivered over to the hands of sinners, be crucified and on the third day be raised again.'" ⁸Then they remembered his words. Mt 28:1-8

⁹When they came back from the tomb, they told all these

^a 46 Psalm 31:5

things to the Eleven and to all the others. [10]It was Mary Magdalene, Joanna, Mary the mother of James, and the others with them who told this to the apostles. [11]But they did not believe the women, because their words seemed to them like nonsense. [12]Peter, however, got up and ran to the tomb. Bending over, he saw the strips of linen lying by themselves, and he went away, wondering to himself what had happened.   Mk 16:1-8; Jn 20:1-8

On the Road to Emmaus

[13]Now that same day two of them were going to a village called Emmaus, about seven miles[a] from Jerusalem. [14]They were talking with each other about everything that had happened. [15]As they talked and discussed these things with each other, Jesus himself came up and walked along with them; [16]but they were kept from recognizing him.   Jn 20:14; 21:4

[17]He asked them, "What are you discussing together as you walk along?"

They stood still, their faces downcast. [18]One of them, named Cleopas, asked him, "Are you the only one visiting Jerusalem who does not know the things that have happened there in these days?"   Jn 19:25

[19]"What things?" he asked.

"About Jesus of Nazareth," they replied. "He was a prophet, powerful in word and deed before God and all the people. [20]The chief priests and our rulers handed him over to be sentenced to death, and they crucified him; [21]but we had hoped that he was the one who was going to redeem Israel. And what is more, it is the third day since all this took place. [22]In addition, some of our women amazed us. They went to the tomb early this morning [23]but didn't find his body. They came and told us that they had seen a vision of angels, who said he was alive. [24]Then some of our companions went to the tomb and found it just as the women had said, but they did not see Jesus."   Mt 21:11; Mk 1:24

[25]He said to them, "How foolish you are, and how slow to believe all that the prophets have spoken! [26]Did not the Messiah have to suffer these things and then enter his glory?" [27]And beginning with Moses and all the Prophets, he explained to them what was said in all the Scriptures concerning himself.   Jn 1:45

[28]As they approached the village to which they were going, Jesus continued on as if he were going farther. [29]But they urged him strongly, "Stay with us, for it is nearly evening; the day is almost over." So he went in to stay with them.

[30]When he was at the table

[a] 13 Or about 11 kilometers

with them, he took bread, gave thanks, broke it and began to give it to them. [31] Then their eyes were opened and they recognized him, and he disappeared from their sight. [32] They asked each other, "Were not our hearts burning within us while he talked with us on the road and opened the Scriptures to us?"   Ps 39:3; Mt 14:19

[33] They got up and returned at once to Jerusalem. There they found the Eleven and those with them, assembled together [34] and saying, "It is true! The Lord has risen and has appeared to Simon." [35] Then the two told what had happened on the way, and how Jesus was recognized by them when he broke the bread.   1Co 15:5

Jesus Appears to the Disciples

[36] While they were still talking about this, Jesus himself stood among them and said to them, "Peace be with you."   Jn 20:19,21,26

[37] They were startled and frightened, thinking they saw a ghost. [38] He said to them, "Why are you troubled, and why do doubts rise in your minds? [39] Look at my hands and my feet. It is I myself! Touch me and see; a ghost does not have flesh and bones, as you see I have."   Mk 6:49; Jn 20:27

[40] When he had said this, he showed them his hands and feet. [41] And while they still did not believe it because of joy and amazement, he asked them, "Do you have anything here to eat?" [42] They gave him a piece of broiled fish, [43] and he took it and ate it in their presence.   Ac 10:41

[44] He said to them, "This is what I told you while I was still with you: Everything must be fulfilled that is written about me in the Law of Moses, the Prophets and the Psalms."   Mt 18:31-33

[45] Then he opened their minds so they could understand the Scriptures. [46] He told them, "This is what is written: The Messiah will suffer and rise from the dead on the third day, [47] and repentance for the forgiveness of sins will be preached in his name to all nations, beginning at Jerusalem. [48] You are witnesses of these things. [49] I am going to send you what my Father has promised; but stay in the city until you have been clothed with power from on high."   Ac 1:4,8

The Ascension of Jesus

[50] When he had led them out to the vicinity of Bethany, he lifted up his hands and blessed them. [51] While he was blessing them, he left them and was taken up into heaven. [52] Then they worshiped him and returned to Jerusalem with great joy. [53] And they stayed continually at the temple, praising God.   2Ki 2:11; Ac 2:46

John

The Word Became Flesh

1 In the beginning was the Word, and the Word was with God, and the Word was God. ²He was with God in the beginning. ³Through him all things were made; without him nothing was made that has been made. ⁴In him was life, and that life was the light of all mankind. ⁵The light shines in the darkness, and the darkness has not overcome*ᵃ* it.   Jn 3:19; 5:26; Php 2:6

⁶There was a man sent from God whose name was John. ⁷He came as a witness to testify concerning that light, so that through him all might believe. ⁸He himself was not the light; he came only as a witness to the light.

⁹The true light that gives light to everyone was coming into the world. ¹⁰He was in the world, and though the world was made through him, the world did not recognize him. ¹¹He came to that which was his own, but his own did not receive him. ¹²Yet to all who did receive him, to those who believed in his name, he gave the right to become children of God— ¹³children born not of natural descent, nor of human decision or a husband's will, but born of God.   Jn 3:6; 1Pe 1:23

¹⁴The Word became flesh and made his dwelling among us. We have seen his glory, the glory of the one and only Son, who came from the Father, full of grace and truth.   Gal 4:4; 1Ti 3:16

¹⁵(John testified concerning him. He cried out, saying, "This is the one I spoke about when I said, 'He who comes after me has surpassed me because he was before me.'") ¹⁶Out of his fullness we have all received grace in place of grace already given. ¹⁷For the law was given through Moses; grace and truth came through Jesus Christ. ¹⁸No one has ever seen God, but the one and only Son, who is himself God and*ᵇ* is in closest relation-

---

ᵃ 5 Or *understood*   *ᵇ 18* Some manuscripts *but the only Son, who* ship with the Father, has made him known. Ex 33:20; 1Jn 4:9

John the Baptist Denies Being the Messiah

¹⁹Now this was John's testimony when the Jewish leaders[a] in Jerusalem sent priests and Levites to ask him who he was. ²⁰He did not fail to confess, but confessed freely, "I am not the Messiah." Lk 3:15-16; Jn 2:18 ²¹They asked him, "Then who are you? Are you Elijah?" Mt 11:14

He said, "I am not."

"Are you the Prophet?" Dt 18:15

He answered, "No."

²²Finally they said, "Who are you? Give us an answer to take back to those who sent us. What do you say about yourself?" ²³John replied in the words of Isaiah the prophet, "I am the voice of one calling in the wilderness, 'Make straight the way for the Lord.'"[b] Isa 40:3; Mt 3:1 ²⁴Now the Pharisees who had been sent ²⁵questioned him, "Why then do you baptize if you are not the Messiah, nor Elijah, nor the Prophet?"

²⁶"I baptize with[c] water," John replied, "but among you stands one you do not know. ²⁷He is the one who comes after me, the straps of whose sandals I am not worthy to untie." Mk 1:4,7 ²⁸This all happened at Beth-

any on the other side of the Jordan, where John was baptizing.

John Testifies About Jesus

²⁹The next day John saw Jesus coming toward him and said, "Look, the Lamb of God, who takes away the sin of the world! ³⁰This is the one I meant when I said, 'A man who comes after me has surpassed me because he was before me.' ³¹I myself did not know him, but the reason I came baptizing with water was that he might be revealed to Israel." Isa 53:7; 1Pe 1:19 ³²Then John gave this testimony: "I saw the Spirit come down from heaven as a dove and remain on him. ³³And I myself did not know him, but the one who sent me to baptize with water told me, 'The man on whom you see the Spirit come down and remain is the one who will baptize with the Holy Spirit.' ³⁴I have seen and I testify that this is God's Chosen One."[d] Mt 3:11,16; Mk 1:10

John's Disciples Follow Jesus

1:40-42pp — Mt 4:18-22; Mk 1:16-20; Lk 5:2-11

³⁵The next day John was there again with two of his disciples. ³⁶When he saw Jesus passing by, he said, "Look, the Lamb of God!" ver 29 ³⁷When the two disciples heard

[a] 19 The Greek term traditionally translated the Jews (hoi Ioudaioi) refers here and elsewhere in John's Gospel to those Jewish leaders who opposed Jesus; also in 5:10, 15, 16; 7:1, 11, 13; 9:22; 18:14, 28, 36; 19:7, 12, 31, 38; 20:19. [b] 23 Isaiah 40:3 [c] 26 Or in; also in verses 31 and 33 (twice) [d] 34 See Isaiah 42:1; many manuscripts is the Son of God.

him say this, they followed Jesus. [38]Turning around, Jesus saw them following and asked, "What do you want?"

They said, "Rabbi" (which means "Teacher"), "where are you staying?" Mt 23:7

[39]"Come," he replied, "and you will see."

So they went and saw where he was staying, and they spent that day with him. It was about four in the afternoon.

[40]Andrew, Simon Peter's brother, was one of the two who heard what John had said and who had followed Jesus. [41]The first thing Andrew did was to find his brother Simon and tell him, "We have found the Messiah" (that is, the Christ). [42]And he brought him to Jesus. Jn 4:25

Jesus looked at him and said, "You are Simon son of John. You will be called Cephas" (which, when translated, is Peter[a]).

Jesus Calls Philip and Nathanael

[43]The next day Jesus decided to leave for Galilee. Finding Philip, he said to him, "Follow me." Mt 10:3; Jn 14:8-9

[44]Philip, like Andrew and Peter, was from the town of Bethsaida. [45]Philip found Nathanael and told him, "We have found the one Moses wrote about in the Law, and about whom the proph-

ets also wrote — Jesus of Nazareth, the son of Joseph." Mt 2:23

[46]"Nazareth! Can anything good come from there?" Nathanael asked. Jn 7:41-42,52

"Come and see," said Philip.

[47]When Jesus saw Nathanael approaching, he said of him, "Here truly is an Israelite in whom there is no deceit." Ps 32:2

[48]"How do you know me?" Nathanael asked.

Jesus answered, "I saw you while you were still under the fig tree before Philip called you."

[49]Then Nathanael declared, "Rabbi, you are the Son of God; you are the king of Israel." Mt 4:3

[50]Jesus said, "You believe[b] because I told you I saw you under the fig tree. You will see greater things than that." [51]He then added, "Very truly I tell you,[c] you[c] will see 'heaven open, and the angels of God ascending and descending on'[d] the Son of Man." Ge 28:12; Mt 3:16; 8:20

Jesus Changes Water Into Wine

2 On the third day a wedding took place at Cana in Galilee. Jesus' mother was there, [2]and Jesus and his disciples had also been invited to the wedding. [3]When the wine was gone, Jesus' mother said to him, "They have no more wine." Mt 12:46; Jn 4:46

[4]"Woman,[e] why do you involve

---

[a] 42 Cephas (Aramaic) and Peter (Greek) both mean rock.   [b] 50 Or Do you believe . . . ?
[c] 51 The Greek is plural.   [d] 51 Gen. 28:12   [e] 4 The Greek for Woman does not denote any disrespect.

me?" Jesus replied. "My hour has not yet come." Jn 7:6; 19:26

⁵His mother said to the servants, "Do whatever he tells you."

⁶Nearby stood six stone water jars, the kind used by the Jews for ceremonial washing, each holding from twenty to thirty gallons.ᵃ

⁷Jesus said to the servants, "Fill the jars with water"; so they filled them to the brim.

⁸Then he told them, "Now draw some out and take it to the master of the banquet."

They did so, ⁹and the master of the banquet tasted the water that had been turned into wine. He did not realize where it had come from, though the servants who had drawn the water knew. Then he called the bridegroom aside ¹⁰and said, "Everyone brings out the choice wine first and then the cheaper wine after the guests have had too much to drink; but you have saved the best till now."

¹¹What Jesus did here in Cana of Galilee was the first of the signs through which he revealed his glory; and his disciples believed in him. Ex 14:31; Jn 1:14

¹²After this he went down to Capernaum with his mother and brothers and his disciples. There they stayed for a few days. Mt 12:46

Jesus Clears the Temple Courts

2:14-16pp — Mt 21:12,13; Mk 11:15-17; Lk 19:45,46

¹³When it was almost time for the Jewish Passover, Jesus went up to Jerusalem. ¹⁴In the temple courts he found people selling cattle, sheep and doves, and others sitting at tables exchanging money. ¹⁵So he made a whip out of cords, and drove all from the temple courts, both sheep and cattle; he scattered the coins of the money changers and overturned their tables. ¹⁶To those who sold doves he said, "Get these out of here! Stop turning my Father's house into a market!" ¹⁷His disciples remembered that it is written: "Zeal for your house will consume me."ᵇ Ps 69:9

¹⁸The Jews then responded to him, "What sign can you show us to prove your authority to do all this?" Mt 12:38

¹⁹Jesus answered them, "Destroy this temple, and I will raise it again in three days." Mt 26:61

²⁰They replied, "It has taken forty-six years to build this temple, and you are going to raise it in three days?" ²¹But the temple he had spoken of was his body. ²²After he was raised from the dead, his disciples recalled what he had said. Then they believed the scripture and the words that Jesus had spoken. Lk 24:5-8; 1Co 6:19

²³Now while he was in Jerusalem at the Passover Festival, many people saw the signs he was performing and believed in his name.ᶜ ²⁴But Jesus would not entrust himself to them, for

ᵃ 6 Or from about 75 to about 115 liters   ᵇ 17 Psalm 69:9   ᶜ 23 Or in him he knew all people. [25] He did not need any testimony about mankind, for he knew what was in each person. *Jn 6:61,64; 13:11*

Jesus Teaches Nicodemus

3 Now there was a Pharisee, a man named Nicodemus who was a member of the Jewish ruling council. [2] He came to Jesus at night and said, "Rabbi, we know that you are a teacher who has come from God. For no one could perform the signs you are doing if God were not with him." *Jn 9:16,33; Ac 2:22*

[3] Jesus replied, "Very truly I tell you, no one can see the kingdom of God unless they are born again.[a]" *Jn 1:13; 1Pe 1:23*

[4] "How can someone be born when they are old?" Nicodemus asked. "Surely they cannot enter a second time into their mother's womb to be born!"

[5] Jesus answered, "Very truly I tell you, no one can enter the kingdom of God unless they are born of water and the Spirit. [6] Flesh gives birth to flesh, but the Spirit[b] gives birth to spirit. [7] You should not be surprised at my saying, 'You[c] must be born again.' [8] The wind blows wherever it pleases. You hear its sound, but you cannot tell where it comes from or where it is going.

So it is with everyone born of the Spirit."[d] *Jn 1:13; Tit 3:5*

[9] "How can this be?" Nicodemus asked. *Jn 6:52,60*

[10] "You are Israel's teacher," said Jesus, "and do you not understand these things? [11] Very truly I tell you, we speak of what we know, and we testify to what we have seen, but still you people do not accept our testimony. [12] I have spoken to you of earthly things and you do not believe; how then will you believe if I speak of heavenly things? [13] No one has ever gone into heaven except the one who came from heaven — the Son of Man.[e] [14] Just as Moses lifted up the snake in the wilderness, so the Son of Man must be lifted up,[f] [15] that everyone who believes may have eternal life in him."[g] *Nu 21:8-9; Jn 8:28*

[16] For God so loved the world that he gave his one and only Son, that whoever believes in him shall not perish but have eternal life. [17] For God did not send his Son into the world to condemn the world, but to save the world through him. [18] Whoever believes in him is not condemned, but whoever does not believe stands condemned already because they have not believed in the name of God's one and only Son. [19] This is the ver-

---

[a] 3 The Greek for *again* also means *from above*; also in verse 7.   [b] 6 Or *but spirit*
[c] 7 The Greek is plural.   [d] 8 The Greek for *Spirit* is the same as that for *wind*.   [e] 13 Some manuscripts *Man, who is in heaven*   [f] 14 The Greek for *lifted up* also means *exalted*.
[g] 15 Some interpreters end the quotation with verse 21.

dict: Light has come into the world, but people loved darkness instead of light because their deeds were evil. [20] Everyone who does evil hates the light, and will not come into the light for fear that their deeds will be exposed. [21] But whoever lives by the truth comes into the light, so that it may be seen plainly that what they have done has been done in the sight of God.   Ro 5:8; 1Jn 4:9-10

John Testifies Again About Jesus

[22] After this, Jesus and his disciples went out into the Judean countryside, where he spent some time with them, and baptized. [23] Now John also was baptizing at Aenon near Salim, because there was plenty of water, and people were coming and being baptized. [24] (This was before John was put in prison.) [25] An argument developed between some of John's disciples and a certain Jew over the matter of ceremonial washing. [26] They came to John and said to him, "Rabbi, that man who was with you on the other side of the Jordan — the one you testified about — look, he is baptizing, and everyone is going to him."   Jn 1:7; 4:2

[27] To this John replied, "A person can receive only what is given them from heaven. [28] You yourselves can testify that I said, 'I am not the Messiah but am sent ahead of him.' [29] The bride belongs to the bridegroom. The friend who attends the bridegroom waits and listens for him, and is full of joy when he hears the bridegroom's voice. That joy is mine, and it is now complete. [30] He must become greater; I must become less."[a]   Jn 1:20,23; 16:24

[31] The one who comes from above is above all; the one who is from the earth belongs to the earth, and speaks as one from the earth. The one who comes from heaven is above all. [32] He testifies to what he has seen and heard, but no one accepts his testimony. [33] Whoever has accepted it has certified that God is truthful. [34] For the one whom God has sent speaks the words of God, for God[b] gives the Spirit without limit. [35] The Father loves the Son and has placed everything in his hands. [36] Whoever believes in the Son has eternal life, but whoever rejects the Son will not see life, for God's wrath remains on them.   Mt 28:18; Jn 5:20,22; 17:2

Jesus Talks With a Samaritan Woman

4 Now Jesus learned that the Pharisees had heard that he was gaining and baptizing more disciples than John — [2] although in fact it was not Jesus who baptized, but his disciples. [3] So he left Judea and went back once more to Galilee.   Jn 3:22,26

[4] Now he had to go through

---

[a] 30 Some interpreters end the quotation with verse 36.   [b] 34 Greek *he*

Samaria. ⁵So he came to a town in Samaria called Sychar, near the plot of ground Jacob had given to his son Joseph. ⁶Jacob's well was there, and Jesus, tired as he was from the journey, sat down by the well. It was about noon.   Ge 33:19

⁷When a Samaritan woman came to draw water, Jesus said to her, "Will you give me a drink?" ⁸(His disciples had gone into the town to buy food.)   Ge 24:17; 1Ki 17:10

⁹The Samaritan woman said to him, "You are a Jew and I am a Samaritan woman. How can you ask me for a drink?" (For Jews do not associate with Samaritans.ᵃ)

¹⁰Jesus answered her, "If you knew the gift of God and who it is that asks you for a drink, you would have asked him and he would have given you living water."   Isa 44:3; Rev 21:6; 22:1,17

¹¹"Sir," the woman said, "you have nothing to draw with and the well is deep. Where can you get this living water? ¹²Are you greater than our father Jacob, who gave us the well and drank from it himself, as did also his sons and his livestock?"   ver 6

¹³Jesus answered, "Everyone who drinks this water will be thirsty again, ¹⁴but whoever drinks the water I give them will never thirst. Indeed, the water I give them will become in them a spring of water welling up to eternal life."   Jn 6:35; 7:38

¹⁵The woman said to him, "Sir, give me this water so that I won't get thirsty and have to keep coming here to draw water."   Jn 6:34

¹⁶He told her, "Go, call your husband and come back."

¹⁷"I have no husband," she replied.

Jesus said to her, "You are right when you say you have no husband. ¹⁸The fact is, you have had five husbands, and the man you now have is not your husband. What you have just said is quite true."

¹⁹"Sir," the woman said, "I can see that you are a prophet. ²⁰Our ancestors worshiped on this mountain, but you Jews claim that the place where we must worship is in Jerusalem."   Dt 11:29

²¹"Woman," Jesus replied, "believe me, a time is coming when you will worship the Father neither on this mountain nor in Jerusalem. ²²You Samaritans worship what you do not know; we worship what we do know, for salvation is from the Jews. ²³Yet a time is coming and has now come when the true worshipers will worship the Father in the Spirit and in truth, for they are the kind of worshipers the Father seeks. ²⁴God is spirit, and his worshipers must worship in the Spirit and in truth."   Mal 1:11; Php 3:3

²⁵The woman said, "I know that Messiah" (called Christ) "is coming. When he comes, he will explain everything to us."   Mt 1:16

ᵃ 9 Or *do not use dishes Samaritans have used*

26 Then Jesus declared, "I, the one speaking to you — I am he." Jn 8:24; 9:35-37

The Disciples Rejoin Jesus

27 Just then his disciples returned and were surprised to find him talking with a woman. But no one asked, "What do you want?" or "Why are you talking with her?" ver 8 **28** Then, leaving her water jar, the woman went back to the town and said to the people, **29** "Come, see a man who told me everything I ever did. Could this be the Messiah?" **30** They came out of the town and made their way toward him. Jn 7:26,31 **31** Meanwhile his disciples urged him, "Rabbi, eat something." Mt 23:7 **32** But he said to them, "I have food to eat that you know nothing about." Job 23:12; Mt 4:4; Jn 6:27 **33** Then his disciples said to each other, "Could someone have brought him food?"

34 "My food," said Jesus, "is to do the will of him who sent me and to finish his work. **35** Don't you have a saying, 'It's still four months until harvest'? I tell you, open your eyes and look at the fields! They are ripe for harvest. **36** Even now the one who reaps draws a wage and harvests a crop for eternal life, so that the sower and the reaper may be glad together. **37** Thus the saying 'One sows and another reaps' is true. **38** I sent you to reap what you have not worked for. Others have done the hard work, and you have reaped the benefits of their labor." Mt 9:37; Jn 6:38; Ro 1:13

Many Samaritans Believe

39 Many of the Samaritans from that town believed in him because of the woman's testimony, "He told me everything I ever did." **40** So when the Samaritans came to him, they urged him to stay with them, and he stayed two days. **41** And because of his words many more became believers. ver 5,29

42 They said to the woman, "We no longer believe just because of what you said; now we have heard for ourselves, and we know that this man really is the Savior of the world." Lk 2:11; 1Jn 4:14

Jesus Heals an Official's Son

43 After the two days he left for Galilee. **44** (Now Jesus himself had pointed out that a prophet has no honor in his own country.) **45** When he arrived in Galilee, the Galileans welcomed him. They had seen all that he had done in Jerusalem at the Passover Festival, for they also had been there. Mt 13:57; Jn 2:23

46 Once more he visited Cana in Galilee, where he had turned the water into wine. And there was a certain royal official whose son lay sick at Capernaum. **47** When this man heard that Jesus had arrived in Galilee from Judea, he went to him and begged him to come and heal his son, who was close to death. Jn 2:1-11

⁴⁸"Unless you people see signs and wonders," Jesus told him, "you will never believe." Da 4:2-3

⁴⁹The royal official said, "Sir, come down before my child dies."

⁵⁰"Go," Jesus replied, "your son will live."

The man took Jesus at his word and departed. ⁵¹While he was still on the way, his servants met him with the news that his boy was living. ⁵²When he inquired as to the time when his son got better, they said to him, "Yesterday, at one in the afternoon, the fever left him."

⁵³Then the father realized that this was the exact time at which Jesus had said to him, "Your son will live." So he and his whole household believed. Ac 11:14

⁵⁴This was the second sign Jesus performed after coming from Judea to Galilee. Jn 2:11

The Healing at the Pool

5 Some time later, Jesus went up to Jerusalem for one of the Jewish festivals. ²Now there is in Jerusalem near the Sheep Gate a pool, which in Aramaic is called Bethesdaᵃ and which is sur-rounded by five covered colonnades. ³Here a great number of disabled people used to lie — the blind, the lame, the paralyzed. [4]ᵇ ⁵One who was there had been an invalid for thirty-eight years. ⁶When Jesus saw him lying there and learned that he had been in this condition for a long time, he asked him, "Do you want to get well?" Ne 3:1; 12:39; Jn 19:13,17,20

⁷"Sir," the invalid replied, "I have no one to help me into the pool when the water is stirred. While I am trying to get in, someone else goes down ahead of me."

⁸Then Jesus said to him, "Get up! Pick up your mat and walk." ⁹At once the man was cured; he picked up his mat and walked. Mt 9:5-6; Mk 2:11; Lk 5:24

The day on which this took place was a Sabbath, ¹⁰and so the Jewish leaders said to the man who had been healed, "It is the Sabbath; the law forbids you to carry your mat." Ne 13:15-22; Mt 12:2

¹¹But he replied, "The man who made me well said to me, 'Pick up your mat and walk.'"

¹²So they asked him, "Who is this fellow who told you to pick it up and walk?"

¹³The man who was healed had no idea who it was, for Jesus had slipped away into the crowd that was there.

ᵃ 2 Some manuscripts *Bethzatha*; other manuscripts *Bethsaida*   ᵇ 3,4 Some manuscripts include here, wholly or in part, *paralyzed — and they waited for the moving of the waters.* ⁴*From time to time an angel of the Lord would come down and stir up the waters. The first one into the pool after each such disturbance would be cured of whatever disease they had.*

¹⁴Later Jesus found him at the temple and said to him, "See, you are well again. Stop sinning or something worse may happen to you." ¹⁵The man went away and told the Jewish leaders that it was Jesus who had made him well. Jn 1:19; 8:11

The Authority of the Son

¹⁶So, because Jesus was doing these things on the Sabbath, the Jewish leaders began to persecute him. ¹⁷In his defense Jesus said to them, "My Father is always at his work to this very day, and I too am working." ¹⁸For this reason they tried all the more to kill him; not only was he breaking the Sabbath, but he was even calling God his own Father, making himself equal with God. Jn 7:1; 10:30,33

¹⁹Jesus gave them this answer: "Very truly I tell you, the Son can do nothing by himself; he can do only what he sees his Father doing, because whatever the Father does the Son also does. ²⁰For the Father loves the Son and shows him all he does. Yes, and he will show him even greater works than these, so that you will be amazed. ²¹For just as the Father raises the dead and gives them life, even so the Son gives life to whom he is pleased to give it. ²²Moreover, the Father judges no one, but has entrusted all judgment to the Son, ²³that all may honor the Son just as they honor the Father. Whoever does not honor the Son does not honor the Father, who sent him. Ac 10:42; 1Jn 2:23

²⁴"Very truly I tell you, whoever hears my word and believes him who sent me has eternal life and will not be judged but has crossed over from death to life. ²⁵Very truly I tell you, a time is coming and has now come when the dead will hear the voice of the Son of God and those who hear will live. ²⁶For as the Father has life in himself, so he has granted the Son also to have life in himself. ²⁷And he has given him authority to judge because he is the Son of Man. Jn 3:18; 1Jn 3:14

²⁸"Do not be amazed at this, for a time is coming when all who are in their graves will hear his voice ²⁹and come out—those who have done what is good will rise to live, and those who have done what is evil will rise to be condemned. ³⁰By myself I can do nothing; I judge only as I hear, and my judgment is just, for I seek not to please myself but him who sent me. Da 12:2; Mt 25:46; 26:39

Testimonies About Jesus

³¹"If I testify about myself, my testimony is not true. ³²There is another who testifies in my favor, and I know that his testimony about me is true. Jn 8:14

³³"You have sent to John and he has testified to the truth. ³⁴Not that I accept human testimony; but I mention it that you may be saved. ³⁵John was a lamp

that burned and gave light, and you chose for a time to enjoy his light. Jn 1:7; 2Pe 1:19

36 "I have testimony weightier than that of John. For the works that the Father has given me to finish—the very works that I am doing—testify that the Father has sent me. 37 And the Father who sent me has himself testified concerning me. You have never heard his voice nor seen his form, 38 nor does his word dwell in you, for you do not believe the one he sent. 39 You study[a] the Scriptures diligently because you think that in them you have eternal life. These are the very Scriptures that testify about me, 40 yet you refuse to come to me to have life. Jn 8:18; 10:25; Ro 2:17-18

41 "I do not accept glory from human beings, 42 but I know you. I know that you do not have the love of God in your hearts. 43 I have come in my Father's name, and you do not accept me; but if someone else comes in his own name, you will accept him. 44 How can you believe since you accept glory from one another but do not seek the glory that comes from the only God[b]? Ro 2:29

45 "But do not think I will accuse you before the Father. Your accuser is Moses, on whom your hopes are set. 46 If you believed Moses, you would believe me, for he wrote about me. 47 But since you do not believe what he wrote, how are you going to believe what I say?" Lk 16:29,31; Jn 9:28; Ro 2:17

Jesus Feeds the Five Thousand

6:1-13pp — Mt 14:13-21; Mk 6:32-44; Lk 9:10-17

6 Some time after this, Jesus crossed to the far shore of the Sea of Galilee (that is, the Sea of Tiberias), 2 and a great crowd of people followed him because they saw the signs he had performed by healing the sick. 3 Then Jesus went up on a mountainside and sat down with his disciples. 4 The Jewish Passover Festival was near. Jn 2:11; 11:55

5 When Jesus looked up and saw a great crowd coming toward him, he said to Philip, "Where shall we buy bread for these people to eat?" 6 He asked this only to test him, for he already had in mind what he was going to do. Jn 1:43

7 Philip answered him, "It would take more than half a year's wages[c] to buy enough bread for each one to have a bite!"

8 Another of his disciples, Andrew, Simon Peter's brother, spoke up, 9 "Here is a boy with five small barley loaves and two small fish, but how far will they go among so many?" 2Ki 4:43; Jn 1:40

10 Jesus said, "Have the people sit down." There was plenty of grass in that place, and they sat

[a] 39 Or 39 Study   [b] 44 Some early manuscripts the Only One   [c] 7 Greek take two hundred denarii

down (about five thousand men were there). [11] Jesus then took the loaves, gave thanks, and distributed to those who were seated as much as they wanted. He did the same with the fish. Mt 14:19

[12] When they had all had enough to eat, he said to his disciples, "Gather the pieces that are left over. Let nothing be wasted." [13] So they gathered them and filled twelve baskets with the pieces of the five barley loaves left over by those who had eaten. Mt 14:13-21; Mk 6:32-44

[14] After the people saw the sign Jesus performed, they began to say, "Surely this is the Prophet who is to come into the world." [15] Jesus, knowing that they intended to come and make him king by force, withdrew again to a mountain by himself. Mt 14:23

Jesus Walks on the Water

6:16-21pp — Mt 14:22-33; Mk 6:47-51

[16] When evening came, his disciples went down to the lake, [17] where they got into a boat and set off across the lake for Capernaum. By now it was dark, and Jesus had not yet joined them. [18] A strong wind was blowing and the waters grew rough. [19] When they had rowed about three or four miles,[a] they saw Jesus approaching the boat, walking on the water; and they were frightened. [20] But he said to them, "It is I; don't be afraid." [21] Then they

were willing to take him into the boat, and immediately the boat reached the shore where they were heading. Mt 14:22-33; Mk 6:47-51

[22] The next day the crowd that had stayed on the opposite shore of the lake realized that only one boat had been there, and that Jesus had not entered it with his disciples, but that they had gone away alone. [23] Then some boats from Tiberias landed near the place where the people had eaten the bread after the Lord had given thanks. [24] Once the crowd realized that neither Jesus nor his disciples were there, they got into the boats and went to Capernaum in search of Jesus.

Jesus the Bread of Life

[25] When they found him on the other side of the lake, they asked him, "Rabbi, when did you get here?" Mt 23:7

[26] Jesus answered, "Very truly I tell you, you are looking for me, not because you saw the signs I performed but because you ate the loaves and had your fill. [27] Do not work for food that spoils, but for food that endures to eternal life, which the Son of Man will give you. For on him God the Father has placed his seal of approval." Isa 55:2; Jn 4:14; Ro 4:11

[28] Then they asked him, "What must we do to do the works God requires?"

[29] Jesus answered, "The work

---

a 19 Or about 5 or 6 kilometers

of God is this: to believe in the one he has sent." Jn 3:17; 1Jn 3:23

30 So they asked him, "What sign then will you give that we may see it and believe you? What will you do? **31** Our ancestors ate the manna in the wilderness; as it is written: 'He gave them bread from heaven to eat.'*a*" Ex 16:4,15; Nu 11:7-9; Mt 12:38

32 Jesus said to them, "Very truly I tell you, it is not Moses who has given you the bread from heaven, but it is my Father who gives you the true bread from heaven. **33** For the bread of God is the bread that comes down from heaven and gives life to the world." Jn 3:13,31

34 "Sir," they said, "always give us this bread." Jn 4:15

35 Then Jesus declared, "I am the bread of life. Whoever comes to me will never go hungry, and whoever believes in me will never be thirsty. **36** But as I told you, you have seen me and still you do not believe. **37** All those the Father gives me will come to me, and whoever comes to me I will never drive away. **38** For I have come down from heaven not to do my will but to do the will of him who sent me. **39** And this is the will of him who sent me, that I shall lose none of all those he has given me, but raise them up at the last day. **40** For my Father's will is that everyone who looks to the Son and believes in him shall

have eternal life, and I will raise them up at the last day." Jn 3:15-16

41 At this the Jews there began to grumble about him because he said, "I am the bread that came down from heaven." **42** They said, "Is this not Jesus, the son of Joseph, whose father and mother we know? How can he now say, 'I came down from heaven'?" Lk 4:22; Jn 7:27-28

43 "Stop grumbling among yourselves," Jesus answered. **44** "No one can come to me unless the Father who sent me draws them, and I will raise them up at the last day. **45** It is written in the Prophets: 'They will all be taught by God.'*b* Everyone who has heard the Father and learned from him comes to me. **46** No one has seen the Father except the one who is from God; only he has seen the Father. **47** Very truly I tell you, the one who believes has eternal life. **48** I am the bread of life. **49** Your ancestors ate the manna in the wilderness, yet they died. **50** But here is the bread that comes down from heaven, which anyone may eat and not die. **51** I am the living bread that came down from heaven. Whoever eats this bread will live forever. This bread is my flesh, which I will give for the life of the world." Isa 54:13; Jn 1:18; Heb 10:10

52 Then the Jews began to argue sharply among themselves,

a 31 Exodus 16:4; Neh. 9:15; Psalm 78:24,25   *b 45* Isaiah 54:13

"How can this man give us his flesh to eat?" Jn 9:16; 10:19

⁵³Jesus said to them, "Very truly I tell you, unless you eat the flesh of the Son of Man and drink his blood, you have no life in you. ⁵⁴Whoever eats my flesh and drinks my blood has eternal life, and I will raise them up at the last day. ⁵⁵For my flesh is real food and my blood is real drink. ⁵⁶Whoever eats my flesh and drinks my blood remains in me, and I in them. ⁵⁷Just as the living Father sent me and I live because of the Father, so the one who feeds on me will live because of me. ⁵⁸This is the bread that came down from heaven. Your ancestors ate manna and died, but whoever feeds on this bread will live forever." ⁵⁹He said this while teaching in the synagogue in Capernaum. 1Jn 3:24; 4:15; Jn 3:36

Many Disciples Desert Jesus

⁶⁰On hearing it, many of his disciples said, "This is a hard teaching. Who can accept it?"

⁶¹Aware that his disciples were grumbling about this, Jesus said to them, "Does this offend you? ⁶²Then what if you see the Son of Man ascend to where he was before! ⁶³The Spirit gives life; the flesh counts for nothing. The words I have spoken to you—they are full of the Spirit*a* and life. ⁶⁴Yet there are some of you who do not believe." For Jesus had known from the beginning which of them did not believe and who would betray him. ⁶⁵He went on to say, "This is why I told you that no one can come to me unless the Father has enabled them." Jn 2:25; 3:13; 2Co 3:6

⁶⁶From this time many of his disciples turned back and no longer followed him. ver 60

⁶⁷"You do not want to leave too, do you?" Jesus asked the Twelve. Mt 10:2

⁶⁸Simon Peter answered him, "Lord, to whom shall we go? You have the words of eternal life. ⁶⁹We have come to believe and to know that you are the Holy One of God." Mk 8:29; Lk 9:20

⁷⁰Then Jesus replied, "Have I not chosen you, the Twelve? Yet one of you is a devil!" ⁷¹(He meant Judas, the son of Simon Iscariot, who, though one of the Twelve, was later to betray him.) Jn 13:27; 15

Jesus Goes to the Festival of Tabernacles

7 After this, Jesus went around in Galilee. He did not want*b* to go about in Judea because the Jewish leaders there were looking for a way to kill him. ²But when the Jewish Festival of Tabernacles was near, ³Jesus' brothers said to him, "Leave Galilee and go to Judea, so that your disciples there may see the works you do. ⁴No one who wants to become a public figure acts in secret. Since

---

a 63 Or *are Spirit*; or *are spirit*   *b* 1 Some manuscripts *not have authority* you are doing these things, show yourself to the world." ⁵For even his own brothers did not believe in him. Mt 12:46; Jn 5:18; Lev 23:34

⁶Therefore Jesus told them, "My time is not yet here; for you any time will do. ⁷The world cannot hate you, but it hates me because I testify that its works are evil. ⁸You go to the festival. I am not*a* going up to this festival, because my time has not yet fully come." ⁹After he had said this, he stayed in Galilee. Mt 26:18; Jn 3:19-20

¹⁰However, after his brothers had left for the festival, he went also, not publicly, but in secret. ¹¹Now at the festival the Jewish leaders were watching for Jesus and asking, "Where is he?" Jn 11:56

¹²Among the crowds there was widespread whispering about him. Some said, "He is a good man."

Others replied, "No, he deceives the people." ¹³But no one would say anything publicly about him for fear of the leaders. Jn 9:22; 12:42; 19:38

Jesus Teaches at the Festival

¹⁴Not until halfway through the festival did Jesus go up to the temple courts and begin to teach. ¹⁵The Jews there were amazed and asked, "How did this man get such learning without having been taught?" Mt 13:54; Jn 1:19; Ac 26:24

¹⁶Jesus answered, "My teaching is not my own. It comes from the one who sent me. ¹⁷Anyone who chooses to do the will of God will find out whether my teaching comes from God or whether I speak on my own. ¹⁸Whoever speaks on their own does so to gain personal glory, but he who seeks the glory of the one who sent him is a man of truth; there is nothing false about him. ¹⁹Has not Moses given you the law? Yet not one of you keeps the law. Why are you trying to kill me?" Jn 5:41; 8:50,54

²⁰"You are demon-possessed," the crowd answered. "Who is trying to kill you?"

²¹Jesus said to them, "I did one miracle, and you are all amazed. ²²Yet, because Moses gave you circumcision (though actually it did not come from Moses, but from the patriarchs), you circumcise a boy on the Sabbath. ²³Now if a boy can be circumcised on the Sabbath so that the law of Moses may not be broken, why are you angry with me for healing a man's whole body on the Sabbath? ²⁴Stop judging by mere appearances, but instead judge correctly." Jn 8:15,48; 10:20

Division Over Who Jesus Is

²⁵At that point some of the people of Jerusalem began to ask, "Isn't this the man they are trying to kill? ²⁶Here he is, speaking publicly, and they are not saying a word to him. Have the au-

a 8 Some manuscripts *not yet*

thorities really concluded that he is the Messiah? ²⁷But we know where this man is from; when the Messiah comes, no one will know where he is from." Mt 13:55; Lk 4:22

²⁸Then Jesus, still teaching in the temple courts, cried out, "Yes, you know me, and you know where I am from. I am not here on my own authority, but he who sent me is true. You do not know him, ²⁹but I know him because I am from him and he sent me." Mt 11:27; Jn 8:14,26,42

³⁰At this they tried to seize him, but no one laid a hand on him, because his hour had not yet come. ³¹Still, many in the crowd believed in him. They said, "When the Messiah comes, will he perform more signs than this man?" Jn 2:11; 8:30

³²The Pharisees heard the crowd whispering such things about him. Then the chief priests and the Pharisees sent temple guards to arrest him.

³³Jesus said, "I am with you for only a short time, and then I am going to the one who sent me. ³⁴You will look for me, but you will not find me; and where I am, you cannot come." Jn 8:21; 13:33

³⁵The Jews said to one another, "Where does this man intend to go that we cannot find him? Will he go where our people live scattered among the Greeks, and teach the Greeks? ³⁶What did he mean when he said, 'You will look for me, but you will not find me,' and 'Where I am, you cannot come'?" Jas 1:1; 1Pe 1:1

³⁷On the last and greatest day of the festival, Jesus stood and said in a loud voice, "Let anyone who is thirsty come to me and drink. ³⁸Whoever believes in me, as Scripture has said, rivers of living water will flow from within them."ᵃ ³⁹By this he meant the Spirit, whom those who believed in him were later to receive. Up to that time the Spirit had not been given, since Jesus had not yet been glorified. Isa 55:1; Joel 2:28; Jn 12:23

⁴⁰On hearing his words, some of the people said, "Surely this man is the Prophet." Mt 21:11; Jn 1:21

⁴¹Others said, "He is the Messiah."

Still others asked, "How can the Messiah come from Galilee? ⁴²Does not Scripture say that the Messiah will come from David's descendants and from Bethlehem, the town where David lived?" ⁴³Thus the people were divided because of Jesus. ⁴⁴Some wanted to seize him, but no one laid a hand on him. Mic 5:2; Jn 9:16

Unbelief of the Jewish Leaders

⁴⁵Finally the temple guards went back to the chief priests and the Pharisees, who asked them, "Why didn't you bring him in?"

⁴⁶"No one ever spoke the way

ᵃ 37,38 Or me. And let anyone drink ³⁸who believes in me." As Scripture has said, "Out of him (or them) will flow rivers of living water."

this man does," the guards replied.   Mt 7:28

⁴⁷ "You mean he has deceived you also?" the Pharisees retorted. ⁴⁸ "Have any of the rulers or of the Pharisees believed in him? ⁴⁹ No! But this mob that knows nothing of the law — there is a curse on them."   Jn 12:42

⁵⁰ Nicodemus, who had gone to Jesus earlier and who was one of their own number, asked, ⁵¹ "Does our law condemn a man without first hearing him to find out what he has been doing?" Jn 3:1

⁵² They replied, "Are you from Galilee, too? Look into it, and you will find that a prophet does not come out of Galilee."

[The earliest manuscripts and many other ancient witnesses do not have John 7:53 — 8:11. A few manuscripts include these verses, wholly or in part, after John 7:36, John 21:25, Luke 21:38 or Luke 24:53.]

8 ⁵³ Then they all went home, ¹ but Jesus went to the Mount of Olives.

² At dawn he appeared again in the temple courts, where all the people gathered around him, and he sat down to teach them. ³ The teachers of the law and the Pharisees brought in a woman caught in adultery. They made her stand before the group ⁴ and said to Jesus, "Teacher, this woman was caught in the act of adultery. ⁵ In the Law Moses commanded us to stone such wom-

en. Now what do you say?" ⁶ They were using this question as a trap, in order to have a basis for accusing him.   Lev 20:10; Dt 22:22; Mt 12:10

But Jesus bent down and started to write on the ground with his finger. ⁷ When they kept on questioning him, he straightened up and said to them, "Let any one of you who is without sin be the first to throw a stone at her." ⁸ Again he stooped down and wrote on the ground.   Dt 17:7

⁹ At this, those who heard began to go away one at a time, the older ones first, until only Jesus was left, with the woman still standing there. ¹⁰ Jesus straightened up and asked her, "Woman, where are they? Has no one condemned you?"

¹¹ "No one, sir," she said.

"Then neither do I condemn you," Jesus declared. "Go now and leave your life of sin."   Jn 3:17; 5:14

Dispute Over Jesus' Testimony

¹² When Jesus spoke again to the people, he said, "I am the light of the world. Whoever follows me will never walk in darkness, but will have the light of life."   Jn 1:4; 6:35; Pr 4:18; Mt 5:14

¹³ The Pharisees challenged him, "Here you are, appearing as your own witness; your testimony is not valid."   Jn 5:31

¹⁴ Jesus answered, "Even if I testify on my own behalf, my testimony is valid, for I know where I came from and where I am going. But you have no idea where I come from or where I

am going. [15] You judge by human standards; I pass judgment on no one. [16] But if I do judge, my decisions are true, because I am not alone. I stand with the Father, who sent me. [17] In your own Law it is written that the testimony of two witnesses is true. [18] I am one who testifies for myself; my other witness is the Father, who sent me." Mt 18:16; Jn 5:37; 7:28

[19] Then they asked him, "Where is your father?"

"You do not know me or my Father," Jesus replied. "If you knew me, you would know my Father also." [20] He spoke these words while teaching in the temple courts near the place where the offerings were put. Yet no one seized him, because his hour had not yet come. Mk 12:41; Jn 16:3; 1Jn 2:23

Dispute Over Who Jesus Is

[21] Once more Jesus said to them, "I am going away, and you will look for me, and you will die in your sin. Where I go, you cannot come." Jn 7:34; 13:33

[22] This made the Jews ask, "Will he kill himself? Is that why he says, 'Where I go, you cannot come'?"

[23] But he continued, "You are from below; I am from above. You are of this world; I am not of this world. [24] I told you that you would die in your sins; if you do not believe that I am he, you will indeed die in your sins." Jn 3:31; 4:26

[25] "Who are you?" they asked.

"Just what I have been telling you from the beginning," Jesus replied. [26] "I have much to say in judgment of you. But he who sent me is trustworthy, and what I have heard from him I tell the world." Jn 3:32; 7:28; 15:15

[27] They did not understand that he was telling them about his Father. [28] So Jesus said, "When you have lifted up[a] the Son of Man, then you will know that I am he and that I do nothing on my own but speak just what the Father has taught me. [29] The one who sent me is with me; he has not left me alone, for I always do what pleases him." [30] Even as he spoke, many believed in him. Jn 4:34; 7:31; 12:32

Dispute Over Whose Children Jesus' Opponents Are

[31] To the Jews who had believed him, Jesus said, "If you hold to my teaching, you are really my disciples. [32] Then you will know the truth, and the truth will set you free." Jn 15:7; Ro 8:2; Jas 2:12

[33] They answered him, "We are Abraham's descendants and have never been slaves of anyone. How can you say that we shall be set free?" Mt 3:9

[34] Jesus replied, "Very truly I tell you, everyone who sins is a slave to sin. [35] Now a slave has no permanent place in the family, but a son belongs to it forever.

[a] 28 The Greek for *lifted up* also means *exalted*.

³⁶So if the Son sets you free, you will be free indeed. ³⁷I know that you are Abraham's descendants. Yet you are looking for a way to kill me, because you have no room for my word. ³⁸I am telling you what I have seen in the Father's presence, and you are doing what you have heard from your father.ᵃ" Jn 5:19,30; Ro 6:16

³⁹"Abraham is our father," they answered.

"If you were Abraham's children," said Jesus, "then you wouldᵇ do what Abraham did. ⁴⁰As it is, you are looking for a way to kill me, a man who has told you the truth that I heard from God. Abraham did not do such things. ⁴¹You are doing the works of your own father." Ro 9:7; Gal 3:7

"We are not illegitimate children," they protested. "The only Father we have is God himself."

⁴²Jesus said to them, "If God were your Father, you would love me, for I have come here from God. I have not come on my own; God sent me. ⁴³Why is my language not clear to you? Because you are unable to hear what I say. ⁴⁴You belong to your father, the devil, and you want to carry out your father's desires. He was a murderer from the beginning, not holding to the truth, for there is no truth in him. When he lies, he speaks his native language, for he is a liar and the father of lies. ⁴⁵Yet because I tell the truth, you do not believe me! ⁴⁶Can any of you prove me guilty of sin? If I am telling the truth, why don't you believe me? ⁴⁷Whoever belongs to God hears what God says. The reason you do not hear is that you do not belong to God." Jn 18:37; 1Jn 4:6

Jesus' Claims About Himself

⁴⁸The Jews answered him, "Aren't we right in saying that you are a Samaritan and demon-possessed?" Mt 10:5; Jn 7:20

⁴⁹"I am not possessed by a demon," said Jesus, "but I honor my Father and you dishonor me. ⁵⁰I am not seeking glory for myself; but there is one who seeks it, and he is the judge. ⁵¹Very truly I tell you, whoever obeys my word will never see death." Jn 5:41; 11:26

⁵²At this they exclaimed, "Now we know that you are demon-possessed! Abraham died and so did the prophets, yet you say that whoever obeys your word will never taste death. ⁵³Are you greater than our father Abraham? He died, and so did the prophets. Who do you think you are?" Mk 3:22; Jn 4:12

⁵⁴Jesus replied, "If I glorify myself, my glory means nothing. My Father, whom you claim as your God, is the one who glorifies me. ⁵⁵Though you do not know him, I know him. If I said I did not, I

ᵃ 38 Or presence. Therefore do what you have heard from the Father. ᵇ 39 Some early manuscripts "If you are Abraham's children," said Jesus, "then would be a liar like you, but I do know him and obey his word. [56] Your father Abraham rejoiced at the thought of seeing my day; he saw it and was glad." Jn 7:28-29

[57] "You are not yet fifty years old," they said to him, "and you have seen Abraham!"

[58] "Very truly I tell you," Jesus answered, "before Abraham was born, I am!" [59] At this, they picked up stones to stone him, but Jesus hid himself, slipping away from the temple grounds. Ex 3:14; Jn 10:31

Jesus Heals a Man Born Blind

9 As he went along, he saw a man blind from birth. [2] His disciples asked him, "Rabbi, who sinned, this man or his parents, that he was born blind?" Ex 20:5

[3] "Neither this man nor his parents sinned," said Jesus, "but this happened so that the works of God might be displayed in him. [4] As long as it is day, we must do the works of him who sent me. Night is coming, when no one can work. [5] While I am in the world, I am the light of the world." Jn 8:12; 12:46

[6] After saying this, he spit on the ground, made some mud with the saliva, and put it on the man's eyes. [7] "Go," he told him, "wash in the Pool of Siloam" (this word means "Sent"). So the man went and washed, and came home seeing. Mk 7:33; 8:23; Jn 11:37

[8] His neighbors and those who had formerly seen him begging asked, "Isn't this the same man who used to sit and beg?" [9] Some claimed that he was. Ac 3:2,10

Others said, "No, he only looks like him."

But he himself insisted, "I am the man."

[10] "How then were your eyes opened?" they asked.

[11] He replied, "The man they call Jesus made some mud and put it on my eyes. He told me to go to Siloam and wash. So I went and washed, and then I could see." ver 7

[12] "Where is this man?" they asked him.

"I don't know," he said.

The Pharisees Investigate the Healing

[13] They brought to the Pharisees the man who had been blind. [14] Now the day on which Jesus had made the mud and opened the man's eyes was a Sabbath. [15] Therefore the Pharisees also asked him how he had received his sight. "He put mud on my eyes," the man replied, "and I washed, and now I see." Jn 5:9

[16] Some of the Pharisees said, "This man is not from God, for he does not keep the Sabbath."

But others asked, "How can a sinner perform such signs?" So they were divided. Jn 7:43; 10:19

[17] Then they turned again to the blind man, "What have you to say about him? It was your eyes he opened."

The man replied, "He is a prophet." Mt 21:11

¹⁸ They still did not believe that he had been blind and had received his sight until they sent for the man's parents. ¹⁹ "Is this your son?" they asked. "Is this the one you say was born blind? How is it that now he can see?" Jn 1:19

²⁰ "We know he is our son," the parents answered, "and we know he was born blind. ²¹ But how he can see now, or who opened his eyes, we don't know. Ask him. He is of age; he will speak for himself." ²² His parents said this because they were afraid of the Jewish leaders, who already had decided that anyone who acknowledged that Jesus was the Messiah would be put out of the synagogue. ²³ That was why his parents said, "He is of age; ask him." Jn 7:13; 12:42

²⁴ A second time they summoned the man who had been blind. "Give glory to God by telling the truth," they said. "We know this man is a sinner." ver 16

²⁵ He replied, "Whether he is a sinner or not, I don't know. One thing I do know. I was blind but now I see!"

²⁶ Then they asked him, "What did he do to you? How did he open your eyes?"

²⁷ He answered, "I have told you already and you did not listen. Why do you want to hear it again? Do you want to become his disciples too?"

²⁸ Then they hurled insults at him and said, "You are this fellow's disciple! We are disciples of Moses! ²⁹ We know that God spoke to Moses, but as for this fellow, we don't even know where he comes from." Jn 5:45; 8:14

³⁰ The man answered, "Now that is remarkable! You don't know where he comes from, yet he opened my eyes. ³¹ We know that God does not listen to sinners. He listens to the godly person who does his will. ³² Nobody has ever heard of opening the eyes of a man born blind. ³³ If this man were not from God, he could do nothing." Ps 34:15-16; Pr 15:29

³⁴ To this they replied, "You were steeped in sin at birth; how dare you lecture us!" And they threw him out. Isa 66:5

Spiritual Blindness

³⁵ Jesus heard that they had thrown him out, and when he found him, he said, "Do you believe in the Son of Man?" Mt 8:20

³⁶ "Who is he, sir?" the man asked. "Tell me so that I may believe in him." Ro 10:14

³⁷ Jesus said, "You have now seen him; in fact, he is the one speaking with you." Jn 4:26

³⁸ Then the man said, "Lord, I believe," and he worshiped him.

³⁹ Jesus said,ᵃ "For judgment I have come into this world, so that

---

ᵃ 38,39 Some early manuscripts do not have *Then the man said . . . ³⁹Jesus said.*

the blind will see and those who see will become blind." Mt 13:13

⁴⁰Some Pharisees who were with him heard him say this and asked, "What? Are we blind too?" Ro 2:19

⁴¹Jesus said, "If you were blind, you would not be guilty of sin; but now that you claim you can see, your guilt remains. Jn 15:22,24

The Good Shepherd and His Sheep

10 "Very truly I tell you Pharisees, anyone who does not enter the sheep pen by the gate, but climbs in by some other way, is a thief and a robber. ²The one who enters by the gate is the shepherd of the sheep. ³The gatekeeper opens the gate for him, and the sheep listen to his voice. He calls his own sheep by name and leads them out. ⁴When he has brought out all his own, he goes on ahead of them, and his sheep follow him because they know his voice. ⁵But they will never follow a stranger; in fact, they will run away from him because they do not recognize a stranger's voice." ⁶Jesus used this figure of speech, but the Pharisees did not understand what he was telling them. Mk 9:32; Jn 16:25

⁷Therefore Jesus said again, "Very truly I tell you, I am the gate for the sheep. ⁸All who have come before me are thieves and robbers, but the sheep have not listened to them. ⁹I am the gate; whoever enters through me will be saved.ᵃ They will come in and go out, and find pasture. ¹⁰The thief comes only to steal and kill and destroy; I have come that they may have life, and have it to the full. Jn 1:4; Ro 5:17

¹¹"I am the good shepherd. The good shepherd lays down his life for the sheep. ¹²The hired hand is not the shepherd and does not own the sheep. So when he sees the wolf coming, he abandons the sheep and runs away. Then the wolf attacks the flock and scatters it. ¹³The man runs away because he is a hired hand and cares nothing for the sheep. Isa 40:11; Eze 34:11-16,23; Heb 13:20

¹⁴"I am the good shepherd; I know my sheep and my sheep know me— ¹⁵just as the Father knows me and I know the Father—and I lay down my life for the sheep. ¹⁶I have other sheep that are not of this sheep pen. I must bring them also. They too will listen to my voice, and there shall be one flock and one shepherd. ¹⁷The reason my Father loves me is that I lay down my life—only to take it up again. ¹⁸No one takes it from me, but I lay it down of my own accord. I have authority to lay it down and authority to take it up again. This command I received from my Father." Mt 11:27; Jn 15:10; Eph 2:11-19

¹⁹The Jews who heard these

ᵃ 9 Or kept safe

words were again divided. **20** Many of them said, "He is demon-possessed and raving mad. Why listen to him?" Jn 7:20,43 **21** But others said, "These are not the sayings of a man possessed by a demon. Can a demon open the eyes of the blind?" Ex 4:11

Further Conflict Over Jesus' Claims

22 Then came the Festival of Dedication[a] at Jerusalem. It was winter, **23** and Jesus was in the temple courts walking in Solomon's Colonnade. **24** The Jews who were there gathered around him, saying, "How long will you keep us in suspense? If you are the Messiah, tell us plainly." Jn 16:25,29; Ac 3:11

25 Jesus answered, "I did tell you, but you do not believe. The works I do in my Father's name testify about me, **26** but you do not believe because you are not my sheep. **27** My sheep listen to my voice; I know them, and they follow me. **28** I give them eternal life, and they shall never perish; no one will snatch them out of my hand. **29** My Father, who has given them to me, is greater than all[b]; no one can snatch them out of my Father's hand. **30** I and the Father are one." Jn 17:21-23

31 Again his Jewish opponents picked up stones to stone him, **32** but Jesus said to them, "I have shown you many good works from the Father. For which of these do you stone me?" Jn 8:59

33 "We are not stoning you for any good work," they replied, "but for blasphemy, because you, a mere man, claim to be God." Lev 24:16; Jn 5:18

34 Jesus answered them, "Is it not written in your Law, 'I have said you are "gods"'[c]? **35** If he called them 'gods,' to whom the word of God came—and Scripture cannot be set aside— **36** what about the one whom the Father set apart as his very own and sent into the world? Why then do you accuse me of blasphemy because I said, 'I am God's Son'? **37** Do not believe me unless I do the works of my Father. **38** But if I do them, even though you do not believe me, believe the works, that you may know and understand that the Father is in me, and I in the Father." **39** Again they tried to seize him, but he escaped their grasp. Jn 14:10-11,20; 15:24

40 Then Jesus went back across the Jordan to the place where John had been baptizing in the early days. There he stayed, **41** and many people came to him. They said, "Though John never performed a sign, all that John said about this man was true." **42** And in that place many believed in Jesus. Jn 1:28; 7:31

a 22 That is, Hanukkah   *b* 29 Many early manuscripts *What my Father has given me is greater than all*   *c* 34 Psalm 82:6

The Death of Lazarus

11 Now a man named Lazarus was sick. He was from Bethany, the village of Mary and her sister Martha. ²(This Mary, whose brother Lazarus now lay sick, was the same one who poured perfume on the Lord and wiped his feet with her hair.) ³So the sisters sent word to Jesus, "Lord, the one you love is sick."   Lk 10:38; Jn 12:3

⁴When he heard this, Jesus said, "This sickness will not end in death. No, it is for God's glory so that God's Son may be glorified through it." ⁵Now Jesus loved Martha and her sister and Lazarus. ⁶So when he heard that Lazarus was sick, he stayed where he was two more days, ⁷and then he said to his disciples, "Let us go back to Judea."   Jn 9:3; Jn 10:40

⁸"But Rabbi," they said, "a short while ago the Jews there tried to stone you, and yet you are going back?"   Mt 23:7; Jn 10:31

⁹Jesus answered, "Are there not twelve hours of daylight? Anyone who walks in the daytime will not stumble, for they see by this world's light. ¹⁰It is when a person walks at night that they stumble, for they have no light."   Jn 9:4; 12:35

¹¹After he had said this, he went on to tell them, "Our friend Lazarus has fallen asleep; but I am going there to wake him up."   Ac 7:60

¹²His disciples replied, "Lord, if he sleeps, he will get better." ¹³Jesus had been speaking of his death, but his disciples thought he meant natural sleep.   Mt 9:24

¹⁴So then he told them plainly, "Lazarus is dead, ¹⁵and for your sake I am glad I was not there, so that you may believe. But let us go to him."

¹⁶Then Thomas (also known as Didymus[a]) said to the rest of the disciples, "Let us also go, that we may die with him."   Mt 10:3; Jn 14:5

Jesus Comforts the Sisters of Lazarus

¹⁷On his arrival, Jesus found that Lazarus had already been in the tomb for four days. ¹⁸Now Bethany was less than two miles[b] from Jerusalem, ¹⁹and many Jews had come to Martha and Mary to comfort them in the loss of their brother. ²⁰When Martha heard that Jesus was coming, she went out to meet him, but Mary stayed at home.   Job 2:11; Lk 10:38-42

²¹"Lord," Martha said to Jesus, "if you had been here, my brother would not have died. ²²But I know that even now God will give you whatever you ask."Jn 9:31

²³Jesus said to her, "Your brother will rise again."

²⁴Martha answered, "I know he will rise again in the resurrection at the last day."   Jn 5:28-29; Ac 24:15

²⁵Jesus said to her, "I am the resurrection and the life. The

---

a 16 *Thomas* (Aramaic) and *Didymus* (Greek) both mean *twin*.   *b* 18 Or about 3 kilometers one who believes in me will live, even though they die; ²⁶and whoever lives by believing in me will never die. Do you believe this?" Jn 1:4; 3:15

²⁷"Yes, Lord," she replied, "I believe that you are the Messiah, the Son of God, who is to come into the world." Mt 16:16; Jn 6:14

²⁸After she had said this, she went back and called her sister Mary aside. "The Teacher is here," she said, "and is asking for you." ²⁹When Mary heard this, she got up quickly and went to him. ³⁰Now Jesus had not yet entered the village, but was still at the place where Martha had met him. ³¹When the Jews who had been with Mary in the house, comforting her, noticed how quickly she got up and went out, they followed her, supposing she was going to the tomb to mourn there. Mt 26:18; Jn 13:13

³²When Mary reached the place where Jesus was and saw him, she fell at his feet and said, "Lord, if you had been here, my brother would not have died."

³³When Jesus saw her weeping, and the Jews who had come along with her also weeping, he was deeply moved in spirit and troubled. ³⁴"Where have you laid him?" he asked. Jn 12:27

"Come and see, Lord," they replied.

³⁵Jesus wept. Lk 19:41

³⁶Then the Jews said, "See how he loved him!"

³⁷But some of them said, "Could not he who opened the eyes of the blind man have kept this man from dying?" Jn 9:6-7

Jesus Raises Lazarus From the Dead

³⁸Jesus, once more deeply moved, came to the tomb. It was a cave with a stone laid across the entrance. ³⁹"Take away the stone," he said. Mt 27:60; Lk 24:2; Jn 20:1

"But, Lord," said Martha, the sister of the dead man, "by this time there is a bad odor, for he has been there four days."

⁴⁰Then Jesus said, "Did I not tell you that if you believe, you will see the glory of God?" ver 23-25

⁴¹So they took away the stone. Then Jesus looked up and said, "Father, I thank you that you have heard me. ⁴²I knew that you always hear me, but I said this for the benefit of the people standing here, that they may believe that you sent me." Jn 3:17; 12:30

⁴³When he had said this, Jesus called in a loud voice, "Lazarus, come out!" ⁴⁴The dead man came out, his hands and feet wrapped with strips of linen, and a cloth around his face. Jn 19:40; 20:7

Jesus said to them, "Take off the grave clothes and let him go."

The Plot to Kill Jesus

⁴⁵Therefore many of the Jews who had come to visit Mary, and had seen what Jesus did, believed in him. ⁴⁶But some of

them went to the Pharisees and told them what Jesus had done. ⁴⁷ Then the chief priests and the Pharisees called a meeting of the Sanhedrin.   Mt 26:3; Jn 2:23; 7:31

"What are we accomplishing?" they asked. "Here is this man performing many signs. ⁴⁸ If we let him go on like this, everyone will believe in him, and then the Romans will come and take away both our temple and our nation."   Jn 2:11

⁴⁹ Then one of them, named Caiaphas, who was high priest that year, spoke up, "You know nothing at all! ⁵⁰ You do not realize that it is better for you that one man die for the people than that the whole nation perish."   Mt 26:3

⁵¹ He did not say this on his own, but as high priest that year he prophesied that Jesus would die for the Jewish nation, ⁵² and not only for that nation but also for the scattered children of God, to bring them together and make them one. ⁵³ So from that day on they plotted to take his life.   Isa 49:6; Mt 12:14; Jn 10:16

⁵⁴ Therefore Jesus no longer moved about publicly among the people of Judea. Instead he withdrew to a region near the wilderness, to a village called Ephraim, where he stayed with his disciples.   Jn 7:1

⁵⁵ When it was almost time for the Jewish Passover, many went up from the country to Jerusalem for their ceremonial cleansing before the Passover. ⁵⁶ They kept looking for Jesus, and as they stood in the temple courts they asked one another, "What do you think? Isn't he coming to the festival at all?" ⁵⁷ But the chief priests and the Pharisees had given orders that anyone who found out where Jesus was should report it so that they might arrest him.   2Ch 30:17-18; Mk 14:1; Jn 7:11

Jesus Anointed at Bethany
12:1-8Ref — Mt 26:6-13; Mk 14:3-9;
     Lk 7:37-39

12 Six days before the Passover, Jesus came to Bethany, where Lazarus lived, whom Jesus had raised from the dead. ² Here a dinner was given in Jesus' honor. Martha served, while Lazarus was among those reclining at the table with him. ³ Then Mary took about a pint[a] of pure nard, an expensive perfume; she poured it on Jesus' feet and wiped his feet with her hair. And the house was filled with the fragrance of the perfume.   Jn 11:2,55

⁴ But one of his disciples, Judas Iscariot, who was later to betray him, objected, ⁵ "Why wasn't this perfume sold and the money given to the poor? It was worth a year's wages.[b]" ⁶ He did not say this because he cared about the poor but because he was a thief; as keeper of the money bag, he

a 3 Or about 0.5 liter   b 5 Greek three hundred denarii

used to help himself to what was put into it. Mt 10:4; Jn 13:29

⁷ "Leave her alone," Jesus replied. "It was intended that she should save this perfume for the day of my burial. ⁸You will always have the poor among you,ᵃ but you will not always have me." Mt 26:6-13; Mk 14:3-9

⁹Meanwhile a large crowd of Jews found out that Jesus was there and came, not only because of him but also to see Lazarus, whom he had raised from the dead. ¹⁰So the chief priests made plans to kill Lazarus as well, ¹¹for on account of him many of the Jews were going over to Jesus and believing in him. Jn 7:31; 11:43-44

Jesus Comes to Jerusalem as King

12:12-15pp — Mt 21:4-9; Mk 11:7-10; Lk 19:35-38

¹²The next day the great crowd that had come for the festival heard that Jesus was on his way to Jerusalem. ¹³They took palm branches and went out to meet him, shouting, Lev 23:40

"Hosanna!ᵇ"

"Blessed is he who comes
   in the name of the
   Lord!"ᶜ Ps 118:25-26

"Blessed is the king of Israel!"

¹⁴Jesus found a young donkey and sat on it, as it is written:

¹⁵ "Do not be afraid, Daughter Zion;
   see, your king is coming,
   seated on a donkey's
   colt."ᵈ Mt 21:4-9; Mk 11:7-10

¹⁶At first his disciples did not understand all this. Only after Jesus was glorified did they realize that these things had been written about him and that these things had been done to him. Jn 7:39; 14:26

¹⁷Now the crowd that was with him when he called Lazarus from the tomb and raised him from the dead continued to spread the word. ¹⁸Many people, because they had heard that he had performed this sign, went out to meet him. ¹⁹So the Pharisees said to one another, "See, this is getting us nowhere. Look how the whole world has gone after him!" Jn 11:42,47-48

Jesus Predicts His Death

²⁰Now there were some Greeks among those who went up to worship at the festival. ²¹They came to Philip, who was from Bethsaida in Galilee, with a request. "Sir," they said, "we would like to see Jesus." ²²Philip went to tell Andrew; Andrew and Philip in turn told Jesus. Mt 11:21; Jn 1:44; 7:35

²³Jesus replied, "The hour has come for the Son of Man to be glorified. ²⁴Very truly I tell you,

---

ᵃ 8 See Deut. 15:11.   ᵇ 13 A Hebrew expression meaning "Save!" which became an exclamation of praise   ᶜ 13 Psalm 118:25,26   ᵈ 15 Zech. 9:9

unless a kernel of wheat falls to the ground and dies, it remains only a single seed. But if it dies, it produces many seeds. ²⁵Anyone who loves their life will lose it, while anyone who hates their life in this world will keep it for eternal life. ²⁶Whoever serves me must follow me; and where I am, my servant also will be. My Father will honor the one who serves me. Mt 10:39; Jn 13:32; 14:3

²⁷"Now my soul is troubled, and what shall I say? 'Father, save me from this hour'? No, it was for this very reason I came to this hour. ²⁸Father, glorify your name!" Mt 26:38-39; Jn 11:33,38

Then a voice came from heaven, "I have glorified it, and will glorify it again." ²⁹The crowd that was there and heard it said it had thundered; others said an angel had spoken to him. Mt 3:17

³⁰Jesus said, "This voice was for your benefit, not mine. ³¹Now is the time for judgment on this world; now the prince of this world will be driven out. ³²And I, when I am lifted up*ᵃ* from the earth, will draw all people to myself." ³³He said this to show the kind of death he was going to die.

³⁴The crowd spoke up, "We have heard from the Law that the Messiah will remain forever, so how can you say, 'The Son of Man must be lifted up'? Who is this 'Son of Man'?" Ps 110:4; Eze 37:25

³⁵Then Jesus told them, "You are going to have the light just a little while longer. Walk while you have the light, before darkness overtakes you. Whoever walks in the dark does not know where they are going. ³⁶Believe in the light while you have the light, so that you may become children of light." When he had finished speaking, Jesus left and hid himself from them. Jn 8:59

Belief and Unbelief Among the Jews

³⁷Even after Jesus had performed so many signs in their presence, they still would not believe in him. ³⁸This was to fulfill the word of Isaiah the prophet:

"Lord, who has believed our message
and to whom has the arm of the Lord been revealed?"ᵇ Ro 10:16

³⁹For this reason they could not believe, because, as Isaiah says elsewhere:

⁴⁰"He has blinded their eyes
and hardened their hearts,
so they can neither see with their eyes,
nor understand with their hearts,
nor turn—and I would heal them."ᶜ

⁴¹Isaiah said this because he saw Jesus' glory and spoke about him. Isa 6:1-4; Mt 13:13,15

ᵃ 32 The Greek for *lifted up* also means *exalted.*   ᵇ 38 Isaiah 53:1   ᶜ 40 Isaiah 6:10

⁴²Yet at the same time many even among the leaders believed in him. But because of the Pharisees they would not openly acknowledge their faith for fear they would be put out of the synagogue; ⁴³for they loved human praise more than praise from God. Jn 5:44; 7:13; 9:22

⁴⁴Then Jesus cried out, "Whoever believes in me does not believe in me only, but in the one who sent me. ⁴⁵The one who looks at me is seeing the one who sent me. ⁴⁶I have come into the world as a light, so that no one who believes in me should stay in darkness. Mt 10:40; Jn 3:19; 14:9

⁴⁷"If anyone hears my words but does not keep them, I do not judge that person. For I did not come to judge the world, but to save the world. ⁴⁸There is a judge for the one who rejects me and does not accept my words; the very words I have spoken will condemn them at the last day. ⁴⁹For I did not speak on my own, but the Father who sent me commanded me to say all that I have spoken. ⁵⁰I know that his command leads to eternal life. So whatever I say is just what the Father has told me to say." Jn 3:17; 14:31

Jesus Washes His Disciples' Feet

13 It was just before the Passover Festival. Jesus knew that the hour had come for him to leave this world and go to the Father. Having loved his own who were in the world, he loved them to the end. Jn 11:55; 16:28

²The evening meal was in progress, and the devil had already prompted Judas, the son of Simon Iscariot, to betray Jesus. ³Jesus knew that the Father had put all things under his power, and that he had come from God and was returning to God; ⁴so he got up from the meal, took off his outer clothing, and wrapped a towel around his waist. ⁵After that, he poured water into a basin and began to wash his disciples' feet, drying them with the towel that was wrapped around him. Mt 28:18; Jn 8:42

⁶He came to Simon Peter, who said to him, "Lord, are you going to wash my feet?"

⁷Jesus replied, "You do not realize now what I am doing, but later you will understand."

⁸"No," said Peter, "you shall never wash my feet."

Jesus answered, "Unless I wash you, you have no part with me."

⁹"Then, Lord," Simon Peter replied, "not just my feet but my hands and my head as well!"

¹⁰Jesus answered, "Those who have had a bath need only to wash their feet; their whole body is clean. And you are clean, though not every one of you." ¹¹For he knew who was going to betray him, and that was why he said not every one was clean. Jn 15:3

¹²When he had finished wash-

ing their feet, he put on his clothes and returned to his place. "Do you understand what I have done for you?" he asked them. [13]"You call me 'Teacher' and 'Lord,' and rightly so, for that is what I am. [14]Now that I, your Lord and Teacher, have washed your feet, you also should wash one another's feet. [15]I have set you an example that you should do as I have done for you. [16]Very truly I tell you, no servant is greater than his master, nor is a messenger greater than the one who sent him. [17]Now that you know these things, you will be blessed if you do them.   Mt 10:24; Php 2:11; Jas 1:25

Jesus Predicts His Betrayal

[18]"I am not referring to all of you; I know those I have chosen. But this is to fulfill this passage of Scripture: 'He who shared my bread has turned[a] against me.'[b]   Ps 41:9; Jn 6:70; 15:16,19
[19]"I am telling you now before it happens, so that when it does happen you will believe that I am who I am. [20]Very truly I tell you, whoever accepts anyone I send accepts me; and whoever accepts me accepts the one who sent me."   Lk 10:16; Jn 14:29; 16:4
[21]After he had said this, Jesus was troubled in spirit and testified, "Very truly I tell you, one of you is going to betray me." Mt 26:21
[22]His disciples stared at one another, at a loss to know which of them he meant. [23]One of them, the disciple whom Jesus loved, was reclining next to him. [24]Simon Peter motioned to this disciple and said, "Ask him which one he means."   Jn 19:26; 20:2; 21:7,20
[25]Leaning back against Jesus, he asked him, "Lord, who is it?"
[26]Jesus answered, "It is the one to whom I will give this piece of bread when I have dipped it in the dish." Then, dipping the piece of bread, he gave it to Judas, the son of Simon Iscariot. [27]As soon as Judas took the bread, Satan entered into him.   Lk 22:3

So Jesus told him, "What you are about to do, do quickly." [28]But no one at the meal understood why Jesus said this to him. [29]Since Judas had charge of the money, some thought Jesus was telling him to buy what was needed for the festival, or to give something to the poor. [30]As soon as Judas had taken the bread, he went out. And it was night.   Lk 22:53; Jn 12:6

Jesus Predicts Peter's Denial

13:37,38pp — Mt 26:33-35; Mk 14:29-31;
   Lk 22:33,34

[31]When he was gone, Jesus said, "Now the Son of Man is glorified and God is glorified in him. [32]If God is glorified in him,[c] God will glorify the Son in himself, and will glorify him at once.   Jn 14:13; 1Pe 4:11

a 18 Greek *has lifted up his heel*   *b 18* Psalm 41:9   *c 32* Many early manuscripts do not have *If God is glorified in him.*

33 "My children, I will be with you only a little longer. You will look for me, and just as I told the Jews, so I tell you now: Where I am going, you cannot come. Jn 7:33-34

34 "A new command I give you: Love one another. As I have loved you, so you must love one another. **35** By this everyone will know that you are my disciples, if you love one another." Lev 19:18; 1Jn 2:7-11

36 Simon Peter asked him, "Lord, where are you going?"

Jesus replied, "Where I am going, you cannot follow now, but you will follow later." Jn 21:18-19

37 Peter asked, "Lord, why can't I follow you now? I will lay down my life for you."

38 Then Jesus answered, "Will you really lay down your life for me? Very truly I tell you, before the rooster crows, you will disown me three times! Mt 26:33-35

Jesus Comforts His Disciples

14 "Do not let your hearts be troubled. You believe in God^a; believe also in me. **2** My Father's house has many rooms; if that were not so, would I have told you that I am going there to prepare a place for you? **3** And if I go and prepare a place for you, I will come back and take you to be with me that you also may be where I am. **4** You know the way to the place where I am going." Jn 12:26; 13:33,36

Jesus the Way to the Father

5 Thomas said to him, "Lord, we don't know where you are going, so how can we know the way?" Jn 11:16

6 Jesus answered, "I am the way and the truth and the life. No one comes to the Father except through me. **7** If you really know me, you will know^b my Father as well. From now on, you do know him and have seen him." Jn 1:14; 10:9

8 Philip said, "Lord, show us the Father and that will be enough for us." Jn 1:43

9 Jesus answered: "Don't you know me, Philip, even after I have been among you such a long time? Anyone who has seen me has seen the Father. How can you say, 'Show us the Father'? **10** Don't you believe that I am in the Father, and that the Father is in me? The words I say to you I do not speak on my own authority. Rather, it is the Father, living in me, who is doing his work. **11** Believe me when I say that I am in the Father and the Father is in me; or at least believe on the evidence of the works themselves. **12** Very truly I tell you, whoever believes in me will do the works I have been doing, and they will do even greater things than these, because I am going to the Father. **13** And I will do whatever you ask in my name, so that the Father may be glorified in

---

^{a} 1 Or *Believe in God* ^{b} 7 Some manuscripts *If you really knew me, you would know* the Son. ¹⁴You may ask me for anything in my name, and I will do it. Jn 10:38; 12:45

Jesus Promises the Holy Spirit

¹⁵ "If you love me, keep my commands. ¹⁶And I will ask the Father, and he will give you another advocate to help you and be with you forever — ¹⁷the Spirit of truth. The world cannot accept him, because it neither sees him nor knows him. But you know him, for he lives with you and will be*a* in you. ¹⁸I will not leave you as orphans; I will come to you. ¹⁹Before long, the world will not see me anymore, but you will see me. Because I live, you also will live. ²⁰On that day you will realize that I am in my Father, and you are in me, and I am in you. ²¹Whoever has my commands and keeps them is the one who loves me. The one who loves me will be loved by my Father, and I too will love them and show myself to them." Jn 15:10; 1Jn 5:3

²²Then Judas (not Judas Iscariot) said, "But, Lord, why do you intend to show yourself to us and not to the world?" Lk 6:16; Ac 10:41

²³Jesus replied, "Anyone who loves me will obey my teaching. My Father will love them, and we will come to them and make our home with them. ²⁴Anyone who does not love me will not obey my teaching. These words you hear are not my own;

they belong to the Father who sent me. Jn 7:16; 1Jn 2:24

²⁵ "All this I have spoken while still with you. ²⁶But the Advocate, the Holy Spirit, whom the Father will send in my name, will teach you all things and will remind you of everything I have said to you. ²⁷Peace I leave with you; my peace I give you. I do not give to you as the world gives. Do not let your hearts be troubled and do not be afraid. Jn 15:26; Php 4:7

²⁸ "You heard me say, 'I am going away and I am coming back to you.' If you loved me, you would be glad that I am going to the Father, for the Father is greater than I. ²⁹I have told you now before it happens, so that when it does happen you will believe. ³⁰I will not say much more to you, for the prince of this world is coming. He has no hold over me, ³¹but he comes so that the world may learn that I love the Father and do exactly what my Father has commanded me. Jn 10:18; 12:31; 13:19

"Come now; let us leave.

The Vine and the Branches

15 "I am the true vine, and my Father is the gardener. ²He cuts off every branch in me that bears no fruit, while every branch that does bear fruit he prunes*b* so that it will be even more fruitful. ³You are already clean because of the word I have spoken to you. ⁴Remain in me, as

---

a 17 Some early manuscripts *and is*   *b* 2 The Greek for *he prunes* also means *he cleans.*

I also remain in you. No branch can bear fruit by itself; it must remain in the vine. Neither can you bear fruit unless you remain in me. Isa 5:1-7; 1Jn 2:6

5 "I am the vine; you are the branches. If you remain in me and I in you, you will bear much fruit; apart from me you can do nothing. 6 If you do not remain in me, you are like a branch that is thrown away and withers; such branches are picked up, thrown into the fire and burned. 7 If you remain in me and my words remain in you, ask whatever you wish, and it will be done for you. 8 This is to my Father's glory, that you bear much fruit, showing yourselves to be my disciples.

9 "As the Father has loved me, so have I loved you. Now remain in my love. 10 If you keep my commands, you will remain in my love, just as I have kept my Father's commands and remain in his love. 11 I have told you this so that my joy may be in you and that your joy may be complete. 12 My command is this: Love each other as I have loved you. 13 Greater love has no one than this: to lay down one's life for one's friends. 14 You are my friends if you do what I command. 15 I no longer call you servants, because a servant does not know his master's business. Instead, I have called you friends, for everything that I learned from my Father I have made known to you. 16 You did not choose me, but I chose you and appointed you so that you might go and bear fruit—fruit that will last—and so that whatever you ask in my name the Father will give you. 17 This is my command: Love each other. Jn 13:18,34; 14:15

The World Hates the Disciples

18 "If the world hates you, keep in mind that it hated me first. 19 If you belonged to the world, it would love you as its own. As it is, you do not belong to the world, but I have chosen you out of the world. That is why the world hates you. 20 Remember what I told you: 'A servant is not greater than his master.'ᵃ If they persecuted me, they will persecute you also. If they obeyed my teaching, they will obey yours also. 21 They will treat you this way because of my name, for they do not know the one who sent me. 22 If I had not come and spoken to them, they would not be guilty of sin; but now they have no excuse for their sin. 23 Whoever hates me hates my Father as well. 24 If I had not done among them the works no one else did, they would not be guilty of sin. As it is, they have seen, and yet they have hated both me and my Father. 25 But this is to fulfill what is written in their Law: 'They hated me without reason.'ᵇ Jn 9:41; 1Jn 3:13

ᵃ 20 John 13:16   ᵇ 25 Psalms 35:19; 69:4

The Work of the Holy Spirit

26 "When the Advocate comes, whom I will send to you from the Father — the Spirit of truth who goes out from the Father — he will testify about me. 27 And you also must testify, for you have been with me from the beginning.   Jn 14:17; 1Jn 5:7

16 "All this I have told you so that you will not fall away. 2 They will put you out of the synagogue; in fact, the time is coming when anyone who kills you will think they are offering a service to God. 3 They will do such things because they have not known the Father or me. 4 I have told you this, so that when their time comes you will remember that I warned you about them. I did not tell you this from the beginning because I was with you, 5 but now I am going to him who sent me. None of you asks me, 'Where are you going?' 6 Rather, you are filled with grief because I have said these things. 7 But very truly I tell you, it is for your good that I am going away. Unless I go away, the Advocate will not come to you; but if I go, I will send him to you. 8 When he comes, he will prove the world to be in the wrong about sin and righteousness and judgment: 9 about sin, because people do not believe in me; 10 about righteousness, because I am going to the Father, where you can see me no longer; 11 and about judgment, because the prince of this world now stands condemned.   Jn 7:33,39

12 "I have much more to say to you, more than you can now bear. 13 But when he, the Spirit of truth, comes, he will guide you into all the truth. He will not speak on his own; he will speak only what he hears, and he will tell you what is yet to come. 14 He will glorify me because it is from me that he will receive what he will make known to you. 15 All that belongs to the Father is mine. That is why I said the Spirit will receive from me what he will make known to you."   Jn 14:17,26; 17:10

The Disciples' Grief Will Turn to Joy

16 Jesus went on to say, "In a little while you will see me no more, and then after a little while you will see me."   Jn 14:18-24

17 At this, some of his disciples said to one another, "What does he mean by saying, 'In a little while you will see me no more, and then after a little while you will see me,' and 'Because I am going to the Father'?" 18 They kept asking, "What does he mean by 'a little while'? We don't understand what he is saying."

19 Jesus saw that they wanted to ask him about this, so he said to them, "Are you asking one another what I meant when I said, 'In a little while you will see me no more, and then after a little

while you will see me'? ²⁰ Very truly I tell you, you will weep and mourn while the world rejoices. You will grieve, but your grief will turn to joy. ²¹ A woman giving birth to a child has pain because her time has come; but when her baby is born she forgets the anguish because of her joy that a child is born into the world. ²² So with you: Now is your time of grief, but I will see you again and you will rejoice, and no one will take away your joy. ²³ In that day you will no longer ask me anything. Very truly I tell you, my Father will give you whatever you ask in my name. ²⁴ Until now you have not asked for anything in my name. Ask and you will receive, and your joy will be complete. Mt 7:7; Jn 15:11,16

²⁵ "Though I have been speaking figuratively, a time is coming when I will no longer use this kind of language but will tell you plainly about my Father. ²⁶ In that day you will ask in my name. I am not saying that I will ask the Father on your behalf. ²⁷ No, the Father himself loves you because you have loved me and have believed that I came from God. ²⁸ I came from the Father and entered the world; now I am leaving the world and going back to the Father." Jn 10:6; 14:21,23

²⁹ Then Jesus' disciples said, "Now you are speaking clearly and without figures of speech. ³⁰ Now we can see that you know all things and that you do not even need to have anyone ask you questions. This makes us believe that you came from God." Jn 13:3

³¹ "Do you now believe?" Jesus replied. ³² "A time is coming and in fact has come when you will be scattered, each to your own home. You will leave me all alone. Yet I am not alone, for my Father is with me. Mt 26:31; Jn 8:16,29

³³ "I have told you these things, so that in me you may have peace. In this world you will have trouble. But take heart! I have overcome the world." Jn 14:27; Ro 8:37

Jesus Prays to Be Glorified

17 After Jesus said this, he looked toward heaven and prayed: Jn 11:41

"Father, the hour has come. Glorify your Son, that your Son may glorify you. ² For you granted him authority over all people that he might give eternal life to all those you have given him. ³ Now this is eternal life: that they know you, the only true God, and Jesus Christ, whom you have sent. ⁴ I have brought you glory on earth by finishing the work you gave me to do. ⁵ And now, Father, glorify me in your presence with the glory I had with you before the world began. Jn 1:2; Php 2:6

Jesus Prays for His Disciples

6 "I have revealed you[a] to those whom you gave me out of the world. They were yours; you gave them to me and they have obeyed your word. 7 Now they know that everything you have given me comes from you. 8 For I gave them the words you gave me and they accepted them. They knew with certainty that I came from you, and they believed that you sent me. 9 I pray for them. I am not praying for the world, but for those you have given me, for they are yours. 10 All I have is yours, and all you have is mine. And glory has come to me through them. 11 I will remain in the world no longer, but they are still in the world, and I am coming to you. Holy Father, protect them by the power of[b] your name, the name you gave me, so that they may be one as we are one. 12 While I was with them, I protected them and kept them safe by[c] that name you gave me. None has been lost except the one doomed to destruction so that Scripture would be fulfilled. Jn 6:39,70; 7:33 13 "I am coming to you now, but I say these things while I am still in the world, so that they may have the full measure of my joy within them. 14 I have given them your word and the world has hated them, for they are not of the world any more than I am of the world. 15 My prayer is not that you take them out of the world but that you protect them from the evil one. 16 They are not of the world, even as I am not of it. 17 Sanctify them by[d] the truth; your word is truth. 18 As you sent me into the world, I have sent them into the world. 19 For them I sanctify myself, that they too may be truly sanctified. Jn 8:23; 20:21

Jesus Prays for All Believers

20 "My prayer is not for them alone. I pray also for those who will believe in me through their message, 21 that all of them may be one, Father, just as you are in me and I am in you. May they also be in us so that the world may believe that you have sent me. 22 I have given them the glory that you gave me, that they may be one as we are one — 23 I in them and you in me — so that they may be brought to complete unity. Then the world will know that you sent me and

---

a 6 Greek *your name*   *b* 11 Or *Father, keep them faithful to*   *c* 12 Or *kept them faithful to*
d 17 Or *them to live in accordance with*

have loved them even as you have loved me. Jn 10:38; 14:20

²⁴ "Father, I want those you have given me to be with me where I am, and to see my glory, the glory you have given me because you loved me before the creation of the world. Jn 12:26

²⁵ "Righteous Father, though the world does not know you, I know you, and they know that you have sent me. ²⁶ I have made you[a] known to them, and will continue to make you known in order that the love you have for me may be in them and that I myself may be in them." Jn 15:9,21; 16:27

Jesus Arrested

18:3-11pp — Mt 26:47-56; Mk 14:43-50; Lk 22:47-53

18 When he had finished praying, Jesus left with his disciples and crossed the Kidron Valley. On the other side there was a garden, and he and his disciples went into it. 2Sa 15:23; Mt 21:1

²Now Judas, who betrayed him, knew the place, because Jesus had often met there with his disciples. ³So Judas came to the garden, guiding a detachment of soldiers and some officials from the chief priests and the Pharisees. They were carrying torches, lanterns and weapons. Lk 21:37; 22:39; Ac 1:16

⁴Jesus, knowing all that was going to happen to him, went out and asked them, "Who is it you want?" Jn 6:64; 13:1,11

⁵ "Jesus of Nazareth," they replied. Mk 1:24

"I am he," Jesus said. (And Judas the traitor was standing there with them.) ⁶When Jesus said, "I am he," they drew back and fell to the ground.

⁷Again he asked them, "Who is it you want?"

"Jesus of Nazareth," they said.

⁸Jesus answered, "I told you that I am he. If you are looking for me, then let these men go." ⁹This happened so that the words he had spoken would be fulfilled: "I have not lost one of those you gave me."[b] Jn 17:12

¹⁰Then Simon Peter, who had a sword, drew it and struck the high priest's servant, cutting off his right ear. (The servant's name was Malchus.)

¹¹Jesus commanded Peter, "Put your sword away! Shall I not drink the cup the Father has given me?" Mt 26:47-56; Mk 14:43-50

¹²Then the detachment of soldiers with its commander and the Jewish officials arrested Jesus. They bound him ¹³and brought him first to Annas, who was the father-in-law of Caiaphas, the high priest that year. ¹⁴Caiaphas was the one who had advised the Jewish leaders that it would be good if one man died for the people.

a 26 Greek *your name*   b 9 John 6:39

Peter's First Denial

18:16-18pp — Mt 26:69,70; Mk 14:66-68;
Lk 22:55-57

15 Simon Peter and another disciple were following Jesus. Because this disciple was known to the high priest, he went with Jesus into the high priest's courtyard, **16** but Peter had to wait outside at the door. The other disciple, who was known to the high priest, came back, spoke to the servant girl on duty there and brought Peter in. *Mt 26:58; Mk 14:54; Lk 22:54*

17 "You aren't one of this man's disciples too, are you?" she asked Peter.

He replied, "I am not."

18 It was cold, and the servants and officials stood around a fire they had made to keep warm. Peter also was standing with them, warming himself. *Mt 26:69-70*

The High Priest Questions Jesus

18:19-24pp — Mt 26:59-68; Mk 14:55-65;
Lk 22:63-71

19 Meanwhile, the high priest questioned Jesus about his disciples and his teaching.

20 "I have spoken openly to the world," Jesus replied. "I always taught in synagogues or at the temple, where all the Jews come together. I said nothing in secret. **21** Why question me? Ask those who heard me. Surely they know what I said." *Mt 26:55; Jn 7:26*

22 When Jesus said this, one of the officials nearby slapped him in the face. "Is this the way you answer the high priest?" he demanded. *Jn 19:3*

23 "If I said something wrong," Jesus replied, "testify as to what is wrong. But if I spoke the truth, why did you strike me?" **24** Then Annas sent him bound to Caiaphas the high priest. *Mt 26:59-68*

Peter's Second and Third Denials

18:25-27pp — Mt 26:71-75; Mk 14:69-72;
Lk 22:58-62

25 Meanwhile, Simon Peter was still standing there warming himself. So they asked him, "You aren't one of his disciples too, are you?"

He denied it, saying, "I am not."

26 One of the high priest's servants, a relative of the man whose ear Peter had cut off, challenged him, "Didn't I see you with him in the garden?" **27** Again Peter denied it, and at that moment a rooster began to crow. *Mt 26:71-75*

Jesus Before Pilate

18:29-40pp — Mt 27:11-18,20-23;
Mk 15:2-15; Lk 23:2,3,18-25

28 Then the Jewish leaders took Jesus from Caiaphas to the palace of the Roman governor. By now it was early morning, and to avoid ceremonial uncleanness they did not enter the palace, because they wanted to be able to eat the Passover. **29** So Pilate came out to them and asked, "What charges are you bringing against this man?" Mt 27:2; Mk 15:1; Jn 11:55

30 "If he were not a criminal," they replied, "we would not have handed him over to you."

31 Pilate said, "Take him yourselves and judge him by your own law."

"But we have no right to execute anyone," they objected. 32 This took place to fulfill what Jesus had said about the kind of death he was going to die. Mt 20:19

33 Pilate then went back inside the palace, summoned Jesus and asked him, "Are you the king of the Jews?" Lk 23:3; Jn 19:9

34 "Is that your own idea," Jesus asked, "or did others talk to you about me?"

35 "Am I a Jew?" Pilate replied. "Your own people and chief priests handed you over to me. What is it you have done?"

36 Jesus said, "My kingdom is not of this world. If it were, my servants would fight to prevent my arrest by the Jewish leaders. But now my kingdom is from another place." Mt 26:53; Jn 6:15

37 "You are a king, then!" said Pilate.

Jesus answered, "You say that I am a king. In fact, the reason I was born and came into the world is to testify to the truth. Everyone on the side of truth listens to me." Jn 8:47; 1Jn 4:6

38 "What is truth?" retorted Pilate. With this he went out again to the Jews gathered there and said, "I find no basis for a charge against him. 39 But it is your custom for me to release to you one prisoner at the time of the Passover. Do you want me to release 'the king of the Jews'?" Lk 23:4

40 They shouted back, "No, not him! Give us Barabbas!" Now Barabbas had taken part in an uprising. Ac 3:14

Jesus Sentenced to Be Crucified
19:1-16pp — Mt 27:27-31; Mk 15:16-20

19 Then Pilate took Jesus and had him flogged. 2 The soldiers twisted together a crown of thorns and put it on his head. They clothed him in a purple robe 3 and went up to him again and again, saying, "Hail, king of the Jews!" And they slapped him in the face. Mt 27:26,29; Jn 18:22

4 Once more Pilate came out and said to the Jews gathered there, "Look, I am bringing him out to you to let you know that I find no basis for a charge against him." 5 When Jesus came out wearing the crown of thorns and the purple robe, Pilate said to them, "Here is the man!" Lk 23:4

6 As soon as the chief priests and their officials saw him, they shouted, "Crucify! Crucify!"

But Pilate answered, "You take him and crucify him. As for me, I find no basis for a charge against him." Lk 23:4; Ac 3:13

7 The Jewish leaders insisted, "We have a law, and according to that law he must die, be-

cause he claimed to be the Son of God." Lev 24:16; Mt 26:63-66

⁸When Pilate heard this, he was even more afraid, ⁹and he went back inside the palace. "Where do you come from?" he asked Jesus, but Jesus gave him no answer. ¹⁰"Do you refuse to speak to me?" Pilate said. "Don't you realize I have power either to free you or to crucify you?" Mk 14:61

¹¹Jesus answered, "You would have no power over me if it were not given to you from above. Therefore the one who handed me over to you is guilty of a greater sin." Jn 18:28-30; Ac 3:13; Ro 13:1

¹²From then on, Pilate tried to set Jesus free, but the Jewish leaders kept shouting, "If you let this man go, you are no friend of Caesar. Anyone who claims to be a king opposes Caesar." Lk 23:2

¹³When Pilate heard this, he brought Jesus out and sat down on the judge's seat at a place known as the Stone Pavement (which in Aramaic is Gabbatha). ¹⁴It was the day of Preparation of the Passover; it was about noon. Mt 27:62

"Here is your king," Pilate said to the Jews.

¹⁵But they shouted, "Take him away! Take him away! Crucify him!"

"Shall I crucify your king?" Pilate asked.

"We have no king but Caesar," the chief priests answered.

¹⁶Finally Pilate handed him over to them to be crucified.

The Crucifixion of Jesus

19:17-24pp — Mt 27:33-44; Mk 15:22-32; Lk 23:33-43

So the soldiers took charge of Jesus. ¹⁷Carrying his own cross, he went out to the place of the Skull (which in Aramaic is called Golgotha). ¹⁸There they crucified him, and with him two others—one on each side and Jesus in the middle. Lk 23:26,32-33; Jn 5:2

¹⁹Pilate had a notice prepared and fastened to the cross. It read: JESUS OF NAZARETH, THE KING OF THE JEWS. ²⁰Many of the Jews read this sign, for the place where Jesus was crucified was near the city, and the sign was written in Aramaic, Latin and Greek. ²¹The chief priests of the Jews protested to Pilate, "Do not write 'The King of the Jews,' but that this man claimed to be king of the Jews." Mk 1:24; Heb 13:12

²²Pilate answered, "What I have written, I have written."

²³When the soldiers crucified Jesus, they took his clothes, dividing them into four shares, one for each of them, with the undergarment remaining. This garment was seamless, woven in one piece from top to bottom. ²⁴"Let's not tear it," they said to one another. "Let's decide by lot who will get it."

This happened that the scripture might be fulfilled that said,

"They divided my clothes
among them
and cast lots for my
garment."[a]   Ps 22:18

So this is what the soldiers did. Mt 27:33-44; Mk 15:22-32; Lk 23:33-43

²⁵Near the cross of Jesus stood his mother, his mother's sister, Mary the wife of Clopas, and Mary Magdalene. ²⁶When Jesus saw his mother there, and the disciple whom he loved standing nearby, he said to her, "Woman,[b] here is your son," ²⁷and to the disciple, "Here is your mother." From that time on, this disciple took her into his home. Mk 15:40-41

The Death of Jesus
19:29,30pp — Mt 27:48,50; Mk 15:36,37; Lk 23:36

²⁸Later, knowing that everything had now been finished, and so that Scripture would be fulfilled, Jesus said, "I am thirsty." ²⁹A jar of wine vinegar was there, so they soaked a sponge in it, put the sponge on a stalk of the hyssop plant, and lifted it to Jesus' lips. ³⁰When he had received the drink, Jesus said, "It is finished." With that, he bowed his head and gave up his spirit.   Mt 27:48,50

³¹Now it was the day of Preparation, and the next day was to be a special Sabbath. Because the Jewish leaders did not want the bodies left on the crosses during the Sabbath, they asked Pilate to have the legs broken and the bodies taken down. ³²The soldiers therefore came and broke the legs of the first man who had been crucified with Jesus, and then those of the other. ³³But when they came to Jesus and found that he was already dead, they did not break his legs. ³⁴Instead, one of the soldiers pierced Jesus' side with a spear, bringing a sudden flow of blood and water. ³⁵The man who saw it has given testimony, and his testimony is true. He knows that he tells the truth, and he testifies so that you also may believe. ³⁶These things happened so that the scripture would be fulfilled: "Not one of his bones will be broken,"[c] ³⁷and, as another scripture says, "They will look on the one they have pierced."[d]   1Jn 5:6,8; Rev 1:7

The Burial of Jesus
19:38-42pp — Mt 27:57-61; Mk 15:42-47; Lk 23:50-56

³⁸Later, Joseph of Arimathea asked Pilate for the body of Jesus. Now Joseph was a disciple of Jesus, but secretly because he feared the Jewish leaders. With Pilate's permission, he came and took the body away. ³⁹He was accompanied by Nicodemus, the man who earlier had visited Jesus at night. Nicodemus brought a mixture of myrrh and aloes, about seventy-

[a] 24 Psalm 22:18   [b] 26 The Greek for *Woman* does not denote any disrespect.
[c] 36 Exodus 12:46; Num. 9:12; Psalm 34:20   [d] 37 Zech. 12:10

five pounds.*a* ⁴⁰Taking Jesus' body, the two of them wrapped it, with the spices, in strips of linen. This was in accordance with Jewish burial customs. ⁴¹At the place where Jesus was crucified, there was a garden, and in the garden a new tomb, in which no one had ever been laid. ⁴²Because it was the Jewish day of Preparation and since the tomb was nearby, they laid Jesus there.   Mt 27:57-61; Mk 15:42-47

The Empty Tomb

20:1-8pp — Mt 28:1-8; Mk 16:1-8;
Lk 24:1-10

20 Early on the first day of the week, while it was still dark, Mary Magdalene went to the tomb and saw that the stone had been removed from the entrance. ²So she came running to Simon Peter and the other disciple, the one Jesus loved, and said, "They have taken the Lord out of the tomb, and we don't know where they have put him!"

³So Peter and the other disciple started for the tomb. ⁴Both were running, but the other disciple outran Peter and reached the tomb first. ⁵He bent over and looked in at the strips of linen lying there but did not go in. ⁶Then Simon Peter came along behind him and went straight into the tomb. He saw the strips of linen lying there, ⁷as well as the cloth that had been wrapped around

Jesus' head. The cloth was still lying in its place, separate from the linen. ⁸Finally the other disciple, who had reached the tomb first, also went inside. He saw and believed. ⁹(They still did not understand from Scripture that Jesus had to rise from the dead.) ¹⁰Then the disciples went back to where they were staying.   Mt 28:1-8

Jesus Appears to Mary Magdalene

¹¹Now Mary stood outside the tomb crying. As she wept, she bent over to look into the tomb ¹²and saw two angels in white, seated where Jesus' body had been, one at the head and the other at the foot.   Mk 16:5; Lk 24:4; Ac 5:19

¹³They asked her, "Woman, why are you crying?"

"They have taken my Lord away," she said, "and I don't know where they have put him." ¹⁴At this, she turned around and saw Jesus standing there, but she did not realize that it was Jesus.   Mk 16:9; Jn 21:4

¹⁵He asked her, "Woman, why are you crying? Who is it you are looking for?"

Thinking he was the gardener, she said, "Sir, if you have carried him away, tell me where you have put him, and I will get him."

¹⁶Jesus said to her, "Mary."

She turned toward him and cried out in Aramaic, "Rabboni!" (which means "Teacher").   Mt 23:7

a 39 Or about 34 kilograms

[17] Jesus said, "Do not hold on to me, for I have not yet ascended to the Father. Go instead to my brothers and tell them, 'I am ascending to my Father and your Father, to my God and your God.'"

[18] Mary Magdalene went to the disciples with the news: "I have seen the Lord!" And she told them that he had said these things to her. Lk 24:10,22-23

Jesus Appears to His Disciples

[19] On the evening of that first day of the week, when the disciples were together, with the doors locked for fear of the Jewish leaders, Jesus came and stood among them and said, "Peace be with you!" [20] After he said this, he showed them his hands and side. The disciples were overjoyed when they saw the Lord. Lk 24:36-39

[21] Again Jesus said, "Peace be with you! As the Father has sent me, I am sending you." [22] And with that he breathed on them and said, "Receive the Holy Spirit. [23] If you forgive anyone's sins, their sins are forgiven; if you do not forgive them, they are not forgiven."

Jesus Appears to Thomas

[24] Now Thomas (also known as Didymus[a]), one of the Twelve, was not with the disciples when Jesus came. [25] So the other disciples told him, "We have seen the Lord!" Jn 11:16

But he said to them, "Unless I see the nail marks in his hands and put my finger where the nails were, and put my hand into his side, I will not believe." Mk 16:11

[26] A week later his disciples were in the house again, and Thomas was with them. Though the doors were locked, Jesus came and stood among them and said, "Peace be with you!" [27] Then he said to Thomas, "Put your finger here; see my hands. Reach out your hand and put it into my side. Stop doubting and believe." Lk 24:40; Jn 14:27

[28] Thomas said to him, "My Lord and my God!"

[29] Then Jesus told him, "Because you have seen me, you have believed; blessed are those who have not seen and yet have believed." Jn 3:15; 1Pe 1:8

The Purpose of John's Gospel

[30] Jesus performed many other signs in the presence of his disciples, which are not recorded in this book. [31] But these are written that you may believe[b] that Jesus is the Messiah, the Son of God, and that by believing you may have life in his name. Jn 3:15; 21:25

Jesus and the Miraculous Catch of Fish

21 Afterward Jesus appeared again to his disciples, by the Sea of Galilee.[c] It happened

---

[a] 24 Thomas (Aramaic) and Didymus (Greek) both mean twin.   [b] 31 Or may continue to believe   [c] 1 Greek Tiberias

this way: ²Simon Peter, Thomas (also known as Didymus*a*), Nathanael from Cana in Galilee, the sons of Zebedee, and two other disciples were together. ³"I'm going out to fish," Simon Peter told them, and they said, "We'll go with you." So they went out and got into the boat, but that night they caught nothing. Mt 4:21; Lk 5:5

⁴Early in the morning, Jesus stood on the shore, but the disciples did not realize that it was Jesus. Lk 24:16; Jn 20:14

⁵He called out to them, "Friends, haven't you any fish?"

"No," they answered.

⁶He said, "Throw your net on the right side of the boat and you will find some." When they did, they were unable to haul the net in because of the large number of fish. Lk 5:4-7

⁷Then the disciple whom Jesus loved said to Peter, "It is the Lord!" As soon as Simon Peter heard him say, "It is the Lord," he wrapped his outer garment around him (for he had taken it off) and jumped into the water. ⁸The other disciples followed in the boat, towing the net full of fish, for they were not far from shore, about a hundred yards.*b* ⁹When they landed, they saw a fire of burning coals there with fish on it, and some bread. Jn 13:23; 18:18

¹⁰Jesus said to them, "Bring some of the fish you have just caught." ¹¹So Simon Peter climbed back into the boat and dragged the net ashore. It was full of large fish, 153, but even with so many the net was not torn. ¹²Jesus said to them, "Come and have breakfast." None of the disciples dared ask him, "Who are you?" They knew it was the Lord. ¹³Jesus came, took the bread and gave it to them, and did the same with the fish. ¹⁴This was now the third time Jesus appeared to his disciples after he was raised from the dead. Jn 20:19,26

Jesus Reinstates Peter

¹⁵When they had finished eating, Jesus said to Simon Peter, "Simon son of John, do you love me more than these?"

"Yes, Lord," he said, "you know that I love you." Mt 26:33,35; Jn 13:37

Jesus said, "Feed my lambs."

¹⁶Again Jesus said, "Simon son of John, do you love me?"

He answered, "Yes, Lord, you know that I love you."

Jesus said, "Take care of my sheep." Ac 20:28; 1Pe 5:2-3

¹⁷The third time he said to him, "Simon son of John, do you love me?"

Peter was hurt because Jesus asked him the third time, "Do you love me?" He said, "Lord, you know all things; you know that I love you." Jn 16:30

Jesus said, "Feed my sheep. ¹⁸Very truly I tell you, when you were younger you dressed

a 2 *Thomas* (Aramaic) and *Didymus* (Greek) both mean *twin*.   *b* 8 Or about 90 meters yourself and went where you wanted; but when you are old you will stretch out your hands, and someone else will dress you and lead you where you do not want to go." **19**Jesus said this to indicate the kind of death by which Peter would glorify God. Then he said to him, "Follow me!" 2Pe 1:14

20Peter turned and saw that the disciple whom Jesus loved was following them. (This was the one who had leaned back against Jesus at the supper and had said, "Lord, who is going to betray you?") **21**When Peter saw him, he asked, "Lord, what about him?" Jn 13:23,25

22Jesus answered, "If I want him to remain alive until I return, what is that to you? You must follow me." **23**Because of this, the rumor spread among the believers that this disciple would not die. But Jesus did not say that he would not die; he only said, "If I want him to remain alive until I return, what is that to you?" Mt 16:27; Ac 1:16

24This is the disciple who testifies to these things and who wrote them down. We know that his testimony is true. Jn 19:35

25Jesus did many other things as well. If every one of them were written down, I suppose that even the whole world would not have room for the books that would be written. Jn 20:30

Acts

Jesus Taken Up Into Heaven

1 In my former book, Theophilus, I wrote about all that Jesus began to do and to teach ²until the day he was taken up to heaven, after giving instructions through the Holy Spirit to the apostles he had chosen. ³After his suffering, he presented himself to them and gave many convincing proofs that he was alive. He appeared to them over a period of forty days and spoke about the kingdom of God. ⁴On one occasion, while he was eating with them, he gave them this command: "Do not leave Jerusalem, but wait for the gift my Father promised, which you have heard me speak about. ⁵For John baptized with*ᵃ* water, but in a few days you will be baptized with*ᵃ* the Holy Spirit."   Lk 1:1-4; Jn 14:16

⁶Then they gathered around him and asked him, "Lord, are you at this time going to restore the kingdom to Israel?"   Mt 17:11

⁷He said to them: "It is not for you to know the times or dates the Father has set by his own authority. ⁸But you will receive power when the Holy Spirit comes on you; and you will be my witnesses in Jerusalem, and in all Judea and Samaria, and to the ends of the earth."   Mt 24:36; Lk 24:48

⁹After he said this, he was taken up before their very eyes, and a cloud hid him from their sight. ¹⁰They were looking intently up into the sky as he was going, when suddenly two men dressed in white stood beside them. ¹¹"Men of Galilee," they said, "why do you stand here looking into the sky? This same Jesus, who has been taken from you into heaven, will come back in the same way you have seen him go into heaven."   Mt 16:27; Jn 20:12

Matthias Chosen to Replace Judas

¹²Then the apostles returned to Jerusalem from the hill called the Mount of Olives, a Sabbath

ᵃ 5 Or *in*

day's walk[a] from the city. [13]When they arrived, they went upstairs to the room where they were staying. Those present were Peter, John, James and Andrew; Philip and Thomas, Bartholomew and Matthew; James son of Alphaeus and Simon the Zealot, and Judas son of James. [14]They all joined together constantly in prayer, along with the women and Mary the mother of Jesus, and with his brothers. Ac 2:42; 9:37

[15]In those days Peter stood up among the believers (a group numbering about a hundred and twenty) [16]and said, "Brothers and sisters,[b] the Scripture had to be fulfilled in which the Holy Spirit spoke long ago through David concerning Judas, who served as guide for those who arrested Jesus. [17]He was one of our number and shared in our ministry."

[18](With the payment he received for his wickedness, Judas bought a field; there he fell headlong, his body burst open and all his intestines spilled out. [19]Everyone in Jerusalem heard about this, so they called that field in their language Akeldama, that is, Field of Blood.) Mt 26:14-15; 27:3-10

[20]"For," said Peter, "it is written in the Book of Psalms:

> " 'May his place be deserted;
>   let there be no one to dwell
>   in it,'[c]   Ps 69:25

and,

> " 'May another take his place
>   of leadership.'[d]

[21]Therefore it is necessary to choose one of the men who have been with us the whole time the Lord Jesus was living among us, [22]beginning from John's baptism to the time when Jesus was taken up from us. For one of these must become a witness with us of his resurrection."   Mk 1:4; Lk 24:48

[23]So they nominated two men: Joseph called Barsabbas (also known as Justus) and Matthias. [24]Then they prayed, "Lord, you know everyone's heart. Show us which of these two you have chosen [25]to take over this apostolic ministry, which Judas left to go where he belongs." [26]Then they cast lots, and the lot fell to Matthias; so he was added to the eleven apostles.   1Sa 16:7; Jer 17:10; Rev 2:23

The Holy Spirit Comes at Pentecost

2 When the day of Pentecost came, they were all together in one place. [2]Suddenly a sound like the blowing of a violent wind came from heaven and filled the whole house where they were sitting. [3]They saw what seemed to be tongues of fire that separated and came to rest on each of them. [4]All of them were filled with the

---

[a] 12 That is, about 5/8 mile or about 1 kilometer   [b] 16 The Greek word for *brothers and sisters* (*adelphoi*) refers here to believers, both men and women, as part of God's family; also in 6:3; 11:29; 12:17; 16:40; 18:18, 27; 21:7, 17; 28:14, 15.   [c] 20 Psalm 69:25   [d] 20 Psalm 109:8

Holy Spirit and began to speak in other tongues[a] as the Spirit enabled them. Mk 16:17; 1Co 12:10

⁵Now there were staying in Jerusalem God-fearing Jews from every nation under heaven. ⁶When they heard this sound, a crowd came together in bewilderment, because each one heard their own language being spoken. ⁷Utterly amazed, they asked: "Aren't all these who are speaking Galileans? ⁸Then how is it that each of us hears them in our native language? ⁹Parthians, Medes and Elamites; residents of Mesopotamia, Judea and Cappadocia, Pontus and Asia,[b] ¹⁰Phrygia and Pamphylia, Egypt and the parts of Libya near Cyrene; visitors from Rome ¹¹(both Jews and converts to Judaism); Cretans and Arabs — we hear them declaring the wonders of God in our own tongues!" ¹²Amazed and perplexed, they asked one another, "What does this mean?" Ac 1:11; 16:6

¹³Some, however, made fun of them and said, "They have had too much wine." 1Co 14:23

Peter Addresses the Crowd

¹⁴Then Peter stood up with the Eleven, raised his voice and addressed the crowd: "Fellow Jews and all of you who live in Jerusalem, let me explain this to you; listen carefully to what I say.

¹⁵These people are not drunk, as you suppose. It's only nine in the morning! ¹⁶No, this is what was spoken by the prophet Joel: 1Th 5:7

¹⁷" 'In the last days, God says,
    I will pour out my Spirit on
        all people.   Jn 7:37-39
Your sons and daughters will
        prophesy,   Ac 21:9
    your young men will see
        visions,
    your old men will dream
        dreams.
¹⁸Even on my servants, both
        men and women,
    I will pour out my Spirit in
        those days,
    and they will prophesy.
¹⁹I will show wonders in the
        heavens above
    and signs on the earth
        below,
    blood and fire and billows
        of smoke.
²⁰The sun will be turned to
        darkness
    and the moon to blood
    before the coming of the
        great and glorious day
        of the Lord.
²¹And everyone who calls
    on the name of the Lord will
        be saved.'[c] Ro 10:13; 2Ti 2:22

²²"Fellow Israelites, listen to this: Jesus of Nazareth was a man accredited by God to you by miracles, wonders and signs, which God did among you through

---

[a] 4 Or *languages*; also in verse 11   [b] 9 That is, the Roman province by that name
[c] 21 Joel 2:28-32

him, as you yourselves know. ²³This man was handed over to you by God's deliberate plan and foreknowledge; and you, with the help of wicked men,ᵃ put him to death by nailing him to the cross. ²⁴But God raised him from the dead, freeing him from the agony of death, because it was impossible for death to keep its hold on him. ²⁵David said about him:

Jn 4:48; 2Co 4:14; Eph 1:20

> " 'I saw the Lord always
>   before me.
> Because he is at my right
>   hand,
> I will not be shaken.
> ²⁶Therefore my heart is glad
>   and my tongue rejoices;
> my body also will rest in
>   hope,
> ²⁷because you will not abandon
>   me to the realm of the
>   dead,
> you will not let your holy
>   one see decay.   Ac 13:35
> ²⁸You have made known to me
>   the paths of life;
> you will fill me with joy in
>   your presence.'ᵇ Ps 16:8-11

²⁹"Fellow Israelites, I can tell you confidently that the patriarch David died and was buried, and his tomb is here to this day. ³⁰But he was a prophet and knew that God had promised him on oath that he would place one of his descendants on his throne.

³¹Seeing what was to come, he spoke of the resurrection of the Messiah, that he was not abandoned to the realm of the dead, nor did his body see decay. ³²God has raised this Jesus to life, and we are all witnesses of it. ³³Exalted to the right hand of God, he has received from the Father the promised Holy Spirit and has poured out what you now see and hear. ³⁴For David did not ascend to heaven, and yet he said,

Ac 10:45; 13:36

> " 'The Lord said to my Lord:
> "Sit at my right hand
> ³⁵until I make your enemies
>   a footstool for your feet." 'ᶜ

³⁶"Therefore let all Israel be assured of this: God has made this Jesus, whom you crucified, both Lord and Messiah."   Lk 2:11

³⁷When the people heard this, they were cut to the heart and said to Peter and the other apostles, "Brothers, what shall we do?"   Lk 3:10,12,14

³⁸Peter replied, "Repent and be baptized, every one of you, in the name of Jesus Christ for the forgiveness of your sins. And you will receive the gift of the Holy Spirit. ³⁹The promise is for you and your children and for all who are far off—for all whom the Lord our God will call."   Lk 24:47

⁴⁰With many other words he warned them; and he pleaded

ᵃ 23 Or *of those not having the law* (that is, Gentiles)   ᵇ 28 Psalm 16:8-11 (see Septuagint)
ᶜ 35 Psalm 110:1

with them, "Save yourselves from this corrupt generation." [41] Those who accepted his message were baptized, and about three thousand were added to their number that day. Dt 32:5; Php 2:15

The Fellowship of the Believers

[42] They devoted themselves to the apostles' teaching and to fellowship, to the breaking of bread and to prayer. [43] Everyone was filled with awe at the many wonders and signs performed by the apostles. [44] All the believers were together and had everything in common. [45] They sold property and possessions to give to anyone who had need. [46] Every day they continued to meet together in the temple courts. They broke bread in their homes and ate together with glad and sincere hearts, [47] praising God and enjoying the favor of all the people. And the Lord added to their number daily those who were being saved. Ac 5:14; Ro 14:18

Peter Heals a Lame Beggar

3 One day Peter and John were going up to the temple at the time of prayer — at three in the afternoon. [2] Now a man who was lame from birth was being carried to the temple gate called Beautiful, where he was put every day to beg from those going into the temple courts. [3] When he saw Peter and John about to enter, he asked them for money.

[4] Peter looked straight at him, as did John. Then Peter said, "Look at us!" [5] So the man gave them his attention, expecting to get something from them. Ps 55:17; Ac 14:8

[6] Then Peter said, "Silver or gold I do not have, but what I do have I give you. In the name of Jesus Christ of Nazareth, walk." [7] Taking him by the right hand, he helped him up, and instantly the man's feet and ankles became strong. [8] He jumped to his feet and began to walk. Then he went with them into the temple courts, walking and jumping, and praising God. [9] When all the people saw him walking and praising God, [10] they recognized him as the same man who used to sit begging at the temple gate called Beautiful, and they were filled with wonder and amazement at what had happened to him. Ac 4:10,16,21

Peter Speaks to the Onlookers

[11] While the man held on to Peter and John, all the people were astonished and came running to them in the place called Solomon's Colonnade. [12] When Peter saw this, he said to them: "Fellow Israelites, why does this surprise you? Why do you stare at us as if by our own power or godliness we had made this man walk? [13] The God of Abraham, Isaac and Jacob, the God of our fathers, has glorified his servant Jesus. You handed him over to be killed, and

you disowned him before Pilate, though he had decided to let him go. [14]You disowned the Holy and Righteous One and asked that a murderer be released to you. [15]You killed the author of life, but God raised him from the dead. We are witnesses of this. [16]By faith in the name of Jesus, this man whom you see and know was made strong. It is Jesus' name and the faith that comes through him that has completely healed him, as you can all see. Mk 1:24; Jn 10:23; Ac 2:24

[17]"Now, fellow Israelites, I know that you acted in ignorance, as did your leaders. [18]But this is how God fulfilled what he had foretold through all the prophets, saying that his Messiah would suffer. [19]Repent, then, and turn to God, so that your sins may be wiped out, that times of refreshing may come from the Lord, [20]and that he may send the Messiah, who has been appointed for you — even Jesus. [21]Heaven must receive him until the time comes for God to restore everything, as he promised long ago through his holy prophets. [22]For Moses said, 'The Lord your God will raise up for you a prophet like me from among your own people; you must listen to everything he tells you. [23]Anyone who does not listen to him will be completely cut off from their people.'[a] Dt 18:15,18; Ac 7:37

[24]"Indeed, beginning with Samuel, all the prophets who have spoken have foretold these days. [25]And you are heirs of the prophets and of the covenant God made with your fathers. He said to Abraham, 'Through your offspring all peoples on earth will be blessed.'[b] [26]When God raised up his servant, he sent him first to you to bless you by turning each of you from your wicked ways." Ac 13:46; Ro 1:16

Peter and John Before the Sanhedrin

4 The priests and the captain of the temple guard and the Sadducees came up to Peter and John while they were speaking to the people. [2]They were greatly disturbed because the apostles were teaching the people, proclaiming in Jesus the resurrection of the dead. [3]They seized Peter and John and, because it was evening, they put them in jail until the next day. [4]But many who heard the message believed; so the number of men who believed grew to about five thousand. Lk 22:4; Ac 5:18

[5]The next day the rulers, the elders and the teachers of the law met in Jerusalem. [6]Annas the high priest was there, and so were Caiaphas, John, Alexander and others of the high priest's family. [7]They had Peter and John brought before them and be-

[a] 23 Deut. 18:15,18,19   [b] 25 Gen. 22:18; 26:4

gan to question them: "By what power or what name did you do this?" Mt 26:3; Lk 3:2; 23:13

⁸Then Peter, filled with the Holy Spirit, said to them: "Rulers and elders of the people! ⁹If we are being called to account today for an act of kindness shown to a man who was lame and are being asked how he was healed, ¹⁰then know this, you and all the people of Israel: It is by the name of Jesus Christ of Nazareth, whom you crucified but whom God raised from the dead, that this man stands before you healed. ¹¹Jesus is Lk 23:13; Ac 2:24

" 'the stone you builders rejected,
which has become the cornerstone.'^a

¹²Salvation is found in no one else, for there is no other name under heaven given to mankind by which we must be saved." Mt 1:21

¹³When they saw the courage of Peter and John and realized that they were unschooled, ordinary men, they were astonished and they took note that these men had been with Jesus. ¹⁴But since they could see the man who had been healed standing there with them, there was nothing they could say. ¹⁵So they ordered them to withdraw from the Sanhedrin and then conferred together. ¹⁶"What are we going to do with these men?" they asked.

"Everyone living in Jerusalem knows they have performed a notable sign, and we cannot deny it. ¹⁷But to stop this thing from spreading any further among the people, we must warn them to speak no longer to anyone in this name." Mt 11:25; Jn 11:47; Ac 3:6-10

¹⁸Then they called them in again and commanded them not to speak or teach at all in the name of Jesus. ¹⁹But Peter and John replied, "Which is right in God's eyes: to listen to you, or to him? You be the judges! ²⁰As for us, we cannot help speaking about what we have seen and heard." Ac 5:29,40

²¹After further threats they let them go. They could not decide how to punish them, because all the people were praising God for what had happened. ²²For the man who was miraculously healed was over forty years old.

The Believers Pray

²³On their release, Peter and John went back to their own people and reported all that the chief priests and the elders had said to them. ²⁴When they heard this, they raised their voices together in prayer to God. "Sovereign Lord," they said, "you made the heavens and the earth and the sea, and everything in them. ²⁵You spoke by the Holy Spirit through the mouth of your servant, our father David: Ac 1:16

^a 11 Psalm 118:22

" 'Why do the nations rage
and the peoples plot in
vain?
²⁶ The kings of the earth rise up
and the rulers band
together
against the Lord
and against his anointed
one.ᵃʹᵇ

²⁷ Indeed Herod and Pontius Pilate met together with the Gentiles and the people of Israel in this city to conspire against your holy servant Jesus, whom you anointed. ²⁸ They did what your power and will had decided beforehand should happen. ²⁹ Now, Lord, consider their threats and enable your servants to speak your word with great boldness. ³⁰ Stretch out your hand to heal and perform signs and wonders through the name of your holy servant Jesus." Lk 4:18; Ac 2:23; 10:38

³¹ After they prayed, the place where they were meeting was shaken. And they were all filled with the Holy Spirit and spoke the word of God boldly. Ac 2:2; Heb 4:12

The Believers Share Their Possessions

³² All the believers were one in heart and mind. No one claimed that any of their possessions was their own, but they shared everything they had. ³³ With great power the apostles continued to testify to the resurrection of the Lord Jesus. And God's grace was so powerfully at work in them all ³⁴ that there were no needy persons among them. For from time to time those who owned land or houses sold them, brought the money from the sales ³⁵ and put it at the apostles' feet, and it was distributed to anyone who had need. Ac 2:44-45; 6:1

³⁶ Joseph, a Levite from Cyprus, whom the apostles called Barnabas (which means "son of encouragement"), ³⁷ sold a field he owned and brought the money and put it at the apostles' feet. Ac 5:2

Ananias and Sapphira

5 Now a man named Ananias, together with his wife Sapphira, also sold a piece of property. ² With his wife's full knowledge he kept back part of the money for himself, but brought the rest and put it at the apostles' feet. Ac 4:35,37

³ Then Peter said, "Ananias, how is it that Satan has so filled your heart that you have lied to the Holy Spirit and have kept for yourself some of the money you received for the land? ⁴ Didn't it belong to you before it was sold? And after it was sold, wasn't the money at your disposal? What made you think of doing such a thing? You have not lied just to human beings but to God." Lev 6:2

⁵ When Ananias heard this, he fell down and died. And great fear

---

ᵃ 26 That is, Messiah or Christ   ᵇ 26 Psalm 2:1,2

seized all who heard what had happened. ⁶Then some young men came forward, wrapped up his body, and carried him out and buried him.   Jn 19:40

⁷About three hours later his wife came in, not knowing what had happened. ⁸Peter asked her, "Tell me, is this the price you and Ananias got for the land?"

"Yes," she said, "that is the price."

⁹Peter said to her, "How could you conspire to test the Spirit of the Lord? Listen! The feet of the men who buried your husband are at the door, and they will carry you out also."

¹⁰At that moment she fell down at his feet and died. Then the young men came in and, finding her dead, carried her out and buried her beside her husband. ¹¹Great fear seized the whole church and all who heard about these events.   Ac 19:17

The Apostles Heal Many

¹²The apostles performed many signs and wonders among the people. And all the believers used to meet together in Solomon's Colonnade. ¹³No one else dared join them, even though they were highly regarded by the people. ¹⁴Nevertheless, more and more men and women believed in the Lord and were added to their number. ¹⁵As a result, people brought the sick into the streets and laid them on beds and mats so that at least Peter's shadow might fall on some of them as he passed by. ¹⁶Crowds gathered also from the towns around Jerusalem, bringing their sick and those tormented by impure spirits, and all of them were healed.   Ac 2:47; 3:11; 19:12

The Apostles Persecuted

¹⁷Then the high priest and all his associates, who were members of the party of the Sadducees, were filled with jealousy. ¹⁸They arrested the apostles and put them in the public jail. ¹⁹But during the night an angel of the Lord opened the doors of the jail and brought them out. ²⁰"Go, stand in the temple courts," he said, "and tell the people all about this new life." Jn 6:63,68; Ac 4:1

²¹At daybreak they entered the temple courts, as they had been told, and began to teach the people.

When the high priest and his associates arrived, they called together the Sanhedrin—the full assembly of the elders of Israel—and sent to the jail for the apostles. ²²But on arriving at the jail, the officers did not find them there. So they went back and reported, ²³"We found the jail securely locked, with the guards standing at the doors; but when we opened them, we found no one inside." ²⁴On hearing this report, the captain of the temple guard and the chief priests were at a loss, wondering what this might lead to. Ac 4:1,5-6

²⁵ Then someone came and said, "Look! The men you put in jail are standing in the temple courts teaching the people." ²⁶ At that, the captain went with his officers and brought the apostles. They did not use force, because they feared that the people would stone them. Ac 4:21

²⁷ The apostles were brought in and made to appear before the Sanhedrin to be questioned by the high priest. ²⁸ "We gave you strict orders not to teach in this name," he said. "Yet you have filled Jerusalem with your teaching and are determined to make us guilty of this man's blood." Mt 23:35; Ac 2:23,36

²⁹ Peter and the other apostles replied: "We must obey God rather than human beings! ³⁰ The God of our ancestors raised Jesus from the dead—whom you killed by hanging him on a cross. ³¹ God exalted him to his own right hand as Prince and Savior that he might bring Israel to repentance and forgive their sins. ³² We are witnesses of these things, and so is the Holy Spirit, whom God has given to those who obey him." Jn 15:26; Ac 3:13; 4:19

³³ When they heard this, they were furious and wanted to put them to death. ³⁴ But a Pharisee named Gamaliel, a teacher of the law, who was honored by all the people, stood up in the Sanhedrin and ordered that the men be put outside for a little while. ³⁵ Then he addressed the Sanhedrin: "Men of Israel, consider carefully what you intend to do to these men. ³⁶ Some time ago Theudas appeared, claiming to be somebody, and about four hundred men rallied to him. He was killed, all his followers were dispersed, and it all came to nothing. ³⁷ After him, Judas the Galilean appeared in the days of the census and led a band of people in revolt. He too was killed, and all his followers were scattered. ³⁸ Therefore, in the present case I advise you: Leave these men alone! Let them go! For if their purpose or activity is of human origin, it will fail. ³⁹ But if it is from God, you will not be able to stop these men; you will only find yourselves fighting against God." Ac 7:51; 11:17

⁴⁰ His speech persuaded them. They called the apostles in and had them flogged. Then they ordered them not to speak in the name of Jesus, and let them go. Mt 10:17

⁴¹ The apostles left the Sanhedrin, rejoicing because they had been counted worthy of suffering disgrace for the Name. ⁴² Day after day, in the temple courts and from house to house, they never stopped teaching and proclaiming the good news that Jesus is the Messiah. Jn 15:21; Ac 2:46

The Choosing of the Seven

6 In those days when the number of disciples was increasing, the Hellenistic Jews[a] among them complained against the Hebraic Jews because their widows were being overlooked in the daily distribution of food. [2]So the Twelve gathered all the disciples together and said, "It would not be right for us to neglect the ministry of the word of God in order to wait on tables. [3]Brothers and sisters, choose seven men from among you who are known to be full of the Spirit and wisdom. We will turn this responsibility over to them [4]and will give our attention to prayer and the ministry of the word." Ac 4:35; 9:29

[5]This proposal pleased the whole group. They chose Stephen, a man full of faith and of the Holy Spirit; also Philip, Procorus, Nicanor, Timon, Parmenas, and Nicolas from Antioch, a convert to Judaism. [6]They presented these men to the apostles, who prayed and laid their hands on them. Ac 1:24; 9:17; 1Ti 4:14

[7]So the word of God spread. The number of disciples in Jerusalem increased rapidly, and a large number of priests became obedient to the faith. Ac 12:24; 19:20

Stephen Seized

[8]Now Stephen, a man full of God's grace and power, performed great wonders and signs among the people. [9]Opposition arose, however, from members of the Synagogue of the Freedmen (as it was called) — Jews of Cyrene and Alexandria as well as the provinces of Cilicia and Asia — who began to argue with Stephen. [10]But they could not stand up against the wisdom the Spirit gave him as he spoke. Lk 21:15; Jn 4:48

[11]Then they secretly persuaded some men to say, "We have heard Stephen speak blasphemous words against Moses and against God." Mt 26:59-61; 1Ki 21:10

[12]So they stirred up the people and the elders and the teachers of the law. They seized Stephen and brought him before the Sanhedrin. [13]They produced false witnesses, who testified, "This fellow never stops speaking against this holy place and against the law. [14]For we have heard him say that this Jesus of Nazareth will destroy this place and change the customs Moses handed down to us." Mt 5:22; Ac 15:1

[15]All who were sitting in the Sanhedrin looked intently at Stephen, and they saw that his face was like the face of an angel.

Stephen's Speech to the Sanhedrin

7 Then the high priest asked Stephen, "Are these charges true?"

[2]To this he replied: "Brothers

---

[a] 1 That is, Jews who had adopted the Greek language and culture

and fathers, listen to me! The God of glory appeared to our father Abraham while he was still in Mesopotamia, before he lived in Harran. ³'Leave your country and your people,' God said, 'and go to the land I will show you.'ᵃ   Ac 22:1; Ge 11:31; 15:7

⁴"So he left the land of the Chaldeans and settled in Harran. After the death of his father, God sent him to this land where you are now living. ⁵He gave him no inheritance here, not even enough ground to set his foot on. But God promised him that he and his descendants after him would possess the land, even though at that time Abraham had no child. ⁶God spoke to him in this way: 'For four hundred years your descendants will be strangers in a country not their own, and they will be enslaved and mistreated. ⁷But I will punish the nation they serve as slaves,' God said, 'and afterward they will come out of that country and worship me in this place.'ᵇ ⁸Then he gave Abraham the covenant of circumcision. And Abraham became the father of Isaac and circumcised him eight days after his birth. Later Isaac became the father of Jacob, and Jacob became the father of the twelve patriarchs.   Ge 29:31-35; Ex 3:12

⁹"Because the patriarchs were jealous of Joseph, they sold him as a slave into Egypt. But God was with him ¹⁰and rescued him from all his troubles. He gave Joseph wisdom and enabled him to gain the goodwill of Pharaoh king of Egypt. So Pharaoh made him ruler over Egypt and all his palace.   Ge 41:37-43; Ps 105:20-22

¹¹"Then a famine struck all Egypt and Canaan, bringing great suffering, and our ancestors could not find food. ¹²When Jacob heard that there was grain in Egypt, he sent our forefathers on their first visit. ¹³On their second visit, Joseph told his brothers who he was, and Pharaoh learned about Joseph's family. ¹⁴After this, Joseph sent for his father Jacob and his whole family, seventy-five in all. ¹⁵Then Jacob went down to Egypt, where he and our ancestors died. ¹⁶Their bodies were brought back to Shechem and placed in the tomb that Abraham had bought from the sons of Hamor at Shechem for a certain sum of money.   Ge 45:1-4

¹⁷"As the time drew near for God to fulfill his promise to Abraham, the number of our people in Egypt had greatly increased. ¹⁸Then 'a new king, to whom Joseph meant nothing, came to power in Egypt.'ᶜ ¹⁹He dealt treacherously with our people and oppressed our ancestors by forcing them to throw out their newborn babies so that they would die.   Ex 1:10-22

²⁰"At that time Moses was

ᵃ 3 Gen. 12:1   ᵇ 7 Gen. 15:13,14   ᶜ 18 Exodus 1:8

born, and he was no ordinary child.*a* For three months he was cared for by his family. ²¹When he was placed outside, Pharaoh's daughter took him and brought him up as her own son. ²²Moses was educated in all the wisdom of the Egyptians and was powerful in speech and action. 1Ki 4:30

²³"When Moses was forty years old, he decided to visit his own people, the Israelites. ²⁴He saw one of them being mistreated by an Egyptian, so he went to his defense and avenged him by killing the Egyptian. ²⁵Moses thought that his own people would realize that God was using him to rescue them, but they did not. ²⁶The next day Moses came upon two Israelites who were fighting. He tried to reconcile them by saying, 'Men, you are brothers; why do you want to hurt each other?'

²⁷"But the man who was mistreating the other pushed Moses aside and said, 'Who made you ruler and judge over us? ²⁸Are you thinking of killing me as you killed the Egyptian yesterday?'*b* ²⁹When Moses heard this, he fled to Midian, where he settled as a foreigner and had two sons.

³⁰"After forty years had passed, an angel appeared to Moses in the flames of a burning bush in the desert near Mount Sinai. ³¹When he saw this, he was amazed at the sight. As he went over to get a closer look, he heard the Lord say: ³²'I am the God of your fathers, the God of Abraham, Isaac and Jacob.'*c* Moses trembled with fear and did not dare to look. Ex 3:1-4,6

³³"Then the Lord said to him, 'Take off your sandals, for the place where you are standing is holy ground. ³⁴I have indeed seen the oppression of my people in Egypt. I have heard their groaning and have come down to set them free. Now come, I will send you back to Egypt.'*d* Ex 3:5,7-10

³⁵"This is the same Moses they had rejected with the words, 'Who made you ruler and judge?' He was sent to be their ruler and deliverer by God himself, through the angel who appeared to him in the bush. ³⁶He led them out of Egypt and performed wonders and signs in Egypt, at the Red Sea and for forty years in the wilderness. Ex 12:41; 14:21

³⁷"This is the Moses who told the Israelites, 'God will raise up for you a prophet like me from your own people.'*e* ³⁸He was in the assembly in the wilderness, with the angel who spoke to him on Mount Sinai, and with our ancestors; and he received living words to pass on to us. Dt 18:15,18

³⁹"But our ancestors refused to obey him. Instead, they rejected him and in their hearts turned

a 20 Or *was fair in the sight of God*   *b 28* Exodus 2:14   *c 32* Exodus 3:6
d 34 Exodus 3:5,7,8,10   *e 37* Deut. 18:15

back to Egypt. ⁴⁰They told Aaron, 'Make us gods who will go before us. As for this fellow Moses who led us out of Egypt—we don't know what has happened to him!'ᵃ ⁴¹That was the time they made an idol in the form of a calf. They brought sacrifices to it and reveled in what their own hands had made. ⁴²But God turned away from them and gave them over to the worship of the sun, moon and stars. This agrees with what is written in the book of the prophets:

"'Did you bring me sacrifices
        and offerings
    forty years in the
        wilderness, people of
        Israel? Ex 32:4-6; Ps 106:19-20
⁴³You have taken up the
        tabernacle of Molek
    and the star of your god
        Rephan,
    the idols you made to
        worship.
Therefore I will send you into
        exile'ᵇ beyond Babylon.

⁴⁴"Our ancestors had the tabernacle of the covenant law with them in the wilderness. It had been made as God directed Moses, according to the pattern he had seen. ⁴⁵After receiving the tabernacle, our ancestors under Joshua brought it with them when they took the land from the nations God drove out before them. It remained in the land until the time of David, ⁴⁶who enjoyed God's favor and asked that he might provide a dwelling place for the God of Jacob.ᶜ ⁴⁷But it was Solomon who built a house for him. Jos 3:14-17; 2Sa 7:8-16

⁴⁸"However, the Most High does not live in houses made by human hands. As the prophet says: 1Ki 8:27; 2Ch 2:6

⁴⁹"'Heaven is my throne,
    and the earth is my
        footstool. Mt 5:34-35
What kind of house will you
        build for me?
            says the Lord.
    Or where will my resting
        place be?
⁵⁰Has not my hand made all
        these things?'ᵈ Isa 66:1-2

⁵¹"You stiff-necked people! Your hearts and ears are still uncircumcised. You are just like your ancestors: You always resist the Holy Spirit! ⁵²Was there ever a prophet your ancestors did not persecute? They even killed those who predicted the coming of the Righteous One. And now you have betrayed and murdered him— ⁵³you who have received the law that was given through angels but have not obeyed it." Ac 3:14

The Stoning of Stephen

⁵⁴When the members of the Sanhedrin heard this, they were

ᵃ 40 Exodus 32:1   ᵇ 43 Amos 5:25-27 (see Septuagint)   ᶜ 46 Some early manuscripts *the house of Jacob*   ᵈ 50 Isaiah 66:1,2 furious and gnashed their teeth at him. [55] But Stephen, full of the Holy Spirit, looked up to heaven and saw the glory of God, and Jesus standing at the right hand of God. [56] "Look," he said, "I see heaven open and the Son of Man standing at the right hand of God." Mt 3:16; Ac 5:33

[57] At this they covered their ears and, yelling at the top of their voices, they all rushed at him, [58] dragged him out of the city and began to stone him. Meanwhile, the witnesses laid their coats at the feet of a young man named Saul. Lev 24:14,16; Dt 13:9

[59] While they were stoning him, Stephen prayed, "Lord Jesus, receive my spirit." [60] Then he fell on his knees and cried out, "Lord, do not hold this sin against them." When he had said this, he fell asleep. Ps 31:5; Ac 9:40

8 And Saul approved of their killing him. Ac 7:58

The Church Persecuted and Scattered

On that day a great persecution broke out against the church in Jerusalem, and all except the apostles were scattered throughout Judea and Samaria. [2] Godly men buried Stephen and mourned deeply for him. [3] But Saul began to destroy the church. Going from house to house, he dragged off both men and women and put them in prison. Ac 11:19; 1Co 15:9

Philip in Samaria

[4] Those who had been scattered preached the word wherever they went. [5] Philip went down to a city in Samaria and proclaimed the Messiah there. [6] When the crowds heard Philip and saw the signs he performed, they all paid close attention to what he said. [7] For with shrieks, impure spirits came out of many, and many who were paralyzed or lame were healed. [8] So there was great joy in that city. Ac 6:5; 15:35

Simon the Sorcerer

[9] Now for some time a man named Simon had practiced sorcery in the city and amazed all the people of Samaria. He boasted that he was someone great, [10] and all the people, both high and low, gave him their attention and exclaimed, "This man is rightly called the Great Power of God." [11] They followed him because he had amazed them for a long time with his sorcery. [12] But when they believed Philip as he proclaimed the good news of the kingdom of God and the name of Jesus Christ, they were baptized, both men and women. [13] Simon himself believed and was baptized. And he followed Philip everywhere, astonished by the great signs and miracles he saw. Ac 13:6; 19:11

[14] When the apostles in Jerusalem heard that Samaria had accepted the word of God, they

sent Peter and John to Samaria. [15]When they arrived, they prayed for the new believers there that they might receive the Holy Spirit, [16]because the Holy Spirit had not yet come on any of them; they had simply been baptized in the name of the Lord Jesus. [17]Then Peter and John placed their hands on them, and they received the Holy Spirit. Ac 6:6; 19:2

[18]When Simon saw that the Spirit was given at the laying on of the apostles' hands, he offered them money [19]and said, "Give me also this ability so that everyone on whom I lay my hands may receive the Holy Spirit."

[20]Peter answered: "May your money perish with you, because you thought you could buy the gift of God with money! [21]You have no part or share in this ministry, because your heart is not right before God. [22]Repent of this wickedness and pray to the Lord in the hope that he may forgive you for having such a thought in your heart. [23]For I see that you are full of bitterness and captive to sin." 2Ki 5:16; Mt 10:8; Ac 2:38

[24]Then Simon answered, "Pray to the Lord for me so that nothing you have said may happen to me." Ex 8:8; Nu 21:7; 1Ki 13:6

[25]After they had further proclaimed the word of the Lord and testified about Jesus, Peter and John returned to Jerusalem, preaching the gospel in many Samaritan villages. Ac 13:48

Philip and the Ethiopian

[26]Now an angel of the Lord said to Philip, "Go south to the road — the desert road — that goes down from Jerusalem to Gaza." [27]So he started out, and on his way he met an Ethiopian[a] eunuch, an important official in charge of all the treasury of the Kandake (which means "queen of the Ethiopians"). This man had gone to Jerusalem to worship, [28]and on his way home was sitting in his chariot reading the Book of Isaiah the prophet. [29]The Spirit told Philip, "Go to that chariot and stay near it." Jn 12:20; Ac 5:19

[30]Then Philip ran up to the chariot and heard the man reading Isaiah the prophet. "Do you understand what you are reading?" Philip asked.

[31]"How can I," he said, "unless someone explains it to me?" So he invited Philip to come up and sit with him.

[32]This is the passage of Scripture the eunuch was reading:

"He was led like a sheep to the
    slaughter,
  and as a lamb before its
    shearer is silent,
  so he did not open his
    mouth.
[33]In his humiliation he was
    deprived of justice.

---

[a] 27 That is, from the southern Nile region

Who can speak of his
    descendants?
For his life was taken from
    the earth."[a]   Isa 53:7-8

[34] The eunuch asked Philip, "Tell me, please, who is the prophet talking about, himself or someone else?" [35] Then Philip began with that very passage of Scripture and told him the good news about Jesus.   Lk 24:27; Ac 18:28

[36] As they traveled along the road, they came to some water and the eunuch said, "Look, here is water. What can stand in the way of my being baptized?" [37][b] [38] And he gave orders to stop the chariot. Then both Philip and the eunuch went down into the water and Philip baptized him. [39] When they came up out of the water, the Spirit of the Lord suddenly took Philip away, and the eunuch did not see him again, but went on his way rejoicing. [40] Philip, however, appeared at Azotus and traveled about, preaching the gospel in all the towns until he reached Caesarea.   1Ki 18:12; 2Ki 2:16; Ac 10:47

Saul's Conversion
9:1-19pp — Ac 22:3-16; 26:9-18

9 Meanwhile, Saul was still breathing out murderous threats against the Lord's disciples. He went to the high priest [2] and asked him for letters to the synagogues in Damascus, so that if he found any there who belonged to the Way, whether men or women, he might take them as prisoners to Jerusalem. [3] As he neared Damascus on his journey, suddenly a light from heaven flashed around him. [4] He fell to the ground and heard a voice say to him, "Saul, Saul, why do you persecute me?"Ac 8:3; 19:9,23; 1Co 15:8

[5] "Who are you, Lord?" Saul asked.

"I am Jesus, whom you are persecuting," he replied. [6] "Now get up and go into the city, and you will be told what you must do."   Eze 3:22

[7] The men traveling with Saul stood there speechless; they heard the sound but did not see anyone. [8] Saul got up from the ground, but when he opened his eyes he could see nothing. So they led him by the hand into Damascus. [9] For three days he was blind, and did not eat or drink anything.   Da 10:7; Ac 22:9

[10] In Damascus there was a disciple named Ananias. The Lord called to him in a vision, "Ananias!"   Ac 10:3,17,19

"Yes, Lord," he answered.

[11] The Lord told him, "Go to the house of Judas on Straight Street and ask for a man from Tarsus named Saul, for he is praying. [12] In a vision he has seen a man

---

[a] 33 Isaiah 53:7,8 (see Septuagint)   [b] 37 Some manuscripts include here *Philip said, "If you believe with all your heart, you may." The eunuch answered, "I believe that Jesus Christ is the Son of God."*

named Ananias come and place his hands on him to restore his sight." _{Ac 21:39; 22:3}

Ac 21:39; 22:3

[13] "Lord," Ananias answered, "I have heard many reports about this man and all the harm he has done to your holy people in Jerusalem. [14] And he has come here with authority from the chief priests to arrest all who call on your name." Ro 1:7; 16:2,15

[15] But the Lord said to Ananias, "Go! This man is my chosen instrument to proclaim my name to the Gentiles and their kings and to the people of Israel. [16] I will show him how much he must suffer for my name." Ac 13:2

[17] Then Ananias went to the house and entered it. Placing his hands on Saul, he said, "Brother Saul, the Lord — Jesus, who appeared to you on the road as you were coming here — has sent me so that you may see again and be filled with the Holy Spirit." [18] Immediately, something like scales fell from Saul's eyes, and he could see again. He got up and was baptized, [19] and after taking some food, he regained his strength. Ac 22:4-16; 26:9-18

Saul in Damascus and Jerusalem

Saul spent several days with the disciples in Damascus. [20] At once he began to preach in the synagogues that Jesus is the Son of God. [21] All those who heard him were astonished and asked, "Isn't he the man who raised havoc in Jerusalem among those who call on this name? And hasn't he come here to take them as prisoners to the chief priests?" [22] Yet Saul grew more and more powerful and baffled the Jews living in Damascus by proving that Jesus is the Messiah. Ac 8:3; 18:5,28

[23] After many days had gone by, there was a conspiracy among the Jews to kill him, [24] but Saul learned of their plan. Day and night they kept close watch on the city gates in order to kill him. [25] But his followers took him by night and lowered him in a basket through an opening in the wall. 1Sa 19:12; Ac 20:3,19

[26] When he came to Jerusalem, he tried to join the disciples, but they were all afraid of him, not believing that he really was a disciple. [27] But Barnabas took him and brought him to the apostles. He told them how Saul on his journey had seen the Lord and that the Lord had spoken to him, and how in Damascus he had preached fearlessly in the name of Jesus. [28] So Saul stayed with them and moved about freely in Jerusalem, speaking boldly in the name of the Lord. [29] He talked and debated with the Hellenistic Jews,[a] but they tried to kill him. [30] When the believers learned of this, they took him down to Caesarea and sent him off to Tarsus. Ac 6:1; 22:17

[a] 29 That is, Jews who had adopted the Greek language and culture

³¹ Then the church throughout Judea, Galilee and Samaria enjoyed a time of peace and was strengthened. Living in the fear of the Lord and encouraged by the Holy Spirit, it increased in numbers. Ac 8:1

Aeneas and Dorcas

³² As Peter traveled about the country, he went to visit the Lord's people who lived in Lydda. ³³ There he found a man named Aeneas, who was paralyzed and had been bedridden for eight years. ³⁴ "Aeneas," Peter said to him, "Jesus Christ heals you. Get up and roll up your mat." Immediately Aeneas got up. ³⁵ All those who lived in Lydda and Sharon saw him and turned to the Lord.

³⁶ In Joppa there was a disciple named Tabitha (in Greek her name is Dorcas); she was always doing good and helping the poor. ³⁷ About that time she became sick and died, and her body was washed and placed in an upstairs room. ³⁸ Lydda was near Joppa; so when the disciples heard that Peter was in Lydda, they sent two men to him and urged him, "Please come at once!" 1Ti 2:10; Tit 3:8 ³⁹ Peter went with them, and when he arrived he was taken upstairs to the room. All the widows stood around him, crying and showing him the robes and other clothing that Dorcas had made while she was still with them. Ac 6:1

⁴⁰ Peter sent them all out of the room; then he got down on his knees and prayed. Turning toward the dead woman, he said, "Tabitha, get up." She opened her eyes, and seeing Peter she sat up. ⁴¹ He took her by the hand and helped her to her feet. Then he called for the believers, especially the widows, and presented her to them alive. ⁴² This became known all over Joppa, and many people believed in the Lord. ⁴³ Peter stayed in Joppa for some time with a tanner named Simon. Lk 7:14; Ac 7:60; 10:6

Cornelius Calls for Peter

10 At Caesarea there was a man named Cornelius, a centurion in what was known as the Italian Regiment. ² He and all his family were devout and God-fearing; he gave generously to those in need and prayed to God regularly. ³ One day at about three in the afternoon he had a vision. He distinctly saw an angel of God, who came to him and said, "Cornelius!" Ac 3:1; 5:19

⁴ Cornelius stared at him in fear. "What is it, Lord?" he asked.

The angel answered, "Your prayers and gifts to the poor have come up as a memorial offering before God. ⁵ Now send men to Joppa to bring back a man named Simon who is called Peter. ⁶ He is staying with Simon the tanner, whose house is by the sea." Ac 9:43; Rev 8:4

[7]When the angel who spoke to him had gone, Cornelius called two of his servants and a devout soldier who was one of his attendants. [8]He told them everything that had happened and sent them to Joppa. Ac 9:36

Peter's Vision

10:9-32Ref — Ac 11:5-14

[9]About noon the following day as they were on their journey and approaching the city, Peter went up on the roof to pray. [10]He became hungry and wanted something to eat, and while the meal was being prepared, he fell into a trance. [11]He saw heaven opened and something like a large sheet being let down to earth by its four corners. [12]It contained all kinds of four-footed animals, as well as reptiles and birds. [13]Then a voice told him, "Get up, Peter. Kill and eat." Mt 24:17; Ac 22:17

[14]"Surely not, Lord!" Peter replied. "I have never eaten anything impure or unclean."

[15]The voice spoke to him a second time, "Do not call anything impure that God has made clean." Ro 14:14,17,20; 1Co 10:25; 1Ti 4:3-4

[16]This happened three times, and immediately the sheet was taken back to heaven.

[17]While Peter was wondering about the meaning of the vision, the men sent by Cornelius found out where Simon's house was and stopped at the gate. [18]They called out, asking if Simon who was known as Peter was staying there.

[19]While Peter was still thinking about the vision, the Spirit said to him, "Simon, three[a] men are looking for you. [20]So get up and go downstairs. Do not hesitate to go with them, for I have sent them." Ac 8:29; 15:7-9

[21]Peter went down and said to the men, "I'm the one you're looking for. Why have you come?"

[22]The men replied, "We have come from Cornelius the centurion. He is a righteous and God-fearing man, who is respected by all the Jewish people. A holy angel told him to ask you to come to his house so that he could hear what you have to say." [23]Then Peter invited the men into the house to be his guests. Ac 11:14

Peter at Cornelius's House

The next day Peter started out with them, and some of the believers from Joppa went along. [24]The following day he arrived in Caesarea. Cornelius was expecting them and had called together his relatives and close friends. [25]As Peter entered the house, Cornelius met him and fell at his feet in reverence. [26]But Peter made him get up. "Stand up," he said, "I am only a man myself." Rev 19:10

[27]While talking with him, Peter went inside and found a large

---

[a] 19 One early manuscript *two*; other manuscripts do not have the number.

gathering of people. [28] He said to them: "You are well aware that it is against our law for a Jew to associate with or visit a Gentile. But God has shown me that I should not call anyone impure or unclean. [29] So when I was sent for, I came without raising any objection. May I ask why you sent for me?" Jn 4:9; Ac 15:8-9

[30] Cornelius answered: "Three days ago I was in my house praying at this hour, at three in the afternoon. Suddenly a man in shining clothes stood before me [31] and said, 'Cornelius, God has heard your prayer and remembered your gifts to the poor. [32] Send to Joppa for Simon who is called Peter. He is a guest in the home of Simon the tanner, who lives by the sea.' [33] So I sent for you immediately, and it was good of you to come. Now we are all here in the presence of God to listen to everything the Lord has commanded you to tell us." Ac 11:5-14

[34] Then Peter began to speak: "I now realize how true it is that God does not show favoritism [35] but accepts from every nation the one who fears him and does what is right. [36] You know the message God sent to the people of Israel, announcing the good news of peace through Jesus Christ, who is Lord of all. [37] You know what has happened throughout the province of Judea, beginning in Galilee after the baptism that John preached — [38] how God anointed Jesus of Nazareth with the Holy Spirit and power, and how he went around doing good and healing all who were under the power of the devil, because God was with him. Mt 28:18; Jn 3:2

[39] "We are witnesses of everything he did in the country of the Jews and in Jerusalem. They killed him by hanging him on a cross, [40] but God raised him from the dead on the third day and caused him to be seen. [41] He was not seen by all the people, but by witnesses whom God had already chosen — by us who ate and drank with him after he rose from the dead. [42] He commanded us to preach to the people and to testify that he is the one whom God appointed as judge of the living and the dead. [43] All the prophets testify about him that everyone who believes in him receives forgiveness of sins through his name." Isa 53:11; Ac 2:24; 5:30

[44] While Peter was still speaking these words, the Holy Spirit came on all who heard the message. [45] The circumcised believers who had come with Peter were astonished that the gift of the Holy Spirit had been poured out even on Gentiles. [46] For they heard them speaking in tongues[a] and praising God. Mk 16:17; Ac 11:18

Then Peter said, [47] "Surely no one can stand in the way of their

[a] 46 Or other languages

being baptized with water. They have received the Holy Spirit just as we have." ⁴⁸So he ordered that they be baptized in the name of Jesus Christ. Then they asked Peter to stay with them for a few days. Ac 2:38; 8:36; 11:17

Peter Explains His Actions

11 The apostles and the believers throughout Judea heard that the Gentiles also had received the word of God. ²So when Peter went up to Jerusalem, the circumcised believers criticized him ³and said, "You went into the house of uncircumcised men and ate with them." Ac 10:25,28

⁴Starting from the beginning, Peter told them the whole story: ⁵"I was in the city of Joppa praying, and in a trance I saw a vision. I saw something like a large sheet being let down from heaven by its four corners, and it came down to where I was. ⁶I looked into it and saw four-footed animals of the earth, wild beasts, reptiles and birds. ⁷Then I heard a voice telling me, 'Get up, Peter. Kill and eat.' Ac 10:9-32

⁸"I replied, 'Surely not, Lord! Nothing impure or unclean has ever entered my mouth.'

⁹"The voice spoke from heaven a second time, 'Do not call anything impure that God has made clean.' ¹⁰This happened three times, and then it was all pulled up to heaven again. Ac 10:15

¹¹"Right then three men who had been sent to me from Caesarea stopped at the house where I was staying. ¹²The Spirit told me to have no hesitation about going with them. These six brothers also went with me, and we entered the man's house. ¹³He told us how he had seen an angel appear in his house and say, 'Send to Joppa for Simon who is called Peter. ¹⁴He will bring you a message through which you and all your household will be saved.' Ac 8:29; 15:9

¹⁵"As I began to speak, the Holy Spirit came on them as he had come on us at the beginning. ¹⁶Then I remembered what the Lord had said: 'John baptized with[a] water, but you will be baptized with[a] the Holy Spirit.' ¹⁷So if God gave them the same gift he gave us who believed in the Lord Jesus Christ, who was I to think that I could stand in God's way?" Ac 2:4; 10:45,47

¹⁸When they heard this, they had no further objections and praised God, saying, "So then, even to Gentiles God has granted repentance that leads to life."

The Church in Antioch

¹⁹Now those who had been scattered by the persecution that broke out when Stephen was killed traveled as far as Phoenicia, Cyprus and Antioch, spreading the word only among Jews. ²⁰Some of them, however, men

ª 16 Or in

from Cyprus and Cyrene, went to Antioch and began to speak to Greeks also, telling them the good news about the Lord Jesus. [21] The Lord's hand was with them, and a great number of people believed and turned to the Lord. Lk 1:66; Ac 2:47 [22] News of this reached the church in Jerusalem, and they sent Barnabas to Antioch. [23] When he arrived and saw what the grace of God had done, he was glad and encouraged them all to remain true to the Lord with all their hearts. [24] He was a good man, full of the Holy Spirit and faith, and a great number of people were brought to the Lord. Ac 5:14; 13:43 [25] Then Barnabas went to Tarsus to look for Saul, [26] and when he found him, he brought him to Antioch. So for a whole year Barnabas and Saul met with the church and taught great numbers of people. The disciples were called Christians first at Antioch. Ac 9:11; 26:28; 1Pe 4:16 [27] During this time some prophets came down from Jerusalem to Antioch. [28] One of them, named Agabus, stood up and through the Spirit predicted that a severe famine would spread over the entire Roman world. (This happened during the reign of Claudius.) [29] The disciples, as each one was able, decided to provide help for the brothers and sisters living in Judea. [30] This they did, sending their gift to the elders by Barnabas and Saul. Ac 12:25; Ro 15:26

Peter's Miraculous Escape From Prison

12 It was about this time that King Herod arrested some who belonged to the church, intending to persecute them. [2] He had James, the brother of John, put to death with the sword. [3] When he saw that this met with approval among the Jews, he proceeded to seize Peter also. This happened during the Festival of Unleavened Bread. [4] After arresting him, he put him in prison, handing him over to be guarded by four squads of four soldiers each. Herod intended to bring him out for public trial after the Passover. Ex 12:15; 23:15; Mt 4:21

[5] So Peter was kept in prison, but the church was earnestly praying to God for him. Eph 6:18 [6] The night before Herod was to bring him to trial, Peter was sleeping between two soldiers, bound with two chains, and sentries stood guard at the entrance. [7] Suddenly an angel of the Lord appeared and a light shone in the cell. He struck Peter on the side and woke him up. "Quick, get up!" he said, and the chains fell off Peter's wrists. Ac 5:19; 16:26 [8] Then the angel said to him, "Put on your clothes and sandals." And Peter did so. "Wrap your cloak around you and follow me," the angel told him. [9] Peter

followed him out of the prison, but he had no idea that what the angel was doing was really happening; he thought he was seeing a vision. [10]They passed the first and second guards and came to the iron gate leading to the city. It opened for them by itself, and they went through it. When they had walked the length of one street, suddenly the angel left him. Ac 16:26

[11]Then Peter came to himself and said, "Now I know without a doubt that the Lord has sent his angel and rescued me from Herod's clutches and from everything the Jewish people were hoping would happen." Da 3:28; 6:22

[12]When this had dawned on him, he went to the house of Mary the mother of John, also called Mark, where many people had gathered and were praying. [13]Peter knocked at the outer entrance, and a servant named Rhoda came to answer the door. [14]When she recognized Peter's voice, she was so overjoyed she ran back without opening it and exclaimed, "Peter is at the door!" Lk 24:41; Jn 18:16-17

[15]"You're out of your mind," they told her. When she kept insisting that it was so, they said, "It must be his angel." Mt 18:10

[16]But Peter kept on knocking, and when they opened the door and saw him, they were astonished. [17]Peter motioned with his hand for them to be qui-

et and described how the Lord had brought him out of prison. "Tell James and the other brothers and sisters about this," he said, and then he left for another place. Ac 13:16; 19:33

[18]In the morning, there was no small commotion among the soldiers as to what had become of Peter. [19]After Herod had a thorough search made for him and did not find him, he cross-examined the guards and ordered that they be executed. Ac 16:27

Herod's Death

Then Herod went from Judea to Caesarea and stayed there. [20]He had been quarreling with the people of Tyre and Sidon; they now joined together and sought an audience with him. After securing the support of Blastus, a trusted personal servant of the king, they asked for peace, because they depended on the king's country for their food supply. 1Ki 5:9,11; Eze 27:17; Ac 8:40

[21]On the appointed day Herod, wearing his royal robes, sat on his throne and delivered a public address to the people. [22]They shouted, "This is the voice of a god, not of a man." [23]Immediately, because Herod did not give praise to God, an angel of the Lord struck him down, and he was eaten by worms and died. 1Sa 25:38; 2Sa 24:16-17

[24]But the word of God continued to spread and flourish. Ac 6:7

Barnabas and Saul Sent Off

²⁵When Barnabas and Saul had finished their mission, they returned from^a Jerusalem, taking with them John, also called

13 Mark. ¹Now in the church at Antioch there were prophets and teachers: Barnabas, Simeon called Niger, Lucius of Cyrene, Manaen (who had been brought up with Herod the tetrarch) and Saul. ²While they were worshiping the Lord and fasting, the Holy Spirit said, "Set apart for me Barnabas and Saul for the work to which I have called them." ³So after they had fasted and prayed, they placed their hands on them and sent them off. Ac 14:26; 22:21

On Cyprus

⁴The two of them, sent on their way by the Holy Spirit, went down to Seleucia and sailed from there to Cyprus. ⁵When they arrived at Salamis, they proclaimed the word of God in the Jewish synagogues. John was with them as their helper. Ac 12:12; Heb 4:12

⁶They traveled through the whole island until they came to Paphos. There they met a Jewish sorcerer and false prophet named Bar-Jesus, ⁷who was an attendant of the proconsul, Sergius Paulus. The proconsul, an intelligent man, sent for Barnabas and Saul because he wanted

to hear the word of God. ⁸But Elymas the sorcerer (for that is what his name means) opposed them and tried to turn the proconsul from the faith. ⁹Then Saul, who was also called Paul, filled with the Holy Spirit, looked straight at Elymas and said, ¹⁰"You are a child of the devil and an enemy of everything that is right! You are full of all kinds of deceit and trickery. Will you never stop perverting the right ways of the Lord? ¹¹Now the hand of the Lord is against you. You are going to be blind for a time, not even able to see the light of the sun." 1Sa 5:6-7; Ac 4:8; 6:7

Immediately mist and darkness came over him, and he groped about, seeking someone to lead him by the hand. ¹²When the proconsul saw what had happened, he believed, for he was amazed at the teaching about the Lord.

In Pisidian Antioch

¹³From Paphos, Paul and his companions sailed to Perga in Pamphylia, where John left them to return to Jerusalem. ¹⁴From Perga they went on to Pisidian Antioch. On the Sabbath they entered the synagogue and sat down. ¹⁵After the reading from the Law and the Prophets, the leaders of the synagogue sent word to them, saying, "Brothers, if you have a word of

^a 25 Some manuscripts *to*

exhortation for the people, please speak." Ac 14:19,21; 16:13

16 Standing up, Paul motioned with his hand and said: "Fellow Israelites and you Gentiles who worship God, listen to me! **17** The God of the people of Israel chose our ancestors; he made the people prosper during their stay in Egypt; with mighty power he led them out of that country; **18** for about forty years he endured their conduct[a] in the wilderness; **19** and he overthrew seven nations in Canaan, giving their land to his people as their inheritance. **20** All this took about 450 years. Dt 1:31; 7:6-8; Jos 19:51

"After this, God gave them judges until the time of Samuel the prophet. **21** Then the people asked for a king, and he gave them Saul son of Kish, of the tribe of Benjamin, who ruled forty years. **22** After removing Saul, he made David their king. God testified concerning him: 'I have found David son of Jesse, a man after my own heart; he will do everything I want him to do.' 1Sa 13:14

23 "From this man's descendants God has brought to Israel the Savior Jesus, as he promised. **24** Before the coming of Jesus, John preached repentance and baptism to all the people of Israel. **25** As John was completing his work, he said: 'Who do you suppose I am? I am not the one you are looking for. But there is one coming after me whose sandals I am not worthy to untie.' Mt 1:21; 3:11

26 "Fellow children of Abraham and you God-fearing Gentiles, it is to us that this message of salvation has been sent. **27** The people of Jerusalem and their rulers did not recognize Jesus, yet in condemning him they fulfilled the words of the prophets that are read every Sabbath. **28** Though they found no proper ground for a death sentence, they asked Pilate to have him executed. **29** When they had carried out all that was written about him, they took him down from the cross and laid him in a tomb. **30** But God raised him from the dead, **31** and for many days he was seen by those who had traveled with him from Galilee to Jerusalem. They are now his witnesses to our people. Mt 28:16

32 "We tell you the good news: What God promised our ancestors **33** he has fulfilled for us, their children, by raising up Jesus. As it is written in the second Psalm: Ac 5:42; Ro 4:13

" 'You are my son;
  today I have become your
   father.'[b]

34 God raised him from the dead so that he will never be subject to decay. As God has said,

" 'I will give you the holy and
  sure blessings promised
   to David.'[c]

---

[a] 18 Some manuscripts *he cared for them*   [b] 33 Psalm 2:7   [c] 34 Isaiah 55:3

³⁵ So it is also stated elsewhere:

" 'You will not let your holy
one see decay.'ᵃ   Ps 16:10

³⁶ "Now when David had served God's purpose in his own generation, he fell asleep; he was buried with his ancestors and his body decayed. ³⁷ But the one whom God raised from the dead did not see decay. Ac 2:24,29; 1Ki 2:10
³⁸ "Therefore, my friends, I want you to know that through Jesus the forgiveness of sins is proclaimed to you. ³⁹ Through him everyone who believes is set free from every sin, a justification you were not able to obtain under the law of Moses. ⁴⁰ Take care that what the prophets have said does not happen to you: Lk 24:47

⁴¹ " 'Look, you scoffers,
wonder and perish,
for I am going to do
something in your days
that you would never
believe,
even if someone told
you.'ᵇ   Hab 1:5

⁴² As Paul and Barnabas were leaving the synagogue, the people invited them to speak further about these things on the next Sabbath. ⁴³ When the congregation was dismissed, many of the Jews and devout converts to Judaism followed Paul and Barnabas, who talked with them and urged them to continue in the grace of God.   Ac 11:23; 14:22
⁴⁴ On the next Sabbath almost the whole city gathered to hear the word of the Lord. ⁴⁵ When the Jews saw the crowds, they were filled with jealousy. They began to contradict what Paul was saying and heaped abuse on him.   Ac 18:6; 1Th 2:16
⁴⁶ Then Paul and Barnabas answered them boldly: "We had to speak the word of God to you first. Since you reject it and do not consider yourselves worthy of eternal life, we now turn to the Gentiles. ⁴⁷ For this is what the Lord has commanded us: Ac 3:26; 18:6; 28:28

" 'I have made youᶜ a light for
the Gentiles,
that youᶜ may bring
salvation to the ends of
the earth.'ᵈ" Lk 2:32; Isa 49:6

⁴⁸ When the Gentiles heard this, they were glad and honored the word of the Lord; and all who were appointed for eternal life believed.   Ac 8:25
⁴⁹ The word of the Lord spread through the whole region. ⁵⁰ But the Jewish leaders incited the God-fearing women of high standing and the leading men of the city. They stirred up persecution against Paul and Barnabas, and expelled them from their region. ⁵¹ So they shook the dust off their feet as a warning to them

ᵃ 35 Psalm 16:10 (see Septuagint)   ᵇ 41 Hab. 1:5   ᶜ 47 The Greek is singular.
ᵈ 47 Isaiah 49:6

1746 | ACTS 13:52

and went to Iconium. ⁵²And the disciples were filled with joy and with the Holy Spirit. Mt 10:14; Lk 1:15

In Iconium

14 At Iconium Paul and Barnabas went as usual into the Jewish synagogue. There they spoke so effectively that a great number of Jews and Greeks believed. ²But the Jews who refused to believe stirred up the other Gentiles and poisoned their minds against the brothers. ³So Paul and Barnabas spent considerable time there, speaking boldly for the Lord, who confirmed the message of his grace by enabling them to perform signs and wonders. ⁴The people of the city were divided; some sided with the Jews, others with the apostles. ⁵There was a plot afoot among both Gentiles and Jews, together with their leaders, to mistreat them and stone them. ⁶But they found out about it and fled to the Lycaonian cities of Lystra and Derbe and to the surrounding country, ⁷where they continued to preach the gospel. Jn 4:48; Heb 2:4

In Lystra and Derbe

⁸In Lystra there sat a man who was lame. He had been that way from birth and had never walked. ⁹He listened to Paul as he was speaking. Paul looked directly at him, saw that he had faith to be healed ¹⁰and called out, "Stand up on your feet!" At that, the man jumped up and began to walk. Mt 9:28-29; Ac 3:8

¹¹When the crowd saw what Paul had done, they shouted in the Lycaonian language, "The gods have come down to us in human form!" ¹²Barnabas they called Zeus, and Paul they called Hermes because he was the chief speaker. ¹³The priest of Zeus, whose temple was just outside the city, brought bulls and wreaths to the city gates because he and the crowd wanted to offer sacrifices to them. Ac 8:10; 28:6

¹⁴But when the apostles Barnabas and Paul heard of this, they tore their clothes and rushed out into the crowd, shouting: ¹⁵"Friends, why are you doing this? We too are only human, like you. We are bringing you good news, telling you to turn from these worthless things to the living God, who made the heavens and the earth and the sea and everything in them. ¹⁶In the past, he let all nations go their own way. ¹⁷Yet he has not left himself without testimony: He has shown kindness by giving you rain from heaven and crops in their seasons; he provides you with plenty of food and fills your hearts with joy." ¹⁸Even with these words, they had difficulty keeping the crowd from sacrificing to them. Ac 10:26; Jas 5:17; Ro 1:20

¹⁹Then some Jews came from Antioch and Iconium and won the crowd over. They stoned

Paul and dragged him outside the city, thinking he was dead. [20] But after the disciples had gathered around him, he got up and went back into the city. The next day he and Barnabas left for Derbe. Ac 13:45; 2Co 11:25; 2Ti 3:11

The Return to Antioch in Syria

[21] They preached the gospel in that city and won a large number of disciples. Then they returned to Lystra, Iconium and Antioch, [22] strengthening the disciples and encouraging them to remain true to the faith. "We must go through many hardships to enter the kingdom of God," they said. [23] Paul and Barnabas appointed elders[a] for them in each church and, with prayer and fasting, committed them to the Lord, in whom they had put their trust. [24] After going through Pisidia, they came into Pamphylia, [25] and when they had preached the word in Perga, they went down to Attalia. 2Ti 3:12; Tit 1:5

[26] From Attalia they sailed back to Antioch, where they had been committed to the grace of God for the work they had now completed. [27] On arriving there, they gathered the church together and reported all that God had done through them and how he had opened a door of faith to the Gentiles. [28] And they stayed there a long time with the disciples. Ac 13:1,3; 1Co 16:9; 2Co 2:12

The Council at Jerusalem

15 Certain people came down from Judea to Antioch and were teaching the believers: "Unless you are circumcised, according to the custom taught by Moses, you cannot be saved." [2] This brought Paul and Barnabas into sharp dispute and debate with them. So Paul and Barnabas were appointed, along with some other believers, to go up to Jerusalem to see the apostles and elders about this question. [3] The church sent them on their way, and as they traveled through Phoenicia and Samaria, they told how the Gentiles had been converted. This news made all the believers very glad. [4] When they came to Jerusalem, they were welcomed by the church and the apostles and elders, to whom they reported everything God had done through them. Ac 14:27; Gal 5:2-3

[5] Then some of the believers who belonged to the party of the Pharisees stood up and said, "The Gentiles must be circumcised and required to keep the law of Moses." Ac 5:17

[6] The apostles and elders met to consider this question. [7] After much discussion, Peter got up and addressed them: "Brothers, you know that some time ago God made a choice among you that the Gentiles might hear

---

[a] 23 Or *Barnabas ordained elders*; or *Barnabas had elders elected*

from my lips the message of the gospel and believe. [8]God, who knows the heart, showed that he accepted them by giving the Holy Spirit to them, just as he did to us. [9]He did not discriminate between us and them, for he purified their hearts by faith. [10]Now then, why do you try to test God by putting on the necks of Gentiles a yoke that neither we nor our ancestors have been able to bear? [11]No! We believe it is through the grace of our Lord Jesus that we are saved, just as they are." Mt 23:4; Ac 10:44,47; Ro 3:24

[12]The whole assembly became silent as they listened to Barnabas and Paul telling about the signs and wonders God had done among the Gentiles through them. [13]When they finished, James spoke up. "Brothers," he said, "listen to me. [14]Simon[a] has described to us how God first intervened to choose a people for his name from the Gentiles. [15]The words of the prophets are in agreement with this, as it is written: Ac 12:17; 14:27

[16]" 'After this I will return
      and rebuild David's fallen
         tent.
   Its ruins I will rebuild,
      and I will restore it,
[17]that the rest of mankind may
      seek the Lord,
   even all the Gentiles who
      bear my name,

says the Lord, who does these
         things'[b] — Am 9:11-12
[18]   things known from long
      ago.[c] Isa 45:21

[19]"It is my judgment, therefore, that we should not make it difficult for the Gentiles who are turning to God. [20]Instead we should write to them, telling them to abstain from food polluted by idols, from sexual immorality, from the meat of strangled animals and from blood. [21]For the law of Moses has been preached in every city from the earliest times and is read in the synagogues on every Sabbath." Ac 13:15; 1Co 10:14-28

The Council's Letter to Gentile Believers

[22]Then the apostles and elders, with the whole church, decided to choose some of their own men and send them to Antioch with Paul and Barnabas. They chose Judas (called Barsabbas) and Silas, men who were leaders among the believers. [23]With them they sent the following letter: Ac 16:19,25,29

The apostles and elders,
your brothers,

To the Gentile believers in Antioch, Syria and Cilicia:
Greetings. Jas 1:1

[24]We have heard that some

---

[a] 14 Greek Simeon, a variant of Simon; that is, Peter   [b] 17 Amos 9:11,12 (see Septuagint)
[c] 17,18 Some manuscripts things' — / [18]the Lord's work is known to him from long ago

went out from us without our authorization and disturbed you, troubling your minds by what they said. 25 So we all agreed to choose some men and send them to you with our dear friends Barnabas and Paul — 26 men who have risked their lives for the name of our Lord Jesus Christ. 27 Therefore we are sending Judas and Silas to confirm by word of mouth what we are writing. 28 It seemed good to the Holy Spirit and to us not to burden you with anything beyond the following requirements: 29 You are to abstain from food sacrificed to idols, from blood, from the meat of strangled animals and from sexual immorality. You will do well to avoid these things. Ac 14:19; 21:25

Farewell.

30 So the men were sent off and went down to Antioch, where they gathered the church together and delivered the letter. 31 The people read it and were glad for its encouraging message. 32 Judas and Silas, who themselves were prophets, said much to encourage and strengthen the believers. 33 After spending some time there, they were sent off by the believers with the blessing of peace to return to those who had

sent them. [34] a 35 But Paul and Barnabas remained in Antioch, where they and many others taught and preached the word of the Lord. Ac 8:4; 1Co 16:11

Disagreement Between Paul and Barnabas

36 Some time later Paul said to Barnabas, "Let us go back and visit the believers in all the towns where we preached the word of the Lord and see how they are doing." 37 Barnabas wanted to take John, also called Mark, with them, 38 but Paul did not think it wise to take him, because he had deserted them in Pamphylia and had not continued with them in the work. 39 They had such a sharp disagreement that they parted company. Barnabas took Mark and sailed for Cyprus, 40 but Paul chose Silas and left, commended by the believers to the grace of the Lord. 41 He went through Syria and Cilicia, strengthening the churches. Ac 12:12; 13:13; 16:5

Timothy Joins Paul and Silas

16 Paul came to Derbe and then to Lystra, where a disciple named Timothy lived, whose mother was Jewish and a believer but whose father was a Greek. 2 The believers at Lystra and Iconium spoke well of him. 3 Paul wanted to take him along on the journey, so he circumcised him because of the Jews who lived

a 34 Some manuscripts include here *But Silas decided to remain there.*

in that area, for they all knew that his father was a Greek. [4]As they traveled from town to town, they delivered the decisions reached by the apostles and elders in Jerusalem for the people to obey. [5]So the churches were strengthened in the faith and grew daily in numbers. Ac 9:31; 11:30; 15:28-29

Paul's Vision of the Man of Macedonia

[6]Paul and his companions traveled throughout the region of Phrygia and Galatia, having been kept by the Holy Spirit from preaching the word in the province of Asia. [7]When they came to the border of Mysia, they tried to enter Bithynia, but the Spirit of Jesus would not allow them to. [8]So they passed by Mysia and went down to Troas. [9]During the night Paul had a vision of a man of Macedonia standing and begging him, "Come over to Macedonia and help us." [10]After Paul had seen the vision, we got ready at once to leave for Macedonia, concluding that God had called us to preach the gospel to them. Ac 9:10; Ro 8:9; 2Co 2:12

Lydia's Conversion in Philippi

[11]From Troas we put out to sea and sailed straight for Samothrace, and the next day we went on to Neapolis. [12]From there we traveled to Philippi, a Roman colony and the leading city of that district[a] of Macedonia. And we stayed there several days. Php 1:1

[13]On the Sabbath we went outside the city gate to the river, where we expected to find a place of prayer. We sat down and began to speak to the women who had gathered there. [14]One of those listening was a woman from the city of Thyatira named Lydia, a dealer in purple cloth. She was a worshiper of God. The Lord opened her heart to respond to Paul's message. [15]When she and the members of her household were baptized, she invited us to her home. "If you consider me a believer in the Lord," she said, "come and stay at my house." And she persuaded us. Lk 24:45; Ac 13:14

Paul and Silas in Prison

[16]Once when we were going to the place of prayer, we were met by a female slave who had a spirit by which she predicted the future. She earned a great deal of money for her owners by fortune-telling. [17]She followed Paul and the rest of us, shouting, "These men are servants of the Most High God, who are telling you the way to be saved." [18]She kept this up for many days. Finally Paul became so annoyed that he turned around and said to the spirit, "In the name of Jesus Christ I command you to come out of her!" At that moment the spirit left her. Mk 16:17; 1Sa 28:3,7

[a] 12 The text and meaning of the Greek for *the leading city of that district* are uncertain.

¹⁹When her owners realized that their hope of making money was gone, they seized Paul and Silas and dragged them into the marketplace to face the authorities. ²⁰They brought them before the magistrates and said, "These men are Jews, and are throwing our city into an uproar ²¹by advocating customs unlawful for us Romans to accept or practice." Ac 17:6; 19:25-26

²²The crowd joined in the attack against Paul and Silas, and the magistrates ordered them to be stripped and beaten with rods. ²³After they had been severely flogged, they were thrown into prison, and the jailer was commanded to guard them carefully. ²⁴When he received these orders, he put them in the inner cell and fastened their feet in the stocks. Jer 20:2-3; 2Co 11:25; 1Th 2:2

²⁵About midnight Paul and Silas were praying and singing hymns to God, and the other prisoners were listening to them. ²⁶Suddenly there was such a violent earthquake that the foundations of the prison were shaken. At once all the prison doors flew open, and everyone's chains came loose. ²⁷The jailer woke up, and when he saw the prison doors open, he drew his sword and was about to kill himself because he thought the prisoners had escaped. ²⁸But Paul shouted, "Don't harm yourself! We are all here!" Ac 4:31; 12:19; Eph 5:19

²⁹The jailer called for lights, rushed in and fell trembling before Paul and Silas. ³⁰He then brought them out and asked, "Sirs, what must I do to be saved?" Ac 2:37

³¹They replied, "Believe in the Lord Jesus, and you will be saved—you and your household." ³²Then they spoke the word of the Lord to him and to all the others in his house. ³³At that hour of the night the jailer took them and washed their wounds; then immediately he and all his household were baptized. ³⁴The jailer brought them into his house and set a meal before them; he was filled with joy because he had come to believe in God—he and his whole household. Jn 3:15; Ro 11:14

³⁵When it was daylight, the magistrates sent their officers to the jailer with the order: "Release those men." ³⁶The jailer told Paul, "The magistrates have ordered that you and Silas be released. Now you can leave. Go in peace." Ac 15:33

³⁷But Paul said to the officers: "They beat us publicly without a trial, even though we are Roman citizens, and threw us into prison. And now do they want to get rid of us quietly? No! Let them come themselves and escort us out." Ac 22:25-29

³⁸The officers reported this to the magistrates, and when they heard that Paul and Silas

were Roman citizens, they were alarmed. [39]They came to appease them and escorted them from the prison, requesting them to leave the city. [40]After Paul and Silas came out of the prison, they went to Lydia's house, where they met with the brothers and sisters and encouraged them. Then they left. Mt 8:34; Ac 1:16

In Thessalonica

17 When Paul and his companions had passed through Amphipolis and Apollonia, they came to Thessalonica, where there was a Jewish synagogue. [2]As was his custom, Paul went into the synagogue, and on three Sabbath days he reasoned with them from the Scriptures, [3]explaining and proving that the Messiah had to suffer and rise from the dead. "This Jesus I am proclaiming to you is the Messiah," he said. [4]Some of the Jews were persuaded and joined Paul and Silas, as did a large number of God-fearing Greeks and quite a few prominent women. Ac 15:22

[5]But other Jews were jealous; so they rounded up some bad characters from the marketplace, formed a mob and started a riot in the city. They rushed to Jason's house in search of Paul and Silas in order to bring them out to the crowd.[a] [6]But when they did not find them, they dragged Jason and some other believers before the city officials, shouting: "These men who have caused trouble all over the world have now come here, [7]and Jason has welcomed them into his house. They are all defying Caesar's decrees, saying that there is another king, one called Jesus." [8]When they heard this, the crowd and the city officials were thrown into turmoil. [9]Then they made Jason and the others post bond and let them go. Lk 23:2; Ro 16:21

In Berea

[10]As soon as it was night, the believers sent Paul and Silas away to Berea. On arriving there, they went to the Jewish synagogue. [11]Now the Berean Jews were of more noble character than those in Thessalonica, for they received the message with great eagerness and examined the Scriptures every day to see if what Paul said was true. [12]As a result, many of them believed, as did also a number of prominent Greek women and many Greek men. Lk 16:29; Jn 5:39; Ac 20:4

[13]But when the Jews in Thessalonica learned that Paul was preaching the word of God at Berea, some of them went there too, agitating the crowds and stirring them up. [14]The believers immediately sent Paul to the coast, but Silas and Timothy stayed at Berea. [15]Those who escorted Paul brought him to Athens and then

[a] 5 Or the assembly of the people

left with instructions for Silas and Timothy to join him as soon as possible. Ac 16:1; 18:5

In Athens

16 While Paul was waiting for them in Athens, he was greatly distressed to see that the city was full of idols. 17 So he reasoned in the synagogue with both Jews and God-fearing Greeks, as well as in the marketplace day by day with those who happened to be there. 18 A group of Epicurean and Stoic philosophers began to debate with him. Some of them asked, "What is this babbler trying to say?" Others remarked, "He seems to be advocating foreign gods." They said this because Paul was preaching the good news about Jesus and the resurrection. 19 Then they took him and brought him to a meeting of the Areopagus, where they said to him, "May we know what this new teaching is that you are presenting? 20 You are bringing some strange ideas to our ears, and we would like to know what they mean." 21 (All the Athenians and the foreigners who lived there spent their time doing nothing but talking about and listening to the latest ideas.) Ac 4:2; 9:20

22 Paul then stood up in the meeting of the Areopagus and said: "People of Athens! I see that in every way you are very reli-gious. 23 For as I walked around and looked carefully at your objects of worship, I even found an altar with this inscription: TO AN UNKNOWN GOD. So you are ignorant of the very thing you worship — and this is what I am going to proclaim to you. Jn 4:22

24 "The God who made the world and everything in it is the Lord of heaven and earth and does not live in temples built by human hands. 25 And he is not served by human hands, as if he needed anything. Rather, he himself gives everyone life and breath and everything else. 26 From one man he made all the nations, that they should inhabit the whole earth; and he marked out their appointed times in history and the boundaries of their lands. 27 God did this so that they would seek him and perhaps reach out for him and find him, though he is not far from any one of us. 28 'For in him we live and move and have our being.'[a] As some of your own poets have said, 'We are his offspring.'[b] Dt 32:8; Ac 14:17

29 "Therefore since we are God's offspring, we should not think that the divine being is like gold or silver or stone — an image made by human design and skill. 30 In the past God overlooked such ignorance, but now he commands all people everywhere to repent. 31 For he has

---

[a] 28 From the Cretan philosopher Epimenides   [b] 28 From the Cilician Stoic philosopher Aratus

set a day when he will judge the world with justice by the man he has appointed. He has given proof of this to everyone by raising him from the dead." Lk 24:47

32 When they heard about the resurrection of the dead, some of them sneered, but others said, "We want to hear you again on this subject." 33 At that, Paul left the Council. 34 Some of the people became followers of Paul and believed. Among them was Dionysius, a member of the Areopagus, also a woman named Damaris, and a number of others. ver 19,22

In Corinth

18 After this, Paul left Athens and went to Corinth. 2 There he met a Jew named Aquila, a native of Pontus, who had recently come from Italy with his wife Priscilla, because Claudius had ordered all Jews to leave Rome. Paul went to see them, 3 and because he was a tentmaker as they were, he stayed and worked with them. 4 Every Sabbath he reasoned in the synagogue, trying to persuade Jews and Greeks. Ro 16:3; 1Co 16:19; 2Ti 4:19

5 When Silas and Timothy came from Macedonia, Paul devoted himself exclusively to preaching, testifying to the Jews that Jesus was the Messiah. 6 But when they opposed Paul and became abusive, he shook out his clothes in protest and said to them, "Your blood be on your own heads! I am innocent of it. From now on I will go to the Gentiles." Ac 13:46; 20:26

7 Then Paul left the synagogue and went next door to the house of Titius Justus, a worshiper of God. 8 Crispus, the synagogue leader, and his entire household believed in the Lord; and many of the Corinthians who heard Paul believed and were baptized.

9 One night the Lord spoke to Paul in a vision: "Do not be afraid; keep on speaking, do not be silent. 10 For I am with you, and no one is going to attack and harm you, because I have many people in this city." 11 So Paul stayed in Corinth for a year and a half, teaching them the word of God. Mt 28:20

12 While Gallio was proconsul of Achaia, the Jews of Corinth made a united attack on Paul and brought him to the place of judgment. 13 "This man," they charged, "is persuading the people to worship God in ways contrary to the law." Ro 15:26; 1Co 16:15

14 Just as Paul was about to speak, Gallio said to them, "If you Jews were making a complaint about some misdemeanor or serious crime, it would be reasonable for me to listen to you. 15 But since it involves questions about words and names and your own law— settle the matter yourselves. I will not be a judge of such things." 16 So he drove them off. 17 Then the crowd there turned on Sos-

thenes the synagogue leader and beat him in front of the proconsul; and Gallio showed no concern whatever. Ac 23:29; 1Co 1:1

Priscilla, Aquila and Apollos

18 Paul stayed on in Corinth for some time. Then he left the brothers and sisters and sailed for Syria, accompanied by Priscilla and Aquila. Before he sailed, he had his hair cut off at Cenchreae because of a vow he had taken. 19 They arrived at Ephesus, where Paul left Priscilla and Aquila. He himself went into the synagogue and reasoned with the Jews. 20 When they asked him to spend more time with them, he declined. 21 But as he left, he promised, "I will come back if it is God's will." Then he set sail from Ephesus. 22 When he landed at Caesarea, he went up to Jerusalem and greeted the church and then went down to Antioch. Ac 11:19; 1Co 4:19

23 After spending some time in Antioch, Paul set out from there and traveled from place to place throughout the region of Galatia and Phrygia, strengthening all the disciples. Ac 14:22; 16:6

24 Meanwhile a Jew named Apollos, a native of Alexandria, came to Ephesus. He was a learned man, with a thorough knowledge of the Scriptures. 25 He had been instructed in the way of the Lord, and he spoke with great fervor[a] and taught about Jesus accurately, though he knew only the baptism of John. 26 He began to speak boldly in the synagogue. When Priscilla and Aquila heard him, they invited him to their home and explained to him the way of God more adequately. Ac 19:3; 1Co 1:12

27 When Apollos wanted to go to Achaia, the brothers and sisters encouraged him and wrote to the disciples there to welcome him. When he arrived, he was a great help to those who by grace had believed. 28 For he vigorously refuted his Jewish opponents in public debate, proving from the Scriptures that Jesus was the Messiah. Ac 9:22; 17:2

Paul in Ephesus

19 While Apollos was at Corinth, Paul took the road through the interior and arrived at Ephesus. There he found some disciples 2 and asked them, "Did you receive the Holy Spirit when[b] you believed?" Ac 18:1,19

They answered, "No, we have not even heard that there is a Holy Spirit."

3 So Paul asked, "Then what baptism did you receive?"

"John's baptism," they replied.

4 Paul said, "John's baptism was a baptism of repentance. He told the people to believe in the one coming after him, that is, in Jesus." 5 On hearing this, they were baptized in the name of the

---

[a] 25 Or with fervor in the Spirit   [b] 2 Or after

Lord Jesus. ⁶When Paul placed his hands on them, the Holy Spirit came on them, and they spoke in tongues*ᵃ* and prophesied. ⁷There were about twelve men in all. Ac 2:4; 6:6; 10:46

⁸Paul entered the synagogue and spoke boldly there for three months, arguing persuasively about the kingdom of God. ⁹But some of them became obstinate; they refused to believe and publicly maligned the Way. So Paul left them. He took the disciples with him and had discussions daily in the lecture hall of Tyrannus. ¹⁰This went on for two years, so that all the Jews and Greeks who lived in the province of Asia heard the word of the Lord. Ac 1:3

¹¹God did extraordinary miracles through Paul, ¹²so that even handkerchiefs and aprons that had touched him were taken to the sick, and their illnesses were cured and the evil spirits left them. Ac 5:15; 8:13

¹³Some Jews who went around driving out evil spirits tried to invoke the name of the Lord Jesus over those who were demon-possessed. They would say, "In the name of the Jesus whom Paul preaches, I command you to come out." ¹⁴Seven sons of Sceva, a Jewish chief priest, were doing this. ¹⁵One day the evil spirit answered them, "Jesus I know, and Paul I know about, but who

are you?" ¹⁶Then the man who had the evil spirit jumped on them and overpowered them all. He gave them such a beating that they ran out of the house naked and bleeding. Mt 12:27; Mk 9:38

¹⁷When this became known to the Jews and Greeks living in Ephesus, they were all seized with fear, and the name of the Lord Jesus was held in high honor. ¹⁸Many of those who believed now came and openly confessed what they had done. ¹⁹A number who had practiced sorcery brought their scrolls together and burned them publicly. When they calculated the value of the scrolls, the total came to fifty thousand drachmas.*ᵇ* ²⁰In this way the word of the Lord spread widely and grew in power. Ac 5:5,11; 6:7; 12:24

²¹After all this had happened, Paul decided*ᶜ* to go to Jerusalem, passing through Macedonia and Achaia. "After I have been there," he said, "I must visit Rome also." ²²He sent two of his helpers, Timothy and Erastus, to Macedonia, while he stayed in the province of Asia a little longer. Ro 15:25; 16:23

The Riot in Ephesus

²³About that time there arose a great disturbance about the Way. ²⁴A silversmith named Demetrius, who made silver shrines of Artemis, brought in a lot of business for the craftsmen

ᵃ 6 Or *other languages*   ᵇ 19 A drachma was a silver coin worth about a day's wages.
ᶜ 21 Or *decided in the Spirit*

there. ²⁵ He called them together, along with the workers in related trades, and said: "You know, my friends, that we receive a good income from this business. ²⁶ And you see and hear how this fellow Paul has convinced and led astray large numbers of people here in Ephesus and in practically the whole province of Asia. He says that gods made by human hands are no gods at all. ²⁷ There is danger not only that our trade will lose its good name, but also that the temple of the great goddess Artemis will be discredited; and the goddess herself, who is worshiped throughout the province of Asia and the world, will be robbed of her divine majesty." Ps 115:4; Isa 44:10

²⁸ When they heard this, they were furious and began shouting: "Great is Artemis of the Ephesians!" ²⁹ Soon the whole city was in an uproar. The people seized Gaius and Aristarchus, Paul's traveling companions from Macedonia, and all of them rushed into the theater together. ³⁰ Paul wanted to appear before the crowd, but the disciples would not let him. ³¹ Even some of the officials of the province, friends of Paul, sent him a message begging him not to venture into the theater. Ac 20:4; 27:2; Col 4:10

³² The assembly was in confusion: Some were shouting one thing, some another. Most of the people did not even know why they were there. ³³ The Jews in the crowd pushed Alexander to the front, and they shouted instructions to him. He motioned for silence in order to make a defense before the people. ³⁴ But when they realized he was a Jew, they all shouted in unison for about two hours: "Great is Artemis of the Ephesians!" Ac 12:17; 21:34

³⁵ The city clerk quieted the crowd and said: "Fellow Ephesians, doesn't all the world know that the city of Ephesus is the guardian of the temple of the great Artemis and of her image, which fell from heaven? ³⁶ Therefore, since these facts are undeniable, you ought to calm down and not do anything rash. ³⁷ You have brought these men here, though they have neither robbed temples nor blasphemed our goddess. ³⁸ If, then, Demetrius and his fellow craftsmen have a grievance against anybody, the courts are open and there are proconsuls. They can press charges. ³⁹ If there is anything further you want to bring up, it must be settled in a legal assembly. ⁴⁰ As it is, we are in danger of being charged with rioting because of what happened today. In that case we would not be able to account for this commotion, since there is no reason for it." ⁴¹ After he had said this, he dismissed the assembly. Ac 18:19; Ro 2:22

Through Macedonia and Greece

20 When the uproar had ended, Paul sent for the disciples and, after encouraging them, said goodbye and set out for Macedonia. ²He traveled through that area, speaking many words of encouragement to the people, and finally arrived in Greece, ³where he stayed three months. Because some Jews had plotted against him just as he was about to sail for Syria, he decided to go back through Macedonia. ⁴He was accompanied by Sopater son of Pyrrhus from Berea, Aristarchus and Secundus from Thessalonica, Gaius from Derbe, Timothy also, and Tychicus and Trophimus from the province of Asia. ⁵These men went on ahead and waited for us at Troas. ⁶But we sailed from Philippi after the Festival of Unleavened Bread, and five days later joined the others at Troas, where we stayed seven days. Ac 9:23-24; 16:9

Eutychus Raised From the Dead at Troas

⁷On the first day of the week we came together to break bread. Paul spoke to the people and, because he intended to leave the next day, kept on talking until midnight. ⁸There were many lamps in the upstairs room where we were meeting. ⁹Seated in a window was a young man named Eutychus, who was sinking into a deep sleep as Paul talked on and on. When he was sound asleep, he fell to the ground from the third story and was picked up dead. ¹⁰Paul went down, threw himself on the young man and put his arms around him. "Don't be alarmed," he said. "He's alive!" ¹¹Then he went upstairs again and broke bread and ate. After talking until daylight, he left. ¹²The people took the young man home alive and were greatly comforted. Mt 9:23-24; Ac 1:13; 1Co 16:2

Paul's Farewell to the Ephesian Elders

¹³We went on ahead to the ship and sailed for Assos, where we were going to take Paul aboard. He had made this arrangement because he was going there on foot. ¹⁴When he met us at Assos, we took him aboard and went on to Mitylene. ¹⁵The next day we set sail from there and arrived off Chios. The day after that we crossed over to Samos, and on the following day arrived at Miletus. ¹⁶Paul had decided to sail past Ephesus to avoid spending time in the province of Asia, for he was in a hurry to reach Jerusalem, if possible, by the day of Pentecost. Ac 2:1; 19:21

¹⁷From Miletus, Paul sent to Ephesus for the elders of the church. ¹⁸When they arrived, he said to them: "You know how I lived the whole time I was with you, from the first day I came into

the province of Asia. ¹⁹I served the Lord with great humility and with tears and in the midst of severe testing by the plots of my Jewish opponents. ²⁰You know that I have not hesitated to preach anything that would be helpful to you but have taught you publicly and from house to house. ²¹I have declared to both Jews and Greeks that they must turn to God in repentance and have faith in our Lord Jesus. Ac 2:38; 18:5

²² "And now, compelled by the Spirit, I am going to Jerusalem, not knowing what will happen to me there. ²³I only know that in every city the Holy Spirit warns me that prison and hardships are facing me. ²⁴However, I consider my life worth nothing to me; my only aim is to finish the race and complete the task the Lord Jesus has given me — the task of testifying to the good news of God's grace. Ac 21:13; Gal 1:1

²⁵ "Now I know that none of you among whom I have gone about preaching the kingdom will ever see me again. ²⁶Therefore, I declare to you today that I am innocent of the blood of any of you. ²⁷For I have not hesitated to proclaim to you the whole will of God. ²⁸Keep watch over yourselves and all the flock of which the Holy Spirit has made you overseers. Be shepherds of the church of God,ᵃ which he bought with his own blood.ᵇ ²⁹I know that after I

leave, savage wolves will come in among you and will not spare the flock. ³⁰Even from your own number men will arise and distort the truth in order to draw away disciples after them. ³¹So be on your guard! Remember that for three years I never stopped warning each of you night and day with tears. Ac 19:10; 1Pe 5:2

³² "Now I commit you to God and to the word of his grace, which can build you up and give you an inheritance among all those who are sanctified. ³³I have not coveted anyone's silver or gold or clothing. ³⁴You yourselves know that these hands of mine have supplied my own needs and the needs of my companions. ³⁵In everything I did, I showed you that by this kind of hard work we must help the weak, remembering the words the Lord Jesus himself said: 'It is more blessed to give than to receive.' " Ac 18:3; 1Co 9:12; Col 1:12

³⁶When Paul had finished speaking, he knelt down with all of them and prayed. ³⁷They all wept as they embraced him and kissed him. ³⁸What grieved them most was his statement that they would never see his face again. Then they accompanied him to the ship. Lk 15:20; Ac 21:5

On to Jerusalem

21 After we had torn ourselves away from them, we

ᵃ 28 Many manuscripts *of the Lord*   ᵇ 28 Or *with the blood of his own Son.*

put out to sea and sailed straight to Kos. The next day we went to Rhodes and from there to Patara. [2]We found a ship crossing over to Phoenicia, went on board and set sail. [3]After sighting Cyprus and passing to the south of it, we sailed on to Syria. We landed at Tyre, where our ship was to unload its cargo. [4]We sought out the disciples there and stayed with them seven days. Through the Spirit they urged Paul not to go on to Jerusalem. [5]When it was time to leave, we left and continued on our way. All of them, including wives and children, accompanied us out of the city, and there on the beach we knelt to pray. [6]After saying goodbye to each other, we went aboard the ship, and they returned home.   Ac 20:23,36

[7]We continued our voyage from Tyre and landed at Ptolemais, where we greeted the brothers and sisters and stayed with them for a day. [8]Leaving the next day, we reached Caesarea and stayed at the house of Philip the evangelist, one of the Seven. [9]He had four unmarried daughters who prophesied.   Ac 6:5; Eph 4:11; 2Ti 4:5

[10]After we had been there a number of days, a prophet named Agabus came down from Judea. [11]Coming over to us, he took Paul's belt, tied his own hands and feet with it and said, "The Holy Spirit says, 'In this way the Jewish leaders in Jerusalem will bind the owner of this belt and will hand him over to the Gentiles.'"   1Ki 22:11; Ac 11:28

[12]When we heard this, we and the people there pleaded with Paul not to go up to Jerusalem. [13]Then Paul answered, "Why are you weeping and breaking my heart? I am ready not only to be bound, but also to die in Jerusalem for the name of the Lord Jesus." [14]When he would not be dissuaded, we gave up and said, "The Lord's will be done."   Ac 9:16

[15]After this, we started on our way up to Jerusalem. [16]Some of the disciples from Caesarea accompanied us and brought us to the home of Mnason, where we were to stay. He was a man from Cyprus and one of the early disciples.   Ac 8:40; 19:21

Paul's Arrival at Jerusalem

[17]When we arrived at Jerusalem, the brothers and sisters received us warmly. [18]The next day Paul and the rest of us went to see James, and all the elders were present. [19]Paul greeted them and reported in detail what God had done among the Gentiles through his ministry.   Ac 1:17; 15:4

[20]When they heard this, they praised God. Then they said to Paul: "You see, brother, how many thousands of Jews have believed, and all of them are zealous for the law. [21]They have been informed that you teach all the Jews who live among the Gentiles to turn away from Moses,

telling them not to circumcise their children or live according to our customs. [22]What shall we do? They will certainly hear that you have come, [23]so do what we tell you. There are four men with us who have made a vow. [24]Take these men, join in their purification rites and pay their expenses, so that they can have their heads shaved. Then everyone will know there is no truth in these reports about you, but that you yourself are living in obedience to the law. [25]As for the Gentile believers, we have written to them our decision that they should abstain from food sacrificed to idols, from blood, from the meat of strangled animals and from sexual immorality." Ac 18:18; 22:3; 1Co 7:18-19

[26]The next day Paul took the men and purified himself along with them. Then he went to the temple to give notice of the date when the days of purification would end and the offering would be made for each of them.

Paul Arrested

[27]When the seven days were nearly over, some Jews from the province of Asia saw Paul at the temple. They stirred up the whole crowd and seized him, [28]shouting, "Fellow Israelites, help us! This is the man who teaches everyone everywhere against our people and our law and this place. And besides, he has brought Greeks into the tem-

ple and defiled this holy place." [29](They had previously seen Trophimus the Ephesian in the city with Paul and assumed that Paul had brought him into the temple.) Ac 20:4; 24:18

[30]The whole city was aroused, and the people came running from all directions. Seizing Paul, they dragged him from the temple, and immediately the gates were shut. [31]While they were trying to kill him, news reached the commander of the Roman troops that the whole city of Jerusalem was in an uproar. [32]He at once took some officers and soldiers and ran down to the crowd. When the rioters saw the commander and his soldiers, they stopped beating Paul. Ac 23:27; 26:21

[33]The commander came up and arrested him and ordered him to be bound with two chains. Then he asked who he was and what he had done. [34]Some in the crowd shouted one thing and some another, and since the commander could not get at the truth because of the uproar, he ordered that Paul be taken into the barracks. [35]When Paul reached the steps, the violence of the mob was so great he had to be carried by the soldiers. [36]The crowd that followed kept shouting, "Get rid of him!" Lk 23:18; Ac 22:22

Paul Speaks to the Crowd

22:3-16pp — Ac 9:1-22; 26:9-18

[37]As the soldiers were about to

take Paul into the barracks, he asked the commander, "May I say something to you?"

"Do you speak Greek?" he replied. 38 "Aren't you the Egyptian who started a revolt and led four thousand terrorists out into the wilderness some time ago?"

39 Paul answered, "I am a Jew, from Tarsus in Cilicia, a citizen of no ordinary city. Please let me speak to the people." Ac 9:11; 22:3

40 After receiving the commander's permission, Paul stood on the steps and motioned to the crowd. When they were all silent, he said to them in Aramaic[a]:

22 1 "Brothers and fathers, listen now to my defense."

2 When they heard him speak to them in Aramaic, they became very quiet. Jn 5:2; Ac 21:40

Then Paul said: 3 "I am a Jew, born in Tarsus of Cilicia, but brought up in this city. I studied under Gamaliel and was thoroughly trained in the law of our ancestors. I was just as zealous for God as any of you are today. 4 I persecuted the followers of this Way to their death, arresting both men and women and throwing them into prison, 5 as the high priest and all the Council can themselves testify. I even obtained letters from them to their associates in Damascus, and went there to bring these people as prisoners to Jerusalem to be punished. Ac 21:20; 26:5

6 "About noon as I came near Damascus, suddenly a bright light from heaven flashed around me. 7 I fell to the ground and heard a voice say to me, 'Saul! Saul! Why do you persecute me?'

8 " 'Who are you, Lord?' I asked.

" 'I am Jesus of Nazareth, whom you are persecuting,' he replied. 9 My companions saw the light, but they did not understand the voice of him who was speaking to me. Ac 9:7; 26:13

10 " 'What shall I do, Lord?' I asked.

" 'Get up,' the Lord said, 'and go into Damascus. There you will be told all that you have been assigned to do.' 11 My companions led me by the hand into Damascus, because the brilliance of the light had blinded me. Ac 9:8; 16:30

12 "A man named Ananias came to see me. He was a devout observer of the law and highly respected by all the Jews living there. 13 He stood beside me and said, 'Brother Saul, receive your sight!' And at that very moment I was able to see him. Ac 9:17; 10:22

14 "Then he said: 'The God of our ancestors has chosen you to know his will and to see the Righteous One and to hear words from his mouth. 15 You will be his witness to all people of what you have seen and heard. 16 And now what are you waiting for? Get up, be baptized

a 40 Or possibly Hebrew; also in 22:2

and wash your sins away, calling on his name.' Ac 9:1-22; 26:9-18

17 "When I returned to Jerusalem and was praying at the temple, I fell into a trance 18 and saw the Lord speaking to me. 'Quick!' he said. 'Leave Jerusalem immediately, because the people here will not accept your testimony about me.' Ac 9:26; 10:10

19 " 'Lord,' I replied, 'these people know that I went from one synagogue to another to imprison and beat those who believe in you. 20 And when the blood of your martyr*a* Stephen was shed, I stood there giving my approval and guarding the clothes of those who were killing him.' Ac 8:1,3

21 "Then the Lord said to me, 'Go; I will send you far away to the Gentiles.' " Ac 9:15; 13:46

Paul the Roman Citizen

22 The crowd listened to Paul until he said this. Then they raised their voices and shouted, "Rid the earth of him! He's not fit to live!" Ac 21:36; 25:24

23 As they were shouting and throwing off their cloaks and flinging dust into the air, 24 the commander ordered that Paul be taken into the barracks. He directed that he be flogged and interrogated in order to find out why the people were shouting at him like this. 25 As they stretched him out to flog him, Paul said to the centurion standing there, "Is it legal for you to flog a Roman citizen who hasn't even been found guilty?" 2Sa 16:13; Ac 16:37

26 When the centurion heard this, he went to the commander and reported it. "What are you going to do?" he asked. "This man is a Roman citizen."

27 The commander went to Paul and asked, "Tell me, are you a Roman citizen?"

"Yes, I am," he answered.

28 Then the commander said, "I had to pay a lot of money for my citizenship."

"But I was born a citizen," Paul replied.

29 Those who were about to interrogate him withdrew immediately. The commander himself was alarmed when he realized that he had put Paul, a Roman citizen, in chains. Ac 16:38

Paul Before the Sanhedrin

30 The commander wanted to find out exactly why Paul was being accused by the Jews. So the next day he released him and ordered the chief priests and all the members of the Sanhedrin to assemble. Then he brought Paul and had him stand before them. Mt 5:22; Ac 23:28

23 Paul looked straight at the Sanhedrin and said, "My brothers, I have fulfilled my duty to God in all good conscience to this day." 2 At this the high priest Ananias ordered those stand-

a 20 Or *witness*

ing near Paul to strike him on the mouth. ³Then Paul said to him, "God will strike you, you whitewashed wall! You sit there to judge me according to the law, yet you yourself violate the law by commanding that I be struck!"

⁴Those who were standing near Paul said, "How dare you insult God's high priest!"

⁵Paul replied, "Brothers, I did not realize that he was the high priest; for it is written: 'Do not speak evil about the ruler of your people.'ᵃ" Ex 22:28

⁶Then Paul, knowing that some of them were Sadducees and the others Pharisees, called out in the Sanhedrin, "My brothers, I am a Pharisee, descended from Pharisees. I stand on trial because of the hope of the resurrection of the dead." ⁷When he said this, a dispute broke out between the Pharisees and the Sadducees, and the assembly was divided. ⁸(The Sadducees say that there is no resurrection, and that there are neither angels nor spirits, but the Pharisees believe all these things.) Mt 22:23; Ac 22:5; 26:5

⁹There was a great uproar, and some of the teachers of the law who were Pharisees stood up and argued vigorously. "We find nothing wrong with this man," they said. "What if a spirit or an angel has spoken to him?" ¹⁰The dispute became so violent that the commander was afraid Paul

would be torn to pieces by them. He ordered the troops to go down and take him away from them by force and bring him into the barracks. Ac 21:34; 22:7,17-18

¹¹The following night the Lord stood near Paul and said, "Take courage! As you have testified about me in Jerusalem, so you must also testify in Rome." Ac 18:9

The Plot to Kill Paul

¹²The next morning some Jews formed a conspiracy and bound themselves with an oath not to eat or drink until they had killed Paul. ¹³More than forty men were involved in this plot. ¹⁴They went to the chief priests and the elders and said, "We have taken a solemn oath not to eat anything until we have killed Paul. ¹⁵Now then, you and the Sanhedrin petition the commander to bring him before you on the pretext of wanting more accurate information about his case. We are ready to kill him before he gets here." Ac 22:30

¹⁶But when the son of Paul's sister heard of this plot, he went into the barracks and told Paul.

¹⁷Then Paul called one of the centurions and said, "Take this young man to the commander; he has something to tell him." ¹⁸So he took him to the commander.

The centurion said, "Paul, the prisoner, sent for me and asked

ᵃ 5 Exodus 22:28

me to bring this young man to you because he has something to tell you." Eph 3:1

¹⁹ The commander took the young man by the hand, drew him aside and asked, "What is it you want to tell me?"

²⁰ He said: "Some Jews have agreed to ask you to bring Paul before the Sanhedrin tomorrow on the pretext of wanting more accurate information about him. ²¹ Don't give in to them, because more than forty of them are waiting in ambush for him. They have taken an oath not to eat or drink until they have killed him. They are ready now, waiting for your consent to their request." ver 14-15

²² The commander dismissed the young man with this warning: "Don't tell anyone that you have reported this to me."

Paul Transferred to Caesarea

²³ Then he called two of his centurions and ordered them, "Get ready a detachment of two hundred soldiers, seventy horsemen and two hundred spearmen[a] to go to Caesarea at nine tonight. ²⁴ Provide horses for Paul so that he may be taken safely to Governor Felix." Ac 24:1-3,10

²⁵ He wrote a letter as follows:

²⁶ Claudius Lysias,

To His Excellency, Governor Felix: Ac 24:3

Greetings. Ac 15:23

²⁷ This man was seized by the Jews and they were about to kill him, but I came with my troops and rescued him, for I had learned that he is a Roman citizen. ²⁸ I wanted to know why they were accusing him, so I brought him to their Sanhedrin. ²⁹ I found that the accusation had to do with questions about their law, but there was no charge against him that deserved death or imprisonment. ³⁰ When I was informed of a plot to be carried out against the man, I sent him to you at once. I also ordered his accusers to present to you their case against him. Ac 24:19; 26:31

³¹ So the soldiers, carrying out their orders, took Paul with them during the night and brought him as far as Antipatris. ³² The next day they let the cavalry go on with him, while they returned to the barracks. ³³ When the cavalry arrived in Caesarea, they delivered the letter to the governor and handed Paul over to him. ³⁴ The governor read the letter and asked what province he was from. Learning that he was from Cilicia, ³⁵ he said, "I will hear your case when your accusers get here." Then he ordered

a 23 The meaning of the Greek for this word is uncertain.

that Paul be kept under guard in Herod's palace. Ac 21:39; 24:27; 25:16

Paul's Trial Before Felix

24 Five days later the high priest Ananias went down to Caesarea with some of the elders and a lawyer named Tertullus, and they brought their charges against Paul before the governor. ²When Paul was called in, Tertullus presented his case before Felix: "We have enjoyed a long period of peace under you, and your foresight has brought about reforms in this nation. ³Everywhere and in every way, most excellent Felix, we acknowledge this with profound gratitude. ⁴But in order not to weary you further, I would request that you be kind enough to hear us briefly. Ac 23:2,24

⁵"We have found this man to be a troublemaker, stirring up riots among the Jews all over the world. He is a ringleader of the Nazarene sect ⁶and even tried to desecrate the temple; so we seized him. [7]ᵃ ⁸By examining him yourself you will be able to learn the truth about all these charges we are bringing against him." Ac 16:20; 21:28

⁹The other Jews joined in the accusation, asserting that these things were true. 1Th 2:16

¹⁰When the governor motioned for him to speak, Paul replied: "I know that for a number of years you have been a judge over this nation; so I gladly make my defense. ¹¹You can easily verify that no more than twelve days ago I went up to Jerusalem to worship. ¹²My accusers did not find me arguing with anyone at the temple, or stirring up a crowd in the synagogues or anywhere else in the city. ¹³And they cannot prove to you the charges they are now making against me. ¹⁴However, I admit that I worship the God of our ancestors as a follower of the Way, which they call a sect. I believe everything that is in accordance with the Law and that is written in the Prophets, ¹⁵and I have the same hope in God as these men themselves have, that there will be a resurrection of both the righteous and the wicked. ¹⁶So I strive always to keep my conscience clear before God and man. Ac 9:2; 23:1; 25:8

¹⁷"After an absence of several years, I came to Jerusalem to bring my people gifts for the poor and to present offerings. ¹⁸I was ceremonially clean when they found me in the temple courts doing this. There was no crowd with me, nor was I involved in any disturbance. ¹⁹But there are some Jews from the province of Asia, who ought to be here be-

---

ᵃ 6-8 Some manuscripts include here *him, and we would have judged him in accordance with our law. ⁷But the commander Lysias came and took him from us with much violence, ⁸ordering his accusers to come before you.*

fore you and bring charges if they have anything against me. [20] Or these who are here should state what crime they found in me when I stood before the Sanhedrin — [21] unless it was this one thing I shouted as I stood in their presence: 'It is concerning the resurrection of the dead that I am on trial before you today.'" Ac 11:29-30; 23:6; 2Co 8:1-4

[22] Then Felix, who was well acquainted with the Way, adjourned the proceedings. "When Lysias the commander comes," he said, "I will decide your case." [23] He ordered the centurion to keep Paul under guard but to give him some freedom and permit his friends to take care of his needs. Ac 27:3; 28:16

[24] Several days later Felix came with his wife Drusilla, who was Jewish. He sent for Paul and listened to him as he spoke about faith in Christ Jesus. [25] As Paul talked about righteousness, self-control and the judgment to come, Felix was afraid and said, "That's enough for now! You may leave. When I find it convenient, I will send for you." [26] At the same time he was hoping that Paul would offer him a bribe, so he sent for him frequently and talked with him. Ac 20:21; 2Pe 1:6

[27] When two years had passed, Felix was succeeded by Porcius Festus, but because Felix wanted to grant a favor to the Jews, he left Paul in prison. Ac 12:3; 25:1,4,9,14

Paul's Trial Before Festus

25 Three days after arriving in the province, Festus went up from Caesarea to Jerusalem, [2] where the chief priests and the Jewish leaders appeared before him and presented the charges against Paul. [3] They requested Festus, as a favor to them, to have Paul transferred to Jerusalem, for they were preparing an ambush to kill him along the way. [4] Festus answered, "Paul is being held at Caesarea, and I myself am going there soon. [5] Let some of your leaders come with me, and if the man has done anything wrong, they can press charges against him there." Ac 24:1,23

[6] After spending eight or ten days with them, Festus went down to Caesarea. The next day he convened the court and ordered that Paul be brought before him. [7] When Paul came in, the Jews who had come down from Jerusalem stood around him. They brought many serious charges against him, but they could not prove them. Mk 15:3

[8] Then Paul made his defense: "I have done nothing wrong against the Jewish law or against the temple or against Caesar." Ac 6:13

[9] Festus, wishing to do the Jews a favor, said to Paul, "Are you willing to go up to Jerusalem and stand trial before me there on these charges?" Ac 12:3; 24:27

[10] Paul answered: "I am now standing before Caesar's court,

where I ought to be tried. I have not done any wrong to the Jews, as you yourself know very well. [11] If, however, I am guilty of doing anything deserving death, I do not refuse to die. But if the charges brought against me by these Jews are not true, no one has the right to hand me over to them. I appeal to Caesar!" Ac 26:32; 28:19

[12] After Festus had conferred with his council, he declared: "You have appealed to Caesar. To Caesar you will go!"

Festus Consults King Agrippa

[13] A few days later King Agrippa and Bernice arrived at Caesarea to pay their respects to Festus. [14] Since they were spending many days there, Festus discussed Paul's case with the king. He said: "There is a man here whom Felix left as a prisoner. [15] When I went to Jerusalem, the chief priests and the elders of the Jews brought charges against him and asked that he be condemned. Ac 24:1,27

[16] "I told them that it is not the Roman custom to hand over anyone before they have faced their accusers and have had an opportunity to defend themselves against the charges. [17] When they came here with me, I did not delay the case, but convened the court the next day and ordered the man to be brought in. [18] When his accusers got up to speak, they did not charge him

with any of the crimes I had expected. [19] Instead, they had some points of dispute with him about their own religion and about a dead man named Jesus who Paul claimed was alive. [20] I was at a loss how to investigate such matters; so I asked if he would be willing to go to Jerusalem and stand trial there on these charges. [21] But when Paul made his appeal to be held over for the Emperor's decision, I ordered him held until I could send him to Caesar." Ac 18:15; 23:29

[22] Then Agrippa said to Festus, "I would like to hear this man myself."

He replied, "Tomorrow you will hear him." Ac 9:15

Paul Before Agrippa
26:12-18pp — Ac 9:3-8; 22:6-11

[23] The next day Agrippa and Bernice came with great pomp and entered the audience room with the high-ranking military officers and the prominent men of the city. At the command of Festus, Paul was brought in. [24] Festus said: "King Agrippa, and all who are present with us, you see this man! The whole Jewish community has petitioned me about him in Jerusalem and here in Caesarea, shouting that he ought not to live any longer. [25] I found he had done nothing deserving of death, but because he made his appeal to the Emperor I decided to send him to Rome.

26 But I have nothing definite to write to His Majesty about him. Therefore I have brought him before all of you, and especially before you, King Agrippa, so that as a result of this investigation I may have something to write. 27 For I think it is unreasonable to send a prisoner on to Rome without specifying the charges against him." Ac 22:22; 23:9

26 Then Agrippa said to Paul, "You have permission to speak for yourself." Ac 9:15

So Paul motioned with his hand and began his defense: 2 "King Agrippa, I consider myself fortunate to stand before you today as I make my defense against all the accusations of the Jews, 3 and especially so because you are well acquainted with all the Jewish customs and controversies. Therefore, I beg you to listen to me patiently. Ac 6:14; 25:19

4 "The Jewish people all know the way I have lived ever since I was a child, from the beginning of my life in my own country, and also in Jerusalem. 5 They have known me for a long time and can testify, if they are willing, that I conformed to the strictest sect of our religion, living as a Pharisee. 6 And now it is because of my hope in what God has promised our ancestors that I am on trial today. 7 This is the promise our twelve tribes are hoping to see fulfilled as they earnestly serve God day and night. King Agrippa, it is because of this hope that these Jews are accusing me. 8 Why should any of you consider it incredible that God raises the dead? 1Th 3:10; 1Ti 5:5; Jas 1:1

9 "I too was convinced that I ought to do all that was possible to oppose the name of Jesus of Nazareth. 10 And that is just what I did in Jerusalem. On the authority of the chief priests I put many of the Lord's people in prison, and when they were put to death, I cast my vote against them. 11 Many a time I went from one synagogue to another to have them punished, and I tried to force them to blaspheme. I was so obsessed with persecuting them that I even hunted them down in foreign cities. Ac 8:3; 1Ti 1:13

12 "On one of these journeys I was going to Damascus with the authority and commission of the chief priests. 13 About noon, King Agrippa, as I was on the road, I saw a light from heaven, brighter than the sun, blazing around me and my companions. 14 We all fell to the ground, and I heard a voice saying to me in Aramaic,*a* 'Saul, Saul, why do you persecute me? It is hard for you to kick against the goads.' Ac 9:7

15 "Then I asked, 'Who are you, Lord?'

" 'I am Jesus, whom you are persecuting,' the Lord replied. 16 'Now get up and stand on your

a 14 Or *Hebrew*

feet. I have appeared to you to appoint you as a servant and as a witness of what you have seen and will see of me. ¹⁷I will rescue you from your own people and from the Gentiles. I am sending you to them ¹⁸to open their eyes and turn them from darkness to light, and from the power of Satan to God, so that they may receive forgiveness of sins and a place among those who are sanctified by faith in me.' Isa 35:5; 42:7,16

¹⁹"So then, King Agrippa, I was not disobedient to the vision from heaven. ²⁰First to those in Damascus, then to those in Jerusalem and in all Judea, and then to the Gentiles, I preached that they should repent and turn to God and demonstrate their repentance by their deeds. ²¹That is why some Jews seized me in the temple courts and tried to kill me. ²²But God has helped me to this very day; so I stand here and testify to small and great alike. I am saying nothing beyond what the prophets and Moses said would happen— ²³that the Messiah would suffer and, as the first to rise from the dead, would bring the message of light to his own people and to the Gentiles." Lk 2:32; Ac 21:27,30

²⁴At this point Festus interrupted Paul's defense. "You are out of your mind, Paul!" he shouted. "Your great learning is driving you insane." Jn 10:20

²⁵"I am not insane, most excellent Festus," Paul replied. "What I am saying is true and reasonable. ²⁶The king is familiar with these things, and I can speak freely to him. I am convinced that none of this has escaped his notice, because it was not done in a corner. ²⁷King Agrippa, do you believe the prophets? I know you do." Ac 23:26

²⁸Then Agrippa said to Paul, "Do you think that in such a short time you can persuade me to be a Christian?" Ac 11:26

²⁹Paul replied, "Short time or long—I pray to God that not only you but all who are listening to me today may become what I am, except for these chains." Ac 21:33

³⁰The king rose, and with him the governor and Bernice and those sitting with them. ³¹After they left the room, they began saying to one another, "This man is not doing anything that deserves death or imprisonment." Ac 23:9; 25:23

³²Agrippa said to Festus, "This man could have been set free if he had not appealed to Caesar."

Paul Sails for Rome

27 When it was decided that we would sail for Italy, Paul and some other prisoners were handed over to a centurion named Julius, who belonged to the Imperial Regiment. ²We boarded a ship from Adramyttium about to sail for ports along the coast of the province of Asia,

and we put out to sea. Aristarchus, a Macedonian from Thessalonica, was with us. Ac 19:29; 25:12

³The next day we landed at Sidon; and Julius, in kindness to Paul, allowed him to go to his friends so they might provide for his needs. ⁴From there we put out to sea again and passed to the lee of Cyprus because the winds were against us. ⁵When we had sailed across the open sea off the coast of Cilicia and Pamphylia, we landed at Myra in Lycia. ⁶There the centurion found an Alexandrian ship sailing for Italy and put us on board. ⁷We made slow headway for many days and had difficulty arriving off Cnidus. When the wind did not allow us to hold our course, we sailed to the lee of Crete, opposite Salmone. ⁸We moved along the coast with difficulty and came to a place called Fair Havens, near the town of Lasea. Ac 24:23; 28:11

⁹Much time had been lost, and sailing had already become dangerous because by now it was after the Day of Atonement.ᵃ So Paul warned them, ¹⁰"Men, I can see that our voyage is going to be disastrous and bring great loss to ship and cargo, and to our own lives also." ¹¹But the centurion, instead of listening to what Paul said, followed the advice of the pilot and of the owner of the ship. ¹²Since the harbor was un-

suitable to winter in, the majority decided that we should sail on, hoping to reach Phoenix and winter there. This was a harbor in Crete, facing both southwest and northwest. Lev 23:27-29; Nu 29:7

The Storm

¹³When a gentle south wind began to blow, they saw their opportunity; so they weighed anchor and sailed along the shore of Crete. ¹⁴Before very long, a wind of hurricane force, called the Northeaster, swept down from the island. ¹⁵The ship was caught by the storm and could not head into the wind; so we gave way to it and were driven along. ¹⁶As we passed to the lee of a small island called Cauda, we were hardly able to make the lifeboat secure, ¹⁷so the men hoisted it aboard. Then they passed ropes under the ship itself to hold it together. Because they were afraid they would run aground on the sandbars of Syrtis, they lowered the sea anchorᵇ and let the ship be driven along. ¹⁸We took such a violent battering from the storm that the next day they began to throw the cargo overboard. ¹⁹On the third day, they threw the ship's tackle overboard with their own hands. ²⁰When neither sun nor stars appeared for many days and the storm continued raging, we finally gave up all hope of being saved. Jnh 1:5; Mk 4:37

ᵃ 9 That is, Yom Kippur   ᵇ 17 Or the sails

²¹After they had gone a long time without food, Paul stood up before them and said: "Men, you should have taken my advice not to sail from Crete; then you would have spared yourselves this damage and loss. ²²But now I urge you to keep up your courage, because not one of you will be lost; only the ship will be destroyed. ²³Last night an angel of the God to whom I belong and whom I serve stood beside me ²⁴and said, 'Do not be afraid, Paul. You must stand trial before Caesar; and God has graciously given you the lives of all who sail with you.' ²⁵So keep up your courage, men, for I have faith in God that it will happen just as he told me. ²⁶Nevertheless, we must run aground on some island." Ac 23:11; 28:1

The Shipwreck

²⁷On the fourteenth night we were still being driven across the Adriatic*ᵃ* Sea, when about midnight the sailors sensed they were approaching land. ²⁸They took soundings and found that the water was a hundred and twenty feet*ᵇ* deep. A short time later they took soundings again and found it was ninety feet*ᶜ* deep. ²⁹Fearing that we would be dashed against the rocks, they dropped four anchors from the stern and prayed for daylight. ³⁰In an attempt to escape from the ship, the sailors let the lifeboat down into the sea, pretending they were going to lower some anchors from the bow. ³¹Then Paul said to the centurion and the soldiers, "Unless these men stay with the ship, you cannot be saved." ³²So the soldiers cut the ropes that held the lifeboat and let it drift away. ver 16,24

³³Just before dawn Paul urged them all to eat. "For the last fourteen days," he said, "you have been in constant suspense and have gone without food—you haven't eaten anything. ³⁴Now I urge you to take some food. You need it to survive. Not one of you will lose a single hair from his head." ³⁵After he said this, he took some bread and gave thanks to God in front of them all. Then he broke it and began to eat. ³⁶They were all encouraged and ate some food themselves. ³⁷Altogether there were 276 of us on board. ³⁸When they had eaten as much as they wanted, they lightened the ship by throwing the grain into the sea. Mt 10:30; 14:19

³⁹When daylight came, they did not recognize the land, but they saw a bay with a sandy beach, where they decided to run the ship aground if they could. ⁴⁰Cutting loose the anchors, they left them in the sea and at the same time untied the ropes that held the rudders. Then they hoisted the

---

ᵃ 27 In ancient times the name referred to an area extending well south of Italy.
ᵇ 28 Or about 37 meters *ᶜ 28* Or about 27 meters

foresail to the wind and made for the beach. ⁴¹But the ship struck a sandbar and ran aground. The bow stuck fast and would not move, and the stern was broken to pieces by the pounding of the surf. Ac 28:1; 2Co 11:25

⁴²The soldiers planned to kill the prisoners to prevent any of them from swimming away and escaping. ⁴³But the centurion wanted to spare Paul's life and kept them from carrying out their plan. He ordered those who could swim to jump overboard first and get to land. ⁴⁴The rest were to get there on planks or on other pieces of the ship. In this way everyone reached land safely. ver 22,31

Paul Ashore on Malta

28 Once safely on shore, we found out that the island was called Malta. ²The islanders showed us unusual kindness. They built a fire and welcomed us all because it was raining and cold. ³Paul gathered a pile of brushwood and, as he put it on the fire, a viper, driven out by the heat, fastened itself on his hand. ⁴When the islanders saw the snake hanging from his hand, they said to each other, "This man must be a murderer; for though he escaped from the sea, the goddess Justice has not allowed him to live." ⁵But Paul shook the snake off into the fire and suffered no ill effects. ⁶The people expected him to swell up or suddenly fall dead; but after waiting a long time and seeing nothing unusual happen to him, they changed their minds and said he was a god. Lk 10:19; Ac 14:11

⁷There was an estate nearby that belonged to Publius, the chief official of the island. He welcomed us to his home and showed us generous hospitality for three days. ⁸His father was sick in bed, suffering from fever and dysentery. Paul went in to see him and, after prayer, placed his hands on him and healed him. ⁹When this had happened, the rest of the sick on the island came and were cured. ¹⁰They honored us in many ways; and when we were ready to sail, they furnished us with the supplies we needed. Ac 9:40; Jas 5:14-15

Paul's Arrival at Rome

¹¹After three months we put out to sea in a ship that had wintered in the island — it was an Alexandrian ship with the figurehead of the twin gods Castor and Pollux. ¹²We put in at Syracuse and stayed there three days. ¹³From there we set sail and arrived at Rhegium. The next day the south wind came up, and on the following day we reached Puteoli. ¹⁴There we found some brothers and sisters who invited us to spend a week with them. And so we came to Rome. ¹⁵The brothers and sisters there had

heard that we were coming, and they traveled as far as the Forum of Appius and the Three Taverns to meet us. At the sight of these people Paul thanked God and was encouraged. [16]When we got to Rome, Paul was allowed to live by himself, with a soldier to guard him.   Ac 1:16; 24:23; 27:6

Paul Preaches at Rome Under Guard

[17]Three days later he called together the local Jewish leaders. When they had assembled, Paul said to them: "My brothers, although I have done nothing against our people or against the customs of our ancestors, I was arrested in Jerusalem and handed over to the Romans. [18]They examined me and wanted to release me, because I was not guilty of any crime deserving death. [19]The Jews objected, so I was compelled to make an appeal to Caesar. I certainly did not intend to bring any charge against my own people. [20]For this reason I have asked to see you and talk with you. It is because of the hope of Israel that I am bound with this chain."   Ac 25:11; 26:6-7

[21]They replied, "We have not received any letters from Judea concerning you, and none of our people who have come from there has reported or said anything bad about you. [22]But we want to hear what your views are, for we know that people everywhere are talking against this sect."   Ac 22:5; 24:5,14

[23]They arranged to meet Paul on a certain day, and came in even larger numbers to the place where he was staying. He witnessed to them from morning till evening, explaining about the kingdom of God, and from the Law of Moses and from the Prophets he tried to persuade them about Jesus. [24]Some were convinced by what he said, but others would not believe. [25]They disagreed among themselves and began to leave after Paul had made this final statement: "The Holy Spirit spoke the truth to your ancestors when he said through Isaiah the prophet: Ac 14:4; 19:8

[26]" 'Go to this people and say,
    "You will be ever hearing but
        never understanding;
    you will be ever seeing but
        never perceiving."
[27]For this people's heart has
        become calloused;
    they hardly hear with their
        ears,
    and they have closed their
        eyes.
Otherwise they might see
        with their eyes,
    hear with their ears,
    understand with their
        hearts
    and turn, and I would heal
        them.'[a]   Mt 13:15

---

[a] 27 Isaiah 6:9,10 (see Septuagint)

[28] "Therefore I want you to know that God's salvation has been sent to the Gentiles, and they will listen!" [29] *a*   Ac 13:46

[30] For two whole years Paul stayed there in his own rented house and welcomed all who came to see him. [31] He proclaimed the kingdom of God and taught about the Lord Jesus Christ — with all boldness and without hindrance!   Ac 4:29

---

a 29 Some manuscripts include here *After he said this, the Jews left, arguing vigorously among themselves.*

Romans

1 Paul, a servant of Christ Jesus, called to be an apostle and set apart for the gospel of God— ²the gospel he promised beforehand through his prophets in the Holy Scriptures ³regarding his Son, who as to his earthly life*a* was a descendant of David, ⁴and who through the Spirit of holiness was appointed the Son of God in power*b* by his resurrection from the dead: Jesus Christ our Lord. ⁵Through him we received grace and apostleship to call all the Gentiles to the obedience that comes from*c* faith for his name's sake. ⁶And you also are among those Gentiles who are called to belong to Jesus Christ. Ac 6:7; 9:15

⁷To all in Rome who are loved by God and called to be his holy people: Ro 8:39

Grace and peace to you from God our Father and from the Lord Jesus Christ. 1Co 1:3; 1Pe 1:2

Paul's Longing to Visit Rome

⁸First, I thank my God through Jesus Christ for all of you, because your faith is being reported all over the world. ⁹God, whom I serve in my spirit in preaching the gospel of his Son, is my witness how constantly I remember you ¹⁰in my prayers at all times; and I pray that now at last by God's will the way may be opened for me to come to you. Ro 15:32; 2Ti 1:3

¹¹I long to see you so that I may impart to you some spiritual gift to make you strong— ¹²that is, that you and I may be mutually encouraged by each other's faith. ¹³I do not want you to be unaware, brothers and sisters,*d* that I planned many times to come to you (but have been prevented from doing so until now) in order that I might have a harvest among you, just as I have had among the other Gentiles. Ro 15:22-23

---

a 3 Or *who according to the flesh*   *b 4* Or *was declared with power to be the Son of God*
c 5 Or *that is*   *d 13* The Greek word for *brothers and sisters* (*adelphoi*) refers here to believers, both men and women, as part of God's family; also in 7:1, 4; 8:12, 29; 10:1; 11:25; 12:1; 15:14, 30; 16:14, 17.

¹⁴I am obligated both to Greeks and non-Greeks, both to the wise and the foolish. ¹⁵That is why I am so eager to preach the gospel also to you who are in Rome. Ro 15:20

¹⁶For I am not ashamed of the gospel, because it is the power of God that brings salvation to everyone who believes: first to the Jew, then to the Gentile. ¹⁷For in the gospel the righteousness of God is revealed—a righteousness that is by faith from first to last,^a just as it is written: "The righteous will live by faith."^b Ro 3:21

God's Wrath Against Sinful Humanity

¹⁸The wrath of God is being revealed from heaven against all the godlessness and wickedness of people, who suppress the truth by their wickedness, ¹⁹since what may be known about God is plain to them, because God has made it plain to them. ²⁰For since the creation of the world God's invisible qualities—his eternal power and divine nature—have been clearly seen, being understood from what has been made, so that people are without excuse. Ps 19:1-6; Ac 14:17

²¹For although they knew God, they neither glorified him as God nor gave thanks to him, but their thinking became futile and their foolish hearts were darkened. ²²Although they claimed to be wise, they became fools ²³and

exchanged the glory of the immortal God for images made to look like a mortal human being and birds and animals and reptiles. Ps 106:20; Jer 2:5

²⁴Therefore God gave them over in the sinful desires of their hearts to sexual impurity for the degrading of their bodies with one another. ²⁵They exchanged the truth about God for a lie, and worshiped and served created things rather than the Creator—who is forever praised. Amen. Jer 10:14; Eph 4:19

²⁶Because of this, God gave them over to shameful lusts. Even their women exchanged natural sexual relations for unnatural ones. ²⁷In the same way the men also abandoned natural relations with women and were inflamed with lust for one another. Men committed shameful acts with other men, and received in themselves the due penalty for their error. Lev 18:22; 1Th 4:5

²⁸Furthermore, just as they did not think it worthwhile to retain the knowledge of God, so God gave them over to a depraved mind, so that they do what ought not to be done. ²⁹They have become filled with every kind of wickedness, evil, greed and depravity. They are full of envy, murder, strife, deceit and malice. They are gossips, ³⁰slanderers, God-haters, insolent, arrogant and boastful; they invent ways

^a 17 Or *is from faith to faith*   ^b 17 Hab. 2:4

of doing evil; they disobey their parents; [31] they have no understanding, no fidelity, no love, no mercy. [32] Although they know God's righteous decree that those who do such things deserve death, they not only continue to do these very things but also approve of those who practice them. Ro 6:23; 2Ti 3:2

God's Righteous Judgment

2 You, therefore, have no excuse, you who pass judgment on someone else, for at whatever point you judge another, you are condemning yourself, because you who pass judgment do the same things. [2] Now we know that God's judgment against those who do such things is based on truth. [3] So when you, a mere human being, pass judgment on them and yet do the same things, do you think you will escape God's judgment? [4] Or do you show contempt for the riches of his kindness, forbearance and patience, not realizing that God's kindness is intended to lead you to repentance? Ex 34:6; Ro 3:25; 2Pe 3:9

[5] But because of your stubbornness and your unrepentant heart, you are storing up wrath against yourself for the day of God's wrath, when his righteous judgment will be revealed. [6] God "will repay each person according to what they have done." [a] [7] To those who by persistence in doing good seek glory, honor and immortality, he will give eternal life. [8] But for those who are self-seeking and who reject the truth and follow evil, there will be wrath and anger. [9] There will be trouble and distress for every human being who does evil: first for the Jew, then for the Gentile; [10] but glory, honor and peace for everyone who does good: first for the Jew, then for the Gentile. [11] For God does not show favoritism. Ac 10:34; 2Th 2:12

[12] All who sin apart from the law will also perish apart from the law, and all who sin under the law will be judged by the law. [13] For it is not those who hear the law who are righteous in God's sight, but it is those who obey the law who will be declared righteous. [14] (Indeed, when Gentiles, who do not have the law, do by nature things required by the law, they are a law for themselves, even though they do not have the law. [15] They show that the requirements of the law are written on their hearts, their consciences also bearing witness, and their thoughts sometimes accusing them and at other times even defending them.) [16] This will take place on the day when God judges people's secrets through Jesus Christ, as my gospel declares. Ac 10:42; Jas 1:22-23,25

The Jews and the Law

[17] Now you, if you call yourself

[a] 6 Psalm 62:12; Prov. 24:12

a Jew; if you rely on the law and boast in God; [18]if you know his will and approve of what is superior because you are instructed by the law; [19]if you are convinced that you are a guide for the blind, a light for those who are in the dark, [20]an instructor of the foolish, a teacher of little children, because you have in the law the embodiment of knowledge and truth— [21]you, then, who teach others, do you not teach yourself? You who preach against stealing, do you steal? [22]You who say that people should not commit adultery, do you commit adultery? You who abhor idols, do you rob temples? [23]You who boast in the law, do you dishonor God by breaking the law? [24]As it is written: "God's name is blasphemed among the Gentiles because of you."[a]   Isa 52:5; Mic 3:11

[25]Circumcision has value if you observe the law, but if you break the law, you have become as though you had not been circumcised. [26]So then, if those who are not circumcised keep the law's requirements, will they not be regarded as though they were circumcised? [27]The one who is not circumcised physically and yet obeys the law will condemn you who, even though you have the[b] written code and circumcision, are a lawbreaker.   Mt 12:41-4

[28]A person is not a Jew who is one only outwardly, nor is circumcision merely outward and physical. [29]No, a person is a Jew who is one inwardly; and circumcision is circumcision of the heart, by the Spirit, not by the written code. Such a person's praise is not from other people, but from God.   2Co 10:18; Gal 6:15

God's Faithfulness

3 What advantage, then, is there in being a Jew, or what value is there in circumcision? [2]Much in every way! First of all, the Jews have been entrusted with the very words of God. Dt 4:8

[3]What if some were unfaithful? Will their unfaithfulness nullify God's faithfulness? [4]Not at all! Let God be true, and every human being a liar. As it is written: Ps 116:11; Heb 4:2

> "So that you may be proved
>   right when you speak
> and prevail when you
>   judge."[c]
>   Ps 51:4

[5]But if our unrighteousness brings out God's righteousness more clearly, what shall we say? That God is unjust in bringing his wrath on us? (I am using a human argument.) [6]Certainly not! If that were so, how could God judge the world? [7]Someone might argue, "If my falsehood enhances God's truthfulness and so increases his glory, why

---

[a] 24 Isaiah 52:5 (see Septuagint); Ezek. 36:20,22   [b] 27 Or who, by means of a

[c] 4 Psalm 51:4

am I still condemned as a sinner?" **8**Why not say — as some slanderously claim that we say — "Let us do evil that good may result"? Their condemnation is just! Ge 18:25; Gal 3:15

No One Is Righteous

9What shall we conclude then? Do we have any advantage? Not at all! For we have already made the charge that Jews and Gentiles alike are all under the power of sin. **10**As it is written: Gal 3:22

"There is no one righteous,
not even one;
11 there is no one who
understands;
there is no one who seeks
God.
12All have turned away,
they have together become
worthless;
there is no one who does
good,
not even one."[a] Ps 14:1-3
13 "Their throats are open
graves;
their tongues practice
deceit."[b] Ps 5:9
"The poison of vipers is on
their lips."[c] Ps 140:3
14 "Their mouths are full
of cursing and
bitterness."[d] Ps 10:7
15 "Their feet are swift to shed
blood;

16 ruin and misery mark their
ways,
17and the way of peace they do
not know."[e] Isa 59:7-8
18 "There is no fear of God
before their eyes."[f] Ps 36:1

19Now we know that whatever the law says, it says to those who are under the law, so that every mouth may be silenced and the whole world held accountable to God. **20**Therefore no one will be declared righteous in God's sight by the works of the law; rather, through the law we become conscious of our sin. Ac 13:39; Ro 7:7

Righteousness Through Faith

21But now apart from the law the righteousness of God has been made known, to which the Law and the Prophets testify. **22**This righteousness is given through faith in[g] Jesus Christ to all who believe. There is no difference between Jew and Gentile, **23**for all have sinned and fall short of the glory of God, **24**and all are justified freely by his grace through the redemption that came by Christ Jesus. **25**God presented Christ as a sacrifice of atonement,[h] through the shedding of his blood — to be received by faith. He did this to demonstrate his righteousness, because in his forbearance he had left the

---

[a] 12 Psalms 14:1-3; 53:1-3; Eccles. 7:20   [b] 13 Psalm 5:9   [c] 13 Psalm 140:3
[d] 14 Psalm 10:7 (see Septuagint)   [e] 17 Isaiah 59:7,8   [f] 18 Psalm 36:1   [g] 22 Or through the faithfulness of   [h] 25 The Greek for sacrifice of atonement refers to the atonement cover on the ark of the covenant (see Lev. 16:15,16).

sins committed beforehand unpunished — ²⁶he did it to demonstrate his righteousness at the present time, so as to be just and the one who justifies those who have faith in Jesus. Ro 1:17; 4:16; 10:12

²⁷Where, then, is boasting? It is excluded. Because of what law? The law that requires works? No, because of the law that requires faith. ²⁸For we maintain that a person is justified by faith apart from the works of the law. ²⁹Or is God the God of Jews only? Is he not the God of Gentiles too? Yes, of Gentiles too, ³⁰since there is only one God, who will justify the circumcised by faith and the uncircumcised through that same faith. ³¹Do we, then, nullify the law by this faith? Not at all! Rather, we uphold the law. 1Co 1:29-31

Abraham Justified by Faith

4 What then shall we say that Abraham, our forefather according to the flesh, discovered in this matter? ²If, in fact, Abraham was justified by works, he had something to boast about — but not before God. ³What does Scripture say? "Abraham believed God, and it was credited to him as righteousness."*a* Ge 15:6

⁴Now to the one who works, wages are not credited as a gift but as an obligation. ⁵However, to the one who does not work but trusts God who justifies the ungodly, their faith is credited as righteousness. ⁶David says the same thing when he speaks of the blessedness of the one to whom God credits righteousness apart from works: Ro 11:6

⁷"Blessed are those
  whose transgressions are
    forgiven,
  whose sins are covered.
⁸Blessed is the one
  whose sin the Lord will
    never count against
    them."*b* Ps 32:1-2; 2Co 5:19

⁹Is this blessedness only for the circumcised, or also for the uncircumcised? We have been saying that Abraham's faith was credited to him as righteousness. ¹⁰Under what circumstances was it credited? Was it after he was circumcised, or before? It was not after, but before! ¹¹And he received circumcision as a sign, a seal of the righteousness that he had by faith while he was still uncircumcised. So then, he is the father of all who believe but have not been circumcised, in order that righteousness might be credited to them. ¹²And he is then also the father of the circumcised who not only are circumcised but who also follow in the footsteps of the faith that our father Abraham had before he was circumcised. Ge 17:10-11; Lk 19:9

¹³It was not through the law that Abraham and his offspring received the promise that he

a 3 Gen. 15:6; also in verse 22   *b 8* Psalm 32:1,2

would be heir of the world, but through the righteousness that comes by faith. ¹⁴For if those who depend on the law are heirs, faith means nothing and the promise is worthless, ¹⁵because the law brings wrath. And where there is no law there is no transgression. Ro 3:20; 7:7-25; Gal 3:18

¹⁶Therefore, the promise comes by faith, so that it may be by grace and may be guaranteed to all Abraham's offspring—not only to those who are of the law but also to those who have the faith of Abraham. He is the father of us all. ¹⁷As it is written: "I have made you a father of many nations."ᵃ He is our father in the sight of God, in whom he believed—the God who gives life to the dead and calls into being things that were not. Ro 3:24

¹⁸Against all hope, Abraham in hope believed and so became the father of many nations, just as it had been said to him, "So shall your offspring be."ᵇ ¹⁹Without weakening in his faith, he faced the fact that his body was as good as dead—since he was about a hundred years old—and that Sarah's womb was also dead. ²⁰Yet he did not waver through unbelief regarding the promise of God, but was strengthened in his faith and gave glory to God, ²¹being fully persuaded that God had power to do what he had promised. ²²This is why "it was credited to him as righteousness." ²³The words "it was credited to him" were written not for him alone, ²⁴but also for us, to whom God will credit righteousness—for us who believe in him who raised Jesus our Lord from the dead. ²⁵He was delivered over to death for our sins and was raised to life for our justification. Ac 2:24; Ro 15:4; Heb 11:19

Peace and Hope

5 Therefore, since we have been justified through faith, weᶜ have peace with God through our Lord Jesus Christ, ²through whom we have gained access by faith into this grace in which we now stand. And weᵈ boast in the hope of the glory of God. ³Not only so, but weᵈ also glory in our sufferings, because we know that suffering produces perseverance; ⁴perseverance, character; and character, hope. ⁵And hope does not put us to shame, because God's love has been poured out into our hearts through the Holy Spirit, who has been given to us. Eph 2:18; Jas 1:2-3

⁶You see, at just the right time, when we were still powerless, Christ died for the ungodly. ⁷Very rarely will anyone die for a righteous person, though for a good person someone might possibly dare to die. ⁸But God demonstrates his own love for us in

ᵃ 17 Gen. 17:5   ᵇ 18 Gen. 15:5   ᶜ 1 Many manuscripts *let us*   ᵈ 2,3 Or *let us* this: While we were still sinners, Christ died for us. Jn 15:13; 1Pe 3:18 ⁹Since we have now been justified by his blood, how much more shall we be saved from God's wrath through him! ¹⁰For if, while we were God's enemies, we were reconciled to him through the death of his Son, how much more, having been reconciled, shall we be saved through his life! ¹¹Not only is this so, but we also boast in God through our Lord Jesus Christ, through whom we have now received reconciliation. Ro 11:28; 2Co 5:18-19

Death Through Adam, Life Through Christ

¹²Therefore, just as sin entered the world through one man, and death through sin, and in this way death came to all people, because all sinned —

¹³To be sure, sin was in the world before the law was given, but sin is not charged against anyone's account where there is no law. ¹⁴Nevertheless, death reigned from the time of Adam to the time of Moses, even over those who did not sin by breaking a command, as did Adam, who is a pattern of the one to come. Ge 2:17; 1Co 15:22,45

¹⁵But the gift is not like the trespass. For if the many died by the trespass of the one man, how much more did God's grace and the gift that came by the grace of the one man, Jesus Christ, over-flow to the many! ¹⁶Nor can the gift of God be compared with the result of one man's sin: The judgment followed one sin and brought condemnation, but the gift followed many trespasses and brought justification. ¹⁷For if, by the trespass of the one man, death reigned through that one man, how much more will those who receive God's abundant provision of grace and of the gift of righteousness reign in life through the one man, Jesus Christ! Ac 15:11

¹⁸Consequently, just as one trespass resulted in condemnation for all people, so also one righteous act resulted in justification and life for all people. ¹⁹For just as through the disobedience of the one man the many were made sinners, so also through the obedience of the one man the many will be made righteous. Ro 4:25; Php 2:8

²⁰The law was brought in so that the trespass might increase. But where sin increased, grace increased all the more, ²¹so that, just as sin reigned in death, so also grace might reign through righteousness to bring eternal life through Jesus Christ our Lord. Gal 3:19; 1Ti 1:13-14

Dead to Sin, Alive in Christ

6 What shall we say, then? Shall we go on sinning so that grace may increase? ²By no means! We are those who have

died to sin; how can we live in it any longer? ³Or don't you know that all of us who were baptized into Christ Jesus were baptized into his death? ⁴We were therefore buried with him through baptism into death in order that, just as Christ was raised from the dead through the glory of the Father, we too may live a new life. Col 2:12; 3:10

⁵For if we have been united with him in a death like his, we will certainly also be united with him in a resurrection like his. ⁶For we know that our old self was crucified with him so that the body ruled by sin might be done away with,[a] that we should no longer be slaves to sin— ⁷because anyone who has died has been set free from sin. Ro 7:24; Gal 2:20

⁸Now if we died with Christ, we believe that we will also live with him. ⁹For we know that since Christ was raised from the dead, he cannot die again; death no longer has mastery over him. ¹⁰The death he died, he died to sin once for all; but the life he lives, he lives to God. Ac 2:24; Rev 1:18

¹¹In the same way, count yourselves dead to sin but alive to God in Christ Jesus. ¹²Therefore do not let sin reign in your mortal body so that you obey its evil desires. ¹³Do not offer any part of yourself to sin as an instrument of wickedness, but rather offer yourselves to God as those who have been brought from death to life; and offer every part of yourself to him as an instrument of righteousness. ¹⁴For sin shall no longer be your master, because you are not under the law, but under grace. Ro 3:24; Gal 5:18

Slaves to Righteousness

¹⁵What then? Shall we sin because we are not under the law but under grace? By no means! ¹⁶Don't you know that when you offer yourselves to someone as obedient slaves, you are slaves of the one you obey—whether you are slaves to sin, which leads to death, or to obedience, which leads to righteousness? ¹⁷But thanks be to God that, though you used to be slaves to sin, you have come to obey from your heart the pattern of teaching that has now claimed your allegiance. ¹⁸You have been set free from sin and have become slaves to righteousness. Jn 8:34; Ro 8:2; 2Ti 1:13

¹⁹I am using an example from everyday life because of your human limitations. Just as you used to offer yourselves as slaves to impurity and to ever-increasing wickedness, so now offer yourselves as slaves to righteousness leading to holiness. ²⁰When you were slaves to sin, you were free from the control of righteousness. ²¹What benefit did you reap at that time from the things you are now ashamed of? Those

[a] 6 Or *be rendered powerless*

things result in death! ²² But now that you have been set free from sin and have become slaves of God, the benefit you reap leads to holiness, and the result is eternal life. ²³ For the wages of sin is death, but the gift of God is eternal life in^a Christ Jesus our Lord. Ro 5:12; Gal 6:7-8

Released From the Law, Bound to Christ

7 Do you not know, brothers and sisters — for I am speaking to those who know the law — that the law has authority over someone only as long as that person lives? ² For example, by law a married woman is bound to her husband as long as he is alive, but if her husband dies, she is released from the law that binds her to him. ³ So then, if she has sexual relations with another man while her husband is still alive, she is called an adulteress. But if her husband dies, she is released from that law and is not an adulteress if she marries another man. Ro 1:13; 1Co 7:39

⁴ So, my brothers and sisters, you also died to the law through the body of Christ, that you might belong to another, to him who was raised from the dead, in order that we might bear fruit for God. ⁵ For when we were in the realm of the flesh,^b the sinful passions aroused by the law were at work in us, so that we bore fruit for death. ⁶ But now, by dying to what once bound us, we have been released from the law so that we serve in the new way of the Spirit, and not in the old way of the written code. Ro 2:29; 6:13

The Law and Sin

⁷ What shall we say, then? Is the law sinful? Certainly not! Nevertheless, I would not have known what sin was had it not been for the law. For I would not have known what coveting really was if the law had not said, "You shall not covet."^c ⁸ But sin, seizing the opportunity afforded by the commandment, produced in me every kind of coveting. For apart from the law, sin was dead. ⁹ Once I was alive apart from the law; but when the commandment came, sin sprang to life and I died. ¹⁰ I found that the very commandment that was intended to bring life actually brought death. ¹¹ For sin, seizing the opportunity afforded by the commandment, deceived me, and through the commandment put me to death. ¹² So then, the law is holy, and the commandment is holy, righteous and good. Lev 18:5; 1Ti 1:8

¹³ Did that which is good, then, become death to me? By no means! Nevertheless, in order

---

^a 23 Or *through*   ^b 5 In contexts like this, the Greek word for *flesh* (*sarx*) refers to the sinful state of human beings, often presented as a power in opposition to the Spirit.
^c 7 Exodus 20:17; Deut. 5:21

that sin might be recognized as sin, it used what is good to bring about my death, so that through the commandment sin might become utterly sinful. Ro 6:23

¹⁴We know that the law is spiritual; but I am unspiritual, sold as a slave to sin. ¹⁵I do not understand what I do. For what I want to do I do not do, but what I hate I do. ¹⁶And if I do what I do not want to do, I agree that the law is good. ¹⁷As it is, it is no longer I myself who do it, but it is sin living in me. ¹⁸For I know that good itself does not dwell in me, that is, in my sinful nature.ᵃ For I have the desire to do what is good, but I cannot carry it out. ¹⁹For I do not do the good I want to do, but the evil I do not want to do — this I keep on doing. ²⁰Now if I do what I do not want to do, it is no longer I who do it, but it is sin living in me that does it. 2Ki 17:17; Gal 5:17

²¹So I find this law at work: Although I want to do good, evil is right there with me. ²²For in my inner being I delight in God's law; ²³but I see another law at work in me, waging war against the law of my mind and making me a prisoner of the law of sin at work within me. ²⁴What a wretched man I am! Who will rescue me from this body that is subject to death? ²⁵Thanks be to God, who delivers me through Jesus Christ our Lord! Ro 6:6; Gal 5:17.

So then, I myself in my mind am a slave to God's law, but in my sinful natureᵇ a slave to the law of sin. Ro 6:16,22

Life Through the Spirit

8 Therefore, there is now no condemnation for those who are in Christ Jesus, ²because through Christ Jesus the law of the Spirit who gives life has set youᶜ free from the law of sin and death. ³For what the law was powerless to do because it was weakened by the flesh,ᵈ God did by sending his own Son in the likeness of sinful flesh to be a sin offering.ᵉ And so he condemned sin in the flesh, ⁴in order that the righteous requirement of the law might be fully met in us, who do not live according to the flesh but according to the Spirit. 1Co 15:45

⁵Those who live according to the flesh have their minds set on what the flesh desires; but those who live in accordance with the Spirit have their minds set on what the Spirit desires. ⁶The mind governed by the flesh is death, but the mind governed by the Spirit is life and peace. ⁷The mind governed by the flesh is hostile to God; it does not submit to God's law, nor can it do so. ⁸Those who

ᵃ 18 Or my flesh   ᵇ 25 Or in the flesh   ᶜ 2 The Greek is singular; some manuscripts me   ᵈ 3 In contexts like this, the Greek word for flesh (sarx) refers to the sinful state of human beings, often presented as a power in opposition to the Spirit; also in verses 4-13.   ᵉ 3 Or flesh, for sin are in the realm of the flesh cannot please God. Gal 6:8; Jas 4:4

⁹You, however, are not in the realm of the flesh but are in the realm of the Spirit, if indeed the Spirit of God lives in you. And if anyone does not have the Spirit of Christ, they do not belong to Christ. ¹⁰But if Christ is in you, then even though your body is subject to death because of sin, the Spirit gives life[a] because of righteousness. ¹¹And if the Spirit of him who raised Jesus from the dead is living in you, he who raised Christ from the dead will also give life to your mortal bodies because of[b] his Spirit who lives in you. Ac 2:24; Gal 4:6

¹²Therefore, brothers and sisters, we have an obligation — but it is not to the flesh, to live according to it. ¹³For if you live according to the flesh, you will die; but if by the Spirit you put to death the misdeeds of the body, you will live.

¹⁴For those who are led by the Spirit of God are the children of God. ¹⁵The Spirit you received does not make you slaves, so that you live in fear again; rather, the Spirit you received brought about your adoption to sonship.[c] And by him we cry, *"Abba,[d] Father."* ¹⁶The Spirit himself testifies with our spirit that we are God's children. ¹⁷Now if we are children, then we are heirs — heirs of God and co-heirs with Christ, if indeed we share in his sufferings in order that we may also share in his glory. Gal 4:7; 1Pe 4:13

Present Suffering and Future Glory

¹⁸I consider that our present sufferings are not worth comparing with the glory that will be revealed in us. ¹⁹For the creation waits in eager expectation for the children of God to be revealed. ²⁰For the creation was subjected to frustration, not by its own choice, but by the will of the one who subjected it, in hope ²¹that[e] the creation itself will be liberated from its bondage to decay and brought into the freedom and glory of the children of God. Ac 3:21; 2Pe 3:13; Jn 1:12

²²We know that the whole creation has been groaning as in the pains of childbirth right up to the present time. ²³Not only so, but we ourselves, who have the firstfruits of the Spirit, groan inwardly as we wait eagerly for our adoption to sonship, the redemption of our bodies. ²⁴For in this hope we were saved. But hope that is seen is no hope at all. Who hopes for what they already have? ²⁵But if we hope for

---

[a] 10 Or *you, your body is dead because of sin, yet your spirit is alive*   [b] 11 Some manuscripts *bodies through*   [c] 15 The Greek word for *adoption to sonship* is a term referring to the full legal standing of an adopted male heir in Roman culture; also in verse 23.   [d] 15 Aramaic for *father*   [e] 20,21 Or *subjected it in hope.* ²¹*For*

what we do not yet have, we wait for it patiently. 2Co 5:2,4; Gal 5:5

²⁶In the same way, the Spirit helps us in our weakness. We do not know what we ought to pray for, but the Spirit himself intercedes for us through wordless groans. ²⁷And he who searches our hearts knows the mind of the Spirit, because the Spirit intercedes for God's people in accordance with the will of God. Eph 6:18

²⁸And we know that in all things God works for the good of those who love him, who*ᵃ* have been called according to his purpose. ²⁹For those God foreknew he also predestined to be conformed to the image of his Son, that he might be the firstborn among many brothers and sisters. ³⁰And those he predestined, he also called; those he called, he also justified; those he justified, he also glorified. 1Co 6:11; Eph 1:5,11

More Than Conquerors

³¹What, then, shall we say in response to these things? If God is for us, who can be against us? ³²He who did not spare his own Son, but gave him up for us all — how will he not also, along with him, graciously give us all things? ³³Who will bring any charge against those whom God has chosen? It is God who justifies. ³⁴Who then is the one who

condemns? No one. Christ Jesus who died — more than that, who was raised to life — is at the right hand of God and is also interceding for us. ³⁵Who shall separate us from the love of Christ? Shall trouble or hardship or persecution or famine or nakedness or danger or sword? ³⁶As it is written: Ps 118:6; Jn 3:16; Heb 7:25

> "For your sake we face death
>   all day long;
>   we are considered as sheep
>   to be slaughtered."*ᵇ*

³⁷No, in all these things we are more than conquerors through him who loved us. ³⁸For I am convinced that neither death nor life, neither angels nor demons,*ᶜ* neither the present nor the future, nor any powers, ³⁹neither height nor depth, nor anything else in all creation, will be able to separate us from the love of God that is in Christ Jesus our Lord. Ps 44:22; 1Co 15:57; 2Co 4:11

Paul's Anguish Over Israel

9 I speak the truth in Christ — I am not lying, my conscience confirms it through the Holy Spirit — ²I have great sorrow and unceasing anguish in my heart. ³For I could wish that I myself were cursed and cut off from Christ for the sake of my people, those of my own race, ⁴the

---

ᵃ 28 Or *that all things work together for good to those who love God, who;* or *that in all things God works together with those who love him to bring about what is good — with those who*
ᵇ 36 Psalm 44:22   *ᶜ 38* Or *nor heavenly rulers*

people of Israel. Theirs is the adoption to sonship; theirs the divine glory, the covenants, the receiving of the law, the temple worship and the promises. [5] Theirs are the patriarchs, and from them is traced the human ancestry of the Messiah, who is God over all, forever praised![a] Amen. Jn 1:1; Heb 9:1

God's Sovereign Choice

[6] It is not as though God's word had failed. For not all who are descended from Israel are Israel. [7] Nor because they are his descendants are they all Abraham's children. On the contrary, "It is through Isaac that your offspring will be reckoned."[b] [8] In other words, it is not the children by physical descent who are God's children, but it is the children of the promise who are regarded as Abraham's offspring. [9] For this was how the promise was stated: "At the appointed time I will return, and Sarah will have a son."[c] Ge 18:10,14; Gal 6:16

[10] Not only that, but Rebekah's children were conceived at the same time by our father Isaac. [11] Yet, before the twins were born or had done anything good or bad—in order that God's purpose in election might stand: [12] not by works but by him who calls—she was told, "The older

will serve the younger."[d] [13] Just as it is written: "Jacob I loved, but Esau I hated."[e] Ge 25:21,23; Ro 8:28

[14] What then shall we say? Is God unjust? Not at all! [15] For he says to Moses, 2Ch 19:7

"I will have mercy on whom I
  have mercy,
and I will have compassion
  on whom I have
  compassion."[f]

[16] It does not, therefore, depend on human desire or effort, but on God's mercy. [17] For Scripture says to Pharaoh: "I raised you up for this very purpose, that I might display my power in you and that my name might be proclaimed in all the earth."[g] [18] Therefore God has mercy on whom he wants to have mercy, and he hardens whom he wants to harden. Ex 4:21; 9:16; 33:19

[19] One of you will say to me: "Then why does God still blame us? For who is able to resist his will?" [20] But who are you, a human being, to talk back to God? "Shall what is formed say to the one who formed it, 'Why did you make me like this?' "[h] [21] Does not the potter have the right to make out of the same lump of clay some pottery for special purposes and some for common use? 2Ti 2:20

[22] What if God, although choosing to show his wrath and

a 5 Or Messiah, who is over all. God be forever praised! Or Messiah. God who is over all be forever praised! b 7 Gen. 21:12 c 9 Gen. 18:10,14 d 12 Gen. 25:23 e 13 Mal. 1:2,3 f 15 Exodus 33:19 g 17 Exodus 9:16 h 20 Isaiah 29:16; 45:9

make his power known, bore with great patience the objects of his wrath—prepared for destruction? ²³What if he did this to make the riches of his glory known to the objects of his mercy, whom he prepared in advance for glory— ²⁴even us, whom he also called, not only from the Jews but also from the Gentiles? ²⁵As he says in Hosea: Ro 3:29; 8:30

> "I will call them 'my people'
>   who are not my people;
> and I will call her 'my loved
>   one' who is not my
>   loved one,"^a

²⁶and,

> "In the very place where it was
>   said to them,
> 'You are not my people,'
>   there they will be called
>   'children of the living
>   God.'"^b   Mt 16:16; Ro 8:14

²⁷Isaiah cries out concerning Israel:

> "Though the number of the
>   Israelites be like the
>   sand by the sea,   Ge 22:17
> only the remnant will be
>   saved.   Ro 11:5
> ²⁸For the Lord will carry out
>   his sentence on earth
> with speed and
>   finality."^c   Isa 10:22-23

²⁹It is just as Isaiah said previously:

> "Unless the Lord Almighty
>   had left us descendants,
> we would have become like
>   Sodom,
> we would have been like
>   Gomorrah."^d   Isa 13:19

Israel's Unbelief

³⁰What then shall we say? That the Gentiles, who did not pursue righteousness, have obtained it, a righteousness that is by faith; ³¹but the people of Israel, who pursued the law as the way of righteousness, have not attained their goal. ³²Why not? Because they pursued it not by faith but as if it were by works. They stumbled over the stumbling stone. ³³As it is written: Ro 1:17; 10:2-3; Gal 5:4

> "See, I lay in Zion a stone
>   that causes people to
>   stumble
> and a rock that makes them
>   fall,
> and the one who believes in
>   him will never be put to
>   shame."^e   Isa 28:16; Ro 10:11

10 Brothers and sisters, my heart's desire and prayer to God for the Israelites is that they may be saved. ²For I can testify about them that they are zealous for God, but their zeal is not based on knowledge. ³Since they did not know the righteousness of God and sought to establish their own, they did not

^a 25 Hosea 2:23   ^b 26 Hosea 1:10   ^c 28 Isaiah 10:22,23 (see Septuagint)
^d 29 Isaiah 1:9   ^e 33 Isaiah 8:14; 28:16

submit to God's righteousness. [4] Christ is the culmination of the law so that there may be righteousness for everyone who believes.

Ac 21:20; Ro 1:17; Gal 3:24

[5] Moses writes this about the righteousness that is by the law: "The person who does these things will live by them." [a] [6] But the righteousness that is by faith says: "Do not say in your heart, 'Who will ascend into heaven?'" [b] (that is, to bring Christ down) [7] "or 'Who will descend into the deep?'" [c] (that is, to bring Christ up from the dead). [8] But what does it say? "The word is near you; it is in your mouth and in your heart," [d] that is, the message concerning faith that we proclaim: [9] If you declare with your mouth, "Jesus is Lord," and believe in your heart that God raised him from the dead, you will be saved. [10] For it is with your heart that you believe and are justified, and it is with your mouth that you profess your faith and are saved. [11] As Scripture says, "Anyone who believes in him will never be put to shame." [e] [12] For there is no difference between Jew and Gentile—the same Lord is Lord of all and richly blesses all who call on him, [13] for, "Everyone who calls on the name of the Lord will be saved." [f]

Ac 2:21

[14] How, then, can they call on the one they have not believed in? And how can they believe in the one of whom they have not heard? And how can they hear without someone preaching to them? [15] And how can anyone preach unless they are sent? As it is written: "How beautiful are the feet of those who bring good news!" [g]

Isa 52:7; Na 1:15

[16] But not all the Israelites accepted the good news. For Isaiah says, "Lord, who has believed our message?" [h] [17] Consequently, faith comes from hearing the message, and the message is heard through the word about Christ. [18] But I ask: Did they not hear? Of course they did:

Col 3:16; Gal 3:2,5

"Their voice has gone out into
    all the earth,
  their words to the ends of
    the world." [i]

[19] Again I ask: Did Israel not understand? First, Moses says,

"I will make you envious by
    those who are not a
    nation;   Ro 11:11,14
  I will make you angry by
    a nation that has no
    understanding." [j]

[20] And Isaiah boldly says,

"I was found by those who did
    not seek me;

---

[a] 5 Lev. 18:5   [b] 6 Deut. 30:12   [c] 7 Deut. 30:13   [d] 8 Deut. 30:14   [e] 11 Isaiah 28:16
(see Septuagint)   [f] 13 Joel 2:32   [g] 15 Isaiah 52:7   [h] 16 Isaiah 53:1   [i] 18 Psalm 19:4
[j] 19 Deut. 32:21

I revealed myself to those
who did not ask
for me."[a]

21 But concerning Israel he says,

"All day long I have held out
my hands
to a disobedient and
obstinate people."[b]

The Remnant of Israel

11 I ask then: Did God reject his people? By no means! I am an Israelite myself, a descendant of Abraham, from the tribe of Benjamin. 2 God did not reject his people, whom he foreknew. Don't you know what Scripture says in the passage about Elijah—how he appealed to God against Israel: 3 "Lord, they have killed your prophets and torn down your altars; I am the only one left, and they are trying to kill me"[c]? 4 And what was God's answer to him? "I have reserved for myself seven thousand who have not bowed the knee to Baal."[d] 5 So too, at the present time there is a remnant chosen by grace. 6 And if by grace, then it cannot be based on works; if it were, grace would no longer be grace.   Ro 4:4; 9:27

7 What then? What the people of Israel sought so earnestly they did not obtain. The elect among them did, but the others were hardened, 8 as it is written: Ro 9:18,31

"God gave them a spirit of
stupor,
eyes that could not see
and ears that could not
hear,   Mt 13:13-15
to this very day."[e]

9 And David says:

"May their table become a
snare and a trap,
a stumbling block and a
retribution for them.
10 May their eyes be darkened so
they cannot see,
and their backs be bent
forever."[f]   Ps 69:22-23

Ingrafted Branches

11 Again I ask: Did they stumble so as to fall beyond recovery? Not at all! Rather, because of their transgression, salvation has come to the Gentiles to make Israel envious. 12 But if their transgression means riches for the world, and their loss means riches for the Gentiles, how much greater riches will their full inclusion bring!   Ac 13:46; Ro 10:19

13 I am talking to you Gentiles. Inasmuch as I am the apostle to the Gentiles, I take pride in my ministry 14 in the hope that I may somehow arouse my own people to envy and save some of them. 15 For if their rejection brought reconciliation to the world, what will their acceptance be but life from the dead? 16 If the part of

---

[a] 20 Isaiah 65:1   [b] 21 Isaiah 65:2   [c] 3 1 Kings 19:10,14   [d] 4 1 Kings 19:18
[e] 8 Deut. 29:4; Isaiah 29:10   [f] 10 Psalm 69:22,23

the dough offered as firstfruits is holy, then the whole batch is holy; if the root is holy, so are the branches. Lk 15:24,32; Ac 9:15 ^17 If some of the branches have been broken off, and you, though a wild olive shoot, have been grafted in among the others and now share in the nourishing sap from the olive root, ^18 do not consider yourself to be superior to those other branches. If you do, consider this: You do not support the root, but the root supports you. ^19 You will say then, "Branches were broken off so that I could be grafted in." ^20 Granted. But they were broken off because of unbelief, and you stand by faith. Do not be arrogant, but tremble. ^21 For if God did not spare the natural branches, he will not spare you either. 1Co 10:12; 1Ti 6:17; 1Pe 1:17 ^22 Consider therefore the kindness and sternness of God: sternness to those who fell, but kindness to you, provided that you continue in his kindness. Otherwise, you also will be cut off. ^23 And if they do not persist in unbelief, they will be grafted in, for God is able to graft them in again. ^24 After all, if you were cut out of an olive tree that is wild by nature, and contrary to nature were grafted into a cultivated olive tree, how much more readily will these, the natural branches,

be grafted into their own olive tree! Jn 15:2; 1Co 15:2; 2Co 3:16

All Israel Will Be Saved

^25 I do not want you to be ignorant of this mystery, brothers and sisters, so that you may not be conceited: Israel has experienced a hardening in part until the full number of the Gentiles has come in, ^26 and in this way^a all Israel will be saved. As it is written: Lk 21:24; Isa 45:17

> "The deliverer will come from Zion;
>   he will turn godlessness away from Jacob.
> ^27 And this is^b my covenant with them
>   when I take away their sins."^c Heb 8:10,12

^28 As far as the gospel is concerned, they are enemies for your sake; but as far as election is concerned, they are loved on account of the patriarchs, ^29 for God's gifts and his call are irrevocable. ^30 Just as you who were at one time disobedient to God have now received mercy as a result of their disobedience, ^31 so they too have now become disobedient in order that they too may now^d receive mercy as a result of God's mercy to you. ^32 For God has bound everyone over to disobedience so that he may have mercy on them all. Dt 7:8; Ro 3:9; Heb 7:21

---

^a 26 Or and so   ^b 27 Or will be   ^c 27 Isaiah 59:20,21; 27:9 (see Septuagint); Jer. 31:33,34
^d 31 Some manuscripts do not have now.

Doxology

³³Oh, the depth of the riches
of the wisdom and^a
knowledge of God! Ps 92:5
How unsearchable his
judgments,
and his paths beyond
tracing out! Job 11:7
³⁴"Who has known the mind of
the Lord?
Or who has been his
counselor?"^b Isa 40:13-14
³⁵"Who has ever given to God,
that God should repay
them?"^c Job 35:7
³⁶For from him and through
him and for him are all
things. 1Co 8:6; Col 1:16
To him be the glory forever!
Amen. Ro 16:27

A Living Sacrifice

12 Therefore, I urge you, brothers and sisters, in view of God's mercy, to offer your bodies as a living sacrifice, holy and pleasing to God—this is your true and proper worship. ²Do not conform to the pattern of this world, but be transformed by the renewing of your mind. Then you will be able to test and approve what God's will is—his good, pleasing and perfect will. Eph 4:23

Humble Service in the Body of Christ

³For by the grace given me I say to every one of you: Do not think of yourself more highly than you ought, but rather think of yourself with sober judgment, in accordance with the faith God has distributed to each of you. ⁴For just as each of us has one body with many members, and these members do not all have the same function, ⁵so in Christ we, though many, form one body, and each member belongs to all the others. ⁶We have different gifts, according to the grace given to each of us. If your gift is prophesying, then prophesy in accordance with your^d faith; ⁷if it is serving, then serve; if it is teaching, then teach; ⁸if it is to encourage, then give encouragement; if it is giving, then give generously; if it is to lead,^e do it diligently; if it is to show mercy, do it cheerfully. Ac 15:32; 2Co 9:5-13

Love in Action

⁹Love must be sincere. Hate what is evil; cling to what is good. ¹⁰Be devoted to one another in love. Honor one another above yourselves. ¹¹Never be lacking in zeal, but keep your spiritual fervor, serving the Lord. ¹²Be joyful in hope, patient in affliction, faithful in prayer. ¹³Share with the Lord's people who are in need. Practice hospitality. 1Ti 3:2; Heb 10:32,36 ¹⁴Bless those who persecute you; bless and do not curse.

---

^a 33 Or *riches and the wisdom and the*   ^b 34 Isaiah 40:13   ^c 35 Job 41:11   ^d 6 Or *the*
^e 8 Or *to provide for others*

¹⁵Rejoice with those who rejoice; mourn with those who mourn. ¹⁶Live in harmony with one another. Do not be proud, but be willing to associate with people of low position.ᵃ Do not be conceited. Mt 5:44; Ro 15:5

¹⁷Do not repay anyone evil for evil. Be careful to do what is right in the eyes of everyone. ¹⁸If it is possible, as far as it depends on you, live at peace with everyone. ¹⁹Do not take revenge, my dear friends, but leave room for God's wrath, for it is written: "It is mine to avenge; I will repay,"ᵇ says the Lord. ²⁰On the contrary: Lev 19:18; Ro 14:19; 2Co 8:21

"If your enemy is hungry, feed him;
if he is thirsty, give him something to drink.
In doing this, you will heap burning coals on his head."ᶜ Mt 5:44; Lk 6:27

²¹Do not be overcome by evil, but overcome evil with good.

Submission to Governing Authorities

13 Let everyone be subject to the governing authorities, for there is no authority except that which God has established. The authorities that exist have been established by God. ²Consequently, whoever rebels against the authority is rebelling against what God has instituted, and those who do so will bring judgment on themselves. ³For rulers hold no terror for those who do right, but for those who do wrong. Do you want to be free from fear of the one in authority? Then do what is right and you will be commended. ⁴For the one in authority is God's servant for your good. But if you do wrong, be afraid, for rulers do not bear the sword for no reason. They are God's servants, agents of wrath to bring punishment on the wrongdoer. ⁵Therefore, it is necessary to submit to the authorities, not only because of possible punishment but also as a matter of conscience. 1Th 4:6; 1Pe 2:14

⁶This is also why you pay taxes, for the authorities are God's servants, who give their full time to governing. ⁷Give to everyone what you owe them: If you owe taxes, pay taxes; if revenue, then revenue; if respect, then respect; if honor, then honor. Mt 22:17,21; Lk 23:2

Love Fulfills the Law

⁸Let no debt remain outstanding, except the continuing debt to love one another, for whoever loves others has fulfilled the law. ⁹The commandments, "You shall not commit adultery," "You shall not murder," "You shall not steal," "You shall not covet,"ᵈ and whatever other command

---

ᵃ *16* Or *willing to do menial work*   ᵇ *19* Deut. 32:35   ᶜ *20* Prov. 25:21,22
ᵈ *9* Exodus 20:13-15,17; Deut. 5:17-19,21

there may be, are summed up in this one command: "Love your neighbor as yourself."[a] [10]Love does no harm to a neighbor. Therefore love is the fulfillment of the law. Mt 19:19; 22:39-40

The Day Is Near

[11]And do this, understanding the present time: The hour has already come for you to wake up from your slumber, because our salvation is nearer now than when we first believed. [12]The night is nearly over; the day is almost here. So let us put aside the deeds of darkness and put on the armor of light. [13]Let us behave decently, as in the daytime, not in carousing and drunkenness, not in sexual immorality and debauchery, not in dissension and jealousy. [14]Rather, clothe yourselves with the Lord Jesus Christ, and do not think about how to gratify the desires of the flesh.[b] Gal 3:27; 5:19-21

The Weak and the Strong

14 Accept the one whose faith is weak, without quarreling over disputable matters. [2]One person's faith allows them to eat anything, but another, whose faith is weak, eats only vegetables. [3]The one who eats everything must not treat with contempt the one who does not, and the one who does not eat everything must not judge the one who does, for God has accepted them. [4]Who are you to judge someone else's servant? To their own master, servants stand or fall. And they will stand, for the Lord is able to make them stand. Lk 18:9

[5]One person considers one day more sacred than another; another considers every day alike. Each of them should be fully convinced in their own mind. [6]Whoever regards one day as special does so to the Lord. Whoever eats meat does so to the Lord, for they give thanks to God; and whoever abstains does so to the Lord and gives thanks to God. [7]For none of us lives for ourselves alone, and none of us dies for ourselves alone. [8]If we live, we live for the Lord; and if we die, we die for the Lord. So, whether we live or die, we belong to the Lord. [9]For this very reason, Christ died and returned to life so that he might be the Lord of both the dead and the living. Gal 2:20; Php 1:20

[10]You, then, why do you judge your brother or sister[c]? Or why do you treat them with contempt? For we will all stand before God's judgment seat. [11]It is written: Mt 7:1

"'As surely as I live,' says the Lord, Isa 49:18

---

[a] 9 Lev. 19:18   [b] 14 In contexts like this, the Greek word for *flesh* (*sarx*) refers to the sinful state of human beings, often presented as a power in opposition to the Spirit.   [c] 10 The Greek word for *brother or sister* (*adelphos*) refers here to a believer, whether man or woman, as part of God's family; also in verses 13, 15 and 21.

'every knee will bow
  before me;
every tongue will
  acknowledge God.' "[a]

¹²So then, each of us will give an account of ourselves to God.

¹³Therefore let us stop passing judgment on one another. Instead, make up your mind not to put any stumbling block or obstacle in the way of a brother or sister. ¹⁴I am convinced, being fully persuaded in the Lord Jesus, that nothing is unclean in itself. But if anyone regards something as unclean, then for that person it is unclean. ¹⁵If your brother or sister is distressed because of what you eat, you are no longer acting in love. Do not by your eating destroy someone for whom Christ died. ¹⁶Therefore do not let what you know is good be spoken of as evil. ¹⁷For the kingdom of God is not a matter of eating and drinking, but of righteousness, peace and joy in the Holy Spirit, ¹⁸because anyone who serves Christ in this way is pleasing to God and receives human approval. Ro 15:13; 1Co 8:8; 2Co 8:21

¹⁹Let us therefore make every effort to do what leads to peace and to mutual edification. ²⁰Do not destroy the work of God for the sake of food. All food is clean, but it is wrong for a person to eat anything that causes someone else to stumble. ²¹It is better not to eat meat or drink wine or to do anything else that will cause your brother or sister to fall. 1Co 8:9-13

²²So whatever you believe about these things keep between yourself and God. Blessed is the one who does not condemn himself by what he approves. ²³But whoever has doubts is condemned if they eat, because their eating is not from faith; and everything that does not come from faith is sin.[b]

15 We who are strong ought to bear with the failings of the weak and not to please ourselves. ²Each of us should please our neighbors for their good, to build them up. ³For even Christ did not please himself but, as it is written: "The insults of those who insult you have fallen on me."[c] ⁴For everything that was written in the past was written to teach us, so that through the endurance taught in the Scriptures and the encouragement they provide we might have hope. Ro 14:1,19; 1Co 10:33

⁵May the God who gives endurance and encouragement give you the same attitude of mind toward each other that Christ Jesus had, ⁶so that with one mind and one voice you may glorify the God and Father of our Lord Jesus Christ. Ps 34:3; Ro 12:16; Rev 1:6

⁷Accept one another, then, just

---

[a] 11 Isaiah 45:23   [b] 23 Some manuscripts place 16:25-27 here; others after 15:33.
[c] 3 Psalm 69:9

as Christ accepted you, in order to bring praise to God. **8**For I tell you that Christ has become a servant of the Jews*a* on behalf of God's truth, so that the promises made to the patriarchs might be confirmed **9**and, moreover, that the Gentiles might glorify God for his mercy. As it is written: Mt 15:24; Ro 14:1

"Therefore I will praise
     you among the
     Gentiles;
  I will sing the praises of
     your name."*b*

10Again, it says,

"Rejoice, you Gentiles, with
   his people."*c*

11And again,

"Praise the Lord, all you
     Gentiles;
  let all the peoples extol
     him."*d*

12And again, Isaiah says,

"The Root of Jesse will
     spring up,   Rev 5:5
  one who will arise to rule
     over the nations;
  in him the Gentiles will
     hope."*e*   Dt 32:43; 2Sa 22:50

13May the God of hope fill you with all joy and peace as you trust in him, so that you may overflow with hope by the power of the Holy Spirit.   Ro 14:17; 1Th 1:5

Paul the Minister to the Gentiles

14I myself am convinced, my brothers and sisters, that you yourselves are full of goodness, filled with knowledge and competent to instruct one another. **15**Yet I have written you quite boldly on some points to remind you of them again, because of the grace God gave me **16**to be a minister of Christ Jesus to the Gentiles. He gave me the priestly duty of proclaiming the gospel of God, so that the Gentiles might become an offering acceptable to God, sanctified by the Holy Spirit.   Ro 1:1; 12:3

17Therefore I glory in Christ Jesus in my service to God. **18**I will not venture to speak of anything except what Christ has accomplished through me in leading the Gentiles to obey God by what I have said and done — **19**by the power of signs and wonders, through the power of the Spirit of God. So from Jerusalem all the way around to Illyricum, I have fully proclaimed the gospel of Christ. **20**It has always been my ambition to preach the gospel where Christ was not known, so that I would not be building on someone else's foundation. **21**Rather, as it is written: Ac 21:19

"Those who were not told
     about him will see,

a 8 Greek *circumcision*   *b 9* 2 Samuel 22:50; Psalm 18:49   *c 10* Deut. 32:43
d 11 Psalm 117:1   *e 12* Isaiah 11:10 (see Septuagint)

and those who have
   not heard will
   understand."[a]

[22] This is why I have often been hindered from coming to you.

Isa 52:15; Ro 1:13

Paul's Plan to Visit Rome

[23] But now that there is no more place for me to work in these regions, and since I have been longing for many years to visit you, [24] I plan to do so when I go to Spain. I hope to see you while passing through and to have you assist me on my journey there, after I have enjoyed your company for a while. [25] Now, however, I am on my way to Jerusalem in the service of the Lord's people there. [26] For Macedonia and Achaia were pleased to make a contribution for the poor among the Lord's people in Jerusalem. [27] They were pleased to do it, and indeed they owe it to them. For if the Gentiles have shared in the Jews' spiritual blessings, they owe it to the Jews to share with them their material blessings. [28] So after I have completed this task and have made sure that they have received this contribution, I will go to Spain and visit you on the way. [29] I know that when I come to you, I will come in the full measure of the blessing of Christ.

Ro 1:10-11; 1Co 9:11

[30] I urge you, brothers and sisters, by our Lord Jesus Christ and by the love of the Spirit, to join me in my struggle by praying to God for me. [31] Pray that I may be kept safe from the unbelievers in Judea and that the contribution I take to Jerusalem may be favorably received by the Lord's people there, [32] so that I may come to you with joy, by God's will, and in your company be refreshed. [33] The God of peace be with you all. Amen.

Ro 16:20; 2Co 13:11; Php 4:9

Personal Greetings

16 I commend to you our sister Phoebe, a deacon[b,c] of the church in Cenchreae. [2] I ask you to receive her in the Lord in a way worthy of his people and to give her any help she may need from you, for she has been the benefactor of many people, including me.

Ac 18:18; Php 2:29

[3] Greet Priscilla[d] and Aquila, my co-workers in Christ Jesus. [4] They risked their lives for me. Not only I but all the churches of the Gentiles are grateful to them.

Ac 18:2

[5] Greet also the church that meets at their house. 1Co 16:19
   Greet my dear friend Epenetus, who was the first convert to Christ in the province of Asia.

1Co 16:15

---

[a] 21 Isaiah 52:15 (see Septuagint)   [b] 1 Or *servant*   [c] 1 The word *deacon* refers here to a Christian designated to serve with the overseers/elders of the church in a variety of ways; similarly in Phil. 1:1 and 1 Tim. 3:8,12.   [d] 3 Greek *Prisca*, a variant of *Priscilla*

[6]Greet Mary, who worked very hard for you.

[7]Greet Andronicus and Junia, my fellow Jews who have been in prison with me. They are outstanding among[a] the apostles, and they were in Christ before I was. ver 11,21

[8]Greet Ampliatus, my dear friend in the Lord.

[9]Greet Urbanus, our co-worker in Christ, and my dear friend Stachys. ver 3

[10]Greet Apelles, whose fidelity to Christ has stood the test.ver 3 Greet those who belong to the household of Aristobulus.

[11]Greet Herodion, my fellow Jew. Greet those in the household of Narcissus who are in the Lord. Ac 11:14

[12]Greet Tryphena and Tryphosa, those women who work hard in the Lord.

Greet my dear friend Persis, another woman who has worked very hard in the Lord.

[13]Greet Rufus, chosen in the Lord, and his mother, who has been a mother to me, too. Mk 15:21

[14]Greet Asyncritus, Phlegon, Hermes, Patrobas, Hermas and the other brothers and sisters with them.

[15]Greet Philologus, Julia, Nereus and his sister, and Olympas and all the Lord's people who are with them. Ac 9:13

[16]Greet one another with a holy kiss.

All the churches of Christ send greetings. 1Co 16:20; 2Co 13:12

[17]I urge you, brothers and sisters, to watch out for those who cause divisions and put obstacles in your way that are contrary to the teaching you have learned. Keep away from them. [18]For such people are not serving our Lord Christ, but their own appetites. By smooth talk and flattery they deceive the minds of naive people. [19]Everyone has heard about your obedience, so I rejoice because of you; but I want you to be wise about what is good, and innocent about what is evil. Mt 10:16; 1Co 14:20

[20]The God of peace will soon crush Satan under your feet.

The grace of our Lord Jesus be with you. 1Th 5:28

[21]Timothy, my co-worker, sends his greetings to you, as do Lucius, Jason and Sosipater, my fellow Jews. Ac 13:1; 16:1; 17:5

[22]I, Tertius, who wrote down this letter, greet you in the Lord.

[23]Gaius, whose hospitality I and the whole church here enjoy, sends you his greetings. Ac 19:29

Erastus, who is the city's director of public works, and our brother Quartus send you their greetings. [24][b] Ac 19:22; 2Ti 4:20

[a] 7 Or are esteemed by   [b] 24 Some manuscripts include here May the grace of our Lord Jesus Christ be with all of you. Amen.

25 Now to him who is able to establish you in accordance with my gospel, the message I proclaim about Jesus Christ, in keeping with the revelation of the mystery hidden for long ages past, 26 but now revealed and made known through the prophetic writings by the command of the eternal God, so that all the Gentiles might come to the obedience that comes from*a* faith — 27 to the only wise God be glory forever through Jesus Christ! Amen.

Ro 11:36

a 26 Or *that is*

1 Corinthians

1 Paul, called to be an apostle of Christ Jesus by the will of God, and our brother Sosthenes,   Ro 1:1; Eph 1:1

²To the church of God in Corinth, to those sanctified in Christ Jesus and called to be his holy people, together with all those everywhere who call on the name of our Lord Jesus Christ — their Lord and ours: Ac 18:1; Ro 1:7

³Grace and peace to you from God our Father and the Lord Jesus Christ.   Ro 1:7

Thanksgiving

⁴I always thank my God for you because of his grace given you in Christ Jesus. ⁵For in him you have been enriched in every way—with all kinds of speech and with all knowledge— ⁶God thus confirming our testimony about Christ among you. ⁷Therefore you do not lack any spiritual gift as you eagerly wait for our Lord Jesus Christ to be revealed. ⁸He will also keep you firm to the end, so that you will be blameless on the day of our Lord Jesus Christ. ⁹God is faithful, who has called you into fellowship with his Son, Jesus Christ our Lord.   Isa 49:7

A Church Divided Over Leaders

¹⁰I appeal to you, brothers and sisters,ᵃ in the name of our Lord Jesus Christ, that all of you agree with one another in what you say and that there be no divisions among you, but that you be perfectly united in mind and thought. ¹¹My brothers and sisters, some from Chloe's household have informed me that there are quarrels among you. ¹²What I mean is this: One of you says, "I follow Paul"; another, "I follow Apollos"; another, "I follow Cephasᵇ"; still another, "I follow Christ."   Jn 1:42; 1Co 3:4,22

¹³Is Christ divided? Was Paul

ᵃ 10 The Greek word for *brothers and sisters* (*adelphoi*) refers here to believers, both men and women, as part of God's family; also in verses 11 and 26; and in 2:1; 3:1; 4:6; 6:8; 7:24, 29; 10:1; 11:33; 12:1; 14:6, 20, 26, 39; 15:1, 6, 50, 58; 16:15, 20.   ᵇ 12 That is, Peter crucified for you? Were you baptized in the name of Paul? ¹⁴I thank God that I did not baptize any of you except Crispus and Gaius, ¹⁵so no one can say that you were baptized in my name. ¹⁶(Yes, I also baptized the household of Stephanas; beyond that, I don't remember if I baptized anyone else.) ¹⁷For Christ did not send me to baptize, but to preach the gospel—not with wisdom and eloquence, lest the cross of Christ be emptied of its power. Jn 4:2

Christ Crucified Is God's Power and Wisdom

¹⁸For the message of the cross is foolishness to those who are perishing, but to us who are being saved it is the power of God. ¹⁹For it is written: Ro 1:16; 2Co 2:15

"I will destroy the wisdom of
   the wise;
the intelligence of the
   intelligent I will
   frustrate."[a] Isa 29:14

²⁰Where is the wise person? Where is the teacher of the law? Where is the philosopher of this age? Has not God made foolish the wisdom of the world? ²¹For since in the wisdom of God the world through its wisdom did not know him, God was pleased through the foolishness of what was preached to save those who believe. ²²Jews demand signs and Greeks look for wisdom,

²³but we preach Christ crucified: a stumbling block to Jews and foolishness to Gentiles, ²⁴but to those whom God has called, both Jews and Greeks, Christ the power of God and the wisdom of God. ²⁵For the foolishness of God is wiser than human wisdom, and the weakness of God is stronger than human strength. 2Co 13:4; Col 2:3

²⁶Brothers and sisters, think of what you were when you were called. Not many of you were wise by human standards; not many were influential; not many were of noble birth. ²⁷But God chose the foolish things of the world to shame the wise; God chose the weak things of the world to shame the strong. ²⁸God chose the lowly things of this world and the despised things—and the things that are not—to nullify the things that are, ²⁹so that no one may boast before him. ³⁰It is because of him that you are in Christ Jesus, who has become for us wisdom from God—that is, our righteousness, holiness and redemption. ³¹Therefore, as it is written: "Let the one who boasts boast in the Lord."[b] 2Co 10:17; Eph 1:7,14; 2:9

2 And so it was with me, brothers and sisters. When I came to you, I did not come with eloquence or human wisdom as I proclaimed to you the testimony about God.[c] ²For I

---

[a] 19 Isaiah 29:14 [b] 31 Jer. 9:24 [c] 1 Some manuscripts *proclaimed to you God's mystery*

resolved to know nothing while I was with you except Jesus Christ and him crucified. ³I came to you in weakness with great fear and trembling. ⁴My message and my preaching were not with wise and persuasive words, but with a demonstration of the Spirit's power, ⁵so that your faith might not rest on human wisdom, but on God's power. Ro 15:19; 2Co 4:7; 6:7

God's Wisdom Revealed by the Spirit

⁶We do, however, speak a message of wisdom among the mature, but not the wisdom of this age or of the rulers of this age, who are coming to nothing. ⁷No, we declare God's wisdom, a mystery that has been hidden and that God destined for our glory before time began. ⁸None of the rulers of this age understood it, for if they had, they would not have crucified the Lord of glory. ⁹However, as it is written: Ac 7:2; 1Co 1:20; Eph 4:13

> "What no eye has seen,
>   what no ear has heard,
> and what no human mind has
>   conceived"ᵃ—
>   the things God has
>   prepared for those who
>   love him—

¹⁰these are the things God has revealed to us by his Spirit. Isa 65:17

The Spirit searches all things, even the deep things of God.

¹¹For who knows a person's thoughts except their own spirit within them? In the same way no one knows the thoughts of God except the Spirit of God. ¹²What we have received is not the spirit of the world, but the Spirit who is from God, so that we may understand what God has freely given us. ¹³This is what we speak, not in words taught us by human wisdom but in words taught by the Spirit, explaining spiritual realities with Spirit-taught words.ᵇ ¹⁴The person without the Spirit does not accept the things that come from the Spirit of God but considers them foolishness, and cannot understand them because they are discerned only through the Spirit. ¹⁵The person with the Spirit makes judgments about all things, but such a person is not subject to merely human judgments, ¹⁶for, 1Co 1:17-18

> "Who has known the mind of
>   the Lord
>   so as to instruct him?"ᶜ

But we have the mind of Christ.

The Church and Its Leaders

3 Brothers and sisters, I could not address you as people who live by the Spirit but as people who are still worldly—mere infants in Christ. ²I gave you milk, not solid food, for you were not yet ready for it. Indeed, you

---

ᵃ 9 Isaiah 64:4   ᵇ 13 Or *Spirit, interpreting spiritual truths to those who are spiritual*
ᶜ 16 Isaiah 40:13

are still not ready. ³You are still worldly. For since there is jealousy and quarreling among you, are you not worldly? Are you not acting like mere humans? ⁴For when one says, "I follow Paul," and another, "I follow Apollos," are you not mere human beings? Gal 5:20

⁵What, after all, is Apollos? And what is Paul? Only servants, through whom you came to believe — as the Lord has assigned to each his task. ⁶I planted the seed, Apollos watered it, but God has been making it grow. ⁷So neither the one who plants nor the one who waters is anything, but only God, who makes things grow. ⁸The one who plants and the one who waters have one purpose, and they will each be rewarded according to their own labor. ⁹For we are co-workers in God's service; you are God's field, God's building. 2Co 6:1; Eph 2:20-22

¹⁰By the grace God has given me, I laid a foundation as a wise builder, and someone else is building on it. But each one should build with care. ¹¹For no one can lay any foundation other than the one already laid, which is Jesus Christ. ¹²If anyone builds on this foundation using gold, silver, costly stones, wood, hay or straw, ¹³their work will be shown for what it is, because the Day will bring it to light. It will be revealed with fire, and the fire will test the quality of each

person's work. ¹⁴If what has been built survives, the builder will receive a reward. ¹⁵If it is burned up, the builder will suffer loss but yet will be saved — even though only as one escaping through the flames. 2Th 1:7-10; Jude 23

¹⁶Don't you know that you yourselves are God's temple and that God's Spirit dwells in your midst? ¹⁷If anyone destroys God's temple, God will destroy that person; for God's temple is sacred, and you together are that temple. 2Co 6:16

¹⁸Do not deceive yourselves. If any of you think you are wise by the standards of this age, you should become "fools" so that you may become wise. ¹⁹For the wisdom of this world is foolishness in God's sight. As it is written: "He catches the wise in their craftiness"ᵃ; ²⁰and again, "The Lord knows that the thoughts of the wise are futile."ᵇ ²¹So then, no more boasting about human leaders! All things are yours, ²²whether Paul or Apollos or Cephasᶜ or the world or life or death or the present or the future — all are yours, ²³and you are of Christ, and Christ is of God. 2Co 10:7

The Nature of True Apostleship

4 This, then, is how you ought to regard us: as servants of Christ and as those entrusted with the mysteries God has revealed. ²Now it is required that

ᵃ 19 Job 5:13   ᵇ 20 Psalm 94:11   ᶜ 22 That is, Peter

those who have been given a trust must prove faithful. [3]I care very little if I am judged by you or by any human court; indeed, I do not even judge myself. [4]My conscience is clear, but that does not make me innocent. It is the Lord who judges me. [5]Therefore judge nothing before the appointed time; wait until the Lord comes. He will bring to light what is hidden in darkness and will expose the motives of the heart. At that time each will receive their praise from God.   Ro 2:1,29

[6]Now, brothers and sisters, I have applied these things to myself and Apollos for your benefit, so that you may learn from us the meaning of the saying, "Do not go beyond what is written." Then you will not be puffed up in being a follower of one of us over against the other. [7]For who makes you different from anyone else? What do you have that you did not receive? And if you did receive it, why do you boast as though you did not? Jn 3:27; 1Co 1:12

[8]Already you have all you want! Already you have become rich! You have begun to reign—and that without us! How I wish that you really had begun to reign so that we also might reign with you! [9]For it seems to me that God has put us apostles on display at the end of the procession, like those condemned to die in the arena. We have been made a spectacle to the whole universe, to angels as well as to human beings. [10]We are fools for Christ, but you are so wise in Christ! We are weak, but you are strong! You are honored, we are dishonored! [11]To this very hour we go hungry and thirsty, we are in rags, we are brutally treated, we are homeless. [12]We work hard with our own hands. When we are cursed, we bless; when we are persecuted, we endure it; [13]when we are slandered, we answer kindly. We have become the scum of the earth, the garbage of the world—right up to this moment.   Ac 17:18; Ro 8:35

Paul's Appeal and Warning

[14]I am writing this not to shame you but to warn you as my dear children. [15]Even if you had ten thousand guardians in Christ, you do not have many fathers, for in Christ Jesus I became your father through the gospel. [16]Therefore I urge you to imitate me. [17]For this reason I have sent to you Timothy, my son whom I love, who is faithful in the Lord. He will remind you of my way of life in Christ Jesus, which agrees with what I teach everywhere in every church.   1Co 7:17; 1Th 1:6; 2:11

[18]Some of you have become arrogant, as if I were not coming to you. [19]But I will come to you very soon, if the Lord is willing, and then I will find out not only how these arrogant people are talking, but what power they have. [20]For the kingdom of God is not a mat-

ter of talk but of power. ²¹What do you prefer? Shall I come to you with a rod of discipline, or shall I come in love and with a gentle spirit?   Ro 15:13; 2Co 1:15-16

Dealing With a Case of Incest

5 It is actually reported that there is sexual immorality among you, and of a kind that even pagans do not tolerate: A man is sleeping with his father's wife. ²And you are proud! Shouldn't you rather have gone into mourning and have put out of your fellowship the man who has been doing this? ³For my part, even though I am not physically present, I am with you in spirit. As one who is present with you in this way, I have already passed judgment in the name of our Lord Jesus on the one who has been doing this. ⁴So when you are assembled and I am with you in spirit, and the power of our Lord Jesus is present, ⁵hand this man over to Satan for the destruction of the flesh,ᵃ,ᵇ so that his spirit may be saved on the day of the Lord.   1Ti 1:20; 2Th 3:6

⁶Your boasting is not good. Don't you know that a little yeast leavens the whole batch of dough? ⁷Get rid of the old yeast, so that you may be a new unleavened batch—as you really are.

For Christ, our Passover lamb, has been sacrificed. ⁸Therefore let us keep the Festival, not with the old bread leavened with malice and wickedness, but with the unleavened bread of sincerity and truth.   Gal 5:9; 1Pe 1:19

⁹I wrote to you in my letter not to associate with sexually immoral people — ¹⁰not at all meaning the people of this world who are immoral, or the greedy and swindlers, or idolaters. In that case you would have to leave this world. ¹¹But now I am writing to you that you must not associate with anyone who claims to be a brother or sisterᶜ but is sexually immoral or greedy, an idolater or slanderer, a drunkard or swindler. Do not even eat with such people.   1Co 10:27; Eph 5:11

¹²What business is it of mine to judge those outside the church? Are you not to judge those inside? ¹³God will judge those outside. "Expel the wicked person from among you."ᵈ   Mk 4:11; 1Co 6:1-4

Lawsuits Among Believers

6 If any of you has a dispute with another, do you dare to take it before the ungodly for judgment instead of before the Lord's people? ²Or do you not know that the Lord's people will judge the world? And if you are

---

ᵃ 5 In contexts like this, the Greek word for *flesh* (*sarx*) refers to the sinful state of human beings, often presented as a power in opposition to the Spirit.   ᵇ 5 Or *of his body*
ᶜ 11 The Greek word for *brother or sister* (*adelphos*) refers here to a believer, whether man or woman, as part of God's family; also in 8:11, 13.   ᵈ 13 Deut. 13:5; 17:7; 19:19; 21:21; 22:21,24; 24:7

to judge the world, are you not competent to judge trivial cases? ³Do you not know that we will judge angels? How much more the things of this life! ⁴Therefore, if you have disputes about such matters, do you ask for a ruling from those whose way of life is scorned in the church? ⁵I say this to shame you. Is it possible that there is nobody among you wise enough to judge a dispute between believers? ⁶But instead, one brother takes another to court—and this in front of unbelievers! Mt 19:28; 2Co 6:14-15

⁷The very fact that you have lawsuits among you means you have been completely defeated already. Why not rather be wronged? Why not rather be cheated? ⁸Instead, you yourselves cheat and do wrong, and you do this to your brothers and sisters. ⁹Or do you not know that wrongdoers will not inherit the kingdom of God? Do not be deceived: Neither the sexually immoral nor idolaters nor adulterers nor men who have sex with men*ᵃ* ¹⁰nor thieves nor the greedy nor drunkards nor slanderers nor swindlers will inherit the kingdom of God. ¹¹And that is what some of you were. But you were washed, you were sanctified, you were justified in the name of the Lord Jesus Christ and by the Spirit of our God. 1Co 1:2; Gal 5:21

Sexual Immorality

¹²"I have the right to do anything," you say—but not everything is beneficial. "I have the right to do anything"—but I will not be mastered by anything. ¹³You say, "Food for the stomach and the stomach for food, and God will destroy them both." The body, however, is not meant for sexual immorality but for the Lord, and the Lord for the body. ¹⁴By his power God raised the Lord from the dead, and he will raise us also. ¹⁵Do you not know that your bodies are members of Christ himself? Shall I then take the members of Christ and unite them with a prostitute? Never! ¹⁶Do you not know that he who unites himself with a prostitute is one with her in body? For it is said, "The two will become one flesh."*ᵇ* ¹⁷But whoever is united with the Lord is one with him in spirit.*ᶜ* Jn 17:21-23; Gal 2:20

¹⁸Flee from sexual immorality. All other sins a person commits are outside the body, but whoever sins sexually, sins against their own body. ¹⁹Do you not know that your bodies are temples of the Holy Spirit, who is in you, whom you have received from God? You are not your own; ²⁰you were bought at a price. Therefore honor God with your bodies. Ro 6:12; Heb 13:4; Rev 5:9

ᵃ 9 The words *men who have sex with men* translate two Greek words that refer to the passive and active participants in homosexual acts.   *ᵇ 16* Gen. 2:24   *ᶜ 17* Or *in the Spirit*

Concerning Married Life

7 Now for the matters you wrote about: "It is good for a man not to have sexual relations with a woman." [2]But since sexual immorality is occurring, each man should have sexual relations with his own wife, and each woman with her own husband. [3]The husband should fulfill his marital duty to his wife, and likewise the wife to her husband. [4]The wife does not have authority over her own body but yields it to her husband. In the same way, the husband does not have authority over his own body but yields it to his wife. [5]Do not deprive each other except perhaps by mutual consent and for a time, so that you may devote yourselves to prayer. Then come together again so that Satan will not tempt you because of your lack of self-control. [6]I say this as a concession, not as a command. [7]I wish that all of you were as I am. But each of you has your own gift from God; one has this gift, another has that. 1Co 9:5; 12:4,11

[8]Now to the unmarried[a] and the widows I say: It is good for them to stay unmarried, as I do. [9]But if they cannot control themselves, they should marry, for it is better to marry than to burn with passion. 1Ti 5:14

[10]To the married I give this command (not I, but the Lord): A wife must not separate from her husband. [11]But if she does, she must remain unmarried or else be reconciled to her husband. And a husband must not divorce his wife. Mal 2:14-16; Mt 5:32; Lk 16:18

[12]To the rest I say this (I, not the Lord): If any brother has a wife who is not a believer and she is willing to live with him, he must not divorce her. [13]And if a woman has a husband who is not a believer and he is willing to live with her, she must not divorce him. [14]For the unbelieving husband has been sanctified through his wife, and the unbelieving wife has been sanctified through her believing husband. Otherwise your children would be unclean, but as it is, they are holy. Mal 2:15

[15]But if the unbeliever leaves, let it be so. The brother or the sister is not bound in such circumstances; God has called us to live in peace. [16]How do you know, wife, whether you will save your husband? Or, how do you know, husband, whether you will save your wife? Ro 14:19; 1Pe 3:1

Concerning Change of Status

[17]Nevertheless, each person should live as a believer in whatever situation the Lord has assigned to them, just as God has called them. This is the rule I lay down in all the churches. [18]Was a man already circumcised

---

[a] 8 Or *widowers*

when he was called? He should not become uncircumcised. Was a man uncircumcised when he was called? He should not be circumcised. ¹⁹Circumcision is nothing and uncircumcision is nothing. Keeping God's commands is what counts. ²⁰Each person should remain in the situation they were in when God called them.

²¹Were you a slave when you were called? Don't let it trouble you—although if you can gain your freedom, do so. ²²For the one who was a slave when called to faith in the Lord is the Lord's freed person; similarly, the one who was free when called is Christ's slave. ²³You were bought at a price; do not become slaves of human beings. ²⁴Brothers and sisters, each person, as responsible to God, should remain in the situation they were in when God called them.   1Co 6:20; Eph 6:6

Concerning the Unmarried

²⁵Now about virgins: I have no command from the Lord, but I give a judgment as one who by the Lord's mercy is trustworthy. ²⁶Because of the present crisis, I think that it is good for a man to remain as he is. ²⁷Are you pledged to a woman? Do not seek to be released. Are you free from such a commitment? Do not look for a wife. ²⁸But if you do marry, you have not sinned; and if a virgin marries, she has not sinned. But those who marry will face many troubles in this life, and I want to spare you this.   1Ti 1:13,16

²⁹What I mean, brothers and sisters, is that the time is short. From now on those who have wives should live as if they do not; ³⁰those who mourn, as if they did not; those who are happy, as if they were not; those who buy something, as if it were not theirs to keep; ³¹those who use the things of the world, as if not engrossed in them. For this world in its present form is passing away.   Ro 13:11-12; 1Jn 2:17

³²I would like you to be free from concern. An unmarried man is concerned about the Lord's affairs—how he can please the Lord. ³³But a married man is concerned about the affairs of this world—how he can please his wife— ³⁴and his interests are divided. An unmarried woman or virgin is concerned about the Lord's affairs: Her aim is to be devoted to the Lord in both body and spirit. But a married woman is concerned about the affairs of this world—how she can please her husband. ³⁵I am saying this for your own good, not to restrict you, but that you may live in a right way in undivided devotion to the Lord.   Ps 86:11; 1Ti 5:5

³⁶If anyone is worried that he might not be acting honorably toward the virgin he is engaged to, and if his passions are too

strong[a] and he feels he ought to marry, he should do as he wants. He is not sinning. They should get married. [37]But the man who has settled the matter in his own mind, who is under no compulsion but has control over his own will, and who has made up his mind not to marry the virgin — this man also does the right thing. [38]So then, he who marries the virgin does right, but he who does not marry her does better.[b]

[39]A woman is bound to her husband as long as he lives. But if her husband dies, she is free to marry anyone she wishes, but he must belong to the Lord. [40]In my judgment, she is happier if she stays as she is — and I think that I too have the Spirit of God. Ro 7:2-3

Concerning Food Sacrificed to Idols

8 Now about food sacrificed to idols: We know that "We all possess knowledge." But knowledge puffs up while love builds up. [2]Those who think they know something do not yet know as they ought to know. [3]But whoever loves God is known by God.[c]

[4]So then, about eating food sacrificed to idols: We know that "An idol is nothing at all in the world" and that "There is no God but one." [5]For even if there are so-called gods, whether in heaven or on earth (as indeed there are many "gods" and many "lords"), [6]yet for us there is but one God, the Father, from whom all things came and for whom we live; and there is but one Lord, Jesus Christ, through whom all things came and through whom we live. Ro 11:36; Mal 2:10

[7]But not everyone possesses this knowledge. Some people are still so accustomed to idols that when they eat sacrificial food they think of it as having been sacrificed to a god, and since their conscience is weak, it is defiled. [8]But food does not bring us near to God; we are no worse if we do not eat, and no better if we do. Ro 14:14,17

[9]Be careful, however, that the exercise of your rights does not become a stumbling block to the weak. [10]For if someone with a weak conscience sees you, with all your knowledge, eating in an idol's temple, won't that person be emboldened to eat what is sacrificed to idols? [11]So this weak brother or sister, for whom Christ

---

[a] 36 Or *if she is getting beyond the usual age for marriage* [b] 36-38 Or *[36]If anyone thinks he is not treating his daughter properly, and if she is getting along in years* (or *if her passions are too strong*), *and he feels she ought to marry, he should do as he wants. He is not sinning. He should let her get married. [37]But the man who has settled the matter in his own mind, who is under no compulsion but has control over his own will, and who has made up his mind to keep the virgin unmarried — this man also does the right thing. [38]So then, he who gives his virgin in marriage does right, but he who does not give her in marriage does better.* [c] 2,3 An early manuscript and another ancient witness *think they have knowledge do not yet know as they ought to know. [3]But whoever loves truly knows.*

died, is destroyed by your knowledge. [12] When you sin against them in this way and wound their weak conscience, you sin against Christ. [13] Therefore, if what I eat causes my brother or sister to fall into sin, I will never eat meat again, so that I will not cause them to fall. Mt 18:6; Ro 14:21; Gal 5:13

Paul's Rights as an Apostle

9 Am I not free? Am I not an apostle? Have I not seen Jesus our Lord? Are you not the result of my work in the Lord? [2] Even though I may not be an apostle to others, surely I am to you! For you are the seal of my apostleship in the Lord. 1Co 3:6; 2Co 3:2-3

[3] This is my defense to those who sit in judgment on me. [4] Don't we have the right to food and drink? [5] Don't we have the right to take a believing wife along with us, as do the other apostles and the Lord's brothers and Cephas[a]? [6] Or is it only I and Barnabas who lack the right to not work for a living? Ac 4:36; 1Th 2:6

[7] Who serves as a soldier at his own expense? Who plants a vineyard and does not eat its grapes? Who tends a flock and does not drink the milk? [8] Do I say this merely on human authority? Doesn't the Law say the same thing? [9] For it is written in the Law of Moses: "Do not muzzle an ox while it is treading out the grain."[b] Is it about oxen that God is concerned? [10] Surely he says this for us, doesn't he? Yes, this was written for us, because whoever plows and threshes should be able to do so in the hope of sharing in the harvest. [11] If we have sown spiritual seed among you, is it too much if we reap a material harvest from you? [12] If others have this right of support from you, shouldn't we have it all the more? Ro 15:27; 2Ti 2:6

But we did not use this right. On the contrary, we put up with anything rather than hinder the gospel of Christ.

[13] Don't you know that those who serve in the temple get their food from the temple, and that those who serve at the altar share in what is offered on the altar? [14] In the same way, the Lord has commanded that those who preach the gospel should receive their living from the gospel. Mt 10:10

[15] But I have not used any of these rights. And I am not writing this in the hope that you will do such things for me, for I would rather die than allow anyone to deprive me of this boast. [16] For when I preach the gospel, I cannot boast, since I am compelled to preach. Woe to me if I do not preach the gospel! [17] If I preach voluntarily, I have a reward; if not voluntarily, I am simply discharging the trust committed to me. [18] What then is my reward? Just this: that in preach-

---

[a] 5 That is, Peter   [b] 9 Deut. 25:4

ing the gospel I may offer it free of charge, and so not make full use of my rights as a preacher of the gospel. 1Co 3:8,14; Gal 2:7

Paul's Use of His Freedom

¹⁹Though I am free and belong to no one, I have made myself a slave to everyone, to win as many as possible. ²⁰To the Jews I became like a Jew, to win the Jews. To those under the law I became like one under the law (though I myself am not under the law), so as to win those under the law. ²¹To those not having the law I became like one not having the law (though I am not free from God's law but am under Christ's law), so as to win those not having the law. ²²To the weak I became weak, to win the weak. I have become all things to all people so that by all possible means I might save some. ²³I do all this for the sake of the gospel, that I may share in its blessings. Ro 2:12,14

The Need for Self-Discipline

²⁴Do you not know that in a race all the runners run, but only one gets the prize? Run in such a way as to get the prize. ²⁵Everyone who competes in the games goes into strict training. They do it to get a crown that will not last, but we do it to get a crown that will last forever. ²⁶Therefore I do not run like someone running aimlessly; I do not fight like a boxer beating the air. ²⁷No, I strike a blow to my body and make it my slave so that after I have preached to others, I myself will not be disqualified for the prize. Ro 8:13; 2Ti 4:7

Warnings From Israel's History

10 For I do not want you to be ignorant of the fact, brothers and sisters, that our ancestors were all under the cloud and that they all passed through the sea. ²They were all baptized into Moses in the cloud and in the sea. ³They all ate the same spiritual food ⁴and drank the same spiritual drink; for they drank from the spiritual rock that accompanied them, and that rock was Christ. ⁵Nevertheless, God was not pleased with most of them; their bodies were scattered in the wilderness. Nu 14:29; Heb 3:17

⁶Now these things occurred as examples to keep us from setting our hearts on evil things as they did. ⁷Do not be idolaters, as some of them were; as it is written: "The people sat down to eat and drink^a and got up to indulge in revelry."^a ⁸We should not commit sexual immorality, as some of them did—and in one day twenty-three thousand of them died. ⁹We should not test Christ,^b as some of them did—and were killed by snakes. ¹⁰And do not grumble, as some of them did—and were killed by the destroying angel. Ex 12:23; Nu 21:5-6

---

^a 7 Exodus 32:6   ^b 9 Some manuscripts *test the Lord*

¹¹These things happened to them as examples and were written down as warnings for us, on whom the culmination of the ages has come. ¹²So, if you think you are standing firm, be careful that you don't fall! ¹³No temptation[a] has overtaken you except what is common to mankind. And God is faithful; he will not let you be tempted[a] beyond what you can bear. But when you are tempted,[a] he will also provide a way out so that you can endure it. Ro 11:20; 2Pe 2:9

Idol Feasts and the Lord's Supper

¹⁴Therefore, my dear friends, flee from idolatry. ¹⁵I speak to sensible people; judge for yourselves what I say. ¹⁶Is not the cup of thanksgiving for which we give thanks a participation in the blood of Christ? And is not the bread that we break a participation in the body of Christ? ¹⁷Because there is one loaf, we, who are many, are one body, for we all share the one loaf. Mt 26:26-28

¹⁸Consider the people of Israel: Do not those who eat the sacrifices participate in the altar? ¹⁹Do I mean then that food sacrificed to an idol is anything, or that an idol is anything? ²⁰No, but the sacrifices of pagans are offered to demons, not to God, and I do not want you to be participants with demons. ²¹You cannot drink the cup of the Lord and the cup of demons too; you cannot have a part in both the Lord's table and the table of demons. ²²Are we trying to arouse the Lord's jealousy? Are we stronger than he? Dt 32:16,21; Isa 45:9

The Believer's Freedom

²³"I have the right to do anything," you say—but not everything is beneficial. "I have the right to do anything"—but not everything is constructive. ²⁴No one should seek their own good, but the good of others. Ro 15:1-2

²⁵Eat anything sold in the meat market without raising questions of conscience, ²⁶for, "The earth is the Lord's, and everything in it."[b] Ps 24:1; Ac 10:15

²⁷If an unbeliever invites you to a meal and you want to go, eat whatever is put before you without raising questions of conscience. ²⁸But if someone says to you, "This has been offered in sacrifice," then do not eat it, both for the sake of the one who told you and for the sake of conscience. ²⁹I am referring to the other person's conscience, not yours. For why is my freedom being judged by another's conscience? ³⁰If I take part in the meal with thankfulness, why am I denounced because of something I thank God for? Lk 10:7; Ro 14:6

---

[a] 13 The Greek for *temptation* and *tempted* can also mean *testing* and *tested*.
[b] 26 Psalm 24:1

[31] So whether you eat or drink or whatever you do, do it all for the glory of God. [32] Do not cause anyone to stumble, whether Jews, Greeks or the church of God — [33] even as I try to please everyone in every way. For I am not seeking my own good but the good of many, so that they may

11 be saved. [1] Follow my example, as I follow the example of Christ. Ro 11:14; 15:2

On Covering the Head in Worship

[2] I praise you for remembering me in everything and for holding to the traditions just as I passed them on to you. [3] But I want you to realize that the head of every man is Christ, and the head of the woman is man,[a] and the head of Christ is God. [4] Every man who prays or prophesies with his head covered dishonors his head. [5] But every woman who prays or prophesies with her head uncovered dishonors her head — it is the same as having her head shaved. [6] For if a woman does not cover her head, she might as well have her hair cut off; but if it is a disgrace for a woman to have her hair cut off or her head shaved, then she should cover her head. 1Co 4:17; 15:2-3

[7] A man ought not to cover his head,[b] since he is the image and glory of God; but woman is the glory of man. [8] For man did not come from woman, but woman from man; [9] neither was man created for woman, but woman for man. [10] It is for this reason that a woman ought to have authority over her own[c] head, because of the angels. [11] Nevertheless, in the Lord woman is not independent of man, nor is man independent of woman. [12] For as woman came from man, so also man is born of woman. But everything comes from God. Ge 2:21-23; Jas 3:9

[13] Judge for yourselves: Is it proper for a woman to pray to God with her head uncovered? [14] Does not the very nature of things teach you that if a man has long hair, it is a disgrace to him, [15] but that if a woman has long hair, it is her glory? For long hair is given to her as a covering. [16] If anyone wants to be contentious about this, we have no other practice — nor do the churches of God. Ro 11:36; 1Co 7:17

Correcting an Abuse of the Lord's Supper

11:23-25pp — Mt 26:26-28; Mk 14:22-24; Lk 22:17-20

[17] In the following directives I

---

a 3 Or *of the wife is her husband*   *b 4-7* Or *4Every man who prays or prophesies with long hair dishonors his head. 5But every woman who prays or prophesies with no covering of hair dishonors her head — she is just like one of the "shorn women." 6If a woman has no covering, let her be for now with short hair; but since it is a disgrace for a woman to have her hair shorn or shaved, she should grow it again. 7A man ought not to have long hair*   *c 10* Or *have a sign of authority on her* have no praise for you, for your meetings do more harm than good. [18] In the first place, I hear that when you come together as a church, there are divisions among you, and to some extent I believe it. [19] No doubt there have to be differences among you to show which of you have God's approval. [20] So then, when you come together, it is not the Lord's Supper you eat, [21] for when you are eating, some of you go ahead with your own private suppers. As a result, one person remains hungry and another gets drunk. [22] Don't you have homes to eat and drink in? Or do you despise the church of God by humiliating those who have nothing? What shall I say to you? Shall I praise you? Certainly not in this matter!   1Co 1:10-12; 1Jn 2:19

[23] For I received from the Lord what I also passed on to you: The Lord Jesus, on the night he was betrayed, took bread, [24] and when he had given thanks, he broke it and said, "This is my body, which is for you; do this in remembrance of me." [25] In the same way, after supper he took the cup, saying, "This cup is the new covenant in my blood; do this, whenever you drink it, in remembrance of me." [26] For whenever you eat this bread and drink this cup, you proclaim the Lord's death until he comes.   Mt 26:26-28; Mk 14:22-24

[27] So then, whoever eats the bread or drinks the cup of the Lord in an unworthy manner will be guilty of sinning against the body and blood of the Lord. [28] Everyone ought to examine themselves before they eat of the bread and drink from the cup. [29] For those who eat and drink without discerning the body of Christ eat and drink judgment on themselves. [30] That is why many among you are weak and sick, and a number of you have fallen asleep. [31] But if we were more discerning with regard to ourselves, we would not come under such judgment. [32] Nevertheless, when we are judged in this way by the Lord, we are being disciplined so that we will not be finally condemned with the world.   Ps 94:12

[33] So then, my brothers and sisters, when you gather to eat, you should all eat together. [34] Anyone who is hungry should eat something at home, so that when you meet together it may not result in judgment.   ver 21-22

And when I come I will give further directions.   1Co 4:19

Concerning Spiritual Gifts

12 Now about the gifts of the Spirit, brothers and sisters, I do not want you to be uninformed. [2] You know that when you were pagans, somehow or other you were influenced and led astray to mute idols. [3] Therefore I want you to know that no one who is speaking by the Spirit of God says, "Jesus be cursed," and

no one can say, "Jesus is Lord," except by the Holy Spirit. Ro 1:11

⁴There are different kinds of gifts, but the same Spirit distributes them. ⁵There are different kinds of service, but the same Lord. ⁶There are different kinds of working, but in all of them and in everyone it is the same God at work. Ro 12:4-8; Eph 4:11; Heb 2:4

⁷Now to each one the manifestation of the Spirit is given for the common good. ⁸To one there is given through the Spirit a message of wisdom, to another a message of knowledge by means of the same Spirit, ⁹to another faith by the same Spirit, to another gifts of healing by that one Spirit, ¹⁰to another miraculous powers, to another prophecy, to another distinguishing between spirits, to another speaking in different kinds of tongues,ᵃ and to still another the interpretation of tongues.ᵃ ¹¹All these are the work of one and the same Spirit, and he distributes them to each one, just as he determines. Eph 4:12; 1Co 2:6

Unity and Diversity in the Body

¹²Just as a body, though one, has many parts, but all its many parts form one body, so it is with Christ. ¹³For we were all baptized byᵇ one Spirit so as to form one body—whether Jews or Gentiles, slave or free—and we were all given the one Spirit to drink. ¹⁴Even so the body is not made up of one part but of many. Gal 3:28

¹⁵Now if the foot should say, "Because I am not a hand, I do not belong to the body," it would not for that reason stop being part of the body. ¹⁶And if the ear should say, "Because I am not an eye, I do not belong to the body," it would not for that reason stop being part of the body. ¹⁷If the whole body were an eye, where would the sense of hearing be? If the whole body were an ear, where would the sense of smell be? ¹⁸But in fact God has placed the parts in the body, every one of them, just as he wanted them to be. ¹⁹If they were all one part, where would the body be? ²⁰As it is, there are many parts, but one body. Ro 12:5

²¹The eye cannot say to the hand, "I don't need you!" And the head cannot say to the feet, "I don't need you!" ²²On the contrary, those parts of the body that seem to be weaker are indispensable, ²³and the parts that we think are less honorable we treat with special honor. And the parts that are unpresentable are treated with special modesty, ²⁴while our presentable parts need no special treatment. But God has put the body together, giving greater honor to the parts that lacked it, ²⁵so that there should be no division in the body, but that its parts should have equal

ᵃ 10 Or languages; also in verse 28   ᵇ 13 Or with; or in

concern for each other. [26]If one part suffers, every part suffers with it; if one part is honored, every part rejoices with it.

[27]Now you are the body of Christ, and each one of you is a part of it. [28]And God has placed in the church first of all apostles, second prophets, third teachers, then miracles, then gifts of healing, of helping, of guidance, and of different kinds of tongues. [29]Are all apostles? Are all prophets? Are all teachers? Do all work miracles? [30]Do all have gifts of healing? Do all speak in tongues[a]? Do all interpret? [31]Now eagerly desire the greater gifts.
1Co 14:1,39; Eph 4:11

Love Is Indispensable

And yet I will show you the most excellent way.

13 If I speak in the tongues[b] of men or of angels, but do not have love, I am only a resounding gong or a clanging cymbal. [2]If I have the gift of prophecy and can fathom all mysteries and all knowledge, and if I have a faith that can move mountains, but do not have love, I am nothing. [3]If I give all I possess to the poor and give over my body to hardship that I may boast,[c] but do not have love, I gain nothing.
Mt 6:2; 1Co 14:2

[4]Love is patient, love is kind. It does not envy, it does not boast, it is not proud. [5]It does not dishonor others, it is not self-seeking, it is not easily angered, it keeps no record of wrongs. [6]Love does not delight in evil but rejoices with the truth. [7]It always protects, always trusts, always hopes, always perseveres.
1Co 10:24; 2Jn 4

[8]Love never fails. But where there are prophecies, they will cease; where there are tongues, they will be stilled; where there is knowledge, it will pass away. [9]For we know in part and we prophesy in part, [10]but when completeness comes, what is in part disappears. [11]When I was a child, I talked like a child, I thought like a child, I reasoned like a child. When I became a man, I put the ways of childhood behind me. [12]For now we see only a reflection as in a mirror; then we shall see face to face. Now I know in part; then I shall know fully, even as I am fully known.
1Co 8:3; 2Co 5:7; 1Jn 3:2

[13]And now these three remain: faith, hope and love. But the greatest of these is love.
1Co 16:14

Intelligibility in Worship

14 Follow the way of love and eagerly desire gifts of the Spirit, especially prophecy. [2]For anyone who speaks in a tongue[d] does not speak to people but to God. Indeed, no one understands them; they utter mysteries by the

---

[a] 30 Or *other languages*   [b] 1 Or *languages*   [c] 3 Some manuscripts *body to the flames*
[d] 2 Or *in another language*; also in verses 4, 13, 14, 19, 26 and 27

Spirit. ³But the one who prophesies speaks to people for their strengthening, encouraging and comfort. ⁴Anyone who speaks in a tongue edifies themselves, but the one who prophesies edifies the church. ⁵I would like every one of you to speak in tongues,ᵃ but I would rather have you prophesy. The one who prophesies is greater than the one who speaks in tongues,ᵃ unless someone interprets, so that the church may be edified.   Nu 11:29; 1Co 12:31

⁶Now, brothers and sisters, if I come to you and speak in tongues, what good will I be to you, unless I bring you some revelation or knowledge or prophecy or word of instruction? ⁷Even in the case of lifeless things that make sounds, such as the pipe or harp, how will anyone know what tune is being played unless there is a distinction in the notes? ⁸Again, if the trumpet does not sound a clear call, who will get ready for battle? ⁹So it is with you. Unless you speak intelligible words with your tongue, how will anyone know what you are saying? You will just be speaking into the air. ¹⁰Undoubtedly there are all sorts of languages in the world, yet none of them is without meaning. ¹¹If then I do not grasp the meaning of what someone is saying, I am a foreigner to the speaker, and the speaker is a foreigner to me. ¹²So it is with you. Since you are eager for gifts of the Spirit, try to excel in those that build up the church.   Nu 10:9; Jer 4:19

¹³For this reason the one who speaks in a tongue should pray that they may interpret what they say. ¹⁴For if I pray in a tongue, my spirit prays, but my mind is unfruitful. ¹⁵So what shall I do? I will pray with my spirit, but I will also pray with my understanding; I will sing with my spirit, but I will also sing with my understanding. ¹⁶Otherwise when you are praising God in the Spirit, how can someone else, who is now put in the position of an inquirer,ᵇ say "Amen" to your thanksgiving, since they do not know what you are saying? ¹⁷You are giving thanks well enough, but no one else is edified.   1Ch 16:36; 1Co 11:24

¹⁸I thank God that I speak in tongues more than all of you. ¹⁹But in the church I would rather speak five intelligible words to instruct others than ten thousand words in a tongue.   ver 6

²⁰Brothers and sisters, stop thinking like children. In regard to evil be infants, but in your thinking be adults. ²¹In the Law it is written: Jn 10:34; Eph 4:14

"With other tongues
  and through the lips of
   foreigners

ᵃ 5 Or *in other languages*; also in verses 6, 18, 22, 23 and 39   ᵇ 16 The Greek word for *inquirer* is a technical term for someone not fully initiated into a religion; also in verses 23 and 24.

I will speak to this people,
    but even then they will not
        listen to me, Isa 28:11-12
        says the Lord."[a]

[22] Tongues, then, are a sign, not for believers but for unbelievers; prophecy, however, is not for unbelievers but for believers. [23] So if the whole church comes together and everyone speaks in tongues, and inquirers or unbelievers come in, will they not say that you are out of your mind? [24] But if an unbeliever or an inquirer comes in while everyone is prophesying, they are convicted of sin and are brought under judgment by all, [25] as the secrets of their hearts are laid bare. So they will fall down and worship God, exclaiming, "God is really among you!" Isa 45:14; Zec 8:23; Ac 2:13

Good Order in Worship

[26] What then shall we say, brothers and sisters? When you come together, each of you has a hymn, or a word of instruction, a revelation, a tongue or an interpretation. Everything must be done so that the church may be built up. [27] If anyone speaks in a tongue, two — or at the most three — should speak, one at a time, and someone must interpret. [28] If there is no interpreter, the speaker should keep quiet in the church and speak to himself and to God. Ro 14:19; 1Co 12:7-10

[29] Two or three prophets should speak, and the others should weigh carefully what is said. [30] And if a revelation comes to someone who is sitting down, the first speaker should stop. [31] For you can all prophesy in turn so that everyone may be instructed and encouraged. [32] The spirits of prophets are subject to the control of prophets. [33] For God is not a God of disorder but of peace — as in all the congregations of the Lord's people. 1Co 12:10

[34] Women[b] should remain silent in the churches. They are not allowed to speak, but must be in submission, as the law says. [35] If they want to inquire about something, they should ask their own husbands at home; for it is disgraceful for a woman to speak in the church.[c] 1Ti 2:11-12

[36] Or did the word of God originate with you? Or are you the only people it has reached? [37] If anyone thinks they are a prophet or otherwise gifted by the Spirit, let them acknowledge that what I am writing to you is the Lord's command. [38] But if anyone ignores this, they will themselves be ignored.[d] 2Co 10:7; 1Jn 4:6

[39] Therefore, my brothers and sisters, be eager to prophesy, and do not forbid speaking

---

[a] 21 Isaiah 28:11,12   [b] 33,34 Or peace. As in all the congregations of the Lord's people, [34] women   [c] 34,35 In a few manuscripts these verses come after verse 40.   [d] 38 Some manuscripts But anyone who is ignorant of this will be ignorant

in tongues. **40**But everything should be done in a fitting and orderly way. 1Co 12:31

The Resurrection of Christ

15 Now, brothers and sisters, I want to remind you of the gospel I preached to you, which you received and on which you have taken your stand. **2**By this gospel you are saved, if you hold firmly to the word I preached to you. Otherwise, you have believed in vain. Ro 1:16; 11:22

3For what I received I passed on to you as of first importance*a*: that Christ died for our sins according to the Scriptures, **4**that he was buried, that he was raised on the third day according to the Scriptures, **5**and that he appeared to Cephas,*b* and then to the Twelve. **6**After that, he appeared to more than five hundred of the brothers and sisters at the same time, most of whom are still living, though some have fallen asleep. **7**Then he appeared to James, then to all the apostles, **8**and last of all he appeared to me also, as to one abnormally born. Ac 1:3-4; 9:3-6,17

9For I am the least of the apostles and do not even deserve to be called an apostle, because I persecuted the church of God. **10**But by the grace of God I am what I am, and his grace to me was not without effect. No, I worked harder than all of them—yet not I, but the grace of God that was

with me. **11**Whether, then, it is I or they, this is what we preach, and this is what you believed. 2Co 11:23

The Resurrection of the Dead

12But if it is preached that Christ has been raised from the dead, how can some of you say that there is no resurrection of the dead? **13**If there is no resurrection of the dead, then not even Christ has been raised. **14**And if Christ has not been raised, our preaching is useless and so is your faith. **15**More than that, we are then found to be false witnesses about God, for we have testified about God that he raised Christ from the dead. But he did not raise him if in fact the dead are not raised. **16**For if the dead are not raised, then Christ has not been raised either. **17**And if Christ has not been raised, your faith is futile; you are still in your sins. **18**Then those also who have fallen asleep in Christ are lost. **19**If only for this life we have hope in Christ, we are of all people most to be pitied.Ac 2:24; Ro 4:25

20But Christ has indeed been raised from the dead, the firstfruits of those who have fallen asleep. **21**For since death came through a man, the resurrection of the dead comes also through a man. **22**For as in Adam all die, so in Christ all will be made alive. **23**But each in turn: Christ, the firstfruits; then, when he

---

a 3 Or *you at the first*   *b* 5 That is, Peter

comes, those who belong to him. ²⁴Then the end will come, when he hands over the kingdom to God the Father after he has destroyed all dominion, authority and power. ²⁵For he must reign until he has put all his enemies under his feet. ²⁶The last enemy to be destroyed is death. ²⁷For he "has put everything under his feet."ᵃ Now when it says that "everything" has been put under him, it is clear that this does not include God himself, who put everything under Christ. ²⁸When he has done this, then the Son himself will be made subject to him who put everything under him, so that God may be all in all.   1Co 3:23; Php 3:21

²⁹Now if there is no resurrection, what will those do who are baptized for the dead? If the dead are not raised at all, why are people baptized for them? ³⁰And as for us, why do we endanger ourselves every hour? ³¹I face death every day—yes, just as surely as I boast about you in Christ Jesus our Lord. ³²If I fought wild beasts in Ephesus with no more than human hopes, what have I gained? If the dead are not raised,   2Co 1:8; 11:26

"Let us eat and drink,
    for tomorrow we die."ᵇ

³³Do not be misled: "Bad company corrupts good character."ᶜ ³⁴Come back to your senses as you ought, and stop sinning; for there are some who are ignorant of God—I say this to your shame.   Isa 22:13; Lk 12:19

The Resurrection Body

³⁵But someone will ask, "How are the dead raised? With what kind of body will they come?" ³⁶How foolish! What you sow does not come to life unless it dies. ³⁷When you sow, you do not plant the body that will be, but just a seed, perhaps of wheat or of something else. ³⁸But God gives it a body as he has determined, and to each kind of seed he gives its own body. ³⁹Not all flesh is the same: People have one kind of flesh, animals have another, birds another and fish another. ⁴⁰There are also heavenly bodies and there are earthly bodies; but the splendor of the heavenly bodies is one kind, and the splendor of the earthly bodies is another. ⁴¹The sun has one kind of splendor, the moon another and the stars another; and star differs from star in splendor.   Eze 37:3; Jn 12:24

⁴²So will it be with the resurrection of the dead. The body that is sown is perishable, it is raised imperishable; ⁴³it is sown in dishonor, it is raised in glory; it is sown in weakness, it is raised in power; ⁴⁴it is sown a natural body, it is raised a spiritual body.   Mt 13:43

If there is a natural body, there

ᵃ 27 Psalm 8:6   ᵇ 32 Isaiah 22:13   ᶜ 33 From the Greek poet Menander is also a spiritual body. ⁴⁵So it is written: "The first man Adam became a living being"ᵃ; the last Adam, a life-giving spirit. ⁴⁶The spiritual did not come first, but the natural, and after that the spiritual. ⁴⁷The first man was of the dust of the earth; the second man is of heaven. ⁴⁸As was the earthly man, so are those who are of the earth; and as is the heavenly man, so also are those who are of heaven. ⁴⁹And just as we have borne the image of the earthly man, so shall weᵇ bear the image of the heavenly man.   Ge 5:3; Ro 8:29

⁵⁰I declare to you, brothers and sisters, that flesh and blood cannot inherit the kingdom of God, nor does the perishable inherit the imperishable. ⁵¹Listen, I tell you a mystery: We will not all sleep, but we will all be changed — ⁵²in a flash, in the twinkling of an eye, at the last trumpet. For the trumpet will sound, the dead will be raised imperishable, and we will be changed. ⁵³For the perishable must clothe itself with the imperishable, and the mortal with immortality. ⁵⁴When the perishable has been clothed with the imperishable, and the mortal with immortality, then the saying that is written will come true: "Death has been swallowed up in victory."ᶜ   Mt 24:31; 2Co 5:2,4

⁵⁵"Where, O death, is your victory?
    Where, O death, is your sting?"ᵈ

⁵⁶The sting of death is sin, and the power of sin is the law. ⁵⁷But thanks be to God! He gives us the victory through our Lord Jesus Christ.   Hos 13:14; Ro 4:15; 8:37

⁵⁸Therefore, my dear brothers and sisters, stand firm. Let nothing move you. Always give yourselves fully to the work of the Lord, because you know that your labor in the Lord is not in vain.   1Co 16:10

The Collection for the Lord's People

16 Now about the collection for the Lord's people: Do what I told the Galatian churches to do. ²On the first day of every week, each one of you should set aside a sum of money in keeping with your income, saving it up, so that when I come no collections will have to be made. ³Then, when I arrive, I will give letters of introduction to the men you approve and send them with your gift to Jerusalem. ⁴If it seems advisable for me to go also, they will accompany me.   Ac 20:7; 24:17

Personal Requests

⁵After I go through Macedonia, I will come to you — for I will

---

ᵃ 45 Gen. 2:7   ᵇ 49 Some early manuscripts *so let us*   ᶜ 54 Isaiah 25:8
ᵈ 55 Hosea 13:14

be going through Macedonia. ⁶Perhaps I will stay with you for a while, or even spend the winter, so that you can help me on my journey, wherever I go. ⁷For I do not want to see you now and make only a passing visit; I hope to spend some time with you, if the Lord permits. ⁸But I will stay on at Ephesus until Pentecost, ⁹because a great door for effective work has opened to me, and there are many who oppose me.   Ac 18:21; 1Co 4:19

¹⁰When Timothy comes, see to it that he has nothing to fear while he is with you, for he is carrying on the work of the Lord, just as I am. ¹¹No one, then, should treat him with contempt. Send him on his way in peace so that he may return to me. I am expecting him along with the brothers.   1Co 15:58; 1Ti 4:12

¹²Now about our brother Apollos: I strongly urged him to go to you with the brothers. He was quite unwilling to go now, but he will go when he has the opportunity.   Ac 18:24; 1Co 1:12

¹³Be on your guard; stand firm in the faith; be courageous; be strong. ¹⁴Do everything in love.   1Co 14:1; Php 1:27

¹⁵You know that the household of Stephanas were the first converts in Achaia, and they have devoted themselves to the service of the Lord's people. I urge you, brothers and sisters, ¹⁶to submit to such people and to everyone who joins in the work and labors at it. ¹⁷I was glad when Stephanas, Fortunatus and Achaicus arrived, because they have supplied what was lacking from you. ¹⁸For they refreshed my spirit and yours also. Such men deserve recognition.   2Co 11:9; Php 2:29

Final Greetings

¹⁹The churches in the province of Asia send you greetings. Aquila and Priscilla[a] greet you warmly in the Lord, and so does the church that meets at their house. ²⁰All the brothers and sisters here send you greetings. Greet one another with a holy kiss.   Ro 16:5,16

²¹I, Paul, write this greeting in my own hand.   Gal 6:11; Col 4:18

²²If anyone does not love the Lord, let that person be cursed! Come, Lord[b]!   Ro 9:3; Eph 6:24

²³The grace of the Lord Jesus be with you.   Ro 16:20

²⁴My love to all of you in Christ Jesus. Amen.[c]

---

[a] 19 Greek *Prisca*, a variant of *Priscilla*   [b] 22 The Greek for *Come, Lord* reproduces an Aramaic expression (*Marana tha*) used by early Christians.   [c] 24 Some manuscripts do not have *Amen.*

2 Corinthians

1

Paul, an apostle of Christ Jesus by the will of God, and Timothy our brother, Col 1:1; 2Ti 1:1

To the church of God in Corinth, together with all his holy people throughout Achaia: Ac 18:12

²Grace and peace to you from God our Father and the Lord Jesus Christ. Ro 1:7

Praise to the God of All Comfort

³Praise be to the God and Father of our Lord Jesus Christ, the Father of compassion and the God of all comfort, ⁴who comforts us in all our troubles, so that we can comfort those in any trouble with the comfort we ourselves receive from God. ⁵For just as we share abundantly in the sufferings of Christ, so also our comfort abounds through Christ. ⁶If we are distressed, it is for your comfort and salvation; if we are comforted, it is for your comfort, which produces in you patient endurance of the same sufferings we suffer. ⁷And our hope for you is firm, because we know that just as you share in our sufferings, so also you share in our comfort. 2Co 4:10,15; Eph 1:3

⁸We do not want you to be uninformed, brothers and sisters,ᵃ about the troubles we experienced in the province of Asia. We were under great pressure, far beyond our ability to endure, so that we despaired of life itself. ⁹Indeed, we felt we had received the sentence of death. But this happened that we might not rely on ourselves but on God, who raises the dead. ¹⁰He has delivered us from such a deadly peril, and he will deliver us again. On him we have set our hope that he will continue to deliver us, ¹¹as you help us by your prayers. Then many will give thanks on

---

ᵃ 8 The Greek word for *brothers and sisters* (*adelphoi*) refers here to believers, both men and women, as part of God's family; also in 8:1; 13:11.

our behalf for the gracious favor granted us in answer to the prayers of many. Ro 15:30; 2Co 4:15

Paul's Change of Plans

[12] Now this is our boast: Our conscience testifies that we have conducted ourselves in the world, and especially in our relations with you, with integrity[a] and godly sincerity. We have done so, relying not on worldly wisdom but on God's grace. [13] For we do not write you anything you cannot read or understand. And I hope that, [14] as you have understood us in part, you will come to understand fully that you can boast of us just as we will boast of you in the day of the Lord Jesus. 1Co 1:8; 2:1,4,13

[15] Because I was confident of this, I wanted to visit you first so that you might benefit twice. [16] I wanted to visit you on my way to Macedonia and to come back to you from Macedonia, and then to have you send me on my way to Judea. [17] Was I fickle when I intended to do this? Or do I make my plans in a worldly manner so that in the same breath I say both "Yes, yes" and "No, no"?

[18] But as surely as God is faithful, our message to you is not "Yes" and "No." [19] For the Son of God, Jesus Christ, who was preached among you by us — by me and Silas[b] and Timothy — was not "Yes" and "No," but in him it has always been "Yes." [20] For no matter how many promises God has made, they are "Yes" in Christ. And so through him the "Amen" is spoken by us to the glory of God. [21] Now it is God who makes both us and you stand firm in Christ. He anointed us, [22] set his seal of ownership on us, and put his Spirit in our hearts as a deposit, guaranteeing what is to come. 2Co 5:5; 1Jn 2:20,27

[23] I call God as my witness — and I stake my life on it — that it was in order to spare you that I did not return to Corinth. [24] Not that we lord it over your faith, but we work with you for your joy, because it is by faith you stand firm. [2:1] So I made up my mind that I would not make another painful visit to you. [2] For if I grieve you, who is left to make me glad but you whom I have grieved? [3] I wrote as I did, so that when I came I would not be distressed by those who should have made me rejoice. I had confidence in all of you, that you would all share my joy. [4] For I wrote you out of great distress and anguish of heart and with many tears, not to grieve you but to let you know the depth of my love for you. 2Co 7:8,12; 12:21

Forgiveness for the Offender

[5] If anyone has caused grief, he has not so much grieved me as he has grieved all of you to some extent — not to put it too severe-

a 12 Many manuscripts holiness   b 19 Greek Silvanus, a variant of Silas ly. ⁶The punishment inflicted on him by the majority is sufficient. ⁷Now instead, you ought to forgive and comfort him, so that he will not be overwhelmed by excessive sorrow. ⁸I urge you, therefore, to reaffirm your love for him. ⁹Another reason I wrote you was to see if you would stand the test and be obedient in everything. ¹⁰Anyone you forgive, I also forgive. And what I have forgiven — if there was anything to forgive — I have forgiven in the sight of Christ for your sake, ¹¹in order that Satan might not outwit us. For we are not unaware of his schemes.   2Co 10:6; Gal 6:1

Ministers of the New Covenant

¹²Now when I went to Troas to preach the gospel of Christ and found that the Lord had opened a door for me, ¹³I still had no peace of mind, because I did not find my brother Titus there. So I said goodbye to them and went on to Macedonia.   Ac 16:8; 2Co 7:5-6,13

¹⁴But thanks be to God, who always leads us as captives in Christ's triumphal procession and uses us to spread the aroma of the knowledge of him everywhere. ¹⁵For we are to God the pleasing aroma of Christ among those who are being saved and those who are perishing. ¹⁶To the one we are an aroma that brings death; to the other, an aroma that brings life. And who is equal to such a task? ¹⁷Unlike

so many, we do not peddle the word of God for profit. On the contrary, in Christ we speak before God with sincerity, as those sent from God.   Lk 2:34; 2Co 1:12

3 Are we beginning to commend ourselves again? Or do we need, like some people, letters of recommendation to you or from you? ²You yourselves are our letter, written on our hearts, known and read by everyone. ³You show that you are a letter from Christ, the result of our ministry, written not with ink but with the Spirit of the living God, not on tablets of stone but on tablets of human hearts.   Jer 31:33

⁴Such confidence we have through Christ before God. ⁵Not that we are competent in ourselves to claim anything for ourselves, but our competence comes from God. ⁶He has made us competent as ministers of a new covenant — not of the letter but of the Spirit; for the letter kills, but the Spirit gives life.   Jn 6:63

The Greater Glory of the New Covenant

⁷Now if the ministry that brought death, which was engraved in letters on stone, came with glory, so that the Israelites could not look steadily at the face of Moses because of its glory, transitory though it was, ⁸will not the ministry of the Spirit be even more glorious? ⁹If the ministry that brought condemnation

was glorious, how much more glorious is the ministry that brings righteousness! [10] For what was glorious has no glory now in comparison with the surpassing glory. [11] And if what was transitory came with glory, how much greater is the glory of that which lasts! Ex 34:29-35; Ro 1:17

[12] Therefore, since we have such a hope, we are very bold. [13] We are not like Moses, who would put a veil over his face to prevent the Israelites from seeing the end of what was passing away. [14] But their minds were made dull, for to this day the same veil remains when the old covenant is read. It has not been removed, because only in Christ is it taken away. [15] Even to this day when Moses is read, a veil covers their hearts. [16] But whenever anyone turns to the Lord, the veil is taken away. [17] Now the Lord is the Spirit, and where the Spirit of the Lord is, there is freedom. [18] And we all, who with unveiled faces contemplate[a] the Lord's glory, are being transformed into his image with ever-increasing glory, which comes from the Lord, who is the Spirit. Ro 8:29; 1Co 13:12

Present Weakness and Resurrection Life

4 Therefore, since through God's mercy we have this ministry, we do not lose heart.

[2] Rather, we have renounced secret and shameful ways; we do not use deception, nor do we distort the word of God. On the contrary, by setting forth the truth plainly we commend ourselves to everyone's conscience in the sight of God. [3] And even if our gospel is veiled, it is veiled to those who are perishing. [4] The god of this age has blinded the minds of unbelievers, so that they cannot see the light of the gospel that displays the glory of Christ, who is the image of God. [5] For what we preach is not ourselves, but Jesus Christ as Lord, and ourselves as your servants for Jesus' sake. [6] For God, who said, "Let light shine out of darkness,"[b] made his light shine in our hearts to give us the light of the knowledge of God's glory displayed in the face of Christ. Ge 1:3; 2Pe 1:19

[7] But we have this treasure in jars of clay to show that this all-surpassing power is from God and not from us. [8] We are hard pressed on every side, but not crushed; perplexed, but not in despair; [9] persecuted, but not abandoned; struck down, but not destroyed. [10] We always carry around in our body the death of Jesus, so that the life of Jesus may also be revealed in our body. [11] For we who are alive are always being given over to death for Jesus' sake, so that his life may also be revealed in our

a 18 Or reflect   b 6 Gen. 1:3

mortal body. [12] So then, death is at work in us, but life is at work in you. 1Co 2:5; 2Co 7:5; Heb 13:5

[13] It is written: "I believed; therefore I have spoken."[a] Since we have that same spirit of[b] faith, we also believe and therefore speak, [14] because we know that the one who raised the Lord Jesus from the dead will also raise us with Jesus and present us with you to himself. [15] All this is for your benefit, so that the grace that is reaching more and more people may cause thanksgiving to overflow to the glory of God. 2Co 1:11; Eph 5:27

[16] Therefore we do not lose heart. Though outwardly we are wasting away, yet inwardly we are being renewed day by day. [17] For our light and momentary troubles are achieving for us an eternal glory that far outweighs them all. [18] So we fix our eyes not on what is seen, but on what is unseen, since what is seen is temporary, but what is unseen is eternal. Ro 8:24; Heb 11:1

Awaiting the New Body

5 For we know that if the earthly tent we live in is destroyed, we have a building from God, an eternal house in heaven, not built by human hands. [2] Meanwhile we groan, longing to be clothed instead with our heavenly dwelling, [3] because when we are clothed, we will not be found naked. [4] For while we are in this tent, we groan and are burdened, because we do not wish to be unclothed but to be clothed instead with our heavenly dwelling, so that what is mortal may be swallowed up by life. [5] Now the one who has fashioned us for this very purpose is God, who has given us the Spirit as a deposit, guaranteeing what is to come. Ro 8:23; 1Co 15:53-54

[6] Therefore we are always confident and know that as long as we are at home in the body we are away from the Lord. [7] For we live by faith, not by sight. [8] We are confident, I say, and would prefer to be away from the body and at home with the Lord. [9] So we make it our goal to please him, whether we are at home in the body or away from it. [10] For we must all appear before the judgment seat of Christ, so that each of us may receive what is due us for the things done while in the body, whether good or bad. Ro 14:10; Eph 6:8

The Ministry of Reconciliation

[11] Since, then, we know what it is to fear the Lord, we try to persuade others. What we are is plain to God, and I hope it is also plain to your conscience. [12] We are not trying to commend ourselves to you again, but are giving you an opportunity to take pride in us, so that you can answer those who take pride in

---

[a] 13 Psalm 116:10 (see Septuagint)   [b] 13 Or *Spirit-given*

what is seen rather than in what is in the heart. [13] If we are "out of our mind," as some say, it is for God; if we are in our right mind, it is for you. [14] For Christ's love compels us, because we are convinced that one died for all, and therefore all died. [15] And he died for all, that those who live should no longer live for themselves but for him who died for them and was raised again. Ro 14:7-9; Gal 2:20

[16] So from now on we regard no one from a worldly point of view. Though we once regarded Christ in this way, we do so no longer. [17] Therefore, if anyone is in Christ, the new creation has come:[a] The old has gone, the new is here! [18] All this is from God, who reconciled us to himself through Christ and gave us the ministry of reconciliation: [19] that God was reconciling the world to himself in Christ, not counting people's sins against them. And he has committed to us the message of reconciliation. [20] We are therefore Christ's ambassadors, as though God were making his appeal through us. We implore you on Christ's behalf: Be reconciled to God. [21] God made him who had no sin to be sin[b] for us, so that in him we might become the righteousness of God. 1Pe 2:22,24; 1Jn 3:5

6 As God's co-workers we urge you not to receive God's grace in vain. [2] For he says, 1Co 3:9

"In the time of my favor I
heard you,
and in the day of salvation I
helped you."[c]

I tell you, now is the time of God's favor, now is the day of salvation. Ps 69:13; Isa 55:6

Paul's Hardships

[3] We put no stumbling block in anyone's path, so that our ministry will not be discredited. [4] Rather, as servants of God we commend ourselves in every way: in great endurance; in troubles, hardships and distresses; [5] in beatings, imprisonments and riots; in hard work, sleepless nights and hunger; [6] in purity, understanding, patience and kindness; in the Holy Spirit and in sincere love; [7] in truthful speech and in the power of God; with weapons of righteousness in the right hand and in the left; [8] through glory and dishonor, bad report and good report; genuine, yet regarded as impostors; [9] known, yet regarded as unknown; dying, and yet we live on; beaten, and yet not killed; [10] sorrowful, yet always rejoicing; poor, yet making many rich; having nothing, and yet possessing everything. Ro 8:32; 2Co 1:8-10

[11] We have spoken freely to you, Corinthians, and opened wide our hearts to you. [12] We are not withholding our affection from you,

---

a 17 Or *Christ, that person is a new creation.*   *b* 21 Or *be a sin offering*   *c* 2 Isaiah 49:8

but you are withholding yours from us. ¹³As a fair exchange — I speak as to my children — open wide your hearts also.   1Co 4:14

Warning Against Idolatry

¹⁴Do not be yoked together with unbelievers. For what do righteousness and wickedness have in common? Or what fellowship can light have with darkness? ¹⁵What harmony is there between Christ and Belial[a]? Or what does a believer have in common with an unbeliever? ¹⁶What agreement is there between the temple of God and idols? For we are the temple of the living God. As God has said:

"I will live with them
    and walk among them,
and I will be their God,
    and they will be my
        people."[b]   1Co 3:16; 5:9-10

¹⁷Therefore,

"Come out from them   Rev 18:4
    and be separate,
        says the Lord.
Touch no unclean thing,
    and I will receive you."[c]

¹⁸And,

"I will be a Father to you,
    and you will be my sons
        and daughters,
        says the Lord Almighty."[d]

7 Therefore, since we have these promises, dear friends, let us purify ourselves from everything that contaminates body and spirit, perfecting holiness out of reverence for God.   2Co 6:17-18

Paul's Joy Over the Church's Repentance

²Make room for us in your hearts. We have wronged no one, we have corrupted no one, we have exploited no one. ³I do not say this to condemn you; I have said before that you have such a place in our hearts that we would live or die with you. ⁴I have spoken to you with great frankness; I take great pride in you. I am greatly encouraged; in all our troubles my joy knows no bounds.   2Co 6:10-13

⁵For when we came into Macedonia, we had no rest, but we were harassed at every turn — conflicts on the outside, fears within. ⁶But God, who comforts the downcast, comforted us by the coming of Titus, ⁷and not only by his coming but also by the comfort you had given him. He told us about your longing for me, your deep sorrow, your ardent concern for me, so that my joy was greater than ever.   2Co 2:13; 4:8

⁸Even if I caused you sorrow by my letter, I do not regret it. Though I did regret it — I see that my letter hurt you, but only for a

_a 15_ Greek _Beliar_, a variant of _Belial_   _b 16_ Lev. 26:12; Jer. 32:38; Ezek. 37:27
_c 17_ Isaiah 52:11; Ezek. 20:34,41   _d 18_ 2 Samuel 7:14; 7:8

little while — [9]yet now I am happy, not because you were made sorry, but because your sorrow led you to repentance. For you became sorrowful as God intended and so were not harmed in any way by us. [10]Godly sorrow brings repentance that leads to salvation and leaves no regret, but worldly sorrow brings death. [11]See what this godly sorrow has produced in you: what earnestness, what eagerness to clear yourselves, what indignation, what alarm, what longing, what concern, what readiness to see justice done. At every point you have proved yourselves to be innocent in this matter. [12]So even though I wrote to you, it was neither on account of the one who did the wrong nor on account of the injured party, but rather that before God you could see for yourselves how devoted to us you are. [13]By all this we are encouraged.   1Co 5:1-2; 2Co 2:2,4

In addition to our own encouragement, we were especially delighted to see how happy Titus was, because his spirit has been refreshed by all of you. [14]I had boasted to him about you, and you have not embarrassed me. But just as everything we said to you was true, so our boasting about you to Titus has proved to be true as well. [15]And his affection for you is all the greater when he remembers that you were all obedient, receiving him with fear and trembling. [16]I am glad I can have complete confidence in you.   2Co 2:9; Php 2:12

The Collection for the Lord's People

8 And now, brothers and sisters, we want you to know about the grace that God has given the Macedonian churches. [2]In the midst of a very severe trial, their overflowing joy and their extreme poverty welled up in rich generosity. [3]For I testify that they gave as much as they were able, and even beyond their ability. Entirely on their own, [4]they urgently pleaded with us for the privilege of sharing in this service to the Lord's people. [5]And they exceeded our expectations: They gave themselves first of all to the Lord, and then by the will of God also to us. [6]So we urged Titus, just as he had earlier made a beginning, to bring also to completion this act of grace on your part. [7]But since you excel in everything — in faith, in speech, in knowledge, in complete earnestness and in the love we have kindled in you[a] — see that you also excel in this grace of giving.   1Co 1:5; 2Co 9:8

[8]I am not commanding you, but I want to test the sincerity of your love by comparing it with the earnestness of others. [9]For you know the grace of our Lord Jesus Christ, that though he was

---

[a] 7 Some manuscripts *and in your love for us*

rich, yet for your sake he became poor, so that you through his poverty might become rich. 1Co 7:6

[10] And here is my judgment about what is best for you in this matter. Last year you were the first not only to give but also to have the desire to do so. [11] Now finish the work, so that your eager willingness to do it may be matched by your completion of it, according to your means. [12] For if the willingness is there, the gift is acceptable according to what one has, not according to what one does not have. Mk 12:43-44

[13] Our desire is not that others might be relieved while you are hard pressed, but that there might be equality. [14] At the present time your plenty will supply what they need, so that in turn their plenty will supply what you need. The goal is equality, [15] as it is written: "The one who gathered much did not have too much, and the one who gathered little did not have too little."[a] Ex 16:18

Titus Sent to Receive the Collection

[16] Thanks be to God, who put into the heart of Titus the same concern I have for you. [17] For Titus not only welcomed our appeal, but he is coming to you with much enthusiasm and on his own initiative. [18] And we are sending along with him the brother who is praised by all the churches for

his service to the gospel. [19] What is more, he was chosen by the churches to accompany us as we carry the offering, which we administer in order to honor the Lord himself and to show our eagerness to help. [20] We want to avoid any criticism of the way we administer this liberal gift. [21] For we are taking pains to do what is right, not only in the eyes of the Lord but also in the eyes of man. Ro 12:17; 14:18; 1Co 16:3-4

[22] In addition, we are sending with them our brother who has often proved to us in many ways that he is zealous, and now even more so because of his great confidence in you. [23] As for Titus, he is my partner and co-worker among you; as for our brothers, they are representatives of the churches and an honor to Christ. [24] Therefore show these men the proof of your love and the reason for our pride in you, so that the churches can see it. 2Co 9:2; Php 2:25

9 There is no need for me to write to you about this service to the Lord's people. [2] For I know your eagerness to help, and I have been boasting about it to the Macedonians, telling them that since last year you in Achaia were ready to give; and your enthusiasm has stirred most of them to action. [3] But I am sending the brothers in order that our boasting about you in this matter should not prove hollow, but

---

[a] 15 Exodus 16:18

that you may be ready, as I said you would be. [4]For if any Macedonians come with me and find you unprepared, we — not to say anything about you — would be ashamed of having been so confident. [5]So I thought it necessary to urge the brothers to visit you in advance and finish the arrangements for the generous gift you had promised. Then it will be ready as a generous gift, not as one grudgingly given. Php 4:17

Generosity Encouraged

[6]Remember this: Whoever sows sparingly will also reap sparingly, and whoever sows generously will also reap generously. [7]Each of you should give what you have decided in your heart to give, not reluctantly or under compulsion, for God loves a cheerful giver. [8]And God is able to bless you abundantly, so that in all things at all times, having all that you need, you will abound in every good work. [9]As it is written: Eph 3:20; Php 4:19

"They have freely scattered
their gifts to the poor;
their righteousness endures
forever."[a]

[10]Now he who supplies seed to the sower and bread for food will also supply and increase your store of seed and will enlarge the harvest of your righteousness. [11]You will be enriched in every way so that

you can be generous on every occasion, and through us your generosity will result in thanksgiving to God. Ps 112:9; Isa 55:10; Hos 10:12

[12]This service that you perform is not only supplying the needs of the Lord's people but is also overflowing in many expressions of thanks to God. [13]Because of the service by which you have proved yourselves, others will praise God for the obedience that accompanies your confession of the gospel of Christ, and for your generosity in sharing with them and with everyone else. [14]And in their prayers for you their hearts will go out to you, because of the surpassing grace God has given you. [15]Thanks be to God for his indescribable gift! Mt 9:8; Ro 5:15-16

Paul's Defense of His Ministry

10 By the humility and gentleness of Christ, I appeal to you — I, Paul, who am "timid" when face to face with you, but "bold" toward you when away! [2]I beg you that when I come I may not have to be as bold as I expect to be toward some people who think that we live by the standards of this world. [3]For though we live in the world, we do not wage war as the world does. [4]The weapons we fight with are not the weapons of the world. On the contrary, they have divine power to demolish strongholds. [5]We demolish arguments

[a] 9 Psalm 112:9

and every pretension that sets itself up against the knowledge of God, and we take captive every thought to make it obedient to Christ. [6]And we will be ready to punish every act of disobedience, once your obedience is complete. Jer 1:10; 2Co 2:9

[7]You are judging by appearances.[a] If anyone is confident that they belong to Christ, they should consider again that we belong to Christ just as much as they do. [8]So even if I boast somewhat freely about the authority the Lord gave us for building you up rather than tearing you down, I will not be ashamed of it. [9]I do not want to seem to be trying to frighten you with my letters. [10]For some say, "His letters are weighty and forceful, but in person he is unimpressive and his speaking amounts to nothing." [11]Such people should realize that what we are in our letters when we are absent, we will be in our actions when we are present. 1Co 1:17; 2:3

[12]We do not dare to classify or compare ourselves with some who commend themselves. When they measure themselves by themselves and compare themselves with themselves, they are not wise. [13]We, however, will not boast beyond proper limits, but will confine our boasting to the sphere of service God himself has assigned to us, a sphere that also includes you. [14]We are not going too far in our boasting, as would be the case if we had not come to you, for we did get as far as you with the gospel of Christ. [15]Neither do we go beyond our limits by boasting of work done by others. Our hope is that, as your faith continues to grow, our sphere of activity among you will greatly expand, [16]so that we can preach the gospel in the regions beyond you. For we do not want to boast about work already done in someone else's territory. [17]But, "Let the one who boasts boast in the Lord."[b] [18]For it is not the one who commends himself who is approved, but the one whom the Lord commends. Ro 2:29; 1Co 4:5

Paul and the False Apostles

11 I hope you will put up with me in a little foolishness. Yes, please put up with me! [2]I am jealous for you with a godly jealousy. I promised you to one husband, to Christ, so that I might present you as a pure virgin to him. [3]But I am afraid that just as Eve was deceived by the serpent's cunning, your minds may somehow be led astray from your sincere and pure devotion to Christ. [4]For if someone comes to you and preaches a Jesus other than the Jesus we preached, or if you receive a different spirit from the Spirit you received, or a different gospel from the one you

a 7 Or *Look at the obvious facts*   b 17 Jer. 9:24

accepted, you put up with it easily enough.

[5] I do not think I am in the least inferior to those "super-apostles."[a] [6] I may indeed be untrained as a speaker, but I do have knowledge. We have made this perfectly clear to you in every way. [7] Was it a sin for me to lower myself in order to elevate you by preaching the gospel of God to you free of charge? [8] I robbed other churches by receiving support from them so as to serve you. [9] And when I was with you and needed something, I was not a burden to anyone, for the brothers who came from Macedonia supplied what I needed. I have kept myself from being a burden to you in any way, and will continue to do so. [10] As surely as the truth of Christ is in me, nobody in the regions of Achaia will stop this boasting of mine. [11] Why? Because I do not love you? God knows I do! 1Co 1:17; Eph 3:4

[12] And I will keep on doing what I am doing in order to cut the ground from under those who want an opportunity to be considered equal with us in the things they boast about. [13] For such people are false apostles, deceitful workers, masquerading as apostles of Christ. [14] And no wonder, for Satan himself masquerades as an angel of light. [15] It is not surprising, then, if his servants also masquerade as servants of righteousness. Their end will be what their actions deserve. Php 3:19; Rev 2:2

Paul Boasts About His Sufferings

[16] I repeat: Let no one take me for a fool. But if you do, then tolerate me just as you would a fool, so that I may do a little boasting. [17] In this self-confident boasting I am not talking as the Lord would, but as a fool. [18] Since many are boasting in the way the world does, I too will boast. [19] You gladly put up with fools since you are so wise! [20] In fact, you even put up with anyone who enslaves you or exploits you or takes advantage of you or puts on airs or slaps you in the face. [21] To my shame I admit that we were too weak for that! 1Co 4:10; Php 3:3-4

Whatever anyone else dares to boast about—I am speaking as a fool—I also dare to boast about. [22] Are they Hebrews? So am I. Are they Israelites? So am I. Are they Abraham's descendants? So am I. [23] Are they servants of Christ? (I am out of my mind to talk like this.) I am more. I have worked much harder, been in prison more frequently, been flogged more severely, and been exposed to death again and again. [24] Five times I received from the Jews the forty lashes minus one. [25] Three times I was beaten with rods, once I was pelted with stones, three

---

[a] 5 Or *to the most eminent apostles*

times I was shipwrecked, I spent a night and a day in the open sea, ²⁶I have been constantly on the move. I have been in danger from rivers, in danger from bandits, in danger from my fellow Jews, in danger from Gentiles; in danger in the city, in danger in the country, in danger at sea; and in danger from false believers. ²⁷I have labored and toiled and have often gone without sleep; I have known hunger and thirst and have often gone without food; I have been cold and naked. ²⁸Besides everything else, I face daily the pressure of my concern for all the churches. ²⁹Who is weak, and I do not feel weak? Who is led into sin, and I do not inwardly burn? Ro 9:4; 1Co 15:10

³⁰If I must boast, I will boast of the things that show my weakness. ³¹The God and Father of the Lord Jesus, who is to be praised forever, knows that I am not lying. ³²In Damascus the governor under King Aretas had the city of the Damascenes guarded in order to arrest me. ³³But I was lowered in a basket from a window in the wall and slipped through his hands. Ac 9:24-25; 1Co 2:3

Paul's Vision and His Thorn

12 I must go on boasting. Although there is nothing to be gained, I will go on to visions and revelations from the Lord. ²I know a man in Christ who fourteen years ago was caught up to the third heaven. Whether it was in the body or out of the body I do not know—God knows. ³And I know that this man—whether in the body or apart from the body I do not know, but God knows— ⁴was caught up to paradise and heard inexpressible things, things that no one is permitted to tell. ⁵I will boast about a man like that, but I will not boast about myself, except about my weaknesses. ⁶Even if I should choose to boast, I would not be a fool, because I would be speaking the truth. But I refrain, so no one will think more of me than is warranted by what I do or say, ⁷or because of these surpassingly great revelations. Therefore, in order to keep me from becoming conceited, I was given a thorn in my flesh, a messenger of Satan, to torment me. ⁸Three times I pleaded with the Lord to take it away from me. ⁹But he said to me, "My grace is sufficient for you, for my power is made perfect in weakness." Therefore I will boast all the more gladly about my weaknesses, so that Christ's power may rest on me. ¹⁰That is why, for Christ's sake, I delight in weaknesses, in insults, in hardships, in persecutions, in difficulties. For when I am weak, then I am strong. 2Co 13:4; 2Th 1:4

Paul's Concern for the Corinthians

¹¹I have made a fool of myself,

but you drove me to it. I ought to have been commended by you, for I am not in the least inferior to the "super-apostles,"ᵃ even though I am nothing. ¹²I persevered in demonstrating among you the marks of a true apostle, including signs, wonders and miracles. ¹³How were you inferior to the other churches, except that I was never a burden to you? Forgive me this wrong! 1Co 9:12,18

¹⁴Now I am ready to visit you for the third time, and I will not be a burden to you, because what I want is not your possessions but you. After all, children should not have to save up for their parents, but parents for their children. ¹⁵So I will very gladly spend for you everything I have and expend myself as well. If I love you more, will you love me less? ¹⁶Be that as it may, I have not been a burden to you. Yet, crafty fellow that I am, I caught you by trickery! ¹⁷Did I exploit you through any of the men I sent to you? ¹⁸I urged Titus to go to you and I sent our brother with him. Titus did not exploit you, did he? Did we not walk in the same footsteps by the same Spirit? 2Co 8:18; 11:9

¹⁹Have you been thinking all along that we have been defending ourselves to you? We have been speaking in the sight of God as those in Christ; and everything we do, dear friends, is for your strengthening. ²⁰For I am afraid that when I come I may not find you as I want you to be, and you may not find me as you want me to be. I fear that there may be discord, jealousy, fits of rage, selfish ambition, slander, gossip, arrogance and disorder. ²¹I am afraid that when I come again my God will humble me before you, and I will be grieved over many who have sinned earlier and have not repented of the impurity, sexual sin and debauchery in which they have indulged. 1Co 14:33; 2Co 13:2

Final Warnings

13 This will be my third visit to you. "Every matter must be established by the testimony of two or three witnesses."ᵇ ²I already gave you a warning when I was with you the second time. I now repeat it while absent: On my return I will not spare those who sinned earlier or any of the others, ³since you are demanding proof that Christ is speaking through me. He is not weak in dealing with you, but is powerful among you. ⁴For to be sure, he was crucified in weakness, yet he lives by God's power. Likewise, we are weak in him, yet by God's power we will live with him in our dealing with you. Ro 1:4; Php 2:7-8

⁵Examine yourselves to see whether you are in the faith; test yourselves. Do you not realize that Christ Jesus is in you—un-

ᵃ 11 Or *the most eminent apostles*   ᵇ 1 Deut. 19:15

less, of course, you fail the test? [6]And I trust that you will discover that we have not failed the test. [7]Now we pray to God that you will not do anything wrong—not so that people will see that we have stood the test but so that you will do what is right even though we may seem to have failed. [8]For we cannot do anything against the truth, but only for the truth. [9]We are glad whenever we are weak but you are strong; and our prayer is that you may be fully restored. [10]This is why I write these things when I am absent, that when I come I may not have to be harsh in my use of authority—the authority the Lord gave me for building you up, not for tearing you down. 1Co 11:28; 2Co 10:8

Final Greetings

[11]Finally, brothers and sisters, rejoice! Strive for full restoration, encourage one another, be of one mind, live in peace. And the God of love and peace will be with you.   Ro 15:33; Eph 6:23

[12]Greet one another with a holy kiss. [13]All God's people here send their greetings.   Ro 16:16

[14]May the grace of the Lord Jesus Christ, and the love of God, and the fellowship of the Holy Spirit be with you all.   Ro 16:20

Galatians

1 Paul, an apostle — sent not from men nor by a man, but by Jesus Christ and God the Father, who raised him from the dead — ²and all the brothers and sisters*a* with me, Ac 2:24; Php 4:21

To the churches in Galatia:

³Grace and peace to you from God our Father and the Lord Jesus Christ, ⁴who gave himself for our sins to rescue us from the present evil age, according to the will of our God and Father, ⁵to whom be glory for ever and ever. Amen. Mt 20:28; Ro 4:25; Php 4:20

No Other Gospel

⁶I am astonished that you are so quickly deserting the one who called you to live in the grace of Christ and are turning to a different gospel — ⁷which is really no gospel at all. Evidently some people are throwing you into confusion and are trying to pervert the gospel of Christ.

⁸But even if we or an angel from heaven should preach a gospel other than the one we preached to you, let them be under God's curse! ⁹As we have already said, so now I say again: If anybody is preaching to you a gospel other than what you accepted, let them be under God's curse! Ro 9:3; 16:17

¹⁰Am I now trying to win the approval of human beings, or of God? Or am I trying to please people? If I were still trying to please people, I would not be a servant of Christ. Ro 2:29; 1Th 2:4

Paul Called by God

¹¹I want you to know, brothers and sisters, that the gospel I preached is not of human origin. ¹²I did not receive it from any man, nor was I taught it; rather, I received it by revelation from Jesus Christ. 1Co 11:23; 15:1

¹³For you have heard of my previous way of life in Judaism, how intensely I persecuted the church

a 2 The Greek word for *brothers and sisters* (*adelphoi*) refers here to believers, both men and women, as part of God's family; also in verse 11; and in 3:15; 4:12, 28, 31; 5:11, 13; 6:1, 18.

of God and tried to destroy it. ¹⁴I was advancing in Judaism beyond many of my own age among my people and was extremely zealous for the traditions of my fathers. ¹⁵But when God, who set me apart from my mother's womb and called me by his grace, was pleased ¹⁶to reveal his Son in me so that I might preach him among the Gentiles, my immediate response was not to consult any human being. ¹⁷I did not go up to Jerusalem to see those who were apostles before I was, but I went into Arabia. Later I returned to Damascus. Mt 15:2; 16:17

¹⁸Then after three years, I went up to Jerusalem to get acquainted with Cephas*a* and stayed with him fifteen days. ¹⁹I saw none of the other apostles — only James, the Lord's brother. ²⁰I assure you before God that what I am writing you is no lie.

²¹Then I went to Syria and Cilicia. ²²I was personally unknown to the churches of Judea that are in Christ. ²³They only heard the report: "The man who formerly persecuted us is now preaching the faith he once tried to destroy." ²⁴And they praised God because of me. Ro 9:1; 1Th 2:14

Paul Accepted by the Apostles

2 Then after fourteen years, I went up again to Jerusalem, this time with Barnabas. I took Titus along also. ²I went in response to a revelation and, meeting privately with those esteemed as leaders, I presented to them the gospel that I preach among the Gentiles. I wanted to be sure I was not running and had not been running my race in vain. ³Yet not even Titus, who was with me, was compelled to be circumcised, even though he was a Greek. ⁴This matter arose because some false believers had infiltrated our ranks to spy on the freedom we have in Christ Jesus and to make us slaves. ⁵We did not give in to them for a moment, so that the truth of the gospel might be preserved for you. Ac 15:1; 2Co 11:26

⁶As for those who were held in high esteem — whatever they were makes no difference to me; God does not show favoritism — they added nothing to my message. ⁷On the contrary, they recognized that I had been entrusted with the task of preaching the gospel to the uncircumcised,*b* just as Peter had been to the circumcised.*c* ⁸For God, who was at work in Peter as an apostle to the circumcised, was also at work in me as an apostle to the Gentiles. ⁹James, Cephas*d* and John, those esteemed as pillars, gave me and Barnabas the right hand of fellowship when they recognized the grace given

a 18 That is, Peter   *b 7* That is, Gentiles   *c 7* That is, Jews; also in verses 8 and 9
d 9 That is, Peter; also in verses 11 and 14

to me. They agreed that we should go to the Gentiles, and they to the circumcised. [10]All they asked was that we should continue to remember the poor, the very thing I had been eager to do all along. Ac 24:17; Ro 12:3

Paul Opposes Cephas

[11]When Cephas came to Antioch, I opposed him to his face, because he stood condemned. [12]For before certain men came from James, he used to eat with the Gentiles. But when they arrived, he began to draw back and separate himself from the Gentiles because he was afraid of those who belonged to the circumcision group. [13]The other Jews joined him in his hypocrisy, so that by their hypocrisy even Barnabas was led astray. Ac 4:36; 11:3

[14]When I saw that they were not acting in line with the truth of the gospel, I said to Cephas in front of them all, "You are a Jew, yet you live like a Gentile and not like a Jew. How is it, then, that you force Gentiles to follow Jewish customs? Ac 10:28

[15]"We who are Jews by birth and not sinful Gentiles [16]know that a person is not justified by the works of the law, but by faith in Jesus Christ. So we, too, have put our faith in Christ Jesus that we may be justified by faith in[a]

Christ and not by the works of the law, because by the works of the law no one will be justified.

[17]"But if, in seeking to be justified in Christ, we Jews find ourselves also among the sinners, doesn't that mean that Christ promotes sin? Absolutely not! [18]If I rebuild what I destroyed, then I really would be a lawbreaker.

[19]"For through the law I died to the law so that I might live for God. [20]I have been crucified with Christ and I no longer live, but Christ lives in me. The life I now live in the body, I live by faith in the Son of God, who loved me and gave himself for me. [21]I do not set aside the grace of God, for if righteousness could be gained through the law, Christ died for nothing!"[b] 2Co 5:15; 1Pe 4:2

Faith or Works of the Law

3 You foolish Galatians! Who has bewitched you? Before your very eyes Jesus Christ was clearly portrayed as crucified. [2]I would like to learn just one thing from you: Did you receive the Spirit by the works of the law, or by believing what you heard? [3]Are you so foolish? After beginning by means of the Spirit, are you now trying to finish by means of the flesh?[c] [4]Have you experienced[d] so much in vain — if it really was in vain? [5]So again I

---

[a] 16 Or *but through the faithfulness of . . . justified on the basis of the faithfulness of*
[b] 21 Some interpreters end the quotation after verse 14.   [c] 3 In contexts like this, the Greek word for *flesh* (*sarx*) refers to the sinful state of human beings, often presented as a power in opposition to the Spirit.   [d] 4 Or *suffered*

ask, does God give you his Spirit and work miracles among you by the works of the law, or by your believing what you heard? [6]So also Abraham "believed God, and it was credited to him as righteousness."[a]   Ro 10:17; 1Co 12:10

[7]Understand, then, that those who have faith are children of Abraham. [8]Scripture foresaw that God would justify the Gentiles by faith, and announced the gospel in advance to Abraham: "All nations will be blessed through you."[b] [9]So those who rely on faith are blessed along with Abraham, the man of faith.   Ac 3:25; Ro 4:3

[10]For all who rely on the works of the law are under a curse, as it is written: "Cursed is everyone who does not continue to do everything written in the Book of the Law."[c] [11]Clearly no one who relies on the law is justified before God, because "the righteous will live by faith."[d] [12]The law is not based on faith; on the contrary, it says, "The person who does these things will live by them."[e] [13]Christ redeemed us from the curse of the law by becoming a curse for us, for it is written: "Cursed is everyone who is hung on a pole."[f] [14]He redeemed us in order that the blessing given to Abraham might come to the Gentiles through Christ Jesus, so that by faith we might receive the promise of the Spirit.   Ac 2:33; Ro 4:9,16

The Law and the Promise

[15]Brothers and sisters, let me take an example from everyday life. Just as no one can set aside or add to a human covenant that has been duly established, so it is in this case. [16]The promises were spoken to Abraham and to his seed. Scripture does not say "and to seeds," meaning many people, but "and to your seed,"[g] meaning one person, who is Christ. [17]What I mean is this: The law, introduced 430 years later, does not set aside the covenant previously established by God and thus do away with the promise. [18]For if the inheritance depends on the law, then it no longer depends on the promise; but God in his grace gave it to Abraham through a promise.   Ex 12:40; Ro 4:14

[19]Why, then, was the law given at all? It was added because of transgressions until the Seed to whom the promise referred had come. The law was given through angels and entrusted to a mediator. [20]A mediator, however, implies more than one party; but God is one.   Ac 7:53; Heb 8:6

[21]Is the law, therefore, opposed to the promises of God? Absolutely not! For if a law had been given that could impart life, then righteousness would certainly have come by the law. [22]But Scripture has locked up everything under the control of sin,

---

[a] 6 Gen. 15:6   [b] 8 Gen. 12:3; 18:18; 22:18   [c] 10 Deut. 27:26   [d] 11 Hab. 2:4
[e] 12 Lev. 18:5   [f] 13 Deut. 21:23   [g] 16 Gen. 12:7; 13:15; 24:7

so that what was promised, being given through faith in Jesus Christ, might be given to those who believe. Ro 11:32; Gal 2:17

Children of God

23 Before the coming of this faith,[a] we were held in custody under the law, locked up until the faith that was to come would be revealed. 24 So the law was our guardian until Christ came that we might be justified by faith. 25 Now that this faith has come, we are no longer under a guardian. Ro 10:4; 11:32

26 So in Christ Jesus you are all children of God through faith, 27 for all of you who were baptized into Christ have clothed yourselves with Christ. 28 There is neither Jew nor Gentile, neither slave nor free, nor is there male and female, for you are all one in Christ Jesus. 29 If you belong to Christ, then you are Abraham's seed, and heirs according to the promise. Ro 8:14; Eph 2:14-15

4 What I am saying is that as long as an heir is underage, he is no different from a slave, although he owns the whole estate. 2 The heir is subject to guardians and trustees until the time set by his father. 3 So also, when we were underage, we were in slavery under the elemental spiritual forces[b] of the world. 4 But when the set time had fully come, God sent his Son, born of a woman, born under the law, 5 to redeem those under the law, that we might receive adoption to sonship.[c] 6 Because you are his sons, God sent the Spirit of his Son into our hearts, the Spirit who calls out, *"Abba,[d] Father."* 7 So you are no longer a slave, but God's child; and since you are his child, God has made you also an heir. Ro 5:5; 8:15-17

Paul's Concern for the Galatians

8 Formerly, when you did not know God, you were slaves to those who by nature are not gods. 9 But now that you know God—or rather are known by God—how is it that you are turning back to those weak and miserable forces[e]? Do you wish to be enslaved by them all over again? 10 You are observing special days and months and seasons and years! 11 I fear for you, that somehow I have wasted my efforts on you. Eph 2:12; 1Th 3:5; 4:5

12 I plead with you, brothers and sisters, become like me, for I became like you. You did me no wrong. 13 As you know, it was because of an illness that I first preached the gospel to you, 14 and even though my illness was a trial to you, you did not treat me with contempt or scorn. Instead, you

a 22,23 Or *through the faithfulness of Jesus . . .* 23*Before faith came* b 3 Or *under the basic principles* c 5 The Greek word for *adoption to sonship* is a legal term referring to the full legal standing of an adopted male heir in Roman culture. d 6 Aramaic for *Father* e 9 Or *principles* welcomed me as if I were an angel of God, as if I were Christ Jesus himself. [15]Where, then, is your blessing of me now? I can testify that, if you could have done so, you would have torn out your eyes and given them to me. [16]Have I now become your enemy by telling you the truth? 1Co 2:3; Gal 6:18

[17]Those people are zealous to win you over, but for no good. What they want is to alienate you from us, so that you may have zeal for them. [18]It is fine to be zealous, provided the purpose is good, and to be so always, not just when I am with you. [19]My dear children, for whom I am again in the pains of childbirth until Christ is formed in you, [20]how I wish I could be with you now and change my tone, because I am perplexed about you! 1Co 4:15; Eph 4:13

Hagar and Sarah

[21]Tell me, you who want to be under the law, are you not aware of what the law says? [22]For it is written that Abraham had two sons, one by the slave woman and the other by the free woman. [23]His son by the slave woman was born according to the flesh, but his son by the free woman was born as the result of a divine promise. Ro 9:7-8; Heb 11:11

[24]These things are being taken figuratively: The women represent two covenants. One covenant is from Mount Sinai and bears children who are to be slaves: This is Hagar. [25]Now Hagar stands for Mount Sinai in Arabia and corresponds to the present city of Jerusalem, because she is in slavery with her children. [26]But the Jerusalem that is above is free, and she is our mother. [27]For it is written: Heb 12:22; Rev 3:12

"Be glad, barren woman,
  you who never bore a
    child;
shout for joy and cry aloud,
  you who were never in
    labor;
because more are the children
    of the desolate woman
  than of her who has a
    husband."[a] Isa 54:1

[28]Now you, brothers and sisters, like Isaac, are children of promise. [29]At that time the son born according to the flesh persecuted the son born by the power of the Spirit. It is the same now. [30]But what does Scripture say? "Get rid of the slave woman and her son, for the slave woman's son will never share in the inheritance with the free woman's son."[b] [31]Therefore, brothers and sisters, we are not children of the slave woman, but of the free woman. Ge 21:9-10

Freedom in Christ

5 It is for freedom that Christ has set us free. Stand firm, then, and do not let yourselves

be burdened again by a yoke of slavery. 1Co 16:13; Gal 2:4 ²Mark my words! I, Paul, tell you that if you let yourselves be circumcised, Christ will be of no value to you at all. ³Again I declare to every man who lets himself be circumcised that he is obligated to obey the whole law. ⁴You who are trying to be justified by the law have been alienated from Christ; you have fallen away from grace. ⁵For through the Spirit we eagerly await by faith the righteousness for which we hope. ⁶For in Christ Jesus neither circumcision nor uncircumcision has any value. The only thing that counts is faith expressing itself through love. Ro 8:23-24; Heb 12:15

⁷You were running a good race. Who cut in on you to keep you from obeying the truth? ⁸That kind of persuasion does not come from the one who calls you. ⁹"A little yeast works through the whole batch of dough." ¹⁰I am confident in the Lord that you will take no other view. The one who is throwing you into confusion, whoever that may be, will have to pay the penalty. ¹¹Brothers and sisters, if I am still preaching circumcision, why am I still being persecuted? In that case the offense of the cross has been abolished. ¹²As for those agitators, I wish they would go the whole way and emasculate themselves! Gal 1:7; 6:12

Life by the Spirit

¹³You, my brothers and sisters, were called to be free. But do not use your freedom to indulge the flesh*a*; rather, serve one another humbly in love. ¹⁴For the entire law is fulfilled in keeping this one command: "Love your neighbor as yourself."*b* ¹⁵If you bite and devour each other, watch out or you will be destroyed by each other. Mt 22:39; 1Co 9:19

¹⁶So I say, walk by the Spirit, and you will not gratify the desires of the flesh. ¹⁷For the flesh desires what is contrary to the Spirit, and the Spirit what is contrary to the flesh. They are in conflict with each other, so that you are not to do whatever*c* you want. ¹⁸But if you are led by the Spirit, you are not under the law.

¹⁹The acts of the flesh are obvious: sexual immorality, impurity and debauchery; ²⁰idolatry and witchcraft; hatred, discord, jealousy, fits of rage, selfish ambition, dissensions, factions ²¹and envy; drunkenness, orgies, and the like. I warn you, as I did before, that those who live like this will not inherit the kingdom of God. Ro 13:13; 1Co 6:18

²²But the fruit of the Spirit is love, joy, peace, forbearance,

---

a 13 In contexts like this, the Greek word for *flesh* (*sarx*) refers to the sinful state of human beings, often presented as a power in opposition to the Spirit; also in verses 16, 17, 19 and 24; and in 6:8.   *b* 14 Lev. 19:18   *c* 17 Or *you do not do what* kindness, goodness, faithfulness, [23] gentleness and self-control. Against such things there is no law. [24] Those who belong to Christ Jesus have crucified the flesh with its passions and desires. [25] Since we live by the Spirit, let us keep in step with the Spirit. [26] Let us not become conceited, provoking and envying each other. Eph 5:9; Php 2:3; Col 3:12-15

Doing Good to All

6 Brothers and sisters, if someone is caught in a sin, you who live by the Spirit should restore that person gently. But watch yourselves, or you also may be tempted. [2] Carry each other's burdens, and in this way you will fulfill the law of Christ. [3] If anyone thinks they are something when they are not, they deceive themselves. [4] Each one should test their own actions. Then they can take pride in themselves alone, without comparing themselves to someone else, [5] for each one should carry their own load. [6] Nevertheless, the one who receives instruction in the word should share all good things with their instructor. 1Co 9:11,14

[7] Do not be deceived: God cannot be mocked. A man reaps what he sows. [8] Whoever sows to please their flesh, from the flesh will reap destruction; whoever sows to please the Spirit, from the Spirit will reap eternal life. [9] Let us not become weary in doing good, for at the proper time we will reap a harvest if we do not give up. [10] Therefore, as we have opportunity, let us do good to all people, especially to those who belong to the family of believers.

Not Circumcision but the New Creation

[11] See what large letters I use as I write to you with my own hand! [12] Those who want to impress people by means of the flesh are trying to compel you to be circumcised. The only reason they do this is to avoid being persecuted for the cross of Christ. [13] Not even those who are circumcised keep the law, yet they want you to be circumcised that they may boast about your circumcision in the flesh. [14] May I never boast except in the cross of our Lord Jesus Christ, through which[a] the world has been crucified to me, and I to the world. [15] Neither circumcision nor uncircumcision means anything; what counts is the new creation. [16] Peace and mercy to all who follow this rule — to[b] the Israel of God. Ro 6:2,6; Gal 5:11

[17] From now on, let no one cause me trouble, for I bear on my body the marks of Jesus. Isa 44:

[18] The grace of our Lord Jesus Christ be with your spirit, brothers and sisters. Amen. Ro 16:20

[a] 14 Or *whom*   [b] 16 Or *rule and to*

Ephesians

1 Paul, an apostle of Christ Jesus by the will of God, 1Co 1:1

To God's holy people in Ephesus,*a* the faithful in Christ Jesus:

2 Grace and peace to you from God our Father and the Lord Jesus Christ. Ro 1:7

Praise for Spiritual Blessings in Christ

3 Praise be to the God and Father of our Lord Jesus Christ, who has blessed us in the heavenly realms with every spiritual blessing in Christ. 4 For he chose us in him before the creation of the world to be holy and blameless in his sight. In love 5 he*b* predestined us for adoption to sonship*c* through Jesus Christ, in accordance with his pleasure and will— 6 to the praise of his glorious grace, which he has freely given us in the One he loves. 7 In him we have redemption through his blood, the forgiveness of sins, in accordance with the riches of God's grace 8 that he lavished on us. With all wisdom and understanding, 9 he*d* made known to us the mystery of his will according to his good pleasure, which he purposed in Christ, 10 to be put into effect when the times reach their fulfillment—to bring unity to all things in heaven and on earth under Christ. Ro 8:29-30; 2Co 1:3

11 In him we were also chosen,*e* having been predestined according to the plan of him who works out everything in conformity with the purpose of his will, 12 in order that we, who were the first to put our hope in Christ, might be for the praise of his glory. 13 And you also were included in Christ when you heard the message of truth, the gospel of your salvation. When you believed, you were marked in him

---

a 1 Some early manuscripts do not have *in Ephesus.*   *b 4,5* Or *sight in love.* *5 He*   *c 5* The Greek word for *adoption to sonship* is a legal term referring to the full legal standing of an adopted male heir in Roman culture.   *d 8,9* Or *us with all wisdom and understanding.* *9 And he*   *e 11* Or *were made heirs* with a seal, the promised Holy Spirit, [14] who is a deposit guaranteeing our inheritance until the redemption of those who are God's possession — to the praise of his glory. Eph 3:11; 4:30

Thanksgiving and Prayer

[15] For this reason, ever since I heard about your faith in the Lord Jesus and your love for all God's people, [16] I have not stopped giving thanks for you, remembering you in my prayers. [17] I keep asking that the God of our Lord Jesus Christ, the glorious Father, may give you the Spirit[a] of wisdom and revelation, so that you may know him better. [18] I pray that the eyes of your heart may be enlightened in order that you may know the hope to which he has called you, the riches of his glorious inheritance in his holy people, [19] and his incomparably great power for us who believe. That power is the same as the mighty strength [20] he exerted when he raised Christ from the dead and seated him at his right hand in the heavenly realms, [21] far above all rule and authority, power and dominion, and every name that is invoked, not only in the present age but also in the one to come. [22] And God placed all things under his feet and appointed him to be head over everything for the church, [23] which is his body, the fullness of him who fills everything in every way. Php 2:9-10; Col 1:4,9

Made Alive in Christ

2 As for you, you were dead in your transgressions and sins, [2] in which you used to live when you followed the ways of this world and of the ruler of the kingdom of the air, the spirit who is now at work in those who are disobedient. [3] All of us also lived among them at one time, gratifying the cravings of our flesh[b] and following its desires and thoughts. Like the rest, we were by nature deserving of wrath. [4] But because of his great love for us, God, who is rich in mercy, [5] made us alive with Christ even when we were dead in transgressions — it is by grace you have been saved. [6] And God raised us up with Christ and seated us with him in the heavenly realms in Christ Jesus, [7] in order that in the coming ages he might show the incomparable riches of his grace, expressed in his kindness to us in Christ Jesus. [8] For it is by grace you have been saved, through faith — and this is not from yourselves, it is the gift of God — [9] not by works, so that no one can boast. [10] For we are God's handiwork, created in Christ Jesus to do good works, which God prepared in advance for us to do. Isa 29:23; Eph 4:24; Tit 2:14

---

[a] 17 Or *a spirit*   [b] 3 In contexts like this, the Greek word for *flesh* (*sarx*) refers to the sinful state of human beings, often presented as a power in opposition to the Spirit.

Jew and Gentile Reconciled Through Christ

11 Therefore, remember that formerly you who are Gentiles by birth and called "uncircumcised" by those who call themselves "the circumcision" (which is done in the body by human hands)— 12 remember that at that time you were separate from Christ, excluded from citizenship in Israel and foreigners to the covenants of the promise, without hope and without God in the world. 13 But now in Christ Jesus you who once were far away have been brought near by the blood of Christ. Ac 2:39; Col 1:20

14 For he himself is our peace, who has made the two groups one and has destroyed the barrier, the dividing wall of hostility, 15 by setting aside in his flesh the law with its commands and regulations. His purpose was to create in himself one new humanity out of the two, thus making peace, 16 and in one body to reconcile both of them to God through the cross, by which he put to death their hostility. 17 He came and preached peace to you who were far away and peace to those who were near. 18 For through him we both have access to the Father by one Spirit.

19 Consequently, you are no longer foreigners and strangers, but fellow citizens with God's people and also members of his household, 20 built on the foundation of the apostles and prophets, with Christ Jesus himself as the chief cornerstone. 21 In him the whole building is joined together and rises to become a holy temple in the Lord. 22 And in him you too are being built together to become a dwelling in which God lives by his Spirit. Mt 16:18

God's Marvelous Plan for the Gentiles

3 For this reason I, Paul, the prisoner of Christ Jesus for the sake of you Gentiles — Ac 23:18

2 Surely you have heard about the administration of God's grace that was given to me for you, 3 that is, the mystery made known to me by revelation, as I have already written briefly. 4 In reading this, then, you will be able to understand my insight into the mystery of Christ, 5 which was not made known to people in other generations as it has now been revealed by the Spirit to God's holy apostles and prophets. 6 This mystery is that through the gospel the Gentiles are heirs together with Israel, members together of one body, and sharers together in the promise in Christ Jesus. Gal 3:29; Eph 2:15-16

7 I became a servant of this gospel by the gift of God's grace given me through the working of his power. 8 Although I am less than the least of all the Lord's people, this grace was given me: to preach to the Gentiles

the boundless riches of Christ, [9] and to make plain to everyone the administration of this mystery, which for ages past was kept hidden in God, who created all things. [10] His intent was that now, through the church, the manifold wisdom of God should be made known to the rulers and authorities in the heavenly realms, [11] according to his eternal purpose that he accomplished in Christ Jesus our Lord. [12] In him and through faith in him we may approach God with freedom and confidence. [13] I ask you, therefore, not to be discouraged because of my sufferings for you, which are your glory. *Eph 2:18; Heb 4:16*

A Prayer for the Ephesians

[14] For this reason I kneel before the Father, [15] from whom every family[a] in heaven and on earth derives its name. [16] I pray that out of his glorious riches he may strengthen you with power through his Spirit in your inner being, [17] so that Christ may dwell in your hearts through faith. And I pray that you, being rooted and established in love, [18] may have power, together with all the Lord's holy people, to grasp how wide and long and high and deep is the love of Christ, [19] and to know this love that surpasses knowledge — that you may be filled to the measure of all the fullness of God.

[20] Now to him who is able to do immeasurably more than all we ask or imagine, according to his power that is at work within us, [21] to him be glory in the church and in Christ Jesus throughout all generations, for ever and ever! Amen. *Ro 11:36; 16:25*

Unity and Maturity in the Body of Christ

4 As a prisoner for the Lord, then, I urge you to live a life worthy of the calling you have received. [2] Be completely humble and gentle; be patient, bearing with one another in love. [3] Make every effort to keep the unity of the Spirit through the bond of peace. [4] There is one body and one Spirit, just as you were called to one hope when you were called; [5] one Lord, one faith, one baptism; [6] one God and Father of all, who is over all and through all and in all. *Ro 11:36; Col 1:10*

[7] But to each one of us grace has been given as Christ apportioned it. [8] This is why it[b] says:

> "When he ascended on high, he took many captives *Col 2:15* and gave gifts to his people."[c]

[9] (What does "he ascended" mean except that he also descended to the lower, earthly regions[d]? [10] He who descended is the very one who ascended higher than

---

[a] 15 The Greek for *family* (*patria*) is derived from the Greek for *father* (*pater*). [b] 8 Or *God*
[c] 8 Psalm 68:18   [d] 9 Or *the depths of the earth*

all the heavens, in order to fill the whole universe.) [11] So Christ himself gave the apostles, the prophets, the evangelists, the pastors and teachers, [12] to equip his people for works of service, so that the body of Christ may be built up [13] until we all reach unity in the faith and in the knowledge of the Son of God and become mature, attaining to the whole measure of the fullness of Christ.

1Co 12:27-28; Col 1:28

[14] Then we will no longer be infants, tossed back and forth by the waves, and blown here and there by every wind of teaching and by the cunning and craftiness of people in their deceitful scheming. [15] Instead, speaking the truth in love, we will grow to become in every respect the mature body of him who is the head, that is, Christ. [16] From him the whole body, joined and held together by every supporting ligament, grows and builds itself up in love, as each part does its work.

1Co 14:20; Eph 1:22

Instructions for Christian Living

[17] So I tell you this, and insist on it in the Lord, that you must no longer live as the Gentiles do, in the futility of their thinking. [18] They are darkened in their understanding and separated from the life of God because of the ignorance that is in them due to the hardening of their hearts.

[19] Having lost all sensitivity, they have given themselves over to sensuality so as to indulge in every kind of impurity, and they are full of greed.

Ro 1:21; 1Ti 4:2

[20] That, however, is not the way of life you learned [21] when you heard about Christ and were taught in him in accordance with the truth that is in Jesus. [22] You were taught, with regard to your former way of life, to put off your old self, which is being corrupted by its deceitful desires; [23] to be made new in the attitude of your minds; [24] and to put on the new self, created to be like God in true righteousness and holiness.

[25] Therefore each of you must put off falsehood and speak truthfully to your neighbor, for we are all members of one body. [26] "In your anger do not sin"[a]: Do not let the sun go down while you are still angry, [27] and do not give the devil a foothold. [28] Anyone who has been stealing must steal no longer, but must work, doing something useful with their own hands, that they may have something to share with those in need.

Zec 8:16; Lk 3:11

[29] Do not let any unwholesome talk come out of your mouths, but only what is helpful for building others up according to their needs, that it may benefit those who listen. [30] And do not grieve the Holy Spirit of God, with whom you were sealed for

[a] 26 Psalm 4:4 (see Septuagint)

the day of redemption. ³¹Get rid of all bitterness, rage and anger, brawling and slander, along with every form of malice. ³²Be kind and compassionate to one another, forgiving each other, just as in Christ God forgave you. ¹Follow God's example, therefore, as dearly loved children ²and walk in the way of love, just as Christ loved us and gave himself up for us as a fragrant offering and sacrifice to God.

Lk 6:36; 2Co 2:15

³But among you there must not be even a hint of sexual immorality, or of any kind of impurity, or of greed, because these are improper for God's holy people. ⁴Nor should there be obscenity, foolish talk or coarse joking, which are out of place, but rather thanksgiving. ⁵For of this you can be sure: No immoral, impure or greedy person—such a person is an idolater—has any inheritance in the kingdom of Christ and of God.ᵃ ⁶Let no one deceive you with empty words, for because of such things God's wrath comes on those who are disobedient. ⁷Therefore do not be partners with them.

Ro 1:18; 1Co 6:9

⁸For you were once darkness, but now you are light in the Lord. Live as children of light ⁹(for the fruit of the light consists in all goodness, righteousness and truth) ¹⁰and find out what pleases the Lord. ¹¹Have nothing to do with the fruitless deeds of darkness, but rather expose them. ¹²It is shameful even to mention what the disobedient do in secret. ¹³But everything exposed by the light becomes visible—and everything that is illuminated becomes a light. ¹⁴This is why it is said:

Lk 16:8; Gal 5:22

"Wake up, sleeper,   Ro 13:11
   rise from the dead,   Jn 5:25
and Christ will shine on
   you."   Isa 60:1

¹⁵Be very careful, then, how you live—not as unwise but as wise, ¹⁶making the most of every opportunity, because the days are evil. ¹⁷Therefore do not be foolish, but understand what the Lord's will is. ¹⁸Do not get drunk on wine, which leads to debauchery. Instead, be filled with the Spirit, ¹⁹speaking to one another with psalms, hymns, and songs from the Spirit. Sing and make music from your heart to the Lord, ²⁰always giving thanks to God the Father for everything, in the name of our Lord Jesus Christ.

Ps 34:1; Col 3:16

Instructions for Christian Households

5:22-6:9pp — Col 3:18-4:1

²¹Submit to one another out of reverence for Christ.   Gal 5:13

²²Wives, submit yourselves to your own husbands as you do to the Lord. ²³For the husband is

ᵃ 5 Or *kingdom of the Messiah and God*

the head of the wife as Christ is the head of the church, his body, of which he is the Savior. [24]Now as the church submits to Christ, so also wives should submit to their husbands in everything.

[25]Husbands, love your wives, just as Christ loved the church and gave himself up for her [26]to make her holy, cleansing[a] her by the washing with water through the word, [27]and to present her to himself as a radiant church, without stain or wrinkle or any other blemish, but holy and blameless. [28]In this same way, husbands ought to love their wives as their own bodies. He who loves his wife loves himself. [29]After all, no one ever hated their own body, but they feed and care for their body, just as Christ does the church— [30]for we are members of his body. [31]"For this reason a man will leave his father and mother and be united to his wife, and the two will become one flesh."[b] [32]This is a profound mystery—but I am talking about Christ and the church. [33]However, each one of you also must love his wife as he loves himself, and the wife must respect her husband.

Mt 19:5; Col 1:22

6 Children, obey your parents in the Lord, for this is right. [2]"Honor your father and mother"—which is the first commandment with a promise— [3]"so that it may go well with you

and that you may enjoy long life on the earth."[c]

Ex 20:12; Col 3:20

[4]Fathers,[d] do not exasperate your children; instead, bring them up in the training and instruction of the Lord.

Ge 18:19

[5]Slaves, obey your earthly masters with respect and fear, and with sincerity of heart, just as you would obey Christ. [6]Obey them not only to win their favor when their eye is on you, but as slaves of Christ, doing the will of God from your heart. [7]Serve wholeheartedly, as if you were serving the Lord, not people, [8]because you know that the Lord will reward each one for whatever good they do, whether they are slave or free.

Col 3:22,24

[9]And masters, treat your slaves in the same way. Do not threaten them, since you know that he who is both their Master and yours is in heaven, and there is no favoritism with him. Col 3:18-4:1

The Armor of God

[10]Finally, be strong in the Lord and in his mighty power. [11]Put on the full armor of God, so that you can take your stand against the devil's schemes. [12]For our struggle is not against flesh and blood, but against the rulers, against the authorities, against the powers of this dark world and against the spiritual forces of evil in the heavenly realms. [13]Therefore put on the full armor of God, so

[a] 26 Or having cleansed   [b] 31 Gen. 2:24   [c] 3 Deut. 5:16   [d] 4 Or Parents

that when the day of evil comes, you may be able to stand your ground, and after you have done everything, to stand. [14] Stand firm then, with the belt of truth buckled around your waist, with the breastplate of righteousness in place, [15] and with your feet fitted with the readiness that comes from the gospel of peace. [16] In addition to all this, take up the shield of faith, with which you can extinguish all the flaming arrows of the evil one. [17] Take the helmet of salvation and the sword of the Spirit, which is the word of God.

[18] And pray in the Spirit on all occasions with all kinds of prayers and requests. With this in mind, be alert and always keep on praying for all the Lord's people. [19] Pray also for me, that whenever I speak, words may be given me so that I will fearlessly make known the mystery of the gospel, [20] for which I am an ambassador in chains. Pray that I may declare it fearlessly, as I should.   2Co 3:12; 5:20

Final Greetings

[21] Tychicus, the dear brother and faithful servant in the Lord, will tell you everything, so that you also may know how I am and what I am doing. [22] I am sending him to you for this very purpose, that you may know how we are, and that he may encourage you.

[23] Peace to the brothers and sisters,[a] and love with faith from God the Father and the Lord Jesus Christ. [24] Grace to all who love our Lord Jesus Christ with an undying love.[b]   Gal 6:16; 1Pe 5:14

---

[a] 23 The Greek word for *brothers and sisters* (*adelphoi*) refers here to believers, both men and women, as part of God's family.   [b] 24 Or *Grace and immortality to all who love our Lord Jesus Christ.*

Philippians

1 Paul and Timothy, servants of Christ Jesus,   Ac 16:1; 2Co 1:1

To all God's holy people in Christ Jesus at Philippi, together with the overseers and deacons[a]:

[2] Grace and peace to you from God our Father and the Lord Jesus Christ.   Ro 1:7

Thanksgiving and Prayer

[3] I thank my God every time I remember you. [4] In all my prayers for all of you, I always pray with joy [5] because of your partnership in the gospel from the first day until now, [6] being confident of this, that he who began a good work in you will carry it on to completion until the day of Christ Jesus.   Ac 16:12-40; 1Co 1:8

[7] It is right for me to feel this way about all of you, since I have you in my heart and, whether I am in chains or defending and confirming the gospel, all of you share in God's grace with me. [8] God can testify how I long for all of you with the affection of Christ Jesus.   Ro 1:9; 2Pe 1:13

[9] And this is my prayer: that your love may abound more and more in knowledge and depth of insight, [10] so that you may be able to discern what is best and may be pure and blameless for the day of Christ, [11] filled with the fruit of righteousness that comes through Jesus Christ — to the glory and praise of God.   1Co 1:8; 1Th 3:12

Paul's Chains Advance the Gospel

[12] Now I want you to know, brothers and sisters,[b] that what has happened to me has actually served to advance the gospel. [13] As a result, it has become clear throughout the whole palace guard[c] and to everyone else that

---

[a] 1 The word *deacons* refers here to Christians designated to serve with the overseers/elders of the church in a variety of ways; similarly in Romans 16:1 and 1 Tim. 3:8,12.   [b] 12 The Greek word for *brothers and sisters* (*adelphoi*) refers here to believers, both men and women, as part of God's family; also in verse 14; and in 3:1, 13, 17; 4:1, 8, 21.   [c] 13 Or *whole palace*

I am in chains for Christ. [14]And because of my chains, most of the brothers and sisters have become confident in the Lord and dare all the more to proclaim the gospel without fear.   Ac 4:29; 21:33

[15]It is true that some preach Christ out of envy and rivalry, but others out of goodwill. [16]The latter do so out of love, knowing that I am put here for the defense of the gospel. [17]The former preach Christ out of selfish ambition, not sincerely, supposing that they can stir up trouble for me while I am in chains. [18]But what does it matter? The important thing is that in every way, whether from false motives or true, Christ is preached. And because of this I rejoice.   Php 2:3

Yes, and I will continue to rejoice, [19]for I know that through your prayers and God's provision of the Spirit of Jesus Christ what has happened to me will turn out for my deliverance.[a] [20]I eagerly expect and hope that I will in no way be ashamed, but will have sufficient courage so that now as always Christ will be exalted in my body, whether by life or by death. [21]For to me, to live is Christ and to die is gain. [22]If I am to go on living in the body, this will mean fruitful labor for me. Yet what shall I choose? I do not know! [23]I am torn between the two: I desire to depart and be with Christ, which is better by far;

[24]but it is more necessary for you that I remain in the body. [25]Convinced of this, I know that I will remain, and I will continue with all of you for your progress and joy in the faith, [26]so that through my being with you again your boasting in Christ Jesus will abound on account of me.   2Co 5:8; 2Ti 4:6

Life Worthy of the Gospel

[27]Whatever happens, conduct yourselves in a manner worthy of the gospel of Christ. Then, whether I come and see you or only hear about you in my absence, I will know that you stand firm in the one Spirit,[b] striving together as one for the faith of the gospel [28]without being frightened in any way by those who oppose you. This is a sign to them that they will be destroyed, but that you will be saved — and that by God. [29]For it has been granted to you on behalf of Christ not only to believe in him, but also to suffer for him, [30]since you are going through the same struggle you saw I had, and now hear that I still have.   Ac 16:19-40; 1Th 2:2

Imitating Christ's Humility

2 Therefore if you have any encouragement from being united with Christ, if any comfort from his love, if any common sharing in the Spirit, if any tenderness and compassion, [2]then make my joy complete by

---

[a] 19 Or *vindication*; or *salvation*   [b] 27 Or *in one spirit*

being like-minded, having the same love, being one in spirit and of one mind. ³Do nothing out of selfish ambition or vain conceit. Rather, in humility value others above yourselves, ⁴not looking to your own interests but each of you to the interests of the others. Ro 12:10; Gal 5:26

⁵In your relationships with one another, have the same mindset as Christ Jesus: Mt 11:29

⁶Who, being in very nature*ᵃ*
  God, Jn 1:1; 14:9
did not consider equality
  with God something
  to be used to his own
  advantage; Jn 5:18
⁷rather, he made himself
  nothing 2Co 8:9
by taking the very nature*ᵇ*
  of a servant, Mt 20:28
being made in human
  likeness. Jn 1:14; Heb 2:17
⁸And being found in
  appearance as a man,
he humbled himself
by becoming obedient to
  death — Mt 26:39; Heb 5:8
  even death on a cross!

⁹Therefore God exalted him to
  the highest place Ac 2:33
and gave him the name
  that is above every
  name, Eph 1:20-21
¹⁰that at the name of Jesus every
  knee should bow, Ro 14:11
in heaven and on earth and
  under the earth, Mt 28:18

¹¹and every tongue
  acknowledge that Jesus
  Christ is Lord, Jn 13:13
to the glory of God the
  Father.

Do Everything Without Grumbling

¹²Therefore, my dear friends, as you have always obeyed — not only in my presence, but now much more in my absence — continue to work out your salvation with fear and trembling, ¹³for it is God who works in you to will and to act in order to fulfill his good purpose. 2Co 7:15; Ezr 1:5

¹⁴Do everything without grumbling or arguing, ¹⁵so that you may become blameless and pure, "children of God without fault in a warped and crooked generation."*ᶜ* Then you will shine among them like stars in the sky ¹⁶as you hold firmly to the word of life. And then I will be able to boast on the day of Christ that I did not run or labor in vain. ¹⁷But even if I am being poured out like a drink offering on the sacrifice and service coming from your faith, I am glad and rejoice with all of you. ¹⁸So you too should be glad and rejoice with me. Ro 15:16; 2Ti 4:6

Timothy and Epaphroditus

¹⁹I hope in the Lord Jesus to send Timothy to you soon, that I also may be cheered when I receive news about you. ²⁰I have no

---

ᵃ 6 Or *in the form of*   *ᵇ* 7 Or *the form*   *ᶜ* 15 Deut. 32:5

one else like him, who will show genuine concern for your welfare. [21] For everyone looks out for their own interests, not those of Jesus Christ. [22] But you know that Timothy has proved himself, because as a son with his father he has served with me in the work of the gospel. [23] I hope, therefore, to send him as soon as I see how things go with me. [24] And I am confident in the Lord that I myself will come soon. 1Co 10:24

[25] But I think it is necessary to send back to you Epaphroditus, my brother, co-worker and fellow soldier, who is also your messenger, whom you sent to take care of my needs. [26] For he longs for all of you and is distressed because you heard he was ill. [27] Indeed he was ill, and almost died. But God had mercy on him, and not on him only but also on me, to spare me sorrow upon sorrow. [28] Therefore I am all the more eager to send him, so that when you see him again you may be glad and I may have less anxiety. [29] So then, welcome him in the Lord with great joy, and honor people like him, [30] because he almost died for the work of Christ. He risked his life to make up for the help you yourselves could not give me. 1Co 16:17-18; 1Ti 5:17

No Confidence in the Flesh

3 Further, my brothers and sisters, rejoice in the Lord! It is no trouble for me to write the same things to you again, and it is a safeguard for you. [2] Watch out for those dogs, those evildoers, those mutilators of the flesh. [3] For it is we who are the circumcision, we who serve God by his Spirit, who boast in Christ Jesus, and who put no confidence in the flesh— [4] though I myself have reasons for such confidence. Ps 22:16,20

If someone else thinks they have reasons to put confidence in the flesh, I have more: [5] circumcised on the eighth day, of the people of Israel, of the tribe of Benjamin, a Hebrew of Hebrews; in regard to the law, a Pharisee; [6] as for zeal, persecuting the church; as for righteousness based on the law, faultless.

[7] But whatever were gains to me I now consider loss for the sake of Christ. [8] What is more, I consider everything a loss because of the surpassing worth of knowing Christ Jesus my Lord, for whose sake I have lost all things. I consider them garbage, that I may gain Christ [9] and be found in him, not having a righteousness of my own that comes from the law, but that which is through faith in[a] Christ—the righteousness that comes from God on the basis of faith. [10] I want to know Christ—yes, to know the power of his resurrection and participation in his sufferings, becoming like him in his death, [11] and so,

---

[a] 9 Or *through the faithfulness of*

somehow, attaining to the resurrection from the dead. Ro 6:3-5; 8:17

[12] Not that I have already obtained all this, or have already arrived at my goal, but I press on to take hold of that for which Christ Jesus took hold of me. [13] Brothers and sisters, I do not consider myself yet to have taken hold of it. But one thing I do: Forgetting what is behind and straining toward what is ahead, [14] I press on toward the goal to win the prize for which God has called me heavenward in Christ Jesus. Lk 9:62; Heb 6:1

Following Paul's Example

[15] All of us, then, who are mature should take such a view of things. And if on some point you think differently, that too God will make clear to you. [16] Only let us live up to what we have already attained. 1Co 2:6; Gal 5:10

[17] Join together in following my example, brothers and sisters, and just as you have us as a model, keep your eyes on those who live as we do. [18] For, as I have often told you before and now tell you again even with tears, many live as enemies of the cross of Christ. [19] Their destiny is destruction, their god is their stomach, and their glory is in their shame. Their mind is set on earthly things. [20] But our citizenship is in heaven. And we eagerly await a Savior from there, the Lord Jesus Christ, [21] who, by the power that enables him to bring everything under his control, will transform our lowly bodies so that they will be like his glorious body. 1Co 15:43-53; Eph 1:19

Closing Appeal for Steadfastness and Unity

4 Therefore, my brothers and sisters, you whom I love and long for, my joy and crown, stand firm in the Lord in this way, dear friends! Php 1:8,27

[2] I plead with Euodia and I plead with Syntyche to be of the same mind in the Lord. [3] Yes, and I ask you, my true companion, help these women since they have contended at my side in the cause of the gospel, along with Clement and the rest of my coworkers, whose names are in the book of life. Php 2:2,25

Final Exhortations

[4] Rejoice in the Lord always. I will say it again: Rejoice! [5] Let your gentleness be evident to all. The Lord is near. [6] Do not be anxious about anything, but in every situation, by prayer and petition, with thanksgiving, present your requests to God. [7] And the peace of God, which transcends all understanding, will guard your hearts and your minds in Christ Jesus. Jn 14:27; Col 3:15

[8] Finally, brothers and sisters, whatever is true, whatever is noble, whatever is right, whatever is pure, whatever is lovely,

whatever is admirable—if anything is excellent or praiseworthy—think about such things. [9]Whatever you have learned or received or heard from me, or seen in me—put it into practice. And the God of peace will be with you. Ro 15:33; Php 3:17

Thanks for Their Gifts

[10]I rejoiced greatly in the Lord that at last you renewed your concern for me. Indeed, you were concerned, but you had no opportunity to show it. [11]I am not saying this because I am in need, for I have learned to be content whatever the circumstances. [12]I know what it is to be in need, and I know what it is to have plenty. I have learned the secret of being content in any and every situation, whether well fed or hungry, whether living in plenty or in want. [13]I can do all this through him who gives me strength.

[14]Yet it was good of you to share in my troubles. [15]Moreover, as you Philippians know, in the early days of your acquaintance with the gospel, when I set out from Macedonia, not one church

shared with me in the matter of giving and receiving, except you only; [16]for even when I was in Thessalonica, you sent me aid more than once when I was in need. [17]Not that I desire your gifts; what I desire is that more be credited to your account. [18]I have received full payment and have more than enough. I am amply supplied, now that I have received from Epaphroditus the gifts you sent. They are a fragrant offering, an acceptable sacrifice, pleasing to God. [19]And my God will meet all your needs according to the riches of his glory in Christ Jesus. Ps 23:1; Ro 2:4

[20]To our God and Father be glory for ever and ever. Amen.

Final Greetings

[21]Greet all God's people in Christ Jesus. The brothers and sisters who are with me send greetings. [22]All God's people here send you greetings, especially those who belong to Caesar's household. Ac 9:13; Gal 1:2

[23]The grace of the Lord Jesus Christ be with your spirit. Amen.[a] Ro 16:20

[a] 23 Some manuscripts do not have *Amen*.

Colossians

1 Paul, an apostle of Christ Jesus by the will of God, and Timothy our brother, 1Co 1:1; 2Co 1:1

[2]To God's holy people in Colossae, the faithful brothers and sisters[a] in Christ:

Grace and peace to you from God our Father.[b]   Ro 1:7; Col 4:18

Thanksgiving and Prayer

[3]We always thank God, the Father of our Lord Jesus Christ, when we pray for you, [4]because we have heard of your faith in Christ Jesus and of the love you have for all God's people — [5]the faith and love that spring from the hope stored up for you in heaven and about which you have already heard in the true message of the gospel [6]that has come to you. In the same way, the gospel is bearing fruit and growing throughout the whole world — just as it has been doing among you since the day you heard it and truly understood God's grace. [7]You learned it from Epaphras, our dear fellow servant,[c] who is a faithful minister of Christ on our[d] behalf, [8]and who also told us of your love in the Spirit.   Ro 15:30; 1Th 5:8

[9]For this reason, since the day we heard about you, we have not stopped praying for you. We continually ask God to fill you with the knowledge of his will through all the wisdom and understanding that the Spirit gives,[e] [10]so that you may live a life worthy of the Lord and please him in every way: bearing fruit in every good work, growing in the knowledge of God, [11]being strengthened with all power according to his glorious might so that you may have great endurance and patience, [12]and giving

---

[a] 2 The Greek word for *brothers and sisters* (*adelphoi*) refers here to believers, both men and women, as part of God's family; also in 4:15.   [b] 2 Some manuscripts *Father and the Lord Jesus Christ*   [c] 7 Or *slave*   [d] 7 Some manuscripts *your*   [e] 9 Or *all spiritual wisdom and understanding*

joyful thanks to the Father, who has qualified you[a] to share in the inheritance of his holy people in the kingdom of light. 13 For he has rescued us from the dominion of darkness and brought us into the kingdom of the Son he loves, 14 in whom we have redemption, the forgiveness of sins. Eph 1:7; 6:12

The Supremacy of the Son of God

15 The Son is the image of the invisible God, the firstborn over all creation. 16 For in him all things were created: things in heaven and on earth, visible and invisible, whether thrones or powers or rulers or authorities; all things have been created through him and for him. 17 He is before all things, and in him all things hold together. 18 And he is the head of the body, the church; he is the beginning and the firstborn from among the dead, so that in everything he might have the supremacy. 19 For God was pleased to have all his fullness dwell in him, 20 and through him to reconcile to himself all things, whether things on earth or things in heaven, by making peace through his blood, shed on the cross. 2Co 5:18; Eph 2:13

21 Once you were alienated from God and were enemies in your minds because of[b] your evil behavior. 22 But now he has reconciled you by Christ's physical body through death to present you holy in his sight, without blemish and free from accusation — 23 if you continue in your faith, established and firm, and do not move from the hope held out in the gospel. This is the gospel that you heard and that has been proclaimed to every creature under heaven, and of which I, Paul, have become a servant. Ro 10:18; 1Co 3:5; Eph 3:17

Paul's Labor for the Church

24 Now I rejoice in what I am suffering for you, and I fill up in my flesh what is still lacking in regard to Christ's afflictions, for the sake of his body, which is the church. 25 I have become its servant by the commission God gave me to present to you the word of God in its fullness — 26 the mystery that has been kept hidden for ages and generations, but is now disclosed to the Lord's people. 27 To them God has chosen to make known among the Gentiles the glorious riches of this mystery, which is Christ in you, the hope of glory. Ro 8:10; Eph 3:2

28 He is the one we proclaim, admonishing and teaching everyone with all wisdom, so that we may present everyone fully mature in Christ. 29 To this end I strenuously contend with all the energy Christ so powerfully works in me. 1Co 15:10; Eph 1:19; Col 2:1

2 I want you to know how hard I am contending for you and for those at Laodicea, and for all who have not met me personally. ²My goal is that they may be encouraged in heart and united in love, so that they may have the full riches of complete understanding, in order that they may know the mystery of God, namely, Christ, ³in whom are hidden all the treasures of wisdom and knowledge. ⁴I tell you this so that no one may deceive you by fine-sounding arguments. ⁵For though I am absent from you in body, I am present with you in spirit and delight to see how disciplined you are and how firm your faith in Christ is. 1Co 14:40; 1Th 2:17

Spiritual Fullness in Christ

⁶So then, just as you received Christ Jesus as Lord, continue to live your lives in him, ⁷rooted and built up in him, strengthened in the faith as you were taught, and overflowing with thankfulness. Eph 3:17; Col 1:10

⁸See to it that no one takes you captive through hollow and deceptive philosophy, which depends on human tradition and the elemental spiritual forces*a* of this world rather than on Christ. Gal 4:3; 1Ti 6:20

⁹For in Christ all the fullness of the Deity lives in bodily form, ¹⁰and in Christ you have been brought to fullness. He is the head over every power and authority. ¹¹In him you were also circumcised with a circumcision not performed by human hands. Your whole self ruled by the flesh*b* was put off when you were circumcised by*c* Christ, ¹²having been buried with him in baptism, in which you were also raised with him through your faith in the working of God, who raised him from the dead. Ac 2:24; Ro 2:29; 6:5

¹³When you were dead in your sins and in the uncircumcision of your flesh, God made you*d* alive with Christ. He forgave us all our sins, ¹⁴having canceled the charge of our legal indebtedness, which stood against us and condemned us; he has taken it away, nailing it to the cross. ¹⁵And having disarmed the powers and authorities, he made a public spectacle of them, triumphing over them by the cross.*e* Eph 2:15; 6:12

Freedom From Human Rules

¹⁶Therefore do not let anyone judge you by what you eat or drink, or with regard to a religious festival, a New Moon celebration or a Sabbath day. ¹⁷These are a shadow of the things that were to come; the reality, however, is found in Christ. ¹⁸Do

---

a 8 Or *the basic principles*; also in verse 20   *b* 11 In contexts like this, the Greek word for *flesh* (*sarx*) refers to the sinful state of human beings, often presented as a power in opposition to the Spirit; also in verse 13.   *c* 11 Or *put off in the circumcision of*
d 13 Some manuscripts *us*   *e* 15 Or *them in him*

not let anyone who delights in false humility and the worship of angels disqualify you. Such a person also goes into great detail about what they have seen; they are puffed up with idle notions by their unspiritual mind. ¹⁹They have lost connection with the head, from whom the whole body, supported and held together by its ligaments and sinews, grows as God causes it to grow. Eph 1:22; 4:16

²⁰Since you died with Christ to the elemental spiritual forces of this world, why, as though you still belonged to the world, do you submit to its rules: ²¹"Do not handle! Do not taste! Do not touch!"? ²²These rules, which have to do with things that are all destined to perish with use, are based on merely human commands and teachings. ²³Such regulations indeed have an appearance of wisdom, with their self-imposed worship, their false humility and their harsh treatment of the body, but they lack any value in restraining sensual indulgence. Mt 15:9; 1Co 6:13; Tit 1:14

Living as Those Made Alive in Christ

3 Since, then, you have been raised with Christ, set your hearts on things above, where Christ is, seated at the right hand of God. ²Set your minds on things above, not on earthly things. ³For you died, and your life is now hidden with Christ in God. ⁴When Christ, who is your*ᵃ* life, appears, then you also will appear with him in glory. Ro 6:2; 1Jn 3:2

⁵Put to death, therefore, whatever belongs to your earthly nature: sexual immorality, impurity, lust, evil desires and greed, which is idolatry. ⁶Because of these, the wrath of God is coming.*ᵇ* ⁷You used to walk in these ways, in the life you once lived. ⁸But now you must also rid yourselves of all such things as these: anger, rage, malice, slander, and filthy language from your lips. ⁹Do not lie to each other, since you have taken off your old self with its practices ¹⁰and have put on the new self, which is being renewed in knowledge in the image of its Creator. ¹¹Here there is no Gentile or Jew, circumcised or uncircumcised, barbarian, Scythian, slave or free, but Christ is all, and is in all. Ro 12:2; Gal 3:28; Eph 1:23

¹²Therefore, as God's chosen people, holy and dearly loved, clothe yourselves with compassion, kindness, humility, gentleness and patience. ¹³Bear with each other and forgive one another if any of you has a grievance against someone. Forgive as the Lord forgave you. ¹⁴And over all these virtues put on love,

ᵃ 4 Some manuscripts *our*   *ᵇ 6* Some early manuscripts *coming on those who are disobedient* which binds them all together in perfect unity. Eph 4:3; Php 2:3

[15] Let the peace of Christ rule in your hearts, since as members of one body you were called to peace. And be thankful. [16] Let the message of Christ dwell among you richly as you teach and admonish one another with all wisdom through psalms, hymns, and songs from the Spirit, singing to God with gratitude in your hearts. [17] And whatever you do, whether in word or deed, do it all in the name of the Lord Jesus, giving thanks to God the Father through him. 1Co 10:31; Eph 5:19

Instructions for Christian Households

3:18-4:1pp — Eph 5:22-6:9

[18] Wives, submit yourselves to your husbands, as is fitting in the Lord. Eph 5:22

[19] Husbands, love your wives and do not be harsh with them.

[20] Children, obey your parents in everything, for this pleases the Lord.

[21] Fathers,[a] do not embitter your children, or they will become discouraged.

[22] Slaves, obey your earthly masters in everything; and do it, not only when their eye is on you and to curry their favor, but with sincerity of heart and reverence for the Lord. [23] Whatever you do, work at it with all your heart, as working for the Lord, not for human masters, [24] since you know that you will receive an inheritance from the Lord as a reward. It is the Lord Christ you are serving. [25] Anyone who does wrong will be repaid for their wrongs, and there is no favoritism. Ac 10:34; 20:32

4 Masters, provide your slaves with what is right and fair, because you know that you also have a Master in heaven.

Further Instructions

[2] Devote yourselves to prayer, being watchful and thankful. [3] And pray for us, too, that God may open a door for our message, so that we may proclaim the mystery of Christ, for which I am in chains. [4] Pray that I may proclaim it clearly, as I should. [5] Be wise in the way you act toward outsiders; make the most of every opportunity. [6] Let your conversation be always full of grace, seasoned with salt, so that you may know how to answer everyone. Mk 9:50; Eph 5:16; 1Pe 3:15

Final Greetings

[7] Tychicus will tell you all the news about me. He is a dear brother, a faithful minister and fellow servant[b] in the Lord. [8] I am sending him to you for the express purpose that you may know about our[c] circumstances and that he may encourage

---

[a] 21 Or *Parents*   [b] 7 Or *slave*; also in verse 12   [c] 8 Some manuscripts *that he may know about your*

your hearts. ⁹He is coming with Onesimus, our faithful and dear brother, who is one of you. They will tell you everything that is happening here.   Eph 6:21-22

¹⁰My fellow prisoner Aristarchus sends you his greetings, as does Mark, the cousin of Barnabas. (You have received instructions about him; if he comes to you, welcome him.) ¹¹Jesus, who is called Justus, also sends greetings. These are the only Jews*a* among my co-workers for the kingdom of God, and they have proved a comfort to me. ¹²Epaphras, who is one of you and a servant of Christ Jesus, sends greetings. He is always wrestling in prayer for you, that you may stand firm in all the will of God, mature and fully assured. ¹³I vouch for him that he is working hard for you and for those at Laodicea and Hierapolis. ¹⁴Our dear friend Luke, the doctor, and Demas send greetings. ¹⁵Give my greetings to the brothers and sisters at Laodicea, and to Nympha and the church in her house.   Ac 4:36; Ro 15:30

¹⁶After this letter has been read to you, see that it is also read in the church of the Laodiceans and that you in turn read the letter from Laodicea.   2Th 3:14

¹⁷Tell Archippus: "See to it that you complete the ministry you have received in the Lord." 2Ti 4:5

¹⁸I, Paul, write this greeting in my own hand. Remember my chains. Grace be with you.

---

a 11 Greek *only ones of the circumcision group*

1 Thessalonians

1 Paul, Silas[a] and Timothy,

To the church of the Thessalonians in God the Father and the Lord Jesus Christ: Ac 17:1

Grace and peace to you.   Ro 1:7

Thanksgiving for the Thessalonians' Faith

[2] We always thank God for all of you and continually mention you in our prayers. [3] We remember before our God and Father your work produced by faith, your labor prompted by love, and your endurance inspired by hope in our Lord Jesus Christ.   Ro 1:8; 8:25

[4] For we know, brothers and sisters[b] loved by God, that he has chosen you, [5] because our gospel came to you not simply with words but also with power, with the Holy Spirit and deep conviction. You know how we lived among you for your sake. [6] You became imitators of us and of the Lord, for you welcomed the message in the midst of severe suffering with the joy given by the Holy Spirit. [7] And so you became a model to all the believers in Macedonia and Achaia. [8] The Lord's message rang out from you not only in Macedonia and Achaia — your faith in God has become known everywhere. Therefore we do not need to say anything about it, [9] for they themselves report what kind of reception you gave us. They tell how you turned to God from idols to serve the living and true God, [10] and to wait for his Son from heaven, whom he raised from the dead — Jesus, who rescues us from the coming wrath.   Ac 2:24; Ro 5:9

Paul's Ministry in Thessalonica

2 You know, brothers and sisters, that our visit to you was not without results. [2] We had previously suffered and been treated outrageously in Philippi, as

---

[a] 1 Greek *Silvanus*, a variant of *Silas*   [b] 4 The Greek word for *brothers and sisters* (*adelphoi*) refers here to believers, both men and women, as part of God's family; also in 2:1, 9, 14, 17; 3:7; 4:1, 10, 13; 5:1, 4, 12, 14, 25, 27.

you know, but with the help of our God we dared to tell you his gospel in the face of strong opposition. ³For the appeal we make does not spring from error or impure motives, nor are we trying to trick you. ⁴On the contrary, we speak as those approved by God to be entrusted with the gospel. We are not trying to please people but God, who tests our hearts. ⁵You know we never used flattery, nor did we put on a mask to cover up greed — God is our witness. ⁶We were not looking for praise from people, not from you or anyone else, even though as apostles of Christ we could have asserted our authority. ⁷Instead, we were like young children[a] among you.

Gal 1:10; 1Th 1:5,9

Just as a nursing mother cares for her children, ⁸so we cared for you. Because we loved you so much, we were delighted to share with you not only the gospel of God but our lives as well. ⁹Surely you remember, brothers and sisters, our toil and hardship; we worked night and day in order not to be a burden to anyone while we preached the gospel of God to you. ¹⁰You are witnesses, and so is God, of how holy, righteous and blameless we were among you who believed. ¹¹For you know that we dealt with each of you as a father deals with his own children, ¹²encouraging, comforting and urging you to live lives worthy of God, who calls you into his kingdom and glory.

Eph 4:1; 1Th 1:5

¹³And we also thank God continually because, when you received the word of God, which you heard from us, you accepted it not as a human word, but as it actually is, the word of God, which is indeed at work in you who believe. ¹⁴For you, brothers and sisters, became imitators of God's churches in Judea, which are in Christ Jesus: You suffered from your own people the same things those churches suffered from the Jews ¹⁵who killed the Lord Jesus and the prophets and also drove us out. They displease God and are hostile to everyone ¹⁶in their effort to keep us from speaking to the Gentiles so that they may be saved. In this way they always heap up their sins to the limit. The wrath of God has come upon them at last.[b]

Mt 23:32; Ac 13:45,50

Paul's Longing to See the Thessalonians

¹⁷But, brothers and sisters, when we were orphaned by being separated from you for a short time (in person, not in thought), out of our intense longing we made every effort to see you. ¹⁸For we wanted to come to you — certainly I, Paul, did, again and again — but Satan blocked our way. ¹⁹For what is our hope, our joy, or the crown in which we

---

[a] 7 Some manuscripts *were gentle*   [b] 16 Or *them fully*

will glory in the presence of our Lord Jesus when he comes? Is it not you? [20] Indeed, you are our glory and joy. 2Co 1:14; 1Th 3:10

3 So when we could stand it no longer, we thought it best to be left by ourselves in Athens. [2] We sent Timothy, who is our brother and co-worker in God's service in spreading the gospel of Christ, to strengthen and encourage you in your faith, [3] so that no one would be unsettled by these trials. For you know quite well that we are destined for them. [4] In fact, when we were with you, we kept telling you that we would be persecuted. And it turned out that way, as you well know. [5] For this reason, when I could stand it no longer, I sent to find out about your faith. I was afraid that in some way the tempter had tempted you and that our labors might have been in vain. Ac 9:16; Gal 2:2

Timothy's Encouraging Report

[6] But Timothy has just now come to us from you and has brought good news about your faith and love. He has told us that you always have pleasant memories of us and that you long to see us, just as we also long to see you. [7] Therefore, brothers and sisters, in all our distress and persecution we were encouraged about you because of your faith. [8] For now we really live, since you are standing firm in the Lord. [9] How can we thank God enough for you in return for all the joy we have in the presence of our God because of you? [10] Night and day we pray most earnestly that we may see you again and supply what is lacking in your faith. 1Th 1:2; 2Ti 1:3

[11] Now may our God and Father himself and our Lord Jesus clear the way for us to come to you. [12] May the Lord make your love increase and overflow for each other and for everyone else, just as ours does for you. [13] May he strengthen your hearts so that you will be blameless and holy in the presence of our God and Father when our Lord Jesus comes with all his holy ones. 1Co 1:8

Living to Please God

4 As for other matters, brothers and sisters, we instructed you how to live in order to please God, as in fact you are living. Now we ask you and urge you in the Lord Jesus to do this more and more. [2] For you know what instructions we gave you by the authority of the Lord Jesus. 2Co 5:9

[3] It is God's will that you should be sanctified: that you should avoid sexual immorality; [4] that each of you should learn to control your own body[a] in a way that is holy and honorable, [5] not in passionate lust like the pagans, who do not know God; [6] and that in this matter no one

---

[a] 4 Or *learn to live with your own wife*; or *learn to acquire a wife*

should wrong or take advantage of a brother or sister.[a] The Lord will punish all those who commit such sins, as we told you and warned you before. [7] For God did not call us to be impure, but to live a holy life. [8] Therefore, anyone who rejects this instruction does not reject a human being but God, the very God who gives you his Holy Spirit.   Ro 5:5; Gal 4:6

[9] Now about your love for one another we do not need to write to you, for you yourselves have been taught by God to love each other. [10] And in fact, you do love all of God's family throughout Macedonia. Yet we urge you, brothers and sisters, to do so more and more, [11] and to make it your ambition to lead a quiet life: You should mind your own business and work with your hands, just as we told you, [12] so that your daily life may win the respect of outsiders and so that you will not be dependent on anybody.   Eph 4:28

Believers Who Have Died

[13] Brothers and sisters, we do not want you to be uninformed about those who sleep in death, so that you do not grieve like the rest of mankind, who have no hope. [14] For we believe that Jesus died and rose again, and so we believe that God will bring with Jesus those who have fallen asleep in him. [15] According to the Lord's word, we tell you that we who are still alive, who are left until the coming of the Lord, will certainly not precede those who have fallen asleep. [16] For the Lord himself will come down from heaven, with a loud command, with the voice of the archangel and with the trumpet call of God, and the dead in Christ will rise first. [17] After that, we who are still alive and are left will be caught up together with them in the clouds to meet the Lord in the air. And so we will be with the Lord forever. [18] Therefore encourage one another with these words.   1Co 15:52; Ac 1:9; Rev 11:12

The Day of the Lord

5 Now, brothers and sisters, about times and dates we do not need to write to you, [2] for you know very well that the day of the Lord will come like a thief in the night. [3] While people are saying, "Peace and safety," destruction will come on them suddenly, as labor pains on a pregnant woman, and they will not escape.

[4] But you, brothers and sisters, are not in darkness so that this day should surprise you like a thief. [5] You are all children of the light and children of the day. We do not belong to the night or to the darkness. [6] So then, let us not be like others, who are asleep, but let us be awake and sober.

[a] 6 The Greek word for *brother or sister* (*adelphos*) refers here to a believer, whether man or woman, as part of God's family.

⁷For those who sleep, sleep at night, and those who get drunk, get drunk at night. ⁸But since we belong to the day, let us be sober, putting on faith and love as a breastplate, and the hope of salvation as a helmet. ⁹For God did not appoint us to suffer wrath but to receive salvation through our Lord Jesus Christ. ¹⁰He died for us so that, whether we are awake or asleep, we may live together with him. ¹¹Therefore encourage one another and build each other up, just as in fact you are doing. 1Th 4:18; Eph 4:29

Final Instructions

¹²Now we ask you, brothers and sisters, to acknowledge those who work hard among you, who care for you in the Lord and who admonish you. ¹³Hold them in the highest regard in love because of their work. Live in peace with each other. ¹⁴And we urge you, brothers and sisters, warn those who are idle and disruptive, encourage the disheartened, help the weak, be patient with everyone. ¹⁵Make sure that nobody pays back wrong for wrong, but always strive to do what is good for each other and for everyone else. Eph 4:32

¹⁶Rejoice always, ¹⁷pray continually, ¹⁸give thanks in all circumstances; for this is God's will for you in Christ Jesus. Php 4:4

¹⁹Do not quench the Spirit. ²⁰Do not treat prophecies with contempt ²¹but test them all; hold on to what is good, ²²reject every kind of evil. 1Co 14:29; Eph 4:30

²³May God himself, the God of peace, sanctify you through and through. May your whole spirit, soul and body be kept blameless at the coming of our Lord Jesus Christ. ²⁴The one who calls you is faithful, and he will do it. 1Co 1:9; Php 1:6

²⁵Brothers and sisters, pray for us. ²⁶Greet all God's people with a holy kiss. ²⁷I charge you before the Lord to have this letter read to all the brothers and sisters.

²⁸The grace of our Lord Jesus Christ be with you. Ro 16:20

2 Thessalonians

1

Paul, Silas[a] and Timothy,

To the church of the Thessalonians in God our Father and the Lord Jesus Christ: *Ac 17:1*

[2] Grace and peace to you from God the Father and the Lord Jesus Christ. *Ro 1:7*

Thanksgiving and Prayer

[3] We ought always to thank God for you, brothers and sisters,[b] and rightly so, because your faith is growing more and more, and the love all of you have for one another is increasing. [4] Therefore, among God's churches we boast about your perseverance and faith in all the persecutions and trials you are enduring. *1Th 3:12; 2:14*

[5] All this is evidence that God's judgment is right, and as a result you will be counted worthy of the kingdom of God, for which you are suffering. [6] God is just: He will pay back trouble to those who trouble you [7] and give relief to you who are troubled, and to us as well. This will happen when the Lord Jesus is revealed from heaven in blazing fire with his powerful angels. [8] He will punish those who do not know God and do not obey the gospel of our Lord Jesus. [9] They will be punished with everlasting destruction and shut out from the presence of the Lord and from the glory of his might [10] on the day he comes to be glorified in his holy people and to be marveled at among all those who have believed. This includes you, because you believed our testimony to you. *1Th 4:16; Jude 14*

[11] With this in mind, we constantly pray for you, that our God may make you worthy of his calling, and that by his power he may bring to fruition your every desire for goodness and your every deed prompted by faith. [12] We pray this so that the name of our Lord Jesus may be glorified in you, and you in him, according to the grace of our God and the Lord Jesus Christ.[c]

---

[a] 1 Greek *Silvanus*, a variant of *Silas*   [b] 3 The Greek word for *brothers and sisters* (*adelphoi*) refers here to believers, both men and women, as part of God's family; also in 2:1, 13, 15; 3:1, 6, 13.   [c] 12 Or *God and Lord, Jesus Christ*

The Man of Lawlessness

2 Concerning the coming of our Lord Jesus Christ and our being gathered to him, we ask you, brothers and sisters, ²not to become easily unsettled or alarmed by the teaching allegedly from us — whether by a prophecy or by word of mouth or by letter — asserting that the day of the Lord has already come. ³Don't let anyone deceive you in any way, for that day will not come until the rebellion occurs and the man of lawlessness*ᵃ* is revealed, the man doomed to destruction. ⁴He will oppose and will exalt himself over everything that is called God or is worshiped, so that he sets himself up in God's temple, proclaiming himself to be God. Isa 14:13-14; 1Co 8:5

⁵Don't you remember that when I was with you I used to tell you these things? ⁶And now you know what is holding him back, so that he may be revealed at the proper time. ⁷For the secret power of lawlessness is already at work; but the one who now holds it back will continue to do so till he is taken out of the way. ⁸And then the lawless one will be revealed, whom the Lord Jesus will overthrow with the breath of his mouth and destroy by the splendor of his coming. ⁹The coming of the lawless one will be in accordance with how Satan works. He will use all sorts of displays of power through signs and wonders that serve the lie, ¹⁰and all the ways that wickedness deceives those who are perishing. They perish because they refused to love the truth and so be saved. ¹¹For this reason God sends them a powerful delusion so that they will believe the lie ¹²and so that all will be condemned who have not believed the truth but have delighted in wickedness. Jn 4:48; Ro 1:32

Stand Firm

¹³But we ought always to thank God for you, brothers and sisters loved by the Lord, because God chose you as firstfruits*ᵇ* to be saved through the sanctifying work of the Spirit and through belief in the truth. ¹⁴He called you to this through our gospel, that you might share in the glory of our Lord Jesus Christ.

¹⁵So then, brothers and sisters, stand firm and hold fast to the teachings*ᶜ* we passed on to you, whether by word of mouth or by letter. 1Co 11:2; 16:13

¹⁶May our Lord Jesus Christ himself and God our Father, who loved us and by his grace gave us eternal encouragement and good hope, ¹⁷encourage your hearts and strengthen you in every good deed and word. Jn 3:16; 1Th 3:2

ᵃ 3 Some manuscripts *sin*   *ᵇ 13* Some manuscripts *because from the beginning God chose you*   *ᶜ 15* Or *traditions*

Request for Prayer

3 As for other matters, brothers and sisters, pray for us that the message of the Lord may spread rapidly and be honored, just as it was with you. [2] And pray that we may be delivered from wicked and evil people, for not everyone has faith. [3] But the Lord is faithful, and he will strengthen you and protect you from the evil one. [4] We have confidence in the Lord that you are doing and will continue to do the things we command. [5] May the Lord direct your hearts into God's love and Christ's perseverance. 1Ch 29:18

Warning Against Idleness

[6] In the name of the Lord Jesus Christ, we command you, brothers and sisters, to keep away from every believer who is idle and disruptive and does not live according to the teaching[a] you received from us. [7] For you yourselves know how you ought to follow our example. We were not idle when we were with you, [8] nor did we eat anyone's food without paying for it. On the contrary, we worked night and day, laboring and toiling so that we would not be a burden to any of you. [9] We did this, not because we do not have the right to such help, but in order to offer ourselves as a model for you to imitate. [10] For even when we were with you, we gave you this rule: "The one who is unwilling to work shall not eat."

[11] We hear that some among you are idle and disruptive. They are not busy; they are busybodies. [12] Such people we command and urge in the Lord Jesus Christ to settle down and earn the food they eat. [13] And as for you, brothers and sisters, never tire of doing what is good. Gal 6:9; 1Ti 5:13

[14] Take special note of anyone who does not obey our instruction in this letter. Do not associate with them, in order that they may feel ashamed. [15] Yet do not regard them as an enemy, but warn them as you would a fellow believer. Gal 6:1; 1Th 5:14

Final Greetings

[16] Now may the Lord of peace himself give you peace at all times and in every way. The Lord be with all of you. Ro 15:33

[17] I, Paul, write this greeting in my own hand, which is the distinguishing mark in all my letters. This is how I write. 1Co 16:21

[18] The grace of our Lord Jesus Christ be with you all. Ro 16:20

---

[a] 6 Or *tradition*

1 Timothy

1 Paul, an apostle of Christ Jesus by the command of God our Savior and of Christ Jesus our hope, Col 1:27; Tit 1:3

2 To Timothy my true son in the faith: Ac 16:1; 2Ti 1:2

Grace, mercy and peace from God the Father and Christ Jesus our Lord. Ro 1:7

Timothy Charged to Oppose False Teachers

3 As I urged you when I went into Macedonia, stay there in Ephesus so that you may command certain people not to teach false doctrines any longer 4 or to devote themselves to myths and endless genealogies. Such things promote controversial speculations rather than advancing God's work — which is by faith. 5 The goal of this command is love, which comes from a pure heart and a good conscience and a sincere faith. 6 Some have departed from these and have turned to meaningless talk. 7 They want to be teachers of the law, but they do not know what they are talking about or what they so confidently affirm. 2Ti 2:22; Tit 1:14

8 We know that the law is good if one uses it properly. 9 We also know that the law is made not for the righteous but for lawbreakers and rebels, the ungodly and sinful, the unholy and irreligious, for those who kill their fathers or mothers, for murderers, 10 for the sexually immoral, for those practicing homosexuality, for slave traders and liars and perjurers — and for whatever else is contrary to the sound doctrine 11 that conforms to the gospel concerning the glory of the blessed God, which he entrusted to me. Gal 2:7; 2Ti 4:3

The Lord's Grace to Paul

12 I thank Christ Jesus our Lord, who has given me strength, that he considered me trustworthy, appointing me to his service. 13 Even though I was once a blasphemer and a persecutor and a

violent man, I was shown mercy because I acted in ignorance and unbelief. ¹⁴ The grace of our Lord was poured out on me abundantly, along with the faith and love that are in Christ Jesus. Ac 8:3

¹⁵ Here is a trustworthy saying that deserves full acceptance: Christ Jesus came into the world to save sinners—of whom I am the worst. ¹⁶ But for that very reason I was shown mercy so that in me, the worst of sinners, Christ Jesus might display his immense patience as an example for those who would believe in him and receive eternal life. ¹⁷ Now to the King eternal, immortal, invisible, the only God, be honor and glory for ever and ever. Amen.

The Charge to Timothy Renewed

¹⁸ Timothy, my son, I am giving you this command in keeping with the prophecies once made about you, so that by recalling them you may fight the battle well, ¹⁹ holding on to faith and a good conscience, which some have rejected and so have suffered shipwreck with regard to the faith. ²⁰ Among them are Hymenaeus and Alexander, whom I have handed over to Satan to be taught not to blaspheme. 1Ti 4:14

Instructions on Worship

2 I urge, then, first of all, that petitions, prayers, interces-sion and thanksgiving be made for all people — ² for kings and all those in authority, that we may live peaceful and quiet lives in all godliness and holiness. ³ This is good, and pleases God our Savior, ⁴ who wants all people to be saved and to come to a knowledge of the truth. ⁵ For there is one God and one mediator between God and mankind, the man Christ Jesus, ⁶ who gave himself as a ransom for all people. This has now been witnessed to at the proper time. ⁷ And for this purpose I was appointed a herald and an apostle — I am telling the truth, I am not lying — and a true and faithful teacher of the Gentiles. 1Co 1:6; Gal 3:20

⁸ Therefore I want the men everywhere to pray, lifting up holy hands without anger or disputing. ⁹ I also want the women to dress modestly, with decency and propriety, adorning themselves, not with elaborate hairstyles or gold or pearls or expensive clothes, ¹⁰ but with good deeds, appropriate for women who profess to worship God. Pr 31:13; 1Pe 3:3

¹¹ A woman[a] should learn in quietness and full submission. ¹² I do not permit a woman to teach or to assume authority over a man;[b] she must be quiet. ¹³ For Adam was formed first, then Eve. ¹⁴ And Adam was not the one deceived; it was the woman who was deceived and became a sinner. ¹⁵ But

a 11 Or wife; also in verse 12   b 12 Or over her husband

women[a] will be saved through childbearing—if they continue in faith, love and holiness with propriety.   Ge 3:1-6,13; 1Co 11:8

Qualifications for Overseers and Deacons

3 Here is a trustworthy saying: Whoever aspires to be an overseer desires a noble task. [2]Now the overseer is to be above reproach, faithful to his wife, temperate, self-controlled, respectable, hospitable, able to teach, [3]not given to drunkenness, not violent but gentle, not quarrelsome, not a lover of money. [4]He must manage his own family well and see that his children obey him, and he must do so in a manner worthy of full[b] respect. [5](If anyone does not know how to manage his own family, how can he take care of God's church?) [6]He must not be a recent convert, or he may become conceited and fall under the same judgment as the devil. [7]He must also have a good reputation with outsiders, so that he will not fall into disgrace and into the devil's trap.   1Ti 6:4; 2Ti 2:26

[8]In the same way, deacons[c] are to be worthy of respect, sincere, not indulging in much wine, and not pursuing dishonest gain. [9]They must keep hold of the deep truths of the faith with a clear conscience. [10]They must first be tested; and then if there is nothing against them, let them serve as deacons.   1Ti 1:19; Tit 2:3

[11]In the same way, the women[d] are to be worthy of respect, not malicious talkers but temperate and trustworthy in everything.

[12]A deacon must be faithful to his wife and must manage his children and his household well. [13]Those who have served well gain an excellent standing and great assurance in their faith in Christ Jesus.

Reasons for Paul's Instructions

[14]Although I hope to come to you soon, I am writing you these instructions so that, [15]if I am delayed, you will know how people ought to conduct themselves in God's household, which is the church of the living God, the pillar and foundation of the truth. [16]Beyond all question, the mystery from which true godliness springs is great: Ro 16:25; Eph 2:21

He appeared in the flesh, Jn 1:14
    was vindicated by the
        Spirit,[e]
was seen by angels,
    was preached among the
        nations,   Col 1:23
was believed on in the world,
    was taken up in glory. Mk 16:19

---

[a] 15 Greek she   [b] 4 Or him with proper   [c] 8 The word deacons refers here to Christians designated to serve with the overseers/elders of the church in a variety of ways; similarly in verse 12; and in Romans 16:1 and Phil. 1:1. are deacons   [d] 11 Possibly deacons' wives or women who are deacons   [e] 16 Or vindicated in spirit

4 The Spirit clearly says that in later times some will abandon the faith and follow deceiving spirits and things taught by demons. ²Such teachings come through hypocritical liars, whose consciences have been seared as with a hot iron. ³They forbid people to marry and order them to abstain from certain foods, which God created to be received with thanksgiving by those who believe and who know the truth. ⁴For everything God created is good, and nothing is to be rejected if it is received with thanksgiving, ⁵because it is consecrated by the word of God and prayer. Ro 14:14-18

⁶If you point these things out to the brothers and sisters,ᵃ you will be a good minister of Christ Jesus, nourished on the truths of the faith and of the good teaching that you have followed. ⁷Have nothing to do with godless myths and old wives' tales; rather, train yourself to be godly. ⁸For physical training is of some value, but godliness has value for all things, holding promise for both the present life and the life to come. ⁹This is a trustworthy saying that deserves full acceptance. ¹⁰That is why we labor and strive, because we have put our hope in the living God, who is the Savior of all people, and especially of those who believe. 1Ti 1:15

¹¹Command and teach these things. ¹²Don't let anyone look down on you because you are young, but set an example for the believers in speech, in conduct, in love, in faith and in purity. ¹³Until I come, devote yourself to the public reading of Scripture, to preaching and to teaching. ¹⁴Do not neglect your gift, which was given you through prophecy when the body of elders laid their hands on you. 1Ti 1:14,18; Tit 2:7

¹⁵Be diligent in these matters; give yourself wholly to them, so that everyone may see your progress. ¹⁶Watch your life and doctrine closely. Persevere in them, because if you do, you will save both yourself and your hearers. Ro 11:14

Widows, Elders and Slaves

5 Do not rebuke an older man harshly, but exhort him as if he were your father. Treat younger men as brothers, ²older women as mothers, and younger women as sisters, with absolute purity. Lev 19:32; Tit 2:6

³Give proper recognition to those widows who are really in need. ⁴But if a widow has children or grandchildren, these should learn first of all to put their religion into practice by caring for their own family and so repaying their parents and grandparents, for this is pleasing

---

ᵃ 6 The Greek word for *brothers and sisters* (*adelphoi*) refers here to believers, both men and women, as part of God's family.

to God. [5] The widow who is really in need and left all alone puts her hope in God and continues night and day to pray and to ask God for help. [6] But the widow who lives for pleasure is dead even while she lives. [7] Give the people these instructions, so that no one may be open to blame. [8] Anyone who does not provide for their relatives, and especially for their own household, has denied the faith and is worse than an unbeliever. 1Ti 4:11; Tit 1:16

[9] No widow may be put on the list of widows unless she is over sixty, has been faithful to her husband, [10] and is well known for her good deeds, such as bringing up children, showing hospitality, washing the feet of the Lord's people, helping those in trouble and devoting herself to all kinds of good deeds. Lk 7:44; 1Pe 2:12

[11] As for younger widows, do not put them on such a list. For when their sensual desires overcome their dedication to Christ, they want to marry. [12] Thus they bring judgment on themselves, because they have broken their first pledge. [13] Besides, they get into the habit of being idle and going about from house to house. And not only do they become idlers, but also busybodies who talk nonsense, saying things they ought not to. [14] So I counsel younger widows to marry, to have children, to manage their homes and to give the enemy no opportunity for slander. [15] Some have in fact already turned away to follow Satan. 1Co 7:9; 2Th 3:11

[16] If any woman who is a believer has widows in her care, she should continue to help them and not let the church be burdened with them, so that the church can help those widows who are really in need. ver 3-5

[17] The elders who direct the affairs of the church well are worthy of double honor, especially those whose work is preaching and teaching. [18] For Scripture says, "Do not muzzle an ox while it is treading out the grain,"[a] and "The worker deserves his wages."[b] [19] Do not entertain an accusation against an elder unless it is brought by two or three witnesses. [20] But those elders who are sinning you are to reprove before everyone, so that the others may take warning. [21] I charge you, in the sight of God and Christ Jesus and the elect angels, to keep these instructions without partiality, and to do nothing out of favoritism. 1Ti 6:13; 2Ti 4:1

[22] Do not be hasty in the laying on of hands, and do not share in the sins of others. Keep yourself pure. Ac 6:6; Eph 5:11

[23] Stop drinking only water, and use a little wine because of your stomach and your frequent illnesses. 1Ti 3:8

[24] The sins of some are obvi-

---

[a] 18 Deut. 25:4   [b] 18 Luke 10:7

ous, reaching the place of judgment ahead of them; the sins of others trail behind them. ²⁵In the same way, good deeds are obvious, and even those that are not obvious cannot remain hidden forever.

6 All who are under the yoke of slavery should consider their masters worthy of full respect, so that God's name and our teaching may not be slandered. ²Those who have believing masters should not show them disrespect just because they are fellow believers. Instead, they should serve them even better because their masters are dear to them as fellow believers and are devoted to the welfare*a* of their slaves.

False Teachers and the Love of Money

These are the things you are to teach and insist on. ³If anyone teaches otherwise and does not agree to the sound instruction of our Lord Jesus Christ and to godly teaching, ⁴they are conceited and understand nothing. They have an unhealthy interest in controversies and quarrels about words that result in envy, strife, malicious talk, evil suspicions ⁵and constant friction between people of corrupt mind, who have been robbed of the truth and who think that godliness is a means to financial gain.   1Ti 1:10; Tit 1:15

⁶But godliness with content-ment is great gain. ⁷For we brought nothing into the world, and we can take nothing out of it. ⁸But if we have food and clothing, we will be content with that. ⁹Those who want to get rich fall into temptation and a trap and into many foolish and harmful desires that plunge people into ruin and destruction. ¹⁰For the love of money is a root of all kinds of evil. Some people, eager for money, have wandered from the faith and pierced themselves with many griefs.   1Ti 3:3; Heb 13:5

Final Charge to Timothy

¹¹But you, man of God, flee from all this, and pursue righteousness, godliness, faith, love, endurance and gentleness. ¹²Fight the good fight of the faith. Take hold of the eternal life to which you were called when you made your good confession in the presence of many witnesses. ¹³In the sight of God, who gives life to everything, and of Christ Jesus, who while testifying before Pontius Pilate made the good confession, I charge you ¹⁴to keep this command without spot or blame until the appearing of our Lord Jesus Christ, ¹⁵which God will bring about in his own time—God, the blessed and only Ruler, the King of kings and Lord of lords, ¹⁶who alone is immortal and who lives in unapproachable

a 2 Or *and benefit from the service*

light, whom no one has seen or can see. To him be honor and might forever. Amen. Jn 18:33-37

[17] Command those who are rich in this present world not to be arrogant nor to put their hope in wealth, which is so uncertain, but to put their hope in God, who richly provides us with everything for our enjoyment. [18] Command them to do good, to be rich in good deeds, and to be generous and willing to share. [19] In this way they will lay up treasure for themselves as a firm foundation for the coming age, so that they may take hold of the life that is truly life. Lk 12:20-21; Ac 14:17

[20] Timothy, guard what has been entrusted to your care. Turn away from godless chatter and the opposing ideas of what is falsely called knowledge, [21] which some have professed and in so doing have departed from the faith. 2Ti 1:12,14; 2:18

Grace be with you all. Col 4:18

2 Timothy

1 Paul, an apostle of Christ Jesus by the will of God, in keeping with the promise of life that is in Christ Jesus, 2Co 1:1

² To Timothy, my dear son:

Grace, mercy and peace from God the Father and Christ Jesus our Lord. Ro 1:7

Thanksgiving

³ I thank God, whom I serve, as my ancestors did, with a clear conscience, as night and day I constantly remember you in my prayers. ⁴ Recalling your tears, I long to see you, so that I may be filled with joy. ⁵ I am reminded of your sincere faith, which first lived in your grandmother Lois and in your mother Eunice and, I am persuaded, now lives in you also.

Appeal for Loyalty to Paul and the Gospel

⁶ For this reason I remind you to fan into flame the gift of God, which is in you through the laying on of my hands. ⁷ For the Spirit God gave us does not make us timid, but gives us power, love and self-discipline. ⁸ So do not be ashamed of the testimony about our Lord or of me his prisoner. Rather, join with me in suffering for the gospel, by the power of God. ⁹ He has saved us and called us to a holy life — not because of anything we have done but because of his own purpose and grace. This grace was given us in Christ Jesus before the beginning of time, ¹⁰ but it has now been revealed through the appearing of our Savior, Christ Jesus, who has destroyed death and has brought life and immortality to light through the gospel. ¹¹ And of this gospel I was appointed a herald and an apostle and a teacher. ¹² That is why I am suffering as I am. Yet this is no cause for shame, because I know whom I have believed, and am convinced that he is able to guard what I have entrusted to him until that day. 1Ti 2:7; 6:20

¹³What you heard from me, keep as the pattern of sound teaching, with faith and love in Christ Jesus. ¹⁴Guard the good deposit that was entrusted to you—guard it with the help of the Holy Spirit who lives in us. 1Ti 1:14

Examples of Disloyalty and Loyalty

¹⁵You know that everyone in the province of Asia has deserted me, including Phygelus and Hermogenes. 2Ti 4:10-11,16 ¹⁶May the Lord show mercy to the household of Onesiphorus, because he often refreshed me and was not ashamed of my chains. ¹⁷On the contrary, when he was in Rome, he searched hard for me until he found me. ¹⁸May the Lord grant that he will find mercy from the Lord on that day! You know very well in how many ways he helped me in Ephesus. 2Ti 4:19; Heb 6:10

The Appeal Renewed

2 You then, my son, be strong in the grace that is in Christ Jesus. ²And the things you have heard me say in the presence of many witnesses entrust to reliable people who will also be qualified to teach others. ³Join with me in suffering, like a good soldier of Christ Jesus. ⁴No one serving as a soldier gets entangled in civilian affairs, but rather tries to please his commanding officer. ⁵Similarly, anyone who competes as an athlete does not receive the victor's crown except by competing according to the rules. ⁶The hardworking farmer should be the first to receive a share of the crops. ⁷Reflect on what I am saying, for the Lord will give you insight into all this. 1Co 9:25; 1Ti 1:18

⁸Remember Jesus Christ, raised from the dead, descended from David. This is my gospel, ⁹for which I am suffering even to the point of being chained like a criminal. But God's word is not chained. ¹⁰Therefore I endure everything for the sake of the elect, that they too may obtain the salvation that is in Christ Jesus, with eternal glory. Ro 2:16 ¹¹Here is a trustworthy saying: 1Ti 1:15

If we died with him,
  we will also live with him;
¹²if we endure,
  we will also reign with
    him. Ro 8:17; 1Pe 4:13
If we disown him,
  he will also disown us;
¹³if we are faithless,
  he remains faithful, Nu 23:19
  for he cannot disown
    himself.

Dealing With False Teachers

¹⁴Keep reminding God's people of these things. Warn them before God against quarreling about words; it is of no value, and only ruins those who listen.

¹⁵Do your best to present yourself to God as one approved, a worker who does not need to be ashamed and who correctly handles the word of truth. ¹⁶Avoid godless chatter, because those who indulge in it will become more and more ungodly. ¹⁷Their teaching will spread like gangrene. Among them are Hymenaeus and Philetus, ¹⁸who have departed from the truth. They say that the resurrection has already taken place, and they destroy the faith of some. ¹⁹Nevertheless, God's solid foundation stands firm, sealed with this inscription: "The Lord knows those who are his," and, "Everyone who confesses the name of the Lord must turn away from wickedness." Jn 10:14; 1Co 1:2

²⁰In a large house there are articles not only of gold and silver, but also of wood and clay; some are for special purposes and some for common use. ²¹Those who cleanse themselves from the latter will be instruments for special purposes, made holy, useful to the Master and prepared to do any good work. Ro 9:21; 2Ti 3:17

²²Flee the evil desires of youth and pursue righteousness, faith, love and peace, along with those who call on the Lord out of a pure heart. ²³Don't have anything to do with foolish and stupid arguments, because you know they produce quarrels. ²⁴And the Lord's servant must not be quarrelsome but must be kind to everyone, able to teach, not resentful. ²⁵Opponents must be gently instructed, in the hope that God will grant them repentance leading them to a knowledge of the truth, ²⁶and that they will come to their senses and escape from the trap of the devil, who has taken them captive to do his will. 1Ti 1:5; 3:7

3 But mark this: There will be terrible times in the last days. ²People will be lovers of themselves, lovers of money, boastful, proud, abusive, disobedient to their parents, ungrateful, unholy, ³without love, unforgiving, slanderous, without self-control, brutal, not lovers of the good, ⁴treacherous, rash, conceited, lovers of pleasure rather than lovers of God— ⁵having a form of godliness but denying its power. Have nothing to do with such people. Ro 1:30; 1Ti 4:1

⁶They are the kind who worm their way into homes and gain control over gullible women, who are loaded down with sins and are swayed by all kinds of evil desires, ⁷always learning but never able to come to a knowledge of the truth. ⁸Just as Jannes and Jambres opposed Moses, so also these teachers oppose the truth. They are men of depraved minds, who, as far as the faith is concerned, are rejected. ⁹But they will not get very far because, as in the case of those

men, their folly will be clear to everyone. Ex 7:12; 1Ti 6:5

A Final Charge to Timothy

¹⁰You, however, know all about my teaching, my way of life, my purpose, faith, patience, love, endurance, ¹¹persecutions, sufferings—what kinds of things happened to me in Antioch, Iconium and Lystra, the persecutions I endured. Yet the Lord rescued me from all of them. ¹²In fact, everyone who wants to live a godly life in Christ Jesus will be persecuted, ¹³while evildoers and impostors will go from bad to worse, deceiving and being deceived. ¹⁴But as for you, continue in what you have learned and have become convinced of, because you know those from whom you learned it, ¹⁵and how from infancy you have known the Holy Scriptures, which are able to make you wise for salvation through faith in Christ Jesus. ¹⁶All Scripture is God-breathed and is useful for teaching, rebuking, correcting and training in righteousness, ¹⁷so that the servant of God*a* may be thoroughly equipped for every good work. 2Pe 1:20-21

4 In the presence of God and of Christ Jesus, who will judge the living and the dead, and in view of his appearing and his kingdom, I give you this charge: ²Preach the word; be prepared in season and out of season; cor-

rect, rebuke and encourage—with great patience and careful instruction. ³For the time will come when people will not put up with sound doctrine. Instead, to suit their own desires, they will gather around them a great number of teachers to say what their itching ears want to hear. ⁴They will turn their ears away from the truth and turn aside to myths. ⁵But you, keep your head in all situations, endure hardship, do the work of an evangelist, discharge all the duties of your ministry. Ac 21:8; 1Ti 1:10

⁶For I am already being poured out like a drink offering, and the time for my departure is near. ⁷I have fought the good fight, I have finished the race, I have kept the faith. ⁸Now there is in store for me the crown of righteousness, which the Lord, the righteous Judge, will award to me on that day—and not only to me, but also to all who have longed for his appearing. 1Ti 1:18; 2Ti 1:12

Personal Remarks

⁹Do your best to come to me quickly, ¹⁰for Demas, because he loved this world, has deserted me and has gone to Thessalonica. Crescens has gone to Galatia, and Titus to Dalmatia. ¹¹Only Luke is with me. Get Mark and bring him with you, because he is helpful to me in my ministry. ¹²I sent Tychicus to Ephe-

a 17 Or that you, a man of God,

sus. [13]When you come, bring the cloak that I left with Carpus at Troas, and my scrolls, especially the parchments.   Col 4:14; 2Ti 1:15

[14]Alexander the metalworker did me a great deal of harm. The Lord will repay him for what he has done. [15]You too should be on your guard against him, because he strongly opposed our message.

[16]At my first defense, no one came to my support, but everyone deserted me. May it not be held against them. [17]But the Lord stood at my side and gave me strength, so that through me the message might be fully proclaimed and all the Gentiles might hear it. And I was delivered from the lion's mouth. [18]The Lord will rescue me from every evil attack and will bring me safely to his heavenly kingdom. To him be glory for ever and ever. Amen.   Ps 121:7; Ro 11:36

Final Greetings

[19]Greet Priscilla[a] and Aquila and the household of Onesiphorus. [20]Erastus stayed in Corinth, and I left Trophimus sick in Miletus. [21]Do your best to get here before winter. Eubulus greets you, and so do Pudens, Linus, Claudia and all the brothers and sisters.[b]   Ac 19:22; 20:4

[22]The Lord be with your spirit. Grace be with you all.   Gal 6:18

---

[a] 19 Greek *Prisca*, a variant of *Priscilla*   [b] 21 The Greek word for *brothers and sisters* (*adelphoi*) refers here to believers, both men and women, as part of God's family.

Titus

1 Paul, a servant of God and an apostle of Jesus Christ to further the faith of God's elect and their knowledge of the truth that leads to godliness — ²in the hope of eternal life, which God, who does not lie, promised before the beginning of time, ³and which now at his appointed season he has brought to light through the preaching entrusted to me by the command of God our Savior,

⁴To Titus, my true son in our common faith: 2Co 2:13

Grace and peace from God the Father and Christ Jesus our Savior.   Ro 1:7

Appointing Elders Who Love What Is Good

1:6-8Ref — 1Ti 3:2-4

⁵The reason I left you in Crete was that you might put in order what was left unfinished and appoint*ᵃ* elders in every town, as I directed you. ⁶An elder must be blameless, faithful to his wife, a man whose children believe*ᵇ* and are not open to the charge of being wild and disobedient. ⁷Since an overseer manages God's household, he must be blameless — not overbearing, not quick-tempered, not given to drunkenness, not violent, not pursuing dishonest gain. ⁸Rather, he must be hospitable, one who loves what is good, who is self-controlled, upright, holy and disciplined. ⁹He must hold firmly to the trustworthy message as it has been taught, so that he can encourage others by sound doctrine and refute those who oppose it.   1Ti 3:2-4

Rebuking Those Who Fail to Do Good

¹⁰For there are many rebellious people, full of meaningless talk and deception, especially those of the circumcision group. ¹¹They must be silenced, because they are disrupting whole households by teaching things they ought not to teach — and that for the sake of dishon-

---

ᵃ 5 Or *ordain*   *ᵇ 6* Or *children are trustworthy*

est gain. [12]One of Crete's own prophets has said it: "Cretans are always liars, evil brutes, lazy gluttons."[a] [13]This saying is true. Therefore rebuke them sharply, so that they will be sound in the faith [14]and will pay no attention to Jewish myths or to the merely human commands of those who reject the truth. [15]To the pure, all things are pure, but to those who are corrupted and do not believe, nothing is pure. In fact, both their minds and consciences are corrupted. [16]They claim to know God, but by their actions they deny him. They are detestable, disobedient and unfit for doing anything good. 1Ti 1:4; 1Jn 2:4

Doing Good for the Sake of the Gospel

2 You, however, must teach what is appropriate to sound doctrine. [2]Teach the older men to be temperate, worthy of respect, self-controlled, and sound in faith, in love and in endurance. 1Ti 1:10; Tit 1:13

[3]Likewise, teach the older women to be reverent in the way they live, not to be slanderers or addicted to much wine, but to teach what is good. [4]Then they can urge the younger women to love their husbands and children, [5]to be self-controlled and pure, to be busy at home, to be kind, and to be subject to their husbands,

so that no one will malign the word of God. Eph 5:22; 1Ti 6:1

[6]Similarly, encourage the young men to be self-controlled. [7]In everything set them an example by doing what is good. In your teaching show integrity, seriousness [8]and soundness of speech that cannot be condemned, so that those who oppose you may be ashamed because they have nothing bad to say about us. 1Ti 4:12; 1Pe 2:12

[9]Teach slaves to be subject to their masters in everything, to try to please them, not to talk back to them, [10]and not to steal from them, but to show that they can be fully trusted, so that in every way they will make the teaching about God our Savior attractive. Mt 5:16; Eph 6:5

[11]For the grace of God has appeared that offers salvation to all people. [12]It teaches us to say "No" to ungodliness and worldly passions, and to live self-controlled, upright and godly lives in this present age, [13]while we wait for the blessed hope — the appearing of the glory of our great God and Savior, Jesus Christ, [14]who gave himself for us to redeem us from all wickedness and to purify for himself a people that are his very own, eager to do what is good.

[15]These, then, are the things you should teach. Encourage and rebuke with all authority. Do not let anyone despise you.

---

[a] 12 From the Cretan philosopher Epimenides

Saved in Order to Do Good

3 Remind the people to be subject to rulers and authorities, to be obedient, to be ready to do whatever is good, [2] to slander no one, to be peaceable and considerate, and always to be gentle toward everyone. Eph 4:31

[3] At one time we too were foolish, disobedient, deceived and enslaved by all kinds of passions and pleasures. We lived in malice and envy, being hated and hating one another. [4] But when the kindness and love of God our Savior appeared, [5] he saved us, not because of righteous things we had done, but because of his mercy. He saved us through the washing of rebirth and renewal by the Holy Spirit, [6] whom he poured out on us generously through Jesus Christ our Savior, [7] so that, having been justified by his grace, we might become heirs having the hope of eternal life. [8] This is a trustworthy saying. And I want you to stress these things, so that those who have trusted in God may be careful to devote themselves to doing what is good. These things are excellent and profitable for everyone. 1Ti 1:15; Tit 2:14

[9] But avoid foolish controversies and genealogies and arguments and quarrels about the law, because these are unprofitable and useless. [10] Warn a divisive person once, and then warn them a second time. After that, have nothing to do with them. [11] You may be sure that such people are warped and sinful; they are self-condemned. 1Ti 1:4; 2Ti 2:14

Final Remarks

[12] As soon as I send Artemas or Tychicus to you, do your best to come to me at Nicopolis, because I have decided to winter there. [13] Do everything you can to help Zenas the lawyer and Apollos on their way and see that they have everything they need. [14] Our people must learn to devote themselves to doing what is good, in order to provide for urgent needs and not live unproductive lives. Ac 18:24; 20:4

[15] Everyone with me sends you greetings. Greet those who love us in the faith. 1Ti 1:2

Grace be with you all. Col 4:18

Philemon

[1] Paul, a prisoner of Christ Jesus, and Timothy our brother,   Eph 3:1

To Philemon our dear friend and fellow worker — [2] also to Apphia our sister and Archippus our fellow soldier — and to the church that meets in your home: Ro 16:5; Php 2:25; Col 4:17

[3] Grace and peace to you[a] from God our Father and the Lord Jesus Christ.   Ro 1:7

Thanksgiving and Prayer

[4] I always thank my God as I remember you in my prayers, [5] because I hear about your love for all his holy people and your faith in the Lord Jesus. [6] I pray that your partnership with us in the faith may be effective in deepening your understanding of every good thing we share for the sake of Christ. [7] Your love has given me great joy and encouragement, because you, brother, have refreshed the hearts of the Lord's people.   2Co 7:4,13; Col 1:4

Paul's Plea for Onesimus

[8] Therefore, although in Christ I could be bold and order you to do what you ought to do, [9] yet I prefer to appeal to you on the basis of love. It is as none other than Paul — an old man and now also a prisoner of Christ Jesus — [10] that I appeal to you for my son Onesimus,[b] who became my son while I was in chains. [11] Formerly he was useless to you, but now he has become useful both to you and to me.   1Co 4:15; Col 4:9

[12] I am sending him — who is my very heart — back to you. [13] I would have liked to keep him with me so that he could take your place in helping me while I am in chains for the gospel. [14] But I did not want to do anything without your consent, so that any favor you do would not seem forced but would be voluntary. [15] Perhaps the reason he was separated from you for a little while was that you might have him back forever — [16] no longer as a slave, but better

---

[a] 3 The Greek is plural; also in verses 22 and 25; elsewhere in this letter "you" is singular.
[b] 10 Onesimus means useful.

than a slave, as a dear brother. He is very dear to me but even dearer to you, both as a fellow man and as a brother in the Lord. 2Co 9:7; 1Ti 6:2

¹⁷So if you consider me a partner, welcome him as you would welcome me. ¹⁸If he has done you any wrong or owes you anything, charge it to me. ¹⁹I, Paul, am writing this with my own hand. I will pay it back—not to mention that you owe me your very self. ²⁰I do wish, brother, that I may have some benefit from you in the Lord; refresh my heart in Christ. ²¹Confident of your obedience, I write to you, knowing that you will do even more than I ask. 2Co 2:3; 8:23

²²And one thing more: Prepare a guest room for me, because I hope to be restored to you in answer to your prayers. 2Co 1:11

²³Epaphras, my fellow prisoner in Christ Jesus, sends you greetings. ²⁴And so do Mark, Aristarchus, Demas and Luke, my fellow workers. Ac 12:12; Col 1:7

²⁵The grace of the Lord Jesus Christ be with your spirit. 2Ti 4:22

Hebrews

God's Final Word: His Son

1 In the past God spoke to our ancestors through the prophets at many times and in various ways, ²but in these last days he has spoken to us by his Son, whom he appointed heir of all things, and through whom also he made the universe. ³The Son is the radiance of God's glory and the exact representation of his being, sustaining all things by his powerful word. After he had provided purification for sins, he sat down at the right hand of the Majesty in heaven. ⁴So he became as much superior to the angels as the name he has inherited is superior to theirs.   Php 2:9-10; Heb 7:27

The Son Superior to Angels

⁵For to which of the angels did God ever say,

"You are my Son;
today I have become your
        Father"ᵃ?   Ps 2:7

Or again,

"I will be his Father,
and he will be my Son"ᵇ?

⁶And again, when God brings his firstborn into the world, he says,   Heb 10:5

"Let all God's angels worship
        him."ᶜ   Ps 97:7

⁷In speaking of the angels he says,

"He makes his angels spirits,
and his servants flames of
        fire."ᵈ   Ps 104:4

⁸But about the Son he says,

"Your throne, O God, will last
        for ever and ever;   Lk 1:33
a scepter of justice will
        be the scepter of your
        kingdom.

ᵃ 5 Psalm 2:7   ᵇ 5 2 Samuel 7:14; 1 Chron. 17:13   ᶜ 6 Deut. 32:43 (see Dead Sea Scrolls and Septuagint)   ᵈ 7 Psalm 104:4

⁹You have loved righteousness
    and hated wickedness;
  therefore God, your God,
    has set you above your
    companions   Php 2:9
  by anointing you with the
    oil of joy."ᵃ   Isa 61:1,3

¹⁰He also says,

  "In the beginning, Lord, you
    laid the foundations of
    the earth,
  and the heavens are the
    work of your hands.Ps 8:6
¹¹They will perish, but you
    remain;
  they will all wear out like a
    garment. Isa 34:4; Heb 12:27
¹²You will roll them up like a
    robe;
  like a garment they will be
    changed.
  But you remain the same,
    and your years will never
    end."ᵇ   Ps 102:25-27

¹³To which of the angels did God
ever say,

  "Sit at my right hand   Mk 16:19
    until I make your enemies
    a footstool for your feet"ᶜ?

¹⁴Are not all angels ministering
spirits sent to serve those who
will inherit salvation?   Jos 10:24

Warning to Pay Attention

2 We must pay the most care-
    ful attention, therefore, to
what we have heard, so that we
do not drift away. ²For since the
message spoken through angels
was binding, and every violation and disobedience received
its just punishment, ³how shall
we escape if we ignore so great a
salvation? This salvation, which
was first announced by the Lord,
was confirmed to us by those
who heard him. ⁴God also testified to it by signs, wonders and
various miracles, and by gifts of
the Holy Spirit distributed according to his will. Lk 1:2; Heb 10:29

Jesus Made Fully Human

⁵It is not to angels that he has
subjected the world to come,
about which we are speaking.
⁶But there is a place where someone has testified: Heb 4:4

  "What is mankind that you
    are mindful of them,
  a son of man that you care
    for him?   Job 7:17; Ps 144:3
⁷You made them a littleᵈ lower
    than the angels;
  you crowned them with
    glory and honor
⁸   and put everything under
    their feet."ᵉ,ᶠ   1Co 15:25

In putting everything under
them,ᵍ God left nothing that is not
subject to them.ᵍ Yet at present we
do not see everything subject to
them.ᵍ ⁹But we do see Jesus, who

ᵃ 9 Psalm 45:6,7   ᵇ 12 Psalm 102:25-27   ᶜ 13 Psalm 110:1   ᵈ 7 Or *them for a little while*
ᵉ 6-8 Psalm 8:4-6   ᶠ 7,8 Or *⁷You made him a little lower than the angels;/ you crowned him
with glory and honor/ ⁸and put everything under his feet."*   ᵍ 8 Or *him*

was made lower than the angels for a little while, now crowned with glory and honor because he suffered death, so that by the grace of God he might taste death for everyone. Jn 3:16; Ac 2:33; Php 2:7-9

¹⁰ In bringing many sons and daughters to glory, it was fitting that God, for whom and through whom everything exists, should make the pioneer of their salvation perfect through what he suffered. ¹¹ Both the one who makes people holy and those who are made holy are of the same family. So Jesus is not ashamed to call them brothers and sisters.ᵃ ¹² He says, Jn 20:17; Ro 11:36

"I will declare your name to
    my brothers and sisters;
in the assembly I will sing
    your praises."ᵇ

¹³ And again,

"I will put my trust in him."ᶜ

And again he says,

"Here am I, and the children
    God has given me."ᵈ

¹⁴ Since the children have flesh and blood, he too shared in their humanity so that by his death he might break the power of him who holds the power of death — that is, the devil — ¹⁵ and free those who all their lives were held in slavery by their fear of death. ¹⁶ For surely it is not angels he helps, but Abraham's descendants. ¹⁷ For this reason he had to be made like them,ᵉ fully human in every way, in order that he might become a merciful and faithful high priest in service to God, and that he might make atonement for the sins of the people. ¹⁸ Because he himself suffered when he was tempted, he is able to help those who are being tempted. Heb 4:15; 1Jn 3:8

Jesus Greater Than Moses

3 Therefore, holy brothers and sisters, who share in the heavenly calling, fix your thoughts on Jesus, whom we acknowledge as our apostle and high priest. ² He was faithful to the one who appointed him, just as Moses was faithful in all God's house. ³ Jesus has been found worthy of greater honor than Moses, just as the builder of a house has greater honor than the house itself. ⁴ For every house is built by someone, but God is the builder of everything. ⁵ "Moses was faithful as a servant in all God's house,"ᶠ bearing witness to what would be spoken by God in the future. ⁶ But Christ is faithful as the Son over God's house. And we are his

---

ᵃ 11 The Greek word for *brothers and sisters* (*adelphoi*) refers here to believers, both men and women, as part of God's family; also in verse 12; and in 3:1, 12; 10:19; 13:22.
ᵇ 12 Psalm 22:22   ᶜ 13 Isaiah 8:17   ᵈ 13 Isaiah 8:18   ᵉ 17 Or *like his brothers*
ᶠ 5 Num. 12:7

house, if indeed we hold firmly to our confidence and the hope in which we glory. Heb 2:11,17

Warning Against Unbelief

[7] So, as the Holy Spirit says:

"Today, if you hear his voice,
[8] do not harden your
hearts Heb 4:7
as you did in the rebellion,
during the time of testing in
the wilderness,
[9] where your ancestors tested
and tried me,
though for forty years they
saw what I did. Ac 7:36
[10] That is why I was angry with
that generation;
I said, 'Their hearts are
always going astray,
and they have not known
my ways.'
[11] So I declared on oath in my
anger, Dt 1:34-35
'They shall never enter my
rest.'" [a] Ps 95:7-11; Heb 4:3,5

[12] See to it, brothers and sisters, that none of you has a sinful, unbelieving heart that turns away from the living God. [13] But encourage one another daily, as long as it is called "Today," so that none of you may be hardened by sin's deceitfulness. [14] We have come to share in Christ, if indeed we hold our original conviction firmly to the very end. [15] As has just been said: Eph 4:22

"Today, if you hear his voice,
do not harden your hearts
as you did in the rebellion." [b]

[16] Who were they who heard and rebelled? Were they not all those Moses led out of Egypt? [17] And with whom was he angry for forty years? Was it not with those who sinned, whose bodies perished in the wilderness? [18] And to whom did God swear that they would never enter his rest if not to those who disobeyed? [19] So we see that they were not able to enter, because of their unbelief. Jn 3:36; Nu 14:20-23

A Sabbath-Rest for the People of God

4 Therefore, since the promise of entering his rest still stands, let us be careful that none of you be found to have fallen short of it. [2] For we also have had the good news proclaimed to us, just as they did; but the message they heard was of no value to them, because they did not share the faith of those who obeyed. [c] [3] Now we who have believed enter that rest, just as God has said, 1Th 2:13; Heb 12:15

"So I declared on oath in my
anger,
'They shall never enter my
rest.'" [d] Ps 95:11; Heb 3:11

And yet his works have been finished since the creation of the

---

[a] 11 Psalm 95:7-11   [b] 15 Psalm 95:7,8   [c] 2 Some manuscripts *because those who heard did not combine it with faith*   [d] 3 Psalm 95:11; also in verse 5

world. ⁴For somewhere he has spoken about the seventh day in these words: "On the seventh day God rested from all his works."*a* ⁵And again in the passage above he says, "They shall never enter my rest." Ex 20:11; Ps 95:11

⁶Therefore since it still remains for some to enter that rest, and since those who formerly had the good news proclaimed to them did not go in because of their disobedience, ⁷God again set a certain day, calling it "Today." This he did when a long time later he spoke through David, as in the passage already quoted: Heb 3:18

"Today, if you hear his voice,
    do not harden your
        hearts."*b*

⁸For if Joshua had given them rest, God would not have spoken later about another day. ⁹There remains, then, a Sabbath-rest for the people of God; ¹⁰for anyone who enters God's rest also rests from their works,*c* just as God did from his. ¹¹Let us, therefore, make every effort to enter that rest, so that no one will perish by following their example of disobedience. Heb 1:1; 3:18

¹²For the word of God is alive and active. Sharper than any double-edged sword, it penetrates even to dividing soul and spirit, joints and marrow; it judges the thoughts and atti-

tudes of the heart. ¹³Nothing in all creation is hidden from God's sight. Everything is uncovered and laid bare before the eyes of him to whom we must give account. Ps 33:13-15; 1Co 14:24-25

Jesus the Great High Priest

¹⁴Therefore, since we have a great high priest who has ascended into heaven,*d* Jesus the Son of God, let us hold firmly to the faith we profess. ¹⁵For we do not have a high priest who is unable to empathize with our weaknesses, but we have one who has been tempted in every way, just as we are—yet he did not sin. ¹⁶Let us then approach God's throne of grace with confidence, so that we may receive mercy and find grace to help us in our time of need. 2Co 5:21; Heb 3:1

5 Every high priest is selected from among the people and is appointed to represent the people in matters related to God, to offer gifts and sacrifices for sins. ²He is able to deal gently with those who are ignorant and are going astray, since he himself is subject to weakness. ³This is why he has to offer sacrifices for his own sins, as well as for the sins of the people. ⁴And no one takes this honor on himself, but he receives it when called by God, just as Aaron was. Heb 7:27-28

⁵In the same way, Christ did not take on himself the glory of

---

a 4 Gen. 2:2   *b* 7 Psalm 95:7,8   *c* 10 Or *labor*   *d* 14 Greek *has gone through the heavens* becoming a high priest. But God said to him, Jn 8:54; Heb 1:1

"You are my Son;
today I have become your
Father."[a]

[6] And he says in another place,

"You are a priest forever,
in the order of
Melchizedek."[b] Ps 110:4

[7] During the days of Jesus' life on earth, he offered up prayers and petitions with fervent cries and tears to the one who could save him from death, and he was heard because of his reverent submission. [8] Son though he was, he learned obedience from what he suffered [9] and, once made perfect, he became the source of eternal salvation for all who obey him [10] and was designated by God to be high priest in the order of Melchizedek. Mk 14:36

Warning Against Falling Away
6:4-6Ref — Heb 10:26-31

[11] We have much to say about this, but it is hard to make it clear to you because you no longer try to understand. [12] In fact, though by this time you ought to be teachers, you need someone to teach you the elementary truths of God's word all over again. You need milk, not solid food! [13] Anyone who lives on milk, being still an infant, is not acquainted with the teaching about righteousness. [14] But solid food is for the mature, who by constant use have trained themselves to distinguish good from evil. 1Co 2:6; 3:2

[6] Therefore let us move beyond the elementary teachings about Christ and be taken forward to maturity, not laying again the foundation of repentance from acts that lead to death,[c] and of faith in God, [2] instruction about cleansing rites,[d] the laying on of hands, the resurrection of the dead, and eternal judgment. [3] And God permitting, we will do so. Php 3:12-14; Heb 5:12

[4] It is impossible for those who have once been enlightened, who have tasted the heavenly gift, who have shared in the Holy Spirit, [5] who have tasted the goodness of the word of God and the powers of the coming age [6] and who have fallen[e] away, to be brought back to repentance. To their loss they are crucifying the Son of God all over again and subjecting him to public disgrace. [7] Land that drinks in the rain often falling on it and that produces a crop useful to those for whom it is farmed receives the blessing of God. [8] But land that produces thorns and thistles is worthless and is in danger of being cursed. In the end it will be burned. Ge 3:17-18; Isa 5:6

[9] Even though we speak like

---

[a] 5 Psalm 2:7   [b] 6 Psalm 110:4   [c] 1 Or *from useless rituals*   [d] 2 Or *about baptisms*
[e] 6 Or *age,* [6] *if they fall*

this, dear friends, we are convinced of better things in your case — the things that have to do with salvation. ¹⁰God is not unjust; he will not forget your work and the love you have shown him as you have helped his people and continue to help them. ¹¹We want each of you to show this same diligence to the very end, so that what you hope for may be fully realized. ¹²We do not want you to become lazy, but to imitate those who through faith and patience inherit what has been promised. 1Th 1:3; Heb 3:6

The Certainty of God's Promise

¹³When God made his promise to Abraham, since there was no one greater for him to swear by, he swore by himself, ¹⁴saying, "I will surely bless you and give you many descendants."ᵃ ¹⁵And so after waiting patiently, Abraham received what was promised.

¹⁶People swear by someone greater than themselves, and the oath confirms what is said and puts an end to all argument. ¹⁷Because God wanted to make the unchanging nature of his purpose very clear to the heirs of what was promised, he confirmed it with an oath. ¹⁸God did this so that, by two unchangeable things in which it is impossible for God to lie, we who have fled to take hold of the hope set before us may be greatly encouraged. ¹⁹We

have this hope as an anchor for the soul, firm and secure. It enters the inner sanctuary behind the curtain, ²⁰where our forerunner, Jesus, has entered on our behalf. He has become a high priest forever, in the order of Melchizedek. Heb 2:17; 4:14; 5:6

Melchizedek the Priest

7 This Melchizedek was king of Salem and priest of God Most High. He met Abraham returning from the defeat of the kings and blessed him, ²and Abraham gave him a tenth of everything. First, the name Melchizedek means "king of righteousness"; then also, "king of Salem" means "king of peace." ³Without father or mother, without genealogy, without beginning of days or end of life, resembling the Son of God, he remains a priest forever. Ge 14:18-20

⁴Just think how great he was: Even the patriarch Abraham gave him a tenth of the plunder! ⁵Now the law requires the descendants of Levi who become priests to collect a tenth from the people — that is, from their fellow Israelites — even though they also are descended from Abraham. ⁶This man, however, did not trace his descent from Levi, yet he collected a tenth from Abraham and blessed him who had the promises. ⁷And without doubt the lesser is

ᵃ 14 Gen. 22:17

blessed by the greater. **8**In the one case, the tenth is collected by people who die; but in the other case, by him who is declared to be living. **9**One might even say that Levi, who collects the tenth, paid the tenth through Abraham, **10**because when Melchizedek met Abraham, Levi was still in the body of his ancestor.   Ro 4:13; Heb 5:6; 6:20

Jesus Like Melchizedek

11If perfection could have been attained through the Levitical priesthood—and indeed the law given to the people established that priesthood—why was there still need for another priest to come, one in the order of Melchizedek, not in the order of Aaron? **12**For when the priesthood is changed, the law must be changed also. **13**He of whom these things are said belonged to a different tribe, and no one from that tribe has ever served at the altar. **14**For it is clear that our Lord descended from Judah, and in regard to that tribe Moses said nothing about priests. **15**And what we have said is even more clear if another priest like Melchizedek appears, **16**one who has become a priest not on the basis of a regulation as to his ancestry but on the basis of the power of an indestructible life. **17**For it is declared: Isa 11:1; Lk 3:33

"You are a priest forever,
  in the order of
  Melchizedek."[a]   Ps 110:4

18The former regulation is set aside because it was weak and useless **19**(for the law made nothing perfect), and a better hope is introduced, by which we draw near to God.   Ro 3:20; Heb 4:16

20And it was not without an oath! Others became priests without any oath, **21**but he became a priest with an oath when God said to him:

"The Lord has sworn
  and will not change his
    mind: 1Sa 15:29; Ro 11:29
  'You are a priest forever.' "[a]

22Because of this oath, Jesus has become the guarantor of a better covenant.   Heb 5:6; 8:6

23Now there have been many of those priests, since death prevented them from continuing in office; **24**but because Jesus lives forever, he has a permanent priesthood. **25**Therefore he is able to save completely[b] those who come to God through him, because he always lives to intercede for them.   Ro 8:34; 11:14

26Such a high priest truly meets our need—one who is holy, blameless, pure, set apart from sinners, exalted above the heavens. **27**Unlike the other high priests, he does not need to offer sacrifices day after day, first

---

[a] 17,21 Psalm 110:4   [b] 25 Or *forever*

for his own sins, and then for the sins of the people. He sacrificed for their sins once for all when he offered himself. ²⁸ For the law appoints as high priests men in all their weakness; but the oath, which came after the law, appointed the Son, who has been made perfect forever. Heb 2:10; 5:2

The High Priest of a New Covenant

8 Now the main point of what we are saying is this: We do have such a high priest, who sat down at the right hand of the throne of the Majesty in heaven, ² and who serves in the sanctuary, the true tabernacle set up by the Lord, not by a mere human being. Heb 9:11,24

³ Every high priest is appointed to offer both gifts and sacrifices, and so it was necessary for this one also to have something to offer. ⁴ If he were on earth, he would not be a priest, for there are already priests who offer the gifts prescribed by the law. ⁵ They serve at a sanctuary that is a copy and shadow of what is in heaven. This is why Moses was warned when he was about to build the tabernacle: "See to it that you make everything according to the pattern shown you on the mountain."*a* ⁶ But in fact the ministry Jesus has received is as superior to theirs as the covenant of which he is mediator is

superior to the old one, since the new covenant is established on better promises. Ex 25:40; Lk 22:20

⁷ For if there had been nothing wrong with that first covenant, no place would have been sought for another. ⁸ But God found fault with the people and said*b*: Heb 7:11

"The days are coming,
    declares the Lord,
when I will make a new
    covenant   Jer 31:31
with the people of Israel
    and with the people of
        Judah.
⁹ It will not be like the covenant
    I made with their ancestors
when I took them by the hand
    to lead them out of Egypt,
because they did not remain
    faithful to my covenant,
    and I turned away from
        them,
        declares the Lord.
¹⁰ This is the covenant I will
    establish with the
        people of Israel   Ro 11:27
    after that time, declares the
        Lord.
I will put my laws in their
    minds
    and write them on their
        hearts.   Heb 10:16
I will be their God,
    and they will be my people.
¹¹ No longer will they teach their
    neighbor,
    or say to one another, 'Know
        the Lord,'

---

a 5 Exodus 25:40   *b* 8 Some manuscripts may be translated *fault and said to the people.*

because they will all
know me,
from the least of them to the
greatest.   Isa 54:13; Jn 6:45
¹²For I will forgive their
wickedness
and will remember their
sins no more."ᵃ   Ro 11:27

¹³By calling this covenant
"new," he has made the first one
obsolete; and what is obsolete
and outdated will soon disappear.   2Co 5:17

Worship in the Earthly Tabernacle

9 Now the first covenant had
regulations for worship and
also an earthly sanctuary. ²A
tabernacle was set up. In its first
room were the lampstand and
the table with its consecrated
bread; this was called the Holy
Place. ³Behind the second curtain was a room called the Most
Holy Place, ⁴which had the gold-
en altar of incense and the gold-
covered ark of the covenant. This
ark contained the gold jar of manna, Aaron's staff that had budded,
and the stone tablets of the covenant. ⁵Above the ark were the
cherubim of the Glory, overshadowing the atonement cover. But
we cannot discuss these things
in detail now.   Ex 25:8,23-29
⁶When everything had been
arranged like this, the priests

entered regularly into the outer room to carry on their ministry. ⁷But only the high priest
entered the inner room, and
that only once a year, and never
without blood, which he offered
for himself and for the sins the
people had committed in ignorance. ⁸The Holy Spirit was
showing by this that the way
into the Most Holy Place had not
yet been disclosed as long as the
first tabernacle was still func-
tioning. ⁹This is an illustration
for the present time, indicating
that the gifts and sacrifices being offered were not able to clear
the conscience of the worshiper.
¹⁰They are only a matter of food
and drink and various ceremonial washings — external regulations applying until the time
of the new order.   Col 2:16; Heb 7:16

The Blood of Christ

¹¹But when Christ came as
high priest of the good things
that are now already here,ᵇ he
went through the greater and
more perfect tabernacle that is
not made with human hands,
that is to say, is not a part of this
creation. ¹²He did not enter by
means of the blood of goats and
calves; but he entered the Most
Holy Place once for all by his own
blood, thus obtainingᶜ eternal redemption. ¹³The blood of goats
and bulls and the ashes of a heifer

ᵃ 12 Jer. 31:31-34   ᵇ 11 Some early manuscripts *are to come*   ᶜ 12 Or *blood, having obtained* sprinkled on those who are ceremonially unclean sanctify them so that they are outwardly clean. [14] How much more, then, will the blood of Christ, who through the eternal Spirit offered himself unblemished to God, cleanse our consciences from acts that lead to death,[a] so that we may serve the living God! Heb 6:1; 1Pe 3:18

[15] For this reason Christ is the mediator of a new covenant, that those who are called may receive the promised eternal inheritance — now that he has died as a ransom to set them free from the sins committed under the first covenant. 1Ti 2:5; Heb 7:22

[16] In the case of a will,[b] it is necessary to prove the death of the one who made it, [17] because a will is in force only when somebody has died; it never takes effect while the one who made it is living. [18] This is why even the first covenant was not put into effect without blood. [19] When Moses had proclaimed every command of the law to all the people, he took the blood of calves, together with water, scarlet wool and branches of hyssop, and sprinkled the scroll and all the people. [20] He said, "This is the blood of the covenant, which God has commanded you to keep."[c] [21] In the same way, he sprinkled with the blood both the tabernacle and everything used in its ceremonies. [22] In fact, the law requires that nearly everything be cleansed with blood, and without the shedding of blood there is no forgiveness. Ex 24:8; Mt 26:28

[23] It was necessary, then, for the copies of the heavenly things to be purified with these sacrifices, but the heavenly things themselves with better sacrifices than these. [24] For Christ did not enter a sanctuary made with human hands that was only a copy of the true one; he entered heaven itself, now to appear for us in God's presence. [25] Nor did he enter heaven to offer himself again and again, the way the high priest enters the Most Holy Place every year with blood that is not his own. [26] Otherwise Christ would have had to suffer many times since the creation of the world. But he has appeared once for all at the culmination of the ages to do away with sin by the sacrifice of himself. [27] Just as people are destined to die once, and after that to face judgment, [28] so Christ was sacrificed once to take away the sins of many; and he will appear a second time, not to bear sin, but to bring salvation to those who are waiting for him. 2Co 5:10

Christ's Sacrifice Once for All

10 The law is only a shadow of the good things that are coming — not the realities

---

[a] 14 Or *from useless rituals*   [b] 16 Same Greek word as *covenant*; also in verse 17
[c] 20 Exodus 24:8

themselves. For this reason it can never, by the same sacrifices repeated endlessly year after year, make perfect those who draw near to worship. ² Otherwise, would they not have stopped being offered? For the worshipers would have been cleansed once for all, and would no longer have felt guilty for their sins. ³ But those sacrifices are an annual reminder of sins. ⁴ It is impossible for the blood of bulls and goats to take away sins.   Heb 9:7,11,23

⁵ Therefore, when Christ came into the world, he said: Heb 1:6

"Sacrifice and offering you
   did not desire,
but a body you prepared
   for me;   1Pe 2:24
⁶ with burnt offerings and sin
   offerings
you were not pleased.
⁷ Then I said, 'Here I am — it is
   written about me in the
   scroll —   Jer 36:2
I have come to do your will,
   my God.' "ᵃ

⁸ First he said, "Sacrifices and offerings, burnt offerings and sin offerings you did not desire, nor were you pleased with them" — though they were offered in accordance with the law. ⁹ Then he said, "Here I am, I have come to do your will." He sets aside the first to establish the second. ¹⁰ And by that will, we have been made holy through the sacrifice of the body of Jesus Christ once for all.   Jn 17:19; Heb 7:27; 1Pe 2:24

¹¹ Day after day every priest stands and performs his religious duties; again and again he offers the same sacrifices, which can never take away sins. ¹² But when this priest had offered for all time one sacrifice for sins, he sat down at the right hand of God, ¹³ and since that time he waits for his enemies to be made his footstool. ¹⁴ For by one sacrifice he has made perfect forever those who are being made holy.   Eph 5:26; Heb 1:13

¹⁵ The Holy Spirit also testifies to us about this. First he says: Heb 3:7

¹⁶ "This is the covenant I will
      make with them
   after that time, says the
      Lord.
I will put my laws in their
   hearts,
   and I will write them on
      their minds."ᵇ

¹⁷ Then he adds:

"Their sins and lawless acts
   I will remember no more."ᶜ

¹⁸ And where these have been forgiven, sacrifice for sin is no longer necessary.   Jer 31:33; Heb 8:10,12

A Call to Persevere in Faith

¹⁹ Therefore, brothers and sisters, since we have confidence to enter the Most Holy Place

ᵃ 7 Psalm 40:6-8 (see Septuagint)   ᵇ 16 Jer. 31:33   ᶜ 17 Jer. 31:34

by the blood of Jesus, ²⁰by a new and living way opened for us through the curtain, that is, his body, ²¹and since we have a great priest over the house of God, ²²let us draw near to God with a sincere heart and with the full assurance that faith brings, having our hearts sprinkled to cleanse us from a guilty conscience and having our bodies washed with pure water. ²³Let us hold unswervingly to the hope we profess, for he who promised is faithful. ²⁴And let us consider how we may spur one another on toward love and good deeds, ²⁵not giving up meeting together, as some are in the habit of doing, but encouraging one another—and all the more as you see the Day approaching. Ac 2:42; 1Co 1:9

²⁶If we deliberately keep on sinning after we have received the knowledge of the truth, no sacrifice for sins is left, ²⁷but only a fearful expectation of judgment and of raging fire that will consume the enemies of God. ²⁸Anyone who rejected the law of Moses died without mercy on the testimony of two or three witnesses. ²⁹How much more severely do you think someone deserves to be punished who has trampled the Son of God underfoot, who has treated as an unholy thing the blood of the covenant that sanctified them, and who has insulted the Spirit of grace? ³⁰For we know him who said, "It is mine to avenge; I will repay,"[a] and again, "The Lord will judge his people."[b] ³¹It is a dreadful thing to fall into the hands of the living God. Eph 4:30; Heb 6:6

³²Remember those earlier days after you had received the light, when you endured in a great conflict full of suffering. ³³Sometimes you were publicly exposed to insult and persecution; at other times you stood side by side with those who were so treated. ³⁴You suffered along with those in prison and joyfully accepted the confiscation of your property, because you knew that you yourselves had better and lasting possessions. ³⁵So do not throw away your confidence; it will be richly rewarded. 1Co 4:9; Php 1:29-30

³⁶You need to persevere so that when you have done the will of God, you will receive what he has promised. ³⁷For,

"In just a little while, Lk 21:19
    he who is coming will come
    and will not delay."[c] Mt 11:3

³⁸And,

"But my righteous[d] one will
    live by faith. Ro 1:17
And I take no pleasure
    in the one who shrinks
    back."[e]

---

[a] 30 Deut. 32:35   [b] 30 Deut. 32:36; Psalm 135:14   [c] 37 Isaiah 26:20; Hab. 2:3
[d] 38 Some early manuscripts *But the righteous*   [e] 38 Hab. 2:4 (see Septuagint)

³⁹ But we do not belong to those who shrink back and are destroyed, but to those who have faith and are saved.   Hab 2:3-4

Faith in Action

11 Now faith is confidence in what we hope for and assurance about what we do not see. ² This is what the ancients were commended for.   Ro 8:24

³ By faith we understand that the universe was formed at God's command, so that what is seen was not made out of what was visible.   Ge 1; 2Pe 3:5

⁴ By faith Abel brought God a better offering than Cain did. By faith he was commended as righteous, when God spoke well of his offerings. And by faith Abel still speaks, even though he is dead.   Ge 4:4; Heb 12:24

⁵ By faith Enoch was taken from this life, so that he did not experience death: "He could not be found, because God had taken him away."ᵃ For before he was taken, he was commended as one who pleased God. ⁶ And without faith it is impossible to please God, because anyone who comes to him must believe that he exists and that he rewards those who earnestly seek him.   Ge 5:21-24; Heb 7:19

⁷ By faith Noah, when warned about things not yet seen, in holy fear built an ark to save his family. By his faith he condemned the world and became heir of the righteousness that is in keeping with faith.   Ge 6:13-22; 1Pe 3:20

⁸ By faith Abraham, when called to go to a place he would later receive as his inheritance, obeyed and went, even though he did not know where he was going. ⁹ By faith he made his home in the promised land like a stranger in a foreign country; he lived in tents, as did Isaac and Jacob, who were heirs with him of the same promise. ¹⁰ For he was looking forward to the city with foundations, whose architect and builder is God. ¹¹ And by faith even Sarah, who was past childbearing age, was enabled to bear children because sheᵇ considered him faithful who had made the promise. ¹² And so from this one man, and he as good as dead, came descendants as numerous as the stars in the sky and as countless as the sand on the seashore.   Ge 22:17; Ro 4:19

¹³ All these people were still living by faith when they died. They did not receive the things promised; they only saw them and welcomed them from a distance, admitting that they were foreigners and strangers on earth. ¹⁴ People who say such things show that they are looking for a country of their own. ¹⁵ If they had been thinking of the country they had

---

ᵃ 5 Gen. 5:24   ᵇ 11 Or *By faith Abraham, even though he was too old to have children — and Sarah herself was not able to conceive — was enabled to become a father because he* left, they would have had opportunity to return. [16] Instead, they were longing for a better country—a heavenly one. Therefore God is not ashamed to be called their God, for he has prepared a city for them.   Ex 3:6,15; Heb 13:14

[17] By faith Abraham, when God tested him, offered Isaac as a sacrifice. He who had embraced the promises was about to sacrifice his one and only son, [18] even though God had said to him, "It is through Isaac that your offspring will be reckoned."[a] [19] Abraham reasoned that God could even raise the dead, and so in a manner of speaking he did receive Isaac back from death.   Ge 22:1-10

[20] By faith Isaac blessed Jacob and Esau in regard to their future.   Ge 27:27-29,39-40

[21] By faith Jacob, when he was dying, blessed each of Joseph's sons, and worshiped as he leaned on the top of his staff.   Ge 48:1

[22] By faith Joseph, when his end was near, spoke about the exodus of the Israelites from Egypt and gave instructions concerning the burial of his bones.   Ge 50:24-25

[23] By faith Moses' parents hid him for three months after he was born, because they saw he was no ordinary child, and they were not afraid of the king's edict.   Ex 1:16,22; 2:2

[24] By faith Moses, when he had grown up, refused to be known as the son of Pharaoh's daughter. [25] He chose to be mistreated along with the people of God rather than to enjoy the fleeting pleasures of sin. [26] He regarded disgrace for the sake of Christ as of greater value than the treasures of Egypt, because he was looking ahead to his reward. [27] By faith he left Egypt, not fearing the king's anger; he persevered because he saw him who is invisible. [28] By faith he kept the Passover and the application of blood, so that the destroyer of the firstborn would not touch the firstborn of Israel.   Ex 12:21-23; Heb 13:13

[29] By faith the people passed through the Red Sea as on dry land; but when the Egyptians tried to do so, they were drowned.   Ex 14:21-31

[30] By faith the walls of Jericho fell, after the army had marched around them for seven days.

[31] By faith the prostitute Rahab, because she welcomed the spies, was not killed with those who were disobedient.[b]   Jos 6:22-25

[32] And what more shall I say? I do not have time to tell about Gideon, Barak, Samson and Jephthah, about David and Samuel and the prophets, [33] who through faith conquered kingdoms, administered justice, and gained what was promised; who shut the mouths of lions, [34] quenched the fury of the flames, and escaped the edge of the sword; whose weakness

a 18 Gen. 21:12   *b 31* Or *unbelieving*

was turned to strength; and who became powerful in battle and routed foreign armies. ³⁵ Women received back their dead, raised to life again. There were others who were tortured, refusing to be released so that they might gain an even better resurrection. ³⁶ Some faced jeers and flogging, and even chains and imprisonment. ³⁷ They were put to death by stoning;ᵃ they were sawed in two; they were killed by the sword. They went about in sheepskins and goatskins, destitute, persecuted and mistreated — ³⁸ the world was not worthy of them. They wandered in deserts and mountains, living in caves and in holes in the ground.

³⁹ These were all commended for their faith, yet none of them received what had been promised, ⁴⁰ since God had planned something better for us so that only together with us would they be made perfect. Heb 2:10

12 Therefore, since we are surrounded by such a great cloud of witnesses, let us throw off everything that hinders and the sin that so easily entangles. And let us run with perseverance the race marked out for us, ² fixing our eyes on Jesus, the pioneer and perfecter of faith. For the joy set before him he endured the cross, scorning its shame, and sat down at the right hand of the throne of God. ³ Consider him who endured such opposition from sinners, so that you will not grow weary and lose heart. Gal 6:9; Php 2:8-9

God Disciplines His Children

⁴ In your struggle against sin, you have not yet resisted to the point of shedding your blood. ⁵ And have you completely forgotten this word of encouragement that addresses you as a father addresses his son? It says, Heb 10:32-34

> "My son, do not make light of
>   the Lord's discipline,
> and do not lose heart when
>   he rebukes you,
> ⁶ because the Lord disciplines
>   the one he loves, Ps 94:12
> and he chastens everyone
>   he accepts as his son."ᵇ

⁷ Endure hardship as discipline; God is treating you as his children. For what children are not disciplined by their father? ⁸ If you are not disciplined — and everyone undergoes discipline — then you are not legitimate, not true sons and daughters at all. ⁹ Moreover, we have all had human fathers who disciplined us and we respected them for it. How much more should we submit to the Father of spirits and live! ¹⁰ They disciplined us for a little while as they thought best; but God disciplines us for our

---

ᵃ 37 Some early manuscripts *stoning; they were put to the test;*   ᵇ 5,6 Prov. 3:11,12 (see Septuagint) good, in order that we may share in his holiness. [11]No discipline seems pleasant at the time, but painful. Later on, however, it produces a harvest of righteousness and peace for those who have been trained by it. Isa 38:16; Jas 3:17-18

[12]Therefore, strengthen your feeble arms and weak knees. [13]"Make level paths for your feet,"[a] so that the lame may not be disabled, but rather healed. Pr 4:26

Warning and Encouragement

[14]Make every effort to live in peace with everyone and to be holy; without holiness no one will see the Lord. [15]See to it that no one falls short of the grace of God and that no bitter root grows up to cause trouble and defile many. [16]See that no one is sexually immoral, or is godless like Esau, who for a single meal sold his inheritance rights as the oldest son. [17]Afterward, as you know, when he wanted to inherit this blessing, he was rejected. Even though he sought the blessing with tears, he could not change what he had done. Ge 25:29-34; 27:30-40

The Mountain of Fear and the Mountain of Joy

[18]You have not come to a mountain that can be touched and that is burning with fire; to darkness, gloom and storm; [19]to a trumpet blast or to such a voice speaking words that those who heard it begged that no further word be spoken to them, [20]because they could not bear what was commanded: "If even an animal touches the mountain, it must be stoned to death."[b] [21]The sight was so terrifying that Moses said, "I am trembling with fear."[c] Ex 20:19; Dt 5:5,25

[22]But you have come to Mount Zion, to the city of the living God, the heavenly Jerusalem. You have come to thousands upon thousands of angels in joyful assembly, [23]to the church of the firstborn, whose names are written in heaven. You have come to God, the Judge of all, to the spirits of the righteous made perfect, [24]to Jesus the mediator of a new covenant, and to the sprinkled blood that speaks a better word than the blood of Abel. Php 3:12; Heb 11:4

[25]See to it that you do not refuse him who speaks. If they did not escape when they refused him who warned them on earth, how much less will we, if we turn away from him who warns us from heaven? [26]At that time his voice shook the earth, but now he has promised, "Once more I will shake not only the earth but also the heavens."[d] [27]The words "once more" indicate the removing of what can be shaken—that is, created things—so that what cannot be shaken may remain. 1Co 7:31

[28]Therefore, since we are receiving a kingdom that cannot

be shaken, let us be thankful, and so worship God acceptably with reverence and awe, [29]for our "God is a consuming fire."[a]

Concluding Exhortations

13 Keep on loving one another as brothers and sisters. [2]Do not forget to show hospitality to strangers, for by so doing some people have shown hospitality to angels without knowing it. [3]Continue to remember those in prison as if you were together with them in prison, and those who are mistreated as if you yourselves were suffering.   Ge 18:1-33

[4]Marriage should be honored by all, and the marriage bed kept pure, for God will judge the adulterer and all the sexually immoral. [5]Keep your lives free from the love of money and be content with what you have, because God has said,   1Co 6:9; Php 4:11

"Never will I leave you;
    never will I forsake you."[b]

[6]So we say with confidence,

"The Lord is my helper; I will
    not be afraid.
What can mere mortals do
    to me?"[c]   Dt 31:6,8; Jos 1:5

[7]Remember your leaders, who spoke the word of God to you. Consider the outcome of their way of life and imitate their faith. [8]Jesus Christ is the same yesterday and today and forever. Heb 1:12

[9]Do not be carried away by all kinds of strange teachings. It is good for our hearts to be strengthened by grace, not by eating ceremonial foods, which is of no benefit to those who do so. [10]We have an altar from which those who minister at the tabernacle have no right to eat. 1Co 9:13; Eph 4:14

[11]The high priest carries the blood of animals into the Most Holy Place as a sin offering, but the bodies are burned outside the camp. [12]And so Jesus also suffered outside the city gate to make the people holy through his own blood. [13]Let us, then, go to him outside the camp, bearing the disgrace he bore. [14]For here we do not have an enduring city, but we are looking for the city that is to come.   Php 3:20

[15]Through Jesus, therefore, let us continually offer to God a sacrifice of praise — the fruit of lips that openly profess his name. [16]And do not forget to do good and to share with others, for with such sacrifices God is pleased.   Php 4:18; Hos 14:2

[17]Have confidence in your leaders and submit to their authority, because they keep watch over you as those who must give an account. Do this so that their work will be a joy, not a burden, for that would be of no benefit to you.   Isa 62:6; Ac 20:28

[18]Pray for us. We are sure that we have a clear conscience and

[a] 29 Deut. 4:24   [b] 5 Deut. 31:6   [c] 6 Psalm 118:6,7

desire to live honorably in every way. [19] I particularly urge you to pray so that I may be restored to you soon. 1Th 5:25; Phm 22

Benediction and Final Greetings

[20] Now may the God of peace, who through the blood of the eternal covenant brought back from the dead our Lord Jesus, that great Shepherd of the sheep, [21] equip you with everything good for doing his will, and may he work in us what is pleasing to him, through Jesus Christ, to whom be glory for ever and ever. Amen. Php 2:13; Jn 3:22

[22] Brothers and sisters, I urge you to bear with my word of exhortation, for in fact I have written to you quite briefly. 1Pe 5:12

[23] I want you to know that our brother Timothy has been released. If he arrives soon, I will come with him to see you. Ac 16:1

[24] Greet all your leaders and all the Lord's people. Those from Italy send you their greetings. Ac 18:2

[25] Grace be with you all. Col 4:18

James

whom be glory for ever and ever. Amen.

Brothers and sisters, I urge you to bear with my word of exhortation, for in fact I have written to you quite briefly. I want you to know that our brother Timothy has been released. If he arrives soon, I will come with him to see you.

Greet all your leaders and all the Lord's people. Those from Italy send you their greetings.

Grace be with you all.

desire to live honorably in every way. I particularly urge you to pray so that I may be restored to you soon.

Benediction and Final Greetings

Now may the God of peace, who through the blood of the eternal covenant, brought back from the dead our Lord Jesus, that great Shepherd of the sheep,

1

James, a servant of God and of the Lord Jesus Christ,

To the twelve tribes scattered among the nations: Jn 7:35; 1Pe 1:1

Greetings.   Ac 15:23

Trials and Temptations

[2] Consider it pure joy, my brothers and sisters,[a] whenever you face trials of many kinds, [3] because you know that the testing of your faith produces perseverance. [4] Let perseverance finish its work so that you may be mature and complete, not lacking anything. [5] If any of you lacks wisdom, you should ask God, who gives generously to all without finding fault, and it will be given to you. [6] But when you ask, you must believe and not doubt, because the one who doubts is like a wave of the sea, blown and tossed by the wind. [7] That person should not expect to receive anything from the Lord. [8] Such a person is double-minded and unstable in all they do.   1Ki 3:9-10; Mk 11:24

[9] Believers in humble circumstances ought to take pride in their high position. [10] But the rich should take pride in their humiliation—since they will pass away like a wild flower. [11] For the sun rises with scorching heat and withers the plant; its blossom falls and its beauty is destroyed. In the same way, the rich will fade away even while they go about their business.   Ps 102:4,11

[12] Blessed is the one who perseveres under trial because, having stood the test, that person will receive the crown of life that the Lord has promised to those who love him.   1Co 9:25; Jas 2:5

[13] When tempted, no one should say, "God is tempting me." For God cannot be tempted by evil, nor does he tempt anyone; [14] but each person is tempted when they are dragged away by their own evil desire and en-

---

[a] 2 The Greek word for *brothers and sisters* (*adelphoi*) refers here to believers, both men and women, as part of God's family; also in verses 16 and 19; and in 2:1, 5, 14; 3:10, 12; 4:11; 5:7, 9, 10, 12, 19.

ticed. ¹⁵Then, after desire has conceived, it gives birth to sin; and sin, when it is full-grown, gives birth to death. Job 15:35; Ps 7:14 ¹⁶Don't be deceived, my dear brothers and sisters. ¹⁷Every good and perfect gift is from above, coming down from the Father of the heavenly lights, who does not change like shifting shadows. ¹⁸He chose to give us birth through the word of truth, that we might be a kind of firstfruits of all he created. Jn 1:13; Rev 14:4

Listening and Doing

¹⁹My dear brothers and sisters, take note of this: Everyone should be quick to listen, slow to speak and slow to become angry, ²⁰because human anger does not produce the righteousness that God desires. ²¹Therefore, get rid of all moral filth and the evil that is so prevalent and humbly accept the word planted in you, which can save you. Eph 1:13; 4:22

²²Do not merely listen to the word, and so deceive yourselves. Do what it says. ²³Anyone who listens to the word but does not do what it says is like someone who looks at his face in a mirror ²⁴and, after looking at himself, goes away and immediately forgets what he looks like. ²⁵But whoever looks intently into the perfect law that gives freedom, and continues in it — not forgetting what they have heard, but

doing it — they will be blessed in what they do. Jn 13:17; Jas 2:12 ²⁶Those who consider themselves religious and yet do not keep a tight rein on their tongues deceive themselves, and their religion is worthless. ²⁷Religion that God our Father accepts as pure and faultless is this: to look after orphans and widows in their distress and to keep oneself from being polluted by the world. Isa 1:17,23; 1Pe 3:10

Favoritism Forbidden

2 My brothers and sisters, believers in our glorious Lord Jesus Christ must not show favoritism. ²Suppose a man comes into your meeting wearing a gold ring and fine clothes, and a poor man in filthy old clothes also comes in. ³If you show special attention to the man wearing fine clothes and say, "Here's a good seat for you," but say to the poor man, "You stand there" or "Sit on the floor by my feet," ⁴have you not discriminated among yourselves and become judges with evil thoughts? Jn 7:24; 1Co 2:8

⁵Listen, my dear brothers and sisters: Has not God chosen those who are poor in the eyes of the world to be rich in faith and to inherit the kingdom he promised those who love him? ⁶But you have dishonored the poor. Is it not the rich who are exploiting you? Are they not the ones who are dragging you into court?

⁷Are they not the ones who are blaspheming the noble name of him to whom you belong? Lk 12:21

⁸If you really keep the royal law found in Scripture, "Love your neighbor as yourself,"ᵃ you are doing right. ⁹But if you show favoritism, you sin and are convicted by the law as lawbreakers. ¹⁰For whoever keeps the whole law and yet stumbles at just one point is guilty of breaking all of it. ¹¹For he who said, "You shall not commit adultery,"ᵇ also said, "You shall not murder."ᶜ If you do not commit adultery but do commit murder, you have become a lawbreaker. Mt 5:19; Gal 3:10

¹²Speak and act as those who are going to be judged by the law that gives freedom, ¹³because judgment without mercy will be shown to anyone who has not been merciful. Mercy triumphs over judgment. Mt 5:7; Jas 1:25

Faith and Deeds

¹⁴What good is it, my brothers and sisters, if someone claims to have faith but has no deeds? Can such faith save them? ¹⁵Suppose a brother or a sister is without clothes and daily food. ¹⁶If one of you says to them, "Go in peace; keep warm and well fed," but does nothing about their physical needs, what good is it? ¹⁷In the same way, faith by itself, if it is not accompanied by action, is dead.

¹⁸But someone will say, "You have faith; I have deeds."

Show me your faith without deeds, and I will show you my faith by my deeds. ¹⁹You believe that there is one God. Good! Even the demons believe that— and shudder. Mt 8:29; Jas 3:13

²⁰You foolish person, do you want evidence that faith without deeds is uselessᵈ? ²¹Was not our father Abraham considered righteous for what he did when he offered his son Isaac on the altar? ²²You see that his faith and his actions were working together, and his faith was made complete by what he did. ²³And the scripture was fulfilled that says, "Abraham believed God, and it was credited to him as righteousness,"ᵉ and he was called God's friend. ²⁴You see that a person is considered righteous by what they do and not by faith alone. 2Ch 20:7; Ro 4:3

²⁵In the same way, was not even Rahab the prostitute considered righteous for what she did when she gave lodging to the spies and sent them off in a different direction? ²⁶As the body without the spirit is dead, so faith without deeds is dead. Heb 11:31

Taming the Tongue

3 Not many of you should become teachers, my fellow believers, because you know

---

ᵃ 8 Lev. 19:18   ᵇ 11 Exodus 20:14; Deut. 5:18   ᶜ 11 Exodus 20:13; Deut. 5:17   ᵈ 20 Some early manuscripts *dead*   ᵉ 23 Gen. 15:6

that we who teach will be judged more strictly. ²We all stumble in many ways. Anyone who is never at fault in what they say is perfect, able to keep their whole body in check. Mt 12:37; Jas 1:26

³When we put bits into the mouths of horses to make them obey us, we can turn the whole animal. ⁴Or take ships as an example. Although they are so large and are driven by strong winds, they are steered by a very small rudder wherever the pilot wants to go. ⁵Likewise, the tongue is a small part of the body, but it makes great boasts. Consider what a great forest is set on fire by a small spark. ⁶The tongue also is a fire, a world of evil among the parts of the body. It corrupts the whole body, sets the whole course of one's life on fire, and is itself set on fire by hell. Pr 16:27; Mt 15:11,18-19

⁷All kinds of animals, birds, reptiles and sea creatures are being tamed and have been tamed by mankind, ⁸but no human being can tame the tongue. It is a restless evil, full of deadly poison. Ps 140:3; Ro 3:13

⁹With the tongue we praise our Lord and Father, and with it we curse human beings, who have been made in God's likeness. ¹⁰Out of the same mouth come praise and cursing. My brothers and sisters, this should not be. ¹¹Can both fresh water and salt water flow from the same spring? ¹²My brothers and sisters, can a fig tree bear olives, or a grapevine bear figs? Neither can a salt spring produce fresh water. Ge 1:26-27; Mt 7:16

Two Kinds of Wisdom

¹³Who is wise and understanding among you? Let them show it by their good life, by deeds done in the humility that comes from wisdom. ¹⁴But if you harbor bitter envy and selfish ambition in your hearts, do not boast about it or deny the truth. ¹⁵Such "wisdom" does not come down from heaven but is earthly, unspiritual, demonic. ¹⁶For where you have envy and selfish ambition, there you find disorder and every evil practice. 1Ti 4:1; Jas 2:18

¹⁷But the wisdom that comes from heaven is first of all pure; then peace-loving, considerate, submissive, full of mercy and good fruit, impartial and sincere. ¹⁸Peacemakers who sow in peace reap a harvest of righteousness. Pr 11:18; Ro 12:9

Submit Yourselves to God

4 What causes fights and quarrels among you? Don't they come from your desires that battle within you? ²You desire but do not have, so you kill. You covet but you cannot get what you want, so you quarrel and fight. You do not have because you do not ask God. ³When you ask, you do not receive, because

you ask with wrong motives, that you may spend what you get on your pleasures. Ro 7:23; 1Jn 3:22

[4] You adulterous people,[a] don't you know that friendship with the world means enmity against God? Therefore, anyone who chooses to be a friend of the world becomes an enemy of God. [5] Or do you think Scripture says without reason that he jealously longs for the spirit he has caused to dwell in us[b]? [6] But he gives us more grace. That is why Scripture says: Jn 15:19; 1Jn 2:15

> "God opposes the proud
> but shows favor to the
> humble."[c]   Pr 3:34; Mt 23:12

[7] Submit yourselves, then, to God. Resist the devil, and he will flee from you. [8] Come near to God and he will come near to you. Wash your hands, you sinners, and purify your hearts, you double-minded. [9] Grieve, mourn and wail. Change your laughter to mourning and your joy to gloom. [10] Humble yourselves before the Lord, and he will lift you up. Isa 1:16; 1Pe 5:6-9

[11] Brothers and sisters, do not slander one another. Anyone who speaks against a brother or sister[d] or judges them speaks against the law and judges it. When you judge the law, you are not keeping it, but sitting in judgment on it. [12] There is only one Lawgiver and Judge, the one who is able to save and destroy. But you—who are you to judge your neighbor? Mt 10:28; Ro 14:4

Boasting About Tomorrow

[13] Now listen, you who say, "Today or tomorrow we will go to this or that city, spend a year there, carry on business and make money." [14] Why, you do not even know what will happen tomorrow. What is your life? You are a mist that appears for a little while and then vanishes. [15] Instead, you ought to say, "If it is the Lord's will, we will live and do this or that." [16] As it is, you boast in your arrogant schemes. All such boasting is evil. [17] If anyone, then, knows the good they ought to do and doesn't do it, it is sin for them. Lk 12:47; 1Co 5:6

Warning to Rich Oppressors

5 Now listen, you rich people, weep and wail because of the misery that is coming on you. [2] Your wealth has rotted, and moths have eaten your clothes. [3] Your gold and silver are corroded. Their corrosion will testify against you and eat your flesh like fire. You have hoarded wealth in the last days. [4] Look! The wages you failed to pay the

---

[a] 4 An allusion to covenant unfaithfulness; see Hosea 3:1.   [b] 5 Or that the spirit he caused to dwell in us envies intensely; or that the Spirit he caused to dwell in us longs jealously   [c] 6 Prov. 3:34   [d] 11 The Greek word for brother or sister (adelphos) refers here to a believer, whether man or woman, as part of God's family.

workers who mowed your fields are crying out against you. The cries of the harvesters have reached the ears of the Lord Almighty. [5] You have lived on earth in luxury and self-indulgence. You have fattened yourselves in the day of slaughter.[a] [6] You have condemned and murdered the innocent one, who was not opposing you. Heb 10:38; Jas 4:2

Patience in Suffering

[7] Be patient, then, brothers and sisters, until the Lord's coming. See how the farmer waits for the land to yield its valuable crop, patiently waiting for the autumn and spring rains. [8] You too, be patient and stand firm, because the Lord's coming is near. [9] Don't grumble against one another, brothers and sisters, or you will be judged. The Judge is standing at the door! Mt 24:33; Jas 4:11

[10] Brothers and sisters, as an example of patience in the face of suffering, take the prophets who spoke in the name of the Lord. [11] As you know, we count as blessed those who have persevered. You have heard of Job's perseverance and have seen what the Lord finally brought about. The Lord is full of compassion and mercy. Job 42:10,12-17; Mt 5:12

[12] Above all, my brothers and sisters, do not swear — not by heaven or by earth or by anything else. All you need to say is a simple "Yes" or "No." Otherwise you will be condemned. Mt 5:34-37

The Prayer of Faith

[13] Is anyone among you in trouble? Let them pray. Is anyone happy? Let them sing songs of praise. [14] Is anyone among you sick? Let them call the elders of the church to pray over them and anoint them with oil in the name of the Lord. [15] And the prayer offered in faith will make the sick person well; the Lord will raise them up. If they have sinned, they will be forgiven. [16] Therefore confess your sins to each other and pray for each other so that you may be healed. The prayer of a righteous person is powerful and effective. Jn 9:31; 1Pe 2:24

[17] Elijah was a human being, even as we are. He prayed earnestly that it would not rain, and it did not rain on the land for three and a half years. [18] Again he prayed, and the heavens gave rain, and the earth produced its crops. 1Ki 18:41-45; Ac 14:15

[19] My brothers and sisters, if one of you should wander from the truth and someone should bring that person back, [20] remember this: Whoever turns a sinner from the error of their way will save them from death and cover over a multitude of sins. Mt 18:15; Ro 11:14; 1Pe 4:8

[a] 5 Or *yourselves as in a day of feasting*

1 Peter

1 Peter, an apostle of Jesus Christ, 2Pe 1:1

To God's elect, exiles scattered throughout the provinces of Pontus, Galatia, Cappadocia, Asia and Bithynia, ²who have been chosen according to the foreknowledge of God the Father, through the sanctifying work of the Spirit, to be obedient to Jesus Christ and sprinkled with his blood: 2Th 2:13; Heb 10:22

Grace and peace be yours in abundance. Ro 1:7

Praise to God for a Living Hope

³Praise be to the God and Father of our Lord Jesus Christ! In his great mercy he has given us new birth into a living hope through the resurrection of Jesus Christ from the dead, ⁴and into an inheritance that can never perish, spoil or fade. This inheritance is kept in heaven for you, ⁵who through faith are shielded by God's power until the coming of the salvation that is ready to be revealed in the last time.

⁶In all this you greatly rejoice, though now for a little while you may have had to suffer grief in all kinds of trials. ⁷These have come so that the proven genuineness of your faith—of greater worth than gold, which perishes even though refined by fire—may result in praise, glory and honor when Jesus Christ is revealed. ⁸Though you have not seen him, you love him; and even though you do not see him now, you believe in him and are filled with an inexpressible and glorious joy, ⁹for you are receiving the end result of your faith, the salvation of your souls. Jn 20:29; Ro 6:22

¹⁰Concerning this salvation, the prophets, who spoke of the grace that was to come to you, searched intently and with the greatest care, ¹¹trying to find out the time and circumstances to which the Spirit of Christ in them was pointing when he predicted the sufferings of the Messiah and the glories that would follow. ¹²It was revealed to them that they were not serving themselves but you, when they spoke

of the things that have now been told you by those who have preached the gospel to you by the Holy Spirit sent from heaven. Even angels long to look into these things. *Lk 24:49; 2Pe 1:21*

Be Holy

[13] Therefore, with minds that are alert and fully sober, set your hope on the grace to be brought to you when Jesus Christ is revealed at his coming. [14] As obedient children, do not conform to the evil desires you had when you lived in ignorance. [15] But just as he who called you is holy, so be holy in all you do; [16] for it is written: "Be holy, because I am holy."[a] *Ro 12:2; Eph 4:18*

[17] Since you call on a Father who judges each person's work impartially, live out your time as foreigners here in reverent fear. [18] For you know that it was not with perishable things such as silver or gold that you were redeemed from the empty way of life handed down to you from your ancestors, [19] but with the precious blood of Christ, a lamb without blemish or defect. [20] He was chosen before the creation of the world, but was revealed in these last times for your sake. [21] Through him you believe in God, who raised him from the dead and glorified him, and so your faith and hope are in God. *1Co 6:20; Heb 12:28*

[22] Now that you have purified yourselves by obeying the truth so that you have sincere love for each other, love one another deeply, from the heart.[b] [23] For you have been born again, not of perishable seed, but of imperishable, through the living and enduring word of God. [24] For, *Jn 1:13*

"All people are like grass,
  and all their glory is like the
    flowers of the field;
the grass withers and the
    flowers fall,
[25] but the word of the Lord
    endures forever."[c]

And this is the word that was preached to you.

2 Therefore, rid yourselves of all malice and all deceit, hypocrisy, envy, and slander of every kind. [2] Like newborn babies, crave pure spiritual milk, so that by it you may grow up in your salvation, [3] now that you have tasted that the Lord is good. *1Co 3:2*

The Living Stone and a Chosen People

[4] As you come to him, the living Stone — rejected by humans but chosen by God and precious to him — [5] you also, like living stones, are being built into a spiritual house[d] to be a holy priesthood, offering spiritual sacrifices acceptable to God through Jesus Christ. [6] For in Scripture it says:

---

[a] 16 Lev. 11:44,45; 19:2 40:6-8 (see Septuagint)   [b] 22 Some early manuscripts *from a pure heart*   [c] 25 Isaiah   [d] 5 Or *into a temple of the Spirit*

"See, I lay a stone in Zion,
  a chosen and precious
    cornerstone,   Eph 2:20
and the one who trusts in him
  will never be put to
    shame."[a]

⁷Now to you who believe, this
stone is precious. But to those
who do not believe,   2Co 2:16

"The stone the builders
    rejected
has become the
    cornerstone,"[b]

⁸and,

"A stone that causes people to
    stumble
  and a rock that makes them
    fall."[c]

They stumble because they disobey the message—which is
also what they were destined for.
⁹But you are a chosen people,
a royal priesthood, a holy nation,
God's special possession, that
you may declare the praises of
him who called you out of darkness into his wonderful light.
¹⁰Once you were not a people,
but now you are the people of
God; once you had not received
mercy, but now you have received mercy.   Hos 1:9-10; Ac 26:18

Living Godly Lives in a
Pagan Society

¹¹Dear friends, I urge you, as
foreigners and exiles, to abstain

from sinful desires, which wage
war against your soul. ¹²Live
such good lives among the pagans that, though they accuse
you of doing wrong, they may see
your good deeds and glorify God
on the day he visits us.   Mt 5:16
¹³Submit yourselves for the
Lord's sake to every human authority: whether to the emperor,
as the supreme authority, ¹⁴or to
governors, who are sent by him
to punish those who do wrong
and to commend those who do
right. ¹⁵For it is God's will that
by doing good you should silence the ignorant talk of foolish people. ¹⁶Live as free people,
but do not use your freedom as
a cover-up for evil; live as God's
slaves. ¹⁷Show proper respect to
everyone, love the family of believers, fear God, honor the emperor.   Ro 12:10; 13:7; 1Pe 3:17
¹⁸Slaves, in reverent fear of
God submit yourselves to your
masters, not only to those who
are good and considerate, but
also to those who are harsh.
¹⁹For it is commendable if someone bears up under the pain of
unjust suffering because they
are conscious of God. ²⁰But how
is it to your credit if you receive a
beating for doing wrong and endure it? But if you suffer for doing
good and you endure it, this is
commendable before God. ²¹To
this you were called, because
Christ suffered for you, leaving

---

[a] 6 Isaiah 28:16   [b] 7 Psalm 118:22   [c] 8 Isaiah 8:14

you an example, that you should follow in his steps. Mt 16:24; Eph 6:5

²² "He committed no sin,
 and no deceit was found in
 his mouth." [a]   Isa 53:9

²³ When they hurled their insults at him, he did not retaliate; when he suffered, he made no threats. Instead, he entrusted himself to him who judges justly. ²⁴ "He himself bore our sins" in his body on the cross, so that we might die to sins and live for righteousness; "by his wounds you have been healed." ²⁵ For "you were like sheep going astray," [b] but now you have returned to the Shepherd and Overseer of your souls. Isa 53:6

3 Wives, in the same way submit yourselves to your own husbands so that, if any of them do not believe the word, they may be won over without words by the behavior of their wives, ² when they see the purity and reverence of your lives. ³ Your beauty should not come from outward adornment, such as elaborate hairstyles and the wearing of gold jewelry or fine clothes. ⁴ Rather, it should be that of your inner self, the unfading beauty of a gentle and quiet spirit, which is of great worth in God's sight. ⁵ For this is the way the holy women of the past who put their hope in God used to adorn themselves. They submitted themselves to their own husbands, ⁶ like Sarah, who

obeyed Abraham and called him her lord. You are her daughters if you do what is right and do not give way to fear.   Ge 18:12; 1Ti 5:5

⁷ Husbands, in the same way be considerate as you live with your wives, and treat them with respect as the weaker partner and as heirs with you of the gracious gift of life, so that nothing will hinder your prayers.   Eph 5:25-33

Suffering for Doing Good

⁸ Finally, all of you, be likeminded, be sympathetic, love one another, be compassionate and humble. ⁹ Do not repay evil with evil or insult with insult. On the contrary, repay evil with blessing, because to this you were called so that you may inherit a blessing. ¹⁰ For,   Heb 6:14; 1Pe 2:21

"Whoever would love life
 and see good days
must keep their tongue from
 evil
 and their lips from deceitful
 speech.
¹¹ They must turn from evil and
 do good;
 they must seek peace and
 pursue it.
¹² For the eyes of the Lord are on
 the righteous
 and his ears are attentive to
 their prayer,
 but the face of the Lord is
 against those who do
 evil." [c]   Ps 34:12-16

a 22 Isaiah 53:9   b 24,25 Isaiah 53:4,5,6 (see Septuagint)   c 12 Psalm 34:12-16

¹³Who is going to harm you if you are eager to do good? ¹⁴But even if you should suffer for what is right, you are blessed. "Do not fear their threats*ᵃ*; do not be frightened."*ᵇ* ¹⁵But in your hearts revere Christ as Lord. Always be prepared to give an answer to everyone who asks you to give the reason for the hope that you have. But do this with gentleness and respect, ¹⁶keeping a clear conscience, so that those who speak maliciously against your good behavior in Christ may be ashamed of their slander. ¹⁷For it is better, if it is God's will, to suffer for doing good than for doing evil. ¹⁸For Christ also suffered once for sins, the righteous for the unrighteous, to bring you to God. He was put to death in the body but made alive in the Spirit. ¹⁹After being made alive,*ᶜ* he went and made proclamation to the imprisoned spirits — ²⁰to those who were disobedient long ago when God waited patiently in the days of Noah while the ark was being built. In it only a few people, eight in all, were saved through water, ²¹and this water symbolizes baptism that now saves you also — not the removal of dirt from the body but the pledge of a clear conscience toward God.*ᵈ* It saves you by the resurrection of Jesus Christ, ²²who has gone into heaven and is at God's right hand — with angels, authorities and powers in submission to him. Ro 8:38; 1Pe 1:3

Living for God

4 Therefore, since Christ suffered in his body, arm yourselves also with the same attitude, because whoever suffers in the body is done with sin. ²As a result, they do not live the rest of their earthly lives for evil human desires, but rather for the will of God. ³For you have spent enough time in the past doing what pagans choose to do — living in debauchery, lust, drunkenness, orgies, carousing and detestable idolatry. ⁴They are surprised that you do not join them in their reckless, wild living, and they heap abuse on you. ⁵But they will have to give account to him who is ready to judge the living and the dead. ⁶For this is the reason the gospel was preached even to those who are now dead, so that they might be judged according to human standards in regard to the body, but live according to God in regard to the spirit. Ac 10:42; 1Pe 3:19

⁷The end of all things is near. Therefore be alert and of sober mind so that you may pray. ⁸Above all, love each other deeply, because love covers over a multitude of sins. ⁹Offer hospitality to one another without grum-

---

ᵃ 14 Or *fear what they fear*   *ᵇ* 14 Isaiah 8:12   *ᶜ* 18,19 Or *but made alive in the spirit,* ¹⁹*in which also*   *ᵈ* 21 Or *but an appeal to God for a clear conscience* bling. ¹⁰Each of you should use whatever gift you have received to serve others, as faithful stewards of God's grace in its various forms. ¹¹If anyone speaks, they should do so as one who speaks the very words of God. If anyone serves, they should do so with the strength God provides, so that in all things God may be praised through Jesus Christ. To him be the glory and the power for ever and ever. Amen.   Pr 10:12; Ro 12:6-7

Suffering for Being a Christian

¹²Dear friends, do not be surprised at the fiery ordeal that has come on you to test you, as though something strange were happening to you. ¹³But rejoice inasmuch as you participate in the sufferings of Christ, so that you may be overjoyed when his glory is revealed. ¹⁴If you are insulted because of the name of Christ, you are blessed, for the Spirit of glory and of God rests on you. ¹⁵If you suffer, it should not be as a murderer or thief or any other kind of criminal, or even as a meddler. ¹⁶However, if you suffer as a Christian, do not be ashamed, but praise God that you bear that name. ¹⁷For it is time for judgment to begin with God's household; and if it begins with us, what will the outcome be for those who do not obey the gospel of God? ¹⁸And,   Ac 5:41; Ro 8:17

"If it is hard for the righteous
    to be saved,
what will become of the
    ungodly and the
    sinner?"ᵃ

¹⁹So then, those who suffer according to God's will should commit themselves to their faithful Creator and continue to do good.   1Pe 2:15; 3:17

To the Elders and the Flock

5 To the elders among you, I appeal as a fellow elder and a witness of Christ's sufferings who also will share in the glory to be revealed: ²Be shepherds of God's flock that is under your care, watching over them — not because you must, but because you are willing, as God wants you to be; not pursuing dishonest gain, but eager to serve; ³not lording it over those entrusted to you, but being examples to the flock. ⁴And when the Chief Shepherd appears, you will receive the crown of glory that will never fade away.   1Co 9:25

⁵In the same way, you who are younger, submit yourselves to your elders. All of you, clothe yourselves with humility toward one another, because,   Eph 5:21

"God opposes the proud
    but shows favor to the
    humble."ᵇ

⁶Humble yourselves, therefore,

ᵃ 18 Prov. 11:31 (see Septuagint)   ᵇ 5 Prov. 3:34

under God's mighty hand, that he may lift you up in due time. [7] Cast all your anxiety on him because he cares for you.   Heb 13:5; Jas 4:6,10

[8] Be alert and of sober mind. Your enemy the devil prowls around like a roaring lion looking for someone to devour. [9] Resist him, standing firm in the faith, because you know that the family of believers throughout the world is undergoing the same kind of sufferings.   Ac 14:22; Col 2:5

[10] And the God of all grace, who called you to his eternal glory in Christ, after you have suffered a little while, will himself restore you and make you strong, firm and steadfast. [11] To him be the power for ever and ever. Amen.   Ro 11:36; 2Co 4:17

Final Greetings

[12] With the help of Silas,[a] whom I regard as a faithful brother, I have written to you briefly, encouraging you and testifying that this is the true grace of God. Stand fast in it.   2Co 1:19; Heb 13:22

[13] She who is in Babylon, chosen together with you, sends you her greetings, and so does my son Mark. [14] Greet one another with a kiss of love.   Ac 12:12; Ro 16:16

Peace to all of you who are in Christ.   Eph 6:23

---

[a] 12 Greek *Silvanus*, a variant of *Silas*

2 Peter

1 Simon Peter, a servant and apostle of Jesus Christ, Ro 1:1

To those who through the righteousness of our God and Savior Jesus Christ have received a faith as precious as ours: Ro 3:21-26

[2] Grace and peace be yours in abundance through the knowledge of God and of Jesus our Lord. Php 3:8

Confirming One's Calling and Election

[3] His divine power has given us everything we need for a godly life through our knowledge of him who called us by his own glory and goodness. [4] Through these he has given us his very great and precious promises, so that through them you may participate in the divine nature, having escaped the corruption in the world caused by evil desires. 2Co 7:1; 1Pe 1:5

[5] For this very reason, make every effort to add to your faith goodness; and to goodness, knowledge; [6] and to knowledge, self-control; and to self-control, perseverance; and to perseverance, godliness; [7] and to godliness, mutual affection; and to mutual affection, love. [8] For if you possess these qualities in increasing measure, they will keep you from being ineffective and unproductive in your knowledge of our Lord Jesus Christ. [9] But whoever does not have them is nearsighted and blind, forgetting that they have been cleansed from their past sins. 1Jn 2:11; Eph 5:26

[10] Therefore, my brothers and sisters,[a] make every effort to confirm your calling and election. For if you do these things, you will never stumble, [11] and you will receive a rich welcome into the eternal kingdom of our Lord and Savior Jesus Christ. 2Pe 3:17

Prophecy of Scripture

[12] So I will always remind you of these things, even though you

---

[a] 10 The Greek word for *brothers and sisters* (*adelphoi*) refers here to believers, both men and women, as part of God's family.

know them and are firmly established in the truth you now have. ¹³I think it is right to refresh your memory as long as I live in the tent of this body, ¹⁴because I know that I will soon put it aside, as our Lord Jesus Christ has made clear to me. ¹⁵And I will make every effort to see that after my departure you will always be able to remember these things.   2Co 5:1,4; 1Jn 2:21

¹⁶For we did not follow cleverly devised stories when we told you about the coming of our Lord Jesus Christ in power, but we were eyewitnesses of his majesty. ¹⁷He received honor and glory from God the Father when the voice came to him from the Majestic Glory, saying, "This is my Son, whom I love; with him I am well pleased."ᵃ ¹⁸We ourselves heard this voice that came from heaven when we were with him on the sacred mountain.   Mt 3:17; 17:1-8

¹⁹We also have the prophetic message as something completely reliable, and you will do well to pay attention to it, as to a light shining in a dark place, until the day dawns and the morning star rises in your hearts. ²⁰Above all, you must understand that no prophecy of Scripture came about by the prophet's own interpretation of things. ²¹For prophecy never had its origin in the human will, but prophets, though human, spoke from God as they were carried along by the Holy Spirit.   Ac 1:16; 2Ti 3:16

False Teachers and Their Destruction

2 But there were also false prophets among the people, just as there will be false teachers among you. They will secretly introduce destructive heresies, even denying the sovereign Lord who bought them — bringing swift destruction on themselves. ²Many will follow their depraved conduct and will bring the way of truth into disrepute. ³In their greed these teachers will exploit you with fabricated stories. Their condemnation has long been hanging over them, and their destruction has not been sleeping.   2Co 2:17; Jude 4

⁴For if God did not spare angels when they sinned, but sent them to hell,ᵇ putting them in chains of darknessᶜ to be held for judgment; ⁵if he did not spare the ancient world when he brought the flood on its ungodly people, but protected Noah, a preacher of righteousness, and seven others; ⁶if he condemned the cities of Sodom and Gomorrah by burning them to ashes, and made them an example of what is going to happen to the ungodly; ⁷and if he rescued Lot, a righteous man, who was distressed

ᵃ 17 Matt. 17:5; Mark 9:7; Luke 9:35   ᵇ 4 Greek *Tartarus*   ᶜ 4 Some manuscripts *in gloomy dungeons* by the depraved conduct of the lawless [8] (for that righteous man, living among them day after day, was tormented in his righteous soul by the lawless deeds he saw and heard)— [9] if this is so, then the Lord knows how to rescue the godly from trials and to hold the unrighteous for punishment on the day of judgment. [10] This is especially true of those who follow the corrupt desire of the flesh[a] and despise authority.   1Co 10:13

Bold and arrogant, they are not afraid to heap abuse on celestial beings; [11] yet even angels, although they are stronger and more powerful, do not heap abuse on such beings when bringing judgment on them from[b] the Lord. [12] But these people blaspheme in matters they do not understand. They are like unreasoning animals, creatures of instinct, born only to be caught and destroyed, and like animals they too will perish.   Jude 8-10

[13] They will be paid back with harm for the harm they have done. Their idea of pleasure is to carouse in broad daylight. They are blots and blemishes, reveling in their pleasures while they feast with you.[c] [14] With eyes full of adultery, they never stop sinning; they seduce the unstable; they are experts in greed—an accursed brood! [15] They have left the straight way and wandered off to follow the way of Balaam son of Bezer,[d] who loved the wages of wickedness. [16] But he was rebuked for his wrongdoing by a donkey—an animal without speech—who spoke with a human voice and restrained the prophet's madness.   Nu 22:21-30

[17] These people are springs without water and mists driven by a storm. Blackest darkness is reserved for them. [18] For they mouth empty, boastful words and, by appealing to the lustful desires of the flesh, they entice people who are just escaping from those who live in error. [19] They promise them freedom, while they themselves are slaves of depravity—for "people are slaves to whatever has mastered them." [20] If they have escaped the corruption of the world by knowing our Lord and Savior Jesus Christ and are again entangled in it and are overcome, they are worse off at the end than they were at the beginning. [21] It would have been better for them not to have known the way of righteousness, than to have known it and then to turn their backs on the sacred command that was passed on to them. [22] Of them the proverbs are true: "A dog returns

---

a 10 In contexts like this, the Greek word for *flesh* (*sarx*) refers to the sinful state of human beings, often presented as a power in opposition to the Spirit; also in verse 18.   *b 11* Many manuscripts *beings in the presence of*   *c 13* Some manuscripts *in their love feasts*   *d 15* Greek *Bosor* to its vomit,"[a] and, "A sow that is washed returns to her wallowing in the mud." Mt 12:45; Heb 6:4-6

The Day of the Lord

3 Dear friends, this is now my second letter to you. I have written both of them as reminders to stimulate you to wholesome thinking. [2]I want you to recall the words spoken in the past by the holy prophets and the command given by our Lord and Savior through your apostles. 2Pe 1:13

[3]Above all, you must understand that in the last days scoffers will come, scoffing and following their own evil desires. [4]They will say, "Where is this 'coming' he promised? Ever since our ancestors died, everything goes on as it has since the beginning of creation." [5]But they deliberately forget that long ago by God's word the heavens came into being and the earth was formed out of water and by water. [6]By these waters also the world of that time was deluged and destroyed. [7]By the same word the present heavens and earth are reserved for fire, being kept for the day of judgment and destruction of the ungodly. Eze 12:22; 2Pe 2:10

[8]But do not forget this one thing, dear friends: With the Lord a day is like a thousand years, and a thousand years are like a day. [9]The Lord is not slow in keeping his promise, as some understand slowness. Instead he is patient with you, not wanting anyone to perish, but everyone to come to repentance. Ps 90:4; Heb 10:37

[10]But the day of the Lord will come like a thief. The heavens will disappear with a roar; the elements will be destroyed by fire, and the earth and everything done in it will be laid bare.[b] Mt 24:35; Rev 21:1

[11]Since everything will be destroyed in this way, what kind of people ought you to be? You ought to live holy and godly lives [12]as you look forward to the day of God and speed its coming.[c] That day will bring about the destruction of the heavens by fire, and the elements will melt in the heat. [13]But in keeping with his promise we are looking forward to a new heaven and a new earth, where righteousness dwells. Isa 65:17; 1Co 1:7

[14]So then, dear friends, since you are looking forward to this, make every effort to be found spotless, blameless and at peace with him. [15]Bear in mind that our Lord's patience means salvation, just as our dear brother Paul also wrote you with the wisdom that God gave him. [16]He writes the same way in all his letters, speaking in them of these matters. His letters contain some things that are hard to under-

---

[a] 22 Prov. 26:11   [b] 10 Some manuscripts *be burned up*   [c] 12 Or *as you wait eagerly for the day of God to come*

stand, which ignorant and unstable people distort, as they do the other Scriptures, to their own destruction. Eph 3:3; 2Pe 2:14

[17] Therefore, dear friends, since you have been forewarned, be on your guard so that you may not be carried away by the error of the lawless and fall from your secure position. [18] But grow in the grace and knowledge of our Lord and Savior Jesus Christ. To him be glory both now and forever! Amen. 2Pe 1:11; Rev 2:5

1 John

The Incarnation of the Word of Life

1 That which was from the beginning, which we have heard, which we have seen with our eyes, which we have looked at and our hands have touched — this we proclaim concerning the Word of life. [2]The life appeared; we have seen it and testify to it, and we proclaim to you the eternal life, which was with the Father and has appeared to us. [3]We proclaim to you what we have seen and heard, so that you also may have fellowship with us. And our fellowship is with the Father and with his Son, Jesus Christ. [4]We write this to make our[a] joy complete. Jn 3:29; 1Jn 2:1

Light and Darkness, Sin and Forgiveness

[5]This is the message we have heard from him and declare to you: God is light; in him there is no darkness at all. [6]If we claim to have fellowship with him and yet walk in the darkness, we lie and do not live out the truth. [7]But if we walk in the light, as he is in the light, we have fellowship with one another, and the blood of Jesus, his Son, purifies us from all[b] sin. Heb 9:14; Rev 1:5

[8]If we claim to be without sin, we deceive ourselves and the truth is not in us. [9]If we confess our sins, he is faithful and just and will forgive us our sins and purify us from all unrighteousness. [10]If we claim we have not sinned, we make him out to be a liar and his word is not in us.

2 My dear children, I write this to you so that you will not sin. But if anybody does sin, we have an advocate with the Father — Jesus Christ, the Righteous One. [2]He is the atoning sacrifice for our sins, and not only for ours but also for the sins of the whole world. Ro 3:25; Heb 7:25

Love and Hatred for Fellow Believers

[3]We know that we have come to know him if we keep his commands. [4]Whoever says, "I know him," but does not do what he

---

a 4 Some manuscripts *your*   *b 7* Or *every*

commands is a liar, and the truth is not in that person. **5**But if anyone obeys his word, love for God*a* is truly made complete in them. This is how we know we are in him: **6**Whoever claims to live in him must live as Jesus did. 1Pe 2:21

7Dear friends, I am not writing you a new command but an old one, which you have had since the beginning. This old command is the message you have heard. **8**Yet I am writing you a new command; its truth is seen in him and in you, because the darkness is passing and the true light is already shining. Jn 1:9; 13:34 **9**Anyone who claims to be in the light but hates a brother or sister*b* is still in the darkness. **10**Anyone who loves their brother and sister*c* lives in the light, and there is nothing in them to make them stumble. **11**But anyone who hates a brother or sister is in the darkness and walks around in the darkness. They do not know where they are going, because the darkness has blinded them. Jn 12:35; 1Jn 3:14

Reasons for Writing

12I am writing to you, dear children,
   because your sins have
      been forgiven on
      account of his name.

13I am writing to you, fathers,
   because you know him who
      is from the beginning.
I am writing to you, young
      men,
   because you have overcome
      the evil one. Mt 5:37

14I write to you, dear children,
   because you know the
      Father.
I write to you, fathers,
   because you know him who
      is from the beginning.
I write to you, young men,
   because you are strong,
   and the word of God lives in
      you, Jn 5:38; 1Jn 1:10
   and you have overcome the
      evil one. ver 13

On Not Loving the World

15Do not love the world or anything in the world. If anyone loves the world, love for the Father*d* is not in them. **16**For everything in the world—the lust of the flesh, the lust of the eyes, and the pride of life—comes not from the Father but from the world. **17**The world and its desires pass away, but whoever does the will of God lives forever. Pr 27:20; Ro 12:2; 1Co 7:31

Warnings Against Denying the Son

18Dear children, this is the

---

a 5 Or *word, God's love*   *b* 9 The Greek word for *brother or sister* (*adelphos*) refers here to a believer, whether man or woman, as part of God's family; also in verse 11; and in 3:15, 17; 4:20; 5:16.   *c* 10 The Greek word for *brother and sister* (*adelphos*) refers here to a believer, whether man or woman, as part of God's family; also in 3:10; 4:20, 21.   *d* 15 Or *world, the Father's love* last hour; and as you have heard that the antichrist is coming, even now many antichrists have come. This is how we know it is the last hour. ¹⁹They went out from us, but they did not really belong to us. For if they had belonged to us, they would have remained with us; but their going showed that none of them belonged to us. 1Co 11:19; 1Jn 4:1

²⁰But you have an anointing from the Holy One, and all of you know the truth.*ᵃ* ²¹I do not write to you because you do not know the truth, but because you do know it and because no lie comes from the truth. ²²Who is the liar? It is whoever denies that Jesus is the Christ. Such a person is the antichrist—denying the Father and the Son. ²³No one who denies the Son has the Father; whoever acknowledges the Son has the Father also. 2Pe 1:12; 1Jn 4:15

²⁴As for you, see that what you have heard from the beginning remains in you. If it does, you also will remain in the Son and in the Father. ²⁵And this is what he promised us—eternal life. Jn 14:23

²⁶I am writing these things to you about those who are trying to lead you astray. ²⁷As for you, the anointing you received from him remains in you, and you do not need anyone to teach you. But as his anointing teaches you about all things and as that anointing is real, not counterfeit—just as it has taught you, remain in him. 2Jn 7

God's Children and Sin

²⁸And now, dear children, continue in him, so that when he appears we may be confident and unashamed before him at his coming. 1Jn 3:2; 4:17

²⁹If you know that he is righteous, you know that everyone who does what is right has been born of him.

3 See what great love the Father has lavished on us, that we should be called children of God! And that is what we are! The reason the world does not know us is that it did not know him. ²Dear friends, now we are children of God, and what we will be has not yet been made known. But we know that when Christ appears,*ᵇ* we shall be like him, for we shall see him as he is. ³All who have this hope in him purify themselves, just as he is pure. Jn 1:12; 16:3

⁴Everyone who sins breaks the law; in fact, sin is lawlessness. ⁵But you know that he appeared so that he might take away our sins. And in him is no sin. ⁶No one who lives in him keeps on sinning. No one who continues to sin has either seen him or known him. 2Co 5:21; 1Jn 5:17

⁷Dear children, do not let anyone lead you astray. The one who does what is right is righteous,

---

ᵃ 20 Some manuscripts *and you know all things*   *ᵇ* 2 Or *when it is made known* just as he is righteous. ⁸The one who does what is sinful is of the devil, because the devil has been sinning from the beginning. The reason the Son of God appeared was to destroy the devil's work. ⁹No one who is born of God will continue to sin, because God's seed remains in them; they cannot go on sinning, because they have been born of God. ¹⁰This is how we know who the children of God are and who the children of the devil are: Anyone who does not do what is right is not God's child, nor is anyone who does not love their brother and sister.   1Jn 4:8; 5:18

More on Love and Hatred

¹¹For this is the message you heard from the beginning: We should love one another. ¹²Do not be like Cain, who belonged to the evil one and murdered his brother. And why did he murder him? Because his own actions were evil and his brother's were righteous. ¹³Do not be surprised, my brothers and sisters,ᵃ if the world hates you. ¹⁴We know that we have passed from death to life, because we love each other. Anyone who does not love remains in death. ¹⁵Anyone who hates a brother or sister is a murderer, and you know that no murderer has eternal life residing in him.   Mt 5:21-22; Gal 5:20-21

¹⁶This is how we know what love is: Jesus Christ laid down his life for us. And we ought to lay down our lives for our brothers and sisters. ¹⁷If anyone has material possessions and sees a brother or sister in need but has no pity on them, how can the love of God be in that person? ¹⁸Dear children, let us not love with words or speech but with actions and in truth.

¹⁹This is how we know that we belong to the truth and how we set our hearts at rest in his presence: ²⁰If our hearts condemn us, we know that God is greater than our hearts, and he knows everything. ²¹Dear friends, if our hearts do not condemn us, we have confidence before God ²²and receive from him anything we ask, because we keep his commands and do what pleases him. ²³And this is his command: to believe in the name of his Son, Jesus Christ, and to love one another as he commanded us. ²⁴The one who keeps God's commands lives in him, and he in them. And this is how we know that he lives in us: We know it by the Spirit he gave us.   1Jn 2:6; 4:13

On Denying the Incarnation

4 Dear friends, do not believe every spirit, but test the spirits to see whether they are from God, because many false prophets

---

ᵃ 13 The Greek word for *brothers and sisters* (*adelphoi*) refers here to believers, both men and women, as part of God's family; also in verse 16.

have gone out into the world. ²This is how you can recognize the Spirit of God: Every spirit that acknowledges that Jesus Christ has come in the flesh is from God, ³but every spirit that does not acknowledge Jesus is not from God. This is the spirit of the antichrist, which you have heard is coming and even now is already in the world. 1Co 12:3; 2Jn 7

⁴You, dear children, are from God and have overcome them, because the one who is in you is greater than the one who is in the world. ⁵They are from the world and therefore speak from the viewpoint of the world, and the world listens to them. ⁶We are from God, and whoever knows God listens to us; but whoever is not from God does not listen to us. This is how we recognize the Spirit[a] of truth and the spirit of falsehood. Jn 8:47; 14:17

God's Love and Ours

⁷Dear friends, let us love one another, for love comes from God. Everyone who loves has been born of God and knows God. ⁸Whoever does not love does not know God, because God is love. ⁹This is how God showed his love among us: He sent his one and only Son into the world that we might live through him. ¹⁰This is love: not that we loved God, but that he loved us and sent his Son as an atoning sacrifice for our sins. ¹¹Dear friends, since God so loved us, we also ought to love one another. ¹²No one has ever seen God; but if we love one another, God lives in us and his love is made complete in us. 1Jn 2:2,5

¹³This is how we know that we live in him and he in us: He has given us of his Spirit. ¹⁴And we have seen and testify that the Father has sent his Son to be the Savior of the world. ¹⁵If anyone acknowledges that Jesus is the Son of God, God lives in them and they in God. ¹⁶And so we know and rely on the love God has for us. Ro 10:9

God is love. Whoever lives in love lives in God, and God in them. ¹⁷This is how love is made complete among us so that we will have confidence on the day of judgment: In this world we are like Jesus. ¹⁸There is no fear in love. But perfect love drives out fear, because fear has to do with punishment. The one who fears is not made perfect in love. Ro 8:15

¹⁹We love because he first loved us. ²⁰Whoever claims to love God yet hates a brother or sister is a liar. For whoever does not love their brother and sister, whom they have seen, cannot love God, whom they have not seen. ²¹And he has given us this command: Anyone who loves God must also love their brother and sister. Mt 5:43; 1Jn 2:4

[a] 6 Or spirit

Faith in the Incarnate Son of God

5 Everyone who believes that Jesus is the Christ is born of God, and everyone who loves the father loves his child as well. [2] This is how we know that we love the children of God: by loving God and carrying out his commands. [3] In fact, this is love for God: to keep his commands. And his commands are not burdensome, [4] for everyone born of God overcomes the world. This is the victory that has overcome the world, even our faith. [5] Who is it that overcomes the world? Only the one who believes that Jesus is the Son of God. Jn 14:15; 16:33

[6] This is the one who came by water and blood—Jesus Christ. He did not come by water only, but by water and blood. And it is the Spirit who testifies, because the Spirit is the truth. [7] For there are three that testify: [8] the[a] Spirit, the water and the blood; and the three are in agreement. [9] We accept human testimony, but God's testimony is greater because it is the testimony of God, which he has given about his Son. [10] Whoever believes in the Son of God accepts this testimony. Whoever does not believe God has made him out to be a liar, because they have not believed the testimony God has given about his Son.

[11] And this is the testimony: God has given us eternal life, and this life is in his Son. [12] Whoever has the Son has life; whoever does not have the Son of God does not have life. Jn 3:15-16,36; 1Jn 2:25

Concluding Affirmations

[13] I write these things to you who believe in the name of the Son of God so that you may know that you have eternal life. [14] This is the confidence we have in approaching God: that if we ask anything according to his will, he hears us. [15] And if we know that he hears us—whatever we ask—we know that we have what we asked of him. Jn 20:31; 1Jn 3:21

[16] If you see any brother or sister commit a sin that does not lead to death, you should pray and God will give them life. I refer to those whose sin does not lead to death. There is a sin that leads to death. I am not saying that you should pray about that. [17] All wrongdoing is sin, and there is sin that does not lead to death. Jas 5:15; 1Jn 3:4

[18] We know that anyone born of God does not continue to sin; the One who was born of God keeps them safe, and the evil one cannot harm them. [19] We know that we are children of God, and that the whole world is under the control of the evil

---

[a] 7,8 Late manuscripts of the Vulgate *testify in heaven: the Father, the Word and the Holy Spirit, and these three are one.* [8] *And there are three that testify on earth: the* (not found in any Greek manuscript before the fourteenth century)

one. [20]We know also that the Son of God has come and has given us understanding, so that we may know him who is true. And we are in him who is true by being in his Son Jesus Christ. He is the true God and eternal life.   Lk 24:45; Jn 17:3

[21]Dear children, keep yourselves from idols.   1Co 10:14; 1Th 1:9

2 John

¹The elder,

¹The elder,

3Jn 1

To the lady chosen by God and to her children, whom I love in the truth—and not I only, but also all who know the truth— ²because of the truth, which lives in us and will be with us forever:

³Grace, mercy and peace from God the Father and from Jesus Christ, the Father's Son, will be with us in truth and love.   Ro 1:7

⁴It has given me great joy to find some of your children walking in the truth, just as the Father commanded us. ⁵And now, dear lady, I am not writing you a new command but one we have had from the beginning. I ask that we love one another. ⁶And this is love: that we walk in obedience to his commands. As you have heard from the beginning, his command is that you walk in love.   1Jn 2:5; 3:11

⁷I say this because many deceivers, who do not acknowl- edge Jesus Christ as coming in the flesh, have gone out into the world. Any such person is the deceiver and the antichrist. ⁸Watch out that you do not lose what we*ᵃ* have worked for, but that you may be rewarded fully. ⁹Anyone who runs ahead and does not continue in the teaching of Christ does not have God; whoever continues in the teaching has both the Father and the Son. ¹⁰If anyone comes to you and does not bring this teaching, do not take them into your house or welcome them. ¹¹Anyone who welcomes them shares in their wicked work.   Ro 16:17; 1Jn 2:23

¹²I have much to write to you, but I do not want to use paper and ink. Instead, I hope to vis- it you and talk with you face to face, so that our joy may be com- plete.   3Jn 13-14

¹³The children of your sister, who is chosen by God, send their greetings.   ver 1

ᵃ 8 Some manuscripts *you*

3 John

¹The elder,   2Jn 1

To my dear friend Gaius, whom I love in the truth.

²Dear friend, I pray that you may enjoy good health and that all may go well with you, even as your soul is getting along well. ³It gave me great joy when some believers came and testified about your faithfulness to the truth, telling how you continue to walk in it. ⁴I have no greater joy than to hear that my children are walking in the truth.   1Co 4:15; 2Jn 4

⁵Dear friend, you are faithful in what you are doing for the brothers and sisters,ᵃ even though they are strangers to you. ⁶They have told the church about your love. Please send them on their way in a manner that honors God. ⁷It was for the sake of the Name that they went out, receiving no help from the pagans. ⁸We ought therefore to show hospitality to such people so that we may work together for the truth.   Ac 20:33,35; Ro 12:13

⁹I wrote to the church, but Diotrephes, who loves to be first, will not welcome us. ¹⁰So when I come, I will call attention to what he is doing, spreading malicious nonsense about us. Not satisfied with that, he even refuses to welcome other believers. He also stops those who want to do so and puts them out of the church.   Jn 9:22,34; 2Jn 12

¹¹Dear friend, do not imitate what is evil but what is good. Anyone who does what is good is from God. Anyone who does what is evil has not seen God. ¹²Demetrius is well spoken of by everyone — and even by the truth itself. We also speak well of him, and you know that our testimony is true.   Jn 21:24; 1Ti 3:7

¹³I have much to write you, but I do not want to do so with pen and ink. ¹⁴I hope to see you soon, and we will talk face to face.   2Jn 12

Peace to you. The friends here send their greetings. Greet the friends there by name.   Jn 10:3

ᵃ 5 The Greek word for *brothers and sisters* (*adelphoi*) refers here to believers, both men and women, as part of God's family.

Jude

¹Jude, a servant of Jesus Christ and a brother of James,   Ac 1:13

To those who have been called, who are loved in God the Father and kept for[a] Jesus Christ: Jn 17:12

²Mercy, peace and love be yours in abundance.   2Pe 1:2

The Sin and Doom of Ungodly People

³Dear friends, although I was very eager to write to you about the salvation we share, I felt compelled to write and urge you to contend for the faith that was once for all entrusted to God's holy people. ⁴For certain individuals whose condemnation was written about[b] long ago have secretly slipped in among you. They are ungodly people, who pervert the grace of our God into a license for immorality and deny Jesus Christ our only Sovereign and Lord.   Gal 2:4; 2Pe 2:1

⁵Though you already know all this, I want to remind you that the Lord[c] at one time delivered his people out of Egypt, but later destroyed those who did not believe. ⁶And the angels who did not keep their positions of authority but abandoned their proper dwelling—these he has kept in darkness, bound with everlasting chains for judgment on the great Day. ⁷In a similar way, Sodom and Gomorrah and the surrounding towns gave themselves up to sexual immorality and perversion. They serve as an example of those who suffer the punishment of eternal fire. Dt 29:23

⁸In the very same way, on the strength of their dreams these ungodly people pollute their own bodies, reject authority and heap abuse on celestial beings. ⁹But even the archangel Michael, when he was disputing with the devil about the body of Moses, did not himself dare to condemn him for slander but said, "The Lord rebuke you!"[d] ¹⁰Yet these people slander whatever they do not understand, and the very

things they do understand by instinct—as irrational animals do—will destroy them. 2Pe 2:10,12

¹¹Woe to them! They have taken the way of Cain; they have rushed for profit into Balaam's error; they have been destroyed in Korah's rebellion. Nu 16:1-3,31-35

¹²These people are blemishes at your love feasts, eating with you without the slightest qualm—shepherds who feed only themselves. They are clouds without rain, blown along by the wind; autumn trees, without fruit and uprooted—twice dead. ¹³They are wild waves of the sea, foaming up their shame; wandering stars, for whom blackest darkness has been reserved forever.

¹⁴Enoch, the seventh from Adam, prophesied about them: "See, the Lord is coming with thousands upon thousands of his holy ones ¹⁵to judge everyone, and to convict all of them of all the ungodly acts they have committed in their ungodliness, and of all the defiant words ungodly sinners have spoken against him."^a ¹⁶These people are grumblers and faultfinders; they follow their own evil desires; they boast about themselves and flatter others for their own advantage. Dt 33:2

A Call to Persevere

¹⁷But, dear friends, remember what the apostles of our Lord Jesus Christ foretold. ¹⁸They said to you, "In the last times there will be scoffers who will follow their own ungodly desires." ¹⁹These are the people who divide you, who follow mere natural instincts and do not have the Spirit. 1Ti 4:1; 2Pe 2:1

²⁰But you, dear friends, by building yourselves up in your most holy faith and praying in the Holy Spirit, ²¹keep yourselves in God's love as you wait for the mercy of our Lord Jesus Christ to bring you to eternal life. Tit 2:13

²²Be merciful to those who doubt; ²³save others by snatching them from the fire; to others show mercy, mixed with fear—hating even the clothing stained by corrupted flesh.^b Am 4:11

Doxology

²⁴To him who is able to keep you from stumbling and to present you before his glorious presence without fault and with great joy— ²⁵to the only God our Savior be glory, majesty, power and authority, through Jesus Christ our Lord, before all ages, now and forevermore! Amen. Ro 11:36

^a 14,15 From the Jewish *First Book of Enoch* (approximately the first century B.C.)
^b 22,23 The Greek manuscripts of these verses vary at several points.

Revelation

Prologue

1 The revelation from Jesus Christ, which God gave him to show his servants what must soon take place. He made it known by sending his angel to his servant John, ²who testifies to everything he saw—that is, the word of God and the testimony of Jesus Christ. ³Blessed is the one who reads aloud the words of this prophecy, and blessed are those who hear it and take to heart what is written in it, because the time is near.   Lk 11:28

Greetings and Doxology

⁴John,

To the seven churches in the province of Asia: ver 11,20

Grace and peace to you from him who is, and who was, and who is to come, and from the seven spirits*a* before his throne, ⁵and from Jesus Christ, who is the faithful witness, the firstborn from the dead, and the ruler of the kings of the earth.   Col 1:18; Rev 17:14

To him who loves us and has freed us from our sins by his blood, ⁶and has made us to be a kingdom and priests to serve his God and Father—to him be glory and power for ever and ever! Amen.   Ro 11:36; 1Pe 2:5

⁷"Look, he is coming with the clouds,"*b*   Da 7:13
and "every eye will see him, even those who pierced him";
and all peoples on earth
"will mourn because of him."*c*
So shall it be! Amen.

⁸"I am the Alpha and the Omega," says the Lord God, "who is, and who was, and who is to come, the Almighty."   Rev 4:8; 21:6

John's Vision of Christ

⁹I, John, your brother and companion in the suffering and

---

a 4 That is, the sevenfold Spirit   *b* 7 Daniel 7:13   *c* 7 Zech. 12:10

kingdom and patient endurance that are ours in Jesus, was on the island of Patmos because of the word of God and the testimony of Jesus. **10**On the Lord's Day I was in the Spirit, and I heard behind me a loud voice like a trumpet, **11**which said: "Write on a scroll what you see and send it to the seven churches: to Ephesus, Smyrna, Pergamum, Thyatira, Sardis, Philadelphia and Laodicea."   2Ti 2:12; Rev 4:1

12I turned around to see the voice that was speaking to me. And when I turned I saw seven golden lampstands, **13**and among the lampstands was someone like a son of man,[a] dressed in a robe reaching down to his feet and with a golden sash around his chest. **14**The hair on his head was white like wool, as white as snow, and his eyes were like blazing fire. **15**His feet were like bronze glowing in a furnace, and his voice was like the sound of rushing waters. **16**In his right hand he held seven stars, and coming out of his mouth was a sharp, double-edged sword. His face was like the sun shining in all its brilliance. Heb 4:12; Rev 2:12,16

17When I saw him, I fell at his feet as though dead. Then he placed his right hand on me and said: "Do not be afraid. I am the First and the Last. **18**I am the Living One; I was dead, and now look, I am alive for ever and ever!

And I hold the keys of death and Hades.   Ro 6:9; Rev 20:1

19"Write, therefore, what you have seen, what is now and what will take place later. **20**The mystery of the seven stars that you saw in my right hand and of the seven golden lampstands is this: The seven stars are the angels[b] of the seven churches, and the seven lampstands are the seven churches.   Mt 5:14-15

To the Church in Ephesus

2 "To the angel[c] of the church in Ephesus write: Ac 18:19

These are the words of him who holds the seven stars in his right hand and walks among the seven golden lampstands. **2**I know your deeds, your hard work and your perseverance. I know that you cannot tolerate wicked people, that you have tested those who claim to be apostles but are not, and have found them false. **3**You have persevered and have endured hardships for my name, and have not grown weary.   1Jn 4:1; Rev 1:16

4Yet I hold this against you: You have forsaken the love you had at first. **5**Consider how far you have fallen! Repent and do the things you did at first. If you do not repent, I will come to you and

---

[a] 13 See Daniel 7:13.   [b] 20 Or messengers   [c] 1 Or messenger; also in verses 8, 12 and 18

remove your lampstand from its place. [6]But you have this in your favor: You hate the practices of the Nicolaitans, which I also hate. Mt 24:12

[7]Whoever has ears, let them hear what the Spirit says to the churches. To the one who is victorious, I will give the right to eat from the tree of life, which is in the paradise of God. Ge 2:9

To the Church in Smyrna

[8]"To the angel of the church in Smyrna write: Rev 1:11

These are the words of him who is the First and the Last, who died and came to life again. [9]I know your afflictions and your poverty — yet you are rich! I know about the slander of those who say they are Jews and are not, but are a synagogue of Satan. [10]Do not be afraid of what you are about to suffer. I tell you, the devil will put some of you in prison to test you, and you will suffer persecution for ten days. Be faithful, even to the point of death, and I will give you life as your victor's crown. Da 1:12,14; Jas 2:5

[11]Whoever has ears, let them hear what the Spirit says to the churches. The one who is victorious will not be hurt at all by the second death. Rev 21:8

To the Church in Pergamum

[12]"To the angel of the church in Pergamum write: Rev 1:11

These are the words of him who has the sharp, double-edged sword. [13]I know where you live — where Satan has his throne. Yet you remain true to my name. You did not renounce your faith in me, not even in the days of Antipas, my faithful witness, who was put to death in your city — where Satan lives.

[14]Nevertheless, I have a few things against you: There are some among you who hold to the teaching of Balaam, who taught Balak to entice the Israelites to sin so that they ate food sacrificed to idols and committed sexual immorality. [15]Likewise, you also have those who hold to the teaching of the Nicolaitans. [16]Repent therefore! Otherwise, I will soon come to you and will fight against them with the sword of my mouth. 2Th 2:8; Rev 1:16

[17]Whoever has ears, let them hear what the Spirit says to the churches. To the one who is victorious, I will give some of the hidden manna. I will also give that person a white stone with a new name written on it, known only to the one who receives it. Rev 19:12

To the Church in Thyatira

18 "To the angel of the church in Thyatira write: Rev 1:11

These are the words of the Son of God, whose eyes are like blazing fire and whose feet are like burnished bronze. 19 I know your deeds, your love and faith, your service and perseverance, and that you are now doing more than you did at first. Rev 1:14-15

20 Nevertheless, I have this against you: You tolerate that woman Jezebel, who calls herself a prophet. By her teaching she misleads my servants into sexual immorality and the eating of food sacrificed to idols. 21 I have given her time to repent of her immorality, but she is unwilling. 22 So I will cast her on a bed of suffering, and I will make those who commit adultery with her suffer intensely, unless they repent of her ways. 23 I will strike her children dead. Then all the churches will know that I am he who searches hearts and minds, and I will repay each of you according to your deeds.

24 Now I say to the rest of you in Thyatira, to you who do not hold to her teaching and have not learned Satan's so-called deep secrets, 'I will not impose any other burden on you, 25 except to hold on to what you have until I come.' Ac 15:28; Rev 9:20

26 To the one who is victorious and does my will to the end, I will give authority over the nations— 27 that one 'will rule them with an iron scepter and will dash them to pieces like pottery'*a*—just as I have received authority from my Father. 28 I will also give that one the morning star. 29 Whoever has ears, let them hear what the Spirit says to the churches. Rev 22:16

To the Church in Sardis

3 "To the angel*b* of the church in Sardis write: Rev 1:11

These are the words of him who holds the seven spirits*c* of God and the seven stars. I know your deeds; you have a reputation of being alive, but you are dead. 2 Wake up! Strengthen what remains and is about to die, for I have found your deeds unfinished in the sight of my God. 3 Remember, therefore, what you have received and heard; hold it fast, and repent. But if you do not wake up, I will come like a thief, and you will not know

a 27 Psalm 2:9   *b 1* Or *messenger;* also in verses 7 and 14   *c 1* That is, the sevenfold Spirit at what time I will come to you. 2Pe 3:10; Rev 1:4,16

⁴Yet you have a few people in Sardis who have not soiled their clothes. They will walk with me, dressed in white, for they are worthy. ⁵The one who is victorious will, like them, be dressed in white. I will never blot out the name of that person from the book of life, but will acknowledge that name before my Father and his angels. ⁶Whoever has ears, let them hear what the Spirit says to the churches. Mt 10:32; Rev 2:7

To the Church in Philadelphia

⁷"To the angel of the church in Philadelphia write: Rev 1:11

These are the words of him who is holy and true, who holds the key of David. What he opens no one can shut, and what he shuts no one can open. ⁸I know your deeds. See, I have placed before you an open door that no one can shut. I know that you have little strength, yet you have kept my word and have not denied my name. ⁹I will make those who are of the synagogue of Satan, who claim to be Jews though they are not, but are liars — I will make them come and fall down at your feet and ac-

knowledge that I have loved you. ¹⁰Since you have kept my command to endure patiently, I will also keep you from the hour of trial that is going to come on the whole world to test the inhabitants of the earth. Rev 6:10; 17:8

¹¹I am coming soon. Hold on to what you have, so that no one will take your crown. ¹²The one who is victorious I will make a pillar in the temple of my God. Never again will they leave it. I will write on them the name of my God and the name of the city of my God, the new Jerusalem, which is coming down out of heaven from my God; and I will also write on them my new name. ¹³Whoever has ears, let them hear what the Spirit says to the churches. Gal 2:9; Rev 22:4

To the Church in Laodicea

¹⁴"To the angel of the church in Laodicea write: Rev 1:11

These are the words of the Amen, the faithful and true witness, the ruler of God's creation. ¹⁵I know your deeds, that you are neither cold nor hot. I wish you were either one or the other! ¹⁶So, because you are lukewarm — neither hot nor cold — I am about to spit you out of my mouth. ¹⁷You say, 'I am rich;

I have acquired wealth and do not need a thing.' But you do not realize that you are wretched, pitiful, poor, blind and naked. [18] I counsel you to buy from me gold refined in the fire, so you can become rich; and white clothes to wear, so you can cover your shameful nakedness; and salve to put on your eyes, so you can see. Hos 12:8

[19] Those whom I love I rebuke and discipline. So be earnest and repent. [20] Here I am! I stand at the door and knock. If anyone hears my voice and opens the door, I will come in and eat with that person, and they with me. Lk 12:36; Heb 12:5-6

[21] To the one who is victorious, I will give the right to sit with me on my throne, just as I was victorious and sat down with my Father on his throne. [22] Whoever has ears, let them hear what the Spirit says to the churches." Mt 19:28

The Throne in Heaven

4 After this I looked, and there before me was a door standing open in heaven. And the voice I had first heard speaking to me like a trumpet said, "Come up here, and I will show you what must take place after this." [2] At once I was in the Spirit, and there before me was a throne in heaven with someone sitting on it. [3] And the one who sat there had the appearance of jasper and ruby. A rainbow that shone like an emerald encircled the throne. [4] Surrounding the throne were twenty-four other thrones, and seated on them were twenty-four elders. They were dressed in white and had crowns of gold on their heads. [5] From the throne came flashes of lightning, rumblings and peals of thunder. In front of the throne, seven lamps were blazing. These are the seven spirits[a] of God. [6] Also in front of the throne there was what looked like a sea of glass, clear as crystal. Rev 11:16; 15:2

In the center, around the throne, were four living creatures, and they were covered with eyes, in front and in back. [7] The first living creature was like a lion, the second was like an ox, the third had a face like a man, the fourth was like a flying eagle. [8] Each of the four living creatures had six wings and was covered with eyes all around, even under its wings. Day and night they never stop saying: Isa 6:2; Eze 1:10

" 'Holy, holy, holy
is the Lord God Almighty,'[b]
who was, and is, and is
to come."

[9] Whenever the living creatures give glory, honor and thanks to

---

[a] 5 That is, the sevenfold Spirit   [b] 8 Isaiah 6:3

him who sits on the throne and who lives for ever and ever, ¹⁰the twenty-four elders fall down before him who sits on the throne and worship him who lives for ever and ever. They lay their crowns before the throne and say: Rev 5:8,14

¹¹ "You are worthy, our Lord and God,
to receive glory and honor and power, Rev 5:12
for you created all things,
and by your will they were created
and have their being." Rev 10:6

The Scroll and the Lamb

5 Then I saw in the right hand of him who sat on the throne a scroll with writing on both sides and sealed with seven seals. ²And I saw a mighty angel proclaiming in a loud voice, "Who is worthy to break the seals and open the scroll?" ³But no one in heaven or on earth or under the earth could open the scroll or even look inside it. ⁴I wept and wept because no one was found who was worthy to open the scroll or look inside. ⁵Then one of the elders said to me, "Do not weep! See, the Lion of the tribe of Judah, the Root of David, has triumphed. He is able to open the scroll and its seven seals." Ge 49:9; Isa 11:1,10

⁶Then I saw a Lamb, looking as if it had been slain, standing at the center of the throne, encircled by the four living creatures and the elders. The Lamb had seven horns and seven eyes, which are the seven spirits[a] of God sent out into all the earth. ⁷He went and took the scroll from the right hand of him who sat on the throne. ⁸And when he had taken it, the four living creatures and the twenty-four elders fell down before the Lamb. Each one had a harp and they were holding golden bowls full of incense, which are the prayers of God's people. ⁹And they sang a new song, saying: Ps 40:3; Rev 14:2

"You are worthy to take the scroll Rev 4:11
and to open its seals,
because you were slain,
and with your blood you purchased for God
persons from every tribe and language and people and nation.
¹⁰You have made them to be a kingdom and priests to serve our God, 1Pe 2:5
and they will reign[b] on the earth."

¹¹Then I looked and heard the voice of many angels, numbering thousands upon thousands, and ten thousand times ten thousand. They encircled the throne and the living creatures

and the elders. [12]In a loud voice they were saying: Da 7:10; Heb 12:22

"Worthy is the Lamb, who was
        slain,   ver 9,13
    to receive power and wealth
        and wisdom and
        strength
    and honor and glory and
        praise!"   Rev 4:11

[13]Then I heard every creature in heaven and on earth and under the earth and on the sea, and all that is in them, saying: Php 2:10

"To him who sits on the
        throne and to the Lamb
    be praise and honor and
        glory and power,
    for ever and ever!"

[14]The four living creatures said, "Amen," and the elders fell down and worshiped.   1Ch 29:11; Rev 4:10

The Seals

6 I watched as the Lamb opened the first of the seven seals. Then I heard one of the four living creatures say in a voice like thunder, "Come!" [2]I looked, and there before me was a white horse! Its rider held a bow, and he was given a crown, and he rode out as a conqueror bent on conquest. Zec 6:11; Rev 19:11

[3]When the Lamb opened the second seal, I heard the second living creature say, "Come!" [4]Then another horse came out, a fiery red one. Its rider was given power to take peace from the earth and to make people kill each other. To him was given a large sword.   Rev 4:7

[5]When the Lamb opened the third seal, I heard the third living creature say, "Come!" I looked, and there before me was a black horse! Its rider was holding a pair of scales in his hand. [6]Then I heard what sounded like a voice among the four living creatures, saying, "Two pounds[a] of wheat for a day's wages,[b] and six pounds[c] of barley for a day's wages,[b] and do not damage the oil and the wine!"   Rev 4:7; 9:4

[7]When the Lamb opened the fourth seal, I heard the voice of the fourth living creature say, "Come!" [8]I looked, and there before me was a pale horse! Its rider was named Death, and Hades was following close behind him. They were given power over a fourth of the earth to kill by sword, famine and plague, and by the wild beasts of the earth.

[9]When he opened the fifth seal, I saw under the altar the souls of those who had been slain because of the word of God and the testimony they had maintained. [10]They called out in a loud voice, "How long, Sovereign Lord, holy and true, until you judge the inhabitants of the earth and avenge our blood?" [11]Then each of them was given a white robe, and they were told to wait a little longer,

---

[a] 6 Or about 1 kilogram   [b] 6 Greek *a denarius*   [c] 6 Or about 3 kilograms

until the full number of their fellow servants, their brothers and sisters,[a] were killed just as they had been. Heb 11:40; Rev 20:4

[12] I watched as he opened the sixth seal. There was a great earthquake. The sun turned black like sackcloth made of goat hair, the whole moon turned blood red, [13] and the stars in the sky fell to earth, as figs drop from a fig tree when shaken by a strong wind. [14] The heavens receded like a scroll being rolled up, and every mountain and island was removed from its place. Jer 4:24

[15] Then the kings of the earth, the princes, the generals, the rich, the mighty, and everyone else, both slave and free, hid in caves and among the rocks of the mountains. [16] They called to the mountains and the rocks, "Fall on us and hide us[b] from the face of him who sits on the throne and from the wrath of the Lamb! [17] For the great day of their[c] wrath has come, and who can withstand it?" Ps 76:7; Zep 1:14-15

144,000 Sealed

7 After this I saw four angels standing at the four corners of the earth, holding back the four winds of the earth to prevent any wind from blowing on the land or on the sea or on any tree. [2] Then I saw another angel coming up from the east, having the seal of the living God. He called out in a loud voice to the four angels who had been given power to harm the land and the sea: [3] "Do not harm the land or the sea or the trees until we put a seal on the foreheads of the servants of our God." [4] Then I heard the number of those who were sealed: 144,000 from all the tribes of Israel. Rev 9:16; 14:1,3

[5] From the tribe of Judah 12,000 were sealed,
from the tribe of Reuben 12,000,
from the tribe of Gad 12,000,
[6] from the tribe of Asher 12,000,
from the tribe of Naphtali 12,000,
from the tribe of Manasseh 12,000,
[7] from the tribe of Simeon 12,000,
from the tribe of Levi 12,000,
from the tribe of Issachar 12,000,
[8] from the tribe of Zebulun 12,000,
from the tribe of Joseph 12,000,
from the tribe of Benjamin 12,000.

The Great Multitude in White Robes

[9] After this I looked, and there

---

[a] 11 The Greek word for *brothers and sisters* (*adelphoi*) refers here to believers, both men and women, as part of God's family; also in 12:10; 19:10.   [b] 16 See Hosea 10:8.   [c] 17 Some manuscripts *his*

before me was a great multitude that no one could count, from every nation, tribe, people and language, standing before the throne and before the Lamb. They were wearing white robes and were holding palm branches in their hands. [10] And they cried out in a loud voice: Rev 5:9

> "Salvation belongs to our
>   God,   Ps 3:8; Rev 12:10; 19:1
> who sits on the throne,   Rev 5:1
> and to the Lamb."

[11] All the angels were standing around the throne and around the elders and the four living creatures. They fell down on their faces before the throne and worshiped God, [12] saying: Rev 4:4,6,10

> "Amen!
> Praise and glory
> and wisdom and thanks and
>   honor
> and power and strength
> be to our God for ever and
>   ever.
> Amen!"   Rev 5:12-14

[13] Then one of the elders asked me, "These in white robes — who are they, and where did they come from?"   Rev 3:4

[14] I answered, "Sir, you know."

And he said, "These are they who have come out of the great tribulation; they have washed their robes and made them white in the blood of the Lamb. [15] Therefore,   Heb 9:14; 1Jn 1:7

> "they are before the throne of
>   God   ver 9
> and serve him day and
>   night in his temple;
> and he who sits on the throne
>   will shelter them with his
>   presence.   Rev 21:3

[16] 'Never again will they hunger;
>   never again will they thirst.
> The sun will not beat down on
>   them,'[a]
> nor any scorching heat.

[17] For the Lamb at the center of
>   the throne
> will be their shepherd;   Ps 23:1
> 'he will lead them to springs
>   of living water.'[a]   Jn 4:10
> 'And God will wipe away
>   every tear from their
>   eyes.'[b]"   Isa 25:8; Rev 21:4

The Seventh Seal and the Golden Censer

8 When he opened the seventh seal, there was silence in heaven for about half an hour. [2] And I saw the seven angels who stand before God, and seven trumpets were given to them.

[3] Another angel, who had a golden censer, came and stood at the altar. He was given much incense to offer, with the prayers of all God's people, on the golden altar in front of the throne. [4] The smoke of the incense, together with the prayers of God's people, went up before God from the angel's hand. [5] Then the angel took the censer, filled it with fire from the altar,

[a] 16,17 Isaiah 49:10   [b] 17 Isaiah 25:8

and hurled it on the earth; and there came peals of thunder, rumblings, flashes of lightning and an earthquake. Ex 30:1-6

The Trumpets

⁶Then the seven angels who had the seven trumpets prepared to sound them. ver 2

⁷The first angel sounded his trumpet, and there came hail and fire mixed with blood, and it was hurled down on the earth. A third of the earth was burned up, a third of the trees were burned up, and all the green grass was burned up. Eze 38:22; Rev 9:4

⁸The second angel sounded his trumpet, and something like a huge mountain, all ablaze, was thrown into the sea. A third of the sea turned into blood, ⁹a third of the living creatures in the sea died, and a third of the ships were destroyed. Jer 51:25; Rev 16:3

¹⁰The third angel sounded his trumpet, and a great star, blazing like a torch, fell from the sky on a third of the rivers and on the springs of water — ¹¹the name of the star is Wormwood.ᵃ A third of the waters turned bitter, and many people died from the waters that had become bitter. Isa 14:12

¹²The fourth angel sounded his trumpet, and a third of the sun was struck, a third of the moon, and a third of the stars, so that a third of them turned dark. A third of the day was with-

out light, and also a third of the night. Ex 10:21-23; Rev 6:12-13

¹³As I watched, I heard an eagle that was flying in midair call out in a loud voice: "Woe! Woe! Woe to the inhabitants of the earth, because of the trumpet blasts about to be sounded by the other three angels!" Rev 9:12; 14:6

9 The fifth angel sounded his trumpet, and I saw a star that had fallen from the sky to the earth. The star was given the key to the shaft of the Abyss. ²When he opened the Abyss, smoke rose from it like the smoke from a gigantic furnace. The sun and sky were darkened by the smoke from the Abyss. ³And out of the smoke locusts came down on the earth and were given power like that of scorpions of the earth. ⁴They were told not to harm the grass of the earth or any plant or tree, but only those people who did not have the seal of God on their foreheads. ⁵They were not allowed to kill them but only to torture them for five months. And the agony they suffered was like that of the sting of a scorpion when it strikes. ⁶During those days people will seek death but will not find it; they will long to die, but death will elude them. Jer 8:3; Rev 8:7

⁷The locusts looked like horses prepared for battle. On their heads they wore something like crowns of gold, and their faces resembled human faces. ⁸Their

ᵃ 11 Wormwood is a bitter substance.

hair was like women's hair, and their teeth were like lions' teeth. [9]They had breastplates like breastplates of iron, and the sound of their wings was like the thundering of many horses and chariots rushing into battle. [10]They had tails with stingers, like scorpions, and in their tails they had power to torment people for five months. [11]They had as king over them the angel of the Abyss, whose name in Hebrew is Abaddon and in Greek is Apollyon (that is, Destroyer). Joel 1:6; 2:5

[12]The first woe is past; two other woes are yet to come. Rev 8:13

[13]The sixth angel sounded his trumpet, and I heard a voice coming from the four horns of the golden altar that is before God. [14]It said to the sixth angel who had the trumpet, "Release the four angels who are bound at the great river Euphrates." [15]And the four angels who had been kept ready for this very hour and day and month and year were released to kill a third of mankind. [16]The number of the mounted troops was twice ten thousand times ten thousand. I heard their number. Rev 7:4; 16:12

[17]The horses and riders I saw in my vision looked like this: Their breastplates were fiery red, dark blue, and yellow as sulfur. The heads of the horses resembled the heads of lions, and out of their mouths came fire, smoke and sulfur. [18]A third of mankind was killed by the three plagues of fire, smoke and sulfur that came out of their mouths. [19]The power of the horses was in their mouths and in their tails; for their tails were like snakes, having heads with which they inflict injury. Rev 11:5

[20]The rest of mankind who were not killed by these plagues still did not repent of the work of their hands; they did not stop worshiping demons, and idols of gold, silver, bronze, stone and wood—idols that cannot see or hear or walk. [21]Nor did they repent of their murders, their magic arts, their sexual immorality or their thefts. Ps 115:4-7; 1Co 10:20

The Angel and the Little Scroll

10 Then I saw another mighty angel coming down from heaven. He was robed in a cloud, with a rainbow above his head; his face was like the sun, and his legs were like fiery pillars. [2]He was holding a little scroll, which lay open in his hand. He planted his right foot on the sea and his left foot on the land, [3]and he gave a loud shout like the roar of a lion. When he shouted, the voices of the seven thunders spoke. [4]And when the seven thunders spoke, I was about to write; but I heard a voice from heaven say, "Seal up what the seven thunders have said and do not write it down." Da 8:26; Mt 17:2

[5]Then the angel I had seen standing on the sea and on the land raised his right hand to

heaven. [6] And he swore by him who lives for ever and ever, who created the heavens and all that is in them, the earth and all that is in it, and the sea and all that is in it, and said, "There will be no more delay! [7] But in the days when the seventh angel is about to sound his trumpet, the mystery of God will be accomplished, just as he announced to his servants the prophets." Rev 4:11; 16:17

[8] Then the voice that I had heard from heaven spoke to me once more: "Go, take the scroll that lies open in the hand of the angel who is standing on the sea and on the land." ver 2,4

[9] So I went to the angel and asked him to give me the little scroll. He said to me, "Take it and eat it. It will turn your stomach sour, but 'in your mouth it will be as sweet as honey.'[a]" [10] I took the little scroll from the angel's hand and ate it. It tasted as sweet as honey in my mouth, but when I had eaten it, my stomach turned sour. [11] Then I was told, "You must prophesy again about many peoples, nations, languages and kings." Jer 15:16; Eze 2:8-3:3

The Two Witnesses

11 I was given a reed like a measuring rod and was told, "Go and measure the temple of God and the altar, with its worshipers. [2] But exclude the outer court; do not measure it, because it has been given to the Gentiles. They will trample on the holy city for 42 months. [3] And I will appoint my two witnesses, and they will prophesy for 1,260 days, clothed in sackcloth." [4] They are "the two olive trees" and the two lampstands, and "they stand before the Lord of the earth."[b] [5] If anyone tries to harm them, fire comes from their mouths and devours their enemies. This is how anyone who wants to harm them must die. [6] They have power to shut up the heavens so that it will not rain during the time they are prophesying; and they have power to turn the waters into blood and to strike the earth with every kind of plague as often as they want. Rev 13:5; Zec 4:14

[7] Now when they have finished their testimony, the beast that comes up from the Abyss will attack them, and overpower and kill them. [8] Their bodies will lie in the public square of the great city—which is figuratively called Sodom and Egypt—where also their Lord was crucified. [9] For three and a half days some from every people, tribe, language and nation will gaze on their bodies and refuse them burial. [10] The inhabitants of the earth will gloat over them and will celebrate by sending each other gifts, because these two prophets had tormented those who live on the earth. Est 9:19,22; Da 7:21

a 9 Ezek. 3:3   b 4 See Zech. 4:3,11,14.

[11] But after the three and a half days the breath[a] of life from God entered them, and they stood on their feet, and terror struck those who saw them. [12] Then they heard a loud voice from heaven saying to them, "Come up here." And they went up to heaven in a cloud, while their enemies looked on. Eze 37:5,9-10,14; Ac 1:9

[13] At that very hour there was a severe earthquake and a tenth of the city collapsed. Seven thousand people were killed in the earthquake, and the survivors were terrified and gave glory to the God of heaven. Rev 6:12; 16:11

[14] The second woe has passed; the third woe is coming soon.

The Seventh Trumpet

[15] The seventh angel sounded his trumpet, and there were loud voices in heaven, which said:

"The kingdom of the world
    has become
  the kingdom of our Lord
    and of his Messiah,
  and he will reign for ever
    and ever."

[16] And the twenty-four elders, who were seated on their thrones before God, fell on their faces and worshiped God, [17] saying: Rev 4:4

"We give thanks to you, Lord
    God Almighty, Rev 1:8
  the One who is and who
    was, Rev 1:4

because you have taken your
    great power
  and have begun to reign.
[18] The nations were angry, Ps 2:1
  and your wrath has come.
The time has come for judging
    the dead,
  and for rewarding your
    servants the prophets
and your people who revere
    your name,
  both great and small—
and for destroying those who
    destroy the earth."

[19] Then God's temple in heaven was opened, and within his temple was seen the ark of his covenant. And there came flashes of lightning, rumblings, peals of thunder, an earthquake and a severe hailstorm. Rev 15:5,8; 16:21

The Woman and the Dragon

12 A great sign appeared in heaven: a woman clothed with the sun, with the moon under her feet and a crown of twelve stars on her head. [2] She was pregnant and cried out in pain as she was about to give birth. [3] Then another sign appeared in heaven: an enormous red dragon with seven heads and ten horns and seven crowns on its heads. [4] Its tail swept a third of the stars out of the sky and flung them to the earth. The dragon stood in front of the woman who was about to give birth, so

---

[a] 11 Or *Spirit* (see Ezek. 37:5,14)

that it might devour her child the moment he was born. [5] She gave birth to a son, a male child, who "will rule all the nations with an iron scepter."[a] And her child was snatched up to God and to his throne. [6] The woman fled into the wilderness to a place prepared for her by God, where she might be taken care of for 1,260 days. Da 8:10; Rev 11:2

[7] Then war broke out in heaven. Michael and his angels fought against the dragon, and the dragon and his angels fought back. [8] But he was not strong enough, and they lost their place in heaven. [9] The great dragon was hurled down — that ancient serpent called the devil, or Satan, who leads the whole world astray. He was hurled to the earth, and his angels with him. Jn 12:31; Rev 20:3,8,10

[10] Then I heard a loud voice in heaven say: Rev 11:15

"Now have come the salvation
        and the power
    and the kingdom of our
        God, Rev 7:10
    and the authority of his
        Messiah.
For the accuser of our
        brothers and sisters,
    who accuses them before
        our God day and night,
        has been hurled down.
[11] They triumphed over him
    by the blood of the Lamb

and by the word of their
        testimony; Rev 6:9
they did not love their lives so
        much
    as to shrink from death.
[12] Therefore rejoice, you
        heavens Ps 96:11; Rev 18:20
    and you who dwell in them!
But woe to the earth and the
        sea, Rev 10:6
    because the devil has gone
        down to you!
He is filled with fury,
    because he knows that his
        time is short."

[13] When the dragon saw that he had been hurled to the earth, he pursued the woman who had given birth to the male child. [14] The woman was given the two wings of a great eagle, so that she might fly to the place prepared for her in the wilderness, where she would be taken care of for a time, times and half a time, out of the serpent's reach. [15] Then from his mouth the serpent spewed water like a river, to overtake the woman and sweep her away with the torrent. [16] But the earth helped the woman by opening its mouth and swallowing the river that the dragon had spewed out of his mouth. [17] Then the dragon was enraged at the woman and went off to wage war against the rest of her offspring — those who keep God's commands and hold fast their testimony about Jesus.

[a] 5 Psalm 2:9

The Beast out of the Sea

13 The dragon[a] stood on the shore of the sea. And I saw a beast coming out of the sea. It had ten horns and seven heads, with ten crowns on its horns, and on each head a blasphemous name. [2]The beast I saw resembled a leopard, but had feet like those of a bear and a mouth like that of a lion. The dragon gave the beast his power and his throne and great authority. [3]One of the heads of the beast seemed to have had a fatal wound, but the fatal wound had been healed. The whole world was filled with wonder and followed the beast. [4]People worshiped the dragon because he had given authority to the beast, and they also worshiped the beast and asked, "Who is like the beast? Who can wage war against it?" Da 7:1-6; Rev 17:8

[5]The beast was given a mouth to utter proud words and blasphemies and to exercise its authority for forty-two months. [6]It opened its mouth to blaspheme God, and to slander his name and his dwelling place and those who live in heaven. [7]It was given power to wage war against God's holy people and to conquer them. And it was given authority over every tribe, people, language and nation. [8]All inhabitants of the earth will worship the beast—all whose names have not been written in the Lamb's book of life, the Lamb who was slain from the creation of the world.[b] Mt 25:34; Rev 20:12

[9]Whoever has ears, let them hear. Rev 2:7

[10]"If anyone is to go into captivity,
into captivity they will go.
If anyone is to be killed[c] with the sword,
with the sword they will be killed."[d] Jer 15:2; 43:11

This calls for patient endurance and faithfulness on the part of God's people. Heb 6:12; Rev 14:12

The Beast out of the Earth

[11]Then I saw a second beast, coming out of the earth. It had two horns like a lamb, but it spoke like a dragon. [12]It exercised all the authority of the first beast on its behalf, and made the earth and its inhabitants worship the first beast, whose fatal wound had been healed. [13]And it performed great signs, even causing fire to come down from heaven to the earth in full view of the people. [14]Because of the signs it was given power to perform on behalf of the first beast, it deceived the inhabitants of the earth. It ordered them to set up an image in honor of the beast who was wounded by the sword and yet lived. [15]The second beast was

given power to give breath to the image of the first beast, so that the image could speak and cause all who refused to worship the image to be killed. ¹⁶It also forced all people, great and small, rich and poor, free and slave, to receive a mark on their right hands or on their foreheads, ¹⁷so that they could not buy or sell unless they had the mark, which is the name of the beast or the number of its name.   Rev 12:9; 14:11

¹⁸This calls for wisdom. Let the person who has insight calculate the number of the beast, for it is the number of a man.ᵃ That number is 666.   Rev 15:2; 17:9

The Lamb and the 144,000

14 Then I looked, and there before me was the Lamb, standing on Mount Zion, and with him 144,000 who had his name and his Father's name written on their foreheads. ²And I heard a sound from heaven like the roar of rushing waters and like a loud peal of thunder. The sound I heard was like that of harpists playing their harps. ³And they sang a new song before the throne and before the four living creatures and the elders. No one could learn the song except the 144,000 who had been redeemed from the earth. ⁴These are those who did not defile themselves with women, for they remained virgins. They follow the Lamb

wherever he goes. They were purchased from among mankind and offered as firstfruits to God and the Lamb. ⁵No lie was found in their mouths; they are blameless.   Ps 32:2; Eph 5:27

The Three Angels

⁶Then I saw another angel flying in midair, and he had the eternal gospel to proclaim to those who live on the earth—to every nation, tribe, language and people. ⁷He said in a loud voice, "Fear God and give him glory, because the hour of his judgment has come. Worship him who made the heavens, the earth, the sea and the springs of water."   Rev 8:10; 15:4

⁸A second angel followed and said, " 'Fallen! Fallen is Babylon the Great,'ᵇ which made all the nations drink the maddening wine of her adulteries."   Isa 21:9

⁹A third angel followed them and said in a loud voice: "If anyone worships the beast and its image and receives its mark on their forehead or on their hand, ¹⁰they, too, will drink the wine of God's fury, which has been poured full strength into the cup of his wrath. They will be tormented with burning sulfur in the presence of the holy angels and of the Lamb. ¹¹And the smoke of their torment will rise for ever and ever. There will be no rest day or night for those who

ᵃ 18 Or *is humanity's number*   ᵇ 8 Isaiah 21:9

worship the beast and its image, or for anyone who receives the mark of its name." [12] This calls for patient endurance on the part of the people of God who keep his commands and remain faithful to Jesus. Isa 34:10; Rev 13:10

[13] Then I heard a voice from heaven say, "Write this: Blessed are the dead who die in the Lord from now on." 1Co 15:18; 1Th 4:16

"Yes," says the Spirit, "they will rest from their labor, for their deeds will follow them." Rev 2:7

Harvesting the Earth and Trampling the Winepress

[14] I looked, and there before me was a white cloud, and seated on the cloud was one like a son of man[a] with a crown of gold on his head and a sharp sickle in his hand. [15] Then another angel came out of the temple and called in a loud voice to him who was sitting on the cloud, "Take your sickle and reap, because the time to reap has come, for the harvest of the earth is ripe." [16] So he who was seated on the cloud swung his sickle over the earth, and the earth was harvested. Jer 51:33

[17] Another angel came out of the temple in heaven, and he too had a sharp sickle. [18] Still another angel, who had charge of the fire, came from the altar and called in a loud voice to him who had the sharp sickle, "Take your sharp sickle and gather the clusters of grapes from the earth's vine, because its grapes are ripe." [19] The angel swung his sickle on the earth, gathered its grapes and threw them into the great winepress of God's wrath. [20] They were trampled in the winepress outside the city, and blood flowed out of the press, rising as high as the horses' bridles for a distance of 1,600 stadia.[b] Heb 13:12; Rev 19:15

Seven Angels With Seven Plagues

15 I saw in heaven another great and marvelous sign: seven angels with the seven last plagues — last, because with them God's wrath is completed. [2] And I saw what looked like a sea of glass glowing with fire and, standing beside the sea, those who had been victorious over the beast and its image and over the number of its name. They held harps given them by God [3] and sang the song of God's servant Moses and of the Lamb: Rev 4:6; 13:14

"Great and marvelous are
    your deeds, Ps 111:2
Lord God Almighty. Rev 1:8
Just and true are your ways,
    King of the nations.[c]
[4] Who will not fear you, Lord,
    and bring glory to your
      name? Ps 86:9

---

[a] 14 See Daniel 7:13.   [b] 20 That is, about 180 miles or about 300 kilometers   [c] 3 Some manuscripts *ages*

For you alone are holy.
All nations will come
    and worship before you,
for your righteous acts have
    been revealed."[a] Rev 19:8

5 After this I looked, and I saw in heaven the temple — that is, the tabernacle of the covenant law — and it was opened. 6 Out of the temple came the seven angels with the seven plagues. They were dressed in clean, shining linen and wore golden sashes around their chests. 7 Then one of the four living creatures gave to the seven angels seven golden bowls filled with the wrath of God, who lives for ever and ever. 8 And the temple was filled with smoke from the glory of God and from his power, and no one could enter the temple until the seven plagues of the seven angels were completed. Ex 40:34-35; Rev 4:6

The Seven Bowls of God's Wrath

16 Then I heard a loud voice from the temple saying to the seven angels, "Go, pour out the seven bowls of God's wrath on the earth." Rev 15:1

2 The first angel went and poured out his bowl on the land, and ugly, festering sores broke out on the people who had the mark of the beast and worshiped its image. Rev 8:7; 13:15-17

3 The second angel poured out his bowl on the sea, and it turned into blood like that of a dead person, and every living thing in the sea died. Ex 7:17-21; Rev 8:8-9

4 The third angel poured out his bowl on the rivers and springs of water, and they became blood. 5 Then I heard the angel in charge of the waters say: Ex 7:17-21; Rev 8:10

"You are just in these
    judgments, O Holy One,
you who are and who were;
6 for they have shed the blood
    of your holy people and
    your prophets, Lk 11:49-51
and you have given them
    blood to drink as they
    deserve."

7 And I heard the altar respond:

"Yes, Lord God Almighty, Rev 1:8
true and just are your
    judgments." Isa 49:26

8 The fourth angel poured out his bowl on the sun, and the sun was allowed to scorch people with fire. 9 They were seared by the intense heat and they cursed the name of God, who had control over these plagues, but they refused to repent and glorify him. Rev 11:13

10 The fifth angel poured out his bowl on the throne of the beast, and its kingdom was plunged into darkness. People gnawed their tongues in agony

[a] 3,4 Phrases in this song are drawn from Psalm 111:2,3; Deut. 32:4; Jer. 10:7; Psalms 86:9; 98:2.

[11] and cursed the God of heaven because of their pains and their sores, but they refused to repent of what they had done. Rev 9:2; 13:2

[12] The sixth angel poured out his bowl on the great river Euphrates, and its water was dried up to prepare the way for the kings from the East. [13] Then I saw three impure spirits that looked like frogs; they came out of the mouth of the dragon, out of the mouth of the beast and out of the mouth of the false prophet. [14] They are demonic spirits that perform signs, and they go out to the kings of the whole world, to gather them for the battle on the great day of God Almighty. 1Ti 4:1; Rev 17:14

[15] "Look, I come like a thief! Blessed is the one who stays awake and remains clothed, so as not to go naked and be shamefully exposed."

[16] Then they gathered the kings together to the place that in Hebrew is called Armageddon.

[17] The seventh angel poured out his bowl into the air, and out of the temple came a loud voice from the throne, saying, "It is done!" [18] Then there came flashes of lightning, rumblings, peals of thunder and a severe earthquake. No earthquake like it has ever occurred since mankind has been on earth, so tremendous was the quake. [19] The great city split into three parts, and the cities of the nations collapsed. God remembered Babylon the Great and gave her the cup filled with the wine of the fury of his wrath. [20] Every island fled away and the mountains could not be found. [21] From the sky huge hailstones, each weighing about a hundred pounds,[a] fell on people. And they cursed God on account of the plague of hail, because the plague was so terrible. Ex 9:23-25; Rev 14:10

Babylon, the Prostitute on the Beast

17 One of the seven angels who had the seven bowls came and said to me, "Come, I will show you the punishment of the great prostitute, who sits by many waters. [2] With her the kings of the earth committed adultery, and the inhabitants of the earth were intoxicated with the wine of her adulteries." Jer 51:13

[3] Then the angel carried me away in the Spirit into a wilderness. There I saw a woman sitting on a scarlet beast that was covered with blasphemous names and had seven heads and ten horns. [4] The woman was dressed in purple and scarlet, and was glittering with gold, precious stones and pearls. She held a golden cup in her hand, filled with abominable things and the filth of her adulteries. [5] The name written on her forehead was a mystery: Jer 51:7; 12:6,14

[a] 21 Or about 45 kilograms

BABYLON THE GREAT
THE MOTHER OF PROSTITUTES
AND OF THE ABOMINATIONS
OF THE EARTH.

[6] I saw that the woman was drunk with the blood of God's holy people, the blood of those who bore testimony to Jesus.   Rev 18:24

When I saw her, I was greatly astonished. [7] Then the angel said to me: "Why are you astonished? I will explain to you the mystery of the woman and of the beast she rides, which has the seven heads and ten horns. [8] The beast, which you saw, once was, now is not, and yet will come up out of the Abyss and go to its destruction. The inhabitants of the earth whose names have not been written in the book of life from the creation of the world will be astonished when they see the beast, because it once was, now is not, and yet will come. Rev 13:3,10

[9] "This calls for a mind with wisdom. The seven heads are seven hills on which the woman sits. [10] They are also seven kings. Five have fallen, one is, the other has not yet come; but when he does come, he must remain for only a little while. [11] The beast who once was, and now is not, is an eighth king. He belongs to the seven and is going to his destruction.   Rev 13:18

[12] "The ten horns you saw are ten kings who have not yet re-ceived a kingdom, but who for one hour will receive authority as kings along with the beast. [13] They have one purpose and will give their power and authority to the beast. [14] They will wage war against the Lamb, but the Lamb will triumph over them because he is Lord of lords and King of kings — and with him will be his called, chosen and faithful followers." 1Ti 6:15; Rev 16:14

[15] Then the angel said to me, "The waters you saw, where the prostitute sits, are peoples, multitudes, nations and languages. [16] The beast and the ten horns you saw will hate the prostitute. They will bring her to ruin and leave her naked; they will eat her flesh and burn her with fire. [17] For God has put it into their hearts to accomplish his purpose by agreeing to hand over to the beast their royal authority, until God's words are fulfilled. [18] The woman you saw is the great city that rules over the kings of the earth."   Rev 10:7; 16:19

Lament Over Fallen Babylon

18 After this I saw another angel coming down from heaven. He had great authority, and the earth was illuminated by his splendor. [2] With a mighty voice he shouted: Eze 43:2; Rev 17:1

"'Fallen! Fallen is Babylon the
     Great!'[a]   Rev 14:8

She has become a dwelling
  for demons
and a haunt for every impure
  spirit,   Rev 16:13
a haunt for every unclean
  bird,
a haunt for every unclean
  and detestable animal.
³For all the nations have drunk
  the maddening wine of her
  adulteries.   Rev 14:8
The kings of the earth
  committed adultery
  with her,   Rev 17:2
and the merchants of the
  earth grew rich from
  her excessive luxuries."

Warning to Escape Babylon's Judgment

⁴Then I heard another voice
from heaven say:

" 'Come out of her, my
  people,'ᵃ   Jer 50:8; 2Co 6:17
so that you will not share in
  her sins,
so that you will not receive
  any of her plagues;
⁵for her sins are piled up to
  heaven,   Jer 51:9
and God has remembered
  her crimes.   Rev 16:19
⁶Give back to her as she has
  given;
pay her back double for
  what she has
  done.   Ps 137:8; Jer 50:15,29
Pour her a double portion
  from her own cup.

⁷Give her as much torment and
  grief
as the glory and luxury she
  gave herself.   Eze 28:2-8
In her heart she boasts,
  'I sit enthroned as queen.
I am not a widow;ᵇ
  I will never mourn.'   Zep 2:15
⁸Therefore in one day her
  plagues will overtake
  her: Isa 47:9
death, mourning and
  famine.
She will be consumed by fire,
  for mighty is the Lord God
  who judges her.

Threefold Woe Over Babylon's Fall

⁹"When the kings of the earth
who committed adultery with
her and shared her luxury see the
smoke of her burning, they will
weep and mourn over her. ¹⁰Ter-
rified at her torment, they will
stand far off and cry: Eze 26:17-18

" 'Woe! Woe to you, great city,
  you mighty city of Babylon!
In one hour your doom has
  come!'   Rev 17:12

¹¹"The merchants of the earth
will weep and mourn over her because no one buys their cargoes
anymore — ¹²cargoes of gold, silver, precious stones and pearls;
fine linen, purple, silk and scarlet
cloth; every sort of citron wood,
and articles of every kind made
of ivory, costly wood, bronze, iron

ᵃ 4 Jer. 51:45   ᵇ 7 See Isaiah 47:7,8.

and marble; ¹³cargoes of cinnamon and spice, of incense, myrrh and frankincense, of wine and olive oil, of fine flour and wheat; cattle and sheep; horses and carriages; and human beings sold as slaves. Eze 27:13; Rev 17:4

¹⁴ "They will say, 'The fruit you longed for is gone from you. All your luxury and splendor have vanished, never to be recovered.' ¹⁵The merchants who sold these things and gained their wealth from her will stand far off, terrified at her torment. They will weep and mourn ¹⁶and cry out: Eze 27:31

"'Woe! Woe to you, great city,
    dressed in fine linen, purple
        and scarlet,
    and glittering with gold,
        precious stones and
            pearls! Rev 17:4
¹⁷In one hour such great wealth
    has been brought to
        ruin!' Rev 17:12,16

"Every sea captain, and all who travel by ship, the sailors, and all who earn their living from the sea, will stand far off. ¹⁸When they see the smoke of her burning, they will exclaim, 'Was there ever a city like this great city?' ¹⁹They will throw dust on their heads, and with weeping and mourning cry out: Eze 27:28-30

"'Woe! Woe to you, great city,
    where all who had ships on
        the sea

became rich through her
    wealth!
In one hour she has been
    brought to ruin!' Rev 17:16

²⁰ "Rejoice over her, you
        heavens! Jer 51:48
    Rejoice, you people of God!
    Rejoice, apostles and
        prophets!
For God has judged her
    with the judgment she
        imposed on you." Rev 19:2

The Finality of Babylon's Doom

²¹Then a mighty angel picked up a boulder the size of a large millstone and threw it into the sea, and said: Jer 51:63; Rev 5:2

"With such violence
    the great city of Babylon
        will be thrown down,
    never to be found again.
²²The music of harpists and
        musicians, pipers and
            trumpeters,
    will never be heard in you
        again. Eze 26:13
No worker of any trade
    will ever be found in you
        again.
The sound of a millstone
    will never be heard in you
        again. Jer 25:10
²³The light of a lamp
    will never shine in you
        again.
The voice of bridegroom and
        bride
    will never be heard in you
        again. Jer 7:34

Your merchants were the
    world's important
    people.   Isa 23:8
By your magic spell all the
    nations were led astray.
²⁴ In her was found the blood of
    prophets and of God's
    holy people,   Rev 17:6
of all who have been
    slaughtered on the
    earth."   Jer 51:49

Threefold Hallelujah Over Babylon's Fall

19 After this I heard what
    sounded like the roar of a
great multitude in heaven shouting: Rev 11:15

"Hallelujah!
Salvation and glory and
    power belong to our
    God,   Rev 4:11; 7:10
²   for true and just are his
    judgments.   Rev 16:7
He has condemned the great
    prostitute   Rev 17:1
who corrupted the earth by
    her adulteries.
He has avenged on her the
    blood of his servants."

³ And again they shouted:

"Hallelujah!
The smoke from her goes up
    for ever and ever."   Isa 34:10

⁴ The twenty-four elders and
the four living creatures fell
down and worshiped God, who
was seated on the throne. And
they cried: Rev 4:4,6; 5:14

"Amen, Hallelujah!"

⁵ Then a voice came from the
throne, saying:

"Praise our God,
    all you his servants,   Ps 134:1
you who fear him,
    both great and small!" Rev 11:18

⁶ Then I heard what sounded
like a great multitude, like the
roar of rushing waters and like
loud peals of thunder, shouting:

"Hallelujah!
For our Lord God Almighty
    reigns.   Rev 1:8
⁷ Let us rejoice and be glad
    and give him glory!   Rev 11:13
For the wedding of the Lamb
    has come,   Mt 22:2; Eph 5:32
and his bride has made
    herself ready.   Rev 21:2,9
⁸ Fine linen, bright and clean,
    was given her to wear."
(Fine linen stands for the righteous acts of God's holy people.)

⁹ Then the angel said to me,
"Write this: Blessed are those
who are invited to the wedding
supper of the Lamb!" And he
added, "These are the true words
of God."   Lk 14:15; Rev 1:19
¹⁰ At this I fell at his feet to
worship him. But he said to me,
"Don't do that! I am a fellow servant with you and with your
brothers and sisters who hold to
the testimony of Jesus. Worship
God! For it is the Spirit of prophecy who bears testimony to Jesus."

The Heavenly Warrior Defeats the Beast

[11] I saw heaven standing open and there before me was a white horse, whose rider is called Faithful and True. With justice he judges and wages war. [12] His eyes are like blazing fire, and on his head are many crowns. He has a name written on him that no one knows but he himself. [13] He is dressed in a robe dipped in blood, and his name is the Word of God. [14] The armies of heaven were following him, riding on white horses and dressed in fine linen, white and clean. [15] Coming out of his mouth is a sharp sword with which to strike down the nations. "He will rule them with an iron scepter."[a] He treads the winepress of the fury of the wrath of God Almighty. [16] On his robe and on his thigh he has this name written: Isa 11:4; Rev 6:2

KING OF KINGS AND
LORD OF LORDS.

[17] And I saw an angel standing in the sun, who cried in a loud voice to all the birds flying in midair, "Come, gather together for the great supper of God, [18] so that you may eat the flesh of kings, generals, and the mighty, of horses and their riders, and the flesh of all people, free and slave, great and small." Eze 39:17-20

[19] Then I saw the beast and the kings of the earth and their armies gathered together to wage war against the rider on the horse and his army. [20] But the beast was captured, and with it the false prophet who had performed the signs on its behalf. With these signs he had deluded those who had received the mark of the beast and worshiped its image. The two of them were thrown alive into the fiery lake of burning sulfur. [21] The rest were killed with the sword coming out of the mouth of the rider on the horse, and all the birds gorged themselves on their flesh. Da 7:11; Rev 13:12

The Thousand Years

20 And I saw an angel coming down out of heaven, having the key to the Abyss and holding in his hand a great chain. [2] He seized the dragon, that ancient serpent, who is the devil, or Satan, and bound him for a thousand years. [3] He threw him into the Abyss, and locked and sealed it over him, to keep him from deceiving the nations anymore until the thousand years were ended. After that, he must be set free for a short time. Da 6:17; Rev 12:9

[4] I saw thrones on which were seated those who had been given authority to judge. And I saw the souls of those who had been beheaded because of their testimony about Jesus and because of the word of God. They[b] had not

---

[a] 15 Psalm 2:9   [b] 4 Or *God; I also saw those who*

worshiped the beast or its image and had not received its mark on their foreheads or their hands. They came to life and reigned with Christ a thousand years. [5] (The rest of the dead did not come to life until the thousand years were ended.) This is the first resurrection. [6] Blessed and holy are those who share in the first resurrection. The second death has no power over them, but they will be priests of God and of Christ and will reign with him for a thousand years. Rev 1:6; 2:11

The Judgment of Satan

[7] When the thousand years are over, Satan will be released from his prison [8] and will go out to deceive the nations in the four corners of the earth—Gog and Magog—and to gather them for battle. In number they are like the sand on the seashore. [9] They marched across the breadth of the earth and surrounded the camp of God's people, the city he loves. But fire came down from heaven and devoured them. [10] And the devil, who deceived them, was thrown into the lake of burning sulfur, where the beast and the false prophet had been thrown. They will be tormented day and night for ever and ever. Eze 38:9,16; Rev 14:10-11

The Judgment of the Dead

[11] Then I saw a great white throne and him who was seated on it. The earth and the heavens fled from his presence, and there was no place for them. [12] And I saw the dead, great and small, standing before the throne, and books were opened. Another book was opened, which is the book of life. The dead were judged according to what they had done as recorded in the books. [13] The sea gave up the dead that were in it, and death and Hades gave up the dead that were in them, and each person was judged according to what they had done. [14] Then death and Hades were thrown into the lake of fire. The lake of fire is the second death. [15] Anyone whose name was not found written in the book of life was thrown into the lake of fire. Mt 16:27; 1Co 15:26

A New Heaven and a New Earth

21 Then I saw "a new heaven and a new earth," [a] for the first heaven and the first earth had passed away, and there was no longer any sea. [2] I saw the Holy City, the new Jerusalem, coming down out of heaven from God, prepared as a bride beautifully dressed for her husband. [3] And I heard a loud voice from the throne saying, "Look! God's dwelling place is now among the people, and he will dwell with them. They will be his people,

[a] 1 Isaiah 65:17

and God himself will be with them and be their God. [4]'He will wipe every tear from their eyes. There will be no more death'[a] or mourning or crying or pain, for the old order of things has passed away." Isa 35:10; 1Co 15:26

[5]He who was seated on the throne said, "I am making everything new!" Then he said, "Write this down, for these words are trustworthy and true." Rev 4:9

[6]He said to me: "It is done. I am the Alpha and the Omega, the Beginning and the End. To the thirsty I will give water without cost from the spring of the water of life. [7]Those who are victorious will inherit all this, and I will be their God and they will be my children. [8]But the cowardly, the unbelieving, the vile, the murderers, the sexually immoral, those who practice magic arts, the idolaters and all liars — they will be consigned to the fiery lake of burning sulfur. This is the second death." Rev 1:8; 16:17

The New Jerusalem, the Bride of the Lamb

[9]One of the seven angels who had the seven bowls full of the seven last plagues came and said to me, "Come, I will show you the bride, the wife of the Lamb." [10]And he carried me away in the Spirit to a mountain great and high, and showed me the Holy City, Jerusalem, coming down out of heaven from God. [11]It shone with the glory of God, and its brilliance was like that of a very precious jewel, like a jasper, clear as crystal. [12]It had a great, high wall with twelve gates, and with twelve angels at the gates. On the gates were written the names of the twelve tribes of Israel. [13]There were three gates on the east, three on the north, three on the south and three on the west. [14]The wall of the city had twelve foundations, and on them were the names of the twelve apostles of the Lamb. Eze 48:30-34; Rev 15:1,6-7

[15]The angel who talked with me had a measuring rod of gold to measure the city, its gates and its walls. [16]The city was laid out like a square, as long as it was wide. He measured the city with the rod and found it to be 12,000 stadia[b] in length, and as wide and high as it is long. [17]The angel measured the wall using human measurement, and it was 144 cubits[c] thick.[d] [18]The wall was made of jasper, and the city of pure gold, as pure as glass. [19]The foundations of the city walls were decorated with every kind of precious stone. The first foundation was jasper, the second sapphire, the third agate, the fourth emerald, [20]the fifth onyx, the sixth ruby, the seventh chrysolite, the eighth beryl, the ninth topaz, the

---

[a] 4 Isaiah 25:8   [b] 16 That is, about 1,400 miles or about 2,200 kilometers   [c] 17 That is, about 200 feet or about 65 meters   [d] 17 Or high

tenth turquoise, the eleventh jacinth, and the twelfth amethyst.[a] ²¹The twelve gates were twelve pearls, each gate made of a single pearl. The great street of the city was of gold, as pure as transparent glass. Isa 54:11-12; Rev 11:1

²²I did not see a temple in the city, because the Lord God Almighty and the Lamb are its temple. ²³The city does not need the sun or the moon to shine on it, for the glory of God gives it light, and the Lamb is its lamp. ²⁴The nations will walk by its light, and the kings of the earth will bring their splendor into it. ²⁵On no day will its gates ever be shut, for there will be no night there. ²⁶The glory and honor of the nations will be brought into it. ²⁷Nothing impure will ever enter it, nor will anyone who does what is shameful or deceitful, but only those whose names are written in the Lamb's book of life. Isa 24:23; 52:1; Rev 22:14-15

Eden Restored

22 Then the angel showed me the river of the water of life, as clear as crystal, flowing from the throne of God and of the Lamb ²down the middle of the great street of the city. On each side of the river stood the tree of life, bearing twelve crops of fruit, yielding its fruit every month. And the leaves of the tree are for the healing of the nations.

³No longer will there be any curse. The throne of God and of the Lamb will be in the city, and his servants will serve him. ⁴They will see his face, and his name will be on their foreheads. ⁵There will be no more night. They will not need the light of a lamp or the light of the sun, for the Lord God will give them light. And they will reign for ever and ever. Eze 47:1; Zec 14:11; Rev 21:23

John and the Angel

⁶The angel said to me, "These words are trustworthy and true. The Lord, the God who inspires the prophets, sent his angel to show his servants the things that must soon take place." Rev 1:1

⁷"Look, I am coming soon! Blessed is the one who keeps the words of the prophecy written in this scroll." Rev 1:3; 3:11

⁸I, John, am the one who heard and saw these things. And when I had heard and seen them, I fell down to worship at the feet of the angel who had been showing them to me. ⁹But he said to me, "Don't do that! I am a fellow servant with you and with your fellow prophets and with all who keep the words of this scroll. Worship God!" Rev 19:10

¹⁰Then he told me, "Do not seal up the words of the prophecy of this scroll, because the time is near. ¹¹Let the one who does

---

^a 20 The precise identification of some of these precious stones is uncertain.

wrong continue to do wrong; let the vile person continue to be vile; let the one who does right continue to do right; and let the holy person continue to be holy."

Eze 3:27; Da 8:26

Epilogue: Invitation and Warning

¹²"Look, I am coming soon! My reward is with me, and I will give to each person according to what they have done. ¹³I am the Alpha and the Omega, the First and the Last, the Beginning and the End.

Isa 40:10; Rev 1:8; 21:6

¹⁴"Blessed are those who wash their robes, that they may have the right to the tree of life and may go through the gates into the city. ¹⁵Outside are the dogs, those who practice magic arts, the sexually immoral, the murderers, the idolaters and everyone who loves and practices falsehood.

Gal 5:19-21; Php 3:2

¹⁶"I, Jesus, have sent my angel to give you[a] this testimony for the churches. I am the Root and the Offspring of David, and the bright Morning Star."

2Pe 1:19; Rev 1:1

¹⁷The Spirit and the bride say, "Come!" And let the one who hears say, "Come!" Let the one who is thirsty come; and let the one who wishes take the free gift of the water of life.

Rev 2:7

¹⁸I warn everyone who hears the words of the prophecy of this scroll: If anyone adds anything to them, God will add to that person the plagues described in this scroll. ¹⁹And if anyone takes words away from this scroll of prophecy, God will take away from that person any share in the tree of life and in the Holy City, which are described in this scroll.

Dt 4:2; Pr 30:6

²⁰He who testifies to these things says, "Yes, I am coming soon."

Rev 1:2

Amen. Come, Lord Jesus.

²¹The grace of the Lord Jesus be with God's people. Amen.

---

[a] 16 The Greek is plural.

Table of Weights and Measures

Biblical Unit		Approximate American Equivalent	Approximate Metric Equivalent
Weights	talent (60 minas)	75 pounds	34 kilograms
	mina (50 shekels)	1 $1/4$ pounds	560 grams
	shekel (2 bekas)	$2/5$ ounce	11.5 grams
	pim ($2/3$ shekel)	$1/4$ ounce	7.8 grams
	beka (10 gerahs)	$1/5$ ounce	5.7 grams
	gerah	$1/50$ ounce	0.6 gram
	daric	$1/3$ ounce	8.4 grams
Length	cubit	18 inches	45 centimeters
	span	9 inches	23 centimeters
	handbreadth	3 inches	7.5 centimeters
	stadion (pl. stadia)	600 feet	183 meters
Capacity			
Dry Measure	cor [homer] (10 ephahs)	6 bushels	220 liters
	lethek (5 ephahs)	3 bushels	110 liters
	ephah (10 omers)	$3/5$ bushel	22 liters
	seah ($1/3$ ephah)	7 quarts	7.5 liters
	omer ($1/10$ ephah)	2 quarts	2 liters
	cab ($1/18$ ephah)	1 quart	1 liter
Liquid Measure	bath (1 ephah)	6 gallons	22 liters
	hin ($1/6$ bath)	1 gallon	3.8 liters
	log ($1/72$ bath)	$1/3$ quart	0.3 liter

The figures of the table are calculated on the basis of a shekel equaling 11.5 grams, a cubit equaling 18 inches and an ephah equaling 22 liters. The quart referred to is either a dry quart (slightly larger than a liter) or a liquid quart (slightly smaller than a liter), whichever is applicable. The ton referred to in the footnotes is the American ton of 2,000 pounds. These weights are calculated relative to the particular commodity involved. Accordingly, the same measure of capacity in the text may be converted into different weights in the footnotes.

This table is based upon the best available information, but it is not intended to be mathematically precise; like the measurement equivalents in the footnotes, it merely gives approximate amounts and distances. Weights and measures differed somewhat at various times and places in the ancient world. There is uncertainty particularly about the ephah and the bath; further discoveries may shed more light on these units of capacity.

Dictionary-Concordance

A

Aaron — the brother of Moses; he served as Moses' spokesman before Pharaoh (Ex 4:14 – 16, 27 – 31; 7:1 – 2); he was Israel's first high priest (Ex 28:1; Nu 17; Heb 5:1 – 4).

abandon — to leave completely; to desert.

Abba — the word for *father* in Aramaic, one of the three languages Jesus spoke.

> Ro 8:15 And by him we cry, "*A*, Father."
>
> Gal 4:6 the Spirit who calls out, "*A*, Father."

Abel — the second son of Adam (Ge 4:2); he offered a pleasing sacrifice to God (Ge 4:4; Heb 11:4) but was murdered by his brother Cain (Ge 4:8; Mt 23:35; 1Jn 3:12).

abhor — to hate or to turn away from.

> Ps 26:5 I *a* the assembly of evildoers
>
> Am 6:8 "I *a* the pride of Jacob

Abigail — the wife of Nabal; she helped save David's life (1Sa 25:14 – 35) and later became his wife (1Sa 25:36 – 42).

abolish — to destroy completely; to put an end to.

abomination — a thing to be hated.

abound — to be more than enough; to overflow.

> Ex 34:6 slow to anger, *a* in love
>
> Php 1:9 that your love may *a* more

Abraham — the father of the Jewish nation and of all believers. God promised that he would make a mighty nation of Abraham's children and would give them the land of Canaan (Ge 15; 17; 22; Ro 4; Heb 6:13 – 15). As a test, God told him to offer his son Isaac as a sacrifice (Ge 22; Heb 11:17 – 19) but withdrew this command when Abraham showed that he would trust God and obey him.

Absalom — a son of David (2Sa 3:3); he plotted to take David's throne. He died when his long hair became tangled in an oak tree and Joab, David's commander, plunged javelins into his heart (2Sa 14 – 18).

abstain — to keep from doing something.

abundance, abundant — having plenty; more than enough.

> Jude 2 Mercy, peace and love be yours in *a*.

Abyss — the place of the dead; the place where evil spirits live.

Achan — an Israelite who kept spoil from the conquest of Jericho for himself; as a result of Achan's stealing what belonged to God, the Israelites were defeated at Ai and he and his family were stoned to death (Jos 7; 22:20).

acknowledge — to know and to say that something is true; to recognize.

> Mt 10:32 I will also *a* before my Father in heaven.
>
> 1Jn 4:3 spirit that does not *a* Jesus is not from God.

acts — deeds.

> Ps 150:2 Praise him for his *a* of power
>
> Isa 64:6 all our righteous *a* are like filthy rags

Adam — the first person God created (Ge 1:26 – 2:25); he sinned by disobeying God (Ge 3) and in that way brought all people under the curse of sin (Ro 5:12 – 21).

admonish — to give warning or advice in a caring way.

adorn — to make more beautiful.

adultery — having sexual relations with someone other than one's husband or wife. Spiritual adultery means being unfaithful to God (Jer 3).

> Ex 20:14 You shall not commit *a*.
>
> Mt 5:28 lustfully has already committed *a*

adversary — enemy; opponent.

advice — an opinion given about a decision to be made.

> 1Ki 12:14 he followed the *a* of the young men
>
> Pr 20:18 Plans are established by seeking *a*;

advocate — 1. (*v.*) to speak in favor of; 2. (*n.*) someone who speaks in another person's defense; 3. (*n.*) another name for the Holy Spirit.

> Jn 14:16 he will give you another *a* to help you
>
> Jn 14:26 But the *A*, the Holy Spirit,
>
> Jn 15:26 "When the *A* comes, whom I will

affliction — trouble or pain that lasts a long time.

Ro 12:12 patient in *a*, faithful in prayer.

agony — extreme pain of mind or body.

Ahab — a wicked king of Israel; the husband of Jezebel (1Ki 16:31). He caused Israel to worship Baal rather than God (1Ki 16:31 – 33) and was opposed by God's prophet Elijah (1Ki 17:1; 18; 21).

alabaster — a hard marble like material that can be made into jars, vases or sculptures.

alienate — to make unfriendly; to turn a person's interest or affection away from another person or thing.

allot — to divide and give away in parts. In Old Testament times the land of Canaan was allotted to the twelve tribes of Israel.

Almighty — a name used to show how strong and powerful God is.

Ge 17:1 "I am God *A*; walk before me

Isa 6:3 "Holy, holy, holy is the LORD *A*;

altar — a raised platform made of stones, metal, dirt or wood, on which sacrifices were made.

ambush — the act of hiding in order to attack by surprise.

Amen — Hebrew word that means "so be it" or "let it become true."

Amos — a prophet of Israel who lived about the same time as Hosea and Jonah; he spoke about God's justice and righteousness.

Ananias — 1. the husband of Sapphira; he was struck dead for lying to God (Ac 5:1 – 11); 2. the disciple who baptized Saul (Ac 9:10 – 19); 3. the high priest before whom Paul was tried in Jerusalem (Ac 22:30 – 24:1).

ancestor — a person from whom someone is descended.

Ps 78:5 commanded our *a* to teach their children,

ancient — very old.

Andrew — one of the twelve apostles; the brother of Peter (Mt 4:18; 10:2; Ac 1:13).

angel — a heavenly being.

Ps 34:7 The *a* of the LORD encamps

Heb 1:14 Are not all *a* ministering spirits

Heb 2:7 made them a little lower than the *a*;

1Pe 1:12 Even *a* long to look

anger — a strong feeling of displeasure; rage; fury.

Ps 103:8 slow to *a*, abounding in love.

Jas 1:20 human *a* does not produce the righteousness

anguish — extreme pain or distress of mind or body.

Jer 49:24 *a* and pain have seized her;

annihilate — to destroy completely.

anoint — to pour oil on a person's head, either for a physical benefit (Jas 5:14) or to set someone apart for service to God (Ex 28:41).

antichrist — a person who is against Christ.

1Jn 2:18 you have heard that the *a* is coming,

1Jn 2:22 Such a person is the *a*

anxiety — worry.

1Pe 5:7 Cast all your *a* on him

Apollos — a Christian from Alexandria who knew the Scriptures well (Ac 18:24 – 28) and helped Paul to minister in Corinth (Ac 19:1; 1Co 1:12).

apostle — 1. any of the twelve men Jesus chose to work with him during his earthly ministry; after being equipped by the Holy Spirit, they were sent out to preach about Jesus; 2. later, someone who had been with Jesus, had seen his miracles and then taught others about him.

Mt 10:2 These are the names of the twelve *a*:

1Co 12:28 God has placed in the church first of all *a*,

1Co 15:9 For I am the least of the *a*

appalled — overcome with shock or horror.

appeal — to make an earnest request.

1Pe 5:1 I *a* as a fellow elder

appoint — to assign someone officially to a job or position.

Aquila — the husband of Priscilla; Aquila and Priscilla were co-workers with Paul in Corinth (Ac 18; Ro 16:3).

Aramaic — the language that was commonly spoken in the countries east of the Mediterranean Sea during Jesus' earthly ministry.

ark of the covenant law — also called the ark of the covenant; a large gold-covered box, which contained the Ten Commandments (tablets of the covenant law), a jar of manna and Aaron's staff, and was kept inside the Most Holy Place in the tabernacle (tent of meeting). It was a reminder to the Israelites of God's presence with them.

armor — protective clothing worn in battle, usually made of metal.

Eph 6:11 Put on the full *a* of God

aroma — an odor or smell, usually pleasant.

arouse — to excite; to stir to action.

arrest — to officially or lawfully make a prisoner of someone.

arrogant — proud; conceited.

arrow — See bow.

ascend — to go up. Jesus ascended to heaven to return to God the Father.

ascribe — to think of as caused by, coming from or belonging to.

1Ch 16:28 *a* to the LORD glory and strength,

Ashera poles — wooden poles honoring Ashera, the Canaanite goddess of love and war.

Dt 12:3 burn their *A* in the fire;

assemble — to bring a group of people together; to meet together.

Assyria — one of the powerful nations of Biblical times; it often attacked the Israelites; its capital was Nineveh.

astray — mistaken; not on the right path; lost.

Isa 53:6 We all, like sheep, have gone *a*,

atone — to make right, by paying the penalty, the relationship between God and humans that was broken through sin. In the Old Testament people atoned symbolically for their sins by offering sacrifices to God. In the New Testament Jesus corrected the relationship between God and people once and for all by dying to take away sins.

atonement — the payment that corrects the relationship between God and humans that was broken through sin.

Lev 17:11 it is the blood that makes *a*

Lev 23:27 this seventh month is the Day of *A*.

Ro 3:25 God presented Christ as a sacrifice of *a*,

Heb 2:17 that he might make *a* for the sins

attack — to set upon with force, as in a battle.

authority — the right and power to give orders.

Mt 9:6 the Son of Man has *a* on earth

Mt 28:18 "All *a* in heaven and on earth has

Ro 13:1 for there is no *a* except that which

Heb 13:17 your leaders and submit to their *a*,

avenge — to get back at or punish someone who has done wrong.

Dt 32:35 It is mine to *a*; I will repay.

avoid — to keep away from.

Pr 20:19 *a* anyone who talks too much.

awe — respect and wonder; a holy fear of God because of his great power.

Ps 65:8 earth is filled with *a* at your wonders;

B

Baal — the name of many false gods in Canaan.

1Ki 18:25 Elijah said to the prophets of *B*,

Babel — a tower built soon after the flood; the builders were attempting to reach up to God, but God confused their language so that the building was stopped.

Babylon — the beautiful capital of Babylonia; it was a powerful and influential city in the Near East from the eighteenth to the sixth centuries B.C. In the New Testament, Babylon represents the godless city.

Ps 137:1 By the rivers of *B* we sat and wept

Rev 14:8 Fallen is *B* the Great,

Balaam — a seer who tried to curse Israel during their journey to the promised land, but God would not allow it (Nu 22 – 24).

balm — a skin cream used to heal sores and relieve pain.

Jer 8:22 Is there no *b* in Gilead?

banish — to force a person away from a place.

banquet — a formal meal, usually for a large group of people.

baptize — a religious ceremony in which water is used as a symbol of cleansing from sin. Churches today baptize by sprinkling or pouring or immersing in water. Baptism is a sign that sin is washed away.

Mk 1:9 and was *b* by John in the Jordan.

Ac 1:5 but in a few days you will be *b*

Ac 2:38 "Repent and be *b*, every one of you,

Barabbas — the Jews chose this criminal, rather than Jesus, to be released by Pilate (Mt 27:26).

Barnabas — an apostle; he was a co-worker with Paul on his first missionary journey (Ac 9:27; Ac 13 – 15).

barren — 1. unable to have children; 2. unable to produce crops.

Bartholomew — one of the twelve apostles (Mt 10:3; Ac 1:13). He was also probably known as Nathanael (Jn 1:45 – 49; 21:2).

Bathsheba — the wife of Uriah; she committed adultery with David and later became his wife (2Sa 11); she was the mother of Solomon (2Sa 12:24).

Beelzebul — the prince of demons; Satan.

Lk 11:19 if I drive out demons by *B*,

Beersheba — an important town that marked the southern boundary of Judah.

believe — to accept as true; to trust; to have faith.

Mk 1:15 Repent and *b* the good news!"
Mk 9:24 "I do *b*; help me overcome my
Jn 1:7 that through him all might *b*.
Jn 3:18 does not *b* stands condemned
Jn 20:27 Stop doubting and *b*."
Ac 16:31 They replied, "*B* in the Lord Jesus,
Ro 3:22 faith in Jesus Christ to all who *b*.
1Th 4:14 we *b* that Jesus died and rose again

Benjamin — the twelfth son of Jacob. Rachel was his mother, and he was the younger brother of Joseph (Ge 35:16 – 24; Ge 42 – 45).

besiege — to surround a city or town completely with an army, so that nothing can go in or out.

bestow — to give.

Bethlehem — the city in Judea where Jesus was born (Mt 2:1).

betray — to turn a friend over to his or her enemies; to be unfaithful to.

Mt 27:3 When Judas, who had *b* him,
1Co 11:23 on the night he was *b*, took bread,

betroth — to promise to marry.

bewildered — confused; puzzled.

bind — 1. to tie with a rope or string; 2. to make tight or firm.

Dt 6:8 and *b* them on your foreheads.
Mt 16:19 whatever you *b* on earth will be

birthright — the special rights of the firstborn son. In the Old Testament, after the father died, the oldest son received the father's power and right to make decisions for the entire family. He also got twice as much money and property as each of his brothers.

bitter — having harsh or hateful feelings.

Eph 4:31 Get rid of all *b*, rage
Heb 12:15 and that no *b* root grows up

blameless — without fault.

Ge 17:1 walk before me faithfully and be *b*.
1Co 1:8 so that you will be *b* on the day

blaspheme — to speak carelessly, falsely or insultingly about God or holy things.

Mk 3:29 whoever *b* against the Holy Spirit

blemish — a spot or mark that makes something imperfect.

1Pe 1:19 a lamb without *b* or defect.

bless — 1. to make holy; 2. to show favor to; 3. to ask God to show favor to.

Ge 2:3 Then God *b* the seventh day
Ge 12:3 I will *b* those who *b* you,
Mt 5:3 "*B* are the poor in spirit
Ro 12:14 *b* those who persecute you; *b*

blight — a disease in plants that makes them shrivel up and die.

blind — unable to see. Spiritual blindness is an inability to understand the things of God.

Mt 11:5 The *b* receive sight, the lame walk,
Jn 9:25 I was *b* but now I see!"

blood — as the life-giving fluid in the body, it represents life itself. In the Old Testament, the blood of sacrifices symbolized the giving of life for life. Through the blood of Jesus on the cross, believers are saved from death for their sins.

Ex 12:13 and when I see the *b*, I will pass
Lev 17:11 For the life of a creature is in the *b*,
Mt 26:28 This is my *b* of the covenant,
Eph 1:7 we have redemption through his *b*,
Heb 9:12 once for all by his own *b*,

blot — to erase or get rid of.

Ex 32:32 then *b* me out of the book you have
Ps 51:1 *b* out my transgressions.

boast — to brag; to call attention to.

Ps 44:8 In God we make our *b*
Gal 6:14 May I never *b* except in the cross

Boaz — a wealthy man who lived in Bethlehem in the days of the judges; he married Ruth (Ru 2; 4).

body — 1. physical part of a person; 2. a group working as a unit.

Pr 3:8 This will bring health to your *b*

Ro 12:1 to offer your *b* as a living
sacrifice,
1Co 6:19 not know that your *b* are
temples
Eph 5:30 for we are members of his *b*.

bondage — slavery.
Ezr 9:9 God has not forsaken us in our *b*.

born again — refers to the experience of
salvation; entering God's family through
faith in Christ.
Jn 3:3 no one can see the kingdom of God
unless they are *b*.
1Pe 1:23 For you have been *b*,

bow — a weapon made of a strip of flexible
material with a cord connecting the two
ends and holding the strip bent; used to
shoot arrows.

branch — an extension of another body or
system.
Jer 33:15 I will make a righteous *B* sprout
Jn 15:5 "I am the vine; you are the *b*.

bread — in Bible times the most important
food in the diet.
Dt 8:3 that man does not live on *b* alone
Mt 6:11 Give us today our daily *b*.
Jn 6:35 Jesus declared, "I am the *b* of life.

breastpiece — a decorated square of linen
cloth worn by the high priest when he entered the Holy Place.

breastplate — a chest-covering made of
metal or leather, worn by soldiers for protection.

bribe — money or favor given to influence
judgment or conduct.
Ex 23:8 "Do not accept a *b*,

bride — a woman who is about to get married. The church is called Jesus' bride.

bridegroom — a man who is about to get
married. Christ is called the church's bridegroom.

bronze — a metal, the combination of copper and tin, used to make tools, weapons
and ornamental articles.

brother — a male who has the same parents
as another person.
Ge 4:9 "Am I my *b* keeper?"
Mt 18:15 "If your *b* or sister sins,
2Co 13:11 Finally, *b* and sisters, rejoice!

burden — a heavy load.
Mt 11:30 my yoke is easy and my *b* is
light.
Gal 6:2 Carry each other's *b*,

burnt offering — in the Old Testament a

sacrifice to the Lord that expressed devotion and complete surrender (Ge 8:20; Ex
29:18).

C

Caesar — the title of many Roman emper-
ors.
Lk 2:1 In those days *C* Augustus
Mt 22:21 "Give back to *C* what is Caesar's,

Cain — Adam and Eve's firstborn son; he
murdered his brother Abel (Ge 4:1 – 16).

calamity — a disaster, usually causing great
loss and suffering.

Caleb — one of the twelve men who was
sent to spy on Canaan. He came back with a
positive report and encouraged the Israelites to take possession of Canaan (Nu
13:6 — 14:38; Dt 1:36).

call — 1. (*v*.) to ask to come; 2. to give a name
to; 3. (*n*.) a summons for a particular purpose or job.
2Ch 7:14 if my people, who are *c*
Ps 145:18 near to all who *c* on him,
Mt 9:13 not come to *c* the righteous,
Ro 8:30 And those he predestined, he
also *c*;
Ro 11:29 gifts and his *c* are irrevocable.
1Pe 2:9 of him who *c* you out of darkness

camel — a large animal, able to travel long
distances and used for transportation of
people and goods.

Canaan — 1. the land God promised to the
nation of Israel; 2. the promised land.

capstone — the stone that holds two walls
together; the stone that finishes a wall.
1Pe 2:7 has become the *c*,"

care — to show concern for.
Ps 8:4 human beings that you *c* for them?
1 Pe 5:7 on him because he *c* for you.

cavalry — a group of soldiers riding horses.

censer — a bowl or dish used for carrying
hot coals or for burning incense.

census — a count of the population of a
group of people.

centurion — a Roman army officer in
charge of one hundred soldiers.

chaff — the seed covering of a grain such as
wheat. In Bible times, the grain and chaff
were separated by tossing the grain into the
air so the wind could blow the chaff away.
Ps 1:4 They are like *c*
Mt 3:12 up the *c* with unquenchable fire."

chariot — a two-wheeled vehicle pulled by horses.

2Ki 6:17 and *c* of fire all around Elisha.

cheerful — full of joy; pleasant.

Pr 15:13 A happy heart makes the face *c*,
2Co 9:7 for God loves a *c* giver.

cherub (pl. cherubim) — an angel, with an appearance something like a human being.

children — sons and daughters.

Mt 19:14 "Let the little *c* come to me,
Eph 6:1 *C*, obey your parents in the Lord,
1Jn 3:1 that we should be called *c* of God!

choose (chosen) — to select.

Jos 24:15 then *c* for yourselves this day
Mt 22:14 "For many are invited, but few are *c*."
Jn 15:16 You did not *c* me,
Eph 1:4 he *c* us in him before the creation
1Pe 2:9 But you are a *c* people, a royal

Christ — the official title of Jesus, meaning "the Anointed One." It is a Greek word, and it means the same as the Hebrew word *Messiah*.

Jn 1:17 grace and truth came through Jesus *C*.
Ac 3:6 name of Jesus *C* of Nazareth, walk."
Ro 5:8 While we were still sinners, *C* died
Eph 5:23 as *C* is the head of the church,
Php 1:21 to live is *C* and to die is gain.

Christian — a believer in or follower of Christ.

Ac 11:26 The disciples were called *C* first
1Pe 4:16 as a *C*, do not be ashamed,

chronicles — a history of events in the order in which they took place.

church — the entire group of people who believe in Christ.

Mt 16:18 and on this rock I will build my *c*,
Eph 5:23 as Christ is the head of the *c*,
Col 1:24 the sake of his body, which is the *c*.

circumcision — the cutting off of the loose fold of skin at the end of the penis; it symbolized the agreement God made with the Israelites, and they came to be known as "the circumcision" (Eph 2:11).

Ge 17:10 Every male among you shall be *c*.

cistern — a pit dug into the ground for storing rainwater.

citadel — a tower or building, especially in a city, equipped for war.

city of refuge — one of six cities set aside by Moses and Joshua for those who had accidentally killed someone. Such people would be safe there until a fair trial could be held (Nu 35:9 – 15).

clan — a group of people belonging to the same extended family.

Ge 24:38 to my father's family and to my own *c*,
Zec 12:12 The land will mourn, each *c* by itself,

clean animals — animals God allowed the Israelites to sacrifice and eat.

cleanse — to make clean; to wash.

cloak — a loose-fitting coat without sleeves.

comfort — to relieve from distress; to console.

Ps 23:4 rod and your staff, they *c* me.
2Co 1:4 so that we can *c* those

commandment — an order given by God. God gave the Ten Commandments to the Israelites while they were encamped in the area of Mount Sinai.

Ex 20:6 who love me and keep my *c*.
Ecc 12:13 Fear God and keep his *c*,
Mt 22:38 This is the first and greatest *c*.

commend — 1. to praise; 2. to hand over to someone for safekeeping.

Ps 145:4 One generation *c* your works

companion — one who is a friend or associate or helper.

compassion (compassionate) — sympathy; pity.

Ne 9:17 gracious and *c*, slow to anger
Ps 103:4 and crowns you with love and *c*,
Mt 9:36 When he saw the crowds, he had *c*
Ro 9:15 and I will have *c* on whom I have *c*."
Col 3:12 clothe yourselves with *c*, kindness,

conceive — 1. to become pregnant; 2. to think up or imagine.

Mt 1:20 what is *c* in her is from the Holy
1Co 2:9 no human mind has *c*

concubine — in Bible times, a woman who belonged to a man but did not have the rights of a wife. She was often one of the spoils of war, and her primary purpose was to bear children for the man.

condemn (condemnation) — to punish; to pronounce guilty.

Jn 3:17 Son into the world to *c* the world,

Ro 8:1 there is now no *c* for those who are

confess — 1. to say what you believe; 2. to tell your sins to someone.

2Ti 2:19 "Everyone who *c* the name of the Lord

1Jn 1:9 If we *c* our sins, he is faithful

conform — to agree with and try to be like someone; to do what others say to do.

Ro 8:29 predestined to be *c* to the image

1Pe 1:14 do not *c* to the evil desires you had

conscience — the sense of knowing if something is good or bad; a sense of right and wrong.

Ro 2:15 their *c* also bearing witness,

Tit 1:15 their minds and *c* are corrupted.

Heb 9:14 cleanse our *c* from acts that lead

consecrate — to set aside or dedicate for God's use.

Ex 13:2 "*C* to me every firstborn male.

Lev 20:7 "*C* yourselves and be holy,

consider — to think about carefully.

Ps 8:3 When I *c* your heavens,

console — to comfort.

conspire — to plan together to do wrong.

consult — to ask the advice or opinion of someone.

consume — 1. to use up or eat up; 2. to destroy completely.

Jn 2:17 "Zeal for your house will *c* me."

Heb 12:29 for our "God is a *c* fire."

contempt — lack of respect; looking down on someone or something as being worthless.

Pr 14:31 Whoever oppresses the poor shows *c*

1Th 5:20 Do not treat prophecies with *c*

contend — to struggle, as in a contest or against difficulties.

content — satisfied.

Php 4:11 to be *c* whatever the circumstances.

Heb 13:5 and be *c* with what you have,

contrite — to feel sorry for one's sins; to feel repentant.

Ps 51:17 a broken and *c* heart,

Isa 66:2 those who are humble and *c* in spirit,

convert — a person who has changed from one belief to another.

1Ti 3:6 He must not be a recent *c*,

convict — 1. to prove one guilty; 2. to make a person feel sorrow.

Jas 2:9 and are *c* by the law as lawbreakers.

copper — a common metal, easy to work with; often used to make coins.

Cornelius — a Roman to whom Peter preached the gospel; he became the first Gentile Christian (Ac 10).

cornerstone — the first or most important stone laid when constructing a building.

Eph 2:20 with Christ Jesus himself as the chief *c*.

corrupt — 1. (*v.*) to change something from good to bad; 2. (*adj.*) wicked.

Ge 6:11 Now the earth was *c* in God's sight

1Co 15:33 "Bad company *c* good character."

counsel — to give advice to.

Pr 15:22 Plans fail for lack of *c*,

covenant — 1. an agreement between two people or two groups of people, in which both usually make specific promises; 2. the promises of God for salvation.

Ge 9:9 "I now establish my *c* with you

Ex 19:5 if you obey me fully and keep my *c*,

Jer 31:31 "when I will make a new *c*

1Co 11:25 "This cup is the new *c* in my blood;

Heb 9:15 Christ is the mediator of a new *c*,

covet — to want for oneself something that belongs to another person.

Ex 20:17 "You shall not *c* your neighbor's

crafty — sly, clever.

Ge 3:1 Now the serpent was more *c*

crave — to desire strongly; to feel a deep need for.

1Pe 2:2 newborn babies, *c* pure spiritual

create — to make; to bring into being.

Ge 1:1 In the beginning God *c* the heavens

Ps 51:10 *C* in me a pure heart, O God,

Col 1:16 For in him all things were *c*:

Rev 10:6 who *c* the heavens and all that is

crime — an unlawful act.

criminal — someone who commits an unlawful act.

Lk 23:32 Two other men, both *c*,

cripple — a disabled person or animal.

cross—a tall beam with a crossbar on which a criminal was hung or tied to die.
  Mt 10:38 Whoever does not take up their *c*
  Gal 6:14 in the *c* of our Lord Jesus Christ,
  Php 2:8 even death on a *c*!
  Col 2:14 taken it away, nailing it to the *c*.
  Heb 12:2 set before him he endured the *c*,
crown—a headpiece worn to symbolize glory, honor and victory.
  1Co 9:25 it to get a *c* that will last forever.
  2Ti 4:8 store for me the *c* of righteousness,
  Rev 2:10 life as your victor's crown.
crucify—to put to death by nailing or tying a person's body to a cross.
  Mt 27:22 They all answered, "*C* him!"
  1Co 1:23 but we preach Christ *c*: a stumbling
  Gal 2:20 I have been *c* with Christ
cruel—causing envy, grief or pain.
cubit—a measure of length in Bible times; about 18 inches.
cupbearer—an officer of considerable responsibility who tasted the king's food and wine before serving them to him (Ne 1:11).
curse—1. (*v.*) to ask God to bring evil or injury to; 2. (*n.*) a prayer or desire that evil or injury come upon someone.
  Lev 20:9 "Anyone who *c* their father or mother
  Lk 6:28 bless those who *c* you, pray
  Gal 3:13 "*C* is everyone who is hung on a pole."
custom—a practice common to a particular place or group of people.
  Mk 15:6 Now it was the *c* at the festival
  Ac 17:2 As was his *c*, Paul went into the synagogue
cymbals—a musical instrument; round metal disks either struck with a stick or struck together to produce a clanging sound.
cypress—an evergreen tree of the pine family.

D

Daniel—a young Jewish exile; he lived in Babylon during the reign of several kings, including Nebuchadnezzar. He prayed to God rather than obey an order to pray only to the king and was thrown into a lion's den (Da 1–6).

daughter—a female descendant.
  Job 1:2 He had seven sons and three *d*,
David—the son of Jesse; anointed by Samuel to become king of Israel (1Sa 16:1–13); killed the giant Goliath (1Sa 17); during his reign Israel's place in the land of Canaan was made secure.
day—1. the period of time between dawn and darkness; 2. a specified time.
  Ge 1:5 God called the light "*d*,"
  Ecc 12:1 Creator in the *d* of your youth,
  Joel 2:31 and dreadful *d* of the LORD.
  Mic 4:1 In the last *d*
  Lk 11:3 Give us each *d* our daily bread.
  Lk 18:33 On the third *d* he will rise
  Heb 1:2 in these last *d* he has spoken to us
  2Pe 3:8 With the Lord a *d* is like
deacon—a church officer whose qualifications are given in 1 Ti 3:8–13.
death—the end of physical life; also the penalty for sin (Ro 6:23).
  Ecc 7:2 for *d* is the destiny of everyone;
  Isa 25:8 he will swallow up *d* forever.
  1Co 15:21 For since *d* came through a man,
  1Co 15:55 Where, O *d*, is your sting?"
  Rev 21:4 There will be no more *d*
debauchery—living an immoral life or a life without religion; living to please only oneself.
Deborah—a prophetess who led Israel to victory over the Canaanites (Jdg 4–5).
debt—something that one person owes another.
  Mt 6:12 And forgive us our *d*,
deceive—to fool or trick; to lie.
  Ge 3:13 "The serpent *d* me, and I ate."
  Gal 6:7 Do not be *d*: God cannot be
  1Jn 1:8 we *d* ourselves and the truth is not
declare—to make known formally; to state forcefully.
  Ps 19:1 The heavens *d* the glory of God;
  Eph 6:20 Pray that I may *d* it fearlessly,
decree—1. (*v.*) to order or command; 2. (*n.*) an order or law given by someone with power and authority.
dedicate—to set apart for a special purpose, often for God's use.
defect—imperfection; fault.
defile—to make something that is good and pure into something impure or unclean.

defraud — to cheat someone by trickery.

Deity — God.

Col 2:9 of the *D* lives in bodily form,

delight — something that gives great pleasure.

Ps 119:47 for I *d* in your commands

Mt 12:18 the one I love, in whom I *d*;

deliver — to rescue; to set free.

demon — evil spirit. A demon-possessed person is one who is controlled by evil spirits.

Mk 5:15 possessed by the legion of *d*,

Jas 2:19 Good! Even the *d* believe that

denarius — a small Roman coin made of silver. During Jesus' earthly ministry, one denarius was the payment for about one day's work.

denounce — to say a person or thing is evil.

deposit — something pledged or given as part of the payment.

Eph 1:14 who is a *d* guaranteeing our

depraved (depravity) — evil or sinful.

2Ti 3:8 They are men of *d* minds,

2Pe 2:19 they themselves are slaves of *d*

deprive — to take something away from.

Am 5:12 and *d* the poor of justice

depths — the deepest part of a thing.

Ps 130:1 Out of the *d* I cry

La 3:55 from the *d* of the pit.

descendant — a member of a particular family line.

desecrate — to treat without respect or reverence.

desolate — not lived in; lonely; deserted.

despise — to look down on with contempt.

Pr 1:7 but fools *d* wisdom

Tit 2:15 Do not let anyone *d* you.

destiny — a predetermined course of events.

Php 3:19 Their *d* is destruction,

destitute — not having necessary things such as money and food.

destroy — to ruin completely.

detest — to hate.

devastate — to bring to ruin by violent action.

Jer 19:8 I will *d* this city

devil — the great enemy of God and tempter of people.

Lk 4:2 forty days he was tempted by the *d*.

Eph 6:11 stand against the *d* schemes.

2Ti 2:26 and escape from the trap of the *d*,

Jas 4:7 Resist the *d*, and he will flee

1Pe 5:8 Your enemy the *d* prowls

devote — to set apart for a special person or for a special reason; to set apart for God's use.

devour — 1. to eat up greedily; 2. to destroy.

1Pe 5:8 looking for someone to *d*.

devout — religious; giving much time to prayer and worship.

die — 1. to lose life; 2. to become insensitive to, as to die to the law (Gal 2:19).

Ge 2:17 when you eat from it you will certainly *d*."

Ecc 3:2 a time to be born and a time to *d*,

Eze 18:4 one who sins is the one who will *d*.

Jn 11:26 by believing in me will never *d*.

1Co 15:22 in Adam all *d*, so in Christ all will

Php 1:21 to live is Christ and to *d* is gain.

diligence (diligent) — characterized by hard work or earnest effort.

disaster — a sudden event bringing great damage, loss or destruction.

Dt 31:29 *d* will fall on you

discern — to understand; to come to know the difference between two or more things.

Php 1:10 you may be able to *d* what is best

disciple — a follower or student, especially one who believes what the leader teaches. Anyone who believes in Jesus is his disciple.

Lk 14:27 and follow me cannot be my *d*.

Jn 13:35 everyone will know that you are my *d*,

discipline — 1. (*v.*) to correct; to teach what is right; 2. (*n.*) training that corrects, molds or perfects moral character.

Pr 29:17 *D* your children, and they will give you

Heb 12:6 the Lord *d* the one he loves,

Rev 3:19 Those whom I love I rebuke and *d*.

disgrace — to bring shame to.

disobey (disobedient) — to fail to obey.

1Pe 2:8 because they *d* the message

disown — to reject someone or something so completely that it no longer belongs to you.

Mt 26:34 you will *d* me three times."

2Ti 2:12 If we *d* him,

disperse — to scatter; to spread around.

dispute — to argue irritably.

dissension — disagreement; quarreling.

distress — suffering, misery, agony.

Ps 57:6 I was bowed down in *d*.

Ro 2:9 There will be trouble and *d*

divination — seeing into the future by magic.

Lev 19:26 "Do not practice *d* or seek omens.

divine — given by God; belonging to God.

Ro 1:20 his eternal power and *d* nature

divorce — to legally dissolve a marriage.

Mal 2:16 who hates and *d* his wife,"

Mt 19:3 for a man to *d* his wife for any

1Co 7:11 And a husband must not *d* his wife.

doctrine — teachings or beliefs about God.

1Ti 4:16 Watch your life and *d* closely.

Tit 2:1 what is appropriate to sound *d*.

dominion — power; rule.

Ps 22:28 for *d* belongs to the LORD

Eph 1:21 far above all rule and authority, power and *d*,

doom — 1. (*v*.) to make certain something will fail or be destroyed; 2. (*n*.) fate; condemnation; ruin.

Rev 18:10 In one hour your *d* has come!'

door — a barrier that can be opened and closed; Christians open the doors of their hearts to Jesus.

Mt 7:7 and the *d* will be opened to you.

Rev 3:20 I stand at the *d* and knock.

doubt — uncertainty.

Mt 21:21 if you have faith and do not *d*,

Mk 11:23 and does not *d* in their heart

Jas 1:6 you must believe and not *d*,

dread — great fear.

dream — thoughts, images or emotion occurring during sleep; God sometimes spoke to his people through dreams.

Da 2:4 Tell your servants the *d*,

dross — the impure scum that floats on the surface of molten metals; sometimes used as a picture of the wicked.

Ps 119:119 you discard like *d*;

drought — a long period of time without rain.

drunkard — a person who is often or usually drunk.

Pr 23:21 for *d* and gluttons become poor,

dwelling — place in which people live; house; in Scripture usually refers to the place where God lives.

1Ki 8:30 Hear from heaven, your *d* place,

Ps 84:1 How lovely is your *d* place,

E

earth — the place that God created for human beings to live.

Ge 1:1 God created the heavens and the *e*.

Ps 24:1 *e* is the LORD's, and everything

Mt 6:10 done, on *e* as it is in heaven.

Mt 24:35 Heaven and *e* will pass away,

Lk 2:14 on *e* peace to those

Php 2:10 in heaven and on *e* and under the *e*,

2Pe 3:13 to a new heaven and a new *e*,

Eden — the location of the beautiful garden God created for Adam and Eve.

edict — an order or law made by a person who has the power to enforce it.

Est 2:8 the king's order and *e*

edify — to teach someone to live a godly life, or to help someone to live in such a way.

1Co 14:4 but the one who prophesies *e* the church.

Egypt — one of the most powerful nations of ancient times, located in the northeast corner of Africa; the Israelites were captives in Egypt at the beginning of the book of Exodus.

elders — 1. the older men of a town or nation; they were the leaders of their community and made all the important decisions; 2. the leaders of the church.

1Ti 5:17 The *e* who direct the affairs

Tit 1:5 and appoint *e* in every town,

election — the choosing of Christians by God, as people who belong to him. Christians are called "the elect" (2Ti 2:10).

Ro 9:11 God's purpose in *e* might stand:

2Pe 1:10 to confirm your calling and *e*.

Eli — the high priest with whom Samuel spent the early years of his life (1Sa 2:11 - 26).

Elijah — a prophet of the Lord who predicted a famine in Israel (1Ki 17:1) and defeated the prophets of Baal in the test of whose God would set fire to the altar (1Ki 18:16 - 46).

Elisha — the prophet who succeeded Elijah. He was present when God took Elijah to heaven, and he took his place as prophet to Israel (2Ki 2:1 - 18).

Elizabeth — the mother of John the Baptist. Mary went to visit her when she found out she, too, was pregnant (Lk 1:5 - 58).

enchanter — a magician or snake charmer.

encourage — to inspire with courage or hope.

2Sa 19:7 Now go out and *e* your men.

1Th 4:18 Therefore *e* one another with these words.

endure — to continue; to keep on going; to bear something that is difficult or painful.

Ps 136:1 His love *e* forever.

Mal 3:2 who can *e* the day of his coming?

1Co 10:13 so that you can *e* it.

enemy — a person who opposes another person or a cause.

Mt 5:44 Love your *e* and pray

Php 3:18 many live as *e* of the cross of Christ.

enjoy — to take pleasure in.

Jdg 19:9 Stay and *e* yourself.

Jer 33:6 and will let them *e* abundant peace

3Jn 2 I pray that you may *e* good health

enmity — a feeling of antagonism, hostility or hatred.

Ge 3:15 put *e* between you and the woman,

Enoch — a man who "walked with God." Later in life, God "took him away" (Ge 5:18–24).

entice — to tempt or lure.

envoy — a person who represents one government in its dealings with another.

envy — to want for oneself something that belongs to another person.

1Co 13:4 It does not *e*, it does not boast,

ephod — a linen apron worn by a priest over his robe. It was decorated with gold, blue, purple and scarlet yarns.

Ephraim — 1. one of Joseph's sons; 2. the tribe of Israel whose members were descendants of Ephraim; 3. a name for the northern kingdom of Israel after the ten tribes of Israel and the two tribes of Judah separated from each other.

Esau — the firstborn son of Isaac and twin of Jacob (Ge 25:21–26). He sold his birthright to Jacob for a pot of stew (Ge 25:29–34) and was tricked out of his blessing by this same brother (Ge 27).

esteem — 1. (*v.*) to value; to consider important; 2. (*n.*) high regard or respect.

Pr 22:1 to be *e* is better than silver or gold.

Isa 53:3 and we held him in low *e*.

Esther — a Jewish woman who lived in Persia (Est 2:7) and became queen (Est 2:8–18).

Upon being told of a plot to kill the Jews, she went to the king and pleaded for the Jewish people and thus saved them (Est 3–4; 7–9).

eternal — without beginning or end; forever; timeless.

Dt 33:27 The *e* God is your refuge,

Jn 3:16 him shall not perish but have *e* life.

Ro 6:23 but the gift of God is *e* life

1Jn 5:13 you may know that you have *e* life.

eunuch — a man whose sex organs have been removed so that he cannot produce children. Often in Bible times these men were important officials in royal palaces.

Eve — the first woman God created (Ge 2:20–24). Her name means "mother of all the living" (Ge 3:20).

everlasting — forever; without end.

Ps 90:2 from *e* to *e* you are God.

Isa 9:6 *E* Father, Prince of Peace.

Isa 55:3 I will make an *e* covenant with you,

2Th 1:9 punished with *e* destruction

evil — wicked; doing things against God's will.

Ge 2:9 of the knowledge of good and *e*.

Ps 23:4 I will fear no *e*,

Mt 6:13 but deliver us from the *e* one.

Ro 12:9 Hate what is *e*; cling

Ro 12:17 Do not repay anyone *e* for *e*.

Eph 6:16 all the flaming arrows of the *e* one.

exalt — to praise; to raise to an important position.

Ps 118:28 you are my God, and I will *e* you.

Ps 148:13 for his name alone is *e*;

Pr 14:34 Righteousness *e* a nation,

Mt 23:12 For those who *e* themselves

examine — to look over carefully; to test.

1Co 11:28 Everyone ought to *e* themselves

exclaim — to cry out or speak in sudden or strong emotion.

Lk 1:42 In a loud voice she *e*: "Blessed

exclude — to leave out.

execute — to put to death, especially as punishment for an illegal act.

Lk 23:32 were also led out with him to be *e*.

exile — 1. (*v.*) to force someone to leave his or her country or home; 2. (*n.*) forced removal from one's country or home.

Ezr 6:19 the *e* celebrated the Passover.

1Pe 1:1 To God's elect, *e* scattered

exodus — the departure of a large group of people from one place to go to another. The book of Exodus is the story of the Israelites' journey from Egypt to Canaan.

exploit — to take unfair advantage of.

Pr 22:22 Do not *e* the poor

extol — to praise.

Ps 34:1 I will *e* the Lord at all times;

Ps 95:2 and *e* him with music and song.

extortion — something gotten from a person by force or by using other illegal means.

Ezekiel — a priest who was called to be a prophet to the Jewish people when they were in exile in Babylon (Eze 1 – 3). He had many visions from the Lord (Eze 37; 40).

Ezra — a priest and teacher of the Law; he led a group of Jewish exiles back to Israel and helped them reestablish the temple of God and restore proper worship (Ezr 7 – 8).

F

fail — to be unsuccessful.

Ecc 6:6 but *f* to enjoy his prosperity.

1Co 13:8 Love never *f*.

faint — 1. (*adj.*) lacking courage; 2. (*v.*) to lose courage.

Ps 142:3 When my spirit grows *f* within me,

Lk 21:26 People will *f* from terror,

faith — belief and trust in God; knowing that God is real, even though one can't see him.

Mt 17:20 if you have *f* as small as a mustard

Lk 7:9 I have not found such great *f*

Ro 1:17 "The righteous will live by *f*."

Ro 3:22 given through *f* in Jesus Christ

1Co 13:2 and if I have a *f* that can move

2Co 5:7 we live by *f*, not by sight.

Eph 6:16 to all this, take up the shield of *f*,

1Ti 6:12 Fight the good fight of the *f*.

Heb 11:1 *f* is confidence in what we hope for

Heb 11:8 By *f* Abraham, when called to go

Heb 12:2 the pioneer and perfecter of *f*

Jas 2:26 so *f* without deeds is dead.

faithful (faithfulness) — trustworthy; loyal.

Ps 145:13 and *f* in all he does.

La 3:23 great is your *f*.

Mt 25:21 'Well done, good and *f* servant!

Ro 12:12 patient in affliction, *f* in prayer.

1Co 10:13 And God is *f*; he will not let you

1Jn 1:9 he is *f* and just and will forgive us

Rev 1:5 who is the *f* witness, the firstborn

false (falsehood) — a lie.

Ex 20:16 "You shall not give *f* testimony

family — a group of people who are related to each other.

Ps 68:6 God sets the lonely in *f*,

Lk 9:61 go back and say goodbye to my *f*."

1Ti 3:4 He must manage his own *f* well

famine — 1. a time when there is not enough food; 2. any severe shortage.

Am 8:11 but a *f* of hearing the words

Mt 24:7 There will be *f* and earthquakes

fast — 1. (*adj.*) firmly fixed; not movable; 2. (*v.*) to go without food for a period of time.

Ps 139:10 your right hand will hold me *f*.

Mt 6:16 "When you *f*, do not look somber

father — a male parent; God is also known as one's father.

Ge 2:24 why a man leaves his *f*

Ge 17:4 You will be the *f* of many nations.

Ex 20:12 "Honor your *f* and your mother,

Mt 6:9 " 'Our *F* in heaven,

Lk 11:11 "Which of you *f*, if your son asks

Jn 10:30 I and the *F* are one."

Jn 14:6 No one comes to the *F*

favor — goodwill; a positive attitude toward another person.

1Sa 20:3 I have found *f* in your eyes,

fear — (*v.*) 1. to respect highly; to feel reverence and awe for; 2. to be afraid of; (*n.*) 1. profound reverence toward God; 2. anticipation or awareness of danger.

Dt 6:13 *F* the Lord your God, serve him

Ps 91:5 You will not *f* the terror of night,

Ps 111:10 *f* of the Lord is the beginning

Isa 41:10 So do not *f*, for I am with you;

Php 2:12 to work out your salvation with *f*

fellowship — companionship or friendship.

1Jn 1:6 claim to have *f* with him yet walk

1Jn 1:7 we have *f* with one another,

fertile — producing fruit in great quantities; productive.

Nu 13:20 How is the soil? Is it *f* or poor?

festival — a religious celebration.

Nu 29:12 Celebrate a *f* to the Lord

Ezr 6:22 with joy the *F* of Unleavened Bread,

Jn 4:45 in Jerusalem at the Passover *F*,

fig — 1. a brownish pear-shaped fruit that

grows in countries near the Mediterranean Sea; 2. the tree that grows this fruit.

Joel 2:22 the *f* tree and the vine yield their riches.

firstborn — a family's first child. The first-born son in an Israelite family became the head of the family when his father died, and he received twice as much money and property as each of his brothers.

Ex 11:5 Every *f* son in Egypt will die,

firstfruits — the first vegetables, fruits and grains harvested from the field.

Ex 23:19 "Bring the best of the *f* of your soil

flesh — 1. the soft parts of the bodies of humans and animals; 2. the believer's sinful nature.

Job 6:12 Is my *f* bronze?

Php 3:3 put no confidence in the *f*

Ro 8:13 live according to the *f*, you will die;

Ro 13:14 gratify the desires of the *f*.

flock — a collection of sheep under the care of a shepherd.

Ps 65:13 The meadows are covered with *f*

Isa 40:11 He tends his *f* like a shepherd:

flog — to beat with a stick or a whip.

flood — a large amount of water that covers the ground, as in the time of Noah (Ge 6 – 8).

foe — an enemy.

Ps 61:3 a strong tower against the *f*.

folly — foolishness; the lack of wisdom.

Pr 26:5 Answer a fool according to his *f*,

2Ti 3:9 their *f* will be clear to everyone.

fool — a person who is not wise.

Ps 14:1 The *f* says in his heart,

Lk 12:20 "But God said to him, 'You *f*!

forbearance — patient endurance; self-control; not enforcing a right.

Gal 5:22 love, joy, peace, *f*, kindness,

forefather — a male ancestor.

forever — for a limitless time.

Dt 32:40 As surely as I live *f*,

Ps 136:1 His love endures *f*.

forgive — to pardon or excuse; to no longer blame or be angry with someone who has done you wrong.

Mt 6:14 For if you *f* other people

Lk 23:34 Jesus said, "Father, *f* them,

Col 3:13 *F* as the Lord forgave you.

1Jn 1:9 and just and will *f* us our sins

forsake — to leave another completely alone; to abandon

Jos 1:5 I will never leave you nor *f* you.

Isa 55:7 Let the wicked *f* their ways

Mt 27:46 my God, why have you *f* me?"

fortified — to make strong, such as a town with a wall.

fortress — a city that is fortified.

fragrance (fragrant) — a sweet or pleasant odor.

SS 4:10 the *f* of your perfume

Php 4:18 They are a *f* offering,

free (freedom) — not bound; liberated.

Jn 8:32 and the truth will set you *f*."

Ro 6:18 You have been set *f* from sin

2Co 3:17 the Spirit of the Lord is, there is *f*.

friend — a person who loves and respects another person.

Pr 18:24 there is a *f* who sticks closer

Jn 15:13 to lay down one's life for one's *f*.

Jas 4:4 Anyone who chooses to be a *f*

fruitful — productive; yielding much fruit.

Ge 1:22 "Be *f* and increase in number

Jn 15:2 prunes so that it will be even more *f*.

fulfill (fulfillment) — to complete a promise or project.

Ps 116:14 I will *f* my vows to the LORD

Mk 14:49 But the Scriptures must be *f*."

Ro 13:10 Therefore love is the *f* of the law.

fury — intense anger.

Pr 6:34 jealousy arouses a husband's *f*,

G

Gabriel — the angel who announced the births of John the Baptist and Jesus (Lk 1:11 – 20, 26 – 38).

Galilee — the northern part of Palestine. Jesus grew up, preached and did most of his miracles there. Today this area is in northern Israel.

gall — 1. a plant with an extremely bitter-tasting fruit; 2. the liquid made by the liver.

Mt 27:34 mixed with *g*; but after tasting it,

genealogy — a list of a person's ancestors or descendants; a family tree.

generation — the entire number of people born and living at about the same time. Grandparents, parents and children are three different generations.

Ps 102:12 your renown endures through all *g*.

Lk 1:48 now on all *g* will call me blessed,

Gentile — anyone who is not a Jew.

Ro 3:9 and *G* alike are all under

Ro 11:13 as I am the apostle to the *G*,

Gideon — a judge who freed Israel from the rule and terror of the Midianites (Jdg 6 – 8). He asked for a sign from God, and God showed him his will by means of dew and a fleece (Jdg 6:36 – 40).

gift — 1. a present; 2. a talent or ability.

Ro 6:23 but the *g* of God is eternal life

1Co 12:4 There are different kinds of *g*,

2Co 9:15 be to God for his indescribable *g!*

glean — to pick up the grain or fruit left behind after harvesting; usually a way for the poor to get food.

Ruth 2:8 Don't go and *g* in another field

gloat — to look at or think about something or someone with malicious satisfaction.

Mic 7:8 Do not *g* over me, my enemy!

glorify — to praise and honor in worship.

Ps 34:3 *G* the Lord with me;

Jn 17:1 *G* your Son, that your Son may

glory — 1. honor; praise; 2. a source of pride or worthiness.

Ps 8:5 and crowned them with *g* and honor.

Ps 19:1 The heavens declare the *g* of God;

Lk 2:14 "*G* to God in the highest heaven,

Jn 1:14 We have seen his *g*, the *g* of the one

1Co 10:31 whatever you do, do it all for the *g*

Rev 4:11 to receive *g* and honor and power,

glutton — a person who eats too much.

Dt 21:20 He is a *g* and a drunkard."

gnash — to grind (one's teeth) together.

Mt 8:12 there will be weeping and *g* of teeth."

goat — an animal raised for its meat and milk; sometimes used in religious sacrifices.

God — the supreme creator and the powerful force of the universe; the one who is to be worshiped.

Ge 1:1 In the beginning *G* created

Ex 20:5 the Lord your *G*, am a jealous *G*,

Nu 23:19 *G* is not human, that he should lie,

Dt 6:4 Lord our *G*, the Lord is one.

Dt 6:5 Love the Lord your *G*

Ps 46:1 *G* is our refuge and strength,

Jn 1:18 ever seen *G*, but the one

Jn 3:16 For *G* so loved the world that he

Jn 4:24 *G* is spirit, and his worshipers must

1Jn 4:16 *G* is love.

Rev 4:8 holy is the Lord *G* Almighty,

godly — to be devoted and loving toward God, wanting to do his will.

1Ti 4:7 train yourself to be *g*.

2Pe 3:11 live holy and *g* lives

Golgotha — the hill outside Jerusalem where Jesus was hung on a cross.

Goliath — the Philistine giant who was killed by David (1Sa 17; 21:9).

gospel — 1. the good news that Jesus died for sins and rose again; 2. any of the first four books of the New Testament.

Ro 1:16 I am not ashamed of the *g*,

1Co 9:16 Woe to me if I do not preach the *g!*

1Co 15:2 By this *g* you are saved,

gossip — to talk too much about others, especially in a way that is hurtful.

2Co 12:20 slander, *g*, arrogance and disorder.

grace — an undeserved favor or gift; the undeserved forgiveness, kindness and mercy that God gives us.

Ro 3:24 all are justified freely by his *g*

Ro 5:20 where sin increased, *g* increased all

2Co 12:9 "My *g* is sufficient for you,

Eph 2:5 it is by *g* you have been saved.

Tit 3:7 having been justified by his *g*,

greed — selfish desire for more money or possessions than one needs.

Lk 12:15 on your guard against all kinds of *g*;

Col 3:5 evil desires and *g*, which is idolatry.

grieve — to cause someone pain or sorrow.

Jn 16:20 You will *g*, but your grief will turn

Eph 4:30 do not *g* the Holy Spirit of God,

guarantee — a pledge that something will take place.

Eph 1:14 who is a deposit *g* our inheritance

guardian-redeemer — in Old Testament times a close male relative who had the responsibility to marry a widow and buy her husband's property (Dt 25:5 – 6).

Ruth 3:9 since you are a *g* of our family.

guide — to direct or point out the way.

Ps 23:3 He *g* me along the right paths

guilty — deserving punishment for having broken a law or commandment.

Ex 34:7 does not leave the *g* unpunished;

Heb 10:22 to cleanse us from a *g* conscience

Jas 2:10 at just one point is *g* of breaking all

H

Hades — hell; the place where the spirits of the dead live.

Mt 16:18 the gates of *H* will not overcome

Hagar — a slave of Sarah and one of Abraham's wives; the mother of Ishmael (Ge 16:1 – 6; 25:12).

Haggai — a prophet who encouraged the Israelites returning from exile in Babylon to rebuild the temple (Ezr 5:1; Hag 1 – 2).

hallelujah — praise the Lord; a song of praise.

Rev 19:1 "*H!* Salvation and glory and power

hallowed — holy; sacred.

Mt 6:9 *h* be your name,

Ham — the youngest of Noah's three sons (Ge 5:32).

Hannah — she prayed for a son, and God gave her Samuel. She dedicated him to God; he lived in the temple as a boy and became a prophet and judge (1Sa 1 – 2).

harp — a musical instrument with twelve strings for strumming; frequently used in religious ceremonies.

Ps 71:22 I will praise you with the *h*

harvest — the season for gathering in crops.

Ge 8:22 "As long as the earth endures, seedtime and *h*,

hate — to detest, to have extreme dislike for.

Ps 5:5 You *h* all who do wrong;

Mk 13:13 Everyone will *h* you because of me,

haughty — proud.

Pr 16:18 a *h* spirit before a fall.

heal — to make well again.

Lk 8:43 but no one could *h* her.

Ac 28:27 and I would *h* them.'

heart — the center of a person's life, including the mind, the will and the emotions.

Dt 6:5 LORD your God with all your *h*

1Sa 16:7 but the LORD looks at the *h*."

Ps 51:10 Create in me a pure *h*, O God,

Ps 119:11 I have hidden your word in my *h*

Ps 139:23 Search me, O God, and know my *h*;

Eze 36:26 I will give you a new *h*

Mt 5:8 Blessed are the pure in *h*,

heaven — 1. the place where God lives; 2. the sky.

Ge 14:19 Creator of *h* and earth.

Mt 19:23 to enter the kingdom of *h*.

Lk 24:51 and was taken up into *h*.

Php 3:20 But our citizenship is in *h*.

Rev 21:1 Then I saw "a new *h* and a new earth,"

Hebrew — 1. another name for an Israelite; a descendant of Abraham; 2. the language spoken by the Jews. The Old Testament was written in Hebrew.

heir — someone who receives the property or blessings of a person who has died.

Ro 8:17 then we are *h* — *h* of God

Eph 3:6 gospel the Gentiles are *h* together

herd — a large number of animals of one kind kept together in a group.

Herod — the family name of five kings who ruled Palestine under the Roman emperor: Herod the Great (Mt 2:16); Herod Antipas (Mk 6:14 – 29); Herod Philip (Mt 14:3; Mk 6:17); Herod Agrippa I (Ac 12:1 – 4, 19 – 23); Herod Agrippa II (Ac 23:35; 25:13 — 26:32).

Herodias — the wife of Herod Antipas; she persuaded her daughter to ask Antipas for the head of John the Baptist (Mk 6:17).

Hezekiah — a king of Judah; he restored the temple, reinstituted proper worship and sought the Lord's help against the Assyrians.

high priest — the chief religious official in the Jewish religion. In the Old Testament he offered the most important sacrifices to God in behalf of the people.

Heb 4:14 a great high *p* who has ascended

Heb 7:26 a high *p* truly meets our need

hinder — to hold back; to prevent; to delay.

Mt 19:14 come to me, and do not *h* them,

holy — set apart for God; belonging to God; pure; godly.

Ex 20:8 the Sabbath day by keeping it *h*.

Lev 11:44 and be *h*, because I am *h*.

Isa 6:3 "*H, h, h* is the LORD Almighty;

Ro 12:1 as a living sacrifice, *h* and pleasing

Rev 4:8 "*H, h, h* is the Lord God Almighty,

Holy Spirit — the third person of the Trinity; he lives and works in the hearts and minds of believers; he came at Pentecost in a powerful way (Ac 2). Other names are: the Spirit, Counselor and Comforter.

Ps 51:11 or take your *H* from me.

Jn 14:26 But the Advocate, the *H*,

Jn 20:22 and said, "Receive the *H*.

Ac 2:4 of them were filled with the *H*

Gal 5:22 But the fruit of the *S* is love, joy,

honor — to show respect to; to give credit to.

Ex 20:12 "*H* your father and your mother,

Ps 8:5 and crowned them with glory and *h*.

hope — the anticipation of something good.

Ps 42:5 Put your *h* in God,

Isa 40:31 but those who *h* in the LORD

Ro 8:24 But *h* that is seen is no *h* at all.

1Co 15:19 for this life we have *h* in Christ,

Heb 11:1 faith is confidence in what we *h* for

hordes — a loosely organized or disorderly crowd of people; usually committing harmful acts.

Hab 1:9 Their *h* advance like a desert wind

horror — strong and painful fear or dread.

Jer 8:21 I mourn, and *h* grips me.

hosanna — a Hebrew word of praise meaning "save."

Mt 21:9 "*H* in the highest heaven!"

hospitality — welcoming people into one's home; sharing one's home and food with others.

Ro 12:13 Practice *h*.

1Pe 4:9 Offer *h* to one another

hostile — like an enemy; unfriendly.

human — like people rather than animals, in actions or thoughts or appearance.

humble — 1. (*v.*) to make lower; 2. (*adj.*) not proud; not pretending to be important.

Ps 147:6 The LORD sustains the *h*

Mt 23:12 who exalt themselves will be *h*,

Jas 4:10 *H* yourselves before the Lord,

humiliate — to make humble; to reduce to a lower position; to make ashamed.

1Co 11:22 by *h* those who have nothing?

humility — the absence of pride.

Php 2:3 but in *h* value others above

1Pe 5:5 clothe yourselves with *h*

hymn — a song of praise to God.

Eph 5:19 with psalms, *h*, and songs

hypocrite — a person who pretends to be better than he or she is.

Mt 6:5 when you pray, do not be like the *h*,

Mt 7:5 You *h*, first take the plank out

hyssop — a plant used to sprinkle water or blood for religious cleansing.

Ps 51:7 with *h*, and I will be clean;

I

idle — 1. lacking worth or basis; 2. lazy.

Dt 32:47 They are not just *i* words

1Th 5:14 warn those who are *i*

idol — a statue made by people and worshiped as if it had the power of a god; anything that takes the place of God in a person's life. Worshiping idols is called idolatry.

1Co 8:4 We know that "An *i* is nothing at all

Col 3:5 evil desires and greed, which is *i*.

image — likeness.

Ge 1:27 God created mankind in his own *i*,

Da 3:12 nor worship the *i* of gold you have set up."

Immanuel — a name for Jesus meaning "God with us."

Mt 1:23 and they will call him *I*"

immoral (immorality) — wicked; not living by right standards.

1Co 6:18 Flee from sexual *i*.

Eph 5:5 No *i*, impure or greedy person

immortal (immortality) — free from death; not able to die.

1Co 15:53 and the mortal with *i*.

1Ti 1:17 Now to the King eternal, *i*,

imperishable — not able to die or to be destroyed.

1Pe 1:23 not of perishable seed, but of *i*,

impure — not pure; not clean.

Ac 10:15 not call anything *i* that God has

1Th 4:7 For God did not call us to be *i*,

incense — 1. spices burned to make a sweet-smelling smoke, as a way of worshiping God; 2. the sweet smell or the smoke of burning spices.

Ps 141:2 my prayer be set before you like *i*;

Rev 8:3 He was given much *i* to offer,

indignation — anger.

Na 1:6 Who can withstand his *i*?

infirmity — physical weakness; disease.

Lk 13:12 set free from your *i*."

inflict — to cause to be endured.

Eze 5:8 I will *i* punishment on you

2Co 2:6 The punishment *i* on him by

inhabitant — one who lives in a particular place.

Nu 33:55 drive out all the *i* of the land

Rev 6:10 the *i* of the earth and avenge

inherit — to receive money, property or keepsakes from a person after his or her death.

Mt 5:5 for they will *i* the earth.

Mk 10:17 "what must I do to *i* eternal life?"

inheritance — money, property or keepsakes received from a person after his or her death.

Dt 4:20 to be the people of his *i*,

1Pe 1:4 and into an *i* that can never perish,

iniquity — sin; wickedness.

Ps 51:2 Wash away all my *i*

Ps 103:10 or repay us according to our *i*.

Isa 53:6 the *i* of us all.

injustice — unfairness.

Pr 22:8 Whoever sows *i* reaps calamity.

inscription — 1. the writing on a coin; 2. a written title or message.

instruct — to give knowledge or information; to teach.

Pr 9:9 *I* the wise and they will be wiser

1Th 4:1 we *i* you how to live

instruction — the action of a teacher; a lesson.

Ac 1:2 after giving *i* through the Holy Spirit

2Ti 4:2 with great patience and careful *i*

insult — 1. (*v.*) to treat with contempt by word or action; to offend; 2. (*n.*) an act or speech of contempt.

Ps 69:9 the *i* of those who *i* you have fallen

Mt 5:11 "Blessed are you when people *i* you,

insurrection — revolt or rebellion against a government.

integrity — complete honesty.

Ps 25:21 May *i* and uprightness protect me,

intercede — to beg or plead for another person.

Ro 8:26 but the Spirit himself *i* for us

intercession — the plea made on behalf of another person.

Isa 53:12 and made *i* for the transgressors.

intermarry — to marry someone from a different race or religion.

Dt 7:3 Do not *i* with them.

interpret — to explain the meaning of.

Mt 16:3 you cannot *i* the signs of the times.

1Co 12:30 Do all speak in tongues? Do all *i*?

invoke — to call for help or support.

Ac 19:13 to *i* the name of the Lord Jesus

Isaac — the promised son of Abraham and Sarah (Ge 17:19; 21:1 - 7); offered as a sacrifice by Abraham (Ge 22); married Rebekah (Ge 24) and was the father of Esau and Jacob (Ge 25).

Isaiah — a prophet called by God (Isa 6) to prophesy to Judah (Isa 1:1). Some of his prophesies were about the coming Messiah (Isa 53).

Ishmael — the son of Abraham and Hagar (Ge 16); he was not to be the son of the covenant (Ge 17:18 - 21).

Israel — 1. the new name God gave to Jacob (Ge 32:28); 2. the nation made up of descendants of the twelve sons of Jacob; 3. the northern ten tribes after they separated from Judah and Benjamin.

Ge 37:3 Now *I* loved Joseph more than

Dt 6:4 Hear, O *I*: The LORD our God,

Lk 22:30 judging the twelve tribes of *I*.

Eph 3:6 Gentiles are heirs together with *I*,

Israelites — the people of Israel.

Ex 14:22 and the *I* went through the sea

Ro 9:27 the number of the *I* be like the sand

J

Jacob — the son of Isaac and Rebekah; he was the twin brother of Esau (Ge 25:21 - 26); he bought Esau's birthright for a pot of stew (Ge 25:29 - 34); he wrestled with God, and his name was changed to Israel (Ge 32:22 - 32); the descendants of his twelve sons became the nation of Israel.

James — 1. one of the twelve apostles; the brother of John (Mt 4:21 - 22); 2. one of the twelve apostles; the son of Alphaeus (Mt 10:3); 3. the brother of Jesus (Mk 6:3); the author of the letter of James (Jas 1:1).

Japheth — one of the sons of Noah (Ge 5:32); he was blessed because he covered his father's nakedness (Ge 9:18 - 28).

jealous (jealousy) — 1. afraid of losing someone's love or affection; 2. angry or unhappy because of what someone else has; 3. careful to guard or keep what one has.

Joel 2:18 Then the LORD was *j* for his land

2Co 11:2 I am *j* for you with a godly *j.*

Gal 5:20 hatred, discord, *j*, fits of rage,

Jeremiah — a prophet called by God to prophesy to Judah (Jer 1:1 – 3). He is often referred to as the prophet of gloom, because he prophesied about the destruction of Judah.

Jericho — the ancient city destroyed by Joshua when the Hebrews entered Canaan (Jos 6).

Jeroboam — an official in Solomon's court; he rebelled and became the first king of the northern ten tribes of Israel (1Ki 11:26 – 40; 12:1 – 20).

Jerusalem — the political and religious center of the Jews; it was the site of many important events in the Bible; also called "Zion" and "the City of David."

2Ki 23:27 and I will reject *J*, the city I chose,

Ne 2:17 Come, let us rebuild the wall of *J*,

Ps 137:5 If I forget you, O *J*,

Jn 4:20 where we must worship is in *J*."

Rev 21:2 I saw the Holy City, the new *J*,

Jesse — the father of David, king of Israel (1Sa 16:10 – 13).

Jesus — the Son of God; the Savior of the world; the Messiah, through whom people can be saved.

Mt 1:21 you are to give him the name *J*,

Mk 11:22 "Have faith in God," *J* answered.

Php 2:10 name of *J* every knee should bow,

Jew — an Israelite; one of the chosen people of God; a descendant of Abraham through Jacob.

Mt 2:2 who has been born king of the *J*?

Ro 3:29 Or is God the God of *J* only?

Gal 3:28 There is neither *J* nor Gentile,

Jezebel — the wife of King Ahab (1Ki 16:31). She promoted Baal worship in Israel (1Ki 16:32 – 33), had many prophets of God killed (1Ki 18:4,13) and opposed the prophet Elijah (1Ki 19:1 – 2).

Joab — the commander of the armies of King David.

Joash — the boy-king of Judah; he repaired the temple (2Ki 12).

Job — a wealthy man from the land of Uz who feared God (Job 1:1 – 5). His righteousness was tested by disaster (Job 1:6 – 22) and personal affliction (Job 2), but in the end God restored wealth and honor to him (Job 42).

John — 1. the Baptist (Mk 1:2 – 8); the son of Zechariah and Elizabeth (Lk 1). He preached in the desert, preparing the people for Jesus (Mt 3:11 – 12); baptized Jesus in the Jordan River (Mt 3:13 – 17); executed by Herod (Mk 6:14 – 29); 2. one of the twelve apostles; brother of the apostle James (Lk 5:1 – 10); wrote the Gospel of John, the letters of John (2Jn 1; 3Jn 1) and the book of Revelation (Rev 1:1; 22:8).

John Mark (see Mark, John).

Jonah — a prophet who was called to preach to Nineveh but instead fled to Tarshish (Jnh 1:1 – 3). While at sea a great storm arose because of his disobedience; he was thrown into the sea and was swallowed by a large fish (Jnh 1:4 – 17). He then repented and went to Nineveh and preached, telling the people to repent (Jnh 3).

Jonathan — a son of King Saul (1Sa 13:16) who had a close friendship with David (1Sa 18:1 – 4; 19 – 20; 23:16 – 18). When he was killed (1Sa 31) David mourned greatly for him (2Sa 1).

Joppa — an ancient walled town on the coast of Palestine.

Jordan — a river in Palestine that flows between the Sea of Galilee and the Dead Sea.

Jos 4:22 'Israel crossed the *J* on dry ground.'

Mt 3:6 baptized by him in the *J* River.

Joseph — 1. the son of Jacob and Rachel (Ge 30:24), who was favored by his father but hated by his brothers (Ge 37:3 – 4). He was sold into slavery (Ge 37:12 – 36), taken to Egypt and eventually given a high position under Pharaoh (Ge 41:41 – 57); 2. the husband of Mary and childhood father of Jesus (Mt 1:16 – 24; 2:13 – 19); 3. a disciple of Jesus from Arimathea; he gave his tomb for Jesus' burial (Mt 27:57 – 61); 4. the original name of Barnabas (Ac 4:36).

Joshua — 1. the son of Nun (Nu 13:8); Moses' aide and later his successor (Dt 31:1 – 18); he led the Israelites across the

Jordan River into Canaan (Jos 3 – 4); was the commander in the conquest of Jericho (Jos 6), Ai (Jos 7 – 8), and a large part of Canaan (Jos 10 – 12); oversaw the dividing up of the promised land among the twelve tribes of Israel (Jos 13 – 22); 2. the high priest in Israel during the rebuilding of both the temple (Hag 1 – 2) and the altar (Ezr 3:2,8); also called Jeshua.

Josiah — godly king of Judah for thirty-one years shortly before the destruction of Jerusalem.

Judah — 1. Jacob's fourth son; 2. the tribe of Israel whose members were descendants of Judah; 3. a name for the southern kingdom after Judah and Benjamin separated from the northern ten tribes.

Ge 29:35 So she named him *J.*

Zec 10:4 From *J* will come the cornerstone,

Mt 2:6 Bethlehem, in the land of *J,*

Rev 5:5 See, the Lion of the tribe of *J,*

Judaism — the teachings of the Jewish religion.

Judas — 1. one of the twelve apostles (Lk 6:16; Ac 1:13); was probably also called Thaddaeus (Mt 10:3); 2. one of the brothers of Jesus (Mt 13:55); author of the last letter in the New Testament (Jude 1); 3. one of the twelve apostles, also called Iscariot; he betrayed Jesus (Mk 3:19; 14:10 – 50) and then hung himself (Mt 27:3 – 5).

Judea — the area of Palestine where the tribe of Judah lived after the exile.

Mk 10:1 into the region of *J* and across the Jordan.

Gal 1:22 to the churches of *J* that are in Christ.

judge — to decide if something is good or bad; to condemn.

Ps 9:8 and *j* the peoples with equity.

Mt 7:1 "Do not *j,* or you too will be judged.

2Ti 4:1 who will *j* the living and the dead,

judgment — 1. a decision or opinion; 2. a decision of guilt or innocence made by a judge in a court of law; punishment decided on by a court; 3. a decision from God, especially the final judgment when God will reward those who believe in him and condemn all others to hell.

Dt 1:17 of anyone, for *j* belongs to God.

Ps 119:66 Teach me knowledge and good *j,*

Isa 66:16 the LORD will execute *j*

Mt 5:21 who murders will be subject to *j.'*

Mt 12:36 have to give account on the day of *j*

Jn 5:22 but has entrusted all *j* to the Son,

Ro 14:10 stand before God's *j* seat.

2Co 5:10 appear before the *j* seat of Christ,

just — righteous, legally correct.

Ps 111:7 The works of his hands are faithful and *j*;

Rev 16:7 true and *j* are your judgments."

justice — fairness.

Isa 30:18 For the LORD is a God of *j.*

Isa 61:8 "For I, the LORD, love *j*;

Zec 7:9 'Administer true *j*; show mercy

Lk 11:42 you neglect *j* and the love of God.

justify (justification) — to erase someone's sins; to declare righteous.

Ac 13:39 a *j* you were not able to obtain

Ro 3:24 and all are *j* freely by his grace

Ro 4:25 and was raised to life for our *j.*

Ro 5:1 since we have been *j* through faith,

Gal 3:24 Christ came that we might be *j* by faith.

K

kind — considerate, loving.

Eph 4:32 Be *k* and compassionate

king — ruler over a country or kingdom; Christ is often referred to as the King of kings.

1Ki 22:3 The *k* of Israel had said

1 Ti 6:15 the *K* of *k* and Lord of lords,

kingdom — an area or group of people headed by a king; God's kingdom, or the kingdom of heaven, is made up of all believers.

Ex 19:6 you will be for me a *k* of priests

Mt 3:2 "Repent, for the *k* of heaven has come

Mt 5:3 for theirs is the *k* of heaven.

Mt 6:33 But seek first his *k* and his

Mt 16:19 the keys of the *k* of heaven;

Jn 18:36 "My *k* is not of this world.

1Co 15:24 hands over the *k* to God the Father

Rev 11:15 "The *k* of the world has become the *k*

Kish — the father of King Saul, the first king of Israel.

knowledge — possessing the facts, understanding.

Pr 1:7 of the LORD is the beginning of *k*,
Hos 4:6 are destroyed from lack of *k*.
1Co 8:1 *k* puffs up while love builds up.

L

Laban — the brother of Rebekah (Ge 24:29–51) and father of Rachel and Leah (Ge 29—31).

labor — 1. (*v.*) to work; 2. (*n.*) a task; 3. (*n.*) the time just before giving birth.

Ge 5:29 the *l* and painful toil of our hands
Ex 20:9 Six days you shall *l* and do all your work,
Jer 13:21 like that of a woman in *l*?

lack — 1. (*v.*) to stand in need of; 2. (*n.*) the state of being in need of something.

Ps 34:9 those who fear him *l* nothing.

lamb — a principal sacrificial animal in the Old Testament; since Jesus is the supreme sacrifice of God, he is called the "Lamb of God."

Isa 53:7 he was led like a *l* to the slaughter,
Jn 1:29 *L* of God, who takes away the sin
1Co 5:7 our Passover *l*, has been sacrificed.
Rev 5:6 Then I saw a *L*, looking

lament, lamentation — a cry of grief.

Ps 5:1 LORD, consider my *l*.

law — 1. God's rules, which help his people know what is right and wrong (the Ten Commandments are part of God's law); 2. (cap.) the first five books of the Bible, written by Moses.

Ps 1:2 and who meditates on his *l*
Ps 19:7 The *l* of the LORD is perfect,
Ps 119:97 Oh, how I love your *l*!
Mt 22:40 All the *L* and the Prophets hang
Ro 8:3 For what the *l* was powerless to do
Ro 13:10 love is the fulfillment of the *l*.
Gal 3:24 So the *l* was our guardian

Lazarus — 1. the poor man in one of Jesus' parables (Lk 16:19–31); 2. the brother of Mary and Martha; Jesus raised him from the dead (Jn 11:1–12:19).

Leah — the wife of Jacob; she had six sons and one daughter (Ge 29:16—30:21).

leprosy — a word used in the Bible for many different skin diseases and infections.

Mk 1:42 Immediately the *l* left him

Levite — a member of the tribe of Levi. The Levites took care of the temple. Only Levites could become priests, but not all Levites were priests.

lewd — indecent; wicked.

life — the total substance of a person's existence; can refer to both physical and spiritual existence.

Ge 2:7 into his nostrils the breath of *l*,
Jn 3:16 shall not perish but have eternal *l*.
Jn 11:25 "I am the resurrection and the *l*.
Jn 14:6 am the way and the truth and the *l*.
Ro 6:23 but the gift of God is eternal *l*

light — the form of energy that allows a person to see; in the Old Testament it symbolized life and blessing.

Ge 1:3 "Let there be *l*," and there was *l*.
Ps 27:1 The LORD is my *l* and my salvation
Ps 119:105 a *l* on my path.
Isa 9:2 have seen a great *l*;
Mt 5:16 let your *l* shine before others,
Jn 8:12 he said, "I am the *l* of the world.
1Jn 1:5 God is *l*; in him there is no

linen — cloth made from the fiber of flax plants.

live — to be alive; may refer to both physical and spiritual existence.

Ex 20:12 so that you may *l* long
Ro 1:17 "The righteous will *l* by faith."
2Co 5:7 For we *l* by faith, not by sight.
Php 1:21 to *l* is Christ and to die is gain.

loathe — to feel disgust or hatred.

Job 10:1 "I *l* my very life;

locusts — a type of grasshopper. When they settle in a grain field, orchard or other cultivated area, they can destroy the crop.

Lord — refers to God as the master. (See also LORD.)

Mt 3:3 'Prepare the way for the *L*,
Lk 2:9 glory of the *L* shone around them,
Ac 16:31 replied, "Believe in the *L* Jesus,
Ro 10:13 on the name of the *L* will be saved."
Php 2:11 acknowledge that Jesus Christ is *L*,
2Pe 1:16 the coming of our *L* Jesus Christ,
Rev 17:14 he is *L* of lords and King of kings
Rev 22:20 Come, *L* Jesus.

LORD (Yahweh) — the intimate and personal name of God; it emphasizes his role as

Israel's Redeemer and covenant Lord. (See also Lord.)

Ge 2:4 when the *L* God made the earth

Ex 20:2 "I am the *L* your God, who

Ps 23:1 The *L* is my shepherd, I lack

Ps 103:1 Praise the *L*, my soul;

Pr 1:7 The fear of the *L* is the beginning

Isa 6:3 "Holy, holy, holy is the *L* Almighty;

Isa 55:6 Seek the *L* while he may be found;

Lot — the nephew of Abraham (Ge 12:5). He chose to live in Sodom (Ge 13); Abraham pleaded with God for Lot's life when God was about to destroy Sodom (Ge 19:1 – 29).

lot — one of the ways used in Bible times to find out God's will about something. It is somewhat like drawing straws.

Mt 27:35 divided up his clothes by casting *l*.

Ac 1:26 Then they cast *l*, and the *l* fell

love — wanting good to come to another person; being concerned and willing to work for another person's benefit.

Ex 20:6 showing *l* to a thousand generations

Ps 23:6 Surely your goodness and *l* will follow

Ps 136:1 – 26 His *l* endures forever.

Mt 3:17 "This is my Son, whom I *l*;

Mt 5:44 *l* your enemies and pray

Mt 19:19 and '*l* your neighbor as yourself.' "

Jn 13:34 I give you: *L* one another.

Jn 15:13 Greater *l* has no one than this:

Ro 13:10 Therefore *l* is the fulfillment

Gal 5:22 But the fruit of the Spirit is *l*, joy,

Eph 1:4 – 5 In *l* he predestined us

1Jn 3:10 anyone who does not *l* their brother.

1Jn 3:16 This is how we know what *l* is:

1Jn 4:7 for *l* comes from God.

1Jn 4:10 This is *l*: not that we loved God,

1Jn 4:16 God is *l*.

Luke — a co-worker with Paul; he wrote the books of Luke and Acts (Col 4:14).

lust — a strong desire for something wrong.

Pr 6:25 Do not *l* in your heart

Ro 1:26 God gave them over to shameful *l*.

lyre — a small lap harp with three to twelve strings.

1Sa 18:10 David was playing the *l*,

M

Macedonia — a Roman province; the first part of Europe to receive Christianity.

Magi — men of Arabia and Persia who studied the stars. People thought they had the power to tell the meaning of dreams.

Mt 2:1 *M* from the east came to Jerusalem

maimed — crippled; having lost a part of one's body, such as an arm or leg.

majestic (majesty) — great and powerful.

Ex 15:6 was *m* in power.

Ps 8:1 how *m* is your name in all the earth!

Ps 111:3 Glorious and *m* are his deeds,

malice — hatred; wishing harm on someone else.

1Pe 2:1 rid yourselves of all *m*

Manasseh — 1. the older son of Joseph and the tribe descended from him (Ge 41:51; Nu 1:34); 2. one of the kings of Judah (2Ki 21:1).

manger — a feed box for cows or other animals.

Lk 2:7 placed him in a *m*, because there

maniac — an insane person; an overly enthusiastic person.

2Ki 9:20 he drives like a *m*."

manna — the special food God gave daily to the Israelites until they reached the promised land.

Ex 16:31 people of Israel called the bread *m*.

Jn 6:49 Your ancestors ate the *m*

Mark, John — the cousin of Barnabas (Col 4:10); a helper to Paul and Barnabas (Ac 13:5); later a co-worker with Barnabas (Ac 15:39) and then Paul (Phm 24); author of the second Gospel, according to early church tradition.

marriage — the joining together before God and other people of a man and a woman to form a new family.

Ge 29:26 younger daughter in *m* before the older

Mt 22:30 neither marry nor be given in *m*;

Heb 13:4 by all, and the *m* bed kept pure,

Martha — the sister of Mary and Lazarus, the man whom Jesus raised from the dead (Jn 11; 12:2).

marvelous — something that surprises, that fills one with wonder.

Ps 118:23 and it is *m* in our eyes.

Rev 15:3 "Great and *m* are your deeds,

Mary — 1. the mother of Jesus (Mt 1:16 – 25); 2. Mary Magdalene — a woman whom Jesus freed from demons (Lk 8:2), who was present at the cross (Mk 15:40) and who came on Easter morning to the tomb (Mt 27:61); 3. the sister of Martha and Lazarus; she washed Jesus' feet with expensive perfume (Jn 12:1 – 8).

master — one who rules over others.

Mt 6:24 "No one can serve two *m*.

Jn 13:16 no servant is greater than his *m*,

Matthew — a tax collector who became one of the twelve apostles (Mt 9:9 – 13); also called Levi (Mk 2:14 – 17).

mediator — one who makes peace between two people or two groups who are displeased and/or angry with each other. Jesus is the mediator between us and God.

1Ti 2:5 and one *m* between God and mankind,

Heb 9:15 For this reason Christ is the *m*

meditate — to think seriously and carefully.

Ps 1:2 who *m* on his law day and night.

Ps 119:15 I *m* on your precepts

medium — a person who can supposedly talk with the spirits of people who have died.

1Sa 28:7 "Find me a woman who is a *m*,

meek — patient; mild; gentle.

Ps 37:11 But the *m* will inherit the land

Mt 5:5 Blessed are the *m*,

Melchizedek — a priest and king of early Salem (Jerusalem); Jesus was said to be a priest like Melchizedek (Heb 5:6).

Mephibosheth — son of Jonathan and grandson of Saul; he lived out his life under King David's protection (2Sa 9:11).

mercy — kindness and forgiveness, especially when given to a person who doesn't deserve it.

Mic 6:8 To act justly and to love *m*

Ro 9:15 "I will have *m* on whom I have *m*,

1Pe 1:3 In his great *m* he has given us new

Messiah — the "Anointed One"; Christ; the one the Jews expected to come and be their king.

Lk 9:20 Peter answered, "God's *M*."

Jn 1:41 "We have found the *M*"

Methuselah — a man in early Bible times who lived 969 years (Ge 5:27).

Michal — daughter of Saul, wife of David, both of whom were kings of Israel.

midwives — women who helped with the birth of a baby.

Ex 1:17 The *m*, however, feared God

millstone — one of a pair of stones used to crush grain for flour.

Lk 17:2 sea with a *m* tied around their neck

minister — 1. (*v.*) to serve; to give care or attention to; 2. (*n.*) one who serves others as God directs.

2Co 3:6 as *m* of a new covenant

1Ti 4:6 you will be a good *m*

miracle — an unusual event, one that goes against the normal laws of nature. Miracles are done by the power of God.

Ps 77:14 You are the God who performs *m*;

Mk 6:2 What are these remarkable *m* he is

Ac 2:22 accredited by God to you by *m*,

Heb 2:4 it by signs, wonders and various *m*,

Miriam — the sister of Moses and Aaron (Nu 26:59); led the Israelites in praising God in dance and song after he had parted the waters of the Red Sea (Ex 15:20 – 21); later temporarily struck with leprosy because she criticized Moses (Nu 12).

Moab — 1. a son of Lot whose descendants became bitter enemies of the Israelites; 2. the land occupied by the Moabites, to the east of the Dead Sea.

money — a medium of exchange.

Ecc 5:10 Whoever loves *m* never has

Mt 6:24 You cannot serve both God and *m*.

1Co 16:2 set aside a sum of *m* in keeping

1Ti 6:10 For the love of *m* is a root

Mordecai — cousin of Esther, queen of Persia; he and Esther saved the Jews from a plot to put them all to death.

mortal — human; able to die.

Ps 9:20 the nations know they are only *m*.

Ps 103:15 The life of *m* is like grass,

1Co 15:53 and the *m* with immortality,

Moses — the leader of Israel in the exodus out of Egypt, ending in their passing through the Red Sea (Ex 12 – 14). He received the law of God at Sinai (Ex 19 – 23) and gave it to the people of Israel. Moses was allowed to view the land of Canaan from the top of Mount Nebo, but he died without entering it (Nu 20:1 – 13; Dt 34:5 – 12).

mother — the female parent.

Ge 2:24 and *m* and is united to his wife,

Dt 5:16 "Honor your father and your *m*,

mourn — to feel deep sorrow; to grieve.

Mt 5:4 Blessed are those who *m*,

murder — to kill someone illegally.

Ex 20:13 "You shall not *m*.

muster — to gather together, especially to gather soldiers for war.

mute — unable to speak.

Mt 9:33 the man who had been *m* spoke.

myrrh — the sweet-smelling sap of the myrrh bush. It was used to make the sacred anointing oil.

Mt 2:11 gifts of gold, frankincense and *m*.

N

Nabal — a rich sheepherder in Judah who insulted David; when David planned to take revenge, Nabal's wife Abigail brought gifts to calm David; Nabal died shortly afterwards, and Abigail married David (1Sa 25:1 – 42).

Naboth — owner of a vineyard that King Ahab wanted and gained by having Naboth accused of blasphemy and stoned (1Ki 21:1 – 29).

Naomi — the mother-in-law of Ruth (Ru 1); she advised Ruth to seek marriage with Boaz (Ru 2 – 4).

Naphtali — a son of Jacob and father of the tribe of Naphtali (Nu 1:42 – 43).

nard — an expensive, pleasant-smelling oil from the spikenard, a plant that grew in India.

Mk 14:3 perfume, made of pure *n*.

Nathan — the prophet of God who exposed David's sin with Bathsheba, causing David to repent (2Sa 12:1 – 25).

Nathanael — one of the twelve apostles (Jn 1:45 – 49); was probably also called Bartholomew (Mt 10:3).

Nazarene — a person who lived in or came from the town of Nazareth in Galilee.

Mk 16:6 looking for Jesus the *N*,

Nazirite — a person who separated himself or herself by taking a vow to do special work for God. This included a promise not to cut one's hair and not to drink wine.

Jdg 16:17 I have been a *N* dedicated to God

Nebuchadnezzar — king of Babylon who took Judah into captivity.

Negev — the desert region south of Judea.

Ge 24:62 for he was living in the *N*.

Nehemiah — the Jewish cupbearer of King Artaxerxes of Persia (Ne 2:1); while in Jerusalem rebuilt the walls of the city (Ne 2 — 6) and with Ezra reestablished the worship of God there after the exile in Babylon (Ne 8).

neighbor — 1. someone who lives nearby; 2. any fellow human being.

Lev 19:18 but love your *n* as yourself.

Lk 10:36 of these three do you think was a *n*

Nicodemus — a Pharisee who visited Jesus at night (Jn 3) and learned about being born again.

Nile — the primary river in Egypt.

Nineveh — the city to which Jonah was sent to preach (Jnh 1:2); the ancient capital of Assyria.

Noah — "a righteous man" in early Bible times; he built an ark, as God commanded him (Ge 6 – 8). God made a covenant with him never again to cover the entire earth with a flood (Ge 9).

nullify — to make of no value; to make unimportant.

Mk 7:13 Thus you *n* the word of God

O

oath — a promise in which one asks God to witness that something is true.

Dt 10:20 take your *o* in his name.

obey (obedience) — to do as asked; to follow someone's commands or wishes.

Dt 6:3 careful to *o* so that it may go well

1Sa 15:22 To *o* is better than sacrifice,

Jn 14:23 who loves me will *o* my teaching.

Ac 5:29 "We must *o* God rather than human

Eph 6:1 Children, *o* your parents in the Lord,

offense — an act that makes someone angry by what was done.

offering — 1. something given to God as an act of worship; 2. the sacrifice of an animal to make the relationship between God and human beings right again. In the Old Testament, animals and grains were regularly used as offerings in an attempt to bring the people closer to God.

Ge 22:8 provide the lamb for the burnt *o*,

Isa 53:10 the LORD makes his life an *o*

Mk 12:33 is more important than all
burnt *o*

Eph 5:2 as a fragrant *o* and sacrifice to
God.

offspring—children.

Ge 3:15 and between your *o* and hers;

Ge 12:7 "To your *o* I will give this land."

oil—almost always refers to olive oil; used
to anoint someone for a physical benefit or
to set someone apart for service.

2Ki 9:6 prophet poured the *o* on Jehu's
head

Lk 7:46 You did not put *o* on my head,

olive—a tree whose fruit gives olive oil,
which was used for varied purposes.

oppress—to control people unfairly and
cruelly by the use of one's power.

Isa 53:7 He was *o* and afflicted,

Zec 7:10 Do not *o* the widow

oracle—1. a saying or answer; 2. the word
of the Lord.

ordain—1. to set apart for a specific office
or duty; 2. to order or command.

Ps 111:9 he *o* his covenant forever

ordinance—1. an official law; 2. a law
made or commanded by God.

1Sa 30:25 a statute and *o* for Israel

ornate—elaborately decorated or adorned.

Ge 37:3 he made an *o* robe for him.

overseer—one of the terms used for leaders in the early church.

Ac 20:28 the Holy Spirit has made you *o*.

1Ti 3:2 Now the *o* is to be above
reproach,

oxen—strong animals that were used in
various ways in farming communities.

P

pagan—a person who does not worship
God, especially someone who worships
idols.

1Pe 2:12 such good lives among the
p that,

papyrus—1. a large water plant, similar to
the reed, which grows in marshes and
lakes. Moses' mother put him in a basket
made from papyrus (Ex 2:3); 2. a paper
made from this plant.

parable—a story that tells a special lesson
or truth. Jesus told many parables.

paralyzed—unable to move certain parts
of one's body.

Mk 2:3 bringing to him a *p* man,

parents—fathers and mothers.

Pr 17:6 and *p* are the pride of their
children.

Eph 6:1 Children, obey your *p* in the Lord,

Col 3:20 obey your *p* in everything,

Passover—an annual holiday that still today reminds the Jewish people of how God
freed them from slavery in Egypt. The Lord
"passed over" the homes marked with the
blood of a lamb on their doorframes, but he
killed all the other firstborn in Egypt.

Ex 12:11 Eat it in haste; it is the LORD's *P*.

Passover lamb—the lamb killed on the
Passover as a sacrifice. Jesus is our Passover
lamb, because he was sacrificed for our deliverance from sin, in the same way a lamb
was sacrificed when the Israelites were delivered from Egypt.

1Co 5:7 our *P* lamb, has been sacrificed.

pasture—a plot or section of grassy land
used for grazing cattle.

patient (patience)—able to put up with
problems or pain without complaining or
becoming angry.

Ro 12:12 Be joyful in hope, *p* in affliction,

1Co 13:4 Love is *p*, love is kind.

Col 3:12 kindness, humility, gentleness
and *p*.

patriarch—the father and ruler of a family;
the head of a tribe.

Paul—a Pharisee from Tarsus (Ac 9:11);
named Saul at birth (Ac 13:9). Jesus appeared to him on the road to Damascus (Ac
9:4–9), and he became a powerful apostle
(Gal 1). His writings make up a large part of
the New Testament, ranging from intricate
theology to passionate letters to struggling
churches.

peace—freedom from disturbance; calm.

Isa 9:6 Everlasting Father, Prince of *P*.

Lk 2:14 on earth *p* to those on whom his

Jn 14:27 *P* I leave with you; my *p*

Ro 5:1 we have *p* with God

Gal 5:22 joy, *p*, forbearance, kindness,

Pentecost—a Jewish feast celebrated fifty
days after the Passover. Today the Christian
church celebrates Pentecost because it was
the day the Holy Spirit came to dwell with
Christ's followers (Ac 2:1–4).

people—a collective group.

2Ch 7:14 if my *p*, who are called by my
name,

1Pe 2:9 you are a chosen *p*,

perfect — flawless; without defect.

Mt 5:48 Be *p*, therefore, as your heavenly

perish — to spoil; to be destroyed.

Ps 102:26 They will *p*, but you remain;

persecute (persecution) — to continually treat someone cruelly and unfairly, even though that person has done nothing wrong. The early Christians were persecuted for believing in Jesus as the Son of God.

Jn 15:20 they *p* me, they will *p* you

Ac 26:14 'Saul, Saul, why do you *p* me?

Ro 12:14 Bless those who *p* you; bless

persevere (perseverance) — to refuse to give up; to keep on trying; to continue in one's actions or beliefs in spite of problems.

Ro 5:3 know that suffering produces *p*;

Heb 10:36 You need to *p* so that

Heb 12:1 let us run with *p* the race

Persia — ancient geographical area and kingdom located north of the Persian Gulf.

pervert — to use wrongly; to turn from what is right.

pestilence — a plague; a disease that spreads quickly and kills many people.

Ps 91:3 snare and from the deadly *p*.

Peter — one of the twelve apostles; the brother of Andrew; also called Simon (Lk 6:14) and Cephas (Jn 1:42); he denied Jesus three times (Mk 14:66–72) but became a bold evangelist. He wrote the books of 1 and 2 Peter.

petition — to make a formal request.

pharaoh — the title given to the ruler of Egypt.

Pharisees — a group of Jews who obeyed very strictly both God's laws and all their own rules about God's laws.

Mt 5:20 surpasses that of the *P*

Philip — 1. one of the twelve apostles (Mt 10:3); 2. a deacon (Ac 6:1–7) and evangelist in Samaria; he witnessed to an Ethiopian (Ac 8:4–40).

Philistines — enemies of the Israelites throughout much of Old Testament history; they were especially powerful during the reigns of Saul and David.

Pilate — the governor of Judea who questioned Jesus (Lk 22:66–23:25) and then sent him to Herod (Lk 23:6–12). Pilate finally consented to Jesus' crucifixion when the crowds chose Barabbas rather than Jesus to be released (Lk 23:13–25).

pity — a sympathy or sorrow for the suffering of another.

Mk 9:22 take *p* on us and help us."

plague — 1. a disease that kills many people, such as the plague of boils; 2. an event that causes much suffering or loss, such as the plague of locusts.

plead — to appeal earnestly; to beg.

Job 16:21 he *p* with God as one *p* for a friend.

pledge — a binding promise or agreement.

1Ti 5:12 they have broken their first *p*.

plot — to plan, usually secretly; to scheme.

Ps 83:5 With one mind they *p* together;

plowshare — the pointed part of the plow; it cuts into the soil to make rows.

Mic 4:3 will beat their swords into *p*

plunder — 1. (*v.*) to loot or rob during a war; 2. (*n.*) property taken by plundering.

pomegranate — a reddish fruit about the size of an orange. It has many seeds and a juicy pulp.

poor — those who have little money.

Dt 15:4 there need be no *p* people

Isa 61:1 me to proclaim good news to the *p*.

Mt 26:11 The *p* you will always have

1Co 13:3 If I give all I possess to the *p*

2Co 8:9 yet for your sake he became *p*,

portico — a porch, usually at the front of a building.

2Ch 3:4 The *p* at the front of the temple

praise — 1. (*v.*) to glorify; to say good things about someone or something; 2. (*n.*) approval; worship.

Ex 15:2 He is my God, and I will *p* him,

Ps 119:175 Let me live that I may *p* you,

Eph 1:12 might be for the *p* of his glory.

pray — to talk with God.

2Ch 7:14 will humble themselves and *p*

Mt 6:5 "And when you *p*, do not be like

Ro 8:26 do not know what we ought to *p*

1Th 5:16–17 Rejoice always, *p* continually,

preach — to tell the message of the gospel in public; to deliver a sermon.

Mt 11:1 and *p* in the towns of Galilee.

Ro 10:15 how can they *p* unless they are sent?

precept — command; law; rule.

Ps 19:8 The *p* of the LORD are right,

Ps 119:69 I keep your *p* with all my heart.

precious — valuable; of great worth.

Ps 139:17 How *p* to me are your thoughts,

predestine — to decide or decree ahead of time.

Ro 8:30 And those he *p*, he also called;

Eph 1:5 he *p* us for adoption

pregnant — carrying an unborn child within a woman's body.

Lk 1:24 his wife Elizabeth became *p*

prevail — to triumph or succeed.

pride — 1. (negative) the attitude that one is better than others; 2. (positive) a healthy self-respect or sense of satisfaction.

Pr 16:18 *P* goes before destruction,

Gal 6:4 they can take *p* in themselves

priest (priesthood) — a Levite who offered sacrifices and prayers to God for the people.

1Pe 2:9 you are a chosen people, a royal *p*,

prince — a male member of a royal family.

prison — a building where people are held, usually for committing a crime.

proclaim — to announce or declare.

1Ch 16:23 *p* his salvation day after day.

Ps 19:1 the skies *p* the work of his hands.

Isa 61:1 to *p* good news to the poor.

1Co 11:26 you *p* the Lord's death

profane — to make a holy thing impure by treating it with disrespect or irreverence.

Lev 22:32 Do not *p* my holy name,

prophecy — a message from God that a prophet brings to the people.

1Co 13:8 where there are *p*, they will cease;

2Pe 1:20 you must understand that no *p*

prophesy — to give the message of God to the people.

Joel 2:28 Your sons and daughters will *p*,

1Co 14:39 brothers and sisters, be eager to *p*,

prophet — a person who receives messages from God to tell to his people. A prophet is called by God to speak for him.

Dt 18:18 up for them a *p* like you

Lk 24:25 believe all that the *p* have spoken!

Ac 10:43 All the *p* testify about him that

Heb 1:1 through the *p* at many times

prosper — to succeed; achieve economic success.

Pr 11:25 A generous person will *p*;

prostitute — a person who lets someone use his or her body for sexual relations in exchange for money.

Jos 2:1 house of a *p* named Rahab

prostrate — lying facedown on the ground.

proud — to have pride.

Ro 12:16 Do not be *p*, but be willing

Jas 4:6 "God opposes the *p*

proverbs — 1. wise sayings; 2. (Proverbs) a book of the Bible that contains many wise sayings.

1Ki 4:32 He spoke three thousand *p*

provoke — to make angry; to cause trouble.

prudent — wise.

Pr 19:14 a *p* wife is from the LORD.

psalms — 1. poetry written to praise God; 2. (Psalms) a book of the Bible that contains many psalms.

Eph 5:19 speaking to one another with *p*,

punish (punishment) — to cause someone to suffer for doing wrong.

Ge 4:13 "My *p* is more than I can bear.

Ex 20:5 jealous God, *p* the children for the sin

pure — perfectly free from fault or blemish.

Ps 51:10 Create in me a *p* heart, O God,

purify — to make pure or clean.

1Jn 1:7 of Jesus, his Son, *p* us from all sin.

1Jn 1:9 and *p* us from all unrighteousness.

Purim — an annual Jewish holiday celebrating Queen Esther's rescue of the Jews when Haman plotted to destroy them.

pursue — 1. to follow in order to overtake; to chase; 2. to seek a goal.

Lev 26:7 You will *p* your enemies,

1Ti 6:11 and *p* righteousness, godliness,

Q

quail — a small spotted bird similar to the partridge; God provided quail and manna to the Israelites when they wandered in the wilderness.

Nu 11:32 people went out and gathered *q*.

quake — 1. (*v.*) to shake or tremble; 2. (*n.*) an earthquake.

Ps 75:3 the earth and all its people *q*,

Rev 16:18 so tremendous was the *q*.

queen — 1. the female ruler of a country; 2. the wife of a king.

R

Rabbi — a teacher of Jewish law.

Rachel — the daughter of Laban (Ge 29:16); she became Jacob's wife (Ge 29:28) and bore him two sons, Joseph and Benjamin (Ge 30:22 – 24; 35:16 – 24).

rage — a fit of anger.

Eph 4:31 Get rid of all bitterness, r

ram — a male sheep.

ransom — the price paid to get back a person who is held as a slave. Because people are slaves of sin, a ransom had to be paid, which was the death of the sinless one, Jesus.

Mt 20:28 and to give his life as a r for many."

Heb 9:15 as a r to set them free

reap — 1. to cut down grain at harvest time; to gather a crop together; 2. to get as a result or reward.

Gal 6:7 A man r what he sows.

Rebekah — Isaac's wife (Ge 24); the mother of Esau and Jacob (Ge 25:19 - 26). With her encouragement, Jacob tricked his father into giving him the blessing that belonged to Esau (Ge 27:1 - 17).

rebel — 1. (v.) to disobey and turn against those in authority; 2. (n.) a person who disobeys and flaunts authority.

Ro 13:2 whoever r against the authority

rebuke — to scold sharply.

2Ti 4:2 correct, r and encourage

Rev 3:19 Those whom I love I r

reconcile (reconciliation) — to return to friendship after a quarrel; human beings are "reconciled" to God through Christ.

Mt 5:24 First go and be r to them;

Ro 5:10 we were r to him through the death

2Co 5:18 and gave us the ministry of r:

redeem (redemption) — 1. to free from evil by paying a price (Gal 3:13); 2. to buy back.

Ex 21:30 the owner may r his life

Gal 3:13 Christ r us from the curse

Eph 1:7 In him we have r through his blood,

Col 1:14 in whom we have r, the forgiveness

Red Sea — the body of water the Israelites crossed in a miraculous way when they were escaping from slavery in Egypt.

refuge — a place of shelter and safety.

Ps 46:1 God is our r and strength,

regard — to pay attention to.

Ps 41:1 Blessed are those who have r for the weak;

regulations — rules dealing with procedure or ceremony.

Rehoboam — the son of Solomon; he be-

came king after his father's death (1Ki 11:43). Because of his harsh treatment of the people, Israel was divided into two kingdoms (1Ki 12:1 - 24; 14:21 - 31).

reign — the time during which a king or other official rules.

rejoice — to express joy or gladness.

Ps 118:24 let us r today be glad.

Lk 1:47 my spirit r in God my Savior,

Php 4:4 R in the Lord always.

remnant — a small part remaining; a small surviving group.

Isa 10:21 A r will return,

repent (repentance) — to turn away from sin; to be sorry for what one has done and to promise not to do it again.

Mt 4:17 "R, for the kingdom of heaven

Lk 3:8 Produce fruit in keeping with r.

Ac 2:38 Peter replied, "R and be baptized,

reproach — 1. (v.) to blame or accuse; 2. (n.) something for which one can be blamed or criticized.

Job 27:6 my conscience will not r me

require (requirement) — to demand as necessary.

1Ki 8:31 is r to take an oath

Zec 3:7 obedience to me and keep my r,

rescue — to save or deliver.

Ps 140:1 R me, LORD from evildoers;

respect — to look up to or hold in high esteem.

1Pe 2:17 Show proper r to everyone,

restitution — to restore or pay back for damage, loss or injury.

Nu 5:7 must make full r for the wrong

restore — to bring back; to return something to its former condition.

Ps 51:12 R to me the joy of your salvation

Ac 3:21 time comes for God to r everything,

resurrection — the act of coming back to life after being dead.

Jn 11:25 Jesus said to her, "I am the r

Ro 1:4 in power by his r from the dead:

1Co 15:12 some of you say that there is no r

retribution — punishment for doing wrong.

Jer 51:56 For the LORD is a God of r;

Reuben — oldest son of Jacob and founder of the tribe of the same name.

revelation — the act of making known or telling about.

Gal 1:12 I received it by *r* from Jesus Christ.

Rev 1:1 *r* from Jesus Christ, which God gave

revenge — to hurt or punish a person who has wronged you; to get back at someone who has hurt you.

Lev 19:18 " 'Do not seek *r* or bear a grudge

Ro 12:19 Do not take *r*, my dear friends,

reverence (revere) — a deep respect, honor and awe.

Ps 5:7 in *r* I bow down

Col 3:22 of heart and *r* for the Lord.

reward — 1. (*v.*) to repay with good for something someone has done; 2. (*n.*) the gift one receives for good behavior or character.

Ps 127:3 offspring a *r* from him.

Jer 17:10 to *r* each person according to

Mt 5:12 because great is your *r* in heaven,

Mt 6:5 they have received their *r* in full.

righteous (righteousness) — being in a right relationship to God; not guilty before God.

Isa 64:6 and all our *r* acts are like filthy rags;

Ro 3:10 "There is no one *r*, not even one;

Rome — 1. the empire that controlled much of the known world at the time of Christ; 2. the capital city of the Roman Empire, located in Italy.

royal — of or belonging to the ruler of a country and his family.

Ruth — a Moabite widow who went with her mother-in-law Naomi to Bethlehem (Ru 1). There she gathered the gleanings from the field of Boaz (Ru 2), whom she later married (Ru 3:1 – 4:12). She was an ancestor of David (Ru 4:13 – 22) and of Jesus (Mt 1:5).

ruthless — merciless; cruel.

Ps 54:3 *r* people are trying to kill me

Hab 1:6 that *r* and impetuous people,

S

Sabbath — the seventh day of the week; the Jewish day of rest and worship. It extended from Friday sunset until Saturday sunset.

Ex 20:8 "Remember the *S* day

sackcloth — a rough cloth, usually woven from goats' hair. Clothing made of sackcloth was worn as a sign of mourning for the dead or as a sign that a person was sorry for his or her sins.

sacred — holy; set apart for God in a special way.

1Co 3:17 God's temple is *s*,

sacrifice — 1. (*v.*) to offer something as a gift to God; 2. (*n.*) an offering given to God. In the Old Testament God commanded the people to pay for their sins by sacrificing the blood of cattle, lambs, goats, doves or pigeons. These sacrifices were pictures of Jesus' coming as a once-for-all sacrifice for sinners.

Ex 12:27 'It is the Passover *s* to the LORD,

1Sa 15:22 To obey is better than *s*,

Ro 12:1 to offer your bodies as a living *s*,

Heb 9:28 so Christ was *s* once

1Jn 2:2 He is the atoning *s* for our sins,

Sadducees — a group of Jewish leaders, many of them priests. Unlike the Pharisees, the Sadducees did not believe in a resurrection of the dead, but they agreed with the Pharisees in their hatred of Jesus.

Mk 12:18 *S*, who say there is no resurrection,

salvation — deliverance from the guilt and power of sin. By his death and resurrection, Jesus brings salvation to people who believe in him.

Ps 27:1 The LORD is my light and my *s*

Lk 2:30 For my eyes have seen your *s*,

Ac 4:12 *S* is found in no one else,

2Co 7:10 brings repentance that leads to *s*

Php 2:12 to work out your *s* with fear

Heb 2:3 escape if we ignore so great a *s*?

Samaritan — a person who lived in or came from Samaria. Because the Samaritans were only partly Jewish and worshiped God differently from the Jews, Jews from Judea and Galilee hated the Samaritans. They would go out of their way to travel around Samaria (Lk 10:30 – 37).

Samson — an Israelite judge who was known for his great strength. He was betrayed by Delilah but in the end was used by God to punish the Philistines (Jdg 16).

Samuel — often called the last of Israel's judges and the first of Israel's prophets (see also Heb 11:32). His birth was earnestly prayed for by his mother Hannah (1Sa 1:10 – 18), and when he was old enough, she brought him to the temple and he was dedicated to the Lord (1Sa 1:21 – 28). There he was raised by Eli (1Sa 2:11; 18 – 26) and was called to be a prophet (1Sa 3).

sanctify (sanctification) — to make holy; sanctification is the ongoing work of the Holy Spirit in the hearts of believers.

Ro 15:16 to God, *s* by the Holy Spirit.

1Th 5:23 *s* you through and through.

2Th 2:13 through the *s* work of the Spirit

sanctuary — a place where God is worshiped; a holy place.

Ps 150:1 Praise God in his *s*;

Sanhedrin — the ruling council of the Jews in Jesus' time. It was made up of seventy men, and the leader was the high priest. The Sanhedrin could decide whether someone was innocent or guilty of breaking a Jewish law, but it could not put anyone to death without the permission of the Roman governor.

Mk 14:55 the whole *S* were looking for evidence

Sarah — the wife of Abraham and mother of Isaac; first called Sarai (Ge 11:29 – 31). God promised her that, though she had been barren throughout her life, she would give birth to a son in her old age (Ge 17:15 – 21; 18:10 – 15).

Satan — the devil; the leader of the fallen spirits; the most powerful enemy of God and humans.

Mk 4:15 *S* comes and takes away the word

2Co 11:14 for *S* himself masquerades

Rev 12:9 serpent called the devil, or *S*,

satisfy — 1. to please, to make happy; 2. to fulfill a condition.

Ps 103:5 who *s* your desires with good things

satrap — the governor of a province in ancient Persia.

Saul — 1. the first king of Israel (1Sa 9 – 10). He was anointed by Samuel but was later rejected by God because of disobedience; David was chosen to be his successor; 2. see Paul.

saved — 1. (*v.*) rescued from danger; 2. (*n.*) people who acknowledge that by Jesus' death they have been rescued from the punishment of death that their sins deserve.

Ro 10:13 on the name of the Lord will be *s*."

Eph 2:8 For it is by grace you have been *s*,

Savior — a name for Jesus that means he saves his people from sin.

Lk 1:47 and my spirit rejoices in God my *S*,

1Ti 4:10 who is the *S* of all people,

1Jn 4:14 Son to be the *S* of the world.

scarlet — the color bright red.

scepter — a rod or stick held by a king or queen as a sign of royal power and authority.

Ge 49:10 The *s* will not depart from Judah,

scoff — to mock or sneer at.

Ps 2:4 the Lord *s* at them.

scorn — to despise, to reject with anger or contempt.

Ps 69:20 *S* has broken my heart

scorpion — a spider-like animal with a poisonous stinger at the end of its tail.

scoundrel — a mean, worthless person; a villain.

Pr 16:27 A *s* plots evil,

scourge — to whip.

2Ch 10:11 My father *s* you with whips;

scribe — a person with the important task of copying letters, books and legal papers.

Scripture — all or part of the Bible. When the Bible uses this word it means the Old Testament, since the New Testament had not yet been written. Today we call the Old and New Testaments the Bible or Scripture.

Jn 10:35 and *S* cannot be set aside

2Ti 3:16 All *S* is God-breathed

2Pe 1:20 that no prophecy of *S* came about

scroll — a book made of a long piece of leather or paper that was rolled around a stick at both ends.

Jos 18:9 They wrote its description on a *s*,

seal — 1. a tool with a design raised on it or cut into it; 2. the mark made by pressing this tool onto wax, paper or other soft material. A seal was used to close a letter or legal paper or to prove the authority of the paper.

2Co 1:22 set his *s* of ownership on us,

Rev 5:2 "Who is worthy to break the *s*

sect — a group of people who hold one or more beliefs in common; especially, a small religious group that has separated from a larger group.

seer — a prophet; a person who, with God's help, can see what will happen in the future.

1Sa 9:19 "I am the *s*," Samuel replied.

self-control — the ability to control one's own actions and feelings.

Gal 5:23 gentleness and *s*.

2Pe 1:6 and to knowledge, *s*; and to *s*,

selfish — centered on oneself; not interested in others.

Php 2:3 Do nothing out of *s* ambition

Sennacherib — an Assyrian king who raided Judah during the time of Hezekiah.

sexual immorality — using sex in ways God says are wrong.

1Co 6:13 body, however, is not meant for *s*,

1Th 4:3 that you should avoid *s*;

shame — a painful emotion caused by an awareness of guilt or shortcoming.

Pr 19:26 a child who brings *s* and disgrace.

1Co 15:34 I say this to your *s*.

sheep — the animal most often mentioned in Scripture, probably because it was the animal most often raised in Bible times; used for meat, for cloth, and for religious sacrifice.

Isa 53:6 We all, like *s*, have gone astray,

shekel — a specific weight of silver, used as money.

Shem — one of the three sons of Noah (Ge 5:32). He, along with his brother Japheth, covered his father when he was naked (Ge 9:21 – 31). Abraham was one of his descendants (Ge 11:10 – 32).

shepherd — someone who takes care of a flock of sheep. It is often used in the Bible as a figure of speech for anyone who cares for a group of people.

Ps 23:1 The LORD is my *s*, I lack nothing.

Jer 31:10 will watch over his flock like a *s*.'

Jn 10:11 The good *s* lays down his life

Ac 20:28 Be *s* of the church of God,

shield — a piece of defensive armor, usually carried on the arm; often a figure of speech in the Bible used to describe God's protection of his people.

Ps 7:10 My *s* is God Most High,

shrine — a dwelling for a god.

sickle — a tool with a long, curved blade and a short handle, used for cutting grain.

siege — see besiege.

signet — a ring with a design on it. The design was stamped in wax to seal a letter or legal paper. Signet rings were usually worn by people in authority.

Silas — a member of the church in Jerusalem; he traveled with Paul.

Simon — 1. see Peter; 2. one of the twelve apostles; also called the Zealot (Mt 10:4; Ac 1:13); 3. a sorcerer in Samaria who had great influence on the Samaritan people during the early days of the church; he was severely rebuked by Peter (Ac 8:9 – 24) for attempting to buy the power of the Holy Spirit.

sin — 1. (*v.*) to break the law of God; 2. (*n.*) the act of not doing what God wants.

Nu 32:23 be sure that your *s* will find you

Ps 51:2 and cleanse me from my *s*.

Ps 119:11 that I might not *s* against you.

Isa 1:18 "Though your *s* are like scarlet,

Mt 1:21 he will save his people from their *s*."

Lk 11:4 Forgive us our *s*,

Jn 1:29 who takes away the *s* of the world!

Ro 3:23 for all have *s* and fall short

Ro 6:23 For the wages of *s* is death,

2Co 5:21 God made him who had no *s* to be *s*

1Jn 1:9 If we confess our *s*, he is faithful

Sinai, Mount — the mountain where Moses received the Ten Commandments (Ex 19 — 20).

sinner — a person who breaks the law of God.

Ps 1:1 or stand in the way that *s* take

Mt 9:13 come to call the righteous, but *s*."

Lk 15:7 in heaven over one *s* who repents

Lk 18:13 'God, have mercy on me, a *s*.'

Ro 5:8 While we were still *s*, Christ died

slander — 1. (*v.*) saying untrue things about another person in order to hurt him or her; 2. (*n.*) false charges or misrepresentations about another person.

Lev 19:16 " 'Do not go about spreading *s*

Titus 3:2 to *s* no one, to be peaceable

slaughter — 1. the butchering of livestock for food; 2. the killing of great numbers of human beings, as in a battle.

slave — 1. a person who is owned by another; 2. a person who is dominated or controlled by an outside force.

Ro 7:14 I am unspiritual, sold as a *s* to sin.

Gal 3:28 *s* nor free, male nor female,

slay, slain — to kill violently or in great numbers.

sluggard — a lazy person.

Pr 19:24 A *s* buries his hand in the dish;

slumber — to sleep.

snare — a trap; something risky that tempts or endangers a person.

snatch — to grab suddenly, often without permission or right.

Sodom and Gomorrah — the two cities destroyed by God because the people were so wicked.

Ge 19:24 rained down burning sulfur on S

Solomon — the son of David and Bathsheba (2Sa 12:24). He became king of Israel after David died (1Ki 1). He asked God for wisdom and was given it (1Ki 3), and he built the temple (1Ki 5 – 7). His many foreign wives turned his heart away from God (1Ki 11:1 – 13).

son — a male descendant.

Pr 10:1 A wise *s* brings joy to his father,

Joel 2:28 Your *s* and daughters will prophesy,

2Co 6:18 you will be my *s* and daughters,

Heb 2:10 many *s* and daughters to glory,

1Jn 4:9 only *S* into the world that we might

Son of Man — a title Jesus used for himself to show his humanity as distinct from his divinity. It was also a reference to the Messiah prophesied about in Daniel 7:13.

Mt 20:18 and the *S* will be delivered

Mk 14:62 you will see the *S* sitting

Lk 19:10 For the *S* came to seek

Jn 3:14 so the *S* must be lifted up,

sorcery — the use of magic and supernatural powers that are evil; witchcraft.

Dt 18:10 practices divination or *s*,

soul — the spiritual part of a person; the part of a person that does not die.

Dt 6:5 with all your *s* and with all your

Ps 23:3 he refreshes my *s*.

Mt 10:28 kill the body but cannot kill the *s*.

Mt 11:29 and you will find rest for your *s*.

Mt 16:26 yet forfeit their *s*? Or what can

Mt 22:37 with all your *s* and with all your

sovereign — having authority over everything; often used in Scripture as a descriptive title for God, "Sovereign LORD."

sow — to plant seeds. In Jesus' time seeds were sown by scattering them by hand over the ground.

Job 4:8 and those who *s* trouble reap it.

Mk 4:3 A farmer went out to *s* his seed.

Gal 6:7 A man reaps what he *s*.

spear — a weapon with a long handle and a sharp point, usually thrown.

spirit — 1. the part of a person that is not the body; the soul; 2. a being who does not have a body; 3. (cap.) see Holy Spirit.

Ps 31:5 Into your hands I commit my *s*;

Eze 36:26 you a new heart and put a new *s*

Mt 5:3 "Blessed are the poor in *s*,

Mt 26:41 *s* is willing, but the flesh is weak."

1Jn 4:1 Dear friends, do not believe every *s*,

splendor — something magnificent or splendid.

spoils — booty or plunder taken from an enemy in war.

springs — a source of water coming up from the ground.

Dt 8:7 streams, and deep *s* gushing out

Rev 7:17 lead them to *s* of living water.

staff — a stick used to lean on; a rod used by a shepherd.

Ps 23:4 your rod and your *s*,

starry hosts — the stars and other heavenly bodies.

2Ki 21:3 He bowed down to all the *s*

statutes — established rules or laws.

Ps 19:7 *s* of the LORD are trustworthy,

steadfast — settled; not changing or wavering.

Ps 51:10 and renew a *s* spirit within me.

steal — to rob; to take what belongs to someone else.

Ex 20:15 "You shall not *s*.

Eph 4:28 must *s* no longer,

stench — a terrible smell.

Stephen — one of the first seven men to serve the Jerusalem church (Ac 6:5); he became the first Christian martyr (Ac 7:60).

stiff-necked — stubborn.

Ac 7:51 "You *s* people!

stone — to kill or to try to kill someone by throwing rocks or stones.

strength — power; forcefulness.

Ex 15:2 "The LORD is my *s* and my defense;

Dt 6:5 all your soul and with all your *s*.

Ps 46:1 God is our refuge and *s*,

Isa 40:31 will renew their *s*.

Php 4:13 through him who gives me *s*.

strife — bitter and sometimes violent conflict.

Pr 30:33 stirring up anger produces *s*."

stronghold — a fortified place; a place of security.

1Sa 24:22 David and his men went up to the *s*.

Ps 27:1 The LORD is the *s* of my life

subdue — to bring under control; to conquer.

Ps 81:14 how quickly I would *s* their enemies

submission — humbleness; obedience.

1Co 14:34 but must be in *s*, as the law says.

1Ti 2:11 learn in quietness and full *s*.

submit — to willingly yield to another.

Pr 3:6 in all your ways *s* to him,

Eph 5:21 *S* to one another out of reverence

Col 3:18 Wives, *s* yourselves to your husbands,

Jas 4:7 *S* yourselves, then, to God.

succeed — 1. to turn out well; 2. to follow another as heir or successor of a title or rank.

suffer — to bear or endure something painful.

Mk 8:31 the Son of Man must *s* many things

Lk 24:26 the Messiah have to *s* these things

1Co 12:26 If one part *s*, every part *s* with it;

suffering — the experience of enduring pain.

Isa 53:3 of *s*, and familiar with *pain*.

Ac 5:41 worthy of *s* disgrace for the Name.

Ro 8:17 share in his *s* in order that we may

2Ti 1:8 Rather, join with me in *s* for the gospel,

summon — to issue a call to come together; to send for.

Isa 43:1 I have *s* you by name; you are mine.

sustain — to give support; to help; to comfort.

Ps 18:35 and your right hand *s* me;

Ps 146:9 and *s* the fatherless and the widow,

swear — to promise forcefully or earnestly.

1Sa 30:15 "*S* to me before God that you will

swindler — someone who cheats another person out of money or other possessions.

1Co 6:10 nor *s* will inherit the kingdom

sword — a weapon with a long blade for cutting or thrusting.

symbol — an object or action that stands for or suggests something else. The cross is a symbol of Jesus' death.

synagogue — the Jewish place of worship and religious teaching.

Lk 4:16 the Sabbath day he went into the *s*,

Ac 17:2 his custom, Paul went into the *s*,

T

tabernacle — the tent used by the Israelites for meeting with God; the place where God chose to show his presence. The tabernacle was made by God's command and according to his plans. It is described in detail in Exodus 26. Also call the tent of meeting.

Ex 40:34 the glory of the LORD filled the *t*.

talent — a large amount of silver or gold, worth very much money.

Ex 25:39 A *t* of pure gold is to be used

tax — money a government requires its citizens to pay.

Mt 22:19 the coin used for paying the *t*."

teach — to instruct; to help someone learn.

Ex 33:13 *t* me your ways so I may know you

Ps 90:12 *T* us to number our days,

Lk 11:1 said to him, "Lord, *t* us to pray,

Jn 14:26 will *t* you all things and will remind

tempest — a violent storm.

temple — 1. the place where the Jewish people worshiped and sacrificed in Jerusalem; the first temple was built by King Solomon as a house for God; 2. any place of worship. In this sense, the human body is referred to as a temple (1Co 6:19).

1Ki 8:27 How much less this *t* I have built!

Ac 17:24 not live in *t* built by human hands.

2Co 6:16 For we are the *t* of the living God.

tempt (temptation) — trying to get someone to do wrong.

Mt 4:1 the wilderness to be *t* by the devil.

1Co 10:13 No *t* has overtaken you except

tenant — one who rents land or a house from a landlord.

testimony — a statement made by a witness to prove that something is true.

Lk 18:20 not give false *t*, honor your father

tetrarch — a ruler over one-fourth of a kingdom.

Thaddaeus — one of the twelve apostles (Mk 3:18); son of James and probably also known as Judas (Lk 6:16; Ac 1:13).

thanks — the expression of gratitude.

1Ch 16:34 Give *t* to the LORD, for

Ps 100:4 give *t* to him and praise his name.

1Co 15:57 *t* be to God! He gives us the victory

2Co 9:15 *T* be to God for his indescribable

1Th 5:18 give *t* in all circumstances;

thanksgiving — recognizing and thanking the one who has provided a gift.

Ps 100:4 Enter his gates with *t*

Php 4:6 by prayer and petition, with *t*,

Thomas — one of the twelve apostles (Lk 6:15; Ac 1:13); at first he doubted Jesus' resurrection, but when he saw Jesus, he believed (Jn 20:24 – 28).

thrive — to grow vigorously.

Thummim — see Urim.

threshing floor — the place where grain was trampled by oxen or beaten with a stick to separate it from the stalk.

Ru 3:6 So she went down to the *t*

Timothy — fellow-traveler and official representative of the apostle Paul. He joined Paul on his second missionary journey (Ac 16 – 20), and at one point in this journey Paul sent him to minister to the church at Corinth (1Co 4:17; 16:10). He was the leader of the church at Ephesus (1Ti 1:3) and a co-writer with Paul (1Th 1:1; 2Th 1:1; Phm 1).

tithe — the giving to God of one-tenth of what one earns.

Lev 27:30 " 'A *t* of everything from the land,

Mal 3:10 the whole *t* into the storehouse,

Titus — a Gentile co-worker with Paul (Gal 2:1 – 3; 2Ti 4:10). Paul sent him to Corinth to help solve some of the problems there (2Co 2:13; 7 – 8; 12:18).

toil — 1. (*n.*) strenuous and tiring work; 2. (*v.*) to work long and hard.

Ecc 3:9 What do workers gain from their *t*?

tomb — a burial place. In Bible times, a tomb was often either a cave or a cavity dug into a stone cliff, with a large stone rolled in front to close it.

Mt 27:65 make the *t* as secure as you know

Lk 24:2 the stone rolled away from the *t*,

Jn 11:17 been in the *t* for four days.

tongue — 1. the organ of speech in the mouth; 2. a language.

Ps 39:1 and keep my *t* from sin;

Ac 2:4 and began to speak in other *t*

Php 2:11 every *t* acknowledge that Jesus

Jas 1:26 do not keep a tight rein on their *t*

torment — extreme pain or anguish; agony.

2Co 12:7 a messenger of Satan, to *t* me.

tradition — the handing down of information and beliefs from one generation to another.

Mt 15:2 break the *t* of the elders?

trample — to walk heavily causing injury or damage.

Ps 60:12 he will *t* down our enemies.

transfigure — to change the appearance of; to make bright and glorious.

Mt 17:2 There he was *t* before them.

transgression — sin; disobeying the law of God.

Ps 32:1 whose *t* are forgiven,

Isa 53:5 But he was pierced for our *t*,

Eph 2:1 you were dead in your *t* and sins,

treacherous — untrustworthy, unreliable, faithless.

tread — to step or walk on or over.

Job 24:11 they *t* the winepresses,

treasure — 1. (*n.*) wealth that is stored up or hidden away; 2. (*v.*) to hold or keep something precious, something of value; to cherish.

Mt 6:21 your *t* is, there your heart will be also.

treaty — an agreement between two people or groups or nations.

Ex 34:12 Be careful not to make a *t*

trespass — sin; wrongdoing.

Ro 5:17 For if, by the *t* of the one man,

tribe — a social group made up of a particular branch of a family.

tribute — payment by one ruler or nation to another as an act of submission or in order to guarantee protection.

Isa 16:1 Send lambs as *t* to the ruler

triumph — a victory; a notable success.

Pr 28:12 the righteous *t*, there is great elation;

true — certain; exactly right.

Ps 119:160 All your words are *t*;

Jn 17:3 the only *t* God, and Jesus Christ,

Ro 3:4 Let God be *t*, and every human
Php 4:8 whatever is *t*, whatever is noble,

trust — firm belief or faith in another.

Ps 37:3 *T* in the LORD and do good;
Pr 3:5 *T* in the LORD with all your heart
Isa 26:3 because they *t* in you.
Isa 30:15 in quietness and *t* is your strength,
1Co 4:2 been given a *t* must prove faithful.

trustworthy — deserving of trust; reliable.

Ps 19:7 The statutes of the LORD are *t*,
1Ti 1:15 Here is a *t* saying that deserves full

truth — that which conforms to the facts.

Ps 145:18 to all who call on him in *t*.
Zec 8:16 are to do: Speak the *t* to each other,
Jn 8:32 know the *t*, and the *t*
Jn 14:6 I am the way and the *t* and the life.
Ro 1:25 They exchanged the *t* about God
1Co 13:6 in evil but rejoices with the *t*.
Eph 4:15 Instead, speaking the *t* in love,
Heb 10:26 received the knowledge of the *t*,
1Jn 1:6 we lie and do not live out the *t*.
1Jn 1:8 deceive ourselves and the *t* is not

tunic — a long shirt worn by men in Bible times.

Ezr 9:3 When I heard this, I tore my *t*

turban — a head-covering made by winding a cloth around the head.

U

unbelief — doubt.

Mk 9:24 help me overcome my *u*!"

unbeliever — one who does not believe in Jesus.

2Co 6:14 Do not be yoked together with *u*.

unclean — morally or spiritually impure; unclean animals were those which the Israelites were not allowed to sacrifice or to eat.

unity — being one.

Ps 133:1 God's people live together in *u*!
Col 3:14 them all together in perfect *u*.

unleavened bread — bread made without yeast. It is usually flat, like a pancake or cracker.

Ex 12:17 "Celebrate the Festival of *U*,

uphold — to give support to.

Ps 37:17 the LORD *u* the righteous.

upright — honest; doing what is right and good.

Urim and Thummim — objects that were placed on the vest of the high priest; used to determine God's will for the nation of Israel.

utter — to pronounce, to speak.

Ps 78:2 I will *u* hidden things,
Jer 15:19 if you *u* worthy, not worthless, words,

utterly — completely, totally.

V

vain — worthless; unsuccessful; foolish. "In vain" means without success or result.

valiant — courageous.

vast — very great in size or amount; huge.

vault — the atmosphere or sky as seen from the earth.

Ge 1:8 God called the *v* "sky."

vengeance — hurt or punishment done to another person who has done something wrong against another.

Isa 34:8 For the LORD has a day of *v*,

vigor — strength and health in the body and its growth.

Job 20:11 The youthful *v* that fills his bones

vile — disgusting, evil.

Rev 22:11 let the *v* person continue to be *v*;

vindicate — to defend; to provide justice for; to set free.

Ps 135:4 For the LORD will *v* his people

violate — 1. to rape; 2. to make something unholy; 3. to fail to obey.

viper — 1. a venomous snake; 2. a treacherous or vicious person.

virgin — a woman or girl who has never had sexual intercourse.

Isa 7:14 The *v* will conceive
Mt 1:23 "The *v* will conceive

vision — a dream from God.

Nu 12:6 reveal myself to them in *v*,
Joel 2:28 your young men will see *v*.
Ac 26:19 disobedient to the *v* from heaven.

vow — a solemn promise made before God or to God.

Jdg 11:30 Jephthah made a *v* to the LORD:
Ps 116:14 I will fulfill my *v* to the LORD

wages — payment received for work completed.

Ro 6:23 For the *w* of sin is death,

wail — to cry loudly.

walk — to follow a certain course.

Ps 1:1 who does not *w* in step

Isa 2:5 let us *w* in the light of the LORD.

Mic 6:8 and to *w* humbly with your God.

2Jn 6 his command is that you *w* in love.

wander — to move about without a fixed course.

Nu 32:13 he made them *w* in the wilderness

Jas 5:19 if one of you should *w* from the truth

warn — to give notice beforehand of danger or evil.

warrior — a soldier.

Isa 9:3 as *w* rejoice when dividing

wash — to clean.

Ps 51:7 *w* me, and I will be whiter

Ac 22:16 be baptized and *w* your sins away,

watch — to be on the lookout for someone or something.

Jer 31:10 will *w* over his flock like a shepherd.'

Mt 26:41 "*W* and pray so that you will not fall

way — the means of getting somewhere; the path.

2Sa 22:31 "As for God, his *w* is perfect:

Ps 1:1 or stand in the *w* that sinners

Ps 37:5 Commit your *w* to the LORD;

Isa 53:6 each of us has turned to our own *w*;

Jn 14:6 "I am the *w* and the truth

1Co 12:31 will show you the most excellent *w*.

wean — to help a child or animal begin to eat solid food rather than his or her mother's milk.

weapon — an object used for fighting.

weary — 1. tired; 2. having one's patience or tolerance exhausted.

Dt 25:18 When you were *w* and worn out,

Zec 11:8 and I grew *w* of them

weep, **wept** — to cry.

Jn 11:35 Jesus *w*.

welcome — 1. to greet a person pleasantly; 2. to make a person feel at home.

Jdg 19:20 "You are *w* at my house,"

wholehearted — sincere; devoted without holding anything back.

wicked — sinful.

Ps 1:1 walk in step with the *w*

Isa 55:7 Let the *w* forsake their ways

widow — a woman whose husband has died.

will — desire; seeking God's will means looking for what God wants to be done.

Ps 143:10 Teach me to do your *w*,

Isa 53:10 Yet it was the LORD's *w*

Mt 6:10 your *w* be done,

Mt 26:39 Yet not as I *w*, but as you *w*."

Ro 12:2 and approve what God's *w* is

Eph 5:17 understand what the Lord's *w* is.

1Jn 5:14 we ask anything according to his *w*,

Rev 4:11 and by your *w* they were created

winepress — a vat or tub in which the juice of grapes is pressed out. Used in the Bible as a symbol for the anger of God against wickedness.

Rev 14:19 into the great *w* of God's wrath.

wisdom — the understanding that comes from God.

Lk 2:52 And Jesus grew in *w* and stature,

Jas 1:5 of you lacks *w*, you should ask God,

witchcraft — practices using evil spirits, magic, or sorcery.

Mic 5:12 I will destroy your *w*

wither — to dry or shrivel up, usually from a lack of moisture.

witness — one who personally sees an event take place.

Ac 22:15 You will be his *w* to all people

woe — great misery; distress.

Isa 6:5 "*W* to me!" I cried.

Lk 11:42 "*W* to you Pharisees, because you

womb — the organ within a woman's body where a child grows before birth.

Lk 1:44 the baby in my *w* leaped for joy.

word — 1. the means of expressing oneself through language; 2. the Bible, as God's written message to people; 3. (cap.) Jesus is the Word sent from God because his life on earth told the message of God.

Jn 1:14 The *W* became flesh and made his

Heb 4:12 For the *w* of God is alive

work — 1. (*n.*) employment; duty; 2. (*v.*) to bring about; to try to achieve a goal.

Ex 23:12 "Six days do your *w*,

Jn 9:4 we must do the *w* of him who sent

Php 2:12 continue to *w* out your salvation

2Ti 3:17 equipped for every good *w*.

world — 1. the earth and those who live in it; 2. the secular, as opposed to the spiritual or religious.

Mt 5:14 "You are the light of the *w*.

Jn 1:29 who takes away the sin of the *w!*

Jn 3:16 so loved the *w* that he gave his one

Jn 8:12 he said, "I am the light of the *w*.

Ro 12:2 Do not conform to the pattern of this *w*,

1Jn 2:15 not love the *w* or anything in the *w*.

worldly — loving the things of the world more than the things of God.

Tit 2:12 to ungodliness and *w* passions,

worry — to feel anxious and uneasy.

Mt 6:25 I tell you, do not *w* about your life,

worship — 1. (*v.*) to give praise, honor and respect to God; 2. (*n.*) reverence given to God.

Ps 95:6 Come, let us bow down in *w*,

Jn 4:24 his worshipers must *w* in the Spirit

worthy — having value; honorable; deserving.

1Ch 16:25 For great is the LORD and most *w*

Eph 4:1 to live a life *w* of the calling you

Rev 5:2 "Who is *w* to break the seals

wrath — great anger; the strong anger of God.

Pr 15:1 A gentle answer turns away *w*,

Ro 5:9 saved from God's *w* through him!

X

Xerxes — king of Persia; he made Esther, a young Jewess, his queen (Est 2:15 – 18).

Y

yearn — to long for; to want very much.

yeast — the ingredient that makes dough rise; sometimes a figure of speech for the influence someone has over others.

Mt 16:6 guard against the *y* of the Pharisees

Gal 5:9 little *y* works through the whole

yield — 1. to submit; 2. to grow or produce fruit.

Ps 67:6 The land *y* its harvest;

Isa 48:11 I will not *y* my glory to another.

yoke — 1. (*v.*) to join together; 2. (*n.*) a wooden bar that goes over the necks of two animals, usually oxen. The yoke holds the animals together as they pull an object, such as a plow or a cart.

Mt 11:29 Take my *y* upon you and learn

2Co 6:14 Do not be *y* together

youth — the time when a person is young.

Ecc 12:1 Creator in the days of your *y*,

Z

Zacchaeus — a tax collector who climbed a tree in order to see Jesus.

zeal — eagerness; strong desire.

Ro 12:11 Never be lacking in *z*,

Zealot — a member of the Jewish group that wanted to fight against and overthrow the Roman government.

Zechariah — a prophet and priest who returned to Jerusalem from the Babylonian captivity; he encouraged the Jews to rebuild the temple (Ezr 5:1; 6:14; Zec 1:1).

Zerubbabel — a descendant of David (1Ch 3:19); he led the return of the Jews from the Babylonian captivity (Ezr 1 – 3; Ne 7:7; Hag 1 – 2; Zec 4).

Zion — 1. the hill on which the city of Jerusalem first stood; David's royal palace and the temple were both built on Mount Zion; 2. the entire city of Jerusalem.

Jer 50:5 They will ask the way to *Z*

Ro 11:26 "The deliverer will come from *Z*;

WORLD OF THE PATRIARCHS

Caspian Sea

Araxes R.

Lake Urmia

Mt. Ararat

Black Sea

Persian Gulf

BABYLONIANS

Ur

Uruk

Nippur

Babylon

Ashur

Tigris R.

Nuzi

Nineveh

Mari

Harran

Euphrates R.

PADDAN ARAM

Tadmor

ARABIA

HITTITES

Carchemish

Aleppo

Ebla

Hattusa

Taurus Mts.

Ugarit

Gebal aka Byblos

Damascus

Shechem

Hazor

Ai

Hebron

Megiddo

Dothan

Bethel

Beersheba

Gerar

Kadesh Barnea

Zoar

Sinai

Red Sea

Sukkoth

Zoan

Heliopolis

Memphis

EGYPTIANS

Nile R.

Kittim (Cyprus)

Mediterranean Sea
(The Great Sea)

Troy

Knossos

Caphtor (Crete)

Aegean Sea

Mycenae

Possible location of Biblical "Ur of the Chaldeans," where Abraham's migration began.

Possible location of Sodom and Gomorrah.

→ Abraham's journey

0   100 km.
0   100 miles

10,000 ft   3050 m
5000 ft   1525 m
2000 ft   610 m
1000 ft   305 m
0 (sea level)   0 (sea level)
-1640 ft   -500 m

EXODUS AND CONQUEST OF CANAAN

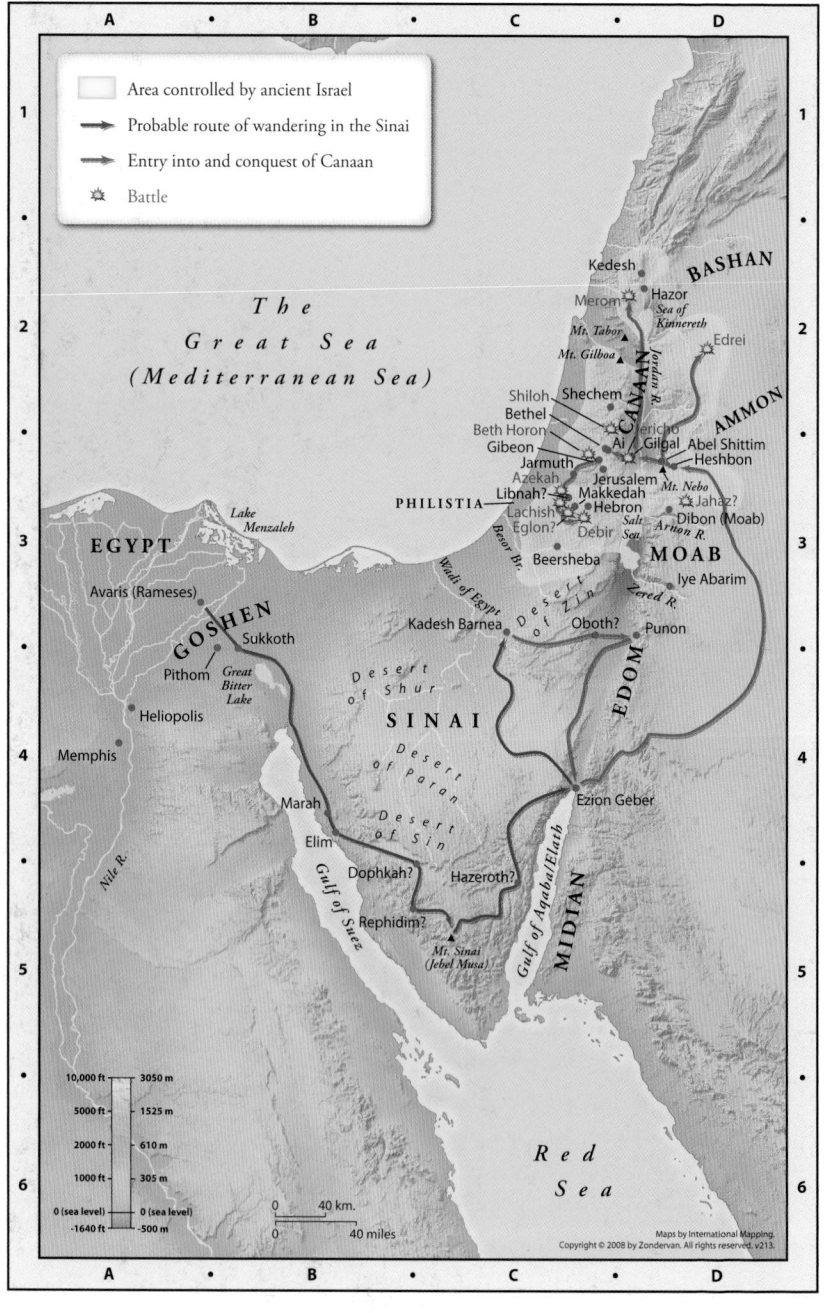

Area controlled by ancient Israel

Probable route of wandering in the Sinai

Entry into and conquest of Canaan

Battle

The Great Sea (Mediterranean Sea)

BASHAN

Kedesh
Merom
Hazor
Sea of Kinnereth
Mt. Tabor
Mt. Gilboa
Edrei

CANAAN

Jordan R.

AMMON

Shiloh
Shechem
Bethel
Beth Horon
Gibeon
Jericho
Ai
Gilgal
Abel Shittim
Heshbon
Jarmuth
Azekah
Libnah?
Lachish?
Eglon?
Makkedah
Jerusalem
Hebron
Debir
Mt. Nebo
Jahaz?
Dibon (Moab)
Salt Sea
Arnon R.

PHILISTIA

Lake Menzaleh

EGYPT

GOSHEN

Avaris (Rameses)
Sukkoth
Pithom
Great Bitter Lake
Heliopolis

Memphis

Nile R.

Marah
Elim
Dophkah?
Rephidim?
Gulf of Suez

Mt. Sinai (Jebel Musa)

Hazeroth?

SINAI

Desert of Shur
Desert of Paran
Desert of Sin

Wadi of Egypt
Besor Br.
Beersheba
Desert of Zin
Kadesh Barnea
Oboth?
Punon

MOAB
Iye Abarim
Zered R.

EDOM

Ezion Geber

Gulf of Aqaba/Elath

MIDIAN

Red Sea

10,000 ft — 3050 m
5000 ft — 1525 m
2000 ft — 610 m
1000 ft — 305 m
0 (sea level) — 0 (sea level)
-1640 ft — -500 m

0 — 40 km.
0 — 40 miles

LAND OF THE TWELVE TRIBES

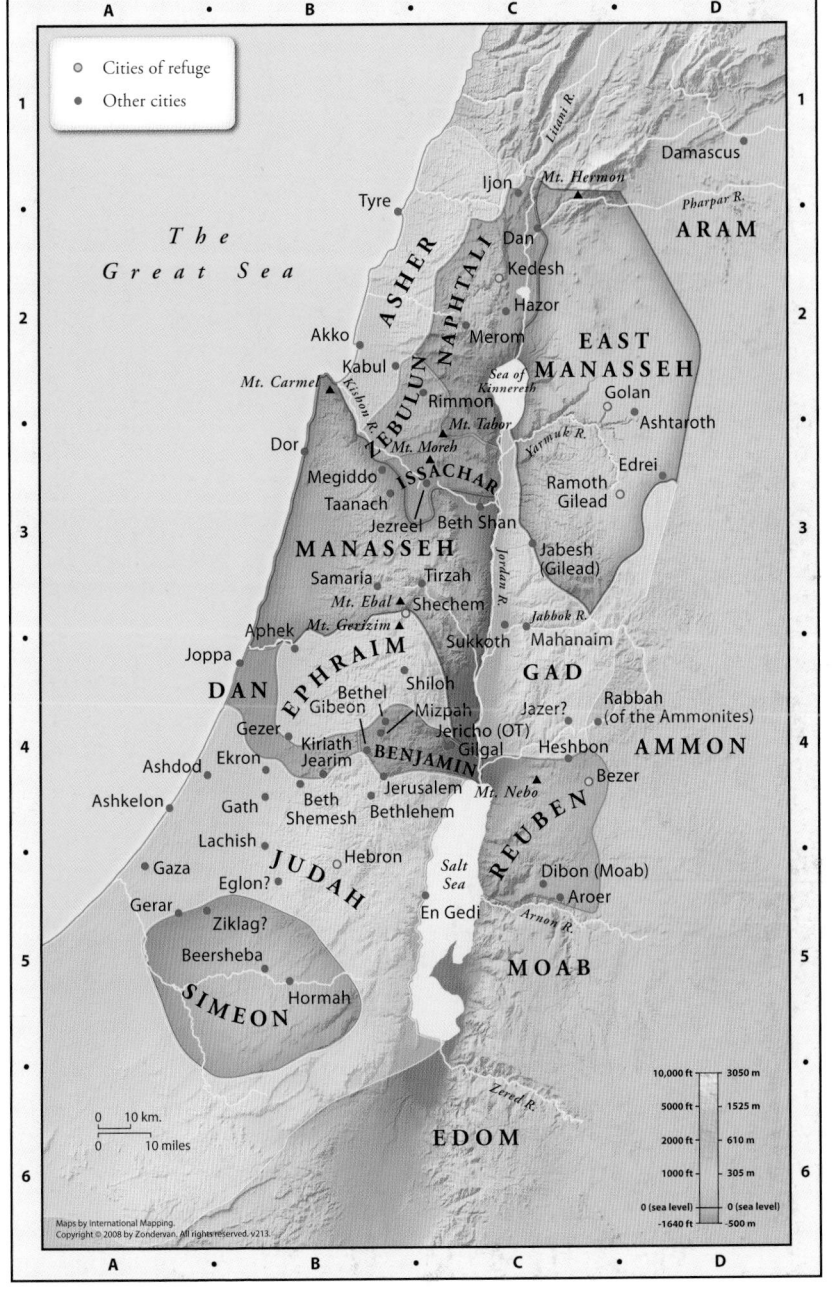

Maps by International Mapping.
Copyright © 2008 by Zondervan. All rights reserved. v213

KINGDOM OF DAVID AND SOLOMON

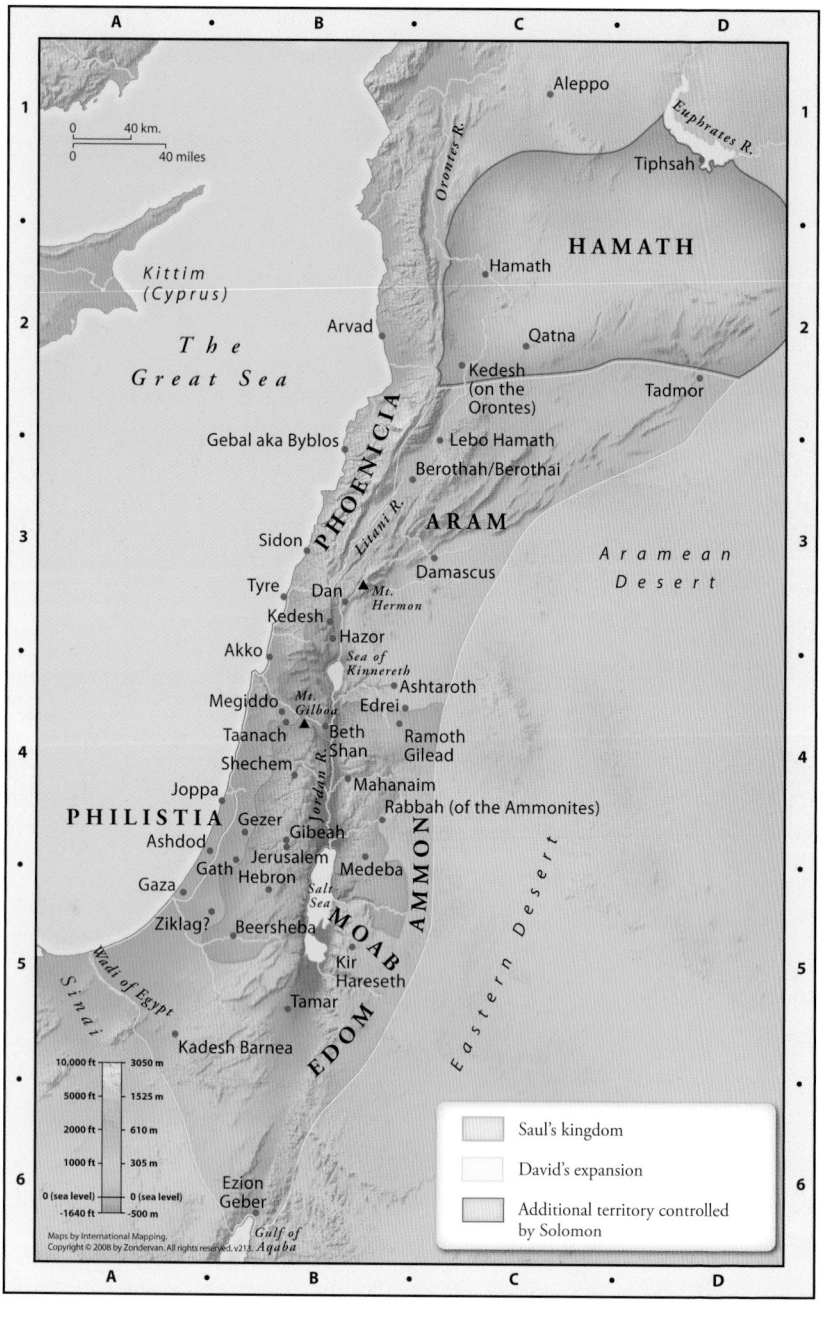

Aleppo

Euphrates R.

Tiphsah

HAMATH

Hamath

Kittim
(Cyprus)

Arvad

Qatna

Orontes R.

The
Great Sea

Kedesh
(on the
Orontes)

Tadmor

Gebal aka Byblos

Lebo Hamath

Berothah/Berothai

PHOENICIA

Litani R.

ARAM

Sidon

Damascus

Aramean
Desert

Tyre

Dan

Mt.
Hermon

Kedesh

Hazor

Akko

Sea of
Kinnereth

Ashtaroth

Megiddo

Mt.
Gilboa

Edrei

Taanach

Beth
Shan

Ramoth
Gilead

Shechem

Jordan R.

Joppa

Mahanaim

PHILISTIA

Gezer

Rabbah (of the Ammonites)

Ashdod

Gibeah

Jerusalem

AMMON

Gath

Hebron

Medeba

Gaza

Salt
Sea

Ziklag?

Beersheba

MOAB

Eastern Desert

Kir
Hareseth

Tamar

EDOM

Kadesh Barnea

Wadi of Egypt

Sinai

10,000 ft	3050 m
5000 ft	1525 m
2000 ft	610 m
1000 ft	305 m
0 (sea level)	0 (sea level)
-1640 ft	-500 m

Saul's kingdom

David's expansion

Additional territory controlled
by Solomon

Ezion
Geber

Gulf of
Aqaba

Maps by International Mapping.
Copyright © 2008 by Zondervan. All rights reserved. v213.

0   40 km.
0   40 miles

JESUS' MINISTRY

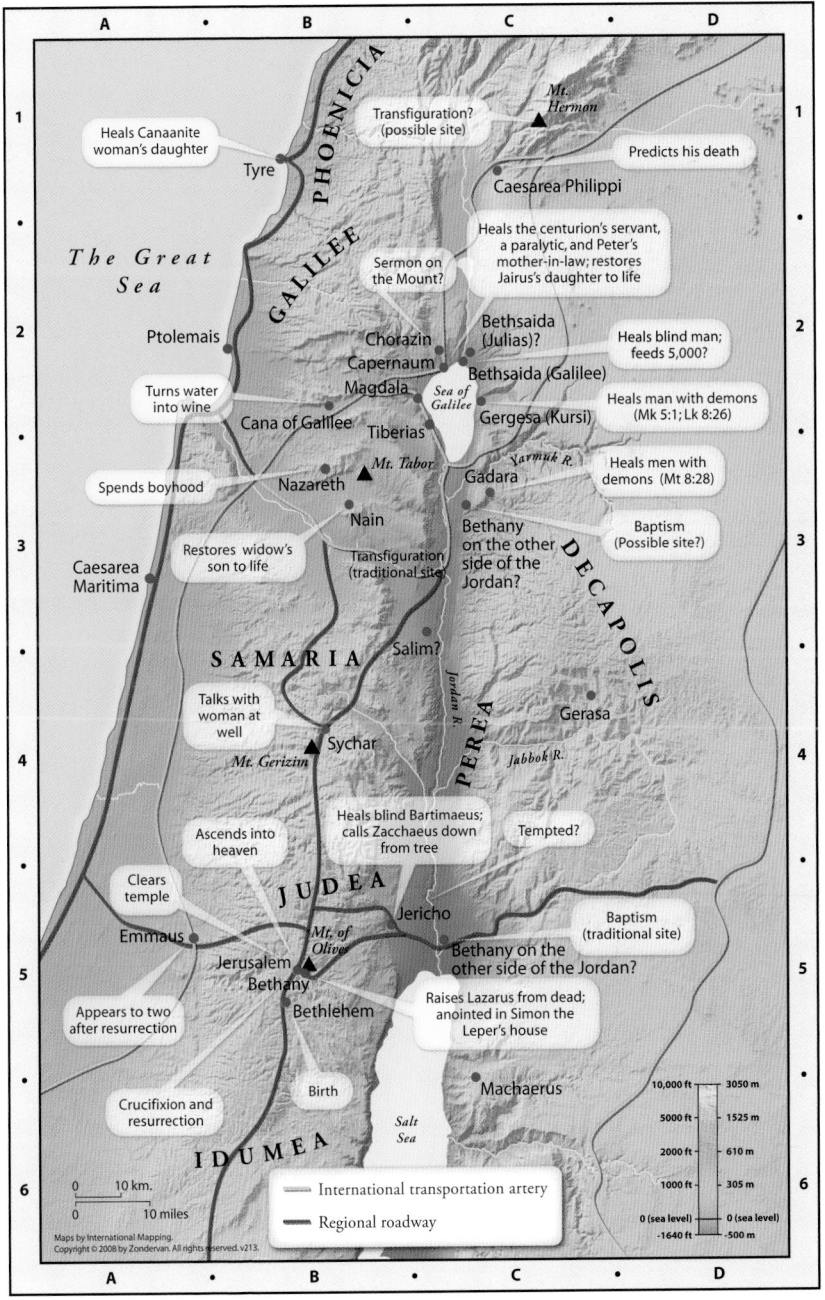

Heals Canaanite woman's daughter — Tyre

Transfiguration? (possible site)

Mt. Hermon

Predicts his death

Caesarea Philippi

PHOENICIA

GALILEE

The Great Sea

Sermon on the Mount?

Heals the centurion's servant, a paralytic, and Peter's mother-in-law; restores Jairus's daughter to life

Ptolemais

Chorazin
Capernaum
Magdala

Bethsaida (Julias)?

Bethsaida (Galilee)

Heals blind man; feeds 5,000?

Turns water into wine

Cana of Galilee

Sea of Galilee

Gergesa (Kursi)

Heals man with demons (Mk 5:1; Lk 8:26)

Tiberias

Mt. Tabor

Yarmuk R.

Heals men with demons (Mt 8:28)

Spends boyhood

Nazareth

Gadara

Nain

Transfiguration (traditional site)

Bethany on the other side of the Jordan?

Baptism (Possible site?)

DECAPOLIS

Restores widow's son to life

Caesarea Maritima

SAMARIA

Salim?

Jordan R.

Talks with woman at well

Sychar

Mt. Gerizim

PEREA

Jabbok R.

Gerasa

Ascends into heaven

Heals blind Bartimaeus; calls Zacchaeus down from tree

Tempted?

Clears temple

JUDEA

Jericho

Emmaus

Mt. of Olives

Baptism (traditional site)

Jerusalem
Bethany

Bethany on the other side of the Jordan?

Appears to two after resurrection

Bethlehem

Raises Lazarus from dead; anointed in Simon the Leper's house

Crucifixion and resurrection

Birth

Machaerus

IDUMEA

Salt Sea

10,000 ft	3050 m
5000 ft	1525 m
2000 ft	610 m
1000 ft	305 m
0 (sea level)	0 (sea level)
-1640 ft	-500 m

0   10 km.
0   10 miles

International transportation artery

Regional roadway

PAUL'S MISSIONARY JOURNEYS

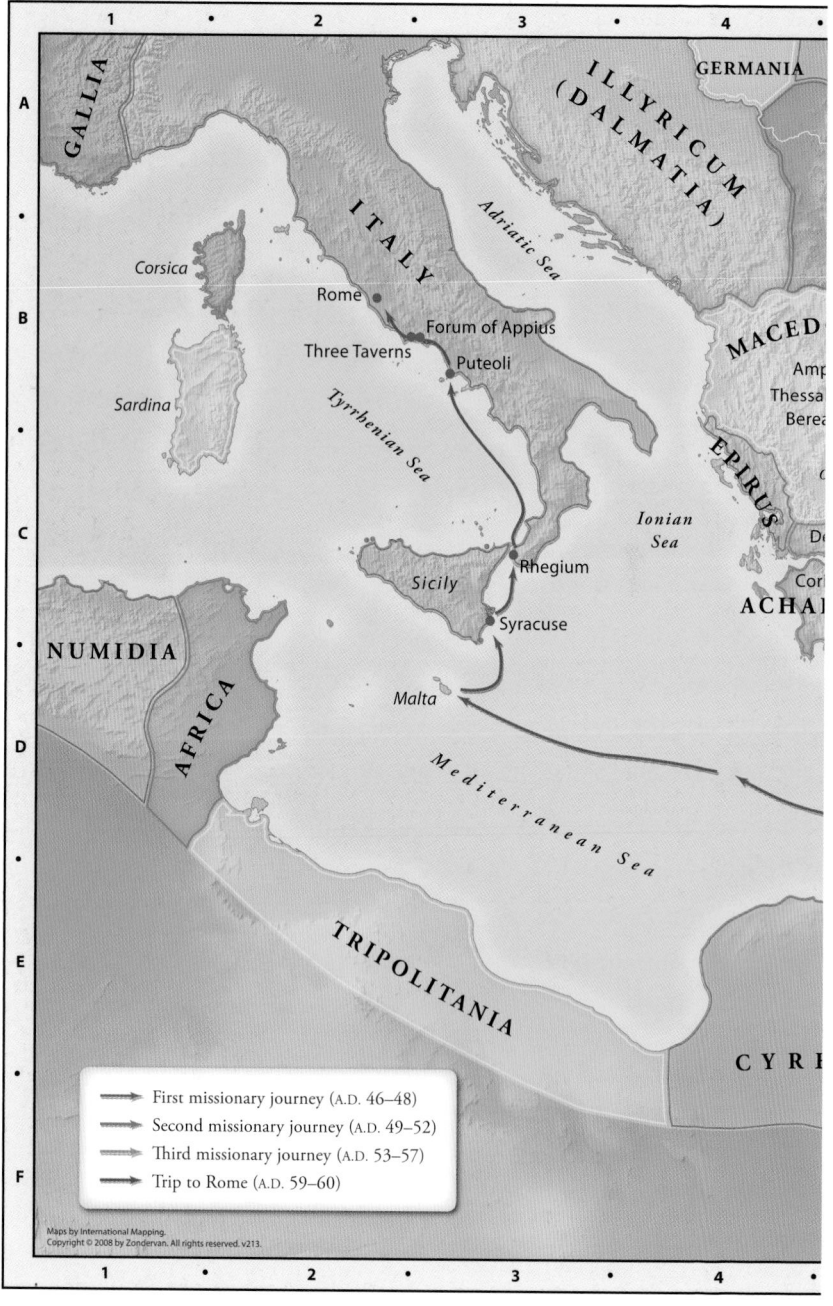

GALLIA

GERMANIA

ILLYRICUM (DALMATIA)

ITALY

Adriatic Sea

Corsica

Rome

MACED

Forum of Appius

Amp

Three Taverns

Thessa

Puteoli

Berea

Sardina

Tyrrhenian Sea

EPIRUS

Ionian Sea

Rhegium

D

Sicily

ACHA

Syracuse

Cor

NUMIDIA

Malta

AFRICA

Mediterranean Sea

TRIPOLITANIA

CYR

➤ First missionary journey (A.D. 46–48)
➤ Second missionary journey (A.D. 49–52)
➤ Third missionary journey (A.D. 53–57)
➤ Trip to Rome (A.D. 59–60)

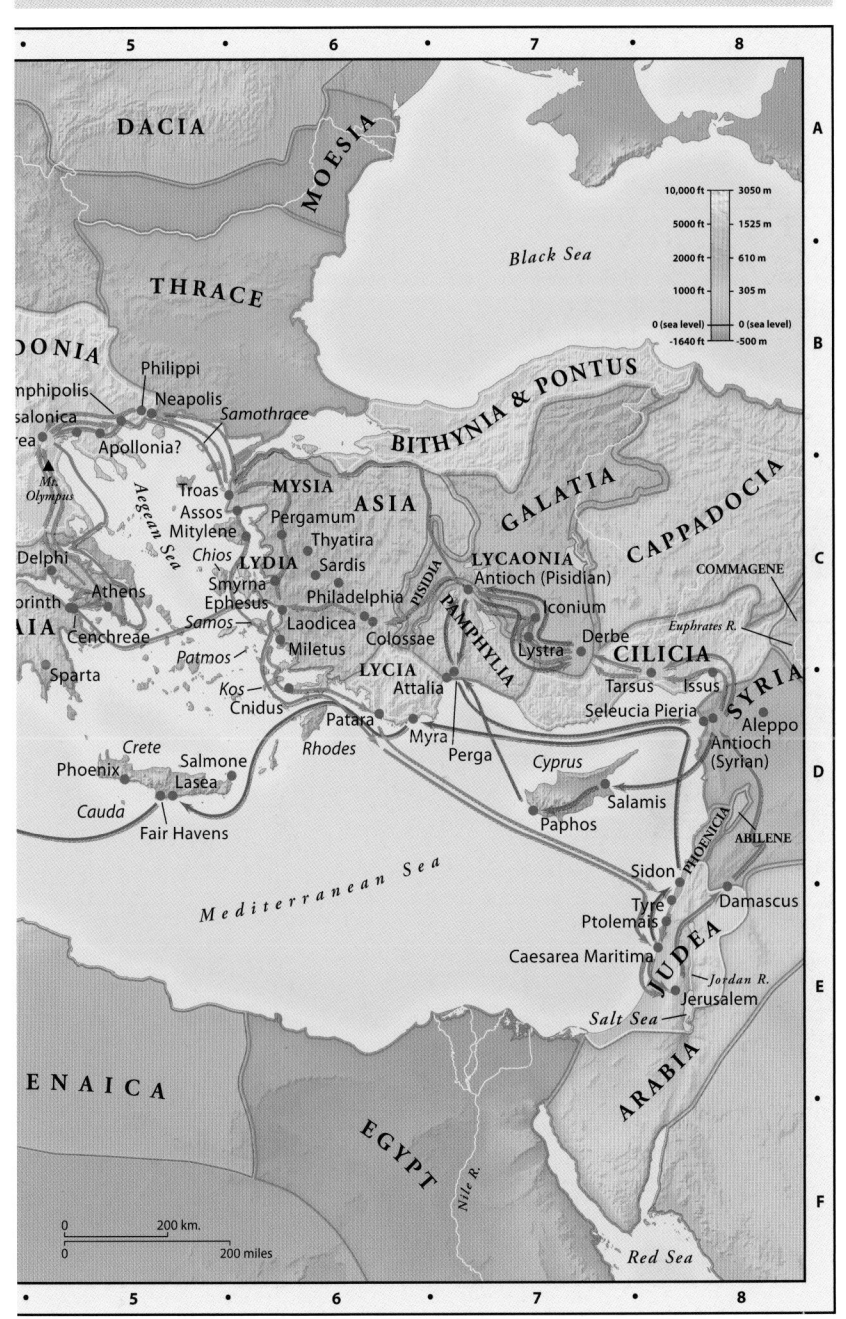

5 6 7 8

Rows: A B C D E F

DACIA

MOESIA

THRACE

Black Sea

10,000 ft — 3050 m
5000 ft — 1525 m
2000 ft — 610 m
1000 ft — 305 m
0 (sea level) — 0 (sea level)
-1640 ft — -500 m

Philippi
Neapolis
Amphipolis
Samothrace
Thessalonica
Berea
Apollonia?

BITHYNIA & PONTUS

Mt. Olympus

Aegean Sea

Troas
Assos
Mitylene
Chios

MYSIA
Pergamum
Thyatira

ASIA

GALATIA

CAPPADOCIA

COMMAGENE

Delphi
Athens
Corinth
Cenchreae

LYDIA
Smyrna
Ephesus
Samos

Sardis
Philadelphia
Laodicea
Miletus
Colossae

PISIDIA

LYCAONIA
Antioch (Pisidian)
Iconium

Euphrates R.

Lystra
Derbe

CILICIA

SYRIA

ACHAIA

Patmos

Sparta

Kos
Cnidus

LYCIA
Attalia

PAMPHYLIA

Patara
Myra
Perga

Tarsus
Seleucia Pieria

Issus
Aleppo
Antioch (Syrian)

Crete
Phoenix
Cauda
Salmone
Lasea
Fair Havens

Rhodes

Cyprus

Paphos

Salamis

PHOENICIA
ABILENE

Mediterranean Sea

Sidon
Tyre
Ptolemais
Caesarea Maritima

Damascus

JUDEA
Jordan R.
Jerusalem
Salt Sea

CYRENAICA

EGYPT

Nile R.

ARABIA

Red Sea

0 — 200 km.
0 — 200 miles

JERUSALEM IN THE TIME OF JESUS

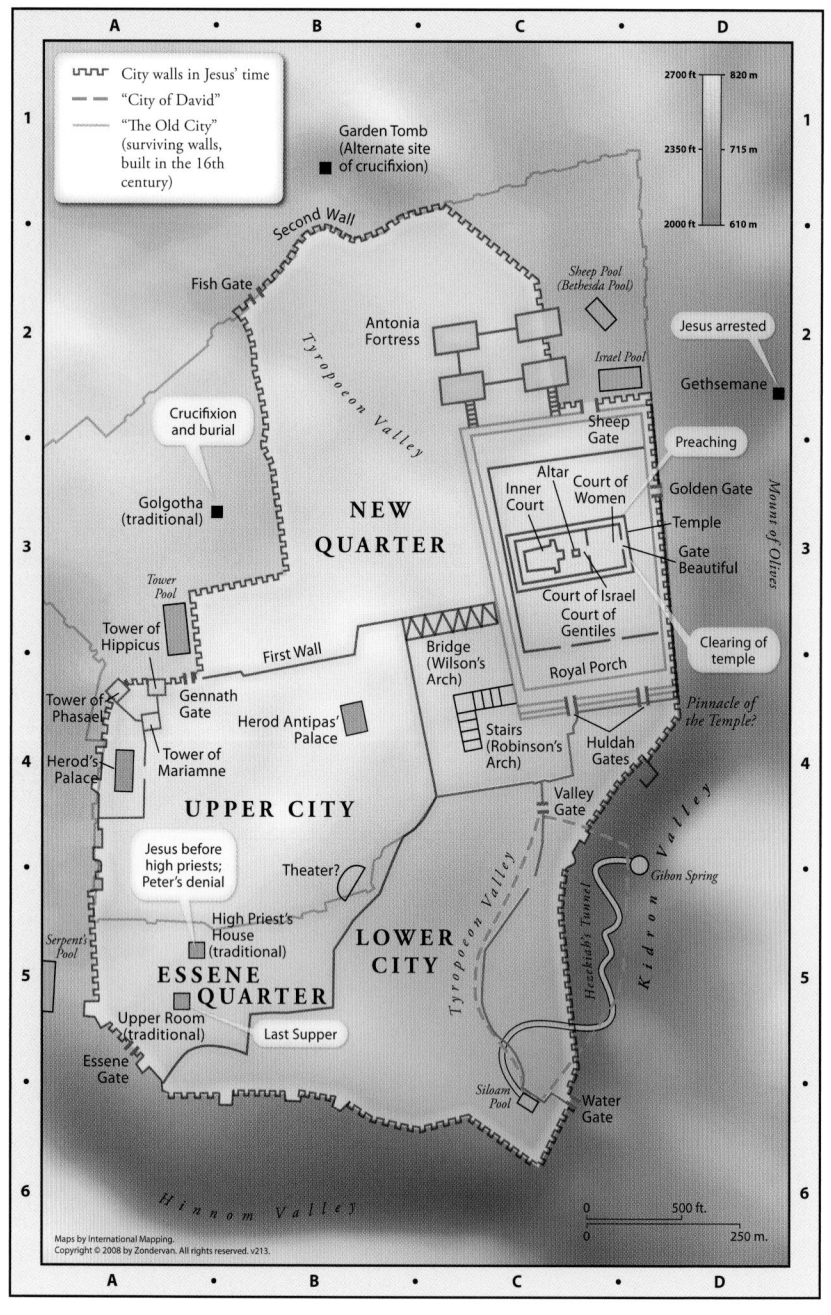

City walls in Jesus' time
--- "City of David"
"The Old City" (surviving walls, built in the 16th century)

Garden Tomb (Alternate site of crucifixion)

2700 ft — 820 m
2350 ft — 715 m
2000 ft — 610 m

Second Wall

Sheep Pool (Bethesda Pool)

Fish Gate

Antonia Fortress

Israel Pool

Jesus arrested

Gethsemane

Tyropoeon Valley

Crucifixion and burial

Sheep Gate

Preaching

Golgotha (traditional)

Altar
Inner Court
Court of Women

Golden Gate

Temple

NEW QUARTER

Court of Israel
Court of Gentiles

Gate Beautiful

Clearing of temple

Mount of Olives

Tower Pool

Tower of Hippicus

First Wall

Bridge (Wilson's Arch)

Royal Porch

Pinnacle of the Temple?

Tower of Phasael

Gennath Gate

Herod Antipas' Palace

Stairs (Robinson's Arch)

Huldah Gates

Tower of Mariamne

Herod's Palace

UPPER CITY

Valley Gate

Kidron Valley

Jesus before high priests; Peter's denial

Theater?

Gihon Spring

Serpents' Pool

High Priest's House (traditional)

LOWER CITY

Tyropoeon Valley

Hezekiah's Tunnel

ESSENE QUARTER

Upper Room (traditional)

Last Supper

Essene Gate

Siloam Pool

Water Gate

Hinnom Valley

0   500 ft.
0   250 m.

Maps by International Mapping.
Copyright © 2008 by Zondervan. All rights reserved. v213.